Baseball America®

DRAFT ALMANAC

A complete listing of every player ever drafted, 1965–2009

2009 EDITION

BASEBALL AMERICA INC. · DURHAM, N.C.

Baseball America
DRAFT ALMANAC

Editor
Will Lingo

Database Programming
Greg Levine, Brent Lewis

Assistant Editors
Matt Eddy, Josh Leventhal, Jim Shonerd

Contributing Editors
Ben Badler, Jim Callis, J.J. Cooper, Aaron Fitt, Conor Glassey, John Manuel

Photo Editor
Nathan Rode

Design & Production
Sara Hiatt McDaniel, Tiffany Schwarz, Linwood Webb

Jacket Photo
Stephen Strasburg by Jesse Soll

Baseball America

President/Publisher: Lee Folger
Editors in Chief: Will Lingo, John Manuel
Executive Editor: Jim Callis
Design & Production Director: Sara Hiatt McDaniel

Distributed by Baseball America
ISBN-13: 978-1-932391-27-5

BaseballAmerica.com

Introduction

Sometimes you have to wonder what all the fuss is about. After poring over 45 draft lists, something in the neighborhood of 60,000 selections, you come across a lot—a *lot*—of people you have never heard of. People whose selection in the draft is interesting only to friends and family at this point.

You realize that if a team gets one solid big leaguer out of a draft, then it has done pretty well for itself. So why all the fuss about the baseball draft?

Because of Albert Pujols in the 13th round.

Check out the Cardinals' 1999 draft class. You'll see they lost a few picks, gained a few picks, ended up with a passable big leaguer in Chris Duncan, and a few other guys who were once interesting to the Baseball America reader.

Then you come to Pujols, and realize that a 13th-round pick can change the course of a franchise. That's why the draft is so fascinating to us and to you when it rolls around every year, and it's why looking back on the history of the draft—both to try to glean lessons and just to have fun looking back over the lists—never gets old.

For Baseball America it all began with our seminal book, "The Baseball Draft: The First 25 Years," which covered the drafts from 1965-89 in amazing detail. Ever since the book was published, our readers have clamored for more.

Actually, it all began with the beginning of Baseball America in 1981. Before that, coverage of the baseball draft had been sporadic and spotty, but it has been an essential part of the magazine's mission from the start.

The first draft book accurately gathered and captured the early history of the draft in one volume. Since then, the profile of and interest in the baseball draft has increased exponentially. A process that used to be conducted by telephone in obscurity now draws national media attention, gets broadcast on television and attracts huge traffic on the Internet.

Baseball America has been there every step of the way. The draft has always the busiest day of the year for us, and we still consider ourselves the essential source for draft information.

We used to be busy because players, friends, family and fans would call us to find out where they had been drafted. The draft was a secret process (you can learn more about why by reading our draft overviews in this book) and Baseball America was the only place to find the complete list of the draft.

Now we're busy because thousands of people visit our Website on draft day to get the latest news. They want to find out who was picked right away and they want to know why.

NOTES ON STYLE

A few notes about our style for the draft lists you'll find in this book:

- The number in parentheses after each phase indicate the team's place in the draft order
- Players who signed are listed in bold
- Positions listed are those given when the player was drafted
- High schools are designated with an HS (or Prep, Academy or Institute in a few rare cases) and the city where the school is, if that's not part of the school name; Canadian high schools are sometimes designated by SS (for secondary school)
- Two-year colleges are designated with a JC or CC, with a state designation if that's not part of the school name
- Four-year colleges are designated simply with the school's name (without the word College or University); colleges below the Division I level include a state designation if that's not part of the school name
- Players with no school designation are listed with a city and state
- Picks gained or lost for whatever reason are indicated in parentheses, with an explanation

They also want a single volume that allows them to review every draft, and here's the latest version. It includes every pick of every draft, with every signing as well.

This is the most comprehensive review of draft data that we've conducted since the first draft book was assembled 20 years ago. We went back through every draft, line by line, double-checking data we already had and plugging in new information. We think it's the best collection of draft data ever assembled.

We undertook this process to create a great book, which you hold in your hands, but also to create the first truly comprehensive online draft database, which we hope to unveil at BaseballAmerica.com in 2010. This was an important step in that process.

But we know our data can always get better. So if you find errors or omissions, please notify us at draft@baseballamerica.com. Just as an example, we tracked down every draft-and-follow signing we could find, but we feel sure there are some that have been overlooked. If you see one we overlooked, please notify us. And if you don't know what a draft-and-follow is, then you will after you read the book.

As long as you have an appetite for draft information, we'll be here to feed it.

The Baseball Draft: An Overview

The selection of Ken Griffey in 1987 almost single-handedly turned around the Mariners

As the notoriety of the baseball draft has evolved over the years, so too has its function.

The draft was originally intended to spread talent more evenly to major league organizations and to put a clamp on bonus payments. It accomplished that goal for a time, but by the 1990s bonuses were spiraling out of control. With a brief interruption, the trend continued after the turn of the century, prompting the most serious calls yet for significant changes to the draft process.

With players (and their agents, another twist added along the way) using their financial demands to manipulate the process, teams frequently based their selections on whether they could sign players, meaning the best talent didn't always go to the neediest teams.

Major League Baseball finally took an active role in dealing with the issue in the early 2000s, suggesting bonuses for each draft slot and (strongly) encouraging teams to hold the line. Bonuses actually slowed down and started to decline.

But the trend gradually reversed itself as baseball entered an unprecedented time of financial prosperity, and the commissioner's office took even more action, altering compensation for unsigned picks and free agents and trying to use an even heavier hand to enforce its bonus recommendations. Most significantly, beginning with the 2007 draft baseball finally had a signing deadline, meaning negotiations couldn't drag out for months.

All this was supposed to give leverage back to teams, but bonuses only went up more as teams scrambled to sign players by the deadline. And with no penalty for breaking MLB's slot recommendations, savvy teams realized that spending more in the draft gave them a leg up on competitors who were toeing the line.

So after years of talk about meaningful changes to the draft process, the astronomical bonus payments of the '00s finally made it a front-burner issue. Going into a new round of labor negotiations, Commissioner Bud Selig said legislated, mandatory bonus slots were a priority, as well as other changes to the draft such as expanding it to include international players.

That the changes will continue in coming years is inarguable. The most amazing feature of the baseball draft is that it has proven flexible enough to handle those changes over 45 years of use.

There have been January and June drafts, regular and secondary phases, American Legion drafts, supplemental picks, compensation picks, and everyone's favorite, the draft-and-follow process.

Through it all, the core purpose of the draft has remained: to bring new talent into baseball as cheaply and fairly as possible. The process has been bent and twisted over the years, but it has never broken.

It all began in 1964, with a complaint that has also stood the test of time: the Yankees and some of the game's wealthier clubs were outspending teams to sign players, and baseball executives were worried about competitive balance. The Yankees had won nine of the previous 10 American League pennants and other teams were spending wildly to try to keep up. The fledgling Los Angeles Angels opened owner Gene Autry's saddlebags that year and paid untested outfielder Rick Reichardt a record $205,000 bonus—at the time, more than the annual salary of most major leaguers.

The more money spent on amateur prospects, the less there was to prop up a sagging player-development system. Once vibrant and self-sustaining with 460 teams in 1949, the minor leagues were falling apart and began to depend on major league subsidization for survival.

Not coincidentally, 1964 was the year baseball instituted a much-debated, much-awaited draft of amateur players. It would begin in 1965 and became the way all but a few amateurs made their way into professional baseball.

And for many years it did its job—to hold down bonuses. No one (at least in 1964 dollars) approached the bonus Reichardt received until the 1990s. But as history shows us, teams can't help but look for any way to get an advantage over their competition.

In simpler times, players were happy just for the chance to play professional baseball and paid little attention to money. There was little competition among clubs for a player's services. World War II created shortages in many aspects of American life, including baseball talent. Competition drove the Tigers to sign outfielder Dick Wakefield for a bonus of $52,000. Suddenly, the rush was on.

Baseball also gained in popularity, resulting in more teams, more money and fierce competition for players. At the 1946 Winter Meetings, baseball made its first effort to curtail bonuses. An agreement between the two major leagues and the National Association (the governing body for the minor leagues) designated a bonus player as anyone signed to a contract that exceeded a fixed level. Teams were fined if they paid out an amount that exceeded an imposed limit.

For the next two decades, major league officials tried various other solutions to control spending and competition for talent. None worked.

Beginning in 1958, baseball tried a first-year rule that required teams to retain bonus babies on major league rosters in their first two full seasons, or expose them to waivers. But that didn't work either.

Bonuses continued to escalate. In 1957, the Milwaukee Braves spent a record $120,000 for power-hitting outfielder Dave Nicholson, then topped that record a few months later by handing $125,000 to shortstop Denis Menke.

In 1964, led by Reichardt's deal, teams paid more than $7 million to amateur players, more than was spent on major league salaries. Teams such as the Yankees and Dodgers were buying up much of the talent and were prospering.

All the other major team sports used a draft to distribute amateur talent. Football introduced the concept in 1936, basketball followed in 1947 and hockey adopted a draft in 1963. Baseball officials were reluctant to follow suit. Some said a draft would penalize the industrious teams and was a form of socialism. Others opposed the draft for legal reasons, arguing that it would restrict a player's bargaining power, which in turn could jeopardize baseball's antitrust exemption. Teams like the Dodgers and Yankees opposed it more for selfish reasons. Opponents, however, were in the minority.

Baseball adopted its draft at the 1964 Winter Meetings. It was to function in a manner similar to football and basketball. The baseball draft, however, introduced several notable differences. First, three drafts would be held each year instead of one: one in January, one in June and a third draft, limited to American Legion players, in late summer. The Legion phase lasted only one year and the winter session was phased out in 1986.

The new amateur draft, officially known as the Rule 4 draft, initially was open to residents of the United States only, with a focus on high school graduates and college players who were sophomores or age 21. By 1990, players from Canada, Puerto Rico and other U.S. territories had become subject to selection. Now a single annual draft in June features high school seniors, junior-college players and college juniors and seniors, with a few exceptions, such as sophomores who are 21.

A baseball clubs' negotiating rights lasted until 15 days before the next draft session, later amended to one week (and then moved to Aug. 15 with the establishment of the signing deadline in 2007). If a player didn't sign by the closed period, he went back into a

THE BONUS RECORD

Rick Monday, the No. 1 overall pick in baseball's first-ever draft in 1965, signed with the Athletics for $100,000—a bonus record that lasted for a decade. The mark has been broken much more frequently since, most recently with Nationals righthander Stephen Strasburg's $7.5 million bonus.

The figures below represent cash bonuses and don't include guaranteed money from major league contracts, college scholarship plans or incentives. They also don't factor in discount rates for bonuses spread over multiple years for two-sport athletes, such as Justin Upton. The list considers only players who signed with the clubs that drafted them and does not include the four loophole free agents from 1996. Among that group is former Devil Rays righthander Matt White, who established a bonus standard that still stands when he signed for $10.2 million.

Year	Player, Pos., Club (Round)	Bonus
1965	Rick Monday, of, Athletics (1)	$100,000
1975	Danny Goodwin, c, Angels (1)	$125,000
1978	Kirk Gibson, of, Tigers (1)	$150,000
	*Bob Horner, 3b, Braves (1)	$162,000
1979	Bill Bordley, lhp, Giants (1#)	$200,000
	Todd Demeter, 1b, Yankees (2)	$208,000
1988	Andy Benes, rhp, Padres (1)	$235,000
1989	Tyler Houston, c, Braves (1)	$241,500
	*Ben McDonald, rhp, Orioles (1)	$350,000
	*John Olerud, 1b, Blue Jays (3)	$575,000
1991	Mike Kelly, of, Braves (1)	$575,000
	Brien Taylor, lhp, Yankees (1)	$1,550,000
1994	Paul Wilson, rhp, Mets (1)	$1,550,000
	Josh Booty, 3b, Marlins (1)	$1,600,000
1996	Kris Benson, rhp, Pirates (1)	$2,000,000
1997	Rick Ankiel, lhp, Cardinals (2)	$2,500,000
	Matt Anderson, rhp, Tigers (1)	$2,505,000
1998	*J.D. Drew, of, Cardinals (1)	$3,000,000
	*Pat Burrell, 3b, Phillies (1)	$3,150,000
	Mark Mulder, lhp, Athletics (1)	$3,200,000
	Corey Patterson, of, Cubs (1)	$3,700,000
1999	Josh Hamilton, of, Devil Rays (1)	$3,960,000
2000	Joe Borchard, of, White Sox (1)	$5,300,000
2005	Justin Upton, ss, Diamondbacks (1)	$6,100,000
2008	Buster Posey, c, Giants (1)	$6,200,000
2009	Stephen Strasburg, rhp, Nationals (1)	$7,500,000

*Major league contract.

special secondary pool for the next draft. The secondary phase of the draft was eliminated in 1987.

One of the immediate benefits of a draft, most clubs agreed, would be an improved game at the major league level. No longer would clubs be forced to clutter their rosters with untested youngsters. In 1964, major league teams had been forced to protect 77 first-year players on their winter rosters.

While most of the emphasis in the early years of the draft was on raw high school talent, a gradual transition took place in the mid-1970s. College players became more and more attractive to scouts as college programs around the country took on a new commitment to fielding competitive teams.

In 1977, for the first time, more college players than high school players were selected, a trend that has never reversed itself.

No matter what the source of talent, the baseball draft remained an inexact science. Unlike in football and basketball, whose drafts deal with more finished products, the best players drafted in baseball, even the top college players, usually need to develop and refine their skills for several seasons in the minor leagues.

Astute drafting, though, has been a major factor for many successful franchises in the draft era. Since its inception, the draft has largely achieved its two underlying goals. Payments to amateur players were held down for a long time, while helping competitive balance.

It wasn't until the Tigers signed outfielder Kirk Gibson in 1978 and the Mets signed Darryl Strawberry two years later that players began to approach, in real dollars, the bonus Reichardt received. By then, inflation had reduced those figures to a fraction of Reichardt's windfall. As late as 1987, Seattle paid a mere $160,000 to sign Ken Griffey Jr., the first overall pick.

It was only in 1988 and 1989—when Baltimore signed No. 1 overall pick Ben McDonald to an $800,000 major league contract that provided for a $350,000 bonus, and Toronto later went to $575,000 for first baseman John Olerud—that players regularly topped the $200,000 barrier. By then, teams had enough money that spending lavishly on amateurs wasn't considered as dangerous as it was in 1964.

In the early 1990s, however, the money in baseball took a quantum leap. Not only were major league players starting to get multimillion-dollar contracts, but bonus payments to draft picks also went off the board.

Atlanta refused to select Texas high school pitcher Todd Van Poppel with the first selection in 1990 because he said he was going to college at Texas—but as a practical matter because of his bonus demands.

Oakland swooped in and drafted Van Poppel 14th overall. He signed a record $1.2 million major league contract that provided for a $500,000 bonus.

A year later, the Yankees stunned the baseball world by signing pitcher Brien Taylor to a $1.55 million bonus—more than double the previous record. Average bonus payments to first-round picks took off. In 1994, with a strike looming, No. 1 pick Paul Wilson tied Taylor's record bonus by signing with the Mets for $1.55 million. Within weeks, that record was broken when the Marlins coughed up $1.6 million to sign shortstop Josh Booty.

Booty's record bonus held up until 1996, when four players found a draft loophole that made them free agents, able to offer their services to all 30 major league clubs. They ended up signing contracts worth a total of nearly $30 million. The No. 1 pick, righthander Kris Benson, became a mere footnote as he signed with the Pirates for $2 million.

After that, teams closed the draft loophole and took a more cautious approach to drafting. Signability became a major factor. Beginning in 1997, first-round picks often reached contract agreements before the draft, a technically illegal but widespread tactic. Other players were passed over because their asking price was deemed too steep.

Still, bonus records continued to get broken. Talented Florida high school lefthander Rick Ankiel—selected 72nd overall by the Cardinals because of his signability—cut a deal for $2.5 million in '97, followed by No. 1 pick Matt Anderson signing with the Tigers for $2.505 million deal.

Agent Scott Boras, who helped negotiate many of the record deals, said the developments of 1996 proved conclusively that a draft system artificially stunts bonuses. And in outfielder J.D. Drew he had a player who was willing to go to the limit to test the system. Drew was the consensus top player in the 1997 draft and was selected second overall by Philadelphia. He set his price at $10 million before the draft and told every club not to draft him unless it was prepared to pay that amount. The Phillies took him anyway and negotiations went nowhere. Drew signed a contract with St. Paul of the independent Northern League and played the summer there.

Drew filed two grievances to try to become a free agent. Both failed, and he was simply thrown back into the pool, eligible again for selection. He went with the fifth pick overall, where he was selected by the Cardinals—and signed quickly to a major league contract with a $3 million signing bonus and potential total value to $8.5 million. The Phillies then signed No. 1 pick Pat Burrell to a major league deal with a $3.15 million bonus and guarantees that brought the total value to $8 million.

One important factor that the Burrell and Drew contracts introduced into other players' negotiations in 1998 was the major league contract that allowed payments to be spread over several years. Teams also exploited a rule that allowed them to spread payments to two-sport athletes (a rule very liberally applied) over five years, reducing their up-front cost.

Records fell again in 1999, as No. 1 pick Josh Hamilton signed with the Devil Rays for $3.96 million. The White Sox followed in 2000 by signing outfielder Joe Borchard to a $5.3 million bonus, in a year when other teams actually made progress in starting to hold the line on bonuses.

A rare crop of talent in 2001 drove prices up again, led by college standouts Mark Prior and Mark Teixeira. Both signed major league deals: Prior with the Cubs for a potential value of $10.5 million, Teixeira with the Rangers for a potential value of $9.5 million.

At the same time, baseball was taking action to slow down bonuses. Sandy Alderson, who took over as MLB's executive vice president of baseball operations in 1998, spearheaded the effort. MLB held a negotiating seminar for teams before the 2000 draft, the first time it had given teams unified direction in how to approach the process. Over the next few years, MLB recommended bonuses for each draft slot, and by 2002, bonuses actually went down for the first time since Baseball America had started tracking them in the 1980s.

But teams couldn't resist competing with each other. Bonuses slowly started climbing up again, and then when teams realized they could benefit by going over MLB's slot recommendations to get premium talent, the system started to fall apart.

Borchard's bonus record actually held up for five years, until high school shortstop Justin Upton signed with the Diamondbacks for a $6.1 million bonus as the No. 1 pick in the 2005 draft. That record fell in 2008, when Florida State catcher Buster Posey signed with the Giants for a $6.2 million bonus.

At the same time, teams were handing out major league contracts with more frequency—another way to circumvent the slotting process—and giving huge bonuses to players beyond the first round.

And then came Stephen Strasburg. Regarded as a once-in-a-generation talent, he was the No. 1 overall pick in the 2009 draft. The Nationals reached a deal with him just before the signing deadline, giving him a $7.5 million bonus as part of a $15.1 million major league deal. And he was just the highlight of a draft that showed teams spending wildly to bring in talent, with all 30 signing at least one player for more than MLB's slot recommendation for the first time.

For some people, Strasburg was a Reichardt for a new generation, the symbol of a system that no longer worked. As it always has, the rules will evolve, and the draft will survive.

1965 ATHLETICS KICK OFF FIRST-EVER DRAFT WITH OUTFIELDER MONDAY, AS TALENT FALLS TO LATER ROUNDS

Most major league teams didn't know what to expect from baseball's first amateur draft, but the Kansas City A's went in prepared. The A's had the first pick because they finished last in the American League the previous year.

"We don't want to pat ourselves on the back, but we did study the system," said Hank Peters, then the A's assistant general manager. "I think we organized ourselves well. I remember clubs talked to us about it after the draft, asking how we did it."

The A's used the initial selection, to no one's surprise, on 19-year-old Arizona State outfielder Rick Monday. It had been speculated for days that Monday would be the first choice.

"Every now and then a player comes along who's head and shoulders above the crowd," Peters said. "We really didn't have much trouble selecting him. We zeroed in on him pretty early. We had Art Lilly, one of our top scouts at the time, following him. It was a case where we didn't have to argue the merits of three or four players."

At a time when college sophomores were eligible for the draft and freshmen ineligible to play varsity sports, Monday hit .359 with 11 homers in his only season at Arizona State. Four days after his selection, with A's owner Charles O. Finley in the stands, Monday led the Sun Devils to their first College World Series championship. He homered as ASU beat Ohio State, 2-1.

On June 15, Finley flew to Monday's Santa Monica, Calif., home and signed Monday to a $104,000 bonus contract, an amount that was little more than half what Rick Reichardt earned from the Los Angeles Angels a year earlier when competitive bidding for players was allowed.

Led by Monday, Kansas City had an excellent draft, claiming 10 players who would play in the big leagues. The list included third baseman Sal Bando, Monday's Arizona State teammate who was the Most Outstanding Player of the College World Series. ASU (54-8), the first college team to win 50 games in a season, had more draft selections (eight) than any other college.

The New York Mets, picking second, went for lefthander Les Rohr, a Billings, Mont., high school product. Rohr won just two big league games, although the Mets would gain a measure of redemption in their draft efforts with the selection nine rounds later of Nolan Ryan.

Two of the next three picks were Boston high school products, both with intriguing backgrounds. Righthander Joe Coleman Jr., whose father won 52 major league games from 1942-55, was claimed by the Washington Senators with the third pick overall. A $75,000 signee, he would be in the big leagues by September.

Nolan Ryan, a 10th-round steal for the Mets, found greater fame with other teams

The Red Sox went for outfielder Billy Conigliaro, brother of emerging star Tony. Boston officials badly wanted the younger Conigliaro and expressed elation when they were able to get him with the fifth pick. The signed him two days after the draft for a reported $60,000 bonus.

Two players from the first round went unsigned. Minnesota, selecting ninth and offering less than $20,000, failed to come to terms with 18-year-old Arizona shortstop Eddie Leon. It would be two more years before Leon, who became a three-time all-American at Arizona, would sign a contract. The Twins also didn't sign their second-round pick, Mississippi State outfielder Del Unser.

Meanwhile, Philadelphia failed to sign its first pick, pitcher Mike Adamson, a San Diego high school product who went to Southern California when the Phillies wouldn't cough up a $100,000 bonus. Adamson, who went just 6-6 as a high school senior, would later go directly to the big leagues, when drafted by Baltimore in 1967.

Ken Plesha, a 19-year-old sophomore who was academically ineligible to play at Notre Dame in the spring of 1965, became the first drafted player to sign a contract. The 17th selection overall, Plesha came to terms with the White Sox for a reported $25,000 just hours after being selected.

College Players Overlooked

There was much predraft speculation among officials gathered at New York's Commodore Hotel about who would be the top picks in baseball's first draft. Monday and Rohr were a consensus 1-2, but there was a wide range of opinion after that.

An indication of what a crapshoot the first draft was came when such talents as Ryan, Tom Seaver and Carlton Fisk weren't even among the first 150 players drafted. Johnny Bench lasted until the second round.

Some of the top-rated talent in the first draft also went in later rounds because of questions about signability.

Steve Arlin, an Ohio State sophomore, merited first-round consideration. He led the nation with a 13-2 record and 165 strikeouts in 141 innings and beat Washington State, 1-0, while striking out 20 in 15 innings, in a classic College World Series contest. But he was a straight-A student in dentistry at Ohio State, which caused teams to pass on him until Detroit in the 12th round. He signed a year later with Philadelphia for a bonus in excess of $100,000.

The Dodgers gambled a second-round pick on righthander Alan Foster, the son of a wealthy Beverly Hills doctor. The gamble paid off, even though it cost the Dodgers $100,000—second only to the bonus Monday received. Foster reached the big leagues by 1967.

The Dodgers missed out on another righthander from their own backyard, however, in Seaver, who would win 263 more games than Foster. The Dodgers selected Seaver in the eighth round, but he chose to return to Southern California—even though he never pitched another game for the Trojans. Seaver became entwined in a draft controversy the next year and eventually wound up with the Mets.

Bill Dobbs, a high school lefthander from Oklahoma City who was drafted in the fifth round by the White Sox, also proved to be an elusive sign. Over the next five years, Dobbs would be drafted six more times out of Oklahoma State. He never did sign.

In addition to the regular June draft, a special American Legion draft was held Aug. 24 for Legion players who completed summer play and became eligible for selection for the first time. Players were ineligible for selection in June if they had yet to reach age 17 and had Legion eligibility remaining. Just 11 players were selected in the Legion phase. Robert Yodice, 16, a catcher from Brooklyn, N.Y., was the first pick in the Legion phase. He signed quickly with the Mets for $17,000.

A proposal went before major league general managers in October to abolish the Legion draft and incorporate it with the regular June draft. It was rejected, but a year later, after just eight players were selected, the Legion draft was phased out.

DRAFT 65: FIRST-ROUND PICKS

No.	Club	Player, Pos.	School	Hometown	Ht.	Wt.	B-T	Age
1.	Athletics	Rick Monday, of	Arizona State	Santa Monica, Calif.	6-2	190	L-L	19
2.	Mets	Les Rohr, lhp	West HS	Billings, Mont.	6-5	200	L-L	19
3.	Senators	Joe Coleman, rhp	Natick HS	Natick, Mass.	6-3	165	R-R	18
4.	Astros	Alex Barrett, ss	Atwater HS	Winton, Calif.	6-0	175	R-R	18
5.	Red Sox	Billy Conigliaro, of	Swampscott HS	Swampscott, Mass.	6-0	175	R-R	17
6.	Cubs	Rick James, rhp	Coffee HS	Florence, Ala.	6-2	200	R-R	17
7.	Indians	Ray Fosse, c	Marion HS	Marion, Ill.	6-3	210	R-R	18
8.	Dodgers	John Wyatt, ss	Bakersfield HS	Bakersfield, Calif.	6-2	200	L-R	17
9.	Twins	*Eddie Leon, ss	Arizona	Tucson, Ariz.	5-11	165	R-R	18
10.	Pirates	Doug Dickerson, of	Ensley HS	Birmingham, Ala.	6-1	178	L-L	17
11.	Angels	Jim Spencer, 1b	Andover HS	Glen Burnie, Md.	6-2	190	L-L	18
12.	Braves	Dick Grant, 1b	Watertown HS	Watertown, Mass.	6-4	205	L-L	18
13.	Tigers	Gene Lamont, c	Hiawatha HS	Kirkland, Ill.	6-1	180	L-R	18
14.	Giants	Al Gallagher, 3b	Santa Clara	Daly City, Calif.	6-0	180	R-R	19
15.	Orioles	Scott McDonald, rhp	Marquette HS	Yakima, Wash.	6-1	195	R-R	18
16.	Reds	Bernie Carbo, 3b	Livonia HS	Garden City, Mich.	5-11	170	L-R	17
17.	White Sox	Ken Plesha, c	Notre Dame	McCook, Ill.	5-11	185	R-R	19
18.	Phillies	*Mike Adamson, rhp	Point Loma HS	San Diego	6-2	175	R-R	17
19.	Yankees	Bill Burbach, rhp	Wahlert HS	Dickeyville, Wis.	6-4	205	R-R	17
20.	Cardinals	Joe DiFabio, rhp	Delta State	Cranford, N.J.	5-11	195	R-R	21

*Did not sign.

1965

CLUB-BY-CLUB SELECTIONS

BALTIMORE ORIOLES

June—Regular Phase

Major League and Class AAA Selections (15)

1. **Scott McDonald, rhp, Marquette HS, Yakima, Wash.**
2. **Richard Horton, c, Dartmouth**
3. **Frank Tepedino, 1b, Wingate HS, Brooklyn, N.Y.**

Class AA Selections (18)

4. **Ken Purvis, of, Nelson County HS, Lovingston, Va.**
5. James Taylor, 3b/of, Southern Methodist
6. **Bill Dillman, rhp, Wake Forest**
7. Frank Chambers, rhp, Mississippi State

Class A Selections

8th Round

8. **Don Roth, of, Spring Arbor (Mich.)**
9. **Dave Halford, ss, Plainfield HS, Hancock, Wis.**
10. Gordon Weir, c, Brigham Young
11. Tom Chiles, rhp, Texas A&M

9th Round

12. Tom Lawton, rhp, Connecticut
13. Bob Schaefer, ss, Connecticut
14. Ronnie Paul, lhp, Texas Christian

10th Round

15. **Quash Thompson, rhp, Jones HS, Orlando, Fla.**
16. Jimmy Carter, ss/3b, Trinity (Texas)
17. Dick Hicks, rhp, Fair Park HS, Shreveport, La.
18. **Will Beauchemin, rhp, Holy Spirit HS, Point Pleasant, N.J.**

11th Round

19. Dave Grangaard, 3b, Camelback HS, Phoenix
20. **Harry Brown, lhp, Baltimore City HS, Baltimore**
21. **Charlie Sands, c, Newport News (Va.) HS**

12th Round

22. **John Rawls, rhp, East Carolina**
23. Lowell Palmer, rhp, Norte Del Rio HS, Sacramento, Calif.
24. **Brent Vines, rhp, Mound City (Ill.) HS**
25. John McCall, ss, Clemson

13th Round

26. Dennis Lamb, 3b, Brigham Young
27. Ron Lanza, of, Maine
28. Frank Antone, rhp, Lawton HS, Fort Sill, Okla.

14th Round

29. **Cliff Matthew, c, North Carolina A&T**
30. **Dave Coleman, c, Northeastern**
31. Steve Garman, ss, Caldwell (Idaho) HS
32. Leroy McDonald, ss, Las Cruces (N.M.) HS

15th Round

33. Allie Prescott, p, Kingsbury HS, Memphis, Tenn.
34. **Robert Jones, ss, Grambling**
35. Ray Frank, of, Southern

16th Round

36. Mike Burns, of, Mississippi State
37. **Dan DeVito, 1b, Stamford (Conn.) HS**
38. Larry Linville, of, Bellingham (Wash.) HS
39. **Stanley Bowen, of/1b, Knox City HS, Novelity, Mo.**

17th Round

40. **Dennis Denning, c/3b, St. Thomas (Minn.)**
41. Henry Tenney, ss/of, Vista (Calif.) HS
42. James Brown, lhp, Englewood (Colo.) HS

18th Round

43. **Mike Hebert, lhp, Terrebonny HS, Thibodeaux, La**
44. Leonard Sheflott, rhp, Vermont
45. **Charles Van Camp, 1b, Minot (N.D.) State**
46. Dale Ehler, c, Oregon

19th Round

47. **Bill Grimes, rhp, Northwest Classen HS, Oklahoma City.**
48. Carlton Fisk, c, New Hampshire
49. Greg Riddoch, ss, Colorado State
50. Jim Wendell, of, La Habra (Calif.) HS

20th Round

51. Percy Sensabaugh, rhp, Virginia Military Institute
52. Bob Malloy, rhp, Shenandoah (Va.) JC
53. Charles Drediger, rhp, Bordentown (N.J.) Military Academy
54. **John Stephens, of, Loyola (La.)**

21st Round

55. **Rich Thoms, lhp, Austin (Texas) CC**
56. Wayne Britton, of, East Carolina
57. Steve Lough, of, Patapsco HS, Baltimore
58. Glen Wallace, rhp, Butler HS, Florence, Ala.

22nd Round

59. Steve Andragia, of, Notre Dame HS, Bridgeport, Conn.
60. **Gary Carnegie, 3b/of, Connelly HS, Pittsburgh**
61. Dale Dulaney, rhp, Chicago Teachers College
62. Gary Smith, rhp, Alpena (Mich.) CC

23rd Round

63. John Rockwell, rhp, Santa Ana (Calif.) HS
64. Paul Knight, lhp, Avon Lake HS, Lorain, Ohio
65. Michael Kenyon, lhp, Ithaca
66. Roger Hansen, lhp, Muskegon (Mich.) HS

24th Round

67. Ed Southard, of, Arizona
68. **Carl Cmejrek, 1b/of, Michigan**
69. Tom Moeller, 2b, Denver
70. George Gazegorek, ss, St. Edwards (Texas)

August—Legion Phase (16)

No selection

BOSTON RED SOX

June—Regular Phase

Major League and Class AAA Selections (5)

1. **Billy Conigliaro, of, Swampscott (Mass.) HS**
2. John Hetrick, of, Hershey (Pa.) HS
3. **Ken Poulsen, 3b, Birmingham HS, Van Nuys, Calif.**

Class AA Selections (15)

4. **Fred Marden, lhp, Brandeis**
5. **Amos Otis, ss, Williamson HS, Mobile, Ala.**
6. **Jim L. Thomas, lhp, Cal State Sacramento**
7. **Jim Hutto, 3b/rhp, Pensacola (Fla.) HS**

Class A Selections

8th Round

8. **Doug Shores, c, Northeast HS, Greensboro, N.C.**
9. Ron Shotts, 3b, Chaffey HS, Ontario, Calif.
10. **Tony Ciarpelli, lhp, Genessee HS, Syracuse, N.Y.**

9th Round

11. Dennis Best, of, Gillepsie (Ill.) HS
12. Manuel Washington, ss, Paragould (Ark.) HS
13. Michael Weber, rhp, Greenville HS, Pocohontas, Ill.

10th Round

14. **Wayne Fuzzard, lhp, McCarthy HS, Fort Pierce, Fla.**
15. **Bill Farmer, rhp, Choctaw (Okla.) HS**
16. Reid Braden, 1b, Cerritos (Calif.) JC

11th Round

17. **Brian Edgerly, of, Colgate**
18. **Ray Jarvis, rhp, Hope HS, Providence, R.I.**
19. **John Iannelli, rhp, East Boston (Mass.) HS**

12th Round

20. **William Barkley, ss, Sam Houston State**

August—Legion Phase (6)

1. Mike McCall, ss, Greenville (S.C.) HS

CALIFORNIA ANGELS

June—Regular Phase

Major League and Class AAA Selections (11)

1. **Jim Spencer, 1b, Andover HS, Glen Burnie, Md.**
2. Sandy Vance, rhp, Pasadena (Calif.) HS
3. Dick Baney, rhp, Anaheim (Calif.) HS

Class AA Selections (7)

4. **John Olerud, c, Washington State**
5. **Joe Henderson, 3b/rhp, Edison HS, Fresno, Calif.**
6. **Clyde Wright, of/lhp, Carson-Newman (Tenn.)**
7. **Marty Pattin, rhp, Eastern Illinois**

Class A Selections

8th Round

8. **Tom Soderstrom, ss, Lexington (Mass.) HS**
9. Craig Schell, rhp, Monterey (Calif.) HS

9th Round

10. Bob Crosby, rhp, Monroe HS, Bronx, N.Y.
11. **Gus Gregory, of, Illinois**

10th Round

12. Gary Wormelduff, rhp, Sunset HS, Hayward, Calif.
13. Jack Glover, lhp, Banks HS, Birmingham

11th Round

14. **John Enos, ss, Millikan HS, Lakewood, Calif.**
15. **Sam Gafford, lhp, South HS, Bakersfield, Calif.**

12th Round

16. **Jarvis Tatum, of, Edison HS, Fresno, Calif.**
17. **Bob Smithson, rhp, Everett (Wash.) CC**

13th Round

18. **Terry Thompson, 3b/rhp, Newport Harbor HS, Newport Beach, Calif.**
19. **George Dugan, lhp, Murray State**

14th Round

20. **Richard Totten, 2b, Coachella HS, Thermal, Calif.**
21. **Doug Griffin, 2b, El Monte HS, La Puente, Calif.**

August—Legion Phase (12)

No selection

CHICAGO CUBS

June—Regular Phase

Major League and Class AAA Selections (6)

1. **Rick James, rhp, Coffee HS, Florence, Ala.**
2. **Ken Rudolph, c, Los Angeles CC**
3. **Greg Werdick, ss, Crawford HS, San Diego**

Class AA Selections (1)

4. **Ken Holtzman, lhp, Illinois**
5. **Ronald Webb, of, Hillcrest HS, Springfield, Mo.**
6. Ron Drake, c, Long Beach (Calif.) CC
7. **Garry Jestadt, ss, Fremont HS, Sunnyvale, Calif.**

Class A Selections

8th Round

8. **Richard Johnson, rhp, Mount San Antonio (Calif.) JC**
9. **Joe Decker, rhp, Petaluma (Calif.) HS**
10. **Duane Rossman, ss, Washington State**

9th Round

11. Tom House, lhp, Nogales HS, La Puente, Calif.
12. **David Amman, rhp, Cocoa Beach (Fla.) HS**

10th Round

13. Darrell Evans, 3b, Muir HS, Altadena, Calif.
14. John Thomas, of, Morehouse HS, Bastrop, La.
15. **Henry Knittel, rhp, Holy Cross**

11th Round

16. **Johnny Hairston, c, Southern**
17. **Craig Glassco, rhp, Glendora (Calif.) HS**

12th Round

18. Robert Rossi, 2b/3b, Loyola (Md.)
19. **John Burnett, 1b, Skyline HS, Oakland**
20. **Jim Williams, of, Harry Ells HS, Richmond, Calif.**

13th Round

21. **Joseph Doerr, 3b, West Liberty State (W.Va.)**
22. Robert Beran, of, Bishop Amat HS, Rosemead, Calif.

14th Round

23. Lamar LaBauve, 1b, Southeastern Louisiana
24. **Thomas Finnegan, ss, Washington (Pa.)**
25. **Lawrence Lobb, lhp, Bangor (Pa.) HS**

15th Round

26. Steve Wright, rhp, Andrew Hill HS, San Jose, Calif.
27. **Nathaniel Perkins, ss, Benedict (S.C.)**

16th Round

28. **John Hermanek, rhp, Bradley**
29. John Bacot, of, Alabama A&M (Selection voided)
30. **Ronald Renner, c, West Virginia**

August—Legion Phase (5)

No selection

CHICAGO WHITE SOX

June—Regular Phase

Major League and Class AAA Selections (17)

1. **Ken Plesha, c, Notre Dame**
2. **Fred Kovner, of, Old Dominion**
3. **Mickey Abarbanel, lhp, Monmouth**

Class AA Selections (20)

4. **Fred Rath, rhp, Baylor**
5. Bill Dobbs, lhp, Marshall HS, Oklahoma City
6. **Emmett Molisee, of, Western HS, Las Vegas**
7. Allan Smith, lhp, Manual HS, Peoria, Ill.

Class A Selections

8th Round

8. **Ron Markowski, of/ss, Central Catholic HS, Pittsburgh**
9. **Richard Newhart, ss, San Clemente HS, San Juan Capistrano, Calif.**
10. **Ron Lolich, 3b/of, Central Catholic HS, Portland, Ore.**

9th Round

11. **John Sluka, 2b, Western Michigan**
12. **Robert Bladek, lhp, Rich East HS, Matteson, Ill.**
13. **Greg Howell, c, Austin Catholic HS, Detroit**

10th Round

14. Richard Noffke, rhp, Boylan HS, Rockford, Ill.
15. John Montague, rhp, Newport HS, Newport News, Va.
16. Richard Slicker, lhp, Edison HS, Tulsa, Okla.

11th Round

17. Clifford Foster, 1b, Sexton HS, Lansing, Mich.
18. Jimmie Carroll, 2b, Georgia Tech
19. Dave Barton, inf, Ithaca (N.Y.)

12th Round

20. Ronald Davini, c, Anaheim (Calif.) HS
21. **Paul Edmondson, rhp, Cal State Northridge**
22. Dewey Weaver, rhp, Pasco HS, Dade City, Fla.

13th Round

23. **Thomas Cottrell, of/3b, Cal State Northridge**
24. Bob Hergenrader, lhp, Nebraska

25. Robert Karlblom, of, Augustana (S.D.)

14th Round

26. **Lawrence Lembo, of/1b, Manhattan**
27. Elvatous Peters, of, Southern
28. Jim Hogan, rhp, Redlands (Calif.)

15th Round

29. **Robert Chandler, rhp/of, Wilson HS, Easton, Pa.**
30. **Jim Ackley, rhp, Hayward (Wis.) HS**
31. **Danny Lazar, lhp, Indiana State**

16th Round

32. John Miklos, lhp, Valparaiso
33. Pete Ciganovich, rhp, Bowen HS, Chicago
34. **Paul Lovrich, rhp, Eisenhauer HS, Blue Island, Ill.**

17th Round

35. Joe Bloom, lhp, Notre Dame HS, North Hollywood, Calif.
36. **Leland White, lhp, Hueneme HS, Oxnard, Calif.**
37. Michael White, c, Costa Mesa (Calif.) HS

18th Round

38. Robert Lawler, lhp, Manatee (Fla.) JC
39. **Timothy McLain, rhp, Bremen HS, Chicago**
40. Joe Holliday, ss, Duncan (Okla.) HS

19th Round

41. **Ken Eby, 3b, Purdue**

August—Legion Phase (18)

No selection

CINCINNATI REDS

June—Regular Phase

Major League and Class AAA Selections (16)

1. **Bernie Carbo, 3b, Livonia HS, Garden City, Mich.**
2. **Johnny Bench, c, Anadarko HS, Binger, Okla.**
3. John Olagues, rhp, Tulane

Class AA Selections (17)

4. **Carl Richardson, ss, Taft HS, Cincinnati**
5. **Louis Keller, c, Oconomowoc (Wis.) HS**
6. **Hal McRae, ss, Florida A&M**
7. **Lester Fulleylove, lhp, Edgewood HS, Atco, N.J.**

Class A Selections @

8th Round

8. John Morlan, of, West HS, Columbus, Ohio
9. **Tom Murphy, ss, Lufkin (Texas) HS**

9th Round

10. **Mike Tyler, c, El Camino HS, San Francisco**
11. James Scheschuk, c, Texas
12. Arthur Boyd, rhp, Escambia HS, Pensacola, Fla.

10th Round

13. Patrick Brown, of, Permian HS, Odessa, Texas
14. **Jerry Baker, rhp, Elgin (Ill.) CC**

11th Round

15. **Joseph Barnes, lhp, Pfeiffer (N.C.)**
16. **Norman Singleton, c, Grandview (Iowa) JC**
17. **Tom Ford, of, Fair Park HS, Shreveport, La.**

12th Round

18. Oscar Brown, of, Poly HS, Long Beach, Calif.
19. Charles Kline, lhp, Western Michigan

13th Round

20. Bill Frost, rhp, California
21. **George Nichols, rhp, Parker HS, Birmingham**
22. **Alan Baur, c, Christian Brothers HS, Memphis, Tenn**

14th Round

23. Ron Rowell, of, Central HS, Tulsa, Okla.
24. **Larry Holly, rhp, Northeast HS, St. Petersburg, Fla.**

15th Round

25. **Glen Flake, rhp, Assumption HS, East St. Louis, Ill.**
26. Paul Reuschel, rhp, Central HS, Camp Point, Ill.
27. Ken Williams, c, East Lansing (Mich.) HS

16th Round

28. **Lynn Coleman, of, Potosi (Mo.) HS**
29. **Carlton Barnes, ss, East Carolina**

17th Round

30. Vic Prather, of, Rogers HS, Tulsa, Okla.
31. **Harlan Hinds, of, Odessa (Texas) JC**
32. Larry McWherter, of, El Camino (Calif.) JC

August—Legion Phase (15)

No selection

CLEVELAND INDIANS

June—Regular Phase

Major League and Class AAA Selections (7)

1. **Ray Fosse, c, Marion (Ill.) HS**
2. **John Sandknop, ss/2b, Knox County HS, Edina, Mo.**
3. **Ronald Constantino, rhp, Monson (Mass.) HS**

Class AA Selections (9)

4. **William Perry, of, Palatka (Fla.) HS**
5. Fred Kampf, rhp, Shore Regional HS, Monmouth Beach, N.J.
6. Phillip ONeil, lhp/1b, St. Peters HS, Worcester, Mass.
7. **John Fouse, of/rhp, Arizona**

Class A Selections

8th Round

8. **Ron Arnold, rhp, Northwestern State**
9. **Vic Albury, 1b/lhp, Key West (Fla.) HS**

9th Round

10. Greg Washburn, rhp, Coal City (Ill.) HS
11. Lou Pieserb, lhp, Brother Rice HS, Chicago

10th Round

12. Ronnie Matney, of, Duncan (Okla.) HS
13. Dave Flettrich, ss, Tulane

11th Round

14. Frank Favia, c/of, West Leyden HS, Franklin Park, Ill.
15. **Harold Joyce, of, Kaimuki HS, Honolulu**

12th Round

16. James Baker, of, McKinley HS, Columbus, Ohio (Selection voided)
17. James Goodwin, rhp, Southwest HS, Miami

13th Round

18. Frank Borgia, ss/3b, Central HS, Scranton, Pa.
19. Fred Kos, 1b, Northeastern

14th Round

20. **James Renfro, rhp, Red Bank HS, Chattanooga, Tenn.**
21. Kenneth Suzawa, lhp, Baldwin HS, Kahului, Hawaii

15th Round

22. Tom Lundgren, lhp, Forest View HS, Rolling Meadows, Ill.
23. Charles Bottom, ss, Lincoln (Ill.) JC

16th Round

24. Tom Schweitzer, lhp, Fairmont State (W.Va.) (Selection voided)
25. Howard Arndt, rhp, Republic (Mo.) HS

17th Round

26. Harold Burke, rhp/of, Parsippany (N.J.) HS
27. Ray DeRiggi, lhp/of, Vailsburg HS, Newark, N.J. (Selection voided)

18th Round

28. Thomas Lomack, of, Lincoln HS, Tallahassee, Fla.
29. Dennis Malseed, rhp/3b, St. James HS, Woodlyn, Pa.

19th Round

30. Mark Devitt, c, Dartmouth (Mass.) HS
31. Harry McCarthy, of, Huntington (W.Va.) HS

20th Round

32. Eugene Sidor, c, Nassau (N.Y.) CC

33. Frank Spaziani, rhp, Clark (N.J.) Regional HS

21st Round

34. Larry Hansen, of/3b, Jefferson HS, Portland, Ore.

August—Legion Phase (8)

1. Daniel Ford, of, Hamden (Conn.) HS
2. Donald Melville, lhp, Saegertown (Pa.) HS
3. Joel McMasters, rhp, Bay HS, Lake City, Ark.

DETROIT TIGERS

June—Regular Phase

Major League and Class AAA Selections (13)

1. **Gene Lamont, c, Hiawatha HS, Kirkland, Ill.**
2. Doug Carson, ss, Bishop Armstrong HS, Sacramento, Calif.
3. Andy Messersmith, rhp, California

Class AA Selections (11)

4. Bob Reed, rhp, Michigan
5. **Thomas White, 3b, Dorman HS, Spartanburg, S.C**
6. **Dennis Grossini, lhp, Lompoc (Calif.) HS**
7. William Bradley, ss, Palestine (Texas) HS

Class A Selections

8th Round

8. **David Bike, c, Notre Dame HS, Bridgeport, Conn.**
9. James Young, lhp, Cherry Hill HS, Inkster, Mich.
10. **Gary Taylor, rhp, Central Michigan**

9th Round

11. **Ronald Kirk, of/inf, Bloomsburg**
12. Kris Krebs, ss, Dykes HS, Atlanta
13. Dennis Deptula, inf, Michigan
14. Vince Bigone, 3b/of, St. Ignatius HS, San Francisco

10th Round

15. **Nick Ross, rhp, Divine Child HS, Inkster, Mich.**
16. Kenneth Hall, lhp, Nassau (N.Y.) CC
17. **Shelburn Morton, rhp, Oak Grove HS, Paragould, Ark.**

11th Round

18. **Neil Branch, inf, Thomas Jefferson HS, Elizabeth, N.J.**
19. Thomas Kelly, of, Holy Cross
20. **Thomas Hamm, of, Georgetown**
21. **Darrell Hollar, inf/of, Lima (Ohio) Senior HS**

12th Round

22. Rick Austin, lhp, Lakes HS, Tacoma, Wash.
23. Steve Arlin, rhp, Ohio State
24. Arnie Chonko, 1b, Ohio State

13th Round

25. **Robert Felber, inf, CC of Baltimore**
26. Danny Talbott, 1b/of, North Carolina
27. Joe Hauptman, c, Granite City (Ill.) HS
28. Ray Peters, rhp, Nickols HS, Buffalo, N.Y.

14th Round

29. **Milton Bender, inf, Northern HS, Detroit**
30. Terry Ley, lhp, Madison HS, Portland, Ore.
31. Neil Pittman, rhp, Park View HS, Springfield, Mo.

15th Round

32. Edward Staron, of, Western Michigan
33. Martin Brown, rhp, Edison HS, Tulsa, Okla.
34. Harold White, rhp, Rutgers
35. Tom Brown, ss, Juniper (Fla.) HS

16th Round

36. Steve Kokor, rhp, Alta Loma (Calif.) HS
37. **Bill Butler, lhp, Herndon (Va.) HS**
38. Robert Yodice, c, Lafayette HS, Brooklyn, N.Y. (Selection voided)

17th Round

39. **John Huizenga, c, Western Michigan**
40. Craig Bozich, of, Aurora Central HS, Denver
41. **Steve Vanderlip, rhp, West Ottawa HS, Holland, Mich.**
42. **Vic Sorrell, ss, North Carolina State**

18th Round

43. Robert Bixler, rhp, Miami (Ohio)
44. **Ralph Foytack, rhp, Moscow (Pa.) HS**

August—Legion Phase (14)

No selection

HOUSTON ASTROS

June—Regular Phase

Major League and Class AAA Selections (4)

1. **Alex Barrett, ss, Atwater HS, Winton, Calif.**
2. **Keith Lampard, of, Oregon**
3. **Jim Monin, ss, Kentucky**

Class AA Selections (16)

4. Pat Jacquez, rhp, Stagg HS, Stockton, Calif.
5. Billy Martin, of/inf, Colonial Heights (Va.) HS
6. **David Fyfe, rhp, Hillsborough HS, Tampa**
7. **Ken Chelini, lhp, Galileo HS, San Francisco**

Class A Selections

8th Round

8. Dan Rudanovich, of, Missouri
9. **Larry Hall, of, Centreville HS, Church Hill, Md.**
10. **Danny Walton, of, Bishop Amat HS, La Puente, Calif.**

9th Round

11. Gary Gentry, rhp, Phoenix (Ariz.) JC
12. **Carl Ergenzinger, c/3b, Dover (Del.) HS**
13. **Jerry Causey, 1b, Denver**

10th Round

14. **Richard Perini, rhp, Fresno State**
15. Bill Seinsoth, 1b/lhp, Arcadia (Calif.) HS
16. Bill Tsoukalas, lhp, Lincoln HS, Seattle

11th Round

17. Jay Armstrong, ss, Arizona State
18. Tom Murphy, rhp, Ohio
19. John Hurst, of, Live Oak (Fla.) HS

12th Round

20. J.B. Jackson, 1b, Roxton HS, Honey Grove, Texas
21. **Dave Anderson, 3b, Western Michigan**
22. **Joseph Vari, 3b/c, William Penn HS, New Castle, Del.**

13th Round

23. **John Francis, c, Bakersfield (Calif.) JC**
24. Joseph Borowy, rhp, Baltimore
25. Buzz Stephen, rhp, Fresno State

14th Round

26. Rusty Adkins, 1b, Clemson
27. Michael Willis, lhp, Alameda HS, Denver
28. Steve Barrett, of, Artesia (N.M.) HS

15th Round

29. Gary Hughes, rhp, Monterrey HS, Lubbock, Texas
30. Paul Suchow, rhp, York HS, Elmhurst, Ill.
31. Berry Cohen, rhp, Senn HS, Chicago

16th Round

32. Pascal Renn, rhp, Wake Forest
33. **Eugene Garritt, of, Delaware**
34. Robert Yingling, ss/2b, St. Joseph HS, West New York, N.J.

17th Round

35. **Ralph Barrier, rhp/1b, Hillsdale (Va.) HS**
36. Jerry DaVanon, of, San Diego Mesa JC
37. **Louis McKown, lhp, Wichita Falls (Texas) HS**

18th Round

38. **Stephen Molberg, 1b, Pampa (Texas) HS**
39. Paul Alderete, of, Los Angeles Pierce JC
40. Doug Parsons, c, Bishop Armstrong HS, Sacramento, Calif. (Selection voided)

19th Round

41. **Wayne Miller, ss, Lambuth (Tenn.)**

42. **Don Sessions, c, Colorado**
43. Gary Butcher, rhp, Los Angeles Harbor JC

20th Round

44. Arthur Gainous, 1b, Moore HS, Waco, Texas
45. **Edward Earlywine, 2b, New Mexico**
46. Mel Behney, lhp, Verona (N.J.) HS

21st Round

47. **Jack Goings, 3b, White Haven HS, Memphis, Tenn.**
48. Patrick Kendig, rhp, South Hunterdon HS, Ringoes, N.J.
49. **Harry Mohr, 3b, Colorado**

22nd Round

50. **Robert Grzymala, lhp, St. Mary's HS, East Northport, N.Y.**
51. **Alfred Pettes, of, Las Cruces (N.M.) HS**
52. Scott Long, ss, Auburn

23rd Round

53. **Henry Boykin, 1b/rhp, Phillips (Texas) HS**
54. Lionel Jones, of, Southern
55. **Gary Fields, inf, Northeast Louisiana**

24th Round

56. Rich Nye, lhp, California
57. Richard Bechtel, ss, Rider
58. Jerry Day, c, Midwest City (Okla.) HS

25th Round

59. Roy Myers, of, Overton HS, Memphis, Tenn.
60. Jon Ives, rhp, Berner HS, Massapequa, N.Y.
61. Jan Adelman, of, Mississippi

26th Round

62. Jimmy Harris, ss, Wilmington (N.C.) JC
63. **John Vignone, of, Susquehanna (Pa.)**
64. **Joe Entiero, c, St. Gabriel HS, Hazelton, Pa.**

27th Round

65. Glen Borkhuis, of, Syracuse (Selection voided)
66. Mario Gillio, c, Don Bosco HS, East Paterson, N.J.
67. Dale Fincher, c, Waxahachie (Texas) HS

28th Round

68. **Otis Thornton, c/rhp, Westfield HS, Docena, Ala.**
69. Jerry Borga, 3b/c, Easton (Md.) HS
70. **Ralph Gonzales, c, Atwater (Calif.) HS**

29th Round

71. Richard Licini, 1b/of, Iona Prep HS, Eastchester, N.Y.
72. **Reginald Thomas, of, Los Angeles**

August—Legion Phase (3)

No selection

KANSAS CITY ATHLETICS

June—Regular Phase

Major League and Class AAA Selections (1)

1. **Rick Monday, of, Arizona State**
2. **Joe Keough, 1b, Mount San Antonio (Calif.) JC**
3. Bob Stinson, of, Miami HS

Class AA Selections (19)

4. **Peter Koegel, of/1b, Seaford (N.Y.) HS**
5. **Richard Suggs, ss, Hart HS, Saugus, Calif.**
6. **Sal Bando, 3b, Arizona State**
7. Scott Reid, of, Cerritos (Calif.) JC

Class A Selections

8th Round

8. Frank Riggins, of/p, Centralia (Kan.) HS
9. Don Lando, of, Ithaca (N.Y.)
10. **George Lauzerique, rhp, George Washington HS, New York**
11. **John Dunn, rhp, Bryant HS, Woodside, N.Y.**

9th Round

12. **Donald Weeks, rhp, Minor HS, Adamsville, Ala.**
13. Terry L'Ange, rhp, Missouri
14. **Craig Gambs, 1b, Richmond (Calif.) HS**
15. **Bob Brooks, of, Los Angeles Harbor JC**

10th Round

16. John Thomas, lhp, Westmont (Calif.)
17. **Donald Arp, rhp, Berry (Ga.)**
18. **Larry Vlasin, 2b/ss, Madrid (Neb.) HS**
19. Jerry Burgess, c, North Tonawanda (N.Y.) HS

11th Round

20. **Gene Tenace, ss, Valley HS, Lucasville, Ohio**
21. **James Buker, rhp, Weymouth (Mass.) HS**
22. **Mike Strode, 2b, Missouri**
23. Troy Garey, ss, Bullard HS, Fresno, Calif.

12th Round

24. **Hugh Britton, 3b, Virginia**
25. Brandt Jackson, c, Buena HS, Ventura, Calif.
26. **James Blakeney, c, William Carey (Miss.)**
27. Stephen Nelson, rhp, Natick HS, Braintree, Mass.

13th Round

28. Greg Garrett, lhp, Hart HS, Newhall, Calif.
29. Darryl Hester, lhp, Byng HS, Ada, Okla.
30. **James Gibney, rhp, Susquehanna (Pa.)**
31. Roger Jackson, rhp, North Kansas City (Mo.) HS

14th Round

32. Jackie Creel, rhp, Phillips HS, Birmingham
33. Peter Middlekauff, 1b, Stanford
34. Bob Biletnikoff, of, Miami
35. Gary Shephard, of, Duffy HS, Niagara Falls, N.Y.

15th Round

36. Ronald Pietila, ss, Sweetwater Union HS, National City, Calif.
37. Mike Koritko, ss, Notre Dame HS, Stratford, Conn.
38. Charles Casey, rhp, Florida
39. **David Sellers, rhp, Independence, Mo.**

16th Round

40. Jeff Herter, rhp, Kansas City
41. **John Fleischaur, c/of, Ventura, Calif.**
42. **Victor Majewski, rhp, Villanova**
43. **Gene Barisano, ss, Ben Franklin HS, New York**

17th Round

44. Gary Avery, of, Fremont HS, Los Angeles
45. **James Watts, ss, Howard**
46. Ron Gorey, rhp/of, San Clemente (Calif.) HS
47. Ronnie Hillman, lhp, Ada (Okla.) HS

18th Round

48. **John Budnick, rhp, Bound Brook (N.J.) HS**

August—Legion Phase (2)

1. Ray DeRiggi, lhp/of, Vailsburg HS, Newark, N.J

LOS ANGELES DODGERS

June—Regular Phase

Major League and Class AAA Selections (8)

1. **John Wyatt, ss, Bakersfield (Calif.) HS**
2. **Alan Foster, rhp, Los Altos HS, Hacienda Heights, Calif.**
3. **Mike Criscione, c, Syracuse**

Class AA Selections (10)

4. **George Mercado, of, Bishop Dubois HS, New York**
5. **John Radosevich, lhp, West Virginia**
6. Peter Barnes, of, Southern
7. **Gary Griffith, rhp, Anadarko (Okla.) HS**

Class A Selections

8th Round

8. **James Johnson, of, Las Vegas HS**
9. Paul Dennenbaum, 1b, Syracuse
10. Tom Seaver, rhp, Southern California

9th Round

11. **Joe Austin, 1b, Southern California**
12. Richard Binder, lhp, Waterloo (Ill.) HS

13. Terrance Derringer, rhp, Southwest HS, Miami

10th Round

14. **Stephen McGreevy, 1b/of, Kansas**
15. **Leon Everitt, rhp, Pemberton HS, Marshall, Texas**
16. Mike McCall, ss, Greenville (S.C.) HS (Selection voided)

11th Round

17. Johnny Alexander, inf, Whitmire (S.C.) HS
18. Rod Austin, of, Santa Clara
19. George Lewark, ss, Colorado

12th Round

20. William Maxwell, rhp, Central HS, Tulsa, Okla.
21. Daro Quiring, rhp, Stanford
22. Eric Krumlauf, 3b, Shaker Heights (Ohio) HS

13th Round

23. Rich Hinton, lhp, Marana (Ariz.) HS
24. **Fred Moulder, ss, Oklahoma State**
25. John Keirns, of, Edmond (Okla.) HS

14th Round

26. **Robert Harvey, 3b, Marshall HS, Oklahoma City**
27. **Rhett Thompson, 3b, Del Mar HS, San Jose, Calif.**
28. **Gary Moore, of, Texas**

15th Round

29. **Kyle Carlin, rhp, Sulphur (La.) HS**
30. **Dennis Jensen, ss, Jacksonville**

August—Legion Phase (7)

1. Barry Snyder, c, Little Rock, Ark. (Selection voided)
2. Frank Stanek, 1b, Omaha, Neb. (Selection voided)

MILWAUKEE BRAVES

June—Regular Phase

Major League and Class AAA Selections (12)

1. **Dick Grant, 1b, Watertown (Mass.) HS**
2. **Don Johnson, c, Southern California**
3. **Douglas King, of, Northeastern HS, Manchester, Pa.**

Class AA Selections (4)

4. **Charles Vaughn, lhp, Brownsville (Texas) HS**
5. **William Bates, rhp, Washington (Pa.)**
6. **Wayne Garrett, ss, Sarasota (Fla.) HS**
7. **Steve Godfrey, ss, Stonewall, Okla.**

Class A Selections

8th Round

8. **Jeff Albies, 2b, Long Island**
9. **Albert Thompson, of, Narbonne HS, Harbor City, Calif.**

9th Round

10. **Thomas Randecker, rhp, Lock Haven, Pa.**
11. **Nick Van Lue, 1b, Carson HS, Wilmington, Calif.**

10th Round

12. Craig Scoggins, of, Cerritos (Calif.) JC
13. **Bobby Christensen, ss, Cal State Northridge**

11th Round

14. Earl Lombardo, inf/of, Rider
15. **Ted Bashore, 1b, UCLA**

12th Round

16. Kenneth Lohnes, c, Mayfair HS, Lakewood, Calif.
17. **David Lobb, rhp, Pacelli HS, Austin, Minn.**

13th Round

18. John Respondek, rhp, Yorktown, Texas
19. Daniel Hootstein, of, Harvard

14th Round

20. John Noriega, rhp, Utah
21. Ken Tatum, rhp, Mississippi State

15th Round

22. **Monte Sharp, lhp, Auburn**
23. **Douglas H. King, of, Connecticut**

16th Round

24. George Girard, lhp, Marblehead (Mass.) HS
25. Peter Lentine, 1b/p, Birmingham HS, Encino, Calif.

17th Round

26. **Darryl Wilkins, 2b/ss, Southern California**
27. William Ferguson, c, Ray HS, Corpus Christi, Texas

18th Round

28. Jerry Foglia, rhp, Woodbridge (N.J.) HS
29. **Richard Small, of, Long Island**

19th Round

30. Steve Wrenn, 1b, Wake Forest
31. William Craig, rhp, Williamson (W.Va.) HS

20th Round

32. John Reynolds, c, Grosse Pointe (Mich.) HS
33. Bill Zepp, rhp, Michigan

21st Round

34. Richard Schaffer, c/3b, Birmingham HS, Encino, Calif.
35. **Joe Beck, 1b, Kansas State**

22nd Round

36. James McFarland, rhp, North Platte, Neb.
37. **Daniel Waraksa, 2b/ss, Seton Hall**

23rd Round

38. Duffy Dyer, c/of, Arizona State
39. Dan Frisella, rhp, Washington State

24th Round

40. Glen Wallace, rhp, Butler HS, Florence, Ala. (Selection voided)

August—Legion Phase (11)

1. **Earl Williams, rhp, Montclair (N.J.) HS**
2. William Speaks, 1b, Newark (Ohio) HS

MINNESOTA TWINS

June—Regular Phase

Major League and Class AAA Selections (9)

1. Eddie Leon, ss, Arizona
2. Del Unser, of, Mississippi State
3. John Dow, of, Bemidji (Minn.) HS

Class AA Selections (14)

4. **Graig Nettles, 3b, San Diego State**
5. **Neil McPhee, ss, Northeastern**
6. **Terry Graham, 1b, Carson City (Nev.) HS**
7. **Mickey Johnston, c, Drewry Mason HS, Ridgeway, Va.**

Class A Selections

8th Round

8. **Ron Keller, rhp, Indiana**
9. William Drummond, rhp, Buena Vista (Iowa)
10. **Johnnie Johnson, c, Americus (Ga.) HS**
11. **John Healy, rhp, Lane Tech HS, Chicago**
12. Tom Burgess, rhp, Phoenix JC

9th Round

13. Jack Palmer, lhp, Cretin HS, St. Paul, Minn.
14. Kenneth Holt, lhp, Campbell HS, Brookneal, Va.
15. Paul Coleman, rhp, Cal Poly Pomona
16. John Herbst, lhp, Southern California
17. **Alan Nordberg, rhp/of, Massachusetts**

10th Round

18. James Vopicka, ss, Illinois
19. Fred Mazurek, of, Pittsburgh
20. Ronald Van Dyke, rhp, Hilltop HS, Chula Vista, Calif.
21. **Louis Smith, 3b, Cal Poly Pomona**
22. **Gary Finch, lhp, Memorial HS, Eau Claire, Wis.**

11th Round

23. Carl Merrill, c, Maine
24. **Joseph Racer, c, Madison HS, Aroda, Va.**
25. Steven Waters, c, Whittier (Calif.)
26. **Jim Mack, lhp, Cicero (Ill) HS**

27. Randy Humphrey, lhp, Carson HS, Torrance, Calif.

12th Round

28. **Bill Ferrell, rhp, Tennessee**
29. Steve Kokor, rhp/of, Baseline HS, Alta Loma, Calif. (Selection voided)
30. **Alvin Hazewinkle, rhp, Eau Claire HS, Columbia, S.C.**
31. **Paul Mankowski, 2b, Buffalo (N.Y.) HS**
32. **Joe Romary, 2b/ss, Wisconsin**

13th Round

33. **Walter Harrison, rhp, Male HS, Louisville**
34. **Craig MacKay, 2b, Utah**
35. John Tartera, 1b, Vermont
36. Joseph Braithwaite, 1b, Atlantic City (N.J.) HS
37. **Bill Gray, of, Arkansas**

14th Round

38. Frank Brosseau, rhp/of, Minnesota
39. **Bob Purkhiser, rhp, Purdue**
40. **Conrad Bradison, ss, Memorial HS, Eau Claire, Wis.**
41. **Doug Dobrei, 1b/lhp, Michigan State**
42. **Jim Duffy, of, Westmont (Ill.) HS**

15th Round

43. **Jerome Cawley, 3b, Minnesota**
44. **Bob Gebhard, rhp, Iowa**
45. Walter Manuel, ss, Lafayette
46. **Jerry Gleisner, rhp, Cathedral HS, New Ulm, Minn.**
47. Gary Bodak, of/1b, Sayreville (N.J.) HS

16th Round

48. **Luis Lagunas, 2b, Arizona State**
49. Rick Manning, 2b, Holy Cross
50. **Larry Deaton, rhp, Edgewater HS, Orlando**
51. **Aubrey Clore, rhp, Madison (Va.) HS**
52. **Robert Rommes, rhp, Mabel (Minn.) HS**

August—Legion Phase (10)

No selection

NEW YORK METS

June—Regular Phase

Major League and Class AAA Selections (2)

1. **Les Rohr, lhp, West HS, Billings, Mont.**
2. **Randy Kohn, c, Greenville (S.C.) HS**
3. **Joe Moock, ss, Louisiana State**

Class AA Selections (6)

4. **Ken Boswell, 2b, Sam Houston State**
5. Doug Britelle, rhp, Massapequa (N.Y.) HS
6. **Harold Roberson, rhp, Central Michigan**
7. **Mike McClure, 3b/ss, Texas A&M**

Class A Selections

8th Round

8. **Roger Harrington, rhp, Fremont HS, Sunnyvale, Calif.**
9. **Louis Williams, c, Patterson HS, Baltimore**

9th Round

10. Roger Stevens, of, Pasadena (Calif.) CC.
11. **Jim McAndrew, rhp, Iowa**

10th Round

12. **Nolan Ryan, rhp, Alvin (Texas) HS**
13. **Dave Hayes, 2b/of, Balboa HS, San Francisco**

11th Round

14. **Gary Burnett, c, East Central (Okla.) JC**
15. **Jack Stroud, lhp, Missouri**

12th Round

16. Wayne Drier, of, Billings (Mont.) HS
17. John Ferguson, rhp, Union HS, DeSoto, Ga.

13th Round

18. **Carl Nicholsen, 2b, Columbia Basin (Wash.) CC**
19. Kenneth Brownell, lhp, Watsonville (Calif.) HS

14th Round

20. Herbert Hofvendahl, of, Miramonte HS, Orinda, Calif.
21. **Kenneth Williamson, of/1b, Orange (Va.) HS**

15th Round

22. John Sauerbier, rhp, Christman HS, Independence, Mo.
23. Al Thomas, of, Narbonne HS, Torrance, Calif. (Selection voided)

16th Round

24. **Steve Renko, 1b/rhp, Kansas**
25. **Gerald Bark, lhp, Maryland**

17th Round

26. Jim Hibbs, c, Stanford
27. **Wayne Burdette, inf, Bowling Green State**

18th Round

28. **Jim Nichols, rhp, Arizona**
29. John Green, rhp/1b, Jones Valley HS, Birmingham

19th Round

30. **Tom Garrett, ss, Lincoln HS, San Diego**
31. James Moore, rhp, Homer (La.) HS

20th Round

32. **Frank Pickens, of, Washburn (Kan.)**
33. Rudolph Luehs, 1b, Lincoln HS, San Francisco

21st Round

34. Michael Carty, of, Downey (Calif.) HS
35. **Don Shaw, lhp, San Diego State**

22nd Round

36. Ron Kyner, of, Arvin (Calif.) HS
37. Dave Aldrich, rhp, Mount Diablo HS, Concord, Calif.

23rd Round

38. **Ray Stadler, c, Arizona State**
39. James Lawson, ss, Antioch (Calif.) HS

24th Round

40. **James Dix, of, Saint Louis**
41. Malcolm Petty, rhp, Tennessee

25th Round

42. **Andrew Shea, 2b, St. Helena HS, Bronx, N.Y.**
43. Jerry Boehmer, 3b, Saint Louis

26th Round

44. **Joe Campbell, of, Morehead State**
45. Toby Frymire, c, Penn State

27th Round

46. **Gary Strom, rhp, San Jose State**
47. **Barry Raziano, rhp/of, East Jefferson HS, Kenner, La.**

28th Round

48. Ron Delplanche, 3b, Oregon
49. Robert Oliver, lhp, Texas

29th Round

50. Mike Welton, c, Billings (Mont.) HS
51. **Antonio Liberti, c, Adams HS, Ozone Park, N.Y.**

30th Round

52. Alexander MacLean, of, Horton Watkins HS, Ladue, Mo.

August—Legion Phase (1)

1. **Robert Yodice, c, Lafayette HS, Brooklyn, N.Y.**
2. **Ed Johnson, of, New Dorp HS, Staten Island, N.Y.**

NEW YORK YANKEES

June—Regular Phase

Major League and Class AAA Selections (19)

1. **Bill Burbach, rhp, Wahlert HS, Dickeyville, Wis.**
2. Danny Thompson, ss, Capren (Okla) HS
3. Dennis Baldridge, of, Oregon

Class AA Selections (8)

4. **Stan Bahnsen, rhp, Nebraska**
5. **Louis Howell, c, Kentucky Wesleyan**
6. John Hurley, rhp, Port Richmond HS, Staten Island, N.Y.

7. Darcy Fast, lhp, North Thurston HS, Olympia, Wash.

Class A Selections

8th Round

8. Scott Lund, rhp, West HS, Davenport, Iowa
9. **Gary Girouard, rhp, Nebraska-Omaha**
10. **Fred Dawson, of, Henderson State (Ark.)**

9th Round

11. **James Alvey, of/1b, Leitchfield (Ky.) HS**
12. Donald Alley, c, Adams State (Colo.)
13. **Robert Hall, 3b, Villanova**

10th Round

14. **Dwain Davidson, 3b, Mountain Home (Ark.) HS**
15. Steve Mezich, c, Seattle
16. **Morton Zenor, 1b/of, Lawton (Iowa) HS**

11th Round

17. **Mickey Scott, lhp, Newburg (N.Y.) Free Academy**
18. **Kerby Compton, lhp, Pittsburg State (Kan.)**
19. **Larry Shawn, rhp, Owensboro (Ky.) HS**

12th Round

20. **Richard Ruggles, 2b, Kansas**
21. Clifton Sisco, of, College HS, Bartlesville, Okla.
22. **James Bidwell, rhp, Holy Cross**

13th Round

23. Bert Gramly, rhp, San Angelo (Texas) JC
24. **James Eubanks, lhp, Arkansas AM&N**
25. **James Rees, of, Southern California**

14th Round

26. Steve Rudanovich, of, Utah
27. Harry Wright, of, Cheshire Academy, Great Neck, N.Y.
28. **George Blaum, 1b, Bellport (N.Y.) HS**

15th Round

29. **Lewis Lawson, 3b, Tech HS, Terre Haute, Ind.**
30. **Jim Fink, rhp, Richmond (Calif.) HS**
31. **Tommy Porter, of, The Citadel**

16th Round

32. Jeff Burns, c, Plattsburg (N.Y.) HS
33. **Paul Bruinsma, 2b, Sioux Center (Iowa) HS**
34. **Tom Shopay, of, Dean (Mass.) JC**

17th Round

35. James N. Smith, rhp, Denmark (S.C.) HS
36. Terry Childers, c, Richmond Academy, Augusta, Ga.
37. Terry Harrison, rhp, Pendleton (Ore.) HS

18th Round

38. Dennis Trame, rhp, Quincy (Mass.)
39. Neil Weber, rhp, Appleton (Wis.) HS
40. Dick Such, rhp, Elon

August—Legion Phase (20)

No selection

PHILADELPHIA PHILLIES

June—Regular Phase

Major League and Class AAA Selections (18)

1. Mike Adamson, rhp, Point Loma HS, San Diego
2. **Larry Hisle, of, Portsmouth (Ohio) HS**
3. **Billy Champion, rhp, Shelby (N.C.) HS**

Class AA Selections (5)

4. **John Parker, rhp, Davie County HS, Cooleemee, N.C.**
5. **Terry Harmon, ss, Ohio**
6. Bob Chlupsa, rhp, Manhattan
7. Stephen Sharp, rhp, Washington HS, Kansas City, Kan.

Class A Selections

8th Round

8. **Del Wilber, ss, Purdue**
9. Orville Hollrah, rhp, Missouri
10. Ken Szotkiewicz, 2b, Salesianum HS, Wilmington, Del.
11. **Thomas Capowski, ss, Fordham**
12. Donald Cook, rhp, Long Island

9th Round

13. Dick Mills, rhp, Parsons College
14. **Richard Trolliet, rhp, Wisconsin State Teachers College**
15. **Thomas Chapman, lhp, Clemson**
16. **Gordon Knutson, lhp, Glendale, Calif.**
17. **Gilbert Barnett, 2b, California (Pa.)**

10th Round

18. Edward Cott, c, Nichols HS, Buffalo, N.Y.
19. **Dan Crothers, of, Jackson (Ohio) HS**
20. **Terry Craven, of, Cal State Northridge**
21. James Cain, 3b, Madison Central HS, Waco, Ky.
22. **Charles Brown, of, Brown HS, Atlanta**

11th Round

23. Jan Fait, of, New Philadelphia (Ohio) HS
24. **Lloyd Ennis, 1b, Wicomico HS, Salisbury, Md.**
25. **Michael Mathias, rhp, Hunter (N.Y.)**
26. **George Fowlkes, rhp, Cal Poly Pomona**
27. Len Zandy, p/1b, Fordham

12th Round

28. Charles Shreve, rhp, Cathedral Prep HS, Erie, Pa.
29. **Don Novick, of, New York**
30. **Terry Ricketts, rhp, Hillsdale (Mich.) HS**
31. **Ken Huebner, of, Florida Southern**
32. Dale Blazure, of, North Hunterdon HS, Pottersville, N.J.

13th Round

33. **Lavis York, 1b, West Georgia**

August—Legion Phase (17)

1. No selection
2. **Ricky Fuller, c, Hoover HS, Fresno, Calif.**

PITTSBURGH PIRATES

June—Regular Phase

Major League and Class AAA Selections (10)

1. **Doug Dickerson, of, Ensley HS, Birmingham**
2. **Roger Hayward, rhp, Pontiac (Mich.) North HS**
3. **Richard Hendrix, rhp, Princeton HS, Cincinnati**

Class AA Selections (2)

4. **Edward Berube, 3b, Colby (Maine)**
5. **Robert Settle, rhp, Wilson HS, Portsmouth, Va**
6. **Ronald Young, lhp, Canton (Ohio) South HS**
7. Stephen Schneider, ss, Minnesota

Class A Selections

8. Terry Thompson, 1b, Sunset HS, Beaverton, Ore.
9. **Larry Killingsworth, rhp, Jordan HS, Long Beach**
10. Kerry Dean, rhp, Mansfield (Ohio) HS

9th Round

11. **Zelman Jack, of, Pittsburg (Calif.) HS**
12. **Douglas Watkins, lhp, Bloomsburg HS, Cheverly, Md.**
13. **Jack Clark, of, St. Charles (Mo.) HS**

10th Round

14. **Terry Sparks, rhp, Minford (Ohio) HS**
15. **Irvin Melton, rhp, Aulander (N.C.) HS**
16. **Paul Giglio, of, Flushing HS, Whitestone, N.Y.**

11th Round

17. **Sam Angott, inf/rhp, Ohio**
18. **Bob Moose, rhp, Franklin Area HS, Export, Pa.**
19. Bob Shannon, of, Natchez, Miss.

12th Round

20. **Gene Garber, rhp, Elizabethtown (Pa.) HS**
21. Jophrey Brown, rhp, Grambling
22. **Fred Patek, ss, Seguin, Texas**

13th Round

23. **Ralph Custer, rhp, Madison HS, Vienna, Va.**
24. **Virgil Bentley, of, Washington (Ohio) HS**

25. **Roger Banze, rhp, Hall HS, St. Louis**

14th Round

26. Tom Dettore, rhp, McMillan HS, Canonsburg, Pa.
27. Alan Putz, 3b, Rockville (Conn.) HS
28. **David Tolley, 3b/c, Grove City (Pa.)**

15th Round

29. Gregory Chlan, p, Westfield (N.J.) HS
30. **Lou Marone, lhp, San Diego Mesa JC**
31. **Jim Nelson, rhp, Burbank HS, Sacramento, Calif.**

16th Round

32. **Benny Grove, inf, Frederick (Md.) HS**
33. **Robert Roadarmel, rhp, Florida Southern**
34. Mike Nickels, lhp, Pulaski HS, Milwaukee

17th Round

35. **David Warmbrod, rhp, Jackson, Tenn.**
36. **Gregory Marotz, rhp, Colgate**
37. Glen Borkhuis, rhp, Syracuse

18th Round

38. **Rich Jackson, rhp, Rockhurst (Mo.)**
39. Berke Reichenbach, 3b, Ohio
40. **Dennis Pierce, lhp, Conserega HS, Swain, N.Y.**

19th Round

41. Mike Garrett, of, Southern California

August—Legion Phase (9)

No selection

ST. LOUIS CARDINALS

June—Regular Phase

Major League and Class AAA Selections (20)

1. **Joe DiFabio, rhp, Delta State (Miss.)**
2. **Terry Milani, 1b, Lewis (Ill.)**
3. **Billy Wolff, of, Cincinnati**

Class AA Selections (13)

4. **Harry Parker, rhp, Collinsville (Ill.) HS**
5. **Jerome Pruett, of/rhp, Lehman HS, Canton, Ohio**
6. Frank Portera, c, Mississippi State
7. Dave Renkiewicz, of, Mt. Carmel HS, Wyandotte, Mich.

Class A Selections

8th Round

8. **Mike Hensley, 3b, Del City (Okla.) HS**
9. **Theodore Friel, rhp, Dartmouth**
10. **Fred Van Iten, c, Dubuque (Iowa)**

9th Round

10. **Fred Brigham, ss, Wyoming**
11. William Close, rhp, St. Mary's HS, Waltham, Mass.
12. **C.A. McGowan, rhp, Memphis State**

10th Round

13. **Michael Davis, ss, Galesburg (Ill.) HS**
14. Ray Henningsen, 2b, Santa Clara
15. **Louis Fiore, rhp, Glendale (Calif.) HS**

11th Round

16. **Edward Tivis, 3b, Kansas City, Mo.**
17. Bruce Hinkel, rhp, Mar-Mack HS, McGregor, Iowa
18. Jay Schloemer, lhp, Lincoln (Ill.) JC

12th Round

19. **Jack Singer, of, Princeton**
20. Eugene Breinig, rhp, Merced (Calif.) HS
21. Dan McGinn, lhp, Notre Dame

13th Round

22. James Townsend, ss, Shasta Union HS, Redding, Calif.
23. Robert Bender, 1b, Goodlettsville, Tenn.
24. Mike Kistner, lhp, Jackson (Mo.) HS

14th Round

25. Robert Carlson, rhp, American International (Mass.)
26. **Ron Jancek, lhp, Weber State**
27. **Jerry Robertson, rhp, Washburn (Kan.)**

15th Round

28. Duane Freemon, 1b, Utah
29. Bobby Smith, 3b, Bacone (Okla.) JC
30. William Carino, c, Revere (Mass.) Immaculate HS

16th Round

31. John Frye, of/3b, Manatee (Fla.) JC
32. **Joe Gegg, c, Saint Louis**
33. Mel Workman, rhp, Moweaqua (Ill.) HS

17th Round

34. Robert Gustafson, of, Rollins (Fla.)
35. William Lierman, rhp, Granite City, Ill.
36. Ronald Masterson, rhp, Soddy (Tenn.) HS

18th Round

37. **Robert Cox, of, Stanford**
38. Isaac Barnes, c, North Chattanooga (Tenn.) HS
39. Rich Hacker, ss, New Athens (Ill.) HS

19th Round

40. Richard Devarney, ss, Maine
41. Peter Hamm, rhp, Soquel (Calif.) HS
42. William Ray, 2b, Lee HS, Brownsboro, Ala.

20th Round

43. **John Olander, of/c, Cal State Sacramento**
44. **Jesse Cleveland, of, Alabama State**
45. David Hanbury, 1b, Oswego (N.Y.) HS

21st Round

46. **James Gretta, 1b/of, Arizona State**
47. Raymond Glinsky, rhp, Akron
48. John Pierce, rhp, Bacone (Okla.) JC

22nd Round

49. Trenton Jackson, of, Illinois
50. Archie Roberts, ss/3b, Columbia
51. Sanford Marks, rhp, Beverly Hills (Calif.) HS

23rd Round

52. **Robert Schanze, 3b, Fresno State**
53. **Marlyn Baum, rhp, Luther (Iowa)**
54. Tommy Thompson, ss/3b, El Cajon (Calif.) HS

24th Round

55. **John Sipin, ss, Watsonville (Calif.) HS**
56. **Ernie DeFilippis, of, Long Island**
57. William Monroe, lhp, Napa, Calif.

25th Round

58. Dale Ford, 1b/of, Washington State
59. **Michael Thompson, c, Texas**
60. Paul DeLoca, rhp, St. Francis (N.Y.)

August—Legion Phase (19)

1. No selection
2. **Robert Sankey, ss, Phillipsburg (Pa.) HS**

SAN FRANCISCO GIANTS

June—Regular Phase

Major League and Class AAA Selections (14)

1. **Alan Gallagher, 3b, Santa Clara**
2. Glen Smith, of, Arizona State
3. **Ken Fila, lhp, Archbishop Ryan HS, Omaha**

Class AA Selections (12)

4. **Hal Jeffcoat, rhp/of, Robinson HS, Tampa**
5. **Rich Robertson, rhp, Santa Clara**
6. **John Marsden, 3b/of, West Torrance (Calif.) HS**
7. **Douglas McMillan, rhp, Santa Monica HS, Malibu, Calif.**

Class A Selections

8th Round

8. **John Matthews, rhp, Reading (Pa.) HS**
9. Richard Hardiman, c, Mortimer Jordan HS, Warrior, Ala.
10. Dick White, 1b/of, South Torrance HS, Torrance, Calif.

9th Round

11. **Chris Arnold, ss, Arcadia (Calif.) HS**
12. Michael Smith, of, Whitehaven HS, Memphis, Tenn.
13. **Seth Marty, c, Sierra HS, Whittier, Calif.**

10th Round

14. **Howard Martin, of, Santa Clara**
15. Albert Strane, ss, St. Elizabeth HS, East Oakland, Calif.
16. Jon Baker, rhp, Sunset HS, Portland, Ore.

11th Round

17. **Jay Reed, of, Washington Union HS, Easton, Calif.**
18. Gary Ford, lhp, Bullis Prep HS, Walnut Creek, Calif.
19. **John Guthrie, of/inf, Alhambra HS, Phoenix**

12th Round

20. **Larry Tolliver, rhp, Bakersfield (Calif.) JC**
21. **Noel Finley, 2b, Roosevelt HS, Fresno, Calif.**
22. **Ron Bryant, lhp, Davis (Calif.) HS**

13th Round

23. **Val Bush, of, Eastern Illinois**
24. Alan Diamond, c, California
25. John Biedenbach, inf/of, Michigan State

14th Round

26. **Joe Pollack, rhp, Minnesota**
27. Mike Perkins, ss, Dorsey HS, Los Angeles
28. Gene Vidoni, c, Eastern Illinois

15th Round

29. James Jordan, 2b, Ouachita Baptist (Ark.)
30. Richard Kwasny, lhp, La Canada (Calif.) HS
31. **Mike Hutson, c, Reedley (Calif.)**

16th Round

32. **Ralph Durgin, rhp, Rancho HS, North Las Vegas, Nev.**
33. **Al Deravin, of, Sierra HS, Torrance, Calif.**
34. **Mike Zink, 1b/c, Wilson HS, Tacoma, Wash.**

17th Round

35. Richard Roberts, lhp, Southwest HS, St. Louis
36. Alvin Strane, 2b, St. Elizabeth HS, East Oakland, Calif.
37. Mark Schaeffer, lhp, Cleveland HS, Los Angeles (Selection voided)

18th Round

38. **Joe Madden, rhp, Iowa**
39. **Ron Grossmiller, inf, Phoenix JC**
40. **Windy Currie, 1b/of, Olympia HS, Columbia, S.C.**

August—Legion Phase (13)

No selection

WASHINGTON SENATORS

June—Regular Phase

Major League and Class AAA Selections (3)

1. **Joe Coleman, rhp, Natick (Mass.) HS**
2. Stanley Bell, rhp, Headland HS, College Park, Ga.
3. **Gene Martin, of, Dougherty HS, Albany, Ga.**

Class AA Selections (3)

4. Richard Zank, lhp, Neillsville (Wis.) HS
5. Arthur Pauls, rhp, St. Rita HS, Chicago
6. **John Taylor, ss, Alleghany HS, Clifton Forge, Va.**
7. **Fred Jacobs, 2b, Carleton (Minn.)**

Class A Selections

8th Round

8. **Edward Lupton, lhp, Notre Dame**
9. Garry Hill, rhp, Garinger HS, Charlotte, N.C.

9th Round

10. Dennis McKernan, of, Kutztown (Pa.)
11. **Richard Hense, of, Wisconsin**

10th Round

12. Richard Koslick, ss, Bishop Egan HS, Levittown, Pa.
13. Gil Torres, of, Morris HS, New York (Selection voided)

11th Round

14. **John Cashman, rhp, St. Joseph's**
15. **Tom Ragland, ss, North HS, Detroit**

12th Round

16. **Gary Dameron, ss, Battle Creek (Mich.) HS**
17. Dick Tidrow, rhp, Mt. Eden (Calif.) HS

13th Round

18. **Bill Gogolewski, rhp, Oshkosh (Wis.) HS**
19. **Richard Drew, c, North HS, Detroit**

14th Round

20. Kenneth Jones, rhp, Forrest HS, Jacksonville, Fla.
21. **Ronald Rosenow, ss, Bonduel HS, Shawano, Wis.**

15th Round

22. Thomas Cook, rhp/c, Sarasota (Fla.) HS
23. Richard Jones, rhp, Valparaiso

16th Round

24. Larry Price, lhp, Racine HS, Portland, Ohio
25. **Dick Billings, of, Michigan State**

August—Legion Phase (4)

No selection

1966 Mets put need first in taking Chilcott first overall, leaving Jackson for Kansas City

Eleven years after the Mets took catcher Steve Chilcott with the No. 1 pick in the 1966 draft, Reggie Jackson vividly reminded the Mets of their great mistake.

Playing for the crosstown rival Yankees, Jackson hit the pinnacle of his illustrious career by slamming three home runs in Game Six of the 1977 World Series to power the Yankees to the first of consecutive titles. Across town the Mets were left wondering what could have been. They had a chance to take Jackson in the 1966 draft, but went instead for Chilcott in one of the most disastrous decisions of the draft era.

As Jackson celebrated his ultimate glory, Chilcott had been out of baseball for five years, having never played a single game in the big leagues. Jackson, picked second, went on to become one of the most colorful and accomplished players in baseball history. He set records for draft-era players for games (2,820) and home runs (563), and played on five World Series champions in the 1970s.

Chilcott and Jackson were rated dead even on the eve of the 1966 draft. They were the consensus top two players on almost every team's list.

"It was a position pick," said Joe McDonald, who was in the Mets' front office at the time. "We did not feel that we had an adequate catching prospect in the organization."

Chilcott's career was plagued by injuries. Over a seven-year minor league career, he played in just 331 games, an average of 47 games a year. He was released by the Yankees in 1972.

There was no doubt the Mets did their homework on Chilcott, 17, who hit .500 with 11 homers and 38 RBIs in 25 games in the spring of 1966 at Antelope Valley High in Lancaster, Calif. They sent Casey Stengel, then the club's vice president of Western scouting, in to see him play. Chilcott went 4-for-4, leading Stengel to say: "One look is enough for me. This boy has all the tools to become a major league hitter."

Several other Mets officials went in to take a look at Chilcott, though Stengel was most instrumental in the decision and was the person who contacted the young catcher to let him know the Mets drafted him. Chilcott, who passed up a number of offers to play quarterback in college, signed two weeks later for a $75,000 bonus.

Jackson, 20, was a sophomore outfielder at Arizona State and a starting defensive back on the football team. He hit .327 and set school records for home runs (15) and RBIs (65). Jackson signed with Kansas City for $84,000.

Kansas City got a huge break when Reggie Jackson was available with the No. 2 pick

It was the second straight year the A's went for an Arizona State product, though Jackson never played on the same team in college as Rick Monday, the first player selected in the 1965 draft. Jackson played on the freshman team at ASU that year.

The 1966 draft year featured three drafts for the first and only time. In addition to the June draft, which Chilcott and Johnson were eligible for, and the obscure September American Legion draft, which would be abolished at the 1966 Winter Meetings, a new January phase was introduced due to fears of possible legal action.

Some owners and front office officials worried that the entire draft process could be ruled illegal because it deprived players of the right to bargain on the open market. They said the opportunity to be drafted every six months would demonstrate that players wouldn't be bound to one organization long-term.

The January draft, one of the first official orders of business for new commissioner Spike Eckert, featured a regular phase for recent high school graduates, junior college players and others who were 21, and a secondary phase for players who had been drafted and were eligible for re-selection.

Eckert also had to make a special ruling on pitcher

Tom Seaver, 21, who was drafted by Atlanta and improperly signed to a $40,000 bonus a month later. Eckert nullified the contract and in an unprecedented move set up a special draft for Seaver that gave the Mets the rights to a player who would become one of the most successful in franchise history.

A total of 197 players were selected in the first January draft, including 95 in the regular phase, which would be the fewest ever. Neither Don Lohse, picked first in the regular phase by Kansas City, nor Stan Bell, selected first by Detroit in the secondary phase, signed.

Great Expectations

The June draft, conducted over two days at New York's Roosevelt Hotel, was also split into two phases. Veteran scouts said the talent in the regular phase was the deepest it had been in years.

"There is more quality this year than in any year since World War II," said veteran scout Paul Richards, who worked for the Phillies. "Give me the entire 20 of the first round and in three years, I guarantee you that team would make trouble for anybody. And I mean anybody."

Of the 20 first-round picks, 12 played in the big leagues—none faster than high school pitchers Gary Nolan, who opened the 1967 season with Cincinnati and strike out 206, and Boston's Ken Brett, who pitched in the 1967 World Series.

Just four college players were selected in the first round, with some of the better college talent going in the secondary phase. California's Bill Frost, who led the nation with 169 strikeouts in 128 innings, was the first player selected, but the most notable—and most expensive—was Steve Arlin of College World Series champion Ohio State. Arlin, who signed for a $105,000 bonus with Philadelphia, was the 13th player selected.

For the second year in a row, a lefthander selected by the Cubs became the first player to reach the big leagues. Rich Nye, a 14th-round pick from California, was promoted that September. Nye was regarded as just the No. 3 pitcher in his own college rotation, behind Frost and Andy Messersmith, who was drafted by the Angels and went on to become one of the key figures in bringing free agency to baseball 10 years later with the Dodgers.

The top playres in college football and basketball were also draft in 1966. Mike Garrett, the 1965 Heisman Trophy winner who also was an outfielder for Southern California, was selected by the Dodgers in the January draft but went on the play for the Kansas City Chiefs.

Cazzie Russell, the No. 1 pick in the 1966 NBA draft by the New York Knicks, never played baseball while at Michigan, but he worked out for the White Sox before the draft and hit several balls into the seats at Comiskey Park. Kansas City took a shot at him in the 27th round in June but did not sign him.

The annual Legion draft was held Aug. 24, but iuts short chapter in baseball history ended when just eight players were selected. It was in this draft that catcher Pete Varney, who would be drafted a record seven times, was first introduced.

DRAFT 66: FIRST-ROUND PICKS

No.	Club	Player, Pos.	School	Hometown	Ht.	Wt.	B-T	Age
1.	Mets	Steve Chilcott, c	Antelope Valley HS	Lancaster, Calif.	5-11	185	L-R	17
2.	Athletics	Reggie Jackson, of	Arizona State	Wyncote, Pa.	6-0	197	L-L	20
3.	Astros	Wayne Twitchell, rhp	Wilson HS	Portland, Ore.	6-6	220	R-R	18
4.	Red Sox	Ken Brett, lhp/of	El Segundo HS	El Segundo, Calif.	6-0	175	L-L	17
5.	Cubs	Dean Burk, rhp	Highland HS	Highland, Ill.	6-5	205	R-R	18
6.	Senators	Tom Grieve, of	Pittsfield HS	Pittsfield, Mass.	6-2	185	R-R	18
7.	Cardinals	Leron Lee, of	Grant HS	Sacramento, Calif.	6-1	195	L-R	18
8.	Angels	Jim DeNeff, ss	Indiana	Holland, Mich.	6-2	190	R-R	19
9.	Phillies	Mike Biko, rhp	Samuel HS	Dallas	6-1	185	R-R	17
10.	Yankees	Jim Lyttle, of	Florida State	Harrison, Ohio	6-0	173	L-R	20
11.	Braves	Al Santorini, rhp	Union HS	Union, N.J.	6-1	190	R-R	18
12.	Indians	*John Curtis, lhp	Central HS	Smithtown, N.Y.	6-2	180	L-L	18
13.	Reds	Gary Nolan, rhp	Oroville HS	Oroville, Calif.	6-3	190	R-R	18
14.	Tigers	*Rick Konik, 1b	St. Andrews HS	Detroit	6-1	175	L-L	18
15.	Pirates	Richie Hebner, ss	Norwood HS	Norwood, Mass.	6-1	210	L-R	18
16.	Orioles	Ted Parks, ss	California	Berkeley, Calif.	5-11	185	R-R	19
17.	Giants	Bob Reynolds, rhp	Ingraham HS	Seattle	5-11	195	R-R	19
18.	White Sox	Carlos May, of	Parker HS	Birmingham, Ala.	6-0	205	B-R	18
19.	Dodgers	Larry Hutton, rhp	Greenfield HS	Greenfield, Ind.	6-1	185	R-R	18
20.	Twins	Bob Jones, 3b	—	Dawson, Ga.	5-10	185	L-R	18

*Did not sign.

1966

CLUB-BY-CLUB SELECTIONS

ATLANTA BRAVES

January—Regular Phase (12)

1. **Robert Ritchie, of, Bryant & Stratton (Mass.)**
2. **Pete Rivera, lhp, Wilson HS, Los Angeles**
3. **Jack Crist, ss, Los Angeles Harbor JC**
4. Jack Patterson, 1b, William Jewell (Mo.) JC
5. **Ray Burner, rhp, Jersey City, N.J.**
6. **Greg Rineer, ss, Jersey City, N.J.**

January—Secondary Phase (20)

1. Tom Seaver, rhp, Southern California (Selection voided)
2. Donald Lando, of, Ithaca (N.Y.)
3. Orville Hollrah, rhp, Missouri
4. **Darryl Hester, lhp, Byne HS, Ada, Okla.**
5. Peter Middlekauff, 1b/rhp, Stanford

June—Regular Phase (11)

1. **Al Santorini, rhp, Union (N.J.) HS**
2. **Fabian Mang, lhp/1b, Jesuit HS, New Orleans**
3. Frank Duffy, ss, Stanford
4. **John Laberrique, c, Loyola Marymount**
5. **George Stone Jr., lhp/1b, Louisiana Tech**
6. Reid Braden, 1b, Cerritos (Calif.) JC
7. Charles Koselke, 1b, Western Michigan
8. Jerald Hurt, rhp, Missouri
9. Samuel Narron, c, East Carolina
10. **William Cupp, c/1b, Banning HS, Wilmington, Calif.**
11. Pat Harrison, ss, Southern California
12. **Chet Bergalowski, c, Mississippi State**
13. Buddy Harris, rhp, Roxborough (Pa.) HS
14. **John Stewart, rhp, Southern California**
15. **William Toney, 3b, Oklahoma State**
16. Roger Cain, of, Roosevelt HS, Los Angeles
17. Charlie Brown, rhp, Central Connecticut State
18. **Rudolph Green, c, Douglas HS, Oklahoma City, Okla.**
19. Rodney O'Brien, 3b, Lakewood HS, Long Beach, Calif.
20. Bill Hanley, of, Sacred Heart HS, Waterbury, Conn.
21. **John Guest, 1b/of, Parker HS, Greenville, S.C.**
22. **Kenneth Smith, c, Central HS, Phenix City, Ala.**
23. Walter Peto, 2b, Seton Hall
24. Glenn Lusk, 1b, Mississippi State
25. Dana Halvorson, 1b/of, Rogers HS, Spokane, Wash.
26. **Raymond Allen, rhp, El Camino (Calif.) JC**
27. David Wright, c, Anniston (Ala.) HS
28. **Vincent Petrarca, ss, St. Peter's (N.J.)**
29. Stanley Rand, 1b/of, Wheatley HS, San Antonio, Texas
30. Kenneth Perrin, rhp, Texas A&M
31. Jimmy Gruber, ss, Edgewater HS, Orlando, Fla.
32. Jimmy Jackson, lhp, Grambling
33. Gary Ross, rhp, Liberty-Portvue HS, Portvue, Pa.
34. Brian Bach, rhp, Kingston (N.Y.) HS
35. Larry McGary, c, Hillsborough HS, Tampa
36. Brantley Jones, lhp/1b, Kingsbury HS, Memphis, Tenn.
37. **Bobby Buckner, 2b, Napa (Calif.) HS**
38. **Jim O'Loughlin, lhp, Chicago**
39. Peter Riffle, lhp, Adams HS, Adamstown, Pa.
40. **Ralph Wells, 3b, Auburn**
41. **Marvin Murphy, 1b, Southeast Lauderdale HS, Meridian, Miss.**
42. **John Lee, 1b, Webster HS, Minden, La.**
43. Richard Allred, ss, Tulsa, Okla.
44. **Leroy Brown, of, Emporia State (Kan.)**
45. Ron Romaniello, c, Torrington (Conn.) HS
46. Terry Kirkpatrick, c, Mona Shores HS, Muskegon, Mich.
47. **Roe Skidmore, c/1b, Millikin**
48. Richard Sauget, c, Notre Dame
49. **Stan Evans, c, Bowling Green State**
50. **John Pitrulis, c, St. Procopius**
51. **William Matusz, rhp, Seton Hall**
52. Thomas Tidball, ss, Southeast HS, Lincoln, Neb.
53. Larry Brown, rhp, Wichita (Kan.) HS
54. Robert Schnietz, ss, Christian Brothers
55. **James Conklin, rhp, Tuxedo (N.Y.) HS**
56. Ronald Schroeder, 1b/of, Cleo Springs (Okla.) HS
57. Patrick Colombo, 3b, Nassau (N.Y.) CC

June—Secondary Phase (7)

1. **Oscar Brown, of, Southern California**
2. **Gary Neibauer, rhp, Nebraska**
3. Reid Braden, 1b, Lakewood (Calif.) JC (Selection voided)
4. Daniel Hootstein, of, Harvard
5. Frank Portera, c, Mississippi State
6. Dennis Trame, rhp, Quincy

August—Legion Phase (12)

1. Guy McTheny, rhp/c, Sarasota, Fla.
2. Jack Goldberg, 2b, Union, N.J.

BALTIMORE ORIOLES

January—Regular Phase (15)

1. Russell Vitallo, rhp, Schenectady, N.Y. (Selection voided)
2. **Carlos Evans, c, Wisconsin**
3. **Alonzo Harris, 3b, Fremont HS, Los Angeles**
4. James Dumais, lhp, Holy Cross
5. Edward Maras, rhp, South Dakota State
6. Steve Melfa, rhp, Edgewood, Mo.
7. **Bert Jones, c, Buffalo State**
8. Richard Wieczezak, ss, Seton Hall
9. **Doug Ward, rhp, Annapolis (Md.) HS**
10. **Dan Prebenda, lhp, Livonia, Mich.**
11. Harry Stelly, lhp, Lafayette, La.
12. **Paul Fleshner, ss, Kankakee, Ill.**

January—Secondary Phase (7)

1. Gary Gentry, rhp, Phoenix JC
2. Carl Merrill, c, Maine
3. Steve Wright, rhp, San Jose (Calif.) CC
4. Paul Dennenbaum, 1b, Syracuse
5. Larry Linville, of, Mesa (Colo.)
6. Fred Kos, 1b, Northeastern
7. **Alan Diamond, c, California**
8. Herbert Hofvendahl, of, Diablo Valley (Calif.) JC

June—Regular Phase (16)

1. **Ted Parks, ss, California**
2. **James Kelly, c, Ensley HS, Birmingham, Ala.**
3. Wayne Francingues, ss, Jesuit HS, New Orleans
4. **Randolph Coon, ss, Dover Plains (N.Y.) HS**
5. Jan Dukes, lhp, Santa Clara
6. Stephen Rogers, lhp, Bethlehem Central HS, Delmar, N.Y.
7. **Ron Norris, rhp, Hillcrest HS, Springfield, Mo.**
8. **Louis Coccia, c, Toledo**
9. **Leon Brown, ss, Grant HS, Sacramento, Calif.**
10. Scott Morton, lhp, Iowa State
11. **Terry Crowley, 1b/of, Long Island**
12. **Dan Kerns, 3b/of, Maryland**
13. Jack Johnson, 3b/of, West Virginia Wesleyan
14. Minton White, 1b/of, Texas
15. **Richard Rhine, rhp, Penn State**
16. Bill Borelli, 1b, Serra HS, Burlingame, Calif.
17. Edward Turnbull, lhp, Virginia
18. Ellsworth Jones, lhp/1b, James Monroe HS, Bronx, N.Y.
19. **Henry Medlin, lhp, Robinson (Texas) HS**
20. Lawrence Pyle, of, Parsippany HS, Tabor, N.J.
21. Glenn Bisbing, 3b, Rider
22. Daniel Beard, rhp, Lakewood (Calif.) HS
23. **Larry Blixt, c, Parsons**

24. Jim Skeins, ss, Ranger (Texas) JC
25. Preston Nash, ss, City College HS, Baltimore
26. Tommy Campbell, of, Jackson State
27. **Richard Pecore, rhp, St. Joseph's HS, Baltimore**
28. **Donald Genussa, 1b, Loyola (La.)**
29. Frank Bon Vardo, rhp, Maryland
30. Bruce Taylor, of, Perth Amboy (N.J.) HS
31. Larry Kleem, lhp, Elder HS, Cincinnati
32. Hugh Hamilton, lhp, Lamar HS, Houston
33. **Richard Stevenson, rhp, Parkville HS, Baltimore**
34. Charles Moore, 1b, Long Beach (Calif.) Poly HS
35. Fred Fagan, c, San Francisco
36. Robert Guerrera, rhp, Crosby HS, Waterbury, Conn.
37. **Donald Atkins, lhp, Housatonic Valley HS, Falls Village, Conn.**
38. Larry Piquet, ss, North Eugene (Ore.) HS
39. **Ronnie Shelton, lhp, Johnson City (Ill.) HS**
40. Billy Ferguson, rhp, Holy Cross HS, New Orleans
41. Steve Corpuel, 1b, Poly HS, Pacoima, Calif.
42. Ronald Soucie, lhp, John Baptist HS, Brewer, Maine
43. **Vaughn Kovach, rhp, West Virginia**
44. Jim Magnuson, of, JC of San Mateo (Calif.)
45. Jeff Slipp, of/lhp, Las Vegas, Nev.
46. Colby Howe, 2b/3b, Menlo-Atherton HS, Menlo Park, Calif.
47. Norm Angelini, lhp, JC of San Mateo (Calif.)
48. John Shafer, c, Madison HS, Portland, Ore.
49. **Gary Holt, lhp, New Bern (N.C.) HS**

June—Secondary Phase (8)

1. **Buddy White, rhp, Rutgers**
2. Jim Scheschuk, c, Texas
3. Greg Riddoch, ss, Colorado State
4. **Edward Maras, 1b/rhp, South Dakota State**
5. Herbert Hofvendahl, of, Diablo Valley (Calif.) JC

August—Legion Phase (15)

No selection

BOSTON RED SOX

January—Regular Phase (3)

1. Jim Rife, c, Lebanon Valley
2. **Mark Schaeffer, lhp, Cleveland HS, Canoga Park, Calif.**
3. **Donald Fox, rhp, Colley HS, Detroit, Mich.**
4. **Donald Peters, p, Tusculum**

January—Secondary Phase (9)

1. **Dick Baney, rhp, Anaheim HS**
2. **Daniel Rudanovich, of, Missouri**
3. Kenneth Hall, lhp, Nassau (N.Y.) CC
4. Jophrey Brown, rhp, Grambling

June—Regular Phase (4)

1. **Ken Brett, lhp/of, El Segundo (Calif.) HS**
2. **Joseph McCullough, inf, Dickinson HS, Jersey City, N.J.**
3. **Rick Hoban, lhp, West HS, Cleveland**
4. Skip Jutze, c, Central Connecticut State
5. **Wayne McGhee, c, Fresno State**
6. **Mike Nagy, rhp, St. Helena HS, Bronx, N.Y.**
7. **Daniel Smith, ss, Red Lion HS, Windsor, Pa.**
8. **Roger McComas, p, Odessa, Texas**
9. Ernie Aguirre, c, Bakersfield (Calif.) HS
10. Nicholas DeFlorio, ss, Carey HS, Franklin Square, N.Y.
11. **William Hathaway, c, Palm Springs (Calif.) HS**
12. **Thomas Stephenson, rhp, Anaheim, Calif.**
13. **Richard Guy, 3b, Jemison (Ala.) HS**
14. **Harry Greenfield, of, Husson**
15. **Bernard Burns, of, Indiana (Pa.)**
16. **Ed Phillips, rhp, Colby**
17. **Dennis Udy, rhp, Utah**
18. **William O'Neill, c, Windsor Locks (Conn.) HS**
19. **John Frye, of, Michigan State**
20. **Bernard Linn, rhp, Grossmont HS, El Cajon, Calif.**
21. Eugene Collins, rhp, Choctawhatchee HS, Fort Walton Beach, Fla.
22. **James Chenevert, of, Redemptorist HS, Baton Rouge, La.**
23. Jack Fulmer, 3b, Arkansas State
24. James Whinery, 3b, Thomas Downey HS, Modesto, Calif.
25. Steve Egan, c, Pittsburg State
26. **Richard Goedert, 1b, Mira Costa (Calif.) JC**
27. **Otis Griggs, c, Andalusia (Ala.) HS**
28. **Louis Inman, 3b, Mississippi College**

June—Secondary Phase (14)

1. **Donald Cook, rhp, Long Island**
2. **Jim Rife, c, Lebanon Valley**
3. **Dick Mills, rhp, Parsons**
4. George Girard, lhp, Marblehead, Mass.

August—Legion Phase (3)

No selection

CALIFORNIA ANGELS

January—Regular Phase (7)

1. Ronald Cherry, c, John Francis Poly HS, Sun Valley, Calif.
2. **Vern Geishert, rhp, Wisconsin**
3. Randy Bobb, c, Verdugo Hills HS, Sunland, Calif.

January—Secondary Phase (5)

1. **James Vopicka, ss, Illinois**
2. **Paul Alderette, of/c, Los Angeles Pierce JC**
3. Randy Humphrey, lhp, Los Angeles Harbor JC
4. Kenneth Suzawa, lhp, Fresno (Calif.) CC
5. Oscar Brown, of, Compton (Calif.) JC

June—Regular Phase (8)

1. **Jim DeNeff, ss, Indiana**
2. **David Frost, rhp, Lawton (Okla.) HS**
3. Bill Gillean, rhp, Mayfair HS, Lakewood, Calif.
4. Jim Suskiewich, lhp, Beaver Falls (Pa.) HS
5. **Buddy Lawhorn, ss, West Haven HS, Memphis, Tenn.**
6. **John Dickson, c/of, Edison HS, Fresno, Calif.**
7. Robert Smith, rhp, St. John's
8. **Michael Floyd, of, Fullerton (Calif.) JC**
9. Ken Forsch, rhp, Sacramento (Calif.) CC
10. **Tim Hewes, c, Bakersfield (Calif.) JC**
11. Jim Barr, rhp, Lynwood (Calif.) HS
12. Larry Bishop, c, Howe HS, Indianapolis
13. **Anthony Mitchell, rhp, Lincoln HS, San Diego**
14. **Paul Devaney, rhp, DeSales HS, Geneva, N.Y.**
15. **John McCall, ss, Clemson**
16. Glenn Pickren, rhp, Seminole HS, St.Petersburg, Fla.
17. **Bruce Christensen, ss, Chatsworth HS, Canoga Park, Calif.**
18. **Randy Brown, c, Florida State**
19. Alan Jackson, lhp, St. Clements HS, Somerville, Mass.
20. Dave LaRoche, lhp, West Torrance (Calif.) HS
21. Irl Davis, rhp, Bishop Montgomery HS, Redondo Beach, Calif.
22. Louis Mellini, rhp, Beverly Hills (Calif.) HS (Selection voided)
23. **William Moray, 3b, Santa Monica (Calif.) HS**
24. Thomas Buchenberger, rhp, St. John's
25. Clarence Smith, rhp, St. Francis College (N.Y.)
26. Dan Stolingrosz, 3b, Cleveland HS, Canoga Park, Calif.
27. **Richard Well, rhp, Bakersfield (Calif.) HS**
28. **Kelly Gaston, c, Ventura (Calif.) JC**
29. **Daniel Pollard, 1b, Fresno State**
30. Forest Hartline, 2b, Pasadena (Calif.) CC
31. Bill Bonham, rhp, Francis Poly HS, Pacoima, Calif.
32. **Jon Lervig, lhp, San Fernando HS, Mission Hills, Calif.**
33. **Richard Ganulin, 1b, UCLA**
34. Marvin Madruga, ss, Mount Whitney HS, Visalia, Calif.
35. **Steve Hovley, of, Stanford**

June—Secondary Phase (12)

1. **Andy Messersmith, rhp, California**
2. **Ken Tatum, rhp, Mississippi State**
3. **Stephen Schneider, ss, Minnesota**

August—Legion Phase (7)

1. Louis Mellini, rhp/3b, Beverly Hills, Calif.

CHICAGO CUBS

January—Regular Phase (6)

1. **John Dudek, c, Tuley HS, Chicago**

2. **John Killebrew, of, Arizona Western JC**
3. **Frank White, c, South Carolina Area Trade School**
4. **William Johns, 1b, Virginia Tech**

January—Secondary Phase (15)

1. No selection
2. Sanford Marks, lhp, Los Angeles CC

June—Regular Phase (5)

1. **Dean Burk, rhp, Highland (Ill.) HS**
2. C.E. Bryson, of, Findlay (Ohio) HS
3. **Robert Owens, c, Henderson HS, West Chester, Pa.**
4. **Richard Curbow, of, Central HS, Springfield, Mo.**
5. **Marcus Rhaney, lhp, Middleton HS, Tampa**
6. **Edward Bruksch, 3b, Minnesota**
7. Pat O'Brien, lhp, Arizona
8. **Jerry Szukala, 1b, Illinois**
9. John Miller, rhp, I.H.M. Academy, Coeur DAlene, Idaho
10. Clyde Kuehn, of, Belleville (Ill.) HS
11. **Elby Bushong, c, California Western**
12. **Elvatous Peters, of, Southern**
13. **Robert Eyer, ss, Loyola HS, Los Angeles**
14. **Rich Nye, lhp, California**
15. **Jeff Rude, of, Southern Oregon State**
16. Charles Jones, lhp, Central HS, Mobile, Ala.
17. Ron Del Planche, ss, Oregon
18. James Silestrini, of, Bullard HS, Fresno, Calif.
19. **Rick Davis, c, Park View HS, Springfield, Mo.**
20. **Dale Ford, 1b, Washington State**
21. **Thomas Whelan, c/1b, San Diego State**
22. Michael Nichols, lhp, Bakersfield (Calif.) HS
23. **Dana Freudeman, lhp, Central HS, Canton, Ohio**
24. Steve Hanson, rhp, Saratoga (Calif.) HS
25. Adrian Kent, rhp, Hillsborough HS, Tampa
26. **David McKelvey, c/3b, Rider**
27. **Bruce Carmichael, 2b/ss, Santa Clara**
28. **Dean Klahr, ss, Albright**
29. William Grogan, rhp, Clarkston (Wash.) HS
30. Patrick Hartigan, rhp, Columbia Basin (Wash.) CC
31. **Bill Stoneman, rhp, Idaho**
32. **Dale Ehler, c, Oregon**
33. **Ronald Pearson, of, Phoenix (Ariz.) JC**
34. **Earl Lombardo, 2b, Rider**
35. **James Nealey, rhp, Corona (Calif.) HS**
36. **Bruce Johnson, of, Wilson HS, Portland, Ore.**
37. **Fred Rodriguez, 2b, East Carolina**
38. **Archie Reynolds, rhp, Paris (Texas) JC**

June—Secondary Phase (3)

1. Eddie Leon, ss, Arizona
2. **Jophrey Brown, rhp, Grambling**
3. **Joe Niekro, rhp, West Liberty State**
4. Ray Henningsen, 2b, Santa Clara

August—Legion Phase (6)

No selection

CHICAGO WHITE SOX

January—Regular Phase (17)

1. Howard Gordon, 1b/of, Southern California
2. **James Barton, rhp, Akron**
3. **Ronald Ellis, rhp/of, Portsmouth, Va.**
4. **Dean DeBuhr, rhp, Wayne State (Mich.)**
5. Al Crawford, 3b, Miami-Dade North CC
6. Richard Schryer, of, Michigan
7. Stephen Moates, rhp, Miami-Dade North CC

January—Secondary Phase (11)

1. Clifford Foster, 1b/of, Lansing (Mich.) CC
2. **Steven Kokor, rhp, Alta Loma (Calif.) JC**
3. **Peter Lentine, 1b/lhp, Los Angeles Pierce JC**
4. Gerald Boehmer, 3b, Saint Louis
5. Bill Drummond, rhp, Buena Vista
6. Robert Hergenrader, lhp, Nebraska
7. Joe Bloom, rhp, Los Angeles Pierce JC

June—Regular Phase (18)

1. **Carlos May, of, Parker HS, Birmingham, Ala.**
2. Johnny Oates, c, Virginia Tech
3. **Jim Magnuson, lhp, Wisconsin-Oshkosh**
4. **Karl Simon, of, Central HS, South Bend, Ind.**
5. **Ken Frailing, lhp, Marion (Wis.) HS**
6. **Gary Lewis, c, Colton (Calif.) HS**
7. David Speas, ss, Clairemont HS, San Diego
8. Randy Coley, 1b, Providence HS, Lockport, Ill.
9. Dennis Jones, lhp, Jetmore (Kan.) HS
10. Mike Adams, inf, Loara HS, Anaheim
11. **Robert Mewes, c, Colorado State**
12. **Gary Kirtlan, 1b/of, Clarksburg (Calif.) HS**
13. John Posen, 3b/of, Morton East HS, Cicero, Ill.
14. William Hess, lhp, Roncalli HS, Aurora, Ill.
15. Mike Thompson, rhp, Ponca City (Okla.) HS
16. **Chuck Brinkman, c, Ohio State**
17. Samuel Watts, ss, Froebel HS, Gary, Ind.
18. Robert Mitchell, c, Lynwood (Calif.) HS
19. Thomas Tutko, inf, Hastings (Neb.)
20. Stephen Vaughn, of/1b, Southeast Missouri State
21. **Jerry Florence, of, East HS, Wichita, Kan.**
22. Greg Garrett, lhp, Los Angeles Pierce JC
23. Andrew Thomas, rhp, Indiana State
24. **John Marcum, lhp, Saint Louis**
25. Jim Limke, rhp, Minot State
26. John Zotz, rhp, Danville (Ill.) HS
27. Bobby Fenwick, inf/of, Minnesota
28. **James Daun, rhp/of, Chilton (Wis.) HS**
29. Marvin Galliher, inf, Lincoln HS, San Diego
30. **Melvin McCoy, lhp, Magnolia HS, Stanton, Calif.**
31. Paul Faust, of, Minnesota
32. **David Smith, rhp, Schaghticoke (N.Y.) HS**
33. John Davsko, rhp, Saint Louis
34. Geoff Zahn, lhp, Michigan
35. **Thomas Henvey, inf, Lincoln HS, Yonkers, N.Y.**
36. Robert Breitzman, inf, Glenbrook North HS, Northbrook, Ill.
37. **Art Kusnyer, c, Kent State**
38. Earl Kennedy, inf, Bakersfield (Calif.) JC (Selection voided)
39. Lawrence Hammer, rhp, Fenger HS, Chicago
40. Edmond Curran, rhp, Saint Louis
41. Ken Kozil, rhp, Glenbrook North HS, Northbrook, Ill.

June—Secondary Phase (4)

1. **Berke Reichenbach, inf, Ohio**
2. James Armstrong, ss, Arizona State
3. Clifford Foster, 1b/of, Lansing (Mich.) CC
4. **Orville Hollrah, rhp, Missouri**
5. **Gerald Boehmer, 3b, Saint Louis**
6. **Frank Chambers, rhp, Mississippi State**

August—Legion Phase (17)

No selection

CINCINNATI REDS

January—Regular Phase (14)

No selection

January—Secondary Phase (10)

1. **Dan McGinn, lhp, Notre Dame**
2. **Joseph Braithwaite, 1b, Atlantic City, N.J.**
3. Walter Manuel, ss, Lafayette
4. **John Noriega, rhp, Utah**
5. Archie Roberts, ss, Holyoke, Mass.

June—Regular Phase (13)

1. **Gary Nolan, rhp, Oroville (Calif.) HS**
2. **Darrell Chaney, ss, Morton HS, Hammond, Ind.**
3. **Mike Oates, rhp, Glenbard West HS, Glen Ellyn, Ill.**
4. Thomas Williams, c, Mount Carmel HS, Los Angeles
5. Richard Washburn, rhp, St. Thomas (Minn.)
6. Steve Steitz, rhp/1b, East Long Meadow (Mass.) HS
7. **David Grawe, rhp, Elder HS, Cincinnati**
8. **James Cartlidge, of, Livingston**
9. David Reeves, rhp, Americus (Ga.) HS
10. Jeffrey Pryor, rhp, Evans HS, Orlando, Fla.

11. Ricky Schwartz, of, Texas A&M
12. Edward Robbins, rhp, Hillsboro (Ohio) HS
13. Thomas Dryja, of/lhp, Riverside HS, Buffalo, N.Y.
14. **Donell Goodwin, ss, Edison HS, Stockton, Calif.**
15. Thomas Henderson, rhp, Northeastern Oklahoma A&M JC
16. James Babyak, ss, Massachusetts
17. **Claude Passeau, rhp, Mississippi State**
18. Larry Housley, 2b/3b, Colton (Calif.) HS
19. **Robert Orange, rhp, Morgan Park HS, Chicago**
20. Rick Henninger, rhp, Hastings (Neb.) HS
21. David Smith, 3b/ss, Red Lion HS, Windsor, Pa. (Selection voided)
22. **Isaac Fuggett, of, Douglas HS, Oklahoma City, Okla.**
23. Robert Leatherwood, 2b, California
24. Timothy White, c, Denton (Texas) HS
25. Donald Van Deusen, ss, Concord
26. Mickey Smith, c, Illinois
27. Conrad DeNeault, rhp, Missouri

June—Secondary Phase (11)

1. John Dow, of, Bemidji, Minn.
2. Dick Tidrow, rhp, Hayward, Calif.
3. Stan Bell, rhp, Manatee (Fla.) JC
4. Thomas Kelly, of, Holy Cross
5. Steve Radulovich, 1b, Utah

August—Legion Phase (14)

No selection

CLEVELAND INDIANS

January—Regular Phase (11)

1. **Ted Ford, of/ss, Richland, N.J.**
2. **Kenneth Showalter, ss, New Martinsville, W. Va**
3. **Dave Singerman, rhp, Cuyahoga (Ohio) CC**
4. **Phil Hennigan, rhp, Sam Houston State**
5. **Wilma Evans, of, Pittsburgh**
6. Dave Pratt, lhp, Tennessee Tech
7. Joe Niekro, of/rhp, West Liberty State
8. Gary Neibauer, rhp, Nebraska

January—Secondary Phase (3)

1. Kris Krebs, ss, Manatee (Fla.) JC
2. **J.B. Jackson, of/1b, Kilgore (Texas) JC**
3. Jackie Kreel, rhp, Gulf Coast (Fla.) JC
4. Arnold Chonko, 1b, Ohio State
5. **Dennis Deptula, 2b, Detroit**
6. Michael Burns, of, Mississippi State
7. Robert Bixler, rhp, Miami (Ohio)
8. **Richard Zank, lhp, Neilsville, Wis.**

June—Regular Phase (12)

1. John Curtis, lhp, Smithtown (N.Y.) Central HS
2. **Billy Lynch, lhp/of, Paul Blazer HS, Ashland, Ky.**
3. **Terry Taylor, of, Soquel HS, Belmont, Calif.**
4. **William Kyle, 1b, University HS, Beverly Hills, Calif.**
5. **William Davis, 3b, Pembroke State (N.C.)**
6. **Gary Sprague, ss/2b, Florida State**
7. Harold Harris, 3b/ss, Hewitt Trussville HS, Birmingham, Ala.
8. **Stephen Reid, ss, DeSales HS, Geneva, N.Y.**
9. Daniel McNulty, 2b/ss, Waterloo (N.Y.) HS
10. **Ollie Coffey, c, East Tech HS, Cleveland**
11. **Clifford Lee, 2b, Campbell HS, Smyrna, Ga.**
12. **Jackson Sexton, of, Titusville (Fla.) HS**
13. William Palmer, rhp, Rice
14. **Russ Nagelson, 1b, Ohio State**
15. **James Wingate, rhp, Trinity**
16. **Gerald Kremer, ss, Maryland**
17. **Ronald Hart, ss, Frederick (Md.) HS**
18. Michael Hastings, of, Ithaca (N.Y.) HS
19. Robert Bossom, 1b, Columbia
20. **Jerry Clark, ss, Rose HS, Greenville, N.C.**
21. Richard Holliday, rhp, Westminster
22. Michael Brannan, of, Broughton HS, Raleigh, N.C.
23. **Robert Biscan, rhp, Morton HS, Hammond, Ind.**
24. **Larry Edwards, rhp, Erskine**
25. Mike Carruthers, 1b, Pembroke State (N.C.)
26. Seaton Daly, c, Santa Clara
27. **Billy Harris, ss/2b, UNC Wilmington**
28. Ronald Henson, lhp, Rice
29. **Donald Del'Mazzio, of, Norwalk, Conn.**
30. John Vance, c, Glasgow (Ky.) HS
31. Jack Lind, 3b, Arizona State
32. William Kollman, 3b, Chamberlin HS, Twinsburg, Ohio
33. Dale Dunham, rhp, Central HS, Bay City, Mich.
34. Dennis Hall, rhp, Memphis (Tenn.) Catholic HS

June—Secondary Phase (16)

1. **John Olagues, rhp, Tulane**
2. **Terry Thompson, 1b, Columbia Basin (Wash.) CC**
3. Scott Reid, ss/of, Cerritos (Calif.) JC
4. **Tommy Gramly, rhp, Texas Christian**
5. Stephen Moates, rhp, Miami-Dade North CC
6. **James Carroll, 2b, Georgia Tech**
7. Charles Watson, rhp, Clemson

August—Legion Phase (11)

No selection

DETROIT TIGERS

January—Regular Phase (13)

1. **Tim Marting, ss, Hillsborough (Fla.) JC**
2. Robert Bellemare, rhp, Post (Conn.) JC (Selection voided)
3. **Kenneth Youngblood, c, Little Rock, Ark.**
4. **Jon Warden, lhp, Harrisburg, Ohio**

January—Secondary Phase (1)

1. Stan Bell, rhp, Manatee (Fla.) JC
2. Ray Glinsky, rhp, Akron
3. Steve Schneider, ss, Minnesota
4. **Jerry Foglia, rhp, Woodridge (N.J.) HS**
5. Glen Borkhuis, rhp, Syracuse
6. Ken Tatum, rhp, Mississippi State
7. Frederick Manning, 2b, Holy Cross
8. Dennis Trame, rhp, Quincy
9. Edward Staron, of, Western Michigan

June—Regular Phase (14)

1. Rick Konik, 1b, St. Andrews HS, Detroit
2. Scott Fields, lhp, Elgin HS, Larue, Ohio
3. **Robert Gilhooley, inf, Michigan**
4. **Les Cain, lhp, El Cerrito (Calif.) HS**
5. **Eugene Spatz, 3b, Alexander HS, Elmsford, N.Y.**
6. **Robert Welz, 1b, Harvard**
7. **Hagen Anderson, inf, Massachusetts**
8. **Mike Irish, c, Grand Ledge (Mich.) HS**
9. **Dan Bootcheck, lhp/1b, Michigan City (Ind.) HS**
10. **Brian Cusino, rhp, Monroe Catholic Central HS, Erie, Mich.**
11. Bob Kloss, rhp/3b, St. Ladislaus HS, Detroit
12. **Chandler Simonds, 1b, Michigan**
13. Vic Pilar, lhp, Thurston HS, Redford Township, Mich.
14. **Herbert Doebler, rhp, Utica (Mich.) HS**
15. Gary Krupinski, c, St. Hedwige HS, Detroit
16. Rodney Pryor, lhp, McLainsboro (Ill.) HS
17. **Randy Hooper, of, Pacific HS, San Bernardino, Calif.**
18. John Mayer, lhp, Western Michigan
19. **Jim Blight, rhp, Michigan State**
20. Ronald Allen, ss, Scott HS, Toledo, Ohio
21. **Robert Buchanan, rhp, East HS, Buffalo, N.Y.**
22. Richard Schlesinger, lhp, Kansas State
23. Thomas Lomicky, inf, St. Joseph's HS, West New York, N.J.
24. John Johnson, c, Northwest Classen HS, Oklahoma City, Okla.
25. **James Martin, lhp, East Brunswick (N.J.) HS**
26. **Nathaniel Dixon, rhp, Tuskegee (Ala.) HS**
27. **Vincent Ammerata, ss, Ossining (N.Y.) HS**
28. Ronald Kohler, lhp, Bellville (Ill.) Township HS
29. Harry Gonso, c, Findlay (Ohio) HS
30. Ron Timko, rhp, Plains (Pa.) HS
31. **Ron Goulet, of, Flint (Mich.) JC**
32. Tom Lee, of, Poindexter Legion HS, Springfield, Mo.
33. Charles Haje, of, Wheaton (Md.) HS
34. Mark Kenney, 3b/of, Jamaica HS, Long Island, N.Y.
35. Frank Sullivan, rhp, Piscataway HS, New Market, N.J.

36. Jim Johnson, lhp/of, Western Michigan

June—Secondary Phase (2)

1. **Richard Devarney, ss, Maine**
2. **Bob Reed, rhp, Michigan**
3. **Paul Coleman, rhp, Cal Poly Pomona**
4. George Grzegorek, ss, St. Edward's (Texas)
5. Darrell Evans, inf, Pasadena (Calif.) CC
6. Alan Putz, 3b, Cheshire (Conn.) Academy
7. Rusty Adkins, 2b/of, Clemson
8. Bill Zepp, rhp, Michigan

August—Legion Phase (13)

No selection

HOUSTON ASTROS

January—Regular Phase (4)

1. **Tom Griffin, rhp, Grant HS, Sun Valley, Calif.**
2. **Herman Johnson, 1b, Jefferson HS, Los Angeles**
3. **Stanley Robinson, rhp, Jefferson HS, Los Angeles**
4. Joe Dawkins, 1b, Fremont HS, Los Angeles
5. Oliver Kozloski, c/of, Blinn (Texas) JC
6. **Robert Santee, rhp, Carverdale HS, Houston**
7. Timothy Ware, ss, Spring Branch HS, Houston

January—Secondary Phase (4)

1. **Joel McMasters, rhp/1b, Southern Baptist (Ark.) JC**
2. **John Respondek, rhp, Texas A&I**

June—Regular Phase (3)

1. **Wayne Twitchell, rhp, Wilson HS, Portland, Ore.**
2. **Ronald Crook, lhp, Georgia Tech**
3. John D'Auria, rhp, Arcadia (Calif.) HS
4. Elliott Maddox, inf, Union (N.J.) HS
5. **Cliff Johnson Jr., c, Wheatley HS, San Antonio, Texas**
6. **Thomas Koziol, inf, La Salle HS, Miami**
7. **Richard Lynn, inf, Edwardsville (Ill.) HS**
8. **Fred Stanley, inf, Monte Vista HS, Whittier, Calif.**
9. **Sli Harvey, 1b, Aransas Pass (Texas) HS**
10. J.D. Hill, of, Edison HS, Stockton HS
11. John Caruso, rhp, Franklin K. Lane HS, Ozone Park, N.Y.
12. **Robert Dickman, c, Rutgers**
13. Douglas Hansen, rhp, Hoover HS, Fresno, Calif.
14. **Alan Pauska, 1b/of, Phillipsburg (N.J.) HS**
15. **Mike Cole, rhp, Southern Baptist (Ark.) JC**
16. James Kobi, ss, Kings College (Pa.)
17. William Green, 3b, Central Missouri State
18. Cyrus Lee, lhp, Jones HS, Little Rock, Ark.
19. **William Steinkamp, c, Highland HS, Albuquerque, N.M.**
20. Ed Goodson, ss, Fries HS, Ivanhoe, Va.
21. Frank Van Devender, rhp, San Diego Mesa JC
22. **Bob Watkins, rhp, Compton (Calif.) HS**
23. William Wright, rhp, South Park HS, Beaumont, Texas
24. John Fletcher, c, Lee HS, Columbus, Miss.
25. Dan Monzon, 2b, Buena Vista
26. Robert Anderson, c, Boulder (Colo.) HS
27. Benny Looper, c, Granite (Okla.) HS
28. Jerry Marion, of, Wyoming
29. Edmund Mantie, rhp, Syracuse
30. **Robert Cassady, inf, Neshaminy HS, Langhorne, Pa.**
31. **Boyd Van Patten, of, Springville (Utah) HS**
32. Steve Evans, rhp, Northville (Mich.) HS
33. **James Moore, 3b, Halifax County HS, South Boston, Va.**
34. Jeffrey Bowman, rhp, Downey HS, Modesto, Calif.
35. **Patrick Warren, of, Miami (Ohio)**
36. Phillip Jones, lhp, Jasper (Texas) HS
37. **Mark Scally, rhp, Curley HS, Miami, Fla.**
38. **Herbert Peterson, c, Rosenwald HS, Panama City, Fla.**
39. Jerome Hall, of, Arlington HS, Fort Worth, Texas

June—Secondary Phase (5)

1. Larry Linville, of, Mesa (Colo.)
2. Al Crawford, of, Miami-Dade North CC
3. **Paul Dennenbaum, 1b, Syracuse**
4. Stephen Lohrer, inf, Nassau (N.Y.) CC

August—Legion Phase (4)

1. Gerald Johnson, lhp, Newberg, Ore.

KANSAS CITY ATHLETICS

January—Regular Phase (1)

1. **Don Lohse, rhp, Indiana**
2. **Bill Geiger, rhp, Keyport (N.J.) HS**
3. **James Shotton, rhp, Marion, Ill.**
4. Jeff Hansen, 1b, SUNY Farmingdale JC
5. David Ray, rhp, Alabama
6. Charles Watson, rhp, Clemson

January—Secondary Phase (19)

1. Ron Drake, c, Long Beach (Calif.) CC
2. **Leonard Zandy, rhp, Fordham**
3. Frank Chambers, rhp, Mississippi State
4. Frank Portera, c, Mississippi State

June—Regular Phase (2)

1. **Reggie Jackson, of, Arizona State**
2. **Roger Washington, of, Los Angeles**
3. **John Greene, of, Brigham Young**
4. Billy Joe Cotton, c, McCook (Neb.) HS
5. **Dave Hamilton, lhp, Edmonds (Wash.) HS**
6. Warren Bogle, lhp, Miami
7. **Clarence Vaughns, 3b, Jordon HS, Los Angeles**
8. **Tom Brooks, rhp, St. James HS, Chester, Pa.**
9. **Frank Fall, rhp, McClatchy HS, Sacramento, Calif.**
10. Nick Radakovic, rhp, Michigan
11. Tom Binkowski, 1b, Michigan State
12. **Edward Howell, lhp, Florida State**
13. Jack Gehrke, ss, Utah
14. Ronald Berta, c, Moravian (Pa.)
15. **Darrell Baker, rhp, Holbrook (Mass.) HS**
16. **John Shearer, lhp, Carlisle (Pa.) HS**
17. **Joseph Tassone, c, Port Chester (N.Y.) HS**
18. **Ed Green, of, San Diego**
19. Robert Rogers, 3b, Salem, Ore.
20. Larry Burchart, rhp, Oklahoma State
21. **Bruce Ocken, rhp, Turlock (Calif.) HS**
22. Clarence Cleveland, 1b/of, Albany (Ga.) HS
23. Michael Lisetski, ss, Rider
24. Allen Ramsey, 3b, Somerville (N.J.) HS
25. Rex Hein, rhp, Rockhurst HS, Kansas City, Mo.
26. Steve Smith, 2b, Long Beach (Calif.) Poly HS
27. Cazzie Russell, 1b, Michigan
28. Norbert Beddow, rhp/of, Aurora (Colo.) HS
29. John Sellers, inf, Northeastern Oklahoma A&M JC
30. **Henry Gunther, of, New London (Conn.) HS**
31. Eli Lyles, of, City College HS, Baltimore
32. Russell Hyder, ss, Boulder (Colo.) HS
33. **Thomas Matakanski, c, Hyde Park, Mass.**
34. Harold Werntz, rhp, Temple
35. **Charles Lynch, rhp, Sayreville HS, Morgan, N.J.**
36. Tom Binder, rhp, Ganesha HS, Pomona, Calif.

June—Secondary Phase (20)

1. **Dennis McKernan, 1b/of, Kutztown**
2. Charles Kline, lhp, Western Michigan
3. **Paul Dumais, lhp, Holy Cross**
4. **Don Lando, of, Ithaca (N.Y.)**

August—Legion Phase (1)

1. Pete Varney Jr., rhp, North Quincy, Mass.
2. **Bruce Bates, rhp/of, Billings, Mont.**

LOS ANGELES DODGERS

January—Regular Phase (20)

1. **James Roberts, rhp/inf, Alabama**
2. **Ivey Armstrong, 2b/of, Miami-Dade North CC**
3. **Robert Childress, 3b, Mothacton HS, Norristown, Pa.**
4. **Albert Choate, rhp, Sam Houston State**
5. **Jorge Benitez, 1b, Miami-Dade North CC**

January—Secondary Phase (14)

1. John Herbst, lhp, Southern California
2. **Henry Tenney, of, Vista HS, Valley Center, Calif.**
3. **Jim Hibbs, c, Stanford**
4. Mike Garrett, of, Southern California

June—Regular Phase (19)

1. **Larry Hutton, rhp, Greenfield (Ind.) HS**
2. **John Gamble, ss, Carson City (Nev.) HS**
3. **Richard Thompson, 2b, Pembroke State (N.C.)**
4. **Jerry Bagwell, ss, Wrens HS, Liberty, S.C.**
5. Gordon Allen, of, Ludlow (Mass.) HS
6. **Dennis James, lhp, Albany (Ga.) HS**
7. James Doran, of, Madison Township HS, Parlin, N.J.
8. **Charlie Hough, inf/rhp, Hialeah (Fla.) HS**
9. **Bill Russell, of, Pittsburg (Kan.) HS**
10. **Dennis Thornton, 1b, Eisenhower HS, Decatur, Ill.**
11. Kenneth Burrow, c, DeAnza HS, Pinole, Calif.
12. **Billy Grabarkewitz, 3b, St. Mary's (Texas)**
13. **Romel Canada, of, Chester (Pa.) HS**
14. **James Raynor, rhp, East Carolina**
15. **Ted Sizemore, c, Michigan**
16. **Allen Shiflet, c, McCallum HS, Austin, Texas**
17. **Kenneth Raab, rhp, Northview HS, Covina, Calif.**
18. Craig Menzl, 1b, Islip HS, Long Island, N.Y.
19. **Martin Parker, rhp/of, King HS, Tampa**
20. Loyd Colson, rhp/inf, Gould (Okla.) HS
21. **John Jiles, of, North Cobb HS, Acworth, Ga.**
22. **Charles Sutton, rhp, Tate HS, Molino, Fla.**
23. **James Frye, rhp, Northern HS, Pontiac, Mich.**
24. **William Ralston, 2b, Cal Poly Pomona**
25. Robert Perruchon, of, Vallejo (Calif.) JC
26. Kenneth Danson, c/of, Forrest HS, Jacksonville, Fla.
27. Lawrence Land, rhp, Bamberg (S.C.) HS
28. **Thomas Alger, lhp, Hudson (N.Y.) HS**
29. Michael Pierce, lhp, Rincon HS, Tucson, Ariz.
30. **Steven Howder, of, CC of San Francisco**
31. Radford Mawhinney, of/1b, Santa Maria (Calif.) HS
32. **James Arkell, of, Claremont**
33. **Donald Reece, rhp, Campbell HS, Smyrna, Ga.**
34. **James McCray, of, San Diego State**
35. David Nitchke, c, Fresno State
36. Mark Harris, rhp, Maryland
37. **Rob Johnson, lhp, Trenton (Mo.) HS**
38. **Steven Hockensmith, 1b, Florida Southern**
39. William Carthel, of/inf, Sul Ross State
40. **Ray Lamb, rhp, Southern California**
41. **Donald Spain, rhp, Eisenhower HS, Decatur, Ill.**
42. **Donny Tidwell, rhp, New Diana (Texas) HS**
43. **Julio Guerrero, ss, Centralia HS, San Angelo, Texas**
44. Richard Shulock, 3b, Vero Beach (Fla.) HS
45. Dicky Shaw, ss, Central State (Okla.)
46. **Jeffrey King, rhp, Mainland HS, Daytona Beach (Fla.) HS**
47. **Richard LeBlanc, lhp, Forrest HS, Jacksonville, Fla.**
48. **Lamar Haynes, lhp, Chipola (Fla.) JC**
49. Jody Gioffoni, rhp, Santa Monica HS, Malibu, Calif.
50. Kenneth Wiedemann, 2b, West Covina (Calif.) HS
51. Mark Johnson, of, New Mexico
52. **Walter Pierce, of, William Carey (Miss.)**
53. Jack Butorac, rhp, Montebello (Calif.) HS
54. David Lindsey, lhp, Fremont HS, Los Angeles
55. Bob Randall, ss, Gove (Kan.) HS
56. **Frank Staab, rhp, Hays (Kan.) HS**
57. John Thurston, c/ss, Bishop Molloy HS, Bronx, N.Y.
58. Adrian Zabala, rhp, Florida
59. William Scott, ss, Germantown Academy, Philadelphia
60. Thomas Smith, rhp, Foley (Ala.) HS
61. **Reed Raynor, rhp, Hamilton HS, Robbinsville, N.J.**
62. Robert Chandler, 2b, Rollins (Fla.)

June—Secondary Phase (15)

1. **Bob Stinson III, c/of, Miami-Dade North CC**
2. **Richard Schryer, of, Michigan**
3. **James Carter, 3b, Trinity**
4. **John Green, rhp, Gulf Coast (Fla.) CC**
5. John Herbst, lhp, Southern California

August—Legion Phase (20)

No selection

MINNESOTA TWINS

January—Regular Phase (19)

1. **Charles Chase, of, JC of San Mateo (Calif.)**
2. Antone Cardoza, rhp, JC of the Sequoias (Calif.)
3. **Tom Hall, lhp, Riverside, Calif.**
4. **Michael Sheftall, rhp, Jones HS, Houston**
5. Barry Kubishta, rhp, Gardena (Calif.) HS
6. **Harold Steinback, 3b, Vallejo (Calif.) JC**
7. Fred Shuey, of, Southern California
8. Tom Cole, of, Wake Forest
9. Richard Holmes, rhp, Michigan State

January—Secondary Phase (15)

1. Robert Crosby, rhp, New York
2. Buzz Stephen, rhp, Fresno State
3. Tom Cook, c, Manatee (Fla.) JC
4. **Joseph Borowy, rhp, Baltimore**
5. **Glen Smith, of, Arizona State**

June—Regular Phase (20)

1. **Bob Jones, 3b, Dawson, Ga.**
2. **Leo Pinnick, lhp, Billings (Mont.) HS**
3. Steve Garvey, 3b, Chamberlain HS, Tampa
4. Robert Desjardins, c, La Habra (Calif.) HS
5. Dale Campbell, 1b/of, Pepperdine
6. Richard Gouin, of, Pomona (Calif.) Catholic HS
7. **Robert Weisenberg, rhp, North HS, Omaha, Neb.**
8. **Raymond Huett, ss/rhp, Palomar (Calif.) JC**
9. James Needham, rhp/of, Loomis Prep School, South Windsor, Conn.
10. **Steve Braun, ss/2b, Hopewell Valley HS, Titusville, N.J.**
11. **Mike Holbrook, of, Hoover HS, Fresno, Calif.**
12. **Ron Chesebro, lhp, Mayfair HS, Lakewood, Calif.**
13. **Thomas Maurer, lhp, St. Thomas (Minn.)**
14. Bruce Wade, rhp, North HS, Torrance, Calif.
15. **Claude Fontenot, ss, San Fernando HS, Pacoima, Calif.**
16. **Joseph Proctor, c, Beckmonton HS, Plattsburg, N.Y.**
17. Chuck Scrivener, ss, Poly HS, Baltimore
18. Mike Sigman, rhp, Kearney HS, San Diego
19. Thomas Stack, c, Calvert Hall HS, Baltimore
20. Denny Brady, 1b, Purdue
21. Dan Vossler, rhp/1b, Porterville (Calif.) HS
22. **Dennis Moran, ss, University HS, Waco, Texas**
23. **Ronnie Barr, inf, Phoenix JC**
24. **Mike Colin, rhp, Washington**
25. **Robert Ziegler, rhp, Iowa State**
26. **Larry Walters, rhp, Santiago HS, Garden Grove, Calif.**
27. **Larry Jerrel, of, Montana State**
28. Tommy Moore, of, John Glenn HS, Norwalk, Calif.
29. Steve Sueeters, of, Loyola HS, Los Angeles
30. Robert Bentley, rhp, Notre Dame
31. **Dave Hoffman, of, Minnesota**
32. **Robert Castiglione, rhp, New York**
33. **William Hahn, of, Saint Louis**
34. **Ralph Perez, 3b, Washington HS, Los Angeles**
35. Steven Wood, lhp, Kansas State
36. **Phil Johnson, rhp, Iowa Teachers**
37. **Richard Barnes, 3b, South Dakota State**
38. Roger Freed, of, Mount San Antonio (Calif.) JC (Selection voided)
39. **Neil Baskin, 3b, Long Island**
40. Bill Farmer, lhp/1b, Seton HS, Endwell, N.Y.
41. John Clifton, lhp, Chapman (Calif.)
42. **Henry Dennis, rhp, Chatham (N.Y.) HS**
43. Rob Vaughn, rhp, Cerritos (Calif.) JC
44. **Richard Erisman, rhp, Lenape HS, Vincetown, N.J.**
45. **Steve Kadison, 3b, Brown**
46. **Willis Lancaster, c, Franklin HS, New York**
47. Thomas Staach, rhp, Iowa
48. Roger Zahn, lhp, New Ulm (Minn.) HS
49. **James Koosa, 1b, Cardinal Newman HS, Columbia, S.C.**

June—Secondary Phase (6)

1. **Buzz Stephen, rhp, Fresno State**
2. Gary Smith, rhp, Alpena (Mich.) CC
3. **Steven Waters, c, Whittier**
4. **Richard Holmes, rhp, Michigan State**
5. **Robert Hergenrader, lhp, Nebraska**
6. **Peter Middlekauff, 1b, Stanford**
7. **Tom Cole, of, Wake Forest**

August—Legion Phase (19)

No selection

NEW YORK METS

January—Regular Phase (2)

1. **Barry Carter, ss, Chambersburg (Pa.) HS**
2. **Robert Sabo, rhp, Ohio**
3. **Mike Griffith, lhp, Fresno State**
4. Tim Keely, ss, Chatham (N.J.) HS
5. John Cervi, 1b/3b, Erie (N.Y.) CC

January—Secondary Phase (18)

1. James Taylor, of, Southern Methodist
2. **Michael Kenyon, lhp, Ithaca (N.Y.)**
3. **Dewey Weaver, rhp, Pasco HS, Dade City, Fla.**
4. Gary Smith, rhp, Alpena (Mich.) CC
5. **Ron Kyner, of, Arvin (Calif.) HS**
6. Scott Reid, 3b/of, Cerritos (Calif.) JC

June—Regular Phase (1)

1. **Steve Chilcott, c, Antelope Valley HS, Lancaster, Calif.**
2. **Byron Von Hoff, rhp, Batavia (Ill.) HS**
3. **Donald Linehan, lhp, Mount Vernon HS, Lorton, Va.**
4. **Mike Jorgensen, 1b/of, Francis Lewis HS, Queens, N.Y.**
5. **Richard Dost, rhp, James Madison HS, Vienna, Va.**
6. **Eddie Lindblad, rhp, Piper (Kan.) HS**
7. **Wayne Ryan, 2b, Hillcrest HS, Springfield, Mo.**
8. **Simon Ashbrook, c, Wellsburg (W.Va.) HS**
9. Gary Matz, ss/3b, Loyola HS, Baltimore
10. Russell Vitallo, rhp, Berkshire (Mass.) CC
11. **Nyal Leslie, 3b, Arizona**
12. **Mike Minster, c, Fairfax HS, Los Angeles**
13. **Michael Eppler, of/2b, Tulsa**
14. **Edward Palat, of, Grainger HS, Kinston, N.C.**
15. **Dave Rose, c, River Local HS, Hannibal, Ohio**
16. Charles Lelas, 1b, Springfield (Mass.)
17. **Richard Summers, c, Texas**
18. Rod Gaspar, of, Cal State Long Beach
19. Ron Cey, 3b, Mount Tacoma (Wash.) HS
20. **Ernie McAnally, rhp, Paris (Texas) JC**
21. **James Gravley, 1b, Cal State Los Angeles**
22. **William Blucher, 3b, Towson State**
23. John Herzing, lhp, Washington (Mo.)
24. **Frank Lolich, rhp, Brigham Young**
25. Terrence Parks, lhp, Fremont HS, Sunnyvale, Calif.
26. Walter Lampmann, of, Manatee (Fla.) JC
27. **Christopher Putnam, of, Cal State Los Angeles**
28. **Mike Martin, of, Florida State**
29. Arnold Nyulassy, 1b, Eastern Kentucky
30. **Richard Adams, rhp, Chesterfield (S.C.) HS**
31. **Willie Richardson, rhp/ss, Burnet (Texas) HS**
32. Kurt Bevacqua, 2b, Miami-Dade North CC
33. Ron Pinsenschaun, of, Eastern Kentucky
34. James Beck, c, Durham (N.C.) HS
35. Robert Walter, lhp, Santa Clara
36. John Meyer, c, Cincinnati
37. Neil Rivenburg, of, Southern Oregon State
38. **John Smith, rhp, Irondequoit HS, Rochester, N.Y.**
39. George Sutton, of, Clemson
40. **Robert Willet, 3b, Ohio**
41. Franklin Stover, rhp, William Carey (Miss.)
42. Thomas Schweitzer, lhp, Fairmont State (W.Va.)
43. **James Zerilla, rhp/1b, Parsons**
44. **Maury Hopkins, 3b, Florida State**
45. John Mispagel, c, Santa Clara
46. Steve Brasher, rhp, Arizona
47. **Robert Haines, rhp, Columbia Basin (Wash.) CC**
48. **Billy Haynes, rhp, East Rowan County HS, Granite Quarry, N.C.**
49. Gary Marion, ss, Pioneer HS, San Jose, Calif.
50. Owen Toy, of, Nevada-Reno
51. John Hilts, rhp, Wyoming
52. Steve Seale, c, Hillcrest HS, Springfield, Mo.

June—Secondary Phase (9)

1. **Duffy Dyer, c, Arizona State**
2. **Ron Paul, lhp, Texas Christian**
3. **Danny Frisella, rhp, Washington State**
4. **Steve Wright, rhp, San Jose (Calif.) CC**
5. **Roger Stevens, of, California**
6. Rod Austin, of, Santa Clara
7. Tim Keeley, ss, Chatham (N.J.) HS
8. Henry Urbanowicz, 1b, Southwest Missouri State

August—Legion Phase (2)

1. Robert Moore, rhp/1b, Klamath Falls, Ore.

NEW YORK YANKEES

January—Regular Phase (9)

1. **Thomas Matheson, c, Eagle Rock HS, Los Angeles**
2. Dennis Pearson, rhp, Pasadena (Calif.) CC
3. **Michael Bruckner, rhp, Bakersfield (Calif.) JC**

January—Secondary Phase (17)

1. **Bob Biletnikoff, of, Miami**
2. Darrell Evans, inf, Pasadena (Calif.) CC
3. John Ferguson, rhp, Abraham Baldwin Agricultural (Ga.) JC
4. Alan Putz, of, Cheshire Prep School, Rockville, Conn.
5. Edward Long, ss, Auburn
6. Paul Coleman, rhp, Cal Poly Pomona

June—Regular Phase (10)

1. **Jim Lyttle Jr., of, Florida State**
2. **Gary Timberlake, lhp, Meade County HS, Bradenburg, Ky.**
3. **Dave Wolfe, inf, Buena Vista**
4. **Robert Starr, of, Fullerton (Calif.) HS**
5. **Carl Black, rhp, Central Missouri State**
6. **Alvis Hodges, of, Yanceyville (N.C.) HS**
7. **Steve Kline, rhp, Lake Chelan (Wash.) HS**
8. Michael McFarland, rhp, Missouri
9. Gary Laney, inf, Clinton (S.C.) HS
10. Ken Stabler, lhp, Alabama
11. **Roger Dutton, of, Northern Illinois**
12. **Bill Fisher, rhp, Tahlequah HS, Hulbert, Okla.**
13. Ken O'Brien, rhp, Hewlett HS, Woodmere, N.Y.
14. **David Ross, c/of, Pittsburg State**
15. Richard Donnelly, c, Xavier
16. **Jerry Matney, lhp, Northside HS, Vernon, Texas**
17. Richard Buff, inf, Rossville (Ga.) HS
18. **Joe Pactwa, lhp/of, North Thornton HS, Calumet, Ill.**
19. **Earl Hash, of, Richmond**
20. **Jeff Hopkins, of, Wesleyan (Conn.)**
21. Julian Karp, rhp, Washington State
22. Marvin Tucker, inf, Truman HS, Independence, Mo.
23. Clarence Stoner, 1b/of, Penn State
24. Tom Porter, inf, Zephyr Hills (Fla.) HS
25. **Robert Dearrah, rhp, Tulane**
26. **Louie Bunch, c, Central HS, Springfield, Mo.**
27. Lamar Davis, 1b, Maryland
28. **Dallas Jones, c, Belhaven**
29. John Lee, inf/of, Linfield (Ore.)
30. Tim Marks, rhp/of, Manual HS, Peoria, Ill.
31. Tommie Iseminger, 1b, Hillcrest HS, Springfield, Mo.
32. Jim Smith, inf, Lewiston (Idaho) HS
33. Fred Keimel, lhp, Berkeley Heights (N.J.) HS
34. Freddie Dukes, lhp, Central HS, Chattanooga, Tenn.
35. Robert Robbins, lhp, Gowanda (N.Y.) Senior HS
36. Gary Washington, 1b, Mississippi State
37. **Carl Ingrim, c, Glenville State**
38. Bobby Bryant, lhp, South Carolina
39. **Richard Olsen, inf, Iowa State**
40. James Price, rhp, Skyline HS, Salt Lake City

41. **Louis Polisano, of, Glassboro State (N.J.)**
42. **David Steen, rhp, Elk Horn, Iowa**
43. Michael Karkut, lhp, Bayonne (N.J.) HS
44. **William Mason, of, American**
45. Jim Pope, rhp, Pasco (Wash.) HS
46. Robert Parker, c, Duval HS, Lanham, Md.
47. **Robert Height, of, Shaw (N.C.)**
48. Roy Waye, 1b, Lynnview HS, Kingsport, Tenn.
49. William Shepherd, rhp, Rogers HS, Spokane, Wash.
50. Al Simmons, rhp, Idaho
51. Roger Banks, c, Mars Hill (N.C.)
52. Steven Richman, inf, Columbia
53. Luis Flores, c, Lafayette HS, Brooklyn, N.Y.
54. **Rusty Torres, of, New York Vocational HS, Jamaica, N.Y.**
55. Gil Scharringhausen, rhp, Portland State
56. **Thomas Bongiorno, c, Seton Hall**
57. **Ron Lewis, 1b, Temple**
58. **Ernest Recob, of, Kansas State**
59. Kelly Prior, rhp, Florida
60. **Tom Bettecher, lhp, Buffalo State**
61. Richard Carlson, of, Buffalo State
62. Frank Brennan, rhp, Fairleigh Dickinson
63. **Matt Galante, inf, St. John's**

June—Secondary Phase (10)

1. **Walter Manuel, ss, Lafayette**
2. Steve Wrenn, 1b, Wake Forest
3. **Dennis Baldridge, of, Oregon**
4. Terry L'Ange, rhp, Missouri
5. **Steven Mezich, c, Seattle**
6. **John Patterson, 1b, William Jewell**
7. **Glen Borkhuis, rhp, Syracuse**

August—Legion Phase (9)

1. Gregory Croft, rhp, Glenview, Ill.

PHILADELPHIA PHILLIES

January—Regular Phase (10)

1. **John Vukovich, 3b/ss, American River (Calif.) JC**

January—Secondary Phase (6)

1. **Lowell Palmer, rhp, American River (Calif.) JC**
2. John Green, rhp, Gulf Coast (Fla.) JC

June—Regular Phase (9)

1. **Michael Biko, rhp, Samuel HS, Dallas**
2. Patrick Skrable, of, Bakersfield (Calif.) HS
3. Patrick Amos, ss, Arlington Heights HS, Fort Worth, Texas
4. **Ken Reynolds, lhp, New Mexico Highlands**
5. Charles West, of, Texas-El Paso
6. **Michael Beaver, rhp, Worland (Wyo.) HS**
7. William Camp, rhp, Nathan Hale HS, Tulsa, Okla.
8. **Marty Meagher, ss, Rolling Hills (Calif.) HS**
9. Randy Moseley, lhp, Waxahachie (Texas) HS
10. **David Myers, 1b, Chambersburg (Pa.) HS**
11. **Gregg Hansen, c, Wagner**
12. **James Jones, of, Moore HS, Waco, Texas**
13. **Gaston Holland, rhp, The Citadel**
14. **Jack Foreman, rhp, Shelby (Ohio) HS**
15. Frederick Grooms, rhp/of, Wilson HS, San Francisco (Selection voided)
16. **Barry Miller, 2b, Hampfield Area HS, Youngswood, Pa.**
17. Philip MacDonald, of, Crescenta HS, La Crescenta, Calif.
18. Thomas Schleer, lhp, Wayne (N.J.) HS
19. Richard Corsetto, rhp, Gannon
20. **James McNeil, c, North Plainfield (N.J.) HS**
21. Ronald Fournier, 1b, Pasadena (Calif.) CC
22. James Sanders, rhp, Southside HS, Florence, S.C.
23. Earl Vickers, of, Fresno State
24. **Richard Seminoff, rhp, Arizona**
25. **Ben Farrell, rhp, Lipscomb**
26. Jodie Beeler, c, Samuels HS, Dallas

June—Secondary Phase (13)

1. **Steve Arlin, rhp, Ohio State**
2. **Carl Merrill, c, Maine**
3. **Richard Johnson, rhp, Arizona**
4. Tom Cook, c, Manatee (Fla.) JC

August—Legion Phase (10)

No selection

PITTSBURGH PIRATES

January—Regular Phase (16)

1. **Kent Smith, of, Sacramento (Calif.) CC**
2. James Minnette, inf, Columbia Basin (Wash.) CC
3. Willard Somerset, inf/of, Duquesne

January—Secondary Phase (8)

1. Fred Mazurek, of, Pittsburgh
2. Frank Brosseau, of, Minnesota
3. **Dennis Malseed, rhp/inf, Woodlynne, Pa.**
4. Del Unser, of/1b, Mississippi State
5. Richard Devarney, ss, Maine
6. Dick Mills, rhp, Parsons
7. Danny Talbott, 1b/of, North Carolina
8. David Barton, ss, Ithaca (N.Y.)

June—Regular Phase (15)

1. **Richie Hebner, ss, Norwood (Mass.) HS**
2. **Jim Minshall, rhp, Newport Catholic HS, Melbourne, Ky.**
3. **Richard Grimaldi, rhp, Proctor HS, Utica, N.Y.**
4. **Dave Lambert, of, Washington**
5. **Dave Cash Jr., ss, Proctor HS, Utica, N.Y.**
6. **Gene Clines, 2b/of, Ells HS, Richmond, Calif.**
7. **Bill Laxton, lhp, Audubon (N.J.) HS**
8. **Stanley Baker, c, 71st HS, Fayetteville, N.C.**
9. **Paul Pierce, of, Pittsfield (Mass.) HS**
10. **Robert McKee, lhp, Etna HS, Pittsburgh**
11. **Dave Arrington, rhp/of, DeAnza HS, El Sobrante, Calif.**
12. Ron Schueler, rhp, Hays HS, Catherine, Kan.
13. **Raymond Heller, rhp, Wicomico HS, Salisbury, Md.**
14. **Robert Sherry, inf, Washington**
15. William Stone, of, Warren Easton HS, New Orleans
16. James Kovalsky, c, Washington (N.J.) HS
17. James Lawrence, c, Deep Creek HS, Chesapeake, Va.
18. **Jim Palm, of, Carlmont HS, Belmont, Calif.**
19. **Michael Fuchs, lhp, Parkersburg (W.Va.) HS**
20. **Robert Butkus, lhp, Bowdoin**
21. **Wilbert Murphy, of, McCloud, Calif.**
22. **Larry Stout, rhp, Huntington**
23. **Calvin Bailey, rhp, West Virginia State**
24. **Robin Porter, c/of, Virginia Military Institute**
25. **Douglas Stanley, of, West Virginia**
26. Taylor Toomey, lhp, Colorado
27. Paul Mann, rhp, Afton HS, St. Louis
28. **Walter Joyner, of/lhp, Western Maryland**
29. **Gary McCabe, rhp/of, Cripple Creek-Victor HS, Victor, Colo.**
30. Edwin Figueroa, c, George Washington HS, New York
31. James Engel, rhp, Bensenville, Ill.
32. Gary Johnson, inf, Idaho
33. Michael Horn, rhp, Boone County HS, Florence, Ky.
34. Richard Jaggars, rhp, Gonzaga
35. James Skovron, rhp, Pentucket Regional HS, West Newbury, Mass.
36. **Donald Messinese, lhp, Crossland HS, Washington, Md.**
37. **Joe Johnson, rhp, Loyal Sock HS, Williamsport, Pa.**
38. Rich Hand, rhp, Lincoln HS, Seattle
39. Ronald Epperson, rhp, Hudson Bay HS, Vancouver, Wash.
40. Charles Dupuis, of, Evergreen, Wash.
41. Philip Scarpellino, 1b, New Haven (Conn.)

June—Secondary Phase (19)

1. **Frank Brosseau, of, Minnesota**
2. Kenneth Lohnes, c, Cerritos (Calif.) JC
3. David Barton, ss, Ithaca (N.Y.)
4. James Minnette, inf, Columbia Basin (Wash.) CC
5. Danny Talbott, 1b/of, North Carolina

August—Legion Phase (16)

No selection

ST. LOUIS CARDINALS

January—Regular Phase (8)

1. Henry Urbanowitz, 1b, Jasper (Mo.) JC
2. **Jessie DuBose, lhp, Smith HS, Ozark, Ala.**
3. **James Moore, 2b/ss, El Dorado, Ark.**

January—Secondary Phase (2)

1. **Raymond Baker, rhp, Columbia Basin (Wash.) CC**
2. Kenneth Lohnes, c, Cerritos (Calif.) JC
3. William Carino, c, Mount Hermon (Mass.) HS

June—Regular Phase (7)

1. **Leron Lee, inf/of, Grant HS, Sacramento, Calif.**
2. **Dan Barrett, ss, Hillcrest HS, Springfield, Mo.**
3. **Clay Kirby Jr., rhp, Washington HS, Arlington, Va.**
4. Bob Spence, 1b, Santa Clara
5. **Donald Cooksey, rhp/of, OFallon Tech HS, St. Louis**
6. Edward Bauer, lhp, Columbus HS, Bronx, N.Y.
7. **Jerry Bartee, ss, Central HS, Omaha, Neb.**
8. **Samuel Stewart, of, Oklahoma Baptist**
9. **Gary Ford, 3b, Ventura (Calif.) HS**
10. Coie Shumaker, lhp, Maben (Miss.) HS
11. **Dewayne Wendt, ss, Deshler (Ohio) HS**
12. **Joe Atilee, rhp, B.C. Almore HS, Houston**
13. **Terrence Murphy, 2b, Cardinal Mooney HS, Rochester, N.Y.**
14. **Douglas Lukens, rhp, Washington State**
15. Frank Patterson, of, Grambling
16. **Monty Little, ss, Ayden (N.C.) HS**
17. Dale Reed, lhp, Glendale HS, Springfield, Mo.
18. Jerry Paetzhold, lhp, Sparta HS, Ellis Grove, Ill.
19. Gary Ratliff, of, Tulsa, Okla.
20. **Clement Nowakowski, rhp, Washington HS, Chicago**
21. Michael Noonan, lhp, Foothill (Calif.) JC
22. Robert Sharp, rhp, Torrance (Calif.) HS
23. Jerry Meadows, rhp, West Virginia
24. **Larry Wright, rhp, College Park HS, Pleasant Hill, Calif.**
25. **Dale Hill, 3b/c, Iowa City (Iowa) HS**
26. Jim Panther, rhp, Southern Illinois
27. **George Bruns, 2b, Manhattan**
28. **Robert Schaffer, ss, Connecticut**
29. **Robert Moone, 1b, St. Ritas HS, Chicago**
30. Jerry Sabourin, lhp, Cleveland HS, St. Louis
31. Stephen Dean, 1b, Mount Whitney HS, Visalia, Calif.
32. **William Cheslock, 1b/of, Hofstra**
33. **Eddie Dixon, 3b/rhp, Hiwasee (Tenn.) JC**
34. **Frederick Covey, rhp, Phillipsburg (Pa.) HS**
35. **Earl Nursement, of, Nevada-Reno**
36. **Kenneth Kurtz, 2b, Arizona**
37. William Flood, of/c, Connecticut
38. John Manginelli, 3b, Irvington (N.J.) HS (Selection voided)
39. Phillip Trombino, 1b, Iona
40. Mike Pruett, lhp, Ritenour HS, Overland, Mo.
41. **Bruce MacLean, rhp, Bowdoin**
42. **James Smith, rhp, Chipola (Fla.) JC**
43. **Lanny Guyer, 2b, Southern Oregon State**
44. Jan Biggs, c, Bullard HS, Fresno, Calif.
45. **Michael Steele, 1b, San Diego State**
46. **Larry Azevedo, rhp, Hilman (Calif.) HS**

June—Secondary Phase (17)

1. **Jerry DaVanon, 2b, Westmont**
2. Bob Chlupsa, rhp/1b, Manhattan
3. Bruce Hinkel, lhp, Upper Iowa

August—Legion Phase (8)

No selection

SAN FRANCISCO GIANTS

January—Regular Phase (18)

1. **Gary Bowman, of, Garden City, Mich.**
2. Stephen Lohrer, of, Nassau (N.Y.) CC
3. Tony Muser, 1b/p, San Diego Mesa JC

January—Secondary Phase (12)

1. Dick Tidrow, p, Chabot (Calif.) JC

June—Regular Phase (17)

1. **Bob Reynolds, rhp, Ingraham HS, Seattle**
2. **Joseph Hebert, ss, Baton Rouge (La.) HS**
3. **James Carroll, rhp, Mississippi State**
4. Rich Folkers, lhp, Ellsworth (Iowa) JC
5. Dave Lemonds, of/lhp, Garinger HS, Charlotte, N.C.
6. **Keith Wade, of, Muir HS, Pasadena, Calif.**
7. **John Beaton, rhp, Murray State**
8. Steve Barnhill, of, Hinkley HS, Aurora, Colo.
9. Gerald Christman, lhp, Deshler (Ohio) HS
10. Jack Grasing, lhp, Villanova
11. **Bernie Williams, of, St. Elizabeth HS, Oakland, Calif.**
12. Mike Sadek, c, Minnesota
13. **Gary Ryerson, lhp, Rolling Hills HS, Palos Verdes, Calif.**
14. Gary Kollman, ss, Wyoming
15. Robert Hoey, 3b, Assumption HS, East St. Louis, Ill.
16. **Robert DeLong, lhp, Willow Glen HS, San Jose, Calif.**
17. **Don Hahn, of, Campbell HS, San Jose, Calif.**
18. **Dale Spier, rhp, Arizona State**
19. Clifford Farmer, rhp, Hillcrest HS, Springfield, Mo.
20. Ted Rohde, of, Sierra HS, Toll House, Calif.
21. Daniel Blood, 2b, Arcadia (Calif.) HS
22. Frank Baker, ss, Southern Mississippi
23. **Charles Hopkins, rhp, Oregon**
24. Michael Babler, rhp, St. Elizabeths HS, San Lorenzo, Calif.
25. **Marc Michel, of, Iowa**
26. **Michael Wysocki, rhp, Georgia**
27. Donald Kirkland, rhp/inf, Southern Illinois
28. Terrence Stofer, of, Key West (Fla.) HS
29. **Roy Johnson, rhp, Canoga Park HS, Woodland Hills, Calif.**
30. Tom Burgess, rhp, Phoenix JC
31. **John Harrell, c, West Valley (Calif.) JC**
32. **Gerald Anding, rhp, Cal State Northridge**
33. Phillip Thomas, rhp/inf, Tonganoxie (Kan.) HS
34. Ray Strable, rhp, JC of the Sequoias (Calif.)
35. James Dew, c, Mayville, N.D.
36. **Brad Dodge, of, Jordan HS, Long Beach, Calif.**
37. **Rusty York, of, Phoenix JC**
38. Richard Wanless, rhp, Quincy (Mass.) HS
39. Mike Ford, c, Lewis (Ill.)
40. Bob Garcia, of, JC of the Sequoias (Calif.)

June—Secondary Phase (1)

1. **Bill Frost, rhp, California**
2. Kris Krebs, ss, Manatee (Fla.) JC
3. Gary Gentry, rhp, Phoenix JC
4. Tom Murphy, rhp, Ohio
5. David Pratt, lhp, Tennessee Tech

August—Legion Phase (18)

No selection

WASHINGTON SENATORS

January—Regular Phase (5)

1. **Timothy Zajeski, rhp, South Holland, Ill.**
2. **Gary Kolumbus, of, Waller HS, Chicago**

January—Secondary Phase (13)

1. Bob Stinson III, of/c, Miami HS
2. Bob Reed, rhp, Michigan
3. John Miklos, lhp, Valparaiso
4. Percy Sensabaugh, rhp, Virginia Military Institute
5. Terry L'Ange, rhp, Missouri
6. George Gazegorek, ss, Houston
7. John Biedenbach, 3b, Michigan State
8. **Dick Such, rhp, Elon**
9. Lionel Jones, of, Southern

June—Regular Phase (6)

1. **Tom Grieve, of/c, Pittsfield (Mass.) HS**
2. **O.L. Bowers, ss, John Marshall HS, Oklahoma City, Okla.**
3. Lou Camilli, 3b, Texas A&M
4. **Wallace Smallwood, rhp, Martinsburg (W.Va.) HS**

5. **Gerald Merlet, ss/3b, Beloit (Wis.) HS**
6. Kim Hillstrom, rhp, Central Michigan
7. John Fryer, rhp, Brevard (Fla.) CC (Selection voided)
8. John Bowman, lhp, Trinity
9. **Robert Miller, 3b, Lewis (Ill.)**
10. Larry Herring, lhp, Dillon (S.C.) HS
11. **Wayne Brescher, c, Southeastern Louisiana**
12. **Jack Merlet, 2b, Northern Illinois**
13. **John Michael, ss, Morrow (Ohio) HS**
14. Dan Neumeier, rhp, Gresham (Wis.) HS
15. Geoff Petrie, rhp, Springfield (Pa.) HS
16. **LeRoy Visor, ss, Park HS, Racine, Wis.**
17. Nick Furlong, rhp, Iona Prep School, New Rochelle, N.Y.
18. **Dwayne Kalmer, c, Quincy**
19. Edward Cook, ss/of, Bridgewater (Va.)
20. Mickey Yates, of, Texas Christian
21. Charles Miller, rhp, Waynesville (Ohio) HS
22. William Kelley, rhp, Archbishop Curley HS, Baltimore
23. William Wright, lhp, Montgomery (Md.) JC
24. Mike Flanagan, rhp, North Carolina
25. **Gerry Schoen, rhp, Loyola (La.)**
26. Gerry Pirtle, rhp, Hale HS, Tulsa, Okla.
27. **Walter Collins, rhp, Norview HS, Norfolk, Va.**
28. **Richard Bucholtz, rhp, Burlington (Wis.) HS**
29. Richard Wicks, lhp, Lake Charles (La.) HS
30. Dick Snyder, of, Davidson
31. Charley Baudier, rhp, Louisiana State
32. **Jerry Etheridge, of, Bamberg (S.C.) HS**
33. Chris Kougias, 1b, Fort Hunt HS, Alexandria, Va.
34. Dave Cichon, c, Eastern HS, Bristol, Conn.

June—Secondary Phase (18)

1. **Del Unser, of/1b, Mississippi State**
2. **John Biedenbach, 3b, Michigan State**
3. **John Miklos, lhp, Valparaiso**
4. **Fred Shuey, of, Southern California**

August—Legion Phase (5)

No selection

1967

TEAMS FIND OUT EARLY IN DRAFT HISTORY THAT DRAFTING FOR NEED USUALLY DOESN'T WORK OUT WELL

The fall was sudden and dramatic. The Yankees, the most successful franchise in baseball history, found themselves on the bottom looking up just two years after winning their ninth American League title in 10 years.

Their consolation prize: the No. 1 pick in the 1967 draft, one of just two times the Yankees owned the dubious distinction.

The Yankees knew right away what kind of player they were looking for. Trying to elicit memories of Mickey Mantle, they went after 18-year-old Ron Blomberg, a power-hitting center fielder. It was no coincidence that Blomberg was also Jewish; the Yankees hoped he would appeal to the large Jewish population in New York.

"The Yankees have always been my favorite team," Blomberg said, "and Mantle my favorite player."

Blomberg, primarily a pitcher/first baseman at Druid Hills High in Atlanta, hit .472 with five homers and 45 RBIs that spring, and signed with the Yankees for $75,000.

"I feel Ronnie is the best pro prospect to come along in several years," said Yankees general manager Lee MacPhail, in announcing Blomberg's signing. "We had six of our scouts watch Ronnie and they unanimously agreed that he was the one we should sign. I figure it will take him about three years to reach the majors."

Blomberg reached New York on schedule, but he became little more than a platoon player with the Yankees, hitting .295 in 461 games spread over seven seasons. He was much more widely noted as the first player to appear in a big league game as a designated hitter, when the AL adopted the rule in 1973.

Many thought the Yankees, plagued by problems at shortstop since the retirement of Tony Kubek after the 1965 season, would go for Terry Hughes, a slick-fielding shortstop from Spartanburg, S.C. When they passed, the Cubs got their man, making him the first player from the June draft to sign, for a $65,000 bonus.

"Our report on this boy," Cubs vice president John Holland said, "is that he has no faults. He could step onto the field right now and hold his own with the glove. He is a tremendous shortstop."

Hughes, a .615 hitter as a high school senior, hit just .209 in 54 big league games—just two with the Cubs.

Righthander Mike Garman from Caldwell, Idaho, was the other member of a clearly defined top three

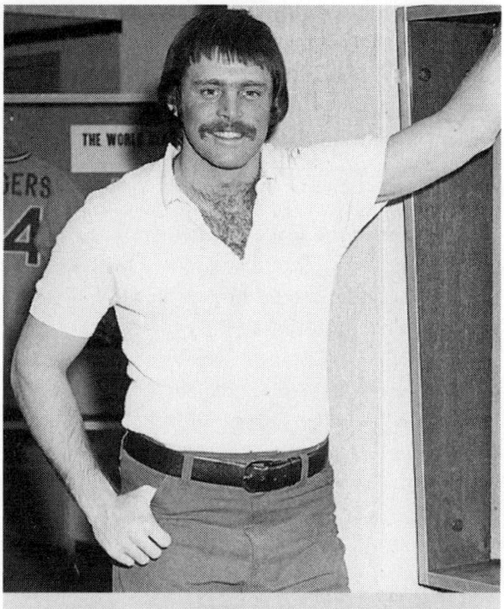

Ron Blomberg was better known for being the first DH than for standout performance

prospects. The Red Sox took him with the third pick and signed him for $50,000.

A total of 1,162 selections were made in the June draft, making it the busiest single draft until 1987, when the January phase was abolished and all players were selected in June.

The 1967 draft also had a decided high school flavor to it. Of the 40 players selected in the first two rounds of the regular phase, 39 were high school products. The lone exception was Southern Methodist third baseman Don Denbow, selected by the Dodgers with the last pick in the first round.

A change in the college rule, restricting the selection of college players to graduates or those who had turned 21, resulted in even more high school selections in the regular phase. The old college rule allowed the signing of college sophomores, but it was amended at the 1966 Winter Meetings. The new rule generally provided protection for colleges until a player completed his junior year, though the player much have turned 21 by Aug. 1 to be eligible that June.

A grandfather clause in the new college rule permitted players who had previously been drafted and would have been eligible for selection in the secondary phase under the old rule to still be drafted. One such player was Southern California sophomore righthander Mike Adamson, an unsigned first-round pick from the 1965 draft. Adamson, selected No. 1 overall after striking out 143 in 101 innings for the Trojans, stepped right into the Orioles rotation. He proved to be overmatched, however, and never won a game in the major leagues.

A draft-record 194 players were selected in the secondary phase of the June draft, including a record 17 by the Dodgers. Among the picks was righthander Gary Gentry, the ace for College World Series champion Arizona State. Gentry, drafted in the third round by the Mets, set a college record with 229 strikeouts in 174 innings, while posting a 17-1 record and 1.14 ERA.

Arizona State and USC, which began a run of eight consecutive College World Series titles between them in 1967, had the greatest impact on the June draft, with eight selections apiece.

For college players, 1967 was also a historic year because freshmen became eligible to play baseball for the first time. Combined with the provisions of the draft's new college rule, the typical college player would play three years in college before being draft eligible. In the past, most of the top college players left after a single varsity season.

The Epstein Factor

Seldom has an active major leaguer had such a profound effect on the draft as first baseman Mike Epstein did in 1967.

At the time, Epstein was one of the most noted young players in the game. A 6-foot-4, 230-pound slugger who signed for a $50,000 bonus with Baltimore following the 1964 Olympics, Epstein piled up some of the best numbers in the minor leagues in 1965 and '66, narrowly missing out on back-to-back triple crowns.

But Epstein balked when Baltimore attempted to option him to the minor leagues after a slow start in 1967, and the Orioles were forced to shop Epstein around. He was traded to Washington about a week before the June draft.

The Yankees had a strong interest in Epstein but were unwilling to part with ace pitcher Mel Stottlemyre to acquire him. So they made their minds up to go for Blomberg.

Epstein's influence didn't stop there. The Senators, drafting fifth, were set to take first baseman John Mayberry with that selection. But having just dealt for Epstein, they decided against taking another first baseman.

Instead the Senators decided to take a sleeper, catcher John Jones, who had hit no homers that spring for a Tennessee high school team that won one game. Jones went on to hit a meager .150 in a four-year pro career that never advanced past Class A.

Mayberry? He was the next pick and went on to hit 255 home runs in a 15-year big league career.

"It was between Jones and Mayberry," Senators general manager George Selkirk said. "We decided to go with the catcher because of the Epstein deal."

Not only did the Senators miss out on Mayberry, but Epstein also fizzled and the Senators continued to bring up the rear in the American League for years to come.

DRAFT 67: FIRST-ROUND PICKS

No.	Club	Player, Pos.	School	Hometown	Ht.	Wt.	B-T	Age
1.	Yankees	Ron Blomberg, 1b	Druid Hills HS	Atlanta	6-1	185	L-R	18
2.	Cubs	Terry Hughes, ss	Dorman HS	Spartanburg, S.C.	6-1	185	R-R	18
3.	Red Sox	Mike Garman, rhp	Caldwell HS	Caldwell, Idaho	6-3	200	R-R	17
4.	Mets	Jon Matlack, lhp	Henderson HS	West Chester, Pa.	6-3	185	L-L	17
5.	Senators	John Jones, c	Loretto HS	St. Joseph, Tenn.	6-1	195	L-R	17
6.	Astros	John Mayberry, 1b	Northwestern HS	Detroit	6-3	207	L-L	17
7.	Athletics	Brian Bickerton, lhp	Santana HS	Santee, Calif.	6-2	190	L-L	17
8.	Reds	Wayne Simpson, rhp	Centennial HS	Los Angeles	6-5	205	R-R	18
9.	Angels	Mike Nunn, c	Smith HS	Greensboro, N.C.	6-0	178	L-R	18
10.	Cardinals	Ted Simmons, c	Southfield HS	Southfield, Mich.	6-0	185	B-R	17
11.	Indians	Jack Heidemann, ss	Brenham HS	Brenham, Texas	6-0	165	R-R	17
12.	Braves	Andrew Finlay, of	Burbank HS	Sacramento, Calif.	6-0	185	R-R	17
13.	White Sox	Dan Haynes, 3b	Headland HS	East Point, Ga.	6-2	210	R-R	17
14.	Phillies	Phil Meyer, lhp	Pius X HS	Downey, Calif.	6-1	185	L-L	18
15.	Tigers	Jim Foor, lhp	McCluer HS	Ferguson, Mo.	6-2	165	L-L	17
16.	Pirates	Joe Grigas, of	Coyle HS	Brockton, Mass.	6-0	170	L-L	18
17.	Twins	Steve Brye, 3b/of	St. Elizabeth HS	Oakland, Calif.	6-1	190	R-R	18
18.	Giants	Dave Rader, c	South HS	Bakersfield, Calif.	5-11	165	L-R	18
19.	Orioles	Bobby Grich, ss	Wilson HS	Long Beach, Calif.	6-2	180	R-R	18
20.	Dodgers	Don Denbow, 3b	Southern Methodist	Dallas	6-2	185	R-R	21

1967

CLUB-BY-CLUB SELECTIONS

ATLANTA BRAVES

January—Regular Phase (11)

1. Travis Washington, of, Bacone (Okla.) JC
2. **Charles Swanson, rhp, Los Angeles Valley JC**
3. **William Adelman, 1b, Broward (Fla.) CC**
4. James O'Leary, rhp/of, Dutchess (N.Y.) CC
5. **John Simmers, rhp, Buena Park, Calif.**
6. **Mike Gutierrez, 2b, Los Angeles CC**
7. Phillip Cardwell, inf/of, Manatee (Fla.) JC
8. John Brett, 3b/of, El Camino (Calif.) JC
9. Donald Smith, rhp/1b, CC of Baltimore
10. Frank Slaton, 1b/lhp, Antelope Valley (Calif.) JC
11. Mark Loper, 3b/of, American River (Calif.) JC
12. **Lee Larson, 3b, Los Angeles Pierce JC**
13. Frederich Senger, c, CC of Baltimore
14. C.T. Coe, c, Navarro (Texas) JC
15. **Edward Silverman, lhp, Fairleigh Dickinson**
16. **Larry Goldberg, c, Trenton (Mo.) JC**

January—Secondary Phase (3)

1. Bill Gillean, rhp, Cerritos (Calif.) JC
2. **Stan Bell, rhp, Manatee (Fla.) JC**
3. **Ron Schueler, rhp, Catherine, Kan.**
4. Chuck Scrivener, ss, CC of Baltimore
5. Frank Patterson, of, Grambling
6. Kurt Bevacqua, 2b, Miami-Dade North CC
7. Gerry Pirtle, rhp, Bacone (Okla.) JC
8. Marvin Tucker, 2b, Independence, Mo.
9. Jerry Marion, of, Wyoming
10. Greg Garrett, lhp, Newhall, Calif.

June—Regular Phase (12)

1. **Andrew Finlay, of, Burbank HS, Sacramento, Calif.**
2. **Dennis Dalton, rhp, Altavista (Va.) HS**
3. **Ralph Garr, 2b, Grambling**
4. **Bob Didier, c, Glen Oaks HS, Baton Rouge, La.**
5. Harold Ziegler, 3b, Coatesville (Pa.) HS
6. **Ronald Owens, rhp, Lake Hamilton HS, Pearcy, Ark.**
7. Bobby Croswell, ss, Central HS, Jackson, Miss.
8. Dave Elmendorf, of, Westbury HS, Houston
9. William Hodge, c, Austin HS, Bryan, Texas
10. Edward Rios, of/lhp, Burbank HS, Sacramento, Calif.
11. **Terry Hankins, ss, Canoga Park HS, Woodland Hills, Calif.**
12. Chester Patterson, rhp, Newark Academy, Far Hills, N.J.
13. **Byron Kennedy, c, Page HS, Greensboro, N.C.**
14. **Richard Wurstner, ss/2b, Turner HS, Buffalo, N.Y.**
15. **Mark Vanderwater, c, Parsippany (N.J.) HS**
16. **Robert Andrews, lhp, San Jose, Calif.**
17. **Robert Wiswell, lhp, UCLA**
18. John Wilmouth, 1b, McClure HS, St. Louis
19. Carl Mayfield, c, Kennedy HS, Denver
20. Edward Fisher, ss, Campbell
21. **James Brittan, lhp, Maplewood HS, St. Louis**
22. Howard Hall, 1b/of, Bogalusa, La.
23. Gary Moleberg, 3b/1b, Pampa (Texas) HS
24. **Forest Patterson, 2b/ss, Altamont (Ill.) HS**
25. **Mike Testa, of, Morris Hills Regional HS, Parsippany, N.J.**
26. **Dusty Baker Jr., of, Del Campo HS, Carmichael, Calif.**
27. Donald Autry, ss, Blair HS, Pasadena, Calif.
28. **Wayne Boatman, of, Murphy HS, Mobile, Ala.**
29. Thomas Urquhart, rhp, Marriam (Kan.) HS
30. David Byerly, of, Permian HS, Odessa, Texas
31. **Robert Churchich, 3b, Nebraska**
32. **Joseph Fanning, c, Central Connecticut State**
33. Gene Rinaldi, ss, Miami-Dade North CC
34. **George Sahadi, 1b, Lafayette HS, Brooklyn, N.Y.**
35. Michael Magness, rhp, Cedartown (Ga.) HS
36. Willie Frazier, ss, Meridian (Miss.) HS
37. Derk Hoving, c, Tascosa HS, Amarillo, Texas
38. William Wright, rhp, Marysville, Calif.
39. Craig Lown, rhp, Roncillo HS, Pueblo, Colo.
40. Russell Ross, ss, Fairfax (Va.) HS
41. **Keith Walters, rhp, Saratoga, Calif.**
42. Gerald Burton, of, Ritenour HS, St. Louis
43. Archie Manning, ss, Drew (Miss.) HS
44. Alan Bush, lhp, Quincy (Ill.) HS
45. **Allen Jillison, lhp, Southern Regional HS, Manalawki, N.J.**
46. Charles Atkinson, ss, Hillside (N.J.) HS
47. Harry Brinson, lhp, Harding HS, Oklahoma City, Okla.
48. Thomas Trailer, of, Robert E. Lee HS, Montgomery, Ala.

June—Secondary Phase (8)

1. **Garry Hill, rhp, North Carolina**
2. Bill Dobbs, lhp, Oklahoma State
3. **Tom House, lhp, Southern California**
4. Harold Harris, 3b, Gulf Coast (Fla.) CC
5. Dennis Parks, of, Long Beach (Calif.) CC
6. **William Craig, rhp, Morehead State**
7. Luis Flores, c, Gardner-Webb

BALTIMORE ORIOLES

January—Regular Phase (20)

1. **Brent Nickoloff, inf, Torrance (Calif.) HS**
2. **Lew Beasley, of, Sparta, Va.**
3. **Herman Grant, rhp, Riverview HS, Boykins, Va.**
4. **Stanley Martin, ss, Los Angeles Valley JC**
5. William Kirkpatrick, rhp, CC of San Francisco
6. **Tom Kober, rhp, Allentown, Pa.**
7. Thomas Keyser, c, Allegheny (Md.) CC
8. Michael Jones, ss, Washington HS, San Francisco
9. Howard Casey, lhp, Treasure Valley (Ore.) CC
10. Joe Arnold, rhp, Miami-Dade North CC
11. **Lawrence Korpisch, 1b, Southeastern Illinois JC**
12. **Frank Joyal, c, Freyburg Academy HS, Burlington, Ver**
13. **Tommy Williams, rhp, Thomasville, Ga.**

January—Secondary Phase (10)

1. **Johnny Oates, c, Virginia Tech**
2. Steve Steitz, 3b, East Longmeadow, Mass.
3. **John Montague, rhp, Newport News, Va.**
4. Alfred Crawford, of, Miami-Dade North CC
5. Greg Riddoch, ss, Colorado State
6. James Skeins, ss, Ranger (Texas) JC
7. Jodie Beeler, c, Dallas
8. **Daniel Beard, rhp, Lakewood, Calif.**
9. **John Hilts, rhp, Wyoming**
10. Michael Noonan, lhp, Foothill (Calif.) JC
11. **Larry Piquet, of, Eugene, Ore.**
12. Herbert Hofvendahl, of, Orinda, Calif. (Selection voided)
13. William Farmer, lhp, Endwell, N.Y.
14. Taylor Toomey, lhp, Colorado

June—Regular Phase (19)

1. **Bobby Grich, ss, Wilson HS, Long Beach, Calif.**
2. **Don Baylor, of, Austin (Texas) HS**
3. **Greg Arnold, rhp, Southern HS, Baltimore**
4. Chris Farasopolous, 2b, North HS, Torrance, Calif.
5. **Dave Johnson, rhp, Cooper HS, Abilene, Texas**
6. **Ronny Stewart, of, Balboa HS, San Francisco**
7. **Wayne Hoots, of, Hendersonville (N.C.) HS**
8. Lou Lanehardt, lhp, Patapsco HS, Baltimore
9. Fred Kuppers, c, Los Angeles Valley JC
10. Robert Blakely, of/1b, Griffin HS, Springfield, Ill.
11. **William Ray, lhp, Belleville (Mich.) HS**
12. **Robert Sorrentino, lhp, Notre Dame HS, Bridgeport, Conn.**
13. Michael Wertz, ss, McCallum HS, Austin, Texas

14. Dave Schmid, of, St. Joseph HS, Baltimore
15. James Reynolds, rhp, Messick HS, Memphis, Tenn.
16. Dave Kropfelter, c, Mount St. Joseph HS, Baltimore
17. **Mike Duggan, 2b, Bishop Barry HS, St. Petersburg, Fla.**
18. **Winston Presley, rhp, Jefferson HS, Los Angeles**
19. Sam Cook, of, San Bernardino (Calif.) HS
20. Doug Rau, lhp, Columbus (Texas) HS
21. Earl Nance, lhp, George Wythe HS, Richmond, Va.
22. Terry Wedgewood, ss/3b, Bosse HS, Evansville, Ind.
23. Billy DeMars, ss, Irondequoit HS, Rochester, N.Y.
24. **David Ekelund, 1b, Wilton (Conn.) HS**
25. Robert Williams, of, Snammish HS, Kirkland, Wash.
26. Ronald Hale, rhp, Highland Springs (Va.) HS
27. Roy Swanson, rhp, Warren (Pa.) HS
28. James Davies, of, Brookston (Ind.) HS
29. Larry Mongillo, of, Serra HS, San Mateo, Calif.
30. **Dave Harter, lhp, Cardinal Doughtery HS, Buffalo, N.Y.**
31. Dan Ryan, 1b, Columbia Basin (Wash.) JC
32. Joe Crocker, c, Goldendale HS, Centerville, Wash.
33. Richard Wagener, lhp, Andover HS, Linthicum Heights, Md.
34. William Carroll, of, Cal State Los Angeles
35. **Edward Watts, 3b, Maggie Walker HS, Richmond, Va.**
36. Watkins Blane, 1b, Georgia Tech
37. **Edward Gilkes, of, Northeast HS, St. Petersburg, Fla.**
38. Bill Borelli, 1b, JC of San Mateo (Calif.)
39. Lee Chilton, rhp, Edison HS, Stockton, Calif.
40. James Cherwa, rhp, Frank W. Cox HS, Virginia Beach, Va.
41. Dave Dingman, c, Churchill HS, Eugene, Ore.
42. Henry Hoxit, rhp, John F. Kennedy HS, Willingboro, N.J.
43. **Doug Hatten, lhp, Naches (Wash.) HS**
44. **John Gonzales, lhp, Metropolitan State**
45. James Snyder, of, East Carolina
46. Robert Wilczynski, 1b/of, St. Francis HS, Toledo, Ohio
47. Robert Taylor, rhp, Colonial Heights (Va.) HS
48. **Len Pupo, of, Gonzaga**
49. **Charles Sylvester, 2b, St. Petersburg (Fla.) HS**
50. Hunter Hollar, rhp, Broadway HS, Singers Glen, Va.
51. Joseph MacDonald, of, Bishop Hendrickson HS, Warwick, R.I.
52. Phil Honeycutt, 3b, Shawnee (Okla.) HS
53. **Allen Kwiatkowski, lhp, Airport (Mich.) CC**
54. George Ferguson, ss, Maine
55. Gene Ammann, rhp, Lakeside HS, Decatur, Ga.
56. Carl Bennett, c, Edison HS, Stockton, Calif.
57. Jimmy Blackmon, rhp, Rock Hill (S.C.) HS (Selection voided)
58. Richard Coble, rhp, Jacksonville (Ill.) HS
59. Mike Ehlers, c, Centerville (Iowa) JC
60. **James Thomas, inf/of, Colby**
61. Steve Webber, rhp, Muscatine (Iowa) CC
62. Barry Woodruff, lhp, Woodside (Calif.) HS
63. Mike Young, rhp, JC of San Mateo (Calif.)
64. Tom Skendarian, of, Brown

June—Secondary Phase (1)

1. **Mike Adamson, rhp, Southern California**
2. **Gil Scharringhausen, rhp, Portland State**
3. Danny Talbott, 3b, North Carolina
4. Dayle Campbell, of, Pepperdine
5. **Jerry Meadows, rhp, West Virginia**
6. William Ferguson, c, Texas Christian
7. Michael McFarland, rhp, Missouri
8. Gary Smith, rhp, Michigan State (Selection voided)
9. Bill Seinsoth, 1b, Southern California
10. Dan Enger, 1b/of, Birmingham HS, Van Nuys, Calif.
11. Robert Walter, lhp, Santa Clara
12. Steve Garman, ss/rhp, Idaho

BOSTON RED SOX

January—Regular Phase (4)

1. **Carlton Fisk, c, Charlestown, N.H.**
2. **Don Newhauser, rhp, Broward (Fla.) CC**
3. Craig Skok, lhp, Broward (Fla.) CC

January—Secondary Phase (18)

1. Harold Harris, ss, Huitt-Trussville HS, Birmingham, Ala.
2. **Michael Koritko, inf, Stratford, Conn.**
3. Bob Bryant, lhp, South Carolina
4. Jack Fulmer, 3b, Arkansas State
5. Geoff Zahn, lhp, Michigan
6. Charles Kline, lhp, Michigan State
7. Bill Zepp, rhp, Michigan

June—Regular Phase (3)

1. **Mike Garman, rhp, Caldwell (Idaho) HS**
2. Danny Graham, ss, Bishop Montgomery HS, Torrance, Calif.
3. **Christopher Cross, c, Englewood HS, Jacksonville, Fla.**
4. Dudley Mitchell, of/1b, Thomas Jefferson HS, Denver
5. Michael Witt, of, McLane HS, Fresno, Calif.
6. **Samuel Phillips, rhp, Eastern Hills HS, Fort Worth, Texas**
7. **Alan Wolfenbarger, ss, Rutledge (Tenn.) HS**
8. Steven Salata, c/of, Trinity Pawling Prepartory HS, Oneonta, N.Y.
9. Floyd Meier, ss, Grossmont (Calif.) JC
10. **Mark Kleibl, 3b, Norland HS, Miami**
11. Ronald Sheppard, 3b, Altus (Okla.) HS
12. **John Newton, ss, Manteca (Calif.) HS**
13. **Lawrence Bellm, rhp, Southern Illinois-Edwardsville**
14. James Thurston, 3b/ss, Central HS, Little Rock, Ark.
15. **James Powers, c, St. Bernard HS, Waterford, Conn.**
16. **Michael Spellman, lhp, St. Bernard HS, Waterford, Conn.**
17. Michael James, of/ss, McKinney (Texas) HS
18. Tommy Harmon, c, Eastern Hills HS, Fort Worth, Texas
19. **Walter Povlick, rhp, East Central HS, Tulsa, Okla.**

June—Secondary Phase (5)

1. **Kris Krebs, ss, Manatee (Fla.) JC**
2. **Ray Henningsen, 2b, Santa Clara**
3. **Rod Austin, of, Santa Clara**
4. **John Clifton, lhp, Chapman (Calif.)**
5. **Neil Rivenburg, of, Southern Oregon State**
6. **Stephen Eagan, c, Pittsburg State**

CALIFORNIA ANGELS

January—Regular Phase (10)

1. **David McCormick, rhp, El Camino (Calif.) JC**
2. **Gary Butcher, rhp, Santa Monica (Calif.) CC**
3. **Michael Brown, c, Porterville (Calif.) JC**
4. **Bruce Davis, inf, Los Angeles Pierce JC**
5. **Wayne Kjorvestad, ss, Mount San Antonio (Calif.) JC**
6. Kenneth Pfau, rhp, El Camino (Calif.) JC
7. Dennis Parks, c/of, Long Beach (Calif.) CC

January—Secondary Phase (6)

1. **Tom Murphy, rhp, Ohio**
2. **Edward Bauer, lhp, Gulf Coast (Fla.) CC**
3. Seaton Daly, c, Santa Clara
4. Bill Bonham, rhp, Los Angeles Valley JC
5. **Dave LaRoche, lhp, Torrance, Calif.**
6. Norbert Beddow, of/rhp, Mesa (Colo.)
7. Rod Austin, of, Santa Clara
8. Dan Stoligrosz, 3b, Los Angeles Valley JC
9. Marvin Madruga, ss, JC of the Sequoias (Calif.)
10. Minton White, rhp/of, Texas

June—Regular Phase (9)

1. **Mike Nunn, c, Ben L. Smith HS, Greensboro, N.C.**
2. Dave Kingman, rhp, Mount Prospect (Ill.) HS
3. Bruce Harkey, rhp, La Habra (Calif.) HS
4. **David Biber, of, Ramona HS, Riverside, Calif.**
5. Stanley Zawacki, of, Weequahic HS, Newark, N.J.
6. Rudolph Kinard, 2b, Druid Hills HS, Decatur, Ga.
7. **Terrance Thompson, rhp, Plant City (Fla.) HS**
8. Thomas Tikker, c, Los Angeles CC
9. Douglas Ross, lhp, Cranford (N.J.) HS
10. **Gerald Lanning, lhp, Brookville (Ind.) HS**
11. **Lawrence Rybicki, rhp, Niagara Falls (N.Y.) HS**
12. **James Englehardt, lhp, Brigham Young**
13. **Charles Oakes, 1b/c, Cal State Los Angeles**
14. Edward Fields, rhp, Sunnyside (Wash.) HS
15. Steven Elliott, lhp, Highland HS, Yakima, Wash.
16. **John Lyles, ss, Bethel (Tenn.)**
17. Steve Moore, of, San Marcos HS, Goleta, Calif.

18. **Greg Smith, lhp, Thousand Oaks (Calif.) HS**
19. Richard David, 1b, UC Santa Barbara
20. **Robert Foderaro, lhp, Brigham Young**
21. **Craig Baker, rhp, Dayton, Ohio**
22. Michael Derrington, lhp/1b, Reitz HS, Evansville, Ind.
23. **Richard Shibley, ss/2b, Cal State Los Angeles**
24. **Dennis Heberlein, 1b, Eisenhower HS, Yakima, Wash.**
25. **John Jackson, 3b, Southwestern (Calif.) JC**
26. **Donald Peracchi, 1b, Fresno State**
27. Ed Crosby, 2b, Wilson HS, Long Beach, Calif.
28. **Roy Lee, c/1b, Edison HS, Fresno, Calif.**
29. Carl Wright, rhp, Holt HS, Cottondale, Ala.

June—Secondary Phase (19)

1. **Greg Washburn, rhp, Lewis (Ill.)**
2. Marvin Galliher, 2b/of, San Diego Mesa JC
3. **Tim Hewes, c, Bakersfield (Calif.) JC**
4. Craig Schell, rhp, UC Santa Barbara
5. Stephen Dean, 1b/of, JC of the Sequoias (Calif.)
6. Brent Strom, lhp, Southern California
7. **Robert Perruchon, of, Fresno State**
8. Michael Babler, rhp, Chabot (Calif.) JC

CHICAGO CUBS

January—Regular Phase (1)

1. **Alec Distaso, rhp, Wilson HS, Los Angeles**
2. **Jim Dunegan, rhp, Bacone (Okla.) JC**
3. **Earl Stephenson, lhp, Benson, N.C.**
4. **Edward Howell, c, Olanta, Pa.**
5. **Theodore Marcopulos, ss, Washington, D.C.**

January—Secondary Phase (7)

1. **Gary Ross, rhp, Portvue, Pa.**
2. **Jay Armstrong, ss, Arizona State**
3. Michael Lisetski, ss, Rider
4. **Pat Jacquez, rhp, San Joaquin Delta (Calif.) JC**
5. David Barton, ss, Ithaca (N.Y.)

June—Regular Phase (2)

1. **Terry Hughes, ss, Dorman HS, Spartanburg, S.C.**
2. **Jimmy McMath, of, Druid HS, Tuscaloosa, Ala.**
3. **Terry Bongiovanni, rhp, Platt HS, South Meridien, Conn.**
4. **Tom Krawczyk, ss, Central Michigan**
5. **Terrell Jones, c, Parkersburg HS, Washington, W.Va.**
6. **Bruce Dixon, of, Jones HS, Washington Shores, Fla.**
7. Michael Redling, rhp, Pleasant Hill (Calif.) HS
8. **Allen Robinson, of, Tennessee State**
9. Edward Thomas, 1b, Pioneer HS, Whittier, Calif.
10. **Joseph Reyda, lhp, Upsala**
11. **John Lung, 3b, UCLA**
12. **Charles Pollock, lhp, Farmington HS, Racheal, W.Va.**
13. David Classen, 3b/c, St. Louis (Mo.) HS
14. **Richard Arbogast, rhp, South Harrison HS, West Milford, W.Va.**
15. **Lloyd Kingfisher, rhp, Bacone (Okla.) JC**
16. Richard Tekavec, c, Jefferson-Morgan HS, Jefferson, Pa.
17. **John Merten, rhp, Rider**
18. **Thomas Brown, rhp, Washington State**
19. **Q.V. Lowe, rhp, Auburn**
20. Gary Lance, rhp, Dentville HS, Columbia, S.C.
21. Allen Dukate, rhp, Admiral King HS, Lorain, Ohio
22. **Martin Miller, of, DePaul HS, Chicago**
23. Bruce Olson, rhp, Montclair (Calif.) HS
24. **John Johnson, of, North Chicago (Ill.) HS**
25. David Stone, lhp, Kittanning (Pa.) HS
26. Leonard Bible, c, Murrah HS, Jackson, Miss.
27. **Dennis Rockwell, 1b, Pacific Grove (Calif.) HS**
28. Larry Sheffield, lhp, Gainesville (Fla.) HS
29. Donald Davis, 3b, Randleman (N.C.) HS
30. **Charles Hunt, rhp, Washington HS, Portland, Ore.**

June—Secondary Phase (2)

1. **Randy Bobb, c, Arizona State**
2. Douglas Hansen, rhp, Fresno (Calif.) CC
3. Larry Hanson, 3b, Oregon
4. Ken Forsch, rhp, Oregon State
5. Joe Arnold, rhp, Miami-Dade North CC
6. **Darcy Fast, lhp, Warner Pacific**
7. **Michael Flanagan, lhp, Yakima Valley (Wash.) JC**

CHICAGO WHITE SOX

January—Regular Phase (14)

1. John Jacobson, c, Bloom (Ill.) JC

January—Secondary Phase (4)

1. **Bob Spence, 1b/of, Santa Clara**
2. **Robert Desjardins, c, Fullerton (Calif.) JC**
3. Rich Folkers, lhp, Ellsworth (Iowa) JC
4. **Thomas Tutko, of/inf, Hastings (Neb.)**
5. Jack Gehrke, ss, Utah

June—Regular Phase (13)

1. **Dan Haynes, 3b, Headland HS, East Point, Ga.**
2. **Stuart Singleton, ss/of, Hudson Bay HS, Vancouver, Wash.**
3. Chris Ward, of, Arrojo HS, San Lorenzo, Calif.
4. **Martin Morrison, 1b/3b, Center Township HS, Monaca, Pa.**
5. Michael Slade, rhp, Washington & Lee HS, Arlington, Va.
6. **Dennis O'Toole, rhp, De LaSalle HS, Chicago**
7. **Stephen Krull, rhp, Purdue**
8. Norman Kraft, 3b/of, Father Judge HS, Philadelphia
9. **William Cooper, rhp, Edison HS, Miami, N.J.**
10. James Rafferty, ss, Groves HS, Birmingham, Mich.
11. Kurt Aschermann, c, Ossining (N.Y.) HS
12. Thomas Wright, of, Santa Ana (Calif.) Valley HS
13. **Steven Agerton, 3b/ss, Foothill HS, Bakersfield, Calif.**
14. **Gerald Hall, c/of, Western HS, Anaheim**
15. Joseph Bowen, 3b/1b, Robinson HS, Norfolk, Va.
16. Kent Calderan, ss, Castro Valley (Calif.) HS
17. **George Weimer, rhp, East Aurora HS, Aurora, Ill.**
18. John Amoroso, lhp, Orange (Calif.) HS
19. **Martin Sauble, 1b, North Hagerstown (Md.) HS**
20. **Kenneth Valentine, ss, South French Broad HS, Asheville, N.C.**
21. Gary Cook, of, Magnolia HS, Anaheim
22. Craig Perkins, c, Western HS, Rossmore, Calif.
23. Victor LaDuna, ss, Williamson HS, Mobile, Ala.
24. Frank Grundler, ss, Thornton Fractional South HS, Lansing, Ill.
25. Richard Hanselman, lhp, St. Johns River (Fla.) CC
26. **Steve Ostrowski, lhp, Lyons Township HS, La Grange, Ill.**
27. Ken Ottoson, rhp, Chadron State
28. Leon Filbeck, rhp, Santa Ana (Calif.) Valley HS
29. **Steve Humphrey, 1b/of, Fullerton (Calif.) JC**
30. Charlie Wolfe, lhp, Bethel HS, Colquitt, Ga.
31. Jim Norris, of, Seaford (N.Y.) HS
32. Lee Jacobsen, of, Kearney State
33. **John Hankammer, rhp, Gibault HS, Waterloo, Ill.**
34. **Harold Jones, rhp, Miami (Ohio)**
35. **Tim Foy, c, Father Judge HS, Philadelphia**
36. Thomas Gehrke, 3b/of, St. Joseph's HS, Westchester, Ind.
37. **Willie Garrison, lhp, Alabama State**
38. **Kenneth Quarles, of, Gardena HS, Los Angeles**
39. Earl Vickers, of, Fresno State (Selection voided)
40. Al Fritz, rhp, Maine West HS, Des Plaines, Ill.
41. **Larry Stewart, rhp, Wilson HS, Tifton, Ga.**
42. Albert Holland, of, Brevard (Fla.) JC
43. Toby Heath, lhp, Santa Ana (Calif.) HS
44. **Richard Ortner, c, San Luis Obispo (Calif.) HS**
45. **Bob DeFries, rhp, Brother Rice HS, Oaklawn, Ill.**
46. David Rusco, 2b/ss, San Luis Obispo (Calif.) HS
47. Douglas McGrath, rhp, Ossining (N.Y.) HS
48. Mike McCarter, c/of, Arcadia Valley HS, Ironton, Mo.
49. Thomas Fuller, c, Point Loma HS, San Diego
50. Lawrence Ulanski, rhp, St. Laurence HS, Chicago
51. **Roger Benko, lhp, Northwestern**
52. **Gary Hoskins, of, Union (Tenn.)**

June—Secondary Phase (11)

1. Herbert Hofvendahl, of, St. Mary's
2. Sandy Vance, rhp, Stanford
3. Pat Harrison, 2b, Southern California
4. **Charles Kline, lhp, Western Michigan**

5. Vincent Bigone, of/3b, Santa Clara
6. Dave Renkiewicz, rhp, Michigan
7. Charles Koselke, 1b, Western Michigan
8. **James Limke, rhp, Minot State (N.D.)**
9. **Neil Weber, rhp, Minnesota**
10. John Hurley, rhp, Michigan
11. Richard Licini, 1b, Notre Dame

CINCINNATI REDS

January—Regular Phase (7)

1. **Marvin Branscomb, of, Gardena (Calif.) HS**
2. Don Enger, of, Birmingham HS, Van Nuys, Calif.
3. Bill Sims, c, Oak Hill, Va.
4. **Donald Hacker, ss, West Chester (Pa.)**
5. David Gunter, rhp, Bacone (Okla.) JC
6. Larry Stroman, 2b, San Antonio (Texas) JC

January—Secondary Phase (11)

1. David Speas, inf, San Diego Mesa JC
2. Gordon Allen, of, Deerfield Academy, Ludlow, Mass.
3. Frank Bon Vardo, rhp, Maryland
4. Gary Ratliff, of, Bacone (Okla.) JC
5. Robert Robbins, lhp, Gowanda, N.Y.
6. John Sellers, ss, Northeastern Oklahoma A&M JC
7. **Edward Curran, rhp, St. Louis CC-Meramec**
8. Norm Angelini, lhp, JC of San Mateo (Calif.)

June—Regular Phase (8)

1. **Wayne Simpson, rhp, Centennial HS, Los Angeles**
2. **Wayne Holsopple, rhp, Bedford (Ohio) HS**
3. **Dick Pooschke, ss, Benson HS, Portland, Ore.**
4. **Fred Kendall, c, Torrance (Calif.) HS**
5. Robert Watts, of, Eastern HS, Bristol, Conn.
6. **Michael Pstragowski, rhp, Central HS, Manchester, N.H.**
7. **James Lewis, c, Gardena (Calif.) HS**
8. **Steve Cochran, lhp, New Palestine (Ind.) HS**
9. **Bob DeGrate, lhp/of, Moore HS, Waco, Texas**
10. **Jerry Cole, 1b, Glen Oaks HS, Baton Rouge, La.**
11. Art Ramsey, lhp, St. Albans (W.Va.) HS
12. Gordon Longmire, ss, Tracy (Calif.) HS
13. John Hale, c, Huntington (W.Va.) HS
14. **Samuel Greenwood, of, Villanova**
15. Patrick Martin, lhp, Palmetto HS, Miami
16. Robert Cramer, rhp, New London (Conn.) HS
17. **William Mottershead, rhp, Boca Cieca HS, St. Petersburg, Fla.**
18. **Kenneth Geiger, rhp, Perkins HS, Sandusky, Ohio**
19. Paul Walton, rhp, Amesbury (Mass.) HS
20. Rick Farizo, rhp, De LaSalle HS, New Orleans
21. **Keith Pridgen, ss, South Greene HS, Snow Hill, N.C.**
22. Terry Wilshusen, 3b, Carson HS, Lakewood, Calif.
23. Edgar Avila, 1b/lhp, Miami-Dade North CC
24. **James Angelo, 2b, Southern HS, Philadelphia**
25. **Sheldon Andrens, of, Southern California**
26. Robert Beck, lhp, East Brunswick (N.J.) HS
27. John Young, 1b, Mount Carmel HS, Los Angeles
28. **Daniel Hootstein, of, Harvard**
29. **Dave Tomlin, lhp, West Union (Ohio) HS**
30. John Lynn, 1b, Creston (Iowa) HS
31. Chris Chambliss, 1b, Mira Costa (Calif.) JC
32. Billy Robertson, 2b, Cisco (Texas) JC
33. Reuben Halliburton, rhp, Moore HS, Waco, Texas
34. Roger Menaugh, of, John Marshall HS, Oklahoma City, Okla.
35. Edward Bravo, 3b, Miami-Dade North CC
36. **Thomas Hooper, 3b, Texas Christian**
37. Jerome Thomas, rhp, Hamburg (Iowa) HS
38. **Johnnie Williamson, lhp/1b, Childersburg (Ala.) HS**
39. Roger Tipton, lhp, Cisco (Texas) JC
40. Paul Simon, of, Cardinal OHara HS, Havertown, Pa.
41. Leo Bouvet, rhp, Boys HS, Brooklyn, N.Y.
42. Robert Zavorskas, ss, Bucknell
43. **Jerry Flick, rhp, New Miami HS, Hamilton, Ohio**
44. Joel Green, ss, Memorial HS, Tulsa, Okla.
45. **Robert Renninger, lhp, Keystone HS, LaGrange, Ohio**
46. Alfred Lee, of, Rice Lake (Wis.) HS
47. Terry Edwards, of, Memorial HS, Tulsa, Okla.
48. Ray Nygard, 3b, Superior (Wis.) HS
49. Mike Mores, rhp, Holy Cross HS, Norridge, Ill.
50. Greg Wilcox, lhp, West Bend (Wis.) HS
51. William Povia, ss, Hamilton East HS, Trenton, N.J.
52. Ron Spain, ss, Rayburn HS, Houston
53. Donald Sasso, 1b, Sacred Heart HS, Waterbury, Conn.
54. **Thomas Peppler, c, Princeton**
55. **Franklin Thompson, lhp, Manatee (Fla.) JC**
56. Joseph Gavel, 3b/1b, Gulf Coast (Fla.) CC
57. **David Abell, 1b, Ridgway (Ill.) HS**
58. **Larry Broeman, lhp, Reitz HS, Evansville, Ind.**
59. Ralph Kirkland, of, Waco (Texas) HS
60. **Kenneth Jones, 2b, Kashmere HS, Houston**
61. William Barr, 1b, Dover (Okla.) HS
62. Timothy Boese, rhp, Lake Forest HS, Lake Bluff, Ill.
63. Donald Churchwell, of, Mark Smith HS, Macon, Ga.
64. Larry Phillippe, rhp, Fort Myers (Fla.) HS
65. Wendell Starrick, ss, Marion (Ill.) HS
66. Danny Peelman, 1b/of, North Posey HS, Poseyville, Ind.
67. Richard Moss, of, Lakeland (Fla.) HS
68. Wayne Church, rhp, Gardner-Webb
69. Fred Steinmark, ss, Denver (Colo.) HS
70. John Fodor, c, Southern California
71. **Bill Sluka, of, Denver**
72. Allen Criswell, lhp, Bucknell

June—Secondary Phase (6)

1. **Frank Duffy, ss, Stanford**
2. **Al Crawford, of, Miami-Dade North CC**
3. **Greg Riddoch, ss, Colorado State**
4. Danny Thompson, ss, Oklahoma State
5. Richard Wanless, rhp, Lakemont Academy HS, Quincy, Mass.
6. Thomas Kelly, of, Holy Cross
7. William Kirkpatrick, rhp, CC of San Francisco
8. William Close, rhp, Holy Cross
9. Edward Cott, c, Cornell
10. James O'Leary, rhp, Dutchess (N.Y.) CC
11. Roger Jackson, rhp, Kansas
12. **Kurt Bevacqua, 2b, Miami-Dade North CC**

CLEVELAND INDIANS

January—Regular Phase (12)

1. **Roger Sexton, 3b, Ohio State**
2. **John Kasper, 3b, Western Michigan**
3. **David Beber, of, Fort Wayne, Ind.**
4. **James Underhill, of, Dinwiddie (Va.) HS**
5. **James Randall, rhp, Columbia Basin (Wash.) CC**
6. **William Hutchens, c, Beckley (W.Va.)**
7. Dennis Droege, rhp, Highland (Kan.) CC
8. Max Winfield, rhp, Panola (Texas) JC
9. **Leslie Williams, of/inf, West Virginia**
10. John Ferguson, rhp, Abraham Baldwin Agricultural (Ga.) JC
11. **James Braxton, rhp, UNC Wilmington**

January—Secondary Phase (16)

1. **Ron Allen, 2b/of, Toledo (Ohio) JC**
2. **Steve Wrenn, 1b, Wake Forest**
3. David Reeves, rhp, South Georgia JC (Selection voided)
4. **Dick Tidrow, rhp, Chabot (Calif.) JC**
5. Luis Flores, c, Gardner-Webb
6. **Robert Bender, 1b/of, Goodlettsville, Tenn.**
7. John Meyer, c, Cincinnati
8. **Billy Ray Palmer, rhp, Rice**
9. **Michael Pierce, lhp, Eastern Arizona JC**
10. **Adrian Zabala, rhp, Florida**
11. George Grzegorek, ss, St. Edward's (Texas)
12. Robert Guerrera, rhp, Cheshire Academy, Waterbury, Conn.
13. Richard Snyder, of, North Canton, Ohio
14. William Carthel, of/inf, Sul Ross State
15. **Ronald Masterson, rhp, Soddy, Tenn.**

June—Regular Phase (11)

1. **Jack Heidemann, ss, Brenham (Texas) HS**
2. **Mark Ballinger, rhp, Thousand Oaks HS, Newbury Park, Calif.**
3. **Charles Cichosz, c, Benilde HS, St. Louis Park, Minn.**
4. **Lawrence Crossan, rhp, Clark (Wash.) JC**
5. **Ed Farmer, rhp, St. Rita HS, Chicago**
6. William Reuss, of, UC Santa Barbara
7. **Timothy Sanders, rhp, Tehachapi (Calif.) HS**
8. **Ronald Zuber, rhp, Colorado State**
9. **Vic Correll, c, Georgia Southern**
10. Thomas Jenner, ss, Lake Mills (Wis.) HS
11. Richard Ogle, rhp, Bozeman (Mont.) HS
12. **Richard Dickinson, 2b, Milford (Conn.) Academy**
13. **Ray Cox, c, Auburn**
14. Jay Ray Rokey, of, Westwood HS, Mesa, Ariz.
15. Charles Sprinkle, ss, Arizona Western JC
16. **Larry Gallagher, rhp, Garfield HS, Terre Haute, Ind.**
17. **Ronald Butterfield, lhp, Murray HS, Salt Lake City**
18. **Michael Schroeder, rhp, Waco (Texas) HS**
19. **William Kohl, lhp, Gnadenhutten (Ohio) HS**
20. **Mike Paul, lhp, Arizona**
21. **Richard Pack, 1b, Stow (Ohio) HS**
22. William Gray, 2b, Randleman HS, High Point, N.C.
23. Ronald Hunt, ss, Miami-Dade North CC
24. **Ed Southard, of, Arizona**
25. **Kevin Casey, of, Avondale HS, Avondale Estates, Ga.**
26. **Tom Taylor, ss, Compton (Calif.) CC**
27. Phillip Still, 2b, DeKalb HS, Decatur, Ga.
28. **Jerry McConnell, rhp, Ohio**
29. John Hathaway, rhp, Fredonia (N.Y.) HS
30. **Larry McDivitt, rhp, Buckeye HS, Medina, Ohio**
31. Tim Huntley, of, Creek County HS, Prineville, Ore.
32. **Mike Yetter, 3b, Hemet (Calif.) HS**
33. Thomas Callan, ss, CC of San Francisco
34. **Jack Brohamer Jr., ss, Huntington Beach (Calif.) HS**
35. Bill Moynier, rhp, Bakersfield (Calif.) JC
36. Elwood Walker, rhp, Salt Lake City
37. **Fred Reedy, lhp, Northeast HS, St. Petersburg, Fla.**
38. Joe Staples, c, Texas A&M
39. **Ladon Green, of, Jordon HS, Columbus, Ga.**
40. **Bo Rein, ss, Ohio State**
41. Michael Burns, of, Oklahoma
42. Brad Lawson, ss, Boardman HS, Youngstown, Ohio
43. Charles Paparone, ss, Ellet HS, Akron, Ohio
44. Craig Erbland, 1b, Mount Union (Ohio)
45. **Robert Brooder, rhp, Southern Connecticut State**
46. William Bright, rhp, Cocoa (Fla.) HS
47. Terry Blitz, rhp, McMahon HS, Norwalk, Conn.
48. John Walker, c, Sacramento (Calif.) CC
49. **John Stephenson, 3b, Ben L. Smith HS, Greensboro, N.C.**
50. Michael Leppa, 3b, Costa Mesa (Calif.) HS
51. Gary Zipfel, of/1b, Tinora HS, Defiance, Ohio
52. Gilbert Marrujo, c, Coachella Valley HS, Indio, Calif.
53. **Bob Dorn, lhp, Cal Poly San Luis Obispo**
54. Gerald Robert, rhp, Brevard (Fla.) CC
55. **James McMahon, c, Iona**
56. William Hendricks, lhp, Brush HS, Cleveland
57. **Kenneth Dean, rhp, Wichita State**
58. Alex Duncan, rhp, Poland (Ohio) Seminary
59. Kenneth Burt, rhp, Chaffey (Calif.) JC
60. Ron Opatkiewicz, ss, Covina (Calif.) HS
61. Dave Phares, c, Hemet (Calif.) HS
62. Joseph Bienko, rhp, Dunkirk (N.Y.) HS

June—Secondary Phase (15)

1. **Ronald Henson, lhp, Rice**
2. **Eddie Leon, ss, Arizona**
3. **Lou Camilli, 3b, Texas A&M**
4. **Dennis Brady, 1b, Purdue**
5. Rich Hinton, lhp, Arizona
6. **Stephen Lohrer, of, Parsons**
7. James Goodwin, rhp, Miami
8. **John Meyer, c, Cincinnati**
9. **Max Winfield, rhp, Panola (Texas) JC**

DETROIT TIGERS

January—Regular Phase (16)

1. James Carter, 3b, Golden West (Calif.) JC
2. **Michael Kotzin, 1b, Fullerton (Calif.) JC**
3. **Mike Murray, c, Cypress (Calif.) JC**
4. Terry Schofield, c, Fullerton (Calif.) JC

January—Secondary Phase (2)

1. **Mike Adams, ss, Fullerton (Calif.) JC**
2. Danny Talbott, 1b/3b, North Carolina
3. **John D'Auria, rhp, Arcadia (Calif.) HS**
4. Ken Lohnes, c, Cerritos (Calif.) JC
5. **Michael Hastings, of, Ithaca (N.Y.)**
6. Robert Smith, rhp, St. John's
7. Roger Banks, c, Mars Hill (N.C.)

June—Regular Phase (15)

1. **Jim Foor, lhp, McCluer HS, Ferguson, Mo.**
2. **Robert Ware, rhp, Hugenot HS, Richmond, Va.**
3. **James Tanner, of, Robinson HS, Tampa**
4. **Leslie Tanona, of, Michigan**
5. **Paul Jata, c, Long Island City (N.Y.) HS**
6. **Dennis Saunders, rhp, Pioneer HS, Whittier, Calif.**
7. **Lynn Adams, ss, St. Elizabeth HS, Oakland, Calif.**
8. **James Wosman, c/1b, Augustinian Academy HS, St. Louis**
9. Larry Fritz, lhp, Whiting (Ind.) HS
10. Mike Deniro, 3b, Chaney HS, Campbell, Ohio
11. **Gary McGhee, 2b, East HS, Knoxville, Tenn.**
12. Henry Bunnell, of/lhp, St. Peters Catholic HS, Scranton, Pa.
13. Jerry Killian, lhp, St. Matthews HS, Flint, Mich.
14. Gilbert LaHaine, 1b, Everett HS, Lansing, Mich.
15. **Ike Blessitt, of, Hamtramck (Mich.) HS**
16. Steve Allen, of, Berkeley (Calif.) HS
17. Marvin Gurley, rhp, MacKenzie HS, Detroit
18. Richard Szal, rhp, Chaminade HS, Long Island, N.Y.
19. William Castle, ss, Southeast HS, Oklahoma City, Okla.
20. **Doug Swiss, c, Northville (Mich.) HS**
21. Danny Fife, rhp, Clarkston (Mich.) HS
22. **Jess Rossiter, rhp, Evart (Mich.) HS**
23. Donald Honne, lhp, Richfield HS, Waco, Texas
24. **Ricky Sayle, of, Memphis State**
25. **Dale Scilley, ss, Washington State**
26. Jim Burton, lhp, Rochester (Mich.) HS
27. Peter Perpich, rhp, O'Rafferty HS, Lansing, Mich.
28. Lanny Yost, ss, Clintondale HS, Mount Clemens, Mich.
29. Jack McCloud, lhp, Kettering HS, Drayton, Mich.
30. Richard Highduke, ss, Chaminade HS, Long Island, N.Y.
31. Daniel Carroll, 1b, Grand Island (N.Y.) HS
32. **Carl Schulz, ss, Toledo**
33. **George McKenzie, 2b, Auburn**
34. **Lee Sage, lhp, Ada (Ohio) HS**
35. **Darrell Schneller, rhp, Sturgeon (Mo.) HS**
36. **Gary Ignasiak, lhp, St. Mary's HS, Anchorville, Mich.**
37. **Mike Marshall, ss, Mount Healthy HS, Cincinnati**
38. **Marvin Isensee, 1b, Sparta (Wis.) HS**
39. Richard Miceli, c, Waterford-Kettering HS, Drayton Plains, Mich.
40. Greg Plant, 2b/ss, Sylvania (Ohio) HS
41. **Dan Rounds, rhp, Arroyo HS, San Lorenzo, Calif.**
42. Ralph Darin, rhp, River Rouge (Mich.) HS
43. Philip Rashead, c, St. Agnes HS, Flint, Mich.
44. **William Mullins, of, Paintsville (Ky.) HS**
45. Thomas Jackson, ss, Citrus (Calif.) JC
46. **Robert Counterman, c, Linden (N.J.) HS**
47. **James Sangregario, of, St. Ladislaus HS, Hamtramck, Mich.**
48. Richard Cutler, ss/3b, Bayside HS, Whitestone, N.Y.
49. Richard Wacheli, rhp, Die-Ruff HS, Allentown, Pa.
50. Richard Shirk, 3b/rhp, Cocalico HS, Denver, Pa.
51. Dan Jackson, inf/rhp, Scott HS, Toldeo, Ohio

June—Secondary Phase (17)

1. **John Hetrick, of, Maryland**
2. Geoff Zahn, lhp, Michigan
3. Skip Jutze, c, Central Connecticut State

4. Mel Behney, lhp, Michigan State
5. Tom Lundgren, lhp, Missouri
6. Tom Binkowski, 1b/of, Michigan State
7. **Louis Ganious, 1b, Southern**
8. John Herzing, lhp, Washington (Mo.)
9. Kenneth Danson, of, Gulf Coast (Fla.) CC
10. Roy Myers, of, Memphis State

HOUSTON ASTROS

January—Regular Phase (5)

1. **Jack Van Vleck, rhp, Everett (Wash.) CC**
2. James Kinds, rhp, Kashmere HS, Houston
3. John Thomas, c, Barbers Hills HS, Mount Belview, Texas

January—Secondary Phase (1)

1. Pete Varney Jr., c, Deerfield (Mass.) Academy
2. **Nikola Radakovic, rhp, Michigan**
3. Jim Johnson, lhp, Western Michigan
4. Jerry Meadows, rhp, West Virginia
5. Frank Vandevender, rhp, San Diego Mesa JC

June—Regular Phase (6)

1. **John Mayberry, 1b/of, Northwestern HS, Detroit**
2. **Jay Schlueter, of, Central HS, Phoenix**
3. **Craig Hilden, lhp, Bellarmine HS, Tacoma, Wash.**
4. **Lewis Brown, 3b, Laney (Calif.) JC**
5. **Douglas Olson, rhp, Bergenfield (N.J.) HS**
6. **Forrest Weatherford, c, William Chrisman HS, Independence, Mo.**
7. **John Kryczkowski, lhp, Hamtramck (Mich.) HS**
8. **Gary Long, c, Byng HS, Ada, Okla.**
9. **Jeffery Morrell, of/3b, Byng (Okla.) HS**
10. **Daniel Evans, lhp, Irvington HS, Fremont, Calif.**
11. George Hunt, 1b, Clearwater (Fla.) HS
12. **Gerald Johnson, rhp, Merced (Calif.) HS**
13. John Ritter, rhp, Kimball HS, Royal Oak, Mich.
14. **Steve Grover, lhp, Calvert HS, Prince Frederick, Md.**
15. **Thomas Suchanek, rhp, Greenfield (Mass.) CC**
16. **Kenneth Hovance, of, Toms River (N.J.) HS**
17. **Ricky Wilson, 3b, Denison HS, Pottsboro, Texas**
18. **Richard Hartzog, of, Provine HS, Jackson, Miss.**
19. Don Jumper, rhp, Jasper (Texas) HS
20. **Wayne Brechtel, rhp, Johnsonburg (Pa.) HS**
21. George Shaw, rhp, Panola (Texas) JC
22. **Kenneth McCary, of, Wayne HS, Byars, Okla.**
23. Paul Greer, c, Prestonburg (Ky.) HS
24. **Emmitt Money, rhp, Avon Park (Fla.) HS**
25. **Larry Franklin, rhp, Central HS, Springfield, Mo.**
26. Larry Caldwell, of, Mission (Texas) HS
27. Michael Cahill, lhp, St. Xavier HS, Cincinnati
28. Jerry Proctor, inf, Muir HS, Pasadena, Calif.
29. James Evans, rhp, Christian Brothers HS, Memphis, Tenn.
30. Donald Paulsen, of, Lyman HS, Casselberry, Fla.
31. Pat McKean, lhp, Palo Duro HS, Amarillo, Texas
32. Robert Danaher, rhp, Montpelier (Vt.) HS
33. **Rory Hummell, c, Washington Township HS, Blackwood, N.J.**
34. David Buchanan, 3b, Muir HS, Pasadena, Calif.
35. Robert Warner, rhp, Stroudsburg (Pa.) HS
36. **Steven Ritchie, lhp, Boca Ciega HS, Treasure Island, Fla.**
37. Glen Hassell, lhp, Rusk (Texas) HS
38. Carl Hayes, ss, Robstown (Texas) HS
39. **Geoff Price, 2b, Muir HS, Pasadena, Calif.**
40. Louie Gavrell, rhp/of, Tyler (Texas) JC
41. John Burger, c, Forest Park HS, Beaumont, Texas
42. Bruce Haynes, rhp, Hopkins (Minn.) HS

June—Secondary Phase (4)

1. **Kim Hillstrom, rhp, Central Michigan**
2. **Gordon Allen, of, Deerfield (Mass.) Academy HS**
3. Pete Varney Jr., c, Deerfield (Mass.) Academy HS
4. **Michael Flanagan, rhp, North Carolina**
5. Raymond DeRiggi, of/1b, Seton Hall
6. Thomas Schweitzer, lhp, Fairmont State (W.Va.)
7. Jack Lind, ss, Arizona State
8. Stephen Hanson, rhp, West Valley (Calif.) JC

KANSAS CITY ATHLETICS

January—Regular Phase (8)

1. Ken Hottman, of, Sacramento (Calif.) CC
2. Walter Adey, lhp, Hudson Valley (N.Y.) CC
3. George Stephanos, lhp, Arizona Western JC
4. Hubert Perkins, of, Iowa State

January—Secondary Phase (12)

1. Rick Konik, 1b, Detroit
2. **Roger Cain, of, East Los Angeles JC**
3. Walter Lampmann, of, Manatee (Fla.) JC
4. **Nicholas DeFlorio, ss, New York Tech**
5. **Jim Panther, rhp, Southern Illinois**
6. **Russell Vitallo, rhp, Massachusetts**
7. William Adkins, 2b, Clemson
8. Walter Prior, rhp, Florida
9. James Gruber, ss, Seminole (Fla.) JC
10. Richard Allred, ss/rhp, Mesa (Ariz.) CC

June—Regular Phase (7)

1. **Brian Bickerton, lhp, Santana HS, Santee, Calif.**
2. **Vida Blue, lhp, DeSoto HS, Mansfield, La.**
3. **Gary Coleman, c, Colonial HS, Orlando, Fla.**
4. **Victor Sciamarelli, of, Hillside (N.J.) HS**
5. Gene Dusan, c, Lakewood (Calif.) HS
6. **Carl Ives, rhp, Plantation HS, Fort Lauderdale, Fla.**
7. **Joseph Robinson, ss, Mineola (N.Y.) HS**
8. Bruce Raible, rhp, Western Hills HS, Cincinnati
9. **Donald Camy, rhp, Alisal HS, Salinas, Calif.**
10. **Lazaro Mata, c, Miami (Fla.) HS**
11. Eric Soderholm, inf, South Georgia JC
12. Steve Mikulic, ss, Thornridge HS, Dolton, Ill.
13. William Harkins, rhp, Holbrook (Mass.) HS
14. **Bill Aubertin, rhp, Washington HS, Keller, Wash.**
15. **Ray Elder, 3b, Rubidoux (Calif.) HS**
16. Rex Kern, 3b, Lancaster (Ohio) HS
17. **Robert Pirnik, c, Woodbridge (N.J.) HS**
18. Mark Resser, lhp, Skyline HS, Oakland, Calif.
19. **Samuel Lovelace, ss/2b, Burbank HS, Sacramento, Calif.**
20. Steve Zimmerman, lhp, Fortune HS, Dearborn, Mich.
21. **David Rhodenbaugh, rhp, Fort Lauderdale (Fla.) HS**
22. John Austin, rhp, Northeast Guilford HS, Greensboro, N.C.
23. **Ron Gordon, of, Pasadena (Calif.) CC**
24. **Joe Grace, 3b, St. Joseph's**
25. **Sheldon Spicher, ss, Clark (Wash.) JC**
26. **Robert Stickels, rhp, Nebraska**
27. **Clyde Steele, lhp, Bakersfield HS, Costa Mesa, Calif.**
28. **Clarence Stoner, 1b, Penn State**
29. Moody Jackson, of, South Mountain HS, Phoenix
30. **Donald Ruris, 2b, Hofstra**
31. Robert Schiffner, lhp, Morris Hills HS, Rockaway, N.J.
32. Thomas Kaehler, of, Cleveland HS, Reseda, Calif.
33. Randy Smith, 1b, Lincoln Land (Ill.) JC
34. **Douglas Ross, rhp, Crown Point (N.Y.) Central HS**
35. **Parke Davidson, ss, Texas Christian**
36. **Michael Heinitz, c, Sacramento (Calif.) HS**
37. Larry Gonsalves, rhp, Fresno State
38. **Ron Fisher, c, Elizabethtown (Pa.)**
39. Allen Simas, rhp, Sacramento (Calif.) CC
40. Ernest Fimbres, of, Tucson (Ariz.) HS
41. **David Margolius, c, Lexington (Mass.) HS**
42. Gregory Hill, of, Los Angeles
43. Reggie Sanders, of, Venice (Calif.) HS (Selection voided)
44. Ed Assaf, rhp, Southern Mississippi
45. **Joe Emanuel, c/1b, North Bend (Neb.) HS**
46. **Mark Pena, rhp, Nicholls State**
47. **Garland Godwin, 1b, Alcorn State**
48. **James Burns, of, Lafayette**
49. James Veryzer, of, Islip (N.Y.) HS

June—Secondary Phase (13)

1. Fred Kampf, rhp, Miami
2. **LaDon Boyd, rhp, Florida State**

3. Ronnie Shotts, of, Stanford
4. **Warren Bogle, lhp, Miami**
5. Ray Peters, rhp, Harvard
6. **William Adkins, 2b, Clemson**
7. **Darrell Evans, 3b, Pasadena (Calif.) CC**
8. **Walter Prior, rhp, Florida**
9. **Ronald Berta, c, Moravian (Pa.)**
10. **Robert Yingling, 2b/of, Miami**

LOS ANGELES DODGERS

January—Regular Phase (19)

1. **Travis King, rhp, South Georgia JC**
2. **James Herbert, lhp, Southern**

January—Secondary Phase (17)

1. Larry Burchart, rhp, Oklahoma State
2. **James Doran, of, Staunton (Va.) Military Academy**
3. Jeffrey Bowman, rhp, Modesto (Calif.) JC
4. **Maurice Smith, c/of, Illinois**
5. **Paul Devaney, rhp, Rochester (N.Y.) Business Institute**
6. Michael Babler, rhp, Chabot (Calif.) JC
7. Eldon Jones, lhp, Trinidad State (Colo.) JC (Selection voided)

June—Regular Phase (20)

1. **Don Denbow, 3b, Southern Methodist**
2. **Thomas Harris, ss, Central Gwinett HS, Lawrenceville, Ga.**
3. **William Rainer, of, Southern Methodist**
4. **Steve Yeager, c, Meadow Dale HS, Dayton, Ohio**
5. Ron Cash, ss, Lakeside HS, Decatur, Ga.
6. Ken Hansen, rhp, Maryvale HS, Phoenix
7. Russell Bodkin, of, Fort Lauderdale (Fla.) HS
8. **Aubrey Saxon, lhp, Pelzer, S.C.**
9. **Gary Wedel, 3b, Gardena (Calif.) HS**
10. **Carmine Marceno, 1b, Christopher Columbus HS, Bronx, N.Y.**
11. **Charles Boggs, c, West Virginia**
12. **Robert Lamber, lhp, New York City Technical JC**
13. **Kara Hall, inf, Dos Palos HS, Los Banos, Calif.**
14. James Loll, 1b/rhp, Crespi HS, Reseda, Calif.
15. Glenn Woodruff, c, Aliceville (Ala.) HS
16. John Donovan, rhp, St. Peter's HS, Staten Island, N.Y.
17. Robert Knight, 2b/ss, King HS, Temple Terrace, Fla.
18. **Don Stoulil, 3b, Alemany HS, Sunland, Calif.**
19. **Abraham Sears, ss/of, Perry (Okla.) HS**
20. **Larry King, rhp, Willingham HS, Macon, Ga.**
21. Bruce Matte, rhp, Miami (Ohio)
22. Leon Murray, 1b, Fremont HS, Los Angeles
23. **Malcolm Bass, 2b/3b, Gulf Coast (Fla.) CC**
24. **Norman Dermody, rhp, Seton Hall**
25. **James Hughes, ss, Okawville (Ill.) HS**
26. James Norton, c, Alemany HS, San Fernando, Calif.
27. Michael Rapkin, lhp, Monroe HS, Sepulveda, Calif.
28. Greg Smith, rhp, Sierra HS, Whittier, Calif.
29. **James Flynn, rhp, Roosevelt HS, Fresno, Calif.**
30. **James Brunnworth, rhp, Edwardsville (Ill.) HS**
31. Ronald Thompson, rhp/1b, Roosevelt HS, Atlanta
32. David Thompson, of, Santa Barbara (Calif.) HS
33. John Brannigan, lhp, Cliffside Park HS, Fairview, N.J.
34. Robert Huellemeier, rhp, Mount DeSalles HS, Macon, Ga.
35. William Wright, c, Carson-Newman (Tenn.)
36. **Chava Flores, ss, Artesia (N.M.) HS**
37. Greg Mattinson, of, Grossmont (Calif.) JC
38. Charles Kingsbury, 3b, Claremont (Calif.) HS
39. Willie Strickland, of, Fremont HS, Los Angeles
40. Gene Martin, 3b, Santa Monica (Calif.) HS
41. **Larry Tingle, rhp, Yerington (Nev.) HS**
42. Douglas Barker, rhp/of, Davis (Calif.) HS
43. **Dennis Murphy, rhp, Southwest HS, Miami**
44. James O'Brien, of, Sacred Heart HS, San Francisco
45. Phillip Cabibi, 2b, Garey HS, Pomona, Calif.
46. James Southworth, rhp, Los Angeles Valley JC
47. **Gene Willetts, c, Johnson-Wales (Mass.) CC**
48. William Susa, rhp, Reseda (Calif.) HS
49. Steven Napoli, of, Alemany HS, San Fernando, Calif.
50. John Marino, c, Los Angeles Valley JC
51. **David Conway, of/1b, Los Angeles Valley JC**
52. **William Graves, rhp, Westmont**
53. Harold Armstrong, ss, Hueneme HS, Oxnard, Calif.
54. Steven Lee, lhp, Monroe HS, Granada Hills, Calif.
55. Joe Jacobsen, c, Roosevelt HS, Fresno, Calif.
56. Michael McPartlin, 3b, Niagara County (N.Y.) CC
57. David Dale, rhp, Culver Military Academy, Pittsburgh
58. Steven Easton, lhp, Sierra HS, Whittier, Calif.
59. David Lloyd, of, Jefferson HS, Los Angeles
60. **Patrick Manahan, 3b, Sylmar (Calif.) HS**
61. Albert Rossi, 2b, St. Francis HS, Pasadena, Calif.
62. Frank Rucker, lhp, Ensley HS, Birmingham, Ala.
63. **Bruce Ellingsen, lhp, Lakewood (Calif.) HS**
64. Francis Karmelich, c, Fermen Lasuen HS, San Pedro, Calif.
65. Tom Lundstedt, c, Prospect HS, Arlington Heights, Ill.
66. Antonio Latour, lhp, Indian River (Fla.) CC
67. Craig Fox, lhp, Ithaca (N.Y.)
68. Bart Bell, 2b, Mesa (Ariz.) CC (Selection voided)
69. Harold Murray, c, Smith Cotton HS, Sedalia, Mo.
70. Keith Lieppman, ss, Southwest HS, Kansas City, Mo.

June—Secondary Phase (14)

1. David Brown, of, Texas
2. Robert Bosson, 1b, Columbia
3. **Larry Burchart, rhp, Oklahoma State**
4. **Randolph Kohn, c, Georgia**
5. **Jim Scheschuk, c, Texas**
6. **Jackie Creel, rhp, Gulf Coast (Fla.) CC**
7. **David Speas, 3b, San Diego Mesa JC**
8. Walter Adey, lhp, Hudson Valley (N.Y.) CC
9. Jon Keirns, of, Central State (Okla.)
10. Lucky Thompson, ss, San Diego
11. Clarence Cleveland, of/3b, Chipola (Fla.) JC
12. Larry Linville, of, Arizona State
13. Patrick O'Brien, lhp, Arizona
14. Bruce Wade, rhp, El Camino (Calif.) JC
15. Richard Binder, lhp, Illinois
16. Douglas Brittele, rhp, Rutgers
17. Glenn Bisbing, 3b, Rider

MINNESOTA TWINS

January—Regular Phase (18)

1. **Leonard Weems, of, Ecorse (Mich.) HS**
2. Jack Nelson, rhp, Fullerton (Calif.) JC
3. Joe Miller, rhp, Orange Coast (Calif.) JC
4. **Gerald Ruettiman, rhp, St. Paul, Minn.**
5. **Marv Danielson, 3b, Silver Bay, Minn.**

January—Secondary Phase (14)

1. **Clifford Foster, of/1b, Sexton HS, Lansing, Mich.**
2. Rod O'Brien, 3b, Long Beach (Calif.) CC
3. **Edwin Figueroa, c, George Washington HS, New York**
4. **Larry Housley, 3b, San Bernardino Valley (Calif.) JC**
5. Douglas Hansen, rhp, Fresno (Calif.) CC
6. Scott Morton, lhp, Iowa State
7. Ted Rohde, of, Fresno (Calif.) CC
8. John Herbst, lhp, Southern California
9. Thomas Kelly, of, Holy Cross

June—Regular Phase (17)

1. **Steve Brye, 3b/of, St. Elizabeth HS, Oakland, Calif.**
2. **Robert Storm, 3b, Adams HS, South Bend, Ind.**
3. **Tom Norman, 3b, Truman HS, Independence, Mo.**
4. **William Perkins, c, Montclair (Calif.) HS**
5. **Dave Goltz, rhp, Rothsay (Minn.) HS**
6. **Mark Strader, c, Jefferson HS, Lafayette, Ind.**
7. **Daniel Mellars, ss, Penn Hills HS, Verona, Pa.**
8. **Anthony Serenelli, ss/3b, Trenton Cathedral HS, Morrisville, Pa.**
9. **Steve Simon, rhp, Pius X HS, Lynwood, Calif.**
10. **Danny Long, c, Calhoun (Tenn.) HS**
11. Al Hrabosky, lhp, Savanna HS, Anaheim
12. **Don Brown, rhp, Clarksville (Tenn.) HS**
13. **Steve Luebber, rhp, Joplin (Mo.) HS**
14. Nils Lambert, lhp, Curtis HS, Staten Island, N.Y.

15. **Rick Dempsey, c, Crespi HS, Simi Valley, Calif.**
16. **Dan Humay, ss, Illinois**
17. **Ray Shoup, of, Ohio State**
18. Keith Spicer, of, Michigan
19. **Robert Gamache, rhp, West HS, Garden City, Mich.**
20. **Gary Reierson, of, Minnesota**
21. **Larry Rathje, of, Iowa**
22. James Enlund, rhp, West Allis (Wis.) Central HS
23. **John Shuloch, 3b, Brevard (Fla.) CC**
24. **Jim Obradovich, 2b, Fort Knox (Ky.) HS**
25. **Michael Shields, lhp, Waukesha (Wis.) Memorial HS**
26. **Frank Archuleta, of, Hanford (Calif.) HS**
27. **Kenneth Gill, rhp/of, Brevard (Fla.) CC**
28. Louis Billmeier, rhp, Kuempter HS, Carroll, Iowa
29. **Robert Fitzner, c, Denver**
30. Daniel Adams, 3b/ss, West Allis (Wis.) Central HS
31. **Walter Evanik, of, Kearney (N.J.) HS**
32. **Patrick Smith, 2b/ss, Robersonville (N.C.) HS**
33. Jake Brown, c, Wheatley HS, Houston
34. **Mike Cichon, rhp, Pomona (Calif.) HS**
35. William Templeton, rhp, Elmira, N.Y.
36. Ronald Pritchett, rhp, Ganesha HS, Pomona, Calif.
37. **Larry Agrella, ss/3b, Camden HS, San Jose, Calif.**
38. Mel Bannon, ss, St. Francis HS, Pasadena, Calif.
39. **William Rahm, rhp, Iowa State**
40. Patrick Knutzen, lhp, El Camino (Calif.) JC
41. **Mike Ford, c, Lewis (Ill.)**
42. Henry Baker, 3b, Liberty HS, Hinesville, Ga.
43. Neal Kalberer, lhp, St. Mary's Central HS, Bismarck, N.D.
44. Gary Hohman, c, Steinert HS, Trenton, N.J.
45. Tim Bodle, rhp, Lancaster (Texas) HS
46. Robert Berezowitz, c, Whitewater State
47. **Lloyd Brunick, rhp, Yankton (S.D.) HS**
48. **Vern Gove, of, Randolph (Wis.) HS**
49. **Robert Meyer, lhp, Wartburg (Iowa)**
50. Michael Vogel, ss, St. Thomas Academy, St. Paul, Minn.
51. Rick Pope, rhp, El Rancho HS, Pico Rivera, Calif.

June—Secondary Phase (3)

1. Ken Szotkiewicz, ss, Georgia Southern
2. **Dan Monzon, ss, Buena Vista**
3. David Grangaard, 3b, Arizona State
4. **Steve Richman, ss, Columbia**
5. **Mike Sadek, c, Minnesota**
6. Michael Noonan, lhp, Foothill (Calif.) JC
7. **Clifford Farmer, rhp, Crowder (Mo.) JC**
8. **James Townsend, inf/of, Santa Clara**
9. **Pete Hamm, rhp, Stanford**
10. Craig Skok, lhp, Broward (Fla.) CC

NEW YORK METS

January—Regular Phase (3)

1. **Ken Singleton, of, Mount Vernon, N.Y.**
2. Daniel DeMichele, of/3b, Vermont Academy, Cranston, R.I.
3. **Thomas Grubb, rhp, Lexington, N.C.**
4. Ike Blessitt, of, Hamtramck (Mich.) HS
5. Arnie Chonko, 1b, Ohio State

January—Secondary Phase (19)

1. **Tommy Campbell, of, Jackson State**
2. Scott Reid, 3b/of, Cerritos (Calif.) JC
3. **Richard Carlson, 1b/of, Buffalo State**
4. John Mispagel, c, Santa Clara
5. Bob Chlupsa, rhp, Manhattan
6. Jim Whinery, 3b, Modesto (Calif.) JC
7. **Dennis Trame, rhp, Trenton, Ill.**
8. Terry Stofer, of, Key West, Fla.
9. **Charles Haje, of, Montgomery (Md.) JC**
10. **Tommy Moore, of, Cerritos (Calif.) JC**
11. Ken Stabler, lhp, Alabama
12. Reid Braden, 1b, Cerritos (Calif.) JC

June—Regular Phase (4)

1. **Jon Matlack, lhp, Henderson HS, West Chester, Pa.**
2. **Daniel Carey, lhp, Hastings (Minn.) HS**
3. Gary Myers, of, Hoover HS, Fresno, Calif.
4. **Gary King, ss, El Segundo (Calif.) HS**
5. **Jackie Adams, of, Monrovia (Calif.) HS**
6. **Russell Seals, rhp, Calhoun (Tenn.) HS**
7. Barry Sheldon, rhp, Batavia (N.Y.) HS
8. **Mike McCready, rhp, El Segundo (Calif.) HS**
9. **Fred Howard, 1b, Hoover HS, Fresno, Calif.**
10. **Charlie Hudson, lhp/of, Tupelo (Okla.) HS**
11. **Jesse Hudson, lhp, DeSoto HS, Mansfield, La.**
12. **Tom Horne, lhp, Puyallup (Wash.) HS**
13. Tim Bograkos, 1b, Central HS, Flint, Mich.
14. Wendell Franke, ss/rhp, Hooper (Neb.) HS
15. **Charles Landis, of, Wisconsin-La Crosse**
16. John Frilling, of, Covington (Ky.) Catholic HS
17. **Forrest Dover, rhp, High Point (N.C.)**
18. **Warren Holmes, of, Norland HS, Miami**
19. Joseph Tillman, 3b, Murphy HS, Mobile, Ala.
20. Steve Broege, lhp, Westlake HS, Thornwood, N.Y.
21. Donald Russell, 3b, Southern HS, Baltimore
22. **Dennis Lingenfelter, rhp, Atwater HS, Winton, Calif.**
23. Michael Lersch, lhp, Hinckley HS, Aurora, Colo.
24. **Bob Bryant, c, Chico (Calif.) HS**
25. **Peter Cappelli, c, Highland HS, Albuquerque, N.M.**
26. Jerry Perkins, lhp, Wirt HS, Miller, Ind.
27. Eugene Salmon, 1b, Del Rio (Texas) H.S
28. **Steve McMillan, 2b, Cerritos (Calif.) JC**
29. **Roger Spagnuolo, ss, Lansing (Mich.) Sexton HS**
30. Larry Kiser, lhp, Dobbyns-Bennett HS, Kingsport, Tenn.
31. Mike Pietrantonio, ss, Bordentown (N.J.) Military Academy
32. Dan Pastorini, ss, Bellarmine Prep HS, San Jose, Calif.
33. **Del Corral, of, Foothill (Calif.) JC**
34. William Luftig, ss, Wantaugh (N.Y.) HS
35. Bill Olsen, lhp, Eureka (Calif.) HS
36. **David Lipp, 2b, Mount Tacoma (Wash.) HS**
37. **John Bachman, c, Edison Tech HS, Rochester, N.Y.**
38. **Dave Schneck, lhp/of, White Hall (Pa.) HS**
39. **Mark Crandall, lhp, Washington State**
40. Robert Thomas, 1b, Dartmouth (Selection voided)
41. **Joseph Abene, 3b, Hillsborough HS, Tampa**
42. Ken Henderson, 1b, Long Beach (N.Y.) HS
43. Robert Larson, rhp/ss, Alhambra (Calif.) HS
44. Melvin McNeil, of, Grambling
45. Michael Swenton, of, Ward HS, Kansas City, Kan.
46. Frank Alfano, ss, Crawford HS, San Diego
47. **Allen Clements, rhp, Texas**
48. Roy Myers, 3b, Youngstown State
49. James Bergholtz, ss, Hicksville (N.Y.) HS
50. **Tom Robson, 1b, Utah State**
51. **Frank Ujcich, rhp, Wellsburg, W.Va.**
52. George Carter, of, St. Bonaventure
53. Harry Saferight, c, Meadowbrook HS, Richmond, Va.
54. **Martin Gearhart, of, Xenia (Ohio) HS**
55. **Gary Coombs, lhp, Cordova HS, Rancho Cordova, Calif.**
56. William Seyfert, 1b, Newfield HS, Selden, N.Y.
57. **Charles Merlo, ss, Morehead State**
58. Robert Shearer, of, Newport (Ky.) Public HS
59. Timothy Uraskevich, rhp, SUNY Buffalo
60. **Richard Shelly, c, Zanesville (Ohio) HS**

June—Secondary Phase (20)

1. **Rich Folkers, lhp, Parsons**
2. **Rod Gaspar, of, Cal State Long Beach**
3. **Gary Gentry, rhp, Arizona State**
4. **Steve Brasher, rhp, Arizona**
5. **Ronald Matney, lhp, Sam Houston State**
6. Neil Pittman, rhp, Missouri
7. James Brown, lhp, Arizona State
8. **Rich Hacker, ss, Southern Illinois**
9. **David Nitschke, c, Fresno State**
10. William Maxwell, rhp, Oklahoma State
11. Franklin Riggins, of/lhp, Kansas
12. **Samuel Narron, c, East Carolina**

13. **Frederick Senger, c, CC of Baltimore**
14. Reid Braden, 1b/of, Southern California

NEW YORK YANKEES

January—Regular Phase (2)

1. Michael Flanagan, lhp, Yakima Valley (Wash.) JC
2. **Charles Burton, rhp, Dallas Baptist**
3. Michael Bertrand, c, Columbia Basin (Wash.) JC
4. Kenneth Carmack, rhp, Yakima Valley (Wash.) JC
5. Stanley Sass, c/3b, Skagit Valley (Wash.) CC
6. Gary Sauer, lhp, Columbia Basin (Wash.) CC

January—Secondary Phase (20)

1. **Harry Wright, of, Pennsylvania**
2. Bruce Wade, rhp, El Camino (Calif.) JC
3. **Terry Ley, lhp, Clark (Wash.) JC**
4. William Shepherd, rhp, Columbia Basin (Wash.) CC
5. **James Babyak, ss, Westfield State**
6. Al Simmons, rhp, Idaho
7. **Patrick Hartigan, rhp, Columbia Basin (Wash.) CC**
8. Wayne Danson, Gulf Coast (Fla.) CC

June—Regular Phase (1)

1. **Ron Blomberg, 1b, Druid Hills HS, Atlanta, Ga.**
2. **Alphonso Neal, 3b, Womack HS, Longview, Texas**
3. **Jimmy Yawn, 2b, Mississippi**
4. **Larry Gowell, rhp, Edward Little HS, Auburn, Maine**
5. **Billy Barlow, c/3b, Kingsburry HS, Memphis, Tenn.**
6. Tim Feldhaus, inf, Bonita HS, La Verne, Calif.
7. **Phillip Ranneberger, of/rhp, Frederick HS, Buckeystown, Md.**
8. **Stanton Evenhus, rhp, Eastmont HS, Rock Island, Wash.**
9. **Robert Carson, inf, Federal Way (Wash.) HS**
10. **Les Gibbens, lhp, Vallivue HS, Caldwell, Idaho**
11. Donnie Davis, 3b, Pascagoula (Miss.) HS
12. **Brian Engle, ss, Lewiston (Idaho) HS**
13. Michael Gomez, rhp, University HS, Spokane, Wash.
14. **Daniel Bohannon, ss, Stagg HS, Stockton, Calif.**
15. **Jim Deidel, c, Mullen HS, Denver**
16. **Craig Fellows, rhp, Fort Hamilton HS, Brooklyn, N.Y.**
17. **David Gunderman, 2b/ss, Mater Dei HS, Fullerton, Calif.**
18. Richard Cross, ss, Carson HS, Torrance, Calif.
19. Mike Ball, 3b, Hoover HS, San Diego
20. **Gerald Wickman, lhp, Minnesota**
21. Daniel Bina, rhp, West Salem (Wis.) HS
22. Robert Vaught, rhp, Santa Ana (Calif.) JC
23. **Barney Scholl, of, Chapman (Calif.)**
24. **Richard Ordway, rhp, Maine**
25. **Joseph Gill, of, San Francisco**
26. Ronald Watts, lhp, Wichita (Kan.) West HS
27. **Thomas Porthen, rhp, Foster HS, Riverton Heights, Wash.**
28. **Loyd Colson, rhp/inf, Bacone (Okla.) JC**
29. **Robby Hefflinger, 1b, Cleveland HS, Portland, Ore.**
30. **Ken Johnson, rhp, Idaho**
31. Douglas Braun, c, Salinas (Calif.) JC
32. **Willie Elmore, c, Livingston**
33. Tommy Monroe, c, Shades Valley HS, Birmingham, Ala.
34. Michael Baier, ss, Calvert Hall HS, Baltimore
35. David Gonzalez, ss, St. Augustine HS, San Diego
36. Jerry McCollough, of/1b, La Puente (Calif.) HS
37. **Walter Peto, ss, Seton Hall**
38. **Joseph Hindelang, rhp, Temple**
39. James Corcoran, ss, Gonzaga Prep HS, Spokane, Wash.
40. Jerre Algeo, inf, Central HS, Springfield, Mo.
41. John Wiley, rhp, Lincoln HS, Portland, Ore.
42. **Nelson Straley, c, Bishop Montgomery HS, Hawthorne, Calif.**
43. Mike Reinbach, of, Granite Hills HS, El Cajon, Calif.
44. Dana Ryan, 2b, Arkansas State
45. Sam Ewing, 1b/of, Overton HS, Nashville, Tenn.
46. **Gerry Vanaman, 2b, Chapman (Calif.)**
47. Dennis Gideon, lhp, Chaffey (Calif.) JC
48. **Jerry Schultz, 2b/3b, North Dakota**
49. Walter Failor, rhp/1b, Aberdeen (Wash.) HS
50. **Dennis Murray, lhp, Cal Poly Pomona**
51. **Jeffery Mason, ss, Deerfield (Ill.) HS**
52. **Dale Braumberger, rhp, Cal Poly Pomona**
53. Atheophilus Jermany, rhp, Roosevelt HS, Portland, Ore.
54. Randy Nelson, 3b, Magnolia HS, Anaheim
55. Randy Vataha, ss, Rancho Alamitas HS, Garden Grove, Calif.
56. **Andrew Bottin, of/1b, Meadowdale HS, Edmonds, Wash.**
57. **Donald Keeler, 1b, Snohomish (Wash.) HS**
58. **Craig Keister, lhp, Marysville (Wash.) HS**
59. Gerald Bosch, of, CC of San Francisco
60. Steve Rogers, rhp, Glendale HS, Springfield, Mo.
61. **Michael Fowler, lhp, Columbia HS, Richland, Wash.**
62. Steve Wiencek, ss, Claremont (Calif.) HS
63. **Paul Branca, c, Brentwood (N.Y.) HS**
64. John Pavlik, of, Springfield (Ore.) HS
65. Charles Zecco, lhp, Burlington HS, Edgewater Park, N.J.
66. Frank Whigham, ss, Seminole HS, Sanford, Fla.
67. **Roger Hambright, rhp, Columbia River HS, Vancouver, Wash.**
68. Wayne Stephens, ss, Charter Oaks HS, Covina, Calif.
69. Michael Hunt, rhp, Kennewick (Wash.) HS
70. Kelly Godfrey, rhp/of, South Hills HS, Covina, Calif.
71. Larry McClenny, rhp, Shadle Park HS, Spokane, Wash.
72. Michael Bubalo, of/1b, Lincoln HS, Portland, Ore.
73. Robert Scott, c, Rossville (Ga.) HS
74. **Thomas Gill, ss, St. Francis (N.Y.)**
75. Greg Wellman, lhp, Forest Hills HS, West Palm Beach, Fla.
76. **David Walsh, ss, Enterprise HS, Reading, Calif.**
77. **Donald Vandeusen, ss, Concord**

June—Secondary Phase (9)

1. **Charles Lelas, 1b/of, Springfield**
2. **Frank Baker, ss, Southern Mississippi**
3. Ronald Davini, c, Arizona State
4. **Gary Washington, 1b, Mississippi State**
5. **Bruce Baudier, rhp, Louisiana State**
6. William Shepherd, rhp, Columbia Basin (Wash.) CC
7. **Gerry Pirtle, rhp, Bacone (Okla.) JC**
8. Norm Angelini, lhp, JC of San Mateo (Calif.)
9. Richard Donnelly, c, Xavier (Selection voided)
10. Harold Werntz, rhp, Temple
11. Stephen Sharp, rhp, Missouri
12. **Al Simmons, rhp, Idaho**

PHILADELPHIA PHILLIES

January—Regular Phase (13)

1. **Michael Coble, rhp, Long Beach (Calif.) CC**

January—Secondary Phase (15)

1. **Pat Skrable, of, Bakersfield (Calif.) JC**
2. **Ernest Aguirre, inf, Bakersfield (Calif.) JC**
3. Darrell Evans, 3b/rhp, Pasadena (Calif.) CC
4. Stephen Smith, 3b, Long Beach (Calif.) Poly HS
5. Richard Corsetto, rhp/of, Harford (Md.) CC

June—Regular Phase (14)

1. **Phil Meyer, lhp, Pius X HS, Downey, Calif.**
2. **Larry Keener, rhp, Wheeler HS, Marietta, Ga.**
3. **Bob McLachlin, lhp, Tenafly (N.J.) HS**
4. **Nicholas Graybeal, c, Tennessee HS, Bristol, Tenn.**
5. Joseph Daniels, of, Las Cruces (N.M.) HS
6. Terry Mathis, ss, Clear Creek HS, League City, Texas
7. **Bruce Hotchkiss, of, Ellsworth (Iowa) JC**
8. **Robert Stevens, lhp, St. Viator HS, Mount Prospect, Ill.**
9. Michael Schomaker, of/c, Stanford
10. **Terry Howarth, 1b, Westchester (Calif.) HS**
11. **Donald Thomson, rhp, Newell (Iowa) HS**
12. **Frank Odum, c, Jessup HS, Odum, Ga.**
13. **Dennis Davies, c, Murray (Utah) HS**
14. Eugene Stack, rhp, Harding HS, Oklahoma City, Okla.
15. **Joseph Sanchez, rhp, Coachella Valley HS, Indio, Calif.**
16. **Jeff Beattie, rhp, Warwick (N.Y.) HS**
17. **Henry Jacquez, of, Stagg HS, Stockton, Calif.**
18. **Robert Kenny, rhp, Parsons**
19. **Joseph Anderson, of, Rahway HS, Winfield Park, N.J.**
20. John Maczuga, of, Franklin (N.J.) HS

21. Milton Jackson, rhp, Tulsa
22. Donald Keenan, c, Pensacola (Fla.) HS
23. **Kenneth Bangsberg, lhp, San Diego Mesa JC**
24. **Anthony Giresi, lhp, Fair Lawn (N.J.) HS**

June—Secondary Phase (18)

1. Douglas Sandstedt, lhp, Benson HS, Omaha, Neb.
2. **Scott Reid, of, Arizona State**
3. **Robert Leatherwood, 2b, California**
4. Tom Cook, c, Manatee (Fla.) JC
5. Steve Smith, ss/3b, Long Beach (Calif.) CC
6. **James Magnuson, of, California**

PITTSBURGH PIRATES

January—Regular Phase (15)

1. Ronald Ritter, rhp, Shelby HS, Shelbyville, Ky.
2. Joseph Staton, 1b/of, Seattle (Wash.) CC
3. Edward Lemmon, rhp/inf, Robert Morris
4. Richard Wieczezak, 3b, Seton Hall
5. **David Etter, 1b, Chambersburg (Pa.) Area HS**
6. **Bobby Herring, rhp, Gainesville (Ga.) JC**

January—Secondary Phase (13)

1. Kris Krebs, ss, Manatee (Fla.) JC
2. **James Minnette, inf, Columbia Basin (Wash.) CC**
3. Frank Brennan, rhp, Fairleigh Dickinson
4. Richard Wanless, rhp, North Quincy (Mass.) HS
5. Bill Tsoukalas, lhp, Everett (Wash.) CC
6. Clifford Farmer, rhp, Hillcrest HS, Springfield, Mo.

June—Regular Phase (16)

1. **Joe Grigas, of, Coyle HS, Brockton, Mass.**
2. **David Sells, rhp, Sullivan HS, Kingsport, Tenn.**
3. **Richie Zisk, of, Parsippany (N.J.) HS**
4. **Mike Roberts, 3b, Mount Eden HS, Hayward, Calif.**
5. William McBrayer, ss, Williamson (W.Va.) HS
6. **Harry Tobergate, rhp, Baden HS, Hamilton, Ohio**
7. **Dennis Vaughn, c, Los Gatos (Calif.) HS**
8. **John Landry, 1b, Istrouma HS, Baton Rouge, La.**
9. **Theodore Taylor, 3b/of, Florida A&M**
10. **Darrell Brown, ss/3b, East Bank HS, Handley, W.Va.**
11. **William Spikes, of, Central Memorial HS, Bogalusa, La.**
12. **Charles Helms, ss, Clemson**
13. **Meredith Cox, rhp, Centennial HS, Compton, Calif.**
14. **Thomas Saunches, c, DuQuoin (Ill.) HS**
15. **Tyrone Hines, ss, Mount Pleasant HS, Schenectady, N.Y.**
16. **Charles Malitz, of/1b, Texas A&M**
17. **Howard Deacon, c, Wayland (Mass.) HS**
18. **Paul Strauch, rhp, Danvers (Mass.) HS**
19. Jack Burns, of/rhp, George Washington HS, Denver
20. **Paul Keany, 3b, Maine**
21. **James Iglehart, of, Castlemont HS, Oakland, Calif.**
22. Michael Derrig, lhp, Lincoln-Way HS, Makena, Ill.
23. George Arnott, 2b, Santa Cruz (Calif.) HS
24. James Topping, lhp, Maine Central Institute, Lewiston, Maine
25. Dave Rose, rhp, San Carlos (Calif.) HS
26. Lee Lamb, rhp, Bremen HS, Midlothian, Ill.
27. Donald Schroeder, rhp, Long HS, Longview, Wash.
28. Donald Barnes, rhp, Marietta (Ohio) HS
29. **Lewis Green, ss, Healdsburg (Calif.) HS**
30. **J.T. Ingram, rhp, Dos Palos (Calif.) HS**
31. **Terry Gardner, rhp, McNary HS, Salem, Ore.**
32. Lyle Wilber, rhp, Goldendale (Wash.) HS
33. Don Anderson, rhp, Pennington Prep HS, Westfield, N.J.
34. Jerald Vitatoe, 3b/of, St. Joseph's HS, Oakland, Calif.
35. **Perry Dunn, ss/3b, Blanchard HS, Augusta, Ga.**
36. Thomas Grayson, inf, Guilford (N.C.)
37. **Lorenzo Lanier, of, John Adams HS, Cleveland**
38. Bob Auriegemma, rhp, South City HS, San Francisco
39. **Daryl French, rhp, Bainbridge HS, Winslow, Wash.**
40. Danny Brown, 2b, Benton HS, St. Joseph, Mo.
41. William Hager, lhp, West Allegheny HS, Imperial, Pa.
42. Edward Perry, of/1b, Bethlehem Central HS, Delmar, N.Y.

June—Secondary Phase (12)

1. John Morlan, of, Ohio
2. Mike Lisetski, ss, Rider
3. **Doug Carson, c, Santa Clara**
4. **Frank Brennan, rhp, Fairleigh Dickinson**
5. **Thomas Buchenberger, rhp, St. John's**
6. Taylor Toomey, lhp, Colorado
7. Rick Austin, lhp, Washington State
8. Edward Mantie, rhp, Syracuse
9. Tom Dettore Jr., rhp, Juniata

ST. LOUIS CARDINALS

January—Regular Phase (9)

1. **Fred Grooms, rhp, Wilson HS, San Francisco**
2. Douglas Sandstedt, lhp, Benson HS, Omaha, Neb.
3. Ronald Lemery, c, Jefferson (Mo.) HS
4. Jackie Creel, rhp, Gulf Coast (Fla.) CC

January—Secondary Phase (9)

1. Jim Scheschuk, c, Texas
2. Stephen Dean, 1b, JC of the Sequoias (Calif.)
3. Clarence Cleveland, rhp, Chipola (Fla.) JC
4. Tom Cook, c, Manatee (Fla.) JC
5. **Bruce Hinkel, lhp, Marquette, Iowa**

June—Regular Phase (10)

1. **Ted Simmons, c/of, Southfield (Mich.) HS**
2. **Jerry Reuss, lhp, Ritenour HS, Overland, Mo.**
3. Bart Johnson, rhp, Torrance (Calif.) HS
4. **Ronald McCollum, c, Shaker HS, Latham, N.Y.**
5. Matt Sterling, rhp, Thomas Jefferson HS, Denver
6. Paul Womble, ss, Wyandotte HS, Kansas City, Kan.
7. **John Polovina, rhp, St. Francis HS, Altadena, Calif.**
8. **Lawrence Koch, rhp, Nassau (N.Y.) CC**
9. James Braxton, 1b/of, Connellsville (Pa.) HS
10. Len Randle, ss, Centennial HS, Compton, Calif.
11. **Alfred Buchta, rhp, New York**
12. **Jeffrey Ice, rhp, Treadwell HS, Memphis, N.Y.**
13. Raymond Wood, of/1b, Central HS, Omaha, Neb.
14. William Kelly, rhp/1b, Reading (Mass.) HS
15. **David Polcari, of, Medford (Mass.) HS**
16. **Melvin Pettigrew, of, Hanford (Calif.) Union HS**
17. **John Carroll, rhp, Fordham**
18. **Ronnie Roberts, lhp, Hay Long HS, Mount Pleasant, Tenn.**
19. Richard Wilson, rhp, Milliken HS, Long Beach, Calif.
20. Thomas Dunn, 1b, Arroyo HS, San Lorenzo, Calif.
21. **Stanley Dyson, 3b/of, Santa Fe HS, Santa Fe Springs, Calif.**
22. **John Howard, 1b/lhp, Assumption HS, East St. Louis, Ill.**
23. **Glenn Marshall, 1b, Los Angeles (Calif.) HS**
24. **Robert Richardson, rhp, Weymouth (Mass.) HS**
25. **Freddy Jamison, rhp, Carver HS, Memphis, Tenn.**
26. **Thomas Kuczynski, lhp/of, Braintree (Mass.) HS**
27. **Paul Kacera, 3b, Granite City (Ill.) HS**
28. **Bob Bonalewicz, c, Parsons**
29. **James Scieres, c, Arkansas State**
30. Wesley Rutledge, rhp, Troy State
31. Randolph Siebert, rhp, Glendale (Calif.) HS
32. Richard McHale, lhp, Villa Park (Calif.) HS
33. Pat Osburn, lhp/1b, Clearwater (Fla.) HS
34. Joel Hall, c, Waukegan (Ill.) HS
35. Orlando Ortega, of, Cypress (Calif.) JC
36. **Freddie Smith, c, Jefferson HS, Los Angeles**
37. Mark Driscoll, 2b, Arlington (Mass.) HS
38. **Benny Haynie, rhp, Northeast Mississippi JC**
39. Richard Householder, ss/of, Fontana (Calif.) HS
40. **Richard Rix, of, University Lake HS, Hartland, Wis.**
41. Malcolm Beard, ss, Dartmouth
42. Robert Olszewski, of, St. Anthony HS, Long Beach, Calif.

June—Secondary Phase (10)

1. **Jimmie Jackson, lhp, Grambling**
2. Charlie West, of, Texas-El Paso
3. **Phillip Trombino, 1b, Iona**
4. Stephen Steitz, lhp/of, Worchester (Mass.) Academy
5. **Bob Chlupsa, rhp, Manhattan**
6. **Jerry Sabourin, lhp, Saint Louis**
7. William Holt, lhp, Lynchburg (Va.)
8. Phillip O'Neil, of, Holy Cross

SAN FRANCISCO GIANTS

January—Regular Phase (17)

1. Von Joshua, of, Chabot (Calif.) JC
2. Brent Strom, lhp, San Diego (Calif.) CC
3. **Fred Fegen, c, San Francisco**
4. William Price, of, Fremont HS, Los Angeles

January—Secondary Phase (5)

1. Marvin Galliher, inf, San Diego Mesa JC
2. John Dow, of, Bemidji, Minn.
3. Ray Strable, rhp, JC of the Sequoias (Calif.)
4. Bobby Garcia, of/rhp, JC of the Sequoias (Calif.)
5. Daniel Blood, 2b, Citrus (Calif.) JC
6. James Magnuson, c/of, JC of San Mateo (Calif.) (Selection voided)
7. Michael Pruett, lhp, Overland, Mo.

June—Regular Phase (18)

1. **Dave Rader, c, South Bakersfield (Calif.) HS**
2. **Michael Roby, 1b, East Waterloo (Iowa) HS**
3. **Don Carrithers, rhp, Lyndale HS, Lynwood, Calif.**
4. Steve Busby, rhp, Fullerton (Calif.) HS
5. **Marty Pfenninger, ss, Central Hunterdon HS, Flemington, N.J.**
6. **Michael Welker, lhp, Pleasant Valley HS, Chico, Calif.**
7. Larry Price, of, Coachella (Calif.) Valley HS
8. Davey Lopes, of, Washburn (Kan.)
9. James Gasbarro, inf, Catholic Memorial HS, Hyde Park, Mass.
10. Robert Tate, ss, Bacone (Okla.) HS
11. **Jim Willoughby, rhp, Gustine (Calif.) HS**
12. **Osvaldo Bosch, of, Haaren HS, New York**
13. **Rosendo Cedeno, 1b/of, DeWitt Clinton HS, Bronx, N.Y.**
14. **Eugene Cook, 2b, Redondo Beach (Calif.) HS**
15. Pat Westley, ss, North HS, Phoenix
16. **Anthony Ketelsleger, rhp, Rio Hondo (Calif.) JC**
17. Gary Houston, lhp, James Lick HS, San Jose, Calif.
18. **Fred Glass, rhp, Alabama**
19. **Larry Iten, c, Calexico (Calif.) HS**
20. **Gary Lavelle, lhp, Liberty HS, Bethlehem, Pa.**
21. **Van Fixico, 2b, Bacone (Okla.) JC**
22. **Garry Pinnow, of/1b, Wisconsin**
23. Danny Guerrero, c, El Rancho HS, Pico Rivera, Calif.
24. Glen Davis, 2b, North HS, Phoenix
25. John Floyd, 1b, Gordo (Ala.) HS
26. Bobby Wade, c, Mississippi
27. Martin Downen, rhp, Brigham Young
28. Gregory Yarbrough, lhp, Shaw (Miss.) HS
29. Rick Sawyer, rhp, Bakersfield (Calif.) JC
30. Donald Elam, rhp, San Francisco State
31. **Michael Newsom, inf/rhp, Western HS, Las Vegas**
32. Robert Huddleston, of, Cataline HS, Tucson, Ariz.
33. **David Voss, 1b, Wilson HS, Tacoma, Wash.**
34. **Jeff Campbell, rhp, Livingston**
35. Wayne Mitchell, of, Richmond (Calif.) Union HS
36. **Leonard Cargill, rhp, Fresno (Calif.) CC**
37. Vache Bahadurian, 1b, Forest Hills (N.Y.) HS
38. **Robert Kenney, rhp, Rutgers**
39. Donald Weber, lhp, Highland Park HS, St. Paul, Minn.
40. John Terista, ss, Ithaca (N.Y.)
41. Robert Graczyk, rhp, Proviso West HS, Bellwood, Ill.
42. **Douglas Theriault, lhp, Puyallup (Wash.) HS**
43. Michael Miller, 1b, West Chester (Pa.) HS
44. Mickey Cureton, of, Centennial HS, Compton, Calif.
45. Dave Gillette, c/of, Alhambra HS, Phoenix
46. **Martin Coil, 1b, San Francisco State**
47. Lynn Sparks, lhp, Cal State Chico
48. Gary Shade, 2b, Reynoldsburg (Ohio) HS
49. **Joe Wischnowski, rhp, Illinois State**

June—Secondary Phase (16)

1. **Bobby Fenwick, ss, Minnesota**
2. Ken Hottman, of, Sacramento (Calif.) CC
3. **Jim Johnson, lhp/of, Western Michigan**
4. **Earl Vickers, of, Fresno State**
5. Thomas Brown, ss, Miami
6. Michael Willis, lhp, Colorado
7. **Jack Fulmer, 3b, Arkansas State**
8. Chuck Scrivener, ss, CC of Baltimore
9. Jerald Hurt, rhp, Missouri
10. Arthur Pauls, rhp, Lewis (Ill.)

WASHINGTON SENATORS

January—Regular Phase (6)

1. **Robert Stach, 1b, Southern HS, West River, Md.**

January—Secondary Phase (8)

1. **Jan Dukes, lhp, Santa Clara**
2. Gary Washington, 1b, Mississippi State
3. Ray Henningsen, 2b, Santa Clara
4. Michael Weber, lhp, Southern Illinois-Edwardsville
5. Richard Narron, c, East Carolina
6. Lamar Davis, 1b, Maryland
7. Charles Watson, lhp, Clemson
8. Terry L'Ange, p, Missouri (Selection voided)

June—Regular Phase (5)

1. **John Jones, c, Loretto HS, St. Joseph, Tenn.**
2. **Dexter Baker, lhp/of, St. Catherine HS, Racine, Wis.**
3. **Mike Thompson, rhp, Ponca City (Okla.) HS**
4. Ken Caldwell, 3b, Mecklenburg HS, Huntersville, N.C.
5. **Ike Brookens, rhp, Chambersburg HS, Fayetteville, Pa.**
6. **Michael Schooff, lhp, Woodbridge (Va.) HS**
7. **Melvin Lowe, of, Lakewood (N.J.) HS**
8. Thomas Elgin, lhp, North Hagerstown (Md.) HS
9. Chris Cammack, 3b, Fayetteville (N.C.) HS
10. **Robert Koehler, rhp, Rider**
11. **Rick Stelmaszek, c, Mendel HS, Chicago**
12. Richard Eisenacher, rhp, Albert Einstein HS, Wheaton, Md.
13. **Wayne Stack, ss, St. John's**
14. Ray Bare, rhp, Southwest HS, Miami
15. Joseph Frye, rhp, Fairmont (N.C.) HS
16. Bruce Kinder, ss, Broward (Fla.) CC
17. **Robert George, lhp, Brooklyn Park HS, Baltimore**
18. **Gordon Steinbach, of, Ripon**
19. Richard Astor, 3b, New Brunswick HS, Milltown, N.J.
20. **Robert Gambill, 2b/rhp, Clearwater (Fla.) HS**
21. **Gary Carter, rhp, Brunswick (Md.) HS**
22. **Jeffrey Drexler, rhp, Oshkosh (Wis.) HS**
23. **Roger Sheridan, of, Quincy**
24. **Thomas Worthington, 3b, Fairmont East HS, Kettering, Ohio**
25. Ralph Owens, ss, Falls Church (Va.) HS
26. Lyle Edwards, of, Western Carolina
27. **Richard Bechtel, ss/2b, Rider**
28. Howard Williams, 3b, Garfield HS, Terre Haute, Ind.
29. **Robert Corwin, c, Little Miami HS, Morrow, Ohio**
30. Donald Burkhalter, rhp, Pensacola (Fla.) HS
31. **Dale Hillard, c/of, Clinton-Massie HS, Clarksville, Ohio**
32. **Richard Baldwin, of, Bradley**
33. Edwin Mossman, 3b, William Chrisman HS, Independence, Mo.
34. **George Hubal, rhp, Trenton (N.J.) Catholic HS**
35. **Delbert Marcus, c, Elkton (Md.) HS**
36. **Bob Jones, 1b, Elkton (Md.) HS**
37. Frank Fillman, lhp, DuVal HS, Lanham, Md.
38. **Lawrence Mischik, lhp, Rider**
39. William Metcalf, lhp, Ripon
40. William Wood, rhp, Warren County HS, Front Royal, Va.
41. **Terry Brecher, ss, Western Illinois**
42. **John Wockenfuss, 3b/rhp, Dickinson HS, Wilmington, Del.**

June—Secondary Phase (7)

1. **Gary Ratliff, of, Bacone (Okla.) JC**
2. **Larry Herring, lhp, Baptist**
3. Paul Reuschel, rhp, Western Illinois
4. Edward Cook, of, Bridgewater
5. Rick Konik, 1b, Detroit
6. Richard Hicks, rhp, Louisiana State
7. Billy Martin, of, Randolph Macon
8. Donald Kirkland, rhp, Southern Illinois

1968 METS' PICK OF JOURNEYMAN FOLI WITH TOP PICK EXEMPLIFIES DRAFT SHORT ON PREMIUM TALENT

Tim Foli was a career .251 hitter, a journeyman infielder who stuck around for 16 seasons and was better known for his volatile temperament than his performance.

Fittingly, Foli was the No. 1 pick in a 1968 draft that was billed as short on top-drawer talent and over the years proved it. Just 11 of 20 first-round picks from the June phase reached the majors, tying a record low. The college crop in particular was thing, and it took more than a year for the first member of the Class of '68 to reach the big leagues.

Foli, whose older brother Ernie signed a sizable bonus contract with the Angels in 1962 but never reached the big leagues, was drafted out of Notre Dame High in Canoga Park, Calif. It was the second time in three years the Mets had the No. 1 selection, and they signed Foli for a $75,000 bonus, the same figure they paid catcher Steve Chilcott two years earlier.

"We didn't decide until after midnight (10 hours before the draft), and we had to make a late call to the coast to check on Foli's availability and his physical condition," Mets farm director Nelson Burbrink said. "We had been undecided between Foli and Lloyd Allen, (a righthander selected 12th overall by the Angels), but the fact that we might need a little hitting in the organization made the difference and we took Foli.

"Foli has good power, good hands, a good arm, but only average speed. He reminds me of Jim Fregosi, except Fregosi can run a little better. I wasn't the only one to see him. Bob Scheffing scouted him, too. Each time Scheffing saw him he hit a home run."

It proved to be Foli's folly. The light-hitting shortstop never homered in 102 games for the Mets. Shortly after he got into a clubhouse altercation with coach Joe Pignatano, the Mets packaged Foli to Montreal in a deal that brought outfielder Rusty Staub to New York.

Had he indicated a willingness to sign out of high school, righthander Pete Broberg may have been the first pick. Broberg committed to Dartmouth, however, and his father Gus, a three-time all-American basketball player at Dartmouth from 1939-41, was determined for his son to get an Ivy League education.

Picking second, the Athletics gambled on Broberg. Despite offers that went as high as $175,000, Broberg went to Dartmouth for three years and signed with the Washington Senators for $150,000 in 1971.

Tim Foli had a long major league career, but he was never more than a role player

Houston had the No. 3 selection, also finding little success. With Thurman Munson available, the Astros took high school receiver Marty Cott, who never advanced past Class A after a two-game stint in Triple-A his first season.

"We think Cott is just a shade away from being a major league catcher right now," said Tal Smith, Astros director of player personnel. "He's that fine a receiver."

Houston promoted both of its first two selections, Cott and outfielder Rich Chiles, to Triple-A in their first seasons, even though both were high school picks.

Munson, who hit .413 at Kent State and was praised for his quick release, was the fourth player picked. He broke in at Double-A and less than 100 games later was in the big leagues. He hit .292 over an 11-year career before dying in the crash of his private plane in 1979.

While Munson and Steve Garvey (Michigan State) would prove to be considerable talents, the overall quality of the 1968 college crop was poor.

North Carolina lefthander Dave Lemonds, selected first by the Cubs in the secondary phase in June, was The Sporting News college player of the year, even though he won just six games, going 6-1, 1.49 with 96 strikeouts in 72 innings. He wasn't a big winner in the major leagues, either, winning four major league games, none with the Cubs.

The Dodgers made the most of it, however. In a below-average year overall, the Dodgers found 15 players (12 in June, three in January) who would play in the big leagues. The nucleus of Garvey, Ron Cey, Bill Buckner, Doyle Alexander, Joe Ferguson and Dave Lopes played on four National League West champions and a future World Series winner.

Little Time To Prepare

With expansion of the major leagues from 20 to 24 teams coming in 1969, the four new clubs participated in the 1968 draft in order to begin building a talent base. They took part in the June proceedings only, and were not allowed to start selecting until the end of the fourth round of both the regular and secondary phases.

Because the American League had committed to expanding to Kansas City and Seattle in October 1967, the Royals and Pilots were much better prepared than their National League counterparts. Expansion franchises weren't awarded to Montreal and San Diego until about a week before the 1968 draft.

By that time, both Kansas City and Seattle had farm teams in the New York-Penn League where drafted players would be assigned. The Expos and Padres had no time to make similar arrangements. They were also required to being negotiations with players within 15 days of their selection, or the players would become free agents.

The Expos' selections were made by Gerry Snyder, the chief drumbeater in Montreal's bid to land an expansion team and the No. 3 man in the Montreal municipal government. The team had not had time to hire a single front-office employee, so Snyder worked from scouting reports that other teams were willing to share with him.

Montreal selected 15 players, signing six. None played in the big leagues. The Expos even drafted a Canadian, outfielder Richard Trembecki, who was better known at the University of Denver for his hockey skills. The selection was later voided because Canadians weren't subject to the draft.

San Diego signed five of the 19 players it drafted. Seattle signed 13 players, most notably future Twins manager Tom Kelly.

Kansas City was the best prepared and signed 26 players, including lefthander Paul Splittorff, who would go on to win 166 major league games.

While the Athletics failed to sign their first two picks in the June draft, they scored in the January draft with the selection of outfielder George Hendrick with the No. 1 pick overall. Hendrick had graduated from Fremont High in Los Angeles the previous week, making him eligible. He didn't play baseball in high school and was spotted playing on weekends with a Pittsburgh Pirates-sponsored semipro team in the Los Angeles area.

The January draft saw a then-record 290 selections made, including three by the poorly prepared Cubs that were voided. Their first selection in the regular phase, pitcher Dave Baldwin, had been signed the previous November by Detroit.

DRAFT 68: FIRST-ROUND PICKS

No.	Club	Player, Pos.	School	Hometown	Ht.	Wt.	B-T	Age
1.	Mets	Tim Foli, ss	Notre Dame HS	Canoga Park, Calif.	5-11	185	R-R	17
2.	Athletics	*Pete Broberg, rhp	Palm Beach HS	Palm Beach, Fla.	6-3	195	R-R	18
3.	Astros	Marty Cott, c	Hutchinson Tech. HS	Buffalo, N.Y.	6-3	185	L-R	17
4.	Yankees	Thurman Munson, c	Kent State	Canton, Ohio	5-11	185	R-R	19
5.	Dodgers	Bobby Valentine, of	Rippowam HS	Stamford, Conn.	5-10	185	R-R	18
6.	Indians	Robert Weaver, ss	Paxon HS	Jacksonville, Fla.	6-1	180	L-R	18
7.	Braves	Curtis Moore, of	Denison HS	Denison, Texas	6-1	180	L-R	18
8.	Senators	Donnie Castle, lhp/of	Coldwater HS	Coldwater, Miss.	6-1	190	L-L	18
9.	Pirates	Dick Sharon, of	Sequoia HS	Redwood City, Calif.	6-2	185	R-R	18
10.	Orioles	Junior Kennedy, ss	Arvin HS	Arvin, Calif.	6-0	180	R-R	17
11.	Phillies	Greg Luzinski, 1b	Notre Dame HS	Prospect Heights, Ill.	6-1	200	R-R	17
12.	Angels	Lloyd Allen, rhp	Selma HS	Selma, Calif.	6-1	180	R-R	18
13.	Reds	Tim Grant, rhp	Riverview HS	Boykins, Va.	6-0	185	L-R	18
14.	White Sox	Rich McKinney, ss	Ohio	Troy, Ohio	6-0	185	R-R	21
15.	Cubs	Ralph Rickey, of	Oklahoma	Oklahoma City, Okla.	6-4	200	B-R	21
16.	Twins	Alex Rowell, of	Luther (Iowa)	North Chicago, Ill.	6-1	195	R-R	21
17.	Giants	Gary Matthews, of	San Fernando HS	Pacoima, Calif.	6-2	185	R-R	17
18.	Tigers	Robert Robinson, of	Thomas Dale HS	Chester, Va.	6-1	190	L-R	18
19.	Cardinals	James Hairston, of	Roth HS	Dayton, Ohio	6-0	175	L-R	17
20.	Red Sox	Tom Maggard, of/c	John Glenn HS	Norwalk, Calif.	6-6	215	R-R	18

*Did not sign.

1968

CLUB-BY-CLUB SELECTIONS

ATLANTA BRAVES

January—Regular Phase (8)

1. **Jim Breazeale, c, Houston**
2. Arnold Murillo, 1b, Canoga Park, Calif.
3. **Michael McCammon, rhp, Indian River (Fla.) CC**
4. Daniel Ketcherside, rhp, St. Louis CC-Meramec
5. Robert Fendlor, lhp, Miami-Dade North CC
6. James Lancaster, 1b, Odessa, Texas
7. Robert Hooper, of, Sardis, Texas

January—Secondary Phase (20)

1. Doug Ross, lhp, Arizona Western JC
2. David Byerly, of, Odessa (Texas) JC
3. Mike Witt, of, Fresno (Calif.) CC
4. Richard Wilson, rhp, Long Beach (Calif.) CC
5. Richard Cross, inf, Los Angeles CC
6. Mike Rapkin, lhp, Los Angeles Valley JC
7. Derk Hoving, c, Amarillo, Texas
8. Stanley Zawacki, of, Newark, N.J.

June—Regular Phase (7)

1. **Curtis Moore, of, Denison (Texas) HS**
2. **Danny Landis, rhp, Franklin Heights HS, Columbus, Ohio**
3. **Clint Compton, lhp, Robert E. Lee HS, Montgomery, Ala.**
4. **Mike McQueen, lhp, Spring Branch HS, Houston**
5. **Roger Reid, ss, Weber State**
6. **John Burns, c, Eastern Illinois**
7. **Lee Grotelueschen, ss, Southeast HS, Lincoln, Neb.**
8. Cecil Johnson, 3b, Dorsey HS, Los Angeles
9. James Shebesta, lhp, Paschal HS, Fort Worth, Texas
10. Mike Beard, lhp, Little Rock, Ark.
11. **John Fuller, 1b, Lynwood (Calif.) HS**
12. **Johnny Brown, 3b, North Jefferson HS, Warrior, Ala.**
13. Sylvan Rothschild, ss, Coronado HS, El Paso, Texas
14. David Thornton, of, Grant HS, Sacramento, Calif.
15. **Grady Little, c, Garinger HS, Charlotte, N.C.**
16. Richard Perry, lhp, William Chrisman HS, Independence, Mo.
17. **Calvin Kelley, ss/2b, Richmond (Calif.) Union HS**
18. **Charles Townson, ss/2b, Waxahachie (Texas) HS**
19. **Robin Ostebo, lhp, Johnson HS, St. Paul, Minn.**
20. Danny Heck, ss, Leuzinger HS, Hawthorne, Calif.
21. Mose Adolph, of, Manual Arts HS, Los Angeles
22. **Richard Sandate, lhp, West Oso HS, Corpus Christi, Texas**
23. **Ron Taylor, rhp, Bonneville (Utah)**
24. **William McEntire, lhp, Alpine (Texas) HS**
25. John Conover, rhp, Santa Ana (Calif.) HS
26. **Webster Muck, 2b, Bethel (Minn.)**
27. Gary Robson, rhp, John Burroughs HS, Los Angeles
28. Richard Law, lhp, Owensboro, Ky.
29. Frank Saenz, rhp, Los Angeles (Calif.) HS
30. **Harold Burke, rhp/of, Villanova**
31. Rudy Arroyo, lhp, Mountainview (Calif.) HS
32. Kenneth Hess, rhp, Dixie HS, New Lebanon, Ohio
33. Dale Burch, rhp, DeLaSalle HS, New Orleans
34. David Kaster, rhp, South HS, Omaha, Neb.
35. **Rowland Houston, of/inf, Poly HS, Long Beach, Calif.**
36. Glen Gilmore, rhp, Burke HS, Omaha, Neb.
37. Johnny Glover, lhp, Appling HS, Macon, Ga.

June—Secondary Phase (7)

1. Larry Pyle, of, Miami
2. Douglas Ross, lhp, Arizona Western JC
3. **James Sanders, rhp, UNC Wilmington**
4. Ron Cash, ss, Manatee (Fla.) JC
5. **Richard Wilson, rhp, Long Beach (Calif.) CC**
6. Bob Bridges, lhp, Arizona Western JC

BALTIMORE ORIOLES

January—Regular Phase (9)

1. **Tom Walker, rhp, Brevard (Fla.) CC**
2. Edward Northrup, rhp, George Mason
3. Tom Hannibal, lhp, Clark (Wash.) JC
4. Leonard Scott, rhp, Baltimore
5. **John Gage, c/1b, Wheeling**
6. William Campbell, lhp, Warrenton, Va.
7. Larry Lorenz, of/1b, Santa Clara, Calif.
8. Michael Houck, lhp, Hudson Valley (N.Y.) CC

January—Secondary Phase (9)

1. Dave Kingman, rhp/of, Mount Prospect, Ill.
2. Ron Cash, ss, Manatee (Fla.) CC
3. Leon Murray, 1b, Los Angeles CC
4. Joe Arnold, rhp, Miami-Dade North CC
5. George Ferguson, 3b, Maine
6. Joe Crocker, c, Spokane (Wash.) CC
7. William Close, rhp, Holy Cross
8. Carl Bennett, c, San Joaquin Delta (Calif.) JC
9. Michael Ehlers, c, Centerville JC
10. James O'Brien, of/c, San Francisco

June—Regular Phase (10)

1. **Junior Kennedy, ss, Arvin (Calif.) HS**
2. **Michael Herson, rhp, Maryland**
3. **Conrad Herrman, rhp, Sterling HS, Somerdale, N.J.**
4. **Jesse Jefferson, rhp, Carver HS, Midlothian, Va.**
5. **Ron Dunn, 2b, Hoover HS, Fresno, Calif.**
6. **Richard Wurkits, c, Hoover HS, Fresno, Calif.**
7. **Danny Hart, ss, Troup County HS, LaGrange, Ga.**
8. Gerald Tassa, lhp, Washington & Lee HS, Arlington, Va.
9. **Larry Jones, rhp, Oak Park HS, Kansas City, Mo.**
10. Lloyd Lightfoot, ss, North Carolina A&T State
11. **Al Bumbry, of, Virginia State**
12. **Arnold Tielke, rhp, West Columbia (Texas) HS**
13. Bill Fahey, c, Redford (Mich.) Union HS
14. Donald Henderson, lhp, Tucker (Ga.) HS
15. **Robert Roth, lhp, Bowen HS, Chicago**
16. Johnny Spriggs, 1b, Luling (Texas) HS
17. **Walter Hamm, of, South Dakota**
18. **George Manz, rhp, Maryland**
19. Larry Tipton, ss/2b, Robstown (Texas) HS
20. **Leonard Finch, 3b, Napa (Calif.) HS**
21. **Rich Coggins, of, Garey HS, Pomona, Calif.**
22. **Robert Bosley, lhp, Essex (Md.) CC**
23. Larry Schutzius, of, Aurora (Colo.) Hinckley HS
24. Ken Wamble, ss, South Houston (Texas) HS
25. Fred Williams, rhp, Soller Point HS, Baltimore
26. **Wayne Zaskoda, ss, El Campo (Texas) HS**
27. **Harold Warden, of, R.L. Turner HS, Carrolton, Texas**
28. **John Blanchard, c, Colorado State**
29. James Kechura, inf/of, James Monroe HS, Bronx, N.Y.
30. Roger Mayer, c/1b, Englewood (Colo.) HS
31. Bill Bonham, rhp, Los Angeles Valley JC
32. **Ricky Gray, ss, Mumford HS, Detroit**
33. Bill Stein, 2b, Brevard (Fla.) CC
34. John Stephens, of/rhp, Gulf Coast (Fla.) CC
35. **Norman Seidel, rhp, Kenwood HS, Baltimore**
36. **Jerrold Szostak, rhp, Quigley South HS, Chicago**
37. **Pennington Hebron, ss, Hanover, Md.**
38. **Charles Lacy, inf, Odessa (Texas) JC**
39. James Latouralle, ss, East Long Meadow (Mass.) HS
40. Robert Bower, 1b/3b, Ypsilanti (Mich.) HS
41. **Joseph Bartlett, of, New Hampshire**
42. Ronald Bennett, lhp, Wayne County HS, Jesup, Ga.
43. **Eddie Williams, lhp, Oklahoma**
44. Stan Gatto, lhp, Suffolk (N.Y.) CC

45. **Lonnie Teasley, lhp, Lincoln HS, Taylor, S.C.**
46. **William Pierce, rhp, Griffin (Ga.) HS**
47. Paul McGlain, lhp, Lincoln HS, San Francisco
48. Glenn Wallace, rhp, Mississippi State
49. Tom Boland, rhp, South Georgia JC
50. Al Cleveland, rhp, Chipola (Fla.) JC

June—Secondary Phase (4)

1. **Derk Hoving, c, Amarillo (Texas) JC**
2. Charles Jones, lhp, Grambling
3. **Eldon Jones, lhp, Southern Colorado**
4. **William Kelley, rhp, Virginia**
5. **Michael Houck, lhp, Hudson Valley (N.Y.) CC**
6. Steven Rogers, of/lhp, Massachusetts
7. William Hunt, ss, Louisiana State

BOSTON RED SOX

January—Regular Phase (19)

1. **Walter Ransom, ss, South Gate, Calif.**
2. Thomas Combs, of, American River (Calif.) JC
3. **Ronald Falls, rhp, Grossmont (Calif.) JC**
4. **Mickey Whitson, rhp, Gulf Coast (Fla.) CC**

January—Secondary Phase (15)

1. **Douglas Sandstedt, lhp, Omaha, Neb.**
2. Wendell Franke, inf, Mesa (Ariz.) CC
3. John Walker, c, Sacramento (Calif.) CC
4. **Thomas Skendarian, of, Brown**
5. Gerald Burton, of, St. Louis CC-Meramec
6. Larry Gonsalves, rhp, Fresno State
7. David Brown, of, Texas

June—Regular Phase (20)

1. **Tom Maggard, of/c, John Glenn HS, Norwalk, Calif.**
2. **Curtis Suchan, inf/of, Jesuit HS, Tampa**
3. **Lynn McGlothen, rhp, Grambling HS, Simsboro, La.**
4. **Allen Collins, c, Glendora (Calif.) HS**
5. Manny Crespo, ss, Miami Senior HS
6. **Cecil Cooper, 1b, Brenham (Texas) HS**
7. **Harold Kurtzman, inf, University HS, Beverly Hills, Calif.**
8. **Roy Handel, c, Columbus (Ga.) HS**
9. **Edward Baird, rhp, Connecticut**
10. Michael O'Banion, c, Dos Palos (Calif.) HS
11. **Ben Oglivie, inf/of, Roosevelt HS, Bronx, N.Y.**
12. **Robert Overmiller, 3b/1b, Red Lion HS, Sexton, Pa.**
13. **Frank Mannerino, of, Oak Lawn (Ill.) Community HS**
14. **Terry Williams, rhp, Davenport (Iowa) West HS**
15. Thomas King, lhp, Acton-Boxboro HS, West Acton, Mass.
16. **William Brown, inf, Fresno State**
17. **Michael Collins, lhp, West Covina (Calif.) HS**
18. **Lonnie Keeter, inf, David Douglas HS, Portland, Ore.**
19. Curtis Jordan, of, Middle Georgia JC
20. **Donald Grate, ss, Harvard**
21. **Frank Addonizo, c, St. John's**
22. **Bill Lee III, lhp, Southern California**
23. **John Moss, inf, Alabama**
24. Doug Miller, c/of, Klamath Union HS, Klamath Falls, Ore.
25. Robert Hoepfinger, of, Timon HS, Buffalo, N.Y.
26. **William Croken, c, Malden (Mass.) HS**
27. **Roger Ward, lhp, Chaminade HS, Fort Lauderdale, Fla.**
28. Felix Skalski, 3b, Kalamazoo Valley (Mich.) JC
29. **Thomas Walsh, rhp, Tilton-Northfield HS, Tilton, N.H.**
30. **Blaine Young, lhp, Bishop Stang HS, Fairhaven, Mass.**
31. **Michael Neal, lhp, Shasta (Calif.) JC**
32. **Michael Harvison, inf, Polytechnical HS, Fort Worth, Texas**
33. **Richard Perry, c/1b, St. Johnsville (N.Y.) HS**
34. **George Reebe, of, Natick (Mass.) HS**
35. **Jeff Guenther, rhp, Katella HS, Anaheim**
36. Michael Comuso, rhp, Lawrence (Mass.) Central HS

June—Secondary Phase (10)

1. **John Curtis, lhp, Clemson**
2. Ronald Soucie, lhp, Husson
3. **Richard Wicks, lhp, McNeese State**
4. **Allen Truskowski, lhp, St. Clair County (Mich.) CC**
5. Nicholas Furlong, rhp, Notre Dame

CALIFORNIA ANGELS

January—Regular Phase (11)

1. Rob Johnson, rhp, Los Angeles Pierce JC
2. **James Cesario, 3b, Torrance, Calif.**
3. James Stern, lhp, South Georgia JC
4. David Landress, 2b, Los Angeles Pierce JC
5. James Eichmeier, lhp, Arizona Western JC
6. Richard Leavitt, of, Cerritos (Calif.) JC
7. Thomas Tanner, of, Cerritos (Calif.) JC
8. Rusty Swisher, rhp, Los Angeles Pierce JC

January—Secondary Phase (13)

1. **Dayle Campbell, 1b, Pepperdine**
2. **Patrick Knutzen, lhp, El Camino (Calif.) JC**
3. Paul Reuschel, rhp, Western Illinois
4. **David Thompson, of, Santa Barbara (Calif.) CC**
5. Ronald Pritchett, rhp, Mount San Antonio (Calif.) JC
6. William Susa, rhp, Los Angeles Pierce JC
7. Lee Chilton, of, San Joaquin (Calif.) Delta JC
8. Jim Pope, rhp, Columbia Basin (Wash.) CC

June—Regular Phase (12)

1. **Lloyd Allen, rhp, Selma (Calif.) HS**
2. Gordon Carter, of, Sunny Hills HS, Fullerton, Calif.
3. John Harbin, ss, Berea HS, Greenville, S.C.
4. **Richard Hansen, rhp, McLane HS, Fresno, Calif.**
5. Dennis Wallin, c, Rio-Americano HS, Sacramento, Calif.
6. **Gregory Dehn, c, Anoka (Minn.) HS**
7. **Tom Bradley, rhp, Maryland**
8. **Randy Niles, ss, Santa Monica (Calif.) JC**
9. **Gilbert McCord, ss, South Carolina**
10. **Harvey Shank, rhp, Stanford**
11. **Jose Quinones, of, Staten Island (N.Y.)**
12. **Brian Nelson, lhp, Cal State Los Angeles**
13. Rick Auerbach, ss, Taft HS, Woodland Hills, Calif.
14. **Damion Howell, ss, Edison HS, Fresno, Calif.**
15. Robert Hubbard, rhp, Spenceport (N.Y.) HS
16. **James Malloney, rhp, Sacred Heart Academy, Cumberland, R.I.**
17. William Jenkins, 2b, Orange Coast (Calif.) JC
18. **Frank Russo, lhp, Everett (Mass.) HS**
19. **Gerald Carr, rhp, Bolsa Grande HS, Garden Grove, Calif.**
20. **Constantine Cirasuolo, of, Whitesboro (N.Y.) HS**
21. Gary Addio, 1b/of, Pius X HS, Downey, Calif.
22. Gene Tate, ss, Turlock (Calif.) HS
23. Richard Mahlmann, lhp, Hanford (Calif.) HS
24. Van Winters, rhp, McLane HS, Fresno, Calif.
25. **Stephen Romero, rhp, Simi (Calif.) HS**
26. **Daniel Loomer, ss, Golden State (Calif.) JC**
27. Rodney Sooter, rhp, Menard HS, Alexandria, Va.
28. **John Schroeder, rhp, UC Santa Barbara**
29. Lionel Schoebridge, 1b/c, Lyndhurst (N.J.) HS
30. Bobby Wheeler, 1b, Sunny Hills HS, Fullerton, Calif.
31. **Jerry Feldman, 1b, Cal State Los Angeles**
32. **Craig Hansen, 1b, Denver**
33. **Ronald St. Clair, rhp, Bakersfield (Calif.) JC**
34. Glenn Spicer, rhp, Grant HS, North Hollywood, Calif.
35. Thomas Utman, ss, Menlo (Calif.) JC
36. **Matthew Moschetti, 3b, Cal State Fullerton**
37. Dennis Gallagher, ss, East Nicholas (Calif.) HS
38. **Greg Henard, ss/3b, Tulare (Calif.) HS**
39. Verdell Adams, of, Jefferson HS, Portland, Ore.

June—Secondary Phase (14)

1. **Larry Hanson, ss, Oregon**
2. **Michael Schomaker, c, Stanford**
3. **Martin Pavlik, lhp, Wilson (Ill.) JC**
4. **James Suskiewich, lhp, Indiana**
5. Michael Babler, rhp, Chabot (Calif.) JC
6. **Michael Lersch, lhp, Mesa (Ariz.) CC**
7. Charles Kurkjian, 3b, Fresno (Calif.) CC
8. Craig Schell, rhp, UC Santa Barbara

CHICAGO CUBS

January—Regular Phase (16)

1. Dave Baldwin, lhp, Manatee (Fla.) JC (Selection voided)
2. Darryl Thomas, lhp, Long Beach (Calif.) CC
3. Steve Simonian, rhp, Fresno (Calif.) CC
4. Jake Molina, ss, San Diego CC
5. **Curtis Barto, ss, Montgomery, Pa.**
6. Robert Petretta, of, San Diego CC
7. N.D. Bingham, rhp, Texas Christian (Selection voided)
8. Patrick Roark, of, San Diego Mesa JC
9. Thomas Palmer, rhp, Delaware (Selection voided)

January—Secondary Phase (10)

1. **Steven Salata, c, Oneonta, N.Y.**
2. Dennis Parks, of, Southern California
3. **Michael Lisetski, ss, Rider**
4. William Grogan, rhp, Yakima (Wash.) Valley JC
5. **Tim Feldhaus, ss, Mount San Antonio (Calif.) JC**
6. Thomas Kaehler, of, Los Angeles Valley JC
7. **Dennis Gideon, lhp, Chaffey (Calif.) JC**

June—Regular Phase (15)

1. **Ralph Rickey, of, Oklahoma**
2. **Matt Alexander, 3b, Grambling**
3. Jeff Pederson, of, Fermin Lausen HS, San Pedro, Calif.
4. **Michael Roe, rhp, East Providence HS, Riverside, R.I.**
5. Eldridge Blake, of, St. Thomas, Virgin Islands (Selection voided)
6. **Randolph Richardson, c, Pfeiffer (N.C.)**
7. Thomas McDermott, ss, Northwest HS, St. Louis
8. **Joseph Biercevicz, rhp, Shelton HS, Huntington, Conn.**
9. **Ronald Jones, lhp, Covina HS, West Covina, Calif.**
10. Don Henrichs, rhp, Enumclaw (Wash.) HS
11. Nicholas Eichelberger, ss, Trinity Prep, Allentown, Pa.
12. Scott Taylor, rhp, Mansfield (Pa.)
13. **Richard Barnes, lhp, Lane Tech HS, Chicago**
14. Kim West, rhp, St. Albans (W.Va.) HS
15. Wayne Anderson, 1b, Lakes HS, Tacoma, Wash.
16. **Oscar Gamble, of, Montgomery, Ala.**
17. Robert Johnston, lhp, Fike HS, Wilson, N.C.
18. Tim Gurp, of, Phoenix JC
19. **Phil Brown, rhp, Manteca (Calif.) HS**
20. **Robert Micheletti, c, Minnesota**
21. **Paul Zahn, rhp, Parsons**
22. **Richard Nye, of, Ribualt HS, Jacksonville, Fla.**
23. James Mottine, rhp, Red Bank (N.J.) HS
24. **Merle Taylor, lhp, West Virginia**
25. **James Bryan, of, Guilford (N.C.)**
26. Herbert Sikes, 3b, Leon HS, Tallahassee, Fla.
27. **Jimmy Walters, ss, Georgia Southern**
28. **Terry Childers, c, Georgia Southern**
29. **Paul Starman, rhp, Iowa**
30. Bill Dorothy, 2b, Bacone (Okla.) JC
31. Ken Wastradowski, lhp, Centralia (Wash.) HS
32. Mike Hetman, c, Hudson Valley (N.Y.) CC

June—Secondary Phase (1)

1. **Dave Lemonds, lhp, North Carolina**
2. **Robert Breitzman, 2b, Illinois State**
3. **Chris Ward, of, Chabot (Calif.) JC**
4. **Paul Reuschel, rhp, Western Illinois**
5. **Allen Simas, of, Sacramento (Calif.) CC**
6. Gary Houston, lhp, San Jose (Calif.) CC
7. **Tom Binkowski, 1b, Michigan State**

CHICAGO WHITE SOX

January—Regular Phase (13)

1. Mickey Rivers, of, Miami-Dade North CC
2. Martin Pavlik, lhp, Wilson (Ill.) JC

January—Secondary Phase (19)

1. Chris Ward, of, Chabot (Calif.) JC
2. Bill Dobbs, lhp, Oklahoma State
3. Richard Hanselman, lhp, St. Johns River (Fla.) CC
4. **Joseph Bowen, 3b/1b, Norfolk, Va.**
5. Jerre Algeo, 2b, Poteau (Mo.) JC
6. Don Lamb, rhp, Thornton (Ill.) CC

June—Regular Phase (14)

1. **Rich McKinney, ss/3b, Ohio**
2. **Hugh Yancy, ss, Sarasota (Fla.) HS**
3. **Lamar Johnson Sr., c, Wenonah HS, Birmingham, Ala.**
4. **Dennis Deck, lhp, Magnolia HS, Anaheim**
5. **Thomas Wittum, 3b, Round Lake (Ill.) HS**
6. **Robert Giesler, lhp, LaPorte (Ind.) HS**
7. Collis James, c, Mobile County Training School, Prichard, Ala.
8. **Leonard Massaro, rhp, Richmond (Calif.) HS**
9. William Menk, lhp, Lincoln HS, Philadelphia
10. **Lawrence Jackson, of/1b, Wenonah HS, Birmingham, Ala.**
11. James Kiley, ss, Reading (Mass.) HS
12. **James Redmon, ss, Western Michigan**
13. Garrett Berry, c, Sunny Hills HS, Fullerton, Calif.
14. **Richie Moloney, rhp, Brookline (Mass.) HS**
15. **Richard Propson, lhp, Stockbridge (Wis.) HS**
16. **Stan Perzanowski, rhp, Morton HS, Hammond, Ind.**
17. Thomas Heinrich, of, Hayward (Wis.) HS
18. **William Hansen, 1b, Long Island**
19. Bobby Lail, lhp, Crest HS, Shelby, N.C.
20. **Kenny Brooks, rhp, Wilkes Central HS, Wilkesboro, N.C.**
21. **Rod Pommes, of/3b, Santa Clara**
22. Robert Kleinholz, 1b/lhp, Loara HS, Anaheim
23. **John Fiene, c, Westside HS, Omaha, Neb.**
24. **Larry Bashford, 3b, Anaheim HS**
25. **Dana Ryan, 2b, Arkansas State**
26. **Stephen Spanich, rhp, Quincy**
27. Mark Jones, 1b, Crowder (Mo.) JC
28. Bruce Finkbeiner, inf/of, Colorado State
29. Dale Reed, lhp, Crowder (Mo.) JC
30. **Charles Auchmutey, rhp, Avondale HS, Avondale Estates, Ga.**
31. **Nathander Pettaway, 1b, St. Elmore HS, Theodore, Ala.**

June—Secondary Phase (2)

1. **Bart Johnson, rhp, Torrance, Calif.**
2. **Ken Hottman, of, Sacramento (Calif.) CC**
3. **Dan Neumeier, rhp, Wisconsin-Oshkosh**
4. Dave Renkiewicz, rhp, Michigan
5. Michael Nichols, 1b/lhp, Biola
6. **Larry Linville, of, Arizona State**
7. Franklin Riggins, of, Kansas

CINCINNATI REDS

January—Regular Phase (14)

1. Donald Shrum, rhp, Houston
2. Freddie Howard, 1b/of, Paris (Texas) JC
3. **William Morton, c, Pittsburgh**
4. **Charles Beck, rhp, Summit, Mo.**
5. David Ward, rhp, Eastern Oklahoma State JC
6. **Jerry Turk, rhp, Fort Valley State**
7. **Charles Higgins, rhp, Jefferson State (Ala.) JC**
8. William Davis, c, Midway, Pa.

January—Secondary Phase (16)

1. **Charles West, of, Texas-El Paso**
2. Chris Chambliss, 1b, Mira Costa (Calif.) JC
3. Michael Wertz, ss, Wharton County (Texas) JC
4. **Michael James, 2b, Dallas Baptist**
5. **Michael Willis, lhp, Colorado**
6. Edward Stack, rhp, Cameron
7. Donald Jumper, rhp, Jasper, Texas
8. **Glenn Bisbing, c, Rider**

June—Regular Phase (13)

1. **Timothy Grant, rhp, Riverview HS, Boykins, Va.**
2. **Milt Wilcox, rhp, Crooked Oak HS, Oklahoma City, Okla.**
3. Richard Lenard, rhp, LaPorte (Ind.) HS
4. **Edward May, lhp, McLain HS, North Tulsa, Okla.**
5. **Edward Upstone, rhp, Walter Lutheran HS, Lyons, Ill.**
6. **Albert Faix, lhp, Pennsylvania Ridge HS, Sellersville, Pa.**
7. **Phillip Freeman, of/1b, Wasson HS, Colorado Springs, Colo.**
8. **William Hoelzer, of, Clinton (Mich.) HS**

9. **Carl Williamson, rhp, El Rancho HS, Pico Rivera, Calif.**
10. **Edward Street, lhp, Horace Scott HS, Modena, Pa.**
11. **Henry Kopps, of, Brazosport HS, Lake Jackson, Texas**
12. **Thomas Dittmat, of/1b, Belleville (Texas) HS**
13. **Vincent Coleman, 1b/3b, St.Joseph HS, Jackson, Miss.**
14. **Robert Flint, rhp, Provine HS, Jackson, Miss.**
15. **Doug Dreier, rhp, Red Bluff (Calif.) HS**
16. **Robert Welsh, ss, Cathedral HS, Trenton, N.J.**
17. Don Sweetland, c, William S. Hart HS, Saugus, Calif.
18. **Jeffrey Brelsford, c, Mainland HS, Daytona Beach, Fla.**
19. **Theodore Bryand, 2b, South French HS, Asheville, N.C.**
20. James Kleckley, rhp, Brookland-Cayce HS, Lexington, S.C.
21. **Benjamin Williams, c/of, Grambling**
22. **Gregory Siereveld, inf, Taft HS, Hamilton, Ohio**
23. **Keith West, of, Gustine (Calif.) HS**
24. Jonathan Tate, rhp, Tompkins HS, Savannah, Ga.
25. Mike Willis, lhp, Hillsboro HS, Nashville, Tenn.
26. Russell Davis, lhp, Capitol Hill HS, Oklahoma City, Okla.
27. Craig White, of, Fairfax (Va.) HS
28. John Mindell, rhp, Okarchee (Okla.) HS
29. James Kelley, 2b, Arlington (Texas) HS
30. Kenneth Burke, rhp, William Bryant HS, Moultrie, Ga.
31. Gregory Faux, rhp, Provo (Utah) HS
32. **Larry Feltner, rhp, High Point HS, College Park, Md.**
33. Ronald Fisher, rhp, Olympus HS, Salt Lake City
34. Gerald Daugherty, c, Cy-Fair HS, Houston
35. Michael O'Connor, lhp, Anderson HS, Cincinnati
36. Michael Carter, ss/3b, John Tyler HS, Tyler, Texas
37. Glen Olsen, rhp, Wilson HS, Sinking Springs, Pa.
38. Bobby Thompson, rhp, Edmond (Okla.) HS
39. **Gregg Slape, of, Sul Ross State**
40. Stephen Boron, rhp, George Washington HS, Philadelphia
41. Kent Estep, rhp, Grandfield (Okla.) HS
42. **Bobby Lemley, inf/2b, Marshall**
43. James Mertens, 1b, Fairmont State (W.Va.)
44. Patrick Korsnick, of, Wheeling (W.Va.) Central HS

June—Secondary Phase (5)

1. **Mel Behney, lhp, Michigan State**
2. Paul Pryor, rhp, Florida Southern (Selection voided)
3. Darrel Thomas, lhp, Long Beach (Calif.) CC
4. Donald Schroeder, rhp, Grays Harbor (Wash.) JC
5. Freddie Howard, 1b/lhp, Paris (Texas) JC
6. David Reeves, rhp, Georgia
7. Dolan Church, rhp, East Tennessee State (Selection voided)

CLEVELAND INDIANS

January—Regular Phase (5)

1. Lambert Ford, of, Richland, N.J.
2. Rick Dierker, rhp, Woodland Hills, Calif.
3. **Bruce Killion, rhp, North Charleston, S.C.**
4. Donald Barnum, rhp, Chabot (Calif.) JC
5. **Allen Boyd, c, Baltimore**
6. Clarence Smith, rhp, St. Francis (N.Y.)
7. Jeff Fuller, 2b, Canoga Park, Calif.
8. **Thomas Penders, of/inf, Connecticut**

January—Secondary Phase (5)

1. Ray Bare, rhp, Miami-Dade North CC
2. **Harold Harris, 3b/ss, Gulf Coast (Fla.) CC**
3. **Rick Sawyer, rhp, Bakersfield (Calif.) JC**
4. Leonard Filbeck, rhp, Santa Ana (Calif.) JC
5. **Kenneth Danson, of, Gulf Coast (Fla.) CC**
6. **Edwin Staples, c, Texas A&M**
7. **Robert Cramer, rhp, Mitchell (Conn.) JC**
8. Taylor Toomey, lhp, Colorado
9. William Moynier, rhp, Bakersfield (Calif.) JC
10. Roy Waye, 1b, Kingsport, Tenn.
11. Roger Jackson, rhp, Kansas
12. Larry Phillippe, rhp, Edison (Fla.) CC

June—Regular Phase (6)

1. **Robert Weaver, ss/of, Paxon HS, Jacksonville, Fla.**
2. **John Parks, 3b, Lakewood (Calif.) HS**
3. **Bob Kaiser, lhp, Weber HS, Ogden, Utah**
4. **Dan Covert, 1b, Austin (Texas) HS**
5. **Larry Shaw, of/1b, Matawan (N.J.) HS**
6. **John Howell, lhp, Lee HS, Midland, Texas**
7. **Richard Napolitano, rhp, St. John's**
8. **Ken Stauffer, c, Margretta HS, Castalia, Ohio**
9. **Larry Johnson, c, East Tech HS, Cleveland**
10. Ken Conlin, 2b, East Valley HS, Yakima, Wash.
11. **Vince Colbert, rhp, East Carolina**
12. **Chuck Machemehl, rhp, Texas Christian**
13. **Cecil Bankhorn, ss, Lipscomb**
14. Dana Baltzer, ss, Hoover HS, San Diego
15. **Mike Carruthers, 1b, Pembroke State (N.C.)**
16. Steve Stone, rhp, Kent State
17. **Robert Shaps, of, Shaker Heights (Ohio) HS**
18. **John Lowenstein, ss, UC Riverside**
19. **Jimmy Hobgood, lhp, Pensacola (Fla.) HS**
20. George Gibson, ss, Tate HS, Cantemont, Fla.
21. **Donald Hayward, rhp, Pontiac (Mich.) Northern HS**
22. Robert Shearer, ss, Indian River (Fla.) CC
23. **Gary Lear, c, Columbia, Mo.**
24. Douglas Bozeman, 2b, Fremont HS, Los Angeles
25. Mickey McCarty, lhp, Texas Christian
26. Steve Fahsbender, lhp, North Bakersfield (Calif.) HS
27. Frank Hagen, of, Napa (Calif.) HS
28. **Richard Schwartz, lhp, St. John's**
29. Doug Bird, rhp, Pomona (Calif.) HS
30. **Walter Hallberg, 3b, Pascagoula (Miss.) HS**
31. Robert Eriksen, rhp, Bullard HS, Fresno, Calif.
32. **Jerry Stitt, of, Arizona**
33. Dave Augustine, c, Miami-Dade South CC
34. **Michael Selland, 3b, DeAnza HS, El Sobrante, Calif.**
35. **Robert Love, rhp, Baldwin-Wallace**
36. Tim Mackin, rhp, Hudson Bay HS, Vancouver, Wash.
37. James Gailey, of, Lake Wales (Fla.) HS
38. **James Bogard, c, Mohawk HS, Sycamore, Ohio**
39. Franco Garcia, inf/of, Westfield (Mass.) HS
40. Alan White, rhp/ss, Buckeye Central HS, New Washington, Ohio
41. William Becker, of, Bowling Green State
42. Harold Smith, ss, Elwood City (Pa.) HS
43. Marvin Knight, rhp, Michigan State
44. Dan Miller, rhp, Sandusky (Ohio) HS
45. Bruce Cannon, 3b, Oberlin (Ohio) HS
46. Walter Sharrock, rhp, Jupiter (Fla.) HS
47. Gary Harover, of/1b, Pendleton (Ore.) HS
48. Wayne Milan, rhp, Stranahan HS, Fort Lauderdale, Fla.

June—Secondary Phase (6)

1. **Rick Austin, lhp, Washington State**
2. David Brown, of, Texas
3. Dale Dunham, rhp, Central Michigan
4. John Morlan, of, Ohio
5. **Leonard Filbeck, rhp, Santa Ana (Calif.) JC**
6. Ray Bare, rhp, Miami-Dade North CC
7. Ronald Davini, c, Arizona State
8. William Moynier, rhp, Bakersfield (Calif.) HS
9. **Larry Price, of, JC of the Desert (Calif.)**

DETROIT TIGERS

January—Regular Phase (17)

1. James Carter, 3b, Golden West (Calif.) JC
2. Thomas Jackson, ss, Citrus (Calif.) JC (Selection voided)
3. Richard Garner, c, Santa Rosa (Calif.) JC
4. James Poole, c, Detroit
5. Nicholas Parilla, rhp, Staunton (Va.) Military Academy
6. **George Moore, of, Detroit**
7. **Bill Slayback, rhp, Glendale (Calif.) JC**
8. **Arthur Clifford, rhp, Quincy, Mass.**
9. **Rod Beckman, ss, Muskegon (Mich.) CC**

January—Secondary Phase (3)

1. **Ken Szotkiewicz, ss, Georgia Southern**
2. **Chuck Scrivener, ss, CC of Baltimore**
3. **Thomas Grayson, 2b, Guilford (N.C.)**
4. Bob O'Brien, lhp, Arizona

5. Steve Smith, 3b, Long Beach (Calif.) CC
6. **Jerry Killian, lhp, Flint (Mich.) JC**
7. Harry Saferight, c, Manatee (Fla.) JC
8. Terry Wilshusen, rhp, Torrance, Calif.
9. **Vache Bahadurian, 1b, New York CC**
10. William Carroll, of, Alhambra, Calif.

June—Regular Phase (18)

1. **Robert Robinson, of, Thomas Dale HS, Chester, Va.**
2. **Bob Molinaro, of, Essex Catholic HS, Newark, N.J.**
3. **Raymond Blosse, rhp, High Point (N.C.)**
4. **Thomas Castellar, rhp, Kennedy HS, Taylor, Mich.**
5. Thomas Miller, of, Reading (Pa.) HS
6. **Frank Fisher, rhp, Wayne (Mich.) HS**
7. **Daryl Busen, rhp, Fordson HS, Dearborn, Mich.**
8. Ross Grimsley II, lhp, Frayser HS, Memphis, Tenn.
9. John Hyde, lhp, Loyola Academy, Chicago
10. **Marvin Lane, of, Pershing HS, Detroit**
11. **Mark Grove, of, Anchor Bay HS, New Baltimore, Mich.**
12. Terry Rutledge, 3b/of, McLain HS, Tulsa, Okla.
13. **Howard Johnson, ss, Milton**
14. **Robert Cole, 1b, West Portsmouth (Ohio) HS**
15. Rex Campbell, c, Beaver Local HS, East Liverpool, Ohio
16. **Spencer Horn, ss, Fort Cobb (Okla.) HS**
17. **Robert LaFrance, c, Natick (Mass.) HS**
18. **Bob Strampe, rhp, Janesville (Wis.) HS**
19. Matthew Rockwood, of, Grand Rapids (Mich.) JC
20. Barry Perteler, rhp, Swartz Creek HS, Gaines, Mich.
21. **Anthony Amendola, rhp, Aviation Tech HS, New York**
22. Michael Crim, rhp, Hickman HS, Columbia, Mo.
23. **Donald Leshnock, lhp, Youngstown State**
24. **Bill Puryear, rhp, Highland Park (Mich.) HS**
25. **Edward Laborio, rhp, Cranston (R.I.) HS**
26. **John Bevil, lhp, Baylor**
27. **Donald Murphy, c, St. Mary's HS, Sacramento, Calif.**
28. John Zbercot, c, South Lake HS, St. Clair Shores, Mich.
29. **Lary Lohse, lhp, Seaman (Ohio) HS**
30. Terry Greene, inf, Republic (Mo.) HS
31. **Richard Foulk, lhp, South Torrance (Calif.) HS**
32. **Wayne Hamilton, inf, Airport HS, New Boston, Mich.**
33. **Stephen Cushmore, lhp, Princeton**
34. Keith Kasparovitch, lhp, Punahou HS, Honolulu
35. John Cabral, lhp, Kaimuki HS, Honolulu
36. Dennis Primeau, inf, Northville HS, Novi, Mich.
37. **Mark Pratt, rhp, Monroe (Mich.) HS**
38. Michael Longstreth, ss, Harding HS, Oklahoma City, Okla.
39. **Thomas Breving, of, Xavier**
40. **Arthur Grassing, rhp, Bourne HS, Flushing, N.Y.**
41. Alfred LiVecchi, rhp, Lane HS, Queens Village, N.Y.
42. Shawn Howitt, 1b, Central HS, Battle Creek, Mich.
43. Robert Hileman, rhp, Staunton (Va.) Military Academy
44. **Joseph Pellechi, inf, Fordham**
45. **Joseph Martin, rhp, Shippensburg (Pa.) HS**

June—Secondary Phase (20)

1. **Elliott Maddox, inf/of, Michigan**
2. John Hurley, rhp, Michigan
3. Ronald Wayne, lhp, Laney (Calif.) JC
4. **Steve Smith, 3b, Long Beach (Calif.) CC**
5. Barry Sheldon, rhp, Genesee (N.Y.) CC

HOUSTON ASTROS

January—Regular Phase (4)

1. **Glenn Adams, of, Springfield**
2. Ken Stabler, lhp, Alabama

January—Secondary Phase (12)

1. **Michael McFarland, rhp, Missouri**
2. Sandy Vance, rhp, Stanford
3. Robert Williams, of, Yakima Valley (Wash.) JC
4. Ronald Shepard, 3b/of, Altus, Okla.

June—Regular Phase (3)

1. **Martin Cott, c, Hutchinson Technical HS, Buffalo, N.Y.**
2. **Rich Chiles, of, Winters (Calif.) HS**
3. **Bill Greif, rhp, Reagan HS, Austin, Texas**
4. **Larry Mansfield, 1b, Tennessee**
5. **Larry Yount, rhp, Taft HS, Woodland Hills, Calif.**
6. **John Grant, lhp, Westchester HS, Los Angeles**
7. Greg Pavlick, rhp/3b, Thomas A. Edison HS, Alexandria, Va.
8. **Raylan Hoellwarth, c, Lodi (Calif.) HS**
9. **Andrew Williams, inf, Jesuit HS, New Orleans**
10. **Carlos Alfonso, inf, Naples (Fla.) HS**
11. **Kenneth Barnes, rhp, Skyline HS, Idaho Falls, Idaho**
12. Henry Yeargan, ss, Wayne County HS, Jesup, Ga.
13. **Lester Roos, ss, Temple**
14. Wendall Clowers, lhp, City HS, Chattanooga, Tenn.
15. **Clinton Burr, rhp, Cocoa HS, Rockledge, Fla.**
16. Curtis Boans, of, Dunedin HS, Clearwater, Fla.
17. David Snow, 3b, Bellflower (Calif.) HS
18. **Ken Forsch, rhp, Oregon State**
19. **Rodney Clabo, of, Temple**
20. **James Baasse, ss, Hammond-Morton HS, Hammond, Ind.**
21. **Edward Ontiveros, rhp, Bakersfield (Calif.) HS**
22. Don Hager, c, Sherman HS, Seth, W.Va.
23. John Euller, rhp, Milford Mill HS, Baltimore
24. Darrell Jones, rhp, Comanche (Okla.) HS
25. **John Canty, lhp, Massachusetts**
26. **Steven Miller, lhp, Dowling HS, Des Moines, Iowa**
27. **Harmon Bove, c, Burlington (Vt.) HS**
28. **John Fox, c/of, Lansdowne HS, Baltimore**
29. **David Doyle, ss, Lynwood (Calif.) HS**
30. Clifford Powers, inf, South Broward HS, Dania, Fla.
31. Steven Griffith, rhp, Pacifica HS, Garden Grove, Calif.
32. Phil Corddry, lhp, Maryland
33. **Alan Peters, rhp, Verbum Dei HS, Los Angeles**
34. Ronald Garlin, of, McArthur HS, Hollywood, Fla.
35. Gary Klass, ss, Reitz Memorial HS, Evansville, Ind.
36. James Fallers, lhp/of, Mount Pleasant HS, Wilmington, Del.

June—Secondary Phase (15)

1. **Buddy Harris, rhp, Miami**
2. **David Grangaard, 3b, Arizona State**
3. **Joseph Arnold, rhp, Arizona State**
4. **Richard Hicks, rhp, Louisiana State**
5. **Lambert Ford, of, Vineland HS, Richland, N.J.**

KANSAS CITY ROYALS

January—Regular Phase

Did not participate (expansion franchise)

January—Secondary Phase

Did not participate (expansion franchise)

June—Regular Phase (24)

1. No selection
2. No selection
3. No selection
4. **Kenneth O'Donnell, ss, Neptune (N.J.) HS**
5. **John Nelson, of, Duarte (Calif.) HS**
6. Mark Tanner, 1b/rhp, Neshannock HS, New Castle, Pa.
7. **Lance Clemons, lhp/of, West Chester (Pa.)**
8. Clark Ullom, lhp, Shawnee Mission (Kan.) South HS
9. **Monty Montgomery, rhp, Pfeiffer (N.C.)**
10. **Robert Lawson, rhp, Cox HS, Virginia Beach, Va.**
11. Robert Nelson, rhp, Roosevelt HS, Seattle
12. **Cornelius Drew, of, Dendron (Va.) HS**
13. **James Hannah, c, Washington State**
14. **Thomas Crichton, 2b, Santa Cruz (Calif.) HS**
15. **Michael Ginn, c, Bakersfield (Calif.) HS**
16. Dane Iorg, ss, Arcata (Calif.) HS
17. **Verbon Walker, rhp, Colorado School of Mines**
18. Mark Fuller, lhp, Chatham (La.) HS
19. Vincent Shawver, rhp, Shawnee Mission (Kan.) North HS
20. Joe Pupo, rhp, Gonzaga HS, Spokane, Wash.
21. Ron Botica, rhp, Shreveport, La.
22. Mike Proffit, lhp, Ensley HS, Birmingham, Ala.
23. **Andrew Chandler, rhp, Prince Edward Academy, Farmville, Va.**
24. **Greg With, 3b, New Mexico**
25. **Paul Splittorff Jr., lhp, Morningside (Iowa)**
26. Patrick Smith, ss, Bellarmine HS, Tacoma, Wash.

27. Jerry Merchant, ss, San Bernardino (Calif.) HS
28. **Bruce Pomeroy, c, James Madison HS, Vienna, Va.**
29. **Richard Long, rhp, Kansas State**
30. Thomas Cason, of, South Georgia JC
31. Gary Rainbow, rhp, North Syracuse (N.Y.) HS
32. **Thomas Moore, rhp, Rider**
33. **Roland Panepinto, ss/2b, Fort Union (Va.) Military HS**
34. James Walker, rhp, San Bernardino (Calif.) HS
35. James Steele, 1b/of, Downey (Calif.) HS
36. James Masters, rhp, Jesuit HS, Carmichael, Calif.
37. Steve Noriega, rhp/of, Jesuit HS, Tampa
38. Stephen Metro, inf/of, Arvada West HS, Golden, Colo.
39. John Medlin, of, William & Mary
40. **Donald Hacker, ss, West Chester (Pa.)**
41. Steve Patchin, c, Joplin (Mo.) HS
42. **Norman Taylor, rhp, Green Central HS, Snow Hill, N.C.**
43. Kurt Lohrke, ss, Jesuit HS, Carmichael, Calif.
44. David Edson, ss, Terra Linda HS, San Rafael, Calif.
45. **Walter Tobler, of, Wilson HS, Portsmouth, Va.**
46. **Greg Chlan, rhp, Rider**
47. **John Marshall, ss, Arkansas**
48. **Terry Schofield, c, San Diego State**
49. Michael McDonald, c/1b, Vermont Academy HS, Rutland, Vt.
50. **Allen Flanagan, 3b, Loudon Valley HS, Leesburg, Va.**
51. James Reid, lhp, T.C. Williams HS, Alexandria, Va.
52. Pete Gigonovich, of, Butler
53. **Larry Largent, rhp, Kansas State**

June—Secondary Phase (22)

1. No selection
2. No selection
3. No selection
4. **Rex Hein, rhp, Missouri**
5. Gary Hohman, c, Bordentown (N.J.) Military Academy
6. Jack Gehrke, ss/2b, Utah
7. Thomas Lundgren, lhp, Missouri
8. William Maxwell, rhp, Oklahoma State
9. John Walker, c, Sacramento (Calif.) CC

LOS ANGELES DODGERS

January—Regular Phase (6)

1. **Larry Hall, 1b/of, Broward (Fla.) CC**
2. Bonnie Smith, c/3b, Los Angeles
3. Craig Brown, 1b, Chipola (Fla.) JC
4. **Ted Rohde, of, Fresno (Calif.) CC**
5. Ronnie Hilton, 2b, Gulf Coast (Fla.) CC
6. Tommy Graham, of, Harbor City, Calif.
7. Lynn Morrison, of, Long Beach (Calif.) CC
8. **Gordon Crook, of, Arizona State**
9. **Vernon Price, lhp, Chaffey (Calif.) JC**
10. **Donald Pierce, 1b, San Francisco**

January—Secondary Phase (6)

1. **Marvin Galliher, inf, San Diego Mesa JC**
2. **Davey Lopes, of, Washburn (Kan.)**
3. Steve Moore, of, Santa Barbara (Calif.) CC
4. **Randy Smith, of, Lincoln Land (Ill.) JC**
5. **Geoff Zahn, lhp, Michigan**
6. David Grangaard, 3b, Arizona State
7. **Gregory Wellman, lhp, Palm Beach (Fla.) JC**
8. James Loll, inf, Los Angeles Pierce JC
9. Thomas Jackson, ss, Citrus (Calif.) JC
10. Ed Crosby, 2b, Long Beach (Calif.) CC
11. John Marino, c, Los Angeles Valley JC
12. Gregory Smith, rhp, Rio Hondo (Calif.) JC
13. William Templeton, rhp, Elmira, N.Y.

June—Regular Phase (5)

1. **Bobby Valentine, of, Rippowam HS, Stamford, Conn.**
2. **Bill Buckner, 1b, Napa HS, Vallejo, Calif.**
3. **Paul Johnson, of, South Carolina State**
4. Mike Pazik, lhp, Lynn (Mass.) English HS
5. **Tom Paciorek, of/1b, Houston**
6. Robert Auger, 1b, Putnam (Conn.) HS
7. Joe Barkauskas, c, Piscataway (N.J.) HS
8. **Joe Ferguson, of, Pacific (Ore.)**
9. **Doyle Alexander, rhp, Woodlawn HS, Birmingham, Ala.**
10. Richard Anderson, rhp, Trumbull (Conn.) HS
11. **Robert Baxter, c, Lower Dauphin HS, Hummelstown, Pa.**
12. Charles Land, of, Midwest City (Okla.) HS
13. Tommy Pratt, lhp, Righetti HS, Santa Maria, Calif.
14. **Frederick Willard, 3b/1b, San Francisco, Calif.**
15. Jeff Port, 3b, Birmingham HS, Encino, Calif.
16. Arthur Brown, rhp, New York
17. **Bob Gallagher, of, Stanford**
18. **Fred Nelson, 2b, Arizona State**
19. Jeff Stout, ss, LaPuente (Calif.) HS
20. **Ted Gilje, lhp, College Park HS, Pleasant Hill, Calif.**
21. **James Rich, of, Centennial HS, Compton, Calif.**
22. **Brooks Anderson, of/1b, Cardinal McCloskey HS, Albany, N.Y.**
23. **Danny Copeland, of/c, West Newton (Pa.) HS**
24. Milton Guggia, 2b, Santa Maria (Calif.) HS
25. **Thomas Sowinski, rhp, St. John's**
26. Robert Baxter, of, Southampton (N.Y.) HS
27. Albert Strane, ss, Santa Clara
28. Alvin Strane, 2b, Santa Clara
29. Bob Wissler, of/2b, Cal Poly Pomona
30. Roy Nelson, lhp, Vigor HS, Mobile, Ala. (Selection voided)
31. Richard Breese, rhp, Port Chester (N.Y.) HS
32. Dennis Major, 1b, Laney (Calif.) JC
33. **Michael St. John, rhp, West Valley (Calif.) JC**
34. Alan Blair, ss/of, Leeds HS, Odenville, Ala.
35. **William Estey, ss, New Hampshire**
36. **Roger Wallace, rhp/of, Englewood HS, Jacksonville, Fla.**
37. **Danny Nichols, 3b, Kansas State**
38. James Curnow, c, Morristown HS, Morris Plains, N.J.
39. Thomas Joyce, ss, Solano (Calif.) CC
40. James Mueller, of, Arkansas State
41. Samuel Pasquatonio, c, Franklin (Mass.) HS
42. **Richard Dorsch, rhp, Valparaiso**
43. Peter Brown, rhp, Hayward (Calif.) HS
44. John Rushing, lhp, Tuscaloosa HS, Northport, Ala.
45. **Kenneth Van Bell, rhp, Richmond Hill (N.Y.) HS**
46. Gary Whittemore, lhp, New Mexico
47. Gary Weese, rhp, Midwest City (Okla.) HS
48. John Fargnoci, 1b, Bryant HS, Astoria, N.Y.
49. **Edward Ott, lhp, Rutgers**
50. Kenneth Pfau, rhp, El Camino (Calif.) JC
51. **Robert Woodruff, of, Portchester (N.Y.) HS**
52. Bob Sheldon, ss, Montebello (Calif.) HS
53. Charles Elwis, lhp, Marshall HS, Los Angeles
54. Beau Robinson, 1b, Central HS, Springfield, Mo.
55. Tod Rush, lhp, Montebello (Calif.) HS
56. Anthony Embessi, rhp, Bristol (Pa.) HS
57. Steven Angelo, inf, Montebello HS, Pico Rivera, Calif.
58. Douglas Blake, of, Hackettstown (N.J.) HS
59. Jeff Paquette, c/of, Lincoln HS, San Francisco
60. Gary Welch, of/c, San Rafael (Calif.) HS
61. **Merritt Barnes, ss, San Francisco**
62. Chester Teklinski, rhp, Tarentum (Pa.) HS
63. **Malcolm Driggers, of, Colonial HS, Orlando, Fla.**
64. Jeffrey Burns, c, Rollins (Fla.)
65. **Charles Cochrane, ss, Lincoln HS, San Francisco**
66. **William Homik, c, Southern California**
67. **Charles Calver, rhp, Cal Poly Pomona**
68. **Peter Scarpati, rhp, St. Francis (N.Y.)**
69. **Stephen Krines, 3b, Villanova**
70. **John DeBrino, rhp, Bishop Gibbons HS, Schenectady, N.Y.**
71. Carl Amendola, c, Plainedge HS, Massapequa, N.Y.

June—Secondary Phase (13)

1. **Steve Garvey, 3b, Michigan State**
2. **Sandy Vance, rhp, Stanford**
3. **Ron Cey, 3b, Washington State**
4. Bruce Kinder, ss, Florida Southern
5. Bill Seinsoth, 1b, Southern California
6. Ellsworth Jones, lhp, New York
7. Bob Randall, ss, Kansas State

MINNESOTA TWINS

January—Regular Phase (15)

1. Daved Hoot, of, Houston
2. Bob Bridges, lhp, Arizona Western JC
3. **Allen Fenchel, of, Laney (Calif.) JC**
4. Larry Klein, lhp, Venice, Calif.
5. **Danny Humphries, rhp, Pico Rivera, Calif.**
6. Louis Rodriguez, 1b, New York

January—Secondary Phase (1)

1. **Eric Soderholm, inf, South Georgia JC**
2. William Borelli, 1b, JC of San Mateo (Calif.)
3. Joe Jacobson, c, Fresno (Calif.) CC
4. Eugene Rinaldi, ss, Miami-Dade North CC
5. Barry Sheldon, rhp, Batavia, N.Y.
6. Edgardo Avila, 1b, Miami-Dade North CC
7. Robert Huddleston, of, Arizona Western JC

June—Regular Phase (16)

1. **Alex Rowell, of, Luther (Iowa)**
2. John Langerhans, 1b, South San Antonio (Texas) HS
3. **Michael Cavanaugh, ss, Birmingham HS, Van Nuys, Calif.**
4. **Jim Nettles, of, San Diego State**
5. Harvey Winn, 2b, Loara HS, Anaheim
6. **Avery Morris, of, Franklin County HS, Estill Springs, Tenn.**
7. John Roatche, c, Hatboro (Pa.) HS
8. Tim Evans, ss, Littleton (Colo.) HS
9. **Mike Brooks, ss, West Covina (Calif.) HS**
10. Gary Bradshaw, rhp, Lake Worth (Fla.) HS
11. **Ron Oglesby, rhp, Ramona HS, Riverside, Calif.**
12. Mike Morrison, lhp/of, La Vista HS, Brea, Calif.
13. Frank Cordaro, rhp, Teaneck (N.J.) HS
14. Paul Commando, c, Columbus HS, Bronx, N.Y.
15. Frank Tokash, rhp, Westfield (N.J.) HS
16. Thomas Fast, rhp, Brighton (Colo.) HS
17. **Gary Majdoch, lhp, Wisconsin-Eau Claire**
18. **Jerry Terrell, 2b, Mankato State (Minn.)**
19. **Samuel Faria, of, Hingham (Mass.) HS**
20. Michael Pivec, of, Calvert Hall HS, Baltimore
21. **Russ Rolandson, ss/2b, Minnesota**
22. **James Hansen, c, Wisconsin-Stevens Point**
23. **Mark Hartig, rhp, Mullen HS, Denver**
24. **Buryl Hemerick, rhp, Costa Mesa HS, Huntington Beach, Calif.**
25. **Gregory Wendorf, lhp, Wisconsin-Stevens Point**
26. Thomas Lolos, c, Parsons
27. John Kiefer, ss, Princess Anne HS, Virginia Beach, Va.
28. **Thomas Bryan, c, Seminole HS, Sanford, Fla.**
29. **Phil Edwards, 2b, East Mecklenburg HS, Charlotte, N.C.**
30. Daniel Patrovich, lhp, Valdosta State (Ga.)
31. **Lee Ware, of, Glassboro State (N.J.)**
32. Nicholas Nicosia, of, Florida
33. **David Skog, lhp, St. Louis Park HS, Minneapolis**
34. **Kenneth Meek, ss, Montclair State (N.J.)**

June—Secondary Phase (18)

1. **Danny Thompson, ss, Oklahoma State**
2. **Gary Matz, 3b/of, Boston College**
3. William Camp, rhp, Oklahoma State
4. Bill Dobbs, lhp, Oklahoma State
5. Jerry Paetzhold, lhp, Southern Illinois-Edwardsville

MONTREAL EXPOS

January—Regular Phase

Did not participate (expansion franchise)

January—Secondary Phase

Did not participate (expansion franchise)

June—Regular Phase (21)

1. No selection
2. No selection
3. No selection
4. Michael Swain, rhp, Ohio State
5. William Ward, rhp, Southern Tech Institute (Fla.)
6. **Roger Nelson, c, Lincoln (Neb.) HS**
7. Kevin Bryant, ss, Winter Haven (Fla.) HS
8. William Kendall, 3b, Minnesota
9. **Ross Hoffman, 1b, UCLA**
10. Carlton Exum, rhp, Maynard Evans HS, Orlando, Fla.
11. **Dave Hartman, lhp, Iowa State**
12. John Palmer, lhp, St. Paul, Minn.
13. **Larry Woltz, 3b/of, DeKalb (Ga.) JC**
14. **Joseph Marecki, ss, Miami-Dade North CC**
15. Richard Trembecki, of, Denver (Selection voided)
16. **Richard Turner, rhp, Eau-Gallie (Fla.) HS**
17. William Seagraves, rhp/1b, Edgewater HS, Orlando
18. Michael Fulford, 3b, Miami-Dade South CC

June—Secondary Phase (23)

No selections

NEW YORK METS

January—Regular Phase (2)

1. **George Kazmarek, of/1b, Baltimore Institute**
2. Larry Sozzi, inf/c, CC of San Francisco

January—Secondary Phase (4)

1. **Bruce Harkey, rhp, La Habra, Calif.**
2. **Michael Derrig, lhp, Joliet (Ill.) JC**
3. Frederick Kampf, rhp, Miami
4. William Bright, rhp/of, Brevard (Fla.) CC
5. Michael Lersch, lhp, Mesa (Ariz.) CC
6. **Bruce Matte, rhp, Miami (Ohio)**
7. Reid Braden, 1b, Southern California
8. Timothy Uraskevich, rhp, SUNY Buffalo
9. Bob Danaher, rhp, Miami-Dade North CC
10. Moody Jackson, of, Phoenix JC
11. Charles Kingsbury, inf/of, San Diego CC

June—Regular Phase (1)

1. **Tim Foli, ss, Notre Dame HS, Canoga Park, Calif.**
2. **Donald Dickerson, 1b, Ensley HS, Birmingham, Ala.**
3. Bernard Boehmer, c, St. Dominic HS, OFallon, Ill.
4. **Alan Dodson, rhp, Sweetwater HS, National City, Calif.**
5. Burt Hooton, rhp, King HS, Corpus Christi, Texas
6. Robert Masteller, lhp, Midwest City (Okla.) HS
7. **Charlie Williams, rhp, Parsons (Iowa)**
8. **Marvin Leonard, lhp, DeWitt Clinton HS, Bronx, N.Y.**
9. Jack Pierce, of, San Jose (Calif.) HS
10. **Hank Webb, rhp, Copaique (N.Y.) HS**
11. **Don Rose, rhp, Stanford**
12. **James Ziegler, of, Colorado State**
13. Stuart Pugh, lhp/of, Mascoutah (Ill.) HS
14. **John Milner, of, South Fulton HS, East Point, Ga.**
15. Ken Dempsey, of, Ensley HS, Birmingham, Ala.
16. **John Gurganus, rhp, Westwood HS, Palestine, Texas**
17. **Leonard Carroll, c, Bergen Catholic HS, Oradell, N.J.**
18. Harley House, rhp, Piedmont Hills HS, San Jose, Calif.
19. John Penn, 1b, Ferrum (Va.) JC
20. **Scott Goodwin, rhp, Reseda (Calif.) HS**
21. John Severs, of, West Mecklenburg HS, Charlotte, N.C.
22. Steve Turigliatto, c, Long Beach (Calif.) CC
23. Wayne Young, c, Sleepy Hollow HS, Tarrytown, N.Y.
24. Daniel Misko, lhp, Tuscaloosa (Ala.) HS
25. Paul Patterson, rhp, Canton (N.Y.) HS
26. **Terry DeWald, 2b, Arizona**
27. **Glenn Stitzel, 2b, Millersville**
28. **Daniel Murphy, rhp, Technical HS, Springfield, Mass.**
29. Charles Covey, 3b, Pasadena (Calif.) CC
30. Frank Szoke, ss, Whitehall HS, Cementon, Pa.
31. Gary Morgan, 1b, Austin (Minn.) HS
32. Greg Archer, lhp/1b, Corcoran (Calif.) HS
33. Frederick Donaldson, ss, Loudon County HS, Leesburg, Va.
34. **Edward Young, 3b, Johnson HS, Savannah, Ga.**
35. Harold Wilkerson, c, Fike HS, Wilson, N.C.
36. Michael Bettega, lhp, Menlo (Calif.) JC
37. **Eugene Zawatski, lhp, Boston**
38. **Charles Carr, of, North Carolina**
39. Joe Kilby, of, Lincoln HS, Tacoma, Wash.

40. **David Colon, rhp, Reicher HS, Waco, Texas**
41. **James Malone, rhp, Union (Utah) HS**
42. **Gary Hill, of, Sacramento (Calif.) CC**
43. Bill Todd, lhp, Ritenour HS, St. Louis
44. Richard Seymour, c, St. Mary's HS, Ogdensburg, N.Y.

June—Secondary Phase (11)

1. Billy Cotton, c, Arizona State
2. **Thomas Williams, c, East Los Angeles JC**
3. Ray Peters, rhp, Harvard
4. John Whitehurst, c, Albemarle (N.C.) JC
5. Rich Hand, rhp, Puget Sound (Wash.)
6. Mickey Wertz, ss, Wharton County (Texas) JC
7. Mike Sigman, rhp, Santa Clara
8. Mickey Rivers, of, Miami-Dade North CC
9. Vincent Bigone, of, Santa Clara

NEW YORK YANKEES

January—Regular Phase (3)

1. **Robert Elliot, rhp, Massapequa, N.Y.**
2. Robert Singer, of/lhp, Los Angeles CC
3. **Harry McCandless, rhp, Kansas City, Mo.**
4. Ron Wayne, lhp, Laney (Calif.) JC
5. John Andrews, of/lhp, Pasadena (Calif.) CC
6. Ken Carmack, rhp, Yakima Valley (Wash.) JC
7. Raleigh Rhodes, p, De Anza (Calif.) JC
8. Melvin Oden, rhp/c, Wenatchee Valley (Wash.) CC
9. **Douglas Duncan, rhp, Spokane (Wash.) CC**
10. **John Manginelli, 3b, Irvington, N.Y.**

January—Secondary Phase (7)

1. **William Olsen, lhp, Eureka, Calif.**
2. **Douglas Hansen, rhp, Fresno (Calif.) CC**
3. Thomas Tikker, c, Los Angeles CC
4. **Bruce Olson, rhp, Chaffey (Calif.) JC**
5. William Shepherd, rhp, Spokane (Wash.) CC
6. Gary Houston, lhp, San Jose (Calif.) CC

June—Regular Phase (4)

1. **Thurman Munson, c, Kent State**
2. **Kenneth Johnson, ss, Redwood HS, Larkspur, Calif.**
3. Richard Trapp, ss, Florida
4. **Steven Kogut, c, Upland (Calif.) HS**
5. **George Zeber, ss, Loara HS, Anaheim**
6. **Adrian Kent, of, Parsons**
7. **Wayne Nordhagen, of, Treasure Valley (Ore.) CC**
8. **Patrick Denning, c, Schurz HS, Chicago**
9. Howard Casey, lhp, Treasure Valley (Ore.) CC
10. **Alonzo Ramirez, rhp, El Campo (Texas) HS**
11. Steven Hanzlik, rhp, David Douglas HS, Portland, Ore.
12. Duane Kuiper, ss, Racine Cast HS, Sturtevant, Wis.
13. Rickie Clements, lhp, Sadler HS, Whitesboro, Texas
14. **Robert McDaniel, of, Missouri**
15. Pat Sonneman, inf/of, Mount Tacoma (Wash.) HS
16. Ronnie Saunders, 1b/c, Burt HS, Clarksville, Tenn.
17. **Lee Choate, 1b, Chattanooga (Tenn.) Central HS**
18. **Patrick Cluney, 1b, Trinity**
19. Jeff Carpenter, ss, Owensboro (Ky.) Catholic HS
20. Mike Siani, ss, New Dorp HS, Staten Island, N.Y.
21. Vernon Gilmore, of, Willamette
22. Terry Pollreicz, of, Portland
23. **Ken Lange, rhp, Glassboro State (N.J.)**
24. Jim Hefflinger, lhp, Cleveland HS, Portland, Ore.
25. **David Reid, lhp, Sessar (Ill.) HS**
26. **Richard Monroe, c, Colton (Calif.) HS**
27. **Richard Koslick, 3b/ss, Tennessee Tech**
28. **Julius Bender, 3b, Ellsworth (Iowa) JC**
29. Charles Keigley, 3b, St. Joseph HS, Greenville, Miss.
30. **John Pogonelski, rhp, Hamden (Conn.) HS**
31. **Timothy O'Connell, of/1b, Xavier**
32. **Daniel Schirrips, rhp, Lafayette HS, Brooklyn, N.Y.**
33. Jeff Geach, ss, Del Campo HS, Carmichael, Calif.
34. Eddie Pyatt, rhp, Glendale HS, Springfield, Mo.
35. Daniel Velander, rhp, Franklin HS, Portland, Ore.
36. John Mills, rhp, Wanatchee (Wash.) HS
37. **Douglas D'Addario, of, Kensington HS, Buffalo, N.Y.**
38. Rich Schoener, of/1b, Marinette (Wis.) HS
39. James Huff, rhp/of, Del Valle HS, Walnut Creek, Calif.
40. Billy Jones, rhp, El Cerrito (Calif.) HS
41. William McDermott, 1b, Moorpark (Calif.) HS
42. **Michael Miller, of, Kaupau HS, Wichita, Kan.**
43. Bruce Zimmerman, rhp, Ukiah (Calif.) HS

June—Secondary Phase (8)

1. **Raymond DeRiggi, lhp, Seton Hall**
2. **George Ferguson, ss/3b, Maine**
3. John Fletcher, c, Mississippi State
4. William Ferguson, c, Texas Christian
5. Thomas Hannibal, lhp, Clark (Wash.) JC
6. Jerre Algeo, 2b, Poteau (Mo.) JC
7. **Richard Buff, 3b, Rossville, Ga.**

OAKLAND ATHLETICS

January—Regular Phase (1)

1. **George Hendrick Jr., rhp, Fremont HS, Los Angeles**
2. **Reggie Sanders, of, Venice (Calif.) HS**
3. Michael Prieto, of, JC of San Mateo (Calif.)
4. Paul Williams, c, Mitchell (Conn.) JC
5. William Coppola, rhp, Hudson Valley (N.Y.) CC
6. **John Luman, rhp/of, Vermont Technical JC**
7. Jack Gehrke, ss, Utah

January—Secondary Phase (17)

1. **Gene Dusan, c, Long Beach (Calif.) CC**
2. Ray Peters, rhp, Harvard
3. Glenn Woodruff, c, Marion (Ala.) Military Institute
4. Michael Magness, rhp, Manatee (Fla.) JC
5. Mark Reeser, lhp, Laney (Calif.) JC
6. **Charles Sprinkle, ss, Arizona Western JC**
7. Gerald Hurt, rhp, Missouri
8. Edward Cook, of, Bridgewater
9. Tom Binkowski, of, Michigan State
10. Gary Hohman, c, Bordertown Military Institute, Trenton, N.J.
11. Allen Simas, rhp, Sacramento (Calif.) CC

June—Regular Phase (2)

1. Pete Broberg, rhp, Palm Beach (Fla.) HS
2. John Shelley, of/inf, Casady HS, Oklahoma City, Okla.
3. **Charles Chaney, c/3b, Los Angeles**
4. Steven Tingle, ss, Pleasure Ridge Park (Ky.) HS
5. **William Lucas, 3b, Westfield (Mass.) HS**
6. Rich Troedson, lhp, Camden HS, San Jose, Calif.
7. **Buddy Copeland, rhp, Georgia**
8. **Edward Bacak, rhp, Carroll HS, Corpus Christi, Texas**
9. **Greg Schubert, of, Washington State**
10. **Patrick Tatum, rhp, Roger Ludlow HS, Fairfield, Conn.**
11. Robert Koeppel, lhp/of/1b, Limestone HS, Bartonville, Ill.
12. Gene Stohs, lhp, Grand Island (Neb.) HS
13. **Phillip Murnahan, rhp, Ironton (Ohio) HS**
14. Charles Walker, of, Lakeside HS, Atlanta
15. **Paul Mastin, rhp, Florida State**
16. Steve Wilmet, lhp, St. Norbert HS, West DePere, Wis.
17. **Stephen Cooley, of/1b, North Dakota**
18. **Michael Peden, c, Auburn**
19. **William Ingram, rhp, Idaho State**
20. **Augusta Massingill, ss, Englewood HS, Jacksonville, Fla.**
21. **Alan Hefferon, rhp, Brown**
22. Mark Arnold, rhp, William Chrisman HS, Independence, Mo.
23. **Mason Elvrom, c/of, Clover Park HS, Tacoma, Wash.**
24. **Robert Gibble, rhp, Bloomsburg**
25. Mark Tschopp, rhp, Jefferson HS, Cedar Rapids, Iowa
26. **John Strohmayer, rhp, Pacific (Ore.)**
27. James Jachym, lhp, Westfield (Mass.) HS
28. John Renhow, of, North Dakota State
29. Ernie Henrickson, rhp/of, Snohomish (Wash.) HS
30. Jerry Devins, rhp/of, Owensboro (Ky.) Catholic HS
31. Douglas Smith, ss/2b, Buena Vista

June—Secondary Phase (12)

1. **Thomas Cook, c, Florida State**
2. **Thomas Smith, rhp, Auburn**

3. Herbert Hofvendahl, of, St. Mary's
4. **Fred Kampf, rhp, Miami**

PHILADELPHIA PHILLIES

January—Regular Phase (12)

1. **Stephen Cates, lhp, Sunland, Calif.**
2. Edward Kelly, rhp, Dayton, Ohio
3. **James Alviso, rhp, Livermore, Calif.**
4. Lawrence Hardin, 2b, Polk (Fla.) CC
5. Carl London, of, Coatesville, Pa.
6. Charles Kurkjian, 3b, Fresno (Calif.) CC

January—Secondary Phase (8)

1. Pat Harrison, 2b, Southern California
2. **David Rusco, ss, Cuesta (Calif.) JC**
3. **Louis Lanehardt, lhp, Baltimore**
4. Donald Burkhalter, ss/rhp, Gulf Coast (Fla.) CC
5. Michael Schomaker, of/c, Stanford

June—Regular Phase (11)

1. **Greg Luzinski, 1b, Notre Dame HS, Prospect Heights, Ill.**
2. **Jeff Wang, of, South Torrance (Calif.) HS**
3. **William Lash, rhp/of, Windsor Locks (Conn.) HS**
4. Buddy Schultz, lhp, Shaw HS, East Cleveland, Ohio
5. **Allen Bowers, of, Mount Vernon HS, Fort Belvoir, Va.**
6. **Willie Jones, of, Southern HS, Philadelphia**
7. **Brian Hansen, c, SUNY Buffalo**
8. **Edward Goldstone, inf, Yale**
9. Phillip Harvey, rhp, Washington HS, Kansas City, Kan.
10. **Wilbur Cole, of, Southside HS, Florence, S.C.**
11. **William Geitz, lhp, West Depthford (N.J.) HS**
12. **Roger Noble, lhp, Troutwood (Ohio) HS**
13. **John Lee, rhp, Great Falls, Mont.**
14. **Jerry Coker, ss, Manning (S.C.) HS**
15. **Robert Cunningham, rhp, Middle Tennessee State**
16. Harry Rogers, of, Curwensville (Pa.) HS
17. **Richard Lang, of, Santa Clara HS, Oxnard, Calif.**
18. **Robert Keister, rhp, Sayerville (N.J.) HS**
19. **Daniel Brigham, ss, Berlin (N.H.) HS**
20. **Robert Maltsberger, c, Shoreline HS, Seattle**
21. **Patrick Locanto, 2b, Western Michigan**
22. Robert Coultas, of, Alhambra HS, Martinez, Calif.
23. **Ronald Carnutt, of, Camden HS, San Jose, Calif.**
24. Charles Janes, rhp, Kingston (N.Y.) HS
25. Larry Robertson, lhp, Lower Dauphin HS, Hummelstown, Pa.
26. Ronald Collier, rhp, Mansfield (Pa.)
27. Larry Tarver, c, Arvin (Calif.) HS
28. Michael Brown, inf, Wilmington (Del.) HS
29. John Malone, 3b, Maine-Endwell HS, Endwell, N.Y.
30. **Charles Pesce, c, Delaware**

June—Secondary Phase (9)

1. Pat Harrison, 2b, Southern California
2. Edgardo Avila, lhp, Miami-Dade North CC
3. Jim Barr, rhp, Southern California
4. **Tom Schleer, lhp, Kentucky Wesleyan**
5. **Reid Braden, 1b/3b, Southern California**

PITTSBURGH PIRATES

January—Regular Phase (10)

1. Sam Viney, 1b/rhp, San Joaquin Delta (Calif.) JC
2. Kevin Crain, rhp, Cabrillo (Calif.) JC
3. **Mark McLeod, c/3b, California, Md.**
4. **Steve Lewis, rhp, Bakersfield, Calif.**
5. **Thomas Davis, of, San Jose (Calif.) CC**
6. **Rob Johnson, lhp, Salem (W.Va.)**
7. Peter Poldiak, rhp, Gulf Coast (Fla.) CC

January—Secondary Phase (18)

1. Robert Taylor, rhp, Richard Bland (Va.) JC
2. James Snyder, of, East Carolina
3. **Tom Dettore Jr., rhp/c, Juniata**
4. Edward Mantie, rhp, Syracuse
5. Jerald Vitatoe, 3b/of, Oakland, Calif.
6. Donald Schroeder, rhp, Grays Harbor (Wash.) JC

June—Regular Phase (9)

1. **Dick Sharon, of, Sequoia HS, Redwood City, Calif.**
2. **Brad Gratz, lhp, George Sclafer HS, Southgate, Mich.**
3. James Sams, rhp, Cuyahoga Falls (Ohio) HS
4. **Mike Marine, rhp, Warren HS, Downey, Calif.**
5. Wayne Garland, rhp, Cohn HS, Nashville, Tenn.
6. Peter Halfman, of, Jesuit HS, Sacramento, Calif.
7. David Van Volkenburg, lhp, Cathedral Prep, Erie, Pa.
8. **Michael Cooper, rhp, Kokomo (Ind.) HS**
9. **Frank Barlew, 3b, Montour HS, Pittsburgh**
10. Ray Borowicz, ss, Huntington (N.Y.) HS
11. **Milt May, ss, St. Petersburg (Fla.) HS**
12. **Thomas Fratto, of, Cambridge (Mass.) Latin HS**
13. David Entrekin, c, Coatesville (Pa.) Area HS
14. **Bruce Kison, rhp, Pasco (Wash.) HS**
15. **Rudolph Brooks, 1b, Berkeley (Calif.) HS**
16. Richard Hurt, rhp, Lihon HS, Nashville, Tenn.
17. **Charles Hines, 3b, Florida State**
18. Paul Mitchell Jr., rhp, Worcester (Mass.) Academy
19. Mike Groves, of, Seminole HS, Largo, Fla.
20. **Steve McFarland, inf, Sammamish HS, Bellevue, Wash.**
21. Joseph Urbanovitch, c, Villanova
22. **Thomas Whalan, 2b/ss, Lowell (Mass.) HS**
23. Dennis Franklin, rhp, Gonzalez Tate HS, Cantonment, Fla.
24. **Randy Beringer, ss, Tigard (Ore.) HS**
25. **Gary Conboy, rhp, Genesee (N.Y.) CC**
26. Keith Scruggs, rhp, Allegheny City HS, Iron Gate, Va.
27. Marvin Tucker, of, Central Missouri State
28. Anthony Girodano, c, Most Holy Trinity HS, Brooklyn, N.Y.
29. Stanley Grout, rhp, Perry (Iowa) Senior HS
30. **Larry Barefoot, rhp, Hallsboro HS, Whiteville, N.C.**
31. **Scott Roswald, of, San Juan HS, Citrus Heights, Calif.**
32. **Robert Hessler, rhp, Hampton (Va.) HS**
33. **Stephen Bentley, rhp, Stoneham (Mass.) HS**
34. Paul Marcek, rhp, Rummell HS, Omaha
35. Roger Wright, c, Northeast Lauderdale HS, Meridian, Miss.
36. **Thomas Rambeau, lhp, York**
37. Michael Price, ss/of, Technical HS, Oakland, Calif.
38. **Barry Houser, lhp, West Chester (Pa.)**

June—Secondary Phase (19)

1. **Edward Northrop, rhp, Alexandria, Va.**
2. **James Skovron, rhp, West Newbury, Mass.**
3. Alan Putz, 1b, Springfield
4. Wayne Harlan, inf, Yakima Valley (Wash.) JC

ST. LOUIS CARDINALS

January—Regular Phase (20)

1. **Michael Maselbas, rhp, Swampscott, Mass.**
2. Frank Buchan, of, Marshalltown (Iowa) CC
3. James Pettee, 2b/of, Manatee (Fla.) JC
4. Elmer Dize, rhp, Mount Olive (N.C.) JC

January—Secondary Phase (14)

1. Ken Hottman, of, Sacramento (Calif.) CC
2. Michael Babler, rhp, Chabot (Calif.) JC
3. Rick Austin, lhp, Washington State
4. **Skip Jutze, c, Central Connecticut State**
5. Douglas Braun, c, Vallejo (Calif.) JC
6. **Russell Bodkin, of, Broward (Fla.) CC**

June—Regular Phase (19)

1. **James Hairston, of, Roth HS, Dayton, Ohio**
2. Wade Boyett, rhp/ss, Davidson HS, Mobile, Ala.
3. Mark Kitchell, of, Mamaroneck (N.Y.) HS
4. **Dick McVay, rhp/of, Norway (Iowa) HS**
5. **David Sagasar, lhp, Taft (Calif.) HS**
6. **Jack Stripling, rhp/ss, Holdenville (Okla.) HS**
7. **Tom Heintzelman, 2b, Parsons**
8. **Ted Hemenway, rhp, Mehlville (Mo.) HS**
9. **Lawrence Hebert, 3b, Sacramento (Calif.) CC**
10. **Donald Picard, lhp, Lyndon State**
11. **Bill Caudell, c, Manchester HS, Richmond, Va.**
12. Harold Wall, rhp, Skaneateles (N.Y.) HS
13. Michael Larkin, rhp, Plantation (Fla.) HS

14. **Don Kirkland, ss, Southern Illinois**
15. Paul Arendt, 3b/ss, Thomas Jefferson HS, Denver
16. Mike Douglas, 1b, Dominguez HS, Paramount, Calif.
17. **George Greer, of, Connecticut**
18. Darrell Downey, ss/c, Ventura (Calif.) HS
19. **Ben Farley, lhp/1b, Cleveland HS, St. Louis**
20. **Guy Gaumont, of, Loyola HS, Los Angeles**
21. **David Hansen, rhp, Ygnova Valley HS, Concord, Calif.**
22. **Ernest Vierra, c/of, Sacramento (Calif.) CC**
23. Craig Swan, rhp, Milliken HS, Long Beach, Calif.
24. Gary Howard, c, Yuba City (Calif.) HS
25. **Gerald Bryant, lhp, Amherst County HS, Madison Heights, Va.**
26. **Bob Forsch, 3b/rhp, Hiram Johnson HS, Sacramento, Calif.**
27. Mark Lopinot, rhp, St. Louis CC-Meramec
28. James Martin, c, Jones Valley HS, Birmingham, Ala.
29. John Davsko, rhp, Saint Louis
30. Nicholas Stipanovich, rhp, Boston
31. **Glenn Essman, c, Riverview HS, St. Louis**
32. Albert Johnson, of, Los Angeles (Calif.) HS
33. **Tim Plodinec, rhp, Arizona**
34. **Steven Frohman, of, Long Island**
35. **Daniel Ford, rhp/of, Quinnipiac**
36. **Chester Jackson, of, Kirkwood (Mo.) HS**
37. **George Newman, ss, Hartnell (Calif.) CC**
38. Ed Halicki, rhp, Kearney (N.J.) HS
39. **Gerald Aanonsen, ss, Wittenberg (Wis.) HS**
40. John Hathaway, c, Lewiston (Idaho) HS
41. Eric Maitland, inf, Gettysburg (Pa.) HS
42. Wayne Johnson, lhp, Brewer HS, Fort Worth, Texas
43. Ronnie Diggle, ss/2b, Dominguez HS, Paramount, Calif.
44. **Scott Sulprizio, 1b, Diablo Valley (Calif.) JC**
45. Michael Dickens, ss, Central Catholic HS, Melbourne, Fla.
46. Stephen Brassey, inf, San Leandro (Calif.) HS

June—Secondary Phase (17)

1. **Steve Evans, rhp, Michigan**
2. **Benny Looper, c, Southwestern Oklahoma State**
3. **Dennis Parks, of, Cal State Long Beach**
4. Brian Bach, rhp, Connecticut
5. **David Cichon, c/rhp, Amherst (Mass.)**
6. **Mike Ehlers, c, Ellsworth (Iowa) JC**
7. Ron Pritchett, rhp, Mount San Antonio (Calif.) JC

SAN DIEGO PADRES

January—Regular Phase

Did not participate (expansion franchise)

January—Secondary Phase

Did not participate (expansion franchise)

June—Regular Phase (23)

1. No selection
2. No selection
3. No selection
4. Luciano Hernandez, rhp, Solana Beach (Calif.) HS
5. **John Preston, rhp, Sweetwater HS, Chula Vista, Calif.**
6. Bob McRoberts, of, Crawford HS, El Cajon, Calif.
7. **Dave Robinson, of, San Diego State**
8. Alan Hansen, rhp, La Mesa (Calif.) HS
9. Dale Davis, lhp, Kearny HS, San Diego
10. William Hancock, c, Furman
11. Matthew Rosiek, rhp, Indian River (Fla.) CC
12. Dave Moates, of, Manatee (Fla.) JC
13. Robert Thompson, inf, Clairemont HS, San Diego
14. Jim Crawford, lhp, Tucson (Ariz.) HS
15. **Ronnie McGarity, c/rhp, North Cobb HS, Kenesaw, Ga.**
16. Nacho Bracamontes, lhp, Sweetwater HS, Chula Vista, Calif.
17. Theodore Tomasovich, of, Georgia Tech
18. **Ronald Drake, c, Southern California**
19. Earl Altschuler, 3b, Crawford HS, San Diego

June—Secondary Phase (21)

1. No selection
2. No selection
3. No selection
4. Rich Hinton, lhp, Arizona
5. **Bob O'Brien, lhp/1b, Arizona**
6. Richard Gouin, of, Pomona, Calif.

SAN FRANCISCO GIANTS

January—Regular Phase (18)

1. **Steve Sibley, lhp, El Camino (Calif.) JC**
2. **Garry Maddox, of, San Pedro (Calif.) HS**
3. **George Foster, of, El Camino (Calif.) JC**
4. Allen Truskowski, lhp, Wallace (Mich.) JC
5. Wayne Harlan, 3b, Yakima Valley (Wash.) JC
6. Jim Bianchi, ss, Las Vegas, Nev.
7. Lawrence Haynes, of, Baton Rouge, La.

January—Secondary Phase (2)

1. **Steve Garman, rhp/ss, Idaho**
2. Tim Huntley, of, Spokane (Wash.) CC
3. **Donald Paulsen, of, Altamonte Springs, Fla.**
4. Pat Westley, ss, Phoenix JC
5. Tom Schweitzer, lhp, Fairmont State (W.Va.)
6. **Edgar Thomas, 1b/lhp, Whittier, Calif.**
7. John Frilling, of, Indian River (Fla.) CC
8. Ed Assaf, rhp, Southern Mississippi
9. Martin Pfenninger, ss, Flemington, N.J.

June—Regular Phase (17)

1. **Gary Matthews Sr., of, San Fernando HS, Pacoima, Calif.**
2. Andrew Dudish, ss/of, Avondale HS, Avondale Estates, Ga.
3. **Allen Cowgill, rhp, Bradley**
4. Ken Rutkowski, of/rhp, SUNY Buffalo
5. **Kerry Horn, of/3b, Fairfield (Ala.) HS**
6. **Thomas Impliazzo, c, Eagle Rock (Calif.) HS**
7. **Gary Jacobson, c, Hamline (Minn.)**
8. **Jim Howarth, of, Mississippi State**
9. Richard McKinley, rhp, Pittsburg (Calif.) HS
10. **Keith Haney, c, California State Teachers (Pa.)**
11. Tommie Nichols, ss, Mississippi
12. Jose Basterrechea, rhp, Flushing (N.Y.) HS
13. **Gary Schafer, ss, Mount Rubidoux HS, Riverside, Calif.**
14. **Todd Martin, ss, Del Mar HS, San Jose, Calif.**
15. William Fitzgerald, c, Tulane
16. **Kenneth Cornell, 3b/of, Roosevelt HS, Wyandotte, Mich.**
17. Michael Ward, 2b, Marion, S.C.
18. James LaRusso, 3b, Monmouth College (N.J.)
19. Robert Horton, c, Dean Attendance Center, Leland, Miss.
20. Pat Bekeza, of/inf, Southern Colorado
21. Doug Balne, lhp, New Caanan (Conn.) HS
22. Cary Livingston, of, West Jefferson HS, Gretna, La.
23. Pat Cech, rhp, Maryvale HS, Phoenix
24. **John Petrock, ss, Somerville (N.J.) HS**
25. Robert McLeod, rhp, Georgetown (Ky.)
26. Joseph Campanario, rhp/of, St. Elizabeth HS, Oakland, Calif.
27. Mike Balogh, rhp, OHara HS, Buffalo, N.Y.
28. Michael Koski, 2b, Las Plumas HS, Oroville, Calif.
29. Kent Corley, 2b, Sandy Springs HS, Atlanta
30. Ralph Dick, of, Mesa (Ariz.) CC
31. **Hugh Woolridge, of, John Harris HS, Harrisburg, Pa.**
32. Steve Holdren, of, Mountain Home (Idaho) HS
33. **George Bochow, 1b/of, New York**
34. Rob Ellis, inf/of, Ottawa Hills HS, Grand Rapids, Mich.
35. Allen Weendone, rhp, Hicks Memorial HS, Selma, Ala.
36. **Tommy Hanegan, ss, Ocala, Fla.**
37. **Tommy Palmertree, lhp, Burbank HS, Sacramento, Calif.**

June—Secondary Phase (3)

1. **Ed Goodson, ss, East Tennessee State**
2. Harry Saferight, c, Manatee (Fla.) JC
3. Patrick Roark, of, San Diego Mesa JC
4. **Edmund Mantie, rhp, Syracuse**
5. Tom Schweitzer, lhp, Fairmont State (W.Va.) (Selection voided)
6. Gerald Christman, lhp, Michigan
7. **Dick Hanselman, lhp, St. John's River (Fla.) CC**

SEATTLE PILOTS

January—Regular Phase

Did not participate (expansion franchise)

January—Secondary Phase

Did not participate (expansion franchise)

June—Regular Phase (22)

1. No selection
2. No selection
3. No selection
4. **Marty West, c, Rock Hill (S.C.) HS**
5. Greg Brosterhous, ss/rhp, Klamath Falls (Ore.) HS
6. Roger McSwain, of, Crest HS, Shelby, N.C.
7. **Bill Parsons, rhp, Riverside (Calif.) CC**
8. **Tom Kelly, of, St. Mary's HS, South Amboy, N.J.**
9. **Milton Jordan, 3b, Lanier HS, Macon, Ga.**
10. **Larry Pickett, rhp, Chaffey HS, Ontario, Calif.**
11. **Frankie Kimball, c, Trinity**
12. Mike Baldwin, lhp, Sacramento (Calif.) CC
13. Ronnie Slingerman, 3b, James Madison HS, Vienna, Va.
14. James Laughridge, rhp, Rock Hill (S.C.) HS
15. Phillip Basler, 1b, Truman HS, Independence, Mo.
16. Roger Sizoo, c, Citrus (Calif.) JC
17. Mike Staffieri, ss, Sunny Hills HS, Fullerton, Calif.
18. Jim Silvey, 2b, Ritenour HS, St. Louis
19. **Wilbur Howard, of, Holbrook HS, Lowell, N.C.**
20. Henry Talbot, of, Boise, Idaho
21. **Gary Upton, c, Bradley**
22. **Wayne Sullivan, rhp, Belmont Abbey (N.C.)**
23. Dario Pini, ss/3b, Sequoia HS, Redwood City, Calif.
24. **Nelson Gibson, rhp, Clemson**
25. Larry Angell, rhp, Shoreline HS, Seattle
26. Ronald Kelam, of, Southwest HS, St. Louis
27. Mitch Laird, rhp, Woodward (Okla.) HS
28. Perry Allen, rhp, Sulphur (Okla.) HS
29. Steve Downs, 3b, Taft HS, Chicago
30. Barry Herron, c, Kansas State
31. **Wayne Vincent, lhp, Florida State**
32. **Larry Nero, rhp, Los Angeles**

June—Secondary Phase (24)

1. No selection
2. No selection
3. No selection
4. **David Etter, of/1b, Shippensburg**

WASHINGTON SENATORS

January—Regular Phase (7)

1. **Jimmy Blackmon, rhp, Rock Hill, S.C.**
2. John Whitehurst, c, Albemarle (N.C.) JC
3. Richard Myers, c, Manasquan, N.J.
4. **DeWayne Chambers, of, Florida Memorial**

January—Secondary Phase (11)

1. Danny Thompson, ss, Oklahoma State
2. Kent Calderan, ss, Chabot (Calif.) JC
3. **William Holt, lhp, Lynchburg (Va.)**
4. **David Schmid, lhp, Catonsville (Md.) CC**
5. Donald Keenan, c/of, Gulf Coast (Fla.) CC
6. **Charles Koselke, 1b, Western Michigan**
7. Bruce Kinder, ss, Florida Southern (Selection voided)
8. Robert Knight, ss, South Georgia JC

June—Regular Phase (8)

1. **Don Castle, lhp/1b, Coldwater (Miss.) HS**
2. **Jim Mason, ss, Murphy HS, Mobile, Ala.**
3. **Rickey Rogers, ss, New Carlisle (Ohio) HS**
4. Alan Schwartz, rhp, McArthur HS, Wantaugh, N.Y.
5. **Jeff Terpko, rhp, Sayre (Pa.) HS**
6. Mike Cubbage, ss/3b, Lane HS, Charlottesville, Va.
7. Harold Richmond, rhp, Travis HS, Austin, Texas
8. **Gene Wiley, rhp, Threadgill HS, Greenwood, Miss.**
9. Bruce Clarke, rhp/of, Pawtucket (R.I.) West HS
10. **Larry Biittner, lhp/1b, Buena Vista**
11. Chris Speier, ss, Alameda (Calif.) HS
12. Richard Oliver, of/3b, Patapsco HS, Baltimore
13. Robert Eldridge, rhp, Robert Morris JC
14. Sherwood Hahn, of, Virginia Tech
15. **Jeffrey Janek, lhp, Harold Richards HS, Oak Lawn, Ill.**
16. **Darrel Hetzler, 1b, Xenia (Ohio) Central HS**
17. **Roy Adams, of/c, Roth HS, Dayton, Ohio**
18. **Robert Shutts, rhp, Northwestern**
19. **Ralph Davidson, rhp, King HS, Tampa**
20. **Jeffrey Vollweiler, rhp, American**
21. Berry McQueen, rhp, Gerrett HS, Charleston, S.C.
22. Alan Lobb, lhp, Bangor (Pa.) HS
23. Jerry Tagge, inf/c, Green Bay (Wis.) West HS
24. Jim Cox, ss, Bloomington (Ill.) HS
25. **Pat Kuehner, 1b, Southern California**
26. **Richard Guarnera, ss, Baltimore**
27. **Gary Sargent, lhp, Indiana**
28. Harold Graff, c, Illinois Wesleyan
29. Elmer Yelvington, rhp, Lee Woodward HS, Black Creek, N.C.
30. **Albert Richards, ss, Maryland**
31. Kenneth McGregor, ss, Gulf Coast (Fla.) CC

June—Secondary Phase (16)

1. **Rick Henninger, rhp, Missouri**
2. Glenn Pickren, rhp, Florida
3. Donald Burkhalter, rhp, Gulf Coast (Fla.) CC
4. Paul Williams, c, Mitchell (Conn.) JC
5. Edward Cott, c, Cornell
6. William Bright, of/rhp, Brevard (Fla.) CC

1969 SENATORS FIND FUTURE MVP WITH FIRST PICK, FOLLOWED BY HEALTHY CROP OF PITCHING

Jeff Burroughs was so highly regarded as a hitter out of high school that no less an authority than Ted Williams called him the best 18-year-old hitter he had ever seen.

Williams was the manager of the Washington Senators at the time and was instrumental in the club's selection of Burroughs as the No. 1 pick in the 1969 draft.

"He doesn't have an outstanding arm nor outstanding speed, but he has an outstanding bat," Williams said. "He has everything it takes to be one of the finest righthanded hitters in the game in three or four years."

Burroughs, 18, signed for an $88,000 bonus, to that point the largest paid to a Senators player. Most clubs agreed he was the best player available in the Class of 1969.

Jack Sheehan, Washington's chief scout, said Burroughs "has the best power of any 18-year-old I've ever seen."

"He was the best all-around hitter available," Senators farm director Hal Keller agreed.

Burroughs impressed Williams and other Senators officials with five batting-practice home runs in a predraft workout at Anaheim Stadium.

"Working out with Ted Williams was quite an experience," said Burroughs, who hit .569 as a high school senior at Woodrow Wilson High in Long Beach. "I've always been a Williams fan. You could say he's been my idol. I was a little boy when he was playing."

Burroughs played for Williams briefly in Washington, but he enjoyed his greatest success as a member of the Rangers after the franchise moved to Arlington following the 1971 season. Burroughs, a .261 hitter in 16 major league seasons, was American League MVP in 1974 when he hit .301 with 25 homers and 118 RBIs.

It was against Williams' better judgment that Burroughs was promoted to Washington in 1970, his first full professional season. Impatient owner Bob Short, who would later exploit top draft picks Pete Broberg (1971) and David Clyde (1973) by starting them in the big leagues, called on Burroughs from Triple-A Denver for an ill-fated two-week stint. It would be another year before he set foot in the big leagues again.

"We realize it was a bad mistake to call Burroughs up last year," Senators vice president Joe Burke said after Burroughs was called up for good.

PAMELA SMITH

Bert Blyleven won 149 games for the Twins in two stints with the organization

Two high school pitchers from the Class of '69 were already solidly entrenched in the big leagues by the time Burroughs broke in, however.

Cincinnati's Don Gullett, who opened the 1970 season in the Reds bullpen, posted a 5-2 record and 2.42 ERA in 44 appearances for the National League champions. Minnesota's Bert Blyleven, a third-round pick, moved into the Twins rotation two months after his 19th birthday and went on to pile up 287 big league wins.

The big-name high school pitcher in the 1969 draft, though, was 6-foot-8 James Rodney Richard, selected second overall by Houston. Richard was 11-0 his senior year and 28-0 overall in his high school career in Ruston, La., and he was hotly pursued for more than just his pitching skills.

An all-America high school basketball player who had offers from more than 100 schools, Richard was also quarterback of his high school team for four years. For added measure, he homered four times in one game in a lopsided 48-0 victory his senior year.

"Our scouts feel that Richard has a Bob Gibson fastball," said Tal Smith, Houston's director of player personnel. "He's the top pitching prospect in the country."

Richard would go on to become one of the game's top power pitchers, twice striking out 300 in a season, before mysteriously being struck down on July 30, 1980 by a stroke. He never pitched in the big leagues again.

The two Chicago teams, both with an eye on inexpensive talent, made surprise first-round selections. Picking third, the White Sox went for 20-year-old third baseman Ted Nicholson. The 6-foot-5 Nicholson had missed a year of school because of a childhood illness, so he was the oldest high school product ever drafted in the first round. He never advanced past Class A in a career that was frequently interrupted by military service.

The Cubs went for shortstop Roger Metzger from tiny St. Edwards (Texas) College. Metzger, a .447 hitter in college, signed with the Cubs for $25,000. He ended up playing 11 major league seasons before his career was curtailed when he lost the tips off several fingers in an accident at his home.

Kuhn In Command

The June 1969 draft was the first conducted under the leadership of commissioner Bowie Kuhn after he took over from Spike Eckert, who resigned under fire the previous December. Eckert's last official duty was to oversee the January draft.

The June draft produced the greatest number of high school selections ever: 723, more than three times the number of high school players picked in the 1985 draft.

Kansas City, stocking six new farm clubs, selected a draft-record 98 players, including 90 in the regular phase. But they couldn't sign their first-round selection, shortstop John Simmons, a .517 hitter at Childersburg (Ala.) High who went on to play football at Auburn. Simmons would never play pro ball, becoming one of four first-round picks never to do so. The Royals, however, landed the equivalent of a first-rounder in the 75th round, when they found outfielder Al Cowens, who played 13 years.

Unlike expansion cousins Kansas City and San Diego, which shared a Double-A farm club in 1969, neither Montreal nor Seattle had a Double-A affiliation, so they couldn't make third-round selections in both phases of the January and June drafts.

According to the draft rules at the time, major league teams made picks in the third round on behalf of their Double-A affiliates. With no Double-A clubs, the Expos and Pilots had to pass in the third round.

Arizona State, the dominant college program of the time, had more players drafted (eight) than any other college and won the College World Series again. The first college player taken in the June regular phase was Sun Devils outfielder Paul Ray Powell, who led the nation with 164 total bases and set a college record with 89 hits. He was selected seventh overall by the Twins and had an unproductive professional career.

DRAFT 69: FIRST-ROUND PICKS

No.	Club	Player, Pos.	School	Hometown	Ht.	Wt.	B-T	Age
1.	Senators	Jeff Burroughs, of	Wilson HS	Long Beach, Calif.	6-1	200	R-R	18
2.	Astros	J.R. Richard, rhp	Lincoln HS	Ruston, La.	6-8	225	R-R	19
3.	White Sox	Ted Nicholson, 3b	Oak Park HS	Laurel, Miss.	6-5	200	R-R	20
4.	Mets	Randy Sterling, rhp	Key West HS	Key West, Fla.	6-3	193	L-R	18
5.	Angels	*Alan Bannister, ss	Kennedy HS	Buena Park, Calif.	6-0	175	R-R	17
6.	Phillies	Mike Anderson, 1b	Timmonsville HS	Timmonsville, S.C.	6-3	187	R-R	17
7.	Twins	Paul Ray Powell, of	Arizona State	Eloy, Ariz.	6-0	190	R-R	20
8.	Dodgers	Terry McDermott, c	St. Agnes HS	West Hempstead, N.Y.	6-4	205	R-R	18
9.	Athletics	Don Stanhouse, rhp/ss	DuQuoin HS	DuQuoin, Ill.	6-2	185	R-R	18
10.	Pirates	Bob May, rhp	Merritt Island HS	Merritt Island, Fla.	6-0	175	R-R	17
11.	Yankees	Charlie Spikes, 3b/of	Central Memorial HS	Bogalusa, La.	6-2	195	R-R	18
12.	Braves	Gene Holbert, c	Palmyra HS	Campbelltown, Pa.	6-1	210	B-R	17
13.	Red Sox	Noel Jenke, of	Minnesota	Owatonna, Minn.	6-1	215	L-L	22
14.	Reds	Don Gullett, lhp	McKell HS	Lynn, Ky.	6-0	190	R-L	18
15.	Indians	Alvin McGrew, of	Parker HS	Fairfield, Ala.	6-2	175	R-R	17
16.	Cubs	Roger Metzger, ss	St. Edwards	San Antonio, Texas	6-0	165	L-R	21
17.	Orioles	Don Hood, lhp	Southside HS	Florence, S.C.	6-2	175	L-L	19
18.	Giants	Mike Phillips, ss	McArthur HS	Irving, Texas	6-0	170	L-R	18
19.	Tigers	Lenny Baxley, 1b	Enterprise HS	Redding, Calif.	6-2	185	L-L	18
20.	Cardinals	Charles Minott, lhp	Royal Oak HS	Covina, Calif.	6-4	200	L-L	17
21.	Pilots	Gorman Thomas, ss	James Island HS	Charleston, S.C.	6-2	190	R-R	18
22.	Expos	Balor Moore, lhp	Deer Park HS	Deer Park, Texas	6-3	185	L-L	18
23.	Royals	*John Simmons, ss	Childersburg HS	Childersburg, Ala.	5-11	165	R-R	18
24.	Padres	Randy Elliott, 1b	Camarillo HS	Camarillo, Calif.	6-2	190	R-R	18

*Did not sign.

1969

CLUB-BY-CLUB SELECTIONS

ATLANTA BRAVES

January—Regular Phase (11)

1. Robert Beach, rhp, Cabrillo (Calif.) JC
2. **Michael Magness, rhp, Manatee (Fla.) JC**
3. William Clark, rhp, San Francisco State
4. William Rhoden, rhp, Palm Beach (Fla.) JC
5. Steven Hembree, ss, Navarro (Texas) JC
6. Curtis Dockery, rhp, Houston
7. David Allen, lhp, Westark (Ark.) CC
8. John Haarmeyer, rhp, Blinn (Texas) JC
9. **Charles Lecroy, 3b, Gardner-Webb**

January—Secondary Phase (15)

1. Harry Saferight, c, Manatee (Fla.) JC
2. **Jeffrey Geach, 2b, American River (Calif.) JC**
3. Jack Pierce, 1b, San Jose (Calif.) CC
4. Peter Halfman, of, American River (Calif.) JC
5. William Fitzgerald, c, Tulane
6. Bobby Lail, lhp, Gardner-Webb
7. Roger McSwain, of, Gardner-Webb

June—Regular Phase (12)

1. **Gene Holbert, c, Palmyra HS, Campbelltown, Pa.**
2. **Leo Foster, ss, Holmes HS, Covington, Ky.**
3. **Larvell Blanks, ss, San Felipe HS, Del Rio, Texas**
4. **Russell Dillon, lhp, Novato (Calif.) HS**
5. **Howard Duckworth, c, Boerne (Texas) HS**
6. **Jimmy Freeman, lhp, Hale HS, Tulsa, Okla.**
7. **Mike Walseth, 1b, Minnesota**
8. Michael Rusk, rhp, Gunn HS, Los Altos, Calif.
9. James Gardner, rhp, Martinsville, Va.
10. Steven Gardner, 3b, Weber State
11. Alan Rome, rhp, Warren Easton HS, New Orleans
12. **Gary Hagen, rhp, Alton (Ill.) HS**
13. **Tom Heierle, c, Santiago HS, Garden Grove, Calif.**
14. Walter Sumner, of, Florida State
15. Leroy Thomas, c/1b, Sam Houston HS, San Antonio, Texas
16. **Charles Westerhouse, rhp, Duquoin (Ill.) HS**
17. John Nickerson, c, Pittsburg (Texas) HS
18. Gil Untemeyer, 3b, Andrew Jackson HS, Jacksonville, Fla.
19. **Marc Mengo, 1b/3b, Blackford HS, San Jose, Calif.**
20. **Bucky Guth, ss, West Virginia**
21. **David Gourieux, rhp, Murray State**
22. George Horton, c/of, Upsala
23. John Yeglinski, of, Sheepshead Bay HS, Brooklyn, N.Y.
24. John LiBrandi, of, Ribault HS, Jacksonville, Fla.
25. Raymond Coley, c, Valparaiso
26. **James Nagel, of, Covington, Ky.**
27. Ronald Middleton, rhp, Lake Land (Ill.) JC
28. Cecil Walley, lhp, Favitdale (Ala.) HS
29. **Stan Babieracki, lhp, St. John's**
30. **Richard Dahlgren, 1b, Indiana (Pa.)**
31. **Richard Atkinson, 2b/3b, Greenville (Ill.)**
32. James Toms, rhp, Lawton (Okla.) HS
33. Michael LaMacchia, of, Antonian HS, San Antonio, Texas
34. Al Ryan, ss, De LaSalle HS, New Orleans
35. Robert Roemer, c/3b, Thornridge HS, South Holland, Ill.

June—Secondary Phase (16)

1. Gary Robson, rhp, Los Angeles CC
2. **Mickey Rivers, of, Miami-Dade North CC**
3. Bert Yeargan, ss, Brewton-Parker (Ga.) JC
4. Sigmund Gancasz, c, Queensborough (N.Y.) CC

BALTIMORE ORIOLES

January—Regular Phase (18)

1. Rick Dierker, rhp, Los Angeles Pierce JC
2. Rudi Strickland, lhp, Indian River (Fla.) CC
3. **Robert Fields, rhp, Allegany (Md.) CC**
4. Ken Caudle, c/3b, East Los Angeles JC
5. Victor Sutherland, lhp, Brevard (Fla.) CC
6. Carl Bennett, c, San Joaquin Delta (Calif.) JC
7. Michael Morris, rhp, CC of San Francisco
8. Roger Carmine, lhp, JC of San Mateo (Calif.)
9. **James Edgar, rhp, Solano (Calif.) CC**
10. **Joseph Walsh, rhp, Maine**

January—Secondary Phase (18)

1. Richard Wanless, rhp, Quincy, Mass.
2. Phillip Corddry, lhp, Maryland
3. **Kirk Berger, rhp, Greensboro, N.C.**
4. Peter Perpich, rhp, Lansing (Mich.) CC
5. Bruce Cannon, 3b, Oberlin, Ohio
6. **Terry Pollreisz, inf/of, Portland**
7. Stephen Boland, rhp, South Georgia JC
8. Michael Babler, rhp, Chabot (Calif.) JC
9. Michael Balough, rhp, Niagara
10. Glen Pickren, rhp, Florida
11. Stan Gatto, lhp, Selden, N.Y.

June—Regular Phase (17)

1. **Don Hood, lhp, Southside HS, Florence, S.C.**
2. **James Stafford, 1b, San Pedro (Calif.) HS**
3. **Terry Clapp, ss, Southeast Guilford HS, Liberty, N.C.**
4. **James Winters, of/1b, St. Francis HS, Mountain View, Calif.**
5. **Mark Weems, rhp, La Puente HS, Azusa, Calif.**
6. **Dave Skaggs, c, North Torrance HS, Lawndale, Calif.**
7. **William O'Connor, 2b, Mount Miguel HS, Lemon Grove, Calif.**
8. **Greg Simendinger, rhp, Brandywine (Del.) JC**
9. **Frank Coleman, rhp/3b, Clearwater (Fla.) HS**
10. **Walter Harrison, c/of, King George (Va.) HS**
11. Ralph Radtke, c, Waukegan (Ill.) East HS
12. Richard Fillings, lhp, Catonsville (Md.) HS
13. Gary Szakacs, 1b/of, Mira Loma HS, Sacramento, Calif.
14. **Jeffrey Bonardel, rhp, Whippany (N.J.) Park HS**
15. Charles Clanton, of, Bradshaw HS, Florence, Ala.
16. Kent Murdock, ss, Clearfield (Utah) HS
17. **Daniel Yaccarino, rhp, Port Richmond HS, Staten Island, N.Y.**
18. John Tatem, rhp, Pocomoke HS, Pocomoke City, Md.
19. **Marvin Hines, of, North Lenoir HS, La Grange, N.C.**
20. Dick Ruthven, rhp, Irvington HS, Fremont, Calif.
21. **Oscar Delbusto, c, Jackson HS, Miami**
22. **Gregory Hansen, rhp, Utah**
23. **Brian Swasey, 2b, Portland, Maine**
24. John Saunders, c, Campolinda HS, Lafayette, Calif.
25. Greg Parrish, lhp, Glendale (Ariz.) CC
26. Mike Barlow, rhp, Syracuse
27. **Kay Patterson, of, Dominquez HS, Compton, Calif.**
28. Walter Wolfe, lhp, Lawrenceville (Ill.) HS
29. Willie Jones, 1b, Bowen HS, Chicago
30. Jay Anderson, c, Chico (Calif.) HS
31. Fred Yilling, c, Mississippi State
32. Michael Jones, lhp, Hazel Park (Mich.) HS
33. **Thomas Souza, ss, Alhambra HS, Martinez, Calif.**
34. Douglas Cash, ss, DeKalb (Ga.) JC
35. Michael Thompson, of, Phillips (Okla.)
36. Robert Wilson, ss, Mountain Lakes (N.J.) HS
37. John Shaw, 2b, Mississippi
38. **Donald Finch, ss, Gloucester (N.J.) HS**
39. Michael Timms, 3b, Arline HS, Bossier City, La.
40. Dave Winfield, rhp/of, Central HS, St. Paul, Minn.
41. Kenneth Bauer, 3b, North Bergen (N.J.) HS
42. James Pikula, of/c, Fernandina Beach (Fla.) HS
43. Robert Boddie, rhp, Woodlawn HS, Shreveport, La.
44. Richard Stevens, rhp, Berkeley HS, Oakland, Calif.

45. **Michael Beitty, rhp/of, Vancouver (Wash.) HS**
46. Donald Sever, 2b, St. Francis HS, Redwood City, Calif.
47. Charles Stone, c, East Los Angeles JC
48. Michael Chitwood, rhp, South Mountain HS, Phoenix
49. **William Wooten, c, Logan HS, Stallings, W.Va.**
50. Richard Brown, of, Sunnyvale, Calif. (Selection voided)

June—Secondary Phase (5)

1. **Wayne Garland, rhp, Gulf Coast (Fla.) CC**
2. Gary Bradshaw, rhp, Miami-Dade North CC
3. David Kropfelder, c, CC of Baltimore
4. **Steven Turigliatto, c, Southern California**
5. Michael Pivec, of, CC of Baltimore

BOSTON RED SOX

January—Regular Phase (14)

1. **William Norton, 1b, Merrimack**
2. **Richard Licini, 1b, Notre Dame**
3. Johnny Grubb Jr., of, Manatee (Fla.) JC
4. William Hamilton, c, Broward (Fla.) CC

January—Secondary Phase (4)

1. **Gary Myers, of, JC of San Mateo (Calif.)**
2. Kenneth Rutkowski, c/rhp, SUNY Buffalo
3. **John Zbercot, c, St. Clair Shores, Mich.**
4. Ronald Garlin, of, Miramar Isles, Fla.
5. Wayne Milan, rhp, Broward (Fla.) CC
6. **John Stephens, of, Gulf Coast (Fla.) CC**
7. **Gerald Daughtry, c, Blinn (Texas) JC**

June—Regular Phase (13)

1. **Noel Jenke, of, Minnesota**
2. **Rick Miller, of, Michigan State**
3. **Buddy Hunter, inf, Pershing**
4. **Jim Wright, rhp, Coopersville (Mich.) HS**
5. **Dwight Evans, 3b/of, Chatsworth HS, Northridge, Calif.**
6. **Michael Cummings, ss, Grambling**
7. **Steve Barr, lhp, Carson HS, Torrance, Calif.**
8. Eric Brown, c, Morristown (Tenn.) East HS
9. **Robert Kerr, rhp, Arvada HS, Denver**
10. William Hernandez, of/c, George Washington HS, New York
11. **Clark Adkins, of, Ray HS, Corpus Christi, Texas**
12. Lindsay Graham, rhp, Dulaney HS, Timonium, Md.
13. Vaughan Sykes, rhp, Mebane, N.C.
14. Greg McCollum, 1b, Meadowdale HS, Lynwood, Wash.
15. **David Klastava, rhp/inf, Scotch Plains (N.J.) HS**
16. James Torres, of, Arlington Heights HS, Fort Worth, Texas
17. **Donald Small, 1b/rhp, Southwestern HS, DeLeon Springs, Fla.**
18. **Dave Coleman, inf, Stebbins HS, Dayton, Ohio**
19. Perry Renfro, lhp, Butler HS, Huntsville, Ala.
20. Larry Smith, of, Tennessee Tech
21. **Thomas Kramer, c, Dieruff HS, Allentown, Pa.**
22. **Fernando Santiago, 1b, Monroe HS, Bronx, N.Y.**
23. Scott Sholbe, ss, Grand Junction (Colo.) HS
24. Donald Rhoden, ss, Franklin County HS, Winchester, Tenn.
25. **James Bryant, rhp, Columbia State (Tenn.) CC**

June—Secondary Phase (9)

1. **William Ward, rhp, Southern Tech Institute (Fla.)**
2. **Phillip Corddry, lhp, Maryland**
3. **John Fletcher, c, Mississippi State**
4. David Allen, lhp, Westark (Ark.) CC

CALIFORNIA ANGELS

January—Regular Phase (4)

1. Randall Bayer, 1b, Mesa (Ariz.) CC
2. Robert Singer, of, Los Angeles CC
3. **Terry Logan, 1b, Panola (Texas) JC**
4. Thomas Thomas, 3b, Menlo (Calif.) JC
5. John Andrews, of/lhp, Pasadena (Calif.) CC
6. Gary McEwen, lhp, Torrance, Calif.
7. Robert Wolf, rhp, Cerritos (Calif.) JC
8. Richard Leavitt, of, Cerritos (Calif.) JC
9. Thor Skogan, of, Sierra (Calif.) JC
10. Donald Pfister, c, Pasadena (Calif.) CC
11. Dwight Johnson, of, De Anza (Calif.) JC
12. Kent Calderan, ss, Chabot (Calif.) JC
13. Bruce Rosenthal, c/3b, Pasadena (Calif.) CC
14. **Terry Tulley, rhp, Chaffey (Calif.) JC**

January—Secondary Phase (14)

1. Sherwood Hahn, rhp/of, Virginia Tech
2. Franklin Riggins, of, Kansas
3. **Charles Elwis, lhp, Los Angeles (Calif.) CC**
4. Ron Diggle, of, Cerritos (Calif.) JC
5. Pat Sonneman, 3b, Columbia Basin (Wash.) CC
6. David Edson, ss, Menlo (Calif.) JC
7. Lawrence Schutzius, of, Mesa (Colo.)
8. Kenneth Pfau, rhp, Torrance, Calif.
9. Dale Davis, lhp, San Diego CC
10. William Kendall, 3b, Minnesota

June—Regular Phase (5)

1. Alan Bannister, ss, Kennedy HS, Buena Park, Calif.
2. **David Chorley, of, Millikan HS, Long Beach, Calif.**
3. **Samuel Ashford, ss, Western HS, Ensley, Ala.**
4. **Rudy Meoli, ss, Royal Oak HS, Covina, Calif.**
5. **James Erautt, rhp, Helix HS, Lemon Grove, Calif.**
6. **Richard Bailey, of, Millikan HS, Long Beach, Calif.**
7. **Michael Martorella, 1b, Monterey Peninsula (Calif.) JC**
8. Murphy Eppinette, rhp, Chalmette HS, Arabi, La.
9. **John Schroeder, ss, Magnolia HS, Anaheim**
10. David Bishop, lhp, Mountain Lakes (N.J.) HS
11. Jim Wohlford, 2b, Mount Whitney HS, Visalia, Calif.
12. **Richard Young, lhp, Larkin HS, Streamwood, Ill.**
13. **Larry Hunt, of, Arcadia HS, Temple City, Calif.**
14. **Eric Shiffer, 3b, Lakewood (Calif.) HS**
15. **David Marikos, c, El Segundo (Calif.) HS**
16. Steve Dix, of, Normandy HS, St. Louis
17. David Babcock, c, Springfield HS, Battle Creek, Mich.
18. **Thomas Benedict, lhp, Chaffey (Calif.) JC**
19. Anthony Piraino, c, Lakewood (Calif.) HS
20. Thomas Lundgren, lhp, Missouri
21. Noel Sweeney, c, Katella HS, Anaheim
22. **Louis Pasierb, lhp, Bradley**
23. **Joseph Muto, ss, San Juan HS, Carmichael, Calif.**
24. Jeffrey Wingert, c/of, Chaffey HS, Ontario, Calif.
25. **Andy Hassler, lhp, Palo Verde HS, Phoenix**
26. Bruce Patras, ss, Hogan HS, Vallejo, Calif.
27. Bob Beyn, rhp, Taft (Calif.) HS
28. **Donald Neugebauer, 1b, Cal State Fullerton**
29. **Anthony Spano, of, Chapman (Calif.)**
30. Gregory Sikora, of, Lincoln HS, San Francisco
31. **James Langrill, lhp, Saddleback (Calif.) CC**
32. Gary Wann, rhp, Orange (Calif.) HS
33. Paul Husband, of, Wingfield HS, Jackson, Miss.
34. **Jared Holve, 1b/lhp, Clovis (Calif.) HS**
35. **Stephen Rosen, of, El Rancho HS, Pico Rivera, Calif.**
36. Richard Cox, lhp, Cal State Fullerton
37. **Phil Rose, c, Houston**
38. Joseph Mecca, of/rhp, Dunmore (Pa.) HS

June—Secondary Phase (23)

1. Robert Beach, rhp, Cabrillo (Calif.) JC
2. **Bruce Heinbechner, lhp, Los Angeles Pierce JC**
3. **Charles Jones, lhp, Grambling**

CHICAGO CUBS

January—Regular Phase (15)

1. Edgar Pate, lhp, Gardena, Calif.
2. Donald Highstreet, rhp, Cerritos (Calif.) JC
3. Edward Spell, rhp, Louisburg (N.C.) JC
4. **Robert Woods, 2b, Atlantic (N.J.) CC**
5. Willie Mims, of, Spoon River (Ill.) JC
6. **Dennis King, c, Claremont-Mudd (Calif.)**

January—Secondary Phase (11)

1. **Joseph Urbanovich, c, Villanova**
2. Douglas Ross, lhp, Arizona Western JC
3. Dana Baltzer, ss, San Diego

4. **Nacho Bracomontes, lhp, Chula Vista, Calif.**

June—Regular Phase (16)

1. **Roger Metzger, ss, St. Edward's (Texas)**
2. **Larry Gura, lhp, Arizona State**
3. **Gary James, lhp, Channel Islands HS, Oxnard, Calif.**
4. **James Davis, 1b, McKinley HS, Canton, Ohio**
5. **Daniel Corder, rhp, El Cajon (Calif.) HS**
6. Kevin Kooyman, c, St. Mary's HS, Lodi, Calif.
7. **James Brunette, 3b, Lewis (Ill.)**
8. **Robert White, of, Fort Cherry HS, Hickory, Pa.**
9. Edwin McLarty, 1b, Mississippi
10. **Jim Todd Jr., rhp, Millersville (Pa.)**
11. Robert Crain, ss, Muir HS, Altadena, Calif.
12. **Billy North, of, Central Washington**
13. Curtis Zimmerman, 1b, De LaSalle HS, New Orleans
14. Dan Hansen, ss, Western HS, Anaheim
15. **Steve Eckert, rhp, Moline (Ill.) HS**
16. Jay Smith, rhp, Boca Ciega HS, Treasure Island, Fla.
17. **Arthur Ganious, 1b, Southern**
18. **Thomas Hulderman, of, Monongah HS, Carolina, W.Va.**
19. Steve Kemnitzer, of, Klamath Falls (Ore.) HS
20. **Rufus Holton, of, St. Johns River (Fla.) CC**
21. **Gary Canepa, rhp, Lodi (Calif.) HS**
22. Dave Oliver, 2b, Franklin HS, Stockton, Calif.
23. **Horace Porter, 2b, Pfeiffer (N.C.)**
24. **James Johnson, 3b, Cal State Chico**
25. **Ralph Pipes, rhp, Fresno (Calif.) HS**
26. Carlos Suarez, lhp, Miami Beach (Fla.) HS
27. Randy Benson, lhp, East Rowan HS, Granite Quarry, N.C.
28. Andy Nelson, rhp, Everett (Wash.) HS
29. **Richard Bennett, rhp, East Meadow HS, Long Island, N.Y.**
30. **Michael Derr, ss, Mansfield (Pa.)**
31. Gary Ghidinelli, c, Santa Cruz (Calif.) HS
32. Carl Shumaker, of, Seminole (Fla.) JC
33. **Pat Bourque, of, Holy Cross**
34. **William Mansfield, rhp, Jacksonville**
35. **Phil Reser, of, Idaho**
36. Thomas Rosa, ss, Coral Park HS, Miami
37. Richard Gold, 2b, Florida State
38. **Arthur Oordt, 1b, Westmar (Iowa)**

June—Secondary Phase (24)

1. **Douglas Ross, lhp, Arizona Western JC**
2. Richard Wanless, rhp, Quincy, Mass.
3. **John Meyer, lhp, Ocean County (N.J.) JC**

CHICAGO WHITE SOX

January—Regular Phase (6)

1. **Richard Motsinger, ss/3b, Wingate (N.C.) JC**
2. Russell Almquist, lhp, Los Angeles Pierce JC
3. **Robert Ebersole, c/1b, Hagerstown (Md.) JC**
4. Larry Sisk, of, Gardner-Webb
5. Kirk Berger, rhp, York (Pa.)
6. Gerald Kelly, 3b, Gulf Coast (Fla.) JC

January—Secondary Phase (20)

1. **Ron Davini, c/of, Arizona State**
2. Pat Osborn, lhp, Manatee (Fla.) JC
3. Gary Bradshaw, rhp, Miami-Dade North CC
4. **Louis Billmeier, rhp, Nebraska-Omaha**
5. Ronald Kelam, of, Saint Louis
6. Douglas Smith, inf, Buena Vista

June—Regular Phase (3)

1. **Ted Nicholson, 3b, Oak Park HS, Laurel, Miss.**
2. **Pat Osburn, rhp, Carol City HS, Miami**
3. Richard Soriano, of, Hialeah HS, Miami
4. **Bill Clark, 3b, Southern Illinois**
5. Pedro Beato, rhp, Joliet (Ill.) West HS
6. Douglas Wessel, rhp, Webster Grove (Mo.) HS
7. **Bruce Kimm, c, Norway (Iowa) HS**
8. **Anthony Rodriguez, ss, St. Philip HS, Chicago**
9. Ruben Garcia, lhp, Brownfield (Texas) HS
10. **Wayne Francinques, ss, Tulane**
11. **Duane Shaffer, rhp, Garden Grove (Calif.) HS**
12. **Steven Tiemeier, lhp, Indian Hills (Iowa) CC**
13. Wayne Pitcock, of/1b, Arkansas State
14. **Thomas Fuller, c, San Diego CC**
15. Richard Austin, 2b, Coronado HS, Scotsdale, Ariz.
16. Thomas Cain, rhp, Wartburg (Iowa)
17. David Breshers, 2b, Iowa
18. **Jim MacDonnell, lhp, Wyoming**
19. **Glenn Redmon, 3b, Michigan**
20. **Barry O'Sullivan, 1b, Southern Illinois**
21. Patrick Sullivan, 1b, Verona (N.J.) HS
22. Timm Moore, of, Ellsworth (Iowa) JC
23. **Charlie Cromer, rhp, Appalachian State**
24. Alan Lindsay, lhp, Cherryville (N.C.) HS
25. **Mark Marquess, 1b, Stanford**
26. **Cleothus Jackson, lhp, Jackson State**
27. **Dan Rourke, ss, Upper Iowa**
28. Timothy Peden, c, Kermit (Texas) HS
29. **Gregg Boehning, lhp, Jefferson HS, Lafayette, Ind.**
30. **Lewis Braddy, ss, Stillman (Ala.)**
31. **Kenneth Samuels, rhp, Stillman (Ala.)**
32. **Gary Isakson, of/rhp, Elmwood Park (Ill.) HS**
33. James Pratt, of, Chataro HS, Indianapolis
34. **Allen Rajanen, c, Superior (Wis.) HS**
35. **Fred Norton, of, Connellsville (Pa.) HS**
36. Louis Lodigiani, of, South San Francisco HS

June—Secondary Phase (17)

1. **Michael Baldwin, lhp, Sacramento (Calif.) CC**
2. Tom Thomas, 3b, Menlo (Calif.) JC
3. **Rich Hinton, lhp, Arizona**
4. **Jim Mueller, of, Arkansas State**

CINCINNATI REDS

January—Regular Phase (13)

1. **John Jackson, rhp, Mount San Antonio (Calif.) JC**
2. Buford Woods, rhp, Bacone (Okla.) JC
3. Andrew Brown, of/3b, Blinn (Texas) JC
4. Orman Warren, rhp, East Los Angeles JC
5. Benton Ragland, 3b, Ranger (Texas) JC
6. **Timothy White, c, Arizona**
7. **Frederick Sarazen, 1b/of, North Texas State**
8. Michael Campbell, rhp, Hill (Texas) JC

January—Secondary Phase (17)

1. **Ross Grimsley II, lhp, Jackson State (Tenn.) CC**
2. **Theodore Tomasovich, 1b, Georgia Tech**
3. David Barnes, rhp, Murray State (Okla.) JC
4. Daniel Misko, lhp, Gulf Coast (Fla.) CC
5. Nicholas Furlong, rhp, Notre Dame
6. James Mertens, 1b, Fairmont State (W.Va.)

June—Regular Phase (14)

1. **Don Gullett, lhp, McKell HS, Lynn, Ky.**
2. **Kent Burdick, of, Parker HS, Janesville, Wis.**
3. **Rawly Eastwick, rhp, Haddonfield (N.J.) HS**
4. **Mike Ruddell, ss/rhp, Lakewood (Calif.) HS**
5. **Clarence Cooper, lhp/1b, Frederick (Md.) HS**
6. **Barry Powell, ss, Pleasanton (Texas) HS**
7. **Ronald Steele, of, Heights HS, Wichita, Texas**
8. **Robert Gallagher, of, Pennsville (N.J.) HS**
9. Emery Mitchell, c, Encina HS, Sacramento, Calif.
10. **Phillip Babcock, rhp, Fort Ann HS, Comstock, N.Y.**
11. **Steven Miller, rhp, Marshall**
12. **Nardi Contreras, rhp, Tampa Catholic HS**
13. **Tim Bolton, lhp, Minor HS, Birmingham, Ala.**
14. William Guy, rhp, Thomson (Ga.) HS
15. **Robert Dreher, c, Springdale (Pa.) HS**
16. Mike Cosgrove, lhp, Bourgade HS, Phoenix
17. **Richard Homan, rhp, Springfield (Mass.) Tech HS**
18. Ronald Procter, c, Frederick (Md.) HS
19. **Kerry Hardiman, rhp, St. Bernard Parish (La.) CC**
20. Tom Spencer, of, Gallia Academy HS, Gallipolis, Ohio
21. Larry O'Brien, 1b, Lakewood HS, Long Beach, Calif.
22. Jackie Brown, ss/of, Starmount-Boonville HS, Jonesville, N.C.
23. Roger Gregg, c, Southwestern (Calif.) JC

24. Robert McConnaugh, ss, West Liberty State
25. Michael Couzzi, inf/of, Trenton State (N.J.)
26. Mac Scarce, lhp, Manatee (Fla.) JC
27. **DeWayne Kerr, of/rhp, Corsicana (Texas) HS**
28. Randall Fowler, c, Eunice (N.M.) HS
29. **Ken Griffey Sr., of, Donora (Pa.) HS**
30. Stephen Klinger, lhp, Bloomsburg
31. **Ronald Swaim, lhp, Sparkman HS, Madison, Ala.**
32. Ronald Hayes, rhp, Monahans (Texas) HS
33. **Robert Young, ss, Rutgers**
34. Melvin Robinson, lhp, Tarboro (N.C.) HS
35. Michael Clancy, c, Bishop Kelley HS, Tulsa, Okla.
36. **Rowe Miller, c, O.D. Wyatt HS, Fort Worth, Texas**

June—Secondary Phase (14)

1. Johnny Grubb Jr., of, Manatee (Fla.) JC
2. **William Ferguson, c, Texas Christian**
3. **Andrew Brown, of, Blinn (Texas) JC**
4. **Carl Bennett, c, San Joaquin Delta (Calif.) JC**
5. James Mertens, 1b, Fairmont State (W.Va.)

CLEVELAND INDIANS

January—Regular Phase (16)

1. Steve Wahl, 2b/ss, Los Angeles
2. Allen Hardin, ss, Polk (Fla.) CC
3. Rocky Jackson, 2b, Yakima Valley (Wash.) JC
4. David Chaffee, lhp/1b, Newman Prep, Melrose, Mass.
5. Barry Parker, c, Southern Tech Institute (Fla.)
6. **Donald Gray, inf, CC of Baltimore**
7. William Hall, of/lhp, San Joaquin Delta (Calif.) JC
8. Christopher Scott, 2b, Cleveland
9. Steven Woods, lhp, Kansas State
10. John Meyer, lhp, Ocean County (N.J.) JC
11. Peter Poldiak, rhp, Gulf Coast (Fla.) CC
12. Stanley Charzewski, c, Staten Island (N.Y.)

January—Secondary Phase (6)

1. William Ward, rhp, Southern Tech Institute (Fla.)
2. Bill Jenkins, ss, Orange Coast (Calif.) JC
3. Freddie Howard, of/1b, Paris (Texas) JC
4. Rich Hinton, lhp, Arizona
5. Craig Schell, rhp, UC Santa Barbara
6. Alex Duncan, rhp, Cuyahoga (Ohio) CC
7. Ken Conlin, inf, Columbia Basin (Wash.) CC
8. Barry Herron, c, Kansas State
9. William Hunt, ss, Louisiana State
10. Larry Tipton, ss/2b, Blinn (Texas) JC
11. Johnny Rushing, lhp, John C. Calhoun (Ala.) CC
12. Mitchell Laird, rhp, Oklahoma Military Academy

June—Regular Phase (15)

1. **Alvin McGrew, of, Parker HS, Fairfield, Ala.**
2. **Victor Ambrose, 2b, Albuquerque**
3. **Alan Ashby, c, San Pedro (Calif.) HS**
4. **Rich Hinton, rhp, Laffette HS, Lexington, Ky.**
5. Michael Ellwood, rhp, West Bloomfield HS, Orchard Lake, Mich.
6. **Michael Pompili, rhp, Toledo**
7. **Jerry Bond, of, Southern Illinois**
8. **Rob Belloir, ss, Mercer**
9. **William Duffy, lhp, Kimball HS, Dallas, Texas**
10. **Michael Young, 2b, Timmonsville (S.C.) HS**
11. **Thomas Sullivan, rhp, Dover (Del.) HS**
12. Robert Perkins, lhp, Lake Wales (Fla.) HS
13. **Richard Magnante, 3b, UC Santa Barbara**
14. **Richard Ray, of, Prosser (Wash.) HS**
15. Stanley Hamlin, rhp, Taft (Calif.) HS
16. **Buddy Bell, 2b, Moeller HS, Cincinnati**
17. **Gary Gloede, of, Parker HS, Janesville, Wis.**
18. **Daniel Maluzhinsky, rhp, Lamphere HS, Madison Heights, Mich.**
19. **Carl Wiggins, of, Latta HS, Sellers, S.C.**
20. Robert Verbeck, c, Ward HS, Kansas City, Kan.
21. **Roger Williams, 3b/ss, Raytown (Mo.) HS**
22. **Joseph Ruby, lhp, Arizona State**
23. **Mike Easom, 3b, Florida State**
24. **Nicholas Hockett, lhp, Northeast HS, St. Petersburg, Fla.**
25. **Ernest McMahan, rhp, Garret HS, Charleston Heights, S.C.**
26. **John Wheeler, rhp, Tampa, Fla.**
27. **Jerry Haggard, 2b, Texas Tech**
28. Dennis Smith, 1b, Bowling Green HS, Weston, Ohio
29. Ken Kravec, lhp, Mid Park HS, Middleburgh Heights, Ohio
30. **Vincent Pope, of, Glenville HS, Cleveland**
31. **Mike Bradley, c, Notre Vista HS, Riverside, Calif.**
32. **Bill Tsoukalas, lhp, Seattle**
33. **Denny Thomas, lhp, Perkins HS, Sandusky, Ohio**
34. **Harry Fry, rhp, Marion (Ohio) Harding HS**
35. Rex Carrow, 2b, East Lansing (Mich.) HS
36. **Tommie Bozich, ss, Northeast HS, St. Petersburg, Fla.**
37. **James Koch, c, St. Mary's (Texas)**
38. **Raymond Johnson, of/1b, Mount San Antonio (Calif.) JC**
39. James Smith, of, Montebello HS, Monterey Park, Calif.
40. **William Dew, of, UNC Wilmington**
41. **Perry Yearwood, rhp, Randolph-Macon**
42. **James Sanders, 3b, Ledford HS, Thomasville, N.C.**
43. Donald Wallace, 1b/of, San Bernardino Valley (Calif.) JC

June—Secondary Phase (1)

1. **Rich Hand, rhp, Puget Sound (Wash.)**
2. Robert Eldridge, rhp, Southern Illinois
3. **Stephen Boland, rhp, South Georgia JC**
4. Bill Dobbs, lhp, Oklahoma State
5. William Camp, rhp, Oklahoma State

DETROIT TIGERS

January—Regular Phase (20)

1. Ralph Edwards, c/of, Miami-Dade North CC
2. **Michael Belcik, c, Toledo**
3. Michael Chaney, of, Chabot (Calif.) JC
4. William Knight, c, Port Huron (Mich.) JC
5. **Jack Nelson, rhp, Fullerton (Calif.) JC**
6. **Joe McIlvaine, rhp, St. Charles Seminary, Narbeth, Pa.**

January—Secondary Phase (16)

1. John Young, 1b, Fullerton (Calif.) JC
2. **Bruce Finkbeiner, of, Colorado**
3. Peter Brown, rhp, Chabot (Calif.) JC
4. **Nils Lambert, lhp, Staten Island (N.Y.)**
5. Edwin Mossman, 3b, Central Missouri State

June—Regular Phase (19)

1. **John Young, 1b, Enterprise HS, Redding, Calif.**
2. **Harry Kendrick, c, Michigan State**
3. **Bill Gilbreth, lhp, Abilene Christian**
4. **James Newhook, of, St. Helena HS, Whitestone, N.Y.**
5. **Hether Hether, ss, Norwood**
6. **Lerrin LaGrow, rhp, Arizona State**
7. Daniel Bielski, rhp, Michigan State
8. **James Smith, rhp, Connecticut**
9. **Mark Giegler, ss, Milford (Mich.) HS**
10. **Robert Service, ss, Central HS, Ilion, N.Y.**
11. Wayne Miller, lhp, Newark (Calif.) HS
12. **Michael Fremuth, rhp, Princeton**
13. Kris Silverthorn, of, Thomas Jefferson HS, Dallas
14. Brad Van Pelt, rhp, Owosso (Mich.) HS
15. Eugene LaFave, rhp, St. Francis DeSales HS, Detroit
16. **Dave DuBois, lhp, Elsie HS, Ovid, Mich.**
17. Bruce Vida, rhp, Ecorse (Mich.) HS
18. **Richard Schroellucke, ss, Algonac (Mich.) HS**
19. **Richard Krumm, rhp, Eastern Michigan**
20. Daniel Gibson, rhp, Hazlewood (Mo.) HS
21. Gary Gentle, c, Belleville (Mich.) HS
22. Frank Crachiolo, c, St. Ambrose HS, Detroit
23. Doug Konieczny, rhp, St. Ladislaus HS, Detroit
24. **Mike Jacobs, of, Ohio Northern**
25. Timothy Dean, inf/rhp, Mansfield (Ohio) HS
26. John Scotto, of/rhp, Holy Cross HS, Queens Village, N.Y.
27. Daniel Ruth, 1b, Colorado
28. John Womack, c, Ecorse (Mich.) HS
29. **Stephen Knowlton, lhp, Genesee (Mich.) HS**
30. Anthony Aquila, rhp, Woodbridge HS, Avenel, N.J.

31. **Daniel McGraw, 2b, Cass Tech HS, Detroit**
32. Robert Dillow, c, Loyola HS, Bayside, N.Y.
33. Robert Moug, 3b, Red Ford HS, Detroit
34. Edward Plomer, c, Red Ford HS, Detroit

June—Secondary Phase (21)

1. William Bright, of, Brevard (Fla.) CC
2. George Pugh, lhp, Mesa (Ariz.) CC
3. Stephen Steitz, 3b/of, Springfield (Mass.)

HOUSTON ASTROS

January—Regular Phase (1)

1. **Derrel Thomas, ss, Dorsey HS, Los Angeles**
2. Craig Caskey, lhp, Yakima Valley (Wash.) JC
3. Charles Benjamin, c, St. Petersburg (Fla.) JC

January—Secondary Phase (3)

1. **Bob McRoberts, of, Grossmont (Calif.) JC**
2. **Gary Howard, of, Yuba (Calif.) CC**
3. **Herman Jordan, of, Middle Georgia JC**
4. William Bright, inf/of, Brevard (Fla.) CC

June—Regular Phase (2)

1. **J.R. Richard, rhp, Lincoln HS, Ruston, La.**
2. **Stan Papi, ss, Bullard HS, Fresno, Calif.**
3. **Harlon Keller, c, Taft (Calif.) HS**
4. **Larry Elenes, rhp, Western HS, Buena Park, Calif.**
5. **Robert Fernley, ss, Torrance (Calif.) HS**
6. Willard Ester, rhp, Carver HS, Houston
7. **Bruce Thomas, rhp, Queen Annes HS, Centerville, Md.**
8. **John Dolinsek, of, Arizona State**
9. **Anthony Sturtevant, of, McGill Institute HS, Mobile, Ala.**
10. **Leroy Martin, rhp, Alisal HS, Salinas, Calif.**
11. Thomas White, lhp, Amherst (Mass.) HS
12. Charles Bates, ss/3b, Dominquez HS, Compton, Calif.
13. **Mark Keller, lhp, Wilson HS, Long Beach, Calif.**
14. **Mike Easler, 3b, Benedictine HS, Cleveland**
15. **Jerome Hutchinson, rhp, Raines HS, Jacksonville, Fla.**
16. Vernon Davis, rhp, Tucson (Ariz.) HS
17. Jack Rhine, c, Riviera Beach (Fla.) HS
18. **Henry Moore, lhp, Centennial HS, Los Angeles**
19. Michael Nelson, 1b, Eisenhower HS, Yakima, Wash.
20. Albert Hughes, ss, Beckley, W.Va. (Selection voided)
21. Cecil Norris, of, South Park HS, Beaumont, Texas
22. James Hooks, ss, Jones (Okla.) HS
23. **Kyle Shook, rhp, Beaumont (Texas) HS**
24. **Charles Taylor, rhp, Eastern Kentucky**
25. **Thomas Lehman, lhp, Miami**
26. **Alan Schmidt, 2b, Dayton**
27. **Adolph Carter, ss, Courter Tech, Cincinnati**
28. Arnold Alaniz, inf, Kingsville (Texas) HS
29. Gary Bullion, rhp, Weslaco (Texas) HS

June—Secondary Phase (22)

1. **Matthew Rosiek, rhp, Indian River (Fla.) CC**

KANSAS CITY ROYALS

January—Regular Phase (22)

1. **Ronald Opatkiewicz, ss, Mount San Antonio (Calif.) JC**
2. Dennis Nicholson, rhp, JC of the Sequoias (Calif.)
3. Steve Lee, lhp, Los Angeles Valley JC
4. Edward Hopkins, 1b, Kansas State
5. Larry Prieto, 2b, Fresno (Calif.) CC
6. **Steve Moore, of, Santa Barbara (Calif.) CC**
7. Reginald Carney, 1b, Fork Union (Va.) Military Academy
8. John Jackson, of, Pasadena (Calif.) CC

January—Secondary Phase (24)

1. Darrell Downey, c, Ventura (Calif.) JC
2. Charles Kurkjian, 3b, Fresno (Calif.) CC
3. **Lloyd Lightfoot, ss, North Carolina A&T State**
4. **Van Winters, rhp, Fresno (Calif.) CC**
5. Dennis Gallagher, ss, Yuba (Calif.) CC
6. **Dave Thornton, of, American River (Calif.) JC**
7. **Paul Walton, rhp, Amesbury, Mass.**
8. No selection
9. Steve Griffith, rhp, Golden West (Calif.) JC
10. **James Kleckley, rhp, Columbia, S.C.**
11. **Tom Pratt, lhp, Hancock (Calif.) JC**
12. Richard Trapp, ss, Florida

June—Regular Phase (23)

1. John Simmons, ss/rhp, Childersburg (Ala.) HS
2. **Howard Phillips, ss, Fresno (Calif.) HS**
3. A.C. Moseley, 1b, Mobile (Ala.) County Training HS
4. **Al Autry, rhp, Grace Davis HS, Modesto, Calif.**
5. **Keith Marshall, of, Loara HS, Anaheim**
6. **Edward Siracusa, of, Los Gatos (Calif.) HS**
7. Gerald Mantlo, c, Poly HS, Long Beach, Calif.
8. **Tom Lugo, ss, Sweetwater Union HS, National City, Calif.**
9. Doug Bridges, lhp, Andalusia (Ala.) HS
10. **James Smith, c, Centennial HS, Compton, Calif.**
11. **Thomas Luck, lhp, Spotsylvania HS, Bumpass, Va.**
12. Eric Raich, rhp, Dominguez HS, South Gate, Calif.
13. **James Buzzard, ss, Glynn Academy, Brunswick, Ga.**
14. **Michael McGrath, lhp, Pershing**
15. David Sasser, 1b, Groves HS, Garden City, Ga.
16. **Jim York, rhp, UCLA**
17. Murry Parish, rhp, Carroll HS, Corpus Christi, Texas
18. David Bewley, rhp, Sarasota (Fla.) HS
19. **James Pappas, c, Kennedy HS, Bethpage, N.Y.**
20. **Ron Clark, rhp, Santa Fe HS, Norwalk, Calif.**
21. **Toby Heath, 1b, Santa Ana (Calif.) JC**
22. **Louis Crua, rhp, Southern State (Ohio) CC**
23. Robert Maneely, rhp, St. Joseph HS, Deptford, N.J.
24. **John Stankey, of, Westmont**
25. **Hugh Waln, of, Fauquier HS, Warrenton, Va.**
26. John Jones, lhp, Russell (Ky.) HS
27. **Art Demery, rhp, Wasco (Calif.) Union HS**
28. **Randy Hammon, rhp, Serra HS, Gardena, Calif.**
29. **Greg Kinder, rhp, La Habra (Calif.) HS**
30. **Victor Price, of, Langley HS, McLean, Va.**
31. **Michael Prieto, of, JC of San Mateo (Calif.)**
32. **Gary Sanserino, ss, UCLA**
33. Kenneth Comer, ss, Minnetonka HS, Excelsior, Minn.
34. **Nathaniel Riggin, ss, Highland Springs (Va.) HS**
35. Lou Berthelson, c, Simi (Calif.) HS
36. Dan Knight, c, Darlington Prep, Lyndale, Ga.
37. **Edward McFarland, 2b, Bowdoin**
38. George Chavez, rhp, Delano (Calif.) HS
39. George Wheeler, rhp, Lanier HS, Montgomery, Ala.
40. **Timothy Pickering, 3b, Camarillo (Calif.) HS**
41. **Lloyd Gladden, rhp, Cal State Los Angeles**
42. **Mike Witt, of, Fresno (Calif.) CC**
43. Wesley Jermyn, ss, Los Angeles Baptist HS
44. **Guy Hansen, rhp, UCLA**
45. John Varga, ss/2b, Queen Anne HS, Seattle
46. Mike Fitzsimmons, of, Monterey Union HS, Del Ray Oaks, Calif.
47. **Frank Ortenzio, of, San Joaquin Memorial HS, Fresno, Calif.**
48. Joseph Borchard, of, Moorpark (Calif.) JC
49. **Charles Burt, rhp, Southwest Missouri State**
50. **Larry Newton, ss, Roxboro HS, Hurdle Mills, N.C.**
51. **Gerald Metivier, 3b, Cal State Los Angeles**
52. **Steven Lizak, 2b, St. John's**
53. **Dean Owens, 3b, West Torrance (Calif.) HS**
54. Gene Kerr, rhp, Montebello (Calif.) HS
55. **Mike Ballantine, rhp, Anaheim HS**
56. **Michael Patrick, rhp, Rancho Alamitos HS, Garden Grove, Calif.**
57. John Helfrick, 3b, Hoover HS, San Diego
58. Glen Berberet, 1b, Long Beach (Calif.) CC
59. **Frank Wright, 1b, Cal State Los Angeles**
60. Aaron Braithwaite, rhp, Long Beach (Calif.) CC
61. Charles Dickinson, ss, Hattiesburg (Miss.) HS
62. Robert McKeel, rhp, Harding
63. Robert Spohr, rhp, Hilltop HS, Chula Vista, Calif.
64. David Hazelip, rhp, Trezevant HS, Memphis, Tenn.
65. James Lasher, rhp, Kennedy HS, Utica, N.Y.
66. Robert Lopresti, rhp, Birmingham HS, Encino, Calif.

67. **Kim Giffoni, rhp, Santa Monica HS, Malibu, Calif.**
68. James Richardson, 1b, Churchland HS, Chesapeake, Va.
69. Robert Williams, rhp, Pius X HS, Downey, Calif.
70. David Brunell, rhp, Bell (Calif.) HS
71. Larry Klein, lhp, Santa Monica (Calif.) JC
72. Steve Bisceglia, rhp, Bullard HS, Fresno, Calif.
73. Donald Shaw, 3b, Pacific Palisades (Calif.) HS
74. Richard Auckland, 1b, West Chester (Pa.)
75. **Al Cowens Jr., ss, Centennial HS, Los Angeles**
76. John Behrens, 2b, San Joaquin Memorial HS, Fresno, Calif.
77. Robert Proechel, c, Franklin Academy, Malone, N.Y.
78. Bill Akers, c, Burlington (Colo.) HS
79. Gary Mack, 2b, Western HS, Los Alamitos, Calif.
80. **Donald Weir, rhp, Nevada**
81. **Mark Stoner, ss, Burroughs HS, Ridgecrest, Calif.**
82. **William Olin, 2b, Pasadena (Calif.) CC**
83. Gary Rausch, lhp, Girard HS, Lake City, Pa.
84. Richard Haderer, rhp, Mills HS, Burlingame, Calif.
85. **Steven Nielsen, lhp, Cal Poly Pomona**
86. **Brian Smith, rhp, North Torrance (Calif.) HS**
87. Mike Seberger, rhp, Bellflower (Calif.) HS
88. Gregory Hopkins, of, Darlington Prep HS, Lyndale, Ga.
89. Roy Petersen, of/1b, Somerville (Mass.) HS
90. James Beal, 2b, Westchester HS, Los Angeles

June—Secondary Phase (15)

1. **Michael Nichols, lhp, Biola**
2. **Stanley Grout, rhp, Perry, Iowa**
3. **Doug Bird, rhp, Mount San Antonio (Calif.) JC**
4. **Thomas Joyce, ss/2b, San Francisco State**
5. **Jeff Stout, 3b/ss, Mount San Antonio (Calif.) JC**
6. Gary Addeo, rhp, Cerritos (Calif.) JC
7. Stephen Griffith, rhp, Golden West (Calif.) JC
8. Larry Diel, ss, Cerritos (Calif.) JC

LOS ANGELES DODGERS

January—Regular Phase (5)

1. **Michael Kimbrell, 2b, Birmingham, Ala.**
2. **Lee Lacy, 3b, Laney (Calif.) JC**
3. Carl Salyers, rhp, Southwestern Christian (Texas) JC
4. **Bob O'Brien, lhp, Fresno (Calif.) CC**
5. Dean Voegerl, lhp, Trinidad State (Colo.) JC
6. Dave Maas, 2b, Fullerton (Calif.) JC

January—Secondary Phase (9)

1. **Pat Harrison, inf, Southern California**
2. William Camp, rhp, Oklahoma State
3. George Pugh, lhp, Mesa (Ariz.) CC
4. William Ferguson, 1b/c, Texas Christian
5. Alan Putz, 1b, Springfield (Mass.)

June—Regular Phase (8)

1. **Terry McDermott, c, St. Agnes HS, West Hempstead, N.Y.**
2. **Lee Lacy, lhp, Putnam City HS, Bethany, Okla.**
3. **Albert Dawson, rhp, Lyndhurst (N.J.) HS**
4. **Bob O'Brien, of, Texas A&M**
5. **Mark Mechuk, rhp, St. Bernards HS, El Segundo, Calif.**
6. **Stan Wall, lhp, Raytown (Mo.) South HS**
7. **James Cardasis, of, New York**
8. **Kenneth Bruno, ss, Cliffside Park HS, Palisades Park, N.J.**
9. **Larry President, lhp, Temple (Texas) HS**
10. **Ron Mitchell, of, Agua Fria HS, Avondale, Ariz.**
11. **John Hughes, 1b, Parkwood HS, Joplin, Mo.**
12. **Stanley Russell, rhp/1b, Villa Park HS, Anaheim**
13. Ronald Dolan, 2b, Seton Hall
14. **Arthur Pauls, rhp, Lewis (Ill.)**
15. Roy Staiger, ss, Bacone (Okla.) JC
16. Jimmy Page, rhp, Hardesty (Okla.) HS
17. Edgar Bellamy, ss/2b, Fort Cobb (Okla.) HS
18. Mark Pastrovich, lhp, Mascoutah (Ill.) HS
19. Anthony Blakely, ss, Sullivan West HS, Kingsport, Tenn.
20. Donald Sweetland, c, Saddleback (Calif.) CC
21. **Joseph Szewezyk, 1b/of, New York**
22. **Royle Stillman, of, North Torrance (Calif.) HS**
23. **Manuel Washington, of, Mississippi State**
24. **David Allen, lhp, California Western**
25. Blake Owen, 3b, Willington (Tenn.) HS
26. Jim Fuller, of, San Diego CC
27. Johnny Hatcher, rhp, Andrews (Texas) HS
28. Harry Chapman, rhp, Sarasota (Fla.) HS
29. George Horman, c/3b, Crawford HS, San Diego
30. Nick Devirgilis, of, Sarasota (Fla.) HS
31. Jeffrey Hogan, ss, Florida State
32. Raymond Ippolito, ss, New York
33. Robert Cox, rhp, Southeast HS, Wichita, Kan.
34. **Vince D'Amico, 1b, Albuquerque**
35. **Jerry Arnold, lhp, Woodward (Okla.) HS**
36. William Wyles, lhp, New Mexico Military Institute JC
37. Gary Granville, of, El Camino (Calif.) JC
38. Johnny Rodgers, inf/of, Tech HS, Omaha, Neb.
39. Gary Erskine, of/lhp, Anderson (Ind.) HS
40. **Dennis Haren, of, Bishop Montgomery HS, Torrance, Calif.**
41. Rodney Boone, c, Crawford HS, San Diego
42. **Robert Sicilia, of, Rogers HS, Spokane, Wash.**
43. **Robert Payne, of, UC Riverside**

June—Secondary Phase (8)

1. **Bill Seinsoth, 1b, Southern California**
2. **Bob Randall, ss, Kansas State**
3. **Steven Wilmet, lhp, St. Norbert**
4. **Randall Bayer, of/1b, Mesa (Ariz.) CC**

MINNESOTA TWINS

January—Regular Phase (8)

1. **Gary Wilburn, c, Gardena, Calif.**
2. **Jimmy Smith, 1b, Van Nuys, Calif.**
3. Gorman Erickson, of, Northridge, Calif.
4. **Marc Scoville, ss, Riverside (Calif.) CC**
5. John Gaylord, lhp, Chaffey (Calif.) JC
6. **Kelly Godfrey, of, Mount San Antonio (Calif.) JC**
7. **Ralph Zuniga, rhp, Chaffey (Calif.) JC**
8. Barry Woodruff, lhp, JC of San Mateo (Calif.)
9. **Ray Strable, rhp, Fresno State**
10. **Ronald Shotts, of/3b, Stanford**
11. Leroy McDonald, ss, Grand Canyon (Ariz.)

January—Secondary Phase (10)

1. John Hurley, rhp, Michigan
2. **Tom Nichols, ss, Mississippi**
3. **Richard Perry, rhp, Independence, Mo.**
4. Gary Addeo, rhp, Paramount, Calif.
5. **Bob Wissler, ss, Cal Poly Pomona**
6. **Ronald Pritchett, rhp, Mount San Antonia (Calif.) JC**
7. **Roger Mayer, c, Colorado**
8. Mike Douglas, 1b, Cerritos (Calif.) JC
9. Jim Mueller, of, Arkansas State
10. **Richard Gouin, of, California Western**
11. Robert Shearer, ss/2b, Indian River (Fla.) CC

June—Regular Phase (7)

1. **Paul Powell, of, Arizona State**
2. **Ron McDonald, 3b, South HS, Covina, Calif.**
3. **Bert Blyleven, rhp, Santiago HS, Garden Grove, Calif.**
4. **Ronald Adams, lhp, Jefferson HS, Carter Lake, Iowa**
5. **Byron Emick, of, Grandledge (Mich.) HS**
6. **Richard Osentowski, of, Kearney State**
7. **Greg Jaycox, rhp/1b, Channel Island HS, Oxnard, Calif.**
8. Rick Burleson, ss, Warren HS, South Gate, Calif.
9. **John Braun, rhp, Marion (Wis.) HS**
10. Gary Atwell, of, Kennedy HS, Buena Park, Calif.
11. **Thomas Schmidt, rhp, Central HS, La Crosse, Wis.**
12. Gregory Bero, c, Ferra HS, Gardena, Calif.
13. **Bill Barnes, lhp, South Hills HS, Covina, Calif.**
14. **Mike Dion, c, St. Paul HS, Santa Fe Springs, Calif.**
15. **Reynold Lyczak, 3b/ss, Burlington HS, Burlington Township, N.J.**
16. **Dan Vossler, rhp, UC Riverside**
17. **James Koering, rhp, Iowa**
18. Rand Rasmussen, ss, Millikan HS, Long Beach, Calif.
19. **Ted Remington, rhp, Parsons**

20. Gregory Zail, rhp, St. Paul HS, Santa Fe Springs, Calif.
21. **Kenneth Knight, of, Victoria HS, Telferner, Texas**
22. **Joseph Bochy, c, Jefferson HS, Falls Church, Va.**
23. **William Giffin, rhp, Eastern Michigan**
24. **Greg Gustafson, c, Bellingham (Wash.) HS**
25. Jerry Johnson, lhp, Oregon State
26. Brent Estee, lhp, Pershing
27. **Thomas Thompson, 3b, Fairfax (Va.) HS**
28. Terry Evans, lhp, Woodbridge (Va.) HS
29. **Robert Love, 3b, Hixon HS, Chattanooga, Tenn.**
30. Daniel Boettcher, rhp, Radnor HS, Rosemont, Pa. (Selection voided)
31. **Arthur Gordon, rhp, Washington HS, Cairo, Ga.**
32. **Richard Judkins, rhp, Goffstown (N.H.) HS**
33. **Jim Hughes, rhp, St. Bernards HS, Los Angeles**
34. **James Michael, rhp, Loras**
35. **David Schmidt, ss, Fresno State**
36. **Wayne Parks, rhp, St. Cloud State**
37. **Charles Wheeler, ss, Buena Vista (Ga.) HS**
38. Wilson Raines, rhp, Johnson HS, Laurinburg, N.C. (Selection voided)
39. **Steven Hardin, rhp, Pisgah HS, Camton, N.C.**
40. **David Nieman, of, Augustana**
41. **Jeff Snowdon, lhp, Jefferson HS, Denver**
42. **Keith Sonnichen, of/rhp, Carthage (Wis.)**
43. Craig Barnes, lhp, South Hills HS, Covina, Calif.
44. **Neal Emerson, lhp, Coon Rapids (Minn.) HS**
45. **Lee Palas, lhp, Elvader HS, St. Olaf, Iowa**
46. Michael Dlugach, c, Overton HS, Memphis, Tenn.
47. James Skogstad, rhp, Metropolitan State
48. Jim Otto, ss, North Hennepin (Minn.) CC

June—Secondary Phase (3)

1. **Ralph Dick, of, Arizona State**
2. **Leroy McDonald, ss, Grand Canyon (Ariz.)**
3. Peter Halfman, of, American River (Calif.) JC
4. **Patrick Bezeka, of, Southern Colorado**
5. George Swanson, of/1b, Miami-Dade North CC
6. Ron Cash, 3b/ss, Manatee (Fla.) JC

MONTREAL EXPOS

January—Regular Phase (21)

1. Larry Diel, ss, Cerritos (Calif.) JC
2. Robert Flynn, of/2b, Miami-Dade North CC
3. No selection
4. William Greener, of, Hill (Texas) JC
5. **Keith Lefevre, rhp, Marrero, La.**
6. Mike Henderson, rhp, Mount San Antonio (Calif.) JC
7. **Steve Wagner, 1b/of, Mount San Antonio (Calif.) JC**
8. Norman Boles, c, Springfield, Mo.
9. Charles Ramshaw, ss, Southern California

January—Secondary Phase (23)

1. **Gene Salmon, 1b, Texas**
2. Alan Hansen, rhp, Grossmont (Calif.) JC
3. No selection
4. Roger Sizoo, c, Citrus (Calif.) JC
5. Jeff Stout, 3b, Mount San Antonio (Calif.) JC
6. **Steve Angelo, rhp/3b, Rio Hondo (Calif.) JC**

June—Regular Phase (22)

1. **Balor Moore, lhp, Deer Park (Texas) HS**
2. James Kocoloski, ss, Shadyside Academy, Monroeville, Pa.
3. No selection
4. **John Reid, ss, Colgate**
5. **Elisco Pompa, of, Mission (Texas) HS**
6. Harry Conlan, of, West Haven (Conn.) HS
7. **Todd Brentlinger, rhp, Los Altos (Calif.) HS**
8. Bill Sanford, c, Los Altos (Calif.) HS
9. Timothy Coffin, rhp, Palos Verde HS, Rolling Hills, Calif.
10. Robert Mollenhauer, 2b, St. Mary's HS, Elizabeth, N.J.
11. **Lincoln Clark, ss, Northwestern HS, Detroit**
12. Richard Brown, of/1b, DeAnza (Calif.) JC
13. **Stephen Keller, rhp, Loyola Marymount**
14. **Robert Schleider, rhp, A&M Consolidated HS, College Station, Texas**
15. **Orval Vickery, rhp, Ben Crain HS, Mobile, Ala.**
16. **James Sparkman, of/rhp, Houston**
17. Bradford Graff, ss, Appleton (Wis.) HS
18. **John Reen, c, Seminole (Fla.) JC**
19. **Randolph Brunner, 1b/rhp, Westminster HS, Atlanta**
20. Jack Garrett, rhp, Eastern Hills HS, Fort Worth, Texas
21. David Fressa, rhp, Clawson (Mich.) HS
22. **Gerard Castaldo, c/ss, Bayonne (N.J.) HS**
23. **Brian Abraham, lhp, Biloxi (Miss.) HS**
24. Thomas Mims, of, Drew (Miss.) HS
25. **Donald Klinger, 2b, Rider**
26. **Patrick Russell, rhp, Nazareth HS, Brooklyn, N.Y.**
27. Joseph Flannery, of/rhp, South Plainfield (N.J.) HS
28. James Ellison, lhp, Peterson HS, Santa Clara, Calif.
29. **James Rispoli, of, New Haven (Conn.)**
30. **Mike Popevec, c, San Jose State**
31. James Hatfield, rhp, Hydro (Okla.) HS
32. Mike Kedulich, c, Workman HS, La Puente, Calif.
33. Albert Nocciolo, c, Hart HS, Saugus, Calif.
34. Steve Gulloti, ss/3b, Sierra HS, Whittier, Calif.
35. **Boris Kopylow, rhp, Sierra HS, Whittier, Calif.**
36. **James McClain, rhp, Santa Clara**
37. Paul Ray Meaut, lhp, Notre Dame HS, Biloxi, Miss.
38. Daniel Cook, 3b, Southwest Missouri State
39. **Terry Humphrey, c/1b, Los Angeles CC**
40. **Ed Fisher, rhp, Valdosta State (Ga.)**
41. Henry Holmes, 1b, Forest Hill HS, West Palm Beach, Fla.
42. Martin Henderson, 1b, Nassau (N.Y.) CC
43. **Robert Williams, rhp, St. Louis CC-Meramec**
44. Gerald Mosley, 2b, Kirkwood (Mo.) HS
45. William Borelli, of/1b, Santa Clara
46. **Terry Tuck, of, San Antonio, Texas**
47. **Jack Robinson, of, Cincinnati**
48. Lee Pelekoudas, rhp, Homestead HS, Sunnyvale, Calif.
49. **Dave LaPointe, ss, Vermont**
50. Steve Fanning, 3b, South Hampton (N.Y.) HS
51. Lawrence Bock, ss, Riviera Beach (Fla.) HS
52. Lloyd DeFoor, c, Calhoun (Ga.) HS
53. Arnold Braden, lhp, Orange Park (Fla.) HS
54. Steve Whitaker, rhp, Brevard (Fla.) JC
55. **Gary Wilhelm, 2b/of, Cherry Hills HS, Inkster, Mich.**
56. Timothy Williams, of, Courter Tech HS, Cincinnati
57. Andrew Calufetti, c, Harrisburg (Ill.) HS
58. Dennis Holmberg, inf, Baker HS, Columbus, Ga.
59. Benny Howard, rhp, B.C. Rains HS, Mobile, Ala.
60. **Sam Kershaw, 1b, Levittown, Pa.**
61. Francis Serrano, rhp/of, Clifton HS, Bronx, N.Y.
62. Jeffrey Peoples, of/rhp, Montgomery Bell Academy, Nashville, Tenn.
63. Steve Loiselle, c, Channel Island HS, Oxnard, Calif.
64. Eugene McElwain, lhp, Manhattan Prep, Bronx, N.Y.
65. Arthur Simon, ss, Hialeah (Fla.) HS
66. Patrick Moore, c, Mira Costa HS, Manhattan Beach, Calif.
67. Francis Slayer, 3b, Ferndale (Wash.) HS
68. Thomas Peavey, rhp, Ingraham HS, Seattle
69. John Spelaliere, ss, Erasmus Hall HS, Brooklyn, N.Y.
70. Frank Zawatski, c, Boundbrook (N.J.) HS
71. **Tony Scott, of, Withrow HS, Cincinnati**
72. **John Gentile, c, CC of Baltimore**
73. Linwood Forte, ss, Munford HS, Detroit
74. **Rick Down, of, Southgate (Mich.) HS**
75. Butch Stinson, lhp, Cohn HS, Nashville, Tenn.
76. Lavery Hiegel, c, St. Francis HS, Palo Alto, Calif.

June—Secondary Phase (10)

1. Mike Weathers, 2b, Cerritos (Calif.) JC
2. Ron Diggle, c/of, Cerritos (Calif.) JC
3. No selection
4. **James LaRusso, 2b, Monmouth (N.J.)**

NEW YORK METS

January—Regular Phase (3)

1. Bruce Heinbechner, lhp, Pacoima, Calif.
2. **Ken Esposito, lhp, Nassau (N.Y.) CC**
3. Doug Britelle, rhp, Rutgers
4. Dave Carey, rhp, Hastings, Minn.

January—Secondary Phase (13)

1. Billy Cotton, c, Arizona State
2. **Jerry Perkins, lhp, Indiana**
3. Greg Archer, 1b, JC of the Sequoias (Calif.)
4. Joseph Kilby, of, Big Bend (Wash.) CC
5. Ryan Bailey, of/3b, Santa Clara
6. Mike Sigman, rhp, Santa Clara
7. **Robert McLeod, rhp, Georgetown (Ky.)**

June—Regular Phase (4)

1. **Randy Sterling, rhp, Key West (Fla.) HS**
2. **Joe Nolan Jr., c, Southwest HS, St. Louis**
3. **Garnett Davis, c/of, East HS, Columbus, Ohio**
4. Boris Kleiber, ss, Vandalia-Butler HS, Vandalia, Ohio
5. **Michael Kowalski, rhp, Stratford (Conn.) HS**
6. **Cecil Reynolds, rhp, New Hanover HS, Wilmington, N.C.**
7. **Joseph Murray, rhp, St. Bernards HS, New London, Conn.**
8. Kenneth Ossola, 3b, Saint Louis
9. Vernon Temple, c, Beaumont (Texas) HS
10. Clifford Kershaw, rhp, Granada Hills (Calif.) HS
11. **John Tregligus, ss, Lawton (Okla.) HS**
12. Al Arthur, ss, Sheepshead Bay HS, Brooklyn, N.Y.
13. **Gary Betts, 1b, Easton (Pa.) HS**
14. Paul Caffrey, of/rhp, Seton Hall Prep, South Orange, N.J.
15. Baylor Alexander, rhp, Orange-Stark HS, Orange, Texas
16. Kevin Tennant, c, Molloy HS, Queens, N.Y.
17. Elroy Othold, rhp, St. Paul HS, Shiner, Texas
18. **Gerald Davis, ss, Parker HS, Janesville, Wis.**
19. **Victor Worry, lhp, Pfeiffer (N.C.)**
20. Scotty Kurtz, lhp, Northwest Missouri State
21. **Lute Barnes, 2b, Oregon State**
22. **John Main, rhp, Lyons (N.Y.) HS**
23. Doug Farrell, rhp/of, Mooney HS, Rochester, N.Y.
24. Bruce Swanson, rhp, Rio Americano HS, Sacramento, Calif.
25. Vic Harris, ss, Los Angeles Valley JC
26. Richard Kelly, c, Brighton (Colo.) HS
27. **Buzz Capra, rhp, Illinois State**
28. **Von Opolous, lhp, West HS, Salt Lake City**
29. **George Leckrone, rhp/ss, Dover (Pa.) HS**
30. Robert Steinberg, 1b/of, Scranton (Pa.)
31. **George Theodore, 1b/of, Utah**
32. Harold Hess, of, Seaford HS, Wantagh, N.Y.
33. **Greg Allen, c, Pembroke State (N.C.)**
34. Robert Murphy, 1b/c, Tulsa
35. **Edmond Robinson, lhp, Webber HS, Eastover, S.C.**
36. Joseph Panele, lhp, LaSalle HS, Niagara Falls, N.Y.
37. **Thomas Kilgore, 3b, Utah**
38. Randall Shipp, rhp/c, South Sevier HS, Joseph, Utah
39. Dave Nelson, rhp, Viewmont HS, Bountiful, Utah
40. Larry Burke, ss, Marietta (Ohio) HS
41. John Monick, lhp/of, Wyoming Prep School, Kingston, Pa.
42. **Ed LaBorde, c, Bethany**
43. Bruce Clouser, of, St. Joseph's
44. James Newman, lhp, Big Springs (Texas) HS
45. Donald McLeod, rhp, Niagara-Wheatfield HS, Niagara Falls, N.Y.
46. Ronald Drews, rhp, Old Dominion
47. Steve Jasinski, rhp, Chicopee (Mass.) Comprehensive HS
48. Craig Menzl, of, Adelphi (N.Y.)
49. Jerry Goode, lhp, Marist HS, Bayonne, N.J.
50. Robert Cary, ss, Greenwood (S.C.) HS
51. Charles Prorok, rhp, Newman HS, Checktowaca, N.Y.
52. Jack MacKay, ss, Valley Stream HS, Franklin Square, N.Y.

June—Secondary Phase (12)

1. **Billy Cotton, c, Arizona State**
2. **Mark Kitchell, of, Larchmont, N.Y.**
3. **Larry Fritz, 1b, Arizona State**
4. **Richard Breese, rhp, Albuquerque**
5. Michael Balogh, rhp, Niagara County (N.Y.) CC
6. **Nicholas Furlong, rhp, Notre Dame**
7. John Andrews, lhp, Pasadena (Calif.) CC

NEW YORK YANKEES

January—Regular Phase (12)

1. Gregory Marshall, of, Laney (Calif.) JC
2. Gary Marks, lhp, Golden West (Calif.) JC
3. **Reinaldo Ramos, of, Chicago**
4. **John Schlesinger, ss/3b, JC of the Redwoods (Calif.)**
5. Michael Warwick, c, Contra Costa (Calif.) JC
6. Toni Breckel, rhp, Centralia (Wash.) JC

January—Secondary Phase (2)

1. Larry Pyle, of, Miami
2. Dennis Wallin, c, American River (Calif.) JC
3. Rickie Clements, lhp, Grayson County (Texas) JC
4. **Donald Schroeder, rhp, Grays Harbor (Wash.) JC**
5. Jim Barr, rhp, Southern California
6. Gary Robson, rhp, Los Angeles CC
7. James LaRusso, 3b/2b, Monmouth College (N.J.)
8. Ken Wastradowski, lhp, Centralia (Wash.) JC

June—Regular Phase (11)

1. **Charlie Spikes, 3b/of, Central Memorial HS, Bogalusa, La.**
2. Peter Helt, lhp, Morristown (N.J.) HS
3. John LaRose, lhp, Cumberland (R.I.) HS
4. **Fred Frazier, 2b, Hoover HS, Fresno, Calif.**
5. **Jim Barr, of, Marshall HS, Chicago**
6. **Marion Prince, ss/rhp, Walker HS, Atlanta**
7. **Jorge Maduro, c, Miami**
8. Todd Sprecher, c, South Eugene (Ore.) HS
9. **David Kilgore, 1b, Beloit (Wis.) Memorial HS**
10. **Ken Crosby, rhp, Brigham Young**
11. **Paul Jenious, rhp, Booker T. Washington HS, Memphis, Tenn.**
12. Eric Long, rhp, Stagg HS, Stockton, Calif.
13. **Thomas O'Connor, of, South Hills Catholic HS, Pittsburgh**
14. **William Colunio, ss, Ashland**
15. John Tamargo, c, Tampa Catholic HS
16. Robert Finley, rhp, Darlington (Wis.) HS
17. **Charles Combs, c, North Carolina State**
18. **William Gardner, of, Bacone (Okla.) JC**
19. **Alan Tetrault, of/1b, Technical HS, Springfield, Mass.**
20. Keith Harding, of, Lewiston (Idaho) HS
21. John McLean, rhp, Overton HS, Nashville, Tenn.
22. Donald Greenough, lhp, South Eugene (Ore.) HS
23. **Rick Kriz, of, Northern Iowa**
24. **David Brown, of, Texas**
25. Larry Hardy, rhp, Texas
26. Henry Garcia, ss, Grant HS, Sacramento, Calif.
27. James Gorton, rhp, Chaminade HS, Rosedale, N.Y.
28. **Terry Vargason, lhp, Borah HS, Boise, Idaho**
29. **Paul Swanson, rhp, Milford (Conn.) HS**
30. Duane Donahoo, inf/of, Christian Brothers HS, Memphis, Tenn.
31. **Donald Palmer, 1b, David Douglas HS, Portland, Ore.**
32. **Paul Baretta, ss, Southern Connecticut State**
33. Michael Venable, rhp/of, Blanchet HS, Seattle
34. **Greg Buys, 1b/c, Kennett (Mo.) HS**
35. **Oliver Lyons, of, Pilgrim HS, Warwick, R.I.**
36. Christopher Boyle, ss, East HS, Wichita, Kan.
37. **Danny Dalonzo, rhp, Lincoln HS, Stockton, Calif.**
38. Stephen Connolly, 1b, Central Catholic HS, Norwalk, Conn.
39. Brian Cogan, lhp, Saratoga Springs, N.Y.
40. Tom Farrias, rhp, New Bedford (Mass.) HS
41. James Linnin, c, Port Chester (N.Y.) HS
42. Jack McDonald, rhp, Pullman (Wash.) HS
43. Gregory Branum, 3b/of, LaCrosse HS, Hooper, Wash.
44. Joel DeTray, rhp, Clarkston (Wash.) HS
45. **Christopher Barker, rhp, McNary HS, Salem, Ore.**
46. Dean Mick, ss/3b, Foster HS, Seattle
47. Kenneth O'Brien, rhp, Villanova
48. **Kenneth Bennett, 1b, West HS, Wichita, Kan.**
49. **Arthur Cooper, 1b, Rodeo (Calif.) HS**

50. Prentice McGray, of, Edison HS, Stockton, Calif.

June—Secondary Phase (13)

1. Joe Kilby, of, Big Bend (Wash.) CC
2. **Ronald Collier, rhp, Mansfield (Pa.)**
3. Daniel Velander, rhp, Portland, Ore.
4. Wayne Adkinson, 2b, Yakima Valley (Wash.) JC
5. **Beau Robinson, of/1b, Bacone (Okla.) JC**

OAKLAND ATHLETICS

January—Regular Phase (10)

1. **Marshall Crossan, rhp, San Jose (Calif.) CC**
2. Daniel Pritchett, of, El Camino (Calif.) JC
3. Reggie Treadway, 3b, Sul Ross State
4. Doug McCoy, rhp, Miami-Dade South CC

January—Secondary Phase (12)

1. **Darryl Thomas, lhp, Long Beach (Calif.) CC**
2. Steve Wilmet, lhp, St. Norbert
3. Pat Bekeza, of/inf, Southern Colorado
4. Jerre Algeo, 2b, Poteau (Mo.) JC
5. Gary Houston, lhp, San Jose (Calif.) CC

June—Regular Phase (9)

1. **Don Stanhouse, rhp/ss, DuQuoin (Ill.) HS**
2. **Tommy Sandt, ss, Pacifica HS, Garden Grove, Calif.**
3. **Steve Lawson, lhp, San Lorenzo HS, San Leandro, Calif.**
4. **Bob Williams, c, Washington State**
5. **Joseph Williamson, 1b, Bartlett Yancey HS, Yanceyville, N.C.**
6. Jim Sundberg, c, Galesburg (Ill.) HS
7. Dave Wiggins, of, McLane HS, North Fresno, Calif.
8. **Glenn Abbott, rhp, North Little Rock (Ark.) HS**
9. Michael Hanson, rhp, Walla Walla (Wash.) HS
10. Ivan Dempsey, c, Science Hill HS, Johnson City, Tenn.
11. Michael Logelin, 2b, Loyola Marymount
12. John Adeimy, ss, Forest Hill HS, West Palm Beach, Fla.
13. John Stearns, c, Thomas Jefferson HS, Denver
14. **Samuel LeClair, of, Bridegewater-Raynham Regional HS, Bridgewater, Mass.**
15. **Billy Swope, rhp, Forest Park HS, Beaumont, Texas**
16. John Lenahan, rhp, Salesianum HS, Wilmington, Del.
17. **Richard Meier, of, Central HS, Davenport, Iowa**
18. **James Capehart, of, Bertie HS, Windsor, N.C.**
19. **Charlie Chant, ss, Narbonne HS, Harbor City, Calif.**
20. Chris Vella, lhp, Notre Dame HS, Van Nuys, Calif.
21. **Wilson Rainer, rhp, Johnson HS, Laurinburg, N.C.**
22. Andrew Bielanskie, c, Savanna HS, Anaheim
23. **David Cavazza, rhp, Milford (Mass.) HS**
24. Michael McKinney, rhp, St. James HS, Chester, Pa.
25. **Joseph Lasorsa, rhp, Boston**
26. **Michael Foyer, c, Sierra (Calif.) JC**
27. Clare Leifer, of, Washington
28. **Ronnie Wynne, ss, Williamston (N.C.) HS**
29. **Dennis Myers, 1b, American River (Calif.) JC**
30. Brian Applegate, ss, El Cajon (Calif.) HS
31. **Alan Castro, c, Cabrillo (Calif.) JC**
32. Terry Mayer, 1b/3b, La Sierra HS, Carmichael, Calif.
33. **William Linehan, lhp, Peabody (Mass.) HS**
34. **Jack Knutson, rhp, Hudson Bay HS, Vancouver, Wash.**

June—Secondary Phase (7)

1. **William Fitzgerald, c, Tulane**
2. Dennis Wallin, c, American River (Calif.) JC
3. **Russell Almquist, lhp, Los Angeles Pierce JC**
4. Larry Prieto, 2b, Fresno (Calif.) CC

PHILADELPHIA PHILLIES

January—Regular Phase (7)

1. Terry Enyart, lhp, Chipola (Fla.) JC
2. **Dennis Weiner, 1b, Philadelphia**
3. John Clear, 1b/of, Wilmington, Calif.
4. **Richard Kelly, 2b, St. Joseph's**

January—Secondary Phase (7)

1. **Douglas Barker, rhp, Sacramento (Calif.) CC**
2. **Frank Hagen, inf, Napa Valley (Calif.) JC**
3. Michael Wertz, ss, Dallas Baptist
4. Lawrence Tarver, c, Bakersfield (Calif.) JC
5. Robert Coultas, rhp, Diablo Valley (Calif.) JC
6. Kevin Bryant, inf, Valencia (Fla.) CC

June—Regular Phase (6)

1. **Mike Anderson, 1b, Timmonsville (S.C.) HS**
2. **Mike Rogodzinski, of, Southern Illinois**
3. **Bobby Wiltshire, rhp, Coahoma County HS, Clarksdale, Miss.**
4. **Mike Wallace, lhp, James Madison HS, Vienna, Va.**
5. **Robert Malcolm, rhp, Tennessee Tech**
6. **Bob Boone, 3b, Stanford**
7. **Craig Sciramuzzo, rhp, St. Phillips HS, Chicago**
8. Allan Matson, of, St. John's
9. **Dennis Iverson, rhp, Winona State**
10. **Daniel Benoit, c, Western Michigan**
11. Roger Pattillo, ss, Ouachita Baptist
12. **Joseph Emer, 2b, St. Norbert**
13. **Richard Giallella, of, Rider**
14. Patrick Rusco, 1b, San Luis Obispo (Calif.) HS
15. Richard Magner, c, Xavier HS, Middletown, Conn.
16. **Ron Diorio, rhp, New Haven (Conn.)**
17. **Willie Sledge, of, Basic HS, Henderson, Nev.**
18. **Ken Ward, rhp/of, Seton Hall**
19. **Lloyd Hutchinson, of/inf, Colorado**
20. **Michael Whalin, lhp, Hughes HS, Cincinnati**
21. **Thomas Coplin, lhp, Laton (Calif.) HS**
22. **Charles Paglierani, of, American International**
23. **Phillip Morgan, 3b, Ohio State**
24. David Merchant, ss, Harding HS, Marion, Ohio
25. **Charles Kniffen, lhp, Nassau (N.Y.) CC**
26. **Donald Kinzel, 2b, San Jose State**
27. **Fred Ruben, 3b, Delaware State**
28. Ellsworth Jones, lhp, New York (Selection voided)
29. Daryl Arenstein, 1b, Rolling Hills (Calif.) HS
30. **Larry Coffin, ss, Oakton HS, Vienna, Va.**
31. **James Dietz, c, Moravian**

June—Secondary Phase (6)

1. **Allen Joyce, ss, Scranton, Pa.**
2. Cal Meier, ss, Southern California
3. Rudy Arroyo, lhp, Foothill (Calif.) JC
4. Ellsworth Jones, lhp, New York

PITTSBURGH PIRATES

January—Regular Phase (9)

1. **Arthur Meza, c, Stockton, Calif.**
2. **Mack McKay, ss, New Orleans**
3. William Woodruff, rhp, Georgia State
4. William Shepherd, rhp, Spokane (Wash.) CC
5. Bruce Irvin, c/rhp, St. Petersburg (Fla.) JC
6. **Thomas Fitzgerald, ss, Rahway, N.J.**
7. **Paul Giroux, inf, Ithaca (N.Y.)**
8. William Updergraff, c, Hagerstown (Md.) JC
9. George Swanson, of, Miami-Dade North CC
10. Allen Joyce, ss, North Scranton, Pa.
11. Sigmund Gancasz, c, Queensborough (N.Y.) CC

January—Secondary Phase (5)

1. **John Morlan, of/rhp, Ohio**
2. Matthew Rosiek, rhp, Indian River (Fla.) CC
3. Wayne Harlan, inf, Yakima Valley (Wash.) JC
4. Gerald Bryant, lhp, Lynchburg (Va.) JC
5. John Mills, rhp, Wenatchee Valley (Wash.) CC

June—Regular Phase (10)

1. **John Morlan, rhp, Merritt Island (Fla.) HS**
2. **James Johnson, of, Brandywine HS, Niles, Mich.**
3. **Fred Cambria, rhp, St. Leo**
4. **Jim McKee, rhp, Otterbein**
5. John Doherty, of, Reading (Mass.) HS
6. Ed Ratleff, rhp, East HS, Columbus, Ohio

7. **Michael Semp, of, Macomb (Mich.) CC**
8. **Donzell McDonald, of, Long Beach (Calif.) Poly HS**
9. **John Griggs, ss, Central HS, Phenix City, Ala.**
10. William Robinson, of/rhp, North Carolina A&T State
11. James Horton, lhp, Ypsilanti (Mich.) HS
12. Dennis Odom, ss, Kearny HS, San Diego
13. **Gary Meyer, rhp, Merritt Island (Fla.) HS**
14. Ronald Van Saders, c, Woodridge HS, Moonachie, N.J.
15. Walter Biercevicz, lhp/of, Norwalk State Tech (Conn.) JC
16. **David Lee, rhp, Wottermark HS, Boyce, La.**
17. Donald Boettger, rhp/1b, Radnor-Delaware County HS, Radnor, Pa. (Selection voided)
18. Frank Shimerola, lhp, Bishop Ryan HS, Omaha, Neb.
19. Jack Baker, 1b/lhp, Maury HS, Norfolk, Va.
20. Edward Munoz, of/ss, Miller HS, Corpus Christi, Texas
21. **Peter Hughes, ss, Southbridge (Mass.) HS**
22. **Daniel Quinn, rhp, Buffalo State**
23. Robert Polinsky, rhp, Panther Valley HS, Lansford, Pa.
24. **James Clark, ss, Catholic HS, Owensboro, Ky.**
25. **Scott Dwyer, 2b/3b, Burbank HS, Sacramento, Calif.**
26. **George Stanley, rhp, Bridgewater HS, Raynham, Mass.**
27. Robert Kowalski, rhp, Cocoa (Fla.) HS
28. Dennis Chambliss, rhp, Sidney Lanier HS, Macon, Ga.
29. Stafford Branch, rhp, Scotia (N.Y.) Senior HS
30. **Brian Blaney, rhp, Methuen (Mass.) HS**
31. **Douglas Storum, c, Brevard (Fla.) CC**
32. Doug Ault, of/lhp, Panola (Texas) JC
33. Michael Smollen, c, Lake Worth (Fla.) HS
34. Eugene Sackett, c, McClatchy HS, Sacramento, Calif.
35. Dave Pyles, inf, East HS, East Bremerton, Wash.
36. David Krull, inf/of, Iowa
37. **Michael Snipes, ss, Martin County HS, Stuart, Fla.**
38. Larry Green, 3b, Deane
39. Joseph Levulis, lhp, Frontier Central HS, Blasdell, N.Y.
40. David Kegris, c, John Harris HS, Harrisburg, Pa.
41. **William Maher, lhp, Johnstown (Pa.) HS**
42. Leonard Jankiewicz, 1b, Lancaster (N.Y.) HS
43. **Dennis Slagle, rhp, Beth-Center HS, Richeyville, Pa.**
44. Gary Gaiser, rhp, West Seneca (N.Y.) HS
45. Victor Sharek, 3b/rhp, Lincoln HS, Wampum, Pa.
46. John Waffle, ss, Cardinal Mooney HS, Rochester, N.Y.
47. Edward Spoth, 1b/ss, DeSales Catholic HS, East Amherst, N.Y.
48. **Joseph Secor, rhp/of, Elkton (Md.) HS**

June—Secondary Phase (4)

1. **Rudy Strickland, lhp, Indian River (Fla.) CC**
2. Glenn Borgmann, c, Miami-Dade North CC
3. Jim Barr, rhp, Southern California
4. Gerald Bryant, lhp, Madison Heights, Va.
5. **Ken Wastradowski, lhp, Centralia (Wash.) JC**
6. William Jenkins, ss, Orange Coast (Calif.) JC

ST. LOUIS CARDINALS

January—Regular Phase (19)

1. **Al Hrabosky, lhp, Fullerton (Calif.) JC**
2. **Ed Crosby, 2b, Long Beach (Calif.) CC**
3. David Jakubs, 3b/ss, Cincinnati
4. John Phillips, rhp, Moorpark (Calif.) JC
5. **Jack Butorac, rhp, Cal State Los Angeles**
6. Glenwood Arbuckle, lhp, Trenton (Mo.) JC

January—Secondary Phase (1)

1. Wayne Garland, rhp, Gulf Coast (Fla.) CC
2. **Arthur Brown, rhp, New York**
3. **Ray Bare, rhp, Miami-Dade North CC**
4. **Robert Auger, 1b/rhp, Putnam, Conn.**
5. **Nicholas Stipanovich, rhp, Boston**
6. **Herbert Hofvendahl, of, St. Mary's**
7. Brian Bach, rhp, Connecticut

June—Regular Phase (20)

1. **Charles Minott, lhp, Royal Oak HS, Covina, Calif.**
2. **Ed Crosby, ss, New Hanover HS, Wilmington, N.C.**
3. **Mick Kelleher, ss, Puget Sound (Wash.)**
4. **Bill Stein, ss, Southern Illinois**
5. **John Heenan, of, Lincoln HS, San Jose, Calif.**
6. **Gregory Millikan, lhp, Occidental**
7. **Stanley Templeton, of, Weatherford (Okla.) HS**
8. **Russell Caldarella, of/ss, Millikan HS, Long Beach, Calif.**
9. Bucky Dent, 3b, Hialeah (Fla.) HS
10. **Barry Poris, 1b/lhp, City College of New York**
11. Bill Madlock Jr., 3b, Eisenhower HS, Decatur, Ill.
12. **Garrett Collins, 1b, Southern Illinois-Edwardsville**
13. **Paul Sheehan, rhp, Burlington (Mass.) HS**
14. Michael Timmel, rhp, Terra Lenda HS, San Rafael, Calif.
15. George Coval, c, Philipsburg (Pa.) HS
16. **Gary Barakat, 2b, Cliffside Park HS, Palisades, N.J.**
17. Andres Frank, of, Castro Valley (Colo.) HS
18. Alex West, c, Fairfax HS, Los Angeles
19. **Henry Daugherty, 3b, South Alabama**
20. Roger Schmuck, of/1b, Mesa (Ariz.) CC
21. Joe Krsnich, of/inf, Ka Paun Memorial HS, Wichita, Kan.
22. Maurice Robert, of/rhp, Richfield HS, Waco, Texas
23. **Jim Ciotti, rhp, Salem (Ohio) HS**
24. **Joseph Partin, rhp, North Hampton HS, Cape Charles, Va.**
25. **Raymond Colin, of, Long Beach (Calif.) CC**
26. **Ronald Dyson, c/3b, Technical HS, Oakland, Calif.**
27. Robert Munson, rhp, Choate Prep, Wallingford, Conn.
28. **John Kitchen, rhp, Massachusetts**
29. Joaquin Saiz, of, Fort Lee (N.J.) HS
30. **Brad Plant, lhp, Mound (Minn.) HS**
31. **Ken Reitz, ss, Jefferson HS, Daly City, Calif.**
32. Robert Dance, c, Colonial Heights (Va.) HS
33. **John Sawatski, c, Hall HS, Little Rock, Ark.**
34. **Timothy McEnderfer, c, Cornell**
35. William Hall, lhp, San Joaquin Delta (Calif.) JC
36. **Lonnie Croslow, ss, Modesto (Calif.) JC**
37. Michael Mantorella, 1b, Monterey Peninsula (Calif.) JC (Selection voided)
38. John Herzing, lhp, Washington (Pa.)
39. **Robert Fulewider, 2b, California Lutheran**
40. **John St. George, 2b/ss, Whittier**

June—Secondary Phase (18)

1. **Gary Marks, of, Golden West (Calif.) JC**
2. **Alan Putz, of, Springfield (Mass.)**
3. Gary Houston, lhp, San Jose (Calif.) CC
4. John Jackson, 3b/of, California (Selection voided)
5. **Kent Calderan, ss, Chabot (Calif.) JC**

SAN DIEGO PADRES

January—Regular Phase (23)

1. Don Keenan, c, Gulf Coast (Fla.) CC
2. Willis Buchanon, of/inf, Mira Costa (Calif.) JC
3. Gary Dunkelberger, rhp, Orange Coast (Calif.) JC
4. Eric Swanson, rhp, San Diego CC
5. David Dowdy, c, Lower Columbia (Wash.) JC
6. **Thomas O'Day, ss, Fort Lauderdale, Fla.**
7. **John Baca, c, Los Angeles**
8. Ronnie Helton, rhp, Gulf Coast (Fla.) CC
9. Charles Taylor, rhp, Vallejo, Calif.

January—Secondary Phase (21)

1. **Jose Basterrechea, rhp, Flushing, N.Y.**
2. Ron Cash, ss, Manatee (Fla.) JC
3. Rudy Arroyo, lhp, Foothill (Calif.) JC
4. **Kenneth McGregor, ss, Gulf Coast (Fla.) CC**
5. **Luciano Hernandez, rhp, Del Mar, Calif.**
6. Beau Robinson, 1b/of, Muskogee JC
7. William Hancock, c, Furman

June—Regular Phase (24)

1. **Randy Elliott, 1b, Camarillo (Calif.) HS**
2. **Ron Cash, rhp, Thomas Jefferson HS, San Antonio, Texas**
3. No selection
4. **Rudy Arroyo, of, Lamar**
4. **Edward Rundle, of, Lamar**
5. **Gilbert Vidrio, ss, Sweetwater HS, National City, Calif.**
6. **Richard Longhurst, of, Pocatello (Idaho) HS**
7. Stephen Peck, rhp, DeAnza HS, Richmond, Calif.

8. William Berkes, 3b/c, Robinson HS, Tampa
9. **Aubrey Anderson, rhp, Escambia HS, Pensacola, Fla.**
10. John Dean, 2b, Calhoun (Ga.) HS
11. **Grant Steer, of, San Francisco**
12. Dennis Loewe, rhp, Pershing
13. **Guy Eargle, of, South Carolina**
14. **Danny Young, rhp, Lodi HS, Stockton, Calif.**
15. **Wayne Zurburg, c, Broward (Fla.) CC**
16. **Gregory Sinclair, rhp, San Francisco**
17. James Kirkland, of, Savannah (Ga.) HS
18. Doug DeCinces, 3b, Los Angeles Pierce JC
19. David Fussell, c, Chattanooga
20. Richard Horn, of, Avondale HS, Decatur, Ga.
21. **David Kostival, 3b, Athens HS, Chauncey, Ohio**
22. **Brian Brown, of/c, James Monroe HS, Bronx, N.Y.**
23. John Blue, lhp, Tempe (Ariz.) HS
24. **Michael Anders, of, Gonzaga**
25. **Marvin Sherzer, rhp, South Florida**
26. Rick Simmons, rhp, Rogers HS, Spokane, Wash.
27. **Richard Zinniger, lhp, Brigham Young**
28. Gregory Prickett, of, Middle Georgia JC
29. Kenneth Robinson, rhp/of, Oakland (Calif.) HS
30. Michael Dishman, 3b, Washington HS, Portland, Ore.
31. **Lawrence Whiteside, rhp, Dixie Hollins HS, St. Petersburg, Fla.**
32. Earl Austin, 3b, Dos Palos (Calif.) HS
33. Michael Wells, ss/of, Normal (Ill.) Community HS

June—Secondary Phase (20)

1. **David Jakubs, 3b, Parma, Ohio**
2. Willis Buchanan, of, Mira Costa (Calif.) JC
3. Freddie Howard, of/1b, Paris (Texas) JC

SAN FRANCISCO GIANTS

January—Regular Phase (17)

1. Daniel Bondon, of/inf, San Pedro, Calif.
2. James Stedman, rhp, Mesa (Ariz.) CC
3. Joseph Jacobsen, c/1b, Fresno (Calif.) CC
4. Robert Garcia, of/rhp, JC of the Sequoias (Calif.)
5. William Wolfe, 2b, JC of the Sequoias (Calif.)
6. Glenn Borgmann, c/1b, Miami-Dade North CC
7. Larry Dierks, lhp, JC of the Sequoias (Calif.)
8. Randall Shroll, rhp, JC of Southern Idaho

January—Secondary Phase (19)

1. Thomas Frye, of/rhp, Fairmont, N.C.
2. Howard Casey, lhp, Umpqua (Ore.) CC
3. Pat Cech, rhp, Glendale (Ariz.) CC
4. **Steve Stone, rhp, Kent State**
5. Edgardo Avila, lhp/of, Miami-Dade North CC

June—Regular Phase (18)

1. **Mike Phillips, ss, McArthur HS, Irving, Texas**
2. **Jack Woolsey, of, Kansas State**
3. **Horace Speed, of, Banning HS, Compton, Calif.**
4. **Steve Stone, ss, Taylor**
5. **Raymond Lombardo, c, Crespi HS, Encino, Calif.**
6. **Steve Ontiveros, 3b, Bakersfield (Calif.) HS**
7. **Gary Thomasson, of, Oceanside (Calif.) HS**
8. **Guy Homoly, of, Illinois State**
9. Peter Franklin, of/ss, Morristown (N.J.) Prep HS
10. **Mike Fisher, of/inf, El Centro (Calif.) HS**
11. **Skip Pitlock, lhp, Southern Illinois**
12. **John Sielicki, lhp, Hartford (Conn.) Public HS**
13. **Rich Miller, 3b, Ithaca (N.Y.)**
14. John Conners, of, Gardena (Calif.) HS
15. Derek Bryant, of, Henry Clay HS, Lexington, Ky.
16. **Michael Murphy, 1b, Ohio**
17. **Randy Kapano, of, Citrus (Calif.) JC**
18. **Mike O'Brien, rhp, Phoenix JC**
19. **Rick Carden, lhp, Hawthorne (Calif.) HS**
20. David Marshall, 1b, Solano (Calif.) CC
21. **Rick Gallagher, 1b, Cal Poly Pomona**
22. Manuel Zepeda, 1b, El Monte (Calif.) HS
23. Eubulus Marshall, of, Solano (Calif.) CC
24. Larry Ike, rhp, Ottawa Hills HS, Grand Rapids, Mich.
25. **Michael Powers, c, Henderson State (Ark.)**
26. William Lazzerini, lhp, Notre Dame HS, Sherman Oaks, Calif.
27. **Jim Hoggarth, c, Oglethorpe**
28. Donald Crew, of, Alabama Christian
29. **Edgar Ward, of, Arlington (Texas) HS**
30. **Edward Hart, c, Westmont HS, San Jose, Calif.**
31. Dominic Herness, rhp, Springfield Gardens HS, Jamaica, N.Y.
32. Mike McCormick, rhp, Boise (Idaho) HS
33. Allen Thomas, rhp, Rochester (Mich.) HS
34. Jerry Vitatoe, 1b/3b, Laney (Calif.) JC
35. Jim Chapados, 1b, Chehalis (Wash.) HS
36. **Joseph Sadelfeld, lhp, Ohio State**
37. **Cephus Mayo, 2b/3b, Treasure Valley (Ore.) CC**
38. Jeffrey Bouton, rhp, Nutley (N.J.) HS
39. **Mark Brewster, of, Northern Arizona**
40. Richard Binder, lhp, Illinois

June—Secondary Phase (2)

1. **Jake Brown, c, Southern**
2. Daniel Ragland, 3b, Ranger (Texas) JC
3. Dave Carey, rhp, Hastings, Minn.
4. Rick Dierker, rhp, Los Angeles Pierce JC

SEATTLE PILOTS

January—Regular Phase (24)

1. Mike Weathers, 2b, Cerritos (Calif.) JC
2. **Jerry Bell, rhp, Southwestern (Tenn.)**
3. No selection
4. Lloyd Breshers, rhp, Centerville JC
5. **Jeffrey Lemon, rhp, Long Beach, Calif.**
6. Randall Brown, of, Sacramento (Calif.) CC

January—Secondary Phase (22)

1. **Ray Peters, rhp, Harvard**
2. Henry Yeargan, ss, Brewton-Parker (Ga.) JC
3. No selection
4. Bill Dobbs, lhp, Oklahoma State
5. Bonnie Smith, 1b, Los Angeles
6. Bruce Kinder, ss, Florida Southern
7. **Rick Auerbach, ss, Los Angeles Pierce JC**
8. Doug Bird, rhp, Mount San Antonio (Calif.) JC
9. Duane Kuiper, ss, Indian Hills (Iowa) CC
10. Michael Longstreth, ss, Eastern Oklahoma A&M JC
11. **David Renkiewicz, rhp, Michigan**
12. Nicholas Nicosia, of, Florida

June—Regular Phase (21)

1. **Gorman Thomas, ss/rhp, James Island HS, Charleston, S.C.**
2. **Jerry Bell, 1b, Jesup (Ga.) HS**
3. No selection
4. **Stephen Harvey, rhp, Ingraham HS, Seattle**
5. **Gary Martz, of/rhp, West Valley HS, Spokane, Wash.**
6. Larry Hollyfield, of, Compton (Calif.) HS
7. **Rick Auerbach, rhp, Estancia HS, Costa Mesa, Calif.**
8. Doug Bird, ss, DuPont Manual HS, Louisville, Ky.
9. Duane Kuiper, c/1b, Western Kentucky
10. Gary King, ss, Clay HS, South Bend, Ind.
11. James Kinsley, rhp, Herricks HS, New Hyde Park, N.Y.
12. **William Gilbert, rhp/of, Pascagoula (Miss.) HS**
13. Dwane Doel, of, Plantation HS, Fort Lauderdale, Fla.
14. **Robert Green, 3b, Boston College**
15. **Jim Slaton, rhp, Antelope Valley (Calif.) JC**
16. Jeffrey Ryser, ss, Bellaire HS, Houston
17. **Bob Coluccio, of/inf, Centralia (Wash.) HS**
18. Jerry Lewis, 1b, Palm Springs (Calif.) HS
19. **John Terranova, lhp, McKean HS, Wilmington, Del.**
20. **Charles Williams, of, Locke HS, Los Angeles**
21. **Bob Hansen, 1b/of, Massachusetts**
22. James Juniel, of, Richmond (Calif.) HS
23. Richard Jones, lhp, Davidson HS, Mobile, Ala.
24. **Billy Turner, rhp, East HS, Des Moines, Iowa**
25. Marc Rhea, ss, Sehome HS, Bellingham, Wash.
26. **Rudolph Toth, 1b, Northampton (Pa.) HS**
27. Steve Cain, rhp, North Kansas City (Mo.) HS

28. Michael Lynch, lhp, Norman (Okla.) HS
29. **John Pankow, lhp, Washington**
30. James Greggerson, lhp, Yaleta HS, El Paso, Texas
31. Bruce Maxwell, c, Madison HS, Portland, Ore.
32. **Virgil Smith, of, Sacramento (Calif.) HS**
33. **Norman Hill, 2b, Mobile County Training School, Magazine, Ala.**
34. Gene Moser, of, Edmonds (Wash.) HS
35. Jack Wilson, of, Sarasota (Fla.) HS
36. **Johnny Martin, 3b, Union (Tenn.)**
37. **John Conzatti, rhp, Centralia (Wash.) HS**
38. Zack Rogers, 1b/lhp, Butler (Ala.) HS
39. William Fuller, lhp, Great Neck (N.Y.) South HS
40. Ricky Patrylo, rhp, Manville (N.J.) HS
41. Herbert Williams, c, Sacramento (Calif.) HS
42. **James Spencer, 1b/3b, Falls Church (Va.) HS**
43. **Bobby Cook, inf, Latta (S.C.) HS**
44. **James Walton, lhp/of, Spartanburg (S.C.) HS**
45. John Petronaci, rhp, Montclair (N.J.) HS
46. Michael Weaver, 2b, Maplewood HS, Richmond Heights, Mo.
47. **Albert Strane, of, Santa Clara**

June—Secondary Phase (11)

1. Pat Osburn, lhp, Manatee (Fla.) JC
2. **Edgar Pate, lhp, Los Angeles CC**
3. No selection
4. Ernie Henrickson, rhp/of, Everett, Wash.
5. **Donald Schmonsky, rhp, Jamestown (N.Y.) CC**

WASHINGTON SENATORS

January—Regular Phase (2)

1. **Joe Lovitto Jr., c, San Pedro, Calif.**
2. Lyn Martin, ss, St. Johns River (Fla.) CC
3. Tim Martin, 2b, St. Johns River (Fla.) CC
4. Daniel Baker, c/of, Montgomery (Md.) JC
5. Rick Cassata, 3b, Syracuse
6. Donald Schmonsky, rhp, Jamestown (N.Y.) CC
7. Jon Roth, lhp, Niagara County (N.Y.) CC
8. **James Bottoms, of, Seabrook, Md.**
9. Brian Moore, 1b, Waterloo, Iowa
10. Michael Pich, c, Salisbury, Md.

January—Secondary Phase (8)

1. Mickey Rivers, of, Miami-Dade North CC
2. Gerald Tassa, lhp/of, Wingate (N.C.) JC
3. **Fred Williams, rhp, Baltimore**
4. Bill Seinsoth, 1b, Southern California
5. Scott Taylor, rhp, Mansfield (Pa.)
6. Ronald Collier, rhp, Mansfield (Pa.)
7. Michael Pivec, of, Baltimore

June—Regular Phase (1)

1. **Jeff Burroughs, rhp, Woodrow Wilson HS, Long Beach, Calif.**
2. **Johnny Brown, rhp, O'Connell HS, Arlington, Va.**
3. Jim Officer, lhp, Madison HS, Portland, Ore.
4. **Pete Mackanin, 3b/ss, Brother Rice Catholic HS, Chicago**
5. **Dave Criscione, c, Dunkirk (N.Y.) HS**
6. Geoffrey Brandt, of/rhp, El Camino HS, Carmichael, Calif.
7. **Melvin Williams, of, Pembroke State (N.C.)**
8. Eric Florence, c, Waynesville (Ohio) HS
9. **Ricky Rowe, ss, Georgetown (S.C.) HS**
10. Claude Renfro, rhp/1b, Red Bank HS, Chattanooga, Tenn.
11. **Eugene Lightfoot, of, Boys HS, Brooklyn, N.Y.**
12. **Vernon Saatzer, lhp, St. Thomas Military HS, St. Paul, Minn.**
13. James Sullivan, lhp, LaJunta (Colo.) HS
14. Darrell Darrow, ss, Jordan HS, Long Beach, Calif.
15. **Donald Shields, rhp, Northwestern State**
16. Randall Goede, lhp, Valparaiso
17. David Cooper, rhp, Wallace HS, Gary, Ind.
18. **Michael Pettit, rhp, St. Catherines Catholic HS, Racine, Wis.**
19. **Gordon Broseker, of/rhp, Northern HS, Baltimore**
20. Daniel Tracy, rhp, Muskogee (Okla.) HS
21. **Farley Banks, ss/c, Gwynn Park HS, Aquasco, Md.**
22. Steven Hegens, rhp, Spingarn HS, Washington, D.C.
23. Charles Krause, lhp, Palo Alto (Calif.) HS
24. **Jack Crable, of, Moeller HS, Cincinnati**
25. Norman Jones, ss, Haddonfield (N.J.) HS
26. Gabriel Padilla, rhp, Johnston HS, Austin, Texas
27. Kristian Sorensen, rhp, Santa Cruz (Calif.) HS
28. **James Herzog, 2b, St. Catherines Catholic HS, Racine, Wis.**
29. John Hickey, c, Belmont Abbey
30. **Jerry Ginter, rhp, Falls HS, International Falls, Minn.**
31. Chuck Seelbach, rhp, Dartmouth
32. **William Brykczynski, rhp, Thornridge HS, Dolton, Ill.**
33. Joseph Cork, ss, Manhattan Prep HS, Bronx, N.Y.
34. Paul Burton, lhp, Archbishop Kennedy HS, Conshohocken, Pa.
35. Tippy Martinez, of/lhp, LaJunta (Colo.) HS
36. **Roger Gifford, c/of, Lewis (Ill.)**
37. **James Cleary, of, Mitchelville, Md.**
38. **Robert Ormond, lhp, Princeton (N.C.) HS**
39. **Edward Layman, rhp, Belmont Abbey**
40. Robert Guinan, 2b, Manhattan Prep HS, New York
41. Daniel Wolfe, rhp, Cardinal Mindszenty HS, Dunkirk, N.Y.
42. James Callison, of, Wake Forest
43. **Steve Foucault, 3b/rhp, South Georgia**
44. **Edward Hose, rhp/of, Williamsport (Md.) HS**
45. Randy Kerstein, 2b, Central HS, Naperville, Ill.
46. Harry Martell, 3b/rhp, Archbishop Curley HS, Baltimore
47. William Eckler, of, SUNY Fredonia
48. Loren Marz, of, Cassadaga Central HS, Sinclairville, N.Y.

June—Secondary Phase (19)

1. Sherwood Hahn, p/1b, Virginia Tech
2. Pete Varney Jr., c, Harvard
3. Bruce Irvin, c, St. Petersburg (Fla.) JC
4. **Dave Moates, of, Florida State**
5. Douglas Smith, 2b, Buena Vista

1970 — No. 1 pick Ivie's obsession with perfection gets best of him in disappointing majors career

The Padres were so proud of Mike Ivie, the No. 1 draft pick in 1970, that they brought the 17-year-old catcher and his parents to San Diego to let him work out with the major league team. It was the beginning of the end for the talented youngster.

Ivie was introduced to the San Diego press, then went behind the plate to catch batting practice before a Padres game. The pitcher had a protective screen in front of him, with a slot cut out on his right side. Ivie's first few throws back to the pitcher were crisp and precise. His next throw hit the screen.

"That, rook, is why they're sending you to Tri-Cities," said veteran catcher Chris Cannizzaro, the regular Padres catcher.

Ivie took the remark to heart. A few days later he made his pro debut at Tri-Cities of the short-season Northwest League, and immediately something wasn't right.

"He was afraid to throw the ball back to the pitcher," said Ivie's father Bill, who had been his coach in Connie Mack ball in Decatur, Ga. "Mike always had a strong, accurate arm in high school, but it became a psychological thing with him."

Ivie, who signed for an $80,000 bonus, never overcame his mental block. Twice he bolted the organization, partly out of humiliation and frustration, partly out of fear of failure. Later he simply refused to catch.

Ivie admitted he was burdened by expectations, both in high school and professional baseball. Ivie's big league career spanned 11 seasons. Yet it was one of the most disappointing of the draft era because he caught just nine games.

"I was the No. 1 draft choice, I set certain standards for the No. 1 choice and I didn't think I was living up to them," he said. "As a No. 1 draft choice, I thought I was supposed to be perfect—hit a home run every time up and throw out everybody who tried to steal. I wasn't doing that, so I thought I was failing."

Padres farm director Peter Bavasi said the Padres narrowed their choice to Ivie and Stanford right-hander Steve Dunning, who went No. 2 to Cleveland. The Indians called him to the big leagues 10 days after his selection.

Veteran scout Lloyd Christopher called Dunning the best prospect he'd ever signed. "Steve Dunning throws as fast as anybody on the Indians staff except Sam McDowell," Christopher said. "And he'll match Sam every once in a while."

LOU SAURITCH

Darrell Porter was considered a notch below Mike Ivie but outperformed him

Like Ivie, Dunning's career went unfulfilled. He posted a 23-41 record in seven seasons.

The next two choices in the June regular phase were high school catchers. Montreal, drafting third, went for Barry Foote, while Milwaukee claimed Darrell Porter. Neither was considered the equal of Ivie going into the draft, but both enjoyed lengthy big league careers behind the plate.

Beyond the three young catchers, most of the attention in the 1970 draft was concentrated on a trio of Pacific-8 Conference players. Dunning, the Stanford ace, electrified scouts by beating No. 1-ranked Southern California twice in a week. Overall, he went 13-2 with a 1.83 ERA, striking out 144 in 108 innings.

Cleveland also had the No. 1 pick in the January secondary phase, and went for former UCLA first baseman Chris Chambliss. A year earlier Chambliss led the Pac-8 with 15 homers, then teamed with Dunning that summer to lead the semipro Anchorage Glacier Pilots to the National Baseball Congress championship.

USC's Dave Kingman, meanwhile, may have been the most sought-after college player of all in 1970. Kingman, selected first in the June secondary phase by the Giants, became one of the most prodigious sluggers in major league history, hitting 442 homers in 16 seasons.

Not surprisingly, USC had more players drafted in June than any four-year college, but greater focus was placed on the junior college ranks in 1970. Florida's Miami-Dade North Community College had the most players drafted in both January (12) and June (six).

USC went a long way toward maintaining its college dominance by landing a pair of unsigned first-round picks from the 1970 draft: pitcher Randy Scarbery (Astros) and shortstop George Ambrow (Mets). The Trojans added to their recruiting haul by nabbing outfielder Fred Lynn, who was picked in the third round by the Yankees.

Draft In Jeopardy?

The June 1970 draft was conducted in the midst of Curt Flood's suit against Major League Baseball, which challenged the reserve clause but also likely would have brought down the draft as well if he had been successful. Flood, the former Cardinals outfielder who was traded against his will following the 1969 season and sat out the 1970 season, lost his case, however, preserving the status quo in baseball and the draft.

Also in 1970, a team other than a major league club participated in the draft for the first time. Bend, a member of the Northwest League, was entitled to make selections at the Class A level on behalf of the Hawaii Islanders of the Pacific Coast League. Bend had a partial working agreement with the Triple-A club, which hoped to bring a major league franchise to Hawaii in future years.

"Hawaii is going to develop its own farm system, and Bend is the first team in the system," said Northwest League president John Carbray, who made the selections on Bend's behalf. "Hawaii is projecting five years ahead, when it hopes to have a major league franchise."

Bend picked three players in January and six in June, though the franchise was not permitted to select until the fourth round in any phase.

The Dodgers raised eyebrows by taking a stab at running back Mike Garrett of the Super Bowl champion Kansas City Chiefs, who was in the final year of his football contract. Garrett, the 1965 Heisman Trophy winner who was also drafted by the Dodgers in 1966, played in the outfield at Southern California and said he wanted to give baseball a try once his football contract ran out, but he never did.

The Pirates drafted the most players in both January (37) and June (65). None of the 28 players the Pirates selected in the January regular phase would play in the big leagues, and only two of their 102 picks saw service in Pittsburgh. In the 14th round, however, the Pirates selected future star Dave Parker.

DRAFT 70: FIRST-ROUND PICKS

No.	Club	Player, Pos.	School	Hometown	Ht.	Wt.	B-T	Age
1.	Padres	Mike Ivie, c	Walker HS	Decatur, Ga.	6-2	198	R-R	17
2.	Indians	Steve Dunning, rhp	Stanford	San Diego	6-2	205	R-R	21
3.	Expos	Barry Foote, c	Selma HS	Smithfield, N.C.	6-3	205	R-R	18
4.	Brewers	Darrell Porter, c	Southeast HS	Oklahoma City, Okla.	6-0	193	L-R	18
5.	Phillies	Mike Martin, lhp	Olympia HS	Columbia, S.C.	6-1	185	L-L	18
6.	White Sox	Lee Richard, ss	Southern	Port Arthur, Texas	6-0	160	R-R	21
7.	Astros	*Randy Scarbery, rhp	Roosevelt HS	Fresno, Calif.	6-1	180	R-R	17
8.	Royals	Rex Goodson, c	Pine Tree HS	Longview, Texas	5-11	190	R-R	18
9.	Dodgers	Jim Haller, rhp	Creighton Prep HS	Omaha, Neb.	6-5	205	R-R	18
10.	Angels	Paul Dade, 3b/of	Nathan Hale HS	Seattle	5-11	175	R-R	18
11.	Cardinals	Jim Browning, rhp	Emma Sansom HS	Gadsden, Ala.	6-0	180	R-R	18
12.	Yankees	Dave Cheadle, lhp	Asheville HS	Asheville, N.C.	6-2	180	L-L	19
13.	Pirates	John Bedard, rhp	Tech HS	Springfield, Mass.	6-2	195	R-R	17
14.	Senators	Charles Maxwell, 3b/ss	Zane Trace HS	Kingston, Ohio	6-1	195	L-R	17
15.	Reds	Gary Polczynski, ss	Nathan Hale HS	West Allis, Wis.	6-0	169	R-R	18
16.	Red Sox	*Jimmy Hacker, ss	Temple HS	Temple, Texas	5-11	170	L-R	18
17.	Giants	John DAcquisto, rhp	St. Augustine HS	San Diego	6-2	205	R-R	18
18.	Athletics	Dan Ford, of	Fremont HS	Los Angeles	6-2	185	R-R	18
19.	Cubs	Gene Hiser, of	Maryland	Baltimore	5-10	175	L-L	21
20.	Tigers	Terry Mappin, c	Durrett HS	Louisville, Ky.	6-0	200	L-R	18
21.	Braves	Ron Broaddus, rhp	Brazosport HS	Freeport, Texas	6-4	190	R-R	17
22.	Twins	Bob Gorinski, ss	Mount Pleasant HS	Calumet, Pa.	6-3	215	R-R	18
23.	Mets	*George Ambrow, ss	Poly HS	Long Beach, Calif.	6-0	190	R-R	18
24.	Orioles	James West, c	Vashon HS	St. Louis	6-3	190	B-R	17

*Did not sign.

1970

CLUB-BY-CLUB SELECTIONS

ATLANTA BRAVES

January—Regular Phase (22)

1. Curran Percival, rhp, San Diego Mesa JC
2. **Jack Pierce, 1b, San Jose (Calif.) CC**
3. William Collins, rhp, Manatee (Fla.) JC
4. Willie Harper, rhp, Douglasville, Ga.
5. **Ray McGhee, 2b, Jersey City, N.J.**
6. Pat Cech, rhp, Glendale (Ariz.) CC

January—Secondary Phase (20)

1. Dennis Loewe, rhp, Pershing (Iowa)
2. Ronald Dolan, of/3b, Seton Hall
3. Steve Steitz, 3b, Springfield (Mass.)
4. **Sigmund Gancasz, c, Queensborough (N.Y.) CC**
5. Kenneth Wamble, 3b, Lamar

June—Regular Phase (21)

1. **Ron Broaddus, rhp, Brazosport HS, Freeport, Texas**
2. **Adrian Devine, rhp, Galveston, Texas**
3. **Rod Gilbreath, ss/rhp, Watkins HS, Laurel, Miss.**
4. **Rowland Office, of, McClatchy HS, Sacramento**
5. James Summers, rhp, Memorial HS, Tulsa, Okla.
6. William Lawrence, rhp, Ramsey HS, Birmingham, Ala.
7. **Michael Knox, rhp, West Waterloo (Iowa) HS**
8. Andy Johnson, ss, Athens (Ga.) HS
9. **David Bogacki, lhp, New Jersey HS, Woodbury, N.J.**
10. Jerry Simmons, lhp, Webster HS, Tulsa, Okla.
11. William Griffith, 1b, Wade Hampton HS, Greenville, S.C.
12. Gary Knuckles, 3b, Richmond (Calif.) HS
13. **Lendon Brookins, 3b, Texas Southern**
14. Merle Jordan, lhp/of, Roseville (Calif.) HS
15. **Wallace Jones, rhp, Tampa**
16. Gary Cavallo, rhp, Seton Hall
17. Ronald Robinson, ss/rhp, St. Augustine HS, New Orleans
18. **Perry Chapple, rhp, Erwin HS, Center Point, Ala.**
19. **Thomas Watson, rhp/of, Deering HS, Portland, Maine**
20. Ray Huard, inf, Princeton
21. **Scotty Selph, c, Lee HS, Montgomery, Ala.**
22. George Howay, lhp, Imbay (Mich.) HS
23. Gaylin Papst, ss/of, Danville (Ill.) HS
24. **Wilson Stallworth, rhp, North Carolina A&T**
25. **Terry Smythe, rhp, North Torrance (Calif.) HS**
26. Gary Ellefson, rhp/inf, Dell Rapids (S.D.) HS
27. **Glenn Landesberg, lhp, Bridgeport (Conn.)**
28. Lyman Willis, rhp, North Hampton HS, Eastville, Va.
29. Michael Morrison, ss, Sam Houston HS, San Antonio, Texas
30. Mike Dorn, lhp, Corinth (Miss.) HS

June—Secondary Phase (13)

1. William Hodge, c, Texas A&M
2. Robert Jones, of, Amherst (Mass.)
3. Johnny Grubb Jr., of, Florida State
4. Keith Leippman, 3b, Kansas

BALTIMORE ORIOLES

January—Regular Phase (23)

1. **William Seltzer, c, Hagerstown (Md.) JC**
2. **Nathaniel Turner, 3b, Southside HS, Effingham, S.C.**
3. **Terrence Jones, of, Lower Columbia (Wash.) JC**
4. Gerald Tassa, lhp, Wingate (N.C.) JC
5. Gerard Fell, of/1b, CC of Baltimore
6. William Cameron, of, Gulf Coast (Fla.) CC
7. William Pierce, lhp, Glassboro (N.J.) HS
8. John Stenglein, of/1b, Miami-Dade North CC
9. **Lynn Murdock, of, Tarrant County (Texas) JC**
10. Bruce Mierkowicz, 1b, St. Clair County (Mich.) CC
11. **Ronald Kavanaugh, lhp, Panhandle State (Okla.)**
12. **Michael Pittruzello, of, Central Connecticut State**

January—Secondary Phase (17)

1. **Mike Reinbach, of, UCLA**
2. **Jim Fuller, 1b, San Diego Mesa JC**
3. **Doug DeCinces, 3b, Los Angeles Pierce JC**
4. Mike Cuozzi, 2b/of, Trenton State (N.J.)
5. **Robert McConnaughy, ss, West Liberty State**
6. **James Juniel, of, Contra Costa (Calif.) JC**
7. Jay Smith, rhp, Treasure Island, Fla. (Selection voided)
8. Dan Pritchett, of, El Camino (Calif.) JC (Selection voided)
9. **Gerald Bryant, lhp, Madison Heights, Va.**

June—Regular Phase (24)

1. **James West, c, Vashon HS, St. Louis**
2. **Michael Satterlee, c, Roosevelt HS, Portland, Ore.**
3. **Edward Blake, rhp, Assumption HS, East St. Louis, Ill.**
4. **Dan Beerbower, 3b, Taft (Calif.) HS**
5. **Edward House, lhp, Parker HS, Birmingham, Ala.**
6. Ron Hodges, c, Appalachian State
7. **Don Hickey, c/ss, High Point (N.C.)**
8. **Anthony Leopoldi, inf/of, Bloomfield (N.J.) HS**
9. **Tim Nordbrook, ss, Loyola (Md.)**
10. **Rob Andrews, of, South Torrance (Calif.) HS**
11. **Sylvester Caudle, of, Dorsey HS, Los Angeles**
12. **Herb Hutson, rhp, Georgia Southern**
13. **George Underwood, rhp, Logan (W.Va.) HS**
14. **Olen Bartley, ss, Artesia HS, Lakewood, Calif.**
15. **Randy Lee, lhp, Laurel (Del.) HS**
16. Robert Loughery, rhp, Northeast HS, Pasadena, Md.
17. Jacky Akin, 1b, Panola (Texas) JC
18. **Michael Ivancin, lhp, Bishop Barry HS, St. Petersburg, Fla.**
19. Huntington Batjer, lhp, Central HS, San Angelo, Texas
20. Casey Ortez, of, Stagg HS, Stockton, Calif.
21. Oren Myers, 1b, R.H. Watkins HS, Laurel, Miss.
22. Steve Prestridge, rhp, Central HS, Jackson, Miss.
23. **Hugh Platt, c, La Puente (Calif.) HS**
24. Floyd Hartley, 2b, CC of Baltimore
25. Ronald Hancock, of, Cocoa (Fla.) HS
26. George Boggan, lhp, Calloway HS, Jackson, Miss.
27. **James Blackwood, 2b, Pfeiffer (N.C.)**
28. Thomas Seybold, lhp, Florida
29. Bob Myrick, lhp, Blair HS, Hattiesburg, Miss.
30. John Jeter, of, Spingarn HS, Washington, D.C.
31. Gary Boyajian, rhp, Riverdell HS, River Edge, N.J.
32. Reginald Leonard, of, Princeton HS, Cincinnati
33. Gary Brown, rhp, Elon
34. **Douglas Felderman, c, North Torrance (Calif.) HS**
35. **Ross Miller, rhp, Wyoming**
36. **Martin Pfenninger, ss, Temple**
37. Darrell Devitt, rhp, Billings, Mont.
38. **Rich May, 1b, SUNY Buffalo**
39. **Peter Miller, ss, Grand Rapids (Mich.) JC**
40. Dan Parma, of, Kennedy HS, Buena Park, Calif.
41. Randy Delerio, c, Dos Palos (Calif.) HS
42. Michael Ginocchio, rhp, Santa Monica HS, Los Angeles
43. John Marzulla, rhp/1b, Belmar HS, Spring Lake, N.J.
44. Preston Douglas, of, Pembroke State (N.C.)
45. Al Ryan, 2b, Gulf Coast (Fla.) CC
46. Robert Cobb, rhp, Fresno (Calif.) CC
47. Guy Robinette, 3b, Jefferson HS, Roanoke, Va.
48. **James Fields, of, Georgia Southern**
49. Ricardo Urbano, lhp, Los Gatos (Calif.) HS
50. Daniel Ferguson, c, Sahuaro HS, Tucson, Ariz.
51. Thomas Nelson, ss, Lakewood (Colo.) HS
52. Michael Buchelman, ss, Wilcox HS, Santa Clara, Calif.
53. David Ellis, of, New London (Conn.) HS
54. Michael Rzepiennik, rhp, Dundalk HS, Baltimore
55. Mike Bacsik, rhp, Bishop Dunne HS, Dallas
56. **Greg Montgomery, c, Lincoln HS, Denver**

57. **Donald Belluomini, lhp, JC of San Mateo (Calif.)**

June—Secondary Phase (24)

1. **Claude Renfro, rhp/1b, Gulf Coast (Fla.) CC**
2. **William Wood, c, Los Angeles Valley JC**
3. Michael Cuozzi, 2b/of, Trenton State (N.J.)
4. Richard Fillings, lhp, Indian River (Fla.) CC
5. John LiBrandi, of, Manatee (Fla.) JC
6. Richard Eisenacher, rhp, Auburn
7. **Gene Salmon, 1b, Texas**
8. Gerard Fell, 1b/c, CC of Baltimore
9. Kevin Bryant, 2b, Valencia (Fla.) CC
10. Phill Still, 3b, Mississippi State

BOSTON RED SOX

January—Regular Phase (15)

1. **John Klitsner, 1b, Birmingham HS, Encino, Calif.**
2. **Wayne Milam, rhp, Broward (Fla.) CC**
3. **Steve Miller, c, Virginia**
4. Larry Patton, of/lhp, Columbia State (Tenn.) CC
5. James Paul, rhp, Henry Ford (Mich.) CC
6. **Shawn Harris, rhp, Johnson & Wales (R.I.) JC**
7. **James Jackson, rhp, Fullerton (Calif.) JC**

January—Secondary Phase (5)

1. **Rick Burleson, ss, Warren HS, South Gate, Calif.**
2. Robert Perkins, lhp, Manatee (Fla.) JC
3. **Harry Chapman, rhp, Sarasota (Fla.) HS**
4. Edgar Bellamy, 2b, Fort Cobb (Okla.) HS
5. Donald Rhoton, ss, Columbia State (Tenn.) CC

June—Regular Phase (16)

1. Jimmy Hacker, 3b, Temple (Texas) HS
2. **Fred Wegner, of, Fresno (Calif.) HS**
3. John Schmidt, 3b/rhp, Lutheran HS, Denver
4. **Charles Ross, lhp, Wilson HS, Long Beach, Calif.**
5. **Donald Dudley, rhp, St. Joseph (Mo.) Central HS**
6. **Tom Jones, rhp, Carson-Newman (Tenn.)**
7. **Jerry Spencer, rhp, Southwest Texas State**
8. **Keith Durant, of/rhp, Rippowan HS, Stamford, Conn.**
9. **Kenneth Watkins, rhp, Southwest Missouri State**
10. **Mike Mooney, c, Cardinal Dougherty HS, Buffalo, N.Y.**
11. **Ramsey Koschak, of, Central HS, San Angelo, Texas**
12. John Binks, lhp, Forest Park HS, Beaumont, Texas
13. **Tim Blackwell, 3b/c, Crawford HS, San Diego**
14. **Leo Veleas, of, New Haven (Conn.)**
15. **Peter Peckham, lhp, Mount Pleasant HS, Providence, R.I.**
16. **Anthony McLin, of, Stillman (Ala.)**
17. **William Kouns, rhp, William Carey (Miss.)**
18. **Jack Wick, ss, San Pedro (Calif.) HS**
19. Bruce Kombrinck, p, Gulf Coast (Fla.) CC
20. **Robert Caballero, of, Loyola (La.)**
21. Kenneth Kollmyer, rhp, Hoover HS, San Diego
22. **Karl King, rhp/of, Ansonia (Conn.) HS**
23. **Chad Nielsen, 1b, Ogden (Utah) HS**
24. Jerry DeWitt, rhp/of, El Dorado HS, Orange, Calif.
25. **Dave Barton, 1b, Costa Mesa HS, Santa Ana, Calif.**
26. **Richard Nichols, 2b, Florida State**
27. George Maldonado, of, Nevada-Reno (Selection voided)
28. James Duckhorn, of, Reedley (Calif.) JC
29. **John Sinclair, of, Husson (Maine)**
30. Frank Johnstone, p, Alvin (Texas) HS

June—Secondary Phase (14)

1. **John LaRose, lhp, Cumberland (R.I.) HS**
2. Dave Elmendorf, of, Texas A&M
3. **Larry O'Brien, 1b/of, Long Beach (Calif.) CC**
4. **Alan Jackson, lhp, Northeastern**
5. Charles Bates, 3b/ss, Los Angeles CC

CALIFORNIA ANGELS

January—Regular Phase (9)

1. Paul Sands, rhp, Lakewood (Calif.) HS
2. **Morris Nettles, of, Venice (Calif.) HS**
3. Jim Chapman, ss, Columbia Basin (Wash.) CC (Selection voided)
4. Thomas Williams, of, Solano (Calif.) CC
5. **Albert Borchetta, lhp, Greenwich, Conn.**
6. Alan Gomez, ss, Foothill (Calif.) JC
7. Jerry Reasonover, 2b, Gulf Coast (Fla.) CC
8. **John Clear, 1b/of, Los Angeles Harbor JC**

January—Secondary Phase (7)

1. **John Doherty, of, Reading, Mass.**
2. Gary Granville, of, El Camino (Calif.) JC
3. Robert Beyn, rhp, Taft (Calif.) JC
4. Sherwood Hahn, 1b/of, Virginia Tech
5. **Thomas Lundgren, lhp, Missouri**
6. Walter Sumner, of, Florida State
7. **Darrell Darrow, 2b, Long Beach (Calif.) CC**

June—Regular Phase (10)

1. **Paul Dade, 3b/of, Nathan Hale HS, Seattle**
2. **Dan Briggs, lhp/1b, Sonoma (Calif.) HS**
3. **Gary Talley, lhp, South Garland (Texas) HS**
4. David Freeborn, ss, Shafter HS, Buttonwillow, Calif.
5. **John Balaz, of, San Diego CC**
6. **Michael Browne, rhp, Sterling HS, Houston**
7. **Dick Lange, rhp, Central Michigan**
8. **Doug Howard, 1b, Brigham Young**
9. Bradley Duncan, rhp, El Camino HS, Sacramento
10. Allen Baker, c, Erwin HS, Birmingham, Ala.
11. Gene Delyon, 3b, Los Altos (Calif.) HS
12. **Ronald Marquez, of/ss, Lakewood (Calif.) HS**
13. **William Rothan, rhp, Western Hills HS, Cincinnati**
14. **Richard Case, rhp, Park Ridge (N.J.) HS**
15. Steve Stroughter, of, Redwood HS, Visalia, Calif.
16. **Antonio Barbosa, lhp, Texas-Pan American**
17. John Bush, rhp, San Gabriel (Calif.) HS
18. Mike Edwards, ss, Jefferson HS, Los Angeles
19. Mark Robinson, rhp, Key West (Fla.) HS
20. **Brian Woodward, rhp, Woodland (Wash.) HS**
21. **Robert Groth, of, Fresno State**
22. Walt Kaczmarek, rhp, Santa Clara (Calif.) HS
23. John Bush, of, Central HS, Miami
24. **Sid Monge, lhp, Brawley (Calif.) HS**
25. Dennis Nadeau, ss, Alvirne HS, Hudson, N.H.
26. Rayford Hall, ss/2b, Roosevelt HS, Fresno, Calif.
27. Richard Hennes, of, Huntington Park (Calif.) HS
28. **Laron Matlock, of, Ventura (Calif.) JC**
29. **Willie Goldwire, c, John Kennedy HS, Riviera Beach, Fla.**
30. Everett Turner, of, San Lorenzo (Calif.) HS
31. Patrick Daniels, lhp, Idaho
32. Mike Krukow, c/rhp, San Gabriel (Calif.) HS
33. Walt Sweeney, lhp, Petaluma (Calif.) HS
34. **Rob Johnson, rhp, Cal State Northridge**
35. Dana Dismukes, rhp, Foothill (Calif.) JC
36. Richard Adkins, rhp, MacArthur HS, Pasadena, Texas (Selection voided)
37. Dennis Palla, of, Shafter HS, Buttonwillow, Calif.
38. Doug Colvard, of, Lincoln HS, Stockton, Calif.
39. Gene Moreau, of, Edison HS, Fresno, Calif.

June—Secondary Phase (22)

1. Richard Soriano, of, Miami-Dade North CC
2. Pat Cech, rhp, Glendale (Ariz.) CC
3. Kenneth Harris, of, Pasadena (Calif.) CC
4. Michael Potter, of, Mount San Antonio (Calif.) JC
5. Todd Sprecher, c, Yakima Valley (Wash.) JC
6. Rick Dierker, rhp, Los Angeles Pierce JC

CHICAGO CUBS

January—Regular Phase (20)

1. **Pete LaCock, 1b, Taft HS, Woodland Hills, Calif.**
2. Greg Gaffey, 1b, Lincoln Land (Ill.) JC
3. Ronald Hardin, of, Polk (Fla.) CC
4. **Walter Hirsh, of, Ocean County (N.J.) JC**
5. Ronald Kendall, ss, Forest Hill HS, West Palm Beach, Fla.

January—Secondary Phase (22)

1. **Bruce Clouser, of, St. Joseph's**

2. **Dennis Odom, ss, San Diego CC**
3. **Robert Maneely, rhp, St. Joseph's HS, Deptford, N.J.**
4. Larry Green, c, Doane (Neb.)
5. Chuck Seelbach, rhp, Dartmouth
6. Ellsworth Jones, lhp, New York
7. Angelo Mecca, of, Keystone (Pa.) JC
8. Jack Wilson, of, Sarasota (Fla.) HS

June—Regular Phase (19)

1. **Gene Hiser, of, Maryland**
2. **Dyain Frazier, lhp, Elmore HS, Houston**
3. **Rick Reuschel, rhp, Western Illinois**
4. Tim Doerr, ss, Granite Hills HS, El Cajon, Calif.
5. **Walter Badcock, lhp, Springfield (Mass.)**
6. **William Butts, of, Fowler (Calif.) HS**
7. **Thomas O'Brien, of, Hoover HS, Fresno, Calif.**
8. **Calvin White, 1b, Maggie (Calif.) HS**
9. **Jimmy Kelly, lhp, Brazosport HS, Freeport, Texas**
10. Jeff Oscarson, ss, Saguaro HS, Scottsdale, Ariz.
11. Jackson Todd, rhp, Will Rogers HS, Tulsa, Okla.
12. Mike Sylvester, rhp, Moeller HS, Cincinnati
13. **Bill Huisman, 2b, Kansas State**
14. **Nicholas McKenzie, c, Moses Lake (Wash.) HS**
15. **Robert Watson, of, Western Illinois**
16. **Craig Schwerman, rhp, Western Illinois**
17. Bernardo Castillo, 2b, Coral Park HS, Miami
18. Jeff Schneider, lhp, Alleman HS, Rock Island, Ill.
19. **Michael Fink, ss, Middlesex (N.J.) HS**
20. **Donald Schuldies, of, Granite Hills HS, El Cajon, Calif.**
21. **Gary Guenther, inf, Modesto (Calif.) JC**
22. James Riddell, rhp, Hillsborough HS, Tampa
23. Gerald Fahland, c, Libby (Mont.) HS
24. Gregg Schnurr, of, Troy HS, Fullerton, Calif.
25. Kevin McNichol, inf, James Monroe HS, Bronx, N.Y.
26. James Walton, rhp, Alleghany HS, Cumberland, Md.
27. **Clinton Henderson, of/rhp, Bethune HS, Shreveport, La.**
28. Dean Boger, lhp, Falls Church (Va.) HS
29. **Mark Thomas, rhp, McMurray (Texas)**
30. **Michael Weiss, rhp, Quincy (Ill.) HS**
31. Glenn Bryant, rhp, Aldine HS, Houston
32. Robert Vandersluis, rhp, Northwest Nazarene (Idaho)
33. **Jimmy Bianchi, ss, Boise State**
34. **Robert Schell, ss, Clay HS, South Bend, Ind.**
35. **Glenn Stinson, of, McMurray (Texas)**
36. **Bruce Hildebrandt, rhp, Pace (N.Y.)**
37. David Landers, of, St. Joseph's
38. Cecil Evans, lhp, Carlsbad (N.M.) HS
39. Thomas Amanti, rhp, New London (Conn.) HS
40. **Gary McKenna, rhp, Providence**
41. Bill Capps, 2b, Arlington (Texas) HS
42. **Gary Hogan, rhp, Broward (Fla.) CC**
43. **Charles Benjamin, 1b, St. Petersburg (Fla.) JC**
44. **Lawrence Pratt, c, South Broward HS, Hollywood, Fla.**
45. Thomas Stafford, of, Lee HS, Jacksonville, Fla.
46. **Thomas McBean, of, Husson (Maine)**
47. **Michael Clampitt, ss, Hobbs (N.M.) HS**

June—Secondary Phase (17)

1. **Tom Lundstedt, c, Michigan**
2. **Steve Steitz, 3b, Springfield (Mass.)**
3. **Kurt Ascherman, c, Springfield (Mass.)**

CHICAGO WHITE SOX

January—Regular Phase (5)

1. Duane Kuiper, ss, Indian Hills (Iowa) CC
2. Archibald Cameron, rhp, Miami-Dade North CC
3. **Barry Curlee, of, East Rowan HS, Granite Quarry, N.C.**
4. **Dan McDonough, c, Indian Hills (Iowa) CC**
5. Joel Sexton, rhp, Indian Hills (Iowa) CC
6. **James Rice, c, Fullerton (Calif.) JC**
7. Michael Misler, lhp, Miami-Dade North CC
8. Daniel Hinzman, lhp, Indian Hills (Iowa) CC
9. **Larry Shoup, of, Cypress (Calif.) JC**
10. Bruce Meredith, lhp, Ellsworth (Iowa) JC

January—Secondary Phase (21)

1. Rick Dierker, rhp, Los Angeles Pierce JC
2. **Emery Mitchell, c, American River (Calif.) JC**
3. Gary Mack, 2b, Cypress (Calif.) JC
4. John Tamargo, c, Miami-Dade North CC

June—Regular Phase (6)

1. **Lee Richard, ss, Southern**
2. **Terry Forster, lhp, Santana HS, Santee, Calif.**
3. **Jerry Hairston Sr., of/inf, Gardendale HS, Birmingham, Ala.**
4. **Harold McClain, lhp, Beaver Falls (Pa.) HS**
5. Dale Lydecker, of, Nyack (N.Y.) HS
6. **Jim Geddes, rhp, Ohio State**
7. **Dennis Weidman, of, Lampeter Strasburg HS, South Lancaster, Pa.**
8. Steve Foran, lhp, Denver
9. **Rich Gossage, rhp, Wasson HS, Colorado Springs, Colo.**
10. Lyn Hamilton, c, Headland HS, East Point, Ga.
11. Mike Hefftner, lhp, Erie (Colo.) HS
12. **Mike Drewett, 3b, Pine Bluff (Ark.) HS**
13. **Steven Houck, of, Oklahoma State**
14. Gary Wagner, rhp, Maine East HS, Niles, Ill.
15. Jimmy Collins, rhp, Southern
16. **Dennis Smith, of, Neshaminy HS, Levittown, Pa.**
17. **Richard Lucke, of, Notre Dame**
18. Arnold Costell, lhp, McArthur HS, South Wantagh, N.Y.
19. **Gregory Mathey, rhp/of, Thornton HS, Harvey, Ill.**
20. **Bruce Miller, ss, Indiana**
21. **Gene Duhe, rhp, Nicholls State**
22. Jay Parker, c, Clay HS, South Bend, Ind.
23. Joseph Lang, c/3b, Cardinal Dougherty HS, Buffalo, N.Y.
24. **Allan Paganucci, rhp, San Francisco**
25. **Cliff Hayes, of/inf, Jackson State**
26. **Michael Reynolds, c, Catawba (N.C.)**
27. Stephen Hazan, lhp, Mission Viejo (Calif.) HS
28. **Bill Bourg, rhp, Arkansas State**
29. **Richard Demay, rhp, Elgin (Ill.) HS**
30. Bruce Mitchell, inf, Little Rock (Ark.) Central HS
31. Stephen Sroba, of, Neshaminy HS, Trevose, Pa.
32. **Frank Buchan, of, Upper Iowa**

June—Secondary Phase (6)

1. **Bucky Dent, 3b, Miami-Dade North CC**
2. Henry Baker, 3b, Southern
3. Archie Manning, ss, Mississippi

CINCINNATI REDS

January—Regular Phase (16)

1. Dale Harrington, rhp, Odessa (Texas) JC
2. **Joel Youngblood, c/ss, Stephen F. Austin HS, Houston**
3. **Frank Martin, lhp, San Joaquin Delta (Calif.) JC**
4. Larry Wondercheck, lhp, Long Beach (Calif.) CC
5. Charles Haymes, c/2b, Chicago, Ill.
6. Larry Hammer, rhp, New Mexico Highlands
7. Stephen Thompson, lhp, Jackson, Tenn.
8. Mark Fouse, rhp, Connors State (Okla.) JC

January—Secondary Phase (18)

1. **Harold Wall, rhp, Auburn (N.Y.) JC**
2. **James Kirkland, of, South Georgia JC**
3. Anthony Blakley, ss/2b, Brewton-Parker (Ga.) JC
4. Johnny Spriggs, of, Angelo State (Texas)
5. **Stephen Klinger, lhp, Bloomsburg (Pa.)**
6. Norman Jones, inf, Atlantic (N.J.) CC

June—Regular Phase (15)

1. **Gary Polczynski, ss, Nathan Hale HS, West Allis, Wis.**
2. **Rex Jackson, rhp, Rubidoux HS, Riverside, Calif.**
3. **Barry Ulsh, 1b, Middletown (Pa.) Area HS**
4. **Leslie Pinkham, c, Jeffersonville (Ind.) HS**
5. Huey Rice, rhp, Leon HS, Tallahassee, Fla.
6. **Tom Carroll, rhp, North Allegheny HS, Pittsburgh**
7. Eugene Quirk, of, Wahconah Regional HS, Dalton, Mass.
8. **Will McEnaney, lhp, Springfield (Ohio) North HS**
9. Greg Sinatro, ss/3b, LaSalle Academy, Hartford, Conn.

10. **Ray Knight, rhp/3b, Dougherty HS, Albany, Ga.**
11. **Ira Damren, 1b, East Carteret HS, Beaufort, N.C.**
12. **William Smith, c, Hope Mills (N.C.) HS**
13. **Chris Jones, of, Azusa Pacific (Calif.)**
14. **David Hill, rhp, North Carolina**
15. **Pat McGehee, of, Oceanside (Calif.) HS**
16. Douglas Kotar, of, Cannor-McMillan HS, Muse, Pa.
17. **Jesse Helton, ss, East Texas Baptist**
18. **David Hagadorn, rhp, Mansfield (Pa.)**
19. **Pat Zachry, rhp, Richfield HS, Waco, Texas**
20. Don Golden, of, Valdosta (Ga.) HS
21. Don Kreke, rhp, Mater Dei HS, Bartelso, Ill.
22. Richard Williams, rhp, Mercid HS, El Nido, Calif.
23. **Rick DeFelice, c, Cincinnati**
24. John Maier, rhp, Laurel Valley HS, New Florence, Pa.
25. **Lawrence Basey, of, Martinsburg (W.Va.) HS**
26. **Stan Norman, of, Fairfield**
27. **Eric Boyd, 1b/c, CC of Baltimore**
28. **James Mavroleon, rhp, West Virginia**
29. **Richard Blackstone, of, Fairmont State (W.Va.)**
30. Victor Mantoni, 3b, Hopedale (Mass.) HS
31. Jack Risdon, lhp, Edmond (Okla.) HS
32. Burke Suter, rhp, Towson (Md.) Senior HS
33. Robert Steinberg, 1b, Scranton (Pa.)
34. Lawrence Gustafson, c/3b, Oakcrest HS, Mays Landing, N.J.
35. David Moharter, lhp, Bloomsburg (Pa.)
36. Stephen Carrigan, ss, Archbishop Curley HS, Baltimore
37. Mark Hoffman, lhp, Titusville (Fla.) HS
38. Gary Richter, 2b, Pleasanton (Texas) HS
39. Stephen Parker, of, Mainland HS, Northfield, N.J.
40. Jeffrey Bradford, rhp, Dundalk HS, Baltimore
41. John Wiggins, rhp, Plant City (Fla.) HS
42. **Thomas Collins, rhp, New York**
43. Larry Cole, ss, Weber State
44. **Ronald Williamson, of/inf, Hallsboro (N.C.) HS**
45. Michael Racobaldo, rhp, Woodrow Wilson HS, Camden, N.J.
46. Charles Cundari, lhp, Westlake HS, Hawthorne, N.Y.
47. Richard Ryan, rhp, Iowa Central CC

June—Secondary Phase (9)

1. **Pat Osburn, lhp, Florida State**
2. Jim Norris, of, Maryland
3. Duane Kuiper, ss, Indian Hills (Iowa) CC
4. Mike Dickens, 3b, Catawba (N.C.)

CLEVELAND INDIANS

January—Regular Phase (1)

1. **Chris Chambliss, 1b, UCLA**
2. Brian Lieckfelt, rhp, St. Clair County (Mich.) CC
3. **Dennis Queen, lhp, St. Clair County (Mich.) CC**
4. **John Detter, rhp, Nickerson (Kan.) HS**
5. **Michael Burger, 3b, Brewton-Parker (Ga.) JC**
6. William Smith, lhp, Mount San Antonio (Calif.) JC
7. **James Valenty, 3b/of, St. Petersburg (Fla.) JC**

January—Secondary Phase (15)

1. **Gary King, ss, South Bend, Ind.**
2. **William Hernandez, c, Staten Island (N.Y.)**
3. Bernie Boehmer, c, St. Louis CC-Meramec
4. **William Hendricks, lhp, Miami (Ohio)**
5. **Carlos Suarez, lhp, Miami-Dade North CC**
6. Randall Goede, lhp, Valparaiso

June—Regular Phase (2)

1. **Steve Dunning, rhp, Stanford**
2. **Burnell Flowers, of, Courter Tech HS, Cincinnati**
3. **Harry Shaughnessy, of, Western Michigan**
4. **Jeff Baker, rhp, Charter Oaks HS, Glendora, Calif.**
5. **Tommy Smith, of, North Carolina State**
6. **Ron Salyers, lhp, Admiral King HS, Lorain, Ohio**
7. Jim Kremmel, lhp, New Mexico
8. Paul Miles, of, Paulding (Ohio) HS
9. **Gary Tucker, 1b, Leto HS, Tampa**
10. **Dennis Kinney, lhp, Bedford HS, Temperance, Mich.**
11. David Hasbach, rhp, Palentine (Ill.) HS
12. **James Beyersdorf, rhp, Freeland HS, Saginaw, Mich.**
13. Richard Katz, 3b, Platt HS, Meriden, Conn.
14. **Dan Stoligrosz, 3b, Southern California**
15. **Randy Peterson, c, Warren HS, Downey, Calif.**
16. **Thomas Burkert, lhp, Eastern Michigan**
17. Byron Florence, of, Roosevelt HS, East Chicago, Ind.
18. Mike Kavanaugh, ss/c, Patterson HS, Baltimore
19. **Dave Jacome, ss, Arizona**
20. **Dave Ruhe, of/1b, St. Joseph's (Ind.)**
21. Craig Paterniti, rhp, Falconer (N.Y.) HS
22. **Dean Schneider, 1b, Capital (Ohio)**
23. **Thomas Kelley, rhp, Aurora (Colo.) HS**
24. Steven Schultz, lhp, Rancho HS, North Las Vegas, Nev.
25. Sam Bowen, of/rhp, Glenn Academy HS, Brunswick, Ga.
26. **Jeff Newman, c/1b, Texas Christian**
27. **Michael Green, 3b, East HS, Atlanta**
28. Mel Cuckovich, 3b/ss, Hiram Johnson HS, Sacramento
29. Ward Glazebrook, 1b, Coalinga (Calif.) HS
30. James Robertson, c, Bay HS, Bay Village, Ohio
31. James Street, rhp, Texas
32. Robert Brough, lhp, Woodmore HS, Woodville, Ohio
33. John Pilewski, rhp, Bowsher HS, Toledo, Ohio
34. **Jack Darnell, rhp, Monterrey HS, Lubbock, Texas**
35. **Donald Kennedy, lhp, Hiram (Ohio)**

June—Secondary Phase (4)

1. Mike Swenton, of, Oklahoma
2. Curran Percival, rhp, San Diego Mesa JC
3. **Robert Eldridge, rhp, Southern Illinois**
4. Doug Ault, of/lhp, Panola (Texas) JC

DETROIT TIGERS

January—Regular Phase (19)

1. James Steele, 1b, Cerritos (Calif.) JC
2. **Douglas Brittelle, rhp, Rutgers**
3. Mike Potter, of, Mount San Antonio (Calif.) JC
4. Raymond Kennett, rhp, Connors State (Okla.) JC
5. John Orr, of, Finney HS, Detroit
6. Michael Strickland, of, Northwestern HS, Detroit

January—Secondary Phase (23)

1. Steven Cash, ss, DeKalb (Ga.) JC
2. **Jeffrey Hogan, 3b, Florida State**
3. **Michael Pivec, of, CC of Baltimore**
4. Rand Rasmussen, ss, Long Beach (Calif.) CC
5. Richard Auckland, 1b/of, West Chester (Pa.)

June—Regular Phase (20)

1. **Terry Mappin, c, Durrett HS, Louisville, Ky.**
2. Mike Ibarguen, rhp, Sam Rayburn HS, Pasadena, Texas
3. James Chamberlain, lhp, Ben Smith HS, Greensboro, N.C.
4. **Daniel Grant, c, Westchester HS, Los Angeles**
5. **Tom Lantz, rhp, Akron (Ohio) East HS**
6. **Alan Locasio, c, St. Francis (N.Y.)**
7. Paul Spivey, of, Lee HS, Montgomery, Ala.
8. **John Knox, 2b, Bowling Green State**
9. **Phil Mankowski, 3b, Bishop Turner HS, Cheektowaga, N.Y.**
10. **Fernando Arroyo, rhp, Burbank HS, Sacramento**
11. William Smith, ss, Mozano HS, Albuquerque, N.M.
12. Gary Hampton, of, Fresno (Calif.) HS
13. **James Bebout, of, Morgan HS, Stockport, Ohio**
14. **David Baye, rhp, Southern Connecticut State**
15. **Ted Brazell, of, St. Louis CC-Meramec**
16. Glenn Knight, rhp, Allen Park (Mich.) HS
17. **Albert Kaminski, ss, Minnesota**
18. Charles Coe, ss, St. Louis CC-Meramec
19. Curt Grote, ss, Hoyletown (Ill.) HS
20. **David Deluca, rhp, Syracuse**
21. **Fred Holdsworth, rhp, Northville (Mich.) HS**
22. **Kenneth Forfar, rhp, Kearny (N.J.) HS**
23. Dennis Hindman, rhp, Brethren (Mich.) HS
24. **Carl Cavanaugh, rhp, Tampa**
25. **Richard Fairbanks, of, Brigham Young**
26. Dean Jones, lhp, Warden HS, Bristol, Va.
27. **Carmine Perotta, rhp, Florida Southern**

28. Thomas DeBeche, rhp, St. Agnes Cathedral HS, Massapequa Park, N.Y.
29. **Steven Strack, ss, Niagara Falls (N.Y.) Senior HS**
30. **Randy Brady, of, Zeeland HS, Holland, Mich.**
31. **Fred Bruntager, lhp, SUNY Cortland**
32. Tim Pierce, rhp, Kenmore East HS, Tonawanda, N.Y.
33. **William Crowley, 3b, Holy Cross**
34. **Jonathan Golden, of, Monmouth**

June—Secondary Phase (12)

1. **Chuck Seelbach, rhp, Dartmouth**
2. **James Bergholz, ss, King's College (N.Y.)**
3. Jerry Reasonover, ss, Gulf Coast (Fla.) CC
4. William Collins, rhp, Manatee (Fla.) JC

HOUSTON ASTROS

January—Regular Phase (8)

1. William Wood, c, Los Angeles Valley JC
2. Kent Froede, of, Southwestern (Calif.) JC
3. Kenneth Doria, 3b, Gulf Coast (Fla.) CC
4. Mason Bean, c, South Georgia JC
5. Larry Carino, 2b, Ridgewood, N.J. (Selection voided)

January—Secondary Phase (14)

1. Robert Masteller, lhp, Grayson County (Texas) JC
2. **Mike Cosgrove, lhp, Phoenix JC**
3. **Steven Gardner, 3b, Weber State**
4. **Jerry Lewis, 1b, JC of the Desert (Calif.)**

June—Regular Phase (7)

1. Randy Scarbery, rhp, Roosevelt HS, Fresno, Calif.
2. **John Williams, ss, Webb HS, Oxford, N.C.**
3. **Robert Stratton, rhp, Los Altos (Calif.) HS**
4. **Greg Gross, of, Red Land HS, Etters, Pa.**
5. **Ronald DeJean, p, Aurora (Colo.) Central HS**
6. **Richard Busby, ss, Bessemer (Ala.) HS**
7. **John McLaren, c, Westbury HS, Houston**
8. **Rick Sanderlin, of, Mission Bay HS, San Diego**
9. **Tom Wise, inf, Madison HS, Portland, Ore.**
10. **Gordon Crane, rhp, Birmingham HS, Van Nuys, Calif.**
11. **Lennard Davis, of, Daytona Mainland HS, Daytona Beach, Fla.**
12. Lonnie Kruger, rhp, Silver Lake (Kan.) HS
13. **William Horne, rhp, Daugherty HS, Albany, Ga.**
14. **William Gardner, rhp, DeLand (Fla.) HS**
15. Joe Wallis, of, McClure HS, Florissant, Mo.
16. Lawrence Kimm, lhp, New Riegel (Ohio) HS
17. Joseph Chelli, rhp, Linden (Calif.) HS
18. Richard Marcet, rhp, McGill HS, Mobile, Ala.
19. **Brad McRoberts, rhp, Santana HS, El Cajon, Calif.**
20. **David Wing, ss, Will Rogers HS, Tulsa, Okla.**
21. **Anthony Lang, of, Central HS, Mobile, Ala.**
22. **James Provenzeno, lhp, Arizona**
23. Thomas Walsh, lhp, St. Maria Goretti HS, Hagerstown, Md.
24. Brad Omlid, inf, Cleveland HS, Seattle
25. **James Streleski, lhp, Puyallup (Wash.) HS**

June—Secondary Phase (11)

1. **Donald Russell, inf, Clemson**
2. Jim Burnes, rhp, Glendale (Ariz.) CC
3. Stan Butkus, rhp, Miami-Dade North CC

KANSAS CITY ROYALS

January—Regular Phase (7)

1. Jack Peres, rhp, Los Angeles Harbor JC
2. **James Webb, lhp, Western Kentucky**
3. **Greg Minton, rhp, San Diego Mesa JC**
4. Wayne Currin, of, Louisburg (N.C.) JC
5. **John Joseph, of, Chabot (Calif.) JC**
6. Larry McDaniel, c, Bacone (Okla.) JC
7. Rick Halsey, 3b, San Diego Mesa JC
8. Joe Meyers, ss, James Monroe HS, Mission Hills, Calif.
9. **Gary Hubbs, c, Cal Poly Pomona**
10. Steven Shaw, of, Prince George's (Md.) CC

January—Secondary Phase (13)

1. Ron Diggle, of, Cerritos (Calif.) JC
2. Cal Meier, ss, Southern California
3. **Jim Wohlford, ss, JC of the Sequoias (Calif.)**
4. Gary Wann, rhp, Fullerton (Calif.) JC
5. Dean Mick, ss, Yakima Valley (Wash.) JC

June—Regular Phase (8)

1. **Rex Goodson, c, Pine Tree HS, Longview, Texas**
2. **John Johnson, ss, Little Rock (Ark.) Central HS**
3. **David Allen, lhp, Haverford Township HS, Havertown, Pa.**
4. **Tom Poquette, of, Memorial HS, Eau Claire, Wis.**
5. Arthur Grzeskowiak, 1b, Sterling Morton East HS, Cicero, Ill.
6. **Paul Pelz, rhp, Neff HS, La Mirada, Calif.**
7. **Richard Lashmet, ss, Chatsworth HS, Canoga Park, Calif.**
8. **Bruce Griggs, rhp, Thornridge HS, Thornton, Ill.**
9. **Arthur Payne, rhp, Arkansas A&M**
10. **Noel Paulson, 2b, Golden West (Calif.) JC**
11. **Stanley Jackson, 1b, Thornton HS, Harvey, Ill.**
12. Ed Bowman, 3b, Santa Barbara (Calif.) HS
13. James Ferguson, of, Kennedy HS, Richmond, Calif.
14. **Brad Rooker, lhp, North Torrance (Calif.) HS**
15. **John Hurst, 2b, Shrewsbury (Mass.) HS**
16. **Robert McDonald, c, Chambersburg (Pa.) HS**
17. Alvin Harper, ss, Webster HS, Minden, La.
18. Allan Houston, rhp, Woburn (Mass.) HS
19. **Darrell Gambero, rhp, Fresno State**
20. **Lonne Reed, of, Fremont HS, Los Angeles**
21. Marv Chamberlain, c, Mark Morris HS, Longview, Wash.
22. Jack Winchester, 3b, Inglewood (Calif.) HS
23. Rick Bloomer, of, Oak Park HS, Kansas City, Mo.
24. Steve Taylor, lhp, Pasadena (Calif.) CC
25. **Gerald Clark, c, Wahama HS, New Haven, W.Va.**
26. **Chris Crews, ss, Westside HS, Omaha, Neb.**
27. Rudy Sgontz, c, Loara HS, Anaheim
28. **Scott McManis, rhp, Sunset HS, Portland, Ore.**
29. Donald Jones, lhp, Arcadia (Calif.) HS
30. John Rowley, lhp, Buffalo (Okla.) HS
31. Stephen Lee, lhp, Cal State Northridge
32. **James Feiler, lhp, Unionville HS, West Chester, Pa.**
33. **Gary Schlagenhauf, of, UC Davis**
34. **Don Campbell, lhp, Western Montana**
35. John Stefanski, ss, New London (Conn.) HS
36. **Peter Dunn, c, Stetson**
37. James Streleski, lhp, Puyallup (Wash.) HS (Selection voided)
38. Joseph Lewandowski, of, Plainedge HS, North Massapequa, N.Y.

June—Secondary Phase (2)

1. **Tom Harmon, c, Texas**
2. **Carl Meier, ss, Southern California**
3. **John Gaylord, c, Chaffey (Calif.) JC**
4. **Gary Houston, lhp, San Jose State**
5. James Steele, 1b, Cerritos (Calif.) JC
6. Bruce Mierkowicz, 1b, St. Clair County (Mich.) CC
7. **Jack Burns, rhp, Denver**

LOS ANGELES DODGERS

January—Regular Phase (10)

1. Jim Burnes, rhp, Glendale (Ariz.) CC
2. Edward Womboldt, c, Indian Hills (Iowa) CC
3. David Holmes, c, Glendale (Ariz.) CC
4. **Ralph Davis, rhp, Alice (Texas) HS**
5. Kenneth Harris, 1b, Pasadena (Calif.) CC

January—Secondary Phase (10)

1. John LaRose, lhp, Cumberland, R.I.
2. Kevin Kooyman, c, Grossmont (Calif.) JC
3. **Bruce Raible, rhp, Cincinnati**
4. Mike Barlow, rhp, Syracuse

June—Regular Phase (9)

1. **Jim Haller, rhp, Creighton Prep HS, Omaha, Neb.**
2. **Randy Fairbanks, lhp, Satellite (Fla.) HS**
3. **Lance Rautzhan, lhp, Blue Mountain HS, Pottsville, Pa.**
4. **Ricky Nitz, rhp, Hoover HS, Glendale, Calif.**

5. **Dewey Forry, of, Terra Linda HS, San Rafael, Calif.**
6. James Vaeth, rhp, Seaford (N.Y.) HS
7. **Thomas Jenkins, of, Tulsa**
8. Rex Peters, 1b, Midland Park (N.J.) HS
9. **John Snider, 3b/of, Fairfield Union HS, Pleasantville, Ohio**
10. **Wayne Ristig, 2b, Chapman (Calif.)**
11. Creighton Tevlin, of, Canoga Park (Calif.) HS
12. Pat Paulson, lhp, East Haven (Conn.) HS
13. **Norman Brown, of, California**
14. **Thomas Corder, ss, San Jose State**
15. John Cosmos, 1b/lhp, Sacred Heart HS, San Francisco
16. **Mike Plunkett, rhp, Emporia State (Kan.)**
17. Mike Vail, ss, Mitty HS, San Jose, Calif.
18. Larry Tolbert, rhp, East Central HS, Tulsa, Okla.
19. **Paul Barnes, of, Middle Georgia JC**
20. **Phil Keller, rhp, Stanford**
21. **Albert Taylor, rhp, Kearny HS, San Diego**
22. **Oscar Burney, 1b, Northeast Louisiana**
23. **Les Rogers, 3b, Tulsa**
24. Francisco Suarez, ss, Hialeah (Fla.) HS
25. Dennis Abel, of, San Francisco State
26. **Thomas Gleason, lhp, Cleveland HS, Reseda, Calif.**
27. John Wade, c, Pasadena (Calif.) HS
28. **Ronald Hall, lhp, Oklahoma**
29. **Steve Wilson, rhp, South Georgia JC**
30. James Ivey, lhp, East Point, Ga.
31. Bruce Collins, rhp, South San Francisco HS
32. Thaddeus Rowe, inf, Brookland-Cayce HS, West Columbia, S.C.
33. **Greg Shanahan, rhp, Humboldt State (Calif.)**
34. Chris Kinsel, c, St. Augustine HS, Bonita, Calif.
35. Mike Garrett, of, Marina del Rey, Calif.
36. Mark Andresen, of, Garden Grove (Calif.) HS
37. Michael Sanders, 3b, Daniel HS, Clemson, S.C.
38. Maury Damkroger, c, Northeast HS, Lincoln, Neb.
39. **Vandon Mattison, lhp, Kennedy HS, Sacramento**
40. Scott Waltermate, rhp, Steeleville (Ill.) HS

June—Secondary Phase (7)

1. **Doug Rau, lhp, Texas A&M**
2. George Pugh, lhp, Mesa (Ariz.) CC
3. **Joe Daniels, of, New Mexico**
4. **Ken O'Brien, rhp, Villanova**
5. Paul Womble, 3b, Kansas

MILWAUKEE BREWERS

January—Regular Phase (3)

1. George Bacher, of, Quincy (Mass.) JC
2. James Timmons, c, Arizona Western JC
3. **Guy McTheny, of/c, Florida**
4. William Bell, ss, Jefferson State (Ala.) JC
5. Dennis Clark, c, Chaffey (Calif.) JC
6. Gary Malcolm, of, Elkhart (Ind.) HS

January—Secondary Phase (19)

1. **Gary Bradshaw, rhp, Miami-Dade North CC**
2. Charles Bates, 3b, Cerritos (Calif.) JC
3. Robert Crain, ss, Pasadena (Calif.) CC
4. Earl Austin, 3b, Dos Palos, Calif.
5. **Dennis Holmberg, 3b, Brewton-Parker (Ga.) JC**
6. Bruce Irvin, c, St. Petersburg (Fla.) JC
7. **David Kropfelder, c, CC of Baltimore**
8. Gilbert Untermeyer, 3b, St. John's River (Fla.) CC

June—Regular Phase (4)

1. **Darrell Porter, c, Southeast HS, Oklahoma City, Okla.**
2. Ken Pape, ss, MacArthur HS, San Antonio, Texas
3. **Price Thomas, of, Shaw HS, Mobile, Ala.**
4. **Gerald O'Neill, lhp, St. Agnes HS, Baldwin Park, N.Y.**
5. **Carl Austerman, rhp, Glendale (Ariz.) HS**
6. **Bill Travers, lhp, Norwood (Mass.) HS**
7. **Duane Espy, 2b, Santa Monica (Calif.) HS**
8. **Marion Jackson, of, Jackson HS, Miami**
9. John Nunnenkamp, rhp, Freeport (N.Y.) HS
10. **Ken Collins, rhp, Clackamas (Ore.) CC**
11. Steve Behlen, lhp, Clovis (Calif.) HS
12. **Darryl Steen, rhp, Jefferson HS, Los Angeles**
13. Richard Baker, lhp, Parker HS, Jacksonville, Fla.
14. **Charles Capello, lhp, Long Island**
15. Charles Manley, of, Springfield (Mass.) Tech HS
16. **Brian Muir, of, Douglas HS, Portland, Ore.**
17. Pat Marble, rhp, Yucca Valley (Calif.) HS
18. William Varner, lhp, Roberts HS, Decorah, Iowa
19. Andrew Kemp, rhp, Pasadena (Calif.) HS
20. Frank Dziadul, 3b, Seminole (Fla.) HS
21. John McMillan, rhp, Parkton HS, North Red Springs, N.C.
22. **Michael Seufer, of, Franklin Heights HS, Columbus, Ohio**
23. **Dennis Yard, rhp, Northridge, Calif.**
24. Donald Cooke, lhp, Monsignor Pace HS, Opalocka, Fla.
25. **Paul Lang, rhp, SUNY Buffalo**
26. Victor Zaremba, of/p, Colorado Springs (Colo.) HS
27. Rex Landis, c, Franklin Heights HS, Columbus, Ohio
28. **Thomas Steadman, ss, Archbishop Carroll HS, Washington, D.C.**
29. **Ronald Harred, c, Southwest Missouri State**

June—Secondary Phase (8)

1. **Dan Adams, 3b, Mississippi**
2. Richard Nance, lhp, Auburn
3. **Gene Ammann, rhp, Florida State**
4. John Tamargo, c, Miami-Dade North CC

MINNESOTA TWINS

January—Regular Phase (21)

1. Sayle Brown, rhp, Glendale (Calif.) JC
2. Stanley Butkus, rhp, Miami-Dade North CC
3. Daniel Hensley, rhp, JC of the Sequoias (Calif.)
4. Perry Yawn, of, Alabama
5. **Tom Wayne, 2b, Miami Shores, Fla.**
6. James Curtis, c, Newhall (Calif.) JC

January—Secondary Phase (11)

1. George Pugh, lhp, Mesa (Ariz.) CC
2. **Thomas Cain, rhp, Wartburg (Iowa)**
3. **Mark Pastrovich, lhp, Three Rivers (Mo.) CC**
4. **Frank Tokash, rhp, Fairleigh Dickinson**
5. Glenn Borgman, c, Miami-Dade North CC (Selection voided)
6. Jim Barr, rhp, Southern California
7. **Mel Bannon, ss, Santa Clara**

June—Regular Phase (22)

1. **Bob Gorinski, ss, Mount Pleasant HS, Calumet, Pa.**
2. **Mark Wiley, rhp, LaMesa, Calif.**
3. **John Hasbrouck, c, Albany (Minn.) HS**
4. **Peter Meyers, lhp, James Monroe HS, Sepulveda, Calif.**
5. Ron Herring, rhp, Greenville (Ala.) HS
6. **Randy Beach, ss, North Torrance (Calif.) HS**
7. Mike Hughes, p, Lynwood (Calif.) HS
8. Dennis Allar, rhp/c, Minnetonka HS, Excelsior, Minn.
9. **Gregory Goularte, of/c, Gavilan (Calif.)**
10. **Samuel Hess, c, Turner Ashby HS, Dayton, Va.**
11. **Dave Saylor, c, Granada Hills (Calif.) HS**
12. **Michael Wagner, rhp, Robertsdale (Ala.) HS**
13. Manny Estrada, ss, Bishop Amat HS, Covina, Calif.
14. Steve Staggs, inf, Cerritos (Calif.) JC
15. **Harold Allen, lhp, Highland Springs HS, Richmond, Va.**
16. **Frank Schuster, lhp, East Aurora (Ill.) HS**
17. **Frank Ciaramella, 3b, St. John's**
18. Sylvester Washington, 1b/of, Locke HS, Los Angeles
19. **Paul Haugen, rhp, Granada Hills (Calif.) HS**
20. **Robert Gause, rhp, Cal State Fullerton**
21. **Edmund Savold, rhp, St. Francis (N.Y.)**
22. Robert Kelly, lhp, Greeley (Colo.) Central HS
23. Daniel Koontz, ss, Hoover HS, Fresno, Calif.
24. **John Geitner, of, Sturgeon Bay (Wis.) HS**
25. **Derry Deguire, ss, Los Angeles Harbor JC**
26. **William Letsom, lhp, Tremper HS, Kenosha, Wis.**
27. **Nicholas Metz, c, Denmark HS, Maribel, Wis.**
28. Kevin Hunt, of, Doane (Neb.)
29. **George Dixon, lhp, Springfield (Mass.)**
30. **Bruce Wachutka, rhp, St. Louis Park (Minn.) HS**

31. **Harold Brown, of/1b, Holdenville (Okla.) HS**
32. **Barry Roderick, ss, Amherst (Mass.)**
33. Gregg Klee, lhp, Port Richmond HS, Staten Island, N.Y.
34. Brad Van Mierlo, lhp, Royal Oak HS, Covina, Calif.
35. Chris Charnish, of, Wisconsin-Platteville
36. **Phillip Flodin, c, Minnesota**
37. Dennis Cline, ss, Conrad HS, Wilmington, Del.
38. Lindsay Hoyer, c, Edina (Minn.) HS
39. **Dan Blood, 2b, Cal Poly Pomona**
40. William Finck, rhp, Tennyson HS, Hayward, Calif.
41. **Michael Ladd, c, Deering HS, Portland, Maine**
42. **Terry Cupples, rhp, Wayne State (Neb.)**
43. Barry Traynor, rhp, Gahr HS, Norwalk, Calif.
44. **Joe Hanzlik, lhp, Edison HS, Minneapolis**
45. **Ronald Davison, ss/rhp, Springfield (Minn.) HS**
46. Lawrence Siedow, of, Shakopee (Minn.) HS

June—Secondary Phase (18)

1. **Dan Guerrero, c, Pico Rivera, Calif.**
2. **Dennis Loewe, rhp, Pershing (Iowa)**
3. Tom Rosa, ss, Miami-Dade South CC
4. Stan Hamlin, rhp, Bakersfield (Calif.) JC

MONTREAL EXPOS

January—Regular Phase (4)

1. **Frank Hale, c, Mount San Antonio (Calif.) JC**
2. Craig Park, rhp, Venice (Calif.) HS
3. John Wilhoit, rhp, DeKalb (Ga.) JC
4. Gary Crawford, rhp, Lamar (Colo.) CC
5. Dirk Dunbar, 1b, Southeastern (Iowa) CC
6. Neil Mersch, rhp, Arizona Western JC

January—Secondary Phase (8)

1. Larry O'Brien, 1b/of, Long Beach (Calif.) CC
2. **Clifford Ker, rhp, Los Angeles Valley JC**
3. Arthur Simon, ss, Miami-Dade North CC
4. George Horton, c, Upsala (N.J.)
5. Ken O'Brien, rhp, Villanova
6. James Curnow, c, Morristown, N.J.
7. **David Krull, of, Iowa**
8. Carlton Exum, rhp, Orlando, Fla.

June—Regular Phase (3)

1. **Barry Foote, c, Smithfield-Selma HS, Smithfield, N.C.**
2. **Chip Lang, rhp, North Hills HS, Pittsburgh**
3. **Randy Viefhaus, 1b, Lafayette HS, Ellisville, Miss.**
4. **James Horsch, rhp, Bellaire HS, Houston**
5. **Pat Scanlon, 3b, Richfield (Minn.) HS**
6. **Ray Mullinax, 3b, Will Rogers HS, Tulsa, Okla.**
7. **Cannon Smith, 1b, Walker HS, Atlanta**
8. Phil Garner, inf, Tennessee
9. **Joe Gilbert, lhp, Newton HS, Jasper, Texas**
10. **Mike Liebeck, of, Long Beach (Calif.) CC**
11. Richard Carter, rhp, North Arlington (N.J.) HS
12. **Wallace Wright, ss/rhp, Mickens HS, Dade City, Fla.**
13. Jeff Hooper, lhp, Granada Hills (Calif.) HS
14. **Jerry White, of, Washington HS, San Francisco**
15. James Healy, ss, Parsippany HS, Lake Hiawatha, N.J.
16. Theodore Schelmay, c, Bayonne (N.J.) HS
17. **James Sloan, ss, William Penn Charter HS, Philadelphia**
18. **Dale Murray, rhp, Blinn (Texas) JC**
19. **Ray Valenzuela, of, Bassett HS, LaPuente, Calif.**
20. Daniel Tripp, lhp, West Ottawa HS, Holland, Mich.
21. **Michael McCord, rhp, Westport HS, Louisville, Ky.**
22. Bernard Kirschner, of/ss, Yorkton HS, Arlington, Va.
23. John Stansik, rhp, St. Alphonsus HS, Dearborn, Mich.
24. **Lee Collins, c, Mountain Lakes (N.J.) HS**
25. **Craig Van Bogelen, rhp, Arlington HS, Poughkeepsie, N.Y.**
26. Embry Pendarvis, ss, Northeast HS, Oklahoma City, Okla.
27. **Robert Patin, rhp, St. Joseph HS, Jackson, Miss.**
28. **Charlie Jackson, 3b/rhp, Crockett (Texas) HS**
29. Alex Pastore, of/3b, Hightstown (N.J.) HS
30. Gene Allen, ss, Biloxi (Miss.) HS
31. William Berryhill, c, Bartlesville (Okla.) HS
32. Anthony Buckley, rhp/of, Ridley Township HS, Swarthmore, Pa. (Selection voided)
33. Stephen Marino, c, Winthrop (Mass.) HS
34. John McLish, of, John Marshall HS, Edmond, Okla.
35. Roy Smalley, ss, Westchester HS, Los Angeles
36. Wade Fatheree, 1b, Rickdale (Texas) HS
37. Max Goldstein, 1b, Turlock (Calif.) HS
38. Horace Holmes, lhp, McComb-Gibson HS, Summit, Miss.

June—Secondary Phase (5)

1. Sam Ewing, of, Tennessee
2. Jim Corcoran, ss/2b, California
3. **Dale Harrington, rhp, Odessa (Texas) JC**
4. **Douglas Balne, lhp, New Canaan, Conn.**

NEW YORK METS

January—Regular Phase (24)

1. **Richard Avalos, of, San Fernando HS, Pacoima, Calif.**
2. **David Chew, of/3b, Contra Costa (Calif.) JC**
3. Clarence Bass, of, Southwood (N.C.) JC
4. John Fargnoli, c, Brevard (Fla.) CC
5. Ronald Burns, rhp, North Greenville (S.C.) JC
6. **Marvin Tucker, of/2b, Southern Colorado**
7. James Gailey, c, Manatee (Fla.) JC

January—Secondary Phase (24)

1. **Roy Staiger, ss, Bacone (Okla.) JC**
2. Larry Prieto, 2b, Fresno (Calif.) CC
3. Gary Breshears, 2b, Iowa
4. Craig Menzl, 1b, Adelphi (N.Y.)

June—Regular Phase (23)

1. George Ambrow, ss, Poly HS, Long Beach, Calif.
2. Gary Nevinger, rhp, Vandalia (Ill.) HS
3. **Michael Graham, of, Pershing (Iowa)**
4. **Ronnie Collins, ss, Pembroke State (N.C.)**
5. George Schneider, lhp, Cold Spring Harbor HS, Lloyds Harbor, N.Y.
6. **Steven Warden, rhp/3b, Sullivan East HS, Bluff City, Tenn.**
7. **Rex Phelps, rhp, Cooper Basin HS, Farner, Tenn.**
8. **Randy Pugh, rhp, Calistoga (Calif.) HS**
9. **Thomas Hallums, 1b, South Carolina State**
10. James Pittman, rhp, Messick HS, Memphis, Tenn.
11. **David Barb, rhp, Elkins (W.Va.) HS**
12. **Bryan Hartman, rhp, Trinity**
13. Jesse Carter, c, Central HS, Murfreesboro, Tenn.
14. William Bishop, 1b, Monroe HS, Bronx, N.Y.
15. **Robert Bartlett, rhp, Arkansas Tech**
16. **Roman Schmidt, c, Riverview HS, Sarasota, Fla.**
17. **Thomas Sheppard, rhp, Cal State Los Angeles**
18. Steven Carp, rhp/inf, Canarsie HS, Brooklyn, N.Y.
19. Russell Cauley, lhp, Hooks HS, Leary, Texas
20. **Bruce Boisclair, of, Killingly HS, Danielson, Conn.**
21. Lawrence Neal, of, Laney (Calif.) JC
22. **Richard Wustefeld, rhp, Wantagh (N.Y.) HS**
23. **Edward Grady, of, Nichols (Ga.) HS**
24. **Allan Rommes, rhp, Caledonia (Minn.) HS**
25. **Carroll Talbert, 3b, Boonsboro (Md.) HS**
26. Robert Sherman, rhp, Seminole (Fla.) JC
27. **Richard Williams, rhp, Chariho HS, Carolina, R.I.**
28. Nicholas Welshmeyer, rhp, Bishop O'Doud HS, Castro Valley, Calif.
29. **Terry Deremer, ss, Fairmont State (W.Va.)**
30. Dennis Zimmerman, of, Albright (Pa.)
31. **Jeff Anderson, of, Jackson State**
32. **Timothy DeCaminada, 1b, Portland**
33. **Daryl Tollinche, of, William Allan HS, Allentown, Pa.**
34. John Lonchar, c, Euclid (Ohio) HS
35. Steve Bossi, of, Contra Costa (Calif.) JC
36. Michael McGuire, of, Amherst HS, Snyder, N.Y.
37. Dave Williams, rhp, Coshocton (Ohio) HS
38. Ron Lyons, of, Mason County (Ky.) HS
39. John Mullins, rhp, Paul Blazer HS, Ashland, Ky.
40. **Larry Potash, lhp, Gannon (Pa.)**
41. Michael Basinger, 3b/1b, Los Banos (Calif.) HS

June—Secondary Phase (3)

1. **Brent Strom, lhp, Southern California**
2. Andrew Bielanski, c, Fullerton (Calif.) JC
3. **Ken Wamble, 2b, Odessa (Texas) JC**
4. Stephen Cash, ss, Dekalb (Ga.) JC

NEW YORK YANKEES

January—Regular Phase (11)

1. **Ron Hinckley, rhp, St. John's River (Fla.) CC**
2. **John Mercado, 1b/3b, Ranger (Texas) JC**
3. John Gaylord, lhp, Chaffey (Calif.) JC
4. Lawrence Knight, rhp, Ranger (Texas) JC
5. Robert Coultas, rhp, Diablo Valley (Calif.) JC
6. James Henley, lhp, Eagle Rock HS, Los Angeles
7. Gary Leach, rhp, Yakima Valley (Wash.) JC (Selection voided)
8. **Jim Hefflinger, rhp, Mount Hood (Ore.) CC**

January—Secondary Phase (3)

1. **Wayne Pitcock, 1b, Arkansas State**
2. Todd Sprecher, c, Yakima Valley (Wash.) JC
3. **David Hazelip, rhp, Columbia State (Tenn.) CC**
4. **Joel DeTray, rhp, Columbia Basin (Wash.) CC**
5. **Dan Velander, rhp, Lower Columbia (Wash.) JC**
6. Jack McDonald, rhp, Spokane (Wash.) CC
7. **Eugene Moser, of, Bellevue (Wash.) CC**

June—Regular Phase (12)

1. **Dave Cheadle, lhp, Asheville (N.C.) HS**
2. **Richard Earle, rhp, Highland Park (N.J.) HS**
3. Fred Lynn, of, El Monte (Calif.) HS
4. **David Lawson, rhp, Germantown Academy, Flourtown, Pa.**
5. **Ned Jayjack, c, Normandy HS, Parma, Ohio**
6. **Doug Stodgel, ss, Cal State Los Angeles**
7. **Don Demola, rhp, Commack (N.Y.) South HS**
8. **Frank Rossi, 1b, Montclair State (N.J.)**
9. **Tom Robbins, of, Belhaven (Miss.)**
10. **Julio Hernandez, ss, Miami Senior HS**
11. Kevin Rusnak, of, Ohio State (Selection voided)
12. **Wes Vandenborg, of, Hastings (Mich.) HS**
13. **Thomas Hannibal, lhp, Portland**
14. Mike McNeilly, rhp/ss, Lower Columbia (Wash.) CC
15. **Richard Bianchi, c, St. Anthony's HS, Trenton, N.J.**
16. Duane Wirth, rhp, St. Mary's HS, Mesa, Ariz.
17. **Dick Clark, c, Anderson (Mo.) HS**
18. **Robert Behar, rhp, Monroe HS, New York**
19. **Bill Sheets, lhp, Eastern Oregon State**
20. **John Shaw, 2b, Mississippi**
21. **George Beattie, ss, South Portland (Maine) HS**
22. **Carlos Rodriguez, ss, Brandeis HS, New York**
23. **Irving Homs, c/of, Lehman (N.Y.)**
24. **Clark Babbitt, rhp, Western Washington**
25. Tom Martell, lhp, Taft HS, Lincoln City, Ore.
26. **Clyde Armstrong, lhp, Capital Hill HS, Oklahoma City**
27. **William Kostbra, lhp, Reynolds HS, Troutdale, Ore.**
28. Randy Fink, lhp, Columbia River HS, Vancouver, Wash.
29. Willie Morales, c, Tucson (Ariz.) HS
30. **Doc Medich, rhp, Pittsburgh**
31. Byron Burns, rhp, Kelso (Wash.) HS
32. Oscar James, of, Owensboro (Ky.) HS
33. Jim Cody, rhp, Big Bend (Wash.) CC
34. **Robin Hippi, rhp, Central Washington**
35. Richard Ralston, rhp, Spokane (Wash.) CC
36. Joe Krsnich, inf/of, Wichita (Kan.) HS
37. Kyle Johnson, 2b, Helena (Mont.) HS
38. **Tom Couples, rhp, Seattle**
39. **Robert Nielsen, of, Minnesota**
40. **John Bakis, 3b, Norwich (Vt.)**
41. Jerry Schuster, lhp, West HS, Billings, Mont.
42. Dave Michael, lhp/of, Pendleton (Ore.) HS
43. Randy Brummitt, lhp, McNary HS, Salem, Ore.
44. John Wade, lhp, West Seattle HS
45. Keith Metheny, rhp, Kentridge HS, Kent, Wash.
46. Charles Gardinier, ss, Oregon College of Education

June—Secondary Phase (16)

1. **Greg Gaffey, 1b, Lincoln Land (Ill.) JC**
2. **Jerry Johnson, lhp, Oregon State**

OAKLAND ATHLETICS

January—Regular Phase (17)

1. **Phil LaGore, rhp, Monroe HS, Panorama City, Calif.**
2. Mary Owen, of, Fullerton (Calif.) JC
3. Jack Brushart, of, Chapman (Calif.) (Selection voided)
4. Mitchell Page, of, Compton (Calif.) CC
5. **Michael Morrison, lhp, Fullerton (Calif.) JC**
6. Mark Wiley, rhp, Cal Poly Pomona (Selection voided)
7. Carl Jones, 2b, Los Angeles CC
8. John Vaught, rhp, Chapman (Calif.) (Selection voided)
9. **John Phillips, rhp, Thousand Oaks HS, Newbury Park, Calif.**
10. Lois Ridley, c/3b, Santa Monica (Calif.) JC
11. Jerry McCullough, of/1b, Mount San Antonio (Calif.) JC
12. Darrell Cox, rhp, Locke HS, Compton, Calif.
13. Allan Wise, of, Chapman (Calif.) (Selection voided)

January—Secondary Phase (9)

1. **Vic Harris, ss, Los Angeles Valley JC**
2. Robert Eldridge, rhp, Southern Illinois
3. John LiBrandi, of, Manatee (Fla.) JC
4. Mike Seberger, rhp, Cerritos (Calif.) JC
5. **Mike Logelin, 2b, Loyola Marymount**

June—Regular Phase (18)

1. **Dan Ford, of, Fremont HS, Los Angeles**
2. Dale Holland, 2b, Riverview HS, Sarasota, Fla.
3. **David Murphy, 3b/ss, Ceres (Calif.) HS**
4. **Dale Sanner, of, Rubidoux HS, Riverside, Calif.**
5. David Wooley, c, Bellaire (Texas) HS
6. Darroll Phillips, rhp/of, Lincoln HS, Stockton, Calif.
7. **Steve Cole, rhp, Carson HS, Torrance, Calif.**
8. **Bill Van Bommet, rhp, Menasha (Wis.) HS**
9. Mark Hamilton, 1b, Ruston (La.) HS
10. **Mike Kowalik, rhp, Kennedy HS, Sacramento**
11. **Alan Griffin, rhp, Mira Costa HS, Hermosa Beach, Calif.**
12. Paul Bagnasco, 3b, Cabrillo (Calif.) JC
13. Daryl Fuchs, c, Evansville (Wis.) HS
14. **Steve Tomasetti, c/of, North Quincy (Mass.) HS**
15. Frank Baumgardner, rhp, Carol City HS, Opalocka, Fla.
16. Ron Corbett, rhp, Suffolk (Mass.)
17. **David Smith, c, St. James HS, Brookhaven, Pa.**
18. Michael McManus, 1b/of, Mount San Antonio (Calif.) JC
19. Jack Brushert, of, Chapman (Calif.)
20. Jim Golden, lhp, Portland
21. **Ron Brenner, rhp, Morningside (Iowa)**
22. Russ Schroeder, ss, Sam Rayburn HS, Pasadena, Texas
23. **Eldon Jones, lhp, Southern Colorado**
24. Doug Cornett, c, Madison Central HS, Richmond, Ky.
25. Mike Gerakos, 3b, Fullerton (Calif.) JC

June—Secondary Phase (20)

1. **Bernie Boehmer, c, St. Louis CC-Meramec**
2. Ronnie Diggle, of, Cerritos (Calif.) JC
3. **Dennis Primeau, ss, St. Clair County (Mich.) CC**
4. James Gailey, of, Manatee (Fla.) JC

PHILADELPHIA PHILLIES

January—Regular Phase (6)

1. **Russ Klobas, of, Laney (Calif.) JC**
2. **James Goodwin, rhp, Georgia Southern**
3. **George Hodge, 3b, Sacramento (Calif.) CC**
4. **Ken Fuller, rhp, Chabot (Calif.) JC**

January—Secondary Phase (16)

1. **Allan Matson, of, St. John's**
2. Claude Renfro, rhp/1b, Gulf Coast (Fla.) CC
3. William Menk, lhp, Philadelphia, Pa.
4. Gary Szakacs, 1b, American River (Calif.) JC

June—Regular Phase (5)

1. **Mike Martin, lhp, Olympia HS, Columbia, S.C.**
2. Roger Choate, c, Allegheny HS, Sparta, N.C.

3. **David Selinsky, lhp, Klamath Falls (Ore.) HS**
4. **Ken Fowler, rhp, Red Springs (N.C.) HS**
5. **Bruce Butler, 1b/of, Elk Grove HS, Sacramento**
6. **Dave Downs, rhp, Viewmont HS, Bountiful, Utah**
7. **Dan Field, c, St. Joseph HS, West Chester, Pa.**
8. **Fred Andrews, ss, Lincoln Heights (Ohio) HS**
9. **Lawrence Utz, rhp, Cypress Lodes HS, Cape Coral, Fla.**
10. **David Yates, 2b, Delaware**
11. **Craig Robinson, ss, Wake Forest**
12. **Fred Thomason, lhp, Ball State**
13. Robert Worthington, 2b, Calvert Hall HS, Timonium, Md.
14. **John Dusenbury, c, Asheville (N.C.) HS**
15. William Emerson, rhp, Haddonfield (N.J.) HS
16. **Robert Wilson, rhp/of, JC of the Redwoods (Calif.)**
17. James Dennor, of/1b, Northern Illinois
18. **Richard Fusari, of/rhp, Central Connecticut State**
19. Eric Wharton, of, Delaware State
20. Scott Ferguson, 3b, Wauwatosa (Wis.) HS
21. **William McGonigle, inf, Santa Clara**
22. **Erskine Thomason, rhp, Erskine (S.C.)**
23. Stanley Sweitham, ss, Polytechnic HS, Baltimore
24. **Chris Bradford, rhp, Diablo Valley (Calif.) JC**
25. Jeff Kalish, 3b, New York
26. Tom Jones, rhp, Carson-Newman (Tenn.) (Selection voided)
27. **Mark Brown, rhp, Delaware**
28. **Bob Beall, of/1b, Oregon State**
29. **Malcolm Smoot, c, Ohio**
30. **Kevin Rusnak, of, Ohio State**

June—Secondary Phase (19)

1. **Thomas Urquardt, rhp, Phillips (Okla.)**
2. **James Jones, ss, Spokane (Wash.) CC**
3. **Robert Masteller, lhp, Grayson County (Texas) JC**
4. **Gary Szakacs, 1b, American River (Calif.) JC**
5. Chris Cammack, 3b, North Carolina State

PITTSBURGH PIRATES

January—Regular Phase (14)

1. Alan Jackson, lhp, Northeastern
2. Ronald Erion, 3b/1b, San Joaquin Delta (Calif.) JC
3. Steven Darden, rhp, South Georgia JC
4. Clinton Olson, rhp, Big Bend (Wash.) CC
5. Charlie Roberts, rhp, Bellevue (Wash.) CC
6. Richard Counts, ss, St. Petersburg (Fla.) JC
7. James Heard, ss, Dalton (Ga.) JC
8. Steve Hunter, c, Yakima Valley (Wash.) JC
9. Peter Castle, rhp, Niagara County (N.Y.) CC
10. Stephen Dorsch, lhp, Concordia (N.Y.)
11. **Ken Fulton, c, Duquesne**
12. Robbie Harms, c, Lakeland (Ill.) CC
13. Ted Cooper, 2b, Morgan State
14. **Joseph Say, c/of, Kenmore East HS, Sterling Heights, Mich.**
15. David Sosnoskie, c/3b, Shamokin (Pa.) HS
16. Kirk Berger, rhp/of, York (Pa.) (Selection voided)
17. Robert Deremer, of, Allegany HS, Cumberland, Md.
18. Robert Brown, rhp, Connellsville Area HS, South Connellsville, Pa.
19. Mark Mooney, rhp, Catonsville (Md.) CC
20. Terry Derfler, c, Pine Grove (Pa.) HS
21. **Stephen Bosley, rhp, Catonsville (Md.) CC**
22. Barry Barns, rhp/of, West Perry HS, Blain, Pa.
23. Anthony Joseph, lhp, Lincoln HS, Ellwood City, Pa.
24. Carl Woolford, lhp/1b, Anne Arundel (Md.) CC
25. William Beauchamp, 1b/lhp, Overlea HS, Baltimore
26. Edward Griffin, rhp, Montgomery (Md.) JC
27. Bruce James, of/1b, Woodlawn HS, Baltimore
28. Kyle Roher, c, Wesley (Del.)

January—Secondary Phase (4)

1. Richard Soriano, of, Miami-Dade North CC
2. Richard Wanless, rhp, Quincy, Mass. (Selection voided)
3. **John Vance, c, Western Kentucky**
4. **Henry Hyde, lhp, Amundson (Ill.) JC**
5. **Frank Shimerdla, lhp, Bishop Ryan HS, Omaha, Neb.**
6. Gary Gaiser, rhp, SUNY Buffalo
7. David Pyles, ss/2b, Olympic (Wash.) JC
8. Eddie Munoz, of/ss, Miller HS, Corpus Christi, Texas
9. Allen Lindsay, lhp, Gaston (N.C.) CC

June—Regular Phase (13)

1. **John Bedard, rhp/c, Springfield (Mass.) Tech HS**
2. **Kenneth Waiss, rhp, DePew (N.Y.) HS**
3. **Wendell Johnson, rhp, Millersburg Military Institute, Florence, Ky.**
4. **Edward Sherlin, of/2b, Gallatin (Tenn.) Senior HS**
5. **Chester Gunter, rhp, Edison HS, Fresno, Calif.**
6. **Gary Gandy, of, Westbury HS, Houston**
7. **Brad Albertson, ss, Cascade HS, Everett, Wash.**
8. John Simontacchi, c, Fremont HS, Sunnyvale, Calif.
9. **Richard Stuart, c, Central Kitsap HS, Bremerton, Wash.**
10. **Richard Standart, ss, St. Mary's HS, Stockton, Calif.**
11. John Caneira, rhp, Naugatuck (Conn.) HS
12. **Jim Sanderson, 1b, Charter Oaks HS, Covina, Calif.**
13. **Richard DeMaria, 1b, Springfield (Mass.) Tech HS**
14. **Dave Parker, c/of, Courter Tech HS, Cincinnati**
15. **Gary Kelley, of, McClatchy HS, Sacramento**
16. **Theodia Johnson, 3b/of, Allen Carver HS, Cincinnati**
17. **Robert Stewart, ss, Westwood (N.J.) HS**
18. **Gary Abram, rhp, Union HS, Tulsa, Okla.**
19. **Richard Swinchock, lhp, Beth Center Senior HS, Clarksville, Pa.**
20. **Charles Arrendale, rhp, Marion (Ind.)**
21. **Edward Robbins, rhp, Ohio**
22. Ken St. Pierre, c, Danvers (Mass.) HS
23. **Ed Ott, 3b/c, Muncy (Pa.) HS**
24. **Kenneth Stollmeyer, of, Charter Oak HS, Glendora, Calif.**
25. Ron Hooks, of, Far Rockaway (N.Y.) HS
26. Greg Van Gaver, rhp, O'Dea HS, Seattle
27. Charles Ringer, ss, Dearborn Heights, Mich.
28. Bennie Allison, 3b/1b, Ursuline HS, Youngstown, Ohio
29. **Richard Berry, ss, Washtenaw (Mich.) CC**
30. Calvin Jones, 3b/ss, Edison HS, Philadelphia
31. **Pat Cassaday, of/rhp, Miles (Iowa) Community HS**
32. **Terry Bowman, 1b, Pensacola (Fla.) HS**
33. David Keigan, rhp, Braintree (Mass.) HS
34. Paul Kurpiel, of, Chaminade HS, Dayton, Ohio
35. John Keough, rhp, Rockland (Mass.) HS
36. Greg Bish, rhp, Northeastern Oklahoma A&M JC
37. Carlos Hughes, lhp, Aurora (N.C.) HS
38. Stan Rosenbrock, ss, Brighton (Colo.) HS
39. Robert Clites, rhp, Mapletown HS, Bobtown, Pa.
40. Mark Whiting, 3b/of, Grand Junction (Colo.) HS
41. Stephen Jarrard, 2b, Bellaire HS, Houston
42. Michael Wood, of, Brookhaven HS, Columbus, Ohio
43. **Arthur Rousseau, rhp, Washtenaw (Mich.) CC**
44. **Carl Hewlett, rhp, Marshall**
45. **Steve Evert, of, Washington State**
46. **Richard Stephenson, of/1b, Idaho State**
47. **John Sullivan, c, Washington State**
48. Michael Rollins, 1b/c, Beaver Falls (Pa.) HS
49. Ray Parr, lhp, Shorecrest HS, Seattle
50. David Mroczkowski, ss, Bridgeport (Ohio) HS
51. Edwin McGraw, rhp, Downington (Pa.) HS
52. Jeff Silfies, 1b, Northampton County Area (Pa.) CC
53. James Caviglia, c, Santa Clara
54. Dave Chambers, rhp, Puget Sound (Wash.)
55. Stew Casterline, c/rhp, Mansfield (Pa.)
56. John Bowling, lhp, LaRue County HS, Hodgensville, Ky.
57. Jerry Gomez, lhp, Bishop Ryan HS, Omaha, Neb.
58. Dennis Peters, rhp, Turner HS, Beloit, Wis.
59. Ray Baye, rhp, Northampton (Mass.) HS
60. **Anthony Buckley, rhp/of, Ridley Township HS, Swarthmore, Pa.**

June—Secondary Phase (15)

1. **Richard Astor, of/3b, Edinboro (Pa.)**
2. **Clinton Olson, rhp, Big Bend (Wash.) CC**
3. Peter Castle, rhp, Monroe (N.Y.) CC
4. James Heard, ss, Dalton (Ga.) JC
5. Steve Hunter, c, Yakima Valley (Wash.) JC

ST. LOUIS CARDINALS

January—Regular Phase (12)

1. **Donald Reed, rhp, Wilson HS Easton, Pa.**
2. **David Fitzmaurice, 1b, St. John's**
3. **Mike Tyson, ss, Indian River (Fla.) CC**
4. **Pascal Johnson, 1b/of, Eastern Oklahoma State JC**
5. Edwin Steverson, of, San Diego Mesa JC
6. **Greg Garver, of, Chaffey (Calif.) JC**
7. Van Winters, rhp, Fresno (Calif.) CC
8. Luis Jiminez, ss, Chaffey (Calif.) JC
9. Darrell Cederlind, 3b, Chaffey (Calif.) JC

January—Secondary Phase (6)

1. Bucky Dent, 3b, Miami-Dade North CC
2. Bill Dobbs, lhp, Oklahoma State
3. Richard Fillings, lhp, Indian River (Fla.) CC
4. **Rudy Arroyo, lhp, Foothill (Calif.) JC**
5. **Richard Branch, rhp, Hudson Valley (N.Y.) CC**
6. Wayne Miller, lhp, Ohlone (Calif.) JC
7. George Chavez, rhp, Delano (Calif.) HS
8. **Richard Brown, of, Cal Poly San Luis Obispo**
9. Peter Halfman, of, American River (Calif.) JC

June—Regular Phase (11)

1. **Jim Browning, rhp/ss, Emma Sansom HS, Gadsden, Ala.**
2. **Ron Kinner, c/of, Dunbar HS, Lubbock, Texas**
3. **Ed Wheeler, inf/of, Sarasota (Fla.) HS**
4. **Mark Covert, rhp, Boulder (Colo.) HS**
5. **Greg Terlecky, rhp, West Covina (Calif.) HS**
6. **Robin Sievers, 3b, Hazelwood HS, St. Louis**
7. **Don Durham, rhp/of, Western Kentucky**
8. Bob Allietta, c, Lawrence HS, Falmouth, Mass.
9. **Fred Warner, rhp, Lake Forest (Ill.)**
10. **Marc Hill, c, Elsberry (Mo.) HS**
11. Paul Dyer, lhp, St. Ignacius HS, San Francisco
12. **John Hund, ss/2b, Wilson HS, Long Beach, Calif.**
13. Thomas Kennedy, ss, Northport (N.Y.) HS
14. **Ray Cingle, 1b, Bald Eagle HS, Clarence, Pa.**
15. **Dennis Duhan, rhp, Stark HS, Orange, Texas**
16. Zane Grubbs, lhp, Brenham (Texas) HS
17. Joe Ford, inf, Elk City HS, Woodward, Okla.
18. Bruce Madden, ss, Danvers (Mass.) HS
19. **Rickey Shepard, lhp, Gorham (Ill.) HS**
20. **Mark Hale, 1b, Blinn (Texas) JC**
21. Richard Wilson, lhp/of, Pendleton (S.C.) HS
22. **Virgil Erickson, c, Wartburg (Iowa)**
23. Stan Kerby, rhp/of, Meridian HS, Mound City, Ill.
24. Farrell Vincent, rhp, Christian Brothers HS, Memphis, Tenn.
25. **Ken Faria, 1b, Mission HS, San Jose, Calif.**
26. Dennis Bean, lhp, Newport Harbor HS, Costa Mesa, Calif.
27. Ed Orizzi, c, Shrewsbury (Mass.) HS
28. Eugene Reinke, 1b, Mesa (Ariz.) CC
29. **John Denny, rhp, Prescott (Ariz.) HS**
30. Roy Meisner, of, West Valley (Calif.) JC
31. **John Davis, rhp, Russellville (Ark.) HS**
32. Wilmer Aaron, ss, Manual Arts HS, Los Angeles
33. **Mark Gasperino, 1b, Pasadena (Calif.) CC**
34. **Willie Farrow, lhp/of, Fremont HS, Los Angeles**
35. Cliff Holland, lhp, San Carlos (Calif.) HS
36. Clint Myers, 3b, Lakewood (Calif.) HS
37. **Bake McBride, lhp/of, Westminster (Mo.)**
38. Robert Jurgensen, rhp, Lakeland Regional HS, Ringwood, N.J.
39. **Jos-Anthony Kimak, rhp, Pequannock (N.J.) HS**
40. **Stephen Yetsko, 3b, Lakeland Regional HS, Skyline Lake, N.J.**
41. **Danny Reynolds, c, Hollywood (Fla.) HS**

June—Secondary Phase (23)

1. Paul Sands, p, Bacone (Okla.) JC
2. **William Bright, of, Louisiana State**
3. David Breshears, 2b, Iowa
4. Craig Barnes, 1b, Mount San Antonio (Calif.) JC
5. Craig Menzl, lhp, Adelphi (N.Y.)

SAN DIEGO PADRES

January—Regular Phase (2)

1. **John Scott, inf, Centennial HS, Los Angeles**
2. **Mike Chapman, of, San Diego Mesa JC**
3. Barry Parker, c/1b, Southern Tech Institute (Fla.)
4. Kevin Bryant, ss, Valencia (Fla.) CC
5. Larry Sweat, lhp/of, Grossmont (Calif.) JC

January—Secondary Phase (12)

1. **Dan Bielski, rhp, Michigan State**
2. Doug Ault, of, Panola (Texas) JC
3. Robert Beach, rhp, Cabrillo (Calif.) JC
4. **Henry Yeargan, ss, Brewton-Parker (Ga.) JC**
5. **Roger Gregg, c, Southwestern (Calif.) JC**

June—Regular Phase (1)

1. **Mike Ivie, c, Walker HS, Decatur, Ga.**
2. **Dan Spillner, rhp, Federal Way (Wash.) HS**
3. **Fred Seibly, rhp, Granada Hills (Calif.) HS**
4. **Steve Simpson, rhp, Washburn (Kan.)**
5. **Ulysses Wilson, ss, Florida A&M**
6. **Bob Davis, rhp/ss, Locust Grove (Okla.) HS**
7. **Richard Arendell, 3b, Mayfair HS, Bellflower, Calif.**
8. **Wayne Rettig, lhp, Davenport (Iowa) Central HS**
9. **Robert Gibson, rhp, McLain HS, Tulsa, Okla.**
10. **Ed Evilsizor, inf/of, Kearny HS, San Diego**
11. Marvin Webb, 2b, Kennedy HS, San Pablo, Calif.
12. **Ronald Olson, rhp, Clayton Valley HS, Concord, Calif.**
13. Steve Dillard, ss, Saltillo (Miss.) HS
14. **Nick Perlozza, 1b, High Point (N.C.)**
15. **John Krawiecki, rhp, New Haven (Conn.)**
16. **Doug Hunt, of, San Diego State**
17. Ron Scott, of, Eastern Oregon State
18. **Ralph Garcia, rhp, Nevada-Las Vegas**
19. **William Morrell, lhp, Ferris State (Mich.)**
20. Thomas Hurn, of/1b, Central HS, Cedar Rapids, Iowa
21. Terry Farmer, rhp, Jordan HS, Columbus, Ga.
22. Roger Keilig, c, San Carlos HS, Redwood City, Calif.
23. **Larry Hardy, rhp, Texas**
24. **Michael Smith, of, Pacific (Ore.)**
25. **Dick Brown, lhp, Oklahoma**

June—Secondary Phase (21)

1. **Bob Graczyk, rhp, Illinois State**
2. Stephen Easton, lhp, Brigham Young
3. William Bell, ss, Jefferson State (Ala.) JC

SAN FRANCISCO GIANTS

January—Regular Phase (18)

1. **Randy Moffitt, rhp, Cal State Long Beach**
2. **Charles Erickson, of, Los Angeles Pierce JC**
3. Bruce Frankum, rhp, Valencia (Fla.) CC
4. **Steve Faria, c/1b, Ohlone (Calif.) JC**
5. Mike Hanson, rhp, San Diego CC
6. **Terry Nelson, inf/of, Antelope Valley (Calif.) JC**
7. Russ Atterbery, c, JC of the Siskiyous (Calif.)
8. Dennis Primeau, ss, St. Clair County (Mich.) CC
9. Arthur Carpenter, lhp, Lower Columbia (Wash.) JC
10. James Whaley, 3b/of, St. Clair County (Mich.) CC
11. Charles Berg, of, Bakersfield (Calif.) JC
12. Lamar Crook, of, JC of the Sequoias (Calif.)
13. Bruce Courtmanch, rhp, Bellevue (Wash.) CC
14. **Gary Williams, rhp, Shoreline (Wash.) CC**
15. James Jones, inf, Spokane (Wash.) CC
16. Steven Schrader, inf, El Camino (Calif.) JC
17. **Robert Ulrich, rhp, Fresno State**

January—Secondary Phase (2)

1. **Chris Speier, ss, Laney (Calif.) JC**
2. Stan Hamlin, rhp, Bakersfield (Calif.) JC
3. **Andrew Nelson, rhp, Everett (Wash.) CC**
4. Brian Applegate, ss, San Diego Mesa JC
5. Craig Barnes, 1b/lhp, Mount San Antonio (Calif.) JC
6. **Clare Leifer, 2b, Marysville, Wash.**
7. Ernie Henrickson, rhp, Washington State
8. John Behrens, inf, Fresno (Calif.) CC

June—Regular Phase (17)

1. **John D'Acquisto, rhp, St. Augustine HS, San Diego**

2. **Butch Metzger, rhp, Kennedy HS, Sacramento**
3. **Kyle Hypes, lhp/of, Santana HS, Lakeside, Calif.**
4. Mark Lucich, 1b, Eureka (Calif.) HS
5. Jim Otten, rhp, Mesa (Ariz.) CC
6. Mark Hance, 1b, South Bakersfield (Calif.) HS
7. **Michael Haynes, of, San Diego HS**
8. Bill Taylor, inf, San Dieguito HS, Encinitas, Calif.
9. **Bill Bates, rhp, Eisenhower HS, Rialto, Calif.**
10. **John Parslow, rhp, Fermin Lasuen HS, San Pedro, Calif.**
11. **John Ogden, rhp, Far Rockaway HS, Broad Channel, N.Y.**
12. **Eugene Alim, inf, Imperial Beach (Calif.) HS**
13. Stan Mann, ss, Southwest HS, St. Louis
14. Jim Hogan, of, Golden West (Calif.) JC
15. Robert Miller, of, Grant Union HS, Sacramento
16. Vern Wilkins, 1b, Mesa (Ariz.) CC
17. **Thomas Smith, ss, Lincoln HS, San Diego**
18. Ray Cocco, 2b, Sequoia HS, Redwood City, Calif.
19. **Glenn Milani, 1b, Mendel Catholic HS, Chicago**
20. Bill Sero, ss, Garfield Heights (Ohio) HS
21. **Steven Tener, rhp, Stagg HS, Stockton, Calif.**
22. Michael Hall, rhp, Mesa (Colo.)
23. **Richard Schroeder, 2b, Wisconsin-Oshkosh**
24. Mark Crane, ss, Flint (Mich.) Central HS
25. **Doug Capilla, lhp, Westmont HS, Campbell, Calif.**
26. John Fuzak, 3b, Alma (Mich.)
27. Warren Brusstar, rhp, Napa (Calif.) HS
28. Tom Hofer, c, Mount Home (Idaho) HS
29. **Dale Dunham, rhp, Central Michigan**
30. **Steve Franceschi, rhp, Pacific**
31. **Jim Vaughn, rhp, Seton HS, Chandler, Ariz.**
32. Paul Djakanow, 3b/1b, Chadsey HS, Detroit
33. Ernest Moen, ss, Golden West (Calif.) JC
34. Eric Geister, rhp, East Detroit HS
35. Ben Heise, ss, Vacaville (Calif.) HS
36. Mike Henley, lhp, Vacaville (Calif.) HS
37. David Whitney, lhp, Astoria (Ore.) HS
38. Steve Borsczwski, c, Seton Hall
39. Samuel Shea, rhp, Winona State (Minn.)
40. **Kenneth Danielson, of/1b, Wagner**

June—Secondary Phase (1)

1. **Dave Kingman, rhp/of, Southern California**
2. Pete Varney Jr., 1b, Harvard
3. **Jim Barr, rhp, Southern California**

WASHINGTON SENATORS

January—Regular Phase (13)

1. Julian Hines, rhp, Tryon, N.C. (Selection voided)
2. Guy Freeland, rhp, Mount San Antonio (Calif.) JC
3. Mardie Cornejo, rhp, Miami (Ohio)
4. **David Wisniewski, ss, SUNY Alfred JC**
5. Don Thomas, rhp, Olar HS, Denmark, S.C. (Selection voided)

January—Secondary Phase (1)

1. **Bill Fahey, rhp, St. Clair County (Mich.) CC**
2. Bill Borelli, 1b, Santa Clara
3. David Carey, rhp, Minnesota
4. Ray Coley, c, Valparaiso
5. **Bill Madlock Jr., ss/3b, Southeastern (Iowa) CC-Keokuk**
6. Arnold Braden, lhp, Orange Park, Fla.
7. James Kiley, ss, Massachusetts
8. Walt Biercevicz, of/lhp, Norwalk (Conn.) CC
9. Tom Rosa, ss, Miami-Dade South CC

June—Regular Phase (14)

1. **Charles Maxwell, 3b/ss, Zane Trace HS, Kingston, Ohio**
2. **Art DeFilippis, lhp/of, Stamford (Conn.) Catholic HS**
3. Steve Baumiller, rhp, Forest Hills HS, West Palm Beach, Fla.
4. **Gary Jackson, lhp, Hicksville (N.Y.) HS**
5. **Rick Waits, lhp, Therrell HS, Atlanta**
6. Richard Baker, rhp, Holy Cross HS, Lynchburg, Va.
7. **Richard Kemp, lhp, Kankakee (Ill.) CC**
8. Paul Stombaugh, of, High Point HS, College Park, Md.
9. **David Daniels, ss, Union (N.J.) HS**
10. Harvey Willis, ss, George Washington HS, Danville, Va.
11. **Tim French, lhp, South Charleston (W.Va.) HS**
12. Edgar DeFore, rhp, Lanier HS, Macon, Ga.
13. **Edward Szado, lhp, Providence**
14. Joe Simpson, of, Norman (Okla.) HS
15. Mike Kirchoff, of, Miami-Dade South CC
16. **Francis Obermeier, 3b, Saint Louis**
17. **Steve Greenberg, 1b, Yale**
18. Rick Colzie, rhp/ss, Miami-Dade South CC
19. Jerry Remy, 2b, Somerset (Mass.) HS
20. **Larry Brooks, rhp, David Douglas HS, Portland, Ore.**
21. Bruce Sutter, rhp, Donegal HS, Mount Joy, Pa.
22. Les Kozlowski, lhp, Quigley Prep HS, Chicago
23. Dave Cosgrove, rhp, Minnesota
24. **James Redmon, rhp/of, Washburn (Kan.)**
25. William Robbins, rhp, Calhoun (Ga.) HS
26. Greg Baldwin, of, Dykes HS, Atlanta
27. George McCollum, lhp, Edgewater HS, Orlando, Fla.
28. **Bobby Billings, of, Appalachian State**
29. Fred Gianiny, lhp, Wheaton (Md.) HS
30. Brad Fulk, 2b, South HS, Hagerstown, Md.
31. **Sam Miller, rhp, Appalachian State**
32. Tim Sherrill, 1b, Miami-Dade South CC
33. John O'Connor, c, Hammond HS, Alexandria, Va.
34. **Sylvester Swindler, of, Southwestern Louisiana**
35. Danny Evans, rhp, Miami-Dade South CC
36. **Ken Rhyne, c, Pfeiffer (N.C.)**
37. Gordon Slade, of, Davidson
38. Robert Boschulte, 2b, Wisconsin
39. Todd Brenizer, lhp, Greenville (Tenn.) HS
40. **Bruce Sydnor, c, Peary HS, Rockville, Md.**
41. **John Bennett, rhp, Coral Park HS, Miami**
42. Anthony Giordano, c/of, Miami-Dade North JC
43. **Mark Munoz, c, Carol City HS, Miami**
44. Roger Mammen, of, Hartsburg-Emden HS, Emden, Ill.
45. Brian Lovett, rhp, Coral Park HS, Miami
46. Robert Woodland, rhp, Suitland (Md.) HS
47. **Johnny Gasque, rhp/ss, Latta HS, Dillon, S.C.**

June—Secondary Phase (10)

1. **Len Randle, inf, Arizona State**
2. Mardie Cornejo, rhp, Wellington, Kan.
3. **Francis Karmelich, c, UC Riverside**
4. **Archie Cameron, rhp, Miami-Dade North CC**
5. **Richard Auckland, 1b, West Chester (Pa.)**
6. Larry Prieto, 2b, Fresno (Calif.) CC
7. **Mike Slade, rhp, Arlington, Va.**
8. Shawn Harris, rhp, Johnson & Wales (R.I.) JC

BEND RAINBOWS (NORTHWEST LEAGUE)

January—Regular Phase

1. No selection
2. No selection
3. No selection
4. Kenneth Suzawa, lhp, Baldwin HS, Kahului, Hawaii

January—Secondary Phase

1. No selection
2. No selection
3. No selection
4. Jeffrey Wingert, c, Chaffey (Calif.) JC
5. Gary Addeo, rhp, Cerritos (Calif.) JC

June—Regular Phase

1. No selection
2. No selection
3. No selection
4. Tom Boyd, lhp, Wilcox HS, Santa Clara, Calif.
5. Charles Chatham, lhp, Ramona HS, Riverside, Calif.
6. **Tom Trebelhorn, c/inf, Portland State**
7. **Jim Van Wyck, ss, Oregon**
8. **Phil Bushman, of, Oregon**
9. **Allan Wise, of, Chapman (Calif.)**
10. Gary Roma, 3b/of, Chaffey (Calif.) JC

June—Secondary Phase

No selection

1971 Teams find little talent at top of draft, but uncover plenty of gems beyond first round

The regular phase of the June 1971 draft got off on the wrong foot when the White Sox selected catcher Danny Goodwin No. 1 but never signed the 17-year-old Peoria, Ill., product.

By the time the top half of the first round was complete, the talent was so thin that journeyman infielder Tom Veryzer, a career .241 hitter drafted 12th by Detroit, would become the most productive big leaguer.

But it got better. Much better.

Frank Tanana and Jim Rice were among those selected later in the first round. George Brett and Mike Schmidt, two of the best third basemen in baseball history, were called in the second round. Future Cy Young Award winner Ron Guidry went a round later. And future MVP Keith Hernandez was a 42nd-rounder.

There never has been a baseball draft where the talent was so misread as this one. The 1971 draft also was the last when higher-risk high school selections made up the entire first round. It wasn't until the White Sox led off the second round by drafting Ohio State outfielder Bill Sharp that a college player was taken in the regular phase.

The fact that no college players went in the first round was not an indictment of the 1971 college crop. Quite the contrary.

It's just that high-profile college selections like pitchers Pete Broberg and Burt Hooton were picked in the 1968 draft out of high school, so they weren't eligible for selection in the regular phase. They would have gone 1-2 in the regular phase had they been available, just as they did in the secondary phase.

Broberg, Hooton and outfielder Rob Ellis, the No. 3 pick in the secondary phase, were so advanced coming out of college that they all began their careers in the big leagues.

Broberg, the fireballing Dartmouth righthander, was picked by the Washington Senators. His father, a judge in West Palm Beach, Fla., negotiated a draft-record $150,000 bonus with Senators owner Bob Short and Broberg made his debut 12 days later.

Short had been expected to go after Ellis with the No. 1 pick, but went for Broberg because he said he could give the club immediate help.

"He has a real good fastball," Senators farm director Hal Keller said. "He's had some problems with control but he can make it in any league as long as he throws strikes with his fastball. He's as fine a pitcher as I've seen in a long, long time."

Danny Godwin saw his name come across the wire as the No. 1 pick in 1971 and '75

For Broberg, it was the second time record bonus money flashed his way. Three years earlier the Athletics took him in the regular phase, but he turned down offers that reached $175,000 in favor of an Ivy League education.

Hooton broke in with the Cubs June 17, but was shipped out to Triple-A after one outing. The three-time Texas all-American returned in September to beat the Mets twice—the first time on a three hit, 15-strikeout effort, the second on a two-hit shutout. He continued his torrid pitching by no-hitting the Phillies the following April, but he never quite lived up to his early billing with the Cubs, who dealt him to the Dodgers in 1975.

Ellis stepped right off the Michigan State campus into a Brewers uniform. Said Brewers scouting director Bobby Mattick: "He was our No. 1 pick all along. He had the most power of any player we scouted."

Ellis never homered in 64 big league games and spent most of his 10-year career in the minor leagues.

The 1971 draft marked the last time college players who were drafted out of high school would be subject to automatic selection in the secondary phase. In the future, all college players not drafted in the previous 13 months would be included in the regular phase.

As a transitional step, the secondary phase was split into two segments: an active phase, for players drafted as recently as January, and a delayed phase, for players drafted prior to 1971. Broberg and Hooton were eligible for the delayed phase.

The White Sox had first selection in the active phase and went for Harvard's two-time All-America catcher Pete Varney, drafted a record seventh time. With his college eligibility finally exhausted, Varney signed with Chicago.

Played Their Cards Wrong

Goodwin, who hit .494 at Peoria (Ill.) Central High, was heavily scouted by just three teams that spring but was generally regarded as the top player available in the regular phase. The White Sox announced two days before the draft that they planned to take Goodwin.

"We've been getting questions from all sides about the choice and rather than dodge them, we decided to make the announcement," player personnel director Roland Hemond said. "After all the hours we've spent in making the decision, we'd look pretty stupid if we hadn't made up our minds by at least 48 hours before the draft."

The White Sox made the pick without knowing Goodwin's bonus demands, however. From their initial meeting after the draft, the team realized Goodwin would be a tough sign.

Goodwin sought more than $100,000 and the White Sox, who were so pressed financially that they failed to sign 20 of their 34 June draft picks, could not close the gap. Goodwin opted for Southern University, where he played for four years before he was drafted No. 1 again in 1975 by the California Angels.

Besides Goodwin, two other first-round picks went unsigned in 1971. Both decided to play quarterback in the Southeastern Conference. The Expos failed to sign shortstop Condredge Holloway, who played both baseball and football at Tennessee but never played baseball professionally. Holloway spent his entire pro career in the Canadian Football League. Mike Miley turned down the Reds to play football at Louisiana State. He quarterbacked the Tigers for three years and later signed with the Angels, again as a first-round pick. He was killed in a car accident early in his major league career.

A total of 938 players were selected in the June draft's three phases. That continued a spiral from the 1,139 players that were drafted two years earlier. The trend would bottom out in 1974, with just 725 selections.

For the first time, the January draft was conducted by telephone from commissioner Bowie Kuhn's office at a cost of $4,000, saving clubs the expense of traveling to New York.

It would be several years before the June draft would go to a telephone conference call.

DRAFT 71: FIRST-ROUND PICKS

No.	Club	Player, Pos.	School	Hometown	Ht.	Wt.	B-T	Age
1.	White Sox	*Danny Goodwin, c	Central HS	Peoria, Ill.	6-1	195	L-R	17
2.	Padres	Jay Franklin, rhp	James Madison HS	Vienna, Va.	6-2	185	R-R	18
3.	Brewers	Tom Bianco, ss	Sewanhaka HS	Elmont, N.Y.	5-11	185	B-R	18
4.	Expos	*Condredge Holloway, ss	Lee HS	Huntsville, Ala.	6-0	175	R-R	17
5.	Royals	Roy Branch, rhp	Beaumont HS	St. Louis	5-11	180	R-R	17
6.	Phillies	Roy Thomas, rhp	Lompoc HS	Lompoc, Calif.	6-5	195	R-R	17
7.	Senators	Roger Quiroga, rhp	Ball HS	Galveston, Texas	6-1	180	R-R	18
8.	Cardinals	Ed Kurpiel, 1b/lhp	Archbishop Molloy HS	Hollis, N.Y.	6-3	210	L-L	17
9.	Indians	David Sloan, rhp	Santa Clara HS	Santa Clara, Calif.	6-1	175	R-R	19
10.	Braves	Taylor Duncan, ss	Grant HS	Sacramento	5-10	165	R-R	18
11.	Tigers	Tom Veryzer, ss	Islip HS	Islip, N.Y.	6-2	175	R-R	18
12.	Astros	Neil Rasmussen, ss	Arcadia HS	Arcadia, Calif.	6-2	185	R-R	18
13.	Angels	Frank Tanana, lhp	Catholic Central HS	Detroit	6-2	180	L-L	17
14.	Mets	Rich Puig, 2b	Hillsborough HS	Tampa	5-11	165	L-R	18
15.	Red Sox	Jim Rice, of	Hannah HS	Anderson, S.C.	6-1	200	R-R	18
16.	Cubs	Jeff Wehmeier, rhp	Brebeuf HS	Indianapolis	6-4	185	R-R	18
17.	Athletics	Sugar Bear Daniels, rhp	MacKenzie HS	Detroit	6-4	195	R-R	17
18.	Giants	Frank Riccelli, lhp	Christian Brothers HS	Syracuse, N.Y.	6-2	185	L-L	18
19.	Yankees	Terry Whitfield, of	Palo Verde HS	Blythe, Calif.	6-2	190	L-R	18
20.	Dodgers	Rick Rhoden, rhp	Atlantic HS	Boynton Beach, Fla.	6-3	195	R-R	18
21.	Twins	Dale Soderholm, ss	Coral Park HS	Miami	6-3	165	R-R	18
22.	Pirates	Craig Reynolds, ss	Regan HS	Houston	6-0	170	L-R	18
23.	Orioles	Randy Stein, rhp	Ganesha HS	Pomona, Calif.	6-4	200	R-R	18
24.	Reds	*Mike Miley, ss	East Jefferson HS	New Orleans	6-1	180	B-R	18

*Did not sign

1971

CLUB-BY-CLUB SELECTIONS

ATLANTA BRAVES

January—Regular Phase (9)

1. **Joseph Turnbullm, of/1b, Seminole (Fla.) JC**

January—Secondary Phase (20)

1. Pete Varney Jr., 1b, Harvard
2. John Adeimy, ss, Miami-Dade South CC
3. Jerry Gomez, lhp, Omaha, Neb.
4. **Jimmy Collins, rhp, Southern**

June—Regular Phase (10)

1. **Taylor Duncan, ss, Grant Union HS, Sacramento**
2. **Jamie Easterly, lhp, Crockett (Texas) HS**
3. Dennis Lewallyn, rhp, Escambia HS, Pensacola, Fla.
4. **Pat McKean, lhp, Texas Tech**
5. **Rob Pitre, rhp, Rosemead (Calif.) HS**
6. Brian Stone, of, El Camino HS, Sacramento
7. **Larry Smith, lhp, Arroyo HS, El Monte, Calif.**
8. Jerry Willeford, of/c, Sam Houston HS, Houston
9. Mike Stanton, rhp, Santa Fe HS, Lakeland, Calif.
10. Jon Dempsey, rhp, Grimsley HS, Greensboro, N.C.
11. **Junior Moore, 3b, Kennedy HS, Richmond, Calif.**
12. James Foxwell, ss, Bridgewater-Raritan East HS, Martinsville, N.J.
13. Larry Silveira, c, San Luis Obispo (Calif.) HS
14. George Gilbreath, rhp, North Greenville (S.C.) JC
15. **Larry Hendrickson, rhp, Santa Rosa (Calif.) JC**
16. **Calvin Smith, ss, Harper HS, Atlanta**
17. **Biff Pocoroba, c, Canoga Park (Calif.) HS**
18. William Daves, c, Guthrie (Okla.) HS
19. Peter Dann, rhp, Metuchen (N.J.) HS
20. Rod Spence, 3b, St. Augustine HS, San Diego
21. **William Lorillard, lhp, Robert E. Lee HS, San Antonio, Texas**
22. Scott McHenry, rhp, Bridgewater-Raritan East HS, Somerville, N.J.
23. Larry Liedy, ss, Staten Island (N.Y.)
24. Rick Dively, of, Saguarao HS, Scottsdale, Ariz.
25. **Roger Williams, of, Texas Christian**

June—Secondary (Active) Phase (10)

1. Ron Hodges, c, Appalachian State

June—Secondary (Delayed) Phase (18)

1. **Mike Beard, lhp, Texas**

BALTIMORE ORIOLES

January—Regular Phase (24)

1. **Edward Jordan, c, Los Angeles Pierce JC**
2. **Richard David, 1b, Honululu, Hawaii**
3. **Allan Wyatt, of/1b, Los Angeles Pierce JC**
4. James Martin, of, Glendale (Calif.) JC
5. Mike Pulaski, of, Indian River (Fla.) CC
6. **Dennis Silvey, 1b, Mount Hood (Ore.) CC**
7. **Harry Bilyeu, c, Glendale (Calif.) JC**
8. **Curt Daniels, 2b, Oregon State**
9. Perry Kozlowski, rhp, Santa Rosa (Calif.) JC
10. Larry Hartman, rhp, JC of San Mateo (Calif.)
11. Robert Brassea, ss, Canada (Calif.) JC

January—Secondary Phase (19)

1. **Wilmer Aaron, ss, Los Angeles Valley JC**
2. **John Euler, rhp, North Carolina**
3. Richard Baker, rhp, Lynchburg, Va.
4. Robert Sherman, rhp, Seminole (Fla.) JC
5. Darrell Devitt, rhp, Billings, Mont.
6. **Tom Seybold, lhp, Florida**
7. John O'Connor, c, Alexandria, Va.
8. Chris Cammack, 3b, North Carolina State
9. Randy Delerio, c, Dos Palos, Calif.

June—Regular Phase (23)

1. **Randy Stein, rhp, Ganesha HS, Pomona, Calif.**
2. **Steve Patterson, rhp, Stark HS, Orange, Texas**
3. **Kiko Garcia, ss, Ygnacio Valley HS, Walnut Creek, Calif.**
4. **Myrl Smith, lhp, Franklin Senior HS, Reisterstown, Md.**
5. **Mark Pettit, ss, Bishop Montgomery HS, Lomita, Calif.**
6. **Tim Hoyles, rhp, Princeton HS, Cincinnati**
7. Hank Small, of, Dykes HS, Atlanta
8. Anthony Davis, of, San Fernando HS, Pacoima, Calif.
9. **Peter Quinlan, of, North Reading (Mass.) HS**
10. **Russell Parker, of/rhp, Southside HS, Effingham, S.C.**
11. Stephen Johnson, ss, Barboursville HS, Huntington, W.Va.
12. Michael Arrington, rhp, Bethel HS, Hampton, Va.
13. **Horace Richardson, lhp/of, William & Mary**
14. Larry Meekins, rhp, Franklin HS, Owings Mills, Md.
15. William Bollman, c, Westbury HS, Houston
16. Roger McSwain, of, Gardner-Webb
17. **Billy Hamilton, lhp, Dumas (Texas) HS**
18. Dan Marple, of, Hueneme HS, Oxnard, Calif.
19. Otis Zagorski, of, Havelock (N.C.) HS
20. **Kim Hall, ss, Maryland-Eastern Shore**
21. **Cary Shea, c, Georgia Southern**
22. **Frank Bowling, of/3b, Cleveland HS, Reseda, Calif.**
23. **Charles Heil, 1b, Serra HS, Hawthorne, Calif.**
24. **Paul Kreins, 1b, College Park HS, Pleasant Hill, Calif.**
25. Leo Szarek, lhp, Whitehouse HS, Somerville, N.J.
26. Donald Rogers, c, Louisburg (N.C.) JC
27. James Thompson, rhp, Lake Havasu (Ariz.) HS
28. John Paull, c, Laurel Highlands HS, Lemont Furnace, Pa.
29. David Christiansen, lhp, Grant HS, Sherman Oaks, Calif.
30. Dennis Watson, rhp, Van Nuys HS, Arleta, Calif.
31. John Kelly, 3b/of, Crenshaw HS, Los Angeles
32. Robert Keller, rhp, Xenia (Ohio) HS
33. Thomas Foster, ss, Aloha (Ore.) HS
34. Tyrus Neely, ss, Macomb (Mich.) CC
35. Brian Jones, c, Edmondson HS, Baltimore
36. Steve Cannady, c, Bellarmine Prep, Campbell, Calif.
37. Frank Kunnen, c, Clearwater (Fla.) Catholic HS
38. Ken Bruchanski, rhp, St. Clement HS, Centerline, Mich.
39. Rocky Manuel, ss, Portage (Mich.) Northern HS
40. Richard Cahill, lhp, Tigard (Ore.) HS
41. Chandler Myers, rhp, Narbonne HS, Harbor City, Calif.
42. Timothy Fox, rhp, Gulf Coast (Fla.) CC

June—Secondary (Active) Phase (9)

1. **Robert Sekel, rhp, Niagara County (N.Y.) CC**
2. Rod Walker, rhp, Mississippi Gulf Coast JC
3. Robert Loughery, rhp, Anne Arundel (Md.) CC
4. Rick Colzie, rhp/ss, Miami-Dade South CC

June—Secondary (Delayed) Phase (7)

1. **Paul Mitchell Jr., rhp, Old Dominion**
2. Robert Koepell, lhp/of, Bradley
3. **Joe Pupo, rhp, Santa Clara**

BOSTON RED SOX

January—Regular Phase (16)

1. Howard Echols, 3b, Columbia State (Tenn.) CC
2. Craig Kimball, c, San Francisco
3. **Dwayne Mayberry, of, San Francisco**
4. Eric Rasmussen, rhp, Indian Hills (Iowa) CC
5. **Michael Averill, of, Fullerton (Calif.) JC**
6. Elliott Jones, rhp, Vanderbilt
7. **Dale Bjerke, rhp, St. Clair County (Mich.) CC**

January—Secondary Phase (21)

1. Jim Otten, rhp, Mesa (Ariz.) CC

2. **Steve Foran, lhp, Denver, Colo.**
3. John Tamargo, c, Miami-Dade North CC
4. Roy Smalley, ss, Los Angeles, Calif.
5. Steve Boryczewski, c, Seton Hall

June—Regular Phase (15)

1. **Jim Rice, of, Hannah HS, Anderson, S.C.**
2. **Milt Jefferson, 3b, Manual Arts HS, Los Angeles**
3. **James Vosk, rhp, Middletown HS, Red Bank, N.J.**
4. **Tom Pokarski, lhp, Northview HS, Covina, Calif.**
5. **Tom Cassell, ss, Mansfield (Pa.)**
6. **Terry Stokes, ss, Pittsburgh**
7. **Paul Flanagan, of, Columbus HS, Dorchester, Mass.**
8. **James Snypes, inf/of, South Alabama**
9. **Bill Moran II, rhp, Louisburg (N.C.) JC**
10. **Michael Sherwood, ss, Bella Vista HS, Fair Oaks, Calif.**
11. **Paul Smith, c/of, South HS, Framingham, Mass.**
12. **David Sauve, 2b, Maryland**
13. **Clyde Zimmerman, ss, Southern Columbia HS, Catawissa, Pa.**
14. **James Barrineau, rhp, South Boston (Mass.) HS**
15. **Thomas Cason, of, Jacksonville State**
16. **Chester Lucas, of, Citronelle (Ala.) HS**
17. Richard Wehner, lhp, St. Clement HS, Detroit
18. **Stephen Chapman, lhp, Minnesota**
19. **Kelly Jones, rhp, Boise (Idaho) HS**
20. **Kenneth Nicar, c, Sam Houston HS, Houston**
21. Jerry Stamps, c, Jess Lanier HS, Bessemer, Ala.
22. **John Seymour, c/3b, St. Lawrence (N.Y.)**
23. **Ken Inglis, lhp, Montclair State (N.J.)**
24. Richard Seid, c, Oak Park (Mich.) HS
25. **Mark Bomback, rhp, Durfee HS, Fall River, Mass.**
26. **Jack Baker, 1b, Auburn**
27. Ronnie Goodman, c/of, Port Jefferson HS, Mount Sinai, N.Y.
28. Steve Kooshkalis, rhp, Peabody (Mass.) HS

June—Secondary (Active) Phase (7)

1. Lynn McKinney, rhp, Rio Hondo (Calif.) JC
2. **Earl Nance, lhp, Auburn**
3. **Henry Baker, 3b, Southern**

June—Secondary (Delayed) Phase (5)

1. **Jim Burton, lhp, Michigan**
2. **Ed Scruggs, rhp, Lynchburg (Va.)**
3. **Kurt Lohrke, ss, Santa Clara**
4. Duane Kuiper, ss, Southern Illinois
5. **Mike Hansen, rhp, Arizona State**
6. Steve Prestridge, rhp, Delta State (Miss.)
7. **Bill Todd, lhp, Missouri**

CALIFORNIA ANGELS

January—Regular Phase (14)

1. **Earl Austin, 3b, West Hills (Calif.) JC**
2. **Larry Dierks, lhp, Arizona**
3. Darold Nogle, of, Rio Hondo (Calif.) JC
4. Alan Cox, rhp, Fullerton (Calif.) JC
5. Dan Everts, rhp, Rio Hondo (Calif.) JC
6. William Weyl, lhp/1b, Santa Rosa (Calif.) JC

January—Secondary Phase (7)

1. **Bob Allietta, c, Falmouth, Mass.**
2. Michael McManus, 1b/of, Mount San Antonio (Calif.) JC
3. Robert Loughery, rhp, Pasadena, Md.
4. Mike Edwards, ss, Los Angeles, Calif.
5. Craig Barnes, 1b, Mount San Antonio (Calif.) JC
6. John Wade, c, Seattle, Wash.
7. Mitch Fahland, c, Libby, Mont.
8. **Jerry Remy, 2b, Roger Williams (R.I.)**

June—Regular Phase (13)

1. **Frank Tanana, lhp, Catholic Central HS, Detroit**
2. **Ron Jackson, 3b, Wenonah HS, Birmingham, Ala.**
3. **Billy Smith, ss, John Jay HS, San Antonio**
4. **David Christiansen, c, Inglewood (Calif.) HS**
5. **Charles Gibbon, lhp, Luezinger-Lawndale HS, Hawthorne, Calif.**
6. **Jeff Kalil, of, Isaac Elston HS, Michigan City, Ind.**
7. **Frank George, of, St. Augustine HS, San Diego**
8. **Steve Miller, rhp/of, Atwater HS, Winton, Calif.**
9. **David Evans, rhp, Sparta (N.C.) HS**
10. **Thomas Whiteley, rhp, Temple City (Calif.) HS**
11. **Ed Romager, rhp, Erwin HS, Birmimgham**
12. Steve Trella, rhp, Servite HS, Anaheim
13. **Mark Block, c, Bellarmine Prep HS, Los Gatos, Calif.**
14. **Jim Uruburu, lhp, Cal Poly Pomona**
15. David Barnes, 2b/ss, East Valley HS, Yakima, Wash.
16. **Charles Wade, rhp, Cave Springs HS, Roanoke, Va.**
17. **Melvin Aaron, of, Los Angeles**
18. Michael Martinez, rhp, Montevello (Calif.) HS
19. **Steve Wiencek, 2b, Cal Poly Pomona**
20. **Peter Levin, lhp, UCLA**
21. Steve Kelley, rhp, Cupertino (Calif.) HS
22. Steve Ross, of, UC Santa Barbara
23. **Thomas Smith, 1b/of, Ohio**
24. Michael Payne, rhp, Mississippi Delta JC
25. Michael Gleason, of, Gonzaga Prep HS, Spokane, Wash.
26. Mike Gatlin, ss, Chaffey HS, Ontario, Calif.
27. **Randy Wilson, 1b, Sylmar (Calif.) HS**
28. **Ken Barker, rhp, Claremont (Calif.) HS**
29. Michael Daley, 1b, Marion (Wis.) HS
30. **Oscar Fisher, of, Southern**
31. Edward Gale, lhp, Peoria (Ill.) Central HS
32. Joe Cipriano, rhp, Delsea Regional HS, Franklinville, N.J.
33. Dennis O'Connor, c, Soquel HS, Santa Cruz, Calif.
34. **Frank Kenyon, lhp, Bonita HS, San Dimas, Calif.**
35. Joe Groetsch, rhp/ss, North Catholic HS, Pittsburgh
36. Jesse Mendoza, of/c, Bishop Amat HS, La Puente, Calif.
37. **Thomas Floyd, rhp, Baptist Christian (La.)**
38. John Palmer, lhp, Corona Del Mar HS, Newport Beach, Calif.
39. Ron Wrigley, rhp, St. Augustine HS, San Diego
40. Frank Welch, rhp, Walterboro (S.C.) HS
41. Alan Brumfield, inf/c, George Washington HS, Danville, Va.
42. David Judnick, rhp, Novato (Calif.) HS
43. Ed Piecynski, rhp, Pittston (Pa.) HS
44. Carl Peternell, c, Miraleste HS, Rolling Hills, Calif.
45. Ray Bolton, rhp, Moorpark (Calif.) JC

June—Secondary (Active) Phase (3)

1. **Jim Officer, lhp, Oregon**
2. **Darroll Phillips, rhp/of, Laney (Calif.) JC**
3. Gary Hampton, 2b/of, Fresno (Calif.) CC
4. Tom Martell, lhp, Linn-Benton (Ore.) CC

June—Secondary (Delayed) Phase (11)

1. **John Donovan, rhp, Seton Hall**
2. **Ron Botica, rhp, Louisiana Tech**
3. Steve Fahsbender, lhp, Claremont-Mudd (Calif.)

CHICAGO CUBS

January—Regular Phase (15)

1. Perry Danforth, ss, Indian Hills (Iowa) CC
2. Richard Koch, lhp, Indian Hills (Iowa) CC
3. James Kick, rhp, St. Louis CC-Meramec

January—Secondary Phase (22)

1. **Gary Brown, rhp, Elon**
2. Steve Stroughter, of, Visalia, Calif.
3. William Bishop, 1b, Bronx, N.Y.

June—Regular Phase (16)

1. **Jeff Wehmeier, rhp, Brebeuf HS, Indianapolis**
2. **Steven Haug, c, Wood River (Ill.) HS**
3. **Dennis Lamp, rhp, St. John Bosco HS, Los Alamitos, Calif.**
4. **Max Stewart, of, Hilltop HS, Chula Vista, Calif.**
5. **Rob Sperring, 3b/ss, Pacific**
6. **Johnnie Jenkins, ss, Riverview HS, Sarasota, Fla.**
7. **Jim Tyrone, of, Texas-Pan American**
8. William Stark, c, Chaffey HS, Ontario, Calif.
9. David Bartholomew, 1b, Kearny HS, San Diego
10. Randy Davidson, 2b, Robert E. Lee HS, Huntsville, Ala.
11. Curtis Wright, rhp, Edison HS, Fresno
12. Dave Bergman, 1b, Maine South HS, Park Ridge, Ill.

13. **Danny Humble, of, Central Greene HS, Waynesburg, Pa.**
14. Gary Hunt, rhp, Ravenswood (W.Va.) HS
15. William Smith, of, Hoggard HS, Wilmington, N.C.
16. **John Anderson, lhp, John Brown (Ark.)**
17. Dwight Ausbon, ss, Locke HS, Los Angeles
18. **Robert Kleen, 3b, Central HS, St. Louis**
19. Terry Teale, c, McClatchy HS, Sacramento
20. **Michael Gutierrez, ss, Merced (Calif.) HS**
21. **Walt Barnes, 2b, Gunn HS, Palo Alto, Calif.**
22. Mike Denevi, ss, Los Gatos (Calif.) HS
23. Guy Hollingsworth, lhp, South Natchez (Miss.) HS
24. **Terry Thompson, rhp, Pillow Academy, Greenwood, Miss.**
25. **Cameron Jury, rhp, William Jewell (Mo.)**

June—Secondary (Active) Phase (18)

1. Jim Otten, rhp, Mesa (Ariz.) CC

June—Secondary (Delayed) Phase (2)

1. **Burt Hooton, rhp, Texas**
2. **Joel Green, ss, Miami**

CHICAGO WHITE SOX

January—Regular Phase (2)

1. Larry O'Brien, rhp, Indian Hills (Iowa) CC
2. Gary Conley, of, Miami-Dade North CC
3. Joe Wolf, c/1b, Northern Iowa

January—Secondary Phase (5)

1. **Sam Ewing, of/1b, Tennessee**
2. **Paul Sands, rhp, Bacone (Okla.) JC**
3. Earl Nance, lhp, Auburn
4. James Hamilton, c, East Point, Ga.

June—Regular Phase (1)

1. Danny Goodwin, c, Peoria (Ill.) Central HS
2. **Bill Sharp, of, Ohio State**
3. Paul Zobeck, lhp, Central HS, Pueblo, Colo.
4. Steve Hergenrader, c, McLane HS, Fresno
5. **Eddie Holly, rhp, Unaka HS, Elizabethton, Tenn.**
6. Jack Kucek, rhp, Newton Falls (Ohio) HS
7. Warren Cromartie, of, Jackson HS, Miami
8. Barry Bonnell, 2b, Milford (Ohio) HS
9. **Kurt Best, rhp, Austin (Minn.) HS**
10. Robert Willis, of, Monroe HS, Pacoima, Calif.
11. **David Leisman, rhp, Michigan State**
12. Ricardo Fuentes, ss, Miami Senior HS
13. Jay Kuhnie, rhp, Eastern Michigan
14. Benny McGrumby, ss/of, Centennial HS, Los Angeles
15. **Don Bolte, lhp, Canoga Park (Calif.) HS**
16. Randy Braxton, 2b, Clairemont HS, San Diego
17. **Jeff Holly, lhp, Aviation HS, Redondo Beach, Calif.**
18. **Rey Santiago, 1b, Washington HS, East Chicago, Ind.**
19. Frank Klancer, rhp, Barberton (Ohio) HS
20. Mike Curran, 3b, Jefferson HS, Cedar Rapids, Iowa
21. Douglas Blue, lhp, Gering (Neb.) HS
22. William Choat, lhp, Huffman HS, Birmingham, Ala.
23. **John Friess, of, Wisconsin State**
24. **Michael McConnell, c, Whiting (Ind.) HS**
25. **James Davis, lhp, Woodrow Wilson HS, Camden, N.J.**
26. Robert Bianco, ss, Norton East HS, Cicero, Ill.

June—Secondary (Active) Phase (1)

1. **Pete Varney Jr., rhp, Harvard**
2. William Taylor, inf, Mira Costa (Calif.) JC
3. Archie Manning, ss, Mississippi
4. Frank Baumgardner, rhp, Miami-Dade North CC

June—Secondary (Delayed) Phase (23)

1. **Craig Lown, rhp, Southern Colorado**
2. Ralph Darin, rhp, Central Michigan

CINCINNATI REDS

January—Regular Phase (23)

1. **Eddie Tobin, of, Baptist Christian (La.)**
2. **Edward Munoz, of/1b, Bacone (Okla.) JC**
3. **Brian Williams, of/1b, Cynthiana, Ky.**
4. Mike Pfitzer, rhp, Mesa (Ariz.) CC
5. Charles Haymes, of/inf, Chicago, Ill.
6. Tom Rima, of, Indian Hills (Iowa) CC
7. Dan Hinzman, lhp, Indian Hills (Iowa) CC

January—Secondary Phase (12)

1. Gaylin Pabst, ss/of, Danville Area (Ill.) CC
2. Chris Charnish, of, Wisconsin-Platteville
3. William Hodge, c, Texas A&M
4. **Richard Soriano, of, Miami-Dade North CC**
5. Gary Ellefson, rhp, Dell Rapids, S.D.

June—Regular Phase (24)

1. Mike Miley, ss, East Jefferson HS, New Orleans
2. **William Covert, 1b, Meridian (Miss.) HS**
3. **Richard Coleman, of, Lane Tech HS, Chicago**
4. **Ernie Pupo, rhp, Gonzaga Prep, Spokane, Wash.**
5. **Don Werner, c, East HS, Appleton, Wis.**
6. **Paul Howland, lhp, McClain HS, Greenfield, Ohio**
7. **Dave Revering, 1b, Bella Vista HS, Fair Oaks, Calif.**
8. Pat Williams, rhp, Camden HS, San Jose
9. **Gary Myers, rhp, Flat River HS, Esther, Mo.**
10. **Frank Ford, 1b/of, North HS, Minneapolis**
11. Scott Torosian, rhp, Hoover HS, Fresno
12. **Allen Knight, c, Bossier City (La.) HS**
13. **Jerry Bowles, rhp, Southeastern Louisiana**
14. Randy Johnston, c/3b, Wichita (Kan.) West HS
15. Doug Horton, rhp, Virginia Tech
16. Dennis Simon, rhp, Monongahela Valley Catholic HS, Findleyville, Pa.
17. Edward Burzo, of, Levittown (N.Y.) Division HS
18. **Michael Heintz, lhp, Lower Moreland HS, Huntington Valley, Pa.**
19. **John Hale, c, West Virginia**
20. **Andre Delgado, rhp, George Washington HS, New York**
21. **Mike Marchovecchio, of/3b, Roncalli HS, Pueblo, Colo.**
22. Carl Person, of, Miami-Dade South CC
23. Dave Collins, 1b/of, Stevens HS, Rapid City, S.D.
24. Pat Tormey, ss, St. Augustine HS, La Mesa, Calif.
25. **Robert Edmond, 2b, Fort Valley State**
26. Gary Mashburn, rhp, Fulton HS, Knoxville, Tenn.
27. **Larry Cole, of, Salem (W.Va.)**
28. Lorenzo Ladaga, c, Hialeah (Fla.) HS
29. Robin Ogle, 1b, Tallawanda HS, Oxford, Ohio
30. Craig Kliebl, rhp, Norland HS, Miami Beach, Fla.
31. Melvin Barkham, ss, Gulfport (Miss.) HS

June—Secondary (Active) Phase (20)

1. **Darrell Devitt, rhp, Mesa (Ariz.) CC**
2. Tom Rima, of, Indian Hills (Iowa) CC

June—Secondary (Delayed) Phase (6)

1. **Robert Borowicz, ss, Ithaca (N.Y.)**
2. **Ken Hansen, rhp, Arizona State**
3. Alan Schwartz, rhp, Duke

CLEVELAND INDIANS

January—Regular Phase (10)

1. William Malacrida, of/c, Valencia (Fla.) CC
2. Bill Dancy, ss, Seminole (Fla.) JC

January—Secondary Phase (23)

1. Steve Behlen, lhp, Fresno (Calif.) CC
2. Dan Tripp, lhp, Holland, Mich.
3. Gary Cavallo, rhp, Seton Hall
4. Mark Robison, rhp, Key West, Fla.
5. **Jim Norris, of, Maryland**

June—Regular Phase (9)

1. **David Sloan, rhp, Santa Clara (Calif.) HS**
2. Jim Umbarger, lhp, Grant HS, Van Nuys, Calif.
3. **Wayne Cage, lhp/1b, Ruston HS, Choudrant, La.**
4. **Donnie Howse, 3b, Central HS, Murfreesboro, Tenn.**
5. John Novak, lhp, Padua HS, Middleburgh Heights, Ohio
6. **Jamie Traber, of, McLane HS, Fresno**
7. **Larry Andersen, rhp, Interlake HS, Bellevue, Wash.**
8. **Delmas Culp, c, West HS, Columbus, Ohio**

9. **Larry Marshall, of, San Fernando (Calif.) HS**
10. **Terry Wedgewood, 3b, Purdue**
11. Stephen Clancy, c, Bacone (Okla.) JC
12. **Jimmy Johnson, c/inf, Rosamond (Calif.) HS**
13. **Donald Cordonnier, 1b, Russia (Ohio) HS**
14. Mark Rogers, of, Rancho Alamitos HS, Garden Grove, Calif.
15. **Jimmy Denny, of, Columbus (Ga.) HS**
16. **Richard Kavanaugh, rhp, Troy (Miss.) HS**
17. Ken Harbin, 2b, Parker HS, Greenville, S.C.
18. **Thomas Roberts, 1b, Toledo**
19. **Anthony Manning, of, Shaker Heights (Ohio) HS**
20. **Brian Sullivan, rhp, Western Michigan**
21. **Ron Ellis, ss, Ohio State**
22. **Richard Langdon, lhp, Southern Illinois**
23. Jeffrey Roser, rhp, Okaloosa-Walton (Fla.) JC
24. Lawrence Longa, 1b/of, Central Catholic HS, Cleveland (Selection voided)
25. Donald Reece, 3b/rhp, Cordova HS, Rancho Cordova, Calif.
26. Lamar Jones, rhp, Roswell (Ga.) HS
27. Mike Eden, 3b, Southern Illinois

June—Secondary (Active) Phase (21)

1. Keith Metheny, rhp, Green River (Wash.) CC

June—Secondary (Delayed) Phase (17)

1. Jim Cox, ss, Iowa
2. **James Sams, rhp, Miami (Ohio)**
3. **Steve Mikulic, ss, Arizona**

DETROIT TIGERS

January—Regular Phase (12)

1. **James Cates, 1b, Fullerton (Calif.) JC**
2. **George Hart, c, Brookdale (N.J.) CC**
3. **Gary Bond, rhp, Los Angeles CC**
4. **Fred Strine, rhp, Ohio State**

January—Secondary Phase (11)

1. Gary Rausch, lhp, Lake City, Pa.
2. Don Kreke, rhp, Bartelso, Ill.
3. Ron Herring, rhp, Greenville, Ala.
4. Ray Huard, ss, Princeton
5. Richard Eisenacher, rhp, Auburn

June—Regular Phase (11)

1. **Tom Veryzer, ss, Islip (N.Y.) HS**
2. **Dennis DeBarr, lhp, Kennedy HS, Fremont, Calif.**
3. **Benjamin Hunt, ss, Bel Air HS, El Paso, Texas**
4. **Ramon Gimenez, c, New York City Technical JC**
5. **William Michael, of, Stonewall Jackson HS, Charleston, W.Va.**
6. **Jeff Natchez, of, Southwestern HS, Flint, Mich.**
7. **Gene Pentz, rhp, Johnstown (Pa.) HS**
8. David Bowden, ss, Kathleen HS, Lakeland, Fla.
9. **Don Leslie, rhp, Jefferson HS, Lafayette, Ind.**
10. Frank Catalano, of, East Meadow (N.Y.) HS
11. **Robert Nemcek, rhp, Central HS, Little Falls, N.Y.**
12. **Lawrence Bracco, rhp, Deer Lakes HS, Creighton, Pa.**
13. **Gary Christenson, lhp, New Hyde Park (N.Y.) Memorial HS**
14. Mitch Lukevics, rhp, Bethlehem (Pa.) Liberty HS
15. Vince Buszko, rhp, South River (N.J.) HS
16. Marvin Otto, c, Starpoint HS, Lockport, N.Y.
17. Dennis McLain, lhp, Southeastern HS, Detroit
18. **Maurice Horton, ss, East St. Louis (Ill.) HS**
19. **Robert Shortell, rhp, St. John's**
20. Curtis Bishop, lhp, Roswell (N.M.) HS
21. John Gutowski, rhp, Piscataway (N.J.) HS
22. Michael Johnson, lhp, Robinson (Ill.) HS
23. **Robert Flanders, of, Brown**
24. **Glenn Faulk, lhp, Rosemead HS, El Monte, Calif.**
25. **Scott Thompson, 3b, Manchester (N.H.) Memorial HS**
26. **Jim Eschen, inf, Wake Forest**
27. **Andy Kanoza, ss, Central Michigan**
28. **Stewart Sims, 3b, Snyder (Texas) HS**
29. **Richard Miceli, rhp, Western New Mexico**
30. **Roberto Perez, 3b, Miami Senior HS**
31. **Michael Corbett, of, Liverpool (N.Y.) HS**
32. Paul Bock, lhp, Mishawka (Ind.) HS
33. Edmund Besch, rhp, Orchard Park (N.Y.) HS
34. **Greg Gromek, ss, Florida State**
35. Robert Brown, rhp, Brother Rice HS, Birmingham, Mich.
36. **Mark Palmer, rhp, La Quinta HS, Westminster, Calif.**
37. Kent Marsh, ss, Caledonia (Mich.) HS

June—Secondary (Active) Phase (11)

1. **Arnold Costell, lhp, Nassau (N.Y.) CC**

June—Secondary (Delayed) Phase (21)

1. **Charles Coe, ss, Kansas State**
2. **Danny Fife, rhp, Michigan**
3. **Ron Cash, ss, Florida State**

HOUSTON ASTROS

January—Regular Phase (11)

1. **Tim Green, rhp, Bakersfield (Calif.) JC**
2. Richard Bubash, rhp, Boyce (Pa.) CC

January—Secondary Phase (4)

1. **Doug Konieczny, rhp, St. Clair County (Mich.) CC**
2. William Horne, rhp, Albany, Ga.
3. Rick Colzie, inf/rhp, Miami-Dade South CC
4. William Taylor, inf, Encinitas, Calif.

June—Regular Phase (12)

1. **Neil Rasmussen, ss, Arcadia (Calif.) HS**
2. **Art Gardner, lhp/of, South Leake HS, Walnut Grove, Miss.**
3. **Paul Siebert, lhp, Edina (Minn.) HS**
4. **David Warburton, rhp, Hale HS, Tulsa, Okla.**
5. James Donker, rhp, Arcadia HS, Phoenix
6. **Marc Cochran, c, Hayfield HS, Alexandria, Va.**
7. **William McLaurine, lhp, Laverne (Okla.) HS**
8. Joe Yocum, rhp, Bullard HS, Fresno, Calif.
9. **Michael Hart, c, Westmont HS, San Jose**
10. **Gary Smith, lhp, Concord HS, Gilman, Vt.**
11. **John Kimbley, of, Dumas (Texas) HS**
12. Mike Patrick, lhp, St. Joseph's HS, Wickliffe, Ohio
13. Michael Galloway, lhp, W.A. Berry HS, Birmingham
14. William Sutton, lhp, Laverne (Okla.) HS
15. Mike Flanagan, lhp, Memorial HS, Manchester, N.H.
16. **John Cook, ss, Mount Everett HS, Sheffield, Mass.**
17. **Gil Stafford, c, Maryvale HS, Phoenix**
18. James Baker, ss, Camden County HS, Waverly, Ga.
19. **James Todd, rhp, Connersville (Ind.) HS**

June—Secondary (Active) Phase (4)

1. **David Kaster, rhp, Nebraska-Omaha**

June—Secondary (Delayed) Phase (8)

1. Rich Troedson, lhp, Santa Clara
2. **Robert Blakley, of/1b, Southern Illinois**
3. Ray Guy, rhp, Southern Mississippi

KANSAS CITY ROYALS

January—Regular Phase (4)

1. **John Wathan, c, San Diego**
2. Michael Bauer, rhp, Wisconsin
3. Billy Simmons, 1b/of, Westark (Ark.) CC

January—Secondary Phase (15)

1. Ron Hodges, c, Appalachian State
2. Archie Manning, ss, Mississippi
3. Gary Roma, 3b/of, Chaffey (Calif.) JC

June—Regular Phase (5)

1. **Roy Branch, rhp, Beaumont HS, St. Louis**
2. **George Brett, ss, El Segundo (Calif.) HS**
3. **Charles Smith, of, Sherwood HS, Olney, Md.**
4. **Joe Zdeb, 3b, Maine South HS, Park Ridge, Ill.**
5. **David Masser, of, Pueblo (Colo.) County HS**
6. **George Feeley, of, West HS, Rockford, Ill.**
7. **Greg Marshall, of, San Jose State**
8. **Gary Dunkleberger, rhp, Chapman (Calif.)**
9. **James Ross, rhp, Sam Houston HS, Houston**
10. Jerry Maddox, ss, Neff HS, La Mirada, Calif.
11. Michael McGee, ss, Gerstmeyer HS, Terre Haute, Ind.

12. **Mark Littell, rhp, Gideon (Mo.) HS**
13. Samuel Howell, rhp, Cardinal Newman HS, West Palm Beach, Fla.
14. **Craig Perkins, c, Southern California**
15. **Gerald Mifsud, of, Edinboro (Pa.)**
16. Tim Ryan, lhp, San Joaquin Memorial HS, Fresno, Calif.
17. **Tim Howard, lhp, Wahama HS, New Haven, W.Va.**
18. **Charles Butler, rhp, Saddleback HS, Santa Ana, Calif.**
19. Mike DuPree, of, Roosevelt HS, Fresno
20. **Ricky Romans, lhp, Jeffersonville (Ind.) HS**
21. David Cargo, 1b, Concord (Calif.) HS
22. Larry Demery, rhp, Locke HS, Los Angeles
23. **Kent Agler, rhp, Cal Poly San Luis Obispo**
24. **Joe Carbone, 2b, Ohio**
25. **Steve Hudson, rhp, Mayfair HS, Lakewood, Calif.**
26. **Randy Johnson, rhp, Aviation HS, Manhattan Beach, Calif.**
27. Mike Walsh, rhp, Neff HS, La Mirada, Calif.
28. Steven Ingram, rhp, Maryvale HS, Phoenix
29. Tom Apa, c, Jesuit HS, Portland, Ore.
30. James Housley, of, Taft HS, Tarzana, Calif.
31. Steven Jones, 1b, Garden Grove (Calif.) HS
32. Ron Hill, 2b, David Douglas HS, Portland, Ore.
33. Steve Bartkowski, 1b, Buchser HS, Santa Clara, Calif.
34. Charles Cleveland, rhp, Bibb HS, Centerville, Ala.

June—Secondary (Active) Phase (13)

1. Gary Anglin, lhp, Ventura (Calif.) JC
2. **Steve Staggs, inf, Cerritos (Calif.) JC**

June—Secondary (Delayed) Phase (15)

1. **Roger Schmuck, of/1b, Arizona State**
2. **Steve Busby, rhp, Southern California**
3. **Mark Arnold, rhp, Kansas State**

LOS ANGELES DODGERS

January—Regular Phase (19)

1. **Steven Olsen, lhp, American River (Calif.) JC**
2. **Don Standley, rhp, Fullerton (Calif.) JC**
3. Paul Few, rhp, Chipola (Fla.) JC

January—Secondary Phase (14)

1. **James Corcoran, inf, California**
2. **David Freeborn, ss, Buttonwillow, Calif.**
3. Francisco Suarez, ss, Hialeah, Fla.

June—Regular Phase (20)

1. **Rick Rhoden, rhp, Atlantic HS, Boynton Beach, Fla.**
2. **Greg Reinecker, rhp, Edgewood HS, La Puente, Calif.**
3. **Rick Green, rhp, Chino (Calif.) HS**
4. Michael Frazier, c, Elmore HS, Houston
5. **Rex Hudson, rhp, Hale HS, Tulsa, Okla.**
6. **Chris Mayo, lhp, Hillsdale HS, San Mateo, Calif.**
7. Chuck Redmon, ss, Moore (Okla.) HS
8. Terry Stupy, c, Los Alamitos (Calif.) HS
9. **Thad Philyaw, of, Gunn HS, Palo Alto, Calif.**
10. **Thomas Urban, rhp, Mount Miguel HS, La Mesa, Calif.**
11. **Stan Watkins, lhp, Pacifica HS, Garden Grove, Calif.**
12. Terry Senn, 2b, San Francisco
13. Robert Sans, 1b, Texas A&M
14. **John Hale, of/3b, Wasco (Calif.) HS**
15. **Leon Wood, 2b/ss, Polk (Fla.) CC**
16. Al Arthur, rhp, Lake Oswego (Ore.) HS
17. **James Conn, ss, Vanderbilt**
18. Pat McNally, 1b, Redlands (Calif.) HS
19. Robert Austin, rhp, Cleveland HS, Northridge, Calif.
20. **Hiawatha Roberson, of, Canada (Calif.) JC**
21. Larry Wolfe, ss/rhp, Cordova HS, Rancho Cordova, Calif.
22. **Curtis Hires, c, Thomas Jefferson HS, Brooklyn, N.Y.**
23. **Ed Carroll, lhp, El Segundo HS, Hawthorne, Calif.**
24. William Hattis, rhp, New Trier East HS, Glencoe, Ill.
25. **Michael Harrelson, of/2b, Georgia**
26. **Dana Hendershott, lhp, San Francisco**
27. **Bobby Johnson, of/c, Southern**
28. John Coon, rhp/of, Las Vegas HS
29. **Kevin Pasley, c, Chaminade HS, Bethpage, N.Y.**
30. **Doug Radestock, lhp, Santana HS, San Diego**
31. Kim Andrew, ss, Monroe HS, Sepulveda, Calif.
32. Steve Rhodin, 1b, Ypsilanti (Mich.) HS
33. **Michael Vinci, 3b/ss, Lakeland HS, Peekskill, N.Y.**
34. Ted Schultz, ss, Escondido (Calif.) HS
35. Tom Hume, rhp, Northeast HS, St. Petersburg, Fla.
36. Willis Gallop, rhp, Santa Fe HS, Alachua, Fla.
37. **Michael Thomas, of, Kirkman HS, Chattanooga, Tenn.**
38. Mike Sudduth, lhp, Holtville (Calif.) HS
39. Keath Chauncey, of, Polk (Fla.) CC
40. Sam Ceci, c, Southern California
41. **Randy Hoppe, c, Santa Rosa (Calif.) JC**
42. **Michael Collins, lhp, Long Beach State**
43. Richard Rogers, 3b, McLain HS, Tulsa, Okla.
44. Ron Wrona, ss, Bishop Keeley HS, Tulsa, Okla.
45. Eddie Ford, ss, Great Neck (N.Y.) South HS
46. Joe Camp, 1b, North Florida JC
47. Mike Trifiolis, 1b, West Orange (N.J.) HS
48. Don Stackpole, c, Elsinore (Calif.) HS

June—Secondary (Active) Phase (14)

1. Mike Pfitzer, rhp, Mesa (Ariz.) CC
2. **Roger Keilig, c, Canada (Calif.) JC**

June—Secondary (Delayed) Phase (20)

1. **Steve Patchin, c, Missouri**
2. **Tim Evans, ss, Colorado**
3. **Pat Paulson, lhp, New Haven (Conn.)**
4. **Roy Petersen, of/1b, Southern Colorado**
5. Mike Siani, ss, Villanova

MILWAUKEE BREWERS

January—Regular Phase (6)

1. Don Collins, lhp, South Georgia JC
2. Douglas David, rhp, Providence
3. No selection
4. Dean Mick, 3b, Yakima Valley (Wash.) JC

January—Secondary Phase (17)

1. **Richard Oliver, of/3b, CC of Baltimore**
2. Mark Hance, 1b, Bakersfield, Calif.
3. Tom Rosa, ss, Miami-Dade North CC
4. John LiBrandi, of, Manatee (Fla.) JC
5. **John Bush, of, Miami**

June—Regular Phase (3)

1. **Tommy Bianco, ss, Sewanhaka HS, Elmont, N.Y.**
2. **Larry Anderson, rhp, El Rancho HS, Pico Rivera, Calif.**
3. No selection
4. **Robert Dunn, of, Kennett Square (Pa.) HS**
5. **Charlie Moore Jr., c/3b, Minor HS, Birmingham, Ala.**
6. **Edwin Kurtz, rhp, Duncan Fletcher HS, Atlantic Beach, Fla.**
7. Dan Boitano, rhp, Hoover HS, Fresno
8. **Jerry Devins, of, South Alabama**
9. **Freddie Tate, of, Minor HS, Birmingham**
10. **Tom Hausman, rhp, La Verne (Calif.) HS**
11. **Kevin Kobel, lhp, St. Francis HS, Colden, N.Y.**
12. James McCutchin, rhp, Levelland (Texas) HS
13. Stephen Tinsley, 1b/of, Roxanna (Ill.) HS
14. **Paul Minton, lhp, Northeastern**
15. Mike Merritt, rhp, New Hanover HS, Wilmington, N.C.
16. **Scott Mork, ss, Eastern Hills HS, Fort Worth, Texas**
17. Robert Tyler, lhp, Ribault HS, Jacksonville, Fla.
18. Donald Fisher, lhp, Pennridge HS, Perkasie, Pa.
19. Robert Steif, rhp, Wausau (Wis.) HS
20. Steve Kendall, rhp, McKean HS, Wilmington, Del.
21. Duane Bickel, rhp, Orchard View HS, Muskegon, Mich.
22. Michael Schrader, ss, Sam Houston HS, Houston
23. Walter Pierson, lhp, Delaware Valley HS, Milford, N.J.
24. Larry Riddle, rhp, Banks HS, Birmingham

June—Secondary (Active) Phase (23)

1. **Gary Cavallo, rhp, Seton Hall**

June—Secondary (Delayed) Phase (3)

1. **Rob Ellis, inf/of, Michigan State**
2. **Scott Larson, rhp/ss, Occidental (Calif.)**
3. John Langerhans, 1b, Texas

MINNESOTA TWINS

January—Regular Phase (22)

1. Jerry Mayberry, rhp, San Jose, Calif.
2. Gary Anglin, lhp, Ventura (Calif.) JC
3. Rulon Herren, of, Cabrillo (Calif.) JC
4. **William Osborne, rhp, Lynchburg (Va.)**
5. Cary Wifler, rhp, Denver, Colo.

January—Secondary Phase (13)

1. **Geoffrey Hooper, lhp, Los Angeles Valley JC**
2. Stephen Hazan, lhp, Mission Viejo, Calif.
3. Stephen Easton, lhp, Brigham Young
4. Richard Hunt, of, Doane (Neb.)

June—Regular Phase (21)

1. **Dale Soderholm, ss, Coral Park HS, Miami**
2. **Michael Uremovich, c, Waukegan (Ill.) HS**
3. **Scott Marchael, lhp, Wilson HS, Long Beach**
4. **Robert Gallagher, of, Mount Miguel HS, Spring Valley, Calif.**
5. **Steve Marquardt, rhp, Poly Tech HS, North Hollywood, Calif.**
6. **William Kissell, ss, Royal Oak HS, Covina, Calif.**
7. **Dave Edwards, c, Jefferson HS, Los Angeles**
8. **Marty Hulse, rhp, Santiago HS, Garden Grove, Calif.**
9. Claude Westmoreland, of, Washington Union HS, Fresno
10. Rick Bethke, lhp, Bellflower (Calif.) HS
11. **Stephen Blood, rhp, Woodsville (N.H.) HS**
12. **Mark Burris, 3b, Wood River (Ill.) HS**
13. **Rob Wilfong, 2b, Northview HS, Covina, Calif.**
14. **Thomas Finch, c, Fairfield (Conn.)**
15. **Greg Rogers, ss, Northview HS, Covina, Calif.**
16. **Jerry Lundin, ss, Iowa State**
17. Phil Convertino, of, Bishop Amat HS, Arcadia, Calif.
18. **Edward Goldbaum, of, Francis Poly HS, North Hollywood, Calif.**
19. James Patterson, rhp, Ithaca (N.Y.) (Selection voided)
20. Randy Young, rhp, West Torrance (Calif.) HS
21. Terry Nance, rhp, Monterey Peninsula (Calif.) JC
22. **Mark Connor, rhp, Manhattan**
23. Thomas Mace, inf/of, CC of Baltimore
24. **Stuart Friedman, c, Lynchburg HS, River Edge, N.J.**
25. **James Bachtell, 2b/ss, Randolph-Macon (Va.)**
26. **Reginald Rowe, rhp, Tulsa**
27. **Jack Maloof, of, La Verne (Calif.)**
28. **Lon Galli, lhp, Wisconsin**
29. **Bruce Skoglund, c/of, Central HS, Duluth, Minn.**
30. **Louis Anemone, 2b, St. Francis (N.Y.)**
31. Steve Shimek, ss, Little Falls HS, Fort Ripley, Minn.
32. Robert Mayhew, lhp, Arcadia (Calif.) HS
33. Rex Hendricks, lhp, Littleton (Colo.) HS
34. **Randy Atchison, ss, Kerkhoven (Minn.) HS**
35. Thomas Carpenter, rhp/ss, Craig HS, Janesville, Wis.
36. Chuck Baker, ss, Orange HS, Garden Grove, Calif.
37. **Dan Solters, rhp, Cal Poly Pomona**
38. **John Katrosh, 1b/of, Trenton State (N.J.)**
39. Joe Theismann, ss, Notre Dame

June—Secondary (Active) Phase (15)

1. Randy Delerio, c, West Hills (Calif.) JC
2. Dan Everts, rhp, Rio Hondo (Calif.) JC
3. **Jeff Kalish, 3b, New York**
4. **Francisco Suarez, 3b, Miami-Dade North CC**
5. Richard Eisenacher, rhp, Auburn
6. Ray Hall, ss/2b, Fresno CC

June—Secondary (Delayed) Phase (9)

1. **Glenn Borgmann, c/1b, South Alabama**
2. John Roatche, c, Florida State
3. **Ken Dempsey, of, Auburn**
4. **Ken Braun, ss, Western Kentucky**
5. **Richard Mahlmann, lhp, Fresno State**
6. **Mike Ball, 3b, Southern California**
7. **Clark Ullom, lhp/of, Kansas**

MONTREAL EXPOS

January—Regular Phase (3)

1. **John Scalia, rhp, Brentwood, N.Y.**
2. Christ Hall, of, Bacone (Okla.) JC
3. Harvey Smith, ss, Cincinnati, Ohio
4. Terry Ray, rhp, Blinn (Texas) JC
5. Ward Lyons, 3b, Mount San Antonio (Calif.) JC
6. Dale Fell, lhp, Palm Beach (Fla.) JC
7. Ron Mahood, of, Houston Baptist

January—Secondary Phase (6)

1. **Harry Conlan, of, West Haven, Conn.**
2. **Richard Baker, lhp, Jacksonville, Fla.**
3. Vern Wilkins, 1b, Mesa (Ariz.) CC
4. Gary Hampton, c, Fresno, Calif.
5. **Michael Lynch, lhp, Grayson County (Texas) JC**
6. Duane Wirth, rhp, Mesa, Ariz.
7. John Wiggins, rhp, Plant City, Fla.
8. Mike Cuozzi, inf/of, Trenton State (N.J.)
9. Williams Collins, rhp, Manatee (Fla.) JC

June—Regular Phase (4)

1. Condredge Holloway, ss, Lee HS, Huntsville, Ala.
2. **Dan Warthen, lhp, Omaha (Neb.) North HS**
3. **Glen Tackitt, lhp, Ryder HS, Wichita Falls, Texas**
4. **David Carey, rhp, Army**
5. **Otto Kemper, 2b, Brenham (Texas) HS**
6. **Larry Lintz, ss/2b, San Jose State**
7. Dan Marrelli, 2b, West HS, Salt Lake City
8. **Walter Rothe, of/1b, Texas**
9. **Steven Ayers, lhp, Walker HS, Decatur, Ga.**
10. **Sam Viney, of/3b, UC Davis**
11. Ken Daughty, of/inf, Lamar (Colo.) CC
12. Wayne Pinkerton, inf, Humphreys Academy, Hollandale, Miss.
13. Steve Cline, rhp, Hagerstown (Md.) JC
14. John Andrews, ss, Lincoln (Ill.) HS
15. Samuel Moore, rhp, Western Hills HS, Cincinnati
16. Dale Brock, of, St. Augustine HS, New Orleans
17. Earl Moran, inf, Biloxi (Miss.) HS
18. John Van Brunt, c, Crawford (N.J.) HS
19. Eugene Martin, 2b, Covington (Ky.) Catholic HS
20. Jeffrey Washington, of, Ypsilanti (Mich.) HS
21. Ken Ward, ss, Calhoun HS, Merrick, N.Y.
22. **Steve Tucker, rhp, Warren HS, Downey, Calif.**
23. Gary Alexander, c, Los Angeles Harbor JC
24. Michael Grover, of, El Cajon (Calif.) HS
25. Tom Cusick, ss/2b, MacArthur HS, San Antonio
26. **David Drumright, rhp, Kansas HS, Ottawa, Kan.**
27. Ralph Petrillo, 3b/of, Newburgh (N.Y.) HS
28. John Pierson, of, Washington HS, Phoenix
29. **Edward Riley, ss, Neshaminy HS, Levittown, Pa.**
30. Robert Lucy, 1b, Lee (Mass.) HS
31. Thomas Joyce, lhp, Clawson (Mich.) HS
32. Al Woods, 1b, St. Elizabeth HS, Oakland
33. **Leonard Bonk, ss/2b, Catholic Central HS, Monroe, Mich.**
34. Thomas Jones, of/rhp, Douglas HS, Oklahoma City, Okla.
35. Samuel Guarino, c, Stamford (Conn.) Catholic HS
36. Ernest Bessette, ss, Naugatuck (Conn.) HS
37. **Peter Finnerty, c/1b, Pace (N.Y.)**
38. **Rich Sanfillipo, ss, Montclair State (N.J.)**

June—Secondary (Active) Phase (8)

1. Ron Herring, rhp, Chipola (Fla.) JC
2. Larry O'Brien, rhp, Indian Hills (Iowa) CC

June—Secondary (Delayed) Phase (4)

1. **Steve Rogers, rhp, Tulsa**
2. **Robert Croswell, ss, Mississippi State**
3. Sam Bowen, of/rhp, Brunswick (Ga.) JC

NEW YORK METS

January—Regular Phase (13)

1. Dan Pettyjohn, c, Yavapai (Ariz.) JC
2. **Joel Elderkin, 3b, Chabot (Calif.) JC**
3. Keith Buckingham, rhp, Lincoln Land (Ill.) JC
4. Steve Janosik, rhp, Wenatchee Valley (Wash.) CC

5. **Frank Estrada, rhp, Cuesta (Calif.) JC**
6. **Victor Rose, lhp, Connors State (Okla.) JC**

January—Secondary Phase (10)

1. **James Evans, rhp, Memphis, Tenn.**
2. **Richard Wagener, lhp, West Virginia**
3. Mardie Cornejo, rhp, Wellington, Kan.
4. Steve Bossi, of, Contra Costa (Calif.) JC
5. **Paul Womble, 3b, Kansas**

June—Regular Phase (14)

1. **Rich Puig, 2b, Hillsborough HS, Tampa**
2. **James Kidder, 2b, Jay HS, San Antonio**
3. **John Busco, ss, Mount St. Michael HS, Bronx, N.Y.**
4. **Earnest Page, of, Carver HS, Birmingham**
5. Terrell Grantham, rhp, McClenegham HS, Florence, S.C.
6. **Isaac Small, of, Deland HS, DeLeon Springs, Fla.**
7. **Clarence Burgy, rhp, Bellaire (Ohio) HS**
8. **Carlos Sagredo, of, Taft HS, Bronx, N.Y.**
9. **Rick Baldwin, of/rhp, Downey HS, Modesto, Calif.**
10. **Ernie DiStasi, c, Ansonia (Conn.) HS**
11. Ralph Darin, rhp, Central Michigan (Selection voided)
12. **Tommy Scott, 1b, Herbert Hoover HS, Elkview, W.Va.**
13. Michael Bahnick, rhp, Rider
14. Michael Aldridge, of, East Carolina
15. Ray Forgie, rhp, Coronado HS, Scottsdale, Ariz.
16. Bob Hampton, of, Leigh HS, San Jose
17. Ron Beaurivage, 1b, Memorial HS, Manchester, N.H.
18. Pat McMahon, lhp, Bishop Kennedy HS, Jacksonville, Fla.
19. Steve Marlow, 1b, Skyline HS, Salt Lake City
20. **Michael Anderson, lhp, Hollywood Hills HS, West Hollywood, Fla.**
21. Aaron Randall, 1b, Vigor HS, Whistler, Ala.
22. Robert Frisby, lhp, McClure HS, Ferguson, Mo.
23. **Mark DeJohn, 3b, Wilson HS, Middletown, Conn.**
24. William Roche, rhp, Jackson HS, Jacksonville, Fla.
25. Roger Danson, ss, Wolfson HS, Jacksonville, Fla.
26. **Richard Holman, rhp, Milton (Wis.)**
27. **Gil Hodges Jr., 1b, C.W. Post (N.Y.)**
28. Paul Kreke, rhp, Mater Dei HS, New Baden, Ill.
29. **Tony Maya, rhp, Ajo (Ariz.) HS**
30. **Scott Stevens, lhp, Lakewood (Calif.) HS**
31. **Steve Pierce, lhp, Gainesville (Ga.) JC**
32. **Don Pooschke, of, Benson HS, Portland, Ore.**
33. Glen Canfield, c, Glendale (Calif.) JC
34. David Levet, of, Bountiful (Utah) HS
35. **William Leeper, c, Fernandina HS, Fernandina Beach, Fla.**

June—Secondary (Active) Phase (12)

1. **Edgar DeFore, rhp, Macon, Ga.**
2. Don Collins, lhp, South Georgia JC
3. **Michael McManus, rhp, Mount San Antonio (Calif.) JC**
4. Dan Pettyjohn, c, Yavapai (Ariz.) JC
5. **Joel Elderkin, 3b, Chabot (Calif.) JC**

June—Secondary (Delayed) Phase (24)

1. Richard Anderson, rhp, New Haven (Conn.)
2. **Greg Pavlick, rhp/3b, North Carolina**
3. **Paul Bagnasco, 3b, Santa Clara**
4. **John Severs, of, Clemson**
5. Alan Lobb, lhp, Elizabethtown (Pa.)

NEW YORK YANKEES

January—Regular Phase (20)

1. Steve Bissett, 2b/ss, JC of San Mateo (Calif.)
2. Roscoe Goehring, rhp, Diablo Valley (Calif.) JC
3. **Jim Alexander, rhp, Yakima Valley (Wash.) JC**

January—Secondary Phase (25)

1. Dave Elmendorf, of, Texas A&M
2. Roger Keilig, c, Redwood City, Calif.
3. **Russ Cauley, lhp, Leary, Texas**
4. Tom Martell, lhp, Lincoln City, Ore.
5. **Jim Golden, lhp, Portland**
6. Michael Venable, rhp/of, Bellevue (Wash.) CC
7. Byron Burns, rhp, Kelso, Wash.
8. Keith Metheny, rhp, Kent, Wash.
9. Dennis Cline, ss, Wilmington, Del.

June—Regular Phase (19)

1. **Terry Whitfield, of, Palo Verde HS, Blythe, Calif.**
2. **Stephen Lindsey, 3b, McLane HS, Fresno**
3. **Ron Guidry, lhp, Southwest Louisiana**
4. **John Williams, of, Tulare (Calif.) Union HS**
5. **Larry Murray, of/inf, Phillips HS, Chicago**
6. **Larry Walker, c, Ramona (Calif.) HS**
7. **Robert Arnold, rhp, West Snyder HS, McClure, Pa.**
8. **Joe Blake, rhp, Simpson (Iowa)**
9. **Phil Still, 3b, Mississippi State**
10. **Kevin Carr, rhp/of, Colgan HS, Pittsburg, Kan.**
11. **Tony Sevy, lhp, Hillcrest HS, Springfield, Mo.**
12. Steven Gullotti, ss, Rio Hondo (Calif.) JC
13. Mike Paxton, rhp/inf, Oakhaven HS, Memphis
14. **James Dodson, lhp, Washburn HS, Topeka, Kan.**
15. Mickey Beard, rhp, French HS, Beaumont, Texas
16. **Larry Raschke, rhp, Gonzaga**
17. **Joel Hall, c, Northwestern**
18. **Jeffrey Davis, 1b, Harwich HS, West Harwich, Mass.**
19. Stephen Burks, lhp, Cabot (Ark.) HS
20. Joe Eberhard, ss, Memorial HS, Joplin, Mo.
21. Michael Berger, rhp, Tacoma (Wash.) HS
22. **Roger Johanson, rhp, Eastmont HS, East Wenatchee, Wash.**
23. Gerald Collins, lhp, Warren HS, Downey, Calif.
24. Michael Guischer, rhp, Mount Hood (Ore.) CC
25. Ken Swygard, lhp, Portland, Ore.
26. Brad Trickey, inf, Jefferson HS, Cedar Rapids, Iowa
27. **Bill Stearns, c/inf, Wyoming**
28. Gary Owens, inf, College of the Ozarks (Mo.)
29. **Roger Adams, 2b, Tulsa**
30. **Jerry Anderson, rhp, McGuire AFB, N.J.**
31. Vince Doherty, rhp, Linfield (Ore.)
32. Greg Branum, 3b/of, Spokane Falls (Wash.) CC

June—Secondary (Active) Phase (17)

1. **David Bishop, lhp, Mountain Lakes, N.J.**
2. Steve Hunter, c, Yakima Valley (Wash.) JC
3. Greg Van Gaver, rhp, Bellevue (Wash.) CC
4. Byron Burns, rhp, Lower Columbia (Wash.) JC
5. **Steve Janosik, rhp, Wenatchee Valley (Wash.) CC**

June—Secondary (Delayed) Phase (13)

1. **Mike Pazik, lhp, Holy Cross**
2. **Robert Schiffner, lhp, Princeton**
3. **Phil Honeycutt, 3b, Tulsa**

OAKLAND ATHLETICS

January—Regular Phase (18)

1. Lynn McKinney, rhp, Rio Hondo (Calif.) JC
2. **Lynn Minner, 1b, Louisville, Ky.**
3. Roger Whitley, rhp, Foothill (Calif.) JC
4. Dan Fitzgerald, c, Solvang, Calif.
5. Rich Dauer, ss, San Bernardino Valley (Calif.) JC
6. Duane Roberts, 1b/of, Ventura (Calif.) JC

January—Secondary Phase (3)

1. **Phil Garner, inf, Tennessee**
2. **Keith Lieppman, 3b, Kansas**
3. Steve Staggs, inf, Cerritos (Calif.) JC
4. John Cosmos, lhp, San Francisco
5. Terry Farmer, rhp, Columbus, Ga.
6. Charles Bates, 3b/ss, Compton (Calif.) CC
7. Doug Cornett, c, Richmond, Ky.
8. **Rudy Sgontz, c, Anaheim, Calif.**
9. **Ron Corbett, rhp, Suffolk (Mass.)**
10. Stan Hamlin, rhp, Bakersfield (Calif.) JC
11. Dan Parma, of, Buena Park, Calif.

June—Regular Phase (17)

1. **Sugar Bear Daniels, rhp, MacKenzie HS, Detroit**
2. **Ron Williamson, of/c, Asher (Okla.) HS**
3. Ken Huizenga, of, Glendora (Calif.) HS
4. **Stan Bockewitz, lhp, Pana (Ill.) HS**
5. **Kirk Thomas, rhp, Kennewick (Wash.) HS**
6. **Ron Lollis, c, Gonzaga Prep HS, Spokane, Wash.**

7. **Charles Gipson, 1b, Santa Ana (Calif.) HS**
8. **Kirk Allison, of, El Segundo (Calif.) HS**
9. John Beckman, lhp, Springfield (Ill.) HS
10. **Ray Leavitt, ss, Charter Oak HS, Glendora, Calif.**
11. Tim Hamilton, 2b, Edmonds (Wash.) HS
12. **Nicholas Parrilla, rhp, Parsons (Iowa)**
13. **James George, rhp, Southern California**
14. **Ron Roller, of, Bellevue (Wash.) CC**
15. **Richard Keller, of, Nashville (Ill.) HS**
16. **Billy Matthews, c/3b, Kirkland Tech HS, Chattanooga, Tenn.**
17. Jeff Reinke, lhp, Pasadena (Calif.) HS
18. Jeff DeBell, rhp/ss, Sammamish HS, Bellevue, Wash.
19. Michael Kee, of, Palo Verde HS, Tucson, Ariz.
20. Greg Sanossian, rhp, St. Anthony HS, Long Beach
21. Greg Kessler, of/inf, Laguna Beach (Calif.) HS
22. Stephen Chipp, rhp, Santa Clara
23. **Ronald Wilson, rhp/1b, Charter Oak HS, Glendora, Calif.**
24. **Robert Wolf, rhp, Chapman (Calif.)**
25. Ben Heise, ss, Yavapai (Ariz.) JC
26. Richard Harris, ss, Westwood HS, Mesa, Ariz.
27. Ricky Holoubek, ss, Wilson HS, Los Angeles

June—Secondary (Active) Phase (19)

1. Stephen Easton, lhp, Brigham Young
2. **Ron Corbett, rhp, Suffolk (Mass.)**
3. Charles Bates, 3b, Los Angeles CC

June—Secondary (Delayed) Phase (19)

1. **Mike Weathers, 2b, Chapman (Calif.)**
2. Mike McNeilly, rhp/ss, Gonzaga
3. James Horton, lhp, Eastern Michigan

PHILADELPHIA PHILLIES

January—Regular Phase (5)

No selection

January—Secondary Phase (18)

1. **Thomas Boyd, lhp, West Valley (Calif.) JC**
2. David Bishop, lhp, West Chester (Pa.)
3. Henry Baker, 3b, Southern
4. Gary Boyajian, rhp, River Edge, N.J.
5. George McCollum, lhp, Orlando, Fla.

June—Regular Phase (6)

1. **Roy Thomas, rhp, Lompoc (Calif.) HS**
2. **Mike Schmidt, ss, Ohio**
3. **Willard Kinard, rhp, North Charleston (S.C.) HS**
4. Greg Cochran, rhp, Lowell HS, Whittier, Calif.
5. **Robert Ray, rhp/of, Alleghany County HS, Iron Gate, Va.**
6. **Jan Barber, rhp, James Lick HS, San Jose**
7. **Larry Dombkowski, of, Elston HS, Michigan City, Ind.**
8. **Mac Scarce, lhp, Florida State**
9. **Allen McLaughlin, 2b, Eastern Michigan**
10. Mike Girazian, rhp, Selma HS, Kingsburg, Calif.
11. **William Letsch, lhp, St. Catherine HS, Racine, Wis.**
12. Robert Barr, lhp, Van Horn HS, Independence, Mo.
13. **Alfonso Rodriguez, rhp/of, Miami Senior HS**
14. **Pat Lowrey, lhp, JC of Lake County (Ill.)**
15. **Roger Skalisky, rhp, Wenatchee (Wash.) HS**
16. Mike Hannah, 1b, Ohio
17. **Ken Kurtz, lhp, Lincoln HS, Stockton, Calif.**
18. **Gary Poteet, rhp, Hiwassee (Tenn.) JC**
19. **John Boyd, c, Bell HS, Hurst, Texas**
20. **Gary Thornton, 3b, Boone HS, Orlando, Fla.**
21. **Terry Periman, lhp, Missouri**
22. Billy Olsen, rhp, Mineral Area (Mo.) JC
23. Greg Ferguson, rhp, Arlington Heights HS, Fort Worth, Texas
24. **Dan Greenhalgh, rhp, Folsom (Calif.) HS**
25. **Mike White, c, Rutgers**
26. **Mike Walsh, rhp, Broward (Fla.) CC**
27. **Terry Ford, ss, Middle Georgia JC**
28. **Billy Anderson, ss, South Carolina**
29. **Jerome Johnson, rhp, Ben Eielson HS, Fairbanks, Alaska**
30. **Randy Smith, rhp, Wahama HS, New Haven, W.Va.**
31. Mark Gehrig, 1b, Diablo Valley (Calif.) JC
32. Dan Hebel, rhp/1b, Senior HS, Lima, Ohio
33. Charles Franklin, 3b, Santa Clara
34. Doug Dickmann, c, St. Mary's HS, St. Louis
35. **Harry Saferight, c, Richmond, Va.**
36. **David Croft, rhp, Monte Vista HS, Danville, Calif.**
37. Edmond Peres, of/3b, Fort Myers (Fla.) HS
38. **Thomas Higgins, 2b, Wilkes (Pa.)**
39. David Quay, rhp, Penn Highlands HS, Lewistown, Pa.

June—Secondary (Active) Phase (16)

1. **Don Kreke, rhp, Belleville Area (Ill.) CC**
2. **Steve Bissett, 2b/ss, JC of San Mateo (Calif.)**
3. Tom Rosa, ss, Miami-Dade South CC

June—Secondary (Delayed) Phase (22)

1. **Dane Iorg, ss, Brigham Young**
2. **James Greggerson, lhp, Texas-El Paso**
3. **Larry Kiser, lhp, North Carolina**

PITTSBURGH PIRATES

January—Regular Phase (21)

1. Alejandro Lopez, 2b, New Brunswick, N.J.
2. **Randy Richards, rhp, Akron**
3. Ron Harrison, rhp, American River (Calif.) JC
4. Michael Meseberg, of, Yakima Valley (Wash.) JC
5. Robert Sekel, rhp, Niagara (N.Y.)
6. **Anthony Blakley, ss, Brewton-Parker (Ga.) JC**
7. Dan DeBattista, 3b, Allegheny (Pa.)
8. Davis May, rhp, Gulf Coast (Fla.) CC

January—Secondary Phase (2)

1. **Robert Jones, of, Amherst (Mass.)**
2. Robert Miller, of, Sacramento, Calif.
3. Jim Cody, rhp, Big Bend (Wash.) CC
4. James Healy, ss, Lake Hiawatha, N.J.
5. John Wade, lhp, Seattle, Wash.
6. Rich Ralston, rhp, Spokane (Wash.) CC
7. Tim Pierce, rhp, Tonawanda, N.Y.
8. **David Landers, of, St. Joseph's**
9. Steve Hunter, c, Yakima Valley (Wash.) JC
10. **Ronald Robinson, ss/rhp, New Orleans**
11. Ray Hall, ss/2b, Fresno, Calif.
12. Greg Van Gaver, rhp, Seattle, Wash.
13. Carlos Hughes, lhp, Aurora, N.C.

June—Regular Phase (22)

1. **Craig Reynolds, ss, Regan HS, Houston**
2. **Doug Bair, rhp, Bowling Green State**
3. **Ron Knaub, 1b, Anaheim HS**
4. **Mike Scaglione, rhp, Mindzenty HS, Dunkirk, N.Y.**
5. Steve Gerlecz, 3b, Sedalia (Mo.) HS
6. **Ray Lilley, rhp, Tarboro (N.C.) HS**
7. **George Whileyman, rhp, Sam Houston State**
8. Ron Bell, rhp, Sunny Hills HS, Fullerton, Calif.
9. **Rodney Davis, rhp, Whetstone HS, Columbus, Ohio**
10. James McKinney, ss, Ensley HS, Birmingham
11. **Thomas Prazych, rhp, Central HS, Scranton, Pa.**
12. **Elliott Jones, rhp, Vanderbilt**
13. **Oscar Johnson, lhp, Dos Palos (Calif.) HS**
14. Richard Prior, of, Trinity-Pawling Prep, Peabody, Mass.
15. **Luther Anderson, of, Jefferson HS, Los Angeles**
16. **Paul Bostic, c, Carson-Newman (Tenn.)**
17. **Bruce Westbrook, rhp, Southeast HS, Bradenton, Fla.**
18. **Richard Bedard, inf, Amherst (Mass.)**
19. **Terry Collins, ss, Eastern Michigan**
20. **John Darnell, lhp/1b, R.L. Osborne HS, Marietta, Ga.**
21. **Allen Dukate, rhp, Miami (Ohio)**
22. Bob Lesslie, rhp, St. Louis CC-Meramec
23. Edward Smith, ss/3b, Washington State
24. **Danny Waelchli, rhp, Kutztown (Pa.)**
25. David Naberezny, ss, Oliver HS, Pittsburgh
26. **John Herrscher, rhp, Central Catholic HS, Kingston, Pa.**
27. **Charles Flint, rhp, Danvers (Mass.) HS**
28. Herman Maston, 2b, Wasco (Calif.) HS
29. **Richard Thomas, rhp, North Hills HS, Pittsburgh**
30. **John Caruso, ss/2b, Regis (Mass.)**
31. **Joe Nagy, of, Keystone (Pa.) JC**

June—Secondary (Active) Phase (24)

No selection

June—Secondary (Delayed) Phase (14)

1. **Thomas Thomas, 3b, Washington State**
2. Doug Farrell, rhp/of, Niagara
3. **Gary Shade, 2b, Ohio**

ST. LOUIS CARDINALS

January—Regular Phase (7)

1. Rand Rasmussen, ss, Long Beach CC
2. Tom Zimmerman, rhp, Nebraska
3. **Mark Cresse, c, Golden West (Calif.) JC**
4. Tommy Zimmer, 2b/c, Manatee (Fla.) JC
5. Gary Matthews, lhp, Columbia State (Tenn.) CC
6. John Behrens, ss/1b, Fresno CC
7. **Bob Kennedy Jr., rhp, Mesa (Ariz.) CC**
8. Edward Hora, lhp, Brigham Young
9. John Alesci, ss, Miami-Dade CC
10. Jeff Neal, lhp, Fresno CC
11. Rick Langford, of/rhp, Manatee (Fla.) JC
12. Rod Walker, rhp, Pascagoula, Miss.
13. Mike Sinovich, 1b, St. Louis CC-Florissant Valley

January—Secondary Phase (16)

1. Mike Ibarguen, rhp, San Jacinto (Texas) JC
2. Al Ryan, 2b, Gulf Coast (Fla.) CC
3. **Mark Andresen, of, Garden Grove, Calif.**
4. **Mike Vail, ss, San Jose, Calif.**
5. William Finck, rhp, Hayward, Calif.
6. **Mike Potter, of, Mount San Antonio (Calif.) JC**
7. **Robert Cobb, rhp, Fresno (Calif.) CC**
8. Marvin Webb, 2b, San Pablo, Calif.

June—Regular Phase (8)

1. **Ed Kurpiel, 1b/of, Archbishop Molloy HS, Hollis, N.Y.**
2. **Gary Christophel, lhp, Mount Healthy HS, Cincinnati**
3. **Larry Herndon, of, Douglas HS, Memphis**
4. **Jerry Mumphrey, ss/of, Chapel Hill HS, Tyler, Texas**
5. Steven Copeland, lhp, St. Patricks HS, Vallejo, Calif.
6. **Charles Blakley, c, Northeast Missouri State**
7. **Gary Trumbauer, lhp, Thousand Oaks (Calif.) HS**
8. Steven Greene, 2b, Fremont HS, Los Angeles
9. **Leon Lee, 3b, Grant HS, Sacramento**
10. **Greg LaMendola, rhp, Western HS, Buena Park, Calif.**
11. **Jim Dwyer, of, Southern Illinois**
12. **John Grijalva, 3b/c, Pasadena HS, Sierra Madre, Calif.**
13. Mark Wogan, rhp, Saguaro HS, Scottsdale, Ariz.
14. **Fred Zwiefel, inf, Missouri-St. Louis**
15. **Shelby Hill, rhp, West HS, Morristown, Tenn.**
16. **Gary Raco, inf, Reedley (Calif.) JC**
17. John Park, rhp, Hale HS, Tulsa, Okla.
18. William Poe, rhp, Waterford HS, Pontiac, Mich.
19. Donald Redoglia, ss, Pasadena (Calif.) HS
20. Arthur Adams, lhp, Wellesley (Mass.) HS
21. **Monte Bolinger, 1b, Lompoc (Calif.) HS**
22. **Marty DeMerritt, rhp, South San Francisco HS**
23. **Charles Voskovitch, lhp, South HS, Commack, N.Y.**
24. **James Walthour, 3b, St. Louis CC-Meramec**
25. **Jethroe Mills, lhp/of, Newton (Mass.) HS**
26. **Mark Penbarthy, c, Los Angeles Baptist**
27. James Hinkleman, rhp, Bowen HS, Lansing, Ill.
28. Mark Mazzucco, rhp, Raritan HS, Hazlet, N.J.
29. Rickey Ritschel, rhp, Rogers HS, Tulsa, Okla.
30. Alan Gifford, rhp/inf, Wayne (N.J.) Hills HS
31. Steve Walsh, lhp, St. Louis University HS
32. William Lankford, of, Mark Twain HS, New London, Mo.
33. Roger Walton, rhp, Hannibal (Mo.) HS
34. **Mark Mueller, 3b/ss, St. Louis CC-Florissant Valley**
35. Sam Hinds, rhp/ss, International School, Hague, Holland
36. **James Linehan, rhp, Peabody (Mass.) HS**
37. Milton Holt, lhp, Phillips Andover Prep, Honolulu
38. William Drescher, c, Clarkston HS, Congers, N.Y.
39. Forrest Meek, rhp, Roosevelt HS, Fresno
40. James Fiack, c, UC Davis
41. Lee Daney, rhp, Army
42. **Keith Hernandez, 1b, Capuchino HS, Millbrae, Calif.**
43. Don Hairston, rhp, Channel Island HS, Oxnard, Calif.
44. Michael Laurent, rhp, Valley HS, Albuquerque, N.M.
45. **William Kelly, rhp, Harvard**

June—Secondary (Active) Phase (2)

1. **Mike Swenton, of, Oklahoma**
2. Roy Smalley, ss, Los Angeles CC
3. **Tommy Zimmer, c/2b, Manatee (Fla.) JC**

June—Secondary (Delayed) Phase (16)

1. Rick Pope, rhp, UCLA
2. **Jim Silvey, 2b, Tulsa**
3. **Steve Broege, lhp, Iona (N.Y.)**
4. James Jachym, lhp, Connecticut

SAN DIEGO PADRES

January—Regular Phase (1)

1. **Dave Hilton, 3b, Southwest Texas JC**
2. **Anthony Glassman, of, Rochester (N.Y.)**
3. No selection
4. William Sims, 1b, San Joaquin Delta (Calif.) JC
5. Wendell Stephens, rhp, East Los Angeles JC

January—Secondary Phase (24)

1. **Johnny Grubb Jr., of, Florida State**
2. **Robert Johnston, lhp, Atlanta Christian**
3. **Marc Rhea, ss, Mesa (Ariz.) CC**
4. Ricardo Urbano, lhp, Los Gatos, Calif.

June—Regular Phase (2)

1. **Jay Franklin, rhp, James Madison HS, Vienna, Va.**
2. **Bill Boynton, rhp, Springfield HS, Skowhegan, Maine**
3. No selection
4. **Craig Settles, ss/3b, Point Loma HS, San Diego**
5. **Dave Freisleben, rhp, Sam Rayburn HS, Pasadena, Texas**
6. **Don Elliott, ss, Norway (Iowa) HS**
7. **Frank Snook, rhp, Grand Canyon (Ariz.)**
8. **Joe Goddard, c, Marshall**
9. Johnny Green, c, Grant HS, Sacramento
10. **Melvin Lord, 1b, Fresno (Calif.) HS**
11. Bill Almon, ss, Veterans Memorial HS, Warwick, R.I.
12. **Mike Caldwell, lhp, North Carolina State**
13. Willie Mims, of, Iowa
14. **Robert Hill, 1b/rhp, Bowling Green State**
15. Greg Richards, rhp, Palos Verdes HS, Palos Verdes Estates, Calif.
16. **Robert Marshall, of, Davidson HS, Mobile, Ala.**
17. **Duane Larson, 2b, Santa Clara**
18. **Gary Myron, rhp, San Diego**
19. Jeff Spagnola, of, El Modina HS, Orange, Calif.
20. **Anthony Ponticelli, rhp, Johnston (R.I.) HS**

June—Secondary (Active) Phase (22)

1. **William Hodge, c, Texas A&M**

June—Secondary (Delayed) Phase (12)

1. **Charlie Dudish, ss/of, Georgia Tech**
2. Frank Rucker, lhp, Alabama
3. Dudley Mitchell, of/1b, Colorado

SAN FRANCISCO GIANTS

January—Regular Phase (17)

1. Robert Makoski, 1b, St. Clair County (Mich.) CC
2. **Richard Thompson, lhp, Cypress (Calif.) JC**
3. Joseph Remcisz, ss, St. Clair County (Mich.) CC
4. David Harness, 1b/of, El Camino (Calif.) JC
5. **Matt Werderber, rhp, Lower Columbia (Wash.) JC**
6. David Bryant, ss, Mount Hood (Ore.) CC
7. **George Maldonado, of, Nevada**
8. Chris Tust, of, Lower Columbia (Wash.) JC
9. Michael Ferney, rhp, Yavapai (Ariz.) JC
10. Robert Burton, rhp/of, JC of the Sequoias (Calif.)
11. James Cannon, rhp, JC of the Sequoias (Calif.)

January—Secondary Phase (8)

1. Mike Swenton, of, Oklahoma
2. Rudy Kinard, 2b, Tennessee
3. Tim Sherrill, 1b, Miami-Dade South CC

4. **Stephen Lee, lhp, Cal State Northridge**
5. Paul Djakonow, 3b, Detroit, Mich.
6. Warren Brusstar, rhp, Napa, Calif.
7. **Robert Vandersluis, rhp, Northwest Nazarene (Idaho)**
8. David Whitney, lhp, Astoria, Ore.

June—Regular Phase (18)

1. **Frank Riccelli, lhp, Christian Brothers HS, Syracuse, N.Y.**
2. **Charles Pepper, 1b/of, Grant HS, Sacramento**
3. **Willie Prall, lhp, Upsala (N.J.)**
4. Rick Anderson, rhp, Southern California Christian HS, Inglewood, Calif.
5. **Skip James, 1b/of, Kansas**
6. Ed Gilliam, of, Locke HS, Los Angeles
7. **William Wolfe, 2b, Fresno State**
8. **Frederic Smith, of, Adrian (Mich.)**
9. **David Walski, inf, UC Santa Barbara**
10. Craig Caskey, lhp, Puget Sound (Wash.)
11. Charles Bordes, ss, Southwestern Louisiana
12. Terry Cornutt, rhp, Linn-Benton (Ore.) CC
13. Gerard Thomas, lhp, West Scranton (Pa.) HS
14. Greg Lyon, lhp, Sayreville HS, Parlin, N.J.
15. Rick Duncan, c, Central HS, Chattanooga, Tenn.
16. Brian Masella, of/1b, Peddie HS, Bordentown, N.J.
17. Michael Rankin, c, Bartlett HS, Memphis
18. Pedro Santiago, of, James Monroe HS, Bronx, N.Y.
19. Mark Servais, 2b, St. Mary's (Minn.)
20. **Jay Dillard, rhp, Branham HS, San Jose, Calif.**
21. **Phil Beall, ss, Baylor**
22. Steve Miller, rhp, Miramonte HS, Orinda, Calif.
23. **Frank Reyes, rhp, Hancock (Calif.) JC**
24. Terry Brown, lhp, Miami
25. David Chapman, rhp, Newark (Del.) HS
26. James Snoots, 3b, Johnson HS, Thurmond, Md.
27. **Bruce Wright, of, Richmond**
28. Francis Sansosti, rhp/1b, Curley HS, Baltimore
29. Connie Smith, ss/rhp, East Texas Baptist
30. Robert Schaeffer, c, El Segundo (Calif.) HS
31. **David Fuqua, rhp, Bend (Ore.) HS**
32. **Greg Thayer, rhp, St. Cloud State**
33. James Howard, of, North Central HS, Indianapolis
34. William Wesley, rhp, Moeller HS, Cincinnati
35. Tim Kampa, rhp, Lewiston (Idaho) HS
36. Juan Eichelberger, rhp, Balboa HS, San Francisco
37. Craig Clark, 2b/ss, Foothill (Calif.) JC
38. Roy Hadden, rhp, Mountain View (Calif.) HS
39. Kenneth Roberts, rhp, Lawndale (Calif.) HS
40. John Chapman, rhp, Fort Myers (Fla.) HS
41. Donald Cooke, lhp, Miami-Dade North CC
42. **Harold Ingle, ss, Campbell**
43. Seldon Morton, 1b/lhp, Jefferson HS, Daly City, Calif.
44. John Fennell, rhp, Minico HS, Rupert, Idaho

June—Secondary (Active) Phase (6)

1. **Steve Stroughter, of, JC of the Sequoias (Calif.)**
2. Terry Farmer, rhp, Chipola (Fla.) JC

June—Secondary (Delayed) Phase (10)

1. Paul Patterson, rhp, Ithaca (N.Y.)
2. **Gordon Carter, of, Southern California**
3. **Bill Adkison, inf, Central Washington**

WASHINGTON SENATORS

January—Regular Phase (8)

1. **Steven Raines, rhp, Tennessee**
2. Mike Coronado, ss, San Diego CC
3. Raleigh Riddle, 2b/ss, Miami-Dade North CC
4. Kenneth Benson, lhp, West Valley (Calif.) JC
5. Terry Dreamer, rhp, Pershing
6. Greg Ojeda, ss, West Valley (Calif.) JC
7. Peter Catalanotte, 1b, Phoenix JC

January—Secondary Phase (9)

1. **Jim Kremmel, lhp, New Mexico**
2. Curran Percival, rhp, San Diego Mesa JC
3. Frank Baumgardner, rhp, Opalocka, Fla.
4. Jeff Kalish, 3b, New York
5. **David Moharter, lhp, Bloomsburg (Pa.)**

June—Regular Phase (7)

1. **Roger Quiroga, rhp, Ball HS, Galveston, Texas**
2. **William Amason, rhp, Lake Worth (Fla.) HS**
3. Ed Putman, c, Northview HS, Covina, Calif.
4. **David Harper, rhp, Boone HS, Orlando, Fla.**
5. Joe Burgess, lhp, Davenport (Okla.) HS
6. **Greg Pryor, 2b, Florida Southern**
7. Leslie Clark, ss, Prince Edward County HS, Farmville, Va.
8. Michael Agosto, of, Clairemont HS, San Diego
9. **James Penner, rhp, McLane HS, Fresno**
10. **Alberto Zamora, rhp, Miami Senior HS**
11. James Lamoure, ss, Bullard HS, Fresno
12. **Steven Eckinger, 3b, Central Missouri State**
13. Gary Kelson, rhp, Miami Beach (Fla.) HS
14. Rick Tomlin, lhp, George Wythe HS, Richmond, Va.
15. William Carleton, lhp, Miami-Dade South CC
16. **Robert Spinner, of, Emporia State (Kan.)**
17. Tom Stoddard, c, Lake Worth (Fla.) HS
18. Mark Rott, c/of, Ynagcio Valley HS, Concord, Calif.
19. Marcelino Huerta, 3b, Plant HS, Tampa
20. **Robert Frye, rhp, Ashbrook HS, Gastonia, N.C.**
21. John Herman, of, Overton HS, Nashville
22. **Gary Boyce, of, Michigan State**
23. Walt Rzepiennik, rhp, CC of Baltimore
24. **Ken Flowers, lhp, Littlefield HS, Lumberton, N.C.**
25. James Van Der Beek, rhp, Lafayette (Pa.)
26. **Richard Revta, c, Lehigh**
27. Stan Thomas, rhp, New Haven (Conn.)
28. **Larry Mohme, 3b, Highland HS, New Douglas, Ill.**
29. Frank Weisse, of, Lafayette (Pa.)
30. Jesse Campbell, c, Jackson HS, Miami
31. Dan Domski, lhp, Rockford (Ill.) West HS
32. **Bruce Cease, 1b, Miami-Dade South CC**
33. Selven Watts, of, Colonial Beach (Va.) HS
34. **Royce Hayes, of, Western Carolina**
35. Lawrence Rettenmund, 2b, Michigan State

June—Secondary (Active) Phase (5)

1. **Vern Wilkins, 1b, Mesa (Ariz.) CC**
2. Steve Behlen, lhp, Fresno (Calif.) CC

June—Secondary (Delayed) Phase (1)

1. **Pete Broberg, rhp, Dartmouth**
2. **Mike Cubbage, ss/3b, Virginia**
3. **Henry Bunnell, of/rhp, George Washington**
4. Joe Barkauskas, c, Lafayette (Pa.)

BEND RAINBOWS (NORTHWEST LEAGUE)

January—Regular Phase

1. No selection
2. No selection
3. No selection
4. Wayne Kiefer, Golden West (Calif.) JC
5. Dean Lyman, Fullerton (Calif.) JC

January—Secondary Phase

1. **James Hogan, of, Golden West (Calif.) JC**

June—Regular Phase

1. No selection
2. No selection
3. No selection
4. **Bill Bolden, rhp, Santa Ana (Calif.) Valley HS**
5. **Mike Lacheur, c, Bonita HS, La Verne, Calif.**
6. **Fred Morgan, 1b/c, Pomona (Calif.) HS**
7. Greg Clark, inf, Fullerton (Calif.) JC
8. Bill Hobbs, of, Fullerton (Calif.) JC
9. Norm Kepner, c, Fullerton (Calif.) JC
10. **Thomas Turner, 3b, Fullerton (Calif.) JC**

June—Secondary (Active) Phase

No selection

June—Secondary (Delayed) Phase

No selection

1972

Class of '72 gets remembered not for big leaguers but for line of tragedy it produced

Dave Roberts began his career with high expectations. A day after he was drafted No. 1 overall by San Diego, he started for the Padres at third base against the Pirates. No drafted player ever began his big league career with such haste.

A year later Roberts demonstrated he belonged by hitting .286 with 21 home runs, including 18 in the second half of the season. He was being touted as one of the game's rising young power hitters.

But Roberts, signed out of the University of Oregon to a $60,000 bonus, never again fulfilled the hopes the Padres held for him. A mysterious back ailment sidelined him to start the 1974 season and he never fully recovered. He hit .167 in 113 games and his career began a downhill slide.

Even though he became an accomplished catcher and later played every position on the field except pitcher during his 10-year career, his relationship with the Padres became a rocky one.

"When you're in an organization a long time," Roberts said later, "people in the organization, coaches, managers, the front office . . . they all made me feel I wasn't appreciated. They look at you and see the negative things you do instead of all the things you do well."

It all ended for Roberts in 1982, in Philadelphia as a backup catcher. His career average: .239.

Roberts' disappointing career set the tone for a 1972 draft that was scarred by tragedy.

Danny Thomas, the second college player selected in June, emerged as a top prospect in the Brewers system in 1976 when he won the Eastern League triple crown. He made his big league debut late that season, but then had a radical change in behavior.

A self-proclaimed wild man, Thomas became extremely religious and eventually refused to play between sundown Friday and sundown Saturday. He soon played his way out of the big leagues. His baseball career and his life in shambles, Thomas later committed suicide in a Mobile, Ala., jail cell.

Lyman Bostock, whose .311 career average was the best of any player from the Class of '72, was gunned down late in the 1978 season in Gary, Ind., a victim of mistaken identity. Bostock had just signed a lucrative contract with the Angels after gaining his free agency from the Twins.

Los Angeles picked shortstop John Harbin with its No. 1 pick, but a knee injury limited him to only one year in the Dodgers system. Despondent over his misfortune, Harbin later was a suicide victim.

The shooting death of Lyman Bostock occurred six years after he was drafted

Not a single player received a bonus of $100,000 in the 1972 draft. The largest reported bonus was the $85,000 the New York Yankees paid lefthander Scott McGregor, the 14th player selected. McGregor never won a game with the Yankees, but had 138 career victories after being traded to Baltimore.

Scouts generally regarded the talent in the 1972 draft as substandard, but the Indians were convinced they found their man in shortstop Rick Manning, a .614 hitter from LaSalle High in Niagara Falls, N.Y., who didn't strike out a single time his senior year.

"Manning is the best-looking kid we've seen in many years," Indians farm director Paul O'Dea said. "He's got a great swing and could come fast. He has the batting potential to hit 30 or more home runs a year in the big leagues."

Manning, who was signed to a $65,000 bonus, proved to be an exceptional defensive center fielder during his 13-year career, but was hardly the power hitter the Indians envisioned. He hit only .257 with 56 home runs.

Montreal, drafting fifth, went for Bobby Goodman, generally regarded as the best catching prospect in the draft. He signed with the Expos for $75,000. He never reached the big leagues in an injury-plagued career. The Expos' next two picks were also catchers.

Strong-armed Ellis Valentine did make it as a right fielder, but what the Expos didn't get in Goodman they got in Gary Carter, their third-round selection and the best catcher in Expos history. He caught 11 seasons for the Expos and became the highest-paid athlete in Canadian history before he was dealt away to the Mets in 1984.

Change For College Players

For the first time in 1972, players who had been drafted previously were eligible for selection again in the regular phase, provided they had not been drafted in the previous 13 months. Just two such players went in the first round of the regular phase. Both were college players who had been drafted out of high school. One, Fresno State pitcher Dick Ruthven (Twins), again elected not to sign. The other was Harbin.

Ruthven, who struck out 153 in 1972 and 171 in 1971 for Fresno State, did not return to school for his senior year and was picked first overall the following January (secondary phase) by Philadelphia.

The 1972 draft was the first time two players from the same high school became first-round picks. The White Sox chose outfielder Mike Ondina, while the Tigers went for shortstop Jerry Manuel, both from Rancho Cordova High near Sacramento.

Another Sacramento-area product, Joel Bishop, was selected in the first round by Boston. He was an all-state quarterback his junior year at McClatchy High but gave up football to concentrate on baseball. His professional career fizzled after just 120 games.

They were among a total of 849 players drafted in June, the lowest total since the first draft in 1965. The January draft also suffered from attrition. The 267 players selected were the fewest since 1966.

There was continued talk that the January phase might be abandoned, but fear of legal action kept it alive. The January draft gave players an opportunity to be drafted a second time each year, thus not unduly restricting their right to earn a living, at least in the eyes of baseball officials. The January draft would linger until 1987.

The Athletics won the 1972 World Series but had another in a string of unproductive drafts that would doom the franchise in the coming years. Oakland selected 15-year major league veteran Chet Lemon with its first pick, but he was dealt to the White Sox before he ever played a big league game in Oakland. After Lemon, the A's failed to sign their next four picks and seven of their first 11.

Two of the most celebrated players to go unsigned in 1972 were Texas recruits Rich Wortham, who had been touted as a potential first-rounder but slipped through to the White Sox in the fifth round; and Jim Gideon, Detroit's third-round selection. Wortham went on to post 50 wins (then an NCAA record) and went 17-0 for a national championship team in 1975.

DRAFT 72: FIRST-ROUND PICKS

No.	Club	Player, Pos.	School	Hometown	Ht.	Wt.	B-T	Age
1.	Padres	Dave Roberts, 3b	Oregon	Corvallis, Ore.	6-3	215	R-R	21
2.	Indians	Rick Manning, ss	LaSalle HS	Niagara Falls, N.Y.	6-0	175	L-R	17
3.	Phillies	Larry Christenson, rhp	Marysville HS	Marysville, Wash.	6-4	215	R-R	18
4.	Rangers	Roy Howell, 3b	Lompoc HS	Lompoc, Calif.	6-1	190	L-R	18
5.	Expos	Bobby Goodman, c	Bishop Byrne HS	Memphis	6-2	195	R-R	18
6.	Brewers	Danny Thomas, 1b	Southern Illinois	East Carondelet, Ill.	6-2	190	R-R	21
7.	Reds	Larry Payne, rhp	Huntsville HS	Bedias, Texas	6-0	180	R-R	18
8.	Twins	*Dick Ruthven, rhp	Fresno State	Fremont, Calif.	6-2	185	R-R	21
9.	Astros	Steve Englishbey, of	South Houston HS	Houston	6-1	193	L-L	17
10.	Angels	Dave Chalk, 3b	Texas	Dallas	5-10	175	R-R	21
11.	Braves	Preston Hanna, rhp	Escambia HS	Pensacola, Fla.	6-1	180	R-R	17
12.	White Sox	Mike Ondina, of	Rancho Cordova HS	Rancho Cordova, Calif.	6-2	190	L-R	18
13.	Mets	Richard Bengston, c	Richwoods HS	Peoria, Ill.	6-3	195	R-R	18
14.	Yankees	Scott McGregor, lhp	El Segundo HS	El Segundo, Calif.	6-0	180	L-L	18
15.	Cubs	Brian Vernoy, lhp	LaQuinta HS	Westminster, Calif.	6-3	180	L-L	18
16.	Red Sox	Joel Bishop, ss	McClatchy HS	Sacramento	6-2	180	R-R	18
17.	Dodgers	John Harbin, ss	Newberry (S.C.)	Greenville, S.C.	6-1	195	R-R	21
18.	Royals	Jamie Quirk, ss	St. Paul HS	Whittier, Calif.	6-3	180	B-R	17
19.	Giants	Rob Dressler, rhp	Madison HS	Portland, Ore.	6-3	175	R-R	18
20.	Tigers	Jerry Manuel, ss	Rancho Cordova HS	Rancho Cordova, Calif.	5-11	165	R-R	18
21.	Cardinals	Dan Larson, rhp	Alhambra HS	Alhambra, Calif.	6-1	180	R-R	17
22.	Athletics	Chet Lemon, ss	Fremont HS	Los Angeles	5-11	175	R-R	17
23.	Pirates	Dwayne Peltier, ss	Servite HS	Anaheim	6-1	180	R-R	17
24.	Orioles	Ken Thomas, c	Clear Fork HS	Bellville, Ohio	5-11	180	R-R	18

*Did not sign.

1972

CLUB-BY-CLUB SELECTIONS

ATLANTA BRAVES

January—Regular Phase (12)

1. Ray Humphries, rhp, San Bernardino Valley (Calif.) JC
2. Laconia Graham, rhp, Ranger (Texas) JC
3. **Kenneth Miller, rhp, Bellevue (Wash.) CC**
4. Barry Rawls, of/rhp, Bronx (N.Y.) CC
5. David Fillipone, c, Seton Hall

January—Secondary Phase (10)

1. Mike McNeilly, rhp/ss, Gonzaga
2. Sam Bowen, of/rhp, Brunswick (Ga.) JC
3. Jeff DeBell, rhp/ss, Bellevue (Wash.) CC

June—Regular Phase (11)

1. **Preston Hanna, rhp, Escambia HS, Pensacola, Fla.**
2. **George Lusic, rhp, San Pedro (Calif.) HS**
3. **Bobby Jack, 1b, Oklahoma**
4. Mickey Lashley, rhp, College HS, Bartlesville, Okla.
5. Denny Martindale, 2b/rhp, North HS, Torrance, Calif.
6. Stephen Cook, 3b, North Miami (Fla.) HS
7. **Gary Scavone, rhp, Meyers HS, Wilkes-Barre, Pa.**
8. Ken Phelps, 1b, Ingraham HS, Seattle
9. **Bobby Buford, rhp, New Hope (Ala.) HS**
10. **Charles Hammond, of, Lee Summit (Mo.) HS**
11. Jan Ehemann, lhp, Glen Este HS, Batavia, Ohio
12. **Ken Alfred, lhp, Nicholls State**
13. **George Tydings, rhp, West Palm Beach, Fla.**
14. Anton Rosentritt, c, St. Edward's (Texas)
15. Dwayne Wilson, 2b, Shamrock HS, Decatur, Ga.
16. Greg McCollum, 1b, Puget Sound (Wash.)
17. Ray Guy, rhp, Southern Mississippi
18. **Conrad Pressley, of, Roberson Skyland HS, Asheville, N.C.**
19. James Yaeger, lhp, Northwest Classen HS, Oklahoma City, Okla.
20. **Pat Herring, rhp, Raytown (Mo.) HS**
21. Charles Leonard, rhp, East HS, Memphis
22. **William Fitzgerald, 1b, Tennessee-Chattanooga**
23. **Ken Zarski, rhp, Wake Forest**
24. Steve Renner, rhp, Woodale HS, Memphis
25. **John Travis, rhp, West Georgia**
26. Timothy Fox, rhp, Gulf Coast (Fla.) CC

June—Secondary Phase (11)

1. **Mike Bahnick, rhp, Rider**
2. **Don Collins, lhp, South Georgia JC**
3. Jim Gattis, 3b, Los Angeles Valley JC

BALTIMORE ORIOLES

January—Regular Phase (23)

1. **Cass Safrit, ss, Pfeiffer (N.C.)**
2. **Larry Green, rhp, Tyler (Texas) JC**
3. Martin Bladen, c, Southwood (Md.) JC
4. Jim Gattis, 3b, Los Angeles Valley JC
5. **Ricardo Urbano, lhp, Los Gatos, Calif.**
6. Carroll Palmer, lhp, Treasure Valley (Ore.) CC
7. Jeff McKay, rhp, Treasure Valley (Ore.) CC
8. **Jack Winchester, 3b, El Camino (Calif.) JC**
9. Mickey Hall, rhp, Santa Monica (Calif.) JC
10. **William Siebler, 1b/c, Antelope Valley (Calif.) JC**
11. **Dan Tippit, rhp, Antelope Valley (Calif.) JC**
12. Terry Bernard, rhp, Los Angeles Valley JC
13. Don Hurst, of, Phoenix JC

January—Secondary Phase (11)

1. **Leslie Clark, ss, Farmville, Va.**
2. Rick Tomlin, lhp, Manatee (Fla.) JC
3. Ricky Holoubek, ss, Pasadena (Calif.) CC
4. Walt Rzepiennik, rhp, CC of Baltimore
5. David Barnes, 2b/ss, Bellevue (Wash.) CC
6. David Christiansen, lhp, Los Angeles Valley JC
7. Richard Cahill, lhp, Mount Hood (Ore.) CC
8. Thomas Foster, ss, Treasure Valley (Ore.) CC
9. Dennis Watson, rhp, Los Angeles Valley JC
10. Frank Kunnen, c, Miami-Dade North CC

June—Regular Phase (24)

1. **Ken Thomas, c, Clear Fork HS, Bellville, Ohio**
2. **John O'Rear, ss, Tarrant (Ala.) HS**
3. **Randy Benson, lhp, Pfeiffer (N.C.)**
4. **Blake Doyle, 2b, Caverna HS, Cave City, Ky.**
5. **Gary Robson, rhp, UCLA**
6. **Rodney Lee, of, Highlands HS, North Highlands, Calif.**
7. **Nathaniel Clayton, of, Atlanta Baptist**
8. Joseph Miller, of, Brandywine HS, Wilmington, Del.
9. **John Adam, rhp, Gardena (Calif.) HS**
10. Don Henley, of, Ewing HS, Trenton, N.J.
11. **Bobby Brown, of/3b, Northampton HS, Eastville, Va.**
12. **Greg Patterson, lhp, Royal HS, Simi, Calif.**
13. **Henry Holmes, lhp, Belmont Abbey**
14. Rick Honeycutt, lhp, Lakeview HS, Fort Oglethorpe, Ga.
15. James Joiner, c, Deland (Fla.) HS
16. Jeff Grantz, ss, Bel Air (Md.) HS
17. **David Garcia, rhp, Royal HS, Thousand Oaks, Calif.**
18. Nate Snell, rhp, Roberts HS, Vance, S.C.
19. John Tatem, rhp, Virginia Tech
20. **Mike Willis, lhp, Vanderbilt**
21. Kenny Califano, lhp/of, Essex (Md.) CC
22. **Willie Royster, c, Spingarn HS, Washington, D.C.**
23. Donald Broom, of, Buna (Texas) HS
24. Larry Pike, lhp, St. Petersburg (Fla.) JC
25. William Sempsrott, rhp, Danville (Ill.) HS
26. **Dale Vineyard, ss, Mehlville HS, St. Louis**
27. John Riehs, lhp, La Grange (Texas) HS
28. John Flinn, rhp, Monroe HS, Sepulvada, Calif.
29. **Jim Buckner, of, Yavapai (Ariz.) JC**
30. Lee Heath, of, Taylor HS, Barberville, Fla.
31. **Howard McPike, rhp, Bowling Green (Mo.) HS**
32. Kevin Gilmartin, ss, Alemany HS, Sepulvada, Calif.
33. **Michael Kroll, c, Tampa Catholic HS**
34. Don Lyons, 1b, Riordan HS, San Francisco
35. **Clarence Laubach, of/1b, Central Columbia HS, Mifflinville, Pa.**
36. John Kennedy, ss, Arvin (Calif.) HS
37. Tony Milledge, 3b, Manatee HS, Palmetto, Fla.
38. **William Fraser, of, Thurston HS, Detroit**
39. Robert Wood, 2b, St. Petersburg (Fla.) JC
40. Eric Peterson, lhp, Mount Lebanon (Pa.) HS
41. Rufus Cook, 1b, Silsbee (Texas) HS
42. Scott Margolin, c, Gardena (Calif.) HS
43. Stan Shoaf, rhp, St. Petersburg (Fla.) HS
44. Eugene Cunningham, 1b, James Monroe HS, Fredericksburg, Va.

June—Secondary Phase (22)

1. Mel Washington, c/of, Los Angeles Valley JC
2. Steve Cline, rhp, Hagerstown (Md.) JC
3. Richard Cahill, lhp, Mount Hood (Ore.) CC
4. Chris Wibberley, rhp, El Camino (Calif.) JC
5. Thomas Forster, ss, Treasure Valley (Ore.) CC
6. David Christiansen, lhp, Los Angeles Valley JC
7. Keath Chauncey, of, Polk (Fla.) CC

BOSTON RED SOX

January—Regular Phase (15)

1. Cliff Holland, lhp, Canada (Calif.) JC
2. Jimmie Williams, rhp, Indian Hills (Iowa) CC

3. **Harold Stutte, rhp, Contra Costa (Calif.) JC**
4. **John Webb, inf, Seminole (Fla.) JC**

January—Secondary Phase (3)

1. **Ken Daughty, of/inf, Lamar (Colo.) CC**
2. Joe Burgess, lhp, Eastern Oklahoma State JC
3. Larry Meekins, rhp, Louisburg (N.C.) JC
4. Ralph Darin, rhp, Central Michigan
5. Roy Smalley, ss, Los Angeles CC

June—Regular Phase (16)

1. **Joel Bishop, ss, McClatchy HS, Sacramento**
2. **Steve Dillard, ss, Mississippi**
3. **Randy Markley, of, Lynwood HS, Long Beach**
4. **Ronnie Sims, rhp, Dorman HS, Una, S.C.**
5. **William Fewox, rhp, Truman HS, Kansas City**
6. **Don Aase, rhp, Savanna HS, Anaheim**
7. **Steven Samuelson, rhp, St. Thomas (Minn.)**
8. **Mark Jones, inf, Arlington Heights HS, Fort Worth, Texas**
9. **Ludwig Benedetti, ss, Long Island**
10. **Andy Merchant, c, Auburn**
11. **Steve Tarbell, c, Upland (Calif.) HS**
12. Donnie Moore, of/rhp, Monterey HS, Lubbock, Texas
13. Joseph Spaulding, of, Connors State (Okla.) JC
14. William Bohne, ss, Blinn (Texas) JC
15. **Ernie Whitt, c, Macomb (Mich.) CC**
16. Ray Boneschans, rhp, Oak Ridge HS, Orlando, Fla.
17. **Albert Ryan, 2b, South Alabama**
18. **Robert Leonard, 3b, Panola (Texas) JC**
19. **Herb Loveless, rhp, Ionia (Mich.) HS**
20. David Chapman, inf, Compton (Calif.) HS
21. Richard Marshall, rhp, South Park HS, Beaumont, Texas
22. **Barry Sbragia, rhp, Washington State**

June—Secondary Phase (20)

1. **Brad Hanson, ss, Valencia (Fla.) CC**

CALIFORNIA ANGELS

January—Regular Phase (9)

1. **Tom Donohue, of, Nassau (N.Y.) CC**
2. **Tim Burns, rhp, Austin Peay**
3. Paul Levar, rhp, Spokane Falls (Wash.) CC
4. Robert Perkins, rhp, St. Clair County (Mich.) CC
5. Michael Lee, rhp, Miami-Dade North CC
6. Craig White, of, Clemson
7. Darrell Dickens, rhp, Contra Costa (Calif.) JC

January—Secondary Phase (23)

1. Craig Caskey, lhp, Puget Sound (Wash.)
2. Jeff Spagnola, of, Santa Ana (Calif.) JC
3. Mike Bahnick, rhp, Rider
4. Jerry Stamps, c, Gulf Coast (Fla.) CC
5. James Jachym, lhp, Connecticut
6. Larry Liedy, ss, Staten Island (N.Y.)
7. Michael Roche, rhp, Seminole (Fla.) JC

June—Regular Phase (10)

1. **Dave Chalk, 3b, Texas**
2. **Bruce Bochte, 1b/of, Santa Clara**
3. **Alan Dopfel, rhp, MIT**
4. **Dave Machemer, ss, Central Michigan**
5. **Michael Elwood, rhp, Michigan**
6. George Milke, rhp, Marion HS, San Diego
7. Donald Houston, c, Murphy HS, Los Angeles
8. **George Lugosan, ss, Washington HS, Chicago, Ind.**
9. **Anthony Gilcrease, c, Patrick Henry HS, San Diego**
10. **Dennis Barry, 1b/of, Ball State**
11. **Kevin Thiel, lhp, Marion (Wis.) HS**
12. Bill Paschall, rhp, Kempsville HS, Virginia Beach
13. Brad Van Pelt, rhp, Michigan State
14. **John Stoffel, lhp, Wisconsin**
15. **Richard Laubert, 3b, Palos Verdes HS, Palos Verdes Estates, Calif.**
16. Dan Lahoue, 1b, Henry Ford (Mich.) CC
17. **Jeff Brock, rhp, California Lutheran**
18. James Kopatz, c, Lamphier HS, Springfield, Ill.
19. Alfred Myer, rhp, Bakersfield (Calif.) HS
20. **Judge Tassone, 2b, San Francisco**
21. Michael Perkins, 1b/of, Cohn HS, Nashville
22. James Hallowell, 1b/of, Buena HS, Ventura, Calif.
23. Brian Smith, c, Calhoun HS, Merrick, N.Y.
24. Mark Barr, rhp, Golden West (Calif.) JC
25. Patrick Pridy, ss, Excelsior HS, Norwalk, Calif.
26. **William McCorkle, 1b/c, Azusa Pacific (Calif.)**

June—Secondary Phase (6)

1. **Dave Collins, 1b/of, Mesa (Ariz.) CC**
2. Sam Bowen, 2b, Brunswick (Ga.) JC

CHICAGO CUBS

January—Regular Phase (16)

1. Rex Peters, 1b, Lafayette
2. **Dana Corey, of, Maine**
3. **Tom Myette, 2b/of, Nassau (N.Y.) CC**
4. Mark Miller, 2b, Ranger (Texas) JC

January—Secondary Phase (20)

1. Greg Van Gaver, rhp, Bellevue (Wash.) CC
2. **Johnny Green, c, Central Arizona JC**
3. John Langerhans, 1b, Texas
4. Mark Rogers, of, Golden West (Calif.) JC

June—Regular Phase (15)

1. **Brian Vernoy, lhp, LaQuinta HS, Westminster, Calif.**
2. **Clifford Hall, of, Tamalpais HS, Marin City, Calif.**
3. **Mike Gordon, c, Brockton (Mass.) HS**
4. Blair Stouffer, 3b/ss, Alamo Heights HS, San Antonio
5. Thomas West, of/1b, Gainesville (Ga.) HS
6. **Buddy Schultz, lhp, Miami (Ohio)**
7. **Stanley Buky, ss, Avondale HS, Avondale Estates, Ga.**
8. **Bill Droege, of, Kansas State**
9. **Craig Cerratani, 1b/of, Melrose (Mass.) HS**
10. **Doug Carvalho, of, Durfee HS, Fall River, Mass.**
11. **Peter Dresser, lhp, New Hampshire**
12. **John Repetto, rhp, Arlington (Mass.) HS**
13. **Robert Ott, rhp, Quincy (Ill.)**
14. **Mark Monaghan, c, Middletownship HS, Highlands, N.J.**
15. **Gary Young, lhp, Texas Wesleyan**
16. **Fred Kreiger, rhp, Allegany HS, Cresaptown, Md.**
17. **Ray Burris, rhp, Southwestern Oklahoma State**
18. **Randy Gettman, of, Adams State (Colo.)**
19. **James Conroy, lhp, Penn State**
20. **Wayne Tyrone, 2b, Texas-Pan American**
21. **Mark Tanner, 1b/rhp, Penn State**
22. James Skripko, rhp, North Hunterdon Regional HS, Hampton, N.J.
23. **Robert McCowan, ss, McMinn County HS, Athens, Tenn.**
24. Harry Martell, rhp, Maryland
25. **Theodore Echols, 1b, Fairmont State (W.Va.)**
26. Mike Ramsey, ss, Roswell (Ga.) HS
27. **Joe Patterson, of, College of Idaho**

June—Secondary Phase (15)

1. Bob Brescher, rhp, Miami-Dade South CC
2. Paul Levar, rhp, Spokane Falls (Wash.) CC

CHICAGO WHITE SOX

January—Regular Phase (11)

1. **Murphy Eppinette, rhp, Northeast Louisiana**
2. Bob Brescher, rhp, Miami-Dade South CC
3. **Postell Johnson, rhp, Miami-Dade North CC**
4. Dennis Aderholt, rhp, Mitchell (N.C.) CC
5. Don Boyer, 1b/of, Miami-Dade South CC

January—Secondary Phase (7)

1. **Paul Patterson, rhp, Ithaca (N.Y.)**
2. Jay Kuhnie, rhp, Eastern Michigan
3. **Roger McSwain, of, Gardner-Webb**
4. Frank Baumgardner, rhp, Miami-Dade North CC

June—Regular Phase (12)

1. **Mike Ondina, of, Rancho Cordova (Calif.) HS**

2. **Cleo Kilpatrick, of, Washington HS, Tulsa**
3. Gene Stohs, lhp/of, Nebraska
4. Bruce Robinson, c, La Jolla (Calif.) HS
5. **Thomas King, lhp, LaPorte HS, Hamlet, Ind.**
6. **George Enright, c, Hialeah (Fla.) HS**
7. **Eric Thomas, ss, West End HS, Birmingham**
8. Mike Overy, rhp, Olivet Nazarene (Ill.)
9. **John Shermer, rhp, Appalachian State**
10. **Glen Bryant, rhp, San Jacinto (Texas) JC**
11. **David Sandoval, rhp, Norte Vista HS, Riverside, Calif.**
12. Gary Parks, lhp, Noblesville (Ind.) HS
13. **Eddie Echols, 3b, Jacksonville State**
14. **Joseph Pomykala, of, Lewis (Ill.)**
15. Wayne Horkey, c, Spalding HS, Granville, Iowa
16. **Nyls Nyman, of, Rancho Cordova (Calif.) HS**
17. **Tate Easton, lhp, Birmingham Southern**
18. Mike Umfleet, ss, Lafayette HS, Ballwin, Mo.
19. Rick Dominik, rhp, St. Louis Park (Minn.) HS
20. **Ron Slingerman, 3b/rhp, High Point**
21. **Gary Whaley, 3b/1b, Birmingham Southern**
22. Alan Wasik, c, Lewis (Ill.)
23. Douglas May, of/1b, West HS, Greeley, Colo.
24. Jim Lentine, of, Sierra HS, Whittier, Calif.

June—Secondary Phase (16)

1. Cliff Holland, lhp, Canada (Calif.) JC

CINCINNATI REDS

January—Regular Phase (8)

1. **Greg Sinatro, ss/3b, Miami-Dade South CC**
2. **Tommy Mutz, c, Cochise County (Ariz.) CC**
3. Bert Francks, rhp, CC of Morris (N.J.)
4. Farrell Vincent, rhp, Southwest Texas JC
5. Keith Overbeck, rhp, Dana (Neb.)
6. Lewis Reasonover, ss, Gulf Coast (Fla.) CC
7. Gary Erskine, of/lhp, Texas
8. **Perry Renfroe, lhp, Jacksonville State**

January—Secondary Phase (16)

1. **Tom Hume, rhp, Manatee (Fla.) JC**
2. **Larry O'Brien, rhp, Indian Hills (Iowa) CC**
3. Ron Herring, rhp, Chipola (Fla.) JC

June—Regular Phase (7)

1. **Larry Payne, rhp, Huntsville HS, Bedias, Texas**
2. Randy Wallace, 3b/of, Englewood HS, Jacksonville
3. **David Embree, inf, Bishop Gallagher HS, Harper Woods, Mich.**
4. **Keith Joseph, lhp, Skyline HS, Salt Lake City**
5. Bernard Hittner, rhp, Bishop Amat HS, West Covina, Calif.
6. **Mike Staffieri, ss, Brigham Young**
7. **David Moore, rhp, Lafayette HS, Lexington, Ky.**
8. **Robert Cummings, 3b, West HS, Phoenix**
9. James Petersen, lhp, Waupun (Wis.) Senior HS
10. **Michael Westerman, ss, Freeport (Pa.) HS**
11. **Wallace Lester, rhp, Carlsbad (N.M.) HS**
12. **Keith Halgerson, rhp, Sioux Falls (S.D.) Lincoln HS**
13. **Gene Phipps, lhp, Yuma (Ariz.) HS**
14. **Pat Sylvester, 3b/2b, JC of the Desert (Calif.)**
15. **Ben Castillo, rhp, Iolani HS, Kailua, Hawaii**
16. Matth Polinski, c, Evanston (Ill.) Senior HS
17. **Donald Lewis, of/3b, Claremont-Mudd (Calif.)**
18. Lonnie Salyers, rhp, Texas
19. Mark Kilmurray, ss, New Haven (Conn.)
20. **Peter Savute, 2b/3b, Heights HS, Wichita**
21. Dan Dumoulin, rhp, Kokoma (Ind.) HS
22. Marty O'Malley, c, Winner (S.D.) Senior HS
23. Ron Hassey, ss, Tucson (Ariz.) HS
24. Dennis Miscik, 1b, Mount Pleasant HS, Calumet, Pa.
25. **Ron Van Saders, c, William Paterson (N.J.)**
26. **Andre Rabouin, c, Texas-Pan American**
27. Jay Toubl, rhp, Milton
28. Johnny Williams, of, Talladega (Ala.) HS
29. Steve Nichols, lhp, Jacksonville
30. David Logan, ss/rhp, Wheat Ridge (Colo.) HS
31. **William Davis, rhp, Central HS, Knoxville, Tenn.**

June—Secondary Phase (9)

No selection

CLEVELAND INDIANS

January—Regular Phase (1)

1. **Eric Raich, rhp, Southern California**
2. **Anthony Giammaresis, ss, Broward (Fla.) CC**
3. **Clyde Fink, of, East Rowan HS, Salisbury, N.C.**
4. Michael Smith, rhp, DeAnza (Calif.) JC
5. Charles Petrillo, 2b, St. Clair County (Mich.) CC
6. John Keough, p, Miami-Dade North CC
7. Michael Johnson, rhp, Bacone (Okla.) JC

January—Secondary Phase (21)

1. **Duane Kuiper, ss, Southern Illinois**
2. Don Collins, lhp, South Georgia JC
3. William Taylor, inf, Mira Costa (Calif.) JC
4. Mike Hannah, 1b, Ohio
5. **Edward Burzo, of, Nassau (N.Y.) CC**
6. Alan Lobb, lhp, Elizabethtown (Pa.)
7. Ben Heise, ss, Yavapai (Ariz.) JC

June—Regular Phase (2)

1. **Rick Manning, ss, LaSalle HS, Niagara Falls, N.Y.**
2. **Bob Grossman, rhp, Maryland**
3. **Dennis Eckersley, rhp, Washington Union HS, Fremont, Calif.**
4. John Sciarra, inf, Bishop Amat HS, Alhambra, Calif.
5. Jeff Feramisco, inf/of, Fresno HS
6. **Rex Bynum, of/inf, Alabama**
7. **Kris Yoder, c, Savanna HS, Buena Park, Calif.**
8. **Robert Hickey, inf, High Point (N.C.)**
9. Mike Armstrong, rhp, North Shore HS, Sea Cliff, N.Y.
10. Pete Redfern, rhp, Sylmar (Calif.) HS
11. **Ken Kirchner, lhp, Richmond Heights (Ohio) HS**
12. **Dick Combs, c, Lakeland (Fla.) HS**
13. James Eden, rhp, Solon (Ohio) HS
14. Dan Shaw, rhp, Stanford
15. **Larry Unser, inf/of, Marion (Ind.)**
16. George Gospodinoff, lhp, Norte Vista HS, Riverside, Calif.
17. Manuel Alfonsin, inf/of, Miami Springs HS, Hialeah, Fla.
18. Thomas Lyons, rhp, Notre Dame HS, Biloxi, Miss.
19. Kent Juday, inf, Clay HS, South Bend, Ind.
20. David Mandell, lhp, Maumee (Ohio) HS
21. **Brian Dingess, lhp, Garden Grove (Calif.) HS**
22. **Dan Van Auken, rhp, St. Petersburg (Fla.) JC**
23. **Ed Arsenault, rhp/1b, Robinson HS, Tampa**
24. Phillip Francis, rhp, Solon (Ohio) HS
25. Greg Redding, rhp, Hillsborough HS, Tampa
26. Michael Melvin, ss, Deep Creek HS, Chesapeake, Fla.
27. Dan O'Brien, rhp, Bishop Berry HS, St. Petersburg, Fla.
28. James Shade, rhp, Reynoldsburg (Ohio) HS
29. **Steve Rametta, inf, Gladstone HS, Covina, Calif.**
30. Ken Bolek, of, University HS, Chardon, Ohio
31. Ken Grolle, rhp, Los Altos (Calif.) HS
32. Robert Rossi, rhp, Corning (N.Y.) West HS
33. Bob Purkey, rhp, Bethel Park (Pa.) HS
34. Steve Meisner, inf/of, Fontana HS, Alta Loma, Calif.
35. Dennis Smith, 1b, Miami (Ohio)
36. Rick Langford, of, Manatee (Fla.) JC
37. **Robert Meyer, 3b, Aurora, Ind.**

June—Secondary Phase (2)

1. Rich Dauer, ss/2b, San Bernardino Valley (Calif.) JC
2. **John Langerhans, 1b, Texas**
3. **Michael Smith, rhp, De Anza (Calif.) JC**
4. Rick Bethke, lhp, Cerritos (Calif.) JC
5. **Charles Hendrix, rhp, Grossmont (Calif.) JC**

DETROIT TIGERS

January—Regular Phase (19)

1. **Alfred Callis, lhp, Fullerton (Calif.) JC**
2. **Dan Gonzales, of, Fullerton (Calif.) JC**

3. Brian Sheekey, rhp, Union County (N.J.) JC
4. Ronald Horgett, c, DeKalb (Ga.) JC
5. **Daniel Kaupla, rhp, Fullerton (Calif.) JC**
6. **Art James, of, Macomb (Mich.) CC**
7. Carl Benson, of, Lamar (Colo.) CC
8. **John Davies, rhp, Toledo**
9. David Lloyd, rhp, Macomb (Mich.) CC

January—Secondary Phase (19)

1. Curtis Bishop, lhp, Bacone (Okla.) JC
2. Mitch Lukevics, rhp, Bethlehem, Pa.
3. John Van Brunt, c, Mesa (Ariz.) CC
4. **Frank Weisse, of, Lafayette (Pa.)**

June—Regular Phase (20)

1. **Jerry Manuel, ss, Rancho Cordova (Calif.) HS**
2. **John Valle, 3b, Holy Cross HS, New York**
3. Jim Gideon, rhp, Bellaire HS, Houston
4. **Dan Meyer, 2b, Santa Ana (Calif.) JC**
5. **James Murray, lhp, St. Mary's (Mich.)**
6. Jeffrey Potter, lhp, Lincoln HS, Elwood City, Pa.
7. **Roy Haney, c, Byng HS, Ada, Okla.**
8. **Nat Calamis, ss, St. John's**
9. **Gary Stollar, c, Westmoor HS, Daly City, Calif.**
10. **Leon Roberts, of, Michigan**
11. Alan Satriano, of, C.W. Post (N.Y.)
12. **Stephen Litras, ss, Floral Park (N.Y.) HS**
13. **John Larkin, lhp, Syracuse**
14. Gary Kennedy, of, Dacula (Ga.) HS
15. **Douglas Ratford, of, St. John's**
16. **Dave Lemanczyk, rhp, Hartwick (N.Y.)**
17. **Vern Ruhle, rhp, Olivet (Mich.)**
18. Philip Vaden, rhp, Western HS, Detroit
19. **Mark Wagner, ss, Harbor HS, Ashtabula, Ohio**
20. **John Petrolla, 3b, Cardinal Mooney HS, Poland, Ohio**
21. **Fred Winner, lhp, Lycoming (Pa.)**
22. Steve Bartolin, lhp, Youngstown State
23. **Greg Kuhl, rhp, Jefferson Davis HS, Montgomery, Ala.**
24. **Allen Szaroleta, rhp, St. Joseph's HS, Perth Amboy, N.J.**
25. Paul Cormier, rhp, New Hampshire
26. **Dennis Ray, of, Garden City (Mich.) East HS**
27. **George Cappuzzello, lhp, Ursuline Catholic HS, Girard, Ohio**
28. Lloyd Sprockett, ss, Warren (Ohio) Reserve HS
29. Bruce Fitzma, rhp, Grand Rapids (Mich.) Central Christian HS
30. Charles Morrison, lhp, Parkview HS, Springfield, Mo.
31. **Richard McDonagh, lhp, Walter Whitman HS, Huntington Station, N.Y.**
32. **John Yalden, rhp, St. John's**
33. Rick Wolff, 2b, Harvard

June—Secondary Phase (12)

1. **Michael McGuire, of, Cornell**

HOUSTON ASTROS

January—Regular Phase (10)

1. William Meyer, ss, Indian River (Fla.) CC
2. Howard Ashlock, lhp, Palm Beach (Fla.) JC
3. David Meites, lhp, Bowling Green State

January—Secondary Phase (14)

1. Rick Bethke, lhp, Cerritos (Calif.) JC

June—Regular Phase (9)

1. **Steve Englishbey, of, South Houston HS**
2. **Stan Floyd, c, George Wythe HS, Richmond**
3. **Lonnie Newland, ss, Hobbs (N.M.) HS**
4. **David Brooks, rhp, Merced (Calif.) HS**
5. **Kenny Reed, 2b, Arizona State**
6. **Donnie Sims, of, Dorman HS, Spartanburg, S.C.**
7. Michael Odum, of, Tucson HS
8. Wayne Williams, ss, Abilene (Texas) HS
9. Wymon Winton, c, Cotaco HS, Sommerville, Ala.
10. **David Ralstin, of, Homestead HS, Palo Alto, Calif.**
11. Pete Padgett, rhp, Del Valle HS, Walnut Creek, Calif.
12. Roy Lee Jackson, rhp, Opelika (Ala.) HS
13. Kevin Stephenson, rhp, Lyman HS, North Orlando, Fla.
14. **Jim Crawford, lhp, Arizona State**
15. Richard Koenig, of, Cardinal Newman HS, West Palm Beach, Fla.
16. **Michael Markl, 2b, Texas**
17. **Paul Dillard, ss, Douglas HS, Oklahoma City, Okla.**
18. Alexander Taylor, rhp, Blair HS, Hattiesburg, Miss.
19. John Revere, of, Patterson Co-op HS, Dayton, Ohio
20. Ted Yoak, rhp/inf, Hamilton Community HS, Dorr, Mich.
21. **Tom Changnon, lhp, Stanford**
22. **John Calzia, rhp, La Verne (Calif.)**
23. **Dennis Nagel, rhp, Cincinnati**
24. **Ben Ochoa, rhp, La Verne (Calif.)**
25. Gary Addeo, rhp, Cal State Los Angeles
26. Robert Diliberto, rhp/of, Mansfield (Pa.)

June—Secondary Phase (7)

1. Bob Gerdes, rhp, Miami-Dade South CC
2. Lawrence Lee, c, Martinez, Calif.

KANSAS CITY ROYALS

January—Regular Phase (17)

1. **Kenzie Davis, of, Chaffey (Calif.) JC**
2. Ron McDonald, rhp, Louisburg (N.C.) JC
3. **Jerry Gomez, lhp, Yavapai (Ariz.) JC**

January—Secondary Phase (9)

1. Dave Collins, 1b/of, Mesa (Ariz.) CC
2. Mike Stanton, rhp, Miami-Dade South CC
3. Byron Burns, rhp, Lower Columbia (Wash.) JC
4. Michael Walsh, rhp, Cerritos (Calif.) JC
5. Mike DuPree, of, Fresno CC
6. Jerry Maddox, ss, Cerritos (Calif.) JC
7. Steven Jones, 1b, Garden Grove, Calif.

June—Regular Phase (18)

1. **Jamie Quirk, ss, St. Paul HS, Whittier, Calif.**
2. **Dennis Leonard, rhp, Iona**
3. Paul Adams, c, Castlewood HS, Dante, Va.
4. Doug Wessel, rhp, Vanderbilt
5. **Karl Jacobsen, c, Valley Central HS, Montgomery, N.Y.**
6. **John Rockwell, 2b, Lane (Tenn.)**
7. **Dale Stevener, of, Francis Howell HS, New Melle, Mo.**
8. **Stan Butkus, rhp, South Alabama**
9. **Shawn Howitt, of, Michigan State**
10. **Kevin Bova, of, Long Branch (N.J.) HS**
11. **Rodney Scott, 3b, Arlington HS, Indianapolis**
12. Scott Gardner, rhp, Riverview HS, Sarasota, Fla.
13. Michael Bartell, ss, Encinal HS, Alameda, Calif.
14. **Jeff Grossick, lhp, Monominee (Mich.) HS**
15. **Joseph McNamara, rhp, Betlehem Central HS, Delmar, N.Y.**
16. **George Throop, rhp, Long Beach State**
17. Pat Curran, of, Golden West (Calif.) JC
18. **Craig Bowser, rhp, La Verne (Calif.)**
19. **David Bradford, ss, Murray State**
20. **Juan Quesada, 3b/1b, DeWitt Clinton HS, New York**
21. John Keisler, rhp, Cal State Long Beach
22. **Reginald Knapper, rhp, Chartiers Houston HS, Houston, Pa.**
23. Robert Glass, 3b, Lakeland (Fla.) HS
24. Doug Duncan, c, Hillcrest HS, Dallas
25. **Roman Bailey, rhp, Union (Tenn.)**
26. **Dennis Gallagher, of, Chapman (Calif.)**
27. Thomas Davis, rhp, Loara HS, Anaheim
28. **Mark Brown, c, Gloucester (Mass.) HS**
29. **Doug Buchanan, c, Eastern (Pa.)**
30. **Don Spare, ss, Chapman (Calif.)**
31. Greg Fairbanks, rhp, Satellite Beach (Fla.) HS
32. **Bernard Hunting, 3b/ss, Rockford (Mich.) HS**
33. James Auringer, ss/rhp, Corcoran HS, Syracuse, N.Y.
34. **Mike Roberts, c, North Carolina**
35. **Rod Boone, of, Stanford**
36. **John Urzi, 2b/ss, San Jose State**
37. **Eric Littell, c, Gideon (Mo.) HS**

June—Secondary Phase (8)

1. Mike Payne, rhp, Delta State (Miss.)
2. Jerry Maddox, ss, Cerritos (Calif.) JC

LOS ANGELES DODGERS

January—Regular Phase (18)

1. **John Adams, rhp, Phoenix, Ariz.**
2. Tim Hosler, of/3b, South Georgia JC
3. Allen Polofsky, lhp, Miami-Dade South CC

January—Secondary Phase (8)

1. **Dennis Lewallyn, rhp, Chipola (Fla.) JC**
2. James Van Der Beek, rhp, Lafayette (Pa.)
3. Francis Sansosti, rhp/1b, Essex (Md.) CC
4. Mike Siani, ss, Villanova
5. **Robert Sans, 1b, Texas A&M**

June—Regular Phase (17)

1. **John Harbin, ss, Newberry (S.C.)**
2. **Cleo Smith, 1b/of, Harry Ells HS, Richmond, Calif.**
3. **Bob Detherage, rhp/of, Hillcrest HS, Springfield, Mo.**
4. **Larry Corrigan, c, Iowa State**
5. **Mitch Bobinger, lhp, Chico (Calif.) Senior HS**
6. **Alton Torregano, c, Southwestern Louisiana**
7. James Fleming, ss, St. Peters HS, New Brunswick, N.J.
8. **Stephen Plut, of, St. Francis HS, San Carlos, Calif.**
9. **Robert Stewart, rhp, Magnolia HS, Anaheim**
10. **William Kooyman, 3b, St. Mary's**
11. **Terry Zorger, 3b, Huntington (Ind.)**
12. **Jere Nolan, of, California**
13. Henry Boguszewski, rhp, Glen Cove (N.Y.) HS
14. **Michael Rushde, of, Fontana (Calif.) HS**
15. Jason Thompson, lhp/1b, Apple Valley (Calif.) HS
16. Doug Schaefer, rhp, Lindberg HS, Afton, Mo.
17. **Glenn Burke, of, Merritt (Calif.) JC**
18. **Richard Magner, c, Rollins (Fla.)**
19. **Leonard Wouters, rhp, Hampton Bays (N.Y.) HS**
20. John Littlefield, rhp, Azusa (Calif.) HS
21. John Freedman, 3b, Claremont (Calif.) HS
22. Richard Jacobs, lhp, Oklahoma
23. Dale Forchetti, ss, Neshaminy HS, Levittown, Pa.
24. Don Redoglia, ss/2b, Pasadena (Calif.) CC
25. Kenneth Smith, of, Jefferson HS, Daly City, Calif.
26. Buff White, lhp, Folsom HS, Orangevale, Calif.
27. David Rothermel, 3b, Hillcrest HS, Springfield, Mo.
28. **Steven O'Brien, rhp, Maryvale HS, Phoenix**
29. Samuel Roberts, 1b, Tennessee HS, Bristol, Tenn.
30. **Brian Felda, of, Wisconsin-Oshkosh**
31. **Michael Parnow, 2b, JC of Marin (Calif.)**
32. **James Fiack, c, UC Davis**
33. **Charles Walker, of, Atlanta Baptist**
34. Jeff Chandler, lhp, Davis (Calif.) HS
35. Craig Minetto, lhp, A.A. Stagg HS, Stockton, Calif.
36. David Baker, c, Pacific HS, San Leandro, Calif.
37. Tom Haley, c, Binger (Okla.) HS
38. Bob Shirley, lhp, Putnam City HS, Oklahoma City, Okla.
39. Tim Lewis, lhp/1b, Germantown Academy, Norristown, Pa.

June—Secondary Phase (1)

1. **Bob Lesslie, rhp, Kansas State**
2. **Walt Rzepiennik, rhp, CC of Baltimore**
3. Robin Ogle, 1b, Miami-Dade South CC

MILWAUKEE BREWERS

January—Regular Phase (5)

1. **Robert Alexander, rhp, St. Clair County (Mich.) CC**
2. **Vincent Roberto, of, Miami**

January—Secondary Phase (17)

1. Terry Cornutt, rhp, Linn-Benton (Ore.) CC
2. **Tim Hamilton, 2b, Mesa (Ariz.) CC**
3. Willie Mims, of, Iowa

June—Regular Phase (6)

1. **Dan Thomas, 1b, Southern Illinois**
2. **Jerry Mantlo, c, Arizona State**
3. **Roger Alexander, rhp, Norman (Okla.) HS**
4. Ronald Pearce, rhp, Gordon HS, Douglasville, Ga.
5. **James Richardson, 1b/of, North Carolina State**
6. **Thomas Diedel, lhp, Mullen HS, Denver**
7. **Kent Jackson, of, Arizona State**
8. **James Blaine, rhp, Midwest City HS, Oklahoma City, Okla.**
9. Henry McGowan, 3b/of, Grandfield (Okla.) HS
10. **Victor Sanchez, ss, Pentucket HS, West Newbury, Mass.**
11. **David Simplot, rhp/c, Sehome HS, Bellingham, Wash.**
12. **Sam Killingsworth, c, Cleveland (Miss.) HS**
13. Kip Coughlan, 3b, Highland Springs (Va.) HS
14. **William Davidson, rhp, Chaffey HS, Ontario, Calif.**
15. **Roger Miller, rhp, Uniontown HS, Mill Run, Pa.**
16. Thomas Sohns, ss/2b, Dunmore (Pa.) HS
17. **Mark Young, lhp, Roswell (N.M.) HS**
18. **Wayne Politelli, 3b, Pilgrim HS, Warwick, R.I.**
19. **Mike Duncan, rhp, Arvin HS, Lamont, Calif.**
20. Greg Marshall, rhp, Northmont HS, Englewood, Ohio
21. **William Collins, c, George Washington**
22. **Bob Sheldon, ss, Loyola Marymount**
23. Carl Sapp, rhp, Dominguez HS, Compton, Calif.
24. **Greg Erardi, rhp, Liverpool (N.Y.) HS**
25. **Charles Solano, rhp, Wayne State (Neb.)**
26. **Al Widmar, rhp, Tulsa**
27. Robert Jantz, of, Shattuck (Okla.) HS
28. Fred Nachbar, c, Rockhurst HS, Shawnee, Kan.

June—Secondary Phase (10)

1. **John Danson, ss, Seminole (Fla.) JC**

MINNESOTA TWINS

January—Regular Phase (7)

1. **Lew Lerner, rhp, Panorama City, Calif.**
2. William Bishop, 1b, Yavapai (Ariz.) JC
3. **John Pangle, rhp, Parsons (Iowa)**
4. Tom Mitterholzer, of, LaCrescenta, Calif.

January—Secondary Phase (1)

1. Bob Koeppel, lhp/of, Bradley
2. **Joseph Yocum, rhp, Fresno CC**
3. Warren Cromartie, of, Miami-Dade North CC

June—Regular Phase (8)

1. Dick Ruthven, rhp, Fresno State
2. Clay Westlake, c/1b, Loara HS, Anaheim
3. **Willie Norwood, of, La Verne (Calif.)**
4. **William Daniels, rhp, Montebello (Calif.) HS**
5. **Tommy Franklin, c, T.C. Roberson HS, Arden, N.C.**
6. **Doug Clarey, ss, Homestead (Calif.) HS**
7. **Randy Bass, 1b, Lawton (Okla.) HS**
8. William Cowens, ss, Centennial HS, Compton, Calif.
9. Michael Baier, ss/2b, Maryland
10. Dave Stegman, of, Lompoc (Calif.) HS
11. **Kevin Cooney, rhp, Montclair State (N.J.)**
12. William Stiegemeier, rhp, Kansas
13. Pete Falcone, lhp, Lafayette HS, Brooklyn, N.Y.
14. **Dan Kelly, c/ss, Unionville HS, Chester, Pa.**
15. Mike Nelson, of, Stanford
16. **Thomas Boettcher, 3b, Madison, Wis.**
17. Steve Wilkins, of, The Dalles (Ore.) HS
18. Kenneth Wright, of, Centennial HS, Compton, Calif.
19. **Mike Gerakos, 3b, UCLA**
20. Lindsay Hoyer, c, Minnesota
21. James Saunders, 3b, Prince Edward HS, Crene, Va.
22. Gary Sargent, inf, Bemidji (Minn.) HS
23. John Brooks, of, Northwestern
24. **Lee Sturtevant, rhp, Laconia (N.H.) HS**
25. Kevin Hanzlik, c, Edison HS, Minneapolis
26. **Lyman Bostock Jr., of, Cal State Northridge**
27. Michael Thissen, rhp, Columbus HS, Waterloo, Iowa
28. **David Morrison, of/rhp, Mission Bay HS, San Diego**
29. Richard Metzger, ss, Hoover HS, Fresno
30. **Michael Coronado, ss, Cal State Los Angeles**
31. Carlos Moreno, lhp, Lennox HS, Inglewood, Calif.
32. **William O'Connor, rhp, Kingsborough (N.Y.) CC**
33. **David Anna, rhp, Jefferson HS, Edgewater, Colo.**
34. **Gary Martin, lhp, Alpaugh (Calif.) HS**
35. Terry Ryan, lhp, Parker HS, Janesville, Wis.

36. Michael Hickman, rhp, Tustin (Calif.) HS

June—Secondary Phase (18)

1. John Eicholtz, rhp, Fresno CC
2. **Al Woods, 1b, Laney (Calif.) JC**

MONTREAL EXPOS

January—Regular Phase (6)

1. **Wayne Piper, rhp, Omaha, Neb.**
2. **Carl Baker, of, LaPuente, Calif.**
3. Rhinehart Dallas, of, Baltimore
4. James Hamilton, c, Middle Georgia JC
5. Mike Edwards, ss, Los Angeles CC
6. Richard Davidson, c, Columbia State (Tenn.) CC

January—Secondary Phase (2)

1. **Jim Cox, ss, Iowa**
2. Steve Hergenrader, c, Fresno CC
3. William Daves, c, Motlow State (Tenn.) CC
4. Steve Cline, rhp, Hagerstown (Md.) JC
5. Edward Gale, lhp, Palm Beach (Fla.) JC

June—Regular Phase (5)

1. **Bobby Goodman, c, Bishop Byrnes HS, Memphis**
2. **Ellis Valentine, c/of, Crenshaw HS, Los Angeles**
3. **Gary Carter, c, Sunny Hills HS, Fullerton, Calif.**
4. **Roger DeLazzer, of, Lake Park HS, Itasca, Ill.**
5. **Dennis Blair, rhp, Eisenhower HS, Rialto, Calif.**
6. Terrence Mackey, rhp, MacArthur HS, San Antonio
7. Thomas Wise, lhp/of, Bayonne (N.J.) HS
8. **Luis Jonas, of, Erasmus Hall HS, Brooklyn**
9. **Gary Bryant, rhp, Madison HS, San Diego**
10. David Bedrosian, 2b, McLane HS, Fresno
11. **Mike Hart, 1b/of, Kalamazoo Valley (Mich.) CC**
12. Rickey Ferguson, rhp, Haskel (Okla.) HS
13. **Michael Criss, rhp, Los Altos HS, Reseda, Calif.**
14. Kevin Morel, ss, Oxen Hill (Md.) HS
15. **Larry Lein, c, Green River (Wash.) CC**
16. Rick Matula, rhp, Wharton (Texas) HS
17. Mark Mercer, lhp, West HS, Minneapolis
18. Keith Drumright, 2b, Hillcrest HS, Springfield, Mo.
19. Don Flanagan, c/rhp, Stephen F. Austin HS, Houston
20. **Kevin Young, of, Portage (Pa.) HS**
21. Scott Mackey, lhp, Marengo (Ill.) HS
22. Michael Amatulli, 3b/of, Wayne Hills Regional HS, Wayne, N.J.
23. **Mario Hewitt, 3b/of, St. John's**
24. Kevin Carney, c, Burlington (Vt.) HS
25. Randy Johnson, rhp, Brooklyn Center (Minn.) HS
26. Glenn Smith, ss/3b, Bordentown (N.J.) Regional HS
27. Mike Williamson, rhp, Hillsdale HS, San Mateo, Calif.
28. Dennis Connally, c, Redondo Beach (Calif.) HS
29. Lawrence Groover, lhp, Temple (Texas) JC
30. Vollon Dixon, of, Morningside HS, Inglewood, Calif.

June—Secondary Phase (13)

1. **Craig Caskey, lhp, Puget Sound (Wash.)**
2. Laconia Graham, rhp, Ranger (Texas) JC

NEW YORK METS

January—Regular Phase (14)

1. **Ron Diggle, of, UCLA**
2. **John Lenahan, rhp, Villanova**
3. **John Blue, lhp, Tempe, Ariz.**
4. Steven Kennedy, rhp, San Jacinto (Texas) JC
5. **Randy Tate, rhp, John C. Calhoun (Ala.) CC**
6. Robert Youse, rhp, Glendale (Ariz.) CC

January—Secondary Phase (24)

1. **Michael Agosto, of, San Diego Mesa JC**
2. **Ron Hodges, c, Appalachian State**
3. John Danson, ss, Seminole (Fla.) JC
4. **Ernest Bessette, ss, Post (Conn.) JC**
5. **Terry Senn, 2b, San Francisco**

June—Regular Phase (13)

1. **Richard Bengston, c, Richwoods HS, Peoria, Ill.**
2. **Craig Skoglund, of, Clairemont HS, San Diego**
3. **Craig Swan, rhp, Arizona State**
4. Andy Replogle, rhp, Snider HS, Fort Wayne, Ind.
5. Randy McGilberry, rhp, Satsuma HS, Saraland, Ala.
6. **Brock Pemberton, 1b, Marina HS, Huntington Beach, Calif.**
7. Jeff Kleinbaum, 1b/of, Martin Van Buren HS, Bayside, N.Y.
8. Larry Ike, rhp, Michigan State
9. **Craig Cacek, of, Monroe HS, Sepulvada, Calif.**
10. **Gary Perritt, lhp, Hanford (Calif.) HS**
11. Bob Polinsky, rhp, Delaware Valley
12. **Ken Perry, ss, Abbeyville (La.) HS**
13. **Dennis Solari, rhp, Irvington HS, Fremont, Calif.**
14. **Jeffrey Grose, lhp, Colonia HS, Iselin, N.J.**
15. David Wiggins, of, San Diego State
16. **Glenn Harper, of, San Pedro (Calif.) HS**
17. **George Marshall, lhp, Northwest Cabarrus HS, Concord, N.C.**
18. Timothy Huff, rhp, West Forsyth HS, Winston-Salem, N.C.
19. Clyde Lineberry, of, Parry-McCluer HS, Buena Vista, Va.
20. Duke Ribar, rhp, Steubenville (Ohio) HS
21. **Gregory Dobson, of/lhp, Bethune-Cookman**
22. **Robert Cheesman, of, Ledyard (Conn.) HS**
23. Eric Magee, rhp, Haddonfield (N.J.) HS
24. Craig Mitchell, rhp, Shadle Park HS, Spokane, Wash.
25. Greg Vogel, inf, Northampton HS, Cherryville, Pa.
26. Tom Swenson, rhp, Rio Linda (Calif.) HS
27. Bruce Caldwell, rhp, DeKalb (Ga.) JC
28. **John Trevisan, c, Elizabethtown (Pa.)**
29. Bo Kleiber, ss, Ohio
30. Randall Owens, rhp, Bamberg (S.C.) HS
31. **Gregory Hill, c, Santa Monica (Calif.) JC**
32. **August Garbatini, rhp, Connecticut**
33. Ray Davis, rhp, Southeast Bulloch HS, Brooklet, Ga.
34. Michael Hasley, lhp, Oakdale (Calif.) HS
35. Chuck Rogers, rhp, Findlay (Ohio) HS
36. **Michael Henderson, rhp, Azusa Pacific (Calif.)**
37. **John Slosar, 1b/of, Connecticut**
38. William Robinson, of, Delaware State
39. Charles Steffen, lhp/1b, Jefferson HS, Rochester, N.Y.
40. Paul Stombaugh, of, Clemson
41. Alex Pastore, of, Miami-Dade North CC
42. Bryan Jones, ss, Haddonfield (N.J.) HS
43. Dan Forsythe, rhp, St. Paul (Minn.) North HS
44. **Tim Juran, lhp, Valparaiso**
45. **Kirk Berger, of, Millersville (Pa.) HS**

June—Secondary Phase (3)

1. **Mike McNeilly, rhp, Gonzaga**

NEW YORK YANKEES

January—Regular Phase (13)

1. Joe Krsnich, inf/of, Wichita State
2. Mike Lester, 3b, Bellevue (Wash.) CC
3. **Fred Luzzi, 2b, Sacramento CC**
4. Lawrence Lee, c, Broward (Fla.) CC
5. Richard Green, 3b, Mesa (Ariz.) CC

January—Secondary Phase (5)

1. **Rick Anderson, rhp, Los Angeles Valley JC**
2. **Steven Greene, 2b, Los Angeles Valley JC**
3. John Herman, of, Motlow State (Tenn.) CC
4. Larry Wolfe, ss/rhp, Sacramento CC
5. Pat Williams, rhp, West Valley (Calif.) JC

June—Regular Phase (14)

1. **Scott McGregor, lhp, El Segundo (Calif.) HS**
2. **Ken Clay, rhp, E.C. Glass HS, Lynchburg, Va.**
3. **Dennis Irwin, c, Hanford (Calif.) HS**
4. **Mickey Klutts, ss, El Rancho HS, Pico Rivera, Calif.**
5. **Darryl Jones, ss, Westminster (Pa.)**
6. **Edward Ricks, rhp, Grambling**
7. **Earl Howell, c, Blair HS, Hattiesburg, Miss.**
8. **John Yeglinski, of, Long Island**
9. **Donald White, of/3b, Grambling HS, Simsboro, La.**
10. **Gaylord Browne, ss, John Brown (Ark.)**

11. Michael Rusk, rhp, San Jose State
12. **Terry Quinn, c, Nevada**
13. **Alfred Alwurm, lhp, Glendale (Calif.) HS**
14. Doug Slocum, rhp, Mesa (Ariz.) CC
15. **Daniel Elko, of, Woodrow Wilson HS, Levittown, Pa.**
16. **James Lawler, rhp, Buena Vista**
17. Michael Milligan, c, East Jefferson HS, Metairie, La.
18. Paul Burnett, 1b/rhp, Temple HS, Vicksburg, Miss.
19. **Bob Artemenko, rhp, Northwestern**
20. Bradley Davis, rhp, Milwaukie (Ore.) HS
21. **Bob Kammeyer, rhp, Stanford**
22. Larry Hart, 1b, Darien (Conn.) HS
23. **Scott Rahl, 1b, New Haven (Conn.)**
24. **Linwood Fisher, 1b, Newburgh (N.Y.) Free Academy**
25. **Raymond Ventura, ss, Seekonk (Mass.) HS**
26. Len Glowzenski, rhp, Mater Dei HS, New Monmouth, N.J.
27. **Robert Wilson, of, William Paterson (N.J.)**
28. **Ronald Spann, 1b, Western Connecticut State**
29. Paul Caffrey, of, Seton Hall
30. **Pete Lancaster, c, Ouachita Baptist**
31. Bill Simpson, ss, Cleveland HS, Portland, Ore.
32. John Varga, 2b/ss, Seattle
33. **Tim Wanner, 3b, Denver**

June—Secondary Phase (13)

1. **Joe Barkauskas, c, Lafayette (Pa.)**
2. Greg Van Gaver, rhp, Bellevue (Wash.) CC
3. **Brian Stone, of, Sacramento, Calif.**

OAKLAND ATHLETICS

January—Regular Phase (21)

1. Charles Hendrix, rhp, Grossmont (Calif.) JC
2. Sylvester Washington, of/1b, Los Angeles CC
3. Marvin Thompson, ss/of, Rio Hondo (Calif.) JC
4. **Joe Lindsey, c/of, Compton, Calif.**
5. Don Lewis, of, Claremont-Mudd (Calif.)
6. Robert Franks, rhp, Glendale (Calif.) JC
7. Chris Wibberly, rhp, El Camino (Calif.) JC
8. **David Love, rhp, San Bernardino Valley (Calif.) JC**
9. Rich Dauer, ss/2b, San Bernardino Valley (Calif.) JC
10. **Bob Lacey Jr., lhp, Central Arizona JC**
11. Greg Motter, rhp, Imperial Valley (Calif.) JC

January—Secondary Phase (13)

1. Steve Trella, rhp, Fullerton (Calif.) JC
2. Bill Hobbs, of, Fullerton (Calif.) JC
3. Gary Anglin, lhp, Ventura (Calif.) JC
4. Steven Ingram, rhp, Glendale (Ariz.) CC

June—Regular Phase (22)

1. **Chet Lemon, ss, Fremont HS, Los Angeles**
2. Garrett Strong, of, Fontana (Calif.) HS
3. Jim Willis, 1b, The Dalles (Ore.) HS
4. Ken McKinney, 3b, Hazelgreen (Ala.) HS
5. R.J. Harrison, c, Milliken HS, Long Beach
6. **Tim Indie, rhp, Camarillo (Calif.) HS**
7. **Clarence Harrell, rhp, Montevallo HS, Wilton, Ala.**
8. **Jack Bastable, 3b/c, Missouri**
9. Dennis Littlejohn, c, North Torrance (Calif.) HS
10. Richard Olson, c, Washington HS, Fresno
11. Don Saulnier, lhp, Waltham (Mass.) HS
12. **Chris Batton, rhp, St. Bernards HS, Los Angeles**
13. David Gronlund, 3b, Norte Vista HS, Riverside, Calif.
14. **Ricky Tronerud, rhp/of, Hoover HS, San Diego**
15. Bob Pate, 3b/of, Compton HS, Gardena, Calif.
16. **Randy Taylor, rhp, Antelope Valley HS, Lancaster, Calif.**
17. **John Brownlee, rhp, South Wichita (Kan.) HS**
18. Jim Rollins, rhp, Glendale (Calif.) HS
19. Chester Franklin, ss, Channel Isles HS, Oxnard, Calif.
20. Bob Mosco, ss, Ganesha HS, Pomona, Calif.
21. James Chellis, c, Bishop Hartley HS, Columbus, Ohio
22. David Hamilton, of, Locke HS, Los Angeles
23. **Ken Templeton, of, Santa Ana (Calif.) Valley HS**
24. Ray Anderson, 2b/ss, Bonita HS, Claremont, Calif.
25. Cliff Goodknight, rhp, Venice (Calif.) HS
26. Dennis Sherow, of, Compton (Calif.) HS
27. Mark Davison, rhp/of, Kennedy HS, Buena Park, Calif.
28. **Thomas Tessar, rhp/c, Central Missouri State**
29. **Charles Barnes, of, Dominguez HS, Compton, Calif.**
30. **Dennis Root, lhp, Cal Poly Pomona**
31. **Albert Curtis, ss, Sir Francis Drake HS, Mill Valley, Calif.**
32. Ronald Ward, inf, El Cerrito HS, Richmond, Calif.

June—Secondary Phase (24)

1. John Pierson, of, Glendale (Ariz.) CC

PHILADELPHIA PHILLIES

January—Regular Phase (4)

1. **Ricky Knepper, 3b, Boonsboro, Md.**
2. **Ernest Gonzalez, of, Polk (Fla.) CC**
3. Brad Hanson, ss, Valencia (Fla.) CC
4. Tom Gallo, rhp/of, Ulster (N.Y.) CC
5. Michael Jacobsen, 2b, Fresno CC
6. Michael Lucide, of, Diablo Vallley (Calif.) JC

January—Secondary Phase (22)

1. **Mark Rott, c/of, Diablo Valley (Calif.) JC**
2. Keath Chauncey, of, Polk (Fla.) CC
3. **Randy Delerio, c, West Hills (Calif.) JC**
4. Mike Girazian, rhp, Fresno CC
5. **Charles Franklin, 3b, Encino, Calif.**

June—Regular Phase (3)

1. **Larry Christenson, rhp, Marysville (Wash.) HS**
2. **Tom Underwood, lhp, Kokomo (Ind.) HS**
3. **Rickey White, 2b, Fresno HS**
4. **John Guarnaccia, of, Downers Grove (Ill.) HS**
5. **Elliott Morton, c, Peachtree HS, Atlanta**
6. **Bill Nahorodny, c, St. Clair County (Mich.) CC**
7. **Randal Hill, lhp, Bryan Adams HS, Dallas**
8. Wayne Krenchicki, ss, Ewing HS, Ewing Township, N.J.
9. **Kevin Bryant, 3b, Florida Southern**
10. **Ronald DeFeo, 3b, Bridgeport**
11. **Eddie Grime, lhp, Archbold (Ohio) HS**
12. Randy Davidson, 2b, Columbia State (Tenn.) CC
13. Kerry Getter, rhp, Pennsylvania
14. **Jeff Wilson, c/of, McLane HS, Fresno, Calif.**
15. **William Dennis, lhp/of, Havre De Grace (Md.) HS**
16. **James Meerpohl, rhp, Bowling Green State**
17. **Billy Beverly, lhp, Georgiana (Ala.) HS**
18. **Walt Stolzenthaler, of, Staten Island (N.Y.)**
19. **Rex Carrow, 2b, Michigan State**
20. David Lockett, rhp, Cleburne (Texas) HS
21. **Matthew Allison, of, Morris Knolls HS, Denville, N.J.**
22. **Dennis Lee, of, Cleburne (Texas) HS**
23. **Pat McCoy, rhp, Northern Colorado**
24. William Zisk, rhp/of, Roseville (Calif.) HS
25. Raymond Kennett, rhp, Tulsa

June—Secondary Phase (17)

1. Dan Boitano, rhp, Fresno CC
2. Richard Davidson, c, Columbia State (Tenn.) CC

PITTSBURGH PIRATES

January—Regular Phase (24)

1. Dennis Bolden, rhp, Chipola (Fla.) JC
2. **David Gaynor, 1b, New Mexico Highlands**
3. Joel Misler, rhp, Miami-Dade North CC
4. Jerry Goode, rhp, Bayonne, N.J.
5. Jim Morrison, 3b, South Georgia JC
6. Ken Donaldson, c, Bellevue (Wash.) CC
7. Alan Drechsler, lhp, Monroe (N.Y.) CC
8. Michael Kirkpatrick, rhp, Bucks County (Pa.) CC
9. Joe Blandford, of, Charles County (Md.) CC
10. Michael McGuire, of, Cornell
11. Tom Holliday, c, Yavapai (Ariz.) JC

January—Secondary Phase (4)

1. **Richard Anderson, rhp, New Haven (Conn.)**
2. **Gerard Thomas, lhp, Scranton, Pa.**

3. Doug Farrell, rhp/of, Niagara (N.Y.)
4. Don Fisher, lhp, Polk (Fla.) CC
5. Keith Metheny, rhp, Green River (Wash.) CC
6. John Paul, c, Lemont Furnace, Pa.
7. **Larry Demery, rhp, Los Angeles CC**

June—Regular Phase (23)

1. **Dwayne Peltier, ss, Servite HS, Anaheim**
2. **John Candelaria, lhp, La Salle Academy, Brooklyn**
3. John Poloni, lhp, Lutheran West HS, Allen Park, Mich.
4. **Tim Jones, rhp, Ponderosa HS, El Dorado Hills, Calif.**
5. Gary Anderson, rhp, Thornridge HS, South Holland, Ill.
6. **Ken Macha, 1b/3b, Pittsburgh**
7. **Willie Randolph, ss/c, Tilden HS, Brooklyn, N.Y.**
8. **Michael Redden, rhp, Brother Rice HS, Chicago**
9. **Robert Mazur, of, Charleroi (Pa.) HS**
10. Scott Gunderson, rhp, Marysville HS, Stanwood, Wash.
11. Michael Cones, ss, San Jacinto (Texas) JC
12. Craig Allegrezza, rhp, Milford (Mass.) HS
13. **Kim West, rhp, West Virginia**
14. **Mike Skinner, of/3b, Potomac State (W.Va.) JC**
15. **Michael Gipaya, lhp, St. Louis HS, Honolulu**
16. **William Estes, lhp, Rockford, Ill.**
17. **Ray Castaldi, of, St. James HS, Parkside, Pa.**
18. **Tim Flaherty, rhp, Rockville (Conn.) HS**
19. **Wayne Eckert, 3b, Goose Creek HS, Hanahan, S.C.**
20. **Robert Rudi, rhp, South Philadelphia (Pa.) HS**
21. **Alan Albert, lhp, Clear Springs (Md.) HS**
22. John Hoffman, rhp, Snohomish HS, Lake Stevens, Wash.
23. **Michael Busby, ss, Bessemer (Ala.) HS**
24. **Charles Janes, rhp, Dartmouth**
25. **Michael Gonzalez, rhp, Kelly HS, Chicago**
26. **Paul Burton, lhp, Villanova**
27. **Joel Sexton, rhp, Louisiana State**
28. **Butch Alberts, 3b, Cincinnati**
29. Richard Hudson, rhp, Century (Fla.) HS
30. **Larry Snowden, lhp/of, Monroe County HS, Monroeville, Ala.**
31. Evan Edge, c, Gadsden (Ala.) HS
32. Brian Bochow, ss, Duke
33. Stan Boskovich, lhp, Albert Aallatin HS, Masontown, Pa.
34. Mike Gannon, c, Central Washington
35. **Michael Burgess, rhp, Lee HS, Baytown, Texas**
36. Doug Zimmerman, c, Slippery Rock (Pa.)
37. **Luther Wrenn, of, Seymour (Ind.) HS**
38. Doug Zavodny, of, McKinley HS, Buffalo, N.Y.
39. Jerome Yankrick, lhp/1b, Greater Latrobe HS, Hostetter, Pa.
40. Gil Kubski, 3b, Granada Hills (Calif.) HS

June—Secondary Phase (23)

1. Jim Morrison, 3b, South Georgia JC
2. **Dennis Simon, rhp, Findleyville, Pa.**
3. Donald Fisher, lhp, Polk (Fla.) CC

ST. LOUIS CARDINALS

January—Regular Phase (22)

1. Bob Gerdes, rhp, Miami-Dade South CC
2. John Eicholtz, rhp, Fresno CC
3. Mark Klein, rhp, Broward (Fla.) CC
4. Charles Ellis, of, Los Angeles Valley JC
5. Richard Chapman, rhp/1b, St. Petersburg (Fla.) JC
6. Mel Washington, c/of, Los Angeles Valley JC
7. Keith Smith, of, Manatee (Fla.) JC
8. **Collier Black, rhp, Middle Georgia JC**

January—Secondary Phase (18)

1. Dan Boitano, rhp, Fresno CC
2. **Scott Torosian, rhp, Fresno CC**
3. Ricardo Fuentes, ss, Miami-Dade North CC
4. **William Poe, rhp, Pontiac, Mich.**

June—Regular Phase (21)

1. **Dan Larson, rhp, Alhambra (Calif.) HS**
2. **Gary Blackwell, ss, Rains HS, Mobile, Ala.**
3. **John Crider, of, Carlsbad (N.M.) HS**
4. Dave Bialas, c, Bellaire (Texas) HS
5. **Rick Hetherington, ss, Fresno HS**
6. **Tommy Washington, ss, Snyder (Texas) HS**
7. **Ray Scott, lhp, Hardaway HS, Columbus, Ga.**
8. **Fred McGaha, of/inf, Louisiana Tech**
9. **Mike Proly, rhp, St. John's**
10. **Dan Radison, inf/c, Southern Illinois**
11. **Lawrence Aubel, rhp, South Alabama**
12. **Rick Simmons, rhp, Idaho**
13. Chris Lynch, rhp, Columbus HS, Miami
14. **Michael Camuso, rhp, Lowell (Mass.)**
15. **David Proffitt, lhp, Mississippi State**
16. Harold Harsh, of, Blairsville (Pa.) HS
17. **Gary Hernandez, 1b/of, California**
18. Steve King, c, Hoggard HS, Wilmington, N.C.
19. Danny Starr, c/rhp, White Station HS, Memphis
20. **James Gorton, rhp, Manhattan**
21. **John Jacobs, of, Metropolis (Ill.) Community HS**
22. Michael Hill, rhp, Puxico (Miss.) HS
23. Michael Murphy, rhp, Hoover HS, Fresno
24. **Bert Nordstrom, rhp, Humboldt State (Calif.)**
25. **James Romanosky, rhp, Columbia**
26. Ted Milton, of, Mississippi State
27. Phil Willingham, 2b, Satsuma HS, Saraland, Ala.
28. **William Bird, inf, Edgewood HS, West Covina, Calif.**
29. **Stan Allison, ss, Central HS, Little Rock, Ark.**
30. James Martinez, c, Cosumnes River (Calif.) JC
31. **Blake Zimmerman, c, Weber State**
32. **Philip McCollough, rhp, Harriman (Tenn.) HS**
33. Greg Wolk, rhp, Crystal City (Mo.) HS
34. **Patrick Hamman, rhp, Canoga Park (Calif.) HS**
35. **Joseph Kubeck, rhp, Springfield (Mass.)**
36. **Johnny Glenn, of/2b, Arizona**
37. Robert Matzenbacher, of, Marissa (Ill.) HS
38. Charles Mitchell, of, Barstow (Calif.) CC
39. Steve Allietta, ss/2b, Lawrence HS, Falmouth, Mass.
40. **Bruce Henderson, 1b, Long Island**
41. Joseph Rezzuti, of, Northeastern

June—Secondary Phase (21)

1. Ray Humphries, rhp, San Bernardino Valley (Calif.) JC

SAN DIEGO PADRES

January—Regular Phase (2)

1. **Cliff Butcher, rhp, Tulsa**
2. **Mike Heftner, lhp, Southern Colorado**
3. Clarence Poitier, 3b/2b, Miami-Dade South CC

January—Secondary Phase (6)

1. **Rich Troedson, lhp, Santa Clara**
2. **Mark Servais, 2b, St. Mary's (Minn.)**

June—Regular Phase (1)

1. **Dave Roberts, 3b, Oregon**
2. **Michael Allen, rhp, Marple-Newtown HS, Newtown Square, Pa.**
3. **Gary Walls, ss, Birmingham HS**
4. **Charles Brown, of, South Leake HS, Walnut Grove, Miss.**
5. **Randy Jones, lhp, Chapman (Calif.)**
6. **Bill Hall, 2b, Virginia**
7. **Edward Arkema, rhp, Morton East HS, Cicero, Ill.**
8. **Don Leege, c, Furman**
9. Dave Heaverlo, rhp, Central Washington
10. **Jerry Turner, of, Venice HS, Culver City, Calif.**
11. Stephen Conley, rhp, Deering HS, Portland, Maine
12. **Rusty Gerhardt, lhp, Clemson**
13. Dennis Whitehead, c, South Alabama
14. Guy Todd, rhp, Richfield HS, Waco, Texas
15. **Thomas Armstrong, 2b, Denver**
16. **William Dorsey, rhp, Fitch HS, Mystic, Conn.**
17. **Craig Bromann, rhp, Denver**
18. **Gary Phillips, 3b/of, Helix HS, Lemon Grove, Calif.**
19. Marvin Owen, of, San Diego State

June—Secondary Phase (5)

1. Warren Cromartie, of, Miami-Dade North CC

SAN FRANCISCO GIANTS

January—Regular Phase (20)

1. **Ken Kollmeyer, lhp, San Diego CC**
2. **Reggie Walton, 1b, Compton (Calif.) JC**
3. Mike Labare, of, Bakersfield (Calif.) JC
4. Craig Cornwell, rhp, Pasadena (Calif.) CC
5. **James Emery, lhp, JC of San Mateo (Calif.)**
6. Harold Sinclair, 3b, Bee County (Texas) JC
7. **Barry Moss, of, Pierce (Calif.) JC**
8. Kevin Darke, p, Chaffey (Calif.) JC
9. Lou Irwin, p, JC of the Sequoias (Calif.)
10. Mark Hance, 1b, Bakersfield (Calif.) JC
11. Michael Turk, 1b, Vallejo (Calif.) JC
12. Michael Supernak, p, Miami-Dade North CC
13. Jeff Bartelt, p, Treasure Valley (Ore.) CC
14. Greg Brinkley, of, Treasure Valley (Ore.) CC
15. **Henry Jones, inf, Lower Columbia (Wash.) JC**

January—Secondary Phase (12)

1. **Ken Roberts, rhp, El Camino (Calif.) JC**
2. **Gary Alexander, c, Los Angeles Harbor JC**
3. Joe Barkauskas, c, Lafayette (Pa.)
4. Terry Farmer, rhp, Chipola (Fla.) JC
5. John Pierson, of, Glendale (Ariz.) CC
6. **Seldon Morton, 1b/lhp, Skyline (Calif.) JC**
7. Lamar Jones, rhp, DeKalb (Ga.) JC

June—Regular Phase (19)

1. **Rob Dressler, rhp, Madison HS, Portland, Ore.**
2. **Bob Knepper, lhp, Calistoga (Calif.) HS**
3. Mike Kirkland, 3b, Pasadena (Texas) HS
4. **Jerry Scarcella, rhp, Walt Whitman HS, Huntington Station, N.Y.**
5. **Joe Meade, inf, Chandler (Ariz.) HS**
6. James Crosta, ss, Union (N.J.) HS
7. Brian Asselstine, of/inf, Hancock (Calif.) JC
8. **William Adams, c, Rider**
9. **R.J. Englert, of, Texas A&M**
10. John Racanelli, p, Terra Nova HS, Pacifica, Calif.
11. **Tim Bull, 1b/of, St. Louis CC-Meramec**
12. **Tim Day, c, San Jose State**
13. Orlando Gonzalez, 1b, Miami-Dade South CC
14. Lenn Sakata, 2b, Treasure Valley (Ore.) CC
15. **Don Greenough, lhp, Oregon**
16. **John Harrison, of, Los Angeles Pierce JC**
17. Isaac Giminez, ss, Bronx (N.Y.) CC
18. **Thomas O'Donnell, lhp, Arroyo HS, El Monte, Calif.**
19. Paul Parker, p, Montclair State (N.J.)
20. John Lacey, 1b, Bergenfield (N.J.) HS
21. Mike Gillespie, p, Iowa State
22. **Charles Polk, of, Narbonne HS, Harbor City, Calif.**
23. **Roger Rasmussen, rhp, Monrovia HS, Newport Beach, Calif.**
24. **Ed Halicki, rhp, Monmouth**
25. Robert Alonzo, inf, Hayden HS, Phoenix
26. Doug Cushman, p, Lee HS, Springfield, Va.
27. Roberto Ayala, 3b, Chandler (Ariz.) HS
28. Michael Younce, ss, Millington (Tenn.) HS
29. **William Binder, c, Princeton**
30. Thomas Boutin, of, Melvindale (Mich.) HS
31. **Harlan Highfill, rhp, Central HS, Little Rock, Ark.**
32. Jackie Johnson, ss, Salem (N.J.) CC
33. **Wendell Stephens, rhp, Los Angeles CC**
34. **Richard Glazebrook, 1b, Arizona State**
35. **Gene Lanthorn, p, Oregon College of Education**
36. **Ken Conlin, ss, Eastern Washington**
37. Ray Mallott, of, Findlay
38. William Przygocki, rhp, Central HS, Bay City, Mich.
39. Rick Burley, lhp, San Jacinto (Texas) JC
40. Peter Cervantes, c/3b, Lincoln HS, Los Angeles
41. Reland McFadden, 1b, Evander Child HS, Bronx, N.Y.
42. Stan Jakubowski, rhp, Union (N.J.) HS
43. Rogelio Dominguez, of/c, Miami HS
44. **Greg Brust, 3b, Arizona State**
45. **Mike Rupcich, c, Arizona State**
46. **Carl Wesley, of, East Texas Baptist**

June—Secondary Phase (19)

1. **Lewis Reasonover, ss, Gulf Coast (Fla.) CC**
2. **Jeff McKay, rhp, Treasure Valley (Ore.) CC**
3. Sylvester Washington, of/1b, Los Angeles CC
4. **Terry Cornutt, rhp, Linn-Benton (Ore.) CC**
5. Craig Cornwell, rhp, Pasadena (Calif.) CC

TEXAS RANGERS

January—Regular Phase (3)

1. James Owen, rhp, San Jose CC
2. **Vincent Ujdur, c, Diablo Valley (Calif.) JC**
3. Bob Tompkins, p, Mesa (Ariz.) CC
4. James Lacey, inf/rhp, Cabrillo (Calif.) JC

January—Secondary Phase (15)

1. **Charles Bordes, ss, Southwestern Louisiana**
2. Ron Bell, rhp, Fullerton (Calif.) JC
3. Michael Rankin, c, Columbia State (Tenn.) CC
4. Ray Forgie, rhp, Mesa (Ariz.) CC
5. Robin Ogle, 1b, Miami-Dade South CC

June—Regular Phase (4)

1. **Roy Howell, 3b, Lompoc (Calif.) HS**
2. **Ron Pruitt, c/of, Michigan State**
3. **Jeff Scott, rhp/c, Eastridge-Kankakee HS, St. Anne, Ill.**
4. **Brian Doyle, ss, Caverna HS, Cave City, Ky.**
5. Rich Wortham, lhp, Odessa (Texas) HS
6. **Mel Barrow, inf, Harlan HS, Chicago**
7. Mark Ackerman, rhp, Sunny Hills HS, Fullerton, Calif.
8. Jim Sundberg, c, Iowa
9. Steve Correll, rhp, Blue Island HS, New Ringgold, Pa.
10. **Wayne Popiolek, rhp, Reavis HS, Chicago**
11. Bo McLaughlin, rhp, Amelia (Ohio) HS
12. Robert Allinder, of, Truman HS, Independence, Mo.
13. George Frazier, rhp, Hillcrest HS, Springfield, Mo.
14. Gil Rondon, rhp, DeWitt Clinton HS, New York
15. Perry Pryor, rhp, Evans HS, Orlando
16. **Charles Fowke, ss, Manatee (Fla.) JC**
17. Donnelly Douglas, lhp, Amherst (Mass.)
18. Sam Leonard, rhp, St. Michaels HS, Royal Oak, Mich.
19. **Bobby Thompson, ss, Harding HS, Charlotte**
20. Dennis Thornbury, lhp, Palomar (Calif.) JC
21. **Mark Mullen, c, Amelia (Ohio) HS**
22. Garry Hancock, of, Brandon HS, Seffner, Fla.
23. **James Pascarella, 2b, New Haven (Conn.)**
24. Wesley Goodale, rhp, Forest Hills HS, West Palm Beach, Fla.
25. **Mike Hargrove, 1b, Northwestern Oklahoma State**
26. Tom Farias, rhp, American International
27. **Stephen Cartier, of, Jupiter (Fla.) HS**
28. Michael Collodi, of/c, Colorado School of Mines
29. Brian Herosian, lhp/1b, Connecticut
30. **James Raynor, rhp, Rollins (Fla.)**
31. Larry Sisk, of, Gardner-Webb
32. **Lawrence Chapman, ss/rhp, Fort Pierce (Fla.) Central HS**
33. Joseph Setticase, of, Miami HS
34. James Brittain, c, Escambia HS, Pensacola, Fla.
35. Edward Mock, rhp, Escambia HS, Pensacola, Fla.
36. **Kevin Murtha, 1b, St. Mary's**
37. Samuel Thomas, rhp, Chamberlain HS, Tampa
38. Barry Redmond, ss, Brandon HS, Seffner, Fla.
39. **Joseph LaRocca, 1b, Notre Dame**
40. **Nelson King, rhp/of, Colorado School of Mines**
41. **Bill Skeens, of/rhp, Indian Hills HS, Oakland, N.J.**
42. Jack Rhine, c, Florida Southern
43. John Butler, of, Miami-Dade South CC
44. Richard Mallman, rhp, Prospect HS, Saratoga, Calif.

June—Secondary Phase (4)

1. Ron Bell, rhp, Fullerton (Calif.) JC
2. Mike Stanton, rhp, Miami-Dade South CC
3. Ron Herring, rhp, Chipola (Fla.) JC
4. **Keith Smith, of, Manatee (Fla.) JC**
5. Terry Farmer, rhp, Chipola (Fla.) JC
6. William Meyer, ss, Indian River (Fla.) CC
7. Mike Siani, ss, Villanova

1973 NO. 1 PICK CLYDE LEADS PARADE OF QUICK MAJOR LEAGUE DEBUTS, BUT CLASS LACKS OVERALL QUALITY

David Clyde was 18. A Texan. Baseball's No. 1 draft pick. The most gifted young pitcher to come along in years. To Rangers owner Bob Short, he was like a gift from heaven.

Three weeks after Clyde completed what may have been the greatest high school pitching career ever, Short auditioned his prized lefthander against the Twins. With bands, amusement shows and grass-skirted dancers as a backdrop, Clyde's June 27 debut was a smashing success, both artistically and financially.

Clyde walked the first two hitters in the first inning, then struck out the side. He pitched five innings and allowed only one hit. He flashed his 95 mph fastball. He won.

Most important to Short, at least, Clyde's debut marked the first sellout since the struggling Rangers franchise moved from Washington, D.C., after the 1971 season. For the first time, people were talking about baseball instead of the Dallas Cowboys.

"We needed something like this to stay in business," Short said after Clyde wowed a sellout crowd of 35,698. "You don't want to read too much into one five-inning performance, but we think David is the kind of player the people of this area can identify with. He's young, he's a Texan, and a winner.

"Isn't it ironic that it took an 18-year-old high school pitching star to pack the house even when the debut of major league baseball two years ago wouldn't do it?"

No debut in draft history attracted more attention. Clyde, signed for a reported $125,000, was featured in Sports Illustrated before he was drafted.

At Houston's Westchester High, Clyde went 18-0 as a senior and struck out a high school record 328 batters in 148 innings. For his career, Clyde was 53-13, 0.65. He struck out a national-record 843 in 475 innings.

"The pressure on the 18-year-old kid was tremendous," then-Rangers manager Whitey Herzog said. "We held up the game for 30 minutes to let the crowd in. At 18, he was as good as any kid I ever saw, including Nolan Ryan, Gary Gentry, Jon Matlack and Tug McGraw."

Clyde wasn't the only draft pick from 1973 to debut in the big leagues.

Days after Dave Winfield was named Most Outstanding Player of the College World Series with Minnesota, the Padres started him at the major league level. The Twins did the same July 4 with their No. 1 pick, lefthander Eddie Bane, who like Clyde attracted a sellout crowd to his debut.

Better known as a pitcher in college, Dave Winfield hit his way to the Hall of Fame

Winfield is one of the greatest athletes ever drafted. By the time the 6-foot-6 Minnesota product was selected by the Padres, he had already been drafted by the NBA, ABA and NFL. And he was better known as a pitcher coming out of college than as an outfielder. In fact it was for two remarkable pitching feats that he was saluted as the CWS hero, though he hit .467 at Omaha.

And it was his bat that intrigued the Padres. As a senior, Winfield hit .385 with eight homers and 33 RBIs in 43 games. He went on to collect 3,110 hits and 465 homers in 22 major league seasons on his way to the Hall of Fame.

Scouts agreed that Clyde was head and shoulders above the rest of the talent in the '73 draft, even though his career never measured up to the three players who were selected after him: all-stars John Stearns, Robin Yount and Winfield.

"You have Clyde far above everybody else and then there's a big dropoff down to whatever comes after him," said Lou Fitzgerald, the Southwest area scout for the Phillies, who picked second. "We'd love to have him, but we don't see any way Texas can pass him by. Everybody I've talked to said he is by far the best talent available."

Veteran Pirates scout Howie Haak also saw Clyde

and was convinced he was the real thing. "His curve is outstanding," Haak said before the draft. "His fastball is better than a great many pitchers in the major leagues today. In fact, it is my opinion that this boy could pitch in the major leagues right now."

Led by Clyde and Winfield, the top four picks in the June regular phase reached the big leagues faster than any quartet in history. Yount was 18 when he opened the 1974 season at shortstop for the Brewers. Stearns, a power-hitting catcher from the University of Colorado, was up with Philadelphia later in the '74 season.

Stearns had led the nation's collegiate ranks with 15 home runs and an .819 slugging percentage in 1973, while hitting .413. He was also an all-Big Eight Conference safety who was drafted by the Buffalo Bills earlier in the year.

Despite the abundance of talent at the top, the 1973 draft was one of the leanest ever. A record-low 107 players selected in June reached the big leagues. There was growing concern among baseball officials that overall talent was beginning to dry up, as only 785 players were selected. That total would bottom out a year later.

Philadelphia had the first pick in both the regular and secondary phases of the January draft and scooped up the two players who would have been first-round picks in June had they elected to return to school. In the regular phase, the Phillies went for shortstop Alan Bannister, Arizona State's two-time All-American. In the secondary phase, the Phils landed righthander Dick Ruthven, who got $80,000 to sign. He was Minnesota's No. 1 pick the previous June as a junior, but went unsigned and chose not to return to Fresno State.

Two selections after the Phillies took Ruthven, the Cubs selected righthander Donnie Moore, who became one of the game's top relievers. Moore's 14-year major league career ended in 1988 and a year later he committed suicide, blamed largely on his depression after giving up the last-strike home run to Boston's Dave Henderson in the 1985 American League Championship Series for the Angels.

Southern California won its fourth consecutive College World Series in 1973, beating Arizona State in the championship game, 4-3, for the second year in a row. The Trojans featured righthander Randy Scarbery (15-2, 1.83), the first player of the draft era to be selected in the first round of the June regular phase twice. He was drafted by Oakland after rejecting an $85,000 offer from Houston out of high school three years earlier.

USC outfielder Fred Lynn was a second-round pick, an obvious oversight considering he became the American League MVP just two years later. Scouts backed off on Lynn during his junior season when he failed to hit .300, and his home run production fell from 14 to seven.

DRAFT 73: FIRST-ROUND PICKS

No.	Club	Player, Pos.	School	Hometown	Ht.	Wt.	B-T	Age
1.	Rangers	David Clyde, lhp	Westchester HS	Houston	6-1	180	L-L	18
2.	Phillies	John Stearns, c	Colorado	Denver	6-0	195	R-R	21
3.	Brewers	Robin Yount, ss	Taft HS	Woodland Hills, Calif.	6-0	165	R-R	17
4.	Padres	Dave Winfield, rhp/of	Minnesota	St. Paul, Minn.	6-6	195	R-R	21
5.	Indians	Glenn Tufts, 1b	Raynham HS	Bridgewater, Mass.	6-3	200	R-R	18
6.	Giants	Johnnie LeMaster, ss	Paintsville HS	Paintsville, Ky.	6-3	165	R-R	17
7.	Angels	Billy Taylor, of	Windsor Forest HS	Savannah, Ga.	5-11	190	L-R	18
8.	Expos	Gary Roenicke, ss	Edgewood HS	West Covina, Calif.	6-3	195	R-R	18
9.	Royals	Lew Olsen, rhp	San Ramon HS	Alamo, Calif.	6-5	220	R-R	18
10.	Braves	Pat Rockett, ss	Robert E. Lee HS	San Antonio	5-10	165	R-R	18
11.	Twins	Eddie Bane, lhp	Arizona State	Westminster, Calif.	5-9	160	R-L	21
12.	Cardinals	Joe Edelen, 3b/rhp	Gracemont HS	Gracemont, Okla.	6-0	175	R-R	17
13.	Yankees	Doug Heinhold, rhp	Stroman HS	Victoria, Texas	6-3	175	R-R	19
14.	Mets	Lee Mazzilli, of	Lincoln HS	Brooklyn	6-1	175	B-R	18
15.	Orioles	Mike Parrott, rhp	Camarillo HS	Camarillo, Calif.	6-4	200	R-R	18
16.	Cubs	Jerry Tabb, 1b	Tulsa	Altus, Okla.	6-2	190	L-R	21
17.	Red Sox	Ted Cox, ss	Midwest City HS	Midwest City, Okla.	6-3	190	R-R	18
18.	Dodgers	Ted Farr, c	Shadle Park HS	Spokane, Wash.	6-0	187	R-R	18
19.	Tigers	Charles Bates, 1b	Cal State Los Angeles	Los Angeles	6-0	210	B-R	21
20.	Astros	Calvin Portley, ss	Longview HS	Longview, Texas	5-10	165	R-R	18
21.	White Sox	Steve Swisher, c	Ohio	Parkersburg, W.Va.	6-2	200	R-R	21
22.	Reds	Charles Kessler, of	Claremont HS	Claremont, Calif.	6-1	200	R-R	17
23.	Athletics	Randy Scarbery, rhp	Southern California	Fresno	6-1	180	R-R	20
24.	Pirates	Steve Nicosia, c	North Miami Beach HS	Miami	5-11	195	R-R	17

1973

CLUB-BY-CLUB SELECTIONS

ATLANTA BRAVES

January—Regular Phase (9)

1. Mike Kirkpatrick, p, Bucks County (Pa.) CC
2. Mike Vernier, 3b, Aquinas (Mich.)
3. Robert Kraft, 1b, Bellevue (Wash.) CC
4. Mike Trifiolis, 1b, Lafayette

January—Secondary Phase (15)

1. **Brian Asselstine, of/inf, Hancock (Calif.) JC**
2. Pete Falcone, lhp, Kingsborough (N.Y.) CC
3. **John Lacey, 1b, Bergen (N.J.) CC**

June—Regular Phase (10)

1. **Pat Rockett, 2b/ss, Robert E. Lee HS, San Antonio, Texas**
2. **Steve Stone, c, Doherty HS, Worcester, Mass.**
3. Jim Gaudet, c, Jesuit HS, New Orleans
4. **Bill Downing, ss, San Francisco**
5. **Paul Wagner, ss, Dickinson**
6. **James Arline, of, Wilby HS, Waterbury, Conn.**
7. Alvin Jones, of, Seguin (Texas) HS
8. Randy Quintrell, lhp, Newton County HS, Covington, Ga.
9. **Greg Kastner, rhp, Missouri Western State**
10. **Roger Cador, of, Southern**
11. Mark Knose, rhp, Harrison (Ohio) HS
12. Gary Atwell, of, Arizona State
13. Charles Phillips, lhp, La Quinta HS, Garden Grove, Calif.
14. **George Ban, c, Kennedy HS, Sacramento**
15. Adam Smith, rhp, Southland Academy, Americus, Ga.
16. **Terry Harper, rhp/of, Douglas County HS, Douglasville, Ga.**
17. Steve Barlow, lhp, Morehouse
18. David Whitehurst, of/rhp, Walker HS, Decatur, Ga.
19. **Larry Bradford, lhp, Clark HS, Chicago**
20. Rick Hays, rhp, Charter Oak HS, Glendora, Calif.
21. Craig Hillard, of, Salisbury (N.C.) HS
22. Steve Barrett, 2b, Murray State
23. **Michael Yates, rhp, Fairfield**
24. **Bobby Malone, c, Sullivan East HS, Piney Flats, Tenn.**
25. **Leland Byrd, ss, Gainesville (Ga.) HS**
26. **William King, rhp, Southwest DeKalb HS, Decatur, Ga.**
27. **John McLean, rhp, Vanderbilt**
28. Mark Hamilton, 1b, North Springs HS, Sandy Springs, Ga.
29. Jim Busby, lhp/of, Leesburg HS, Yahala, Fla.
30. **Anthony Taylor, of, Clark**

June—Secondary Phase (14)

No selection

BALTIMORE ORIOLES

January—Regular Phase (16)

1. **Cleve Reed, of, Southeastern Oklahoma State**
2. **Richard Cuoco, 2b, Los Angeles Valley JC**
3. Martin Fleming, rhp, Cypress (Calif.) JC
4. Jeff Budrick, p, Los Angeles Valley JC
5. Rickey Holoubek, ss, Pasadena (Calif.) CC
6. Mark Lee, rhp, El Camino (Calif.) JC
7. Michael Manns, p, El Camino (Calif.) JC
8. Tom Kotchman, c, Chipola (Fla.) JC
9. Alton Caesar, 3b/of, Sierra (Calif.) JC

January—Secondary Phase (16)

1. **Alfred Aulwurm, lhp, Glendale (Calif.) JC**
2. **John Flinn, rhp, Los Angeles Valley JC**
3. **Gil Rondon, rhp, New York**
4. James Joiner, c, Seminole (Fla.) JC
5. Richard Cahill, p, Mount Hood (Ore.) CC
6. Rufus Cook, 1b, Panola (Texas) JC
7. Don Lyons, 1b, CC of San Francisco
8. Scott Margolin, c, East Los Angeles JC

June—Regular Phase (15)

1. **Mike Parrott, rhp, Camarillo (Calif.) HS**
2. **Jerry Guinn, rhp, Maud (Okla.) HS**
3. **Eddie Murray, c/1b, Locke HS, Los Angeles**
4. **Don Whiting, of, Lincoln HS, San Diego**
5. **Michael Hile, lhp, Venice HS, Los Angeles**
6. **Ricky Ryser, rhp, Texas Wesleyan**
7. **Mike Flanagan, lhp, Massachusetts**
8. Ed Bowman, 3b/c, Southern California
9. **David Obal, c, St. John's College HS, Washington**
10. Steven Ramsey, ss, Westchester HS, Houston
11. Mike Hilderbrandt, c, Woodland (Calif.) HS
12. Kenny Alderman, ss, Radford (Va.) HS
13. Errect Ridley, of, Venice (Calif.) HS
14. Greg Davis, of, Oral Roberts
15. **Russ Peach, lhp, Murray State**
16. **Robert George, rhp, Poly HS, Arleta, Calif.**
17. Jerry Garvin, lhp, Merced (Calif.) HS
18. **Martin Parrill, 3b, Findlay (Ohio)**
19. **Dennis McMillan, rhp, Hermitage HS, Richmond**
20. Brett Terrell, 1b, Bowie (Md.) HS
21. **Michael Perez, rhp, Armijo HS, Fairfield, Calif.**
22. **David Highmark, lhp, Dartmouth**
23. Dan Beitey, rhp, Clark (Wash.) JC
24. **Vernon Snyder, of, Northern HS, Grantsville, Md.**
25. Tim Smith, 3b, Bishop Montgomery HS, Hermosa Beach, Calif.
26. Robert Ehrig, c, Los Angeles Valley JC
27. Robert Davis, lhp, Albemarle (N.C.) JC
28. Chuck Porter, rhp, Perry Hall (Md.) HS

June—Secondary Phase (7)

1. **Doug Wessel, rhp, Vanderbilt**
2. **Richard Cuoco, 2b, Los Angeles Valley JC**
3. James Diventi, rhp, Essex (Md.) CC
4. Bob Pate, 3b/of, Mesa (Ariz.) CC

BOSTON RED SOX

January—Regular Phase (18)

1. Lloyd Thompson, 3b, Blinn (Texas) JC (Selection voided)
2. William Daves, c, Motlow State (Tenn.) CC
3. Brian McCune, p, Clark (Wash.) JC
4. Larry Howser, ss/2b, Manatee (Fla.) JC
5. Ted Updike, 1b, San Diego Mesa JC

January—Secondary Phase (22)

1. Mike Payne, p, Delta State (Miss.)
2. Bob Pate, 3b/of, San Diego Mesa JC
3. Michael Hill, p, Three Rivers (Mo.) CC
4. Kevin Stephenson, p, Seminole (Fla.) JC
5. **Greg McCollum, 1b, Puget Sound (Wash.)**
6. **Mark Kilmurray, ss, New Haven (Conn.)**
7. **Tom Farias, rhp, American International**
8. Glen Smith, ss/3b, Bordentown, N.J.

June—Regular Phase (17)

1. **Ted Cox, ss, Midwest City (Okla.) HS**
2. **Fred Lynn, of, Southern California**
3. **Charles Meyers, 2b, Oklahoma State**
4. **Curran Percival, rhp, Chapman (Calif.)**
5. **Rick Jones, lhp, Forrest HS, Jacksonville, Fla.**
6. **Glenn Bannister, c, Oklahoma**
7. William St. Claire, lhp, Springfield (Mass.) Technical HS
8. **Butch Hobson, 3b, Alabama**
9. **Rick Berg, of, Apple Valley HS, Hesperia, Calif.**
10. **Roswell Brayton, rhp, Harvard**
11. Chris DiLorenzo, rhp, West Rome (Ga.) HS
12. **Barrett Jackson, of/1b, Piscataway HS, Plainfield, N.J.**

13. **Jack Medick, c, Nebraska**
14. **James Lease, rhp, William Carey (Miss.)**
15. Carmen Coppol, rhp, Claymont (Del.) HS
16. **Lanny Phillips, 3b/of, Oklahoma**
17. **James Bodinski, c, North Attleboro (Mass.) HS**
18. Mike Cunico, ss, Pueblo (Colo.) Central HS
19. **Michael Bennett, of, Western Illinois**
20. **Collin Youtz, lhp, Lebanon (Pa.) HS**
21. **Greg Eastin, lhp, Ridge HS, Basking Ridge, N.J.**
22. **Larry Morello, of, Lafayette HS, Brooklyn**

June—Secondary Phase (5)

No selection

CALIFORNIA ANGELS

January—Regular Phase (8)

1. **Randy Smith, p, Three Rivers (Mo.) CC**
2. Marvin Townsend, ss, Albemarle (N.C.) JC
3. Pat Perrino, 3b/c, Henry Ford (Mich.) CC
4. Paul Zobeck, p, Yavapai (Ariz.) JC
5. Larry Eubanks, of, Glendale (Ariz.) CC
6. **Gary Beese, c, Lewis (Ill.)**
7. Len Patterson, c, Laney (Calif.) JC
8. Tim Hurley, 3b/of, Spokane (Wash.) CC
9. Art Bordley, p, El Camino (Calif.) JC
10. Larry Hutton, p, Long Beach CC
11. Clark Maynard, 1b, Greenfield (Mass.) CC

January—Secondary Phase (4)

1. Jeff Feramisco, inf/of, Fresno CC
2. **Mike Overy, rhp, Olivet (Mich.)**
3. **Melvin Washington, c/of, Los Angeles Valley JC**
4. Kevin Carney, c, Burlington, Vt.
5. Ron Ward, inf, Contra Costa (Calif.) JC
6. Ken McKinney, 3b, Columbia State (Tenn.) CC
7. Ken Nelson, of, Stanford
8. James Yaeger, p, Connors State (Okla.) JC
9. Mike Mulligan, c, Chipola (Fla.) JC
10. Ted Milton, of, Mississippi State
11. Tom Rezzuti, of, Northeastern

June—Regular Phase (7)

1. **Billy Taylor, of, Windsor Forest HS, Savannah, Ga.**
2. Bruce Tonascia, of/c, Napa (Calif.) HS
3. **Pat Kelly, c, Santa Maria (Calif.) HS**
4. **Doug Slettvet, rhp, Lakewood (Calif.) HS**
5. **Rob Johnson, of, Lakewood (Calif.) HS**
6. **Steve Brisbin, c, Lakewood (Calif.) HS**
7. Carl Gardner, 3b, Miami-Dade North CC
8. Steve Burke, rhp, Tokay HS, Lodi, Calif.
9. Lee Overton, c, Sacramento HS
10. **Clinton Sander, of, Nathan Hale HS, Seattle**
11. **Lawrence Rush, 1b, Venice HS, Culver City, Calif.**
12. Brian Kingman, rhp, Santa Monica (Calif.) JC
13. **Glenn Prichard, rhp, Verdugo HS, Tugunga, Calif.**
14. **Bob Makoski, 1b, Ohio**
15. Danny Boone, lhp, Cerritos (Calif.) JC
16. Bob DiPietro, lhp, Stanford
17. **Roger Smith, ss, Florida State**
18. Mitchell Delmonico, ss, Napa (Calif.) HS
19. **Rhordick Wallace, of, South San Francisco HS**
20. Brian Rhode, lhp, East HS, Wichita, Kan.
21. Jim Dorsey, rhp, Cleveland HS, Los Angeles
22. Raymond Smith, 1b, Lincoln HS, San Diego
23. **William Berger, 2b, Arizona State**
24. Tim Brill, c, Olney (Pa.) HS
25. **Keith McVicker, ss, Leigh HS, San Jose**
26. **Dean Jelmini, of, Loyola Marymount**
27. Willie McIntyre, of, Hueneme HS, Oxnard, Calif.
28. **Robert Verbeck, c, Missouri Western State**
29. David Farley, rhp, Yucaipa (Calif.) HS
30. Zackary Butler, c, Lee HS, Huntsville, Ala.
31. Wilson Plunkett, of, Southern Mississippi

June—Secondary Phase (21)

1. David Bedrosian, 2b, Fresno CC
2. Kevin Morel, ss, Indian River (Fla.) CC
3. Martin Fleming, rhp, Cypress (Calif.) JC
4. Dennis Sherow, of, Compton, Calif.

CHICAGO CUBS

January—Regular Phase (15)

1. Wayne Benson, inf/of, Ranger (Texas) JC
2. Charles Pfab, inf, Middle Georgia JC
3. **Travis Roberts, rhp, South Georgia JC**

January—Secondary Phase (3)

1. **Donnie Moore, rhp/of, Ranger (Texas) JC**
2. **Lawrence Groover, lhp, Temple (Texas) JC**
3. Paul Levar, p, Spokane Falls (Wash.) CC

June—Regular Phase (16)

1. **Jerry Tabb, 1b, Tulsa**
2. **Darrell Turner, rhp, Ocoee (Fla.) HS**
3. **Earl Chew, of, Temple**
4. **William Burleson, rhp/1b, Pine Bluff (Ark.) HS**
5. **Dave Geisel, lhp/1b, Tonawanda (N.Y.) HS**
6. **Joe Wallis, of, Southern Illinois**
7. **August Juricic, 2b, Joliet (Ill.) Central HS**
8. **Mike Krukow, rhp, Cal Poly San Luis Obispo**
9. **Greg Collins, c, Vanderbilt**
10. Emeel Salem, ss, Mountain Brook (Ala.) HS
11. **Byron Wilkerson, rhp, Harrison HS, Evansville, Ind.**
12. **Stephen Pearsall, of, Assumption (Mass.)**
13. **Byron Loomans, ss, Central (Iowa)**
14. **Steve Haglund, 2b, Cleveland HS, Reseda, Calif.**
15. **Richard Meek, of, Ponderosa HS, Shingle Springs, Calif.**
16. **Kevin Markert, c, Albany (Ga.) HS**
17. **Richard Ware, lhp, Southern Illinois**
18. George Sullivan, rhp, Hueytown (Ala.) HS
19. **Vernon Temple, rhp, Rice**
20. John Barnfield, lhp, Niles North HS, Glenview, Ill.
21. **Stephen Clancy, c, Texas**
22. **Mack Parker, 1b, South Leake HS, Walnut Grove, Miss.**
23. Ralph Chafin, of, Northeast HS, Macon, Ga.
24. Robert Lehtola, ss, Rio Americano HS, Sacramento
25. Michael Giobbi, rhp, Deering HS, Portland, Maine
26. **Richard Poythress, ss, South Georgia JC**
27. **Ken Kral, of, Southern Illinois**
28. **Robbie Hatfield, ss, Mount Pleasant (Texas) JC**
29. Marvin Wooten, 1b, Rocky Mount (N.C.) HS
30. Rocky Thompson, c, Thomas Jefferson HS, San Antonio
31. Vincent Hillyer, lhp, Thayer Academy, Weymouth, Mass.

June—Secondary Phase (9)

1. Ken McKinney, 3b, Yavapai (Ariz.) JC

CHICAGO WHITE SOX

January—Regular Phase (22)

1. **Elmer Yelverton, rhp, UNC Wilmington**
2. **Joseph Hickerson, 2b, North Carolina**
3. **Kenny Bagwell, 2b, Clemson**

January—Secondary Phase (24)

1. Stephen Cook, 3b, Miami-Dade North CC

June—Regular Phase (21)

1. **Steve Swisher, c, Ohio**
2. **Jim Otten, rhp, Arizona State**
3. **Ken Kravec, lhp, Ashland (Ohio)**
4. **William Kautzer, rhp, McKoosa (Wis.) HS**
5. **Curt Minges, 3b, Concord (Calif.) HS**
6. **Robert Palmer, c, Corona del Mar HS, Newport Beach, Calif.**
7. Philip Nerone, 3b, Baldwin HS, Pittsburgh
8. **Manny Estrada, ss/3b, Cal State Los Angeles**
9. Julio Alonso, lhp, Power Memorial HS, Bronx, N.Y.
10. **James Barrett, of, Hillcrest HS, Springfield, Mo.**
11. **Douglas Fortune, of/1b, New Haven (Conn.)**
12. **William Lehman, rhp, Edison HS, Edison Township, N.J.**
13. **Robert Klein, rhp, Memorial HS, Beloit, Wis.**

14. Michael Cross, ss/2b, Oklahoma State
15. **Bobby Tucker, of, Tennessee**
16. Monte Kruse, lhp, Little Rock (Iowa) HS
17. William Tucker, lhp, Bloom HS, Chicago Heights, Ill.
18. **Mike Squires, of/1b, Western Michigan**
19. Andrew Gallo, rhp, Magnolia HS, Anaheim
20. **Jeff Sovern, 3b/c, Central Michigan**
21. Chris Nyman, ss, Cordova HS, Rancho Cordova, Calif.
22. **Michael Wolf, ss, Hart HS, Saugus, Calif.**
23. **Nicholas Medrano, of, Cal State Dominguez Hills**
24. Nicholas Bandow, of, Jacobs HS, Stevens Point, Wis.
25. Don Davis, 3b, Portage (Mich.) Northern HS
26. David Rende, lhp, Eisenhower HS, Blue Island, Ill.
27. Greg Klette, rhp, Washburn HS, Minneapolis
28. **Barry Smith, rhp, Cummings HS, Burlington, N.C.**
29. **Elbert Coulter, lhp, Creiger HS, Chicago**
30. **David Vanderloop, ss, Kaukauna (Wis.) HS**
31. **Don Bridges, rhp, Hoggard HS, Wilmington, N.C.**
32. Glenn Bright, rhp, Western Carolina
33. **Michael Dlugach, c, Memphis State**
34. Randy Davidson, 2b, Columbia State (Tenn.) CC
35. **Donald Miller, rhp, Thornwood HS, South Holland, Ill.**
36. Terry Hough, rhp, Glendale HS, Springfield, Mo.
37. **Phillip Mullen, lhp, Methodist (N.C.)**
38. **Tony Johnson, of, Vallejo (Calif.) HS**
39. Phil Klimas, 3b, Hubbard HS, Chicago
40. Tom Mee, ss/rhp, Prior Lake (Minn.) HS

June—Secondary Phase (11)

1. **Mark Jackson, c, Long Beach CC**

CINCINNATI REDS

January—Regular Phase (21)

1. Gary Lucas, lhp, Riverside (Calif.) CC
2. **Jonathon Ellefson, rhp, North Dakota**
3. John Higgins, of/p, Indian Hills (Iowa) CC
4. Steven Hargest, p, Suffolk County (N.Y.) CC
5. Terry Willis, p, Lake-Sumter (Fla.) CC

January—Secondary Phase (9)

1. **Jeff Chandler, lhp, Sacramento CC**
2. Paul Parker, p, Montclair State (N.J.)
3. Ray Guy, p, Southern Mississippi

June—Regular Phase (22)

1. **Charles Kessler, of, Claremont (Calif.) HS**
2. **Richard Jensen, lhp, Tooele (Utah) HS**
3. **Wallace Williams, c, Merritt Island (Fla.) HS**
4. **Pat Garvey, rhp, Ashtabula (Ohio) HS**
5. **Marlon Styles, c, Aiken HS, Cincinnati**
6. Reed Schielke, lhp, Boulder (Colo.) HS
7. **James Kulina, lhp, Lower Dauphin HS, Hummelstown, Pa.**
8. Stephan Jackson, 2b, Wesleyan Academy, Chatom, Pa.
9. **George Meier, c, Mercy HS, University City, Mo.**
10. **Joseph Nichols, rhp, Central Catholic HS, Pittsburgh**
11. Richard Barrett, rhp, Goochland (Va.) HS
12. Jay Howell, rhp, Fairview HS, Boulder, Colo.
13. **Richard Kuhn, lhp, Swissvale HS, Pittsburgh**
14. Jeff Lang, lhp, McNicholas HS, Cincinnati
15. Alfred Henkel, lhp, Churchland HS, Portsmouth, Va.
16. **Donald Hawkins, c, Buffalo Gap HS, Churchville, Va.**
17. Robert Ferber, of, Sahuaro HS, Tucson
18. **Curtis Runyon, of/inf, Temple (Texas) JC**
19. **James McNeil, rhp, Bacone (Okla.) JC**
20. **Ronald Reagan, of, Southeastern Oklahoma State**
21. Joseph Waugh, of/1b, Barboursville HS, Huntington, W.Va.
22. **John Underwood, rhp, Royal Oak HS, Covina, Calif.**
23. Jeff Scheumack, rhp, Springwoods HS, Houston
24. Phil Bittle, 1b/of, Douglas (Ariz.) HS
25. Paul Downey, lhp, Columbia State (Tenn.) CC
26. Michael Knight, of, Mainland HS, Holly Hills, Fla.
27. **Sammy Heasley, lhp, Lamar (Colo.) CC**
28. **Pierre Lyons, rhp, Riverdale HS, Murfreesboro, Tenn.**
29. **Jerry Rodgers, of, Gonzaga**
30. **George Knowles, rhp, Rider**
31. Chester Czaplicki, rhp, Rider
32. Mark Unsoeld, c, Charter Oak HS, Glendora, Calif.
33. **Rick Colzie, of, Florida State**
34. William Martin, rhp, Shaw HS, Mobile, Ala.

June—Secondary Phase (22)

1. Gary Lucas, lhp, Riverside (Calif.) CC

CLEVELAND INDIANS

January—Regular Phase (6)

1. **James McCutchin, rhp, Level Land, Texas**
2. Jerry Devine, of/inf, Rose State (Okla.) JC
3. Don Sasser, inf/c, Middle Georgia JC
4. William Tiedemann, inf, Yavapai (Ariz.) JC
5. Paul Faulk, of, Seminole (Fla.) JC
6. Danny Howell, c, Brunswick (Ga.) JC
7. James Postel, p, Orange Coast (Calif.) JC

January—Secondary Phase (12)

1. Don Saulnier, p, Massachusetts Bay CC
2. Gene Stohs, lhp/of, Nebraska
3. Manuel Alfonsin, inf/of, Miami-Dade North CC
4. Clyde Lineberry, of, Southwood (Md.) JC
5. Dennis Whitehead, c, South Alabama

June—Regular Phase (5)

1. **Glenn Tufts, inf, Raynham HS, Bridgewater, Mass.**
2. **Tom McMillan, inf, Jacksonville**
3. **Dave Oliver, inf, Cal Poly San Luis Obispo**
4. **Thomas McGouch, rhp, Greater Johnstown (Pa.) HS**
5. **Vassie Gardner, of, Dorsey HS, Los Angeles**
6. **Norman Werd, lhp, Indiana**
7. **Rock Weeks, c, Western HS, Buena Park, Calif.**
8. **Earl Moran, ss, Gulf Coast (Fla.) CC**
9. Gary Ezell, ss/rhp, Elgin (Okla.) HS
10. Les Hemby, c, Blinn (Texas) JC
11. **Don Flanagan, rhp, San Jacinto (Texas) JC**
12. **Joseph Bodine, lhp, Emma Sanson HS, Gadsden, Ala.**
13. **Tim Holden, lhp, Cleveland State**
14. **John Conover, rhp, Humboldt (Calif.) State**
15. **Joseph Cork, ss, Fordham**
16. **Steve Baumiller, rhp, Florida Southern**
17. Stephen Lee, rhp, Hattiesburg (Miss.) HS
18. Tom Hinrichs, 3b, Yuba City (Calif.) HS
19. Dan Walker, rhp, Malone (Ohio)
20. **Robert Daub, c, Hicksville (N.Y.) HS**
21. Donald Carr, rhp/of, Lufkin (Texas) HS
22. Cliff Mays, rhp, Central Catholic HS, Portland, Ore.
23. Danny Miller, rhp/inf, Los Angeles Pierce JC
24. **Curtis Zimmerman, 1b, Tulane**
25. Billy Sorrell, rhp, Andrew HS, High Point, N.C.
26. Mark Wezet, rhp, Evansville (Ind.) Memorial HS
27. Danny Rollin, of, Petal (Miss.) HS
28. Steve Scott, rhp, East Ridge HS, St. Ann, Ill.
29. James Boulter, lhp, King Phillip Regional HS, Norfolk, Mass.
30. Richard Chappell, 3b, Griffith (Ind.) HS
31. Edward Wright, 2b, Churchland HS, Portsmouth, Va.
32. **Stephen Proniewych, 1b, Idaho State**
33. Robert Wilmot, rhp, Clintondale HS, Mount Clemons, Mich.
34. Bradford Hoch, ss/3b, North Florida JC
35. Ron Harrington, c, Petal (Miss.) HS
36. Gary Smith, of, Deering HS, Portland, Maine
37. Vincent Degrouttola, rhp, Rummel HS, Metairie, La.
38. Frank Toups, inf, Brother Martin HS, New Orleans
39. Danny White, inf, Arizona State
40. Douglas Dye, of, Wooster (Ohio)
41. **Wilbert Avery, ss, Baldwin-Wallace (Ohio)**
42. Michael Rachuba, lhp, Start HS, Toledo, Ohio

June—Secondary Phase (15)

1. Alex Pastore, of, South Alabama

DETROIT TIGERS

January—Regular Phase (20)

1. Steve Trella, p, Fullerton (Calif.) JC

2. Dino Hloros, p, St. Clair County (Mich.) CC
3. Larry Graves, p, Washentaw (Mich.) JC
4. Francis Sansosti, p, Essex (Md.) CC

January—Secondary Phase (8)

1. **Larry Ike, rhp, Michigan State**
2. Gary Kennedy, of, Brewton-Parker (Ga.) JC
3. Phil Vaden, p, Detroit

June—Regular Phase (19)

1. **Charles Bates, 3b, Cal State Los Angeles**
2. **Kevin Slattery, ss, Oceanside (N.Y.) HS**
3. **Bob Adams, 3b, UCLA**
4. **Robert Trudo, of, Brookfield HS, Masury, Ohio**
5. **Michael Elders, rhp, Clay HS, Oregon, Ohio**
6. **Greg Shippy, c, Garrett HS, Auburn, Ind.**
7. Robert Stadnika, rhp, Eisenhower HS, Saginaw, Mich.
8. **Elliott Moore, lhp, Michigan State**
9. **Joseph Simbolick, c, Seymour (Conn.) HS**
10. Joseph Carroll, rhp, Rogers HS, Tulsa, Okla.
11. Ken Gregory, of, North Plainfield (N.J.) HS
12. **Michael Ray, rhp, Cairo (Ga.) HS**
13. Charlie Puleo, rhp, Bloomfield (N.J.) HS
14. **Ronald Jones, of, Highland Park (Mich.) HS**
15. **Thomas Butler, ss, Texas Christian**
16. **Curtis Morgan, 1b, Western HS, Detroit**
17. **Thomas Walko, of, Cardinal Mooney HS, Poland, Ohio**
18. Michael St. Louis, lhp, Ithaca (N.Y.)
19. **Anthony Jonas, of, Long Island**
20. **Charles Moore, c, Northeast HS, Macon, Ga.**
21. **William Madden, rhp, St. Joseph's HS, Pittsfield, Mass.**
22. **Michael Hughes, lhp, Lamar**
23. **Roy Marks, rhp, Parsons (Iowa)**
24. **Jeff Bouton, rhp, Monmouth**
25. Richard Flynn, rhp, Keyport HS, Union Beach, N.J.
26. Richard Sherkel, c, Penn State
27. Frederick Petersen, rhp, Commack (N.Y.) South HS
28. **Fred Swanson, of, Pine River HS, Tustin, Mich.**

June—Secondary Phase (23)

No selection

HOUSTON ASTROS

January—Regular Phase (19)

1. Robert Nickeson, ss, West Valley (Calif.) JC

January—Secondary Phase (5)

1. **Mike Stanton, rhp, Miami-Dade South CC**
2. Donald Broom, of, McNeese State

June—Regular Phase (20)

1. **Calvin Portley, ss, Longview (Texas) HS**
2. **Scott Gregory, rhp, Palos Verdes HS, Palos Verdes Estates, Calif.**
3. **David Aloi, rhp, Edgewood HS, West Covina, Calif.**
4. **Michael Jones, of, Fremont HS, Inglewood, Calif.**
5. **Mike Mendoza, rhp, McClintock HS, Tempe, Ariz.**
6. Stephen Williams, rhp, Milton (Fla.) HS
7. **Eric Brown, c, Tennessee Tech**
8. Ken Landreaux, of, Dominguez HS, Compton, Calif.
9. **Michael Holland, 1b, Charter Oak HS, Covina, Calif.**
10. **Steven Oberweather, ss, Lees Summit (Mo.) HS**
11. **Ron Roznovsky, rhp, Texas**
12. **Nathan Stewart, of, Le Tourneau (Texas)**
13. Kelly Cordes, lhp, Prescott (Ariz.) HS
14. Bobby Clark, ss, Perris (Calif.) HS
15. Steve Woitock, 2b, Dana (Neb.)
16. Richard Nesloney, rhp, Tuloso Midway HS, Corpus Christi, Texas
17. **Joe Sambito, lhp, Adelphi (N.Y.)**
18. Mike Davey, lhp, Gonzaga
19. Jerry Halstead, 1b, St. Petersburg (Fla.) JC

June—Secondary Phase (20)

No selection

KANSAS CITY ROYALS

January—Regular Phase (10)

1. Marty French, rhp, Grossmont (Calif.) JC
2. **Karel Deleeuw, of, Glendale (Ariz.) CC**

January—Secondary Phase (20)

1. **John Pierson, of, Glendale (Ariz.) CC**
2. **Bradley Davis, rhp, Mount Hood (Ore.) CC**

June—Regular Phase (9)

1. **Lew Olsen, rhp, San Ramon HS, Alamo, Calif.**
2. **Brian Trifiolis, c, West Orange (N.J.) HS**
3. **Ruppert Jones, of, Berkeley (Calif.) HS**
4. **Ron Sutler, ss, Buckingham HS, Dillwyn, Va.**
5. Mike Colbern, c, Hawthorne (Calif.) HS
6. **Bob Kellison, of, San Diego State**
7. **Danny Link, rhp, North Davidson HS, Lexington, N.C.**
8. **Bob Falcon, lhp, Texas A&M**
9. Ron Miles, lhp, Marion (S.C.) HS
10. **Jim Peterson, rhp, St. Mary's HS, Gaylord, Mich.**
11. **Willie Clark, rhp, Jackson State**
12. **Chris Evers, rhp, Wayzata (Minn.) HS**
13. Sandy Wihtol, rhp, Homestead HS, Sunnyvale, Calif.
14. John Yandle, lhp, Lake Oswego (Ore.) HS
15. **Jeff White, of, Wakefield HS, Arlington, Va.**
16. **Ruben Garcia, lhp, Texas Tech**
17. Tom Ricks, ss, Valencia HS, Placentia, Calif.
18. **Gary Williams, lhp, Fenger HS, Chicago**
19. **Richard Rich, rhp, Loara HS, Anaheim**
20. Xavier Dixson, of, St. Mary's
21. **Greg Kuhnke, of, Nekoosa (Wis.) HS**
22. Charles Stevens, of, Princeton (N.C.) HS
23. Robert MacHale, ss, Villa Park HS, Orange, Calif.
24. **Clyde Athman, c, Healy HS, Pierz, Minn.**
25. Dan Burns, c, St. Bernard HS, Hawthorne, Calif.
26. Chuck Baker, ss, Santa Ana (Calif.) JC
27. Manny Chavez, 2b, Whittier (Calif.) HS
28. Robert Bechtelheimer, rhp, Herndon HS, Fairfax, Va.
29. **Dwight Favors, 1b, Manual Arts HS, Los Angeles**
30. **Alex Gorgie, rhp, Rancho Alamitos HS, Garden Grove, Calif.**
31. Robert Sellers, 1b, W.T. Woodson HS, Annandale, Va.
32. **Dwayne Taggart, of, Los Angeles Southwest CC**
33. **Brian Slagle, rhp, Huntington Beach (Calif.) HS**
34. **Marvell McKinney, inf, East HS, Memphis**
35. **Darrell Parker, of, Woodside HS, Palo Alto, Calif.**
36. Mark Gesquiere, rhp, Aviation HS, Manhattan Beach, Calif.
37. **David Bewley, rhp, La Verne (Calif.)**
38. Bob Goodyear, lhp, Lutheran HS, Inglewood, Calif.
39. **Jim Lemon, 2b, Creighton**
40. Mike Ongarato, of, Rolling Hills HS, Palos Verdes, Calif.
41. Robert Price, ss, Eastern Wayne HS, Goldsboro, N.C.
42. **Elvin Lowe, 2b, Parkview HS, Little Rock, Ark.**
43. **Ellis Clayton, ss, Springfield (Ore.) HS**
44. **Kenneth Wright, lhp, Kailua (Hawaii) HS**
45. Dale Cline, rhp, Bridgeton (N.J.) HS
46. **Steven Barnes, rhp, Willamette HS, Eugene, Ore.**
47. Mike Gatlin, 3b, Chaffey (Calif.) JC
48. **William Heigel, c, San Jose State**
49. **Jimmy Kelley, c, Texas**
50. **Michael Larkin, rhp, Wyoming**
51. Dave Klungreseter, lhp, Cal State Fullerton
52. Robert Allen, 3b, Arizona

June—Secondary Phase (19)

1. Cliff Holland, lhp, Southern California
2. **Paul Caffrey, of, Seton Hall**
3. **Bob McClure, lhp, JC of San Mateo (Calif.)**
4. Rob Picciolo, inf, Santa Monica (Calif.) JC

LOS ANGELES DODGERS

January—Regular Phase (17)

1. **Wesley Moore, rhp, Yavapai (Ariz.) JC**
2. Michael Boyd, of, Chipola (Fla.) JC

3. Bob McClure, lhp, JC of San Mateo (Calif.)
4. Jeff Moore, 1b/3b, Middle Georgia JC
5. Jeff Hill, of, Phoenix JC
6. Terry Nance, p, Monterey Peninsula (Calif.) JC

January—Secondary Phase (17)

1. **Guy Todd, rhp, Blinn (Texas) JC**
2. Bob Purkey, rhp, Gulf Coast (Fla.) CC
3. Craig Minetto, lhp, San Joaquin Delta (Calif.) JC

June—Regular Phase (18)

1. **Ted Farr, c, Shadle Park HS, Spokane, Wash.**
2. **Mike Paciorek, ss, St. Mary's HS, Detroit**
3. **Joe Simpson, of, Oklahoma**
4. **Mark Hance, 3b, Fresno State**
5. Tom Steinmetz, ss, Canevin Catholic HS, Carnegie, Pa.
6. **Mike Dimmel, of, Logansport (Ind.) HS**
7. **David Richards, c, Proviso East HS, Forest Park, Ill.**
8. **Brad Drysdale, rhp, Brawley (Calif.) Union HS**
9. Bob Stanley, rhp, Kearny (N.J.) HS
10. Mark Wilson, of/3b, Ashland (Ore.) HS
11. **Charles Barrett, rhp, Rancho HS, North Las Vegas, Nev.**
12. **William Collins, rhp, South Alabama**
13. **Daniel Smith, rhp, Covina HS, West Covina, Calif.**
14. **James Mitchell, ss, Cardinal Mooney HS, Rochester, N.Y.**
15. Kelly Snider, 1b, Hillcrest HS, Springfield, Mo.
16. **Edward Davis, 3b/of, West Jefferson HS, Marrera, La.**
17. **Robert Arceneaux, c, Manual Arts HS, Los Angeles**
18. Tom Dixon, rhp/3b, Boone HS, Orlando, Fla.
19. Charles James, of, Manual Arts HS, Los Angeles
20. Marty Kunkler, lhp, Lindbergh HS, St. Louis
21. **Russell Holland, rhp, Parksley (Va.) HS**

June—Secondary Phase (16)

1. **William Meyer, ss, Michigan**

MILWAUKEE BREWERS

January—Regular Phase (4)

1. **Michael Robinson, of, Shoreline (Wash.) CC**
2. James Diventi, rhp, Essex (Md.) CC

January—Secondary Phase (6)

1. Scott Gunderson, rhp, Bellevue (Wash.) CC

June—Regular Phase (3)

1. **Robin Yount, ss, Taft HS, Woodland Hills, Calif.**
2. **Joe Slaymaker, lhp, Newport HS, Bellevue, Wash.**
3. **Gary Conn, rhp, Bentley HS, Flint, Mich.**
4. **Mark Plunkett, rhp, Edmonds (Wash.) HS**
5. **Michael Gilbert, 2b, Hartsville (S.C.) HS**
6. **John Buffamoyer, c, Berea HS, Greenville, S.C.**
7. Cary Scarborough, ss/2b, Bishopville (S.C.) HS
8. **Jerry Costain, 1b/of, Toms River (N.J.) South HS**
9. **Jeffrey Barker, rhp, Claremont (Calif.) HS**
10. **Charles Moore, c, Western Branch HS, Chesapeake, Va.**
11. **Terry Ervin, of, Wilson HS, Los Angeles**
12. **Jack Chilton, lhp, Maryvale HS, Phoenix**
13. **James Bendick, of, Shenendahowa HS, Ballston Lake, N.Y.**
14. **Paul Ausman, lhp, Regis HS, Eau Claire, Wis.**
15. Terry Unruh, rhp, Enid (Okla.) HS
16. **Terry Frawley, lhp, Bodley HS, Fulton, N.Y.**
17. **Perry Danforth, ss/2b, New Mexico**
18. **Raymond Rudolph, ss/c, Tottenville (N.Y.) HS**
19. **Richard Baker, lhp, Monte Vista HS, La Mesa, Calif.**
20. **William Smith, ss, Dominican HS, Milwaukee**
21. Michael Schisler, rhp, Georgia Tech

June—Secondary Phase (12)

1. Scott Gunderson, rhp, Bellevue (Wash.) CC

MINNESOTA TWINS

January—Regular Phase (12)

1. **Joseph Honce, of, West Virginia**
2. Dan Argee, of, Cosumnes River (Calif.) JC
3. Scott Wilson, 3b, Golden West (Calif.) JC
4. **Arthur Castillo, of, Fullerton (Calif.) JC**
5. **William Brock, lhp, Manatee (Fla.) JC**
6. David Morris, of, Citrus (Calif.) JC

January—Secondary Phase (18)

1. Dennis Sherow, of, Compton (Calif.) CC
2. Ron Bell, rhp, Fullerton (Calif.) JC
3. Jerry Maddox, 3b, Cerritos (Calif.) JC

June—Regular Phase (11)

1. **Eddie Bane, lhp, Arizona State**
2. **Eddie McMahon, ss, Massachusetts**
3. **Russ Noah, of, Loyola Marymount**
4. **Michael Beck, ss, Oakton HS, Vienna, Va.**
5. **Richard Tintor, c, Hibbing (Minn.) HS**
6. Darrell Jackson, lhp, Locke HS, Los Angeles
7. **Luis Gomez, ss, UCLA**
8. Sam Donabedian, of, McLane HS, Fresno
9. **Larry Wolfe, ss, Sacramento (Calif.) CC**
10. Ken Schrom, rhp, Grangeville (Idaho) HS
11. Jerry Reed, rhp, Enka HS, Asheville, N.C.
12. **Archie Amerson, ss, Morse HS, San Diego**
13. James Worth, rhp, Edgewood HS, West Covina, Calif.
14. Rob Klebba, 3b, La Crescenta (Calif.) HS
15. **Mike Seberger, rhp, Cal Poly Pomona**
16. **Michael Dodd, c, Golden West (Calif.) JC**
17. Gary Bishop, 1b, Poly Institute, Baltimore
18. Rick Peters, inf, Dominguez HS, Compton, Calif.
19. Dan Grimm, rhp, Fresno State
20. Richard Douglass, rhp/1b, San Clemente (Calif.) HS
21. **Michael Messman, rhp, Marshall HS, Portland, Ore.**
22. Frank Meyers, lhp, De LaSalle HS, Minneapolis
23. **Dave Garcia, rhp, Stevens Institute of Technology (N.Y.)**
24. **Robert Daniels, 2b, Long Island**
25. **Brad Duncan, rhp, Fresno State**
26. **Paul Franco, rhp, Cal State Los Angeles**
27. Gary Woods, of, Santa Barbara (Calif.) CC (Selection voided)
28. Robbert Henderson, ss, Clairemont HS, San Diego
29. **Jerry Matejka, lhp, Breckenridge (Minn.) HS**
30. Bill Sanford, c, Washington State

June—Secondary Phase (9)

1. Wayne Williams, ss, Ranger (Texas) JC
2. Bob Nickeson, ss, West Valley (Calif.) JC
3. Michael Buckingham, rhp, Gulf Coast (Fla.) CC
4. Marty French, rhp, Grossmont (Calif.) JC

MONTREAL EXPOS

January—Regular Phase (7)

1. **Thomas Ford, lhp, Eastern Michigan**
2. **Mark Cunningham, inf, Diablo Valley (Calif.) JC**
3. Hubert Hewitt, inf, Merritt (Calif.) JC
4. **Steve Melton, 3b, John Brown (Ark.)**
5. **Jack Spence, lhp, Alamogordo, N.M.**
6. Dan Henry, ss/of, San Bernardino Valley (Calif.) JC
7. Jay Seccombe, ss, Chabot (Calif.) JC
8. Thomas Slater, c, Mesa (Ariz.) CC
9. Kenneth Snyder, p, Chabot (Calif.) JC
10. Greg Ballard, rhp, Pomona, Calif.
11. Stephen Gooding, 1b, Catonsville (Md.) CC
12. Lee Sneath, p, Foothill (Calif.) JC
13. **Jimmy Williams, rhp, Indian Hills (Iowa) CC**
14. Robert Willis, p, Valencia (Fla.) CC

January—Secondary Phase (21)

1. David Bedrosian, 2b, Fresno CC
2. Dan Boitano, rhp, Fresno CC
3. **William Bohne, ss, Blinn (Texas) JC**
4. **David Gronlund, 3b, Riverside (Calif.) CC**

June—Regular Phase (8)

1. **Gary Roenicke, ss, Edgewood HS, West Covina, Calif.**
2. **Pat Creech, ss, Mercer**
3. **Rickey Hughes, 1b/of, Gaston HS, Gadsden, Ala.**
4. **Daniel Smith, of/3b, Westchester HS, Los Angeles**
5. **Richard Shannon, 3b, Jacksonville**
6. Pat Kelleher, rhp, Servite HS, Los Alamitos, Calif.

7. Dennis Doss, rhp, Memorial HS, Joplin, Mo.
8. **Michael Marvelle, of, Quincy (Mass.) HS**
9. **David Heffner, of, Gardner-Webb**
10. Mark Carpenter, lhp, Los Alamitos (Calif.) HS
11. Earl Thornton, lhp, Holtville HS, Deatsville, Ala.
12. **Greg Biagini, 1b/of, Iowa State**
13. Greg Chandler, c, Everett (Wash.) HS
14. Eugene Frey, of, Redwood HS, Corte Madero, Calif.
15. Greg Ballard, rhp, Pomona, Calif.
16. David Koza, lhp/of, Torrington, Wyo.
17. Terry Kieffer, lhp, Indian Hills (Iowa) CC
18. Bill Harris, lhp, St. Francis HS, Mountain View, Calif.
19. Mike Henderson, ss, Lincoln HS, Stockton, Calif.
20. Jerry Keller, c/1b, Seaholm HS, Birmingham, Mich.
21. **Larry Brown, rhp, Morningside HS, Inglewood, Calif.**
22. **Matt Dinkle, rhp, Nicholls State**
23. Jeff Reardon, rhp, Wahconah HS, Dalton, Mass.
24. **Elgin Battles, rhp, Waianae (Hawaii) HS**
25. **Tim Ireland, 2b, Chabot (Calif.) JC**
26. Scott Moffitt, 3b, Cottonwood HS, Salt Lake City
27. Robin Robinson, of, Centennial HS, Los Angeles
28. **Paul Joyce, rhp, Louisiana State**
29. Bruce Freeberg, rhp, Edgewood HS, West Covina, Calif.
30. David Steck, rhp, Patrick Henry HS, San Diego
31. Steve Viefhaus, ss, Ellisville, Mo.

June—Secondary Phase (6)

1. **Warren Cromartie, of, Miami-Dade North CC**

NEW YORK METS

January—Regular Phase (13)

1. **James Johnson, rhp, Little Rock, Ark.**
2. Melvin Anderson, of/1b, Los Angeles CC
3. Andrew Jackson, ss, Yakima Valley (Wash.) JC
4. Thomas Guess, 1b, Hillsborough (Fla.) CC
5. Mark Kramer, of, Yakima Valley (Wash.) JC
6. **Eduardo Oliveros, ss, Miami-Dade North CC**

January—Secondary Phase (11)

1. Doug Wessel, rhp, Vanderbilt
2. Bob Gerdes, rhp, Miami-Dade South CC
3. Chris Lynch, p, Miami-Dade South CC
4. Michael Hasley, p, Modesto (Calif.) JC
5. Charles Steffen, p/1b, Monroe (N.Y.) CC

June—Regular Phase (14)

1. **Lee Mazzilli, of, Lincoln HS, Brooklyn, N.Y.**
2. **Jackson Todd, rhp, Oklahoma**
3. **Gary Nevinger, rhp, Georgia**
4. Tom Kinkelaar, rhp, Mundelein (Ill.) HS
5. **John Williams, of, Robinson HS, Tampa**
6. **Richard Miller, of, West Chester (Pa.)**
7. **Michael Papa, of, Lafayette HS, Brooklyn, N.Y.**
8. Thomas Baxter, rhp, Bayonne (N.J.) HS
9. **John Courtney, rhp, Corrigan (Texas) HS**
10. John Brass, rhp, West HS, Bakersfield, Calif.
11. **Gary Blaylock, 1b, Union (Tenn.)**
12. **David Lozano, ss, San Joaquin Delta (Calif.) JC**
13. **James Matthews, ss, Luling (Texas) HS**
14. **Gary Albert, rhp, Elco HS, Myerstown, Pa.**
15. Ronald Reynolds, ss, Savannah (Tenn.) Central HS
16. **Dennis Jackson, 1b, Tottenville (N.Y.) HS**
17. **Chris Ryba, rhp, SUNY Stony Brook**
18. **Ron King, rhp, Redmond (Wash.) HS**
19. Ronnie Hildreth, rhp, Vigor HS, Prichard, Ala.
20. **Richard Harris, of, Arizona State**
21. **Mardie Cornejo, rhp, Tulsa**
22. Garnett Houghton, rhp, Ohlone (Calif.) JC
23. **Robert Salinger, c, St. Leo (Fla.)**
24. **Randy Trapp, of, Eastern Illinois**
25. **Brian Canfield, 3b, Louisiana-Lafayette**
26. Harry Tabler, c, Elder HS, Cincinnati
27. Colin Leisher, ss, Summit (N.J.) HS
28. **Larry Calufetti, c, Southern Illinois**
29. **Paul Dyer, lhp, California**
30. **Alan Osmundson, c, Tottenville HS, Staten Island, N.Y.**
31. Matt Gondak, of, Redwood HS, Larkspur, Calif.
32. Charles Fore, rhp, Flomaton (Ala.) HS
33. Warren Brusstar, rhp, Fresno State
34. **Kevin Meistickle, rhp, Thiel (Pa.)**
35. **Ed Wallace, ss, Southern Tech Institute (Fla.)**
36. **Michael Neumann, rhp, Kennedy HS, Chicago**

June—Secondary Phase (24)

No selection

NEW YORK YANKEES

January—Regular Phase (14)

1. Greg Kane, c, Yavapai (Ariz.) JC
2. **Steve Hergenrader, c/of, Fresno CC**
3. **Dean Engler, p, Clark (Wash.) JC**
4. David Jost, inf, Foothill (Calif.) JC
5. Joe Eberhard, ss, Crowder (Mo.) JC
6. Michael Lester, 3b, Bellevue (Wash.) CC

January—Secondary Phase (14)

1. **Bob Polinsky, rhp, Delaware**
2. Wayne Horkey, c, Granville, Iowa
3. Craig Mitchell, rhp, Spokane Falls (Wash.) CC
4. Brian Herosian, p/1b, Connecticut

June—Regular Phase (13)

1. **Doug Heinhold, rhp, Stroman HS, Victoria, Texas**
2. **Mike Heath, ss, Hillsborough HS, Tampa**
3. **Howard Shoff, rhp, William Penn HS, York, Pa.**
4. **Kerry Dineen, of, San Diego**
5. **LaMarr Hoyt, rhp, Keenan HS, Columbia, S.C.**
6. **Sheldon Gill, c, Jordan HS, Long Beach**
7. **Steve Coulson, 3b/of, Murray State**
8. **Garth Iorg, ss, Arcata (Calif.) HS**
9. Marion Harvey, rhp/c, Laverne (Okla.) HS
10. **Jack Shupe, 1b, Wayne State (Neb.)**
11. Barry Barritt, c, Thomas Jefferson HS, Council Bluffs, Iowa
12. **Craig White, of/1b, Clemson**
13. **Jim Sullivan, lhp, Colorado State**
14. Don Lenhof, rhp, Erlanger (Ky.) HS
15. **Lee Boettchner, rhp, Winona State (Minn.)**
16. **Tim Grice, 3b/c, Minnesota**
17. James Roach, rhp, West Bakersfield (Calif.) HS
18. Ron Pederson, lhp, Rock Valley (Iowa) Community HS
19. **Bob Majczan, rhp, Villanova**
20. David Hasbach, rhp, Miami (Ohio)
21. **Gary Blevins, rhp, Princeton**
22. **Donald Moore, c/3b, Green Hills (Ohio) Community HS**
23. Mark Erickson, 1b, Clark (Wash.) JC
24. James Hill, of, Belleville HS, Millstant, Ill.
25. Collin Morrison, lhp, Livermore (Calif.) HS
26. **Richard Melts, c/rhp, Yonkers (N.Y.) HS**
27. **Robert Wasilak, c, Kearny (N.J.) HS**
28. Jack Patchin, c, Crowder (Mo.) JC

June—Secondary Phase (3)

1. Wayne Benson, inf, Ranger (Texas) JC
2. **Dean Engler, rhp, Clark (Wash.) JC**
3. Kevin Nelson, lhp, JC of Southern Idaho
4. Greg Kane, c, Arcata, Calif.

OAKLAND ATHLETICS

January—Regular Phase (24)

1. **Mike Norris, rhp, San Francisco**
2. John Morris, p, Cypress (Calif.) JC
3. Clark Beam, rhp/2b, Mitchell (N.C.) CC
4. Steven Williams, p, Golden West (Calif.) JC
5. Gordon Blakeley, of/inf, Golden West (Calif.) JC

January—Secondary Phase (10)

1. Warren Cromartie, of, Miami-Dade North CC
2. **Carl Sapp, rhp, Compton, Calif.**
3. John Freedman, 3b, Citrus (Calif.) JC

June—Regular Phase (23)

1. **Randy Scarbery, rhp, Southern California**
2. **James Tuttle, rhp, Roger Bacon HS, Cincinnati**
3. Floyd Bannister, lhp, Kennedy HS, Seattle
4. **Ransom Voelkel, lhp, DeKalb HS, Auburn, Ind.**
5. **Charles Staniland, rhp, Santa Clara**
6. **Mack Harrison, ss/2b, Watkins HS, Laurel, Miss.**
7. **Matt Keough, 3b/rhp, Corona Del Mar (Calif.) HS**
8. **Derek Bryant, of, Kentucky**
9. **Wayne Gross, 1b, Cal Poly Pomona**
10. Scott Freebairn, c, Detroit County Day HS, Royal Oak, Mich.
11. **Richard Zoss, lhp, East Detroit HS, Warren, Mich.**
12. Danny Hall, 2b, Federal-Hocking HS, Coolville, Ohio
13. **David Moore, rhp, Marshall HS, West Sacramento, Calif.**
14. Stan Skidgel, rhp, Oakmont HS, Roseville, Calif.
15. **Dwayne Murphy, of, Antelope Valley HS, Lancaster, Calif.**
16. Monty Hannah, of, Eastmoor HS, Columbus, Ohio
17. **Gary Rump, c, Lahser HS, Bloomfield, Mich.**
18. **James Biehl, rhp/of, Garden Grove (Calif.) HS**
19. **Marty Stajduhar, 3b, La Verne (Calif.)**
20. **Scott Gilchrist, c, Granada Hills HS, Northridge, Calif.**
21. **Bill Hobbs, of/1b, UCLA**
22. **William Zedalis, rhp, Eisenhower HS, Rialto, Calif.**
23. Jeff Rineer, lhp, Penn Manor HS, Pequea, Pa.
24. William Dwyer, ss, Arlington (Mass.) HS
25. **William Undegaff, c, High Point (N.C.)**
26. James Dobens, rhp/ss, Bishop Guertin HS, Nashua, N.H.
27. **Robert Mollenhauer, 2b, Lafayette (Pa.)**
28. **Gary Williams, rhp, Los Alamitos HS, Cypress, Calif.**
29. John Boggan, rhp, Manhattan Academy, Jackson, Miss.
30. **David Sparks, ss, Ohio**
31. **Rick Ingalls, of/2b, Cal State Los Angeles**

June—Secondary Phase (1)

1. **Craig Mitchell, rhp, Spokane Falls (Wash.) CC**
2. Don Lyons, 1b, CC of San Francisco

PHILADELPHIA PHILLIES

January—Regular Phase (1)

1. **Alan Bannister, ss, Arizona State**
2. **Greg Gold, rhp, Diablo Valley (Calif.) JC**
3. **Andrew Russo, c, LeMoyne**
4. Errol Moore, of, Sacramento CC
5. Rick Talley, p, San Jacinto (Texas) JC
6. Joseph Griffin, c, Polk (Fla.) CC
7. **Rick Bosetti, 2b, Shasta (Calif.) JC**
8. **Dennis Perry, p, Ranger (Texas) JC**
9. Gene Litle, p, West Valley (Calif.) JC

January—Secondary Phase (1)

1. **Dick Ruthven, rhp, Fresno State**
2. Don Fisher, p, Polk (Fla.) CC
3. Paul Caffrey, of, Seton Hall
4. **William Zisk, rhp/of, Roseville, Calif.**

June—Regular Phase (2)

1. **John Stearns, c, Colorado**
2. **Todd Cruz, ss, Western HS, Detroit**
3. **Ronald Jackson, 3b, Central HS, St. Joseph, Mo.**
4. **John Hughes, c, Hale HS, Tulsa, Okla.**
5. **Jim Wright, rhp, Benton HS, St. Joseph, Mo.**
6. **Manny Seoane, rhp, Tampa Catholic HS**
7. Steve Kesses, of, North Haven (Conn.) HS
8. **Randy Lerch, lhp, Rancho Cordova (Calif.) HS**
9. **Dan Fitzgerald, of, New Mexico**
10. **Lawrence Hicks, of, Texas-Arlington**
11. Jeff Malinoff, 1b, UC Irvine
12. Glen Halverson, of, Edmonds (Wash.) HS
13. **Mark Crane, ss, Michigan**
14. **Darrell Flowers, lhp, Cairo (Ill.) HS**
15. Bruce Hodges, rhp, Sarasota (Fla.) HS
16. **Stephen Thornton, lhp, Pearl HS, Nashville**
17. **Oliver Bell, lhp, Encina HS, Sacramento**
18. **Mark Ammons, 1b/of, Bowling Green State**
19. **Mark Klein, rhp, Broward (Fla.) CC**
20. Ken Bourque, lhp, Fermi HS, Enfield, Conn.
21. James Cullen, rhp, Farmingdale (N.Y.) HS
22. **Joseph O'Brien, rhp, Tennessee**

June—Secondary Phase (12)

1. **Dan Boitano, rhp, Fresno CC**

PITTSBURGH PIRATES

January—Regular Phase (23)

1. **Paul Nelson, p, Sacramento CC**
2. Michael Buckingham, p, Gulf Coast (Fla.) CC
3. Ray Parr, p, Bellevue (Wash.) CC
4. Larry Prewitt, p, Sierra (Calif.) JC
5. David Quay, p, Tennessee Tech
6. Paul Risso, p, JC of San Mateo (Calif.)
7. Harold Flewelling, p, Shippensburg, Pa.
8. **John Hall, rhp/2b, Mineral Area (Mo.) JC**
9. Ron Sciarro, p, Kentucky
10. **Steve Gerlecz, of, State Fair (Mo.) CC**
11. William Muoio, p, Monroe (N.Y.) CC
12. Dale Przybysz, p, Erie (N.Y.) CC
13. Frank Jarosiewicz, rhp/3b, Staunton (Va.) Military Academy

January—Secondary Phase (19)

1. **Richard Olson, c, Fresno CC**
2. Sam Leonard, p, Yavapai (Ariz.) JC
3. Harry Martell, 3b/rhp, Maryland
4. John Hoffman, p, Lamar (Colo.) CC
5. Richard Hudson, p, Chipola (Fla.) JC
6. Mike Collodi, of/c, Colorado School of Mines

June—Regular Phase (24)

1. **Steve Nicosia, c, North Miami Beach (Fla.) HS**
2. **Jim Nelson, lhp, Manatee (Fla.) JC**
3. **Mitchell Page, of, Cal Poly Pomona**
4. **Randy Sealy, rhp, Brazoswood HS, Clute, Texas**
5. **Randy Brandt, lhp/1b, Frazier HS, Newell, Pa.**
6. **Dennis Davis, rhp, Martin County HS, Stuart, Fla.**
7. **Henry Welty, c, Whitesboro (N.Y.) HS**
8. **Robert Hall, ss, Concord HS, Wilmington, Del.**
9. **Thomas Frizzi, of, Mira Loma HS, Sacramento**
10. **Ken Barnes, ss, Gulf Coast (Fla.) CC**
11. **Larry Kinn, lhp, Eastern Michigan**
12. **Nicholas Bredy, of, Hiram Johnson HS, Sacramento**
13. **Randy Hopkins, lhp, Livingston (Ala.)**
14. **Wesley Edwards, ss, Berea HS, Greenville, S.C.**
15. Richard Rhodes, lhp, Vanderbilt
16. **Joe Turnbull, of, High Point (N.C.)**
17. **Vincent Frye, lhp/of, Monessen (Pa.) HS**
18. **Joseph Corrado, rhp/of, Deer Lakes HS, Gibsonia, Pa.**
19. **Joseph Neal, lhp, St. Joseph's**
20. **Dennis Blomberg, rhp, Hibbing (Minn.) HS**
21. **Stephen Dorsch, lhp, Concordia (N.Y.)**
22. **Robert Cecil, of, High Point (N.C.)**
23. **Michael Kavanagh, rhp, Villanova**
24. David Chappell, of/1b, West Allegheny HS, Imperial, Pa.
25. **Joseph Piscotty, of, SUNY Buffalo**
26. **Stanley Schroer, lhp, Louisiana State**
27. Michael Williams, lhp, Brazoswood HS, Clute, Texas
28. Lawrence Jones, rhp, Seminole (Fla.) HS
29. Paul Anthony, lhp, Lancaster (N.Y.) HS
30. Tom Kettinger, of, Michigan
31. Craig Cordt, rhp, Marshalltown (Iowa) HS

June—Secondary Phase (2)

1. **Mark Mercer, lhp, Hill (Texas) JC**
2. **Charles Steffen, lhp/1b, Monroe (N.Y.) CC**
3. William Sempsrott, rhp, Danville, Ill.
4. Marvin Townsend, ss, Albemarle (N.C.) CC
5. Brad Van Pelt, rhp, Michigan State

ST. LOUIS CARDINALS

January—Regular Phase (11)

1. **Larry Storti, 2b, Long Beach CC**
2. Don Hogestyn, of, Broward (Fla.) CC

3. Mark Jackson, c, Long Beach CC
4. Chris Loafman, p, DeAnza (Calif.) JC
5. Richard Smith, p, Miami-Dade North CC
6. Lynn Merrell, p, Bakersfield (Calif.) JC
7. Dean Cummings, p, Ohlone (Calif.) JC
8. John Smith, p, Ohlone (Calif.) JC
9. Roger Parker, p, Pascagoula, Miss.
10. Bill Beno, p, Manatee (Fla.) JC

January—Secondary Phase (7)

1. Brad Van Pelt, rhp, Michigan State
2. **Kip Coughlan, 3b, Richmond, Va.**
3. **Tony Milledge, 3b, Manatee (Fla.) JC**
4. Paul Cormier, rhp, New Hampshire

June—Regular Phase (12)

1. **Joe Edelen, 3b, Gracemont (Okla.) HS**
2. **Ron Selak, rhp, El Cerrito (Calif.) HS**
3. **Paul Husband, of, Mississippi**
4. **Clint Myers, 3b, Arizona State**
5. **Randy Wiles, lhp, Louisiana State**
6. **John Tamargo, c, Georgia Southern**
7. Richard Hand, c, Union (N.J.) HS
8. James Bradford, lhp, Pine Bluff (Ark.) HS
9. Steve Whitehead, ss, Ramona HS, Riverside, Calif.
10. **Steve Pasternak, rhp, Missouri**
11. **David Martin, 1b/of, Kennedy-King (Ill.) JC**
12. Thomas Cook, 1b, Lenoir City (Tenn.) HS
13. **John Stosz, of, Amherst (Mass.) Regional HS**
14. Jim Peterson, rhp, Sonora HS, Fullerton, Calif.
15. **Donald Boyd, of, Meridian (Miss.) HS**
16. Gene Laguna, 3b, Union (N.J.) HS
17. **Ronald Aront, ss, Union (N.J.) HS**
18. **Frank Nuzzo, 3b, Everett (Mass.) HS**
19. **Jimmy Wise, rhp, Iowa**
20. **Ricky Steen, ss, Big Spring (Texas) HS**
21. **David Sandlin, lhp/of, UNC Wilmington**
22. **Joe Ford, 3b/c, Oklahoma**
23. **William Starr, c, Mississippi**
24. **James Beal, of, La Verne (Calif.)**
25. Dick Jauron, ss, Yale
26. Don Walker, 1b/of, Centralia (Ill.) HS
27. Dana Pearson, lhp, Cobden (Ill.) HS
28. Carmen Caldwell, 1b/of, Jay HS, San Antonio
29. **Robert Corcoran, rhp, Yale**
30. Don Cardoza, of, JC of the Sequoias (Calif.)
31. Dana McManus, rhp, Palomar (Calif.) CC
32. **Eric Rasmussen, rhp, Louisiana State**
33. **Keith Cochran, 2b, Arkansas**
34. **Ernie Rosseau, of, South Alabama**
35. Gerald Ako, rhp, Aiea HS, Honolulu
36. **Kris Sorenson, rhp, San Jose State**
37. **Jeff Peeples, rhp, Vanderbilt**
38. **Gary Walker, rhp, Nebraska-Omaha**
39. **George Chisolm, 1b, Callaway HS, Jackson, Miss.**
40. **Steve Sherrill, c, Pacific**
41. Tim Hotop, rhp, Mexico (Miss.) HS
42. Gil Patterson, of/rhp, Norland HS, North Miami Beach, Fla.
43. James Burress, rhp, Valley HS, Las Vegas
44. Rickey Scarbery, rhp, Roosevelt HS, Fresno
45. **Thurman Smith, of, Arkansas**
46. Russell Hamilton, of/rhp, Reedley (Calif.) JC
47. **Tommy Neal, of, Arkansas**
48. **Stephen Ballard, 1b, Arkansas**
49. Bryn Smith, rhp, Santa Maria (Calif.) HS
50. **Richard Shaw, 3b, Tuskegee (Ala.)**
51. John Dominianni, 3b, Upsala (N.J.)
52. **Bert Francks, rhp, CC of Morris (N.J.)**

June—Secondary Phase (8)

1. **William Daves, c, Motlow State (Tenn.) CC**

SAN DIEGO PADRES

January—Regular Phase (3)

1. **Dave Wehrmeister, rhp, Northeast Missouri State**
2. Phil Williams, c, Saddleback (Calif.) CC
3. Mike Parkinson, ss, Mount San Antonio (Calif.) JC
4. **Mike DuPree, rhp/of, Fresno CC**

January—Secondary Phase (13)

1. **Dan Shaw, rhp, Stanford**
2. Wayne Williams, ss, Ranger (Texas) JC

June—Regular Phase (4)

1. **Dave Winfield, rhp/of, Minnesota**
2. **Mike Champion, ss/3b, Foothill HS, Santa Ana, Calif.**
3. Steve Day, ss, Lufkin (Texas) HS
4. **Jerry Stone, c, Loyola Marymount**
5. **Nathaniel Harmon, rhp, Taft HS, Cincinnati**
6. Steven Hogan, of/inf, Grant HS, Sacramento
7. Butch Stinson, lhp/of, Lipscomb
8. **Jay Smith, rhp, Florida Southern**
9. **John McAllen, lhp, Cal State Los Angeles**
10. **Peter Cusick, c, Monmouth**
11. **Aldrich Adams, c, Los Angeles (Calif.) HS**
12. **Dale Torcato, 3b, Woodland (Calif.) HS**
13. **Joe McIntosh, rhp, Washington State**
14. **Bob Polock, 2b, Illinois**
15. **Gregory Zail, rhp, UCLA**
16. Samuel Nicholson, rhp, Texas
17. Glen Johnson, c/of, Stanford
18. Tim Pettorini, of, Bowling Green State
19. Gregory Kruciak, lhp, St. Gerards HS, San Antonio
20. Ray Crawford, ss/of, Santa Ana (Calif.) HS
21. **Scott Brown, 1b, UC Santa Barbara**

June—Secondary Phase (18)

No selection

SAN FRANCISCO GIANTS

January—Regular Phase (5)

1. **John Andrews, ss, Lincoln Land (Ill.) JC**
2. Rob Picciolo, inf, Santa Monica (Calif.) JC
3. Bill Malpass, ss/2b, West Valley (Calif.) JC
4. **James Davidson, rhp/of, Linn-Benton (Ore.) CC**
5. William Kolarik, p, Los Angeles Valley JC
6. Kevin Nelson, p, JC of Southern Idaho
7. Mark Weldon, inf, Green River (Wash.) CC
8. Thomas Park, p, Bellevue (Wash.) CC
9. Stephen Corn, p/1b, Spokane Falls (Wash.) CC
10. Doug Johnson, p, Scottsdale (Ariz.) CC

January—Secondary Phase (23)

1. **Dave Heaverlo, rhp, Central Washington**
2. Steve Wilkins, of, Treasure Valley (Ore.) CC
3. **Dennis Smith, 1b, Miami (Ohio)**
4. Robert Alonzo, inf, Phoenix JC
5. William Przygocki, p, St. Clair County (Mich.) CC
6. Craig Cornwell, p, Pasadena (Calif.) CC
7. Peter Cervantes, c/3b, Los Angeles CC

June—Regular Phase (6)

1. **Johnnie LeMaster, ss, Paintsville (Ky.) HS**
2. **Ernest Young, c, Denby HS, Detroit**
3. **Jeff Little, lhp, Woodmore HS, Woodville, Ohio**
4. **Terry Coomer, rhp, Novlesville (Ind.) HS**
5. Bobby Mitchell, of, Chatsworth (Calif.) HS
6. **Tommy Toms, rhp, East Carolina**
7. **Steve Grimes, inf, Point Loma HS, San Diego**
8. **Tony Cabrera, 3b, Hialeah (Fla.) HS**
9. Bobby McClellan, c, Emma Sanson HS, Gadsden, Ala.
10. **Ed Plank, rhp, Nevada-Reno**
11. Tommy Jarmon, of, Edison HS, Stockton, Calif.
12. **Gerald Anderson, of, Edgewood HS, West Covina, Calif.**
13. **Jack Clark, rhp/of, Gladstone HS, Covina, Calif.**
14. Karl Gordon, ss, Montclair State (N.J.)
15. Robert Simons, c, Logansport (Ind.) HS
16. **Arturo Marin, 2b, Pasadena (Calif.) CC**
17. **Stephen Williams, lhp, Swanton (Ohio) HS**
18. Jeffrey Ross, lhp, Cubberley HS, Palo Alto, Calif.
19. **Frank Zawatski, c, Lehigh**

20. **Carroll Palmer, lhp, Treasure Valley (Ore.) CC**
21. Dan Graham, 3b, Mesa (Ariz.) CC
22. James Schak, rhp, Newark College of Engineering
23. Kevin Tennant, c, Seton Hall
24. James Bertram, rhp, La Jolla (Calif.) HS
25. Darnell Waters, inf, Fremont HS, Oakland
26. **Robert Sparks, of, Castlemont HS, Oakland**
27. George Hahn, c, Campbell (Calif.) HS
28. **Lee Cook, lhp, Treasure Valley (Ore.) CC**
29. Stewart Bringhurst, rhp/c, Crestmoor HS, San Bruno, Calif.
30. Gavin Long, rhp, Westmoor HS, Pacifica, Calif.

June—Secondary Phase (4)

1. **Pete Falcone, lhp, Kingsborough (N.Y.) CC**

TEXAS RANGERS

January—Regular Phase (2)

1. **Brad Fulk, 2b, Hagerstown, Md.**
2. Jeff Schneider, lhp, Iowa State
3. Zane Grubbs, p, Texas

January—Secondary Phase (2)

1. **Jim Sundberg, c, Iowa**
2. Rick Bethke, lhp, Cerritos (Calif.) JC
3. Kevin Morel, ss, Indian River (Fla.) CC
4. Donnelly Douglas, lhp, Amherst (Mass.)
5. Ray Boneschans, p, Valencia (Fla.) CC
6. Richard Mallman, p, West Valley (Calif.) JC
7. William Robinson, of, Delaware

June—Regular Phase (1)

1. **David Clyde, lhp, Westchester HS, Houston**
2. **Richard Shubert, lhp, Bryant HS, Astoria, N.Y.**
3. **Len Barker III, rhp, Neshaminy HS, Trevose, Pa.**
4. Lynn Garrett, ss, Berkeley (Calif.) HS
5. **Ken Pape, ss, Texas**
6. Andrew Mason, 3b, Charter Oak HS, Covina, Calif.
7. **Drew Nickerson, rhp, Reseda (Calif.) HS**
8. Wayne Steele, lhp, Hoover HS, San Diego
9. **Don Thomas, 3b, California**
10. **Steven Strickland, lhp, Fort Myers (Fla.) HS**
11. **John Weber, ss/of, LaSalle HS, Niagara Falls, N.Y.**
12. **Ray Rainboldt, rhp, Cleveland (Okla.) HS**
13. Eugene Norman, rhp, San Gorgonio HS, Highland, Calif.
14. Gerald Erb, rhp, Wahconah Regional HS, Dalton, Mass.
15. **Gary Wright, of/1b, Albert Einstein HS, Kensington, Md.**
16. Mark Peters, rhp, Morton HS, Hammond, Ind.
17. **Gary Hubka, 3b, Beloit (Wis.) Memorial HS**
18. Walt Kaczmarak, rhp, Santa Clara
19. Roland Keys, ss, Morristown (N.J.) HS
20. Mike Merritt, rhp, North Carolina
21. **Walter Gawaluch, ss, Texas Wesleyan**
22. **Greg Keen, rhp, Miami-Dade South CC**
23. **Jonathan Astroth, of, Southern Methodist**
24. Barry Mollencupp, c, Harlem HS, Loves Park, Ill.
25. **Gene Delyon, 3b, Santa Clara**
26. **Lindsey Graham, rhp, Clemson**
27. Nick Peterson, lhp, Stanford
28. Billy Sample, 3b, Andrew Lewis HS, Salem, Va.
29. **Rudy Jaramillo, of, Texas**
30. **Dan Duran, 1b, Foothill (Calif.) JC**
31. **Don Bodenhamer, 3b, Texas Christian**
32. Mark Hance, 3b, Fresno State (Selection voided)
33. **Michael Mehaffie, rhp/of, Kimball HS, Dallas**
34. Frederic Wade, 3b, Columbus HS, Miami
35. Steve Polan, ss, El Camino HS, Sacramento
36. Gary Wiencek, c, Citrus (Calif.) JC

June—Secondary Phase (17)

1. Jeff Feramisco, inf/of, Fresno CC

1974

Padres finally get their man in Almon, but other teams worry about future of young talent

When Bill Almon was graduating from Warwick (R.I.) High in 1971, scouts from every major league team wanted the young shortstop, and the Brewers were one of the teams willing to draft him in the first round. But Brown University won the Almon sweepstakes.

Prior to the draft, Almon wrote to every major league club and explained that he was going to college to get an Ivy League education. The San Diego Padres still took a chance in the 10th round of the '71 draft, and Almon turned them down.

"I knew I wasn't going to sign then, and the Padres knew it too," Almon said. "But they weren't drafting too many people then and they thought it was worth the risk. Frankly, I didn't think I was mature enough, either mentally or physically, for professional baseball at the time."

Three years later, the Padres finally got their man. They had the first pick in the June 1974 draft and grabbed the Brown shortstop, signing Almon to a $90,000 bonus. Almon hit .362 as a junior with a school-record 10 home runs and 31 RBIs.

"I'm really pleased to be with San Diego," Almon said at the time of his signing. "I like the organization and the people I've dealt with. I couldn't be happier if I had been drafted by any other club."

Almon expressed a desire to start his career in the major leagues, as previous Padres first-rounders like Dave Roberts and Dave Winfield had done, but he acceded to the Padres' wishes and started his career with Triple-A Hawaii instead after working out with the major league club.

But Almon languished on the bench there because Hawaii owned many of its own players at the time and had a say in who would play. Almon hit .222 in 14 games. Sent to Double-A Alexandria in the Texas League, he hit .186 in 25 contests before receiving a September callup to San Diego.

Over a 15-year career, the 6-foot-3, 170-pounder never did hit with much authority. He batted .254 with 36 homers, playing for eight different teams.

If it was a familiar face that the Padres went for in Almon, the Rangers, drafting second, also went for more of the same.

A year after taking David Clyde No. 1, the Rangers went for another hard-throwing Texan, righthander Tommy Boggs from Austin. The Rangers were more patient with Boggs and resisted the temptation to send Boggs straight to the big leagues.

"Boggs isn't as refined as Clyde," team president Bobby Brown said. "It's not every kid who can step into the major leagues right away. But Boggs may throw harder than Clyde."

Royals star Willie Wilson was one player who decided to pick baseball over football

It wasn't until two years later that Boggs, 20, reached the big leagues. He went 1-10 in his career with the Rangers before he was dealt to Atlanta following the 1977 season. Rotator-cuff surgery finished Boggs' 20-44 career.

Beyond the individual players, however, the 1974 draft was most notable because it featured the fewest players ever drafted in June (725).

"The apparent reduction in the quality of talent available at the free-agent level has to raise serious questions as to the quality of our product at the major league level 10 or 15 years from today," said Lou Gorman, then the farm director for the Royals. "If this alarming trend continues, I shudder to think what we will be marketing as Major League Baseball in the future.

"We must do everything humanly and financially possible to revitalize, rejuvenate and redirect the high school baseball programs in this country."

Baseball, however, did its part in steering athletes away from other sports—specifically football—in the '74 draft.

In the first round, the California Angels went after Louisiana State quarterback Mike Miley, who the previous January led LSU to victory over Penn State in the Orange Bowl. It took a $90,000 bonus to get Miley, one of the top quarterbacks in college football, to give up his senior year of football. Three years later, Miley was killed in a car accident.

Another Angels draft pick took advantage of the new NCAA rule that allowed players to be professionals in one sport and remain amateurs in another. High school basketball sensation Mark Wulfmeyer, the leading prep scorer in Southern California history, signed with the Angels and played basketball at the University of Southern California, though he never fulfilled his potential in either sport.

Meanwhile, the Royals paid $90,000, the largest bonus in club history, to get first-round pick Willie Wilson, who had been recruited to play football by some 200 colleges.

Houston got its first-round selection, Kevin Drake, to give up a football career at UCLA by starting him at Triple-A. That was the highest level he reached in his career. Another UCLA football recruit, linebacker Lance Parrish, was Detroit's first pick.

The Orioles weren't so fortunate. They drafted four players in the first 20 rounds who later played in the NFL, including California first baseman Steve Bartkowski, who became the No. 1 pick in the 1975 NFL draft. Bartkowski had once been a top major league prospect, but his disappointment at being drafted so low (19th round) caused him to quit baseball and concentrate solely on football.

The Orioles also took Georgia quarterback Andy Johnson, who had already been drafted and signed by the New England Patriots.

Baseball also continued its pursuit of Brad Van Pelt, once a top pitching prospect at Michigan State. Even though Van Pelt had a year under his belt with the New York Giants, he was drafted in January by St. Louis, the fifth time he had been selected.

In a year when the designated hitter and aluminum bats were introduced to the college game, there were fewer college players selected (300) than in any June draft ever.

In the January draft, it was a foregone conclusion that shortstop Roy Smalley, who contributed to two NCAA championships at USC, would be the No. 1 pick. The only question was whether the Rangers, drafting first in the regular phase, would start Smalley immediately in the big leagues.

Smalley, the nephew of Expos manager Gene Mauch, had dropped out of school the previous fall to make himself eligible. He signed with the Rangers for $100,000, and they sent him to Double-A to begin his career.

"A lot of people think Smalley can play major league ball right now," Rangers owner Bob Short said. "We thought, just as we thought about David Clyde last summer, that he was head and shoulders above the rest of the eligibles."

DRAFT 74: FIRST-ROUND PICKS

No.	Club	Player, Pos.	School	Hometown	Ht.	Wt.	B-T	Age
1.	Padres	Bill Almon, ss	Brown	Warwick, R.I.	6-3	170	R-R	21
2.	Rangers	Tommy Boggs, rhp	Lanier HS	Austin	6-2	201	R-R	18
3.	Phillies	Lonnie Smith, of	Centennial HS	Compton, Calif.	5-9	177	R-R	18
4.	Indians	Tom Brennan, rhp	Lewis	Oaklawn, Ill.	6-1	180	R-R	21
5.	Braves	Dale Murphy, c	Wilson HS	Portland, Ore.	6-4	195	R-R	18
6.	Brewers	Butch Edge, rhp	El Camino HS	Sacramento	6-3	195	R-R	17
7.	Cubs	Scot Thompson, of	Knox HS	Renfrew, Pa.	6-2	160	L-L	18
8.	White Sox	Larry Monroe, rhp	Forest View HS	Mount Prospect, Ill.	6-4	200	R-R	17
9.	Expos	Ron Sorey, 3b	Stebbins HS	Dayton, Ohio	6-1	200	R-R	19
10.	Angels	Mike Miley, ss	Louisiana State	Metairie, La.	6-1	180	B-R	21
11.	Pirates	Rod Scurry, lhp	Proctor Hug HS	Sparks, Nev.	6-2	180	L-L	18
12.	Yankees	Dennis Sherrill, ss	South Miami HS	Miami	6-0	165	R-R	18
13.	Cardinals	Garry Templeton, ss	Valley HS	Santa Ana, Calif.	5-11	170	R-R	18
14.	Twins	Ted Shipley, ss	Vanderbilt	Chattanooga, Tenn.	6-1	170	R-R	21
15.	Astros	Kevin Drake, of	Cabrillo HS	Lompoc, Calif.	6-3	200	R-R	18
16.	Tigers	Lance Parrish, 3b	Walnut HS	Diamond Bar, Calif.	6-4	215	R-R	17
17.	Mets	Cliff Speck, rhp	Beaverton HS	Beaverton, Ore.	6-3	190	R-R	17
18.	Royals	Willie Wilson, of	Summit HS	Summit, N.J.	6-3	195	R-R	18
19.	Giants	Terry Lee, 2b	San Luis Obispo HS	San Luis Obispo, Calif.	6-1	175	L-R	18
20.	Red Sox	Eddie Ford, ss	South Carolina	Great Neck, N.Y.	6-1	165	B-R	20
21.	Dodgers	Rick Sutcliffe, rhp	Van Horn HS	Kansas City	6-5	205	L-R	17
22.	Athletics	*Jerry Johnson, c	McCallum HS	Austin	6-2	185	R-R	18
23.	Reds	Steve Reed, rhp	Fort Wayne HS	Fort Wayne, Ind.	6-1	185	R-R	18
24.	Orioles	Rich Dauer, 3b	Southern California	Colton, Calif.	6-0	175	R-R	21

*Did not sign.

1974

CLUB-BY-CLUB SELECTIONS

ATLANTA BRAVES

January—Regular Phase (6)

1. **Larry McWilliams, lhp, Paris (Texas) JC**
2. Tim Graven, lhp, Columbia State (Tenn.) CC
3. John Anderson, ss, South Georgia JC
4. **Tom Westlake, 2b, Sacramento CC**
5. Steven Watson, 1b/of, Spokane Falls (Wash.) CC
6. John Schott, rhp, Blinn (Texas) JC
7. **Patrick Hobbs, lhp, Miami-Dade North CC**

January—Secondary Phase (8)

1. Mike Williams, lhp, Temple (Texas) JC
2. **Mike Davey, lhp, Gonzaga**
3. Michael Schisler, rhp, Georgia Tech

June—Regular Phase (5)

1. **Dale Murphy, c, Wilson HS, Portland, Ore.**
2. **Joey McLaughlin, rhp, McLain HS, Tulsa, Okla.**
3. **Robert Long, of, Redwood Larkspur HS, Corte Madera, Calif.**
4. **Donald Fletcher, ss, Blount HS, Mobile, Ala.**
5. **Jimmy Hacker, 3b, Texas A&M**
6. **Steven Van Kerns, rhp, San Jacinto (Texas) JC**
7. **Rick Camp, rhp, West Georgia**
8. **Steve Oliva, of, Kennedy HS, Granada Hills, Calif.**
9. **Eric Cervantes, of, Hiram Johnson HS, Sacramento**
10. **Mickey Mahler, lhp, Trinity (Texas)**
11. Tim Costello, lhp, Central Hower HS, Akron, Ohio
12. **Daniel Newell, 2b, Green River (Wash.) CC**
13. David Reed, 1b/lhp, Corner HS, Dora, Ala.
14. Marshall Justice, rhp, South Georgia JC
15. Joe McClain, rhp/1b, Happy Valley HS, Johnson City, Tenn.
16. **Glenn Smith, 2b, Lipscomb**
17. William Taylor, rhp, Ridgeview HS, Atlanta

June—Secondary Phase (11)

1. Scott McGlamory, rhp, Gulf Coast (Fla.) CC

BALTIMORE ORIOLES

January—Regular Phase (23)

1. Lee Brownell, c, Hancock (Calif.) JC
2. **Ed Pebley, 3b, Hancock (Calif.) JC**
3. Sherwin Rogers, 2b, Adrian (Mich.)
4. Alex Torres, ss, JC of the Sequoias (Calif.)
5. Billy De'Yo, lhp, East Los Angeles JC
6. Donald Gardner, lhp, Hancock (Calif.) JC
7. Edward Montes, of, Bellflower, Calif.
8. Alton Caesar, ss, Sierra (Calif.) JC
9. Mark Lee, rhp, El Camino (Calif.) JC
10. John Edwards, c, Carmichael, Calif.
11. Walt Mason, of, Central Arizona JC
12. James Lugo, rhp, Mount San Jacinto (Calif.) JC
13. Richard Martinez, of, Mira Costa (Calif.) JC
14. Wilburt Ellis, rhp, East Los Angeles JC
15. Terry Gray, rhp, Merced (Calif.) JC

January—Secondary Phase (3)

1. **Brad Drysdale, rhp, Arizona Western JC**
2. Robbie Henderson, ss, San Diego Mesa JC
3. Steve Hogan, of/inf, Central Arizona JC
4. Edward Wright, 2b, Albemarle (N.C.) JC

June—Regular Phase (24)

1. **Rich Dauer, ss/2b, Southern California**
2. **Craig Ryan, 1b/of, Cal State Northridge**
3. **Michael Brown, rhp, Crescenta Valley HS, La Crescenta, Calif.**
4. **Mike Darr, rhp, Norco (Calif.) HS**
5. **Randy Miller, rhp, UC San Diego**
6. Andy Johnson, ss, Georgia
7. John Sciarra, inf, UCLA
8. **Joseph Villa, c, Cantwell HS, Pico Rivera, Calif.**
9. Kenny Washington, 1b/of, Morningside HS, Los Angeles
10. **James Bryan, of, Merced (Calif.) JC**
11. **Richard Rickman, ss, Ragsdale HS, Greensboro, N.C.**
12. Dean Phillips, rhp, Paschal HS, Fort Worth, Texas
13. **John Gordy, rhp, James Bennett HS, Salisbury, Md.**
14. **James Evans, of, Booker T. Washington HS, Norfolk, Va.**
15. Anthony Davis, of, Southern California
16. **John Cline, c, Campbell**
17. **Robert Volk, rhp, Lambuth (Tenn.)**
18. Marvin Saunders, of, Deep Creek HS, Chesapeake, Va.
19. Steve Bartkowski, 1b, California
20. **Bernard Bumbrey, of, Stafford HS, Hartwood, Va.**
21. Alan Willett, rhp, Patchogue-Medford HS, Patchogue, N.Y.
22. Marvin Townsend, ss, Campbell (Selection voided)
23. Richard Hudson, rhp, Chipola (Fla.) JC
24. **Creighton Tevlin, of, Southern California**
25. **Dan Marple, of, Cal Poly San Luis Obispo**
26. Michael Croswell, ss, Manhattan HS, Jackson, Miss.
27. Mark Naehring, 1b, La Salle HS, Cincinnati
28. **Tom Kibbee, rhp, Mendocino (Calif.) CC**
29. Robert Hamilton, of, Suitland HS, District Heights, Md.
30. **Ricky Ford, inf, Texas Wesleyan**
31. Bernard Menapace, c, Broad Run HS, Sterling Park, Va.
32. **Richard Katz, 3b, Jacksonville**
33. Vernon Crockett, 2b, Huguenot HS, Richmond
34. Scott Winston, lhp, Windsor Forest HS, Savannah, Ga.
35. **Richard Reichle, 3b, Miami**
36. **Gus Quiros, rhp, Los Angeles, Calif.**
37. Mark Trapani, rhp, Poly HS, North Hollywood, Calif.
38. **William Bird, rhp, Oklahoma State**
39. **Gary Brandenburg, c, Oklahoma State**
40. Randy Johnson, 3b, San Diego Mesa JC
41. **Ron DeGrande, of, Stagg HS, Stockton, Calif.**

June—Secondary Phase (14)

1. **Charles James, of, Los Angeles Valley JC**
2. **Jeff Feramisco, inf/of, Fresno CC**
3. Robbie Henderson, ss, San Diego Mesa JC
4. **Tom Chism, of, Brandywine (Del.) JC**
5. Alex Torres, ss, JC of the Sequoias (Calif.)

BOSTON RED SOX

January—Regular Phase (19)

1. **Chuck Rainey, rhp, San Diego Mesa JC**
2. Ralph Russo, 1b, Quinnipiac
3. Stephen Kolenda, 2b, Stetson
4. James Wargo, ss, Gulf Coast (Fla.) CC
5. Brad Liedtke, of/rhp, Fullerton (Calif.) JC

January—Secondary Phase (7)

1. **Bob Stanley, rhp, Kearny (N.J.) HS**
2. **Steve Burke, rhp, Merritt (Calif.) JC**
3. **Greg Kane, c, Yavapai (Ariz.) JC**

June—Regular Phase (20)

1. **Eddie Ford, ss, South Carolina**
2. **Jimmy Schankle, c, Lubbock (Texas) Monterey HS**
3. **Ronny Patrick, lhp, Castlewood (Va.) HS**
4. **Charles Reilly, 2b, Adelphi (N.Y.)**
5. Craig Brooks, of, Richmond (Calif.) HS
6. **Robert Klass, rhp, Southern Illinois**
7. **Sam Bowen, 2b, Valdosta State (Ga.)**
8. **Paul McClure, inf, Wyoming**
9. **Joel Finch, rhp, Washington HS, South Bend, Ind.**
10. Lee Roy Russell, rhp, Bibb County HS, Brent, Ala.
11. **Charles Pinkney, of, Kingsborough (N.Y.) CC**

12. **John Tagliarino, rhp, Tampa Catholic HS**
13. Michael Wholey, rhp, Lakes HS, Tacoma, Wash.
14. **Mark Barr, rhp, Southern California**
15. **Burke Suter, rhp, High Point (N.C.)**
16. Jeff Hardy, ss, Gulf Coast (Fla.) CC
17. Jackie Snell, lhp, George Wallace (Ala.) CC
18. **Jerome Register, of, Valdosta State (Ga.)**

June—Secondary Phase (20)

1. **Marvin Townsend, ss, Campbell**
2. **David Koza, lhp, Eastern Oklahoma State JC**

CALIFORNIA ANGELS

January—Regular Phase (9)

1. Larry Howser, ss, Manatee (Fla.) JC
2. **Pat Cristelli, rhp, Puget Sound (Wash.)**
3. Owen Prather, lhp, Cypress (Calif.) JC
4. Steve Hammond, of, Gulf Coast (Fla.) CC
5. Edward Nuss, rhp, Valencia (Fla.) CC
6. **Frank Panick, rhp, UCLA**
7. William Sundquist, 1b, JC of the Redwoods (Calif.)
8. James Davis, rhp, Long Beach CC
9. Scott McGlamory, rhp, Gulf Coast (Fla.) CC
10. **David Drevnak, of, Gulf Coast (Fla.) CC**
11. Mike Holt, rhp, JC of the Canyons (Calif.)
12. Gary Wilburn, c, Riverside (Calif.) CC
13. Keith Ulrich, lhp, El Camino (Calif.) JC
14. **Juan Delgado, 1b, San Bernardino Valley (Calif.) JC**
15. Steve Fenoglio, of, Long Beach (Calif.) CC
16. Leon Smith, lhp, Hartnell (Calif.) CC
17. William Felt, c, American River (Calif.) JC
18. George Ambrow, ss/rhp, Southern California

January—Secondary Phase (23)

1. David Bedrosian, 2b, Fresno CC
2. Charles James, of, Los Angeles Valley JC
3. Steve Barrett, 2b, Murray State
4. **Danny Miller, rhp/inf, Los Angeles Pierce JC**
5. Danny Boone, lhp, Cerritos (Calif.) JC

June—Regular Phase (10)

1. **Mike Miley, ss, Louisiana State**
2. **Mike Martinson, c, Lakewood (Calif.) HS**
3. **Rance Mulliniks, ss, Monache HS, Woodville, Calif.**
4. **Thad Bosley Jr., of, Oceanside (Calif.) HS**
5. **Stan Cliburn, c, Forrest Hill HS, Jackson, Miss.**
6. **Gary Wheelock, rhp, UC Irvine**
7. **Ralph Botting, lhp, Burbank (Calif.) HS**
8. Floyd Chiffer, rhp, Lakewood (Calif.) HS
9. **Mark Wulfemeyer, rhp/of, Troy HS, Fullerton, Calif.**
10. Greg Harris, rhp, Los Alamitos (Calif.) HS
11. **Bryant Fahrow, ss, Kankakee (Ill.) CC**
12. **John Verhoeven, rhp, La Verne (Calif.)**
13. Curtis Anderson, ss, Deerfield (Ill.) HS
14. **Russ McQueen, rhp, Southern California**
15. David Anderson, rhp, Gresham HS, Portland, Ore.
16. **William Case, rhp, Antelope Valley (Calif.) JC**
17. Jackie Smith, lhp, Manatee (Fla.) JC
18. **Donald Johnson, lhp, Palomar (Calif.) JC**
19. Steve Vaughn, of, Palisades HS, Pacific Palisades, Calif.
20. **Kenneth Wright, of, Compton (Calif.) CC**
21. **Lamar Wright, lhp, Shorter (Ga.)**
22. Carl Spikes, of, Bogalusa (La.) HS
23. Barry Acquistapace, rhp, Dos Pueblos HS, Goleta, Calif.
24. Daniel Owen, rhp, Miami-Dade North CC
25. **Arthur Lorick, of, Florida Air Academy, Melbourne, Fla.**
26. Erol Akchurin, 3b, Burlingame (Calif.) HS
27. Paul Kolesnikow, of, Burlingame (Calif.) HS
28. Joseph Ducey, c, Foothill HS, Santa Ana, Calif.
29. Paul Stefan, rhp, Drake
30. Dennis Hawkins, of, Chaffey (Calif.) JC
31. Randall Bonner, c, Wheeler HS, Marietta, Ga.
32. **John Picone, c, UC Santa Barbara**
33. James Billuris, of/inf, Del Mar HS, San Jose
34. Tim Cashman, ss, Santa Barbara (Calif.) CC
35. Larry Marsh, ss, South Hills HS, Covina, Calif.
36. **Gregory Kulesza, rhp, Royal Oak (Mich.) HS**
37. Gary Wiencek, c, Citrus (Calif.) JC

June—Secondary Phase (2)

1. **John Caneira, rhp, Eastern Connecticut State**
2. **Jeff Malinoff, 1b, UC Irvine**

CHICAGO CUBS

January—Regular Phase (8)

1. **Eric Grandy, 1b/of, Essex (Md.) CC**

January—Secondary Phase (16)

1. **Karl Gordon, ss, Montclair State (N.J.)**

June—Regular Phase (7)

1. **Scot Thompson, of, Knox HS, Renfrew, Pa.**
2. **Mike Sember, ss, Tulsa**
3. John Henderson, c, Mount DeSales HS, Macon, Ga.
4. **George Riley, lhp, South Philadelphia HS**
5. **Kevin Drury, ss, Glynn Academy, Brunswick, Ga.**
6. **David Wood, rhp, Washington HS, South Bend, Ind.**
7. Craig McGinnis, lhp, Powers HS, Flint, Mich.
8. **Thomas Deskins, 2b, Paintsville (Ky.) HS**
9. **Jeffrey Collins, rhp, Ironton (Ohio) HS**
10. **Ken Christensen, rhp/c, Wisconsin Lutheran HS, Cudahy, Wis.**
11. David Hall, of, New Trier HS, Winnetka, Ill.
12. **Harvey Selnik, ss, Hart HS, Saugus, Calif.**
13. **Jack Uhey, rhp, Hart HS, Newhall, Calif.**
14. Bob Welch, rhp, Hazel Park HS, Ferndale, Mich.
15. **Steve Hamrick, lhp, Cornell**
16. **Gary Howard, of, Williamson HS, Mobile, Ala.**
17. **Ronald Hill, c, Delano (Calif.) HS**
18. Jeff Rowlands, c, Howland HS, Warren, Ohio
19. **Marion Massee, ss, Fitzgerald (Ga.) HS**
20. Michael Tucker, rhp, Great Falls (Mont.) HS
21. Joe Budiselish, c, Linden HS, Stockton, Calif.
22. Greg Stitzinger, 2b, Mesa (Ariz.) CC
23. **Aaron Randall, 1b, Grambling**
24. William Miles, rhp, East HS, Nashville
25. John Harris, of, Jackson HS, Miami

June—Secondary Phase (17)

No selection

CHICAGO WHITE SOX

January—Regular Phase (7)

1. **Kevin Bell, 3b, Mount San Antonio (Calif.) JC**
2. Richard Swanson, rhp, Triton (Ill.) JC
3. **Jay Attardi, lhp, Miami-Dade North CC**
4. Ed Devalasco, rhp, Miami-Dade North CC
5. **Cas Sledzik, c, Mayfair (Ohio) JC**

January—Secondary Phase (9)

1. **Butch Stinson, lhp/of, Vanderbilt**
2. Carl Gardner, 3b, Miami-Dade North CC
3. Garnett Houghton, rhp, Ohlone (Calif.) JC

June—Regular Phase (8)

1. **Larry Monroe, rhp, Forest View HS, Mount Prospect, Ill.**
2. **Jack Kucek, rhp, Miami (Ohio)**
3. **Pete Vuckovich, rhp, Clarion (Pa.)**
4. **Harris Price, c, Shaler Township HS, Glenshaw, Pa.**
5. **Ray Katts, of, Southside HS, Sardis, Ala.**
6. **Thomas Toman, of, Gateway Senior HS, Monroeville, Pa.**
7. **Tony Komadina, lhp, Arizona State**
8. **Donn Seidholz, 3b, Indiana**
9. Jim Farr, rhp, Athens (Pa.) HS
10. **Dennis Sandoval, rhp, Servite HS, Placentia, Calif.**
11. **Michael Smith, c/rhp, Carver HS, Birmingham**
12. **Paul Bock, lhp, Western Michigan**
13. **Phil Trucks, c, Carol City HS, Opalocka, Fla.**
14. **Edward Olszta, c/of, Providence HS, New Lenox, Ill.**
15. Lawrence Berkery, 1b/lhp, Riverview HS, Sarasota, Fla.
16. Bill Swiacki, rhp, Choate Prep School, Sturbridge, Mass.

17. **Scott Richartz, ss, Chino (Calif.) HS**
18. **Dave Frost, rhp, Stanford**
19. James Roach, rhp, Lincolnway HS, Mokena, Ill.
20. **Ted Loehr, rhp, Stetson**
21. **Marland Easley, c/of, Santa Ana (Calif.) Valley HS**
22. Joseph Nahay, lhp, Garden Grove HS, Pacifica, Calif.
23. Albert Paglione, rhp, St. Anthony HS, Trenton, N.J.

June—Secondary Phase (18)

1. **Phil Nerone, 3b, Miami-Dade North CC**
2. Michael St. Louis, lhp, Ithaca (N.Y.)

CINCINNATI REDS

January—Regular Phase (24)

1. **Mike Armstrong, rhp, Miami**
2. Dennie Gentry, rhp, Rose State (Okla.) JC
3. Bruce Ryals, of, Florida CC
4. Scott Miller, of, St. Petersburg (Fla.) JC
5. Alan Kunick, of, Bismarck (N.D.) JC
6. Ronnie Corder, ss/3b, Highland Community (Kan.) JC
7. Kevin Gallinari, rhp, Nassau (N.Y.) CC
8. Tom Kotchman, 3b, Chipola (Fla.) JC

January—Secondary Phase (22)

1. **James Diventi, rhp, Essex (Md.) CC**
2. Richard Barrett, rhp, Manatee (Fla.) JC

June—Regular Phase (23)

1. **Steve Reed, rhp, Fort Wayne (Ind.) HS**
2. **Mike Grace, 3b, Waterford Mott HS, Pontiac, Mich.**
3. **Mike LaCoss, rhp, Mount Whitney HS, Visalia, Calif.**
4. **Jim Reeves, of, Texas**
5. **Steve Henderson, ss/3b, Prairie View A&M**
6. **Mark Pearson, rhp, Alton (Ill.) HS**
7. **Bradley Bush, c, Paris (Texas) HS**
8. Jeff Hansen, of, El Camino HS, Sacramento
9. **Ron Oester, ss, Withrow HS, Cincinnati**
10. **Lynn Jones, of, Thiel (Pa.)**
11. **Jerry Christensen, rhp, Manzano HS, Albuquerque**
12. **Charles Renneau, rhp, Granite Hills HS, El Cajon, Calif.**
13. **Paul Marshall, of, Sheridan (Wyo.) HS**
14. **Robert Constantine, 3b, Lyman HS, Altamonte Springs, Fla.**
15. **Dan Norman, 1b/of, Barstow (Calif.) CC**
16. Kevin Waldrop, rhp, Herrin (Ill.) HS
17. **Randy Walraven, lhp, Alvarado (Texas) HS**
18. **Tim Doerr, 3b/1b, UCLA**
19. **Brice Kinnamon, c, Cambridge (Md.) HS**
20. **William Baggett, of, Rose Sterling HS, Houston**
21. **Charles Neal, rhp/1b, Smiley HS, Houston**
22. John Barron, rhp, Cameron (Texas) HS
23. **Dean Graumann, 2b/ss, Tulsa**
24. **Tim Dull, rhp, Johnstown (Pa.) Vocational Tech HS**
25. Scott Burk, ss/rhp, Cherry Creek HS, Englewood, Colo.
26. **John Fuller, c, Florida**
27. George McLean, rhp, New Albany (Ind.) HS
28. **James Turner, ss, Georgia**
29. James Russell, 1b/3b, Helix HS, La Mesa, Calif.
30. **Stephen Hughes, rhp, Cal State Los Angeles**
31. David Pugh, ss/of, Highland Park HS, St. Paul, Minn.
32. Keith Lloyd, lhp, Waltrip HS, Houston
33. Timothy Rappe, of/2b, Wisconsin
34. John Crane, rhp, Martin County HS, Stuart, Fla.
35. Julian Rodriguez, 3b, Twin Lake HS, West Palm Beach, Fla.
36. Andy McGaffigan, rhp, Twin Lake HS, West Palm Beach, Fla.

June—Secondary Phase (1)

1. Mike Gatlin, 3b, Arizona

CLEVELAND INDIANS

January—Regular Phase (3)

1. Stephen Cook, of/3b, Miami-Dade North CC
2. Francis Legath, ss, St. Petersburg (Fla.) JC
3. Steven Gorthy, c, Fresno CC
4. Jamie Baby, lhp, Cuyahoga (Ohio) CC
5. Paul Moskau, 3b/rhp, Arizona State
6. **Robert Fulgham, lhp/of, Holmes (Miss.) JC**
7. Joe Griffin, c, Polk (Fla.) CC
8. Glen Lamas, c, Southeastern Louisiana
9. **Michael Dolf, 2b/ss, JC of the Redwoods (Calif.)**
10. Garry Hancock, of, Hillsborough (Fla.) CC
11. Robert Glass, 3b, Manatee (Fla.) JC
12. Mark Clemons, ss/2b, Itawamba (Miss.) JC
13. John Webster, ss/2b, Panola (Texas) JC

January—Secondary Phase (19)

1. Mike Merritt, rhp, North Carolina
2. Gary Ezell, ss/rhp, Connors State (Okla.) JC
3. Brad Van Pelt, rhp, Michigan State

June—Regular Phase (4)

1. **Tom Brennan, rhp, Lewis (Ill.)**
2. **Ricky Howerton, c, Taft HS, Canoga Park, Calif.**
3. **John Arnold, lhp, Effingham (Ill.) HS**
4. Stanley Mann, ss, Southern Illinois
5. Earl Bass, rhp, South Carolina
6. Karl Schroeder, lhp, John Marshall HS, Oklahoma City, Okla.
7. **Steven Hanson, rhp, Andover HS, North Linthicum, Md.**
8. Michael Frazier, c, Texas A&M
9. Ward Wilson, c, Dunedin (Fla.) HS
10. **Ben Heise, ss, Arizona**
11. David Gallino, ss, El Sabrante (Calif.) HS
12. Steven Van Deren, c, JC of the Redwoods (Calif.)
13. **Thomas Sowles, of, Albion (Mich.)**
14. **Steven Widner, lhp, Gibbs HS, Corryton, Tenn.**
15. **Stanley Maffey, of, Treasure Valley (Ore.) CC**
16. David Adeimy, c, Forest Hill HS, West Palm Beach, Fla.
17. **Steven Huusfeldt, rhp, Lowell HS, Whittier, Calif.**
18. **Orlando Gonzalez, 1b, Miami**
19. **Hurley Mitchell, rhp, Coeburn (Va.) HS**
20. Jerry Stamps, c/1b, South Alabama
21. **Michael Jones, rhp, Colonial HS, Orlando, Fla.**
22. James McBride, rhp, Blair HS, Hattiesburg, Miss.
23. Kevin Kopp, c, Sylmar (Calif.) HS
24. **Carlos Brooks, c, North Carolina**
25. **Timothy Fox, rhp, Oklahoma**

June—Secondary Phase (12)

1. Ron Montgomery, of, East Los Angeles JC
2. **Sandy Wihtol, rhp, DeAnza (Calif.) JC**
3. Danny White, inf, Arizona State

DETROIT TIGERS

January—Regular Phase (15)

1. Randy Nall, of, Citrus (Calif.) JC
2. William Crawford, lhp, Gulf Coast (Fla.) CC
3. David Delenick, 1b, St. Clair, Pa.

January—Secondary Phase (17)

1. Bob Pate, 3b/of, Mesa (Ariz.) JC

June—Regular Phase (16)

1. **Lance Parrish, inf, Walnut HS, Diamond Bar, Calif.**
2. **James Taylor, lhp, Franklin County HS, Decherd, Tenn.**
3. **Steve Viefhaus, inf, St. Louis CC-Meramec**
4. **Melvin Jackson, ss, LeMoyne-Owen (Tenn.)**
5. **Ronald Martinez, of, Buena HS, Ventura, Calif.**
6. William Poland, lhp, Crescenta Valley HS, Glendale, Calif.
7. **David Balbierz, rhp, Hilbert (N.Y.) JC**
8. Dan Morogiello, lhp, Milford Academy, Brooklyn, N.Y.
9. Jake Battle, c, Western HS, Detroit
10. **Mark Fidrych, rhp, Worcester Academy HS, Northboro, Mass.**
11. **Stephen Gamby, rhp, Carey (Ohio) HS**
12. **William Coury, c, Durfee HS, Fall River, Mass.**
13. **Brian Kelly, ss, Churchill HS, Livonia, Mich.**
14. Richard Spanton, lhp, Chathard HS, Indianapolis
15. Greg Keatley, c, Miami-Dade North CC
16. **Steven Harris, lhp, Connally HS, West, Texas**
17. **Greg Kline, of, Northeastern HS, Mount Wolf, Pa.**
18. John Stocker, 3b, Custer HS, Milwaukee

19. **Bob Sykes, lhp, Miami-Dade North CC**
20. **Calvin Jones, ss, Delaware State**
21. John Crabtree, lhp, John Marshall HS, Indianapolis
22. **Clifford Irwin, rhp, California**
23. Terry O'Hearn, of, Catholic Central HS, Grand Rapids, Mich.
24. **Robert LaLonde, rhp, Mohawk Valley (N.Y.) CC**
25. **John Johnson, rhp, South Carolina**
26. **Patrick Murphy, lhp, Pepperdine**
27. **Richard Fulton, rhp, Gardner-Webb (N.C.)**
28. **Edward Carroll, of, Raritan HS, Hazlet, N.J.**
29. David Hollifield, of, Kenwood HS, Baltimore

June—Secondary Phase (6)

1. Rob Picciolo, inf, Pepperdine

HOUSTON ASTROS

January—Regular Phase (16)

1. **Joe Cannon, of, Pensacola (Fla.) JC**
2. Robert Starks, lhp, Canada (Calif.) JC

January—Secondary Phase (24)

1. Danny White, inf, Arizona State

June—Regular Phase (15)

1. **Kevin Drake, of, Cabrillo HS, Lompoc, Calif.**
2. **Jeff Smith, ss, Hoggard HS, Wilmington, N.C.**
3. **Alan Knicely, rhp, Turner Ashby HS, Bridgewater, Va.**
4. **Fay Thompson, 1b, Vallejo (Calif.) HS**
5. **David Buckley, lhp, Bellevue (Wash.) CC**
6. **Ken LaHonta, of, Serra HS, Millbrae, Calif.**
7. Don Kainer, rhp, Milby HS, Houston
8. **Richard Haynes, inf, Clemson**
9. **Tom Twellman, inf, Southern Illinois-Edwardsville**
10. **Greg Jurgenson, lhp, Oregon State**
11. Gaylon Austin, lhp, Klein HS, Spring, Texas
12. **Larry Matula, rhp, Temple (Texas) JC**
13. Tony Johnson, of, Northside HS, Memphis
14. Mickey Hatcher, of, Mesa (Ariz.) HS
15. **Tom Rima, of, New Orleans**
16. **Michael Hasley, lhp, Modesto (Calif.) JC**

June—Secondary Phase (3)

1. Gil Patterson, of/rhp, Miami-Dade South CC
2. Chuck Baker, ss, Loyola Marymount

KANSAS CITY ROYALS

January—Regular Phase (17)

1. **Mark Souza, lhp, JC of San Mateo (Calif.)**
2. **Harold Thomasson, 3b/ss, Laney (Calif.) JC**
3. Phil Doktor, ss, Citrus (Calif.) JC
4. Mike Scott, lhp, Central Arizona JC
5. Dale King, rhp, Miami-Dade South CC
6. **Bobby Castillo Jr., rhp, Los Angeles Valley JC**
7. Rowland George, rhp, Atlantic (N.J.) CC
8. Wayne Carmichael, lhp, Atlantic (N.J.) CC
9. **Craig Husband, lhp, Oregon**

January—Secondary Phase (1)

1. **David Hasbach, rhp, Miami (Ohio)**
2. **Xavier Dixson, of, St. Mary's**
3. **Dan Walker, rhp, Malone (Ohio)**
4. Steve Woitock, 2b, Dana (Neb.)

June—Regular Phase (18)

1. **Willie Wilson, of, Summit (N.J.) HS**
2. **Robert Edmondson, c, Lakeview HS, Fort Oglethorpe, Ga.**
3. Everett Murray, of, North College Hill HS, Cincinnati
4. **Pat Curran, of, Chapman (Calif.)**
5. **Thomas Laseter, of, San Jacinto (Texas) JC**
6. Craig Eaton, rhp, Miami-Dade North CC
7. **Kevin Lahey, rhp, Newburgh (N.Y.) Free Academy**
8. **Ed Sempsrott, lhp, Danville (Ill.) HS**
9. Russ Francis, rhp, Oregon
10. Jeff Campbell, lhp, Unicoi HS, Erwin, Tenn.
11. Scott Sanderson, rhp, North HS, Glenbrook, Ill.
12. **Keith Bridges, of, UC Irvine**
13. Charles McLean, 3b, Richmond Senior HS, Rockingham, N.C.
14. **Ray Humphries, rhp, UC Irvine**
15. Lawrence Pekarcik, rhp, Damien HS, Pomona, Calif.
16. Bobby Gabriesheski, of, Raleigh-Egypt HS, Memphis
17. Gregg Foster, rhp, Marina HS, Huntington Beach, Calif.
18. David McIntyre, c, Polk Central HS, Tryon, N.C.
19. Jeff Hemm, c, Hale HS, Tulsa, Okla.
20. **Jerry Peterson, rhp, Ocoee (Fla.) HS**
21. **Gary Wright, lhp, Miami (Ohio)**
22. **William Wilson, lhp, Montclair (N.J.) HS**
23. Thomas Perkins, rhp, Cal State Los Angeles
24. Tim O'Neill, rhp, North Torrance (Calif.) HS
25. **John Affinito, of, Linton HS, Schenectady, N.Y.**
26. Mike Parker, 3b, Start HS, Toledo, Ohio
27. Douglas Warrick, 3b, Louisburg (N.C.) JC
28. Sammy Stewart, rhp, Montreat-Anderson (N.C.) JC
29. **Stewart Colton, lhp, Nevada-Reno**
30. **Craig Lloyd, 1b, Southern Utah State**
31. **Dale Hrovat, rhp, Arizona State**
32. **Huey Fleming, of, Leon Godchaux HS, Reserve, La.**
33. Michael McLellan, rhp, Kennedy HS, Denver
34. Larry Goldetsky, ss, St. Louis Park (Minn.) HS
35. Daniel Gans, 3b, Torrance (Calif.) HS

June—Secondary Phase (8)

1. **Mike Williams, lhp, Temple (Texas) JC**
2. **Randy Nall, of, Citrus (Calif.) JC**

LOS ANGELES DODGERS

January—Regular Phase (22)

1. **Claude Westmoreland, of, California**
2. Dale Forchetti, ss, Southern Mississippi
3. Henry Boguszewski, rhp, Nassau (N.Y.) CC
4. Shane Rawley, lhp, Indian Hills (Iowa) CC

January—Secondary Phase (6)

1. **Don Cardoza, of, JC of the Sequoias (Calif.)**
2. Jim Dorsey, rhp, Los Angeles Valley JC

June—Regular Phase (21)

1. **Rick Sutcliffe, rhp, Van Horn HS, Kansas City**
2. **Steve Shirley, lhp, Terra Nova HS, Pacifica, Calif.**
3. **Freddie Tisdale, ss, Centennial HS, Los Angeles**
4. **Jim Riggleman, 2b/3b, Frostburg State (Md.)**
5. **Alvin Harper, ss, Southern**
6. **James Delvecchio, 2b, Andrew Ward HS, Fairfield, Conn.**
7. Chris Gandy, of, Christian Brothers HS, Sacramento
8. **Randall Rogers, ss, Texas HS, Texarkana, Texas**
9. **Joseph Keller, rhp, Clover Park HS, Tacoma, Wash.**
10. **Rick Ollar, of, Oklahoma State**
11. Scott Anderson, rhp, Lake Oswego (Ore.) HS
12. Dwayne Wright, c, Berkeley (Calif.) HS
13. Leslie Pearsey, ss, Brethren HS, Los Angeles
14. Jackie Schuman, 2b, Putnam City (Okla.) HS
15. **Richard Oliver, 3b, Bishop Fallon HS, Buffalo, N.Y.**
16. **Billy Wilson, rhp, Emporia State (Kan.)**
17. **Michael Laurent, rhp, New Mexico**
18. Ray Murillo, rhp, Agua Fria HS, Avondale, Ariz.
19. Brian Heublein, lhp, Southern California
20. Chris Lynch, rhp, Miami-Dade North CC
21. Ron Wrobel, lhp, Quigley HS, Chicago
22. **Doug Slocum, rhp, Arizona State**

June—Secondary Phase (5)

1. **Robert Glass, 3b, Manatee (Fla.) JC**

MILWAUKEE BREWERS

January—Regular Phase (5)

1. John Caneira, rhp, Eastern Connecticut State
2. Tom Chism, of, Brandywine (Del.) JC

January—Secondary Phase (21)

1. Robert Nickeson, ss, West Valley (Calif.) JC

June—Regular Phase (6)

1. **Butch Edge, rhp, El Camino HS, Sacramento**

2. **Moose Haas, rhp, Franklin HS, Owings Mills, Md.**
3. Tom Van Der Meersche, rhp, Everett (Wash.) HS
4. **Barry Cort, rhp, King HS, Tampa**
5. **Gary Beare, rhp, Cal State Long Beach**
6. Mike Denevi, ss, Santa Clara
7. **Steve Bowling, of, Tulsa**
8. **David Sylvia, rhp, Lakewood HS, Long Beach**
9. William Taylor, of, St. Augustine HS, San Diego
10. **Carl Pohlman, lhp, Central Michigan**
11. Paul Bain, rhp, South Torrance (Calif.) HS
12. **Jim Gantner, ss, Wisconsin-Oshkosh**
13. **Tom Farina, ss, Pulaski HS, Milwaukee**
14. Dan Morgan, rhp, Superior (Wis.) HS
15. **Jerry Augustine, lhp, Wisconsin-La Crosse**
16. David Pencille, rhp, Stagg HS, Stockton, Calif.

June—Secondary Phase (10)

1. **Richard Scarborough, ss/2b, Clemson**

MINNESOTA TWINS

January—Regular Phase (13)

1. **Mark Lockwood, lhp, Fullerton (Calif.) JC**
2. William Nelson, lhp, Miami-Dade North CC
3. Doug Thomson, rhp, Rio Hondo (Calif.) JC
4. Brian Pulliam, of, Fullerton (Calif.) JC
5. John Batton, rhp, Los Angeles Pierce JC
6. Neal Patton, rhp, Southwestern (Calif.) JC
7. Frank Terriogo, ss, St. Peter's (N.J.)
8. Sam Floyd, ss, Canada (Calif.) JC
9. **Donald Cross, rhp, Fremont, Calif.**
10. **Wayne Caughey, ss, St. Cloud State (Minn.)**

January—Secondary Phase (11)

1. **Jerry Garvin, lhp, Merced (Calif.) JC**
2. Richard Douglass, rhp/1b, Saddleback (Calif.) CC
3. Kevin Morel, ss, Indian River (Fla.) CC

June—Regular Phase (14)

1. **Ted Shipley, ss, Vanderbilt**
2. **Butch Wynegar Jr., c, Red Lion HS, York, Pa.**
3. **Dean Olson, lhp, Nogales HS, LaPuente, Calif.**
4. Michael Lambert, lhp, Culver City (Calif.) HS
5. **John Maier, rhp, Penn State**
6. Curtis Etchandy, ss, Santiago HS, Garden Grove, Calif.
7. **John Lonchar, c, Michigan**
8. Howard McCann, ss, Oswego (N.Y.) HS
9. **Steven Flores, of, La Habra (Calif.) HS**
10. Steve Kruzelock, c, Venice HS, Mar Vista, Calif.
11. Tom Costello, p, Newberg HS, Dundee, Ore.
12. John Helfrick, 3b, San Diego State
13. Dartt Wagner, of, Buchser HS, Santa Clara, Calif.
14. **Bud Bulling, c, Cal State Los Angeles**
15. **William Bitter, c, Fresno (Calif.) HS**
16. **Randy Lee, lhp, Bell Gardens (Calif.) HS**
17. **Robb Mayhew, lhp, La Verne (Calif.)**
18. **Theodore Groff, lhp, Lampeter-Strasburg HS, Willow, Pa.**
19. **Frank Quintero, rhp, Buena Park (Calif.) HS**
20. Brett Houser, p, Millikan HS, Long Beach
21. Ronnie Mears, ss, Pinole (Calif.) HS
22. David Enos, ss, Troy HS, Yorba Linda, Calif.
23. **Michael Angione, rhp, Iona**
24. **James Volkmar, c, Ithaca (N.Y.)**
25. Bill Foley, c, Bowie (Md.) HS
26. **Jesus Lopez, 3b/2b, East Side HS, Newark, N.J.**
27. Gary Armstrong, ss, El Capitan HS, Lakeside, Calif.
28. David Pearce, lhp, Kearns HS, Salt Lake City
29. Fred Westfall, rhp, Madison HS, San Diego
30. **Charles Alonso, 1b, La Verne (Calif.)**
31. **Mike Heinen, rhp, Cal Poly Pomona**
32. Bill Hughes, ss, Notre Dame HS, North Hollywood, Calif.
33. **Douglas Gildenzoph, rhp, Nekoosa (Wis.) HS**
34. **John Torreano, lhp, Albany HS, Berkeley, Calif.**
35. Larry Randel, ss, Magnolia HS, Anaheim
36. Eric Show, rhp, Ramona HS, Riverside, Calif.
37. Tom Jahnke, of, Richfield HS, Minneapolis
38. **Tom Channel, rhp, Washington HS, Portland, Ore.**
39. Benjamin Chrin, rhp, Whitehall (Pa.) HS
40. **Kent Mariska, of, Jefferson HS, Bloomington, Minn.**
41. Robert Blake, lhp, Cretin HS, St. Paul, Minn.

June—Secondary Phase (24)

1. Gary Bishop, 1b, Indian River (Fla.) CC

MONTREAL EXPOS

January—Regular Phase (10)

1. **Joe Kerrigan, rhp, Temple**
2. Ned Yost, c, Chabot (Calif.) JC
3. Bill Przygocki, rhp, St. Clair County (Mich.) CC
4. Kent Taylor, ss, East Los Angeles JC
5. Randy Niemann, lhp, JC of the Redwoods (Calif.)
6. John Bass, 3b, Laney (Calif.) JC
7. **Mike Uebbing, rhp, Grossmont (Calif.) JC**
8. **Ronald Edwards, rhp, Detroit**
9. Gary Gronowski, rhp, Valencia (Fla.) CC
10. **Kenneth Snyder, rhp, Chabot (Calif.) JC**
11. **William Wood, of, South Georgia JC**
12. David Oliver, of, Grossmont (Calif.) JC
13. Doug Heinz, rhp, San Joaquin Delta (Calif.) JC
14. Kevin Kearney, 1b, Laney (Calif.) JC

January—Secondary Phase (10)

1. Michael St. Louis, rhp, Ithaca (N.Y.)
2. Steve Williams, lhp, St. Clair County (Mich.) CC
3. Dan Grimm, rhp, Fresno State
4. David Koza, lhp/of, Eastern Oklahoma State JC

June—Regular Phase (9)

1. **Ron Sorey, 3b, Stebbins HS, Dayton, Ohio**
2. **Jerry Fry, ss, Springfield (Ill.) HS**
3. Dave Tobik, rhp, Ohio
4. **Godfrey Evans, ss, Morningside HS, Compton, Calif.**
5. **Norm Fierbaugh, rhp, Ashland (Ohio)**
6. **David Frederickson, rhp, Santa Barbara (Calif.) CC**
7. **Bobby Ramos, c, Jackson HS, Miami**
8. **Marv Chamberlain, 1b/3b, Washington State**
9. **John Novak, lhp, Ohio**
10. Bobby Bonner, 3b, King HS, Corpus Christi, Texas
11. Tim Richards, c, Westminster (Calif.) HS
12. **Robert Woodland, of, Howard**
13. **Dave Whiteaker, c, Gonzaga**
14. **Bob Bohr, rhp, Central Dauphin HS, Harrisburg, Pa.**
15. **Joe Meir, rhp, Hillsboro (Ore.) HS**
16. **Michael Curran, 3b, Iowa State**
17. **Joe Gonzalez, of/1b, Blinn (Texas) JC**
18. Robert Dinges, of/1b, Gunn HS, Palo Alto, Calif.
19. Hubie Brooks, ss, Dominguez HS, Compton, Calif.
20. **William Welsh, ss, St. Anthony's HS, Trenton, N.J.**
21. Stanley Butler, ss, Long Beach Poly HS
22. Gregg Bemis, lhp, Puget Sound (Wash.)
23. Lawrence Kalmus, rhp, Gonzalez (Texas) HS
24. **Gary Horstmann, rhp, Blinn (Texas) JC**
25. Randall Esker, rhp, Valmeyer (Ill.) HS
26. Robert Weis, c, Eastmont HS, East Wenatchee, Wash.
27. Larry Kowalishen, rhp, Chabot (Calif.) JC
28. **Rodney Hampton, 1b/of, Henry Ford (Mich.) CC**
29. David Thieneman, rhp, Chalmette HS, Meraux, La.
30. Steve Wilkins, of, Treasure Valley (Ore.) CC
31. Gerry Greene, c, Essex (Vt.) HS
32. Ronald Irwin, rhp, Pontiac (Mich.) Northern HS
33. Cleveland Porter, rhp, Ganesha HS, Pomona, Calif.
34. Richard Casillas, c, San Bernardino (Calif.) HS
35. Ted Smith, p/of, San Leandro (Calif.) HS
36. Randy Toogood, c, Kailua (Hawaii) HS
37. John Riffle, rhp/of, Palisades (Calif.) HS
38. Ronald Goodman, lhp, Santa Barbara (Calif.) HS
39. Waldo Winborn, of, Buena HS, Sierra Vista, Ariz.

June—Secondary Phase (13)

1. **Jamie Baby, lhp, Cuyahoga (Ohio) CC**
2. **Shane Rawley, lhp, Indian Hills (Iowa) CC**

NEW YORK METS

January—Regular Phase (18)

1. Robert Carroll, rhp, East Los Angeles JC
2. **Stan Hough, of, McLennan (Texas) JC**
3. James Eble, lhp, Roane State (Tenn.) CC
4. **Edward Hicks, ss, Brewton-Parker (Ga.) JC**
5. Antonio Castro, of, Southwestern (Calif.) JC
6. Richie Howard, 3b, Middle Georgia JC
7. **Gerald Tenge, rhp, Scottsdale (Ariz.) CC**
8. Randy Peterson, c, Green River (Wash.) CC

January—Secondary Phase (20)

1. Charles Fore, rhp, Faulkner State (Ala.) JC
2. Colin Leisher, ss, Valencia (Fla.) CC

June—Regular Phase (17)

1. **Cliff Speck, rhp, Beaverton (Ore.) HS**
2. **Dwight Bernard, rhp, Belmont**
3. **Keith Bodie, of, South Shore HS, Brooklyn, N.Y.**
4. **John Pacella, rhp, Connetquot HS, Oakdale, N.Y.**
5. **James Mills, 1b, Baker (La.) HS**
6. **Darrell Lakey, rhp, Redwood HS, Visalia, Calif.**
7. **Don Driskill, rhp, Jordan HS, Long Beach**
8. **Ed Cipot, of, Highland HS, Highland Park, N.J.**
9. **Steve Garrison, of, St. Augustine HS, San Diego**
10. Brian Cherevko, rhp, Buchser HS, Santa Clara, Calif.
11. John McBride, ss, Utah
12. Pat Putnam, 1b, Miami-Dade North CC
13. **Stephen Lott, of, Jefferson HS, Tampa**
14. **Randy Frankum, rhp, Wharton (Texas) HS**
15. Ray Cardinalli, of, Monterey (Calif.) HS
16. **William Gifford, ss, Whitehaven HS, Memphis**
17. **David Richardson, rhp, Alhambra HS, Martinez, Calif.**
18. Steve Baker, rhp, Monte Vista HS, La Mesa, Calif.
19. Joe Grajewski, rhp, Central Catholic HS, Steubenville, Ohio
20. **Bob Myrick, lhp, Mississippi State**
21. **Lowell Jacobsen, rhp, Grand View (Iowa) JC**
22. **Bruce Gustafson, c, Minnesota**
23. **William Beno, of, Manatee (Fla.) JC**
24. **William Daly, 3b, Richmond**
25. **David Butler, rhp, Cal State Stanislaus**
26. Michael O'Connor, lhp, Christ the King HS, Glendale, N.Y.
27. Ralph Jiminez, c, Stevenson HS, Bronx, N.Y.
28. **Wayne Bauers, of, Sonoma State (Calif.)**
29. **Robert Leonard, rhp, Salinas (Calif.) HS**
30. **Greg Boos, rhp, Wayne State (Neb.)**
31. Gene Krug, 1b, Lamar (Colo.) CC
32. Tim Glines, c, Central Catholic HS, Modesto, Calif.
33. **Gene Felts, of, Valdosta State (Ga.)**
34. Stewart Bringhurst, c, JC of San Mateo (Calif.)
35. Gene Little, rhp, California
36. Steve Marlowe, 1b, Utah
37. Jim Lysgaard, rhp, JC of San Mateo (Calif.)
38. Scott Lankford, rhp, Downey HS, Modesto, Calif.

June—Secondary Phase (7)

1. **Ned Yost, c, Chabot (Calif.) JC**
2. **Antonio Castro, of, Southwestern (Calif.) JC**

NEW YORK YANKEES

January—Regular Phase (11)

1. Ken Phelps, of, Mesa (Ariz.) CC
2. Ron Montgomery, of, East Los Angeles JC
3. Jason Tanneberg, lhp, Bellevue (Wash.) CC

January—Secondary Phase (5)

1. Gene Delyon, 3b, Santa Clara
2. Scott Gunderson, rhp, Bellevue (Wash.) CC
3. **Leon Plunkett, of, Southern Mississippi**

June—Regular Phase (12)

1. **Dennis Sherrill, ss, South Miami (Fla.) HS**
2. **Dave Bergman, 1b/of, Illinois State**
3. **Jose Alvarez, ss, St. Patrick's HS, Elizabeth,N.J**
4. **Terry Bevington, c, Santa Monica (Calif.) HS**
5. **David Carter, of, Glassboro State (N.J.)**
6. **Jerry Narron, c, Goldsboro (N.C.) HS**
7. Jeff Jens, rhp, Kennedy HS, Granada Hills, Calif.
8. **Richard Fleshman, rhp, American**
9. **Scott Norris, of, Arizona**
10. **Joe Kwasny, rhp, Kellam HS, Virginia Beach, Va.**
11. **Edward O'Rick, lhp, Reading (Ohio) HS**
12. Billy Severns, of, Oklahoma
13. **Robert Gagg, rhp/ss, Butler HS, Bloomingdale, N.J.**
14. **Pat Peterson, ss, Southern Illinois-Edwardsville**
15. **Charles Jones, rhp, Walpole (Mass.) HS**
16. Orville Rhuems, rhp, Colgan HS, Pittsburg, Kan.
17. **Sam Mishmash, rhp, Colgan HS, Pittsburg, Kan.**
18. **Sabah Mendez, rhp, Julia Richmond HS, New York**
19. **Dennis Werth, c/1b, Southern Illinois-Edwardsville**
20. **Kevin McNichol, inf, New York**
21. **Gary McMurtry, lhp, Metcalf (Ga.)**
22. **Greg Diehl, rhp, Delaware**
23. Robert Giapponi, of, Sheenan HS, Wellingford, Conn.

June—Secondary Phase (22)

No selection

OAKLAND ATHLETICS

January—Regular Phase (23)

1. Steven Williams, rhp, Golden West (Calif.) JC
2. Kevin LanFranco, lhp, Santa Ana (Calif.) JC
3. Eddie White, rhp, Riverside (Calif.) CC
4. Michael Tennant, rhp, Neosho County (Kan.) JC
5. Ronald Smith, 2b, Los Angeles CC
6. Robert McKelvey, of/1b, Cerritos (Calif.) JC
7. Rodney Brown, 2b, Golden West (Calif.) JC
8. Clark Beam, of, Mitchell (N.C.) CC
9. **Richard Peregud, rhp, Saddleback (Calif.) CC**

January—Secondary Phase (15)

1. David Steck, rhp, San Diego Mesa JC
2. Wayne Steele, lhp, San Diego State
3. Errect Ridley, of, Santa Monica (Calif.) JC

June—Regular Phase (22)

1. Jerry Johnson, c, McCallum HS, Austin
2. Jim Loftin, lhp, Rains HS, Mobile, Ala.
3. David Wendt, lhp, Shawnee Mission North HS, Merriam, Kan.
4. **Dennis Haines, c, Arizona**
5. Don Walker, ss/rhp, Pecos (Texas) HS
6. **Don Petrie, rhp/inf, Pem Day HS, Overland Park, Kan.**
7. Ron Roenicke, 1b, Edgewood HS, West Covina, Calif.
8. **James Oldham, rhp, Fox HS, Arnold, Mo.**
9. Tom Ruegger, of, Hawthorne (Calif.) HS
10. Jerry Ennis, ss, South HS, Bakersfield, Calif.
11. **James Moldenhauer, c, Minnesota**
12. **Darrell Woodard, inf, Bell HS, Los Angeles**
13. Michael Wirwas, ss, Inglewood (Calif.) HS
14. Richard Brewster, 2b, San Bernardino (Calif.) HS
15. **Nolan Ramirez, ss, Whittier**
16. **Robert Argenti, ss, Lafayette**
17. **Ronald Beaurivage, 1b, Massachusetts**
18. **Michael Rodriguez, c, Grand Island (N.Y.) HS**
19. **Rick Lysander, rhp, Cal State Los Angeles**
20. Larry Buckle, rhp, Wilson HS, Long Beach
21. **Chris Wibberley, rhp, Loyola Marymount**
22. Anthony Williams, of, Santa Monica (Calif.) HS
23. **Robert Salas, rhp, Nogales HS, LaPuente, Calif.**
24. Leonard Johnson, of, El Camino (Calif.) JC
25. Larry Rosin, rhp, Niles North HS, Skokie, Ill.

June—Secondary Phase (16)

1. Phil Doktor, ss, Citrus (Calif.) JC

PHILADELPHIA PHILLIES

January—Regular Phase (4)

1. **Morris Cooper, rhp, Texas Wesleyan**
2. **Robert Keller, rhp, Austin Peay**
3. **Donald Ballenger, lhp, Merced (Calif.) JC**

4. Fernando Tarin, rhp, Mount San Antonio (Calif.) JC
5. **Ed Oliveros, 2b, Miami-Dade North CC**
6. **Jerry Houston, rhp, San Jose CC**
7. Ken Berger, of, Valencia (Fla.) CC
8. Ron Estes, rhp, JC of Southern Idaho
9. Steve Wyatt, lhp, Mesa (Ariz.) CC
10. Michael Rector, rhp, San Diego CC
11. Harold Adams, of, Bellevue (Wash.) CC
12. Dennis Luquet, 2b, Diablo Valley (Calif.) JC

January—Secondary Phase (14)

1. **Wayne Williams, ss, Ranger (Texas) JC**
2. Jeff Malinoff, 1b, UC Irvine
3. Dan Graham, 3b, Mesa (Ariz.) CC
4. **Warren Brusstar, rhp, Fresno State**
5. Walt Kaczmarek, rhp, Santa Clara

June—Regular Phase (3)

1. **Lonnie Smith, of, Centennial HS, Compton, Calif.**
2. **Kevin Saucier, lhp, Escambia HS, Warrington, Fla.**
3. **Frank Ciammachilli, rhp, Oceanside (Calif.) HS**
4. **Don McCormack, c, Omak (Wash.) HS**
5. **Jim Morrison, 3b, Georgia Southern**
6. **Keefe Perkins, c, East HS, Denver**
7. David Tyler, 3b, Lane HS, Charlottesville, Va.
8. **Mark Clear, rhp, Northview HS, Covina, Calif.**
9. **Doyle Sheets, rhp, Grace (Ind.)**
10. **Tim Ryan, lhp, Santa Clara**
11. **John Gibson, lhp, Georgia Southern**
12. David Caldwell, of, Northwest Cabarrus HS, Kannapolis, N.C.
13. **Todd Brenizer, lhp, Furman**
14. **Larry Wertz, lhp, Las Lomas HS, Walnut Creek, Calif.**
15. **Doug Harrison, rhp, Adams HS, Rochester, Mich.**
16. Freddie Van Bever, 3b, Brevard (Fla.) CC
17. **John Gambrell, of, South Carolina**
18. **Vincent Monti, lhp, Lafayette HS, Brooklyn, N.Y.**
19. **Larry Silveira, c, Cal Poly San Luis Obispo**
20. Jeffrey Brown, of, Air Force
21. **Joseph DiBenedetto, lhp, James Madison HS, Brooklyn, N.Y.**
22. **Jerome Reedy, ss, UC Davis**
23. **John Hill, of, Bridgeport (Conn.) HS**
24. **Dave Smith, ss, Union HS, Tulare, Calif.**
25. Mike Morrissey, rhp, Schenectady, N.Y.
26. Derek Botelho, ss, Boca Raton (Fla.) HS
27. David Stevens, of, Jesuit HS, Citrus Heights, Calif.
28. Randy Owens, rhp, Spartanburg Methodist (S.C.) JC
29. **Alan Franklin, 2b, Catawba (N.C.)**
30. Steve Kaia, rhp, Bullard HS, Fresno
31. **Nicolas Ysursa, ss, Idaho State**
32. William Heberle, 2b, Encina HS, Sacramento

June—Secondary Phase (19)

1. Ken Phelps, of, Mesa (Ariz.) CC

PITTSBURGH PIRATES

January—Regular Phase (12)

1. Dan Bishop, rhp, Green River (Wash.) CC
2. Dennis Bolden, rhp, South Alabama
3. **Fred Breining, rhp, JC of San Mateo (Calif.)**
4. John Pilato, of, Monroe (N.Y.) CC
5. Robert Harold, rhp, Monroe (N.Y.) CC
6. James Del Re, lhp, Monroe (N.Y.) CC
7. Eric Peterson, lhp, Gulf Coast (Fla.) CC
8. Edward Todd, of, Marion (Ala.) Military Institute
9. Stephen Tanner, lhp, Gulf Coast (Fla.) CC
10. Randy Law, ss, Monroe (N.Y.) CC
11. John Hoffman, rhp, Lamar (Colo.) CC
12. Sam Leonard, rhp, Yavapai (Ariz.) JC

January—Secondary Phase (2)

1. **Bob DiPietro, lhp, Stanford**
2. Glen Halvorson, of, Bellevue (Wash.) CC
3. Richard Sherkel, c, Penn State
4. William Martin, rhp, Chipola (Fla.) JC

June—Regular Phase (11)

1. **Rod Scurry, lhp, Proctor Hug HS, Sparks, Nev.**
2. **Gary Hargis, inf, Cabrillo HS, Lompoc, Calif.**
3. LaMart Harris, of, Abilene (Texas) HS
4. **Ray Price, rhp, Washington**
5. **Roger Wick, c, Hermiston (Ore.) Senior HS**
6. **Ed Whitson, rhp, Unicoi County HS, Erwin, Tenn.**
7. **Mike Edwards, inf, UCLA**
8. **Joseph Isaac, rhp, East Laurens HS, Dublin, Ga.**
9. **Phil Scaffidi, ss, St. Joseph's HS, Buffalo, N.Y.**
10. **Bryan Clark, lhp, Madera (Calif.) HS**
11. **Marion Higgins, c, Minor HS, Birmingham**
12. Victor Holmes, rhp, Shoreline HS, Seattle
13. Wayne Anderson, lhp, Crenshaw HS, Los Angeles
14. Richard Murray, 3b, O'Fallon (Ill.) HS
15. **Claude Smith, rhp, Mercer**
16. Robert McIlwain, of, Bainbridge Island (Wash.) HS
17. Michael McLeod, rhp, Middle Georgia JC
18. **James Leverenz, rhp, Indianapolis**
19. Jonathon Walton, 1b/of, Buffalo State
20. **John Bowling, lhp, Kentucky**
21. Timothy Size, rhp, Spring Hill (Ala.)
22. **Alfred Rein, of, Martin County HS, Stuart, Fla.**
23. **Mitchell Nowicki, c, Illinois State**
24. **Walter Cieply, rhp, Monessen (Pa.) HS**
25. Albert Kissner, rhp, Hamden (Conn.) HS
26. **Ronald Barlow, ss, Shenandoah (Pa.) HS**
27. William Yarbrough, inf, Sebring (Fla.) HS
28. Robert Turner, rhp, Fruitland (Idaho) HS
29. Bruce Hunter, ss, Yakima Valley (Wash.) JC
30. **Gregory Yoken, of, Poudre HS, Fort Collins, Colo.**
31. Rick Sweet, c, Gonzaga
32. **Greg Ferguson, rhp, Oklahoma State**
33. Tim Burman, lhp, Cincinnati
34. Charles Ledbetter, rhp, Clearwater (Fla.) HS
35. **Frederick Neeland, rhp, Cherryfield (Maine) HS**
36. **Tim Hogle, lhp, Moon HS, Coraopolis, Pa.**
37. James Stoeckel, inf, Harvard

June—Secondary Phase (21)

1. Alton Caesar, ss, Sierra (Calif.) JC
2. William Cranford, lhp, Gulf Coast (Fla.) CC

ST. LOUIS CARDINALS

January—Regular Phase (14)

1. **John Urrea, rhp, Rio Hondo (Calif.) JC**
2. Bill Simpson, ss, Long Beach CC
3. **Michael Stone, c, Watertown, Conn.**
4. Gerald Hynko, c, South Georgia JC
5. **Calvin Barr, c/of, Broward (Fla.) CC**
6. James Weil, rhp, Grand View (Iowa) JC
7. **William Lobdell, rhp, Broome (N.Y.) CC**
8. **James McGuffin, c, Pasadena (Calif.) CC**
9. Logan Clark, lhp, Mount San Antonio (Calif.) JC
10. Michael Antone, of, Chabot (Calif.) JC

January—Secondary Phase (18)

1. **Alex Pastore, of, South Alabama**
2. **Ed Bowman, inf/of, Southern California**
3. Cliff Holland, lhp, Southern California

June—Regular Phase (13)

1. **Garry Templeton, ss, Santa Ana (Calif.) Valley HS**
2. **Robert Hrapman, ss, Northwestern State**
3. **Gregory Herman, lhp, Lakewood (Calif.) HS**
4. **Kenneth Grassano, rhp, Springfield Garden HS, Rosedale, N.Y.**
5. **Joe Crockett, of, Southern Illinois**
6. David Perez, ss, Hillsdale HS, San Mateo, Calif.
7. Jack Lawson, rhp, Scottsdale (Ariz.) HS
8. **Bill Caudill, rhp, Aviation HS, Redondo Beach, Calif.**
9. Michael Cameron, rhp, Council Rock HS, Ivyland, Pa.
10. Stephen Makwinski, rhp, Sayreville-Warrenton Memorial HS, South Amboy, N.J.
11. **Harold Witt, ss/3b, Stebbins HS, Dayton, Ohio**

12. Charles Maynard, rhp, South San Francisco HS
13. **Dale Carr, 1b/of, Birmingham HS, Encino, Calif.**
14. **Hugh Mendenhall, of, Cottonwood HS, Salt Lake City**
15. **Stan Meek, lhp, Oklahoma**
16. Randy Rodgers, 1b, North Riverside (Calif.) HS
17. **Michael Murphy, rhp/of, St. Louis CC-Meramec**
18. James Buggy, lhp, Power Memorial HS, Ozone Park, N.Y.
19. **William Cowens, ss, Compton (Calif.) JC**
20. Peter Rankowitz, rhp, Tolman HS, Pawtucket, R.I.
21. **Lonnie Kruger, rhp, Kansas State**
22. Neil Fiala, 2b, Vianney HS, St. Louis
23. Dave Baker, ss, Granada Hills HS, Northridge, Calif.
24. **Len Strelitz, rhp, Temple City (Calif.) HS**
25. **Scott Hohensinner, lhp, Puyallup (Wash.) HS**
26. Pat Wathall, rhp, Loara HS, Anaheim
27. Glenn Comoletti, lhp, Braintree (Mass.) HS
28. Paul Molitor, ss, Cretin HS, St. Paul, Minn.
29. **Thomas Valdes, lhp, Baldwin HS, Maui, Hawaii**
30. Phil Marty, ss, El Camino HS, San Francisco
31. **David Boyer, 3b, Hermann (Mo.) HS**

June—Secondary Phase (23)

1. **Terry Kieffer, lhp, Louisiana State**

SAN DIEGO PADRES

January—Regular Phase (2)

1. **Tucker Ashford, 3b/ss, Shelby State (Tenn.) CC**
2. Witt Beckman, of, Miami
3. **Rodney Jett, lhp, Cypress (Calif.) JC**
4. Bobby Hottinger, c, Butte (Calif.) JC
5. Richard Boss, of, JC of San Mateo (Calif.)

January—Secondary Phase (4)

1. Gil Patterson, of/rhp, Miami-Dade South CC
2. Ray Crawford, ss/of, Santa Ana, Calif.

June—Regular Phase (1)

1. **Bill Almon, ss, Brown**
2. **Donnie Alfano, 1b/lhp, Mount Whitney HS, Visalia, Calif.**
3. **Roger Coe, lhp, Toledo**
4. Brandt Humphry, rhp/3b, North Torrance (Calif.) HS
5. Lenn Sakata, 2b, Gonzaga
6. **Galen McSpadden, lhp, Southeast Missouri State**
7. **Jim Wilhelm, 1b/of, Santa Clara**
8. **Stuart McCoy, of, Bullard HS, Fresno**
9. **Robert Taylor, ss, Nicholls State**
10. **Lyn Hamilton, c, Clemson**
11. **Carl Mayberry, 1b, Floresville (Texas) HS**
12. Bump Wills, 2b, Arizona State
13. **Ron Gill, rhp, UC Riverside**
14. **Rodney Leisle, 2b, Bullard HS, Fresno**
15. **Rod Bovee, lhp, Pacific**
16. **Bill Delormier, rhp, San Diego State**
17. Steven Roak, rhp, San Pedro (Calif.) HS
18. **Byron Burns, rhp, Gonzaga**
19. **Mark Carroll, rhp, San Jose State**
20. James Wilson, rhp/of, Compton (Calif.) HS

June—Secondary Phase (9)

1. **Gene Delyon, 3b, Santa Clara**
2. **Steve Barrett, 2b, Murray State**

SAN FRANCISCO GIANTS

January—Regular Phase (20)

1. **Daniel Smith, lhp/1b, Los Angeles Valley JC**
2. Arthur Spann, of, Alcorn State
3. Larry Nevarez, rhp, Ventura (Calif.) JC
4. Tyrone Osborne, rhp/1b, Berkeley, Calif.
5. Mark Miggins, 1b, Miami-Dade South CC
6. Steven Turner, p, Treasure Valley (Ore.) CC
7. Dale Yraguen, rhp, Treasure Valley (Ore.) CC

January—Secondary Phase (12)

1. Clifford Mays, rhp, Clark (Wash.) JC
2. Les Hemby, c, Blinn (Texas) JC
3. **Gary Atwell, of, Arizona State**
4. **Dan Beitey, rhp, Clark (Wash.) JC**
5. **Mark Erickson, 1b, Clark (Wash.) JC**

June—Regular Phase (19)

1. **Terry Lee, 2b, San Luis Obispo (Calif.) HS**
2. Kenny Kolkhorst, c/1b, Waltrip HS, Houston
3. **Alan Wirth, rhp, St. Mary's HS, Mesa, Ariz.**
4. Rob Lory, lhp, Buena HS, Ventura, Calif.
5. **John Proud, ss, San Luis Obispo (Calif.) HS**
6. **Steve Cline, rhp, Clemson**
7. Chris Raper, 3b, Austin (Texas) HS
8. Denny Walling, of, Brookdale (N.J.) CC
9. **Michael Kenney, of, SUNY Albany**
10. **Guy Sularz, of/rhp, North Hollywood (Calif.) HS**
11. **Steve LaFerrara, c, Molloy HS, Bayside, N.Y.**
12. **Michael Wilbins, 1b, Southern Illinois**
13. **James Ray, of, Ashland (Ohio)**
14. **Steve Ryan, 1b/rhp, Widener (Pa.)**
15. **John Henry Johnson, lhp, Sonoma (Calif.) HS**
16. Stew Cliburn, rhp/ss, Forrest Hills HS, Jackson, Miss.
17. **Joe Zagarino, of/1b, Cal Poly San Luis Obispo**
18. Mike Tulacz, lhp, Wappingers Falls HS, Poughkeepsie, N.Y.
19. **Monroe Greenfield, rhp, Gonzaga**
20. David Morgan, rhp, Mehlville HS, St. Louis
21. Randy Brandt, rhp, Minnesota Lake (Minn.) HS
22. Dave Rozema, rhp, Central HS, Grand Rapids, Mich.
23. Denis Froehlich, ss, Creighton
24. **Jeff Yurak, c, Citrus (Calif.) JC**
25. **Joseph Small, ss, New Haven (Conn.)**
26. John Shoemaker, ss, Waverly (Ohio) HS
27. **Mike Cash, 2b, Georgia Southern**

June—Secondary Phase (15)

No selection

TEXAS RANGERS

January—Regular Phase (1)

1. **Roy Smalley, ss, Southern California**
2. **Glenn Purvis, of, Mesa (Ariz.) CC**
3. **John Sutton, rhp, Plano (Texas) JC**
4. Tim Pagnozzi, inf, Mesa (Ariz.) CC

January—Secondary Phase (13)

1. Jeff Feramisco, inf/of, Fresno CC
2. **Rick Hays, rhp, Mount San Antonio (Calif.) JC**
3. **Glenn Bright, rhp, Western Carolina**
4. Gary Bishop, 1b, Indian River (Fla.) CC

June—Regular Phase (2)

1. **Tommy Boggs, rhp, Lanier HS, Austin**
2. **Jeff Byrd, rhp, El Capitan HS, Lakeside, Calif.**
3. **Joseph Russell, c, Miami Lakes HS, Hialeah, Fla.**
4. **Jim Clancy, rhp, St. Rita HS, Chicago**
5. **Ron Norman, lhp, Pembroke State (N.C.)**
6. **David McCarthy, lhp, Bourgade HS, Phoenix**
7. **William Patten, lhp, Northrope HS, Fort Wayne, Ind.**
8. **Ward Smith, lhp, Mira Loma HS, Sacramento**
9. **Eddie Holman, lhp, Louisiana Tech**
10. Ronald Smith, ss, Elkhart (Ind.) Memorial HS
11. Ken O'Brien, ss, Widener (Pa.)
12. **Denny Tidwell, rhp, Atlantic HS, Delray, Fla.**
13. **Rick Lisi, 3b, Pittsfield (Mass.) HS**
14. **James Crall, c, Northrop HS, Fort Wayne, Ind.**
15. **Keath Chauncey, of, Georgia Southern**
16. **Jim Umbarger, lhp, Arizona State**
17. Mike Massa, 2b, La Salle HS, Cincinnati
18. **Gary Gray, 3b, Southeastern Oklahoma State**
19. **Terry Pyka, of, Texas**
20. **Richard Getter, rhp, Texas Wesleyan**
21. Dale Brock, of, Southern
22. Charles Faubion, rhp, Alhambra HS, Glendale, Ariz.
23. Wade Leitch, rhp, Sahuaro HS, Tucson
24. Derrick Jackson, of, Wheaton (Ill.) Central HS
25. Tim Stoddard, rhp, North Carolina State
26. **Darrel Frolin, rhp, Phillips (Okla.)**

27. Steven Murray, rhp, Hoover HS, Fresno, Calif.
28. **Dave Braden, lhp, Franklin, Ohio**
29. **Bobby Cuellar, rhp, Texas**
30. Al Holland, lhp, North Carolina A&T
31. **Robert Worthington, 2b, High Point (N.C.)**
32. Johnny Brown, ss, Hartsville (S.C.) HS
33. Keith Snider, 1b/ss, New Castle HS, Newport, Va.
34. Larry Shelton, c, Tunstall HS, Dry Fork, Va.
35. **Thomas Smith, ss, Walter Johnson HS, Bethesda, Md.**
36. John Bell, c, Brookville HS, Lynchburg, Va.

June—Secondary Phase (4)

1. Garry Hancock, of, Hillsborough (Fla.) JC
2. **Robert Carroll, rhp, East Los Angeles JC**

1975 STRANGE DRAFT CLASS MARKED BY FAILURES FROM THE FIRST ROUND AND SUCCESS FROM LATE PICKS

Danny Goodwin says he never received a fair opportunity. Neither, apparently, did most other first-round picks from the Class of 1975.

In a draft that may have yielded the weakest talent ever, only one of the first five picks and 12 of 24 first-rounders played in the big leagues. Twelve years later, only Rick Cerone, Clint Hurdle and Dale Berra were active, all in utility roles. As for Goodwin, he played parts of seven seasons in the big leagues, but never regularly.

"I just don't think I was given a fair chance," said Goodwin, drafted No. 1 overall by California. "As a catcher, the Angels gave up on me. And can you call 159 at-bats a fair opportunity? That's the most at-bats I got in a big league season. Anytime I've been able to get 300 at-bats in the minor leagues, I've produced."

Goodwin twice was the first player selected in the draft, making his failure to become a star—or at least a big league regular—all the more puzzling. The White Sox also drafted him first in 1971, but he rejected their offer and enrolled at Southern University for four years.

"It's always remained a mystery to me why he threw so well in high school and college, then couldn't throw in the pros," then-Angels scouting director Walter Shannon said. "Looking back, I guess we made a mistake, but I was sure when we drafted him that he was going to be a major league catcher for a long time."

Goodwin was full of promise when the Angels spent the No. 1 pick on him in the June regular phase and signed him to a reported $125,000 bonus.

Expectations were also high for the No. 1 picks of several other clubs. Four, including Goodwin, were already in the big leagues by September. No draft, before or after, saw so many players rise to the top so quickly.

But attrition and injuries hit quickly. Arm problems short-circuited the careers of pitchers Mike Lentz, selected second overall by the Padres, and Jim Gideon, the two-time all-American at Texas who was drafted by the Rangers. Lentz never advanced past Double-A, while Gideon pitched one game in the big leagues.

And in one of the most bizarre injuries ever to hit a first-rounder, Montreal's Art Miles broke his neck when he dove off a pier into shallow water. He was celebrating a league championship with teammates in 1977 when the accident occurred, and it partially paralyzed him.

An 11th-round pick, Andre Dawson went on to win an MVP with the Cubs in 1987

Hurdle, Kansas City's first-round pick, had the makings of a star. Sports Illustrated featured him on a cover in the spring of 1978, but he fell out of favor with the Royals and his career declined rapidly. He found more success as a manager, taking over as the Rockies' skipper in 2002 and remaining at their helm until getting fired early in the 2009 season.

The 1975 draft was not without treasures, however. The Cubs found ace reliever Lee Smith in the second round. The Angels made up for Goodwin by tabbing third baseman Carney Lansford in the third. The Tigers got first baseman Jason Thompson and second baseman Lou Whitaker in rounds four and five.

The best evidence to point out how twisted the draft was in 1975 involved Montreal's Andre Dawson. He was an obscure 11th-rounder from Florida A&M, but his talent was obvious from the start of his professional career. In 186 minor league games, Dawson hit .343 with 41 homers, and then he went on to a 21-year big league career that included an MVP award in 1987 with the Cubs.

"He was a natural," Shannon said. "But he was from a small school and very few scouts saw him play. I'm sure if we had it to do over again, he'd have been the No. 1 pick. But that's hindsight."

In many ways, the January draft was more productive than June. The Padres took outfielder Gene Richards with the first pick in the regular phase and he launched an eight-year major league career with one of the most spectacular seasons by a first-year pro in the draft era.

Richards won the California League batting title with a .381 average, and led the league with 148 runs and 85 stolen bases. Two years later, he set a major league record for rookies by stealing 56 bases.

In the secondary phase, outfielder Barry Bonnell was the first pick, and he too won a batting title in his first season, leading the Western Carolinas League with a .324 average.

Richards and South Carolina State teammate Willie Aikens established a draft first when they were selected 1-2 in the January regular phase. Only one other time (Southern California, 1976) did a school produce the first two picks in a draft. The pair became eligible when South Carolina State dropped its baseball program in the fall of 1974.

Rise Of College Baseball

The 1975 draft signaled a turning point in the impact college baseball would have in the future. A record-low total of 188 high school players were signed as clubs began to focus on the more proven talent the college ranks were providing. Two years later, more college players would be drafted than high school players for the first time ever, a trend that never reversed itself.

A centralized scouting combine, the forerunner to the Major League Scouting Bureau, was established prior to the 1975 draft. Membership was optional, and a total of 17 clubs coughed up $115,000 apiece to join. Most teams viewed a central scouting concept as a chance to cut costs, and scouts were dropped from the payrolls of several clubs.

The June draft also was conducted for the first time in 1975 by a conference call originating from the commissioner's office. The January draft had been conducted that way for several years.

The first amendment in eight years to baseball's college rule was passed in 1975, to go into effect the following year. It provided for all college players, regardless of age, to be subject to the draft after their junior season. Previously a player had to be 21 no later than 45 days after the June draft to be eligible.

The requirement affected Goodwin, who was not eligible to sign in 1974 after his junior year of college. It also affected three prominent Southern Cal juniors—pitcher Pete Redfern, catcher Dennis Littlejohn and outfielder Steve Kemp—who weren't eligible in 1975 and were forced to drop out of school that fall to be eligible for the January 1976 draft. Kemp was the first player selected in the regular phase; Redfern and Littlejohn went 1-2 in the secondary phase.

DRAFT 75: FIRST-ROUND PICKS

No.	Club	Player, Pos.	School	Hometown	Ht.	Wt.	B-T	Age
1.	Angels	Danny Goodwin, c	Southern	Peoria, Ill.	6-1	195	L-R	21
2.	Padres	Mike Lentz, lhp	Juanita HS	Kirkland, Wash.	6-0	185	R-L	18
3.	Tigers	Les Filkins, of	George Washington HS	Chicago	5-11	185	L-L	18
4.	Cubs	Brian Rosinski, of	Evanston HS	Evanston, Ill.	6-2	205	L-R	18
5.	Brewers	Rich O'Keefe, lhp	Yorktown Heights HS	Yorktown Heights, N.Y.	6-6	210	L-L	17
6.	Mets	Butch Benton, c	Godby HS	Tallahassee, Fla.	6-1	190	R-R	17
7.	Indians	Rick Cerone, c	Seton Hall	Newark, N.J.	5-11	190	R-R	21
8.	Giants	Ted Barnicle, lhp	Jacksonville State	Sudbury, Mass.	5-11	170	L-L	21
9.	Royals	Clint Hurdle, of	Merritt Island HS	Merritt Island, Fla.	6-3	195	L-R	17
10.	Expos	Art Miles, ss	Crockett HS	Austin, Texas	6-2	175	L-R	18
11.	White Sox	Chris Knapp, rhp	Central Michigan	St. Joseph, Mich.	6-5	200	R-R	21
12.	Phillies	Sam Welborn, rhp	Wichita Falls HS	Wichita Falls, Texas	6-4	195	L-R	18
13.	Twins	Rick Sofield, ss	Morristown HS	Morristown, N.J.	6-1	195	L-R	18
14.	Astros	Bo McLaughlin, rhp	Lipscomb	Amelia, Ohio	6-5	185	R-R	21
15.	Red Sox	Otis Foster, 1b	High Point	High Point, N.C.	6-0	210	R-R	21
16.	Cardinals	David Johnson, lhp	Gaylord HS	Gaylord, Mich.	6-1	175	R-L	18
17.	Rangers	Jim Gideon, rhp	Texas	Houston	6-3	190	R-R	21
18.	Braves	Donald Young, c	Dos Pueblos HS	Goleta, Calif.	6-3	190	R-R	18
19.	Yankees	Jim McDonald, 1b	Verbum Dei HS	Los Angeles	6-2	190	L-L	17
20.	Pirates	Dale Berra, ss	Montclair HS	Montclair, N.J.	6-0	180	R-R	18
21.	Athletics	Bruce Robinson, c	Stanford	LaJolla, Calif.	6-1	185	L-R	21
22.	Reds	Tony Moretto, of	Harrison HS	Evansville, Ind.	6-2	170	L-R	18
23.	Orioles	Dave Ford, rhp	Lincoln West HS	Cleveland	6-4	190	R-R	18
24.	Dodgers	Mark Bradley, ss	Elizabethtown HS	Elizabethtown, Ky.	6-0	178	R-R	18

1975

CLUB-BY-CLUB SELECTIONS

ATLANTA BRAVES

January—Regular Phase (17)

1. Ernie Mauritson, rhp, Chabot (Calif.) JC
2. **Gary Caraletto, of, Hancock (Calif.) JC**
3. **William Bowman, of, Hancock (Calif.) JC**
4. **Dennis Shambaugh, rhp, Mechanicsburg, Pa.**

January—Secondary Phase (21)

1. Keith Lloyd, p, Blinn (Texas) JC
2. **William Cranford, lhp, Gulf Coast (Fla.) CC**

June—Regular Phase (18)

1. **Donald Young, c, Dos Pueblos HS, Goleta, Calif.**
2. **Larry Whisenton, of, Central HS, St. Louis**
3. **Gary Cooper, of, Grove HS, Garden City, Calif.**
4. **Hank Small, of, South Carolina**
5. Bob Skube, of, Simi Valley (Calif.) HS
6. **James Doherty, ss, Ithaca (N.Y.)**
7. John Semarod, of, Monsignor Ferrell HS, Staten Island, N.Y.
8. **Jerry Maddox, ss, Arizona State**
9. **Mike Reynolds, of, Blinn (Texas) JC**
10. Condredge Holloway, ss, Tennessee
11. **Ricky Carriger, rhp, Elizabethton (Tenn.) HS**
12. **Duane Theiss, rhp, Marietta (Ohio)**
13. **Kevin Connolly, c, Rider**
14. **Michael Park, rhp, Mississippi**
15. Donald Eagan, 3b, Glacier HS, Burien, Wash.
16. **Dean Marietta, rhp, St. Bonaventure HS, Ventura, Calif.**
17. William Pye, lhp, Avondale HS, Avondale Estates, Ga.
18. **William Stewart, 3b, Verbum Dei HS, Compton, Calif.**
19. **James Shanks, rhp, Harlem (Ga.) HS**
20. **Glenn Hubbard, 2b, Ben Lomond HS, Ogden, Utah**
21. Gary Skow, of, Yavapai (Ariz.) JC
22. Nate Snell, rhp, Tennessee State
23. Michael Wooten, 2b, West HS, Knoxville, Tenn.

June—Secondary Phase (16)

1. **David Stevens, of, American River (Calif.) JC**

BALTIMORE ORIOLES

January—Regular Phase (24)

1. **Ricky Mayo, rhp, Merced (Calif.) JC**
2. Donald Kuhnoff, ss, Los Angeles Valley JC
3. **Greg Broomis, rhp, Los Angeles Valley JC**
4. Doug Stokke, ss, Long Beach (Calif.) CC
5. Scott Hefner, p, Central Arizona JC
6. Stephen Maehl, p, Foothill (Calif.) JC
7. Michael Kelly, 1b/of, Hancock (Calif.) JC
8. Russell Mitchell, p, San Diego Mesa JC
9. Tim Feickert, of, Antelope Valley (Calif.) JC
10. Julio Acosta, of, Miami-Dade North CC
11. **Mike Pagnozzi, lhp, Tucson, Ariz.**
12. Paul Mize, 2b, Sierra (Calif.) JC
13. Scott Frazier, 3b, Sacramento CC
14. James Rogers, p, JC of Southern Idaho
15. Joseph Romero, c/3b, Yavapai (Ariz.) JC
16. Edward Ribera, p, Yavapai (Ariz.) JC

January—Secondary Phase (16)

1. **Mark Gesquiere, rhp, El Camino (Calif.) JC**
2. Paul Bain, rhp, El Camino (Calif.) JC
3. David Stevens, of, American River (Calif.) JC
4. Stan Skidgel, p, Cal Poly San Luis Obispo
5. Mark Trapani, p, Los Angeles Pierce JC

June—Regular Phase (23)

1. **Dave Ford, rhp/of, Lincoln West HS, Cleveland**
2. **John Dyer, lhp, McLain HS, Tulsa, Okla.**
3. **Steve Lake, c, Lennox (Calif.) HS**
4. **Samuel Gierhan, rhp, Lakewood (Calif.) HS**
5. **Vernon Thomas, of, Harlem HS, Thompson, Ga.**
6. **Darryl Cias, c, Kennedy HS, Granada Hills, Calif.**
7. **George Mitchell, ss, Laudon HS, Chevy Chase, Md.**
8. Robert Theoudele, rhp, Kennedy HS, Richmond, Calif.
9. **Darwin Luna, rhp, St. Louis HS, Pearl City, Hawaii**
10. **Vincent White, of, Kennedy HS, Sacramento**
11. **Mike Ornest, 3b, Beverly Hills (Calif.) HS**
12. Jim Skaalen, 1b/3b, San Diego State
13. **Greg Ward, rhp, South Carolina**
14. Thomas Vitale, lhp, Belle Vernon, Pa.
15. Jarrell Wilkerson, lhp, Smithfield (Va.) HS
16. Chris Nurse, ss, Bel Air HS, Fallston, Md.
17. **Richard McCarthy, ss, New Orleans**
18. **Porter Wyatt, rhp, Inglewood HS, Compton, Calif.**
19. Alfred Blank, c, Morrisville (Pa.) HS
20. Mark Esser, lhp, Ketcham HS, Poughkeepsie, N.Y.
21. Randy Kwist, 1b, Springfield (Mass.) Tech HS
22. Bobby Knezevich, rhp, Jefferson HS, Council Bluffs, Iowa
23. **Jack Neimeyer, rhp, Long Beach, Calif.**
24. Bruce Hardy, c/1b, Arizona State
25. **Henry Vanderhook, c/3b, Bellflower, Calif.**
26. **Randy Checkos, rhp, Notin HS, Buena Park, Calif.**
27. Charles Moore, rhp, Bayside HS, Virginia Beach, Va.
28. **Charles Fletcher, rhp, Manhattan Beach, Calif.**
29. **David Hogg, c, Jeanette (Pa.) HS**
30. **Chris Smith, c, Bishop Montgomery HS, Hermosa Beach, Calif.**
31. **Doug Thiel, 1b/2b, Merced (Calif.) JC**
32. **Edwin Lashley, of, Wicomico HS, Salisbury, Md.**
33. **Robert Ehrig, c, Hawaii**
34. Ben Hines, ss, Mesa (Ariz.) CC
35. **Robert Walker, rhp, North Central (Ill.)**

June—Secondary Phase (5)

1. **Everett Murray, of, Kentucky**
2. **Donald Kuhnoff, ss, Los Angeles Valley JC**
3. **Jeff Rineer, lhp, Franklin & Marshall (Pa.)**
4. Erik Hendricks, rhp, Chabot (Calif.) JC

BOSTON RED SOX

January—Regular Phase (16)

1. **Walter Bigos, rhp, Cerritos (Calif.) JC**
2. Tim Vranich, ss, St. Petersburg (Fla.) JC
3. **Edward Nuss, rhp, Valencia (Fla.) CC**
4. James McKenzie, p, Solano (Calif.) CC
5. David Isaacson, p, JC of the Redwoods (Calif.)

January—Secondary Phase (14)

1. **Ken Huizenga, of, Southern California**
2. Jerry Ennis, ss, Bakersfield (Calif.) JC
3. Chris Gandy, of, Sacramento CC
4. Jerry Stamps, c/1b, South Alabama
5. Mike Morrissey, p, Schenectady, N.Y.

June—Regular Phase (15)

1. **Otis Foster, 1b, High Point**
2. **Dave Schmidt, c, Mission Viejo (Calif.) HS**
3. **Ed Jurak, ss, San Pedro (Calif.) HS**
4. **Michael Moore, rhp, Oak Park HS, Kansas City, Mo.**
5. **Larry Hyman, 3b, Irwin County HS, Mystic, Ga.**
6. **Mike Howard, rhp, South Portland (Maine) HS**
7. Larry Littleton, of, Georgia
8. **Bob Hampton, of, Stanford**
9. Dave Stegman, of, Arizona
10. **Dave Stapleton, 2b, South Alabama**
11. **Gary Purcell, of, New Orleans**
12. **Carlton Steele, of, Westfield State (Mass.)**
13. **Breen Newcomer, lhp, Oklahoma**

14. **Phllip Welch, rhp, Providence**
15. **Richard Waller, rhp, Montclair State (N.J.)**
16. **David Schoppee, rhp, Deering HS, Portland, Maine**
17. **Richard McAlister, c, Louisiana Tech**
18. **Happy Vincent, 3b, Palm Springs (Calif.) HS**
19. **Thomas Streightiff, of, Juniata (Pa.)**
20. Larry Ennis, of, Fairleigh Dickinson
21. **Timothy Clemmons, of, Southeastern HS, Chillicothe, Ohio**
22. **Mike O'Berry, c, South Alabama**
23. **Mike Paxton, rhp/inf, Memphis State**
24. Peter Khoury, of, Durfee HS, Fall River, Mass.

June—Secondary Phase (11)

1. **Ronald Evans, 3b, North Carolina State**

CALIFORNIA ANGELS

January—Regular Phase (2)

1. **Willie Aikens, 1b, South Carolina State**
2. **Jim Dorsey, rhp, Los Angeles Valley JC**
3. **Gary Hinshaw, ss, Modesto (Calif.) JC**
4. Jim Raska, p, CC of Baltimore
5. Bob Walk, rhp, JC of the Canyons (Calif.)
6. James Roach, p, Bakersfield (Calif.) JC
7. Bob Meadows, p, Seminole (Fla.) JC
8. Andy Schardt, 1b, Fullerton (Calif.) JC
9. Rodger Bills, p, Idaho Falls, Idaho
10. **Carl Meche, rhp, Northwestern State**
11. Hal Jeffrey, p, JC of the Canyons (Calif.)
12. Mark Miller, p, Central Arizona JC
13. David Rhinehart, of, Riverside, Calif.

January—Secondary Phase (12)

1. **Gil Kubski, 3b, Cal State Northridge**
2. **Richard Brewster, 2b, San Bernardino Valley (Calif.) JC**
3. **Terry Stupy, c, UC Irvine**
4. Derek Botelho, ss, Miami-Dade South CC
5. **Bobby Clark, ss, Riverside (Calif.) CC**
6. Paul Kolesnikow, of, JC of San Mateo (Calif.)
7. William McIntyre, of, Cal State Northridge
8. Albert Paglione, p, Valencia (Fla.) CC

June—Regular Phase (1)

1. **Danny Goodwin, c, Southern**
2. **Jim Anderson, ss, Kennedy HS, Granada Hills, Calif.**
3. **Carney Lansford, ss, Wilcox HS, Santa Clara, Calif.**
4. **Floyd Rayford, c, Manual Arts HS, Los Angeles**
5. Gene Ransom, 2b, Berkeley (Calif.) HS
6. **Steve Kelley, rhp, Santa Clara**
7. Marvin Cobb, 2b, Southern California
8. **Jimmy Brown, rhp, Bogalusa (La.) HS**
9. **John Flannery, ss, Lakewood (Calif.) HS**
10. **Paul Hartzell, rhp, Lehigh**
11. Steve King, c, South Carolina
12. **Mike Merritt, rhp, North Carolina**
13. **Robert Boyd, rhp, Brooklyn Park HS, Baltimore**
14. Columbus Duncan, of, McDonogh HS, Baltimore
15. **David Hollifield, lhp, Seminole (Fla.) JC**
16. **Wayne Williams, of, King George (Va.) HS**
17. **Gary Boyle, rhp, Torrance (Calif.) HS**
18. **Jerry Quigley, rhp, Lewis (Ill.)**
19. **Steve Eddy, rhp, United Township HS, Moline, Ill.**
20. **Robert LaFave, of, Carmen HS, Flint, Mich.**
21. Kim Mason, rhp, Arizona Western JC
22. Ron Musselman, rhp, Louisburg (N.C.) JC
23. Jim Capoferi, c, Lakeview HS, St. Clair Shores, Mich.
24. Clarence Syers, rhp, Sylmar (Calif.) HS
25. James Morphis, rhp, Ells HS, Richmond, Calif.
26. Jim Watkins, of, Pike HS, Indianapolis
27. James Schwanke, ss, Yavapai (Ariz.) JC
28. Brian Sweet, rhp, Highland HS, Salt Lake City

June—Secondary Phase (21)

1. Garry Hancock, of, South Carolina
2. Randy Rogers, 1b, UC Riverside

CHICAGO CUBS

January—Regular Phase (3)

1. **Wayne Doland, rhp, Fairleigh Dickinson**
2. **William Mullins, 1b, St. Petersburg (Fla.) JC**
3. Jeffrey Robinson, ss, Blinn (Texas) JC

January—Secondary Phase (3)

1. **Ed Putman, c, Southern California**
2. **Michael Perkins, 1b/of, Belmont**
3. **Michael Cameron, rhp, Ivyland, Pa.**

June—Regular Phase (4)

1. **Brian Rosinski, of, Evanston (Ill.) HS**
2. **Lee Smith, rhp, Northwestern State**
3. Randy Wallace, of, Tennessee
4. **Charles Peoples, c, Columbia HS, Richland, Wash.**
5. **Michael Taylor, rhp, Scotlandville HS, Baton Rouge, La.**
6. **Willis Stewart, inf, Sam Houston State**
7. Bill Hainline, ss, Rogers HS, Spokane, Wash.
8. **Chuck Rogers, rhp, Michigan**
9. Ron Kainer, rhp, Sam Houston State
10. Morris Wilmer, of, Louisiana College
11. **Mike Umfleet, ss, Oklahoma**
12. **Jeffrey Lucchesi, lhp, JC of Marin (Calif.)**
13. **Michael Moore, rhp, Tennessee Tech**
14. **Mike Anderson, of, Texas**
15. Richard Alexander, of, Myers Park HS, Charlotte
16. Scott Green, rhp, Kennedy HS, Granada Hills, Calif.
17. **Dwight Bryant, of, Decatur (Ga.) HS**
18. Sam Marsi, rhp, Tomales HS, Pt. Reyes Station, Calif.
19. **Ryan Weber, lhp, New Mexico**
20. **William Von Ahen, lhp, Kingsborough (N.Y.) CC**
21. **Rick Brockaway, inf, Texas-Pan American**
22. Del Leutbecher, 1b, Katella HS, Anaheim
23. Steve Winfield, rhp, San Augustine (Texas) HS
24. Chris Hartig, rhp, Mullen HS, Lakewood, Colo.
25. Timothy Huff, rhp, Gardner-Webb
26. **Joe Hernandez, of, Texas-Pan American**
27. Steve Bush, ss, Kentucky
28. **James Travis, ss, Whitworth (Wash.)**
29. James Hackney, 1b, Michigan

June—Secondary Phase (4)

1. John Henderson, c, Georgia
2. **Charles Ledbetter, rhp, Valencia (Fla.) CC**

CHICAGO WHITE SOX

January—Regular Phase (12)

1. James Dyer, ss, Arizona Western JC
2. John MacAuley, 2b, Golden West (Calif.) JC
3. Monty Bothwell, of, Cypress (Calif.) JC
4. **Robert Madden, rhp, Golden West (Calif.) JC**
5. **Marshall Harper, of/inf, Brevard (Fla.) CC**
6. **Kent Hunziker, rhp, Golden West (Calif.) JC**
7. **Gary Eagle, inf, Miami-Dade North CC**
8. Bruce Bochy, c, Brevard (Fla.) CC
9. **Michael Farrell, rhp, Miami-Dade North CC**
10. Willie Lee, of, Southwestern Oklahoma State (Selection voided)

January—Secondary Phase (20)

1. Scott Anderson, p, Mesa (Ariz.) CC
2. **Tim Stoddard, rhp, North Carolina State**
3. **Curtis Etchandy, ss, Golden West (Calif.) JC**
4. **Bobby McClellan, c, Gadsden State (Ala.) JC**
5. Mike Tulacz, lhp, Miami-Dade North CC
6. Dan Gans, 3b, Mount San Antonio (Calif.) JC
7. Michael Wirwas, ss, Mesa (Ariz.) CC

June—Regular Phase (11)

1. **Chris Knapp, rhp, Central Michigan**
2. **Mitch Lukevics, rhp, Penn State**
3. **Thomas Bright, inf, Alto Loma (Calif.) HS**
4. John Wells, of, Hoover HS, San Diego
5. **Phillip Bauer, ss, Joliet (Ill.) Central HS**

6. Robert Cochran, lhp, Royal Oak HS, Covina, Calif.
7. **Edward Yesenchak, c, Cannon-McMillan HS, Cannonsburg, Pa.**
8. Mickey Lashley, rhp, Oklahoma
9. **Randy Seitzer, lhp, Parkland HS, Wescoville, Pa.**
10. **Leo Elter, ss, Shaler HS, Pittsburgh**
11. Don Hanna, rhp, Yavapai (Ariz.) JC
12. **Ted Schultz, ss, San Diego**
13. David Daniels, of, Edgewood HS, West Covina, Calif.
14. Jon Dempsey, rhp, North Carolina State
15. **Peter Maropis, ss, Allegheny (Pa.)**
16. Dan O'Brien, rhp, Florida State
17. **Marv Foley, c, Kentucky**
18. Jeff Simons, lhp, Brevard (Fla.) CC
19. **James Handley, rhp, Auburn**
20. Clark Langdon, 3b, Lamar (Colo.) CC
21. Harry Chappas, ss, Nova HS, Lauderhill, Fla.
22. Ronald Russell, 3b/of, Christian Brothers HS, Memphis
23. Roger Mayo, rhp, Jacksonville State
24. Stephen Walsh, lhp, Saint Louis
25. Greg Johnson, rhp, Santiago HS, Santa Ana, Calif.
26. James Green, rhp, Maplesville (Ala.) HS
27. **Thomas Joyce, lhp, Michigan**
28. **Wayne Gottleber, rhp, St. Clair County (Mich.) CC**
29. Michael Ryan, lhp, Bellaire HS, Houston
30. Mark Reese, of, Atherton HS, Louisville
31. Brian Zapalac, lhp, Sealy (Texas) HS

June—Secondary Phase (9)

1. Mike Tulacz, lhp, Miami-Dade North CC
2. **James Crosta, ss, Miami**
3. Thomas Baxter, rhp, Miami-Dade South CC

CINCINNATI REDS

January—Regular Phase (21)

1. James Slaughter, c, Pasadena (Calif.) CC
2. Teddy Asbill, p, Bunch, Okla.
3. **Bernard Plent, rhp, Arizona State**
4. Mark Clark, of, Antelope Valley (Calif.) JC

January—Secondary Phase (5)

1. **Lawrence Pekarcik, rhp, Mount San Antonio (Calif.) JC**
2. **Mark Unsoeld, c, Mount San Antonio (Calif.) JC**
3. Thomas Baxter, rhp, Miami

June—Regular Phase (22)

1. **Tony Moretto, of, Harrison HS, Evansville, Ind.**
2. **Frank Pastore, rhp, Damien HS, Upland, Calif.**
3. **Paul Moskau, rhp, Azusa Pacific (Calif.)**
4. **Scott Brown, rhp, DeQuincy (La.) HS**
5. **Mark Miller, c, El Capitan HS, Lakeside, Calif.**
6. **Sal Ferrara, rhp, Tampa Catholic HS**
7. **Frederick Warren, rhp, Sam Houston State**
8. Ed Skribiski, ss, Frontier Regional HS, Sunderland, Mass.
9. **Randy Davidson, 2b, Florida State**
10. Don Welchel, rhp, Lake Highland HS, Dallas
11. **Marti Wolever, of, St. Albert HS, Bludes, Iowa**
12. **Mark Hopper, ss, Florida Southern**
13. **Lawrence Groves, ss, Encinal HS, Alameda, Calif.**
14. **Tony Grana, rhp, Bishop Gorman HS, Las Vegas**
15. James McArdle, 3b, Brevard (Fla.) CC
16. **Evan Edge, c, Jacksonville State**
17. **Kelly Jensen, rhp, Utah Technical JC**
18. Michael Bretz, rhp, Eastern Hills HS, Fort Worth, Texas
19. **Reggie Waller, of, San Diego CC**
20. Mark Copeland, rhp, Eastern Hills HS, Fort Worth, Texas
21. **John Huntington, lhp/of, Rancho HS, North Las Vegas, Nev.**
22. **Charles Moore, rhp, Paxon HS, Jacksonville, Fla.**
23. **Gary Richter, 2b, Grayson County (Texas) JC**
24. Stephen Muccio, ss, DeWitt Clinton HS, Bronx, N.Y.
25. **Robert Adams, rhp, East Bay HS, Ruskin, Fla.**
26. Stanley Cannon, of/1b, Woodham HS, Pensacola, Fla.
27. Bill Paschall, rhp, North Carolina

June—Secondary Phase (14)

1. Scott Burk, ss/rhp, Oklahoma State

CLEVELAND INDIANS

January—Regular Phase (8)

1. **Michael Vaughn, rhp, West Valley (Calif.) JC**
2. John Hills, p, Moorpark (Calif.) JC
3. **Stephen Klein, rhp, Queens (N.Y.)**
4. Alfonso Williams, 3b/c, Lawson State (Ala.) CC
5. Gary Talbert, c/of, Faulkner State (Ala.) JC
6. **Patrick Washko, inf/of, Cleveland State**

January—Secondary Phase (8)

1. **Marion Harvey, rhp/c, Laverne, Okla.**
2. **Ralph Jiminez, c, Bronx (N.Y.) CC**
3. Steven Van Deren, c, JC of the Redwoods (Calif.)
4. Michael Massa, 2b, Miami-Dade South CC
5. Danny White, inf, Arizona State
6. David Adeimy, c, Miami-Dade North CC

June—Regular Phase (7)

1. **Rick Cerone, c, Seton Hall**
2. **Daniel Skiba, rhp, South Houston (Texas) HS**
3. **William Hiss, ss, Queens (N.Y.)**
4. **Larkin Bullard, rhp, Lee HS, Springfield, Va.**
5. Mike Macha, 3b, Rice
6. **Jeff Tomski, c, Thomas More HS, Milwaukee**
7. Casey Lindsey, lhp, Billings (Mont.) Senior HS
8. **Larry Harmon, ss, Clover Hill HS, Midlothian, Va.**
9. Jerry Schmidt, rhp, Lewis-Clark State (Idaho)
10. **Dave Schuler, lhp, New Haven (Conn.)**
11. Marvin Hammock, ss, Carol City HS, Opalocka, Fla.
12. William Wilborn, of, McClatchy HS, Sacramento
13. David Erickson, rhp, Escambia HS, Pensacola, Fla.
14. Roderick Ingram, of, Linfield (Ore.)
15. **Gary Melson, rhp, Middle Tennessee State**
16. Leo Sutherland, of, Santiago HS, Garden Grove, Calif.
17. **Angelo Logrande, 1b, Sehome HS, Bellingham, Wash.**
18. **Thomas Amenita, rhp, Rider**
19. Dennis Firenza, of, Elk Grove HS, Sacramento
20. **Earl Jordan, of, Virginia Wesleyan**
21. Jerome Miller, of, Leland HS, Elizabeth, Miss.
22. Ronald Rippee, c, Alhambra HS, Martinez, Calif.
23. Michael Hrnyak, ss, Euclid (Ohio) HS
24. **Richard Ezell, ss, Virginia Wesleyan**
25. Ricky Connell, rhp, Indian Hills (Iowa) CC
26. **Barry Glabman, ss, Homewood, Ill.**

June—Secondary Phase (13)

1. **Johnny Brown, of, South Georgia JC**
2. Jackie Snell, lhp, George Wallace (Ala.) CC

DETROIT TIGERS

January—Regular Phase (4)

1. **Tom Brookens, ss, Mansfield (Pa.)**
2. Eric Mustad, p, Citrus (Calif.) JC
3. Mike Parkinson, inf, Mount San Antonio (Calif.) JC
4. **Frederick DiPietro, c, San Jose CC**
5. **Frank Harris, rhp, Fullerton (Calif.) JC**
6. **John Romero, inf, Santa Monica (Calif.) CC**
7. Brian Rusca, p, West Valley (Calif.) JC
8. Christopher O'Brien, p, Central Arizona JC
9. Pat Callahan, c, Broward (Fla.) CC

January—Secondary Phase (2)

1. **Dave Tobik, rhp, Ohio**
2. **Thomas Perkins, rhp, Cal State Los Angeles**
3. Dean Phillips, p, Panola (Texas) JC
4. **Dave Rozema, rhp, Grand Rapids (Mich.) JC**

June—Regular Phase (3)

1. **Les Filkins, of, George Washington HS, Chicago**
2. **John Murphy, lhp, St. Francis Prep HS, Brooklyn, N.Y.**
3. Bob Grandas, ss, Central HS, Flint, Mich.
4. **Jason Thompson, lhp/1b, Cal State Northridge**

5. **Lou Whitaker Jr., 3b, Martinsville (Va.) HS**
6. **Jeff Reinke, lhp, Southern California**
7. **Dana McManus, rhp, Chapman (Calif.)**
8. Steve Powers, rhp, Arizona
9. Andrew Lopez, ss, UCLA
10. **Vince Diaz, c, Jackson HS, Miami**
11. **Paul Vavruska, rhp, St. Johns River (Fla.) CC**
12. Chuck Black, ss, Shawnee HS, Lima, Ohio
13. John Racanelli, rhp, Southern California
14. Steve Morrison, 2b, Farmington-Harrison HS, Farmington, Mich.
15. **Don Thomas, rhp, North Baltimore (Ohio) HS**
16. Karl Boesch, rhp, Clackamas (Ore.) CC
17. **Mike Bartell, ss, Santa Clara**
18. John Phipps, c, Central HS, Flint, Mich.
19. Bruce Berenyi, rhp, Glen Oaks (Mich.) CC
20. Derek Carrier, ss, Science Hill HS, Johnson City, Tenn.
21. **Venoy Garrison, c, UCLA**
22. **David Bowden, ss, Florida**
23. **Julio Alonso, lhp, Lamar**
24. **Wynn Sherman, c/of, Cal Poly Pomona**
25. Scott McLeod, rhp, Riverview (Mich.) HS
26. **Dexter Redd, of, Hoover HS, San Diego**

June—Secondary Phase (17)

1. **Phil Doktor, ss, Southern California**
2. Mike Parkinson, inf, Mount San Antonio (Calif.) JC
3. Brian Rusca, rhp, West Valley (Calif.) JC

HOUSTON ASTROS

January—Regular Phase (13)

1. Darrell Brown, ss, East Los Angeles JC
2. **John Goetz, c, Rollins (Fla.)**
3. Michael Hopkins, p, Shelby State (Tenn.) CC

January—Secondary Phase (7)

1. **Jim Willis, 1b, Oregon**
2. Steven Murray, p, Fresno CC
3. James Crosta, ss, Miami-Dade South CC

June—Regular Phase (14)

1. **Bo McLaughlin, rhp, Lipscomb**
2. **Edward Andersen, rhp, Redwood HS, Greenbrae, Calif.**
3. **Robert Hallgren, of, Adams HS, Clarkston, Wash.**
4. **John Cloherty, rhp, St. Patrick's HS, Watertown, Mass.**
5. **Joe Pittman, 3b, Southern**
6. **Michael Lally, of, Peoria (Ariz.) HS**
7. Arnold McCrary, of, Muir HS, Altadena, Calif.
8. Frank Aranco, rhp, Union (N.J.) HS
9. Jimmy Hickman, of/3b, Loris (S.C.) HS
10. **Scott Makela, 3b, Rochester Institute of Technology**
11. **Gerald Taylor, 1b, Huston-Tillotson (Texas)**
12. Lance Gore, lhp, Katella HS, Anaheim
13. **Donald Pisker, of, Rider**
14. **Michael Tyler, c, St. John's**
15. **Richard Miller, lhp, Arkansas**
16. Phillip Pundt, rhp, Mount St. Joseph HS, Baltimore
17. **Brian Woltman, 3b, Clawson (Mich.) HS**
18. **Robert Blank, rhp, Arkansas**
19. Daniel Newell, rhp, Cardington-Lincoln HS, Cardington, Ohio
20. Greg Vogel, inf, Penn State
21. **Robert Wood, 2b, Birmingham-Southern**
22. **Al Osofsky, of, St. John's**
23. Kim Seaman, lhp, Live Oak Academy HS, Moss Point, Miss.
24. Mark Champagne, rhp, Port Neches HS, Groves, Texas

June—Secondary Phase (24)

1. **Bruce Bochy, c, Brevard (Fla.) CC**
2. Gerald Green, rhp, Lower Columbia (Wash.) JC

KANSAS CITY ROYALS

January—Regular Phase (10)

1. Steven Manley, p, Kingsborough (N.Y.) CC
2. **Frank Mastrangelo, c, Shippensburg (Pa.)**
3. Scott Boras, p, Golden West (Calif.) JC
4. Timothy Hayes, ss, Cypress (Calif.) JC
5. Steven Brooks, p, Huntington Beach, Calif.

January—Secondary Phase (24)

1. **Tim Richards, c, Golden West (Calif.) JC**
2. Jake Battle, c, Miami-Dade North CC
3. Larry Randel, ss, Fullerton (Calif.) JC

June—Regular Phase (9)

1. **Clint Hurdle, of, Merritt Island (Fla.) HS**
2. Pat Gillie, rhp, Alhambra HS, Phoenix
3. **Bryan Jones, ss, Iowa**
4. **David Winters, rhp, Bonnabel HS, Kenner, La.**
5. **Rich Gale, rhp, New Hampshire**
6. **Jack Hudson, c, South Charleston (W.Va.) HS**
7. **Kevin Gillen, of, Niles West HS, Skokie, Ill.**
8. James Murphy, c, Port Clinton (Ohio) HS
9. **Steve Lacy, ss, Louisiana Tech**
10. **Ron Smith, rhp, Wilcox HS, Santa Clara, Calif.**
11. **Danny Garcia, of, Baruch (N.Y.)**
12. **Don Rothwell, c, Oak Hills HS, Cincinnati**
13. **David Burroughs, c, Ketchum (Okla.) HS**
14. **Randy McGilberry, rhp, Louisiana Tech**
15. **Henry Greene, lhp, McCracken HS, Bluffton, S.C.**
16. Frank Shellenback, c, Barrington HS, Barrington Hills, Ill.
17. **Kent Cvejdlik, rhp, Thomas Jefferson HS, Carter Lake, Iowa**
18. Larry Brown, c, Niceville (Fla.) HS
19. **John Hart, rhp, Mercer**
20. John Ferrell, 3b, Northern HS, Durham, N.C.
21. **John Sebastian, rhp, Columbus (Ga.) HS**
22. Ron Hassey, 3b, Arizona
23. **Greg Schuller, c, Independence, Mo.**
24. Gordon Blakeley, 3b, Chapman (Calif.)
25. Mike Hankins, 3b, South Raytown (Mo.) HS

June—Secondary Phase (19)

1. **Mike Denevi, ss, Santa Clara**
2. William Yarbrough, inf, Manatee (Fla.) JC
3. Denny Martindale, 2b/rhp, Southern California (Selection voided)

LOS ANGELES DODGERS

January—Regular Phase (23)

1. **Donald Washington, of, Laney (Calif.) JC**
2. Dale Emmer, of, Santa Monica (Calif.) JC
3. Gavin Long, p, JC of San Mateo (Calif.)
4. Patrick Buckner, c, Sacramento CC
5. Steven Watson, p, Midland (Texas) JC
6. **Michael Tennant, rhp, Crowder (Mo.) JC**
7. **Ron Weirum, 2b, Santa Barbara (Calif.) CC**
8. Terry Watkins, p, Sacramento CC

January—Secondary Phase (23)

1. Gil Patterson, of/rhp, Miami-Dade South CC
2. William Yarbrough, inf, Manatee (Fla.) JC
3. Earl Bass, rhp, South Carolina

June—Regular Phase (24)

1. **Mark Bradley, ss, Elizabethtown (Ky.) HS**
2. **Myron White, of, Santa Ana (Calif.) Valley HS**
3. **Rodney Scheller, rhp, Greeley (Colo.) West HS**
4. **James Evans, lhp, East Technical HS, Cleveland**
5. **Marvin Garrison, of, Verbum Dei HS, Compton, Calif.**
6. **Robert Adams, ss/2b, Fairview HS, Camden, Ark.**
7. **Kenneth Townsend, rhp, Sonora (Calif.) HS**
8. **Jacky Parish, c, Oklahoma**
9. Arthur Toal, ss, Tottenville HS, Staten Island, N.Y.
10. **Charles Martin, of, Wheaton (Ill.) North HS**
11. **Michael Lake, lhp, Hueneme (Calif.) HS**
12. Robert Healey, rhp, Roosevelt HS, St. Louis
13. **Robert Lowman, rhp, Mamaroneck HS, Larchmont, N.Y.**
14. Samuel Roberts, 1b, Carson-Newman (Tenn.)
15. **Robert Stoffle, rhp, Kennedy HS, Sacramento**
16. **Dave Stewart, rhp, St. Elizabeth HS, Oakland**
17. **Brad Gulden, c, Chaska HS, Carver, Minn.**

18. Mike Walters, rhp, Alta Loma (Calif.) HS
19. Robert Dove, rhp, Tustin (Calif.) HS
20. William Seney, rhp, Apple Valley (Calif.) HS
21. Stephen Youngman, 1b, North Brunswick (N.J.) HS
22. Paul Jacobs, of/3b, Kennedy HS, Sacramento
23. Paul Touchstone, rhp, Galveston
24. Robert Newman, rhp, Mount Hood (Ore.) CC
25. Kris Kaminska, rhp, Peoria (Ariz.) HS
26. Jay Nelson, rhp, Chaska HS, Carver, Minn.
27. Mitch Dean, rhp, Concord (Calif.) HS
28. **Arthur Fischetti, 2b/3b, Lafayette**
29. Michael Otto, rhp, Kennedy HS, Sacramento
30. Paul Lanier, c/3b, Moultrie (Ga.) HS
31. Rudy Rufer, ss, Valley Stream HS, Malverne, N.Y.
32. James Black, ss, Camden (Ark.) HS
33. Alan Clark, rhp, Hiawatha HS, Kirkland, Ill.

June—Secondary Phase (18)

No selection

MILWAUKEE BREWERS

January—Regular Phase (6)

1. Gerald Green, rhp, Lower Columbia (Wash.) JC
2. James Parker, p, Yakima Valley (Wash.) JC

January—Secondary Phase (10)

1. **Lenn Sakata, 2b, Gonzaga**
2. Mike Denevi, ss, Santa Clara

June—Regular Phase (5)

1. **Richard O'Keefe, lhp, Yorktown Heights (N.Y.) HS**
2. **Robert Ross, c, Tates Creek HS, Lexington, Ky.**
3. **Alvin Edge, rhp, Crawford HS, San Diego**
4. **Gregory Anderson, of, North HS, Riverside, Calif.**
5. Robert Hely, ss, Fort Lauderdale (Fla.) HS
6. Brian Hayes, lhp, Savanna HS, Buena Park, Calif.
7. **John Hannon, rhp, Jacksonville**
8. Greg Jemison, of, Seton Hall
9. **Talmadge Tanks, 1b, George Washington Carver HS, Martinsville, Va.**
10. **Richard Ford, lhp, Lynn (Mass.) Technical**
11. **Elliot Franklin, ss, Ranger (Texas) JC**
12. **Bradley Meagher, lhp, Adirondack Central HS, Forestport, N.Y.**
13. **Stephen Ruling, rhp, South Florida**
14. **Gary LaRocque, 2b, Hartford**
15. **John Morris, rhp, Cal State Los Angeles**
16. Frank Miloszewski, lhp, Beaver Falls (Pa.) HS
17. Jeff Kenaga, of, Lutheran West HS, Dearborn Heights, Mich.
18. **Raymond Hallgren, ss, Cal State Chico**
19. Bob Stoddard, rhp, Live Oak HS, Morgan Hill, Calif.
20. **David Marino, ss, Carthage (Wis.)**
21. **William Dick, lhp, Cleveland Heights (Ohio) HS**
22. Walter Passmore, of, Colonial HS, Orlando, Fla.

June—Secondary Phase (15)

1. **Billy Severns, of, Oklahoma**
2. Jeff Hardy, ss, Gulf Coast (Fla.) CC

MINNESOTA TWINS

January—Regular Phase (14)

1. Vic Bernal, p, Cal Poly Pomona (Selection voided)
2. Donald Albares, 2b, George Wallace (Ala.) CC
3. Randy Niemann, lhp, JC of the Redwoods (Calif.)
4. Steve Ross, of, San Jose CC
5. Steve Lund, p, Mount Hood (Ore.) CC
6. Vance McHenry, ss, Butte (Calif.) JC
7. Robert Milostan, of/1b, Ataksa, Ill.

January—Secondary Phase (22)

1. **Mark Wilson, of/3b, Linn-Benton (Ore.) CC**
2. **Rick Duncan, c, Vanderbilt**
3. Dale Brock, of, Southern
4. Anthony Davis, of, Southern California
5. **Mike Gatlin, 3b, Arizona**

June—Regular Phase (13)

1. **Rick Sofield, ss, Morristown (N.J.) HS**
2. **Stephen Parrott, rhp, Camarillo (Calif.) HS**
3. **Stephen Douglas, 3b, T.C. Williams HS, Alexandria, Va.**
4. **Greg Field, rhp, Lake Worth HS, West Palm Beach, Fla.**
5. **Dan Graham, c, La Verne (Calif.)**
6. Bruce Humphrey, 1b, Hale HS, Tulsa, Okla.
7. **Donald Yarborough, c, Lake Worth HS, Fort Pierce, Fla.**
8. Larry Reynolds, 2b, Corvallis (Ore.) HS
9. **Mike Bacon, 3b, LaSierra HS, Riverside, Calif.**
10. **Robert Franz, of, Kennedy HS, Granada Hills, Calif.**
11. Joseph Smith, of, Hogan HS, Vallejo, Calif.
12. **Frank Estes, of, Cal State Fullerton**
13. **Dennis Mantick, 2b, Western Illinois**
14. Peter Brown, lhp, Glens Falls, N.Y.
15. **Ronald Jones, rhp, Missouri Western State**
16. Paul Mirabella, lhp, Montclair State (N.J.)
17. **Joseph Kordosku, ss, Minnesota**
18. **Gregg Gaughran, c, Kennedy HS, Bloomington, Minn.**
19. Gary Bowers, rhp, Anaheim HS
20. **Steve Wagner, rhp, Hazen HS, Renton, Wash.**
21. Marty Castillo, 3b, Savanna HS, Anaheim
22. Wilbert Haslip, 2b, Santa Ana Valley HS, Santa Ana, Calif.
23. **Gary Grunsky, lhp, Delano (Calif.) HS**
24. **Davis May, rhp, Auburn**
25. Gilbert Ramirez, c, Savanna HS, Buena Park, Calif.
26. Mark Grier, c, Severna Park (Md.) HS
27. **Charles Carvis, rhp, Wilcox HS, Santa Clara, Calif.**
28. George Rath, lhp, Bella Vista HS, Orangevale, Calif.
29. Steven Rice, rhp, San Joaquin Delta (Calif.) JC
30. Mike Arlotta, lhp, Norland HS, Miami
31. Walter Podgurski, 2b, Union (N.J.) HS
32. Gary Spies, c, Anne Arundel (Md.) CC
33. Steve Christmas, 3b, Colonial HS, Orlando, Fla.
34. Roger Dirkes, ss, Washington State
35. **Dan Petrowitz, lhp, Edison HS, Minneapolis**
36. **Gregg Bemis, lhp, Puget Sound (Wash.)**
37. **Al Arthur, rhp, Stanford**

June—Secondary Phase (3)

1. **Hosken Powell, of, Chipola (Fla.) JC**
2. Scott Anderson, rhp, Mesa (Ariz.) CC
3. Dirk Blankenship, rhp, Blinn (Texas) JC

MONTREAL EXPOS

January—Regular Phase (9)

1. Johnny Brown, of, South Georgia JC
2. Ken Lelek, p, Monroe (N.Y.) CC
3. **Randy Eickenhorst, 3b, Gulf Coast (Fla.) CC**
4. Kevin LaFranco, p, Santa Ana (Calif.) JC
5. Peter Peltz, ss, Brookdale (N.J.) CC
6. Jack Hudson, c, Golden West (Calif.) JC
7. Dirk Blankenship, p, Blinn (Texas) JC
8. **Larry Horn, rhp/3b, Blinn (Texas) JC**

January—Secondary Phase (13)

1. **Mark Knose, rhp, Toledo**
2. Jeff Hardy, ss, Gulf Coast (Fla.) CC
3. **Larry Goldetsky, ss, Indian Hills (Iowa) CC**
4. Brian Cherevko, p, West Valley (Calif.) JC
5. Ronald Goodman, p, Santa Barbara (Calif.) CC

June—Regular Phase (10)

1. **Art Miles, ss, Crockett HS, Austin**
2. **Dale McMullen, of, St. Pius HS, Houston**
3. **Mitch Cipolla, c, Martin Van Buren HS, Bellrose, N.Y.**
4. **Andrew Dyes, of, Fresno State**
5. **Dale Halvorson, rhp, Essex Junction, Vt.**
6. **Ronald Staggs, 1b, East Carolina**
7. Rodney Feight, rhp, Everett (Pa.) HS
8. Mike Boddicker, rhp, Norway (Iowa) HS
9. **Walter Johnson, c, Anderson HS, Austin**
10. **Jeff Gingrich, rhp, San Jose State**
11. **Andre Dawson, of, Florida A&M**
12. **Bob Weatherford, rhp, MacArthur HS, Decatur, Ill.**

13. **Mark Ewell, rhp, Iowa**
14. Alphonso Eiland, ss, Inglewood (Calif.) HS
15. Craig Smith, lhp, Fort Vancouver (Wash.) HS
16. Chick Valley, lhp, San Diego CC
17. **Lloyd Thompson, ss/2b, New Mexico**
18. John Marquardt, of, Alamogordo (N.M.) HS
19. Robert Powell, rhp, Bloomington (Calif.) HS
20. **Michael Cooper, c, El Camino (Calif.) JC**
21. Rickey Keeton, rhp, West Hills HS, Cincinnati
22. **Tim Stuthard, rhp, Henderson State (Ark.)**
23. Ronald Keyes, rhp, Watkins HS, Laurel, Miss.
24. William Evers, c, Eckerd (Fla.)
25. **Ray Crowley, 1b, Lewis (Ill.)**
26. Michael Krill, lhp, Irvington (N.J.) HS
27. Tom Teuchert, rhp, Chapparel HS, Scottsdale, Ariz.
28. Tom McLish, rhp, Edmond (Okla.) HS
29. Manuel Mayer, 3b, Irvington (N.J.) HS
30. Mark Hredzak, of, Keystone Oaks HS, Pittsburgh

June—Secondary Phase (12)

1. Del Bender, of, Miami-Dade South CC
2. Mark Liber, lhp, Mesa (Ariz.) CC
3. Frank Williams, c, Louisburg (N.C.) JC

NEW YORK METS

January—Regular Phase (5)

1. Dave Hudgens, 1b, Oroville, Calif.
2. Fritz Lagergren, 2b, Seminole (Fla.) JC
3. **Rick Sander, rhp, San Bernardino Valley (Calif.) JC**
4. **Marshall Brant, 1b, Santa Rosa (Calif.) JC**
5. Robert Simmons, p, Broward (Fla.) CC
6. Karl Pagel, 1b, Glendale (Ariz.) CC

January—Secondary Phase (9)

1. **Stanley Mann, ss, Southern Illinois**
2. Gene Krug, 1b, Lamar (Colo.) CC
3. Jackie Smith, p, Manatee (Fla.) JC
4. Greg Harris, rhp, Long Beach CC
5. **John McBride, ss, Utah**
6. **Gene Litle, p, California**
7. Steve Marlowe, 1b, Utah
8. Stewart Bringhurst, c, JC of San Mateo (Calif.)
9. Michael Wholey, p, Green River (Wash.) CC

June—Regular Phase (6)

1. **Butch Benton, c, Godby HS, Tallahassee, Fla.**
2. Rodney Boxberger, rhp, Foothill HS, Santa Ana, Calif.
3. **George Milke, rhp, Southern California**
4. **Larry Prewitt, rhp, Pacific**
5. **Robert Grant, c, Westchester HS, Los Angeles**
6. **George Bradbury, 2b, Pinole (Calif.) Valley HS**
7. **Randy Brown, rhp, Seminole HS, Sanford, Fla.**
8. Steve Houlberg, ss, Southwest HS, Miami
9. Frank McCann, inf, Delaware
10. Chuck McMichael, lhp, Hoover HS, Glendale, Calif.
11. Guy Jones, rhp, Shasta HS, Redding, Calif.
12. **Gene Bardot, rhp, Southwestern (Calif.) JC**
13. Richter Armer, of, Fremont HS, Sunnyvale, Calif.
14. Rich Wortham, lhp, Texas
15. Charlie Lea, rhp/1b, Kingsbury HS, Memphis
16. **Paul Cacciatore, rhp, Waltham (Mass.) HS**
17. **Russell Clark, rhp, Mississippi Gulf Coast JC**
18. James Noonan, ss, Cordova HS, Rancho Cordova, Calif.
19. David Pfeiffer, rhp, Green City HS, Winigan, Mo.
20. **Gilbert Joseph, rhp, Brownsville HS, Hiller, Pa.**
21. John Tudor, lhp, Georgia Southern
22. John Tillema, rhp, Cupertino (Calif.) HS
23. Robert Bonnette, ss, Wellington Academy HS, Neeses, S.C.
24. **Jeff Carter, 3b/of, Memphis State**
25. **James Howard, of, Stetson**
26. **Anthony Wylie, of, Salinas (Calif.) HS**
27. **Kevan Aman, of, Kamiakan HS, Kennewick, Wash.**

June—Secondary Phase (20)

1. **Ward Wilson, c, Valencia (Fla.) CC**
2. **James Dyer, ss, Arizona Western JC**

NEW YORK YANKEES

January—Regular Phase (20)

1. Patrick McGehee, p, Carson, Calif.

January—Secondary Phase (18)

1. Larry Buckle, rhp, Long Beach CC
2. Ward Wilson, c, Valencia (Fla.) CC

June—Regular Phase (19)

1. **Jim McDonald, 1b, Verbum Dei HS, Los Angeles**
2. **Benny Lloyd, of, Manual Arts HS, Los Angeles**
3. **Nate Chapman, of, Jarvis Christian (Texas)**
4. **Jim Beattie, rhp, Dartmouth**
5. **Willie Upshaw, 1b, Blanco (Texas) HS**
6. **Leon Laurent, rhp, Lutcher HS, Gramercy, La.**
7. **Mike Fischlin, ss, Cosumnes River (Calif.) JC**
8. Alex Kager, rhp, Permian HS, Odessa, Texas
9. Len Glowzenski, rhp, Seton Hall
10. Larry Brown, rhp, Norwood (Mass.) HS
11. Kent Nicar, rhp, Morgan City (La.) HS
12. James Kopatz, c, Illinois
13. John Hoscheidt, of, Southern Illinois
14. Danny Boone, lhp, Cal State Fullerton
15. Greg Sanossian, 1b, St. John's
16. **Robert Cahall, rhp, Atlantic (N.J.) CC**
17. Henry Campbell, ss, Yazoo City (Miss.) HS
18. **Robert Smith, of, Philadelphia College of Textiles**

June—Secondary Phase (7)

1. **Gil Patterson, of/rhp, Miami-Dade South CC**
2. **Randy Niemann, lhp, JC of the Redwoods (Calif.)**

OAKLAND ATHLETICS

January—Regular Phase (22)

1. Del Bender, of, Miami-Dade South CC
2. **Gary Medeiros, c, Chabot (Calif.) JC**
3. Erik Hendricks, p, Chabot (Calif.) JC
4. Ray Dimick, p, Los Angeles Pierce JC

January—Secondary Phase (4)

1. **Rob Picciolo, inf, Pepperdine**
2. Pat Kelleher, p, Fullerton (Calif.) JC
3. Brian Heublein, p, Southern California
4. **David Gallino, ss, Contra Costa (Calif.) JC**

June—Regular Phase (21)

1. **Bruce Robinson, c, Stanford**
2. **Greg Cochran, rhp, Arizona State**
3. **Clarence Green, rhp, Ketchum (Okla.) HS**
4. Mike Wright, c, Father Ryan HS, Nashville
5. Robert Heuck, lhp, John Marshall HS, San Antonio
6. Steven Splitt, of, Clairemont HS, San Diego
7. **Steven Malito, of, Central Valley HS, Spokane, Wash.**
8. **Guy Murphy, rhp, Meridian (Miss.) HS**
9. Jeffrey Marson, lhp, Logan HS, La Crosse, Wis.
10. Tom Wieghaus, c, Rich East HS, Park Forest, Ill.
11. Thomas Underhill, rhp, Central HS, Bristol, Wis.
12. Mark Paradise, lhp, Marblehead (Mass.) HS
13. **Kenneth Hunter, c, Muir HS, Altadena, Calif.**
14. Robert Harris, rhp, Montgomery Bell Academy HS, Nashville
15. Bob Horner, ss, Apollo HS, Glendale, Ariz.
16. Steve Benson, ss, Culver City (Calif.) HS
17. Kenneth Robinson, of, Ypsilanti (Mich.) HS
18. Albert Dunn, c, South San Francisco (Calif.) HS
19. George Mahan, rhp, Michigan State
20. George Robins, of/rhp, Manual Arts HS, Los Angeles
21. **Howard Robinson, 3b/ss, Dorsey HS, Los Angeles**
22. Michael Hilliard, 3b, Lincoln HS, San Diego
23. **John Hagman, rhp, St. Olaf (Minn.)**
24. Mike Chris, 1b, Venice HS, Los Angeles
25. Robert Hardaway, c/of, Inglewood (Calif.) HS

June—Secondary Phase (1)

1. **Denny Walling, of, Clemson**
2. **Monty Bothwell, of, Cypress (Calif.) JC**

PHILADELPHIA PHILLIES

January—Regular Phase (11)

1. Richard Nesloney, p, Ranger (Texas) JC
2. **Joseph Daniels, ss, Murray Wright HS, Detroit**
3. **David Roper, ss, Spartanburg Methodist (S.C.) JC**
4. Chris Carstensen, of, Moorpark (Calif.) JC
5. Michael Benfield, p, Spartanburg Methodist (S.C.) JC
6. Mark Liber, lhp, Mesa (Ariz.) CC
7. **Cubb Stokes, 1b, Tennessee**
8. Jack Lazorko, 3b/rhp, Miami-Dade South CC

January—Secondary Phase (1)

1. **Barry Bonnell, of, Ohio State**
2. **Ken O'Brien, ss, Widener (Pa.)**
3. **Dennis Hawkins, of, Chaffey (Calif.) JC**
4. **Steve Kruzelock, c, Santa Monica (Calif.) JC**

June—Regular Phase (12)

1. **Sam Welborn, rhp, Wichita Falls (Texas) HS**
2. **Joe Jones, c, Columbus (Ga.) HS**
3. **Ray LaPointe, rhp, Baptist (Fla.)**
4. **Dickie Noles, rhp, Harding HS, Charlotte, N.C.**
5. **Roberto Roman, c, Manhattan Vocational HS, New York**
6. **Dave Baker, c, Stanford**
7. **Keith Moreland, 3b, Texas**
8. **Greg Bradford, lhp, Legrand (Calif.) HS**
9. Dave Van Gorder, c, Chandler (Ariz.) HS
10. DeVallon Harper, rhp, Alhambra HS, Martinez, Calif.
11. Rick Leach, of, Southwestern HS, Flint, Mich.
12. **Mark Rogers, of, Azusa Pacific (Calif.)**
13. Greg Norris, rhp, Whiteville HS, Brunswick, N.C.
14. **Martin Robinson, rhp, Penn HS, Osceola, Ind.**
15. **Raymond Schmidt, ss, Bishop McNamara HS, Kankakee, Ill.**
16. Jeffrey Brisson, of, Iowa Western CC
17. **James Smoak, of, Baptist (Fla.)**
18. **James Nickerson, rhp, Pittsburgh HS**
19. Dave Rucker, lhp, Eisenhower HS, Rialto, Calif.
20. Kenneth Young, of, Amityville (N.Y.) HS
21. **Gregory Stone, rhp, South Alabama**
22. Richard Lipp, of, Grant Island (N.Y.) HS
23. Allan Ramirez, rhp, Victoria (Texas) HS
24. Marc Thomas, c/of, San Luis Obispo (Calif.) HS
25. **Don Fowler, rhp, Dana Hill HS, Dana Point, Calif.**
26. **Jeffrey Johnson, ss, Christian Brothers HS, Quincy, Ill.**
27. **James Lasak, rhp, Black Hawk (Ill.) JC**
28. **Louis Reyes, c/3b, Hillsborough (Fla.) CC**
29. Roger Slagle, rhp, Kansas

June—Secondary Phase (8)

1. **Joe Berriatus, 1b/of, JC of San Mateo (Calif.)**
2. **Tim Pagnozzi, ss, Mesa (Ariz.) CC**

PITTSBURGH PIRATES

January—Regular Phase (19)

1. Hosken Powell, of, Chipola (Fla.) JC
2. **Ray Negron, ss, New York Tech**
3. John Tolan, ss, Big Bend (Wash.) CC
4. Frank Williams, c, Louisburg (N.C.) JC
5. **Richard Ferrell, p, Charleston, W.Va.**
6. Mark Corey, 1b, Central Arizona JC
7. Russell Aldrich, c, Chipola (Fla.) JC
8. Daniel Bishop, p, Green River (Wash.) CC
9. James Keough, p, Ricks (Idaho) JC
10. Francis Spetter, c, Three Rivers (Mo.) CC

January—Secondary Phase (15)

1. Charles Ledbetter, p, Valencia (Fla.) CC
2. Michael Frazier, c, Texas A&M
3. Gary Smith, of, Valencia (Fla.) CC
4. **Timothy Burman, p, Cincinnati**

June—Regular Phase (20)

1. **Dale Berra, ss, Montclair (N.J.) HS**
2. **Jeff Pinkus, rhp, Hingham (Mass.) HS**
3. **Don Robinson, rhp, Ceredo-Kenova HS, Kenova, W.Va.**
4. **Larry Olson, c, Katella HS, Anaheim**
5. **Jerry McDonald, of, Banks HS, Birmingham**
6. Rob Simond, lhp, Barrington (Ill.) HS
7. **Heyward Edrington, c, McCrory-Liston HS, Blair, S.C.**
8. **Jim Busby, of, Florida State**
9. **James Johnston, rhp, Shorter (Ga.)**
10. **Steven Fleming, of, Sale HS, Chester, Va.**
11. Greg Stahl, ss, Rolling Hills HS, Rancho Palos Verdes, Calif.
12. Ernie Camacho, rhp, Hartnell (Calif.) CC
13. Ron Pearce, rhp, Lake Brantley HS, Altamonte, Fla.
14. **David Joyner, 3b, Dalton (Ga.) HS**
15. David Aronow, rhp, Taft HS, Canoga Park, Calif.
16. **Mark Tapia, rhp, South Alabama**
17. Charles Dorgan, lhp, Meadowdale HS, Lynwood, Wash.
18. Paul Smith, 1b, Clearwater (Fla.) HS
19. Frank Lucarelli, rhp, Newport HS, Bellevue, Wash.
20. **Mark Saber, ss/3b, Georgia**
21. **Joe Daniel, c, Mercer**
22. **Robert Semerano, rhp, Orange County (N.Y.) CC**
23. **James Burkett, rhp, Mortimer Jordan HS, Morris, Ala.**
24. **Vaughn Robbins, 1b, Shorter (Ga.)**
25. Paul Tasker, c/3b, Dunedin HS, Clearwater, Fla.
26. **Harry Summers, c, Shorter (Ga.)**
27. Craig Thorpe, rhp, Miami
28. **Jeffrey Woods, ss, West Branch HS, Beloit, Ohio**
29. Richard Holloway, rhp, Mount Lebanon HS, Pittsburgh
30. William Krampe, rhp, Shaler HS, Pittsburgh
31. Robert Sims, ss, Lafayette-Jefferson HS, Lafayette, Ind.
32. Larry McIver, of, Power Memorial HS, New York
33. Michael Munns, rhp, Caldwell, Idaho
34. John Pennington, ss, Bell (Calif.) HS

June—Secondary Phase (6)

1. LaMart Harris, of, Ranger (Texas) JC
2. Ernie Mauritson, rhp, Chabot (Calif.) JC
3. Steve Wilkins, of, Oregon State

ST. LOUIS CARDINALS

January—Regular Phase (15)

1. **Terry Gray, rhp, Merced (Calif.) JC**
2. Ray Gault, p, Manatee (Fla.) JC
3. Randall Hagerty, 1b, San Diego Mesa JC
4. Peter Tereschuk, p, Long Beach CC
5. Richard Lacey, ss, Anderson (S.C.) JC

January—Secondary Phase (11)

1. **Jerry Johnson, c, Temple (Texas) JC**
2. **Chuck Redmon, ss, Oklahoma**
3. Erol Akchurin, 3b, JC of San Mateo (Calif.)
4. **Brett Houser, rhp, Long Beach CC**
5. Scott Lankford, p, Modesto (Calif.) JC
6. Jackie Snell, lhp, George Wallace (Ala.) CC
7. Tim Glines, c, JC of the Sequoias (Calif.)

June—Regular Phase (16)

1. **David Johnson, lhp, Gaylord (Mich.) HS**
2. **Kelly Paris, ss, Taft HS, Woodland Hills, Calif.**
3. **Mike Ramsey, ss, Appalachian State**
4. **James Propst, rhp, West HS, Columbus, Ohio**
5. **Steve Schartzer, of, Southern Illinois**
6. Dale Eiler, c, Clairemont HS, San Diego
7. **Ralph Costanzo, 3b, Capuchino HS, Millbrae, Calif.**
8. **Richard Montejano, rhp, Imperial (Calif.) HS**
9. **Andy Replogle, rhp, Kansas State**
10. Mark Nipp, rhp, Aptos (Calif.) HS
11. Scott Stranski, rhp, Mount Vernon (Ill.) HS
12. **Jim Lentine, of, La Verne (Calif.)**
13. **Al Olmsted, lhp, Hazelwood East HS, St. Louis**
14. **Robert Frantz, lhp, Clarion (Pa.)**
15. Steve Romine, of, Wheeler HS, Marietta, Ga.
16. **Karl Rieger, lhp, Sam Houston State**
17. Randy Rhodes, 2b, Canada (Calif.) JC
18. **David Oliver, rhp, Belleville East HS, Fairview Heights, Ill.**
19. Robert Stephens, ss, Fayetteville (Ark.) HS

20. Kell Schmidt, lhp, San Leandro (Calif.) HS
21. **Alfred Meyer, rhp, Southern California**
22. Randy Evans, rhp, Catalina HS, Tucson
23. **R.J. Harrison, c, Arizona State**
24. **Nick Leyva, ss, La Verne (Calif.)**
25. **Anthony Dennard, rhp, Chipola (Fla.) JC**
26. Anthony Tornincasa, c/of, Hillsdale HS, San Mateo, Calif.
27. Michael Finch, lhp, El Capitan HS, Lakeside, Calif.
28. **Jeff Borges, ss, San Leandro (Calif.) HS**
29. Michael Bungarz, lhp, Moreau HS, Hayward, Calif.
30. **David Lundsford, 1b, Monte Vista HS, San Diego**
31. **George Shuford, of, Kailua (Hawaii) HS**

June—Secondary Phase (2)

1. **Earl Bass, rhp, South Carolina**
2. Karl Pagel, 1b, Glendale (Ariz.) CC

SAN DIEGO PADRES

January—Regular Phase (1)

1. **Gene Richards Jr., of, South Carolina State**
2. John Savage, p, West Valley (Calif.) JC
3. Regindo Wilkerson, p, St. Johns River (Fla.) CC
4. Michael Swingle, p, Lincoln Land (Ill.) JC

January—Secondary Phase (19)

1. **Juan Eichelberger, rhp, California**
2. **Chuck Baker, ss, Loyola Marymount**
3. **Rick Sweet, c, Gonzaga**
4. Al Holland, lhp, North Carolina A&T

June—Regular Phase (2)

1. **Mike Lentz, lhp, Juanita HS, Kirkland, Wash.**
2. **Harold Drake, ss, Bonita HS, La Verne, Calif.**
3. **Tony Castillo, c, James Lick HS, San Jose**
4. **Tim Derryberry, of, Chino (Calif.) HS**
5. Tom Willette, lhp, Plymouth State (Mich.)
6. **Victor Bernal, rhp, Cal Poly Pomona**
7. **William Joseph, lhp, Kearny HS, San Diego**
8. **Walter Segrest, c, Vallejo (Calif.) HS**
9. **Robert Mitchell, ss/of, Richmond**
10. **Carl Maglio, inf, Edgewood HS, Madison, Wis.**
11. Ron Driver, lhp, Sam Rayburn HS, Pasadena, Texas
12. **Joseph Hicks, of, San Pedro (Calif.) HS**
13. Brian Savidge, of, San Mateo (Calif.) HS
14. **Gene Menees, 3b, Vanderbilt**
15. Samuel Albert, ss, Toulimsville HS, Mobile, Ala.
16. **Guy Hollingsworth, lhp, Louisiana State**
17. **Alan Brumfield, ss, High Point**
18. **Don Reynolds, of, Oregon**
19. Michael Koppess, rhp, Chino (Calif.) HS
20. **Kurt Wittmeyer, ss, San Diego State**
21. **Greg Wilkes, rhp, San Diego State**
22. Dave Crutcher, rhp, Woodland (Calif.) HS
23. James Ridenour, rhp, Vincennes (Ind.) JC
24. James Harris, rhp, Bossier HS, Bossier City, La.
25. **Marty French, rhp, San Diego State**

June—Secondary Phase (22)

1. Larry Buckle, rhp, Long Beach CC

SAN FRANCISCO GIANTS

January—Regular Phase (7)

1. **Gene Schmidt, rhp, El Camino (Calif.) JC**
2. **Rick Steen, rhp, Ventura (Calif.) JC**
3. Frank Marini, of, Mount San Antonio (Calif.) JC
4. Dave Hostetler, 1b, Citrus (Calif.) JC
5. John Guarino, of/1b, Pepperdine
6. **Alan Ayres, of, Citrus (Calif.) JC**
7. **Dennis Lee, 2b, Mount San Antonio (Calif.) JC**
8. **Pat Ryan, inf/c, Pasadena (Calif.) CC**
9. Harold Rowe, ss, West Valley (Calif.) JC
10. Joe Berriatus, 1b/of, JC of San Mateo (Calif.)
11. **Luis Pereiro, inf, Tampa, Fla.**
12. Tom Pagnozzi, ss, Mesa (Ariz.) CC
13. John Braas, p, Bakersfield (Calif.) JC
14. **Steve Watson, rhp/of, Spokane Falls (Wash.) CC**
15. Robert Dahlquist, p/1b, Everett (Wash.) CC
16. Mace Magruder, p/of, Bellevue (Wash.) CC

January—Secondary Phase (17)

1. **David Anderson, rhp, Arizona Western JC**
2. Jeffrey Ross, p, Fresno State
3. Billy Severns, of, Oklahoma

June—Regular Phase (8)

1. **Ted Barnicle, lhp, Jacksonville State**
2. **Rick Bradley, c, Texas**
3. **Jose Barrios, 1b, South Miami HS**
4. **Garrett Strong, of, Arizona State**
5. Bob Shirley, lhp, Oklahoma
6. **Rich Murray, 1b, Locke HS, Los Angeles**
7. **George Davis, of, Scottsdale (Ariz.) HS**
8. Gregg Fisher, 3b, Pleasant Hill HS, Concord, Calif.
9. **Tom Bhagwatt, of, Hawaii**
10. Dan Massari, 1b, Oklahoma State
11. **Ted Schoenhaus, of, Seton Hall**
12. **Greg Johnston, of, Citrus (Calif.) JC**
13. **Steve Osborne, of, CC of San Francisco**
14. **Mark Woodbrey, 2b, Amherst (Mass.)**
15. **Doug Schaefer, rhp, Oklahoma**
16. Charles Wyatt, rhp, Foothill (Calif.) JC
17. **Bryan Boyne, ss, Rice**
18. James English, 2b, Hazelwood Central HS, St. Louis
19. Dan Hartwig, rhp, Quartz Hill HS, Lancaster, Calif.
20. **Mark Daugherty, 3b, Hoggard HS, Wilmington, N.C.**
21. **Howard Mitchell, 2b, Southern Illinois**
22. **Mike Rowland, rhp, Millikin (Ill.)**
23. **Martin Flores, lhp, Texas**
24. **Bret Paris, ss, Los Angeles Pierce JC**
25. John Holcomb, of, Carroll HS, Corpus Christi, Texas
26. Javiar Fierro, 3b, Mount San Antonio (Calif.) JC
27. William Eve, 1b, North Miami Beach HS, Opalocka, Fla.
28. **Timothy Peterson, rhp, Bellevue (Wash.) CC**
29. Ron Roenicke, of/1b, Mount San Antonio (Calif.) JC
30. Mark Clifford, rhp, Harrison County HS, Cynthiana, Ky.
31. Cyrus Smith, of, Callaway HS, Jackson, Miss.
32. **Steven Sherman, lhp, Patrick Henry HS, San Diego**
33. Ty Waller, inf, Hoover HS, San Diego
34. Duane Walker, lhp/of, Deer Park HS, Pasadena, Texas
35. Mike Zouras, 3b, El Camino (Calif.) JC
36. Kevin Kopp, c, Los Angeles Pierce JC
37. Robert Cramer, rhp, Long HS, Longview, Wash.

June—Secondary Phase (10)

1. Darrell Brown, ss, East Los Angeles JC
2. Ray Gault, rhp, Manatee (Fla.) JC

TEXAS RANGERS

January—Regular Phase (18)

1. **Tim Brookens, of, Shenandoah (Va.)**
2. Ron Evans, 3b, Greensboro, N.C.
3. Greg Fairbanks, p, Brevard (Fla.) CC
4. Michael MacDonald, p, Columbia State (Tenn.) CC

January—Secondary Phase (6)

1. **Bump Wills, 2b, Arizona State**
2. Tony Johnson, of, Shelby State (Tenn.) CC
3. Andrew Mason, 3b, Oregon State (Selection voided)

June—Regular Phase (17)

1. **Jim Gideon, rhp, Texas**
2. **Eddie Miller, of, Ells HS, Richmond, Calif.**
3. Kem Wright, rhp, Paris (Texas) HS
4. **Victor Mabee, ss, Sunnyvale (Calif.) HS**
5. **Blair Stouffer, 3b/ss, Texas**
6. **John Poloni, lhp, Arizona State**
7. **David Rivera, of, King City HS, Greenfield, Calif.**
8. John Shouse, 1b, Chamberlain HS, Tampa
9. **Randall Reynolds, c, York (Pa.)**
10. Richard Comeau, rhp, Leominster (Mass.) HS
11. Hal Hutchens, rhp, New Hanover HS, Wilmington, N.C.

12. **Richard Couch, lhp, Berkeley HS, Oakland**
13. **Wayne Pinkerton, inf, Mississippi State**
14. **John Takacs, ss/2b, West Haven (Conn.) HS**
15. Glenn Ballard, c, Satellite Beach HS, Indian Harbor Beach, Fla.
16. **Mike Bucci, of, West Chester (Pa.)**
17. **Joseph Stewart, of, Burbank HS, Sacramento**
18. Dennis Doyle, c, St. Peters HS, Worcester, Mass.
19. Michael Smith, rhp, Norwood (Ohio) HS
20. Peter Alfano, rhp, Ensley HS, Birmingham
21. **Harold Kelly, rhp, Plant City (Fla.) HS**
22. **Pat Moock, rhp, Louisiana State**
23. **La Rue Washington, ss, Cal State Dominguez Hills**
24. Mark Brisker, of, Colerain HS, Cincinnati
25. **David Chapman, 1b, UCLA**
26. David Lockett, rhp, Texas A&M
27. **James Thomas, c, Texas Wesleyan**
28. **William Stone, ss, Toronto (Ohio) HS**
29. **Lawrence Burgess, lhp, American Christian HS, Fort Worth, Texas**
30. Thomas Crain, 1b, Texas Christian
31. Mickey Reichenbach, 1b, Texas
32. Bruce Poole, lhp, South Alabama
33. George Tebbetts, 3b, Bradenton HS, Anna Maria, Fla. (Selection voided)

June—Secondary Phase (23)

1. **Pat Putnam, 1b, South Alabama**

1976 BANNISTER HIGHLIGHTS STRONG GROUP OF SOUTHPAWS, AS TIGERS REBOUND AFTER FIRST-ROUND PICK

When the Astros selected Floyd Bannister with the No. 1 pick in the 1976 draft, both parties dashed speculation that the Arizona State lefthander would begin his career in the major leagues.

"I've talked to Houston about starting out in the majors and I don't want to. I want to go to the minor leagues first and prove myself there," Bannister said. "It will give me a chance to get accustomed to professional baseball and not move up too quickly. I've seen too many cases of people starting out in the big leagues and having it hurt them. I'd like to start off low and build my confidence."

If there was a player who seemed ready to start in the big leagues, it was Bannister. He led the nation in strikeouts two years in a row, fanning 217 in 157 innings as a sophomore in 1975 and 213 more in an NCAA-record 186 innings as a junior in 1976. He tied the all-time college record for wins (19) in 1976, while posting a 1.45 ERA and completing an NCAA-record 17 games.

"Bannister is not far removed from the major league level now," Astros general manager Tal Smith said, "but we feel that when he comes to the major leagues, it will be to stay. He will be ready when he does pitch for the Astros."

Bannister started at the bottom rung of the Astros system, but seven games later he was in the big leagues to stay. Over the next 13 seasons, he won 133 games.

Bannister's selection—which coincidentally came on the same day that the Houston Rockets used the No. 1 overall pick in the NBA draft on Maryland guard John Lucas—set the tone for a draft that was deep in lefthanded pitching and had a heavy Arizona State flavor. Four of the first five picks in the June regular phase were lefthanders, and a record 13 Sun Devils were selected.

The Tigers had the second selection and wanted a local product, Eastern Michigan lefthander Bob Owchinko, who beat Bannister 2-1 in a classic matchup at the College World Series. But the Tigers and Owchinko weren't close on contract terms, so Detroit went for another lefthander, Pat Underwood, younger brother of Philadelphia pitcher Tom Underwood.

"The Tigers called me before the draft, but they weren't talking enough money," Owchinko said. "They wouldn't give me a few certain things I wanted."

Underwood made the big leagues in his fourth season but won just 13 games in a four-year career.

CULF PHOTO

Floyd Bannister didn't spend much time in the minors on his way to Houston

His brother Tom lasted 11 seasons, winning 86 games. Owchinko went fifth overall to San Diego. He was in the big leagues with the Padres by September.

If Detroit bungled its first-round pick, it made up for it later. The Tigers took shortstop Alan Trammell in the second round, and pitchers Dan Petry and Jack Morris in rounds four and five. They even selected shortstop Ozzie Smith in the seventh round, but couldn't sign him.

The fourth lefthander of the group was Bill Bordley, who never signed with the Brewers. He was one of three first-round picks from the '76 draft who did not sign.

Third baseman Jamie Allen rebuffed a $50,000 offer from the Twins to attend Arizona State. Allen had indicated that he would go to college, but the Twins drafted him anyway. Oakland also couldn't sign lefthander Mike Sullivan, not to mention its second-round pick and five of its first 10 picks. Sullivan went to college at Clemson and three years later was picked in the first round again, by Cincinnati. He never played in the big leagues.

Arizona State (65-10) didn't reach the final game of the 1976 College World Series, but it may have fielded the most talented college team ever assembled. The Sun Devils' 65 wins were an NCAA record; so were their 87 home runs.

With 13 players drafted, the Sun Devils had more than twice as many selections as the next-highest team. They became the first school ever to hit double figures, and 13 members of the '76 Sun Devil team reached the big leagues—another record.

If Arizona State was the dominant college team of 1976, then California's Lakewood High was the best high school team. Four Lakewood High players were selected in '76, and 15 from that team eventually went on to play professional baseball. One, Mike Fitzgerald, made the big leagues.

Changes On The Way

Just three college players were selected in the first round of the June regular phase: Bannister, Owchinko and Arizona State's Ken Landreaux. But 65 more college players were picked than the previous year, and 1976 became the last year that more high school players were drafted than college.

A change in baseball's college rule was partially responsible. Previously only juniors were eligible if they had their 21st birthday within 45 days of the draft. That rule was rescinded and made all juniors, regardless of age, eligible.

Also in 1976, pitchers Dave McNally and Andy Messersmith successfully challenged baseball's reserve clause, paving the way for free agency. Free agency had implications on the draft. As major leaguers were permitted to play out their options and sign as free agents, their former clubs were awarded draft picks as compensation.

The January 1976 draft had some unusually strong talent, thanks to three University of Southern California dropouts. Pitcher Pete Redfern (Twins) and catcher Dennis Littlejohn (Giants) were the first two picks in the regular phase, while Steve Kemp (Tigers) was the No. 1 pick in the secondary phase. All three had dropped out of school the previous fall to be eligible.

All were juniors but none was 21 within 45 days of the June 1975 draft. The change in the draft rule came too late to benefit them.

Kemp set USC's single-season batting record in 1975, hitting .435 with 13 homers and 67 RBIs. He hit .386 in a 52-game trial with Triple-A Evansville in 1976 and went on to hit .278 in 10 big league seasons. His career effectively ended in 1983 when he was hit in the head by a batting-practice drive that knocked him unconscious and left him with blurred vision.

Redfern's career ended when he broke his neck prior to the 1983 season in a swimming accident.

Texas lefthander Rich Wortham was also selected in the January draft and signed with the White Sox after posting a 14-2, 1.70 record for the Longhorns. His 14 wins enabled him to finish with 50 career wins, eclipsing the NCAA record of 47.

DRAFT 76: FIRST-ROUND PICKS

No.	Club	Player, Pos.	School	Hometown	Ht.	Wt.	B-T	Age
1.	Astros	Floyd Bannister, lhp	Arizona State	Seattle	6-1	185	L-L	20
2.	Tigers	Pat Underwood, lhp	Kokomo HS	Kokomo, Ind.	6-0	175	L-L	19
3.	Braves	Ken Smith, 3b	East HS	Youngstown, Ohio	6-2	190	L-R	18
4.	Brewers	*Bill Bordley, lhp	Bishop Montgomery HS	Rolling Hills Estates, Calif.	6-3	185	R-L	18
5.	Padres	Bob Owchinko, lhp	Eastern Michigan	Detroit	6-2	190	L-L	21
6.	Angels	Ken Landreaux, of	Arizona State	Compton, Calif.	5-11	170	L-R	21
7.	Cubs	Herm Segelke, rhp	El Camino HS	South Sacramento, Calif.	6-5	215	R-R	18
8.	White Sox	Steve Trout, lhp	Thornwood HS	South Holland, Ill.	6-4	195	L-L	18
9.	Expos	Bob James, rhp	Verdugo Hills HS	Sunland, Calif.	6-3	220	R-R	17
10.	Twins	*Jamie Allen, 3b/rhp	Davis HS	Yakima, Wash.	5-11	195	R-R	18
11.	Giants	Mark Kuecker, ss	Brenham HS	Brenham, Texas	5-10	152	R-R	18
12.	Rangers	Billy Simpson, of	Lakewood HS	Lakewood, Calif.	6-2	180	B-R	18
13.	Mets	Tom Thurberg, of/rhp	South Weymouth HS	South Weymouth, Mass.	6-1	185	R-R	18
14.	Indians	Tim Glass, c	South HS	Springfield, Ohio	6-2	215	R-R	18
15.	Cardinals	Leon Durham, 1b	Woodward HS	Cincinnati	6-1	200	L-L	18
16.	Yankees	Pat Tabler, of	McNicholas HS	Cincinnati	6-3	185	R-R	18
17.	Phillies	Jeff Kraus, ss	Colerain HS	Cincinnati	6-1	175	R-R	17
18.	Royals	Ben Grzybek, rhp	Hialeah HS	Hialeah, Fla.	6-5	200	L-R	18
19.	Dodgers	Mike Scioscia, c	Springfield HS	Morton, Pa.	6-2	200	L-R	17
20.	Orioles	Dallas Williams, of	Lincoln HS	Brooklyn, N.Y.	5-11	170	L-L	18
21.	Pirates	Jim Parke, rhp	Henry Ford II HS	Sterling Heights, Mich.	6-4	215	R-R	18
22.	Red Sox	Bruce Hurst, lhp	Dixie HS	St. George, Utah	6-4	185	L-L	18
23.	Reds	Mark King, rhp	Owensboro HS	Owensboro, Ky.	6-1	185	R-R	18
24.	Athletics	*Mike Sullivan, rhp	Garfield HS	Woodbridge, Va.	5-11	173	R-R	17

*Did not sign.

1976

CLUB-BY-CLUB SELECTIONS

ATLANTA BRAVES

January—Regular Phase (4)

1. **William Free, rhp, Tuskegee (Ala.)**
2. Carl Pankratz, rhp, Temple (Texas) JC
3. Larry Wright, lhp, DeKalb (Ga.) JC

January—Secondary Phase (10)

1. **Mike Macha, 3b, Rice**
2. Dave Stegman, of, Arizona
3. Bob Stoddard, rhp, Gavilan (Calif.) JC
4. Condredge Holloway, ss, Tennessee

June—Regular Phase (3)

1. **Ken Smith, 3b, Youngstown (Ohio) East HS**
2. **Dom Chiti, lhp, Raleigh-Egypt HS, Memphis**
3. **Dan Morogiello, lhp, Seton Hall**
4. **Gordon Guzenski, rhp, Benedictine**
5. **Bruce Benedict, c, Nebraska-Omaha**
6. **Jim Wessinger, ss, LeMoyne**
7. Glynn Tschirhart, ss, St. Mary's (Texas)
8. Anthony Jordan, rhp, Rolling Hills HS, Rancho Palos Verdes, Calif.
9. **Clayton Elliott, ss, Liberty**
10. **Jerry Keller, c/1b, Eastern Michigan**
11. **James Bagley, of, San Jacinto (Texas) JC**
12. Rick Peters, inf, Arizona State
13. **David Long, of, Loyola Marymount**
14. **Rick Matula, rhp, Sam Houston State**
15. David Duff, c, Menchville HS, Newport News, Va.
16. **William Tucker, lhp, Eastern Illinois**
17. **Jeffrey Culbreth, rhp, Sylvan HS, Atlanta**
18. Ricky Jones, rhp/ss, Towers HS, Decatur, Ga.
19. Eugene Wisniewski, ss, Holy Ghost Prep HS, Philadelphia
20. **Wyatt Tonkin, rhp, Washington**
21. **Isaac Seoane, c, Dade HS, Miami**
22. **Aaron Hudson, 3b, West Montgomery HS, Mount Gilead, N.C.**
23. **Bob Brasher, of, Louisiana Tech**
24. Robert McGraw, 1b, Huffman HS, Birmingham
25. **Eldgre Huddleston, of, Southwest Missouri State**
26. Richard Volz, ss, Antonian HS, San Antonio
27. Clayton Stotle, rhp, Highlands HS, San Antonio
28. Richard Montoni, of, Miami

June—Secondary Phase (1)

1. Gerald Price, 2b, Diablo Valley (Calif.) JC
2. Ron Roenicke, of/1b, Mount San Antonio (Calif.) JC
3. John Butcher, rhp, Yavapai (Ariz.) JC

BALTIMORE ORIOLES

January—Regular Phase (19)

1. Raphael Hampton, of, Detroit
2. **Mark Corey, of, Central Arizona JC**
3. Craig Robinson, c/1b, Chipola (Fla.) JC
4. **Howard Ashlock, lhp/1b, Cal Poly Pomona**
5. Michael Moore, rhp, Cleveland State (Tenn.) CC
6. **Michael Long, rhp, Central Arizona JC**
7. **Paul Burgess, rhp, Lancaster, Calif.**
8. **Patrico Espinosa, rhp, UCLA**

January—Secondary Phase (7)

1. **Wayne Krenchicki, ss, Miami**
2. Erik Hendricks, rhp, Chabot (Calif.) JC
3. William Yarbrough, inf, Manatee (Fla.) JC
4. Stephen Vaughan, of, Arizona
5. **Jim Skaalen, 1b/3b, San Diego State**
6. **Randy Johnson, 3b, San Diego State**
7. Paul Tasker, c/3b, Clearwater, Fla.

June—Regular Phase (20)

1. **Dallas Williams, of, Abraham Lincoln HS, Brooklyn, N.Y.**
2. Jerry Don Gleaton, lhp, Brownwood (Texas) HS
3. **Andrew Davis, 2b, Southeastern Louisiana**
4. **Michael Lindal, lhp, Libertyville (Ill.) HS**
5. **Kevin Jondle, rhp, St. John Bosco HS, Long Beach**
6. **Jim Smith, ss, Cal State Long Beach**
7. Ronald Adkins, ss, Grambling State
8. **Kevin Kennedy, c, San Diego State**
9. **Pedro Torrez, lhp, Dallas Baptist**
10. **Michael Ithier, 1b, Washington HS, Milwaukee**
11. **Robert Welch, rhp, Copiague HS, Lindenhurst, N.J.**
12. John Isley, 1b/of, Hoggard HS, Wilmington, N.C.
13. Darrell Guillory, rhp, LaGrange HS, Lake Charles, La.
14. **Steven Fedoris, rhp, Allderdice HS, Pittsburgh**
15. **Evon Martinson, c, Point Loma Nazarene**
16. **Craig Allegrezza, rhp, Massachusetts**
17. **Anthony Zentgraf, 3b, Virginia**
18. Mark Poehlman, of, Loyola HS, Baltimore
19. Don Carfino, ss, St. John Bosco HS, Bellflower, Calif.
20. Daniel Prior, rhp, Gulf Coast (Fla.) CC
21. **Edward Blankmeyer, 2b, Seton Hall**
22. Fred Benham, c, Abramson HS, New Orleans

June—Secondary Phase (16)

No selection

BOSTON RED SOX

January—Regular Phase (21)

1. Nate Puryear, rhp, Stillman (Ala.)
2. **Dennis Burtt, rhp, Santa Ana (Calif.) JC**
3. **Steven Schneck, rhp, Kalamazoo Valley (Mich.) CC**
4. Gary Hoyle, c, Broward (Fla.) CC
5. Roscoe Alburtis, 1b, Blinn (Texas) JC
6. Jeffrey Spahr, rhp, Gulf Coast (Fla.) CC
7. Terry Leach, rhp, Auburn (Selection voided)
8. Russell Cain, c, George Wallace (Ala.) CC

January—Secondary Phase (9)

1. **David Tyler, 3b, Vanderbilt**
2. Greg Jemison, of, Seton Hall
3. **John Tudor, lhp, Georgia Southern**
4. **Bruce Poole, lhp, South Alabama**

June—Regular Phase (22)

1. **Bruce Hurst, lhp, Dixie HS, St. George, Utah**
2. **Glenn Hoffman, ss, Savanna HS, Anaheim**
3. **Mark Twogood, of, Loara HS, Anaheim**
4. Larry Jones, rhp, Florida State
5. **Mike Smithson, rhp, Tennessee**
6. Ron Kovach, lhp, Grand Junction (Colo.) HS
7. **Wade Boggs, ss, Plant HS, Tampa**
8. **Ronald Harrington, c, William Carey (Miss.)**
9. **Gary Allenson, c, Arizona State**
10. **Danny Parks, rhp, Memphis State**
11. **David Denton, 2b, Nevada-Las Vegas**
12. **Reid Nichols, 2b, Ocala (Fla.) Forest HS**
13. **John Edwards, c, La Verne (Calif.)**
14. Larry Edwards, lhp, Bishop Walsh HS, Lavale, Md.
15. Dan Swanson, lhp, Aragon HS, San Mateo, Calif.
16. **Byron Ormsby, ss, Arkansas**
17. **Jack Sauer, rhp, Northwestern Business (Ohio) JC**
18. **Glenn Fisher, ss, Mansfield (Pa.)**
19. **John Kidd, 3b, SUNY Buffalo**
20. **Mike Ongarato, of, Cal Poly San Luis Obispo**
21. Frederick Opper, 1b, Mount St. Michaels HS, Mount Vernon, N.Y.
22. **Chico Walker, 2b, Tilden Tech HS, Chicago**
23. Peter Reilly, c, Trinity HS, Manchester, N.H.

24. **Jerome King, rhp, San Diego HS**
25. **Randy Lamprecht, c, Rice**
26. **John Faccinto, 3b, Bishop Gorman HS, Las Vegas**

June—Secondary Phase (22)

1. **Steve Miller, rhp, Lower Columbia (Wash.) JC**

CALIFORNIA ANGELS

January—Regular Phase (5)

1. **Steve Tebbetts, of, Florida State**
2. **Stephen Lettric, rhp, San Jose CC**
3. **Kenneth Gooch, ss, Yuba (Calif.) CC**
4. **Mark Brouhard, c, Los Angeles Pierce JC**
5. **Keith Comstock, lhp, Canada (Calif.) JC**
6. Howard Herl, rhp, Essex (Md.) CC
7. Dan Gausepohl, c/of, Long Beach CC
8. Thomas Crisler, rhp, South Georgia JC
9. Jim Christiansen, 3b/of, Fullerton (Calif.) JC
10. Michael Shipley, lhp, Barstow (Calif.) CC
11. **Don Jones, c, Barstow (Calif.) CC**
12. Marty Serrano, ss, San Jose CC
13. Ron Johnson, 1b, Fullerton (Calif.) JC
14. Charles Cassell, rhp, Barstow (Calif.) CC
15. Steven Balla, p, Gavilan (Calif.) JC
16. Lawrence Cole, p, Butte (Calif.) JC

January—Secondary Phase (15)

1. **Greg Johnson, rhp, Santa Ana (Calif.) JC**
2. Mike Chris, 1b, Los Angeles Pierce JC
3. Steve King, c, South Carolina
4. Ernie Camacho, rhp, Hartnell (Calif.) CC
5. Greg Stahl, ss, Los Angeles Harbor JC

June—Regular Phase (6)

1. **Ken Landreaux, of, Arizona State**
2. **Bob Ferris, rhp, Maryland**
3. **Craig Hendrickson, ss, Woodson HS, Annandale, Va.**
4. **Bill Ewing, of, Wyoming**
5. Mickey Palmer, of/lhp, West Covina (Calif.) HS
6. **Steve Whitehead, ss, UC Irvine**
7. **Chuck Porter, rhp, Clemson**
8. **Bob Slater, 2b, Cal State Northridge**
9. Joseph Powell, 1b, Overlea HS, Baltimore
10. **David Moore, 2b, Sahuaro HS, Tucson**
11. Rick Schwenn, rhp, Cal Poly Pomona
12. **Mike Bishop, 3b, Righetti HS, Santa Maria, Calif.**
13. Joe Carroll, rhp, Tulsa
14. Jeffrey Gilbert, of, Cal State Northridge
15. **Don Lyons, 1b, Gonzaga**
16. **William Douglas, c, Sylmar (Calif.) HS**
17. **Ken Schrom, rhp, Idaho**
18. Larry Owen, c, Bowling Green State
19. Peter Chapin, rhp, Troy HS, Fullerton, Calif.
20. **Greg Moffitt, 3b, Utah**
21. Jon Hansen, of, Santa Barbara (Calif.) HS
22. Stan Edmonds, of, Needles (Calif.) HS
23. **Jeffrey Wolf, rhp, Dixie (Utah) JC**
24. William Sylvester, rhp, Rancho Alamitos HS, Garden Grove, Calif.
25. Robert Luitwieler, lhp, La Habra (Calif.) HS
26. **David DaCosta, 3b, Santana-Santee HS, San Diego**
27. Tommy Montgomery, lhp, Lee HS, Thomaston, Ga.
28. Jeff Calhoun, lhp, Parklane Academy HS, McComb, Miss.
29. **John Harris, 1b, Lubbock Christian**
30. Keith Vranesh, 3b, Arlington HS, Riverside, Calif.
31. Bruce Ferguson, rhp, Arizona
32. Dave Garcia, ss, El Cajon (Calif.) HS
33. Monte Pries, rhp, Corona Del Mar HS, Newport Beach, Calif.
34. Bruce Tonascia, of/c, Southern California

June—Secondary Phase (10)

1. **John Racanelli, rhp, Southern California**
2. **Danny Boone, lhp, Cal State Fullerton**
3. William Eve, 1b, Miami-Dade North CC
4. Michael Shipley, lhp, Barstow (Calif.) CC
5. **Thomas Crisler, rhp, South Georgia JC**
6. Joseph Ward, of, Manatee (Fla.) JC
7. Charles Cassell, rhp, Barstow (Calif.) CC

CHICAGO CUBS

January—Regular Phase (8)

1. **John Faley, rhp, Camden County (N.J.) CC**
2. **Bryan Johnson, c, Bellevue (Wash.) CC**
3. **Ron Davis, rhp, Blinn (Texas) JC**
4. **Ray Dimick, rhp, Los Angeles Pierce JC**

January—Secondary Phase (24)

1. **Peter Brown, lhp, Glens Falls, N.Y.**
2. Steven Winfield, rhp, Panola (Texas) JC

June—Regular Phase (7)

1. **Herman Segelke, rhp, El Camino HS, South San Francisco**
2. **Donald Lowe, rhp, Sarasota (Fla.) HS**
3. **Kurt Seibert, ss, Clemson**
4. **Keith Drumright, 2b, Oklahoma**
5. **Greg Keatley, c, South Carolina**
6. **Daniel England, rhp, High Point**
7. Odie Davis, ss, Prairie View A&M
8. **Robert Clark, lhp, Pleasant Hill HS, Concord, Calif.**
9. Frank D'Antico, rhp, Upsala (N.J.)
10. **Duane Gustavson, c, Wisconsin**
11. Donald Fusari, lhp, Eastern Connecticut State
12. **Gordon Hodgson, 3b, Terra Linda HS, San Rafael, Calif.**
13. **Laverne Jark, 2b, Northern State (S.D.)**
14. **Steve Davis, ss, Stanford**
15. **Edwin Mohr, of, Rib Lake (Wis.) HS**
16. James Funderberk, lhp, Bell HS, Huntington Park, Calif.
17. Edward Szymanski, lhp, Salesianum HS, Wilmington, Del.
18. **Denzel Palmer, ss, Cal State Los Angeles**
19. **Joseph Thompson, 1b, Knock HS, Renfrew, Pa.**
20. **Richard Herendeen, lhp, Chardon (Ohio) HS**
21. **Daniel Brown, lhp, New Haven (Ind.) HS**
22. **Douglas McCracken, of, Sunset HS, Portland, Ore.**
23. **Jared Martin, of, St. Mary's**
24. Felix Oroz, lhp, Manogue HS, Reno, Nev.
25. Brian Snitker, c, New Orleans
26. **Tony Messer, 3b, Virginia HS, Bristol, Va.**
27. **Melvin Godard, 1b, Williamston (N.C.) HS**
28. **Richard McClure, rhp, Los Medanos (Calif.) JC**
29. **Raymond Powell, lhp, Etowah HS, Attalla, Ala.**
30. **Bert Newman, 2b, Southern Illinois**

June—Secondary Phase (21)

1. **Karl Pagel, 1b, Texas**
2. **John Reiter, rhp, St. Louis CC-Meramec**
3. Mark Post, lhp, Keystone (Pa.) JC
4. Ken Lelek, rhp, Monroe (N.Y.) CC
5. Gary Skow, of, Yavapai (Ariz.) JC
6. **William Evers, c, Eckerd (Fla.)**

CHICAGO WHITE SOX

January—Regular Phase (7)

1. Jesse Baez, c, Cerritos (Calif.) JC
2. John Reiter, rhp, St. Louis CC-Meramec
3. Mike Estes, rhp, Manatee (Fla.) JC
4. Robert Kocol, of, Brevard (Fla.) CC
5. Andy McGaffigan, rhp, Palm Beach (Fla.) JC
6. **Fred Howard, rhp, Miami-Dade South CC**

January—Secondary Phase (3)

1. **Leo Sutherland, of, Golden West (Calif.) JC**
2. **Rich Wortham, lhp, Texas**
3. Dennis Sandoval, rhp, Fullerton (Calif.) CC
4. Mike Tulacz, lhp, Miami-Dade North CC
5. Michael Otto, rhp, Sacramento CC
6. **Harry Chappas, ss, Miami-Dade North CC**
7. Mark Esser, lhp, Miami-Dade North CC
8. John Racanelli, rhp, Southern California
9. Robert Healey, rhp, St. Louis CC-Meramec
10. Karl Schroeder, lhp, Oklahoma

June—Regular Phase (8)

1. **Steve Trout, lhp, Thornwood HS, South Holland, Ill.**
2. **Mike Colbern, c, Arizona State**
3. **A.J. Hill, ss, Hollywood HS, Los Angeles**
4. James Stehle, lhp, Wilkes (Pa.)
5. Jerry Stovall, rhp, Hoover HS, Fresno
6. **Clay Hicks, rhp, Edmond (Okla.) HS**
7. Willie McGee, of, Harry Ells HS, Richmond, Calif.
8. **Lorenzo Gray, ss, Lynwood (Calif.) HS**
9. **Ken Hamman, ss, Detroit**
10. **Jim Gabella, 2b, Deerfield Beach (Fla.) HS**
11. **Richard Thoren, lhp, Northern Colorado**
12. Jeff Wick, lhp, Verdugo Hills HS, Tujunga, Calif.
13. Pat Keedy, 1b, Gardendale HS, Birmingham
14. Stephen Collins, rhp, CC of San Francisco
15. **Paul Soth, rhp, Marini HS, Westminster, Calif.**
16. **John Martin, rhp, Big Bend (Ore.) CC**
17. Mark Blumenschein, lhp, Tecsoma HS, New Carlisle, Ohio
18. **William Parmenter, ss, San Marin HS, Novato, Calif.**
19. **Keith Rokosz, of, Troy HS, Fullerton, Calif.**
20. **Andy Pasillas, c, Cal State Fullerton**
21. Ed Olwine, lhp, Greenville (Ohio) HS
22. John Thetford, rhp, Bartlett HS, Memphis
23. Glen Watson, of, Maine West HS, Des Plaines, Ill.
24. Paul Stefan, rhp, Louisiana State
25. **David Greenway, 2b, Sterling HS, Magnolia, N.J.**
26. Eugene Zurowski, of, Martin (Tenn.) JC

June—Secondary Phase (14)

1. Hubie Brooks, ss, Mesa (Ariz.) CC
2. Greg Stahl, ss, Los Angeles Harbor JC
3. Robert Kocol, of, Brevard (Fla.) CC

CINCINNATI REDS

January—Regular Phase (24)

1. Roderick Patterson, rhp, Santa Monica (Calif.) JC
2. Dwayne Mikemann, rhp, Rose State (Okla.) JC
3. **Thomas McClendon, ss, George Wallace (Ala.) CC**
4. Gary Hill, lhp, Indian Hills (Iowa) CC
5. **Glenn Bonnell, ss, Milford (Ohio) HS**
6. **Alfred Nichols, of, Bakersfield (Calif.) JC**
7. David Froelich, rhp, Indian Hills (Iowa) CC
8. Jerry Veale, lhp, Jefferson State (Ala.) JC

January—Secondary Phase (22)

1. **Duane Walker, lhp/of, San Jacinto (Texas) JC**
2. **Clarence Syers, rhp, JC of the Canyons (Calif.)**

June—Regular Phase (23)

1. **Mark King, rhp, Owensboro (Ky.) Senior HS**
2. **Paul Householder, of, North Haven (Conn.) HS**
3. **Gregory Meyer, lhp, Kennedy HS, Ballwin, Mo.**
4. Mark Bingham, ss/1b, Hastings on the Hudson HS, Hastings, N.Y.
5. **Mark Breitenbach, rhp, Shaler HS, Glenshaw, Pa.**
6. Steve Renfroe, of, Berkmar HS, Liliburn, Ga.
7. **Bill Dawley, rhp, Griswold HS, Lisbon, Conn.**
8. **Michael Kopsky, 3b, Christian Brothers HS, St. Louis**
9. Peter Rowe, c, Oregon State
10. **Ronnie Stryker, rhp, Tate HS, Pensacola, Fla.**
11. **Alfred Welch, of, Seminole (Fla.) HS**
12. Derek Tatsuno, lhp, Aiea (Hawaii) HS
13. **Robert Mayer, lhp, Florida State**
14. **Thomas Norko, c, Shelton (Conn.) HS**
15. **Paul Herring, of, Mary Hardin-Baylor (Texas)**
16. Gary Pickert, lhp, Emporia State (Kan.)
17. **Thomas Dimino, ss, Monroe (N.Y.) CC**
18. **Randy Brinkley, lhp, Blanchester (Ohio) HS**
19. Michael Barrett, rhp, Forest Park HS, Beaumont, Texas
20. **Kevin Jensen, of, Southern Utah State**
21. **Eddie Milner, of, Central State (Ohio)**
22. Paul Homrig, of, San Pedro (Calif.) HS
23. **Wiley Harris, of/3b, Wingate (N.C.) JC**
24. **John Gosse, rhp, Lower Columbia (Wash.) JC**
25. **Thomas Sohns, ss, Scranton (Pa.)**
26. Abner Johnson, rhp, Creighton
27. James Jones, of, Milby HS, Houston
28. **Donald Carr, of, Texas Wesleyan**
29. **Robert Harold, rhp, Illinois**
30. Douglas Smith, rhp, Southwestern Oklahoma State
31. **Jay Howell, rhp, Colorado**
32. Dominic Antonini, c, Glassboro State (N.J.)
33. Tim Laudner, c, Park Center HS, Minneapolis
34. **David Goodman, c, Coral Park HS, Miami**
35. Scotti Madison, ss, Tate HS, Pensacola, Fla.
36. Pat Sheridan, of, Wayne (Mich.) Memorial HS
37. Greg Johnson, inf, Taft HS, Hamilton, Ohio
38. James Snyder, 1b, Stevenson HS, Livonia, Mich.

June—Secondary Phase (3)

1. **Bruce Berenyi, rhp, Northeast Missouri State**
2. **Rickey Lear, rhp, Valencia (Fla.) CC**
3. Jeff Hardy, ss, Florida State
4. Dwayne Mikemann, rhp, Rose State (Okla.) JC

CLEVELAND INDIANS

January—Regular Phase (13)

1. **Julian Rodriguez, rhp, Palm Beach (Fla.) JC**
2. Jaime Lopez, 1b, Yavapai (Ariz.) JC
3. Reginald Pearman, 1b, Davidsonville, Md.
4. Cleo DeWitt, c/of, South Florida JC
5. Steven Turco, ss, Broward (Fla.) CC
6. Kenneth Jarahek, of, Pensacola (Fla.) JC
7. Victor Herold, 1b, Broward (Fla.) CC
8. Jeffrey Muehling, lhp, Lincoln Land (Ill.) JC
9. Douglas Hogan, rhp, Indian Hills (Iowa) CC
10. Jerry Valentine, 3b, Westark (Ark.) CC
11. James Johnson, inf, Monroe (N.Y.) CC

January—Secondary Phase (17)

1. **Garry Hancock, of, South Carolina**
2. **George Mahan, rhp, Michigan State**
3. Thomas Egan, 2b, Burien, Wash.
4. **Dan Massari, 1b, Oklahoma**
5. William Evers, c, Eckerd (Fla.)

June—Regular Phase (14)

1. **Tim Glass, c, Springfield (Ohio) South HS**
2. **Sam Spence, rhp, Brandon HS, Mango, Fla.**
3. **Craig Adams, of, Boone HS, Orlando, Fla.**
4. Robert Scott, of, Gunn HS, Palo Alto, Calif.
5. **David Fowlkes, c, Decatur (Ga.) HS**
6. Bill Scherrer, lhp, Bishop O'Hara HS, Tonawanda, N.Y.
7. Gary Hardie, ss, Georgia Military Academy, Milledgeville, Ga.
8. Steven Nielsen, rhp, Penn State
9. **John Teising, lhp, St. Bernard Parish (La.) CC**
10. Dennis Doss, rhp, American Christian (Okla.)
11. **William Mitchell, lhp, East Texas Baptist**
12. Joe Beckwith, rhp, Auburn
13. **Kevin Jeansenne, of, Southwestern Louisiana**
14. **John Buszka, of, SUNY Buffalo**
15. **Duane Wilson, 1b, Georgia**
16. **Terry Tyson, ss, Toledo**
17. Matthew Schaper, ss/of, Texas City (Texas) HS
18. **Ron Hassey, c, Arizona**
19. **Troy Wilder, lhp, Oak Harbor (Wash.) HS**
20. Rob Johnson, ss, Binger (Okla.) HS
21. **Kenneth Preseren, ss, Baldwin-Wallace (Ohio)**
22. Randy Puckett, ss, Dinuba (Calif.) HS
23. Todd Heimer, lhp, Seton Hall
24. Jim Haggerty, lhp, Grand Junction (Colo.) HS
25. Jack Lopez, ss, Sandalwood HS, Jacksonville, Fla.
26. **Frank Toups, inf, Louisiana State**
27. Joseph Keohane, rhp, Burlington (Mass.) HS
28. Gary Hinson, ss, Hillsborough (Fla.) JC
29. Morgan Lester, lhp, Sterling HS, Houston
30. **Michael Rowe, 1b, Palm Beach (Fla.) JC**
31. Charles Gwynn, of, Poly HS, Long Beach
32. Thomas Cook, lhp, Hamilton-Wenham HS, Hamilton, Mass.
33. Michael Lynes, lhp, Rolling Hills HS, Rancho Palos Verdes, Calif.

34. Timothy Newtson, c, Pendleton (Ore.) HS
35. **Reggie Smith, rhp/3b, Judson (Ill.)**

June—Secondary Phase (8)

1. **Ray Gault, rhp, Manatee (Fla.) JC**
2. **Nate Puryear, rhp, Stillman (Ala.)**
3. Victor Jacobsen, 3b, Big Bend (Wash.) CC
4. Bill Springman, 2b, Cerritos (Calif.) JC
5. **Paul Tasker, c/3b, Edison (Fla.) CC**
6. Dave Hostetler, 1b, Citrus (Calif.) JC

DETROIT TIGERS

January—Regular Phase (1)

1. **Steve Kemp, of, Southern California**
2. Gerald Price, 2b, Diablo Valley (Calif.) JC
3. Mike Yackee, rhp, Citrus (Calif.) JC
4. Larry Randel, ss, Fullerton (Calif.) JC
5. Brian McCaslin, rhp, Yavapai (Ariz.) JC
6. **Garry Grafton, rhp, Slippery Rock (Pa.)**
7. **Albert Wilson, of, Concordia (Mich.)**

January—Secondary Phase (23)

1. Ray Gault, rhp, Manatee (Fla.) JC
2. Mike Walters, rhp, Chaffey (Calif.) JC
3. Ron Roenicke, of/1b, Mount San Antonio (Calif.) JC
4. Ben Hines, ss, Cypress (Calif.) JC

June—Regular Phase (2)

1. **Pat Underwood, lhp, Kokomo (Ind.) HS**
2. **Alan Trammell, ss, Kearny HS, San Diego**
3. **Scott Johnson, c, Bonita HS, La Verne, Calif.**
4. **Dan Petry, rhp, El Dorado HS, Placentia, Calif.**
5. **Jack Morris, rhp, Brigham Young**
6. **Lawrence Douglas, ss, Salem (N.H.) HS**
7. Ozzie Smith, ss, Cal Poly San Luis Obispo
8. **Glenn Gulliver, ss, Eastern Michigan**
9. Charles Farmer, c, Hernando County HS, Brooksville, Fla.
10. **Michael Burns, rhp, Alma (Mich.)**
11. **Robert Castleberry, of, Norte Del Rio HS, Sacramento**
12. **Gary Wiencek, c, Southern California**
13. **John Ward, lhp, Westmont (Calif.)**
14. Rod Booker, ss, Pasadena (Calif.) HS
15. **John Northrup, of, Central Michigan**
16. **Roger Weaver, rhp, SUNY Oneonta**
17. **Herbert Krul, c, Toledo**
18. **John Sauer, rhp, St. John Vienney Seminary HS, Falls Church, Va.**
19. **Gordon Blakely, 3b, Chapman (Calif.)**
20. **Larry Corr, rhp, Belmont**
21. Robert Jenkins, of, Fairfax HS, Los Angeles
22. Ken Castles, lhp, Santa Theresa (Calif.) HS
23. **Kip Young, rhp, Bowling Green State**
24. **Ken Bolek, of, Arizona**
25. **Scott Bradley, lhp, Lincoln Park (Mich.) HS**
26. Thomas Schultz, of, Union HS, Grand Rapids, Mich.
27. **Gabriel Hernandez, lhp, Flushing HS, Bayside, N.Y.**
28. Brian Francisco, 2b, UC Riverside
29. Tracy Harris, rhp, Washington State

June—Secondary Phase (2)

1. **Dave Stegman, of, Arizona**
2. **Stephen Vaughan, of, Los Angeles Valley JC**
3. **Larry Randel, ss, Fullerton (Calif.) JC**

HOUSTON ASTROS

January—Regular Phase (2)

1. **Gary Wilson, rhp, Southern Arkansas**
2. Thomas Offerman, lhp, Nassau (N.Y.) CC
3. Mark Post, lhp, Keystone (Pa.) JC

January—Secondary Phase (18)

1. Rodney Feight, rhp, Indian River (Fla.) CC
2. Randy Wallace, 3b/of, Tennessee

June—Regular Phase (1)

1. **Floyd Bannister, lhp, Arizona State**
2. **Phil Klimas, 3b, St. Xavier (Ill.)**
3. **Reggie Baldwin, c, Grambling State**
4. **Jim Pankovits, 3b, South Carolina**
5. Joe Isaacs, rhp, Asher HS, Ada, Okla.
6. **Douglas Jackson, rhp, Madison HS, Houston**
7. **Tom Wiedenbauer, of, Sahuaro HS, Tucson**
8. **Dave Smith, rhp, San Diego State**
9. **George Ploucher, lhp, Middle Tennessee State**
10. **Jerry Williford, c, Houston**
11. **Gary Rajsich, 1b/of, Arizona State**
12. Ronnie Estes, rhp, Boise State
13. **Charles Gardner, ss, John Brown (Ark.)**
14. **Randolph Lamb, ss, Ouachita Baptist (Ark.)**
15. Ronald Lee, ss, Sharpstown HS, Houston
16. Jimmy Johnson, of, Sam Rayburn HS, Pasadena, Texas
17. **Bert Roberge, rhp, Maine**
18. Steven Lerner, lhp, Miami-Dade New World Center CC
19. Mike Villegas, rhp, East HS, Phoenix
20. **Jeff Ellison, of, San Diego State**
21. **Randy Rouse, c, John Brown (Ark.)**
22. **Dennis Miscik, lhp, Indiana (Pa.)**
23. **Thomas McCann, 1b, Washington Township HS, Turnersville, N.J.**
24. Douglas Welenc, rhp, Greenfield (Mass.) HS
25. Steven Mueller, c, Hondo (Texas) HS

June—Secondary Phase (7)

1. Robert Healey, rhp, St. Louis CC-Meramec
2. Ron Musselman, rhp, Clemson

KANSAS CITY ROYALS

January—Regular Phase (17)

1. **Stephen Beene, c, Central Arkansas**
2. Matt Mullins, ss/rhp, Los Angeles Harbor JC
3. Charles Maynard, rhp, JC of San Mateo (Calif.)

January—Secondary Phase (5)

1. Hubie Brooks, ss, Mesa (Ariz.) CC
2. Ron Wrobel, lhp, Yavapai (Ariz.) JC
3. **Bill Paschall, rhp, North Carolina**
4. **Ron Kainer, rhp, Houston**
5. Alphonso Eiland, ss, Los Angeles Harbor JC
6. George Robins, of/p, Santa Monica (Calif.) JC

June—Regular Phase (18)

1. **Ben Grzybek, rhp, Hialeah (Fla.) HS**
2. Tim Brandenburg, lhp, Elizabethtown (Ky.) HS
3. **Rich Dubee, rhp, Bridgewater-Raynham HS, Bridgewater, Mass.**
4. **Thomas Close, c, Canton HS, Plymouth, Mich.**
5. **Brad Simmons, lhp, Glendale HS, Springfield, Mo.**
6. **Jim Gaudet, c, Tulane**
7. **Darrell Vosejpka, 3b, Montgomery HS, Lonsdale, Minn.**
8. **Tim Riley, 3b, Nevada-Reno**
9. **Timmy Gowen, lhp, Niles (Mich.) HS**
10. **Philip Pulido, rhp, Tampa Catholic HS**
11. **Juan Rodriguez, of, Paterson (N.J.) HS**
12. **John Krattli, 3b, Kansas**
13. Theodore French, of, Waterloo (N.Y.) HS
14. **Raymond Prince, rhp, Altus (Okla.) HS**
15. **Ken Phelps, of, Arizona State**
16. **Paul Stevens, 2b, Lewis (Ill.)**
17. **Robert Lizarraga, rhp, UCLA**
18. **Edward Cowan, rhp, UCLA**
19. Clyde Simmons, ss, Western HS, Detroit
20. **Victor Mendez, ss, Yonkers (N.Y.) HS**
21. Galen Cisco, 3b, St. Mary's HS, St. Mary, Ohio
22. Gary Guisness, 3b/c, Corona Del Mar (Calif.) HS

June—Secondary Phase (4)

1. **Frank McCann, ss, Delaware**
2. **William Yarbrough, inf, Manatee (Fla.) JC**
3. **Marty Serrano, ss, San Jose CC**
4. Javier Fierro, 3b, Cal State Los Angeles

LOS ANGELES DODGERS

January—Regular Phase (20)

1. Michael Wetklow, of, Sacramento CC
2. **Dave Patterson, rhp, Cerritos (Calif.) JC**
3. **Paul Bain, rhp, El Camino (Calif.) JC**
4. Mookie Wilson, of, Spartanburg Methodist (S.C.) JC
5. Timothy DeWald, rhp, Cypress (Calif.) JC
6. Robert Weis, rhp, Sacramento CC
7. Mark Garber, rhp, Antelope Valley (Calif.) JC
8. Richard Barnhart, rhp, Green River (Wash.) CC
9. Rickey Lear, rhp, Valencia (Fla.) CC
10. Robert Benda, ss/2b, Palm Beach (Fla.) JC
11. Charles Young, rhp/3b, Los Angeles Pierce JC

January—Secondary Phase (12)

1. **Jack Lawson, rhp, Phoenix JC**
2. **Charles Dorgan, lhp, Green River (Wash.) CC**
3. Larry Buckle, rhp, Long Beach CC

June—Regular Phase (19)

1. **Mike Scioscia, c, Springfield HS, Morton, Pa.**
2. **Don Ruzek, ss, Lakewood (Calif.) HS**
3. **Max Venable, of, Cordova HS, Rancho Cordova, Calif.**
4. **Marty Kunkler, lhp, Oklahoma**
5. **Ted Power, rhp, Kansas State**
6. **Mike Howard, of/3b, Sacramento HS**
7. **Kelly Snider, 1b, Oklahoma**
8. **Robert Kownacki, ss, Fairfield**
9. **Charles Phillips, lhp, Southern California**
10. **Calvin Swoope, c, Norfolk (Va.) Catholic HS**
11. **William Martin, rhp, William Carey (Miss.)**
12. **Jimmy Giles, of, Alcorn State**
13. **Jim Peterson, rhp, Arizona State**
14. Doug Elliott, 2b, Fullerton (Calif.) HS
15. **Keith Macwhorter, rhp, Bryant (R.I.)**
16. **Jack Perconte, 2b, Murray State**
17. **Miguel Rodriguez, rhp, Adlai Stephenson HS, Bronx, N.Y.**
18. **Timothy Jones, c/of, Wooster (Ohio) HS**
19. **Eric Schmidt, lhp, Mission Viejo (Calif.) HS**
20. **Dan Henry, 3b, Loyola Marymount**
21. **Jeffrey Albert, rhp, C.W. Post (N.Y.)**
22. **Robert Amico, 1b/of, SUNY Buffalo**
23. Richard Martini, of, UC Davis
24. **Mickey Lashley, rhp, Oklahoma**
25. Jose Martinez, ss, South San Francisco HS
26. **George Kaage, 1b, Kankakee (Ill.) CC**
27. **Mark Kryka, rhp, Antigo (Wis.) HS**
28. Steven Silagi, rhp, El Rancho HS, Pico Rivera, Calif.
29. Mickey Martin, c, U.S. Grant HS, Oklahoma City
30. **Douglas Foster, of, Compton (Calif.) HS**
31. John Holland, rhp, South Florence (S.C.) HS
32. Stephen Nelson, rhp, Wilson HS, Tacoma, Wash.
33. Jeff Hunter, 3b, Millard HS, Omaha
34. Mark Wychopen, c, South Houston HS
35. Scott Fletcher, ss, Wadsworth (Ohio) HS
36. Bruce Scheidegger, rhp, Chadwick (Ill.) HS
37. **Donald Brodell, of, Arkansas-Little Rock**
38. James Riedel, rhp, SUNY Buffalo
39. Gerald Snow, rhp, Madras (Ore.) HS

June—Secondary Phase (11)

1. Joe Ferri, of, Pasadena (Calif.) CC
2. Mike Walters, rhp, Chaffey (Calif.) JC

MILWAUKEE BREWERS

January—Regular Phase (3)

1. **David Globig, of, Minnesota**
2. Victor Jacobsen, 3b, Big Bend (Wash.) CC
3. William LaRosa, rhp, Cuyahoga (Ohio) CC

January—Secondary Phase (19)

1. **Jason Passmore, of, Orlando, Fla.**
2. **Jon Dempsey, rhp, Greensboro, N.C.**

June—Regular Phase (4)

1. Bill Bordley, lhp, Bishop Montgomery HS, Rolling Hills, Calif.
2. **Melvin Manning, ss, Hopewell (Va.) HS**
3. Ken Gardner, rhp, Monterey HS, Lubbock, Texas
4. **Terry Shoebridge, c, Lyndhurst (N.J.) HS**
5. **John Roesch, lhp, El Capitan HS, El Cajon, Calif.**
6. **Andrew Pascarella, 2b, Wisconsin**
7. **Ronald Jacobs, c, Texas**
8. **Lary Sorensen, rhp, Michigan**
9. **George Frazier, rhp, Oklahoma**
10. Steven Guengerich, of, Homestead HS, Cupertino, Calif.
11. **Larry Montgomery, rhp, Sharpstown HS, Houston**
12. **Garry Pyka, 2b, Texas**
13. **Gary Holle, 1b, Siena**
14. **James Quinn, rhp, New Caney HS, Porter, Texas**
15. **Jeffrey Harryman, lhp, North HS, Riverside, Calif.**
16. **Richard Thurman, rhp, Springfield (Mich.) HS**
17. Tim Peerenboom, 1b, Kimberly HS, Combined Locks, Wis.
18. **Eric Restin, ss, St. John's**
19. **Gary Donovan, ss, Portland State**
20. **Chester Nelson, c, Nicholls HS, New Orleans**
21. George Hill, c, Virginia Tech
22. **Garry Fritch, rhp, Wisconsin-Superior**
23. William Henley, of, Arcadia HS, Temple City, Calif.

June—Secondary Phase (6)

1. Darrell Brown, ss, Cal State Los Angeles
2. **Thomas Offerman, lhp, Nassau (N.Y.) CC**

MINNESOTA TWINS

January—Regular Phase (9)

1. **Bob Veselic, rhp, Mount San Antonio (Calif.) JC**
2. Jim Leicht, rhp, Fullerton (Calif.) JC
3. **John Breaux, rhp, Mount San Antonio (Calif.) JC**
4. **John Altman, rhp, Linn-Benton (Ore.) CC**
5. **Eugene Montgomery, of/p, JC of San Mateo (Calif.)**
6. Joe Charboneau, of, West Valley (Calif.) JC
7. **Kevin Stanfield, lhp, San Bernardino Valley (Calif.) JC**
8. Lloyd Ard, rhp, Chipola (Fla.) JC

January—Secondary Phase (1)

1. **Pete Redfern, rhp, Southern California**
2. **Steve Benson, ss, Arizona Western JC**
3. Mike Arlotta, lhp, Miami-Dade North CC
4. Gary Bowers, rhp, Fullerton (Calif.) JC
5. Robert Dinges, of/1b, Foothill (Calif.) JC
6. Robert Knezerich, rhp, Council Bluffs, Iowa

June—Regular Phase (10)

1. Jamie Allen, 3b/rhp, Davis HS, Yakima, Wash.
2. **Terry Felton, rhp, Baker (La.) HS**
3. **John Castino, 3b, Rollins (Fla.)**
4. **Warren Allen, ss, Richmond County HS, Hamlet, N.C.**
5. Tony Cameron, lhp, Pepperdine
6. **Bill Harris, lhp, Santa Clara**
7. **Paul Cantanese, of, Cupertino HS, Sunnyvale, Calif.**
8. **Michael Gustave, of, Harford (Md.) CC**
9. Greg Sporrer, ss, Troy-Fullerton HS, Yorba Linda, Calif.
10. John Violette, c, St. Bernard HS, Playa Del Rey, Calif.
11. **Steve Christian, ss, Piedmont Hills HS, San Jose**
12. Ronald Moore, lhp, Troy HS, Yorba Linda, Calif.
13. Glenn Wendt, ss, Temple (Texas) JC
14. Randy Ingle, ss/2b, East Rutherford HS, Forest City, N.C.
15. **Steven Hypes, rhp, Milligan (Tenn.)**
16. **Mark Funderburk, of, Louisburg (N.C.) JC**
17. **Mark Tomasiak, rhp, Lafayette HS, Chesterfield, Mo.**
18. Joseph Sekora, rhp, Newton Falls (Ohio) HS
19. **John Jones, lhp, Baldwin HS, Milledgeville, Ga.**
20. Tim Byelland, ss, Millikan HS, Long Beach
21. **Bruce MacPherson, rhp, Cal Poly Pomona**
22. **Tom McWillams, lhp, Morningside (Iowa)**
23. **Wallace McMakin, rhp, Louisiana State**
24. Preston Banks, 3b, Manual Arts HS, Los Angeles
25. **Donald Tryon, ss, Orange Coast (Calif.) JC**
26. Jim Brooks, ss, El Rancho HS, Pico Rivera, Calif.

27. **Gary Dobbs, lhp, Warren HS, Downey, Calif.**
28. **Daniel Spain, of, Orange Coast (Calif.) JC**
29. **Eric Barstad, lhp, Salinas (Calif.) HS**
30. **Bret Williams, rhp, Yucaipa (Calif.) HS**
31. Michael Davis, ss, Rio Hondo (Calif.) JC
32. Joe Scherger, of, Billings (Mont.) HS

June—Secondary Phase (24)

1. **Greg Vogel, inf, Penn State**
2. David Froelich, rhp, Indian Hills (Iowa) CC

MONTREAL EXPOS

January—Regular Phase (10)

1. Steve Miller, rhp, Lower Columbia (Wash.) JC
2. Scott Winston, lhp, Chipola (Fla.) JC
3. **Doug Simunic, c, St. Clair County (Mich.) CC**
4. Michael Mann, p, St. Clair County (Mich.) CC
5. Gary Weiss, 2b, Blinn (Texas) JC
6. Matthew Gaglione, of, Chipola (Fla.) JC
7. Ronnie Mears, 2b/ss, Contra Costa (Calif.) JC
8. Robert Volk, c, Cerritos (Calif.) JC
9. John Thiele, c, Pasadena (Calif.) CC
10. **Robert Watkins, rhp, Grossmont (Calif.) JC**
11. Kevin Minter, rhp, Moorpark (Calif.) JC

January—Secondary Phase (4)

1. **LaMart Harris, of, Ranger (Texas) JC**
2. **Stephen Walsh, lhp, Saint Louis**
3. **Kurt Boesch, rhp, Clackamas (Ore.) CC**
4. **Daniel Newell, rhp, Ohio Dominican**

June—Regular Phase (9)

1. **Bob James, rhp, Verdugo Hills HS, Sunland, Calif.**
2. **Dennis Sherow, rhp, Cal Poly Pomona**
3. **Dan Schatzeder, lhp/of, Denver**
4. **Bob Pate, of, Arizona State**
5. **Carlton Roberts, lhp, Cabrillo HS, Lompoc, Calif.**
6. Anthony Zahradnick, lhp, Arkport (N.Y.) HS
7. **Johnnie Walker, ss, Sacramento HS**
8. **John Scoras, c, Montclair State (N.J.)**
9. **Jack O'Connor, lhp, Yucca Valley (Calif.) HS**
10. **Michael Trembla, 3b, Connellsville HS, Champion, Pa.**
11. **Michael Brooks, rhp, Jackson State**
12. Nick Capra, 2b, Lincoln HS, Denver, Colo.
13. Ed Irvine, of, Jordan HS, Long Beach, Calif.
14. **Michael Sullivan, rhp, Elder HS, Cincinnati**
15. **Clay Westlake, c/1b, Arizona State**
16. John Evans, 1b, St. Bernard HS, Los Angeles
17. Ray Bozich, of, St. Petersburg (Fla.) JC
18. James Gibson, lhp, Texas A&M
19. Tom Chamberlain, rhp, Oregon State
20. Andrew Walker, c, East St. Louis HS
21. **David Palmer, rhp, Glens Falls (N.Y.) HS**

June—Secondary Phase (17)

1. **Don Hanna, rhp, Arizona State**
2. Jim Leicht, rhp, Fullerton (Calif.) JC

NEW YORK METS

January—Regular Phase (14)

1. Dean Moranda, lhp, Fresno CC
2. Mickey Hatcher, of, Mesa (Ariz.) CC
3. **Jody Davis, 1b/c, Middle Georgia JC**
4. Theron Baker, c/3b, DeKalb (Ga.) JC
5. Kendall Driggers, rhp, Florida CC
6. Alvin Moore, of, South Georgia JC
7. Greg Harris, rhp, Long Beach CC
8. **Fred Westfall, rhp, San Diego Mesa JC**
9. **Theodore O'Neil, rhp, Rollins (Fla.)**
10. **Gary Corrado, lhp, Luzerne County (Pa.) CC**

January—Secondary Phase (16)

1. **Steven Kesses, of, Duke**
2. Greg Fisher, inf, Diablo Valley (Calif.) JC
3. Michael Coppess, rhp, Chaffey (Calif.) JC
4. **Kim Seaman, lhp, Mississippi Gulf Coast JC**

June—Regular Phase (13)

1. **Tom Thurberg, of/rhp, South Weymouth (Mass.) HS**
2. **Mike Scott, rhp, Pepperdine**
3. **Curtis Baker, 3b, Fullerton (Calif.) HS**
4. **Robert Pappageorgas, ss, Pacific Grove HS, Pebble Beach, Calif.**
5. **David Riehl, lhp, Deer Park (Texas) HS**
6. Scott Brantley, of, Forest HS, Ocala, Fla.
7. Brian Hurse, rhp, Engelwood HS, Jacksonville, Fla.
8. Barry Evans, ss/3b, West Georgia JC
9. **Curtis Fisher, 1b, Georgia Southern**
10. **Elmer Cardwell, 3b, Normandy HS, St. Louis**
11. **Neil Allen, rhp, Ward HS, Kansas City, Kan.**
12. **Robert Grote, rhp, Wright State**
13. **Donald Pearson, rhp, Delphi (Ind.) HS**
14. Charles Clarke, of, Nicholls HS, New Orleans
15. **Charles Warren, of/3b, Brunswick (Ga.) JC**
16. **David Owen, lhp, Lynchburg (Va.)**
17. **Dave Von Ohlen, lhp, Flushing HS, College Point, N.Y.**
18. Willie Harmon, inf, Kosciusko (Miss.) HS
19. Anthony Guralas, ss/1b, Redwood HS, Larkspur, Calif.
20. Billy Lott, c, Wayne County HS, Jesup, Ga.
21. Martin Chargin, inf, Monte Vista HS, San Jose
22. **Robert Bryant, of, Methodist (N.C.)**
23. Marty Kain, rhp, LaQuinta HS, Westminster, Calif.
24. Rob Kauffman, inf, Hale HS, Tulsa, Okla.
25. **Michael Mitchell, lhp, West Muskingum HS, Zanesville, Ohio**
26. Michael Matlock, rhp/3b, Laytonville (Calif.) HS
27. **James Murphy, 3b/ss, Wittenberg (Ohio)**
28. **Tonus Thomas, of, Franklin, Ill.**
29. Mike Mitskavich, rhp, Central Catholic HS, DuBois, Pa.
30. **Keith Shermeyer, inf, Dover (Pa.) HS**
31. **Carman Coppol, rhp, Elizabethtown (Pa.)**
32. Terry Sutcliffe, rhp, Van Horn HS, Kansas City, Mo.

June—Secondary Phase (9)

1. **Richter Farmer, of, DeAnza (Calif.) JC**
2. Dennis Sandoval, rhp, Fullerton (Calif.) JC
3. Michael Coppess, rhp, Chaffey (Calif.) JC

NEW YORK YANKEES

January—Regular Phase (15)

1. John Fulgham, rhp, Yavapai (Ariz.) JC
2. James Smith, of, Chabot (Calif.) JC
3. **Darnell Waters, ss, Chabot (Calif.) JC**
4. Jay Elmore, rhp, Longview (Mo.) CC

January—Secondary Phase (11)

1. William Wilborn, of, Cosumnes River (Calif.) JC
2. Frank McCann, ss, Delaware

June—Regular Phase (16)

1. **Pat Tabler, of, McNicholas HS, Cincinnati**
2. **Calvin Riggar, lhp, Lennox (Calif.) HS**
3. **Johnny Crawford, of, Fremont HS, Los Angeles**
4. **Ted Wilborn, of, McClatchy HS, Sacramento**
5. Bill Knudson, rhp, University HS, Spokane, Wash.
6. Dwight Harris, of, Blair HS, Pasadena, Calif.
7. **Fred Atkins, rhp, Technical HS, Oakland**
8. **Tim Lewis, lhp, South Carolina**
9. Gordon Hahn, 2b, Santa Clara
10. **Mark Thiel, c, Missouri**
11. Warren Hollier, rhp, Muir HS, Altadena, Calif.
12. Pat Callahan, c, Miami
13. **Garry Smith, of, South Florida**
14. Randy Whistler, c, Lakewood HS, Long Beach
15. Daniel Teel, c, Ridgefield Park (N.J.) HS
16. **Donald Fisk, rhp, Nevada-Reno**
17. Frank Wren, of, Northeast HS, St. Petersburg, Fla.
18. **Mark Softy, rhp, Princeton**
19. Paul Semall, rhp, Ohio State
20. Joseph Portale, c, St. Edward HS, North Olmsted, Ohio
21. Harry Tabler, c, Ohio State

22. Richard Clowson, lhp, Ohio State
23. **Peter Eshelman, lhp, Williams (Mass.)**
24. Chris Welsh, lhp, South Florida
25. **Donald Hogestyn, 2b, South Florida**

June—Secondary Phase (20)

1. **Roger Slagle, rhp, Kansas**
2. Mike Estes, rhp, Manatee (Fla.) JC

OAKLAND ATHLETICS

January—Regular Phase (23)

1. Colin Danielsen, rhp, Pasadena (Calif.) CC
2. **Christian Jensen, 2b, Trenton State (N.J.)**
3. **Barton Braun, rhp, Solano (Calif.) CC**
4. Robert Bohnet, 3b, Solano (Calif.) CC
5. Joe Ferri, of, Pasadena (Calif.) CC
6. Greg Fite, rhp, Laney (Calif.) JC

January—Secondary Phase (13)

1. **Thomas Baxter, rhp, Hudson County (N.J.) JC**
2. **Donald Henley, of, Mercer County (N.J.) CC**
3. Stephen Muccio, ss, Valencia (Fla.) CC

June—Regular Phase (24)

1. Mike Sullivan, rhp, Garfield HS, Woodbridge, Va.
2. Brian Duffy, lhp/1b, Serra HS, Foster City, Calif.
3. **Allan Minker, 1b, Glasgow HS, Newark, Del.**
4. **Rickey Henderson, of, Technical HS, Oakland**
5. **Dave Hornacek, of, Beaver Falls (Pa.) HS**
6. Jeff Walsh, rhp, Mitty HS, Santa Clara, Calif.
7. Jerry Joyce, of, Monterey HS, Seaside, Calif.
8. **Vernon Armstead, of, Jefferson HS, Los Angeles**
9. **Dom Scala, 3b, St. John's**
10. Stan Levi, of, Locke HS, Los Angeles
11. **Bobby Moore, rhp, Kennedy HS, Sepulveda, Calif.**
12. **Jim Bennett, of/1b, Edison Street HS, Stockton, Calif.**
13. **Bryan Meyl, rhp, SUNY Brockport**
14. **Timothy Spaulding, rhp, Montrose (Mich.) HS**
15. Dale Crummie, c, Locke HS, Los Angeles
16. **Donald Schubert, rhp, Fox Chapel HS, Sharpsburg, Pa.**
17. Mike Myerchin, lhp, Mira Costa HS, Manhattan Beach, Calif.
18. **Thomas Wright, c, Belmont**
19. **Ken McKinney, 2b, Memphis State**
20. **John Kniss, 2b, San Joaquin Delta (Calif.) JC**
21. Eric Prevost, lhp, San Fernando (Calif.) HS
22. Tom Beyers, 1b, Harbor HS, Santa Cruz, Calif.
23. Jarvis Redwine, of, Inglewood (Calif.) HS
24. **Richard Dziemiela, 3b/ss, Elmhurst (Ill.)**
25. **Michael Nipert, c, Hazen HS, Renton, Wash.**
26. Kevin Darst, 2b, Vallejo (Calif.) HS
27. **Michael Billington, 2b, Forest Park (Mo.) JC**
28. **Ron McNeely, of, Memphis State**
29. Charles Love, of, Banning HS, Long Beach
30. Philip Tyson, lhp, Centennial HS, Compton, Calif.
31. John Hanley, c, Grant HS, Van Nuys, Calif.
32. Elijah Risper, of, Crenshaw HS, Los Angeles
33. Michael Hunter, lhp, Vintage HS, Napa, Calif.
34. **Brian Bullas, of/2b, San Diego**

June—Secondary Phase (18)

1. **Ernie Camacho, rhp, Hartnell (Calif.) CC**
2. **Jim Smith, of, Chabot (Calif.) JC**
3. Bob Stoddard, rhp, Gavilan (Calif.) JC
4. **Roderick Patterson, rhp, Santa Monica (Calif.) JC**
5. Mike Chris, 1b, Los Angeles Pierce JC

PHILADELPHIA PHILLIES

January—Regular Phase (18)

1. Jack Lazorko, rhp, Miami-Dade South CC
2. **Derek Botelho, rhp, Miami-Dade South CC**
3. **Ricky Burdette, lhp, Chipola (Fla.) JC**
4. Robert Casanova, 2b, Grossmont (Calif.) JC
5. Bob Walk, p, JC of the Canyons (Calif.)
6. Tony Dorsey, of/2b, Ranger (Texas) JC
7. Michael Glenn, lhp, Ranger (Texas) JC
8. Thomas Popovich, 2b/ss, Battle Creek, Mich.
9. Frank Horak, rhp, Pasadena (Calif.) CC
10. Mark Taylor, rhp, St. John's River (Fla.) CC
11. **Erik Nelson, of, Diablo Valley (Calif.) JC**
12. Jeff Lahti, rhp, Treasure Valley (Ore.) CC

January—Secondary Phase (20)

1. **Glenn Ballard, c, Valencia (Fla.) CC**
2. Stephen Powers, rhp, Arizona
3. **Marvin Hammock, ss, Miami-Dade North CC**

June—Regular Phase (17)

1. **Jeff Kraus, ss, Colerain HS, Cincinnati**
2. **Eddie Williams, c, Northwestern HS, Detroit**
3. **Richard Whaley, lhp, Jacksonville (N.C.) HS**
4. **Randy Curtis, ss, Pine Bluff (Ark.) HS**
5. **Len Matuszek, of, Toledo**
6. **Ozzie Virgil Jr., c, Moon Valley HS, Glendale, Ariz.**
7. **Wallace Nunn, rhp, Holland Hall HS, Tulsa, Okla.**
8. **Michael Kruzelock, rhp, Venice HS, Mar Vista, Calif.**
9. Duane Evans, 1b, Yuma (Ariz.) HS
10. **William Buchan, 3b, South Weymouth (Mass.) HS**
11. **Randy Black, of, Guilford (N.C.)**
12. **Lee Wilson, rhp, Seaside (Ore.) HS**
13. **Henry Mack, rhp, George Rogers Clark HS, Winchester, Ky.**
14. **Brian Watts, rhp, Caseville (Mich.) HS**
15. **Brent Adams, rhp, Sonora HS, Jamestown, Calif.**
16. **Charles Davis, rhp, Richmond County HS, Rockingham, N.C.**
17. Eugene Norman, rhp, UC Irvine
18. **Frank Lucy, c, Arizona State**
19. **Elijah Bonaparte, of, Kennedy HS, Paterson, N.J.**
20. Steven Safranski, of, Putman HS, Mark, Ill.
21. **Louis Packer, of, Marshall**
22. **Stephen Hagen, lhp, Elk Grove (Calif.) HS**
23. **Thomas Brunswick, ss, Coldwater (Ohio) HS**
24. George Bertstrom, c, Faulkner State (Ala.) JC
25. **Shawn Kuhn, rhp, Morro Bay HS, Baywood Park, Calif.**
26. John Lohse, 3b, Hamilton City HS, Glenn, Calif.
27. Stephen Brown, rhp, Morris Harvey HS, Charleston, W.Va.
28. Keith Walker, lhp, Arlington (Texas) HS

June—Secondary Phase (13)

1. Jack Lazorko, 3b, Miami-Dade South CC
2. **Joe Charboneau, of, West Valley (Calif.) JC**
3. **Bob Walk, rhp, JC of the Canyons (Calif.)**
4. Gary Bowers, rhp, Fullerton (Calif.) JC

PITTSBURGH PIRATES

January—Regular Phase (22)

1. **Michael Imhoff, of, Polk (Fla.) CC**
2. Joseph Ward, of, Manatee (Fla.) JC
3. Ken Lelek, rhp, Monroe (N.Y.) CC
4. Hillary Nelson, lhp, Chipola (Fla.) JC
5. Chris Keyes, c, Big Bend (Wash.) CC
6. John Duda, rhp, Yakima Valley (Wash.) JC (Selection voided)

January—Secondary Phase (6)

1. **Larry Littleton, of, Georgia**
2. Jerry Schmidt, rhp, Lewis-Clark State (Idaho)
3. Tim Huff, rhp, Gardner-Webb
4. Phillip Pundt, rhp, Miami-Dade North CC
5. Richard Hand, c, Brown
6. Gerald Green, rhp, Lower Columbia (Wash.) JC
7. Albert Kissner, rhp, New Haven (Conn.)

June—Regular Phase (21)

1. **Jim Parke, rhp, Henry Ford II HS, Sterling Heights, Mich.**
2. **Doe Boyland, of, Wisconsin-Oshkosh**
3. Mike Madden, lhp, Palmer HS, Colorado Springs, Colo.
4. **George Goodrich, of, Lincoln HS, Wisconsin Rapids, Wis.**
5. **James Smith, rhp, University HS, Waco, Texas**
6. **Charles Rouse, 2b, Fulton HS, Knoxville**
7. Don Crow, c, Davis HS, Yakima, Wash.
8. **Robert Rock, rhp, Mount Vernon HS, Alexandria, Va.**
9. **Brian Schwerman, rhp, Libertyville (Ill.) HS**

10. Don Davisson, of, Rock Hill HS
11. Pat Shackelford, rhp, Buchholz HS Gainesville, Fla.
12. **Allen Leech, ss, West Chester (Pa.)**
13. **James Rogers, rhp, Cleveland State (Tenn.) CC**
14. **Robert Stadnika, rhp, Central Michigan**
15. **Jeff Greenhalgh, 1b, Valdosta State (Ga.)**
16. **Marvin Evans, 1b, Seminole (Fla.) CC**
17. **Rick Honeycutt, 1b/lhp, Tennessee**
18. David Banes, ss, Buchholz HS, Gainesvile, Fla.
19. **Dick Walterhouse, 2b, Michigan**
20. Jeff Mincey, c, Liberty
21. **Eric Peterson, lhp, Jacksonville**
22. **George Renfroe, c, Lompoc (Calif.) HS**
23. **Terry Burkholder, 2b, West Chester (Pa.)**
24. **Bob Long, rhp/of, Shorter (Ga.)**
25. **Lenny Spicer, of, Walton-Verona HS, Verona, Ky.**
26. **Gary Fulton, of, Murphy HS, Atlanta**
27. Ray Dahlmann, c/1b, Cabrillo HS, Lompoc, Calif.
28. **Ritchie Howard, 3b, Auburn**
29. **Thomas Burke, of/inf, Northwestern**
30. Wade Manning, of, Ohio State
31. **Laurence Kienzle, lhp, Clarion (Pa.)**
32. **Gene Gentile, of, Allderdice HS, Pittsburgh**
33. **Mark Howars, rhp, South Alabama**
34. Scott Kuvinka, 3b/c, Hopewell HS, Aliquippa, Pa.
35. Ledell Lowe, 1b, South Alabama
36. **Richard Baker, c, Scranton (Pa.)**

June—Secondary Phase (19)

1. **Steve Powers, rhp, Arizona**
2. Mike Zouras, 3b, Cal State Long Beach
3. Thomas Eagan, 3b, Green River (Wash.) CC

ST. LOUIS CARDINALS

January—Regular Phase (16)

1. **Fulvio Bertolotti, c, Merced (Calif.) JC**
2. John Butcher, rhp, Yavapai (Ariz.) JC
3. James Harskamp, inf, Merced (Calif.) JC
4. **William Schopp, rhp, Moorpark (Calif.) JC**
5. John Zalopany, rhp, Grossmont (Calif.) JC
6. Randy Toogood, c, Glendale (Ariz.) CC
7. **Roger Nolan, of/1b, North Hills HS, Pittsburgh**
8. David Mobley, ss, Chipola (Fla.) JC
9. **Ronald Swanson, of, Contra Costa (Calif.) JC**
10. Mark Hoffman, lhp, Harvard

January—Secondary Phase (14)

1. Michael Bungarz, lhp, Chabot (Calif.) JC
2. Gary Skow, 1b, Yavapai (Ariz.) JC
3. **Dan O'Brien, rhp, Florida State**
4. James Kopatz, c, Illinois

June—Regular Phase (15)

1. **Leon Durham, 1b/lhp, Woodward HS, Cincinnati**
2. **Walt Pierce, 3b, Wilcox HS, Santa Clara, Calif.**
3. **Jere Schuler, lhp, Lampeter-Strasburg HS, Lancaster, Pa.**
4. **Randy Thomas, ss, Lynchburg (Va.)**
5. **Paul Keck, of, San Mateo (Calif.) HS**
6. Larry Kuhn, rhp, North Torrance (Calif.) HS
7. Bryan Hardy, lhp, Bingham HS, West Jordan, Calif.
8. **Denny Martindale, 2b/rhp, Cal Poly San Luis Obispo**
9. **Daniel Winslow, c, Buena HS, Sierra Vista, Ariz.**
10. **Billy Meza, rhp, San Gabriel HS, San Marino, Calif.**
11. Stan Williams, of, Lakewood (Calif.) HS
12. **Gene Roof, ss, St. Mary's HS, Paducah, Ky.**
13. David Harrigan, ss, Altus (Okla.) HS
14. **John Fedorko, rhp, Bethel (Conn.) HS**
15. Billy Minor, of/rhp, New Chaney (Texas) HS
16. **Jeff Toothman, 1b/of, Edgewood HS, West Covina, Calif.**
17. **Frank Marsalan, c, Greensberg Catholic HS, Apollo, Pa.**
18. Keith Gradwohl, rhp, Yakima Valley (Wash.) JC
19. **Kenneth Given, of, Morris Harvey (W.Va.)**
20. **Bill Simpson, 3b, Arizona**
21. **Ray Williams, rhp, Thousand Oaks (Calif.) HS**
22. **Ray Searage, lhp, West Liberty State**
23. Greg Moyer, rhp, La Mirada (Calif.) HS
24. **Mike Calise, 3b, Mesa (Ariz.) CC**
25. Anthony Hudson, rhp, San Bernardino (Calif.) HS
26. **Terry Jacob, rhp, Arizona State**
27. Steve Schefsky, rhp, Hillsdale HS, San Mateo, Calif.
28. **Mark Bumstead, inf, Cal State Northridge**
29. **Frank Hunsaker, c, Southern Illinois**
30. **John Littlefield, rhp, Azusa Pacific (Calif.)**
31. Russell McDonald, rhp, Monte Vista HS, San Jose, Calif.
32. Garry Lewis, of/rhp, Dixon (Mo.) HS
33. Larry Navilhon, rhp, Crestmoor HS, San Bruno, Calif.
34. **David Benoit, ss, Assumption (Mass.)**

June—Secondary Phase (15)

1. **John Fulgham, rhp, Yavapai (Ariz.) JC**
2. Charlie Lea, rhp/inf, Shelby State (Tenn.) CC
3. Steve Winfield, rhp, Panola (Texas) JC

SAN DIEGO PADRES

January—Regular Phase (6)

1. **Keith Miller, c, New Orleans**
2. Bill Springman, 2b, Cerritos (Calif.) JC
3. Stephen Conner, c, Volunteer State (Tenn.) CC
4. Milton Smith, 3b, Southwestern (Calif.) JC

January—Secondary Phase (8)

1. **Bob Shirley, lhp, Oklahoma**
2. Danny Boone, lhp, Cal State Fullerton
3. Stanley Cannon, of/1b, Pensacola (Fla.) JC
4. Roger Slagle, rhp, Kansas

June—Regular Phase (5)

1. **Bob Owchinko, lhp, Eastern Michigan**
2. **Steve Mura, rhp, Tulane**
3. **Ted Olson, ss, Atwater (Calif.) HS**
4. **Paul O'Neill, 3b, Texas Wesleyan**
5. **Jim Beswick, of, East Allegheny HS, North Versailles, Pa.**
6. **Mark Spatz, ss, Wilson HS, Hacienda Heights, Calif.**
7. **Daniel Keen, lhp, Coral Park HS, Miami**
8. Pat Blamey, rhp, Buchser HS, Santa Clara, Calif.
9. **Craig Stimac, c, Denver**
10. Mark Daly, lhp, Florida Southern
11. **Tom Tellmann, rhp, Grand Canyon (Ariz.)**
12. **Ronnie Barnett, of, Texas-Arlington**
13. **Mark Lee, rhp, Pepperdine**
14. **Earl Battey, 3b, UCLA**
15. Broderick Perkins, 1b, St. Mary's
16. Tim Muser, ss, Clairemont HS, San Diego
17. **William Hallstrom, ss, Grand Canyon HS, Scottsdale, Ariz.**
18. Steve Glaum, rhp, UC Riverside
19. **Gary Lucas, lhp, Chapman (Calif.)**
20. **Mike Bullock, rhp, St. Mary's**
21. **Dane Ilertson, 1b, Point Loma Nazarene (Calif.)**
22. Larry Kowalishen, rhp, California
23. **Bobby DuPree, rhp, Grambling State**
24. **Steven Smith, ss, Pepperdine**
25. Johnny Jones, of, Lampassa (Calif.) HS
26. Robert Denton, of, La Jolla (Calif.) HS

June—Secondary Phase (5)

1. **William Wilborn, of, Cosumnes River (Calif.) JC**
2. **Jerry Schmidt, rhp, Lewis-Clark State (Idaho)**

SAN FRANCISCO GIANTS

January—Regular Phase (12)

1. **Lazando Washington, of, Los Angeles Harbor JC**
2. **John Harper, lhp, Los Angeles Pierce JC**
3. **Fred Shourds, of, Garden Grove, Calif.**
4. Dave Hostetler, 1b, Citrus (Calif.) JC
5. Jim Wilson, 3b, Cerritos (Calif.) JC
6. **Stephen McKown, rhp, Hutchinson (Kan.) CC**
7. Steve Huff, rhp, Phoenix JC
8. Eric Mustad, rhp, Citrus (Calif.) JC
9. Robert Ruth, rhp, Centralia (Wash.) JC
10. Robert Turner, rhp, Treasure Valley (Ore.) CC

January—Secondary Phase (2)

1. **Dennis Littlejohn, c, Southern California**
2. Roderick Ingram, of/c, Linfield (Ore.)
3. Daniel Hartwig, rhp, Antelope Valley (Calif.) JC
4. Richard Holloway, rhp, Gulf Coast (Fla.) CC
5. **William Krampe, p, Pittsburgh**
6. William Eve, 1b, Miami-Dade North CC
7. Robert Cramer, rhp, Columbia Basin (Wash.) CC
8. Greg Vogel, inf, Penn State

June—Regular Phase (11)

1. **Mark Kuecker, ss, Brenham (Texas) HS**
2. Tom Hawk, rhp, Fairmont West HS, Kettering, Ohio
3. **John Sylvester, of, Tampa**
4. Kevin Rostenkowski, lhp, Perry Meridian HS, Indianapolis
5. **Jeffrey O'Donnell, c, North Hollywood (Calif.) HS**
6. John Fenwick, ss, Anoka (Minn.) HS
7. **Richard Farrell, c, St. Xavier (Ill.)**
8. Dean Gottler, c, Tates Creek HS, Lexington, Ky.
9. Renie Martin, rhp, Richmond
10. Jerome Ahlert, ss, Aiken HS, Cincinnati
11. **Danny Held, of, JC of the Desert (Calif.)**
12. **Mike Wardlow, of, Southern California Christian HS, Inglewood, Calif.**
13. Raymond Mass, rhp, Bellevue (Wash.) CC
14. **William Tullish, of, North Florida**
15. **Steve Stumpff, 1b, Iowa**
16. **Ray Cosio, rhp, Miami (Fla.) Senior HS**
17. Frank Ferroni, lhp, Redwood HS, Mill Valley, Calif.
18. **Mike Rex, ss, Linfield (Ore.)**
19. **David Schwartz, of, Shaker Heights (Ohio) HS**
20. Johnny Hamilton, p, Navajo HS, Altus, Okla.
21. Robert Pettit, inf, Chandler (Ariz.) HS
22. Jeff Ahearn, lhp, St. Genevieve HS, Reseda, Calif.
23. Mike Couchee, rhp, Los Gatos (Calif.) HS
24. **Mike Walker, of, Victor Valley (Calif.) CC**
25. **Wayne Pechek, of, Oklahoma**
26. **Jeff Stember, rhp, Westfield (N.J.) HS**
27. David Meyer, 2b, Mira Costa (Calif.) JC
28. Steve Macko, 3b, Baylor
29. George Hawkins, of, Shorter (Ga.)
30. Michael Stover, rhp, JC of Southern Idaho
31. **Mike Glinatsis, rhp, Youngstown State**
32. Robert Jester, rhp, Trenton State (N.J.)
33. Samuel Dittoe, rhp, Sheridan HS, Somerset, Ohio
34. Mike Bates, rhp, Apollo HS, Phoenix
35. Robert Everling, rhp, Marion (Ind.) HS
36. Steve Day, ss, Texas
37. Leslie Ream, 2b, Ohio
38. **James Pryor, c, Cal Poly Pomona**
39. **Thomas Boutin, of, Eastern Michigan**
40. Sammy Bickham, rhp, Plano HS, Richardson, Texas

June—Secondary Phase (23)

1. Jim Wilson, 3b, Cerritos (Calif.) JC
2. **Dan Hartwig, rhp, Antelope Valley (Calif.) JC**
3. Robert Ruth, rhp, Centralia (Wash.) JC

TEXAS RANGERS

January—Regular Phase (11)

1. Jerome Hojnacki, 1b, Northwestern
2. Paul Givens, lhp, San Jose CC
3. **John Phenix, of, Reno, Nevada**

January—Secondary Phase (21)

1. **Paul Mirabella, lhp, Montclair State (N.J.)**
2. Richard Comeau, rhp, Manatee (Fla.) JC
3. **Len Glowzenski, rhp, Seton Hall**
4. James Watkins, of, Valencia (Fla.) CC

June—Regular Phase (12)

1. **Billy Simpson, of, Lakewood (Calif.) HS**
2. **Steve Finch, rhp, Cordova HS, Rancho Cordova, Calif.**
3. **Mike Griffin, rhp, Woodland (Calif.) HS**
4. **Brian Allard, rhp, Henry Senachwine HS, Henry, Ill.**
5. Paul Rudiman, rhp, Duval HS, Lanham, Md.
6. **David Peterson, c, Wilson HS, Portland, Ore.**
7. **Ted Davis, rhp, Fairmont Heights HS, Cheverly, Maine**
8. **Kevin Keenan, rhp, Slippery Rock (Pa.)**
9. **Alphonso Lewis, of/c, Pensacola (Fla.) HS**
10. **Billy Sample, 3b/of, James Madison**
11. **Peter Zilonis, ss, Rindge Tech HS, Cambridge, Mass.**
12. Andre Robertson, ss, West Orange (Texas) HS
13. Michael Guman, lhp, Bethlehem (Pa.) Catholic HS
14. **James Capowski, ss, Roosevelt HS, Yonkers, N.Y.**
15. Greg Eason, lhp, Escambia HS, Pensacola, Fla.
16. Brian Snyder, lhp, Chantilly (Va.) HS
17. **Glenn Williams, of, San Jose State**
18. Richard Hereth, c, Colerain HS, Cincinnati
19. **Mike Jaccar, inf, Southern Methodist**
20. **Doug Duncan, c, Texas**
21. **Mike Williamson, rhp, Stanford**
22. **Wayne Wilkerson, 3b/of, American**
23. Gordon Hawkins, rhp, Surrathville HS, Clinton, Md.
24. Monte McAbee, of, Medford (Ore.) HS
25. Vincent Merolla, rhp, James Madison HS, Brooklyn, N.Y.
26. Timothy Bjelland, ss, Milliken HS, Long Beach (Selection voided)
27. Paul Adams, 1b, Virginia Tech
28. Timothy Knight, of, Daytona Mainland HS, Holly Hill, Fla.

June—Secondary Phase (12)

1. **Greg Jemison, of, Seton Hall**

1977 MAVERICK VEECK GOES AGAINST CONSENSUS WITH BAINES, WHILE COLLEGE PLAYERS GAIN INFLUENCE

Bill Gullickson was supposed to be the No. 1 pick of the White Sox in the 1977 draft. He was a hometown boy, a hard-throwing right-hander from Joliet, Ill., and was rated No. 1 in the country by the Major League Scouting Bureau.

But White Sox owner Bill Veeck wasn't known as one of the game's most colorful and unpredictable characters for nothing. Sure enough, Veeck crossed everyone up by having his team go for first baseman Harold Baines, whom Veeck began scouting personally some six years earlier when Baines was a Little Leaguer.

Prior to acquiring the White Sox in 1976, Veeck lived in Easton, on Maryland's Eastern Shore. Baines lived 10 miles away, in St. Michaels, and was making a name for himself as a young hitter. Intrigued, Veeck often went over to watch him play.

"He's got good speed, and he's a natural hitter," Veeck said. "I saw him play in Little League, and he impressed me even then."

Baines, who hit .532 with two home runs that spring at St. Michaels High, was rated the fifth-best player in the country by the scouting bureau, though most scouts agreed he was the best hitting prospect available.

"Our choice was universal," Veeck said. "We scouted him as thoroughly as we scouted anybody, even Gullickson and others. Whenever our scouts looked at Baines, the first line in the report was, 'He has one of the greatest natural swings we've ever seen. He's an all-around athlete.' "

Veeck was so determined to take Baines that he went to St. Michaels himself and signed Baines the night before the draft to a reported $40,000 deal, the lowest bonus ever paid a No. 1 pick.

Three days later, Baines drove an hour from his home in Baltimore to join the White Sox for a weekend series against the Orioles. He took batting practice with the big leaguers but was so in awe of his surroundings that he didn't hit a single ball out of the infield in three turns in the batting cage.

That had little bearing on his future outlook, though, as Baines spent 22 seasons in the major leagues. He spent the majority of his time with the White Sox, getting traded away in 1989 but coming back twice more, and finished his career with 2,866 hits and 384 home runs.

Leading up to the 1977 draft, scouts had singled out Gullickson as the top young prospect in the nation. He was clocked at 96 mph and went unbeaten his senior year, with a 12-0, 0.48 mark, so it surprised Gullickson when the Sox went for Baines. He had thought either he or Florida State catcher Terry Kennedy would be the No. 1 pick.

Harold Baines was a gamble that paid off big for the White Sox and Bill Veeck

Gullickson and Baines both earned regular work in the big leagues in 1980. Gullickson had the more spectacular rookie season, striking out 18 Cubs in one game, but he was stricken by diabetes that season and his career never took off. Baines, meanwhile, became one of the best hitters of his generation.

Kennedy, whose father Bob was general manager of the Cubs, ended up going sixth overall to St. Louis. As a boy, Kennedy regularly worked out with the Cardinals when his dad was that club's farm director. Kennedy became the first of six consecutive Cardinals picks in June to reach the big leagues, tying a draft record.

The first college player selected, Minnesota shortstop Paul Molitor, went third to the Brewers, despite the presence of Robin Yount at shortstop in Milwaukee.

Molitor played a half-season in the Midwest League, then jumped all the way from Class A to the big leagues. He started the 1978 season at second base in Milwaukee, the beginning of a 21-year major league career that saw him finish with 3,319 hits and 234 home runs.

A total of five college players were selected in the first round of the June regular phase. For the first time in draft history, more college (438) than high school players (392) were selected in June. The trend would widen over the years as clubs placed more emphasis on older and more proven college players.

Changing Philosophy

If teams were looking for evidence to justify switching away from untested high school talent, the 1977 draft had plenty of it. Of 19 high school players selected in the first round, six never even advanced past Class A.

Baseball did win over football in a battle over four California two-sport stars: Brian Greer and Craig Landis, both of whom passed up a scholarship at UCLA; Drungo Hazewood, signed by the Orioles away from Southern California; and Dave Henderson, who signed with the Mariners instead of attending Fresno State. Only Henderson had notable success as a baseball player.

Expansion teams in Toronto and Seattle made their debuts in 1977, but a favorable draft position was not part of the $10 million expansion price. The Blue Jays and Mariners began selecting talent in January, in the Nos. 25 and 26 positions. The same order held in June.

Atlanta, meanwhile, had to challenge commissioner Bowie Kuhn to keep its first-round pick in June. Kuhn declared the Braves guilty of tampering in their 1976 courtship of Giants outfielder Gary Matthews, who played without a contract and signed as a free agent with the Braves following the 1976 season.

Punishment was suspension of Braves owner Ted Turner for a year, a $10,000 fine and loss of their first-round draft picks in the January and June regular phases. After losing their January pick, the Braves had Kuhn's ruling overturned in the courts. They won reinstatement of their June first-round pick and went for lefthander Tim Cole, who never reached the big leagues.

The courts would also get involved four years later in a tug-of-war between the Blue Jays and the NBA's Boston Celtics over Danny Ainge, a 15th-round pick of the Blue Jays in 1977.

Ainge would have been a top-round selection if not for his basketball prowess and his commitment to Brigham Young. For the next four years, Ainge played professional baseball during the summer while developing into one of the nation's best college basketball players at Brigham Young. When it came time to decide whether he would pursue baseball or basketball, the courts ruled in favor of the Celtics despite a three-year deal Ainge had with Toronto.

DRAFT 77: FIRST-ROUND PICKS

No.	Club	Player, Pos.	School	Hometown	Ht.	Wt.	B-T	Age
1.	White Sox	Harold Baines, 1b/of	St. Michaels HS	St. Michaels, Md.	6-2	175	L-L	18
2.	Expos	Bill Gullickson, rhp	Joliet Catholic HS	Orland Park, Ill.	6-3	200	R-R	18
3.	Brewers	Paul Molitor, ss	Minnesota	St. Paul, Minn.	6-0	185	R-R	20
4.	Braves	Tim Cole, lhp	Saugerties HS	Saugerties, N.Y.	6-0	185	L-L	18
5.	Tigers	Kevin Richards, rhp	Roosevelt HS	Wyandotte, Mich.	6-2	175	R-R	19
6.	Cardinals	Terry Kennedy, c	Florida State	Mesa, Ariz.	6-3	220	L-R	21
7.	Angels	Richard Dotson, rhp	Anderson HS	Cincinnati	6-1	182	R-R	18
8.	Padres	Brian Greer, of	Sonora HS	Brea, Calif.	6-3	210	R-R	18
9.	Rangers	David Hibner, ss	Howell HS	Howell, Mich.	5-10	180	R-R	18
10.	Giants	Craig Landis, ss	Vintage HS	Napa, Calif.	6-2	200	R-R	18
11.	Indians	Bruce Compton, of	Norman HS	Norman, Okla.	6-2	185	R-R	18
12.	Cubs	Randy Martz, rhp	South Carolina	Elizabethville, Pa.	6-4	210	L-R	21
13.	Red Sox	Andrew Madden, rhp	New Hartford HS	New Hartford, N.Y.	6-7	225	R-R	17
14.	Astros	Ricky Adams, ss	Montclair HS	Montclair, Calif.	6-1	175	R-R	18
15.	Twins	Paul Croft, of	Morristown HS	Morristown, N.J.	6-0	175	R-R	17
16.	Mets	Wally Backman, ss	Aloha HS	Beaverton, Ore.	5-10	160	B-R	17
17.	Athletics	Craig Harris, rhp	Buena HS	Sierra Vista, Ariz.	6-5	185	R-R	18
18.	Pirates	Anthony Nicely, of	Meadowdale HS	Dayton, Ohio	6-0	180	R-R	17
19.	Orioles	Drungo Hazewood, of	Sacramento HS	Sacramento	6-3	205	R-R	17
20.	Dodgers	Bob Welch, rhp	Eastern Michigan	Ferndale, Mich.	6-4	190	R-R	20
21.	Royals	Mike Jones, lhp	Sutherland HS	Pittsford, N.Y.	6-6	215	L-L	17
22.	Phillies	Scott Munninghoff, rhp	Purcell HS	Cincinnati	6-0	175	R-R	18
23.	Yankees	Steve Taylor, rhp	Delaware	Newark, Del.	6-4	200	R-R	21
24.	Reds	Tad Venger, 3b	Hart HS	Newhall, Calif.	6-2	175	L-R	18
25.	Blue Jays	Tom Goffena, ss	Sidney HS	Sidney, Ohio	6-0	160	R-R	17
26.	Mariners	Dave Henderson, of	Dos Palos HS	Dos Palos, Calif.	6-2	210	R-R	18

1977

CLUB-BY-CLUB SELECTIONS

ATLANTA BRAVES

January—Regular Phase (3)

1. (Selection lost as penalty for tampering with Gary Matthews prior to 1976 major league re-entry draft.)
2. **Romel Beck, ss, East Los Angeles JC**
3. Mark Garber, rhp, Antelope Valley (Calif.) JC
4. Walter Parmenter, of, Middle Georgia JC

January—Secondary Phase (14)

1. Gerald Price, 3b, Diablo Valley (Calif.) JC

June—Regular Phase (4)

1. **Tim Cole, lhp, Saugerties (N.Y.) HS**
2. **Tony Brizzolara, rhp, Texas**
3. **Bob Porter, of, Napa (Calif.) HS**
4. Allen Wesolowski, rhp, La Porte (Ind.) HS
5. **Richard Wieters, rhp, The Citadel**
6. **Albert Hall, ss, Jones Valley HS, Birmingham**
7. **George Ramos, of, Seton Hall**
8. Reggie King, c, Morgan Park HS, Chicago
9. Phil Deriso, lhp, Westover HS, Albany, Ga.
10. **Jeffrey Matthews, ss/2b, Mankato State (Minn.)**
11. Greg Cypret, ss, Missouri
12. **Tom Mee, of, Minnesota**
13. Cody Whitt, rhp, North Springs HS, Atlanta
14. Daniel Hejl, c, Johnson HS, Austin, Texas
15. **Terry Abbott, rhp, Jacksonville State**
16. **Daniel Ballard, rhp, St. Francis (N.Y.)**
17. **Larry Owen, c, Bowling Green State**
18. **Daniel Lucia, rhp, JC of Marin (Calif.)**
19. Quinton Lloyd, of, L.B. Johnson HS, Austin, Texas
20. Mike Brown, rhp, Marshall HS, Vienna, Va.
21. Charlie Locke, rhp, Corrigan (Texas) HS
22. **Daryl Logan, 3b, Asheville (N.C.) HS**
23. **Brady Baldwin, c, Cincinnati**
24. Tod Carter, rhp, Washington & Lee HS, Arlington, Va.
25. **Thomas LaGrave, rhp, American**
26. Daniel England, of, North Eugene (Ore.) HS

June—Secondary Phase (23)

1. Mark Martin, c, San Jacinto (Texas) JC
2. Billy Bowen, of, Grayson County (Texas) JC

BALTIMORE ORIOLES

January—Regular Phase (20)

1. **John Shelby, ss, Columbia State (Tenn.) CC**
2. **Tom Rowe, rhp, Rockland (N.Y.) CC**
3. **Gerald Coleman, of, Baltimore, Md.**
4. Frederick Lund, rhp, Sacramento CC
5. Mike Otto, of, Sacramento CC
6. **Terrence Swinton, ss, Philadelphia CC**
7. **Thomas McWilliams, c, Oakland (Mich.) CC**
8. Michael Smoot, 3b/c, DeKalb (Ga.) JC

January—Secondary Phase (23)

1. **Joseph Powell, 1b/3b, Valencia (Fla.) CC**
2. Gary Bozich, 2b, St. Petersburg (Fla.) JC

June—Regular Phase (19)

1. **Drungo Hazewood, c/of, Sacramento (Calif.) HS**
2. **Dan Logan, 1b, West Georgia**
3. **Richard Moore, c, South Dorcester HS, Cambridge, Md.**
4. **David Caldwell, of, Clemson**
5. **Larry Jones, rhp, Florida State**
6. **Will George, lhp, Pensauken (N.J.) HS**
7. **Mark Van Bever, 2b, South Carolina**
8. **John Denman, of, American**
9. **Mark Smith, rhp, American**
10. **Russ Brett, 3b, Santa Clara**
11. **Michael Sherman, c, Goldsboro (N.C.) HS**
12. **Steven Polan, 3b, La Verne (Calif.)**
13. **William Marrero, of, Hauppauge HS, Smithtown, N.Y.**
14. **David Lankster, ss, Middle Tennessee State**
15. Mike Martin, 3b/c, Milwaukie HS, Troutdale, Ore.
16. Mark Bolton, rhp, Longview (Texas) HS
17. **Tom Eaton, 2b, Tulsa**
18. **Michael Lacasse, 2b, James Madison**
19. **Steve Lesser, rhp, Alderson-Broaddus (W.Va.)**
20. **David Emala, 3b, Johns Hopkins (Md.)**
21. **Robert Whitfield, ss, Alderson-Broaddus (W.Va.)**
22. Lorenzo Bundy, ss, Essex HS, Tappahannock, Va.
23. Chris Jones, of, Grossmont (Calif.) JC

June—Secondary Phase (9)

1. **Steve Lerner, lhp, Miami**
2. Earl Robinson, of, Gulf Coast (Fla.) CC

BOSTON RED SOX

January—Regular Phase (14)

1. Marcus Bell, rhp, Cleveland State (Tenn.) CC
2. Carl Pankratz, rhp, Temple (Texas) JC
3. **John Morgan, 3b, Chelmsford, Mass.**
4. Rodney Feight, rhp, Indian River (Fla.) CC
5. **Stephen Annarummo, of, Rhode Island College**
6. Ron Koenigsfeld, ss, Indian Hills (Iowa) CC

January—Secondary Phase (17)

1. **Jim Wilson, 3b, Cerritos (Calif.) JC**

June—Regular Phase (13)

1. **Andrew Madden, rhp, New Hartford (N.Y.) HS**
2. **Bobby Sprowl, lhp, Alabama**
3. Scott Sullivan, of, Cupertino HS, Los Gatos, Calif.
4. **Erwin Bryant, ss, Columbia State (Tenn.) CC**
5. **Mark Baum, rhp, Northland HS, Columbus, Ohio**
6. **Scott Burk, 3b, Oklahoma State**
7. **Richard Parr, of, Greenville (Ill.)**
8. **Roger LaFrancois, c, Oklahoma**
9. **Charles Thompson, c, DeKalb (Ga.) JC**
10. **Steve Shields, rhp, Hokes Bluff HS, Gadsden, Ala.**
11. Bill Swiacki, rhp, Amherst (Mass.)
12. **Frank Gill, 2b, Fairfield**
13. **Richard Colbert, c, Joliet (Ill.) Catholic HS**
14. **Barry Butera, ss/3b, Tulane**
15. **Alvin Hulbert, rhp, Westboro (Mass.) HS**
16. **Mark Saunders, rhp, Allderdice HS, Pittsburgh**
17. Gary Redus, ss/of, Athens State (Ga.)
18. Bruce Alexander, rhp, Kokomo (Ind.) HS
19. **Rosaire Viens, rhp, Sacred Heart (Conn.)**
20. Eli Roberson, of, Lee HS, Baytown, Texas
21. **Russell Laribee, of, Connecticut**
22. Gerry Davis, 3b, Ewing HS, Trenton, N.J.
23. **Richard Nesloney, rhp, Lamar**
24. **Mark Kaeterle, ss, Vocational HS, New Bedford, Mass.**
25. **Pete Ladd, rhp, Massachusetts**
26. **Lee Graham, of, Lake Weir HS, Belleview, Fla.**

June—Secondary Phase (7)

1. **Stephen Collins, rhp, Fresno State**
2. **Ronald Lee, ss, Blinn (Texas) JC**

CALIFORNIA ANGELS

January—Regular Phase (8)

1. **Alan Wiggins, inf, Pasadena (Calif.) CC**
2. **Guy Jones, rhp, JC of the Sequoias (Calif.)**
3. **Daryl Sconiers, 1b, Orange Coast (Calif.) JC**
4. Steve England, c, Mineral Area (Mo.) JC

5. Brian Winship, inf, Yuba (Calif.) CC
6. John Hartnell, lhp, El Camino (Calif.) JC
7. Barry Acquistapace, rhp, Santa Barbara (Calif.) CC
8. Marty Castillo, 3b, Santa Ana (Calif.) JC
9. Ron Cooper, rhp, Orange Coast (Calif.) JC
10. David Bertulli, 3b, Valencia (Fla.) CC
11. Marty Barrett, 2b, Mesa (Ariz.) CC

January—Secondary Phase (8)

1. **Robert Healy, rhp, St. Louis CC-Meramec**
2. Monte Pries, rhp, Orange Coast (Calif.) JC

June—Regular Phase (7)

1. **Richard Dotson, rhp, Anderson HS, Cincinnati**
2. **Gary Johnson, rhp, Deep Creek HS, Chesapeake, Va.**
3. **Jeff Conner, lhp, Trevor Browne HS, Phoenix**
4. **Brian Harper, c, San Pedro HS, Rolling Hills, Calif.**
5. **Rick Steirer, rhp, Maryland-Baltimore County**
6. Brian Hayes, lhp, Southern California
7. **Doug Thomson, rhp, La Verne (Calif.)**
8. **Brad Havens, lhp, Kimball HS, Royal Oak, Mich.**
9. **Brandt Humphry, 3b, Arizona State**
10. Kevin Dukes, lhp, Sahuaro HS, Tucson, Ariz.
11. **Michael Heaton, rhp, Butte (Calif.) JC**
12. **George Tucker, lhp, Narbonne HS, Culver City, Calif.**
13. John Garcia, rhp, Hayden HS, Phoenix
14. Brian Denman, 1b/rhp, Minnesota
15. Mark Reeves, c, Spokane Falls (Wash.) CC
16. **Melvin Quarles, of, UC Riverside**
17. Joseph Plummer, of, St. Anthony's HS, Long Beach, Calif.
18. **Steve Trumbauer, c, California Lutheran**
19. **Filiberto Gonzalez, lhp, Sierra (Calif.) JC**
20. Neal Herrick, rhp, Arundel HS, Jessop, Md.
21. **Monte Mendenhall, rhp, Nevada-Las Vegas**
22. Reggie West, of, Santa Ana (Calif.) Valley HS
23. **Jessie Plummer, of, Salisbury State (Md.)**
24. **Jim Vallone, lhp, La Verne (Calif.)**
25. **Joey Blyleven, rhp, Santiago HS, Garden Grove, Calif.**
26. Kim Nelson, 3b, Brigham Young
27. **Art Miller, lhp, Northwest Missouri State**
28. Les Pearsey, ss, Arizona
29. John Flares, rhp, Glendale (Ariz.) CC
30. Brett Baumann, lhp, Colton (Calif.) HS
31. Dave Meier, ss, Bullard HS, Fresno, Calif.
32. La Schelle Tarver, of, Madera (Calif.) HS
33. James Watkins, of, Valencia (Fla.) CC

June—Secondary Phase (20)

1. **Mike Walters, rhp, Chaffey (Calif.) JC**
2. **Michael Stover, rhp, Brigham Young**
3. Lyle Brackenridge, ss, Pasadena (Calif.) CC

CHICAGO CUBS

January—Regular Phase (11)

1. Blane McDonald, c, South Florida JC
2. **Lawrence Panella, of, Saugerties, N.Y.**
3. **Charles Tewell, lhp, Chelmsford, Mass.**
4. **Jim Tracy, of, Fairfield, Ohio**
5. **James Messmer, 3b, Point Park (Pa.)**
6. Vincent Noldon, of, Porterville (Calif.) JC
7. Tim Mueller, rhp, JC of Southern Idaho
8. Randall Carter, ss, Arizona Western JC

January—Secondary Phase (11)

1. **Jeff Hardy, ss, Florida State**
2. **Billy Joe Minor, rhp, Angelina (Texas) JC**

June—Regular Phase (12)

1. **Randy Martz, rhp, South Carolina**
2. Terry Francona, 1b, New Brighton (Pa.) HS
3. **Randy Clark, rhp, Point Loma HS, San Diego**
4. **Dan Rohn, 2b, Central Michigan**
5. **Steve Macko, 3b/2b, Baylor**
6. **Mike Turgeon, ss, Eastern Connecticut State**
7. **Carl Spikes, of, Southern**
8. **Thomas Spino, lhp, Maine East HS, Niles, Ill.**
9. **Michael Shepston, c, Phoenix JC**
10. **John Hartin, 1b/of, Missouri Baptist**
11. **Kenneth Veenema, 2b, Cornell**
12. **Michael Wright, lhp, Pattonville HS, Bridgeton, Mo.**
13. **Joseph Stethers, lhp, Coastal Carolina**
14. **Javier Fierro, 3b, Cal State Los Angeles**
15. **Todd Winterfeldt, of, James Madison**
16. **Mark Obal, ss, Northeastern Illinois**
17. Dave Weatherman, rhp, West Torrance (Calif.) HS
18. **Joey Cole, rhp, Halifax HS, Vernon Hills, Va.**
19. **William Ross, rhp, Borah HS, Boise, Idaho**
20. Stephen Maral, c, Marina HS, San Leandro, Calif.
21. Carl Carlson, 1b/of, Cahokia (Ill.) HS
22. Louis Rojas, of, Kennedy HS, New York
23. Jay Schwamberger, lhp, Independence HS, Charlotte, N.C.
24. James Robinson, of, Lake Washington HS, Kirkland, Wash.
25. **Paul Brownlee, ss, Fairmont State (W.Va.)**
26. **Eric Robertson, of, Stillman (Ala.)**
27. **Vincent Valentini, rhp, Fairleigh Dickinson**
28. Wendell Henderson, c, Leon Godchaux HS, Mount Airy, La.
29. **Gene Krug, 1b, Oklahoma**
30. **Richard DeLoach, 3b, Stephenville (Texas) HS**
31. **John Bargfeldt, rhp/of, Anderson (Ind.)**
32. Anthony Veith, 1b, Brainerd, Minn.
33. Jackie Snell, lhp, Tulane
34. **Will Morgan, of, Alief Hastings HS, Houston**
35. Jon Putnam, rhp, King HS, Tampa
36. **Philip Rossi, ss, Millersville (Pa.)**
37. **Wilfred Puentes, of, Monmouth**

June—Secondary Phase (8)

1. David Sullivan, c, Yavapai (Ariz.) JC
2. **Jerome Ahlert, ss, Cincinnati**
3. Marcus Bell, rhp, Cleveland State (Tenn.) CC

CHICAGO WHITE SOX

January—Regular Phase (2)

1. Simon Glenn, of, Blinn (Texas) JC
2. **Handsome Roundtree, rhp, Orange Coast (Calif.) JC**
3. **Jeff Vuksan, c, Miami-Dade South CC**
4. Pat Rubino, c, JC of the Canyons (Calif.)
5. Michael Selwood, 3b/c, Golden West (Calif.) JC
6. Phillip Francis, rhp, Kent State (Selection voided)
7. Martin McDermott, ss/2b, Palm Beach (Fla.) JC
8. **Mark Esser, lhp, Miami-Dade North CC**
9. **Alex Suarez, c/of, Los Angeles Pierce JC**
10. Pete Teixeira, rhp, Miami-Dade South CC
11. Rodolfo Arias, c, Miami-Dade South CC
12. Michael Powell, rhp, Manatee (Fla.) JC
13. **Joseph Netzler, rhp, Wautoma, Wis.**
14. Ted May, of, Cleveland State (Tenn.) CC

January—Secondary Phase (19)

1. Gary Bowers, rhp, Fullerton (Calif.) JC
2. **John Hanley, c, Los Angeles Pierce JC**
3. Robert Kocol, of, Brevard (Fla.) CC
4. Charlie Lea, rhp, Shelby State (Tenn.) CC

June—Regular Phase (1)

1. **Harold Baines, 1b/of, St. Michael's (Md.) HS**
2. **Rich Barnes, lhp, Lake Worth (Fla.) HS**
3. **Mark Naehring, 1b, Miami (Ohio)**
4. Dan Hanggie, ss/3b, Brea (Calif.) Olinda HS
5. Paul Fox, rhp, San Mateo (Calif.) HS
6. **Rod Allen, of, Santa Monica (Calif.) HS**
7. Perry Swanson, rhp, Rancho HS, North Las Vegas, Nev.
8. **Ron Woods, rhp, UC Santa Barbara**
9. Fred Williams, lhp, Fremont HS, Sunnyvale, Calif.
10. **Steve Tipa, of, New Haven (Conn.)**
11. **Rusty Kuntz, of, Cal State Stanislaus**
12. Dennis Mark, of, West Valley (Calif.) JC
13. James Tjader, 2b, Iowa Western CC
14. **Richard Montoni, of, Miami**
15. **Mike Johnson, of, Cal State Dominguez Hills**
16. Bob Volk, 3b, Oral Roberts
17. Terry Bogener, of, Oklahoma
18. **Jackie Smith, lhp, Florida State**

19. **Dewey Robinson, rhp, Southern Illinois**
20. **Ross Baumgarten, lhp, Florida**
21. **Ed Bahns, 1b, Florida Southern**
22. Alvin Ruben, 1b, Lee HS, Baytown, Texas
23. **David Pencille, rhp, Cal Poly San Luis Obispo**
24. Orlando Quiroga, rhp, Pima (Ariz.) CC
25. Rick Keeler, c, DeSoto (Texas) HS
26. Steven Mobley, rhp, DeSoto (Texas) HS

June—Secondary Phase (3)

1. Hubie Brooks, of, Arizona State
2. **David Daniels, of, West Covina, Calif.**
3. Greg Moyer, of, Cerritos (Calif.) JC

CINCINNATI REDS

January—Regular Phase (23)

1. **Gregg Lorenz, lhp, Inddian Hills (Iowa) CC**
2. Jack Holmes, lhp, Temple (Texas) JC
3. David Hanna, rhp, Phoenix JC
4. **Kevin Knuth, of, Monroe (N.Y.) CC**
5. **Walter Paluch, of, Triton (Ill.) JC**
6. Mike Schultz, rhp, Yakima Valley (Wash.) JC
7. Robert Potts, of, Yakima Valley (Wash.) JC
8. Ronnie Driver, lhp, San Jacinto (Texas) JC
9. Kevin Williams, of, Edmonds (Wash.) CC
10. Norman Walker, of, San Jacinto (Texas) JC
11. Michael Gouch, rhp, Kingsborough (N.Y.) CC
12. Bob Dernier, of, Longview (Mo.) CC

January—Secondary Phase (1)

1. **Bill Scherrer, lhp, Las Vegas, Nev.**

June—Regular Phase (24)

1. **Tad Venger, 3b, Hart HS, Newhall, Calif.**
2. **Ray Corbett, c, Samuel Clemons HS, Schertz, Texas**
3. **Kevin Mulholland, lhp, Don Bosco Tech HS, Paterson, N.J.**
4. **Joe Price, lhp, Oklahoma**
5. **Jack Hudson, c, Chapman (Calif.)**
6. Kevin Shannon, c, Sharpstown HS, Houston
7. **Tom Foley, ss, Palmetto HS, Miami**
8. **Tony Walker, ss, San Marcos HS, Martindale, Texas**
9. **William Kuchar, of, Manden HS, Hamden, Conn.**
10. **Joel Willett, rhp, Aloha (Ore.) HS**
11. **Ricky Arnold, rhp, Ceres HS, Modesto, Calif.**
12. **John Halasz, of, Climax Scott HS, Scotts, Mich.**
13. **Larry Jackson, rhp, Rockledge (Fla.) HS**
14. **Chris Wells, rhp, Bellport (N.Y.) HS**
15. **Richard Lombardo, lhp, Florida Southern**
16. **Roger Glynn, lhp, Iowa Western CC**
17. **Kelly Becker, lhp, Scottsbluff (Neb.) HS**
18. Greg Korbe, of, Kansas State
19. Donald Minnick, lhp, Liberty HS, Bedford, Va.
20. **Robert Umdenstock, rhp, Lincoln HS, Des Moines, Iowa**
21. **Michael Norman, rhp, California**
22. **Greg Hughes, rhp, Sharpstown HS, Houston**
23. **Larry Jensen, rhp, Mankato State (Minn.)**
24. **Wayne Pizer, of, Tigard HS, Tualatin, Ore.**
25. **Jeff Mihlbachler, rhp, St. Anthony HS, Effingham, Ill.**
26. **Theophilus Stokes, inf, Guilford (N.C.)**
27. Daniel Flattery, rhp, St. Edmond HS, Vincent, Iowa
28. Mark Abrusley, rhp, Oakdale (La.) HS
29. Carlos Matamoras, 2b, South Miami (Fla.) HS
30. Dennis Trompeter, rhp, Northwestern
31. **Robert Morrison, 2b, St. Olaf (Minn.)**
32. Dave Perez, ss/2b, Stanford
33. Jeff Morrison, lhp, Atlantic Delray HS, Delray Beach, Fla.
34. Jeffrey Ayers, rhp, Lake Washington HS, Kirkland, Wash.
35. Olice King, lhp/1b, Bowen HS, Chicago

June—Secondary Phase (15)

1. **Robert Potts, of, Yakima Valley (Wash.) JC**
2. Blane McDonald, c, South Florida JC

CLEVELAND INDIANS

January—Regular Phase (11)

1. **Michael Elliott, lhp, West Hills (Calif.) JC**
2. Earl Robinson, of, Gulf Coast (Fla.) CC
3. **Bobby McCormick, of, Porterville (Calif.) JC**
4. **Norm Churchill, lhp, Hillsborough (Fla.) CC**
5. **Robert Costa, of, Lakeland (Ohio) CC**
6. **Kendall Driggers, rhp, Florida CC**
7. Aurelio Cadahia, 1b/c, Miami-Dade New World Center CC
8. **Donald Hubbard, 1b/3b, Seminole State (Okla.) JC**
9. Steven Robbins, 2b/3b, South Georgia JC
10. **Ernest Gibson, ss/of, South Georgia JC**

January—Secondary Phase (6)

1. Frank Ferroni, lhp, Central Arizona JC
2. Tim Knight, of, Valencia (Fla.) CC
3. Pete Alfano, rhp, Jefferson State (Ala.) JC
4. James Harris, rhp, Mississippi State
5. Thomas Underhill, rhp, Wisconsin
6. Jack Lopez, ss, Gulf Coast (Fla.) CC

June—Regular Phase (11)

1. **Bruce Compton, of, Norman (Okla.) HS**
2. **Samuel Davis, of, Jacksonville State**
3. Bret Baynham, lhp, Columbus HS, Miami
4. Michael Sanford, rhp, Childersburg (Ala.) HS
5. Tim Lollar, lhp, Arkansas
6. **Eric Wilkins, rhp, Washington State**
7. **John Dubeau, lhp, Dos Palos HS, Firebaugh, Calif.**
8. **Scott Dwyer, rhp, Eau Gallie HS, Melbourne, Fla.**
9. **Stephen McMurray, c, Polk (Fla.) CC**
10. **Albert Rausch, ss, Jacksonville**
11. **Lynn Garrett, of, Arizona**
12. **Glenn Wendt, ss, Arizona**
13. **Ricky Borchers, lhp, Southeastern Oklahoma State**
14. **Kevin Rhomberg, 3b, St. Francis (Ill.)**
15. **Jerry Dybzinski, ss, Cleveland State**
16. **Brent Hurley, of, Cuyahoga (Ohio) CC**
17. **Ben Curry, 1b, Florida State**
18. **Kenneth Rogers, rhp, Faulkner State (Ala.) JC**
19. **James Neely, rhp, Iowa Western CC**
20. **Greg Johnson, rhp, Cal State Fullerton**
21. **Tim Brill, c, St. Joseph's**
22. William Musser, rhp, Yorktown HS, Arlington, Va.
23. David Jaffe, lhp, Keppel HS, Monterey Park, Calif.
24. **Reggie Walker, 2b, Tuskegee (Ala.)**
25. Mitchell Denson, lhp, Tyler (Texas) JC
26. William Klank, rhp, Ewing HS, Trenton, N.J.
27. James Souder, rhp, Bourgade HS, Phoenix
28. **Sal Rende, 1b, St. Xavier (Ill.)**

June—Secondary Phase (16)

1. **John Shouse, inf, Tampa, Fla.**
2. **Steven Robbins, 2b/3b, South Georgia JC**

DETROIT TIGERS

January—Regular Phase (6)

1. **Raphael Hampton, of, Jackson (Mich.) CC**
2. David Witty, rhp, Yavapai (Ariz.) JC
3. John Tillema, rhp, DeAnza (Calif.) JC
4. Michael Rostas, rhp, Central Arizona JC
5. Roy Naas, rhp, Citrus (Calif.) JC
6. **Allan Bauman, lhp, Lakeland (Ohio) CC**
7. **Larry Marsh, ss, Mount San Antonio (Calif.) JC**
8. Bill Laskey, rhp, Monroe County (Mich.) CC
9. Michael Murphy, rhp, Macomb (Mich.) CC
10. **Michael Bateman, ss, Riverside (Calif.) CC**

January—Secondary Phase (10)

1. **Mike Chris, 1b, West Los Angeles JC**
2. Duane Evans, 1b, Yavapai (Ariz.) JC
3. **Larry Kowalishen, rhp, California**

June—Regular Phase (5)

1. **Kevin Richards, rhp, Roosevelt HS, Wyandotte, Mich.**
2. **Jeff Jackowiak, rhp, St. Joseph HS, South Bend, Ind.**
3. **Darrell Brown, of, Cal State Los Angeles**
4. Mark McKinney, of, Tennessee HS, Bristol, Tenn.
5. **Donald Taylor, 3b, Fair Park HS, Shreveport, La.**

6. **Dave Steffen, rhp, Flat Rock (Mich.) HS**
7. **Rick Peters, of, Arizona State**
8. **Kurt Hall, c, Cape Elizabeth (Maine) HS**
9. **John Upshaw, c, Emporia State (Kan.)**
10. **Michael Beecroft, rhp, Kennedy HS, Sacramento**
11. Bobby Supel, 3b, East Carolina
12. **Gary Armstrong, ss, San Diego State**
13. **Clifton Wilder, of, Manchville HS, Newport News, Va.**
14. **Bruce Robbins, lhp, Blackford HS, Dunkirk, Ind.**
15. **Dale Reis, lhp, UC Riverside**
16. Willie Hardwick, rhp, Berkeley (Calif.) HS
17. **John Flynn, rhp, Kings Park (N.Y.) HS**
18. Willie Lozado, ss, Thomas Jefferson HS, Brooklyn, N.Y.
19. **Joe Janton, rhp, UC Santa Barbara**
20. **Ted Dasen, 3b, Eastern Michigan**
21. **Gary Champagne, of, Northwood (Texas)**
22. **Charles Irving, rhp, Wake Forest**
23. **Bert Geiger, rhp, Palmetto HS, Miami**
24. Kevin Balogh, rhp, Toledo
25. William Crews, of, Memorial HS, Wayne, Mich.
26. Rod Hodde, 1b, Burton (Texas) HS
27. Theodore Geer, c, Park Ridge (N.J.) HS
28. **Ronnie Reasonover, of, Troy State**
29. **Juan Gomez, c, Union HS, Union City, N.J.**

June—Secondary Phase (24)

1. Bill Laskey, rhp, Monroe (N.Y.) CC
2. David Witty, rhp, Yavapai (Ariz.) JC
3. Pete Padgett, rhp, Nevada-Reno

HOUSTON ASTROS

January—Regular Phase (13)

1. Victor Walters, rhp, Miami-Dade South CC
2. **Don Harkness, ss, Lynn, Mass.**
3. Stephen McLaughlin, rhp, Cleveland State (Tenn.) CC

January—Secondary Phase (5)

1. John Butcher, rhp, Yavapai (Ariz.) JC
2. Mark Grier, c, Anne Arundel (Md.) CC

June—Regular Phase (14)

1. **Ricky Adams, ss, Montclair (Calif.) HS**
2. **Stan Leland, rhp, Wabash (Ind.) HS**
3. **Kevin Houston, lhp, Liberty (Mo.) HS**
4. Terry Byrum, ss, Madison HS, Houston
5. **Scott Loucks, of, Southeastern Oklahoma State**
6. **James MacDonald, rhp, Woodsville (N.H.) HS**
7. Steven Holman, rhp, Old Main HS, North Little Rock, Ark.
8. **George Gross, 3b, Delaware**
9. **Paul Cooper, of, Jackson State**
10. Wayne Guinn, rhp, Druid Hills HS, Decatur, Ga.
11. **Fred Morris, lhp, La Salle**
12. **Eddie Curry, lhp, Jackson State**
13. **Joseph Miller, of, Widener (Pa.)**
14. **Billy Smith, rhp, Sam Houston State**
15. Stephen Martin, rhp, Palo Verde HS, Tucson, Ariz.
16. **Charles White, rhp, DeKalb (Texas) HS**
17. Donald Robinson, rhp, Mississippi State
18. **Steven Sitek, rhp, Hot Springs (Ark.) HS**

June—Secondary Phase (19)

1. Vic Walters, rhp, Miami-Dade South CC

KANSAS CITY ROYALS

January—Regular Phase (22)

1. **Cliff Roberts, of, Brevard (Fla.) CC**
2. Jeff Musser, of, Ferrum (Va.)
3. **Robert Engelmeyer, lhp, Baltimore**
4. Brad Coxon, ss, Central Arizona JC

January—Secondary Phase (25)

1. James Funderburk, lhp, Orange Coast (Calif.) JC
2. **Mark Daly, lhp, Florida Southern**

June—Regular Phase (21)

1. **Mike Jones, lhp, Sutherland HS, Pittsford, N.Y.**
2. **Michael Morley, lhp, Eisenhower HS, Saginaw, Mich.**
3. Russ Davis, rhp, Meridian (Miss.) HS
4. **William Miller, rhp, Madison HS, Portland, Ore.**
5. **Phil Westendorf, 1b, Washington State**
6. Donald Oliver, rhp, Victoria (Texas) HS
7. **Kelly Heath, ss, Louisburg (N.C.) JC**
8. **Gerald Ako, rhp, Hawaii**
9. Bobby Bonner, ss, Texas A&M
10. **Bret Mitchell, 3b, Clay HS, South Bend, Ind.**
11. Bill Earley, lhp, Miami (Ohio)
12. **Kevin Staley, rhp, Louisburg (N.C.) JC**
13. **Elwaine Hardike, rhp, Glenbard East HS, Lombard, Ill.**
14. **Mickey Reichenbach, rhp, Texas**
15. **Geoffrey Nash, of, Arthur Hill HS, Saginaw, Mich.**
16. **Rick McGlone, c, Florida State**
17. **Dennis Webb, of, Northwest Missouri State**
18. **Culpepper Smith, c, Leesburg (Fla.) HS**
19. **Renie Martin, rhp, Richmond**
20. **Daniel Weiser, ss, Southeast Missouri State**
21. Ronn Dixon, lhp, Glenn Oaks HS, Baton Rouge, La.
22. Stephen Smith, of, Trenton (N.J.) Central HS
23. Ken Martinson, c, West HS, Billings, Mont.
24. Daniel Graham, c, Raytown (Mo.) South HS

June—Secondary Phase (22)

1. Mike Bates, rhp, Phoenix JC

LOS ANGELES DODGERS

January—Regular Phase (19)

1. Tim Gloyd, ss, Sacramento CC
2. **Jessie Daniels, 2b, Louisburg (N.C.) JC**
3. **Rocky Cordova, rhp, Sacramento CC**
4. Daniel Forer, lhp, Iowa Western CC
5. **Larry Wright, rhp, DeKalb (Ga.) JC**
6. Ronald Grout, 1b, Wingate (N.C.)
7. Randall May, rhp, Yakima Valley (Wash.) JC

January—Secondary Phase (16)

1. Mark Wychopen, c, San Jacinto (Texas) JC

June—Regular Phase (20)

1. **Bob Welch, rhp, Eastern Michigan**
2. **Joe Beckwith, rhp, Auburn**
3. **Doug Harrison, rhp, Central Michigan**
4. **John Bush, ss, Ogden (Utah) HS**
5. **Mickey Hatcher, of, Oklahoma**
6. **Mark Elliott, 1b, Silver Lake (Kan.) HS**
7. **Bobby Mitchell, of, Southern California**
8. **James Nobles, lhp, Kentucky Wesleyan**
9. **Henry Noble, ss, McIntosh Academy, Darien, Ga.**
10. **Danny Coulon, rhp, JC of the Sequoias (Calif.)**
11. **Jack Littrell, rhp, Oldham County HS, Crestwood, Ky.**
12. **Ken Likewise, lhp, Chapparal HS, Scottsdale, Ariz.**
13. Dennis Delany, c, UCLA
14. **Jerry Bass, rhp, Georgia Tech**
15. **Joe Purpura, lhp, West Leyden HS, Melrose Park, Ill.**
16. **Jesse Baez, c, Cerritos (Calif.) JC**
17. Ed Reilly, rhp, Fanwood HS, Scotch Plains, N.J.
18. Sam Favata, 2b, Edgewood HS, Baldwin Park, Calif.
19. Richard Ross, of, Santa Teresa HS, San Jose, Calif.
20. Steven Green, rhp, Pepperell HS, Rome, Ga.
21. Mike Ledna, ss, Buffalo Grove (Ill.) HS
22. **Bobby Brown, of, John Brown (Ark.)**
23. **Mitch Webster, of, Larned (Kan.) HS**
24. **Victor Woods, of, El Cerrito HS, Richmond, Calif.**
25. **Mike Zouras, 3b, Cal State Long Beach**
26. **Michael Holt, rhp, East Forsyth HS, Kernersville, N.C.**
27. Mark Jakway, of, Hemet (Calif.) HS
28. **Douglas Hogan, rhp, Mineral Area (Mo.) JC**
29. Melvin Freemen, 3b, Easley (S.C.) HS
30. Anthony Bolla, c, Crestmoor HS, San Bruno, Calif.
31. Scott Hadley, rhp, Central HS, Hinsdale, Ill.
32. Ronald Kiene, rhp, Stuyvesant HS, Brooklyn, N.Y.
33. Jeffrey Jordan, rhp, Orangeville (Ill.) HS
34. Ken Duckett, of, Reynolds HS, Winston-Salem, N.C.

35. **John Shoemaker, ss, Miami (Ohio)**
36. Tom Niedenfuer, rhp, Redmond (Wash.) HS
37. Todd Roddy, inf, Bellevue (Neb.) HS

June—Secondary Phase (17)
1. **Ron Roenicke, of, UCLA**
2. Rick Kranitz, rhp, Yavapai (Ariz.) JC
3. Kevin Williams, of/1b, Edmonds (Wash.) CC

MILWAUKEE BREWERS

January—Regular Phase (4)
1. **Daryl Bailey, rhp, Monroe (N.Y.) CC**
2. **Dale LaBar, 3b, New Castle, Del.**
3. Stephen Ibarguen, rhp, Panola (Texas) JC
4. **Richard Nicholson, rhp, St. Petersburg, Fla.**

January—Secondary Phase (4)
1. **Steve Splitt, of, UCLA**
2. **Larry Edwards, lhp, Allegany (Md.) CC**
3. Steven Winfield, rhp, Panola (Texas) JC

June—Regular Phase (3)
1. **Paul Molitor, ss, Minnesota**
2. **Kevin Bass, of, Menlo HS, Menlo Park, Calif.**
3. **Stan Davis, 1b, Halifax HS, Nathalie, Va.**
4. **Jerry Jenkins, rhp, Royal HS, Simi Valley, Calif.**
5. Michael Breslin, rhp, Bellaire HS, Houston
6. **Bill Foley, c, Clemson**
7. Alan Page, 1b, Menlo HS, Redwood City, Calif.
8. **Steve Day, ss, Texas**
9. **Chris Carstensen, of, Cal State Los Angeles**
10. **Dave LaPoint, lhp, Glens Falls (N.Y.) HS**
11. **Mike Henderson, ss, Arizona State**
12. **Steve Manderfield, lhp, Kimball HS, Royal Oak, Mich.**
13. **John Skorochocki, ss, Trenton (N.J.) HS**
14. **Joe Bob Mitchell, of, Prairie View A&M**
15. **Richard Bross, lhp, Tonawanda (N.Y.) HS**
16. Larry Groves, rhp/of, Shawnee Mission West HS, Overland Park, Kan.
17. **Tim Jordan, of, Edward Little HS, Auburn, Maine**
18. Dave Hudgens, 1b, Arizona State
19. Ron Pisel, rhp, Southeastern Illinois JC
20. **Brian Fisher, ss, Tonawanda (N.Y.) HS**
21. Charles Beverly, rhp, Kelly HS, Wise, Va.
22. Chris Bando, c, Arizona State
23. Larry Reasonover, 3b, Gulf Coast (Fla.) CC

June—Secondary Phase (14)
1. **Ron Driver, lhp, San Jacinto (Texas) JC**
2. Curt Reade, rhp, Hancock (Calif.) JC

MINNESOTA TWINS

January—Regular Phase (16)
1. **Lance Hallberg, ss, San Bernardino Valley (Calif.) JC**
2. Craig Kornfeld, ss, Miami-Dade North CC
3. **Stan Cannon, of, Pensacola (Fla.) JC**
4. **Dean Moranda, lhp, Fresno (Calif.) CC**
5. **Tim Savage, c, San Bernardino Valley (Calif.) JC**
6. Russell Fowler, 2b, San Diego Mesa (Calif.) JC
7. Brad Lesley, rhp, Merced (Calif.) JC
8. Everett Rey, c, San Joaquin Delta (Calif.) JC
9. Richard Holloway, rhp, Gulf Coast (Fla.) CC
10. Casey Hagan, lhp, Los Angeles Harbor JC
11. **Mark Clapham, rhp, North Carolina State**
12. Manuel Adams, of/c, Fresno CC
13. Dale Adair, inf, Mount San Antonio (Calif.) JC
14. David Free, rhp, San Diego Mesa (Calif.) JC
15. Russ Penfold, lhp, Cypress (Calif.) JC
16. Brad Mills, 3b/1b, JC of the Sequoias (Calif.)

January—Secondary Phase (21)
1. Mike Walters, rhp, Chaffey (Calif.) JC
2. Greg Stahl, ss, Los Angeles Harbor JC
3. Greg Moyer, of, Cerritos (Calif.) JC
4. Tom Costello, rhp, Oregon State

June—Regular Phase (15)
1. **Paul Croft, of, Morristown (N.J.) HS**
2. **Bart Nieuwenhuis, lhp, Tombstone HS, Huachuca City, Ariz.**
3. **Roger Erickson, rhp, New Orleans**
4. **Kevin McWhirter, of, San Diego State**
5. Rich Bordi, rhp, El Camino HS, San Francisco
6. **Steve Herz, c, Cal State Fullerton**
7. Tom Jagiela, c, Minnesota
8. Eduardo Rodriguez, ss/2b, Miami HS
9. **Darrell Jackson, lhp, Arizona State**
10. **George Slembecker, ss, Overlea HS, Baltimore**
11. Mark Mauer, c, Harding HS, St. Paul, Minn.
12. **Jose Rodriguez, ss, Flushing HS, Corono, N.Y.**
13. **Steve McManaman, of, Nebraska**
14. **Gary Hall, c, Columbus (Ga.)**
15. **Gary Adair, of, Cal State Los Angeles**
16. **Michael O'Connor, lhp, St. John's**
17. **Rick Cyburt, ss, Rider**
18. **Scott Ullger, ss, St. John's**
19. **Ken Angulo, lhp/of, Edgewood HS, West Covina, Calif.**
20. **Rubio Malone, lhp, Compton (Calif.) HS**
21. Anthony Torrez, rhp, Lemoore (Calif.) HS
22. Jim David, ss, Bishop Diego HS, Santa Barbara, Calif.
23. Curt Burkhead, rhp, Crawford HS, San Diego
24. **Eugene Robinson, rhp, New Orleans**
25. **Timothy Loberg, of/inf, Minnesota**
26. **Joseph Bennett, 2b, New Orleans**
27. **Abner Johnson, rhp, Creighton**
28. **Charles Aldridge, rhp, Las Vegas HS**
29. **Joseph Tarver, ss, Arvin (Calif.) HS**
30. Dominic Perry, 2b, Gahr HS, Lakewood, Calif.
31. Robert Crissman, ss, Gahr HS, Cerritos, Calif.
32. David Montanari, 2b, Santa Monica (Calif.) HS
33. Floyd Brennecke, ss, Azusa Pacific (Calif.)
34. **Dwight Lewis, rhp, Cal State Fullerton**
35. **Gary Bishop, 1b/of, Maryland**
36. **Jeff Brueggemann, rhp, Stetson**
37. Glenn Cupstid, of, Windsor Forest HS, Savannah, Ga.
38. David Fowke, 2b, Brandon (Fla.) HS

June—Secondary Phase (1)
1. Frank Ferroni, lhp, Central Arizona JC
2. **Gary Bozich, 2b, St. Petersburg (Fla.) JC**

MONTREAL EXPOS

January—Regular Phase (1)
1. Calvin Adams, c/3b, Central Arizona JC
2. **Robert Sagers, inf/of, Cincinnati**
3. Christian Loeffler, c, Wharton County (Texas) JC
4. Clifford Mackey, lhp, Linn-Benton (Ore.) CC
5. Michael Hobbs, of, Southeastern (N.C.) CC
6. William Eady, rhp, Temple (Texas) JC
7. Dan Firova, c, Beeville (Texas) JC
8. **Richard Heidorn, ss, Ohio State**
9. David Waddell, rhp, Trinidad State (Colo.) JC
10. Michael Mann, rhp, St. Clair County (Mich.) CC
11. **Gregory Cox, rhp, Cincinnati**
12. Gregory Charzanowski, ss, St. Clair County (Mich.) CC

January—Secondary Phase (22)
1. Allen Pye, lhp, DeKalb (Ga.) JC

June—Regular Phase (2)
1. **Bill Gullickson, rhp, Joliet Catholic HS, Orland Park, Ill.**
2. **Greg Staffon, rhp, Hawthorne (Calif.) HS**
3. **Scott Sanderson, rhp, Vanderbilt**
4. **Scott Anderson, rhp, Oregon State**
5. **Tim Raines, ss, Seminole HS, Sanford, Fla.**
6. Chris Day, lhp, Sharpstown HS, Houston
7. **David Hall, of, Rollins (Fla.)**
8. **Bruce McAllister, ss, Rollins (Fla.)**
9. **Thomas Haggerty, 1b, Maryvale HS, Phoenix**
10. Ronald Brower, 1b, Appalachian State
11. **Don Simmons, ss/2b, Osborne HS, Marietta, Ga.**

12. **Jeff Roberts, c, Newark (Ohio) Catholic HS**
13. **Randy Trumbull, rhp, Taft HS, Hamilton, Ohio**
14. **John Treadway, 1b, Jacksonville State**
15. **Daniel Morgan, rhp, Minnesota**
16. **Mark Steenken, c, Northern Kentucky**
17. **Steve King, lhp, Middletown (Ohio) JC**
18. **John Willis, rhp, Kecoughtan HS, Hampton, Va.**
19. Rob Pietroburgo, lhp, Missouri
20. **Harvey Kuenn, 1b, Central HS, Milwaukee**
21. **Tommy Joe Shimp, rhp, Rose State (Okla.) JC**
22. **Walter Coppol, lhp, Claymont (Del.) HS**
23. **Tom Steinmetz, 2b, Iowa**
24. Michael Kelly, of, Cordova HS, Rancho Cordova, Calif.
25. **Richard Phillips, of/1b, Kentucky State**
26. **Tony Johnson, of, LeMoyne-Owen (Tenn.)**
27. **Dave Hensil, c/1b, Illinois**
28. **Jeff Wilson, rhp, Cincinnati**
29. Michael Ruelas, rhp, Alvin (Texas) HS

June—Secondary Phase (10)

1. **Calvin Adams, of/3b, Central Arizona JC**

NEW YORK METS

January—Regular Phase (15)

1. David Sullivan, c, Yavapai (Ariz.) JC
2. **Robert Rossen, of, St. Petersburg (Fla.) JC**
3. Donald Hess, c, Lamar (Colo.) CC
4. David Vickers, rhp, Lamar (Colo.) CC
5. John Hessler, rhp, Crowder (Mo.) JC
6. William Wrightson, 1b, DeAnza (Calif.) JC
7. Randall Cashore, rhp, Butte (Calif.) JC

January—Secondary Phase (3)

1. Ronald Lee, ss, Blinn (Texas) JC
2. Brian Hurse, rhp, Florida CC
3. Michael Matlock, rhp/3b, Concordia (Ala.) JC
4. Anthony Guralas, ss/1b, Cuesta (Calif.) JC

June—Regular Phase (16)

1. **Wally Backman, ss, Aloha HS, Beaverton, Ore.**
2. **Mookie Wilson, of, South Carolina**
3. Steve McQueen, ss, Fernandina Beach (Fla.) HS
4. **Ray Lewis, c, Southern**
5. **Alfredo Martinez, rhp, Cal State Los Angeles**
6. **Brent Gaff, rhp, Churubusco (Ind.) HS**
7. **William Chamberlain, of, Wilson HS, Long Beach, Calif.**
8. **Jeff Franklin, rhp, South Carroll HS, Mount Airy, Md.**
9. **Randy Bozeman, rhp, Thomasville (Ga.) Central HS**
10. **August Garrett, of, Locust Valley (N.Y.) HS**
11. Jean Donalaya, rhp, El Camino HS, San Francisco
12. **Stephen Golden, rhp, Paulding County HS, Rockmart, Ga.**
13. **Robert Healy, ss, Cal State Hayward**
14. **Herbert Kizer, 1b, Georgia Tech**
15. **Michael Supczenski, of, Wilkes (Pa.)**
16. Michael Foster, lhp, Atwater (Calif.) HS
17. **Ron MacDonald, 2b, Kansas**
18. **Scott Allen, rhp, Mercer**
19. Craig Chamberlain, rhp, Long Beach CC
20. **James Olinger, rhp, St. Edward's HS, Elgin, Ill.**
21. Dan Gausepohl, of, Long Beach (Calif.) CC
22. **William Nafziger, c, Woodland (Calif.) HS**
23. **Michael Lowry, rhp, Madera (Calif.) HS**
24. Jack Lambeth, lhp, Hillcrest HS, Springfield, Mo.
25. Chris Wilmes, 3b, St. Dominic HS, O'Fallon, Mo.
26. **Doug Mizzi, lhp, Hicksville (N.Y.) HS**
27. **Henri Jones, of, Iowa State**
28. Mike McCain, ss, Edmonds (Wash.) HS
29. **Greg Charleston, ss, Florida CC**
30. **Duane Howard, rhp/of, Wichita, Kan.**
31. **Michael Brown, of, Southern Illinois-Edwardsville**
32. Sean Mays, ss, Dublin (Calif.) HS
33. Brad Jordison, lhp, Hillcrest HS, Sandy, Utah
34. Richard Finn, lhp, Northeast HS, St. Petersburg, Fla.
35. Mark Raust, 1b, Campbell (Calif.) HS

June—Secondary Phase (25)

1. **Allen Pye, lhp, DeKalb (Ga.) JC**
2. Bud Black, lhp, Lower Columbia (Wash.) JC

NEW YORK YANKEES

January—Regular Phase (24)

1. Robert Moncur, of, Utah Technical JC
2. **Eddie Mickelsen, ss, Snow (Utah) JC**
3. Peter Padgett, rhp, Nevada-Reno
4. James Harper, rhp, Los Medanos (Calif.) JC
5. **Jeffrey Thornton, of, Scottsdale (Ariz.) CC**

January—Secondary Phase (15)

1. **Willie McGee, of, Diablo Valley (Calif.) JC**

June—Regular Phase (23)

1. **Steve Taylor, rhp, Delaware**
2. Jeff White, c, Bryan Station HS, Lexington, Ky.
3. **Joe Lefebvre, of, Eckerd (Fla.)**
4. **Roger Holt, ss, Florida**
5. **Buck Showalter, of, Mississippi State**
6. Michael Ickowski, rhp, Kennedy HS, Cheektowage, N.Y.
7. Erik Hendricks, rhp, Chapman (Calif.)
8. **Pat Callahan, c, Miami**
9. **Jamie Werly, rhp, Harvard**
10. Chuck Hensley, lhp, Tulare (Calif.) Union HS
11. **Daniel Moroff, 3b, Valencia (Fla.) CC**
12. **Paul Semall, rhp, Ohio State**
13. Andy Marston, of/rhp, Dunedin (Fla.) HS
14. **John Farrior, c, Jesuit HS, Tampa**
15. **Rowland Keys, 2b, Rollins (Fla.)**
16. Gerald Weller, 1b/of, Michigan State
17. **Kenny Baker, of, Wake Forest**
18. **Kevin Murphy, 1b/of, Bates (Maine)**
19. **Mike McLeod, rhp, Florida State**
20. **Dan Schmitz, 2b, Eastern Michigan**
21. **Chris Welsh, lhp, South Florida**
22. Morris Schrimsher, rhp, Florida CC
23. **Thomas Bonfield, 1b, St. Leo (Fla.)**
24. Juan Bonilla, 2b, Florida State (Selection voided)
25. **Ron Hess, inf, Iowa**
26. **Gene Laguna, 3b, Seton Hall**
27. **Stan Saleski, rhp, Eckerd (Fla.)**

June—Secondary Phase (11)

1. **Byron Ballard, rhp, Miami-Dade North CC**
2. Jack Lazorko, rhp, Mississippi State

OAKLAND ATHLETICS

January—Regular Phase (18)

1. **Dennis Wyszynski, rhp, Mercer County (N.J.) CC**
2. **Pat Dempsey, c, Columbia State (Tenn.) CC**
3. Doug Hunt, rhp, Taft (Calif.) JC
4. William Haley, p, Solano (Calif.) CC
5. Larry Adams, rhp, Southern California (Selection voided)
6. Robert Bradford, rhp, Yavapai (Ariz.) JC
7. James Evans, lhp, Santa Monica (Calif.) JC
8. Michael Boyd, of, Los Angeles Pierce JC
9. Ricky Allen, of, Southwestern (Calif.) JC

January—Secondary Phase (2)

1. Hubie Brooks, ss/of, Mesa (Ariz.) CC
2. **Thomas Eagan, 3b, Green River (Wash.) CC**
3. Kevin Darst, 2b, Solano (Calif.) CC
4. Preston Banks, 3b, Southwestern (Calif.) JC

June—Regular Phase (17)

1. **Craig Harris, rhp, Buena HS, Sierra Vista, Ariz.**
2. Keith Creel, rhp, Duncanville (Texas) HS
3. **Mike Davis, of, Hoover HS, San Diego**
4. **Dana Berry, 1b, Morgantown (W.Va.) HS**
5. Willie Davis, of, Jefferson HS, Portland, Ore.
6. **Dave Beard, rhp, Sequoyah HS, Chamblee, Ga.**
7. **Scott Inbach, lhp, Chaparral HS, Las Vegas**
8. Bill Repass, c, T.C. Roberson HS, Arden, N.C.
9. Jay Erdahl, of, Lincoln HS, Seattle
10. **Robert Markham, 1b, Porterville (Calif.) JC**
11. **Leroy Robbins, of, Kentucky**
12. **Ted Nowakowski, c, SUNY Farmingdale JC**

13. **Jeff Jones, rhp, Bowling Green State**
14. **Paul Mize, ss, Hawaii**
15. Maury Ornest, 1b, Beverly Hills (Calif.) HS
16. Michael Munns, rhp, JC of Southern Idaho
17. David Curran, rhp, Pepperdine
18. David Malloy, lhp, Heightstown HS, East Winsor, N.J.
19. Kerry Sabo, rhp, West Geauga HS, Chesterland, Ohio
20. Edward Long, rhp, Fairfax HS, Los Angeles
21. **Dan Donovan, c, Morris Harvey (W.Va.)**
22. Steve Shields, ss/rhp, Ranger (Texas) JC
23. **Rob Klebba, 2b, Pepperdine**
24. Michael Campbell, 3b, North Mesquite (Texas) HS
25. **Shooty Babitt, inf, Berkeley (Calif.) HS**
26. Harold Washington, of, Manual Arts HS, Los Angeles
27. Rondal Rollin, of, Carson (Calif.) HS
28. Ron Nickerson, 3b, Jordan HS, Los Angeles
29. Harry Brown, rhp, San Bernardino (Calif.) HS
30. David McClain, ss/3b, JC of the Canyons (Calif.)
31. Mendez Davis, of, Centennial HS, Los Angeles
32. Gary Aguirre, ss, Foothill HS, Bakersfield, Calif.
33. Michael Davis, ss/of, Compton, Calif.
34. **Mike Yesenchak, lhp, Canon McMillan HS, Canonsburg, Pa.**
35. Stephen Dicarlo, rhp, Revere (Mass.) HS
36. Tom Riley, ss, Blanchet HS, Seattle
37. Joe Madrigal, rhp, Ganesha HS, Pomona, Calif.

June—Secondary Phase (5)

1. Richard Holloway, rhp, Gulf Coast (Fla.) CC
2. **Jack Holmes, lhp, Temple (Texas) JC**
3. Dave Morgan, 3b, Fresno (Calif.) CC
4. Michael Mann, rhp, St. Clair County (Mich.) CC
5. **Frederick Lund, rhp, Sacramento CC**
6. Rob Dondero, rhp, Mesa (Ariz.) CC

PHILADELPHIA PHILLIES

January—Regular Phase (21)

1. Michael Childs, c, Ranger (Texas) JC
2. Byron Ballard, rhp, Miami-Dade North CC
3. Doug Laufer, rhp, Paris (Texas) JC
4. **Armando Abreu, lhp, Newark, N.J.**
5. Eddie Bonine, rhp, Mesa (Ariz.) CC
6. **Gary Mitchell, rhp, Holyoke (Mass.) CC**
7. Ernest Lee, of/ss, Ranger (Texas) JC
8. Scott Job, rhp, JC of Southern Idaho
9. John Freed, rhp, Miami-Dade South CC
10. Eric Snider, rhp/c, Diablo Valley (Calif.) JC
11. David Labrum, rhp, JC of Southern Idaho

January—Secondary Phase (9)

1. **John Lohse, 3b, Butte (Calif.) JC**
2. Ray Mass, rhp, Bellevue (Wash.) CC
3. Tony Dorsey, of/2b, Fort Worth, Texas

June—Regular Phase (22)

1. **Scott Munninghoff, rhp, Purcell HS, Cincinnati**
2. **Earl Neal, 1b, San Bernardino (Calif.) HS**
3. **Andres Romero, of/1b, Miami HS**
4. **George Vukovich, of, Southern Illinois**
5. **Keith Washington, of, Atlantic HS, Boynton Beach, Fla.**
6. **John Quijada, ss, Trevor Browne HS, Phoenix**
7. **Robert Volkerding, of, Central HS, Cape Girardeau, Mo.**
8. **Gregory Moore, rhp, East Bakersfield (Calif.) HS**
9. **Ronald Smith, ss, Furman**
10. Lawrence Davila, rhp, Key West (Fla.) HS
11. **Michael Pace, of, Oklahoma**
12. **John Daynor, 1b/of, Bradley**
13. **Steve Swain, of, Redondo HS, Redondo Beach, Calif.**
14. **Collin Sullivan, of, Christian Brothers HS, Sacramento**
15. Martin Little, rhp, Ashe Central HS, West Jefferson, N.C.
16. **Ernest Gause, lhp, Kingstree HS, Georgetown, S.C.**
17. Roger Godwin, rhp, Fernandina Beach (Fla.) HS
18. **Tom Lombarski, ss, Livingston (N.J.) HS**
19. Gregory DeHart, rhp, North Hollywood (Calif.) HS
20. **Greg Walker, c, Coffee HS, Douglas, Ga.**
21. **Anthony Capps, c, Jacksonville (N.C.) HS**
22. **Jerry Reed, rhp, Western Carolina**
23. **Dennis Becker, rhp, Saint Louis**
24. Tim Geddes, rhp, Quartz Hill (Calif.) HS
25. **Wally Goff, lhp, William Penn HS, Bear, Del.**
26. **Steve Curry, inf, Scottsdale (Ariz.) JC**
27. **Jose Castro, ss, Jackson HS, Miami**
28. Jim Adduci, of, Brother Rice HS, Oaklawn, Ill.
29. **Stuart Miller, c, Portola (Calif.) HS**
30. **Edward Cuervo, c/2b, Angelina (Texas) JC**
31. Kerry Nash, rhp, Miami-Dade South CC
32. Randy Wroten, of, Novi HS, Northville, Mich.
33. **Chris Bouchee, of, Des Plaines, Ill.**

June—Secondary Phase (6)

1. **Aurelio Cadahia, 1b/c, Miami-Dade New World Center CC**

PITTSBURGH PIRATES

January—Regular Phase (17)

1. **Tom Fiesthumel, lhp, Utica, N.Y.**
2. **Randy Cooney, lhp, Austin, Pa.**
3. Joe Kubit, of, Valencia (Fla.) CC
4. Mark Endriss, 2b, Central Arizona JC
5. **Robert Ferguson, lhp, Point Park (Pa.)**
6. Joel Pyfrom, rhp, Miami-Dade South CC

January—Secondary Phase (18)

1. **Paul Rudiman, rhp, Lanham, Md.**
2. David Banes, ss, Manatee (Fla.) JC
3. Timothy Newtson, c, Mesa (Ariz.) CC

June—Regular Phase (18)

1. **Anthony Nicely, of, Meadowdale HS, Dayton, Ohio**
2. **Mike Pill, rhp, Edgewood HS, West Covina, Calif.**
3. **Lance Dodd, rhp, Atholton HS, Laurel, Md.**
4. **Stew Cliburn, rhp, Delta State (Miss.)**
5. **Jim Poff, of, Workman HS, Covina, Calif.**
6. Randy Smith, rhp, Childersburg (Ala.) HS
7. **Charles Powell, lhp, Fullerton (Calif.) HS**
8. **Paul Moore, of, Fort Chiswell HS, Maxmeadows, Va.**
9. **Michael Shoaf, lhp, Carson City (Nev.) HS**
10. **Phillip Cyburt, lhp, Brea (Calif.) Olinda HS**
11. **Rick Lancellotti, of, Glassboro State (N.J.)**
12. Wayne Tolleson, ss, Western Carolina
13. Mike Davis, 2b, Parker HS, Janesville, Wis.
14. **Gerald Busby, rhp, Chapparal HS, North Las Vegas, Nev.**
15. **Ben Wiltbank, rhp, CC of Baltimore**
16. Mark Beuclear, rhp, Dickinson (Texas) HS
17. Mark Gray, 2b/ss, Gallatin HS, Warshaw, Ky.
18. Dennis Rasmussen, lhp, Bear Creek HS, Lakewood, Colo.
19. **Wendell Hibbett, of, Texas**
20. **Casey Clark, ss, San Diego**
21. Robert Shelton, rhp/c, Gretna HS, Hunt, Va.
22. Lawrence Dotson, of, San Bernardino (Calif.) HS
23. **Jessie Jones, c, Jackson State**
24. Ronald Thurston, c, Wilson HS, Long Beach
25. Fulton Walker, of, Martinsburg (W.Va.) HS
26. Mark Haley, c, Cabrillo HS, Lompoc, Calif.
27. Kurt Kingsolver, c, Long Beach CC
28. Marvin Fowler, rhp, Madison HS, San Diego
29. Paul Doty, rhp, Santana HS, Santee, Calif.
30. **Chick Valley, 1b/lhp, San Diego State**
31. **Edward Baker, 2b, DeKalb (Ga.) CC**
32. Michael Ferguson, rhp, Northview HS, Covina, Calif.
33. Robert Wicks, rhp, Amador HS, Pleasanton, Calif.
34. William Metil, 3b, Northgate HS, Bellevue, Pa.
35. **Timothy Ganch, 1b, Point Park (Pa.)**
36. **George Hill, of, Virginia Tech**
37. **Steven Hawes, c, Tennessee Wesleyan**
38. Rick Witt, 3b, Spokane (Wash.) CC

June—Secondary Phase (2)

1. Bill Springman, 2b, Oral Roberts
2. **Michael Selwood, 3b/c, Golden West (Calif.) JC**
3. Michael Childs, c, Ranger (Texas) JC
4. **Casey Hagan, lhp, Los Angeles Harbor JC**

ST. LOUIS CARDINALS

January—Regular Phase (5)

1. Curt Reade, rhp, Hancock (Calif.) JC
2. Rob Dondero, rhp, Mesa (Ariz.) CC
3. Rick Kranitz, rhp, Yavapai (Ariz.) JC
4. **Ty Waller, 3b, San Diego CC**
5. Randy Wiens, rhp, Merced (Calif.) JC (Selection voided)
6. Randy Evans, rhp, Central Arizona JC
7. Jesse Orosco, lhp, Santa Barbara (Calif.) CC
8. Greg Dees, c, San Bernardino (Calif.) JC
9. James Harskamp, ss, Merced (Calif.) JC
10. Terry Mixon, 2b, DeKalb South (Ga.) CC

January—Secondary Phase (7)

1. **Randy Puckett, ss, Reedley (Calif.) JC**
2. Larry Navilhon, rhp, JC of San Mateo (Calif.)
3. James Snyder, of/1b, St. Clair County (Mich.) CC

June—Regular Phase (6)

1. **Terry Kennedy, c, Florida State**
2. Ricky Wright, lhp, Paris (Texas) HS
3. **Joe DeSa, 1b, Damien HS, Honolulu**
4. **Jim Gott, of/rhp, San Marino (Calif.) HS**
5. **Andy Rincon, rhp, St. Paul HS, Pico Rivera, Calif.**
6. **Jeff Doyle, ss, Oregon State**
7. **Donald Moore, rhp, El Camino Real HS, Woodland Hills, Calif.**
8. **Leroy Grossini, ss, Santa Barbara (Calif.) CC**
9. **Randy Howell, of, Furman**
10. Tom Heckman, rhp, Helias HS, Jefferson City, Mo.
11. **Tom Chamberlain, rhp, Oregon State**
12. Stan Younger, of, Santa Monica (Calif.) HS
13. Don Tracey, rhp, Yonkers (N.Y.) HS
14. **Tom Vasche, rhp, Corvallis (Ore.) HS**
15. **Kelly Miller, ss, Elon**
16. **Jim Reeves, of, Southern Illinois**
17. **Richard Murray, 3b, Southern Illinois**
18. Paul Grame, rhp, Los Altos (Calif.) HS
19. **Mark David, of, Houston**
20. Kernan Ronan, rhp, Brophy Prep HS, Phoenix
21. **Brooks Whitehead, lhp, Westmont**
22. **Rick Cheshire, c, Middle Tennessee State**
23. Floyd Chiffer, rhp, UCLA
24. Charles Montgomery, rhp, Chipola (Fla.) JC
25. **Barry Cheesman, c, Galesburg (Ill.) HS**
26. **Darnell Barnett, of, Cal State Los Angeles**
27. **Richard Hay, rhp, Lower Dauphin HS, Middletown, Pa.**
28. **Dennis Morton, lhp, Helix HS, Lemon Grove, Calif.**
29. John Cherney, rhp, Los Angeles Pierce JC
30. Mike Jeffcoat, lhp, Pine Bluff (Ark.) HS
31. **Dennis Cirbo, c, Colorado**
32. **Neil Fiala, inf, Southern Illinois**
33. Otis Metz, of, New Rochelle (N.Y.) HS
34. Kenneth Erickson, rhp, Glendora (Calif.) HS
35. **Jimmy Hickman, of, Newberry (S.C.)**
36. **Vaughn Yadao, lhp, McKinney HS, Honolulu**
37. Steve Lane, lhp, Vanderbilt
38. **Joe Baciotti, of, West Chester (Pa.)**
39. Richard Stewart, lhp, Fillmore (Calif.) HS
40. **William Thomas, rhp, Kecoughtan HS, Hampton, Va.**
41. **Jerry Poston, 1b/of, South Alabama**
42. Deron Thomas, inf, McCluer HS, Ferguson, Mo.

June—Secondary Phase (12)

1. Simon Glenn, of, Blinn (Texas) JC
2. Greg Pastors, inf, Yavapai (Ariz.) JC
3. **Michael Rostas, rhp, Central Arizona JC**
4. **Randall Bonner, c, Marietta, Ga.**

SAN DIEGO PADRES

January—Regular Phase (7)

1. **Kevin Chapman, rhp, Mount San Antonio (Calif.) JC**
2. **James Haight, lhp, Wilmington (Del.)**
3. Michael Bungarz, lhp, Chabot (Calif.) JC
4. Mark Boggs, rhp, Cleveland State (Tenn.) CC

January—Secondary Phase (20)

1. Frank Araneo, rhp, Valencia (Fla.) CC

June—Regular Phase (8)

1. **Brian Greer, of, Sonora HS, Brea, Calif.**
2. **Barry Evans, ss, West Georgia**
3. Rick Foley, rhp, Santa Clara
4. **Ozzie Smith, ss, Cal Poly San Luis Obispo**
5. **James Stehle, lhp, Wilkes (Pa.)**
6. Nick Harsh, rhp, Mater Dei HS, Santa Ana, Calif.
7. **Michael Vint, rhp, Granite Hills HS, El Cajon, Calif.**
8. **Troy Dixon, rhp, Leuzinger HS, Hawthorne, Calif.**
9. **Bob Blakley, of, Southwest Missouri State**
10. **Ron Tingley, of, Ramona HS, Riverside, Calif.**
11. **John Yandle, lhp, Stanford**
12. **George Hahn, c, Santa Clara**
13. **John Alvarez, 3b, Cal State Fullerton**
14. **Joe Carroll, rhp, Tulsa**
15. **Eric Mustad, rhp, Cal State Fullerton**
16. **Frank Hardy, 1b, Cal State Long Beach**
17. **Eric Clark, of, Hoover HS, San Diego**
18. **Curtis Reed, ss, Joliet (Ill.) West HS**
19. **John Almon, of, Rhode Island College**
20. **Gary Pickert, lhp, Emporia State (Kan.)**
21. **Larry Bowie, c, Jacksonville State**
22. **Gary Ashby, 1b, Texas Tech**
23. Gary Weiss, 2b, Houston
24. **Glynn Tschirhart, ss/2b, St. Mary's (Texas)**
25. **Bob Sherwood, rhp, Washington State**
26. **William Wesserman, lhp, Glassboro State (N.J.)**
27. Harley Woody, lhp, Lookout Valley HS, Tiftonia, Tenn.
28. Rob Hertel, 2b, Southern California

June—Secondary Phase (21)

No selection

SAN FRANCISCO GIANTS

January—Regular Phase (9)

1. **Gareth Ledbetter, c, Santa Ana (Calif.) JC**
2. Lyle Brackenridge, ss, Pasadena (Calif.) CC
3. Bud Black, lhp, Lower Columbia (Wash.) JC
4. Randy Meyer, rhp, Mount Hood (Ore.) CC
5. Jeff Evans, inf, Golden West (Calif.) JC
6. Dennis Gonsalves, rhp, El Camino (Calif.) JC
7. Jeff Lahti, rhp, Treasure Valley (Ore.) CC
8. Jay Pettibone, rhp, Fullerton (Calif.) JC
9. **Bart Bass, rhp, San Diego**
10. Dave Morgan, 3b, Fresno (Calif.) CC

January—Secondary Phase (24)

1. Mike Bates, rhp, Phoenix JC
2. Jeff Ahern, lhp, Arizona Western JC
3. Stephen Youngman, 1b, Trenton State (N.J.)

June—Regular Phase (10)

1. **Craig Landis, ss, Vintage HS, Napa, Calif.**
2. **Phil Huffman, rhp, Brazoswood HS, Lake Jackson, Texas**
3. **Mike Fox, ss, Fontana (Calif.) HS**
4. **Darnell Baker, of/c, Bishop Gibbon HS, Schenectady, N.Y.**
5. Jon Reelhorn, rhp, Edison HS, Stockton, Calif.
6. **Scott Budner, lhp, Eastern Connecticut State**
7. **George Torassa, c, St. Ignatius HS, San Francisco**
8. **Louis Marietta, rhp, St. Bonaventure HS, Ventura, Calif.**
9. **Glenn Goya, 1b, Colorado State**
10. Larry Fobbs, inf, Southern California
11. **Chili Davis, of, Dorsey HS, Los Angeles**
12. **Bob Tufts, lhp, Princeton**
13. Ron Batter, c, JC of San Mateo (Calif.)
14. **Bob Kearney, c, Texas**
15. Jim Farr, lhp, Penn State
16. **Jeff Stadler, rhp, Mission Bay HS, Pacific Beach, Calif.**
17. Daryl Adams, rhp, Willows (Calif.) HS
18. Norm Christensen, rhp, Claremont HS, San Diego
19. Joseph Ward, of, Florida (Selection voided)

20. Ricky Horton, lhp, Roosevelt HS, Hyde Park, N.Y.
21. James Keyte, lhp, Verdugo Hills HS, Tujunga, Calif.
22. Albert Ward, rhp, Escambia HS, Pensacola, Fla.
23. Steve Espinoza, ss, Los Altos HS, Mountainview, Calif.
24. Joe Lentsch, c, Creighton
25. Weston Mitchell, ss, Campbell (Calif.) HS
26. Dan Siler, lhp, Shoreline (Wash.) CC
27. Rodney Hudson, c, Portland State

June—Secondary Phase (4)

1. **John Fenwick, ss, Anoka, Minn.**
2. Dave Hostetler, 1b, Southern California

SEATTLE MARINERS

January—Regular Phase (25)

1. **Paul Givens, lhp, Fresno (Calif.) CC**
2. **Mark Schuster, 1b, Central Arizona JC**
3. **Jeff Cary, rhp, Pensacola (Fla.) JC**
4. Dan Townsend, of, Yavapai (Ariz.) JC
5. **Alphonso Eiland, of/ss, Palomar (Calif.) JC**
6. Don Keener, 3b, Chipola (Fla.) JC
7. Glen Moon, of, Santa Monica (Calif.) JC
8. Porter Wyatt, of, Palomar (Calif.) JC
9. Michael Tice, of, DeKalb South (Ga.) CC
10. **James Hall, 2b/ss, Los Angeles, Calif.**

January—Secondary Phase (26)

1. Dom Antonini, c, Glassboro State (N.J.)
2. **John Evans, 1b, Los Angeles Harbor JC**

June—Regular Phase (26)

1. **Dave Henderson, of, Dos Palos (Calif.) HS**
2. **Henry Bender, c, Wilson HS, Tacoma, Wash.**
3. **Bud Anderson, rhp, Rutgers**
4. **Kyle Koke, ss, South Grand Prairie (Texas) HS**
5. **Ron Musselman, rhp, Clemson**
6. **Tony Cameron, lhp, Pepperdine**
7. **Michael Moore, 1b, Davis HS, Yakima, Wash.**
8. **Rodney Hobbs, of, Renton HS, Seattle**
9. **Tracy Harris, rhp, Washington State**
10. John Haley, of, Anacortes (Wash.) HS
11. Bill Latham, lhp, Huffman HS, Birmingham
12. **Karl Best, rhp, Kent Meridian HS, Kent, Wash.**
13. **Mark Oestreich, of, Florida International**
14. **Tim Hallgren, rhp, Adams HS, Clarkston, Wash.**
15. **Greg Biercevicz, rhp, Connecticut**
16. Tony Phillips, ss, Roswell (Ga.) HS
17. **James Knight, lhp, Hillsborough (Fla.) CC**
18. **Loyd Ard, rhp, Florida International**
19. **Al Weston, of, Michigan State**
20. **Gary McDonnell, 2b, Nicholls State**
21. **Larry Patterson, 3b, Gonzaga**
22. **Calvin King, ss, Southern-New Orleans**
23. Rick Ramos, rhp, Lewis (Ill.)
24. Thomas Bloemke, rhp, Missouri
25. Jack Hills, lhp, Cal State Los Angeles
26. **Scott Miller, of, South Florida**
27. Del Curtis, of, Central Arizona JC
28. Larry Eiler, lhp, Arizona State
29. Rick Santarone, c, Cherry Hill (N.J.) HS
30. **Tom Fitzgerald, rhp, Florida International**
31. Juan Corey, c, Central HS, Miami
32. John Jordan, c, Mount St. Joseph HS, Glen Burnie, Md.

June—Secondary Phase (26)

1. **Rodolfo Arias, c, Miami-Dade South CC**

TEXAS RANGERS

January—Regular Phase (10)

1. **Dave Righetti, lhp, San Jose CC**
2. Phil Cordova, c, Colby (Kan.) CC
3. Billy Bowen, of, Grayson County (Texas) JC
4. Greg Pastors, ss, Yavapai (Ariz.) JC
5. **Ronald Johnson, 1b, Central Arizona JC**
6. **Steve Righetti, 3b, San Jose (Calif.) CC**
7. Frankie Meason, 1b, Paris (Texas) JC

January—Secondary Phase (12)

1. **Arnold McCrary, of, Los Angeles CC**
2. **Dennis Doyle, c, Assumption (Mass.)**
3. Rob Johnson, rhp, Southwestern Oklahoma State

June—Regular Phase (9)

1. **David Hibner, ss, Howell (Mich.) HS**
2. **Linvel Mosby, rhp, Pecos (Texas) HS**
3. Jerry Vasquez, rhp, Arizona State
4. **George Wright, of, Capitol Hill HS, Oklahoma City, Okla.**
5. **Mike Jirschele, ss, Clintonville (Wis.) HS**
6. **Patrick Nelson, rhp, Carol City HS, Cooper City, Fla.**
7. **Odie Davis, ss, Prairie View A&M**
8. Joseph Knight, rhp, Texas HS, Texarkana, Texas
9. **Bob Johnson, c, Kimball HS, Dallas**
10. **Chuck Lamson, lhp, Gloucester County (N.J.) JC**
11. **Steven Nielsen, rhp, Penn State**
12. **Ronald Carney, of, Texas Wesleyan**
13. **Don Kainer, rhp, Texas**
14. **Glenn Hollands, lhp, Santa Clara**
15. James Sutton, rhp, Colton (Calif.) HS
16. **William LaRosa, rhp, Dallas Baptist**
17. Ken Jones, rhp, Lennox (Calif.) HS
18. Richard Martini, of, UC Davis
19. **James Barbe, 3b, James Madison**
20. **Joseph Carroll, of, Lehigh**
21. Terry Mixon, ss, Georgia Southern
22. **Ed Lynch, rhp, South Carolina**
23. John White, rhp, Millikan HS, Long Beach
24. Thad Reece, ss, Porterville (Calif.) HS
25. **Marty Scott, 3b, Dallas Baptist**
26. Dewey Porter, c, Munford HS, Detroit
27. Douglas Myers, 3b, Indian Lake HS, Huntsville, Ohio
28. Jeff Taylor, c, Delaware

June—Secondary Phase (18)

1. **John Butcher, rhp, Yavapai (Ariz.) JC**
2. Steve Winfield, rhp, Panola (Texas) JC

TORONTO BLUE JAYS

January—Regular Phase (26)

1. Bradford Ross, of, Blinn (Texas) JC
2. Tom Penney, c, Blinn (Texas) JC
3. **Jay Robertson, rhp, Sacramento CC**
4. Michael Wright, rhp, Fresno CC

January—Secondary Phase (13)

1. Jerry Stovall, rhp, Fresno CC
2. Michael Barrett, rhp, San Jacinto (Texas) JC

June—Regular Phase (25)

1. **Tom Goffena, ss, Sidney (Ohio) HS**
2. Dave Hodgins, c, Buchser HS, Santa Clara, Calif.
3. Jim Teahan, rhp, Esperanza HS, Yorba Linda, Calif.
4. **Daryl Hill, 2b, Peterson HS, Sunnyvale, Calif.**
5. **Rich Hertel, inf, Southern California**
6. **David Rohm, rhp, Fresno State**
7. **Scott Gregory, rhp, Southern California**
8. **Jack Hollis, rhp, New Mexico**
9. **Jesse Barfield, of, Central HS, Joliet, Ill.**
10. Mark Armstrong, rhp, Chesterton (Ind.) HS
11. **Pete Rowe, c, Oregon State**
12. **Dwayne Wright, c, St. Mary's**
13. **Rocket Wheeler, 2b, Houston**
14. Randy Brown, rhp, MacArthur HS, Houston
15. **Danny Ainge, ss, North Eugene (Ore.) HS**
16. Steve Leppert, c, Avon Worth HS, Pittsburgh

June—Secondary Phase (13)

1. Tom Penney, c, Blinn (Texas) JC

1978 BRAVES REAP IMMEDIATE DIVIDEND WITH SELECTION OF HORNER, BUT TIGERS SCORE BIG WITH GIBSON

Bob Horner set an NCAA record for home runs. He homered in his first game with the Braves and became the National League rookie of the year in 1978—the same year he was drafted.

But if the Braves had their way, Horner would not have been the No. 1 pick in the 1978 draft. Michigan State's Kirk Gibson was the man the Braves really wanted.

"Gibson stands out. The rest are a box entry," Atlanta scouting director Paul Snyder said on the eve of the 1978 draft. "If I had to compare him with anybody, he's like Mickey Mantle. You don't see that combination of speed and power very often."

The Braves and 10 other teams passed on Gibson at the top of the June draft, however, because they weren't sure they'd be able to sign him. Gibson was an outstanding wide receiver at Michigan State and a likely first-round pick in the 1979 NFL draft. He had a year of eligibility remaining in college, and most teams thought he there was no way he would give that up.

"I definitely want to play my senior year of football," Gibson said. "I'm not going to leave Michigan State. Being an athlete and a student here have been the best experiences of my life, and I want it to last as long as possible."

The Tigers, who worked Gibson out at Tiger Stadium two weeks before the draft and watched him hit several balls into the upper deck, gambled on Gibson with the 12th pick, and eventually worked out a deal that allowed him to return for his senior year of football. It cost them a bonus in excess of $200,000, the largest in baseball history at the time.

While the Braves passed on Gibson, they were happy with Horner, who hit .412 with 25 homers and 100 RBIs for College World Series runner-up Arizona State. Horner, a career .386 hitter who set an NCAA record with 56 homers, played all four infield positions at Arizona State. He was a second baseman most of the 1978 season, but switched to his natural position of third base in early May.

Horner's career got off to an auspicious start, and he had 138 career home runs by the end of the 1982 season, but injuries struck him down and he ended up playing 10 seasons and hitting 218 home runs. It took Gibson longer to establish himself in the majors, but he played 17 seasons and won the National League MVP award in 1988 with the Dodgers, not to mention hitting one of the most dramatic home runs in World Series history against the Athletics.

RUSS REED

Oakland's Mike Morgan was one of four picks who went straight to the majors

When they drafted him and started negotiations, the Braves had no intention of taking Horner directly to the big leagues, but Horner persuaded Braves general manager Bill Lucas to give him a shot.

"Bob talked me into him being here," Lucas said. "He feels like he can play here now and were going to give him a shot. If we can talk manager Bobby Cox into it, he'll start right away. It's up to Cox, but I may lean on him a little bit to make it happen."

Horner started three days later and in his third at-bat homered against Pittsburgh's Bert Blyleven, setting off a wild celebration among 18,572 Braves fans who had cheered his every move.

"There hasn't been this much feeling in the crowd since the day Henry hit 715," Snyder said. "It's a shame we had to lose because this is the biggest day I've ever experienced. When you work seven days a week for three months toward something like this, this reward is hard to describe."

Four players from the 1978 draft began their careers in the big leagues. Horner proved he was ready for the challenge, but none of the other three, all high school selections, lasted more than three games before they returned to the minor leagues.

For Athletics owner Charles Finley, starting 18-year-old pitchers Mike Morgan and Tim Conroy at the top was his way of recouping his investment in his club's two first-round picks. Morgan made his debut against the Orioles, attracting a crowd of 23,123 to Oakland's Alameda County Coliseum. He held his own, scattering 10 hits in a complete game, though he lost 3-0.

Two starts later, the A's shipped a confused Morgan and his 0-3 record to the minor leagues. His spot on the roster was taken by Conroy, a lefthander from Monroeville, Pa., who made his debut before 39,000 fans in Kansas City.

The fourth member of the Class of '78 to debut in the big leagues was Toronto catcher Brian Milner. Milner was considered likely to attend Arizona State on a football scholarship, so he still was available when the Blue Jays turn came up in the seventh round. Dangling first-round money (a reported $140,000) and the big league offer, they were able to steer Milner away from college.

First-Round Failures

For the second year in a row, six first-round picks from the June regular phase never advanced beyond Class A. One was Baltimore's Bob Boyce, who hit .318 his first pro season. A .221 average thereafter sent him packing. Not all was lost for the Orioles, however. In the second round they picked Cal Ripken Jr.

Much of the top high school talent wasn't taken early, however, because those players began to regard college as a more viable option. Such talents as Mike Moore, Kevin McReynolds, Mark Langston and Frank Viola were paid only passing interest, while three years later they became the cornerstones of a draft whose emphasis in the early rounds swung dramatically to college talent.

The 1978 draft had special significance because it was the first one when compensation was awarded to teams that lost free agents. Teams signing free agents compensated the player's former club with a draft pick. A total of 11 free agents changed clubs following the 1977 season, so 11 picks changed hands. Distinctions were made between the quality of free agent lost. If a player's negotiating rights were claimed by less than two teams in the re-entry draft, no compensation was required.

The Yankees lost pitcher Mike Torrez and outfielder Ron Blomberg, so they got the first-round picks of the Red Sox and White Sox. That's a trend they would frequently reverse in the coming years, when they rarely participated in the draft's first round. Of the team's three first-rounders, only Rex Hudler ever reached New York.

Boston forfeited its picks in the first three rounds of the 1978 draft and didn't select for the first time until the 99th pick. The Red Sox got a single game out of their only selection to reach the big leagues, catcher John Lickert, a 13th-round pick.

DRAFT 78: FIRST-ROUND PICKS

No.	Club	Player, Pos.	School	Hometown	Ht.	Wt.	B-T	Age
1.	Braves	Bob Horner, 3b	Arizona State	Glendale, Ariz.	6-1	190	R-R	20
2.	Blue Jays	Lloyd Moseby, 1b	Oakland HS	Oakland	6-3	190	L-R	18
3.	Mets	Hubie Brooks, ss	Arizona State	Tempe, Ariz.	6-0	180	R-R	21
4.	Athletics	Mike Morgan, rhp	Valley HS	Las Vegas	6-3	195	R-R	18
5.	Padres	Andy Hawkins, rhp	Midway HS	Waco, Texas	6-5	205	R-R	18
6.	Mariners	Tito Nanni, of/1b	Chestnut Hill Academy	Philadelphia	6-4	205	L-L	18
7.	Giants	Bob Cummings, c	Brother Rice HS	Chicago	6-2	180	R-R	17
8.	Brewers	Nick Hernandez, c	Hialeah HS	Hialeah, Fla.	6-4	195	R-R	18
9.	Expos	Glenn Franklin, ss	Chipola (Fla.) JC	St. Louis	5-10	175	L-R	20
10.	Indians	Phil Lansford, ss	Wilcox HS	Santa Clara, Calif.	6-3	195	R-R	18
11.	Astros	Rod Boxberger, rhp	Southern California	Santa Ana, Calif.	6-3	185	R-R	20
12.	Tigers	Kirk Gibson, of	Michigan State	Waterford, Mich.	6-2	212	L-L	21
13.	Cubs	Bill Hayes, c	Indiana State	North Platte, Neb.	6-1	190	R-R	20
14.	Angels	Tom Brunansky, of	West Covina HS	West Covina, Calif.	6-4	210	R-R	17
15.	Cardinals	Robert Hicks, 1b	Tate HS	Pensacola, Fla.	6-3	190	R-R	17
16.	Twins	Lenny Faedo, ss	Jefferson HS	Tampa	6-0	170	R-R	18
17.	Reds	Nick Esasky, ss	Carol City HS	Carol City, Fla.	6-3	190	R-R	18
18.	Yankees	Rex Hudler, ss	Bullard HS	Fresno, Calif.	6-1	175	R-R	17
19.	Pirates	Brad Garnett, 1b	DeSoto HS	DeSoto, Texas	6-4	205	L-L	17
20.	Athletics	Tim Conroy, lhp	Gateway HS	Monroeville, Pa.	6-0	178	L-L	18
21.	Pirates	Gerry Aubin, of	Dougherty HS	Albany, Ga.	6-2	195	R-R	17
22.	Orioles	Robert Boyce, 3b	Deer Park HS	Cincinnati	6-1	175	R-R	18
23.	Phillies	Rip Rollins, 1b/rhp	Alleghany HS	Sparta, N.C.	6-2	200	R-R	18
24.	Yankees	Matt Winters, of	Williamsville HS	Williamsville, N.Y.	6-3	195	L-R	18
25.	Royals	Buddy Biancalana, ss	Redwood HS	Greenbrae, Calif.	5-11	150	B-R	18
26.	Yankees	Brian Ryder, rhp	Shrewsbury HS	Shrewsbury, Mass.	6-5	200	R-R	18

1978

CLUB-BY-CLUB SELECTIONS

ATLANTA BRAVES

January—Regular Phase (2)

1. Joe Housey, rhp, Miami-Dade North CC
2. **Ronald Rudd, 3b, Sacramento CC**
3. **James Rogers, rhp, Murray State (Okla.) JC**
4. Jack McMahon, rhp, Cypress (Calif.) JC
5. Howard Scott, rhp, DeKalb (Ga.) JC

January—Secondary Phase (4)

1. **Mark Martin, c, San Jacinto (Texas) JC**
2. Stephen Maral, c, Chabot (Calif.) JC

June—Regular Phase (1)

1. **Bob Horner, 3b, Arizona State**
2. **Matt Sinatro, c, Conrad HS, West Hartford, Conn.**
3. **Steve Bedrosian, rhp, New Haven (Conn.)**
4. **Rick Behenna, rhp, South Ridge HS, Cutler Ridge, Fla.**
5. **Michael Miller, ss, Louisville**
6. **Ken Scanlon, ss, Granada Hills HS, Northridge, Calif.**
7. Doyle Wilson, ss, Shorter (Ga.)
8. **Jose Alvarez, rhp, Southwestern Louisiana**
9. Gary Friedrich, lhp, Gavit HS, Hammond, Ind.
10. **Jimmy Matthews, 3b, Georgia Southern**
11. **Gerald Perry, of, McCracken HS, Hilton Head, S.C.**
12. **Bobby Supel, 3b, East Carolina**
13. Robert Elsea, lhp, Cleveland State (Tenn.) CC
14. **Lance Gore, lhp, Cal State Fullerton**
15. **William Aldridge, rhp, Tennessee**
16. **Daniel Lopez, of, Houston**
17. **James Van Deventer, of, Catholic (D.C.)**
18. Charles Shearer, rhp, Weber HS, Chicago
19. James Harris, lhp, Thomas Jefferson HS, Brooklyn, N.Y.
20. **Kevin Balogh, rhp, Toledo, Ohio**
21. **Gil Ryan, rhp, Blinn (Texas) JC**
22. Larry Brown, rhp, Harvard
23. **Michael Smith, rhp, Massachusetts Bay CC**
24. Hubert Taylor, rhp, Georgia Southwestern
25. **Mark Roush, rhp, Cincinnati**
26. Lawrence Dugger, rhp, Eastwood HS, El Paso, Texas
27. **Brad Campbell, rhp, West Georgia**
28. Paul Robinson, 3b, Bishop Nolan HS, Fort Worth, Texas
29. Kerry Cox, of, Tarrant HS, Birmingham

June—Secondary Phase (1)

1. Jim Watkins, c, Florida
2. **Blane McDonald, c, Florida State**
3. Jimmy Boring, rhp, DeKalb South (Ga.) CC

BALTIMORE ORIOLES

January—Regular Phase (21)

1. Kenny Kurtz, lhp, Seminole (Fla.) CC
2. **Daniel Keck, of, Central Arizona JC**
3. David Jensen, lhp, Edmonds (Wash.) CC
4. **Stanley Hendrickson, of/1b, Philadelphia CC**
5. **George Paul, rhp, Manatee (Fla.) JC**
6. Curt Kowalski, rhp, Seminole (Fla.) CC
7. Ted Dixon, rhp, Angelina (Texas) JC
8. John Wood, 3b, Abraham Baldwin Agricultural (Ga.) JC
9. **Charles Proviano, ss, Pittsburgh**
10. Robert Pigford, rhp, Philadelphia CC

January—Secondary Phase (3)

1. **Eduardo Rodriguez, ss, Miami-Dade South CC**
2. **Mark Bolton, rhp, Longview, Texas**
3. Lawrence Davila, rhp, Key West, Fla.

June—Regular Phase (22)

1. **Robert Boyce, 3b, Deer Park HS, Cincinnati**
2. **Larry Sheets, of, Lee HS, Staunton, Va.** (Pick from Mets as compensation for free agent Elliott Maddox)
2. **Edwin Hook, rhp, Point Loma HS, San Diego** (Pick from Expos as compensation for free agent Ross Grimsley)
2. **Cal Ripken Jr., 3b, Aberdeen (Md.) HS**
2. **Cecil Whitehead, c, Valdosta State (Ga.)** (Pick from Red Sox as compensation for free agent Dick Drago)
3. **Bobby Bonner, ss, Texas A&M**
4. **Tim Norris, rhp, Archbishop Curley HS, Baltimore**
5. Tony Herron, lhp, Sanger (Calif.) HS
6. **Mike Boddicker, rhp, Iowa**
7. **Don Welchel, rhp, Sam Houston State**
8. Scott Collins, ss, Plymouth-Canton HS, Canton, Ohio
9. **Kurt Fabrizio, 1b, Edmonds (Wash.) CC**
10. **Brooks Carey, lhp, Florida State**
11. Robin Dreizler, c, Redondo Beach (Calif.) HS
12. **Charles Salagan, lhp, St. Clair County (Mich.) CC**
13. **William Purdy, rhp, Niagara**
14. **Jim Loftin, lhp, South Alabama**
15. John Mortillaro, lhp, Smithtown East HS, Nesconset, N.Y.
16. **Michael Byars, ss, Canyon HS, Orange, Calif.**
17. **James Delmonico, of, West Hempstead, N.Y.**
18. **Marion Thackston, lhp, Huntington (W.Va.) HS**
19. William Butler, ss, Rossville (Ga.) HS

June—Secondary Phase (22)

1. **Juan Corey, c, Miami-Dade North CC**

BOSTON RED SOX

January—Regular Phase (23)

1. Bruce Kastelic, ss, Ranger (Texas) JC
2. Matt Young, lhp, Pasadena (Calif.) CC
3. Milton Ondracek, rhp, San Jacinto (Texas) JC
4. **Daniel Weppner, lhp, Palm Beach (Fla.) JC**
5. Howard Brodsky, c, Miami North Beach HS
6. James Funderburk, lhp, Orange Coast (Calif.) JC

January—Secondary Phase (13)

1. **Brian Denman, 1b/rhp, Richfield, Minn.**
2. **Mark Paradise, lhp, Marblehead, Mass.**

June—Regular Phase (24)

1. (Pick to Yankees as compensation for free agent Mike Torrez)
2. (Pick to Orioles as compensation for free agent Dick Drago)
3. (Pick to White Sox as compensation for free agent Jack Brohamer)
4. **Edward Connors, 3b, North Bergen (N.J.) HS**
5. **Del Bender, of/inf, Mississippi State**
6. **Steve Schaefer, rhp, Alhambra (Calif.) HS**
7. **Ken Hagemann, 1b, Tottenville HS, Staten Island, N.Y.**
8. **Ken Young, of, New Haven (Conn.)**
9. **Russ Quetti, ss, Maine**
10. **Donald Hayford, rhp, Lakeland (Fla.) HS**
11. **Craig Vandersteen, lhp, Grand Ledge (Mich.) HS**
12. **James Fabiano, ss, Westwood, Maine**
13. **John Lickert, c, Langley HS, Pittsburgh**
14. **Lloyd Bessard, of, Abbeville (La.) HS**
15. **Robert Parker, of, William Carey (Miss.)**
16. Mark Mitchell, rhp, North Hills HS, Pittsburgh
17. Steve Reish, rhp, Union City (Ind.) HS
18. **Gary Givens, rhp, Georgia Southern**
19. **Harold Nataupsky, c, Marblehead (Mass.) HS**
20. **Keith Pecka, lhp, Kankakee (Ill.) CC**

June—Secondary Phase (20)

1. Marty Barrett, inf, Mesa (Ariz.) CC

CALIFORNIA ANGELS

January—Regular Phase (13)

1. Rick Evans, lhp, El Camino (Calif.) JC
2. Steven Norman, of, Barstow (Calif.) CC
3. **Anthony Dailey, of, Valencia (Fla.) CC**
4. **Mark Nocciolo, c, JC of the Canyons (Calif.)**
5. Jeff Hanslovan, lhp, Linn-Benton (Ore.) CC
6. Mark Seeger, of, Mesa (Ariz.) CC
7. Trent Smith, rhp, Seminole (Fla.) CC
8. Arthur Maebe, rhp, Mission (Calif.) JC
9. Billy Blizzard, rhp, Barstow (Calif.) CC
10. Dave Yobs, 1b, Los Angeles Valley JC

January—Secondary Phase (25)

1. Simon Glenn, of, Blinn (Texas) JC
2. Stephen Martin, rhp, Pima (Ariz.) CC

June—Regular Phase (14)

1. **Tom Brunansky, of, West Covina (Calif.) HS**
2. (Pick to Padres as compensation for free agent Merv Rettenmund)
3. **Dave Engle, 3b, Southern California**
4. **Mike Witt, rhp, Servite HS, Buena Park, Calif.**
5. **Rick Foley, rhp, Santa Clara**
6. **Gary Clevenger, 3b, Buena HS, Ventura, Calif.**
7. **Bill Springman, 2b, Oral Roberts**
8. Tim Wallach, 1b, Cal State Fullerton
9. **Preston Freeman, ss, Chandler (Ariz.) HS**
10. Terry Marshall, lhp, Riverside Christian HS, Mira Loma, Calif.
11. **Perry Morrison, rhp, Phoenix JC**
12. Jeff Schattinger, rhp, Southern California
13. Peter Otero, c, Yavapai (Ariz.) JC
14. **Dan Whitmer, c, Cal State Fullerton**
15. **Richard Rommel, rhp, Cal State Fullerton**
16. John Christensen, of, Troy HS, Fullerton, Calif.
17. Brian Owens, rhp, Mesa (Ariz.) HS
18. Walter Hagerty, c, Altus (Okla.) HS
19. **John Soderman, rhp, Santa Ana, Calif.**
20. Steve Muccio, of, New Mexico
21. Howard Dashefsky, c, El Camino Real HS, Canoga Park, Calif.
22. Thomas Saatzer, c, West Brady HS, St. Paul, Minn.

June—Secondary Phase (6)

1. Paul Homrig, 1b, San Pedro, Calif.
2. Karl Jastrow, lhp, West Los Angeles JC

CHICAGO CUBS

January—Regular Phase (14)

1. **Joe Hicks, 3b, Indianapolis, Ind.**
2. **Craig Kornfeld, ss, Miami-Dade North CC**
3. Richard Aspenleiter, rhp, Grossmont (Calif.) JC
4. Matt Stilwell, of, Linn-Benton (Ore.) CC
5. John Kossick, lhp, Houston CC
6. Kevin Shuster, c, Pasadena (Calif.) CC
7. Todd Wilson, lhp, Mount San Antonio (Calif.) JC

January—Secondary Phase (22)

1. Michael Campbell, 3b, Panola (Texas) JC
2. **Andrew Walker, c, East St. Louis, Ill.**

June—Regular Phase (13)

1. **Bill Hayes, c, Indiana State**
2. **Mel Hall, of, Port Byron HS, Cayuga, N.Y.**
3. **Bubba Kizer, ss, Georgia**
4. Dave Seiler, lhp, Manzano HS, Albuquerque, N.M.
5. Jon Perlman, rhp, Baylor
6. **Robert Triplett, c, Phillips HS, Chicago**
7. **Mark Parker, rhp, Huntington (Ind.)**
8. Dave Klipstein, ss, Marshall HS, Milwaukee
9. Jeff Groth, of, Bowling Green State
10. **John Stockstill, ss, Hurley HS, Crane, Mo.**
11. Mark Lohuis, rhp, Fresno State
12. **Glenn Swaggerty, rhp, Carter HS, Knoxville**
13. Dave Govea, 1b/of, Poly HS, Arleta, Calif.
14. **Mark Gilbert, of, Florida State**
15. Mark Langston, lhp, Buchser HS, Santa Clara, Calif.
16. **James Mitchell, ss, James Madison**
17. Scott Stranski, rhp, Northwestern
18. Matt Elser, 1b/lhp, Poly HS, Arleta, Calif.
19. **Joe McClain, rhp, Milligan (Tenn.)**
20. **Mark Vaji, lhp, Marshall HS, Cleveland**
21. Chris Adomanis, rhp, Bowie (Md.) HS
22. Darrel White, of, Southwest HS, St. Louis
23. Joe Beason, rhp, Taylor HS, Kokomo, Ind.
24. **Mike Godley, of, Jackson State**
25. Richard Raphael, rhp, San Jose State
26. **Tim Carroll, of, Nebraska**
27. **Kevin Kirby, rhp, Santa Clara**
28. **Eric Gorman, lhp, West Morris HS, Chester, N.J.**
29. **Mike Weakman, 3b, Meredian HS, Sanford, Mich.**
30. **Mike Diaz, 1b, Terra Nova HS, Pacifica, Calif.**
31. Wayne Stone, of, Oral Roberts

June—Secondary Phase (14)

1. Jim McManus, rhp, Triton (Ill.) JC
2. Jeff Stottlemyre, rhp, Yakima Valley (Wash.) JC
3. Greg Moyer, of, Cerritos (Calif.) JC (Selection voided)

CHICAGO WHITE SOX

January—Regular Phase (17)

1. Mark Christy, rhp, Miami-Dade North CC
2. John Wolfer, rhp, Miami-Dade North CC
3. Jeffrey Orville, rhp, Santa Ana (Calif.) JC
4. Duane Dewey, c/1b, Miami-Dade North CC
5. Don Brownell, rhp, Seminole (Fla.) CC
6. Russ Fowler, inf, San Diego Mesa JC
7. Ken Hallin, rhp, Southwestern (Calif.) JC

January—Secondary Phase (7)

1. **Vic Walters, rhp, Miami-Dade South CC**
2. Randy Brown, rhp, San Jacinto (Texas) JC

June—Regular Phase (18)

1. (Pick to Yankees as compensation for free agent Ron Blomberg)
2. **David White, 3b, Valdosta (Ga.) HS** (Pick from Padres as compensation for free agent Oscar Gamble)
2. Buck Belue, of, Valdosta (Ga.) HS
3. **Britt Burns, lhp, Huffman HS, Birmingham**
3. **Mike Maitland, lhp, Pace HS, Miami** (Pick from Red Sox as compensation for free agent Jack Brohamer)
4. Mike Rubel, c, Banning (Calif.) HS
5. **Dennis Keating, of, Marin Catholic HS, San Rafael, Calif.**
6. Dom Fucci, 1b/of, Auburn
7. Michael Schoeller, c/1b, Florida Southern
8. **Ivan Mesa, ss, Miami Springs HS, Hialeah, Fla.**
9. Preston Williams, 1b, Indiana State
10. Brian Stemberger, ss, Eastern Michigan
11. **Ramon Murillo, rhp, Arizona**
12. **Mark Platel, rhp, Veghany HS, Del Mor, N.Y.**
13. Rick Witt, ss/3b, Spokane Falls (Wash.) CC
14. Bob Meacham, ss, Mater Dei HS, Westminster, Calif.
15. Andrew Dawson, ss, Waxahachie (Texas) HS
16. William Stroope, 1b, Waxahachie (Texas) HS
17. Larry Doby, of, Duke
18. **Thomas Kokas, of/2b, Northwestern**

June—Secondary Phase (18)

1. Mark Christy, rhp, Miami-Dade North CC
2. Duane Dewey, c/inf, Miami-Dade North CC
3. Gary Gaetti, inf, Lincoln Land (Ill.) CC

CINCINNATI REDS

January—Regular Phase (18)

1. Brad Lesley, rhp, Merced (Calif.) JC
2. **Larry Buckel, rhp, Long Beach CC**
3. **Paul Gibson, lhp, Center Moriches (N.Y.) HS**
4. Larry Mikesell, lhp, Brevard (Fla.) CC
5. **Dan Sarrett, c, Valencia (Fla.) CC**
6. Tim Muench, rhp, Seminole (Fla.) CC

7. Kevin Wiebold, rhp, McLennan (Texas) CC
8. Robert Day, 3b/ss, North Idaho JC
9. James McManus, rhp, Triton (Ill.) JC
10. Jeff Fiechtner, rhp, Des Moines Area (Iowa) CC

January—Secondary Phase (16)

1. **Wayne Guinn, rhp, DeKalb (Ga.) JC**
2. Jeff Ayers, rhp, Bellevue (Wash.) CC

June—Regular Phase (17)

1. **Nick Esasky, ss, Carol City (Fla.) HS**
2. **Dave Van Gorder, c, Southern California**
3. **Esky Viltz, of, Notre Dame HS, North Hollywood, Calif.**
4. **Mike Kripner, c, Texas Lutheran**
5. **Jeff Lahti, rhp, Portland State**
6. Ray Townsend, 2b, UCLA
7. Tim Greene, lhp, River North Academy, Macon, Ga.
8. **Charles McKinney, rhp, Baden HS, Hamilton, Ohio**
9. **Charlie Leibrandt Jr., lhp, Miami (Ohio)**
10. **Chris Stropolo, of, John Curtis HS, Metairie, La.**
11. John Warren, c/of, Wayne County HS, Jesup, Ga.
12. **Mike Sullivan, c, Northwest Regional HS, Colebrook, Conn.**
13. **Byron Jackson, rhp, Rider HS, Wichita Falls, Texas**
14. James Thomas, ss, Southeast HS, Wichita, Kan.
15. **Gary Redus, ss, Athens State (Ga.)**
16. **Skeeter Barnes, 2b, Cincinnati**
17. **Tom Lawless, ss/2b, Penn State**
18. Mitch Dean, rhp, Arizona State
19. David Anderson, rhp, Western HS, Las Vegas
20. **James Taylor, c, Harding HS, Charlotte**
21. Otis Nixon, inf, Louisburg (N.C.) JC
22. John Cook, of, Washington State
23. Kevin Maroney, of, Oakwood HS, Dayton, Ohio
24. **Richard Jendra, ss/2b, Florida International**
25. **Lee Hover, of, Oklahoma**
26. Alan Deratt, rhp, North Carolina
27. **James Mugele, inf, High Point**
28. Bill Bakewell, p, Arkansas
29. **Alex Neely, p, Phillips (Okla.)**
30. Joe Stafani, p, Dowling HS, Des Moines, Iowa
31. Ronald Walling, lhp, Westmont HS, Johnstown, Pa.
32. **Cary Hornaman, of, Northern State (S.D.)**
33. James Johnson, c, Wake Forest
34. **Charles Engel, rhp, St. Cloud State (Minn.)**
35. Kurt Moody, lhp, Hoover HS, Des Moines, Iowa
36. **John LoCascio, lhp, St. Francis DeSales HS, Toledo**
37. **Patrick Chester, ss, South Dorchester HS, Cambridge, Md.**

June—Secondary Phase (9)

1. **Brad Lesley, rhp, Merced (Calif.) JC**
2. Ralph Citarella, rhp, Brevard (Fla.) CC
3. Kevin Niewulis, lhp, Louisburg (N.C.) JC
4. Gary Kempton, c, Triton (Ill.) JC

CLEVELAND INDIANS

January—Regular Phase (9)

1. **Thomas Anderson, 1b, South Florida JC**
2. **Robert Conley, ss, Enterprise State (Ala.) JC**
3. **Lloyd Turner, ss, Middle Georgia JC**
4. **Robin Fuson, rhp, Valencia (Fla.) CC**
5. **Keith Hendry, rhp, South Florida JC**
6. Robert Payne, of, St. Johns River (Fla.) CC
7. **Ralph Henriguez, c, Indian River (Fla.) CC**
8. **Russell Cain, c, George Wallace (Ala.) CC**
9. James Gardner, c, Miami-Dade North CC
10. Joseph Kelihar, 1b/of, St. Petersburg (Fla.) JC

January—Secondary Phase (17)

1. Mike Bates, rhp, Phoenix JC
2. Kernan Ronan, rhp, Glendale (Ariz.) CC

June—Regular Phase (10)

1. **Phil Lansford, ss, Wilcox HS, Santa Clara, Calif.**
2. **Chris Bando, c, Arizona State**
3. **Michael Taylor, of, Columbia State (Tenn.) CC**
4. **Dane Anthony, rhp, James Buchanan HS, St. Thomas, Pa.**
5. **John Asbell, rhp, Southwest HS, Macon, Ga.**
6. **Tom Owens, rhp, Michigan**
7. Mike Young, of, Hayward (Calif.) HS
8. Eric Porter, c, Waseca (Mich.) HS
9. **Peter Peltz, 3b, Clemson**
10. **Kenneth Henderson, 2b, Worthington, Ohio**
11. **Gordon Glaser, rhp, Louisiana College**
12. Casey Lindsey, lhp, Arizona State
13. **Robert Hussey, rhp, St. Xavier**
14. Mark Meleski, ss, J.R. Tucker HS, Richmond
15. **Gerald Stutzriem, lhp, Rich Central HS, County Club Hills, Ill.**
16. **Richard Barnhart, rhp, Puget Sound (Wash.)**
17. **Jerald Hammermeister, 3b, Ellensburg (Wash.) HS**
18. Howard Lukehardt, lhp, Norwin HS, Huntingdon, Fla.
19. James McBride, rhp, Jackson State
20. Bob Bonnette, inf, Clemson
21. **Robert Pfeffer, rhp, Glassboro State (N.J.)**
22. Phillip Preliezo, lhp, Christopher Columbus HS, Miami
23. **Chris Barker, of, St. Catherine HS, Racine, Wis.**
24. **Louis Ganci, rhp, New York Tech**
25. **Reid Cassidy, rhp, Colby (Maine)**
26. **Randy Rambis, rhp, San Jose State**
27. **Kenneth Gilmore, 2b/3b, Troy State**
28. **Tom Van Der Meersche, rhp, Arizona State**
29. Kenneth Smith, rhp, North Carolina
30. Tim Behler, lhp, La Verne (Calif.)
31. Warner Crumb, rhp, Northampton HS, Cheriton, Va.
32. Jay Waid, c, Hewitt HS, Trussville, Ala.
33. Mike Brecht, lhp, Hazel Park (Mich.) HS
34. Ronald Kollmann, rhp, Nampa (Idaho) HS
35. Scott August, lhp, Potomac HS, Oxon Hill, Md.
36. **Richard Hille, rhp, St. John's**
37. George White, rhp, Ballard HS, Seattle
38. John Shrewsberry, rhp, Palm Beach (Fla.) JC
39. **Lawrence Beck, lhp, Occidental (Calif.)**
40. **Ron Wrobel, lhp, Grand Canyon (Ariz.)**
41. Michael Culbert, rhp, Bonanza HS, Las Vegas (Selection voided)
42. **George Ravanis, rhp, Boston College**
43. Michael Mowrey, rhp, San Gabriel (Calif.) HS
44. **David Warnecke, rhp, McKendree (Ill.)**
45. Michael Yackee, rhp, Cal State Los Angeles
46. David Spamer, rhp, East Allegheny HS, North Versailles, Pa.
47. Ron Reeves, rhp, Monterey HS, Lubbock, Texas
48. Delbert Stacey, rhp, Rutland (Vt.) HS

June—Secondary Phase (13)

1. David Grier, rhp, Valencia (Fla.) CC
2. Doug Wabeke, ss, Grand Rapids (Mich.) JC
3. Richard Evans, lhp, El Camino (Calif.) JC

DETROIT TIGERS

January—Regular Phase (11)

1. **Chris Codiroli, rhp, San Jose CC**
2. **Kevin Fitzhugh, rhp, Orange Coast (Calif.) JC**
3. John Cardinali, ss, DeAnza (Calif.) JC
4. Steve Conroy, lhp, Citrus (Calif.) JC
5. Rich DeVincenzo, lhp, Miami-Dade North CC
6. Donald Pierce, lhp, Chaffey (Calif.) JC
7. **Dan O'Connor, c, Central Florida JC**

January—Secondary Phase (26)

1. **William Klank, rhp, Mercer County (N.J.) CC**
2. Rick Santarone, c, Gulf Coast (Fla.) CC

June—Regular Phase (12)

1. **Kirk Gibson, of, Michigan State**
2. **Craig Johnson, of, UCLA**
3. Fran Mullins, ss, Santa Clara
4. **Jerry Ujdur, rhp, Minnesota**
5. **Marty Castillo, 3b, Chapman (Calif.)**
6. Kevin Martin, ss, Falconer Central HS, Jamestown, N.Y.
7. **Bruce Fields, of, Everett HS, Lansing, Mich.**

8. **Ted Hutson, c, Miami East HS, Fletcher, Ohio**
9. **Mike Wright, of, Vanderbilt**
10. **James Simerly, rhp, Chapman (Calif.)**
11. **Art Toal, 2b/ss, Oklahoma**
12. **Jack Smith, rhp, Glen Oaks (Mich.) CC**
13. **David Cassetto, rhp, Western Michigan**
14. Mike Mason, of/lhp, Normandale (Minn.) CC
15. **Marvin Saunders, rhp, South Alabama**
16. **Dave Rucker, lhp, La Verne (Calif.)**
17. **Todd Ervin, 2b, Stanford**
18. Mark Jacob, rhp, De LaSalle HS, Detroit
19. Edwin Schneider, lhp, Indian River (Fla.) CC
20. **John Crawford, c, Delta State (Miss.)**
21. **Michael Untisz, rhp, Fairleigh Dickinson (N.J.)**
22. **Bob Benda, inf, Florida State**
23. Gary Baker, 3b, Hazel Park (Mich.) HS
24. Tom Grinstead, lhp, Edgewood HS, West Covina, Calif.
25. **John Kelley, of, Simon Kenton HS, Independence, Ky.**
26. **James Wilfong, of, La Verne (Calif.)**
27. **John Martin, lhp, Eastern Michigan**
28. Holden Smith, of, California
29. **Judson Thigpen, rhp, Delta State (Miss.)**
30. **Michael Polvi, rhp, Detroit**
31. **Ben Bonk, rhp, Central Michigan**
32. **Buddy Slemp, of, Oral Roberts**

June—Secondary Phase (12)

1. Pete Chapin, rhp, Fullerton (Calif.) JC

HOUSTON ASTROS

January—Regular Phase (12)

1. **Greg Smith, of, Canada (Calif.) JC**
2. **Pat Perry, lhp, Lincoln Land (Ill.) CC**
3. Joe Collins, rhp, Hillsborough (Fla.) CC

January—Secondary Phase (14)

1. James Tjader, 2b, Iowa Western CC

June—Regular Phase (11)

1. **Rod Boxberger, rhp, Southern California**
2. **Danny Heep, of/lhp, St. Mary's (Texas)**
3. **John Hessler, rhp, Tulsa**
4. **Ron Meridith, lhp, Oral Roberts**
5. **Doug Stokke, ss, Southern California**
6. Bob Palmer, c, Chapman (Calif.)
7. **Greg Cypret, ss, Missouri**
8. **Larry Ashley, Oakland HS**
9. Brad Carlson, 3b, Boone HS, Orlando, Fla.
10. Frank Castro, c, Miami Springs HS, Hialeah, Fla.
11. **Jack Lazorko, 3b/rhp, Mississippi State**
12. **Tim Tolman, of, Southern California**
13. Mike Browning, 1b/rhp, Southridge HS, Miami
14. **Arvis Harper, of, Arkansas**
15. **Thad Troedson, rhp, San Diego State**
16. Michael Buggs, of, Castlemont HS, Oakland
17. Charles Hutchingson, rhp, West Memphis (Ariz.) HS

June—Secondary Phase (5)

1. Scott Fletcher, ss, Valencia (Fla.) CC

KANSAS CITY ROYALS

January—Regular Phase (26)

1. Lee Cline, rhp, JC of Southern Idaho
2. Eugene Picchena, 3b, Edmonds (Wash.) CC
3. **Keith Vranesh, of, Saddleback (Calif.) CC**
4. Doug Wabeke, ss, Grand Rapids (Mich.) JC
5. **Francis Mouse, ss, Allegany (Md.) CC**
6. **Larry Onesi, rhp, Russelton, Pa.**
7. Tom Chevolek, lhp, East Los Angeles JC
8. **John Melody, lhp, Irvington, N.J.**
9. Randy Cornelius, rhp, McKinleyville, Calif.
10. Michael Koch, c, Scottsdale (Ariz.) CC

January—Secondary Phase (5)

1. **Earl Robinson, of, Gulf Coast (Fla.) CC**
2. **Mike Haley, of, Central Arizona JC**
3. Tony Zahradnick, lhp, Valencia (Fla.) CC

June—Regular Phase (25)

1. **Buddy Biancalana, ss, Redwood HS, Greenbrae, Calif.**
2. **Darryl Motley, of, Grant HS, Portland, Ore.**
3. **Mark Ryal, of/lhp, Dewar (Okla.) HS**
4. **David Mangrum, rhp, Bells (Texas) HS**
5. **David Hogg, c, Northwestern**
6. **Jesse Lucious, of, Rich East HS, Park Forest, Ill.**
7. Tim Rodgers, rhp, Bixby HS, Broken Arrow, Okla.
8. **Jeff Cornell, rhp, Mississippi**
9. **Erik Hendricks, rhp, Chapman (Calif.)**
10. Harold Bright, of, Mumford HS, Detroit
11. **Ulises Infante, 3b, St. Patrick's HS, Elizabeth, N.J.**
12. **Robert Ganger, rhp, Pepperdine**
13. **James Davidson, of, Alma**
14. **Ira Turner, 1b, Bethune-Cookman**
15. Don Heinkel, rhp, Horlick HS, Racine, Wis.
16. Frank Viola, lhp, East Meadow (N.Y.) HS
17. **James Canfield, lhp, Wayne (Mich.) Memorial HS**
18. Bob Fiala, 3b, Oklahoma City
19. Bradley Kast, lhp, Reading (Mich.) HS
20. Tom Willette, lhp, North Carolina State
21. **Steven Porter, of, Upsala**
22. **Anthony Washington, of, Southeastern Oklahoma State**
23. **Jim McCoy, rhp, Texas**
24. **Ron Johnson, 1b, Fresno State**
25. **Chris Czarka, rhp, Central Michigan**
26. Welby Bailey, c, Lynchburg (Va.)
27. Mark Terrill, rhp, Gilroy (Calif.) HS
28. John Seneca, rhp, Seton Hall
29. Charles Curry, inf, Southern Illinois
30. **Craig Pippin, rhp, Florida**
31. Gregg Baker, rhp, Marcos de Niza HS, Tampa

June—Secondary Phase (2)

1. **Craig Chamberlain, rhp, Arizona**
2. **Bill Laskey, rhp, Kent State**
3. **Jeff Hanslovan, lhp, Linn-Benton (Ore.) CC**

LOS ANGELES DODGERS

January—Regular Phase (22)

1. **Brian Holton, rhp, Louisburg (N.C.) JC**
2. **Greg Schultz, ss, Sacramento CC**
3. Brad Patterson, rhp, Umpqua (Ore.) CC
4. **Matt Reeves, lhp, Sacramento CC**
5. Bryan Little, ss, Louisburg (N.C.) JC
6. Jimmy Boring, rhp, DeKalb South (Ga.) CC
7. Larry Pittman, 1b, Abraham Baldwin Agricultural (Ga.) JC
8. Anthony Murdaugh, rhp, South Carolina
9. Peter Zorich, rhp, Lower Columbia (Wash.) JC

January—Secondary Phase (8)

1. **Rusty McDonald, rhp, DeAnza (Calif.) JC**
2. Dan Sijer, lhp, Shoreline (Wash.) CC
3. **Stephen Smith, rhp/of, Gulf Coast (Fla.) CC**

June—Regular Phase (21)

1. (Pick to Pirates as compensation for free agent Terry Forster)
2. **Clay Smith, ss, Northwest HS, Oklahoma City**
3. **Augie Ruiz, lhp, Miami**
4. Glenn Gallagher, lhp, Peekskill (N.Y.) HS
5. **John Robbins, of, Lockhart HS, Union, S.C.**
6. **Mike Marshall, 1b/rhp, Buffalo Grove (Ill.) HS**
7. **Mark Nipp, rhp, Oklahoma**
8. **Bill Swiacki, rhp, Amherst (Mass.)**
9. **Steve Sax, ss, Marshall HS, West Sacramento, Calif.**
10. **Rodney Kemp, of, San Jose State**
11. **John Malkin, c, Cardinal Spellman HS, Bronx, N.Y.**
12. **Francis Wilczewski, rhp, Independence HS, San Jose**
13. **Melvin Meadows, of, White Oak HS, Maysville, N.C.**
14. **Jeff Kopjo, of/1b, Lyons Township HS, Brookfield, Ill.**
15. **Stephen Maples, c, Skyline HS, Dallas**
16. **Brian Hayes, lhp, Southern California**
17. **Joe Pocoroba, ss, Crespi HS, Woodland Hills, Calif.**

18. Eric Bullock, of, South Gate HS, Los Angeles
19. **Gary Weiss, inf, Houston**
20. Chris Iwasaki, of, Reedley (Calif.) JC
21. **Dave LaPoint, rhp, Monadnock Regional HS, Troy, N.H.**
22. **Tom Banducci, rhp, William Floyd HS, Mastic, N.Y.**
23. **Chris Gandy, 1b, UC Riverside**
24. **Warren Reeh, lhp, Comfort, Texas**
25. William Murray, ss, Tamalpais HS, Mill Valley, Calif.
26. David Albrecht, lhp, Appleton (Wis.) East HS
27. James Taylor, c, South Carolina
28. **Robert White, lhp, Lake Mills (Wis.) HS**
29. **Joe Herbert, of/c, Columbia (Tenn.) HS**
30. Kevin Patten, of, Miami (Ohio)
31. **Kent Johnson, rhp, Muncie (Ind.) Northside HS**
32. Dan Forer, lhp, Iowa Western CC
33. Michael Vienne, rhp, St. Mary's HS, Natchitoches, La.
34. Mark Pirruccello, c, Servite HS, Anaheim

June—Secondary Phase (7)

1. **Dann Bilardello, c, Cabrillo (Calif.) JC**
2. Morris Schrimsher, rhp, South Florida

MILWAUKEE BREWERS

January—Regular Phase (7)

1. **Weldon Swift, rhp, Baltimore**
2. **Doug Loman, of, Bakersfield (Calif.) JC**
3. **Doug Jones, rhp, Central Arizona JC**
4. Larry May, rhp, Central Arizona JC
5. Roland Atkins, c, Calhoun (Ala.) CC
6. **Porter Wyatt, ss, Palomar (Calif.) JC**
7. Robert Duncan, lhp, Blinn (Texas) JC
8. Greg Robles, 1b, San Jose CC
9. Kyle Farenthold, lhp, Blinn (Texas) JC
10. **Jerry Lewis, of, Central Arizona JC**
11. **Eddie Brunson, of, Miami-Dade North CC**
12. Charles Dinkins, lhp, Miami-Dade New World Center CC

January—Secondary Phase (19)

1. **Greg DeHart, rhp, Los Angeles Valley JC**
2. Maury Ornest, 1b, Central Arizona JC
3. Jerry Joyce, of, West Valley (Calif.) JC

June—Regular Phase (8)

1. **Nick Hernandez, c, Hialeah (Fla.) HS**
2. (Pick to Mariners as compensation for free agent Ray Fosse)
3. **Rickey Keeton, rhp, Southern Illinois**
4. **Rich Olsen, rhp, Hawaii**
5. **Tim Cook, rhp, Newberry (S.C.)**
6. **Steven Gibson, p, Kennedy HS, Granada Hills, Calif.**
7. **Franklin Thomas, 2b, Maryland**
8. **Vince Pone, 3b, El Camino Real HS, Woodland Hills, Calif.**
9. **Dan Gilmartin, ss, Monroe HS, Sepulveda, Calif.**
10. **Lance Ediger, of, Dallas (Ore.) HS**
11. **Columbus Duncan, 1b, Virginia**
12. Jerry DeSimone, ss, Southern Illinois
13. **Steven Norwood, rhp, Virginia**
14. Tom McLish, rhp, Edmond, Okla.
15. Carl Watson, rhp, East Bay HS, Gibsonton, Fla.
16. Tim Teufel, ss, St. Petersburg (Fla.) JC
17. **Mark Lepson, rhp, Lansdown HS, Arbutus, Md.**
18. **Dean Hall, 1b, Hawaii**
19. Kevin McReynolds, of, Sylvan HS, North Little Rock, Ark.
20. Mark Clabough, rhp, Lakewood (Calif.) HS
21. Randy Guerra, inf, Miami
22. Chuckie Canady, c, White Oak HS, Maysville, N.C.
23. Alan Mayles, rhp, Turner Asbey HS, Harrisonburg, Va.
24. **Randy Boyce, lhp, Cal State Dominguez Hills**
25. **Humberto Acosta, of, Miami**
26. **Pat Seegers, of, Wisconsin**
27. Mark Bonner, of, Long Beach CC
28. **James Manship, rhp, Arizona**
29. Rob Murphy, lhp, Columbus HS, Miami
30. Buster Moore, c, Molalia HS, Beaver Creek, Ore.
31. Steve Krueger, lhp, Garden City (Kan.) CC
32. Kevin McKenna, rhp, Lakewood (Calif.) HS
33. Michael Woods, ss, Southern

June—Secondary Phase (4)

1. **Allen Wesolowski, rhp, LaPorte, Ind.**
2. **James Robinson, of, Edmonds (Wash.) CC**
3. Robert Smith, of/inf, Orange Coast (Calif.) JC
4. James Johnson, ss, Edmonds (Wash.) CC
5. **James Padula, c, Chaffey (Calif.) JC**
6. **Daniel Maxson, rhp, DeKalb (Ga.) JC**
7. Stephen Maral, c, Chabot (Calif.) JC

MINNESOTA TWINS

January—Regular Phase (15)

1. Ralph Citarella, rhp, Brevard (Fla.) CC
2. **Jesse Orosco, lhp, Santa Barbara (Calif.) CC**
3. **Harold Rowe, ss, San Jose, Calif.**
4. Timothy Madera, of, JC of Marin (Calif.)
5. **Steven Green, rhp, Modesto (Calif.) JC**
6. Richard Austin, c, Cerritos (Calif.) JC
7. David Dodson, rhp, San Joaquin Delta (Calif.) JC
8. Larry Navilhon, rhp, JC of San Mateo (Calif.)
9. **Ronnie Mears, ss/2b, San Pablo, Calif.**
10. **Art Piccolotti, of, Skyline (Calif.) JC**
11. Tom Paul, of, Treasure Valley (Ore.) CC
12. Gary Forillo, ss, Citrus (Calif.) JC
13. **John Minarcin, rhp, Oneonta, N.Y.**

January—Secondary Phase (1)

1. **Joe Isaacs, rhp, Eastern Oklahoma State JC**
2. Mike Couchee, rhp, San Jose (Calif.) CC
3. Willie Lozado, ss, Miami-Dade New World Center CC
4. **Harold Washington, of/p, Southwestern (Calif.) JC**
5. Steve McQueen, ss, Gulf Coast (Fla.) CC

June—Regular Phase (16)

1. **Lenny Faedo, ss, Jefferson HS, Tampa**
2. **Mike Riley, rhp, Agawam (Mass.) HS**
3. Dave Leeper, lhp/of, Villa Park (Calif.) HS
4. **Wade Adamson, rhp, South Dakota State**
5. **Frank Vilorio, ss, Cal State Fullerton**
6. Nattie George, of, Overfelt HS, San Jose, Calif.
7. **Mark Maher, c, Tulane**
8. **Les Pearsey, 2b, Arizona**
9. Tony Fossas, lhp, South Florida
10. Tom Morris, lhp, Brigham Young
11. **Don Smith, c, Istrouma HS, Baton Rouge, La.**
12. Scott Bradley, c, West Essex HS, Essex Fells, N.J.
13. **Ron Grout, 1b, Wingate (N.C.)**
14. Craig Shumock, 3b, Chestnut Hill Academy, Willow Grove, Pa.
15. **Robert Jones, lhp, Archbishop Curley HS, Baltimore**
16. **Michael Williams, c, Wingate (N.C.)**
17. **Kent Hrbek, 1b, Kennedy HS, Bloomington, Minn.**
18. **Alex Dovalis, 3b, Long Beach CC**
19. Gene Ransom, inf, California
20. **Kevin Sevcik, rhp, St. Olaf (Minn.)**
21. Tom Lounibos, inf, San Francisco
22. **Chris Geason, lhp, Augsburg (Minn.)**
23. William Guinn, rhp, Beaverton (Ore.) HS
24. Edward Castro, rhp, Maryland
25. **Robert Holden, c, Glassboro State (N.J.)**
26. **Rufus Thompson, of, Cal Poly Pomona**
27. Al Mejia, c, Fullerton (Calif.) JC
28. Randy Ramirez, rhp, Katella HS, Anaheim
29. Steven Houlberg, ss, Alabama
30. Randy Filkins, of, West Hills (Calif.)
31. **Robert Waldusky, of, La Verne (Calif.)**
32. Ron Dearth, 3b, Lakewood (Calif.) HS
33. Paul Mancuso, lhp, Shaw HS, Gretna, La.

June—Secondary Phase (25)

1. Bruce Kastelic, ss, Ranger (Texas) JC

MONTREAL EXPOS

January—Regular Phase (10)

1. **Gary Hartsock, rhp, Muscatine (Iowa) CC**

2. Charles Barclift, 1b, Louisburg (N.C.) JC
3. John Maxom, rhp, DeKalb South (Ga.) CC
4. Ken Kellogg, of, Blinn (Texas) JC
5. Louis Stawarz, 1b, Manatee (Fla.) JC
6. Brian Benedict, c, Palm Beach (Fla.) JC
7. **Renardo Richardson, 3b, Cincinnati**
8. **Mark South, rhp, Wright State**
9. John Damon, ss, Sacramento CC
10. **Paul Josephson, rhp, Shrewsbury, Conn.**

January—Secondary Phase (10)

1. **Tony Phillips, ss/2b, New Mexico Military Institute JC**
2. Larry Reasonover, 3b, Hillsborough (Fla.) CC
3. **Gary Aguirre, ss, Bakersfield, Calif.**
4. Michael Kelly, of, Cosumnes River (Calif.) JC

June—Regular Phase (9)

1. **Glenn Franklin, ss, Chipola (Fla.) JC**
2. (Pick to Orioles as compensation for free agent Ross Grimsley)
3. **Steve Michael, of, Arizona State**
4. **Dave Hostetler, 1b, Southern California**
5. **Steve Morrison, 3b, South Alabama**
6. Bill Mooneyham, rhp, Atwater HS, Winton, Calif.
7. Cat Whitfield, of/1b, Middle Georgia JC
8. **David Perez, ss/2b, Stanford**
9. **Charlie Lea, rhp, Memphis State**
10. **Tom Wieghaus, c, Illinois State**
11. Dave Clements, ss, Eastbay HS, Riverview, Fla.
12. **Ronnie Pearce, rhp, Stetson**
13. Jim Deshaies, lhp, Massena (N.Y.) HS
14. **Grayling Tobias, of, Missouri-St. Louis**
15. **Jeff Taylor, lhp, Garfield HS, Garrettsville, Ohio**
16. **Jerry George, c, Louisiana College**
17. **Rick Ramos, rhp, Lewis (Ill.)**
18. **Razor Shines, c, St. Augustine (N.C.)**
19. **Kevin Mendon, rhp, Emporia State (Kan.)**
20. **Pat Rooney, of, Eastern Illinois**
21. Chris Cawthon, inf, Avondale HS, Avondale Estates, Ga.
22. **Steve Lovins, rhp, Northern Kentucky**

June—Secondary Phase (24)

No selection

NEW YORK METS

January—Regular Phase (4)

1. Gerry Miller, 1b, Des Moines Area (Iowa) CC
2. **Michael Cannon, of, Middlesex (Conn.) CC**
3. Marty Barrett, 2b, Mesa (Ariz.) CC
4. Ron Graves, rhp, Modesto (Calif.) JC
5. Ricky Jones, 3b/rhp, Chipola (Fla.) JC
6. Louis D'Amore, rhp, CC of Morris (N.J.)
7. Floyd Gow, lhp, Butte (Calif.) JC
8. **Jamie Nelson, c, Orange Coast (Calif.) JC**
9. Al Hammack, rhp, Bellevue (Wash.) CC
10. Robert Randolph, rhp, Butte (Calif.) JC

January—Secondary Phase (24)

1. Michael Foster, lhp, Merced (Calif.) JC
2. Jack Lambeth, lhp, Westark (Ark.) CC

June—Regular Phase (3)

1. **Hubie Brooks, of, Arizona State**
2. (Pick to Orioles as compensation for free agent Elliott Maddox)
3. **Brian Giles, 2b, Kearny HS, San Diego**
4. **Don Troyan, 1b, St. John's**
5. **Jeff Gossett, ss, Eastern Illinois**
6. **Mike Fitzgerald, c, Lakewood (Calif.) HS**
7. Henry Janssen, c, Scotch Plains (N.J.) HS
8. **James Cooperider, lhp, Central Valley HS, Redding, Calif.**
9. **Glen Johnson, rhp, Lewis-Clark State (Idaho)**
10. **Richard Lane, c, San Jose State**
11. **Randy Johnson, ss, San Jose State**
12. Reggie Whittemore, of, Lipscomb (Tenn.)
13. Jeff Sunderlage, lhp, Elgin (Ill.) HS
14. **Darryl Denby, of, Lincoln HS, San Diego**
15. **John Elder, 3b, Frostburg State (Md.)**
16. **James Beck, 1b, Temple**
17. **Randy Pitts, rhp, Redlands (Calif.)**
18. **Michael Tancredi, rhp, Mansfield (Pa.)**
19. John Wells, of, Southern California
20. **Steve Till, c, Cal State Fullerton**
21. **Michael Viggiano, inf, Bricktown (N.J.) HS**
22. Mark Davis, lhp, Granada Hills HS, Livermore, Calif.
23. Richard Eckleberry, rhp, Flathead HS, Kalispell, Mont.
24. **Rick Anderson, rhp, Washington**
25. Clint Harvey, rhp, Coastal Carolina
26. **Greg Korbe, of, Kansas State**
27. Al Lachowicz, rhp, Canevin HS, McKeesrock, Pa.
28. **Gary Hilton, rhp, Canyon HS, Anaheim**
29. **Ronald Walker, 1b, Benedictine (Kan.)**
30. **David Smith, of, Siena**
31. **Marc Siciliano, c, Iona**

June—Secondary Phase (3)

1. James Tjader, inf, Iowa Western CC

NEW YORK YANKEES

January—Regular Phase (25)

1. **Mark Harris, ss, Manassas, Va.**
2. **John Franks, rhp, Seminole (Fla.) CC**
3. Kevin Niewulis, lhp, Louisburg (N.C.) JC
4. Rusty McNealy, of, JC of Southern Idaho
5. Dean Foes, lhp, Central Arizona JC

January—Secondary Phase (11)

1. **David Garcia, 2b, Grossmont (Calif.) JC**
2. James Robinson, of, Edmonds (Wash.) CC
3. David Fowke, 2b, Manatee (Fla.) JC

June—Regular Phase (26)

1. **Rex Hudler, ss, Bullard HS, Fresno** (Pick from White Sox as compensation for free agent Ron Blomberg)
1. **Matt Winters, of, Williamsville (N.Y.) HS** (Pick from Red Sox as compensation for free agent Mike Torrez)
1. **Brian Ryder, rhp, Shrewsbury (Mass.) HS**
2. **Steve Balboni, 1b, Eckerd (Fla.)**
3. **Mark Johnston, of, South Alabama**
4. **Tim Lollar, lhp/1b, Arkansas**
5. **Pete Khoury, of, Eckerd (Fla.)**
6. **Andy McGaffigan, rhp, Florida Southern**
7. **Kevin Hemphill, 3b, Catawba (N.C.)**
8. **Dan Plante, c, Crespi HS, Woodland Hills, Calif.**
9. **Jeff Taylor, c, Delaware**
10. **Dan Ledduke, rhp, Florida International**
11. **Mark Moore, lhp, South Florida**
12. Randy Kwist, 3b, Eckerd (Fla.)
13. **Claude Sammons, 1b/of, Gonzaga**
14. Andy Beene, rhp, Baylor
15. Dan Peterson, rhp, Great Falls (Mont.) HS
16. **Brian Dayett, 3b, St. Leo (Fla.)**
17. **Don Cooper, rhp, New York Tech**
18. **Rich Carlucci, rhp, Iowa**
19. **Karl Steffen, lhp, Ithaca (N.Y.)**
20. Eric Snider, rhp, Washington State
21. Jerome Burgess, c, Atlantic HS, Delray Beach, Fla.
22. Jeff Ledbetter, 1b, Largo (Fla.) HS
23. Howard Johnson, rhp/3b, Clearwater (Fla.) HS

June—Secondary Phase (15)

1. Joe Housey, rhp, Miami-Dade North CC

OAKLAND ATHLETICS

January—Regular Phase (3)

1. David Grier, rhp, Valencia (Fla.) CC
2. Kendall Greene, rhp, Santa Barbara (Calif.) CC
3. Thomas McGivney, c, Alvin (Texas) CC
4. Karl Jastrow, lhp, West Los Angeles JC
5. Jerry Lane, inf, West Los Angeles JC
6. James Padula, c, Chaffey (Calif.) JC
7. James Johnson, ss, Edmonds (Wash.) CC
8. Robert Parr, of, West Los Angeles JC

9. Kevin Darst, inf, Solano (Calif.) CC
10. Larry White, rhp, Los Angeles Pierce JC
11. John Davis, rhp, Solano (Calif.) CC

January—Secondary Phase (21)

1. Scott Fletcher, ss, Valencia (Fla.) CC
2. Mark Beuclear, rhp, San Jacinto (Texas) JC
3. Edward Long, rhp, Santa Monica (Calif.) JC
4. Joe Madrigal, rhp, Mount San Antonio (Calif.) JC

June—Regular Phase (4)

1. **Mike Morgan, rhp, Valley HS, Las Vegas**
1. **Tim Conroy, lhp, Gateway HS, Monroeville, Pa.**
2. **Keith Atherton, rhp, Mathews (Va.) HS**
3. **Bob Grandas, of, Central Michigan**
4. **Mike Woodard, 2b, Proviso East HS, Maywood, Ill.**
5. **Scott Meyer, c, Western Michigan**
6. **Kelvin Moore, 1b, Jackson State**
7. **Charles Dougherty, lhp, Steubenville (Ohio) HS**
8. Robert Adams, c, Sherrill (N.Y.) Central HS
9. Mike Codiroli, of, Stanford
10. **Stephen Marlowe, rhp, St. Petersburg Christian HS, Pinellas Park, Fla.**
11. **Jay Greb, ss, Eagle Point (Ore.) HS**
12. **Ron Jensen, lhp, Coronado HS, Scottsdale, Ariz.**
13. **Bret Cleland, rhp, Corning (Calif.) HS**
14. **Omar Minaya, of, Newton HS, Elmhurst, N.Y.**
15. Jim Scranton, ss, Palomar (Calif.) JC
16. Daniel Casey, lhp, Edison (N.J.) HS
17. **Donald Morris, of, Oklahoma**
18. **Fred DeVito, 3b, Pace (N.Y.)**
19. Charles Hollowell, lhp, Plant HS, Tampa
20. Tim Byron, rhp, Our Lady of the Valley HS, Florham Park, N.J.
21. Wymon Smith, rhp, JC of Southern Idaho
22. John Lunden, rhp, JC of Southern Idaho
23. Casey Schaefer, rhp, North Salem (Ore.) HS
24. Bud Yanus, rhp, Eastern Michigan
25. Gregg Mayer, of/rhp, Brick Township HS, Lakewood, N.J.
26. Stephen Bricker, rhp, Watkins Memorial HS, Etna, Ohio
27. Jeffrey Way, c, University HS, Spokane, Wash.
28. Carlo Hernandez, lhp, Tampa Catholic HS
29. Greg Key, ss, Citrus HS, Inverness, Fla.
30. Brian Harrison, rhp, Stanford
31. **Steven Oliver, lhp, Cecil (Md.) CC**
32. Greg Booker, 1b/ss, Cummings HS, Burlington, N.C.
33. **Ralph Jean, rhp, Dover (Del.) HS**
34. John Moller, lhp, Brookdale (N.J.) CC
35. George Cecchetti, 1b, Tokay HS, Stockton, Calif.

June—Secondary Phase (26)

1. **Michael Kennedy, ss, Linn-Benton (Ore.) CC**

PHILADELPHIA PHILLIES

January—Regular Phase (24)

1. **Don Woodward, rhp, Central Arizona JC**
2. Steven Russell, rhp, Muskogee (Okla.) HS
3. James Green, of, Panola (Texas) JC
4. **Angelo Ross, of, Pasadena (Calif.) CC**
5. Gary Venner, c, Ranger (Texas) JC
6. **Juan Parker, of, Truman (Ill.) JC**
7. Jeffrey Musser, of, Ferrum (Va.)

January—Secondary Phase (20)

1. **Daryl Adams, rhp, Butte (Calif.) JC**
2. Kevin Williams, of, Edmonds (Wash.) CC

June—Regular Phase (23)

1. **Rip Rollins, 1b, Allegheny HS, Sparta, N.C.**
2. **Anthony McGill, of, Jones HS, Houston**
3. **Dean Martinez, rhp, Pueblo (Colo.) East HS**
4. **Ed Hearn, c, Fort Pierce (Fla.) Central HS**
5. **Darren Burroughs, lhp, Vinitia HS, Langley, Okla.**
6. **Pete Dempsey, ss, Temple**
7. **Paul Kiess, 1b, Granada Hills HS, Northridge, Calif.**
8. **Mike Henson, c, San Mateo HS, Foster City, Calif.**
9. **Dan Prior, rhp, James Madison**
10. **Marty Shoemaker, rhp, Checotah (Okla.) HS**
11. Dwight Taylor, of, Fremont HS, Los Angeles
12. **Michael Culbert, rhp, Bonanza HS, Las Vegas**
13. **Bruce Humphrey, 1b, Tulsa**
14. **Robert Angius, lhp/1b, Lassen HS, Susanville, Calif.**
15. **Charles Marshall, rhp, Floyd County HS, Willis, Va.**
16. Ron Rendleman, rhp, Bloomington (Calif.) HS
17. Michael Kreymborg, rhp, Kelley HS, Tulsa, Okla.
18. **Randy Greer, of, Southern California College**
19. **Jeff Ulrich, c, Fresno (Calif.) CC**
20. **Ryne Sandberg, inf, North Central HS, Spokane, Wash.**
21. **Alvin White, of, Northern Colorado**
22. **Thomas Popovich, inf, Toledo**
23. **John Palmieri, lhp, Pilgrim HS, Warwick, R.I.**
24. Rick Leach, 1b/of, Michigan
25. **Phil Teston, rhp, Land O'Lakes (Fla.) HS**
26. Michael Vojtesak, rhp, Joliet (Ill.) Central HS
27. **John DeVincenzo, rhp, Tampa**
28. **Derek Williams, c, Willingsboro (N.J.) HS**
29. **Steve Harvey, of, Benjamin Franklin HS, Philadelphia**
30. Sammy Bickham, lhp, Southern Methodist

June—Secondary Phase (21)

1. Kendall Greene, rhp, Santa Barbara (Calif.) CC
2. Ken Eriksen, rhp, Citrus (Calif.) JC

PITTSBURGH PIRATES

January—Regular Phase (20)

1. Pete Chapin, rhp, Fullerton (Calif.) JC
2. **Brent Hillenga, 1b, San Diego Mesa JC**
3. Mel Locke, rhp, Pasadena (Calif.) CC
4. Bill Waag, ss, Lower Columbia (Wash.) JC
5. Robert Smith, of, Orange Coast (Calif.) JC
6. **Michael Leveton, 1b, White Park**
7. Courtney Wyrick, rhp, West Los Angeles JC
8. John Garcia, p, Chattahoochee Valley (Ala.) CC
9. Joe Nemeth, 1b, Orange Coast (Calif.) CC

January—Secondary Phase (12)

1. Kurt Kingsolver, c, Long Beach (Calif.) CC
2. Lawrence Dotson, of, Orange Coast (Calif.) CC
3. Marvin Fowler, rhp, San Diego Mesa JC
4. Rob Dondero, rhp, Mesa (Ariz.) CC

June—Regular Phase (19)

1. **Brad Garnett, 1b, DeSoto (Texas) HS**
1. **Gerry Aubin, of, Dougherty HS, Albany, Ga.** (Pick from Dodgers as compensation for free agent Terry Forster)
2. **Brad Palmer, lhp, Escondido (Calif.) HS**
3. **Pat Rubino, c, San Diego State**
4. **Thomas Siebert, rhp, Coeur D'Alene HS, Fernan Hill, Idaho**
5. **Robert Davis, rhp, Utah**
6. Don McCarthy, p, Del City, Okla.
7. Scott Roberts, rhp, Roosevelt HS, Seattle
8. **Donald Cline, rhp, Piqua, Ohio**
9. **Frank Miloszewski, rhp, Indiana**
10. David Rosenhahn, rhp/ss, West Seneca (N.Y.) HS
11. **Tim Florey, rhp, Brooklyn Park HS, Baltimore**
12. **Dennis Jones, of, Kearny HS, Spring Valley, Calif.**
13. Barry Brown, lhp, Lake Worth HS, Fort Worth
14. **Wesley Hair, 3b/2b, Albany State (Ga.)**
15. John Young, c, Henry Ford HS, Sterling Heights, Mich.
16. **Stanton Brown, of, Davidson**
17. **Mike Nedelisky, rhp, Lewis-Clark State (Idaho)**
18. **John Stuper, rhp, Point Park (Pa.)**
19. Jeff Vlha, inf, Fullerton (Calif.) HS
20. **Todd Denby, inf, Fluvanna HS, Scottsvile, Va.**
21. **Dave Dravecky, lhp, Youngstown State**
22. **Thaddeus Reed, of, Glass HS, Lynchburg, Va.**
23. Arbrey Lucas, rhp, Chapparal HS, North Las Vegas, Nev.
24. David McDonald, lhp, Allegheny (Pa.) CC
25. Vince Pellegrini, rhp, Father Judge HS, Philadelphia
26. **John Huey, rhp, Mannington (W.Va.) HS**
27. **Jeff Zaske, rhp, Meadowdale HS, Lynwood, Wash.**
28. David Pascho, rhp, Juanita HS, Kirkland, Wash.

29. Michael O'Boyle, rhp, Northport HS, Long Island, N.Y.
30. Mark Johnson, rhp, Kearns (Utah) HS
31. **Dean Rick, lhp, Wilson HS, Sinking Spring, Pa.**
32. **James Fiori, c, Carlynton HS, Carnegie, Pa.**
33. John West, ss, Granite Falls HS, Marysville, Wash.
34. Kevin Johnson, rhp, CC of Baltimore
35. Geoff Meadows, rhp, Southmoreland HS, Everson, Pa.
36. Tim Ronan, rhp, San Diego
37. Albert Brehm, rhp, Foothills HS, Santa Ana, Calif.
38. Mike Bretz, rhp, Florida State
39. **Vance Law, ss, Brigham Young**
40. Fenton Lebon, p/of, Lincoln Academy, Pemquiz Harbor, Maine

June—Secondary Phase (23)

1. **Bill Waag, ss, Lower Columbia (Wash.) JC**
2. Tim Muench, rhp, Seminole (Fla.) CC

ST. LOUIS CARDINALS

January—Regular Phase (16)

1. Michael Gentry, rhp, Chipola (Fla.) JC
2. Don Sutherland, rhp, Barstow (Calif.) CC
3. **Daniel Pierce, rhp, El Camino (Calif.) JC**
4. Gary Gaetti, 3b, Lincoln Land (Ill.) CC
5. Edward Lindsey, lhp, Broward (Fla.) CC
6. Gary Kempton, c, Triton (Ill.) JC
7. Kevin Coughlon, of, Moorpark (Calif.) JC
8. Robert Weirum, 2b, Santa Barbara (Calif.) CC
9. Matthew Vejar, 3b, Merced (Calif.) JC
10. Kenneth Corzel, rhp, Santa Monica (Calif.) JC
11. Kevin Waller, of, San Diego CC

January—Secondary Phase (18)

1. James David, ss, Santa Barbara (Calif.) CC
2. Ken Eriksen, rhp, Citrus (Calif.) JC
3. Dave Meier, ss, Fresno (Calif.) CC

June—Regular Phase (15)

1. **Bob Hicks, 1b, Tate HS, Pensacola, Fla.**
2. **David Kable, 1b, West HS, Columbus, Ga.**
3. Mike Moore, rhp, Eakly HS, Carnegie, Okla.
4. **George Bjorkman, c, Oral Roberts**
5. Glenn Jones, of, Frankfort (Ky.) HS
6. **Tim Mueller, c, Arroyo HS, San Lorenzo, Calif.**
7. **Dennis Gadowski, rhp, Central Catholic HS, Cleveland**
8. Richard Budweg, lhp, Bloomsburg (Pa.)
9. Marty Wilkerson, ss, Corona (Calif.) HS
10. Marshall Cook, lhp, Dallas Baptist
11. Jeff Sollars, lhp, Wellington (Ill.) HS
12. **Dennis Delany, c, UCLA**
13. **Roosevelt Lett, 3b, Garey HS, Pomona, Calif.**
14. **Martin Little, rhp, West Jefferson, N.C.**
15. Mike Toothman, of, Edgewood HS, West Covina, Calif.
16. **Mike Carpenter, of, UCLA**
17. Mark Smith, rhp, Lipscomb HS, Franklin, Tenn.
18. Bob Skube, of, Southern California
19. Ken Malone, of, Prairie View A&M
20. **Jeff Young, of, Trenton (N.J.) HS**
21. **John Perlongo, inf, Ridgefield Park (N.J.) HS**
22. **Ray Rivas, inf, Santa Clara**
23. John Carter, 1b/of, Bloomfield (N.J.) HS
24. **Robert Russell, rhp, Paducah (Ky.) CC**
25. Tom Sauer, rhp, St. Louis CC-Meramec
26. Les Kakazu, 3b, Waipahu (Hawaii) HS
27. **Everett Smith, 2b, Furman**
28. Gerald Klauser, c, Whitesboro (N.Y.) HS
29. Tim Gloyd, ss/2b, Pepperdine
30. Steven Southerland, rhp, Desmet Catholic HS, Chesterfield, Mo.
31. Armand Villa, rhp, Sunnyslope HS, Phoenix
32. **James Dieters, 3b, Oakland (Mich.)**
33. **Scott Arigoni, lhp, Cape Cod (Mass.) CC**
34. **Paul Wysocki, rhp, Sacred Heart**
35. **Thomas Wertz, rhp, Brighton (Mass.) HS**
36. Randy Ratcliff, 1b, William Carey (Miss.)
37. **Reginald Ward, of, Beaumont HS, St. Louis**
38. Pat Patterson, ss, Miami-Dade North CC
39. Frank Horak, rhp, Loyola Marymount
40. **John Harshbarger, rhp, Illinois**
41. **Kerry Burchett, rhp, East Tennessee State**
42. **David Picconi, lhp, Northern Colorado**
43. Kevin Pyatte, lhp, Portland, Texas
44. **Peter Beattie, of, Wilson HS, Hacienda Heights, Calif.**
45. Curt Wardle, lhp, Norco (Calif.) HS
46. **Thomas Chandler, of, Bryan (Texas) HS**

June—Secondary Phase (19)

1. **Jeff Orville, rhp, Santa Ana (Calif.) JC**
2. Curt Reade, rhp, Fresno State
3. Don Pierce, lhp, Chaffey (Calif.) JC
4. Ed Vande Berg, lhp, San Bernardino Valley (Calif.) JC

SAN DIEGO PADRES

January—Regular Phase (6)

1. **Donald Johnson, lhp, Westland, Mich.**
2. Jeff Stottlemyre, lhp, Yakima Valley (Wash.) JC
3. Ed Vande Berg, lhp, San Bernardino Valley (Calif.) JC
4. James Tunnell, rhp, San Joaquin Delta (Calif.) JC

January—Secondary Phase (6)

1. **Mike Martin, c, Mount Hood (Ore.) CC**
2. **Willie Hardwick, rhp, Laney (Calif.) JC**
3. Reggie West, of, Santa Ana (Calif.) JC
4. Robert Wicks, rhp, Chabot (Calif.) JC

June—Regular Phase (5)

1. **Andy Hawkins, rhp, Midway HS, Waco, Texas**
2. **Doug Gwosdz, c, Madison HS, Houston** (Pick from Angels as compensation for free agent Merv Rettenmund)
3. **George Stablein, rhp, Cal State Dominguez Hills**
4. Larry Reynolds, of, Stanford
5. **Floyd Chiffer, rhp, UCLA**
6. **Tim Flannery, 2b, Chapman (Calif.)**
7. **Steve Fireovid, rhp, Miami (Ohio)**
8. **Mike Parker, of, Michigan**
9. **Tim Hamm, rhp, Soquel HS, Santa Cruz, Calif.**
10. **Mobil Cox, ss, UCLA**
11. **Jack Hills, lhp, Cal State Dominguez Hills**
12. **Brad Shames, c, UC Santa Barbara**
13. **Greg Patton, rhp, Lower Dauphin HS, Elizabethtown, Pa.**
14. **Al Richmond, of, St. Mary's**
15. Ken Harris, 3b/ss, El Cerrito HS, Berkeley, Calif.
16. **Curt Cannedy, 1b, St. Mary's**
17. **Bob Volk, 3b, Oral Roberts**
18. **Eric Show, rhp, UC Riverside**
19. **Anthony McGrue, of, Morse HS, San Diego**
20. **Syd Church, lhp, Pacific**
21. Ken McLemore, inf, Morse HS, San Diego
22. Gregg Sporrer, inf, Cal State Fullerton
23. Aaron Cain, 2b/of, New Mexico
24. Mark Thurmond, lhp, Texas A&M
25. Paul Noce, ss, Sequoia HS, Redwood City, Calif.
26. Randy Kramer, rhp, Oak Grove HS, San Jose, Calif.

June—Secondary Phase (11)

1. **Greg Pastors, ss, Oklahoma State**
2. Rob Hertel, inf, Southern California

SAN FRANCISCO GIANTS

January—Regular Phase (8)

1. Greg Byrd, 1b, Columbia State (Tenn.) CC
2. **Ned Raines, 2b, Seminole (Fla.) CC**
3. **Paul Plinski, inf, Los Angeles Valley JC**
4. James Evans, lhp, West Los Angeles JC
5. Eugene Hernandez, rhp, San Joaquin Delta (Calif.) JC
6. Michael Ott, of, Yavapai (Ariz.) JC
7. Michael Kennedy, ss, Linn-Benton (Ore.) CC
8. Joe Olivas, rhp/inf, San Joaquin Delta (Calif.) JC
9. **Bruce Oliver, 3b/of, San Diego CC**

January—Secondary Phase (2)

1. **Ron Pisel, rhp, Southeastern Illinois JC**
2. **Greg Moyer, of, Cerritos (Calif.) JC**
3. Norm Christensen, rhp, San Diego CC

June—Regular Phase (7)

1. **Bob Cummings, c, Brother Rice HS, Chicago**
2. Steve Raine, rhp, North Salinas (Calif.) HS
3. **David Wiggins, lhp/of, Seminole HS, Sanford, Fla.**
4. **Rob Deer, of, Canyon HS, Anaheim**
5. **Jeff Ransom, c, Berkeley (Calif.) HS**
6. Ken Hall, p, McNicholas HS, Cincinnati
7. **Kelly Anderson, rhp, Ygnacio Valley HS, Concord, Calif.**
8. Alvin Davis, 3b/of, North HS, Riverside, Calif.
9. **Chris Barbone, of/inf, Azusa Pacific (Calif.)**
10. Dwayne Jackson, of, Locke HS, Los Angeles
11. **John Rabb, c, Washington HS, Los Angeles**
12. Charles Everett, rhp, Crowley (Texas) HS
13. **Dale Baldwin, 2b, Boise State**
14. Greg Norris, rhp, North Carolina
15. **Jeff Ahlert, c, Aiken HS, Cincinnati**
16. **Ricky Kittrell, lhp, Vanderbilt**
17. Steve Roberts, 3b, Kentucky
18. Robert Taylor, rhp, Thomas Jefferson HS, Port Arthur, Texas
19. **Richard Doss, inf, Eastern Illinois**
20. Babe Laufenberg, rhp, Crespi HS, Canoga Park, Calif.
21. **Mark Calvert, rhp, Tulsa**
22. **Darius Copley, of, Lubbock Christian (Texas)**
23. Doug Hoppock, rhp/of, Southeast HS, Wichita, Kan.
24. Kem Wright, rhp, Texas
25. **Keith Brooks, of, Martinsburg (W.Va.) HS**
26. Burl Coker, lhp, Baylor
27. **Leotis Butler, of, Georgia Southwestern**
28. Kevin Clinton, of/rhp, Southeast HS, Wichita, Kan.
29. Randy Meyer, of, Mount Hood (Ore.) CC
30. **Richard Casillas, c, Oregon College of Education**
31. Ted Notos, lhp, Grant HS, Portland, Ore.
32. Mark Brewer, rhp, Coronado HS, Tempe, Ariz.
33. John Millholland, 2b, Louisa (Va.) HS

June—Secondary Phase (17)

1. **Kevin Darst, inf, Solano (Calif.) CC**
2. Greg Byrd, inf, Columbia State (Tenn.) CC

SEATTLE MARINERS

January—Regular Phase (5)

1. **Jim Maler, 1b, Miami-Dade South CC**
2. **Anthony Jordan, rhp, Monterey Peninsula (Calif.) JC**
3. Dann Bilardello, c, Cabrillo (Calif.) JC
4. Kirk Komstadius, 3b, Yakima Valley (Wash.) JC
5. Kevin Miller, 1b, Cerritos (Calif.) JC
6. **Teddy Adkins, rhp, Palm Beach (Fla.) JC**

January—Secondary Phase (9)

1. **Richard Alexander, of, Matthews, N.C.**
2. Juan Corey, c, Miami-Dade North CC
3. **Carlos Matamoras, 2b, Miami-Dade North CC**

June—Regular Phase (6)

1. **Tito Nanni, of/1b, Chestnut Hill Academy, Philadelphia**
2. **Dave Valle, c, Holy Cross HS, Bayside, N.Y.**
2. **Rich Naumann, lhp, Bay Village (Ohio) HS** (Pick from Brewers as compensation for free agent Ray Fosse)
3. **Rob Simond, lhp, Southern Illinois**
4. **Ron McGee, rhp, Lincoln HS, San Jose, Calif.**
5. **Werner Lajszky, c, Mater Christi HS, Astoria, N.Y.**
6. **Doug Smith, rhp, Oklahoma**
7. **Jack Hobbs, lhp, Lynchburg (Va.)**
8. **Lazoro Santin, lhp, Rochester Adams HS, Miami**
9. **Richard Graser, lhp/of, Fort Vancouver (Wash.) HS**
10. **Bob Stoddard, rhp, Fresno State**
11. **Vance McHenry, ss, Nevada-Las Vegas**
12. **Terry Mixon, ss, Georgia Southern**
13. Bill Kampen, rhp, Rummel HS, Metairie, La.
14. **Rob Pietroburgo, lhp, Missouri**
15. **Harry Mauch, of, Southern Oregon State**
16. **David Nowland, ss, Tulsa**
17. **Michael Guerra, inf/of, Nevada-Las Vegas**
18. Jerry Vasquez, rhp, Arizona State
19. Calvin Horhn, of, Des Moines Area (Iowa) CC
20. **Rod Hudson, c, Portland (Ore.) State**
21. **Dave Edler, inf, Washington State**
22. **Chris Flammang, inf/of, Sierra HS, Tollhouse, Calif.**

June—Secondary Phase (8)

1. Gerald Miller, inf/of, Des Moines Area (Iowa) CC
2. Scott Benedict, c, Palm Beach (Fla.) JC

TEXAS RANGERS

January—Regular Phase (19)

1. **Michael Vickers, lhp, Hill (Texas) JC**
2. Mark Knowles, lhp, Central Arizona JC
3. Anthony Stevens, of, Seminole (Fla.) CC
4. Richard Derechailo, c, Brookdale (N.J.) CC
5. Edward Bailey, c, Paris (Texas) JC

January—Secondary Phase (23)

1. **Michae Childs, c, Ranger (Texas) JC**
2. **Greg Eason, lhp, Pensacola, Fla.**

June—Regular Phase (20)

1. (Pick to Athletics as compensation for free agent Mike Jorgensen)
2. **Amos Lewis, rhp/inf, Astronaut HS, Mims, Fla.**
3. **David Crutcher, rhp, Arizona**
4. Mitch Zwolensky, rhp, Owosso (Mich.) HS
5. Eric Shellenbeck, of, Barrington HS, Barrington Hills, Ill.
6. **Terry Bogener, of, Oklahoma**
7. **Jerry Neufang, c, Hayfield HS, Lorton, Va.**
8. **Wayne Tolleson, ss, Western Carolina**
9. **Tracy Cowger, of/c, Loyola Marymount**
10. Allan Ramirez, rhp, Rice
11. **Chris Smith, of/inf, Southern California**
12. Rick Misuraca, 3b, Del City (Okla.) HS
13. **Albert Ortiz, of, Baruch**
14. Charlie O'Brien, c, Kelly HS, Tulsa, Okla.
15. Eddie Greene, lhp, Ed White HS, Jacksonville, Fla.
16. **Daniel Dixon, of, Nebraska**
17. Brian Piper, rhp, Buena HS, Sierra Vista, Ariz.
18. **Ron Gooch, 2b, Southeastern Oklahoma State**
19. Howard Shapiro, inf, Miami
20. **Keith Shellings, lhp, Southern**
21. **Charles Kwolek, lhp, Providence**
22. **Andrew Tam, rhp, Texas Wesleyan**
23. Donald Atkins, ss, Parkview HS, Little Rock, Ark.
24. **Stanley Reese, 1b, George Mason**
25. **Cameron Killebrew, of, Brigham Young**
26. **David Miller, of, George Mason**
27. **Jeff Zitek, ss, Illinois State**
28. **Wesley Williams, rhp, New Mexico Highlands**
29. **Jim Farr, rhp, Penn State**
30. **Gene Nelson, rhp, Pasco County HS, Dade City, Fla.**
31. **Steve Paine, of/c, Dallas Baptist**
32. Tommy Blackmon, rhp, South Florence (S.C.) HS
33. **Cecil De Fla Strawn, c, Southern Methodist**
34. James Strum, rhp, St. Marks HS, Wilmington, Del.
35. **Keith Walsh, rhp, John F. Kennedy HS, Suffolk, Va.**
36. Harry Oakley, c, Rogers HS, Newport, R.I.
37. **David Chapman, 3b, Michigan**
38. **John Zisk, of, Delaware Valley**
39. Tim Hulett, ss, Lamphier HS, Springfield, Ill.
40. Jeff Scott, 3b, Port Clinton (Ohio) HS
41. **Alvin Williams, 3b, Jackson State**
42. Moses Kyles, ss, Buchanan (Mich.) HS

June—Secondary Phase (10)

1. **Mike Richardt, 3b, Fresno (Calif.) CC**
2. **Thomas McGivney, c, Alvin (Texas) CC**
3. David Jensen, lhp, Edmonds (Wash.) CC

TORONTO BLUE JAYS

January—Regular Phase (1)

1. **Mike Lebo, c, Middletown, Pa.**
2. Mike Richardt, ss, Fresno CC
3. **Geno Petralli, c, Sacramento CC**
4. **Michael Kelly, of, Santa Barbara, Calif.**

January—Secondary Phase (15)

1. Rob Hertel, 2b/3b, Southern California

June—Regular Phase (2)

1. **Lloyd Moseby, 1b, Oakland HS**
2. **Tim Thompson, 1b, Winter Park (Fla.) HS**
3. **Mike Cullen, rhp, Columbus (Wis.) HS**
4. **Mike Coyne, of, McNicholas HS, Cincinnati**
5. **Dave Stieb, of, Southern Illinois**
6. **Mike Cuellar, rhp, Madison HS, Houston**
7. **Brian Milner, c, Southwest HS, Fort Worth, Texas**
8. **Brad Burger, rhp, North Boone HS, Roscoe, Ill.**
9. Tom Stauffer, lhp, Monsignor Bonner HS, Drexel Hill, Pa.
10. **Alan Montgomery, 3b, Houston**
11. **Dave Baker, 3b, UCLA**
12. **Vincent Williams, of, Sam Houston HS, Houston**
13. **Thomas O'Dowd, rhp, Jackson (Mich.) Lumen Christ HS**
14. **Mark Stoeber, rhp, Northern Kentucky**
15. Rob Irwin, lhp, Stanford
16. **Ronald Harper, of, El Cerrito HS, Richmond, Calif.**
17. **Richard Palmer, c, West Covina (Calif.) HS**
18. Robert Heuck, lhp, Texas
19. **Terry Watkins, rhp, St. Mary's**
20. **Bill Lajoie, inf, St. Clair County (Mich.) CC**
21. Mondel Williams, of, McClatchy HS, Sacramento
22. Russ Dickerson, inf, Harrisonburg (Va.) HS
23. John Moses, lhp, Bellaire HS, Houston
24. Michael Cunningham, rhp, Highlands HS, Sacramento
25. Jimmie Ranson, 1b, San Diego State

June—Secondary Phase (16)

1. Simon Glenn, of, Blinn (Texas) JC

1979

Class of '79 features plenty of gridiron talent, but lots of busts on baseball diamonds

The 1979 draft became a showcase for more than just the baseball players it produced. It also turned out to be a preview of the 1983 NFL draft.

Three players selected in the '79 baseball draft went on to become first-round picks in the NFL four years later: John Elway and Dan Marino, who were drafted by the Royals, and Curt Warner, who was picked by the Phillies.

Elway went to Stanford, played six weeks in the Yankees system in 1982, then used baseball as leverage when he became the first player selected in the 1983 NFL draft by the Baltimore Colts. He insisted on being traded to a team in the West and got his wish, going to Denver and leading the Broncos to five Super Bowl appearances in his career, including back-to-back titles in 1998 and '99.

Jack Thompson, who in 1978 set a then-NCAA record for career passing yardage at Washington State, was drafted by the Mariners and became a first-round NFL pick of the Bengals in 1979.

More notable from a baseball perspective was Jay Schroeder, who was selected third overall in the '79 baseball draft and played football at UCLA while playing baseball in the Blue Jays organization. He gave up baseball when he was drafted by the Washington Redskins in 1984.

Baseball didn't lose out to football on all the two-sport stars who came along in 1979. Rick Leach, the Michigan quarterback who finished third in the 1978 Heisman Trophy balloting, signed with the Tigers as their first-round pick.

The Mariners had the No. 1 overall choice in June and appropriately went for Al Chambers, an all-state defensive end from Pennsylvania. His commitment to Arizona State was seen as a more significant hurdle than his football background, but Chambers, a powerful first baseman, signed with the Mariners a day before the draft, agreeing to a $60,000 bonus.

For the Mariners it was a nice change from the previous year, when protracted negotiations with first-round pick Tito Nanni cost farm director Mel Didier his job.

"I enjoy hitting a baseball much more than getting hit in football," Chambers said of his decision to sign so quickly.

The Mariners went for Chambers primarily because of his power potential. Bob Harrison, a Mariners scout who saw Chambers play and helped engineer his signing, said Chambers was a combination of Dave Parker and Dave Winfield.

Brad Komminsk was one of several touted 1979 draft picks who didn't pan out

"I rated Chambers at 65 (on the 20-80 scouting scale) and I'm conservative," Harrison said. "There's no doubt he's going to have 70 power. And that means 35 to 40 home runs a year, maybe more in our place."

Of course, it didn't work out that way. Chambers struggled in his debut at short-season Bellingham, hitting .247 with two homers, in what was a sign of things to come. The 6-foot-4, 220-pound slugger never showed the power the Mariners projected. His big league career lasted just 57 games and he hit two home runs while batting .208, making him one of the certifiable busts of the draft era.

While the Mariners were convinced Chambers was their man, other teams preferred Schroeder, Tim Leary and Brad Komminsk. Braves scouting director Paul Snyder compared Komminsk's power/speed combination with Kirk Gibson, and the Braves took him fourth overall.

Like Chambers, though, Komminsk never panned out. He and many of the other top picks in 1978 seemed burdened by the weight of high expectations.

Leary, a hard-throwing righthander from UCLA, went No. 2 to the Mets, who touted him as the second coming of Tom Seaver. Leary earned a spot in the Mets rotation to open the 1981 season and made his major league debut in 46-degree weather in Chicago, pitched to seven hitters and blew out his arm. He was never was the same dominant pitcher, though he came back to win 78 games in nearly 1,500 career innings.

Four Go Unsigned

A record four first-round picks from the June regular phase didn't sign. The Giants failed to sign righthander Rick Luecken, who opted to attend Texas A&M, while the White Sox lost out to Stanford on shortstop Steve Buechele.

The Athletics had a pair of first-round selections and came up short on signing both—shortstop Juan Bustabad and outfielder Mike Stenhouse—and they signed just two of their first 10 picks.

Hawaii's record-setting lefthander Derek Tatsuno was passed over in the first round, even after going 20-1 and striking out 234 hitters. The Padres took him in the second round but he pitched in the Japanese industrial leagues instead.

The typically quiet January draft took on an interesting twist in 1979 when lefthander Bill Bordley, 26-2 in two seasons at Southern California and the top commodity in the secondary phase, made it clear that he wanted to pitch for a West Coast club, to be near his family. His father had suffered a heart attack, and an older brother had been badly hurt in a recent motorcycle accident.

Bordley had a predraft agreement with the Angels for a $200,000 signing bonus and a spot on the major league roster. The Angels, however, had the fourth pick. Bordley wrote the clubs ahead of the Angels, requesting they not draft him. The Phillies and Blue Jays complied, but the Reds drafted Bordley. Bordley stuck to his guns and refused to sign with the Reds.

Kuhn fined the Angels $15,000 and granted Cincinnati three draft choices for tampering, charging that the Angels persuaded Bordley not to sign with Cincinnati. Kuhn also set up a special lottery for five teams deemed acceptable by Bordley to vie for his negotiating rights. The Giants won and quickly signed the lefthander to a $200,000 deal.

Bordley encountered rotator-cuff problems early in his career with the Giants and wound up winning just two big league games.

Philadelphia, with the No. 1 pick, had to settle for another lefthander from California, Mark Davis, who enjoyed considerably more success than Bordley. Davis won the National Leagues Cy Young Award as a member of the Padres in 1989.

Another lefthander, Neal Heaton, was the first pick in the regular phase, but he turned down the Mets $38,000 offer for a three-year career at the University of Miami.

DRAFT 79: FIRST-ROUND PICKS

No.	Club	Player, Pos.	School	Hometown	Ht.	Wt.	B-T	Age
1.	Mariners	Al Chambers, of	John Harris HS	Harrisburg, Pa.	6-4	210	L-L	18
2.	Mets	Tim Leary, rhp	UCLA	Santa Monica, Calif.	6-3	195	R-R	20
3.	Blue Jays	Jay Schroeder, c	Palisades HS	Pacific Palisades, Ca.	6-3	195	R-R	17
4.	Braves	Brad Komminsk, of	Shawnee HS	Lima, Ohio	6-3	187	R-R	18
5.	Athletics	*Juan Bustabad, ss	Miami Lakes HS	Hialeah, Fla.	5-9	145	B-R	17
6.	Cardinals	Andy Van Slyke, of	New Hartford HS	New Hartford, N.Y.	6-2	190	L-R	18
7.	Indians	Jon Bohnet, lhp	Hogan HS	Vallejo, Calif.	6-0	180	B-L	18
8.	Astros	John Mizerock, c	Punxsutawney HS	Punxsutawney, Pa.	6-0	180	L-R	18
9.	White Sox	*Steve Buechele, ss	Servite HS	Fullerton, Calif.	6-2	185	R-R	18
10.	Expos	Tim Wallach, 1b	Cal State Fullerton	Tustin, Calif.	6-3	195	R-R	21
11.	Twins	Kevin Brandt, of	Nekoosa HS	Nekoosa, Wis.	6-0	180	R-R	17
12.	Cubs	Jon Perlman, rhp	Baylor	Carthage, Texas	6-3	180	R-R	22
13.	Tigers	Rick Leach, of	Michigan	Flint, Mich.	6-1	180	L-L	22
14.	Padres	Joe Lansford, 1b	Wilcox HS	San Jose, Calif.	6-5	220	R-R	18
15.	Giants	Scott Garrelts, rhp	Buckley-Loda HS	Buckley, Ill.	6-4	200	R-R	17
16.	Dodgers	Steve Howe, lhp	Michigan	Clarkston, Mich.	6-1	180	L-L	21
17.	Rangers	Jerry Don Gleaton, lhp	Texas	Brownwood, Texas	6-3	190	L-L	21
18.	Giants	*Rick Luecken, rhp	Spring-Woods HS	Houston	6-6	218	R-R	17
19.	White Sox	Rick Seilheimer, c	Brenham HS	Brenham, Texas	5-11	185	L-R	18
20.	Reds	Dan Lamar, c	Bellaire HS	Houston	6-1	195	R-R	18
21.	Royals	Atlee Hammaker, lhp	East Tennessee State	Alexandria, Va.	6-2	193	L-L	21
22.	Reds	Mike Sullivan, rhp	Clemson	Woodbridge, Va.	6-0	170	R-R	20
23.	Tigers	Chris Baker, of	Livonia Franklin HS	Dearborn Hts., Mich.	6-3	190	R-R	18
24.	Padres	Bob Geren, c	Clairemont HS	San Diego	6-2	195	R-R	17
25.	Dodgers	Steve Perry, rhp	Michigan	Ann Arbor, Mich.	6-5	215	R-R	22
26.	Athletics	*Mike Stenhouse, of	Harvard	Cranston, R.I.	6-1	185	L-R	21

*Did not sign.

1979

CLUB-BY-CLUB SELECTIONS

ATLANTA BRAVES

January—Regular Phase (3)

1. Kelly Faulk, rhp, Wharton County (Texas) JC
2. **Milt Thompson, of, Gaithersburg, Md.**
3. **Rick Coatney, rhp, Westark (Ark.) CC**
4. Edward Lambeth, lhp, Westark (Ark.) CC
5. Randy Porter, lhp, Linn-Benton (Ore.) CC
6. Benji De La Rosa, of, Murray State (Selection voided)
7. **Brook Jacoby, of, Ventura (Calif.) JC**

January—Secondary Phase (20)

1. Willie Davis, of, Canada (Calif.) JC

June—Regular Phase (4)

1. **Brad Komminsk, of/1b, Shawnee HS, Lima, Ohio**
2. (Pick to Reds as compensation for free agent Mike Lum)
3. **Daniel Church, rhp, San Marin HS, Novato, Calif.**
4. **Ken Ames, rhp, St. Helens HS, Warren, Ore.**
5. **Bob Luzon, 2b, West Lake HS, Thornwood, N.Y.**
6. **Mike Payne, rhp, Williston (Fla.) HS**
7. **Roy North, rhp, Rider**
8. **David Coghill, lhp, Clackamas (Ore.) CC**
9. **Paul Runge, ss, Jacksonville**
10. Keith Belcik, c, Clay HS, Oregon, Ohio
11. **Gary Reiter, lhp, Bowling Green State**
12. **Glenn Bockhorn, 2b, Texas Lutheran**
13. **Steve Stieb, c, Southern Illinois**
14. **Randy Ingle, ss, Appalachian State**
15. **Bret Ferguson, lhp, North Baltimore (Ohio) HS**
16. **Welby Bailey, c, Lynchburg (Va.)**
17. Nick O'Connor, rhp, Reading HS, Cincinnati
18. **Harold Williams, 1b, Virginia Tech**
19. **Pete Teixeira, rhp, Florida**
20. **Randy Whistler, c, Arizona State**
21. **Billy Bowen, of, Southeastern Oklahoma State**
22. **Greg Norris, rhp, North Carolina**
23. **Brett Butler, of, Southeastern Oklahoma State**
24. John Shannon, rhp, Houston
25. **Robert Kennedy, rhp, Cochise County (Ariz.) CC**
26. **Chuck Black, 2b, Bowling Green State**
27. **Mike Garcia, 2b, Cal State Fullerton**
28. **Tommy Thompson, c, Oklahoma**
29. Eric Call, rhp, Miami-Dade South CC
30. **Arcilio Castaigne, rhp, Texas Wesleyan**
31. **Greg Dikos, 3b, Ball State**
32. **DeWayne Kitts, lhp, Lynchburg (Va.)**
33. Jeff Groth, of, Bowling Green State
34. **Kevin Patten, of, Miami (Ohio)**
35. **Arthur Neal, of, Morehouse (Ga.)**
36. Philip Bowie, of, Greenwood (S.C.) HS
37. **Tim Fuller, rhp, Berkmar HS, Norcross, Ga.**
38. **Russell Kerdolff, rhp, Northern Kentucky**
39. Scott Matthews, of, Melbourne HS, India Lantic, Fla.

June—Secondary Phase (24)

No selection

BALTIMORE ORIOLES

January—Regular Phase (20)

1. Darren Dilks, lhp, Chaffey (Calif.) JC
2. **Steve Espinoza, ss, Foothill (Calif.) JC**
3. **Randy Miller, 2b, Florida CC**
4. Bill Bond, 1b/rhp, St. Petersburg (Fla.) JC
5. **Gregg Burtt, of, Quinisigamond (Mass.) CC**
6. Craig Cunard, lhp, Iowa Western CC
7. Antonio Barquin, of, Miami-Dade South CC
8. Kevin Usher, rhp, Bayport (N.Y.) HS

January—Secondary Phase (1)

1. **Andy Marston, of/rhp, St. Petersburg (Fla.) JC**

June—Regular Phase (19)

1. (Pick to White Sox as compensation for free agent Steve Stone)
2. **Tim Maples, rhp, Pinecrest HS, Southern Pines, N.C.**
3. Bob Melvin, c, Menlo-Atherton HS, Menlo Park, Calif.
4. **Greg Dees, inf, Auburndale (Fla.) HS**
5. **Allan Ramirez, rhp, Rice**
6. **Julian Gonzalez, lhp, Tampa Catholic HS**
7. **Storm Davis, rhp, University Christian HS, Jacksonville, Fla.**
8. **Robert Palmer, c, Chapman (Calif.)**
9. Jeff Hunter, 3b, Nebraska
10. Rod Booker, ss, California
11. **Mark Jurena, of, Louisville**
12. **Kenneth Jordan, rhp, William Campbell HS, Brookneal, Va.**
13. **Terry Schriner, of, Harrisburg (Pa.) HS**
14. **David Schuman, of, Seton Hall**
15. **Freddie Smith, rhp, Pasco HS, Dade City, Fla.**
16. Bill Hainline, ss, Gonzaga
17. **Angelo Blake, 2b, Sacramento CC**
18. **Larry Woodhall, lhp, Mankato State (Minn.)**
19. **Lonnie Ivie, c, Blinn (Texas) JC**
20. Thomas Harrell, ss, Columbus (Ga.)
21. **Bruss Bowman, 1b, Walt Whitman HS, Bethesda, Md.**
22. **Manuel Martinez, c, Southwest Texas JC**
23. Greg Schuler, of, Robinson HS, Fairfax, Va.
24. **Gary Zedonak, rhp, Mansfield (Pa.)**
25. **David Pfeiffer, rhp, Northwest Missouri State**
26. **Bill Swaggerty, rhp, Stetson**
27. Chris Newman, 1b, Churchill HS, Eugene, Ore.
28. Scott Gardner, rhp, Oklahoma
29. Cecil Morris, of, Loyola HS, Los Angeles
30. **John DeLeon, 1b, University City HS, Philadelphia**
31. Glenn Davis, 1b/rhp, University Christian HS, Jacksonville, Fla.
32. Kevin Gross, rhp, Fillmore (Calif.) HS
33. Rodney Mason, rhp, High Point HS, Beltsville, Md.
34. **Charles Williams, ss, Apopka HS, Plymouth, Fla.**
35. Charles Tomaselli, lhp, Clearwater (Fla.) HS
36. Jack Leonard, inf, Tucker HS, Richmond

June—Secondary Phase (7)

1. Joe Housey, rhp, Miami-Dade North CC
2. **Fred Conradi, lhp, Centralia (Wash.) JC**

BOSTON RED SOX

January—Regular Phase (25)

1. **Kevin Kane, rhp, Cuesta (Calif.) JC**
2. Michael Dolinar, 3b, Bakersfield (Calif.) JC
3. Harley Woody, lhp, Columbia State (Tenn.) CC
4. Michael Burton, rhp, Mobile, Ala.
5. Kenneth Cox, 1b, Columbia State (Tenn.) CC
6. **Lee Pruitt, of/c, Westark (Ark.) CC**
7. **Scott Gering, rhp/of, St. John's River (Fla.) CC**
8. **Timothy Wadsworth, c/1b, Pensacola, Fla.**

January—Secondary Phase (25)

No selection

June—Regular Phase (26)

1. (Pick to Athletics as compensation for free agent Steve Renko)
2. **Marc Sullivan, c, Florida**
3. **John Ackley, c, Mahopac HS, Carmel, N.Y.**
4. Gib Seibert, of, Sahuaro HS, Tucson
5. **Jim Watkins, of, Florida**
6. Rick Thompson, ss, Glen Oaks HS, Canton, Ohio

7. **Tom McCarthy, rhp, Plymouth (Mass.) Carver HS**
8. Steven True, lhp, Marlow (Okla.) HS
9. **Charles Sandberg, 1b, Florida**
10. **Jerry Miklosi, ss, Western Michigan**
11. Tom Dunbar, of, Middle Georgia JC
12. Ronnie Perry, ss, Holy Cross
13. Glen Kuhn, rhp, Sauquoit (N.Y.) HS
14. Mickey Meister, rhp, Redwood HS, San Rafael, Calif.
15. **Reggie Whittemore, of, Lipscomb**
16. Mark Sewald, rhp, Bishop Montgomery HS, Carson, Calif.
17. John Leonard, rhp, Connellsville HS, Dawson, Pa.
18. **Eddie Lee, of, South Alabama**
19. **Bob Birrell, lhp, Brandeis (Mass.)**
20. **Jay Fredlund, rhp, Lafayette**
21. **David Holt, c, Fresno State**
22. **Glenn Eddins, 3b, Lipscomb**

June—Secondary Phase (1)

1. **Marty Barrett, 2b, Arizona State**
2. **Jeems Teller, of, Sacramento CC**

CALIFORNIA ANGELS

January—Regular Phase (16)

1. Dennis Ivy, of/1b, San Joaquin Delta (Calif.) JC
2. Bill Worden, c, Mission (Calif.) JC
3. Al Newman, ss, Chaffey (Calif.) JC
4. **Edward Lindsey, lhp, Broward (Fla.) CC**
5. Don Freeman, ss, West Los Angeles JC
6. **Gary Pettis, of, Laney (Calif.) JC**
7. Russ Stephans, c, Los Angeles Valley JC
8. Stanford Hill, lhp, McLennan (Texas) CC
9. **Robert Klein, rhp, JC of the Canyons (Calif.)**
10. **Peter Nebrich, 1b, Broward (Fla.) CC**

January—Secondary Phase (4)

1. Otis Nixon, 3b, Louisburg (N.C.) JC
2. Ken Eriksen, rhp, Citrus (Calif.) JC
3. Curt Wardle, lhp, San Bernardino Valley (Calif.) JC
3. **Lawrence Dugger, rhp, Arizona Western JC** (Pick awarded from Montreal)
4. Brian Owens, rhp, Mesa (Ariz.) CC

June—Regular Phase (15)

1. (Pick to Giants as compensation for free agent Jim Barr)
2. (Pick to Reds as penalty for tampering with amateur free agent Bill Bordley)
3. **Mickey Saatzer, rhp, Eisenhower HS, Hopkins, Minn.**
4. Eric Barry, lhp, Mount Whitney HS, Visalia, Calif.
5. **Pat Keedy, 2b, Auburn**
6. **Jackie Skaggs, rhp, William Carey (Miss.)**
7. Stephen Renfroe, of, Auburn
8. **Warren Hollier, rhp, Oral Roberts**
9. **Darrell Miller, c, Cal Poly Pomona**
10. Bob Gunnarsson, lhp, Lake Havasu (Ariz.) HS
11. **Greg Hanson, c, Southern California College**
12. Danny Smith, lhp, Southern HS, Cutler Ridge, Fla.
13. **Marion Hunter, ss, Kearny HS, San Diego**
14. **Jim Celedonia, c, William Carey (Miss.)**
15. Don Carfino, ss, Southern California
16. **Mark Pangborn, rhp, Rio Hondo (Calif.) JC**
17. Galdenio Noda, ss, Bell (Calif.) HS
18. Andrew Pavlovic, rhp, Yavapai (Ariz.) JC
19. Mingo Nunez, ss, Wagner
20. **Brian Buckley, rhp, UC Davis**
21. Maurice Christian, of, Texas Southern
22. **David Duran, rhp, Cal State Los Angeles**
23. **Eli Aldridge, of, Prairie View A&M**
24. **Tim Collins, of, Loyola Marymount**
25. Paul Wirkus, of, San Diego State
26. **Jay Kibbe, rhp, Louisiana Tech**
27. Rod Martin, of, Eisenhower HS, San Bernardino, Calif.
28. Michael Rizzo, ss/2b, Holy Cross HS, Chicago
29. **Frank Pennachio, inf, Southern California**

June—Secondary Phase (19)

1. (Pick to Reds as penalty for tampering with amateur free agent Bill Bordley)
2. (Pick to Reds as penalty for tampering with amateur free agent Bill Bordley)
3. Bill Lindsey, 3b, Broward (Fla.) CC

CHICAGO CUBS

January—Regular Phase (11)

1. **Mark Wilkins, rhp, Eastern Michigan**
2. David Means, of, Winchester, Ky.
3. Steve Podraza, c, Brookdale (N.J.) CC
4. **Terry Austin, of, Ranger (Texas) JC**
5. Michael Maack, lhp, Miami-Dade South CC
6. Michael O'Malley, lhp, Triton (Ill.) JC
7. Todd Wilson, lhp, Mount San Antonio (Calif.) JC

January—Secondary Phase (9)

1. Mark Christy, rhp, Miami-Dade North CC

June—Regular Phase (12)

1. **Jon Perlman, rhp, Baylor**
2. **Shane Allen, inf, Palm Bay HS, Melbourne, Fla.**
3. Chuck Crim, rhp, Thousand Oaks (Calif.) HS
4. **Stan Kyles, rhp, Wendell Phillips HS, Chicago**
5. Steve Gehrke, rhp, Murray (Utah) HS
6. **James Buckley, ss, Lakewood (Calif.) HS**
7. **Randy LaVigne, of, Connecticut**
8. Tim Thompson, rhp, Jordan HS, Long Beach, Calif.
9. **Thomas Morris, lhp, Brigham Young**
10. **Dave Owen, ss, Texas-Arlington**
11. **Ray Soff, rhp, Central Michigan**
12. **James Lockett, of, Missouri**
13. **Joe Fiori, 2b, Point Park (Pa.)**
14. **Jack Upton, 1b/3b, Colorado State**
15. **Kirk Ortega, c, St. Francis (N.Y.)**
16. **Tom Grant, of, New Haven (Conn.)**
17. **Brian Hardy, lhp, Brigham Young**
18. **Mark Scheiwe, rhp, Buckley (Ill.) Loda HS**
19. **Craig Weissmann, rhp, Clairemont HS, San Diego**
20. Bryan Oelkers, lhp, Pattonville HS, Overland, Mo.
21. **Tim Millner, rhp, Illinois State**
22. **Robert Blyth, rhp, Brigham Young**
23. Mark Huismann, rhp, Colorado State
24. **Sidney Smith, of, Patrick Henry HS, San Diego**
25. **Michael Kelley, of, Mississippi State**
26. **Anthony Biafore, ss, Monmouth**
27. Joseph Carter, rhp, Helix HS, El Cajon, Calif.
28. **Dennis Mork, of, UC Riverside**
29. Steve Ziem, rhp, Banning (Calif.) HS
30. **Glenn Millhauser, of, Northern Colorado**
31. Doug Huffman, lhp, North Carolina State
32. **Michael Thompson, lhp, Fairleigh Dickinson**
33. Dave Fabela, c, Aquinas HS, San Bernardino, Calif.
34. Dave McClure, c, Kapaun Mount Carmel HS, Wichita, Kan.
35. **Richard Renwick, rhp, Babson (Mass.)**
36. **Phillip Belmonte, inf, Azusa Pacific (Calif.)**
37. **Howie Shapiro, 2b, Miami**
38. Wes Clements, of/1b, Arizona
39. **William Trapani, lhp, Bellevue (Neb.)**

June—Secondary Phase (6)

1. **Scott Fletcher, ss, Georgia Southern**
2. **Anthony Veith, 1b, Brainerd, Minn.**
3. John Moller, lhp, Seton Hall
4. John Millholland, ss, Louisburg (N.C.) JC
5. **James McManus, rhp, Nebraska**
6. **Pedro Bazan, c, Central Arizona JC**

CHICAGO WHITE SOX

January—Regular Phase (10)

1. Bruce Cooper, rhp, Broward (Fla.) CC
2. Randy Riccardi, c, Miami-Dade North CC
3. **Randy Johnson, 1b/of, Miami-Dade South CC**
4. Tim Kammeyer, rhp, Southwestern (Calif.) JC
5. **Felix Agapay, 1b/of, Chicago**
6. Allen Black, rhp, West Los Angeles JC

7. Robert Brown, ss, Pasadena (Calif.) CC
8. Jim David, ss, JC of the Canyons (Calif.)
9. Richard Kryzsiak, of, Chaffey (Calif.) JC
10. Craig Nelson, rhp, Glendale (Ariz.) CC

January—Secondary Phase (17)

1. **Gary Friedrich, lhp, Wabash Valley (Ill.) JC**
2. Paul Doty, rhp, Grossmont (Calif.) JC

June—Regular Phase (9)

1. Steve Buechele, ss, Servite HS, Fullerton, Calif.
1. **Ricky Seilheimer, c, Brenham (Texas) HS** (Pick from Orioles as compensation for free agent Steve Stone)
2. Scott Glanz, rhp, Edison HS, Tulsa, Okla.
3. **Fran Mullins, ss, Santa Clara**
4. Richard Frazier, c, Butler HS, Huntsville, Ala.
5. **Dom Fucci, 1b, Auburn**
6. **Chuck Johnson, rhp, Iowa**
7. **Mitch Olson, of/inf, Los Alamitos (Calif.) HS**
8. **William Mills, rhp, Marathon (Fla.) HS**
9. Scott Meier, c, Tokay HS, Lodi, Calif.
10. Jimmy Key, lhp/1b, Butler HS, Huntsville, Ala.
11. **Ted Ronshauser, c, San Marin HS, Novato, Calif.**
12. **Randy Evans, rhp, Oklahoma State**
13. Jon Soderberg, rhp, Essex Junction (Vt.) HS
14. **Tom Keating, rhp, University HS, San Diego**
15. Wayne Fugett, rhp, Valdosta (Ga.) HS
16. Darryl Wilks, of, Glenwood HS, Fort Mitchell, Ala.
17. **Jim English, 2b/1b, Missouri**
18. **Mark Jackman, lhp, Birmingham-Southern**
19. **Dennis Vasquez, rhp, La Verne (Calif.)**
20. **Keith Brown, of/1b, Southern California**
21. **Larry Hall, ss, Florida**
22. Chris Johnston, 3b, Corona del Mar HS, Newport Beach, Calif.
23. Tom Dieters, ss, Rochester (Mich.) HS
24. Reggie Fischer, rhp, Mount Carmel HS, Bellmont, Ill.
25. Len Kasper, 1b, Proviso West HS, Bellwood, Ill.
26. **Keefe Davis, rhp, Los Angeles (Calif.) HS**
27. **Dan Williams, 1b, Stetson**
28. Kevin Kristan, rhp, Carmel HS, Mundelein, Ill.
29. **Albert Likely, 1b, Davison HS, Mobile, Ala.**
30. **Ron Nacierio, of, St. John's**
31. Ray Thoma, 2b, Marist HS, Oak Lawn, Ill.
32. **Paul Manieri, 2b, New Orleans**
33. Randy Abel, c, Sealy (Texas) HS
34. **Larry Doby, of, Duke**

June—Secondary Phase (5)

1. **Bob Fallon, lhp, Miami-Dade North CC**
2. Bruce Cooper, rhp, Broward (Fla.) CC
3. Tim Teufel, 2b, Clemson

CINCINNATI REDS

January—Regular Phase (21)

1. **Kevin Waller, of/3b, San Diego CC**
2. Robert Elliott, rhp, Gulf Coast (Fla.) CC
3. Kevin Lindsley, rhp, Linn-Benton (Ore.) CC
4. **Larry Raskin, c/1b, Coastal Carolina**
5. Dale Chatham, lhp, Gulf Coast (Fla.) CC
6. **Tim Stamper, rhp, Spokane Falls (Wash.) CC**
7. Richard Rizzo, of/inf, Suffolk County (N.Y.) CC
8. Tim Henry, lhp, Paris (Texas) JC

January—Secondary Phase (3)

1. **Bill Bordley, lhp, El Camino (Calif.) JC**
2. Gary Kempton, c, Triton (Ill.) JC

June—Regular Phase (22)

1. **Dan Lamar, c, Bellaire HS, Houston** (Pick from Phillies as compensation for free agent Pete Rose)
1. **Mike Sullivan, rhp, Clemson**
2. **Keefe Cato, rhp, Fairfield** (Pick from Braves as compensation for free agent Mike Lum)
2. **Bob Buchanan, lhp, Riverview HS, Sarasota, Fla.** (Pick from Angels as penalty for tampering with amateur free agent Bill Bordley)
2. Richard Wysocki, lhp, Lakewood (N.J.) HS
3. Scott Lindquist, rhp, Kingsburg (Calif.) HS
4. Michael Tolbert, rhp, Phillips HS, Chicago
5. **Jeff Russell, rhp, Wyoming HS, Cincinnati**
6. **Ron Little, of, Asheboro (N.C.) HS**
7. **Robert Lappie, c, Davidson**
8. Bill Crone, inf, West Chester (Pa.)
9. Augie Schmidt, ss, Bradford HS, Kenosha, Wis.
10. **Tony Masone, of, Clemson**
11. **Keith Schrimsher, rhp, South Florida**
12. Tom Edens, of, Fruitland (Idaho) HS
13. Randy Gomez, c, Utah
14. **Rick Myles, lhp, Jackson (Mich.) CC**
15. Eric Jordan, c, Chaparral HS, North Las Vegas, Nev.
16. **Greg Bangert, lhp, Lewis-Clark State (Idaho)**
17. Cary Palmer, rhp, Mesa (Ariz.) CC
18. **Russell Jones, of, Texas**
19. **Kevin Flannery, rhp, Central Michigan**
20. **Jeff Jones, of, Iowa**
21. **Kevin Hinds, 2b, Jackson State**
22. **Steven Daniels, rhp, Texas Wesleyan**
23. **Perry Estep, of, West Virginia State**
24. **Nick Fiorillo, lhp, Texas-El Paso**
25. **Kurt Kepshire, rhp, New Haven (Conn.)**
26. **Mark Miller, of, UCLA**
27. Dave Eldredge, c, Punahou HS, Honolulu
28. **Newton Box, lhp, Phillips (Okla.)**
29. Robert Slavens, lhp, Westbury HS, Houston
30. **Mike Dowless, rhp, Hoggard HS, Wilmington, N.C.**
31. James Vegara, of, Kennedy HS, Old Bethpage, N.Y.
32. Kyle Rutledge, 2b, New Mexico
33. James Melson, rhp, Morgan County HS, Hartselle, Ala.
34. **Bill Boddy, c, Start HS, Toledo, Ohio**
35. **Rodney Johnson, 3b, Temple**
36. Mike Maddux, rhp, Rancho HS, North Las Vegas, Nev.
37. **Jeff Ayers, rhp, Bellevue (Wash.) CC**
38. **Robert Hoover, rhp, New Mexico**
39. Sonny James, of, Fulton (Mo.) HS
40. Randy Reed, c, Tennessee Wesleyan
41. Mike Adkins, c, Caldwell (Idaho) HS
42. Daniel Klosicki, rhp, Spokane Falls (Wash.) CC
43. Mike Fischer, c, Riverview HS, Sarasota, Fla.

June—Secondary Phase (16)

1. Larry Mikesell, lhp, Brevard (Fla.) CC
2. Mark Pederson, rhp, Yakima Valley (Wash.) CC (Pick from Angels as penalty for tampering with amateur free agent Bill Bordley)
3. Robert Elliott, rhp, Gulf Coast (Fla.) CC (Pick from Angels as penalty for tampering with amateur free agent Bill Bordley)

CLEVELAND INDIANS

January—Regular Phase (8)

1. **Francis Regan, rhp, Valencia (Fla.) CC**
2. Jeff Thompson, of, Miami-Dade North CC
3. Rod McDonald, rhp, Cuyahoga (Ohio) CC
4. **Roberto Alvarez, 3b/2b, Miami-Dade North CC**
5. Luis Duarte, c/1b, Miami-Dade North CC
6. Joseph Cazares, ss, Imperial Valley (Calif.) JC
7. Dave Oliva, of, Los Angeles Valley JC
8. **John Napolitano, rhp, Cohoes, N.Y.**
9. Mike Reddish, c, Indian River (Fla.) CC
10. **Alex Christenson, rhp, Merced (Calif.) JC**
11. James Winters, 3b, Cuyahoga (Ohio) CC
12. Mark Lacy, 1b, St. Petersburg (Fla.) JC
13. Larry Pittman, 1b, Abraham Baldwin Agricultural (Ga.) JC
14. **Tommy Martinez, rhp/of, Hialeah, Fla.**
15. **Jack Lopez, ss, Miami-Dade North CC**

January—Secondary Phase (13)

1. **Brad Carlson, of, Edison (Fla.) CC**
2. Michael Sanford, rhp, DeKalb South (Ga.) CC

June—Regular Phase (7)

1. **John Bohnet, lhp, Hogan HS, Vallejo, Calif.**

2. **Chris Rehbaum, of, St. Joseph's Collegiate HS, Buffalo, N.Y.**
3. Eric Hardgrave, 1b, Bullard HS, Fresno, Calif.
4. **John Hoban, rhp, Cal State Dominguez Hills**
5. Ed Brennan, ss, Sweet Home (Ore.) HS
6. Dave Landrith, c, Homestead HS, Sunnyvale, Calif.
7. **Von Hayes, inf, St. Mary's**
8. Charles Melito, 1b, Tulane
9. **Ricky Baker, of, San Francisco State**
10. Len Bradley, rhp, Clemson
11. Brian Butera, of, Tulane
12. **Ron Leach, lhp, Fresno State**
13. **Frank Osmulski, c, Summit (N.J.) HS**
14. **Jerry Larison, rhp, Lafayette HS, Lexington, Ky.**
15. **Jack Nuismer, rhp, Vanderbilt**
16. Mike Hocutt, 3b, Rogers HS, Michigan City, Ind.
17. **Thomas Clancy, rhp, Wilmot HS, Twin Lakes, Wis.**
18. **Lawrence Locascio, c, St. Xavier (Ill.)**
19. **George Cecchetti, of, San Joaquin Delta (Calif.) JC**
20. Larry Smith, ss, Ilion (N.Y.) HS
21. **Kirk Jones, rhp, Nevada-Las Vegas**
22. Ricky Edwards, rhp, Santa Clara
23. Robbie Cobb, inf, Garfield HS, Hamilton, Ohio
24. Gary Whisler, inf, Klamath Union HS, Klamath Falls, Ore.
25. **Larry Hrynko, rhp, St. Xavier (Ill.)**
26. Chris Sigourney, lhp, Larkin HS, Elgin, Ill.
27. **Ralph Hodge, 1b, San Francisco State**
28. Thomas Gilchrist, rhp, Newport HS, Bellevue, Wash.
29. **Todd Richard, lhp, DeSales HS, Walla Walla, Wash.**
30. Allen Peel, c, Davis (Calif.) HS
31. **Larry White, rhp, San Francisco State**
32. **Michael Jakubowicz, rhp, Clarke HS, Hammond, Ind.**
33. Robert Heath, rhp, Maine East HS, Niles, Ill.
34. Jeff Walsh, rhp, Santa Clara
35. Joseph Krisik, lhp, Badger HS, Genoa City, Wis.
36. Stan Osiecki, rhp, Ansonia (Conn.) HS
37. **George Merry, lhp, Ipswich (Mass.) HS**
38. **Donald Nicolet, of/3b, Fort Steilacoom (Wash.) CC**
39. Gerald Drobnick, ss, Euclid (Ohio) HS
40. **Matt Maki, lhp, San Jose State**
41. Gary Joseph, rhp/ss, New Iberia (La.) HS
42. **Brian Meier, 3b, San Joaquin Delta (Calif.) JC**
43. Brian Duffy, lhp, California
44. **Bruce Chaney, inf, Washington State**

June—Secondary Phase (25)

1. **Weston Mitchell, ss, San Jose (Calif.) CC**
2. **Stephen Roche, rhp, Sacramento CC**
3. John Damon, ss, Sacramento CC
4. **Victor Woods, of, Laney (Calif.) JC**
5. James Glenn, of, Texas A&M
6. **Bob Ferris, c/inf, Mesa (Ariz.) CC**

DETROIT TIGERS

January—Regular Phase (14)

1. **Michael Camp, rhp, Eastern Oklahoma State JC**
2. Dave Kirby, of, Citrus (Calif.) JC
3. Brian Stehling, rhp, San Jacinto (Texas) JC
4. **Gary Zelmanski, 1b, St. Clair County (Mich.) CC**
5. Mike Querrey, 1b, Citrus (Calif.) JC
6. Ricky Gomez, ss/2b, Central Arizona JC
7. John Collier, rhp, St. Clair County (Mich.) CC

January—Secondary Phase (12)

1. **Howard Johnson, 3b, St. Petersburg (Fla.) JC**
2. Pat Blamey, rhp, San Jose (Calif.) CC
3. **Eli Roberson, of, Baytown, Texas**

June—Regular Phase (13)

1. **Rick Leach, of, Michigan**
1. **Chris Baker, of, Livonia Franklin HS, Dearborn Heights, Mich.** (Pick from Brewers as compensation for free agent Jim Slaton)
2. **Keith Fisher, c, Apopka (Fla.) HS**
3. **Randy Harvey, of, Riverside (Calif.) Poly HS**
4. **Luis Sanchez, rhp, Pace HS, Miami**
5. **Jon Driver, c, Shelby County HS, Shelbyville, Ky.**
6. David Arnold, ss, La Habra HS, Los Angeles
7. **Charlie Nail, rhp, McClure Academy, Jackson, Miss.**
8. **Vern Followell, ss, UCLA**
9. **Michael Schoeller, 1b, Florida Southern**
10. Winston Ficklin, inf, El Cerrito HS, Richmond, Calif.
11. **Anthony Barraco, c, De La Salle HS, Pittsburg, Calif.**
12. **Mike Warren, rhp, Fullerton HS, Garden Grove, Calif.**
13. Mitch Seoane, 2b, Tampa Catholic HS
14. **Gordon Chretien, rhp, Eastern Michigan**
15. **Jeff Kenaga, of, Western Michigan**
16. **Ron Lindberg, ss, Pace (N.Y.)**
17. **John Lackey, rhp, Florida Southern**
18. Steve Hendrix, lhp, Center Line (Mich.) HS
19. **Steve Dunn, lhp, Southwest Missouri State**
20. Greg Funk, ss, Serra HS, San Bruno, Calif.
21. **Michael Krill, lhp, Irvington, N.J.**
22. **Ken Baldwin, 2b, Rice**
23. Audie Cole, of, Eastern Michigan
24. **John Wells, of, Southern California**
25. **William Hardy, of, Alabama State**
26. Michael Ward, 1b, Alma (Mich.) HS
27. **Robert Bresnen, lhp, Miami (Ohio)**
28. **Scott Vaughn, rhp, Allen Park (Mich.) HS**
29. Terry Schalk, rhp, Lakeshore HS, St. Clair Shore, Mich.
30. **Randy Nelson, rhp, Cal Poly Pomona**
31. **Scott Bollens, rhp, UCLA**
32. **Wilson Tucker, of, Belmont**
33. **Mark McKnight, 2b, Pfeiffer (N.C.)**

June—Secondary Phase (17)

1. **Paul Fox, rhp, Canada (Calif.) JC**
2. **James Good, of, JC of Southern Idaho**

HOUSTON ASTROS

January—Regular Phase (7)

1. Jeff Dedmon, rhp, West Los Angeles JC
2. **Adalio Penate, rhp, Miami-Dade New World Center CC**
3. Jeff Etsell, lhp, Palm Beach (Fla.) JC
4. Gil Robison, rhp, Centralia (Wash.) JC

January—Secondary Phase (5)

1. Edwin Schneider, lhp, Indian River (Fla.) CC
2. Richard Eckleberry, rhp, JC of Southern Idaho

June—Regular Phase (8)

1. **John Mizerock, c, Punxsutawney (Pa.) HS**
2. **Ty Gainey, inf, Cheraw (S.C.) HS**
3. **Cliff Wherry, ss, UC Riverside**
4. **Larry Ray, of, Kentucky Wesleyan**
5. **Mark Strucher, 1b/c, Georgia Southern**
6. **Bill Doran, inf, Miami (Ohio)**
7. **Mark Ross, rhp, Texas A&M**
8. **William Ray, rhp, Oklahoma City**
9. Mark Dempsey, rhp, Ohio State
10. **Marc Thomas, of, Brigham Young**
11. **Greg Peterson, rhp, Brigham Young**
12. **Johnny Ray, 2b, Arkansas**
13. **Doug Welenc, rhp, Massachusetts**
14. **Larry Brown, rhp, Harvard**
15. **Eddie Bonine, rhp, Grand Canyon (Ariz.)**
16. **Ken Smith, rhp, North Carolina**
17. **Val Primante, c, Nebraska**
18. **Steve Quealey, rhp, Washington State**
19. **Andrew Rice, lhp, Murray State**
20. Orlando Fernandez, 3b/of, Miami Lake HS, Hialeah, Fla.
21. **Mark Lohuis, rhp, Fresno State**
22. William Ratterman, lhp, Purcell HS, Cincinnati
23. **Mark Campbell, c, Florida International**
24. **Michael Finch, lhp, San Diego State**
25. **Chris Jones, of, San Diego State**
26. Dana Ynostroza, c, Serramonte HS, Daly City, Calif.

June—Secondary Phase (20)

1. Lemmie Miller, of, Santa Barbara (Calif.) CC

KANSAS CITY ROYALS

January—Regular Phase (22)

1. **Mike Brewer, rhp, Foothill (Calif.) JC**
2. Tim Cates, rhp, DeKalb South (Ga.) CC
3. Alex Christy, 1b, Westerville, Ohio
4. **Roger Patoka, c, Plover, Wis.**
5. Curt Thrasher, lhp, Oxnard (Calif.) JC
6. Mike Bielecki, rhp, Valencia (Fla.) CC

January—Secondary Phase (21)

1. **Jeff Schattinger, rhp, Southern California**
2. David Anderson, rhp, Arizona Western JC

June—Regular Phase (21)

1. **Atlee Hammaker, lhp, East Tennessee State**
2. **John Skinner, rhp, North Carolina State**
3. **Pat Sheridan, of, Eastern Michigan**
4. Dan Marino, rhp, Central Catholic HS, Pittsburgh
5. **Mickey Palmer, of, Cal State Fullerton**
6. **Kenneth Pour, rhp, New Athens (Ill.) HS**
7. Craig Lefferts, lhp, Arizona
8. Doran Perdue, 2b, Murray State
9. **Rob Townley, of, Cal State Long Beach**
10. Bill Moore, of, Covina HS, West Covina, Calif.
11. **Otis Irvin, ss, Phillips HS, Chicago**
12. **Ron Krauss, lhp, Seminole (Fla.) HS**
13. **Ron Batter, c, Miami**
14. Osbe Hoskins, 3b, Grand Rapids (Mich.) Creston HS
15. **Walter Vanderbush, rhp, Wooster (Ohio)**
16. **Johnny Barnette, of, Spartanburg Methodist (S.C.) JC**
17. David Sullivan, c, Oklahoma State
18. John Elway, of, Granada Hills HS, Northridge, Calif.
19. **Daniel St. Clair, rhp, Kansas**
20. **James Atkinson, 3b, North Carolina**
21. **Lawrence Grahek, of, Minnesota**
22. **Dave Luethy, ss, Oklahoma**
23. **Larry Williams, rhp, Central Michigan**
24. **Vin Yuhas, rhp, Manalapan HS, Englishtown, N.J.**
25. **Jeff Twitty, lhp, South Carolina**
26. **Daniel Fischer, rhp, Nevada-Las Vegas**
27. Craig Herberholz, rhp, Catholic Central HS, Farmington Hills, Mich.
28. Bryan Nabors, rhp, South Shores HS, Chicago
29. Andrew Basten, rhp, Ashwaubenon HS, Green Bay, Wis.
30. Mark Wakai, c, Cumberland HS, Seabrook, N.J.
31. **Craig Patterson, 2b, Florida State**
32. **Ken Kurtz, lhp, Mississippi State**
33. James Jones, rhp, Redwood HS, Kentfield, Calif.
34. **Allan Garray, c, Connecticut**
35. Reggie West, of, Santa Ana (Calif.) JC
36. **Leon Vickers, of, Kansas**
37. Greg Housner, c, Bridgeport HS, Saginaw, Mich.

June—Secondary Phase (21)

1. **Duane Dewey, c/1b, Louisiana State**
2. David McDonald, lhp, Allegheny (Pa.) CC
3. David LaBounty, rhp, Yakima Valley (Wash.) JC
4. Gil Robison, rhp, Centralia (Wash.) JC

LOS ANGELES DODGERS

January—Regular Phase (23)

1. **Robert Silicani, 3b/ss, JC of San Mateo (Calif.)**
2. Jeems Teller, of, Sacramento CC
3. Kyle Dunning, rhp, Linn-Benton (Ore.) CC
4. Joseph Siers, rhp, Palm Beach (Fla.) JC
5. Phillip Smith, lhp, DeKalb South (Ga.) CC
6. Eric Stack, rhp, Lane (Ore.) CC
7. James Gleissner, c, Mount San Antonio (Calif.) JC

January—Secondary Phase (16)

1. **Rick Misuraca, 3b, Rose State (Okla.) JC**
2. John Millholland, ss, Louisburg (N.C.) JC
3. Richard Ross, of, San Jose CC
4. Tommy Blackmon, rhp, Spartanburg Methodist (S.C.) JC

June—Regular Phase (24)

1. **Steve Howe, lhp, Michigan** (Pick from Pirates as compensation for free agent Lee Lacy)
1. **Steve Perry, rhp, Michigan** (Pick from Yankees as compensation for free agent Tommy John)
2. **David Lanning, 3b, Georgia**
3. **Don Crow, c, Washington State**
4. **Leo Mann, ss, Missouri**
5. **Terry Sutcliffe, rhp, Kansas**
6. **Dale Holman, of, Louisiana Tech**
7. **Tim Gloyd, ss/2b, Pepperdine**
8. Jeff Dietrich, lhp, Serramonte HS, Daly City, Calif.
9. **Felix Oroz, lhp, Wyoming**
10. **John Houston, c/3b, Kennedy HS, Sacramento**
11. **Mark Sheehy, 2b, UC Riverside**
12. Kerwin Danley, of/1b, Dorsey HS, Los Angeles
13. **Greg Brock, 1b, Wyoming**
14. **Frank Bryant, rhp, North Carolina State**
15. **Tom Beyers, of, Cal Poly San Luis Obispo**
16. **Ken Bullock, lhp, San Francisco**
17. **Orel Hershiser IV, rhp, Bowling Green State**
18. **Keith Mohler, of, South Alabama**
19. **Wayne Kellam, rhp, Indian River HS, Chesapeake, Va.**
20. **Bill Sobbe, c, Northwest Missouri State**
21. **Clint Wickenscheimer, rhp, Ball State**
22. **Glenn Terry, lhp, Kimball HS, Dallas**
23. **David Daniel, rhp, Antelope Valley HS, Hesperia, Calif.**
24. **Morris Madden, lhp, Spartanburg Methodist (S.C.) JC**
25. Leonard Collins, ss/of, Hiram Johnson HS, Sacramento
26. Brian Dillard, of, Bloom Township HS, Chicago Heights, Ill.
27. Harry Kazanjian, c/of, Washington HS, San Francisco
28. Kevin Roddy, inf, Bellevue (Neb.) West HS
29. P.J. Schranz, ss, Bloom Township HS, Chicago Heights, Ill.
30. Ted Salcido, of, Wilson HS, Los Angeles
31. James Garcia, rhp, Bell HS, Huntington Park, Calif.
32. George Page, of, Kennedy HS, Pacoima, Calif.

June—Secondary Phase (18)

1. **Al Mejia, c, Oral Roberts**
2. Thomas McLaughlin, rhp, Los Angeles CC
3. Kyle Dunning, rhp, Linn-Benton (Ore.) CC
4. Bill Worden, c, Mission Hills (Calif.) JC

MILWAUKEE BREWERS

January—Regular Phase (24)

1. **David Thomas, rhp, Lafayette, Ind.**
2. Jeff Heathcock, rhp, Golden West (Calif.) JC
3. Larry Robinson, rhp, Compton (Calif.) CC
4. **Benjie Biggus, rhp, Frederick (Md.) CC**
5. Weston Mitchell, 2b, San Jose CC
6. **Jesse Vasquez, rhp, Los Angeles Harbor JC**
7. Pedro Bazan, c, Central Arizona JC
8. Ricky Daniels, ss, Los Angeles CC
9. James Woodward, ss, Rio Hondo (Calif.) JC
10. **Brian Meadows, rhp, Yavapai (Ariz.) JC**
11. Jeff Ronk, 3b, JC of the Canyons (Calif.)
12. Scott Olshane, rhp, Los Angeles Valley JC
13. Tillmon Crownover, rhp, Central Arizona JC
14. Daniel Anctile, rhp, Los Angeles Valley JC
15. Daryl Pitts, of, Los Angeles CC
16. Tim Sinovich, 1b, Central Arizona JC
17. **Rick Odekirk, lhp, Southern California**
18. **Scott Job, of, JC of Southern Idaho**
19. Pedro Perez, inf, Miami-Dade New World Center CC

January—Secondary Phase (8)

1. **Tony Torres, rhp, JC of the Sequoias (Calif.)**
2. **Ronald Walling, lhp, Johnstown, Pa.**
3. **Todd Freeman, 3b, Spartanburg Methodist (S.C.) JC**
4. Ron Thurston, c, Santa Ana (Calif.) JC
5. Richard Evans, lhp, El Camino (Calif.) JC
6. Karl Watson, rhp, Manatee (Fla.) JC

June—Regular Phase (23)

1. (Pick to Tigers as compensation for free agent Jim Slaton)

2. **Mark Higgins, of, Central Valley HS, Veradale, Wash.**
3. **Jon Hansen, of, Hawaii**
4. **Rick Kranitz, rhp, Oklahoma State**
5. **Andy Beene, rhp, Baylor**
6. **Karl McKay, rhp/of, Lafayette HS, Ballwin, Mo.**
7. **Ed Irvine, of, Arizona State**
8. **Bill Schroeder, c, Clemson**
9. **David Morris, rhp, West Linn (Ore.) HS**
10. **Ron Koenigsfeld, inf, Florida International**
11. Paul Zuvella, 2b, Stanford
12. Tom Mallon, lhp, Woodson HS, Fairfax, Va.
13. **Bob Skube, of, Southern California**
14. Scott Smith, rhp, Polytechnic HS, Baltimore
15. Bruce Hines, 2b, La Verne (Calif.)
16. **Kurt Kingsolver, c, Cal State Fullerton**
17. **Ray Alonzo, of, Grand Canyon (Ariz.)**
18. Chris Glass, 2b, Hagerstown (Md.) CC
19. **Joe Tkac, lhp, Tulane**
20. Don Slaught, c/1b, UCLA
21. Pat Gillie, rhp, Arizona State
22. **Kevin McCoy, rhp, Baltimore**
23. Keith Mucha, 3b, Kennedy HS, Granada Hills, Calif.
24. **Frank Galloway, rhp, The Citadel**
25. James Koontz, rhp, Clarion (Pa.)
26. **Curt Downs, ss, Los Angeles, Calif.**
27. Mike Fulmer, lhp, Antelope Valley HS, Lancaster, Calif.
28. Danny Marshall, lhp, Cheraw HS, Patrick, S.C.
29. Dan Firova, c, Texas-Pan American
30. Randy Poitevint, 3b, Reseda HS, Sunland, Calif.
31. Jorge Reyes, lhp, Southwest Senior HS, Miami
32. Darren Swanson, rhp, Kent (Wash.) Meridian HS
33. Eugene Hering, of, Brookdale (N.J.) CC
34. Andrew Speck, rhp, Beaverton HS, Aloha, Ore.

June—Secondary Phase (26)

1. **David Grier, rhp, Virginia Tech**
2. **Randy Meyer, of, UC Santa Barbara**
3. Chris Cawthon, 1b, DeKalb (Ga.) JC
4. Willie Davis, of, Canada (Calif.) JC
5. Harold Brown, rhp, Chipola (Fla.) JC

MINNESOTA TWINS

January—Regular Phase (12)

1. Joseph McCarthy, of, Seminole (Fla.) CC
2. **Scott Stoltenberg, ss/of, Sacramento CC**
3. Tracy Turner, lhp, El Camino (Calif.) JC
4. John Damon, 2b, Sacramento CC
5. **Ed Hodge, lhp, Cerritos (Calif.) JC**
6. **Alan Jensen, c, South Florida JC**
7. Bruce Amador, 2b, Modesto (Calif.) JC
8. Nelson Page, p, Utah Technical JC
9. Trent Smith, rhp, Seminole (Fla.) CC
10. Ken Rolfe, ss, Lower Columbia (Wash.) JC
11. David Wilson, rhp, Anderson (S.C.) JC
12. **Thomas Paul, of, Treasure Valley (Ore.) CC**
13. Richard King, p, Solano (Calif.) CC
14. **Rick Kyzer, 3b, South Florida JC**
15. Lou Sottile, 3b, Seminole (Fla.) CC
16. **Larry May, rhp, Central Arizona JC**

January—Secondary Phase (19)

1. Joe Plummer, rhp, Long Beach (Calif.) CC
2. Mike Mason, lhp, Normandale (Minn.) CC
3. Jeff Viha, 2b, Fullerton (Calif.) JC
4. Randy Ramirez, rhp, Fullerton (Calif.) JC

June—Regular Phase (11)

1. **Kevin Brandt, of, Nekoosa (Wis.) HS**
2. **Randy Bush, of, New Orleans**
3. **Tim Laudner, c, Missouri**
4. **Sam Arrington, rhp, Taft (Calif.) HS**
5. **Bob Konopa, lhp, Bedford (Ohio) HS**
6. **Rich Shefte, ss, Nebraska-Omaha**
7. David Stokes, 3b, Tulane
8. **Ron Wilkinson, ss, Chapman (Calif.)**
9. **Paul Voigt, rhp, Virginia**
10. **Mike Kinnunen, lhp, Washington State**
11. **Bruce Stocker, of, Pima (Ariz.) CC**
12. **Rick Beswick, 2b, Lewis & Clark (Ill.) JC**
13. Todd Taylor, rhp, Upland (Calif.) HS
14. Andre David, of, Cal State Fullerton
15. **Manny Colletti, ss, New Orleans**
16. **Ken Francingues, rhp, Tulane**
17. **Wayne Palica, rhp, Huntington Beach (Calif.) HS**
18. **Kevin Miller, of, Cerritos (Calif.) JC**
19. **Boyce Orosco, rhp, Monache HS, Porterville, Calif.**
20. **Jack Gurholt, lhp, Wisconsin**
21. Bill Piwnica, ss, Minotonka (Minn.) HS
22. **Richard Austin, c, Cerritos (Calif.) JC**
23. **Tim Fagely, lhp, Winona State (Minn.)**
24. **Bob Mulligan, lhp, John Jay (N.Y.)**
25. **Brandon Rosenberg, of, Glassboro State (N.J.)**
26. Randy Newman, lhp, Cypress (Calif.) JC
27. **Bill Lampey, rhp, New Orleans**
28. **Alfredo Agras, of/c, Miami Springs HS, Hialeah, Fla.**
29. Edward Odin, of, Pacifica HS, Cypress, Calif.
30. Tom Colburn, c, California
31. Tom Nieto, c, Cerritos (Calif.) JC
32. David Zitkus, lhp, JC of Lake County (Ill.)
33. **Derek Bulcock, ss, San Jose State**
34. John Lastinger, of, Valdosta (Ga.) HS

June—Secondary Phase (11)

1. **Gary Gaetti, 3b, Northwest Missouri State**
2. Randy O'Neal, rhp, Palm Beach (Fla.) JC

MONTREAL EXPOS

January—Regular Phase (9)

1. **Stephen Roeder, ss, Columbia State (Tenn.) CC**
2. Jim Weaver, of/1b, Manatee (Fla.) JC
3. Derrell Baker, 2b, Middle Georgia JC
4. Randy O'Neal, rhp, Palm Beach (Fla.) JC
5. Chris Campbell, 3b, Panola (Texas) JC
6. Rory Brown, lhp, Broward (Fla.) CC
7. Steve Mastro, 3b/of, Macomb (Mich.) CC
8. Mike Withrow, rhp, Blinn (Texas) JC
9. Tracy Cohron, lhp, Middle Georgia JC
10. Richard Vitato, inf, Merced (Calif.) JC
11. John Baker, rhp, Manatee (Fla.) JC
12. **Blake Byrket, rhp, Muscatine (Iowa) CC**
13. **Jim Atkinson, of, Western Kentucky**
14. Ric Wilson, c, Mesa (Ariz.) CC
15. **George Keen, c, Wittenberg (Ohio)**

January—Secondary Phase (14)

1. Chris Cawthon, 1b, DeKalb (Ga.) JC
2. **Cat Whitfield, 1b, Middle Georgia JC**

June—Regular Phase (10)

1. **Tim Wallach, 1b, Cal State Fullerton**
2. **Mike Kwiecinski, ss, Shawnee HS, Warren, Mich.** (Pick from Cardinals as compensation for free agent Darold Knowles)
2. (Pick to Athletics as compensation for free agent Elias Sosa)
3. (Pick to Pirates as compensation for free agent Duffy Dyer)
4. John Russell, c, Norman (Okla.) HS
5. **Jim Auten, of, UCLA**
6. **Wallace Johnson, 2b, Indiana State**
7. **Mike Gates, 2b, Pepperdine**
8. **Bill St. John, lhp, Aiken HS, Cincinnati**
9. **Larry Boger, rhp/ss, Del Campo HS, Carmichael, Calif.**
10. Thor Edgel, rhp, Garden Grove (Calif.) HS
11. **Joe Abone, rhp, LeMoyne**
12. **Ronnie Caldwell, rhp/of, McNeese State**
13. **Kirk Forbes, 2b, Tennessee State**
14. John Palica, 1b/of, Torrance HS, Lomita, Calif.
15. Guy Burgess, lhp, Atlantic HS, Delray Beach, Fla.
16. **Bobby Ruiz, lhp, Dupont HS, Hermitage, Tenn.**
17. **Brad Mills, 3b, Arizona**
18. Shayne Hammond, lhp, West Columbus HS, Cerro Gordo, N.C.
19. Jeff McDonald, rhp, Monta Vista HS, Saratoga, Calif.

20. **Chuck Fick, c, Pepperdine**
21. **Keith White, lhp, Jackson State (Tenn.) CC**
22. Thomas Scheer, rhp, Burbank HS, Sacramento
23. **David Flowers, lhp, Methodist (N.C.)**
24. David Flores, rhp, Carroll HS, Corpus Christi, Texas
25. **Bud Yanus, rhp, Eastern Michigan**
26. **David Bradshaw, lhp, Jac Cen Del HS, Osgood, Ind.**
27. **Tommy Montgomery, lhp, Columbus (Ga.)**
28. George Foussianes, ss, Michigan
29. **Bill Sattler, rhp, Youngstown State**
30. Billy Hatcher, of/rhp, Williams (Ariz.) HS
31. John McKeon, 2b, Cummings HS, Burlington, N.C.

June—Secondary Phase (10)

1. Mark Christy, rhp, Miami-Dade North CC
2. Ed Schiavo, rhp, Boyertown, Pa.

NEW YORK METS

January—Regular Phase (1)

1. Neal Heaton, lhp, Sachem HS, Holtsville, N.Y.
2. **Mark Welch, lhp, Indiana Central**
3. **Marcus Cooper, of, Three Rivers (Mo.) CC**
4. Thomas McLaughlin, rhp, Los Angeles CC
5. Michael Befort, rhp, Allen County (Kan.) CC
6. **Ron Souza, ss, Butte (Calif.) JC**
7. **Ron Graves, rhp, Modesto (Calif.) JC**
8. **David Michael, rhp, Dodge City (Kan.) CC**
9. **John Semprini, rhp, Des Moines Area (Iowa) CC**
10. **Rusty Tillman, of, Florida CC**
11. Jesse Anderson, rhp, San Diego CC
12. Mike Sodders, 3b, Orange Coast (Calif.) JC

January—Secondary Phase (11)

1. **John Violette, c, El Segundo, Calif.**
2. **Jeff Sunderlage, lhp, Des Moines Area (Iowa) CC**

June—Regular Phase (2)

1. **Tim Leary, rhp, UCLA**
2. **Jeff Bettendorf, rhp, Lompoc (Calif.) HS**
3. Craig Jones, rhp, Army (Selection voided)
4. **David Howard, of, Wichita State**
5. **Gary Hardie, ss, Georgia Tech**
6. **Ron Gardenhire, inf, Texas**
7. **Mike Hennessy, of, Bogota (N.J.) HS**
8. **David Buttles, rhp, Kearny HS, San Diego**
9. **Lee Shockley, rhp, Parkside HS, Salisbury, Md.**
10. Brooks Wallace, ss, Texas Tech
11. **Bryan Dunbar, c, JC of Marin (Calif.)**
12. Larry Hernandez, of, Jones HS, Orlando, Fla.
13. **Doug Elliott, 2b, San Diego State**
14. Brick Toifel, c, Davidson HS, Mobile, Ala.
15. Walt Terrell, rhp, Morehead State
16. **Bill Hill, of, Brookdale (N.J.) CC**
17. Todd Davidson, of, North Allegheny HS, Wexford, Pa.
18. John Bryant, of, El Toro (Calif.) HS
19. **Mike Anicich, 1b, Arizona State**
20. John Leister, rhp, Russell HS, Great Falls, Mont.
21. **Ted Damiter, rhp, Shippensburg**
22. Joe Scherger, of, Nebraska
23. Joseph Healy, rhp, Judge HS, Philadelphia
24. **Richard Greenfield, ss, La Salle**
25. **Scott LaVielle, c, Olympic (Wash.) JC**
26. Jim Phillips, rhp, Shawnee HS, Shawnee Mission, Kan.
27. **Dave Smith, rhp, Lamar**
28. Darryl Stephens, 1b, Butte (Calif.) JC
29. Clay Christiansen, rhp, Kansas
30. **William Rittweger, 2b, Seton Hall**
31. **Paul Niggebrugge, of, Temple**
32. **Thomas Miller, lhp, Modesto (Calif.) JC**
33. **Michael Privette, rhp, Millikan HS, Long Beach, Calif.**
34. Dan Sprick, of, Saint Louis
35. Terry Byrum, ss, Houston
36. **David Duff, c, Virginia**

June—Secondary Phase (22)

1. Bill Mooneyham, rhp, Merced (Calif.) JC
2. **Joe Plummer, rhp, Long Beach (Calif.) CC**
3. Sheldon Andrews, rhp, Lower Columbia (Wash.) JC

NEW YORK YANKEES

January—Regular Phase (26)

1. **James Campbell, rhp, Orange Coast (Calif.) JC**
2. **Glen Swires, 3b, Mount San Antonio (Calif.) JC**
3. **Jeff Van Der Plass, lhp, Camden County (N.J.) JC**
4. Gary Higgins, rhp, Columbia State (Tenn.) CC
5. Otis Reuban, lhp, Black Hawk (Ill.) JC
6. **George Zimmerer, 2b, San Jose (Calif.) CC**
7. Ed Schiavo, rhp, Boyertown (Pa.) HS
8. **Rich Santarone, c, Camden County (N.J.) JC**

January—Secondary Phase (26)

1. **Carlos Hernandez, lhp, Hillsborough (Fla.) CC**
2. **Alan Mayles, rhp, Louisburg (N.C.) JC**
3. Dan Peterson, rhp, North Idaho JC
4. Jerome Burgess, 1b, Palm Beach (Fla.) JC
5. Charles Beverly, rhp, Wise, Va.

June—Regular Phase (25)

1. (Pick to Dodgers as compensation for free agent Tommy John.)
2. **Todd Demeter, inf, Grant HS, Sacramento**
3. **Freddie Toliver, rhp, San Gorgonio HS, San Bernardino, Calif.**
4. Ted Perkins, 1b, El Cerrito HS, Richmond, Calif.
5. **Greg Gagne, ss, Somerset (Mass.) HS**
6. **Stefan Wever, rhp, UC Santa Barbara**
7. **Mike Echstenkamper, of, Ohio**
8. **Huey Gayden, of, Jackson State**
9. **Pete Filson, lhp, Temple**
10. **Richard Budweg, lhp, Bloomsburg (Pa.)**
11. **George Demaria, rhp, El Segundo (Calif.) HS**
12. **Michael Free, rhp, Chapman HS, San Diego**
13. **David Buffamoyer, c, Clemson**
14. **Randy Guerra, 1b, Miami**
15. **Keith Smith, ss, Canyon HS, Canyon Country, Calif.**
16. **Chris Lein, rhp, Florida International**
17. **Rob Teegarden, of, Florida**
18. Mike Dotterer, of, Edison HS, Huntington Beach, Calif.
19. **Don Mattingly, 1b, Reitz Memorial HS, Evansville, Ind.**
20. Sean Everton, of, Santa Clara
21. **Derwin McNealy, of, Crenshaw HS, Carson, Calif.**
22. Cedric Mack, of, Brazosport HS, Freeport, Texas
23. **Brian Murphy, lhp, Eastern Connecticut State**
24. **Gregg Sporrer, inf, La Verne (Calif.)**
25. **Jeff Rudolph, c/3b, Central Florida**
26. **Frank Ricci, rhp, Rollins (Fla.)**
27. **Kevin Irot, rhp, Cal Poly San Luis Obispo**
28. **John Seneca, rhp, Seton Hall**
29. Rusty Piggott, ss, Rollins (Fla.)
30. **Greg Copeland, rhp, Shaw HS, Cleveland**

June—Secondary Phase (3)

1. **Otis Nixon, 3b, Louisburg (N.C.) JC**
2. **Scott Benedict, c, Georgia**
3. **Mark Ochal, rhp, Brookdale (N.J.) CC**

OAKLAND ATHLETICS

January—Regular Phase (6)

1. Lemmie Miller, of, Santa Barbara (Calif.) CC
2. Bob Fallon, lhp, Miami-Dade North CC
3. David Granger, rhp, Santa Barbara (Calif.) CC
4. Harold Brown, rhp, Chipola (Fla.) JC
5. Frederick Conradi, lhp, Centralia (Wash.) JC
6. Kirk Komstadius, 3b, Yakima Valley (Wash.) JC
7. Al Romero, of, JC of Southern Idaho

January—Secondary Phase (10)

1. Paul Homrig, 1b, Los Angeles Harbor JC
2. Stephen Maral, c, Chabot (Calif.) JC

June—Regular Phase (5)

1. Juan Bustabad, ss, Miami Lakes HS, Hialeah, Fla.
1. Mike Stenhouse, of, Harvard (Pick from Red Sox as compensation for free agent Steve Renko)
2. Tom Dodd, of, Oregon
2. **Mark Ferguson, rhp, West Muskingum HS, Zanesville, Ohio** (Pick from Expos as compensation for free agent Elias Sosa)
3. Ricky McMullen, inf, William Carey (Miss.)
4. Tom Caulfield, lhp, St. Mary's HS, Jersey City, N.J.
5. Ronn Reynolds, c, Arkansas
6. **Oscar Burnett, of/3b, Moravia (N.Y.) Central HS**
7. Robert Ruffus, rhp, Monmouth
8. Jeff Blankenship, rhp, El Dorado HS, Placentia, Calif.
9. Mark Calvert, rhp, Thomas Stone HS, Waldorf, Md.
10. **Paul Spillane, c, Colby (Maine)**
11. Craig Roberson, ss, Highland Springs (Va.) HS
12. Joe Jacowiak, rhp, St. Joseph's HS, South Bend, Ind.
13. Jim Stefanski, c, Long Island
14. Mike McCandless, rhp, San Jose (Calif.) CC
15. **Keith Call, rhp, Hammond (Ind.) Tech HS**
16. **Paul Stockley, ss, American International (Mass.)**
17. Manuel Costa, 3b, Gavilan (Calif.) JC
18. Kevin Olson, rhp, Marina HS, Huntington Beach, Calif.
19. Mike O'Hara, rhp, Covina HS, West Covina, Calif.
20. **Robert Wood, rhp, Northeast Louisiana**
21. **Steven Roberts, 3b, Kentucky**
22. Michael Jefferson, of, Berkeley (Calif.) HS
23. Jordan Berge, ss, Pueblo (Colo.) East HS
24. Hank Landers, of, Somerville (Mass.) HS
25. Ron Sylvia, rhp, Cal State Los Angeles
26. **Ken Corzel, rhp, Cal State Long Beach**
27. **Bert Bradley, rhp, Brigham Young**
28. **Ed Retzer, rhp, SUNY Buffalo**
29. **Joseph Williams, 1b, South Florida**
30. Brian Guinn, ss, Berkeley HS, Richmond, Calif.
31. Greg Hazel, ss, San Jose (Calif.) CC
32. Arthur Sullivan, of, Colby (Maine)
33. Ken Babcock, lhp, Centenary
34. **John Pignotti, c, Claremont-Mudd (Calif.)**

June—Secondary Phase (9)

1. Edwin Schneider, lhp, Indian River (Fla.) CC
2. Scott Patterson, rhp, Mesa (Ariz.) CC
3. Jeff Dedmon, rhp, West Los Angeles JC

PHILADELPHIA PHILLIES

January—Regular Phase (19)

1. **Dean Baugh, of/inf, Butte (Calif.) JC**
2. Robert Fischer, rhp, Panola (Texas) JC
3. **Jon Lindsey, ss, Seminole State (Okla.) JC**
4. Grant Priess, c, Blinn (Texas) JC
5. Ken Schubert, rhp, St. Clair County (Mich.) CC
6. Benny Smith, lhp, Ranger (Texas) JC
7. Robert Culley, 3b, Panola (Texas) JC
8. Nathan Frierson, rhp, Ranger (Texas) JC
9. Don Young, of, Paris (Texas) JC
10. Steve D'Ercole, ss, Seminole (Fla.) CC
11. Donald Wilson, rhp, Salem (N.J.) CC
12. Richard Yraguen, ss, JC of Southern Idaho

January—Secondary Phase (1)

1. **Mark Davis, lhp, Chabot (Calif.) JC**
2. Luis Rojas, of, New York
3. Kem Wright, rhp, Paris (Texas) JC
4. Ron Rendleman, rhp, San Bernardino Valley (Calif.) JC

June—Regular Phase (20)

1. (Pick to Reds as compensation for free agent Pete Rose)
2. **Kyle Money, rhp, Samuell HS, Dallas**
3. **Roy Smith, rhp, Mount Vernon (N.Y.) HS**
4. **Jay Baller, rhp, Canby (Ore.) HS**
5. **Herbert Bennett, rhp, Riverdale HS, Fort Myers, Fla.**
6. **Trent Purcell, of, Trotwood (Ohio) HS**
7. **Ken Ellenberg, 3b, Carl Albert HS, Midwest City, Okla.**
8. **Jeff Nate, ss, Dowagiac (Mich.) HS**
9. **Matthew Dorin, rhp, Miraleste HS, Rolling Hills, Calif.**
10. **Rusty Hamric, 2b, Hardin-Simmons (Texas)**
11. **DeWayne Hutchinson, rhp, Yoncalla (Ore.) HS**
12. **David Harrigan, c, Oklahoma**
13. Jeff Ahern, lhp, Arizona State
14. **Adam Conti, rhp, Chicopee (Mass.) HS**
15. **Willie Darkis, of, Eastern Oklahoma State JC**
16. **Steve Dunnegan, rhp, Kerman (Calif.) HS**
17. **Roger Redmond, rhp, Kelley HS, Tulsa, Okla.**
18. **Michael Hanson, 3b, Woodway HS, Edmonds, Wash.**
19. **Robert Barnett, rhp, Oregon (Ill.) HS**
20. **Michael Lynes, lhp, UC Riverside**
21. Mike Knox, ss, Carlisle (Pa.) HS
22. Randy Foyt, 3b, Beyer HS, Modesto, Calif.
23. **Andrew Owings, ss, Klamath Falls (Ore.) HS**
24. Tim Reynolds, rhp, Skyline HS, Dallas
25. **David Mitchell, rhp, Leesburg HS, Fruitland Park, Fla.**
26. **Kelly Downs, rhp, Viewmont HS, Bountiful, Utah**
27. **Russell Gums, rhp, Rio Linda (Calif.) HS**
28. Brian Henderson, c, South Albany (Ore.) HS
29. Nelson Santovenia, 3b, Southridge HS, Miami
30. **Brad Lenaburg, rhp, Southwestern Oklahoma State**
31. Keith Robinson, 1b, Julian HS, Chicago
32. Curt Warner, of, Pineville HS, Wyoming, W.Va.
33. Deron Gustafson, 2b, Crockett HS, Austin

June—Secondary Phase (4)

1. **Kelly Faulk, rhp, Wharton County (Texas) JC**
2. Mike Withrow, rhp, Blinn (Texas) JC
3. Russ Stephans, c, Los Angeles Valley JC
4. **Ken Martinson, c, Billings, Mont.**

PITTSBURGH PIRATES

January—Regular Phase (15)

1. **William Nice, lhp, JC of Southern Idaho**
2. Chris Goodchild, rhp, Santa Monica (Calif.) JC
3. Carl Taylor, rhp, Camden County (N.J.) JC
4. Rick Ownbey, rhp, Santa Ana (Calif.) JC
5. Todd Dinsmore, of, Treasure Valley (Ore.) CC
6. Sheldon Andrews, rhp, Lower Columbia (Wash.) JC
7. Warren DeLisle, ss, Bellevue (Wash.) CC
8. Chris Fazendine, rhp, Yakima Valley (Wash.) JC
9. Mark Ochal, rhp, Brookdale (N.J.) CC

January—Secondary Phase (18)

1. David McDonald, lhp, Allegheny (Pa.) CC

June—Regular Phase (16)

1. (Pick to Dodgers as compensation for free agent Lee Lacy)
2. **Scott Fiepke, lhp, Elizabethtown (Ky.) HS**
3. **Jose DeLeon, rhp, Perth Amboy, N.J.** (Pick from Expos as compensation for free agent Duffy Dyer)
3. **Scott Kuvinka, 3b, Ohio**
4. **Chris Green, lhp, Dorsey HS, Los Angeles**
5. **Conner McGehee, of, Douglas Freeman HS, Richmond**
6. Craig Fitzpatrick, rhp, Fatima HS, Kolesztown, Mo.
7. John Alvarez, 3b, Helix HS, Lemon Grove, Calif.
8. **Andrew Snaith, 2b, Choctawatchee HS, Fort Walton Beach, Fla.**
9. **Art Ray, rhp, Northern Illinois**
10. **Ken Ford, c, Albany State**
11. **Michael Johnson, rhp, Osseo (Minn.) HS**
12. **Terry Salazar, 1b, Texas**
13. **Wilmot Reedy, 2b, Thomas Jefferson HS, Brooklyn, N.Y.**
14. **Jim Felt, of, DeKalb (Ga.) JC**
15. **Thomas Olszak, of, Pennsylvania**
16. **Ron Wotus, ss, Bacon Academy HS, Colchester, Conn.**
17. Darryl Stephens, of, Gonzaga Prep HS, Spokane, Wash.
18. Philip Fritz, ss, Henrico HS, Richmond
19. Otis Grant, inf/c, Carver HS, Atlanta
20. **Tim Wheeler, 3b, Dupont HS, Charleston, W.Va.**
21. **Larry Nicholson, lhp, Ohio**
22. **Mike Quade, of, New Orleans**
23. Ron Evans, ss, New Hartford (N.Y.) HS

24. Kevin Babb, rhp, Taft HS, Rose Lodge, Ore.
25. Joey Farrill, rhp, Mosely HS, Panama City, Fla.
26. Jeff Metz, rhp, Connellsville (Pa.) HS
27. John Tutt, ss/of, East Rome (Ga.) HS
28. Lance Mason, c, Meadowbrook HS, Richmond
29. Thomas Bart, rhp/of, Burrell HS, Lower Burrell, Pa.
30. Greg Tutt, ss/of, East Rome (Ga.) HS
31. Roger Lorenzen, of, Oregon College of Education
32. Craig Steensen, c, Hotchkiss School, Newark, Del.
33. David Blume, 1b, Lewis-Clark State (Idaho)
34. **Robert Gulaskey, inf, Elizabeth (Pa.) Forward HS**
35. **Lawrence Styles, rhp, Penn State**
36. Paul Bard, c, Tufts (Mass.)
37. **Joel Skinner, c, Mission Bay HS, San Diego**
38. John Peoples, rhp, Dickinson HS, Wilmington, Del.
39. Herm Winningham, of, Wilkinson HS, Orangeburg, S.C.
40. Robert Seames, rhp, Telestar HS, Bethel, Maine
41. Mike Sharperson, ss, Wilkinson HS, Orangeburg, S.C.
42. **Gordon Maki, rhp, Poly HS, Baltimore**
43. Michael Giedlin, rhp, Alford Almond HS, Alfred, N.Y.
44. Paul Cox, lhp, Springbrook HS, Silver Spring, Md.

June—Secondary Phase (8)

1. **Mike Bielecki, rhp, Valencia (Fla.) CC**
2. Nattie George, of, San Jose (Calif.) CC
3. Rick Witt, inf, Gonzaga

ST. LOUIS CARDINALS

January—Regular Phase (5)

1. Bob Ferris, 1b, Mesa (Ariz.) CC
2. **Keith Spreckles, ss, Islip, N.Y.**
3. Mike Evans, lhp, Merced (Calif.) JC
4. Ronald Sloy, 1b, Mount Hood (Ore.) CC
5. Mark Pedersen, rhp, Yakima Valley (Wash.) JC
6. Bill Lindsey, 3b, Broward (Fla.) CC
7. Gary Fradella, 1b, Glendale (Calif.) JC
8. John Mathews, rhp, Rio Hondo (Calif.) JC
9. Kevin Coughlon, of, Oxnard (Calif.) JC
10. Sam Cordero, rhp, Eastern Arizona JC
11. Thomas Kurant, rhp, Miami-Dade North CC
12. Greg Bargar, rhp, El Camino (Calif.) JC
13. **John Rincon, of, Rio Hondo (Calif.) JC**
14. Steve Heslop, lhp, San Bernardino Valley (Calif.) JC

January—Secondary Phase (7)

1. Bill Mooneyham, rhp, Merced (Calif.) JC
2. David Jensen, lhp, Edmonds (Wash.) CC

June—Regular Phase (6)

1. **Andy Van Slyke, of, New Hartford (N.Y.) HS**
2. (Pick to Expos as compensation for free agent Darold Knowles)
3. Ed Vosberg, lhp, Salpointe HS, Tucson, Ariz.
4. **John Del Monte, of, St. Joseph's**
5. Mark Roberts, lhp, Myers Park HS, Charlotte, N.C.
6. **Robert Brooks, rhp, Ithaca (N.Y.)**
7. **Bill Fink, of, Greenfield (Ind.) HS**
8. **Earl Weaver, rhp, Kutztown (Pa.)**
9. **Mike Kopala, c, Hackensack HS, Rochelle Park, N.J.**
10. **Jon Ayers, ss, Cal Poly San Luis Obispo**
11. **Tom Dozier, rhp, Richmond (Calif.) HS**
12. **Jeff Taylor, lhp, Righetti HS, Santa Maria, Calif.**
13. **Jeff Warburton, lhp, Granger HS, Salt Lake City**
14. Tracy Hamilton, ss, Tattnall Square HS, Macon, Ga.
15. **Tim Fish, lhp, Whittier Christian HS, Rowland Heights, Calif.**
16. Steve Stanicek, 1b, Rich East HS, Park Forest, Ill.
17. Tony Hudson, rhp, Cal State Fullerton
18. **Mark Salas, c, Nogales HS, LaPuente, Calif.**
19. Greg Howe, of, Eisenhower HS, Rochester, Mich.
20. Doug Latrenta, of, St. John's
21. Lloyd Martin, lhp, Los Altos HS, Hacienda Heights, Calif.
22. John Krol, 3b, Bishop McGuiness HS, Winston-Salem, N.C.
23. **Terry Clark, rhp, Mount San Antonio (Calif.) JC**
24. Jeff Keeler, rhp, Miami-Dade South CC
25. **Phil Baskerville, of, Elon**
26. **Stan McCauley, 3b, Troy State**
27. Kevin House, of, Southern Illinois

June—Secondary Phase (12)

1. **Ralph Citarella, rhp, Florida Southern**
2. Mike Mason, lhp, Normandale (Minn.) CC

SAN DIEGO PADRES

January—Regular Phase (13)

1. **John Stevenson, inf, Los Angeles Valley JC**
2. Carlos Moreno, rhp, Miami-Dade New World Center CC
3. Victor Woods, of, Laney (Calif.) JC
4. **Greg Tarnow, c/3b, Rolling Prairies, Ind.**
5. Larry See, inf, Cerritos (Calif.) JC

January—Secondary Phase (22)

1. Mondell Williams, of, Sacramento CC

June—Regular Phase (14)

1. **Jody Lansford, 1b, Wilcox HS, San Jose, Calif.**
1. **Bob Geren, c, Clairemont HS, San Diego** (Pick from Dodgers as compensation for free agent Derrel Thomas)
2. Derek Tatsuno, lhp, Hawaii
3. **Steve Johnson, of, Rich East HS, Park Forest, Ill.**
4. **Mark Parent, c, Anderson HS, Cottonwood, Calif.**
5. **Mark Thurmond, lhp, Texas A&M**
6. Harold Reynolds, ss, Corvallis (Ore.) HS
7. **Mike Barba, rhp, Coastal Carolina**
8. **Jim Steels, of, Santa Maria (Calif.) HS**
9. **Courtney Wyrick, rhp, Cal Poly San Luis Obispo**
10. **Dan Gausepohl, of, UCLA**
11. **Jerry DeSimone, ss, Southern Illinois**
12. Larry Navilhon, rhp, Cal State Fullerton
13. **Aaron Cain, 2b/of, New Mexico**
14. **Dave Froelick, rhp, New Orleans**
15. Paul Bradley, c, La Sierra HS, Riverside, Calif.
16. **Dave Wilson, rhp, Bethel HS, Hampton, Va.**
17. **Dan Sijer, lhp, Washington**
18. **Doug Lulay, of, Oregon College of Education**
19. **Alfredo Rodriguez, inf, Miami**
20. **Dan Danielson, rhp, Cal State Long Beach**
21. **Francisco Gonzalez, 2b/ss, Valdosta State (Ga.)**
22. **Thomas Brokaph, rhp, Thornton (Ill.) CC**
23. **Rodney Peterson, rhp, Black Hawk (Ill.) JC**
24. Ronnie Scheer, of, Kentucky HS, Paducah, Ky.
25. Mark Hoffman, lhp, Mount Eden HS, Hayward, Calif.
26. Richard Scott, inf, Gunn HS, Palo Alto, Calif.
27. Donald Canedo, ss, Hoover HS, San Diego

June—Secondary Phase (14)

1. Jeff Heathcock, rhp, Golden West (Calif.) JC

SAN FRANCISCO GIANTS

January—Regular Phase (17)

1. **Kevin Johnson, of, Los Angeles CC**
2. **Matthew Dunn, c, Brookdale (N.J.) CC**
3. Mario Ramirez, p, Los Angeles CC
4. David LaBounty, rhp, Yakima Valley (Wash.) JC
5. Albert Hammack, rhp, Bellevue (Wash.) CC
6. **Ralph Guarante, of, Paterson, N.J.**
7. **Ronald Perodon, of, Los Angeles CC**
8. Kurtis Kemp, c, Linn-Benton (Ore.) CC
9. **Arthur Maebe, rhp, JC of the Desert (Calif.)**
10. **Jerry Lane, c/inf, Santa Monica (Calif.) JC**
11. Eugene Hernandez, rhp, San Joaquin Delta (Calif.) JC
12. Jack Glaze, lhp, Lane (Ore.) CC

January—Secondary Phase (24)

1. Jeff Stottlemyre, rhp, Yakima Valley (Wash.) JC

June—Regular Phase (17)

1. **Scott Garrelts, rhp, Buckley-Loda HS, Buckley, Ill.** (Pick from Angels as compensation for free agent Jim Barr)
1. Rick Luecken, rhp, Spring-Woods HS, Houston
2. **Chris Brown, 3b, Crenshaw HS, Los Angeles**

3. **David Wilhelmi, rhp, Joliet (Ill.) Catholic HS**
4. **Randy Kutcher, ss, Palmdale (Calif.) HS**
5. Louis Burmester, rhp, Herricks HS, Williston Park, N.Y.
6. **James Dunn, 2b/rhp, Portland State**
7. **Darryl McNealy, 1b, Crenshaw HS, Carson, Calif.**
8. **Greg Baker, of, Indiana State**
9. **Charles Curry, 1b, Southern Illinois**
10. Scotti Madison, c, Vanderbilt
11. **Frank Williams, rhp, Lewis-Clark State (Idaho)**
12. **Cordie Dillard, 2b, Crenshaw HS, Los Angeles**
13. Joe Cardwell, ss, East Tennessee State
14. Lance Junker, of, Mission (Calif.) JC
15. Scott Blanke, of, Cypress (Calif.) JC
16. **Tom O'Malley, 2b/inf, Montoursville (Pa.) HS**
17. Steve Murphy, rhp, Grant HS, North Hollywood, Calif.
18. **Michael Woods, ss, Southern**
19. **John Wojcik, of, SUNY Buffalo**
20. Paul Ash, of, Delaware State
21. John Ross, 3b, William Paterson (N.J.)
22. Mark Dacko, rhp, James Madison
23. Jim Wilson, c, Franklin HS, Livonia, Mich.
24. **David Thornton, rhp, St. Joseph's**
25. James Kelly, rhp, Westwood HS, Fort Pierce, Fla.
26. Bill Zempolich, rhp, Roosevelt HS, Lanham, Md.
27. **Jerald Felt, rhp, Mesa (Colo.)**
28. **John Ziccardi, 1b/of, Florida Tech**
29. **Don Jamerson, of, Cal State Hayward**
30. **Joe Lorenz, 3b, Lewis (Ill.)**
31. Tim Thiessen, ss/3b, Roosevelt HS, Fresno, Calif.
32. **Jerrett Turner, c, Texas A&M**
33. David Del Rio, of, Ponderosa HS, Lotus, Calif.
34. Russell Cleland, c/rhp, El Dorado HS, Placerville, Calif.

June—Secondary Phase (2)

1. **Chris Goodchild, rhp, Santa Monica (Calif.) JC**

SEATTLE MARINERS

January—Regular Phase (2)

1. **Michael Hood, c, Washington Academy, Greenville, Miss.**
2. **Don Minnick, lhp, Bedford, Va.**
3. Carlos Diaz, lhp, Hancock (Calif.) JC
4. Steve Lawrence, lhp, Yavapai (Ariz.) JC

January—Secondary Phase (15)

1. Joe Housey, rhp, Miami-Dade North CC

June—Regular Phase (1)

1. **Al Chambers, of, John Harris HS, Harrisburg, Pa.**
2. **Jamie Allen, inf, Arizona State**
3. **Rick Adair, lhp, Western Carolina**
4. **Jim Presley, ss, Escambia HS, Pensacola, Fla.**
5. **Mark Cahill, rhp, East HS, Cranston, R.I.**
6. **Kevin King, of, Chief Sealth HS, Seattle**
7. **Brian Snyder, lhp, Clemson**
8. **Scott Stranski, rhp, Northwestern**
9. **Bob Randolph, rhp, Arizona State**
10. **Chris Henry, c, North Central HS, Spokane, Wash.**
11. **Mark Batten, rhp, Miami**
12. **Mike Codiroli, of, Stanford**
13. **Mike Hart, of, Wisconsin**
14. **Joe Georger, rhp, Kentucky**
15. Brian McDonough, rhp, Tottenville HS, Staten Island, N.Y.
16. **Charles Colby, ss, Westmont (Calif.)**
17. **Bud Black, lhp, San Diego State**
18. Fred Belak, rhp, Cardinal Spellman HS, Bronx, N.Y.
19. **William Gaffney, ss, Adelphi (N.Y.)**
20. Tom Henke, rhp, East Central (Mo.) JC
21. **Brian Harrison, rhp, Stanford**
22. **John Cook, of, Washington State**
23. David Axenfeld, lhp, Fayetteville-Manilius HS, Manilius, N.Y.
24. **Roy Clark, 2b, North Carolina**
25. **Kevin Steger, rhp, New Mexico State**
26. **Jed Murray, rhp, Southern Utah State**
27. **Dale Eiler, c, Arizona State**
28. **Bill Martin, rhp, Quinnipiac (Conn.)**
29. **Chris Hunger, rhp/ss, Edgewood HS, Berlin, N.J.**
30. **Mark Chellette, 3b/ss, Texas**
31. Daniel McFadden, lhp, Kingstree (S.C.) HS
32. Mike Rantz, ss, Moundsview Heights HS, St. Paul, Minn.
33. Edward Kolo, c, St. Mark's HS, Auburn, N.Y.
34. Jack Thompson, of, Washington State

June—Secondary Phase (15)

1. **Carlos Diaz, lhp, Hancock (Calif.) JC**
2. **Jeff Stottlemyre, rhp, Yakima Valley (Wash.) JC**

TEXAS RANGERS

January—Regular Phase (18)

1. Clay Weisinger, rhp, Angelina (Texas) JC
2. **Keith Showell, of, Prince Georges (Md.) CC**
3. Larry Mikesell, lhp, Brevard (Fla.) CC
4. Michael Young, rhp, Trinidad State (Colo.) JC
5. **David Orzel, lhp, Macomb (Mich.) CC**
6. James Good, of, JC of Southern Idaho
7. Lee Cline, rhp, JC of Southern Idaho
8. Perry Kilgo, rhp, McLennan (Texas) CC
9. Michael Williams, c, Hill (Texas) JC
10. Oscar Cardenas, ss, Hill (Texas) JC
11. Randy Jones, of, Wenatchee Valley (Wash.) CC

January—Secondary Phase (6)

1. Arbrey Lucas, rhp, Arizona Western JC
2. **Jerry Vasquez, rhp, Arizona State**
3. **Doyle Wilson, ss, Rome, Ga.**

June—Regular Phase (17)

1. **Jerry Don Gleaton, lhp, Texas**
2. **Donnie Scott, c, Tampa Catholic HS**
3. **Nick Capra, 2b, Oklahoma**
4. **Larry Reynolds, ss, Stanford**
5. Mark Gammage, rhp, Osborn HS, Detroit
6. **Shelton McMath, of, Texas A&M**
7. **Larry D'Onofrio, c, St. Francis (Ill.)**
8. **Michael Roberts, rhp, Baylor**
9. Jeff Johnson, rhp, Muir HS, Pasadena, Calif.
10. **William Goodman, 2b, George Washington**
11. **Mel Gilliam, lhp, Florida A&M**
12. **Tony Fossas, lhp, South Florida**
13. **Bobby Ball, of, Cal State Dominguez Hills**
14. **Mike Behudian, 2b/of, Fairfield**
15. **Pete O'Brien, 1b, Nebraska**
16. **James Hager, rhp, Newberry (S.C.)**
17. Steve Brigante, 2b, Lubbock Christian
18. Joe Kucharski, rhp, Surrattsville HS, Clinton, Md.
19. Larry Hamilton, of, Morehead State
20. James Hawkins, c, Herndon HS, Reston, Va.
21. Homer Moncrief, rhp, Jackson State
22. Steven Davis, of, Middle Georgia JC
23. **James Schaefer, of, Southwest Missouri State**
24. Andy Ortiz, lhp, Roselle (N.J.) Catholic HS
25. **Elwood Zebley, c, Towson State**
26. **Dave Schmidt, rhp, UCLA**
27. **Stanley Baker, ss, Dallas Baptist**
28. **Jorge Gomez, ss, Macomb (Mich.) CC**
29. **Charles Stafford, of, Dallas Baptist**
30. **Jay Pettibone, rhp, Chapman (Calif.)**
31. Daryl Frazier, rhp, Midwestern State
32. **Gordon Ricossa, lhp, Southern Methodist**
33. Joe Dellasega, 1b, Colgan HS, Pittsburg, Kan.
34. **Ray Fontenot, lhp, McNeese State**
35. **Rodger Bastien, ss, Michigan State**
36. Mitch Ashmore, c, Centenary
37. Thomas Smith, rhp, Minnesota
38. **Stephen Romey, 1b/3b, Kent State**

June—Secondary Phase (23)

1. Michael Sanford, rhp, DeKalb South (Ga.) CC
2. Joseph McCarthy, of, Seminole (Fla.) CC
3. Jerome Burgess, 1b, Delray Beach, Fla.

TORONTO BLUE JAYS

January—Regular Phase (4)

1. Scott Patterson, rhp, Valencia (Fla.) CC
2. **Mark Eichhorn, ss/rhp, Cabrillo (Calif.) JC**
3. Stephen Roache, rhp, Sacramento CC
4. Craig Charron, ss, Merced (Calif.) JC
5. Jeff Moronko, inf, San Jacinto (Texas) JC
6. Randy Brown, rhp, San Jacinto (Texas) JC

January—Secondary Phase (2)

1. Nattie George, of, San Jose CC

June—Regular Phase (3)

1. **Jay Schroeder, c, Palisades HS, Pacific Palisades, Calif.**
2. **Ron Shepherd, of, Kilgore (Texas) HS**
3. Ron Romanick, rhp, Newport HS, Bellevue, Wash.
4. **Andre Robertson, 2b, Texas**
5. **Keith Walker, lhp/of, Texas**
6. **Robert Tackitt, rhp, Mount Diablo HS, Concord, Calif.**
7. **John Seiber, rhp, Sweet Home (Ore.) HS**
8. **Mark Lieber, lhp, Pepperdine**
9. **Mark Holton, rhp, Elizabeth Forward HS, Buena Vista, Pa.**
10. Matt Ford, rhp, Bossier City (La.) HS
11. **Randy Ford, lhp, Western Michigan**
12. **Vern Ramie, 1b, Hawaii**
13. **Brian Stemberger, 3b, Eastern Michigan**
14. **Paul White, of, North Carolina State**
15. Tim Cassell, rhp, El Cerrito HS, Pinole, Calif.
16. Jack McMahon, rhp, Cal State Dominguez Hills
17. Jeff Robinson, rhp, Troy HS, Yorba Linda, Calif.
18. **Jeff Vail, 1b/rhp, St. Xavier (Ill.)**
19. **Phillip Turner, 1b, Mott (Mich.) CC**
20. **Lee Wetenkamp, 3b, Wisconsin**

June—Secondary Phase (13)

1. **Kem Wright, rhp, Texas**
2. Darren Dilks, lhp, Chaffey (Calif.) JC

1980

Mets begin new era of success with selection of Strawberry, as clubs try to curb bonuses

In 1980, the Mets were in the middle of a run of five last-place finishes in seven years. But it also marked the start of a remarkable transition, as the Mets began drafting talented young players who formed the foundation of a budding dynasty.

Beginning with the June 1980 draft, the Mets signed 29 players over the next four years who reached the big leagues. No team came close to matching their success during the same period, either in quality or quantity.

It began with the first pick in 1980 in their first year under new ownership, when the Mets went for a strapping high school outfielder from Los Angeles. Darryl Strawberry went on to become one of the best No. 1 picks ever, before his career declined suddenly because of drugs and injuries.

Strawberry reached the big leagues in 1983, winning National League rookie of the year honors, then made eight straight All-Star Game appearances, never hitting fewer than 26 home runs in any of those seasons. His decline began in 1992 after he had signed with the Dodgers as a free agent, and he had only one more productive season—with the Yankees in 1998.

"He's the best prospect I've seen in the last 30 years," veteran Phillies scout Hugh Alexander said before the 1980 draft.

Strawberry was an all-city forward for Crenshaw High's city championship basketball team, and he hit .400 with six homers in 14 games after starting baseball season late. He also pitched on occasion, going 1-1 with three saves.

"He is just a pure hitter with major league power," Mets scout Roger Jongewaard said. "He has good instincts for his age, runs like a deer and his arm is better than adequate."

The Mets got Strawberry to agree to a bonus of $210,000 after he held out for five weeks, baiting the Mets with a basketball offer from the University of Oklahoma.

The Mets' rebuilding efforts got a further boost because they also had two other first-round picks, and four of the first 28. Led by Mets' trio of first-round picks (outfielder Billy Beane and catcher John Gibbons were the others), all of whom reached New York, 20 first-rounders from 1980 eventually played in the big leagues.

Seattle farm director Hal Keller had a good assessment of the talent available when he said on the eve of the draft: "There are more blue-chippers in this draft than we've had for the past few years. There are more good pitchers overall than I've seen in quite a while."

TOM DIPACE

Darryl Strawberry quickly became a star with the Mets before a precipitous decline

One of six first-round picks who failed to reach the big leagues was shortstop Garry Harris, selected second overall by Toronto and a player the Blue Jays began courting as a high school sophomore.

"I'd bet my wife and children that he'll make it to Toronto," said Bob Warner, Harris' high school coach. Harris didn't come close. He peaked at Double-A, hitting .224 in 1983, his final season. In fact, not a single Toronto draft pick made the big leagues.

In spite of the success of the class of '80, Harris was one of three top five picks who were out of the game within four years. The Athletics' Mike King and Padres' Jeff Pyburn also bit the dust early on. Pyburn was the son of Jim Pyburn, one of the top bonus players of 1954 who got $40,000 from Baltimore to sign.

Pyburn was one of two sons of big leaguers drafted in the first round. The other was Terry Francona, the son of 15-year big leaguer Tito Francona, who was selected 22nd by Montreal. He had a successful major league career but became better known as a major league manager, winning two World Series with the Red Sox.

Oakland, in the final year of ownership by Charles Finley, signed just seven of 27 June draft picks. Their

26.9 percent signing rate was the worst in draft history.

And because of the players the A's couldn't sign in previous years, the January draft had more talent than usual available. Five of the first eight picks in the secondary phase were players who had been drafted but not signed by the A's.

Sworn To Secrecy

The January draft marked the first one where an element of secrecy prevailed, a trend that would continue for many years.

As free agency was driving up salaries, clubs sought ways to curb bonuses to amateur players. One was to cut off information, which clubs felt was going to agents and college coaches and helping them identify top players.

Only names of players selected in the first two rounds of the regular phase were made public immediately. Names of remaining players were released a week later. By keeping agents and the colleges in the dark, clubs were able to contact players and negotiate with them for at least a week.

Another reason for tightening the disclosure policy was to police clubs who weren't notifying players who had been drafted within 15 days of selection. Under the new system, the commissioner's office was obligated to notify all players within 24 hours who drafted them in what round, and what their rights were.

The Yankees tried a draft move of their own with Billy Cannon, the son of the 1959 Heisman Trophy winner and a high school shortstop from Baton Rouge, La.

The Yankees had no picks in the first two rounds of the June draft for signing Rudy May and Bob Watson as free agents following the 1979 season. Most clubs expected Cannon to go in the first round.

Shortly before the draft, Cannon's father notified all clubs that his son intended to go to college and indicated only a bonus of at least $250,000 would make him change his mind. That caused him to fall to the Yankees, who took Cannon in the third round.

Four other clubs filed a grievance that in effect charged Yankees owner George Steinbrenner with working with the Cannon family to scare other teams off. Commissioner Bowie Kuhn agreed and nullified the selection of Cannon. A special draft gave Cannon's rights to the Indians for the price of a third-round pick in the 1981 June draft, but he decided to attend Texas A&M and later became a first-round pick of the Dallas Cowboys. Cannon never played professional baseball.

After losing Cannon, the Yankees got little from the 1980 draft. In the first six rounds of the June regular phase, they signed only one player, Brent Gjesdal, who never made it beyond Class A.

DRAFT 80: FIRST-ROUND PICKS

No.	Club	Player,Pos.	School	Hometown	Ht.	Wt.	B-T	Age
1.	Mets	Darryl Strawberry, of	Crenshaw HS	Los Angeles	6-6	180	L-L	18
2.	Blue Jays	Garry Harris, ss	Hoover HS	San Diego	5-9	165	R-R	17
3.	Braves	Ken Dayley, lhp	Portland	The Dalles, Ore.	6-0	180	L-L	21
4.	Athletics	Mike King, lhp	Morningside Coll.	Sioux City, Iowa	6-1	180	L-L	21
5.	Padres	Jeff Pyburn, of	Georgia	Athens, Ga.	6-2	205	R-R	22
6.	Mariners	Darnell Coles, ss	Eisenhower HS	Rialto, Calif.	6-1	180	R-R	18
7.	Giants	Jay Reid, 1b	Lynwood HS	Lynwood, Calif.	6-0	202	L-L	18
8.	White Sox	Cecil Espy, of	Point Loma HS	San Diego	6-3	185	B-R	17
9.	Dodgers	Ross Jones, ss	Miami	Hialeah, Fla.	6-2	185	R-R	20
10.	Indians	Kelly Gruber, ss	Westlake HS	Austin, Texas	6-0	175	R-R	18
11.	Cubs	Don Schulze, rhp	Lake Park HS	Roselle, Ill.	6-3	205	R-R	17
12.	Twins	Jeff Reed, c	West HS	Joliet, Ill.	6-1	183	L-R	18
13.	Phillies	Lebo Powell, c	Pine Forest HS	Pensacola, Fla.	5-11	215	R-R	18
14.	Rangers	Tim Maki, rhp	Carrol HS	Humtertown, Ind.	6-2	210	R-R	18
15.	Cardinals	Don Collins, rhp	Ferguson HS	Newport News, Va.	6-2	190	R-R	17
16.	Royals	Frank Wills, rhp	Tulane	New Orleans	6-2	200	R-R	21
17.	Angels	Dennis Rasmussen, lhp	Creighton	Lakewood, Colo.	6-6	200	L-L	21
18.	Tigers	Glenn Wilson, 3b	Sam Houston State	Channelview, Texas	6-1	195	R-R	21
19.	Reds	Ron Robinson, rhp/ss	Woodlake HS	Woodlake, Calif.	6-4	200	R-R	18
20.	Pirates	Rich Renteria, ss	South Gate HS	South Gate, Calif.	5-9	180	R-R	18
21.	Braves	Jim Acker, rhp	Texas	Freer, Texas	6-2	215	R-R	21
22.	Expos	Terry Francona, of	Arizona	New Brighton, Pa.	6-1	190	L-L	21
23.	Mets	Billy Beane, of	Mount Carmel HS	Rancho Bernardo, Ca.	6-3	185	R-R	18
24.	Mets	John Gibbons, c	MacArthur HS	San Antonio	5-11	190	R-R	17
25.	Brewers	Dion James, of	McClatchy HS	Sacramento	6-1	170	L-L	17
26.	Orioles	Jeff Williams, of	Princeton HS	Cincinnati	6-1	175	L-L	17

1980

CLUB-BY-CLUB SELECTIONS

ATLANTA BRAVES

January—Regular Phase (4)

1. **Craig McMurtry, rhp, McLennan (Texas) CC**
2. David Chiono, rhp, Yuba (Calif.) CC
3. **Donald Haddock, 3b, Valencia (Fla.) CC**
4. Tommy Blackmon, rhp, Spartanburg Methodist (S.C.) JC

January—Secondary Phase (12)

1. **Scott Patterson, rhp, Long Beach (Calif.) CC**
2. Daniel McFadden, lhp, Spartanburg Methodist (S.C.) JC

June—Regular Phase (3)

1. **Ken Dayley, lhp, Portland**
1. **Jim Acker, rhp, Texas** (Pick from Expos as compensation for free agent Rowland Office)
2. **Brian Fisher, rhp, Hinkley HS, Aurora, Colo.**
3. Harry McCulla, c, Central Arizona JC
4. **Craig Jones, rhp, Army**
5. **Ralph Giansanti, 2b, South Windsor (Conn.) HS**
6. Nicholas Brandt, lhp, Oroville (Calif.) HS
7. **Keith Hagman, 1b, New Mexico**
8. **Tom Hayes, of, Texas Wesleyan**
9. Darrel Akerfelds, rhp, Columbine HS, Lakewood, Colo.
10. **Rick Siriano, of, Louisville**
11. **George Hill, of, Santa Ana Valley HS, Santa Ana, Calif.**
12. **John Lee, 3b, Florida Southern**
13. **Quinton Lloyd, of, Texas**
14. **Kevin Rigby, 2b, Duke**
15. **Paul Zuvella, 2b, Stanford**
16. **Dale Weaver, ss, Southern Arkansas**
17. **Glen Germer, rhp, Texas Lutheran**
18. **Gary Wex, rhp, Alabama**
19. **Andre Treadway, rhp, Reynolds HS, Asheville, N.C.**
20. **John Ayers, rhp, West Georgia**
21. **Russell Eagel, c/of, Georgia State**
22. **Mark Bonner, of, Oral Roberts**
23. **James Stefanski, c, Long Island**
24. Derek Edwards, rhp, Northern Kentucky

June—Secondary Phase (5)

1. **Jeff Dedmon, rhp, West Los Angeles JC**
2. Mike Hogan, rhp, Orange Coast (Calif.) JC
3. Timothy Greene, lhp, Middle Georgia JC

BALTIMORE ORIOLES

January—Regular Phase (26)

1. **George Dummas, 1b, Milford, Conn.**
2. Chris Willsher, rhp, JC of San Mateo (Calif.)
3. **Randall Duggan, c/of, Chipola (Fla.) JC**
4. **Steven Gessell, rhp, San Jose (Calif.) CC**
5. Lawrence Lewis, c, Cecil (Md.) CC
6. Ed Wojna, rhp, Indian River (Fla.) CC
7. Joseph Malott, rhp, Murray State (Okla.) JC
8. **Michael Clarkson, of, St. Petersburg (Fla.) JC**
9. David Maschino, lhp, Seminole State (Okla.) JC

January—Secondary Phase (11)

1. **Mike Young, of, Chabot (Calif.) JC**
2. **Michael Kreymborg, rhp, Bacone (Okla.) JC**
3. Chuck Tomaselli, lhp, Manatee (Fla.) JC
4. Steven Davis, of, Middle Georgia JC

June—Regular Phase (26)

1. **Jeff Williams, of, Princeton HS, Cincinnati**
2. **Al Pardo, c, Jefferson HS, Tampa**
3. **Ken Dixon, rhp, Amherst County HS, Monroe, Va.** (Pick from Dodgers as compensation for free agent Don Stanhouse)
3. **Andy Timko, ss, Kennedy HS, McDonald, Ohio**
4. **Carl Nichols, c/ss, Compton (Calif.) HS**
5. **Ron Dillard, ss, Norfolk State**
6. **Mark Brown, rhp, Massachusetts**
7. **Neal Herrick, rhp, Maryland**
8. **William Butler, ss, Cleveland State (Tenn.) CC**
9. **Matt Tyner, of, Miami**
10. Brian McDonough, rhp, Seminole State (Okla.) JC
11. Randy Asadoor, 3b, Bullard HS, Fresno, Calif.
12. Joey Pursell, rhp, Tulane
13. George Cook, 2b, Crenshaw HS, Los Angeles
14. **Rich Cratch, 2b, Bird HS, Chester, Va.**
15. **Ricky Jones, ss, West Georgia**
16. **Dave Griggs, c, Sparrows Point HS, Baltimore**
17. Robert Link, rhp, Brookwood Prep HS, Thomasville, Ga.
18. **Joseph Hughes, 3b, Florida International**
19. **Ron Cashore, of, San Joaquin Delta (Calif.) JC**
20. Ron Kelly, 1b, Chamberlain HS, Lutz, Fla.
21. **Scott Johnson, lhp, Montgomery (Md.) JC**
22. Thomas Harrell, ss, Columbus (Ga.)
23. Tom Funk, lhp, Winnetonka HS, Gladstone, Mo.
24. Michael Casha, of, Marina HS, San Leandro, Calif.
25. Alan Sadler, ss, Crossland HS, Camp Springs, Md.
26. Brent Worcester, lhp, Grant HS, Oklahoma City, Okla.

June—Secondary Phase (24)

1. **Chris Willsher, rhp, JC of San Mateo (Calif.)**
2. **Richard Marshall, rhp/of, Sharpsburg, Md.**
3. **Jeff Spencer, 2b, Lower Columbia (Wash.) JC**
4. John Leonard, rhp, Yavapai (Ariz.) JC

BOSTON RED SOX

January—Regular Phase (23)

1. Ray Krawczyk, rhp, Golden West (Calif.) JC
2. Michael Rosales, rhp, Lamar (Colo.) CC
3. **Brice Cote, rhp, Mercer County (N.J.) CC**
4. Wallace Dulling, lhp, Columbia State (Tenn.) CC
5. **David Frank, ss/2b, Solano (Calif.) CC**
6. **Nathan Banes, rhp, St. Johns River (Fla.) CC**
7. Glenn Davis, 1b/of, Middle Georgia JC

January—Secondary Phase (1)

1. **Juan Bustabad, ss, Miami-Dade North CC**
2. **Guy Burgess, lhp, Palm Beach (Fla.) JC**

June—Regular Phase (24)

1. (Pick to Mets as compensation for free agent Skip Lockwood)
2. **Mike Brown, rhp, Clemson** (Pick from Yankees as compensation for free agent Bob Watson)
2. (Pick to Expos as compensation for free agent Tony Perez)
3. **Mitch Johnson, rhp, Donegal HS, Mount Joy, Pa.**
4. **Jeff Hall, c, Rochester Institute of Technology**
5. **Ronnie Hill, lhp, Dixie HS, Bloomington, Utah**
6. **Pat Dodson, 1b, UCLA**
7. Mark Margis, lhp, Culver City (Calif.) HS
8. **Al Nipper, rhp, Northeast Missouri State**
9. **Michael Bryant, of, Lowell**
10. **Brian Zell, of, Cal Poly Pomona**
11. **Timothy Duncan, ss, Christian Brothers (Tenn.)**
12. Dave Magadan, 3b, Jesuit HS, Tampa
13. **Simon Glenn, of, Texas A&M**
14. **Mark Weinbrecht, lhp, Clairemont HS, San Diego**
15. **Tyrone Herman, rhp, Mankato State (Minn.)**
16. **Oil Can Boyd, rhp, Jackson State**
17. Marcus Handley, rhp, Larue County HS, Hodgenville, Ky.
18. **Robert Sandling, lhp, Crete-Monee HS, Park Forest, Ill.**
19. **Al Bowlin, lhp, Grace Davis HS, Modesto, Calif.**
20. **Tom Bolton, lhp, Antioch HS, Brentwood, Tenn.**
21. **Parker Wilson, 3b, Livingston (Ala.)**
22. **George Mecerod, rhp, Adelphi (N.Y.)**
23. Bobby Falls, 2b, West Mecklenburg HS, Charlotte, N.C.

24. **Mike Ciampa, of, Westfield State**
25. **Jeff Hunter, 3b, Nebraska**
26. William Lowry, rhp, Santa Ynez HS, Goleta, Calif.
27. **George Greco, lhp, Iona**

June—Secondary Phase (22)

1. Clem Freeman, lhp, Manatee (Fla.) JC
2. **Steve Garrett, rhp, Chabot (Calif.) JC**

CALIFORNIA ANGELS

January—Regular Phase (19)

1. **Chris Ray, rhp, San Joaquin Delta (Calif.) JC**
2. Don Fenton, rhp, Lower Columbia (Wash.) JC
3. Kevin Romine, ss/of, Orange Coast (Calif.) JC
4. Timothy Arnold, lhp, Los Angeles Valley JC
5. Ryan Collier, of, Los Angeles CC
6. Steven Ray, lhp, Southwestern (Calif.) JC
7. Richard Diffine, 1b, Cerritos (Calif.) JC
8. David Wilder, of/ss, Contra Costa (Calif.) JC
9. Corey Zawadski, of, Broward (Fla.) CC
10. Greg Dees, c, Cosumnes River (Calif.) JC
11. James Tunell, rhp, Southwestern (Calif.) JC
12. Joseph Mehallow, lhp, Belleville Area (Ill.) JC
13. Billy Donathan, rhp, Edison (Fla.) CC
14. Mario Alos, 2b/3b, Miami-Dade North CC

January—Secondary Phase (21)

1. Thomas McLaughlin, rhp, Los Angeles CC
2. George Page, of, Los Angeles Valley JC

June—Regular Phase (20)

1. **Dennis Rasmussen, lhp, Creighton** (Pick from Astros as compensation for free agent Nolan Ryan)
1. (Pick to Pirates as compensation for free agent Bruce Kison)
2. (Pick to Royals as compensation for free agent Fred Patek)
3. **Jack McMahon, rhp, Cal State Dominguez Hills**
4. **Matt Gundelfinger, of/1b, Kansas**
5. Frank Marrero, rhp, Columbus HS, Miami
6. **Harry Francis, 3b, Texas A&M**
7. **Mike Brown, of, San Jose State**
8. **Duffy Ryan, c, New Mexico**
9. **Ron Sylvia, rhp, Cal State Los Angeles**
10. David Mote, inf, El Segundo (Calif.) HS
11. **Chris Clark, of, Cal Poly Pomona**
12. **John McGaffey, of/c, Point Loma Nazarene (Calif.)**
13. **Joe Brock, 1b, William Paterson (N.J.)**
14. **Bob Bastian, rhp, Miami**
15. **Gregory Hammond, rhp, Phoenix, Ariz.**
16. **Thomas Roen, lhp, Northern Illinois**
17. **Aldo Bagiotti, c, Fort Lauderdale (Fla.)**
18. **Goldie Wright, of, Rio Mesa HS, Camarillo, Calif.**
19. Jeff Salazar, rhp, Sylmar (Calif.) HS
20. Nelson Hayman, of, Belhaven (Miss.)
21. **Thomas Schneider, rhp, Seton Hall**
22. **Dennis Valdes, of, Florida Southern**
23. Orestes Destrade, 1b, Columbus HS, Miami
24. Ricky Nelson, of, Arizona State
25. **Ronald Hunt, 1b, UC Riverside**
26. **Drew Steinbach, lhp, Illinois Tech**
27. **James Christopher, of, Chapman (Calif.)**
28. Douglas Laufer, rhp, Texas
29. Steve Marlin, rhp, Miami HS, Claytool, Ariz.
30. **Dave Burroughs, of/lhp, Phoenix JC**

June—Secondary Phase (10)

1. **Bill Mooneyham, rhp, Merced (Calif.) JC**

CHICAGO CUBS

January—Regular Phase (12)

1. Mike Hogan, rhp, Orange Coast (Calif.) JC
2. **Gary Monroe, of, Seward County (Kan.) CC**
3. **Scott Peterson, c, Margate, Fla.**
4. Ralph Elpin, rhp, CC of Morris (N.J.)
5. Mike Lambert, rhp, Citrus (Calif.) JC
6. Brian Peck, rhp, JC of Southern Idaho
7. **Kevin Schoendienst, of, St. Louis CC-Meramec**
8. **Robert Gilles, c, Jefferson (Mo.) JC**
9. Greg Braunwalder, 3b, Citrus (Calif.) JC
10. **Gary Young, rhp, Ferry, N.Y.**
11. Jim Eppard, 1b, Citrus (Calif.) JC

January—Secondary Phase (24)

1. Tom Henke, rhp, East Central (Mo.) JC
2. **Joseph Carter, rhp, San Diego Mesa JC**

June—Regular Phase (11)

1. **Don Schulze, rhp, Lake Park HS, Roselle, Ill.**
2. **Dan Cataline, of, Archbishop Ryan HS, Philadelphia**
3. **David Pagel, ss, Central Michigan**
4. **Bruce Seid, ss, Oak Park (Mich.) HS**
5. **James Walsh, of, Lewis (Ill.)**
6. **Jeff Remo, c, Mahwah (N.J.) HS**
7. **Fritzie Connally, 3b, Baylor**
8. Tom DiCeglio, ss, Lawrence HS, Cedarhurst, N.Y.
9. **Craig Lefferts, lhp, Arizona**
10. **Brian Roerden, lhp, Adelphi (N.Y.)**
11. **Troy Chestnut, rhp, Marion (S.C.) HS**
12. Dwayne Ellis, rhp, Pasadena (Calif.) CC
13. Mike Knox, rhp, Wooster (Ohio)
14. **Rich Buonantony, rhp, Western HS, Las Vegas**
15. Michael Winbush, rhp, Goldsboro (N.C.) HS
16. **Gary Wayne, c, Marion (La.) HS**
17. **Mike Shulleeta, rhp, Yucaipa (Calif.) HS**
18. Gerald McDermott, c, Fontana (Calif.) HS
19. **Jeff Burton, of, Brigham Young**
20. David Flattery, rhp, Iowa State
21. **Ken Arnerich, ss, Alameda (Calif.) HS**
22. Todd Schulte, lhp, Winfield HS, Old Monroe, Mo.
23. **Rusty Piggott, 3b/ss, Rollins (Fla.)**
24. Thomas Corcoran, rhp, Miami-Dade North CC
25. Ken Scott, rhp, Fontana (Calif.) HS
26. Keith Turnbull, rhp, Winfield (Mo.) HS
27. Rob Amble, of, Bakersfield (Calif.) JC
28. Dick Seidel, rhp, Mira Costa (Calif.) JC
29. **Dwayne Tenney, ss, West Virginia Wesleyan**
30. **Jon MacMillan, of/1b, Azusa Pacific (Calif.)**
31. Gregg Goodman, rhp, Mississippi College
32. **Kenneth Pryce, rhp, Azusa Pacific (Calif.)**
33. Bruce Tanner, rhp, Neshannock HS, New Castle, Pa.

June—Secondary Phase (13)

1. **Darryl Banks, rhp, JC of Southern Idaho**
2. **Joe Housey, rhp, New Orleans**
3. Rick Thurman, rhp, Los Angeles Pierce JC

CHICAGO WHITE SOX

January—Regular Phase (7)

1. **Bill Luzinski, of, Miami-Dade North CC**
2. Dave Malpeso, c, Miami-Dade North CC
3. **Jim Siwy, rhp, Rhode Island**
4. Allen Black, rhp, West Los Angeles JC
5. Billy Wiesler, of, Miami-Dade North CC
6. Mitchell Roe, rhp, Miami-Dade North CC
7. Dave Oliva, of, Los Angeles Valley JC
8. Rick Anderson, ss, Taft (Calif.) JC
9. Lamon Lawrence, lhp, JC of the Sequoias (Calif.)

January—Secondary Phase (3)

1. **Tim Hulett, 2b, Miami-Dade North CC**
2. Derek Tatsuno, lhp, Hawaii

June—Regular Phase (8)

1. **Cecil Espy, of, Point Loma HS, San Diego**
2. **Wes Kent, 1b, Sahuaro HS, Tucson, Ariz.**
2. Turner Gill, ss, Arlington Heights HS, Fort Worth (Pick from Indians as compensation for free agent Jorge Orta)
3. **Allan Heath, lhp, Waukegan (Ill.) West HS** (Pick from Giants as compensation for free agent Milt May)
3. **Ronnie Perry, ss, Holy Cross**
4. **Mark Wiesler, 2b, Chaminade HS, Miramar, Fla.**
5. **Len Bradley, rhp, Clemson**

6. **David Nix, ss, DeSoto (Texas) HS**
7. **Mike Morse, ss, South Plantation (Fla.) HS**
8. Neil Reilly, c, Lake Forest HS, Lake Bluff, Ill.
9. **Wayne Schuckert, lhp, Shaler HS, Pittsburgh**
10. Larry McLane, lhp, Chapman (Calif.)
11. **Mark Seeger, of, Northern Arizona**
12. **Roy Schumacher, rhp, Elgin (Ill.) CC**
13. **Keith Flenior, of, El Camino Real HS, Los Angeles**
14. **Gary Robinette, 3b, East Tennessee State**
15. **Tom Mullen, rhp, Iowa**
16. **Dave Wall, of, Iowa Western CC**
17. Calvin Schiraldi, rhp, Westlake HS, Austin, Texas
18. **Terry McAnnawly, rhp, Gardendale (Ala.) HS**
19. Kevin House, of, Southern Illinois
20. Mark Ridgik, rhp, Cherry Hill (N.J.) East HS

June—Secondary Phase (26)

1. **Jeff Barnard, rhp, Iowa Western CC**

CINCINNATI REDS

January—Regular Phase (20)

1. **Mark Bowden, lhp, San Jacinto (Texas) JC**
2. **Michael Ferguson, rhp, Mount San Antonio (Calif.) JC**
3. Todd Wheeler, lhp, Yakima Valley (Wash.) JC
4. **Andrew Barbee, of, JC of Southern Idaho**
5. Dan Boever, ss, Westark (Ark.) CC
6. Harold Hatcher, c, Mesa (Ariz.) CC
7. **Leroy Wenzel, 1b, West Los Angeles JC**
8. Jeffrey Adams, c, Saddleback (Calif.) CC
9. Broc Higgins, rhp, San Jacinto (Texas) JC
10. **Michael McCardell, c, Cecil (Md.) CC**

January—Secondary Phase (22)

1. Scott Meier, c, San Joaquin Delta (Calif.) JC
2. **Daniel Klosicki, rhp, Spokane Falls (Wash.) CC**

June—Regular Phase (19)

1. **Ron Robinson, rhp/ss, Woodlake (Calif.) HS**
2. **Jim Pettibone, rhp, Saguaro HS, Scottsdale, Ariz.** (Pick from Astros as compensation for free agent Joe Morgan)
2. **Ken Jones, rhp, Arizona State**
2. **Dave Miley, ss/3b, Chamberlain HS, Tampa** (Pick from Expos as compensation for free agent Fred Norman)
3. **Danny Tartabull, 2b, Carol City (Fla.) HS**
4. **Ken Scarpace, of, Western Michigan**
5. **Steve Leppert, c, Jacksonville State**
6. **Miguel Salgueiro, rhp, South Miami (Fla.) HS**
7. **Tom Wesley, 1b, Stillman (Ala.)**
8. **Eric Davis, ss, Fremont HS, Los Angeles**
9. **Tim Hume, ss/2b, Gibbs HS, St. Petersburg, Fla.**
10. Larry Simcox, ss, Mississippi
11. **Thomas Marino, c, McArthur HS, Pembroke Pines, Fla.**
12. **Scott Terry, of, Southwestern (Texas)**
13. **Broderick Walker, of, Bellaire HS, Houston**
14. **Dave Lochner, lhp/1b, Wright State**
15. Stan Edmonds, of, Southern California
16. **Anthony Threatt, rhp, Murray State**
17. **Bill Metil, 3b, Slippery Rock (Pa.)**
18. **Charles Smith, of, Lakewood HS, St. Petersburg, Fla.**
19. **Doug Barba, rhp, University HS, San Diego**
20. **Anthony Delancey, ss, Astronaut HS, Mims, Fla.**
21. **Edward White, 2b, Canal Winchester HS, Winchester, Ohio**
22. **Michael Murray, ss, Western Kentucky**
23. Coe Brier, c, Salisbury (N.C.) HS
24. **Scot Ender, rhp, Winona State (Minn.)**
25. Roger Lewis, rhp, Stevens HS, Rapid City, S.D.
26. Calvin James, 1b/of, American HS, Carol City, Fla.
27. **David Hall, of/3b, Gonzaga**
28. **Thomas Layton, rhp, Bacone (Okla.) JC**
29. **Tim Stout, of, Centralia (Wash.) JC**
30. **Mike Foote, ss, New Mexico**
31. **Sean Severns, c, Eastern Washington**
32. **Curt Heidenreich, rhp, Illinois State**
33. Willie Wilson, rhp, Wayne County HS, Jesup, Ga.
34. David Carter, rhp, Edgewater HS, Orlando, Fla.

June—Secondary Phase (3)

1. **Kevin Maroney, of, Miami Sinclair (Ohio) CC**
2. Edwin Schneider, lhp, Florida State
3. Randy O'Neal, rhp, Palm Beach (Fla.) JC
4. **Jeffrey Adams, c, Saddleback (Calif.) CC**
5. Scott Meier, c, San Joaquin Delta (Calif.) JC

CLEVELAND INDIANS

January—Regular Phase (9)

1. **Marlin Methven, ss, Edmonds (Wash.) CC**
2. **Alan Willis, rhp, Georgia Southern**
3. Tim Cannon, of, Chipola (Fla.) JC
4. **Angelo Gilbert, lhp, Laney (Calif.) JC**
5. **Michael Dixon, lhp, Sacramento CC**
6. **Charles Tillett, lhp/of, Brevard (Fla.) CC**
7. Steve Giovacchini, ss, Modesto (Calif.) JC
8. **Darold Ellison, 3b, Mount Hood (Ore.) CC**
9. Tom Gil, of, Miami-Dade South CC
10. **Florentino Gonzales, ss, Big Bend (Wash.) CC**
11. Tracey Player, lhp, Florida CC
12. **Larry Swann, 1b/lhp, Chipola (Fla.) JC**
13. **Dale Nichols, rhp, Central Florida CC**
14. Phillip Jackson, of, San Joaquin Delta (Calif.) JC
15. **Michael Schwarber, rhp, Cleveland State (Tenn.) CC**
16. Scott Brusse, rhp, Mount Hood (Ore.) CC
17. Michael Wilder, 2b, Contra Costa (Calif.) JC
18. Gordon Gradwohl, lhp, Edmonds (Wash.) CC

January—Secondary Phase (26)

1. **Mark Roberts, lhp, DeKalb (Ga.) JC**
2. **Charles Hollowell, lhp, Hillsborough (Fla.) CC**
3. Mitch Seoane, 2b, Hillsborough (Fla.) CC
4. **Darren Swanson, rhp, Green River (Wash.) CC**

June—Regular Phase (10)

1. **Kelly Gruber, ss, Westlake HS, Austin, Texas**
2. (Pick to White Sox as compensation for free agent Jorge Orta)
3. **Greg Pope, rhp, Sacramento CC** (Pick from Padres as compensation for free agent Rick Wise)
3. **Bart Mackie, c, Meadowdale HS, Lynwood, Wash.**
4. Doug Drabek, rhp, St. Joseph's HS, Victoria, Texas
5. **Eric Jones, of, Burbank HS, Sacramento**
6. **Jeff Moronko, 3b, Texas Wesleyan**
7. Norman Morton, lhp, McArthur HS, Hollywood, Fla.
8. **Rich Thompson, rhp, Amherst (Mass.)**
9. **Ed Tanner, ss, Brookland-Cayce HS, West Columbia, S.C.**
10. **Lawrence Dotson, of, UC Irvine**
11. Limbric Windham, of, Vigor HS, Prichard, Ala.
12. Don Long, ss, Meadowdale HS, Edmonds, Wash.
13. **Mike Jeffcoat, lhp, Louisiana Tech**
14. **Michael Kolodney, rhp, Brooklyn**
15. **Richard Elkin, c, Tacoma (Wash.) CC**
16. Terry Steinbach, 3b, New Ulm (Minn.) HS
17. **Patrick Grady, of, Upsala (N.J.)**
18. **Gary Holden, of, Aragon HS, Burlingame, Calif.**
19. **William Holland, rhp, Ibany (Calif.) HS**
20. Anthony Freeman, of, Albany HS, Berkeley, Calif.
21. Robert Gilchrist, rhp, Sandusky (Ohio) HS
22. **Richard Gebin, lhp, Monterey Peninsula (Calif.) JC**
23. **Steven Jenter, rhp, Southwestern Louisiana**
24. **Matt Minium, of, Miami**
25. **Arthur Sullivan, of, Colby (Maine)**
26. **Thomas Stibora, lhp, Cleveland State**
27. **Dan McInerny, of, California**
28. John Churlin, rhp, Meadowdale HS, Lynwood, Wash.
29. **Jack Fimple, ss/3b, Humboldt State (Calif.)**
30. **James Oros, 3b, St. Xavier**
31. **Michael Crowley, lhp, St. Mary's HS, Lynn, Mass.**
32. Timothy Kelly, c, Wooster (Ohio)
33. **Andy Alvis, c/1b, Washington State**
34. **Richard Saavedra, rhp, Santa Clara (Calif.) HS**
35. **Kevin Malone, 2b, Louisville**
36. **Ricky Lintz, rhp, San Francisco State**
37. **Mark Wright, ss, Newberry (Fla.) HS**
38. Rich Rice, rhp, Lake Worth (Fla.) HS

39. Harvey Heise, 3b, Brookland-Cayce HS, West Columbia, S.C.
40. Thomas Smercynski, rhp, St. John's Prep, Peabody, Mass.
41. William Schoenig, 2b, Montclair State (N.J.)
42. Martin Writt, c, Livingston (N.J.) HS
43. **Luis Duarte, c/1b, Miami**
44. **Shanie Dugas, ss, McNeese State**

June—Secondary Phase (8)

1. **Dave Gallagher, of, Mercer County (N.J.) CC**
2. **Gary Whisler, ss, Canada (Calif.) JC**
3. Steve Ellsworth, rhp, Fresno (Calif.) CC
4. Glenn Edwards, of, Mercer County (N.J.) CC
5. **Tommy Blackmon, rhp, Spartanburg Methodist (S.C.) JC**
6. **Winston Ficklin, 2b, Richmond, Calif.**
7. Nattie George, of, San Jose (Calif.) CC
8. **Ralph Elpin, rhp, CC of Morris (N.J.)**
9. Mike Wilder, 2b, Contra Costa (Calif.) JC

Special Draft

1. Billy Cannon, ss, Broadmoor HS, Baton Rouge, La.

DETROIT TIGERS

January—Regular Phase (17)

1. **Mike Laga, 1b, Bergen (N.J.) CC**
2. Paul Huyck, lhp, Yavapai (Ariz.) JC
3. **Kevin Young, of, Valencia (Fla.) CC**
4. **Guy Hubert, ss, Delgado (La.) JC**
5. Randy Hunt, c, Chattahoochee Valley (Ala.) CC
6. **John Engen, lhp, Minnesota-Duluth**
7. **James Doleski, rhp, Northern Virginia CC**
8. Kenneth Merritt, c, Yavapai (Ariz.) JC

January—Secondary Phase (17)

1. **John Moller, lhp, Old Bridge, N.J.**
2. **Nick O'Connor, rhp, Cumberlands (Ky.) JC**

June—Regular Phase (18)

1. **Glenn Wilson, 3b, Sam Houston State**
2. Charles Reese, ss, Pequannock HS, Pompton Plains, N.J.
3. **Robert Casanovas, of, Mahwah (N.J.) HS**
4. Bob Sebra, rhp, Gloucester Catholic HS, Medford Lakes, N.J.
5. **Lawrence Gilmore, 1b, West Covina (Calif.) HS**
6. **Mark Smith, of, Fairfield (Conn.) HS**
7. **Stan Younger, of, Brigham Young**
8. **Walter Poole, c, Pacific**
9. **Homer Moncrief, rhp, Jackson State**
10. **Chuck Hensley, lhp, California**
11. **Dwight Lowry, c, North Carolina**
12. **Carl Burns, 1b, Chadsey HS, Detroit**
13. **Kevin Perrett, c, Madison HS, San Diego**
14. **Michael Jones, ss, Rome (N.Y.) Free Academy**
15. **Rondal Rollin, of, Cal State Northridge**
16. **Howard Carter, of, Tuskegee (Ala.)**
17. **Thomas Merkle, of, Saginaw Valley State (Mich.)**
18. Jeff Morrison, lhp, Miami
19. **Norman Michaud, lhp, Northeastern**
20. **David Simononis, of, Penn State**
21. **James Clark, rhp, St. Peter's (N.J.)**
22. **Gary Nutter, rhp, Eckerd (Fla.)**
23. **Willie Ward, 1b, Berringer HS, Newark, N.J.**
24. **William Nash, of, Chadsey HS, Detroit**
25. Mark Friedly, rhp, Glenn HS, Norwalk, Calif.
26. David Hage, ss, Amsterdam (N.Y.) HS
27. **Robert Vavrock, rhp, Cal Poly San Luis Obispo**
28. Walter Faber, lhp, Grand Rapids (Mich.) JC
29. **Robert Ruffus, rhp, Monmouth**
30. **Ron Mathis, rhp, Missouri**
31. **Mark Dacko, rhp, James Madison**
32. Dave Kopf, rhp, Kimball HS, Royal Oak, Mich.
33. Mike Tanzi, lhp, Florida Southern
34. Mark Recker, rhp, Oakland (Mich.) CC
35. **Mark Fellows, rhp, Central Michigan**
36. **George Foussianes, ss, Michigan**

June—Secondary Phase (14)

1. Joseph McCarthy, of, South Carolina
2. Mitch Seoane, 2b, Hillsborough (Fla.) CC

HOUSTON ASTROS

January—Regular Phase (18)

1. Jeff Bair, rhp, CC of Morris (N.J.)
2. **Chris Buckley, of, CC of Morris (N.J.)**
3. Pat Shortt, lhp, Eastern Arizona JC
4. Kelly Moore, of, San Diego Mesa JC
5. Donnie Hill, ss, Orange Coast (Calif.) JC

January—Secondary Phase (14)

1. Kevin Olson, rhp, Golden West (Calif.) JC
2. Billy Hatcher, of/rhp, Yavapai (Ariz.) JC

June—Regular Phase (17)

1. (Pick to Angels as compensation for free agent Nolan Ryan)
2. (Pick to Reds as compensation for free agent Joe Morgan)
3. **Jeff Calhoun, lhp, Mississippi**
4. **Ken Elsee, rhp, Nevada-Las Vegas**
5. **Tom Hawk, rhp, Arizona State**
6. **Wes Clements, of/1b, Arizona**
7. **Mike Sheppard, ss/3b, Seton Hall**
8. Tony Arias, rhp, Hialeah (Fla.) HS
9. **Scott Gardner, rhp, Oklahoma**
10. James Miley, c, William Tennant HS, Warminster, Pa.
11. **David Sullivan, c, Oklahoma State**
12. **Tim Meckes, rhp, St. Francis (Ill.)**
13. **Gary D'Onofrio, ss, Oral Roberts**
14. **Neil Simons, of, Clemson**
15. **Jeff Morris, lhp, Arizona**
16. **John Kolacki, lhp, Middletown South HS, Lincroft, N.J.**
17. Jose Rodiles, rhp, Lamar HS, Houston
18. **Roderick Shepard, c, Princeton**
19. Larry Kiesling, ss, Centenary
20. **Billy Weems, of, Clemson**
21. **Joey Squilla, 1b, John Brown (Ark.)**
22. **Ken Babcock, lhp, Centenary**
23. **Dennis Cleveland, 3b, Jacksonville State**
24. **Gary Malinowski, rhp, Rutgers**
25. **Michael Cerefin, rhp, Burnt Hills (N.Y.) HS**

June—Secondary Phase (1)

1. **Jeff Heathcock, rhp, Oral Roberts**

KANSAS CITY ROYALS

January—Regular Phase (15)

1. Tyson Hubbard, rhp, Spartanburg Methodist (S.C.) JC
2. Tim Crews, rhp, Valencia (Fla.) CC
3. **Willie Neal, of, Chicago, Ill.**
4. Kevin Wiggins, of, San Diego Mesa JC
5. **Doug Potestio, rhp, Chabot (Calif.) JC**
6. Kevin Kilstofte, rhp, Des Moines Area (Iowa) CC
7. **James Gleissner, c, Mount San Jacinto (Calif.) JC**
8. Richard Turner, c, Santa Ana (Calif.) JC

January—Secondary Phase (5)

1. **Steve Raine, rhp, Hartnell (Calif.) CC**
2. Richard Scott, inf, Canada (Calif.) JC
3. Mark Hoffman, lhp, Chabot (Calif.) JC

June—Regular Phase (16)

1. **Frank Wills, rhp, Tulane**
2. **Roger Hansen, 3b, Rio Mesa HS, Camarillo, Calif.**
2. **Mike Olson, rhp, St. Louis Park (Minn.) HS** (Pick from Angels as compensation for free agent Fred Patek)
3. **Doug Cook, rhp, Forest Hills HS, West Palm Beach, Fla.**
4. **Lester Strode, lhp, Kentucky State**
5. **Chino Cadahia, c, Hialeah (Fla.) HS**
6. **Rondin Johnson, 2b, Washington**
7. **Don Slaught, c, UCLA**
8. **Cliff Pastornicky, ss, Brigham Young**
9. **Bert Johnson, lhp, Cypress Lake HS, Fort Myers, Fla.**
10. **Ken Swank, lhp, Watsonville (Calif.) HS**
11. **Francis Cutty, rhp, Pepperdine**
12. **Butch Davis, of, East Carolina**

13. **Anthony Notaroberto, of, Trenton State (N.J.)**
14. **Aubrey Johnson, c, Castlemont HS, Oakland, Calif.**
15. **Bob Hegman, ss, St. Cloud State (Minn.)**
16. **Theo Shaw, ss, Proviso East HS, Maywood, Ill.**
17. **Tom Romano, of, Coastal Carolina**
18. Vince Beringhele, ss, Loyola HS, Los Angeles
19. **David Wong, rhp, Willamette (Ore.)**
20. Mitch Hawley, rhp, California
21. John Cox, lhp, Hueneme HS, Oxnard, Calif.
22. Anthony Bartolomucci, lhp, Oak Forest (Ill.) HS
23. **Olice King, lhp/1b, Bradley**
24. Al Romero, c, San Diego State
25. Dan Sehlhorst, c, Oak Hills HS, Cincinnati
26. Jeff Doerr, rhp, Aragon HS, San Mateo, Calif.
27. **Billy Best, 2b, East Carolina**
28. Rich Poznanski, c/of, Eisenhower HS, Yakima, Wash.

June—Secondary Phase (4)

1. **Keith Creel, rhp, Texas**
2. **Bob Ferris, c/1b/3b, Arizona State**
3. **Russ Stephans, c, Arizona State**
4. David Wilder, of/ss, Contra Costa (Calif.) JC
5. Andrew Pavlovic, rhp, Yavapai (Ariz.) JC
6. **Harold Hatcher, c, Mesa (Ariz.) CC**
7. David Bailor, of, Yavapai (Ariz.) JC

LOS ANGELES DODGERS

January—Regular Phase (10)

1. **David Lesch, rhp, Central Arizona JC**
2. **R.J. Reynolds, of, Sacramento CC**
3. Larry See, 3b, Cerritos (Calif.) JC
4. Robbie Allen, ss, Clemson
5. **Ruell Martin, ss, Potomac State (W.Va.) JC**
6. Ralph Bryant, of, Abraham Baldwin Agricultural (Ga.) JC
7. Mark Wenzel, rhp, Fresno CC
8. Damon Hunt, of, Sacramento CC
9. Paul Hagan, of, South Georgia JC
10. David Bailor, of, Yavapai (Ariz.) JC
11. **Brett Wise, rhp, Seminole (Fla.) CC**
12. Richard Lucero, rhp, Phoenix JC
13. Greg Hudson, rhp, DeKalb South (Ga.) CC

January—Secondary Phase (2)

1. **Ricky Wright, lhp, Texas**
2. Jack Leonard, 3b, Louisburg (N.C.) JC
3. Harry Kazanjian, c/of, CC of San Francisco

June—Regular Phase (9)

1. **Ross Jones, ss, Miami**
2. (Pick to Twins as compensation for free agent Dave Goltz)
3. (Pick to Orioles as compensation for free agent Don Stanhouse)
4. (Pick to Padres as compensation for free agent Jay Johnstone)
5. Pete Beall, ss, Mater Dei HS, Santa Ana, Calif.
6. **Paul Bard, c, Tufts (Mass.)**
7. **Todd Gauntlett, c, UCLA**
8. Kevin Sliwinski, of, Santiago HS, Garden Grove, Calif.
9. **Steve Marsden, rhp, Wisconsin**
10. **Ricky Thomas, of, La Verne (Calif.)**
11. **Curt Reade, rhp, Fresno State**
12. **Anthony Lachowetz, of, Springfield (Mass.)**
13. **Greg Smith, 1b, Southern**
14. **Thomas Robinson, 2b, Widener (Pa.)**
15. **Charles Jones, rhp, New Hampshire**
16. **Frank Dente, rhp, Palm Beach (Fla.) JC**
17. **Richard Lloyd, rhp, East Valley HS, Otis Orchards, Wash.**
18. **Pasquale Raimondo, 2b, SUNY Buffalo**
19. **Tom Klawitter, lhp, Wisconsin**
20. **Audie Cole, of, Eastern Michigan**
21. **Jon Debus, of, St. Francis (Ill.)**
22. **Francis McQuade, rhp, Elmhurst (Ill.)**
23. **Phillip Webber, of, San Bernardino Valley (Calif.) JC**
24. Jerry Bendorf, ss, Gonzaga
25. **Bobby Kenyon, rhp, Clemson**
26. Jim Pacanowski, c, Downers Grove HS, Woodbridge, Ill.
27. Cori Ryan, rhp, Colorado State
28. Todd Zacher, 2b, Arkansas
29. Gregory Hull, of, Hiram Johnson HS, Sacramento
30. Tom Woleslagel, ss, Ross HS, Fremont, Ohio
31. **Michael Strawberry, of, Los Angeles Southwest CC**
32. Hank DeMello, c, Roseville (Calif.) HS

June—Secondary Phase (9)

1. **Robbie Allen, ss, Clemson**
2. **Richard Felt, lhp, DeKalb South (Ga.) CC**
3. Michael Carringer, rhp, Bacone (Okla.) JC

MILWAUKEE BREWERS

January—Regular Phase (25)

1. **Michael Orlich, rhp, Central Arizona JC**
2. **Ronald Kollman, rhp, JC of Southern Idaho**
3. **Terry Ragan, of, Chipola (Fla.) JC**
4. Alan Haugen, ss/2b, Centralia (Wash.) JC
5. Ben Donisi, 3b, Broward (Fla.) CC
6. Frank Booker, 2b, Contra Costa (Calif.) JC
7. **Curt Watanabe, 3b, Hawaii**
8. Garrett Nago, c, Pima (Ariz.) CC
9. Ralph Kennedy, rhp, Miami-Dade North CC
10. **David Jensen, rhp, Logan, Utah**
11. Michael Burton, rhp, Enterprise State (Ala.) JC
12. Greg Cottrell, c, Los Angeles Valley JC
13. Rory Brown, lhp, Broward (Fla.) CC
14. Phil Smith, ss, Laney (Calif.) JC
15. John Whitt, of, Los Angeles Harbor JC
16. Kevin Lindsley, rhp, Linn-Benton (Ore.) CC
17. William Palmer, 3b, Laney (Calif.) JC
18. Mike Evans, lhp, Merced (Calif.) JC
19. **Ronnie Jones, of, Central Arizona JC**
20. **Walt Steele, 3b, Pepperdine**
21. Robert Zima, rhp, Central Arizona JC
22. **Steven Mitchell, of, Clifton Park, N.Y.**
23. Joseph Mutt, rhp, Orange Coast (Calif.) JC
24. Gerrett Smith, of, Pasadena (Calif.) CC
25. Michael Mangold, c, Umpqua (Ore.) CC

January—Secondary Phase (19)

1. Herm Winningham, of, DeKalb South (Ga.) CC
2. **Craig Herberholz, rhp, Central Arizona JC**
3. Randy O'Neal, rhp, Palm Beach (Fla.) JC
4. James Jones, rhp, Corte Madera, Calif.
5. Randy Poitevint, 3b, Central Arizona JC
6. Andrew Speck, rhp, Aloha, Ore.

June—Regular Phase (25)

1. **Dion James, of, McClatchy HS, Sacramento**
2. **Bob Schroeck, lhp, Southern Illinois**
3. **Maury Ornest, 3b, UC Santa Barbara**
4. Matt Williams, rhp, Rice (Pick from Giants as compensation for free agent Jim Wohlford)
4. **Butch Kirby, ss/2b, Arundel HS, Severn, Md.**
5. **Gerard Miller, 1b/of, Southern Illinois**
6. **Randy Ready, 2b, Mesa (Colo.)**
7. **Ted Pallas, rhp, Pepperdine**
8. Billy Irions, lhp, Seminole State (Okla.) JC
9. Steve Engel, lhp, Reading HS, Cincinnati
10. Todd Soares, ss, Kingsburg (Calif.) HS
11. Dan Davidsmeier, ss, Southern California
12. Russ Kibler, rhp, Sandalwood HS, Jacksonville, Fla.
13. **Sam Favata, 2b, Cal State Fullerton**
14. **Johnson Wood, 1b/rhp, Oxnard (Calif.) JC**
15. **Jeff Gilbert, lhp, Pasadena, Md.**
16. Audrey Robinson, of, Canada (Calif.) JC
17. **Ricki Bass, of, Hawaii**
18. Gary Adams, lhp, Grass Lake (Mich.) HS
19. Bill Peltola, rhp, Southern California
20. Vic Woods, ss, Centennial HS, Compton, Calif.
21. David Conte, ss, Lakewood HS, Long Beach
22. Richard Wiesner, of, Kennedy HS, Manchester, Mo.
23. Duane Widner, rhp, Hueneme HS, Port Hueneme, Calif.
24. Dean Naylor, rhp, Miami-Dade South CC

25. Terry Coates, 3b, Southern Wayne HS, Mount Olive, N.C.

June—Secondary Phase (6)

1. **Mark Effrig, rhp, Lower Columbia (Wash.) JC**
2. Garrett Nago, c, Pima (Ariz.) CC
3. **Robert Elliott, rhp, Georgia Southern**

MINNESOTA TWINS

January—Regular Phase (11)

1. Jeff Barnard, rhp/1b, Iowa Western CC
2. Timothy Greene, lhp, Middle Georgia JC
3. **Keith Silva, lhp, Lemoore, Calif.**
4. **Harold Jackson, rhp, Solano (Calif.) CC**
5. Jeffrey Spencer, inf, Lower Columbia (Wash.) JC
6. **Al Arrieta, rhp, Pepperdine**
7. Steve Ellsworth, rhp, Fresno CC
8. Ricardo Moreyra, c, Palm Beach (Fla.) JC
9. Ernie Moya, rhp, Hillsborough (Fla.) CC
10. Luis Roche, c, Los Angeles CC
11. Mike Kasprzak, rhp, Manatee (Fla.) JC
12. **David Wilson, rhp, Montreat-Anderson (N.C.) JC**
13. Mike Vanderburg, p/of, Orange Coast (Calif.) JC
14. Gary Klein, rhp, Pasadena (Calif.) CC

January—Secondary Phase (9)

1. Nattie George, of, San Jose CC
2. John Leonard, rhp, Yavapai (Ariz.) JC
3. Daniel Casey, lhp, Edison, N.J.
4. **Brian Butera, of, Tulane**

June—Regular Phase (12)

1. **Jeff Reed, c, Joliet (Ill.) West HS**
2. **Jim Weaver, of, Florida State** (Pick from Dodgers as compensation for free agent Dave Goltz)
2. **Tim Teufel, 2b, Clemson**
3. **Scotti Madison, c, Vanderbilt**
4. **Rod Booker, ss, California**
5. Mike Fuentes, of, Florida State
6. **Lee Belanger, lhp, La Verne (Calif.)**
7. **Kirby Krueger, rhp, New Orleans**
8. **Andre David, of, Cal State Fullerton**
9. **Tony Guerrero, lhp, Cleveland HS, Northridge, Calif.**
10. **Ken Foster, 1b, Cal Poly Pomona**
11. **Kevin Williams, of, Hawaii**
12. Mitch Ashmore, c, Centenary
13. **Lyle Brackenridge, of, California**
14. Dan Clark, ss, Glenn HS, La Mirada, Calif.
15. **Tony Pilla, 2b, Long Island**
16. **Jim Eisenreich, of, St. Cloud State (Minn.)**
17. **Jeffrey Martin, c, Louisa (Va.) County HS**
18. **Mike Cole, 2b, San Diego CC**
19. **Domingo Nunez, ss, Wagner**
20. **Michael Tirella, lhp, Rhode Island**
21. Bryan Price, lhp, Tamalpais HS, Mill Valley, Calif.
22. Reggie Wyatt, lhp, Santa Monica (Calif.) JC
23. Mark Bauer, rhp, Merced (Calif.) HS
24. **Scott Wilhelmy, c, Carleton (Minn.)**
25. Rod Langston, of, Brevard (Fla.) CC
26. **Rich Yett, rhp, Don Lugo HS, Chino, Calif.**
27. **William Price, 2b, Cal State Dominguez Hills**
28. Kurt Reid, of, St. Louis CC-Meramec
29. **Mark Wright, rhp, Boise State**
30. **Frank Rampenn, c/3b, Tampa**
31. Don Smith, rhp, Orange Coast (Calif.) JC
32. Chuck Lusted, rhp, Georgia Southern
33. Robert Elliott, rhp, Georgia Southern (Selection voided)
34. Chuck Yaeger, lhp, Rio Mesa HS, Camarillo, Calif.
35. **David Jackson, rhp, Hogan HS, Vallejo, Calif.**
36. Kenny Kohler, c, North Plainfield (N.J.) HS
37. **Brad Baker, ss, Gustavus Adolphus HS, St. Peter, Minn.**

June—Secondary Phase (25)

1. **John Palica, of, Los Angeles Harbor JC**
2. Steve Watson, rhp, Manatee (Fla.) JC
3. Dave Malpeso, c, Miami-Dade North CC

MONTREAL EXPOS

January—Regular Phase (22)

1. Richard Felt, lhp, DeKalb South (Ga.) CC
2. Richard Marshall, of, Hagerstown (Md.) JC
3. **David Spriggs, of, Ohio**
4. Benny Melares, c, St. Clair County (Mich.) CC
5. Richard Vitato, ss, Merced (Calif.) JC
6. Rich DeVincenzo, lhp, Miami-Dade North CC
7. Steve Janousek, lhp, Middle Georgia JC
8. Bryan Kelly, rhp, Valencia (Fla.) CC
9. **Mike Powers, rhp, Kentucky Wesleyan**
10. **Joe Emery, rhp, Garden City, Mich.**

January—Secondary Phase (4)

1. **Mike Stenhouse, of, Harvard**
2. Mike Sharperson, ss, DeKalb South (Ga.) CC

June—Regular Phase (21)

1. (Pick to Braves as compensation for free agent Rowland Office)
1. **Terry Francona, of, Arizona** (Pick from Yankees as compensation for free agent Rudy May)
1. (Pick to Reds as compensation for free agent Fred Norman)
2. **Joe Hesketh, lhp, SUNY Buffalo** (Pick from Red Sox as compensation for free agent Tony Perez)
3. **Greg Bargar, rhp, Arizona**
4. **Tom Gorman, lhp, Gonzaga**
5. **Roy Johnson, of, Tennessee State**
6. **Bob Valliant, lhp, Oxbow HS, Wells River, Vt.**
7. **Ken Weislak, 3b, Lewis (Ill.)**
8. **David Hoeksema, ss, Iowa**
9. **Bryan Little, ss, Texas A&M**
10. Phil Deriso, lhp, Auburn
11. **Terry Eldridge, of, Anne Arundel (Md.) CC**
12. Julius Anderson, 3b, Nichols (Ga.) HS
13. **Larry Groves, rhp/of, Emporia State (Kan.)**
14. **Pete Chapin, rhp, Cal State Fullerton**
15. Mike Williams, 1b, Western Kentucky
16. Kevin Sumuel, of, Rockdale (Texas) HS
17. Douglas Young, rhp, Glenbard West HS, Glen Ellyn, Ill.
18. **Joel Lepel, c, Mankato State (Minn.)**
19. **Bob Baldrick, lhp, Hughes HS, Cincinnati**
20. **Larry Glasscock, lhp, Western Kentucky**
21. Alvin Ruben, 1b, Houston
22. **Ken Westray, lhp, Eastern Illinois**
23. **Scott Hinson, rhp, Cox HS, Virginia Beach, Va.**
24. **Harry Jones, c, Newton County HS, Covington, Ga.**
25. Don DeLoach, ss, Florida State
26. **Mark Shuler, rhp, Memphis State**
27. **Jeff Whelan, of, Xavier**
28. **Dane Rogers, of, Richland (Texas) JC**
29. **Glen Stachiet, of, South Lake HS, St. Clair Shores, Mich.**
30. Chris Sabo, 3b, Catholic Central HS, Detroit
31. **Steve Dawes, inf, Xavier**
32. Kendall Carter, rhp, Coronado HS, Scottsdale, Ariz.
33. **Rod Nealeigh, 1b/of, Anderson (Ind.)**

June—Secondary Phase (15)

1. Herm Winningham, of, DeKalb South (Ga.) CC

NEW YORK METS

January—Regular Phase (2)

1. **Roger Frash, of, Oxnard (Calif.) JC**
2. Joe Anderson, rhp, Florida CC
3. Charles Nat, rhp, Solano (Calif.) CC
4. Robert Smart, of, Golden West (Calif.) JC
5. Michael Sims, rhp, Johnson County (Kan.) CC
6. Gary Dawson, of, Orange Coast (Calif.) JC
7. Eric Porter, c, Iowa Western CC
8. Michael Paul, 3b, JC of the Sequoias (Calif.)
9. James Harris, of, Butte (Calif.) JC

January—Secondary Phase (16)

1. Chris Johnston, 3b, Costa Mesa (Calif.) JC

June—Regular Phase (1)

1. **Darryl Strawberry, of, Crenshaw HS, Los Angeles**
1. **Billy Beane, of, Mount Carmel HS, Rancho Bernardo, Calif.** (Pick from Pirates as compensation for free agent Andy Hassler)
1. **John Gibbons, c, MacArthur HS, San Antonio, Texas** (Pick from Red Sox as compensation for free agent Skip Lockwood)
2. **Jay Tibbs, rhp, Huffman HS, Birmingham**
3. **Jody Johnston, rhp, Franklin Academy, Burke, N.Y.**
4. **Mike Davis, 2b, Wichita State**
5. **Ronn Reynolds, c, Arkansas**
6. Jay Palma, 3b, Peterson HS, Sunnyvale, Calif.
7. **Jeff Bittiger, rhp, Secaucus (N.J.) HS**
8. **Lloyd McClendon, c, Valparaiso**
9. Anthony Kelley, rhp, Orr HS, Chicago
10. Otis Tramble, ss, Southern
11. **Alex Delano, of, Florida Southern**
12. **Scott Merlack, rhp, North Hills HS, Pittsburgh**
13. **Rick Ownbey, rhp, Santa Ana (Calif.) JC**
14. Carl Ehmann, of, Corona del Mar HS, Newport Beach, Calif.
15. John Hennell, 1b, Arkansas
16. **James Woodward, ss/3b, Cal State Long Beach**
17. **Edward Teate, rhp, Jonesboro (Ga.) HS**
18. Alan Maria, lhp, Texas-Pan American
19. **Donald Magdzuik, rhp, Los Alamitos (Calif.) HS**
20. **Mickey Replogle, rhp, Rose State (Okla.) JC**
21. Mark Pingree, 2b, Lewis-Clark State (Idaho)
22. Trey Brooks, ss, Texas Christian
23. Tony Beal, of, Mainland HS, Daytona Beach, Fla.
24. Steve O'Donnell, ss, Connellsville (Pa.) HS
25. **Kenneth Stelly, lhp, Northwestern State**
26. Keith Jones, of, Wichita State
27. **Chuck Schnoor, ss, Kearney State (Neb.)**
28. Thomas Saenz, lhp, Pacifica HS, Cypress, Calif.
29. Anthony Malloy, lhp, Rider
30. **Jessie Vann, 3b, Johnson County (Kan.) CC**
31. **Stephen Moore, of, Cal State Long Beach**
32. **Duane Evans, 1b, Oklahoma State**
33. **Martin Brophy, c, St. Clair (Pa.) HS**
34. Lance Hudson, ss, San Bernardino HS, Fremont, Calif.
35. Darrel White, of, St. Louis CC-Meramec
36. **Bill Boone, 1b, La Salle**
37. **Ricky Poe, 1b/of, Arkansas State**
38. Nick Esposito, rhp, Los Medanos (Calif.) JC

June—Secondary Phase (11)

1. Bill Worden, c, Stanford
2. Al Newman, 3b, Chaffey (Calif.) JC
3. Derek Tatsuno, lhp, Aiea, Hawaii

NEW YORK YANKEES

January—Regular Phase (21)

1. Clem Freeman, lhp, Manatee (Fla.) JC
2. **Mark Cartwright, rhp, Yuba (Calif.) CC**
3. **Reggie Bratton, rhp, Spartanburg Methodist (S.C.) JC**
4. **Jeff Reynolds, 3b, Potomac State (W.Va.) JC**
5. Randy Graham, rhp, Santa Rosa (Calif.) JC
6. **Daniel O'Regan, of, JC of San Mateo (Calif.)**
7. **Steve Toporek, rhp, JC of Lake County (Ill.)**

January—Secondary Phase (7)

1. **Tom Dodd, of, Oregon**
2. Tod Taylor, rhp, Citrus (Calif.) JC
3. Robert Jackowiak, rhp, Middle Georgia JC

June—Regular Phase (22)

1. (Pick to Expos as compensation for free agent Rudy May)
2. (Pick to Red Sox as compensation for free agent Bob Watson)
3. Billy Cannon, ss, Broadmoor HS, Baton Rouge (Selection voided)
4. Steve Madden, of, New Hartford (N.Y.) HS
5. **Brent Gjesdal, 3b, Reynolds HS, Portland, Ore.**
6. Glenn Braggs, of, San Bernardino (Calif.) HS
7. **Dan Hanggie, ss, Cal State Fullerton**
8. Dave Yobs, of, Oral Roberts
9. **Steve Fincher, lhp, Jefferson HS, Tampa**
10. **Mark Mendez, rhp, San Joaquin Delta (Calif.) JC**
11. **Kenneth Martin, rhp, Burlington HS, Waterbury, Vt.**
12. Jeff Brown, c, Monache HS, Porterville, Calif.
13. **David Bailey, 1b, Florida Southern**
14. **Kevin Shannon, c, Texas**
15. **Clay Christiansen, rhp, Kansas**
16. **David Banes, 3b, Florida**
17. **Glenn Robertson, ss, Cal State Fullerton**
18. Todd Lamb, rhp, Cape Elizabeth (Maine) HS
19. **Michael Foster, lhp, Humboldt State (Calif.)**
20. **Harold DeWitt, rhp, Ball State**
21. **Ken Smith, rhp, Florida State**
22. **John Gaston, rhp, Nevada-Reno**
23. **Doug Latrenta, of, St. John's**
24. **Joe Perna, of, South Florida**
25. **Jeffrey Marks, lhp, Pine Bush (N.Y.) HS**
26. **Kevin Quirk, rhp, St. Joseph's**
27. David Myers, ss, Temple
28. **Randy McDaniel, 2b, Tennessee**
29. **Gerald Kennedy, rhp, Knoxville, Tenn.**
30. Jim Camacho, ss, Cal Poly Pomona
31. **Ben Callahan, 1b, Catawba (N.C.)**
32. Pat Clements, lhp, Pleasant Valley HS, Chico, Calif.
33. **James D'Aloia, ss, St. Leo**
34. **Brad Bennett, of, Fresno State**
35. **James Gross, 3b, Miami (Ohio)**
36. **Randy Filkins, of, Cal State Stanislaus**
37. **Darren Holt, 2b, Fresno State**
38. Don Montgomery, of, Proviso West HS, Bellwood, Ill.
39. **Timothy Knight, of, Florida International**
40. Joseph Portale, c, Baldwin-Wallace (Ohio)
41. **Bob Raftice, lhp, Cape Elizabeth (Maine) HS**
42. Gregory Eskra, rhp, Oak Glen HS, Chester, W.Va.

June—Secondary Phase (20)

1. **John Milholland, ss, Louisburg (N.C.) JC**
2. **Sheldon Andrews, rhp, Lower Columbia (Wash.) JC**
3. Randy Hunt, c, Chattahoochee Valley (Ala.) CC
4. **Joe Stefani, rhp, Iowa Western CC**

OAKLAND ATHLETICS

January—Regular Phase (3)

1. Dave Gallagher, of, Mercer County (N.J.) CC
2. Richard Ousman, rhp, Los Angeles Pierce JC
3. Rick Thurman, rhp, Los Angeles Pierce JC
4. Gail Arnold, rhp, Linn-Benton (Ore.) CC
5. Steven Garrett, rhp, Chabot (Calif.) JC
6. Greg McAnulty, of, Centralia (Wash.) JC
7. Gregory Mine, rhp, Green River (Wash.) CC
8. Greg Monda, 1b, Centralia (Wash.) JC
9. Eric Kuntz, rhp, Big Bend (Wash.) CC
10. Reggie Sells, rhp, Cochise County (Ariz.) CC
11. Michael Schreck, of, Antelope Valley (Calif.) JC

January—Secondary Phase (23)

1. Larry Hernandez, of, Valencia (Fla.) CC

June—Regular Phase (4)

1. **Mike King, lhp, Morningside (Iowa)**
2. Rhett Whisman, ss, Fairfield (Ohio) HS
3. **Rich Bordi, rhp, Fresno State**
4. **Ken Johnson, ss, Garfield HS, Woodbridge, Va.**
5. Brian Myers, rhp, Lakewood (Calif.) HS
6. Terry Bell, c, Fairmont East HS, Kettering, Ohio
7. **John Horner, lhp, Warren Local HS, Belpre, Ohio**
8. John Sullivan, ss, Grand Island (N.Y.) HS
9. John Farrell, rhp, Short Regional HS, Monmouth Beach, N.J.
10. Scott Parsons, of, Livingston (N.J.) HS
11. Scott Kimball, c, Skyline HS, Oakland
12. Robert Shannon, ss, Paul VI HS, Bellmawr, N.J.
13. Randy Ward, 1b, Nevada-Las Vegas
14. Erik Sonberg, lhp, Bishop Kelly HS, Tulsa, Okla.
15. Eric Broersma, rhp, UCLA
16. Scott Anderson, rhp, Newport HS, Bellevue, Wash.

17. **Juan Cruz, ss, Davis HS, Yakima, Wash.**
18. Jim Teahan, rhp, Utah
19. David Couch, c, Asheboro (N.C.) HS
20. **Terry Byrum, 2b, Houston**
21. **Joseph Soprano, of/1b, New York Tech**
22. Barry Koch, rhp, Mesa (Ariz.) CC
23. David Peters, of, Northport, N.Y.
24. Danny Jackson, lhp, Aurora (Colo.) Central HS
25. Bruce Kastelic, ss, Oklahoma State
26. Don O'Connor, rhp, Sunset HS, Hayward, Calif.

June—Secondary Phase (18)

1. Chris Johnston, 3b, Orange Coast (Calif.) JC

PHILADELPHIA PHILLIES

January—Regular Phase (14)

1. **Tony Ghelfi, rhp, Iowa Western CC**
2. **Ron Richardson, rhp, Linn-Benton (Ore.) CC**
3. **Jimmy Darnell, rhp, Seminole (Fla.) CC**
4. Robin Dreizler, c, El Camino (Calif.) JC
5. Daniel Prine, lhp, Mott (Mich.) CC
6. David Vanderleen, rhp, Grand Rapids (Mich.) JC
7. Paul Perez, c, Lassen (Calif.) JC
8. Warren Oliver, ss, Victoria, Texas
9. Tommy George, ss, Bacone (Okla.) JC
10. Harlan Robertson, c, Hill (Texas) JC
11. Joe Dan Petty, rhp, Panola (Texas) JC
12. Kevin Bates, ss, Brevard (Fla.) CC
13. John Proctor, c, Allen County (Kan.) CC
14. Bryan Price, rhp, Ranger (Texas) JC
15. Douglas Scott, of, Grand Rapids (Mich.) JC
16. **Michael Befort, rhp, Allen County (Kan.) CC**
17. Bradley Coker, c, McLennan (Texas) CC
18. Keith Kearney, c, Blinn (Texas) JC
19. Willie Briscoe, rhp, Blinn (Texas) JC
20. Kenneth Myrick, ss/2b, Blinn (Texas) JC
21. **Richard Yraguen, ss, Treasure Valley (Ore.) CC**
22. **Dale Drew, rhp, Joliet (Ill.) JC**

January—Secondary Phase (18)

1. James Harris, lhp, Jefferson HS, Brooklyn, N.Y.
2. **Steven True, lhp, Seminole State (Okla.) JC**
3. Bryon Henderson, c, Linn-Benton (Ore.) CC
4. **Edward Schiave, rhp, Boyertown, Pa.**

June—Regular Phase (13)

1. **Lebo Powell, c, Pine Forest HS, Pensacola, Fla.**
2. **Larry Knight, rhp, Lookout Valley HS, Chattanooga, Tenn.**
3. **Doug Maggio, c, Shaler HS, Pittsburgh**
4. **Jon Reelhorn, rhp, Fresno State**
5. **Yonis Rodriguez, rhp, Eastern District HS, Ozone Park, N.Y.**
6. **Richie Gaynor, of, Bullard HS, Fresno, Calif.**
7. Bobby Hinson, rhp, LaMarque (Texas) HS
8. Greg Lorenzetti, ss, Fortuna (Calif.) HS
9. **Steve Jeltz, ss/2b, Kansas**
10. **Jerome Kovar, c, Southern Methodist**
11. **Craig Musick, ss/of, Seminole State (Okla.) JC**
12. **Johnny McAnally, lhp, Rogers HS, Tulsa, Okla.**
13. **Randy Salava, of, Indiana State**
14. **Bernardo Howard, 3b/ss, Wyandotte HS, Kansas City, Kan.**
15. **Tim Steverson, rhp, Umatilla (Fla.) HS**
16. Mike Brumley, ss, Union HS, Broken Arrow, Okla.
17. John Machin, lhp, Turner HS, Carrolton, Texas
18. Steve Smith, ss, Dallas (Ore.) HS
19. Andy Nossek, lhp, Waltrip HS, Houston
20. **Bryan Hoppie, ss/2b, Santa Ana (Calif.) HS**
21. **Rocky Childress, rhp, Santa Rosa (Calif.) HS**
22. **Ron Ridling, of, Southeastern Oklahoma State**
23. **Marty Decker, rhp, Point Loma Nazarene (Calif.)**
24. Mike Capel, rhp/ss, Spring (Texas) HS
25. **Darren Daulton, c, Arkansas City (Kan.) HS**
26. Douglas LaPlant, rhp, West Columbus HS, Brazoria, Texas
27. **Greg Money, rhp, Samuel HS, Dallas**
28. Scott Wright, rhp, Vintage HS, Napa, Calif.
29. **Andre Mallet, of, Madison HS, Houston**
30. **Dale Cook, rhp, Winfield HS, Calvin, La.**

June—Secondary Phase (21)

1. Kevin Romine, of, Orange Coast (Calif.) JC
2. Tim Lambert, rhp, Citrus (Calif.) JC
3. **Ken Dowell, ss, Sacramento CC**
4. **Paul Perez, c, Lassen (Calif.) JC**
5. **Ed Wojna, rhp, Indian River (Fla.) CC**
6. John Whitt, of, Los Angeles Harbor JC

PITTSBURGH PIRATES

January—Regular Phase (24)

1. Darryl Banks, rhp, JC of Southern Idaho
2. Gerald Eckelberry, rhp, JC of Southern Idaho
3. **James Goff, rhp, Edmonds (Wash.) CC**
4. **Scott Gibson, rhp, Seminole (Fla.) CC**
5. Kyle Johnson, rhp, Seminole State (Okla.) JC
6. Mark Andos, rhp, Cuyahoga (Ohio) CC
7. **Ray Jablonski, c, Canisius**
8. Robert Bailey, 3b/of, Louisburg (N.C.) JC
9. Matthew Shibner, 3b/rhp, Louisburg (N.C.) JC
10. Bill Bathe, c, Fullerton (Calif.) JC

January—Secondary Phase (6)

1. Keith Creel, rhp, Texas
2. Sheldon Andrews, rhp, Lower Columbia (Wash.) JC
3. Tom Nieto, c, Cerritos (Calif.) JC
4. Kevin Babb, rhp, Rose Lodge, Ore.
5. **Jeff Metz, rhp, Yavapai (Ariz.) JC**

June—Regular Phase (23)

1. **Rich Renteria, ss, South Gate (Calif.) HS** (Pick from Angels as compensation for free agent Bruce Kison)
1. (Pick to Mets as compensation for free agent Andy Hassler)
2. **Jeff Horne, rhp, White Oak HS, Jacksonville, N.C.** (Pick from Giants as compensation for free agent Rennie Stennett)
2. **Tim Burke, rhp, Nebraska**
3. **Keith Thibodeaux, rhp, Louisiana Tech**
4. **Mike Berger, c, Central Catholic HS, Pittsburgh**
5. **Alec McCullock, rhp, Birmingham-Southern**
6. **Joe Orsulak, of/1b, Parsippany Hills HS, Parsippany, N.J.**
7. **Robert Adkins, rhp, Texas Wesleyan**
8. **Nick Castaneda, c, San Pedro (Calif.) HS**
9. **Tim Howell, c, Lompoc (Calif.) HS**
10. **Michael Allman, rhp, Forthill HS, Cumberland, Md.**
11. **John Schiave, 1b, New Orleans**
12. Charles Mathison, rhp, Theodore HS, Mobile, Ala.
13. **Christopher Edwards, rhp, Indiana (Pa.) HS**
14. **Robert Nichols, lhp, Delmar (Del.) HS**
15. **Chris Conroyd, lhp, North Carolina State**
16. **Pat McAlurney, lhp, Wagner**
17. Darryl Jones, 1b, Carver HS, Columbus, Ga.
18. **Mark Isbell, of, Texas Lutheran**
19. **Jeff White, lhp, Northridge HS, Johnstown, Ohio**
20. Michael Gray, 2b, Gallatin County HS, Warsaw, Ky.
21. Robert Lackeby, rhp, Grants Pass (Ore.) HS
22. **Meredith Tingler, rhp, Clifton Forge HS, Eagle Rock, Va.**
23. Donald Lawson, of, Bridgeport (Ala.) HS
24. Mark Gabriel, ss, Niagara Catholic HS, Niagara Falls, N.Y.
25. Joe Cipolloni, c, Phoenix JC
26. Rick Hunley, of, Petersburg (Va.) HS
27. George Pugsley, rhp, Miraleste HS, Ranchos Palos Verdes, Calif.
28. **Don Howard, lhp, Norfolk State**
29. **Rob O'Leath, of/1b, Butler**
30. **Barry Maxwell, c, Glencoe, Ky.**
31. Richie Carter, of, Hood River (Ore.) HS
32. Randy Edwards, lhp, Bishop Walsh HS, Lavale, Md.
33. **Bernie Bastian, rhp, Francis Marion (S.C.)**
34. Andrew Baranek, 3b, Allentown (Pa.) Central Catholic HS
35. Hal Nurkka, lhp, Chapparal HS, Scottsdale, Ariz.
36. Bill Merrifield, ss, Rocky Mount (N.C.) HS
37. **Larry Acker, lhp, Manatee (Fla.) JC**
38. Scott Diez, lhp, Riverview HS, Sarasota, Fla.
39. **Matthew Sinnen, c, Virginia Wesleyan**

40. Carl Vasquez, rhp, Marietta (Ohio)
41. Charles Fonville, c, White Oak HS, Jacksonville, N.C.
42. Joseph Cutler, of, Phoenix JC

June—Secondary Phase (17)

1. Dave Chiono, rhp, Yuba (Calif.) CC
2. Tyson Hubbard, rhp, Spartanburg Methodist (S.C.) JC
3. Richard Lucero, rhp, Phoenix JC
4. Brian Peck, rhp, JC of Southern Idaho

ST. LOUIS CARDINALS

January—Regular Phase (16)

1. **Ken Spears, of, Stratford, Conn.**
2. **Brian O'Donnell, lhp, Milroy, Pa.**
3. **Mitch Southern, of, Mount San Antonio (Calif.) JC**
4. **Kevin Hagen, rhp, Bellevue (Wash.) CC**
5. **Donald Hughes, rhp, Pensacola (Fla.) JC**
6. Edward McNamara, rhp, Edmonds (Wash.) CC
7. **James Gonzales, c, Edmonds (Wash.) CC**
8. Barry Aden, rhp, Centralia (Wash.) JC
9. Dan Devers, rhp, Yavapai (Ariz.) JC

January—Secondary Phase (20)

1. Joe Stefani, rhp, Iowa Western CC

June—Regular Phase (15)

1. **Don Collins, rhp, Ferguson HS, Newport News, Va.**
2. Dan Plesac, lhp, Crown Point (Ind.) HS
3. **Dan Stryffler, of, Fitch HS, Youngstown, Ohio**
4. **Ricky Horton, lhp, Virginia**
5. **Brent Milligan, lhp, West Perry HS, Loysville, Pa.**
6. **Russ Davis, rhp, Mississippi**
7. **Jim Adduci, of, Southern Illinois**
8. **Jay North, rhp, Ygnacio Valley HS, Concord, Calif.**
9. Joe Wood, 2b, Herkimer (N.Y.) HS
10. David Page, 3b/rhp, Sunnyside HS, Tucson
11. Dave Droschak, rhp, Pensacola (Fla.) JC
12. Mike Samuel, ss, Pacifica HS, Garden Grove, Calif.
13. Steven Anderson, ss, Kennedy HS, Granada Hills, Calif.
14. **Mike Gambeski, 3b, Hamden (Conn.) HS**
15. **Rick Weems, c, Columbus (Ga.)**
16. **John Martin, rhp, Washington**
17. **Paul Cherry, lhp, Pace HS, Davie, Fla.**
18. Gary Jensen, c, Solano (Calif.) CC
19. Jim Jefferson, rhp, Marcos de Niza HS, Tempe, Ariz.
20. James Allison, of, Ygnacio Valley HS, Concord, Calif.
21. **Greg Dunn, rhp/of, Eisenhower HS, Yakima, Wash.**
22. **Mike Rhodes, lhp, Virginia Tech**
23. **James Stevens, of/3b, Kecoughtan HS, Hampton, Va.**
24. **Perry Redmond, of, University City (Mo.) HS**
25. Mike Santiago, lhp, Baldwin Park (Calif.) HS
26. **Barry Sayler, c, Seattle**
27. Jay Keeler, rhp, Florida State
28. **Kenneth Mohlerm, lhp, South Florida**
29. **Richard Reed, rhp, Lindbergh HS, St. Louis**
30. **Keith Thrower, ss, Texas Wesleyan**
31. **Tom Epple, lhp, Leavitown (N.Y.) Memorial HS**
32. **Kevin Fehr, rhp, Alabama-Birmingham**
33. John Vela, lhp, Poly HS, Riverside, Calif.
34. Joseph Hackett, of, Elon
35. Todd Schulz, of, Tombstone HS, Huachuca City, Ariz.
36. **Raymond Williams, 2b/of, Pinole HS, Richmond, Calif.**
37. Rick Aguilera, rhp, Edgewood HS, West Covina, Calif.

June—Secondary Phase (23)

1. Ray Krawczyk, rhp, Golden West (Calif.) JC
2. Ric Wilson, c, Mesa (Ariz.) CC

SAN DIEGO PADRES

January—Regular Phase (6)

1. Ken Dowell, ss, Sacramento CC
2. Curt Wardle, lhp, San Bernardino Valley (Calif.) JC
3. George Sarkissian, 3b, Mount San Antonio (Calif.) JC
4. Anthony Wadley, rhp, Laney (Calif.) JC
5. Stacy Morgan, rhp, JC of the Redwoods (Calif.)
6. William Deesa, 1b, Chipola (Fla.) JC

January—Secondary Phase (10)

1. **Ricky McMullen, 2b, Slidell, La.**
2. Randy Newman, lhp, Cypress (Calif.) JC

June—Regular Phase (5)

1. **Jeff Pyburn, of, Georgia**
2. (Pick to Giants as compensation for free agent John Curtis)
3. (Pick to Indians as compensation for free agent Rick Wise)
4. **Neil Bryant, lhp, Los Angeles CC**
4. **Dave Christianson, 1b, Kennedy HS, Chicago** (Pick from Dodgers as compensation for free agent Jay Johnstone)
5. **Steve Murray, of, Glassboro State (N.J.)**
6. **Gerry Davis, 3b, Howard (D.C.)**
7. **John White, rhp, Cal State Long Beach**
8. John Tillema, rhp, San Jose State
9. Sam Martin, ss, Louisburg (N.C.) JC
10. **Pat Casey, of, Portland**
11. **George Hinshaw, of, La Verne (Calif.)**
12. Gary Blaine, ss, Livingston HS, Smithland, Ky.
13. **Pat Blamey, rhp, Santa Clara, Calif.**
14. **Andy Krzanik, rhp, Elmhurst (Ill.)**
15. **Rodney Bellamy, ss, Georgia**
16. **Raymie Styons, c, East Carolina**
17. Glen Cook, rhp, Ithaca (N.Y.)
18. **Bruce Hines, 2b, La Verne (Calif.)**
19. **Mike Couchee, rhp, Southern California**
20. **Joe Wood, 3b, Emporia State (Kan.)**
21. **Brian Duffy, rhp, California**
22. **Rick Witt, ss/3b, Gonzaga**
23. **James Coffman, rhp, Portland State (Ore.)**
24. **Mike Bertalot, of, Portland State (Ore.)**
25. **Michael Smith, lhp, Washington**
26. **Joe Scherger, of, Nebraska**
27. Jeff Walsh, rhp, Santa Clara
28. **Jim Thomas, c, UCLA**
29. **Mike Mahoski, rhp, Gonzaga**
30. **Michael Britt, rhp, East Carolina**
31. Terry Raley, ss, St. Mary's (Texas)
32. **Scott Lovekamp, rhp, Concordia (Ill.)**
33. Stan Williams, rhp, Southern California
34. **David Kirk, rhp, North Carolina**
35. **Daniel Wodrich, 2b, Washington State**
36. **Billy Ireland, of/c, Oklahoma State**
37. John Slaughter, of, Southern Alamance HS, Burlington, N.C.
38. Chuck Hartenstein, 2b, Johnson HS, Austin, Texas
39. Brad Ditto, 2b/ss, Rio Hondo (Calif.) JC
40. Jeff Robinson, rhp, Christian HS, El Cajon, Calif.

June—Secondary Phase (7)

1. Ron Romanick, rhp, Arizona State
2. **Tim Cannon, of, Chipola (Fla.) JC**
3. Michael Tolbert, rhp, Triton (Ill.) JC

SAN FRANCISCO GIANTS

January—Regular Phase (8)

1. **Willie Hysaw, rhp, Compton (Calif.) JC**
2. Randy Ebersberger, inf, Los Angeles Pierce JC
3. **Mark McDonald, rhp, Santa Barbara (Calif.) CC**
4. **Joseph Henderson, inf, San Diego Mesa JC**
5. Dennis Ivy, of, San Joaquin Delta (Calif.) JC
6. Pedro LaTorre, 2b, Miami-Dade North CC
7. Andrew Epping, rhp, Indian Hills (Iowa) CC
8. James Oxe, c, Grossmont (Calif.) JC

January—Secondary Phase (8)

1. Jeff Dedmon, rhp, West Los Angeles JC
2. **Bill Hainline, ss, Spokane, Wash.**

June—Regular Phase (7)

1. **Jessie Reid, 1b, Lynwood (Calif.) HS**
2. **Eric Erickson, lhp, La Jolla (Calif.) HS** (Pick from Padres as compensation for free agent John Curtis)
2. (Pick to Pirates as compensation for free agent Rennie Stennett)

3. (Pick to White Sox as compensation for free agent Milt May)
4. (Pick to Brewers as compensation for free agent Jim Wohlford)
5. **Rollo Adams, c/of, Southern California College**
6. Dave Hengel, of, Mission HS, Fremont, Calif.
7. **Mike Wallace, 3b, Nevada-Reno**
8. **Doran Perdue, 2b, Murray State**
9. Ross Kingsley, c, Craig HS, Janesville, Wis.
10. **Alan Fowlkes, rhp, Cal Poly Pomona**
11. Brick Smith, 1b, Wake Forest
12. Mark Shiflett, lhp, Auburn
13. **Kelly Smith, of, Washington State**
14. Mark Johnson, c, San Francisco
15. **Jerome Littman, ss, Milton (Wis.)**
16. **Ben Gallo, lhp, San Diego State**
17. **Joe Banach, lhp, Peabody HS, Pittsburgh**
18. **Sean Toerner, 2b, Cal State Northridge**
19. **Joe Olivas, inf/rhp, San Joaquin Delta (Calif.) JC**
20. **Kenneth Frazier, c, Compton (Calif.) HS**
21. Craig Stevenson, ss, Chatsworth HS, Northridge, Calif.
22. **David Wilson, 3b, Southern California**
23. Tommy Alexander, rhp, Gordon (Ga.) JC
24. **Jeff Trax, rhp, Oakland (Mich.) CC**
25. **Randy Gomez, c, Utah**
26. **Mark Dempsey, rhp, Ohio State**
27. **Mark Sharpe, ss/2b, UC San Diego**
28. **Bill Heimach, 2b, Western Michigan**
29. Gary Green, ss, Taylor-Allderdice HS, Pittsburgh
30. Danny Clay, of, Los Angeles Pierce JC
31. Richard Belli, rhp, Terra Nova HS, Pacifica, Calif.
32. Colin Ward, lhp, Citrus (Calif.) JC
33. John Duval, rhp, San Luis Obispo (Calif.) HS
34. Jeff Anderson, rhp, Nampa (Idaho) HS
35. **James Smith, rhp, Western HS, Las Vegas**
36. **Joseph Cardwell, ss, East Tennessee State**
37. Bob Tumpane, 1b, Lewis (Ill.)
38. **Mike Lenti, 2b, St. Xavier (Ill.)**
39. Louis Zanini, inf, Edison HS, Stockton, Calif.
40. Monico Corral, ss, San Francisco
41. Marlon Warren, ss, Rancho Cotati HS, Rohnert Park, Calif.
42. **Doug Wabeke, 2b, Central Michigan**
43. **Robert Spurlin, c, Northern Illinois**

June—Secondary Phase (19)

1. **Lance Junker, of, Loyola Marymount**
2. Donnie Hill, ss, Orange Coast (Calif.) JC
3. **Daniel McDonald, lhp, Penn State**
4. Harry Kazanjian, c/of, CC of San Francisco
5. **Thomas McLaughlin, rhp, Los Angeles CC**

SEATTLE MARINERS

January—Regular Phase (5)

1. Don Freeman, ss, West Los Angeles JC
2. Mike Reddish, c, Indian River (Fla.) CC
3. Mark Effrig, rhp, Shoreline (Wash.) CC
4. Al Simmons, 2b, Fort Steilacoom (Wash.) CC
5. Ric Wilson, c, Mesa (Ariz.) CC
6. **Michael Howe, lhp, Rochester, Pa.**
7. Bret Elbin, ss, Hagerstown (Md.) JC
8. **Takashi Upshur, 2b, Glassboro State (N.J.)**

January—Secondary Phase (13)

1. Bill Mooneyham, rhp, Merced (Calif.) JC
2. **Dan Firova, c, Refugio, Texas**
3. Chris Glass, rhp, Hagerstown (Md.) JC

June—Regular Phase (6)

1. **Darnell Coles, ss, Eisenhower HS, Rialto, Calif.**
2. **Matt Young, lhp, UCLA**
3. **Robert Hudson, rhp, UC Riverside**
4. **Steve Krueger, lhp, Arkansas**
5. Ken Lynn, rhp, Riverside HS, Greer, S.C.
6. Kevin Dukes, lhp, Arizona State
7. **Bill Crone, ss, West Chester (Pa.)**
8. Tim Kammeyer, rhp, Southern California
9. William Blair, c, Boone HS, Orlando, Fla.
10. **Donell Nixon, of/3b, West Columbus HS, Evergreen, N.C.**
11. **Glen Walker, of, Washington State**
12. **Don McKenzie, rhp, Newberry (S.C.)**
13. **Ed Vande Berg, lhp, Arizona State**
14. **Clark Crist, ss, Arizona**
15. **Kevin McGann, 3b, New Orleans**
16. **John Moses, of, Arizona**
17. **Rusty McNealy, of, Florida International**
18. **David Blume, 1b, Lewis-Clark State (Idaho)**
19. Stan Holmes, of, Arizona State
20. Leo George, c, Southern Methodist
21. Ernest Riles, ss, Middle Georgia JC
22. Darren Mazeroski, 2b, Hempfield HS, Greensburg, Pa.
23. Brian Rice, lhp, Bayside HS, Virginia Beach, Va.

June—Secondary Phase (2)

1. **Harold Reynolds, ss, Canada (Calif.) JC**
2. **Mark Pedersen, rhp, Washington State**
3. Don Freeman, ss, West Los Angeles JC

TEXAS RANGERS

January—Regular Phase (13)

1. Mike Carriger, rhp, Bacone (Okla.) JC
2. **Billy Taylor, rhp, Abraham Baldwin Agricultural (Ga.) JC**
3. Al Newman, 2b, Chaffey (Calif.) JC
4. Dewayne Ward, rhp, Murray State (Texas) JC
5. Hans Herzog, lhp, Louisburg (N.C.) JC
6. **Daryl Smith, rhp, Essex (Md.) CC**
7. Carl Watson, rhp, Manatee (Fla.) JC
8. James Casey, rhp, Miami-Dade North CC
9. **James Maxwell, ss, Mercer County (N.J.) CC**
10. Ronald Caldwell, rhp, CC of Baltimore
11. **Jeffrey Simmons, rhp, Essex (Md.) CC**
12. Glen Edwards, of, Valencia (Fla.) CC

January—Secondary Phase (25)

1. **Tom Dunbar, of, Middle Georgia JC**
2. David McDonald, lhp, Penn State
3. **John Millholland, ss, Louisburg (N.C.) JC**
4. Jeff Groth, of, Chagrin Falls, Ohio

June—Regular Phase (14)

1. **Tim Maki, rhp, Carrol HS, Huntertown, Ind.**
2. **Dwayne Henry, rhp, Middletown HS, Odessa, Del.**
3. **Lindy Duncan, ss, Missouri**
4. **Curtis Wilkerson, ss, Dinwiddie HS, Sutherland, Va.**
5. **Brad Mengwasser, rhp, Southern Methodist**
6. **Al Hartman, rhp, Joliet (Ill.) West HS**
7. Tony Hudson, lhp, Cal State Fullerton
8. **Craig Goodin, ss, Tulare (Calif.) Union HS**
9. Doug Shields, ss, Plant HS, Tampa
10. **Joe Roberts, c, Louisville**
11. **Tim Henry, lhp, Texas Wesleyan**
12. Dion Lowe, of, Lakewood (N.J.) HS
13. **David Stokes, 3b, Tulane**
14. **Stan Haas, of, Nebraska**
15. **Montye Mayfield, rhp, Bell HS, Hurst, Texas**
16. **Dennis Long, rhp, Connecticut**
17. Lorenzo Spencer, of, Tampa Bay Tech HS, Tampa
18. **Dan Murphy, of, Nevada-Las Vegas**
19. **Randal Carter, 2b, Arkansas**
20. **Brett Benza, of, Rhode Island**
21. **Brooks Wallace, inf, Texas Tech**
22. **Andrew Wright, c, Lincoln (R.I.) HS**
23. **George Crum, of, Hillsborough HS, Tampa**
24. Chris Joslin, lhp, Linden HS, Gaines, Mich.
25. **Richard Wilkinson, 1b, Texas-Arlington**
26. **Perry Cliburn, rhp, Mississippi State**
27. **Paul Ondo, 1b, Southern Illinois**
28. Paul Gay, of, North Carolina
29. Chris Oleson, 3b, Hinkley HS, Aurora, Colo.
30. Cameron Young, rhp, Texas Christian
31. **Anthony Garcia, 3b, Plant HS, Tampa**
32. **Gary Venner, c, Texas Wesleyan**
33. **Walt Terrell, rhp, Morehead State**

34. Bill Lucas, ss, Florida A&M

June—Secondary Phase (12)

1. **Mike Mason, lhp, Oral Roberts**
2. Gail Arnold, rhp, Linn-Benton (Ore.) CC
3. Mark Ochal, rhp, North Carolina
4. **Tom Henke, rhp, East Central (Mo.) JC**

TORONTO BLUE JAYS

January—Regular Phase (1)

1. **Colin McLaughlin, rhp, Connecticut**
2. Roger Samuels, lhp, San Jose (Calif.) CC
3. Steven Smith, c, JC of San Mateo (Calif.)
4. Ron Burns, rhp, Centralia (Wash.) JC
5. Michael Lazzeri, of, Bellevue (Wash.) CC
6. Raymond Brown, 3b/rhp, Enterprise State (Ala.) JC

January—Secondary Phase (15)

1. Cary Palmer, rhp, Mesa (Ariz.) CC
2. Andrew Pavlovic, rhp, Yavapai (Ariz.) JC

June—Regular Phase (2)

1. **Garry Harris, ss, Hoover HS, San Diego**
2. **Ken Kinnard, 1b, Claremore (Okla.) HS**
3. **Rico Sutton, of, Lamar**
4. **Bob McNair, 1b, Oregon State**
5. **Dennis Howard, rhp, SUNY Buffalo**
6. **David Trimble, 2b, Davis HS, Yakima, Wash.**
7. John Stevens, rhp, Granada Hills HS, Northridge, Calif.
8. **Matt Nawrocki, rhp, St. Francis (Ill.)**
9. **Kirk Richmond, c, Lansing (Mich.) Everett HS**
10. **Paul Langfield, rhp, Providence**
11. **James Baker, rhp, Bethel (Ind.)**
12. **Sean Everton, of, Santa Clara**
13. **Mike Hurdle, of, Texas A&M**
14. Ben Snyder, rhp, St. Mary's
15. Robert Smith, rhp, Westchester HS, Houston
16. Pete Zeegers, 1b, Tallahassee (Fla.) HS
17. Tom Heckman, rhp, Missouri
18. **John Cosby, c, Portland State (Ore.)**
19. Dennis Tiefenthaler, ss, Armour, S.D.
20. Doug Scherer, rhp, San Jose (Calif.) CC
21. **Steven Smith, rhp, Coastal Carolina**
22. **James Michalec, c, Rice**
23. **Tom Lukish, rhp, Houston**
24. Thomas Penney, c, Houston
25. **David Goffena, rhp/of, Sidney (Ohio) HS**

June—Secondary Phase (16)

1. Michael Jefferson, of, Laney (Calif.) JC

1981 SELECTION OF MOORE WITH FIRST PICK SIGNALS CONTINUING SHIFT TO LOWER-RISK COLLEGE TALENT

Some blamed a poor high school crop. Others cited the impact of major league free agency. More likely it was a sign that college baseball was coming of age as a development source.

Whatever the reason, the early rounds of the 1981 draft represented a sudden and dramatic swing to college talent for the first time.

Historically emphasis in the early rounds had been on high school talent, but of the 26 first-round picks in 1981, 17 were from the college ranks. Never before had more than 10 collegians been taken in the first round.

Of the first 50 players selected, 34 were from college, double the previous record. Twice as many college players as high school players were drafted overall, and just 113 high school players were signed, a record low.

For added measure, the Astros didn't even select a single high school player, the only time in draft history that has happened.

Mets general manager Frank Cashen tried to explain the new philosophy: "For quicker dividends, you go for college players, especially pitchers, because they're more advanced than high school kids. It takes less time for them to develop. Consequently, it's better economically . . . It costs us less money."

For the second time in three years, the Mariners had first pick in the June regular phase. They were set on Oral Roberts righthander Mike Moore most of the spring.

"Once I saw him, he was on the top perch and someone had to knock him off," Mariners farm director Hal Keller said. "I liked his consistency and ability to hold his stuff a long time."

It took one of the most memorable pitching performances in NCAA history, by Yale's Ron Darling, to suddenly make it a two-man race.

With Mariners scouts among those in attendance, Darling went head-to-head against St. John's Frank Viola, who became a second-round pick of Minnesota and later a teammate of Darling's with the Mets. Darling had a no-hitter through 11 innings, struck out 16, and lost when St. John's Steve Scafa singled in the 12th for the only Redmen hit, and scored the game's only run when he stole second, third and home.

"I went back to see Darling in that game because I had heard so many good things," Keller said. "I had no idea we would seriously consider him, but he pitched so good, we had to consider him with Moore."

BERNARD TRONCALE

Mike Moore's price tag helped Seattle decide to make him the No. 1 pick

The key factor that caused the Mariners to back off on Darling was his decision to hire an agent, Steve Kaufman. With rare exceptions, amateur players of the time did not have agents (they lost their NCAA eligibility if they hired one), so this was a new twist.

Moore conducted his own negotiations, and his $100,000 price tag was more in the Mariners' range. As it turned out, both pitchers had solid major league careers. Moore had so-so results in seven seasons with Seattle but became a key member of Oakland's 1989 World Series winner and won 161 big league games in 2,832 career innings. Darling had 136 wins in 2,360 innings.

Moore and Darling, who was picked ninth by Texas, led the unprecedented wave of college selections in the first round. Of the 17 college first-rounders, eight were not drafted out of high school, a testament to the growth of college baseball as a player development system.

The Padres had an outstanding draft, getting Kevin McReynolds with their first-round pick and Tony Gwynn in the third round. McReynolds was a productive big leaguer, and Gwynn became the best Padres player ever and one of the game's great hitters.

Both were considered gambles at the time. McReynolds injured his knee sliding into second base in the weeks before the draft. Gwynn was an all-Western Athletic Conference guard at San Diego State, and clubs were concerned he might opt for basketball, which he had said was his favorite sport.

Gwynn pulled off one of the rare doubles in draft history, getting picked in baseball and basketball on the same day. Both teams, the Padres and Clippers, were in the same city where he played the two sports as a collegiate star.

Braves Have Draft To Forget

While the 1981 draft yielded some of the best talent ever, the Braves didn't quite see it that way. They had one pick in the first three rounds, and not a single Braves pick advanced to the big leagues; only one reached Triple-A.

"It's the leanest year I've ever seen," Atlanta scouting director Paul Snyder said on the eve of the draft. "I'm not trying to degrade the draft, but we've only listed 14 players who we feel are worthy of first-round money."

With players like Gwynn, Viola, Mark Gubicza and Mark Langston available when they picked in the first round, the Braves decided on an obscure outfielder from Centralia, Wash., Jay Roberts, with the 12th pick. Roberts played no baseball that spring in high school and had signed to play football at Washington.

The Angels, who the previous winter had signed free agents John DAcquisto, Geoff Zahn, Juan Beniquez and Bill Travers, had only one pick in the first five rounds. Between Dick Schofield, the third pick overall, and sixth-round pick, Devon White, the Angels sat through 130 selections without making a pick. In White, the wait was worth it.

"He was the rawest professional baseball player I had ever seen," said Gene Mauch, California's director of player personnel. "He didn't know a thing about swinging a bat. He could throw the ball, but he didn't know where it was going. He could do only one thing like a big league ballplayer, and that was run."

He spent six years refining his skills in the minor leagues and developed into one of the most accomplished all-around outfielders in the game, playing 17 seasons in the big leagues.

Two other players who created early-round intrigue were John Elway and Bubby Brister. Both had brief careers in the minors before making names for themselves as NFL quarterbacks.

Elway, who hit .361 with nine homers when not playing football, signed with the Yankees after the football season had started at Stanford. His contract with the Yankees was unique: a $150,000 bonus to play six weeks in the Yankees system in 1982.

Detroit's fourth-round pick was Brister, who played two seasons before he enrolled at Northeast Louisiana, where he launched his football career.

DRAFT 81: FIRST-ROUND PICKS

No.	Club	Player, Pos.	School	Hometown	Ht.	Wt.	B-T	Age
1.	Mariners	Mike Moore, rhp	Oral Roberts	Eakly, Okla.	6-4	205	R-R	21
2.	Cubs	Joe Carter, of	Wichita State	Oklahoma City, Okla.	6-3	215	R-R	21
3.	Angels	Dick Schofield, ss	Griffin HS	Springfield, Ill.	5-11	177	R-R	18
4.	Mets	Terry Blocker, of	Tennessee State	Columbia, S.C.	6-2	185	L-L	20
5.	Blue Jays	Matt Williams, rhp	Rice	Clute, Texas	6-2	197	R-R	21
6.	Padres	Kevin McReynolds, of	Arkansas	Little Rock, Ark.	6-1	200	R-R	21
7.	White Sox	Daryl Boston, of	Woodward HS	Cincinnati	6-4	185	L-L	18
8.	Cardinals	Bobby Meacham, ss	San Diego State	Westminster, Calif.	6-1	185	R-R	20
9.	Rangers	Ron Darling, rhp	Yale	Millbury, Mass.	6-3	205	R-R	20
10.	Giants	Mark Grant, rhp	Catholic HS	Joliet, Ill.	6-2	195	R-R	17
11.	Twins	Mike Sodders, 3b	Arizona State	Westminster, Calif.	6-3	195	R-R	22
12.	Braves	Jay Roberts, of	Centralia HS	Centralia, Wash.	6-3	210	R-R	18
13.	Indians	George Alpert, of	Livingston HS	Livingston, N.J.	6-1	185	L-L	17
14.	Pirates	Jim Winn, rhp	John Brown	Clever, Mo.	6-4	185	R-R	21
15.	Athletics	Tim Pyznarski, 3b/of	Eastern Illinois	Chicago Ridge, Ill.	6-2	190	R-R	21
16.	Cubs	Vance Lovelace, lhp	Hillsborough HS	Tampa	6-5	190	L-L	17
17.	Tigers	Ricky Barlow, rhp	Woodville HS	Woodville, Texas	6-1	160	R-R	18
18.	Expos	Darren Dilks, lhp	Oklahoma State	Ontario, Calif.	6-3	204	L-L	20
19.	Red Sox	Steve Lyons, of/ss	Oregon State	Corvallis, Ore.	6-3	190	L-R	21
20.	Phillies	Johnny Abrego, rhp	Mission HS	San Jose, Calif.	5-11	175	R-R	18
21.	Blue Jays	John Cerutti, lhp	Amherst Coll.	Albany, N.Y.	6-2	185	L-L	21
22.	Dodgers	Dave Anderson, ss	Memphis State	Memphis	6-2	185	R-R	20
23.	Royals	Dave Leeper, of	Southern California	Orange, Calif.	5-11	165	L-L	21
24.	Rangers	Al Lachowicz, rhp	Pittsburgh	McKees Rocks, Pa.	6-3	190	R-R	20
25.	Red Sox	Kevin Burrell, c	Poway HS	Poway, Calif.	6-2	175	R-R	18
26.	Padres	Frank Castro, c	Miami	Hialeah, Fla.	6-0	180	R-R	21

1981

CLUB-BY-CLUB SELECTIONS

ATLANTA BRAVES

January—Regular Phase (11)

1. **Terry Cormack, c, Long Beach (Calif.) CC**
2. **Michael Hinton, lhp, Fenton, Mich.**
3. James McIntosh, rhp, Carl Albert (Okla.) JC
4. Muldrow Lloyd, rhp, Spartanburg Methodist (S.C.) JC
5. Dan Boever, ss, Westark (Ark.) CC
6. **Mark Lance, lhp, Joliet (Ill.) JC**
7. Martin Dean, 1b/c, Carl Albert (Okla.) JC

January—Secondary Phase (13)

1. **Jon Soderberg, rhp, Gulf Coast (Fla.) CC**
2. **Jay Palma, 3b, DeAnza (Calif.) JC**

June—Regular Phase (12)

1. **Jay Roberts, of/rhp, Centralia (Wash.) HS**
2. (Pick to Mets as compensation for free agent Claudell Washington)
3. (Pick to Yankees as compensation for free agent Gaylord Perry)
4. **Clint Brill, c, Humboldt State (Calif.)**
5. **Jerry Ragsdale, c, Turlock (Calif.) HS**
6. **Paul Llewellyn, of/1b, Eastern Hills HS, Fort Worth**
7. **Ken Clark, ss, Bradford HS, Starke, Fla.**
8. **Pat Hodge, of, Vintage HS, Napa, Calif.**
9. **Rudy Torres, rhp, Catalina HS, Tucson**
10. Manny Mantrana, ss, Jackson HS, Miami
11. **Carmine Sperto, rhp, Lincoln HS, Brooklyn**
12. Scott Tabor, rhp, Arkansas
13. Kevin Towers, rhp, Mira Costa (Calif.) JC
14. Steve Gay, rhp, Green River (Wash.) CC
15. Julius McDougal, ss, Callaway HS, Jackson, Miss.
16. John Seitz, rhp, Shippensburg (Pa.)
17. **Steve Chmil, ss, Vanderbilt**
18. Mike Leverette, 3b, Harlem HS, Appling, Ga.
19. **Bruce Heiser, 2b, Oral Roberts**
20. **Bob Tumpane, 1b, Lewis (Ill.)**
21. **Bryan Neal, of, Southwestern (Texas)**
22. **Dave Clay, rhp, West Chester (Pa.)**
23. Frank DeSantis, c, Nevada-Las Vegas
24. **Al Sears, rhp, Old Dominion**
25. **Leonard Klaus, rhp, Missouri-St. Louis**
26. Andy Sherkness, lhp, Catholic HS, McAdoo, Pa.
27. Tony Leonardi, rhp, Aurora (Ill.) West HS
28. Tom Wasilewski, rhp, Wyoming Valley HS, Kingston, Pa.
29. **Jimmy Tompkins, rhp, Texas**
30. **Mike Hamer, rhp, Texas**
31. **Bill Lucas, 2b/ss, Florida A&M**
32. **Lary Aaron, of, Florida A&M**
33. **Larry Moser, of, Parkland HS, Breinigsville, Pa.**
34. **Kyle Sanford, 1b, Texas Wesleyan**
35. **Brad Edelfson, rhp, Montevallo (Ala.)**
36. **Jeff Wagner, of, Round Rock (Texas) HS**

June—Secondary Phase (18)

1. John Wallace, of, Fresno CC
2. David Blair, c, Middle Georgia JC
3. **Keith Street, of, Middle Georgia JC**
4. **Robyn Lynch, 1b, Garden City (Kan.) CC**
5. Mike Fay, rhp, DeAnza (Calif.) JC

BALTIMORE ORIOLES

January—Regular Phase (25)

1. **Dave Corman, 2b, Hagerstown (Md.) JC**
2. **Rocky Cusack, 3b, Florida CC**
3. **David Gray, rhp, San Joaquin Delta (Calif.) JC**
4. **Anthony Wadley, rhp, Laney (Calif.) JC**
5. George Page, of, Los Angeles Valley JC
6. **Frank Ferroni, lhp, Canada (Calif.) JC**
7. Wayne Walker, ss, Florida CC
8. Brad Wheeler, lhp, Indian River (Fla.) CC
9. Michael Bayly, p, Florida CC
10. **Charles Guinn, rhp, Seminole State (Okla.) JC**

January—Secondary Phase (26)

1. **Tommy Alexander, rhp, Gordon (Ga.) JC**
2. Russ Kibler, 1b, Gulf Coast (Fla.) CC
3. Robert Link, rhp, Thomasville, Ga.
4. **Brian McDonough, rhp, Seminole (Okla.) CC**

June—Regular Phase (25)

1. (Pick to Red Sox as compensation for free agent Jim Dwyer)
2. (Pick to Twins as compensation for free agent Jose Morales)
3. **Jeff Lackie, lhp, McKinney (Texas) HS**
4. David Ledbetter, rhp/1b, Chipola (Fla.) JC
5. **Dave Falcone, 1b, Florida**
6. **John Mitcheltree, rhp, Old Dominion**
7. **Mark Butler, lhp, California Lutheran**
8. **John Tutt, of, Auburn**
9. **Don Cole, lhp, Columbus (Ga.)**
10. **Tony Arnold, rhp, Texas**
11. **Ron Cardieri, c, Florida**
12. **Jeff Schaefer, 2b, Maryland**
13. **Rich Rembielak, ss, Miami (Ohio)**
14. **Tandy Charley, lhp, Hoquiam HS, Taholah, Wash.**
15. Jeff Roberts, rhp, Lake Havasu (Ariz.) HS
16. **Charles Bertucio, of/lhp, Laney (Calif.) JC**
17. Alejandro Diaz, c, Jackson HS, Miami
18. **Brett Gold, rhp, La Salle**
19. Mark Dougherty, 2b, Scottsdale (Ariz.) CC
20. DeWayne Rosenbaum, rhp, Lipscomb
21. **Ron Kelly, 1b, Miami-Dade South CC**
22. Mike Snaidach, rhp, South Park HS, Library, Pa.
23. **Ralph Albano, 2b, Jacksonville**
24. Mike Knox, rhp, Memorial HS, Tulsa
25. **Lee Granger, of, UC Irvine**
26. **Oliver Mauli, c, Cape Henlopen HS, Lewes, Del.**
27. **Tim Riche, of, Howard**
28. Ken Sinclair, rhp, St. Francis (N.Y.)
29. Bart Bishop, rhp, Sunset HS, Miami
30. **Hubert Crumley, rhp, Edgewood (Md.) HS**
31. Cecil Fielder, 1b, Nogales HS, La Puente, Calif.
32. Larry Paskiewicz, 2b, Eastern Arizona JC
33. James Thomas, of, Boys Latin HS, Baltimore

June—Secondary Phase (7)

1. **Jim Rooney, lhp, CC of Morris (N.J.)**
2. **Randy Boyd, lhp, Cochise County (Ariz.) CC**
3. Rod Langston, of, Indian River (Fla.) CC

BOSTON RED SOX

January—Regular Phase (20)

1. **Danny Sheaffer, c, Harrisburg Area (Pa.) CC**
2. **Joe Arfstrom, of, Miami-Dade New World Center CC**
3. **David Scheller, lhp, Lewis & Clark (Ill.) JC**
4. Robyn Lynch, 1b, Garden City (Kan.) CC
5. Joey Farrill, rhp, Gulf Coast (Fla.) CC
6. Robert Meyer, rhp, Golden West (Calif.) JC
7. John Wallace, of, Fresno CC
8. **John Sorensen, rhp, Joliet (Ill.) JC**
9. **Steven Seaman, ss, CC of Beaver County (Pa.)**
10. Mark Wenzel, rhp, Fresno CC

January—Secondary Phase (22)

1. **Dave Malpeso, c, Miami-Dade North CC**
2. **Michael Jefferson, of, Contra Costa (Calif.) JC**

June—Regular Phase (19)

1. **Steve Lyons, ss/of, Oregon State**
1. **Kevin Burrell, c, Poway (Calif.) HS** (Pick from Orioles as compensation for free agent Jim Dwyer)
2. **Chris Howard, 2b, Boone HS, Orlando, Fla.**
3. **Rob Woodward, rhp, Lebanon (N.H.) HS**
4. **Todd Benzinger, 1b, New Richmond HS, Cincinnati**
5. **Peter Gonzales, of, San Leandro (Calif.) HS**
6. **Kevin Clinton, rhp, Kansas**
7. Kevin Fowler, ss, Donar HS, Stillwater, Okla.
8. **John Key, rhp, Central HS, Muskogee, Okla.**
9. **Charles Fisher, of, Jacksonville State**
10. **Craig Walck, 3b, Ursinus (Pa.)**
11. Peter Mancini, 2b, Memorial HS, West New York, N.J.
12. **Chuck Davis, rhp, Jacksonville State**
13. **Pat Castiglia, 1b, Eckerd (Fla.)**
14. **Willie Weston, rhp, Mississippi Valley State**
15. **Kevin Johnston, of, Logan HS, La Crosse, Wis.**
16. Troy Howerton, lhp, Arkansas City (Kan.) HS
17. **Bruce Lockhart, lhp, Brunswick (Maine) HS**
18. Jeff Achilles, rhp, Houston
19. **Bill Carpenter, ss, Brandeis (Mass.)**
20. Darryl Menard, rhp, Clearlake HS, Seabrook, Texas
21. Brian Smith, rhp, South HS, Weymouth, Mass.

June—Secondary Phase (9)

1. **Steve Ellsworth, rhp, Cal State Northridge**
2. **Tony Beal, of, Seminole (Fla.) CC**

CALIFORNIA ANGELS

January—Regular Phase (4)

1. **Kevin Price, rhp, Cosumnes River (Calif.) JC**
2. Mike Blair, c, Middle Georgia JC
3. David Velez, ss, Los Medanos (Calif.) JC
4. **Robert Gast, rhp, Clemson**
5. **Gary Robbins, of/rhp, Solano (Calif.) CC**
6. Bruce Hamrick, 3b, Hiwassee (Tenn.) JC
7. Brian Hartsock, c, Riverside (Calif.) CC
8. Ken Rebiejo, rhp, Ohlone (Calif.) JC
9. Darrell Higgs, rhp, Pima (Ariz.) CC
10. Ronald Bachmeier, 2b, Glendale (Calif.) JC
11. Richard Henkemeyer, lhp, Brainerd (Minn.) CC
12. Jeff Mace, of, Scottsdale (Ariz.) CC
13. Jim Sharp, lhp, Gloucester County (N.J.) JC
14. **Curt Mathe, 1b/of, Des Moines Area (Iowa) CC**
15. Bruce Miller, rhp/c, Des Moines Area (Iowa) CC
16. Kent Testerman, c, Los Angeles Valley JC

January—Secondary Phase (4)

1. **Ron Romanick, rhp, Arizona State**
2. Mike Hogan, rhp, Orange Coast (Calif.) JC
3. George Cook, 2b, Los Angeles CC
4. Craig Stevenson, ss, Los Angeles Valley JC

June—Regular Phase (3)

1. **Dick Schofield, ss, Griffin HS, Springfield, Ill.**
2. (Pick to Expos as compensation for free agent John D'Acquisto)
3. (Pick to Twins as compensation for free agent Geoff Zahn)
4. (Pick to Mariners as compensation for free agent Juan Beniquez)
5. (Pick to Brewers as compensation for free agent Bill Travers)
6. **Devon White, 3b, Park West HS, Manhattan, N.Y.**
7. **Lonnie Garza, ss, Texas-Pan American**
8. Joey Meyer, 1b, Punahou HS, Kailua, Hawaii
9. **Rick Turner, c, UC Riverside**
10. **Sap Randall, 1b, Grambling State**
11. **Rick Stromer, 3b, Grand Canyon (Ariz.)**
12. **Tim Kammeyer, rhp, Southern California**
13. **Buck Long, rhp, Texas Southern**
14. **Brad Withrow, rhp, Wyoming**
15. **Doug Lindsey, rhp, La Verne (Calif.)**
16. **Rick Sundberg, c, Santa Clara**
17. **Jeff Kennedy, of, Lamar**
18. **Dave Morris, of, Grand Canyon (Ariz.)**
19. **Bill Worden, c, Stanford**
20. **Craig Gerber, ss, Cal Poly San Luis Obispo**
21. **Mark Smelko, 1b, San Diego State**
22. **Lee Jones, rhp, Southern California**
23. **Scott Oliver, rhp, Bellarmine (Ky.)**
24. **Steve Eakes, ss, Cal State Sacramento**
25. **Joe King, rhp, La Verne (Calif.)**
26. **Darryl Stephens, of, Cal State Fullerton**
27. Kendall Walling, ss, Canyon (Texas) HS
28. **Thomas Dowies, rhp, McNeese State**
29. **Jack Crawford, of, Seminole State (Okla.) JC**
30. Tony DeFrancesco, c, Suffern HS, Monsey, N.Y.

June—Secondary Phase (26)

1. Reggie Montgomery, of, Orange Coast (Calif.) JC
2. Dick Seidel, rhp, Arizona
3. Jeff Mace, of, Scottsdale (Ariz.) CC
4. James Woods, ss, San Jacinto (Texas) JC

CHICAGO CUBS

January—Regular Phase (1)

1. Jim Rooney, lhp, CC of Morris (N.J.)
2. **Greg Trotter, rhp, Westark (Ark.) CC**
3. Craig Jenks, lhp, Butte (Calif.) JC
4. Tim Arnsberg, rhp, Merced (Calif.) JC
5. Clay Carter, rhp, JC of Southern Idaho
6. **Billy Hatcher, of, Yavapai (Ariz.) JC**
7. Robin Emerson, rhp, Bakersfield (Calif.) JC
8. George Martinez, rhp, Pasadena (Calif.) CC

January—Secondary Phase (7)

1. Nick Brandt, lhp, Merced (Calif.) JC
2. Gary Jensen, c, Solano (Calif.) CC
3. Ken Scott, rhp, Chaffey (Calif.) JC

June—Regular Phase (2)

1. **Joe Carter, of, Wichita State**
1. **Vance Lovelace, lhp, Hillsborough HS, Tampa** (Pick from Reds as compensation for free agent Larry Biittner)
2. **Darrin Jackson, of, Culver City (Calif.) HS**
3. **Mitch Cook, rhp, New Hanover HS, Wilmington, N.C.**
4. Randy Whisler, ss, Klamath Union HS, Klamath Falls, Ore.
5. **Rob Schilling, rhp, Pacific**
6. **Dave Rosenhahn, ss, SUNY Buffalo**
7. Steve Rousey, rhp, Crescenta Valley HS, La Crescenta, Calif.
8. **Trey Brooks, 2b, Texas Christian**
9. **Tom Isgett, rhp, McBee HS, Hartsville, S.C.**
10. **Anthony Colbert, of, Murphy (N.C.) HS**
11. Bill Hobbs, lhp, Arroyo HS, El Monte, Calif.
12. **Ken Emmert, 3b, Arcadia (Calif.) HS**
13. **Walter Beede, 1b, Fitchburg (Mass.) HS**
14. **Jim Adamczak, rhp, Arkansas Tech**
15. **Allen Black, rhp, Arizona State**
16. **Stan Webb, rhp, Washington State**
17. **Ron Kaufman, rhp, Davis & Elkins (W.Va.)**
18. **Otis Tramble, ss, Southern**
19. **Lawrence Wilson, of/1b, Redlands (Calif.) HS**
20. Jim Sherman, of, Delaware
21. **Robert Hook, lhp, Victor Valley (Calif.) CC**
22. **Pat Tobin, 1b, Pacific**
23. Mark Walberg, of, Indiana State
24. **Wendell Henderson, c, Grambling State**
25. **Jeff Andrews, rhp, East Tennessee State**
26. **Mark Nowlin, rhp, UC Santa Barbara**
27. **Lawrence Tribble, c, South Point HS, Belmont, N.C.**
28. Derril Lewis, lhp, San Bernardino Valley (Calif.) JC
29. **Lawrence McGee, 3b, Cal State Los Angeles**

June—Secondary Phase (10)

1. **Jeff Rutledge, ss, Fresno CC**
2. **Ron Bachmeier, 2b, Glendale (Calif.) JC**
3. Dean Naylor, rhp, Miami-Dade South CC

CHICAGO WHITE SOX

January—Regular Phase (8)

1. Reggie Montgomery, of, Orange Coast (Calif.) JC
2. Greg Griffin, of, Texas Southmost JC
3. James Twardowski, 3b, Blinn (Texas) JC
4. **John Moses, lhp, Houston**
5. Kevin Kollmansperger, rhp, McLennan (Texas) CC
6. **Ed Sedar, of/inf, JC of Lake County (Ill.)**
7. Bobby Joe Williams, ss, Panola (Texas) JC
8. Charlie Corbell, rhp, Blinn (Texas) JC
9. Mark Dennis, lhp, McLennan (Texas) CC
10. Dave Van Horn, 3b, McLennan (Texas) CC
11. Gary Jones, of, Paris (Texas) JC
12. Curtis Dishman, 1b, Blinn (Texas) JC
13. Alceed Owens, rhp, Texas Southmost JC
14. Michael Edwards, ss, Blinn (Texas) JC
15. Doug Galloway, rhp, Paris (Texas) JC
16. Joe Petty, rhp, Panola (Texas) JC

January—Secondary Phase (20)

1. **Scott Meier, c, San Joaquin Delta (Calif.) JC**
2. Frank Marrero, rhp, Miami-Dade South CC

June—Regular Phase (7)

1. **Daryl Boston, lhp/of, Woodward HS, Cincinnati**
2. (Pick to Athletics as compensation for free agent Jim Essian)
3. **Bill Babcock, lhp, Grosse Point North HS, Grosse Point Woods, Mich.**
4. **Craig Smajstrla, ss, Pearland (Texas) HS**
5. Greg McClain, 3b/of, Pasadena HS, Altadena, Calif.
6. **Max Diaz, 3b/rhp, American HS, Fremont, Calif.**
7. **Mike Withrow, rhp, Texas**
8. **Wade Rowdon, ss, Stetson**
9. **Greg Butler, rhp, Lodi HS, Lockeford, Calif.**
10. **Mike Tanzi, lhp, Florida Southern**
11. **Charles Epperson, of, Jackson State**
12. **Eddie Miles, of, Louisville**
13. **Al Jones, rhp, Alcorn State**
14. **Dave Yobs, of, Oral Roberts**
15. Mike Bertotti, ss, Lassen HS, Susanville, Calif.
16. **Kevin Jones, of, Lincoln HS, San Diego**
17. Richard Smith, ss, Vallejo (Calif.) HS
18. **Michael Buggs, of, California**
19. **Pat Adams, 1b, Detroit**
20. **Don Koch, c, Florida Southern**
21. **Jack Hardy, rhp, Biscayne (Fla.)**
22. **Jim Harris, of, Nevada**
23. Mark Heuer, rhp, Harper (Ill.) JC
24. **Jim Sutton, rhp, Cal State Fullerton**
25. **Mike Ledna, 2b, Purdue**
26. **Mike Nagle, ss, UC Irvine**
27. Steve Iannini, of, Colonial HS, Orlando
28. **Jason Costa, of, Castro Valley (Calif.) HS**
29. **Roger Stevens, of, Elgin (Ill.) CC**
30. La Vel Freeman, 1b, Kennedy HS, Sacramento
31. Richie Hines, 1b, Hill HS, Jackson, Miss.
32. Ed Vidmar, lhp, Arkansas
33. **Art Niemann, rhp, Louisiana Tech**
34. Mark Johnson, c, North Boone HS, Poplar Grove, Ill.
35. Roger Johnson, c, Parkway West HS, Ballwin, Mo.
36. **John Walsh, 2b, Westmount HS, Campbell, Calif.**
37. **Billy Gayton, 3b, Indian Hills (Iowa) CC**
38. Mike Toothman, of, Stanford

June—Secondary Phase (3)

1. Norman Morton, rhp, Miami-Dade North CC
2. John Leonard, p, Yavapai (Ariz.) JC

CINCINNATI REDS

January—Regular Phase (15)

1. Daniel Durst, rhp, Iowa Western CC
2. Damon Farmar, of, West Los Angeles JC
3. Randy Romagna, rhp, Indian River (Fla.) CC
4. Terrell Ayo, 2b, Linn-Benton (Ore.) CC
5. **John Minyard, rhp, Des Moines Area (Iowa) CC**
6. **Jackie Foley, of/1b, Edison (Fla.) CC**
7. **William Kincanon, rhp, Triton (Ill.) JC**

January—Secondary Phase (3)

1. **Rob Murphy, lhp, Miami**
2. **Tyson Hubbard, rhp, Spartanburg Methodist (S.C.) JC**
3. Derek Tatsuno, lhp, Aiea, Hawaii

June—Regular Phase (16)

1. (Pick to Cubs as compensation for free agent Larry Biittner)
2. **Lanell Culver, of, Palmdale (Calif.) HS**
3. **Delwyn Young, ss, Belmont HS, Los Angeles**
4. **Paul O'Neill, of, Brookhaven HS, Columbus, Ohio**
5. **Steve Padia, c, Wharton (Texas) HS**
6. **Guy Findeisen, rhp, South Plantation (Fla.) HS**
7. **Dexter Day, 3b/of, William Carey (Miss.)**
8. **Terry McGriff, c, Westwood HS, Fort Pierce, Fla.**
9. **Richard Johns, rhp, Sebring (Fla.) HS**
10. **Bubba Jennings, 2b, St. Edward's (Texas)**
11. Gerald Burton, rhp, Mater Dei HS, Santa Ana, Calif.
12. **Charlie Colclough, 1b, South Carolina-Aiken**
13. **Joe Stalp, rhp, Portland State**
14. Scott Ruskin, of, Sandalwood HS, Jacksonville, Fla.
15. **Jeff Rhodes, of/rhp, Poly Tech HS, Fort Worth**
16. **Tony Howell, of/1b, Central State (Ohio)**
17. Brian Blakely, 3b, Ambingdon (Va.) HS
18. **John Grier, of, Central Cabarrus HS, Concord, N.C.**
19. **Mark Matzen, 3b, Seton Hall**
20. **Michael Manfre, ss, Kean (N.J.)**
21. Michael Darby, rhp/ss, Rock Island (Ill.) HS
22. **Tom Riley, ss, Washington**
23. Dan Whelan, rhp, Catholic HS, Lexington, Ky.
24. **Gerardo Macias, lhp, New Mexico State**
25. Vince Bargar, lhp, San Joaquin Memorial HS, Firebaugh, Calif.
26. **John Groninger, c, Northern Colorado**
27. Jeff Datz, c, Glassboro State (N.J.)
28. **Tom Pillar, 3b/of, Northern Colorado**
29. Ronald Johnson, of, Garfield HS, Seattle
30. **Tim Dodd, rhp, Cleveland (Tenn.) HS**
31. **Ron Carapezzi, 3b, Fairfield**
32. Alan Koonce, rhp, Robert E. Lee HS, Midland, Texas
33. **Gary Desa, ss, Damien HS, Honolulu**
34. Dana Williams, ss, Davidson HS, Mobile, Ala.
35. Greg Key, 2b, Montevallo (Ala.)
36. Arthur Pigg, 2b, Garfield HS, Seattle

June—Secondary Phase (24)

1. Don Long, ss, Edmonds (Wash.) CC
2. **Don Fenton, rhp, Lower Columbia (Wash.) JC**
3. Randy Romagna, rhp, Indian River (Fla.) CC

CLEVELAND INDIANS

January—Regular Phase (14)

1. **Steve Cushing, lhp, St. Leo (Fla.)**
2. Todd Wenberg, rhp, Waldorf (Iowa) JC
3. Dennis Van Loren, rhp, Cochise County (Ariz.) CC
4. Jim Opie, 3b/of, Valencia (Fla.) CC
5. **Dane Clark, rhp, Gloucester County (N.J.) JC**
6. Anthony Virgo, rhp, Contra Costa (Calif.) JC
7. **James Pool, c, Kansas Newman**

January—Secondary Phase (10)

1. **John Tillema, rhp, San Jose, Calif.**
2. James Miley, c, Montgomery (Md.) JC
3. Alan Peel, c, Sacramento CC

June—Regular Phase (13)

1. **George Alpert, of, Livingston (N.J.) HS**
2. **Neal Heaton, lhp, Miami**
3. (Pick forfeited for right to select Billy Cannon in special 1980 draft)
4. **Randy Washington, of, Stagg HS, Stockton, Calif.**
5. **Rich Doyle, rhp, Neff HS, La Mirada, Calif.**
6. Matt Kinzer, rhp, Norwell HS, Ossian, Ind.
7. **Dwight Taylor, of, Arizona**

8. **Brian Silvas, rhp, Miami**
9. Tommy Gregg, of, Reynolds HS, Winston-Salem, N.C.
10. **Wayne Johnson, lhp, Orange Park (Fla.) HS**
11. Terry Wells, lhp, Westview HS, Kankakee, Ill.
12. Jeff Bassett, of, Willoughby Hills (Ohio) HS
13. Steve Gelmine, lhp, New Providence (N.J.) HS
14. Jim Paciorek, of, Michigan
15. **Scott Collins, 2b, Missouri**
16. Stan Yagiello, ss, Livingston (N.J.) HS
17. **John Merchant, 1b, The Kings (N.J.)**
18. **Phil Deriso, lhp, Auburn**
19. Brad Arnsberg, rhp, Medford (Ore.) HS
20. **Michael Poindexter, rhp, Jackson HS, Charleston, W.Va.**
21. Chuck Jackson, ss, Ingraham HS, Seattle
22. James Warner, of, Friendly HS, Oxon Hill, Md.
23. Bill Cutshall, rhp, Mayo HS, Rochester, Minn.
24. Keith Miller, ss, Bay City (Mich.) All Saints HS
25. Jim O'Dell, 1b, Lower Columbia (Wash.) JC
26. Geoff Redgrave, lhp, Thomas Wooten HS, Rockville, Md.

June—Secondary Phase (23)

1. Ted Perkins, of, El Cerrito, Calif.
2. **Sam Martin, ss, Louisburg (N.C.) JC**

DETROIT TIGERS

January—Regular Phase (18)

1. Jeff Rutledge, ss, Fresno CC
2. Everett Graham, of, Louisburg (N.C.) JC
3. Johnny Hatcher, of, Yavapai (Ariz.) JC
4. Mike Sharperson, ss, DeKalb South (Ga.) CC
5. **Laurence Berthelson, rhp, Los Angeles Valley JC**
6. **James Ross, rhp, Henry Ford (Mich.) CC**
7. Herb McManaway, of/1b, St. Clair County (Mich.) CC

January—Secondary Phase (2)

1. **Bob Melvin, c, Canada (Calif.) JC**
2. **Donald O'Connor, rhp, Chabot (Calif.) JC**

June—Regular Phase (17)

1. **Ricky Barlow, rhp, Woodville (Texas) HS**
2. **Nelson Simmons, of, Madison HS, San Diego**
3. **Bob Williamson, c, Catholic Central HS, Redford, Mich.**
4. **Bubby Brister, ss, Neville HS, Monroe, La.**
5. **Stan Barker, of, Alcorn State**
6. **Bryan Kelly, rhp, Alabama**
7. **Chuck Cary, lhp, California**
8. **Reggie Thomas, of, Arkansas**
9. **George Miguel, lhp, Grady Vocational HS, Brooklyn**
10. David Flattery, rhp, Iowa State
11. **Mark Lockenmeyer, rhp/of, Princeton**
12. **Albert Silva, 1b, Catholic HS, Tampa**
13. Rob Clark, lhp, Southern Illinois
14. **Scott Earl, 2b, Eastern Kentucky**
15. Tom Brassil, ss, Duke
16. **Mark Jacob, rhp, Detroit**
17. **Steve Haynes, of, Alabama Christian**
18. **Robert McFadden, rhp, Wooster (Ohio)**
19. Don Rowland, ss, Bishop Gallagher HS, St. Clair Shores, Mich.
20. **Bryon Horn, 2b, Eastern Michigan**
21. **Kraig Priessman, c, Northwest HS, Cincinnati**
22. **Greg Norman, 1b, UCLA**
23. **Chris Goodyear, 3b, Hillsborough (Fla.) CC**
24. Robert Yeager, 3b, Piscataway (N.J.) HS
25. Barry Lyons, c, Delta State (Miss.)
26. Randal Gorgon, rhp, Eastern Michigan
27. **Dan Phillip, c, Ashland (Ohio)**
28. Jim Phelps, rhp, Saline (Mich.) HS
29. **Bruce Franklin, 2b, Coastal Carolina**
30. **Jim Moriarty, of, South Weymouth (Mass.) HS**
31. Billy DeWitt, rhp, Broadmoor HS, Baton Rouge, La.
32. **Jon Zureich, 1b, Eastern Michigan**

June—Secondary Phase (15)

1. **Randy O'Neal, rhp, Florida**
2. **Ernie Moya, rhp, Hillsborough (Fla.) CC**
3. **Tom Corcoran, rhp, Florida International**

HOUSTON ASTROS

January—Regular Phase (23)

1. Trent Ferrin, rhp, JC of Southern Idaho
2. Michael Fay, rhp, DeAnza (Calif.) JC
3. Johnny Salery, of, Indian River (Fla.) CC
4. John Bryant, of, Santa Ana (Calif.) JC
5. Joe Wendolowski, ss, CC of Morris (N.J.)

January—Secondary Phase (5)

1. **Glenn Davis, 1b/of, Manatee (Fla.) JC**
2. Don Long, ss, Edmonds (Wash.) CC
3. Dean Naylor, rhp, Miami-Dade South CC

June—Regular Phase (24)

1. (Pick to Rangers as compensation for free agent Dave Roberts)
2. (Pick to Dodgers as compensation for free agent Don Sutton)
3. **Curtis Burke, of, Tennessee State**
4. **Ben Snyder, rhp, St. Mary's**
5. **Steve McAllister, ss, Bradley**
6. Mike Rubel, 1b, Cal State Fullerton
7. **Russell Blaylock, 3b, Kansas**
8. **Henry Janssen, c, Seton Hall**
9. **Larry Simcox, ss, Mississippi**
10. **Geoff Meadows, rhp, Slippery Rock (Pa.)**
11. **Don Berti, c, Pfeiffer (N.C.)**
12. **Randy Braun, of, Missouri Southern State**
13. **Phil Smith, 2b, Lewis-Clark State (Idaho)**
14. Stu Foulks, rhp, Mercer County (N.J.) CC
15. **Hank Clark, 3b, Cal State Northridge**
16. **Mike Callahan, rhp, North Adams State (Mass.)**
17. **Mark Clinton, rhp, Michigan**
18. **Mitch Copion, rhp, Oklahoma State**
19. **David Malloy, lhp, Rider**
20. **Don Mundie, rhp, Mississippi State**
21. Jim Harkins, lhp, Eastern Kentucky
22. **Greg Mize, rhp, Broward (Fla.) CC**
23. **Rex Schimpf, rhp, Louisiana Tech**
24. **Joe Ferrante, rhp, San Diego State**
25. **Glenn Carpenter, of, Florida**
26. **Roger Godwin, rhp, Georgia Southern**
27. **Ed Reilly, rhp, Seton Hall**
28. **Ira Lane, of, Texas Southern**

June—Secondary Phase (20)

1. **Eric Bullock, of, Los Angeles Harbor JC**
2. **Bobby Falls, ss, Walters State (Tenn.) CC**

KANSAS CITY ROYALS

January—Regular Phase (24)

1. **Rick Rizzo, of, Mesa State (Colo.)**
2. **Thomas McHugh, 1b, Iowa Western CC**
3. **James Brittman, 1b, Chicago**
4. **James Minor, rhp, Fullerton (Calif.) JC**
5. Dave Johnson, rhp, CC of Baltimore
6. **Tracy Hall, of, Detroit**
7. Russ Morman, of, Iowa Western CC
8. Carl Davis, of, Detroit
9. Jeff Kobernus, lhp, Laney (Calif.) JC
10. **Bill Pecota, 3b, DeAnza (Calif.) JC**
11. **John Antonelli, c, CC of Baltimore**
12. **David Spalt, ss, Patterson HS, Baltimore**
13. Craig Stump, 3b, CC of Baltimore

January—Secondary Phase (24)

1. **Mitch Ashmore, c, Centenary**
2. Steven Anderson, 3b, West Los Angeles JC
3. John Stevens, rhp, Los Angeles Valley JC

June—Regular Phase (23)

1. **Dave Leeper, of, Southern California**
2. **Mark Gubicza, rhp, Penn Charter HS, Philadelphia** (Pick from Cardinals as compensation for free agent Darrell Porter)
2. **Tony Ferreira, lhp, North HS, Riverside, Calif.**
3. **David Cone, rhp, Rockhurst HS, Kansas City, Mo.**
4. Shane Mack, ss, Gahr HS, Cerritos, Calif.

5. **Marty Wilkerson, 3b, Southern California**
6. **Nick Harsh, rhp, San Diego State**
7. **John Davis, rhp, Centennial HS, Pueblo, Colo.**
8. **Warren Skelton, ss, Harrison HS, Evansville, Ind.**
9. **John Bryant, rhp, La Verne (Calif.)**
10. **Randy Smith, c, Vallejo (Calif.) HS**
11. **Warren Oliver, ss, Texas Christian**
12. Mark Williamson, rhp, San Diego State
13. Lex Bleckley, ss, Pennsville (N.J.) HS
14. Robert Merenda, of, San Juan HS, Orangeville, Calif.
15. **Stan Palmore, of, Vocational HS, Chicago**
16. **Joe Citari, 1b, Oak Park (Ill.) HS**
17. Rich Rodriguez, lhp, Mount View HS, El Monte, Calif.
18. Ken Spratke, rhp, Chippewa Valley HS, Mount Clemens, Mich.
19. **Tom Mohr, of, Rib Lake (Wis.) HS**
20. **Mitch Hawley, rhp, California**
21. **Tom Thompson, 1b, Georgia Tech**
22. **Perry Swanson, rhp, Texas A&M**
23. Pat Saitta, rhp, Salesian HS, Bronx, N.Y.
24. **Rick Plautz, of, Grand Canyon (Ariz.)**
25. **Marty Martino, of, Indiana State**
26. Jay Phillips, 2b, Virginia Tech
27. **Mark Bloomfield, lhp, Nevada-Las Vegas**
28. Mark Solz, of, Santana HS, Santee, Calif.
29. Glen Gwaltney, of, Sylvan Hills HS, North Little Rock, Ark.
30. **Meade Langhorne, of, Richmond**
31. **Don Seeker, of, Miami (Ohio)**
32. **Bill Gaunce, c, William Carey (Miss.)**
33. **Allen Peake, 1b, Stafford (Va.) HS**
34. **Richard Sielicki, rhp, Bothell HS, Seattle**

June—Secondary Phase (21)

1. **Reggie Wyatt, rhp, Santa Monica (Calif.) JC**

LOS ANGELES DODGERS

January—Regular Phase (21)

1. Kevin White, rhp, Cosumnes River (Calif.) JC
2. **Robert Seymour, of/3b, Sacramento CC**
3. **Frederick Bass, 3b, Sacramento CC**
4. **John Sylvia, ss, JC of the Sequoias (Calif.)**
5. Jack Lopp, 1b, Pasadena (Calif.) CC
6. **Eugene Steinbach, c, DeKalb South (Ga.) CC**
7. Brad Harlow, ss/3b, Cosumnes River (Calif.) JC
8. Brett Ragland, rhp, Valencia (Fla.) CC
9. Jon Van Dort, of/1b, Chaffey (Calif.) JC
10. Larry Riddle, rhp, Alvin (Texas) CC
11. Andy Hargrove, rhp, Barstow (Calif.) CC
12. James Sewell, of, Sacramento CC
13. Ronnie Chapman, 2b, Louisburg (N.C.) JC
14. James Woods, inf, San Jacinto (Texas) JC
15. Charles Byers, 3b, Chaffey (Calif.) JC
16. Benny Distefano, 1b, Alvin (Texas) CC

January—Secondary Phase (21)

1. **Shayne Hammond, lhp, Southeastern (N.C.) CC**
2. Tom DiCeglio, ss, Gulf Coast (Fla.) CC

June—Regular Phase (22)

1. **Dave Anderson, ss, Memphis State**
2. **Sid Bream, 1b, Liberty**
2. **Lemmie Miller, of, Arizona State** (Pick from Astros as compensation for free agent Don Sutton)
3. **Sid Fernandez, lhp, Kaiser HS, Honolulu**
4. **Steve Boncore, c, La Verne (Calif.)**
5. **John Franco, lhp, St. John's**
6. **Brian Williams, of, South HS, Bakersfield, Calif.**
7. **Mike Beuder, lhp, Santa Clara**
8. **Greg Chinn, of, Cal State Sacramento**
9. **Stu Pederson, of, Southern California**
10. Mark Pirruccello, c, Cal State Fullerton
11. **Greg Carne, rhp, Redondo HS, Torrance, Calif.**
12. **Peyton Mosher, rhp, Georgia**
13. **David Anderson, rhp, Nevada**
14. **Dean Rennicke, rhp, Wisconsin**
15. **Jimmy Guillen, rhp, Roosevelt HS, Los Angeles**
16. **Harold Perkins, ss, Cal State Los Angeles**
17. **Chris Chavez, ss, Nebraska**
18. **Jerry Bendorf, ss, Gonzaga**
19. **Jeff Greene, ss, Vermont**
20. Tim Criswell, rhp, Carrollton (Ga.) HS
21. **John Gregory, 1b, Lake Worth (Fla.) HS**
22. **Craig Thompson, of, Dallas Baptist**
23. **Bill Murray, 2b, San Francisco**
24. **Steve Young, of, Chambersburg (Pa.) HS**
25. Robert Philps, rhp, Carmichaels (Pa.) HS
26. **Charles Beard, rhp/3b, Cal State Sacramento**
27. David Dunlap, inf/of, Cal State Sacramento
28. Brett Davis, of, Pearland (Texas) HS
29. Jeff Carter, inf, Evanston (Ill.) HS
30. Ronnie Robbins, rhp, Louisiana State-Alexandria JC

June—Secondary Phase (22)

1. **Ralph Bryant, of, Abraham Baldwin Agricultural (Ga.) JC**
2. **Mike Moore, c, Edmonds (Wash.) CC**
3. Ethan McHenry, rhp, Yakima Valley (Wash.) JC

MILWAUKEE BREWERS

January—Regular Phase (22)

1. **Dewey James, of, Central Arizona JC**
2. **Tim Crews, rhp, Valencia (Fla.) CC**
3. **Mike Felder, 2b, Contra Costa (Calif.) JC**
4. John Thornton, c, CC of Baltimore
5. Michael Hakala, rhp, Yakima Valley (Wash.) JC
6. **Jeff Schultz, rhp, Atheus, Pa.**
7. Bruce Kipper, 1b, Scottsdale (Ariz.) CC
8. Phillip Chilton, rhp, Scottsdale (Ariz.) CC
9. Gene Morgan, rhp, Middle Georgia JC
10. Phil Lane, 3b, Broward (Fla.) CC
11. **Gary Evans, rhp, Morrisville, Pa.**
12. **Chris Fedor, rhp, Cuyahoga (Ohio) CC**
13. Scott Davis, c, Fullerton (Calif.) JC
14. Irvin Anderson, rhp/of, Mount Olive (N.C.) JC
15. **Don Carfino, 3b, Bellflower, Calif.**
16. Wade Jannsen, rhp, Central Arizona JC
17. Jeffrey Hutchinson, rhp, Indian Hills (Iowa) JC
18. James Kelly, lhp, El Camino (Calif.) JC
19. Ethan McHenry, rhp, Yakima Valley (Wash.) JC

January—Secondary Phase (14)

1. **Mike Samuel, ss, Orange Coast (Calif.) JC**
2. Keith Mucha, 3b, Granada Hills, Calif.
3. **Ernest Riles, ss, Middle Georgia JC**
4. Audrey Robinson, of, Foothill (Calif.) JC
5. Jeffrey Johnson, rhp, Pasadena, Calif.
6. Richie Carter, of, Umpqua (Ore.) CC

June—Regular Phase (21)

1. (Pick to Blue Jays as compensation for free agent Roy Howell)
2. **Scott Roberts, rhp, Hawaii**
3. **Dan Davidsmeier, ss, Southern California**
4. **Bruce Williams, rhp, West Linn (Ore.) HS**
5. **Collin Tanabe, c, Hawaii** (Pick from Angels as compensation for free agent Bill Travers)
5. **Bill Wegman, rhp, Oak Hills HS, Cincinnati**
6. **Rich Embser, lhp, Bloomfield (N.J.)**
7. **Bryan Clutterbuck, rhp, Eastern Michigan**
8. **Dave Hoff, rhp/1b, Pittsburgh-Johnstown**
9. **Dan Burns, rhp, Cal State Fullerton**
10. Todd Morgan, lhp, Dinwiddie HS, Church Road, Va.
11. Ron Sismondo, lhp, Arizona
12. Bobby Alexander, lhp, Cardinal Gibbons HS, Baltimore
13. **Randy McFarlen, of, Cal Poly Pomona**
14. Dean Albany, rhp, Brooklyn (Md.) HS
15. **Mike Villegas, rhp, Grand Canyon (Ariz.)**
16. Jeff Ballard, lhp, Billings (Mont.) West HS
17. Jeff McNally, ss, Billings (Mont.) West HS
18. **Mike Myerchin, lhp, Cal State Dominguez Hills**
19. **Jim Teahan, rhp, Utah**
20. **Stan Borosky, c, Buckeye South HS, Rayland, Ohio**
21. **Barry McPherson, rhp, St. Louis CC-Meramec**

22. **Charles Dinkins, lhp, Southern**
23. **Eric Peyton, of, Cal Poly San Luis Obispo**
24. **Bart Brainard, c/of, San Diego**
25. Scott Campbell, lhp, Los Angeles Pierce JC
26. Greg Brandenburg, rhp, Lafayette HS, Ballwin, Mo.
27. Tom Rasinski, ss, Villa Park (Calif.) HS
28. Bart Elbin, rhp, Southern Fulton HS, Warfordsburg, Pa.
29. Ken Cerf, of, Gilman HS, Baltimore

June—Secondary Phase (19)

1. John Thornton, 1b/c, CC of Baltimore
2. Frank Marrero, rhp, Miami-Dade North CC
3. Rick Knapp, rhp, Indian River (Fla.) CC

MINNESOTA TWINS

January—Regular Phase (12)

1. Peter Kutsukos, rhp, Seminole (Fla.) CC
2. **Cedric Gray, of, Canada (Calif.) JC**
3. **Talbot Aiello, inf/of, Miami-Dade North CC**
4. Robin Thompson, rhp, Santa Monica (Calif.) JC
5. Dan Devers, rhp, Yavapai (Ariz.) JC
6. Steve Shields, of, Santa Monica (Calif.) JC
7. **Art Valencia, rhp, Cerritos (Calif.) JC**
8. **Michael Kribell, lhp, Irene, S.D.**
9. Steve Davis, of, Middle Georgia JC
10. Jeff Sutterfield, rhp, Orange Coast (Calif.) JC
11. Brian Kubala, rhp/3b, Miami-Dade North CC
12. Ignacio Velazquez, inf/c, Miami-Dade North CC
13. Ralph Bryant, of, Abraham Baldwin Agricultural (Ga.) JC
14. Ernie Moya, rhp, Hillsborough (Fla.) CC

January—Secondary Phase (25)

1. **Rhett Whisman, ss, Gulf Coast (Fla.) CC**
2. Mike O'Hara, rhp, West Covina, Calif.

June—Regular Phase (11)

1. **Mike Sodders, 3b, Arizona State**
2. **Frank Viola, lhp, St. John's**
2. **Craig Henderson, lhp, Wisconsin-Oshkosh** (Pick from Orioles as compensation for free agent Jose Morales)
3. John Marzano, c, Central HS, Philadelphia (Pick from Angels as compensation for free agent Geoff Zahn)
3. **Curt Wardle, lhp, UC Riverside** (Pick from Mets as compensation for free agent Mike Cubbage)
3. **Eric Broersma, rhp, UCLA**
4. **Paul Fleming, of, St. John HS, Garyville, La.**
5. **Dave Meier, ss, Stanford**
6. **George Skeens, c, Ramapo (N.J.)**
7. **Jeff Arney, rhp, UC Riverside**
8. **Stan Holmes, of, Arizona State**
9. **Steve Lombardozzi, ss, Florida**
10. **Ken Proctor, of, Cal Poly Pomona**
11. Tom Schubert, lhp, Peekskill (N.Y.) HS
12. **Steve Korczyk, rhp, Upsala (N.J.)**
13. **Herb Carter, of, St. John HS, Garyville, La.**
14. **Mike Weiermiller, lhp, Rochester (N.Y.)**
15. **Sebby Borriello, c, St. John's**
16. **Mike McCain, inf, Arizona State**
17. **Carson Carroll, 2b, UC Irvine**
18. **David Hoyt, of, New Haven (Conn.)**
19. **Jim Flores, ss, Fresno State**
20. **Mike Giordano, rhp, New Haven (Conn.)**
21. **Albert Everett, rhp, Hillsborough HS, Tampa**
22. **Gerry Lomastro, of, Louisiana Tech**
23. **Dean Kappes, c, Breckenridge HS, Kent, Minn.**
24. **Randy Weibel, rhp, Eastern Illinois**
25. Bill Blount, lhp, Hoover HS, San Diego
26. George Flower, 3b, Calvert Hall HS, Baltimore
27. **Robert Heimerl, of, Sibley HS, West St. Paul, Minn.**
28. Rick Hazard, of, UC Riverside
29. **Gary Robertson, 1b, Cal State Stanislaus**
30. Rob Vodvarka, lhp, Montclair HS, Upland, Calif.
31. **Marc Page, rhp, Riverview HS, Sarasota, Fla.**
32. **Mike Piatnik, ss, Florida Southern**
33. Michael Watson, of, Delgado (La.) JC
34. Gary Jost, 2b, Minnesota

June—Secondary Phase (13)

1. **Johnny Salery, of, Indian River (Fla.) CC**
2. Jeff Salazar, rhp, Los Angeles Valley JC

MONTREAL EXPOS

January—Regular Phase (17)

1. Bruce Crabbe, inf, Gulf Coast (Fla.) CC
2. Mark De LaTorre, lhp, Los Angeles Harbor JC
3. Glenn Davis, 1b/of, Middle Georgia JC
4. Steve Oliverio, rhp, Cumberlands (Ky.) JC
5. **Ricky Lemon, of, Paul Quinn (Texas)**
6. Cal Santarelli, rhp, Edison (Fla.) CC
7. Jeffrey French, of, Central Arizona JC
8. **Barry Branam, rhp, Cincinnati**
9. John Olsen, of, St. Clair County (Mich.) CC
10. Albie Scoggins, of, Indian River (Fla.) CC
11. Steve Lusby, 1b, Manatee (Fla.) JC
12. Doug Birkoffer, 2b, Cumberlands (Ky.) JC
13. Shane O'Shea, inf, Indian River (Fla.) CC
14. Frank Russo, inf, Indian River (Fla.) CC
15. **Thomas Fettig, 3b, Pensacola (Fla.) JC**
16. **Paul LeMire, of/1b, Northeastern**
17. **Robert Graves, rhp, Cowley County (Kan.) CC**
18. Jeff Treadway, 2b, Middle Georgia JC

January—Secondary Phase (23)

1. Reggie Wyatt, lhp, Santa Monica (Calif.) JC
2. Michael Winbush, rhp, Winston-Salem State

June—Regular Phase (18)

1. **Darren Dilks, lhp, Oklahoma State**
2. **Jeff Carl, ss, Wisconsin-Oshkosh** (Pick from Angels as compensation for free agent John D'Acquisto)
2. **Mike Fuentes, of, Florida State**
3. Nelson Santovenia, c, Miami-Dade South CC
4. Jeff Ledbetter, 1b, Florida State
5. Phil Stephenson, 1b, Wichita State
6. **Bobby Doerrer, 2b, Southern Illinois**
7. **Steve Yenser, rhp, Northern Kentucky**
8. Mark McGwire, rhp/1b, Damien HS, Claremont, Calif.
9. Marvin Freeman, rhp, Vocational HS, Chicago
10. **Craig Corbett, of, Lenoir-Rhyne (N.C.)**
11. **Mike Norment, c, Middle Tennessee State**
12. **Don Carter, of, Arkansas**
13. **Tom Ellis, of, Southeastern Oklahoma State**
14. Jose Pena, ss, Blair HS, Altadena, Calif.
15. **Dan Hoskins, ss, Falmouth, Ky.**
16. **Mike Vaughn, c, Alabama-Birmingham**
17. Gerry Melillo, c, Eckerd (Fla.)
18. Craig Koslowski, rhp, St. Francis de Sales HS, Chicago
19. **John Damon, 2b, Pepperdine**
20. **Paul Hertzler, 1b, Cal Poly San Luis Obispo**
21. **Derrell Baker, 3b, Georgia Southern**
22. **Randy Budd, rhp, Akron**
23. **Ron Gilbreath, rhp, Southeastern Oklahoma State**
24. **Willie Cooley, of, Cal State Long Beach**
25. Gene Walter, lhp, Eastern Kentucky
26. **Jerome Coleman, of, Jacksonville State**
27. Carlos Hidalgo, rhp, Texas-Pan American
28. **Hardy Dotson, of, Texas Wesleyan**
29. **Dan Flattery, c, Iowa State**
30. Mike King, c, Jackson State
31. **Tyris Suggs, c, Lane (Tenn.)**
32. **Kevin McDaniel, ss, Troy State**
33. **Fred Mitchell, rhp, Cal State Dominguez Hills**
34. Allen Harp, c, Coronado HS, Lubbock, Texas
35. **Elliott Skorupa, rhp, Eastern Illinois**
36. David Czosek, rhp, South Alabama
37. **Charlie Scott, rhp, Jackson State**
38. **Chris Campbell, 1b, Texas**

June—Secondary Phase (12)

1. **Al Newman, 2b, San Diego State**
2. **Jim McIntosh, rhp, Carl Albert (Okla.) JC**

3. Michael Winbush, rhp, Winston-Salem State

NEW YORK METS

January—Regular Phase (3)

1. **Randy Milligan, of, San Diego Mesa JC**
2. **Steve Ray, lhp, Southwestern (Calif.) JC**
3. Rey Tolentino, rhp, Chaffey (Calif.) JC
4. Dodd Hook, 1b, Indian Hills (Iowa) CC
5. **Jim Cazet, ss, Modesto (Calif.) JC**
6. Greg Cary, rhp, Chabot (Calif.) JC
7. Craig Walter, rhp, Waldorf (Iowa) JC
8. **Tim Hampton, rhp, Modesto (Calif.) JC**
9. Brian Pate, inf/of, Columbia State (Tenn.) CC
10. William Bankhead, 3b, Green River (Wash.) CC
11. Roger Lee, of/1b, Garden City (Kan.) CC
12. **Greg Shirley, c, Alabama Christian**
13. **Robert Smith, inf/of, Sanford, Fla.**

January—Secondary Phase (9)

1. **Herm Winningham, of, DeKalb South (Ga.) CC**
2. Billy Irions, lhp, Seminole State (Okla.) JC
3. Nick Esposito, rhp, Los Medanos (Calif.) JC

June—Regular Phase (4)

1. **Terry Blocker, of, Tennessee State**
2. (Pick to Rangers as compensation for free agent Rusty Staub)
2. **John Christensen, of, Cal State Fullerton** (Pick from Braves as compensation for free agent Claudell Washington)
3. (Pick to Twins as compensation for free agent Mike Cubbage)
4. **Dave Cochrane, rhp/3b, Troy HS, Yorba Linda, Calif.**
5. **Steve Phillips, ss, De La Salle HS, Detroit**
6. **Ken Harris, ss/of, La Verne (Calif.)**
7. Jeff Keeler, rhp, Florida State
8. **Mark Carreon, of, Salpointe HS, Tucson, Ariz.**
9. **Rich Webster, rhp, Memphis State**
10. Albert Candelaria, lhp, Yerba Buena HS, San Jose
11. **Steve Walker, rhp, Mount Carmel HS, San Diego**
12. Roger Clemens, rhp, San Jacinto (Texas) JC
13. **Lenny Dykstra, of, Garden Grove (Calif.) HS**
14. Gary Kanwisher, rhp, Pascack HS, Hillsdale, N.J.
15. **Larry McNutt, 1b, Jackson State**
16. Ron Woellert, rhp, Moeller HS, Cincinnati
17. Bryan Olden, 2b, Beaverton (Ore.) HS
18. **Ed Garton, 3b, Iowa**
19. **Lou Thornton, 3b, Jefferson Davis HS, Hopehull, Ala.**
20. Mark Boyd, c, McEachern HS, Powder Springs, Ga.
21. **Steve Slaton, rhp, Long Beach State**
22. **Matthew Fitts, rhp, Lompoc (Calif.) HS**
23. Kurt Griffon, of, Plaquemine (La.) HS
24. **Bob Costello, c, New York Tech**
25. **Russell Orrick, of, Vintage HS, Napa, Calif.**
26. **Randy Hoffman, of, Southeastern Louisiana**
27. **James Oates, lhp, Huntington**
28. **Joe Licata, of/3b, Florida State**
29. Gary Heien, rhp, O'Fallon (Ill.) HS
30. **Michael Franks, 2b, Loyola Marymount**
31. **Mike Harlander, rhp, Nebraska**
32. **Steve DeMatties, c, Ithaca (N.Y.)**
33. Luis Medina, of, Warren HS, Downey, Calif.
34. **Bruce Kastelic, ss, Oklahoma State**
35. **Louis Martinez, c, DeWitt Clinton HS, Bronx, N.Y.**
36. Darrell Rodgers, rhp, Eisenhower HS, Lawton, Okla.
37. **Larry Czeszewski, c, Midwestern State (Texas)**
38. **Scott Holiday, of, Middle Tennessee State**

June—Secondary Phase (14)

1. **John Felice, of, JC of the Canyons (Calif.)**
2. **Gail Arnold, rhp, Brigham Young**
3. Greg Griffin, of, Corpus Christi, Texas
4. Kevin Sliwinski, of, Orange Coast (Calif.) JC
5. Greg Cary, rhp, Chabot (Calif.) JC

NEW YORK YANKEES

January—Regular Phase (26)

1. **Mike Gatlin, of, Lurleen Wallace (Ala.) JC**
2. **Ed Darling, 1b, Millbury, Mass.**
3. Kurt Eskildsen, rhp, Los Angeles Harbor JC
4. **Mark Blaser, 3b, Butte (Calif.) JC**
5. **Johnny Hawkins, c, Pensacola (Fla.) JC**
6. **Boyce Bailey, rhp, Pensacola (Fla.) JC**
7. David Niemiec, rhp, San Jose CC
8. **Howard Maynor, 3b, Merced (Calif.) JC**
9. Millard Williams, 1b, Solano (Calif.) CC
10. David Aragon, ss, Santa Barbara (Calif.) CC
11. **Mike Isherwood, c, JC of the Sequoias (Calif.)**
12. Eric Call, 1b/of, Palm Beach (Fla.) JC
13. Rick Knapp, rhp, Indian River (Fla.) CC
14. Donald Bragg, of, Lurleen Wallace (Ala.) JC
15. Jeffrey Allen, rhp, Truman (Ill.) JC
16. Brent Main, rhp, JC of the Sequoias (Calif.)
17. Kevin Bascue, of/1b, Garden City (Kan.) CC
18. Mike Costello, rhp, Centralia (Wash.) JC
19. Kelly Pfaller, of, Lane (Ore.) CC

January—Secondary Phase (16)

1. Rod Langston, of, Indian River (Fla.) CC
2. Todd Schulz, of, Central Arizona JC
3. Brian Peck, rhp, JC of Southern Idaho
4. Randy Edwards, lhp, Allegany (Md.) CC

June—Regular Phase (26)

1. (Pick to Padres as compensation for free agent Dave Winfield)
2. **John Elway, of, Stanford**
3. **Scott Bradley, c, North Carolina** (Pick from Braves as compensation for free agent Gaylord Perry)
3. **Phil Lombardi, c, Kennedy HS, Granada Hills, Calif.**
4. **Eric Plunk, rhp, Bellflower (Calif.) HS**
5. Dennis Lubert, lhp, South Carolina
6. **Mike Pagliarulo, 3b, Miami**
7. **Andy Swope, rhp, Otterbein**
8. John Fishel, of, Loara HS, Anaheim
9. **Fred McGriff, 1b, Jefferson HS, Tampa**
10. **Matt Gallegos, ss, San Francisco State**
11. **Tom Jones, of, UNC Wilmington**
12. **David Repass, lhp, Louisburg (N.C.) JC**
13. **David Woodworth, lhp, Western Michigan**
14. **Mike Browning, rhp, Miami**
15. **Mike Reddish, c/of, Florida International**
16. **Mike Speeney, ss, Council Rock HS, Holland, Pa.**
17. **Dick Scott, ss, Ellsworth (Maine) HS**
18. **Pat Bone, of, Florida International**
19. **Bob Tewksbury, rhp, St. Leo**
20. **Logan Easley, rhp, JC of Southern Idaho**
21. **Steve Swinney, of, Thornwood HS, Markham, Ill.**
22. **Steve Scafa, 2b, St. John's**
23. **Gary Kempton, c, Southern Illinois**
24. Les Lancaster, rhp, Nimitz HS, Irving, Texas
25. **Mark Silva, rhp, Cal Poly San Luis Obispo**
26. **Paul Doty, rhp, Brigham Young**
27. **Mark Shiflett, lhp, Auburn**
28. **Larry Mikesell, lhp, Florida**
29. **Mike Siwiec, rhp, Triton (Ill.) JC**
30. Ken Reed, rhp, Tuslaw HS, North Lawrence, Ohio
31. **Greg Zunino, of, California**
32. **Bob Bomerito, 3b, Wichita State**
33. **Larry Lewis, rhp, Prospect HS, Mount Prospect, Ill.**
34. Mark Baker, rhp, Palm Beach (Fla.) JC
35. Derek Vanacore, of, Sacramento HS
36. Bill Stevenson, 1b, St. Thomas Aquinas HS, Fort Lauderdale
37. **Meade Palmer, of, Philadelphia College of Pharmacy**
38. **Stan Williams, rhp, Southern California**
39. **Scott Smith, of, Kent County HS, Chestertown, Md.**

June—Secondary Phase (5)

1. Phil Lane, 3b, Broward (Fla.) CC
2. **Trent Ferrin, rhp, JC of Southern Idaho**
3. **Bill Williams, 1b, Solano (Calif.) CC**
4. **David Niemiec, rhp, West Valley (Calif.) JC**
5. **Shane O'Shea, inf, Indian River (Fla.) CC**
6. **John Hughes, 1b, JC of Southern Idaho**

OAKLAND ATHLETICS

January—Regular Phase (16)

1. **Steve Kiefer, ss, Fullerton (Calif.) JC**
2. **Mark Jarrett, rhp, Riverside (Calif.) CC**
3. Wayne Bonham, of, Yavapai (Ariz.) JC
4. **Gary Dawson, of, Fullerton (Calif.) JC**
5. Ricky Daniels, ss, Los Angeles CC
6. Robert Feldhaus, 2b, Chaffey (Calif.) JC
7. Jeffrey Rojas, rhp, San Bernardino Valley (Calif.) JC
8. Lee Mays, rhp, Los Angeles CC
9. Doug Baker, inf, Los Angeles Valley JC
10. **Jay Schellin, of, Arcadia, Calif.**
11. **Gregory Mine, rhp, Green River (Wash.) CC**
12. **Elton Hooker, of, Los Angeles CC**
13. Carter Pittman, ss, Central Arizona JC
14. Paul Felix, of, Fullerton (Calif.) JC
15. **Gene Ransom, 2b, California**
16. **James Sanfilipo, 3b, Kearney, N.J.**
17. Marvin McWhirter, 1b, Los Angeles CC

January—Secondary Phase (6)

1. John Leonard, rhp, Yavapai (Ariz.) JC
2. Robert Lackeby, rhp, Central Arizona JC
3. **John Vela, lhp, Saddleback (Calif.) CC**
4. **Kelvin Hudson, 2b, San Bernardino Valley (Calif.) JC**

June—Regular Phase (15)

1. **Tim Pyznarski, 3b/of, Eastern Illinois**
2. **Mike Gallego, 2b, UCLA** (Pick from White Sox as compensation for free agent Jim Essian)
2. **Rick Rodriguez, rhp, UC Riverside**
3. **John Hotchkiss, 3b, Cal Poly Pomona**
4. **Curt Young, lhp, Central Michigan**
5. **Mickey Tettleton, c/of, Oklahoma State**
6. Alvin Davis, 1b, Arizona State
7. Don Smith, rhp, Orange Coast (Calif.) JC
8. **Bill Bathe, c, Pepperdine**
9. **Jim Camacho, ss, Cal Poly Pomona**
10. **Tony Herron, lhp, Fresno State**
11. Tom Siefert, c, Whitmer HS, Toledo
12. **Tom Heckman, rhp, Missouri**
13. **Dave Weatherman, rhp, Cal State Fullerton**
14. Henry Gatewood, c, McClatchy HS, Sacramento
15. **Luis Rojas, of, Texas Christian**
16. Kevin Madden, rhp, Massanutten Academy, Westmont, N.J.
17. **Thad Reece, 2b, Hawaii**
18. Bo Jordan, rhp, Mississippi College
19. **Phil Strom, 1b, Utah**
20. **Scot Mitchell, c, Cal State Northridge**
21. **Chuck Kolotka, rhp, Northern Illinois**
22. **Tom Copeland, of, UC Riverside**
23. Gary Weinberger, of, Cal State Sacramento
24. **Mike Ashman, 1b, Cal Poly Pomona**
25. **Kevin Coughlin, of, Fresno State**
26. **Bruce Amador, 2b, Cal State Stanislaus**
27. **Bryan Smith, 3b, Rio Hondo (Calif.) JC**
28. Mike Correia, rhp/2b, University HS, San Diego
29. **Pat O'Hara, c, Covina HS, Hesperia, Calif.**
30. **John Michel, 1b, Evergreen HS, Vancouver, Wash.**
31. Steve Clark, of, San Diego CC

June—Secondary Phase (1)

1. **Donnie Hill, ss, Arizona State**
2. Craig Fitzpatrick, rhp, Koeltztown, Mo.
3. Damon Farmar, of, West Los Angeles JC

PHILADELPHIA PHILLIES

January—Regular Phase (19)

1. Eric Schmidt, rhp, Antelope Valley (Calif.) JC
2. **Mark Frishman, of, Los Angeles Valley JC**
3. Herbert Jordan, rhp, Blinn (Texas) JC
4. **Michael Sims, rhp, Johnson County (Kan.) CC**
5. Joe Jordan, c, Seminole State (Okla.) JC
6. **Tommy George, ss, Bacone (Okla.) JC**
7. **Kent Kaiser, of, Mineral Area (Mo.) JC**
8. Kyle Johnson, rhp, Seminole State (Okla.) JC
9. **John Proctor, c/of, Allen County (Kan.) CC**
10. Ron Johnson, rhp, Mission (Calif.) JC
11. Marvin White, lhp, Seminole State (Okla.) JC
12. Donald McCaleb, 2b, Angelina (Texas) JC
13. **Steve Giovacchini, rhp, Modesto (Calif.) JC**
14. Billy Vinson, rhp, Ranger (Texas) JC
15. Tim Middleton, rhp, Bacone (Okla.) JC

January—Secondary Phase (11)

1. **Kevin Gross, rhp, Oxnard (Calif.) JC**
2. Doug Laufer, rhp, Texas
3. Andrew Nossek, lhp, Blinn (Texas) JC

June—Regular Phase (20)

1. **Johnny Abrego, rhp, Mission HS, San Jose, Calif.**
2. **C.L. Penigar, of, Ontario (Calif.) HS**
3. **Vin Soreca, c, Pace (N.Y.)**
4. Jerry Holtz, ss, Atlantic City HS, Margate, N.J.
5. **John Kanter, ss/2b, Camelback HS, Phoenix**
6. **Will Currier, of, Vermont**
7. **Jim Olander, of, Sahuaro HS, Tucson**
8. **Dave Seiler, lhp, Texas**
9. **Troy Berry, 2b, Benson HS, Portland, Ore.**
10. **Mel Williams, of, Lipscomb**
11. **Bud Bartholow, rhp, Oral Roberts**
12. **Charles Hudson, rhp, Prairie View A&M**
13. **Steve Witt, rhp, Servite HS, Buena Park, Calif.**
14. **Jim Reilly, rhp, Longview (Mo.) CC**
15. Todd Simmons, rhp, Bellflower (Calif.) HS
16. **Joe Nemeth, 1b, Cal State Dominguez Hills**
17. David Denny, ss, Humble (Texas) HS
18. Brooks Shumake, ss, Hartsville (S.C.) HS
19. **Todd Smith, c, Wingate (N.C.)**
20. Vince Coleman, of, Florida A&M
21. Ed Augustine, of, Brevard (Fla.) CC
22. **Jay Davisson, rhp, Eastern Michigan**
23. **Ace Oswel, rhp, Texas Wesleyan**
24. Charlie Kerfeld, rhp, Carson City (Nev.) HS
25. Jerry Anderson, rhp, Violet Hill HS, Horseshoe Bend, Ark.
26. **Adolph Crump, c, Prairie View A&M**
27. **Ron Mack, lhp, Crowder (Mo.) JC**
28. **Al LeBoeuf, 1b, Eastern Connecticut State**
29. **Tim Finch, rhp, San Joaquin Delta (Calif.) JC**
30. Jeff Brinson, 2b, Riverview Academy, Albany, Ga.
31. **Frank Rubio, rhp, Midwestern State (Texas)**
32. Todd Ezold, c, Classical HS, Springfield, Mass.
33. Mike Dennis, rhp, Wolfson HS, Jacksonville

June—Secondary Phase (6)

1. **Billy Irions, rhp, Seminole State (Okla.) JC**
2. John Bryant, of, Santa Ana (Calif.) JC
3. John Whitt, of, Cal State Dominguez Hills

PITTSBURGH PIRATES

January—Regular Phase (13)

1. **Brian Reams, rhp, Long Beach (Calif.) CC**
2. **Dickie Scott, 2b, Canada (Calif.) JC**
3. John Kruk, of, Allegany (Pa.) CC
4. **Tim Cassell, rhp, Sacramento CC**
5. Paul Steinert, of, Dundalk (Md.) CC
6. Jeff Bernash, rhp, Yakima Valley (Wash.) JC
7. Scott Reckord, rhp, Bellevue (Wash.) CC
8. **William Daiker, rhp, CC of Baltimore**
9. Randy Graham, rhp, Santa Rosa (Calif.) JC
10. Robert Kaser, rhp, Mount Hood (Ore.) CC

January—Secondary Phase (19)

1. Norman Morton, lhp, Miami-Dade North CC
2. **Todd Davidson, of, Wexford, Pa.**
3. Bobby Falls, ss, Walters State (Tenn.) CC

June—Regular Phase (14)

1. **Jim Winn, rhp, John Brown (Ark.)**
2. **Lee Tunnell, rhp, Baylor**

3. **Craig Brown, of, Goldsboro (N.C.) HS**
4. **Stacey Pettis, of, Castlemont HS, Oakland, Calif.**
5. Bip Roberts, ss/2b, Skyline HS, Oakland
6. **Mike Zamba, rhp, New Haven (Conn.)**
7. Scott Wade, of, Duval HS, Seabrook, Md.
8. **Kevin Battle, 3b, North Lenore HS, Grifton, N.C.**
9. **Ken Brown, inf, Grambling State**
10. **Richard Mott, rhp, Oscar Smith HS, Chesapeake, Va.**
11. **Steve Susce, rhp, Mississippi State**
12. **Jim Churchill, of, Texas Wesleyan**
13. **Tom Gil, of, Miami**
14. **Tony Burley, 2b, Iowa**
15. **Keith Stafford, rhp, Wiley (Texas)**
16. Jeff Fruge, rhp, Menard HS, Alexandria, La.
17. Scott Bankhead, rhp, Reidsville (N.C.) HS
18. Jim Thrift, ss, Oakton HS, Vienna, Va.
19. **Mark Veon, of/c, Point Park (Pa.)**
20. **Steve Kellam, c, Northern Kentucky**
21. **Larry Lamonde, rhp, Pittsburgh**
22. Marvin Parker, c, Baker County HS, MacClenny, Fla.
23. **Bob Loscalzo, of, Villanova**
24. Mark Davis, lhp, Oconomowoc HS, Okawchee, Wis.
25. Geoff Magnuson, of, Eastmont HS, East Wenatchee, Wash.
26. Dale Hurst, rhp, Marietta (Ohio)
27. **Dan Smith, ss, Texas-Arlington**
28. Ray Krieger, of, Sayreville War Memorial HS, South Amboy, N.J.
29. Chris Bosio, rhp, Cordova HS, Rancho Cordova, Calif.
30. Lance Johnson, of, Cincinnati
31. Michael Scarcella, rhp, Roxbury HS, Roxbury Township, N.J.
32. Jim Balmer, rhp, Marple Newton HS, Newton Square, Pa.
33. Gary Butler, rhp, Woodson HS, Annandale, Va.
34. Steve McGuire, rhp, Bayley-Ellard HS, Morris Plains, N.J.
35. James Lane, c, DeKalb South (Ga.) CC
36. Allan Peterson, c/of, Lower Columbia (Wash.) JC
37. Jerry Lillard, 1b, Glencoe (Ky.) HS
38. Ken Bender, of, Wilson HS, Tacoma
39. Steve Hallahan, inf, Penn Hills HS, Pittsburgh
40. Bill Drambel, rhp, Iowa
41. Brian Jones, 2b, Gallatin County HS, Warsaw, Ky.
42. Charles Simpson, 3b, James Hurt HS, Wilson, N.C.
43. Paul Westwood, ss, Peabody HS, Pittsburgh

June—Secondary Phase (4)

1. **Ray Krawczyk, rhp, Oral Roberts**
2. Bruce Crabbe, ss/of, Gulf Coast (Fla.) CC
3. Ken Lynn, rhp, Spartanburg Methodist (S.C.) JC
4. Kelly Simon, rhp, Orange Coast (Calif.) JC

ST. LOUIS CARDINALS

January—Regular Phase (7)

1. **Brad Luther, ss, JC of the Sequoias (Calif.)**
2. Barry Aden, rhp, Centralia (Wash.) JC
3. Dave Griffin, 1b, Thornton (Ill.) CC
4. Oddibe McDowell, of, Miami-Dade North CC
5. **John DiGioia, c, Mount San Antonio (Calif.) JC**
6. **Robert Hayes, rhp, Onondaga (N.Y.) CC**
7. Todd Oakes, rhp, Waldorf (Iowa) JC
8. Gregory Wirth, rhp, Glendale (Ariz.) CC
9. Jerry Eklund, rhp, Eastern Arizona JC

January—Secondary Phase (1)

1. **Harry McCulla, c, Delgado (La.) JC**
2. Jorge Reyes, lhp, Miami-Dade South CC
3. Mike Santiago, lhp, Mount San Antonio (Calif.) JC

June—Regular Phase (8)

1. **Bob Meacham, ss, San Diego State**
2. (Pick to Royals as compensation for free agent Darrell Porter)
3. **Tom Nieto, c, Oral Roberts**
4. **Curt Ford, 2b, Jackson State**
5. **Jeff Lauck, of/1b, McLane HS, Fresno**
6. Reggie Williams, of, Southern
7. **Jeff Keener, rhp, Kentucky**
8. **Willy Finnegan, rhp, Nevada-Las Vegas**
9. **Scott Young, rhp, Delaware**
10. Bruce Walton, rhp, North HS, Bakersfield, Calif.
11. **Bobby Kish, rhp, South Carolina**
12. **Greg Guin, 1b, Clemson**
13. **Danny Cox, rhp, Troy State**
14. Greg Morhardt, of, Gilbert HS, Winsted, Conn.
15. Todd Ostrominski, rhp, Hampton HS, Allison Park, Pa.
16. **Alan Hunsinger, 1b, Oregon State**
17. Keith Gilliam, lhp, Austin Peay
18. **Brian Hopkins, of/rhp, Pottsville (Pa.) HS**
19. Rich Rosemus, lhp, Madison HS, Portland, Ore.
20. **John Adams, rhp, Mississippi**
21. Jeff Edwards, lhp, DuPont HS, Old Hickory, Tenn.
22. Juan Perkins, of, Newton-Conover HS, Conover, N.C.
23. Ron Proctor, rhp, Los Altos HS, Hacienda Heights, Calif.
24. Sal Vaccaro, lhp, Westmore HS, Daly City, Calif.
25. **David Reinhardt, 3b, Utica (N.Y.) Free Academy**
26. Leland Maddox, c, Lincoln HS, San Diego
27. **Dave Bear, rhp, Ben Davis HS, Indianapolis**
28. **Chuck Menzhuber, 2b, Southern California**
29. Bob Fingers, rhp, Saguaro HS, Scottsdale, Ariz.
30. **Steven Roath, of, Manchester (Conn.) CC**
31. David Osteen, ss/p, Anneville-Cleona HS, Anneville, Pa.
32. Jim Cecchini, c, Southern California

June—Secondary Phase (2)

1. **Randy Hunt, c, Alabama**

SAN DIEGO PADRES

January—Regular Phase (5)

1. Eric Bullock, of, Los Angeles Harbor JC
2. Michael Moore, c, Edmonds (Wash.) CC
3. Donald Fenton, rhp, Lower Columbia (Wash.) JC
4. **Pride Evans, inf, Citrus (Calif.) JC**
5. Keith Street, of, Middle Georgia JC
6. **Paul Huyck, lhp, Hancock (Calif.) JC**
7. **Fred Williams, lhp, Mountainview, Calif.**
8. Willard Medley, rhp, Gulf Coast (Fla.) CC

January—Secondary Phase (15)

1. Sam Martin, ss, Louisburg (N.C.) JC
2. Marcus Handley, rhp, Cumberlands (Ky.) JC

June—Regular Phase (6)

1. **Kevin McReynolds, of, Arkansas**
1. **Frank Castro, c, Miami** (Pick from Yankees as compensation for free agent Dave Winfield)
2. **Bill Long, rhp, Miami (Ohio)**
3. **Tony Gwynn, of, San Diego State**
4. **Scott Thompson, of, Lower Dauphin HS, Grantville, Pa.**
5. Burk Goldthorn, c, Texas
6. **Louis Langie, ss, Gardena HS, Compton, Calif.**
7. Craig Holthus, of, Fruita Monument HS, Grand Junction, Colo.
8. **Craig Shumock, inf, North Carolina**
9. **Larry Kiesling, inf, Centenary**
10. **Greg Booker, rhp, Elon**
11. **Mark Gillaspie, of, Mississippi State**
12. **Marc Ochal, rhp, North Carolina**
13. **John Hennell, 1b, Arkansas**
14. **Paul Noce, ss, Washington State**
15. **Steve Schefsky, rhp, San Diego State**
16. **Jim Giacomazzi, rhp, Azusa Pacific (Calif.)**
17. **Lee Purchatzke, rhp, Wisconsin-Oshkosh**
18. **Bobby Macias, rhp, Oral Roberts**
19. Jeff Morrison, lhp, Miami
20. **Bill Solomon, rhp, Iowa State**
21. **Steve Patterson, c, Long Beach State**
22. **Marty Kain, rhp, Washington State**
23. **Jeff Blood, of, Lewis-Clark State (Idaho)**
24. **Jamie Oberbruner, rhp, Wisconsin-Parkside**
25. **Joey Balderston, rhp, Santa Clara**
26. **Mark Christy, rhp, New Orleans**
27. **Jim Leopold, rhp/of, Kentucky**
28. **Bob Gonsoulin, inf, Southeast Missouri State**
29. **Ray Etchebarren, inf, Oklahoma State**
30. **Mark Wedel, 2b, Long Beach State**

31. **Tom Cannon, 3b/rhp, Sayersville HS, Parlin, N.J.**
32. Lynn Mortin, inf, South Alamance HS, Graham, N.C.
33. **Paul Grame, rhp, Stanford**
34. **Jeff Ronk, inf, California**
35. **Wes Smith, rhp, Portland**
36. **Jim Stein, rhp, Washington**
37. Wade Boccard, inf, Bloomfield (Colo.) HS

June—Secondary Phase (16)

1. Everett Graham, of, Louisburg (N.C.) JC
2. **Peter Kutsukos, rhp, Seminole (Fla.) CC**
3. **John Kruk, of, Allegany (Pa.) CC**

SAN FRANCISCO GIANTS

January—Regular Phase (9)

1. Mel White, rhp, Fullerton (Calif.) JC
2. **Louis D'Amore, rhp, CC of Morris (N.J.)**
3. **Gene Lambert, lhp, Los Angeles Valley JC**
4. **Daryl Pitts, of, Los Angeles CC**
5. Chuck Bartlett, c, Cuyahoga (Ohio) CC
6. Al Cardwood, rhp/1b, Ranger (Texas) JC
7. Keith O'Day, rhp, West Valley (Calif.) JC
8. Bob Lockwood, of, Los Angeles Valley JC
9. Terry Quinn, inf, Los Angeles Valley JC
10. Douglas Boren, rhp, Fresno CC
11. Chad Miltenberger, c, JC of the Sequoias (Calif.)
12. James McCann, ss, San Diego Mesa JC
13. **Ted Ladd, ss, St. Andrews, Tenn.**
14. Orlando Blackwell, inf, Sacramento CC
15. Keith Davila, rhp, Sacramento CC
16. Michael Pintar, rhp, JC of Southern Idaho
17. Tony Laird, of/1b, Treasure Valley (Ore.) CC
18. Bradley Mettler, rhp, San Joaquin Delta (Calif.) JC

January—Secondary Phase (17)

1. John Duval, rhp, Cuesta (Calif.) JC
2. Tony Beal, of, Seminole (Fla.) CC
3. Louis Lanini, inf, San Joaquin Delta (Calif.) JC

June—Regular Phase (10)

1. **Mark Grant, rhp, Catholic HS, Joliet, Ill.**
2. **Kelvin Torve, 1b, Oral Roberts**
3. Brad Powell, rhp, Ridge HS, Basking Ridge, N.J.
4. Dan Penner, rhp, Rio Mesa HS, Camarillo, Calif.
5. Dennis Livingston, lhp, North Reading (Mass.) HS
6. **Brian Snyder, of, East Tennessee State**
7. **Bob O'Connor, 2b, Rider**
8. **Randy Ebersberger, ss, Loyola Marymount**
9. **George Spiroff, c, Kent State**
10. Kevin Brown, lhp, Overlea HS, Baltimore
11. **Glenn Barling, inf/rhp, California Baptist**
12. **Marty Baier, of, Elk Grove HS, Sacramento**
13. **Mike Brecht, lhp, Central Michigan**
14. **Glenn Jones, of, Morehead State**
15. **Marty Mathiesen, rhp, Cal State Chico**
16. **Brian Murtha, lhp, Shippensburg (Pa.)**
17. Monico Corral, ss, San Francisco
18. **Kernan Ronan, rhp, Northern Arizona**
19. Bruce Castoria, 1b, Mississippi State
20. **Matt Nokes, c, Patrick Henry HS, San Diego**
21. **Steve Malin, rhp, Elmhurst (Ill.)**
22. **Darrell Pride, of, Ector HS, Odessa, Texas**
23. **Todd Zacher, 3b, Arkansas**
24. **Steve Wilcox, rhp, Fresno State**
25. **Dean Kornacker, ss, St. Xavier (Ill.)**
26. **Chuck Lusted, rhp, Georgia Southern**
27. **Gary Davenport, 2b, Santa Clara**
28. David Rhino, ss, Henderson HS, Atlanta
29. Tim Haller, 2b, San Mateo (Calif.) HS
30. **Mike Spinozzi, 2b, St. Francis (Ill.)**
31. Ricky Hester, of, Southeastern (N.C.) CC
32. Bill Gordon, 3b, Sylmar (Calif.) HS
33. **Randy Gleason, 3b, Cal State Chico**
34. Mark Warren, of, American River (Calif.) JC
35. Clay Harbin, rhp, Johnson HS, Huntsville, Ala.
36. Vince DeBono, rhp, Cupertino (Calif.) HS
37. Jim Rigby, 2b, McCaskey HS, Lancaster, Pa.
38. **Don Pote, of, Juniata (Pa.)**
39. Curtis Zucco, lhp, Greensburg-Salem HS, Delmont, Pa.
40. John Atkinson, lhp, Long Beach (Calif.) Poly HS
41. Steve Stark, rhp, Chaminade HS, Canoga Park, Calif.
42. Mark Michna, of, Blinn (Texas) JC
43. Terry Lawrence, of, Texas A&M
44. **Mark Winters, lhp, Quaker Hill, Conn.**

June—Secondary Phase (8)

1. Craig Stevenson, ss, Los Angeles Valley JC
2. Dave Leiper, lhp, Fullerton (Calif.) JC
3. Mike Hogan, rhp, Orange Coast (Calif.) JC

SEATTLE MARINERS

January—Regular Phase (2)

1. **Bret McAfee, ss, Merced (Calif.) JC**
2. Kelly Simon, rhp, Orange Coast (Calif.) JC
3. John Felice, of, JC of the Canyons (Calif.)
4. Gary Parmenter, rhp, Middle Georgia JC
5. Dennis Werth, lhp/1b, Tacoma CC
6. **Jeff Eldridge, rhp, Olympic (Wash.) JC**
7. Chris Mitchell, rhp, Jefferson State (Ala.) JC
8. John Hughes, 1b, JC of Southern Idaho

January—Secondary Phase (18)

1. Thor Edgell, rhp, Fullerton (Calif.) JC
2. Louis Burmester, rhp, Williston Park, N.Y.

June—Regular Phase (1)

1. **Mike Moore, rhp, Oral Roberts**
2. **Kevin Dukes, lhp, Arizona State**
2. **Mark Langston, lhp, San Jose State** (Pick from Rangers as compensation for free agent Bill Stein)
3. **Phil Bradley, of, Missouri**
4. **Ricky Nelson, of, Arizona State**
4. **Lee Guetterman, lhp, Liberty** (Pick from Angels as compensation for free agent Juan Beniquez)
5. **Brick Smith, 1b, Wake Forest**
6. Brian Howard, ss, Rockville (Md.) HS
7. **Eric Parent, rhp, Anderson (Calif.) HS**
8. **Vic Martin, 1b/rhp, San Diego State**
9. Eric Varoz, 2b, Hillcrest HS, Midvale, Utah
10. **Terry Hayes, lhp, Wichita State**
11. **Ronn Dixon, lhp, New Orleans**
12. **Don Holland, rhp, Holy Family HS, Denver**
13. **Dave Myers, ss, Temple**
14. **Frank Meraz, of, Oklahoma**
15. **Kal Koenig, lhp, Lipscomb**
16. **Stan Edmonds, of, Southern California**
17. **Wayne Kinley, rhp, East Gaston HS, Mount Holly, N.C.**
18. Bob Hallas, rhp, Purdue
19. **Clay Hill, c/3b, Washington State**
20. **Randy Meier, of, Central Michigan**
21. Charlie O'Brien, c, Wichita State
22. **Howie Brodsky, of, New Orleans**
23. Dan Griffin, ss, Niceville (Fla.) HS
24. Brian Rupe, of, Virginia Tech
25. **Jim Aulenbach, c, Massachusetts**

June—Secondary Phase (25)

1. **Ric Wilson, c, Arizona State**
2. Richie Carter, rhp, Umpqua (Ore.) CC

TEXAS RANGERS

January—Regular Phase (10)

1. **Greg Tabor, inf, Chabot (Calif.) JC**
2. Dave Leiper, lhp, Fullerton (Calif.) JC
3. **Barry Bass, of/rhp, Manatee (Fla.) JC**
4. **Oscar Mejia, ss, El Camino (Calif.) JC**
5. Brian Aviles, rhp, Rockland (N.Y.) CC
6. Calvin Gray, of, Angelina (Texas) JC
7. Craig Tice, lhp, Ocean County (N.J.) JC
8. Brian Farley, rhp, St. Petersburg (Fla.) JC

9. Paul Edwards, of, Solano (Calif.) CC
10. Randy Boyd, lhp, Cochise County (Ariz.) CC

January—Secondary Phase (8)

1. Ken Lynn, rhp, Spartanburg Methodist (S.C.) JC
2. Tony Arias, rhp, Miami-Dade North CC
3. Kevin Sliwinski, of, Orange Coast (Calif.) JC
4. **Joseph Hackett, of/1b, Greensboro, N.C.**

June—Regular Phase (9)

1. **Ron Darling, rhp, Yale**
1. **Al Lachowicz, rhp, Pittsburgh** (Pick from Astros as compensation for free agent Dave Roberts)
2. **Chuckie Canady, of, North Carolina State** (Pick from Mets as compensation for free agent Rusty Staub)
3. **Brendan Hennessy, 3b, Bogota (N.J.) HS**
4. **Doug Davis, c, Eastern Michigan**
5. **Frank Brosious, rhp, Mansfield (Pa.)**
6. Barry Jones, rhp, Centerville (Ind.) HS
7. **Marty Leach, rhp, St. Leo (Fla.)**
8. **Mike Schmid, lhp, Lowell (Mass.)**
9. **Larry McLane, lhp, Chapman (Calif.)**
10. **Joe Benes, lhp, Nebraska-Omaha**
11. **Mitch Zwolensky, rhp, Eastern Michigan**
12. **Tony Triplett, ss, Kansas State**
13. **Lew Surratt, 1b, Lamar**
14. **Chris Serazio, of, Southern Colorado**
15. **Keith Jones, of, Wichita State**
16. Wayne Dale, c, Campbell
17. **Kevin Buckley, of, Maine**
18. **Rod Hodde, 1b, Texas A&M**
19. **Bryan Harwell, 2b, Southeastern Oklahoma State**
20. **Gary Sharp, 3b, Southeastern Oklahoma State**
21. **Ray Warren, lhp, CC of Rhode Island**
22. **Randy Thorpe, of, Texas-Arlington**
23. **Curtis Kouba, lhp, Texas-Arlington**
24. **Glen Cook, rhp, Ithaca (N.Y.)**
25. **Scott Perry, 3b, CC of Rhode Island**
26. **Jeff Barnes, rhp, Charleston (W.Va.)**
27. **Ken Gordon, ss, Upsala (N.J.)**
28. Robert Fannin, c/1b, Ranger (Texas) JC
29. Larry Long, of, Texas
30. Keith Hamilton, rhp, Broken Bow (Okla.) HS
31. **Michael Johnson, 2b, Connecticut**
32. Tim Barker, 2b, John Vianny HS, Aberdeen, N.J.
33. **Jim Schult, of, Mercy (N.Y.)**
34. **Jim Jeffries, c/of, American**

June—Secondary Phase (17)

1. Doug Laufer, rhp, Texas
2. Oddibe McDowell, of, Miami-Dade North CC
3. **Todd Schulte, lhp, Old Monroe, Mo.**

TORONTO BLUE JAYS

January—Regular Phase (6)

1. Ken Galloway, lhp, West Valley (Calif.) JC
2. **Richard Fagnani, lhp, Westchester (N.Y.) CC**
3. **Fred Mead, 1b/of, Stamford, Conn.**
4. Mark Hoffman, lhp, Chabot (Calif.) JC
5. Scott Simmons, lhp, Massasoit (Mass.) CC
6. Ed Augustine, lhp, Seminole (Fla.) CC
7. Dave Eichhorn, rhp, Watsonville, Calif.
8. **Jeff Phillips, rhp, Lake Michigan (Mich.) JC**
9. **Steve Stenquist, rhp, Norwalk (Conn.) CC**
10. **Martin Pulley, c, Eastern Illinois**
11. **James Wahlig, of/2b, Iowa State**

January—Secondary Phase (12)

1. **Joey Pursell, rhp, Tulane**
2. **Steve Reish, rhp, Union City, Ind.**

June—Regular Phase (5)

1. **Matt Williams, rhp, Rice**
1. **John Cerutti, lhp, Amherst (Mass.)** (Pick from Brewers as compensation for free agent Roy Howell)
2. **Bill Pinkham, c, San Diego**
3. **Glenn Gallagher, of/rhp, Clemson**
4. **Scott Pleis, c/inf, Wentzville HS, St. Louis**
5. **Jim Bishop, 3b, Lynwood (Calif.) HS**
6. **Stan Clarke, lhp, Toledo**
7. Jeff Kaiser, lhp, Western Michigan
8. Alan Cockrell, of/c, Parkwood HS, Joplin, Mo.
9. **Mark Poole, c, Oklahoma State**
10. **Scot Elam, rhp, Michigan**
11. **Tim Rodgers, rhp, Oklahoma State**
12. **Chuck Faucette, of, Willingboro (N.J.) HS**
13. **Greg Moore, rhp, Texas Christian**
14. **Gary Henderson, rhp, Mount View, Ark.**
15. **Gerry Hool, c, Michigan**
16. Jeff Szczecinski, 2b, Long Island
17. **Ed Schneider, lhp, Florida State**
18. **Myron Gilmore, of, St. Edward's (Texas)**
19. **Chris Phillips, rhp, Centenary**
20. Tom Willerson, rhp, Springfield (Mass.)
21. Jeff Pries, rhp, Corona del Mar HS, Newport Beach, Calif.
22. Jack Del Rio, 1b, Hayward (Calif.) HS
23. Tim Dietz, rhp, Hale HS, Tulsa, Okla.
24. **Terry Raley, ss, St. Mary's (Texas)**

June—Secondary Phase (11)

1. **Mike Sharperson, ss, DeKalb South (Ga.) CC**
2. Benny Distefano, 1b, Alvin (Texas) CC
3. Tim Arnsberg, rhp, Merced (Calif.) JC
4. Dave Eichhorn, rhp, Cabrillo (Calif.) JC
5. Ken Galloway, lhp, West Valley (Calif.) JC
6. Mark Hoffman, lhp, Chabot (Calif.) JC

1982 Cubs get solid player at No. 1 in Dunston, while Mets find breakout star with Gooden

The 1982 draft represented the first big test for the Philadelphia Connection that Dallas Green brought with him to Chicago to boost a sad-sack Cubs franchise.

If the Cubs, who had not won a title of any kind in 37 years, were to become contenders again, astute drafting would be the foundation of the turnaround, the formula Green used during his reign as farm and scouting director in Philadelphia. Green, who managed the Phillies to a World Series victory in 1980, joined the Cubs following the 1981 season and brought a large contingent of Phillies executives and scouts.

The 1982 draft gave the Cubs, with a depleted farm system and the worst record in the strike-shortened 1981 season, an opportunity to catch up in a hurry. They had the first overall pick and two additional first-round selections.

The Cubs had not signed, developed and brought to Wrigley Field a top-flight infielder since Don Kessinger in 1964, so they used the No. 1 selection on Shawon Dunston, a high school shortstop from Brooklyn. They saw a shortstop with a rocket arm who hit .790 his senior year and stole 37 bases in 37 attempts. Dunston also hit 25 homers in four years.

The club planned to eventually move Dunston to third base, which was his position until his senior year of high school.

"He may not be a bona fide shortstop, but we feel he's the best athlete in the crop," Green said. "He's the best hitter in the nation, including college."

Gordon Goldsberry, the new Cubs director of minor leagues and scouting, concurred: "We feel that Shawon has the most physical potential of any player our scouting staff has seen this year. We had five of our people watch him play at various times."

Dunston, 19, signed with the Cubs for $100,000 and promised to be in Chicago by 1986—as a shortstop—which he did right on schedule. He didn't become a top-of-the-line everyday shortstop until 1989, when he led the resurgent Cubs to their second National League East championship of the decade. He went on to an 18-season big league career.

Neither of Chicago's other two first-round picks panned out. Shortstop Tony Wood never reached the major leagues, while outfielder Stan Boderick had a promising rookie season but fizzled thereafter.

For all the hype of the Cubs' picks, though, it was a little-known righthander from talent-rich Tampa who proved to be the real catch of the 1982 draft. Dwight

R & R SPORTS GROUP

No. 1 pick Shawon Dunston spent 12 seasons playing shortstop for the Cubs

Gooden wasn't even regarded as the best high school pitcher in Tampa and wasn't the No. 1 pitcher on his high school team as recently as a year before the draft. He emerged as a true talent in the weeks leading up to the draft, and the Mets nabbed him with the fifth overall pick.

"Gooden was a little bit of a projection," Mets scouting director Joe McIlvaine said. "We surprised a few people when we picked him fifth. I think, yes, it was somewhat of a gamble at that point.

"But I felt in my own mind—and I had scouted Florida for eight years—that he was the best pitching prospect I had ever seen in that state."

Less than a year later, Gooden was the hottest prospect in the game. At Class A Lynchburg, in his first full minor league season, Gooden went 19-4 with a 2.50 ERA. More impressively, he spun a Carolina League-record 300 strikeouts in 191 innings.

In 1984, at age 19, Gooden made one of the most auspicious debuts in major league history, winning 17 games and striking out 276 in 216 innings. In back to back late-season outings, he struck out 16 without walking a batter. He quickly established himself as one of the best pitchers in the game, winning the National League Cy Young Award in 1985.

Like fellow Mets phenom Darryl Strawberry,

however, Gooden's career was devastated by drug abuse, and his decline was precipitous. Still, he pitched in 16 seasons and won 194 games, with a career 3.51 ERA.

Gooden and Dunston were just two of the future major league stars to come through the 1982 draft. The Athletics found Jose Canseco in the 15th round, while the Royals grabbed Bret Saberhagen in the 19th. The Twins got future Hall of Famer Kirby Puckett with the third overall pick in the January draft out of a junior college in Illinois.

High School Resurgence

In contrast to the record 17 college players who were claimed in the first round of the 1981 draft, 1982 saw a swing back to high school picks. Still, 11 college players went in the first round.

While every high school player drafted in the first round signed, no draft in history produced so many premium high school players who went unsigned, which would be felt three years later in a 1985 draft that may have produced the best first-round talent ever.

The Yankees not only failed to sign B.J. Surhoff, who would be the No. 1 pick overall in the '85 draft, but they also didn't sign Bo Jackson, a second-round pick who went to Auburn and won the 1985 Heisman Trophy.

Two other two-sport stars from the class of 1982 were outfielders Kenny Williams and Kevin Murray. Williams was a third-round pick of the White Sox. He signed for a $165,000 bonus and the understanding he would be allowed to play football at Stanford while playing summers in the White Sox system.

Williams gave up football after his freshman season, however, to devote his full attention to baseball. He hit .218 in 1,154 major league at-bats over six seasons, and gained more notoriety later when he became general manager of the White Sox.

Murray was picked in the 11th round by Milwaukee. He played a year, then quit and played quarterback for three seasons at Texas A&M. The Brewers sued to get Murray's $35,000 bonus back, but Murray got to keep it and play college football.

One of the provisions of the 1981 baseball strike settlement was the reclassification of major league free agents as Type A or Type B, which affected draft compensation.

Compensation for the more valued Type A free agents (rated in the top 20 percent at their positions) was a draft pick and an existing minor leaguer. Clubs losing Type B free agents (rated in the 20-30 percentile) were awarded the signing team's first-round pick, and a supplemental selection between the first and second rounds.

DRAFT 82: FIRST-ROUND PICKS

No.	Club	Player, Pos.	School	Hometown	Ht.	Wt.	B-T	Age
1.	Cubs	Shawon Dunston, ss	Thomas Jefferson HS	Brooklyn, N.Y.	6-1	175	R-R	19
2.	Blue Jays	Augie Schmidt, ss	New Orleans	Kenosha, Wis.	6-2	185	R-R	20
3.	Padres	Jimmy Jones, rhp	Thomas Jefferson HS	Dallas	6-1	180	R-R	18
4.	Twins	Bryan Oelkers, lhp	Wichita State	St. Louis	6-2	190	L-L	21
5.	Mets	Dwight Gooden, rhp	Hillsborough HS	Tampa	6-3	183	R-R	17
6.	Mariners	Spike Owen, ss	Texas	Cleburne, Texas	5-9	160	B-R	21
7.	Pirates	Sam Khalifa, ss	Sahuaro HS	Tucson	5-11	170	R-R	18
8.	Angels	Bob Kipper, lhp	Central Catholic HS	Aurora, Ill.	6-2	175	R-L	17
9.	Braves	Duane Ward, rhp	Farmington HS	Farmington, N.M.	6-4	185	R-R	18
10.	Royals	John Morris, of	Seton Hall	Bellmore, N.Y.	6-1	180	L-L	21
11.	Giants	Steve Stanicek, 1b	Nebraska	Park Forest, Ill.	6-3	185	R-R	20
12.	Indians	Mark Snyder, rhp	Beardon HS	Knoxville	6-5	210	R-R	18
13.	Phillies	John Russell, c/of	Oklahoma	Norman, Okla.	6-0	195	R-R	21
14.	White Sox	Ron Karkovice, c	Boone HS	Orlando	6-1	205	R-R	18
15.	Astros	Steve Swain, of	Grossmont HS	El Cajon, Calif.	6-2	180	R-R	18
16.	Red Sox	Sam Horn, 1b	Morse HS	San Diego	6-5	215	L-L	18
17.	Cubs	Tony Woods, ss	Whittier (Calif.)	Oakland	6-2	185	R-R	20
18.	Red Sox	Rob Parkins, rhp	Cerritos HS	Cerritos, Calif.	6-2	185	R-R	18
19.	Dodgers	Franklin Stubbs, 1b	Virginia Tech	Hamlet, N.C.	6-2	200	L-L	21
20.	Tigers	Rich Monteleone, rhp	Tampa Catholic HS	Tampa	6-2	220	R-R	19
21.	Cardinals	Todd Worrell, rhp	Biola (Calif.)	Arcadia, Calif.	6-5	200	R-R	22
22.	Reds	Scott Jones, lhp	South HS	Hinsdale, Ill.	5-11	185	R-L	18
23.	Reds	Billy Hawley, rhp	Brookland Cayce HS	West Columbia, S.C.	6-2	190	L-R	18
24.	Orioles	Joe Kucharski, rhp	South Carolina	Clinton, Md.	6-3	225	R-R	21
25.	Brewers	Dale Sveum, ss	Pinole Valley HS	Pinole, Calif.	6-2	185	B-R	18
26.	Red Sox	Jeff Ledbetter, 1b/of	Florida State	Clearwater, Fla.	6-3	200	L-L	22

1982

CLUB-BY-CLUB SELECTIONS

ATLANTA BRAVES

January—Regular Phase (10)

1. **Johnny Hatcher, of, Yavapai (Ariz.) JC**
2. Larry Riddle, rhp, Alvin (Texas) CC
3. **John Van Gennep, rhp, Thornton, Ill.**
4. **Gregory Mayse, ss/3b, Cecil (Md.) CC**
5. Greg Laniban, lhp, Brevard (Fla.) CC
6. **James Thompson, of, Riverdale (Ga.) HS**
7. **Gary Hall, of, Kings River (Calif.) JC**
8. David Grams, rhp, Mount San Antonio (Calif.) JC

January—Secondary Phase (10)

1. **Albert Candelaria, lhp, San Jose CC**
2. Mark Warren, of, American River (Calif.) JC

June—Regular Phase (9)

1. **Duane Ward, rhp, Farmington (N.M.) HS**
2. **Joe Johnson, rhp, Maine**
3. **Zane Smith, lhp, Indiana State**
4. Randy Johnson, lhp, Livermore (Calif.) HS
5. Mike Campbell, rhp, Newport HS, Seattle
6. **Rich Thompson, of, Texas**
7. **Mike Knox, ss, The Citadel**
8. **Tracy Edwards, c, Mesquite (Texas) HS**
9. Ron Robicheaux, 1b, Lafayette (La.) HS
10. **Dave Van Horn, 2b, Arkansas**
11. **Dennis Lubert, lhp, South Carolina**
12. **Tom Willerson, rhp, Springfield (Mass.)**
13. **Urban Meyer, ss, St. John's HS, Ashtabula, Ohio**
14. Doug Hodo, of, Churchill HS, San Antonio
15. **Jim Rivera, rhp, North Carolina State**
16. **Dave Griffin, 1b, Texas Wesleyan**
17. **Jeff Hentz, rhp, La Salle**
18. Bill Anderson, ss, Point Loma Nazarene (Calif.)
19. **Tony Nuendorff, c/3b, Southwestern (Texas)**
20. **Dale Chatham, lhp, William Carey (Miss.)**
21. **Kurt Moody, lhp, Missouri**
22. **Chip Childress, ss/rhp, Lynchburg (Va.)**
23. **Rusty Uresti, c, Texas**
24. **John Mortillaro, lhp, Jacksonville State**
25. **Tom Reynolds, 3b, Eastern Connecticut State**
26. **Preston Cash, of, Shorter (Ga.)**
27. **Allen Carden, 3b, Northwest Whitfield HS, Rocky Face, Ga.**
28. Steve Cranford, c/3b, DeKalb Central (Ga.) JC
29. **James Morelock, rhp, Fayette County HS, Fayetteville, Ga.**
30. **David Morris, rhp, West Georgia**
31. Mark North, lhp, Huffman HS, Birmingham

June—Secondary Phase (11)

1. John Bryant, of, Santa Ana (Calif.) JC
2. **Ken Lynn, rhp, Spartanburg Methodist (S.C.) JC**

BALTIMORE ORIOLES

January—Regular Phase (23)

1. **Jeff Doerr, 3b, JC of San Mateo (Calif.)**
2. **Dennis Tiefenthaler, ss, Yavapai (Ariz.) JC**
3. Robert Rase, rhp, Indian River (Fla.) CC
4. Romy Cucjen, inf, Southwestern (Calif.) JC
5. **Robert Karjalainen, 1b/of, Florida CC**
6. Scott Russell, of, JC of Southern Idaho
7. Scott Hurst, rhp, Florida CC
8. **Thomas Banner, 3b, New Haven (Conn.)**
9. Rick Hopkins, 2b, Orange Coast (Calif.) JC

January—Secondary Phase (5)

1. **John Leonard, rhp, Dawson, Pa.**
2. Manny Mantrana, ss, Miami-Dade North CC

June—Regular Phase (24)

1. **Joe Kucharski, rhp, South Carolina**
2. Dave Otto, lhp, Elk Grove Village (Ill.) HS
3. **John Habyan, rhp, St. John Baptist HS, Brentwood, N.Y.**
4. **Manuel Miranda, 2b, Sweetwater HS, Chula Vista, Calif.**
5. **Ken Gerhart, of, Middle Tennessee State**
6. **Edward Mason, rhp, Boone HS, Orlando, Fla.**
7. Rick Lockwood, 3b, Georgia Tech
8. **Roger Wilson, rhp, Poly HS, Long Beach**
9. **Eric Bell, lhp, Beyer HS, Modesto, Calif.**
10. Walt Weiss, ss, Suffern (N.Y.) HS
11. **Billy Ripken, rhp/ss, Aberdeen (Md.) HS**
12. **Randy Wilson, rhp, South Florida**
13. **Gerry Melillo, c, Eckerd (Fla.)**
14. **Ron Salcedo, 3b, Arizona State**
15. **Mike Vanderburg, of, Cal State Fullerton**
16. **Scott Lawrence, ss, Chopticon HS, Hollywood, Md.**
17. Marty Lanoux, 2b, Orange Park (Fla.) HS
18. **Chris Holmes, c, Durant (Okla.) HS**
19. **Steve Spalt, ss, Patterson HS, Baltimore**
20. Eric Hohn, lhp, Butler (Pa.) Area HS
21. **Jim Traber, 1b, Oklahoma State**
22. **Greg Beucher, ss, Connellsville (Pa.) HS**
23. **Bill Cowgill, of, North Caroline HS, Goldsboro, Md.**
24. **Carlos Concepcion, rhp, Charlotte, N.C.**
25. Chris Courtright, of, Highlands HS, Blackwood, N.J.
26. Matthew Merriman, 3b, Roswell (Ga.) HS
27. **Gene Dudek, 2b, SUNY Buffalo**
28. Jeff McKnight, ss, Westark (Ark.) CC
29. **Michael Cain, 2b, Jackson State**

June—Secondary Phase (25)

1. Brad Arnsberg, rhp, Merced (Calif.) JC
2. Troy Afenir, c, Palomar (Calif.) JC

BOSTON RED SOX

January—Regular Phase (17)

1. **Mike Rochford, lhp, Santa Fe (Fla.) CC**
2. Curt Kindred, rhp, Fullerton (Calif.) JC
3. **Scott Skripko, rhp, Middle Georgia JC**
4. **Charlie Mitchell, rhp, Columbia State (Tenn.) CC**
5. **John Roth, of, Cypress (Calif.) JC**
6. Mike Gildehaus, rhp, Jefferson (Mo.) JC
7. Ted Langdon, rhp, Brevard (Fla.) CC
8. Irving Weston, c, Kingsborough (N.Y.) CC
9. Kevin Smith, rhp, Seminole (Fla.) CC
10. Gregory Haynes, 1b/c, Jackson State (Tenn.) CC

January—Secondary Phase (13)

1. Jose Rodiles, rhp, Seminole State (Okla.) JC

June—Regular Phase (18)

1. **Sam Horn, 1b, Morse HS, San Diego** (Pick from Rangers as compensation for Type A free agent Frank Tanana)
1. **Rob Parkins, rhp, Cerritos (Calif.) HS**
1. **Jeff Ledbetter, 1b/of, Florida State** (Pick from Athletics as compensation for Type A free agent Joe Rudi)
2. **Kevin Romine, of, Arizona** (Pick from Cubs as compensation for Type A free agent Bill Campbell)
2. **Steve Jongewaard, ss, Fountain Valley (Calif.) HS**
3. **Mike Greenwell, 3b, North Fort Myers (Fla.) HS**
4. **Tim Gordon, 3b, Maryland**
5. **Gary Miller-Jones, 2b, South Alabama**
6. **Sam Nattile, 3b, Central Florida**
7. Jay Grate, rhp/ss, East Noble HS, Avila, Ind.
8. **Jeff Sellers, rhp, Paramount HS, Long Beach**
9. Fred Carter, of, Millwood HS, Oklahoma City
10. **Dave Oliva, of, Santa Clara**
11. Don O'Toole, rhp, Moore Catholic HS, Staten Island, N.Y.

12. **Rob Geels, c, Fresno State**
13. **Mike Mesh, ss, Southern Illinois**
14. **Scott Diez, lhp, Miami-Dade South CC**
15. **Tom Bonk, 1b, La Salle**
16. **Brustor Minor, rhp, Columbus, Miss.**
17. Ed Mondelli, lhp, Neshamini HS, Hulmeville, Pa.
18. **Billy Joe Richardson, c, Southern Illinois**
19. Scott Gay, rhp, Milford (N.H.) HS

June—Secondary Phase (20)

No selection

CALIFORNIA ANGELS

January—Regular Phase (7)

1. **Jay Lewis, rhp, Eastern Oklahoma State JC**
2. Brian Phillips, rhp, Diablo Valley (Calif.) JC
3. Cedric Wright, of, Laney (Calif.) JC
4. Vince Woods, of, Long Beach (Calif.) CC
5. John Johnson, rhp, Mount San Antonio (Calif.) JC
6. Harold Littlejohn, ss/3b, Ranger (Texas) JC
7. Tom Duggan, 3b, Orange Coast (Calif.) JC
8. **John Hudson, rhp, Euless, Texas**
9. Martin Rodriguez, rhp, San Bernardino Valley (Calif.) JC
10. Ty Dabney, 2b, Riverside, Calif. (Selection voided)
11. Ed McCarter, rhp, Umpqua (Ore.) CC
12. Chip Dill, rhp, Cerritos (Calif.) JC
13. Kent Testerman, c, Los Angeles Valley JC

January—Secondary Phase (26)

1. Kendall Walling, ss, Santa Ana (Calif.) JC

June—Regular Phase (8)

1. **Bob Kipper, lhp, Aurora (Ill.) Central Catholic HS**
2. (Pick to Yankees as compensation for Type A free agent Reggie Jackson)
3. **Tony Mack, rhp, Lamar**
4. **Kirk McCaskill, rhp, Vermont**
5. Chris Gwynn, of, Poly HS, Long Beach
6. **David Brady, c, Southeastern Oklahoma State**
7. **Don Timberlake, rhp, South Granville HS, Butner, N.C.**
8. **Scott Suehr, rhp, William Carey (Miss.)**
9. **Mark McLemore, ss, Morse HS, San Diego**
10. **Kevin Davis, ss, West Mecklenburg HS, Charlotte, N.C.**
11. Wade Phillips, rhp, West Orange Stark HS, Orange, Texas
12. **Dave Govea, 1b, Cal State Northridge**
13. **Scott Glanz, rhp, Arkansas**
14. **Billy Wiesler, of, Louisiana State**
15. **Kris Kline, ss/3b, Grand Canyon (Ariz.)**
16. **Greg Key, of, Montevallo (Ala.)**
17. **Doug McKenzie, rhp, Cal State Northridge**
18. **Don Groh, lhp, Nevada-Reno**
19. **Mike Madril, of, Grand Canyon (Ariz.)**
20. **Bob Kilmer, rhp, La Verne (Calif.)**
21. Jeff Norwood, lhp, Northwood Institute (Texas)
22. **Michael Rizzo, 2b, St. Xavier (Ill.)**
23. **Kirk Knowles, rhp, Northeast Louisiana**
24. **Robert Ritchie, 1b, Triton (Ill.) JC**
25. **Alex Christy, of, Indiana**
26. **Dave Heath, c, Auburn**
27. **Bert Adams, c, Hebert HS, Beaumont, Texas**

June—Secondary Phase (14)

1. Mark Bauer, rhp, Merced (Calif.) JC
2. Paul Williams, of, Mesa (Ariz.) CC
3. Keith Bond, rhp, Rose State (Okla.) JC
4. Gerald McDermott, c, Fontana (Calif.) HS
5. **Jeff Salazar, rhp, Los Angeles Valley JC**
6. Chip Dill, rhp, Cerritos (Calif.) JC

CHICAGO CUBS

January—Regular Phase (2)

1. Troy Afenir, c, Palomar (Calif.) JC
2. Alex Madrid, rhp, Yavapai (Ariz.) JC
3. Mike Mazzocco, of, JC of the Canyons (Calif.)
4. Michael Lozano, lhp, Sacramento CC
5. Frank Spear, lhp, Santa Ana (Calif.) JC
6. James Price, rhp, Ranger (Texas) JC
7. Charles Martin, rhp, Merced (Calif.) JC
8. **Steve Cordner, of, Gloucester County (N.J.) JC**
9. **Jim Allen, 1b/3b, Southern California**

January—Secondary Phase (24)

1. **Jeff Fruge, rhp, Panola (Texas) JC**

June—Regular Phase (1)

1. **Shawon Dunston, ss, Thomas Jefferson HS, Brooklyn, N.Y.**
1. **Tony Woods, ss, Whittier** (Pick from Expos as compensation for Type B free agent Tim Blackwell)
1. **Stan Boderick, of, Robinson HS, Tampa** (Supplemental pick—27th—for loss of Blackwell)
2. (Pick to Red Sox as compensation for Type A free agent Bill Campbell)
3. **Juan Velasquez, c, Miami Lakes HS, Hialeah, Fla.**
4. **C.J. Sciacca, ss, LaHabra HS, Whittier, Calif.**
5. **Gary Varsho, 2b, Wisconsin-Oshkosh**
6. Guy Normand, lhp, Gresham (Ore.) HS
7. Eric Nolte, lhp, Hemet (Calif.) HS
8. **Frank DeSantis, c, Nevada-Las Vegas**
9. **Geoff Doggett, of, South Alabama**
10. Ken Harvey, ss, Richmond
11. Mike Birkbeck, rhp, Akron
12. **Rudy Serafini, lhp, Shippensburg (Pa.)**
13. **Stephen Young, lhp, Amadoro HS, Pioneer, Calif.**
14. Joe Dunlap, ss, Haskell (Okla.) HS
15. **Larry Whelan, of, Kearney State (Neb.)**
16. **Joe Pantaleo, rhp, Lamar**
17. **Derrick Smith, 1b, Grambling State**
18. **Steve Roadcap, c, Francis Marion (S.C.)**
19. **Joe Holecek, c, Truman (Ill.) JC**
20. **Steve Burton, of, Southwestern State (Okla.)**
21. Jim Orsag, 1b, Thornton Fractional South HS, Lansing, Ill.
22. **Jim Boudreau, lhp, Arizona State**
23. **Kevin Atwood, of, Cordova HS, Rancho Cordova, Calif.**
24. **Jeff Schwarz, rhp, Fort Pierce (Fla.) West HS**
25. **Charles Stewart, c, William Paterson (N.J.)**
26. Jonathon Baker, c, Valley HS, Sacramento

June—Secondary Phase (21)

1. Byron Kemmerling, rhp, Alvin (Texas) CC
2. **Damon Farmar, of, West Los Angeles JC**
3. Tim Englund, rhp, San Jacinto (Texas) JC

CHICAGO WHITE SOX

January—Regular Phase (13)

1. Rodney McCray, of, Santa Monica (Calif.) JC
2. Stephen Clements, lhp, JC of Marin (Calif.) (Selection voided)
3. Tom Wallace, of, Glendale (Calif.) JC
4. **John Cangelosi, of, Miami-Dade North CC**
5. Randy Robertson, rhp, Citrus (Calif.) JC
6. Chris Beasley, rhp, Orange Coast (Calif.) JC
7. Brian Kubala, rhp, Miami-Dade North CC
8. James Everton, c, Long Beach (Calif.) CC
9. Larry Bentz, of, Kellogg (Mich.) CC
10. Ron Herring, rhp, Southwestern (Calif.) JC
11. Ronald Brown, of, Enterprise State (Ala.) JC

January—Secondary Phase (11)

No selection

June—Regular Phase (14)

1. **Ron Karkovice, c, Boone HS, Orlando, Fla.**
2. **Rolando Pino, 3b/ss, Miami Springs HS, Hialeah, Fla.**
3. **Kenny Williams, of, Mount Pleasant HS, San Jose, Calif.**
4. Scott Kannenberg, rhp, Wheat Ridge HS, Lakewood, Colo.
5. Otis Green, p/1b, Carol City (Fla.) HS
6. Todd Trafton, c, Elk Grove HS, Sacramento
7. **Mike Trujillo, rhp, Northern Colorado**
8. **Mike Hunsucker, 1b, DeSoto (Texas) HS**
9. **Tom Moritz, of, Southern California**
10. Terry Marshall, lhp, California Baptist
11. Twain Freeman, rhp, Simeon Vocational HS, Chicago

12. **Shawn Stacey, rhp, Granite Hills HS, El Cajon, Calif.**
13. **Mike Toothman, of, Stanford**
14. **Dave McLaughlin, of, Montclair State (N.J.)**
15. **Kim Christensen, 3b, Lamar**
16. **Gary Gonzales, rhp, Kerman (Calif.) HS**
17. **Buster Sunde, rhp, Western Michigan**
18. Richard Alvarez, rhp, Blackford HS, San Jose, Calif.
19. **Mark Ruckebeil, rhp, Zion-Benton HS, Winthrop Harbor, Ill.**
20. Matthew Warren, rhp, Mount Eden HS, Hayward, Calif.
21. **Larry McGee, of, Cal State Los Angeles**
22. Todd Oakes, rhp, Nebraska
23. **Bill Sandry, 1b, Kentucky**
24. **Robert Taylor, rhp, Texas A&M**
25. Dan Hamstra, rhp, Illinois
26. **Bryan Koch, c, Muhlenberg HS, Reading, Pa.**
27. **Garry Keeton, inf, Middle Tennessee State**
28. Tim Layana, rhp, Loyola HS, Culver City, Calif.
29. Dan Davies, lhp, Bishop Gallagher HS, Mount Clemens, Mich.

June—Secondary Phase (16)

1. **Joel McKeon, lhp, Miami-Dade North CC**
2. Harold Stewart, rhp, San Jacinto (Texas) JC

CINCINNATI REDS

January—Regular Phase (24)

1. **Orsino Hill, of, Los Angeles CC**
2. **Glenn Spagnola, rhp, Fullerton (Calif.) JC**
3. Randy Myers, lhp, Clark (Wash.) JC
4. Tom DiCeglio, ss, Gulf Coast (Fla.) CC
5. **Jay Munson, of, Shoreline (Wash.) CC**
6. **Steven Stout, rhp, Arizona Western JC**
7. Scott Obert, c, JC of Southern Idaho
8. Kent Schwartz, of, Cloud County (Kan.) CC
9. Louis Burmester, rhp, Nassau (N.Y.) CC
10. Glen Kuiper, ss, Indian Hills (Iowa) CC
11. **Richard Walker, of, Maple Woods (Mo.) CC**

January—Secondary Phase (14)

1. Richie Carter, of, Umpqua (Ore.) CC
2. Ron Johnson, of, Oregon
3. Ken Sinclair, rhp, Bronx, N.Y.

June—Regular Phase (23)

1. **Scott Jones, lhp, Hinsdale (Ill.) South HS** (Pick from Yankees as compensation for Type B free agent Dave Collins)
1. **Billy Hawley, rhp, Brookland Cayce HS, West Columbia, S.C.**
1. Robert Jones, 1b, Proviso East HS, Maywood, Ill. (Supplemental pick—28th—for loss of Collins)
2. Barry Larkin, ss, Moeller HS, Cincinnati
3. **Mike Konderla, rhp, Texas**
4. **Buddy Pryor, c, Arizona State**
5. **James Posillico, of, Clarke HS, Westbury, N.Y.**
6. **Tony Evans, ss, Michigan**
7. Bobby Witt, rhp, Canton (Mass.) HS
8. Mickey Brantley, of, Coastal Carolina
9. **Tom Browning, lhp, Tennessee Wesleyan**
10. **Jeff Spisok, ss, Schlarman HS, Danville, Ill.**
11. **Darryl Wilks, of/1b, Auburn**
12. Rick Luecken, rhp, Texas A&M
13. **Kevin Steinmetz, 3b, Portland State (Ore.)**
14. Robert Farnan, 2b, Texas-El Paso
15. **Michael Romano, c, Suffolk (Mass.)**
16. Ron Bianco, ss, Seminole (Fla.) HS
17. **Jeff Davis, ss, Newberry (S.C.)**
18. **Vin Rover, ss, Loyola Marymount**
19. **Greg Toler, c, Oak Ridge HS, Orlando, Fla.**
20. **William Albino, of, Fairfield**
21. **Tim Scott, rhp, C.W. Post (N.Y.)**
22. **Curtis Culberson, 2b, Texas-Arlington**
23. **Scott Radloff, 1b, Valley City State (N.D.)**
24. Mark Hammond, rhp, Willirod Catholic HS, Chicago
25. John Koontz, ss/2b, Petersburg (W.Va.) HS
26. **Louie Trujillo, rhp, Kansas State**
27. Steve Eager, c, Utah Technical JC
28. **Dave Keller, 1b/of, Northern Colorado**
29. **Paul Farlow, of, Randleman HS, Sophia, N.C.**
30. Hector Limon, ss, Estacado HS, Lubbock, Texas
31. Brad Alvaro, 2b, Caldwell (Idaho) HS
32. Mike Mills, rhp, Trevecca Nazarene (Tenn.)
33. Eric Boudreaux, rhp, Strake Jesuit HS, Houston
34. Larry Herrel, rhp, Rogers HS, Tulsa, Okla.

June—Secondary Phase (7)

1. **Kal Daniels, of, Middle Georgia JC**
2. Alex Madrid, rhp, Yavapai (Ariz.) JC

CLEVELAND INDIANS

January—Regular Phase (11)

1. Tracy Echols, of, DeKalb South (Ga.) CC
2. James Jefferson, rhp, Palm Beach (Fla.) JC
3. **Rod Carraway, inf/of, South Carolina**
4. **Craig Kiley, c, SUNY Farmingdale JC**
5. **Kelvin Stovall, of, DeKalb Central (Ga.) JC**
6. Jeff Gyarmati, rhp, Mercer County (N.J.) CC
7. **Kerry Kohler, c, CC of Morris (N.J.)**
8. Steve White, rhp, Mercer County (N.J.) CC
9. Moses Coleman, 1b, Brewton-Parker (Ga.) JC
10. Paul Williams, of, Mesa (Ariz.) CC
11. John Charboneau, of, Cuyahoga West (Ohio) CC
12. James Hill, lhp, Alabama Christian
13. **Richard Howroyd, c, St. Albans, W.Va.**
14. John Murray, 3b, DeKalb South (Ga.) CC

January—Secondary Phase (17)

1. Craig Holthus, of, Fruita Memorial HS, Grand Junction, Colo.
2. **John Thornton, 1b, CC of Baltimore**
3. **Robert Gilchrist, rhp, Sandusky, Ohio**

June—Regular Phase (12)

1. **Mark Snyder, rhp, Beardon HS, Knoxville, Tenn.**
2. **Jim Wilson, 1b, Oregon State**
3. Chad Squires, c, Gahr HS, Artesia, Calif.
4. **Andrew Ortiz, lhp, Jersey City State (N.J.)**
5. **Pookie Bernstine, of, Lewis-Clark State (Idaho)**
6. **Chris Cawthon, of, Florida State**
7. Carlos Diaz, c, St. Mary of the Assumption HS, Elizabeth, N.J.
8. **Wes Pierorazio, lhp, Long Island**
9. **Andre Holmes, of, Monrovia (Calif.) HS**
10. **Rick Filippo, lhp, Illinois**
11. **Jay Keeler, rhp, Florida State**
12. (Selection voided—player previously selected)
13. **Jeff Barkley, rhp, The Citadel**
14. **Rod Peters, 2b, George Washington**
15. **Charles Mitchell, 2b, West Chester (Pa.)**
16. **Dwight Madison, of, Georgetown**
17. Chris Knabenshue, of, Smokey Hill HS, Aurora, Colo.
18. **Mark Fagan, rhp, Ithaca (N.Y.)**
19. **Dave McCarthy, lhp, Amherst (Mass.)**
20. Casey Close, rhp/of, Worthington (Ohio) HS
21. Paul Beck, rhp, Murray (Utah) HS
22. Doug Little, rhp, North Shore HS, West Palm Beach, Fla.
23. Steve Kordish, rhp, Princeton
24. **Wayne Dale, c, Campbell**
25. Bill McGuire, c, Creighton Prep HS, Omaha, Neb.
26. Joseph Iafelice, ss, Euclid (Ohio) HS
27. Robbie Cobb, 2b, Ohio State
28. Richard Burkett, lhp, Hartville (S.C.) HS
29. **Edward Clark, lhp, Charlottesville (Va.) HS**
30. **Mike Connolly, rhp, East Bridgewater (Mass.) HS**
31. Daniel Neal, lhp, Wyoming

June—Secondary Phase (2)

1. Brian Howard, ss/2b, Rockville, Md.
2. **Edward Emmons, rhp, South Florida JC**
3. Dennis Woods, of, Spartanburg Methodist (S.C.) JC
4. Ricky Hester, of, Clemson
5. **Mark Barbagelata, ss, JC of Southern Idaho**

DETROIT TIGERS

January—Regular Phase (19)

1. **Thor Edgell, rhp, Fullerton (Calif.) JC**
2. Jody Ryan, rhp, Seminole (Fla.) CC
3. **Steve Caito, rhp, Northwest Mississippi JC**
4. **Anthony Long, 2b/of, San Diego Mesa JC**
5. Scott Whaley, rhp, Gadsden State (Ala.) JC
6. **Gary Whaley, of/1b, San Diego Mesa JC**
7. Tod Schulz, of, Central Arizona JC
8. Cordell Ross, of/ss, Central Arizona JC

January—Secondary Phase (25)

1. Dana Williams, ss, Enterprise State (Ala.) JC

June—Regular Phase (20)

1. **Rich Monteleone, rhp, Tampa Catholic HS**
2. Scott Kamieniecki, rhp, St. Mary's HS, Detroit
3. **Colin Ward, lhp, UCLA**
4. **Marc Washington, of, Northwestern HS, Detroit**
5. **Benny Ruiz, ss, Midwestern State (Texas)**
6. **Chris Pittaro, ss, North Carolina**
7. **Kerry Cook, rhp, Bradley**
8. **Jon Furman, rhp, Pepperdine**
9. **Doug Baker, ss, Arizona State**
10. **Walter Faber, lhp, Western Michigan**
11. **Scott Tabor, rhp, Arkansas**
12. Steve Ziem, rhp, Cal Poly Pomona
13. **Randy Conte, rhp, Illinois**
14. Jeff Robinson, rhp, Cal State Fullerton
15. **Ronnie Whitmore, rhp, Covington (Va.) HS**
16. Louis Blanco, c, East Chester HS, Tuckahoe, N.Y.
17. Steve Chumas, 3b, Western Michigan
18. **Craig Mills, ss, Hamilton (Ohio) HS**
19. **John Young, c, Michigan**
20. Mark Novak, rhp, Middle Tennessee State
21. **Kirk Anderson, rhp, Cal State Dominguez Hills**
22. **Paul Sokolowski, 1b, San Diego State**
23. Bert Martinez, 2b, Arizona State
24. **Glen Hobbie, rhp, Greenville (Ill.)**
25. **William Culver, rhp, Loyola Marymount**
26. **James Irwin, of, Eastern Michigan**
27. Jeff Jacobson, 2b, Michigan
28. Doug Starcher, rhp, Miramar (Fla.) HS
29. **Keith Traylor, of, Poly HS, Long Beach**
30. **Don Heinkel, rhp, Wichita State**
31. **Don Gordon, rhp, South Carolina**
32. Robert Nettles, rhp, Orange Coast (Calif.) JC
33. **William Granger, rhp, Alabama Christian**

June—Secondary Phase (4)

1. Doug Sheets, rhp/c, Saddleback (Calif.) CC
2. Tim McMannon, rhp, JC of Southern Idaho
3. Richard Helzer, rhp, JC of Marin (Calif.)

HOUSTON ASTROS

January—Regular Phase (16)

1. Mark Bauer, rhp, Merced (Calif.) JC
2. Randy Kramer, rhp, San Jose (Calif.) CC
3. Jeff Brown, of/1b, Orange Coast (Calif.) JC
4. Andrea Eli, rhp, San Diego CC
5. Jeff Schassler, rhp, Highland Falls, N.Y.
6. **Sam Moore, rhp, Walters State (Tenn.) CC**
7. **Keith Morin, of, Middlesex County (N.J.) JC**
8. Tim Englund, rhp, San Jacinto (Texas) JC
9. Harold Stewart, rhp, San Jacinto (Texas) JC
10. **Orlando Denis, inf, San Jacinto (Texas) JC**

January—Secondary Phase (22)

1. Kevin Sliwinski, of, Orange Coast (Calif.) JC

June—Regular Phase (15)

1. **Steve Swain, of, Grossmont HS, El Cajon, Calif.**
2. **Louie Meadows, 1b, North Carolina State**
3. **Mark Knudson, rhp, Colorado State**
4. **Rick Thompson, ss, Purdue**
5. **Mike Stellern, of, Missouri-St. Louis**
6. **Mark Bailey, 2b, Southwest Missouri State**
7. **Bruce Castoria, 1b, Mississippi State**
8. **Jamey Shouppe, lhp, Florida State**
9. **Jimmy Thomas, 2b, Wichita State**
10. **Rick Bombard, rhp, Florida**
11. **John Miller, 3b, Mission Bay HS, San Diego**
12. **Mike Botkin, of, Kentucky**
13. **Tracy Dophied, of, Texas**
14. **Jim Sherman, of, Delaware**
15. Andy Wortham, lhp, Pasadena (Calif.) HS
16. **Ray Perkins, rhp, Virginia Tech**
17. **Jeff Jacobson, c/of, Houston**
18. **Mike Kasprzak, rhp, Miami**
19. **Jeff Datz, c, Glassboro State (N.J.)**
20. **Arbrey Lucas, rhp, Grand Canyon (Ariz.)**
21. **Richard Strasser, rhp, Florida International**
22. **Jim Ambrose, rhp, Old Dominion**
23. **Neil Lautaret, 3b, Sahuaro HS, Tucson, Ariz.**
24. **James Donnelly, c, Ocean County (N.J.) CC**
25. **B.J. Hinson, 2b, East Tennessee State**
26. **Tom Roarke, c, Jacksonville**
27. Rob Nelson, 1b, South Pasadena (Calif.) HS
28. Karl Dorrell, of, Helix HS, San Diego

June—Secondary Phase (5)

1. **Charlie Kerfeld, rhp, Yavapai (Ariz.) JC**
2. **Mike Hogan, rhp, Arizona State**

KANSAS CITY ROYALS

January—Regular Phase (9)

1. Bob Ralston, 2b, Chabot (Calif.) JC
2. Eric Schmidt, rhp, Antelope Valley (Calif.) JC
3. Craig Reid, ss/2b, Panola (Texas) JC
4. **Jack Shuffield, of, Ventura (Calif.) JC**
5. Scott Groot, ss, Orange Coast (Calif.) JC
6. Chris Schulz, c, Golden West (Calif.) JC
7. **Donald Sparling, 1b, Spokane Falls (Wash.) CC**
8. George Cook, 2b, Los Angeles CC
9. Edward Bass, rhp, Chabot (Calif.) JC
10. James Mecate, of, Rio Hondo (Calif.) JC
11. Mark Berry, 3b, Oxnard (Calif.) JC
12. **Roscoe Palmer, of, Riverhead, N.Y.**

January—Secondary Phase (1)

1. **Danny Jackson, lhp, Trinidad State (Colo.) JC**
2. Damon Farmer, of, West Los Angeles JC
3. Richard Smith, rhp, Diablo Valley (Calif.) JC

June—Regular Phase (10)

1. **John Morris, of, Seton Hall**
2. **Joe Szekely, c, Texas A&M**
3. **Edward Allen, of, Verbum Dei HS, Compton, Calif.**
4. Will Clark, 1b, Jesuit HS, New Orleans
5. Mike Ollom, rhp, Cascade HS, Everett, Wash.
6. **Kevin Stanley, lhp, Oceanview HS, Huntington Beach, Calif.**
7. **Doug Gilcrease, ss, Auburn**
8. **Art Martinez, rhp, Grand Canyon (Ariz.)**
9. **Israel Sanchez, lhp, Von Steuben HS, Chicago**
10. **Jay Phillips, 2b, Virginia Tech**
11. **Eric Monson, 3b, Pacific Lutheran (Wash.)**
12. **Mark Pirruccello, c, Cal State Fullerton**
13. **Darren Sturdivant, c, Cherry Creek HS, Englewood, Calif.**
14. **John Serritella, rhp, Weber HS, Melrose Park, Ill.**
15. **Phillip George, lhp, Plum HS, Pittsburgh**
16. **Bill Wilder, rhp, East Carolina**
17. Gary Bockhorn, rhp/of, Steelville (Ill.) HS
18. **Michael Cusey, rhp, Wilson HS, Hacienda Heights, Calif.**
19. **Bret Saberhagen, ss, Cleveland HS, Northridge, Calif.**
20. **Robert Davis, c, Los Altos HS, Hacienda Heights, Calif.**
21. **Stan Oxner, c, Westark (Ark.) CC**
22. **Jeff Neuzil, ss, Kansas**
23. **Robert DeBord, rhp, Richmond**
24. **Greg Moseley, rhp, Occidental (Calif.)**
25. Darryl Dixon, of, Michigan State

26. Andy Stankiewicz, ss, St. Paul HS, Cerritos, Calif.
27. **Matthew Hall, of, Mesa (Colo.)**
28. **Duane Ware, rhp, Washington**
29. **Willis Whitehurst, ss, Pottstown (Pa.) HS**
30. Loren Hoppes, ss, Wapato (Wash.) HS
31. **Dave Rooker, of, Arizona**

June—Secondary Phase (6)

1. **Tom Wallace, of, Glendale (Calif.) JC**
2. Mark Berry, 3b, Oxnard (Calif.) JC
3. Robert Locke, of, Gordon (Ga.) JC
4. **Cecil Fielder, 1b, LaPuente, Calif.**

LOS ANGELES DODGERS

January—Regular Phase (20)

1. **Michael Kolb, rhp, Sacramento CC**
2. William Wilson, lhp, San Jacinto (Texas) JC
3. Mike Kolovitz, rhp, Triton (Ill.) JC
4. Joey Aragon, ss, Citrus (Calif.) JC
5. Jerald Phillips, c, Taft (Calif.) JC
6. **Mike Pinckard, rhp, Cerritos (Calif.) JC**
7. Bill Geivett, 3b/1b, Sacramento CC
8. Riley Epps, c, McLennan (Texas) CC
9. Greg Wallace, c, Bee County (Texas) JC

January—Secondary Phase (12)

1. **Henry Gatewood, c, Sacramento CC**
2. Derril Lewis, lhp, San Bernardino Valley (Calif.) JC
3. Bart Elbin, rhp, Louisburg (N.C.) JC

June—Regular Phase (19)

1. **Franklin Stubbs, 1b, Virginia Tech**
2. **Richard Flores, ss, Coachella Valley HS, Thermal, Calif.**
3. **Ken Howell, rhp, Tuskegee (Ala.)**
4. Ron McCormack, rhp, Liberty HS, Renton, Wash.
5. **Bill White, 1b, The Citadel**
6. **Brian Innis, rhp, Illinois**
7. **Tim Hill, of/3b, Elk Grove HS, Wilton, Calif.**
8. **Joe Vavra, ss, Wisconsin-Stout**
9. Richard Jennings, 3b, Fenwick HS, Chicago
10. **Ron Burns, rhp, Eastern Washington**
11. **John Diehl, of, Shippensburg, Pa.**
12. Steve Gehrke, rhp, Nebraska
13. **Reggie Williams, of, Southern**
14. **Gary Newsom, 2b, Georgia Tech**
15. **Brian Piper, rhp, Texas-El Paso**
16. **Mark Mangione, ss, Kentucky**
17. Rich Medina, lhp, Lewis-Clark State (Idaho)
18. **Greg Clark, of, North Carolina Wesleyan**
19. **Tim Meeks, rhp, Santa Rosa (Calif.) JC**
20. **Bill Scudder, rhp, San Francisco State**
21. **Edward Williams, 2b/of, Cal State Los Angeles**
22. **Gerald Cain, of, Zion-Benton HS, Zion, Ill.**
23. **Mike Gentle, lhp, North Alabama**
24. Kurt Beamesderfer, c, Troy HS, Yorba Linda, Calif.
25. **Joe Wesley, 3b/of, Silver Creek HS, San Jose, Calif.**
26. Stan Van Muyden, rhp, Elk Grove HS, Wilton, Calif.
27. Gordie Hershiser, rhp, Birmingham Groves HS, Bloomfield Hills, Mich.
28. **Kirk Vucsko, rhp, Lewis (Ill.)**
29. **Jeff Hamilton, ss/of, Flint Carman HS, Davison, Mich.**

June—Secondary Phase (3)

1. **Don Smith, rhp, Arizona State**
2. Matt Rowe, rhp, JC of Marin (Calif.)
3. Jim O'Dell, of/1b, Lewis-Clark State (Idaho)

MILWAUKEE BREWERS

January—Regular Phase (25)

1. **Derek Tatsuno, lhp, Aiea, Hawaii**
2. **Larry Jackson, of, Triton (Ill.) JC**
3. **Robert Sullivan, rhp, Moorpark (Calif.) JC**
4. Sherman Bennett, rhp, Miami-Dade South CC
5. **Mark Delgado, 3b, Alvin (Texas) CC**
6. **Brian Finley, of, Contra Costa (Calif.) JC**
7. Byron Kemmerling, rhp, Alvin (Texas) CC
8. Daniel Aruca, of, Miami-Dade North CC
9. Rex Perozo, rhp, Miami-Dade South CC
10. Joe Grayston, ss, Long Beach (Calif.) CC
11. Terry Repp, 2b/3b, St. Louis CC-Meramec
12. Tyrone Walker, c, Central Arizona JC
13. Brad Goodwin, of, Umpqua (Ore.) CC
14. David Williams, ss/2b, Central Arizona JC
15. Mark Michel, rhp, Ventura (Calif.) JC
16. Tony Blasucci, of/lhp, Broward (Fla.) CC
17. **James Culver, of, Antelope Valley (Calif.) JC**
18. **Fred Williams, of, JC of Lake County (Ill.)**
19. Earl Frishman, 3b, Los Angeles Valley JC
20. Anthony Brown, rhp, Yakima Valley (Wash.) JC
21. Steve Arseneault, ss/2b, Glendale (Calif.) JC
22. Joseph Lozano, lhp, Ventura (Calif.) JC
23. **Billy Smith, rhp, Santa Ana (Calif.) JC**
24. Tom Pagnozzi, 3b, Central Arizona JC
25. Mark Stathas, ss, Linn-Benton (Ore.) CC
26. Fred Perez, c, Ventura (Calif.) JC
27. Michael Russell, rhp, Santa Barbara (Calif.) CC

January—Secondary Phase (21)

1. Curtis Zucco, lhp, Mount Olive (N.C.) JC
2. **Chris Bosio, rhp, Sacramento CC**
3. Frank Marrero, rhp, Miami-Dade North CC

June—Regular Phase (25)

1. **Dale Sveum, ss, Pinole (Calif.) Valley HS**
2. **Bryan Duquette, lhp, Hawaii**
3. **Dan Scarpetta, lhp, Auburn Senior HS, Rockford, Ill.**
4. **Alan Cartwright, of, Southeastern Oklahoma State**
5. **Bill Shamblin, rhp, Mojave HS, Riviera, Ariz.**
6. **Billy Jo Robidoux, 1b, Ware (Mass.) HS**
7. Kevin Sheary, rhp, Roxbury HS, Flanders, N.J.
8. **Jim Paciorek, of, Michigan**
9. **Brian Mignano, rhp, Stanford**
10. **Jay Aldrich, rhp, Montclair State (N.J.)**
11. **Kevin Murray, of, North Dallas HS**
12. **Hank Landers, of, Brown**
13. David Bailey, 1b, Montevallo (Ala.)
14. **Ben Donisi, 3b, Florida International**
15. Greg Burlingame, lhp, Kingsway HS, Mullica Hill, N.J.
16. **Robert Derksen, rhp, Wisconsin**
17. **Chuck Crim, rhp, Hawaii**
18. **Gary Ream, rhp, Eastern Wayne HS, La Grange, N.C.**
19. **Barry Koch, rhp, Arizona State**
20. **Joel Weatherford, of, Newberry (S.C.)**
21. Michael Parsons, rhp, St. Louis CC-Meramec
22. **Michael Meyer, 2b, Cal State Los Angeles**
23. **Matt Sferrazza, of/3b, Cerritos (Calif.) JC**
24. Stan Floyd, of, Houston
25. Greg Bartek, rhp, Roxbury HS, Succasunna, N.J.
26. Paul Togneri, lhp, Nogales HS, LaPuente, Calif.
27. Mark Ciardi, rhp, Maryland
28. Kevin Renz, rhp, Paris (Texas) JC
29. **Dave Klipstein, of, Mississippi State**
30. Rick Abbott, ss/2b, Santa Ana (Calif.) JC

June—Secondary Phase (12)

1. **Tim Utecht, 1b, Lower Columbia (Wash.) JC**
2. **Jeff Gyarmati, rhp, Mercer County (N.J.) CC**
3. John Wallace, of, Southern California
4. Dean Albany, rhp, CC of Baltimore
5. Steve Oswald, lhp, Triton (Ill.) JC
6. Doug Givler, rhp, Frederick (Md.) CC

MINNESOTA TWINS

January—Regular Phase (3)

1. **Kirby Puckett, of, Triton (Ill.) JC**
2. Doug Sheets, rhp/c, Saddleback (Calif.) CC
3. Steve Moses, of, Cerritos (Calif.) JC
4. Matt Rowe, rhp, JC of Marin (Calif.)
5. Brad Seehwaer, ss, Umpqua (Ore.) CC
6. Robert Locke, of, Gordon (Ga.) JC

7. Mark Friedly, rhp, Cerritos (Calif.) JC
8. Bob Grandstaff, 3b, Golden West (Calif.) JC
9. Greg Mathews, lhp, Santa Ana (Calif.) JC
10. Marty Reed, lhp, Hillsborough (Fla.) CC
11. Troy Galloway, lhp, Modesto (Calif.) JC
12. Jeffrey Rojas, rhp, San Bernardino Valley (Calif.) JC
13. Steve Brueggeman, p/of, Kings River (Calif.) JC

January—Secondary Phase (8)

1. Mark Margis, lhp, Culver City, Calif.
2. John Bryant, of, Santa Ana (Calif.) JC
3. **Ted Perkins, of, Richmond, Calif.**

June—Regular Phase (4)

1. **Bryan Oelkers, lhp, Wichita State**
2. **Allan Anderson, lhp, Lancaster (Ohio) HS**
3. **Greg Howe, of, Eastern Michigan**
4. **Robert Ferro, ss, Muhlenberg HS, Reading, Pa.**
5. **Ken Klump, rhp, Southern Illinois**
6. **Bob DeCosta, ss, Stanford**
7. **Brian Rupe, of, Virginia Tech**
8. **Mike Tryon, c, Catholic (D.C.)**
9. Shell Scott, ss, Mount Carmel HS, Poway, Calif.
10. **David Butters, c, Sutherland HS, Pittsford, N.Y.**
11. **Mark Davidson, of, Clemson**
12. Scott Sabo, lhp, Wisconsin
13. **Erez Borowsky, c, Vanderbilt**
14. **Jeff Szczecinski, 2b, Long Island**
15. **Mike Moreno, ss, Lewis-Clark State (Idaho)**
16. Lenny Webster, c, Lutcher (La.) HS
17. **Kiel Higgins, rhp, New Mexico**
18. **Frank Eufemia, rhp, Ramapo (N.J.)**
19. **Marty Pevey, c, Georgia Southern**
20. **Terrill Parham, lhp, Georgia Southern**
21. **Larry Hatley, of, South Stanley HS, Albemarle, N.C.**
22. Mark Cardaci, of, William Paterson (N.J.)
23. **Andrew Lesnak, ss, Southeastern Louisiana**
24. **Brian Hobaugh, rhp, Iowa**
25. **Thomas Cichon, 1b, Kennedy HS, Utica, N.Y.**
26. Andre Crawford, of, Harding HS, Charlotte, N.C.
27. David Turney, of/inf, Mount San Antonio (Calif.) JC
28. **Ronn Van Krevelen, of, Minnesota**
29. **Doug Smith, rhp, Liberty**
30. **Alberto Zappala, inf, Fairfield**
31. **Paul Mancuso, lhp, New Orleans**
32. Eduardo Gonzalez, c, Jackson HS, Miami
33. Robert Cramer, lhp, Highland HS, Bakersfield, Calif.

June—Secondary Phase (18)

1. **Curt Kindred, rhp, Fullerton (Calif.) JC**

MONTREAL EXPOS

January—Regular Phase (18)

1. **Troy McKay, of/rhp, Des Moines Area (Iowa) CC**
2. Scott Prickett, lhp, Des Moines Area (Iowa) CC
3. Blaze Katich, of, Pensacola (Fla.) JC
4. Robert Wright, inf, San Joaquin Delta (Calif.) JC
5. **Julius Anderson, 3b, South Georgia JC**
6. **Rodney Schnatz, rhp, Batavia, Ohio**
7. Roy Campbell, of, Columbia State (Tenn.) CC (Selection voided)
8. Terrill Adams, rhp, Mission (Calif.) JC
9. Robert Thompson, of, JC of Southern Idaho
10. James Bettis, of, Cincinnati
11. **Rick Miller, p/1b, Richmond, Ky.**
12. Curran Hubbard, rhp, St. Louis CC-Meramec
13. **Terry Strickland, 3b, Campbell**
14. Jeffrey Edwards, 3b, Louisburg (N.C.) JC

January—Secondary Phase (6)

1. David Alores, rhp, Blinn (Texas) JC
2. Mark Baker, rhp, Palm Beach (Fla.) JC
3. David Flattery, rhp, Iowa State

June—Regular Phase (17)

1. (Pick to Cubs as compensation for Type B free agent Tim Blackwell).
2. **John Dopson, rhp, Delore Catholic HS, Finksburg, Md.**
3. **Tim Thiessen, ss, Fresno State**
4. Lloyd Martin, lhp, Santa Clara
5. **Rene Gonzales, ss, Cal State Los Angeles**
6. **Buck Belue, of, Georgia**
7. Jeff Peterson, lhp, St. Mary's
8. Wayne Able, of, Davidson HS, Mobile, Ala.
9. Ron Jackson, c, McKinney (Texas) HS
10. **John Glidewell, rhp, Gorham (Ill.) HS**
11. **Jim Cecchini, c, Southern California**
12. Paul Quinzer, rhp, Castle HS, Newburg, Ind.
13. Darryl Stephens, of, Stanford
14. Tom Thompson, 1b/of, Knoch HS, Renfrew, Pa.
15. **Tom Krupa, 1b, Louisiana Tech**
16. **Mark Hall, 2b, Bowling Green State**
17. Lou Brock Jr., ss, Ladue HS, St. Louis
18. Tim Rypien, c, Shadle Park HS, Spokane, Wash.
19. **Keith Washington, ss, Los Angeles CC**
20. Scott Powers, ss, Middle Georgia JC
21. Jeff Parrett, rhp, Kentucky
22. **Tim Nichting, c, Xavier**
23. **Shawn Mielke, rhp, Valley HS, Las Vegas**
24. **Jim Lumpe, 2b, Missouri**
25. Kevin Pour, of/rhp, New Athens (Ill.) HS
26. **Corey Zawadski, of, Southern Illinois**
27. **Daniel Szajko, of, Notre Dame**
28. **Mike Hocutt, 3b, Iowa State**
29. **Gary Weinberger, of, Cal State Sacramento**
30. **Steve Shoemaker, of, Cumberlands (Ky.) JC**
31. **David Duvnjak, c, Ball State**

June—Secondary Phase (19)

1. **Nelson Santovenia, c, Miami**
2. Norman Morton, lhp, Miami-Dade North CC
3. **David Flores, rhp, Texas A&M**
4. **Blaze Katich, of, Pensacola (Fla.) JC**
5. **Curtis Zucco, lhp, Mount Olive (N.C.) JC**
6. Jeffrey Edwards, 3b, Louisburg (N.C.) JC

NEW YORK METS

January—Regular Phase (6)

1. Tim McMannon, rhp, JC of Southern Idaho
2. Bobby Estrada, rhp, San Jacinto (Texas) JC
3. Kal Daniels, of, Middle Georgia JC
4. Greg Selecky, 1b, Brookdale (N.J.) CC
5. **Scott Adams, rhp, Alabama Christian**
6. Brett Harrison, ss, Bacone (Okla.) JC
7. **Kenneth Bodle, of, Orange Coast (Calif.) JC**
8. Steven Oswald, lhp, Triton (Ill.) JC
9. Tim Utecht, 1b, Lower Columbia (Wash.) JC
10. **Edward Groves, rhp, Romulus (Mich.) HS**
11. Timothy Lemons, 3b, Gulf Coast (Fla.) CC
12. **Michael Robair, rhp, Chipola (Fla.) JC**
13. **Nicholas Brandt, lhp, Butte (Calif.) JC**
14. Robert Voydat, ss, DeAnza (Calif.) JC
15. Keith Bond, lhp, Rose State (Okla.) JC
16. **David Wyatt, lhp, Alabama Christian**
17. **John Wilson, of, Bamberg, S.C.**
18. Andrew Sanclers, of, Allen County (Kan.) CC
19. **Ed Pruitt, lhp, Blum, Texas**

January—Secondary Phase (18)

1. **Steven Gay, rhp, Green River (Wash.) CC**
2. Luis Medina, of, Cerritos (Calif.) JC
3. **Marvin Parker, c, Florida CC**

June—Regular Phase (5)

1. **Dwight Gooden, rhp, Hillsborough HS, Tampa**
2. **Floyd Youmans, rhp, Fontana (Calif.) HS**
3. **Roger McDowell, rhp, Bowling Green State**
4. Tracy Jones, 3b, Loyola Marymount
5. **Gerald Young, ss, Santa Ana (Calif.) Valley HS**
6. **Kyle Hartshorn, rhp, Allentown HS, New Egypt, N.J.**
7. **Greg Olson, c, Minnesota**
8. Rafael Palmeiro, of, Jackson HS, Miami

9. **Joe Redfield, ss, UC Santa Barbara**
10. Troy Evers, rhp, West HS, Appleton, Wis.
11. **Alan Carmichael, c, Bailor HS, Signal Mountain, Tenn.**
12. **Mickey Weston, rhp, Eastern Michigan**
13. David Jacas, of, Ramapo HS, Spring Valley, N.J.
14. Scott Tidmore, rhp, Arab (Ala.) HS
15. **Barry Lyons, c, Delta State (Miss.)**
16. Doug Henry, rhp, Tennyson HS, Hayward, Calif.
17. **John Boyles, rhp, Gannon (Pa.)**
18. **Carl Hollis, ss, Stillman (Ala.)**
19. Jeff Richardson, rhp, Northwest HS, Wichita, Kan.
20. **Steve Springer, of, Utah**
21. Jim Phillips, rhp, Kansas
22. **Wes Gardner, rhp, Central Arkansas**
23. **Eugene Hawkins, c, Norfolk State**
24. **Rick Paul, rhp, Saint Louis**
25. **John Metasavage, 3b, Auburn**
26. John Grier, of, Rye (N.Y.) HS
27. John Morgan, ss, Lee HS, Montgomery, Ala.
28. Charles Higson, rhp, Columbia HS, Columbia Falls, Mont.
29. Ricky Kyle, rhp, Northwest HS, Omaha, Neb.

June—Secondary Phase (9)

1. **Randy Myers, lhp, Clark (Wash.) JC**
2. **Stu Foulks, rhp, Jacksonville**
3. Jim Benedict, rhp, Los Angeles Valley JC

NEW YORK YANKEES

January—Regular Phase (21)

1. **George Freeman, rhp, Fresno (Calif.) CC**
2. Charles Hardwick, lhp, Mount Olive (N.C.) JC
3. **Tony Russell, of, Middle Georgia JC**
4. **Earl Nichols, rhp, Allen County (Kan.) CC**
5. Tony Arias, rhp, Miami-Dade South CC
6. Brad Wheeler, lhp, Indian River (Fla.) CC
7. Tim Meacham, rhp, Lurleen B. Wallace State (Ala.) JC
8. Harry Overton, of, Louisburg (N.C.) JC
9. George Pierce, of, Lurleen B. Wallace State (Ala.) JC
10. Lee Boykin, c/of, Quinsigamond (Mass.) CC
11. Donald Johnson, rhp, Rock Valley (Ill.) JC
12. Joseph Orszulak, rhp, Quinsigamond (Mass.) CC
13. Marty Freeman, 2b/of, Indian River (Fla.) CC
14. Joe Fletcher, rhp, Illinois Valley CC
15. David Lenderman, rhp, Linn-Benton (Ore.) CC
16. Marvin White, 3b, JC of Marin (Calif.)
17. Frank Russo, of, Indian River (Fla.) CC
18. Chad Miltenberger, c/dh, JC of the Sequoias (Calif.)
19. John Smolski, rhp, Illinois Valley CC
20. Randy Howard, ss, Illinois Valley CC
21. Ronald Troester, rhp, JC of Southern Idaho
22. Jeffery Franks, c, Umpqua (Ore.) CC
23. Tracy Poulsen, rhp, JC of Southern Idaho
24. Scott Ninneman, rhp, Oxnard (Calif.) JC
25. Paul Osborne, c, DeKalb North (Ga.) JC
26. Ronald Marbrey, 2b, West Covina, Calif.

January—Secondary Phase (9)

1. Oddibe McDowell, of, Miami-Dade North CC
2. Ken Reed, rhp, Crowder (Mo.) JC

June—Regular Phase (22)

1. (Pick to Reds as compensation for Type B free agent Dave Collins).
2. **Tim Birtsas, lhp, Michigan State** (Pick from Angels as compensation for Type A free agent Reggie Jackson)
2. Bo Jackson, ss, McAdory HS, Bessemer, Ala.
3. **Dan Pasqua, of, William Paterson (N.J.)**
4. **James Riggs, 3b, Eastern Michigan**
5. B.J. Surhoff, ss, Rye (N.Y.) HS
6. **Herman Cunningham, of, Danville (Ill.) HS**
7. **Rory Brown, lhp, Florida International**
8. **Bill Ruffner, of, Wake Forest**
9. **Joey MacKay, of, Villa Park HS, Orange, Calif.**
10. **Richard Gumpert, rhp, Lawrence HS, Mashpee, Mass.**
11. **Michael Fennell, c, LeMoyne**
12. **Charles Tomaselli, lhp, St. Leo (Fla.)**
13. **Kirk Bailey, rhp, Appalachian State**
14. **Ronald Inman, lhp, UNC Wilmington**
15. **Stephen George, lhp, Florida Southern**
16. **Fredi Gonzalez, c, Southridge HS, Miami**
17. **Tim Kubacki, ss, Toledo**
18. James Morris, lhp, Brownwood (Texas) HS
19. **Tim Byron, rhp, Seton Hall**
20. **Pete Adams, ss, Maine**
21. **Jim Deshaies, lhp, LeMoyne**
22. **John Bryant, rhp, Alma (Mich.)**
23. **Peter Post, of, Florida International**
24. **Greg Unger, lhp, Pacific**
25. **Jim Corsi, rhp, St. Leo (Fla.)**
26. **Tom Barrett, 2b, Arizona**
27. **Pete Dalena, 1b, Fresno State**
28. **Jeff Wiley, 2b, St. Clair County (Mich.) CC**
29. **Dick Seidel, rhp, Wisconsin-La Crosse**
30. **Steve Compagno, lhp, Cal Poly San Luis Obispo**
31. Richard Lewallen, of, Kansas
32. **Paul Peer, of, Toledo**
33. Wayne Fugett, rhp, Valdosta State (Ga.)
34. **Mark Chestna, of, St. Peter's HS, Worcester, Mass.**
35. Jeff Manto, rhp/3b, Bristol (Pa.) HS
36. **Clayton Stidham, rhp, Central Catholic HS, Toledo, Ohio**
37. Hilario Valdespino, 3b, Carol City HS, Miami
38. **Craig Jobes, 3b, Lakeland Regional HS, Wanaque, N.J.**
39. David Poulos, ss, Middle Georgia JC
40. **Mike York, rhp/of, Argo HS, Justice, Fla.**
41. **Randy White, lhp, Yakima Valley (Wash.) JC**
42. **Stacy Morgan, rhp, Washington State**
43. Andrew Fava, 3b, Loyola HS, Towson, Md.
44. **Glynn Perry, of, Kansas State**
45. **Daniel Gasparino, c, Vermont**
46. **Paul LeSieur, c, St. Leo (Fla.)**
47. **Robert Woodcock, 2b, San Francisco**

June—Secondary Phase (24)

1. Mark Stathas, ss, Linn-Benton (Ore.) CC
2. **Richie Carter, of, Umpqua (Ore.) CC**
3. Luis Medina, of, Cerritos (Calif.) JC
4. **Richard Borowski, 3b, Erie (N.Y.) CC**
5. **Marvin White, 3b, JC of Marin (Calif.)**
6. Jeff Franks, c, Umpqua (Ore.) CC
7. Bob Grandstaff, 3b, Golden West (Calif.) JC

OAKLAND ATHLETICS

January—Regular Phase (26)

1. Richard Helzer, rhp, JC of Marin (Calif.)
2. Robby Thompson, ss, Palm Beach (Fla.) JC
3. Chuck Spiegel, 1b, Golden West (Calif.) JC
4. Jerrald Muldrew, of, Contra Costa (Calif.) JC
5. Stevie Bowens, lhp, Compton (Calif.) CC
6. Larry Schofield, p, Laney (Calif.) JC
7. Jack Reinholtz, lhp, Orange Coast (Calif.) JC
8. **Clemente Oropeza, 3b/rhp, CC of San Francisco**
9. Anthony Huff, rhp/of, Compton, Calif.
10. Michael Fields, rhp, El Camino (Calif.) JC
11. **Rob Currie, of, Paterson, N.J.**
12. **Gary Pool, lhp, Redlands (Calif.)**
13. Fred Dalaine, of, Orange Coast (Calif.) JC
14. Robert Gray, of, Saddleback (Calif.) CC
15. Martin Alejos, 1b, Santa Rosa (Calif.) JC

January—Secondary Phase (23)

1. **Dave Leiper, lhp, Fullerton (Calif.) JC**

June—Regular Phase (26)

1. (Pick to Red Sox as compensation for Type A free agent Joe Rudi)
2. **Steve Ontiveros, rhp, Michigan**
3. **Phil Stephenson, 1b, Wichita State**
4. **Brian Graham, of, UCLA**
5. **Charlie O'Brien, c, Wichita State**
6. **Ray Thoma, ss, Western Michigan**

7. **Glenn Godwin, lhp, San Diego**
8. Mike Dotterer, of, Stanford
9. Pat Griffin, rhp, Northern Illinois
10. **Jeff Kaiser, lhp, Western Michigan**
11. **Bob Bathe, 1b, Cal State Fullerton**
12. **Ed Myers, rhp, Arkansas**
13. **Jim Eppard, 1b, California**
14. **Tony Laurenzi, of, Cal State Long Beach**
15. **Jose Canseco Jr., 3b, Carol City HS, Miami**
16. Todd Welborn, rhp, East Wilkes HS, Ronda, N.C.
17. **Russ Wortmann, c, Texas-El Paso**
18. **Leon Baham, ss, Brigham Young**
19. **Pete Kendrick, lhp, Brigham Young**
20. **Eric Barry, lhp, Cal State Fullerton**
21. **Mike Gorman, rhp, Oregon State**
22. Thomas Walsh, 2b/ss, California Baptist
23. **Tim Lambert, rhp, San Diego State**
24. **Thomas Czuk, 3b, West Florida**
25. **David Peterson, 1b/of, Western Michigan**
26. **Douglas Farrow, rhp, Pomona-Pitzer (Calif.)**
27. **Tom Conquest, rhp, Chapman (Calif.)**
28. **Bob Hallas, rhp, Purdue**
29. Matt Held, c, UC Riverside
30. **Mark Border, rhp, Cal Poly Pomona**
31. Keith Mucha, 3b, Oral Roberts

June—Secondary Phase (26)

1. Jose Rodiles, rhp, Seminole State (Okla.) JC
2. Rodney McCray, of, Santa Monica (Calif.) JC
3. Rich Rosemus, lhp, Linn-Benton (Ore.) CC

PHILADELPHIA PHILLIES

January—Regular Phase (14)

1. Jimmy King, ss, Colorado Springs, Colo.
2. **Vaughn Calloway, c, Pratt (Kan.) CC**
3. **Dan Odgers, 3b/ss, Chipola (Fla.) JC**
4. Dodd Hook, 3b/1b, Indian Hills (Iowa) CC
5. **Ray Ortega, 3b, Bakersfield (Calif.) CC**
6. Darren Loy, c, Seminole State (Okla.) JC
7. **Kirk Burgess, rhp, Seminole State (Okla.) JC**
8. Alejandro Garcia, lhp, San Jacinto (Texas) JC
9. Alan Brown, c, San Jacinto (Texas) JC
10. Joe Jordan, c, Seminole State (Okla.) JC
11. Joe Neely, lhp, Bacone (Okla.) JC
12. Walt Stull, rhp, Sacramento CC
13. **Harris Campbell, of, Van Nuys, Calif.**
14. Jamie Doughty, ss, Seminole State (Okla.) JC
15. Jamie Campbell, rhp, McBee HS, Bethune, S.C.
16. Tony Faryniarz, rhp, Cordova HS, Rancho Cordova, Calif.
17. **Thomas Orsag, rhp, Triton (Ill.) JC**
18. Robert McClanahan, lhp, Mount Olive (N.C.) JC
19. Matt Butcher, 2b, West Los Angeles JC
20. **Rick Surhoff, rhp, St. John's River (Fla.) CC**

January—Secondary Phase (16)

1. **John Machin, lhp, Austin (Texas) CC**
2. Mark Michna, of, Blinn (Texas) JC
3. Craig Fitzpatrick, rhp, Koeltztown, Mo.

June—Regular Phase (13)

1. **John Russell, c/of, Oklahoma**
2. **Lance McCullers, rhp, Tampa Catholic HS**
3. **Kevin Ross, of, Newberry (Fla.) HS**
4. **Gib Seibert, of, Arizona State**
5. **Mike Maddux, rhp, Texas-El Paso**
6. Mike Cook, rhp, St. Andrews HS, Charleston, S.C.
7. **Howard Nichols, 1b/c, Skyline HS, Oakland, Calif.**
8. Billy Bates, 2b/ss, Aldine HS, Houston
9. **Russell Morton, rhp, Kansas Newman**
10. Lance Lincoln, ss, Pullman (Wash.) HS
11. **Kevin Coker, rhp, North Brunswick HS, Leland, N.C.**
12. **Jerry Arnold, lhp, Baylor**
13. **Damon Dombek, lhp, Penny HS, East Hartford, Conn.**
14. **Frank Martinez, 1b, Selma (Calif.) HS**
15. **Terry Dickerson, lhp, Forrest Hill HS, West Palm Beach, Fla.**
16. **Henry Smith, 3b, Forest Brook HS, Houston**
17. **Kevin Walters, c, Santa Clara**
18. Greg Lorenzetti, of, Stanford
19. **Brant Weatherford, rhp, Muskogee (Okla.) HS**
20. Steve Castleberry, 3b, Mount Carmel HS, Poway, Calif.
21. Bernard Walker, of, Corsicana (Texas) HS
22. **Greg Legg, ss, Southeastern Oklahoma State**
23. **Milo Choate, 3b, Texas**
24. **James Vest, of, Holy Cross**
25. **David Vernon, c, Oxnard (Calif.) HS**
26. **Greg Devone, of, Oak Park (Mich.) HS**
27. **Rodger Cole, rhp, Wiley (Texas)**
28. **Byron Beal, rhp, Lewisville (Texas) HS**
29. Ken Patterson, lhp, McGregor (Texas) HS
30. **David Kennard, 2b/ss, Texas A&M**
31. Bruce Ruffin, lhp, Hanks HS, El Paso, Texas
32. **John Powell, rhp, Lewisville (Texas) HS**
33. **Louis Lukes, of, Cajon HS, San Bernardino, Calif.**
34. **Paul Robinson, rhp, Sam Houston State**
35. Wayne Egbert, rhp, Sumner (Wash.) HS

June—Secondary Phase (17)

1. **Ken Jackson, ss, Angelina (Texas) JC**
2. Craig Reid, ss, Panola (Texas) JC
3. Brett Harrison, ss, Bacone (Okla.) JC
4. **Todd Johnson, of, Northwood (Texas)**

PITTSBURGH PIRATES

January—Regular Phase (8)

1. **Charles Cunningham, 3b, Cumberlands (Ky.) JC**
2. Dennis Woods, of, Spartanburg Methodist (S.C.) JC
3. Mark Barbagelata, ss, JC of Southern Idaho
4. Tim Grachen, lhp, Fullerton (Calif.) JC
5. Mike Santiago, lhp, Mount San Antonio (Calif.) JC
6. Jamie Brisco, rhp, Fresno CC
7. Michael Wood, rhp, Frederick (Md.) CC
8. Richard Borowski, 3b, Erie (N.Y.) CC
9. Al Hamilton, 3b, Crowder (Mo.) JC
10. Robert Kline, rhp, Hagerstown (Md.) JC
11. **Gary Grudzinski, rhp, Lackawanna (Pa.) JC**

January—Secondary Phase (4)

1. **Burk Goldthorn, c, Texas**
2. **Benny Distefano, 1b, Alvin (Texas) CC**
3. Tim Barker, 2b, Seminole (Fla.) CC

June—Regular Phase (7)

1. **Sam Khalifa, ss, Sahuaro HS, Tucson, Ariz.**
2. **Jim Opie, 3b, New Orleans**
3. Joe Magrane, lhp, Rowan County HS, Morehead, Ky.
4. **Charles Marty, rhp, Point Loma Nazarene (Calif.)**
5. **Shawn Stone, rhp, Grossmont (Calif.) JC**
6. **Mitch McKelvey, rhp, Groveton HS, Alexandria, Va.**
7. **Brian DeValk, of, New Orleans**
8. **David Coss, of, Centenary**
9. Tom Bryant, 3b, Caldwell (N.J.) HS
10. **David Frederick, of, Anderson (S.C.)**
11. **Tony Bagwell, 3b/ss, Shorter (Ga.)**
12. Ray Hayward, lhp, Oklahoma
13. Barry Shifflett, 1b, Western Albemarle HS, Earlysville, Va.
14. **Shawn Holman, rhp, Ambridge HS, Sewickley, Pa.**
15. Bob D'Agostino, rhp, Southwestern Louisiana
16. **Andy Watson, inf, Centenary**
17. Bryant Robertson, of, Hillcrest HS, Country Club Hills, Ill.
18. **Justin Catlett, rhp, Meridian (Miss.) HS**
19. **Bernard Stanton, rhp, Stillman (Ala.)**
20. Mike Patton, rhp, Seton Hall
21. **James Smith, c, Kelly HS, Wise, Va.**
22. **James Mims, c, Baptist (Fla.)**
23. **John Kenny, ss, Denison (Ohio)**
24. Fred Laningham, ss, West HS, Bakersfield, Calif.
25. Michael Walker, ss, Cerritos (Calif.) HS
26. Mark Barron, rhp, JC of DuPage (Ill.)
27. Ed Veres, ss, West Branch HS, Grassflat, Pa.
28. Randy Foster, lhp, Oxford (N.Y.) HS

29. Jose DeLeon, rhp, Perth Amboy (N.J.) HS
30. **Tom Graziano, 1b/of, New Orleans**
31. Mark Whitman, 3b, Erwin (N.C.) HS
32. Craig Conti, of, McDowell HS, Erie, Pa.
33. Marshall Miller, 3b, Brashear HS, Pittsburgh
34. Tom Snowberger, of, Sylvania Northview HS, Pittsburgh
35. Allen Depew, of, Herculaum HS, Pevely, Mo.

June—Secondary Phase (13)

1. **Bip Roberts, ss, Chabot (Calif.) JC**
2. Frank Russo, 1b/3b, Indian River (Fla.) CC
3. Mike Mazzocco, of, JC of the Canyons (Calif.)
4. **Scott Bailes, lhp, St. Louis CC-Meramec**
5. Marty Freeman, 2b/of, Indian River (Fla.) CC

ST. LOUIS CARDINALS

January—Regular Phase (22)

1. Tom Mauch, of, Mount San Antonio (Calif.) JC
2. David Bond, rhp, Pasadena (Calif.) CC
3. Brent Blum, 1b/lhp, Centralia (Wash.) JC
4. Doug Givler, rhp, Frederick (Md.) CC
5. Victor Walker, rhp, Chipola (Fla.) JC
6. **Ken Mills, lhp, Massasoit (Mass.) CC**
7. Mark Turner, rhp, Louisburg (N.C.) JC
8. **Ron Morander, ss, Massasoit (Mass.) CC**

January—Secondary Phase (20)

1. Brad Arnsberg, rhp, Merced (Calif.) JC
2. Jerry McDermott, c, Fontana, Calif.

June—Regular Phase (21)

1. **Todd Worrell, rhp, Biola (Calif.)**
2. **Tim Wallace, c, Wofford**
3. **John Young, lhp, Bradley**
4. **Mike Shade, rhp, West Chester (Pa.)**
5. Mark Davis, of, Hoover HS, San Diego
6. **Brian Farley, rhp, Vanderbilt**
7. **Terry Pendleton, of, Fresno State**
8. **Gary Gill, 1b, Slippery Rock (Pa.)**
9. **David Clements, ss, Mississippi**
10. **Vince Coleman, of, Florida A&M**
11. Rob Dibble, rhp, Southington (Conn.) HS
12. Bobby Joe Edmonds, of, Lutheran North HS, St. Louis
13. **Vince Russomagno, 1b/of, Brandeis (Mass.)**
14. **Pedro LaTorre, 2b, Troy State**
15. **Billy Donathon, rhp, Louisiana State**
16. **Dennis Seiple, lhp, South Carolina-Aiken**
17. **Ted Carson, rhp, Tennessee**
18. **Tom Rossi, of, Connecticut**
19. John Healey, c, Warren Central HS, Indianapolis
20. Tim Thompson, rhp, Cal State Fullerton
21. **Jeff Pasquale, 3b, Slippery Rock (Pa.)**
22. **Kevin Moon, rhp, Oakland HS**
23. **Brad Blunt, rhp, North County Tech HS, Deslage, Mo.**
24. **Mark Schulte, of, Marissa (Ill.) HS**
25. Steve Routos, ss, Newport HS, Bellevue, Wash.
26. **Pat Wallace, of, Hofstra**
27. **Tom Bocock, ss, James Madison**
28. **Bruce Dunn, rhp, Lewis-Clark State (Idaho)**
29. Kevin Ward, of, Arizona
30. **Bill Packer, c, Sacred Heart**
31. **Paul Russell, c, Sacred Heart HS, San Francisco**
32. Oliver Whitaker, lhp, Brookland Cayce HS, West Columbia, S.C.

June—Secondary Phase (23)

1. Tom Mauch, of, Mount San Antonio (Calif.) JC
2. **Keith Turnbull, rhp, Mineral Area (Mo.) JC**

SAN DIEGO PADRES

January—Regular Phase (4)

1. John Yowler, lhp, Valencia (Fla.) CC
2. Jim Benedict, rhp, Los Angeles Valley JC
3. Glenn Zielinski, of, Taft (Calif.) JC
4. **Craig Estrada, ss, Cuesta (Calif.) JC**
5. Mike Kellog, ss, Spokane Falls (Wash.) CC
6. Randy Ardery, rhp, Allegany (Pa.) CC
7. **Sam Daniels, rhp, Wanchese, N.C.**
8. Timmy Reid, rhp, Taft (Calif.) JC

January—Secondary Phase (2)

1. **Scott Parsons, of, Miami**
2. Dean Albany, rhp, CC of Baltimore
3. **Ken Bender, of, Centralia (Wash.) JC**
4. Jeff Salazar, rhp, Los Angeles Valley JC

June—Regular Phase (3)

1. **Jimmy Jones, rhp, Thomas Jefferson HS, Dallas**
2. **Joe Plesac, rhp, North Carolina State**
3. **Mark Wasinger, 2b, Old Dominion**
4. **Mark Williamson, rhp, San Diego State**
5. **Greg Raymer, rhp, Western Kentucky**
6. **Tom Brassil, ss, Duke**
7. **Osbe Hoskins, of, Western Michigan**
8. **Mitch Williams, lhp, West Linn (Ore.) HS**
9. **John Frierson, c, Oakland (Calif.) HS**
10. **Rigo Rodriguez, 3b, San Diego State**
11. **Al Simmons, 2b, Eastern Washington**
12. **Jeff Dean, rhp, Central Missouri State**
13. **Bob Allinger, of, Evergreen HS, Vancouver, Wash.**
14. **Bob Klusacek, lhp, Stetson**
15. **John Westmoreland, c, California Lutheran**
16. Chris Burgess, rhp, Delta State (Miss.)
17. **Willie Anderson, of, Hoover HS, San Diego**
18. **Greg Steffanich, lhp, JC of Southern Idaho**
19. **Don Freeman, 2b, Oklahoma State**
20. Joe Sickles, of, Florida Southern
21. **Bob Patterson, lhp, East Carolina**
22. **Mark Poston, rhp, Appalachian State**
23. **Lawrence Pott, c, Cal Poly San Luis Obispo**
24. **Dan Jones, 3b, Lewis & Clark (Ore.)**
25. **Greg Crabb, rhp, San Diego State**
26. **Kevin Wiggins, of, San Diego State**
27. **Frank Warner, rhp, Wake Forest**
28. **Jim Harkins, lhp, Eastern Kentucky**
29. **Gene Walter, lhp, Eastern Kentucky**

June—Secondary Phase (1)

1. **Kevin Towers, rhp, Brigham Young**
2. Scott Groot, ss, Orange Coast (Calif.) JC
3. **Ray Nodell, of, Broward (Fla.) CC**

SAN FRANCISCO GIANTS

January—Regular Phase (12)

1. **Mike Jones, of, Arvonia, Va.**
2. Dale Gehringer, inf, Los Angeles Pierce JC
3. Reggie Mosley, of, Laney (Calif.) JC
4. Joel McKeon, lhp, Miami-Dade North CC
5. **David Miller, ss, Walters State (Tenn.) CC**
6. **Charles Norman, rhp, Walters State (Tenn.) CC**
7. **Terry Quinn, 2b, Los Angeles Valley JC**
8. **Ethan Charles, of, Los Angeles Harbor JC**
9. Dave Snell, rhp, Spokane Falls (Wash.) CC
10. Kenneth Schulz, rhp, Fort Steilacoom (Wash.) CC
11. **Orlando Blackwell, ss/2b, Sacramento CC**
12. **Joseph Powell, of, Allegany (Md.) JC**
13. Cesar Hooker, lhp, CC of San Francisco
14. Darrell Freter, 3b/rhp, JC of Southern Idaho
15. Tony Laird, of/1b, Treasure Valley (Ore.) CC
16. **Scott Rainey, c/rhp, Rose State (Okla.) JC**
17. **Randy Saunier, ss/2b, Eastern Oklahoma State JC**
18. Richard Belli, rhp, Canada (Calif.) JC
19. Mark Breining, lhp, CC of San Francisco
20. Lonnie Strickland, rhp, Utah Technical JC
21. **Mark Swenson, lhp, Costa Mesa, Calif.**
22. **Mickey Swenson, inf, Costa Mesa, Calif.**

January—Secondary Phase (8)

1. **Everett Graham, of, Louisburg (N.C.) JC**
2. Ken Lynn, rhp, Spartanburg Methodist (S.C.) JC
3. Bob Merenda, of, Sacramento CC

June—Regular Phase (11)

1. **Steve Stanicek, 1b, Nebraska**
2. Barry Bonds, of, Serra HS, San Carlos, Calif.
3. Gil Villaneuva, lhp, Tehachapi (Calif.) HS
4. Mike Young, lhp, Rolling Hills HS, Rancho Palos Verdes, Calif.
5. David McNeil, of, Narbonne HS, Los Angeles
6. Brian Guinn, ss, California
7. **Lester Mosley, of, Morningside HS, Inglewood, Calif.**
8. Will Schock, rhp, Tamalpais HS, Mill Valley, Calif.
9. Andy Leonard, c, El Camino HS, South San Francisco
10. Pete Incaviglia, 3b/1b, Monterey HS, Pebble Beach, Calif.
11. **Randy Morse, lhp, Central Michigan**
12. Steve Cotter, rhp, Skyline (Calif.) JC
13. **Billy Cabell, ss, Amherst HS, Madison Heights, Va.**
14. **Matt Cimo, of, Eastern Illinois**
15. **Jeff Blobaum, rhp, Cal State Stanislaus**
16. **Billy Loard, c, Norwalk (Calif.) HS**
17. **Jim Stassi, c, Nevada-Reno**
18. Tom Krause, ss, Diablo Valley (Calif.) JC
19. **John Hughes, lhp, Westlake HS, Westlake Valley, Calif.**
20. **Steve Kenney, of, UC Davis**
21. Daniel Morris, of/lhp, Hoover HS, Glendale, Calif.
22. **Rob Brezinski, 2b, Pacific**
23. Ken May, lhp, Los Angeles Pierce JC
24. **Mark Morton, inf, Cal State Northridge**
25. Mike Meyers, 3b, Narbonne HS, Carson, Calif.
26. **Glenn Knudsen, c, California Baptist**
27. Charles Kane, rhp, El Camino (Calif.) JC
28. Rob Holbrook, rhp, Oregon State
29. **Stan Baughn, of, Oklahoma State**
30. **Dean Hummel, lhp, Portland State (Ore.)**
31. Carl Willis, rhp, UNC Wilmington
32. Jeff Gilbert, rhp, Clemson
33. **Mike Empting, c, Oklahoma**
34. **Randy Bockus, of, Kent State**
35. **Brice Proctor, 2b, Southwestern (Calif.) JC**
36. Jose Tolentino, 1b, Seminole State (Okla.) JC
37. Gayron Jackson, of, Banning HS, Carson, Calif.
38. Michael Wilder, 2b, St. Mary's
39. Mark Kane, 3b, Oregon Tech
40. James Doss, of, Cal State Chico
41. **Kelvin Smith, of/inf, Southwestern (Texas)**
42. Jeff Montgomery, of, Cuesta (Calif.) JC
43. **Kevin Bates, 2b, Oklahoma**
44. **Brain Bargerhuff, rhp, Texas Wesleyan**

June—Secondary Phase (15)

1. Jody Reed, ss, Manatee (Fla.) JC

SEATTLE MARINERS

January—Regular Phase (5)

1. **Wray Bergendahl, rhp, Cerritos (Calif.) JC**
2. **Kevin Roy, rhp, Umpqua (Ore.) CC**
3. Ray Nodell, of, Broward (Fla.) CC
4. **Mike Evans, lhp, Merced, Calif.**
5. Jeff Wilpon, c, Roslyn Heights, N.Y.
6. **Scott Roebuck, 3b, Citrus (Calif.) JC**

January—Secondary Phase (3)

1. Charlie Kerfeld, rhp, Yavapai (Ariz.) JC
2. Rich Rosemus, lhp, Linn-Benton (Ore.) CC
3. Vince DeBono, lhp, DeAnza (Calif.) JC

June—Regular Phase (6)

1. **Spike Owen, ss, Texas**
2. **Mike Wishnevski, of, Indiana Central**
3. **Renard Brown, of, Liberty**
4. **Terry Taylor, rhp, Crestview (Fla.) HS**
5. **Jeff McDonald, rhp, UCLA**
6. **Alvin Davis, 1b, Arizona State**
7. **Joe Whitmer, rhp, Brigham Young**
8. Gary Parmenter, rhp, Middle Georgia JC
9. **John Duncan, c, Saint Louis**
10. **Brian David, 2b, Cal State Fullerton**
11. **Darrell Bickers, ss, Charlottesville (Va.) HS**
12. Kirk Killingsworth, rhp, Texas
13. **Ron Sismondo, lhp, Arizona**
14. **Roger Hill, of, Nebraska**
15. **Eric Stewart, c, Cal Poly Pomona**
16. **Randy Newman, lhp, Arizona State**
17. **Scott Barnhouse, rhp, Mercer**
18. **Robbie Vollmer, of, South Carolina**
19. **Ken Briggs, of, Cal State Long Beach**
20. **Randy Ramirez, rhp, Cal State Long Beach**
21. **Greg Bartley, rhp, East Tennessee State**
22. Clay Daniel, lhp, Gulf Coast (Fla.) CC
23. Rich Rice, rhp, Palm Beach (Fla.) JC
24. **Dave Smith, 1b, Southern California**
25. Greg Shirley, c, Huntington Beach (Calif.) HS
26. **Randy Falconer, c, James Madison**
27. Brad Colton, of, Maine
28. Mel Stottlemyre Jr., rhp, Davis HS, Yakima, Wash.
29. **David Rodriguez, 2b, Lake View HS, Chicago**
30. **Todd Francis, 1b, Beaverton (Ore.) HS**
31. Lance Johnson, of, Triton (Ill.) JC
32. Terrance Johnson, 1b, Kearny HS, San Diego
33. Scott DeMarrais, c, Emersen (N.J.) HS
34. Jeb Best, of, Washington

June—Secondary Phase (8)

1. **Tom Duggan, 3b, Orange Coast (Calif.) JC**
2. Jamie Doughty, 3b, Seminole State (Okla.) JC
3. **Kevin Roy, rhp, Umpqua (Ore.) CC**
4. **Larry Paskiewicz, of, Texas-El Paso**
5. **Jeff Schassler, rhp, Francis Marion (S.C.)**
6. Robby Thompson, ss, Palm Beach (Fla.) JC

TEXAS RANGERS

January—Regular Phase (15)

1. **James Allison, rhp, Modesto (Calif.) JC**
2. **Larry McLin, lhp, DeKalb South (Ga.) CC**
3. Jody Reed, ss, Manatee (Fla.) JC
4. Keith Turnbull, rhp, Mineral Area (Mo.) JC
5. John Fryhoff, lhp, San Jose (Calif.) CC
6. Kent Cooper, of, West Valley (Calif.) JC
7. Scott Bailes, lhp, St. Louis CC-Meramec
8. Mike Dotzler, c, DeAnza (Calif.) JC
9. James Mee, c, Seminole (Fla.) CC
10. Todd Johnson, of, Northwood (Texas)
11. Barry Burham, c, Hampton, Va.

January—Secondary Phase (19)

1. **Chris Joslin, lhp, Hillsborough (Fla.) CC**
2. Ed Augustine, of, Brevard (Fla.) CC
3. Michael Winbush, rhp, Winston-Salem State (N.C.)
4. Alex Diaz, c, Miami-Dade North CC

June—Regular Phase (16)

1. (Pick to Red Sox as compensation for Type A free agent Frank Tanana)
2. **Mike Rubel, 1b, Cal State Fullerton**
3. **Clint Curry, 3b, Turner Ashby HS, Bridgewater, Va.**
4. **Terry Johnson, lhp, Michigan State**
5. **Steve Buechele, 2b, Stanford**
6. Rob Walton, rhp, Rutherford (N.J.) HS
7. **Kevin Stock, 3b, Stadium HS, Tacoma, Wash.**
8. Eric Lane, c, Tulane
9. **Eric Dersin, rhp, Frankfort HS, Fort Ashby, W.Va.**
10. **Bob Gergen, ss, Oklahoma City**
11. Mike Oglesbee, 1b, Alamogordo (N.M.) HS
12. Loren Hibbs, of, Wichita State
13. **Eli Ben, of, Seton Hall**
14. **David Hopkins, rhp, Virginia**
15. **Mark Swiski, of, La Salle**
16. **Rob Clark, lhp, Southern Illinois**
17. **Barry Brunenkant, c, New Mexico**
18. **Bob Hausladen, c, Stanford**
19. **Bobby Kohler, of, Texas Tech**
20. **Mark Sutton, 2b, Maine**
21. Regan Bass, rhp, Washington State

22. **Joe Ambrosino, ss, Widener (Pa.)**
23. Bobby McKercher, ss, Serra HS, San Carlos, Calif.
24. **Sam Sorce, rhp, Miami**
25. **Ed Brennan, of, Arizona State**
26. **Jimmy Foit, ss, Virginia Tech**
27. **Warren McReddie, 1b, Massachusetts**
28. **William Porterfield, 1b, Murray State (Okla.) JC**
29. Doug Shields, of, Miami
30. Ricky Darwin, rhp, Bonham (Texas) HS
31. Jordan Stanley, lhp, Sulphur Springs (Texas) HS
32. Jeff Colton, lhp, Bishop Moore HS, Longwood, Fla.
33. **Cecil Brim, of, Drewery Mason HS, Ridgeway, Va.**
34. Woodrow Broussard, lhp, Loreaville HS, St. Martinville, La.
35. Buddy Shaw, rhp, Hollywood (Fla.) Hills HS
36. Robert Williams, rhp, Hodge HS, Jonesboro, La.
37. Dell Curry, rhp, Fort Defiance HS, Grottoes, Va.
38. Rodney Carter, of, Elizabeth (N.J.) HS
39. **Kenny Rogers, lhp/of, Plant City HS, Dover, Fla.**
40. Dave Martinez, 1b/of, Lake Howell HS, Castleberry, Fla.
41. **Mike Esser, of, George Mason**

June—Secondary Phase (10)

1. **Randy Kramer, rhp, San Jose (Calif.) CC**
2. Manny Mantrana, ss, Miami-Dade North CC
3. **Jeff Mace, of, Lewis-Clark State (Idaho)**
4. **Michael Winbush, rhp, Winston-Salem State (N.C.)**

TORONTO BLUE JAYS

January—Regular Phase (1)

1. **Kash Beauchamp, of, Bacone (Okla.) JC**
2. **Ron Johnson, rhp, Los Angeles Pierce JC**
3. Ken Jackson, 3b/ss, Angelina (Texas) JC
4. Tim Owen, c, Palm Beach (Fla.) JC
5. David Hinnrichs, rhp, McLennan (Texas) CC
6. Shawn Holton, rhp, Allegany (Pa.) CC
7. George Jones, of, JC of the Sequoias (Calif.)
8. Leo Cardenas, 3b, Texas Southmost JC
9. Michael Voelkel, rhp, Centralia (Wash.) JC
10. Paul Scholer, c, Miami-Dade North CC
11. Scott Morris, c, Modesto (Calif.) JC
12. Edward Emmons, rhp, South Florida JC
13. Jack Dietrich, ss/2b, Valencia (Fla.) CC
14. Norman Bethel, 3b/1b, Fresno (Calif.) CC

January—Secondary Phase (15)

1. **Randy Romagna, rhp, Indian River (Fla.) CC**
2. Norman Morton, lhp, Miami-Dade North CC
3. Dave Eichhorn, rhp, Cabrillo (Calif.) JC

June—Regular Phase (2)

1. **Augie Schmidt, ss, New Orleans**
2. **David Wells, lhp, Point Loma HS, San Dego**
3. **Jimmy Key, lhp, Clemson**
4. **Chris Johnston, 1b/3b, Arizona State**
5. **Dave Stenhouse, c, Holy Cross**
6. **Pat Borders, 3b/of, Lake Wales (Fla.) HS**
7. **Vernon Rhodes, ss, Arkansas-Monticello**
8. **Chris Shaddy, ss, Arkansas**
9. **Dave Walsh, lhp, UC Santa Barbara**
10. **Ronnie Chapman, 2b, Florida International**
11. Ed Vosberg, lhp, Arizona
12. **Mark Gerard, 1b, Western Michigan**
13. Stan Hilton, rhp, Baylor
14. Ron Jones, of, Seguin (Texas) HS
15. Chuck Bartlett, c, Mississippi State
16. Deric Ladnier, ss, Gonzalez Tate HS, Pensacola, Fla.
17. Vince Lopez, ss, La Quinta HS, Santa Ana, Calif.
18. **Keith Gilliam, lhp, Austin Peay**
19. **Scott Kimball, c, UC Santa Barbara**
20. **John Mason, of, Greenville, Texas**
21. **Steve Davis, lhp, Texas A&M**
22. Randy Byers, of, Cumberland Regional HS, Bridgeton, N.J.
23. Dan Boever, ss, Nebraska
24. **Rusty Rightmire, rhp, Louisiana Tech**
25. Chris Sarmiento, rhp, MacArthur HS, Saginaw, Mich.
26. **Michael Lavery, c, Amherst (Mass.)**
27. Mike Henneman, rhp, Jefferson (Mo.) JC
28. James Jackson, 1b, Fremont HS, Oakland, Calif.
29. Greg Simpson, lhp, Stuart (Okla.) HS
30. **Tim Phillips, rhp, Florida State**
31. James Hudson, 3b, Oklahoma State
32. Jim St. Laurent, of, Manatee (Fla.) JC

June—Secondary Phase (22)

1. David Hinnrichs, rhp, McLennan (Texas) CC
2. Jamie Brisco, rhp, Fresno CC
3. **Kevin Sliwinski, of, Orange Coast (Calif.) JC**
4. **Greg Griffin, of, Midwestern State (Texas)**
5. Oddibe McDowell, of, Miami-Dade North CC
6. Tony Blasucci, of, Broward (Fla.) CC

1983

Belcher emerges as top pick in thin year overall, while Red Sox find major star in Clemens

It was one of the great rags-to-riches stories in draft history. Tim Belcher, a virtual unknown six weeks before the 1983 draft, suddenly shot to the top of the charts and was drafted No. 1 overall by the Twins.

"One scout said he had been in the business for more than 20 years and never saw a situation like mine," said Belcher, a 21-year-old righthander from obscure Mount Vernon Nazarene College in Ohio.

Belcher went unnoticed his first two years at Mt. Vernon Nazarene, going 9-8 with a 4.65 ERA. He began the 1983 season losing four of five decisions, but suddenly turned it around and began attracting scouts in droves, curious about the righthander with the 96 mph fastball.

"A lot has happened to me in the last few months," Belcher said. "At the start of the season, I was hoping to get drafted. I wasn't thinking about the first round. As for being the first player taken, well, I didn't even dream about that."

Belcher became the second player drafted No. 1 overall in June not to sign. He joined catcher Danny Goodwin, who jilted the White Sox in 1971, when he could not come to terms with the Twins.

The Twins also couldn't sign Arizona State outfielder Oddibe McDowell, the first selection in the secondary phase, and Maine pitcher Billy Swift, their second-round pick in the regular phase.

McDowell was offered less than $30,000, returned to Arizona State, was Baseball America's College Player of the Year in 1984 and became a first-round pick of the Rangers.

Swift also went back to school, but the Twins blew the whistle on his use of an agent in his negotiations and he was suspended for the first third of the 1984 college season. He was selected second overall, by Seattle, in the '84 draft.

Belcher, McDowell and Swift all made it to the big leagues within five years, while not a single player the Twins signed in the 1983 draft was active in professional baseball.

Both Baltimore and Los Angeles had drafts nearly as futile as that of the Twins.

The Orioles wasted their first-round pick on high school pitcher Wayne Wilson, who won 21 games in five years and never advanced above Class A. They didn't sign anyone else in the regular phase who reached the big leagues. The Dodgers didn't sign a single pick who played in Los Angeles.

While scouting director George Brophy had little luck signing players for the Twins, he correctly assessed the talent in the 1983 draft, overall one of the leanest ever.

Roger Clemens wasn't his college team's top starter, but Boston saw his talent

"This is the worst draft I've seen since it began in 1965," he said. "It's the weakest in both caliber of the first round and overall depth. I think much of the blame is the poor weather around the country, which didn't give the players a chance to compete and develop their skills."

While the Twins took a hard line on negotiations, the Reds took a renewed, aggressive approach to signing new talent. They selected shortstop Kurt Stillwell with the No. 2 pick, and bought him away from a scholarship to Stanford for $150,000. The Reds also signed their first 23 selections, to that point a draft record for consecutive signings at the start of a draft.

If any team appeared to clean up it was the Mets. By allowing eight-game winner Pete Falcone to sign on with Atlanta as a free agent and getting two draft picks as compensation, the Mets had four of the first 32 selections. They corralled every big name in sight, including Eddie Williams, Stan Jefferson, Calvin Schiraldi and Dave Magadan.

"We're elated with the draft," Mets director of baseball operations Lou Gorman said. "It was a year in which the talent was a bit down by comparison with other years, but overall we came out fine and got what we were after."

In keeping with the general lack of talent in the 1983 draft, only Magadan really made his mark with the Mets. Williams, Jefferson and Schiraldi were all traded away by the Mets before they saw appreciable time in the big leagues, though a draft-high 10 Mets selections reached the big leagues.

Milwaukee signed the most impressive contingent of future big leaguers and landed lefthander Juan Nieves, a Puerto Rican who attended a Connecticut prep school. Because he was from Puerto Rico, Nieves was not subject to the draft, where he would have been a first-round pick. The Brewers won a bidding war over 17 other clubs for Nieves, paying out the largest bonus in club history, a reported $150,000.

The so-called Nieves Rule subsequently made foreign players attending school in the U.S. eligible for the draft.

Clemens Trumps All

Not all the talent in the 1983 draft fell short of expectations. After all, Roger Clemens was drafted that year.

The Red Sox snagged him with the 19th pick overall, after 10 pitchers had been taken before him. Clemens emerged immediately as the draft's dominant pick when he debuted at Class A Winter Haven and didn't walk a batter in 29 innings while striking out 36. Fourteen starts later, he was in Boston taking the wraps off on a career that produced seven Cy Young Awards, 354 wins and 4,672 strikeouts. Of the 10 pitchers taken ahead of Clemens, five never reached the big leagues, and only Belcher had a winning record, going 146-140 in 14 seasons.

Red Sox scouting director Eddie Kasko explained Clemens' availability in the 1983 draft: "It was one of those years where there was no clear-cut No. 1 choice and opinions were varied on a lot of players."

Another factor may have been that Texas coach Cliff Gustafson continued to refer to and use Clemens as the No. 3 pitcher on his staff, behind Calvin Schiraldi and Mike Capel.

"I think they used to say that because they already had their pitching staff set when I came in from junior college," Clemens said.

One of the few scouts who wasn't fooled by the way the Longhorns used Clemens was Red Sox scout Danny Doyle.

"There was no doubt who the best pitcher on the Texas staff was in my mind," Doyle said. "Roger had the best arm and the best makeup. It was a rare kind of makeup and intensity."

DRAFT 83: FIRST-ROUND PICKS

No.	Club	Player, Pos.	School	Hometown	Ht.	Wt.	B-T	Age
1.	Twins	*Tim Belcher, rhp	Mount Vernon Nazarene	Sparta, Ohio	6-3	210	R-R	21
2.	Reds	Kurt Stillwell, ss	Thousand Oaks HS	Thousand Oaks, Calif.	5-11	165	B-R	18
3.	Rangers	Jeff Kunkel, ss	Rider	Leonardo, N.J.	6-2	175	R-R	21
4.	Mets	Eddie Williams, 3b	Hoover HS	San Diego	6-0	170	R-R	18
5.	Athletics	Stan Hilton, rhp	Baylor	Hurst, Texas	6-1	195	R-R	22
6.	Cubs	Jackie Davidson, rhp	Everman HS	Everman, Texas	6-0	175	R-R	18
7.	Mariners	Darrel Akerfelds, rhp	Mesa State (Colo.)	Lakewood, Colo.	6-2	208	R-R	20
8.	Astros	Robbie Wine, c	Oklahoma State	Norristown, Pa.	6-2	195	R-R	20
9.	Blue Jays	Matt Stark, c	Los Altos HS	Hacienda Heights, Calif.	6-4	220	R-R	18
10.	Padres	Ray Hayward, lhp	Oklahoma	Enid, Okla.	6-1	190	L-L	22
11.	Indians	Dave Clark, of	Jackson State	Tupelo, Miss.	6-2	198	L-R	20
12.	Pirates	Ron DeLucchi, of	Campolinda HS	Moraga, Calif.	6-1	180	R-R	18
13.	White Sox	Joel Davis, rhp	Sandalwood HS	Jacksonville, Fla.	6-5	202	R-R	18
14.	Expos	Rich Stoll, rhp	Michigan	Attica, Ind.	5-11	182	R-R	20
15.	Tigers	Wayne Dotson, rhp	Estacado HS	Lubbock, Texas	6-1	175	R-R	18
16.	Expos	Brian Holman, rhp	North HS	Wichita, Kan.	6-4	185	R-R	18
17.	Mariners	Terry Bell, c	Old Dominion	Kettering, Ohio	6-0	195	R-R	20
18.	Dodgers	Erik Sonberg, lhp	Wichita State	Tulsa, Okla.	6-2	195	R-L	21
19.	Red Sox	Roger Clemens, rhp	Texas	Katy, Texas	6-4	205	R-R	20
20.	Mets	Stan Jefferson, of	Bethune-Cookman	Bronx, N.Y.	6-0	175	R-R	20
21.	Royals	Gary Thurman, of	North Central HS	Indianapolis	5-10	170	R-R	18
22.	Phillies	Ricky Jordan, 1b	Grant HS	Sacramento	6-3	190	R-R	18
23.	Angels	Mark Doran, of	Wisconsin	South Holland, Ill.	6-3	210	R-R	21
24.	Cardinals	Jim Lindeman, 3b	Bradley	Des Plaines, Iowa	6-1	200	R-R	21
25.	Orioles	Wayne Wilson, rhp	Redondo Beach HS	Redondo Beach, Calif.	6-3	180	L-R	17
26.	Brewers	Dan Plesac, lhp	North Carolina State	Crown Point, Ind.	6-5	210	L-L	21

*Did not sign.

1983

CLUB-BY-CLUB SELECTIONS

ATLANTA BRAVES

January—Regular Phase (19)

1. **James Bartlett, rhp, Cuyahoga (Ohio) CC**
2. **Jay Reeves, rhp, Pearl River (Miss.) JC**
3. Daryl Brown, rhp, CC of Morris (N.J.)
4. Clarence Perry, 1b, Spartanburg Methodist (S.C.) JC
5. **Sal D'Alessandro, c, Orange Coast (Calif.) JC**
6. Darryl Decker, rhp, Paris (Texas) JC
7. Chris Cron, 1b, Santa Ana (Calif.) JC
8. Tom Prince, c, Kankakee (Ill.) JC
9. Wallace Moore, of, DeKalb (Ga.) JC
10. Melvin Webb, of, Brewton-Parker (Ga.) JC
11. Chuck Williams, 3b, DeKalb (Ga.) JC
12. David Grams, rhp, Mount San Antonio (Calif.) JC

January—Secondary Phase (19)

1. Rob Nelson, 1b, Mount San Antonio (Calif.) JC
2. Bryant Robertson, of, Triton (Ill.) JC
3. Steven Cotter, rhp, Skyline (Calif.) JC

June—Regular Phase (20)

1. (Pick to Mets as compensation for Type B free agent Pete Falcone)
2. (Pick to Dodgers as compensation for Type A free agent Terry Forster)
3. **Marty Clary, rhp, Northwestern**
4. **Ron Gant, ss, Victoria (Texas) HS**
5. Dera Clark, rhp, Artesia (N.M.) HS
6. Chuck Oertli, c, Travis HS, Austin
7. **Joe Scime, 1b, Wisconsin**
8. **Steve Ziem, rhp, Cal Poly Pomona**
9. Jay Buhner, of, McLennan (Texas) CC
10. **Todd Lamb, rhp, Duke**
11. **Kevin Coffman, of/rhp, Victoria (Texas) HS**
12. **Walter Shirley, rhp, Texas Tech**
13. **James Bates, lhp, Kelley HS, Wise, Va.**
14. **David Lebeau, ss, UC Davis**
15. **Kyle Reese, c, North Cobb HS, Acworth, Ga.**
16. **Mike Nipper, 2b, East Tennessee State**
17. **Troy Tomsick, rhp, Ranum HS, Denver**
18. **Brian Aviles, rhp, Coastal Carolina**
19. Huck Hibberd, rhp, San Jose State
20. Robert Huffman, of, Hamilton (Ohio) HS
21. **Ross Kingsley, ss, Wisconsin-Oshkosh**
22. **David Camara, of, San Diego CC**
23. Jim Hunter, rhp, Brookdale (N.J.) CC
24. **Chris Baird, of, North Carolina State**
25. **Phil Nagle, rhp, Garrett (Md.) CC**
26. Arned Hernandez, of, Sunnyside HS, Tucson
27. **Mark Lemke, 2b, Notre Dame HS, Whitesboro, N.Y.**
28. **David Jones, rhp, King HS, Tampa**
29. **Paul Daddario, 2b/ss, SUNY Buffalo**
30. **Louis Newsome, lhp, Cherokee (Ala.) HS**
31. **Mac Rodgers, rhp, Texas Wesleyan**
32. **Warren Bachmann, 1b, Armstrong State**
33. **Wayne Harrison, of, Lynchburg (Va.)**
34. Gerald Wright, ss/of, Regan HS, Austin, Texas
35. Wayne Stephens, rhp, Texas Southern
36. **Bob Berry, 3b, Auburn**
37. **Ron Bunnell, c, Georgia**

June—Secondary Phase (18)

1. Kevin Williamson, rhp, Pima (Ariz.) CC
2. Tim Englund, rhp, Rice
3. **Gary Ballou, of, Long Beach (Calif.) CC**
4. Tom Prince, c, Kankakee (Ill.) CC

BALTIMORE ORIOLES

January—Regular Phase (25)

1. Bill Fulton, rhp, Pensacola (Fla.) JC
2. **Nick Piazza, c/of, Scottsdale (Ariz.) CC**
3. **Scott Ninneman, rhp, Oxnard (Calif.) JC**
4. **Mark Leiter, rhp, Connors State (Okla.) JC**
5. Frank Morrison, rhp, Lower Columbia (Wash.) JC
6. **Steve Morris, of, Fullerton (Calif.) JC**
7. **Anthony Burroughs, rhp, CC of Baltimore**
8. Derrick Richardson, 3b, Westark (Ark.) CC
9. Alan Sontag, rhp, Indian River (Fla.) CC
10. James Pruett, 2b, Florida CC
11. William Benfield, 1b, Florida CC
12. Jerome Rothman, lhp, Indian River (Fla.) CC

January—Secondary Phase (25)

1. Ken Patterson, lhp, McLennan (Texas) CC
2. Chris Courtright, of, CC of Baltimore

June—Regular Phase (25)

1. **Wayne Wilson, rhp, Redondo Beach (Calif.) HS**
2. **Mike Conley, lhp, Hamilton (Ohio) HS**
3. Mike Pavelka, lhp, Hopkins (Minn.) HS
4. **Rick Lockwood, 3b, Georgia Tech**
5. **David Dahse, of, Texas Lutheran**
6. Jim Howard, ss, Siena
7. Bryan Price, lhp, California
8. **Mike Lopez, of, Eckerd (Fla.)**
9. **Marc Heyison, 3b, George Washington**
10. **Tim Smith, of, Mercer**
11. **Jeff Jacobson, 2b, Michigan**
12. **Mike Skinner, rhp, CC of Morris (N.J.)**
13. James Colmer, rhp, Mississippi
14. **Keith Mucha, 3b, Oral Roberts**
15. **Randy King, rhp, Rogers HS, Tulsa**
16. **Rich Medina, lhp, Lewis-Clark State (Idaho)**
17. **Ben Bianchi, rhp, Portland State**
18. **Gerald Adams, rhp, Howard**
19. **Louis Dichiaro, 2b, Seton Hall**
20. Chuck Baldwin, ss, Whiteville (N.C.) HS
21. **Jonathan Black, of, Widener (Pa.)**
22. Chris Bengel, rhp, Calvert Hall HS, Baltimore
23. **Jeff LeRiger, ss, Georgia**
24. **Ty Nichols, ss, Dodge City (Kan.) HS**
25. Keith Felden, rhp, Clearwater (Fla.) HS
26. **Danny Fitzpatrick, c, CC of Baltimore**
27. Bert Pascual, of, Miami-Dade South CC
28. **Ken Wilp, lhp, New Mexico**
29. Robert Squires, c, Dekalb HS, Waterloo, Ind.

June—Secondary Phase (3)

1. **Rich Rice, rhp, Florida**
2. **Bob Milacki, rhp, Yavapai (Ariz.) JC**
3. Alan Sontag, rhp, Indian River (Fla.) CC
4. Chris Courtright, of, CC of Baltimore

BOSTON RED SOX

January—Regular Phase (20)

1. **Ellis Burks, of, Ranger (Texas) JC**
2. **Michael Kane, 3b, Truman (Ill.) JC**
3. **Roy Hall, 2b/3b, Columbia State (Tenn.) CC**
4. **Richard Winfield, c, Truman (Ill.) JC**
5. Eric Hetzel, rhp, Eastern Oklahoma State JC
6. Michael Adams, rhp, Garden City (Kan.) CC
7. Terry Selk, 3b, Las Vegas, Nev.
8. **Kevin Camilli, c, Polk (Fla.) CC**
9. **Laverne Jackson, of, Bethune, S.C.**
10. Craig Gutman, rhp, El Camino (Calif.) JC

January—Secondary Phase (22)

1. Richard Helzer, rhp, JC of Marin (Calif.)

June—Regular Phase (19)

1. **Roger Clemens, rhp, Texas**
2. **Mike Brumley, ss, Texas** (Pick from Athletics as compensation for Type A free agent Tom Burgmeier)
2. **John Toale, 3b, Taravella HS, Coral Springs, Fla.**
3. **Paul Thoutsis, of, Holy Name HS, Worcester, Mass.**
4. **Tony Latham, of, Virginia**
5. **Tim Corder, rhp, Memphis State**
6. **Gary Tremblay, c, Coastal Carolina**
7. **John Mitchell, rhp, Overton HS, Nashville**
8. **Dana Kiecker, rhp, St. Cloud State (Minn.)**
9. **Chris Cannizzaro, 2b, San Diego State**
10. **Alvin Hamilton, 2b, Southwest Missouri State**
11. Steve Beer, rhp, Loara HS, Anaheim
12. Kirt Manwaring, c, Horsehead (N.Y.) Central HS
13. Ray Revak, lhp, Key West (Fla.) HS
14. Billy Sheeks, rhp, Christian Brothers HS, Memphis
15. **Mike Dalton, lhp, DeAnza (Calif.) JC**
16. **Jim Hines, rhp, Crane Hill, Ala.**
17. **DeMarlo Hale, 1b, Southern**
18. Blane Lockley, of, Franklin HS, Baldwin, La.
19. **John Sanderski, rhp, St. Johns HS, Oxford, Mass.**

June—Secondary Phase (11)

1. Randy Byers, of, CC of Baltimore

CALIFORNIA ANGELS

January—Regular Phase (24)

1. **Steve Lee, of, Seminole State (Okla.) JC**
2. Mike Scott, rhp, Southeastern Illinois JC
3. Ted Kockenmeister, lhp, Mercer County (N.J.) CC
4. **Terrence Spellmon, 2b, Hill (Texas) JC**
5. James Gonzales, rhp, Pima (Ariz.) CC
6. Mark Gardner, rhp, Fresno CC
7. **Billy Mitchell, of, Howard (Texas) JC**
8. Troy Dodd, 1b, El Reno (Texas) JC
9. David Chambers, rhp, Ohlone (Calif.) JC
10. Andre Toliver, of, Pima (Ariz.) CC
11. Saul Cortez, rhp, Riverside (Calif.) CC
12. Greg Sparks, 1b, Mesa (Ariz.) CC

January—Secondary Phase (6)

1. Brad Arnsberg, rhp, Merced (Calif.) JC
2. James Jackson, 1b, Laney (Calif.) JC
3. Jeff Franks, c, Ranger (Texas) JC

June—Regular Phase (23)

1. **Mark Doran, of, Wisconsin**
2. **Bill Merrifield, ss, Wake Forest**
3. **Wally Joyner, 1b, Brigham Young** (Pick from Yankees as compensation for Type A free agent Don Baylor)
3. Steve Bast, lhp, Damien HS, Upland, Calif.
4. **Pat Clements, lhp, UCLA**
5. **Mark Lynds, of, Los Medanos (Calif.) JC**
6. **Steve Heatherly, 2b, Morehead State**
7. **Tom Alfredson, ss, Coral Springs (Fla.) HS**
8. **Brian Migliore, rhp, Tulane**
9. **Charles Smith, 1b, Midwestern State (Texas)**
10. **Kenny Grant, ss/3b, Eastside HS, Paterson, N.J.**
11. **Bobby Buchanon, 1b/3b, Jackson State**
12. **Don Tinkey, rhp, Youngstown State**
13. **Scott Cannon, rhp, Texas-Pan America**
14. **Steve Sciacca, c, San Diego**
15. **Doug Reibel, 1b, St. Xavier (Ill.)**
16. **Ray Chadwick, rhp, Winston-Salem State (N.C.)**
17. Matt Sexton, ss, Kansas Newman
18. **Marty Cain, 3b, Anadarko (Okla.) HS**
19. **Don Stanfield, rhp, Northview HS, Covina, Calif.**
20. **Fred Wilburn, rhp, Texas-Arlington**
21. **Mike O'Hara, of, Cal State Northridge**
22. Dirk Tidwell, rhp, Westlake HS, Austin
23. Michael Cutola, lhp, Secaucus (N.J.) HS
24. **Greg Steen, 2b, Arizona State**
25. **Reggie Montgomery, of, Southern California**
26. Shawn Hillegas, rhp, Middle Georgia JC
27. Chris Beasley, rhp, Newport Beach, Calif.

June—Secondary Phase (15)

1. **Byron Kemmerling, rhp, Lamar**
2. **Alex Diaz, c, Middle Georgia JC**

CHICAGO CUBS

January—Regular Phase (5)

1. David Cortez, ss, Lower Columbia (Wash.) JC
2. Derek Vanacore, of, Sacramento CC
3. Kevin Williamson, rhp, Pima (Ariz.) CC
4. Stanley Bryant, c, Modesto (Calif.) JC
5. David Stewart, 1b, Citrus (Calif.) JC
6. Paul Hartwig, p, Yavapai (Ariz.) JC
7. **Jim Doyle, rhp, Queensborough (N.Y.) CC**
8. Carl Hamilton, lhp, Triton (Ill.) JC
9. Chris Ritter, rhp, CC of Baltimore
10. **Derrick Hardamon, of, Fresno CC**
11. Dean Williams, 1b, Shasta (Calif.) JC

January—Secondary Phase (5)

1. **Jonathon Baker, c, Sacramento CC**
2. **James Balmer, rhp, Delaware County (Pa.) CC**
3. **Dave Martinez, of, Valencia (Fla.) CC**

June—Regular Phase (6)

1. **Jackie Davidson, rhp, Everman (Texas) HS**
2. **Rich Amaral, 2b, UCLA**
3. **David Kopf, rhp, Michigan**
4. **Terry Edwards, of, Central State (Ohio)**
5. **Steve Engel, lhp, Eastern Kentucky**
6. **John Cox, lhp, California**
7. **Jacob Brumfield, of, Hammond (La.) HS**
8. **Robert Glendening, c, St. Lawrence (N.Y.)**
9. **David Lenderman, rhp, Southern Utah State**
10. **Jeff Brewer, rhp, Eastern Connecticut State**
11. **Marty Tyson, ss, Ontario (Calif.) HS**
12. **Harold Walck, rhp, Old Dominion**
13. **Mike Capel, rhp, Texas**
14. **Donnie Richardson, of, Campbellsville (Ky.)**
15. **Dean Holmes, rhp, Cal State Los Angeles**
16. **John Turner, of, Xavier**
17. Billy Plante, inf/of, Virginia Tech
18. Eric Bauer, lhp, Clackamas (Ore.) CC
19. **James Dickerson, of, UNC Charlotte**
20. **Jim Phillips, rhp, Kansas**
21. Darrell Clifton, ss, Cal Allen HS, Corpus Christi, Texas
22. Robert Auth, rhp, Westminster Christian HS, Miami
23. Jeff King, ss, Rampart HS, Colorado Springs
24. Anthony Smith, of, East Ascension HS, Gonzales, La.
25. Calvin James, 1b/of, Miami
26. Wade Tobin, rhp, Mineral County HS, Hawthorne, Nev.
27. **Thad Slowik, rhp, Rollins (Fla.)**
28. Mark McMorris, 1b, Delgado (La.) JC

June—Secondary Phase (6)

1. **Gary Parmenter, rhp, South Carolina**
2. **Carl Hamilton, lhp, Triton (Ill.) JC**

CHICAGO WHITE SOX

January—Regular Phase (18)

1. Don Dunster, rhp, Mission (Calif.) JC
2. Clark Lange, 3b, Miami-Dade North CC
3. **William Ottino, 3b, Los Angeles Pierce JC**
4. **Don Devlin, ss, Des Moines Area CC**
5. Bill Geivett, 3b, Sacramento CC
6. Kight Higgins, rhp, Seminole (Fla.) CC
7. Steve Peters, lhp, Seminole (Fla.) CC
8. Robert Koopman, lhp, Harper (Ill.) JC
9. John Koenig, rhp, Blinn (Texas) JC
10. **Jesse Vasquez, of, Mount San Antonio (Calif.) JC**
11. Michael McClear, rhp, Valencia (Fla.) CC
12. **Vincent Woods, of, Long Beach (Calif.) CC**

13. Damon Berryhill, c, Orange Coast (Calif.) JC
14. Jeff Farber, of, Long Beach (Calif.) CC
15. Patrick Dougherty, rhp, Los Angeles Harbor JC
16. Kirk Bates, 2b, Fullerton (Calif.) JC

January—Secondary Phase (24)

1. **Otis Green, inf, Miami-Dade North CC**
2. Matthew Warren, rhp, Chabot (Calif.) JC

June—Regular Phase (17)

1. **Joel Davis, rhp, Sandalwood HS, Jacksonville** (Pick from Yankees as compensation for Type A free agent Steve Kemp)
1. (Pick to Mariners as compensation for Type A free agent Floyd Bannister)
1. **Russ Morman, of/1b, Wichita State** (Supplemental pick—28th—for loss of Type B free agent Bill Almon)
2. **Roger Jensen, of, Sonoma State (Calif.)**
3. **Mike Soper, ss, Palmetto HS, Miami**
4. **Bruce Tanner, rhp, Florida State**
5. **Tim Gourlay, ss, Western Michigan**
6. **Rex Blackwell, of, Colton HS, Grand Terrace, Calif.**
7. **Eric Schmidt, rhp, Oklahoma State**
8. **Charlie Moore, ss, Valdosta State (Ga.)**
9. Paul Fuller, c, St. Lee HS, Chicago
10. **Paul Imig, rhp, Florida Southern**
11. **Doug Drabek, rhp, Houston**
12. **Jeff O'Dell, of, Central Florida**
13. **Jim Hickey, rhp, Texas-Pan America**
14. **Bob D'Agostino, rhp, Southwestern Louisiana**
15. **Joe Sickles, of, Florida Southern**
16. **Richard Johnson, 2b, Harper (Ill.) JC**
17. **Ken Henricks, of/3b, Garey HS, Ontario, Calif.**
18. **Pat Pomeranz, of, Mississippi**
19. **Kirk Gilmore, 3b, Washington HS, Los Angeles**
20. **Michael Taylor, of, Wagner**
21. **Jim Trevathan, c, Baylor**
22. Robert O'Hearn, c, Canada (Calif.) JC
23. **Kevin Kristan, rhp, Creighton**
24. **Kurt Walker, rhp, Fresno State**
25. Lawrence Samuel, ss, Eastern Hills HS, Fort Worth
26. Terry Brown, of, El Cerrito HS, Berkeley, Calif.
27. **Derrel Rector, of, Compton (Calif.) HS**
28. Tom Ard, of, Seton Hall Prep School, Springfield, N.J.
29. Terry Winkelhake, c, Harper (Ill.) JC

June—Secondary Phase (13)

1. Mike Young, lhp, Los Angeles Harbor JC
2. **Troy Thomas, of, Mount San Antonio (Calif.) JC**
3. Robert Koopman, lhp, Harper (Ill.) JC

CINCINNATI REDS

January—Regular Phase (1)

1. **Ted Langdon, rhp, Brevard (Fla.) CC**
2. Jac Hein, p, Southeastern Illinois
3. Mike Duncan, 1b, JC of Southern Idaho
4. David Boston, of, Triton (Ill.) JC
5. Cordell Williams, of, Johnson County (Kan.) CC
6. Paul James, rhp, St. Louis CC-Meramec
7. Thomas Fulkerson, rhp, Rend Lake (Ill.) JC
8. Keith Reinhart, rhp, St. Louis CC-Florissant Valley
9. Mike Westbrook, ss, Johnson County (Kan.) CC
10. Douglas Miller, rhp, Des Moines Area (Iowa) CC
11. Larry Mims, 2b, Indian Hills (Iowa) CC
12. **Rob Ergle, rhp, Santa Fe (Fla.) CC**
13. Jimmy Franklin, rhp, Westark (Ark.) CC
14. **Andre Hamb, of, Thornton HS, Harvey, Ill.**

January—Secondary Phase (1)

1. **Tracy Jones, 3b, Hawthorne, Calif.**
2. Luis Medina, of, Cerritos (Calif.) JC
3. **Mark Hammond, rhp, Willibrod HS, Chicago**

June—Regular Phase (2)

1. **Kurt Stillwell, ss, Thousand Oaks (Calif.) HS**
2. **Chris Sabo, 3b, Michigan**
2. **Joe Oliver, c, Boone HS, Orlando** (Pick from Yankees as compensation for Type A free agent Bob Shirley)
3. **Peter Grimm, rhp, SUNY Buffalo**
4. **Mike Goedde, rhp, Evansville**
5. **Lenny Harris, 3b, Jackson HS, Miami**
6. **James Petties, rhp, Tennessee State**
7. **Ron Henika, 3b, Oral Roberts**
8. **Dan Boever, of, Nebraska**
9. **Jeff Montgomery, rhp, Marshall**
10. **Danny Smith, lhp, Miami**
11. **Scott Loseke, of, Arkansas**
12. **Darren Riley, of, Patrick Henry HS, San Diego**
13. **Hugh Kemp, rhp, Georgia**
14. **Mark Calvert, rhp, South Carolina**
15. **Greg Monda, 1b, Washington State**
16. **Ken Houp, c, Oral Roberts**
17. **Gary Denbo, ss, Oakland (Mich.) CC**
18. **Ronnie Giddens, 2b, Union (Tenn.)**
19. **Scott Middleton, rhp, Southwest Missouri State**
20. **Robert Balaguer, of, Dartmouth**
21. **Steve Oliverio, rhp, South Alabama**
22. **David Salmen, of, Geneva (Pa.)**
23. Tony Walker, of, Henry Ford HS, Detroit
24. Bill Blount, 1b, Proctor HS, Utica, N.Y.
25. **Michael Mattern, of, New Haven (Conn.)**
26. Tim Fernandez, 2b, Pima (Ariz.) CC
27. **Jordan Berge, of, Northern Colorado**
28. **Larry Huggins, of, Mesa State (Colo.)**
29. Anthony Blackmon, ss, West Side HS, Gary, Ind.
30. Ron Marigny, ss, St. Augustine HS, New Orleans
31. William Humes, ss/of, Erwin HS, Asheville, N.C.
32. **Manuel Correa, of, Fairleigh Dickinson**
33. Jeff Mons, c, Bolles HS, Jacksonville

June—Secondary Phase (20)

1. **Rob Dibble, rhp, Southington, Conn.**
2. Greg Schiffelbein, of, Allen County (Kan.) CC
3. Derrick Richardson, 3b, Westark (Ark.) CC
4. Larry Mims, 2b, Indian Hills (Iowa) CC

CLEVELAND INDIANS

January—Regular Phase (12)

1. **Glenn Simmons, rhp, DeKalb Central (Ga.) JC**
2. **Anthony Grande, ss, Rome, N.Y.**
3. Alex Diaz, c, Middle Georgia JC
4. **Robert Kowalski, 2b, Niagara Falls, N.Y.**
5. **Shawn Cisco, rhp, Cypress (Calif.) JC**
6. Ralph Backes, rhp, Monroe (N.Y.) CC
7. Jeff Kitchens, lhp, DeKalb (Ga.) JC
8. Amin David, c, Fullerton (Calif.) JC
9. Richard Belli, of, Canada (Calif.) JC
10. Marion Frazier, c, DeKalb South (Ga.) JC
11. Robert Mortimer, lhp, Ferrum (Va.)

January—Secondary Phase (10)

1. Bob Grandstaff, 3b, Golden West (Calif.) JC
2. Manny Mantrana, ss, Middle Georgia JC
3. Brad Powell, rhp, Basking Ridge, N.J.

June—Regular Phase (11)

1. **Dave Clark, of, Jackson State**
2. **Andy Allanson, c, Richmond**
3. **Cal Santarelli, rhp, Louisiana State**
4. **Glenn Edwards, of, Oklahoma State**
5. **Mike Greer, rhp, Valley HS, Las Vegas**
6. **Stephen Whitmyer, rhp, Notre Dame**
7. **Paul Perry, rhp, Jacksonville**
8. **Richard Browne, lhp, Alabama**
9. **Joe Kramer, of, Cleveland State**
10. **Michael Street, rhp, Rochester Institute of Technology**
11. **Steve Smith, of, Oregon State**
12. **Tom Reynolds, rhp, Chicago State**
13. **Kelly Robinette, inf, East Carolina**
14. Bruce Crabbe, inf, Florida
15. **Vin Martelli, c, Harvard**
16. John Farrell, rhp, Oklahoma State

17. **Jeffery Killings, of, Haworth HS, Kokomo, Ind.**
18. **Mike Murphy, rhp, Manhattan**
19. **Kenneth Connerty, of, Lowell (Mass.)**
20. John Boling, lhp, St. Xavier (Ill.)
21. **Steve Arbogast, rhp, American**
22. **Vic Madden, 1b, Pacific**
23. John Ramos, c, Plant HS, Tampa
24. David Zapien, 1b, Nooksack Valley HS, Sumas, Wash.
25. James Rockey, of, Fremont HS, Sunnyvale, Calif.
26. Andy Leonard, c, Canada (Calif.) JC
27. Erick Rapp, rhp, Weatherwax HS, Aberdeen, Wash.

June—Secondary Phase (19)

1. Richard Belli, rhp, Canada (Calif.) JC

DETROIT TIGERS

January—Regular Phase (16)

1. Jon Leake, 3b, Sacramento CC
2. Wallace Love, rhp, American River (Calif.) JC
3. Joe Bitker, rhp, Sacramento CC
4. Kevin Brockway, rhp, West Los Angeles JC
5. **Larry Goodwin, of, Cleveland State (Tenn.) CC**
6. Walt Stull, rhp, Sacramento CC

January—Secondary Phase (8)

1. Randy Byers, of, CC of Baltimore
2. Gordie Hershiser, rhp, Indian River (Fla.) CC

June—Regular Phase (15)

1. **Wayne Dotson, rhp, Estacado HS, Lubbock, Texas**
2. **Rodney Poissant, rhp, Irvine (Calif.) HS**
3. **Jeff Robinson, rhp, Azusa Pacific (Calif.)**
4. **Alan Dunn, rhp, Alabama**
5. **Bruce Hinz, rhp, Oklahoma**
6. **Rob Baker, of, Indiana State**
7. **Anthony Cunningham, of, Denton (Texas) HS**
8. Rob Mallicoat, lhp, Hillsboro (Ore.) HS
9. **Jim Walewander, 2b, Iowa State**
10. **David McClure, c, Wichita State**
11. Scott Sadler, rhp, Radford HS, Hickam AFB, Hawaii
12. Don Cohoon, 3b, Braintree (Mass.) HS
13. **Alejandro Garcia, lhp, Houston**
14. **Tim Bailey, c, East Tennessee State**
15. Richard Rumbold, rhp, Norland HS, Miami
16. **Joey Millis, of, Old Dominion**
17. Peter Mancini, 2b, Seton Hall
18. D.J. Dozier, ss/of, Kempsville HS, Virginia Beach, Va.
19. **Michael Patterson, rhp, Michigan State**
20. **Jim Scudero, lhp, New York Tech**
21. **Thomas Held, rhp, Defiance (Ohio)**
22. **Brad Wheeler, lhp, St. Joseph, Mich.**
23. **Carl Willis, rhp, UNC Wilmington**
24. Warren Dickey, rhp, Westmont (Calif.)
25. **John Bauldry, rhp, Spring Arbor (Mich.)**
26. **Paul Embry, ss, Lincoln, Ala.**
27. Doug Duke, c, Central HS, Tuscaloosa, Ala.
28. Mike Reitzel, lhp, Handy HS, Bay City, Mich.
29. Kevin Gilles, rhp, Clio (Mich.) HS
30. Gary Peters, 2b, Royal Oak (Mich.) HS
31. **Tyrone Barnes, rhp, Mississippi Valley State**
32. **Michael Ward, 1b, Central Michigan**

June—Secondary Phase (17)

1. **Glenn Simmons, rhp, DeKalb (Ga.) JC**
2. **Scott Baker, rhp, Mesa (Ariz.) CC**
3. Chris Cron, 1b, Santa Ana (Calif.) JC
4. Cyrenius Phillips, 1b, Panola (Texas) JC
5. John Bryant, of, Cal State Fullerton

HOUSTON ASTROS

January—Regular Phase (7)

1. Bob Vodvarka, lhp, Chaffey (Calif.) JC
2. **Steve Verrone, rhp, CC of Morris (N.J.)**
3. Greg Edge, 2b, Sacramento CC
4. Robert Smith, rhp, Miami-Dade South CC
5. Scott Marsh, lhp, Golden West (Calif.) JC
6. Randy Robinson, lhp, CC of Morris (N.J.)
7. Dan Sullivan, 1b, Sacramento CC
8. Brett Gideon, rhp, Bee County (Texas) JC

January—Secondary Phase (11)

1. **Troy Afenir, c, Palomar (Calif.) JC**

June—Regular Phase (8)

1. **Robbie Wine Jr., c, Oklahoma State**
2. (Pick to Pirates as compensation for Type A free agent Omar Moreno)
3. **Mike Friedrich, rhp, Fredericksburg (Texas) HS**
4. **Greg Dube, rhp, Portland**
5. **Rayner Noble, lhp, Houston**
6. **Jim O'Dell, 1b, Lewis-Clark State (Idaho)**
7. Curtis Parham, of, Thornridge HS, Phoenix, Ill.
8. David Carley, rhp, Campolinda HS, Moraga, Calif.
9. David Hensel, of, Powers HS, Flint, Mich.
10. **Roger Samuels, lhp, Santa Clara**
11. **Charles Mathews, rhp, Texas Wesleyan**
12. **Randy Hammond, rhp, Mesa State (Colo.)**
13. **Nelson Rood, ss, Florida Southern**
14. **Rodney Martin, of, Azusa Pacific (Calif.)**
15. **Steve Lipinski, of, Montclair State (N.J.)**
16. **Shane Fairbanks, of, Missouri**
17. **Scott Houp, of, Long Beach State**
18. **Anthony Kelley, rhp, Nebraska**
19. **Doug Snyder, of, Los Medanos (Calif.) JC**
20. **Frank Talotta, 2b, Coastal Carolina**
21. **Glenn Sherlock, c, Rollins (Fla.)**
22. Jeff Hirsch, rhp, Broward (Fla.) CC
23. **Doug Shaab, lhp, Delaware**
24. **Seth Richmond, of, Trevecca Nazarene (Tenn.)**
25. **Peter Mueller, 1b, Upsala (N.J.)**
26. Brian Brooks, lhp, El Cerrito HS, Hercules, Calif.
27. **Jason Johnson, rhp, Altoara (Wis.) HS**
28. **Tom Funk, lhp, Northwest Missouri State**
29. David Lawson, of, Missouri
30. Michael Allen, 2b/of, Lincoln HS, San Diego
31. **Daraka Shaheed, ss, Contra Costa (Calif.) JC**
32. **Ronald Russell, ss, Canoga Park HS, Reseda, Calif.**
33. **Robert Retz, lhp, Tucson, Ariz.**

June—Secondary Phase (22)

1. Paul Williams, of, Oklahoma
2. Scott Sempier, ss/3b, CC of Morris (N.J.)
3. Robert Nettles, rhp, Orange Coast (Calif.) JC

KANSAS CITY ROYALS

January—Regular Phase (22)

1. **Mark Van Blaricom, ss, Orange Coast (Calif.) JC**
2. Brett Adams, rhp, Yakima Valley (Wash.) JC
3. Keith Peterson, of, Edmonds (Wash.) CC
4. Mike Clarkin, rhp, Normandale (Minn.) CC
5. Chris Stull, of, Northeastern Oklahoma A&M JC
6. Larry Schofield, rhp, Laney (Calif.) JC
7. **Keith Williamson, of, Pasadena (Calif.) CC**
8. Steve Echols, of, Sacramento CC
9. **Russell Powers, rhp, North Tarrytown, N.Y.**
10. Steve Vasquez, rhp, Chabot (Calif.) JC
11. Elmer Lewis, 2b, Pasadena (Calif.) CC
12. Tim Jester, of, JC of San Mateo (Calif.)
13. David Miramontes, rhp, Butte (Calif.) JC
14. Craig Moe, rhp, Bellevue (Wash.) CC
15. Dexter McClendon, of, Los Angeles CC
16. Rob Bartlett, of, Citrus (Calif.) JC
17. Robert Orozco, of, Chabot (Calif.) JC
18. Michael David, rhp, Santa Barbara (Calif.) CC
19. **John Rubel, of, Cypress (Calif.) JC**
20. Manny Salinas, ss, Southwestern (Calif.) JC

January—Secondary Phase (16)

1. **Ron McCormack, rhp, Green River (Wash.) CC**
2. **Glen Gwatney, of, North Little Rock, Ark.**

June—Regular Phase (21)

1. **Gary Thurman, of, North Central HS, Indianapolis**
2. **Todd Mabe, ss, Edison HS, Huntington Beach, Calif.**
3. **Joe Jarrell, inf, Ramapo (N.J.)**
4. **Geoff Peterson, of, Clovis West HS, Fresno**
5. Scott Hemond, c, Dunedin (Fla.) HS
6. **Mike Miller, 2b, Washington State**
7. **David Koller, rhp, Peabody HS, Pittsburgh**
8. **Carey Ross, 3b, Central Michigan**
9. Montie Phillips, of, Davis HS, Yakima, Wash.
10. **Jeff Hull, rhp, South Hills HS, Covina, Calif.**
11. **Kevin Seitzer, 3b, Eastern Illinois**
12. **Dave Landrith, c, Arizona**
13. **Tim Richardson, 1b, Illinois**
14. **Tom Edens, rhp, Lewis-Clark State (Idaho)**
15. Vince Shinholster, ss, Loara HS, Anaheim
16. **Gary Klein, rhp, Cal State Northridge**
17. **Ed Bass, rhp, San Jose State**
18. **Kevin Tuck, rhp, Tennessee**
19. **David Velez, of, St. Mary's**
20. **John Yowler, lhp, CC of Baltimore**
21. **Charles Green, 2b, Wiley (Texas)**
22. **John Lutz, 3b, Thomas More HS, Milwaukee**
23. **Jeff Schulz, of, Indiana State**
24. **Dennis Boatright, rhp, William Jewell (Mo.)**
25. **John Zelenka, 2b, Tulane**
26. **Jere Longenecker, 1b, Pepperdine**
27. **Floyd Smith, rhp, Dowagiac (Mich.) HS**
28. Michael Van Mill, of, Bishop McNamara HS, Kankakee, Ill.
29. Darwin Freeman, of, Birmingham HS, Inglewood, Calif.
30. Todd Zeile, c, Hart HS, Valencia, Calif.
31. **Mike Conte, 3b, Cal State Los Angeles**
32. Mark Dudenake, c, Clark HS, Las Vegas
33. **John Devich, of, Long Beach (Calif.) CC**
34. Chris Morgan, of, Georgia Tech

June—Secondary Phase (25)

1. John Nero, of, Fullerton (Calif.) JC
2. **Robert Vodvarka, lhp, Chaffey (Calif.) JC**
3. Rob Bartlett, of, Citrus (Calif.) JC
4. **Scott Campbell, of, Citrus (Calif.) JC**

LOS ANGELES DODGERS

January—Regular Phase (17)

1. **Derek Lee, rhp, Sacramento CC**
2. **Todd Cobbs, rhp, Vincennes (Ind.) JC**
3. Pat Sullivan, c, Sacramento CC
4. Mark Tindall, lhp, Sinclair (Ohio) JC
5. Victor Marin, rhp, Chaffey (Calif.) JC
6. **Randy Hamrick, lhp, Spartanburg Methodist (S.C.) JC**
7. John Partridge, rhp, Alvin (Texas) CC
8. Rob Leary, rhp/c, JC of San Mateo (Calif.)
9. Kenneth Boone, rhp, Citrus (Calif.) JC
10. Ted Parker, of, Spartanburg Methodist (S.C.) JC
11. Scott Campbell, of, Citrus (Calif.) JC
12. **Mark Reynolds, of, Austin (Texas) CC**
13. **Wayne Kirby, of, Newport News, Va.**
14. **Karl Ciamaichelo, ss/3b, Havertown, Pa.**
15. Gerald Robinson, c, Easton, Md.

January—Secondary Phase (23)

1. Dennis Woods, of, Spartanburg Methodist (S.C.) JC
2. Rodney McCray, of, West Los Angeles JC

June—Regular Phase (18)

1. **Erik Sonberg, lhp, Wichita State**
2. **Michael Cherry, rhp, The Citadel** (Pick from Padres as compensation for Type A free agent Steve Garvey)
2. **Bob Hamilton, rhp, Northeast HS, St. Petersburg, Fla.**
2. **Luis Lopez, c, Lafayette HS, Brooklyn, N.Y.** (Pick from Braves as compensation for Type A free agent Terry Forster)
3. **Mitchell Moran, of, Texas-Pan America**
4. **Bert Flores, of, Mount Whitney HS, Visalia, Calif.**
5. **Rick Thurman, rhp, Pepperdine**
6. **Scott May, rhp, Wisconsin-Oshkosh**
7. **Tim Zapolski, 3b, Boulder City (Nev.) HS**
8. **Dave Eichhorn, rhp, Miami**
9. **Curtis Campbell, c, Gardena (Calif.) HS**
10. **Chuck Bartlett, c, Mississippi State**
11. **Joe Karmeris, 3b, Reavis HS, Burbank, Ill.**
12. **Kevin Dotson, c, Memphis State**
13. **Ken Harvey, 2b, Richmond**
14. **Barry Wohler, lhp, Minnesota**
15. Richard Ross, 3b, North Park (Ill.)
16. **Steve Shields, rhp, Cal State Los Angeles**
17. **Michael Blair, c, Jacksonville State**
18. Fred LaGroue, rhp, Holy Cross HS, Chalmette, La.
19. **Chris Chapman, of, Southern**
20. Mark Stevens, of/1b, Citrus (Calif.) JC
21. Shawn Gilbert, ss, Agua Fria HS, Litchfield Park, Ariz.
22. Mike Fetters, rhp, Iolani HS, Ewa Beach, Hawaii
23. **Rob Rowen, lhp, Lassen (Calif.) JC**
24. **Vince Beringhele, of, UCLA**
25. **John Rexrode, rhp, Dallas Baptist**
26. Scott Parrish, rhp, Clemson
27. Dale Hamrick, 3b/c, Spartanburg Methodist (S.C.) JC
28. **Fernando Fernandez, 3b, Lennox (Calif.) HS**
29. Kevin Monk, 1b, Fremont HS, Los Angeles
30. Danny Kapea, lhp/of, Waipahu (Hawaii) HS

June—Secondary Phase (24)

1. Jon Leake, 3b/1b, Sacramento CC
2. Terence Guzman, lhp, Ferrum (Va.)
3. **Tim Criswell, rhp, DeKalb Central (Ga.) JC**

MILWAUKEE BREWERS

January—Regular Phase (26)

1. **La Vel Freeman, of, Sacramento CC**
2. **Steve Anderson, c, Cerritos (Calif.) JC**
3. **Michael Serviente, rhp, Northwood Institute (Texas)**
4. John Griswold, lhp, Mercer County (N.J.) CC
5. Tim Lemmons, rhp, Gulf Coast (Fla.) CC
6. Jeff Graham, of, Gadsden State (Ala.) JC
7. Bobby Thigpen, of, Seminole (Fla.) CC
8. **Tom Kleean, lhp, Palm Beach (Fla.) JC**
9. Mark Stone, p, Sierra (Calif.) JC
10. **Greg Simmons, rhp, Gadsden State (Ala.) JC**
11. Rick Waltman, rhp, South Florida JC
12. **Troy Watkins, rhp, Sacramento CC**
13. Herman Spera, rhp, Endwell, N.Y.
14. Mark Leonette, rhp, Rio Hondo (Calif.) JC
15. Randy Poitevint, 3b, Sunland, Calif.
16. Ken Longman, rhp, Sacramento CC
17. **Gary Appino, of, Sacramento CC**
18. Henry Gonzalez, rhp, Mount San Antonio (Calif.) JC
19. Bret Williamson, of, Central Arizona JC
20. Michael Crawford, of, Moorpark (Calif.) JC
21. Alfred Sapp, of, East Los Angeles JC

January—Secondary Phase (4)

1. **Jim Morris, lhp, Ranger (Texas) JC**
2. Wayne Egbert, rhp, Green River (Wash.) CC
3. **Gerald McDermott, 3b, San Bernardino Valley (Calif.) JC**
4. Paul Togneri, lhp, Citrus (Calif.) JC

June—Regular Phase (26)

1. **Dan Plesac, lhp, North Carolina State**
2. **Glenn Braggs, of, Hawaii**
3. **Jeff Reece, lhp, Oregon State**
4. **Mike Birkbeck, rhp, Akron**
5. **Joey Meyer, 1b, Hawaii**
6. **Kerry Everett, 3b, Point Loma Nazarene (Calif.)**
7. **Mike Gobbo, c, Midwestern State (Texas)**
8. **Derek Diaz, rhp, Hawaii-Hilo**
9. **Jeff Parrett, rhp, Kentucky**
10. **Jeff Gilbert, rhp, Clemson**
11. **John Thompson, rhp, Willamette (Ore.)**
12. Darryl Stephens, of, Stanford
13. **Bobby Fingers, rhp, Scottsdale (Ariz.) CC**
14. **Kyle Selden, lhp, Cerritos (Calif.) HS**

15. **Mark Ciardi, rhp, Maryland**
16. **Terry Derby, 3b, Hawaii**
17. Alan Sadler, rhp, Maryland
18. Chris Kahler, rhp, North Carolina
19. Lindsay Meggs, 3b, UCLA
20. Phil Lane, of, Miami
21. Kendall Carter, rhp, Arizona State
22. Jeff Glover, rhp, Farragut HS, Knoxville
23. Pete Beall, 3b, UCLA
24. **Joe Mitchell, c, Morehead State**
25. **John Beuerlein, c, Arizona**
26. **David Page, 3b/1b, Tucson, Ariz.**
27. **Tom Steinbach, of, Valley Stream (N.Y.) South HS**
28. **Michael Smith, c, Southern Connecticut State**
29. **Bo Shipp, 3b, Morehead State**
30. Todd Azar, rhp, Cherry Hill (N.J.) East HS
31. Dan Gakeler, 1b, Mercer County (N.J.) CC
32. Jeff Pequignot, of, Stetson

June—Secondary Phase (21)

1. **Rick Abbott, 2b, Texas-El Paso**
2. **Alex Madrid, rhp, Yavapai (Ariz.) JC**
3. Saul Cortez, rhp, Riverside (Calif.) CC
4. Bob Bernardo, of/3b, Allegheny (Pa.) CC

MINNESOTA TWINS

January—Regular Phase (2)

1. **Kevin Hammond, rhp, St. Petersburg (Fla.) JC**
2. David Cohen, ss, Fullerton (Calif.) JC
3. Clark Lancet, 3b, Miami-Dade CC (Selection voided)
4. Troy Thomas, of, Mount San Antonio (Calif.) JC
5. **Donnie Iasparro, rhp, Fullerton (Calif.) JC**
6. **Troy Galloway, lhp, Modesto (Calif.) JC**
7. Faustino Diaz, 3b, Miami-Dade New World Center CC
8. Thomas Green, rhp, Fullerton (Calif.) JC
9. Octavio Marante, lhp, Miami-Dade New World Center CC
10. Eric Schou, lhp, JC of San Mateo (Calif.)
11. John Saylor, rhp, JC of San Mateo (Calif.)
12. Alfredo Perez, of, Miami-Dade New World Center CC
13. Hugo Carballoza, rhp, Miami-Dade New World Center CC
14. John Nero, of, Fullerton (Calif.) JC
15. **Leo Cardenas, ss, Taft (Calif.) JC**

January—Secondary Phase (20)

1. **Coe Brier, c/1b, Salisbury, N.C.**
2. Chip Dill, rhp, Cerritos (Calif.) JC
3. Steve Iannini, of, Orlando, Fla.

June—Regular Phase (1)

1. Tim Belcher, rhp, Mount Vernon Nazarene (Ohio)
2. Bill Swift, rhp, Maine
3. **Chris Forgione, of, Salesianum HS, Wilmington, Del.**
4. **Tim Wiseman, rhp, UC Riverside**
5. **Jeff Trout, 2b, Delaware**
6. Steve Wiley, lhp, Myers Park HS, Charlotte
7. **Tim Thompson, rhp, Cal State Fullerton**
8. **Mike Verkuilen, of, Wisconsin**
9. **David Vetsch, of, St. Cloud State (Minn.)**
10. Dwayne Dahl, rhp, Rush City (Minn.) HS
11. **Jim Weiss, c, New York Tech**
12. **Doug Palmer, of/rhp, Creighton**
13. **Greg Cottrell, c, Oral Roberts**
14. **Matt Butcher, ss, Nebraska**
15. Matt Bergeron, ss, Nicholls State
16. Ken Galloway, lhp, Fresno State
17. **Jim Pancake, c, St. Cloud State (Minn.)**
18. **Jeff Schugel, 3b, Mankato State (Minn.)**
19. Kent McBride, of, UC Santa Barbara
20. Doug Emery, of, East Mecklenburg HS, Charlotte
21. **Mike Cloninger, rhp/1b, East Lincolnton (N.C.) HS**
22. **Craig Coppola, 1b, Nicholls State**
23. **Robert Calley, c, Chino HS, Ontario, Calif.**
24. **Serafin Diaz, of, Garden Grove (Calif.) HS**
25. **Jay Johnson, of, St. Thomas (Minn.)**
26. Ron Johnson, rhp, Fruita HS, Grand Junction, Colo.
27. **Shaun Smith, ss, UC Riverside**
28. Mark Brown, rhp, Garden Grove (Calif.) HS
29. **Scott Klingbeil, rhp, Cal State Chico**
30. **Angel Garcia, of, Bell HS, Huntington Beach, Calif.**
31. Joe Giordanella, rhp, Lindenhurst (N.Y.) HS

June—Secondary Phase (1)

1. Oddibe McDowell, of, Arizona State
2. **Henry Gonzales, rhp, Mount San Antonio (Calif.) JC**

MONTREAL EXPOS

January—Regular Phase (13)

1. **Steve Moran, lhp, Triton (Ill.) JC**
2. Chris Huchingson, rhp, Wharton County (Texas) JC
3. **Charles Hilton, rhp, Riverside (Calif.) CC**
4. Joe Neely, lhp, Bacone (Okla.) JC
5. **Rick Smith, c, Antelope Valley (Calif.) JC**
6. John Ackerman, rhp, Labette (Kan.) JC
7. **Tony Nicometi, lhp, Buffalo, N.Y.**
8. William Froelich, rhp, Indian Hills (Iowa) CC
9. Bob Bernardo, of, Allegany (Md.) JC
10. Scott Clemo, ss, Gulf Coast (Fla.) CC
11. Cyrenius Phillips, 1b, Panola (Texas) JC
12. Bret Allen, p, De Anza (Calif.) JC (Selection voided)
13. Tim Swab, lhp, Northeastern Oklahoma A&M JC
14. Cordell Ross, ss, Central Arizona JC
15. Patrick Cummings, c, Delgado (La.) JC
16. **James Hess, rhp, Western Kentucky**
17. **Kevin Birkoffer, inf, Western Kentucky**
18. Gary Wright, of, Alvin (Texas) CC

January—Secondary Phase (17)

1. Robert Nettles, rhp, Orange Coast (Calif.) JC
2. Ron Jones, of, Wharton County (Texas) JC
3. Kevin Pour, of/rhp, Bellevue Area (Ill.) JC
4. **Jeff Wilpon, c, Palm Beach (Fla.) JC**

June—Regular Phase (14)

1. **Rich Stoll, rhp, Michigan**
1. **Brian Holman, rhp, North HS, Wichita, Kan.** (Pick from Giants as compensation for Type A free agent Joel Youngblood)
2. **Jim Jefferson, rhp, Arizona State**
3. **Randy Ray, c, Minden (La.) HS**
4. **Cas Soma, rhp, UC Irvine**
5. **Cliff Young, lhp, Willis (Texas) HS**
6. **Bill Moore, of/1b, Cal State Fullerton**
7. Erik Hanson, rhp, Peddie Prep, Kennelon, N.J.
8. **Don Montgomery, of, Creighton**
9. Tim Meacham, rhp, Alabama
10. **Robbie Cobb, 2b, Ohio State**
11. **Tom Traen, lhp, Creighton**
12. **Gary Mahler, 1b, Rider**
13. Bob Latmore, ss, Deland HS, Osteen, Fla.
14. **Jeff DePiano, of, Jacksonville**
15. **Gary Page, rhp, Point Loma Nazarene (Calif.)**
16. **Alan DeVall, 2b, LaVerne (Calif.)**
17. **Mike Rupp, c, UC Irvine**
18. **Ralph Antone, 1b, Western Kentucky**
19. **Fred Blair, 1b, Wright State**
20. Ed Delzer, lhp, Cal State Fullerton
21. **Norland Claxton, 3b, Jackson State**
22. Loren Hibbs, of, Wichita State
23. Craig Howard, lhp, Iowa State
24. **Gary Brahs, lhp, UC Irvine**
25. **Michael Fisher, rhp, Wright State**
26. **Steven Graf, of, Northwestern State**
27. **H.J. Lopes, 2b, Temple**
28. Randy Riley, 1b, Jacksonville
29. **David Pascho, rhp, Washington**
30. **J.C. Batista, ss, Southridge HS, Miami**
31. **John Dodd, lhp, Canyon HS, Canyon Country, Calif.**
32. **David Lucas, ss, Wichita State**
33. **Shane Reilly, ss, Plantation (Fla.) HS**

June—Secondary Phase (10)

1. **Mark Tindall, lhp, Sinclair (Ohio) CC**

NEW YORK METS

January—Regular Phase (3)

1. **Ralph Adams, rhp, McKeesport, Pa.**
2. Joe Kraemer, lhp, Lower Columbia (Wash.) JC
3. Miles Schuler, rhp, Santa Ana (Calif.) JC
4. James Eurton, c, Citrus (Calif.) JC
5. Henry Robinson, rhp, Lower Columbia (Wash.) JC
6. Rocky Lambourne, rhp, Snow (Utah) JC
7. Kevin Ryan, rhp, Palm Beach (Fla.) JC
8. **Reggie Dobie, rhp, Triton (Ill.) JC**
9. Jerry Mack, 2b, Iowa Western CC
10. **Michael Houston, of, East Los Angeles JC**
11. Carl Coates, rhp, Utah Technical JC
12. Greg Mooneyham, 1b, Palm Beach (Fla.) JC
13. Jeffrey Hintz, of, Merced (Calif.) JC
14. Ken Reed, rhp, Crowder (Mo.) JC
15. Rob Jones, c, Yuba (Calif.) CC
16. **David Jarman, of, JC of the Redwoods (Calif.)**
17. Samuel Thielapape, ss, Northwood Institute
18. **Dennis Glynn, 2b, Eastern Connecticut State**
19. Joseph Morris, rhp, Enterprise State (Ala.) JC

January—Secondary Phase (3)

1. **Kevin Brown, lhp, Ranger (Texas) JC**
2. **Jeff McKnight, ss, Westark (Ark.) CC**

June—Regular Phase (4)

1. **Eddie Williams, 3b, Hoover HS, San Diego**
1. **Stan Jefferson, of, Bethune-Cookman** (Pick from Braves as compensation for Type B free agent Pete Falcone)
1. **Calvin Schiraldi, rhp, Texas** (Supplemental pick—27th—for loss of Falcone)
2. **Dave Magadan, 1b, Alabama**
3. **Rick Aguilera, rhp, Brigham Young**
4. **David West, lhp, Craigmont HS, Memphis**
5. Steve Browning, c, Cook County HS, Adel, Ga.
6. **Marcus Lawton, ss, Harrison Central HS, Gulfport, Miss.**
7. **Eric Stampfl, rhp, St. John's**
8. **William Page, rhp, DeKalb County HS, Smithville, Tenn.**
9. Gar Millay, 2b, University HS, San Diego
10. **Eric Ricketts, of/c, Soddy Daisy (Tenn.) HS**
11. **Jeff Ciszkowski, rhp, Brandywine (Del.) HS**
12. Ryan Virgo, of, Madera (Calif.) HS
13. **Jeff Innis, rhp, Illinois**
14. Bob Caffrey, c, Cal State Fullerton
15. Barry Dacus, rhp, UC Santa Barbara
16. **Jeff Dinkel, of, Grand Canyon (Ariz.)**
17. Mark Gabriel, ss/of, Niagara
18. John D. Martin, rhp, Morro Bay HS, Los Osos, Calif.
19. **Bob Colescott, ss, Deerfield (Fla.) HS**
20. **William Stiles, rhp, Comsewogue HS, Port Jefferson, N.Y.**
21. **Scott Bardwell, rhp, Central Washington**
22. **Charles Huggins, of, Johnson HS, Huntsville, Ala.**
23. Ed West, rhp, Denver
24. Mike Shambaugh, 1b, Jay (Okla.) HS
25. **Charles Friedel, rhp, Glassboro State (N.J.)**
26. Frank Velleggia, c, Alabama
27. Matt Williams, 3b, Carson City (Nev.) HS
28. **Chris Hayes, rhp, Davis HS, Modesto, Calif.**
29. **Desmond Brooks, c, Far Rockaway HS, Queens, N.Y.**
30. Mike Santiago, lhp, Oklahoma
31. Jeff Kantnor, c, Reading (Pa.) HS
32. **Corky Swindell, 2b, Houston**
33. Scott Sellner, ss, Cordova HS, Rancho Cordova, Calif.
34. **Everton Johnson, of, Samuel Gompers HS, Bronx, N.Y.**
35. Roy Caso, ss/2b, Portland (Conn.) HS
36. **Joe Klink, lhp, Biscayne (Fla.)**
37. Mike Young, of, UCLA

June—Secondary Phase (16)

1. Bob Grandstaff, 3b, Golden West (Calif.) JC
2. **Ken Reed, rhp, Crowder (Mo.) JC**

NEW YORK YANKEES

January—Regular Phase (14)

1. Blaine Deabenderfer, rhp, Louisburg (N.C.) JC
2. **Ozzie Canseco, rhp, Miami-Dade South CC**
3. Kevin Torlai, c, Lower Columbia (Wash.) JC
4. **Timothy Williams, rhp, Butte (Calif.) JC**
5. **Scott Todd, 3b, Brevard (Fla.) CC**
6. Lynn Van Every, ss, JC of Southern Idaho
7. Tracy Poulsen, rhp, JC of Southern Idaho
8. **Steven Fingerlow, rhp, North Tonawanda, N.Y.**
9. Philip Laws, c, Blinn (Texas) JC
10. Todd Persico, rhp, Mesa (Ariz.) CC
11. Steve Rollings, of, Edison (Fla.) JC

January—Secondary Phase (26)

1. David Rhino, of, DeKalb Central (Ga.) JC
2. Ed Veres, rhp, Indian River (Fla.) CC

June—Regular Phase (13)

1. (Pick to White Sox as compensation for Type A free agent Steve Kemp)
2. (Pick to Reds as compensation for Type A free agent Bob Shirley)
3. (Pick to Angels as compensation for Type A free agent Don Baylor)
4. **Mitch Lyden, c, Beaverton (Ore.) HS**
5. Todd Stottlemyre, rhp, Davis HS, Yakima, Wash.
6. John Savage, rhp, Reno (Nev.) HS
7. Elanis Westbrooks, 2b/ss, Bellaire HS, Houston
8. **David Smalley, lhp, Florida State**
9. Reggie Farmer, of, Madison HS, San Diego
10. **Ken Rebiejo, rhp, San Jose State**
11. Paul DeJaynes, rhp, Galesburg (Ill.) HS
12. **Anthony Sarno, rhp, CC of Morris (N.J.)**
13. **Richard Mattocks, 2b, North Carolina Wesleyan**
14. **Steve O'Donnell, ss, Oklahoma State**
15. **Steve Frey, lhp, Bucks County (Pa.) CC**
16. **Fernando Davis, lhp, Chicago Vocational HS**
17. Brad Brink, rhp, Downey HS, Modesto, Calif.
18. Turner Gill, ss, Nebraska
19. Mark Ambrose, ss/rhp, Wyoming (Pa.) HS
20. John Hoover, rhp, Fresno State
21. **Isaac Washington, 2b, Albany HS, Berkeley, Calif.**
22. Scott Raziano, 3b, New Orleans
23. **Greg Funk, 2b, Fresno State**
24. **Jeffrey Smith, 1b, Central State**
25. Arnold Issac, lhp, Huntsville (Texas) HS
26. Tommy Gross, ss, Lannier HS, Jackson, Miss.
27. Doug Torborg, lhp, Jonathon Dayton Regional HS, Mountainside, N.J.
28. **Terry Gammage, rhp, DelRay Beach, Fla.**
29. **Louis Monte, rhp, Bishop Turner HS, Buffalo**
30. Mike Dotterer, of, Stanford
31. **Rick Molnar, 3b/ss, Toledo**
32. **Doug Carpenter, of, Florida International**
33. **Stanley Johnson, ss, Texas Southern**
34. **Derrick Cunningham, of, Danville (Ill.) HS**
35. Rob Livchak, lhp, Ohio
36. Jesse Long, rhp, East Lyme (Conn.) HS
37. **Francis Corbin, c, Susquehanna Valley HS, Kirkwood, N.Y.**
38. Gus Torres, of, Temple Heights Christian HS, Tampa
39. Leonard Nichols, c, Temple Heights Christian HS, Tampa
40. Scott Arnold, rhp, Miami (Ohio)
41. **Frank Thomas, rhp, Morton East HS, Cicero, Ill.**
42. Donald Lewis, rhp, Balboa HS, San Francisco
43. Michael Dowdy, of, Marshall HS, Chicago

June—Secondary Phase (9)

1. **Brad Arnsberg, rhp, Merced (Calif.) JC**
2. **Bill Fulton, rhp, Pensacola (Fla.) JC**
3. Derek Vanacore, of, Sacramento CC
4. Greg Burlingame, lhp, CC of Baltimore
5. Blaine Deabenderfer, rhp, Louisburg (N.C.) JC
6. Rod Rush, of, Allen County (Kan.) CC
7. Lynn Van Every, ss, JC of Southern Idaho

8. Chris Ritter, rhp, CC of Baltimore

OAKLAND ATHLETICS

January—Regular Phase (6)

1. **Oscar DeChavez, rhp, Fullerton (Calif.) JC**
2. William Dudek, rhp, Central Arizona JC
3. **Darel Hansen, rhp, Riverside (Calif.) CC**
4. James Reschke, lhp, Imperial Valley (Calif.) JC
5. Dale Johnson, rhp, Citrus (Calif.) JC
6. **Steve Bowens, lhp, Compton (Calif.) JC**
7. Jerry Goff, 1b/c, JC of Marin (Calif.)
8. **Steve Howard, of, Laney (Calif.) JC**
9. Philip Braase, ss, JC of Southern Idaho
10. William Anderson, rhp, Los Angeles Harbor JC
11. **Maurice Castain, of, Napa (Calif.) JC**

January—Secondary Phase (2)

1. Todd Welborn, rhp, Ronda, N.C.
2. Twain Freeman, rhp, Utica (Miss.) JC
3. **Mike Wilder, 2b, St. Mary's**

June—Regular Phase (5)

1. **Stan Hilton, rhp, Baylor**
2. (Pick to Red Sox as compensation for Type A free agent Tom Burgmeier)
3. **John Marquardt, ss, Missouri**
4. **Steve Chasteen, rhp, Patrick Henry HS, San Diego**
5. **Brian Guinn, ss, California**
6. John Leister, rhp, Michigan State
7. **Jose Tolentino, 1b, Texas**
8. Jeff Peterson, lhp, St. Mary's
9. **Terry Steinbach, 3b, Minnesota**
10. **Brian Dorsett, c, Indiana State**
11. **Greg Cadaret, lhp, Grand Valley State (Mich.)**
12. **Jim Jones, c, Pepperdine**
13. **Doug Scherer, rhp, Arizona**
14. **Winford Harris, ss, Long Beach Poly HS, Compton, Calif.**
15. **Scott Whaley, rhp, Jacksonville State**
16. **Orlando Artilles, of, Miami**
17. Robert Ryley, c, St. Francis De Sales HS, Beecher, Ill.
18. David Karasinski, lhp, Utica (Mich.) HS
19. Roger Lewis, rhp, Oral Roberts
20. Jeff Anderson, rhp, Nebraska
21. **Mike Fulmer, lhp, UC Santa Barbara**
22. **Lawrence Smith, lhp, California Baptist**
23. Gary Wayne, lhp, Michigan
24. **Steve Chumas, 3b, Western Michigan**
25. **Larry Beardman, of, Cal Poly Pomona**
26. **Matt Held, c, UC Riverside**
27. Brian Leighton, of, Loyola Marymount
28. **Camilo Pascual, rhp, Miami**
29. **Bob Vantrease, lhp, Delaware**
30. **Steve Gomez, rhp, Cal Poly Pomona**
31. Scott Schultz, 3b, Mira Costa (Calif.) JC
32. **Mike Rantz, 2b/ss, St. Thomas (Minn.)**
33. Steven Maunakea, rhp/of, Balboa HS, San Francisco
34. **Ralph Sheffield, of, Pepperdine**
35. **Scott Wanzer, rhp, UC Riverside**
36. Craig Amerkhanian, lhp, California

June—Secondary Phase (7)

1. **Rob Nelson, 1b, Mount San Antonio (Calif.) JC**
2. **Mark Bauer, rhp, Miami**
3. Luis Medina, of, Cerritos (Calif.) JC
4. **Mark Leonette, rhp, Rio Hondo (Calif.) JC**
5. **Joe Odom, rhp, Laney (Calif.) JC**
6. **James Jackson, 1b, Laney (Calif.) JC**

PHILADELPHIA PHILLIES

January—Regular Phase (21)

1. Danny Sheeley, rhp, Crowder (Mo.) JC
2. **Billy Ferguson, rhp, Angelina (Texas) JC**
3. William Jose, rhp, Mineral Area (Mo.) JC
4. Bill Jester, lhp, Seminole State (Okla.) JC
5. Rod Rush, of, Allen County (Kan.) CC
6. Greg Schiffelbein, of, Allen County (Kan.) CC
7. Herbert Darden, rhp, Jefferson (Mo.) CC
8. Roy Ellis, rhp, Indian Hills (Iowa) CC
9. Louis Kelly, of, Angelina (Texas) JC
10. Chris Moritz, ss, San Jacinto (Texas) JC
11. Arnold Garritano, c, Kalamazoo Valley (Mich.) CC
12. Jeff Stewart, 1b, Kalamazoo Valley (Mich.) CC
13. David Greene, c/3b, Fresno CC
14. **Graylyn Engram, ss, Hammond, La.**

January—Secondary Phase (9)

1. **Jeff Norwood, lhp, Northwood Institute (Texas)**
2. **Darryl Menard, rhp, Austin (Texas) CC**
3. **Harold Stewart, rhp, San Jacinto (Texas) JC**
4. Bernard Walker, of, Navarro (Texas) JC
5. Rich Rosemus, lhp, Taft (Calif.) JC

June—Regular Phase (22)

1. **Ricky Jordan, 1b, Grant HS, Sacramento**
2. **Mike Colpitt, ss, Okmulgee (Okla.) HS**
3. **Wayne Dannenburg, of, East Tennessee State**
4. David Lynch, lhp, Sehome HS, Bellingham, Wash.
5. **Kenneth Lewis, ss/2b, Forestbrook HS, Houston**
6. **Kevin Ward, of, Arizona**
7. **Prince Cousinard, of, Texas Southern**
8. Jeff Bronkey, rhp, Klamath Union HS, Klamath Falls, Ore.
9. **Steve Moses, of, Arizona State**
10. **Brian Householder, lhp, Kofa HS, Yuma, Ariz.**
11. Sherman Collins, rhp, Paden (Okla.) HS
12. **Butch Baccala, rhp, San Francisco State**
13. Kevin Campbell, rhp, Des Arc (Ark.) HS
14. **Max Floyd, c, Texas-El Paso**
15. **Bruce Long, rhp, Southwest Baptist**
16. Greg Brinkman, rhp, Houston
17. Phillip Whitten, ss, Kimball HS, Dallas
18. **Todd Adkins, ss, Elmwood HS, Wayne, Ohio**
19. **Tony Evetts, rhp, Iowa State**
20. **John McLarnon, rhp, San Jose State**
21. Lawrence Grubb, rhp, South Florida
22. **David Cram, rhp, Belmont**
23. **Steven Monson, c, Chesapeake HS, Pasadena, Md.**
24. **Tom Newell, rhp, Lassen (Calif.) JC**
25. **Danny Griffen, of, Hill (Texas) JC**
26. **Randy Collier, lhp, Wabash Valley (Ill.) JC**
27. **Timothy Meert, c, Garces HS, Bakersfield, Calif.**
28. **Randy Maples, c, Bakersfield (Calif.) JC**
29. Mike Jackson, rhp, Forest Brook HS, Houston
30. **Stanley Strutz, rhp, Triton (Ill.) JC**
31. **Daniel Siblerud, rhp, Kalispell (Mont.) HS**

June—Secondary Phase (12)

1. David Hinnrichs, rhp, Rice
2. Mike Henneman, rhp, Oklahoma State
3. Ken Patterson, lhp, McLennan (Texas) CC
4. **Ken Longman, rhp, Sacramento CC**

PITTSBURGH PIRATES

January—Regular Phase (11)

1. Bill Gilmore, rhp, Pasadena (Calif.) CC
2. Ronnie Gideon, 1b, Panola (Texas) JC
3. Van Evans, of, Grossmont (Calif.) JC
4. **Joe Dudek, 1b, St. Clairsville, Ohio**
5. David Leonard, ss, Ferrum (Va.)
6. Todd Fraser, of, Chabot (Calif.) JC
7. John Shouse, c, Cumberlands (Ky.) JC
8. **Peter Davila, of, Alexandria, Va.**
9. **Thomas Hartman, ss, Lancaster, Pa.**
10. **Pat Brown, of, CC of Baltimore**
11. Rich Sauveur, lhp, Manatee (Fla.) JC
12. **Tim Drummond, rhp, Charles County (Md.) CC**
13. Terence Guzman, lhp, Ferrum (Va.)
14. **Dan Smith, inf, Grossmont (Calif.) JC**

January—Secondary Phase (13)

1. **Brian Howard, ss/2b, Rockville, Md.**

2. **Dean Albany, rhp, CC of Baltimore**
3. Michael Walker, ss, Cerritos (Calif.) JC

June—Regular Phase (12)

1. **Ron DeLucchi, of, Campolinda HS, Moraga, Calif.**
2. **Stan Fansler, rhp, Elkins (W.Va.) HS** (Pick from Astros as compensation for Type A free agent Omar Moreno)
2. (Pick to Cardinals as compensation for Type A free agent Gene Tenace)
3. **Andy Hall, c, El Cajon (Calif.) HS**
4. Tom Powers, rhp, Mount Carmel HS, South Holland, Ill.
5. Randy Strijek, ss, Draper HS, Schenectady, N.Y.
6. **Boris King, 1b, Palm Springs (Calif.) HS**
7. **Thad Steele, of, Western Hills HS, Cincinnati**
8. **Jeff Satzinger, rhp, Coon Rapids (Minn.) HS**
9. Matt Siuda, ss, Muskegon (Mich.) HS
10. **Scott Walker, 1b, Pleasant Grove (Vt.) HS**
11. **Jack Welch, rhp, Thornton HS, Riverdale, Ill.**
12. **John Smiley, lhp, Perkiomen HS, Trappe, Pa.**
13. Steve Hecht, 2b, Union HS, Tulsa
14. **Aaron Carlie, lhp, Jackson State**
15. Eric Opron, 3b, St. Johns HS, Geneva, Ohio
16. **Larry Johnson, of, Alabama-Birmingham**
17. Ivan Hyso, rhp, Palm Springs HS, Cathedral, Calif.
18. Oscar Talley, of, Douglas Freeman HS, Richmond
19. David Cross, of/1b, Perth Amboy (N.J.) HS
20. Howard Manzon, of, CC of Morris (N.J.)
21. Steve Carter, of, Albemarle HS, Charlottesville, Va.
22. Ted Williams, of, Caldwell HS, Columbus, Miss.
23. **Kevin Gordon, rhp, Eastern Illinois**
24. **Curtis Thurston, of, Henderson State (Ark.)**
25. Perry Franklin, 3b, Junction City (Ark.) HS
26. Brian Kopetsky, ss, Muhlenberg HS, Laureldale, Pa.
27. Kendall Echols, rhp, Maryland
28. **Kevin Letwin, lhp, Maryland**
29. Lyle Swepson, ss, South Alamance HS, Graham, N.C.
30. Carlos Calderon, c, Narbonne HS, Torrance, Calif.
31. David Hellman, ss, Covington Catholic HS, Edgewood, Ky.
32. **Johnny Cortez, 2b, Oklahoma City**
33. **Bryan Burrows, 3b, Texas**
34. **Charles Carr, 1b, West Virginia State**
35. Wayne Webb, rhp, Mansfield (Pa.)

June—Secondary Phase (4)

1. **Tony Blasucci, lhp, Florida State**
2. **James Eurton, c, Citrus (Calif.) JC**
3. Ronnie Gideon, 1b, Panola (Texas) JC
4. Dennis Wood, of, Spartanburg Methodist (S.C.) JC
5. **Rich Sauveur, lhp, Manatee (Fla.) JC**
6. Michael Walker, ss, Cerritos (Calif.) JC
7. John Shouse, c, Cumberlands (Ky.) JC

ST. LOUIS CARDINALS

January—Regular Phase (23)

1. **Jeff Perry, rhp, JC of the Canyons (Calif.)**
2. Jordan Stevens, 1b, Merced (Calif.) JC
3. Tom Seyler, rhp, Antelope Valley (Calif.) JC
4. Deron Johnson Jr., 3b, Grossmont (Calif.) JC
5. Ronald Vara, 3b, Indian River (Fla.) CC
6. Scott Baker, rhp, Mesa (Ariz.) CC
7. Mike Trapasso, lhp, Jefferson (Mo.) JC
8. Robert Jensen, rhp, Bellevue (Wash.) CC
9. Chris Gaeta, of, New Milford, N.J.

January—Secondary Phase (7)

1. Greg Burlingame, lhp, CC of Baltimore
2. **Jamie Brisco, rhp, Fresno CC**

June—Regular Phase (24)

1. **Jim Lindeman, 3b, Bradley**
2. **Paul Oates, lhp, Alemany HS, Granada Hills, Calif.** (Pick from Pirates as compensation for Type A free agent Gene Tenace)
2. Gary Green, ss, Oklahoma State
3. **John Rigos, of, Coastal Carolina**
4. **Kevin Whitaker, lhp, Millikan HS, Long Beach**
5. **Mike Robinson, of, Arkansas**
6. **Mark Dougherty, 2b, Florida Southern**
7. **Ted Milner, of, Biola (Calif.)**
8. **Tom Pagnozzi, c, Arkansas**
9. **Kurt Kaull, 3b, George Washington**
10. Scott Madden, lhp, Arkansas-Little Rock
11. **James O'Connor, c, George Penney HS, East Hartford, Conn.**
12. **Charles Kinard, 3b, Newberry (S.C.) HS**
13. E.L. Ittner, rhp, U.S. International
14. Justin Gannon, lhp, James Madison
15. Mike Ullian, lhp, Stetson
16. **Mike Behrend, rhp/3b, Tennessee Tech**
17. **Chuck McGrath, rhp, Brown**
18. **Mark Angelo, 1b, Florida Southern**
19. **George Vogel, of, Southern Illinois-Edwardsville**
20. **Jim Reboulet, 2b, Southern Illinois**
21. **Glenn Harris, 1b, Virginia**
22. **Sal Agostinelli, c, Slippery Rock (Pa.)**
23. **Tim Kavanaugh, ss, Missouri**
24. **John Costello, rhp, Mercyhurst (Pa.)**
25. **Jeffrey Gass, rhp, Murray State**
26. Allen Sigler, of, Memphis State
27. **Phil Burwell, rhp, Cal State Los Angeles**
28. Marvin Smith, c, Shaw HS, New Orleans
29. Dennis Hummel, ss, Oak Park HS, Gladstone, Mo.

June—Secondary Phase (8)

1. **Tom Mauch, of, Cal Poly Pomona**
2. **Jac Hein, rhp, Southeastern Illinois JC**
3. Bobby Joe Edmonds, of, Arkansas

SAN DIEGO PADRES

January—Regular Phase (9)

1. Bob Milacki, rhp, Yavapai (Ariz.) JC
2. **Jeff Stewart, rhp, Martin (Tenn.) JC**
3. Richard Murdock, rhp, Merced (Calif.) JC
4. Mike Smith, rhp, Ranger (Texas) JC
5. Robert Green, of, Cochise County (Ariz.) CC
6. Dennis Cook, lhp, Angelina (Texas) JC
7. Dennis Carter, rhp, Middle Georgia JC

January—Secondary Phase (15)

1. John Koontz, ss, Petersburg, W.Va.
2. Robert Cramer, lhp, Bakersfield (Calif.) JC

June—Regular Phase (10)

1. **Ray Hayward, lhp, Oklahoma**
2. (Pick to Dodgers as compensation for Type A free agent Steve Garvey)
3. **Ed Vosberg, lhp, Arizona**
4. Todd Crosby, ss, El Camino Real HS, Woodland Hills, Calif.
5. **Henry Hubbard, of, Wofford**
6. **Eric Hardgrave, 1b, Stanford**
7. **Mike Mills, rhp, Birmingham-Southern**
8. **Jeffrey Parks, rhp, Yakima Valley (Wash.) JC**
9. **Jay Porter, c, Mississippi State**
10. **Ken Clawson, ss, Johnson HS, Sacramento**
11. **Darrin Cloninger, rhp, Campbell**
12. Richard McIntyre, rhp, La Junta (Colo.) HS
13. **Steve Wolff, ss, Oral Roberts**
14. **Jeff Childers, rhp, Marshall HS, Portland, Ore.**
15. **Marlon Hubbard, rhp, Vanderbilt**
16. **Tim McLoughlin, rhp, Davis & Elkins (W.Va.)**
17. **David Dillard, 1b, Washington**
18. **David James, rhp, Northern Kentucky**

June—Secondary Phase (14)

1. **Craig Reid, ss, Oklahoma**
2. **Ted Kockenmeister, lhp, Mercer County (N.J.) CC**
3. William Gillmore, rhp, Pasadena (Calif.) CC

SAN FRANCISCO GIANTS

January—Regular Phase (15)

1. Mike Fitzgerald, c, Middle Georgia JC
2. Ray Rosthenhausler, ss/2b, Pima (Ariz.) CC

3. **Jesse Brew, inf, Santa Monica (Calif.) JC**
4. Tom Meagher, rhp, West Valley (Calif.) JC
5. Jeff Hughes, inf, JC of the Canyons (Calif.)
6. **Brian Wood, lhp, Los Angeles Pierce JC**
7. Peter Palermo, rhp, Monroe (N.Y.) CC
8. Bruce Morrison, 1b, Yavapai (Ariz.) JC
9. Hector Berrios, of/lhp, Connors State (Okla.) JC
10. **Bill Gordon, of, JC of the Canyons (Calif.)**
11. Bob Siegel, rhp, Scottsdale (Ariz.) CC
12. Charles Baumann, rhp, Skyline (Calif.) JC
13. Steve Wood, rhp, Skyline (Calif.) JC
14. Hector Cano, inf, Pasadena (Calif.) CC
15. Eric Pawling, 3b, Moorpark (Calif.) JC

January—Secondary Phase (21)

1. Tim Criswell, rhp, DeKalb Central (Ga.) JC
2. Michael Meyers, 3b, Los Angeles Pierce JC
3. Mike Oglesbee, 1b, Yavapai (Ariz.) JC
4. Gayron Jackson, of, West Los Angeles JC

June—Regular Phase (18)

1. (Pick to Expos as compensation for Type A free agent Joel Youngblood)
2. **Jeff Robinson, rhp, Cal State Fullerton**
3. **Don Long, 3b, Washington State**
4. **Charlie Hayes, 3b, Forrest County Agricultural HS, Hattiesburg, Miss.**
5. **Steve Smith, rhp, Baylor**
6. **John Burkett, rhp, Beaver (Pa.) HS**
7. **Mike Aldrete, 1b/of, Stanford**
8. Michael Fay, of, Bishop Montgomery HS, Manhattan Beach, Calif.
9. **Eric Lane, c, Tulane**
10. **A.J. Jones, of, San Francisco State**
11. **Dan Yokubaitis, lhp, UC Santa Barbara**
12. **Deron McCue, of, Hutchinson (Kan.) CC**
13. **Steve Miller, ss, Hyattsville, Md.**
14. John Reilley, rhp, Westlake HS, Westlake Village, Calif.
15. **Dave Allen, of, Oral Roberts**
16. **Kurt Lee, lhp, Brigham Young**
17. Bobby Ralston, 2b/ss, Arizona
18. Robert Fannin, 1b, Lubbock Christian
19. Mike Pitz, rhp, Colfax (Calif.) HS
20. **Todd Oakes, rhp, Nebraska**
21. **Charlie Corbell, rhp, Arkansas**
22. **Jim Spring, 2b, Wichita State**
23. **George Ferran, rhp, Granada Hills (Calif.) HS**
24. **Phillip Arp, 1b, Georgia College & State**
25. **Kirk Raithel, rhp, Cal State Stanislaus**
26. **Brian Fabun, ss, Mission (Calif.) JC**
27. Michael Rooney, of, St. Viator HS, Arlington Heights, Ill.
28. **Wayne Bonham, of, Arizona**
29. Joey Zellner, 2b, Yakima Valley (Wash.) JC
30. **David Webb, ss, Chatsworth HS, Canoga Park, Calif.**
31. **Todd Thomas, of, Oregon State**
32. **Steve Gehrke, rhp, Nebraska**
33. Jack Pool, 3b/1b, Mercer
34. **Ken Ritter, of, Kennedy HS, Granada Hills, Calif.**
35. John Paye, of, Menlo HS, Atherton, Calif.

June—Secondary Phase (2)

1. **Robby Thompson, ss, Florida**
2. Steve Eagar, c, Brigham Young
3. Kight Higgins, rhp, Seminole State (Okla.) JC

SEATTLE MARINERS

January—Regular Phase (8)

1. **Keith Komeiji, c, Orange Coast (Calif.) JC**
2. Jeff Osterode, p, Orange Coast (Calif.) JC
3. **Sam Haley, of, Front Royal, Va.**
4. Ken Altona, lhp, Bellevue (Wash.) CC
5. Edward Clark, rhp, Golden West (Calif.) JC
6. Joe Mitchum, rhp, Yakima Valley (Wash.) JC

January—Secondary Phase (18)

1. Marty Lanoux, 2b, Santa Fe (Fla.) CC

June—Regular Phase (7)

1. **Darrel Akerfelds, rhp, Mesa State (Colo.)**
1. **Terry Bell, c, Old Dominion** (Pick from White Sox as compensation for Type A free agent Floyd Bannister)
2. **Mickey Brantley, of, Coastal Carolina**
3. **Dave Hengel, of, California**
4. **Bill Wilkinson, lhp, Cherry Creek HS, Englewood, Colo.**
5. **Bob Hinson, rhp, Lubbock Christian (Texas)**
6. **Scott Nielsen, rhp, Brigham Young**
7. **John Wallace, of, Southern California**
8. Mark Hamann, rhp, McNary HS, Salem, Ore.
9. **Bob Gunnarsson, lhp, Southern California**
10. **Billy Wrona, ss, Miami**
11. **Mickey Meister, rhp, Southern California**
12. **Frank Tunnell, ss, Grand Canyon (Ariz.)**
13. Jay Hunt, lhp, Washington State
14. Reggie Hammonds, of, Northwestern
15. **Bob Bruzik, ss, Quinnipiac**
16. **Ed Salazar, lhp, Lewis-Clark State (Idaho)**
17. **Oriol Perez, of, Florida International**
18. **James Bryant, rhp, William Carey (Miss.)**
19. **Tom Steinbach, of, Minnesota**
20. **Brad Colton, of, Maine**
21. **Jeff Lawson, 1b, Phillips (Okla.)**
22. Duane Akerfelds, rhp, Columbine HS, Littleton, Colo.
23. **Doug Swearingen, lhp, Ohio State**
24. **Paul Smith, 1b, UC Santa Barbara**
25. Jeff Kambak, c, Loyola Marymount
26. **George Priftis, 2b, Virginia**
27. **Rick Luecken, rhp, Texas A&M**
28. **Gary Balmer, 3b, Lewis-Clark State (Idaho)**
29. William King, ss, Proviso East HS, Maywood, Ill.
30. Orlando Martinez, of/3b, Rockhurst HS, Castle City, Mo.
31. Mike McIlvaine, rhp, Delaware
32. Randy Luciani, rhp, Windham HS, Willimantic, Conn.
33. **Ben Amaya, 3b, Nebraska**
34. Dan Ducusin, of, Chaparral HS, Scottsdale, Ariz.

June—Secondary Phase (23)

1. Jose Rodiles, rhp, Arizona State
2. Dennis Carter, of, Chipola (Fla.) JC
3. Jerry Mack, 2b, Iowa Western CC

TEXAS RANGERS

January—Regular Phase (4)

1. **Javier Ortiz, 1b, Miami-Dade South CC**
2. **Mike Soper, lhp, Winthrop, Mass.**
3. Gary Ballou, of, Long Beach (Calif.) CC
4. Franklin Brandt, ss, Kankakee (Ill.) CC
5. Joe Odom, rhp, Laney (Calif.) JC
6. Bret Davis, lhp, DeAnza (Calif.) JC
7. **Robin Keathley, rhp, Modesto (Calif.) JC**
8. **John Jones, c, Dallas, Texas**
9. Charles Wood, rhp, Louisburg (N.C.) JC
10. Thomas Arrington, rhp, JC of Marin (Calif.)
11. Kevin Hooper, rhp, Ranger (Texas) JC
12. Thomas Henderson, ss, Spartanburg Methodist (S.C.) JC
13. Mark Higgins, 1b, Chipola (Fla.) JC

January—Secondary Phase (12)

1. Alex Madrid, rhp, Yavapai (Ariz.) JC
2. Eduardo Gonzalez, c, Miami

June—Regular Phase (3)

1. **Jeff Kunkel, ss, Rider**
2. **George Threadgill, of, Whiteville (N.C.) HS**
3. **Randy Asadoor, 3b, Fresno State**
4. **Todd Jackson, ss, Indio HS, Palm Desert, Calif.**
5. **Bob Sebra, rhp, Nebraska**
6. **Bill Hance, c, Missouri**
7. **Kirk Killingsworth, rhp/of, Texas**
8. **John Harrington, rhp, Alcorn State**
9. **Steve Kordish, rhp, Princeton**
10. **Bruce Kipper, lhp, Grand Canyon (Ariz.)**
11. Tim Raley, c, Potomac Senior HS, Triangle, Va.

12. Thomas Kelley, of, Marist HS, Chicago
13. **Kerry Burns, rhp, Oklahoma City**
14. **Greg Bailey, of, Washington State**
15. Eloy Gil, c, Miami Springs HS, Hialeah, Fla.
16. **Anthony Carlucci, c, Rhode Island**
17. **David Linton, lhp, Musselman HS, Innoud, W.Va.**
18. **Reggie Mosley, 1b, Arizona State**
19. **Dan Simpson, of, Southern Colorado**
20. **Vince Sakowski, 3b, Stanford**
21. **Dennis Knight, rhp, James Madison**
22. **Mark Gile, 2b, Kansas**
23. Mike Yastrzemski, of, Florida State
24. **David Hartman, rhp, New Orleans**
25. **Ricky Hester, ss/of, Clemson**
26. **Ron Hansen, c, Santa Clara**
27. **John Andrade, 2b, Towson State**
28. **Mark Cipres, rhp, Pacific**
29. **Roger Lawrence, 1b, Dallas Baptist**
30. **Nick Esposito, rhp, California**
31. **Bret Elbin, 3b, Alabama**
32. Stu Rogers, lhp, Georgia Tech
33. **Regan Bass, rhp, Washington State**
34. **Jim Cesario, of, New Orleans**
35. **Mark Novak, rhp, Middle Tennessee State**
36. William Warren, c, Connors State (Okla.) JC
37. Joe Heeney, 3b, Kansas
38. **James Mart, c, Texas Wesleyan**
39. Les Lancaster, rhp, Arkansas
40. **Wayne King, 1b, Virginia Tech**
41. **Rick Knapp, rhp, Virginia Tech**
42. **Glenn Davis, 1b, Georgia**
43. **John Munley, rhp, James Madison**
44. **Marty Blair, ss, The Citadel**
45. Clay Damon, 3b, Lewis & Clark HS, Spokane, Wash.
46. **Mike Keehn, 2b, Kearney State**
47. **Fred Lovely, of, Central Florida CC**
48. Kevin Penner, of, Wichita State
49. Michael Reeves, of, James Madison
50. Brad Hill, of, Emporia State (Kan.)

June—Secondary Phase (26)

1. Ray Rosthenhausler, ss, Pima (Ariz.) CC
2. Jody Reed, ss, Florida State
3. Mark Higgins, 1b, Chipola (Fla.) JC
4. Marty Lanoux, 2b, Santa Fe (Fla.) CC

TORONTO BLUE JAYS

January—Regular Phase (10)

1. **Howard Akers, of, Gulf Coast (Fla.) CC**
2. Scott Hamilton, rhp, Seminole State (Okla.) JC
3. Scott Sempier, 3b, CC of Morris (N.J.)
4. John Baumgartner, lhp, CC of Morris (N.J.)
5. William Cunningham, c, Chipola (Fla.) JC
6. Mark White, of, Laney (Calif.) JC
7. Eric Tutt, 1b, East Mississippi JC
8. John Hegwood, lhp, San Francisco
9. **Duane Miller, rhp, North Dakota**
10. Keith Hoskison, c, St. Louis CC-Meramec
11. Todd Edwards, ss, Lake Michigan (Mich.) JC
12. Jeff Corbally, of, Lower Columbia (Wash.) JC
13. Paul Mason, of, Chabot (Calif.) JC
14. **Greg Ferlenda, rhp, Onondaga (N.Y.) CC**

January—Secondary Phase (14)

1. Mike Young, lhp, Los Angeles Harbor JC
2. **Rob Holbrook, rhp, Oregon State**

June—Regular Phase (9)

1. **Matt Stark, c, Los Altos HS, Hacienda Heights, Calif.**
2. **Webster Garrison, ss, Ehrat HS, Marrero, La.**
3. **Jeff DeWillis, c, Pearland (Texas) HS**
4. **Jeff Hearron, c, Texas**
5. **Alan McKay, lhp, Baylor**
6. **Tom Linkmeyer, ss, Marian**
7. **Drex Roberts, dh, North Carolina**
8. **Ken Whitfield, ss/of, Mindon (La.) HS**
9. **Glenallen Hill, of, Santa Cruz (Calif.) HS**
10. Durrell Schoenly, lhp, Boyertown (Pa.) HS
11. Mike Raczka, lhp, New Haven (Conn.)
12. **Rob Emerson, rhp, Fresno State**
13. Bruce Carter, of, East St. John HS, Mount Airy, La.
14. **Ronnie Robbins, rhp, Louisiana State**
15. **Jeff Thompson, ss, Mercer**
16. **Robert Murray, rhp, Florida International**
17. Chris Miller, ss, Sheldon HS, Eugene, Ore.
18. Jim Van Houten, rhp, American International (Mass.)
19. **Mark Clemons, rhp, Coastal Carolina**
20. **Mark Dickman, rhp, Houston**
21. **Mike Werner, lhp, South Carolina**
22. Tim Becker, ss, Manheim Central HS, Lititz, Pa.
23. Don Enoch, rhp, Delran (N.J.) HS

June—Secondary Phase (5)

1. **Otis Green, of/1b, Miami-Dade North CC**
2. Mike Clarkin, rhp, Normandale (Minn.) CC
3. Mike Trapasso, lhp, Jefferson (Mo.) CC
4. Charlie Baumann, rhp, Skyline (Calif.) JC
5. Keith Hoskison, c, St. Louis CC-Meramec

1984

Star-studded Olympic squad produces a lot of hype, but no gold and few major leaguers

They were called the best amateur baseball team ever assembled in the United States.

For seven weeks in the summer of 1984, 20 of the nation's best college prospects—many of them recently signed first-round draft picks—were united on a team that went to Los Angeles for the '84 Olympics, where baseball was a demonstration sport. The players enjoyed a wave of success and popularity never before seen in the U.S. at a level beneath the major leagues.

While Team USA was upset by Japan 6-3 in the gold-medal game, there was little mistaking the talent, underscored by the fact that 18 of the 20 players on the roster were first-round picks—13 in 1984; the remaining five a year later.

"I think everyone knows that it was the best amateur baseball team ever put together," said first baseman Mark McGwire, who went on to become a star first with the Athletics and then with the Cardinals. "I don't think there ever has been, or ever will be a team to match it. If you ask anybody on the team, they'll say the same thing."

R & R SPORTS GROUP

Mark McGwire hit 583 home runs in his 16-season major league career

Big league clubs agreed to let drafted players selected to the Olympic squad spend the summer with Team USA before embarking on their professional careers.

"Baseball is an Olympic sport this summer," Rangers farm director Tom Grieve said, "and it's only fitting for the U.S. to put its best team on the field. If we had our choice, of course, we'd like to get all of our kids signed and playing immediately.

"But considering the circumstances, we can make the best of it. I don't think it's a bad situation, a group of young college kids with the opportunity to represent their country. If we put ourselves in the kids' place, I'm sure we'd like to have the same opportunity."

But of the 15 Olympians selected in the 1984 draft, only McGwire, who became one of baseball's most noted home run hitters, and first baseman Will Clark could be regarded as unqualified success stories in the major leagues.

Four players from the team never even reached the big leagues. That included the team's No. 1 starter, John Hoover, who led the nation in wins (18) and strikeouts (205) as a senior at Fresno State but never pitched above Double-A in the pro ranks. Catcher Bob Caffrey and second baseman Flavio Alfaro failed to advance beyond Class A.

Clark, a Mississippi State sophomore, was the unquestioned star of Team USA, leading the team in batting (.397), home runs (16) and RBIs (43). He yielded the first-base job to McGwire and spent most of the summer as a DH.

Clark was not eligible for the 1984 draft, and he became the second overall selection in 1985.

Led by the contingent of Olympic team players, the 1984 draft had more college players selected in the first round (18) than any previous draft, topping the previous record of 17, set in 1981.

Even Cincinnati, which had never used its first draft pick on a college player, took Seton Hall's Pat Pacillo with the fifth pick overall. Pacillo, a reliever for Team USA, had spent much of his career as a hitter and never panned out as a pitcher.

While most of the focus concentrated on members of the Olympic team, the Mets used the first pick overall on high school outfielder Shawn Abner.

The Mets, who were picking No. 1 for the fourth time, narrowed their choice to Abner and McGwire, and decided on Abner when they couldn't get McGwire to make a commitment in a lengthy negotiating session in his home a day before the draft.

Abner had worked out with the Mets the same day at Shea Stadium. Four days later he agreed to a reported $150,000 bonus.

The Mets said Abner had the ability to make it to

the big leagues as a center fielder, but the possibility of a shortstop with Abner's offensive potential was too intriguing not to explore. But he never played a game at shortstop in three years in the Mets system before he was packaged to San Diego following the 1986 season in an eight-player deal that brought Kevin McReynolds to New York.

In a draft when a record-low 253 high school players were selected, the Mets went against the grain. Their first eight selections and 16 of their first 17 were from the high school ranks. By contrast, Seattle took college players with their first 21 selections.

Neither had much success with their different talent mixes. The only player each club signed who reached the big leagues was their first pick: Abner for the Mets, Olympian Billy Swift for Seattle.

January's Last Hurrah

The January draft drew renewed interest in 1984 because of righthander Tim Belcher, whom the Twins drafted No. 1 overall the previous June but couldn't sign. He was snapped up by the Yankees, who had the first pick.

But Belcher was almost immediately lost to Oakland through a loophole in baseball's short-lived compensation draft. The Athletics lost free agent pitcher Tom Underwood to Baltimore, so they could take any player not on the 26-man protection list submitted by the other 25 major league clubs on Jan. 12.

Belcher was drafted Jan. 17 by the Yankees and signed to a $120,000 bonus Jan. 31. Oakland made its compensation pick Feb. 8 and took an unprotected Belcher. The Yankees, who could have avoided losing Belcher if they had signed him after the A's made their compensation selection, protested and were later compensated with a first-round pick in the 1985 draft.

"The unfortunate result of this matter is that it is unfair to the Yankees," commissioner Bowie Kuhn said. A new basic agreement in 1985 wiped out the free-agent compensation draft.

The January draft, three years from being abolished, introduced a new twist for junior college players in 1984. In the past, big league clubs could sign a junior college player, particularly a January draft pick, at any time prior to the start of the spring season. A change protected junior college programs until the team had completed play in the spring.

"The old rule was ridiculous," said Miami-Dade North CC coach Demie Mainieri, who had more players drafted over the life of the January draft than any other coach. "It got to the point where I was losing two or three starters every year. In some cases I'd lose them a day before the season started. I'll still lose some of them in June, but at least I can sleep before the season starts."

DRAFT 84: FIRST-ROUND PICKS

No.	Club	Player, Pos.	School	Hometown	Ht.	Wt.	B-T	Age
1.	Mets	Shawn Abner, of	Mechanicsburg HS	Mechanicsburg, Pa.	6-0	185	R-R	17
2.	Mariners	Billy Swift, rhp	Maine	So. Portland, Maine	6-1	175	R-R	22
3.	Cubs	Drew Hall, lhp	Morehead State	Rush, Ky.	6-5	200	L-L	21
4.	Indians	Cory Snyder, ss	Brigham Young	Canyon Country, Calif.	6-3	175	R-R	21
5.	Reds	Pat Pacillo, rhp	Seton Hall	Rutherford, N.J.	6-2	205	R-R	20
6.	Angels	Erik Pappas, c	Mount Carmel HS	Chicago	6-0	185	R-R	18
7.	Cardinals	Mike Dunne, rhp	Bradley	Bartonville, Ill.	6-4	195	L-R	21
8.	Twins	Jay Bell, ss	Gonzalez Tate HS	Pensacola, Fla.	6-1	175	R-R	18
9.	Giants	Alan Cockrell, of	Tennessee	Knoxville	6-2	210	R-R	21
10.	Athletics	Mark McGwire, 1b	Southern California	Claremont, Calif.	6-5	215	R-R	20
11.	Padres	Shane Mack, of	UCLA	Cerritos, Calif.	6-0	190	R-R	20
12.	Rangers	Oddibe McDowell, of	Arizona State	Hollywood, Fla.	5-9	170	L-L	21
13.	Expos	Bob Caffrey, c	Cal State Fullerton	Fullerton, Calif.	6-1	185	R-R	22
14.	Red Sox	John Marzano, c	Temple	Philadelphia	5-10	180	R-R	21
15.	Pirates	Kevin Andersh, lhp	New Mexico	Albuquerque	6-3	185	R-L	20
16.	Royals	Scott Bankhead, rhp	North Carolina	Reidsville, N.C.	5-10	170	R-R	20
17.	Astros	Don August, rhp	Chapman (Calif.)	Mission Viejo, Calif.	6-3	190	R-R	20
18.	Brewers	Isaiah Clark, ss	Crockett HS	Crockett, Texas	6-1	180	R-R	18
19.	Braves	Drew Denson, 1b/of	Purcell Marion HS	Cincinnati	6-4	195	B-R	18
20.	White Sox	Tony Menendez, rhp	American HS	Carol City, Fla.	6-2	195	R-R	19
21.	Phillies	Pete Smith, rhp	Burlington HS	Burlington, Mass.	6-2	170	R-R	18
22.	Yankees	Jeff Pries, rhp	UCLA	Newport Beach, Calif.	6-5	200	R-R	21
23.	Dodgers	Dennis Livingston, lhp	Oklahoma State	North Reading, Mass.	6-0	180	L-L	21
24.	Giants	Terry Mulholland, lhp	Marietta (Ohio)	Uniontown, Pa.	6-3	200	R-L	21
25.	Orioles	John Hoover, rhp	Fresno State	Fresno	6-3	200	R-R	21
26.	White Sox	Tom Hartley, of	Hudson Bay HS	Vancouver, Wash.	6-5	210	R-R	18

1984

CLUB-BY-CLUB SELECTIONS

ATLANTA BRAVES

January—Regular Phase (20)

1. **Jim Salisbury, rhp, Rio Hondo (Calif.) JC**
2. Scott Kershaw, rhp, Oxnard (Calif.) JC
3. **Bill Glossen, rhp, Rend Lake (Ill.) JC**
4. James Massey, rhp, American River (Calif.) JC
5. Tim Peters, rhp, JC of Southern Idaho
6. Richard Browe, of, Central Arizona JC
7. **James Turner, 2b, Diablo Valley (Calif.) JC**
8. Jose Bennett, of, Arizona Western JC
9. **Keith Burke, of, Iowa Western CC**
10. Edward McIvor, rhp, Texas

January—Secondary Phase (12)

1. **Steve Beer, rhp, Santa Ana (Calif.) JC**
2. **Chris Cron, 1b, Santa Ana (Calif.) JC**
3. **Mike Yastrzemski, of, Highland Beach, Fla.**
4. Arned Hernandez, of, Arizona Western JC
5. **Tony Leonardi, rhp, Aurora, Ill.**

June—Regular Phase (19)

1. **Drew Denson, 1b/of, Purcell Marion HS, Cincinnati**
2. **Tom Glavine, lhp, Billerica HS, North Billerica, Mass.**
3. **Matt Rowe, rhp, Pepperdine**
4. **Flavio Alfaro, ss, San Diego State**
5. **Bob Pfaff, c, Westwood HS, Round Rock, Texas**
6. **Rob Sepanek, 1b, Eastern Michigan**
7. **Greg Johnson, rhp, Southwest Missouri State**
8. **Rick Siebert, rhp, University Heights, Ohio**
9. **Vince Barger, lhp, Fresno State**
10. **Leon Wright, ss, Woodward HS, Cincinnati**
11. Robert Green, of, Florida Southern
12. **Dennis Hood, of, Muir HS, Altadena, Calif.**
13. **Kelly Guthrie, of, McLennan (Texas) CC**
14. **Bob Posey, 3b, Campbell**
15. **Darrell King, 3b, East Los Angeles JC**
16. **Jeff Groves, rhp, Glassboro State (N.J.)**
17. **Scott Powers, ss, Clemson**
18. **Tim Meacham, rhp, Alabama**
19. **Chris Clawson, of, Kansas Newman**
20. **Mike Santiago, lhp, Oklahoma**
21. Tony Bailey, rhp, Grambling State
22. **Greg Tubbs, of, Austin Peay**
23. **Lyle Smith, c, Stanford**
24. **Chuck Martin, rhp, Santa Clara**
25. Mark Gabriel, ss/of, Niagara
26. Ed Fulton, c, Tunstall HS, Dry Fork, Va.
27. **Chuck Williams, 2b, Augusta (Ga.)**
28. **Danny Weems, rhp, North Green HS, Greenville, Tenn.**
29. Tyrone Sims, c, Assumption HS, Bel Rose, La.
30. Joe Ausanio, rhp, Catholic HS, Kingston, N.Y.
31. **Kyle O'Brien, 3b, Amherst (Mass.)**
32. Randy Ralstin, rhp, Foothill (Calif.) JC
33. **Scott James, c, West Chester (Pa.)**

June—Secondary Phase (5)

1. **Jeff Blauser, ss, Sacramento CC**
2. Doug Cox, lhp, DeKalb Central (Ga.) JC
3. **Franklin Hamrick, 3b/c, Spartanburg Methodist (S.C.) JC**
4. David Potts, rhp, Broome (N.Y.) CC
5. Steve Cummings, rhp, Blinn (Texas) JC
6. Scott Ayers, rhp, McLennan (Texas) CC
7. Blaine Deabenderfer, rhp, Louisburg (N.C.) JC
8. Jim Rockey, of, San Jose (Calif.) CC
9. Dodd Johnson, 1b, McLennan (Texas) CC
10. Kevin Williamson, rhp, Arizona State

BALTIMORE ORIOLES

January—Regular Phase (25)

1. **Pedro Llanes, rhp, Los Angeles Harbor JC**
2. Dana Smith, ss, Canada (Calif.) JC
3. William Thompson, lhp, Gloucester County (N.J.) JC
4. Mike Knaflec, lhp, Santa Fe (Fla.) CC
5. Blaine Beatty, lhp, San Jacinto (Texas) JC
6. **Chris Egelston, rhp, Johnson County (Kan.) CC**
7. **Chris Gaeta, of, CC of Morris (N.J.)**
8. James Kinnear, rhp, Central Arizona JC
9. Robert Collum, ss/2b, Mesa (Ariz.) CC
10. Barry Harper, rhp, Rose State (Okla.) JC
11. **Chris Mica, c, Alvin (Texas) CC**
12. **Robert Ricciani, c, Mercer County (N.J.) JC**
13. Ronald Aron, rhp, Camden County (N.J.) JC
14. Terry Moore, c, San Jacinto (Texas) JC
15. Chris Eaton, 1b, Longview (Mo.) CC

January—Secondary Phase (5)

1. **Kurt Beamesderfer, c, Fullerton (Calif.) JC**
2. Jim Hunter, rhp, Brookdale (N.J.) CC

June—Regular Phase (25)

1. **John Hoover, rhp, Fresno State**
2. **Jeff Tackett, c, Camarillo (Calif.) HS**
3. **Greg Talamantez, rhp, Idaho Falls (Idaho) HS**
4. **Gerry Holtz, ss/2b, Villanova**
5. **Mike Raczka, lhp, New Haven (Conn.)**
6. **D.L. Smith, ss, UC Riverside**
7. **Chris Padget, of, Mississippi**
8. Rick Morris, of, Scottsdale (Ariz.) CC
9. **Alan Hixon, rhp, Old Dominion**
10. **Bill Lavelle, rhp, Portland**
11. Randy Mazey, lhp, United HS, Seward, Pa.
12. **Jeff Hubbard, 3b, North Carolina**
13. Pete Stanicek, 2b, Stanford
14. Steve Mumaw, lhp, Tampa
15. Raul Gutierrez, rhp, Mesa (Ariz.) CC
16. **Troy Howerton, lhp, Wichita State**
17. Jay Searcy, 3b, Oklahoma
18. Mike Prior, of, Illinois State
19. **Frank Velleggia, c, Alabama**
20. **Randy Riley, 1b, Jacksonville**
21. Randy Butts, 1b, North Hagerstown (Md.) HS
22. Mike Montagnino, c, Harding HS, Charlotte, N.C.
23. Lem Pilkinton, c, Overton HS, Nashville, Tenn.
24. **Steven Colavito, of, Schuvkill HS, Bernville, Ga.**
25. Rich Bosley, rhp, Appalachian State
26. Brian Thomas, ss, Lewis & Clark (Ore.)
27. Jeff Ballard, lhp, Stanford
28. Dave Haas, rhp, Truman HS, Independence, Mo.

June—Secondary Phase (24)

1. Blaine Beatty, lhp, San Jacinto (Texas) JC
2. Jim Hunter, rhp, Brookdale (N.J.) CC

BOSTON RED SOX

January—Regular Phase (13)

1. Greg Mayberry, rhp, Ferrum (Va.)
2. Mark Winner, rhp, Taft (Calif.) JC
3. Daryl Irvine, rhp, Ferrum (Va.)
4. **Paul Slifko, rhp, DeKalb (Ga.) JC**
5. Charles Bell, of, Nashville, Tenn.
6. Pat Hewes, c, Bakersfield (Calif.) JC
7. **Tary Scott, 1b, Walters State (Tenn.) CC**
8. Jimmy Hitt, rhp, Chipola (Fla.) JC
9. George Creekmore, rhp, JC of the Sequoias (Calif.)

January—Secondary Phase (3)

1. **Dan Gakeler, 1b, Mercer County (N.J.) CC**
2. Larry Herrel, rhp, Tulsa, Okla.
3. **John Leister, rhp, Michigan State**

June—Regular Phase (14)

1. **John Marzano, c, Temple**
2. **Scott Wade, of, Oklahoma State**
3. **Brock Knight, rhp, American Fork (Utah) HS**
4. Sean Berry, ss, West Torrance (Calif.) HS
5. Steve Boyd, c, Southern Illinois
6. Larry Schwartz, lhp, Seton Hall
7. **Steve Curry, rhp, Manatee (Fla.) JC**
8. **Jody Reed, ss, Florida State**
9. **Tony DeFrancesco, c, Seton Hall**
10. **Odie Abril, rhp, Colton (Calif.) HS**
11. **Michael Fenn, rhp, Lipscomb**
12. Brad Powell, rhp, North Carolina
13. **Zach Crouch, lhp, Cordova HS, Sacramento**
14. Mickey Pina, of, Bridgewater (Mass.) HS
15. Derek Lilliquist, lhp, Sarasota (Fla.) HS
16. Scott Jordan, of, Georgia Tech
17. Terry Griffin, rhp, Florrist HS, Jacksonville, Fla.
18. Brian Nichols, c, El Cerrito HS, Richmond, Calif.
19. **Larry Riddle, rhp, Texas-El Paso**
20. Jack McDowell, rhp, Notre Dame HS, Van Nuys, Calif.
21. **Mike Goff, 2b, Alabama-Birmingham**
22. **Dan Sullivan, 1b, UCLA**
23. Tim Weinfurtner, rhp, Palmetto HS, Miami
24. **Joe Stephenson, lhp, Sonoma State (Calif.)**

June—Secondary Phase (26)

1. **Chris Moritz, ss, San Jacinto (Texas) JC**

CALIFORNIA ANGELS

January—Regular Phase (5)

1. **Dave Martinez, rhp, Blinn (Texas) JC**
2. **Doug Jennings, 1b/of, Brevard (Fla.) CC**
3. Billy Bartels, rhp, Fresno (Calif.) CC
4. Darin Mott, rhp, Fullerton (Calif.) JC
5. Gary Alexander, 3b, Laney (Calif.) JC
6. Todd Gedaminski, lhp, Lincoln Land (Ill.) CC
7. **Chris Horrel, rhp, Fullerton (Calif.) JC**
8. Jeff Klukkert, rhp, Linn-Benton (Ore.) CC
9. Lee Stansbury, rhp, Linn-Benton (Ore.) CC
10. Brad Rohde, rhp, Brevard (Fla.) CC
11. Jim Osborne, 1b, Harford (Md.) CC
12. Jack Mayes, of/rhp, Brevard (Fla.) CC
13. Paul Migliore, ss, Delgado (La.) JC
14. Hector Cano, 3b, Pasadena (Calif.) CC
15. Michael Reyna, 3b, West Los Angeles JC
16. Michael Weglein, of, Essex (Md.) CC

January—Secondary Phase (26)

1. Robert Auth, rhp, Miami-Dade North CC
2. Thomas Thompson, of, Renfrew, Pa.
3. Keith Felden, rhp, St. Petersburg (Fla.) JC

June—Regular Phase (6)

1. **Erik Pappas, c, Mount Carmel HS, Chicago**
2. (Pick to Astros as compensation for Type A free agent Frank LaCorte)
3. **Sherman Corbett, lhp, Texas A&M**
4. **Kent Anderson, ss, South Carolina**
5. **Todd Eggertsen, rhp, Brea-Olinda HS, Brea, Calif.**
6. **Brian Brady, of, New York Tech**
7. **Mike Romanovsky, lhp, Maryland**
8. **Bryan Price, lhp, California**
9. **Doug Davis, c, North Carolina State**
10. **Terry Jones, of/1b, San Diego State**
11. **Pete Coachman, inf, South Alabama**
12. **Matt Sexton, ss, Kansas Newman**
13. Joe Lynch, rhp, William Paterson (N.J.)
14. **Marty Reed, lhp, Tampa**
15. Chuck Finley, lhp, Northeast Louisiana
16. **Pete Beall, 1b, UCLA**
17. **Dante Bichette, of, Palm Beach (Fla.) JC**
18. **Allan Peterson, of, Lewis-Clark State (Idaho)**
19. **Gerald Baker, c, College of Boca Raton (Fla.)**
20. **Barry Dacus, rhp, UC Santa Barbara**
21. **Ed Delzer, lhp, Cal State Fullerton**
22. **Mike Campbell, 3b, Cal State Los Angeles**
23. **Michael Butler, lhp, Montclair State (N.J.)**

June—Secondary Phase (6)

1. Eric Tutt, of, Middle Georgia JC
2. Tom Forrester, 1b, Miami-Dade North CC
3. Mark McMorris, 1b, Southeastern Louisiana
4. **Jim Osborne, 1b, Harford (Md.) CC**
5. Larry Allen, of, Laney (Calif.) JC
6. Robert Auth, rhp, Miami-Dade South CC
7. Todd Gedaminski, lhp, Lincoln Land (Ill.) CC

CHICAGO CUBS

January—Regular Phase (4)

1. **Damon Berryhill, c, Orange Coast (Calif.) JC**
2. Chris Moritz, ss, San Jacinto (Texas) JC
3. **Todd Smith, of, Grossmont (Calif.) JC**
4. **Mark Solz, 1b, Grossmont (Calif.) JC**
5. Matt Crouch, rhp, Sacramento CC
6. Jeff Cook, rhp/of, Johnson County (Kan.) CC
7. Theodore Parker, of, Spartanburg Methodist (S.C.) JC
8. **Von Thayer, rhp, Grossmont (Calif.) JC**
9. **Allan Casteel, c, Santa Fe (Fla.) CC**
10. Jeff Yurtin, 3b, Sacramento CC
11. **Dennis Fortner, 2b, Bacone (Okla.) JC**
12. Mike Stanford, rhp/inf, Citrus (Calif.) JC

January—Secondary Phase (24)

1. Rob Bartlett, of, Citrus (Calif.) JC

June—Regular Phase (3)

1. **Drew Hall, lhp, Morehead State**
2. **Greg Maddux, rhp, Valley HS, Las Vegas**
3. **Julius McDougal, ss, Jackson State**
4. **Dave Liddell, c, Rubidoux HS, Riverside, Calif.**
5. **Anthony Lee, rhp, Garner (N.C.) HS**
6. **Jamie Moyer, lhp, St. Joseph's**
7. Al Ashmont, rhp, Union Catholic HS, Winfield Park, N.J.
8. Glenn Twardy, of, Wilson HS, Alhambra, Calif.
9. **Bryan House, 2b, Illinois State**
10. Marshall Bliss, rhp, Palmyra (Pa.) HS
11. Bill Geivett, inf/of, UC Santa Barbara
12. **Jimmie Gardner, rhp, Technical HS, Tampa**
13. **Jeff Pico, rhp, Antioch (Calif.) HS**
14. **Michael O'Connor, c, Bentley (Mass.)**
15. **Myron Hunter, lhp, Springfield (Ill.) HS**
16. **Rick Hopkins, ss/2b, Long Beach State**
17. **Bill Danek, rhp, St. John's**
18. **John Lewis, of, Grambling State**
19. **Bruce Crabbe, ss, Florida**
20. Alex Sanchez, of/rhp, Antioch (Calif.) HS
21. **Frank Spear, lhp, UC Santa Barbara**
22. **Tim Rice, lhp, Clemson**
23. **Matthew Reed, rhp, New Haven (Conn.)**
24. **Dave Amaro, 1b, Duke**
25. **Laddie Renfroe, rhp, Mississippi**
26. **Robert Mandeville, ss/2b, Whitworth (Wash.)**
27. **Parnell Perry, of, Grant HS, Sacramento**
28. Bill Blount, lhp, San Diego State
29. **Jeff Sjoberg, ss, Mankato State (Minn.)**
30. Jim Kating, c/1b, Fremd HS, Rolling Meadows, Ill.

June—Secondary Phase (15)

1. **Steve Maye, rhp, Los Angeles Harbor JC**
2. Derrick Richardson, 3b, Arkansas
3. **Dwight Smith, of, Spartanburg Methodist (S.C.) JC**
4. Rob Tomberlin, 3b, Normandale (Minn.) CC
5. Mike Stanford, rhp, Citrus (Calif.) JC

CHICAGO WHITE SOX

January—Regular Phase (26)

1. Tom Forrester, lhp/1b, Miami-Dade North CC
2. Keith Bennett, ss, Laney (Calif.) JC
3. **Tom Lahrman, rhp, Kishwaukee (Ill.) JC**
4. **Norm Santiago, 3b, Mount San Antonio (Calif.) JC**
5. **Jorge Alcazar, c, Miami-Dade North CC**
6. Adrian Powell, 3b, West Los Angeles JC
7. Kevin Thomas, lhp, Spartanburg Methodist (S.C.) JC
8. Thomas Henderson, ss, Spartanburg Methodist (S.C.) JC
9. Tim Buddenbaum, of, Iowa Western CC

January—Secondary Phase (7)

1. Jeff Richardson, rhp, Connors State (Okla.) JC
2. Mike Clarkin, rhp, Normandale (Minn.) CC
3. **Jim Phelps, rhp, Saline, Mich.**

June—Regular Phase (26)

1. **Tony Menendez, rhp, American HS, Hialeah, Fla.** (Pick from Blue Jays as compensation for Type A free agent Dennis Lamp)
1. **Tom Hartley, of, Hudson Bay HS, Vancouver, Wash.**
2. **Kevin Renz, rhp, Sam Houston State**
3. **Kent Torve, 3b/of, San Diego State**
4. **Todd Simmons, rhp, Cal State Fullerton**
5. **Adam Peterson, rhp, Timpview HS, Provo, Utah**
6. Al Toledo, rhp, Brooklyn (N.Y.) Technical HS
7. **Chris Jefts, rhp, Darlington HS, Rome, Ga.**
8. Terry Wells, lhp, Illinois
9. Rob Swain, ss, Texas A&M
10. **Bill Eveline, ss, Waukegan (Ill.) East HS**
11. Antoine Pickett, of, El Cerrito HS, Oakland, Calif.
12. **Jim Filippi, rhp, Florida International**
13. **Pete Venturini, ss, St. Peter's (N.J.)**
14. Ron Bianco, 2b, Duke
15. John Von Ahnen, of, Wagner
16. **Jeff Anderson, rhp, Nebraska**
17. **Steve Oswald, lhp, New Orleans**
18. **Dan Sehlhorst, c, Kentucky**
19. **Manny Salinas, ss, U.S. International (Nairobi)**
20. Dan Cronkright, 3b, Central Michigan
21. John Selvitella, of/rhp, San Francisco HS, Fairfield, Calif.
22. **Michael Murray, 3b, Kean (N.J.)**
23. **Darren Garrick, rhp, Southern Utah State**
24. **Jerry Bertolani, of, Los Medanos (Calif.) JC**
25. **Eric Campbell, rhp/c, Creighton**
26. Don Samra, 2b, Florida Southern
27. **Walter Lampkin, lhp, Iowa State**
28. **Scott Goss, 1b, Ball State**
29. Brian Osinski, rhp, Proviso West HS, Stone Park, Ill.
30. **John Christy, of, Baylor**
31. **James Byrd, 2b, Florida Memorial**
32. **Darrell Pruitt, 3b, Southern Utah State**
33. **Larry Arrington, c, San Francisco**
34. **James Markert, c, Western Michigan**
35. **Scott Nossek, lhp, Arizona**
36. **David White, rhp, St. Francis (Ill.)**
37. Mike Patterson, lhp, Mount San Antonio (Calif.) JC
38. **Joseph Martinez, of, Mount San Antonio (Calif.) JC**

June—Secondary Phase (20)

1. Tom Powers, rhp, Triton (Ill.) JC

CINCINNATI REDS

January—Regular Phase (6)

1. **Dusty Rogers, lhp, Utica (Miss.) JC**
2. Ron Bennett, rhp, Dundalk (Md.) CC
3. Jeff Marr, rhp, Brevard (Fla.) CC
4. Scott Hamilton, rhp, Seminole State (Okla.) JC
5. **Mike Smith, rhp, Ranger (Texas) JC**
6. Jim Carroll, rhp, Mesa (Ariz.) CC
7. **Ernest Bacon, rhp, Bristol (Mass.) CC**
8. Eddy Yanes, rhp, Brevard (Fla.) CC
9. William Avant, rhp, Blinn (Texas) JC
10. Paul James, rhp, St. Louis CC-Meramec

January—Secondary Phase (22)

1. Fred Carter, 3b, Millwood HS, Oklahoma City, Okla.

June—Regular Phase (5)

1. **Pat Pacillo, rhp, Seton Hall**
2. Curt Krippner, rhp, Cypress Creek HS, Houston
3. **Chris Jones, 3b/1b, Liverpool (N.Y.) HS**
4. **Steve Kennelley, ss/2b, Golden West HS, Visalia, Calif.**
5. **Brooks Shumake, 3b, Clemson**
6. **Mark Berry, c, Arkansas**
7. Allan Stallings, of, Alabama
8. **Charles Donahue, ss, Robinson HS, Tampa**
9. **Doug Kampsen, rhp, Minnesota**
10. **Leon Wilcox, ss, Westwood HS, Fort Pierce, Fla.**
11. Greg LaFever, rhp, Wichita State
12. **Joel Lono, lhp, Hawaii**
13. **Scott Reburn, rhp, Louisville**
14. **Francesco Trasacco, lhp, Quinnipiac**
15. **George Pace, of/lhp, Richmond**
16. **Frank Driver, rhp, Hampton (Va.) HS**
17. **Scott Hughes, rhp, Old Dominion**
18. **Michael Torre, ss, Oak Ridge HS, Orlando, Fla.**
19. **Lalo Berezo, of, Cincinnati**
20. **Clay Daniel, lhp, Florida**
21. **Allen Sigler, of, Memphis State**
22. **Mark Germann, ss/2b, Rutgers**
23. **John Bryant, of, Cal State Fullerton**
24. **Glenn Zielinski, of, Nevada-Las Vegas**
25. **Tim Mirabito, rhp, LeMoyne**
26. Howie Freiling, 1b, Northeast HS, Philadelphia

June—Secondary Phase (11)

No selection

CLEVELAND INDIANS

January—Regular Phase (3)

1. Tommy Hinzo, ss, Southwestern (Calif.) JC
2. **Butch Garcia, c, Palm Beach (Fla.) JC**
3. Michael Redding, rhp, Florida JC
4. Tom Duke, c, CC of Morris (N.J.)
5. Wayne Higginbotham, rhp, Florida JC
6. Frank Taylor, of, DeKalb North (Ga.) JC
7. Kevin Badgett, of, Knoxville, Tenn.
8. Douglas Parton, rhp, Spokane Falls (Wash.) CC
9. Robert Alexander, lhp, DeKalb Central (Ga.) JC
10. Mike Fitzgerald, c/of, Middle Georgia JC
11. Eduardo Gonzalez, of, Chipola (Fla.) JC
12. Steven Polk, 1b, JC of the Canyons (Calif.)
13. **Mark Barineau, 2b/ss, Tallahassee, Fla.**

January—Secondary Phase (17)

1. Blaine Deabenferter, rhp, Louisburg (N.C.) JC
2. Joe Giordanella, rhp, Lindenhurst (N.Y.) HS
3. Erick Rapp, rhp, Centralia (Wash.) JC

June—Regular Phase (4)

1. **Cory Snyder, ss, Brigham Young**
2. **John Farrell, rhp, Oklahoma State**
2. Kurt Dempster, rhp, Esperanza HS, Yorba Linda, Calif.
3. Todd Brown, of, Arizona State
4. **Pete Carganilla, ss, Porterville (Calif.) HS**
5. **Ken Galloway, lhp, Fresno State**
6. **Andrew Robertson, rhp, St. Agatha HS, Detroit**
7. **Chris Kahler, rhp, Winthrop**
8. **Rozier Jordan, of, Howard (D.C.)**
9. **Chris Beasley, rhp, Arizona State**
10. **Bill Leslie, 3b, San Marino (Calif.) HS**
11. Charles Hardwick, lhp, Wilmington, N.C.
12. **Reggie Coker, of, Austin, Texas**
13. **Joe Stephenson, rhp, Campbell**
14. **Mark Hopkins, c, Augusta**
15. Mark Hardy, of, UC Riverside
16. Randy McCament, rhp, Grand Canyon (Ariz.)
17. Mark Gardner, rhp, Fresno State
18. **Rick Sharp, rhp, Loyola Marymount**
19. Mark Malizia, of, Geneva (Ohio) HS

20. **Dain Syverson, ss/c, Oregon State**
21. Sean Grubb, rhp/1b, Norman (Okla.) HS
22. **James McMahan, ss/3b, Montreat-Anderson (N.C.) JC**
23. **Mike Shellnut, rhp, Tennessee Wesleyan**
24. Ward Merdes, lhp, Santa Clara
25. Brian Dodd, lhp, Greenway HS, Glendale, Ariz.
26. Mike Devereaux, of, Arizona State
27. Bob Dombrowski, ss, Coronado HS, Scottsdale, Ariz.
28. Chris Norman, rhp, South Carolina
29. **William Jenkins, of, Southern Tech Institute (Fla.)**
30. **Michael Tolleson, of, Wofford**
31. Scott Fricks, c, Eastern Hills HS, Fort Worth, Texas
32. Tommy Gregg, of, Wake Forest
33. Steve Clinton, ss, San Jose (Calif.) CC
34. Rich Martig, inf, Santa Clara
35. Damon Tyson, ss, Cleveland Central HS, East Cleveland, Ohio
36. Paul List, of, North Hollywood (Calif.) HS
37. Rock Hurst, c, Furman
38. Ken Rahming, 1b/3b, Miami-Dade North CC
39. **Lonnie Phillips, rhp, Cleveland State**
40. **Mark DiFrancisco, rhp, Cleveland State**
41. **Tommy Decker, c, Duke**
42. Charles Wacha, rhp, Edison (Fla.) CC
43. John Pust, ss, Western Carolina
44. **Mark Reed, rhp, Bridgeport (Conn.)**
45. Jeff Plympton, rhp, King Phillip HS, Plainville, Mass.
46. Kevin Chenail, rhp, Drury HS, North Adams, Mass.
47. **David Lelievre, c, Lowell (Mass.)**
48. Brad DeJardin, 1b, St. Francis HS, Pasadena, Calif.

June—Secondary Phase (8)

1. **Mark Higgins, 1b, New Orleans**
2. Joe Giordanella, rhp, Ocean County (N.J.) JC
3. Tim Fortugno, lhp, Golden West (Calif.) JC
4. Tom Duke, c, CC of Morris (N.J.)
5. Terence Guzman, lhp, Ferrum (Va.)

DETROIT TIGERS

January—Regular Phase (23)

1. **Charles McHugh, rhp, Harford (Md.) CC**
2. **Kelly Burton, of, Grossmont (Calif.) JC**
3. Marc D'Andrea, lhp, Southwestern (Calif.) JC
4. Dan Flores, rhp, Oxnard (Calif.) JC
5. Jordan Stevens, 1b/of, Merced (Calif.) JC
6. Joey Seaver, lhp, Walters State (Tenn.) CC
7. Johannes McFarlane, rhp, San Diego CC
8. Richard Solis, rhp, Merced (Calif.) JC
9. Doyle Wilson, c, Mesa (Ariz.) CC
10. Bernard Walker, of, Navarro (Texas) JC

January—Secondary Phase (23)

1. **Scott Schultz, 3b, Mira Costa (Calif.) JC**
2. Don Cohoon, 3b, Chipola (Fla.) JC

June—Regular Phase (24)

1. (Pick to Giants as compensation for Type A free agent Darrell Evans)
2. **Rob Souza, rhp, Miami**
3. **Marty Freeman, of, Maryland**
4. **Mike Henneman, rhp, Oklahoma State**
5. **Al Labozetta, lhp, New York Tech**
6. **Steve Eagar, c, Brigham Young**
7. Damon Allen, rhp, Cal State Fullerton
8. **Gerald Phillion, lhp, Central Michigan**
9. **Jeff Hermann, 1b, St. Francis (Ill.)**
10. **John Roddy, rhp, Southern California**
11. **Chris Morgan, of, Georgia Tech**
12. Kent Murphy, lhp, Western Illinois
13. Miguel Ferradas, c, American HS, Hialeah, Fla.
14. Fred Samson, ss, Cooper City HS, Miramar, Fla.
15. **Kevin Creech, 3b, West Georgia**
16. **John Boling, lhp, St. Xavier (Ill.)**
17. Luis Cedeno, rhp, Memorial HS, West New York, N.J.
18. **Ronald Stock, lhp, St. Francis (Ill.)**
19. Pete Schmidt, c, San Bernardino (Calif.) HS
20. **Tim Newsome, ss, St. Xavier College (Ill.)**
21. **Jeff Peterson, 1b/lhp, St. Mary's**
22. **William Fuggatt, c, Tennessee Wesleyan**
23. Gary Pifer, rhp, Saddleback (Calif.) CC
24. **Allan Kline, rhp, Olivet Nazarene (Ill.)**
25. Rufus Ellis, rhp, Alabama State
26. **Alan Goetz, rhp, Alma (Mich.)**
27. **Cary Colbert, 1b, Kansas State**
28. **David Minnema, rhp, Central Michigan**
29. Bobby Moore, of, Purcell Marion HS, Cincinnati
30. William Kushmaul, of, Midland (Mich.) HS
31. **Donald Bulmer, c, Riverside (Calif.) Poly HS**
32. Greg Lotzar, of, Central Michigan
33. Marc Wolever, of, Lewis Central HS, Council Bluffs, Iowa
34. Bill Shuta, rhp, Michigan

June—Secondary Phase (2)

1. **Ray Rosthenhausler, ss, Pima (Ariz.) CC**
2. Darryl Stephens, of, Stanford
3. **Jerry Mack, 2b, Iowa Western CC**
4. **Keith Nicholson, rhp, Mission (Calif.) JC**
5. Larry Mims, 2b, Indian Hills (Iowa) CC
6. Jeff Forney, of, Roane State (Tenn.) CC

HOUSTON ASTROS

January—Regular Phase (18)

1. **Anthony Hampton, of, Los Angeles Harbor JC**
2. Russ Swan, lhp, Spokane Falls (Wash.) CC
3. Lamonte Bethea, rhp, Scottsdale (Ariz.) CC
4. **John Elliott, 2b, Long Beach (Calif.) CC**
5. Jeff Sutter, rhp, Sacramento CC
6. **Dave Meads, lhp, Middlesex County (N.J.) JC**
7. Ed Ricks, 3b/of, Long Beach (Calif.) CC
8. Greg Hibbard, lhp, Mississippi Gulf Coast JC
9. **Joe Mikulik, of, San Jacinto (Texas) JC**
10. Anthony Ciccione, ss, Mission (Calif.) JC
11. Marc Lopez, rhp, Pasadena (Calif.) CC
12. Thomas Chermany, of, Arizona Western JC
13. Scott Winterburn, c, Citrus (Calif.) JC
14. Jeff Gardner, 2b, Orange Coast (Calif.) JC

January—Secondary Phase (16)

1. **Rob Mallicoat, lhp, Taft (Calif.) JC**
2. Donald Enoch, rhp, Mercer County (N.J.) CC
3. **William King, ss, Chicago, Ill.**

June—Regular Phase (17)

1. **Don August, rhp, Chapman (Calif.)**
2. **Terry Green, ss, Stringtown (Okla.) HS** (Pick from Angels as compensation for Type A free agent Frank LaCorte)
2. **Karl Allaire, ss, Rhode Island College**
3. **Ken Caminiti, 3b, San Jose State**
4. **Don Dunster, rhp, St. Mary's**
5. **Dan Walters, c, Santana HS, Santee, Calif.**
6. **Clarke Lange, 3b, Miami**
7. **Chuck Jackson, of, Hawaii**
8. John Vander Wal, 1b, Hudsonville (Mich.) HS
9. Mike Patton, rhp, Seton Hall
10. **Mike Ullian, lhp, Stetson**
11. **Craig Stevenson, 3b, Southern California**
12. **Gary Chesnoski, rhp, Slippery Rock (Pa.)**
13. **Chris Parker, rhp, Jacksonville State**
14. **Tony Metoyer, 3b, Texas A&M**
15. **Jeff Livin, rhp, Southwestern (Texas)**
16. **John Spazante, rhp, Ramapo (N.J.)**
17. **Norm Brock, of, Morehead State**
18. **Chris Huchingson, rhp, Texas A&M**
19. Ed Shea, c, Palm Beach (Fla.) JC
20. Ken Pennington, ss, Fairfax HS, Los Angeles
21. **Bob Parker, ss, Mississippi State**
22. **Steve Berlin, lhp, Denver**
23. **Ray Paparella, 2b/3b, Villanova**
24. **Joe Kwolek, 3b, Orange Coast (Calif.) JC**
25. **Alfredo Perez, of/c, Florida International**

June—Secondary Phase (9)

1. Luis Medina, 1b, Arizona State
2. Ed Ricks, 3b/of, Long Beach (Calif.) CC
3. Scott Lerner, lhp, Diablo Valley (Calif.) JC
4. **Mark Baker, rhp, Mineral Area (Mo.) JC**
5. Craig Worthington, 3b, Cerritos (Calif.) JC

KANSAS CITY ROYALS

January—Regular Phase (15)

1. **Jeff Redus, of, Snead State (Ala.) JC**
2. Eric Hetzel, rhp, Eastern Oklahoma State JC
3. David S. Miller, rhp/of, Pensacola (Fla.) JC
4. Dirk Veldman, rhp, Moraine Valley (Ill.) CC
5. Peter Carey, of, Rockland (N.Y.) CC
6. **Roy Ellis, rhp, Indian Hills (Iowa) CC**
7. Rob Tomberlin, 3b, Normandale (Minn.) CC
8. Greg Roscoe, rhp, Des Moines Area (Iowa) CC
9. **Henry Robinson, rhp, Lower Columbia (Wash.) JC**
10. Louis Fuentes, c, Mission (Calif.) JC
11. Steven Purdy, rhp, Northeastern Oklahoma A&M JC
12. Scott Volz, rhp, Des Moines Area (Iowa) CC
13. James Sullivan, rhp, Fort Steilacoom (Wash.) CC
14. **Paul Howarth, of, Scottsdale (Ariz.) CC**
15. Robert Fields, rhp, Pima (Ariz.) CC
16. Tim Swob, lhp, Northeastern Oklahoma A&M JC
17. Jeff D. Brown, of, Yucaipa, Calif.

January—Secondary Phase (13)

1. **Andy Leonard, c, Canada (Calif.) JC**
2. Steve Carter, of, Hagerstown (Md.) JC

June—Regular Phase (16)

1. **Scott Bankhead, rhp, North Carolina**
2. **Luis de los Santos, 3b/c, Newtown HS, Elmhurst, N.Y.**
3. **Bobby Bell, of, Gardena (Calif.) HS**
4. **Jim Daniel, rhp, Wichita State**
5. **Rob Van Vuren, rhp, Louisiana Tech**
6. **Chito Martinez, of, Brother Martin HS, Metairie, La.**
7. **Darin Grimes, ss, North HS, Wichita, Kan.**
8. **Kurt Kunz, ss, Wisconsin-Parkside**
9. Bill Cunningham, lhp, Ohio State
10. **John Radtke, rhp, Stanford**
11. **Tom Johnson, 1b, Taylor Allderdice HS, McKees Rock, Pa.**
12. **Jose Rodiles, rhp, Arizona State**
13. **Doug Konruff, rhp, Wisconsin**
14. **Troy Brauchle, rhp, Alabama**
15. **Lindsay Meggs, 3b, UCLA**
16. **Carl Rogers, rhp, Central Arkansas**
17. **Brian McCormack, rhp, San Clemente HS, Capistrano Beach, Calif.**
18. **Maurice Dorsey, c, Marshall HS, Chicago**
19. **Jeffrey M. Brown, 1b, Richmond**
20. **Kevin Koslofski, of, Maroa-Forsyth HS, Maroa, Ill.**
21. Darrin Garner, 2b, Crenshaw HS, Los Angeles
22. Mike Blaskowski, c, Wausau (Wis.) West HS

June—Secondary Phase (12)

1. **Derek Vanacore, of, UC Santa Barbara**
2. **Matt Crouch, rhp, Sacramento CC**
3. **Jeff Bedell, 3b, Montgomery (Md.) JC**
4. **Louis Fuentes, c, Mission (Calif.) JC**

LOS ANGELES DODGERS

January—Regular Phase (24)

1. John Alva, inf, Pima (Ariz.) JC
2. Keith Nicholson, rhp, Mission (Calif.) JC
3. Eddie Citronelli, c, Ranger (Texas) JC
4. **Jovon Edwards, of, SUNY Alfred JC**
5. Kevin Phillips, rhp, Panola (Texas) JC
6. Tim McCoy, lhp, Mount San Antonio (Calif.) JC
7. Ted Brooks, of, Victor Valley (Calif.) CC
8. Brent Bolin, rhp, Central Arizona JC
9. Keith Sheldon, rhp, DeKalb South (Ga.) CC
10. **Daniel Robles, of, Mount San Antonio (Calif.) JC**
11. Kelly Wilson, of, Paris (Texas) JC

January—Secondary Phase (4)

1. **Shawn Hillegas, rhp, Middle Georgia JC**
2. Vince Shinholster, ss, Santa Ana (Calif.) JC

June—Regular Phase (23)

1. **Dennis Livingston, lhp, Oklahoma State**
2. **Tim Scott, rhp, Hanford (Calif.) HS**
3. **Tracy Woodson, 1b, North Carolina State**
4. **David Carlucci, c, Westfield State (Mass.)**
5. **Jim Ward, 2b, Arkansas**
6. **Mike Pesavento, lhp, North Carolina State**
7. **Jeff Edwards, lhp, Vanderbilt**
8. **Jay Hornacek, 3b, Lyons Township HS, La Grange, Ill.**
9. **Jeff L. Brown, of, Southern California**
10. **Jimmy Williams, lhp, Choctaw County HS, Butler, Ala.**
11. **Ted Holcomb, ss/1b, Westchester HS, Playa del Rey, Calif.**
12. **Doug Treadway, rhp, Florida State**
13. **Jack Schlichting, of/c, Minnesota**
14. **Bob Jacobsen, rhp, Fresno State**
15. **Jack Ritch, 2b, Georgia College & State**
16. **Darren Holmes, rhp, Roberson HS, Fletcher, N.C.**
17. Greg Smith, of/1b, Baylor HS, Chattanooga, Tenn.
18. Adrian Adkins, c/of, Jones County HS, Gray, Ga.
19. **Craig Dorsey, of, CC of Baltimore**
20. Brad Freking, lhp, Wauconda (Ill.) HS
21. **Eddie Jacobo, of, Fresno State**
22. **Jeff Nelson, rhp, Catonsville HS, Baltimore**
23. Jerald Clark, of, Lamar
24. John Cowan, of, Montclair State (N.J.)

June—Secondary Phase (3)

1. **Greg Mayberry, rhp, Ferrum (Va.)**
2. **Brian Kopetsky, inf/of, Dundalk (Md.) CC**
3. **John Satnat, lhp, Modesto (Calif.) JC**
4. Scott Clemo, 3b, Gulf Coast (Fla.) CC

MILWAUKEE BREWERS

January—Regular Phase (17)

1. **Matthew Kent, 1b, Chipola (Fla.) JC**
2. Terrence Johnson, of, San Diego Mesa JC
3. Steve Naegle, rhp, Diablo Valley (Calif.) JC
4. Russ Burk, lhp, Middle Georgia JC
5. Peter Davidson, rhp, Miami-Dade North CC
6. Robert Askew, of, Brookdale (N.J.) CC
7. Kevin Kirkman, rhp, JC of the Sequoias (Calif.)
8. **Howard Bowens, 2b, Sacramento CC**
9. **Reggie Dymally, 3b, Los Angeles, Calif.**
10. James Trafton, rhp, Riverside (Calif.) CC
11. Jaime Barragan, 1b, Southwestern (Calif.) JC
12. Gary Stacy, of, Southwestern (Calif.) JC
13. Gary Gorski, 3b, Los Angeles Harbor JC
14. Richard Brown, rhp, Brookdale (N.J.) CC
15. **Richard Sauer, of, Oxnard (Calif.) JC**
16. Joseph McFarland, ss, Los Angeles CC
17. James Cook, of, Mount San Antonio (Calif.) JC
18. Craig Breaux, of, Yavapai (Ariz.) JC
19. Steven Mills, rhp, San Diego CC
20. **Scott Groot, ss, Yorba Linda, Calif.**

January—Secondary Phase (21)

1. Steve Wiley, lhp, Indian River (Fla.) CC
2. Kevin Monk, 1b, Los Angeles CC
3. Carlos Calderon, c, Santa Monica (Calif.) JC
4. Darwin Freeman, of, El Camino (Calif.) JC

June—Regular Phase (18)

1. **Isaiah Clark, ss, Crockett (Texas) HS**
2. **Bob Simonson, of, Taft (Calif.) JC**
3. **Warren Olson, c, Medford (Mass.) HS**
4. **Rod Zeratsky, c, Indiana State**
5. **James Larsen, of, El Dorado HS, Las Vegas**
6. **Mike Frew, rhp, Bradley**
7. **Rob DeWolf, of, Malone (Ohio)**
8. **Frank Mattox, 2b, California**

9. **Tim Casey, of, Portland**
10. **Mike Stanek, 2b, Delaware**
11. **Alan Sadler, rhp, Maryland**
12. **Gary Kanwisher, rhp, Oklahoma State**
13. **Greg Watkins, rhp, Shaw (N.C.)**
14. **John Jaha, 3b/ss, Douglas HS, Portland, Ore.**
15. Robin Torres, lhp/of, Culver City (Calif.) HS
16. Gary Grant, of, McKinley HS, Canton, Ohio
17. Mike Erb, rhp, Madison HS, San Diego
18. **Lloyd Schafer, 2b/ss, Ramona HS, Riverside, Calif.**
19. **Carl Gordon, of, Wingate (N.C.)**
20. Doug Gonring, c, Florida Atlantic
21. Buddy Haney, 1b, Texas A&M
22. Dan Nyssen, of, Eisenhower HS, Yakima, Wash.
23. **Rick Ames, rhp, Florida Institute of Technology**
24. John Keao, rhp, Waialua (Hawaii) HS
25. Herman Spera, rhp, Syracuse
26. Joe Polubeski, 2b, Burbank HS, Sun Valley, Calif.
27. James Gasser, rhp, Newbury Park (Calif.) HS
28. Bryan Luedtke, c, Potomac HS, Triangle, Va.
29. Michael Stewart, of, Bakersfield (Calif.) JC
30. Kenneth Greco, ss, Boys Latin HS, Timonium, Md.

June—Secondary Phase (10)

1. **Darryel Walters, of, Miami-Dade North CC**
2. Gary Alexander, rhp, Laney (Calif.) JC
3. Stephen Bowden, rhp, San Jacinto (Texas) JC
4. Greg Vaughn, of, Sacramento CC
5. Joey Seaver, lhp, Walters State (Tenn.) CC
6. Scott Hamilton, rhp, Seminole State (Okla.) JC
7. Russ Burk, lhp, Middle Georgia JC

MINNESOTA TWINS

January—Regular Phase (7)

1. Doug Cox, lhp, DeKalb Central (Ga.) JC
2. Daryl Boyd, rhp, Palm Beach (Fla.) JC
3. **Greg Hill, c, Proctorville, Ohio**
4. David Lawn, lhp, Laney (Calif.) JC
5. **Phil Wilson, of, Ehrhardt, S.C.**
6. Joe Bitker, rhp, Sacramento CC
7. **Jose Martinez, ss, Miami-Dade North CC**
8. **Bob Lee, rhp, Normandale (Minn.) CC**
9. Steve Janni, c, Allen County (Kan.) CC
10. Robert Cramer, lhp, Bakersfield (Calif.) JC
11. John Lastinger, 1b, Georgia
12. Craig Robison, p/of, Fullerton (Calif.) JC
13. **Joe Gherna, 2b, Three Rivers, Mich.**
14. Randall Comnick, rhp, Olympic (Wash.) JC
15. Mark Grace, 1b, Saddleback (Calif.) CC
16. **Ken DeGroot, 3b, Miami-Dade North CC**

January—Secondary Phase (9)

1. **Alan Sontag, rhp, Indian River (Fla.) JC**
2. Kenneth Shaw, rhp, Miami-Dade North CC

June—Regular Phase (8)

1. **Jay Bell, ss, Gonzalez Tate HS, Pensacola, Fla.**
2. **Greg Morhardt, 1b, South Carolina**
3. John Verducci, ss, Stanford
4. **Larry Blackwell, ss, Dinwiddie (Va.) HS**
5. **Neil Landmark, rhp, North Central Bible**
6. **Bob Ralston, 2b/ss, Arizona**
7. **Mike Ryan, 1b/of, Florida Atlantic**
8. **Ray Velasquez, rhp, La Puente (Calif.) HS**
9. **Chris Calvert, c, Chapman (Calif.)**
10. **Pat Crosby, of, Cordoza HS, Springfield Gardens, N.Y.**
11. **Brian Leighton, of, Loyola Marymount**
12. **Joey Aragon, ss, Chapman (Calif.)**
13. **Brian Honeycutt, rhp, William Penn HS, New Castle, Del.**
14. **Jeff Smith, of, St. Petersburg (Fla.) Catholic HS**
15. **Jeff Rojas, rhp, Chapman (Calif.)**
16. **Perry Husband, 2b, Cal State Northridge**
17. **Tom Thomas, of, Cal State Fullerton**
18. **Robert Richards, rhp, Onondaga (N.Y.) CC**
19. **Juan Yancof, rhp, Miami**
20. **Gene Larkin, 3b/1b, Columbia**
21. Clay Parker, rhp, Louisiana State
22. **Anthony Lopez, c, La Puente (Calif.) HS**
23. **James Dalton, ss, New York Tech**
24. **Dave Williams, ss, Cal State Northridge**
25. **Steve Riley, c, Tulane**
26. **Jose Dominguez, rhp, Cal State Northridge**
27. **Dan Jones, c, Minot State (N.D.)**
28. Bill Voeltz, lhp, Broward (Fla.) CC
29. Dennis Bryant, rhp, Olympic (Wash.) JC
30. **Todd Budke, ss, Kirkwood (Iowa) CC**
31. Dan Raley, ss, Potomac HS, Triangle, Va.
32. Mel Houston, 3b, Laney (Calif.) JC
33. Jamie Acton, c, Forman HS, Topeka, Kan.
34. Jerome Santivasci, rhp, Patapsco HS, Baltimore
35. **Al Cardwood, 1b, Long Island**
36. Mickey Billmeyer, c, Hagerstown (Md.) JC
37. Billy Gardner Jr., 1b, Waterford (Conn.) HS

June—Secondary Phase (22)

1. **Eddy Yanes, of, Brevard (Fla.) CC**
2. Mike Trapasso, lhp, Oklahoma State
3. Vince Shinholster, ss, Santa Ana (Calif.) JC
4. Mike Belanger, lhp, San Joaquin Delta (Calif.) JC

MONTREAL EXPOS

January—Regular Phase (14)

1. Jim Willis, of, Triton (Ill.) JC
2. Thomas Green, rhp, Fullerton (Calif.) JC
3. John Power, rhp, Taft (Calif.) JC
4. Scott Lerner, lhp, Diablo Valley (Calif.) JC
5. **Anson Jones, 3b, Taft (Calif.) JC**
6. **Mike Pierce, rhp, Bossier City, La.**
7. Mike Havers, lhp, Kirkwood (Iowa) CC
8. Mike Sims, ss, Seminole (Fla.) CC
9. Mike Veres, ss, Indian River (Fla.) CC
10. Colt Larson, rhp, JC of Marin (Calif.)
11. Thomas Shurley, rhp, Edmonds (Wash.) CC
12. Keith Seifert, c, DeKalb South (Ga.) CC
13. Mitch Moen, rhp, Indian Hills (Iowa) CC
14. David Zech, ss, Central Arizona JC
15. James Gibbs, rhp/dh, Muscatine (Iowa) CC
16. Roy Calhoun, lhp, Mott (Mich.) CC

January—Secondary Phase (6)

1. Gregg Schiffelbein, of, Allen County (Kan.) CC
2. James Rockey, of, San Jose (Calif.) CC
3. Marty Lanoux, 2b, Santa Fe (Fla.) CC

June—Regular Phase (13)

1. **Bob Caffrey, c, Cal State Fullerton**
1. **Norm Charlton, lhp, Rice** (Supplemental pick—28th—for loss of Type B free agent Manny Trillo)
2. **Dave Graybill, rhp, Arizona State**
3. Kevin Garner, rhp/of, Brazoswood HS, Lake Jackson, Texas
4. **Gary Wayne, lhp, Michigan**
5. **Ben Abner, of, Georgia Southern**
6. **Scott Raziano, 3b, New Orleans**
7. Tim Dulin, 2b, Memphis State
8. **Kent Bachman, 2b/ss, Cal Poly San Luis Obispo**
9. **Bob Slover, ss, Jacksonville**
10. Anthony Young, rhp/of, Furr HS, Houston
11. **Bill Cutshall, rhp, Minnesota**
12. Frank Dominguez, c, Southridge HS, Miami
13. Jeff Brantley, rhp, Mississippi State
14. Mike C. Walker, rhp, Hernando HS, Brooksville, Fla.
15. **Todd Wilkinson, of, North Carolina**
16. **Steve St. Claire, of, Whitehall (N.Y.) Central HS**
17. **Kurt Brauckmiller, rhp, Portland State (Ore.)**
18. **Lex Bleckley, ss, Delaware**
19. Oneri Fleita, lhp, Key West (Fla.) HS
20. **Dave Pregon, 1b, Georgia Southern**
21. **Pete Hardee, rhp, Appalachian State**
22. Mike Scott, rhp, St. Xavier (Ill.)
23. Bob Bretwisch, lhp, Proviso HS, Westchester, Ill.

24. Sal Vaccaro, lhp, Santa Clara
25. **Jeff Cisco, c, Winthrop**
26. **Jeff LaMarr, c, Cordova HS, Rancho Cordova, Calif.**
27. Mike Darby, rhp, Iowa
28. Herman Boddy, rhp, Mississippi Valley State
29. **Doug Shields, of, Miami**
30. Jeff Atha, ss/3b, Central Gwinnett HS, Lawrenceville, Ga.
31. **Ernest Pacheco, rhp/of, Providence**
32. **Greg Hudson, rhp, Southern Tech Institute (Fla.)**
33. **Jeff Doorey, lhp, Baldwin-Wallace (Ohio)**
34. Mark Bond, rhp, St. Mary's (Texas)

June—Secondary Phase (19)

1. Gordie Hershiser, rhp, Indian River (Fla.) CC
2. Jose Alou, of, Canada (Calif.) JC

NEW YORK METS

January—Regular Phase (2)

1. Garry Clark, rhp, St. Louis CC-Forest Park
2. **Kevin Elster, ss, Golden West (Calif.) JC**
3. Mike Westbrook, of/inf, Johnson County (Kan.) CC
4. **Bryant Robertson, of, Triton (Ill.) JC**
5. Richard Yochem, c, Valencia (Fla.) CC
6. Craig Worthington, 3b, Cerritos (Calif.) JC
7. **Scott Little, of, Mineral Area (Mo.) JC**
8. Paul Nicholson, rhp, Rockland (N.Y.) CC
9. Tim Williams, lhp, Crowder (Mo.) JC
10. **Brian Givens, lhp, Trinidad State (Colo.) JC**
11. Jeff Schneeberger, c, Indian Hills (Iowa) CC
12. John Sellick, 1b, Santa Rosa (Calif.) JC
13. **Dale Coles, 1b/of, Clairton, Pa.**
14. **Oscar Moreland, rhp, Seminole State (Okla.) JC**
15. Mark Behny, rhp, Garden City (Kan.) CC
16. William Mulligan, lhp, Indian Hills (Iowa) CC

January—Secondary Phase (20)

1. Larry Mims, 2b, Indian Hills (Iowa) CC
2. Jerry Mack, 2b, Iowa Western CC

June—Regular Phase (1)

1. **Shawn Abner, of, Mechanicsburg (Pa.) HS**
2. **Lorenzo Sisney, c, Washington HS, Gardena, Calif.**
3. **Mark Brunswick, c, Coldwater (Ohio) HS**
4. **Jeff Howes, rhp, Plainville (Conn.) HS**
5. **Brandon Bailey, 1b, Hanna HS, Anderson, S.C.**
6. **David Sanders, rhp, Columbia (Miss.) HS**
7. **Anthony Thompson, of, Marion (Ind.) HS**
8. **Barry Hightower, lhp, Northview HS, Dothan, Ala.**
9. **Rich Rodriguez, lhp, Tennessee**
10. Mike Goff, rhp, Red Bluff HS, Cottonwood, Calif.
11. **Lorin Jundy, rhp, Palmdale HS, Saugus, Calif.**
12. John Wetteland, rhp, Cardinal Newman HS, Santa Rosa, Calif.
13. **Mauro Gozzo, rhp/ss, Berlin (Conn.) HS**
14. Terrel Hansen, rhp, Bremerton (Wash.) HS
15. **Jeff Cooley, ss, El Camino HS, Sacramento**
16. Dan Eskew, rhp, McGavock HS, Nashville, Tenn.
17. John Orton, c, Soquel HS, Santa Cruz, Calif.
18. **Bucky Autry, ss, Indiana**
19. Wendell Harris, of, Pasadena HS, Altadena, Calif.
20. **Marty Crews, 3b/rhp, Fernandina Beach HS, Hule, Fla.**
21. **Shane Young, lhp, Memphis State**
22. Greg Johnson, rhp, Red Bank HS, Hixson, Tenn.
23. Garrett Carter, 3b/of, Walterboro (S.C.) HS
24. George Fowler, c, Delano (Calif.) HS
25. **Ramon Pereira, ss, Concordia (N.Y.)**
26. **Mark Davis, rhp, Cal State Sacramento**
27. **Angelo Cuevas, of, Aviation HS, Long Island City, N.Y.**
28. Dale Snyder, 3b, Soquel (Calif.) HS
29. **Lew Graham, of, San Diego State**
30. **Allen Wilson, c, Memphis State**
31. Steve Brueggemann, rhp, Cal State Sacramento
32. Randy Veres, rhp, Cordova HS, Rancho Cordova, Calif.
33. **Troy James, rhp, Tacoma (Wash.) CC**
34. Gary Canfield, lhp, McLane HS, Fresno, Calif.
35. Eddie Soto, rhp, Lincoln HS, Brooklyn, N.Y.

June—Secondary Phase (1)

1. Tommy Hinzo, 2b, Southwestern (Calif.) JC
2. **Terrance Johnson, of, San Diego Mesa JC**
3. John Alva, 3b, Pima (Ariz.) CC
4. **Mike Westbrook, 2b/3b, Johnson County (Kan.) CC**
5. John Sellick, 1b/3b, Santa Rosa (Calif.) JC

NEW YORK YANKEES

January—Regular Phase (21)

1. **William Smith, of/ss, Virginia Commonwealth**
2. Norman Gates, rhp, Broward (Fla.) CC
3. David Potts, rhp, Broome (N.Y.) CC
4. Dody Rather, rhp, San Jacinto (Texas) JC
5. Dom Atteo, 1b/c, Indian River (Fla.) CC
6. **Kevin Trudeau, rhp, Chabot (Calif.) JC**
7. **Doug Armstrong, rhp, American River (Calif.) JC**
8. **Derek Lane, rhp, Iowa Western CC**
9. Ike Bradley, c, Beloit, Wis.
10. Darrell Hughes, of, Paducah (Ky.) CC
11. Chuck Johnson, of, Laney (Calif.) JC
12. Jerry Goff, 1b/c, JC of Marin (Calif.)
13. Doug Hylton, rhp, Bakersfield (Calif.) JC
14. Tom Brousseau, ss, Butte (Calif.) JC
15. Darren Pearson, rhp, Laney (Calif.) JC
16. **Carl Jones, of, San Joaquin Delta (Calif.) JC**
17. Tim Tucker, of/c, Gavilan (Calif.) JC
18. Michael Trapp, lhp, Richfield, Minn.

January—Secondary Phase (1)

1. **Tim Belcher, rhp, Mount Vernon Nazarene (Ohio)**
2. Tom Bryant, 3b, Caldwell, N.J.
3. **Donald Lewis, rhp, San Francisco**
4. David Zapien, 1b, Centralia (Wash.) JC
5. Mark Dudenake, c, Orange Coast (Calif.) JC

June—Regular Phase (22)

1. **Jeff Pries, rhp, UCLA**
2. **Keith Miller, of, Oral Roberts** (Pick from Padres as compensation for Type A free agent Rich Gossage)
2. **Al Leiter, lhp, Central Regional HS, Pine Beach, N.J.**
3. Mo Sanford, rhp, Starkville (Miss.) HS
4. Randy Hennis, rhp, Patrick Henry HS, San Diego
5. **Corey Viltz, 1b, The Dalles (Ore.) HS**
6. Steve Iannini, of, Georgetown
7. **Randy Foyt, 2b, Texas Wesleyan**
8. **Art Calvert, of, U.S. International (Nairobi)**
9. **Matt Harrison, lhp, LeMoyne**
10. Hardin Brown, of, Red Springs (N.C.) HS
11. **Elmer Robinson, rhp, LaGrange (Ill.) HS**
12. **Dennis Chastain, lhp, Georgia**
13. **Keith Foley, c, Florida Atlantic**
14. **Tony Thomas, rhp, Hillsborough HS, Tampa**
15. Gator Thiesen, ss/2b, Mississippi State
16. **Phil Lane, of, Miami**
17. Bean Stringfellow, lhp, Virginia Tech
18. **Jeff Franks, c, Texas-El Paso**
19. **Frank Shamie, rhp, St. Patricks HS, Chicago**
20. **Gordon Meyer, 2b, Nicholls State**
21. **Darren Mandel, c/1b, Miami**
22. **Dan Greenleaf, rhp, Los Angeles Harbor JC**
23. **Tom Woleslagel, ss, Ohio State**
24. **Bob Davidson, rhp, East Carolina**
25. **Mark DeLaTorre, lhp, Brigham Young**
26. **James Starling, rhp, Delaware State**
27. **Chris Zink, 3b/2b, Lamar**
28. **Pat Dougherty, rhp, Nevada-Reno**
29. **Kevin Blake, ss, Western Orange State (Calif.)**
30. Jeff Livesey, c, Lakeland HS, Ringwood, N.J.
31. **Todd Marston, c, Cal State Sacramento**
32. **Ricardo Rivas, c, La Progresiva HS, Miami**
33. **Gary Cathcart, of, Middle Tennessee State**
34. Braz Davis, rhp, Pearland (Texas) HS
35. Greg Kuzma, lhp, Indian Hills HS, Oakland, N.J.
36. William Wolf, ss, Barron Collier HS, Naples, Fla.
37. Scott Johnson, 3b, Rice

38. **Jeff King, c, Ohio State**
39. Todd Persico, of, Triton (Ill.) JC
40. Todd Krumhever, rhp, Hemet (Calif.) HS
41. Kevin Ryan, rhp, Palm Beach (Fla.) JC
42. Al Quintero, of, Lewis-Clark State (Idaho)
43. **Jeff Ott, rhp, Iowa**
44. **Jay Burton, of, Lamar**
45. Ira Tieul, c, Grambling State
46. Ray Graff, of, Detroit
47. **Tom Gilles, 3b, Indiana State**
48. Greg Iavarone, c, Illinois
49. Frank Ricchey, c, Upper Moreland HS, Willow Grove, Pa.
50. Ty Dabney, of, UC Riverside
51. Don Wakamatsu, c, Arizona State

June—Secondary Phase (16)

1. **Dody Rather, rhp, San Jacinto (Texas) JC**
2. Scott Kershaw, rhp, Oxnard (Calif.) JC
3. **Darren Reed, c, Ventura (Calif.) JC**
4. **Shell Scott, 3b/ss, JC of Southern Idaho**
5. **Ike Bradley, c, Wisconsin**
6. Steve Wiley, lhp, Indian River (Fla.) CC
7. **Fred Carter, of, Connors State (Okla.) JC**

OAKLAND ATHLETICS

January—Regular Phase (9)

1. Tim Fortugno, lhp, Golden West (Calif.) JC
2. Mike Belanger, lhp, San Joaquin Delta (Calif.) JC
3. **Darren Balsley, rhp, Palomar (Calif.) JC**
4. Scott Clemo, 3b, Gulf Coast (Fla.) CC
5. Larry Allen, of/1b, Laney (Calif.) JC
6. Bill Bluhm, 3b, JC of the Canyons (Calif.)
7. **Robert Gould, of, Fullerton (Calif.) JC**
8. Reggie Attaway, rhp/inf, Laney (Calif.) JC
9. Melvin Sisney, rhp, Los Angeles CC
10. Darren Reed, c, Ventura (Calif.) JC

January—Secondary Phase (25)

1. **Michael Walker, ss, Cerritos (Calif.) JC**
2. Arnold Isaac, of, Wharton County (Texas) JC

June—Regular Phase (10)

1. **Mark McGwire, 1b, Southern California**
2. (Pick to Indians as compensation for Type A free agent Lary Sorensen)
3. **Mark Howie, ss, Louisiana State**
4. **Russ Kibler, rhp, Florida**
5. **Victor Figueroa, rhp, Mesa (Colo.)**
6. **Pat Dietrick, of, Purdue**
7. **Todd Burns, rhp, Oral Roberts**
8. **Tony Arias, 3b, Florida International**
9. **Greg Brake, lhp, Western Michigan**
10. David Denny, 3b, Texas
11. **Dan Winters, c, Indiana**
12. **Ed Puikunas, lhp, Chapman (Calif.)**
13. **Kevin Russ, of, Gonzalez Tate HS, Pensacola, Fla.**
14. **George Johnson, 3b, Gonzalez Tate HS, Pensacola, Fla.**
15. **Joe Strong, rhp, UC Riverside**
16. **Mike Eddington, 1b, Michigan State**
17. **Brian Criswell, lhp, Western Michigan**
18. **Cordell Ross, ss, Michigan State**
19. John Fishel, of, Cal State Fullerton
20. Tom Scaletta, ss, Cal Poly Pomona
21. **Scott Parrish, rhp, Clemson**
22. Rod Brunelle, of, Grand Valley State (Mich.) (Selection voided)
23. Mac Siebert, lhp/1b, Gonzalez Tate HS, Pensacola, Fla.
24. Wade Kosakowski, rhp, St. Francis de Sales HS, Calumet City, Ill.
25. **John Gonzalez, rhp, Monroe HS, Sylmar, Calif.**
26. **Mike Cupples, c, Grand Valley State**
27. **Mark Gillespie, lhp, UC Riverside**
28. **Jim Thrift, ss, Winthrop**
29. **Eldridge Armstrong, of, Southern California**
30. Joe Leahey, rhp, Western Michigan
31. **Scott Lavander, rhp, St. Mary's**
32. **Mark Beaver, rhp, Winthrop**
33. **Andy Krause, of, Michigan State**

June—Secondary Phase (18)

1. Tim McCoy, lhp, Mount San Antonio (Calif.) JC
2. James Trafton, rhp, Riverside (Calif.) CC

PHILADELPHIA PHILLIES

January—Regular Phase (22)

1. Jeff Mays, rhp, Crowder (Mo.) JC
2. Dodd Johnson, 3b/of, McLennan (Texas) CC
3. Darryel Walters, of, Miami-Dade North CC
4. Keith Kerns, ss, Bacone (Okla.) JC
5. **Walter Nesbitt, rhp, Bishop State (Ala.) JC**
6. Mark Baker, c, Mineral Area (Mo.) JC
7. Brian Duff, rhp, Bee County (Texas) JC
8. Mike Oglesbee, lhp/1b, Lee (Texas) JC
9. Steve Towey, rhp, Fort Steilacoom (Wash.) CC
10. Jeff Wetherby, of/1b, JC of the Canyons (Calif.)
11. Ken Altona, lhp, Bellevue (Wash.) CC
12. Fred Frazier, rhp, Delgado (La.) JC
13. **Rodney Wheeler, of/1b, Hill (Texas) JC**
14. Scott Shaffer, lhp, Strasburg, Pa.
15. Jon Beuder, of, El Camino (Calif.) JC
16. John Shea, lhp, Worcester Academy, Colchester, Conn.
17. Rich Richardi, ss, Valencia (Fla.) CC
18. Carl Coates, rhp, Utah Technical JC
19. **Todd Herrenbruck, 1b, Rend Lake (Ill.) JC**

January—Secondary Phase (18)

1. **Darrel Clifton, ss, Blinn (Texas) JC**
2. **Mike Jackson, of/rhp, Hill (Texas) JC**
3. Rickey Darwin, rhp, Bonham, Texas

June—Regular Phase (21)

1. **Pete Smith, rhp, Burlington (Mass.) HS**
2. **Marvin Freeman, rhp, Jackson State**
3. **Scott Hufford, of, Pacific Grove (Calif.) HS**
4. **Todd Soares, of, Fresno State**
5. **Jim Fortenberry, of, Wingate (N.C.)**
6. **Roger Johnson, c, Missouri**
7. **Bill Jester, lhp, Seminole State (Okla.) JC**
8. David Johnson, rhp, Seminole State (Okla.) JC
9. **Heath Frazier, 2b, Stringtown (Okla.) HS**
10. **Guy Hardaker, 3b, Central State (Okla.)**
11. **Darren Loy, c, Texas**
12. **Bradley Thomas, rhp, School of the Ozarks (Mo.)**
13. **Todd Frohwirth, rhp, Northwest Missouri State**
14. **Scott Wright, rhp, Cal State Fullerton**
15. David Havley, rhp, Bartelsville (Okla.) HS
16. **Keith Miller, ss, Lubbock Christian (Texas)**
17. **Jeff Knox, rhp, Bothell (Wash.) HS**
18. Ken Adams, rhp, Park Hill HS, Kansas City, Mo.
19. **Mike Miller, lhp, Arkansas Tech**
20. **Isaac Johnson, ss, Cordova HS, Rancho Cordova, Calif.**
21. **Shawn Barton, lhp, Nevada-Reno**
22. **Daryl Evans, rhp, Newport (Wash.) HS**
23. **Robert Gsellman, c, Culver City (Calif.) HS**
24. Ken Morris, rhp, Whitehouse (Texas) HS
25. **Bob Scanlan Jr., rhp, Harvard HS, Beverly Hills, Calif.**
26. **Eric Bennett, c, San Diego**
27. Steven Harris, rhp, Paxon HS, Jacksonville, Fla.
28. **Ray Roman, c, Cal State Fullerton**
29. Ray Carter, ss, Western Oklahoma State JC
30. David Osteen, ss/rhp, Elon
31. Dean Douty, rhp, Ocean View HS, Fountain Valley, Calif.

June—Secondary Phase (23)

1. **Ronnie Gideon, 1b, Panola (Texas) JC**
2. Chris Sarmiento, rhp, Seminole State (Okla.) JC
3. **George Creekmore, rhp, JC of the Sequoias (Calif.)**

PITTSBURGH PIRATES

January—Regular Phase (16)

1. Gil Heredia, rhp, Pima (Ariz.) CC
2. **Michael Edge, rhp, Brewton-Parker (Ga.) JC**

3. Floyd Rossom, rhp, Angelina (Texas) JC
4. James Warner, lhp, Allegany (Md.) CC
5. **Frank Klopp, of, San Diego Mesa JC**
6. Stephen Bowden, rhp, San Jacinto (Texas) JC
7. Oscar Valencia, lhp, Grossmont (Calif.) JC
8. Joe Schueller, of, Kansas City (Kan.) CC
9. **Anthony Stewart, of, Portland, Maine**
10. **Evan Evans, of, Grossmont (Calif.) JC**
11. Alex Cole Jr., of, Manatee (Fla.) JC
12. Michael Campbell, rhp, Dundalk (Md.) CC
13. **Dan Clark, 2b, Grossmont (Calif.) JC**
14. Darrell Smith, 2b, Paris (Texas) JC
15. Rob Russell, lhp, Allegany (Md.) CC
16. Damon Baldwin, 1b, San Jacinto (Texas) JC
17. Danny Wilson, of, Bucks County (Pa.) CC
18. Jeffrey Bonsall, rhp, Cecil (Md.) CC
19. **Carey Cheek, of, CC of Baltimore**
20. Louis Kelly, of, Angelina (Texas) JC
21. Roy Mays, c, Angelina (Texas) JC
22. Mark Maultsby, c, Louisburg (N.C.) JC
23. Jeff Forney, of, Roane State (Tenn.) CC
24. David Miller, ss, Walters State (Tenn.) CC
25. **James Davins, of, Maine**

January—Secondary Phase (10)

1. Ronnie Gideon, 1b, Panola (Texas) JC
2. **Jay Buhner, of, McLennan (Texas) CC**
3. John D. Martin, rhp, Golden West (Calif.) JC
4. **Tom Prince, c, Kankakee (Ill.) CC**
5. Oscar Talley, of, Ferrum (Va.)

June—Regular Phase (15)

1. **Kevin Andersh, lhp, New Mexico**
2. **Tim McMillan, of, Oak Hills HS, Scarboro, W.Va.**
3. **Barry Jones, rhp, Indiana**
4. Scott Mackie, of, Elkton (Md.) HS
5. Wes Chamberlain, of, Simeon HS, Chicago
6. **Greg Stading, rhp, Central HS, Billings, Mont.**
7. **Kevin Helton, rhp, Carson-Newman (Tenn.)**
8. **Greg McClain, ss, California**
9. **Ron Knotts, of, Southeastern Oklahoma State**
10. Gerald Ingram, of, Simeon HS, Chicago
11. **Terrance Smith, c, Simeon HS, Chicago**
12. **Lance Belen, 3b, Hawaii**
13. **Steve Brown, ss/of, South Florence HS, Effingham, S.C.**
14. Bob Orr, lhp, Los Medanos (Calif.) JC
15. Craig Repoz, ss, Katella HS, Anaheim
16. **James Nicholson, ss, Muskingum**
17. **Todd Hansen, 1b/rhp, Idaho Falls (Idaho) HS**
18. **Emmett Robinson, ss/2b, St. Augustines (N.C.)**
19. Stu Cole, ss, South Mecklenburg HS, Charlotte, N.C.
20. Mike Linskey, lhp, Loyola HS, Baltimore
21. **Lindsey Johnson, c, Oregon State**
22. **Eric Bolling, 3b/of, Rollins (Fla.)**
23. **Scott Neal, lhp, Southwestern (Texas)**
24. **Reggie Hammonds, of, Northwestern**
25. Joel Smith, of, Jones County HS, Macon, Ga.
26. Steven Trumbull, of, Pinellas Park (Fla.) HS
27. **John Johnson, of, Chicago State**
28. Frank Thomas, rhp, Triton (Ill.) JC (Selection voided)
29. **Reggie Barringer, ss, Cumberlands (Ky.) JC**
30. **Jeff Wayland, rhp, Rio Grande**
31. **Chris Hill, rhp, Cumberlands (Ky.) JC**
32. Larry Gryskevich, 1b/lhp, Brook HS, Weirton, W.Va.
33. William Savage, ss, Sussex HS, Georgetown, Md.
34. Michael McHugh, lhp, Boonton (N.J.) HS
35. James Agemy, rhp, Divine Child HS, Dearborn Heights, Mich.
36. **Stan Fabre, rhp, Nicholls State**
37. Tommy Kurczewski, rhp, Henry Ford HS, Sterling Heights, Mich.
38. Darrell Rodgers, rhp, Oklahoma
39. **Belgee Falkner, of, Baylor**
40. Jeff Necessary, inf/of, Abingdon HS, Glade Spring, Va.
41. Brent Pless, lhp, Brown HS, Kannapolis, N.C.
42. Spencer Wilkinson, rhp, Muskogee (Okla.) HS

June—Secondary Phase (13)

1. Eric Hetzel, rhp, Eastern Oklahoma State JC
2. **Jon Kolb, rhp, Southwestern (Calif.) JC**
3. Steve DeAngelis, of, Saddleback (Calif.) CC
4. Jim Willis, of, Triton (Ill.) JC
5. Billy Bartels, rhp, Fresno (Calif.) CC
6. Greg Schiffelbein, of, Allen County (Kan.) CC
7. Gordie Dillard, lhp, Connors State (Okla.) JC
8. **Rob Russell, lhp, Allegany (Md.) CC**

ST. LOUIS CARDINALS

January—Regular Phase (8)

1. Jeff Blauser, ss, Sacramento CC
2. Dan Hickey, lhp, JC of Marin (Calif.)
3. Doug Piatt, rhp, Gulf Coast (Fla.) CC
4. Gordie Hershiser, rhp, Indian River (Fla.) CC
5. Greg Vaughn, of, Sacramento CC
6. Scott Willis, rhp, JC of the Sequoias (Calif.)
7. Burt Beattie, c, Crowder (Mo.) JC
8. **John Haynes, rhp, Columbia State (Tenn.) CC**
9. Robert Jensen, rhp, Bellevue (Wash.) CC
10. **Michael Robertson, rhp, Murray State (Okla.) JC**
11. Theron Powell, of, Roane State (Tenn.) CC
12. Sammy Garcia, lhp, Los Angeles CC
13. Greg Bochesa, c, Los Angeles Harbor JC
14. Rene Isenhart, rhp, Citrus (Calif.) JC
15. Pete Roberts, lhp, Mira Costa (Calif.) JC

January—Secondary Phase (14)

1. **Dennis Carter, of, Chipola (Fla.) JC**
2. Shell Scott, 3b, JC of Southern Idaho

June—Regular Phase (7)

1. **Mike Dunne, rhp, Bradley**
2. **Matt Kinzer, rhp, Purdue**
3. **Ron Johns, 1b/3b, Cal Poly Pomona**
4. **Brett Harrison, ss, Arkansas**
5. **Scott Arnold, rhp, Miami (Ohio)**
6. **Lance Johnson, of, South Alabama**
7. **David Crossley, lhp, Eckerd (Fla.)**
8. Phil Goguen, rhp, Southwest HS, San Diego
9. **Jon Billinger, c, Cal State Long Beach**
10. **Greg Mathews, lhp, Cal State Fullerton**
11. Billy Carver, c, Beech HS, Hendersonville, Tenn.
12. Tim Sossamon, of, Louisiana State
13. Carey Nemeth, 3b, James Madison
14. John Rohde, lhp, Carson-Newman (Tenn.)
15. **Tommy Mathews, 1b, Tulane**
16. Ron Rooker, lhp, San Jose State
17. Joe Murtagh, rhp, Downers Grove HS, Woodridge, Ill.
18. **Don Isner, c, Georgetown (Ky.)**
19. **Gary Blaine, of, Murray State**
20. **Craig Wilson, ss/2b, Anne Arundel (Md.) CC**
21. **Jim Van Houten, rhp, American International (Mass.)**
22. **Jeff Fassero, lhp, Mississippi**
23. **John Murphy, 3b, The Citadel**
24. Brad Bierley, of/3b, Pepperdine
25. **Bill Wilson, of/lhp, Texas-Pan American**
26. **Steve Barnard, c, San Diego State**

June—Secondary Phase (21)

1. **Mike Fitzgerald, c/of, Middle Georgia JC**
2. Kevin Thomas, lhp, Spartanburg Methodist (S.C.) JC

SAN DIEGO PADRES

January—Regular Phase (12)

1. **Larry Martin, of, Mississippi Gulf Coast JC**
2. **Richard Scales, ss, Chipola (Fla.) JC**
3. DeJon Watson, of, West Los Angeles JC
4. Dave Satnat, lhp, Modesto (Calif.) JC
5. **Greg Sparks, 1b, Mesa (Ariz.) CC**
6. Ernest May, rhp, Taft (Calif.) JC
7. **Robert Greenlee, lhp, Uniondale, N.Y.**
8. **Robert Perkins, c, Mesa (Ariz.) CC**
9. **Rodney McCray, of, West Los Angeles JC**

January—Secondary Phase (8)

1. **Randy Byers, inf/of, CC of Baltimore**
2. Lynn Van Every, ss, JC of Southern Idaho

June—Regular Phase (11)

1. **Shane Mack, of, UCLA**
1. **Gary Green, ss, Oklahoma State** (Supplemental pick—27th—for loss of Type B free agent Ruppert Jones)
2. (Pick to Yankees as compensation for Type A free agent Rich Gossage).
3. **Brad Pounders, 3b, UC Riverside**
4. Larry Melton, rhp, Portland
5. **Eric Varoz, 2b, Brigham Young**
6. Steve Allen, rhp, Central Valley HS, Veradale, Wash.
7. **Randy Robertson, rhp, Southern California**
8. **Mike DeButch, ss/2b, Bradley**
9. **Trace Czyzewski, rhp, Lewis & Clark (Ore.)**
10. **Mike Costello, rhp, Washington State**
11. **Mickey Kazmierski, rhp, Texas Christian**
12. **Joe Filandino, rhp, West Virginia**
13. Phil Williams, c, Seminole State (Okla.) JC
14. **Michael Visor, rhp, Ballard HS, Seattle**
15. **Terry Forbes, rhp, Long Beach State**
16. **Jeff Gray, of, Muir HS, Pasadena, Calif.**
17. **Russell Ford, rhp, Texas Wesleyan**
18. Mike Harkey, rhp, Ganesha HS, Pomona, Calif.
19. Kevin Gorczyca, c, Hoffman HS, South Amboy, N.J.
20. **Mike Gildehaus, rhp, Missouri Southern State**

June—Secondary Phase (6)

1. **Bob Grandstaff, 3b, Arizona State**
2. **Joe Bitker, rhp, Sacramento CC**
3. Larry Cratsenburg, inf, Orange Coast (Calif.) JC

SAN FRANCISCO GIANTS

January—Regular Phase (10)

1. **Greg Litton, 2b, Pensacola (Fla.) JC**
2. Jose Alou, of, Canada (Calif.) JC
3. Eric Tutt, of, Middle Georgia JC
4. **Greg Schmidt, rhp, Pomona, Calif.**
5. **Mackey Sasser, c, Dothan, Ala.**
6. William Dudek, rhp, Central Arizona JC
7. **John Ackerman, rhp, Labette (Kan.) CC**
8. Dick Canan, ss, Triton (Ill.) JC
9. **Brad Porter, c/1b, Mission (Calif.) JC**
10. Jeff Schow, 2b, JC of Southern Idaho
11. Dion Beck, lhp, Cerritos (Calif.) JC
12. **David Hornsby, c, Chowan (N.C.) JC**

January—Secondary Phase (2)

1. **Lyle Swepson, ss, Louisburg (N.C.) JC**
2. Terence Guzman, lhp, Ferrum (Va.)

June—Regular Phase (9)

1. **Alan Cockrell, of, Tennessee**
1. **Terry Mulholland, lhp, Marietta** (Pick from Tigers as compensation for free agent Darrell Evans)
2. **Joe Olker, lhp, Illinois**
3. **Tony Perezchica, ss, Palm Springs (Calif.) HS**
4. **Keith Silver, rhp, Lamar**
5. **T.J. McDonald, of/3b, Pace (N.Y.)**
6. **Greg Gilbert, rhp, Cal Poly San Luis Obispo**
7. **John Grimes, c, Texas Tech**
8. **Stu Tate, rhp, Auburn**
9. Garrett O'Connor, rhp, Southwestern Louisiana
10. **Loren Hibbs, of, Wichita State**
11. **Darin James, of, Patrick Henry HS, San Diego**
12. **Todd Moriarty, lhp, Southern Utah State**
13. Greg Ehmig, of/1b, Rhea County HS, Dayton, Tenn.
14. **Steve Cottrell, rhp, Stanford**
15. **David Hinnrichs, rhp, Rice**
16. **Charles Culberson, of, Jacksonville State**
17. **Romy Cucjen, ss, Arizona State**
18. Chad Miltenberger, c, Lewis-Clark State (Idaho)
19. John Skurla, of, Washington State
20. **Tom Messier, lhp, Rhode Island**
21. Michael Pirro, 3b, Henniger HS, Syracuse, N.Y.
22. **Michael Cicione, 3b, Los Angeles Valley JC**
23. **Kent Cooper, of, Santa Clara**
24. **James Utley, rhp, Texas-El Paso**
25. **Jim Wasem, ss, Eastern Washington**
26. Aaron Marks, rhp, Glendale (Ariz.) CC

June—Secondary Phase (17)

1. Eric Bauer, lhp, Eastern Washington
2. Mike Blowers, ss, Tacoma (Wash.) CC
3. **Rod Rush, of, Oklahoma City**

SEATTLE MARINERS

January—Regular Phase (1)

1. **Calvin Jones, rhp, Chaffey (Calif.) JC**
2. Larry Cratsenburg, ss, Orange Coast (Calif.) JC
3. Rickie Vogt, rhp, Bellevue (Wash.) CC
4. Steve Maye, rhp, Los Angeles Harbor JC
5. Jeff Osterode, lhp, Orange Coast (Calif.) JC
6. Joe Kraemer, lhp, Lower Columbia (Wash.) JC (Selection voided)
7. David Swolsky, c, Triton (Ill.) JC
8. Mike Blowers, 3b, Tacoma (Wash.) CC

January—Secondary Phase (11)

1. Ray Rosthenhausler, inf, Pima (Ariz.) CC
2. Robert Nettles, rhp, Orange Coast (Calif.) JC

June—Regular Phase (2)

1. **Bill Swift, rhp, Maine**
2. **Mike Christ, rhp, Jacksonville**
3. **Ken Spratke, rhp, Eastern Michigan**
4. **Steve Rousey, rhp, Cal State Fullerton**
5. **Ed West, rhp, Denver**
6. **Don Neufelder, lhp, Murray State**
7. **Bob Gibree, c, St. Leo (Fla.)**
8. **Bob Siegel, rhp, Hawaii**
9. **Bill Mendek, lhp, Temple**
10. **Steve Murray, 2b, Arizona State**
11. **Jim Walker, rhp, Cal State Northridge**
12. **Brad Kinney, rhp, UC Santa Barbara**
13. **Greg Brinkman, rhp, Houston**
14. **Bregg Ray, ss, Texas Wesleyan**
15. Tim Schneider, 3b, Louisiana State
16. **Scott Buss, of, Fresno State**
17. **Jack Reinholtz, lhp, Cal State Fullerton**
18. **David Bresnahan, c, Grand Canyon (Ariz.)**
19. **Nestor Valiente, c, Florida International**
20. **Darrell Higgs, rhp, Grand Canyon (Ariz.)**
21. Anthony Buglione, c, New Haven (Conn.)
22. **Arvid Morfin, ss/3b, Beaverton (Ore.) HS**
23. **Logan White, rhp, Western New Mexico**
24. **John Anderson, of, St. Leo (Fla.)**
25. **Mike Solomon, of, Cal State Northridge**
26. **Mike Carozza, of, Long Beach State**
27. **Paul Steinert, rhp, Florida International**
28. **Richard Hayden, c, El Dorado HS, Placentia, Calif.**
29. **William O'Leary, 3b, Northeastern**
30. **Tom Krause, ss, San Jose State**
31. **Dan Larson, 2b, Houston**
32. Kraig Luckenbill, rhp, Trinity HS, Euless, Texas
33. Rex Peters, 1b, Cherry Creek HS, Denver
34. **Rich Middleton, 3b, Portland State (Ore.)**
35. **Mark Machalec, of, Rice**
36. James King, ss, Oklahoma Baptist
37. **Michael Wood, rhp, Francis Marion (S.C.)**
38. **Charlie Fonville, 1b, Western Carolina**
39. **A.D. Jackson, of, St. Thomas (Fla.)**
40. **Dan Clark, 2b, UC Santa Barbara**

June—Secondary Phase (4)

1. Vince Lopez, ss, Orange Coast (Calif.) JC
2. Russ Swan, lhp, Spokane Falls (Wash.) CC
3. Jeff Marr, rhp, Brevard (Fla.) CC
4. Thomas Green, rhp, Fullerton (Calif.) JC
5. David Miller, ss, Walters State (Tenn.) CC (Selection voided)

TEXAS RANGERS

January—Regular Phase (11)

1. **Kevin Bootay, of, Cerritos (Calif.) JC**
2. Gordie Dillard, lhp, Connors State (Okla.) JC
3. Jon Kolb, rhp, Southwestern (Calif.) JC
4. **Carmelo LoSauro, rhp, Miami-Dade North CC**
5. Steve Cummings, rhp, Blinn (Texas) JC
6. **John Scofield, rhp, Laney (Calif.) JC**
7. Nathaniel Greene, of, Ranger (Texas) JC
8. Jeff Colton, lhp, Valencia (Fla.) CC
9. Patrick Rowe, 2b, Baltimore, Md.
10. Charles Todd, c, Rockland (N.Y.) CC

January—Secondary Phase (19)

1. Dale Hamrick, 3b/c, Spartanburg Methodist (S.C.) JC
2. Darryl Stephens, of, Stanford

June—Regular Phase (12)

1. **Oddibe McDowell, of, Arizona State**
2. **Jimmy Meadows, rhp, Walters State (Tenn.) CC**
3. **Sid Akins, rhp, Southern California**
4. Scott Ruskin, of/lhp, Florida
5. **Dave Darretta, ss, Dunedin (Fla.) HS**
6. **Larry Pardo, rhp, Columbus HS, Miami**
7. **Scott Anderson, rhp, Oregon State**
8. **Huck Hibberd, rhp, San Jose State**
9. **Scott Russell, of, Mount Whitney HS, Visalia, Calif.**
10. **Riley Epps, c, Houston**
11. **Kirk Bates, 2b/1b, Cal State Fullerton**
12. **Larry Klein, ss, Emporia State (Kan.)**
13. **Jamie Doughty, ss, Texas**
14. **Kendall Carter, rhp, Arizona State**
15. **Joe Grayston, ss, Azusa Pacific (Calif.)**
16. **Jeff Paul, 3b, Maine**
17. **Charles Dial, rhp, Middle Tennessee State**
18. **Jim St. Laurent, of, South Carolina**
19. **E.L. Ittner, rhp, U.S. International (Nairobi)**
20. **Michael Grouse, 1b, Phillips (Okla.)**
21. **James Bridges, lhp, Florida Southern**
22. **Mike Fay, rhp, UC Santa Barbara**
23. **Jeff Melrose, 1b/of, Santa Clara**
24. **Rick Poznanski, c, Washington State**
25. **Rob Amble, of, Azusa Pacific (Calif.)**
26. **Steve Cullers, c, James Madison**
27. **Albert Farmer, 2b, William Carey (Miss.)**
28. **Neil Reilly, c, Phillips (Okla.)**
29. **Tim Owen, c, Florida**
30. **Jim Jagnow, 2b, Louisiana Tech**
31. **Billy Sheeks, rhp, Christian Brothers (Tenn.)**
32. **Ronnie King, of, Baylor**
33. **Dan Danelson, rhp, Lewis-Clark State (Idaho)**
34. **Darrell Whitaker, rhp, Dallas Baptist**
35. **Brad Hill, of, Emporia State (Kan.)**
36. Greg Karpuk, rhp, South Glastonbury, Conn.
37. **Matthew Baker, rhp, Jersey City State**
38. **John Schuessler, of, Northeastern**
39. **Rodney Covington, of, Cherokee County HS, Centre, Ala.**
40. **Dale Lanik, 1b, Emporia State (Kan.)**
41. **Mark Kramer, of, Bremen HS, Midlothian, Ill.**
42. Gregg Patterson, lhp, East Ascension HS, Gonzales, La.
43. **Paul Kilgus, lhp, Kentucky**
44. Dave Alvis, 1b, Southwestern Louisiana
45. Walt Guillory, of, Southwestern Louisiana
46. **Marshall Jones, rhp, Palatka (Fla.) HS**
47. Rod Ehrhard, of, Manatee (Fla.) JC

June—Secondary Phase (14)

1. **Thomas Kelley, of, Triton (Ill.) JC**
2. **Robert O'Hearn, c, St. Mary's**
3. David Lawn, lhp, Laney (Calif.) JC

TORONTO BLUE JAYS

January—Regular Phase (19)

1. **Eric Yelding, of/inf, Chipola (Fla.) JC**
2. Scott Ayers, rhp, McLennan (Texas) CC
3. Dwight Smith, of, Spartanburg Methodist (S.C.) JC
4. Keith Swartzlander, rhp, Allegheny (Pa.) CC
5. Jeff Bedell, 3b, Montgomery (Md.) JC
6. **Darryl Landrum, of, Calhoun (Ala.) CC**
7. Robert Smith, rhp, Miami, Fla.
8. Jack Peel, of, Northwest Mississippi JC
9. Steve DeAngelis, of, Saddleback (Calif.) CC
10. **Steve Lounello, rhp, Albany, N.Y.**
11. John Bornhop, of, East Central (Mo.) JC
12. Randy Usenick, rhp, Mishawaka, Ind.

January—Secondary Phase (15)

1. Mark Hamann, rhp, Taft (Calif.) JC
2. **Tim Rypien, c, Spokane Falls (Wash.) CC**
3. Chris Miller, ss, Oregon

June—Regular Phase (20)

1. (Pick to White Sox as compensation for Type A free agent Dennis Lamp)
2. **Dane Johnson, rhp, St. Thomas (Fla.)**
3. **Greg Myers, c, Riverside (Calif.) Poly HS**
4. **Pat Saitta, rhp, Concordia (N.Y.)**
5. **Todd Provence, rhp, Anderson HS, Redding, Calif.**
6. Scott Livingstone, 3b, Lake Highlands HS, Dallas
7. **Gerald Turano, rhp, Mansfield (Pa.)**
8. **Tim Englund, rhp, Rice**
9. **Tom Wasilewski, rhp, Vanderbilt**
10. **Brian Morrison, of, Oakland (Calif.) HS**
11. William Stokes, 1b, Pasadena (Calif.) HS
12. Jeff Oswalt, lhp, Madison HS, San Diego
13. Robert Lipscomb, ss, Pasadena HS, Altadena, Calif.
14. **Norm Tonucci, ss, Waterford (Conn.) HS**
15. Mike C. Jones, of, Valdosta State (Ga.)
16. **Mark Cooper, c, Louisiana State**
17. **Bruce Blake, lhp, Quinsigamond (Mass.) CC**
18. Jeff Mott, ss, Merced (Calif.) HS
19. **Jim Howard, ss, Siena**
20. **Rick Moyer, rhp, Kent State**
21. Russ Elsberry, rhp, Monterey Peninsula (Calif.) JC
22. Eric Fox, of, Fresno State
23. **Willie Shanks, rhp, Missouri-St. Louis**
24. **Thomas Winter, lhp, Siena**
25. Rod Brewer, lhp, Apopka HS, Zellwood, Fla.
26. Anthony Newman, of, Beaverton HS, Portland, Ore.
27. **Greg Lorenzetti, of, Stanford**
28. Jerald Jones, lhp, Vallejo (Calif.) HS
29. **Lawrence Monaco, rhp, Siena**
30. Rodney Peete, ss, Shawnee Mission (Kan.) South HS

June—Secondary Phase (25)

1. **Jeff Richardson, rhp, Wichita, Kan.**
2. Daryl Irvine, rhp, Ferrum (Va.)
3. Paul James, rhp, St. Louis CC-Meramec
4. **Dan Hickey, lhp, JC of Marin (Calif.)**
5. Keith Felden, rhp, St. Petersburg (Fla.) JC

1985

EVEN BEFORE DRAFT TAKES PLACE, CLASS OF '85 LOOKS LIKE SPECIAL CROP OF MAJOR LEAGUE TALENT

Normally, the relative merits of a baseball draft must stand the test of time, but it was clear early that the 1985 draft was something special.

"Eighty-one was pretty good, too," Mets vice president Joe McIlvaine said. "The first 10 guys drafted in '81 all played in the big leagues, but I don't think the caliber of '81 was equal to the caliber of '85.

"An awful lot of them have a good chance to have good careers. And it's probably the fastest group to get to the big leagues. Whether that says something about the outstanding caliber of the players themselves or the caliber of play in the major leagues, I don't know. But it's pretty amazing."

It started with the 1984 Olympic team, which contributed plenty of talent in '84 and then had even more to give to the talent pool for the '85 draft. B.J. Surhoff, Will Clark, Bobby Witt and Barry Larkin—the first four players drafted—were all Olympic teammates, as was Chris Gwynn, selected 10th overall.

"A lot of people would have thought the talent group out of the Olympic year would never be duplicated," Rangers general manager Tom Grieve said. "Well, 1985 came sooner than anyone thought."

"A lot of it was exposure," Surhoff said. "We got a lot of publicity from the Olympic team, and I think the teams that drafted us were willing to take a chance on us because of that. But we were also in the right place at the right time. Some of us just happened to be drafted by teams that needed players right away and we came through when we got the chance."

The seeds for the '85 draft were planted in 1982, when several choice members of the high school crop went unsigned. Three years later they had matured into premium prospects.

Of the first 12 players drafted in 1985, an unprecedented 11 were from the college ranks. In addition to the Olympians, that included outfielders Barry Bonds—who became the most noted player out of the entire loaded draft class—and Pete Incaviglia, shortstop Walt Weiss and pitcher Mike Campbell, all of whom were highly coveted out of high school.

"None was quite at the level where a club would invest the kind of first-round money, $40,000 to $100,000, it took to keep them from going to college, because it would have been overpaying just to buy a player."

Twelve of the 17 college players selected in the first round of the 1985 draft were players who had been selected in the first 10 rounds of the 1982 draft.

Milwaukee took North Carolina's B.J. Surhoff to lead off an amazing first round

There was such a pronounced emphasis on college talent in the 1985 draft that a record-low 232 high school players were selected. The year's signing rate (74.4 percent of the players drafted in the June regular phase) was the highest ever.

The talent was not limited to the top of the draft, either. It spread throughout the first round, where longtime big leaguers Joe Magrane, Gregg Jefferies and Rafael Palmeiro were picked.

With the pick of the litter, the Brewers went for Surhoff, a catcher from the University of North Carolina. His combination of speed, versatility and exceptional bat control led the Brewers to go for Surhoff over players like Clark and Incaviglia. Surhoff signed a $150,000 bonus contract with the Brewers an hour after his selection.

Milwaukee settled on Surhoff as the No. 1 choice, even though three of the most coveted prospects in draft history were available. The trio included: Clark, a sweet-swinging first baseman from Mississippi State who went on to become baseballs first $4 million-a-year player after getting drafted by the Giants; Witt, a hard-throwing righthander who earned the highest grade ever turned in by the Major League Scouting Bureau and was drafted third by the Rangers; and Incaviglia, the most prolific home run hitter in college baseball history. He slid to eighth overall, where he was claimed by Montreal.

And of course that doesn't even include Bonds, who went on to have the most productive career of them all, though the later years of his amazing run were clouded by accusations of steroid use.

No Thanks, Expos

Incaviglia, the powerful Oklahoma State slugger, enjoyed the most phenomenal offensive year in college baseball history, hitting .464 with NCAA records for home runs (48) and RBIs (143). He demanded a two-year big league contract from the Expos with a stipulation that he be placed on the major league roster. It was his way of saying he wasn't thrilled about being drafted by the Expos.

Incaviglia, determined to play for a warm-weather team, held out all summer and most of the fall. The Expos, who didn't want to risk losing him in the January 1986 draft, negotiated a deal to send him to Texas.

Since baseball rules prohibited the trading of draft picks, Montreal signed Incaviglia, then sent him to the Rangers in a deal for pitching prospect Bob Sebra and journeyman infielder Jimmy Anderson.

A rule was passed after that restricting a team from trading its first-round pick for a year following his selection.

The Royals made draft history in 1985 by selecting shortstop Brian McRae with their first-round pick. At the time, Brian's father Hal, was the club's veteran DH. It was the first time that a player was selected by a team for which his father was an active player. The McRaes never had a chance to play together as Hal retired as an active player following the 1987 season.

Talent-filled as the 1985 draft was, scouts generally agreed that the best talent was a player the California Angels took in the 20th round. Auburn's talented Bo Jackson, who hit .401 with 17 homers that spring, would have been a cinch first-round choice had he indicated he wanted to play baseball. Instead, Jackson returned to school and won the 1985 Heisman Trophy as a running back.

Jackson didn't sign with the Angels and became the No. 1 pick of the NFL's Tampa Bay Buccaneers the following spring, though he unexpectedly turned his back on the NFL—temporarily, at least—and signed with Kansas City out of the 1986 baseball draft.

For the first time in 1985, foreign players attending school in the U.S. became subject to the draft. The rule was an outgrowth of the bidding war that took place in 1983 over Puerto Rican lefthander Juan Nieves, who attended prep school in Connecticut for three years. The first foreign player picked in the draft was shortstop Jorge Robles, a Puerto Rico native who attended Miami-Dade New World Center CC.

DRAFT 85: FIRST-ROUND PICKS

No.	Club	Player, Pos.	School	Hometown	Ht.	Wt.	B-T	Age
1.	Brewers	B.J. Surhoff, ss/c	North Carolina	Rye, N.Y.	6-2	185	L-R	20
2.	Giants	Will Clark, 1b	Mississippi State	New Orleans	6-1	170	L-L	21
3.	Rangers	Bobby Witt, rhp	Oklahoma	Canton, Mass.	6-1	185	R-R	21
4.	Reds	Barry Larkin, ss	Michigan	Cincinnati	6-0	175	R-R	21
5.	White Sox	Kurt Brown, c	Glendora HS	Glendora, Calif.	6-2	205	R-R	18
6.	Pirates	Barry Bonds, of	Arizona State	San Carlos, Calif.	6-1	175	L-L	20
7.	Mariners	Mike Campbell, rhp	Hawaii	Seattle	6-3	195	R-R	21
8.	Expos	Pete Incaviglia, of	Oklahoma State	Pebble Beach, Calif.	6-1	225	R-R	21
9.	Indians	Mike Poehl, rhp	Texas	Houston	6-4	195	R-R	20
10.	Dodgers	Chris Gwynn, of	San Diego State	Long Beach	6-0	170	L-L	20
11.	Athletics	Walt Weiss, ss	North Carolina	Suffern, N.Y.	6-0	175	B-R	21
12.	Astros	Cameron Drew, of	New Haven	Yardville, N.J.	6-5	210	L-R	21
13.	Twins	Jeff Bumgarner, rhp	Hanford HS	Richland, Wash.	6-6	210	R-R	18
14.	Braves	Tommy Greene, rhp	Whiteville HS	Whiteville, N.C.	6-5	225	R-R	18
15.	Angels	Willie Fraser, rhp	Concordia (N.Y.)	Newburgh, N.Y.	6-2	185	R-R	20
16.	Phillies	Trey McCall, c	Abingdon HS	Abingdon, Va.	6-3	200	R-R	17
17.	Royals	Brian McRae, ss	Manatee HS	Blue Springs, Fla.	5-10	175	B-R	17
18.	Cardinals	Joe Magrane, lhp	Arizona	Morehead, Ky.	6-5	200	R-L	20
19.	Angels	Mike Cook, rhp	South Carolina	Charleston, S.C.	6-2	180	L-R	21
20.	Mets	Gregg Jefferies, ss	Serra HS	Millbrae, Calif.	5-10	170	B-R	17
21.	Red Sox	Dan Gabriele, rhp	Western HS	Walled Lake, Mich.	6-4	190	B-R	18
22.	Cubs	Rafael Palmeiro, of	Mississippi State	Miami	6-0	170	L-L	20
23.	Padres	Joey Cora, ss	Vanderbilt	Caguas, Puerto Rico	5-8	153	B-R	20
24.	Cubs	Dave Masters, rhp	California	Honolulu	6-9	220	R-R	20
25.	Blue Jays	Greg David, of	Barron Collier HS	Naples, Fla.	6-1	185	L-R	18
26.	Tigers	Randy Nosek, rhp	Chillicothe HS	Chillicothe, Mo.	6-4	200	R-R	18

1985

CLUB-BY-CLUB SELECTIONS

ATLANTA BRAVES

January—Regular Phase (13)

1. **David Seitz, lhp, Birmingham, Ala.**
2. Lionel Gaston, lhp, Triton (Ill.) JC
3. Ken Sebree, rhp, Brevard (Fla.) CC
4. **David Shotkoski, rhp, Kishwaukee (Ill.) JC**
5. Kendrick Bourne, of, Chaffey (Calif.) JC
6. Chris Hawkins, lhp, Anderson (S.C.) JC
7. **Adrian Wills, c, Walters State (Tenn.) CC**
8. **Tom Cantrell, ss, DeKalb South (Ga.) CC**
9. Mike Sander, lhp, Chipola (Fla.) JC
10. Stanley Cook, of, Walters State (Tenn.) CC
11. **Paul Marak, rhp, Trinidad State (Colo.) JC**
12. Barry Pearman, rhp, Brewer State (Ala.) JC
13. Tom Brock, of, Central Arizona JC
14. Duane Crow, rhp, Vincennes (Ind.) JC
15. Douglas Willey, rhp, Essex (Md.) CC

January—Secondary Phase (23)

1. **John Alva, ss, Pima (Ariz.) CC**
2. **James Rockey, of, San Jose (Calif.) CC**

June—Regular Phase (14)

1. **Tommy Greene, rhp, Whiteville (N.C.) HS**
2. (Pick to Cardinals as compensation for Type A free agent Bruce Sutter)
3. **Tom Abrell, rhp, Central HS, Muncie, Ind.**
4. **David Justice, 1b, Thomas More (Ky.)**
5. **Ellis Roby, 2b, Arkansas**
6. **Todd Dewey, c, California Lutheran**
7. **Joe Mullins, of, Yosemite HS, Oakhurst, Calif.**
8. **Al Martin, 1b/of, Rowland HS, West Covina, Calif.**
9. **Mike Scott, rhp, St. Xavier (Ill.)**
10. Stan Royer, c, Charleston (Ill.) HS
11. **Jeff Greene, rhp, Toledo**
12. **Gary Eave, rhp, Grambling State**
13. **Jermaine Casey, of, Rich Central HS, Country Club Hills, Ill.**
14. **Steven Vasquez, rhp, San Jose State**
15. **Dave Ford, 1b, Connecticut**
16. **Mike Trapasso, lhp, Oklahoma State**
17. **Greg Marshall, of, Grant HS, Sacramento, Calif.**
18. **Michael Alfano, 3b, Long Island-C.W. Post**
19. **Robert Burke, rhp, Southern Colorado**
20. **Roger Huff, rhp, Waterville (Maine) HS**
21. **Jeff Wetherby, of, Southern California**
22. **Pat Gliha, rhp, Akron**
23. Milt Hill, rhp, DeKalb Central (Ga.) JC
24. **Bean Stringfellow, lhp, Virginia Tech**
25. Paul McClellan, rhp, Sequoia HS, Redwood City, Calif.
26. **Roger Hackett, of, Southern Tech Institute (Fla.)**
27. Ward Horton, 1b/p, Chamblee (Ga.) HS
28. **Monty Aldrich, of, Eastern Illinois**
29. **David Garrison, 2b, Samford**

June—Secondary Phase (14)

1. **Dodd Johnson, 3b, Texas**
2. John Clements, rhp, Chipola (Fla.) JC
3. Lionel Gaston, lhp, Triton (Ill.) JC

BALTIMORE ORIOLES

January—Regular Phase (20)

1. Tom Gallagher, lhp, Sacramento CC
2. Mike Direnzo, c, Broome (N.Y.) CC
3. DeWayne Coleman, rhp, Chaffey (Calif.) JC
4. Arned Hernandez, of, Arizona Western JC
5. Al Osuna Jr., lhp, Cerritos (Calif.) JC
6. Gil Heredia, rhp, Pima (Ariz.) CC
7. **Ernie Young, of, Essex (Md.) CC**
8. Stephen Kraiss, 1b, Orange Coast (Calif.) JC
9. **Michael Rossano, 1b, Chaffey (Calif.) JC**
10. Patrick Murray, 3b/ss, Queensborough (N.Y.) CC
11. John Horsey, lhp, Essex (Md.) CC
12. Harlan Blackiston, rhp, Camden County (N.J.) JC
13. Orlando Guerra, rhp, Orange Coast (Calif.) JC
14. Jeff Simmelink, c, Lower Columbia (Wash.) JC
15. Vince Ogawa, rhp, El Camino (Calif.) JC
16. John Woodward, of, Santa Fe (Fla.) CC
17. **Johannes McFarlane, rhp, Mesa (Ariz.) CC**
18. John Marchbank, lhp, Centralia (Wash.) CC

January—Secondary Phase (25)

1. Terry Griffin, rhp, Florida JC
2. **Bob Latmore, ss, Indian River (Fla.) CC**
3. Vince Shinholster, ss, Santa Ana (Calif.) JC
4. Mike Blowers, 3b, Tacoma (Wash.) CC

June—Regular Phase (19)

1. (Pick to Angels as compensation for Type A free agent Fred Lynn)
2. (Pick to Pirates as compensation for Type A free agent Lee Lacy)
3. (Pick to Angels as compensation for Type A free agent Don Aase)
4. **Brian Dubois, lhp, Reed Custer HS, Briarwood, Ill.**
5. **Tim Dulin, 2b, Memphis State**
6. **Chuck Stanhope, rhp, Troy State**
7. **Jeff Ballard, lhp, Stanford**
8. **Norm Roberts, of, Arkansas**
9. **Pete Stanicek, 2b, Stanford**
10. **Harry Kline, c, Archbishop HS, Baltimore**
11. Mike Loynd, rhp, Florida State
12. Ty Griffin, ss, King HS, Tampa
13. **Joe Gast, lhp, Calvert Hall HS, Baltimore**
14. Dell Curry, rhp, Virginia Tech
15. **Brad Powell, rhp, North Carolina**
16. **Kenny Sims, of, Lower Columbia (Wash.) JC**
17. **Peter Mancini, ss, Seton Hall**
18. **Jim Sullivan, of, Indiana State**
19. **Rob Santo, 1b, Flagler (Fla.)**
20. **Kevin Burke, 1b, George Mason**
21. **Ray Crone, 2b, Sam Houston State**
22. Joe Bradley, lhp, Batesburg-Leesville (S.C.) HS
23. **Steven St. Hill, of, Long Island**
24. **Robert Bellini, of, St. John's**
25. **Frank Bellino, of, Mount San Antonio (Calif.) JC**
26. **Matt Skinner, c, Texas-Arlington**
27. Steve Muh, lhp, Long Branch (N.J.) HS
28. **Tim Haller, 2b, Regis (Mass.)**
29. **Frederick Ludwig, rhp, Penfield (N.Y.) HS**
30. **Terrell McCall, lhp, Enak HS, Asheville, N.C.**
31. John Albertson, c, Mainland HS, Northfield, N.J.
32. **Robert Dromerhouser, c, Mercy (N.Y.)**
33. **Rico Rossy, ss, Purdue**
34. **Mike Halasz, ss, Chapman (Calif.)**
35. Curry Harden, rhp, A&M Consolidated HS, College Station, Texas
36. Chaeho Chong, c, Chatsworth (Calif.) HS
37. Kevin Smith, of, Eastern Illinois

June—Secondary Phase (11)

1. **Craig Worthington, 3b, Cerritos (Calif.) JC**
2. **Mickey Billmeyer, c, North Carolina State**
3. John Kohli, lhp, Mira Costa (Calif.) JC
4. Joey Seaver, lhp, Tennessee
5. Barry Griffin, lhp, North Idaho JC

BOSTON RED SOX

January—Regular Phase (22)

1. **Tim Speakman, c, Fullerton (Calif.) JC**
2. Rod Simon, rhp, Central Arizona JC
3. Oscar Murphy, rhp, Columbia State (Tenn.) CC
4. **Greg Bochesa, c, Los Angeles Harbor JC**
5. Ricky Carriger, rhp, Northeastern Oklahoma A&M JC
6. Steven Meyer, rhp, Westark (Ark.) CC
7. **Dell Carter, of, Kings River (Calif.) JC**
8. Tom Kane, rhp, Manatee (Fla.) JC
9. Steve Mrowka, 3b, Polk (Fla.) CC
10. Tim Good, c, Angelina (Texas) JC
11. Kevin Edwards, ss, Westark (Ark.) CC

January—Secondary Phase (20)

1. **Daryl Irvine, rhp, Ferrum (Va.)**
2. Ken Morris, rhp, Angelina (Texas) JC

June—Regular Phase (21)

1. **Dan Gabriele, rhp, Western HS, Walled Lake, Mich.**
2. Lance Blankenship, 3b, California
3. Tino Martinez, 1b, Jefferson HS, Tampa
4. **Don McGowan, rhp, Central Missouri State**
5. **Mike Clarkin, rhp, Minnesota**
6. **Todd Pratt, c, Hilltop HS, Chula Vista, Calif.**
7. **Gary Gouldrup, 3b, Oliver Ames HS, North Easton, Mass.**
8. Scott Middaugh, rhp, Patrick Henry HS, San Diego
9. **Jim Orsag, 1b, Illinois**
10. **Brady Anderson, of, UC Irvine**
11. **Chris Bayer, rhp, Pace (N.Y.)**
12. **Greg Lotzar, of, Central Michigan**
13. **Mike Bianco, c, Seminole (Fla.) HS**
14. **Mike Carista, rhp, Saugus, Mass.**
15. **Derek Livernois, rhp, Lyman HS, Altamonte Springs, Fla.**
16. Ron Stephens, ss, Linsly Institute, Wheeling, W.Va.
17. James Boehne, rhp, Louisiana Tech
18. **Kerman Williams, rhp, Vanguard HS, Ocala, Fla.**
19. Gregg Magistri, lhp, Louisiana Tech
20. **Billy Plante, 3b, Virginia Tech**
21. **James Cox, lhp, Harrisburg, Ohio**
22. Tom Hostetler, rhp, East Mississippi JC
23. Cliff Suggs, rhp, Cooper HS, Abilene, Texas
24. **Erik Laseke, 2b, Columbia State (Tenn.) CC**
25. **John Abbott, lhp, Visalia, Calif.**
26. Ed Sprague Jr., c, St. Mary's HS, Stockton, Calif.
27. Grady Hall, lhp, Northwestern

June—Secondary Phase (1)

1. **Eric Hetzel, rhp, Louisiana State**
2. **Bill Zupka, rhp, Queensborough (N.Y.) CC**

CALIFORNIA ANGELS

January—Regular Phase (16)

1. John Wilder, rhp, Walters State (Tenn.) JC
2. John Hoffman, lhp, Glendale (Calif.) JC
3. Lyle Befort, rhp, Butler County (Kan.) CC
4. John Buss, lhp, Triton (Ill.) JC
5. Phillip Lieberher, lhp, Polk (Fla.) CC
6. Martin Robitaille, 1b/of, Cochise County (Ariz.) CC
7. Anthony Venneri, 1b, Dundalk (Md.) CC
8. Darren Peters, rhp, Triton (Ill.) JC
9. Gary Nalls, ss, Garden City (Kan.) CC

January—Secondary Phase (4)

1. **Chuck Finley, lhp, West Monroe, La.**
2. Bill Voeltz, lhp, Broward (Fla.) CC

June—Regular Phase (15)

1. **Willie Fraser, rhp, Concordia (N.Y.)**
1. **Mike Cook, rhp, South Carolina** (Pick from Orioles as compensation for Type A free agent Fred Lynn)
2. **Bob Sharpnack, rhp, Fountain Valley (Calif.) HS**
3. **Jerome Nelson, of, Pine Forest HS, Pensacola, Fla.**
3. **Chris Collins, rhp, Mercer** (Pick from Orioles as compensation for free agent Don Aase)
4. **Scott Marrett, rhp, Pepperdine**
5. **Bobby Rose, ss, San Dimas HS, Glendora, Calif.**
6. **Tim Burcham, rhp, Virginia**
7. **Michael Kesler, lhp, Western New Mexico**
8. **Richard Morehouse, rhp, South Dakota State**
9. **Jim McCollom, 1b, Clemson**
10. **Steve McGuire, rhp, North Carolina**
11. **Kendall Walling, ss, Lubbock Christian (Texas)**
12. **Tim Arnold, c, Nevada-Las Vegas**
13. **Bill Geivett, 3b, UC Santa Barbara**
14. **Jeff Manto, of, Temple**
15. **Frank DiMichele, lhp, Philadelphia CC**
16. **Reggie Lambert, of, Loyola Marymount**
17. Carlos Carrasco, rhp, Live Oak HS, Morgan Hill, Calif.
18. Rick Raether, rhp, Miami
19. Freddie Davis, rhp, Auburndale (Fla.) HS
20. Bo Jackson, of, Auburn
21. Charlie White, of, Woodham HS, Pensacola, Fla.
22. **Mark Ban, of, Cal State Northridge**
23. **Glenn Washington, of, Ramapo (N.J.)**
24. Toby Nivens, rhp, McAllen (Texas) HS
25. Scott Carter, rhp, Brandon (Fla.) HS
26. Dan Grunhard, of, Northwestern
27. Kevin Kunkel, rhp, Stanford
28. Wade Phillips, rhp, Texas

June—Secondary Phase (21)

1. **Gary Nalls, ss, Lamar**
2. **David Johnson, rhp, Oklahoma**
3. Greg Vaughn, of, Sacramento CC

CHICAGO CUBS

January—Regular Phase (23)

1. **Jeff Small, ss, Seattle, Wash.**
2. **Lee Grimes, of, Palm Beach (Fla.) JC**
3. Daryl Boyd, rhp, Palm Beach (Fla.) JC
4. Ron Ewart, of, Cerritos (Calif.) JC
5. Doug Kline, rhp, Blue Mountain (Ore.) CC
6. **Michael Jones, of, Miami-Dade North CC**
7. William O'Neal, 1b, Westark (Ark.) CC
8. **Scott Lochow, c, Edmonds (Wash.) CC**
9. Tim K. Anderson, ss, Sacramento CC
10. Gary Geiger, 3b/rhp, Seminole State (Okla.) JC
11. Mike Siler, rhp, Edmonds (Wash.) CC

January—Secondary Phase (9)

1. Craig Worthington, 3b, Cerritos (Calif.) JC
2. Phil Williams, c, Seminole State (Okla.) JC
3. Glenn Twardy, of, Mount San Antonio (Calif.) JC

June—Regular Phase (22)

1. **Rafael Palmeiro, of, Mississippi State** (Pick from Padres as compensation for Type A free agent Tim Stoddard)
1. **Dave Masters, rhp, California**
2. **Greg Smith, ss, Glenelg HS, Sykesville, Md.**
3. **Mike Miller, c, Paradise Valley HS, Phoenix**
4. **Roger Williams, rhp, North Carolina**
5. **Rick Wrona, c, Wichita State**
6. John Viera, of, Southridge HS, Cutler Ridge, Fla.
7. **Joe Murphy, 1b/of, Wagner**
8. **Bob Bafia, 3b, Fresno State**
9. Kevin Tapani, rhp, Central Michigan
10. **Greg Kallevig, rhp, South Dakota State**
11. **Bryan Anders, c, Ohio Dominican**
12. **Doug Dascenzo, of, Oklahoma State**
13. **Dick Canan, 3b, Illinois**
14. **Fernando Zarranz, rhp, St. Thomas HS, Miami**
15. Sergio Espinal, 2b, Oklahoma State
16. **Joe Kraemer, lhp, Vancouver, Wash.**
17. Don Burke, of, Florida Southern
18. **Robert Strickland, rhp, SUNY Buffalo**
19. **Mark McMorris, 1b, Southeastern Louisiana**
20. **Kelly Mann, c, Santa Monica (Calif.) HS**
21. **Len Damian, rhp, Canyon HS, Anaheim**
22. **Jeff Hirsch, rhp, UCLA**

23. Brent Addison, ss, Auburndale (Fla.) HS
24. **Mark Grace, 1b, San Diego State**
25. **Kris Roth, rhp, Southwestern Oklahoma State**
26. John Peet, 1b/of, Santa Monica (Calif.) HS
27. **Clint Harting, ss, Redlands HS, Glendora, Calif.**
28. **John Horn, lhp, Georgia Tech**
29. **Mark Jefferson, lhp, North Marion HS, Carolina, W.Va.**
30. Bobby DeJardin, ss, Mater Dei HS, Huntington Beach, Calif.
31. Tom Williams, 2b, Elkton (Md.) HS
32. **Tim Wallace, 2b, Cal State Hayward**

June—Secondary Phase (12)

1. **Ron Ewart, 1b/of, Cerritos (Calif.) JC**
2. Robert Chadwick, lhp, Oxnard (Calif.) JC
3. Paul Kuzniar, rhp, Alvin (Texas) CC

CHICAGO WHITE SOX

January—Regular Phase (6)

1. Louis Calvert, rhp, Blinn (Texas) JC
2. Jorge Robles, ss, Miami-Dade New World Center CC
3. **Tony Scruggs, of, Mount San Antonio (Calif.) JC**
4. Robert Wolkoys, 3b, Mount San Antonio (Calif.) JC
5. **Victor Heckman, rhp, Western Michigan**
6. **Jesus Alvarez, of/inf, Miami-Dade South CC**

January—Secondary Phase (22)

1. **Tom Forrester, lhp/1b, Miami-Dade North CC**
2. **Larry Allen, of, Laney (Calif.) JC**

June—Regular Phase (5)

1. **Kurt Brown, c, Glendora (Calif.) HS**
2. **Jose Mota, 2b, Cal State Fullerton**
3. **Glen Braxton, of, Idabel (Okla.) HS**
4. **Bobby Thigpen, rhp, Mississippi State**
5. **Aubrey Waggoner, of, Eisenhower HS, Fontana, Calif.**
6. **John Pawlowski, rhp, Clemson**
7. **James Bledsoe, of, Manual Arts HS, Los Angeles**
8. **Marty Warren, rhp, Campbell**
9. Scott Nelson, lhp, Oak Park (Ill.) River Forest HS
10. **Wayne Edwards, lhp, Azusa Pacific (Calif.)**
11. **Eric Milholland, c, Valparaiso**
12. **John Stein, rhp, Nevada-Las Vegas**
13. **Dan Cronkright, 3b, Central Michigan**
14. **David Sheldon, of, San Francisco**
15. **John Von Ahnen, of, Wagner**
16. **Steve Mehl, ss/2b, North Highlands (Calif.) HS**
17. **Tom Drees, lhp, Creighton**
18. **George Stone, rhp, Clemson**
19. **Randy Velarde, ss, Lubbock Christian (Texas)**
20. **Samuel Ruiz, 2b, Central State (Ohio)**
21. **Michael Moore, of, Cal State Los Angeles**
22. **David Reynolds, ss, Northwestern State**
23. **Donn Pall, rhp, Illinois**
24. **Tom Hildebrand, 2b, Northwestern**
25. **David Lee, rhp, Florida**
26. John Hairston, 3b, Grant HS, Portland, Ore.
27. **Andre Toliver, of, Grand Canyon (Ariz.)**
28. Matt Lagunas, ss, Mesa (Ariz.) HS
29. Dale Roder, rhp, Briar Cliff (N.Y.)
30. **Steve Ruzich, c, St. Francis (Ill.)**

June—Secondary Phase (9)

1. **Scott Kershaw, rhp, UCLA**
2. **Vince Lopez, ss, UCLA**
3. **Ken Rahmine, of, Miami-Dade North CC**

CINCINNATI REDS

January—Regular Phase (3)

1. **Scott Willis, rhp, JC of the Sequoias (Calif.)**
2. **Jack Smith, ss, Seminole (Fla.) CC**
3. Jeff Moe, 3b, Clark (Wash.) CC
4. **Brad Brusky, rhp, Des Moines Area (Iowa) CC**
5. William Parham, 1b, Walters State (Tenn.) CC
6. Mathias Butala, rhp, Willmar (Minn.) CC
7. Ray Schuyler, of, CC of Morris (N.J.)
8. Kevin Pozniak, rhp, North Arkansas CC
9. David Suemnicht, rhp, Indian Hills (Iowa) CC
10. Gary Fonnesbeck, rhp, Lane (Ore.) CC
11. Randy St. Ward, of, Westark (Ark.) CC
12. Mike Grabliauskas, lhp, Rockland (N.Y.) CC
13. Jose Tartabull, of, Miami-Dade North CC

January—Secondary Phase (11)

1. Tom Powers, rhp, Triton (Ill.) JC
2. Shawn Gilbert, ss, Golden West (Calif.) JC

June—Regular Phase (4)

1. **Barry Larkin, ss, Michigan**
2. **Steve Davis, of, Plano (Texas) East HS**
3. **Ken Huseby, rhp, Rolling Meadows (Ill.) HS**
4. **Joe Dunlap, ss, Oral Roberts**
5. Billy St. Peter, 3b, Western HS, Bay City, Mich.
6. **Tim Deitz, rhp, Arkansas**
7. **Ricky Epps, of, Linden-Kildare (Texas) HS**
8. **Tim Watkins, rhp, Mississippi College**
9. **Richard Sapienza, c, Forest HS, Ocala, Fla.**
10. **Pete Beeler, c, Middleburg (Fla.) HS**
11. **Don Wakamatsu, c, Arizona State**
12. **Marty Brown, of/3b, Georgia**
13. **Troy Girdner, rhp, St. Cloud HS, Kissimmee, Fla.**
14. **Larry Schwartz, lhp, Seton Hall**
15. **Don Brown, ss, Vernon (Fla.) HS**
16. **Mike Ramsey, of, Texas Christian**
17. **Mike Roesler, rhp, Ball State**
18. **Jeff Hayward, rhp, Jacksonville State**
19. **Tom Summers, lhp, Cincinnati**
20. **Gary Curtis, ss, Arkansas**
21. Keith Kaiser, rhp, MacArthur HS, San Antonio, Texas
22. **Cal Cain, of, Fresno State**
23. Mike Oglesbee, 1b, Nevada-Las Vegas
24. **Thomas Wilson, c, Jacksonville**
25. **Richard Beaupre, ss, North Carolina Wesleyan**
26. Everett Cunningham, rhp, Waterloo (Iowa) HS
27. James Johnston, rhp, Regis HS, Cedar Rapids, Iowa
28. **Rick Campbell, ss, Kentucky**

June—Secondary Phase (18)

1. **Jeff Forney, of, Florida Atlantic**

CLEVELAND INDIANS

January—Regular Phase (10)

1. Rick Wharf, ss, Centralia (Wash.) JC
2. Jeff Smith, rhp, Cleveland State (Tenn.) CC
3. **Myron Gardner, rhp, Louisburg (N.C.) JC**
4. **Mike Farr, rhp, Dundalk (Md.) CC**
5. Frank Taylor, of, DeKalb North (Ga.) JC
6. Shawn Talbott, rhp, Cochise County (Ariz.) CC
7. **John Githens, rhp, Camden County (N.J.) JC**
8. Ed Stockhousen, 2b, DeKalb North (Ga.) JC
9. James Ryerson, ss, Brookdale (N.J.) CC
10. **Charles Todd, 1b/c, Rockland (N.Y.) CC**
11. Charles Bell, of, Aquinas (Tenn.) JC

January—Secondary Phase (6)

1. Doug Cox, lhp, DeKalb (Ga.) JC
2. Kevin Thomas, lhp, Spartanburg Methodist (S.C.) JC
3. Anthony Newman, of, Oregon

June—Regular Phase (9)

1. **Mike Poehl, rhp, Texas**
2. **Andy Ghelfi, rhp, Indiana State**
3. Scott Ruskin, of/lhp, Florida
4. **Scott Jordan, of, Georgia Tech**
5. **Rod Nichols, rhp, New Mexico**
6. **Charles Scott, rhp, Arizona State**
7. **Greg Williamson, rhp, Western New Mexico**
8. **Glenn Fairchild, ss, Cal State Los Angeles**
9. **Luis Medina, 1b, Arizona State**
10. **Mike Rountree, of, Claremont (Calif.)**
11. **Kent Murphy, lhp, Western Illinois**
12. **Manny Mercado, lhp, St. Mary's HS, Jersey City, N.J.**

13. **Don Lovell, of, Portland State**
14. **Greg LaFever, rhp, Wichita State**
15. **Rock Hurst, c, Furman**
16. **Troy Startoni, c, St. Thomas (Fla.)**
17. **Bill Wilkes, 1b, Campbell**
18. **Greg Karpuk, rhp, North Carolina**
19. **John Power, 1b/lhp, Madison HS, Portland, Ore.**
20. Brian Jordan, ss, Milford Mill HS, Baltimore
21. **Rob Swain, ss, Texas A&M**
22. **Mike Belleman, rhp, Penn State**
23. Brad Smith, rhp, Cleveland State (Tenn.) CC
24. **Casey Webster, 1b, Western Oregon State**
25. **Steve Johnigan, c, Texas A&M**
26. **Jules Franzen, c, Curry (Mass.)**
27. **Robert Link, rhp, St. Leo (Fla.)**
28. Russell Whittle, lhp, North Greenville (S.C.) JC
29. **Donaciano Santos, 1b, Shadle Park HS, Spokane, Wash.**
30. Chris Nabholz, lhp, Pottsville (Pa.) HS
31. **Dave Alvis, 1b, Southwestern Louisiana**
32. Kevin Shea, lhp, Lewis-Clark State (Idaho)
33. Jay Semke, of, Cambridge (Ohio) HS
34. Jeff Mutis, lhp, Allentown (Pa.) Catholic HS
35. Josh Lowery, ss, Oakland (Calif.) Tech HS
36. Gary Zwolinski, lhp, Brother Wright HS, Farmington Hills, Mich.
37. **Michael Vannucci, c, Ohlone (Calif.) JC**
38. **Michael Workman, of, Florida Southern**
39. Clay Parrach, 1b/of, Aurora (Neb.) HS

June—Secondary Phase (19)

1. John Woodward, of, Santa Fe (Fla.) CC
2. John Vuz, c, Keystone (Pa.) JC
3. Greg Briley, ss, Louisburg (N.C.) JC
4. Jorge Robles, ss, Miami-Dade New World Center CC

DETROIT TIGERS

January—Regular Phase (26)

1. **Ken Williams, lhp, Live Oak, Fla.**
2. **Paul Jackson, rhp/ss, Citrus (Calif.) JC**
3. **David Cooper, c, Macomb (Mich.) CC**
4. Jerald Frost, ss, Ocean County (N.J.) JC
5. **Frank Masters, c, Scottsdale (Ariz.) CC**
6. Craig Burns, of, Sacramento CC
7. Robert Fassold, c, Mira Costa (Calif.) JC
8. Tyrone Boseman, ss, Montreat-Anderson (N.C.) JC
9. Rodger Castner, rhp, Arizona Western JC
10. Daniel Cetnar, rhp, Thornton (Ill.) CC
11. Steve Kovensky, rhp, Palomar (Calif.) JC
12. Scott Spurgeon, c/3b, Labette (Kan.) CC
13. Gary Smith, lhp/1b, Brookdale (N.J.) CC
14. Donald Mire, c, Citrus (Calif.) JC

January—Secondary Phase (8)

1. **Gary Pifer, rhp, Santa Ana (Calif.) JC**
2. Ken Pennington, ss, El Camino (Calif.) JC
3. Larry Cratsenberg, inf, Orange Coast (Calif.) JC

June—Regular Phase (26)

1. **Randy Nosek, rhp, Chillicothe (Mo.) HS**
2. **Richard Carter, rhp, Havelock (N.C.) HS**
3. **Steve Searcy, lhp, Tennessee**
4. **Robert Friesen, rhp, Meridian HS, Boise, Idaho**
5. **Gerry Wetherell, rhp, Mount Vernon Nazarene (Ohio)**
6. **Scott Lusader, of, Florida**
7. **Doug Strange, 2b, North Carolina State**
8. **Don Rowland, 2b, Miami**
9. **Derreck Bastinck, c, Ramapo (N.J.)**
10. Lou Frazier, of, Scottsdale (Ariz.) CC
11. **Ruben Jackson, of, Cajon HS, San Bernardino, Calif.**
12. **Joe Slavik, lhp, Eastern Michigan**
13. **Alain Patenaude, rhp, Miami**
14. **Doyle Balthazar, c, Los Angeles (Calif.) HS**
15. **Mark Lee, lhp, Florida International**
16. Jeff Henderson, lhp, Stetson
17. **Allen Liebert, c, West HS, Waukegan, Ill.**
18. Andy Stankiewicz, 2b, Pepperdine
19. **Ted Lawrence, c, Pace (N.Y.)**
20. **Ed Waylock, ss, Bradley**
21. Ted Wiesfuss, ss, Chatsworth (Calif.) HS
22. **John Smoltz, rhp, Waverly HS, Lansing, Mich.**
23. **Thelanious Prioleau, ss, Central State (Ohio)**
24. Craig Good, rhp, Rio Mesa HS, Camarillo, Calif.
25. **Thomas Knapp, of, Ferris State (Mich.)**
26. **Tom Snowberger, of, Iowa**
27. Dan Disher, rhp, Michigan
28. **Ken Gohmann, rhp, Northwestern**
29. Ken Deal, rhp, Trinidad State (Colo.) JC
30. Steve Kern, 3b, Durfee HS, Fall River, Mass.
31. **Adam Dempsay, c, Bradley**
32. **Rob Thomson, c, Kansas**
33. Randy Kotchman, ss, Seminole (Fla.) HS

June—Secondary Phase (26)

1. Pete Roberts, lhp, Mira Costa (Calif.) JC
2. David Miller, rhp, Camden County (N.J.) JC
3. Rob Hartwig, of, Los Angeles Harbor JC
4. **Kevin Ritz, rhp, Indian Hills (Iowa) CC**
5. Gary Alexander, rhp, Laney (Calif.) JC
6. Mike Sisco, ss, St. Louis CC-Meramec
7. Tom Powers, rhp, Triton (Ill.) JC

HOUSTON ASTROS

January—Regular Phase (11)

1. Pete Roberts, lhp, Mira Costa (Calif.) JC
2. **Randy Randle, ss, San Jacinto (Texas) JC**
3. Jimmy Hitt, rhp, Chipola (Fla.) JC
4. Ken Sorensen, rhp, San Jacinto (Texas) JC
5. John Clements, rhp, Chipola (Fla.) JC
6. Mark Lundy, 1b, Mira Costa (Calif.) JC
7. **Carlo Colombino, 3b, Brookdale (N.J.) CC**
8. **Robert Romo, rhp, Ventura (Calif.) JC**
9. **John Sheehan, rhp, Ocean County (N.J.) JC**
10. Mike Sisco, ss, St. Louis CC-Meramec
11. Flynn Carr, c, Cochise County (Ariz.) CC
12. Jeff Piland, lhp, Cerritos (Calif.) JC
13. Don Enoch, rhp, Mercer County (N.J.) CC
14. **Jeff Baldwin, of, Camden County (N.J.) JC**

January—Secondary Phase (3)

1. **Mel Stottlemyre Jr., rhp, Yakima Valley (Wash.) JC**
2. Anthony Blackmon, ss, Seminole State (Okla.) JC
3. Paul James, rhp, St. Louis CC-Meramec

June—Regular Phase (12)

1. **Cameron Drew, of, New Haven (Conn.)**
2. **Bert Hunter, ss, Norte Vista HS, Riverside, Calif.**
3. Mike Hensley, rhp, Latta HS, Ada, Okla.
4. **Blaise Ilsley, lhp, Indiana State**
5. **Troy Aleshire, c, Meadowbrook HS, Byesville, Ohio**
6. **Mike Simms, 1b, Esperanza HS, Yorba Linda, Calif.**
7. **Jeff Edwards, c, Cal Poly Pomona**
8. **Terry Wells, lhp, Illinois**
9. **John Fishel, of, Cal State Fullerton**
10. **James Vike, rhp, Willamette (Ore.)**
11. **Joe Schultz, rhp, Southeast Missouri State**
12. **Wayne Rogalski, inf, New Haven (Conn.)**
13. **Calvin James, of, Miami**
14. **Gary Murphy, rhp, Arkansas**
15. Bryn Kosco, ss, Poland (Ohio) HS
16. Craig Wilson, c, La Mirada (Calif.) HS
17. **Scott Gray, ss, Stetson**
18. **Tim Arnsberg, rhp, San Diego State**
19. **Tim Jester, of, California**
20. **Ron Roebuck, lhp, Southern California**
21. **Steve Gelmine, lhp, Florida State**
22. **Kevin Smith, rhp, Florida State**
23. **Tony Dineen, rhp, Lewis-Clark State (Idaho)**
24. **Stan Fascher, rhp, Florida**
25. Keith Hamilton, rhp, Oklahoma
26. Jeff Reboulet, ss, Louisiana State
27. **Robert Hartman, rhp, Otterbein (Ohio)**

28. **Robert Shepis, of, Seton Hall**
29. Doug Fisher, 1b, Central Michigan
30. **Richard Johnson, 1b, Sam Houston State**
31. Dewitt Cotton, of, Westchester (Calif.) HS
32. Isaac Elder, of, Westchester (Calif.) HS
33. Ron Moore, rhp, UC Riverside
34. Rick Hirtensteiner, of, Buena HS, Ventura, Calif.

June—Secondary Phase (20)

1. **Gayron Jackson, of, El Camino (Calif.) JC**
2. James Willis, of, Triton (Ill.) JC
3. Scott Boudreaux, rhp, Wharton County (Texas) JC
4. Tim Lichty, of/3b, Moorpark (Calif.) JC
5. **Shawn Talbott, rhp, Cochise County (Ariz.) CC**
6. Ed Shea, c, Palm Beach (Fla.) JC

KANSAS CITY ROYALS

January—Regular Phase (18)

1. Scott Boudreaux, rhp, Wharton County (Texas) JC
2. **Peter Carey, of, Rockland (N.Y.) CC**
3. **DeJon Watson, 1b, West Los Angeles JC**
4. Kevin D. Brown, lhp, Sacramento CC
5. Joaquin Contreras, of, Miami-Dade South CC
6. Andy Mota, 2b, Golden West (Calif.) JC
7. Dennis King, ss, Riverside (Calif.) CC
8. Tim John, rhp, JC of Southern Idaho
9. Brad Noe, of, Edmonds (Wash.) CC
10. Mike Aspray, rhp, West Los Angeles JC
11. Blas Minor Jr., rhp, Merced (Calif.) JC
12. **Keith Sheldon, rhp, Brasstown, N.C.**
13. Mike Zuber, rhp, Centralia (Wash.) JC
14. Rob Bartlett, of, Citrus (Calif.) JC
15. Pat Waid, of, Oxnard (Calif.) JC
16. Scott Reaves, ss, JC of the Sequoias (Calif.)
17. Jon Taylor, of, Cuesta (Calif.) JC
18. Steve Hansen, 3b, Kings River (Calif.) JC
19. Joseph Nelms, lhp, Los Medanos (Calif.) JC
20. **Richard Day, 3b, Essex (Md.) CC**
21. **Gerald Smith, c, Essex (Md.) CC**

January—Secondary Phase (16)

1. Mike Reitzel, lhp, Seminole State (Okla.) JC
2. Darrin Garner, ss, Orange Coast (Calif.) JC
3. Charles Wacha, rhp, Edison (Fla.) CC

June—Regular Phase (17)

1. **Brian McRae, ss, Manatee HS, Blue Springs, Fla.**
2. **Chris Jelic, c, Pittsburgh**
3. **Mike Loggins, of, Arkansas**
4. **Mike Macfarlane, c, Santa Clara**
5. **Ricky Rojas, rhp, Miami Lakes HS, Hialeah, Fla.**
6. Deion Sanders, of, North Fort Myers (Fla.) HS
7. **David Tinkle, ss, Ocean View HS, Huntington Beach, Calif.**
8. **Deric Ladnier, 3b, Mississippi**
9. **Kevin Karcher, rhp, Oakland (Mich.) CC**
10. **Randy Goodenough, lhp, Iowa Central CC**
11. Greg S. Harris, lhp, Gonzaga
12. **Ken Crew, rhp, Fresno State**
13. **Tim Lemons, 1b/rhp, Auburn**
14. Carl Shaw, rhp, Bellevue (Wash.) CC
15. **Albert Peluso, rhp, Point Park (Pa.)**
16. **Robert O'Hoppe, ss, Erskine (S.C.)**
17. **Linton Dyer, c, Grady Vocational HS, Brooklyn**
18. **Sal Vaccaro, lhp, Santa Clara**
19. **Dean Duane, rhp, New Mexico**
20. Brett Roach, ss, Lakeview HS, St. Clair Shores, Mich.
21. Tony Welborn, of, Appalachian State
22. **Gene Morgan, rhp, Mississippi State**
23. **Abbie Woyce, rhp, Vanderbilt**
24. **Rufus Ellis, rhp, Alabama State**
25. **Jimmy Franklin, rhp, Arkansas Tech**
26. **Hunter Hoffman, 3b, Hewitt HS, Trussville, Ala.**
27. John Schilling, of, Santa Ana (Calif.) HS
28. Scott Shockey, 1b, El Toro (Calif.) HS
29. **Darren Watkins, rhp, Everett, Wash.**
30. **Russ Stachler, ss, Borah HS, Boise, Idaho**

June—Secondary Phase (23)

1. Todd Ross, 3b/ss, Shasta (Calif.) JC
2. Joe Kemp, of, Citrus (Calif.) JC
3. Curtis Parham, of, Phoenix, Ill.

LOS ANGELES DODGERS

January—Regular Phase (9)

1. **Brad Zeinert, lhp/of, Tigerton, Wis.**
2. **Darren Farley, 3b/of, San Jacinto (Texas) JC**
3. Greg Briley, ss, Louisburg (N.C.) JC
4. Mike Kitz, lhp, JC of San Mateo (Calif.)
5. Paul Kuzniar, rhp, Alvin (Texas) CC
6. Lester Logan, c, Los Angeles CC
7. Gregory Martin, 2b/ss, Middle Georgia JC
8. Mike Fowler, 3b/c, Spartanburg Methodist (S.C.) JC
9. Bruce Powers, of, Skyline (Calif.) JC
10. Chris Graves, rhp, Middle Georgia JC
11. **Kevin Nelson, rhp, Yuba (Calif.) CC**
12. Derek Keathley, rhp, Yuba (Calif.) CC
13. John McEntee, lhp, JC of Marin (Calif.)

January—Secondary Phase (13)

1. **Eric Tutt, 1b/3b, Middle Georgia JC**
2. **John Wetteland, rhp, JC of San Mateo (Calif.)**
3. Adrian Adkins, c, Middle Georgia JC

June—Regular Phase (10)

1. **Chris Gwynn, of, San Diego State**
2. **Mike Watters, 2b, Michigan** (Pick from Rangers as compensation for Type A free agent Burt Hooton)
2. **Dan Smith, c, Morehead State**
3. **Pete Geist, of, Georgia Tech**
4. Mike Prior, of, Illinois State
5. **Mike Devereaux, of, Arizona State**
6. **Walt McConnell, 3b, Georgia Tech**
7. **Rene Garcia, lhp, Hoover HS, Glendale, Calif.**
8. **Jack Savage, rhp, Kentucky**
9. **Walt Stull, rhp, UC Riverside**
10. **Fred Farwell, lhp, Arkansas**
11. **Mike Fiala, rhp, Princeton**
12. **Ken Lambert, c, Portland**
13. **Andy Naworski, rhp, UCLA**
14. **Mike Batesole, 3b, Oral Roberts**
15. **Jay Ray, rhp, Kentucky**
16. **Mike Huff, of, Northwestern**
17. **Bryan Smith, lhp, St. Mary's**
18. **Carl Thomas, lhp, Calhoun County HS, Edison, Ga.**
19. **Mike Burke, 1b, St. Xavier (Ill.)**
20. **Mike Lilly, rhp, West Georgia**
21. **Charles Hardwick, lhp, South Carolina**
22. **Edwin Hart, lhp, Patrick Henry HS, Beaverdam, Va.**
23. **Jeff Hartman, ss, McCaskey HS, Lancaster, Pa.**
24. **Michael White, of, Valdosta State (Ga.)**
25. **Paul Moralez, 1b, UC Riverside**
26. **Douglas Ames, lhp, Columbia, S.C.**
27. **Robert Tucker, c, West Virginia**
28. **Kevin Ayers, ss, North Carolina-Charlotte**
29. **Brett Parker, ss, Sul Ross State (Texas)**
30. **Andrew Anthony, of, Valdosta State (Ga.)**
31. **James Garrison, ss/2b, Plant City (Fla.) HS**
32. **Ron Jackson, c, Huston-Tillotson (Texas)**
33. **William Bluhm, 3b, JC of the Canyons (Calif.)**

June—Secondary Phase (24)

1. **Doug Cox, lhp, DeKalb (Ga.) JC**
2. **Marvin Newton, c, San Bernardino Valley (Calif.) JC**
3. John McEntee, lhp, JC of Marin (Calif.)

MILWAUKEE BREWERS

January—Regular Phase (2)

1. **Oliver Nichols, rhp, Oxnard (Calif.) JC**
2. Steven Michael, of, Big Bend (Wash.) CC
3. Steve Carter, of, Hagerstown (Md.) JC

4. **John Ludy, rhp, Boyertown, Pa.**
5. John Chaffee, ss/2b, Grossmont (Calif.) JC
6. Everett Utter, c, Spartanburg Methodist (S.C.) JC
7. **Oscar Duran, lhp/1b, East Los Angeles JC**
8. Chris Howard, of/lhp, Miami-Dade South CC
9. Ernie Isaac, 2b, Sacramento CC
10. Brian Clark, 1b, Polk (Fla.) CC
11. **Luis Verdugo, c, East Los Angeles JC**
12. Tim Fisher, c, Sacramento CC
13. William Schutt, rhp, Southwestern (Calif.) JC
14. Rusty Covington, rhp, Shelby State (Tenn.) CC
15. Eric Woods, of, Sacramento CC
16. Jim Bowie, 1b, Sacramento CC
17. Brett Bohatuk, rhp, Macomb (Mich.) CC

January—Secondary Phase (2)

1. **Randy Veres, rhp, Sacramento CC**
2. Ed Shea, c, Palm Beach (Fla.) JC
3. Miguel Ferradas, c, Miami-Dade South CC
4. Steve Wiley, lhp, Indian River (Fla.) CC
5. Joe Palubeski, 2b, JC of the Canyons (Calif.)

June—Regular Phase (1)

1. **B.J. Surhoff, ss/c, North Carolina**
2. **Carl Moraw, rhp, Bowling Green State**
3. **Shon Ashley, ss, Meridan HS, Boise, Idaho**
4. **Billy Bates, 2b, Texas**
5. **Todd Brown, of, Arizona State**
6. **Robert Tinkey, 3b, West Liberty State (W.Va.)**
7. **Charles McGrew, c, Southeastern Oklahoma State**
8. **Doug Henry, rhp, Arizona State**
9. Anthony Hill, of, Rhode Island
10. **Rich Bosley, rhp, Appalachian State**
11. **Lance Lincoln, ss, Lewis-Clark State (Idaho)**
12. **Mario Monico, of, Hawaii**
13. **Edward Greene, of, Swarthmore (Pa.)**
14. **Russ McGinnis, 1b, Oklahoma**
15. Colby Ward, rhp, Brigham Young
16. Bob Collum, 3b, Hawaii
17. Enoch Simmons, ss/of, North HS, Riverside, Calif.
18. **Damon Oppenheimer, c, Southern California**
19. **Frank Fazzini, of, Florida State**
20. Russ Burk, lhp, Baltimore, Md.
21. **Eric Pilkington, lhp, Westmont (Calif.)**
22. Robert Clark, of, JC of the Desert (Calif.)
23. Scott Kamieniecki, rhp, Michigan
24. **Don Bridges, c, Arlington HS, Riverside, Calif.**
25. Nikco Riesgo, 3b, Poly HS, Long Beach
26. Bruce Wegman, rhp, Oak Hills HS, Cincinnati
27. Robert Jones, of/1b, Southern Illinois
28. Steven Lee, ss, Fontana (Calif.) HS
29. **Buddy Haney, of, Texas A&M**
30. Mike Ross, ss, Fresno CC
31. Mike Gorman, ss, Bishop Amat HS, Azusa, Calif.
32. Dave Dawson, rhp, Culver City (Calif.) HS
33. Don Arnold, lhp/1b, Hemet (Calif.) HS
34. **Gary Sanchez, of, Alabama-Birmingham**
35. Pedro Borbon, lhp, Dewitt Clinton HS, Bronx, N.Y.

June—Secondary Phase (17)

1. **John Wilder, rhp, Walters State (Tenn.) CC**
2. Tom Gallagher, lhp, Sacramento CC
3. Steve Carter, of, Hagerstown (Md.) JC
4. Joe Palubeski, 2b, JC of the Canyons (Calif.)
5. Rob Bartlett, of, Citrus (Calif.) JC
6. Dennis King, ss, Riverside (Calif.) CC
7. **Jeff Smith, rhp, Cleveland State (Tenn.) CC**

MINNESOTA TWINS

January—Regular Phase (14)

1. Tony Faryniarz, rhp, Sacramento CC
2. **James Cook, rhp, Mount San Antonio (Calif.) JC**
3. **Mike Redding, rhp, Manatee (Fla.) JC**
4. Dan Paradoa, of, Indian River (Fla.) CC
5. **Scott Rohlof, of, Central Arizona JC**
6. Jerald Higby, lhp, Modesto (Calif.) JC
7. Mike Benjamin, 2b, Cerritos (Calif.) JC
8. James Dodds, of, JC of the Sequoias (Calif.)
9. Duane Walker, of, Santa Fe (Fla.) CC
10. James Winkle, c, Umpqua (Ore.) CC
11. **Gary Thomasson, of, Santa Ana (Calif.) JC**
12. Craig McIver, rhp, Fullerton (Calif.) JC

January—Secondary Phase (26)

1. Garrett O'Connor, rhp, Lafayette, La.
2. William Stokes, 1b, Glendale (Calif.) JC

June—Regular Phase (13)

1. **Jeff Bumgarner, rhp, Hanford HS, Richland, Wash.**
2. **Steve Gasser, rhp, New Philadelphia (Ohio) HS**
3. **Paul Abbott, rhp, Sunny Hills HS, Fullerton, Calif.**
4. **Robbie Smith, rhp, Louisiana State**
5. **Brad Bierley, 3b/of, Pepperdine**
6. **Gary Borg, of, Illinois**
7. **Lee Swenson, c, Luther (Iowa)**
8. **Mark Davis, lhp, Nebraska**
9. **Mike Adams, rhp, Phillips (Okla.)**
10. **Julio Delancer, ss, Lehman (N.Y.)**
11. **Howard Manzon, of, Pace (N.Y.)**
12. **Tom Scaletta, ss, Cal Poly Pomona**
13. **Marty Lanoux, 3b, Louisiana State**
14. **Joe Boyce, ss, Coon Rapids (Minn.) HS**
15. Paul Burghardt, 1b/lhp, Normandale (Minn.) CC
16. **Robert Strube, lhp, Luther (Iowa)**
17. David Keating, lhp, North Salinas (Calif.) HS
18. Scott Wilkinson, of, Cerritos (Calif.) JC
19. **Henry Siemers, of/3b, St. John's**
20. **Robert Perry, 1b/3b, UC Irvine**
21. **Lenny Webster, c, Grambling State**
22. Don Snowden, lhp/of, Fountain Valley (Calif.) HS
23. **Mark Casey, 2b, Iona**
24. Mark Hicks, of, Davis (Calif.) HS
25. Derk Madden, rhp, San Mateo (Calif.) HS
26. **William O'Connor, of, Adelphi (N.Y.)**
27. **Lawrence Buzzard, c, LaVerne (Calif.)**
28. Mike Owens, of, Notre Dame HS, Sauquoit, N.Y.
29. Burt Beattie, 3b, Nebraska
30. **Harrison Sherman, of, Santa Monica (Calif.) JC**
31. **Ted Miller, c, Newberry (S.C.)**
32. **Kenneth Wright, rhp, Central Florida**

June—Secondary Phase (13)

1. **DeWayne Coleman, rhp, Chaffey (Calif.) JC**
2. Shawn Gilbert, ss, Golden West (Calif.) JC
3. Philip Price, rhp, Los Angeles Harbor JC

MONTREAL EXPOS

January—Regular Phase (7)

1. **Maurice Bigden, ss, Cuesta (Calif.) JC**
2. Gayron Jackson, of, West Los Angeles JC
3. David Rose, rhp/c, South Georgia JC
4. Frank Ward, lhp, Santa Rosa (Calif.) JC
5. Larry Walsh, lhp, Cabrillo (Calif.) JC
6. **Kenneth Fox, of, Lane (Ore.) CC**
7. Luc Berube, ss, Cochise County (Ariz.) CC
8. Tim Lichty, of, Moorpark (Calif.) JC
9. Mark Berghala, of, Albany, N.Y.
10. Eric Jacques, rhp, San Jose (Calif.) CC
11. George Bargfrede, of, CC of Morris (N.J.)
12. Robert Hartley, of, Clark (Wash.) JC
13. Sean Baker, 3b, CC of Morris (N.J.)
14. Don Cohoon, inf, Indian River (Fla.) CC
15. **William Deboever, rhp, Des Moines Area (Iowa) CC**
16. Robert Slate, lhp, Ferrum (Va.)
17. Tim Demoonie, ss/2b, Middle Georgia JC
18. Kevin Brooks, c/rhp, Jackson State (Tenn.) CC
19. Kurt Soderholm, ss/of, Central Florida CC

January—Secondary Phase (15)

1. Mike C. Walker, rhp, Seminole (Fla.) CC
2. **Mel Houston, ss, Laney (Calif.) JC**

3. Jeff Atha, ss/3b, DeKalb South (Ga.) CC

June—Regular Phase (8)

1. **Pete Incaviglia, 3b, Oklahoma State**
2. **Randy Johnson, lhp, Southern California**
3. **Jeff Oller, ss, Minden (La.) HS**
4. **Anthony Candelino, of, Elizabeth (N.J.) HS**
5. **Leonard Kelly, rhp, Tennessee State**
6. **Bill Cunningham, lhp, Ohio State**
7. **Jeff Fischer, rhp, Florida**
8. **Mark Gardner, rhp, Fresno State**
9. **Bob Sudo, rhp, Ramapo (N.J.)**
10. **Chan Galbato, rhp, SUNY Fredonia**
11. **Paul Martineau, 1b, Eastern Connecticut State**
12. **Tim Barker, of, Central Florida**
13. **Mike Day, c, Oklahoma State**
14. Bobby Jones, of, El Campo HS, Citrus Heights, Calif.
15. **Darren Travels, rhp, Contra Costa (Calif.) JC**
16. Guy Normand, lhp, Washington State
17. **Loren White, c, Illinois State**
18. **Robert Williams, rhp, Morehead State**
19. **Stu Stauffacher, lhp, Houston**
20. Mike Adkisson, of, Interlake HS, Bellevue, Wash.
21. David Dasch, ss, Ithaca (N.Y.)
22. Barry Shifflett, 3b, North Carolina-Charlotte
23. Frank Bolick, ss, Mount Carmel (Pa.) HS
24. Rick Parker, c, John Curtis HS, River Ridge, La.
25. Randy Robinson, rhp, Woodlake (Calif.) HS
26. Mark Arndt, lhp, Spencer (Texas) HS
27. Mike Montagnino, c, North Greenville (S.C.) JC

June—Secondary Phase (10)

1. **Jim Hunter, rhp, Georgia**
2. **Scott Ayers, rhp, New Orleans**
3. Louis Calvert, rhp, Blinn (Texas) JC
4. Frank Taylor, of/1b, DeKalb North (Ga.) JC

NEW YORK METS

January—Regular Phase (19)

1. **Mike Anderson, rhp, Los Angeles Valley JC**
2. **Scott Jaster, of, Trinidad State (Colo.) JC**
3. Robert Doman, lhp, Allegheny (Pa.) CC
4. William Norwood, rhp, Jefferson Davis (Ala.) JC
5. Mark Howell, c, Howard (Texas) JC
6. **Geary Jones, c, Butte (Calif.) JC**
7. Joe Warren, rhp, Scottsdale (Ariz.) CC
8. Shawn McAfee, ss, Angelina (Texas) JC
9. Andy Berg, lhp, Sacramento CC
10. Herbert Nauert, 2b, Angelina (Texas) JC
11. Steve Eckenrode, 1b, Panola (Texas) JC
12. Jerry Nielsen, lhp, Sacramento CC
13. **Randy Tubbleville, of, Angelina (Texas) JC**

January—Secondary Phase (5)

1. **Craig Repoz, ss, Fullerton (Calif.) JC**
2. Steven Harris, rhp, Florida JC
3. John Sellick, 1b/3b, Santa Rosa (Calif.) JC

June—Regular Phase (20)

1. **Gregg Jefferies, ss, Serra HS, Millbrae, Calif.**
2. Scott Servais, c, Westby HS, Coon Valley, Wis.
3. **Rob Lemle, of, Compton (Calif.) HS**
4. **Todd Welborn, rhp, Appalachian State**
5. Tim Layana, rhp, Loyola Marymount
6. Dan Henley, 3b, Southern California
7. Monty Fariss, ss, Leedey (Okla.) HS
8. **Cliff Gonzalez, of/ss, St. Raymond's HS, Bronx, N.Y.**
9. **Rodney Murrell, ss, Skyline HS, Dallas**
10. **Kennedy Farmer, of, Harrison Central HS, Saucier, Miss.**
11. Chris Gallego, ss, Rowland HS, Walnut, Calif.
12. **Ron Narcisse, c, Norfolk State**
13. **Mark Willoughby, lhp, Independence HS, Tickfaw, La.**
14. **Victor Garcia, lhp, Cardinal Hayes HS, Bronx, N.Y.**
15. **Chris Rauth, rhp, Ithaca (N.Y.)**
16. Reggie Garcia, rhp, Hanford (Calif.) HS
17. **David Gelatt, 2b, Washington**
18. **Kevin Armstrong, rhp, Sam Houston State**
19. **Alan Hayden, of, Northern Kentucky**
20. David Jacas, of, San Diego
21. **John Tuozzo, rhp, Hartford**
22. **Jaime Archibald, 1b, Lewis-Clark State (Idaho)**
23. Gary Bockhorn, rhp, Southern Illinois
24. Shannon Jones, rhp, Live Oak HS, Watson, La.
25. Carlton Cochrane, lhp, Central Arizona JC
26. Howard Williams, lhp, Texas Christian
27. **Jeff Jones, ss, Washington HS, Los Angeles**
28. Mark Hudson, rhp, West Valley (Calif.) JC
29. **Arthur Douglas, of, Robert E. Lee HS, Montgomery, Ala.**
30. **Mark Bohne, rhp, Buckholz HS, Gainesville, Fla.**
31. **Bruce McDonald, rhp, Ocala (Fla.) Vanguard HS**
32. Dan Monzon, ss, Cardinal Spellman HS, Bronx, N.Y.
33. **Maury Gooden, of, Huston-Tillotson (Texas)**
34. Erik Judson, 2b, Hemet (Calif.) HS
35. **Steve Brueggeman, lhp/of, Cal State Sacramento**
36. **Kurt DeLuca, 3b, Ithaca (N.Y.)**
37. **Thomas Wachs, lhp, Huntington (Ind.)**

June—Secondary Phase (16)

1. Jerry Nielsen, lhp, Sacramento CC
2. Gordie Dillard, lhp, Oklahoma State
3. Andy Berg, lhp, Sacramento CC
4. **Joaquin Contreras, of, Miami-Dade South CC**
5. Gerald Higby, lhp, Modesto (Calif.) JC

NEW YORK YANKEES

January—Regular Phase (24)

1. **David Clark, lhp, Laney (Calif.) JC**
2. Bill Zupka, rhp, Queensborough (N.Y.) CC
3. Bruce Charlesbois, rhp, Indian River (Fla.) CC
4. Paul Zack, rhp, CC of Morris (N.J.)
5. Darrin Bartel, 3b, San Jacinto (Texas) JC
6. **Dino Johnson, 3b/of, Sacramento CC**
7. **Greg Vella, 1b, JC of San Mateo (Calif.)**
8. Scott Maxwell, of, Cochise County (Ariz.) CC
9. David Martin, rhp, Chaffey (Calif.) JC
10. Greg Wherry, rhp, Los Angeles Harbor JC

January—Secondary Phase (24)

1. Scott Lerner, lhp, Diablo Valley (Calif.) JC
2. Jeff Marr, rhp, Brevard (Fla.) CC
3. Todd Gedaminski, lhp, Lincoln Land (Ill.) CC

June—Regular Phase (23)

1. (Pick to Padres as compensation for Type A free agent Ed Whitson)
1. **Rick Balabon, rhp, Conestoga HS, Berwyn, Pa.** (Supplemental pick—28th—for loss of Tim Belcher in 1984 major league compensation draft)
2. **Troy Evers, rhp, Iowa State**
3. **Ken Patterson, lhp, Baylor**
4. **Scott Gay, rhp, Western Carolina**
5. **Bobby Green, of, Florida Southern**
6. **Shane Turner, ss, Cal State Fullerton**
7. **Mike Christopher, rhp, East Carolina**
8. Brad Hildreth, ss, UMS Prep HS, Mobile, Ala.
9. **Chris Lombardozzi, ss, Florida**
10. **Jason Maas, of, Cal Poly San Luis Obispo**
11. **Scott Shaw, ss/3b, Eckerd (Fla.)**
12. **Neal Cargile, of, Gardner-Webb**
13. **Ed Stanko, 1b, William & Mary**
14. **Greg Iavarone, c, Illinois**
15. **Matt Mainini, of, South Florida**
16. **Brent Blum, lhp, Eastern Washington**
17. **John Shane, rhp, Wisconsin**
18. **Todd Ezold, c, Massachusetts**
19. **John Pleicones, ss, Florida Southern**
20. **Rob Lambert, 2b, Cal Poly San Luis Obispo**
21. Steve Taylor, of, Lincoln HS, Spring Valley, Calif.
22. Mark Razook, ss, South Hills HS, West Covina, Calif.
23. **Ted Higgins, 1b, Nevada**
24. Bill Bean, of, Loyola Marymount

25. **David Banks, 1b, Troy State**
26. **Tim Reker, lhp, Florida International**
27. **Chris Carroll, rhp, Kentucky**
28. Grant Feruto, of, Boulder (Colo.) HS
29. Jeff Ingram, c, Shawnee Mission HS, Overland Park, Kan.
30. Preston Watson, rhp, Luling (Texas) HS
31. **Scott Cantrell, rhp, Toledo**
32. **Dick Sisler, rhp, Tennessee**
33. **Robert Kupfner, 3b, Bloomfield (Colo.) HS**

June—Secondary Phase (5)

1. Mike Belanger, lhp, Cal State Fullerton
2. **Garrett O'Connor, rhp, Southwestern Louisiana**
3. Scott Lerner, lhp, Diablo Valley (Calif.) JC
4. Jeff Marr, rhp, Brevard (Fla.) CC
5. Terry Griffin, rhp, Florida JC

OAKLAND ATHLETICS

January—Regular Phase (12)

1. Allen Wisdom, lhp, San Jacinto (Texas) JC
2. David Ray, c, DeKalb Central (Ga.) JC
3. Marvin Newton, c, San Bernardino Valley (Calif.) JC
4. Robert Chadwick, lhp, Oxnard (Calif.) JC
5. Ralph Lusian, 2b, Mira Costa (Calif.) JC
6. Larry Oedewaldt, 3b, Grossmont (Calif.) JC
7. Philip Price, rhp, Los Angeles Harbor JC
8. Joe Kemp, of, Citrus (Calif.) JC
9. Rob DeYoung, rhp, Fullerton (Calif.) JC
10. Ron Dale, ss/of, Los Angeles Valley JC

January—Secondary Phase (12)

1. **Mark Gabriel, ss, Niagara Falls, N.Y.**
2. **Rich Martig, 3b, Santa Clara**

June—Regular Phase (11)

1. **Walt Weiss, ss, North Carolina**
2. **Dave Otto, lhp/1b, Missouri**
3. **Wally Whitehurst, rhp, New Orleans**
4. **Phil Cundari, rhp, Seton Hall**
5. **Keith Wentz, 3b, York (Pa.)**
6. **Steve Iannini, of, Georgetown**
7. **Kirk McDonald, rhp, Otterbein (Ohio)**
8. Ray Williamson, of, Santa Clara
9. **Pat Britt, c, UC Riverside**
10. **Mike Duncan, 1b, Nebraska**
11. David Richards, lhp, Grossmont HS, El Cajon, Calif.
12. **Shannon Mendenhall, ss, Lake Worth (Fla.) HS**
13. **Joe Xavier, ss, Fresno State**
14. **John Minch, c, Ohio State**
15. Mark Manering, 1b, Miami (Ohio)
16. **Bruce Walton, rhp, Hawaii**
17. Gil Villanueva, lhp, Arizona State
18. **Scott Hyde, c, Missouri-St. Louis**
19. **Mark Tortorice, lhp, Grand Canyon (Ariz.)**
20. **Kevin Williamson, rhp, Arizona State**
21. **Bryan Olden, 2b, Portland**
22. **Jeff Shaver, rhp, SUNY Fredonia**
23. **Gary Cullison, lhp, Portland State**
24. Jim Pena, lhp, Cal State Dominguez Hills
25. **Bob Stocker, rhp, Wisconsin-Oshkosh**
26. **Larry Arndt, inf/of, Bowling Green State**
27. **Frank Groves, rhp, U.S. International**
28. **Martin Hall, rhp, Cochise County (Ariz.) CC**
29. **Reese Lambert, lhp, Oklahoma State**
30. Bob Malloy, rhp, Virginia

June—Secondary Phase (7)

1. **Blaine Deabenderfer, rhp, North Carolina**
2. Ken Sebree, rhp, Brevard (Fla.) CC
3. Russ Elsberry, rhp, San Diego State
4. Jimmy Hitt, rhp, Chipola (Fla.) JC
5. Steve Wapnick, rhp, Moorpark (Calif.) JC
6. Mike Stanford, rhp, Citrus (Calif.) JC

PHILADELPHIA PHILLIES

January—Regular Phase (15)

1. **Scott Steen, 3b, Ventura (Calif.) JC**
2. Clyde Powell, of, Delgado (La.) JC
3. Bruce Carter, ss, Delgado (La.) JC
4. Darwin DeVaughan, rhp, Seminole State (Okla.) JC
5. Chris Burgin, rhp, Tulsa, Okla.
6. **Nathaniel Green, of/3b, Ranger (Texas) JC**
7. Jason Bridges, 3b, McLennan (Texas) CC
8. Brian Shepherd, rhp, Angelina (Texas) JC
9. Joseph Bourque, ss, San Jacinto (Texas) JC
10. Jack Johnson, 3b/ss, Central Arizona JC
11. Mark Shiflett, rhp, McLennan (Texas) CC
12. Scotty George, of, Seminole State (Okla.) JC
13. Kevin Ponder, rhp, McLennan (Texas) CC
14. Andrew Bourne, of, Citrus (Calif.) JC
15. Jimmy Carroll, rhp, Mesa (Ariz.) CC
16. Mike McLeod, rhp, Allen County (Kan.) CC
17. John Barfield, lhp, Crowder (Mo.) JC
18. Dann Howitt, rhp/of, Venice, Calif.
19. Todd Ross, 3b/ss, Shasta (Calif.) JC
20. **Ryan Silva, c, North Idaho JC**
21. Mike Domenick, 1b/of, Triton (Ill.) JC

January—Secondary Phase (7)

1. **Eric Boudreaux, rhp, Austin (Texas) CC**
2. **Steve DeAngelis, of, Dana Point, Calif.**

June—Regular Phase (16)

1. **Trey McCall, c, Abingdon (Va.) HS**
2. **Bruce Ruffin, lhp, Texas** (Pick from Pirates as compensation for free agent Sixto Lexcano)
2. Mike Young, lhp, Arizona
3. **Vince Holyfield, of, Southern Arkansas**
4. **Wally Ritchie, lhp, Glendale (Calif.) JC**
5. Darin Campbell, ss, DeMatha HS, Lanham, Md.
6. **Rick Lundblade, 1b, Stanford**
7. **Jeff Kaye, c, Oklahoma**
8. Jimmy Long, rhp, Oklahoma State
9. **Todd Howey, of, Texas Tech**
10. **Jason Grimsley, rhp, Tarkington HS, Cleveland, Texas**
11. **John McKinney, rhp, Marshall**
12. **Ben Blackman, 3b/ss, San Joaquin Delta (Calif.) JC**
13. Eric Fox, of, Fresno State
14. **Clifton Walker, rhp, Northwestern State**
15. **Rod Brunelle, of, Grand Valley State (Mich.)**
16. **Rick Parker, ss, Texas**
17. **Steve Sharts, lhp, Cal State Northridge**
18. **Tim Collins, rhp, Metropolitan State (Colo.)**
19. **Mario Perez, rhp, St. Mary's (Texas)**
20. **Scott McClanahan, rhp, Lubbock Christian (Texas)**
21. **Derrick Richardson, inf, Arkansas**
22. **Robert Nazabal, rhp, Merced (Calif.) JC**
23. **Dion Beck, lhp, Cal State Fullerton**
24. Robert Hatcher, lhp, Twin Lake HS, West Palm Beach, Fla.
25. Alex Alvarez, c, Garden Grove (Calif.) HS
26. **Bruce Luttrull, rhp, Arlington HS, Dorona, Calif.**
27. Robbie Key, lhp, Broadmoor HS, Baton Rouge, La.
28. **Kenley Graves, of/2b, North Idaho JC**
29. Paul Skorupa, rhp, Eastern Illinois
30. **Greg Suhajda, of/c, Grand Valley State (Mich.)**
31. **David Pruett, rhp, Anderson (S.C.)**
32. Mark Borcherding, p, Rock Island (Ill.) HS
33. **David Denny, 3b/of, Texas**

June—Secondary Phase (8)

1. **Allen Wisdom, lhp, San Jacinto (Texas) JC**
2. **Stephen Bowden, rhp, San Jacinto (Texas) JC**
3. Kevin D. Brown, lhp, Sacramento CC
4. **Steven Harris, rhp, Florida JC**
5. Blas Minor Jr., rhp, Merced (Calif.) JC
6. **Ernie Rodriguez, 2b, Sacramento CC**

PITTSBURGH PIRATES

January—Regular Phase (5)

1. Pat Gilbert, of, Columbia State (Tenn.) CC
2. **Steve Taylor, of, Henry Clay HS, Lexington, Ky.**
3. David Miller, rhp, Camden County (N.J.) JC
4. **Mike Stevanus, ss, Valencia (Fla.) CC**
5. Troy Jackson, of, JC of San Mateo (Calif.)
6. Mitchell Ferrick, rhp, Santa Rosa (Calif.) JC
7. Barry Griffin, lhp, North Idaho JC
8. **Craig Heakins, c, Triton (Ill.) JC**
9. Derek Lee, 3b, Manatee (Fla.) JC
10. James Warner, lhp, Allegany (Md.) CC
11. **Keith Swartzlander, rhp, Allegheny (Pa.) CC**
12. Tom Hoffman, rhp, Pensacola (Fla.) JC
13. John Vuz, c, Keystone (Pa.) JC
14. Brian Warfel, of, Labette Community (Kan.) JC

January—Secondary Phase (19)

1. Greg Vaughn, of, Sacramento CC
2. Ken Rahming, of, Miami-Dade North CC
3. **Chris Ritter, rhp, CC of Baltimore**

June—Regular Phase (6)

1. **Barry Bonds, of, Arizona State**
2. (Pick to Phillies as compensation for Type A free agent Sixto Lezcano)
2. **Damon Hansel, c, Granite Hills HS, El Cajon, Calif.** (Pick from Orioles as compensation for Type A free agent Lee Lacy)
3. Joe Klancnik, rhp, Niles (Ill.) West HS
4. **Robin Vaughn, ss, Crenshaw HS, Los Angeles**
5. **Ondra Ford, of, Ontario (Calif.) HS**
6. **Brett Gideon, rhp, Mary Hardin-Baylor (Texas)**
7. **Tommy Gregg, of, Wake Forest**
8. **Larry Melton, rhp, Portland**
9. **Terry Wakefield, of, Guthrie (Okla.) HS**
10. **Jeff Cook, of, Phillips (Okla.)**
11. **Desmond Scieneaux, 1b, Montclair (Calif.) HS**
12. **Billy Sampen, rhp, MacMurray (Texas)**
13. Brad Robinson, of/1b, Seminole State (Okla.) JC
14. **Kyle Todd, 3b, Baylor**
15. Luis Ramos, ss, Georgia Southern
16. **Ronnell Daniels, of, Utica (Miss.) JC**
17. Brian Zanardelli, rhp, Robert Morris (Ill.)
18. **Juan McWilliams, 3b, Grambling State**
19. **Richard Kiluk, of, Lowell (Mass.)**
20. **John Shouse, c, Cumberlands (Ky.) JC**
21. **Ray Gambino, ss, Point Park (Pa.)**
22. **Mark Koller, rhp, Peabody HS, Pittsburgh**
23. **Ralph Denkenberger, of, Loch Raven HS, Baltimore**
24. **Thomas Pierce, ss, Georgia College & State**
25. **Robert Benkert, c, William Paterson (N.J.)**
26. **Mark Oberholtzer, rhp, Ohio Wesleyan**
27. **Tony Mealy, of, Fayetteville (W.Va.) HS**
28. **Kyle Channing, lhp, Dallas Baptist**
29. **Lawrence Brady, of, Coastal Carolina**
30. **Brian Schaum, ss, California (Pa.)**
31. Buster Lopes, rhp, Notre Dame
32. Greg Shirley, c, Azusa Pacific (Calif.)
33. **Scott Berry, of, Cumberlands (Ky.) JC**
34. **Page Odle, of, Oral Roberts**
35. **Doug Smallwood, 3b, Thomas Johnson HS, Frederick, Md.**
36. Tommy Shields, ss, Notre Dame

June—Secondary Phase (4)

1. Tommy Hinzo, ss, Arizona
2. Jason Bridges, ss/3b, McLennan (Texas) CC
3. **Kirk Barry, of, Mesa (Ariz.) CC**

ST. LOUIS CARDINALS

January—Regular Phase (17)

1. Chris Lee, rhp, Edison (Fla.) CC
2. **Alex Cole Jr., of, Manatee (Fla.) JC**
3. Kip Gross, rhp, Murray State (Okla.) JC
4. Jeff Burkhart, of, Vincennes (Ind.) JC
5. Kirk Barry, of, Mesa (Ariz.) CC

January—Secondary Phase (1)

1. Todd Stottlemyre, rhp, Yakima Valley (Wash.) JC
2. **Steve Boyd, c, Columbus, Ohio**

June—Regular Phase (18)

1. **Joe Magrane, lhp, Arizona**
2. **Jim Fregosi, ss/3b, New Mexico** (Pick from Braves as compensation for Type A free agent Bruce Sutter)
2. **Tim Jones, ss, The Citadel**
3. **Mike Henry, rhp, Chamberlain HS, Lutz, Fla.**
4. **Nate Singletary, of, King HS, Tampa**
5. **Steve Peters, lhp, Oklahoma**
6. **Ray Stephens, c, Troy State**
7. Doug Little, rhp, Florida State
8. **Mark Jackson, of/inf, Arkansas**
9. Bryan Hickerson, lhp, Minnesota
10. **Gator Thiesen, 2b, Mississippi State**
11. **Carey Nemeth, 3b, James Madison**
12. Mike Tresemer, rhp, UC Santa Barbara
13. **Joe Farmer, rhp, Kentucky**
14. **David DeCordova, lhp, UC San Diego**
15. **Mike Robertson, of, Southern Illinois-Edwardsville**
16. **Kerry Griffith, rhp, Louisville**
17. **Jim Puzey, c, Nevada**
18. **Anthony Buglione, c, New Haven (Conn.)**
19. **Shaun McGinnis, of, Chaparral HS, Las Vegas**
20. **Rob Knowles, of, San Diego State**
21. Daven Bond, rhp, Mesa State (Colo.)
22. **Howard Hilton, rhp, Arkansas**
23. Darren Linden, 1b, Southwestern Oklahoma State
24. **Alex Ojea, 2b, Florida International**
25. Brad Rhodes, lhp, North Davidson HS, Clemons, N.C.
26. John McLain, of, Clifton (N.J.) HS
27. **David Turney, ss, Southern California College**
28. Jeff Bonacquista, 1b/of, South HS, Pueblo, Colo.
29. **Ken Warmbler, of, Illinois**
30. Kevin Sheary, rhp, Miami
31. **Mick Freed, rhp, Eastern Illinois**
32. Larry Gonzales, c, Edgewood HS, West Covina, Calif.
33. Ben Webb, rhp, Tate HS, Gonzalez, Fla.
34. **Mike McNeely, rhp, Illinois Wesleyan**

June—Secondary Phase (6)

1. Rick Morris, 2b, Arizona State
2. Blaine Beatty, lhp, Baylor

SAN DIEGO PADRES

January—Regular Phase (21)

1. Rob Hartwig, of, Los Angeles Harbor JC
2. Steve Wapnick, rhp, Moorpark (Calif.) JC
3. Robert Gomez, rhp, JC of the Sequoias (Calif.)
4. Ken Garcia, 2b, JC of the Sequoias (Calif.)
5. **Jim Lewis, rhp, Citrus (Calif.) JC**
6. Michael Herrera, rhp, Modesto (Calif.) JC
7. Jim Bruske, of, Antelope Valley (Calif.) JC
8. David Smith, of, Delgado (La.) JC
9. **Rodney Clark, 1b, Fullerton (Calif.) JC**

January—Secondary Phase (17)

1. Mike Stanford, rhp, Citrus (Calif.) JC
2. Tyrone Sims, c, Western Oklahoma State JC

June—Regular Phase (23)

1. (Pick to Cubs as compensation for Type A free agent Tim Stoddard)
1. **Joey Cora, ss, Vanderbilt** (Pick from Yankees as compensation for Type A free agent Ed Whitson)
2. Mark Cole, ss, Kennedy HS, Sacramento
3. **Jim Tatum, 3b, Santana HS, Santee, Calif.**
4. Greg Burlingame, lhp, Hawaii
5. **Chris Knabenshue, of, Northern Colorado**
6. **Eric Nolte, lhp, UCLA**
7. **Matt Maysey, rhp, Alief Hastings HS, Houston**
8. Troy Cunningham, rhp, East Valley HS, Spokane, Wash.

9. Mark Davis, of, Stanford
10. **Greg Harris, rhp, Elon**
11. **Jay Nieporte, c, Stetson**
12. **Jerald Clark, 3b, Lamar**
13. **Bill Blount, lhp, San Diego State**
14. **Bill Marx, rhp, Bradley**
15. Dana Schmerer, lhp, Eastern Washington
16. **Carl Ferraro, lhp, Florida Southern**
17. **Eric Bauer, lhp, Eastern Washington**
18. **Tom Meagher, rhp, UC Santa Barbara**
19. Willie Forbes, lhp, Gulf Coast (Fla.) CC
20. Bob Lutticken, c, Serra HS, San Mateo, Calif.
21. **Joe Lynch, rhp, William Paterson (N.J.)**
22. **Maurice Morton, 1b, Elon**
23. **Greg Hall, c, New Mexico**
24. **Adam Ging, ss, UC Irvine**
25. **Bill Stevenson, c, Lewis-Clark State (Idaho)**

June—Secondary Phase (22)

1. Tony Faryniarz, rhp, Sacramento CC
2. Al Osuna Jr., lhp, Cerritos (Calif.) JC

SAN FRANCISCO GIANTS

January—Regular Phase (1)

1. **Ricky Nelson, of, Orange Coast (Calif.) JC**
2. **Todd Miller, of, St. Petersburg (Fla.) JC**
3. Randy Ryan, lhp, Harford (Md.) CC
4. Kevin Ritz, rhp, Indian Hills (Iowa) CC
5. **Steve Santora, of, Ventura (Calif.) JC**
6. **Tim Mead, rhp/3b, Mount Hood (Ore.) CC**
7. John Cebuhar, lhp, Eastern Oklahoma State JC
8. Kelvin Dubose, c, Gordon (Ga.) JC
9. **Brian Petty, ss, Moorpark (Calif.) JC**
10. Darryl Robinson, of, Los Angeles Valley JC

January—Secondary Phase (21)

1. Antoine Pickett, of, Contra Costa (Calif.) JC
2. Sherman Collins, rhp, Seminole State (Okla.) JC

June—Regular Phase (2)

1. **Will Clark, 1b, Mississippi State**
2. **Brian Ohnoutka, rhp, Texas Christian**
3. **Doug Robertson, rhp, Cal State Fullerton**
4. **Robert Jackson, 3b, Galesburg (Ill.) HS**
5. **John Verducci, ss, Stanford**
6. **Jeff Brantley, rhp, Mississippi State**
7. **Mike Whitt, 1b/c, Loyola Marymount**
8. **Trevor Wilson, of/lhp, Oregon City, Ore.**
9. **Jeff Carter, of, Nebraska**
10. **Joe Kmak, c, UC Santa Barbara**
11. **Lloyd Jackson, of, Douglass HS, Baltimore**
12. **Darren Pearson, rhp, Cal Poly San Luis Obispo**
13. **Ty Dabney, of, UC Riverside**
14. **George Bonilla, lhp, UC Santa Barbara**
15. **Randy McCament, rhp, Grand Canyon (Ariz.)**
16. **Darrell Rodgers, rhp, Oklahoma**
17. **Steven Van Kempen, p, North Park**
18. **Dennis Cook, of/lhp, Texas**
19. **Joe Jordan, c, Oklahoma**
20. **Howard Townsend, lhp, Cal State Long Beach**
21. **Brad Bambee, rhp, Beaverton (Ore.) HS**
22. Robert Hernandez, 1b/lhp, Los Angeles Valley JC
23. **Tommy Smith, inf, Clemson**
24. **Mike Dandos, ss, Utah**
25. **Billy Smith, of, Oklahoma State**
26. Brian Harrison, lhp/of, Ventura (Calif.) JC
27. **David Blakley, rhp, Santa Clara**
28. Andre London, of, Lithis Springs HS, Douglasville, Ga.
29. **Paul Van Stone, 2b/ss, San Diego**
30. **Tom Ealy, of, Chaparral HS, Las Vegas**

June—Secondary Phase (2)

1. Pat Gilbert, of, Columbia State (Tenn.) CC
2. Mike Reitzel, lhp, Seminole State (Okla.) JC
3. Lance Davis, rhp, Connors State (Okla.) JC

SEATTLE MARINERS

January—Regular Phase (8)

1. Dan Larsen, rhp, Citrus (Calif.) JC
2. Pat Garman, 3b, JC of the Sequoias (Calif.)
3. **Tony Woods, ss, Mount San Jacinto (Calif.) JC**
4. Shane Flores, c, Golden West (Calif.) JC
5. **Chris Miller, ss, Oregon**
6. **Brad Rohde, rhp, Brevard (Fla.) CC**
7. John Turner, of/inf, Walters State (Tenn.) CC
8. Tim McKercher, c, Orange Coast (Calif.) JC

January—Secondary Phase (18)

1. Stephen Bowden, rhp, San Jacinto (Texas) JC
2. Greg Ehmig, lhp, Walters State (Tenn.) CC

June—Regular Phase (7)

1. **Mike Campbell, rhp, Hawaii**
1. **Bill McGuire, c, Nebraska** (Supplemental pick—27th—for loss of Type B free agent Steve Henderson)
2. **Mike Schooler, rhp, Cal State Fullerton**
3. **Clint Zavaras, rhp, Mullin HS, Denver**
4. **Nezi Balelo, ss, Pepperdine**
5. Brad Mengel, ss, Eagle Rock (Calif.) HS
6. Brad Eagar, c, Orem (Utah) HS
7. **Tim McLain, rhp, Auburn**
8. **Barrymore Greaves, of, Cassidy HS, Raynham, Mass.**
9. **Bret Davis, lhp, New Mexico**
10. **Rich Slominski, 1b, Cal State Fullerton**
11. **John Clem, of, Western Kentucky**
12. **Jeff Roberts, rhp, Arizona State**
13. Kevin Pearson, ss, Oklahoma
14. **David Stewart, 1b, UC Santa Barbara**
15. **Clay Parker, rhp, Louisiana State**
16. **Dave McCorkle, rhp, Florida Southern**
17. **George Lopez, 3b, Arizona State**
18. **Mike Simon, of, Texas**
19. **Steve Oizumi, rhp, Western New Mexico**
20. **Dane Quince, rhp/1b, North Brunswick HS, Leland, N.C.**
21. **Doug Givler, rhp, Georgia**
22. **Tom Eccleston, of, Cal State Chico**
23. Scott Johnson, of, North Carolina
24. Mike Scanlin, of, Texas A&M
25. **Bob Bernardo, of, West Virginia**
26. **Mike Darby, rhp, Iowa**
27. Dewayne Jones, ss, Murphy HS, Mobile, Ala.
28. **Brian Thomas, ss, Lewis-Clark State (Idaho)**
29. **Greg Fulton, inf, Atlantic Christian (Ga.)**
30. Michael Florak, 1b, Steubenville Central (Ohio)

June—Secondary Phase (15)

1. Pat Garman, 3b, JC of the Sequoias (Calif.)
2. **Don Cohoon, 3b, Indian River (Fla.) CC**
3. Jim Bruske, rhp/of, Antelope Valley (Calif.) JC

TEXAS RANGERS

January—Regular Phase (4)

1. **David Rolland, 3b/of, Orange Coast (Calif.) JC**
2. Lance Davis, rhp, Connors State (Okla.) JC
3. **Travis Sheffield, of, Los Angeles CC**
4. Mike Papajohn, of, Gulf Coast (Fla.) CC
5. Scott Broadfoot, rhp, Allen County (Kan.) CC
6. **Anthony Clark, of, Los Angeles Harbor JC**
7. Jay Fox, rhp, Spokane Falls (Wash.) CC
8. Michael Gianfrancesco, 3b, Nassau (N.Y.) CC
9. John Fleming, p, East Mississippi JC
10. Mel Sisney, rhp, Los Angeles CC
11. Rafael Bournigal, ss, Canada (Calif.) JC

January—Secondary Phase (10)

1. **Ed Soto, rhp, Miami-Dade North CC**
2. Gary Alexander, rhp, Laney (Calif.) JC

June—Regular Phase (3)

1. **Bobby Witt, rhp, Oklahoma**
2. (Pick to Dodgers as compensation for Type A free agent Burt

Hooton)
3. **Jim Vlcek, rhp, Amos Alonzo Stagg HS, Palos Hills, Ill.**
4. **Steve Wilson, lhp, Portland**
5. **Chad Kreuter, c, Pepperdine**
6. **Mark Seay, of, San Bernardino (Calif.) HS**
7. **Dan Olsson, rhp, Montclair State (N.J.)**
8. **Mitch Thomas, rhp, Northeast Louisiana**
9. **Michael Jackson, of, Appomattox (Va.) HS**
10. **Frank Bryan, rhp, Clovis (Calif.) HS**
11. **Kevin Reimer, 1b, Cal State Fullerton**
12. **Terrill Adams, rhp, San Jose State**
13. **Mike Dotzler, c, Sunnyvale, Calif.**
14. Mike Ollom, rhp, Lewis-Clark State (Idaho)
15. **Warren Busick, rhp, Citrus (Calif.) JC**
16. **Mike Stanley, 1b, Florida**
17. **Rob Mortimer, lhp, James Madison**
18. **Tommy West, rhp, Old Dominion**
19. **Joseph Nannariello, rhp, Pace (N.Y.)**
20. **Steve Lankard, rhp, Cal State Long Beach**
21. **Dan Van Cleve, of, Mississippi State**
22. **Jay Reynolds, rhp, Oklahoma**
23. **Ron Russell, 1b, Brandeis (Mass.)**
24. Randy Snyder, c, Davis HS, Yakima, Wash.
25. **William Booker, rhp, Texas Christian**
26. **Gary Mielke, rhp, Mankato State (Minn.)**
27. Mark Potoshnik, rhp, Kennewick (Wash.) HS
28. **James Browne, 1b, Drexel**
29. Damon Allen, rhp, Cal State Fullerton
30. John Hudek, rhp, Plant HS, Tampa
31. Willie Tatum, 3b, Burbank HS, Sacramento

June—Secondary Phase (25)

1. **Darrin Garner, ss, Orange Coast (Calif.) JC**
2. **Dan Larsen, rhp, Citrus (Calif.) JC**
3. Tim McCoy, lhp, Oral Roberts
4. Anthony Newman, of, Oregon
5. **Paul James, rhp, Missouri**

TORONTO BLUE JAYS

January—Regular Phase (25)

1. Howard Farmer, rhp, Utica (Miss.) JC
2. Brian Veilleux, lhp, Allen County (Kan.) CC
3. John Kohli, lhp, Mira Costa (Calif.) JC
4. **Jim Tracy, rhp, North Shore (Mass.) CC**
5. Craig Bolton, lhp, Santa Fe (Fla.) CC
6. Joe Hollinshed, 1b, Lurleen B. Wallace State (Ala.) JC
7. Michael House, lhp, Bellevue (Wash.) CC
8. **Dennis Jones, lhp, Gadsden State (Ala.) JC**
9. Marvin McBurrows, of, Chipola (Fla.) JC
10. Don Stanford, rhp, Onondaga (N.Y.) CC
11. Rey Vizcaino, rhp, Indian River (Fla.) CC
12. Travis Law, of, San Jose (Calif.) CC
13. Bernard Black, inf/c, Florida JC
14. James Bodace, of, Los Angeles Pierce JC
15. Dan Dondlinger, c, Kings Rivers (Calif.) JC

January—Secondary Phase (14)

1. Oneri Fleita, lhp, Miami-Dade North CC
2. Wendell Harris, of, Pasadena HS, Altadena, Calif.
3. **Keith Felden, rhp, St. Petersburg (Fla.) JC**
4. James Willis, of, Triton (Ill.) JC

June—Regular Phase (25)

1. **Greg David, of, Barron Collier HS, Naples, Fla.**
2. **Kevin Batiste, of, Ball HS, Galveston, Texas**
3. **Joe Humphries, rhp, Western Michigan**
4. **Chris Jones, rhp, Ohio State**
5. **Jeff Mays, rhp, Nebraska**
6. **Jeff Musselman, lhp, Harvard**
7. **Shawn Jeter, of, Woodlawn HS, Shreveport, La.**
8. **Steve Mumaw, lhp, Tampa**
9. Brian Johnson, c, Spring Westfield HS, Houston
10. Erik Boddie, of, West HS, Waukegan, Ill.
11. **Paul Rodgers, of, U.S. Grant HS, Oklahoma City**
12. **Sterling Housley, 2b, Southeastern Louisiana**
13. **Mike C. Jones, of, Valdosta State (Ga.)**
14. **Walter Watford, ss, Troy State**
15. Rich DeLucia, rhp, Tennessee
16. **Glen Kwiatkowski, rhp, Eastern Michigan**
17. Dewayne Martin, rhp, Sandpoint HS, Sagle, Idaho
18. **Roger Marquardt, c, Western Michigan**
19. Kight Higgins, rhp, Texas Christian
20. **Joseph Schlieper, lhp, West Virginia**
21. Scott Runge, rhp, Sacramento CC
22. Tim McKinley, c, Southeastern Illinois JC
23. Blake Butterfield, rhp, Glendora (Calif.) HS
24. **Kerry St. Clair, of, Georgia**
25. Alex Smith, ss, Indiana
26. **John Rohde, lhp, Carson-Newman (Tenn.)**
27. **Randy Whisler, 2b, Oklahoma State**
28. **Richard Anderson, rhp, Florida Memorial**
29. **Dewayne Smith, of, South Young HS, Knoxville, Tenn.**
30. Steven Adams, rhp, Hartnell (Calif.) CC
31. **Pat Sullivan, c, Tennessee**
32. Robert Cuff, rhp, St. Petersburg (Fla.) JC
33. Reggie Ramert, of, Dudley HS, Greensboro, N.C.
34. **Doug Gonring, c, Florida Atlantic**
35. **Derek Ware, of, Christian Brothers HS, Sacramento**
36. Jim Abbott, lhp, Flint (Mich.) Central HS
37. **Greg Dennis, ss, Baylor**

June—Secondary Phase (3)

1. **Todd Stottlemyre, rhp, Yakima Valley (Wash.) JC**
2. Craig Bolton, lhp, Santa Fe (Fla.) CC
3. Chris Lee, rhp, Edison (Fla.) CC
4. Antoine Pickett, 3b, Contra Costa (Calif.) JC
5. Joe Hollinshed, 1b, Lurleen B. Wallace State (Ala.) JC
6. Bruce Powers, of, Skyline (Calif.) JC
7. Oneri Fleita, lhp, Miami-Dade North CC

1986 King goes first, Angels have first draft bonanza, but Royals grab glory by taking Bo

For the California Angels, the 1986 draft provided a potential bonanza.

Under the new compensation rules of the Basic Agreement, the Angels got four extra draft picks for losing free agents, giving them five in the first 28 selections. It was the first first-round windfall in what became a trend in the free-agency era.

"We're in a situation without precedent," Angels scouting director Larry Himes said. "I think the draft this year is the strongest I've been involved with. There's enough talent that even selecting No. 28 there's going to be someone there with baseball ability who is interested in playing professional baseball as a career."

The Angels played it safe, going for five players they knew they would be able to sign.

"The draft did for us just about what we wanted it to," Himes said. "Our emphasis was on pitching. We got two college players to match up with the players we have in our system."

But the Angels got little return on their investment. While three of the players earned significant big league time—pitchers Mike Fetters and Roberto Hernandez and outfielder Lee Stevens—it was not in Anaheim.

The Angels elected not to gamble one of their extra picks on the biggest name of the draft era, outfielder Bo Jackson. Most scouts agreed he would have been a likely No. 1 pick overall if teams knew he wanted to focus on baseball.

Jackson won the 1985 Heisman Trophy at Auburn and was the No. 1 pick in the 1986 NFL draft, and most people thought he would play football. The NFL coveted Jackson even more than it would have based simply on his talent because it had lost the previous three Heisman Trophy winners to the upstart United States Football League.

"I think it's almost cut and dried," Himes said. "He's going to the NFL. I don't think he's going to be able to resist the hoopla and the dollars that go with the NFL draft. I don't think the baseball team that drafts him will be able to compete."

What Himes didn't know was that Jackson harbored ill will against the Tampa Bay Buccaneers, who gave him a free plane ride that cost him most of his senior baseball season at Auburn. He also didn't know that Royals scouts had been cultivating a relationship with Jackson and his mother for months.

The Angels had drafted Jackson in 1985 in the 20th round. This time around he went in the fourth

MEL BAILEY

Bo Jackson shocked most people by signing with the Royals as a fourth-round pick

round to Kansas City. In addition to the Angels, the Royals were one of three clubs Jackson visited prior to the draft. And on the morning of the draft, Jackson telephoned Royals general manager John Schuerholz and indicated his choice of baseball teams was the Royals. He also said he didn't have to be selected in the first round to consider signing.

"Once we selected our first three players," Royals scouting director Art Stewart said, "it was then that we decided to go for Jackson. We felt we could risk a fourth-round pick on him. We knew he had been honest with us in saying he wanted to play for Kansas City when California and Toronto didn't take him in the first round."

He signed with the Royals on June 21, a coup for baseball, and ended up starring in both baseball and football before a hip injury cut his career short.

While Jackson drew most of the attention, the two top picks in the June draft were rival Southwest Conference players: Arkansas third baseman Jeff King, drafted by Pittsburgh, and Texas lefthander Greg Swindell, selected by Cleveland. Both King and Swindell held out into July for identical bonuses of $160,000.

Led by King and Swindell, the first four players drafted were from the college ranks for the second year in a row. San Francisco, drafting third, took Nevada-

Las Vegas shortstop Matt Williams, while Texas took Georgia Tech righthander Kevin Brown.

From that point on, however, there was a sharp swing back to high school talent. Of the remaining 22 picks in the first round, 15 were from the prep ranks, the first time since 1980 that more high school players were selected than college players in the first round.

The first high school player selected was lefthander Kent Mercker, drafted by the Braves. Milwaukee, picking sixth, took shortstop Gary Sheffield, nephew of Mets pitching star Dwight Gooden.

End Of Innocence

The draft took on a different look in 1986. Concerned with agents and college coaches using the draft list to uncover talent, Major League Baseball imposed a news blackout. Other than the players drafted in the first round of the regular phase, no other information was released for a week thereafter, and then only the names of drafted players in alphabetical order, by clubs. The new rule appeared to achieve its desired effect. Less than 10 percent (26 of 263) of the players selected in the first 10 rounds didn't sign, the highest percentage achieved to that time.

More significantly, MLB announced the January draft would end after 1986. Because most players drafted in January were from junior colleges and not eligible to sign immediately, executives agreed that draft had outlived its usefulness. Beginning in 1987, the January and June drafts would be combined. In the final January draft, 420 players were selected, one short of the record.

Overall, there were 331 high school players drafted in 1986, the highest total since 1979 and almost 100 more than the previous year. Clubs now could select a junior college-bound high school player in June, follow his progress and decide before the next year's draft whether to sign him. The new "draft-and-follow" approach became standard practice until the advent of a signing deadline in 2007.

While baseball threw a cross-body block at the NFL by luring Jackson away, it lost a player to football as well. The Red Sox used their first-round pick on outfielder Greg McMurtry, a talented two-sport athlete from nearby Brockton, Mass., even though McMurtry made it clear prior to the draft that he would honor his commitment to Michigan. He went on to become an all-America wide receiver at Michigan and played five seasons in the NFL.

For failing to sign their first-round pick, the Red Sox received a supplemental selection between the first and second rounds in the 1987 draft, another new draft provision of the new Basic Agreement.

DRAFT 86: FIRST-ROUND PICKS

No.	Club	Player, Pos.	School	Hometown	Ht.	Wt.	B-T	Age
1.	Pirates	Jeff King, 3b	Arkansas	Colorado Springs, Colo.	6-0	165	R-R	21
2.	Indians	Greg Swindell, lhp	Texas	Houston	6-2	225	R-L	21
3.	Giants	Matt Williams, ss	Nevada Las Vegas	Carson City, Nev.	6-2	180	R-R	20
4.	Rangers	Kevin Brown, rhp	Georgia Tech	McIntyre, Ga.	6-4	193	R-R	21
5.	Braves	Kent Mercker, lhp	Dublin HS	Dublin, Ohio	6-2	185	L-L	18
6.	Brewers	Gary Sheffield, ss	Hillsborough HS	Tampa	6-0	190	R-R	17
7.	Phillies	Brad Brink, rhp	Southern California	Modesto, Calif.	6-1	185	R-R	21
8.	Mariners	Patrick Lennon, ss	Whiteville HS	Whiteville, N.C.	6-2	200	R-R	18
9.	Cubs	Derrick May, of	Newark HS	Newark, Del.	6-4	205	L-R	17
10.	Twins	Derek Parks, c	Montclair HS	Upland, Calif.	6-0	190	R-R	17
11.	Padres	Thomas Howard, of	Ball State	Germantown, Ohio	6-1	198	B-R	21
12.	Athletics	Scott Hemond, c	South Florida	Dunedin, Fla.	5-11	200	R-R	20
13.	Astros	Ryan Bowen, rhp	Hanford HS	Hanford, Calif.	6-2	185	R-R	18
14.	Red Sox	*Greg McMurtry, of	Brockton HS	Brockton, Mass.	6-2	195	L-R	18
15.	Expos	Kevin Dean, of	Hogan HS	Vallejo, Calif.	6-1	175	R-R	18
16.	Angels	Roberto Hernandez, rhp	South Carolina-Aiken	New York City	6-4	225	R-R	21
17.	Reds	Scott Scudder, rhp	Prairiland HS	Blossom, Texas	6-2	170	R-R	18
18.	Tigers	Phil Clark, c	Crockett HS	Crockett, Texas	6-0	175	R-R	18
19.	Dodgers	Mike White, of	Loudon HS	Loudon, Tenn.	6-2	180	L-R	18
20.	White Sox	Grady Hall, lhp	Northwestern	Findlay, Ohio	6-2	200	R-R	22
21.	Mets	Lee May, of	Purcell Marion HS	Cincinnati	6-2	175	R-R	18
22.	Angels	Lee Stevens, of	Lawrence HS	Lawrence, Kan.	6-4	200	L-L	18
23.	Cardinals	Luis Alicea, 2b	Florida State	Guaynabo, P.R.	5-9	165	B-R	20
24.	Royals	Tony Clements, ss	Don Lugo HS	Chino, Calif.	6-0	180	R-R	17
25.	Angels	Terry Carr, of	Bennett HS	Salisbury, Md.	6-1	172	R-R	18
26.	Blue Jays	Earl Sanders, rhp	Jackson State	Moss Point, Miss.	6-3	210	R-R	21

*Did not sign.

1986

CLUB-BY-CLUB SELECTIONS

ATLANTA BRAVES

January—Regular Phase (6)

1. Bob Jones, lhp, Citrus (Calif.) JC
2. **Richard Longuil, rhp, Iowa Western CC**
3. **Brian Deak, c, Yavapai (Ariz.) JC**
4. Brad Herrel, rhp, Northeastern Oklahoma A&M JC
5. Ed Banasiak, rhp, CC of Morris (N.J.)
6. **Ken Pennington, inf, El Camino (Calif.) JC**
7. Edward Lamando, lhp, DeKalb Central (Ga.) JC
8. Tim Groner, inf, Walters State (Tenn.) CC
9. **Morris Bland, inf, Indian River (Fla.) CC**
10. **Jesse Minton, 1b, Chaffey (Calif.) JC**
11. Jorge Pedre, c, West Los Angeles JC

January—Secondary Phase (2)

1. **Kevin D. Brown, lhp, Sacramento CC**
2. Carlos Carrasco, rhp, Gavilan (Calif.) JC

June—Regular Phase (5)

1. **Kent Mercker, lhp, Dublin (Ohio) HS**
2. **Brian Champion, ss, Corvallis (Ore.) HS**
3. **Chad Smith, lhp, Sullivan HS, Kingsport, Tenn.**
4. **Mike Bell, 1b, Newton (N.J.) HS**
5. **Andy Nezelek, rhp, Bucknell**
6. **Rick Morris, of, Arizona State**
7. **Robert Stuart, ss, Sonora HS, Brea, Calif.**
8. **Sean Ross, of, Hoggard HS, Wilmington, N.C.**
9. **Ralph Meister, rhp, Norman (Okla.) HS**
10. **Jim LeMasters, rhp, West Liberty State**
11. Steve Finley, of, Southern Illinois
12. **Terry Sloan, c, Master's (Calif.)**
13. **Rich Maloney, ss, Western Michigan**
14. Steve Wilson, rhp, St. Xavier (Ill.)
15. **Mark Clark, rhp, St. Mary's HS, St. Louis**
16. **Alex Smith, ss, Indiana**
17. **Walt Williams, lhp, Western Michigan**
18. Tim Salmon, of, Greenway HS, Phoenix
19. **Jay Johnson, 2b, Dallas Baptist**
20. **Dave Butts, 3b, Murray State**
21. **George Naumczik, lhp, Northern Illinois**
22. **Steve Alexander, of, Southern Tech Institute (Fla.)**
23. **Stan Scarborough, rhp, Parkview HS, Milburn, Ga.**
24. **John Stewart, lhp, Georgia Tech**
25. **Lynn Robinson, of, Chicago State**
26. **David Plumb, c, Auburn**
27. Ben McDonald, rhp, Denham Springs (La.) HS
28. **Jeff Weiss, of, California**
29. **Jim Czajkowski, rhp, North Alabama**
30. **Steve O'Quinn, rhp, DeKalb (Ga.) JC**
31. **Arthur Smith, of, Coastal Carolina**
32. **Phil Maldonado, c, Texas Tech**
33. Byron Magee, lhp, Shippensburg (Pa.) HS
34. Richard Pfaff, c, Westwood HS, Round Rock, Texas
35. **Scott Kickbush, c, Iowa State**
36. **Randy Ralstin, rhp/1b, Pacific**
37. **Joe Datin, 1b, South Carolina**
38. Todd Pennington, of, Roswell (Ga.) HS
39. **Ron Huntington, 2b, Western Carolina**
40. Ken Sirak, ss, Camarillo (Calif.) HS
41. Tim Lindsay, lhp, Arcadia (Calif.) HS
42. **David Karasinski, lhp, Michigan**
43. Kerry Cahill, ss, Father Judge HS, Philadelphia

June—Secondary Phase (9)

1. **Carl Jones-Pointer, of, Mount San Antonio (Calif.) JC**
2. **Jerald Frost, inf, Ocean County (N.J.) JC**
3. Paul Keefer, inf, Des Moines Area (Iowa) CC

BALTIMORE ORIOLES

January—Regular Phase (15)

1. Glenn Twardy, of, Cerritos (Calif.) JC
2. Jaime Navarro, rhp, Miami-Dade New World Center CC
3. Joel Smith, of, Middle Georgia JC
4. Paris Hayden, of, Indian River (Fla.) CC
5. David Taylor, rhp, McLennan (Texas) CC
6. Jeff Gidcumb, rhp, Florida CC
7. **Robert Williams, rhp, Buffalo**
8. **Rickey Carriger, rhp, Northeastern Oklahoma A&M JC**
9. Todd Nash, of, Golden West (Calif.) JC
10. Rafael Bournigal, inf, Canada (Calif.) JC

January—Secondary Phase (3)

1. **David Miller, rhp, Camden County (N.J.) JC**

June—Regular Phase (16)

1. (Pick to Angels as compensation for Type A free agent Juan Beniquez)
2. **John Posey, c, Campbell**
3. **Mike Lehman, c, Vallivue HS, Caldwell, Idaho**
4. **Doug Cinnella, rhp, Seton Hall**
5. **Craig Lopez, rhp, Virginia Commonwealth**
6. **Tom Michno, rhp, Columbus**
7. **Bill Kler, of, Milwaukie (Ore.) HS**
8. **Terry Crowley Jr., ss, Dulaney HS, Baltimore**
9. **Blaine Beatty, lhp, Baylor**
10. **Ken Adderley, of, Florida International**
11. **Dale Barry, lhp, Texas A&M**
12. **Walt Harris, of, Stanford**
13. **Steve Sonneberger, rhp, Middle Tennessee State**
14. **Gordie Dillard, lhp, Oklahoma State**
15. William Jones, rhp, Palatka (Fla.) HS
16. **Larry Mims, 2b, Nebraska**
17. **Randy Strijek, ss, Western Kentucky**
18. Bill Narleski, ss, Virginia
19. **Steven Williams, rhp, Upsala (N.J.)**
20. **Walt Wallen, 3b, South Carolina-Aiken**
21. **Richard Winzenread, rhp, Hanover**
22. **Mark Morawski, 2b, Eckerd (Fla.)**
23. Jim Huslig, rhp, Shawnee Mission (Kan.) East HS
24. Daniel Bench, c, Northeast HS, St. Petersburg, Fla.
25. **Rob Walton, rhp, Oklahoma State**
26. **Tracey Pancoski, of, Brookdale (N.J.) CC**
27. Dave Briggs, 1b/of, Rumson Fair Haven (N.J.) HS
28. Mike Shambaugh, 1b, Oral Roberts
29. Charles Tanton, c, Lee (Texas) JC
30. Jim DePalo, c, Harvard
31. **Robert Cox, of/1b, Anne Arundel (Md.) CC**
32. Mark Bookmeyer, of, Lee (Texas) JC
33. **Chris Klyczek, 2b, St. Benedictine HS, Chicago**
34. Tommy Raffo, lhp/1b, Bishop Kenny HS, Jacksonville, Fla.
35. **Matthew Radzik, c, Indian Hills (Iowa) CC**
36. **Matthew Nowak, 3b, Southwest Missouri State**
37. **Rob Lukachyk, ss, Henry Hudson HS, Highlands, N.J.**
38. John Fowler, ss, Brunswick (Md.) HS
39. Darren Villani, 3b, West Windsor HS, Lawrenceville, N.J.
40. Craig Marshall, rhp, Pittsburg (Kan.) HS
41. Dell Ahalt, ss, Hagerstown (Md.) JC
42. Doug Shields, ss, La Salle HS, Cincinnati
43. **Franklin Martz, 2b, Frederick (Md.) CC**
44. Eric Cox, c, Esperanza HS, Yorba Linda, Calif.
45. **Phil Williams, c, Hawaii**
46. Rod Steiner, 3b, Seminole State (Okla.) JC

47. Casey Moore, c, Loupla Academy HS, Glencoe, Ill.
48. David Arendas, ss, West Windsor HS, Lawrenceville, N.J.
49. Daniel Johnston, 2b, Manual HS, Indianapolis

June—Secondary Phase (26)

1. **Paris Hayden, of, Indian River (Fla.) CC**
2. Jaime Navarro, rhp, Miami-Dade New World Center CC
3. Ray Schuyler, of, CC of Morris (N.J.)

BOSTON RED SOX

January—Regular Phase (13)

1. Alan Mills, rhp, Polk (Fla.) CC
2. **Curt Schilling, rhp, Yavapai (Ariz.) JC**
3. Scott Boggs, inf, Columbia State (Tenn.) CC
4. William Rawdon, rhp, Columbia State (Tenn.) CC
5. Michael Whiting, rhp, JC of Eastern Utah
6. Michael Leland, c, San Joaquin Delta (Calif.) JC
7. Thomas McGee, of, San Jacinto (Texas) JC
8. **Glen O'Donnell, inf, Quinsigamond (Mass.) CC**
9. Charlie Holmes, rhp, Mount San Antonio (Calif.) JC
10. Andres Cruz, of, Laredo (Texas) JC
11. **Lem Pilkinton, c, Columbia State (Tenn.) CC**
12. **Kendrick Bourne, of, Chaffey (Calif.) JC**

January—Secondary Phase (7)

1. **Ray Revak, lhp, Key West, Fla.**
2. Mike Bianco, c, Indian River (Fla.) CC

June—Regular Phase (14)

1. Greg McMurtry, of, Brockton (Mass.) HS
2. **Paul Williams, c, Smiley HS, Houston**
3. **Scott Cooper, 3b/rhp, Pattonville HS, St. Louis**
4. **Charles Wacha, rhp, Columbus**
5. **Steve Bast, lhp, Southern California**
6. **Bart Haley, lhp, Grand Canyon (Ariz.)**
7. Mike Garcia, rhp, North HS, Moreno Valley, Calif.
8. **David Milstien, ss, Simi Valley (Calif.) HS**
9. Joe Kelly, lhp, Notre Dame HS, Whitesboro, N.Y.
10. **Jim Morrison, rhp, Jonesboro HS, Anna, Ill.**
11. **Terry Marrs, of, Lake Worth (Fla.) HS**
12. **David Walters, rhp, Campbell**
13. **Joe Marchese, 2b, Mankato State (Minn.)**
14. **Anthony Hill, of, Rhode Island**
15. **Brian Warfel, of, Labette (Kan.) CC**
16. Steven Tucker, lhp, Riverview HS, Sarasota, Fla.
17. Tony Kounas, c, San Gorgonio HS, Highland, Calif.
18. **Ron Warren, lhp, Troy State**
19. **Tim Buheller, of, Virginia Tech**
20. **Mike Baker, 2b, Nevada-Reno**
21. **Tom Sepela, rhp, Lock Haven (Pa.)**
22. **Stu Weidie, of, New Orleans**
23. Chris Hanks, c, Roaring Forks HS, Carbondale, Colo.

June—Secondary Phase (20)

1. **Ed Banasiak, rhp, CC of Morris (N.J.)**

CALIFORNIA ANGELS

January—Regular Phase (21)

1. **Brandy Vann, rhp, Butler County (Kan.) CC**
2. **Scott Kannenberg, rhp, San Diego State**
3. Ken James, of, Mount San Jacinto (Calif.) JC
4. **Bill Vanderwel, rhp, Seminole State (Okla.) JC**
5. Scott Henion, rhp, Crowder (Mo.) JC
6. Robert Cabello, inf, Moorpark (Calif.) JC
7. Richard Hochanadel, lhp, Labette (Kan.) CC
8. Ed Alicea, 2b, Chipola (Fla.) JC
9. Marcus Trammell, inf, Louisburg (N.C.) JC
10. **Tony Rasmus, inf, Enterprise State (Ala.) JC**
11. **Greg Jackson, 1b, Polk (Fla.) CC**
12. Greg Sims, inf, Lee (Texas) JC
13. Israel Gonzales, rhp, Laredo (Texas) JC
14. Lane Mallett, lhp, Panola (Texas) JC
15. Jay Searcy, 3b, Texas

January—Secondary Phase (25)

1. Jeff Marr, rhp, Brevard (Fla.) CC

June—Regular Phase (22)

1. **Roberto Hernandez, rhp, South Carolina-Aiken** (Pick from Orioles as compensation for Type A free agent Juan Beniquez)
1. **Lee Stevens, of, Lawrence (Kan.) HS**
1. **Terry Carr, of, Bennett HS, Salisbury, Md.** (Pick from Yankees as compensation for Type A free agent Al Holland)
1. **Mike Fetters, rhp, Pepperdine** (Supplemental pick—27th—for loss of Beniquez)
1. **Daryl Green, rhp, Nacogdoches (Texas) HS** (Supplemental pick—28th—for loss of Holland)
2. **Jeff Gay, c, Santana HS, Santee, Calif.**
3. **Chris Graves, of, Brenham (Texas) HS**
4. **Paul Sorrento, of, Florida State**
5. **David Grilione, 1b, Selma (Calif.) HS**
6. **Colin Charland, lhp, Dallas Baptist**
7. Tony Scruggs, of, UCLA
8. **Mike Anderson, of, Northern Colorado**
9. Jon Shave, ss, Fernandina Beach (Fla.) HS
10. **Greg Fix, lhp, Columbus HS, Perrysburg, Ohio**
11. **Colby Ward, rhp, Brigham Young**
12. **Jim Bisceglia, lhp, St. John's**
13. **Scott Cerny, 2b, UC Santa Barbara**
14. **Gary Gorski, 3b, UCLA**
15. **Mike Knapp, c, California**
16. **Troy Giles, of, Passaic (N.J.) HS**
17. Mark Carper, rhp, Atholton HS, Highland, Md.
18. **Louis Merejo, rhp, CC of Morris (N.J.)**
19. Stephen Mauldin, of, Leto HS, Tampa
20. Gary Forrester, ss, Sacramento CC
21. **Ken Bandy, of/rhp, Dallas Baptist**

June—Secondary Phase (8)

1. **Alan Mills, rhp, Polk (Fla.) CC**
2. Richard Hochanadel, lhp, Labette (Kan.) CC
3. **Robert Cabello, inf, Moorpark (Calif.) JC**

CHICAGO CUBS

January—Regular Phase (10)

1. **Shawn Boskie, rhp, Modesto (Calif.) JC**
2. **Jerome Walton, of, Enterprise State (Ala.) JC**
3. Ray Lankford, of, Modesto (Calif.) JC
4. **Ken Taylor, c, San Bernardino Valley (Calif.) JC**
5. Derek Lee, of, Manatee (Fla.) JC
6. Ken Ramos, of, Otero (Colo.) JC
7. Paul Aguirre, lhp, Grossmont (Calif.) JC
8. Mark Linden, inf, Bellevue (Wash.) CC
9. John Kuehl, inf, Scottsdale (Ariz.) CC
10. Bobby Hill, inf, McLennan (Texas) CC

January—Secondary Phase (22)

1. Mike Ross, ss, Fresno CC

June—Regular Phase (9)

1. **Derrick May, of, Newark (Del.) HS**
2. Kraig Washington, ss, Diamond Bar (Calif.) HS
3. **Eddie Williams, of, Vallejo (Calif.) HS**
4. **Pat Gomez, lhp, San Juan HS, Citrus Heights, Calif.**
5. **Joe Girardi, c, Northwestern**
6. **Bill Kazmierczak, rhp, Lewis (Ill.)**
7. **Mike Reeder, 1b, Newark (Del.) HS**
8. **Bill Melvin, rhp, Louisburg (N.C.) JC**
9. **Jim Bullinger, ss, New Orleans**
10. **Mike Curtis, lhp, Ohio State**
11. **Darren Eggleston, ss, Martinsville (Va.) HS**
12. **Steve Parker, lhp, Arkansas**
13. **Steve Hill, 2b, San Diego State**
14. Doug Peters, rhp, Shenango HS, New Castle, Pa.
15. Mark Dawn, of, Sarasota (Fla.) HS
16. **Phil Harrison, lhp, Nebraska**
17. **Harry Shelton, of, North Alabama**
18. Al Jorajuria, ss, Kathleen HS, Lakeland, Fla.
19. **Anthony LaPoint, rhp, Oral Roberts**
20. Mike Mahady, rhp, Manasquan HS, Brielle, N.J.

21. **Martin Rivero, ss, Cal Poly Pomona**
22. **Kent Alexander, rhp, Appalachian State**
23. **Rick Wilkins, c, Florida CC**
24. **Sergio Espinal, 2b, Oklahoma State**
25. **Ray Mullino, rhp, Mississippi State**
26. Mike Noel, of, Clovis (Calif.) West HS
27. **David Sommer, rhp, Clark (Wash.) JC**
28. **Greg Jackson, of, Tucson (Ariz.) HS**
29. **Eric Woods, of, San Diego State**
30. Jon Anderson, c, North Shore HS, West Palm Beach, Fla.
31. Greg Burlingame, lhp, Hawaii
32. Eric Hughes, rhp, Hug HS, Hawthorne, Nev.
33. Tom Popplewell, rhp, Fairfield (Ohio) HS

June—Secondary Phase (13)

1. **Tony Faryniarz, rhp, San Diego State**
2. Mike Reitzel, lhp, Hawaii

CHICAGO WHITE SOX

January—Regular Phase (19)

1. **Herman Adames, inf, Miami-Dade South CC**
2. Mike Todd, 1b, San Bernardino Valley (Calif.) JC
3. **Chris Cota, of, JC of the Canyons (Calif.)**
4. **Vincent Harris, of, Triton (Ill.) JC**
5. **Jeff Greene, 1b, Seminole (Fla.) CC**
6. Pete Kuld, c, JC of the Canyons (Calif.)
7. Keith Kaub, 1b, Golden West (Calif.) JC

January—Secondary Phase (11)

1. **Randy Robinson, rhp, JC of the Sequoias (Calif.)**

June—Regular Phase (20)

1. **Grady Hall, lhp, Northwestern**
2. **Carl Sullivan, of, Brenham (Texas) HS**
3. **Scott Radinsky, lhp, Simi Valley (Calif.) HS**
4. **Frank Potestio, rhp, UC Riverside**
5. **Todd Trafton, 1b, Arizona**
6. **Bo Kennedy, rhp, Central HS, Elvins, Mo.**
7. **Matt Merullo, c, North Carolina**
8. **Gil Villanueva, lhp, Cal State Fullerton**
9. **Bryce Hulstrom, lhp, Oregon State**
10. **Doug Little, rhp, Florida State**
11. Terry Brown, of, Southern California
12. **Mark Davis, of, Stanford**
13. Mark Smith, lhp, Waltrip HS, Houston
14. **Todd Hall, lhp, Bowling Green State**
15. **Mike Ollom, rhp, Lewis-Clark State (Idaho)**
16. **Dan Wagner, of, Tulane**
17. **John Becker, c, Arroyo HS, El Monte, Calif.**
18. Don Erickson, ss, JC of the Canyons (Calif.)
19. **Kelly Maebe, lhp, Crescenta Valley HS, La Crescenta, Calif.**
20. Collin Wiley, rhp/c, Cal Poly Pomona
21. Brian Steiner, lhp, Seminole State (Okla.) JC

June—Secondary Phase (24)

1. Dan Rohrmeier, inf, Miami-Dade North CC

CINCINNATI REDS

January—Regular Phase (18)

1. **Ron Wenrich, of, Georgia**
2. **Bill Dodd, rhp, Saddleback (Calif.) CC**
3. **Rainford Harris, of, Brooklyn, N.Y.**
4. Mike Butcher, rhp, Northeastern Oklahoma A&M JC
5. Jesse Ybarra, of, Des Moines Area (Iowa) CC
6. **Chris Hammond, lhp, Gulf Coast (Fla.) CC**
7. Mike Bosco, inf, DeAnza (Calif.) JC
8. Steve Meyer, rhp, Westark (Ark.) CC
9. Tony Floyd, rhp, Three Rivers (Mo.) CC
10. Lonnie Maclin, of, St. Louis CC-Meramec
11. Paul Keefer, inf, Des Moines Area (Iowa) CC
12. Scott Volz, rhp, Des Moines Area (Iowa) CC

January—Secondary Phase (16)

1. Rick Parker, c, Western Oklahoma State JC

June—Regular Phase (17)

1. **Scott Scudder, rhp, Prairiland HS, Blossom, Texas**
2. **Keith Thomas, of, Kenwood HS, Chicago**
3. **Reggie Jefferson, 1b, Lincoln HS, Tallahassee, Fla.**
4. **Mike Moscrey, lhp, Thomas Jefferson HS, Dallas**
5. **Joe Lazor, lhp, Mount Vernon Nazarene (Ohio)**
6. **Eddie Taubensee, c, Lake Howell HS, Casselberry, Fla.**
7. **Jeff Richardson, ss, Louisiana Tech**
8. **Kevin Pearson, ss, Oklahoma**
9. **Chuck Carr, of, Fontana (Calif.) HS**
10. **Tom Novak, rhp, Central Florida**
11. **Keith Lockhart, 2b, Oral Roberts**
12. **Kent Willis, rhp, Southern Mississippi**
13. Derek Heyden, rhp, Corvallis (Ore.) HS
14. **Bernie Walker, of, Texas Christian**
15. Allen Rath, rhp, Highland HS, Riverside, Iowa
16. **John Savage, rhp, Santa Clara**
17. **Sean O'Hare, 1b, Old Dominion**
18. Tom Harms, of, Portland State (Ore.)
19. Tony Terzarial, of, Highland (Ind.) HS
20. **Ken Sims, of, Jackson HS, Jenkinsburg, Ga.**
21. **Keith Brown, rhp, Cal State Sacramento**
22. Pete Young, 3b/c, McComb HS, Summit, Miss.
23. **Quinn Marsh, rhp, Utah Technical JC**
24. **John Stewart, 2b, Northwestern**
25. **Doug Eastman, of, Cal State Sacramento**
26. **Bret Williamson, of, Mesa (Colo.)**
27. Paul Miller, rhp, Carthage (Wis.)
28. **Charles McFadden, c, Lake City (S.C.) HS**
29. Jesse Davis, of, Wooster HS, Reno, Nev.
30. Robert Copeland, c, Waltrip HS, Houston
31. Jim Byrd, ss, Lawton (Okla.) HS
32. Troy Hammell, ss, Lakewood (Calif.) HS
33. Todd Nace, of, Hattiesburg (Miss.) HS
34. Charles Thompson, 2b, Lawton (Okla.) HS
35. Tommy Youngblood, rhp, Auburn (Ala.) HS
36. Mike Taylor, ss, Waltrip HS, Houston
37. Ryan Jackson, rhp, Swansea (S.C.) HS
38. Brett Hendley, 1b, Stratford Academy HS, Macon, Ga.

June—Secondary Phase (7)

1. **Greg Lonigro, inf, Florida CC**
2. Jon Hurst, rhp, Spartanburg Methodist (S.C.) JC

CLEVELAND INDIANS

January—Regular Phase (1)

1. **Jeff Shaw, rhp, Cuyahoga (Ohio) CC**
2. **Mike C. Walker, rhp, Seminole (Fla.) CC**
3. **Jim Baxter, c, Southwestern (Calif.) JC**
4. **Anthony Scaglione, rhp, Morton (Ill.) JC**
5. Benny Castillo, of, CC of Baltimore
6. Kevin Lawson, of, Florida CC
7. Andrew Bourne, of, Citrus (Calif.) JC
8. Randy Ryan, lhp, Miami-Dade North CC
9. **Troy Neel, 1b, Howard (Texas) JC**
10. Thomas Draper, rhp, Monroe (N.Y.) CC
11. Jeff Forgione, lhp, Cecil (Md.) CC
12. Winston Relaford, of, Florida JC
13. Brian Drahman, rhp, Miami-Dade South CC

January—Secondary Phase (15)

1. Lou Frazier, of, Scottsdale (Ariz.) CC
2. **Kraig Luckenbill, rhp, Texas**

June—Regular Phase (2)

1. **Greg Swindell, lhp, Texas**
2. **Kevin Wickander, lhp, Grand Canyon (Ariz.)**
3. **Joe Skalski, rhp, St. Xavier (Ill.)**
4. **Rudy Seanez, rhp, Brawley (Calif.) HS**
5. **Bruce Egloff, rhp, UC Santa Barbara**
6. **Steve Bird, rhp, South Carolina-Aiken**
7. **Tommy Hinzo, 2b, Arizona**
8. Greg Fowble, ss, Granada Hills (Calif.) HS
9. **Ray Williamson, of, Santa Clara**
10. **Doyle Wilson, c, Arkansas**

11. **Tom Lampkin, c, Portland**
12. **Kent Maggard, rhp, Purdue**
13. Dan Davies, lhp, Miami
14. **Kerry Richardson, 3b, Lubbock Christian**
15. **Jeff Battaglia, of, West Virginia**
16. **Kevin Kuykendall, rhp, Western Oregon State**
17. **Carl Chambers, lhp, Chicago State**
18. **Mark Pike, of, South Florida**
19. Steve Hosey, of, Fremont HS, Oakland, Calif.
20. **Jeff Simmelink, c, Lower Columbia (Wash.) JC**
21. **Scott Johnson, of, North Carolina**
22. **Tom Gamba, 3b, Ithica (N.Y.)**
23. **Jim Richardson, 3b, Oklahoma**
24. **Keith Seifert, c, Columbus (Ga.)**
25. **Phil Dillmore, lhp, Florida Southern**
26. **Abraham Walker, 2b, Western Michigan**
27. Kevin Bearse, lhp, Old Dominion
28. **Riley Polk, 2b/ss, South Carolina**
29. **Mike Twardoski, of, Alabama**
30. **John Balis, 3b, North Park (Ill.)**
31. **James Hindulak, lhp, Cleveland State**
32. **Dana Schmerer, lhp, Eastern Washington**
33. Jonathan King, ss, York (Pa.) HS
34. **Brad Wolten, of, Washington State**
35. **Luis Martinez, of, Cleveland State**
36. **Lewis Kent, c, Grand Canyon (Ariz.)**
37. Reggie Farmer, of, Nevada-Las Vegas
38. Tom McGraw, lhp, Battleground HS, Lake Center, Wash.
39. Chad Allen, rhp, Richland (Wash.) HS
40. Shawn Rohrwild, rhp, Andrew Hill HS, San Jose, Calif.

June—Secondary Phase (6)

1. **Jim Bruske, of, Loyola Marymount**
2. **Paul Kuzniar, rhp, Houston**
3. Dan Eskew, rhp, Indian River (Fla.) CC

DETROIT TIGERS

January—Regular Phase (17)

1. Jeff Cesari, rhp, Taft (Calif.) JC
2. **Henry Lott, lhp, Chicago**
3. Ken Weatherby, of, Laney (Calif.) JC
4. Rick Christian, of, Hagerstown (Md.) JC
5. Kevin Higgins, inf, Los Angeles Harbor JC
6. Mike Maksudian, of, CC of Morris (N.J.)
7. Rocky Elli, lhp, Kishwaukee (Ill.) JC
8. **Wayne Housie, of, Riverside (Calif.) CC**
9. Roddy Wilburn, rhp, Southwestern (Calif.) JC
10. Allen Robbins, of, Columbia Basin (Wash.) CC

January—Secondary Phase (26)

1. Jerry Nielsen, lhp, Sacramento CC
2. Lionel Gaston, lhp, Triton (Ill.) JC

June—Regular Phase (18)

1. **Phil Clark, c, Crockett (Texas) HS**
2. **Milt Cuyler Jr., of, Southwest Macon (Ga.) HS**
3. **Zach Doster, of, Robinson HS, Tampa**
4. **Bill Bean, of, Loyola Marymount**
5. **Pat Austin, ss, Wilmington (Ohio)**
6. **Richard Lacko, rhp, Long Island**
7. **Darryl Martin, of, Roberto Clemente HS, Chicago**
8. **Ron Marigny, ss/2b, Tulane**
9. **Wade Phillips, rhp, Texas**
10. **Russ Elsberry, rhp, San Diego State**
11. **Steve Parascand, lhp, Rider**
12. Brian Davis, of, Cleveland (Texas) HS
13. Dante Johnson, of, Academy P.E. HS, Cincinnati
14. Damon Saetre, 1b, Dowagiac (Mich.) Union HS
15. Gary Peters, 2b, Detroit
16. **Scott Aldred, lhp, Montrose (Mich.) HS**
17. **Darrin Hursey, lhp, Urbana (Ill.) HS**
18. Dan Dimascio, of, UC San Diego
19. **Chris Hoiles, c, Eastern Michigan**
20. Mike Hansen, rhp, Central Michigan
21. Brad Stoltenberg, rhp, Sacramento CC
22. Doug Noch, rhp, Central Michigan
23. Robert Bleisch, c, Chula Vista (Calif.) HS
24. Florentino Lozano, of, San Marcos (Calif.) HS
25. Sam Drake, rhp, Charles Henderson HS, Troy, Ala.
26. **Paul Foster, of, Auburn**

June—Secondary Phase (14)

1. Mike Jones, rhp, Cosumnes River (Calif.) JC
2. Robert Cuff, rhp, Florida Southern

HOUSTON ASTROS

January—Regular Phase (14)

1. Ervin Houston, of, Laney (Calif.) JC
2. **Sam August, rhp, Orange Coast (Calif.) JC**
3. **Dan Lewis, of, El Camino (Calif.) JC**
4. James Cartwright, rhp, Walters State (Tenn.) CC
5. Steve Cantu, lhp, San Jacinto (Texas) JC
6. **Robert Simmons, inf, Louisburg (N.C.) JC**
7. Dave Oropeza, rhp, Pima (Ariz.) CC
8. Jack Moore, inf, Itawamba (Miss.) JC
9. Joe Federico, of, Glendale (Calif.) JC
10. **Bryan King, inf, Los Angeles Harbor JC**
11. Jorge Hernandez, inf, Laredo (Texas) JC
12. Gary Murdock, lhp, CC of Morris (N.J.)
13. Paul Garrison, rhp, Los Medanos (Calif.) JC
14. Aaron Rico, rhp, Southwestern (Calif.) JC
15. David Haggard, rhp, Los Angeles Harbor JC
16. Larry Oedenwalt, inf, San Diego Mesa JC
17. Kevin Barker, rhp, Contra Costa (Calif.) JC
18. Frank Isbell, rhp, Alvin (Texas) CC
19. Jeff Massicotte, rhp, Florida JC
20. Gerald Cifarelli, c, Diablo Valley (Calif.) JC
21. Samuel Coston, of, Los Medanos (Calif.) JC
22. Thomas Siau, inf, Texarkana (Texas) CC

January—Secondary Phase (20)

1. Scott Carter, rhp, Manatee (Fla.) JC
2. Mark Potoshnik, rhp, Taft (Calif.) JC
3. Dewitt Cotton, of, West Los Angeles JC
4. Mike Prior, of, Chicago Heights, Ill.

June—Regular Phase (13)

1. **Ryan Bowen, rhp, Hanford (Calif.) HS**
2. **Mike Hook, lhp, Santana HS, Santee, Calif.**
3. **Karl Rhodes, of, Western Hills HS, Cincinnati**
4. **Fred Costello, rhp, Oceana HS, San Bruno, Calif.**
5. **Dave Rohde, ss, Arizona**
6. **Richard Simon, rhp, St. Francis (N.Y.)**
7. **Gary Cooper, of, Brigham Young**
8. **Kevin Hancock, of, Mira Mesa HS, San Diego**
9. **Rusty Kryzanowski, 3b, Wisconsin-Oshkosh**
10. **Mike Beams, of/ss, Lake Brantley HS, Altamonte Springs, Fla.**
11. **Matthew Stennett, of, Pittsburgh**
12. **Trenidad Hubbard, 2b, Southern**
13. **Guy Normand, lhp, Washington State**
14. **Daven Bond, rhp, Mesa (Colo.)**
15. **Kevin Wasilewski, rhp, Stetson**
16. **Brian Meyer, rhp, Rollins (Fla.)**
17. **Mike Boagni, of, Washington HS, Los Angeles**
18. **Ed Whited, 3b, Rider**
19. **James Olson, rhp, Eastern Washington**
20. **Carl Grovom, lhp, U.S. International (Nairobi)**
21. Brian Fleury, c, Morristown HS, Morris Plains, N.J.
22. **Tom Temrowski, inf, Florida Southern**
23. **Joe Estes, lhp, Arizona**
24. **John Murphy, c, Missouri-St. Louis**
25. Steve Stowell, lhp, UCLA
26. Toncie Reed, of, Pleasant Grove HS, Texarkana, Texas
27. Randy Pryor, rhp, Pearland (Texas) HS
28. **Damon Brooks, of, Dayton**
29. Bob Suggs, rhp, Hovatio (Ark.) HS
30. Steven Glass, ss/3b, San Francisco State
31. Jay Garrett, of, Banning HS, Carson, Calif.
32. Gary Cameron, lhp/1b, Mountain View HS, Orem, Utah
33. **Andy Ruscitto, c, Valencia HS, Placentia, Calif.**

34. **Eric Anthony, of, Sharpstown HS, Houston**
35. Don Young, of, Mount Miguel HS, Spring Valley, Calif.
36. Jose Fernandez, c, Palm Beach (Fla.) JC
37. Chris Basso, c, Taravella HS, Coral Springs, Fla.
38. John Jackson, inf, Apopka HS, Tangerine, Fla.
39. Paul Anderson, ss, Morse HS, San Diego
40. Brian Thornbury, inf, Southwestern (Calif.) JC
41. Eric Bridge, rhp, San Diego CC
42. George Fowler, 3b, Bakersfield (Calif.) JC
43. Tim MacNeil, rhp, Esperanza HS, Yorba Linda, Calif.
44. Richard Lodding, rhp, Western HS, Cypress, Calif.
45. Jose Lleneras, rhp, Patrick Henry HS, San Diego
46. Mike Contreras, rhp, Sweetwater HS, National City, Calif.
47. Joe Bellezzo, c, Poway (Calif.) HS
48. Jason Brosnan, lhp, Arroyo HS, San Leandro, Calif.

June—Secondary Phase (5)

1. **Lou Frazier, of, Scottsdale (Ariz.) CC**
2. Craig Wilson, c, Cerritos (Calif.) JC
3. Scott Carter, rhp, Manatee (Fla.) JC
4. Joe Ortiz, of, Scottsdale (Ariz.) CC
5. Brian Bennett, c, JC of the Desert (Calif.)
6. David Haggard, rhp, Los Angeles Harbor JC
7. Mike Peters, rhp, Florida CC
8. Mike Maksudian, of, CC of Morris (N.J.)
9. Mike Pomeranz, lhp, Miami-Dade North CC
10. Julio Morales, 1b, Nassau (N.Y.) CC
11. Tim Lichty, of, Fresno State

KANSAS CITY ROYALS

January—Regular Phase (23)

1. Kevin Moynagh, rhp, Shelton State (Ala.) JC
2. Kevin Knutson, 1b, Big Bend (Wash.) CC
3. **Rafael Jackson, of, Miami-Dade North CC**
4. John Buss, lhp, Triton (Ill.) JC
5. Brian Bennett, c, JC of the Desert (Calif.)
6. **Eugenio Acevedo, rhp, Queensborough (N.Y.) CC**
7. Steve Michael, of, Big Bend (Wash.) CC
8. Rex Barker, inf, Chabot (Calif.) JC
9. Eric Nelson, inf, Chabot (Calif.) JC
10. Ron Tyson, of, Southwestern (Calif.) JC
11. Frank Halcovich, rhp, JC of the Canyons (Calif.)
12. Rene Rivera, inf, Long Beach (Calif.) CC
13. Jerry Daniels, lhp, St. Louis CC-Meramec
14. Kevin Wrice, rhp, St. Louis CC-Forest Park
15. Lorenzo Lesky, inf, West Los Angeles JC
16. Anthony Peterson, rhp, San Joaquin Delta (Calif.) JC
17. **Brian Meyers, rhp, Essex (Md.) CC**
18. Jon Seise, lhp, Essex (Md.) CC
19. John Horsey, lhp, Essex (Md.) CC
20. Jim Hoos, of, Essex (Md.) CC

January—Secondary Phase (9)

1. **Sean Berry, inf, Torrance, Calif.**
2. Carl Shaw, rhp, Bellevue (Wash.) CC

June—Regular Phase (24)

1. **Tony Clements, ss, Don Lugo HS, Chino, Calif.**
2. **Darryl Robinson, of, Whitney Young HS, Chicago**
3. **Harvey Pulliam, ss, McAteer HS, San Francisco**
4. **Bo Jackson, of, Auburn**
5. **Pat Bailey, c, Alabama**
6. **Tom Gordon, rhp, Avon Park (Fla.) HS**
7. **Rob Wolkoys, ss, Chapman (Calif.)**
8. **Mike Oglesbee, 1b, Nevada-Las Vegas**
9. Paul Murphy, 3b, Delaware
10. **Mike Tresemer, rhp, UC Santa Barbara**
11. **Brannon Champagne, rhp, Illinois**
12. **Luke Nocas, rhp, Santa Ynez HS, Solvang, Calif.**
13. **Gary Blouin, rhp, Washington**
14. **Pete Capello, ss, Pace (N.Y.)**
15. **Ben Lee, lhp, Gulfport (Miss.) HS**
16. **Greg Hibbard, lhp, Alabama**
17. **Dennis Moeller, lhp, Los Angeles Valley JC**
18. **Tim Odom, rhp/1b, Hattiesburg (Miss.) HS**
19. Rocky Ynclan, rhp, Tulare (Calif.) Union HS
20. **Anthony Snypes, of, Sullivan East HS, Bristol, Tenn.**
21. Mike Skaggs, of, Henderson County (Ky.) HS
22. **George Jones, rhp, Tennessee Tech**
23. **Tim Goff, c, Middle Tennessee State**
24. **Michael Davis, c, Lake Brantley HS, Longwood, Fla.**
25. Charles Scales, of, Pittsburgh
26. **John Joslyn, 1b, UCLA**
27. Torey Lovullo, 2b, UCLA
28. Miles Bowman, of, Crenshaw HS, Los Angeles
29. **Peter Alborano, of, Brooklyn (N.Y.)**
30. **John Larios, of, Fresno State**
31. Chris Martin, ss, Hamilton HS, Los Angeles
32. David Howard, of, Manatee (Fla.) JC
33. Tom Urbani, 1b, Harbor HS, Santa Cruz, Calif.
34. Pat Fetty, rhp, Soquel HS, Santa Cruz, Calif.
35. Raymond Sanders, of, Skyline HS, West Pittsburg, Calif.
36. Brad Davis, of, Morningside HS, Inglewood, Calif.
37. Chris Schaefer, rhp, Mater Dei HS, Evansville, Ind.
38. Tony Anderson, c, Tuscaloosa County HS, Northport, Ala.
39. Matthew Gillis, c, Orange Coast (Calif.) JC
40. Javier Fimbres, c, Bell Gardens (Calif.) HS
41. Marvin Fight, of, Southwest HS, Kansas City, Mo.
42. Chris Airey, c, Dulaney HS, Monkton, Md.
43. Steven Day, of/rhp, Brooklyn Park HS, Baltimore
44. Richard Pfaff, 1b/of, Archbishop Curley HS, Baltimore

June—Secondary Phase (10)

1. Tim Herrmann, rhp, Blinn (Texas) JC
2. **Mike Butcher, rhp, Northeastern Oklahoma A&M JC**
3. **Antoine Pickett, inf, Contra Costa (Calif.) JC**
4. **James Willis, of, Cumberlands (Ky.) JC**
5. **Charles Mount, rhp, Northeastern Oklahoma A&M JC**
6. Rex Barker, inf, Chabot (Calif.) JC
7. Steve Cantu, lhp, San Jacinto (Texas) JC
8. Jeff Cesari, rhp, Taft (Calif.) JC
9. Bobby Jones, of, Sacramento CC
10. Mark Linden, inf, Bellevue (Wash.) CC

LOS ANGELES DODGERS

January—Regular Phase (20)

1. **Tim K. Anderson, inf, Sacramento CC**
2. Brian Flanagan, of, Citrus (Calif.) JC
3. **Wes Langley, of, Linn-Benton (Ore.) CC**
4. **Adam Brown, c, DeKalb (Ga.) JC**
5. Stephen Carmarda, rhp, San Jacinto (Texas) JC
6. Darren Lewis, of, Chabot (Calif.) JC
7. Mike Bundeson, lhp, Mott (Mich.) CC
8. Keith Hayes, c, Los Angeles CC
9. Brad Freking, lhp, Harper (Ill.) JC
10. Ranfred Johnson, rhp, Los Angeles Harbor JC
11. Mike Bledsoe, lhp, JC of the Sequoias (Calif.)
12. Eliezer Quinones, of, Gulf Coast (Fla.) CC
13. Mike Ripplinger, of, Taft (Calif.) JC
14. Tim M. Anderson, of, DeKalb (Ga.) JC
15. David Downey, of, Muscatine (Iowa) CC
16. David Ray, c, DeKalb (Ga.) JC

January—Secondary Phase (12)

1. **Jim Kating, c, Triton (Ill.) JC**
2. Blake Butterfield, rhp, Mount San Antonio (Calif.) JC
3. Pedro Borbon, lhp, Ranger (Texas) JC

June—Regular Phase (19)

1. **Mike White, of, Loudon (Tenn.) HS**
2. **Dave Hansen, ss, Rowland HS, Rowland Heights, Calif.**
3. **Mike Munoz, lhp, Cal Poly Pomona**
4. **Mike Pitz, rhp, Pacific**
5. **Kevin Campbell, rhp, Arkansas**
6. **Mike Siler, rhp, Portland**
7. **Dan Henley, inf, Southern California**
8. **Joe Kesselmark, of, Pace (N.Y.)**
9. **Henry Goshay, of, Pacelli HS, Phenix City, Ala.**
10. **Ken Riensche, rhp, St. Mary's**
11. **Kenny King, rhp, UNC Wilmington**

12. **Daniel Pena, lhp, Texas**
13. **Chris Cerny, lhp, New Mexico**
14. **Danny Montgomery, 2b, UNC Charlotte**
15. Ted Dyson, 1b, Arizona State
16. **Anthony Ciccone, 2b, Sonoma State (Calif.)**
17. **Eric Mangham, of, Florida State**
18. Clifton Smith, 3b, South San Francisco HS
19. **Billy Brooks, rhp, Georgia Southern**
20. **Stephen Wood, rhp, St. Mary's**
21. **Jeff D. Brown, of, Brigham Young**
22. **Donnie Poteet, 3b, Augusta (Ga.)**
23. **John Knapp, 3b, Iowa**
24. **Billy Bartels, rhp, Fresno State**
25. Tim Brown, of, Monroe (Ga.) HS
26. Paul Quantrill, rhp, Okemos (Mich.) HS
27. **Greg Hornsby, of, King HS, Tampa**
28. Scott Longaker, rhp, Petaluma (Calif.) HS
29. David Proctor, rhp, Topeka (Kan.) HS
30. Craig Stiveson, rhp, Marin Catholic HS, Novato, Calif.
31. Chris Dominque, rhp, Westchester HS, Los Angeles
32. Greg Reid, of, Poly HS, Long Beach

June—Secondary Phase (11)

1. Carlos Carrasco, rhp, Gavilan (Calif.) JC
2. Wade Taylor, rhp, Jefferson Davis (Ala.) JC
3. **Miguel Ferradas, c, Miami-Dade South CC**
4. Adrian Adkins, c, Middle Georgia JC
5. Mike Bundeson, lhp, Mott (Mich.) CC
6. Keith Hayes, c, Los Angeles CC
7. **Andrew Bourne, of, Citrus (Calif.) JC**

MILWAUKEE BREWERS

January—Regular Phase (5)

1. **Edwin Anderson, rhp, DeKalb Central (Ga.) JC**
2. Reid Gunter, rhp, Sacramento CC
3. John Briscoe, rhp, Texarkana (Texas) CC
4. Allen Rutledge, inf, Hillsborough (Fla.) CC
5. **Terry Brown, inf, Hillsborough (Fla.) CC**
6. **Jose Samaniego, inf, South Mountain (Ariz.) CC**
7. Byron Williams, of, Glendale (Calif.) JC
8. **Rob Sobczyk, c, Madison Area Tech (Wis.) JC**
9. **William Rabb, of, San Joaquin Delta (Calif.) JC**
10. Rich Bielski, inf, Miami-Dade North CC
11. Mike Kelly, of, St. Petersburg (Fla.) JC
12. Pat Mackey, inf, Central Arizona JC
13. James Matas, rhp, Modesto (Calif.) JC
14. Ed Beuerlein, c, Scottsdale (Ariz.) CC
15. Miguel Ferradas, c, Miami-Dade South CC
16. Clyde Keller, rhp, Sacramento CC

January—Secondary Phase (17)

1. Dan Eskew, rhp, Indian River (Fla.) CC
2. Don Arnold, lhp, Taft (Calif.) JC
3. Bruce Wegman, rhp, Central Arizona JC

June—Regular Phase (6)

1. **Gary Sheffield, ss, Hillsborough HS, Tampa**
2. **Mark Ambrose, rhp, Vanderbilt**
3. **Tim McIntosh, c/of, Minnesota**
4. **David Woodhouse, rhp, Bonita Vista HS, Chula Vista, Calif.**
5. **Brian Stone, rhp, New Haven (Conn.)**
6. **George Canale, 1b, Virginia Tech**
7. **Jamie Cangemi, rhp, Ithaca (N.Y.)**
8. **Bryan Foster, ss, North Central HS, Indianapolis**
9. **Keith Fleming, rhp, Georgia Tech**
10. Buddy Jenkins, lhp, Starmount HS, Hamptonville, N.C.
11. **Darryl Hamilton, of, Nicholls State**
12. **A.J. Richardson, 3b, Eastern Michigan**
13. Chuck Baldwin, 1b, Clemson
14. **Billy Walker, 1b, Connell (Wash.) HS**
15. **Shane Ogawa, rhp, Hilo (Hawaii) HS**
16. **David Carley, rhp, Arizona**
17. **Joey Seaver, lhp, Tennessee**
18. **James Falzone, c, Cumberlands (Ky.) JC**
19. Jeff Goodale, 3b, Palm Springs (Calif.) HS
20. **Robert Jones, of, Southern Illinois**
21. Scott Drury, c, JC of the Canyons (Calif.)
22. Greg Brown, ss, Taravella HS, Coral Springs, Fla.
23. Stephen Condon, rhp, Davidson
24. Bob Vancho, rhp, Trumbull (Conn.) HS
25. Mitch McDowell, of, Madison Area Tech (Wis.) JC
26. Charlie Montoyo, 3b, Louisiana Tech
27. Steve Cole, lhp, Englewood HS, Jacksonville, Fla.
28. Joe Grahe, rhp, Palm Beach (Fla.) JC
29. **Francis Boreffi, of, Union Endicott (N.Y.) HS**
30. **Troy Holland, of, Malabar HS, Mansfield, Ohio**
31. **Chris Cassels, of, Gonzalez Tate HS, Pensacola, Fla.**
32. Todd Azar, of, Old Dominion
33. Craig Stefan, of, North Central (Ill.)
34. Dennis Tafoya, rhp, Yuba (Calif.) CC
35. Mark Rubini, of, Delaware
36. Jarrod Dossen, rhp, Wayne HS, Fort Wayne, Ind.
37. Michael Hawkins, of, Glenelg HS, Baltimore
38. Calvin Duncan, rhp, Columbus (Ga.)

June—Secondary Phase (4)

1. **Greg Vaughn, of, Miami**
2. **Brian Drahman, rhp, Miami-Dade South CC**
3. David Taylor, rhp, McLennan (Texas) CC
4. Fred Riscen, lhp, Los Angeles Pierce JC
5. Jack Hollis, of, Los Angeles Harbor JC
6. Robert Chadwick, lhp, Arkansas
7. Scott Boggs, inf, Columbia State (Tenn.) CC
8. John Kuehl, inf, Scottsdale (Ariz.) CC
9. Ed Beuerlein, c, Scottsdale (Ariz.) CC

MINNESOTA TWINS

January—Regular Phase (9)

1. **Jarvis Brown, inf, Triton (Ill.) JC**
2. **Larry Johnson, inf, Taft (Calif.) JC**
3. Mike Pomeranz, lhp, Miami-Dade North CC
4. **Mike Dyer, rhp, Citrus (Calif.) JC**
5. John Grove, rhp, Ventura (Calif.) JC
6. Brent Hahn, c, San Jose, Calif.
7. **Robert Hernandez, lhp, Fullerton (Calif.) JC**
8. Mike Schwabe, rhp, Rancho Santiago (Calif.) JC
9. Craig Stamey, c, Spartanburg Methodist (S.C.) JC
10. **Ken Davis, of, San Bernardino Valley (Calif.) JC**
11. Clint Thompson, c, Gulf Coast (Fla.) CC
12. Wade Clark, rhp, Los Angeles CC
13. Ruben Gonzalez, 1b, Rancho Santiago (Calif.) JC
14. **Jorge Hoffner, rhp, Broward (Fla.) CC**

January—Secondary Phase (1)

1. **Toby Nivens, rhp, San Jacinto (Texas) JC**
2. Antoine Pickett, inf, Contra Costa (Calif.) JC

June—Regular Phase (10)

1. **Derek Parks, rhp/c, Montclair HS, Upland, Calif.**
2. **Jeff Bronkey, rhp, Oklahoma State**
3. **Fred White, rhp, Jordan HS, Long Beach**
4. **Park Pittman, rhp, Ohio State**
5. **Chris Martin, of, Nogales (Calif.) HS**
6. **Mike Randle, of, San Jacinto (Texas) JC**
7. **Bryan Hickerson, lhp, Minnesota**
8. **John Eccles, c, Cal State Fullerton**
9. Jeff Lynch, rhp, Tehachapi (Calif.) HS
10. **Jeff Reboulet, ss, Louisiana State**
11. Todd Wilson, lhp/1b, Billings (Mont.) HS
12. Paul DeJaynes, rhp, Bradley
13. **Scott Leius, ss, Concordia (N.Y.)**
14. **David Jacas, of, San Diego**
15. **David Dasch, ss, Ithaca (N.Y.)**
16. **Ira Goldstein, c, New York Tech**
17. **Kenny Morgan, of, UNC Charlotte**
18. **Dana Heinle, rhp, UC Riverside**
19. Kurt Olson, 1b/of, Hinsdale Central HS, Clarendon Hills, Ill.
20. **Kendall Snyder, 1b/3b, Eastern Illinois**
21. **Shawn Courtney, 2b, Northern Colorado**
22. Sam Bland, c, Fenger HS, Chicago

23. **Mike Lexa, 2b, Indiana State**
24. Michael Gianfrancesco, 3b, C.W. Post (N.Y.)
25. **Michael Stolnick, of, Wisconsin-Parkside**
26. Michael Stewart, of, Fresno State
27. Mike Parks, rhp, Miami-Dade North CC
28. **Vern Hildebrandt, ss, Gahr HS, Cerritos, Calif.**
29. **Mike Baer, inf, California**
30. **Burt Beattie, c, Nebraska**

June—Secondary Phase (25)

1. James McClellan, rhp, Ohlone (Calif.) JC
2. Eric Albright, c, Los Angeles Harbor JC
3. Mike Schwabe, rhp, Rancho Santiago (Calif.) JC
4. Scott Hutson, rhp, Mesa (Ariz.) CC

MONTREAL EXPOS

January—Regular Phase (16)

1. **Randy Bouman, rhp, Cypress (Calif.) JC**
2. Mark Helms, c, Panola (Texas) JC
3. Scott McMullen, rhp, Sacramento CC
4. Roy Westbrook, c, Angelina (Texas) JC
5. Brian Branigan, rhp, CC of Morris (N.J.)
6. Brent Saclett, rhp, JC of the Siskiyous (Calif.)
7. Willie Garza, rhp, Laney (Calif.) JC
8. **Kody Duey, 1b, Bakersfield (Calif.) JC**
9. Leo Clouser, rhp, Los Angeles Pierce JC
10. Steve Gray, inf, Cuesta (Calif.) JC
11. Fred Riscen, lhp, Los Angeles Pierce JC
12. James McClellan, rhp, Ohlone (Calif.) JC
13. Fred Schweizer, rhp, Chabot (Calif.) JC
14. Guillermo Herrera, rhp, Laney (Calif.) JC
15. Joe Leonguerrero, rhp, Sacramento CC
16. Chris Morocco, 1b, Middle Georgia JC
17. Brian Lutes, rhp, Bakersfield (Calif.) JC
18. Orlando Cepeda, rhp, JC of the Canyons (Calif.)
19. Steve Eaton, inf, DeKalb Central (Ga.) JC
20. Greg Adelsbach, inf, JC of Southern Idaho
21. Lance Dorsey, ss, CC of Morris (N.J.)
22. Jerald Frost, inf, Ocean County (N.J.) JC
23. **Greg Faught, of, Dallas Baptist**

January—Secondary Phase (8)

1. Scott Ruskin, of, Florida
2. Bobby Jones, of, Sacramento CC
3. Andy Berg, lhp, Sacramento CC

June—Regular Phase (15)

1. **Kevin Dean, of, Hogan HS, Vallejo, Calif.**
2. **Jeff Tabaka, lhp, Kent State**
3. **Tony Welborn, of/rhp, Appalachian State**
4. **Kent Bottenfield, rhp, Madison HS, Portland, Ore.**
5. **Gene Harris, rhp, Tulane**
6. **John Howes, lhp, Indiana State**
7. **Doug Duke, c, Alabama**
8. **Mike Dull, 3b, South Alabama**
9. **Mark Hardy, of, UC Riverside**
10. **Mike Blowers, ss, Washington**
11. **Paul Frye, of, Indiana State**
12. **Rob Leary, c, Louisiana State**
13. **Manuel Alvarez, of, George Washington HS, New York**
14. **Scott Clemo, inf, Florida**
15. **Joe Sims, of, Northeast Louisiana**
16. **Russ Schueler, ss, Kentucky**
17. Reggie Hubbard, ss, Hogan HS, Vallejo, Calif.
18. **Dave Morrow, c, Brigham Young**
19. Chris Dorn, rhp, Cypress Creek HS, Houston
20. **Scott McHugh, 3b, Central Florida**
21. **Don Burke, of, Florida Southern**
22. **Kevin Finigan, of, Claremont-Mudd (Calif.)**
23. **Randy Maville, c, Apollo HS, Glendale, Ariz.**
24. **Bobby Gaylor, inf, Tennessee**
25. **Steven King, rhp, Mississippi State**
26. **Jim McDonald, rhp, Arizona**
27. **Jeff Wedvick, c, Iowa State**
28. **Albert Foster, ss, San Dia HS, Albuquerque, N.M.**
29. **Robert Simmons, 1b, Rollins (Fla.)**
30. **Brad Brian, c, Eastern Kentucky**
31. **John Marino, lhp, Citrus (Calif.) JC**
32. **Dean Rockweiler, lhp, Wisconsin-La Crosse**
33. Vince Fultz, rhp, Salinas (Calif.) HS
34. Johnny Johnson, of, Santa Cruz (Calif.) HS
35. Mike Briley, inf, Cypress Creek HS, Houston
36. Brian Johnson, c, Skyline HS, Oakland, Calif.
37. Mike Funk, of, Fries (Va.) HS

June—Secondary Phase (15)

1. Jeff Oswalt, lhp, San Diego Mesa JC
2. Roy Westbrook, c, Angelina (Texas) JC

NEW YORK METS

January—Regular Phase (22)

1. Mike Thompson, rhp, Mira Costa (Calif.) JC
2. Carl Jones-Pointer, of, Mount San Antonio (Calif.) JC
3. **Ronald Height, inf, Citrus (Calif.) JC**
4. **Marvin Newton, rhp, Pensacola (Fla.) JC**
5. Thomas Henderson, c, Citrus (Calif.) JC
6. **Terry McDaniel, of, Kansas City, Mo.**
7. Kevin Ponder, rhp, Central Florida JC
8. William Norwood, rhp, Jefferson Davis (Ala.) JC
9. Jeff George, rhp, Waubonsee (Ill.) JC
10. Dan Rohrmeier, inf, Miami-Dade North CC
11. Gordon Farmer, rhp, JC of the Siskiyous (Calif.)
12. Dean Hartgraves, lhp, JC of the Siskiyous (Calif.)
13. **Mark DiVincenzo, inf, Mount San Antonio (Calif.) JC**

January—Secondary Phase (18)

1. **Robert Hernandez, lhp, Los Angeles Valley JC**
2. Gerald Higby, lhp, Modesto (Calif.) JC

June—Regular Phase (21)

1. **Lee May Jr., of/1b, Purcell Marion HS, Cincinnati**
2. **Fritz Polka, c, Mankato State (Minn.)**
3. **James Morrisette, of, Fairhope (Ala.) HS**
4. **Kip Gross, rhp, Nebraska**
5. Eddie Zosky, ss, St. Paul HS, Whittier, Calif.
6. **Steve Piskor, c, Plano (Texas) East HS**
7. **Richard Brown, rhp, William Paterson (N.J.)**
8. **Pete Bauer, rhp, St. Paul, Minn.**
9. Rob Fitzpatrick, c, Midland Park (N.J.) HS
10. **Curtis Pride, of, Kennedy HS, Silver Springs, Md.**
11. **Jaime Roseboro, of, Los Angeles CC**
12. **David Crowson, rhp, Brenham (Texas) HS**
13. Tom Peters, rhp, Santa Monica (Calif.) HS
14. **Jason Woods, c, West Orange (Texas) Stark HS**
15. **Mark Fiedler, lhp, St. Thomas (Minn.)**
16. **Archie Corbin, rhp, Charlton Pollar HS, Beaumont, Texas**
17. Darryl Fry, lhp, Texas A&M
18. **Richard Durant, rhp, Huntingdon**
19. Michael Hoog, 1b, Niwot HS, Longmont, Colo.
20. **Andrew Taylor, rhp, Adelphi (N.Y.)**
21. **Richard Lundahl, ss/3b, Southern Utah State**
22. Kevin Miller, c, San Joaquin Delta (Calif.) JC
23. **Bill Robinson, rhp, North Carolina**
24. Titi Roche, of, Miami Lakes HS, Hialeah, Fla.
25. John Thoden, rhp, Patchogue-Medford (N.Y.) HS
26. Cal Eldred, rhp, Urbana Community HS, Center Point, Iowa
27. John Olerud, 1b/lhp, Interlake HS, Bellevue, Wash.
28. **Robert Olah, 1b, Notre Dame HS, Bridgeport, Conn.**
29. James Sloan, lhp, Casa Roble HS, Citrus Heights, Calif.
30. Chris Stiltner, c, Vanden HS, Travis AFB, Calif.
31. Ever Magallanes, ss, Texas A&M
32. Mike Richardson, inf, Glendale (Calif.) JC
33. Anthony Coleman, rhp, Leflore HS, Mobile, Ala.
34. **Lee Johnson, rhp, Beaumont HS, St. Louis**
35. **Cedric Hawkins, ss, Geneva**
36. Scott Erickson, rhp, Homestead HS, Sunnyvale, Calif.
37. Ken Todd, of, Santana HS, Santee, Calif.
38. **Rodney Bond, 1b/of, Dixie Hollins HS, Pinellas Park, Fla.**
39. Todd Hawkins, c, Baylor
40. Brian Beal, c, Harrisburg (Ill.) HS

41. Todd Jones, rhp, Osborne HS, Marietta, Ga.
42. Robert Sneed, rhp, Lassen (Calif.) JC
43. Phil Angelos, rhp, Waukegan (Ill.) HS

June—Secondary Phase (1)

1. **Alex Jimenez, 1b, Miami-Dade South CC**
2. **Rocky Elli, lhp, Kishwaukee (Ill.) JC**
3. **John Wenrich, rhp, Long Beach (Calif.) CC**
4. **Scott Henion, rhp, Crowder (Mo.) JC**
5. Thomas Henderson, c, Citrus (Calif.) JC
6. **Tom Fine, rhp, Northeastern Oklahoma A&M JC**
7. **Kevin Ponder, rhp, Central Florida JC**
8. Jerry Nielsen, lhp, Sacramento CC
9. **Jeff George, rhp, Waubonsee (Ill.) JC**

NEW YORK YANKEES

January—Regular Phase (25)

1. Jay Makemson, rhp, Orange Coast (Calif.) JC
2. **Dean Wilkins, rhp, San Diego Mesa JC**
3. **Luc Berube, inf, Cochise County (Ariz.) CC**
4. Scott Miller, inf, Manatee (Fla.) JC
5. Reggie Glover, inf, Contra Costa (Calif.) JC
6. **Darrin Chapin, rhp, Cuyahoga (Ohio) CC**
7. Shawn Jenkins, 1b, Chabot (Calif.) JC
8. Gary Brown, 1b, Sacramento CC
9. Jeff Jones, of, San Joaquin Delta (Calif.) JC
10. Greg Roth, inf, Cochise County (Ariz.) CC
11. Pete Robertson, of, San Jose (Calif.) CC
12. Andrew Nieman, rhp, Sinclair (Ohio) CC
13. Matt Gruver, of, Sacramento CC

January—Secondary Phase (13)

1. **Mark Manering, 1b, Miami (Ohio)**
2. Jeff Oswalt, lhp, San Diego Mesa JC

June—Regular Phase (25)

1. (Pick to Angels as compensation for Type A free agent Al Holland)
2. **Rich Scheid, lhp, Seton Hall**
3. **Tim Layana, rhp, Loyola Marymount**
4. **Steve Rosenberg, lhp, Florida**
5. **John Ramos, c, Stanford**
6. **Tim Becker, ss, South Alabama**
7. **Casey Close, of, Michigan**
8. **Hal Morris III, 1b, Michigan**
9. **Jerry Rub, rhp, South Alabama**
10. **Ralph Kraus, of, Arkansas**
11. **Chris Byrnes, lhp, Stetson**
12. **Andy Stankiewicz, 2b, Pepperdine**
13. **Bill Voeltz, lhp, St. Thomas (Fla.)**
14. **Scott Kamieniecki, rhp, Michigan**
15. **Steve Adkins, lhp, Pennsylvania**
16. **Dana Ridenour, rhp, UCLA**
17. **Dan Arendas, of, Princeton**
18. **Turner Ward, of, South Alabama**
19. Darius Gash, of, Roane State (Tenn.) CC
20. **Kevin Crofton, c, Hillsborough (Fla.) CC**
21. **Mark Rose, rhp, South Florida**
22. **Kevin Maas, 1b, California**
23. **Robert Hunter, of, Dunellan (Fla.) HS**
24. **Robert Ryan, rhp, Knox (Ill.)**
25. Dana Leibovitz, 1b, United Township HS, Silvis, Ill.
26. Scott Livingstone, 3b, Texas A&M
27. Erik Johnson, ss, UC Santa Barbara
28. Troy Paulsen, ss, La Quinta HS, Fountain Valley, Calif.
29. Steven Livesey, 3b, Springstead HS, Spring Hill, Fla.
30. Greg Torborg, of, Springfield HS, Mountainside, N.J.

June—Secondary Phase (18)

1. **Jay Makemson, rhp, Orange Coast (Calif.) JC**
2. Rich Bielski, inf, Miami-Dade North CC
3. William Norwood, rhp, Jefferson Davis (Ala.) JC
4. Scott Miller, inf, Manatee (Fla.) JC
5. Brad Herrel, rhp, Northeastern Oklahoma A&M JC
6. Kevin Moynagh, rhp, Shelton State (Ala.) JC

OAKLAND ATHLETICS

January—Regular Phase (11)

1. Tim Herrmann, rhp, Blinn (Texas) JC
2. Jeff Kipila, rhp, Brookdale (N.J.) CC
3. Scott Hutson, rhp, Mesa (Ariz.) CC
4. **Dave Veres, rhp, Mount Hood (Ore.) CC**
5. **Eric Albright, c, Los Angeles Angeles Harbor JC**
6. Anthony Toney, of, Orange Coast (Calif.) JC
7. Mark Stancel, rhp, Hinds (Miss.) JC
8. Greg Mannion, of, Cerritos (Calif.) JC
9. Alex Jimenez, 1b, Miami-Dade South CC
10. David Cantrell, rhp, West Los Angeles JC
11. Paul Ellison, c, Orange Coast (Calif.) JC
12. Steven Pratt, c, Saddleback (Calif.) CC
13. William Kehoe, c, Scottsdale (Ariz.) CC
14. Joe Ortiz, of, Scottsdale (Ariz.) CC

January—Secondary Phase (21)

1. **Pat Gilbert, of, Columbia State (Tenn.) CC**
2. Thomas Gallagher, lhp, Sacramento CC

June—Regular Phase (12)

1. **Scott Hemond, c, South Florida**
2. **Kevin Tapani, rhp, Central Michigan**
3. **Darrin Duffy, ss, Grand Canyon (Ariz.)**
4. **David Gavin, of, Central State (Ohio)**
5. **Jeff Glover, rhp, Tennessee**
6. Harold Milliken, rhp, Key West (Fla.) HS
7. Ken Bowen, ss, Oregon State
8. **Drew Stratton, of, Princeton**
9. **Vince Teixeira, 3b, UC Santa Barbara**
10. **Lance Blankenship, 3b, California**
11. **Todd Hartley, of/rhp, Fort Hays State**
12. **Robbie Gilbert, rhp, Mississippi Valley State**
13. **Rod Beck, rhp, Grant HS, Van Nuys, Calif.**
14. **Mark Beavers, lhp, Brigham Young**
15. **Weston Weber, rhp, Mankato State (Minn.)**
16. **Jim Carroll, rhp, Arizona**
17. **Kevin Kunkel, rhp, Stanford**
18. **Dann Howitt, of, Cal State Fullerton**
19. **Billy Reynolds, c, Maine**
20. **Jeff Kopyta, rhp, Creighton**
21. **Jamie Reiser, 2b, Bowling Green State**
22. **Glenn Hoffinger, of, Portland**
23. **Kevin Johnson, inf, California**
24. Anthony Johnson, c/ss, Lincoln HS, San Diego
25. **Larry Ritchey, rhp, Point Park (Pa.)**

June—Secondary Phase (22)

1. Bret Barberie, inf, Cerritos (Calif.) JC
2. Carlton Cochran, lhp, Central Arizona JC
3. Glenn Twardy, of, Cerritos (Calif.) JC

PHILADELPHIA PHILLIES

January—Regular Phase (8)

1. **Jessie Allison, rhp, Labette (Kan.) CC**
2. **Steve Scarsone, inf, Rancho Santiago (Calif.) JC**
3. Dale DeVaughan, rhp, Seminole State (Okla.) JC
4. Jonathan Dukes, rhp, Bacone (Okla.) JC
5. **Chuck Malone Jr., rhp, Three Rivers (Mo.) CC**
6. Charles Mount, rhp, Northeastern Oklahoma A&M JC
7. Rusty Richards, rhp, Austin (Texas) CC
8. Darryl Rowley, lhp, Northeastern Oklahoma A&M JC
9. Gregory Carter, rhp, Seminole State (Okla.) JC
10. Rodney Downey, rhp, McLennan (Texas) CC
11. Troy Garner, rhp, Delgado (La.) JC
12. Mike Peters, rhp, Florida CC
13. Joe Bourque, inf, San Jacinto (Texas) JC
14. Mike Seal, lhp, Delgado (La.) JC
15. Jimmy Wooly, rhp, Seminole State (Okla.) JC
16. Rodney Sitton, of, Connors State (Okla.) JC
17. Anthony Ward, lhp, Seminole State (Okla.) JC
18. Steve Barton, rhp, Connors State (Okla.) JC
19. Mickey House, of, Texarkana (Texas) CC

20. Anthony Miller, of, Aquinas (Tenn.) JC
21. Rob DeYoung, rhp, Fullerton (Calif.) JC
22. Jeff Gremillion, of, Blinn (Texas) JC
23. Todd Ashmore, inf, Carl Albert (Okla.) JC
24. **Joel Faulk, 3b, Merced (Calif.) JC**
25. Daryn Lansdell, rhp, Cochise County (Ariz.) CC
26. Roger Quillen, rhp, Merced (Calif.) JC
27. Dino Ebel, inf, San Bernardino Valley (Calif.) JC
28. Wendell Harris, of, Citrus (Calif.) JC
29. David Lozano, inf, Cerritos (Calif.) JC

January—Secondary Phase (24)

1. Blas Minor Jr., rhp, Merced (Calif.) JC
2. Alex Alvarez, c, Cypress (Calif.) JC

June—Regular Phase (7)

1. **Brad Brink, rhp, Southern California**
2. **Cliff Brantley, rhp, Port Richmond HS, Staten Island, N.Y.**
3. **Rod Robertson, ss, West Orange (Texas) Stark HS**
4. **Dave Brundage, of/lhp, Oregon State**
5. **Todd Crosby, 2b, Hawaii**
6. **Scott Ruckman, ss, Madera (Calif.) HS**
7. **Chris Bennett, rhp, Cal State Sacramento**
8. **Chuck McElroy, lhp, Lincoln HS, Port Arthur, Texas**
9. **Steve Blackshear, lhp, Rice**
10. Franklin Harris, c, Jackson State
11. Greg Hunter, ss, Juanita HS, Kirkland, Wash.
12. **Keith Greene, of, McNeese State**
13. **Harvey Brumfield, of, Fresno State**
14. **Doug Hodo, of, Texas**
15. **Darrell Coulter, rhp, North County HS, Bonne Terre, Mo.**
16. **Martin Foley, ss, Grambling State**
17. Erik Bennett, rhp, Eureka (Calif.) HS
18. Chuck Knoblauch, ss, Bellaire HS, Houston
19. Michael Gregory, rhp, Sarasota (Fla.) HS
20. Mitch DuPlantis, 3b, Vanderbilt HS, Houma, La.
21. **Chris Limbach, lhp, Warren Central HS, Indianapolis**
22. Jon Miller, rhp, McNeese State
23. **Olen Parker, 2b, Grambling State**
24. **Garland Kiser, lhp, Sullivan Central HS, Blountville, Tenn.**
25. **Leroy Vantress, ss, Shady Grove HS, Maringouin, La.**
26. Miah Bradbury, c, Mount Carmel HS, San Diego
27. **Glen Anderson, rhp, Southwestern Louisiana**
28. **Kenny Miller, c, McNeese State**
29. Kevin Van de Brake, ss, Selah (Wash.) HS
30. **Jeff Stark, of, Fresno State**
31. **Jeff Myaer, rhp, Utah**
32. **Mark Sims, lhp, Quachita HS, Monroe, La.**
33. **Tim Peek, rhp, Memorial HS, Elkhart, Ind.**
34. **Ken Jarner, ss, Santa Rosa (Calif.) JC**
35. Wayne Helm, rhp, Laguna Hills (Calif.) HS
36. Jesse Levis, c, Northeast HS, Philadelphia
37. **Steve Ochoa, of, San Jose State**
38. **Gary Berman, 1b/3b, UCLA**
39. Ernie Johnson, lhp, El Dorado (Mo.) Springs HS
40. **Donald Church, ss, East Tennessee State**

June—Secondary Phase (17)

1. Derek Lee, inf, Manatee (Fla.) JC
2. Mark Hudson, rhp, West Valley (Calif.) JC
3. Robert Jones, lhp, Citrus (Calif.) JC
4. Jorge Robles, inf, Miami-Dade New World Center CC

PITTSBURGH PIRATES

January—Regular Phase (2)

1. **Moises Alou, of, Canada (Calif.) JC**
2. **David Rose, rhp, South Georgia JC**
3. **Robert Harris, of, Sacramento CC**
4. Mike Khoury, inf, Brockton, Mass.
5. Michael Patrick, c, Seminole State (Okla.) JC
6. Darryl Knight, of, Seminole State (Okla.) JC
7. Peter Drevline, 1b, Kishwaukee (Ill.) JC
8. Adrian Adkins, c, Middle Georgia JC
9. **Rusty Crockett, inf, Seminole State (Okla.) JC**
10. **David Vasquez, of, San Jacinto (Texas) JC**
11. **Archi Cianfrocco, inf, Onondaga (N.Y.) JC**
12. Mark Dover, rhp, Gavilan (Calif.) JC
13. Tim Sinicki, rhp, Broome (N.Y.) CC
14. Brandon Montler, 1b, Colorado
15. Ray Washington, of, Philadelphia CC
16. James Webb, rhp, Allegheny (Pa.) CC
17. Norman Bromley, inf, Cecil (Md.) CC

January—Secondary Phase (10)

1. **Scott Runge, rhp, Sacramento CC**
2. Jason Bridges, 1b, McLennan (Texas) CC

June—Regular Phase (1)

1. **Jeff King, ss/3b, Arkansas**
2. **Mike Walker, rhp, Houston**
3. **Raymond Doss, rhp, Mount Vernon (Texas) HS**
4. **Joel Forrest, lhp, Mesa (Colo.)**
5. **Steve Moser, 2b, Nevada-Las Vegas**
6. Tom Goodwin, of, Central HS, Fresno, Calif.
7. **Bill Copp, lhp, Iowa State**
8. **Tony Longmire, of, Hogan HS, Vallejo, Calif.**
9. **Tim Vaughn, ss, Gonzaga**
10. **Stan Belinda, rhp, Allegheny (Pa.) CC**
11. **Keith Shepherd, rhp, Wabash (Ind.) HS**
12. **Dean Moran, 3b, Cumberland (Ky.)**
13. **Blane Lockley, of/1b, Northeast Louisiana**
14. **Brian Lipscomb, of, LaPorte HS, Kingsford Heights, Ind.**
15. **Tommy Shields, ss, Notre Dame**
16. **Randy Wilson, rhp, South Florida**
17. **Doug Fisher, 1b, Central Michigan**
18. Andre Redmond, of, Roosevelt HS, Seattle
19. **Al Quintana, ss, Northwestern**
20. **Ed Hartman, ss, Indiana (Pa.)**
21. **Jeff Gurtcheff, c, Iowa**
22. **Garland Slaughter, of, Culpepper HS, Reva, Va.**
23. **Peter Murphy, rhp/3b, Columbia**
24. Lonnie Walker, of, Lee (Texas) JC
25. **Jeff Banister, c/1b, Houston**
26. **Rick Reed, rhp, Marshall**
27. **Daryl Boyd, rhp, Florida**
28. Scott Barczi, c, Northwestern
29. Steve Culkar, rhp, Kentucky
30. **Tim Kirk, lhp, North Carolina**
31. Torre Bowen, ss, Mount Lebanon HS, Pittsburgh
32. **Ron Robicheaux, of, Southwestern Louisiana**
33. Mike Mordecai, ss, Hewitt Trussville HS, Birmingham
34. Michael Olen, c, Crestwood HS, Wapwallopen, Pa.

June—Secondary Phase (21)

1. Steve Michael, of, Big Bend (Wash.) CC
2. **Norm Bromley, inf, Cecil (Md.) CC**
3. **Scott Ruskin, of/lhp, Jacksonville, Fla.**
4. Archi Cianfrocco, inf, Onondaga (N.Y.) CC
5. James Webb, rhp, Allegheny (Pa.) CC

ST. LOUIS CARDINALS

January—Regular Phase (24)

1. **Charlie Barrs, inf, Florida CC**
2. Bret Barberie, inf, Cerritos (Calif.) JC
3. Robert Stiegele, inf, Brevard (Fla.) CC
4. Jack Hollis, of, Los Angeles Harbor JC
5. **Randy Butts, 1b, Hagerstown (Md.) JC**
6. Andrew Schreiver, rhp, Louisburg (N.C.) JC
7. **Michael Alvarez, of, Fullerton (Calif.) JC**
8. Michael Murrie, lhp, Southeastern Illinois JC
9. Baron Bower, c, Fresno (Calif.) CC
10. Joe Jones, of, San Diego CC
11. **Orlando Thomas, c, Aquinas (Tenn.) JC**

January—Secondary Phase (14)

1. Craig Wilson, c, Cerritos (Calif.) JC

June—Regular Phase (23)

1. **Luis Alicea, 2b, Florida State**
2. **Reed Olmstead, 1b/lhp, Blair HS, Pasadena, Calif.**

2\. **Todd Zeile, c, UCLA** (Supplemental pick—55th—for loss of

Type C free agent Ivan DeJesus)
3. **David Sala, lhp, Cincinnati**
4. Mark Guthrie, lhp, Louisiana State
5. **Bien Figueroa, ss, Florida State**
6. Mike Couture, c, Eastern Wayne HS, Goldsboro, N.C.
7. **Vince Kindred, of, Troy State**
8. **Rob Glisson, lhp, Chapman (Calif.)**
9. **Greg Smith, ss, Central State (Ohio)**
10. **Larry Carter, rhp, West Virginia State**
11. **Pat Hewes, c, Houston**
12. **Mike Perez, rhp, Troy State**
13. **Mark Behny, rhp, Wichita State**
14. **Mike Senne, of, Arizona**
15. **William Hershman, rhp, Clarion (Pa.)**
16. **Ted Parker, of, South Carolina-Aiken**
17. **Scott Hamilton, rhp, Oklahoma**
18. **Steve Meyer, 1b, Southwest Missouri State**
19. **Scott Lawrence, rhp, San Diego State**
20. **Ernie Radcliffe, 1b, Central State (Ohio)**
21. **Eddie Looper, 3b, Alabama**
22. **Stan Zaltsman, lhp, Oklahoma**
23. **Mark Grater, rhp, Florida International**
24. **Eric Hohn, lhp, Penn State**
25. **Bobby Nettles, rhp, Cal State Fullerton**
26. Andrew Casano, rhp, St. John's
27. **Ed Carter, of, Parker HS, Jacksonville, Fla.**
28. **Edward Lampe, of, Brentwood (N.Y.) HS**
29. **Tom Baine, of, UC Irvine**
30. **Steve Jeffers, 2b, Western Illinois**

June—Secondary Phase (19)
1. **Rick Christian, of, Hagerstown (Md.) JC**
2. Keith Kaub, 1b, Golden West (Calif.) JC
3. **Lonnie Maclin, of, St. Louis CC-Meramec**
4. Pete Kuld, c, JC of the Canyons (Calif.)

SAN DIEGO PADRES

January—Regular Phase (12)
1. **Doug Brocail, rhp, Lamar (Colo.) CC**
2. **Brian Wood, rhp, Middle Georgia JC**
3. John Patterson, ss, Central Arizona JC
4. **Warren Newson, of, Middle Georgia JC**
5. John Spinapont, rhp, Brookdale (N.J.) CC
6. Hector Cotto, of, Miami-Dade New World Center CC
7. James Matoska, inf, Brookdale (N.J.) CC
8. Vince Herring, lhp, Santa Rosa (Calif.) JC
9. Bob Ayrault, rhp, Moorpark (Calif.) JC
10. Ray Schuyler, of, CC of Morris (N.J.)

January—Secondary Phase (4)
1. **Brian Harrison, of, Ventura (Calif.) JC**
2. **Bob Lutticken, c, JC of San Mateo (Calif.)**

June—Regular Phase (11)
1. **Thomas Howard, of, Ball State**
2. **Will Taylor, of, Alexandria (La.) HS**
3. Joe Lewis, c, St. Amant (La.) HS
4. **Mike Young, lhp, Arizona**
5. **Craig Cooper, 1b, Georgia Southern**
6. **Jim Austin, rhp, Virginia Commonwealth**
7. **Carl Holmes, of, Magnolia HS, Anaheim**
8. **Tom LeVasseur, 3b, San Diego State**
9. **Mike King, c, Middletown South HS, Lincroft, N.J.**
10. **Paul Quinzer, rhp, Indiana State**
11. **Jimmy Dean, inf, Madison HS, San Diego**
12. **Jeff Yurtin, 3b, Louisiana State**
13. **Greg S. Harris, lhp, Gonzaga**
14. **Mark Sampson, lhp, California**
15. **Ron Moore, rhp, UC Riverside**
16. **Brian Brooks, lhp, Southern California**
17. Jeff Barns, ss, South Carolina
18. **Mike Basso, 3b, Houston**
19. **Tony Pellegrino, ss, St. John's**
20. Mike Grimes, rhp, Jesuit HS, Dallas
21. **Keith Harrison, of, Gahr HS, Cerritos, Calif.**
22. **Jim Navilliat, lhp, Providence**
23. Alan Zinter, c, Hanks HS, El Paso, Texas
24. Mark Walker, lhp, Bellarmine HS, Menlo Park, Calif.
25. Woody Smith, ss, Andrews (S.C.) HS
26. Charles Chauvin, c, Vallejo (Calif.) HS
27. **Terry McDevitt, ss, Eastern Illinois**

June—Secondary Phase (3)
1. **Pete Roberts, lhp, Alabama**
2. Mike Ross, ss/2b, Fresno CC

SAN FRANCISCO GIANTS

January—Regular Phase (4)
1. Mike Jones, rhp, Cosumnes River (Calif.) JC
2. **James Jones, inf, Linn-Benton (Ore.) CC**
3. Thayer Swain, of, San Jacinto (Texas) JC
4. **John Barry, inf, Agoura, Calif.**
5. Tom Fine, rhp, Northeastern Oklahoma A&M JC
6. **Jeff Hughes, of, Northridge, Calif.**
7. Mark Diefenderfer, rhp, Butte (Calif.) JC
8. James Gasser, rhp, Moorpark (Calif.) JC
9. John Cebuhar, lhp, Eastern Oklahoma JC
10. **Drew Richer, lhp, Los Angeles Valley JC**
11. Damon Tyson, inf, Los Angeles CC
12. Chris Chavez, lhp, Santa Monica (Calif.) JC
13. John Gleason, rhp, Moorpark (Calif.) JC

January—Secondary Phase (6)
1. **Paul McClellan, rhp, JC of San Mateo (Calif.)**
2. Jorge Robles, inf, Miami-Dade New World Center CC

June—Regular Phase (3)
1. **Matt Williams, 3b, Nevada-Las Vegas**
2. **Kirt Manwaring, c, Coastal Carolina**
3. Jack Armstrong, rhp, Rider
4. **Paul Meyers, of, Nebraska**
5. **Jim McNamara, c, North Carolina State**
6. **Tim McCoy, lhp, Oral Roberts**
7. **Greg Conner, of, Southern Mississippi**
8. **Gregg Ritchie, of, George Washington**
9. **Russ Swan, lhp, Texas A&M**
10. **Matt S. Williams, c, Corvallis (Ore.) HS**
11. **John Toal, 2b, Oklahoma**
12. Gordon Douglas, rhp, North Carolina
13. Chris Haslock, inf, Los Angeles Valley JC
14. **Dave Patterson, 1b, Arkansas**
15. **Kevin Redick, of, Westmont (Calif.)**
16. **Jim Pena, lhp, Cal State Dominguez Hills**
17. **Dee Dixon, of, Norfolk State (Va.)**
18. Lennie McGuire, rhp, Corvallis (Ore.) HS
19. **David Connelly, of/1b, North Hollywood (Calif.) HS**
20. **Craig Colbert, 3b, Oral Roberts**
21. **Charles Higson, rhp, Lewis-Clark State (Idaho)**
22. **Chuck Tate, rhp, Oklahoma State**
23. **Kevin Fitzgerald, 2b, George Washington**
24. **David Nash, of, Central Michigan**
25. **Chris Shultis, 3b, Utah**
26. Carlos Robles, 1b, Pater Noster HS, Los Angeles
27. Derek Scholl, of, Los Angeles Harbor JC
28. Greg Roscoe, rhp, Nevada-Las Vegas
29. **Mark Leonard, of, UC Santa Barbara**
30. **John Rannow, c/of, Concordia (Ore.)**
31. **Keith Krafve, 3b, Oregon State**
32. Jeff Distasio, 1b, Georgia Tech
33. **Robin Riemer, lhp, Monroe (N.Y.) CC**

June—Secondary Phase (23)
1. Jay Searcy, 3b, Texas

SEATTLE MARINERS

January—Regular Phase (7)
1. **Jim Pritikin, of, San Diego Mesa JC**
2. **Jim Blueberg, rhp, Yuba (Calif.) CC**
3. Rod Byerly, lhp, Brevard (Fla.) CC
4. Shawn Butler, lhp, Green River (Wash.) CC

5. Danny Kapea, lhp, Central Arizona JC (Selection voided)
6. **Rudy Webster, rhp, Central Iowa JC**
7. Ken Shamburg, inf, Butte (Calif.) JC
8. Mike Beiras, rhp, El Camino (Calif.) JC
9. Jon Hurst, rhp, Spartanburg Methodist (S.C.) JC
10. David Kandra, rhp, Butte (Calif.) JC

January—Secondary Phase (5)

1. **Eric Fox, of, Fresno State**
2. Mike Montagnino, c, Palm Beach (Fla.) JC

June—Regular Phase (8)

1. **Patrick Lennon, ss, Whiteville (N.C.) HS**
2. **Erik Hanson, rhp, Wake Forest**
3. **Jerry Goff, c, California**
4. **Mike McDonald, ss, Douglas County HS, Douglasville, Ga.**
5. David Lowe, rhp, Satellite HS, Satellite Beach, Fla.
6. **Rich DeLucia, rhp, Tennessee**
7. **Mark Wooden, rhp, Lewis-Clark State (Idaho)**
8. **Ted Williams, of, Alabama**
9. **Michael Brandts, 3b/of, Marietta (Ohio)**
10. **Dan Disher, rhp, Michigan**
11. **Troy Williams, 2b, Eastern Kentucky**
12. **Jim Bowie, 1b, Louisiana State**
13. **Dru Kosco, of, Ball State**
14. **Dave Hartnett, lhp, Creighton**
15. **Jody Ryan, rhp, Troy State**
16. Rusty Harris, ss, Lewis-Clark State (Idaho)
17. Gary Young, rhp, Hoopa (Calif.) HS
18. **Jose Tartabull, of, Miami-Dade North CC**
19. **Wendell Bolar, 3b, Cal State Chico**
20. **Tommy Little, rhp, Tulane**
21. Lanny Phillips, 3b, Lewis-Clark State (Idaho)
22. **Mike Thorpe, rhp, Arizona State**
23. Jamie McAndrew, rhp, Ponderosa HS, Parker, Colo.
24. **Jose Bennett, of, Western New Mexico**
25. Kevin Sheary, rhp, Miami
26. Erick Bryant, rhp, Poly HS, Long Beach
27. Paul Carey, 1b, Boston College HS, Weymouth, Mass.
28. Anthony Carnavale, c, Trinidad (Colo.) HS
29. **Deron Johnson Jr., 1b, San Diego State**

June—Secondary Phase (12)

1. **Greg Briley, 2b, North Carolina State**
2. Larry Oedenwalt, inf, San Diego Mesa JC
3. Gary Alexander, rhp, Arizona
4. Paul Ellison, c, Orange Coast (Calif.) JC
5. Damon Allen, rhp, San Diego

TEXAS RANGERS

January—Regular Phase (3)

1. **Chris Shiflett, rhp, Rancho Santiago (Calif.) JC**
2. Heath Lane, rhp, San Joaquin Delta (Calif.) JC
3. David Boss, rhp, San Jose (Calif.) CC
4. John Wenrich, rhp, Long Beach (Calif.) CC
5. Michael Ferreira, rhp, Chabot (Calif.) JC
6. Brian McSwain, rhp, Spartanburg Methodist (S.C.) JC
7. Julio Morales, 1b, Nassau (N.Y.) CC
8. Angel Caceres, lhp, Arizona Western JC
9. John Burgos, lhp, Arizona Western JC
10. Wesley Holmes, rhp, Garden City (Kan.) CC
11. Dennis Karlin, rhp, Garden City (Kan.) CC

January—Secondary Phase (19)

1. Carlton Cochrane, lhp, Central Arizona JC
2. Damon Allen, rhp, San Diego
3. Louis Cedeno, rhp, West New York, N.J.

June—Regular Phase (4)

1. **Kevin Brown, rhp, Georgia Tech**
2. **Roger Pavlik, rhp, Aldine HS, Houston**
3. **Dean Palmer, ss, Florida HS, Tallahassee, Fla.**
4. Rob Richie, of, Nevada-Reno
5. **Scott Morse, rhp, Maine**
6. **Rick Raether, rhp, Miami**
7. **Mike Loynd, rhp, Florida State**
8. **Brad Fontes, c, McLane HS, Fresno, Calif.**
9. David Howell, lhp, Swampscott (Mass.) HS
10. Mike Belanger, lhp, Cal State Fullerton
11. **John Barfield, lhp, Oklahoma City**
12. **Rick Bernardo, 1b, Maine**
13. **Rey Sanchez, ss, Rio Piedras, Puerto Rico**
14. **Ron Jackson, c, Texas Christian**
15. **Mike Scanlin, of, Texas A&M**
16. **Joe Pearn, c, Fairleigh Dickinson**
17. **Paul Postier, ss, Southeastern Oklahoma State**
18. **James McCutcheon, of, Clovis (Calif.) HS**
19. **Bob Malloy, rhp, Virginia**
20. **Jose Velez, 1b/of, Chipola (Fla.) JC**
21. Mark Juhas, rhp, Arcadia (Calif.) HS
22. William Bomar, c, Coeur dAlene HS, Hayden Lake, Idaho
23. **Gary Lang, ss, Kansas**
24. **Wayne Rosenthal, rhp, St. John's**
25. Luke Sable, of, Geoge Mason
26. Dean Weese, rhp, U.S. International (Nairobi)
27. Glenn Abraham, of, Howard (D.C.)
28. **Gar Millay, 2b, Arizona**
29. **Lucious Cole, of, Monachan HS, Richmond**
30. **Mike Spear, inf, Manchester HS, Richmond**

June—Secondary Phase (2)

1. **Pat Garman, 3b, Cal State Fullerton**
2. David Boss, rhp, San Jose (Calif.) CC
3. Eliezer Quinones, of, Gulf Coast (Fla.) CC
4. Allen Rutledge, inf, Hillsborough (Fla.) CC
5. Brian McSwain, rhp, Spartanburg Methodist (S.C.) JC

TORONTO BLUE JAYS

January—Regular Phase (26)

1. **Morgan Roderick, rhp, DeKalb Central (Ga.) JC**
2. **Lindsay Foster, inf, Louisburg (N.C.) JC**
3. Pat Mehrtens, lhp, Faulkner State (Ala.) JC
4. David Black, rhp, St. Louis CC-Meramec
5. **Mark Whiten, of, Pensacola (Fla.) JC**
6. Peter Brown, rhp, Chipola (Fla.) JC
7. Chuck Johnson, inf, Laney (Calif.) JC
8. Michael Ordez, rhp, Merced (Calif.) JC
9. Wade Taylor, rhp, Jefferson Davis (Ala.) JC
10. Dean DeCillis, inf, Miami-Dade South CC
11. Greg Lonigro, inf, Florida CC
12. Doug DeKock, c, Santa Fe (Fla.) CC
13. Vincent Davis, of, Gulf Coast (Fla.) CC
14. Rodney Brooks, rhp, Lurleen B. Wallace State (Ala.) JC
15. Glenn Moore, inf, Indian River (Fla.) CC

January—Secondary Phase (23)

1. Charlie White, of, Jefferson Davis (Ala.) JC
2. Bruce Powers, of, Skyline (Calif.) JC

June—Regular Phase (26)

1. **Earl Sanders, rhp, Jackson State**
2. **Steve Cummings, rhp, Houston**
3. **Andrew Dziadkowiec, c, Quigley South HS, Chicago**
4. **Xavier Hernandez, rhp, Southwestern Louisiana**
5. **Pat Hentgen, rhp, Fraser (Mich.) HS**
6. **Jerry Schunk, ss, Toledo**
7. Cris Carpenter, rhp, Georgia
8. **Jimmy Long, rhp, Oklahoma State**
9. **Rich DePastino, rhp, Riverview HS, Sarasota, Fla.**
10. **Randy Knorr, c/3b, Baldwin Park (Calif.) HS**
11. **Willie Blair, rhp, Morehead State**
12. Jose Salva, rhp, Southwestern Louisiana
13. Ron Lewis, ss, Raines HS, Jacksonville, Fla.
14. **Carlos Diaz, c, Oklahoma State**
15. Demetrius Smith, of, Gardena HS, Los Angeles
16. Jimmy Rogers, rhp, Seminole State (Okla.) JC
17. **John Shea, lhp, Connecticut**
18. Jason Younker, of, North Bend HS, Coos Bay, Ore.
19. James Moran, c, St. Joseph's
20. Steve Surico, lhp, Tustin (Calif.) HS
21. **Barry Shifflett, of, UNC Charlotte**

22. **Joseph Ward, rhp, Rhode Island**
23. Tony Lewis, rhp, Pepperdine
24. **Robert Watts, ss, West Virginia**
25. **Richard Ironside, c, Nassau (N.Y.) CC**
26. Mark Beck, rhp, Mayfair HS, Lakewood, Calif.
27. **Tom Quinlan, ss, Hill Murray HS, Maplewood, Minn.**
28. **Darren Hall, rhp, Dallas Baptist**
29. **Bob Cavanaugh, rhp, Central Michigan**
30. **Andy Wortham, lhp, California**
31. **Pat Rosenbauer, rhp, Toledo**
32. **Ray McDonald, 3b, San Francisco**
33. Sherman Collins, rhp, Oklahoma
34. Chris Woodfin, rhp, South Irondale HS, Statesville, N.C.
35. **Gary Bockhorn, rhp, Southern Illinois**
36. Warren Holt, rhp, Aptos (Calif.) HS
37. John Dolak, c, Palisades HS, Malibu, Calif.
38. Brian Goodwin, rhp, Frankfort (Ind.) HS
39. Tommy Hardgrove, 1b, Arlington Heights HS, Fort Worth, Texas
40. Glenn Baxley, 3b, Moreau HS, Union City, Calif.
41. Steve Balstad, of, St. John Bosco HS, Buena Park, Calif.
42. **Barry Morphew, ss, Alexandria (Ind.) HS**
43. **Doug Linton, rhp, UC Irvine**
44. David Freese, of, Springboro (Ohio) HS

June—Secondary Phase (16)

1. John Briscoe, rhp, Texarkana (Texas) CC
2. David Keating, of, UCLA
3. Pat Mehrtens, lhp, Faulkner State (Ala.) JC
4. Andrew Nieman, rhp, Sinclair (Ohio) CC
5. Charlie White, of, Jefferson Davis (Ala.) JC
6. Scott Gerner, lhp, St. Mary's

1987 First No. 1 pick with major league father makes an even bigger name for himself

When the Mariners drafted Ken Griffey Jr. in 1987, it was the first time the No. 1 overall pick in June was the son of a big leaguer.

Two years later, when Griffey, then 19, became Seattle's Opening Day center fielder, he and his father, 38, became the first father-son act ever to play in the big leagues simultaneously.

Previously, the highest-drafted players with ties to former big leaguers were Dick Schofield Jr. (selected third overall in 1981) and Jeff Kunkel (who also went third overall, in 1983).

For his part, Griffey Sr. never seemed to have any doubt about who the best player in the family was.

"He's got more power than I'll ever have," he said. "He hits a lot harder. At his age now, he's a lot faster than I ever was.

"I'm very proud of my son because he accomplished this on his own. I really didn't get to see him develop very much because I was away. He learned and he watched me over the years and picked up a few things."

JOHN WILLIAMSON

Ken Griffey Jr. turned out to be one of the best No. 1 picks in draft history

While Griffey and his father agreed to terms with the Mariners on a $160,000 bonus the night before the draft, there was doubt that Seattle, selecting first overall for the third time in its 10-year history, would spend its first pick on Griffey, or any high school player.

Mariners owner George Argyros had announced earlier that spring his intention to sell the Mariners and buy the Padres. As the draft approached with the franchise in limbo, there were questions whether Argyros was committed to paying top dollar to get the best player possible.

"We have sufficient funds to get the top player. And I mean the top player, not the player we can sign," team president Chuck Armstrong said.

The sale of the Mariners never came about, though there were still concerns that Argyros, known for meddling in his team's baseball operations, was reluctant to use the first pick on a high school talent because of the pressing need to obtain a player who could contribute in the short term.

In the end, the wisdom of scouting director Roger Jongewaard and general manager Dick Balderson prevailed, and the choice was Griffey.

"Ken has got great bloodlines and lots of talent," said Jongewaard, who also recommended No. 1 pick successes Darryl Strawberry (Mets, 1980) and Alex Rodriguez (Mariners, 1993). "There's nothing he can't do above-average. But what really sold us were his instincts for the game and his power potential."

Griffey, a .478 hitter with seven homers as a senior at Cincinnati's Moeller High, spent only 129 games in the minor leagues. He took the Mariners' center-field job in 1989 and quickly established himself as one of the game's best young players. He won the American League MVP award in 1997 and from 1997-99 hit 56, 56 and 48 home runs in a season. He also made 11 straight appearances in the All-Star Game.

Injuries dented his career somewhat after that, but he returned to Seattle for the 2009 season—his 21st in the majors—and finished the year with 630 career home runs.

Unlike the previous two years, when the first four players drafted were from the college ranks, the 1987 draft saw a major shift to high school talent. Led by Griffey, the first three selections were from high school.

The first two college players drafted were 6-foot-5 righthanders from California who went to the two Chicago teams. The Cubs, selecting fourth, went for Cal State Fullerton's Mike Harkey, while the White Sox took Jack McDowell, who hurled Stanford to the first of consecutive College World Series titles. McDowell also became the first player from the Class of '87 to reach the big leagues.

Overall, the college pitching crop was unusually strong in 1987. A total of 12 pitchers with college experience were selected by the time Seattle began drafting in the second round.

Had he not been suspended prior to NCAA regional play, temperamental Louisiana State outfielder Joey (née Albert) Belle probably would have been drafted among the first 10. Belle, hitting .349 with 21 homers and 66 RBIs, was suspended by LSU coach Skip Bertman for leaving the field to chase a Mississippi State fan who shouted racial slurs at him during the championship game in the Southeastern Conference tournament in Athens, Ga. The suspension came after other outbursts during the year by Belle, who had a problem controlling his temper.

Cleveland didn't have a first-round pick but took Belle in the second round, and he went on to become one of baseball's top sluggers before a hip injury suddenly ended his career.

At Long Last, One Draft

A total of 1,263 players were selected in 1987, topping the previous record of 1,169 in June 1967. The Royals were the last team to stop picking, bowing out in the 74th round.

The primary reason for the sharp increase was the abolition of the January draft. All players who had normally been eligible for that draft were simply incorporated into the June draft.

In another measure aimed at streamlining the entire selection process, the secondary phase in June was eliminated, resulting in one pool for all players. The change had universal support.

"The big thing about it is you don't have to worry anymore about who's in what phase," Twins scouting director Terry Ryan said.

Unlike 1986, when the Red Sox couldn't sign their first-round pick (outfielder Greg McMurtry), teams chose not to gamble when the same opportunity presented itself in 1987.

Two such players were Mike Mussina, a pitcher from Montoursville, Pa., who took his 4.0 grade-point average to Stanford; and Rick Lantrip, a shortstop from Visalia, Calif., who decided to play for the University of Arizona. Both had projected as top 10 picks based on their ability.

The Orioles took a stab at Mussina in the 11th round, and made little attempt to sign him away from Stanford. Money was not at issue with Lantrip, who let every club know he was not ready for professional baseball and did not want to be drafted. Seattle gambled a fourth-round pick on him, but couldn't persuade him to change his mind.

DRAFT 87: FIRST-ROUND PICKS

No. Club	Player, Pos.	School	Hometown	Ht.	Wt.	B-T	Age
1.Mariners	Ken Griffey, of	Moeller HS	Cincinnati	6-3	185	L-L	18
2.Pirates	Mark Merchant, of	Oviedo HS	Oviedo, Fla.	6-1	185	B-R	18
3.Twins	Willie Banks, rhp	St. Anthonys HS	Jersey City, N.J.	6-1	190	R-R	18
4.Cubs	Mike Harkey, rhp	Cal State Fullerton	Diamond Bar, Calif.	6-5	185	R-R	20
5.White Sox	Jack McDowell, rhp	Stanford	Van Nuys, Calif.	6-5	175	R-R	21
6.Braves	Derek Lilliquist, lhp	Georgia	Sarasota, Fla.	6-0	190	L-L	21
7.Orioles	Chris Myers, lhp	Plant HS	Tampa	6-2	185	L-L	18
8.Dodgers	Dan Opperman, rhp	Valley HS	Las Vegas	6-3	175	R-R	18
9.Royals	Kevin Appier, rhp	Antelope Valley JC	Lancaster, Calif.	6-2	180	R-R	19
10. Padres	Kevin Garner, rhp/of	Texas	Midland, Mich.	6-2	185	R-L	21
11. Athletics	Lee Tinsley, of	Shelby County HS	Shelbyville, Ky.	5-11	175	B-R	18
12. Expos	Delino DeShields, ss/2b	Seaford HS	Seaford, Del.	6-2	180	L-R	18
13. Brewers	Bill Spiers, ss	Clemson	Cameron, S.C.	6-3	192	L-R	21
14. Cardinals	Cris Carpenter, rhp	Georgia	Gainesville, Ga.	6-2	185	R-R	22
15. Orioles	*Brad DuVall, rhp	Virginia Tech	Silver Spring, Md.	6-1	180	R-R	21
16. Giants	Mike Remlinger, lhp	Dartmouth Coll.	Plymouth, Mass.	6-0	195	L-L	21
17. Blue Jays	Alex Sanchez, rhp	UCLA	Antioch, Calif.	6-2	170	R-R	21
18. Reds	Jack Armstrong, rhp	Oklahoma	Neptune, N.J.	6-5	215	R-R	22
19. Rangers	Brian Bohanon, lhp	North Shore HS	Houston	6-3	210	L-L	18
20. Tigers	Bill Henderson, c	Westminster Christian HS	Miami	6-3	200	R-R	18
21. Tigers	Steve Pegues, of	Pontotoc HS	Pontotoc, Miss.	6-2	170	R-R	19
22. Astros	Craig Biggio, c	Seton Hall	Kings Park, N.Y.	5-11	185	R-R	21
23. Rangers	Bill Haselman, c	UCLA	Saratoga, Calif.	6-3	205	R-R	21
24. Mets	Chris Donnels, 3b	Loyola Marymount	Torrance, Calif.	6-0	185	L-R	21
25. Angels	John Orton, c	Cal Poly San Luis Obispo	Santa Cruz, Calif.	6-0	175	R-R	21
26. Red Sox	Reggie Harris, rhp	Waynesboro HS	Waynesboro, Va.	6-2	195	R-R	18

*Did not sign.

1987

CLUB-BY-CLUB SELECTIONS

ATLANTA BRAVES

June—Regular Phase (6)

1. **Derek Lilliquist, lhp, Georgia**
2. **Mike Urman, c, Canoga Park (Calif.) HS**
3. **Tom Redington, ss, Esperanza HS, Anaheim**
4. **Keith Mitchell, of, Lincoln HS, San Diego**
5. **Dennis Burlingame, rhp, Kingsway HS, Mullica Hill, N.J.**
6. John Kosenski, rhp, Fairview HS, Boulder, Colo.
7. **Paulo Reis, ss/2b, Diamond Vocational HS, Fall River, Mass.**
8. **Brian Hunter, 1b, Cerritos (Calif.) JC**
9. **Kevin Kelly, lhp, Wichita State**
10. **Lamar Hall, ss, Pinole Valley HS, San Pablo, Calif.**
11. **Anthony Baldwin, of, McLennan (Texas) CC**
12. **Winston Relaford, of, Florida JC**
13. **Mike Stanton, lhp, Alvin (Texas) CC**
14. **David Nied, rhp, Duncanville (Texas) HS**
15. **Craig Gourlay, rhp, Wake Forest**
16. **Brian Cummings, rhp, Blinn (Texas) JC**
17. **Rich Casarotti, 2b, Santa Rosa (Calif.) JC**
18. Joey Chimelis, ss, Howard (Texas) JC
19. **Darren Cox, lhp, Triton (Ill.) JC**
20. Marc Loeb, c, Eisenhower HS, Rialto, Calif.
21. **Theron Todd, of, CC of Baltimore**
22. **Scott Grove, rhp, Douglas County HS, Littleton, Colo.**
23. **Jeff Allison, of, Purdue**
24. **Richard Duke, c, Oregon State**
25. George Sells, of, Attleboro (Mass.) HS
26. **Pat Tilmon, rhp, South Carolina-Spartanburg**
27. **Seth Reeser, rhp, Shippensburg (Pa.)**
28. Greg Randazza, rhp, Elizabeth (N.J.) HS
29. **John Albertson, c, Camden County (N.J.) JC**
30. **Greg Harper, c, West Georgia**
31. Joseph Pagan, rhp, Chicago State
32. **Kevin McNees, of, Western Michigan**
33. **John Mitchell, 1b, Mississippi State**
34. **Brian Wright, c, South Gate (Calif.) HS**
35. Godfrey Knight, ss, Georgia Southern
36. **Randy Ward, lhp, West Florida**
37. Darrell Wyatt, of, Kishwaukee (Ill.) JC
38. **Steve Glass, ss/3b, San Francisco State**
39. **Greg Cloninger, ss, Campbell**
40. **Scott Bohlke, of, Georgia**
41. **Jeff Dodig, of, Winthrop**
42. John Niekro, rhp, Shiloh HS, Lilburn, Ga.
43. Roger Kinard, lhp, Georgia Tech
44. John Pappas, rhp, Crown Point (Ind.) HS
45. **Paul Opdyke, rhp, Valley HS, Las Vegas**
46. Shawn Buchanan, ss, Horace Mann HS, Gary, Ind.
47. **Greg Ziegler, rhp, Morton (Ill.) JC**
48. Steve Gill, lhp/of, El Dorado HS, Placentia, Calif.
49. Paul Gogo, rhp, Kishwaukee (Ill.) JC
50. Herman Johnson, c, Skyline HS, Dallas

BALTIMORE ORIOLES

June—Regular Phase (7)

1. **Chris Myers, lhp, Plant HS, Tampa**
1. Brad DuVall, rhp, Virginia Tech (Pick from Indians as compensation for Type A free agent Rick Dempsey)
1. **Pete Harnisch, rhp, Fordham** (Supplemental pick—27th—for loss of Dempsey)
2. (Pick to Mets as compensation for Type B free agent Ray Knight)
3. **Anthony Telford, rhp, San Jose State**
4. **Chuck Ricci, rhp, Shawnee HS, Medford, N.J.**
5. **Tim Holland, ss, Rio Americano HS, Sacramento**
6. **Sam Amarena, rhp, Tulane**
7. **Dan Simonds, c, Davidson**
8. **Mike Eberle, c, Indiana State**
9. **Jack Voigt, of/3b, Louisiana State**
10. **Thomas Harms, of, Portland State (Ore.)**
11. Mike Mussina, rhp, Montoursville (Pa.) HS
12. **Bob Shoulders, of, Purdue**
13. **Steve Finley, of, Southern Illinois**
14. **Steve Culkar, rhp, Kentucky**
15. **Chris Pinder, c, Virginia Commonwealth**
16. **Charles Elmore, of, Troy State**
17. **Terry Brown, of, Southern California**
18. **David Segui, 1b, Louisiana Tech**
19. **George Wahlig, 2b, Southwest Missouri State**
20. **Dave Bettendorf, 3b, Kent State**
21. **Steve Browning, c, Valdosta State (Ga.)**
22. Ray Giannelli, 3b, New York Tech
23. **Joe Hartline, of, Methodist (N.C.)**
24. **Steve Williams, lhp, Crescent City HS, Pomana Park, Fla.**
25. Longo Garcia, rhp, Cal State Fullerton
26. **Marcus Pilkinton, rhp, Troy State**
27. Malcolm Jordan, of, Montgomery HS, Santa Rosa, Calif.
28. John Sipple, lhp, Oregon State
29. Terry Melton, c, Charles Owen HS, Swannanoa, N.C.
30. **Jeff Ahr, of, Xavier**
31. **David Esquer, ss, Stanford**
32. **Paul Murphy, 3b, Delaware**
33. **Scott Wallman, c, Sutherland HS, Pittsford, N.Y.**
34. Kirk Dressendorfer, rhp, Pearland (Texas) HS
35. Matt Howard, rhp, Jersey Village HS, Houston
36. Reggie Robinson, of, Hogan HS, Vallejo, Calif.
37. Steve Godin, of, Fauquier HS, Warrenton, Va.
38. Mike Shebek, rhp, Ball State
39. Mike Beall, 1b, St. Thomas (Fla.)
40. Tim Seaton, 2b, Millard North HS, Omaha
41. Jimmy Crowley, 3b, Liberty Road HS, Cockeysville, Md.
42. Dan Martz, ss, Thomas Johnson HS, Frederick, Md.
43. Gerald Santos, rhp, Columbus HS, Miami
44. George Hildreth, of, Monroe (N.Y.) CC
45. Marc Imbasciani, of/c, C.W. Post (N.Y.)
46. Mike Brenner, of, Muscatine (Iowa) CC
47. Shawn Jenkins, of, Southwood HS, Shreveport, La.
48. David Lucchino, c, Central Catholic HS, Pittsburgh
49. Kevin Pleasant, ss, Lake Park HS, Roselle, Ill.
50. Jody Treadwell, rhp, Temple Christian HS, Jacksonville, Fla.
51. Julio Morales, 1b, C.W. Post (N.Y.)
52. Mark Brockell, 3b, James Madison

BOSTON RED SOX

June—Regular Phase (26)

1. **Reggie Harris, rhp, Waynesboro (Va.) HS**
1. **Bob Zupcic, of, Oral Roberts** (Supplemental pick—32nd—for failure to sign 1986 first-rounder Greg McMurtry)
2. **Paul Brown, lhp, Hawaii**
3. **Craig Wilson, c, Cerritos (Calif.) JC**
4. **Scott Powers, ss, Brandeis (Mass.)**
5. **Steve Michael, of, Emporia State (Kan.)**
6. **Ronnie Richardson, rhp, Lee HS, Columbus, Miss.**
7. Scott Vonderlieth, lhp, Mission Bay HS, San Diego
8. **Jim Byrd, ss, Seminole State (Okla.) JC**
9. **Mike Kelly, of, South Florida**
10. **Jeff Plympton, rhp, Maine**
11. **Phil Plantier, 3b, Poway (Calif.) HS**
12. **Pedro Matilla, c, Southridge HS, Miami**
13. **Peter Estrada, rhp, Irvington (N.J.) HS**
14. **Sam Melton, 3b, Columbia State (Tenn.) CC**
15. Desi Wilson, 1b, Glen Cove (N.Y.) HS
16. **Larry Scannell, of, Lewis (Ill.)**
17. **Vince DeGifico, 1b, Southern Maine**

18. Stewart Lee, 3b, Jacksonville State
19. Scott Thompson, of, Westminster (Md.) HS
20. Kevin Digiacomo, c, Ithaca (N.Y.) HS
21. James Wray, lhp, Troy State
22. **Anthony Mosley, lhp, Fort Meade (Fla.) HS**
23. Richard Santiago, lhp, Palm Bay (Fla.) HS
24. Pat Pesavento, ss, Notre Dame
25. Jayhawk Owens, c, Glen Este HS, Cincinnati
26. Stan Spencer, rhp, Columbia River HS, Vancouver, Wash.
27. **Greg McCollum, rhp, Illinois**
28. **Chris Hanks, c, JC of Southern Idaho**
29. Don Redmond, of, Guilford (N.C.)
30. Jesse Cross, rhp, Middle Georgia JC
31. Clint Creed, c, Triton HS, Dunn, N.C.

CALIFORNIA ANGELS

June—Regular Phase (25)

1. **John Orton, c, Cal Poly San Luis Obispo**
1. **David Holdridge, rhp, Ocean View HS, Huntington Beach, Calif.** (Supplemental pick—31st—for loss of Type A free agent Reggie Jackson)
2. **Mike Erb, rhp, San Diego State** (Pick from Athletics as compensation for Jackson)
2. **Kevin Flora, ss, Bonita HS, LaVerne, Calif.**
3. **Chris Threadgill, of, Whiteville (N.C.) HS**
4. **Mark Holzemer, lhp, Mullen HS, Littleton, Colo.**
5. **Wiley Lee, 2b, Old Dominion**
6. **Scott Randolph, rhp, Mount Hood (Ore.) CC**
7. **Ramon Martinez, ss, Franklin HS, Highland Park, Calif.**
8. **Mike Musolino, c, Sacramento CC**
9. **Mario Molina, of, Alhambra (Calif.) HS**
10. Kyle Balch, rhp, Vanderbilt
11. **Ruben Amaro Jr., of, Stanford**
12. **Reed Peters, of, Nevada-Las Vegas**
13. **Ted Dyson, 1b, Arizona State**
14. Ray Harris, lhp, Arkansas
15. **Jeff Barns, ss, South Carolina**
16. **Daniel Ward, rhp, St. Mary's**
17. **James Townsend, lhp, Ohio State**
18. **Jay Bobel, rhp, Michigan State**
19. **Cary Grubb, 3b, Clarion (Pa.)**
20. **Jim McAnany, c, Loyola Marymount**
21. **Rob Wassenaar, rhp, Stanford**
22. **Mark Baca, of, Cal State Fullerton**
23. **Frank Mutz, rhp, Master's (Calif.)**
24. **Tony Mattia, 1b, Arizona State**
25. **Jimmy Long, rhp, Oklahoma State**
26. Brian Sajonia, lhp, Washington State
27. **John Fritz, rhp, Beaver Falls (Pa.) HS**
28. Perry Berry, ss, Cortez (Colo.) HS
29. **Lanny Abshier, 3b, Central Florida**
30. James McDonald, rhp, Deer Park (Texas) HS
31. Andrew McDonald, 2b, Riverview HS, Sarasota, Fla.
32. **Todd James, lhp, Sacramento CC**
33. Scott Schanz, rhp, North HS, Riverside, Calif.
34. Paul Gay, of, South Florida JC
35. **Justin Martin, rhp, McKay HS, Salem, Ore.**
36. Kevin Brown, of, JC of the Sequoias (Calif.)
37. Randy Vollmer, ss, Taravella (Fla.) HS
38. Woody Smith, ss, Spartanburg Methodist (S.C.) JC

CHICAGO CUBS

June—Regular Phase (4)

1. **Mike Harkey, rhp, Cal State Fullerton**
2. (Pick to Expos as compensation for Type A free agent Andre Dawson)
3. **Alex Arias, 3b, George Washington HS, New York**
4. Ronaldo Noriega, inf, Southwest HS, Miami
5. **Gregg Patterson, lhp, Louisiana State**
6. **Frank Castillo, rhp, Eastwood HS, El Paso, Texas**
7. **Matt Franco, 3b, Westlake HS, Thousand Oaks, Calif.**
8. **Matt Walbeck, c, Sacramento (Calif.) HS**
9. Joe Klancnik, rhp, Triton (Ill.) JC
10. Kevin O'Connor, ss, Mater Dei HS, Huntington Beach, Calif.
11. **Jeff Massicotte, rhp, Florida JC**
12. Billy Masse, of, Davidson
13. **Horace Tucker, of, Lincoln HS, San Diego**
14. **Gabby Rodriguez, lhp, UC Irvine**
15. **Eric Perry, 1b, Dos Palos (Calif.) HS**
16. Darin Campbell, ss, North Carolina
17. **Wayne Weinheimer, of, Sacramento (Calif.) HS**
18. **Vaughn Williams, of, Northwestern State**
19. **Scott Taylor, c, Waukegan (Ill.) East HS**
20. Steve Allen, rhp, Massachusetts
21. **Braz Davis, rhp, Baylor**
22. **Derek Stroud, lhp, Fresno State**
23. **Derek Moore, of, Santa Monica (Calif.) JC**
24. **Lenny Bell, 1b/3b, Texas**
25. **Steve Owens, 3b, St. Lawrence (N.Y.)**
26. **John Gardner, rhp, Indiana State**
27. **Warren Arrington, of, Troy State**
28. **Sean Reed, lhp, Linn-Benton (Ore.) CC**
29. **Glenn Sullivan, 1b, Oklahoma**
30. **Danny Carpenter, of, Dallas Baptist**
31. **Michael Boswell, c/ss, Palm Beach (Fla.) JC**
32. Mike Eastley, 3b, Lee (Texas) JC
33. **Fernando Ramsey, of, New Mexico State**
34. Bob Brucato, of, Rancho Santiago (Calif.) JC
35. Bill Lantrip, lhp, Overton HS, Memphis
36. David Zauner, ss, Berkley (Mich.) HS
37. Jeff Cirillo, rhp, Providence HS, North Hollywood, Calif.
38. **Tom Thobe, lhp, Edison HS, Huntington Beach, Calif.**
39. **Anthony Whitson, rhp, Unicoi HS, Erwin, Tenn.**
40. Tracy Smith, 3b/rhp, Miami (Ohio)
41. Kirk Goodson, rhp, Independence (Va.) HS
42. Eric Crawford, of, Venice HS, Los Angeles
43. Johnny Walker, of, Holmes HS, San Antonio
44. **David Hellmann, 3b, Miami (Ohio)**

CHICAGO WHITE SOX

June—Regular Phase (5)

1. **Jack McDowell, rhp, Stanford**
2. **Brent Knackert, rhp, Ocean View HS, Huntington Beach, Calif.**
3. **Kinnis Pledger, of, Garland County CC, Benton, Ark.**
4. **Steve Schrenk, rhp, North Marion HS, Aurora, Ore.**
5. **Dan Rohrmeier, 3b, St. Thomas (Fla.)**
6. **Jerry Kutzler, rhp, William Penn (Iowa)**
7. **Ed Smith, 3b, Pemberton HS, Brown Mills, N.J.**
8. **Bernardo Cruz, ss, Southview HS, Lorain, Ohio**
9. Dan Gil, 3b, Polytechnic HS, North Hollywood, Calif.
10. **Rob Lukachyk, ss, Brookdale (N.J.) CC**
11. **Ken Burroughs, rhp, Northeast HS, St. Petersburg, Fla.**
12. **Buddy Groom Jr., lhp, Mary Hardin-Baylor (Texas)**
13. **Dwayne Hosey, of, Altadena, Calif.**
14. **Ed Walsh, 1b, Providence**
15. Maurice Crum, 1b, Hillsborough HS, Tampa
16. **John Sabatino, rhp, Lewis (Ill.)**
17. **Paul Fuller, c, Southern California**
18. Chris Hansen, rhp, Iona
19. **Ray Payton, of/1b, Southern**
20. **Brad Fella, lhp, Indiana**
21. **Curt Hasler, rhp, Bradley**
22. **Jesus Merejo, ss, CC of Morris (N.J.)**
23. Brian Roberts, c, Loara HS, Anaheim
24. **Franklin Harris, c, Jackson State**
25. **Virgil Cooper, rhp, Labette (Kan.) CC**
26. **Keith Harris, of, Queensborough (N.Y.) CC**
27. **Shaun Doyle, of, Cal State Dominguez Hills**
28. **Dwight Thomas, 1b, Dallas Baptist**
29. Kerry Valrie, of/2b, Robertsdale HS, Loxley, Ala.
30. **Mario Silva, 2b/3b, American HS, Miami**
31. Derek Davis, of, Simeon HS, Chicago
32. **Kevin Murdock, c, Wisconsin-Oshkosh**
33. **Randy Warren, of, Elon**
34. **Paul Colontino, of, Roosevelt HS, Brooklyn**
35. John Kroeger, c, Fairleigh Dickinson
36. **John Morabito, of/inf, Wake Forest**

37. Brian Gennings, rhp, Queen City (Texas) HS
38. Jeff Buell, 1b, Indiana State
39. Phil Doyle, ss, Hueman HS, Birmingham
40. Lawrence Smith, ss, Bethune-Cookman

CINCINNATI REDS

June—Regular Phase (18)

1. **Jack Armstrong, rhp, Oklahoma**
2. **Freddie Benavides, ss, Texas Christian**
3. **Brian Lane, ss, Midway HS, Waco, Texas**
4. **Jeremy Mathews, ss, Sandalwood HS, Jacksonville, Fla.**
5. **Shane Letterio, ss, Lake Mary HS, Longwood, Fla.**
6. Bo Loftin, c, Jacksonville (Ala.) HS
7. **Reggie Sanders, ss/of, Spartanburg Methodist (S.C.) JC**
8. Jimmy Kremers, 3b/of, Arkansas
9. Brian Nichols, c, Southern California
10. **Joe Turek, rhp, West Chester (Pa.)**
11. **Steve McCarthy, lhp, Brown**
12. **Eugene Jones, 1b, Litchfield HS, Gadsden, Ala.**
13. **Steve Hester, rhp, Cedarville HS, Crozet, Va.**
14. **Bill Risley, rhp, Truman (Ill.) JC**
15. **Butch Henry III, lhp, El Paso (Texas) HS**
16. **Scott Jeffery, rhp, Mansfield (Pa.)**
17. **Gary Sloan, of/inf, Long Beach State**
18. **Dante Johnson, of, Santa Fe (Fla.) CC**
19. **Brad Robinson, of, Oral Roberts**
20. **Lavell Cudjo, of, Charlotte HS, Punta Gorda, Fla.**
21. **Scott Economy, rhp, James Madison**
22. John Cebuhar, lhp, Arkansas
23. **Ed Rush, ss, South Florida**
24. Norman Villanueva, c, Tehachapi (Calif.) HS
25. **Paul Kovarick, 1b, Broome (N.Y.) CC**
26. **Scott Sellner, 3b, Cal State Sacramento**
27. **Bryan Ganter, of, Oregon State**
28. **Milt Hill, rhp, Georgia College & State**
29. **Mike Stout, rhp, James Madison**
30. **Steve Storms, rhp, Fairborne (Ohio) HS**
31. **Joey Vierra, rhp, Hawaii**
32. **Mike Shepherd, of, Georgia Southern**
33. **Rick Keen, rhp, Colorado State**
34. Mike Virden, of, Ballinger (Texas) HS
35. **Tori Tomasino, c, Northern Colorado**
36. Bob Gralewski, 1b, Salesian HS, Wilmington, Del.
37. **Keith Beam, of, Southern Arkansas**
38. Tom Mileski, 1b, Willis (Texas) HS
39. Tim Wells, rhp, Mineral Area (Mo.) JC
40. Scott McCarty, lhp, Converse HS, San Antonio
41. Tim Costo, ss, Glenbard HS, Glen Ellyn, Ill.
42. **Brian Whitaker, 2b, Southern Utah State**
43. Mark Faile, of, Lancaster (S.C.) HS
44. **Tony Terzarial, of, Triton (Ill.) JC**
45. **Glenn Sutko, c, Spartanburg Methodist (S.C.) JC**
46. Russell Williams, rhp, Bryan County HS, Pembroke, Ga.
47. Richard Reisdorf, of, Winona (Minn.) HS
48. Todd Mercier, 1b, Manchester (Conn.) CC
49. Kevin Kirk, rhp, Lewisville (Texas) HS
50. Anthony Brown, of, Connellsville (Pa.) HS
51. **Carl Nordstrom, rhp, Allegheny (Pa.) CC**
52. Anthony Fleming, of, Triton (Ill.) JC
53. **Scott Trochim, 3b, Rutgers**
54. **Brian Mershon, of/2b, Illinois**
55. **Robert Riccio, ss/2b, New Haven (Conn.)**
56. **Andy Alvey, 2b, Georgia College & State**
57. Joe White, rhp, Mesa (Colo.)
58. **Mike Mohr, of, Western Illinois**
59. **Reggie Brock, of, Chicago State**
60. **David Hamilton, 2b, Southwest Texas State**
61. Jimmy Armstrong, lhp, Wichita Falls (Texas) HS

CLEVELAND INDIANS

June—Regular Phase (15)

1. (Pick to Orioles as compensation for Type A free agent Rick Dempsey)
2. **Albert Belle, of, Louisiana State**
3. **Tom Kurczewski, rhp, Michigan State**
4. **Carl Keliipuleole, rhp, Brigham Young**
5. **Tom Kramer, rhp, Roger Bacon HS, Cincinnati**
6. **Todd Ogden, rhp, Rice**
7. **Scott Mackie, of, James Madison**
8. **Chris Isaacson, c, Eastern Washington**
9. **Greg Roscoe, rhp, Nevada-Las Vegas**
10. **Ever Magallanes, ss, Texas A&M**
11. **Chuck Baldwin, 2b, Clemson**
12. Gordie Farmer, rhp, Arizona State
13. **Pete Kuld, c, Pepperdine**
14. **Jamie Allison, of, Indiana State**
15. **Bill Narleski, ss, Virginia**
16. **Steve Olin, rhp, Portland State (Ore.)**
17. **John Stitz, rhp, St. Joseph's (Ind.)**
18. Dan Eskew, rhp, Tennessee
19. **Chris Dunham, 1b, Stetson**
20. **Willie Garza, rhp, Laney (Calif.) JC**
21. **Vince Barranco, of, Gonzaga**
22. **Kevin Bearse, lhp, Old Dominion**
23. **Frank Sommerkamp, c, Hillsborough (Fla.) CC**
24. **David Harwell, rhp, Dallas Baptist**
25. **Beau Allred, of, Lamar**
26. **Sam Ferretti, 2b, Rutgers**
27. Kevin Dattola, of, Brevard (Fla.) CC
28. Kevin Farlow, ss, Kennedy HS, Northridge, Calif.
29. **Robbie Rogers, ss, San Diego**
30. Kurt Dempster, rhp, Arizona State
31. David Ferrell, 2b, Palo Alto (Calif.) HS
32. Mark Smith, rhp, San Jacinto (Texas) JC
33. **Ivan McBride, ss, Baptist (Fla.)**
34. **Brent Roberts, of/3b, Snow (Utah) JC**
35. Clyde Samuel, rhp, Mission (Calif.) JC
36. Scott Tedder, of, Ohio Wesleyan
37. **Wayne Bell, of, Pasadena, Calif.**

DETROIT TIGERS

June—Regular Phase (21)

1. **Bill Henderson, c, Westminster Christian HS, Miami** (Pick from Phillies as compensation for Type A free agent Lance Parrish)
1. **Steve Pegues, of, Pontotoc (Miss.) HS**
1. **Travis Fryman, ss, Tate HS, Gonzalez, Fla.** (Supplemental pick—30th—for loss of Parrish)
2. **Rob Richie, of, Nevada**
3. **Jim Hayes, rhp, Topeka, Kan.**
4. **Riccardo Ingram, of, Georgia Tech**
5. **Torey Lovullo, 2b, UCLA**
6. **Dean DeCillis, inf, Miami-Dade South CC**
7. **Chris Harley, 3b, CC of Baltimore**
8. Derek Lee, inf/of, South Florida
9. **Blaine Rudolph, rhp, Fresno (Calif.) CC**
10. **Robert Shipman, of, Winter Haven (Fla.) HS**
11. **Dave Dawson, rhp, Orange Coast (Calif.) JC**
12. **Jody Supak, rhp, Houston**
13. **Paul Nozling, lhp, Lakeland (Ohio) CC**
14. **Don Vesling, lhp, Eastern Michigan**
15. Shane Jackson, rhp/c, Northern HS, Pontiac, Mich.
16. **Hernan Cortes, 1b, San Francisco State**
17. **Mike Wilkins, rhp, Lamar**
18. **Anthony Toney, of, Orange Coast (Calif.) JC**
19. Sean Baron, 1b, San Diego
20. **Larry Coker, lhp, Houston**
21. **Mike Schwabe, rhp, Arizona State**
22. **Chris Schnurbusch, ss, Central Missouri**
23. **Ron Cook, lhp, St. Clair County (Mich.) CC**
24. **Steve Strong, c, Arizona**
25. **Doug Biggs, of, Auburndale (Fla.) HS**
26. Mark Dawn, of, Manatee (Fla.) JC
27. **Dave Richards, lhp, Grossmont (Calif.) JC**
28. Tim McDonald, rhp, Central Michigan
29. **Jay Fox, rhp, Eastern Washington**
30. Eric Methner, rhp, Coleman (Mich.) HS

31. Jeff Tanderys, rhp, Novi (Mich.) HS
32. **Mike Koller, rhp, Glen Este HS, Cincinnati**
33. **Rusty Meacham, rhp, Indian River (Fla.) CC**
34. John Johnson, rhp, Kellogg (Mich.) CC
35. Andy Postema, 3b, Grand Rapids (Mich.) JC
36. Joseph Frias, ss, Elizabeth (N.J.) HS
37. Greg Haeger, lhp, Catholic Central HS, Livonia, Mich.
38. **Edward Ferm, rhp, Long Beach (Calif.) CC**
39. Damon Webb, of, MacKenzie HS, Detroit
40. Mario Linares, c, Colonial HS, Orlando, Fla.
41. Terre Woods, c, West Side HS, Gary, Ind.

HOUSTON ASTROS

June—Regular Phase (22)

1. **Craig Biggio, c, Seton Hall**
2. **Randy Hennis, rhp, UCLA**
3. **David Henderson, ss, McAlester (Okla.) HS**
4. **Roger Locke, rhp, Sparkman HS, Harvest, La.**
5. **Harold Allen, lhp, Indiana State**
6. **Billy Carver, c, Tennessee**
7. **Dan Nyssen, of, Hawaii**
8. **John Massarelli, c, Akron**
9. Mike Ross, ss/2b, Cal State Fullerton
10. **Chris Small, rhp, Troy State**
11. **David Washington, of, Murrah HS, Jackson, Miss.**
12. **Andy Mota, inf/of, Cal State Fullerton**
13. **Rusty Harris, ss, Lewis-Clark State (Idaho)**
14. **Leo Clouser, rhp, Los Angeles Pierce JC**
15. **Chris Hawkins, lhp, South Carolina-Spartanburg**
16. **Al Osuna Jr., lhp, Stanford**
17. **Steve Polverini, rhp, Cal State Los Angeles**
18. **Doug Royalty, rhp, San Diego State**
19. **Greg Johnson, rhp, Middle Tennessee State**
20. **Dean Hartgraves, lhp, JC of the Siskiyous (Calif.)**
21. **Ken Dickson, 3b, South Carolina-Aiken**
22. **Chris Lee, rhp, Miami**
23. **Todd Newman, lhp, Brigham Young**
24. William Parrish, ss, Shorter (Ga.)
25. **Dennis Tafoya, rhp, Cal State Sacramento**
26. **David Panizzi, of, Bradley**
27. Kevin Smothers, 3b, Lincoln HS, San Diego
28. Scott Kirk, of/1b, San Bernardino Valley (Calif.) JC
29. Michael Bible, c, JC of the Canyons (Calif.)
30. **Darryl Kile, rhp, Chaffey (Calif.) JC**
31. **Toncie Reed, of, Seminole State (Okla.) JC**
32. Anthony Manahan, 2b, Horizon HS, Scottsdale, Ariz.
33. Tony Ochs, c, Southeastern Illinois JC
34. Scott Erickson, rhp, San Jose (Calif.) CC
35. Barry Earl, of, Columbus (Ga.)
36. Sam Austin, of, Waukegan (Ill.) East HS
37. Lance Dickson, lhp, Grossmont HS, La Mesa, Calif.
38. Rodney Windes, lhp, Cal State Los Angeles
39. Kevin Bumgarner, rhp, Cypress (Calif.) JC
40. Kevin Nielsen, lhp, JC of the Canyons (Calif.)
41. Dusty Madsen, rhp, Bella Vista HS, Fair Oaks, Calif.
42. Peter Hankinson, ss, Minnesota
43. Todd Pick, rhp, Lassen (Calif.) JC
44. Greg Gistlinck, c, Anaheim HS
45. Dan Donovan, rhp, Freehold Township (N.J.) HS
46. James Elliot, c, Glenbard West HS, Glen Ellen, Ill.

KANSAS CITY ROYALS

June—Regular Phase (9)

1. **Kevin Appier, rhp, Antelope Valley (Calif.) JC**
2. **Terry Shumpert, 2b, Kentucky**
3. **Stu Cole, ss, North Carolina-Charlotte**
4. **Jon Alexander, lhp, South Florida**
5. **Bob Wellington, rhp, Elizabeth (N.J.) HS**
6. **Ken Bowen, ss, Oregon State**
7. **Trey Gainous, of, Auburn**
8. **Kevin Shaw, rhp, Katella HS, Yorba Linda, Calif.**
9. **Bud Adams, rhp, Vanderbilt**
10. **Richie LeBlanc, rhp, Louisiana Tech**
11. **Darron Johnson, of, Boone HS, Orlando, Fla.**
12. **Kevin Pickens, rhp, Louisiana Tech**
13. **Archie Smith, lhp, Vanderbilt**
14. Javier Alvarez, ss, Sacred Heart HS, San Francisco
15. **Bill Drohan, rhp, Brewer State (Ala.) JC**
16. **Bobby Moore, of, Eastern Kentucky**
17. Greg Hammond, c, Chipola (Fla.) JC
18. John Seeburger, 1b, UC Irvine
19. **Doug Nelson, rhp, Pacific**
20. **Don Wright, 1b, San Jacinto (Texas) JC**
21. Darnell Dickerson, of, King HS, Detroit
22. **Jim Hudson, rhp, Los Angeles Harbor JC**
23. **Doug Bock, c, Missouri**
24. **Ben Pierce, lhp, Birmingham-Southern**
25. **Luis Mallea, rhp, St. Francis (N.Y.)**
26. **Keith Shibata, lhp, UCLA**
27. **Lanny Phillips, 3b, Lewis-Clark State (Idaho)**
28. Kelly Boyer, rhp, Shadow Mountain HS, Phoenix
29. **Steve Hoeme, rhp, Pratt (Kan.) CC**
30. **Juan Berrios, c/of, Long Island**
31. Jim Kosnik, lhp, Oakland (Mich.)
32. **Jim Campbell, lhp, San Diego State**
33. **Jorge Pedre, c, Los Angeles Harbor JC**
34. **Bobby Knecht, 2b, Hanover (Ind.)**
35. Scott Weiss, ss/rhp, Quartz Hill HS, Palmdale, Calif.
36. **Darryl Hardwick, of, Redwood HS, Visalia, Calif.**
37. **Derek Sholl, of, Los Angeles Harbor JC**
38. **Jeff Baum, 2b, Dallas Baptist**
39. **Brendan Haugh, of, Cloud County (Kan.) CC**
40. Don Ray, c, Kentucky
41. **Tim Byrnes, ss, Adelphi (N.Y.)**
42. **Pat Bergquist, of, Minnesota-Duluth**
43. Tim Ricks, rhp, Fayetteville HS, Childersburg, Ala.
44. **Doug Hupke, of, San Francisco**
45. **Jeff Cruse, rhp, Eastern Kentucky**
46. **Greg Karklins, rhp, Wright State**
47. **Kent Headley, of, Wichita State**
48. Damon Tyson, ss, Los Angeles CC
49. Tim Laker, c, Simi Valley (Calif.) HS
50. **Billy Gardner Jr., 1b, Mitchell (Conn.) JC**
51. **Fred Russell, ss, Compton (Calif.) HS**
52. Kim Cornist, of, Armijo HS, Suisun City, Calif.
53. Jeff Joseph, 2b, Arizona State
54. **Erwin Houston, of, Laney (Calif.) JC**
55. Henry DeLeon, 1b/of, Lee (Texas) JC
56. Greg Blevins, c, Choctaw (Okla.) HS
57. Fred Maggard, rhp, Cumberland (Ky.) HS
58. **Jeff Conine, 3b/1b, UCLA**
59. Mark Small, rhp, West Seattle HS
60. **Jerry Bentley, lhp, Mason (Ohio) HS**
61. Adam Mokres, of, Cuesta (Calif.) JC
62. Steve Gray, inf, Cuesta (Calif.) JC
63. Merle Gardner, of, Rockhurst HS, Kansas City, Mo.
64. Fred Riscen, lhp, JC of the Canyons (Calif.)
65. Bret Barberie, inf, Cerritos (Calif.) JC
66. Erik Plantenberg, lhp, Newport HS, Bellevue, Wash.
67. Mark Jones, rhp, Lee Davis HS, Mechanicsville, Va.
68. Gary Hymel, c, Belaire HS, Baton Rouge, La.
69. Chris Moock, ss, Baker HS, Greenwell Spring, La.
70. Kevin McGehee, rhp, Tioga HS, Pineville, La.
71. Eric Kuhlman, of, Bradley
72. Peter Hinkle, rhp, King HS, Tampa
73. Jerry Dean, rhp, Northeast HS, Little Rock, Ark.
74. Stewart Anthony, ss, Sparrows Point HS, Baltimore

LOS ANGELES DODGERS

June—Regular Phase (8)

1. **Dan Opperman, rhp, Valley HS, Las Vegas**
2. **Donnie Carroll, of, Granite Hills HS, El Cajon, Calif.**
3. **Chris Nichting, rhp, Northwestern**
4. **Tom DeMerit, of, Dartmouth**
5. **Luis Martinez, ss, Ohio Dominican**
6. **Darrin Fletcher, c, Illinois**
7. **Tony Barron, 3b/of, Willamette (Ore.)**

8. **Howard Freiling, 1b, North Carolina**
9. **Ken Luckham, rhp, Los Amigos HS, Fountain Valley, Calif.**
10. **Doug Noch, rhp, Central Michigan**
11. **Larry Gonzales, rhp, Don Lugo HS, Chino, Calif.**
12. Barry Blackwell, c, Florida State
13. **Sherman Collins, rhp, Oklahoma**
14. **Dan Floyd, c, Chino HS, Ontario, Calif.**
15. **Alan Lewis, ss, Davidson**
16. **John Wanish, rhp, Florida State**
17. **Bruce Dostal, of, William Paterson (N.J.)**
18. **Steve Green, of, Georgia Tech**
19. **Rafael Bournigal, inf, Florida State**
20. **Jose Munoz, ss, Florida JC**
21. **Dennis Springer, rhp, Fresno State**
22. Mike Parks, rhp, Florida
23. **Dan Kreuder, rhp, Pace (N.Y.)**
24. **Randy Wadsworth, c/of, California (Pa.)**
25. **Frank Mustari, 3b, Illinois State**
26. **Brian Emmert, 1b, Pace (N.Y.)**
27. **Dan Piscetta, rhp, Wooster (Ohio)**
28. **David Martin, rhp, Phillips (Okla.)**
29. **Zak Shinall, rhp, El Camino (Calif.) JC**
30. **Todd Melisauskas, c, Shippensburg (Pa.)**
31. **Eric Johnson, of, Cal State Sacramento**
32. **Bill Argo, of, Iowa State**
33. Chris Harding, of/3b, Clover HS, Moseley, Va.
34. Jim Poole, lhp, Georgia Tech
35. **Brian Currie, lhp, South Carolina**
36. Garrett Carter, 3b, South Carolina
37. **Jeff Herman, of, DeAnza (Calif.) JC**
38. Larry Rezny, lhp, Grand Haven (Mich.) HS
39. **Brett Magnusson, of, Santa Rosa (Calif.) JC**
40. Jerry Lutterman, rhp, Lafayette HS, Ellisville, Mo.
41. Jim Robinson, rhp/c, Sullivan HS, Chicago
42. Joe Fernandez, of, Galileo HS, San Francisco
43. **Mike James, rhp, Lurleen Wallace State (Ala.) JC**
44. **Chris Gettler, rhp, Jacksonville**
45. Doug Simons, lhp, Pepperdine
46. **Sam Bland, c, Kishwaukee (Ill.) JC**
47. **Albert Bustillos, rhp, Gavilan (Calif.) JC**
48. Ken Woods, ss, Palisades HS, Pacific Palisades, Calif.
49. Troy Arrington, rhp/ss, Jordan HS, Los Angeles
50. Vince Muldrew, of/lhp, Centennial HS, Compton, Calif.
51. Andre Perkens, c, Blair HS, Altadena, Calif.

MILWAUKEE BREWERS

June—Regular Phase (13)

1. **Bill Spiers III, ss, Clemson**
2. **Chris Johnson, rhp, Red Bank HS, Hixson, Tenn.**
2. **Curt Krippner, rhp, Texas** (Pick from Yankees as compensation for Type B free agent Rick Cerone)
3. **Jaime Navarro, rhp, Miami-Dade New World Center CC**
4. **Larry Carter, rhp, Plant City (Fla.) HS**
5. **Steve Sparks, rhp, Sam Houston State**
6. **Charlie Montoyo, 2b, Louisiana Tech**
7. **Brad Kucera, lhp, Creighton**
8. **Joe Ortiz, c, Pacific**
9. **Frank Bolick, 3b, Georgia Tech**
10. Scott Kimball, rhp, Salem State (Mass.)
11. **Rob Smith, of, Washington State**
12. **Mark Aguilar, 1b, Pima (Ariz.) CC**
13. **Troy O'Leary, of, Cypress (Calif.) HS**
14. **Tony Boze, of, Anderson (S.C.)**
15. **Mike Whitlock, lhp, Cuesta (Calif.) JC**
16. Keith Krenke, of, Owatonna (Minn.) HS
17. Layne Lambert, ss, Arlington HS, Riverside, Calif.
18. **Mark Chapman, rhp, Auburn**
19. **Todd Shiver, rhp, Georgia Tech**
20. Brian Turang, c/of, Long Beach (Calif.) CC
21. **Mark Kiefer, rhp, Fullerton (Calif.) JC**
22. **Dan Russell, 1b, Moorpark (Calif.) JC**
23. **Joe Roebuck, 3b/ss, Bryan (Ohio) HS**
24. Jeromy Burnitz, c/of, Conroe (Texas) HS
25. Chris Haney, lhp, Orange County HS, Barbourville, Va.
26. James Ingram, lhp, Lasanger HS, Hawthorne, Calif.
27. **Tim Raley, c/of, Wichita State**
28. Alfred Mitchell, of, Cuesta (Calif.) JC
29. Odel Stewart, of, Buena HS, Sierra Vista, Ariz.
30. Greg Knowles, rhp, Cardinal Gibson HS, Plantation, Fla.
31. Doug Louden, rhp, Elmhurst HS, Fort Wayne, Ind.
32. **Jeff Kinder, lhp, Randolph Southern HS, Lynn, Ind.**
33. James Henderson, c, Westlake HS, Agoura, Calif.
34. Shane Espitia, rhp, Ventura (Calif.) HS
35. Bart Grubbs, rhp, Carbon HS, Price, Utah
36. **Ron Jefferson, rhp, Kishwaukee (Ill.) JC**
37. Steve Renard, lhp, Preble HS, Green Bay, Wis.
38. Michael Bobala, lhp, Hudson (Fla.) HS
39. Mike Tosar, 2b, Columbus HS, Miami
40. Martin Durkin, 2b, Miami-Dade South CC
41. Troy Chacon, lhp, Pima (Ariz.) CC
42. Kreg Gresham, rhp, Independence HS, Charlotte
43. Ethon Flowers, c, Central Arizona JC
44. Steve Peck, rhp, Mesa (Ariz.) CC
45. Robert Dampier, rhp, Arizona Western JC
46. **David Bates, ss, South Salem (Ore.) HS**
47. **Steve Albillar Diez, c, Righetti HS, Santa Maria, Calif.**

MINNESOTA TWINS

June—Regular Phase (3)

1. **Willie Banks, rhp, St. Anthony's HS, Jersey City, N.J.**
2. **Terry Jorgensen, of, Wisconsin-Oshkosh**
3. **Wade Wacker, ss, Jackson (Minn.) HS**
4. **Mike Mathiot, c, Springfield (Ill.) HS**
5. **David Smith, of, Tulane**
6. **Larry Casian, lhp, Cal State Fullerton**
7. **Mark Guthrie, lhp, Louisiana State**
8. Mike Hinde, of, Brevard (Fla.) CC
9. Tom Lachmann, c, Kiona Benton HS, Benton City, Wash.
10. **David Richardson, lhp, Lone Pine (Calif.) HS**
11. Daren Burns, rhp, Birmingham-Southern
12. **Shawn Gilbert, ss, Fresno State**
13. **Doug Kline, rhp, Portland**
14. **Steve Stowell, lhp, UCLA**
15. Lozzell Mongomery, ss, Roswell (Ga.) HS
16. **Jose Marzan, inf/of, Florida State**
17. **Chip Hale, 2b, Arizona**
18. **Mark Ericson, c, Connecticut**
19. **Ed Alvarez, of, American HS, Miami**
20. **Mike Anthony, lhp, Rancho Santiago (Calif.) JC**
21. **Charles Jones, 1b, UNC Wilmington**
22. Dan Smith, lhp, Apple Valley (Minn.) HS
23. Dennis Burbank, rhp, Valencia HS, Anaheim
24. **Pat Bangston, rhp, Kent State**
25. **Dean Tartarian, ss, Cardozza HS, Bayside, N.Y.**
26. Dan Deville, rhp, Mount San Antonio (Calif.) JC
27. Cord Corbitt, lhp, Leonard HS, West Palm Beach, Fla.
28. Bret Boone, ss, El Dorado HS, Villa Park, Calif.
29. Glen Dallmann, c, Bradley
30. **Walter Watts, rhp, Independence HS, San Jose**
31. Matt Bullock, of, Alta Loma (Calif.) HS
32. **Steve Scanlon, rhp, Pepperdine**
33. **Richard Freeman, c, Dundalk (Md.) CC**
34. Daryl Lancaster, lhp, Whittier (Calif.) Christian HS
35. John Stewart, of, Horace Mann HS, Gary, Ind.
36. Craig Paquette, 3b, Rancho Alamitos HS, Garden Grove, Calif.
37. **Tom Marten, rhp, Long Island**
38. Toi Cook, of, Stanford
39. Charles Guetter, rhp, Pensacola (Fla.) JC
40. Chris Garrett, rhp, Westchester HS, Los Angeles
41. Matt Hattabaugh, c, Marina HS, Huntington Beach, Calif.
42. **Bryan Roskom, ss, Appleton (Wis.) HS**

MONTREAL EXPOS

June—Regular Phase (12)

1. **Delino DeShields, ss, Seaford (Del.) HS**
1. **Tyrone Kingwood, of, Imperial Valley (Calif.) JC** (Supplemental pick—28th—for loss of Type A free agent

Andre Dawson)
2. **Nate Minchey, rhp, Pflugerville (Texas) HS** (Pick from Cubs as compensation for Dawson)
2. **Richie Lewis, rhp, Florida State**
3. **John Vander Wal, of, Western Michigan**
4. **Boi Rodriguez, 3b, Indiana State**
5. **Archi Cianfrocco, ss, Purdue**
6. **Greg Colbrunn, 3b, Fontana (Calif.) HS**
7. **Howard Farmer, rhp, Jackson State**
8. **Trevor Penn, 1b, Cal State Los Angeles**
9. Donovan Osborne, lhp, Carson HS, Carson City, Nev.
10. **Chris Pollack, lhp, Florida State**
11. **Steve Lemuth, of, Pentucket Regional HS, Groveland, Mass.**
12. **Chris Marchok, lhp, Harvard**
13. **Bob Natal, c, UC San Diego**
14. **Terrel Hansen, rhp, Washington State**
15. **Kelvin Shephard, of, Montevallo (Ala.)**
16. Robbie Orndorff, 2b, Connellsville HS, Millrun, Pa.
17. **Javan Reagans, of, Dallas Baptist**
18. **Tim Piechowski, of, St. Mary's (Minn.)**
19. **Jeff Carter, rhp, Tampa**
20. **Matt Shiflett, rhp, Arizona State**
21. **Rob Mason, c, New Orleans**
22. **Tom Giannelli, 1b, Redlands (Calif.)**
23. **Kevin Cavalier, rhp, Northeast Louisiana**
24. **Jeff Atha, 2b, Jacksonville State**
25. Mike Sodders, lhp, Alabama
26. **Bruce Wegman, rhp, Central Arizona JC**
27. **Larry Doss, of, Southwest Missouri State**
28. Bret Davis, rhp, Sacramento CC
29. **Kevin Foster, 3b, Evanston (Ill.) HS**
30. **Steve Overeem, rhp, Southern California College**
31. Mike Lane, 1b, Ely HS, Coral Springs, Fla.
32. Gary Posey, of, Mosley HS, Panama City, Fla.
33. John McGinnis, lhp, Clackamas HS, Milwaukie, Ore.
34. Greg Kennard, rhp, Leonard HS, West Palm Beach, Fla.
35. Jon French, ss, St. Joseph HS, Alameda, Calif.
36. Robert Wilkinson, of, Waukegan (Ill.) West HS
37. Kevin Johnson, of, Taft (Calif.) JC
38. Peter LeBlond, of, Mesa (Ariz.) HS
39. **Roosevelt Walker, of, Selma (Ala.) HS**
40. Mike Seda, of, Shadow Mountain HS, Phoenix
41. **James Faulk, of, Louisburg (N.C.) JC**
42. Arnold Williams, 1b/of, Southeast Guilford HS, Greensboro, N.C.
43. Greg Brown, ss, Indian River (Fla.) CC
44. Bobby Magallanes, ss, Bell HS, Downey, Calif.
45. David Horine, ss/2b, Chandler (Ariz.) HS
46. Chris Grant, of, Crenshaw HS, Los Angeles
47. Hermie Brown, of/1b, Crenshaw HS, Los Angeles
48. Clash Bailey, c, Verbum Dei HS, Compton, Calif.
49. Robert Small, 1b, Compton (Calif.) JC

NEW YORK METS

June—Regular Phase (24)

1. **Chris Donnels, 3b, Loyola Marymount**
2. **Todd Hundley, c, Fremd HS, Palatine, Ill.** (Pick from Orioles as compensation for Type B free agent Ray Knight)
2. **Pete Schourek, lhp, Marshall HS, Falls Church, Va.**
3. **Tim Hines, c, Kishwaukee (Ill.) JC**
4. **Mike Miller, rhp, St. Louis CC-Meramec**
5. Ricky Kimball, rhp, Redan HS, Lithonia, Ga.
6. **Jim Tesmer, of, Fresno CC**
7. **Terry Griffin, rhp, Tennessee Temple HS, Jacksonville**
8. **Tim Bogar, ss, Eastern Illinois**
9. **Pat Howell, of, Vigor HS, Prichard, Ala.**
10. **Steve LaRose, rhp, Crowder (Mo.) JC**
11. **Monte Krogman, rhp, Quincy (Ill.) HS**
12. **Derrick Young, of, Edmonds (Wash.) CC**
13. **Terry Bross, rhp, St. John's**
14. Robert Pickowitz, ss/of, Indio (Calif.) HS
15. Todd Krumm, rhp, Michigan State
16. **Eric Hillman, lhp, Eastern Illinois**
17. Robert Dodd, lhp, River City HS, Sacramento
18. **Denny Harriger, rhp, Ford City (Pa.) HS**
19. **Jim McAnarney, rhp, Fort Hays State (Kan.)**
20. **John Johnstone, rhp, Bishop Ludden HS, Liverpool, N.Y.**
21. Kyle Irvin, rhp, Oral Roberts
22. **David Trautwein, rhp, North Carolina**
23. **Pat Disabato, lhp, Lewis (Ill.)**
24. **Stan Cameron, of, Palo HS, Powell, Tenn.**
25. Gary Forrester, ss, Sacramento CC
26. Dan Wilson, c/rhp, Barrington (Ill.) HS
27. **Doug Myres, rhp, Texas-Arlington**
28. Jon Martin, c/of, Edison HS, Huntington Beach, Calif.
29. **Lonnie Walker, of, Houston**
30. **James Echols, of, East Webster HS, Mantee, Miss.**
31. **Craig Scott, rhp, Franklin County HS, Cowan, Tenn.**
32. **Titi Roche, of, Miami-Dade North CC**
33. Andrew Lumsdon, lhp, Brazil (Ind.) HS
34. **Ryan Richmond, rhp, Bradley Bourbon HS, Bourbonnais, Ill.**
35. Robbie Guzik, of, Latrobe (Pa.) HS
36. **Greg Turtletaub, of, JC of San Mateo (Calif.)**
37. **David Joiner, 3b/of, Vanderbilt**
38. **Anthony Young, rhp, Houston**
39. Brent Bartlett, 3b, Allen County (Kan.) CC
40. Rob Norman, lhp, Tullahoma (Tenn.) HS
41. **Marc Wiese, 3b, Wilson HS, Tacoma**
42. **Chris Hill, lhp, Duncanville (Texas) HS**
43. Barry Johnson, rhp, Joliet (Ill.) Catholic HS
44. Darrin White, c, Cypress (Texas) Fair HS
45. Shaun Lesina, rhp, JC of the Redwoods (Calif.)
46. **Scott Spoolstra, of/1b, Moraine Valley (Ill.) JC**
47. **Dan Segui, rhp, Kansas City (Kan.) CC**
48. Manny Cervantes, 1b, La Serna HS, Whittier, Calif.
49. Jeff Borgese, of, Los Gatos HS, Los Angeles
50. Mike Cornelius, lhp, Fenger HS, Chicago
51. **Richard Ostopowicz, lhp, Northwood Institute (Texas)**
52. William Abernathy, rhp, Bowden (Ga.) HS
53. Keith Dunkel, ss, Topeka (Kan.) West HS
54. Eric Bush, of, Quincy (Ill.) HS
55. Michael Kirk, of, West Valley HS, Cottonwood, Calif.
56. Ryan Hundsdorfer, 3b, Monache HS, Porterville, Calif.
57. Joe Magill, c, Mullin HS, Littleton, Colo.
58. Ken Henderson, of/1b, Saratoga HS, Santa Clara, Calif.
59. Scott Sorenson, rhp, Cloquet (Minn.) HS
60. Terence Harshaw, c, Northeast HS, North Little Rock, Ark.

NEW YORK YANKEES

June—Regular Phase (23)

1. (Pick to Rangers as compensation for Type A free agent Gary Ward)
2. (Pick to Brewers as compensation for Type B free agent Rick Cerone)
3. **Bill DaCosta, rhp, New York Tech**
4. **Doug Gogoleski, rhp, Michigan State**
5. **Anthony Morrison, lhp, High Point (N.C.)**
6. **Tom Popplewell, rhp, Miami-Dade North CC**
7. **Dave Eiland, rhp, South Florida**
8. Doug Tegtmeier, rhp, Beatrice (Neb.) HS
9. **Lewellyn Hill, of, Collingwood HS, Cleveland**
10. **Dean Kelley, 2b, Tampa**
11. **Ed Martel, rhp, De La Salle HS, New Baltimore, Mich.**
12. Mike Mahady, rhp, Brewton-Parker (Ga.)
13. **Vince Phillips, of, Muir HS, Pasadena, Calif.**
14. **Gerald Williams, of, Grambling State**
15. **Darrell Tingle, ss, Louisburg (N.C.) JC**
16. **Rodney Imes, rhp, Old Dominion**
17. Terry Bradshaw, ss, Windsor HS, Zuni, Va.
18. **Royal Clayton, rhp, UC Riverside**
19. **Freddie Hailey, of, Western Carolina**
20. Robert Coffel, c, Bremen (Ind.) HS
21. Rob Bargas, 3b, Sacramento CC
22. **David Turgeon, 3b, Davidson**
23. **Bobby Dickerson, ss, Nicholls State**
24. **Steve Erickson, c, Pepperdine**
25. **Tom Weeks, 1b, Cal Poly Pomona**
26. **David Howell, lhp, Miami-Dade South CC**
27. **Sean Gargin, rhp, John Jay (N.Y.)**

28. Paul Meade, ss, Urbandale (Iowa) HS
29. **Dennis Ryans, ss, LaSalle HS, South Bend, Ind.**
30. Steve Tucker, lhp, Manatee (Fla.) JC
31. Curtis Ralph, rhp, Sacramento CC
32. Brian Faw, rhp, DeKalb Central (Ga.) JC
33. David Sorokowski, rhp, Southridge HS, Miami
34. Todd Ingram, rhp, Sammamish HS, Bellevue, Wash.
35. **Ricky Rhodes, rhp, Navarro (Texas) JC**
36. Joel Sealer, lhp, Nebraska
37. **Todd Brill, lhp, Allen County (Kan.) CC**
38. Jeff Livesey, c, Auburn
39. **Cullen Hartzog, rhp, Mosley HS, Panama City, Fla.**
40. Todd Neibel, rhp, Southern Illinois
41. **Rod Ehrhard, c, Tampa**
42. James Mouton, ss, Burbank HS, Sacramento
43. **Mike Minix, ss, Paintsville, (Ky.) HS**
44. **Joey Blackwell, ss, Donithan (Miss.) HS**
45. Richard Ayers, of, Donithan (Miss.) HS
46. **Dan Roman, ss, Indiana State**
47. Tom Breidenbach, rhp, Concordia (N.Y.)
48. **Brad Ausmus, c, Cheshire (Conn.) HS**
49. David Fitzgerald, lhp, Davidson
50. **Ken Brown, ss, Northeast Louisiana**
51. Jim Agemy, rhp, Michigan
52. Kevin Parrish, rhp, Cleveland State
53. David Taylor, of, Miami
54. Brent McCoy, ss, Howard (D.C.)
55. **Steve Taddeo, of, Florida State**
56. Derrick Pedro, of, King HS, Tampa

OAKLAND ATHLETICS

June—Regular Phase (11)

1. **Lee Tinsley, of, Shelby County HS, Shelbyville, Ky.**
2. (Pick to Angels as compensation for Type A free agent Reggie Jackson)
3. Scott Livingstone, 3b, Texas A&M
4. **Scott Chiamparino, rhp, Santa Clara**
5. **Jim Chenevey, lhp, Harvard**
6. **Marteese Robinson, 1b, Seton Hall**
7. **Joel Smith, of, Tennessee**
8. **Mike Ryser, c, Southern Utah State**
9. **Steve Wilson, rhp, St. Xavier (Ill.)**
10. **Kevin MacLeod, lhp, Toledo**
11. Jerry Nielsen, lhp, Florida State
12. **Rick Berg, rhp, LeMoyne**
13. **Trevor Eldridge, ss, Cerritos (Calif.) HS**
14. **Ron Coomer, 3b, Taft (Calif.) JC**
15. **Pat Wernig, lhp, Texas A&M**
16. **Brian Veilleux, lhp, Texas Christian**
17. **Keith Watkins, of, Southern California**
18. Dan Penner, rhp, Cal State Northridge
19. **Rodney Williams, ss, Waukegan (Ill.) West HS**
20. **Scott Brosius, 3b, Linfield (Ore.)**
21. Jay Knoblauh, of, Rice
22. **Will Schock, rhp, California**
23. **Steven Hosinski, rhp, Bethel (Ind.)**
24. **Roy Hill, rhp, Alcorn State**
25. Howard Landry, lhp, Howard (Texas) JC
26. **Mike Dockery, lhp, Abingdon (Va.) HS**
27. **David Finley, ss, UC Riverside**
28. Chad Kuhn, 1b, New Mexico
29. Andrew Nieman, rhp, Holy Cross
30. Eric Campa, ss, Colton (Calif.) HS
31. **Fred Hanker, 3b, Cal State Dominguez Hills**
32. **Robert Parry, of, San Diego State**
33. Eric Christopherson, c, Ocean View HS, Huntington Beach, Calif.
34. Antonio Adams, 2b, Vanden HS, Vacaville, Calif.
35. Jeff Cesari, rhp, UC Santa Barbara

PHILADELPHIA PHILLIES

June—Regular Phase (20)

1. (Pick to Tigers as compensation for Type A free agent Lance Parrish)
2. **Matt Rambo, lhp, Richland (Texas) JC**
3. **Kim Batiste, ss, St. Amant HS, Prairieville, La.**
4. **Ricky Trlicek, rhp, La Grange (Texas) HS**
5. Roger Dixon, lhp, Antioch HS, Nashville, Tenn.
6. **Doug Lindsey, c, Seminole State (Okla.) JC**
7. **Donnie Elliott, rhp, Deer Park (Texas) HS**
8. **Isaac Galloway, of, Alta Loma (Calif.) HS**
9. **David Allen, rhp, Greece Athena HS, Rochester, N.Y.**
10. Robert LeFebre, of, Miami-Dade South CC
11. Marc Helms, c, Panola (Texas) JC
12. Kevin Castleberry, ss, Conroe (Texas) HS
13. **Dave Willes, 2b, Brigham Young**
14. **Mark Cobb, of, Franklin HS, Columbus, Ohio**
15. **Gary Maasberg, 3b, Santa Clara**
16. **Scott Reaves, 3b, Cal Poly San Luis Obispo**
17. Jeff Williams, rhp, Wichita (Kan.) North HS
18. **Steve Dell'Amico, rhp, Pepperdine**
19. **Jimmy Barragan, 1b, Oklahoma State**
20. **Jim Vatcher, of, Cal State Northridge**
21. **Troy Zerb, 2b, Ephrata (Wash.) HS**
22. **Jeff Scott, c, Butler County (Kan.) CC**
23. **Robert Hurda, lhp, Angelina (Texas) JC**
24. Anthony Ward, lhp, Seminole State (Okla.) JC
25. Jeff Hilleshiem, rhp, Central (Iowa)
26. **Marc Lopez, rhp, Alhambra, Calif.**
27. **Toby Borland, rhp, Quitman (La.) HS**
28. **John LaRosa, lhp, Cal State Northridge**
29. **Steve Bates, of, Fresno State**
30. Jon Degennaro, rhp, Moorpark (Calif.) JC
31. **Royal Thomas, rhp, Westbrook HS, Beaumont, Texas**
32. **Joe Williams, of, San Francisco**
33. **Shelby McDonald, rhp, Alvin (Texas) CC**
34. **Matt Viggiano, rhp, Cousno HS, Warren, Mich.**
35. **Bob Chadwick, lhp, Nevada-Las Vegas**
36. **Greg McCarthy, lhp, Bridgeport (Conn.) HS**
37. **Andy Carter, lhp, Springfield HS, Erdenheim, Pa.**
38. Pete Schmidt, c, Oral Roberts
39. **Phil Fagnana, rhp, South Florida**
40. **Tony Trevino, 2b, Cal State Fullerton**
41. **Eric Enos, c, San Francisco**
42. **Rodney Hampton, of, Fostoria (Ohio) HS**
43. Ken Bean, of, Ranger (Texas) JC
44. Jason DeGroote, c, Granite Hills HS, Ramona, Calif.
45. Bill Lucid, lhp, Alemany HS, Sylmar, Calif.
46. Greg Bicknell, rhp, Bullard HS, Fresno
47. Matt Lundin, ss, Tustin (Calif.) HS
48. Troy Mentzer, c, Allen County (Kan.) CC
49. **Corey Smith, c, McCluer HS, Ferguson, Md.**
50. **Robert Britt, of, Wilmington (Del.)**
51. Kurt Pfeffer, 3b, Drake HS, Forest Knolls, Calif.

PITTSBURGH PIRATES

June—Regular Phase (2)

1. **Mark Merchant, of, Oviedo (Fla.) HS**
2. **Ben Shelton, lhp/1b, Oak Park (Ill.) HS**
3. Brian Williams, ss, Lewisville HS, Fort Lawn, S.C.
4. **Wes Chamberlain, of, Jackson State**
5. **Ben Webb, rhp, Chipola (Fla.) JC**
6. **Mark Thomas, of, Santa Rosa (Calif.) JC**
7. Mickey Morandini, ss, Indiana
8. Kurt Knudsen, rhp, American River (Calif.) JC
9. **Jim Haywood, lhp/1b, Dundee-Crown HS, Carpentersville, Ill.**
10. **Scott Barczi, c/of, Northwestern**
11. **Jose Palos, of, Castle Park HS, Chula Vista, Calif.**
12. **Calvin Duncan, rhp, Columbus (Ga.)**
13. **Jeff Griffith, 3b, Anderson (S.C.)**
14. **Rey Vizcaino, 1b/rhp, Valdosta State (Ga.)**
15. **Craig Lewis, rhp, JC of Southern Idaho**
16. **Anthony Thompson, of, Selma (Ala.) HS**
17. **Steve Carter, of, Georgia**
18. **Kevin Burdick, 2b/ss, Oklahoma**
19. Mike Fyhrie, ss/rhp, Ocean View HS, Westminster, Calif.
20. **Mike Wall, 3b, Norwood (Mass.) HS**
21. **Pete Freeman, c/1b, Georgia**

22. **Ron Downs, rhp, Wyoming**
23. **Mickey Peyton, of/ss, Valdosta State (Ga.)**
24. Jeff Knepper, rhp, Mount Union (Pa.) Area HS
25. **Keith Raisanen, of, Birmingham-Southern**
26. Bob Ayrault, rhp, Nevada-Las Vegas
27. **Doug Torborg, lhp, North Carolina**
28. **Lyle Befort, rhp, Fort Hays State (Kan.)**
29. **Ed Shea, c, Florida**
30. **John Latham, lhp, Spartanburg Methodist (S.C.) JC**
31. **George Spriggs, 2b, Anne Arundel (Md.) CC**
32. **Gary Schmitt, of, Allegheny (Pa.) CC**
33. **Jody Williams, 2b/ss, Hampton-Sydney (Va.)**
34. **Troy Jackson, of/1b, Canada (Calif.) JC**
35. **Tim Holmes, rhp, Valparaiso**
36. Anthony Lee, rhp, Kishwaukee (Ill.) JC
37. **Robert Barnwell, rhp, Henderson County (Texas) JC**
38. Mike Persichini, lhp, Penn State
39. **William Moore, lhp, North Carolina Wesleyan**
40. **Andy Stewart, of, Austin Peay**
41. Jeff Shore, c, UNC Charlotte
42. Troy Trollope, of, Billings (Mont.) HS
43. Jessie Torres, c, Nampa (Idaho) HS
44. Todd McCray, rhp, Santa Fe (Fla.) CC
45. Steve Borris, of, Valencia (Fla.) CC
46. Shawn Purdy, rhp, Valencia (Fla.) CC
47. Alfonso Bryan, of, Dundalk (Md.) CC
48. David Silvernail, rhp, University HS, Spokane, Wash.
49. Reggie Hubbard, ss, Santa Rosa (Calif.) JC
50. **Rodger Castner, rhp, Nevada-Las Vegas**
51. Anthony Brown, inf/of, Highlands HS, North Highland, Calif.
52. Steve Polewski, ss, Triton (Ill.) JC
53. **Paul Miller, rhp, Carthage (Wis.)**

ST. LOUIS CARDINALS

June—Regular Phase (14)

1. **Cris Carpenter, rhp, Georgia**
2. **Jeremy Hernandez, rhp, Cal State Northridge**
3. **Ray Lankford, of, Modesto (Calif.) JC**
4. Mike Ignasiak, rhp, Michigan
5. **Rod Brewer, 1b/of, Florida**
6. **Antron Grier, of, Faulkner (Ala.)**
7. **Dean Weese, rhp, U.S. International (Nairobi)**
8. **Tim Redman, c, Georgetown**
9. David Tripp, rhp/of, Mount St. Joseph HS, Glen Burnie, Md.
10. Paul Splatt, ss, CC of Baltimore
11. **Darren Nelson, of/1b, Chapman (Calif.)**
12. **Alan Biggers, ss, Stratford HS, Goose Creek, S.C.**
13. **Ken Sebree, rhp, Florida**
14. **Brad Harvick, lhp, Oral Roberts**
15. **Jean-Paul Gentleman, ss, Mississippi**
16. **Ed Fulton, c, Florida State**
17. **Kevin Robinson, of, U.S. International (Nairobi)**
18. **Tim Sherrill, lhp, Arkansas**
19. **Chris Houser, rhp, Nevada**
20. **Kris Huffman, ss, Catawba (N.C.)**
21. **Frank Moran, ss/2b, U.S. International (Nairobi)**
22. **Shawn Hathaway, rhp, Washington State**
23. **John Balfanz, 1b, Cal State Northridge**
24. **Mike Hinkle, rhp, Kansas State**
25. **Pat Moore, c, Louisiana Tech**
26. **Joey Fernandez, of, Florida**
27. Ken Deal, rhp, Florida International
28. **John Sellick, 1b, UC Riverside**
29. **Clint Horsley, rhp, Liberty**
30. **Ken Smith, rhp, West Virginia**
31. **Dan Hitt, lhp, St. Louis CC-Meramec**
32. **Scott Halama, rhp, Florida Atlantic**
33. **Jim Gibbs, rhp, Southwest Missouri State**
34. **Tony Russo, rhp, Missouri**
35. **Larry Pierson, rhp, Missouri**
36. Brad Court, ss, Logan HS, Union City, Calif.
37. **Jerry Daniels, lhp, St. Louis CC-Meramec**
38. William Ramirez, of, Anderson HS, Cincinnati
39. David Williams, rhp, Marked Tree (Ark.) HS
40. **Ryan Johnston, of, George Mason**

SAN DIEGO PADRES

June—Regular Phase (10)

1. **Kevin Garner, rhp/of, Texas**
2. **Roger Smithberg, rhp, Bradley**
3. **Bob Sheridan, rhp, Upland (Calif.) HS**
4. **Darrin Reichle, rhp, St. Leo (Fla.)**
5. **David Bond, lhp, Troy State**
6. **Dave Hollins, 3b, South Carolina**
7. **Andy Skeels, c, Arkansas**
8. Marty Cordova, ss, Bishop Gorman HS, Las Vegas
9. **Reggie Farmer, of, Nevada-Las Vegas**
10. **Saul Soltero, rhp, Emporia State (Kan.)**
11. Steve Fitzgerald, ss, Brookdale (N.J.) CC
12. **Ed Jones, rhp, W.T. White HS, Dallas**
13. Glen Gardner, of, Rutgers
14. **Rich Holsman, lhp, San Diego State**
15. **Charles Hillemann, of, Southern Illinois**
16. **William Reed, lhp, Santana HS, Santee, Calif.**
17. Gil Torres, of, Gulf Coast (Fla.) CC
18. **Tony Lewis, rhp, Pepperdine**
19. **Steve Loubier, rhp, Maine**
20. **Terry Gilmore, rhp, Florida Southern**
21. Pedro Gonzalez, c, American HS, Hialeah, Fla.
22. **Kevin Farmer, c, South Alabama**
23. **Paul Faries, ss, Pepperdine**
24. **Monte Brooks, of, San Jose State**
25. Nathan LaDuke, of, Alhambra HS, Phoenix
26. Alan Newman, lhp, La Habra (Calif.) HS
27. **Mike Meyers, rhp, UC Santa Barbara**
28. **Steve Hendricks, of, U.S. International (Nairobi)**
29. **Jay Estrada, rhp, Metropolitan State (Colo.)**
30. Harry Perez, of, Olivet Nazarene (Ill.)
31. William Neverr, rhp, Diamond HS, Anchorage
32. Jason Thornburg, 3b, Golden West HS, Visalia, Calif.
33. Eldridge Olmstead, rhp, Cate HS, Laguna Beach, Calif.
34. Tony Spires, rhp, Anderson (S.C.) JC

SAN FRANCISCO GIANTS

June—Regular Phase (16)

1. **Mike Remlinger, lhp, Dartmouth**
2. **Eric Gunderson, lhp, Portland State (Ore.)**
3. **Mike Benjamin, ss, Arizona State**
4. **Joe Speakes, of, Poly HS, Sun Valley, Calif.**
5. **Steve Hecht, 2b, Oral Roberts**
6. **Jamie Cooper, of, Dallas Baptist**
7. Sylvester Love, of, Southern Mississippi
8. **Tom Hostetler, rhp, Delta State (Miss.)**
9. **Gil Heredia, rhp, Arizona**
10. **John Vuz, c, Jacksonville**
11. David Westwood, 1b, Pittsburgh
12. Bill Gearhart, rhp, Armstrong State (Ga.)
13. **Randy Lind, of, Portland State (Ore.)**
14. Dan Henrikson, lhp/of, Richland (Wash.) HS
15. **Tony Michalak, ss/2b, Illinois**
16. Stan Loewer, rhp, Louisiana State
17. **Doug Messer, lhp, Florida International**
18. **Erik Johnson, ss, UC Santa Barbara**
19. **Markus Owens, c/3b, Hawaii**
20. **Kevin Meier, rhp, Georgia Southern**
21. **Ron McClintock, 1b/of, Concordia (Ore.)**
22. **Mike Greenwood, of, Moorpark (Calif.) JC**
23. **Mark Dewey, rhp, Grand Valley State (Mich.)**
24. **Mike Ham, c, Cal State Fullerton**
25. **Jim Terrill, lhp, Lamar**
26. **Keith James, of, JC of the Desert (Calif.)**
27. **Andy Rohn, 2b, Central Michigan**
28. Robert Somerville, rhp, Charles County (Md.) CC
29. **Steve Lienhard, rhp, Overton HS, Memphis**
30. Adam Smith, c, Oklahoma State
31. **Rich Aldrete, of, California**
32. **Reid Gunter, rhp, Sacramento CC**

33. **Jim Malseed, of, Winthrop**
34. **Lennie McGuire, rhp, Mount Hood (Ore.) CC**
35. **Jimmy Meyers, rhp, Crowder (Okla.) HS**
36. David Klinefelter, lhp, Allegheny (Pa.) CC
37. Mike Meyers, 1b, Washington State
38. **Chris Kocman, 3b, Cal State Chico**
39. **Donn Perno, 2b, Georgia**
40. **Mike Wandler, ss/3b, Point Park (Pa.)**
41. **Rocco Buffolino, rhp, Cal State Sacramento**
42. **Gary Geiger, rhp, Texas A&M**
43. **Robert Wilson, 1b, Sonoma State (Calif.)**
44. **Kip Southland, ss, Central Michigan**
45. **Glenn Abraham, of, Howard (D.C.)**
46. **Todd Hawkins, c, Baylor**
47. **Elanis Westbrooks, ss, Texas**
48. Mike Rooney, rhp, Alemany HS, Granada Hills, Calif.

SEATTLE MARINERS

June—Regular Phase (1)

1. **Ken Griffey Jr., of, Moeller HS, Cincinnati**
2. **Dave Burba, rhp, Ohio State**
3. **Mike Goff, rhp, Fresno State**
4. Rick Lantrip, ss, Golden West HS, Visalia, Calif.
5. **Brian Wilkinson, rhp, Cherry Creek HS, Englewood, Colo.**
6. Joe Slusarski, rhp, New Orleans
7. **Mike McGuire, rhp, Sweeny HS, Old Ocean, Texas**
8. Eric Helfand, c, Patrick Henry HS, San Diego
9. **Ted Eldredge, rhp, California**
10. Tookie Spann, 3b/of, Tulane
11. Bob Bretwisch, lhp, Bradley
12. **Brian Baldwin, rhp, Northeastern**
13. Jim Foley, rhp, Orange Coast (Calif.) JC
14. **Keith Helton, lhp, Arkansas**
15. **Charlie Webb, lhp, Cal Poly Pomona**
16. **Corey Paul, of, Belmont HS, Los Angeles**
17. **Ellerton Maynard, of, Miami-Dade New World Center CC**
18. **Mike Gardiner, rhp, Indiana State**
19. **Dorian Daughtry, of, Kingsborough (N.Y.) CC**
20. **Mike Sisco, ss, Arkansas**
21. **Daryl Burrus, 3b/c, Locke HS, Los Angeles**
22. **Kevin Reichardt, 2b, Wisconsin-Oshkosh**
23. Pat Listach, ss, McLennan (Texas) CC
24. **Greg Burlingame, lhp, Hawaii**
25. **Otis Patrick, of, Edmonds (Wash.) CC**
26. **Anthony Gordon, lhp, Avon Park (Fla.) HS**
27. Randy Rivera, rhp, Ranger (Texas) JC
28. **Tony Cayson, of, Ocala (Fla.) Forest HS**
29. Brian Cisarik, of, Texas
30. **Gary Cameron, lhp/1b, Utah Technical JC**
31. Keith Barrett, of/inf, Cal Poly Pomona
32. **Ranfred Johnson, rhp, El Camino (Calif.) JC**
33. Justin Mitton, ss, Trevor Brown HS, Phoenix
34. **Scott Pitcher, rhp, Hillsborough (Fla.) CC**
35. **Steve Hisey, of, UCLA**
36. **Jeff Hooper, c, Washington State**
37. **Erick Bryant, rhp, Long Beach, Calif.**
38. **Todd Haney, 2b, Texas**
39. **Scott Storck, rhp, Orange Coast (Calif.) JC**
40. **Steve Bieksha, rhp, Lowell (Mass.)**
41. **John Hoffman, c, Ballard HS, Seattle**
42. Gar Finnvold, rhp, Palm Beach (Fla.) JC
43. **Tom Peters, rhp, Santa Monica (Calif.) JC**
44. Jeff Brouelette, 2b, Orange Coast (Calif.) JC
45. Emmitt Cohick, of, Fullerton (Calif.) JC
46. Jeff Darwin, rhp, Bonham (Texas) HS
47. Corey Thomas, rhp, Pinole Valley HS, Pinole, Calif.
48. Florentino Lozano, of, Palomar (Calif.) JC
49. Keith Mays, rhp, Bassett (Va.) HS
50. John Burton, rhp, Bonita HS, LaVerne, Calif.
51. **Ruben Gonzales, 1b, Pepperdine**
52. James Hurst, lhp, South Florida JC
53. David Boss, rhp, San Jose (Calif.) CC
54. **Jeff Keitges, 1b, American River (Calif.) JC**
55. **Jeff Morrison, 1b, Chapman (Calif.)**

TEXAS RANGERS

June—Regular Phase (19)

1. **Brian Bohanon, lhp, North Shore HS, Houston**
1. **Bill Haselman, c, UCLA** (Pick from Yankees as compensation for Type A free agent Gary Ward)
1. **Mark Petkovsek, rhp, Texas** (Supplemental pick—29th—for loss of Ward)
2. **Barry Manuel, rhp, Louisiana State**
3. **Scott Coolbaugh, 3b, Texas**
4. **Jon Hurst, rhp, Spartanburg Methodist (S.C.) JC**
5. **Terry Mathews, rhp, Northeast Louisiana**
6. **Kevin Belcher, of, Navarro (Texas) JC**
7. **Tony Scruggs, of, UCLA**
8. **Gary Alexander, of, Arizona**
9. Bert Heffernan, c, Clemson
10. **Brian Steiner, lhp, Seminole State (Okla.) JC**
11. Bryant Winslow, of, Columbine HS, Littleton, Colo.
12. **Mike Taylor, rhp, McLennan (Texas) CC**
13. **Glen Bruckner, inf, Georgetown**
14. **Spencer Wilkinson, rhp, Arkansas**
15. **Todd Van Horn, ss, St. Edward's (Texas)**
16. **Darren Niethammer, c/of, Evansville, Ind.**
17. **Omar Brewer, of, Houston**
18. **Bill Losa, c, San Jacinto (Texas) JC**
19. **Wayne Ebarb, rhp, Zwolle (La.) HS**
20. **Mike Rogers, of, Missouri**
21. **Rod Lung, c, McNeese State**
22. **David Lynch, lhp, New Orleans**
23. **Adam Lamle, lhp, Southwestern Louisiana**
24. Mike Helm, ss, Carson (Calif.) HS
25. **Randy Boron, rhp, Cleveland State**
26. Greg Logan, rhp, Martin HS, Arlington, Texas
27. **Marvin Rockman, rhp, Oklahoma State**
28. **Luke Sable, of, George Mason**
29. John Morton, rhp, Texas
30. **Todd Schultz, ss, Ferris State (Mich.)**
31. **Kevin Mmahat, lhp, Tulane**
32. **Robb Nen, rhp, Los Alamitos HS, Seal Beach, Calif.**
33. **Thayer Swain, of, San Jacinto (Texas) JC**
34. Manuel Molina, rhp, Arizona Western JC
35. Ed Pierce, of, Glendora HS, San Dimas, Calif.
36. Brad Hebets, rhp, Southwestern Louisiana
37. **Todd Kopczynski, rhp, North Carolina**
38. Elgin Bobo, c, Monta Vista HS, Freedom, Calif.
39. Brian Maize, 1b, Rolling Meadows HS, Arlington Heights, Ill.
40. Michael Brady, rhp, Nassau (N.Y.) JC
41. Gary Ross, rhp, San Diequito HS, Olivehaim, Calif.
42. Kevin Jones, 3b, Seminole State (Okla.) JC
43. Eric Stone, rhp, Seminole State (Okla.) JC
44. Charlton Lynch, inf/of, Lincoln HS, San Diego
45. Mike Burton, 1b, JC of the Sequoias (Calif.)
46. Kevin Weik, rhp/ss, Trinity HS, Bedford, Texas
47. Keith Osik, ss, Wading River (N.Y.) HS
48. Ernie Carr, of, Jacksonville
49. **Angel Caceres, 1b, Arizona Western JC**
50. **Brian Romero, lhp, East Los Angeles JC**
51. Anthony Hicks, of, Maryland

TORONTO BLUE JAYS

June—Regular Phase (17)

1. **Alex Sanchez, rhp, UCLA**
2. **Derek Bell, of, King HS, Tampa**
3. **Bob Wishnevski, rhp, Kishwaukee (Ill.) JC**
4. **Ed Smith, of, Warrior (Ala.) HS**
5. **Mike Timlin, rhp, Southwestern (Texas)**
6. **Matt Gilmore, ss, Reseda HS, Encino, Calif.**
7. **Jason Townley, rhp, Escambia HS, Pensacola, Fla.**
8. **Joe Newcomb, rhp, Memphis State**
9. Kevin King, lhp, Braggs (Okla.) HS
10. Darrell Whitmore, ss, Warren County HS, Front Royal, Va.
11. **Nate Cromwell, lhp, Chaparral HS, Las Vegas**
12. **Chris Lariviere, rhp, Cal State Los Angeles**
13. **Ryan Thompson, of, Kent County HS, Rock Hall, Md.**

14. **Terrence Wilson, of, Clintondale HS, Clemens, Mich.**
15. **Brian Rollins, ss/2b, Crenshaw HS, Los Angeles**
16. **Mark Young, of, UC Riverside**
17. Anton Mobley, of, Fernandina Beach (Fla.) HS
18. Dave Haas, rhp, Wichita State
19. **Bob MacDonald, lhp, Rutgers**
20. **Greg Vella, 1b, UC Santa Barbara**
21. **Mike Chesney, c, New York Tech**
22. Pierre Sylvain, rhp, Nicholls State
23. **Jim Trahey, rhp, Eastern Michigan**
24. Erik Schullstrom, rhp, Alameda HS, San Leandro, Calif.
25. **Steve Baucom, 3b, Clemson**
26. Chris Butterfield, rhp/of, Merced (Calif.) JC
27. **Shawn Scott, of/ss, El Camino HS, Pacifica, Calif.**
28. **Rodney Richey, rhp, South Carolina**
29. **Steven Roberts, of/1b, UC Davis**
30. **Steve Wapnick, rhp, Fresno State**
31. **Allan Silverstein, rhp, New York Tech**
32. Greg Perschke, rhp, Southwestern Michigan JC
33. **Anthony Conliffe, rhp, West Virginia**
34. Joe Summers, of, Royal HS, Simi Valley, Calif.
35. Allen Tyson, rhp, Glen Oak HS, Canton, Ohio
36. Todd Ross, ss, Lassen (Calif.) CC
37. **Dan Etzweiler, 3b, Maine**
38. **Steve Berriatua, ss, San Francisco**
39. Rodney Mills, of, Anderson (Ind.) HS
40. Bruce Bensching, rhp, Clarkston (Wash.) HS
41. Pat Rodgers, of, Pensacola (Fla.) JC
42. **Richard Embry, rhp, Paris (Texas) HS**
43. David Atkinson, of/3b, Waukegan (Ill.) HS
44. **Bob Bevis, rhp, Western Michigan**
45. Darren Lewis, of, Chabot (Calif.) JC
46. **Floyd Wade, 1b, Jackson State**
47. Rick Nowak, rhp, UC San Diego
48. William Abare, 1b, St. Augustine (Fla.) HS
49. Michael Stewart, of, Fresno State
50. Mario Baker, ss, Thomasville (Ga.) HS
51. Jeff Burr, rhp, San Gorgonio HS, Highland, Calif.
52. **Cisco Johnson, 2b, St. Leo (Fla.)**
53. **Mike Taylor, ss, San Jacinto (Texas) JC**
54. Wes Bliven, rhp, Santa Clara
55. John Booth, rhp, Sullivan (Ind.) HS
56. Jeff Beck, rhp, El Camino (Calif.) JC
57. Orlando Palmeiro, of, Southridge HS, Miami
58. Doug McCoy, 2b, Laurel HS, New Castle, Pa.
59. David Keating, of, UCLA
60. Matthew Barker, of, Taylor HS, DeLand, Fla.
61. **Willy Fillard, 3b, Slippery Rock (Pa.)**
62. Michael Roberts, of, North Florida JC
63. Thomas Strabazy, of, Bishop Noll HS, Whiting, Ind.
64. Fausto Tejero, c, Miami-Dade New World Center CC
65. Eugene Nicholas, ss, Utica (Miss.) JC
66. **Terrence Wilson, rhp, Warren (Pa.) HS**
67. Eric Cullens, ss, Hillsborough (Fla.) CC
68. Sergio Guasch, rhp, Miami-Dade North CC
69. Todd Hudson, rhp, Cardinal Mooney HS, Sarasota, Fla.
70. Tom Marsh, rhp, Toledo
71. **Brian Dixon, of/2b, Clearwater (Fla.) HS**

1988 Padres pick Benes over Olson with first selection as bonus payments start to get bigger

It was six days before the 1988 draft and the Padres still weren't sure they were going to take pitcher Andy Benes with the No. 1 pick.

They needed something to cinch the decision, and Benes provided it when he shut out Arizona State 1-0 in the opening round of NCAA regional play, striking out eight. The victory stretched Benes' record to 16-3 and capped a brilliant season for the 6-foot-5, 230-pound righthander from Evansville.

"He was awesome," Padres scouting director Tom Romenesko said. "If Arizona State had been using wood bats, they could have started a bonfire with the broken ones."

Benes was a relative unknown at the start of the 1988 season, but he started to open eyes when he struck out 21 against UNC Wilmington with a fastball clocked at 94 mph. By the time he beat Arizona State nearly three months later, he had struck out a national-best 188 in 146 innings. An NCAA-record eight shutouts contributed to a 1.42 ERA.

Interestingly, it was watching Benes during one of his three losses, early in the season against Purdue, that convinced Romenesko that Benes was a good candidate for the No. 1 pick.

"Every time I'd seen him before there were dozens of scouts," Romenesko said. "This time there was only a guy from Cleveland and myself. It was a real lousy day, and Andy lost the game when he jammed a guy and the wind blew it out of the park.

"He knocked the next guy on his ass. That's when I knew I wanted him. That proved to me he was a real competitor."

San Diego had the No. 1 pick in the draft for the fourth time in its 20-year history. With the three previous picks having achieved only marginal success, the Padres were committed to picking the right man. A total of 14 Padres scouts and front-office officials saw Benes. Almost as many saw Auburn's Gregg Olson, and the decision came down to those two college righthanders.

"They're two very similar pitchers," said San Diego general manager Jack McKeon, who installed himself as manager of the struggling Padres four days before the draft but saw both pitchers several times. "About the only difference between the two is that Olson has a better curveball."

There was general agreement that Benes and Olson, who ended up being drafted fourth overall by Baltimore, were so polished that neither was far from being ready to pitch in the big leagues.

Andy Benes put together a great season at Evansville to become the No. 1 pick

Olson got there first, but only because he passed up an opportunity to play with the U.S. Olympic team. Olson was in Baltimore in September when Team USA, featuring Benes and a handful of other first-round picks, won a gold medal at the 1988 Olympics in Seoul, South Korea.

The Orioles felt they were burned four years earlier when their first-round pick John Hoover, who was the ace of the 1984 Olympic staff, came down with a tired arm and never fulfilled his potential. They did not want Olson to play for the Olympic team, and a $200,000 bonus and a guarantee he would be in the big leagues by September were enough to persuade him to drop off the team.

Benes began the 1989 season in the minor leagues, but was in San Diego by August. He made one All-Star Game appearance and was a solid starter for 14 seasons—winning 155 games and compiling 2,505 career innings—though he never quite achieved stardom.

Unlike 1984, when the 20-man U.S. Olympic team featured 18 eventual first-round draft picks, the 1988 team featured 11 first-rounders: nine from 1988 and two from 1989.

A total of 1,432 players were drafted in 1988, topping the previous record of 1,263 set in 1987. The Yankees were the final team to stop drafting, in the

75th round.

Bonuses Start Their Climb

By agreeing to a $235,000 bonus with San Diego, Benes took bonus payments to a new level in 1988. Two high school pitchers also received bonuses that topped the previous record amounts outfielders Kirk Gibson (1978) and Darryl Strawberry (1980) received.

Lefthander Steve Avery, who had a Stanford scholarship as a bargaining chip, was given a $211,000 bonus by Atlanta after being drafted third overall.

Then Avery's bonus was topped when the Expos startled the baseball world by signing righthander Reid Cornelius, an 11th-round draft pick, to a $225,000 bonus. Cornelius was a strong student and could have been one of the first five players drafted had he not been seen as committed to attending Mississippi State.

"He and Avery were the top two high school pitchers in the draft," Expos scouting director Gary Hughes said. "We were always led to believe he would sign. It was just a case of ownership deciding they wanted to spend the money."

For the ninth time in 10 years, the Yankees did not have a first-round pick. But they made draft history by signing their first 27 picks, topping the previous record of 23 (Cincinnati, 1983) consecutive players signed at the start of a draft.

They also drafted and signed a prime football talent, all-America defensive back Deion Sanders, who did not play baseball in 1988 at Florida State. Sanders agreed to a lucrative deal to play for the summer in the Yankees system, and reached Triple-A before returning to Florida State for his final year of football.

Sanders returned to the Yankees in 1989 and spent the early portion of the season in Double-A. The Atlanta Falcons selected him fifth overall in the 1989 NFL draft, and Sanders set his asking price at $10 million. He continued to play baseball as negotiations with the Falcons bogged down.

Sanders finally did sign with the Falcons, though he continued his flirtation with baseball with the Braves and other teams while putting together a hall of fame-caliber football career.

St. Louis, meanwhile, spent one of its three first-round picks on outfielder Brian Jordan, who played briefly in the Cardinals organization in 1988, then rejoined the football team at the University of Richmond. Jordan was subsequently drafted in the sixth round of the 1989 NFL draft by Buffalo. He played alongside Sanders for the Falcons, but eventually gave up football for a long baseball career.

DRAFT 88: FIRST-ROUND PICKS

No.	Club	Player, Pos.	School	Hometown	Ht.	Wt.	B-T	Age
1.	Padres	Andy Benes, rhp	Evansville	Evansville, Ind.	6-5	230	R-R	20
2.	Indians	Mark Lewis, ss	Hamilton HS	Hamilton, Ohio	6-1	170	R-R	18
3.	Braves	Steve Avery, lhp	Kennedy HS	Taylor, Mich.	6-4	185	L-L	18
4.	Orioles	Gregg Olson, rhp	Auburn	Omaha, Neb.	6-4	210	R-R	21
5.	Dodgers	Bill Bene, rhp	Cal State Los Angeles	Long Beach	6-4	190	R-R	20
6.	Rangers	Monty Fariss, ss	Oklahoma State	Leedey, Okla.	6-4	180	R-R	20
7.	Astros	Willie Ansley, of	Plainview HS	Plainview, Texas	6-2	195	R-R	18
8.	Angels	Jim Abbott, lhp	Michigan	Flint, Mich.	6-3	200	L-L	20
9.	Cubs	Ty Griffin, 2b	Georgia Tech	Tampa, Fla.	6-0	180	B-R	20
10.	White Sox	Robin Ventura, 3b	Oklahoma State	Santa Maria, Calif.	6-1	170	L-R	20
11.	Phillies	Pat Combs, lhp	Baylor	Houston	6-3	200	L-L	21
12.	Red Sox	Tom Fischer, lhp	Wisconsin	West Bend, Wis.	5-11	190	L-L	21
13.	Pirates	Austin Manahan, ss	Horizon HS	Phoenix, Ariz.	6-1	175	R-R	18
14.	Mariners	Tino Martinez, 1b	Tampa	Tampa, Fla.	6-2	190	L-R	20
15.	Giants	Royce Clayton, ss	St. Bernard HS	Playa del Rey, Calif.	6-0	175	R-R	18
16.	Athletics	Stan Royer, 3b	Eastern Illinois	Charleston, Ill.	6-3	195	R-R	20
17.	Indians	Charles Nagy, rhp	Connecticut	Fairfield, Conn.	6-3	200	L-R	21
18.	Royals	Hugh Walker, of	Jacksonville HS	Jacksonville, Ark.	6-1	190	L-R	18
19.	Expos	Dave Wainhouse, rhp	Washington State	Mercer Island, Wash.	6-2	182	R-R	20
20.	Twins	Johnny Ard, rhp	Manatee (Fla.) JC	Hemingway, S.C.	6-5	215	R-R	21
21.	Mets	Dave Proctor, rhp	Allen County (Kan.) CC	Topeka, Kan.	6-3	200	R-R	20
22.	Cardinals	John Ericks, rhp	Illinois	Tinley Park, Ill.	6-7	215	R-R	20
23.	Cardinals	Brad DuVall, rhp	Virginia Tech	Silver Spring, Md.	6-1	185	R-R	22
24.	Brewers	*Alex Fernandez, rhp	Pace HS	Miami	6-1	205	R-R	18
25.	Blue Jays	Ed Sprague, 3b	Stanford	Stockton, Calif.	6-2	190	R-R	20
26.	Tigers	Rico Brogna, 1b	Watertown HS	Watertown, Conn.	6-2	190	R-R	18

*Did not sign.

1988

CLUB-BY-CLUB SELECTIONS

ATLANTA BRAVES

June—Regular Phase (3)

1. **Steve Avery, lhp, Kennedy HS, Taylor, Mich.**
2. **Jimmy Kremers, c, Arkansas**
2. **Matt Murray, rhp, Loomis Chaffee HS, Windsor, Conn.** (Pick from Phillies as compensation for Type B free agent Dave Palmer)
2. **John Kupsey, 3b, Gloucester Catholic HS, Gibbstown, N.J.** (Supplemental pick—57th—for loss of Type C free agent Glenn Hubbard)
3. **Preston Watson, rhp, Texas**
4. **Kevin Tyson, c, Jefferson HS, Lafayette, Ind.**
5. **Turk Wendell, rhp, Quinnipiac**
6. **Jimmie Pullins, of, Tyler (Texas) HS**
7. **Lee Heath, of, La Salle HS, Cincinnati**
8. **Mark Wohlers, rhp, Holyoke (Mass.) HS**
9. **Ed Alicea, 2b, Florida State**
10. Tommy Adams, of, Capistrano Valley HS, Mission Viejo, Calif.
11. **Sean Hutchinson, c, Northview HS, Covina, Calif.**
12. Fred Cooley, rhp, Southern Mississippi
13. **David Waldenberger, 3b, Rowland HS, Rowland Heights, Calif.**
14. Mike Hostetler, rhp, Sprayberry HS, Marietta, Ga.
15. **Tony Tarasco, of, Santa Monica (Calif.) HS**
16. Russell Brock, rhp, Lockland (Ohio) HS
17. **John Greenwood, 1b, San Francisco State**
18. **Tom Rizzo, ss, North Adams State (Mass.)**
19. **Randy Simmons, of, Delaware**
20. Mike Lopez, rhp, Sheridan HS, Denver
21. **Steve Lopez, 3b/of, Vacaville (Calif.) HS**
22. **Donovan Campbell, of, Texas Southern**
23. Greg Perschke, rhp, New Orleans
24. **Ramces Guerrero, 2b, Dominican (N.Y.)**
25. Thomas Neff, of, Magnolia HS, Anaheim
26. Craig Bradshaw, lhp, Alexandria (La.) HS
27. Ron Hazl, of, Alhambra HS, Glendale, Ariz.
28. **Rickey Rigsby, of, Angelina (Texas) JC**
29. Scott Stice, rhp, Wake Forest
30. **Gary Schoonover, ss, Brigham Young**
31. Mark Dressen, rhp, La Serna HS, Whittier, Calif.
32. **James Kortright, rhp, Snow (Utah)**
33. Chris Gaskill, rhp, Westfield HS, Houston
34. Adam Schulhofer, 3b, Canoga Park HS, Woodland Hills, Calif.
35. **Colovito Thomas, of, Ventura (Calif.) JC**
36. Billy Morris, ss, St. Francis HS, Glendale, Calif.
37. **William Lange, lhp, Rio Hondo (Calif.) JC**
38. **Scott Goselin, 2b, Olivet Nazarene (Ill.)**
39. Scott Ruffcorn, rhp, Austin HS
40. Mike Smith, of, Woodward HS, Cincinnati
41. Mike Solar, 1b, Covina HS, West Covina, Calif.
42. John Keller, c, Westwood HS, Austin
43. **Calvain Culberson, of, Armstrong State (Ga.)**
44. **Wallace Gonzales, c, Rosemead (Calif.) HS**
45. **Rodolfo Gardey, rhp, Canada (Calif.) JC**
46. Steve Dailey, of, Ventura (Calif.) HS
47. Jason Gonzales, ss, Cuero (Texas) HS
48. **Mark Eskins, rhp, Jacksonville State**
49. **Chris Jones, 1b, Southern Tech Institute (Fla.)**
50. **Pat Stivers, ss/2b, Mesa (Colo.)**
51. **Brent McCoy, ss, Howard (D.C.)**
52. Doug Kimball, ss/rhp, Shadow Mountain HS, Phoenix
53. David Cronin, of, La Salle HS, Cincinnati
54. **David Piela, c, Western Carolina**
55. Craig Triplett, c/1b, Paradise Valley HS, Phoenix
56. **Marco Paddy, c, Southern**
57. Jeff Blanks, ss, Del Rio (Texas) HS
58. Greg Viks, rhp, DeSoto (Texas) HS
59. **Glen Gardner, of, Rutgers**
60. Roy Gamez, c, Casa Grande (Ariz.) HS
61. **Joe Saccamanno, ss/2b, Bloomfield (N.J.)**
62. **Paul Bacosa, rhp, San Jose State**
63. **Eric Kuhlman, of, Bradley**
64. Drayton Reedy, 1b, Towers HS, Decatur, Ga.
65. Mike Eiffert, of, Lewisville (Texas) HS
66. **Kevin Thomas, rhp, Rockdale HS, Conyers, Ga.**
67. **Kevin Henry, 3b, Auburn**

BALTIMORE ORIOLES

June—Regular Phase (4)

1. **Gregg Olson, rhp, Auburn**
1. Ricky Gutierrez, ss, American HS, Hialeah, Fla. (Supplemental pick—28th—for failure to sign 1987 first-rounder Brad DuVall)
2. **Arthur Rhodes, lhp/of, La Vega HS, Waco, Texas**
3. **Stacy Jones, rhp, Auburn**
4. **Aman Hicks, of, Gardena (Calif.) HS**
5. **Steve Nicosia, of, Bishop Gallagher HS, St. Clair Shores, Mich.**
6. **Tom Martin, lhp, Bay HS, Panama City, Fla.**
7. **Keith Lee, of, Glassboro State (N.J.)**
8. **Mike Deutsch, rhp, Rider**
9. **Mike Linskey, lhp, James Madison**
10. **Doug Robbins, c, Stanford**
11. Cris Allen, 3b, Florida Southern
12. **Pete Rose Jr., 3b, Oak Hills HS, Cincinnati**
13. **Rodney Lofton, ss, Grambling State**
14. Jim Robinson, rhp, Northwestern
15. Gustavo Miranda, 3b/ss, Miami HS
16. **Bob Bretwisch, lhp, Bradley**
17. **Mike Richardson, 1b, Portland State (Ore.)**
18. **Joe Redman, 2b, Paulsboro (N.J.) HS**
19. **Scott McNaney, ss, Elizabethtown**
20. **Robert Doman, lhp, James Madison**
21. Rene Francisco, of, Indian River (Fla.) CC
22. **Roy Gilbert, of, Centenary**
23. **Chris Burgin, rhp, Oklahoma**
24. **Zach Kerr, rhp, New Mexico State**
25. Brian Barnes, lhp, Clemson
26. **Carey Metts, c, Mars Hill (N.C.)**
27. **Chris Shebby, rhp, Georgetown**
28. Joey Hamilton, rhp, Statesboro (Ga.) HS
29. Michael Place, rhp, Seminole (Fla.) HS
30. **Brian Janutolo, ss, Bluefield State**
31. **Mark Withers, of, North Carolina State**
32. Baylor Alexander, c, Wolfson HS, Jacksonville, Fla.
33. **Jeff Champ, c, San Diego State**
34. **Dell Ahalt, 3b, North Carolina State**
35. Bobby Lamm, of, Hunt HS, Wilson, N.C.
36. **John Fowler, 3b, Frederick (Md.) CC**
37. Mark Brockell, 3b, James Madison
38. Aaron Van Scoyoc, ss, Norway (Iowa) HS
39. **Bob Block, of, Southern Arkansas**
40. **Chris LaFollette, of, Southview HS, Fayetteville, N.C.**
41. Brian Cornelius, of, Southern
42. Jason Marshall, ss, Cooper HS, Abilene, Texas
43. Chris Finley, of, Lamar HS, Houston
44. **Earl Williams, c, Catonsville (Md.) CC**
45. **Don Marett, rhp, Owen HS, Black Mountain, N.C.**

BOSTON RED SOX

June—Regular Phase (12)

1. **Tom Fischer, lhp, Wisconsin**
2. **Andy Rush, rhp, Somerset (Pa.) HS**
3. **Mickey Rivers Jr., of, Bacone (Okla.) JC**
4. **Dan Kite, rhp, Louisiana State**
5. **John Valentin, ss, Seton Hall**

6. **Ed Riley, lhp, St. Peter-Marien HS, Worcester, Mass.**
7. **Dave Owen, lhp, Carson-Newman (Tenn.)**
8. **Tim Naehring, ss, Miami (Ohio)**
9. **Willie Tatum, 3b, Pacific**
10. **Meredith Moore, of, Nogales HS, La Puente, Calif.**
11. David Stuart, rhp, Indian River (Fla.) CC
12. **Alan Sanders, rhp, Lower Columbia (Wash.) JC**
13. **Richard Witherspoon, of, Nogales HS, La Puente, Calif.**
14. **Garrett Jenkins, of, Steubenville (Ohio) HS**
15. **Howard Landry, lhp, Southwestern Louisiana**
16. **Bernie Dzafic, rhp, Lincoln Land (Ill.) CC**
17. Eric Slinkard, c, Chula Vista (Calif.) HS
18. **Hilly Hathaway, lhp, Sandalwood HS, Jacksonville, Fla.**
19. **Kevin Crowder, 2b/3b, Keene (N.H.) HS**
20. Corey Powell, of, Patrick Henry HS, San Diego
21. Gary Kinser, rhp, Columbia State (Tenn.) CC
22. **Chris Whitehead, 3b, Middle Tennessee State**
23. Scott Bakkum, rhp, Aquinas HS, La Crosse, Wis.
24. **Bernard Doyle, of, North Newton HS, Morocco, Ill.**
25. **John Flaherty, c, George Washington**
26. Joe Biasucci, ss, South Broward HS, Hollywood, Fla.
27. Mark Mitchelson, lhp, Hillsborough (Fla.) CC
28. **Scott Taylor, lhp, Bowling Green State**
29. **John Spencer, of, Lowell (Mass.)**
30. Andrew Flagler, 1b, Valencia (Fla.) CC
31. Dan Robinson, 3b, San Jacinto (Texas) JC
32. Michael Rebhan, rhp, Lake City (Fla.) CC
33. **Peter Hoy, rhp, LeMoyne**
34. **Barton Moore, 2b, Jefferson State (Ala.) JC**
35. Gary Posey, of, Gulf Coast (Fla.) CC
36. Jim Wiley, of/p, Westark (Ark.) JC
37. Steve Worrell, lhp, Lower Cape May (N.J.) Regional HS
38. Roger Luce, c, San Jacinto (Texas) JC

CALIFORNIA ANGELS

June—Regular Phase (8)

1. **Jim Abbott, lhp, Michigan**
2. (Pick to Giants as compensation for Type A free agent Chili Davis)
3. **Glenn Carter, rhp, Triton (Ill.) JC**
4. **J.R. Phillips, lhp/of, Bishop Amat HS, Rowland Heights, Calif.**
5. **David Neal, lhp, Montgomery HS, Semmes, Ala.**
6. **Gary DiSarcina, ss, Massachusetts**
7. **Jim Edmonds, of, Diamond Bar (Calif.) HS**
8. **David Partrick, of, Tate HS, Cantonment, Fla.**
9. **Jeff Kelso, of, Missouri Western State**
10. **Dave Sturdivant, c, Nevada-Las Vegas**
11. **Scott Lewis, rhp, Nevada-Las Vegas**
12. **Jeff Kipila, of, Elon**
13. Mike Robertson, of, Servite HS, Placentia, Calif.
14. Damon Mashore, of, Clayton Valley HS, Concord, Calif.
15. **Mike Sheehy, of, Penn State**
16. Dirk Skillicorn, of, St. Francis HS, Los Altos, Calif.
17. **Marcus Moore, rhp, Kennedy HS, Richmond, Calif.**
18. L.V. Powell, of, Poly HS, Long Beach
19. Tom Bates, ss, Paris (Texas) JC
20. Kirk Dulom, 3b, Miami
21. **Paul Borse, of, Sacramento CC**
22. **Larry Gonzales, c, Hawaii**
23. Bill Minnis, ss, Mesa (Ariz.) CC
24. **Jeff Oberdank, 2b, UC Irvine**
25. **Gary Cooper, 3b, Scottsdale (Ariz.) CC**
26. **Wes Bliven, rhp, Santa Clara**
27. **Bruce Vegely, lhp, Cal State Dominguez Hills**
28. **Frank Dominguez, c, Miami**
29. **John Marchese, rhp, Grand Canyon (Ariz.)**
30. **Damion Easley, ss/2b, Long Beach (Calif.) CC**
31. Darrin Gleiser, ss, Sandpoint (Idaho) Legion HS
32. Robert Dodd, lhp, Sacramento CC
33. Michael Lloyd, ss, Miami-Dade New World Center CC
34. Jim Henry, lhp, Placer HS, Forest Hill, Calif.
35. **Don Vidmar, rhp, Grand Canyon (Ariz.)**
36. **Steve Kirwin, of, Lewis (Ill.)**
37. Mike Hartnett, c, Borah HS, Boise, Idaho
38. Raul Rodarte, ss, Ganesha HS, Diamond Bar, Calif.
39. **Rodney Eldridge, 1b/of, Scottsdale (Ariz.) CC**
40. Corey Kapano, ss, Azusa (Calif.) HS·
41. Mark Roberts, rhp, Brewton-Parker (Ga.)
42. James Pedicaris, of, Lake Gibson HS, Lakeland, Fla.
43. Todd Marinovich, lhp, Capistrano Valley HS, Mission Viejo, Calif.
44. Jon Anderson, c, Indian River (Fla.) CC
45. **William Jones, c, Triton (Ill.) JC**
46. Brian Goodwin, rhp, Indian River (Fla.) CC
47. Rene Delgado, ss, Miami-Dade North CC

CHICAGO CUBS

June—Regular Phase (9)

1. **Ty Griffin, 2b, Georgia Tech**
2. (Pick to Expos as compensation for Type B free agent Vance Law)
3. **Roberto Smalls, rhp, St. Thomas, Virgin Islands**
4. **Brad Huff, c, Monroe (Ga.) Area HS**
5. **John Salles, rhp, Fresno State**
6. **Troy Bailey, of, Williams HS, Alexandria, Va.**
7. **Billy St. Peter, 3b/ss, Michigan**
8. **Rob Bonneau, ss, Gonzaga Prep HS, Spokane, Wash.**
9. Dennis Gray, lhp, Banning (Calif.) HS
10. **David Goodwin, rhp, Xavier**
11. **Billy Paynter, c, Coronado HS, Tempe, Ariz.**
12. Roger Burnett, ss, Broken Arrow (Okla.) HS
13. **James Murphy, of, Portland State (Ore.)**
14. Rick Hirtensteiner, of, Pepperdine
15. **Todd Borders, c, Lake Wales (Fla.) HS**
16. **Kevin Roberson, of, Parkland (Ill.) JC**
17. **Luis Sierra, of, Dupont HS, Wilmington, Del.**
18. **Daren Burns, rhp, Birmingham-Southern**
19. Andy Croghan, rhp, Servite HS, Yorba Linda, Calif.
20. **Woody Smith, 3b, Spartanburg Methodist (S.C.) JC**
21. **Kraig Washington, of, Rancho Santiago (Calif.) JC**
22. **Mathew Leonard, 3b, Benedictine (Kan.)**
23. **Jason Doss, rhp, Westwood HS, Fort Pierce, Fla.**
24. **George Browder, c, Zephyr Hills (Fla.) HS**
25. **Juan Figueroa, of, Laredo (Texas) JC**
26. **Dan Johnston, rhp, Creighton**
27. **Greg Kessler, rhp, North Idaho JC**
28. **Tim Ellis, lhp, Rosemont (Calif.) JC**
29. **Mike Sodders, lhp, Alabama**
30. **John Jensen, of, Texas**
31. **Albert Stacey, 1b, Cleveland State**
32. **Ronnie Rasp, rhp, Montevallo (Ala.)**
33. **Shannon Jones, rhp, Southeastern Louisiana**
34. **Ben Shreve, ss, West Virginia**
35. Rodney Pedraza, rhp, Cuero (Texas) HS
36. **Richard Mundy, c, Pattonville HS, Bridgeton, Mo.**
37. Chris Pritchett, ss, Central Catholic HS, Modesto, Calif.
38. Bill Judge, 3b, Brother Rice HS, Oak Forest, Ill.
39. **Tracy Smith, rhp, Miami (Ohio)**
40. **Jessie Hollins, rhp, Willis (Texas) HS**
41. **Eric Williams, of, UNC Charlotte**
42. **Marvin Cole, ss, Alexandria (La.) HS**
43. **Chris Lutz, rhp, Michigan**
44. Mathew Johnson, ss, Arvada (Colo.) West HS
45. Peter Gardere, 1b, Robert E. Lee HS, Houston
46. **Rusty Crockett, ss, Texas**

CHICAGO WHITE SOX

June—Regular Phase (10)

1. **Robin Ventura, 3b, Oklahoma State**
2. **Lenny Brutcher, rhp, Cicero-North Syracuse (N.Y.) HS**
3. **Mike Mitchener, rhp, Armstrong State (Ga.)**
4. **Johnny Ruffin, rhp, Choctaw County HS, Butler, Ala.**
5. Joey Eischen, lhp, West Covina (Calif.) HS
6. **Mark Chasey, 1b, Florida Southern**
7. Rich Batchelor, rhp, South Carolina-Aiken
8. **Wayne Moye, of, Princeton HS, Cincinnati**
9. **Jerome Wolak, of, South Hills HS, West Covina, Calif.**
10. **John Hudek, rhp, Florida Southern**

11. **Dennis Walker, 3b/c, Grambling State**
12. **Scott Egan, c, Glen Ridge (N.J.) HS**
13. **Scott Middaugh, rhp, San Diego State**
14. **John Zaksek, of, Cincinnati**
15. **Fred Dabney, lhp, Seminole State (Okla.) JC**
16. **Frank Merigliano, rhp, Pittsburgh**
17. Todd Hobson, of, Lawrence North HS, Indianapolis
18. **John Chafin, rhp, Marshall**
19. **LeWayne Busby, ss, Mississippi College**
20. **James Pague, rhp, Central Florida CC**
21. **Scott Tedder, of, Ohio Wesleyan**
22. **Michael Galvan, lhp, Louisiana Tech**
23. **John Furch, 1b, Duke**
24. Brian Noack, ss, Pensacola (Fla.) JC
25. **Dwayne Harvey, rhp, Sherrills Ford, N.C.**
26. **Arthur Thigpen, rhp, Flagler (Fla.)**
27. **Patrick Hulme, rhp, Hanna HS, Anderson, S.C.**
28. Chris Fruge, rhp, Mississippi Delta JC
29. Anthony Pritchett, c, Mobile County HS, Grand Bay, Ala.
30. John DeSilva, rhp, Brigham Young
31. **James Garrett, rhp, Southern**
32. **Paul Abbatinozzi, c, Flagler (Fla.)**
33. **Craig Teter, of, Seminole State (Okla.) JC**
34. Carl Dorsey, lhp, Hanna HS, Anderson, S.C.
35. Keith Morrison, rhp, North Gwinett HS, Suwanee, Ga.
36. Brian Whittal, rhp/3b, Marysville, Wash.
37. Brian Stephens, of, Hillsborough (Fla.) CC
38. **Scott Fuller, rhp, Wisconsin**
39. Marvin Benard, of, Bell HS, Cudahy, Calif.
40. Jack Johnson, c, St. Rita HS, Chicago
41. Jeff Graff, of, Texarkana (Texas) CC
42. **Derek Lee, inf/of, South Florida**
43. **Jeff Ingram, c, New Orleans**
44. Ozzie Timmons, of, Brandon HS, Tampa
45. **Todd Bargman, 1b, Oklahoma State**
46. **Ronnie Plemmons, of, Spartanburg Methodist (S.C.) JC**
47. **Lane Mallet, of, Houston**
48. Brian Cordero, lhp, St. John's
49. Timothy Sheriff, ss, West Oak HS, Westminster, S.C.
50. **Robert Fletcher, 3b, Alabama**
51. **Robert Thompson, c/of, Indian River (Fla.) CC**
52. **Steve James, 1b, Mississippi Valley State**
53. **Brett Berry, of, Emporia State (Kan.)**
54. Hart Lee Dykes, lhp, Oklahoma State
55. **Jeff Buell, 1b, Indiana State**
56. Alex Alvarez, rhp, Gulf Coast (Fla.) CC
57. Dwayne Wade, of, Washington HS, Greenville, Miss.
58. **Ron Stephens, rhp, Cincinnati**
59. Wayne Johnson, ss, Leuzinger HS, Gardena, Calif.
60. **Brian Gennings, rhp, Texarkana (Texas) CC**
61. Mike Carlsen, ss, St. Anthony's HS, Jersey City, N.J.

CINCINNATI REDS

June—Regular Phase (15)

1. (Pick to Giants as compensation for Type B free agent Eddie Milner)
2. **Jeff Branson, ss, Livingston (Ala.)**
3. Tyler Green, rhp, Thomas Jefferson HS, Denver
4. **Gaetano Gianni, c, Gordon Tech HS, Chicago**
5. **K.C. Gillum, 3b, Westerville (Ohio) North HS**
6. **Kurt Dempster, rhp, Arizona State**
7. **Shane Coker, of, Asher (Okla.) HS**
8. **Carl Stewart, rhp, Plano (Texas) East HS**
9. Kevin Digiacomo, c, Choate College HS, Ithaca, N.Y.
10. **Roosevelt Williams, 3b, Tyler (Texas) HS**
11. **Mark Arland, of, Central Valley HS, Spokane, Wash.**
12. **Steve Foster Jr., rhp, Texas-Arlington**
13. Paul Byrd, rhp, St. Xavier HS, Louisville
14. **Johnny Almaraz, rhp, Southwest Texas State**
15. Craig Rapp, lhp, Red Land HS, Lewisberry, Pa.
16. Scott McCarty, lhp, San Jacinto (Texas) JC
17. **Benny Colvard, of, Southeastern Oklahoma State**
18. **Kyle Reagan, of, East Lyme (Conn.) HS**
19. **Jerry Spradlin, rhp, Fullerton (Calif.) JC**
20. Earl Coachman, 3b, Wallace (Ala.) CC
21. **Brian Nichols, c, Southern California**
22. **Doug Bond, 1b, Quinnipiac**
23. **Chris Keim, lhp, Taft (Calif.) JC**
24. Chris Hart, of, Harrisonburg (Va.) HS
25. **Duane Mulville, c, Bakersfield (Calif.) JC**
26. Charles Sullivan, 3b, Greenwich (Conn.) HS
27. **Jason Satre, rhp, Abilene (Texas) HS**
28. **Agustin Gonzalez, c, Orosi (Calif.) HS**
29. Edward Klamm, lhp, Bishop Ludden HS, Syracuse, N.Y.
30. **John Weeks, c, Miami**
31. **Clarence Thomas, rhp, Western Kentucky**
32. **Mo Sanford, rhp, Alabama**
33. Brett Roberts, rhp, South Webster (Ohio) HS
34. **Dwayne Van Horne, rhp/3b, South Carolina-Spartanburg**
35. Derrick Copes, of, Angelina (Texas) JC
36. **Michael Malley, lhp, Connecticut**
37. Issac Jackson, of, Victor Valley HS, Victorville, Calif.
38. **Jon Fuller, c, Bellevue (Wash.) CC**
39. Dan Cholowsky, ss, Bellarmine Prep HS, San Jose
40. **John Edward, lhp, New Mexico State**
41. **Cary Moore, inf/of, Sulphur Springs (Texas) HS**
42. **Brian Landy, lhp, Quinnipiac**
43. Glenn Osinski, 3b, Triton (Ill.) JC
44. **Mike Mulvaney, 1b, Wyoming**
45. **Jason Cornell, of, Iowa Western CC**
46. Bo Siberz, rhp, Westmar (Iowa)
47. Barry Leavell, of, Washington HS, Chicago
48. David Williams, rhp, Westark (Ark.) CC
49. Brian Carie, rhp, Vincennes (Ind.) JC
50. **Lawrence Moore, of, Rend Lake (Ill.) JC**
51. Adrian Jones, of/rhp, Missouri
52. Mark Healy, rhp/1b, Iowa Western CC
53. Dan Schwader, lhp, Kishwaukee (Ill.) JC
54. Ben Blake, c, Indianola (Ind.) HS
55. Phil Zimmerman, 2b, Regis HS, Denver
56. Tim Boge, c, Dyersville-Beckman HS, Dyersville, Iowa
57. Rick Freehling, of, Regis HS, Denver
58. Sam Austin, of, Triton (Ill.) JC
59. Robert Robinson, rhp, Circleville (Ohio) HS
60. Don Wengert, rhp, Heelan HS, Sioux City, Iowa

CLEVELAND INDIANS

June—Regular Phase (2)

1. **Mark Lewis, ss, Hamilton (Ohio) HS**
1. **Charles Nagy, rhp, Connecticut** (Pick from Giants as compensation for Type A free agent Brett Butler)
1. **Jeff Mutis, lhp, Lafayette** (Supplemental pick—27th—for loss of Butler)
2. **Brian Johnson, c, Texas**
3. **Clyde Pough, rhp/ss, Avon Park (Fla.) HS**
4. **Daren Epley, 1b, Bradley**
5. **Ty Kovach, rhp, Central Arizona JC**
6. **Don Young, of, Grossmont (Calif.) JC**
7. **Greg McMichael, rhp, Tennessee**
8. **Olonzo Woodfin, lhp, Sylmar (Calif.) HS**
9. **Brett Merriman, rhp, Grand Canyon (Ariz.)**
10. Tom Duffin, 3b/of, Miami-Dade North CC
11. Jorge Fabregas, c/1b, Columbus HS, Miami
12. Keith Millay, rhp, Apollo HS, Owensboro, Ky.
13. Tommy Boudreau, rhp, Chaparral HS, Las Vegas
14. Josh Lowery, ss, Laney (Calif.) JC
15. **Charles Alexander, lhp, Western Michigan**
16. **Joey James, of, UCLA**
17. **Barry Blackwell, c, Florida State**
18. Darrin Paxton, lhp, East HS, Wichita, Kan.
19. **Sean Baron, 1b, San Diego**
20. **Zeonare Leger, rhp, Ventura (Calif.) JC**
21. Jason Geis, of, Hudson Bay HS, Vancouver, Wash.
22. **Darin Campbell, 3b, North Carolina**
23. **Bob Kairis, rhp, Northwestern State**
24. **Rick Falkner, of, Portland**
25. **Javier Murillo, 2b, Azusa Pacific (Calif.)**
26. **Martin Eddy, of/1b, Dallas Baptist**

27. **Lawrence Smith, 2b, Bethune-Cookman**
28. **Randy Mazey, of, Clemson**
29. Kraig Constantino, 1b/c, Branham HS, San Jose
30. **William Scarborough, rhp, Ferrum (Va.)**
31. David Keating, of, UCLA
32. **Rouglas Odor, ss, New Orleans**
33. **Alex Ferran, of, Coral Park HS, Miami**
34. **Andrew Baker, rhp, Cook HS, Lenox, Ga.**
35. Troy Eklund, of, Arkansas
36. **Cecil Pettiford, rhp, Jackson State**
37. **Dan Williams, c, Western Oregon State**
38. **Lenny Gilmore, of, Cal State Northridge**
39. **Mark Tepper, 1b, Lubbock Christian (Texas)**
40. **Keith Bevenour, lhp, Penn State**
41. **Brad Hebets, rhp, Southwestern Louisiana**
42. John Abercrombie, c, Eisenhower HS, Houston
43. **Teryl Morrison, rhp, Contra Costa (Calif.) JC**
44. **Jeff Bonchek, 3b, Michigan State**
45. **Steve Harrell, of, Hamilton (Ohio) HS**
46. **Todd Mraz, c, Texas-Arlington**
47. **Brian Cofer, ss, Montevallo (Ala.)**
48. Douglas Egloff, rhp, Denver
49. Greg Fowble, 2b, Arizona
50. **Dean Meddaugh, of/2b, Victor Valley (Calif.) CC**
51. John Eierman, of, Leo HS, Chicago
52. **Michael Ashworth, rhp, Westmont**
53. **Bill Kull, of, Florida Southern**
54. David Ferrell, 2b, DeAnza (Calif.) JC
55. Jason Pfaff, 1b, St. Xavier HS, Cincinnati
56. Michael Bonetto, lhp, Big Bear HS, Big Bear Lake, Calif.
57. Erik Young, of, Baldwin-Wallace (Ohio)
58. Mark Smith, rhp, San Jacinto (Texas) JC

DETROIT TIGERS

June—Regular Phase (26)

1. **Rico Brogna, 1b/lhp, Watertown (Conn.) HS**
2. **Scott Livingstone, 3b, Texas A&M**
3. **Tookie Spann, of, Tulane**
4. **Lance Shebelut, 1b, Fresno State**
5. **Mike Lumley, rhp, Eastern Michigan**
6. **Eric Stone, rhp, Texas**
7. **Tim Brader, lhp, Shelton State (Ala.) JC**
8. **Tom Aldrich, ss, Bowdoin (Maine)**
9. **Kurt Knudsen, rhp, Miami**
10. **Chris Gollehon, rhp, Medical Lake HS, Fairchild, Wash.**
11. Michael Brown, of, Pensacola (Fla.) Catholic HS
12. **Mickey Delas, c, Eastern Michigan**
13. **Mike Rendina, 1b, Grossmont HS, El Cajon, Calif.**
14. **Linty Ingram, rhp, Arizona State**
15. **Dave Haas, rhp, Wichita State**
16. **Brett Roach, c, Eastern Michigan**
17. **Rich Rowland, c, Mendocino (Calif.) CC**
18. **Ron Howard, 2b, Palomar (Calif.) JC**
19. Todd A. Taylor, c, Lakeland (Fla.) HS
20. **Kurt Shea, rhp, Southwestern Michigan JC**
21. **Robert Thomas, rhp, Sonoma State (Calif.)**
22. Willie Warrecker, lhp, California
23. **John Barton, rhp, Nevada-Reno**
24. **Benny Castillo, of, Oklahoma State**
25. **Robert Frassa, of, CC of Morris (N.J.)**
26. Brian Dour, rhp, Bradley
27. Michael Pfeifer, rhp, Stevens HS, Edison, N.J.
28. **Eric Shoup, rhp, Point Park (Pa.)**
29. **Jimmy Hitt, rhp, Florida Southern**
30. **Mike Davidson, of, Michigan State**
31. **James Hill, ss, Pacific**
32. **Joe Niedinger, rhp, Catholic Central HS, Monroe, Mich.**
33. Brian Eubanks, rhp, Marysville (Calif.) HS
34. Ed Bustamonte, of, Fresno State
35. **Mike Jones, rhp, Loyola Marymount**
36. **Travis Kinyoun, c, Royal HS, Simi Valley, Calif.**
37. **Duane Walker, of, South Florida**
38. **Bert Patton, lhp, Eastern Michigan**
39. Todd Winston, c, Marysville (Mich.) HS
40. **Bobby Holley, ss, UCLA**
41. **Don Pedersen, 1b/of, JC of the Canyons (Calif.)**
42. David Brink, rhp, Lake Michigan (Mich.) JC
43. Joe Arredondo, 1b, Bellflower (Calif.) HS
44. Derric Taylor, of, Muir HS, Altadena, Calif.
45. Kirk Piskor, c, Plano (Texas) East HS
46. James Wolfe, c, Spanish River HS, Boca Raton, Fla.
47. Tony Muser Jr., 2b, Los Alamitos (Calif.) HS
48. Robert Welch, c, Horizon HS, Scottsdale, Ariz.
49. Andrew Watson, rhp, Vashon HS, St. Louis
50. Russ Gaston, rhp, Belleville Area (Ill.) CC

HOUSTON ASTROS

June—Regular Phase (7)

1. **Willie Ansley, of, Plainview (Texas) HS**
2. **Mica Lewis, ss, Cal State Los Angeles**
2. **Dave Silvestri, ss, Missouri** (Pick from Yankees as compensation for Type B free agent Jose Cruz)
3. **Scott Servais, c, Creighton**
4. **Luis Gonzalez, 1b, South Alabama**
5. Terry Christopher, rhp, Moline, Ill.
6. **Chris Gardner, rhp, Cuesta (Calif.) JC**
7. **Bernard Jenkins, of, St. Francis (N.Y.)**
8. **Gordy Farmer, rhp, Arizona State**
9. **Brian Griffiths, rhp, Mount Hood (Ore.) CC**
10. **David Klinefelter, lhp, Allegheny (Pa.) CC**
11. **Maurice Jones, of, Edgewater HS, Orlando, Fla.**
12. **Dave Shermet, of, Arizona**
13. **Bill Gearhart, rhp, Armstrong State (Ga.)**
14. **Larry Lamphere, of, Central Michigan**
15. **Wally Trice, lhp, U.S. International (Nairobi)**
16. **Ed Quijada, 3b, Rio Vista (Calif.) HS**
17. **Kenny Lofton, of, Arizona**
18. **Rod Windes, lhp, Cal State Los Angeles**
19. Mike Durant, c, Watterson HS, Columbus, Ohio
20. **Eric Given, c, South Carolina-Spartanburg**
21. **Rick Dunnum, rhp, William Penn (Iowa)**
22. **Ken Morris, rhp, Northwestern State**
23. **Jim Desapio, lhp, St. Francis (N.Y.)**
24. **David Metheney, rhp, Dixie Hollins HS, Seminole, Fla.**
25. Kevin Schula, c, El Dorado HS, Placentia, Calif.
26. **Rod Scheckla, rhp, Oregon State**
27. **Ben Gonzales, rhp, Cypress (Calif.) JC**
28. Mark King, of, Mount Carmel HS, San Diego
29. **Anthony Gutierrez, lhp, Englewood HS, Littleton, Colo.**
30. Mike Kirk, of, Shasta (Calif.) JC
31. **Bob Hurlbutt, c, Monroe (N.Y.) CC**
32. Matthew Lackie, rhp, Rancho Santiago (Calif.) JC
33. Mark Rudis, c, Clear Creek HS, League City, Texas
34. Eric Gray, rhp, Bloomington HS, Rialto, Calif.
35. Dan Tiumalu, 3b/of, Helix HS, Lemon Grove, Calif.
36. **Scott Spurgeon, 3b, Northwest Missouri State**
37. **Duane Brown, rhp, South Umpqua HS, Myrtle Creek, Ore.**
38. Elgin Bobo, c, Cabrillo (Calif.) JC
39. **Mark Hudgins, ss, Plantation (Fla.) HS**
40. Richard Czajkowski, ss, Haverling HS, Bath, N.Y.
41. Chris Tremie, c, South Houston (Texas) HS
42. Billy Wissler, rhp, Central Dauphin HS, Harrisburg, Pa.
43. **Troy Dovey, rhp, Miami-Dade South CC**
44. **Luis Navarro, lhp, Southwest HS, Miami**
45. Heath Daniel, of, Central HS, Phenix City, Ala.
46. Craig Fairbanks, rhp, Morello Prep HS, Boulder Creek, Calif.
47. Scott Mowl, 1b, Bellflower (Calif.) HS
48. David Lacroix, rhp/ss, Los Angeles Harbor JC
49. Placido Vicente, c, Southwest HS, Miami
50. Anthony Dunnahoe, 1b/of, Haines City (Fla.) HS
51. Ross Macaluso, ss, Hillsborough (Fla.) CC
52. James Simpson, of, Lake Worth (Fla.) HS
53. Steven Schuerman, rhp, Spokane Falls (Wash.) CC
54. Joe Burnett, of, Delgado (La.) JC
55. John Hercholcz, rhp, Miami-Dade North CC
56. Patrick King, of/inf, Don Lugo HS, Chino, Calif.
57. Jose Rubiera, of, Howard (Texas) JC
58. Nelson Izquierdo, 2b, Pace HS, Hialeah, Fla.

59. Grady Garrow, rhp, Butte (Calif.) JC
60. Matthew Morgan, of, Creskill (N.J.) HS
61. Jon Newville, rhp, Bishop Montgomery HS, Palos Verdes Estates, Calif.
62. Jim Greenlee, lhp, Pinole Valley HS, San Pablo, Calif.
63. Joe Church, rhp, Santana HS, Santee, Calif.
64. Michael Ballerelli, of, Castle Park HS, San Diego

KANSAS CITY ROYALS

June—Regular Phase (18)

1. **Hugh Walker, of, Jacksonville (Ark.) HS**
2. **Bob Hamelin, 1b, Rancho Santiago (Calif.) JC**
3. **Joel Johnston, rhp, West Chester, Pa.**
4. **Greg Harvey, rhp, Seminole State (Okla.) JC**
5. **Tim Spehr, c, Arizona State**
6. **Jim Smith, rhp, Jacksonville State**
7. **Frankie Watson, of, Longwood (Va.)**
8. **Randy Vaughn, rhp, Shelton State (Ala.) JC**
9. **Jeff Hulse, c, Kansas State**
10. **Jeff Garber, 2b, James Madison**
11. **Mike Magnante, lhp, UCLA**
12. **Steve Otto, rhp, St. Xavier (Ill.)**
13. **David Rolls, c, San Diego**
14. **Victor Cole, rhp, Santa Clara**
15. **Kyle Balch, rhp, Vanderbilt**
16. **Kerwin Moore, of, King HS, Detroit**
17. **John Conner, rhp, Rose State (Okla.) JC**
18. **Stan Bowling, rhp, Desales HS, Louisville**
19. **Marvin Mayberry, c, Cody HS, Detroit**
20. John Cuda, rhp, Penn Hills HS, Verona, Pa.
21. **Milt Richardson, of, Skyline (Calif.) JC**
22. **Frank Halcovich, of/1b, Arizona**
23. **Kyle Irvin, rhp, Oral Roberts**
24. **Kelvin Davis, ss, Longwood**
25. **Zach Kimbell, rhp, Kansas State**
26. **Chad Stombaugh, c, Rend Lake (Ill.) JC**
27. Rich Gonzales, of/1b, Rancho Santiago (Calif.) JC
28. **Gerald Ingram, of, Western Kentucky**
29. **Ronald Collins, 1b, Mount San Jacinto (Calif.) JC**
30. **John Gilcrist, of, Indian River (Fla.) CC**
31. **John McCormick, lhp, Ohio State**
32. **Stephen Osik, rhp, Long Island**
33. **Mike Beall, 1b, St. Thomas**
34. Mike Gillette, c, Michigan
35. **Steve Preston, 2b, Michigan State**
36. **Greg Prusia, of, SUNY Alfred JC**
37. Brad Seitzer, ss/3b, Lincoln Land (Ill.) CC
38. Dean McMillin, lhp, Ventura (Calif.) HS
39. **Brad Hopper, rhp, Fullerton (Calif.) JC**
40. Jim Austin, of, Mater Dei HS, Mission Viejo, Calif.
41. Mickey Kerns, ss, Hancock (Md.) HS
42. Greg Blevins, c, Northeastern Oklahoma A&M JC
43. **John Gross, rhp, Clovis HS, Fresno**
44. William Melvin, of, Pace HS, Milton, Fla.
45. David Fletcher, rhp, Yucca Valley (Calif.) HS
46. **Jerome Beyers, of, Washington HS, Kansas City, Kan.**
47. Kim Cornist, of, Solano (Calif.) CC
48. Jose Fernandez, c, Florida
49. **Jason Bryans, rhp, Macomb (Mich.) CC**

LOS ANGELES DODGERS

June—Regular Phase (5)

1. **Bill Bene, rhp, Cal State Los Angeles**
2. (Pick to Athletics as compensation for Type A free agent Mike Davis)
3. **Billy Ashley, of, Belleville (Mich.) HS**
4. **Anthony Collier, of, Muir HS, Pasadena, Calif.**
5. **Paul Branconier, rhp, Covina (Calif.) HS**
6. **Eric Karros, 1b, UCLA**
7. **Jeff Hartsock, rhp, North Carolina State**
8. Scott Erwin, rhp, Georgia Tech
9. **Jim Poole, lhp, Georgia Tech**
10. **Eddie Pye, ss, Middle Tennessee State**
11. **Brock McMurray, of, Southeastern Louisiana**
12. **Jerry Brooks, of/3b, Clemson**
13. **Chris Morrow, of, Skyline (Calif.) JC**
14. Dana Allison, lhp, James Madison
15. **Lance Rice, c, Oregon State**
16. **Brian Traxler, 1b, New Orleans**
17. **Mike Chiusano, c, Nazareth HS, Brooklyn, N.Y.**
18. Russell Smith, of, Conestoga Valley HS, Talmage, Pa.
19. **James Wray, lhp, Troy State**
20. **Sean McKamie, ss, Central HS, St. Paul, Minn.**
21. **Steve Finken, ss, Michigan**
22. **Michael St. Estaben, lhp, Chino (Calif.) HS**
23. **Bill Wengert, rhp, Iowa State**
24. **Rod Harvell, of, Fairfield (Calif.) HS**
25. **Mike Sampson, rhp, Holyoke (Mass.) CC**
26. **Ernie Carr, 3b/of, Jacksonville**
27. Mike Munson, rhp, Illinois
28. **Eric Ganino, c, Fontana (Calif.) HS**
29. **John Braase, rhp, College of Idaho**
30. **Sean Snedeker, rhp, Texas A&M**
31. **Clayton Enno, lhp, Des Moines Area (Iowa) CC**
32. **Bryan Beals, 2b/of, Chapman (Calif.)**
33. **Cam Biberdorf, rhp, Mayville State (N.D.)**
34. **Napoleon Robinson, rhp, Columbus (Ga.)**
35. **Hector Ortiz, c, Ranger (Texas) JC**
36. **Jeff Castillo, rhp, Mesa (Colo.)**
37. **Brad Boggetto, rhp, Parkland (Ill.) JC**
38. **Wendall Zink, 3b/ss, Dixie (Utah) JC**
39. **K.G. White, of, Georgia Tech**
40. Felix Rios, 3b, George Fox (Ore.)
41. Todd Reische, c, Minooka (Ill.) HS
42. **Eric Blackwell, of, Spartanburg Methodist (S.C.) JC**
43. Garey Ingram, c, Columbus (Ga.) HS
44. Brent Miller, 3b/1b, Jordan HS, Columbus, Ga.
45. Brad Cohen, of, Starkville (Miss.) Academy
46. Wilfred Brown, ss, Lurleen Wallace State (Ala.) JC
47. **Garrett Beard, of/3b, Spartanburg Methodist (S.C.) JC**
48. Terry Miller, of, Compton (Calif.) CC
49. Deon Montgomery, ss, Compton (Calif.) CC
50. Jose Fernandez, of, CC of San Francisco
51. Daniel Hancock, rhp, Bremen HS, Midlothian, Ill.
52. Gaither Bagsby, rhp, Dickson County (Tenn.) HS
53. Michael Emmons, rhp, Pensacola (Fla.) JC
54. Shannon Zerlang, of/3b, JC of the Redwoods (Calif.)
55. Craig Thomas, of, Northside HS, Warner Robins, Ga.
56. Dan Frye, ss/2b, Logansport (Ind.) HS
57. Dennis Frye, 1b/of, Logansport (Ind.) HS
58. Mike Vdovkin, rhp, Merced (Calif.) HS
59. Chris Harding, of, Louisburg (N.C.) JC
60. Robert Hoffman, c, Kennedy HS, Richmond, Calif.
61. **Erik Boddie, of, Creighton**
62. **Mike Piazza, 1b/c, Miami-Dade North CC**

MILWAUKEE BREWERS

June—Regular Phase (24)

1. Alex Fernandez, rhp, Pace HS, Miami
2. **Randy Snyder, c, Washington State**
3. **Joe Andrzejewski, rhp, Chesapeake HS, Pasadena, Md.**
4. **Ken Kremer, 1b, Rider**
5. **Pat Listach, ss, Arizona State**
6. **Greg Landry, rhp, Texas**
7. **Chris George, rhp, Kent State**
8. **Mike Ignasiak, rhp, Michigan**
9. **Bert Heffernan, c, Clemson**
10. Charlie Fiacco, of, UCLA
11. **Danny Kapea, lhp, Hawaii**
12. **Don Meyett, of, Catonsville (Md.) CC**
13. **Leon Glenn, 1b, East Central (Miss.) JC**
14. Ken Hokuf, rhp, Golden West (Calif.) JC
15. **Sylvester Love, of, Southern Mississippi**
16. **Heath Lane, rhp, Arizona**
17. **Robert Scott, of, Mankato (Minn.) West HS**
18. **Stewart Lee, 3b, Jacksonville State**
19. **Dave Voit, rhp, Kentucky**

20. **Ruben Rodriguez, of, Southwestern Louisiana**
21. Brian Dodd, lhp, Arizona State
22. **Robert Muhammad, of, Hawaii**
23. **Tim Snow, 2b, East Carolina**
24. Troy Bradford, rhp, Cochise County (Ariz.) CC
25. **Kevin Carmody, lhp, North Adams State (Mass.)**
26. **Javier Brown, ss/of, Morse HS, San Diego**
27. **David Fitzgerald, lhp, Davidson**
28. Doug Vander Weele, rhp, Bonanza HS, Las Vegas
29. **Rich Pfaff, of, Essex (Md.) CC**
30. **Larry Oedewaldt, c, U.S. International**
31. **Michael Grayson, rhp, Florida International**
32. Robert Jakubik, 1b, St. John Bosco HS, Cerritos, Calif.
33. Chris Norton, c, Lake Howell HS, Maitland, Fla.
34. Donald Culberson, of, Neshoba Central HS, Philadelphia
35. Dwayne Wilson, of, Oceanside (Calif.) HS
36. **Brad Tilly, 2b, Bradley**
37. **John Littlewood, 3b, Brigham Young**
38. **Bryan Parks, c, Catonsville (Md.) CC**
39. Chris Tacik, rhp, Thomas Johnson HS, Frederick, Md.
40. Bryan Hastings, rhp, East Forsyth HS, Kernersville, N.C.
41. Edgar Anderson, of, Logan HS, Dolton, Ill.
42. Scott Craven, 3b, Punahou HS, Kailua, Hawaii

MINNESOTA TWINS

June—Regular Phase (20)

1. **Johnny Ard, rhp, Manatee (Fla.) JC**
2. **Alan Newman, lhp, Fullerton (Calif.) JC**
3. Mike Harrison, c, Campolinda (Calif.) HS
4. **Steve Dunn, 1b, Robinson HS, Fairfax, Va.**
5. Steve Dean, of/rhp, Ada (Okla.) HS
6. **Pat Mahomes, rhp, Lindale (Texas) HS**
7. **Doug Sutton, rhp, Kentucky**
8. **Jay Kvasnicka, of, Minnesota**
9. **Doug Simons, lhp, Pepperdine**
10. **Jody Harrington, lhp, Armijo HS, Fairfield, Calif.**
11. **J.T. Bruett, of, Minnesota**
12. **Deryk Gross, of, Pacific**
13. **Mike Pomeranz, lhp, Clemson**
14. **Steve Muh, lhp, Georgia**
15. **Tony Tucker, of, Tate HS, Cantonment, Fla.**
16. Gary Tatterson, rhp, Glendale (Ariz.) CC
17. **Gary Resetar, c, Rutgers**
18. Vince Palyan, of, Minnesota
19. **Carl Fraticelli, 2b, Loyola Marymount**
20. **Loy McBride, of, Cal State Los Angeles**
21. **Jeff Milene, c, Mayo HS, Rochester, Minn.**
22. **Angel Lugo, ss, Grady HS, Brooklyn, N.Y.**
23. Jeff Edmunds, 1b, Plantation HS, Sunrise, Fla.
24. Jody Hurst, of, Mississippi State
25. **J.P. Wright, of, Washburn (Kan.)**
26. Steve Gill, lhp/of, Cypress (Calif.) JC
27. Scott Stahoviak, rhp/1b, Carmel Mundelin HS, Grays Lake, Ill.
28. Peter Raether, rhp, Edina (Minn.) HS
29. Jon Bellamy, 3b, Lafayette (La.) HS
30. Will Vespe, 1b, Miami
31. Chris Hmielewski, lhp, Leyden HS, Franklin Park, Ill.
32. **Dom Rovasio, rhp, Quinnipiac**
33. Pat Hope, rhp, Oklahoma State
34. George Behr, of, Hill Murray HS, Maplewood, Minn.
35. **Steve Morris, of, Hawaii-Manoa**
36. Michael Teron, rhp, Santa Clara HS, Oxnard, Calif.
37. Aaron Sele, rhp, North Kitsap HS, Poulsbo, Wash.
38. Marc Pak, of, Valley HS, Las Vegas
39. Sheldon Forehand, of, American HS, Fremont, Calif.
40. **Pedro Oliva, of, Kennedy HS, Bloomington, Minn.**
41. David Baine, lhp, San Marin HS, Novato, Calif.
42. **Willie McKinnon, of, Nicholls (Ga.) HS**
43. Jeremy Kendall, lhp, Towns Country HS, Hiwassee, Ga.
44. Carl Johnson, rhp, North Thurston Johnson HS, Frederick, Md.
45. **Troy Hoerner, of, Milaca (Minn.) HS**
46. John Jackson, of, Washington State
47. Jerome McGerry, of/rhp, Liberty Eylau HS, Texarkana, Texas
48. Frederick Smith, rhp, Venice HS, Culver City, Calif.

MONTREAL EXPOS

June—Regular Phase (19)

1. **Dave Wainhouse, rhp, Washington State**
2. **Ben Howze, rhp, Washington HS, Pensacola, Fla.** (Pick from Cubs as compensation for Type B free agent Vance Law)
2. **Chris Nabholz, lhp, Towson State**
3. **Marquis Grissom, of/rhp, Florida A&M**
4. **Scott Davison, rhp/ss, Redondo Union HS, Redondo Beach, Calif.**
5. **Tyrone Woods, 3b, Hernando HS, Brooksville, Fla.**
6. **Tim Laker, c, Oxnard (Calif.) JC**
7. **Bret Barberie, ss, Southern California**
8. **Bryn Kosco, 3b, North Carolina State**
9. **Martin Martinez, rhp, Cochise County (Ariz.) CC**
10. **Joe Klancnik, rhp, Florida**
11. **Reid Cornelius, rhp, Thomasville (Ala.) HS**
12. **Isaac Elder, of, Cal State Los Angeles**
13. **Rod Boddie, of, James Madison**
14. **Dan Archibald, rhp, San Jose State**
15. **Rafael Adame, rhp, Bell HS, Maywood, Calif.**
16. **Steve Whitehead, rhp, Brawley (Calif.) HS**
17. **Dan Freed, rhp, Illinois State**
18. **Darrin Winston, lhp, Rutgers**
19. Richard Busch, c, St. Petersburg (Fla.) HS
20. **Brian Sajonia, lhp, Washington State**
21. **Eric Nelson, 3b/rhp, San Jose State**
22. Brian Pease, lhp, Bonny Eagle HS, Cornish, Maine
23. **Pat Heiderscheit, rhp/c, Iowa State**
24. **Mike Farrell, rhp, LeMoyne**
25. **Dale Buzzard, rhp, La Verne (Calif.)**
26. **David Oropeza, rhp, Alabama**
27. Scott Banton, of, Virginia Commonwealth
28. **Keith Kaub, 1b, Cal State Fullerton**
29. Robert Langer, ss, Carmel HS, Mundelein, Ill.
30. Danny Parente, 1b/lhp, Los Angeles Harbor JC
31. Vernon Slater, of, Brandon HS, Tampa
32. Justin Heinold, lhp, Stroman HS, Victoria, Texas
33. Dan Stanley, ss, Lindberg HS, Renton, Wash.
34. Marvin Cobb, rhp, Oklahoma
35. **Mike Virden, of, Lee (Texas) JC**
36. Antonio Grissom, of, Lakeshore HS, Red Oak, Ga.
37. Todd Manly, rhp, San Jose CC
38. Mike Lane, 1b, Indian River (Fla.) CC
39. **Ken Lake, of, Wyoming**
40. **Ricardo Cartwright, of, Florida A&M**
41. **Paul Hutto, rhp, Auburndale (Fla.) HS**
42. Brad Erdman, 3b, Douglas (Ariz.) HS
43. Gary Young, rhp, San Jacinto (Texas) JC
44. Jesus Molina, lhp, Pima (Ariz.) CC
45. **Jeff Tuss, rhp, Capital HS, Helena, Mont.**
46. Stephen Day, rhp, Indian River (Fla.) CC
47. Cord Corbitt, lhp, Palm Beach (Fla.) JC
48. Frank Giunta, 1b/lhp, Martin County HS, Palm City, Fla.
49. Jared Snyder, c, Saugus (Calif.) HS
50. Norman Montoya, lhp, Newark (Calif.) Memorial HS
51. **Jeff Ramsey, ss/of, Northampton East HS, Rich Square, N.C.**
52. Robert Yonker, rhp, CC of Morris (N.J.)
53. **Doug DeKock, c, Miami**
54. Keith Hopkins, of, Brandon HS, Tampa
55. **Marlon Correa, 2b, Carol City (Fla.) HS**
56. James Wallkvist, rhp, Lincoln HS, San Francisco
57. John Fleischer, rhp, Benedictine HS, Richmond
58. John Halverson, rhp, Brookwood HS, Snellville, Ga.

NEW YORK METS

June—Regular Phase (21)

1. **Dave Proctor, rhp, Allen County (Kan.) CC**
2. Jeff Seale, rhp, Fairview HS, Boulder, Colo.
3. **Doug Saunders, 2b, Esperanza HS, Yorba Linda, Calif.**
3. Derrick Warren, of, Washington HS, Pensacola, Fla. (Pick from Yankees as compensation for Type B free agent John Candelaria)
4. **Dan Furmanik, rhp, Palm Beach (Fla.) JC**
5. **Tim Howard, 2b, Imperial Valley (Calif.) JC**

6. **Kyle Washington, of, Kishwaukee (Ill.) JC**
7. **Kevin Baez, ss, Dominican (N.Y.)**
8. **Mike Lehnerz, rhp, Regis HS, Denver**
9. Pat Leinen, lhp, Nebraska
10. **Andrew Fidler, lhp, Methacton HS, Audubon, Pa.**
11. **Greg Langbehn, lhp, Everest HS, Schofield, Wis.**
12. Doug Bennett, rhp, Hillcrest HS, Springfield, Mo.
13. **Jeff Thompson, ss, Newnan (Ga.) HS**
14. **Mike Anaya, rhp, Valley HS, Albuquerque**
15. **Nicky Davis, 1b, Merritt Island (Fla.) HS**
16. **Andy Reich, rhp, Louisburg (N.C.) JC**
17. **Mason Rudolph, c, Dobson HS, Mesa, Ariz.**
18. **Mike Noelke, 2b, Wisconsin**
19. Beau Campbell, c, Lindberg HS, Renton, Wash.
20. **Jon Hudson, lhp, Kentucky**
21. **Paul Johnson, rhp, Rutgers**
22. **Chris Butler, rhp, McEachern HS, Marietta, Ga.**
23. **Dale Plummer, rhp, Maine**
24. Mike Kelly, of, Los Alamitos (Calif.) HS
25. **Fred Brown, rhp, Navarro (Texas) JC**
26. Sean Lawrence, lhp, River Forest HS, Oak Park, Ill.
27. Paul Perkins, rhp, Fairfield (Calif.) HS
28. **Deron Sample, rhp/of, Paris (Texas) JC**
29. **Chris Dorn, rhp, San Jacinto (Texas) JC**
30. **Robbie Guzik, of, Allegheny (Pa.) CC**
31. Phillip Essex, rhp, McLennan (Texas) CC
32. **Richard Bristow, rhp, Geneva (Ill.) HS**
33. **Brian Zimmerman, lhp, North Central (Ill.)**
34. **David Parouse, c, Dominican (N.Y.)**
35. Gary Wilson, ss/2b, Arcata (Calif.) HS
36. Scott Ellrich, lhp, Crystal Lake (Ill.) South HS
37. **Devren Moore, of, Madison HS, San Antonio**
38. Joe Vitko III, rhp, Central Cambria HS, Ebensburg, Pa.
39. **Bryan Rogers, rhp, Sonoma State (Calif.)**
40. Jeff Herrington, rhp, Northeastern Oklahoma A&M JC
41. **Reid Hartmann, 2b, St. Louis CC-Meramec**
42. Steve Hinton, lhp, Elgin (Ill.) HS
43. **Danny Auchard, lhp, Tracy (Calif.) HS**
44. Brian Buzard, lhp, Neodesha (Kan.) HS
45. **James Harris, c, St. John the Baptist HS, North Babylon, N.Y.**
46. **Tom Becker, ss, Pratt (Kan.) CC**
47. **Joseph McCann, rhp, DeKalb (Ga.) JC**
48. Alex Garces, rhp, Westminster HS, Miami
49. Mark Moore, c, Shawnee Mission East HS, Overland Park, Kan.
50. **Nathaniel Benson, rhp, Leo HS, Country Club Hills, Ill.**
51. John Bentley, rhp, Trinity HS, Weaverville, Calif.
52. Mike Sell, 2b, Capital HS, Helena, Mont.
53. **Wayne Mathis, of, Cuero (Texas) HS**
54. Mark Bonini, of, Pinole Valley (Calif.) HS
55. Pat Kokora, ss, Boulder (Colo.) HS
56. Mike Kundrat, rhp, Thornwood HS, Calumet City, Ill.
57. Greg Akerman, 3b, Bradley-Bourbonnais HS, Bradley, Ill.
58. Perry Amos, of/lhp, Orland HS, Willows, Calif.
59. Chuck Foster, of, San Jacinto (Texas) JC
60. Jerome Tolliver, of, Lincoln Academy HS, Kansas City, Mo.

NEW YORK YANKEES

June—Regular Phase (22)

1. (Pick to Cardinals as compensation for Type A free agent Jack Clark)
2. (Pick to Astros as compensation for Type B free agent Jose Cruz)
3. (Pick to Mets as compensation for Type B free agent John Candelaria)
4. **Todd Malone, lhp, Casa Robles HS, Citrus Heights, Calif.**
5. **Don Sparks, 3b, Loyola Marymount**
6. **Jeff Johnson, lhp, UNC Charlotte**
7. **Billy Masse, of, Wake Forest**
8. **Bobby DeJardin, ss, Loyola Marymount**
9. **Pat Kelly, ss, West Chester (Pa.)**
10. **Kenny Greer, rhp, Massachusetts**
11. **Andy Cook, rhp, Memphis State**
12. **Frank Seminara, rhp, Columbia**
13. **Jeff Livesey, c, Auburn**
14. **Jeff Hoffman, rhp, Vanderbilt**
15. **Bobby Munoz, rhp, Palm Beach (Fla.) JC**
16. **Herb Erhardt, inf/c, Texas-Pan American**
17. **Jay Knoblauh, of, Rice**
18. **Jerry Nielsen, lhp, Florida State**
19. **Steve Perry, lhp, King HS, Detroit**
20. **Craig Brink, rhp, UC Irvine**
21. **Bruce Prybylinski, rhp, Illinois State**
22. **Skip Nelloms, of, Western Carolina**
23. **Bob Zeihen, of, Indiana State**
24. **John Seeburger, 1b, UC Irvine**
25. **Jason Bridges, of, Alabama**
26. **Mike Draper, rhp, George Mason**
27. **Curtis Ralph, rhp, Sacramento CC**
28. **Michael Rhodes, of, Houston**
29. **Russ Davis, ss, Shelton State (Ala.) JC**
30. **Deion Sanders, of, Florida State**
31. Joe Vitiello, 1b/rhp, Stoneham (Mass.) HS
32. John Cummings, lhp, Canyon HS, Anaheim
33. Todd Youngblood, ss, Farmington (N.M.) HS
34. David Tuttle, rhp, Los Gatos (Calif.) HS
35. Mark Kingston, of, Potomac HS, Dumphries, Va.
36. Troy Tallman, c, Napa (Calif.) HS
37. Pat Maloney, of, Lyons Township HS, La Grange, Ill.
38. Deshon Brown, of, Modesto (Calif.) HS
39. Thomas Quinn, rhp, South Florida JC
40. Matthew Barker, of, Brevard (Fla.) CC
41. Chad Ogea, rhp, St. Louis HS, Lake Charles, La.
42. Brian Faw, rhp, DeKalb (Ga.) JC
43. Orlando Palmeiro, of, Miami-Dade South CC
44. Donald Robinson, of, Killian HS, Miami
45. **Brad Stoltenberg, rhp, Cal State Sacramento**
46. **Art Canestro, lhp, New York Tech**
47. Brian Reimsnyder, of, Florida
48. Michael Gonzalez, rhp, Sul Ross State (Texas)
49. Kurt Pfeffer, rhp, JC of Marin (Calif.)
50. Allen Popowitz, rhp, Saddle River County HS, Upper Saddle River, N.J.
51. Fernando Vina, ss/2b, Cosumnes River (Calif.) JC
52. Franklin Lacy, c/of, Laney (Calif.) JC
53. Alex Kuhn, c, Eldorado HS, Albuquerque
54. George Day, 2b, LaGrange HS, Lake Charles, La.
55. Keiver Campbell, of, Greenville (Miss.) HS
56. Joe Smith, rhp, Paris (Texas) JC
57. **Mike Eckert, lhp, Texas-Pan American**
58. **John Broxton, rhp, Mercer**
59. Jeff Pickett, c, Blue Springs (Mo.) HS
60. **Matt Michael, lhp, Morehead State**
61. Rodney Huffman, rhp, Lake Highlands HS, Dallas
62. Phil Mendelson, rhp, Grand Junction (Colo.) HS
63. James Mauldin, rhp, Seminole State (Okla.) JC
64. **Mark Ohlms, rhp, Grand View (Iowa)**
65. Jay Gravens, rhp, Dallas Baptist
66. Mark Futrell, rhp, Miami-Dade South CC
67. **Mark Zeratsky, c, Grand View (Iowa)**
68. Wayne Weinheimer, of, Sacramento CC (Selection voided)
69. **Len Thigpen, of, Monticello, Fla.**
70. Rob Bargas, 3b, Sacramento CC
71. Scott Thoma, rhp, Texas Wesleyan
72. Dan Rambo, rhp, Central Michigan
73. Michael Boyan, rhp, Bradley
74. Oscar Rivas, lhp, San Jacinto (Texas) JC
75. Robert LeFebre, of, Florida Southern

OAKLAND ATHLETICS

June—Regular Phase (16)

1. **Stan Royer, c/3b, Eastern Illinois**
2. **Wynn Beck, c, South Brunswick HS, Southport, N.C.** (Pick from Dodgers as compensation for Type A free agent Mike Davis)
2. **Joe Slusarski, rhp, New Orleans**
3. **John Briscoe, rhp, Texas Christian**
4. **Enoch Simmons, of, Loyola Marymount**
5. Joe Grahe, rhp, Miami
6. **Dan Eskew, rhp, Tennessee**

7. **Ron Witmeyer, 1b, Stanford**
8. **Rich Rozman, rhp, Michigan State**
9. **Nick Venuto, rhp, Kent State**
10. **Tom Carcione, c, Texas A&M**
11. **Joel Chimelis, ss, Texas**
12. **James Lawson, rhp, Huntington (Ind.)**
13. **Mike Messerly, 1b, Middle Tennessee State**
14. Rodney Peete, 3b, Southern California
15. **Rod Correia, ss, Southeastern Massachusetts**
16. Mike Butler, lhp, North Caroline HS, Denton, Md.
17. **Gerard Rizza, rhp, Long Island**
18. **Darren Lewis, of, California**
19. **William Love, of/lhp, Lassen (Calif.) JC**
20. **Dean Borrelli, c, Massachusetts**
21. **Tony Floyd, rhp, Southwest Missouri State**
22. **Ray Harris, lhp, Arkansas**
23. **Bronswell Patrick, rhp, Conley HS, Winterville, N.C.**
24. **Jim Buccheri, of, Golden West (Calif.) JC**
25. **Joe Hillman, of, Indiana**
26. **Tony Ariola, lhp, Northwestern**
27. **Michael Mungin, rhp, Norfolk State**
28. **Greg Ferguson, lhp, Virginia Tech**
29. **Dewayne Jones, 2b, South Alabama**
30. Steve Whitaker, lhp, Atwater (Calif.) HS
31. **Jeff Webber, of, Merced (Calif.) JC**
32. Lyndon Wright, c, Caesar Rodney HS, Camden, Del.
33. Mike Raskind, rhp, Granite Hills HS, El Cajon, Calif.
34. Tim McDonald, rhp, Central Michigan
35. Bobby Jones, of, Cal State Fullerton
36. Chris Butterfield, of, Cal Poly Pomona
37. Eric Gruben, rhp, Citrus (Calif.) JC
38. **Brian Foster, 1b/of, Farragut HS, Knoxville, Tenn.**
39. **Tim Vannaman, of, Rice**
40. **Jim Foley, rhp, Cal State Fullerton**
41. **Graham Miller, rhp, Laney (Calif.) JC**
42. Clifford Jones, lhp/of, Oakland HS, Richmond, Calif.
43. **Steven Peck, rhp, Mesa (Ariz.) CC**
44. Randy Brown, ss, Alief Elsik HS, Houston
45. John Pricher, rhp, Winter Park HS, Orlando, Fla.
46. Pat Tozier, 3b, Clayton Valley HS, Concord, Calif.
47. Pat Sullivan, lhp, Notre Dame HS, Signal Mountain, Tenn.
48. Blase Sparma, rhp, Watterson HS, Columbus, Ohio

PHILADELPHIA PHILLIES

June—Regular Phase (11)

1. **Pat Combs, lhp, Baylor**
2. (Pick to Braves as compensation for Type B free agent David Palmer)
3. **Tim Mauser, rhp, Texas Christian**
4. Joe Ciccarella, 1b, Mater Dei HS, Huntington Beach, Calif.
5. **Mickey Morandini, ss, Indiana**
6. **Albert Bennett, of, Lee (Texas) JC**
7. **Mike Owens, lhp, Massachusetts**
8. **Gary Wilson, rhp, St. Mary's (Texas)**
9. **Anthony Lozinski, c, Pacific**
10. **Jeff Etheredge, of, Panola (Texas) JC**
11. **Mike Sullivan, rhp, North Lake (Texas) JC**
12. **Scott Hatteberg, c, Eisenhower HS, Yakima, Wash.**
13. **Chris Lowe, of, University HS, Johnson City, Tenn.**
14. **Nick Santa Cruz, 2b/ss, Rancho Santiago (Calif.) JC**
15. **Tim Churchill, 1b/of, Cypress (Calif.) JC**
16. **Tom Marsh, of/rhp, Toledo**
17. Brian Walker, lhp, Capistrano Valley HS, Mission Viejo, Calif.
18. **Eric Bratlien, rhp, Cal Poly San Luis Obispo**
19. Sam Colarusso, rhp, Orange Coast (Calif.) JC
20. **Todd Goergen, rhp, Trinidad State (Colo.) JC**
21. David Boss, rhp, UC Santa Barbara
22. **Mathew Current, c, Middletown (Ohio) HS**
23. Mark Steffens, of, Germantown Academy HS, Fort Washington, Pa.
24. **Calvin Talford, of, Castlewood HS, Dante, Va.**
25. **Chris Toney, 3b, Hiram Johnson HS, Sacramento**
26. Jamie Allen, lhp, Hillsborough (Fla.) CC
27. James Short, 1b, Esperanza HS, Yorba Linda, Calif.
28. **Tim Dell, rhp, Huntington (Ind.)**
29. Greg Rehkow, lhp, Blue Springs (Mo.) HS
30. **Brian Harper, lhp, Southeast Missouri State**
31. **Craig Johnston, lhp, Napa (Calif.) HS**
32. **Ray Walker, ss, Madison HS, Houston**
33. **John Marshall, 1b/3b, Kentucky**
34. Darryl Vice, 2b, California
35. **Michael Dafforn, rhp, Fort Wayne, Ind.**
36. Brian Archer, rhp, Kearny HS, San Diego
37. Rod Klopfer, 3b, Fullerton (Calif.) JC
38. **Darrell Lindsey, rhp, Southern Mississippi**
39. Tom Crowley, 2b, Deptford (N.J.) HS
40. **Paul Fletcher, rhp, West Virginia State**
41. **Andrew Barrick, 2b/3b, Elizabethtown (Pa.)**
42. **Joe Tenhunfeld, of, Cincinnati**
43. Paul Anderson, rhp, San Diego Mesa JC
44. **Reggie Garcia, rhp, JC of the Sequoias (Calif.)**
45. Todd Pick, rhp, Lassen (Calif.) JC
46. **Troy Kent, rhp, UC Riverside**
47. **Greg Breaux, 2b, Waltrip HS, Houston**
48. David Willman, c, Hill HS, Boyertown, Pa.
49. **Nick Macaluso, 2b, New Orleans**
50. **Brian Cummings, 1b/of, Panola (Texas) JC**
51. **Thomas Doyle, 1b, Redondo Beach (Calif.) HS**
52. Gary Balderas, 3b, Madison HS, Houston
53. Steve Cooke, lhp, Tigard (Ore.) HS
54. **Chris Walker, 1b, Montevallo (Ala.)**
55. Rodd Hairston, rhp, Angelina (Texas) JC
56. Willie Navarette, lhp, Rancho Santiago (Calif.) JC
57. Dallas Monday, lhp, Jefferson County HS, Strawberry Plains, Tenn.
58. **Jeff Patterson, rhp, Cypress (Calif.) JC**
59. Bubba Smith, rhp, Rubidoux HS, Riverside, Calif.
60. Carey Newton, rhp, Christian Brothers HS, West Sacramento, Calif.
61. James Davis, c, University HS, Johnson City, Tenn.
62. Juan Price, c, Sweetwater HS, San Diego
63. David Richison, ss, Spiro (Okla.) HS
64. Randy Graves, ss, Riverside (Calif.) Poly HS
65. **Gil Valencia, of, Camarillo (Calif.) HS**

PITTSBURGH PIRATES

June—Regular Phase (13)

1. **Austin Manahan, ss, Horizon HS, Scottsdale, Ariz.**
2. **Keith Richardson, rhp, Georgia Southern**
3. **Glen McNabb, 2b/ss, Millikan HS, Long Beach**
4. **Steve Buckholz, rhp, Fresno State**
5. **Daryl Ratliff, of, Santa Cruz (Calif.) HS**
6. **Blas Minor Jr., rhp, Arizona State**
7. **John Wehner, 3b, Indiana**
8. **Tim Wakefield, 1b, Florida Institute of Technology**
9. **Jeff Payne, lhp, University HS, Morgantown, W.Va.**
10. **Jon Martin, of, Golden West (Calif.) JC**
11. **Joe Ausanio, rhp, Jacksonville**
12. **Chris Estep, of, Kentucky**
13. **Mike Huyler, 2b, Golden West (Calif.) JC**
14. Deryk Hudson, 3b, Fullerton (Calif.) JC
15. Mitchell Burke, c, Florida A&M
16. Jim Heins, rhp, Vanderbilt
17. **Bobby Underwood, lhp, South Carolina**
18. **Randy Tomlin, lhp, Liberty**
19. **Mandy Romero, c, Brevard (Fla.) CC**
20. Lawrence Gilligan, ss, Lakeland HS, Ringwood, N.J.
21. **Val Henderson, of, Bellevue (Wash.) CC**
22. Dave Staton, 1b, Orange Coast (Calif.) JC
23. **Renald Datcher, 1b, Lackey HS, Laplata, Md.**
24. **Scott Cowley, of, St. Leo (Fla.)**
25. **Greg Sims, of, St. Leo (Fla.)**
26. Chris Sheffield, 2b, Pine Forest HS, Pensacola, Fla.
27. **Paul McGhay, of, Montana State**
28. **Jeff Osborne, c, Kent State**
29. **Matthew Udell, rhp, Southwestern Michigan JC**
30. **Jeff Kuder, lhp, Mount Vernon Nazarene (Ohio)**
31. **Troy Clemens, c, Foothill (Calif.) JC**
32. Brian Purvis, of, Noblesville (Ind.) HS
33. **Paul Spalt, ss, North Carolina State**
34. **Steve Roeder, rhp, Mishiwaka (Ind.) Penn HS**

35. **Derek Tinnin, of/ss, Anderson (S.C.)**
36. **Al Molina, ss, Texas-Pan American**
37. **Darwin Pennye, of, Southwest Texas State**
38. **Mike Thompson, 1b, North Texas State**
39. **Ken Buksa, c/of, St. Xavier (Ill.)**
40. **Mike Fortuna, of, Coastal Carolina**
41. **Richard Haupt, lhp, Bald Eagle Area HS, Milesburg, Pa.**
42. **Ronald Way, lhp, Henry Ford (Mich.) CC**
43. Mark Hummell, 3b, Arizona Western JC
44. **Rich Wilson, lhp, Columbus (Ga.)**
45. Ben Burlingame, rhp, Newton (Mass.) South HS
46. **Fernando Arguellas, c, Florida Southern**
47. **Craig Juran, lhp, Colorado State**
48. Steve O'Donnell, 3b, La Salle
49. **Wade Lytle, 3b, Bellmont HS, Decatur, Ind.**
50. **Keith Mays, rhp, Louisburg (N.C.) JC**
51. Mike LeBlanc, rhp, Maine
52. **Joe Pagan, rhp, Chicago State**
53. **Bryan Arnold, c/1b, Florida Southern**
54. **Dan Nielson, rhp, Western Michigan**
55. Cary Elston, rhp, Green River (Wash.) CC
56. Scott Sharts, 1b, Simi Valley (Calif.) HS
57. **Bobby West, of, Brewton-Parker (Ga.)**
58. Ken Baurle, rhp, North Allegheny HS, Pittsburgh
59. Troy Trollope, of, Bellevue (Wash.) CC
60. Thomas Owen, c, Brewton-Parker (Ga.)
61. Jon Fisher, c, Brenham (Texas) HS
62. Jerry Summers, of, Beaver County (Pa.) CC
63. David Silvernail, rhp, Columbia Basin (Wash.) CC
64. **Jessie Torres, c, JC of Southern Idaho**
65. Burk Cromer, 3b, Lexington (S.C.) HS
66. Randy Martin, ss/of, Godby HS, Tallahassee, Fla.

ST. LOUIS CARDINALS

June—Regular Phase (23)

1. **John Ericks, rhp, Illinois** (Pick from Yankees as compensation for Type A free agent Jack Clark)
1. **Brad DuVall, rhp, Virginia Tech**
1. **Brian Jordan, of, Richmond** (Supplemental pick—30th—for loss of Clark)
2. **Mike Hensley, rhp, Oklahoma**
3. **Charlie White, of, New Orleans**
4. **Mike Ross, 2b, Cal State Fullerton**
5. **Lee Plemel, rhp, Stanford**
6. **Rheal Cormier, lhp, CC of Rhode Island**
7. **Steve Fanning, ss, Troy State**
8. **Jerry Davis, ss, Lincoln HS, San Diego**
9. **Mark Clark, rhp, Lincoln Land (Ill.) CC**
10. **Joe Hall, 3b, Southern Illinois**
11. **Rod Brooks, rhp, Troy State**
12. **Tom Malchesky, 3b, Western Carolina**
13. **Bill Decker, rhp, Iowa Central CC**
14. **John Cebuhar, lhp, Arkansas**
15. **Mike Fiore, of, Miami**
16. **Steve Corry, rhp, Cedar City (Utah) HS**
17. **David Richardson, lhp, Middle Tennessee State**
18. **Julio Mendez, ss, Florida**
19. **Mark Battell, c, Mercy (N.Y.)**
20. Steve Callahan, lhp, Lewis-Clark State (Idaho)
21. **Fred Langiotti, c, Tampa**
22. **Tim Pettengill, c, Nebraska**
23. **Jeff Shireman, ss, Georgia Southern**
24. **John Lepley, lhp, Nebraska**
25. **Randy Berlin, 1b/3b, Virginia Tech**
26. **Cory Satterfield, rhp, Campbell**
27. **Sean Grubb, rhp, Oral Roberts**
28. **John Stephens, 3b, The Citadel**
29. David D. Adams, rhp, Auburn
30. **Joe Federico, 1b/of, Nebraska**
31. **Richard Hoffman, rhp, Long Island**
32. **Dave Grimes, rhp, Arkansas Tech**
33. **Steve Graham, of, Ithaca (N.Y.)**
34. **Brian Golden, rhp, Gettysburg (Pa.)**
35. **John Kroeger, c, Fairleigh Dickinson**
36. David C. Adams, rhp, Ohio
37. William Henderson, rhp, Volunteer State (Tenn.) CC
38. **David Bell, of, Volunteer State (Tenn.) CC**
39. Scott Buchheit, lhp, St. Dominic HS, St. Peters, Mo.
40. Ken Phillips, of, Pasadena (Calif.) CC
41. Steve DiBartolomeo, rhp, New Haven (Conn.)
42. Jerry Lutterman, rhp, St. Louis CC-Meramec
43. Ray Calhoun, rhp, Spartanburg Methodist (S.C.) JC
44. **Derron Spiller, lhp, Rio Mesa HS, Camarillo, Calif.**
45. Joe Philpot, rhp, Volunteer State (Tenn.) CC
46. David King, 1b/3b, Northeastern Oklahoma A&M JC

SAN DIEGO PADRES

June—Regular Phase (1)

1. **Andy Benes, rhp, Evansville**
2. **Kelly Lifgren, rhp, Glendale (Ariz.) CC**
3. **Ray Holbert III, ss, Jordan HS, Long Beach**
4. **Squeezer Thompson, rhp, Mount Dora (Fla.) HS**
5. **Bryce Florie, rhp, Hanahan (S.C.) HS**
6. **Bob Brucato, rhp, Northwestern**
7. Mike Grace, rhp, Joliet (Ill.) Catholic HS
8. **Nikco Riesgo, 3b/of, San Diego State**
9. **Matt Witkowski, ss, Deer Valley HS, Glendale, Ariz.**
10. **A.J. Sager, rhp, Toledo**
11. **Scott Welish, 1b/of, San Diego Mesa JC**
12. Chris Ebright, of/1b, Oklahoma
13. **J.D. Noland, of, Central Florida CC**
14. **Eric Harris, ss, Roosevelt HS, Dallas**
15. **Mike Humphreys, of, Texas Tech**
16. **Brian Cisarik, 1b/of, Texas**
17. **Vance Tucker, rhp, Seminole State (Okla.) JC**
18. **Joe Murdock, lhp, Southern Arkansas**
19. Greg Ebbert, lhp, Lake Brantley HS, Longwood, Fla.
20. **Brian Span, of, Seminole (Fla.) CC**
21. **Pedro Lopez, c, Arizona Western JC**
22. **Scott Bingham, ss, Willamette (Ore.)**
23. **David Briggs, 3b, Brookdale (N.J.) CC**
24. **Brad Hoyer, lhp, Cal Poly Pomona**
25. **Renay Bryand, lhp, UC Santa Barbara**
26. **Greg Conley, c, Rollins (Fla.)**
27. **Chris Haslock, rhp, Cal State Dominguez Hills**
28. **Stanley Tukes, rhp, Broward (Fla.) CC**
29. **Darrin Hart, ss, Harding HS, Charlotte, N.C.**
30. **Rob Cantwell, lhp, North Idaho JC**
31. **Chad Kuhn, 1b/of, New Mexico**
32. **Craig Pueschner, of, Sahuaro HS, Tucson, Ariz.**
33. **John Kuehl, 1b/3b, California**
34. Randy Tanner, of, Southern California
35. **Bob Curnow, c, Cal Poly Pomona**
36. **Craig Proctor, 2b, Cal Poly Pomona**
37. Jason Farrell, rhp, Kennedy HS, Granada Hills, Calif.
38. Heath Jones, c, El Segundo HS, Hawthorne, Calif.
39. **Walter Wilkerson, rhp, Clermont (Fla.) HS**
40. Ramey Brooks, c, Blanchard (Okla.) HS
41. **Richard Peacock, of, Ernest Ward HS, Walnut Hill, Fla.**
42. **Jeff Hart, rhp, Central Arkansas**
43. Brian Looney, lhp, Cunnery HS, Cheshire, Conn.
44. Mike Basse, of, Mater Dei HS, San Juan Capistrano, Calif.

SAN FRANCISCO GIANTS

June—Regular Phase (17)

1. **Royce Clayton, ss, St. Bernard HS, Playa del Rey, Calif.** (Pick from Reds as compensation for Type B free agent Eddie Milner)
1. (Pick to Indians as compensation for Type A free agent Brett Butler)
1. **Ted Wood, of, New Orleans** (Supplemental pick—29th—for loss of Type A free agent Chili Davis)
2. **Scott Ebert, rhp, Edmond (Okla.) Memorial HS** (Pick from Angels as compensation for Davis)
2. **Chris Hancock, lhp, Fontana (Calif.) HS**
3. **Reuben Smiley, of, Los Angeles CC**
4. **Carl Hanselman, rhp, Merritt Island (Fla.) HS**

5. **Eddie Tucker, c, Delta State (Miss.)**
6. **Jeff Kaiser, ss, Southwest Missouri State**
7. **David Horan, rhp, Eastern Oklahoma State JC**
8. **Gary Sharko, rhp, Grand Canyon (Ariz.)**
9. **Kevin Rogers, lhp, Mississippi Delta JC**
10. Turtle Zaun, 1b, North Carolina State
11. **Longo Garcia, rhp, Cal State Fullerton**
12. Moose Adams, rhp, Juanita HS, Kirkland, Wash.
13. **Andre George, 2b, Mount Hood (Ore.) CC**
14. **Adam Smith, c, Oklahoma State**
15. **Shannon Coppell, of, Eastern Illinois**
16. **Mark Standiford, 2b, Wichita State**
17. **Mitchell Ferrick, rhp, UC Riverside**
18. **Adell Davenport, 3b, Southern**
19. **David Slavin, c, Missouri**
20. **Shane Durham, lhp, Wichita State**
21. **Steve Decker, c, Lewis-Clark State (Idaho)**
22. **Steven Gray, ss, Cuesta (Calif.) JC**
23. **John Patterson, 2b, Grand Canyon (Ariz.)**
24. **George Penrod, of, Florida Atlantic**
25. **Reggie Williams, of, South Carolina-Aiken**
26. **Bill Gibbons, rhp, Delaware**
27. **David Wuthrich, lhp, Troy State**
28. **Adam Hilpert, ss, Cal State Stanislaus**
29. **Ken Brauckmiller, rhp, Portland State (Ore.)**
30. **Glenn Warren, of, Mount Olive (N.C.)**
31. **William Berry, lhp, Glendale (Calif.) JC**
32. **Mike Sanderson, of, Alabama**
33. **David Cantrell, rhp, Chapman (Calif.)**
34. **Pat Brady, of, St. Mary's**
35. **Don Brock, rhp, South Carolina-Spartanburg**
36. **Brett Hewatt, 1b/of, Seward County (Kan.) CC**
37. **David Booth, of, West Virginia State**
38. Rod Billingsley, c, George Mason
39. **Lance Burnett, of, Crowder HS, McAlester, Okla.**
40. **Richard Thompson, of/3b, Los Angeles Valley JC**
41. **Greg Lee, inf, Hancock (Calif.) JC**
42. Basilio Ortiz, of, Buckley HS, Hartford, Conn.
43. Michael Scialo, ss, Saguero HS, Scottsdale, Ariz.
44. Jason Hendricks, rhp, Kincaid HS, Houston
45. Danny Lane, inf, Laguna Beach (Calif.) HS

SEATTLE MARINERS

June—Regular Phase (14)

1. **Tino Martinez, 1b, Tampa**
2. **Greg Pirkl, c, Los Alamitos (Calif.) HS**
3. **Jim Campanis, c, Southern California**
4. **Lee Hancock, lhp, Cal Poly San Luis Obispo**
5. **Willie Romay, of, Miami Senior HS**
6. **Kelvin Thomas, of, Smiley HS, Houston**
7. **Julio Reyan, of, Southridge HS, Miami**
8. Mike Smedes, rhp, Laguna Hills (Calif.) HS
9. Steve Chitren, rhp, Stanford
10. Ted Devore, rhp, Portland
11. Ronnie Allen, rhp, Lake Washington HS, Kirkland, Wash.
12. **Nick Felix, lhp, Texas A&M**
13. **Jeff Darwin, rhp, Alvin (Texas) CC**
14. **Mike Beiras, rhp, Texas Tech**
15. **Scott Taylor, rhp, Kansas**
16. **Mark Razook, ss, Cal State Fullerton**
17. **James Kosnik, lhp, Oakland (Mich.) CC**
18. **Delvin Thomas, ss, Smiley HS, Houston**
19. James Clifford, 1b, Ingraham HS, Seattle
20. **Tom Liss, lhp, Detroit**
21. **Michael McLaughlin, ss, Glassboro State (N.J.)**
22. **Jeff Miller, c, Normandale (Minn.) CC**
23. **Joe White, rhp, Mesa (Colo.)**
24. Todd Krumm, of/rhp, Michigan State
25. Jim Price, rhp, Stanford
26. **Jorge Robles, 2b, Miami**
27. **Doug Davis, 1b/3b, Grossmont (Calif.) JC**
28. Scott Cline, 3b, UCLA
29. **Kerry Woodson, rhp, San Jose CC**
30. Scott Bibee, rhp, Carson City (Nev.) HS
31. Joel Wolfe, 3b, Chatsworth HS, Northridge, Calif.
32. Dusty Madsen, rhp, Sacramento CC
33. **Tim Stargell, 2b, Southern**
34. **Ben Burnau, lhp, Miami (Ohio)**
35. Mike Cloutier, of, Detroit
36. Mike Kerber, c, Canoga Park HS, West Hills, Calif.
37. Shawn Brown, of, Granada Hills HS, Los Angeles
38. **John Kohli, lhp, Nebraska**
39. Glen Raasch, c, Mount San Antonio (Calif.) JC
40. Felix Gurruchaga, lhp, Miami-Dade New World Center CC
41. **Chris Howard, c, Southwestern Louisiana**
42. Dean Haskins, c/3b, Montgomery HS, Santa Rosa, Calif.
43. Rob Callistro, rhp, Concord (Calif.) HS
44. Damian Torino, c, North Marion HS, Sparr, Fla.
45. John Burton, rhp, Mount San Antonio (Calif.) JC
46. **Tom Brock, of, Michigan**
47. Mark Ringkamp, rhp, Palomar (Calif.) JC
48. Eddie Christian, of, Salesian HS, San Pablo, Calif.
49. Arthur Bass, of, Westfield HS, Houston
50. Daniel Donovan, rhp, Brookdale (N.J.) CC
51. **Keith Barrett, of/inf, Cal Poly Pomona**
52. Brent Lutz, 3b, Issaquah (Wash.) HS

TEXAS RANGERS

June—Regular Phase (6)

1. **Monty Fariss, ss, Oklahoma State**
2. **Tim Morrow, of, South Alamance HS, Graham, N.C.**
3. **Darren Oliver, lhp, Rio Linda (Calif.) HS**
4. **Everett Cunningham, rhp, Northwestern**
5. **Cliff Williams, c, East St. Louis HS, Fairview Heights, Ill.**
6. **Rob Maurer, 1b, Evansville**
7. **Dom Pierce, 3b, Skyline (Calif.) JC**
8. **Travis Law, of, Oklahoma State**
9. **Trey McCoy, of, Virginia Tech**
10. **Eric McCray, lhp, Farmerville (La.) HS**
11. David Wallace, ss/of, Brandeis HS, New York
12. **Cedric Shaw, lhp, Grambling State**
13. **Tim MacNeil, rhp, Rancho Santiago (Calif.) JC**
14. **Mike Patrick, c/3b, Texas**
15. Peter Lawrence, of, Logan HS, Union City, Calif.
16. **John Sipple, lhp, Oregon State**
17. **Carl Randle, rhp, Huston-Tillotson (Texas)**
18. **Tom Mileski, rhp, San Jacinto (Texas) JC**
19. **Jim Hvizda, rhp, Old Dominion**
20. **Joey Wardlow, 2b, Tampa**
21. Mark Bowlan, rhp, Memphis State
22. **Doug Cronk, 1b, Southern Mississippi**
23. **Mike Reitzel, lhp, Northeastern Oklahoma A&M JC**
24. Mark Tolbert, rhp, Dixie (Utah) JC
25. **Rod Morris, of, Southeastern Louisiana**
26. **Kyle Spencer, rhp, Missouri Valley**
27. **Jeff Shore, c, UNC Charlotte**
28. **Todd DeVaughan, rhp, Seminole State (Okla.) JC**
29. **Robert Gamez, lhp/1b, Chabot (Calif.) JC**
30. **Jeff Frye, 2b, Southeastern Oklahoma State**
31. **Jonathan Huth, rhp, Waldorf (Iowa) JC**
32. **Lindsey Robinson, 3b, South Carolina-Spartanburg**
33. Shawn Wills, of, Hanford (Calif.) HS
34. Tom Urbani, 1b, Cabrillo (Calif.) JC
35. David Schmidt, 2b, Montgomery HS, San Diego
36. **Tony Berry, of, Rust (Miss.)**
37. **Steve Allen, rhp, Massachusetts**
38. **Jeff Simmons, rhp, Rend Lake (Ill.) JC**
39. **Brian Evans, rhp, Jacksonville**
40. **Ken Penland, lhp, South Carolina-Spartanburg**
41. Anthony Peeler, lhp, Paseo HS, Kansas City, Mo.
42. **Greg Kuzma, lhp, Princeton**
43. **William Shorr, rhp, Nicholls State**
44. Fred Collins, lhp, Manatee (Fla.) JC
45. Americo Loera, rhp, Dallas Baptist (Selection voided)
46. **Ed Ohman, rhp, Auburn**
47. Donald Parker, of, Rangeview HS, Aurora, Colo.
48. **Brian Mouton, of, Hayward HS, Oakland**
49. Pat Underhill, rhp, Valencia (Fla.) CC

50. Shannon Albright, rhp, Fruita HS, Grand Junction, Colo.
51. Mike Easley, 1b, Texas A&M (Selection voided)
52. **Jeff Hainline, 1b, Gonzaga**
53. Dan Robinson, of, Crossett (Ark.) HS
54. Henderson Mosley, ss, H.D. Woodson HS, Washington, D.C.
55. Paul Spyhalski, of, Howard (Texas) JC
56. Brett Snyder, rhp, Rancho Santiago (Calif.) JC
57. Tony Tijerina, c, Long Beach CC
58. **Shannon Penn, ss, Lakeland (Ohio) CC**
59. Joe Caruso, rhp, Casa Grande HS, Petaluma, Calif.

TORONTO BLUE JAYS

June—Regular Phase (25)

1. **Ed Sprague Jr., 3b/c, Stanford**
2. **Tim Hodge, c, Callaway HS, Jackson, Miss.**
3. **David Weathers, rhp, Motlow State (Tenn.) CC**
4. **Eric Brooks, c, LaMirada (Calif.) HS**
5. **Billy Parese, ss, Owasso (Okla.) HS**
6. **Mike Ogliaruso, rhp, Countryside HS, Palm Harbor, Fla.**
7. **Rob Montalvo, ss, Memorial HS, West New York**
8. Tim Pugh, rhp, Oklahoma State
9. Brent Gilbert, rhp, Blinn (Texas) JC
10. **Anthony Ward, lhp, Oral Roberts**
11. Pat Pesavento, ss, Notre Dame
12. William Fuller, rhp, Eau Gallie HS, Melbourne, Fla.
13. **Curtis Johnson, rhp, Washington**
14. Eric Persinger, rhp, Marion (Ind.) HS
15. Greg Kobza, 1b, Blinn (Texas) JC
16. Matthew Wilke, ss, Beaver Dam (Wis.) HS
17. **Mike Brady, rhp, Nassau (N.Y.) CC**
18. **Rick Vaughn, c, Oral Roberts**
19. **Tim Bruzdewicz, lhp, Allegheny (Pa.) CC**
20. Dan Berthel, of, El Camino (Calif.) JC
21. **Rick Holifield, of, Ganesha HS, Montclair, Calif.**
22. Mario Baker, of, Gulf Coast (Fla.) CC
23. **Terrance Jones, ss, Monroe (N.Y.) CC**
24. Mike Daniel, c, Connors State (Okla.) JC
25. **Tim Brown, rhp, St. Petersburg (Fla.) JC**
26. **Rick Nowak, rhp, UC San Diego**
27. **Greg McCutcheon, rhp, Kent State**
28. **Woody Williams, rhp, Houston**
29. **Greg Harding, 1b, Richmond**
30. **Scott Hutson, rhp, Arizona State**
31. Mike Matheny, c, Reynoldsburg (Ohio) HS
32. **Greg O'Halloran, c, Orange Coast (Calif.) JC**
33. George Tsamis, lhp, Stetson
34. Jeff Lawrence, lhp, Fallbrook (Calif.) HS
35. Michael Harris, 1b, Tates Creek HS, Lexington, Ky.
36. **Chris Kerr, rhp, California Baptist**
37. **Jeff Mooney, rhp, Chapman (Calif.)**
38. **Ray Giannelli, 3b, New York Tech**
39. Eric Reichenbach, rhp, Sachem HS, Farmingville, N.Y.
40. **Eric Bradley, rhp, Laney (Calif.) JC**
41. **Andrew Carlton, 1b/rhp, Providence HS, Frankfort, Ill.**
42. Brian Brazier, inf, Hanford (Calif.) HS
43. Matt Sines, rhp, Hillsborough (Fla.) CC
44. Scott Erickson, rhp, San Jose CC
45. **Wayne Williams, c, Chesapeake HS, Pasadena, Md.**
46. Thomas Irwin, rhp, Victor Valley HS, Victorville, Calif.
47. **Eric Carter, rhp, Louisburg (N.C.) JC**
48. Sean Gousha, c, Orange Glen HS, Escondido, Calif.
49. Dax Jones, of, Waukegan (Ill.) West HS
50. Greg Davis, rhp, North Torrance HS, Gardena, Calif.
51. Michael Boyd, ss, Clearwater Catholic HS, Largo, Fla.
52. Gordon Purvis, rhp/ss, Berrien County HS, Ray City, Ga.
53. Jeff Kidwiler, ss, Chapman (Calif.)
54. Terre Woods, of/3b, Utica (Miss.) JC
55. Anthony Mills, inf/of, Taft (Calif.) HS
56. Jason Wood, inf, McLane HS, Fresno
57. David Edwards, of, East St. Louis HS, Brooklyn, Ill.
58. Darrell Whitmore, ss, West Virginia
59. Michael Lustyk, 1b, Interlake HS, Bellevue, Wash.
60. **William Abare, 1b, St. Petersburg (Fla.) JC**
61. Brad Raulston, of, La Jolla (Calif.) HS
62. **Jesse Cross, rhp, Middle Georgia JC**
63. Thomas Hamilton, of, Forest Hills HS, Marshville, N.C.
64. Warren Holt, rhp, Cabrillo (Calif.) JC
65. Walter Heckel, 2b, St. John's
66. Jeff Borgese, ss, San Jose CC
67. Ross Urshan, rhp, Lyman HS, Altamonte Springs, Fla.
68. Louis Williams, rhp, Benton Harbor (Mich.) HS
69. Jerry Worley, of, Miami (Fla.) Springs HS
70. James Lewis, rhp, Terry Parker HS, Jacksonville, Fla.
71. Kenneth Koon, of, Orange Park (Fla.) HS
72. Dennis Stachura, c, Downers Grove (Ill.) North HS
73. **Anton Mobley, of, Yule, Fla.**

1989 McDonald leads record number of picks, as teams use record bonuses to sign them

In its 25th year, the draft proved more popular—and more expensive—than ever. A record 1,490 players were selected in the 1989 draft, and several clubs claimed a record number of players, led by the Astros, who didn't stop drafting until 87 rounds were complete.

Bonuses also went through the roof. Two players, Batimore's Ben McDonald and Toronto's John Olerud, signed three-year major league deals worth more than $800,000.

Only Kansas City's Bo Jackson, in 1986, had ever received a multi-year deal in the past, and his three-year, $1.066 million contract was the inducement needed to buy him away from the NFL. McDonald and Olerud commanded their big deals based strictly on their merits on the baseball field.

McDonald, a two-time All-American and Olympic team star, was the first player selected, and it took more than two months for the Orioles to sign him. His selection marked the first time that the team with the No. 1 pick was in first place at the time the selection was made. He made two minor league starts, then went directly to Baltimore.

Within days of McDonald signing, Olerud signed with the Blue Jays. Because of a near-fatal aneurysm near his brain that required a six-hour operation six months before the draft, the Washington State pitcher/first baseman wasn't selected until the third round. There had been concern that he wouldn't sign until he was 100 percent healthy, but he became the first player from the Class of '89 to reach the big leagues, debuting in Toronto with a base hit in September.

Olerud's career also outstripped McDonald's. McDonald wasn't a bust, but his career was considered a disappointment with a 78-70, 3.91 record in nine major league seasons. Olerud, while never a superstar, was a steady first baseman for 17 seasons, finishing his career with a .295 average and .398 on-base percentage. He won three Gold Gloves and made two All-Star Game appearances.

The 1989 draft marked the first time every first-round pick was offered at least $100,000. Still, three first-rounders did not sign, the most since four didn't sign in 1979.

The Expos never came to terms with catcher Charles Johnson, who went on to Miami and was a first-round pick again three years later; the Indians lost infielder Calvin Murray to the University of Texas; and the Mariners couldn't sign Scott Burrell, who went on to play at Connecticut and became an NBA basketball player.

John Olerud was a two-way star in college but made his name as a pro with the bat

"We're really disappointed," Expos scouting director Gary Hughes said. "He wanted $235,000 from the start and never backed off. It was tied directly to the Cornelius deal." (The Expos signed Reid Cornelius for $225,000 out of the 1988 draft, and Johnson sought that amount plus $10,000 for inflation.)

McDonald almost became a member of that list. McDonald was such a dominant amateur talent that scouts had him pegged as the No. 1 pick in '89 as much as a year before the draft. He rejected the Orioles' first offer of $255,000 and negotiations dragged on all summer with McDonald's father Larry and agent Scott Boras.

"You can't expect Ben to sign for a figure comparable to what high school kids are getting," Boras said. "It's more like an NFL or NBA situation because he's so close to being an impact player in the big leagues. He's a very, very unique talent."

And thus began the Boras Era in the draft, and the first of his unique talents.

The threat of a new baseball league, which planned to begin operating in 1990, complicated things further. Rumors surfaced of McDonald signing a $2 million personal services contract with the new circuit.

"I definitely considered the new league," McDonald said. "Definitely."

But in the end, McDonald signed a deal that included a $350,000 bonus.

More Drafting, Following

With the abolition of the January draft in 1987, teams continued to develop the draft-and-follow approach, securing the rights to a large number of players but not offering them contracts before they attended (or returned to) junior college. Teams had until a week before the next year's draft to sign players that blossomed.

Consequently, the draft signing rate went down significantly from the 74 percent peak figure in 1985. The Astros, for example, did not sign 64 of their 89 draft picks in the summer after the draft, but retained the rights to 53 of those players.

Despite the draft's aim to equalize talent, the defending World Series champion Dodgers had five selections in the first two rounds, more than any other team, for the loss of free agents. In fact, their fifth selection was made before Oakland, which lost to the Dodgers in the 1988 World Series, made its first pick. Of the five players the Dodgers took, though, only outfielder Tom Goodwin had a significant big league career.

An interesting twist to the 1989 draft was the inclusion of the Northwest League's independent Boise Hawks in the selections. The Hawks chose two players, starting in the fourth round. Draft rules provided unaffiliated minor league clubs the opportunity to draft, and the Hawks exercised the option, becoming the first minor league club since Bend (Northwest) in 1971 to do so. The rule has since been changed.

"It was not done for publicity," Hawks director of baseball operations Mal Fichman said. "It was done to help the ballclub.

"Reaction from major league clubs was 99 percent good. A couple of clubs weren't sure what we were doing initially. They were concerned we would draft 30-40 players and resell them. You can't sell or trade drafted players, so obviously that was not our intent at all."

Another significant development was the inclusion of players from U.S. territories in the draft, most notably Puerto Ricans. Previously only such players who attended school in the U.S. were eligible, while others signed on the open market.

The change was made in an effort to curb bonus payments to Puerto Rican players who signed as free agents, and while it accomplished that goal, many in the game cited it as a reason for a decline in the talent Puerto Rico produced in future years. A total of 55 Puerto Ricans were selected in 1989, but none in the first five rounds.

DRAFT 89: FIRST-ROUND PICKS

No.	Club	Player, Pos.	School	Hometown	Ht.	Wt.	B-T	Age
1.	Orioles	Ben McDonald, rhp	Louisiana State	Denham Springs, La.	6-7	215	R-R	21
2.	Braves	Tyler Houston, c	Valley HS	Las Vegas	6-2	210	L-R	18
3.	Mariners	Roger Salkeld, rhp	Saugus HS	Saugus, Calif.	6-5	210	R-R	18
4.	Phillies	Jeff Jackson, of	Simeon HS	Chicago	6-3	180	R-R	17
5.	Rangers	Donald Harris, of	Texas Tech	Lubbock, Texas	6-1	180	R-R	21
6.	Cardinals	Paul Coleman, of	Frankston HS	Frankston, Texas	5-11	200	R-R	18
7.	White Sox	Frank Thomas, 1b	Auburn	Columbus, Ga.	6-5	240	R-R	21
8.	Cubs	Earl Cunningham, of	Lancaster HS	Lancaster, S.C.	6-2	225	R-R	19
9.	Angels	Kyle Abbott, lhp	Long Beach State	Mission Viejo, Calif.	6-4	190	L-L	21
10.	Expos	*Charles Johnson, c	Westwood HS	Ft. Pierce, Fla.	6-3	185	R-R	17
11.	Indians	*Calvin Murray, of	White HS	Dallas	5-11	180	R-R	17
12.	Astros	Jeff Juden, rhp	Salem HS	Salem, Mass.	6-7	240	R-R	18
13.	Royals	Brent Mayne, c	Cal State Fullerton	Costa Mesa, Calif.	6-2	195	L-R	21
14.	Giants	Steve Hosey, of	Fresno State	Inglewood, Calif.	6-3	215	R-R	20
15.	Dodgers	Kiki Jones, rhp	Hillsborough HS	Tampa	5-11	170	R-R	17
16.	Red Sox	Greg Blosser, of	Sarasota HS	Sarasota, Fla.	6-3	190	L-L	18
17.	Brewers	Cal Eldred, rhp	Iowa	Urbana, Iowa	6-4	210	R-R	21
18.	Pirates	Willie Greene, ss	Jones County HS	Haddock, Ga.	5-11	160	L-R	17
19.	Blue Jays	Eddie Zosky, ss	Fresno State	Whittier, Calif.	6-0	170	R-R	21
20.	Reds	Scott Bryant, of	Texas	San Antonio	6-2	215	R-R	21
21.	Tigers	Greg Gohr, rhp	Santa Clara	Campbell, Calif.	6-3	200	R-R	21
22.	Dodgers	Tom Goodwin, of	Fresno State	Fresno	6-0	170	L-R	20
23.	Red Sox	Mo Vaughn, 1b	Seton Hall	Norwalk, Conn.	6-1	220	L-R	21
24.	Mets	Alan Zinter, c	Arizona	El Paso, Texas	6-2	190	B-R	21
25.	Twins	Chuck Knoblauch, ss	Texas A&M	Houston	5-9	170	R-R	20
26.	Mariners	*Scott Burrell, rhp	Hamden HS	Hamden, Conn.	6-5	195	R-R	18

*Did not sign

1989

CLUB-BY-CLUB SELECTIONS

ATLANTA BRAVES

June—Regular Phase (2)

1. **Tyler Houston, c, Valley HS, Las Vegas**
2. **Tab Brown, rhp, St. Xavier HS, Louisville, Ky.**
2. **Brian Boltz, lhp, Catawba (N.C.)** (Supplemental pick—57th—for loss of Type C free agent Rick Mahler)
3. **Kevin Castleberry, 2b, Oklahoma**
4. **George Virgilio, 2b, Elizabeth (N.J.) HS**
5. **Ryan Klesko, lhp/1b, Westminster (Calif.) HS**
6. **Mike Mordecai, ss, South Alabama**
7. **Stuart McMillan, of, Withrow HS, Cincinnati**
8. **Troy Hughes, of, Mount Vernon (Ill.) HS**
9. **Nathan Fults, of/c, Franklin County HS, Decherd, Tenn.**
10. **David Williams, rhp, Westark (Ark.) CC**
11. **Vincent Jiminez, c/ss, Rockdale (Texas) HS**
12. **Brett Grebe, rhp, Westminster (Calif.) HS**
13. **Tony Valle, rhp, Southwest Texas State**
14. Bo Siberz, rhp, Westark (Ark.) CC
15. Billy Morris, ss, Los Angeles Pierce JC
16. **Mark Beck, rhp, Cal State Fullerton**
17. **Dickey Marze, of/2b, Northwestern State (La.)**
18. **Joe Roa, rhp, Hazel Park (Mich.) HS**
19. **Darren Ritter, rhp, Maryland-Baltimore County**
20. John Slate, lhp, Glenn HS, Winston-Salem, N.C.
21. Chris Castro, rhp, Baldwin Park (Calif.) HS
22. **Tony Gallaher, rhp, Waite HS, Toledo**
23. **Jose Olmeda, ss, Oklahoma Baptist**
24. Thomas Niles, rhp, Southern Maine
25. Chris Kughn, of, Virginia
26. **Robert Steinmetz, rhp, Converse Judson HS, San Antonio**
27. Todd Greene, 3b, Evans HS, Martinez, Ga.
28. **Chris Burton, of, Sam Houston State**
29. Gilbert Johnson, of, Fairfax HS, Los Angeles
30. Jason Johnson, rhp, Williamsport (Pa.) HS
31. **Paul Ellis, c, Newton County HS, Conyers, Ga.**
32. **Earl Jewett, rhp, Wagner**
33. **Barry Chiles, rhp, East Wake HS, Raleigh, N.C.**
34. James Dillon, rhp, Maine
35. Robert Compton, rhp, Liberty Eylau HS, Texarkana, Texas
36. David Simon, of, Joplin (Mo.) HS
37. **Daniel Sims, of, Birmingham-Southern**
38. Keith Morrison, rhp, Middle Georgia JC
39. Kevin Walling, 1b, Kankakee (Ill.) CC
40. Brett Misavage, rhp, Allegany (Pa.) CC
41. Joel Heath, ss/rhp, Tarkington HS, Cleveland, Texas
42. John Harris, ss, Southwest HS, Fort Worth
43. William Noweck, rhp, Catonsville (Md.) CC
44. Jared Baker, rhp, Stratford HS, Goose Creek, S.C.
45. Trent Petrie, ss, Memonomee (Wis.) HS
46. David Rollen, c, Panola (Texas) JC
47. Reginald Jackson, of/rhp, Atlanta (Texas) HS
48. Victor McCraney, of, Basic HS, Henderson, Nev.
49. Jason Heath, ss, Tarkington HS, Cleveland, Texas
50. Leron Rogers, 2b, Lutheran HS, Milwaukee
51. **Kevin Haeberle, rhp, Glendale (Ariz.) CC**
52. **Travis Dunlap, rhp, Calallen, HS, Corpus Christi, Texas**
53. Walter Dunson, of, Central HS, Carrollton, Ga.
54. David Hollingsworth, rhp, Memorial Day HS, Savannah, Ga.
55. Willie Brown, of, Calhoun County HS, Edison, Ga.
56. **Anthony Maye, rhp, Withrow HS, Cincinnati**
57. Ken Musacchio, c, Great Bridge HS, Chesapeake, Va.
58. Turner Williams, of, Bayside HS, Virginia Beach, Va.
59. Kevin Cockrell, ss, Montreat-Anderson (N.C.) JC
60. **Alvin Martin, of, Imperial Valley (Calif.) JC**
61. Bryan White, of, Tri Cities HS, Hapeville, Ga.

BALTIMORE ORIOLES

June—Regular Phase (1)

1. **Ben McDonald, rhp, Louisiana State**
2. **Keith Schmidt, of, Burton (Texas) HS**
2. **Tommy Taylor, rhp, Louisa County HS, Mineral, Va.** (Pick from Mariners as compensation for Type B free agent Tom Niedenfuer)
3. **Eric Alexander, rhp, University HS, Los Angeles**
4. **T.R. Lewis, 3b, Sandalwood HS, Jacksonville**
5. **Matt Anderson, lhp, Buena HS, Ventura, Calif.**
6. **Allen Davis, of, Lee County Senior HS, Sanford, N.C.**
7. Dan Melendez, 1b, SL Bernard HS, Mar Vista, Calif.
8. **Shawn Heiden, rhp, Hillcrest HS, Sandy, Utah**
9. Mike Lansing, ss, Wichita State
10. Chad Mottola, of, Aquinas HS, Pembroke Pines, Fla.
11. **Gary Shingledecker, 2b, North Carolina State**
12. **Brad Pennington, lhp, Vincennes (Ind.) JC**
13. **Mike Oquist, rhp, Arkansas**
14. **Aaron Norwood, of, Cerritos (Calif.) HS**
15. **Ed Horowitz, c, Rider**
16. **Dan Berthel, of, Long Beach State**
17. **Gregg Zaun, c, St. Francis HS, Glendale, Calif.**
18. **Brad Hildreth, ss, Mississippi State**
19. **Tony Beasley, ss/2b, Liberty**
20. **David Riddle, rhp, San Diego State**
21. **James Roso, c, Linn-Benton (Ore.) CC**
22. **Pat Hedge, of, Hartford**
23. Chris Bastiste, of, Roosevelt HS, San Bernardino, Calif.
24. Brad Gore, rhp, Taloga (Okla.) HS
25. **Mel Wearing, 1b, Norfolk State**
26. Michael Egelston, rhp, Johnson County (Kan.) CC
27. Henderson Mosley, of, Central State (Ohio)
28. Brian Bark, of, North Carolina State
29. **Pat Leinen, lhp, Nebraska**
30. **Mark Rupp, rhp, New Mexico State**
31. Greg D'Alexander, 3b/c, Arkansas
32. **Robert Wheatcroft, rhp, Cal State Northridge**
33. **Doug Reynolds, c, Liberty**
34. John Burke, rhp, Cherry Creek HS, Englewood, Colo.
35. Vincent Jones, 1b, Nemo Vista HS, Center Ridge, Ark.
36. **Keith Kessinger, ss, Mississippi**
37. Sean Spellecy, of, Mesa (Ariz.) CC
38. Shawn O'Connell, rhp, Campolindo HS, Moraga, Calif.
39. Brian Sackinsky, rhp, South Park HS, Library, Pa.
40. **John Hemmerly, lhp, San Diego State**
41. Michael Wiley, lhp, Conway (Ark.) HS
42. **David Brown, rhp, American International (Mass.)**
43. Anthony Bonifazio, of, Gorman HS, Las Vegas
44. Byron Mathews, of, Lafayette HS, Ballwin, Mo.
45. **Richard Meek, of, Linn-Benton (Ore.) CC**
46. Brian Banks, c, Mountain View HS, Mesa, Ariz.

BOSTON RED SOX

June—Regular Phase (23)

1. **Greg Blosser, of, Sarasota (Fla.) HS** (Pick from Padres as compensation for Type A free agent Bruce Hurst)
1. **Mo Vaughn, 1b, Seton Hall**
1. **Kevin Morton, lhp, Seton Hall** (Supplemental pick—29th—for loss of Hurst)
2. **Jeff McNeely, of, Spartanburg Methodist (S.C.) JC**
3. **Eric Wedge, c, Wichita State**
4. **Jeff Bagwell, 3b, Hartford**
5. **Tim Mitchell, 1b, Culver City HS, Los Angeles**
6. Paul Quantrill, rhp, Wisconsin
7. Paul Anacki, rhp, Sandwich (Mass.) HS
8. Stoney Burke, c, Avon HS, Danville, Ind.

9. **Cedric Santiago, lhp, Yauco, P.R.**
10. **Greg Hansell, rhp, Kennedy HS, La Palma, Calif.**
11. **Jason Freidman, of/1b, Cypress (Calif.) JC**
12. Peter Janicki, rhp, El Dorado HS, Placentia, Calif.
13. Chris Wimmer, 2b, East HS, Wichita
14. Fred Starks, rhp/of, Rockledge (Fla.) HS
15. **James Dennison, lhp, Jacksonville State**
16. **Tim Graham, of, Lancaster (Ohio) HS**
17. **Colin Dixon, 1b, Southeastern Louisiana**
18. **Lawrence Grant, ss, Ballard HS, Seattle**
19. **H.B. Awkard, of, Nelson County HS, Faber, Va.**
20. Billy Wallace, lhp, Monroe Academy HS, Monroeville, Ala.
21. **Ernie Brown, rhp, Catonsville (Md.) CC**
22. **Brian Conroy, rhp, Massachusetts**
23. Dom DeSantis, rhp, Miami-Dade North CC
24. **Troy Vann, of, CC of San Francisco**
25. **Terre Woods, c, Hinds (Mo.) JC**
26. Sean Darrock, of, Mission Bay HS, San Diego
27. Mark Williams, of, Patrick Henry (Ala.) JC
28. Randy Brown, ss, San Jacinto (Texas) JC
29. Tracy Wildes, rhp, Sandalwood HS, Jacksonville
30. **David Ring, rhp, Columbia (Tenn.) Central HS**
31. Jerald Shelton, 3b, Shelton State (Ala.) JC
32. Sean Hickman, lhp, Linn-Benton (Ore.) CC
33. John Lammon, c, Solano (Calif.) CC
34. **Bryan Niemeyer, of, Minster (Ohio) HS**
35. Michael Hickey, ss, Edmond (Okla.) Memorial HS
36. **Willie Dukes, of, Mississippi Delta JC**
37. Michael Canton, ss, San Augustine (Texas) HS
38. **Melvin Gonzales, rhp, Arecibo, P.R.**
39. **John Malzone, of, North Adams State (Mass.)**
40. **John Locker, rhp, Michigan**
41. Roberto Santa, 1b, Arecibo, P.R.

CALIFORNIA ANGELS

June—Regular Phase (9)

1. **Kyle Abbott, lhp, Long Beach State**
2. **Joe Grahe, rhp, Miami**
3. **Tim Salmon, of, Grand Canyon (Ariz.)**
4. **Erik Bennett, rhp, Cal State Sacramento**
5. **Terry Taylor, 2b, Texas A&M**
6. **David Staydohar, of, American River (Calif.) JC**
7. **Marvin Cobb, rhp, Oklahoma**
8. **Rick Hirtensteiner, of, Pepperdine**
9. **Fili Martinez, lhp, Cal State Northridge**
10. **Ron Lewis, of, Florida State**
11. Jeff Rhein, of, Sacramento CC
12. Mike Couture, c, Clemson
13. **Clifton Garrett, lhp/of, Roberto Clemente HS, Chicago**
14. **Kent Williams, of, South Alabama**
15. **Wayne Helm, rhp, Pepperdine**
16. **Eric Martinez, rhp, Mira Mesa HS, San Diego**
17. **Ricky Goode, rhp, Porterville (Calif.) JC**
18. **David C. Adams, rhp, Ohio**
19. **Rick Parker, c, Tulane**
20. **Brian Specyalski, 2b/ss, Connecticut**
21. **Jewell Walker, rhp, University HS, Los Angeles**
22. **David Rice, rhp, Cal Poly Pomona**
23. **Bob Jones, of, Cal State Fullerton**
24. **Willy Warrecker, lhp, California**
25. **Chris Allen, 1b, Florida Southern**
26. Brian Dodd, lhp, Arizona State
27. **Matt Lasher, ss, James Madison**
28. Norman Montoya, lhp, Chabot (Calif.) JC
29. **Paul Swingle, rhp, Grand Canyon (Ariz.)**
30. Joe Randa, ss, Delafield, Wis.
31. **Ron Tallent, c, Wooster Prep, Winthrop, Mass.**
32. **Tim Pinkowski, rhp, Lewis (Ill.)**
33. **Jeff Kilpatrick, of, Florida Southern**
34. **Henry Threadgill, 2b, Clemson**
35. Hilly Hathaway, lhp, Manatee (Fla.) JC
36. **Les Haffner, rhp, South Florida**
37. Chris Gomez, ss, Lakewood (Calif.) HS
38. Ken House, 3b, Cabrillo (Calif.) JC
39. **Douglas Canney, lhp, Salem (Mass.) HS**
40. **Bryan Street, c, Simeon HS, Chicago**
41. **Jose Santana, of, Carolina, P.R.**
42. **James Jones, rhp, Connecticut**
43. **Drew Peterson, 3b, Brighton HS, Sandy, Utah**
44. Glenn Osinski, ss, Triton (Ill.) JC
45. **Chad Curtis, of, Grand Canyon (Ariz.)**
46. John Jackson, of, Southern California
47. Allen Rath, rhp, Iowa
48. Jon Anderson, c, Georgia Tech
49. **Chris Rios, of, Southwest (N.M.)**
50. James Mason, c, Liberty
51. Carlton Davenport, 2b, UC Santa Barbara

CHICAGO CUBS

June—Regular Phase (8)

1. **Earl Cunningham, of, Lancaster (S.C.) HS**
2. **Gary Scott, 3b, Villanova**
3. **Billy White, ss, Kentucky**
4. Jason Evans, ss, Chatsworth (Calif.) HS
5. Darrick Duke, 1b/of, Reagan HS, Houston
6. **Calvin Ford, of, Ontario (Calif.) HS**
7. **Edgardo Larregui, of, Carolina, P.R.**
8. **Travis Willis, rhp, California**
9. **Dave Swartzbaugh, rhp, Miami (Ohio)**
10. Gordon Sanchez, c, San Marcos (Calif.) HS
11. **Richie Grayum, of, Mississippi State**
12. **Timothy Moore, ss, La Habra HS, Whittier, Calif.**
13. David DeMoss, of, North Marion HS, Fairmont, W.Va.
14. Jamie Sepeda, rhp, Sinton (Texas) HS
15. **Aaron Taylor, rhp, Wooster HS, Reno, Nev.**
16. **Mike Little, 1b/of, Biloxi (Miss.) HS**
17. **Brad Erdman, c, Cochise County (Ariz.) CC**
18. **Chris Ebright, of, Oklahoma**
19. Edwin Corps, rhp, Carolina, P.R. (Selection voided)
20. Dave Stevens, rhp, La Habra (Calif.) HS
21. **Steve DiBartolomeo, rhp, New Haven (Conn.)**
22. **Dale Craig, c, Hancock (Calif.) JC**
23. **Fredrick Hill, rhp, Hinds (Miss.) JC**
24. **Kalani Bush, rhp, Loyola Marymount**
25. **Ray Mack, rhp, Sumter (S.C.) HS**
26. **Kevin Dalson, ss, Michigan State**
27. Tony Pena, rhp, Mater Dei HS, Santa Ana, Calif.
28. **Scott Teague, lhp, UNC Asheville**
29. **Eric Jacques, lhp, Indiana**
30. **Micah Murphy, 1b, Lee (Texas) JC**
31. **Mark Linden, 3b, Whitworth (Wash.)**
32. **Doug Welch, of, Lubbock Christian**
33. **Don Gillespie, lhp, Eisenhower HS, Rialto, Calif.**
34. Matthew Hess, 3b, Dixon (Ill.) HS
35. **Randy Sodders, 2b, Hillsborough (Fla.) CC**
36. Charlie Fiacco, 2b, UCLA
37. Joe Wise, rhp, Georgia Tech
38. **Rene Francisco, of, Jacksonville**
39. **Amilcar Correa, rhp, San Sebastian, P.R.**
40. Felix Holguin, rhp, Deming (N.M.) HS
41. Angel Allende, c, Bayamon, P.R.
42. Raymon Martinez, ss, Bayamon, P.R.
43. Juan Debrand, ss, Chipola (Fla.) CC
44. Shawn Gift, of, Gilbert (Ariz.) HS
45. Axel Ortiz, 3b, Loiza, P.R.
46. Bennie Mayberry, of, Pima (Ariz.) CC
47. **Clinton White, of, JC of the Desert (Calif.)**
48. Edwin Zayas, rhp, Luquillo, P.R.
49. Robert Boisvert, of, Housatonic (Conn.) CC
50. Michael Barber, rhp, Elsinore HS, Lake Elsinore, Calif.
51. Lonnie Webb, 3b, South Georgia JC
52. Hector Reyes, rhp, Naranijito, P.R.
53. Gary Goldsmith, rhp, Alamogordo (N.M.) HS
54. Timothy Sharp, rhp, Three Rivers (Mo.) CC

CHICAGO WHITE SOX

June—Regular Phase (7)

1. **Frank Thomas, 1b, Auburn**
2. **Don Sheppard, of, Pittsburg (Calif.) HS**
3. **Todd Martin, ss, Morehead HS, Eden, N.C.**
4. **Dan Matznick, rhp, Sterling (Ill.) HS**
5. **Mike Eatinger, 3b, UC Riverside**
6. **John Smith, rhp, Garrett (Md.) CC**
7. **Mike Mongiello, rhp, Fairleigh Dickinson**
8. John Sutherland, rhp, UCLA
9. **Kevin Tolar, lhp, Mosley HS, Panama City, Fla.**
10. Scotty Pugh, 1b, Cooper HS, Abilene, Texas
11. **Gregory Kobza, 1b, Texas Tech**
12. **David Van Winkle, rhp, Northwestern**
13. **Lance Sanders, ss, Hanover (Ind.)**
14. Keith Johns, ss, Sandalwood HS, Jacksonville
15. Doug Shields, of, Southern Illinois
16. **Rollie Caridad, rhp, Westminster Christian HS, Miami**
17. **Scott Stevens, rhp, Brookdale (N.J.) CC**
18. **Richard Long, lhp, Eastern Washington**
19. **Brian Keyser, rhp, Stanford**
20. **Scott Thoma, rhp, Texas Christian**
21. **Jorge Ruiz, rhp, Rio Piedras, P.R.**
22. **James Robinson, rhp, Northwestern**
23. **Scott Cepicky, 1b, Wisconsin**
24. **Greg Perschke, rhp, New Orleans**
25. **Kevin Conover, lhp, Rutgers**
26. **Randy Norris, of, High Point (N.C.)**
27. **Bobby Hunter, rhp, Mainland HS, South Day, Fla.**
28. **Thomas Borgula, rhp, Northwestern**
29. David Geeve, rhp, Oakton (Ill.) CC
30. John Reece, of, Jersey Village HS, Houston
31. **Michael Potter, rhp, Potterville HS, Dimondale, Mich.**
32. **Joe Borowski, rhp, Bayonne (N.J.) HS**
33. Thomas O'Donnell, 2b/ss, Hazlet (N.J.) HS
34. Dean Locklear, lhp, Seminole State (Okla.) JC
35. Chris Gump, 3b, Westwood HS, Tempe, Ariz.
36. Jon French, ss/2b, Modesto (Calif.) JC
37. Richard Paschal, lhp, Coronado HS, Phoenix
38. Harry Durkin, ss/2b, Cardinal Gibbons HS, Ft. Lauderdale
39. **Horace Gaither, ss/2b, Southern**
40. Matt Klusener, lhp, Shawnee Heights HS, Topeka, Kan.
41. Bobby Reed, rhp, Mississippi State
42. **Michael Davino, rhp, South Carolina-Aiken**
43. **Dan Monzon, 3b/2b, Pace (N.Y.)**

CINCINNATI REDS

June—Regular Phase (20)

1. **Scott Bryant, of/rhp, Texas**
2. **Aaron Goins, of, Owasso (Okla.) HS**
3. **Ross Powell, lhp, Michigan**
4. Paul Jackson, of, Oldham County HS, La Grange, Ky.
5. **Darron Cox, c, Oklahoma**
6. **Tim Pugh, rhp, Oklahoma State**
7. Bert Inman, rhp, Westwood HS, Austin
8. **Charles Wyatt, rhp, Pflugerville HS, Manor, Texas**
9. **Rafael Diaz, lhp, Bayamon, P.R.**
10. **Rick Allen, 3b, Loyola Marymount**
11. **Trevor Hoffman, ss, Arizona**
12. **Jamie Dismuke, 1b, Corcoran HS, Syracuse, N.Y.**
13. **Steve Vondran, 3b/c, Fresno State**
14. **Todd Watson, 3b, Howard (D.C.)**
15. **Noel Velez, 3b/1b, Anasco, P.R.**
16. J.J. Picollo, c, Cherry Hill (N.J.) West HS
17. Kenneth Neal, of, Memphis (Tenn.) Catholic HS
18. **Bob Dombrowski, 3b, Arizona State**
19. **Sean Doty, rhp, Linn-Benton (Ore.) CC**
20. **Harry Henderson, 1b, San Diego State**
21. **Bob Blankenship, rhp, Cal State Sacramento**
22. **Mark Borcherding, rhp, Bradley**
23. **Frank Kremblas, c, Eastern Kentucky**
24. **Dale Stevens, rhp, Seminole (Fla.) CC**
25. **Jack Hollis, of, Stanford**
26. **Mark Cerny, of, Houston**
27. **Gil Galloway, rhp, Northwestern State (La.)**
28. **Carlos Molina, c, Vega Baja, P.R.**
29. Darrin Glenn, 2b, Howard (Texas) CC
30. **Torin Berge, 1b, Metropolitan State (Colo.)**
31. **Eric Bates, rhp, Cal State Sacramento**
32. **Brian Fry, lhp, Monroe (N.Y.) CC**
33. Bruce Smolen, ss, Kishwaukee (Ill.) JC
34. **Scott Pose, of, Arkansas**
35. **James Burns, of, Crockett (Texas) HS**
36. John Kostro, of, Thomas Jefferson HS, Denver
37. Todd Unrein, lhp, Southwestern Louisiana
38. **Andy Duke, of, Texas A&M**
39. **Thomas Aubertin, rhp, St. Louis CC-Meramec**
40. Chris Vasquez, of, Hart HS, Newhall, Calif.
41. Julian Velez, rhp, Bayamon, P.R.
42. Jerry Grider, rhp, Cooper HS, Abilene, Texas
43. Sean Lowe, rhp, Mesquite (Texas) HS
44. Jonathan Bates, ss, Arlington (Texas) HS
45. Scott Dodd, lhp, Glendale (Ariz.) CC
46. Jason Carroll, rhp, Putnam HS, Milwaukie, Ore.
47. Tim Boge, c, Muscatine (Iowa) CC
48. James Nix, ss, Brenham (Texas) HS
49. Donnie Carlisle, rhp, Brewer HS, Fort Worth
50. **Mark Roberts, ss, Dixie (Utah) JC**
51. Thomas Yerly, rhp, Hall HS, Spring Valley, Ill.
52. Shawn Ledet, lhp, H.L. Bourgeois HS, Houma, La.
53. Tim Grieve, rhp, Martin HS, Arlington, Texas
54. Jeffery Leftin, of, Beechwood HS, Fort Mitchell, Ky.
55. Lee Reiber, c, Meridian (Idaho) HS

CLEVELAND INDIANS

June—Regular Phase (11)

1. Calvin Murray, 3b/of, White HS, Dallas
2. (Pick to Dodgers as compensation for Type B free agent Jesse Orosco)
3. **Jerry Dipoto III, lhp, Virginia Commonwealth**
4. **Jesse Levis, c, North Carolina**
5. **Alan Embree, lhp, Prairie HS, Vancouver, Wash.**
6. **Mark Charbonnet, of, Gahr HS, Cerritos, Calif.**
7. **John Martinez, c, Juana Diaz, P.R.**
8. **Curt Leskanic, rhp, Louisiana State**
9. **Chad Allen, rhp, Gonzaga**
10. **John Cotton, 2b, Angelina (Texas) JC**
11. Kelly Stinnett, c, Seminole State (Okla.) JC
12. **Von Wechsberg, rhp, Camarillo (Calif.) HS**
13. **Jim Thome, ss, Illinois Central JC**
14. **Nolan Lane, of, St. Xavier (Ill.)**
15. **Tom Lachmann, c, Columbia Basin (Wash.) CC**
16. Mike Potts, lhp, Lithonia (Ga.) HS
17. **Brian Giles, of, Granite Hills HS, El Cajon, Calif.**
18. **Stacy Hamm, of, Valhalla HS, El Cajon, Calif.**
19. **Marcus Robertson, of, Iowa State**
20. **Dennis Kluss, of, Veneta, Ore.**
21. **Avery Johnson, ss, Texas Southern**
22. **Charles Davis, 1b, West Georgia**
23. Miguel Flores, ss, Burbank HS, San Antonio
24. **Jeffrey Hancock, 2b, Dallas Baptist**
25. **Robert Person, ss/of, Seminole State (Okla.) JC**
26. Billy Brewer, lhp, Dallas Baptist
27. **Tommy Tillman, lhp, UNC Wilmington**
28. **Joseph Perez, of, James Monroe HS, Bronx, N.Y.**
29. **Alan Walden, rhp, Cleveland State (Tenn.) CC**
30. Kraig Constantino, 1b, Mission (Calif.) JC
31. **Bill Wertz, rhp, Ohio State**
32. **James Hurst, lhp, Florida Southern**
33. Andy Sheets, ss, St. Amant (La.) HS
34. **Ronald Young, of, UC Riverside**
35. Jeffrey Weibel, c, North Kitsap HS, Poulsbo, Wash.
36. Jeff Martin, c, Goodpasture HS, Godlettsville, Tenn.
37. **Michael Soper, rhp, Alabama**
38. **Marty Durkin, 2b, Georgia Tech**
39. **Gennaro Mirabella, rhp, Brookdale (N.J.) CC**
40. David Norwood, rhp, Lehigh
41. Barry Shepherd, rhp, Angelina (Texas) JC
42. Clarence Brown, rhp, Connors State (Okla.) JC

43. Chris Johnson, rhp, Red Oak (Texas) HS
44. James Walker, rhp, Connors State (Okla.) JC
45. Jon Shirley, of, Southwestern Michigan JC
46. **Scott Johnson, 1b, Allegheny (Pa.) JC**
47. Cary Conklin, rhp, Washington
48. R.D. Long, ss, Webster HS, Penfield, N.Y.
49. Ken Kaveny, 1b, Linn-Benton (Ore.) CC
50. Gavin Saladino, 3b, McClancy HS, Howard Beach, N.Y.
51. Michael Strobel, 3b, Bonanza HS, Las Vegas
52. Eric Snell, of, Hamilton West HS, Trenton, N.J.
53. Darrin Kotch, lhp, Rutgers
54. **Erik Young, of, Baldwin-Wallace (Ohio)**
55. Barry O'Neil, of, Lower Columbia (Wash.) JC

DETROIT TIGERS

June—Regular Phase (21)

1. **Greg Gohr, rhp, Santa Clara**
2. **Brad Wilson, c, Towns County HS, Hiawassee, Ga.**
3. **Gino Tagliaferri, ss, Kennedy HS, Granada Hills, Calif.**
4. Paul Carey, of, Stanford
5. **David Keating, of, UCLA**
6. Doug Mirabelli, c, Valley HS, Las Vegas
7. **Eric Albright, c, Texas A&M**
8. **John DeSilva, rhp, Brigham Young**
9. **Kelley O'Neal, 2b, Belleville (Mich.) HS**
10. **Jody Hurst, of, Mississippi State**
11. **Ronald Maietta, rhp, Dubois Area (Pa.) HS**
12. **Keith Langston, rhp, Texas A&M**
13. **Jeff Goodale, of, UC Riverside**
14. **Robert Davis, of, Colerain HS, Cincinnati**
15. **Mark Cole, ss, Oklahoma**
16. **Frank Gonzales, lhp, Colorado State**
17. **Pat Pesavento, ss, Notre Dame**
18. **Chris Hall, ss, Don Lugo HS, Chino, Calif.**
19. **John Doherty, rhp, Concordia (N.Y.)**
20. **Keith Kimberlin, ss, Missouri Baptist**
21. **Ken Lewis, of, Cosumnes River (Calif.) JC**
22. **Michael Bowman, rhp, Montreat-Anderson (N.C.) JC**
23. **Jim Heins, rhp, Vanderbilt**
24. Daniel Cruz, of, Bayamon, P.R.
25. **Tim Herrmann, rhp, Texas A&M**
26. Derrick Copes, of, Angelina (Texas) JC
27. **Doug Marcero, lhp, Western Michigan**
28. **Ivan Cruz, 1b, Jacksonville**
29. **Craig Middlekauff, of/1b, Santa Clara**
30. **Bob Reimink, 2b, Western Michigan**
31. David Wilson, rhp, Cal Poly San Luis Obispo
32. **Freddie Gamble, ss, Manning (S.C.) HS**
33. **Mark Ettles, rhp, West Florida**
34. **Kasey McKeon, c, San Diego State**
35. **Stephen Matchett, rhp, Pembroke State (N.C.)**
36. **Mac Seibert, 1b, Jacksonville State**
37. Bradley Lamont, rhp, Michigan State
38. Joel Shapiro, rhp, Jacksonville
39. **Matt Coleman, rhp, Kentucky**
40. Mike Bianco, c, Lousiana State
41. **Brian Rountree, rhp, South Carolina**
42. Randy Rivera, rhp, Oklahoma State
43. **Brian Cornelius, of, Southern**
44. **Mario Moccia, 1b, New Mexico State**
45. Jim Henry, lhp, Sacramento CC
46. **Matt Logue, rhp, Coastal Carolina**
47. Kevin Taylor, rhp, Waukegan (Ill.) East HS
48. Marcus Ortiz, lhp, Bayamon, P.R.
49. Chris Bailey, ss, Garfield HS, Seattle
50. Michael Bond, ss, Walbrook HS, Baltimore
51. Michael Parker, rhp, North Hagerstown (Md.) HS
52. Samuel Ubinas, c, Caguas, P.R.
53. **Brian Dubose, 1b, Redford St. Mary's HS, Detroit**
54. Tony Muser Jr., 2b, Cerritos (Calif.) JC
55. **Mike Garcia, rhp, Riverside (Calif.) JC**
56. **Lance Daniels, of, Clayton Valley HS, Concord, Calif.**
57. Scott Klingenbeck, rhp, Oak Hills HS, Cincinnati
58. Todd Kelly, 1b, Bethel HS, Hampton, Va.
59. Scott Simmons, lhp, Three Rivers (Mo.) CC

HOUSTON ASTROS

June—Regular Phase (12)

1. **Jeff Juden, rhp, Salem (Mass.) HS**
1. **Todd Jones, rhp, Jacksonville State** (Supplemental pick—27th—as compensation for Type A free agent Nolan Ryan)
2. **Brian Hunter, of, Fort Vancouver HS, Vancouver, Wash. (Pick from Rangers as compensation for Ryan)**
2. **Jermaine Swinton, of, Fort Hamilton HS, Brooklyn**
3. **Shane Reynolds, rhp, Texas**
4. **Tyrone Scott, lhp, Leuzinger HS, Palmdale, Calif.**
5. John Stanczak, 1b/3b, LaSalle HS, Philadelphia
6. **Scott Makarewicz, c, Michigan State**
7. **Gershon Dallas, of, Hillsborough (Fla.) CC**
8. **Craig Curtis, of, North Kansas City (Mo.) HS**
9. **Cole Hyson, rhp, Arkansas**
10. **Mark Hampton, rhp, Southwest (Miss.) JC**
11. **Ken Wheeler, rhp, Chillicothe (Ohio) HS**
12. **Lance Madsen, of, Utah**
13. **Glen Reyes, ss, Orange Glen HS, Escondido, Calif.**
14. Robert Ferguson, rhp, Glendale (Ariz.) CC
15. **P.J. Riley, of, Southern Illinois**
16. **Corey Diggs, 3b, Hogan HS, Vallejo, Calif.**
17. **Mark Small, rhp, Washington State**
18. **Donne Wall, rhp, Southwestern Louisiana**
19. Mike Condon, c, Harris County HS, Pine Mountain, Ga.
20. Marcus Lee, of, Mt Carmel HS, San Diego
21. **Anthony Lucin, c, Morton (Ill.) JC**
22. Ricardo Jordan, lhp, Miami-Dade South CC
23. Jeffrey Slider, lhp, San Bernardino Valley (Calif.) JC
24. David Wallace, of, Howard (Texas) CC
25. Brian Fontes, rhp, McLane HS, Fresno
26. Paul Dalzochio, rhp, DeAnza (Calif.) JC
27. Geoff Grenert, rhp, Coronado HS, Scottsdale, Ariz.
28. Michael Houck, rhp, Redondo HS, Redondo Beach, Calif.
29. **David Richison, ss/2b, Texarkana (Texas) CC**
30. Dominic Herness, rhp, San Bernardino Valley (Calif.) JC
31. **Howard Prager, of, Texas-Arlington**
32. **Kevin Scott, c, Washington State**
33. Steve Veit, 1b, Mesa (Ariz.) CC
34. Frank Castillo, rhp, North HS, Denver
35. Gerardo Diaz, of, Carolina, P.R.
36. David Angotti, c, Valhalla HS, El Cajon, Calif.
37. Gregory Almond, c, Bay HS, Panama City, Fla.
38. Robert Henkel, rhp, Irving (Texas) HS
39. David Duplessis, lhp/of, Los Medanos (Calif.) JC
40. Mike Bailey, of, Eisenhower HS, Yakima, Wash.
41. Rodrick McCall, 1b, Rancho Alamitos HS, Stanton, Calif.
42. **Steve Boatman, rhp, Coppell (Texas) HS**
43. Shawn Wills, of, UCLA
44. Matthew Ruoff, 3b, Casa Grande HS, Petaluma, Calif.
45. Ruben Cruz, of, Salinas, P.R.
46. Bryan Smith, of, Texarkana (Texas) CC
47. Clarke Rea, c, Scottsdale (Ariz.) CC
48. Andre Earthly, c, Smiley HS, Houston
49. Chris Gies, rhp, Temple
50. James Henderson, of, Los Angeles Harbor JC
51. Richard Williams, rhp, Lamar HS, Houston
52. John Elder, rhp, Terry Parker HS, Jacksonville
53. **Mike McDowell, rhp, Eastern Washington**
54. Donald Strayer, of, Plant HS, Tampa
55. Carl Stall, ss, Paragould (Ark.) HS
56. Alan Walania, rhp, Notre Dame HS, Derby, Conn.
57. Bradley West, of, Dansville (N.Y.) HS
58. David Maice, c, Weber HS, Chicago
59. Jeff Boatner, of, Columbus (Ga.) HS
60. Darrell McMillin, 3b, Ventura (Calif.) JC
61. Alfred Kermode, rhp, Chandler (Ariz.) HS
62. John Vandemark, lhp, Lockport (N.Y.) HS
63. Marc Claus, ss, Cardinal Gibbons HS, Fort Lauderdale
64. William Brockschmidt, rhp, Mater Dei HS, Tustin, Calif.
65. Chad Phillips, rhp, Orange Coast (Calif.) JC
66. Craig Fairbrother, of, Cerritos (Calif.) JC
67. Rollie Jacobson, of/1b, Palm Desert HS, Rancho Mirage, Calif.
68. Brian Carpenter, rhp, Marble Falls (Texas) HS

69. Floyd White, 1b/of, Jones County HS, Gray, Ga.
70. Clark Cole, 1b, Columbus (Ga.) HS
71. Steve Cromwell, of, Spencer HS, Columbus, Ga.
72. Todd Jarvis, lhp, Drury HS, North Adams, Mass.
73. Ryan Karp, of, Los Angeles Harbor JC
74. Steven Hernandez, ss, Oceanview HS, Huntington Beach, Calif.
75. Gary Christopherson, 3b, Oceanview HS, Huntington Beach, Calif.
76. James Short, 1b, Cypress (Calif.) JC
77. Jason Dailey, 1b/3b, Anderson HS, Austin
78. Scott Mowl, 1b, Cerritos (Calif.) JC
79. William Fitzgerald, rhp, Katella HS, Anaheim
80. John Parr, rhp, JC of the Redwoods (Calif.)
81. Kevin Schula, c, Cypress (Calif.) JC
82. Matthew Lackie, rhp, Rancho Santiago (Calif.) JC
83. John DeRicco, 3b, Nevada
84. Michael Petrich, of, Minnesota-Duluth
85. **Mario Prats, lhp, Coral Park HS, Miami**
86. Dean Haskins, c, Santa Rosa (Calif.) JC
87. Desi Wilson, 1b, Fairleigh Dickinson

KANSAS CITY ROYALS

June—Regular Phase (13)

1. **Brent Mayne, c, Cal State Fullerton**
2. **Rick Tunison, 1b, Brevard (Fla.) JC**
2. **Lance Jennings, c, El Rancho HS, Pico Rivera, Calif.** (Supplemental pick—58th—for loss of Type C free agent Jamie Quirk)
3. **Ed Gerald, of, St. Paul's (N.C.) HS**
4. Ray Suplee, of, Sarasota (Fla.) HS
5. **Brian Ahern, rhp, Central Florida**
6. **Bubba Dunn, rhp, Volunteer State (Tenn.) CC**
7. **Ed Pierce, of, Orange Coast (Calif.) JC**
8. **Matt Karchner, rhp, Bloomsburg State (Pa.)**
9. **Keith Adaway, of, Parkway South HS, Ballwin, Mo.**
10. **Chris Schaefer, rhp, Indiana State**
11. **Clint Foster, rhp, Frankston (Texas) HS**
12. **Edgar Caraballo, 3b, Yauco, P.R.**
13. **Sean Collins, of, Kansas State**
14. **Colin Ryan, c, Maine**
15. **Scott Centala, rhp, Texas A&M**
16. **David King, 1b, Southwestern Louisiana**
17. **Chris Jones, 3b, Serra HS, Lawndale, Calif.**
18. **Kirk Thompson, of, Texas A&M**
19. **Michael Webster, lhp, Grand Canyon (Ariz.)**
20. **Kirk Baldwin, lhp, Central Missouri State**
21. **David Ritchie, ss, East Carolina**
22. **Donald Lindsey, lhp, Michigan State**
23. **Ben Pardo, lhp, Houston**
24. **Louis Talbert, rhp, Lassen (Calif.) JC**
25. Kevin Nielsen, lhp, San Diego State
26. Jay Hassel, rhp, El Dorado HS, Placentia, Calif.
27. **Andres Berumen, rhp, Banning (Calif.) HS**
28. **Darnell Dickerson, of, Pittsburgh**
29. **Patrick Murphy, 3b, Hanover (Ind.)**
30. **David Solseth, c, Grand View (Iowa)**
31. **Kevin Long, of, Arizona**
32. **Herbert Milton, rhp, Smiley HS, Houston**
33. **Javier Alvarez, ss, JC of Marin (Calif.)**
34. Enoc Rosado, c, Humacao, P.R.
35. George Liebert, of, Zion Benton HS, Zion, Ill.
36. Arnie Sambel, of, San Francisco
37. **Eric West, rhp, West Orange Stark HS, Orange, Texas**
38. **Rodney Rodgers, rhp, Iowa**
39. Gabriel Pineda, rhp, San Bernardino Valley (Calif.) JC
40. Torreahno Sweet, of, Serra HS, Los Angeles
41. Jackie Kellogg, of, Clover Park HS, Tacoma
42. Conrad Colby, 1b, Rancho Santiago (Calif.) JC
43. **Jay Andrews, ss, Smiley HS, Houston**
44. Shawn Purdy, rhp, Indian River (Fla.) CC
45. Reginal Ricketts, c, Soddy-Daisy HS, Hixon, Tenn.
46. Cristobal Rodriguez, rhp, Caguas, P.R.
47. Joel Cartagena, rhp, Rio Piedras, P.R.
48. Sean Drinkwater, ss, El Toro (Calif.) HS
49. Ricky Moser, rhp/3b, Lakeland (Fla.) HS
50. Chris Coulter, lhp, Beech HS, Goodlettsville, Tenn.
51. Randall Parks, rhp, Northeastern Oklahoma A&M JC
52. Kevin Ashworth, 1b, Pacifica HS, Garden Grove, Calif.
53. Vic Darensbourg, lhp, Westchester HS, Los Angeles
54. George Day, ss, Northeastern Oklahoma A&M JC
55. Robert Mosser, rhp, Oley Valley HS, Oley, Pa.
56. David Toth, c, Brookdale (N.J.) CC
57. Javier Robles, rhp, Cantera Santurce, P. R
58. Inaldo Marrero, c, Dorado, P.R.
59. John Dean, of, Topeka (Kan.) HS
60. **Rod Stillwell, ss, Arkansas**

LOS ANGELES DODGERS

June—Regular Phase (22)

1. **Kiki Jones, rhp, Hillsborough HS, Tampa** (Pick from Yankees as compensation for Type A free agent Steve Sax)
1. **Tom Goodwin, of, Fresno State**
1. **Jamie McAndrew, rhp, Florida** (Supplemental pick—28th—for loss of Sax)
2. **Bill Lott, of, Petal HS, Hattiesburg, Miss.** (Pick from Indians as compensation for Type B free agent Jesse Orosco)
2. Stan Payne, lhp, Clarke Central HS, Athens, Ga.
3. Phil Nevin, ss, El Dorado HS, Placentia, Calif.
4. **Javier Delahoya, rhp, Grant HS, Van Nuys, Calif.**
5. **John Deutsch, 1b, Montclair State (N.J.)**
6. **Tim Barker, ss, Virginia Commonwealth**
7. **Bryan Baar, c, Western Michigan**
8. **Jason Brosnan, lhp, Fresno State**
9. **Barry Parisotto, rhp, Gonzaga**
10. Kevin Jordan, 2b, Canada (Calif.) JC
11. Dennis Burbank, rhp, Cypress (Calif.) JC
12. **Garett Teel, c, William Paterson (N.J.)**
13. **Lee DeLoach, ss/2b, Rutgers**
14. **Michael Wismer, of, Villanova**
15. **Anthony Daniel, rhp, Pander HS, Currie, N.C.**
16. **Frank Humber, lhp, Wake Forest**
17. **Pedro Gonzalez, c, Miami-Dade North CC**
18. **Audelle Cummings, rhp, Ohio Dominican**
19. **Mike Potthoff, rhp, Missouri**
20. **Gary Forrester, ss, Nevada-Las Vegas**
21. **Mike Galle, 3b, Purdue**
22. **Billy Miller, of, San Diego State**
23. **Craig White, ss/2b, Slippery Rock (Pa.)**
24. **Rex Peters, 1b, Cal State Fullerton**
25. **Javier Puchales, of, Caguas, P.R.**
26. **Craig Bishop, lhp, Erie (N.Y.) CC**
27. **Raymond Bielanin, rhp, Niagara**
28. **George Calhoun, rhp, Spartanburg Methodist (S.C.) JC**
29. **Tim Patrick, lhp, Sacramento CC**
30. Jerome Santivasci, rhp, Clemson
31. **Charles Whims, of, Thomas Johnson HS, Frederick, Md.**
32. **Yale Fowler, of/1b, Cal State San Bernardino**
33. John Farren, c, Villanova
34. **Matt Howard, 2b, Pepperdine**
35. **Albert Drumheller, lhp/of, Shenandoah Area (Pa.) HS**
36. **Steve O'Donnell, 1b, La Salle**
37. **Helmut Bohringer, 3b, Adelphi (N.Y.)**
38. **Daniel Stupur, 2b/3b, George Fox (Ore.)**
39. **Billy Seals, c, Belmont**
40. **Jimmy Brown, ss/2b, Loiza, P.R.**
41. Ross Farnsworth, lhp, Pinole (Calif.) HS
42. Roger Sweeney, of, San Rafael (Calif.) HS
43. **Eric Young, of, Rutgers**
44. Garey Ingram, c, Middle Georgia JC
45. Melvin Warren, of, Fairfield (Calif.) HS
46. Ray Bowen, lhp, San Diego Mesa JC
47. Martin Kilian, rhp, San Jose (Calif.) CC
48. Mark Lundeen, lhp, Napa (Calif.) HS
49. Daniel Poulton, rhp, Minidoka HS, Heyburn, Idaho
50. Brannon Veal, of, Middle Georgia JC
51. Patrick Reed, ss, Castlemont HS, Oakland
52. Don Meyers, 1b/3b, Sacramento CC
53. Gaither Bagsby, rhp, Roane State (Tenn.) CC
54. Robert Hoffman, c, Contra Costa (Calif.) JC
55. Timothy McDermott, c, Millard South HS, Omaha, Neb.

56. Brian Van Horn, lhp, Pinconning HS, Bentley, Mich.
57. Richard Josepher, 1b/3b, St. Rita HS, Chicago
58. Bradley Cohen, of, Meridian (Miss.) JC
59. Charles Williams, of, Lumberton (Miss.) HS
60. Pete Altenberger, rhp, Purdue
61. Brent Prudhomme, 1b, Kaplan (La.) HS
62. Rich Crane, lhp, Fresno State

MILWAUKEE BREWERS

June—Regular Phase (17)

1. **Cal Eldred, rhp, Iowa**
1. **Gordon Powell, 3b, Hughes HS, Cincinnati** (Supplemental pick—30th—for failure to sign 1988 first-rounder Alex Fernandez)
2. **Rusty Rugg, lhp, Downsville (La.) HS**
3. **Bo Dodson, 1b, Christian Brothers HS, Sacramento** (Pick from Mariners as compensation for Type B free agent Jeffrey Leonard)
3. **John Byington, 3b, Texas A&M**
4. **Bill Brakeley, lhp, Delaware**
5. **Jason Zimbauer, rhp, Andrew HS, Orland Hills, Ill.**
6. **Tony Diggs, 2b, North Florida**
7. Daniel Perez, of, Hanks HS, El Paso
8. **Brant McCreadie, rhp, Kaiser HS, Honolulu**
9. **Eric Patton, rhp, Saddleback (Calif.) CC**
10. **John Finn, 3b, Arizona State**
11. **Timothy Wilson, rhp, St. Andrew's (N.C.)**
12. **Daren Cornell, ss, Cal Lutheran**
13. Steven Hegan, of, South Pontotoc (Miss.) HS
14. **Darrin White, c, Blinn (Texas) JC**
15. **Kenneth Harris, of, Taft (Calif.) JC**
16. **Mitch Hannahs, 2b, Indiana State**
17. **Geoff Kellogg, rhp, Mead HS, Spokane, Wash.**
18. **Scott Muscat, rhp, UNC Charlotte**
19. **Kevin Tannahill, c, San Jose State**
20. **Arthur Butcher, of, Texas**
21. **David Weldin, of, Bakersfield (Calif.) JC**
22. Brian Gore, ss, Sterling HS, Baytown, Texas
23. **Bob Vancho, rhp, Housatonic (Conn.) CC**
24. **Sam Drake, rhp, Georgia Tech**
25. Manny Gagliano, ss, Crawford HS, San Diego
26. Scott Cline, 3b, UCLA
27. **Michael Johnson, c, Wisconsin-Milwaukee**
28. Demerius Pittman, of, Workman HS, La Puente, Calif.
29. Derek January, lhp, Bridgeton Academy HS, Swampscott, Mass.
30. Charles Walker, of, Starmount HS, Booneville, N.C.
31. Tim Smith, rhp, Boston College
32. Bill Barber, lhp, St. Petersburg (Fla.) JC
33. Shane Smith, lhp, Hinkley HS, Aurora, Colo.
34. Jay Patterson, of, Cabrillo (Calif.) JC
35. **William Robertson, of, Mesa State (Colo.)**
36. **Rocky Ynclan, rhp, Hawaii**
37. Jesse Villanueva, rhp, Evergreen HS, Vancouver, Wash.
38. **Rusty Charpia, ss, Clemson**
39. Marc Tsitouris, 3b, Wingate (N.C.)
40. **James Walker, of, Carolina, P.R.**
41. **Justin McCray, ss/3b, Cal Poly San Luis Obispo**
42. Donald Culberson, of, East Central (Miss.) JC
43. Jason Giambi, ss, South Hills HS, Covina, Calif.
44. Jason Grabosch, 1b/3b, Coronado HS, Tucson, Ariz.
45. Fausto Tejero, c, Florida International
46. Scott Rose, rhp, Hillsborough (Fla.) CC
47. David Whiteside, 1b/of, West Davidson HS, Lexington, N.C.

MINNESOTA TWINS

June—Regular Phase (25)

1. **Chuck Knoblauch, ss, Texas A&M**
2. **John Gumpf, of, Poly HS, Riverside, Calif.**
3. **Denny Neagle Jr., lhp, Minnesota**
4. **Scott Erickson, rhp, Arizona**
5. Jay Richardson, of, Northside HS, Fort Smith, Ark.
6. **Ken Norman, of, Sweetwater (Texas) HS**
7. **Ray Ortiz, of, Oklahoma State**
8. **Jeff Thelen, rhp, Craig HS, Janesville, Wis.**
9. **Troy Buckley, c, Santa Clara**
10. **Marty Cordova, 3b, Orange Coast (Calif.) JC**
11. **Dan Masteller, 1b, Michigan State**
12. **Alvin Brown, c, Los Angeles CC**
13. **Timmy Moore, of, Rose HS, Greenville, N.C.**
14. **Mike Trombley, rhp, Duke**
15. **George Tsamis, lhp, Stetson**
16. **David Krol, rhp, Toledo**
17. Chad McConnell, of, Ogorman HS, Sioux Falls, S.D.
18. **Mike House, 1b, Hawaii Pacific**
19. **Bob McCreary, rhp, Villanova**
20. **Javier Fimbres, 1b, Cerritos (Calif.) JC**
21. **Tim Nedin, lhp, Florida State**
22. **Rex Delanuez, of, Cal State Los Angeles**
23. Derrick White, 3b, Santa Rosa (Calif.) JC
24. **Ken Briggs, c, Chapman (Calif.)**
25. **Phil Wiese, lhp, New Orleans**
26. Jeff Pearce, of, Mann (Calif.) JC
27. **William Houk, ss, Lincoln Land (Ill.) CC**
28. Ben Lindsey, c, Lakeland HS, Croton, N.Y.
29. Tom Urbani, lhp, Long Beach State
30. **Jody Bryant, of, Twin Falls (Idaho) HS**
31. **Mike Lloyd, ss, St. Leo (Fla.)**
32. **Francisco Ramirez, c, Vega Alta, P.R.**
33. Allen Hayes, of, Forestbrook HS, Houston
34. Gregory Bowles, of, Cleveland State (Tenn.) JC
35. Todd Johnson, c, Bullard HS, Fresno
36. **Bradley Brooks, 1b/rhp, Western New Mexico**
37. **Randy Gentile, 3b, Illinois State**
38. Richard Faulks, lhp, Cal State Fullerton
39. **David Bigham, lhp, West HS, Rogers, Minn.**
40. **Jon Pittenger, 3b, Missouri**
41. **Robert Schiel, ss, St. Cloud State (Minn.)**
42. **John Howard, of, Pasadena (Calif.) CC**
43. **Joe Siwa, c, Auburn**
44. **Bryan Asp, rhp, North Hennepin (Minn.) CC**
45. James Dorough, lhp, Lafayette HS, Lexington, Ky.
46. Steve Stuart, lhp, Prairie HS, Ridgefield, Wash.
47. Michael Jewell, rhp, Sacramento CC
48. Reggie Jackson, lhp/of, Lake Wales (Fla.) HS
49. Charles Wallgren, c, Sacramento CC
50. Christopher Smith, rhp, Baylor HS, Chattanooga
51. Todd Blakeman, 1b, Lakeland (Ohio) CC
52. Dennis Hocking, c, El Camino (Calif.) JC
53. David Shell, 3b, Red Bank HS, Hixon, Tenn.
54. George Spaan, ss, Saddleback (Calif.) CC
55. Mark Burke, rhp, West HS, Rockford, Ill.
56. Sam Vranjes, c, Southern California
57. **Todd Logan, c, Eastern Washington**
58. **Karl King, c, Mount St. Mary's HS, Oklahoma City**
59. Timothy Leppert, c, Brown County HS, Nineveh, Ind.

MONTREAL EXPOS

June—Regular Phase (10)

1. Charles Johnson, c, Westwood HS, Fort Pierce, Fla.
2. **Glenn Murray, c, Manning (S.C.) HS**
3. **Ron Krause, ss, North HS, Eastlake, Ohio**
4. **Brian Barnes, lhp, Clemson**
5. **Dan Hargis, c, Eastern Illinois**
6. **Pete Young, rhp/3b, Mississippi State**
7. Jeff Brohm, ss, Trinity HS, Louisville
8. Walter Camp, rhp, Leonard HS, Lake Worth, Fla.
9. **Doug Bochtler, rhp, Indian River (Fla.) CC**
10. **Mike Fier, lhp, Mankato State (Minn.)**
11. **John Thoden, rhp, North Carolina**
12. **Paul Ciaglo, lhp, Massachusetts**
13. James Martin, of, Eufaula (Okla.) HS
14. **Angelo Santiago, 3b, Buena (N.J.) HS**
15. **Buck Atwater, ss, Southern Alamance HS, Graham, N.C.**
16. Greg Margheim, lhp, Virginia Tech
17. Andrew Swain, rhp, Purdue
18. Kelton Jacobson, rhp, Kennedy HS, Seattle
19. **James Heilgeist, of, Liberty HS, Issaquah, Wash.**
20. **F.P. Santangelo, ss, Miami**
21. Craig Stiveson, rhp, Pepperdine

22. **Rusty Kilgo, lhp, Arizona State**
23. **Michael Regira, rhp, Nicholls State**
24. Hector Rodriguez, 3b, Arroyo, P.R.
25. **Duane Ashley, rhp, Yerba Buena HS, San Jose**
26. Joseph Norris, rhp, Bakersfield (Calif.) JC
27. **Bill Cramer, c, Cal State Sacramento**
28. **Joseph Logan, rhp, Florida Southern**
29. **Pressley Herron, ss/of, West Mecklenburg HS, Charlotte**
30. **Charles Smith, 1b, Tennessee State**
31. Harold Williams, 1b, East St. John HS, Garyville, La.
32. **Todd Mayo, of, California**
33. **Gary Pipik, of, Florida Southern**
34. **Deryk Hudson, 3b, Long Beach State**
35. **Robert Small, c, Chico State**
36. Ronnie Quijada, rhp, Mount Pleasant HS, San Jose
37. John Rodgers, c, Waxahachie (Texas) HS
38. **James Eddy, rhp, Marietta (Ohio)**
39. Chris Stewart, rhp, Christian Brothers HS, Memphis
40. James Bell, c, Mesa (Ariz.) CC
41. Shane Warenski, lhp, Granger HS, West Valley, Utah
42. **Gary Adams, of, Science Hill HS, Johnson City, Tenn.**
43. James Wallkvist, rhp, CC of San Francisco
44. **Roger Horne, of, West Montgomery HS, Troy, N.C.**
45. Todd A. Taylor, c, South Florida JC
46. Todd H. Taylor, lhp, Millikan HS, Long Beach
47. **Michael Romberg, rhp, U.S. International (Nairobi)**
48. **Chris Etheridge, c, Whiteville (N.C.) HS**
49. Shawn Henrichs, rhp, Hermiston (Ore.) HS
50. **Hector Rivera, of, Banonguitas, P.R.**
51. **Gary Young, rhp, San Jacinto (Texas) JC**
52. Richard Greenwell, c, Shelby County HS, Shelbyville, Ky.
53. **Fernando Torres, rhp, Rio Piedras, P.R.**
54. Troy Kopp, c, Mission Viejo (Calif.), HS
55. Christopher Altman, of/ss, Richmond HS, Hamlet, N.C.
56. Alan Beavers, rhp, Scottsdale (Ariz.) CC
57. Todd Hall, ss, El Dorado HS, Placerville, Calif.
58. Corey McCormick, lhp/of, Burbank HS, Sacramento
59. Matt Conley, rhp, Moreno Valley (Calif.) HS
60. Riley McKelvey, ss, North Greenville (S.C.) JC
61. Michael Bieger, rhp, JC of the Desert (Calif.)
62. Michael Morland, c, Canada (Calif.) JC
63. Paul Carpentier, 3b, Montclair (Calif.) HS
64. Corey Powell, of, Grossmont HS, San Diego
65. Chad Dembisky, rhp, Lassen (Calif.) JC
66. Kevin Cerveny, rhp, Palomar (Calif.) JC
67. Cornell Caldwell, of, Independence HS, Charlotte
68. **Christopher Ellis, c/of, Cave Spring HS, Roanoke, Va.**
69. **Abimael Rodriguez, ss, Hatillo, P.R.**

NEW YORK METS

June—Regular Phase (24)

1. **Alan Zinter, c, Arizona**
2. **Tom Engle, rhp, Fairfield Union HS, Lancaster, Ohio**
3. **Brook Fordyce, c, St. Bernards HS, Old Lyme, Conn.**
4. **Tim McClinton, of, Downers Grove North HS, Woodridge, Ill.**
5. **Paul Meyer, c, Patrick Henry HS, Minneapolis**
6. **Robert Rees, rhp, Lake Washington HS, Kirkland, Wash.**
7. **Butch Huskey, 3b, Eisenhower HS, Lawton, Okla.**
8. **Derek Henderson, ss, Tennesee State**
9. Nathaniel Florell, of/rhp, Sullivan HS, Chicago
10. Scot McCloughan, rhp/ss, Loveland (Colo.) HS
11. Ritchie Moody, lhp, Brookville (Ohio) HS
12. **Jay Davis, lhp, Orr HS, Chicago**
13. **Ed Vazquez, rhp, Baruch (N.Y.)**
14. **Chris Butterfield, of, Cal Poly Pomona**
15. Sean Hogan, lhp, Bishop Rosecrans HS, Nashport, Ohio
16. Kendall Rhine, rhp, Parkview HS, Lilburn, Ga.
17. Mark Grudzielanek, ss, Hanks HS, El Paso
18. **Omar Garcia, 1b, Carolina, P.R.**
19. Clint Whitworth, rhp, Frederick (Okla.) HS
20. **Tim Buhe, ss, Northwestern**
21. Jason Angel, rhp, Hermitage HS, Glen Allen, Va.
22. **Marcel Johnson, 1b, Fremont HS, Oakland, Calif.**
23. **Mike Thomas, lhp, Labette (Kan.) JC**
24. **Joe Vitko III, rhp, St. Francis College (N.Y.)**
25. Jeff Hostetler, lhp, Science Hill HS, Johnson City, Tenn.
26. David Hutcheson, rhp, Chamberlain HS, Tampa
27. Todd Harris, lhp, Taft (Calif.) CC
28. Thomas Bates, ss, Paris (Texas) JC
29. William Hunt, lhp, Asher HS, Byars, Okla.
30. Joseph Petcka, rhp, Everest HS, Clintonville, Wis.
31. **Dave Telgheder, rhp, Massachusetts**
32. Ronald Miller, ss, Ruskin HS, Kansas City, Mo.
33. **Steven Graves, c, Southern Mississippi**
34. Robert Dodd, lhp, Sacramento CC
35. **Jerome Tolliver, 1b, Bacone (Okla.) JC**
36. **Arness Rittman, 3b/2b, Shanks HS, Quincy, Fla.**
37. Joe Arredondo, 3b, Cerritos (Calif.) JC
38. **Joe Dellicarri, ss, Pennsylvania**
39. Leon Clay, of, Texas Christian
40. **Eric Thornton, of, Faulkner (Ala.)**
41. **Michael Hemmerich, lhp, Marian (Ind.)**
42. Clayton Klavitter, 3b, Glendale (Ariz.) CC
43. Kevin Magers, of, Nettleton (Miss.) HS
44. Clifford Hamilton, of, Diablo Valley (Calif.) JC
45. **James Scheffler, rhp, Joliet (Ill.) JC**
46. Craig Gienger, of, Douglas County HS, Castle Rock, Colo.
47. Earskine Kelley, ss, Freeport (N.Y.) HS
48. Ottis Smith, lhp, Goodrich HS, Fond du lac, Wis.
49. Ronald Ollison, 2b/ss, Malvern (Ark.) HS
50. **Michael Freitas, rhp, Sacramento CC**
51. Clifford Krull, rhp/of, Bonduel (Wis.) HS
52. Brian Thompson, of, Sunset HS, Hayward, Calif.
53. **Jaime Hoffner, 1b, Mankato State (Minn.)**
54. Timothy Sandy, 1b/of, Fargo, N.D.

NEW YORK YANKEES

June—Regular Phase (15)

1. (Pick to Dodgers as compensation for Type A free agent Steve Sax)
2. **Andy Fox, 3b, Christian Brothers HS, Sacramento**
3. **Jason Robertson, of, Hillcrest HS, Country Club Hills, Ill.**
4. **Adin Lohry, c/3b, Winter Park (Fla.) HS**
5. **J.T. Snow, 1b, Arizona**
6. **Larry Stanford, rhp, Florida International**
7. **Russ Springer, rhp, Louisiana State**
8. **Scott Romano, 3b, Hillsborough HS, Tampa**
9. **Sterling Hitchcock, lhp, Armwood HS, Seffner, Fla.**
10. **Richard Turrentine, rhp, Arkansas HS, Texarkana, Ark.**
11. **James Mauldin, rhp, Texas Tech**
12. **Thomas Wiley, rhp, Westark (Ark.) JC**
13. **Mike Gardella, lhp, Oklahoma State**
14. Ricky Greene, rhp, Coral Gables (Fla.) HS
15. Ernie Yaroshuk, of/1b, Columbus HS, Miami
16. **Brian Johnson, 3b/of, Stanford**
17. **Richard Barnwell, of, Pepperdine**
18. Stuart Seiler, lhp, Virginia
19. **Timothy Cooper, 3b/ss, Hiram Johnson HS, Sacramento**
20. **Richard Polak, rhp, Central Florida**
21. **Aaron Van Scoyoc, ss, Westark (Ark.) JC**
22. **Jose Vazquez, 2b, Florida International**
23. **Peter Gietzen, lhp, Florida International**
24. **James Haller, lhp, Kansas State**
25. **Joel Petlick, rhp, Pfeiffer (N.C.)**
26. Chris Martin, ss, Pepperdine
27. Tony Khoury, c, Bowsher HS, Toledo
28. Dennis Konuszewski, rhp, Bridgeport (Mich.) HS
29. Gary Posey, of, Gulf Coast (Fla.) CC
30. Troy Penix, 1b, Tokay HS, Stockton, Calif.
31. Jeff Asnicar, lhp, Enterprise HS, Redding, Calif.
32. **John Jarvis, c, Southwestern Louisiana**
33. **Todd Devereaux, of, Arizona**
34. **Ricky Strickland, of, Austin Peay State**
35. Bob Baxter, lhp, Harvard
36. **Paul Oster, of, Oklahoma**
37. Agusto Padilla, 1b, Camuy, P.R.
38. Rich Batchelor, rhp, South Carolina-Aiken
39. **James Moody, rhp, Huntingdon (Ind.)**
40. **Brian Turner, of, Grand Valley HS, Orwell, Ohio**
41. Daniel Heidman, rhp, Hoban HS, Akron, Ohio

42. Arthur Johnson, ss, Denham Springs (La.) HS
43. Jorge Posada, ss, Rio Piedras, P.R.
44. Mike Figga, c, Central Florida CC
45. Robert Glenn, lhp, George Wallace (Ala.) CC
46. Timothy Jones, rhp/of, American River (Calif.) JC
47. Shad Mix, 3b, Mission (Calif.) JC
48. **Timothy Garland, of, Pensacola (Fla.) JC**
49. Joel Schaedler, rhp, Holy Name HS, Berea, Ohio
50. Joseph Finley, c, Columbia (Miss.) HS
51. Tim Demerson, of, Howard (Texas) JC
52. Bruce Freeman, c, Clarksdale HS, Meridian, Miss.
53. Jeffrey Stych, of, Southeast HS, Lincoln, Neb.
54. Malcolm Jordan, of, Santa Rosa (Calif.) JC
55. Scott Pace, lhp, Fajardo, P.R.
56. Eric Ford, ss, Brandon (Miss.) HS
57. **Gerald Davis, of, Chadsey HS, Detroit**
58. Brian Jackson, rhp, Bonner Springs (Kan.) HS
59. Jeff Pickett, c, Allen County (Kan.) CC
60. **Rey Noriega, of, Miami**
61. **Sidney Gilliam, of, Florida A&M**

OAKLAND ATHLETICS

June—Regular Phase (26)

1. (Pick to Mariners as compensation for Type B free agent Mike Moore)
2. **Scott Lydy, of, South Mountain (Ariz.) CC**
3. **Mike Grimes, rhp, Michigan**
4. **Darin Kracl, rhp, Brigham Young**
5. **Scott Erwin, rhp, Georgia Tech**
6. **Steve Chitren, rhp, Stanford**
7. **Scott Shockey, 1b, Pepperdine**
8. **Craig Paquette, 3b, Golden West (Calif.) JC**
9. **Gavin Osteen, lhp, Allegany (Md.) CC**
10. **Todd Smith, rhp, Lassen (Calif.) JC**
11. Levon Largusa, lhp, Mount Eden HS, Hayward, Calif.
12. **Russ Cormier, rhp, Northeastern**
13. Rodney Peete, 3b, Southern California
14. **Brett Hendley, 1b, Georgia Southern**
15. **Kurt Abbott, ss, St. Petersburg (Fla.) JC**
16. **Darryl Vice, 2b, California**
17. Andy Beasley, c, Virginia Military institute
18. **Scott McCarty, lhp, San Jacinto (Texas) JC**
19. **Mike Conte, of, Virginia Tech**
20. Matt Mieske, of, Western Michigan
21. **Dana Allison, lhp, James Madison**
22. Walter Rivera, rhp, Chipola (Fla.) JC
23. John Tejeck, ss, Mount Carmel HS, San Diego
24. **Russell Miller, rhp, Anderson (S.C.) JC**
25. **Doug Twitty, of/1b, Nebraska**
26. **Lee Sammons, of, Augusta (Ga.)**
27. Charles McCray, rhp, Florida
28. **Todd Russell, rhp, Pearl River (Miss.) JC**
29. **Trent Weaver, 3b/2b, Baylor**
30. James Wilkie, rhp, Portage (Wis.) HS
31. **Brad Brimhall, rhp, Ricks (Idaho) JC**
32. **Ed Tredway, c, Flagler (Fla.)**
33. **David Latter, rhp, Southern California**
34. Sean Hardwick, rhp, North Myrtle Beach (S.C.) HS
35. Dallas Rhinehart, rhp, Sullivan Central HS, Kingsport, Tenn.
36. Richard Lovan, lhp, Lakewood HS, Long Beach
37. **Fred Cooley, rhp/3b, Southern Mississippi**
38. **Jim Gibbs, rhp, San Diego State**
39. **Mario Lyons, of, Eastern Washington**
40. **Jeffrey Lynch, rhp, UC Santa Barbara**
41. **Brad Eager, c, Brigham Young**
42. Mike Mohler, lhp, Nicholls State
43. **Eric Campa, ss, San Bernadino Valley (Calif.) JC**
44. **James Waggoner, ss, Austin Peay State**
45. **Daniel Orr, rhp, Glendale (Ariz.) CC**
46. **Hugh Gulledge, rhp, Enterprise State (Ala.) JC**
47. **Kevin Lofthus, 1b, Nevada-Las Vegas**
48. **Sean Krokroskia, of, Southwestern Oklahoma State**
49. **Scott Henry, c, South Florida**
50. **Gary Ross, rhp, Grossmont (Calif.) JC**
51. **Ruben Lardizabal, rhp, Cochise County (Ariz.) CC**
52. Clifford Jones, lhp/of, Laney (Calif.) JC
53. Roderick Walker, c, Morristown (Tenn.) West HS
54. Christopher Lohman, 3b/of, Notre Dame HS, Northridge, Calif.
55. Todd Breyfogle, rhp, Scottsdale (Ariz.) CC
56. Chris Kelley, rhp, Lurleen Wallace (Ala.) JC
57. Jason Davis, rhp, Upland (Calif.) HS
58. William Rose, rhp, Hillsborough (Fla.) CC (Selection voided)
59. Robert Richter, of, Arcadia (Calif.) HS
60. Jamie Anderson, of, Hillsborough HS, Tampa
61. Anthony Pritchett, of, Faulkner State (Ala.) JC

PHILADELPHIA PHILLIES

June—Regular Phase (4)

1. **Jeff Jackson, of, Simeon HS, Chicago**
2. Chris Roberts, lhp, Middleburg (Fla.) HS
3. **Lamar Foster, 3b, Bibb County HS, Brent, Ala.**
4. **Julio Vargas, c, Santa Ana (Calif.) HS**
5. **Steve Parris, rhp, St. Francis (Ill.)**
6. Miah Bradbury, c, Loyola Marymount
7. **Corey Thomas, of, Don Lugo HS, Chino, Calif.**
8. **Darrell Goedhart, rhp, Mount San Jacinto (Calif.) JC**
9. **Paul Carson, of, Woodinville (Wash.) HS**
10. **Cary Williams, of, Alabama**
11. **Casey Waller, 3b, Virginia Tech**
12. **Tommy Hardgrove, 1b, Texas Christian**
13. **Robert Mendonca, 3b, Modesto (Calif.) JC**
14. **Sam Taylor, of, Kentucky**
15. **Steven Avent, c, Oklahoma City**
16. James Savage, 3b, Hillsborough (Fla.) CC
17. **Joe Urbon, of, Washington State**
18. Matt Whisenant, lhp, La Canada (Calif.) HS
19. **William Smith, c, Sacramento CC**
20. **Steve Campos, rhp, Venice HS, Los Angeles**
21. **Ismael Cruz, ss, Eckerd (Fla.)**
22. **David Ross, lhp, Saddleback (Calif.) CC**
23. **Mark Randall, rhp, Saddleback (Calif.) CC**
24. Joseph Davis, ss/rhp, Central Arizona JC
25. Sean Teague, c, Judson HS, Converse, Texas
26. Ted Corbin, ss, Barren Collier HS, Naples, Fla.
27. **David Agado, rhp, Tarleton State (Texas)**
28. Thomas Neff, of, Rancho Santiago (Calif.) JC
29. **Matt Stevens, rhp, Le Moyne**
30. **Josh Lowery, ss, Portland**
31. **Brian Adams, c, Otero (Colo.) JC**
32. **Steve Bieser, of/c, Southeast Missouri State**
33. Rafael Charriez, lhp, Bayamon, P.R. (Selection voided)
34. Scott Corliss, rhp, Mater Dei HS, Chino Hills, Calif.
35. **Dana Brown, of, Seton Hall**
36. **John Douglas, of, Oklahoma**
37. **Steven Stocker, c, Washington**
38. **Ken Sirak, ss, Nebraska**
39. Gary Morgan, 3b, JC of the Canyons (Calif.)
40. **Charles Shive, rhp, Southern Mississippi**
41. **Robert Gaddy, lhp, Tennessee**
42. **James Cosman, c, Mississippi**
43. **Elliot Gray, rhp, Wiley (Texas)**
44. **Daniel Welch, of, Christian Brothers (Tenn.)**
45. **Scott Wiegandt, lhp, Bellarmine (Ky.)**
46. Larry Maddox, of, Saddleback (Calif.) CC
47. **Robby Corsaro, rhp, Long Beach State**
48. Leon Whaley, of, St. Cloud (Fla.) HS
49. Coy Baskin, lhp, Cypress Creek (Texas) HS
50. Thomas Heming, lhp, Aquinas (Tenn.) JC
51. Terrance Tewell, c, Cypress (Calif.) JC
52. Gregory Phillips, ss/of, Rutledge HS, Bean Station, Tenn.
53. Alexis Santana, rhp, Caguas, P.R.

PITTSBURGH PIRATES

June—Regular Phase (18)

1. **Willie Greene, ss, Jones County HS, Gray, Ga.**
2. **Rich Aude, 3b, Chatsworth (Calif.) HS**
2. **John Hope, rhp, Stranahan HS, Fort Lauderdale, Fla.** (Supplemental pick—59th—for loss of Type C free agent Dave LaPoint)

3. **Rob Bailey, of, Fullerton (Calif.) JC**
4. Patrick Hicks, c, Overland HS, Aurora, Colo.
5. **Michael Brown, 1b, Vacaville (Calif.) HS**
6. **Kevin Rychel, rhp, Midland (Texas) HS**
7. **Timothy Williams, of, Springboro (Ohio) HS**
8. **Ricardo Ufret, ss, Aquinas (Tenn.) JC**
9. **Joe Ronca, of, Tate HS, Cantonment, Fla.**
10. **David Bird, lhp, Chapman (Calif.)**
11. Joseph McLin, 1b, Riverside HS, Milwaukee, Wis.
12. **Paul Wagner, rhp, Illinois State**
13. Brian Arntzen, c, American River (Calif.) JC
14. **Richard Scoates, rhp, Evans HS, Martinez, Ga.**
15. Joe Russo, 3b, Santa Fe (Fla.) CC
16. Steve Gill, of, Cypress (Calif.) JC
17. **Scott Arvesen, rhp, St. Xavier (Ill.)**
18. **Marcus Hanel, c, Horlick HS, Racine, Wis.**
19. Darren Hedley, of, American River (Calif.) JC
20. Jeff McCurry, rhp, San Jacinto (Texas) JC
21. **Dean Hinson, c/1b, Bloomfield (N.M.) HS**
22. **Eric Parkinson, rhp, Kellogg (Mich.) CC**
23. **Luis Garcia, ss, Levittown, P.R.**
24. **David Howard, c/1b, Siena**
25. **David Watson, lhp, Yavapai (Ariz.) JC**
26. **Bill Holmes, 1b, Marietta (Ohio)**
27. **Ken Trusky, of, Maryland**
28. **Michael Hayes, of, Edmonds (Wash.) CC**
29. Steve Young, of, Van Horn HS, Kansas City, Mo.
30. **Mike Brewington, of, Methodist (N.C.)**
31. Chris Abbe, c/ss, Sycamore HS, Cincinnati
32. **Robert Peterson, c, Wooster (Ohio)**
33. **Nelson Caraballo, c, Florida International**
34. **Tony Mitchell, c, Mumford HS, Detroit**
35. Steve Cooke, lhp, JC of Southern Idaho
36. Derek Wallace, rhp, Chatsworth (Calif.) HS
37. Robert Hinds, ss, Cerritos (Calif.) HS
38. Casey Burrill, c, Hart HS, Newhall, Calif.
39. **Kimberly Broome, lhp, Columbus (Ga.)**
40. **Tom Deller, rhp, Kentucky**
41. **Troy Mooney, rhp, Ashland (Ohio)**
42. Mark Johnson, 1b/rhp, Dartmouth
43. **Shane Sparks, rhp, Campbell County HS, Jacksboro, Tenn.**
44. Chad Trahan, rhp, Tecumseh (Okla.) HS
45. Randy Martin, of, Palm Beach (Fla.) JC
46. David Pearlman, rhp, Los Amigos HS, Fountain Valley, Calif.
47. Todd Johnson, rhp, Cal State Los Angeles
48. William Bates, rhp, Eastern Michigan

ST. LOUIS CARDINALS

June—Regular Phase (6)

1. **Paul Coleman, of, Frankston (Texas) HS**
2. **Mike Milchin, lhp/1b, Clemson**
3. **Tripp Cromer III, ss, South Carolina**
4. John Farrell, of/c, Sandalwood HS, Jacksonville
5. **Tony Ochs, c, Memphis State**
6. Todd Steverson, of, Culver City HS, Venice, Calif.
7. **Tracey Ealy, of, Chaparral HS, Las Vegas**
8. **Anthony Lewis, of, Rancho HS, Las Vegas**
9. **Jeff Fayne, of, Munford HS, Brighton, Tenn.**
10. **John Dempsey, c, Crespi HS, Agoura, Calif.**
11. Kevin Legault, rhp, Watervliet (N.Y.) HS
12. **David Boss, rhp, UC Santa Barbara**
13. **Jeremy McGarity, rhp, El Capitan HS, Lakeside, Calif.**
14. **Jose Fernandez, c, Florida**
15. **Donald Green, lhp, Iowa State**
16. **Ben Ellsworth, ss, Orem (Utah) HS**
17. **Danny Davis, of, Rustburg (Va.) HS**
18. **Joseph Turvey, c, Roxborough HS, Philadelphia**
19. **Mark Bowlan, rhp, Memphis State**
20. Bill Hurst, rhp, Central Florida CC
21. **James Allen, of, Otterbein (Ohio)**
22. **Jeff Oswalt, lhp, U.S. International (Nairobi)**
23. **Alan Botkin, lhp, Clemson**
24. **Tremayne Donald, 2b, Tilghman HS, Paducah, Ky.**
25. **Michael Campas, of, San Francisco**
26. **Jose Trujillo, 2b, Miami**
27. **Albert Pacheco, rhp, Florida International**
28. **Dennis Fletcher, rhp, Arkansas**
29. **Jeffrey Brannon, rhp/of, Kennesaw (Ga.)**
30. **Denny Wiseman, rhp, Florida International**
31. **Steve Dixon, lhp, Paducah (Ky.) CC**
32. **Clyde Keller, rhp, Florida State**
33. **Manuel Rodriguez, rhp, Rio Piedras, P.R.**
34. **Millard Hammond, rhp, Wellston (Ohio) HS**
35. **Anthony Hicks, of, Florida International**
36. **Tim Lata, rhp, Michigan**
37. **Frank Cimorelli, rhp, Dominican (N.Y.)**
38. **David Cassidy, lhp, Arizona State**
39. **John Corona, lhp, Cerritos (Calif.) JC**
40. **William Espinal, rhp, Pace (N.Y.)**
41. William Meury, ss, Maryland
42. **William Fielitz, c, Birmingham-Southern**
43. **Kevin Tahan, 1b/of, U.S. International (Nairobi)**
44. **Larry Merrill, 3b/2b, Vestavia Hills (Ala.) HS**
45. **Tim Jordan, of, Fernandina Beach HS, Yulee, Fla.**
46. **Scott Banton, of, Virginia Commonwealth**
47. **Jarvis French, of, Fernandina Beach HS, Yulee, Fla.**
48. Steven Jackson, c, Sullivan (Mo.) HS
49. **Mark Tolbert, rhp, Dixie (Utah) JC**
50. Brian Cavalli, c, St. Joseph HS, Alameda, Calif.
51. Tim Costa, rhp, LeMoore (Calif.) HS., Calif.
52. Steve Harelson, lhp, Hempfield HS, Landisville, Pa.
53. **Greg Glover, rhp, Junction City (Ark.) HS**
54. Sean Page, of, Volunteer State (Tenn.) CC
55. Stanley Hurt, lhp/of, Jefferson Forest HS, Forest, Va.
56. **Algerian Williams, rhp, King HS, Tampa**

SAN DIEGO PADRES

June—Regular Phase (16)

1. (Pick to Red Sox as compensation for Type A free agent Bruce Hurst)
2. Kenny Felder, of, Niceville (Fla.) HS
3. **Scott Bream, ss, Millard South HS, Omaha**
4. **Russell Garside, lhp, Douglas HS, Garnerville, Nev.**
5. **Dave Staton, 1b, Cal State Fullerton**
6. **Darrell Sherman, of, Long Beach State**
7. **Rick Davis, rhp, Cal State Dominguez Hills**
8. **Billy Johnson, rhp, South Georgia JC**
9. Ray McDavid, of, Clairemont HS, San Diego
10. **Lee Henderson, c, West Covina (Calif.) HS**
11. Pat Clougherty, c, Broughton HS, Raleigh, N.C.
12. **Kevin Higgins, 2b, Arizona State**
13. **Ted Devore, rhp, Portland**
14. **Brian McKeon, rhp, Madison (Wis.) Tech JC**
15. **Shawn Whalen, of, Warner Pacific (Ore.)**
16. **Steve Martin, of, Arizona State**
17. **Terry Rupp, 1b, Tampa**
18. **Kerry Knox, lhp, Texas Christian**
19. **Tony McGee, c, Jacksonville**
20. Tim Worrell, rhp, Biola (Calif.)
21. **Samuel Shannon, 2b, South Mecklenburg HS, Charlotte**
22. **John Phelan, rhp, Eastern Washington**
23. James Hallinan, rhp, Snow (Utah) JC
24. **Jeff Barton, of, Princeton**
25. Scott Vorderlieth, lhp, San Diego Mesa JC
26. **Steve Bethea, ss, Texas**
27. Jeffrey Huber, lhp, Chaparrel HS, Scottsdale, Ariz.
28. **Rod Billingsley, c, George Mason**
29. **Dan Deville, rhp, Cal State Fullerton**
30. **Matt Toole, ss, Santa Clara**
31. Joel Adamson, lhp, Artesia HS, Lakewood, Calif.
32. Rich Robertson, lhp, San Jacinto (Texas) JC
33. **Charles Thompson, rhp, South Johnson HS, Four Oaks, N.C.**
34. Douglas McConathy, 3b, Western HS, Buena Park, Calif.
35. **Mark Gieseke, 1b/lhp, Cal State Sacramento**
36. **Rico Coleman, of, Grambling State**
37. **Brian Beck, of, Hidden Valley HS, Grants Pass, Ore.**
38. **Ed Zinter, rhp, Brigham Young**
39. **Rafael Santiago, lhp, San Lorenzo, P.R.**

40. **James Joyce, c, Seminole HS, Sanford, Fla.**
41. **Jose Davila, rhp, Santurce, P.R.**
42. Alfredo Suarez, c, San Juan, P. R
43. **Troy Cunningham, rhp, Gonzaga**

SAN FRANCISCO GIANTS

June—Regular Phase (14)

1. **Steve Hosey, of, Fresno State**
2. **Clay Bellinger, ss, Rollins (Fla.)**
3. **Jason McFarlin, of, Pensacola (Fla.) HS**
4. **Mike Grahovac, c/1b, Chapman (Calif.)**
5. **Brian Dour, rhp, Bradley**
6. Renaldo Bullock, of, Proviso West HS, Bellwood, Ill.
7. Matt Watson, rhp, Cal State Fullerton
8. **Frank Carey, 2b, Stanford**
9. **Rafael Novoa, lhp, Villanova**
10. Ricky Ward, ss, Chemeketa (Ore.) JC
11. **Greg Brummett, rhp, Wichita State**
12. **John Carrico, lhp, Purdue**
13. Jeff Gidcumb, rhp, Forida
14. **Roger Miller, c, Georgia**
15. **Pat Rapp, rhp, Southern Mississippi**
16. **Dan Rumsey, of, Arizona State**
17. **Steve Callahan, lhp, Lewis-Clark State (Idaho)**
18. **Ed Gustafson, rhp, Washington State**
19. **Steve Willis, 1b, Arizona State**
20. **Kelly Ahrens, c, Newberry (S.C.)**
21. **Daniel Stenz, lhp, Grand Canyon (Ariz.)**
22. **Dave Hocking, lhp, Oklahoma Baptist**
23. **Stewart Hillman, rhp, Detroit**
24. **Greg Lund, rhp, Kutztown (Pa.)**
25. **Steve Rolen, 3b, West Virginia**
26. **Jeff Brauning, ss/2b, Oregon State**
27. **Jon Schiller, rhp, Central Washington**
28. **Dan Rambo, rhp, Central Michigan**
29. **Mike McDonald, of, Wichita State**
30. **Darren Garrison, lhp, Southwest Missouri State**
31. Eugene Thomas, of, Montgomery (Md.) JC
32. **Clark Huntey, c, Central Michigan**
33. Dan Carlson, rhp, Mount Hood (Ore.) CC
34. **Shawn May, ss/2b, Mansfield (Pa.)**
35. Danny Jenkins, 3b, South Torrance HS, Torrance, Calif.
36. **John Chiaramonte, rhp, Moorpark (Calif.) JC**
37. **Gus Vollmer, of, South Florida**
38. **Ronald Crowe, ss/rhp, Cal Poly San Luis Obispo**
39. Cyrus Crosby, rhp, Seminole State (Okla.) JC
40. **Darren Musselwhite, rhp, Mississippi**
41. **Daniel Henrikson, lhp, Clark (Wash.) JC**
42. **Vince Palyan, of, Minnesota**
43. Tyler Williams, c, North HS, Davenport, Iowa
44. Brian McLeod, rhp, Orange Coast (Calif.) CC
45. Lenny Ayres, rhp, Kennewick (Wash.) HS
46. Albie Lopez, rhp, Westwood HS, Mesa, Ariz.
47. **Heath Jones, 1b, El Camino (Calif.) JC**
48. **Matt Harr, 2b, Briar Cliff (N.Y.)**
49. **Jon Pattin, c, Johnson County (Kan.) JC**
50. Michael Sambito, 1b, Seminole (Fla.) HS

SEATTLE MARINERS

June—Regular Phase (3)

1. **Roger Salkeld, rhp, Saugus (Calif.) HS**
1. Scott Burrell, rhp, Hamden (Conn.) HS (Pick from Athletics as compensation for Type B free agent Mike Moore)
2. (Pick to Orioles as compensation for Type B free agent Tom Niedenfuer)
3. (Pick to Brewers as compensation for Type B free agent Jeffrey Leonard)
4. **Kyle Duke, lhp, Newman Smith HS, Carrollton, Texas**
5. **Jim Gutierrez, rhp, Burlington-Edison HS, Burlington, Wash.**
6. **David Evans, rhp, San Jacinto (Texas) JC**
7. **Scott Lodgek, rhp, North Carolina**
8. **Sean Twitty, of, McClancy Memorial HS, Astoria, N.Y.**
9. **William Kostich, lhp, Taylor Center HS, Taylor, Mich.**
10. **Fred McNair, ss, Bleckley County HS, Cochran, Ga.**
11. Charles Greene, c, Killian HS, Miami
12. **Jim Newlin, rhp, Wichita State**
13. **Mark Brakebill, 3b, Glendale (Ariz.) CC**
14. **Valentine Ballesteros, lhp, Southwestern Michigan JC**
15. **Lash Batley, 1b, Long Beach (Calif.) CC**
16. **Richard Lodding, rhp, Cypress (Calif.) JC**
17. **Oscar Rivas, lhp, Arizona State**
18. Keith Tippett, ss, Ocala Forest HS, Ocala, Fla.
19. **Matthew Kluge, c, Hillsborough HS, Tampa**
20. Pat Russo, rhp, Tampa
21. **Damon Saetre, 1b, Western Michigan**
22. **Mike LeBlanc, rhp, Maine**
23. Dave Mlicki, rhp, Oklahoma State
24. **Melvin DeJesus, rhp, Salinas, P.R.**
25. **Richard Hanlin, of, Cal State San Bernardino**
26. **Darin Loe, rhp, Valley City State (N.D.)**
27. **David Smith, of, Southwestern Louisiana**
28. Philip Black, lhp, North Florida
29. **Winston LeBlanc, ss, Mississippi Delta JC**
30. **Tom Duffin, 3b, South Alabama**
31. Jason Ogden, rhp, San Jacinto (Calif.) JC
32. Bryan Hartman, 1b, Turner HS, Leon, Okla.
33. Darryl Boyd, rhp, JC of the Siskiyous (Calif.)
34. **Israel Seda, 2b, Puerto Real, P.R.**
35. Gaylon Johnson, c, Central Valley HS, Redding, Calif.
36. David Hobbs, rhp, Westwood HS, Fort Pierce, Fla.
37. Steve Surico, lhp, Loyola Marymount
38. Todd Youngblood, ss, Cochise County (Ariz.) CC
39. **Keith Bryant, rhp, Mount Vernon Nazarene (Ohio)**
40. James Schultz, c, Cooper HS, Crystal, Minn.
41. Cedric Allen, lhp, Johnston HS, Austin
42. Joseph Madden, ss/of, Salesian HS, Richmond, Calif.
43. Larry Mitchell, rhp, Charlottesville (Va.) HS
44. Andru Small, 3b, San Bernardino Valley (Calif.) JC
45. L.V. Powell, of, Cerritos (Calif.) JC
46. Jesus Gonzalez, c, Triton (Ill.) JC
47. **Tommy Boudreau, of, Cerritos (Calif.) JC**
48. **Alvin Rittman, ss, Bethune-Cookman**
49. **Landon Williams, ss, Grambling State**
50. Bobby Magallanes, ss, Cerritos (Calif.) JC
51. **Brian Turang, of, Loyola Marymount**
52. **Mark Czarkowski, lhp, Hartford**
53. Brian Morrow, of, El Dorado (Kan.) HS
54. John Johnson, ss, Channel Islands HS, Oxnard, Calif.
55. Brian McGlone, ss, Leto HS, Tampa
56. Andre Keene, 1b, Duval HS, Lanham, Md.
57. Thomas Wilson, of, Troy HS, Yorba Linda, Calif.
58. **James Terrell, of, Hogan HS, Vallejo, Calif.**
59. Ryan Lefebvre, of, Loyola HS, Los Angeles
60. James Beauchamp, rhp, Modesto (Calif.) JC
61. David Utz, rhp, Ocean Springs (Miss.) HS
62. D.J. Boston, 1b/of, Woodward HS, Cincinnati
63. Marcus Urban, rhp, Procter Hug HS, Reno, Nev.
64. Matthew Winton, of, Merced (Calif.) JC
65. Clem Barlow, of, Southern Union State (Ala.) JC
66. Walter Rivera, rhp, Chipola (Fla.) JC (Selection voided)
67. Dusty Madsen, of, Sacramento CC
68. Paul Perkins, rhp, Solano (Calif.) CC
69. Del Marine, 3b, El Camino Real HS, Woodland Hills, Calif.
70. Dexter St. George, of, Lanett (Ala.) HS
71. Sidney Stigall, ss, Eau Gallie HS, Melbourne, Fla.

TEXAS RANGERS

June—Regular Phase (5)

1. **Donald Harris, of, Texas Tech**
2. (Pick to Astros as compensation for Type A free agent Nolan Ryan)
3. **Dan Peltier, of, Notre Dame**
4. **Joey Eischen, lhp, Pasadena (Calif.) CC**
5. **Jason Ayala, rhp, Brighton HS, Sandy, Utah**
6. **Ken Powell, of, Poly HS, Long Beach**
7. **Dave Giberti, lhp, Alhambra HS, Martinez, Calif.**
8. **Jay Franklin, rhp, Oral Roberts**

9. **Randy Marshall, of/1b, Le Moyne**
10. **Steve Rowley, rhp, Tulane**
11. Chris Snopek, ss, Harrison County HS, Cynthiana, Ky.
12. **Barry Winford, c, Mississippi State**
13. **Michael Arner, rhp, Clearwater (Fla.) HS**
14. **Geoff Flinn, ss, Indiana**
15. **George Kerfut, rhp, Pace (N.Y.)**
16. **Rob Brown, rhp, San Diego State**
17. **Mike Burton, 1b, Fresno State**
18. **Kevin Keon, rhp, Le Moyne**
19. **Keith McGough, rhp, Neville HS, Monroe, La.**
20. Ron Rico, of, La Mirada (Calif.) HS
21. **Gerald Alexander, rhp, Tulane**
22. **Bryan Gore, lhp, Oklahoma State**
23. **Tyrone Washington, rhp, Southern**
24. **Travis Buckley, rhp, Johnson County (Kan.) CC**
25. **Troy Eklund, of, Arkansas**
26. **Trevor Haughney, of, St. Raymonds HS, New York**
27. **David Perez, rhp, St. Mary's (Texas)**
28. **Todd Abell, ss/3b, Lynchburg (Va.)**
29. **Roberto Camarillo, ss, Magnolia HS, Anaheim**
30. **Brian Crowley, of, Hartford**
31. **James Clinton, ss/2b, Illinois-Chicago**
32. Mark Slobonik, c, Oakton (Ill.) CC
33. **Brian Roper, c, Texas Tech**
34. **Jose Texidor, of, Juana Diaz, P.R.**
35. David Lavallee, 3b/1b, Rhode Island
36. Gilbert Cleveland, rhp, North Alabama
37. **Kevin Fowler, rhp, Montevallo (Ala.)**
38. **Larry Hays, of, Lubbock Christian (Texas)**
39. **John Graves, rhp, Oklahoma City**
40. **Scott Asche, lhp, Cleveland State**
41. Ben O'Connor, lhp, Maryland-Baltimore County
42. **Stacey Parker, of, UC Irvine**
43. Jason Beauchamp, rhp, Rancho Cordova (Calif.) HS
44. **Brian Scheetz, rhp, Illinois-Chicago**
45. **Eric Bickhardt, rhp, St. Joseph's**
46. Bertland Watson, of, Mount San Jacinto (Calif.) JC
47. Danny Patterson, rhp, San Gabriel HS, Rosemead, Calif.
48. **Dick Phillips, rhp, Vernon (Texas) JC**
49. **Victor Reyes, c, Juayanilla, P.R.**
50. Jeff Gyselman, c, Inglemoor HS, Bothell, Wash.
51. Ronald Reams, of, Laney (Calif.) JC
52. Daniel Madsen, c, Newbury Park HS, Thousand Oaks, Calif.
53. Bryan Leiser, rhp, Ventura (Calif.) JC
54. Avery Duval, rhp, Hernando HS, Brooksville, Fla.
55. **Brandon Devereaux, lhp, American Fork (Utah) HS**
56. Gabriel Angulo, of, Miami-Dade South JC
57. David Eggert, lhp, Ventura (Calif.) JC
58. Tory Winrow, ss/3b, Helix HS, Lemon Grove, Calif.
59. Michael Weisenberg, c, St. Francis HS, Pasadena, Calif.

TORONTO BLUE JAYS

June—Regular Phase (19)

1. **Eddie Zosky, ss, Fresno State**
2. Michael Moore, of, Beverly Hills (Calif.) HS
2. **Brent Bowers, of, St. Laurence HS, Burbank, Ill.** (Supplemental pick—60th—for loss of Type C free agent Rick Leach)
3. **John Olerud, 1b/lhp, Washington State**
4. Troy Bradford, rhp, Cochise County (Ariz.) CC
5. **Ricky Steed, rhp, Covina (Calif.) HS**
6. **Marc Loeb, c, San Bernardino (Calif.) Valley JC**
7. **Jeff Irish, c, Milford HS, Highland, Mich.**
8. **Lonell Roberts, of, Bloomington (Calif.) HS**
9. Jeffrey Hammonds, of, Scotch Plains-Fanwood HS, Scotch Plains, N.J.
10. **Shawn Holtzclaw, of, Auburn**
11. Ned Darley, rhp, Manning (S.C.) HS
12. **Walter Heckel, 2b, St. John's**
13. **Michael Taylor, lhp, Hillsborough HS, Tampa**
14. **Robert Blumberg, lhp, Nicholls State**
15. **Scott Gordon, rhp, Xavier**
16. Pat Leahy, rhp, Eisenhower HS, Yakima, Wash.
17. **Dante Reid, of/lhp, Geneva (N.Y.) HS**
18. Kipp Jeffries, ss, Etiwanda HS, Rialto, Calif.
19. **Gerald Crump, of, Upland HS, Fontana, Calif.**
20. **Jeff Kent, ss, California**
21. **Gregg Martin, rhp, Northwestern**
22. **Aaron Small, rhp, South Hills HS, West Covina, Calif.**
23. Angel Reyes, lhp/of, Coamo, P.R.
24. **Sean Hearn, of, Worthing HS, Houston**
25. **Scott Fritz, rhp, Southside HS, Muncie, Ind.**
26. C.J. Kerr, lhp, Cerritos (Calif.) JC
27. **Andrew Rooney, 1b, Ocean County (N.J.) JC**
28. **Sterling Stock, rhp, Pacific Lutheran (Wash.)**
29. **Daren Brown, rhp, Southeastern Oklahoma State**
30. **Allen Tyson, rhp, Gulf Coast (Fla.) CC**
31. Douglas Hekking, rhp, Ohlone (Calif.) JC
32. **Norbert Wilson, of, Renaissance HS, Detroit**
33. Eric Johnson, c, Chatsworth (Calif.) HS
34. Keith Hines, of, Chipola (Fla.) JC
35. Stephen Adams, rhp, Olustee (Okla.) HS
36. **Kristopher Harmes, c, Donegal HS, Mount Joy, Pa.**
37. **Darren Kizziah, rhp, Western Kentucky**
38. **Kenny Kulina, lhp, Jacksonville**
39. **Greg Bicknell, rhp, Fresno CC**
40. **Chris Beacom, 2b/1b, Northwestern**
41. **Kevin Meyers, ss, Southwestern Louisiana**
42. Jason Miller, 3b, Plattsburg (N.Y.) HS
43. **Brad Mengel, 3b, Cal State Los Angeles**
44. Gracia Martinez, ss, Toa Baja, P.R.
45. Vic Merritt, 1b, Nicholls State
46. Shannon Jackson, lhp, Shelton State (Ala.) CC
47. Thomas Leahy, rhp, Howard (Texas) JC
48. Bob Aylmer, lhp, Fordham
49. Jason DeLeon, of, Burroughs HS, Ridgecrest, Calif.
50. Robert Moose, 1b, Lake Howell HS, Maitland, Fla.
51. Robert Barber, c, Sommers, Mont.
52. Thomas Froning, lhp, Sidney (Ohio) HS
53. Randy Powers, rhp, Southern California
54. Jose Flores, ss, Cidra, P.R.
55. Mike Daniel, c, Connors State (Okla.) JC
56. Jon Shave, 2b, Mississippi State
57. Thomas Brown, lhp, Delaware Tech JC
58. David Gray, rhp, Banning (Calif.) HS
59. Ricardo Serpo, of, Bayamon, P.R.
60. Leland Patterson, rhp, Riverside (Calif.) CC
61. Travis Sexton, c/of, Taylor HS, Kokomo, Ind.
62. David Fletcher, rhp, Mount San Jacinto (Calif.) JC
63. Gregory Lewis, of, Newburgh Free Academy HS, Newburgh, N.Y.
64. Thomas Irwin, rhp, Orange Coast (Calif.) JC
65. Ricky Otero, of, Vega Baja, P.R.
66. Jeff Lawrence, lhp, Palomar (Calif.) JC
67. Jeffery Cheek, rhp, Pensacola (Fla.) JC
68. Lee Daniels, ss/3b, Wilcox County HS, Rochelle, Ga.
69. Peter Stacey, c, Granite Hills HS, El Cajon, Calif.
70. LaBradford Smith, rhp, Louisville
71. Robert Tucker, c, Santee, Calif.
72. James Bostock, 2b/ss, De La Salle Collegiate HS, New Baltimore, Mich.
73. Marc Palmieri, rhp, Chaminade HS, Melville, N.Y.
74. Mark St. Claire, c, Whitehall (N.Y.) HS
75. Bert Emanuel, of, Langham Creek HS, Houston

BOISE HAWKS (NORTHWEST LEAGUE)

June—Regular Phase

1. No selection
2. No selection
3. No selection
4. **Paul Cluff, 2b, Brigham Young**
5. **Darrell MacMillan, c, Kennesaw (Ga.)**

1990 VAN POPPEL FALLS TO ATHLETICS AND GETS HIS PAYDAY, BUT BRAVES SCORE BIG WITH BACKUP PLAN

Triggered by a lucrative new television deal, major league teams went on a spending spree in 1990.

They spent freely at the big league level, introducing the huge multi-year, multimillion-dollar contracts that so inflated payrolls in years to come. But they also spent freely on amateur talent, paying out some of the biggest bonuses in draft history.

The biggest jackpot from the 1990 draft went to Texas schoolboy sensation Todd Van Poppel, who signed a major league deal with the defending World Series champion Athletics that included a $500,000 bonus and was worth $1.2 million overall. It was the first multi-year contract ever signed by a high school player and only the fourth in draft history. The $1.2 million package was the largest ever.

Van Poppel's deal raised the average bonus for first-round picks to more than $250,000—up 37 percent from 1989, a year that itself saw a sharp increase. Every first-round pick in 1990 got a bonus of at least $175,000, and for the first time since 1985, every first-round pick signed.

R & R SPORTS GROUP

Todd Van Poppel got his payday but never fulfilled his promise in the big leagues

Van Poppel was singled out as the top prospect in the draft early in the process, but he complicated the picture by saying he did not intend to sign and wanted to attend the University of Texas.

The Braves held the first pick and met frequently with Van Poppel to determine if they would be able to sign him. The last meeting took place a day before the draft. Convinced they couldn't, the Braves took Chipper Jones, a high school shortstop from Pierson, Fla., as their fallback pick.

The next 12 clubs also passed on Van Poppel, and Oakland took him 14th overall. The A's could gamble because they had seven picks in the first two rounds

Van Poppel initially expressed displeasure at being drafted by Oakland.

"If they think they can buy me, they're wrong," he said. "Money's not everything. The things I want to do, money can't buy. I've got to mature as a person and as a ballplayer. I think I can do that in college."

A's officials took a low-pressure approach to negotiations with Van Poppel, his father Hank and agent Scott Boras. About a month after the draft, Van Poppel signed.

As fate would have it, of course, Jones proved to be the much better player, winning a National League MVP award in 1999 and becoming a fixture in the middle of the Braves lineup for years. He established himself as one of the best switch-hitters in baseball history and completed his 15th full season with the Braves in 2009.

Van Poppel, in part burdened by the fast track his major league contract put him on, never made a significant contribution in Oakland and bounced around the big leagues as a middle reliever. The A's, in fact, got little from their draft bonanza.

Oakland got Van Poppel and six other picks in the first two rounds, and spent all but two of the picks on pitchers. Van Poppel and the other three first-rounders—righthander Don Peters, lefthander David Zancanaro and righthander Kirk Dressendorfer—were referred to as the Four Aces, but none made a signifcant contribution in the big leagues. Peters and Zancanaro never even reached the majors.

The Expos had an even bigger windfall, with 10 selections in the first two rounds. They spent more than $1.2 million to sign all 10 picks, and went on to sign every pick through the first 24 rounds, some 22 players in all. The most notable success story from the group was outfielder Rondell White, a first-rounder who played 15 seasons in the major leagues and finished with a .284 career average.

Overall, 1,487 players were drafted in 1990, three fewer than the record number in 1989. The Astros, who picked a record 87 players in '89, topped that figure by taking 100 players in 1990. They signed just 29 of them, but retained the rights to 52 who went to junior colleges.

Bonus Inflation Skyrockets

Van Poppel's rich deal continued the escalation of bonuses, a spending spree in which the 10 largest bonuses of the draft era were paid out in a 12-month period, ending in July 1990.

Alex Fernandez, who two years earlier turned down $150,000 as Milwaukee's first-round pick, signed with the White Sox for $350,000 as the fourth overall pick. The Tigers, with the second pick, went up to $500,000 to sign Tony Clark, while also agreeing to let him play basketball at Arizona. The Indians, drafting eighth, spent $300,000 for Iowa shortstop Tim Costo, regarded as the top power hitter in the college ranks.

The Blue Jays gambled their first two picks on righthander Steve Karsay and third baseman Chris Weinke and spent big money to sign them.

Karsay had asked to have his name taken out of the draft because he wanted to attend Louisiana State, but Toronto picked him anyway and signed him for $325,000.

Weinke was one of the nation's best prep quarterbacks and had already started fall football practice at Florida State when the Jays signed him for $375,000. Weinke never made it to the big leagues with Toronto and returned to Florida State to play football in 1997. He led the Seminoles to a national championship in 1999 and won the Heisman Trophy in 2000 at the age of 28, going on to play in the NFL with the Carolina Panthers.

And after a Northwest League team participated in the 1989 draft, two independent Class A clubs took players in 1990, jumping in beginning with the fourth round, as provided by draft rules at the time.

The New York-Penn League's Erie Sailors took only one player, but the Florida State League's Miami Miracle took 16, including future big leaguer Mike Lansing in the sixth round. Many of the players the Miracle took were legitimate prospects.

Many major league clubs didn't like the Miracle's tactics, but team owner Marv Goldklang said his club could not get enough talent from major league clubs. The Miracle paid out bonuses totaling about $250,000 and signed 15 of their picks, later selling many of their contracts to major league organizations.

"It was absolutely a last resort," Goldklang said. "In life, you do what you have to do. If the help was forthcoming, there's a good chance we would not have participated in the draft."

In large part because of the Miracle, draft rules were changed to prevent minor league clubs from participating.

DRAFT 90: FIRST-ROUND PICKS

No.	Club	Player, Pos.	School	Hometown	Ht.	Wt.	B-T	Age
1.	Braves	Chipper Jones, ss	Bolles School	Jacksonville, Fla.	6-3	185	B-R	18
2.	Tigers	Tony Clark, of	Christian HS	El Cajon, Calif.	6-7	207	B-R	17
3.	Phillies	Mike Lieberthal, c	Westlake HS	Westlake Village, Calif.	6-0	170	R-R	18
4.	White Sox	Alex Fernandez, rhp	Miami-Dade South CC	Miami	6-2	200	R-R	20
5.	Pirates	Kurt Miller, rhp	West HS	Bakersfield, Calif.	6-5	195	R-R	17
6.	Mariners	Marc Newfield, 1b	Marina HS	Hunt. Beach, Calif.	6-4	210	R-R	17
7.	Reds	Dan Wilson, c	Minnesota	Barrington, Ill.	6-3	185	R-R	21
8.	Indians	Tim Costo, ss	Iowa	Glen Ellyn, Ill.	6-5	205	R-R	21
9.	Dodgers	Ron Walden, lhp	Blanchard HS	Blanchard, Okla.	6-3	180	L-L	17
10.	Yankees	Carl Everett, of	Hillsborough HS	Tampa	6-0	190	B-R	18
11.	Expos	Shane Andrews, 3b	Carlsbad HS	Carlsbad, N.M.	6-2	210	R-R	18
12.	Twins	Todd Ritchie, rhp	Duncanville HS	Duncanville, Texas	6-3	180	R-R	18
13.	Cardinals	Donovan Osborne, lhp	Nevada-Las Vegas	Carson City, Nev.	6-2	180	L-L	20
14.	Athletics	Todd Van Poppel, rhp	Martin HS	Arlington, Texas	6-5	195	R-R	18
15.	Giants	Adam Hyzdu, of	Moeller HS	Cincinnati	6-3	210	R-R	18
16.	Rangers	Dan Smith, lhp	Creighton	Apple Valley, Minn.	6-5	190	L-L	20
17.	Mets	Jeromy Burnitz, of	Oklahoma State	Conroe, Texas	6-0	195	B-R	21
18.	Cardinals	Aaron Holbert, ss	Jordan HS	Long Beach	6-0	170	R-R	17
19.	Giants	Eric Christopherson, c	San Diego State	Hunt. Beach, Calif.	6-1	190	R-R	21
20.	Orioles	Mike Mussina, rhp	Stanford	Montoursville, Pa.	6-2	185	R-R	21
21.	Astros	Tom Nevers, ss.	Edina HS	Edina, Minn.	6-1	185	B-R	18
22.	Blue Jays	Steve Karsay, rhp	Christ The King HS	Queens, N.Y.	6-3	185	R-R	18
23.	Cubs	Lance Dickson, lhp	Arizona	La Mesa, Calif.	6-1	185	R-L	20
24.	Expos	Rondell White, of	Jones County HS	Gray, Ga.	6-1	185	R-R	18
25.	Padres	Robbie Beckett, lhp	McCallum HS	Austin, Texas	6-6	225	L-L	17
26.	Athletics	Don Peters, rhp	St. Francis (Ill.)	Crestwood, Ill.	5-11	180	R-R	20

1990

CLUB-BY-CLUB SELECTIONS

ATLANTA BRAVES

June—Regular Phase (1)

1. **Chipper Jones, ss, Bolles School, Jacksonville**
2. (Pick to Red Sox as compensation for Type B free agent Nick Esasky)
3. **Lance Marks, of, Dana Hills HS, Dana Point, Calif.**
4. **Johnny Walker, of, Texas**
5. **Joe Ayrault, c, Sarasota (Fla.) HS**
6. Ken Reed, 3b/1b, Hamilton (Ohio) HS
7. **Ed Giovanola, ss, Santa Clara**
8. **Armando Rodriguez, of, JC of San Mateo (Calif.)**
9. **Brian Kowitz, of, Clemson**
10. **Tony Graffanino, ss, East Islip (N.Y.) HS**
11. Phil Stidham, rhp, Arkansas
12. **Brian Bark, lhp/of, North Carolina State**
13. Damon Lembi, 3b/1b, Burlingame (Calif.) HS
14. **Kian Sly, of/1b, San Diego (Calif.) HS**
15. **Adrian Garcia, c, Elizabeth (N.J.) HS**
16. Michael Tarter, c, Walton HS, Marietta, Ga.
17. **Jerome Koller, rhp, Martinsville (Ind.) HS**
18. **Mike Potts, lhp, Gordon (Ga.) JC**
19. **Juan Williams, of, Ramona HS, Riverside, Calif.**
20. **Ralph Garr, of, Bellaire HS, Missouri City, Texas**
21. James King, rhp, Gordon (Ga.) JC
22. **Stewart Ford, lhp, Ranger (Texas) JC**
23. Matthew Wagner, rhp, Cedar Falls (Iowa) HS
24. **Jason Kempfer, rhp, Sparta HS, Baldwin, Ill.**
25. **Cory Mathis, of, Gonzales (Texas) HS**
26. **Michael Place, rhp, St. Petersburg (Fla.) JC**
27. **Larry Owens, lhp, Armstrong State (Ga.)**
28. **Loren Gross, 1b, Hutchinson (Kan.) JC**
29. **Scott Ryder, rhp, Georgia Southern**
30. David Hollingsworth, rhp, Middle Georgia JC
31. **Gerald Trevino, ss, Pleasanton (Texas) HS**
32. **Kevin O'Connor, of, Illinois**
33. **Doyle Moore, of, Madison Heights HS, Anderson, Ind.**
34. Dustin Longenecker, of, Parkview HS, Stone Mountain, Ga.
35. Scott Watkins, lhp, Seminole State (Okla.) JC
36. **Brian Dare, lhp, Texas**
37. Adrian Jones, of/rhp, Missouri-St. Louis
38. **Don Robinson, of, Haynesville (La.) HS**
39. Jason Wood, ss, Fresno (Calif.) CC
40. Chris Chandler, ss, Beverly Hills (Calif.) HS
41. Amauri Rodriguez, 2b, Caguas, P.R.
42. **John Wilder, rhp/ss, South Florence HS, Florence, S.C.**
43. William Maitland, rhp, Dinwiddie County HS, Sutherland, Va.
44. Christopher Robbins, rhp, Union County HS, Blairsville, Ga.
45. Ja'Rad Hunt, 2b/3b, McNair HS, Atlanta, Ga.
46. **Samuel Rutter, rhp, Abingdon (Va.) HS**
47. **Shannon Ledwick, rhp, Ranger (Texas) JC**
48. Jake Green, ss/rhp, Suwannee HS, Live Oak, Fla.
49. Adan Garcia, rhp, Gadsden HS, Anthony, N.M.
50. Joseph Hiller, rhp, Stratford Academy HS, Macon, Ga.
51. Reed Garwood, 1b, Deerfield Winds HS, Albany, Ga.
52. Mark Beeman, 3b, Carlsbad (N.M.) HS
53. Richard Freeman, 3b, Bellaire HS, Houston, Texas
54. Kelly Wunsch, lhp, Bellaire HS, Houston, Texas
55. **Tommy Owen, c, Georgia**
56. Jason Gonzales, ss, Blinn (Texas) JC
57. Gary Herrmann, lhp, Blinn (Texas) JC
58. Brad Riddle, of, Morton (Ill.) JC
59. Darrett Robinson, of, Bellaire HS, Houston, Texas
60. **James Arendt, of, Montezuma (Iowa) HS**
61. Jamine Adams, of, Canyon Springs HS, Moreno Valley, Calif.
62. **Mark Chambers, of, Northern Iowa**
63. **Anthony Johnson, of, Huston Tillotson (Texas)**
64. Robert Valdez, lhp, El Dorado HS, Albuquerque, N.M.
65. Greg Quinn, of, Shadow Mountain HS, Phoenix
66. Victor McCraney, of, Taft (Calif.) JC
67. James Richardson, of, Westark (Ark.) JC
68. Robert Hooker, ss, Norland HS, Miami

BALTIMORE ORIOLES

June—Regular Phase (20)

1. **Mike Mussina, rhp, Stanford**
2. **Erik Schullstrom, rhp, Fresno State**
2. **Jeff Williams, rhp, Wichita State** (Supplemental pick—69th—for loss of Type C free agent Dave Schmidt).
3. **Mike Thomas, of, Richmond County HS, Rockingham, N.C.**
4. Chris West, 1b/3b, Eastern Wayne HS, Goldsboro, N.C.
5. **Bobby Chouinard, rhp, Forest Grove (Ore.) HS**
6. **Brad Tyler, ss, Evansville**
7. **John Hale, lhp, South Alabama**
8. Mike Daniel, c, Oklahoma State
9. **Roy Hodge, of, St. Thomas, Virgin Islands**
10. **Damon Buford, 2b/of, Southern California**
11. **Gordon Graham, 1b, Hershey (Pa.) HS**
12. **Jason Alstead, of, St. Cloud State (Minn.)**
13. **Kip Yaughn, rhp, Arizona State**
14. **Scott Miley, of, Mission HS, San Jose, Calif.**
15. Duane Page, rhp, Ocean View HS, Westminster, Calif.
16. Willie Speakman, c, Fullerton (Calif.) JC
17. **Steve Godin, of, East Carolina**
18. **Brett Benge, rhp, Rend Lake (Ill.) JC**
19. **Brent Miller, 1b, Middle Georgia JC**
20. **Steve DiMarco, 3b, C.W. Post (N.Y.)**
21. **Daniel Ramirez, ss, Tennessee**
22. **Scott McClain, rhp, Atascadero (Calif.) HS**
23. **Justin Evans, of, Betheny (Okla.) HS**
24. **Scott Sprick, ss, Jacksonville State**
25. **Michael Hebb, rhp, Anne Arundel (Md.) CC**
26. **David Paveloff, rhp, Chapman (Calif.)**
27. **Michael Lamitola, 2b, Seton Hall**
28. Dom DeSantis, rhp, New Orleans
29. Jason Hutchins, rhp, Golden West (Calif.) JC
30. Robin Jennings, of, Annandale HS, Alexandria, Va.
31. **Todd Unrein, lhp, Southwestern Louisiana**
32. **Greg Hays, rhp, Long Beach State**
33. **Jim Dedrick, rhp, Southern California**
34. Matt Jarvis, lhp, La Cueva HS, Albuquerque, N.M.
35. Anthony Simas, rhp, St. Joseph HS, Santa Maria, Calif.
36. Kyle Allred, ss, Murray State (Okla.) JC
37. **Ihosvany Marquez, rhp, Miami Springs HS, Hialeah, Fla.**
38. **Jose Millares, 3b, Azusa Pacific (Calif.)**
39. Jon Nunnally, c, Hargrave Military Academy, Pelham, N.C.
40. Kevin Ryan, rhp, Seminole State (Okla.) JC
41. David McLaughlin, ss, Milwaukie (Ore.) HS
42. Dennis Van Pelt, of/1b, Long Branch (N.J.) HS
43. Doug McConathy, 1b/3b, Cypress (Calif.) JC
44. **Doug Flowers, c, North Carolina Wesleyan**

BOSTON RED SOX

June—Regular Phase (18)

1. (Pick to Cardinals as compensation for Type A free agent Tony Pena)
2. **Frank Rodriguez, rhp/ss, Eastern District HS, Brooklyn, N.Y.** (Pick from Braves as compensation for Type B free agent Nick Esasky)
2. (Pick to Twins as compensation for Type A free agent Jeff Reardon)
3. **Walt McKeel, c, Greene Central HS, Snow Hill, N.C.**
4. Greg Thomas, of, Lake Brantley HS, Altamonte Springs, Fla.
5. **Tim Tackett, c, Waverly (Ohio) HS**
6. **Gar Finnvold, rhp, Florida State**

7. **Todd Miller, rhp, Temple**
8. Aaron Knieper, rhp, Nouvel Catholic HS, Saginaw, Mich.
9. John Collett, rhp, Citrus (Calif.) JC
10. **Rikchy Borrero, c, Hormigueros, P.R.**
11. **Terry Powers, rhp, Volunteer State (Tenn.) CC**
12. **David Schmidt, 2b, Southwestern (Calif.) CC**
13. **Greg Graham, ss, Louisville**
14. **Quinn Feno, 1b/of, New Bedford (Mass.) HS**
15. **Bruce Chick, of, Georgia**
16. **Erik Plantenberg, lhp, San Diego State**
17. Evan Pratte, 2b/ss, Southwest Missouri State
18. Robert Henkel, lhp, San Jacinto (Texas) JC
19. **Brian Young, rhp, Ohio**
20. **Mike DeKneef, ss, Lewis-Clark State (Idaho)**
21. Chad Trahan, rhp, Seminole State (Okla.) JC
22. **David Klvac, lhp, San Jacinto (Texas) JC**
23. **Ryan Maloney, lhp, Lancaster (Ohio) HS**
24. **Tim Smith, rhp, Boston College**
25. **William Norris, 3b, Eckerd (Fla.)**
26. Les Norman, of, St. Francis (Ill.)
27. **Chris Davis, rhp, JC of the Sequoias (Calif.)**
28. **John Crimmins, c, Norwood (Mass.) HS**
29. **Scott Bethea, ss, Louisiana State**
30. Jerry Burns, rhp, Napa Valley (Calif.) JC
31. Jeffrey Johnson, rhp, Fresno (Calif.) CC
32. Joseph Mondello, c, San Jacinto (Texas) JC
33. James Young, of, Weaver (Ala.) HS
34. Nicolas Ortiz, 3b/ss, Cidra, P.R.
35. (Selection voided)
36. **Tim Davis, 2b, Southern Illinois**
37. Greg Sorrell, 1b/of, Poway HS, San Diego

CALIFORNIA ANGELS

June—Regular Phase (24)

1. (Pick to Expos as compensation for Type A free agent Mark Langston)
2. **Phil Leftwich, rhp, Radford**
3. **Brandon Markewicz, ss, Dixie Hollins HS, St. Petersburg, Fla.**
4. **Garret Anderson, of, Kennedy HS, Granada Hills, Calif.**
5. Doug Creek, lhp, Georgia Tech
6. **Troy Percival, c, UC Riverside**
7. **Randy Powers, rhp, Southern California**
8. **Dan Gil, c, Southern California**
9. **Mark Simmons, 3b, Morgan Park HS, Chicago**
10. **J.R. Showalter, ss, Georgia**
11. **Mike Pineiro, 3b, West Covina (Calif.) HS**
12. **Joe Bertucci, 3b, Ridgewood HS, Port Richey, Fla.**
13. Ryan Hancock, rhp, Monta Vista HS, Cupertino, Calif.
14. **Fausto Tejero, c, Florida International**
15. Jermaine Allensworth, ss, Madison Heights HS, Anderson, Ind.
16. **Wayne Johnson, ss, Oklahoma Christian**
17. **Todd McCray, rhp, Florida**
18. **Mark Dalesandro, c, Illinois**
19. **Brian Grebeck, ss, San Diego State**
20. **P.J. Forbes, 2b, Wichita State**
21. **Ken Edenfield, rhp, Western Kentucky**
22. **Brian Guzik, ss, Greater Latrobe (Pa.) HS**
23. **Joe Williams, 3b, New Mexico State**
24. **Don Barbara, 1b, Long Beach State**
25. Drew Christman, of, Midwest City (Okla.) HS
26. **Britt Craven, rhp, Pepperdine**
27. **Vladimiro Alcaraz, 1b, West Valley HS, Spokane, Wash.**
28. Brian Toney-Gay, of, Morritton (Ark.) HS
29. Mark Ledinsky, lhp/of, JC of Lake County (Ill.)
30. Kevin Lewis, c, Indian River (Fla.) CC
31. **Louis Pakele, rhp, Hawaii-Hilo**
32. Dave Berg, 2b, Sacramento CC
33. **Jeff Ball, rhp, Hawaii**
34. Todd Hall, ss, Sacramento CC
35. **Theron Heusman, lhp, El Reno (Okla.) JC**
36. **Joseph Hardwick, of, Nashua (N.H.) HS**
37. **Ronald Watson, rhp, Eckerd (Fla.)**
38. **Elgin Bobo, 1b/c, Sonoma State (Calif.)**
39. Todd Blyleven, rhp, Villa Park (Calif.) HS
40. John Deremer, rhp, San Jose (Calif.) CC
41. Joshua Hurst, ss, Glendale (Ariz.) CC
42. Jay Hassel, rhp, Rancho Santiago (Calif.) JC
43. Tony Gonzales, ss, Rubidoux HS, Mira Loma, Calif.
44. **Todd Refnes, rhp, Cal Poly San Luis Obispo**
45. Alfredo Diaz, ss, El Monte (Calif.) HS
46. Steven Morgan, of, Tate HS, Gonzales, Fla.
47. Earl Partrick, c, Tate HS, Gonzales, Fla.
48. Martin Malloy, ss/2b, Trenton (Fla.) HS
49. **Eric Buechele, c, Fresno State**
50. Tony Rice, c, Notre Dame
51. Jerry McLemore, of, Waxahachie (Texas) HS
52. Brian Duva, 2b/of, Oak Hall HS, Gainesville, Fla.
53. Joe Davis, ss, Central Arizona JC
54. Bimbo Coles, ss, Virginia Tech

CHICAGO CUBS

June—Regular Phase (23)

1. **Lance Dickson, lhp, Arizona**
2. **Ryan Hawblitzel, rhp, Leonard HS, West Palm Beach, Fla.**
2. **Troy Bradford, rhp, Arizona** (Supplemental pick—72nd—for loss of Type C free agent Scott Sanderson)
3. **Tim Parker, rhp, Clemson**
4. **Sean Cheetham, rhp, Woodbridge (Va.) HS**
5. **Tyson Godfrey, rhp, Aberdeen (Wash.) HS**
6. Ronnie Brown, of, Manatee (Fla.) JC
7. **Adrian Sanchez, lhp, Rio Grande HS, Albuquerque, N.M.**
8. **Phil Dauphin, of, Indiana**
9. **Jim Wolff, c, Palm Beach (Fla.) JC**
10. Randy Ortega, c, Lincoln HS, Stockton, Calif.
11. **Michael Young, rhp, Anderson (Ind.)**
12. Pedro Valdes, lhp, Loiza, P.R.
13. Steve Gurtner, rhp, Holy Cross HS, Chalmette, La.
14. **Scott Gardner, rhp, Imperial Valley (Calif.) JC**
15. **Joe Porcelli, lhp, Iona**
16. Travis Woods, of, Santa Monica (Calif.) CC
17. **Willie Gardner, of, Tupelo (Miss.) HS**
18. **Mike Gabbani, c, Cal State Dominguez Hills**
19. **Ken Krahenbuhl, rhp, San Bernardino (Calif.) HS**
20. **Steve Coffey, ss, Massachusetts**
21. **Jim Robinson, c, Mississippi State**
22. **Joe Blasucci, 2b, Palm Beach (Fla.) JC**
23. **Brian Wilson, ss, Modesto (Calif.) JC**
24. Glenn Delafield, of, Denham Springs (La.) HS
25. **John DeRicco, 1b, Nevada-Reno**
26. Kurt Bierek, 3b, Glencoe HS, Hillsboro, Ore.
27. Patrick Huston, 3b, Los Angeles Pierce JC
28. Angel Abreu, rhp, Guaynabo, P.R.
29. Jay Meyer, lhp, Johnson County (Kan.) CC
30. **Andy Hartung, 3b, Maine**
31. **Charles Kirk, rhp, Jacksonville**
32. Benjamin Bryant, rhp, San Jacinto (Texas) JC
33. **J.R. Postiff, 3b, Fresno State**
34. Steven Walker, of, Lee County HS, Leesburg, Ga.
35. Jorge Santiago, 3b, Bayamon, P.R.
36. Ramon Martinez, ss, Toa Alta, P.R.
37. Edwin Zayas, rhp, Luquillo, P.R.
38. Darren Stumberger, 3b/1b, Spanish River HS, Boca Raton, Fla.
39. Mike Schmitz, 1b, Coconut Creek (Fla.) HS
40. James Riggio, rhp, Chamberlain HS, Tampa, Fla.
41. Ricardo Serpa, of/lhp, Bayamon, P.R.
42. **Tommy Helms, 2b, Western Hills HS, Cincinnati**
43. Travis Champion, of, Hibriten HS, Lenoir, N.C.
44. Jeff Mapson, c, Pairndale (Calif.) HS
45. **Rolando Fernandez, of, Northwestern State**

CHICAGO WHITE SOX

June—Regular Phase (4)

1. **Alex Fernandez, rhp, Miami-Dade South CC**
2. **Bob Wickman, rhp, Wisconsin-Whitewater**
2. Eric Maloney, rhp, Carmel HS, Mundelein, Ill. (Supplemental pick—67th—for loss of Type C free agent Richard Dotson)

3. **Robert Ellis, rhp, Panola (Texas) JC**
4. **James Baldwin Jr., rhp, Pinecrest HS, Southern Pines, N.C.**
5. **Ray Durham, 2b, Harding HS, Charlotte, N.C.**
6. **Charles Poe, of, West Covina (Calif.) HS**
7. **Mike Vogel, c/of, Cretin HS, Brooklyn Park, Minn.**
8. **Nathaniel James, of, Lake Mary HS, Altamonte Springs, Fla.**
9. **Doug McGraw, rhp, Duncanville (Texas) HS**
10. **Jonathon Taylor, c, Alcorn Central HS, Corinth, Miss.**
11. **Keith Strange, c, Oregon Tech**
12. **Jimmy Hurst, of, Central HS, Tuscaloosa, Ala.**
13. **Rodney Bolton, rhp, Kentucky**
14. Fred Starks, rhp, Brevard (Fla.) CC
15. **Mike Bradish, 1b, Christ College-Irvine (Calif.)**
16. **Jeff DiNuzzo, rhp, Seton Hall**
17. **Larry Gilligan, 2b, Brookdale (N.J.) CC**
18. **Brandon Wilson, ss, Kentucky**
19. **Kerry Valrie, of, Southern Mississippi**
20. **Jonathan Jenkins, rhp, East Carolina**
21. **Muzzy Jackson, 1b, Mercer**
22. **Terry Marshall, lhp, Sweet Water HS, Nanafalia, Ala.**
23. **Todd Altaffer, lhp, Jacksonville State**
24. Mark Gilreath, rhp, Brevard (Fla.) JC
25. **Jonathan Story, ss/2b, Southern**
26. **Vince Zarate, of, Kennedy HS, New York**
27. **James Coachman, 1b, Troy State**
28. Dennis McCaffery, of, Villanova
29. Dan Magee, lhp, Jackson State
30. **Roosevelt Smith, rhp, Southern**
31. **Todd Hotz, lhp, Texas**
32. Corey Austin, 1b/of, Faulkner State (Ala.) JC
33. Jason Hisey, rhp, Arizona
34. Billy Warner, rhp, Central Private HS, Greenell Springs, La.
35. Cedrick Thomas, lhp, Gulf Coast (Fla.) CC
36. **Jason Bere, rhp, Middlesex (Mass.) CC**
37. Ron Scott, lhp, Sarasota (Fla.) HS
38. **Tim Green-Shornock, 1b, Marlboro HS, Morganville, N.J.**
39. Mike Potter, rhp, Central Arizona JC
40. **Greg McGough, c, Northeast Louisiana**
41. Matt Skrmetta, rhp, Satellite Beach (Fla.) HS
42. Mike Hancock, lhp, Volunteer State (Tenn.) CC
43. **Donald Culberson, rhp, East Central (Texas)**
44. Karun Jackson, ss, Bishop State (Ala.) JC
45. Allen Battle, of, South Alabama
46. Eric Chapman, of, Garrett (Md.) CC
47. Chad Zerbe, lhp, Gaither HS, Tampa
48. Emanuel Hayes, ss, Forest Brook HS, Houston
49. **Andrew Hoey, rhp, Central Washington**
50. John Timko, c, Clearwater (Fla.) HS
51. Clemente Gordon, c, Grambling State
52. Steve Davis, rhp, Angelina (Texas) JC
53. Chris Hitt, lhp, Jersey Village HS, Houston
54. Brad Kantor, 3b/c, Manatee (Fla.) JC
55. Mike Badorek, rhp, Olivet Nazarene (Ill.)
56. Greg Elliott, ss, Pearl River (Miss.) JC
57. Anthony Box, ss/of, Brookwood (Ala.) HS

CINCINNATI REDS

June—Regular Phase (7)

1. **Dan Wilson, c, Minnesota**
2. **Keith Gordon, ss, Wright State**
3. **Dan Tobin, rhp, Dowagiac Union HS, Dowagiac, Mich.**
4. **Mike Ferry, rhp, Auburn**
5. **Kevin Aubin, c, Drury HS, Stamford, Vt.**
6. **Steve Gibralter, of, Duncanville (Texas) HS**
7. **Juan Loyola, of, Canuy, P.R.**
8. **Larry Luebbers, rhp, Kentucky**
9. Ken Carlyle, rhp, Mississippi
10. Clifton Foster, rhp, Angelina (Texas) JC
11. Shannon Jones, ss, Aurora (Colo.) Central HS
12. **John Roper, rhp, Hoke County HS, Raeford, N.C.**
13. **Derick Graham, of, Hoke County HS, Raeford, N.C.**
14. **Bobby Perna, 3b, Cumberland (Tenn.)**
15. Randy Albaladejo, c, Vega Alta, P.R.
16. Shane Halter, ss, Seminole State (Okla.) JC
17. **Tucker Hammargren, 1b/c, Arizona State**
18. Brian Carlin, of, Angelina (Texas) JC
19. **Kevin Berry, rhp, Northwestern State**
20. Marc Valdes, rhp, Jesuit HS, Tampa
21. Mark Fields, of, Washington HS, Los Angeles
22. Martis Aviles, lhp, Levittown, P.R.
23. Joseph Wallace, c, Granite City (Ill.) HS
24. Ryan Towns, rhp, Gonzales (Texas) HS
25. **Greg Margheim, lhp, Virginia Tech**
26. Brian Hierholzer, c, Blue Valley North HS, Overland Park, Kan.
27. Scott Connor, rhp, Gateway HS, Aurora, Colo.
28. **Kevin Riggs, 2b, East Carolina**
29. Mark Mann, rhp, McNicholas HS, Cincinnati
30. Craig Bolcerek, c, Brenham (Texas) HS
31. Jorge Ortiz, rhp, Carolina, P.R.
32. Edwin Corps, rhp, San Juan, P.R.
33. **Charles McClain, rhp, Tennessee**
34. John Gast, 3b, East Carolina
35. **Bo Loftin, c, New Orleans**
36. Chad Hodge, of, Marcus HS, Flower Mound, Texas
37. Michael Carlton, c, Texas City (Texas) HS
38. James Rushworth, rhp, Panola (Texas) JC
39. **Pierre Burris, of/3b, Kansas City Kansas CC**

CLEVELAND INDIANS

June—Regular Phase (8)

1. **Tim Costo, ss, Iowa**
1. **Sam Hence, of, Stone County HS, Wiggins, Miss.** (Supplemental pick—39th—for failure to sign 1989 first-rounder Calvin Murray)
2. **Darrell Whitmore, of, West Virginia** (Pick from Mariners as compensation for Type B free agent Pete O'Brien)
2. **Pat Bryant, of, Cleveland HS, Reseda, Calif.**
3. **Jason Hardtke, ss, Leland HS, San Jose, Calif.**
4. **Jeff Brohm, ss, Louisville**
5. **Oscar Munoz, rhp, Miami**
6. Paul Bako, c, Lafayette (La.) HS
7. **David Bell, 3b, Moeller HS, Cincinnati**
8. **Shawn Bryant, lhp, Oklahoma City**
9. **Rodrick McCall, 1b, Orange Coast (Calif.) JC**
10. **Robert Smith, 2b, Allen County (Kan.) CC**
11. **Carl Johnson, rhp, Lassen (Calif.) JC**
12. **Craig Sides, rhp, Jefferson Davis (Ala.) JC**
13. **Todd Whitehurst, rhp, North Monterey HS, Salinas, Calif.**
14. **Dino Philyaw, of, Southern Wayne HS, Dudley, N.C.**
15. **Samuel Baker, rhp, Hill (Texas) JC**
16. **James Morgan, of, North Marion HS, Sparr, Fla.**
17. **Dave Mlicki, rhp, Oklahoma State**
18. **Steve Gajkowski, rhp, Bellevue (Wash.) CC**
19. **Ricky Powell, of, Tioga HS, Alexandria, La.**
20. **Robert Schultz, of, Walton HS, Marietta, Ga.**
21. Matt Carpenter, c, Euclid (Ohio) Senior HS
22. **Jerry Ashford, 3b/c, Everman (Texas) HS**
23. Baylor Alexander, c, Florida CC
24. Roynal Coleman, of, Kishwaukee (Ill.) JC
25. **Timothy Thomas, 1b/of, Ohio**
26. **Scott Morgan, rhp, Middle Tennessee State**
27. Oscar Resendez, rhp, Texas Southmost JC
28. Bart Peterson, rhp, Brigham Young
29. David Vindivich, of, Mount Tahoma HS, Tacoma, Wash.
30. Eric Trice, of, LaGrande (Ore.) HS
31. **Victor Ramirez, of, Hill (Texas) JC**
32. **Pete Guerra, c, Laredo (Texas) JC**
33. **Kenneth Day, rhp, Washington State**
34. **Larry Minter, of, Harlan HS, Chicago**
35. **Jose Sued, c, Hill (Texas) JC**
36. **Edwin Couvertier, of, Urb Las Virtude, P.R.**
37. Cesar Ramirez, of, Phoenixville (Pa.) Area HS
38. **Joseph Fleet, rhp, Southeastern Louisiana**
39. **Tim Langdon, lhp, East Carolina**
40. Michael Zollars, ss, Western Oklahoma State JC
41. Joseph Frias, 2b, Oklahoma City
42. Mark Martin, of, Connors State (Okla.) JC
43. David Chisum, of, Laredo (Texas) JC

44. John Rodgers, c, Panola (Texas) JC
45. Efrain Montero, lhp, Ponce, P.R.
46. Charles Hickman, 1b, San Jacinto (Texas) JC
47. (Selection voided)
48. Ron Vaught, rhp, Deer Park (Texas) HS
49. Joseph Chastain, lhp, Florida CC
50. **DeWayne Wilson, 2b, Lockhart HS, Sharon, S.C.**
51. **Carlos Crawford, rhp, Montreat-Anderson (N.C.) JC**
52. Chad Brown, lhp, North Gaston HS, Gastonia, N.C.
53. James Warwick, ss, Colfax (Wash.) HS
54. Lance Martin, of, Tumwater (Wash.) HS
55. Brian Coleman, rhp, Bainbridge Island (Wash.) HS
56. **Aaron Morris, of/1b, Lakeland (Ohio) CC**
57. **John Lorms, c, Eastern Kentucky**
58. **Tracy Sanders, of, Limestone (S.C.)**
59. **Frank Monastero, 2b, West Chester (Pa.)**

DETROIT TIGERS

June—Regular Phase (2)

1. **Tony Clark, of, Christian HS, El Cajon, Calif.**
2. (Pick to Athletics as compensation for Type B free agent Tony Phillips)
2. Keith Grunewald, ss, Walton HS, Marietta, Ga. (Pick from Padres as compensation for Type B free agent Fred Lynn)
3. **Vince Bradford, of, Malvern (Ark.) HS**
4. **Jimmy Alder, 3b, Dobyns-Bennett HS, Kingsport, Tenn.**
5. **Shannon Withem, rhp, Willow Run HS, Ypsiianti, Mich.**
6. **Steve Wolf, rhp, Fresno State**
7. Randy Curtis, of, Riverside (Calif.) CC
8. **Dan Rogers, 1b, Missouri Southern**
9. **Greg Coppeta, lhp, Southern Maine**
10. Roger Luce, c, Texas
11. **Sean Sadler, 3b, Missouri Baptist**
12. **Aaron Seja, of, Millikan HS, Long Beach**
13. Charlie Greene, c, Miami-Dade South CC
14. Ben Blomdahl, rhp, Riverside (Calif.) CC
15. Toby McFarland, lhp, Petoskey (Mich.) HS
16. **Brian Nelson, rhp, George Mason**
17. **Tom Drell, rhp, Florida Southern**
18. Keith Kimsey, of, Santa Fe HS, Lakeland, Fla.
19. **Michael Guilfoyle, lhp, St. Peter's**
20. **Warren Sawkiw, 2b, Wake Forest**
21. **Greg Haeger, 1b/lhp, Michigan**
22. **David Mastropietro, of, La Salle**
23. **Douglas Kimbler, ss, St. Rose (N.Y.)**
24. **Brian Saltzgaber, of/2b, Western Michigan**
25. **Gregg Radachowsky, c, Boston College**
26. Kerry Collins, ss/3b, Wilson HS, West Lawn, Pa.
27. Greg McMurtry, of, Michigan
28. Rodney Peete, 3b, Marina Del Ray, Calif.
29. Darwin Traylor, of, Poly HS, Riverside, Calif.
30. John Rosengren, lhp, Rye (N.Y.) HS
31. **Paul Reinisch, 1b, Wake Forest**
32. **Brian Schubert, rhp, Kent State**
33. **Bob Undorf, rhp, South Florida**
34. Thomas Paskievitch, rhp, Central Michigan
35. **Dennis McNamara, of, Central Michigan**
36. **Kirk Mendenhall, ss, Westminster (Mo.)**
37. **Kevin Miller, c, Chico State (Calif.)**
38. **Rob Fazekas, rhp, Rutgers**
39. **Robert Riker, rhp, Central Michigan**
40. **Eric Leimeister, rhp, St. John's**
41. **Tim Kirt, of, Missouri Baptist**
42. **Keith Roberts, of, West Nassau HS, Callahan, Fla.**
43. **Brian Warren, rhp, New Mexico State**
44. Matthew Hammett, lhp, Macomb (Mich.) JC
45. David Bowden, c, Martin Luther King HS, Detroit
46. Rodney Tisdale, of, University Christian HS, Jacksonville, Fla.
47. Steven Hughart, lhp, Brevard (Fla.) JC
48. Arthur Johnson, ss, Texarkana (Texas) CC
49. Gregory Steele, rhp, Homer (Mich.) HS
50. Karry Riley, rhp, Suwannee HS, Live Oak, Fla.
51. Dan Ruff, of, Michigan
52. Willie Adams, rhp, La Serna HS, La Mirada, Calif.
53. Tim Goodwin, of, Burlington (Iowa) HS
54. Doug Newstrom, rhp, Woodson HS, Fairfax, Va.
55. **John Sutey, of, Kentwood HS, Kent, Wash.**
56. Willie Morales, c, Tucson (Ariz.) HS

HOUSTON ASTROS

June—Regular Phase (15)

1. (Pick to Giants as compensation for Type B free agent Ken Oberkfell)
1. **Tom Nevers, ss, Edina (Minn.) HS** (Pick from Giants as compensation for Type A free agent Kevin Bass)
1. **Brian Williams, rhp, South Carolina** (Supplemental pick—31st—for loss of Bass)
2. **Gary Mota, of, Fullerton (Calif.) JC**
3. **Chris Hatcher, of, Iowa**
4. **Perry Berry, 2b, Southwestern Louisiana**
5. **Al Harley, of, Sheldon HS, Eugene, Ore.**
6. **Jimmy White, of, Brandon HS, Tampa**
7. **David Nix, lhp, Harrison HS, Evansville, Ind.**
8. **Tony Gilmore, c, Arkansas**
9. **Jorge Correa, rhp, Miami Senior HS**
10. Brian Boehringer, rhp, Nevada-Las Vegas
11. **Fletcher Thompson, 2b, Nicholls State**
12. **Jeff Ball, 3b, San Jose State**
13. **Ray Montgomery, of, Fordham**
14. James Evans, rhp, Hancock (Calif.) JC
15. **Layne Lambert, 3b, Nevada-Las Vegas**
16. **Marsalis Basey, ss, Martinsburg (W.Va.) HS**
17. **Jon Quaid, lhp, Chabot (Calif.) JC**
18. Frank Jacobs, 1b, Notre Dame
19. **Steven Bottoms, lhp, Overton HS, Nashville, Tenn.**
20. **Juan Martinez, rhp, Huston Tillotson (Texas)**
21. Anthony Griffin, 1b, Washington HS, Hawthorne, Calif.
22. **Dennis Reed, rhp, Cal Poly San Luis Obispo**
23. Jason Varitek, c, Lake Brantley HS, Longwood, Fla.
24. Johnny Mitchell, of, Sprayberry HS, Marietta, Ga.
25. James Martin, of, Seminole State (Okla.) JC
26. Jim Dougherty, rhp, North Carolina
27. **Lincoln Gumbs, ss, Clarke (Miss.) JC**
28. **Douglas Ketchen, rhp, Cal State Fullerton**
29. Bret Hemphill, c, Cupertino HS, Santa Clara, Calif.
30. Chris Singleton, of, Pinole Valley HS, Hercules, Calif.
31. **Michael Irwin, rhp, Portland**
32. **Lance Smith, c, McNeese State**
33. Robert Baldwin, of, DeLand HS, Lake Helen, Fla.
34. Joe Gonzalez, rhp, Miami Senior HS
35. Dax Winslett, rhp, Plano (Texas) Senior HS
36. **Scott Black, rhp, Missouri**
37. Rodney Foster, of/2b, Midwest City (Okla.) HS
38. **Jose Flores, ss, Cidra, P.R.**
39. **Jason Wall, lhp, Louisiana State**
40. **Vincent Roman, of, Ithaca (N.Y.)**
41. **Scott Bullard, rhp, Florida CC**
42. **Stephen McCumiskey, c, Rhode Island**
43. Raymond Dault, rhp, Austin (Texas) HS
44. Robert McCloud, rhp, Palomar (Calif.) JC
45. Steve Williams, of, Santa Cruz HS, Arizona City, Ariz.
46. Christopher Milton, ss, Wilson HS, Hacienda Heights, Calif.
47. Derek Davis, of, Ellison HS, Fort Hood, Texas
48. Greg Almond, c, Middle Georgia JC
49. Cleveland Ladell, 2b/of, Texarkana (Texas) HS
50. Mark Prather, of, McLennan (Texas) CC
51. Malcolm Huckaby, 3b, Bristol (Conn.) Central HS
52. James Davis, 3b, Lincoln HS, San Diego
53. Brian McGlone, ss, Hillsborough (Fla.) CC
54. Todd Coburn, c, Wooster HS, Carson City, Nev.
55. Scott Smith, of, Coppell (Texas) HS
56. Michael Belcher, c, Broad Run HS, Sterling, Va.
57. Carey Landstrom, rhp, Los Angeles Harbor JC
58. David Maize, c, Triton (Ill.) JC
59. William Paragin, c, Hamilton (Ohio) HS
60. Bernard Bellard, rhp, Acadiana HS, Lafayette, La.
61. Johnny Booker, of, Tucson (Ariz.) HS
62. David Angotti, c, Grossmont (Calif.) JC

63. Kevin Ehl, rhp, Cypress (Calif.) JC
64. Kevin Cook, of, Cypress (Calif.) JC
65. Steven Hernandez, ss, Orange Coast (Calif.) JC
66. Brian Thompson, of, Chabot (Calif.) JC
67. Jason Rathburn, rhp, Westlake HS, Austin, Texas
68. Ron Cacini, ss, Triton (Ill.) JC
69. Donald Miller, rhp, Sprayberry HS, Marietta, Ga.
70. Michael Lustyk, rhp/3b, Interlake HS, Bellevue, Wash.
71. Joseph Miller, of, Los Angeles Harbor JC
72. Todd Mancini, of, La Salle Academy, Cranston, R.I.
73. Mike Condon, c, Southern Union State (Ala.) JC
74. William Adams, of, John Jay HS, San Antonio, Texas
75. Jeff Brown, rhp, Schenectady (N.Y.) CC
76. Travis Driskill, rhp, Anderson HS, Austin, Texas
77. Anastoshio Navarro, 3b, El Rancho HS, Pico Rivera, Calif.
78. Darious Carter, ss, Glenn Oaks HS, Baton Rouge, La.
79. Dennis Colon, ss, Manati, P.R.
80. Kenneth Jackson, 1b, Polk (Fla.) CC
81. Eric Mooney, lhp, St. Anthony HS, Long Beach
82. Jose Matos, rhp, Rio Piedras, P.R.
83. Danny Young, lhp, Cannon County HS, Woodbury, Tenn.
84. Patrick Bettancourt, 3b, Mission Bay HS, San Diego
85. Marc Claus, ss, Broward (Fla.) CC
86. George Wyles, c, Permian HS, Odessa, Texas
87. Daniel Pagan, 3b/1b, Rio Piedras, P.R.
88. Greg Guell, lhp, Miami-Dade CC South
89. Adam West, of, Hudson Valley (N.Y.) CC
90. Sean Garrison, lhp, Berlin HS, Kensington, Conn.
91. Geoff Grenert, rhp, Mesa (Ariz.) CC
92. Brian Whyburn, rhp, Ukiah (Calif.) HS
93. Scott Mowl, rhp, Cerritos (Calif.) JC
94. Matthew Martinez, 2b, Sacramento CC
95. Chad Phillips, rhp, Orange Coast (Calif.) JC
96. Michael Houck, rhp, El Camino (Calif.) JC
97. Floyd White, 1b/of, Middle Georgia JC
98. Cedric Moore, of, Westwood HS, Port Pierce, Fla.
99. Jeff Caldwell, of, Bogalusa (La.) HS

KANSAS CITY ROYALS

June—Regular Phase (25)

1. (Pick to Padres as compensation for Type A free agent Mark Davis)
2. (Pick to Athletics as compensation for Type A free agent Storm Davis)
3. **Shayne Rea, rhp, Henry Ford (Mich.) CC**
4. **Doug Harris, rhp, James Madison**
5. **Darren Burton, of, Pulaski County HS, Somerset, Ky.**
6. **Wade Fyock, rhp, Somerset (Pa.) HS**
7. **Tom Smith, inf, Avon Park (Fla.) HS**
8. **Phil Hiatt, 3b, Louisiana Tech**
9. **Anthony Lee, rhp, El Dorado HS, Las Vegas**
10. **Robert Toth, rhp, Pacifica HS, Cypress, Calif.**
11. Chad Drown, ss, La Mirada HS, Placentia, Calif.
12. **Rodney Myers, rhp, Wisconsin**
13. **Chad Strickland, c, Carl Albert HS, Oklahoma City**
14. **Damon Pollard, rhp, Southern Mississippi**
15. **Thomas Lee, rhp, Los Angeles CC**
16. **David Haber, of, Catonsville (Md.) CC**
17. **Raul Gonzalez, 3b/of, Carolina, P.R.**
18. **Donald Harrel, c, Taft (Calif.) JC**
19. **Doug Shields, of, Southern Illinois**
20. **Doug Peters, rhp, Indiana**
21. **Brady Stewart, ss, Ohio State**
22. **William Long, lhp, Montgomery (Md.) JC**
23. **Vernon Slater, of, Polk (Fla.) CC**
24. **Andre Newhouse, ss, Sterling HS, Houston**
25. **Raymond Brooks, c, El Reno (Okla.) JC**
26. **Alan Budnick, rhp, Detroit**
27. **Rafael Gutierrez, rhp, East Los Angeles JC**
28. **Arnie Sambel, of, San Francisco**
29. **Charles Frederick, rhp, Parkland (Ill.) JC**
30. Brian Bevil, rhp, Angelina (Texas) JC
31. **Weddison Ebanks, of, Utah Valley CC**
32. Marcello Hansen, lhp, Olympic (Wash.) JC
33. **Scott Davis, rhp, Adelphi (N.Y.)**
34. **Sean Franceschi, lhp, New Orleans**
35. **Brad Holman, rhp, Auburn**
36. Damon Daniels, of, Texarkana (Texas) CC
37. **John Schreiner, 1b, Penn State**
38. **David Hierholzer, rhp, Kansas State**
39. Kevin Sisk, 3b, James Madison
40. Mitch Simons, 2b, Oklahoma State
41. **Shannon Strong, of, Treasure Valley (Ore.) CC**
42. **Terrance Mays, of, Kaskaskia (Ill.) CC**
43. **Scott Hennessey, of, Johnson County (Kan.) CC**
44. Tyres Blackburn, c/of, Bryan Adams HS, Dallas
45. Chris Moten, rhp, Bellflower (Calif.) HS
46. Brian Gelzheiser, rhp, Baldwin HS, Pittsburgh
47. Sean Strade, rhp, Grant HS, Portland, Ore.
48. Reggie Ingram, of, Coffee HS, Douglas, Ga.
49. Craig Tucker, rhp, Klamath HS, Klamath Falls, Ore.
50. Richard Parker, rhp, Los Angeles CC
51. Gerald Sharko, 1b, Phoenix (Ariz.) JC
52. Brian Parks, rhp, Skagit Valley (Wash.) CC
53. Shane Gilder, 2b, San Jacinto (Texas) JC
54. Lyle Mouton, of, Louisiana State
55. **John Jacobs, rhp, Chino (Calif.) HS**
56. Nick Kaiser, 2b/ss, Cuesta (Calif.) JC
57. Jonathan Mathews, 1b/of, Centerville (Iowa) HS

LOS ANGELES DODGERS

June—Regular Phase (9)

1. **Ron Walden, lhp, Blanchard (Okla.) HS**
2. (Pick to Expos as compensation tor Type A free agent Hubie Brooks)
2. **Leroy Williams, ss, East St. John HS, Reserve, La.** (Supplemental pick—68th—for loss of Type C free agent Dave Anderson)
2. **Scott Freeman, rhp, Wyoming** (Supplemental pick—73rd—for loss of Type C free agent John Tudor)
3. (Pick to Pirates as compensation tor Type A free agent Jim Gott)
4. **Mike Busch, 1b, Iowa State**
5. **Frank Smith, of, Poly HS, Riverside, Calif.**
6. **Alton Pinkney, of, Glynn Academy, Brunswick, Ga.**
7. **Daniel Gray, c, SUNY Binghamton**
8. **C.J. Kerr, lhp, Cerritos (Calif.) JC**
9. **Jake Botts, rhp, North Monterey HS, Salinas, Calif.**
10. **Kenneth Hamilton, rhp, Patrick Henry (Ala.) JC**
11. Eric Mapp, of, Natrona County HS, Casper, Wyo.
12. **Keoki Farrish, of, Ohlone (Calif.) JC**
13. **Greg Davis, rhp, El Camino (Calif.) CC**
14. **Warren Daspit, rhp, Cal State Sacramento**
15. **Tim Griffin, 3b, Stanford**
16. Donn Cunnigan, of, Gahr HS, Los Angeles
17. **Steve Mintz, c, Mount Olive (N.C.)**
18. **Lonnie Webb, ss, South Georgia JC**
19. **Burgess Watts, 3b/rhp, JC of Du Page (Ill.)**
20. **Peter Nurre, c, Cabrillo (Calif.) JC**
21. Wayne Lindemann, lhp, Lower Columbia (Wash.) JC
22. **Michael Racobaldo, rhp, Pennsauken (N.J.) HS**
23. **Ron Maurer, ss, North Carolina**
24. **Mike Mimbs, lhp, Mercer**
25. **Mark Mimbs, lhp, Mercer**
26. **Gordie Tipton, rhp, Oklahoma State**
27. **Jody Treadwell, rhp, Jacksonville**
28. **Randall Graves, ss, Riverside (Calif.) CC**
29. **David Baumann, rhp, Western New England**
30. **Benjamin O'Connor, lhp, Maryland**
31. **Domingo Mota, of, Cal State Fullerton**
32. **Anthony Rodriguez, c, Aguadilla, P.R.**
33. **Albert Maldonado, lhp, Yauco, P.R.**
34. Kurt Ehmann, ss, Mendocino (Calif.)
35. **Steve Matos, c, Chaminade HS, Hollywood, Fla.**
36. **Mike Brady, lhp, Florida State**
37. **Ira Smith, of/2b, Maryland-Eastern Shore**
38. Brady Raggio, rhp, San Ramon HS, Danville, Calif.
39. Mark Sweeney, of, Maine

40. **Larry Jacinto, rhp, Southern California College**
41. John Cranford, 2b, Middle Georgia JC
42. Clint Minear, lhp, East Mississippi JC
43. Charles Williams, of, Meridian (Miss.) JC
44. **Ed Lund, c, Notre Dame**
45. Jason Sengbusch, rhp, Westfield HS, Oxford, Wis.
46. **Thomas Matthews, rhp, Edinboro (Pa.)**
47. Joseph Jacobsen, rhp, Clovis (Calif.) West HS
48. **Robert Sweeney, 3b, Waukesha (Wis.) County Technical JC**
49. **Dirk Gorman, of, SUNY Binghamton**
50. Ismael Castaneda, lhp, Hanford (Calif.) HS
51. Mario Johnson, ss, Simmons HS, Hollandale, Miss.
52. Gordon Hockett, 1b, Union HS, Tulsa, Okla.
53. Robert Calton, lhp, Lehi (Utah) HS
54. **Todd Williams, rhp, Onondaga (N.Y.) CC**
55. Brett Kim, 3b, JC of Marin (Calif.)
56. Joseph Wagner, rhp, Adams Friendship (Wis.) HS
57. Patrick Reed, ss, Mount Hood (Ore.) CC
58. Melvin Warren, of, Solano (Calif.) CC
59. **Daniel Andrews, of, Cal Poly Pomona**
60. David Madsen, 3b, Murray (Utah) HS
61. Greg Raisola, c, Nogales HS, Walnut, Calif.
62. Roger Sweeney, of, JC of Marin (Calif.)
63. Fausto Abad, of, Jupiter (Fla.) HS

MILWAUKEE BREWERS

June—Regular Phase (14)

1. (Pick to Athletics as compensation for Type A free agent Dave Parker)
2. **LaRue Baber, of, Grant HS, Sacramento, Calif.**
3. **Michael Carter, ss, Livingston (Ala.)**
4. **Don Blair, rhp, Wabash (Ind.) HS**
5. **Duane Singleton, of, McKee Vocational Tech, Staten Island, N.Y.**
6. **Tom McGraw, lhp, Washington State**
7. **Bobby Benjamin, 1b/of, Nebraska**
8. **Tim Clark, of, Louisiana State**
9. **Kevin McDonald, rhp, Southwestern Louisiana**
10. **Kurt Archer, rhp, San Diego State**
11. **Brian Souza, rhp, Hawaii**
12. **Marshall Boze, rhp, Southwestern (Calif.) CC**
13. **Dave Wrona, ss, Southern Illinois**
14. **Tim Carter, 1b, Miami (Ohio)**
15. **John Tatum, 3b, Grossmont HS, Santee, Calif.**
16. **Mike Couture, c, Clemson**
17. **Mark Stephens, lhp, Central Arizona JC**
18. **Orlando Barrios, of, High Point (N.C.)**
19. **Patrick Miller, rhp, Detroit**
20. **David White, rhp, South Florida**
21. **Michael Norris, of, Richland (Texas) CC**
22. **Charles Rambadt, c, Dominican**
23. **Don Pruitt, rhp, Arizona**
24. **Orlando Griego, rhp, New Mexico State**
25. **Christopher Wheat, ss, Monmouth**
26. Brendt Newbill, lhp, McNary HS, Salem, Ore.
27. Michael Killimet, of, Fort Walton Beach (Fla.) HS
28. **Anthony Coble, of, Wingate (N.C.)**
29. **Todd Edwards, of, Arizona**
30. Sam Taylor, of, El Cerrito HS, Richmond, Calif.
31. **Mike Lynch, rhp, Rollins (Fla.)**
32. **Julian Salazar, ss, Pasadena (Calif.) CC**
33. **Vince Castaldo, 3b, Kentucky**
34. Alonso Beltran, rhp, Socorro HS, El Paso, Texas
35. Robert Dickerson, of, Harrison Central HS, Gulfport, Miss.
36. **Carlos Flores, ss, Sierra Vista HS, Baldwin Park, Calif.**
37. Luis Melendez, 3b, Ponce, P.R.
38. Steve Boyd, rhp, Central Arizona JC
39. David Repass, 1b/lhp, Forest HS, Ocala, Fla.
40. Ernie Nietzke, of, Saddleback (Calif.) JC
41. **David Acevedo, rhp, San Sebastian, P.R.**
42. Reid Mizuguchi, rhp, Southern California
43. **Steven Sigloch, 2b, Utah**
44. Clinton Brown, rhp, Taft (Calif.) CC

MINNESOTA TWINS

June—Regular Phase (12)

1. **Todd Ritchie, rhp, Duncanville (Texas) HS**
1. **Midre Cummings, of, Edison HS, Miami** (Supplemental pick—29th—for loss of Type A free agent Jeff Reardon)
2. **Jayhawk Owens, c, Middle Tennessee State**
2. **Ron Caridad, rhp, Westminster HS, Miami** (Pick from Red Sox as compensation for Reardon)
3. **Jamie Ogden, lb, White Bear Lake (Minn.) HS** (Pick from Pirates as compensation for Type C free agent Wally Backman)
3. **Rich Becker, of, Aurora West HS, Aurora, Ill.**
4. Silvio Censale, lhp, Catholic HS, Paramus, N.J.
5. **Brent Brede, of, Wesclin HS, Trenton, Ill.**
6. **Craig Hawkins, 2b, Simeon HS, Chicago**
7. **Tim Persing, rhp, Mansfield (Pa.)**
8. James Mouton, of, St. Mary's
9. Trevor Humphry, rhp, Delight (Ark.) HS
10. **Andrew Prater, c, Travis HS, Austin, Texas**
11. **Mark Swope, rhp, Arkansas**
12. **Pat Meares, 3b, Wichita State**
13. Steve Whitaker, lhp, Merced (Calif.) JC
14. Jeff Granger, lhp, Orangefield (Texas) HS
15. **Jon Henry, rhp, Central Florida**
16. **Paul Russo, c/1b, Tampa**
17. Fred Smith, rhp, Roosevelt HS, Brooklyn, N.Y.
18. Scott Weiss, rhp, Stanford
19. **Matt Morse, 2b, Michigan**
20. **Damian Miller, c, Viterbo (Wis.)**
21. **Eddie Guardado, lhp, San Joaquin Delta (Calif.) CC**
22. **John Cohen, of, Mississippi State**
23. David Schwartz, rhp, California
24. **Tom Gavin, 3b, Rider**
25. Clint Jensen, of, Naperville (Ill.) Central HS
26. Robert Welles, rhp, Beverly Hills (Calif.) HS
27. **Dicky Dixon, lhp, Mississippi**
28. **Devin Peppers, of, JC of the Desert (Calif.)**
29. Steve Kimble, of, Mount Zion HS, Decatur, Ill.
30. Charles MacKendrick, rhp, Grand Junction (Colo.) HS
31. **Glenn Evans, ss, Harlan HS, Chicago**
32. **Brian Ewing, of, College of Idaho**
33. Geoff Edsell, rhp, Montoursville (Pa.) HS
34. **Kurt Pfeffer, rhp, JC of Marin (Calif.)**
35. James Belcher, rhp, Spring Hill HS, Olathe, Kan.
36. Alex Pereira, lhp, Southwest HS, Miami
37. Brian Klepper, lhp, Iola (Kan.) HS
38. **Richard Portu, of, Westminster HS, Miami**
39. **Paul Bruno, c, New York Tech**
40. **Matt Brown, c, San Jose State**
41. **Brian Raabe, 2b, Minnesota**
42. **Derrell Rumsey, of, Sonoma State (Calif.)**
43. Mike Neal, ss, Hammond (La.) HS
44. Greg Stephens, rhp, South HS, Fargo, Mo.
45. Hiram Ramirez, c, Ensenada, P.R.
46. Jason Luttges, of, DeAnza (Calif.) CC
47. Chris Gump, 2b, Mesa (Ariz.) CC
48. David Garrow, ss, South Mountain (Ariz.) CC
49. Clarke Rea, c, Scottsdale (Ariz.) CC
50. Anthony Lacy, of/ss, Foothill HS, Sacramento, Calif.
51. Larry Lucchetti, rhp, San Joaquin Delta (Calif.) CC
52. Kevin Rawitzer, lhp, Diablo Valley (Calif.) CC
53. Brian Henderson, of, Boone HS, Orlando, Fla.
54. Blake Byers, c, Seabreeze HS, Daytona Beach, Fla.

MONTREAL EXPOS

June—Regular Phase (11)

1. **Shane Andrews, 3b, Carlsbad (N.M.) HS**
1. **Rondell White, of, Jones County HS, Gray, Ga.** (Pick from Angels as compensation for Type A free agent Mark Langston)
1. **Gabe White, lhp, Sebring (Fla.) HS** (Supplemental pick—28th—for loss of Langston)
1. **Stan Spencer, rhp, Stanford** (Supplemental pick—35th—for loss of Type A free agent Hubie Brooks)
1. **Ben Van Ryn, lhp, East Noble HS, Kendallville, Ind.**

(Supplemental pick—37th—for loss of Type A free agent Pascual Perez)

1. **Stan Robertson, of, Plainview (Texas) HS** (Supplemental pick—40th—for failure to sign 1989 first-rounder Charles Johnson)
2. **Michael Hardge, ss, Ellison HS, Killeen, Texas** (Pick from Dodgers as compensation for Type A free agent Hubie Brooks)
2. **Tavo Alvarez, rhp, Tucson (Ariz.) HS** (Pick from Yankees as compensation for Type A free agent Pascual Perez)
2. **Chris Haney, lhp, UNC Charlotte.**
2. **Chris Martin, ss, Pepperdine** (Pick from Cardinals as compensation for Type B free agent Bryn Smith)
3. **Mike Mathile, rhp, Wright State**
4. **Jeff Barry, of, San Diego State**
5. **Ricky Clelland, rhp, Buckeye North US, Brilliant, Ohio**
6. **Steve Long, rhp, St. Xavier (Ill.)**
7. **Rob Fitzpatrick, c, Georgia Southern**
8. **Javier Pages, c, Stranahan HS, Fort Lauderdale, Fla.**
9. **Craig Clow, 1b, Western Oregon State**
10. **Billy Samples, of, Liberty**
11. **Brian Jones, of, Barstow (Calif.) HS**
12. **Bob Baxter, lhp, Harvard**
13. **Ted Ciesla, ss, Rutgers**
14. **Robbie Katzaroff, of, UCLA**
15. Troy Kopp, c, Pacific
16. **Randy Wilstead, 1b, Brigham Young**
17. Jackie Ross, of, Edison HS, Miami
18. Frederick Collier, 1b, Abbeville (S.C.) HS
19. **Thomas Philips, c, Fresno State**
20. **Perry Sanchez, c, Long Beach State**
21. Scott Brocail, rhp, Lamar (Colo.) HS
22. David Bingham, ss/of, Walla Walla (Wash.) CC
23. **Steve Renko, rhp, Kansas**
24. **Marc Tsitouris, 1b/c, Wingate (N.C.)**
25. Mathew Haas, c, St. Mary's HS, Paducah, Ky.
26. **Ranbir Grewal, rhp, Fresno State**
27. **Darrin Kotch, lhp, Rutgers**
28. **Billy Brewer, lhp, Dallas Baptist**
29. Kenya Hunt, 1b, Oceanside (Calif.) HS
30. **Brian Shehan, rhp, UNC Asheville**
31. Dean Madsen, of, Yuba (Calif.) JC
32. Kelton Jacobson, rhp, Bellevue (Wash.) CC
33. Robert Navarro, rhp, Pomona (Calif.) HS
34. Trenton Hauswirth, c, Palm Desert (Calif.) HS
35. **Ryan Whitman, rhp, Jupiter HS, Lake Park, Fla.**
36. Mike Morland, c, Texas
37. Ben Boulware, of, Los Gatos (Calif.) HS
38. **John Polasek, lhp, Rice**
39. Jose Diaz, of, Guayama, P.R.
40. David Schultz, of, Marina HS, Huntington Beach, Calif.
41. **Doug Noce, c, Cal Poly San Luis Obispo**
42. Jacob Benz, lhp, College Park HS, Pleasant Hill, Calif.
43. John Rogers, lhp, East Los Angeles HS
44. Todd Anderson, of, Lewis-Clark State (Idaho)
45. Alex Miranda, 1b, Columbus HS, Miami
46. Victor Llanos, 3b, Carolina, P.R.
47. Jason Jensen, of, McLane HS, Fresno, Calif.
48. Mark Palfalvi, 1b, Chabot (Calif.) JC
49. Ronald Jones, of, Mesa (Ariz.) CC
50. Jorge Adame, c, Bell HS, Maywood, Calif.
51. Archie Jean, of, Mendocino (Calif.) CC
52. Allen Gallagher, ss, Centennial HS, Gresham, Ore.
53. Charles Lee, of, Currituck HS, Poplar Branch, N.C.
54. Clinton Oltjenbruns, 1b, Willits (Calif.) HS
55. Gregg Press, rhp, Cabrillo (Calif.) JC
56. Stephen Mitchell, rhp, Saratoga HS, Los Gatos, Calif.
57. Brett Brown, c, Mesa (Ariz.) CC
58. Randy Collins, c, Mount San Jacinto (Calif.) JC
59. Christopher Lowen, rhp, Moreno Valley (Calif.) HS
60. Paul Carpentier, rhp, Chaffey (Calif.) JC
61. Martin Colunga, c, Colton (Calif.) HS
62. Matthew Jones, 1b, Red Land HS, Lewisberry, Pa.
63. Michael Grigsby, rhp, Lassen (Calif.) JC

NEW YORK METS

June—Regular Phase (17)

1. **Jeromy Burnitz, of, Oklahoma State**
2. **Aaron Ledesma, ss, Chabot (Calif.) JC**
3. **Micah Franklin, ss, Lincoln HS, San Francisco**
4. **Mike Petrizi, c, Pennsauken (N.J.) HS**
5. **Darwin Davis, 3b, Simeon HS, Chicago**
6. **Demond Smith, of, Eisenhower HS, Rialto, Calif.**
7. **Pete Walker, rhp, Connecticut**
8. **Raul Casanova, c, Ponce, P.R.**
9. **Fernando Vina, 2b, Arizona State**
10. **Michael Quillin, of, Nickerson HS, Buhler, Kan.**
11. Darren Dreifort, of, Wichita (Kan.) Heights HS
12. **Caspar Van Rynbach, rhp, Iowa Western CC**
13. Tom Hamilton, of, South Fork HS, Indiantown, Fla.
14. **Todd Douma, lhp, Arizona State**
15. Steve Soderstrom, rhp, Turlock (Calif.) HS
16. **Eric Corbell, rhp, Incarnate Word (Texas)**
17. **Brian Daubach, 1b, Belleville (Ill.) Township HS**
18. Trey Cheek, rhp, Broughton HS, Raleigh, N.C.
19. Anthony Phillips, rhp, Southern Mississippi
20. **Steven Steele, c, Millikan HS, Long Beach**
21. **Jason King, ss, Washington State**
22. **Brad Schorr, rhp, Columbus (Ga.) HS**
23. **Mike Sciortino, lhp, Central Connecticut State**
24. **Steven Seymour, rhp, Ocean County (N.J.) CC**
25. **Steve Thomas, rhp, Alabama**
26. **Robert Carpenter, rhp, New Hampshire**
27. Englebert Bull, of, Fairfax HS, Los Angeles
28. **Terrell Williams, 3b, Harlan HS, Chicago**
29. Will Brunson, lhp, Eastfield (Texas) JC
30. **Philip Scott, ss, Wittenberg (Ohio)**
31. Joseph Sewell, rhp, UC Irvine
32. Michael Holtz, lhp, Central Cambria HS, Ebensburg, Pa.
33. James Northeimer, c, Sacramento (Calif.) HS
34. Aaron Richards, rhp/ss, Westlake HS Austin, Texas
35. **James Manfred, rhp, Indian Hills (Iowa) CC**
36. Maceo Mitchell, of, Fresno (Calif.) CC
37. Anthony Richardson, 1b, Simeon HS, Chicago
38. Andrew Lorraine, lhp, Hart HS, Valencia, Calif.
39. Thomas King, of, Albany (Ga.) HS
40. Todd Pridy, 1b, Napa Valley (Calif.) JC
41. Shaun Watson, rhp, Southwestern HS, Brighton, Ill.
42. Shane Bushard, 3b, North Idaho JC
43. Karl Carswell, 2b, Shawnee Mission HS, Overland Park, Kan.
44. Douglas Yartz, lhp, Yuba (Calif.) CC
45. **Ricky Otero, of, Vega Baja, P.R.**
46. **Scotty Williams, rhp, Morristown (Tenn.) HS**
47. Thomas Daniel, of, Prairie HS, Vancouver, Wash.
48. **Tom Allison, 2b, Chapman (Calif.) JC**
49. Claude Allen, rhp, Hogan HS, Vallejo, Calif.
50. Rick Helling, rhp, Kishwaukee (Ill.) JC
51. Christopher Eckley, of/1b, Burke HS, Omaha, Neb.
52. Randy Farmer, 2b/ss, Meridian (Miss.) JC

NEW YORK YANKEES

June—Regular Phase (10)

1. **Carl Everett, of, Hillsborough HS, Tampa**
2. **Robert Eenhoorn, ss, Davidson** (Pick from Pirates as compensation for Type B free agent Walt Terrell)
2. (Pick to Expos as compensation for Type A free agent Pascual Perez)
3. **Tate Seefried, 1b, El Segundo (Calif.) HS**
4. **Kirt Ojala, lhp, Michigan**
5. **Rick Lantrip, inf, Fresno State**
6. **Sam Militello Jr., rhp, Tampa**
7. **Jalal Leach, of, Pepperdine**
8. **Tim Rumer, lhp, Duke**
9. Matthew Terrell, of, Sturgis (Mich.) HS
10. **Darren Hodges, rhp, Ferrum (Va.)**
11. **Richard Hines, rhp, Mississippi**
12. **Ron Frazier, rhp, Clemson**
13. **Jeff Motuzas, c, Nashua (N.H.) HS**

14. **Bo Siberz, rhp, Texas A&M**
15. **Michael Smith, rhp, Seekonk HS, Pawtucket, R.I.**
16. **Ricky Ledee, of, Salinas, P.R.**
17. **Bryan Faw, rhp, Clemson**
18. **Bob Deller, of, Texas Wesleyan**
19. **Brent Gilbert, rhp, Texas A&M**
20. **Kevin Jordan, 2b, Nebraska**
21. **Keith Seiler, lhp, Virginia**
22. **Andy Pettitte, lhp, Deer Park (Texas) HS**
23. Tom Wilson, of, Fullerton (Calif.) JC
24. **Jorge Posada, ss, Rio Piedras, P.R.**
25. **Matt Dunbar, lhp, Florida State**
26. Shannon Knighton, 1b, Bleckley County HS, Cochran, Ga.
27. James Musselwhite, rhp/1b, Apopka (Fla.) HS
28. **Shane Spencer, of, Granite Hills HS, El Cajon, Calif.**
29. Corey Hayes, of, Pattonville HS, Florissant, Mo.
30. Brad Stuart, rhp, New Orleans
31. Kent Donnelly, rhp, Foothill HS, Santa Ana, Calif.
32. **Mike Hankins, ss, UCLA**
33. John Sutherland, rhp, UCLA
34. **Pat Morphy, rhp, Northeastern Louisiana**
35. Kevin Ohme, lhp, Indian River (Fla.) CC
36. Brett King, ss, Apopka (Fla.) HS
37. Ernie Yaroshuk, of/1b, Miami-Dade CC South
38. **John Thibert, rhp, Mesa (Ariz.) JC**
39. Mike Heathcott, rhp, Creighton
40. Wesley Hawkins, of, Mansfield (La.) HS
41. John Wasdin, rhp, Godby HS, Tallahassee, Fla.
42. **Barry Smith, 2b, Cumberland (Ky.)**
43. Daniel Redovian, rhp, Brevard (Fla.) JC
44. William Lawrence, lhp, Gulf Breeze (Fla.) HS
45. Albert Perez, rhp, Ohlone (Calif.) JC
46. Matthew Ruoff, 3b, Santa Rosa (Calif.) JC
47. James Ramminger, 1b, Goodrich HS, Fond du Loc, Wis.
48. James Spero, of, Santa Rosa (Calif.) JC
49. Tim Kester, rhp, Coral Springs (Fla.) HS
50. Alex McCoy, of, Culver Military HS, Wilmington, N.C.
51. Rich Haley, of, Rancho Cordova (Calif.) HS
52. Kurt Alderman, c, Sacramento CC
53. Scott Patrick, rhp, Indian River (Fla.) CC
54. Jeff Ciendrich, rhp, Edison (Fla.) CC
55. Franklyn Johnson, 1b, Howard (Texas) JC
56. Mark Saugstad, ss/3b, California
57. Sean Palmer, of, Ganesha HS, Diamond Bar, Calif.
58. Andres Texidor, c, Canovanas, P.R.
59. Tracy Latimer, rhp, Westwood HS, Fort Pierce, Fla.
60. **Scott Kendall, lhp, Central HS, Fort Pierce, Fla.**
61. Joe Smith, rhp, Cardinal Newman HS, West Palm Beach, Fla.
62. Anthony Crueger, lhp, Texarkana (Texas) CC
63. Kortney Paul, c, Southwest HS, Fort Worth, Texas
64. Derek January, lhp, Miami-Dade CC South
65. Joseph Long, rhp, Citrus (Calif.) JC
66. Joel Grimes, 1b, Barbers Hill HS, Mount Bellvieu, Texas
67. Kevin Bosse, 3b/1b, Navasota (Texas) HS
68. Eric Methner, rhp, Michigan State
69. Rodd Kelley, ss, Brandon (Fla.) HS
70. Pedro Lewis, 3b, McClatchy HS, Sacramento, Calif.
71. Terry Vaughn, of, Oceanside (Calif.) HS
72. Danny Rios, rhp, Pace HS, Hialeah, Fla.
73. Ray Gossett, lhp, Glendora HS, San Dimas, Calif.
74. Eric Taylor, lhp, Mingo HS, Mingo Junction, Ohio

OAKLAND ATHLETICS

June—Regular Phase (26)

1. **Todd Van Poppel, rhp, Martin HS, Arlington, Texas** (Pick from Brewers as compensation for Type A free agent Dave Parker)
1. **Don Peters, rhp, St. Francis (Ill.)**
1. **David Zancanaro, lhp, UCLA** (Supplemental pick—34th—for loss of Type A free agent Storm Davis)
1. **Kirk Dressendorfer, rhp, Texas** (Supplemental pick—36th—for loss of Parker)
2. **Curtis Shaw, lhp, Kansas** (Pick from Tigers as compensation for Type B free agent Tony Phillips)
2. **Eric Helfand, c, Arizona State** (Pick from Royals as compensation for Davis)
2. **Gary Hust, of, Petal (Miss.) HS**
3. **Chaon Garland, rhp, Haverford (Pa.)**
4. **Jeff Duncan, 3b, Jackson State (Tenn.) CC**
5. **Chris Hart, of, Auburn**
6. **Creighton Gubanich, c, Phoenixville (Pa.) Area HS**
7. **Dan Vizzini, lhp, Francis Marion**
8. Andy Bruce, 3b, Georgia Tech
9. **Mike Kennedy, c, Elon**
10. **Ernie Young, of, Lewis (Ill.)**
11. **Mark Craft, rhp, Virginia Military Institute**
12. **Bill Picketts, 2b, Cal State Los Angeles**
13. **Eric Myers, rhp, Seminole State (Okla.) JC**
14. **Jim Dillon, rhp, Maine**
15. **Kevin Dattola, of, South Florida**
16. **Doug Johns, lhp, Virginia**
17. Scott Dodd, lhp, Glendale (Ariz.) CC
18. **Greg Reid, of, Cal State Los Angeles**
19. **Carlos Salazar, 1b/c, Azusa Pacific (Calif.)**
20. **Chris Olofson, of, Bakersfield (Calif.) JC**
21. **Rick Miller, lhp, Grand Canyon (Ariz.)**
22. **Izzy Molina, c, Columbus HS, Miami**
23. **Tanyon Sturtze, rhp, Quinsigamond (Mass.) CC**
24. Dwayne Fowler, rhp, Long Beach State
25. **David Tripp, rhp/of, Clemson**
26. Shawn Purdy, rhp, Miami
27. **Eric Booker, of, San Jose State**
28. **Glenn Osinski, ss, New Orleans**
29. **Craig Connolly, rhp, Pennsylvania**
30. **Mike Newson, rhp, Crenshaw HS, Los Angeles**
31. **Scott Rose, rhp, Hillsborough (Fla.) CC**
32. **Craig Sudbury, rhp, Utah**
33. **Jeff Clifford, rhp, Assumption (Mass.)**
34. **Tony Gechter, rhp, Trinidad (Colo.) JC**
35. T.J. Mathews, rhp, St. Louis CC-Meramec
36. **Tony Scharff, rhp, Oklahoma City**
37. **Todd Revenig, rhp, Mankato State (Minn.)**
38. **Reggie Bailey, 1b, Coffee HS, Douglas, Ga.**
39. **Mike Muhlethaler, 3b, California**
40. Chris Oscar, inf, Valley HS, Las Vegas
41. **Tony Fults, lhp, Franklin County HS, Decherd, Tenn.**
42. Carlos James, of, Pine Bluff (Ark.) HS
43. Sean Lowe, rhp, McLennan (Texas) CC
44. Marcus Maple, of, Central HS, Beaumont, Texas
45. Michael Bumpers, of, McCrory (Ark.) HS
46. Marcus Miller, rhp, Bay HS, Panama City, Fla.
47. Oscar Draper, rhp, Johnson HS, Huntsville, Ala.
48. Robert Pierce, rhp, Dixie (Utah) JC
49. John White, 3b, Long Beach (Calif.) CC

PHILADELPHIA PHILLIES

June—Regular Phase (3)

1. **Mike Lieberthal, c, Westlake HS, Westlake Village, Calif.**
2. Timothy Schweitzer, lhp, Reedsport (Ore.) HS
3. **Dan Larson, of, Birmingham (Calif.) HS**
4. **John Ingram, lhp, Los Angeles Harbor JC**
5. **Tom Nuneviller, of, West Chester (Pa.)**
6. **Mike Murphy, of, St. Pius X HS, Albuquerque, N.M.**
7. **Joel Adamson, lhp, Cerritos (Calif.) JC**
8. **Ron Lockett, 1b, Jackson State**
9. Derrick White, 3b, Santa Rosa (Calif.) JC
10. **Jorge Pascual, 2b/3b, Aquinas (Tenn.) JC**
11. **Gary Bennett, c, Waukegan (Ill.) East HS**
12. **Chad Anderson, rhp, Roseburg (Ore.) HS**
13. **Jerome Edwards, of, Jackson State**
14. **Mike Williams, rhp, Virginia Tech**
15. **Scott Coleman, lhp, Orange Glen HS, Valley Center, Calif.**
16. Eric Spann, of, Stamford (Conn.) HS
17. **Maurice Hines, 1b, Rose HS, Greenville, N.C.**
18. **Darren Hedley, of, American River (Calif.) JC**
19. **Antonio Grissom, of, South Georgia JC**
20. Marvin Benard, of, Los Angeles Harbor JC
21. B.J. Waszgis, c, Fort Scott (Kan.) CC

22. Robert Lamb, rhp, Central HS, Tuscaloosa, Ala.
23. James Koehler, 1b, De Anza (Calif.) JC
24. **R.A. Neitzel, 2b, Oregon State**
25. **Steve McGovern, rhp, Cal State Los Angeles**
26. Omar Washington, rhp, Samuell HS, Dallas, Texas
27. **Terrell Smith, ss, Stanhope Elmore HS, Millbrook, Ala.**
28. Mark Graham, lhp, Santa Monica (Calif.) CC
29. **Gary Lance, rhp, American River (Calif.) JC**
30. **Ryan Ridenour, c, Oregon Tech**
31. **Erik Judson, ss/2b, UC San Diego**
32. **Samuel Edwards, rhp, Gateway HS, Kissimmee, Fla.**
33. **Thomas Jones, rhp/of, Sam Houston State**
34. Danny Miller, rhp, Poway (Calif.) HS
35. John Salamon, rhp, Sto-Rox HS, McKees Rocks, Pa.
36. **Bill Higgins, rhp, Clinch Valley County HS, Castlewood, Va.**
37. **Mike Montgomery, rhp, East Tennessee State**
38. **Sean Ryan, 1b, Rutgers**
39. **Troy Paulsen, ss, Stanford**
40. **Jeff Borgese, of, Fresno State**
41. **Steven Hollins, ss, Appalachian State**
42. **Chadwick Silvers, of, Carson-Newman (Tenn.)**
43. **Eric Hill, rhp, Walters State (Tenn.) CC**
44. **Troy Rusk, c/1b, South Florida**
45. **Jeffery Gunn, of, Grambling State**
46. **Pat Cheek, 3b, U.S. International**
47. Patrick Garrigan, ss, Miami (Ohio)
48. Eric Maudlin, of, American River (Calif.) JC
49. Julio Cruz, c, American River (Calif.) JC
50. Lawrence Novey, c, Grant HS, Sacramento, Calif.
51. Jeff Richardson, 3b, St. Bernards HS, Culver City, Calif.
52. Jeffrey Wagner, 3b, Federal Way (Wash.) HS
53. Scott Eggleston, rhp, Maple Woods (Mo.) CC
54. Demetrius Comeaux, of, Gahr HS, Cerritos, Calif.
55. Manuel Evans, of, Pasadena (Calif.) HS
56. Ron Ollison, 2b, Angelina (Texas) JC
57. Michael Myers, of, Donegal HS, Mount Joy, Pa.

PITTSBURGH PIRATES

June—Regular Phase (5)

1. **Kurt Miller, rhp, West HS, Bakersfield, Calif.**
1. **Mike Zimmerman, rhp, South Alabama** (Supplemental pick—27th—for loss of Type A free agent Jim Gott)
2. (Pick to Yankees as compensation for Type B free agent Walt Terrell)
3. (Pick to Twins as compensation for Type B free agent Wally Backman)
3. **John Schulte, of, Brenham (Texas) HS** (Pick from Dodgers as compensation for Gott)
4. **Norm House, c, Castlewood (Va.) HS**
5. **Glenn Coombs, rhp, Cypress Creek HS, Houston**
6. **Tim Edge, c, Auburn**
7. **Kevin Young, 3b, Southern Mississippi**
8. **Jeff Conger, lhp/of, Charlotte (N.C.) Latin HS**
9. **Rich Robertson, lhp, Texas A&M**
10. **Cedrick Peppers, of, Hughes Springs HS, Avinger, Texas**
11. Artis Johnson, of, Delray Beach (Fla.) HS
12. **Wes Grisham, of, Louisiana State**
13. **Brian Shouse, lhp, Bradley**
14. Jeff McCurry, rhp, San Jacinto (Texas) CC
15. **Rick White, rhp, Paducah (Ky.) JC**
16. **Lynn Carlson, rhp, Greenville (Ill.)**
17. **John Douris, rhp, Orange Coast (Calif.) CC**
18. **Charles Tooch, ss, Forest Hill HS, West Palm Beach, Fla.**
19. Jason Leto, of/2b, St. Petersburg (Fla.) JC
20. **Mark Johnson, 1b, Dartmouth**
21. **Shelton Simpson, rhp, Eastern Kentucky**
22. Ben Murray, of, Beaver Dam (Wis.) HS
23. Robin Tumble, of/rhp, Carthage (Texas) HS
24. **Keith Osik, c/3b, Louisiana State**
25. **Troy Hooper, rhp, Shorter (Ga.)**
26. **Cory Schaefer, of, Wisconsin-Oshkosh**
27. **Bradley Davis, c, Columbus (Ga.)**
28. **Dave Tellers, rhp, San Jose State**
29. **Ben Johnson, 3b, Oregon State**
30. **Tom Green, of, Georgia Tech**
31. Mark LaRosa, lhp, Louisiana State
32. Aaron Wofford, ss, Lindhurst HS, Olivehurst, Calif.
33. **David Pike, rhp, Riverview HS, Sarasota, Fla.**
34. Shawn Buchanan, of, Nebraska
35. Angel Delgado, ss/3b, East Chicago (Ind.) Central HS
36. Mike Russell, rhp, Fort Vancouver HS, Vancouver, Wash.
37. John Carter, rhp, Simeon HS, Chicago
38. **Tim French, rhp, Northern Kentucky**
39. **Joe Sondrini, 2b, North Adams State (Mass.)**
40. **Steven Polewski, ss/2b, Chicago State**
41. **Javier Martinez, ss, Levittown, P.R.**

ST. LOUIS CARDINALS

June—Regular Phase (13)

1. **Donovan Osborne, lhp, Nevada-Las Vegas**
1. **Aaron Holbert, ss, Jordan HS, Long Beach** (Pick from Red Sox as compensation for Type A free agent Tony Pena)
1. **Paul Ellis, c, UCLA** (Supplemental pick—30th—for loss of Pena)
2. (Pick to Expos as compensation for Type B free agent Bryn Smith)
3. **Marc Ronan, c/of, Florida State**
4. **Andrew Beasley, c, Virginia Military Institute**
5. Jimmy Lewis, rhp, Florida CC
6. **George Sells, lhp, Old Dominion**
7. **Scott Baker, lhp, Taft (Calif.) JC**
8. **Mark MacArthur, ss, Master's (Calif.)**
9. **Terry Bradshaw, of, Norfolk State**
10. **Mark Smith, of/rhp, Texas**
11. **Jose Velez, of, Mayaguez, P.R.**
12. **Jimmy Davenport, of, Jackson State**
13. **Tom Urbani, lhp, Long Beach State**
14. Keith Adaway, 2b/of, St. Louis CC-Meramec
15. **Brad Beanblossom, ss, Oklahoma State**
16. Pat Treend, rhp, El Camino Real, West Hills, Calif.
17. Ricky Kimball, rhp, Florida State
18. **David Norris, lhp, St. Mary's**
19. **Jimmy Marchesi, rhp, El Capitan HS, Lakeside, Calif.**
20. **Don Prybylinski, c, Illinois State**
21. **Troy Salvior, rhp, Hilisdale (Mich.)**
22. **Steve Dudek, of, Rancho HS, Las Vegas**
23. **Kevin Carpenter, c, West Virginia**
24. **Duff Brumley, rhp, Cleveland (Tenn.) State CC**
25. **Skeets Thomas, of, South Carolina**
26. Joe Wise, rhp, Georgia Tech
27. **Bill Gale, of, Central Connecticut State**
28. **Lorenzo Meza, ss, Sweetwater HS, National City, Calif.**
29. **Anthony Jenkins, of, The Citadel**
30. **Harry Ball, 2b, Rollins (Fla.)**
31. **Brian Sullivan, lhp, Cumberland (Tenn.)**
32. **Rich Gonzalez, of, Cal State Fullerton**
33. **Brian Avram, rhp, JC of Southern Idaho**
34. **John Kelly, rhp, Kennesaw State**
35. **Frank Speek, rhp, Liberty**
36. Kevin Morgan, 2b, Southeastern Louisiana
37. **Tom Fusco, lhp, Long Island**
38. **Darryl Meek, rhp, Parkway South HS, St. Louis**
39. **Michael Jolley, rhp, Dixie (Utah) JC**
40. **Beto Rodriguez, 1b, U.S. International**
41. **Andy Petersen, rhp, San Diego State**
42. **Kevin Nielsen, lhp, San Diego State**
43. Chris Turner, 3b/of, Western Kentucky
44. **Craig Ruyak, rhp, William & Mary**
45. **Joe Aversa, ss, Southern California College**
46. Ryan Martindale, c, Creighton
47. Doak Wishon, of, Seminole State (Okla.) JC
48. John Coletti, lhp, Seminole State (Okla.) JC
49. **Sydney Lowman, c, Draughon's (Tenn.) JC**
50. **Gilberto Torres, of, Florida International**
51. **Matthew Tomso, rhp, Mount Olive (Ill.) HS**
52. **Jonas Hamlin, 1b, JC of Southern Idaho**
53. Bart Evans, rhp, Three Rivers (Mo.) CC
54. **Victor Vargas, 2b, Wyoming**

55. Steven Afenir, c, Escondido HS, San Marcos, Calif.
56. Joseph Merritt, c, Volunteer State (Tenn.) CC
57. Travis Hunter, rhp, JC of Southern Idaho
58. Greg Jones, of, Southeastern Illinois JC
59. Jackie Sosa, 1b/of, Castle Park Heights HS, Chula Vista, Calif.
60. Nicholas DeLuca, ss, Taylorsville HS, Salt Lake City, Utah

SAN DIEGO PADRES

June—Regular Phase (19)

1. (Pick to Giants as compensation tor Type A free agent Craig Lefferts)
1. **Robbie Beckett, lhp, McCallum HS, Austin, Texas** (Pick from Royals as compensation for Type A free agent Mark Davis)
1. **Scott Sanders** (Supplemental pick), rhp, Nicholls State (Supplemental pick—32nd—for loss of Davis)
2. (Pick to Tigers as compensation tor Type B free agent Fred Lynn)
3. **Jerrey Thurston, c, Lake Brantley HS, Altamonte Springs, Fla.**
4. **Rusty Silcox, rhp, Arizona State**
5. **Mark Anthony, 3b, Lancaster (S.C.) HS**
6. **Jeff Pearce, of, Pepperdine**
7. **Craig Bullock, 3b, Aldine HS, Houston**
8. **Keith McKoy, 2b, Southeastern (N.C.) CC**
9. **Tyrone Narcisse, rhp, Lincoln HS, Port Arthur, Texas**
10. **Paul Gonzalez, 3b, Texas Christian**
11. Jay Powell, rhp/3b, West Lauderdale HS, Collinsville, Miss.
12. **David Mowry, 1b, Glendora (Calif.) HS**
13. **Steve Gill, of, Arizona**
14. **Scott Fredrickson, rhp, Texas**
15. **Kevin Farlow, ss, Cal State Fullerton**
16. **Brent Bish, ss, Cal State Los Angeles**
17. **Matt Mieske, of, Western Michigan**
18. Todd Evers, rhp, Wisconsin
19. Keith Stafford, ss/2b, Swainsboro (Ga.) HS
20. **Billy Meury, ss, Maryland**
21. Scott Emerson, lhp, Shadow Mountain HS, Phoenix
22. Jon Ratliff, rhp, Liverpool Central HS, Clay, N.Y.
23. **James Elliott, c, Denver**
24. **Jay Gainer, 1b, South Alabama**
25. **Lance Painter, lhp, Wisconsin**
26. **Bruce Bensching, rhp, Lewis-Clark State (Idaho)**
27. **Jon Bellamy, 3b, Lassen (Calif.) JC**
28. **Reginald Stephens, 2b, St. Louis CC-Forest Park**
29. Greg Cushman, 3b, Monterey HS, Lubbock, Texas
30. **Ryan Ivie, lhp, Tumwater HS, Olympia, Wash.**
31. **Mike Bradley, rhp, Texas**
32. **Darius Gash, of, Middle Tennessee State**
33. **Lawrence Hawks, 1b/c, Central Missouri State**
34. **Paul Martin, rhp, Florida CC-Jacksonville**
35. Thomas Quinn, rhp, Mississippi State
36. **Joseph Waldron, lhp, Southwestern Oklahoma State**
37. Shawn Pagee, c, JC of San Mateo (Calif.)
38. **Jim West, c, San Francisco**
39. **Aaron Frederickson, lhp, Portland**
40. **Aldren Sadler, rhp, Rockdale County HS, Conyers, Ga.**
41. **David Adams, of, Cal State Los Angeles**
42. Stephen Grack, of, Rancho Santiago (Calif.) JC
43. **Thomas DeCareau, of, Harvard**
44. **German Carion Vega, 2b, Gurabo, P.R.**
45. **Steve Siebert, 2b/of, Georgia Southern**
46. **Jeffrey Brown, lhp, Navarro (Texas) JC**
47. Phillip Haney, c, Radford
48. **Tim Ploeger, rhp, Western HS, Las Vegas**
49. Alan Benes, rhp, Lake Forest (Ill.) HS
50. Gary Frank, 2b, La Jolla (Calif.) HS
51. **Robert Hays, rhp, Chico State (Calif.)**
52. **Jeffrey Ordway, ss/2b, Oregon Tech**
53. Alan Levine, rhp, Southern Illinois

SAN FRANCISCO GIANTS

June—Regular Phase (21)

1. **Adam Hyzdu, of, Moeller HS, Cincinnati** (Pick from Astros as compensation for Type B free agent Ken Oberkfell)
1. **Eric Christopherson, c, San Diego State** (Pick from Padres as compensation for Type A free agent Craig Lefferts)
1. (Pick to Astros as compensation for Type A free agent Kevin Bass)
1. **Marcus Jensen, c/rhp, Skyline HS, Oakland** (Supplemental pick—33rd—for loss of Lefferts)
2. Jose Prado, rhp, Coral Gables (Fla.) HS
2. **Joe Rosselli, lhp, Alemany HS, Mission Hills, Calif.** (Supplemental pick—70th—for loss of Type C free agent Candy Maldonado)
3. **Rick Huisman, rhp, Lewis (Ill.)**
4. **Mike Myers, lhp, Iowa State**
5. **Julio Vega, of, Shoreham-Wading River HS, Shoreham, N.Y.**
6. **John Jackson, of, Southern California**
7. Greg Norton, ss, Bishop O'Dowd HS, Orinda, Calif.
8. **Kevin McGehee, rhp, Louisiana Tech**
9. Nate Holdren, of, Richland (Wash.) HS
10. **Derek Reid, of, Triton (Ill.) JC**
11. **Kurt Peltzer, lhp, Wisconsin**
12. **Shelby Hart, of, Golden West (Calif.) JC**
13. Shawn Henrichs, rhp, Linn-Benton (Ore.) JC
14. Stacy Hollins, rhp, Willis (Texas) HS
15. **Mark Yockey, lhp, Lewis-Clark State (Idaho)**
16. Rikkert Faneyte, of, Miami-Dade South CC
17. **Jason Sievers, c, Lee's Summit (Mo.) HS**
18. **Mate Borgogno, 2b, Cal State Fullerton**
19. John Davis, rhp, Georgia Tech
20. **Tony Spires, ss, Coastal Carolina**
21. **Daniel Flanagan, rhp, Virginia Commonwealth**
22. Craig Bauer, rhp, Grand Canyon (Ariz.)
23. **Jim Huslig, rhp, Oklahoma**
24. Jarrod Smith, 3b/of, Winter Haven (Fla.) HS
25. Alan Dosty, c, Grant HS, Sacramento, Calif.
26. Lance Chambers, ss/3b, St. Petersburg (Fla.) JC
27. **Michael Helms, ss/of, Oregon**
28. **Rodney Huffman, rhp, McLennan (Texas) CC**
29. Lou Pote, lhp, Kishwaukee (Ill.) JC
30. Shawn Ramion, c, Lakeland (Ohio) CC
31. Vince Beall, of, Sacramento (Calif.) HS
32. Andre Keene, 1b, Lanham, Md.
33. Marcus Lee, of, U.S. Naval Academy Prep School, San Diego
34. **Daniel Varnell, of, Foothill (Calif.) JC**
35. Matt Castles, lhp, Davis (Calif.) HS
36. **Brian Dakin, c/inf, San Francisco**

SEATTLE MARINERS

June—Regular Phase (6)

1. **Marc Newfield, 1b, Marina HS, Huntington Beach, Calif.**
1. **Anthony Manahan, ss, Arizona State** (Supplemental pick—38th—for failure to sign 1989 first-rounder Scott Burrell)
2. (Pick to Indians as compensation for Type B free agent Pete O'Brien)
3. **Dave Fleming, lhp, Georgia**
4. **Paul Brannon, of, Kings Mountain (N.C.) HS**
5. **Bret Boone, 2b, Southern California**
6. **Mike Hampton, lhp, Crystal River (Fla.) HS**
7. **Kevin King, lhp, Oklahoma**
8. **John Cummings, lhp, Southern California**
9. **David Lawson, 1b/of, West Covina (Calif.) HS**
10. **Stafford Walace, rhp, Lufkin (Texas) HS**
11. **Tommy Robertson, of, Fairfield Central HS, Ridgeway, S.C.**
12. Luis Victoria, rhp, Isla Verde, P.R.
13. Kekoa Kaluhiokalani, rhp, Waianae (Hawaii) HS
14. **Lipso Nava, ss, Miami-Dade New World Center CC**
15. **Scott Schanz, rhp, UCLA**
16. **Jim Converse, rhp, Casa Roble HS, Orangevale, Calif.**
17. **Richard Russell, rhp, Campbell**
18. **David Adam, rhp, Central Connecticut State**
19. Albie Lopez, rhp, Mesa (Ariz.) CC
20. **Jim Neugent, lhp, Mustang HS, Yukon, Okla.**
21. **Tony Kounas, of, Loyola Marymount**
22. Pat Bojcun, rhp, Central Michigan

23. **Greg Hunter, 2b, Washington State**
24. **Willie Wilder, of, Murray State**
25. **Douglas Fitzer, lhp, Detroit**
26. Jeff Tucker, rhp, Allen County (Kan.) CC
27. Christopher Terry, ss, Tokay HS, Stockton, Calif.
28. Brad Gay, c, Dixie Hollins HS, St. Petersburg, Fla.
29. **David McDonald, lhp, Brandeis (Mass.)**
30. Renaldo Bullock, of, Triton (Ill.) JC
31. Damon Bihm, of, University HS, Los Angeles
32. Ron Rico, 1b, Cerritos (Calif.) JC
33. **Dion Gargagriano, lhp, CC of Morris (N.J.)**
34. Michael Bond, ss, Allegany (Md.) CC
35. **Clay Klavitter, 3b, Glendale (Ariz.) CC**
36. **Salvy Urbo, lhp, Plant HS, Tampa**
37. Alfred Rivers, of, Tallassee (Ala.) HS
38. Miguel Nolasco, ss, Lely HS, Naples, Fla.
39. Kenny Williams, rhp, Elk Grove (Calif.) HS
40. Bernard Erhard, ss/2b, Spartanburg Methodist (S.C.) JC
41. Gary Miller, rhp, Penn State
42. Armando Morales, rhp, Indian Hills (Iowa) CC
43. Anthony Maisano, 1b, Georgia Tech
44. Michael Gilmore, of/1b, Broomfield (Colo.) HS
45. Brian Fontes, rhp, Fresno (Calif.) CC
46. **Charles Wiley, rhp, Johnson County (Kan.) CC**
47. Scott Bedford, c, Edmonds (Wash.) CC
48. Rodney Mazion, ss, Hillsborough HS, Tampa
49. George Glinatsis, rhp, Cincinnati
50. Richard Wrobel, of, Upland (Calif.) HS
51. Daniel Stanley, ss, Yakima Valley (Wash.) CC
52. **Jon Halland, 2b, Arizona State**
53. Brian Klomp, rhp, McLane HS, Fresno, Calif.
54. **Rob Nichols, 1b, Washington State**
55. Roger Johnson, c, San Pedro (Calif.) HS
56. Eddie Miller, rhp, Compton (Calif.) CC
57. Dennis Shrum, 3b, Bullard HS, Fresno, Calif.
58. **James Bonnici, ss, Adams HS, Rochester, Mich.**
59. Robert Lewis, c, Los Angeles Harbor JC
60. Marcus Drake, of, Arroyo Grande HS, Oceano, Calif.
61. Ron Stanford, rhp, Crisp County HS, Cordele, Ga.
62. Hector Hernandez, rhp, Carolina, P.R.
63. Thomas Borio, rhp, Plainville (Conn.) HS
64. Brandon Newell, 3b, Nooksack Valley HS, Everson, Wash.
65. Matthew Pontbriant, lhp, St. Bernards HS, Norwich, Conn.
66. Bryan Lundberg, rhp, Glendale (Ariz.) CC
67. Silas Grinstead, c, Cardinal Neumann HS, Lake Worth, Fla.
68. Tim Cornish, of/ss, Camarillo (Calif.) HS
69. Keith Tippett, ss, Indian River (Fla.) CC
70. Dan Ricabal, rhp, San Gabriel HS, Rosemead, Calif.
71. Shawn Sanderfer, 3b, Upland (Calif.) HS
72. Toraino Golston, of, Gateway HS, Aurora, Colo.
73. Craig Gienger, 1b, Otero (Colo.) JC
74. Michael Bruce, c, Canoga Park (Calif.) HS
75. **Tim Roberts, lhp, Duke**

TEXAS RANGERS

June—Regular Phase (16)

1. **Dan Smith, lhp, Creighton**
2. Mike Schiefelbein, rhp, Chatfield HS, Littleton, Colo.
3. **Bobby Reed, rhp, Mississippi State**
4. **Mickey Henson, rhp, South Point HS, Belmont, N.C.**
5. **Jon Shave, ss, Mississippi State**
6. **Kevin Woodall, ss, Georgetown (S.C.) HS**
7. **Terry Burrows, lhp, McNeese State**
8. **Steve Dreyer, rhp, Northern Iowa**
9. **Tim Wells, rhp, Southwest Missouri State**
10. **Rusty Greer III, of, Montevallo (Ala.)**
11. **Efrain Gonzalez, of, Margarita River HS, Gurabo, P.R.**
12. **Andy Watson, rhp, Crowder (Mo.) CC**
13. **David Hulse, of, Schreiner (Texas)**
14. **Brian Mercado, rhp/3b, Eastern Connecticut State**
15. **Greg Blevins, c, Southwestern Louisiana**
16. Harry Berrios, of, Ottawa Hills HS, Grand Rapids, Mich.
17. **Frank Turco, ss, Barry (Fla.)**
18. **Rodney Busha, rhp, North Alabama**
19. **Todd Guggiana, 3b, Long Beach State**
20. Tim Kubinski, lhp, San Luis Obispo (Calif.) HS
21. Jarod Juelsgaard, rhp, Waldorf (Iowa) CC
22. **Marty Posey, c/of, Tulane**
23. **Keith Murray, of, South Alabama**
24. Shawn Kennedy, rhp, El Monte (Calif.) HS
25. **Matt Whiteside, rhp, Arkansas State**
26. **Johnny Johnson, rhp, Birmingham-Southern**
27. **Troy Rhoades, rhp, Greenwood (Ark.) HS**
28. **Chris McMullan, c, Richmond**
29. **Steve Rambarter, lhp, Rice**
30. Noe Najera, lhp, Cypress (Calif.) CC
31. **Scott Erickson, lhp, Kearney State (Neb.)**
32. Bryan Judice, of, Poly HS, Riverside, Calif.
33. **Mark Finney, rhp, Glendale (Ariz.) CC**
34. **Greg Wiseman, of, Crowder (Mo.) CC**
35. **Junior Antoine, of, St. Croix, Virgin Islands**
36. **Lee Hodge, 2b, Mississippi**
37. Chris Alexander, c, Southside HS, Memphis
38. **Chris Gies, rhp, Seminole State (Okla.) JC**
39. **Tim Cain, rhp, Connecticut**
40. Damian Grossie, 3b, Southwestern Louisiana
41. **Tim Stafford, rhp, McNeese State**
42. Brad Haley, 3b/of, El Toro (Calif.) HS
43. Donavon Hopper, rhp, Goldendale (Wash.) HS
44. Reggie Moore, ss, UCLA
45. **Sidney Holland, of, Texas-Pan American**
46. **Lance Jones, of, Texas**
47. **George Evangelista, ss, Merrimack (Mass.)**
48. **Peter Laake, 1b/of, Maryland**
49. **Richard Kunz, lhp, Brigham Young**
50. **Steve Surico, lhp, Loyola Marymount**
51. **Anthony Bouton, rhp, South Carolina**
52. **Paul Matachun, 3b/2b, Eastern Connecticut State**
53. Joe Dawley, rhp, Canyon Springs HS, Moreno Valley, Calif.
54. Ryan Hepworth, of, North Florida CC
55. Richard Juarez, lhp, Fresno (Calif.) CC
56. Donald Aslasken, of, Clear Creek HS, League City, Texas
57. Gary Beashore, 3b/rhp, Kansas City Kansas CC
58. Mark Lummus, lhp, Cleburne (Texas) HS
59. Quran Strane, of, Westmoore HS, Oklahoma City
60. Jerry Garrett, Oceanside (Calif.) HS

TORONTO BLUE JAYS

June—Regular Phase (22)

1. **Steve Karsay, rhp, Christ the King HS, Queens, N.Y.**
2. **Chris Weinke, 3b, Cretin HS, St. Paul, Minn.**
2. **Tim Hyers, 1b/of, Newton County HS, Covington, Ga.** (Supplemental pick—71st—for loss of Type C free agent Lloyd Moseby)
3. **Felipe Crespo, of, Notre Dame HS, Caguas, P.R.**
4. **Howard Battle, of, Mercy Cross HS, Ocean Springs, Miss.**
5. **Scott Burrell, rhp, Connecticut**
6. **David Tollison, 2b, Texas**
7. **Scott Brow, rhp, Washington**
8. **Paul Menhart, rhp, Western Carolina**
9. **Huck Flener, lhp, Cal State Fullerton**
10. **Tom Singer, lhp, St. John's**
11. **Daniel Vittala, of, Northern Michigan**
12. **Mark Choate, ss, North HS, Bakersfield, Calif.**
13. Craig Holman, rhp, Jacksonville State
14. **Matt Watson, rhp, Cal State Fullerton**
15. **Travis Burley, rhp, Miramar HS, Hollywood, Fla.**
16. **Mike Coolbaugh, ss, Roosevelt HS, San Antonio, Texas**
17. **Allen Rhea, lhp, Milligan (Tenn.)**
18. **Ron Reams, of, Laney (Calif.) JC**
19. **Carlos Santiago, of, Comerio, P.R.**
20. **Matthew Wilke, ss, North Dakota**
21. **Rafael Garcia, rhp, Southern California College**
22. **Sam Mandia, rhp, Seton Hall**
23. **Jason Reese, rhp, UC Riverside**
24. Deron Pointer, of, Curtis HS, Tacoma, Wash.
25. **Matthew Hudik, 2b, Ohio**
26. **David Marcon, lhp, Oral Roberts**

27. **Tom Hotchkiss, rhp, Santa Clara**
28. **Robert Adkins, rhp, Manatee HS, Bradenton, Fla.**
29. **Dale Kistaitis, lhp, Nebraska**
30. **Ciro Ambrosio, ss, Long Island**
31. **Greg Wilcox, rhp, Davidson**
32. **Kyle Duey, rhp, Portland**
33. **Bob Aylmer, lhp, Fordham**
34. **Scott Miller, ss/rhp, Elon**
35. **Rusty Filter, rhp, San Diego State**
36. **John Gilligan, rhp, Southern Mississippi**
37. **Ricardo Jordan, lhp, Miami-Dade CC South**
38. **Frank Kower, rhp, UNC Charlotte**
39. **D.J. Boston, 1b, San Jacinto (Texas) JC**
40. Darian Hagan, ss, Colorado
41. **Joe Ganote, rhp, UNC Charlotte**
42. **Roberto Duran, of, Seward Park HS, New York**
43. Patrick Valero, lhp, Kent State
44. Todd Weinberg, lhp, Somerset (Mass.) HS
45. **Travis Baptist, lhp, Hillsboro HS, Aloha, Ore.**
46. Robert Barber, c, American River (Calif.) JC
47. John Allan, lhp, Yakima Valley (Wash.) CC
48. Chris Laiche, lhp, St. Martin's Episcopal HS, Metairie, La.
49. Ryan Henderson, rhp, Citrus (Calif.) JC
50. David Pearlman, rhp, Fullerton (Calif.) JC
51. Jonathan Holsgrove, ss, Mineola HS, Williston Park, N.Y.
52. Martin Thomas, 1b, Kendrick HS, Columbus, Ga.
53. David Burke, rhp, Clay HS, Green Cove Springs, Fla.
54. Jeffery Gatland, rhp, Northport HS, East Northport, N.Y.
55. Bob Ippolito, rhp, Helix HS, La Mesa, Calif.

ERIE SAILORS (NEW YORK-PENN LEAGUE)

June—Regular Phase

1. No selection
2. No selection
3. No selection
4. **Gary Daniels, of, Brigham Young**

MIAMI MIRACLE (FLORIDA STATE LEAGUE)

June—Regular Phase

1. No selection
2. No selection
3. No selection
4. **Paul Carey, of, Stanford**
5. **Micah Bradbury, c, Loyola Marymount**
6. **Mike Lansing, ss, Wichita State**
7. **Greg D'Alexander, 3b, Arkansas**
8. **Tommy Raffo, 1b, Mississippi State**
9. **Brad Gregory, rhp, Florida State**
10. **Ken Whitworth, rhp, UC Irvine**
11. **Mike Czarnetski, of, UC Santa Barbara**
12. **Rod Nettnin, lhp, Nevada**
13. **Tim Rigsby, ss, Clemson**
14. Todd Pick, rhp, New Orleans
15. **John Urcioli, ss, New York Tech**
16. **Mike Ericson, rhp, Michigan State**
17. **Joe Burnett, of, Southwestern Louisiana**
18. **Charlie Rogers, lhp, North Alabama**
19. **Billy Walker, rhp, Gonzaga**

1991 TAYLOR, BORAS, YANKEES COMBINE TO TAKE DRAFT BONUSES TO NEW LEVELS, NEARLY TRIPLING RECORD

Agent Scott Boras emerged as a factor on the draft scene in the late 1980s, and he had helped drive the escalation of draft bonuses in 1989 and '90, but in 1991 he shot them through the roof.

North Carolina high school lefthander Brien Taylor, the No. 1 overall pick by the Yankees, signed for $1.55 million, shattering the previous record of $575,000 (John Olerud, 1989, and Mike Kelly, earlier in 1991) and setting a new standard in draft history. More significantly, Taylor and the Yankees started a wave of bonus inflation that didn't slow down until a decade later.

The Yankees signed Taylor just hours before he was to start classes at Louisburg (N.C.) Junior College, rewarding the patience of Taylor, his mother Bettie and Boras. Most people thought Taylor would sign for something close to the $350,000 the Yankees originally offered. It turned out to be a long, hot summer for the two sides, who at times exchanged heated words but finally sat down to sort out a contract.

When the dust cleared, the Yankees had their player, Taylor had his money and the industry had heartburn. The draft system, which was instituted to curb bonus inflation, was now producing payments that were rising out of control. Taylor's bonus was about 10 times that of Ken Griffey Jr., the No. 1 pick just four years earlier.

"This is not a smart thing," San Diego general manager Joe McIlvaine said. "We've got a workable, fair system that is equitable to clubs and players, and a few teams are trying to jeopardize it. If other clubs use these deals as a barometer, we'll all go out of business."

It should be noted that baseball teams continued to hand out larger and larger bonuses as the years went on, and no one went out of business.

Taylor's huge bonus continued a trend started by Ben McDonald and Todd Van Poppel (also Boras clients) in the two previous drafts. Industry officials hoped those deals would be seen as aberrations, but that proved not to be the case.

Every top 12 pick in 1991 who signed received a bonus of at least $325,000, far more than *any* draft pick got before 1989. When Taylor signed, he became the engine on a runaway train.

The principal cause for this was players threatening to go to college if teams didn't meet their demands. Clubs lose the rights to players who go to four-year colleges, so teams coughed up bundles of money rather than losing players.

R & R SPORTS GROUP

Brien Taylor blew the roof off signing bonuses but never fulfilled his promise

Many clubs proposed a rule change at the 1991 Winter Meetings to allow clubs to keep the rights to high school players for four years after they were drafted—eliminating the leverage players of college—but the rule was never adopted.

The signing had other repercussions for the rest of the draft. Two clubs that didn't want to go along with the inflationary trend didn't sign their first-round picks—two players who were also Boras clients.

The Brewers took Georgia high school righthander Kenny Henderson with the fifth pick but would not meet his $1 million asking price. They offered $500,000 and Henderson ended up at Miami. The Astros had the next pick and took Florida righthander John Burke, who asked for the same $500,000 the Brewers had offered Henderson. Houston declined and Burke returned to school. Neither player ended up having a significant career.

The inability of two smaller-market teams to sign their top picks worried some officials, who feared that rich clubs like the Yankees would price teams out of the market for top talent. It was a worry that would grow in future years as players and agents used bonus demands to manipulate the draft process, and even two decades later baseball had not figured out a mehod to deal with it.

Astros general manager Bill Wood said the players and agents weren't to blame.

"It's a lack of backbone on the clubs' part, to be honest, in not being able to show some common sense," Wood said. "They've convinced themselves that the money doesn't matter and that it's a one-time thing. But these contracts become basepoints . . . And I don't want to become part of these matters of insanity."

More Money

The second-largest bonus of 1991 went to outfielder Shawn Green, who got $700,000 from the Blue Jays. An outstanding student, Green signed a contract that allowed him to attend Stanford for two semesters in each of his first three years before reporting to spring training with the Blue Jays.

Still, Green made it to the big leagues for good in 1995 and went on to become an all-star outfielder, first with the Blue Jays and then with the Dodgers. He and Indians first-rounder Manny Ramirez, one of the cheaper first-round picks at $250,000, were the most successful players from a first round that saw many players not live up to their bonuses.

Taylor, most significantly, never reached the big leagues because of a shoulder injury he sustained after the 1993 season. He was involved in an altercation near his home in Beaufort, N.C., and missed the 1994 season. He never really recovered from the injury, bouncing around the minors for several more seasons before his career ended in 2000.

The Astros didn't participate in the bonus bonanza. They did, however, top their own draft record of sheer numbers of players drafted, taking 101 this time around. It was part of an overall trend that saw a record 1,600 players drafted.

The Astros and Cardinals, because they had lost free agents the previous winter and received compensation picks, made 13 of the first 50 selections. Aside from losing Burke, Houston did sign all of its other top picks, though none of them ended up being much better than Burke was. The Rangers signed their first 28 picks, breaking a record set by the 1988 Yankees, who signed their first 27.

Another contributor to 1991's bonus inflation was Frank Rodriguez, a shortstop/righthander who became the first big-money draft-and-follow signing of the draft era. The Red Sox picked him in the second round in 1990 and he went to Howard (Texas) Junior College instead of signing. Rodriguez was considered a first-round lock had he gone back into the draft, and might have gone as high as second overall, but the Red Sox signed him at the last minute for $425,000.

DRAFT 91: FIRST-ROUND PICKS

No.	Club	Player, Pos.	School	Hometown	Ht.	Wt.	B-T	Age
1.	Yankees	Brien Taylor, lhp	East Carteret HS	Beaufort, N.C.	6-3	195	L-L	19
2.	Braves	Mike Kelly, of	Arizona State	Los Alamitos, Calif.	6-4	195	R-R	21
3.	Twins	David McCarty, 1b	Stanford	Houston	6-5	205	R-L	21
4.	Cardinals	Dmitri Young, 3b	Rio Mesa HS	Oxnard, Calif.	6-2	215	R-R	17
5.	Brewers	*Kenny Henderson, rhp	Ringgold HS	Ringgold, Ga.	6-7	180	R-R	18
6.	Astros	*John Burke, rhp	Florida	Littleton, Colo.	6-4	210	B-R	21
7.	Royals	Joe Vitiello, 1b/of	Alabama	Stoneham, Mass.	6-3	210	R-R	21
8.	Padres	Joey Hamilton, rhp	Georgia Southern	Statesboro, Ga.	6-4	215	R-R	20
9.	Orioles	Mark Smith, of	Southern California	Arcadia, Calif.	6-2	215	R-R	21
10.	Phillies	Tyler Green, rhp	Wichita State	Denver	6-5	185	R-R	21
11.	Mariners	Shawn Estes, lhp	Minden HS	Douglas, Nev.	6-2	175	R-L	18
12.	Cubs	Doug Glanville, of	Pennsylvania	Teaneck, N.J.	6-2	180	R-R	20
13.	Indians	Manny Ramirez, of	George Washington HS	New York	6-1	185	R-R	18
14.	Expos	Cliff Floyd, 1b	Thornwood HS	South Holland, Ill.	6-4	220	L-R	18
15.	Brewers	Tyrone Hill, lhp	Yucaipa HS	Yucaipa, Calif.	6-5	195	L-L	19
16.	Blue Jays	Shawn Green, of	Tustin HS	Tustin, Calif.	6-3	170	L-L	18
17.	Angels	Eduardo Perez, 1b	Florida State	Santurce, P.R.	6-4	205	R-R	21
18.	Mets	Al Shirley, of	George Washington HS	Danville, Va.	6-1	210	R-R	17
19.	Rangers	Benji Gil, ss	Castle Park HS	Chula Vista, Calif.	6-2	180	R-R	18
20.	Reds	Calvin Reese, ss	Lower Richland HS	Hopkins, S.C.	5-9	160	R-R	17
21.	Cardinals	Allen Watson, lhp	New York Tech	Middle Village, NY	6-3	190	L-L	20
22.	Cardinals	Brian Barber, rhp	Dr. Phillips HS	Orlando	6-1	175	R-R	18
23.	Red Sox	Aaron Sele, rhp	Washington State	Poulsbo, Wash.	6-4	195	R-R	20
24.	Pirates	Jon Farrell, c/of	Florida CC	Jacksonville, Fla.	6-2	180	R-R	19
25.	White Sox	Scott Ruffcorn, rhp	Baylor	Austin, Texas	6-4	210	R-R	21
26.	Athletics	Brent Gates, ss	Minnesota	Grandville, Mich.	6-1	175	B-R	21

*Did not sign.

1991

CLUB-BY-CLUB SELECTIONS

ATLANTA BRAVES

June—Regular Phase (2)

1. **Mike Kelly, of, Arizona State**
2. (Pick to Cardinals as compensation for Type A free agent Terry Pendleton)
3. **Blase Sparma, rhp, Ohio State**
4. **Chris Seelbach, rhp, Lufkin (Texas) HS**
5. **Vince Moore, of, Elsik HS, Alief, Texas**
6. **Jose Rodriquez, c, Cayey, P.R.**
7. **Earl Nelson, lhp, Clark HS, San Antonio**
8. **Jason Schmidt, rhp, Kelso (Wash.) HS**
9. **Brad Rippelmeyer, c/rhp, Kansas State**
10. Jerome Jones, 3b, Carthage HS, Beckville, Texas
11. **Ken Giard, rhp, Toll Gate HS, Warwick, R.I.**
12. **Andre Johnson, of, Norfolk State**
13. **Byron Woods, of, Northeastern Oklahoma A&M JC**
14. **Kevin Lomon, rhp, Westark (Ark.) CC**
15. **Eric Lairsey, lhp, Pierce County HS, Blackshear, Ga.**
16. **Willie Havens, rhp, Holmes HS, San Antonio**
17. **Bill Shafer, rhp/1b, South Grand Prairie HS, Grand Prairie, Texas**
18. Jason Noel, of, Edison (Fla.) CC
19. Jes Rathke, rhp, Brownwood (Texas) HS
20. **Javier Rivas, of, Los Angeles CC**
21. **Mike Hostetler, rhp, Georgia Tech**
22. Ryan Karp, lhp, Miami
23. Don Denbow, of/1b, Corsicana (Texas) HS
24. **Sequinn Leichmon, ss, Strong (Ariz.) HS**
25. **Brad James, of, Illinois State**
26. **Pedro Swann, of, Delaware State**
27. **William Maier, c, Raritan Valley (N.J.) CC**
28. **Paul Kelliher, c, Maine**
29. **Kevin Grijak, of, Eastern Michigan**
30. Jason Cash, 1b, Newbury Park HS, Simi Valley, Calif.
31. Alton Huffstetler, rhp, Adairsville (Ga.) HS
32. **Jimmy Armstrong, lhp, Dallas Baptist**
33. Phil Hollis, ss, Purdue
34. **Rick O'Neill, ss, Illinois State**
35. **Craig Rapp, lhp, North Carolina State**
36. **Dirk Blair, rhp, Southeastern Oklahoma State**
37. **Ben Weeks, rhp, Butte (Calif.) JC**
38. **Dwayne Fowler, rhp, Long Beach State**
39. **Augie Vivenzio, c, Boca Raton (Fla.)**
40. Darnell Hendricks, of, Taft HS, Los Angeles
41. **Thomas Coates, of, Austin Peay State**
42. **Scott Behrens, rhp, Illinois State**
43. Leland Macon, of, Kirkwood (Mo.) HS
44. Greg Granger, rhp, Edgewood HS, Ellettsville, Ind.
45. **Michael Weiser, of/3b, Fargo (N.D.) HS**
46. Rinker Robinson, lhp, Tavares (Fla.) HS
47. Kurt Bierek, 3b/1b, Modesto (Calif.) JC
48. Kevin Willingham, rhp, DeSoto (Texas) HS
49. **Ronald York, of, South Carolina State**
50. **Yves Martineau, rhp, Pointe-aux-Trembles, Quebec**
51. Matt Sherwood, rhp, Blinn (Texas) JC
52. Phil Doyle, 3b/of, Alabama
53. **Robert Grob, c, Frederick (Md.) CC**
54. **Carlos Lara, c, New Mexico Highlands**
55. Rodney Close, of, Bainbridge (Ga.) HS
56. Earl Wheeler, rhp, Oklahoma State
57. Jason Garrett, 3b, Bowie HS, Manchaca, Texas
58. Jason Gunter, rhp, Sulphur (La.) HS
59. Jeremy Woods, rhp, Midwest City (Okla.) HS
60. **Ron Lloyd, of, Judson HS, Schertz, Texas**
61. Derek Berschaminski, 1b, North Dakota
62. Robert Valdez, lhp, Central Arizona JC
63. Frank Watts, of, Baker HS, Columbus, Ga.

BALTIMORE ORIOLES

June—Regular Phase (9)

1. **Mark Smith, of, Southern California**
2. **Shawn Curran, c, Corona (Calif.) HS**
3. **Alex Ochoa, of, Miami Lakes HS, Hialeah, Fla.**
4. **Vaughn Eshelman, lhp, Houston**
5. **Jim Wawruck, of, Vermont**
6. **Daniel Fregoso, rhp, Catalina HS, Tucson**
7. **Jimmy Haynes, rhp, Troup County HS, LaGrange, Ga.**
8. **Terry Farrar, lhp, Missouri Baptist**
9. **Chris Lemp, rhp, Sacramento CC**
10. **B.J. Waszgis, c, McNeese State**
11. **Brad Seitzer, 3b, Memphis State**
12. **Curtis Goodwin, of, San Leandro (Calif.) HS**
13. **Jim Audley, of, Wichita State**
14. **Glenn Coleman, of, JC of the Desert (Calif.)**
15. **Lamann Washington, ss, Beaufort (S.C.) HS**
16. **Derek Adams, ss, Louisburg (N.C.) JC**
17. Joel Franklin, rhp, Coronado (Calif.) HS
18. Aaron Lane, lhp, Lincoln Land (Ill.) CC
19. **Trov Tallman, c, Stanford**
20. **Allen Plaster, rhp, UNC Charlotte**
21. **Jeremy Winget, 1b, Murray (Utah) HS**
22. **Chris Chatterton, rhp, High Point (N.C.)**
23. **Rick Krivda, lhp, California (Pa.)**
24. **Glenn Tatro, of, Bryant (R.I.)**
25. **Steven Firsich, rhp, Grossmont (Calif.) JC**
26. **David Forney, rhp, Anne Arundel (Md.) CC**
27. **Jamie Conner, ss, Hedgesville HS, Martinsburg, W.Va.**
28. Angelo Stutts, of, Hammond (La.) HS
29. Orrett Bennett, of, Evanston (Ill.) HS
30. **Basillo Ortiz, of, Eastern Connecticut State**
31. Kyle Kennedy, rhp, Quitman (Miss.) HS
32. Erick Mapp, of, Cochise County (Ariz.) CC
33. **Kris Gresham, c, UNC Charlotte**
34. **Scott Conner, rhp, New Mexico JC**
35. Shane Shallenberger, of, Portales (N.M.) HS
36. Patrick Hicks, c, Mesa (Ariz.) CC
37. Johnny Walker, of, Hillsborough HS, Tampa
38. **Matt Sanders, rhp, Portland**
39. Terry Hawke, of, Putnam City West HS, Oklahoma City
40. Scott Emerson, lhp, Scottsdale (Ariz.) JC
41. Hector Castenada, c, Laredo (Texas) JC
42. Ryan Creek, of, Jefferson HS, Martinsburg, W.Va.
43. Jeff Ferguson, ss, LaSerna HS, LaMirada, Calif.
44. Brett Ames, lhp, Tucson HS
45. Tom Szimanski, rhp, Catonsville (Md.) CC
46. Torn Clarkson, 2b, The Bolles School, Jacksonville
47. Chris Pageau, ss, Schenectady (N.Y.) JC
48. Matthew Reimer, ss, Patapsco HS, Baltimore

BOSTON RED SOX

June—Regular Phase (23)

1. **Aaron Sele, rhp, Washington State**
1. **J.J. Johnson, of, Pine Plains (N.Y.) HS** (Supplemental pick—37th—for loss of Type A free agent Larry Andersen)
1. **Scott Hatteberg, c, Washington State** (Supplemental pick—43rd—for loss of Type A free agent Mike Boddicker)
2. **Terry Horn, rhp, Yukon (Okla.) HS** (Pick from Royals as compensation for Boddicker)
2. **Chad Schoenvogel, rhp, Blinn (Texas) JC**
3. **Joe Caruso, rhp, Loyola Marymount**
4. **Joe Ciccarella, 1b/lhp, Loyola Marymount**
5. Mark Carroll, of, Holliston (Mass.) HS
6. **Donny Jones, of, Poway (Calif.) HS**
7. **Dan Collier, of, Enterprise State (Ala.) JC**

8. **Luis Ortiz, 3b, Union (Tenn.)**
9. Dan McDonald, 3b, Evans HS, Orlando
10. **Tony Rodriguez, ss, Charleston (W.Va.)**
11. **Jimmy Crowley, 3b, Clemson**
12. **Craig Bush, rhp, Lancaster (Ohio) HS**
13. **John Eierman, of, Rice**
14. **Dana LeVangie, c, American International (Mass.)**
15. **Cory Bailey, rhp, Southeastern Illinois JC**
16. **Tony Ferreira, 2b, Manatee (Fla.) CC**
17. **Tim Van Egmond, rhp, Jacksonville State**
18. **Ron Mahay, of, South Suburban (Ill.) JC**
19. **Brian Bright, of, Massachusetts**
20. **Cesar Martinez, lhp, Chula Vista HS, San Diego**
21. **Joel Bennett, rhp, East Stroudsburg (Pa.)**
22. **Jim Lentz, c, Columbia State (Tenn.) CC**
23. **Bryan Brown, of, Tulane**
24. Ryan Beeney, ss, Newark (Ohio) HS
25. Melvin Walker, of, McNair HS, Atlanta
26. Jesus Armendariz, lhp, Howard (Texas) JC
27. Jake Austin, of, Wake Forest
28. Rafael Gutierrez, of, Sandalwood HS, Jacksonville
29. Lance Davis, lhp, Mary Montgomery HS, Semmes, Ala.
30. Chris Wiggs, ss, Santa Fe Catholic HS, Lakeland, Fla.
31. Daren Hobson, rhp, Meridian (Miss.) CC
32. Joshua Stough, rhp, Walker County HS, Jasper, Ala.
33. **Diogenes Baez, of, Connors State (Okla.) JC**
34. **Kevin Becker, rhp, Hilliard HS, Galloway, Ohio**
35. Jerry Taylor, c/of, Goliad (Texas) HS
36. Richie Wyman, of, Central Florida CC
37. Ken Albarado, of, Woodlawn HS, Baton Rouge
38. Steven Carver, ss, Bolles School, Jacksonville
39. Chris Davis, rhp, Northwest Mississippi CC

CALIFORNIA ANGELS

June—Regular Phase (17)

1. **Eduardo Perez, 1b, Florida State**
1. **Jorge Fabregas, 3b/c, Miami** (Supplemental pick—34th—for loss of Type A free agent Chili Davis)
2. **Chris Pritchett, 1b, UCLA**
3. **Mark Ratekin, rhp, Point Loma Nazarene (Calif.)**
4. **John Donati, 1b, De La Salle HS, Concord, Calif.**
5. **David Kennedy, rhp/of, Montclair State (N.J.)**
6. **Brian Williard, rhp, Dixie Hollins HS, St. Petersburg, Fla.**
7. **Chris Turner, 3b/c, Western Kentucky**
8. Kurt Ehmann, ss, Arizona State
9. **Mark Sweeney, of, Maine**
10. **Gary Hagy, ss, UCLA**
11. **Jeff Knox, rhp, Deltona (Fla.) HS**
12. Ken Maire, rhp, Eureka (Calif.) HS
13. **Kyle Sebach, rhp, Grossmont (Calif.) JC**
14. **Fred Young, rhp, Hillsborough HS, Tampa**
15. **Korey Keling, rhp, Oklahoma**
16. **Shawn Purdy, rhp, Miami**
17. **Shad Williams, rhp, Fresno CC**
18. **John Gledhill, rhp, Oklahoma City**
19. **Dennis McCaffery, of, Villanova**
20. Kevin Kloek, rhp, Citrus (Calif.) CC
21. Keith Stafford, ss, South Georgia JC
22. **Ron Martin, of, Downey HS, Compton, Calif.**
23. **Robbie Saitz, rhp, Fresno State**
24. **James Ruocchio, 3b, Long Island-C.W. Post**
25. Jon McGuire, 1b, McIntosh HS, Peachtree City, Ga.
26. Scott Schultz, rhp, Broad Run HS, Sterling, Va.
27. **Mark Mammola, lhp, Pace (N.Y.)**
28. Frank Greely, of, Lassen (Calif.) JC
29. Lyall Barwick, c, Delgado (La.) JC
30. Mike Parisi, rhp, Arcadia (Calif.) HS
31. Michael Monday, c, Orange Coast (Calif.) JC
32. **John Wylie, rhp, Jacksonville**
33. **Orlando Palmeiro, of, Miami**
34. Mike Halperin, lhp, Barron Collier HS, Naples, Fla.
35. Glenn Duckett, ss, Carthage (Mo.) HS
36. Rob Plarski, c, Poway (Calif.) HS
37. Carl Dalton, ss, Cave Spring HS, Roanoke, Va.
38. Richie Blackwell, lhp, Whiteville (N.C.) HS
39. Enrique Ramos, rhp, Luquillo, P.R.
40. David Vindivich, of, Edmonds (Wash.) CC
41. O.J. McDuffie, of, Penn State
42. Alfredo Diaz, ss, Pasadena (Calif.) CC
43. Aaron Boone, ss/3b, Villa Park (Calif.) HS
44. Eric Morgan, rhp, Cocoa (Fla.) HS
45. Jacob Cruz, of, Channel Islands HS, Oxnard, Calif.
46. **Mike Butler, lhp, North Carolina State**
47. Eric Mayo, rhp, Cherokee HS, Canton, Ga.
48. Rudolph Stroud, ss/3b, Brandon (Fla.) HS
49. **Mark Ledinsky, lhp/of, Jacksonville**
50. Allan Parker, ss, Polk (Fla.) CC
51. Browning Nagle, rhp, Louisville
52. Travis Exurn, rhp, Lake Weir HS, Ocklawaha, Fla.
53. John Foran, rhp, Marianna HS, Alford, Fla.

CHICAGO CUBS

June—Regular Phase (12)

1. **Doug Glanville, of, Pennsylvania**
2. (Pick to Blue Jays as compensation for Type A free agent George Bell)
3. **Bill Bliss, lhp, Villanova**
4. **Terry Adams, rhp, Mary Montgomery HS, Semmes, Ala.**
5. **Ozzie Timmons, of, Tampa**
6. **Hector Trinidad, rhp, Pioneer HS, Whittier, Calif.**
7. **Maceo Houston, of, Galileo HS, San Francisco**
8. **Steve Trachsel, rhp, Long Beach State**
9. Jon Lieber, rhp, South Alabama
10. **Scott Weiss, rhp, Stanford**
11. Sean Drinkwater, 2b/ss, Cypress (Calif.) JC
12. **Michael Reeves, of, Arizona State**
13. **Carl Schramm, rhp, Illinois Benedictine**
14. **Ben Burlingame, rhp, Maine**
15. **Devin Chavez, 3b/1b, Riverview HS, Kennewick, Wash.**
16. Chad Tredaway, ss, Seminole State (Okla.) JC
17. **Mitchell Root, ss, Chatsworth (Calif.) HS**
18. Trevor Humphry, rhp, Westark (Ark.) CC
19. **Thomas Walker, 1b, Walla Walla (Wash.) CC**
20. Bryan Garrett, of, Odessa (Texas) JC
21. Chris Clemons, rhp, McGregor (Texas) HS
22. **Kirk Goodson, rhp, Bluefield State (W.Va.)**
23. **Joe Szczepanski, lhp, California Baptist**
24. **Joe Terilli, of, Northwood Institute (Texas)**
25. **Michael Tidwell, lhp, Lenoir-Rhyne (N.C.)**
26. Frank Sanders, of, Dillard HS, Fort Lauderdale
27. Orlando Lopez, lhp, Isabela, P.R.
28. **Randy Belyeu, c, Jacksonville State**
29. **Rudy Gornez, ss, California Baptist**
30. **Brian Kenny, rhp, Villanova**
31. **Steven Davis, rhp, Lenoir-Rhyne (N.C.)**
32. **Frank Sample, rhp, College of the Ozarks (Mo.)**
33. Robin Jennings, of, Manatee (Fla.) JC
34. Jonathan Cornelius, of, Charter Oak HS, Covina, Calif.
35. Robert Nutting, c, Riverton HS, Galena, Kan.
36. Ramon Martinez, ss, Bayamon, P.R.
37. Chad Richardson, rhp, JC of Southern Idaho
38. Curtis Hall, ss, Pocatello (Idaho) HS
39. David Skeels, c, Thousand Oaks (Calif.) HS
40. Kevin Lydon, lhp, Mission HS, Fremont, Calif.
41. Daron Mooneyharn, ss, Mammoth HS, Mammoth Lakes, Calif.
42. Doug Webb, 3b/rhp, Alta HS, Draper, Utah
43. Traver Hunter, rhp, JC of Southern Idaho
44. **Perry Amos, lhp, Butte (Calif.) JC**
45. Eluid Barreto, of, Aguadilla, P.R.
46. Orlando Portalatin, of, Bayamon, P.R.
47. Roque Colon, of/1b, Manati, P.R.

CHICAGO WHITE SOX

June—Regular Phase (25)

1. **Scott Ruffcorn, rhp, Baylor**
2. **Larry Thomas, lhp, Maine**
3. **Mike Robertson, 1b, Southern California**

4. **Brian Boehringer, rhp, Nevada-Las Vegas**
5. **Eric Richardson, of, Brenham (Texas) HS**
6. **Harold Henry, of, Northeast Louisiana**
7. **Steve Olsen, rhp, Eastern Kentucky**
8. Demond Thomas, ss/of, Elizabethtown (Ky.) HS
9. **Troy Fryman, 1b, Jefferson Davis State (Ala.) JC**
10. **Juan Thomas, of, Paul Blazer HS, Ashland, Ky.**
11. **Alan Levine, rhp, Southern Illinois**
12. **Doug Brady, ss, Liberty**
13. **Mike Heathcott, rhp, Creighton**
14. **Glenn DiSarcina, ss, Massachusetts**
15. **Charles Frontera, rhp, Bishop Ford HS, Brooklyn**
16. **Marc Kubicki, rhp, Southern Mississippi**
17. **Demarcus Harris, ss, Caesar Rodney HS, Camden, Del.**
18. **Mike Cameron, of, LaGrange (Ga.) HS**
19. Denis Pujals, rhp, Southwest HS, Miami
20. **Michael Call, rhp, Washington**
21. **Matt Hattabaugh, c, Cal State Fullerton**
22. **David Martorana, 3b/ss, Flagler (Fla.)**
23. **Anthony Milledge, of, Palmetto (Fla.) HS**
24. Paul Crow, rhp, San Jacinto (Texas) JC
25. **Shawn Buchanan, of, Nebraska**
26. **Essex Burton, 2b/of, San Francisco State**
27. **Richard Bowrosen, 2b, Flagler (Fla.)**
28. Clay Hill, of, South Grand Prairie HS, Grand Prairie, Texas
29. **John Herrholz, rhp, New Orleans**
30. Carmine Cappuccio, of, Rollins (Fla.)
31. **Mike Bertotti, lhp, Iona**
32. **Dean Haase, c, Wisconsin-Oshkosh**
33. **Julio Vinas, c, American HS, Hialeah, Fla.**
34. David Marrero, 3b, Miami Lakes HS, Hialeah, Fla.
35. John MacCauley, rhp, Evansville
36. Jason Jordan, 1b, Jefferson Davis HS, Montgomery, Ala.
37. Sean Duncan, of, Martin HS, Arlington, Texas
38. Brandon Wilhite, rhp, Mississippi Delta JC
39. Darin Dreasky, 2b, Central Michigan
40. Mike Schmitz, 1b, Brevard (Fla.) JC
41. Robert Perry, 3b, Sacramento CC
42. Derek Bullock, rhp, Chaparral HS, Las Vegas
43. Michael Eaglin, ss/2b, DeAnza HS, San Pablo, Calif.
44. Tyler Borup, 1b, Sammamish HS, Bellevue, Wash.
45. Shannon Coulter, ss, Grand Prairie HS, Cedar Hill, Texas
46. William King, rhp, Carrol HS, Ozark, Ala.
47. Deloren Corbett, rhp, St. Augustine (Fla.) HS
48. Greg McGraw, rhp, Mortimer-Jordan HS, Gardendale, Ala.
49. Brian Jones, of, St. Augustine (Fla.) HS
50. Bobby Langer, ss, Creighton
51. Robert Lamb, rhp, Mississippi Delta JC
52. Shawn McGinn, ss, Nebraska-Omaha
53. Chris Mader, c, Rollins (Fla.)
54. Lovett Purnell, of, Seaford (Del.) HS

CINCINNATI REDS

June—Regular Phase (20)

1. **Pokey Reese, ss, Lower Richland HS, Hopkins, S.C.**
2. **Toby Rumfield, c, Belton (Texas) HS**
3. **Joe DeBerry, 1b, Clemson**
4. Kevin Bentley, of, Mansfield (Texas) HS
5. **Mike Harrison, c, California**
6. **Dave Tuttle, rhp, Santa Clara**
7. **Chris Reed, rhp, Katella HS, Anaheim**
8. **John Courtright, lhp, Duke**
9. **Damon Montgomery, of, Fremont HS, Los Angeles**
10. **Armando Morales, rhp, New Orleans**
11. **Scott Dodd, lhp, Arizona State**
12. **Rodney Steph, rhp, Texas Tech**
13. Jason Heath, 3b/of, Seminole State (Okla.) JC
14. **Brian Koelling, ss, Bowling Green State**
15. **Ken Cavazzoni, of, Columbia**
16. Bubba Hardwick, lhp, Polk (Fla.) CC
17. **Mike Jones, c/3b, Wichita State**
18. **Mike Coletti, lhp, Oklahoma City**
19. **Gene Taylor, of, Lubbock Christian (Texas)**
20. Jeff Stephens, 3b, Texas-Arlington
21. **Kevin Jarvis, rhp, Wake Forest**
22. Clifton Foster, rhp, Angelina (Texas) JC
23. James Ritchey, c, Copperas Cove (Texas) HS
24. **Rodney Thomas, of, North Marion HS, Reddick, Fla.**
25. **John Gast, 3b, East Carolina**
26. **Wayne Wilkerson, of, Norfolk State**
27. Isaac Burton, 3b, Washington HS, Los Angeles
28. **John Hrusovsky, rhp, Indian River (Fla.) CC**
29. **Scott Snead, ss, North Carolina State**
30. Brian Carlin, of, Northwestern State
31. **George Dreisbach, c, West Liberty State**
32. Matt Cesare, ss, Pearce HS, Richardson, Texas
33. Kevin Zellers, ss/2b, Holy Name HS, Maple Heights, Ohio
34. **Elijah Robinson, of/1b, Central HS, Joliet, Ill.**
35. Doyle Preston, of, Mount Vernon HS, Saltillo, Texas
36. **Matt Martin, 2b, Lubbock Christian (Texas)**
37. **Rossi Morris, of, Madison HS, Houston**
38. John Sherbert, c, Whiteville (N.C.) HS
39. **Yamil Concepcion, 3b, Florida, P.R.**
40. Stephen Larkin, 1b, Moeller HS, Cincinnati
41. Aaron Fultz, lhp, Munford (Tenn.) HS
42. **Demetrish Jenkins, ss, Dreher HS, Columbia, S.C.**
43. Jimmy Rice, ss/2b, McLean County HS, Owensboro, Ky.
44. Brett Backlund, rhp, Iowa
45. James Ethridge, lhp, Marengo Academy, Linden, Ala.
46. Curt Lowry, of, Paris (Texas) HS
47. Saul Bustos, 3b, Odessa (Texas) JC
48. John Gildon, c, Pleasant Grove HS, Texarkana, Texas
49. Rodriguez Sanders, of, Wilson HS, Florence, S.C.
50. Derbe Pearson, rhp, Dayton (Texas) HS
51. Stephen Claybrook, ss, Calallen HS, Robstown, Texas
52. Stuart Downing, of, Fairport (N.Y.) HS

CLEVELAND INDIANS

June—Regular Phase (13)

1. **Manny Ramirez, 3b/of, George Washington HS, New York**
2. **Herb Perry, 3b, Florida**
3. **Chad Ogea, rhp, Louisiana State**
4. **Paul Byrd, rhp, Louisiana State**
5. **Kevin Logsdon, lhp, Linn-Benton (Ore.) CC**
6. **Tom Vantiger, of, Iowa State**
7. **Pep Harris, rhp, Lancaster (S.C.) HS**
8. **Chris Coulter, lhp, Pensacola (Fla.) JC**
9. **Paul Meade, ss, Oral Roberts**
10. **Scott Sharts, 1b/rhp, Cal State Northridge**
11. **Brad Kantor, 2b, Manatee (Fla.) JC**
12. **Jeff Whitaker, ss, Martinsville (Va.) HS**
13. **Ryan Martindale, c, Creighton**
14. **Mike Jewell, rhp, Sacramento CC**
15. **Tommy Bates, ss, Southwestern Louisiana**
16. **Rod Koller, rhp, Southern Arkansas**
17. **Wade Key, rhp, Spartanburg Methodist (S.C.) JC**
18. **Michael Burritt, 3b/rhp, Oak Grove HS, San Jose**
19. **Chris Maffett, rhp, Southport HS, Indianapolis**
20. **Albie Lopez, rhp, Mesa (Ariz.) CC**
21. Jed Hansen, ss, Capitol HS, Olympia, Wash.
22. **Grady Davidson, lhp, Southern**
23. **Greg Knapland, lhp, Washington**
24. **Andre White, of, Laney (Calif.) JC**
25. **Brandon Bluhm, lhp, West HS, Chehalis, Wash.**
26. Rufus Boykin, of, Oviedo (Fla.) HS
27. Denny Vigo, 1b/3b, Cal State Northridge
28. Warren Frierson, 2b, Hartsville HS, Lydia, S.C.
29. **Patrick Maxwell, 2b, Western New Mexico**
30. **Rodd Hairston, 1b, Stephen F. Austin**
31. **Ian Doyle, rhp, Cuyahoga (Ohio) CC**
32. Jeff Seale, rhp, San Jacinto (Texas) JC
33. **Dave Duplesis, 1b, St. Mary's**
34. Dave Majeski, of, Florida
35. **Gary Tatterson, rhp, Arizona State**
36. **Jorge Santiago, 3b, Bayamon, P.R.**
37. **Michael Moore, c, West Virginia**
38. Robert Sherwood, c, Burroughs HS, Burbank, Calif.
39. Jason Elders, rhp, Rocky River (Ohio) HS

40. **Michael Taylor, c, Brookdale (N.J.) CC**
41. **Brian Buzard, lhp, Wichita State**
42. Erik Lane, ss, Russellville (Ark.) HS
43. Damien Crabtree, lhp, Ballard HS, Seattle
44. Damian Jackson, ss, Ygnacio Valley HS, Concord, Calif.
45. Greg Sinner, rhp, Kishwaikee (Ill.) JC
46. James Gatlin, c, Cedar Hills (Texas) HS
47. William Duffie, c, Irmo (S.C.) HS
48. Shannon Jones, ss, New Mexico JC
49. Steve Bourgeois, rhp, Delgado (La.) CC
50. Ryan Post, rhp, Wilson HS, Tacoma
51. Jonathan Stephany, of, Spanaway Lake HS, Tacoma
52. Jay Giardina, rhp, Delgado (La.) CC
53. Dale Dolejsi, rhp, Lindbergh HS, Renton, Wash.
54. John Waters, of, Eastern Wayne HS, La Grange, N.C.
55. Jamie Hanson, c, Kentwood HS, Kent, Wash.
56. Erasmo Velasco, of, Laredo (Texas) JC
57. Robert Augustine, rhp, Cowley County (Kan.) CC
58. Damon Sims, rhp, Belaire HS, Baton Rouge
59. Brian Holter, rhp, Benton (Ark.) HS
60. Ryan Stofer, rhp, Victoria, B.C
61. **Andy Stemler, lhp, Lewis (Ill.)**
62. Tim Thompson, ss, Harding HS, Charlotte

DETROIT TIGERS

June—Regular Phase (15)

1. (Pick to Brewers as compensation for Type A free agent Rob Deer)
1. **Justin Thompson, lhp, Klein Oak HS, Spring, Texas** (Supplemental pick—32nd—for loss of Type A free agent Jack Morris)
1. **Trever Miller, lhp, Trinity HS, Louisville** (Supplemental pick—41st—for loss of Type A free agent Mike Heath).
2. **Tarrik Brock, of, Hawthorne (Calif.) HS.**
3. **Brian Edmondson, rhp, Norte Vista HS, Riverside, Calif.** (Pick from Brewers as compensation for Type B free agent Edwin Nunez)
3. **Justin Mashore, of, Clayton Valley HS, Concord, Calif.**
4. **Sean Bergman, rhp, Southern Illinois**
5. **Paul Megrini, rhp, Wallington (N.J.) HS**
6. **Jason Pfaff, rhp, Michigan**
7. **Arthur Adams, rhp, Laney (Calif.) JC**
8. **Joe Perona, c, Northwestern**
9. **Clint Sodowsky, rhp, Connors State (Okla.) JC**
10. **Thomas Gibson, of, Mission (Calif.) JC**
11. **Brian Sullivan, of, Fordham**
12. **Clarke Rea, c, Arizona State**
13. **Evan Pratte, ss, Southwest Missouri State**
14. **Brian Prichard, c, Cincinnati Academy of Physical Education**
15. **Phil Stidham, rhp, Arkansas**
16. **Todd Bussa, rhp, Palm Beach Gardens (Fla.) HS**
17. Todd Ruyak, lhp, Virginia
18. **Peter Feeley, of, Lowell (Mass.)**
19. **Robin Higginbotham, of, Mississippi Gulf Coast JC**
20. **Rich Kelley, lhp, Jacksonville**
21. **Mark Tillman, of, Loyola Marymount**
22. **Tom Schwarber, rhp, Ohio State**
23. **Robert Grable, 3b, St. John's**
24. **Matt Bauer, lhp, Central Michigan**
25. **Scott Durussel, rhp, Western Michigan**
26. **John Reid, rhp, Stanford**
27. Victor Rodriguez, ss, Woodham HS, Pensacola, Fla,
28. **Robert Lemay, lhp, St. Andrews Presbyterian (N.C.)**
29. **Dan Ruff, of, Michigan**
30. **Kevin Morgan, ss, Southeastern Louisiana**
31. **James Givens, 2b/ss, Kent State**
32. Drew Christman, of, Oklahoma
33. Ray Ricken, rhp, Notre Dame HS, Warren, Mich.
34. **Inaldo Marrero, c, Arizona Western JC**
35. Scott Kennedy, rhp, Plymouth-Canton HS, Plymouth, Mich.
36. James Gordon, rhp, Turner HS, Burneyville, Okla.
37. Del Marine, c, Moorpark (Calif.) JC
38. (Selection voided)
39. Ryan Dedmon, 1b, Gaither HS, Lutz, Fla.
40. Enrique Martinez, ss, JC of the Desert (Calif.)
41. Joshua Kirtlan, 1b, Sacramento CC
42. Sean Hugo, 1b, West Moore HS, Oklahoma City
43. Troy Wachter, of, Miller Place (N.Y.) HS
44. **Doug Martin, rhp, Eastern Michigan**
45. **Dennis Walsh, lhp, Alabama**
46. **Greg Raffo, rhp, Middle Tennessee State**
47. Bobby Hughes, c/3b, Los Angeles Valley JC
48. Tristan Paul, ss, Rolling Hills HS, Rolling Hills Estates, Calif.
49. Brian Shumard, 1b, JC of the Redwoods (Calif.)
50. Michael Jenkins, rhp, Moorpark (Calif.) JC
51. Reggie Jackson, lhp, Hillsborough (Fla.) CC
52. Chris McCarter, of, Gulf Coast (Fla.) CC
53. Curt Bell, c, Indian River (Fla.) CC
54. Robert Dickerson, of, Mississippi Gulf Coast JC
55. Ken Tipton, of, Texarkana (Texas) CC
56. Sean Davisson, c/of, Sacramento CC
57. John Tirnko, c, Polk (Fla.) CC
58. Steven Breland, lhp, Mosley HS, Panama City, Fla.
59. Toby McFarland, lhp, Riverside (Calif.) CC
60. Kerry Collins, ss/3b, Penn State
61. **Robert Yelton, c, Miami (Ohio)**
62. **Greg Prey, of, Ohio State**

HOUSTON ASTROS

June—Regular Phase (6)

1. John Burke, rhp, Florida
1. **Shawn Livsey, ss, Simeon HS, Chicago** (Supplemental pick—28th—for loss of Type A free aqent Danny Darwin)
1. **Jim Gonzalez, c, East Hartford (Conn.) HS** (Supplemental pick—40th—for loss of Type A free agent Dave Smith)
1. **Mike Groppuso, 3b, Seton Hall** (Supplemental pick—44th—for loss of Type A free agent Franklin Stubbs)
2. **Buck McNabb, of, Fort Walton Beach (Fla.) HS** (Pick from Cardinals as compensation for Type B free agent Juan Agosto)
2. **Jimmy Lewis, rhp, Florida State** (Pick from Brewers as compensation for Stubbs)
2. **Eddy Ramos, 3b, American HS, Hialeah, Fla.**
3. **Chris Durkin, of, Youngstown State**
4. **Brian Holliday, rhp, San Diego State**
5. **Dan Grapenthien, 1b/of, Thornton Fractional South HS, Lansing, Ill.**
6. **Todd Hobson, of, Indiana State**
7. **James Mouton, of, St. Mary's**
8. **Tom Anderson, rhp, Iowa**
9. **Angelo Lee, of, Simeon HS, Chicago**
10. **Joshua Spring, rhp, Lebanon (Ohio) HS**
11. **Kevin Webb, 3b, UCLA**
12. **Rod Biehl, lhp, Louisville**
13. **Anthony Miller, lhp, Dayton**
14. **Bryant Winslow, 1b, UC Irvine**
15. **Rich Schulte, of, Central (Iowa)**
16. **Michael Murphy, c, U.S. International (Nairobi)**
17. **Randy Albaladejo, c, Vega Alta, P.R.**
18. **Mario Linares, c, Florida**
19. Carlos Perez, 1b/of, Ellison HS, Killeen, Texas
20. **Chris White, rhp, Cleveland State**
21. **James Waring, rhp, Stetson**
22. **Roger Rumsey, of, Dallas Baptist**
23. Kirk Larson, ss, Homestead HS, Sunnyvale, Calif.
24. **Joe Sewell, rhp, UC Irvine**
25. Jose Flores, ss/2b, Brandeis HS, New York
26. Anthony Dermendziev, of, Santa Teresa HS, San Jose
27. Kyle Wagner, c, Red Land HS, New Cumberland, Pa.
28. Aldren Sadler, rhp, Middle Georgia JC
29. **Mark Loughlin, lhp, Providence**
30. Michael Machado, of, Antioch (Calif.) HS
31. Matt Williams, rhp, Edmond Memorial HS, Edmond, Okla.
32. Bobby Howry, rhp, Deer Valley HS, Glendale, Ariz.
33. Craig Castellanos, lhp, Victor Valley HS, Victorville, Calif.
34. Tony Pruett, c/of, El Camino (Calif.) JC
35. Jermine Adams, of, Riverside (Calif.) CC
36. Keith Davenport, lhp, Michigan State

37. **Jeffrey Miller, rhp, Missouri Baptist**
38. Marlon Gardinera, of, Mission Bay HS, San Diego
39. **Alvin Morman, lhp, Wingate (N.C.)**
40. Mike Metcalfe, ss, Colonial HS, Orlando
41. **Heath Rose, lhp, MacMurray (Ill.)**
42. **Ricky Blest, lhp, Missouri Baptist**
43. **Roy Nieto, rhp, Southwestern (Texas)**
44. Todd Coburn, c, Butte (Calif.) JC
45. Marty Henry, rhp, Treasure Valley (Ore.) CC
46. Donald Smith, rhp, Orange Coast (Calif.) JC
47. Eduardo Fuentes, 2b, Santurce, P.R.
48. Paul Barber, ss, Queen City (Texas) HS
49. James Davis, 3b, San Diego CC
50. Michael Keenan, rhp, Hancock (Calif.) JC
51. Johnny Mitchell, of, Middle Georgia JC
52. Jason Reed, lhp, El Capitan HS, El Cajon, Calif.
53. Sean Tyler, of, Texarkana (Texas) CC
54. Kraig Kupiec, of, Durfee HS, Fall River, Mass.
55. D.C. Olsen, c, Fullerton (Calif.) HS
56. Lou Collier, rhp, Vocational HS, Chicago
57. **Fausto Abad, of, Middle Georgia JC**
58. Jamie Falconer, lhp, LaGrand (Ore.) HS
59. Johnny Isom, of, Crowley HS, Fort Worth
60. Joch Martin, of, Loves Park-Harlem HS, Rockford, Ill.
61. **Sean Fesh, lhp, Bethel (Conn.) HS**
62. Jeff Henry, of, Glenwood HS, Phenix City, Ala.
63. Jay Witasick, rhp, Brevard (Fla.) CC
64. Luis Victoria, rhp, Catano, P.R.
65. Kerry Bertrand, of, Berwick HS, Morgan City, La.
66. Eric Dumas, of, Covington HS, Madisonville, La.
67. Chad Dunavan, of, Everman HS, Fort Worth
68. Trevin Smith, rhp/c, West Mecklenburg HS, Denver, N.C.
69. Alfonso Montoya, of, San Marino (Calif.) HS
70. Chris Briones, c, Brea (Calif.) HS
71. Jeff Beck, c, Mount Vernon HS, Alexandria, Va.
72. Matthew Maffei, 1b, Laguna Hills HS, Dana Point, Calif.
73. Brett Baptist, rhp, Jacksonville (Ill.) HS
74. Matt Beaumont, lhp, Rittman (Ohio) HS
75. Donald Shump, 3b, Northeast HS, Pasadena, Md.
76. Rahasal Buggs, c, Morgan Park HS, Chicago
77. Robert Giannola, c, Ohlone (Calif.) JC
78. Scott Martyka, of/lhp, Incline HS, Incline Village, Nev.
79. Robert Medel, 3b, Waukegan (Ill.) HS
80. Thomas Uptegrove, of, Clear Creek HS, League City, Texas
81. Jeff Latimore, 3b, Vocational HS, Chicago
82. Robert Klemme, 1b, Niles North HS, Skokie, Ill.
83. Koby Stovall, lhp, Skyview HS, Billings, Mont.
84. David Vergara, lhp, Westminster (Calif.) HS
85. Anthony Spivey, rhp, Pacelli HS, Phenix City, Ala.
86. Rodney Ruelas, lhp, Niles North HS, Skokie, Ill.
87. Evan Bailey, rhp, Escambia HS, Pensacola, Fla.
88. Britt Gusmus, of, Cherry Creek HS, Englewood, Colo.
89. Pat Harter, of, Fernandina Beach (Fla.) HS
90. Danny Harris, 3b, Henry County HS, Stockbridge, Ga.
91. Brook Holding, 3b, Blanchard (Okla.) HS
92. Mike Hammer, ss, Willowbrook HS, Villa Park, Ill.
93. Craig Everett, of, Norcast HS, Pasadena, Md.
94. Jose Avina, of, East Union HS, Lathrop, Calif.
95. Daniel Pagan, 3b/1b, Howard (Texas) JC
96. Brian Hudson, rhp, Mater Dei HS, Fountain Valley, Calif.

KANSAS CITY ROYALS

June—Regular Phase (7)

1. **Joe Vitiello, of/1b, Alabama**
1. **Jason Pruitt, rhp, Rockingham County HS, Wentworth, N.C.** (Supplemental pick—30th—for loss of Type A free agent Steve Farr)
2. **Ryan Long, 3b, Dobie HS, Pasadena, Texas** (Pick from Yankees as compensation for Farr)
2. (Pick to Red Sox as compensation for Type A free agent Mike Boddicker)
3. (Pick to Dodgers as compensation for Type B free agent Kirk Gibson)
4. **Dwayne Gerald, ss, St. Paul's (N.C.) HS**
5. **Shane Halter, ss, Texas**
6. **Mike Bovee, rhp, Mira Mesa HS, San Diego**
7. Paul Failla, ss, North Alleghany HS, Wexford, Pa.
8. **Kevin Hodges, rhp, Klein Oak HS, Spring, Texas**
9. **Steve Hinton, of, Creighton**
10. **Mike Sweeney, c, Ontario (Calif.) HS**
11. **Joe Randa, 3b, Tennessee**
12. **Mike Fyhrie, rhp, UCLA**
13. **Rod Myers, of, Conroe (Texas) HS**
14. **Angel Macias, rhp, East Los Angeles JC**
15. **Chris Connolly, lhp, Radford**
16. **Michael Bailey, rhp, Tallahassee (Fla.) CC**
17. **Mark Johnson, of, Arkansas**
18. Brian Teeters, of, Bakersfield (Calif.) JC
19. Michael Currier, rhp, North Harris (Texas) CC
20. **John Downs, rhp, Muscatine (Iowa) CC**
21. **David Farsaci, rhp, High Point (N.C.)**
22. **Matthew Bennett, rhp, Davis HS, Modesto, Calif.**
23. **Andrew Brookens, 2b, Shippensburg (Pa.)**
24. Joe Carrillo, lhp, Southwestern (Calif.) JC
25. **Les Norman, of, St. Francis (Ill.)**
26. **Joel Johnson, rhp, Simpson (Iowa)**
27. **Kris Glaser, rhp, Olney Central (Ill.) JC**
28. **Daniel Servello, of, West Virginia**
29. Justin Craig, rhp, Peabody HS, Pittsburgh
30. Michael McLain, rhp, Sacramento CC
31. **Troy Babbitt, 3b, Cypress (Calif.) JC**
32. **Paul Sanders, c, Oregon State**
33. **Ryan Towns, rhp, Blinn (Texas) JC**
34. **Roger Landress, rhp, Augusta (Ga.)**
35. **Kevin Kobetitsch, lhp, Concordia (N.Y.)**
36. **Paul West, rhp, Garland County (Ark.) CC**
37. **Rodney Williams, of, Palmdale (Calif.) HS**
38. Shandel Curris, of, Cass HS, Detroit
39. Jim Miller, rhp, Michigan State
40. Trenton Hauswirth, c, JC of the Desert (Calif.)
41. Dax Winslett, rhp, McLennan (Texas) CC
42. Jarrod Smith, of/3b, Polk (Fla.) CC
43. **Chris Medrick, lhp, Emporia State (Kan.)**
44. **Jeff Smith, rhp, Oregon State**
45. Ramon Smith, of, Encinal HS, Alameda, Calif.
46. Twaino Moss, of, Hancock Central HS, Sparta, Ga.
47. James Reinecker, rhp, Northview HS, Covina, Calif.
48. Jorge Ortiz, rhp, Carolina, P.R.
49. Jason Chandler, lhp, Burbank (Calif.) HS
50. Chad Bumgarner, rhp, Palm Desert (Calif.) HS
51. Michael Blang, rhp, Monona Grove HS, Monona, Wis.
52. Rex Crosnoe, c, Cape-Central HS, Cape Girardeau, Mo.
53. Derrick Robinson, 3b, Pleasant Grove (Utah) HS
54. Edgar Orta, lhp, San Gabriel HS, Alhambra, Calif.
55. **Thomathon Good, of, Brazoswood HS, Clute, Texas**
56. Scott Harrison, rhp, Texas
57. Roy Marsh, of, Perry Hall HS, Baltimore
58. Michael Mitchell, 1b, Rio Mesa HS, Camarillo, Calif.
59. Jason Guyton, of, Caruthersville (Mo.) HS
60. Ron Rivera, rhp, Cayey, P.R.
61. Francis Rosa, rhp, Arecibo, P.R.
62. Kenneth Phillips, of, Oregon

LOS ANGELES DODGERS

June—Regular Phase (18)

1. (Pick to Mets as compensation for Type A free agent Darryl Strawberry)
2. (Pick to Expos as compensation tor Type B free agent Kevin Gross)
3. **Todd Hollandsworth, of, Newport HS, Bellevue, Wash.** (Pick from Royals as compensation for Type B free agent Kirk Gibson)
3. Todd LaRocca, ss, The Lovett School, Atlanta
4. **Mike Walkden, lhp, Lake Stevens (Wash.) HS**
5. **Doug Bennett, rhp, Arkansas**
6. **Mike Iglesias, rhp, Hayward (Calif.) HS**
7. **Brandon Watts, lhp, Ruston (La.) HS**
8. **Vince Jackson, of, Central HS, Davenport, Iowa**

9. **Dennis Winicki, ss, Mona Shores HS, Muskegon, Mich.**
10. **Lonnie Jackson, of, Washington HS, Oakland**
11. **Chris Latham, ss, Basic HS, Las Vegas**
12. **Carlo Walton, c, East Side HS, Newark, N.J.**
13. **David Fitzpatrick, rhp, Sullivan South HS, Kingsport, Tenn.**
14. **Robert Legendre, rhp, Cypress (Calif.) JC**
15. **Erik Zammarchi, of, JC of Marin (Calif.)**
16. **Chris Sinacori, rhp, Florida International**
17. **Chad Zerbe, lhp, Hillsborough (Fla.) CC**
18. **JoJo Smith, lhp, Vanderbilt**
19. **Rick Gorecki, rhp, Oak Forest (Ill.) HS**
20. **Billy Stephens, rhp, Ringgold (Ga.) HS**
21. **Kevin Zahner, c, Ellington HS, Rockville, Conn.**
22. **Ken Huckaby, c, San Joaquin Delta (Calif.) JC**
23. David Carroll, lhp, Chantilly HS, Fairfax, Va.
24. **Kevin Smith, lhp, Columbus (Ga.) HS**
25. **Murph Proctor, 1b, Southern California**
26. **Chris Crabtree, lhp, Middle Tennessee State**
27. **Todd Soares, of, New Bedford (Mass.) HS**
28. **John Landrum, of, Jacksonville State**
29. **Vern Spearman, of, Fresno State**
30. **Jack Johnson, c, Arizona**
31. **Chris Demetral, 2b, Western Michigan**
32. Travis Hall, lhp, Middle Georgia JC
33. **Jay Kirkpatrick, c, Methodist (N.C.)**
34. Cedric Allen, lhp, McLennan (Texas) CC
35. **Eduardo Acosta, ss, Rock Falls (Ill.) HS**
36. Kenneth Sikes, 1b/rhp, Perry (Ga.) HS
37. Alejandro Periera, lhp, Miami-Dade New World Center CC
38. **Gary Cope, lhp, Motlow State (Tenn.) CC**
39. **Clifton Joyce, lhp, South Stokes HS, Walnut Cove, N.C.**
40. **Michael Sube, lhp, West Virginia**
41. **Carlos Castillo, rhp, Cypress (Calif.) JC**
42. **Carlos Thomas, rhp, Tennessee State**
43. Chris West, 3b, Louisburg (N.C.) JC
44. **Eric Vorbeck, of, Cal State Sacramento**
45. **Marc Tramuta, ss, St. Bonaventure**
46. Mario Moody, ss, Glynn Academy, Brunswick, Ga.
47. Ken Jones, 1b, Pelham (Ga.) HS
48. Matthew Svoboda, rhp, El Dorado HS, Placentia, Calif.
49. **Richard Ware, 2b, Greenville (Ill.)**
50. **German Gonzalez, 3b, JC of the Desert (Calif.)**
51. Dustin Rennsnies, c, Mosley HS, Panama City, Fla.
52. **Cam Aronetz, lhp, Coquitlam, B.C**
53. Chris Vaughn, lhp, John Logan (Ill.) JC
54. Javier Ortiz, rhp, Caguas, P.R.
55. Brian Clark, c, Armijo HS, Fairfield, Calif.
56. Brian Wise, lhp, El Sequndo (Calif.) HS
57. Roger Cropper, of, St. Croix, Virgin Islands
58. William Belcher, of, Fairfax HS, Los Angeles
59. Jonathan Goodnch, rhp, Sonoma (Calif.) HS
60. Steven Kline, lhp, Allegany (Pa.) CC
61. Jareld Dunkin, c, Capitol Hill HS, Oklahoma City
62. Kevin Clark, 3b, Basic HS, Henderson, Nev.
63. Richard Linares, rhp, Cerritos (Calif.) JC
64. David Buhner, 1b, Clear Creek HS, Nassau Bay, Texas
65. David Silvas, ss, San Jacinto HS, Pearland, Texas
66. **Jason Bobb, rhp, Chippewa Falls (Wis.) HS**
67. Derek Ornelas, of, Sylmar (Calif.) HS
68. Chris Kenady, of, Westonka HS, Mound, Minn.
69. Richard Heineman, c, Culver City (Calif.) HS
70. Joseph Jacobsen, rhp, Fresno CC
71. Mark Fraser, rhp, Sudbury, Ontario
72. Kerry Cosgrove, of, Palm Desert (Calif.) HS
73. Stephane DiLauro, ss, Montreal, Quebec
74. Eric Ontiveros, rhp, Bakersfield (Calif.) JC
75. Joshua Hamik, c, Mount Si HS, Fall City, Wash.
76. Brent Crowther, rhp, North Vancouver, B.C.
77. Rich Haley, of, Sacramento CC
78. David Glass, of, Santa Rosa (Calif.) JC
79. Stephen Matyczyk, ss, Southington (Conn.) HS
80. Ismael Castaneda, lhp, Fresno CC
81. Gar Vallone, ss, El Dorado HS, Placentia, Calif.
82. Michael Sanburn, rhp, JC of San Mateo (Calif.)
83. Aaron Wofford, ss, Yuba (Calif.) JC
84. Jose Martinez, rhp, Los Angeles CC
85. Darrell Sutton, rhp, Beverly Hills (Calif.) HS
86. Brett Schafer, 3b, Santa Monica HS, Malibu, Calif.
87. Andy Saltsman, c, Crescenta Valley HS, La Crescenta, Calif.
88. Jarman Leach, of, San Marin HS, Novato, Calif.
89. Martin Meza, rhp, Cerritos (Calif.) JC
90. Todd Blyleven, rhp, Cypress (Calif.) JC
91. Steven Arffa, lhp, Glendora (Calif.) HS
92. Derek Gauthier, 2b, East York (Toronto)
93. William Stroud, c/1b, Dunwoody HS, Atlanta
94. William McNally, ss, Winder Barrow HS, Winder, Ga.

MILWAUKEE BREWERS

June—Regular Phase (5)

1. Kenny Henderson, rhp, Ringgold (Ga.) HS
1. **Tyrone Hill, lhp, Yucaipa (Calif.) HS** (Pick from Tigers as compensation for Type A free agent Rob Deer)
2. (Pick to Astros as compensation for Type A free agent Franklin Stubbs)
2. **Judd Wilstead, rhp, Dixie HS, St. George, Utah** (Supplemental pick—71st—for loss of Type C free agent Bill Krueger)
3. (Pick to Tigers as compensation for Type B free agent Edwin Nunez)
4. **Mike Harris, 1b, Kentucky**
5. Nomar Garciaparra, ss, St. John Bosco HS, Whittier, Calif.
6. **Cecil Rodrigues, of, Indian River (Fla.) CC**
7. **Derek Wachter, of, Iona**
8. **Mike Matheny, c, Michigan**
9. **Bill Dobrolsky, c, Shippensburg (Pa.)**
10. **Jim Wilkie, rhp, Triton (Ill.) JC**
11. **Jeff Cirillo, 3b, Southern California**
12. **Paul Arredondo, ss, Colton HS, Grand Terrace, Calif.**
13. **Byron Browne, rhp, Grand Canyon (Ariz.)**
14. **John Trisler, rhp, Indiana State**
15. **Scott Talanoa, 1b, Long Beach State**
16. **David Preikszas, of, Miami (Ohio)**
17. **Charles O'Laughlin, lhp, Southwestern (Calif.) JC**
18. **Tim Albert, of, Hawaii**
19. **Mike Basse, of, Tennessee**
20. **Michael Hancock, lhp, Volunteer State (Tenn.) CC**
21. **Rob Gorrell, rhp, Arizona State**
22. Scott Morgan, 3b, Lompoc (Calif.) HS
23. **Brian Dennison, lhp, Arkansas**
24. **Andy Fairman, 1b, Michigan**
25. Michael Swenson, lhp, Chamberlain HS, Tampa
26. **Derek Ghostlaw, c, Bentley (Mass.)**
27. **Mark Stillwell, 1b, Kaiser HS, Honolulu**
28. Antonio Valdez, rhp, Miami Beach (Pa.) HS
29. Steven Brown, rhp, Central Arizona JC
30. Mark Sobolewski, c/3b, Florida Southern
31. Brent Simonian, of, Fowler (Calif.) HS
32. **Howard House, of, Howard (D.C.)**
33. Osmel Garcia, rhp/of, American HS, Hialeah, Fla.
34. **Mike Lawn, of, California**
35. Geoff Hughes, of, Naperville North HS, Naperville, Ill.
36. Bobby Jones, of, Arlington HS, Riverside, Calif.
37. Albert Harvell, lhp, San Jose (Calif.) CC
38. **Jason Imperial, 3b, Rutgers**
39. Maurice Crum, c/1b, Miami
40. **Michael Stefanski, c, Detroit**
41. Brad Gay, c, Hillsborough (Fla.) CC
42. Jerry Fisher, rhp, Southern HS, Baltimore
43. Michael Mace, rhp, Gulf Coast (Fla.) CC
44. Bobby Jones, lhp, Chipola (Fla.) JC
45. **Jackie Ross, of, Miami-Dade CC North**
46. **Charles Payne, rhp, Battle Ground Academy, Brenton, Tenn.**
47. Francisco Gonzalez, rhp, Arecibo, P.R.
48. Tommy Schenbeck, rhp, Palm Beach (Fla.) JC
49. Scott Wayne, c, Englewood (Colo.) HS

MINNESOTA TWINS

June—Regular Phase (3)

1. **David McCarty, 1b, Stanford**
1. **Scott Stahoviak, 3b, Creighton** (Supplemental pick—27th—for loss of Type A free agent Gary Gaetti)
2. **Mike Durant, c, Ohio State**
3. **Keith LeGree, ss, Statesboro (Ga.) HS**
4. **Brett Roberts, rhp, Morehead State**
5. **Shawn Miller, rhp, Beyer HS, Modesto, Calif.**
6. **Pedro Grifol, c, Florida State**
7. **LaTroy Hawkins, rhp, West Side HS, Gary, Ind.**
8. **Brad Radke, rhp, Jesuit HS, Tampa**
9. **Neil Stevens, rhp/c, Beekmantown Central HS, Plattsburg, N.Y.**
10. **Anthony Banks, of, Hoover HS, San Diego**
11. **Bill Wissler, rhp, Pennsylvania**
12. **Jeff Mansur, lhp, Portland**
13. **Matt Lawton III, 2b, Mississippi Gulf Coast JC**
14. Robert Neal, of, Westlake HS, Thousand Oaks, Calif.
15. Travis Huenfeld, of, Rockhurst HS, Olathe, Kan.
16. Rob Johnson, rhp, El Toro HS, Mission Viejo, Calif.
17. Eric Kunz, rhp, Keller HS, Wautauga, Texas
18. **David Sartain, lhp, Virginia Commonwealth**
19. **Mike Fernandez, of/3b, New York Tech**
20. **Steve Hazlett, of, Wyoming**
21. **Michael Lewis, lhp, UCLA**
22. Reid Hensley, rhp, Marian HS, Lansing, Ill.
23. **Dennis Sweeney, lhp, Seton Hall**
24. **David Schwartz, rhp, California**
25. **Bob Robinson, rhp, Ohio**
26. Larry Hawkins, of, Mississippi Gulf Coast JC
27. **Rafael Pina, rhp, East Los Angeles JC**
28. **Chad Baucom, c, Hibbing (Minn.) HS**
29. Chris Moten, rhp, Cerritos (Calif.) JC
30. Ryan Kjos, rhp, Hopkins (Minn.) HS
31. Steven Friedrich, c, Troy HS, Yorba Linda, Calif.
32. Matt Petersen, rhp, Iowa State
33. David Baine, lhp, Sonoma State (Calif.)
34. Tim Davis, lhp, Florida State
35. Myron Glass, of, St. Joseph HS, Kenosha, Wis.
36. David Doezie, c, Brighton HS, Sandy, Utah
37. Cesar Barrera, 3b, Ontario (Calif.) HS
38. Tim Mathews, rhp, Nevada
39. Jon Hillis, c, Alvin (Texas) CC
40. Cory Simpson, 3b/of, Red Bank HS, Chattanooga, Tenn.
41. Brad Niedermeier, rhp, Niles West HS, Niles, Ill.
42. German Casillas, lhp, Los Angeles Harbor JC
43. Joe Bergen, c, Mesa (Ariz.) CC
44. Thomas Gourdin, c, Murray (Utah) HS
45. Kevin Allen, rhp, Mountain View HS, Mesa, Ariz.
46. **James Kohl, rhp, Rutgers**
47. **Pat Wright, of, Minnesota**

MONTREAL EXPOS

June—Regular Phase (14)

1. **Cliff Floyd, 1b, Thornwood HS, South Holland, Ill.**
2. **Scott Pisciotta, rhp, Walton HS, Marietta, Ga.**
2. **Rodney Pedraza, rhp, Texas** (Pick from Dodgers as compensation for Type B free agent Kevin Gross)
3. **Jeff Hostetler, rhp, Cleveland State (Tenn.) JC**
4. **Jim Austin, 3b/of, Arizona State**
5. **Mike Daniel, c, Oklahoma State**
6. **Derrick White, 1b, Oklahoma**
7. **Doug O'Neill, of, Cal Poly San Luis Obispo**
8. **Mark LaRosa, rhp, Louisiana State**
9. **Brett Jenkins, 2b, Southern California**
10. **Brian Looney, lhp, Boston College**
11. **Mark Grudzielanek, ss, Trinidad State (Colo.) JC**
12. Shawn Wills, of, UCLA
13. **Khary Heidelberg, of, Princess Anne HS, Virginia Beach**
14. **Gary Hymel, c, Louisiana State**
15. **James Ferguson, rhp, San Diego**
16. **Buddy Jenkins, lhp, Wake Forest**
17. **Stanley Tarutis, rhp, Scranton (Pa.)**
18. **Kirk Rueter, lhp, Murray State**
19. **Stephen Allen, c, Alabama**
20. **Jamal Fastening, rhp, Vintage HS, Vallejo, Calif.**
21. **John White, of, Wagner**
22. Lance Calmus, rhp, Jenks (Okla.) HS
23. **Mitch Simons, 2b, Oklahoma State**
24. Allen Gallagher, rhp, Lower Columbia (Wash.) CC
25. Craig Mattson, rhp, Belvidere (Ill.) HS
26. Bob Henley, c, Mobile County HS, Grand Bay, Ala.
27. **Jim Wynne, rhp, Oklahoma City**
28. Darrell O'Brien, ss/2b, Ontario (Calif.) HS
29. **Nick Sproviero, rhp, New Haven (Conn.)**
30. **Scott Campbell, of, Oklahoma**
31. Omar Fernandez, rhp, Gulliver Prep HS, Coral Gables, Fla.
32. Matt Copp, rhp, Green Mountain HS, Golden, Colo.
33. Dan DeStefano, rhp, Santaluces HS, Boynton Beach, Fla.
34. **Scott Dennison, 2b, San Diego State**
35. Shane McCubbin, c, Western Oklahoma State JC
36. Brian Sosa, 3b, Yucaipa (Calif.) HS
37. Maurio Hanson, of, Spartanburg Methodist (S.C.) JC
38. Ryan Duffy, lhp, Sombra, Ontario
39. **Darrin Paxton, rhp, Wichita State**
40. Kevin Galart, rhp, American River (Calif.) JC
41. William Brabec, of, Glenbard East HS, Lombard, Ill.
42. Mike Cavanaugh, c, Linfield (Ore.)
43. **Fernando DaSilva, rhp, Brossard, Quebec**
44. Vincent Guay, of, Sherbrooke, Quebec
45. Rocky Murray, lhp, North Bend (Ore.) HS
46. **Jason Thorsteinson, 1b, Richmond, B.C.**
47. Jon Valenti, ss, Highland HS, Bakersfield, Calif.
48. Matt Splawn, rhp/1b, Waxahachie (Texas) HS
49. Ron Lewis, rhp, El Molino HS, Forestville, Calif.
50. Swindell Flowers, of, Greene Central HS, Hookerton, N.C.
51. Jeffery Sommer, 1b, Moorpark (Calif.) JC
52. Eduardo Payan, 3b, Fairfax HS, Los Angeles
53. Marlin Hamilton, 1b, Jordan HS, Long Beach
54. Craig Peterson, of, McMinn Central HS, Etowah, Tenn.
55. Jody Crump, lhp, Harrison County HS, Sadieville, Ky.
56. Russ White, ss, Hale HS, Tulsa
57. Daniel Chastain, c, Fort Collins (Colo.) HS
58. Scott Wulfing, 2b, Poly HS, Riverside, Calif.
59. Rodney Weary, 1b, St. Louis CC-Meramec
60. Jason Myers, lhp, Fontana (Calif.) HS
61. Eric White, 2b, Mount San Antonio (Calif.) JC
62. Michael Clayton, c, Mount San Antonio (Calif.) JC
63. Jason Vanheerde, c, Eisenhower HS, Rialto, Calif.
64. Jay Sissener, rhp/1b, Mohave HS, Bullhead City, Ariz.
65. Jason Jenkins, rhp, Henry Clay HS, Lexington, Ky.
66. James Jennings, lhp, George Washington HS, Danville, Va.
67. Robert Hughes, of, Western Oklahoma State JC
68. Dan DiPace, ss, Martin County HS, Palm City, Fla.
69. Troy Walsh, of, Bellport HS, East Patchogue, N.Y.
70. Scott Watkins, lhp, Oklahoma State
71. Shawn Moore, of, Virginia

NEW YORK METS

June—Regular Phase (22)

1. **Al Shirley, of, George Washington HS, Danville, Va.** (Pick from Dodgers as compensation for Type A free agent Darryl Strawberry)
1. **Bobby Jones, rhp, Fresno State** (Supplemental pick—36th—for loss of Strawberry)
2. **Bill Pulsipher, lhp, Fairfax (Va.) HS**
2. **Marc Kroon, rhp, Shadow Mountain HS, Phoenix** (Supplemental pick—72nd—for loss of Type C free agent Pat Tabler)
3. **Jeff Kiraly, 1b, La Cueva HS, Albuquerque**
4. **Erik Hiljus, rhp, Canyon HS, Santa Clarita, Calif.**
5. **Jared Osentowski, 3b, Kearney (Neb.) HS**
6. **Eric Reichenbach, rhp, St. John's**
7. **Frank Jacobs, 1b, Notre Dame**
8. **Randy Curtis, of, Riverside (Calif.) CC**
9. **Dave Swanson, rhp, Berlin HS, Kensington, Conn.**

10. **Dwight Robinson, 3b, Middle Tennessee State**
11. **Todd Fiegel, lhp, Virginia**
12. **Jason Jacome, lhp, Pima (Ariz.) CC**
13. **Tony Tijerina, c, Texas Tech**
14. **Jeff Henderson, rhp, Golden West (Calif.) JC**
15. Chris Petrocella, rhp, Fort Scott (Kan.) CC
16. **Donald White, of, Southeastern (Ill.) CC**
17. **Joe Crawford, lhp, Kent State**
18. **Tyson Young, 1b, Hardin Jefferson HS, Kountze, Texas**
19. James White, of, Florida HS, Tallahassee, Fla.
20. **Andrew Cotner, lhp, Illinois State**
21. **Greg Beals, c, Kent State**
22. **Ervin Collier, rhp, County Central HS, New Madrid, Mo.**
23. **Cliff Jones, lhp, Hawaii Pacific**
24. **James McCready, rhp, Bentley (Mass.)**
25. Kyle Harris, of, Ridgecrest HS, Paragould, Ark.
26. Todd Jackson, rhp, Arizona Western JC
27. **Mark Hokhanson, rhp, Joliet (Ill.) JC**
28. **Mark Wipf, of, San Marcos HS, Santa Barbara, Calif.**
29. Mark Lukasiewicz, lhp, Secaucus (N.J.) HS
30. **Chris George, lhp, Mississippi State**
31. Jerry Hiraldo, of, Carolina, P.R.
32. **Brett Rossler, c/3b, Pearl River (Miss.) JC**
33. Owen Johnson, rhp, St. Pius X HS, Houston
34. Travis Ryan, ss/2b, Labette (Kan.) CC
35. Robert Cardera, lhp, Chabot (Calif.) JC
36. Armando Fernandez, of, Hawthorne (Calif.) HS
37. Brad Talley, rhp, Jefferson Davis HS, Montgomery, Ala.
38. Chris Pialer, rhp, Three Rivers (Mo.) CC
39. Jesus Maldonado, rhp, Roosevelt HS, San Antonio
40. Robert Conway, rhp, Northwestern State
41. Richard Towers, rhp, Paris (Texas) HS
42. Kenneth Bradley, ss, Dollarway HS, Pine Bluff, Ark.
43. Brandon Ford, of, Golden West HS, Visalia, Calif.
44. **Jason Isringhausen, rhp, Lewis & Clark (Ill.) JC**
45. Eric Harris, 1b, Laney (Calif.) JC
46. Brian Fassbender, rhp, West HS, Appleton, Wis.
47. Trevor Blake, of, Greenway HS, Glendale, Ariz.
48. William Abbott, rhp, North Little Rock (Ark.) HS
49. Cory Buck, c, Neligh-Oakdale HS, Oakdale, Neb.
50. Ken Copeland, of, Otero (Colo.) JC
51. Anthony Richardson, 1b, Kishwaukee (Ill.) JC

NEW YORK YANKEES

June—Regular Phase (1)

1. **Brien Taylor, lhp, East Carteret HS, Beaufort, N.C.**
2. (Pick to Royals as compensation for Type A free agent Steve Farr)
3. **Tim Flannelly, 3b, Michigan**
3. **Mark Hubbard, rhp/of, South Florida** (Pick from Giants as compensation for Type B free agent Dave Righetti)
4. **Marc Gipner, c, Dunedin (Fla.) HS**
5. **Lyle Mouton, of, Louisiana State**
6. **Eric Knowles, ss, St. Brenden HS, Miami**
7. **Tommy Carter, lhp, Auburn**
8. **Grant Sullivan, rhp, Mississippi**
9. **Keith Garagozzo, lhp, Delaware**
10. Mike Muncy, ss, Camanllo (Calif.) HS
11. **Jason Wuerch, of, Leamington, Ontario**
12. **Bert Inman, rhp, McLennan (Texas) CC**
13. **Andy Albrecht, of, Auburn**
14. **Ben Short, rhp, Alabama**
15. **Steven Munda, rhp, Illinois**
16. **Andy Croghan, rhp, Long Beach State**
17. Brad Rigby, rhp, Lake Brantley HS, Longwood, Fla.
18. **John Coleman, rhp, Northwood Institute (Texas)**
19. **Roger Burnett, ss, Stanford**
20. **James Lewis, of, Virginia HS, Bristol, Va.**
21. **Scott Gully, rhp, Elon**
22. Scott Baldwin, lhp, Lewis-Clark State (Idaho)
23. **Steve Anderson, ss, San Jose State**
24. **John Quintell, c, Cal State Sacramento**
25. Terry Harvey, rhp, Dacula (Ga.) HS
26. **Dennis Burbank, rhp, Oklahoma State**
27. **Whitney Floren, rhp, South Florida**
28. **Chris Heaps, ss, Gadsden State (Ala.) CC**
29. Fred Rath, rhp, Jefferson HS, Tampa
30. Michael Beresh, rhp, Cardinal Gibbons HS, Lighthouse Point, Fla.
31. Charlie Brown, rhp, John Carroll HS, Fort Pierce, Fla.
32. Arnaldo Espada, of, Coamo, P.R.
33. Todd Harrell, rhp, Gulf Coast (Fla.) CC
34. Matt Parker, rhp, Jesuit HS, Temple Terrace, Fla.
35. **Steve Livesey, 3b/1b, Davidson**
36. Martin Winchester, 1b, Long Beach (Calif.) CC
37. Ron Hollis, ss/rhp, Brighton HS, South Lyon, Mich.
38. Paul Reynolds, 1b, East Lake HS, Tarpon Springs, Fla.
39. David Renteria, ss, Riverside (Calif.) CC
40. Major Hudson, of, St. John's HS, Darlington, S.C.
41. Chris Shafer, rhp, St. Petersburg (Fla.) HS
42. Will Green, 1b/3b, Chipola (Fla.) JC
43. Chris Plonk, rhp, Manatee (Fla.) JC
44. Nick Skuse, rhp, West Valley (Calif.) JC
45. Bronson Heflin, rhp, Central Florida CC
46. William Lawrence, lhp, Pensacola (Fla.) JC
47. Chad Plonk, rhp, Manatee (Fla.) JC
48. Jason Flexen, of, Chabot (Calif.) JC
49. William Friedman, rhp, Eastern Hills HS, Fort Worth
50. Danny Larivee, of, Rio Americano HS, Sacramento
51. Jon Boddy, 1b/3b, Woodham HS, Pensacola, Fla.
52. Michael Cutler, rhp, Orange Coast (Calif.) JC
53. Eric Taylor, lhp, St. Petersburg (Fla.) JC
54. Jason Crum, rhp, Indian River (Fla.) CC
55. Marco Contreras, rhp, Citrus (Calif.) JC
56. Mark Dean, ss, Florida CC-Jacksonville
57. Michael Caldwell, rhp, Columbia Falls (Mont.) HS
58. Lawrence Markham, 2b, Okeechobee (Fla.) HS
59. Tim Kester, rhp, Miami-Dade South CC
60. Kelvin Washington, ss, Westwood HS, Fort Pierce, Fla.
61. David Vance, of, Indian River (Fla.) CC
62. Scott Sorenson, rhp, Palm Beach Lakes HS, West Palm Beach, Fla.
63. Jason Birmingham, ss, Sarnia, Ontario
64. Rob Berryman, rhp, York HS, Yorktown, Va.
65. Jeremy Lewis, c, Jefferson HS, Cedar Rapids, Iowa
66. Alain Fernandez, of, Arroyo HS, San Lorenzo, Calif.
67. Kory Kiper, ss, Wellington HS, West Palm Beach, Fla.
68. Michael McKenna, rhp, Kishwaukee (Ill.) JC
69. Mariano Borges, of, Arecibo, P.R.
70. Bert Martinez, 1b/c, Marian HS, Chula Vista, Calif.
71. Jesse Kerr, rhp, Clear Lake HS, Houston
72. Howard Ferguson, rhp, Hamilton, Ontario
73. Chris Targac, rhp, Sacred Heart HS, Weimer, Texas
74. Joel Irvine, c, Des Moines Area (Iowa) CC
75. Brent Hall, ss, Claresholm, Alberta
76. Tim Borys, lhp, Surrey, B.C
77. Robert Nicholson, of, Calgary, Alberta
78. Brandon Ford, rhp, John Carroll HS, Vero Beach, Fla.
79. Chris Moock, 3b, Louisiana State
80. Rex Pritchard, 3b, Whittier Christian HS, Fullerton, Calif.

OAKLAND ATHLETICS

June—Regular Phase (26)

1. **Brent Gates, ss, Minnesota**
1. **Mike Rossiter, rhp, Burroughs HS, Burbank, Calif.** (Supplemental pick—38th—as compensation for Type A free agent Wllie McGee)
2. **Mike Neill, of, Villanova** (Pick from Giants as compensation for McGee)
2. **Russ Brock, rhp, Michigan**
3. **Joel Wolfe, of, UCLA**
4. **Steve Wojciechowski, lhp, St. Xavier (Ill.)**
5. **Tim Smith, rhp, Ohio State**
6. **Tim Doyle, lhp, Cal State Sacramento**
7. **Ricky Kimball, rhp, Florida State**
8. **Scott Sheldon, ss, Houston**
9. **Damon Mashore, of, Arizona**
10. **Zach Sawyer, rhp, Clinton (Mass.) HS**

11. **Jason Wood, ss, Fresno State**
12. **Miguel Jimenez, rhp, Fordham**
13. **Jeff Light, c/rhp, Stanford**
14. Darrell May, lhp, Sacramento CC
15. **Brent Cookson, of, Long Beach State**
16. **Kurt Endebrock, 2b, Southern Illinois**
17. **Chris Thomson, 1b, Texas Christian**
18. **Rick Norton, 3b, Kentucky**
19. James Henderson, rhp, Purdue
20. Ivan Montane, rhp, Killian HS, Miami
21. **Todd Ingram, rhp, Arizona**
22. William Kingsbury, rhp, Villanova
23. Sean Gavaghan, rhp, Richmond
24. **George Williams, 3b, Texas-Pan American**
25. **Daniel Nerat, rhp, William Penn (Iowa)**
26. **Brian McArn, of, Nebraska**
27. **Robert Leary, 1b, Louisburg (N.C.) JC**
28. **Greg Smock, lhp, Austin Peay State**
29. **Joe Misa, rhp, Lewis-Clark State (Idaho)**
30. **Brad Stowell, rhp, The Citadel**
31. Craig Wagner, of/1b, Broken Arrow (Okla.) HS
32. **Michael Evans, rhp, St. Leo (Fla.)**
33. **Michael Thees, rhp, Carson Newman (Tenn.)**
34. **Brad Parker, 3b, Auburn**
35. **Keith Millay, rhp, Gulf Coast (Fla.) CC**
36. **Dane Walker, of, Portland State**
37. **Brandon Smith, c, Roswell (Ga.) HS**
38. **Sean Scott, of, Pace (N.Y.)**
39. **Thomas Myers, lhp, UC Santa Barbara**
40. **Raymond Sutch, rhp, James Madison**
41. **Steven Shoemaker, rhp, Muscatine (Iowa) JC**
42. **Mark Buckler, of, Vermont**
43. William Bishop, c, Mississippi Gulf Coast JC
44. **Tod Prick, c, Florida Southern**
45. Leland McAfee, of, Mira Mesa HS, San Diego
46. Tom Hamilton, of, Indian River (Fla.) CC
47. Clinton Koppe, rhp, Brazoswood HS, Lake Jackson, Texas
48. David Boone, of, Hickory (N.C.) HS
49. Antonio Fant, of, El Cerrito HS, Richmond, Calif.
50. Rick Braisted, of, Dixie Hollins HS, St. Petersburg, Fla.
51. William Cornish, rhp, Northeast Lauderdale HS, Merion, Miss.
52. Donald Aslasken, of, San Jacinto (Texas) JC
53. Carlos James, of, Seminole State (Okla.) JC
54. Adrian Yots, 1b/3b, Columbia State (Tenn.) CC
55. Frank Campbell, 1b/of, Pasadena (Calif.) CC
56. Jim Bonds, rhp/c, UCLA

PHILADELPHIA PHILLIES

June—Regular Phase (10)

1. **Tyler Green, rhp, Wichita State**
2. **Kevin Stocker, ss, Washington**
3. **Ronnie Allen, rhp, Texas A&M**
4. **Gene Schall, of, Villanova**
5. Steve Verdusco, ss, Bellarmine Prep HS, Scotts Valley, Calif.
6. **Tommy Eason, c, East Carolina**
7. **Dave Tokheim, of, UCLA**
8. **Dave Hayden, ss, Tennessee**
9. **Phil Geisler, of, Portland**
10. **Mike Grace, rhp, Bradley**
11. **Art Ruth, c, Cal State Stanislaus**
12. **John Mallee, ss, Illinois-Chicago**
13. **Brent Bell, 1b/3b, St. John Bosco HS, Downey, Calif.**
14. Andrew Martin, 3b/1b, Master's (Calif.)
15. Demond Thompkins, of, Elsenhower HS, Rialto, Calif.
16. **Pat Bojcun, rhp, Central Michigan**
17. **Joe Jelinek, 2b, Maple Woods (Mo.) CC**
18. Bobby Higginson, of, Temple
19. **John Salamon, rhp, Allegheny (Pa.) CC**
20. **Dom DeSantis, rhp, New Orleans**
21. **Greg Brown, rhp, Tennessee**
22. **Craig Holman, rhp, Jacksonville State**
23. **Tom Vilet, of, Wisconsin**
24. Chad Sweitzer, rhp, American River (Calif.) JC
25. Jerry Whittaker, of, Poly HS, Long Beach
26. **Thane Page, rhp, Crowder (Mo.) JC**
27. **Andrew Sallee, 1b, Claremont McKenna (Calif.)**
28. Curtis Schmidt, rhp, Kansas
29. Tim Pugh, lhp, Cecil (Md.) CC
30. **John Whisonant, lhp, U.S. International (Nairobi)**
31. **Glenn Nevill, lhp, Baylor**
32. Allan Hebbert, rhp, Alta Loma (Calif.) HS
33. **Joel Gilmore, rhp, Dallas Baptist**
34. Aaron Edwards, of, Ontario (Calif.) HS
35. **Dean Hopp, c, Northeastern Oklahoma A&M JC**
36. Paul Reynolds, 3b, Snowflake (Ariz.) HS
37. **Carlton Hardy, 3b/rhp, Grambling State**
38. Dan Vetter, of, Del Campo HS, Fair Oaks, Calif.
39. **Wayne Johnson, of, Compton (Calif.) CC**
40. Steven Afenir, c, Palomar (Calif.) JC
41. **Jason Urbanek, 2b, Westby HS, Coon Valley, Wis.**
42. **Bruce Smolen, 3b, Bradley**
43. **Craig Billeci, 1b, St. Mary's**
44. Nathan LaDuke, of, Arizona State
45. James Gwaltney, lhp, Rancho Santiago (Calif.) JC
46. John Lockett, of, Jordan HS, Long Beach
47. Don Hill, rhp, Westlake HS, Westlake Village, Calif.
48. **Michael Merthie, of, Lake Mary HS, Sanford, Fla.**
49. Marion McKinney, 3b, Poly HS, Sun Valley, Calif.
50. Chris Lee, rhp, Tooele (Utah) HS
51. Chris Witt, rhp, Roger Bacon HS, Cincinnati
52. Bobby Waits, lhp, Fresno CC
53. Michael White, 2b, Anderson (Calif.) HS
54. Alex Figueroa, c, Hawthorne (Calif.) HS

PITTSBURGH PIRATES

June—Regular Phase (24)

1. **Jon Farrell, c/of, Florida CC**
2. **Dave Doorneweerd, rhp, Ridgewood HS, Port Richey, Fla.**
2. **Dan Jones, rhp, Northwestern** (Supplemental pick—73rd—for loss of Type C free agent Sid Bream)
3. **Matt Ruebel, lhp, Oklahoma**
4. **Benjamin Boka, c, Barrington (Ill.) HS**
5. **Marty Neff, of, Oklahoma**
6. Mickey Kerns, of, Alabama
7. **Tony Womack, ss, Guilford (N.C.)**
8. **Matt Pontbriant, lhp, Brevard (Fla.) CC**
9. **Deon Danner, lhp, UNC Charlotte**
10. Chance Sanford, ss/2b, San Jacinto (Texas) JC
11. **Jason Bullard, rhp, Texas A&M**
12. Stacy Hollins, rhp, San Jacinto (Texas) JC
13. **Chris Edmondson, 3b, Alcorn Central HS, Corinth, Miss.**
14. **Jacob Payne, c, Don Lugo HS, Ontario, Calif.**
15. Jason McDonald, of, Sacramento CC
16. **Dan Gernand, rhp, Arizona Western JC**
17. **Todd Schroeder, 1b, Illinois State**
18. Brian Pelka, rhp, Allegany (Pa.) CC
19. **Marc Pisciotta, rhp, Georgia Tech**
20. **Don Garvey, 2b, Wisconsin-Oshkosh**
21. **Victor Bogan, of, Linn-Benton (Ore.) CC**
22. **Mike Maguire, lhp, Northeastern**
23. **Sean Evans, rhp, South Carolina**
24. Ivory Jones, of, Vallejo (Calif.) HS
25. **Ken Fairfax, rhp, Geibel HS, Uniontown, Pa.**
26. Tim Merrick, of, South Florida
27. **Michael Taylor, lhp, Admiral King HS, Lorian, Ohio**
28. **James Martin, lhp, Eastern Michigan**
29. **Ron Ducksworth, ss, Mississippi Gulf Coast JC**
30. **Craig Shotton, of, Florida Atlantic**
31. Ricardo Hermida, rhp, Coral Park HS, Miami
32. **Michael Teich, lhp, Cal State Sacramento**
33. Felix Merced, ss, Guaynabo, P.R.
34. **Marcus Ponder, of, South Georgia JC**
35. Jason Green, rhp, Pinole Valley HS, Hercules, Calif.
36. Neil James, 3b, Lake Mary HS, Altamonte Springs, Fla.
37. **Jim Krevokuch, 3b, Old Dominion**
38. Steve Shoemaker, rhp, Phoenixville (Pa.) HS
39. Dustin Hermanson, rhp, Kenton Ridge HS, Springfield, Ohio
40. Colin Hinds, of, Hamilton HS, Los Angeles

41. Todd Boulanger, lhp, Surrey, B.C
42. Terry Mitchum, 1b, Fairfield (Ohio) HS
43. Andrew Noffke, rhp, Northwestern HS, Springfield, Ohio
44. Jason Moore, c, Sacramento CC
45. **Eugene Knapp, lhp, Osceola HS, Kissimmee, Fla.**
46. Brian Brewer, lhp, Armijo HS, Fairfield, Calif.
47. **Jeff Leatherman, 1b, Auburn**
48. Scott May, c, Manatee HS, Bradenton, Fla.
49. **Ken Bonifay, 1b/of, Georgia Tech**
50. **Clyde Earl, ss, Chicago State**
51. Kenneth Vike, rhp, DeSoto (Texas) HS
52. **O'Brien Cunningham, of, Lancaster (S.C.) HS**
53. **Michael Ragland, of, Belmont**
54. Ryan Huffman, of, Clear Lake HS, Houston
55. Terrance Goree, 2b, Carthage (Texas) HS
56. Jim Brower, rhp, Minnetonka (Minn.) HS
57. Paul Wilson, rhp, Boone HS, Orlando
58. Scott Krause, ss, North HS, Willowick, Ohio

ST. LOUIS CARDINALS

June—Regular Phase (4)

1. **Dmitri Young, 3b/of, Rio Mesa HS, Oxnard, Calif.**
1. **Allen Watson, lhp, New York Tech** (Pick from Blue Jays as compensation for Type A free agent Ken Dayley)
1. **Brian Barber, rhp, Dr. Phillips HS, Orlando, Fla.** (Pick from Mets as compensation for Type B free agent Vince Coleman)
1. **Tom McKinnon, rhp, Jordan HS, Long Beach** (Supplemental pick—28th—for loss of Type A free agent Terry Pendleton)
1. **Dan Cholowsky, 3b, California** (Supplemental pick—39th—for loss of Dayley)
2. **Eddie Williams, c, Edison HS, Miami** (Pick from Braves as compensation for Pendleton)
2. (Pick to Astros as compensation for Type B free agent Juan Agosto)
3. **Basil Shabazz, of, Pine Bluff (Ark.) HS**
4. **Andy Bruce, 3b, Georgia Tech**
5. **Da Rond Stovall, of, Althoff HS, East St. Louis, Ill.**
6. **John Mabry, of, West Chester (Pa.)**
7. **Doug Creek, lhp, Georgia Tech**
8. **Antoine Henry, of, Clairemont HS, San Diego**
9. **Dennis Slininger, rhp, Largo (Fla.) HS**
10. **Allen Battle, of, South Alabama**
11. **Mike DiFelice, c, Tennessee**
12. **Michael Badorek, rhp, Olivet Nazarene (Ill.)**
13. **Scott Simmons, lhp, Southwest Missouri State**
14. **Mike Busby, rhp, Banning HS, Wilmington, Calif.**
15. **Victor Llanos, 3b, Carolina, P.R.**
16. **Kevin Lucero, lhp, Florida International**
17. **Ron Warner, ss, Wyoming**
18. **Darrel Deak, 2b, Loyola Marymount**
19. Terrence McClain, of, Cape HS, Cincinnati
20. **Jason Hisey, rhp, Arizona**
21. Jeff Meszar, ss, Butler County (Kan.) CC
22. **Scott Longaker, rhp, UC Santa Barbara**
23. **Don Slattery, 1b, JC of Southern Idaho**
24. **John Frascatore, rhp, Long Island-C.W. Post**
25. **Garrett Blanton, of, Florida State**
26. **Rigo Beltran, lhp/1b, Wyoming**
27. **Rick Mediavilla, of, Loyola Marymount**
28. **Robert Strehlow, of/2b, Basic HS, Henderson, Nev.**
29. **Tim DeGrasse, rhp, UC Santa Barbara**
30. **Curt Callicot, 3b, Riverside (Calif.) CC**
31. **Larry Lucchetti, rhp, Nevada-Las Vegas**
32. **Michael Cantu, 1b, Tarleton State (Texas)**
33. **Antonio Boone, rhp, Norfolk State**
34. **John O'Brien, 1b, Oral Roberts**
35. Dan Heideman, rhp, Florida CC
36. **Alan Robinson, of, Widener (Pa.)**
37. **Chris Vlasis, of/3b, Virginia Commonwealth**
38. **Paul Romanoli, lhp, Memphis State**
39. **Jerry Santos, rhp, Florida International**
40. **Eric Miller, rhp, JC of Southern Idaho**
41. **Steven Jones, rhp, Memphis State**
42. **Steve Cerio, c, Nevada-Las Vegas**
43. **David Chasin, of, St. Louis CC-Meramec**
44. **Earnest Fisher, rhp, Rider**
45. **Chad Smith, rhp, Lynchburg (Va.)**
46. **Jeff Dillman, rhp, Rider**
47. **Duffy Guyton, rhp, Dallas Baptist**
48. **Doug Radziewicz, 1b, Georgia**
49. **Clint Davis, rhp, Dallas Baptist**
50. **Mike Eicher, of, Wyoming**
51. **Curtis Underwood, 1b, Central State (Okla.)**
52. **Dirk Lindauer, rhp, Southwest Missouri State**
53. **Chad Sumner, 3b/2b, Georgia Southern**
54. **Keith Black, 2b, Troy State**
55. **Gary Taylor, of, Maine**
56. Jeff Twist, c, Highland HS, Bakersfield, Calif.
57. Aaron Gerteisen, of, Leon HS, Tallahassee, Fla.
58. Colby Neal, rhp, North Mecklenburg HS, Davidson, N.C.
59. Jaime Sanjurjo, of, Rio Grande, P.R.
60. Shawn Lopez, of, Fort Scott (Kan.) CC
61. **Ray Davis, rhp, Palatka (Fla.) HS**
62. Daniel Rude, rhp, Skyview HS, Billings, Mont.
63. Hank Crosby, 3b/2b, Kanab (Utah) HS
64. Jason Shanahan, 3b, Sentinel HS, Missoula, Mont.
65. Sean Centeno, 3b, Kelly Walsh HS, Casper, Wyo.
66. Paul Williams, lhp, Mountain Home (Idaho) HS
67. Bryan Donnelly, rhp, St. Louis CC-Meramec

SAN DIEGO PADRES

June—Regular Phase (8)

1. **Joey Hamilton, rhp, Georgia Southern**
1. **Greg Anthony , rhp/of, Tavares (Pla.) HS** (Supplemental pick—31st—for loss of Type A free agent Jack Clark)
2. **Jon Barnes, rhp, Lancaster (S.C.) HS**
3. Antone Williamson, 3b, Torrance (Calif.) HS
4. **Sean Mulligan, c, Illinois**
5. **Joey Long, lhp, Kent State**
6. **Mike Grohs, rhp, Old Dominion**
7. **Homer Bush, ss, East St. Louis (Ill.) HS**
8. **Manuel Cora, ss, Levittown, P.R.**
9. **Craig Hanson, rhp, Triton (Ill.) JC**
10. **John Roberts, of, Watson Chapel HS, Pine Bluff, Ark.**
11. **Scott Pugh, 1b, Texas**
12. **Scott Eggleston, rhp, Maple Woods (Mo.) CC**
13. **Reginald Stewart, of, Fernandina Beach HS, Yulee, Fla.**
14. **Derek Valenzuela, c, St. John Bosco HS, Anaheim, Calif.**
15. Justin Atchley, lhp, Sedro Wooley (Wash.) HS
16. **Alex Rivera, of, Cayey, P.R.**
17. **Billy Hall, 2b, Wichita State**
18. **Robert Compton, rhp, Seminole State (Okla.) JC**
19. **Charlie Greene, c, Miami-Dade CC South**
20. **Paul Thompson, 1b, Blinn (Texas) JC**
21. Michael Weston, lhp, Lower Richland HS, Eastover, S.C.
22. **Joe Grygiel, lhp, Lowell (Mass.)**
23. **Dwight Wyatt, of, Halifax County HS, Scottsburg, Va.**
24. Darrell White, rhp, Bolton HS, Alexandria, La.
25. **John Biancamano, 3b, Fairleigh Dickinson**
26. Alex Andreopoulos, c, Toronto
27. **Derek Vaughn, of, Santa Monica (Calif.) JC**
28. Greg Kennedy, lhp, Meridian (Miss.) CC
29. Bryan Ward, lhp, Morris (N.J.) CC
30. Michael Hermanson, rhp, Kishwaukee (Ill.) JC
31. **Tim Hall, c, Cumberland (Tenn.)**
32. James Garcia, of, San Bernardino Valley (Calif.) JC
33. **Randall Fjeld, rhp, Liberty HS, Renton, Wash.**
34. Sandy McKinnon, of, Coffee HS, Nicholls, Ga.
35. **Brian D'Amato, rhp, Pilgrim HS, Warwick, R.I.**
36. **David Lebak, of, Trenton State (N.J.)**
37. Matt Bentke, of, Brenham (Texas) HS
38. **Rich Loiselle, rhp, Odessa (Texas) JC**
39. Casey Kirkman, rhp, Exeter (Calif.) HS
40. **Joe Frias, 2b, Oklahoma City**
41. John Dettmer, rhp, Missouri
42. **Mel Edwards, 2b/1b, Rider**
43. **Arthur Vazquez, rhp, Miami-Dade CC North**
44. **Ralph Perez, of, Southwest HS, Miami**

45. **Kevin Johnson, c, Mayville State (N.D.)**
46. Kyle White, 1b, Laney (Calif.) JC
47. Leon Bertsch, rhp, Morris (N.J.) CC
48. **Kyle Moody, 2b, Texas**
49. Scott Shores, of, Phoenix JC
50. **Jerrold Rountree, of, UC Santa Barbara**
51. Torri Allen, of, John Jay HS, San Antonio
52. Matthew Spade, rhp, Boyertown (Pa.) HS
53. Robert Hughes, of, Iowa
54. **Tim Goins, c, St. Mary's (Texas)**
55. **Jerry Creer, 2b, East St. Louis (Ill.) HS**
56. **John Nash, of, Princeton**
57. **Jerry Burns, rhp, Napa Valley (Calif.) JC**

SAN FRANCISCO GIANTS

June—Regular Phase (16)

1. (Pick to Blue Jays as compensation for Type A free agent Bud Black)
1. **Steve Whitaker, lhp, Long Beach State** (Supplemental pick—33rd—for loss of Type A free agent Brett Butler)
2. (Pick to Athletics as compensation for Type A free agent Willie McGee)
3. (Pick to Yankees as compensation for Type B free agent Dave Righetti)
4. **Chris Gambs, rhp, Monte Vista HS, Danville, Calif.**
5. **Billy Van Landingham, rhp, Kentucky**
6. **Duane Thielen, 3b, Mount Hood (Ore.) CC**
7. **Julian Frazier, of, Smackover (Ark.) HS**
8. **Dax Jones, of, Creighton**
9. **Doug Vanderweele, rhp, Nevada-Las Vegas**
10. **Jeff Martin, rhp, Hazen HS, Renton, Wash.**
11. Tim Kraus, rhp, Colerain HS, Cincinnati
12. **Tim Luther, rhp, Missouri Southern State**
13. **Marcial Gomez, rhp, Columbus HS, Hialeah, Fla.**
14. **Ray Jackson, of, Tennessee**
15. **Randy Swank, ss, American River (Calif.) JC**
16. David Rosato, ss, South HS, Torrance, Calif.
17. **Frank Charles, c/of, Cal State Fullerton**
18. **Kevin Brown, rhp, North Salem HS, Salem, Ore.**
19. **Matt Brewer, of, Southwest Missouri State**
20. **Eric Stonecipher, rhp, Kansas**
21. George Arias, 3b, Pima (Ariz.) CC
22. Gary Phillips, 3b, Motlow State (Tenn.) CC
23. Craig Wilson, ss, Kansas State
24. **Charles Peysar, rhp, Atascadero (Calif.) HS**
25. **Tim Flores, 2b, Grand Canyon (Ariz.)**
26. **Hiram Ramirez, c, Ensenada, P.R.**
27. **Jarod Juelsgaard, rhp, Iowa State**
28. **Derek Dana, c, Massachusetts**
29. **Al Benavides, rhp, Houston**
30. **Richard Hyde, rhp, Illinois**
31. **Thurman Williams, of, Chatsworth (Calif.) HS**
32. **Adam Benschoter, c, Siena Heights**
33. **Ken Feist, of, Portland State**
34. Juan Johnson, ss, Thomas Stone HS, Waldorf, Md.
35. **Rico Bolivar, 1b/of, Umpqua (Ore.) CC**
36. **Vince Towns, rhp, Suitland HS, Forestville, Md.**
37. Herbert Baxter, lhp, Spartanburg Methodist (S.C.) JC
38. John Fullford, of, Douglas County HS, Castle Rock, Colo.
39. Darvin Traylor, of, Riverside (Calif.) CC
40. **Scott Stroth, rhp, Kansas State**
41. **Don Montgomery, c, Lewis-Clark State (Idaho)**
42. Maurice Taylor, of, Thornwood US, Calumet City, Ill.
43. J.T. Messick, ss, Union HS, Tulsa
44. **Kevin McGonnigal, of, Maryland**
45. **Darren Wittcke, rhp, Portland State**
46. **Dan Calcagno, c, Sonoma State (Calif.)**
47. Chris Kelly, rhp, Tennessee
48. Noe Najera, lhp, Cypress (Calif.) JC
49. Leron Golden, of, American River (Calif.) JC
50. Stephen Gurtner, rhp, Butler County (Kan.) CC
51. Faruq Darcuiel, of, Hoover HS, Fresno
52. Scott Boyle, lhp, San Marin HS, Novato, Calif.
53. **Ken Grundt, lhp, Missouri Southern State**
54. **Jeff Locklear, lhp, Pembroke State (N.C.)**
55. **Tim Casper, 2b, Missouri Southern State**
56. **Kevin Bellomo, of, Western Carolina**
57. Craig Gee, rhp, Fontana HS, Bloomington, Calif.
58. **Ronald Foster, 3b, Indian Hills (Iowa) CC**
59. Lorenzo Hidalgo, rhp, San Joaquin Delta (Calif.) JC
60. **Ken Henderson, of, San Jose State**
61. Jason Beeler, rhp, Farmington (Ark.) HS
62. Chad Breashears, of, Malvern HS, Donaldson, Ark.
63. Douglas Cecil, lhp, Fresno HS
64. Anthony Lacy, of, Sacramento CC
65. Shawn Everett, of, Cosumnes River (Calif.) JC
66. Craig Marcelin, c, St. Louis CC-Forest Park
67. Matthew Meier, 2b/ss, Washington HS, Cedar Rapids, Iowa
68. Samuel Mathis, rhp, El Dorado (Ark.) HS
69. **Demetris Jones, of, Motlow State (Tenn.) CC**

SEATTLE MARINERS

June—Regular Phase (11)

1. **Shawn Estes, lhp, Douglas HS, Minden, Nev.**
2. **Tommy Adams, of, Arizona State**
3. **Jim Mecir, rhp, Eckerd (Fla.)**
4. **Desi Relaford, ss, Sandalwood HS, Jacksonville**
5. **Sean Rees, lhp, Arizona State**
6. **Craig Clayton, rhp/1b, Cal State Northridge**
7. Bruce Thompson, of, Brandon (Fla.) HS
8. **Derek Lowe, rhp, Ford HS, Dearborn, Mich.**
9. **Trey Witte, rhp, Texas A&M**
10. **Jeff Borski, rhp, South Carolina-Aiken**
11. **Peter Weinbaum, rhp, Nassau (N.Y.) CC**
12. **David Lisiecki, rhp, Lake Michigan (Mich.) JC**
13. **Kevin Jenkins, rhp, Riverview (Mich.) HS**
14. **Raul Rodarte, ss, Rancho Santiago (Calif.) JC**
15. **Doug Anderson, lhp, North Florida**
16. **Dan Sullivan, rhp, Indian River (Fla.) CC**
17. **Kenny Winzer, rhp, Southern**
18. **Craig Bryant, ss, North Alabama**
19. **Tony Phillips, rhp, Southern Mississippi**
20. **Erik O'Donnell, rhp, Portland**
21. **Toby Foreman, lhp, St. Mary's**
22. **Darren Bragg, of, Georgia Tech**
23. Joseph Gazarek, of, North Baltimore (Ohio) HS
24. Paul London, ss, Bethel HS, Hampton, Va.
25. **Matt Mantei, rhp, River Valley HS, Sawyer, Mich.**
26. **Bubba Smith, 1b, Illinois**
27. Todd Cady, c, Grossmont HS, La Mesa, Calif.
28. James Riggio, rhp, Hillsborough (Fla.) CC
29. Chad Soden, lhp, Tuckerman (Ark.) HS
30. Edward Odom, ss, Atlantic HS, Delray Beach, Fla.
31. Ryan Black, of, Sam Houston HS, Arlington, Texas
32. **George Glinatsis, rhp, Cincinnati**
33. **Byron Thomas, of, Catonsville (Md.) CC**
34. Michael Martin, ss, Maclay HS, Tallahassee, Fla.
35. Steve McNair, ss, Mount Olive (Miss.) HS
36. Andrew Schope, lhp, Hempstead HS, Dubuque, Iowa
37. Daniel Scutchfield, lhp, Saline (Mich.) HS
38. Damian Cox, of, Victor Valley HS, Victorville, Calif.
39. Kevin Faircloth, ss, Glenn HS, Winston-Salem, N.C.
40. Lance Scott, rhp, Carmel (Calif.) HS
41. Lenny Weber, rhp, Jeanerette (La.) HS
42. **Craig Griffey, of, Ohio State**
43. Ryan Nye, rhp, Cameron (Okla.) HS
44. Chris Gorr, ss, Rancho Buena Vista HS, Vista, Calif.
45. John Thompson, ss, Shadle Park HS, Spokane, Wash.
46. Federico Warner, of, Oceanside (Calif.) HS
47. William Lewis, c, East Carteret HS, Smyrna, N.C.
48. Nicholas Williams, c, Hastings (Mich.) HS
49. Tyson Kimm, ss, Norway HS, Amana, Iowa
50. Jelani Lewis, of, Logan HS, Union City, Calif.
51. Mark Fields, of, Southwestern (Calif.) JC
52. Bryan Pfeifer, lhp, Kennedy HS, Taylor, Mich.
53. Jeff Tucker, rhp, Allen County (Kan.) CC
54. Gregory Theron, rhp, Dobson HS, Mesa, Ariz.
55. Jason Beverlin, rhp, Dondero HS, Royal Oak, Mich.

56. **Jose Cruz, 3b, San Jacinto (Texas) JC**
57. Francisco Antunez, c, Bayamon, P.R.
58. **Scott Bosarge, c, South Alabama**
59. Chris Schmitt, lhp, Manatee (Fla.) JC
60. Rudolph Sasina, c, Overland HS, Aurora, Colo.
61. Edward Davis, of, Cerritos (Calif.) JC
62. James Lezeau, of, Prescott (Ariz.) HS
63. Charles Gipson, of, Loara HS, Anaheim
64. Brian Klomp, rhp, King's River (Calif.) JC
65. Shane Ziegler, rhp, Howard (Texas) JC
66. Brian Fontes, rhp, Fresno CC
67. Darian Hagan, ss, Colorado

TEXAS RANGERS

June—Regular Phase (19)

1. **Benji Gil, ss/of, Castle Park HS, Chula Vista, Calif.**
2. **Terrell Lowery, of, Loyola Marymount**
3. **Lawrence Hanlon, ss, Texas-Arlington**
4. **Chris Curtis, rhp, Blinn (Texas) JC**
5. **Mark O'Brien, lhp, Deering HS, Portland, Maine**
6. **Steve Sadecki, rhp, Vanderbilt**
7. **Bert Gerhart, rhp, New Hope HS, Columbus, Miss.**
8. **Roger Luce, c/rhp, Texas**
9. **Scott Eyre, lhp, JC of Southern Idaho**
10. **Dave Geeve, rhp, Bradley**
11. **Lance Schuermann, lhp, Nevada-Las Vegas**
12. **Lanny Williams, c, Henderson State (Ark.)**
13. **Mike Edwards, 3b, Utah**
14. **Jon Pitts, c, Esperanza HS, Anaheim**
15. **Kerry Lacy, rhp, Chattanooga State (Tenn.) Tech CC**
16. **Chris Starr, rhp, Muskingum (Ohio)**
17. **Todd Gates, of, Loyola Marymount**
18. **Dan Magee, lhp, Jackson State**
19. **Jim Bethke, c, Oak Park HS, Kansas City, Mo.**
20. **Brian Roberts, of, Illinois**
21. **Paul Dalzochio, rhp, California State**
22. **James Koebler, 1b, Oklahoma**
23. **Steve Burton, 1b, Richmond**
24. **Mark Ringkamp, rhp, San Jose State**
25. **Billy Seaton, rhp, Mohave HS, Riviera, Ariz.**
26. **David Gandolph, lhp, Indiana**
27. **Charles Sullivan, 2b, Vanderbilt**
28. **Tom Migliozzi, rhp, St. John's**
29. Tim Beard, lhp, Grace King HS, Metairie, La.
30. **Desi Wilson, of, Fairleigh Dickinson**
31. **Joe Brownholtz, lhp, Pacific**
32. **Scott Buchheit, lhp, Southwest Missouri State**
33. J.J. Thobe, rhp, Rancho Santiago (Calif.) JC
34. **Shelby Shaw, rhp, McNeese State**
35. Daniel Ortiz, lhp, Hoboken (N.J.) HS
36. **Brad Stuart, rhp, New Orleans**
37. **James Kennedy, c, North Florida**
38. Paul Lesch, rhp, Clackamas (Ore.) CC
39. **Kevin Sisk, ss/3b, James Madison**
40. **Jeff Carew, rhp, Kimberly (Wis.) HS**
41. James Smith, rhp, Boyle County HS, Danville, Ky.
42. **Darin Haddock, lhp, Oklahoma Baptist**
43. Joe Raineri, of, Smithtown East HS, Smithtown, N.Y.
44. **Eric Vargas, c, California State**
45. **Harold Vallot, rhp, Arkansas**
46. **Tim Minik, rhp, Austin Peay State**
47. **Keith Nalepka, c/1b, Montgomery (Md.) JC**
48. **Daniel Vaughn, rhp, Crowder (Mo.) CC**
49. Jerry Martin, rhp, Shelby State (Tenn.) CC
50. **Patrick Underhill, rhp, West Florida**
51. Todd Walker, ss, Airline HS, Bossier City, La.
52. David Ullan, c, La Grande (Ore.) HS
53. **Daryl Henderson, lhp, Elgin (Ill.) CC**
54. Raul Ibanez, of, Sunset HS, Miami
55. Trey Moore, lhp, Keller HS, Southlake, Texas
56. Brian Wisler, of, Lynnwood HS, Alderwood Manor, Wash.
57. Teddy Warrecker, c, Allan Hancock (Calif.) JC
58. Kevin Bradley, rhp, San Jose (Calif.) CC
59. Brian Davis, rhp, Corcoran (Calif.) HS
60. Lawrence Vrtiska, rhp, Iowa Western CC
61. Steve Maltaglaiti, rhp, East Islip (N.Y.) HS
62. Jason Rogers, lhp, McQueen HS, Reno, Nev.
63. Pat Flury, rhp, Reed HS, Sparks, Nev.

TORONTO BLUE JAYS

June—Regular Phase (21)

1. **Shawn Green, of, Tustin (Calif.) HS** (Pick from Giants as compensation for Type A free agent Bud Black)
1. (Pick to Cardinals as compensation for Type A free agent Ken Dayley)
1. **Jeff Ware, rhp, Old Dominion** (Supplemental pick—35th—for loss of Type A free agent George Bell)
1. Dante Powell, ss, Millikan HS, Long Beach (Supplemental pick—42nd—for loss of Black)
2. **Trevor Mallory, rhp, Lakewood HS, St. Petersburg, Fla.** (Pick from Cubs as compensation for Bell)
2. **Dennis Gray, lhp, Long Beach State**
3. **Chris Stynes, ss, Boca Raton (Fla.) HS**
4. **Roger Doman, rhp, Joplin (Mo.) HS**
5. **Rickey Cradle, of, Cerritos (Calif.) HS**
6. **Jose Silva, rhp, Hilltop HS, Chula Vista, Calif.**
7. Carlton Loewer, rhp, St. Edmund HS, Eunice, La.
8. **Stoney Briggs, of, Delaware Tech JC**
9. **Pat Thacker, c, Millikan HS, Long Beach**
10. **Kenny Robinson, rhp, Florida State**
11. **Adam Meinershagen, rhp, Oakville HS, St. Louis**
12. **Keiver Campbell, of, Alcorn State**
13. **Alex Gonzalez, ss, Killian HS, Miami**
14. **Alonso Beltran, rhp, New Mexico JC**
15. **Sharnol Adriana, 2b, Martin Methodist (Tenn.) JC**
16. **John Tsoukalas, 3b, Gonzaga**
17. **Mike Carlsen, 2b, Fairleigh Dickinson**
18. **Ryan Griffin, of, Dunedin (Fla.) HS**
19. **Brent Lutz, c, Washington**
20. **Ben Weber, rhp, Houston**
21. **Tim Lindsay, rhp, UCLA**
22. **Andrew Dolson, lhp, Troy State**
23. **Chris Kotes, rhp, Columbia**
24. **Albert Montoya, lhp, New Mexico State**
25. Ryan Franklin, rhp, Spiro (Okla.) HS
26. Jason Maloney, rhp, Bullard HS, Fresno
27. **Paul Barton, lhp, Utah**
28. **Steve Sinclair, lhp, Victoria, B.C**
29. Scott Bartucca, 1b, Onondaga (N.Y.) CC
30. **Joe Lis, 2b, South Florida**
31. **Jim O'Connor, rhp, New York Tech**
32. Mark Voisard, rhp, Mount Vernon Nazarene (Ohio)
33. **Kurt Heble, 1b, McNeese State**
34. **Ted Langowski, 1b, San Francisco**
35. **Darin Nolan, rhp, Washington State**
36. **Thomas Vaught, 3b, Tallassee (Ala.) HS**
37. **Gary Miller, rhp, Penn State**
38. **Alan Ford, rhp, San Francisco State**
39. **Chris Ermis, rhp, San Antonio (Texas) JC**
40. Steve Marr, rhp, Western Kentucky
41. Angel Abreu, rhp, Guaynabo, P.R.
42. Andrew Srebroski, ss, Anne Arundel (Md.) CC
43. **Louis Benbow, 2b, Saddleback (Calif.) JC**
44. **Craig Quinlan, 1b, St. Thomas (Minn.)**
45. **Mike Morland, c, Texas**
46. Rayfield Ragland, of, Chipola (Texas) JC
47. **Peter Polis, c, New York Tech**
48. Ryan Adamo, rhp, Reedsport (Ore.) HS
49. Emanuel Hayes, ss, Odessa (Texas) JC
50. Toraino Golston, of, New Mexico JC
51. Symmion Willis, ss, Mays HS, Atlanta
52. Edsel Ambrosina, 2b, Berrien Springs, Mich.
53. Vick Brown, ss, Grand Ridge HS, Cypress, Fla.
54. Cuba Gregory, ss, Southeastern HS, Detroit
55. Gregg Rinaldi, rhp, Memorial HS, New Hyde Park, N.Y.
56. Les Dennis, ss, West Linn (Ore.) HS
57. Ronald Mason, of, Martin Methodist (Tenn.) JC
58. Patrick Guerrero, 3b, Middle Georgia JC

1992

Signability takes center stage, with Astros passing on Jeter with No. 1 pick to take Nevin

After several years of rapid bonus inflation, the 1992 draft introduced a new buzzword into the forefront of all draft discussions: signability.

As opposed to a player's baseball ability, signability referred to the amount of money it would take to sign a player. The concept wasn't new, but scouting directors' interest reached a new level as bonus records were being broken year after year. It was a concept that became an integral part of any scouting report on a draft-eligible player in future years.

The 1992 draft was the first that featured decisions on several early picks being distinctly altered by teams' outlook on what kind of talent they needed out of the draft: cheap and agreeable. And it resulted in some unfortunate decisions for clubs at the top of the draft order.

Astros owner John McMullen set a $700,000 limit on the team's signing bonus. Cal State Fullerton third baseman Phil Nevin gave the Astros assurances his demands were in that range, so they took him with the No. 1 pick and he signed for that amount.

Astros general manager Bill Wood claimed that Nevin, a third baseman from Cal State Fullerton and Baseball America's College Player of the Year, was the club's first choice all along.

"Signability this year was a factor, but it has been for the last 15 years I've been watching drafts for the Astros," said Wood, who didn't sign first-round pick John Burke in 1991 because he didn't want to get into the escalating bonuses then. "We wanted to get a feel for what some players wanted, so we knew things could get worked out on a reasonable basis."

The Astros were known to be looking at five other players, however, one of whom was Michigan high school shortstop Derek Jeter.

Former Hall of Fame pitcher Hal Newhouser was an area scout for the Astros in Michigan. While the word among scouts was that Jeter, who had a scholarship to Michigan, would take $1 million to sign, Newhouse lobbied for the Astros to draft him and claimed he could sign Jeter for $750,000.

That was $50,000 over the Astros' self-imposed limit, so they instead drafted Nevin, prompting Newhouser to quit. The Yankees grabbed Jeter with the sixth pick—and he signed for the same $700,000 that Nevin got.

Nevin became a solid big league player, though after the Astros essentially gave up on him. But Jeter evolved into an eventual Hall of Famer, the Yankees' all-time hits leader, a franchise icon in addition to an excellent shortstop with offensive ability.

JOE MIXAN

Charles Johnson proved a good choice as the Marlins' first-ever draft selection

And in spite of owners' efforts to hold down bonuses, the average bonus paid to first-round picks in 1992 was $482,000, a sharp increase over the $355,000 average in 1991 and $243,000 in 1990.

If money hadn't been a key issue, Stanford outfielder Jeffrey Hammonds, who was regarded as the consensus best talent in the Class of '92, probably would not have slipped to the Orioles at No. 4. But the budget-conscious Astros, Indians and Expos had the first three picks, and they did not want to get on the bonus elevator.

Hammonds signed with the Orioles for $975,000, more than any of the first three picks.

Owners even tried to implement new draft rules to limit players' negotiating leverage. At a March meeting, they approved a rule that gave teams exclusive negotiating rights to a player until a year after his college class graduated. Players could have dropped out of school more easily to turn pro, and the draft would have been restricted to 50 rounds.

The Players Association filed a grievance and the case was heard a week before the draft. An arbitrator sided with the union, ruling that Major League Baseball could not make changes to the draft without negotiating them with the union as part of the Basic Agreement. Even though amateur players are not members of the union, the arbitrator ruled the union had a say in the draft because draft picks are awarded to teams that lose free agents, affecting the value of major league players.

This affected draft changes for years to come, as ownership realized it could make only minor alterations unilaterally. Significant changes would be collectively bargained with the union.

Expansion Clubs Stock Up

The draft also attracted an unusual level of media attention in Denver and Miami, as fans there celebrated the first draft picks of the expansion Rockies and Marlins, who began play in 1993.

The Rockies took Florida righthander John Burke, who pitched briefly for them in the big leagues, while the Marlins took Miami catcher Charles Johnson, who became a Gold Glove winner and longtime big leaguer.

It took the Marlins until November to sign Johnson, one of 11 first-round picks who played for Team USA in the 1992 Olympics. Marlins general manager Dave Dombrowski and scouting director Gary Hughes also drafted Johnson in 1989 when they were with the Expos. He turned down $200,000 and went to college.

This time around, Johnson asked for a contract matching 1991 No. 1 pick Brien Taylor's $1.55 million bonus. Negotiations dragged until Johnson finally agreed to a $575,000 contract.

Another Olympian who was a first-round pick out of high school, Calvin Murray of Texas, also signed late. The No. 7 pick to the Giants, Murray had an oral agreement to a $500,000 bonus, but he changed his mind after hearing about Hammonds' deal. He also signed in November, for an $825,000 bonus. Both Johnson and Murray were represented by Scott Boras.

As illustrated by most of the top picks, the 1992 draft was the most college-dominated ever. Fifteen of the first 16 players were out of college, and just six high school players went in the first round, the fewest ever.

In another arbitration ruling that affected the '92 draft, the Twins won a battle with the Mariners over the No. 26 overall pick. Minnesota originally lost the pick to Seattle for signing free-agent pitcher Bill Krueger. The Twins argued successfully that Krueger had signed a minor league contract before making the club out of spring training.

DRAFT 92: FIRST-ROUND PICKS

No.	Club	Player, Pos.	School	Hometown	Ht.	Wt.	B-T	Age
1.	Astros	Phil Nevin, 3b	Cal State Fullerton	Placentia, Calif.	6-2	185	R-R	21
2.	Indians	Paul Shuey, rhp	North Carolina	Raleigh, N.C.	6-3	210	R-R	21
3.	Expos	B.J. Wallace, lhp	Mississippi State	Monroeville, Ala.	6-3	195	L-L	21
4.	Orioles	Jeffrey Hammonds, of	Stanford	Scotch Plains, N.J.	6-0	180	R-R	21
5.	Reds	Chad Mottola, of	Central Florida	Pembroke Pines, Fla.	6-3	200	R-R	20
6.	Yankees	Derek Jeter, of	Central HS	Kalamazoo, Mich.	6-3	170	R-R	17
7.	Giants	Calvin Murray, of	Texas	Dallas	5-11	185	R-R	20
8.	Angels	Pete Janicki, rhp	UCLA	Placentia, Calif.	6-4	190	R-R	21
9.	Mets	Preston Wilson, of	Bamberg-Ehrhardt HS	Bamberg, S.C.	6-3	190	R-R	17
10.	Royals	Michael Tucker, ss	Longwood (Va.) Coll.	Chase City, Va.	6-2	185	L-R	20
11.	Cubs	Derek Wallace, rhp	Pepperdine	Oxnard, Calif.	6-3	190	R-R	20
12.	Brewers	Kenny Felder, of	Florida State	Niceville, Fla.	6-3	225	R-R	21
13.	Phillies	Chad McConnell, of	Creighton	Sioux Falls, S.D.	6-1	180	R-R	20
14.	Mariners	Ron Villone, lhp	Massachusetts	Bergenfield, N.J.	6-3	230	L-L	22
15.	Cardinals	Sean Lowe, rhp	Arizona State	Mesquite, Texas	6-2	200	R-R	21
16.	Tigers	Rick Greene, rhp	Louisiana State	Miami	6-5	200	R-R	21
17.	Royals	Jim Pittsley, rhp	DuBois Area HS	DuBois, Pa.	6-7	220	R-R	18
18.	Mets	Chris Roberts, lhp	Florida State	Middleburg, Fla.	6-0	186	L-L	20
19.	Blue Jays	Shannon Stewart, of	Southridge HS	Miami	6-1	185	R-R	18
20.	Athletics	Benji Grigsby, rhp	San Diego State	Lafayette, La.	6-1	195	R-R	21
21.	Braves	Jamie Arnold, rhp	Osceola HS	Kissimmee, Fla.	6-2	185	R-R	18
22.	Rangers	Rick Helling, rhp	Stanford	Fargo, N.D.	6-3	215	R-R	21
23.	Pirates	Jason Kendall, c	Torrance HS	Torrance, Calif.	6-0	180	R-R	17
24.	White Sox	Eddie Pearson, 1b	Bishop State (Ala.) JC	Mobile, Ala.	6-3	225	B-R	18
25.	Blue Jays	Todd Steverson, of	Arizona State	Inglewood, Calif.	6-2	194	R-R	20
26.	Twins	Dan Serafini, lhp	Serra HS	San Mateo, Calif.	6-3	175	L-L	18
27.	Rockies	John Burke, rhp	Florida	Englewood, Colo.	6-4	220	B-R	22
28.	Marlins	Charles Johnson, c	Miami	Fort Pierce, Fla.	6-2	209	R-R	20

1992

CLUB-BY-CLUB SELECTIONS

ATLANTA BRAVES

June—Regular Phase (21)

1. **Jamie Arnold, rhp, Osceola HS, Kissimmee, Fla.**
2. **Jamie Howard, rhp, St. Thomas More HS, Lafayette, La.**
3. **Carey Paige, rhp, Cooper HS, Abilene, Texas**
4. **Damon Hollins, of, Vallejo (Calif.) HS**
5. **Sean Smith, c, Oconomowoc (Wis.) HS**
6. Justin Atchley, lhp, Walla Walla (Wash.) CC
7. **Ken Warner, ss, St. Helena Central HS, Amite, La.**
8. **Maurice Christmas, rhp, Lexington (Mass.) Christian Academy**
9. **Anthony Diieso, of, Copiague HS, Lindenhurst, N.Y.**
10. **Brad Clontz, rhp, Virginia Tech**
11. **Bobby Smith, of/3b, Fremont HS, Oakland**
12. **Chris Brock, of/rhp, Florida State**
13. Mark Hendrickson, lhp, Mount Vernon (Wash.) HS
14. **Shane Bryant, rhp, Hug HS, Reno, Nev.**
15. Jose Cruz Jr., of, Bellaire HS, Houston
16. **Clint Gagnon, rhp, South Suburban (Ill.) JC**
17. **Richard Williams, of, Hesperia (Calif.) HS**
18. Shane Monahan, of, Wheeler HS, Marietta, Ga.
19. **Tyrone Domingo, ss, Los Angeles (Calif.) HS**
20. **Jason Shelley, 1b, Vallejo (Calif.) HS**
21. **Shawn Brennan, of, Moeller HS, Cincinnati**
22. **Mike Warner, of, Florida International**
23. **Tony Stoecklin, lhp, Southern Illinois-Edwardsville**
24. **Aaron Turnier, lhp, Nevada-Las Vegas**
25. **Dan Teran, lhp, Mesa (Ariz.) CC**
26. **Bryan Spetter, ss/2b, Anderson (Ind.)**
27. Mike McKenna, rhp, Kishwaukee (Ill.) JC
28. Chris Wyrick, ss, Missouri
29. **Doug Wollenburg, ss, Ohio State**
30. **Phil Zimmerman, ss, Regis (Colo.)**
31. Derrick Calvin, rhp, Southern
32. **Fernando Benitez, c, Lindsay (Calif.) HS**
33. **Ryan Jacobs, lhp, Glenn HS, Kernersville, N.C.**
34. Cedric Williams, ss, Western Hills HS, Fort Worth
35. Brian Cravey, rhp, Silsbee (Texas) HS
36. **William Paragin, c, Logan (Ill.) CC**
37. **Anthony Ruff, of, Moreno Valley (Calif.) HS**
38. **Terrell Buckley, of, Florida State**
39. **James Stutts, of, San Jacinto (Texas) JC**
40. **James Blaine, rhp, McLennan (Texas) CC**
41. **David Bingham, of, Lewis-Clark State (Idaho)**
42. Corey Ehlers, rhp/3b, Sharpstown HS, Houston
43. Monty Means, of, Union (S.C.) HS
44. Mark Brunell, lhp, Washington
45. John Webb, c, McLennan (Texas) CC
46. **Darrell May, lhp, Sacramento CC**
47. **Chris Church, lhp, Penn State**
48. **Ted Hassan, rhp, Jackson State**
49. **Kevin Nalls, 3b, Grambling State**
50. **John Simmons, lhp, St. Xavier (Ill.)**

BALTIMORE ORIOLES

June—Regular Phase (4)

1. **Jeffrey Hammonds, of, Stanford**
2. **Brian Sackinsky, rhp, Stanford**
3. **Billy Owens, 1b, Arizona**
4. **Hut Smith, rhp, A.L. Brown HS, Kannapolis, N.C.**
5. **Scott Klingenbeck, rhp, Ohio State**
6. **Robert Chancey, of, Stanhope Elmore HS, Millbrook, Ala.**
7. **Keith Eaddy, of, William Paterson (N.J.)**
8. **Cory Brown, rhp/of, Gibbs HS, St. Petersburg, Fla.**
9. **Calvin Lee, rhp, East St. John HS, Garvyille, La.**
10. Roberto Lopez, rhp, Wilcox HS, Santa Clara, Calif.
11. **Angel Pagan, ss, Arecibo, P.R.**
12. **Michael Porter, rhp, Centenary (N.J.)**
13. **Tobias Price, lhp, Lincoln HS, San Diego**
14. **Adam Burton, 2b, Florida CC-Jacksonville**
15. Ryan Minor, ss, Hammon (Okla.) HS
16. Bubba Trammell, 3b, Cleveland State (Tenn.) CC
17. **Carlos Chavez, rhp, New Mexico JC**
18. **Garrett Stephenson, rhp, Ricks (Idaho) JC**
19. Korey Burkhart, rhp, Barton County (Kan.) CC
20. James Esparza, lhp, Cedar Valley (Texas) JC
21. Chris Bauer, ss, Jenks HS, Tulsa, Okla.
22. **Keivi Baker, c, Shanks HS, Gretna, Fla.**
23. **Paul Jones, 1b, Cumberland (Ky.)**
24. **Aaron Lane, lhp, New Orleans**
25. Ron Wallech, rhp, Hagerstown (Md.) JC
26. Brian Scutero, rhp, Valencia (Fla.) CC
27. **Howie Clark, 1b, Huntington Beach (Calif.) HS**
28. Joe Dawley, rhp, Riverside (Calif.) CC
29. **Gregg Castaldo, ss, Central Florida**
30. Dean Kent, of, Jesuit HS, Oldsmar, Fla.
31. Ledowick Johnson, of, Louisburg (N.C.) JC
32. **Joe Lantrip, lhp, Memphis State**
33. Scott Schroeffel, of, North Allegheny HS, Pittsburgh
34. Tony Enard, rhp, Sparks (Nev.) HS
35. Brian Simmons, of, Peters Township HS, McMurray, Pa.
36. Jose Santiago, ss, Dr. Phillips HS, Orlando
37. Rob Gardner, rhp, Carlmont HS, Belmont, Calif.
38. George Arias, 3b, Pirna (Ariz.) CC
39. **Kyle Yeske, of, St. Mary's (Minn.)**
40. **George Freeberger, c, Polytechnic HS, Baltimore**
41. Anthony Marnell, c, Bishop Gorman HS, Las Vegas
42. William Tanksley, rhp, Kemp (Texas) HS
43. Mario Iglesias, rhp, Hayward (Calif.) HS
44. Brad Crede, 3b, Fatima HS, Westphalia, Mo.
45. Mike Drumright, rhp, Valley Center (Kan.) HS
46. Robert Costello, rhp, Watson Chapel HS, Pine Bluff, Ark.
47. Jarvis White, of, Polk (Fla.) CC
48. Marvin Perkins, of, Lake City (Fla.) CC
49. Joe Goodwin, c, South Carroll HS, New Windsor, Md.
50. Michael Thompson, of, Clovis (N.M.) HS

BOSTON RED SOX

June—Regular Phase (18)

1. (Pick to Mets as compensation for Type A free agent Frank Viola)
2. **Tony Sheffield, of, Tullahoma (Tenn.) HS**
3. **Doug Hecker, 1b, Tennessee**
4. **Joe Hamilton, 3b, Dighton-Rehobeth (Mass.) HS**
5. **Steve Rodriguez, 2b, Pepperdine**
6. **Derek Vinyard, of, San Diego State**
7. **Joe DePastino, lhp/of, Riverview HS, Sarasota, Fla.**
8. **J.B. Bowles, 3b, Montgomery HS, Rockville, Md.**
9. **Todd Carey, ss, Brown**
10. **Mark Senkowitz, c, Ohio Wesleyan**
11. **Aaron Rounsifer, ss, Vista (Calif.) HS**
12. **Chad Amos, rhp, Ohio State**
13. **Bill Selby, ss, Southern Mississippi**
14. **James Tyrrell, lhp, Dutchess (N.Y.) CC**
15. **Gettys Glaze, rhp, The Citadel**
16. Ricardo Gama, 2b, Southridge HS, Miami
17. Chris McCranie, ss, Colquitt County HS, Moultrie, Ga.
18. **Eric Norman, ss, Jones County HS, Haddock, Ga.**
19. **Brent Hansen, rhp, California**
20. **Rob Berryman, rhp, Yorktown, Va.**
21. **Leif McKinley, rhp, Chemeketa (Ore.) CC**
22. **Jeff Martin, c, Vanderbilt**
23. **Wes Brooks, rhp, Belleville Area (Ill.) CC**

24. **Bob Juday, ss/2b, Michigan State**
25. **Jeff Faino, lhp, Florida Tech**
26. **Eric Cormier, rhp, Milford (Mass.) HS**
27. **Joe Hudson, rhp, West Virginia**
28. **Rick Milligan, of, San Joaquin Delta (Calif.) JC**
29. **Ricky Craig, rhp, Webb City HS, Jasper, Mo.**
30. **Scott Bakkum, rhp, Minnesota**
31. Wilredo Rivera, of, Vega Alta, P.R. (Selection voided)
32. **Randy Lawrence, rhp, Ferrum (Va.)**
33. **Ethan Faggett, of, Dunbar HS, Burleson, Texas**
34. Marcus Cuper, lhp, Voorhees HS, High Bridge, N.J.
35. **Andrew Moore, 2b, Bridgewater (Va.)**
36. Lou Merloni, ss, Providence
37. **Jason Smith, c, West Florida**
38. **T.J. O'Donnell, ss, Old Dominion**
39. Joe Barksdale, rhp, Southern Union State (Ala.) JC
40. Steve McCollough, c, Eisenhower HS, Lawton, Okla.
41. Reggie Hightower, of, George Wallace (Ala.) CC
42. Gresham Fortune, of, East Central (Miss.) JC
43. Kevin Gibbs, ss, St. John's HS, Davidsonville, Md.
44. Eric DeMoura, ss, Taunton (Mass.) HS
45. Chris Wagner, rhp, Santa Fe (Fla.) CC
46. Allen Williams, 3b, Arkansas
47. Brian Johnson, 1b, Lee County HS, Albany, Ga.
48. Lewis Spencer, ss, Hampton (Va.) HS
49. Rico Wood, 2b, Southern Union State (Ala.) JC
50. Michael Linenberger, of, Mississippi Gulf Coast JC

CALIFORNIA ANGELS

June—Regular Phase (8)

1. **Pete Janicki, rhp, UCLA**
1. **Jeff Schmidt, rhp, Minnesota** (Supplemental pick—29th—for loss of Type A free agent Wally Joyner)
2. **DeShawn Warren, lhp, Choctaw County HS, Butler, Ala.**
2. **Chris Smith, ss/of, Vallejo (Calif.) HS** (Pick from Royals as compensation for Joyner)
2. **Marquis Riley, of, Central Arkansas** (Supplemental pick—67th—for loss of Type C free agent Kirk McCaskill)
3. Brian Powell, rhp, Bainbridge (Ga.) HS
4. **Shawn Holcomb, rhp, El Dorado HS, Placentia, Calif.**
5. **Paxton Briley, rhp, Clemson**
6. **Bill Simas, rhp, Fresno (Calif.) CC**
7. **Larry Hingle, lhp, Stetson**
8. **John Lloyd, rhp, Englewood HS, Jacksonville, Fla.**
9. **Mickey Kerns, of, Alabama**
10. **Travis Thurmond, rhp, Beaverton (Ore.) HS**
11. Travis Driskill, rhp, Blinn (Texas) JC
12. **Morisse Daniels, of, Florida A&M**
13. **John Snyder, rhp, Westlake HS, Thousand Oaks, Calif.**
14. **Jay Simpson, of, South Alabama**
15. **Dallas Rinehart, rhp, East Tennessee State**
16. **Michael Wolff, of, Georgia Tech**
17. Ted Tiffany, of, Cactus HS, Glendale, Ariz.
18. **David Kesster, c, UC Riverside**
19. Ray McWhite, of, Florida CC-Jacksonville
20. **George Dafun, rhp, Baldwin HS, Kihei, Hawaii**
21. Aaron Guiel, of, Langley, B.C
22. **John Pricher, rhp, Florida**
23. Luis Ducasse, of, Kennedy HS, Bronx, N.Y.
24. **Ronald Davis, of, Simeon HS, Chicago**
25. Benny Agbayani, of, Hawaii Pacific
26. Charles Beale, rhp, Dublin (Ga.) HS
27. Juan Henderson, ss, Gulf Coast (Fla.) CC
28. David Krug, rhp, Concordia (N.Y.)
29. Aaron Mayer, c, California HS, San Ramon, Calif.
30. Manuel Mendez, lhp, Washington Union HS, Fresno
31. Seth Brizek, ss, Oley Valley HS, Fleetwood, Pa.
32. Alvie Shepherd, rhp/of, Proviso West HS, Bellwood, Ill.
33. Casey Kirkman, rhp, JC of the Sequoias (Calif.)
34. Todd Singelyn, rhp, Loyola HS, Whittier, Calif.
35. Erik Plaisted, rhp, Minnetonka (Minn.) HS
36. Chad Baker, rhp, Polk (Fla.) CC
37. Felix Merced, ss, Brevard (Fla.) CC
38. James Johnson, of, San Bernardino Valley (Calif.) JC
39. Brandy Bengoechea, ss, Lewis-Clark State (Idaho)
40. Brian Ussery, c, Bloomingdale HS, Brandon, Fla.
41. Dan Ladehoff, ss, Central HS, Davenport, Iowa
42. Michael Cole, of, Monterey (Calif.) HS
43. **Bill Blanchette, lhp, Hawaii**
44. **Marcus Garcia, of, Mount San Antonio (Calif.) JC**
45. **Greg Biley, ss, California Baptist**
46. Ben Duncan, of, Palomar (Calif.) JC
47. David Vindivich, of, Edmonds (Wash.) CC
48. Brad Buenconsejo, rhp, Hawaii Pacific
49. **Joe Urso, 2b, Tampa**
50. **Anthony Chavez, rhp, San Jose State**

CHICAGO CUBS

June—Regular Phase (11)

1. **Derek Wallace, rhp, Pepperdine**
2. (Pick to Dodgers as compensation tor Type A free agent Mike Morgan)
3. **Brant Brown, 1b, Fresno State**
4. **Brandon Pico, of, Rogers HS, Newport, R.I.**
5. Ryan Wilson, c, Cerritos (Calif.) HS
6. **Emilio Mendez, ss, Miami Beach (Fla.) HS**
7. **Darren Dreyer, rhp, Southwest Texas State**
8. **Mike Hubbard, c, James Madison**
9. **Chris Petersen, ss, Georgia Southern**
10. Kris Hanson, rhp, Wisconsin-Stevens Point
11. **Kevin Booker, of, Central Arkansas**
12. **Kennie Steenstra, rhp, Wichita State**
13. **Adam Schulhofer, rhp, UCLA**
14. **David DeMoss, of, West Virginia**
15. **Byron Bradley, 3b, Indiana**
16. Joel Galarza, c, Yabucoa, P.R.
17. Brent Woodall, lhp, California
18. **Billy Childress, lhp, Chowan (N.C.) JC**
19. **Scott Barton, c, Marion County HS, Jasper, Tenn.**
20. **Chuck Daniel, rhp, Mississippi State**
21. **Dan Madsen, of, Nevada-Las Vegas**
22. **Kevin Kessinger, of, Mississippi**
23. **Paul Stojsavjevic, c, Southwestern (Calif.) JC**
24. Shane White, rhp, Jay County HS, Redkey, Ind.
25. **Dan Gustavson, rhp, Mount San Antonio (Calif.) JC**
26. **Chris Plonk, 3b, Manatee (Fla.) JC**
27. **Jason Boehlow, 1b, Saint Louis**
28. **Joshua Simmons, ss, Cuesta (Calif.) CC**
29. **Jon Jarolimek, rhp, Nevada-Las Vegas**
30. **Joe Rino, rhp, New Mexico Highlands**
31. **Coleman Smith, of, Tennessee**
32. Mark Taylor, lhp, Northeast HS, St. Petersburg, Fla.
33. David Caldwell, lhp, Canarsie HS, Brooklyn
34. **Daryle Gavlick, lhp, Armstrong State (Ga.)**
35. **Jay Hassel, rhp, San Diego State**
36. Rich Crowe, of, Oceanview HS, Huntington Beach, Calif.
37. Antonio Leonardi, rhp, Lee HS, Houston
38. **David Dark, lhp, Louisiana Tech**
39. **Andrew Elsbecker, rhp, Boone (Iowa) CC**
40. **Luis Matos, rhp, Cabo Rojo, P.R.**
41. Dion Knighten, of, Los Angeles Harbor JC
42. Justin Baughman, ss, Bellarmine Prep HS, San Jose
43. Charles Leckie, 3b, La Quinta HS, Garden Grove, Calif.
44. Jacob Steinkemper, c, Brophy HS, Phoenix
45. Matt Schafer, c, Northeast HS, St. Petersburg, Fla.
46. Robert Vargas, of, Irvington HS, Fremont, Calif.
47. Andrew Marquardt, of, Kennewick (Wash.) HS
48. **Tim Stutheit, ss/3b, Bellevue (Neb.)**
49. Chad Schroeder, rhp, Larkin HS, Elgin, Ill.
50. David Schmidt, c, Kennewick (Wash.) HS

CHICAGO WHITE SOX

June—Regular Phase (24)

1. **Eddie Pearson, 1b, Bishop State (Ala.) JC**
2. A.J. Hinch, c, Midwest City (Okla.) HS
3. **Byron Mathews, of, Oklahoma**
4. **Scott Patton, of, Capistrano Valley HS, Mission Viejo, Calif.**

5. **Tim Moore, rhp, Stanford**
6. **Chris Snopek, 3b, Mississippi**
7. **Mickey McKinion, rhp, Montgomery HS, Wilmer, Ala.**
8. **Robert Theodile, rhp, San Jacinto (Texas) JC**
9. **Carmine Cappuccio, of, Rollins (Fla.)**
10. **Andrea Levias, of, El Camino (Calif.) JC**
11. David Hutcheson, rhp, South Florida
12. **Jason Evans, 3b, Oklahoma**
13. **Craig Wilson, ss, Kansas State**
14. **Phil Giese, lhp, Joliet (Ill.) JC**
15. **Sean Johnston, lhp, Harvard**
16. Irven Stacy, 3b, Winter Haven (Fla.) HS
17. **David Elsbernd, rhp, Baylor**
18. **Steve Worrell, lhp, Stanford**
19. **Bob Mumma, c, Maryland-Baltimore County**
20. **Wayne Lindemann, lhp, Washington State**
21. **Wayne Faircloth, c, UNC Asheville**
22. Tom Luke, rhp, Mississippi
23. Jose Flores, ss/2b, New Mexico JC
24. **Jason Ogden, of, Rice**
25. **Jason Pierson, lhp, Delaware**
26. **Ty Lynch, 2b/3b, Central Florida**
27. **Brendan Donnelly, rhp, Mesa State (Colo.)**
28. **Ted Rich, 2b, Florida**
29. Geoff Grenert, rhp, Nevada-Reno
30. Kevin Chabot, of, Dr. Phillips HS, Orlando
31. **Yusef Ford, lhp, Cal State Fullerton**
32. Kristren Detmer, lhp, Nokomis (Ill.) HS
33. **Scot Hollrah, rhp, Southeast Missouri State**
34. Shayne Bennett, rhp, Parkland (Ill.) JC
35. Joel Colgrove, rhp, Warrior Academy HS, Boligee, Ala.
36. John Reece, of, Nebraska
37. Jay Veniard, lhp, Bolles HS, Jacksonville
38. **Jim McDermott, rhp, Fordham**
39. **Chris Tremie, c, Houston**
40. **Nelson Izquierdo, 3b, St. Thomas (Fla.)**
41. **Toby Lehman, rhp, Frank Phillips (Texas) JC**
42. Jason Bell, rhp, Boone HS, Orlando
43. Hoby Mork, 3b, Minnetonka HS, Excelsior, Minn.
44. Joseph Freitas, of, Hanford (Calif.) HS
45. Josh Klimek, ss, Vianney HS, Kirkwood, Mo.
46. **Tyres Blackburn, of, New Mexico JC**
47. Jason Santoro, of, El Toro (Calif.) HS
48. Mike Lowell, 2b, Coral Gables (Fla.) HS
49. **Chris Madar, c/3b, Rollins (Fla.)**
50. **Efrain Ventura, of, Florida International**

CINCINNATI REDS

June—Regular Phase (5)

1. **Chad Mottola, of, Central Florida**
2. Chad Alexander, of, Lufkin (Texas) HS
2. **Rick Magdelano, ss, Baldwin Park (Calif.) HS** (Pick from Phillies as compensation for Type B free agent Mariano Duncan)
3. **Todd Etler, rhp, Catholic HS, Covington, Ky.**
4. **Eric Owens, ss, Ferrum (Va.)**
5. **Jason Angel, rhp, Clemson**
6. **Curt Lyons, rhp, Madison Central HS, Richmond, Ky.**
7. **Martin Lister, lhp, Jefferson Davis (Ala.) JC**
8. **Mike Meggers, of, Mary Hardin-Baylor (Texas)**
9. **Brian Silvia, c, Mississippi**
10. **Dan Kopriva, 3b, Louisville**
11. **Brad Keenan, 1b, Concordia (Minn.)**
12. **Justin Towle, c, Inglemoor HS, Bothell, Wash.**
13. **Dan Oyas, of/rhp, San Bernardino Valley (Calif.) JC**
14. **Cleveland Ladell, of, Northwood Institute (Texas)**
15. **Tim Belk, 1b, Lubbock Christian**
16. **Jeff Ashton, 2b, Wright State**
17. **Jason Kummerfeldt, rhp, Wyoming**
18. **Jeff Ramey, of, Indiana**
19. **James Nix, rhp, Texas A&M**
20. **Dan Frye, ss, Indiana State**
21. **Will Brunson, lhp, Southwest Texas State**
22. **John Bess, c, Mesa State (Colo.)**
23. **Chad Fox, rhp, Tarleton State (Texas)**
24. Sean Hogan, lhp, Morehead State
25. **Ray Moon, of, Vincennes (Ind.) JC**
26. **Jeff Manship, of, Nevada-Reno**
27. William Roland, ss, Miller HS, Corpus Christi, Texas
28. **Ricky Pickett, lhp, Northeastern Oklahoma A&M JC**
29. **Jeff Nagy, of, Findlay (Ohio)**
30. **Todd Ruyak, lhp, Virginia**
31. **Mike Collins, ss/2b, Central Florida CC**
32. **Denny Fussell, lhp, Mary Hardin-Baylor (Texas)**
33. **Rodriguez Sanders, 2b, Spartanburg Methodist (S.C.) JC**
34. Fletcher Austin, lhp, Tehachapi (Calif.) HS
35. Tony Darden, ss, Gilmer (Texas) HS
36. Ben Fay, c, Brewer HS, Fort Worth
37. Jeff Keppen, rhp, Central Gwinnett HS, Lawrenceville, Ga.
38. **William Sullivan, rhp, North Florida JC**
39. Steve Schneider, rhp, North Florida JC
40. Charles McQuaig, c, Milledge Academy, Milledgeville, Ga.
41. Mike Henke, rhp, Corning East HS, Big Flats, N.Y.
42. Peter Dellaratta, rhp, Gulf Breeze (Fla.) HS
43. Kevin Beirne, rhp, McCullough HS, Woodlands, Texas
44. **Louis Maberry, rhp, Abilene Christian (Texas)**
45. Brandon Stanley, ss, Clark HS, San Antonio
46. Brad Mulvaney, c, Arvada West HS, Arvada, Colo.
47. David Miller, rhp, Lee County HS, Sanford, N.C.
48. Robbie McIver, ss, Lee County HS, Sanford, N.C.
49. Doug Anderson, rhp, Waubonsie Valley HS, Naperville, Ill.
50. Mark Mapes, c, Corning-Painted Post West HS, Painted Post, N.Y.

CLEVELAND INDIANS

June—Regular Phase (2)

1. **Paul Shuey, rhp, North Carolina**
2. **Mike Matthews, lhp, Montgomery-Rockville (Md.) CC**
3. **Jon Nunnally, of, Miami-Dade CC South**
4. **Matt Williams, lhp, Virginia Commonwealth**
5. **Jamie Taylor, 3b, Ohio State**
6. Jeff Liefer, of, Upland (Calif.) HS
7. **J.J. Thobe, rhp, Rancho Santiago (Calif.) JC**
8. Greg Gregory, lhp, Millikan HS, Long Beach
9. Larry Schneider, c, Tulane
10. Ryan Ritter, ss, Wheeler HS, Marietta, Ga.
11. **Terry Miller, ss, Lincoln HS, Port Arthur, Texas**
12. **Mitch Meluskey, c, Eisenhower HS, Yakima, Wash.**
13. Chris Westcott, rhp, Delgado (La.) JC
14. **Chad Townsend, 1b, UC Riverside**
15. Cerleston Bargman, 3b, Southridge HS, Miami
16. **Fred Smith, rhp, Connors State (Okla.) JC**
17. Cale Carter, of, Mater Dei HS, Orange, Calif.
18. **Curtis George, ss, Florida A&M**
19. **Noe Najera, lhp, North Carolina State**
20. **Damian Leyva, lhp, Miami-Dade CC Wolfson**
21. **Jon Zubiri, rhp, Hanford (Calif.) HS**
22. Joe Parks, of, Pike County HS, Concord, Ga.
23. **Derek Hacopian, of, Maryland**
24. Stephen Randolph, 1b, Bowie HS, Austin, Texas
25. **Leroy Thompson, of, Fernandina Beach (Fla.) HS**
26. **Mike Neilson, lhp, Willamette (Ore.)**
27. **Eric White, 3b, Mount San Antonio (Calif.) JC**
28. **David Welch, rhp, Tulane**
29. Lawyer Milloy, of, Lincoln HS, Tacoma
30. **Allen Gallagher, rhp, Lower Columbia (Wash.) CC**
31. **John Lewandowski, c, South Suburban (Ill.) JC**
32. **Ben Blake, rhp, Simpson (Iowa)**
33. Jason Langolis, lhp, Sanderson HS, Raleigh, N.C.
34. **Epi Cardenas, 2b, Laredo (Texas) JC**
35. Gregg Bitner, rhp, Euclid (Ohio) HS
36. Brian Wisler, rhp, Walla Walla (Wash.) CC
37. Kiko Palacios, c, Castle Park HS, San Diego
38. **Germaine Mayberry, of, Arizona State**
39. Jason Myers, lhp, Chaffey (Calif.) JC
40. Milton Anderson, of, Pasco Hernando (Fla.) CC
41. Johnathan Oram, ss, Tumwater HS, Olympia, Wash.
42. Mack Chambers, ss/2b, Seminole State (Okla.) JC

43. Rodney Tisdale, of, Florida CC-Jacksonville
44. Allan Hebbert, rhp, Chaffey (Calif.) JC
45. Claude Love, of, Plantation HS, Sunrise, Fla.
46. Marvin Pierce, rhp, Twin Falls (Idaho) HS
47. Maft Braughler, c, Lafayette HS, Lexington, Ky.
48. **Roberto Garza, rhp, Laredo (Texas) JC**
49. Jason Rooker, rhp, Edmonds (Wash.) CC
50. Joey Malone, rhp, Tennessee HS, Bristol, Tenn.

COLORADO ROCKIES

June—Regular Phase (27)

1. **John Burke, rhp, Florida**
2. **Mark Thompson, rhp, Kentucky**
3. **Roger Bailey, rhp, Florida State**
4. **Lloyd Peever, rhp, Louisiana State**
5. **Ryan Freeburg, 3b/of, Grand Canyon (Ariz.)**
6. **Bill Scalzitti, c, Miami-Dade CC North**
7. **Jason Bates, ss, Arizona**
8. **Chris Henderson, rhp, Brevard (Fla.) CC**
9. **Mike Eiffert, lhp, Texas-Pan American**
10. **Garvin Alston, rhp, Florida International**
11. **Craig Counsell, ss, Notre Dame**
12. **James Hovey, lhp, Indian Hills (Iowa) CC**
13. **Mark Voisard, rhp, Mount Vernon Nazarene (Ohio)**
14. **Juan Acevedo, rhp, Parkland (Ill.) JC**
15. **Danny Figueroa, of, Rio Piedras, P.R.**
16. **Greg Boyd, of, Essex (Md.) CC**
17. **Angel Echevarria, of, Rutgers**
18. **Jason Hutchins, rhp, Texas A&M**
19. Eric Wulf, c, Washington State
20. **Mike Kotarski, lhp, Duke**
21. **Randy Edwards, of, Bishop Amat HS, West Covina, Calif.**
22. **John Oakland, 1b, Cal Poly San Luis Obispo**
23. **Chris Neier, rhp, Chico State**
24. **Tom Schmidt, 3b, Brevard (Fla.) CC**
25. **Quinton McCracken, 2b, Duke**
26. Thomas Waterman, lhp, Saddleback (Calif.) CC
27. Charles Whitehead, 2b, Pleasure Ridge Park HS, Louisville
28. **Mark Strittmatter, c, Virginia Commonwealth**
29. **Keith Krenke, of, Minnesota**
30. **Richard Hatfield, c, Pineville HS, Marianna, W.Va.**
31. **Jeff Sobkoviak, rhp, Kankakee (Ill.) CC**
32. **Jay Holland, rhp, Hawaii**
33. **Mike Case, of, Long Beach State**
34. Ken Copeland, of, Trinidad State (Colo.) JC
35. James Dixon, rhp, Trinidad State (Colo.) JC
36. **Tim Scott, 3b, Maine**
37. **Mike Machado, of, Diablo Valley (Calif.) JC**
38. **Greg Tafoya, lhp, Holbrook (Ariz.) HS**
39. **Isaac Barnes, lhp, Red Bank HS, Hixson, Tenn.**
40. **Neil Garrett, rhp, West HS, Joliet, Ill.**
41. Matt Chamberlain, rhp, Louisiana State
42. Jason Weiss, rhp, Nevada Union HS, Gass Valley, Calif.
43. **Bill Metzinger, rhp, Cincinnati**
44. Anthony Dermendziev, of, San Jose (Calif.) CC
45. Jayson Sessoyeff, c, Clovis (Calif.) HS
46. **Jonathan Goodrich, rhp, Santa Rosa (Calif.) JC**
47. Matt Pridgen, of, Hayden HS, Phoenix
48. Dan Butcher, rhp, Diablo Valley (Calif.) JC
49. **Lamarr Rogers, 2b, Long Beach State**
50. **Torry Zerilla, ss, Youngstown State**

DETROIT TIGERS

June—Regular Phase (16)

1. **Rick Greene, rhp, Louisiana State**
2. **Yuri Sanchez, ss, Lynn (Mass.) Tech HS**
3. **Chris Gomez, ss, Long Beach State**
4. **Kenny Carlyle, rhp, Mississippi**
5. **David Mysel, rhp, Maryland**
6. **Malvin DeJesus, ss, William Penn (Iowa)**
7. **Pat Ahearne, rhp, Pepperdine**
8. David Reinfelder, lhp, Vassar (Mich.) HS
9. **Lawrence Lopez, rhp, Wyoming**
10. **Frank Catalanotto, 2b, East HS, Smithtown, N.Y.**
11. **Sean Whiteside, lhp, UNC Charlotte**
12. **Bobby Higginson, of, Temple**
13. **Rick Navarro, rhp, San Diego State**
14. **Mike Berlin, rhp, South Carolina**
15. **Corey Parker, 1b, UC Irvine**
16. **Scott Pagano, of, St. Francis (N.Y.)**
17. **Casey Mendenhall, rhp, Oklahoma**
18. **Tim Jones, rhp, Texas-Pan American**
19. **Darren Milne, of, Brigham Young**
20. **Brian Maxcy, rhp, Mississippi**
21. **Moises Ayala, c, Sabana Grande, P.R.**
22. Chris Wilcox, 1b, St. Johns (Mich.) HS
23. **John Rosengren, lhp, North Carolina**
24. **Kevin Lidle, c, Mount San Antonio (Calif.) JC**
25. Scott Timmerman, 2b, Michigan
26. Scott Norman, rhp, Pasco Hernando (Fla.) CC
27. **John Grimm, rhp, Kent State**
28. Beau Campbell, c, Washington State
29. Derek Kraemer, rhp, Madison HS, Madison Heights, Mich.
30. **James Greene, of, Sacramento CC**
31. Thomas Wolff, rhp, Hillsdale (Mich.) HS
32. Rene Justiniano, 1b, Roberto Clemente HS, Chicago
33. **Jeff Brown, rhp, St. John's**
34. **Ken Valdez, of, King HS, Tampa**
35. **David Verduzco, rhp, Yale**
36. **John Lamar, of, Indiana State**
37. Wynter Phoenix, of, Grossmont HS, El Cajon, Calif.
38. Gary Morris, rhp, St. Mary's HS, Orchard Lake, Mich.
39. Francisco Mejia, rhp, University HS, Los Angeles
40. **Eric Weber, rhp, Swan Valley HS, Saginaw, Mich.**
41. Mark Redman, lhp, Escondido (Calif.) HS
42. **Matt Evans, 1b, Grand Canyon (Ariz.)**
43. Scott Kapla, rhp, Catholic Central HS, Redford, Mich.
44. Brian Jacobson, rhp, Perris (Calif.) HS
45. James Castro, rhp, Riverside (Calif.) CC
46. Chris Gonzalez, 3b, Harry Doss HS, Louisville
47. Brian Casey, lhp, East Montgomery HS, Biscoe, N.C.
48. Carlos Yedo, 1b, Columbus HS, Miami
49. David Newhan, 2b, Cypress (Calif.) JC
50. Julian Gaillard, rhp, Florida Southern

FLORIDA MARLINS

June—Regular Phase (28)

1. **Charles Johnson, c, Miami**
2. **John Lynch, rhp, Stanford**
3. **Rich Ireland, lhp, Crater HS, Central Point, Ore.**
4. **Willie Brown, of, Florida A&M**
5. **Alex Aranzamendi, ss, Rio Piedras, P.R.**
6. **Pat Leahy, rhp, Notre Dame**
7. **Reynol Mendoza, rhp, Incarnate Word (Texas)**
8. **Dan Roman, lhp, Brooklyn (N.Y.)**
9. **Scott Samuels, of, Arizona State**
10. **Chris Sheff, of, Pepperdine**
11. **Tony Torres, ss, Nevada-Reno**
12. **Mike Veneziale, rhp, Camden County (N.J.) JC**
13. **Jerry Stafford, lhp, San Diego State**
14. **Jason Tidwell, rhp, Jacksonville State**
15. **Jim Patterson, rhp, Fresno State**
16. **Eddie Christian, of, Long Beach State**
17. **Gavin Baugh, ss, JC of San Mateo (Calif.)**
18. **Mark Skeels, c, Stanford**
19. John Codrington, rhp, Bowie HS, Austin, Texas
20. Rob Steinert, rhp, North Carolina State
21. Chris Clark, of, Smackover (Ark.) HS
22. **Matt Donahue, rhp, North Caroline State**
23. **Todd Pridy, 1b, Long Beach State**
24. Marcus Mays, lhp, McNair HS, Decatur, Ga.
25. **Andy Larkin, rhp, South HS, Medford, Ore.**
26. Brian Loyd, c, El Dorado HS, Placentia, Calif.
27. **Matt Petersen, rhp, Iowa State**
28. **Ken Kendrena, rhp, Cal State Northridge**
29. **Anthony Bonifazio, of, Fresno State**
30. Mark Leber, 1b, Mitty HS, San Jose

31. **Erick Strickland, of, West HS, Bellevue, Neb.**
32. **Lou Lucca, 3b, Oklahoma State**
33. Tim Lanier, c, Catholic HS, Baton Rouge, La.
34. **Bruce Nolte, ss, Pennsauken (N.J.) HS**
35. **Rick Freehling, of, Creighton**
36. Matt Furrey, of, Hilliard (Ohio) HS
37. **Hiram Fantauzzi, of, Arroyo, P.R.**
38. **Jason Frazier, c, Hilton Head HS, Bluffton, S.C.**
39. **Sean Gousha, c, San Diego**
40. **Bob Frazier, lhp, Clarion (Pa.)**
41. **Doug Pettit, rhp, Texas**
42. Matt Wood, rhp, Canyon HS, Anaheim
43. **Greg Reeder, rhp, Christian HS, Panama City, Fla.**
44. **Scott Johnson, rhp, Central HS, Greeley, Colo.**
45. Dan Lyons, rhp, Mullen HS, Littleton, Colo.
46. Chris Altman, rhp, UNC Wilmington
47. **Scott Englehart, rhp, George Fox (Ore.)**
48. **Mitchel Bowen, rhp, JC of the Canyons (Calif.)**
49. Robert Hernandez, c, San Jose (Calif.) CC
50. James Woods, of, San Fernando HS, Pacoima, Calif.

HOUSTON ASTROS

June—Regular Phase (1)

1. **Phil Nevin, 3b, Cal State Fullerton**
1. **Kendall Rhine, rhp, Georgia** (Supplemental pick—37th—for failure to sign 1991 first-rounder John Burke)
2. **David Landaker, ss, Royal HS, Simi Valley, Calif.**
3. **Chris Holt, rhp, Navarro (Texas) JC**
4. Chad Sheffer, ss, Bloomingdale HS, Valrico, Fla.
5. **Sean Runyan, lhp, Urbandale (Iowa) HS**
6. **Jeff Tenbarge, rhp, Evansville**
7. **Mike Rennhack, of, Leland HS, San Jose**
8. **Chris Thomas, of, Boise State**
9. **Greg Elliott, 3b, Southeastern Louisiana**
10. **Jamie Walker, lhp, Austin Peay**
11. **Ray Bowers, of, West Middlesex (Pa.) Area HS**
12. **Doug Mlicki, rhp, Ohio**
13. **Hector Mercado, lhp, Dorado, P.R.**
14. **Donovan Mitchell, 2b, UNC Charlotte**
15. Cade Gaspar, rhp, Saddleback (Calif.) JC
16. **Joseph Witt, 1b, Richfield (Minn.) HS**
17. **Alan Probst, c, Mansfield (Pa.)**
18. Edwin Rodriguez, 2b, Ponce, P.R.
19. **Mike Grzanich, rhp, Parkland (Ill.) JC**
20. **Marvin Billingsley, lhp/of, Odessa (Texas) JC**
21. **Destry Westbrook, rhp, Texas Wesleyan**
22. **Dwayne Dawson, rhp, Cleveland State**
23. **Zak Krislock, rhp, Oklahoma**
24. **Brett Wyngarden, c, Northwestern**
25. Scott Conant, ss, Western Michigan
26. Aaron Wooley, 1b, Fresno (Calif.) CC
27. Chandler Martin, rhp, Sprague HS, Salem, Ore.
28. Jeff Hook, rhp, Newbury Park (Calif.) HS
29. Bobby Howry, rhp, Yavapai (Ariz.) JC
30. Julio Colon, rhp, Los Angeles CC
31. Rob Ramsay, lhp, Mountain View HS, Vancouver, Wash.
32. Joel Garber, lhp, Mira Costa HS, Manhattan Beach, Calif.
33. Darold Brown, of, Laney (Calif.) JC
34. Ryan Creek, rhp, Louisburg (N.C.) JC
35. Ted Warrecker, rhp, Hancock (Calif.) JC
36. Robert Wiemer, 1b, Odessa (Texas) JC
37. Ryan Reynolds, rhp, Tumwater HS, Olympia, Wash.
38. **Anthony Ross, of, St. Pius X HS, Kansas City, Mo.**
39. Brook Holding, 3b, Texarkana (Texas) CC
40. Flint Wallace, rhp, Weatherford (Texas) HS
41. Chris Hitt, lhp, Seminole State (Okla.) JC
42. Travis Biggs, c, Northside HS, Barling, Ark.
43. Rafael Graner, rhp, Guayama, P.R.
44. Brett Baptist, rhp, Lincoln Land (Ill.) CC
45. Andy Weltlinger, lhp, Calvert Hall HS, Randallstown, Md.
46. Steven Martin, rhp, Bridge City (Texas) HS
47. Brian Aylor, of, Midwest City (Okla.) HS
48. Gary Trammell, 2b, Texarkana (Texas) CC
49. Fred Little, ss, Biloxi (Miss.) HS
50. Irving Smith, of, Notre Dame

KANSAS CITY ROYALS

June—Regular Phase (10)

1. **Michael Tucker, ss, Longwood (Va.)**
1. **Jim Pittsley, rhp, Dubois (Pa.) Area HS** (Pick from Padres as compensation for Type A tree agent Kurt Stillwell)
1. **Sherard Clinkscales, rhp, Purdue** (Supplemental pick—31st—for loss of Type A free agent Danny Tartabull)
1. **Johnny Damon, of, Dr. Phillips HS, Orlando** (Supplemental pick—35th—for loss of Stillwell)
2. **Jon Lieber, rhp, South Alabama** (Pick from Yankees as compensation for Tartabull)
2. (Pick to Angels as compensation for Type A free agent Wally Joyner)
3. **Chris Eddy, lhp, Texas Christian**
4. **Steve Murphy, of, Birmingham-Southern**
5. **Jeff Haas, lhp, Houston**
6. **Jelani Brandon, of, Lloyd Memorial HS, Erlanger, Ky.**
7. **Justin Adam, rhp, Holy Names HS, Windsor, Ontario**
8. **Mike Kern, of, Culver City (Calif.) HS**
9. **Bart Evans, rhp, Southwest Missouri State**
10. **John Dickens, lhp, Texas**
11. **Ken Fitzpatrick, rhp, Bell Gardens (Calif.) HS**
12. **David Bladow, rhp, UC Irvine**
13. **Jason Marshall, ss, Texas A&M**
14. **Brian Harrison, rhp, Texas A&M**
15. **Melvin Bunch, rhp, Texarkana (Texas) CC**
16. **Steve Sisco, 2b, Cal State Fullerton**
17. **David Cornell, of, Stanford**
18. **Paul Vindivich, c, Mount Tahoma HS, Tacoma**
19. Jeff Parsons, ss, Dale HS, Shawnee, Okla.
20. **Tom Heming, lhp, Tennessee**
21. **Larry Sutton, of, Illinois**
22. Clemente Sainten, of, Arroyo Grande (Calif.) HS
23. **Sean Delaney, c, North Central (Ill.)**
24. **Paul Fletcher, lhp, Tennessee**
25. Jamie Splittorff, rhp, Blue Springs (Mo.) HS
26. **Troy McAllister, ss, William Paterson (N.J.)**
27. **Chris Sheehan, rhp, Washington State**
28. **Jeff Antoon, 1b/3b, UC Santa Barbara**
29. **Julius Alfonzo, 2b, Kingsborough (N.Y.) CC**
30. **John Weglarz, rhp, Lamar**
31. **Eric Walls, of, Kaskaskia (Ill.) JC**
32. **Aaron Dorlarque, rhp, Stanford**
33. **Richard Bacon, rhp, Cuesta (Calif.) JC**
34. **James Hodgson, rhp, North Dakota**
35. Steven Ashton, of, Sunny Hills HS, Fullerton, Calif.
36. **Ray Solomon, rhp, Windsor, Ontario**
37. **Scott Abell, c, Longwood (Va.)**
38. Brent Coon, of, Troy HS, Yorba Linda, Calif.
39. Mike Muncy, ss, Moorpark (Calif.) JC
40. Brandon Hoalton, rhp, Garden Grove (Calif.) HS
41. Steve Spille, lhp, Purcell Marian HS, Cincinnati
42. Charles Winters, lhp, St. Martin Deporres HS, Detroit
43. Sherroid Blake, of, Kashmere HS, Houston
44. Mike Williamson, 1b, Gilbert HS, Tempe, Ariz.
45. Jason LeBlanc, rhp, LaSerna HS, Whittier, Calif.
46. David Brooks, ss, Blinn (Texas) JC
47. Casey Brookens, rhp, Chambersburg Area HS, Fayetteville, Pa.
48. Jared Janke, rhp, Diamond Bar (Calif.) HS
49. Carlos Williams, of, Rio Grande, P.R.
50. Lamont Williams, of, Georgetown (Texas) HS

LOS ANGELES DODGERS

June—Regular Phase (19)

1. (Pick to Blue Jays as compensation for Type A free agent Torn Candiotti)
1. **Ryan Luzinski, c, Holy Cross HS, Delran, N.J.** (Supplemental pick—32nd—for loss of Type A free agent Eddie Murray)
1. **Michael Moore, of, UCLA** (Supplemental pick—36th—for loss of Type A free agent Mike Morgan)
2. **Dwain Bostic, ss, Morse HS, San Diego** (Pick from Cubs as

compensation for Morgan)
2. **Dan Melendez, 1b, Pepperdine**
3. **Dwight Maness, of, William Penn HS, New Castle, Del.** (Pick from Mets as compensation for Murray)
3. **David Spykstra, rhp, Cherry Creek HS, Englewood, Colo.**
4. **Keith Johnson, ss, Pacific**
5. **Chris Abbe, c, Texas**
6. **Jon Graves, rhp, Long Beach State**
7. **Brian Richardson, 3b, St. Bernard HS, Walnut, Calif.**
8. **Dan Markham, lhp, Diablo Valley (Calif.) JC**
9. **Ryan Henderson, rhp, Southern California**
10. **David Post, 3b, Kingston (N.Y.) HS**
11. **Brent Colson, lhp, Georgia Tech**
12. **Juan Hernaiz, of, Carolina, P.R.**
13. **Jason Butcher, rhp, Albertson (Idaho)**
14. **Reggie Johnson, 3b, Georgia Tech**
15. **Brandon White, rhp, Eastern Michigan**
16. **James Martin, of, Oklahoma State**
17. **Michael Troutman, rhp, Spartanburg Methodist (S.C.) JC**
18. **Ervan Wingate, ss, Redlands (Calif.) HS**
19. **David Pyc, lhp, Charleston (W.Va.)**
20. Widd Workman, rhp/of, Gilbert (Ariz.) HS
21. **Paul Wittig, c, Bremerton (Wash.) HS**
22. **Andre Lewis, ss/2b, Waco Christian HS, Waco, Texas**
23. Will Schleuss, lhp, Mussellman HS, Martinsburg, W.Va.
24. Ryan Duffy, lhp, Northeastern Oklahoma A&M JC
25. Matt Powell, rhp, Southridge HS, Miami
26. Kevin Pitts, of, Kishwaukee (Ill.) JC
27. **Daniel Sarmiento, lhp, Tempe (Ariz.) HS**
28. Jeff Velez, rhp, Greenwich (Conn.) HS
29. Sean Watkins, 1b/of, Notre Dame HS, Peoria Heights, Ill.
30. Kyle Evans, 1b, Katella HS, Anaheim
31. **Kenny Cook, rhp, Spartanburg Methodist (S.C.) JC**
32. **James Breuer, of, Century HS, Bismarck, N.D.**
33. Ken Sikes, 1b/rhp, Middle Georgia JC
34. Ryan Topham, of, Central HS, Portage, Mich.
35. **Joe Vogelgesang, rhp, Eastern Kentucky**
36. John Collins, rhp, Thompson HS, Alabaster, Ala.
37. **Michael Serbalik, 2b, Siena**
38. Sheldon Anderson, of, Washington HS, Los Angeles
39. **Cliff Anderson, ss, Chapman (Calif.)**
40. Twaino Moss, of, Middle Georgia JC
41. Greg Ziesemer, rhp, Larkin HS, Elgin, Ill.
42. **Ken Chapman, 1b, Florida Southern**
43. David Hayman, of, Hillcrest Christian HS, Jackson, Miss.
44. Chris Apodaca, rhp, Lynwood (Calif.) HS
45. Brian Clark, c, Napa (Calif.) JC
46. Dimas Padilla, lhp, Rio Piedras, P.R.
47. Jeff Poor, c, El Segundo (Calif.) HS
48. Stephen Munroe, of, Crescent HS, Thornhill, Ontario
49. **Barry Dunn, ss, East Tennessee State**
50. Tyler Boulo, 3b, St. Paul's Episcopal HS, Mobile, Ala.

MILWAUKEE BREWERS

June—Regular Phase (12)

1. **Kenny Felder, of, Florida State**
1. **Gabby Martinez, ss, Santurce, P.R.** (Supplemental pick—38th—for failure to sign 1991 first-rounder Kenny Henderson)
2. **Bobby Hughes, c, Southern California**
3. **Danan Hughes, of, Iowa**
4. **Kevin Kloek, rhp, Cal State Northridge**
5. **Dan Kyslinger, rhp, Western Carolina**
6. **Scott Karl, lhp, Hawaii**
7. Chris Mayfield, of, McNeese State
8. **Jeff Droll, rhp, Allegany (Md.) CC**
9. **Wes Weger, ss, Stetson**
10. Travis Wilson, c, Rancho Buena Vista (Calif.) HS
11. **Ryan Maloney, rhp, Central HS, Butte, Mont.**
12. **Derrick Cantrell, of, Edison (Fla.) CC**
13. Rayon Reid, rhp, North Miami (Fla.) HS
14. **Scott Richardson, 2b, Cal State Northridge**
15. **Ron Rico, lhp, Cerritos (Calif.) JC**
16. Guy Smith, rhp, Northern HS, Brunswick, Md.
17. **Anthony Pridgen, of, Hallsboro (N.C.) HS**
18. **George Behr, 1b, Minnesota**
19. Danny Kanell, 3b, Westminster Academy HS, Fort Lauderdale, Fla.
20. **Gerry Salzano, 3b, Steinert HS, Trenton, N.J.**
21. **Danny Perez, of, Oklahoma State**
22. **Richard Werner, rhp, Oviedo (Fla.) HS**
23. **Bubba Hardwick, lhp, Polk (Fla.) CC**
24. **Brian Hostetler, c, Western Michigan**
25. Lyle Prempas, lhp, Fenwick HS, Westchester, Ill.
26. Matt Morris, rhp, Valley Central HS, Montgomery, N.Y.
27. **Ruben Cephas, of, Delaware Tech JC**
28. **Tim Unroe, ss, Lewis (Ill.)**
29. **Sid Roberson, lhp, North Florida**
30. **Aldren Sadler, rhp, Middle Georgia JC**
31. **Craig Smith, ss, New Mexico State**
32. **David England, rhp, Augusta (Ga.)**
33. **Kevin Krause, rhp, West Genesee HS, Syracuse**
34. **David Majeski, of, Florida**
35. Kelvin Barnes, ss/of, North Edgecombe HS, Battleboro, N.C.
36. **Steve Maltagliati, rhp, East Islip, N.Y.**
37. **Chris Petrocella, rhp, Western Kentucky**
38. **Gary Rhoda, rhp, East Bladen HS, Elizabethtown, N.C.**
39. Scott Sullivan, rhp, Auburn
40. **Sean Holub, 3b/1b, Johns Hopkins**
41. **Mark Kingston, 1b, North Carolina**
42. **Walter Figueroa, of, Caguas, P.R.**
43. **Derrick Torres, of, Guanica, P.R.**
44. **Chris Thomas, c, Stetson**
45. Scott Morgan, rhp, Hancock (Calif.) JC
46. Todd Woodaz, rhp, King HS, Tampa
47. **Derek Gaskill, rhp, Manor HS, Portsmouth, Va.**
48. Kevin Horton, of, West Carteret HS, Morehead City, N.C.
49. Brian Stanley, 2b, Horizon HS, Scottsdale, Ariz.
50. **Robert Powers, 2b, Marist HS, Bayonne, N.J.**

MINNESOTA TWINS

June—Regular Phase (26)

1. **Dan Serafini, lhp, Serra HS, San Mateo, Calif.**
2. **Chad Roper, ss, Belton-Honea Path HS, Belton, S.C.**
2. **Tom Knauss (Supplemental pick), 3b, Hersey HS, Arlington Heights, Ill.** (Supplemental pick—68th—for loss of Type C free agent Dan Gladden)
3. **Gus Gandarillas, rhp, Miami**
4. **Kevin Pearson, ss, Fergus Falls (Minn.) HS**
5. **Aaron Thatcher, lhp, Mountain Crest HS, Hyrum, Utah**
6. **Keith Linebarger, rhp, Columbus (Ga.)**
7. **Armann Brown, of, Johnston HS, Austin, Texas**
8. Chad Cooley, ss/of, Barbe HS, Lake Charles, La.
9. **Rene Lopez, c, Los Angeles Harbor JC**
10. **Ben Jones, of, Alexandria (La.) HS**
11. **Anthony Byrd, of, Georgia Tech**
12. Steve Rosga, ss, Cretin HS, Roseville, Minn.
13. Dexter McCleon, c, Meridian (Miss.) HS
14. **Dan Naulty, rhp, Cat State Fullerton**
15. **Todd A. Taylor, c, Florida Southern**
16. **Sean Gavaghan, rhp, Richmond**
17. **Javi DeJesus, lhp, Southwestern Louisiana**
18. **Jeff Crick, rhp, Sandalwood HS, Jacksonville**
19. **Todd H. Taylor, lhp, Long Beach State**
20. **Ted Corbin, ss, Clemson**
21. **Ken Tirpack, 1b, Ohio State**
22. **Tom Horincewich, ss, Pace (N.Y.)**
23. **Scott Watkins, lhp, Oklahoma State**
24. **Trevor Cobb, lhp, Cascade HS, Marysville, Wash.**
25. Jeff Cermak, 3b, Riverside-Brookfield HS, Brookfield, Ill.
26. **Robert Debrino, rhp, Northern Valley (N.J.) Regional HS**
27. **Andrew Kontorinis, 1b, South Alabama**
28. **Paul Saccavino, rhp, Richmond**
29. **Adrian Gordon, of, Alexandria (La.) HS**
30. **Jason Tatar, rhp, Rantoul (Ill.) HS**
31. **Marc Claus, 2b, North Florida**
32. **Joe Miller, of, Los Angeles Harbor JC**
33. **Kevin Legault, rhp, Seton Hall**
34. **Butch Burrough, rhp/of, Concordia (N.Y.)**

35. Chris Piggott, of, Stevenson HS, Long Grove, Ill.
36. **Tim Costic, of, Fresno State**
37. **Luis Alvarado, rhp, Cayey, P.R.**
38. Gary Matthews, 2b, Granada Hills HS, Northridge, Calif.
39. Chris Tolbert, of, Enterprise State (Ala.) JC
40. Dwayne Walters, rhp, Hibbing (Minn.) HS
41. George Johnson, ss, Lowndes HS, Quitman, Ga.
42. **Jason Baker, of, Motlow State (Tenn.) CC**
43. Brent Nichols, lhp, Clayton Valley HS, Concord, Calif.
44. Dave Bies, of, Como Park HS, St. Paul, Minn.
45. John Box, lhp, Waltrip HS, Houston
46. **Hiram Cruz, ss, Southwest Miami HS, Miami**
47. **Jeff Horn, c, Wyoming**
48. **Paul Gomez, c, North Florida JC**
49. Bryan Zollman, 3b, Hill-Murray HS, Oakdale, Minn.
50. Craig Dingman, rhp, North HS, Wichita

MONTREAL EXPOS

June—Regular Phase (3)

1. **B.J. Wallace, lhp, Mississippi State**
2. **Rod Henderson, rhp, Kentucky**
3. **Everett Stull, rhp, Tennessee State**
4. **Scott Gentile, rhp, Western Connecticut State**
5. **Jon Saffer, of, Amphitheater HS, Tucson**
6. **Jose Vidro, 2b, Sabana Grande, P.R.**
7. **Luis Martinez, c, Santa Isabel, P.R.**
8. **Tommy Phelps, lhp, Robinson HS, Tampa**
9. John Geis, 1b, Moore HS, Central Square, N.Y.
10. **Steve Falteisek, rhp, South Alabama**
11. **Alfred Kermode, rhp, Grand Canyon (Ariz.)**
12. Kevin Rawitzer, lhp, Arizona State
13. **Matt Rundels, 2b, Kent State**
14. **Matt Raleigh, 3b, Western Carolina**
15. Scott Schoeneweis, lhp, Lenape Valley HS, Mount Laurel, N.J.
16. **Vincent LaChance, of, Charlesbourg, Quebec**
17. **Marc Niethammer, c, Lake Wales (Fla.) HS**
18. **Jim Rushworth, rhp, Florida State**
19. **Arce Vializ, rhp, Aguana, P.R.**
20. **Tom Doyle, 1b, Minnesota**
21. **David Eggert, lhp, Cal State Northridge**
22. **Todd Dreifort, of, Wichita State**
23. Logan Miller, c, Drake HS, Fairfax, Calif.
24. **Danny Lane, ss/3b, UC Santa Barbara**
25. William Markham, rhp, Scottsdale (Ariz.) CC
26. Barry Lunney, lhp, Southside HS, Fort Smith, Ark.
27. **Scott Harrison, rhp, Texas**
28. Charles Bivens, of, Anson HS, Wadesboro, N.C.
29. Lance Calmus, rhp, Seminole State (Okla.) JC
30. **James Hylton, rhp, Diablo Valley (Calif.) JC**
31. **Kevin Northrup, of, Clemson**
32. Brett Weinberger, of, Arizona State
33. **Rocky Ray, rhp, California State**
34. Jonathan Johnson, rhp, Forest HS, Ocala, Fla.
35. Craig Mattson, rhp, Kishwaukee (Ill.) JC
36. Eric Berthelot, lhp, Brother Martin HS, Metairie, La.
37. Rashad Stewart, lhp, Elgin (Ill.) HS
38. Steve Beard, rhp, Woodstock HS, Hebron, Ill.
39. **Kris Foster, rhp, Riverdale HS, Lehigh Acres, Fla.**
40. Jon Valenti, 3b, Bakersfield (Calif.) JC
41. **Curt Schmidt, rhp, Kansas**
42. Quentin Stone, 3b, Sparks (Nev.) HS
43. James Motte, ss, Trinidad State (Colo.) JC
44. **Brad Aurila, 1b/of, Edinboro (Pa.)**
45. Jerome Robinson, of, Anson HS, Wadesboro, N.C.
46. Brandon Anderson, c, Imperial Valley (Calif.) JC
47. Andrew McCormick, of, Scottsdale (Ariz.) CC
48. Eric Harris, 1b, Columbia State (Tenn.) JC
49. Russ Shiels, lhp, Maple Ridge (B.C.) HS
50. Russell Handy, rhp, Arvin HS, Bakersfield, Calif.

NEW YORK METS

June—Regular Phase (9)

1. **Preston Wilson, ss, Bamberg Ehrhardt HS, Bamberg, S.C.**
1. **Chris Roberts, lhp/of, Florida State** (Pick from Red Sox for loss of Type A free agent Frank Viola)
1. Jon Ward, rhp, Huntington Beach (Calif.) HS (Supplemental pick—30th—for loss of Viola)
2. (Pick to Pirates as compensation for Type A free agent Bobby Bonilla)
3. (Pick to Dodgers as compensation for Type A free agent Eddie Murray)
4. **Steve Lyons, rhp, Old Dominion**
5. **Joe Petcka, rhp, Bradley**
6. David Sumner, of, Northport HS, East Northport, N.Y.
7. **Chris Saunders, 3b, Fresno (Calif.) CC**
8. **Robert Spang, rhp, Horlick HS, Racine, Wis.**
9. **Andrew Trumpour, rhp, Cypress (Calif.) JC**
10. **Derek Baker, rhp, Glendale (Calif.) CC**
11. **James Knott, rhp, Cowley County (Kan.) CC**
12. **Heriberto Morales, c, Moca, P.R.**
13. Darin Erstad, of, Jamestown (N.D.) HS
14. Jeff Fry, lhp, Bellwood-Antis HS, Tyrone, Pa.
15. **Scott Williams, rhp, Panola (Texas) JC**
16. **Steve Lackey, ss, Norte Vista HS, Riverside, Calif.**
17. **Jonathen Smith, of, Miami**
18. Toby Smith, rhp, Connors State (Okla.) JC
19. Bill Mobilia, ss, Minnesota
20. **Allen McDill, lhp, Arkansas Tech**
21. **Todd Beckerman, rhp, Lubbock Christian (Texas)**
22. **Josh Haggas, 3b, Virginia Tech**
23. **Tyril Sherman, rhp, San Jose (Calif.) CC**
24. Chris Gobert, lhp, Northside HS, Lafayette, La.
25. Karl Thompson, c, Diamond Bar (Calif.) HS
26. Chris Gump, 2b, Arizona
27. **James Popoff, rhp, Cal State Fullerton**
28. **Alfred Hammell, c, LeMoyne**
29. Clint Hendry, of, Hardee HS, Wauchula, Fla.
30. Mike Biehle, lhp, Kings HS, South Lebanon, Ohio
31. **Brent Hayward, rhp, Henry Ford (Mich.) CC**
32. Brad Schmeh, of, Eaton HS, Greeley, Colo.
33. **Tripp Keister, of, Delaware**
34. **John Harris, rhp, Columbus HS, Duncan, Neb.**
35. Justin Rayment, lhp, Sedro Woolley (Wash.) HS
36. **Greg Stark, rhp, Texas Wesleyan**
37. **Michael Farrell, ss, Grossmont (Calif.) JC**
38. **Mark McGinn, rhp, Millard North HS, Omaha**
39. **Jerry Hiraldo, of, Carolina, P.R.**
40. **Chad Epperson, c, Seminole (Fla.) CC**
41. **Travis Shaffer, rhp, Pittsburg State**
42. **Tom Pinson, lhp, Valdosta State (Ga.)**
43. Brian Cox, of, Grossmont (Calif.) JC
44. Tom Baird, lhp, Carthage (Mo.) HS
45. Dominic Demark, of, Prescott (Ariz.) HS
46. **Jose Flores, of, St. Mary's (Texas)**
47. Keith Bradley, ss, Connors State (Okla.) JC
48. Brian Parten, rhp, Thomasville (Ala.) HS
49. Steven Pack, rhp, Fallbrook (Calif.) HS
50. Beau Champoux, ss, San Diego Mesa JC

NEW YORK YANKEES

June—Regular Phase (6)

1. **Derek Jeter, ss, Central HS, Kalamazoo, Mich.**
2. (Pick to Royals as compensation for Type A free agent Danny Tartabull)
3. (Pick to Athletics as compensation for Type A free agent Mike Gallego)
4. **Mike Buddie, rhp, Wake Forest**
5. **Don Leshnock, c, North Carolina**
6. **Ray Suplee, of, Georgia**
7. **Carlton Fleming, 2b, Georgia Tech**
8. **Matt Luke, of, California**
9. **Ryan Karp, lhp, Florida International**
10. **Robert Hinds, 2b, UCLA**
11. **Mike Gordon, rhp, Shanks HS, Quincy, Fla.**
12. **Kraig Hawkins, of, South Alabama**
13. **Jim Thomforde, rhp, Trinity (Conn.)**
14. **Kent Wallace, rhp, Murray State**

15. **Jeff Antolick, rhp, Lafayette (Pa.)**
16. **Blaise Kozeniewski, ss, Georgia**
17. **Bill Underwood, rhp, Kent State**
18. **Ernie Yaroshuk, of, Stetson**
19. **Gordon Sanchez, c, Long Beach State**
20. **Glenn Delafield, of, Panola (Texas) JC**
21. **Travion Nelson, of, South Hills HS, Covina, Calif.**
22. **Bruce Pool, lhp, Texas-Arlington**
23. **Quivia Samuel, 1b, Washington HS, Redondo Beach, Calif.**
24. **Mike DeJean, rhp, Livingston (Ala.)**
25. **Nick Delvecchio, of, Harvard**
26. Eric Trice, of, Oregon
27. Francis Fucile, ss, St. Thomas Aquinas HS, Hollywood, Fla.
28. Chris Ashby, c, Spanish River HS, Boca Raton, Fla.
29. **Brian McLamb, ss, Florida CC-Jacksonville**
30. Anthony Shelby, lhp, Lockport (Ill.) HS
31. Joshua Gregson, 1b, Dale HS, Shawnee, Okla.
32. Rommel Motley, of, Poly HS, Riverside, Calif.
33. Mike Robbins, lhp, Skyline HS, Oakland
34. Greg Dean, rhp/3b, Ada (Okla.) HS
35. Drew Pearce, rhp, St. Francis HS, Mountain View, Calif.
36. Victor Rodriguez, rhp, Okaloosa-Walton (Fla.) CC
37. Vick Brown, ss, Okaloosa-Walton (Fla.) CC
38. **R.D. Long, ss, Houston**
39. Bryan Richardson, of, Lowe HS, Windsor, Ontario
40. Brad Tayles, rhp, Western Michigan
41. **Tibor Brown, lhp, Stetson**
42. Sean McClellan, rhp, Seminole (Fla.) HS
43. John Ziegelman, of, Placer HS, Auburn, Calif.
44. Andrew Stenger, of, Indian River (Fla.) JC
45. Dale Brandt, lhp, Vero Beach (Fla.) HS
46. Keith Heberling, lhp, Indian River (Fla.) JC
47. Sean Duncan, of, McLennan (Texas) CC
48. Chris Cumberland, lhp, Pasco Hernando (Fla.) CC
49. Reginald Coleman, of, Frankston (Texas) HS
50. Damon Lembi, c/1b, JC of San Mateo (Calif.)

OAKLAND ATHLETICS

June—Regular Phase (20)

1. **Benji Grigsby, rhp, San Diego State**
2. **Jason Giambi, 3b, Long Beach State**
3. Gabe Alvarez, ss, Bishop Amat HS, Santa Ana, Calif. (Pick from Yankees for loss of Type A free agent Mike Gallego)
3. **Scott Miller, rhp, Clemson**
4. **Don Wengert, rhp, Iowa State**
5. **Steve Cox, 1b, Monache HS, Porterville, Calif.**
6. **Clifton Foster, rhp, Oklahoma**
7. **Bob Bennett, rhp, Dartmouth**
8. **Troy Penix, 1b, California**
9. **Marcel Galligani, of, Iona (N.Y.)**
10. **William Urbina, rhp, Pueblo HS, Tucson**
11. **D.T. Cromer, of, South Carolina**
12. **Stan Payne, lhp, Georgia**
13. **Brian Eldridge, 2b, Oklahoma**
14. **Tim Killeen, c, Iowa**
15. Chris Michalak, lhp, Notre Dame
16. **Brian Darwin, of, Gahr HS, Cerritos, Calif.**
17. Kip Schaefer, of, Redwood HS, Greenbrae, Calif.
18. **Richard King, rhp, Tennessee**
19. **Brian Domenico, rhp, Dean (Mass.) JC**
20. **Mark Sobolewski, 3b, Florida Southern**
21. Skye Leibee, of/lhp, Taft (Calif.) JC
22. **Gary Haught, rhp, Southwestern Louisiana**
23. **Chris Keel, of, Motlow State (Tenn.) CC**
24. **Terance Frazier, 3b, Fresno State**
25. **Brian Lesher, 1b, Delaware**
26. **Trent Montgomery, rhp, Baker HS, Mobile, Ala.**
27. Mike Salazar, lhp, Fresno State
28. **Jason White, 1b, Wichita State**
29. **Shawn Sanderfer, c, Riverside (Calif.) CC**
30. Larry Kingsbury, rhp, Villanova
31. **Geoff Loomis, 2b, Portland**
32. **Craig Gienger, rhp, Brigham Young**
33. Harold Williams, of, Livingston (Ala.)
34. **Herman Johnson, c, Northwood Institute (Texas)**
35. Martin Meza, rhp, Los Angeles Harbor JC
36. **Tim Bojan, rhp, St. Francis (Ill.)**
37. **Brendan Hause, 1b/lhp, Mira Mesa HS, San Diego**
38. Bryan Evans, rhp, Brevard (Fla.) JC
39. **James Banks, rhp, Shelby State (Tenn.) CC**
40. **James Byerly, rhp, Montclair State (N.J.)**
41. Jerrod Wong, 1b, Boise (Idaho) HS
42. Ramon Medina, of, American HS, Miami
43. **Stacy Hollins, rhp, San Jacinto (Texas) JC**
44. Donald Machacon, 2b, American HS, Miami
45. Robert Fick, c, Newbury Park HS, Thousand Oaks, Calif.
46. Matthew Curtis, c, Golden West HS, Visalia, Calif.
47. **John Jones, 3b, Laney (Calif.) JC**
48. Michael Jackson, of, San Rafael HS, Tiburon, Calif.
49. **Lauro Felix, ss, New Mexico State**
50. **Mark Moore, c, Oral Roberts**

PHILADELPHIA PHILLIES

June—Regular Phase (13)

1. **Chad McConnell, of, Creighton**
2. (Pick to Reds as compensation for Type A free agent Mariano Duncan)
3. **Trevor Humphry, rhp, Westark (Ark.) CC**
4. **Jason Moler, c, Cal State Fullerton**
5. **Larry Mitchell, rhp, James Madison**
6. **Jamie Sepeda, rhp, Stanford**
7. **Steve Solomon, of, Stanford**
8. **Jon McMullen, 1b, Rio Mesa HS, Oxnard, Calif.**
9. Nate Brown, lhp, California
10. **Stan Evans, of, Seminole (Fla.) CC**
11. Casey Blake, ss, Indianola (Iowa) HS
12. **Jon Zuber, lhp/1b, California**
13. **Alan Burke, 1b/3b, Long Beach State**
14. **David Gomez, 2b, Delaware**
15. **Shawn Wills, of, UCLA**
16. **Tim Costa, rhp, West Hills (Calif.) JC**
17. Grant Hohman, ss, St. Bernard HS, Westchester, Calif.
18. Jon Morris, c, Northeastern Oklahoma A&M JC
19. **Scott Haws, c, Bucks County (Pa.) CC**
20. **Michael Thompson, of, Gulf Coast (Fla.) CC**
21. Joe Scopio, 2b, Gloucester County (N.J.) JC
22. **Tim Cornish, of, Ventura (Calif.) JC**
23. **Bobby Estalella, c, Cooper City HS, Pembroke Pines, Fla.**
24. **Steven Nutt, lhp, Centenary (N.J.)**
25. Brian Brewer, lhp, Sacramento CC
26. **Jeremy Kendall, of, Winona State (Minn.)**
27. **Dell Allen, c/1b, Black Hawk (Ill.) JC**
28. **Tony Fiore, rhp, Triton (Ill.) JC**
29. **David Fisher, 2b, Missouri Southern State**
30. **Eric Smith, rhp, Brigham Young**
31. **Chris Phipps, rhp, Tennessee HS, Bristol, Tenn.**
32. Clint Whitworth, rhp, Oklahoma City
33. **Blake Doolan, rhp, Northeast Louisiana**
34. Bo Gray, rhp, Cherry Hill West HS, Cherry Hill, N.J.
35. **Mark Tranberg, rhp, Cal State Dominguez Hills**
36. **Thomas Irwin, rhp, California State**
37. **E.J. Brophy, c, Alabama-Birmingham**
38. **Ronald Kratz, ss/3b, Kutztown (Pa.)**
39. **Phil Romero, 2b, Fresno State**
40. **Ryan McWilliams, rhp, Southern Illinois**
41. **Ben Martinez, of, Central HS, St. Paul, Minn.**
42. **Shane Hobbs, c, Santana HS, Santee, Calif.**
43. Matthew Kilgore, c, Dobyns Bennett HS, Kingsport, Tenn.
44. Dan McDonald, of, Sarasota (Fla.) HS
45. Matt Rosemeyer, of, Eldorado HS, Las Vegas
46. **Charlton Moore, of, Chicago State**
47. **Michael Shipman, c, Dexter (Mo.) HS**
48. Charles Burns, of, Grapevine (Texas) HS
49. Chris Freeman, rhp, Walters State (Tenn.) CC
50. Angel Aragon, rhp, Channel Islands HS, Oxnard, Calif.

PITTSBURGH PIRATES

June—Regular Phase (23)

1. **Jason Kendall, c, Torrance (Calif.) HS**
1. **Shon Walker (Supplemental pick), of, Harrison County HS, Cynthiana, Ky.** (Supplemental pick—33rd—for loss of Type A free agent Bobby Bonilla)
2. **Danny Clyburn, of, Lancaster (S.C.) HS** (Pick from Mets for loss of Bonilla)
2. **Trey Beamon, of, W.T. White HS, Dallas**
3. **Jamie Keefe, ss, Spaulding HS, Rochester, N.H.**
4. **Tim Leger, of, Acadiana HS, Lafayette, La.**
5. **Brett Backlund, rhp, Iowa**
6. **Sean Lawrence, lhp, St. Francis (Ill.)**
7. **Dennis Konuszewski, rhp, Michigan**
8. **Aaron Cannaday, c, Elon**
9. **Rod Davidson, lhp, Rustburg (Va.) HS**
10. **John Turlais, c, Illinois Math and Science Academy, Aurora, Ill.**
11. **Jeff Hairston, of, Grant HS, Portland, Ore.**
12. **Larry Stahlhoefer, c, Chapman (Calif.)**
13. **Brian Wolf, 1b, Minster (Ohio) HS**
14. **Jason Phillips, rhp, Hughesville HS, Muncy, Pa.**
15. **Ted Klamm, lhp, Seton Hall**
16. **Travis Palmer, of, Camp Verde (Ariz.) HS**
17. **Jake Austin, of, Wake Forest**
18. **Gary Wilson, rhp, Cal State Sacramento**
19. **Rico Gholston, 1b, McNeese State**
20. **John Dillinger, rhp, Manatee (Fla.) JC**
21. **John Cranford, 3b, Georgia**
22. **G.G. Harris, 1b, Lancaster (S.C.) HS**
23. **Sean Nolan, ss, Edison HS, Miami**
24. **Michel Laplante, rhp, East Montreal, Quebec**
25. Steve Connelly, rhp, Wilson HS, Long Beach
26. **Marc Mesewicz, lhp, Ohio State**
27. **Chance Sanford, ss, San Jacinto (Texas) JC**
28. **Matt Jones, 1b, Florida Atlantic**
29. **Stan Wiltz, 1b, Northeast Louisiana**
30. **Kevin Polcovich, ss, Florida**
31. **Lou Collier, ss, Kishwaukee (Ill.) JC**
32. Jeff Meszar, ss, North Carolina State
33. Stephen Bosch, rhp, Norwood (Ohio) HS
34. **Jamie Mackert, c, Community HS, West Chicago**
35. **John Ford, lhp, Southwest Texas State**
36. **Erskine Kelly, of, Richmond**
37. Murray Rutledge, rhp, Seminole State (Okla.) JC
38. **Jon Gendron, rhp, Bishop Kelley HS, Tulsa, Okla.**
39. Phillip King, of, American River (Calif.) JC
40. **Mark Fabela, rhp, Santa Clara**
41. Jason Imrisek, c, Andrew HS, Orland Park, Ill.
42. **Rich Townsend, lhp, Florida Southern**
43. Dan DeStefano, rhp, Palm Beach (Fla.) CC
44. **Riegal Hunt, of, Old Dominion**
45. Tim Cossins, c, Oklahoma
46. Mickey Dutil, rhp, Southern Mississippi
47. **Marc Wilkins, rhp, Toledo**
48. **Adrian Brown, of, McComb (Miss.) HS**
49. Bert Emanuel, of/ss, Rice
50. James Rudolph, rhp, American River (Calif.) JC

ST. LOUIS CARDINALS

June—Regular Phase (15)

1. **Sean Lowe, rhp, Arizona State**
2. **Mike Gulan, 3b, Kent State**
3. **Steve Montgomery, rhp, Pepperdine**
4. **Mark Williams, c, Coral Springs (Fla.) HS**
5. **Jeff Alkire, lhp, Miami**
6. **Keith Johns, ss, Mississippi**
7. Mike Corominas, lhp, Diamond Bar (Calif.) HS
8. **Brian Carpenter, rhp, Baylor**
9. **Donnie Bellum, of, Albertson (Idaho)**
10. Scarborough Green, ss, Lafayette HS, Ballwin, Mo.
11. **Alan Beavers, rhp, Ohio**
12. **Glenn Bowen, c, Chesnee HS, Mayo, S.C.**
13. **Jamie Sailors, lhp, Parkland (Ill.) JC**
14. Todd Greene, of, Georgia Southern
15. **Ron Dicken, ss, Volunteer State (Tenn.) CC**
16. **Brad Owens, 2b, Western Illinois**
17. **Scott Lair, rhp, Parkway Central HS, Chesterfield, Mo.**
18. Frank Lankford, rhp, Virginia
19. **Jeff Murphy, c, Nebraska**
20. **Brady Raggio, rhp, Chabot (Calif.) JC**
21. Mike Pasqualicchio, lhp, McClancy HS, Astoria, N.Y.
22. **Joe Carrillo, lhp, Wyoming**
23. **Michael Henderson, of, Carson Newman (Tenn.)**
24. Michael Blais, rhp, Connecticut
25. **Darren Doucette, 1b, Ulster (N.Y.) CC**
26. Mark Hamlin, of, Evans HS, Augusta, Ga.
27. **Randy Bledsoe, rhp, Angelina (Texas) JC**
28. **Joe McEwing, of/ss, CC of Morris (N.J.)**
29. **John Stutz, 3b, St. Andrews Presbyterian (N.C.)**
30. **Andrew Martin, 1b, Master's (Calif.)**
31. **Jeff Matranga, rhp, Arizona State**
32. **Kirk Bullinger, rhp, Southeastern Louisiana**
33. **Victor Pellot, of, Guaynabo, P.R.**
34. **Jason Stoppello, lhp, JC of Southern Idaho**
35. **David Oehrlein, lhp, St. Cloud State (Minn.)**
36. **T.J. Mathews, rhp, Nevada-Las Vegas**
37. **Trey Ritz, ss, Southern Arkansas**
38. Micah Stovall, lhp, Cypress (Calif.) HS
39. Bryan Garrett, of, Odessa (Texas) JC
40. **Dennis Milius, lhp, Cameron (Okla.)**
41. **Joe Larson, lhp, Bridgewater State (Mass.)**
42. **Jose Vazquez, of, Tennessee**
43. **Brian Rupp, ss, Missouri-St. Louis**
44. **Charlie Anderson, 2b, Mississippi State**
45. **Todd Blake, lhp/1b, Catawba (N.C.)**
46. John Cappelmann, rhp, Northern Valley (N.J.) Regional HS
47. Paul Williams, lhp, Treasure Valley (Ore.) CC
48. Theopolis Frost, of, Wellington (Kan.) HS
49. Derrick Robinson, 3b, JC of Southern Idaho
50. Aaron Gerteisen, of, Tallahassee (Fla.) CC

SAN DIEGO PADRES

June—Regular Phase (17)

1. (Pick to Royals as compensation for Type A free agent Kurt Stillwell)
2. Todd Helton, of, Central HS, Knoxville
3. **Jared Baker, rhp, South Carolina**
4. Brett Laxton, rhp, Audubon (N.J.) HS
5. **Jimmy Baron, lhp, Humble (Texas) HS**
6. **Brad Gennaro, of, San Diego State**
7. **Tom Kindler, rhp, Kent State**
8. Rich Lawrence, ss, Barron Collier HS, Naples, Fla.
9. **Todd Erdos, rhp, Meadville (Pa.) HS**
10. **Ricky Talbott, 3b, Northview HS, Covina, Calif.**
11. **John Fantauzzi, 1b, Florida International**
12. **Troy Gillis, ss, Curtis HS, Tacoma, Wash.**
13. **Aaron Roques, of, Canyon Springs HS, Moreno Valley, Calif.**
14. **Marcus McCoy, of, Meridian (Miss.) HS**
15. **Brian McLain, rhp, Mountain View HS, Vancouver, Wash.**
16. **Luis Arroyo, lhp, Bajaderos, P.R.**
17. **Sean Drinkwater, ss, North Carolina State**
18. **Bobby Bonds Jr., of, Canada (Calif.) JC**
19. **Chris Murphy, rhp, Elon**
20. Brent Bearden, rhp, Texarkana (Texas) CC
21. **Joseph Bowden, ss, Simeon HS, Chicago**
22. **Gabby Martinez, c, Odessa (Texas) JC**
23. **Ken Grzelaczyk, rhp, St. John's**
24. Geoff Jenkins, 3b, Cordova HS, Rancho Cordova, Calif.
25. **Joe Jumonville, rhp, Bishop Noll HS, Hammond, Ind.**
26. Rico Laggattuta, lhp, Westlake HS, Thousand Oaks, Calif.
27. **Jeff Jones, rhp, Vincent Massey HS, Windsor, Ontario**
28. Mark Davis, rhp, Sterling HS, Baytown, Texas
29. **Zaven Luckett, of, Westbury HS, Houston**
30. **Erick Corps, ss, Carolina, P.R.**
31. Jeff Gyselman, c, Portland State (Ore.)

32. **Bill Robbs, of, Grand Canyon (Ariz.)**
33. **Michael Sanders, of, Monroe HS, Bronx, N.Y.**
34. **Martin Winchester, lhp, Long Beach (Calif.) CC**
35. **Mike Stadler, c, El Cajon Valley HS, El Cajon, Calif.**
36. Todd Bartels, rhp, Millard North HS, Omaha
37. Mark Bellhorn, ss, Oviedo (Fla.) HS
38. **Robert Deleon, 2b, Texas**
39. Justin Long, of/ss, Claremont HS, Pomona, Calif.
40. **Scott Singleton, rhp, Westlake HS, Thousand Oaks, Calif.**
41. **Britton Scheibe, of, Mira Costa (Calif.) JC**
42. **Brett Malekovic, 1b, Stagg HS, Palos Hills, Ill.**
43. **Hector Fargas, rhp, Rio Piedras, P.R.**
44. Karl Goins, c, Mira Mesa HS, San Diego
45. **Kevin Minchk, 1b, Iowa**
46. Marcus Willis, rhp, W.T. White HS, Dallas
47. Adam Frost, rhp, Ocean Springs (Miss.) HS
48. Robert Myers, rhp, Long Beach (Calif.) CC
49. **Matthew Goebel, of, Royal HS, Simi Valley, Calif.**
50. Shane Gunderson, c, Faribault (Minn.) HS

SAN FRANCISCO GIANTS

June—Regular Phase (7)

1. **Calvin Murray, of, Texas**
2. **Jim Rosenbohm, rhp, Hutchinson (Kan.) JC**
3. **Benji Simonton, of, Diablo Valley (Calif.) JC**
4. **Kurt Ehmann, ss, Arizona State**
5. **Doug Mirabelli, c, Wichita State**
6. **Aaron Fultz, lhp, North Florida JC**
7. **Mark Pooschke, 3b, Madison HS, Portland, Ore.**
8. **Chris Wimmer, ss, Wichita State**
9. **Petie Roach, 1b/of, Nevada-Reno**
10. **Jamie Brewington, rhp/of, Virginia Commonwealth**
11. **Chad Fonville, ss, Louisburg (N.C.) JC**
12. **Armond Anderson, ss, East St. John HS, LaPlace, La.**
13. **Mark Peterson, lhp, Portland State (Ore.)**
14. **Jeff Myers, lhp, Pepperdine**
15. **Kenny Woods, ss, Lewis-Clark State (Idaho)**
16. Everhard Griffiths, rhp, North Miami (Fla.) HS
17. Rob Welles, 3b, Los Angeles Pierce JC
18. **Kumandae Miller, rhp, Grant HS, Sacramento**
19. **Mark Saugstad, 3b, UC Riverside**
20. **Keith Stafford, ss, South Georgia JC**
21. Josh Deakman, rhp, Beaverton (Ore.) HS
22. Bryant Nelson, rhp, Crossett (Ark.) HS
23. **Papo Ramos, of, Southwestern Louisiana**
24. **Clay King, 3b, Texas**
25. **Kendrick Mitchell, rhp, Madison HS, Portland, Ore.**
26. Dietrich Evans, c, Cibola HS, Yuma, Ariz.
27. **Tom O'Neill, 2b, Northern Illinois**
28. **Craig Mayes, c, Michigan State**
29. John Licea, of, Lindsay (Calif.) HS
30. William Johnson, ss/of, Freedom HS, Morganton, N.C.
31. **David Baine, lhp, Sonoma State (Calif.)**
32. **Andrew Heckman, lhp, UNC Charlotte**
33. **Bobby Gorham, rhp, Howard (D.C.)**
34. Jason Maloney, rhp, Fresno (Calif.) CC
35. **Charles Hicks, rhp, Birmingham-Southern**
36. Darian Hagan, ss, Colorado
37. **Jorge Vazquez, rhp, Comerio, P.R.**
38. Dwayne Crawley, of/lhp, Douglas HS, Upper Marlboro, Md.
39. **Chris Pinder, rhp, Woodbridge (Va.) HS**
40. **James Poyner, c, DeKalb (Ga.) JC**
41. **John Richey, rhp, Louisiana Tech**
42. **Dennis Szczechowski, rhp, Siena Heights (Mich.)**
43. Clay Crossan, rhp, American River (Calif.) JC
44. **Todd Harris, of, Spartanburg Methodist (S.C.) JC**
45. Dan Reed, lhp, Gonzaga HS, McLean, Va.
46. Tista Perri, rhp, Oak Ridge HS, Cameron Park, Calif.
47. Shawn Bowders, of, Martinsburg HS, Kerneysville, W.Va.
48. **Cody McKay, ss, Horizon HS, Scottsdale, Ariz.**
49. **Michael Cavanagh, c, Linfield (Ore.)**
50. **Marvin Benard, of, Lewis-Clark State (Idaho)**

SEATTLE MARINERS

June—Regular Phase (14)

1. **Ron Villone, lhp, Massachusetts**
2. **Bob Wolcott, rhp, North HS, Medford, Ore.**
3. **Chris Widger, c, George Mason**
4. **Andy Sheets, ss, Louisiana State**
5. **John Vanhof, lhp, Southgate Anderson HS, Southgate, Mich.**
6. **Tim Davis, lhp, Florida State**
7. **Chris Dessellier, rhp, Ypsilanti (Mich.) HS**
8. **Brian Doughty, rhp, Juanita HS, Kirkland, Wash.**
9. **Ivan Montane, rhp, Miami-Dade CC South**
10. **Joe Pomierski, 3b, Biloxi (Miss.) HS**
11. Chris Dean, of, Hayward (Calif.) HS
12. **Mike Hickey, 2b, Texas A&M**
13. **Oscar Rivera, rhp, San Jose (Calif.) CC**
14. **Brian Wallace, 3b, Delaware**
15. Todd Johnson, c, Fresno State
16. **Brett Hinchliffe, rhp, Bishop Gallagher HS, Detroit**
17. Jack Stanczak, 3b, Villanova
18. **Jackie Nickell, rhp, Southern California**
19. Brent Smith, rhp, Arizona State
20. **Bobby Worley, rhp, Ohio State**
21. Ray Farmer, of, Glenn HS, Kernersville, N.C.
22. Ryan Nye, rhp, Westark (Ark.) CC
23. **Ryan Franklin, rhp, Seminole State (Okla.) JC**
24. **James Clifford, 1b, Washington**
25. **Derek Bieniasz, rhp, Toronto, Ontario**
26. Chris Sturgeon, rhp, Grant HS, Portland, Ore.
27. Josh Potter, rhp, Rose HS, Greenville, N.C.
28. **Marcus Sturdivant, of, West Stanley HS, Oakboro, N.C.**
29. **Stacey Davis, 1b, Southwest Dekalb HS, Decatur, Ga.**
30. Eric Poullard, of, Sacred Heart HS, Ville Platte, La.
31. **Richard Graham, rhp, Massachusetts**
32. Jason Haynie, lhp, Lakewood HS, St. Petersburg, Fla.
33. Raymond Miller, 3b, Dobson HS, Chandler, Ariz.
34. **Tim Harikkala, rhp, Florida Atlantic**
35. **Ron Cody, rhp, UC Riverside**
36. **Raul Ibanez, of, Miami-Dade CC South**
37. Christian Shewey, c, Redmond (Wash.) HS
38. **Jamon Deal, rhp, UNC Asheville**
39. **Jerry Aschoff, lhp, Pepperdine**
40. Michael Brady, of, Glasgow HS, Newark, Del.
41. Philip Olson, rhp, Riverview HS, Sarasota, Fla.
42. Brian Williams, rhp, Phoenix JC
43. Dennis Regan, c, Loomis Chaffee HS, Windsor, Conn.
44. Jeff Martin, lhp, Mahomet (Ill.) HS
45. **Charles Golden, rhp, Opelika (Ala.) HS**
46. Randall Wilson, rhp, Esperanza HS, Yorba Linda, Calif.
47. Chad Soden, lhp, Westark (Ark.) CC
48. Dax Winslett, rhp, McLennan (Texas) CC
49. **Kevin Stock, lhp, Virginia**
50. Mike Martin, ss, Manatee (Fla.) JC

TEXAS RANGERS

June—Regular Phase (22)

1. **Rick Helling, rhp, Stanford**
2. **Ritchie Moody, lhp, Oklahoma State**
3. **David Manning, rhp, Palm Beach (Fla.) JC**
4. **Ramiro Martinez, lhp, Los Angeles CC**
5. **Mike Smith, ss, Indiana**
6. **Cory Pearson, of, Logan (W.Va.) HS**
7. **Jeff Runion, rhp, Riverdale (Ga.) HS**
8. **Kevin Dunivan, rhp, Captain Shreve HS, Shreveport, La.**
9. **Scott Malone, of, Texas Christian**
10. **Scot Sealy, c, South Alabama**
11. **John Dettmer, rhp, Missouri**
12. **John Tomasello, of, San Francisco**
13. **Del Eggleston, 2b/3b, Pfeiffer (N.C.)**
14. **Earl Hieb, c, South Carolina-Aiken**
15. **Rod Seip, rhp, Egyptian HS, Tamms, Ill.**
16. **Mike Welch, of, George Washington**
17. John Danner, rhp, King HS, Tampa
18. **Chris Kelley, rhp, Tennessee**

19. **Brent Evans, lhp, Southwest Missouri State**
20. Andreaus Lewis, of, McNair HS, Decatur, Ga.
21. **Deshon Brown, of, Biola (Calif.)**
22. **Chris Newcomb, rhp, Indiana**
23. **Daniel Mascia, rhp, Adelphi (N.Y.)**
24. **Rich Aurilia, ss, St. John's**
25. **Chad Wiley, rhp, Kansas City (Kan.) JC**
26. **Mark Brandenburg, rhp, Texas Tech**
27. Craig Bolcerek, c, Blinn (Texas) JC
28. **Wes Shook, of, Texas Tech**
29. **Terry Rosenkranz, lhp, Morton (Ill.) JC**
30. Whitney Shanklin, of, Crenshaw HS, Los Angeles
31. **Ray Williams, 2b, Skyline HS, Dallas**
32. **Jack Kimel, lhp, Western Carolina**
33. Antawan Smith, of, Madison County HS, Madison, Fla.
34. **Michael Anderson, rhp, Northampton (Pa.) CC**
35. **Chris Burr, 1b/of, George Mason**
36. Ted Rose, rhp, St. Clairsville (Ohio) HS
37. Brian Dallimore, ss, Clark HS, Las Vegas
38. Michael Fox, rhp, Cameron (Okla.) HS
39. Tripp Mackay, ss/2b, Mount Pleasant (Texas) HS
40. Frederick Barnes, lhp, Van Horn HS, Kansas City, Mo.
41. Jason Farmer, rhp, Jones HS, Midwest City, Okla.
42. Jason Smith, rhp, Canton (Miss.) Academy HS
43. Jermaine Dye, rhp, Wood HS, Vacaville, Calif.
44. Matt Jones, ss, Rose HS, Greenville, N.C.
45. Robert St. Pierre, rhp, DeMatha HS, Huntingtown, Md.
46. William Reames, c, Seneca (S.C.) HS
47. Larry Ephan, c, Lewis-Clark State (Idaho)
48. Brian Basteyns, rhp, Enumclaw (Wash.) HS
49. Stan Stewart, rhp, North Florida JC
50. Darious Carter, of, Southwest Mississippi JC

TORONTO BLUE JAYS

June—Regular Phase (25)

1. **Shannon Stewart, of, Southridge HS, Miami** (Pick from Dodgers as compensation for Type A free agent Tom Candiotti)
1. **Todd Steverson, of, Arizona State**
1. **Brandon Cromer (Supplemental pick), ss, Lexington (S.C.) HS** (Supplemental pick—34th—for loss of Candiotti)
2. **Tim Crabtree, rhp, Michigan State**
3. **Levon Largusa, lhp, Hawaii**
4. **Tom Evans, rhp/3b, Juanita HS, Kirkland, Wash.**
5. **Jeff Patzke, ss, Klamath Union HS, Klamath Falls, Ore.**
6. Shea Morenz, of, Central HS, San Angelo, Texas
7. **Anthony Sanders, 3b/of, Santa Rita HS, Tucson**
8. Mike Kendzierski, rhp, Union HS, Endicott, N.Y.
9. **Tim Adkins, lhp, Wayne HS, Huntington, W.Va.**
10. **Scot McCloughan, 3b, Wichita State**
11. **Scott Kennedy, rhp, Palm Beach (Fla.) JC**
12. Doug Mientkiewicz, c, Westminster Christian HS, Miami
13. **Richard Halbruner, 1b, Providence HS, Matthews, N.C.**
14. **Pat Moultrie, of, Edison HS, Fresno, Calif.**
15. **Doug Meiners, rhp, Curtis HS, Staten Island, N.Y.**
16. Brian McClure, ss, Glenwood HS, Chatham, Ill.
17. **Mike Stefanoff, rhp, Rowland HS, Rowland Heights, Calif.**
18. **David Becker, c, Elder HS, Cincinnati**
19. **Chad Brown, lhp, North Greenville (N.C.) JC**
20. **Ben Candelaria, of, Hatillo, P.R.**
21. Terry Adams, 3b, Eastern Commerce HS, Toronto
22. Stanley Sanders, of, Stanhope Elmore HS, Millbrook, Ala.
23. **Matt Johnson, ss, Iowa**
24. **Randy Phillips, rhp, Arkansas State**
25. Aaron France, rhp, Loara HS, Anaheim
26. **Chris Chandler, 3b/ss, Moorpark (Calif.) JC**
27. Matt Jones, 3b, Grossmont HS, El Cajon, Calif.
28. John Knight, ss, Leland (Miss.) HS
29. **Derek Brandow, rhp, Oklahoma State**
30. **Jonathan Rivers, 1b, Tallassee (Ala.) HS**
31. Deron Pointer, of, Washington State
32. Tremayne Noles, 1b, Westchester HS, Los Angeles
33. Colin Mattiace, rhp, Jefferson HS, Cedar Rapids, Iowa
34. Carlton Washington, of, Eisenhower HS, Houston
35. **Aaron Hightower, of, Opp (Ala.) HS**
36. **Keilan Smith, rhp, Frayser HS, Memphis**
37. Neil James, 3b, Broward (Fla.) CC
38. Peter Durkovic, lhp, Trinity-Pawling HS, Flushing, N.Y.
39. Darrin Babineaux, rhp, Rayne (La.) HS
40. Michael Schroeder, 3b, Yosemite HS, North Fork, Calif.
41. **Jeff Ladd, c, Toledo**
42. **Kevin King, of, Central HS, St. Croix, Virgin Islands**
43. **Aaron Jersild, lhp, Clemson**
44. Steven Hacker, of/1b, Mehlville HS, St. Louis, Ill.
45. Jeff DaVanon, 2b, Bellaire HS, Houston
46. **Sy Dorsey, rhp, Dorsey HS, Los Angeles**
47. William Abbott, rhp, Westark (Ark.) CC
48. Jason Uhlman, ss, Redondo HS, Redondo Beach, Calif.
49. **Wade Norris, 1b, South Florida**
50. Martin Jones, of, Aiken HS, Cincinnati

1993 MARINERS PASS ON IMMEDIATE GRATIFICATION, MAKE RODRIGUEZ ONE OF BEST NO. 1 PICKS EVER

The baseball world was expecting a curveball in the 1993 draft, but instead got a fastball right down the middle.

People thought the Mariners' selection with the No. 1 pick would be influenced by manager Lou Piniella, who coveted a college pitcher who could contribute in Seattle right away. That would have meant taking Wichita State righthander Darren Dreifort.

High school shortstop Alex Rodriguez was considered the best long-range talent but at least two years away from the big leagues.

"If anything, I learned that you don't go the safe way," scouting director Roger Jongewaard said a week before the draft. "You don't worry about who will get there quickly."

Jongewaard's track record, which included recommending Darryl Strawberry as the No. 1 pick for the Mets in 1980 and Ken Griffey Jr. as the No. 1 pick for the Mariners in 1987, allowed him to convince his organization that Rodriguez was their man.

Many scouts called Rodriguez the best position player they had evaluated in 20 years, with standout skills both offensively and defensively. He quickly proved the Mariners made the right call.

Rodriguez was in the big leagues for good by 1995, at the age of 19, and seemed well on his way to becoming one of the best shortstops in major league history. He also gained notoriety for signing as a free agent with the Rangers after the 2000 season for a record package worth $252 million.

A trade to the Yankees before the 2004 season resulted in a move to third base but didn't change his record of performance. He had already won three American League MVP awards and had 583 career home runs by the end of the 2009 season, at the age of 34.

Signing Rodriguez as an amateur also proved expensive. With Scott Boras as his agent, Rodriguez asked for a $2.5 million bonus and major league contract. Rodriguez let it be known before the draft that he preferred to go to the Dodgers at No. 2, but the Mariners took him anyway.

Seattle's first offer was a $1 million bonus or a $500,000 bonus and a major league contract, with a guaranteed callup in September 1993 worth an additional $500,000.

Negotiations went slowly, and at one point Rodriguez' family and advisers insisted the Mariners communicate with them only by fax. He finally signed just before he was to start classes at the University of Miami, getting a $1 million bonus major league contract with a total value of about $1.3 million.

LARRY GOREN

Story of the 1993 draft begins and ends with A-Rod, perhaps the best No. 1 ever

The Mariners had barely budged off their original proposal, but the intrigue didn't end after Rodriguez signed. Boras prompted the Players Association to file a grievance in October that accused the Mariners of failing to respect Rodriguez' right to an agent and misleading him when they signed him. It asked that Rodriguez' contract be voided, making him a free agent, or renegotiated. The grievance eventually was dropped.

Baseball won another battle against escalating bonuses when Dreifort, who went to the Dodgers with the No. 2 pick, signed about a week after Rodriguez for a $1.3 million bonus. He had sought a major league contract worth about $2 million.

Still, the bonus was the second-highest in draft history, and overall bonus payments still went up markedly. The first-round average for 1993 was $611,000, continuing a trend. The trend of college influence on the draft also continued, as Dreifort was the first of 14 college pitchers taken in the first 28 picks. Pitching in general dominated in '93, with 19 pitchers taken in the first round, though teams shied away from high school arms.

"If they don't have good arm action, and Dwight Gooden was an exception, high school pitching is too risky," one scouting director said. "A college pitcher will at least get to the big leagues faster, which will hold the job of the scouting director. They don't get rid of managers anymore. They fire the general manager and the scouting director."

The lack of position players, particularly from college, was also significant. The only lock for the first round was Georgia Tech catcher Jason Varitek, but his alignment with Boras scared teams off. He went No. 21 to the Twins, who didn't budge from a $450,000 bonus offer and did not sign Varitek.

The Cubs pulled a surprise in taking Texas' Brooks Kieschnick with the 10th pick, and he and Varitek were the only college position players to go in the first round. It was the lowest total since 1976, before college baseball's growth in the early 1980s.

More Twists And Turns

The 1993 draft also included a historic twist as five Cuban defectors were made eligible through a special agreement with Major League Baseball. Teams didn't regard them as premium talents, however, and didn't pick any of the players in the first eight rounds.

Cuba had 26 players on major league rosters when Fidel Castro took power in 1959, but he banned professional sports in the early days of his revolution. By 1961 contract between Cuba and American professional leagues was cut off.

Lefthander Ivan Alvarez was the first Cuban selected, going to the Giants in the ninth round. None of the players made a contribution in the big leagues.

Baseball also made its first effort to establish a signing deadline, setting it on Aug. 15. At the time it was seen as a goodwill gesture to college coaches, who could find out definitively if a player was turning pro. The existing rule gave teams rights to high school and college players until the player entered his first college class, a date that could vary widely.

But the union objected, based on its 1992 victory in challenging sweeping draft alterations. An arbitrator ruled that MLB can change virtually no aspect of the draft without union approval because doing so could alter the value of draft picks used as free-agent compensation.

"They just didn't have their thinking caps on," union general counsel Gene Orza said.

A ruling that limited the number of rounds to 50 in 1992 and would have cut that down to 45 in '93 was also overturned. Free again to draft at will, clubs took a record 1,719 players, led by the Marlins, who drafted into the 91st round.

DRAFT 93: FIRST-ROUND PICKS

No.	Club	Player, Pos.	School	Hometown	Ht.	Wt.	B-T	Age
1.	Mariners	Alex Rodriguez, ss	Westminster Christian HS	Miami	6-3	190	R-R	17
2.	Dodgers	Darren Dreifort, rhp	Wichita State	Wichita	6-2	205	R-R	21
3.	Angels	Brian Anderson, lhp	Wright State	Geneva, Ohio	6-1	195	B-L	21
4.	Phillies	Wayne Gomes, rhp	Old Dominion	Hampton, Va.	6-2	215	R-R	20
5.	Royals	Jeff Granger, lhp	Texas A&M	Orange, Texas	6-4	193	L-L	21
6.	Giants	Steve Soderstrom, rhp	Fresno State	Turlock, Calif.	6-3	220	R-R	21
7.	Red Sox	Trot Nixon, of	New Hanover HS	Wilmington, N.C.	6-2	195	L-L	19
8.	Mets	Kirk Presley, rhp	Tupelo HS	Tupelo, Miss.	6-3	192	R-R	18
9.	Tigers	Matt Brunson, ss	Cherry Creek HS	Englewood, Colo.	5-11	160	B-R	18
10.	Cubs	Brooks Kieschnick, 1b/of	Texas	Corpus Christi, Texas	6-4	228	L-R	21
11.	Indians	Daron Kirkreit, rhp	UC Riverside	Norco, Calif.	6-6	225	R-R	20
12.	Astros	Billy Wagner, lhp	Ferrum (Va.)	Tazewell, Va.	5-11	180	L-L	21
13.	Yankees	Matt Drews, rhp	Sarasota HS	Sarasota, Fla.	6-8	210	R-R	18
14.	Padres	Derrek Lee, 1b	El Camino HS	Sacramento	6-5	195	R-R	17
15.	Blue Jays	Chris Carpenter, rhp	Trinity HS	Manchester, N.H.	6-5	220	R-R	18
16.	Cardinals	Alan Benes, rhp	Creighton	Lake Forest, Ill.	6-4	205	B-R	21
17.	White Sox	Scott Christman, lhp	Oregon State	Tualatin, Ore.	6-3	190	L-L	21
18.	Expos	Chris Schwab, of	Cretin-Derham HS	Eagan, Minn.	6-3	215	L-R	18
19.	Orioles	Jay Powell, rhp	Mississippi State	Collinsville, Miss.	6-4	221	R-R	21
20.	Twins	Torii Hunter, of	Pine Bluff HS	Pine Bluff, Ark.	6-1	190	R-R	17
21.	Twins	*Jason Varitek, c	Georgia Tech	Altamonte Springs, Fla.	6-2	207	B-R	21
22.	Pirates	Charles Peterson, of	Laurens HS	Laurens, S.C.	6-4	200	R-R	19
23.	Brewers	Jeff D'Amico, rhp	Northeast HS	St. Petersburg, Fla.	6-6	235	R-R	17
24.	Cubs	Jon Ratliff, rhp	LeMoyne Coll.	Clay, N.Y.	6-5	195	R-R	21
25.	Athletics	John Wasdin, rhp	Florida State	Tallahassee, Fla.	6-2	190	R-R	20
26.	Brewers	Kelly Wunsch, lhp	Texas A&M	Houston	6-5	192	L-L	20
27.	Marlins	Marc Valdes, rhp	Florida	Tampa	6-0	165	R-R	21
28.	Rockies	Jamey Wright, rhp	Westmoore HS	Oklahoma City	6-6	205	R-R	18

*Did not sign.

1993

CLUB-BY-CLUB SELECTIONS

ATLANTA BRAVES

June—Regular Phase (24)

1. (Pick to Cubs as compensation for Type A free agent Greg Maddux)
2. **Andre King, of, Stranahan HS, Fort Lauderdale**
3. **Carl Schutz, lhp, Southeastern Louisiana**
4. **James Franklin, of, Larue County HS, Hodgenville, Ky.**
5. **Del Mathews, 1b/lhp, Fernandina Beach (Fla.) HS**
6. **Danny Magee, ss, Denham Springs (La.) HS**
7. **Travis Cain, rhp, Hanna HS, Anderson, S.C.**
8. **Micah Bowie, lhp, Kingwood (Texas) HS**
9. **Jason Green, rhp, Contra Costa (Calif.) JC**
10. **Rob Sasser, of, Oakland HS**
11. **Kevin Millwood, rhp, Bessemer City (N.C.) HS**
12. **Jerrod Miller, rhp, Ferris HS, Spokane, Wash.**
13. **Wes Culp, of, Anderson HS, Austin**
14. **Doug Brewer, of, Snowflake (Ariz.) HS**
15. **John Leroy, rhp, Sammamish HS, Bellevue, Wash.**
16. **John Reece, of, Nebraska**
17. **Jermaine Dye, rhp, Cosumnes River (Calif.) CC**
18. **John Rocker, lhp, First Presbyterian Day HS, Macon, Ga.**
19. **David Wells, rhp, Wabash Valley (Ill.) JC**
20. **Roosevelt Brown, of, Vicksburg (Miss.) HS**
21. David Knoerr, of, Mesquite (Texas) HS
22. **Andrew Tolbert, of, John Jay HS, San Antonio**
23. **Darold Brown, lhp, Laney (Calif.) JC**
24. Jarod Erdody, c, Gladstone (Mich.) HS
25. Darren Grass, c, Minnesota
26. **Rich Betti, lhp, Quinsigamond (Mass.) CC**
27. **Casey Burrill, c, Southern California**
28. **Ralph Denman, of, Dallas Baptist**
29. **Michael Warner, rhp, Bellaire HS, Houston**
30. **Wayne Newman, of, American River (Calif.) JC**
31. **Bennie Tillman, of, Jackson (Miss.) State**
32. **Eric Olszewski, rhp, Concordia Lutheran HS, Spring, Texas**
33. **Jason Dailey, of, Lee (Texas) JC**
34. **Chris Cox, 3b, North Carolina**
35. Gregory Feris, rhp, Plainview (Texas) HS
36. **William Faile, rhp, Greenwich (N.Y.) HS**
37. **Gator McBride, 2b, Logan (Ill.) JC**
38. **Charlie Gann, rhp, Jurupa Valley HS, Mira Loma, Calif.**
39. **Rickey Carter, 3b, North Marion HS, Sparr, Fla.**
40. **Adrian Lollie, rhp, Windsor HS, Kirkwood, N.Y.**
41. **Brian Cruz, c, Anderson (Ind.)**
42. Brandon Wooten, lhp, Davidson Academy, Goodlettsville, Tenn.
43. **David Catlett, 1b, Laney (Calif.) JC**
44. **Justin Rigney, lhp, Tallahassee (Fla.) JC**
45. **Marcus Tyner, rhp, Laney (Calif.) JC**
46. **Cam Browder, of, UNC Charlotte**
47. **Jason Simmons, rhp, Bradley**
48. Brent Moore, lhp, Midland Valley HS, Clearwater, S.C.
49. Kenneth Mullen, lhp, Beaufort (S.C.) HS
50. **Wonderful Monds, of, Tennessee State**
51. Pat Murphy, 2b, South Alabama (Selection voided)
52. Steven Lay, rhp, Roane County HS, Kingston, Tenn.
53. John Morris, 1b, Valley Christian HS, Lakewood, Calif.
54. Reginald Swilley, rhp, Santa Teresa HS, San Jose
55. Ryan Martin, c, Highland HS, Pierron, Ill.
56. Brian Steinbach, rhp, Arrowhead HS, Pewaukee, Wis.
57. Andre Shaw, of, Lufkin (Texas) HS

BALTIMORE ORIOLES

June—Regular Phase (19)

1. **Jay Powell, rhp, Mississippi State**
2. **David Lamb, ss, Newbury Park (Calif.) HS**
3. **Jimmy Walker, rhp, Kansas**
4. **Jason Hackett, lhp, Caravel Academy, Bear, Del.**
5. **Mike Gargiulo, c, Bishop McDevitt HS, Harrisburg, Pa.**
6. **Brian Brewer, lhp, Sacramento CC**
7. **John Lombardi, rhp/of, Central Arizona JC**
8. **Harry Berrios, of, Louisiana State**
9. **Edwon Simmons, ss, Leo HS, Chicago**
10. **Wes Hawkins, of, Louisiana Tech**
11. **Tim Karns, rhp, Regis (Colo.)**
12. Eric Mooney, lhp, St. Mary's
13. **Brandon Bridgers, of, Methodist (N.C.)**
14. **Kimera Bartee, of, Creighton**
15. **Kevin Curtis, of, Long Beach State**
16. **Delshon Bowman, of, Brandon (Fla.) HS**
17. **Lincoln Martin, 2b, Birmingham-Southern**
18. **Kenny Reed, 1b, Ball State**
19. Rocky Coppinger, rhp, Coronado HS, El Paso, Texas
20. Mike McKinlay, rhp, Marriott HS, White Rock, B.C
21. **Alex Pena, rhp, New Mexico JC**
22. **Jim Foster, c, Providence**
23. **Jeff Michael, ss, Kentucky**
24. **Michael Lane, rhp, Belmont**
25. John Batts, 2b, Penn Charter HS, Philadelphia
26. **Jesse Garcia, 2b, Lee (Texas) JC**
27. **Trovin Valdez, of, New Mexico JC**
28. **Ron Shankle, ss, Essex (Md.) CC**
29. Robert Conway, rhp, Tallahassee (Fla.) CC
30. **Rocco Cafaro, rhp, Polk (Fla.) CC**
31. **Michael Trimarco, rhp, Aurora (Ill.)**
32. **Bryan Link, of, Austin Peay**
33. Paul Barry, rhp, Sacramento CC
34. James Fritz, c, North Eugene (Ore.) HS
35. Michael Sak, 1b, West Leyden HS, Melrose Park, Ill.
36. Jacques Landry, 3b, San Jacinto North (Texas) JC
37. Dennis Gilich, rhp, Peninsula HS, Gig Harbor, Wash.
38. Jeff Westerman, rhp, Kennedy HS, La Palma, Calif.
39. Aaron France, rhp, Meridian (Miss.) JC
40. Josh Itzoe, ss, Calvert Hall HS, Towson, Md.
41. Mike Bohny, 3b, Baylor
42. **Kendrick Singleton, rhp, Chamberlain HS, Tampa**
43. Tim Giles, 1b, Arundel HS, Gambrills, Md.
44. James Esparza, lhp, Cedar Valley (Texas) CC

BOSTON RED SOX

June—Regular Phase (7)

1. **Trot Nixon, of, New Hanover HS, Wilmington, N.C.**
2. **Jeff Suppan, rhp, Crespi HS, Encino, Calif.**
3. **Ryan McGuire, 1b, UCLA**
4. **Shawn Senior, lhp, North Carolina State**
5. **Kevin Clark, 3b, Cypress (Calif.) JC**
6. Peter Munro, rhp, Cardoza HS, Bayside, N.Y.
7. **David Gibralter, 3b, Duncanville (Texas) HS**
8. Sean DePaula, rhp, Cardinal Cushing Central HS, Derry, Mass.
9. **Dean Peterson, rhp, Allegheny (Pa.) JC**
10. **Lou Merloni, ss, Providence**
11. **Kurt Bogott, lhp, St. Xavier (Ill.)**
12. **Pat Murphy, 2b, South Alabama**
13. **Wilfredo Rivera, of, Vega Alta, P.R.**
14. **David Smith, ss, LeMoyne**
15. **Jacob Cook, rhp, Greenville (Ohio) HS**
16. **Andy Abad, of, Middle Georgia JC**
17. **Greg Patton, ss, George Washington**
18. Keith McDonald, c, Cypress (Calif.) JC
19. **Courtney Arrollado, ss, Valhalla HS, El Cajon, Calif.**
20. Edward Westfall, rhp, Deltona (Fla.) HS
21. **John Graham, of, Massachusetts**
22. **Craig Phillip, rhp, Aurora (Ill.)**

23. Mark Ballard, rhp, Maine
24. **Greg Kennedy, lhp, Southern Mississippi**
25. **Shayne Bennett, rhp, JC of Du Page (Ill.)**
26. Christian McCarter, of, Northeast Louisiana
27. Scotty Hartfield, of, Hattiesburg (Miss.) HS
28. **Steve Hayward, rhp, Seton Hall**
29. Jeff Belcher, of, Calhoun (Ala.) CC
30. **Jim Larkin, 3b, Holy Cross**
31. **Aaron Fuller, 2b, California**
32. **Nathan Tebbs, 2b, JC of Southern Idaho**
33. Ricky Rodriguez, ss, Miami Springs (Fla.) HS
34. **James Fernandes, rhp, Brandeis (Mass.)**
35. **John Walker, 2b, Grand Rapids (Mich.) JC**
36. **Gavin Jackson, ss, Chipola (Fla.) JC**
37. **Mark Dewalt, rhp, Upper Arlington (Ohio) HS**
38. Wayne Slater, of, F.D. Roosevelt HS, Brooklyn
39. **Tony Brannon, 2b, Johnstown-Monroe HS, Johnstown, Ohio**
40. Patrick McLendon, c, Lee HS, Baytown, Texas
41. Danny Ardoin, c, Texarkana (Texas) CC
42. Chad Helmer, rhp, East Bay HS, Ruskin, Fla.
43. **Eric Ford, of, Jacksonville State**
44. Kenneth Davis, lhp, Chipola (Fla.) JC
45. **Joseph Hayward, of, Boston College**
46. Scott Brewer, rhp, Southern Union State (Ala.) JC
47. Alphonso Johnson, ss, Hollandale Simmons HS, Hollandale, Miss.
48. Ricky Joe Redd, of, Mississippi State
49. Michael Davis, rhp, Northwest Whitfield HS, Rocky Face, Ga.
50. Chris Ciraulo, c, Cardinal Newman HS, Santa Rosa, Calif.

CALIFORNIA ANGELS

June—Regular Phase (3)

1. **Brian Anderson, lhp, Wright State**
2. **Ryan Hancock, rhp, Brigham Young**
3. **Matt Perisho, lhp, McClintock HS, Tempe, Ariz.**
4. **Andrew Lorraine, lhp, Stanford**
5. **Jose Cintron, rhp, Yabucoa, P.R.**
6. **Geoff Edsell, rhp, Old Dominion**
7. **George Arias, 3b, Arizona**
8. **Tim Harkrider, ss, Texas**
9. **Jamie Burke, 3b, Oregon State**
10. **Willard Brown, rhp, Stetson**
11. Greg Romo, rhp, Wasco Union HS, Wasco, Calif.
12. **Todd Greene, of, Georgia Southern**
13. **Kevin Ham, of, Eastwood HS, El Paso, Texas**
14. John Pollard, of, Jersey Village HS, Houston
15. Terrance Freeman, 2b, Bloomingdale HS, Brandon, Fla.
16. Sidney Newman, ss, Cordova HS, Rancho Cordova, Calif.
17. **Derrin Doty, of, Washington**
18. **Bryan Harris, lhp, Florida State**
19. **Jeffrey Bawlson, lhp, Hillsborough (Fla.) CC**
20. **Geoff Grenert, rhp, Nevada-Reno**
21. **Aaron Iatarola, of, Stetson**
22. **Aaron Puffer, rhp, Creighton**
23. **Brooks Drysdale, rhp, Santa Clara**
24. **John Bushart, lhp, Cal State Northridge**
25. Carl Caddell, lhp, Wyatt HS, Fort Worth, Texas
26. **Shawn Slade, rhp, Tampa**
27. Kevin Culmo, rhp, Sacramento CC
28. Casey Snow, c, Crespi HS, Encino, Calif.
29. Timothy Moran, 1b, Chabot (Calif.) JC
30. Steven Goodell, ss, Chabot (Calif.) JC
31. Daniel Petroff, rhp, Gulf Coast (Fla.) CC
32. Carlos Pagan, c, Vega Baja, P.R.
33. Keith Luuloa, ss, Modesto (Calif.) JC
34. Brendon Cowsill, 3b, Crescenta Valley HS, La Crescenta, Calif.
35. Scott Rivette, rhp, Citrus (Calif.) JC
36. Todd Stubblefield, rhp/1b, Cooper City (Fla.) HS
37. Bryan Smithson, lhp, Santa Barbara (Calif.) HS
38. Everard Griffiths, rhp, Miami-Dade CC North
39. Adam Brick, c, Brandon (Fla.) HS
40. David Johnson, rhp, Baxter Springs (Kan.) HS
41. Gary Stevenson, rhp, Hart HS, Valencia, Calif.
42. Howard Pride, of, Butler HS, Huntsville, Ala.
43. Marshall Faulk, of, San Diego State
44. Richard Gonzalez, c, Indian River (Fla.) CC
45. Richard Nadeau, of, Kennedy HS, Granada Hills, Calif.
46. Ryan Folmar, c, Chambersburg (Pa.) Area HS
47. Brian Boeth, rhp, Pensacola (Fla.) JC
48. Kyle Richardson, 3b, Casa Grande (Ariz.) HS
49. Randi Mallard, c/of, Gainesville (Ga.) HS
50. Alvin Casillas, rhp, Caguas, P.R.
51. William Perusek, rhp, Hillsborough (Fla.) CC
52. David Robinson, of, Gulf Coast (Fla.) CC
53. Rafael Gutierrez, of, Levittown, P.R.
54. Matt Schafer, c, Hillsborough (Fla.) CC
55. Shawn Coolidge, of, Dunedin (Fla.) HS
56. Daryl Porter, of, St. Thomas Aquinas HS, Fort Lauderdale
57. David Supple, c, Notre Dame HS, Northridge, Calif.

CHICAGO CUBS

June—Regular Phase (10)

1. **Brooks Kieschnick, of/rhp, Texas**
1. **Jon Ratliff, rhp, LeMoyne** (Pick from Braves as compensation for Type A free agent Greg Maddux)
1. **Kevin Orie, ss, Indiana** (Supplemental pick—29th—for loss of Maddux)
2. (Pick to Rangers as compensation for Type A free agent Jose Guzman)
3. **Vee Hightower, of, Vanderbilt**
4. **Miguel Montilla, ss, North Bergen (N.J.) HS**
5. Matt Miller, lhp, Monterey HS, Lubbock, Texas
6. **Pat Cline, c, Manatee HS, Bradenton, Fla.**
7. **Scott Kendrick, rhp, Monroe-Woodbury HS, Central Valley, N.Y.**
8. **Chris Bryant, lhp, Brandon (Fla.) HS**
9. **Bob Morris, 3b, Iowa**
10. Jamey Price, rhp, Texarkana (Texas) CC
11. **Steve Rain, rhp, Walnut (Calif.) HS**
12. **Gabe Whatley, of, Vanderbilt**
13. **Tony Locey, rhp, Columbus (Ga.)**
14. **Jose Molina, c, Vega Alta, P.R.**
15. **Brad Chambers, of/rhp, Midlothian (Va.) HS**
16. **Wade Walker, rhp, Northeast Louisiana**
17. Robert Duncan, 3b, Central Florida CC
18. Nathan Dunn, ss, Vestavia Hills HS, Birmingham
19. **Alfredo Garcia, rhp, Buena Park (Calif.) HS**
20. **Nate Thomas, lhp/1b, First Colonial HS, Virginia Beach**
21. **David Hutcheson, rhp, South Florida**
22. Gary Burnham, of, South Windsor (Conn.) HS
23. **Gilbert Avalos, ss, Alvin (Texas) CC**
24. **John Rodgers, c, Rice**
25. James Hamilton, lhp, Turner Ashby HS, Weyers Cove, Va.
26. **Andrew Devries, lhp, Manatee (Fla.) JC**
27. **Ronald Smith, 1b, Southern**
28. **John Sauer, of, Patterson HS, Baltimore**
29. **Gregory Hillman, lhp, Texas**
30. **David Weber, rhp, Marist HS, Jersey City, N.J.**
31. **Kenneth Jones, of, Middle Georgia JC**
32. **Gabe Duross, 1b/of, Maine**
33. **Doug Alongi, of, Rutgers**
34. **Sean Fric, of, Alvin (Texas) CC**
35. **Jared Snyder, c, Nicholls State**
36. **Frank Cicero, c, La Mirada (Calif.) HS**
37. Adam Robinson, 2b, West Morris Central HS, Long Valley, N.J.
38. **Danny Gil, of, Mission Bay HS, San Diego**
39. Kelvin Barnes, ss/of, Lake City (Fla.) CC
40. **Bo Porter, of, Iowa**
41. **Gary Beashore, rhp, Missouri Western State**
42. **Jose DeJesus, 3b, Patillas, P.R.**
43. **Jason Dunn, rhp, Raritan Valley (N.J.) CC**
44. **Mark Lavenia, lhp, South Carolina-Aiken**
45. **James Young, of, Valdosta State (Ga.)**
46. Jose Peraza, lhp, Norwalk (Calif.) HS
47. **Shawn Hill, rhp, Nicholls State**
48. **William Vielleux, ss, Hartford HS, White River Junction, Vt.**

49. **Gamalier Castro, lhp, Aguadilla, P.R.**
50. **Thomas Ball, lhp, Cal State Dominguez Hills**
51. **Sean Hogan, lhp, Morehead State**
52. **Demetrius Dowler, 2b/of, Indiana State**
53. **Rodd Kurtz, lhp, Texas-Pan American**
54. **Greg Twiggs, lhp, Brewton-Parker (Ga.)**
55. **Stephen Kulpa, ss, Quinnipiac**
56. Javi Herrera, rhp, Miami (Fla.) HS
57. **Michael Gibson, of/2b, Bowie State (Md.)**
58. **Artis Johnson, of, Florida A&M**
59. **Ralph Eusebio, of, Brevard (Fla.) CC**
60. **Joe Biernat, ss, South Carolina**
61. **Brett McCabe, 1b, Centenary**
62. **Thomas King, of, Valdosta State (Ga.)**
63. **Tony Khoury, c/rhp, Ohio State**
64. **Sean Davisson, 2b/of, Long Beach State**
65. Dustin Wilkinson, 3b, Shaw HS, Columbus, Ga.
66. Rob Carpenter, of, Southern Maine
67. Gregory Denly, rhp, Valdosta (Ga.)
68. Scott Stephens, lhp, Eau Gallie HS, Melbourne, Fla.
69. Anthony Dellamano, rhp, Pierce (Calif.) JC
70. Chris Price, rhp, Goddard HS, Roswell, N.M.
71. Cory Lima, 1b/of, Redan HS, Stone Mountain, Ga.
72. Danier Anderson, of, Tioga HS, Pineville, La.
73. Jose Castillo, lhp, Falfurrias (Texas) HS
74. **Jason Maxwell, ss, Middle Tennessee State**
75. Shawn Knight, ss, William & Mary
76. **James Farrow, rhp, Brewton-Parker (Ga.)**
77. **Jamil Cunningham, ss, Bethune-Cookman**
78. Steve Everson, of, Valdosta (Ga.) HS
79. Robert Baldwin, of, Duke
80. Clarence Williams, c/1b, Crescent City (Fla.) HS
81. Anthony Rich, ss, Rollins (Fla.)
82. James Huntley, ss, West Mecklenburg HS, Charlotte, N.C.

CHICAGO WHITE SOX

June—Regular Phase (17)

1. **Scott Christman, lhp, Oregon State**
2. **Greg Norton, 3b, Oklahoma**
3. **Joe Bales, rhp, Reed HS, Sparks, Nev.**
4. Dennis Twombley, c, Patrick Henry HS, San Diego
5. **David Lundquist, rhp, Cochise County (Ariz.) CC**
6. **Craig McClure, of, Columbine HS, Littleton, Colo.**
7. **Ben Boulware, 2b/of, Cal Poly San Luis Obispo**
8. **Jason Goligoski, ss, Western Montana**
9. **Rich Pratt, lhp, South Carolina**
10. **Zane Leiber, rhp, Central Arizona JC**
11. **Tom Fordham, lhp, Grossmont (Calif.) JC**
12. **Sandy McKinnon, of, Middle Georgia JC**
13. **Steve Friedrich, of, Fullerton (Calif.) JC**
14. **Bill Proctor, rhp, Western Oregon State**
15. **Mike Sirotka, lhp, Louisiana State**
16. **Billy Joe Hobert, of, Washington**
17. **Scott Vollmer, c, Pepperdine**
18. Bill Mobilia, ss, Minnesota
19. **Rich Carone, c, Mississippi**
20. **Brian Woods, rhp, Fairleigh Dickinson**
21. **Andrew McCormack, lhp, South Florida**
22. **Curtis Broome, rhp, Evansville**
23. **John Quirk, lhp, Westchester (N.Y.) CC**
24. **Jim Dixon, rhp, New Mexico State**
25. Joel Peters, ss, Lincoln HS, Vincennes, Ind.
26. **Harold Williams, of, Livingston (Ala.)**
27. Chris Olson, lhp, Alvin (Texas) HS
28. Alex Prejean, rhp, Clear Lake HS, Houston
29. Travis Rapp, c, Sebring (Fla.) HS
30. Tim Fuhrman, rhp, Casa Roble HS, Orangevale, Calif.
31. Jory Diamond, rhp, Tallahassee (Fla.) CC
32. Jeff Abbott, of, Kentucky
33. **Jim Schlotter, rhp, Rider**
34. **David Moore, 3b, Dr. Phillips HS, Orlando, Fla.**
35. Ricky Garcia, rhp, Mesa (Ariz.) CC
36. Brad Harker, 1b, Lawrence (Kan.) HS
37. **William Baldwin, rhp, Florida Memorial**
38. Jim Gargiulo, c, Coconut Creek (Fla.) HS
39. Ryan Roberts, ss, Utah Valley CC
40. Joshua Whittenton, 3b, Auburndale (Fla.) HS
41. Brandon Berger, c, Beechwood HS, Fort Mitchell, Ky.
42. Anthony Guerra, c, North Miami HS
43. Carey Schueler, lhp/1b, Campolindo HS, Moraga, Calif.
44. **Todd Hall, ss, Cal State Sacramento**
45. **Frank Menechino, 2b, Alabama**
46. Marty Patterson, c, Croswell-Lexington HS, Croswell, Mich.
47. Gorky Estrella, 3b, George Washington HS, New York
48. Mario Valdez, 1b, Miami HS
49. Placido Polanco, 2b, Miami-Dade CC Wolfson

CINCINNATI REDS

June—Regular Phase (20)

1. (Pick to Twins as compensation for Type A free agent John Smiley)
1. **Pat Watkins, of, East Carolina** (Supplemental pick—32nd—for loss of Type A free agent Greg Swindell)
2. **Scott Sullivan, rhp, Auburn**
3. **Steve Wilkerson, rhp, Grand Canyon (Ariz.)** (Pick from Astros as compensation for Swindell)
3. **Brad Tweedlie, rhp, Western Carolina**
4. **Samuel Osorio, of, Loiza, P.R.**
5. **Paul Bako, c, Southwestern Louisiana**
6. David Caldwell, lhp, Northeast Texas CC
7. **Darran Hall, of, Lincoln HS, San Diego**
8. **Pete Harvell, lhp, Tennessee**
9. John Ambrose, rhp, Memorial HS, Evansville, Ind.
10. **Chris Sexton, of/2b, Miami (Ohio)**
11. **Joel Franklin, rhp, Southwestern (Calif.) JC**
12. **Doug Durrwachter, ss, Texas-Arlington**
13. **James Lofton, ss, Los Angeles CC**
14. J.J. Picollo, c, George Mason
15. Jason Ruskey, lhp, Triton (Ill.) JC
16. **Jackie McCroskey, of, Male HS, Louisville**
17. Matt Purkiss, 3b, Redwood HS, Visalia, Calif.
18. Jeff Niemeier, c, Kansas
19. **Trey Rutledge, rhp, Louisiana State**
20. **Peter Magre, rhp, St. Mary's (Texas)**
21. James Emiliano, rhp, Odessa (Texas) JC
22. **David McKenzie, rhp, Northwood Institute (Texas)**
23. Anthony Johnson, of, Brookdale (N.J.) CC
24. **Stephen Gann, 2b, Dallas Baptist**
25. **David Chandler, rhp, Morehead State**
26. **Donald Broach, of, Cincinnati**
27. Alejandro Sanchez, rhp, Ontario (Calif.) HS
28. **Jason Baker, of, Allegany (Md.) CC**
29. **Jon Hebel, rhp, Auburn**
30. Scott Shores, of, Arizona State
31. **Michael Moses, lhp, Wyoming**
32. **Cobi Cradle, of, Long Beach State**
33. **Steven Eddie, ss, Iowa**
34. **Chad Akers, ss, West Virginia State**
35. Scott Wilson, 3b, San Dieguito HS, Carlsbad, Calif.
36. Brian Jergenson, of/1b, Lacrescent (Minn.) HS
37. Michael Bauder, lhp, Western HS, Las Vegas
38. Chad Allen, of, Duncanville (Texas) HS
39. Rommel Motley, of, Riverside (Calif.) CC
40. **Jonathon Dold, of, St. John's (Minn.)**
41. James Debruin, rhp, Calhoun HS, Seadrift, Texas
42. Damon Miller, c, Washington HS, Cherokee, Iowa
43. **Danny Hagan, lhp, Louisville, Ky.**

CLEVELAND INDIANS

June—Regular Phase (11)

1. **Daron Kirkreit, rhp, UC Riverside**
2. **Casey Whitten, lhp, Indiana State**
3. **J.J. Done, rhp, Pace HS, Miami**
4. **Travis Driskill, rhp, Texas Tech**
5. **Kris Hanson, rhp, Wisconsin-Whitewater**
6. **Matt Hobbie, of, Sarasota (Fla.) HS**
7. Seth Greisinger, rhp, McLean HS, Falls Church, Va.

8. **Steve Kline, lhp, West Virginia**
9. **Greg Thomas, 1b, Vanderbilt**
10. Derrick Cook, rhp, Robert E. Lee HS, Staunton, Va.
11. **Jason Mackey, lhp, Lower Columbia (Wash.) JC**
12. **Jeffrey Haag, c, Florida Southern**
13. **Steven Soliz, c, Cal State Los Angeles**
14. **Todd Betts, 3b, Northeastern Oklahoma A&M JC**
15. **Roland De la Maza, rhp, Cal State Sacramento**
16. **Mike Neal, 3b/ss, Louisiana State**
17. **Robert Lewis, c, Texas A&M**
18. **Todd Johnson, c, Fresno State**
19. **Blair Hodson, 1b, Yale**
20. **Brett Palmer, lhp, Idaho Falls (Idaho) HS**
21. **Eric Chapman, of, South Carolina-Aiken**
22. **Chris Plumlee, rhp, Arkansas State**
23. Steve Hagins, c, University HS, Irvine, Calif.
24. **Richie Sexson, 1b, Prairie HS, Brush Prairie, Wash.**
25. **Robert Kulle, of, LeMoyne**
26. **Norman Williams, of, Chipola (Fla.) JC**
27. **Ryan Lefebvre, of, Minnesota**
28. **Richard Prieto, 2b/ss, Carmel, Calif.**
29. **Richard King, ss, Concordia (Texas)**
30. Greg Tippin, 1b, Cypress (Calif.) JC
31. Jamie Coons, of, Edgewood (Md.) HS
32. **Richard Lemons, of, Arizona**
33. **Gerad Cawhorn, 3b, San Jose State**
34. Ken Westmoreland, rhp, Austin HS, Decatur, Ala.
35. Randy Woodall, rhp, Sheffield (Ala.) HS
36. **Rodney Holland, of, Schriener (Texas)**
37. Ted Warrecker, c, Hancock (Calif.) JC
38. Mike Rodriguez, c/of, Brandeis HS, New York
39. David Townsend, rhp, Hinds (Miss.) CC
40. Ara Petrosian, rhp, Fountain Valley (Calif.) HS
41. **Jason Lyman, 2b, Cal State San Bernardino**
42. Nisam Bean, ss, Kennedy HS, Richmond, Calif.
43. **Dalton Dempsey, lhp, Southwest Texas State**
44. **Marvin Pierce, rhp, Lassen (Calif.) CC**
45. **Darnell Batiste, of, Sam Houston HS, Arlington, Texas**
46. Jeff Bell, ss, Pinson Valley (Ala.) HS
47. Dave Roberts, of, UCLA
48. David Stevenson, of/1b, Los Angeles Valley JC
49. Larry Dobson, of, Putnam City HS, Oklahoma City
50. Poncho Ruiz, 2b, Esperanza HS, Placentia, Calif.
51. Samuel Mitchell, rhp, Navarro (Texas) JC
52. Bret Soverel, rhp, Martin County HS, Palm City, Fla.
53. Aaron Gentry, ss, Claremore (Okla.) HS
54. **Kevin Dinnen, rhp, Barry (Fla.)**
55. Robert Kinnee, rhp, Marshall HS, Portland, Ore.
56. Carlos Arellano, rhp, Granada HS, Livermore, Calif.
57. Angel Rodriguez, rhp, Isabella, P.R.
58. **Tony Runion, rhp, Duke**
59. Brian Basowski, of, Pierce (Calif.) JC
60. Vincent Griffin, of, South Suburban (Ill.) JC
61. Brian Norris, rhp, Stephen F. Austin HS, Port Arthur, Texas
62. Ken Vining, lhp, Cardinal Newman HS, Columbia, S.C.
63. Jeffrey Kober, lhp, Jefferson (Wis.) HS
64. Roger Walker, c, Florida CC-Jacksonville
65. Casey Swingley, rhp, Lower Columbia (Wash.) JC
66. Jason Vorhauer, 1b, Fairfield HS, Suisun City, Calif.
67. **Bryan Garrett, of, Florida International**
68. Keith Cowley, 3b, Westminster (Calif.) HS
69. Joseph Adams, rhp, Freeman HS, Richmond
70. Travis Peterson, of, Edmonds (Wash.) CC
71. **Pedro Marte, 2b/of, Florida Memorial**
72. **Jason Marshall, c, Baylor**

COLORADO ROCKIES

June—Regular Phase (28)

1. **Jamey Wright, rhp, Westmoore HS, Oklahoma City**
2. **Bryan Rekar, rhp, Bradley**
3. **Joel Moore, rhp, Bradley**
4. **Doug Walls, rhp, Muscatine (Iowa) CC**
5. **Mike Zolecki, rhp, St. Mary's (Texas)**
6. **Chad Gambill, of, Clearwater (Fla.) HS**
7. **John Thomson, rhp, Blinn (Texas) JC**
8. **Kyle Houser, ss, Duncanville (Texas) HS**
9. **John Myrow, of, UCLA**
10. **Edgard Velazquez, of, Guaynabo, P.R.**
11. **Jacob Viano, rhp, Long Beach (Calif.) CC**
12. **Keith Grunewald, ss, North Carolina**
13. **Derrick Gibson, of, Haines City (Fla.) HS**
14. **Bob Lasbury, rhp, Manhattanville (N.Y.)**
15. Casey Davis, of, Corsicana (Texas) HS
16. **Nate Holdren, 1b, Michigan**
17. **Kevin Wehn, rhp, Florida International**
18. **Morgan Burdick, rhp, Clovis HS, Dunlap, Calif.**
19. **Jason Johnson, rhp, Auburn**
20. **John Giudice, of, Eastern Connecticut State**
21. **Derrick Calvin, rhp, Southern**
22. **Mike Higgins, c, Rutgers**
23. **Martin Dewitt, lhp, Mesa (Ariz.) CC**
24. **Jason Smith, c, Texas-Arlington**
25. **Jamie Anderson, ss, Hanover (Ind.)**
26. **Curt Conley, lhp, Ball State**
27. **Raymond Hoover, c, Cedar Cliff HS, Camp Hill, Pa.**
28. **Mario Munoz, 3b, Mesa State (Colo.)**
29. **Dan Barry, lhp, West Virginia**
30. Mark Brownson, rhp, Wellington (Fla.) Community HS
31. **Patrick McClinton, lhp, Bellarmine (Ky.)**
32. **Dennis McAdams, rhp, Palomar (Calif.) JC**
33. Dominic Demark, of, Mesa (Ariz.) CC
34. **Ben Ortman, of, Portland**
35. Philip Davis, rhp, Yuma (Ariz.) HS
36. **Dan Butcher, rhp, Diablo Valley (Calif.) JC**
37. **Enrigue Melendez, ss, Ensenada, P.R.**
38. Darin Baugh, ss, Serra HS, San Mateo, Calif.
39. Brandon Nickens, rhp, Pierce (Calif.) JC
40. **Terry Jones, of, North Alabama**
41. Justin Liniak, of, San Dieguito HS, Encinitas, Calif.
42. **Brian Culp, c, Kansas State**
43. Larry Green, c, JC of Eastern Utah
44. Johnathan Delya, rhp, Crescent-Iroquois HS, Crescent City, Ill.
45. Andrew Keehn, rhp, Central Arizona JC
46. Joshua Jensen, rhp, Mountain Crest HS, Providence, Utah
47. Marc D'Allessandro, lhp, St. John Vianney HS, Hazlet, N.J.
48. Bradley Molcak, ss, Cardston (Alberta) HS
49. **Philip Schneider, lhp, Rutgers**
50. William Eden, lhp, Motlow State (Tenn.) CC
51. Michael Dewitt, rhp, Pine Plains (N.Y.) HS
52. Ryan Ware, ss, Jersey Village HS, Houston
53. Marty Remmers, rhp, Riverbank HS, Modesto, Calif.
54. Brett Bibeau, rhp, Bishop Kelly HS, Boise, Idaho
55. Brandon Knight, 2b, Buena HS, Oxnard, Calif.
56. Chris Cooper, 2b, Mesa (Ariz.) CC
57. David Melendez, rhp, Blinn (Texas) JC
58. Anders Stahl, c, Anderson (Calif.) HS
59. Frank Chelbian, lhp, Middlesex (N.J.) CC
60. **David Mineer, rhp, Utah State**

DETROIT TIGERS

June—Regular Phase (9)

1. **Matt Brunson, ss, Cherry Creek HS, Englewood, Colo.**
2. **Tony Fuduric, rhp, Cardinal HS, Middlefield, Ohio**
3. **Cameron Smith, rhp, Ithaca (N.Y.)**
4. **Michael Wilson, rhp, Blinn (Texas) JC**
5. **Jason Bass, of, O'Dea HS, Seattle**
6. **Brian Moehler, rhp, UNC Greensboro**
7. **Greg Granger, rhp, Lake City (Fla.) CC**
8. **Drew Christman, of, Oklahoma**
9. **Lonny Landry, of, Flagler (Fla.)**
10. R.A. Dickey, rhp, Montgomery Bell Academy, Nashville
11. **Glen Barker, of, St. Rose (N.Y.)**
12. **Bryan Corey, ss, Pierce (Calif.) JC**
13. **Eddie Gaillard, rhp, Florida Southern**
14. Keith Foulke, rhp, Galveston (Texas) JC
15. **Bobby Jones, of, Riverside (Calif.) CC**
16. **David Crafton, c, Lyons Township HS, La Grange, Ill.**
17. **Mike Salazar, lhp, Fresno State**

18. **Shawn Wooten, c, Mount San Antonio (Calif.) JC**
19. Javier Cardona, c, Dorado, P.R.
20. Brandon Kent, rhp, Duncanville (Texas) HS
21. **Chris Wyrick, ss, Missouri**
22. **Billy Thompson, c, Kentucky**
23. **Corey Broome, c, UNC Wilmington**
24. Matt Beech, lhp, Houston
25. **Shawn Brown, 2b, Rider**
26. **Matt Skrmetta, rhp, Jacksonville**
27. **Eric Danapilis, of, Notre Dame**
28. **Steve Dietz, ss, San Diego State**
29. **Jason Hamilton, 1b, St. Joseph's**
30. **Joshua Neese, rhp, Southwestern Oklahoma State**
31. **Will Hunt, lhp, Louisiana State**
32. **Roderick Jackson, rhp, Jackson State**
33. **Craig Tupper, c, Cal State Hayward**
34. **Mike Wiseley, of, Eastern Michigan**
35. George Abernathy, of, Pensacola (Fla.) JC
36. **Kirk Ordway, 2b, Portland State (Ore.)**
37. Michael Goralczyk, lhp, Niles (Mich.) HS
38. **Gabe Sollecito, rhp, UCLA**
39. David Malenfant, rhp, Kearsley HS, Flint, Mich.
40. **Samuel Arguto, rhp, Jacksonville**
41. **Adam Rodriguez, c, Oklahoma City**
42. **Scott Conant, ss, Western Michigan**
43. **Michael Richardson, rhp, San Diego State**
44. Joel Hillebrand, rhp, Roosevelt HS, Wyandotte, Mich.
45. **Brandon Reed, rhp, West HS, Lapeer, Mich.**
46. Brian Rios, ss, Riverside (Calif.) CC
47. **Tyrone Dixon, of, South Alabama**
48. Justin Bettencourt, lhp, Cabrillo (Calif.) JC
49. Anthony Jackson, of, Louisburg (N.C.) JC
50. Brian Wilkes, c, Bishop Kenny HS, Jacksonville
51. Michael Martino, rhp, Grand Blanc (Mich.) HS
52. Rich Hartmann, rhp, Long Island
53. **Gary Goldsmith, rhp, New Mexico State**
54. Kiko Palacios, c, Southwestern (Calif.) JC
55. Lloyd Wade, c, Escambia HS, Pensacola, Fla.
56. Bradley Lee, lhp, Delaware Tech JC
57. Jeffrey Barker, rhp, Riverside (Calif.) CC
58. Anthony Williams, rhp, Fort Walton Beach (Fla.) HS
59. **Rob Welles, 1b, Pepperdine**
60. **Graham Koonce, of, Julian (Calif.) HS**
61. Carlton Washington, of, Texas-El Paso
62. Nathan Smith, ss/of, Bonanza HS, Las Vegas
63. Adam Finnieston, of, Gulf Coast (Fla.) CC
64. Justin Duckwiler, c, Bonanza HS, Las Vegas
65. Terry Tripp, ss, Harrisburg (Ill.) HS

FLORIDA MARLINS

June—Regular Phase (27)

1. **Marc Valdes, rhp, Florida**
2. **John Roskos, c, Cibola HS, Rio Rancho, N.M.**
3. **Dan Ehler, rhp, South Hills HS, Covina, Calif.**
4. **Thomas Howard, lhp, Titusville (Fla.) HS**
5. **Ernie Delgado, rhp, Sunnyside HS, Tucson**
6. **Paul Thornton, rhp, Georgia Southern**
7. **Todd Dunwoody, of, Harrison HS, West Lafayette, Ind.**
8. **Billy McMillon, of, Clemson**
9. **Brady Babin, ss, St. Amant HS, Gonzales, La.**
10. **Ryan Filbeck, rhp, Rancho Santiago (Calif.) JC**
11. **Damon Johnson, 3b, Crossett (Ark.) HS**
12. Jason Fawcett, rhp, Robert E. Lee HS, Montgomery, Ala.
13. **David Jefferson, of, Palo Alto (Calif.) HS**
14. **Mike Sims, c, Cal State Northridge**
15. Erik Robinson, of, West Orange HS, Winter Park, Fla.
16. **Scott Southard, ss, South Alabama**
17. **Don Matthews, rhp, Lower Columbia (Wash.) JC**
18. **Tommy Giles, lhp, Thomas Jefferson HS, Carter Lake, Iowa**
19. **Richard Seminoff, lhp, Grand Canyon (Ariz.)**
20. **Bryan Ward, lhp, South Carolina-Aiken**
21. **Greg Mix, rhp, Stanford**
22. **Dan Chergey, rhp, Cal Poly San Luis Obispo**
23. Ivory Jones, of, Contra Costa (Calif.) JC
24. **Ronnie Brown, of, Mississippi State**
25. Richard Dishman, rhp, Archbishop Molloy HS, Jamaica, N.Y.
26. **Matt Martinez, 2b, Cal State Sacramento**
27. **Andy Small, 3b, Cal State Northridge**
28. Tony Darden, ss, Northeast Texas CC
29. **Samuel Minyard, lhp, Master's (Calif.)**
30. Justin Long, ss, Riverside (Calif.) CC
31. Justin Mark, rhp, Lassen (Calif.) JC
32. Matthew Wells, rhp, Quincy (Calif.) HS
33. **Zachary Stark, lhp, Lipscomb**
34. **Jeffrey Lewis, of, Dundalk (Md.) CC**
35. **Eric Genden, of, Taravella HS, Coral Springs, Fla.**
36. Brett Ames, lhp, Pima (Ariz.) CC
37. Brandon Villafuerte, rhp, Live Oak HS, Morgan Hill, Calif.
38. **Dave Berg, 2b, Miami**
39. James Merritt, rhp, South Georgia JC
40. Derrick Johnson, of, Ewing HS, Trenton, N.J.
41. Eric Sees, ss, Santa Margarita HS, San Juan Capistrano, Calif.
42. Chad Phillips, lhp, Clemson
43. Ian Roberts, of, Mountain View HS, Vancouver, Wash.
44. **Greg Hubley, of, JC of San Mateo (Calif.)**
45. Bobby Howry, rhp, Yavapai (Ariz.) JC
46. **Jon Van Zandt, rhp, UCLA**
47. Rafael Corrales, rhp, Niles West HS, Skokie, Ill. (Selection voided)
48. Josh Deakman, rhp, Riverside (Calif.) CC
49. Michael Reyes, of, Wayland Baptist (Texas)
50. Mark Creelman, 1b, Ulster (N.Y.) CC
51. Leslie Sean, lhp, Mendocino (Calif.) CC
52. Ward White, 1b, Hug HS, Reno, Nev.
53. Jason Russell, rhp, Chattahoochee Valley (Ala.) CC
54. Charles Bivens, of, Taft (Calif.) JC
55. Diallo Banks, rhp, West Point (Miss.) HS
56. David Harper, rhp, Mansfield (Texas) HS
57. Michael Myers, c, Gaithersburg (Md.) HS
58. Marc Lee, of, Calvert HS, Tiffin, Ohio
59. Chad Ricketts, rhp, East Lake HS, Palm Harbor, Fla.
60. Daniel Sousa, of, Mendocino (Calif.) CC
61. Michael Rios, rhp, Pacific
62. Casey Baker, of, McLane HS, Fresno
63. Chris Sauritch, ss, Southern Illinois
64. Robert Cowan, rhp, Saugus (Calif.) HS
65. James Gann, rhp, Norman (Okla.) HS
66. Todd Teeter, c, West Orange HS, Winter Park, Fla.
67. Chris Hendrix, c, Oakland HS, Murfreesboro, Tenn.
68. Anthony Longueira, ss, Cooper City (Fla.) HS
69. Larry Barnes, 1b, Bakersfield (Calif.) JC
70. **Brian Deskins, lhp, Nebraska**
71. Cameron Jones, ss, Millwood HS, Oklahoma City
72. **Franklin Roberts, rhp, Seaford (Del.) HS**
73. Brent Yarrow, of, Chemainus (B.C.) HS
74. Brian Reid, 2b, Corona del Sol HS, Phoenix
75. Eric Johnson, of, South Georgia JC
76. David Bernhard, rhp, Monterey Peninsula (Calif.) JC
77. Kenny Williams, of, Independence HS, San Jose
78. Allen Stalvey, of, Columbia HS, Lake City, Fla.
79. Charles Roberson, rhp, Franklin HS, Seattle
80. Dustin Spencer, ss, Santa Barbara (Calif.) HS
81. Michael Logan, rhp, Dougherty HS, Albany, Ga.
82. Richard Bell, rhp, Crater HS, Central Point, Ore.
83. John Woodard, rhp, Cartersville (Ga.) HS
84. Theron Truitt, of, LaGrange (Ga.) HS
85. Jerry Whaley, c, McIntosh Academy, Darien, Ga.
86. Stephen Haggard, rhp, Southern Arkansas
87. Jason Mann, rhp, First Colonial HS, Virginia Beach
88. Cabott Woods, rhp, Princeton (Ind.) Community HS
89. Jason Dyer, of, Shawnee (Okla.) HS
90. Tom Buckman, rhp, Broward (Fla.) CC
91. Shawn Summers, of, Tennessee

HOUSTON ASTROS

June—Regular Phase (12)

1. **Billy Wagner, lhp, Ferrum (Va.)**
2. (Pick to Pirates as compensation for Type A free agent Doug

Drabek)
3. (Pick to Reds as compensation for Type A free agent Greg Swindell)
4. **Steve Verduzco, ss, San Jose, Calif.**
5. **Derek Root, 1b, St. Edward HS, Lakewood, Ohio**
6. **Jamie Saylor, ss, North Garland HS, Garland, Texas**
7. **Jaime Bluma, rhp, Wichita State**
8. **Mike Diorio, rhp, Seward County (Kan.) CC**
9. **Brett Callan, c, San Diego Mesa JC**
10. **Kary Bridges, 3b, Mississippi**
11. **Edward Lewis, rhp, Central Missouri State**
12. **William Hartnett, rhp, Northeastern**
13. Rolando Avila, of, Los Angeles Harbor JC
14. **Tim Forkner, 3b, Seward County (Kan.) CC**
15. **Troy Schulte, rhp, Creighton**
16. **Grant Gosch, of, Serra HS, San Mateo, Calif.**
17. **Mark Dorencz, ss, Illinois State**
18. **Tim Kester, rhp, Florida International**
19. **Jon Phillips, lhp, St. Bonaventure**
20. **John Vindivich, of, Southeastern Louisiana**
21. **Jason Turley, rhp, Brighton HS, Sandy, Utah**
22. Jay Vaught, rhp, Texas
23. Landon Hessler, rhp, Brooksville-Hernando HS, Brooksville, Fla.
24. Jon Cannon, lhp, Gunn HS, Los Altos, Calif.
25. **Michael Walter, rhp, Palomar (Calif.) JC**
26. **Tom Czanstkowski, rhp, Arkansas**
27. **Trevor Froschauer, 1b/c, Lincoln Land (Ill.) CC**
28. **Klint Klaas, 2b, Iowa Western CC**
29. Steven Keen, rhp, Baldwin (Fla.) HS
30. David Green, rhp, Port Hope (Ontario) & District HS
31. **Brock Steinke, rhp, Washington HS, Cedar Rapids, Iowa**
32. Duane Eason, rhp, Hackensack (N.J.) HS
33. **Ted Wieczorek, 1b/3b, Southern California College**
34. Joseph Painich, rhp, West Monroe (La.) HS
35. Jerry Brandon, 2b, Airline HS, Bossier City, La.
36. Ryan Kelly, rhp, Amarillo (Texas) HS
37. Rafael Corrales, rhp, Niles West HS, Skokie, Ill.
38. Joshua Halemanu, of, Mission (Calif.) JC
39. **Daniel Dolney, c, New Trier HS, Wilmette, Ill.**
40. Todd Cook, rhp, Tavares (Fla.) HS
41. Jonathan Lawrence, ss/2b, Columbus (Ga.) HS
42. **Terry Beyna, 3b, Illinois State**
43. Anthony Mack, of, Los Angeles Harbor JC
44. **Bryant Nelson, ss, Texarkana (Texas) JC**
45. Ryan O'Toole, rhp, Irvine (Calif.) HS
46. Mike Bustamonte, lhp, Eisenhower HS, Rialto, Calif.
47. Chris Bowker, rhp, Dillon (Mont.) HS
48. Jeremy Miller, ss, Connelsville HS, Mill Run, Pa.
49. James Sapp, of, Geneva (N.Y.) HS
50. **Ryan Campbell, rhp, Hoover HS, Fresno**
51. Paul Powell, lhp, Denison (Texas) HS
52. Nassim Hijazi, lhp, Downey HS, Bellflower, Calif.
53. **Scott Eidle, of, Yale**
54. Patrick Bell, rhp, Asheboro (N.C.) HS
55. **Shawn Bartle, rhp, McLennan (Texas) CC**
56. **Chad White, of, Maine**
57. **Richard Humphrey, rhp, Liberty**
58. **Yamil Lopez, ss, Puerto Nuevo, P.R.**
59. **Chad Crossley, rhp, South Florida**
60. Pat Maxwell, c, Cherry Creek HS, Englewood, Colo.
61. Dwayne Crawley, of/lhp, Prince George's (Md.) CC
62. Eric Plooy, rhp, Hanford (Calif.) HS
63. Michael Myro, rhp, West Torrance HS, Torrance, Calif.
64. Jeffrey Hook, rhp, Ventura (Calif.) JC
65. Robert Poland, lhp, Southwood HS, Shreveport, La.
66. Carl Franzten, c, Fredericksburg (Texas) HS
67. Leo Nunez, ss, Fresno CC
68. Shaw Casey, ss/3b, Green Valley HS, Henderson, Nev.
69. Colland Felts, c, Brighton HS, Sandy, Utah
70. Robert Slomkowski, rhp, Rutherford (N.J.) HS
71. Jermaine Timberlake, 2b, Louisa County HS, Louisa, Va.
72. Anthony Sciola, c, Bullard HS, Fresno
73. Aaron Martin, lhp, Angelina (Texas) JC
74. Kiwane Garris, of, Westinghouse HS, Chicago
75. Jack Jones, ss, Downey HS, Modesto, Calif.
76. Anthony Peters, c, Cardinal HS, Middlefield, Ohio
77. Aaron Baker, rhp, Bellmont HS, Decatur, Ind.
78. Raphael Baro, lhp, La Salle HS, Miami
79. John Anderson, rhp, Chaffey (Calif.) JC
80. Raul Plasencia, rhp, Jordan HS, Long Beach
81. Chad Pittman, of, Haltom (Texas) HS
82. Kelvin Parker, of, Montgomery (Md.) JC
83. Jason Meier, of, Bluevale HS, Waterloo, Ontario

KANSAS CITY ROYALS

June—Regular Phase (5)

1. **Jeff Granger, lhp, Texas A&M**
2. (Pick to Blue Jays as compensation for Type A free agent David Cone)
3. (Pick to Twins as compensation for Type A free agent Greg Gagne)
4. **Phil Grundy, rhp, Western Carolina**
5. **Phil Brassington, rhp, Lamar**
6. **Tyrone Frazier, of/ss, Woodlawn HS, Shreveport, La.**
7. **Pat Flury, rhp, JC of Southern Idaho**
8. **O.J. Rhone, of, Central Missouri State**
9. Chad Green, of, Mentor (Ohio) HS
10. Tom Buchman, c, Shawnee Mission South HS, Lenexa, Kan.
11. **Larry Smith, of, Broomfield (Colo.) HS**
12. **Kevin Rawitzer, lhp, Arizona State**
13. **Malcolm Cepeda, 1b, Solano (Calif.) CC**
14. **Braxton Hickman, 1b, Texas**
15. **Bill Dunn, 2b, Arizona State**
16. **Dustin Brixey, rhp, Northeastern Oklahoma A&M JC**
17. **Glendon Rusch, lhp, Shorecrest HS, Seattle**
18. **Ken Ray, rhp, Roswell (Ga.) HS**
19. **Jimmie Byington, of, Seminole State (Okla.) JC**
20. **Eric Anderson, rhp, Blue Springs (Mo.) HS**
21. **Kris Ralston, rhp, Central Missouri State**
22. **Michael Evans, c/of, Lubbock (Texas) Christian**
23. **Jeremy Carr, 2b, Cal State Fullerton**
24. **Nevin Brewer, rhp, Southeastern (N.C.) CC**
25. **Leonard Weathersby, of, Hamilton HS, Los Angeles**
26. **Luke Oglesby, of/2b, New Mexico**
27. **Jason Huffman, rhp, Southeastern (N.C.) CC**
28. Gadiel Medero, rhp, Trujillo Alto, P.R.
29. **Justin McCoy, c, Bingham HS, South Jordan, Utah**
30. **Lino Diaz, 3b, Nevada-Las Vegas**
31. Jacque Jones, of, San Diego HS
32. **Toby Smith, 1b/rhp, Wichita State**
33. Brian Meyers, rhp, George Fox (Ore.)
34. **Stephen Wojtkowski, 3b, Montgomery (Md.) JC**
35. **Neil Atkinson, lhp, St. Mary's (Texas)**
36. **Jeff Ramos, c, Power-St. Joseph's HS, Toronto**
37. **Sal Fasano, c, Evansville**
38. **Daron Dondero, ss, Mount San Jacinto (Calif.) JC**
39. Derek Dubois, lhp, Ft. William Collegiate HS, Murillo, Ontario
40. Ryan Stover, 1b, Winter Haven (Fla.) HS
41. **Matt Aminoff, rhp, George Washington**
42. **Cody Kosman, rhp, Nevada-Reno**
43. Frank Stewart, of, Julian (Calif.) HS
44. Thornton Davis, 3b, Liberty County HS, Bristol, Fla.
45. Donovan Delaney, of, Bossier Parish (La.) CC
46. Jeff Terrell, ss, Tri-City Christian HS, Blue Springs, Mo.
47. Ricardo Calderon, 1b, Carolina, P.R.
48. Howard Rosenberry, lhp, Hagerstown (Md.) JC
49. Montrell Pride, 1b, Oak Ridge HS, Orlando
50. Brian Paluk, rhp, Catholic Central HS, Plymouth, Mich.
51. Jess Utecht, of, Kamiakin HS, Richland, Wash.
52. William Roland, 3b, Galveston (Texas) JC
53. Toussaint Waterman, of, Country Day HS, Pontiac, Mich.
54. Patrick Johnson, c, Taylorsville HS, Salt Lake City
55. Jeffrey Peck, lhp, Ryan HS, Denton, Texas
56. Jason Hueth, rhp, Norte Vista HS, Riverside, Calif.
57. David Trentine, rhp, Foothill HS, Santa Ana, Calif.
58. Christopher Jackson, of, Brownsboro HS, Chandler, Texas
59. Sal McCullough, of, Muir HS, Pasadena, Calif.
60. Bubba Dixon, lhp, Seminole State (Okla.) JC
61. Mike Klostermeyer, 1b, Seminole State (Okla.) JC

62. Tremain Mack, of, Chapel Hill HS, Tyler, Texas
63. Andrew Bernard, rhp, Highland HS, Bakersfield, Calif.
64. Anthony Barrett, rhp, Athens (Texas) HS
65. Jeff Phipps, rhp, Palo Verde Valley HS, Blythe, Calif.
66. Scott Seal, of, Irvine (Calif.) HS
67. Gordon Hegeman, 2b, Bakersfield (Calif.) JC

LOS ANGELES DODGERS

June—Regular Phase (2)

1. **Darren Dreifort, rhp, Wichita State**
2. (Pick to Cardinals as compensation tor Type B free agent Todd Worrell)
3. **Dax Winslett, rhp, Arizona State**
4. **Nate Bland, lhp, Mountain Brook (Ala.) HS**
5. **Scott Hunter, c/of, Northeast HS, Philadelphia**
6. Nate Yeskie, rhp, Carson HS, Carson City, Nev.
7. **Doug Newstrom, 1b, Arizona State**
8. **Jose Prado, rhp, Miami**
9. **Matt Schwenke, c, UCLA**
10. **John Vukson, rhp/3b, Sanger HS, Fresno**
11. **Josh Rash, of, Lamar HS, Arlington, Texas**
12. **Craig Scheffler, lhp, Wisconsin-Milwaukee**
13. **Brian Rolocut, rhp, Miami-Dade CC Wolfson**
14. **Brett Binkley, lhp, Georgia Tech**
15. **David Steed, c, Meridian (Miss.) CC**
16. **Dan Hubbs, rhp, Southern California**
17. **Mike Biltimier, 1b, Purdue**
18. **Joe LaGarde, rhp, East Forsyth HS, Winston-Salem, N.C.**
19. **Eric Maloney, rhp, Creighton**
20. **Michael Kinney, of, Texas Tech**
21. Mark Watson, lhp, Marist HS, Atlanta
22. Charlie Nelson, of, Minnesota
23. **Eddie Davis, of, Long Beach State**
24. **Carl South, rhp, Marist HS, Atlanta**
25. **Paul Lo Duca, c, Arizona State**
26. Corey Coggburn, of, Ada (Okla.) HS
27. Bryan Coyle, rhp, Hudson's Bay HS, Vancouver, Wash.
28. Jeffrey Astgen, 2b, El Camino Real HS, Canoga Park, Calif.
29. Anthony Cellars, of, Texas HS, Texarkana, Texas
30. Adrian Black, of, North Brunswick HS, Leland, N.C.
31. Doug Davis, lhp, North Gate HS, Pleasant Hill, Calif.
32. Jordan Zimmerman, lhp, Brenham (Texas) HS
33. Raul Correa, rhp, Juana Diaz, P.R.
34. Dwayne McCray, of, Sumter (S.C.) HS
35. Tracy Johnson, of, Deer Valley HS, Phoenix
36. Matt Wagner, rhp, Iowa State
37. Richard Shaw, rhp, Sandwich HS, LaSalle, Ontario
38. **Mark Manbeck, rhp, Round Rock (Texas) HS**
39. David Propst, of, West Charlotte HS, Charlotte
40. Dion Rhodes, of, Hudson's Bay HS, Vancouver, Wash.
41. Eric Yanz, rhp, Arvada West HS, Golden, Colo.
42. **Bruce Yard, ss, Indiana (Pa.)**
43. Thomas Cody, c, Fort Vancouver HS, Vancouver, Wash.
44. Brian Piddington, rhp, Southwestern HS, Hazel Green, Wis.
45. Ben Padilla, ss, Carson (Calif.) HS
46. Gustavo Rubio, 1b/c, Leuzinger HS, Lawndale, Calif.
47. Jason Smith, rhp, Meridian (Miss.) CC
48. Jeff Falardeau, lhp, Notre Dame HS, Welland, Ontario
49. **Julio Colon, rhp, Long Beach State**
50. Richard Condon, 2b, Crossroads HS, Culver City, Calif.
51. Kendall Hill, rhp, Escambia HS, Pensacola, Fla.
52. **Nathan Rasmussen, 1b, Lakeville (Minn.) HS**
53. Victor Sobieraj, rhp, Catholic Central HS, Windsor, Ontario
54. David Wease, 1b, Chesnee HS, Gaffney, S.C.
55. Jaymie Bane, lhp, Paradise Valley HS, Phoenix
56. Steve Huls, ss, Rocori HS, Cold Spring, Minn.
57. **Brian Carpenter, rhp, Texas**
58. Matthew Powell, rhp, Miami-Dade CC Wolfson

MILWAUKEE BREWERS

June—Regular Phase (23)

1. **Jeff D'Amico, rhp, Northeast HS, St. Petersburg, Fla.**
1. **Kelly Wunsch, lhp, Texas A&M** (Pick from Blue Jays as compensation for Type A free agent Paul Molitor)
1. **Todd Dunn, of, North Florida** (Supplemental pick—35th—for loss of Type A free agent Chris Bosio)
1. **Joe Wagner, rhp, Central Florida** (Supplemental pick—39th—for loss of Molitor)
2. **Brian Banks, c/of, Brigham Young** (Pick from Mariners for loss of Bosio) (Pick from Mariners as compensation for Bosio)
2. **Danny Klassen, ss, John Carrol HS, Port St. Lucie, Fla.**
3. **George Preston, rhp, Brenham (Texas) HS**
4. **Shane Sheldon, rhp, Gordon (Ga.) JC**
5. **Steve Duda, rhp, Pepperdine**
6. **Josh Zwisler, c, St. Vincent-St. Mary HS, Akron, Ohio**
7. **Mark Loretta, ss, Northwestern**
8. **Tano Tijerina, rhp, Navarro (Texas) JC**
9. **Jon Hillis, rhp, Rice**
10. **Chris McInnes, ss, Ricks (Idaho) JC**
11. Chris Junghans, c, McDonough HS, Waldorf, Md.
12. Brian Blessie, rhp, Burke HS, Omaha
13. Brian Luna, 1b, Craigmont HS, Memphis
14. **Peter Benny, rhp, Wooster HS, Carson City, Nev.**
15. **Scott Perkins, rhp, Southwestern Louisiana**
16. James Wallace, rhp, Kellenberg Memorial HS, Wantagh, N.Y.
17. **Chad Kopitzke, rhp, Wisconsin-Oshkosh**
18. **Gabriel Mercado, rhp, Indian Hills (Iowa) CC**
19. **Sean Maloney, rhp, Georgetown**
20. **Pedro Fuertes, 3b, Carolina, P.R.**
21. **Chris Schmitt, lhp, West Florida**
22. Rick Gutierrez, 2b, Oklahoma
23. Ron Wallech, rhp, Hagerstown (Md.) JC
24. **Greg Martinez, of, Barstow (Calif.) JC**
25. **Jarod Fryman, 3b, Jefferson Davis (Ala.) JC**
26. **Allen Mealing, of, Strom Thurmond HS, Edgefield, S.C.**
27. **James Cole, rhp, Mercer**
28. **Matt Murphy, lhp, Vermont**
29. Todd Cutchins, lhp, Westlake (La.) HS
30. **Chris Carter, c, Clemson**
31. **Todd Landry, 1b, Arizona**
32. James Reames, rhp, Seneca (S.C.) HS
33. **Jim Hodge, of, Mercer County (N.J.) CC**
34. Michael Kimbrell, lhp, Jefferson Davis (Ala.) CC
35. Mark Wasikowski, 3b, Pepperdine
36. **Clayton Hill, of, McLennan (Texas) JC**
37. Julio Ayala, lhp, Guaynabo, P.R.
38. Jamie Bass, 2b, Pine Bluff (Ark.) HS
39. Brian Conley, ss, Glen Este HS, Cincinnati
40. Ronald Fawley, c/of, Santaluces HS, Lantana, Fla.
41. Chris Ciaccio, rhp, Georgia
42. Lorne Rosas, of, Hilo (Hawaii) HS
43. Peter Jenkins, c, Redlands (Calif.) HS
44. John Cromwell, rhp, Lake Howell HS, Winter Park, Fla.
45. **Jose Calderon, rhp, San Juan, P.R.**
46. Mandy Jacomino, c, Westminster Christian HS, Miami
47. Joseph Walls, rhp, LaSierra HS, Hesperia, Calif.
48. **Eduardo Acosta, ss/of, Muscatine (Iowa) CC**
49. Jason Greuel, rhp, South HS, Waukesha, Wis.
50. Kerry Mikulski, of, Pope John Paul HS, Boca Raton, Fla.
51. **Miguel Villaran, ss, Loiza, P.R.**
52. **Francisco Garcia, c, Lewistown, P.R.**
53. Daniel Jordan, ss, Thomasville (Ga.) HS
54. Ken Wagner, rhp, Palm Beach (Fla.) JC
55. Anthony Pavlovich, rhp, Thomasville HS, Pavo, Ga.
56. Bret Hemphill, c, Cal State Fullerton
57. Marty Bourgon, c, Central Florida CC
58. Michael Ribaudo, of, Sarasota (Fla.) HS
59. Charlie Ward, ss/of, Florida State
60. Cameron Andrews, 1b, Milton (Fla.) HS
61. Brian Scutero, rhp, Valencia (Fla.) CC

MINNESOTA TWINS

June—Regular Phase (21)

1. **Torii Hunter, of, Pine Bluff (Ark.) HS** (Pick from Reds as compensation for Type A free agent John Smiley)
1. Jason Varitek, c, Georgia Tech
1. **Marc Barcelo, rhp, Arizona State** (Supplemental pick—

33rd—for loss of Smiley)
1. **Kelcey Mucker, of, Lawrenceburg (Ind.) HS** (Supplemental pick—38th—for loss of Type A free agent Greg Gagne)
2. **Dan Perkins, rhp, Westminster Christian HS, Miami**
3. **Troy Carrasco, lhp, Jesuit HS, Tampa** (Pick from Royals as compensation for Gagne)
3. **Jose Valentin, 3b, Manati, P.R.**
4. Toby Dollar, rhp, Graham (Texas) HS
5. Jesse Ibarra, 1b, Loyola Marymount
6. **Benj Sampson, lhp, Ankeny (Iowa) HS**
7. Kelly Dransfeldt, lhp, Morris (Ill.) HS
8. **Ryan Lane, ss, Bellefontaine (Ohio) HS**
9. **Kevin Ohme, lhp, North Florida**
10. Mark Merila, 2b, Minnesota
11. **Troy Fortin, c, Lundar (Manitoba) HS**
12. Alex Cora, ss, Caguas, P.R.
13. Pete Forster, lhp, Oak Park HS, Kansas City
14. **Ryan Radmanovich, of, Pepperdine**
15. Mike Torti, ss, Newman Smith HS, Carrollton, Texas
16. Wylie Campbell, ss, Southwest HS, Fort Worth
17. Dan Kolb, rhp, Walnut (Ill.) HS
18. L.J. Yankosky, rhp, West Springfield HS, Springfield, Va.
19. Chris Granata, rhp, Ohio State
20. **Aaron Santini, ss, New Mexico**
21. **Shane Bowers, rhp, Loyola Marymount**
22. Rob Radlosky, rhp, Central Florida CC
23. **Scott Stricklin, c, Kent State**
24. Ronrico Harris, of, Englewood HS, Jacksonville, Fla.
25. **Brian O'Brien, lhp, Creighton**
26. Mauricio Estavil, lhp, Pepperdine
27. **Russel Lehoisky, rhp, New Haven (Conn.)**
28. **Mike Stadelhofer, rhp, Calistoga (Calif.) HS**
29. Javier Encina, rhp, North Mesquite HS, Mesquite, Texas
30. Doug Rheaume, rhp, Santana HS, Lakeside, Calif.
31. **Jacob Patterson, 1b, Neosho County (Kan.) CC**
32. Jessie Thompson, of, Wingfield HS, Jackson, Miss.
33. Kenny Harrison, c, Hawaii
34. **Deron Dowhower, rhp, Virginia**
35. **James Motte, ss, Arizona**
36. **Daniel Venezia, ss, Concordia (N.Y.)**
37. Emil Brown, of, Harlan HS, Chicago
38. Jason Ford, lhp, North Idaho JC
39. Stephen Watson, rhp, Westwood HS, Austin
40. Douglas Beddinger, rhp, Manatee (Fla.) JC
41. Jason Adge, rhp, Sacramento CC
42. Lance Carter, rhp, Manatee HS, Bradenton, Fla.
43. Robert Landstad, of, Indian Hills (Iowa) CC
44. **Chad Rupp, 1b, Miami**
45. Matt Freeman, c, Seminole (Fla.) HS
46. **Justin Tomberlin, 3b, Maine**
47. Spencer McIntyre, lhp, Texas A&M
48. **Eric Anderson, lhp, Parkland (Ill.) JC**
49. Matthew Gondini, rhp, Green Valley HS, Henderson, Nev.
50. Aaron Sellner, rhp, Naugatuck (Conn.) HS
51. Sandy Lopez, rhp, CC of Morris (N.J.)
52. **Chris Phillips, 2b, Western Kentucky**
53. J.T. Messick, ss, Seminole State (Okla.) JC
54. Anthony Lucca, lhp, South San Francisco HS
55. William Stone, lhp, Delight (Ark.) HS
56. Eddie Medlin, c, Billings (Mont.) HS
57. Andrew Burt, rhp, Wisconsin
58. Christopher Kilen, lhp, Janesville, Wis.
59. Danny Peoples, 1b, Round Rock (Texas) HS
60. **Aaron Schooler, rhp, Columbia Basin (Wash.) CC**

MONTREAL EXPOS

June—Regular Phase (18)

1. **Chris Schwab, of, Cretin HS, Eagan, Minn.**
1. **Josue Estrada, of, Rio Piedras, P.R.** (Supplemental pick—31st—for loss of Type A free agent Spike Owen)
2. **Martin Mainville, rhp, Marquette HS, Montreal** (Pick from Yankees as compensation for Owen)
2. **Brad Fullmer, 3b, Montclair Prep HS, Chatsworth, Calif.**
3. **Jason Baker, rhp, Robert E. Lee HS, Midland, Texas**
4. **Ronnie Hall, of, Tustin (Calif.) HS**
5. **Nate Brown, lhp, California**
6. **Jeff Foster, 3b, Tennessee**
7. Donnie Fowler, rhp, Spring (Texas) HS
8. **Neal Weber, lhp, Cuesta (Calif.) CC**
9. **Jayson Durocher, rhp, Horizon HS, Scottsdale, Ariz.**
10. **Trace Coquillette, of, Sacramento CC**
11. Richard Giannola, rhp, Boca Raton (Fla.) Community HS
12. **Aaron Knieper, rhp, Central Michigan**
13. **Randy Culp, c, Ellison HS, Killeen, Texas**
14. **Tom Schneider, lhp, Centenary**
15. Jason Bond, lhp, St. Mary's HS, Scottsdale, Ariz.
16. **Troy Mattes, rhp, Riverview HS, Sarasota, Fla.**
17. **Angelo Thompson, of/1b, Shaw (N.C.)**
18. Ricardo Spears, of, California
19. Scott Needham, c, Bentonville (Ark.) HS
20. Kevin Nykoluk, c, Simi Valley (Calif.) HS
21. Darryl Monroe, of, Kansas
22. Peter Bezeredi, 1b, Seminole (Fla.) CC
23. Dirk Lewallen, 1b, Hesperia (Calif.) HS
24. **Matt Harrell, c, Duke**
25. Donzell McDonald, of, Cherry Creek HS, Englewood, Colo.
26. Jason Romine, rhp, Omak (Wash.) HS
27. Shane Gift, c, Gilbert (Ariz.) HS
28. Stephan Neill, rhp, John Carroll HS, Port St. Lucie, Fla.
29. Ryan Fisher, lhp, Unity HS, Milltown, Wis.
30. David Moraga, lhp, Armijo HS, Suisun City, Calif.
31. **Chris Grubb, of, Elizabethtown (Pa.)**
32. Daniel Albrecht, lhp, Butler (Kan.) CC
33. **Brian Detwiler, c, William Paterson (N.J.)**
34. **Scott Quade, ss, Austin Peay**
35. George Elmore, rhp, Louisburg (N.C.) JC
36. Robert Lentz, ss, Bloomingdale HS, Brandon, Fla.
37. Shawn Lopez, rhp, Lewis-Clark State (Idaho)
38. Christopher Weidert, rhp, Butler (Kan.) CC
39. Walter Owens, of, Odessa (Texas) JC
40. Nole Elizer, c, Cape Coral (Fla.) HS
41. Scott Kidd, ss, DeAnza (Calif.) JC
42. Stephen Kokinda, ss, Cardinal Newman HS, West Palm Beach, Fla.
43. Shawn Painter, of, Beaconsfield (Quebec) HS
44. **Jeff Mitchell, rhp, Harvard**
45. Brett Rapozo, rhp, American River (Calif.) JC
46. John Portugal, rhp, Oceanside (Calif.) HS
47. Logan Miller, c, JC of Marin (Calif.)
48. Richard Matteson, rhp, Diablo Valley (Calif.) JC
49. Orin Hirschkorn, rhp, Kerman (Calif.) HS
50. Brian Cummings, rhp, Iona Prep HS, East Chester, N.Y.
51. Mike Lincoln, rhp, Casa Roble HS, Orangevale, Calif.
52. Ryan Gause, ss, Temecula (Calif.) HS
53. Brian Downs, c, Don Lugo HS, Chino, Calif.
54. Nason Beckett, c, Port Angeles (Wash.) HS
55. John O'Brien, of, Malvern HS, Chester, Pa.
56. Jeffrey Howard, rhp, Spartanburg Methodist (S.C.) JC
57. Brett Lockwood, 3b, Mesa (Ariz.) CC
58. **Jason Woodring, rhp, Trinidad State (Colo.) JC**
59. **Michael Leon, lhp, Western New Mexico**
60. Greg Morris, 3b, UC Davis
61. **Joseph Tosone, of, Dartmouth**
62. Adam Housley, rhp, Pepperdine

NEW YORK METS

June—Regular Phase (8)

1. **Kirk Presley, rhp, Tupelo (Miss.) HS**
2. **Eric Ludwick, rhp, Nevada-Las Vegas**
3. **Mike Welch, rhp, Southern Maine**
4. Bill Koch, rhp, West Babylon (N.Y.) HS
5. **Fletcher Bates, of, New Hanover HS, Wilmington, N.C.**
6. **Matt Terrell, of, Western Michigan**
7. **Scott Adair, rhp, Norte Vista HS, Riverside, Calif.**
8. **Paul Petrulis, ss, Mississippi State**
9. **Joe Atwater, lhp, South Alamance HS, Graham, N.C.**
10. **Derek Sutton, lhp, Indian Hills (Iowa) CC**
11. Jared Camp, rhp, East HS, Huntington, W.Va.

12. **Ethan McEntire, lhp, Habersham Central HS, Cornelia, Ga.**
13. John Powell, rhp, Auburn
14. **Jeff Cosman, rhp, Mississippi**
15. **Rodney Mazion, of, Nevada-Las Vegas**
16. **Paul Bowman, rhp, Garrett (Md.) CC**
17. **Sean Kenny, rhp, Eastern Michigan**
18. Jason Middlebrook, rhp, Grass Lake (Mich.) HS
19. Ryan Rupe, rhp, Northbrook HS, Houston
20. **Jarrod Patterson, 1b, Jefferson Davis (Ala.) JC**
21. Billy Oliver, rhp/3b, Monta Vista HS, Cupertino, Calif.
22. **Kevin Lewis, c, Florida Atlantic**
23. **David Zuniga, ss, San Jose State**
24. **Brian Mast, rhp, Lipscomb**
25. Brandon Welch, of/1b, Butler County (Kan.) CC
26. **Thomas Wolff, rhp, Kellogg (Mich.) CC**
27. **Robert Gontkosky, lhp, Rider**
28. **Tad Smith, 1b, Eastern Illinois**
29. **Scott Winterlee, c, Michigan**
30. **Benny Agbayani, of, Hawaii Pacific**
31. **David Pellhauer, 1b, Gaither HS, Tampa**
32. Burdette Greeny, rhp, Port Angeles (Wash.) HS
33. **Jesus Morales, ss, East Los Angeles JC**
34. **Ross Ferrier, of, Waterloo (Ontario)**
35. **Gary Collum, of, Pace (N.Y.)**
36. Ken Harrell, c, Alamogordo (N.M.) HS
37. Joseph Robinson, ss, Burlington (Iowa) HS
38. Carlos Morrison, of, Cimarron HS, Las Vegas
39. Keith Maxwell, of, Liberty County HS, Bristol, Fla.
40. Santiago Sanchez, ss, Lodi (Calif.) HS
41. Barrett Short, rhp, Three Rivers (Mo.) CC
42. Michael Ruhmann, lhp, St. Louis CC-Meramec
43. **Brandon Newell, rhp, Washington**
44. **Vance Wilson, c, Mesa (Ariz.) CC**
45. **Michael Johnson, 2b, Union (N.Y.)**

NEW YORK YANKEES

June—Regular Phase (13)

1. **Matt Drews, rhp, Sarasota (Fla.) HS**
2. (Pick to Expos as compensation for Type A free agent Spike Owen)
3. (Pick to Blue Jays as compensation for Type A free agent Jimmy Key)
4. **Sloan Smith, of, Northwestern**
5. **Mike Jerzembeck, rhp, North Carolina**
6. **Kurt Bierek, 1b, Southern California**
7. **Jim Musselwhite, rhp, Georgia**
8. **Rob Trimble, c/rhp, Texas A&M**
9. **Clint Whitworth, rhp, Oklahoma City**
10. **Derek Shumpert, of, Aquinas-Mercy HS, St. Louis**
11. **Jason Rathbun, rhp, Baylor**
12. **Anthony Shelby, lhp, Triton (Ill.) JC**
13. **Shawn Alazaus, lhp, Mount Vernon Nazarene (Ohio)**
14. **Jim Palmer, 3b, St. Thomas Aquinas HS, Fort Lauderdale**
15. **Gregory Resz, rhp, Southwest Missouri State**
16. John Peters, lhp, Texarkana (Texas) JC
17. **Frank Lankford, rhp, Virginia**
18. **Joe Wharton, rhp, Baylor**
19. Terry Harvey, rhp, North Carolina State
20. **Casey Mittauer, rhp, Florida International**
21. Andrew Remala, ss, El Dorado HS, Placentia, Calif.
22. **Mike Schmitz, 1b/of, Florida State**
23. Jason Dietrich, rhp, Rancho Santiago (Calif.) JC
24. **Scott Standish, rhp, Bellevue (Neb.)**
25. Chad Moeller, c, Upland (Calif.) HS
26. **Kent Donnelly, rhp, Southern California**
27. Jason Clark, 1b, Poly HS, Riverside, Calif.
28. Chris Druckrey, rhp, Kankakee HS, St. Anne, Ill.
29. Frisco Parotte, rhp, Toa Baja, P.R.
30. Jay Evans, lhp, Indian River (Fla.) CC
31. Jason Smithberger, rhp, Watkins Mill HS, Gaithersburg, Md.
32. Craig Dour, ss, Tarpon Springs HS, Palm Harbor, Fla.
33. Jarred McAlvain, 1b, Stigler (Okla.) HS
34. Tom Bernhardt, of, Columbus HS, Miami
35. James Kerr, ss, Coral Springs (Fla.) HS
36. **Craig Dingman, rhp, Hutchinson (Kan.) CC**
37. Matthew Aden, of, Northwest HS, Omaha
38. **Jason Berry, rhp, Miami-Dade CC Wolfson**
39. Cade Gaspar, rhp, Saddleback (Calif.) CC
40. Joseph Victery, rhp, Ninnekah (Okla.) HS
41. Eric Knutson, ss/2b, Benson HS, Omaha
42. Brett Schlomann, rhp, Owasso HS, Collinsville, Okla.
43. Dietrich Johnson, of, South Dorchester HS, Cambridge, Md.
44. Eddie Yarnall, lhp, St. Thomas Aquinas HS, Fort Lauderdale, Fla.
45. Dale Brandt, lhp, Indian River (Fla.) CC
46. John Strasser, ss, Greenway HS, Glendale, Ariz.
47. Shawne Ware, of, Sacramento CC
48. Phillip Haigler, rhp, Faulkner State (Ala.) JC
49. Brandon Marsters, c, Sarasota (Fla.) HS
50. Luis Flores, c, Columbus HS, Miami
51. Roy Reis, c, Diman Regional Vocational Tech HS, Fall River, Mass.
52. Oliver Harwas, rhp, Okeechobee (Fla.) HS
53. Brent Southall, 1b/of, Manatee (Fla.) JC
54. Isreal Barnes, rhp, King HS, Tampa
55. Michael Massey, c, Indian River (Fla.) CC
56. Greg Smitherman, of, Hartshorne (Okla.) HS
57. Chris Wright, c, West Jones HS, Laurel, Miss.
58. Ken Shelly, ss, Ely HS, Pompano Beach, Fla.
59. Chris Dickerson, ss, Alvin (Texas) HS
60. Wyley Steelmon, c, Enid (Okla.) HS
61. Chris Halliday, c, Evans HS, Martinez, Ga.
62. Nolan Lofgren, c, East HS, Rockford, Ill.
63. Scott Carley, rhp, Crescent City HS, Milford, Ill.
64. Matt Dornfeld, of, Harding HS, St. Paul, Minn.

OAKLAND ATHLETICS

June—Regular Phase (25)

1. **John Wasdin, rhp, Florida State**
1. **Willie Adams, rhp, Stanford** (Supplemental pick—36th—for loss of Type A free agent Dave Stewart)
2. **Jeff D'Amico, ss, Redmond (Wash.) HS**
2. **Mike Moschetti, ss, La Mirada (Calif.) HS** (Pick from Blue Jays as compensation for Stewart)
3. Tucker Barr, c, Maclay HS, Tallahassee, Fla.
4. **Jason McDonald, ss, Houston**
5. **Andy Smith, rhp, A.L. Brown HS, Kannapolis, N.C.**
6. **Scott Spiezio, 1b, Illinois**
7. **Tim Kubinski, lhp, UCLA**
8. **Leon Hamburg, of, Casa Roble HS, Orangevale, Calif.**
9. **Damon Newman, rhp, Fullerton (Calif.) JC**
10. John Phillips, rhp, Bullard HS, Fresno
11. **Jason Rajotte, lhp, Maine**
12. **Chris Michalak, lhp, Notre Dame**
13. **Scott Baldwin, lhp, Lewis-Clark State (Idaho)**
14. **Willie Morales, c, Arizona**
15. Daniel Choi, rhp, Long Beach State
16. **Mat Reese, of, Indiana State**
17. Stephen Fuller, rhp, St. Charles (Ill.) HS
18. **Brian Whatley, c, Long Beach State**
19. **Pat Sanders, 1b, Cumberland (Tenn.)**
20. **Aaron Huber, rhp, Panola (Texas) JC**
21. **Tony Banks, of, Cal State Fullerton**
22. **Jeff Richardson, of, Long Beach State**
23. **Eric Harris, of, Columbia State (Tenn.) CC**
24. Toby Larson, rhp, Lassen (Calif.) JC
25. Joe Montelongo, rhp, Truett-McConnell (Ga.) JC
26. **Derek Manning, lhp, North Carolina**
27. **Ryan Whitaker, rhp, Arkansas**
28. **Jason Lowe, rhp, Mississippi**
29. Felix Martinez, ss, Rio Piedras, P.R.
30. Jeff Poor, c, Los Angeles Harbor JC
31. **Brandy Bengoechea, ss, Lewis-Clark State (Idaho)**
32. **Michael McLeod, of, South Carolina**
33. **Randy Ortega, c, Santa Clara**
34. Jon Farmer, 1b/lhp, Porterville (Calif.) JC
35. Peter Cervantes, of, Lincoln HS, Los Angeles
36. **Thomas Luft, rhp, Warner Southern (Fla.)**
37. Robert Moore, rhp, Lassen (Calif.) JC

38. Brandon Kolb, rhp, Chabot (Calif.) JC
39. **Matthew Weisbruch, rhp, Bradley**
40. Bryan Warner, of, Monrovia (Calif.) HS
41. **Matt Walsh, rhp, Boston College**
42. **Jeff Carr, c, Mission Viejo (Calif.) HS**
43. **Chad Griffin, 2b, Garinger HS, Charlotte**
44. Santos Cortez, of, Millikan HS, Long Beach
45. Tal Light, 3b, Seminole State (Okla.) JC
46. Eric Fuller, ss, West HS, Bakersfield, Calif.
47. Frank Harmer, c/rhp, Lake Brantley HS, Altamonte Springs, Fla.
48. Jay Wiebe, of, Foothill HS, Bakersfield, Calif.

PHILADELPHIA PHILLIES

June—Regular Phase (4)

1. **Wayne Gomes, rhp, Old Dominion**
2. **Scott Rolen, 3b, Jasper (Ind.) HS**
3. **Josh Watts, of, Ironwood HS, Glendale, Ariz.**
4. **Jeffrey Key, of, Newton County HS, Covington, Ga.**
5. **Thomas Franek, rhp, Mesa State (Colo.)**
6. Blair Fowler, rhp, Everett (Wash.) HS
7. Scott Sladovnik, of, Westside HS, Omaha
8. **Bo Hamilton, rhp, Cleveland (Texas) HS**
9. **Nelson Metheney, rhp, Clinch Valley (Va.)**
10. **Silvio Censale, lhp, Miami**
11. Jarrod Mays, rhp, El Dorado Springs (Mo.) HS
12. **Chris Mayfield, of, McNeese State**
13. **Brian Costello, of, Dr. Phillips HS, Orlando**
14. **Rich Hunter, rhp, The Linfield School, Temecula, Calif.**
15. **Tom Danulevith, lhp, St. John's**
16. **Doug Angeli, ss, New Orleans**
17. Eric Ekdahl, ss, Pepperdine
18. Mark Gardener, lhp, Fountain Valley (Calif.) HS
19. **Jeff Gyselman, c, Portland State (Ore.)**
20. **Charles Tinsley, of, Cumberland HS, Lynch, Ky.**
21. **Nate Rodriquez, ss, Cal State Fullerton**
22. **Andrew Szarko, rhp, Richmond**
23. **Mark Foster, lhp, Richmond**
24. **Tyrone Swan, rhp, La Verne (Calif.)**
25. **Matthew Brainard, c/3b, Wilmington (Del.)**
26. **Derek Stingley, of, Triton (Ill.) JC**
27. **David Doster, 2b, Indiana State**
28. **Neal Murphy, c, Iona**
29. **Brian O'Connor, rhp, Creighton**
30. **Mike Muncy, ss, Ventura (Calif.) CC**
31. **Danton Pierre-Louis, 1b, Dwight HS, New York**
32. **Joseph Madden, of, Cal State Hayward**
33. **Kevin Sefcik, ss, St. Xavier (Ill.)**
34. Shawn Fouch, rhp, Virginia HS, Bristol, Va.
35. Michael Boucher, rhp, Saddleback (Calif.) CC
36. Larry Karpinski, rhp, Eisenhower HS, Rialto, Calif.
37. Darin Wood, c, Redwood HS, Visalia, Calif.
38. Jacob Esteves, rhp, Placer HS, Auburn, Calif.
39. **Barry Fitzgerald, c, West Hills HS, Santee, Calif.**
40. Karl Chatman, of, Nacogdoches (Texas) HS
41. Michael Neal, rhp, Seymour (Tenn.) HS
42. **Daniel Held, c, Waukesha County Technical HS, Neosho, Wis.**

PITTSBURGH PIRATES

June—Regular Phase (22)

1. **Charles Peterson, of, Laurens (S.C.) HS**
1. **Jermaine Allensworth, of, Purdue** (Supplemental pick—34th—for loss of Type A free agent Doug Drabek)
1. **Andy Rice, 1b, Parker HS, Birmingham** (Supplemental pick—42nd—for loss of Type A free agent Barry Bonds)
2. **Kevin Pickford, lhp, West HS, Clovis, Calif.** (Pick from Astros as compensation for Drabek)
2. **Jose Delgado, ss, Carolina, P.R.**
3. **Derek Swafford, of/2b, Ventura (Calif.) HS**
4. **Kerry Ward, rhp, Edison (Fla.) CC**
5. **Jason Temple, rhp, Woodhaven (Mich.) HS**
6. Shane McGill, rhp, Campbell HS, Smyrna, Ga.
7. **Akili Smith, of, Lincoln HS, San Diego**
8. **Sean Hagen, ss, Brighton HS, Sandy, Utah**
9. **Rayon Reid, rhp, Miami-Dade CC North**
10. **T.J. Staton, 1b/lhp, West HS, Elyria, Ohio**
11. **Matt Chamberlain, rhp, Louisiana State**
12. **Joseph Serna, rhp/c, Mount San Antonio (Calif.) JC**
13. **Kane Davis, rhp, Spencer HS, Reedy, W.Va.**
14. **Craig Mattson, rhp, Triton (Ill.) JC**
15. **Kevin Keener, lhp, Arkansas HS, Texarkana, Ark.**
16. **Richard Luna, ss, Cosumnes River (Calif.) JC**
17. Jacob Eye, rhp, Windham (Ohio) HS
18. **Jeff Isom, lhp, Purdue**
19. Francisco Lebron, 1b, Toa Baja, P.R.
20. **Alan Purdy, ss, Vanderbilt**
21. Heath Henderson, rhp, Huffman HS, Birmingham
22. **Jeff Pickich, rhp, Southern Mississippi**
23. **Anthony Sharer, rhp, Tyrone Area (Pa.) HS**
24. Matt Brown, rhp, Boone HS, Orlando
25. **Matt Ryan, rhp, Mississippi**
26. **Matt Torres, c/3b, American River (Calif.) JC**
27. **Ben Goldman, rhp, Sacramento CC**
28. **Ryan Cunningham, 3b, Lancaster (S.C.) HS**
29. Trevor Leppard, rhp, Simi Valley (Calif.) HS
30. **John Yselonia, 1b, Georgia**
31. **Jeffery Henry, rhp, George Wallace (Ala.) CC**
32. **Trevor Skjerpen, rhp, North Dakota**
33. John Brammer, rhp, Logan HS, West Logan, W.Va.
34. **Joel Williamson, c, Texas**
35. Ronald Ricks, rhp, Florida HS, Tallahassee, Fla.
36. Pete Pryor, 1b, Sacramento CC
37. **Chris Peters, lhp, Indiana**
38. Michael Butts, ss/2b, Hillsborough HS, Tampa
39. **Johnny Mitchell, of, South Carolina-Aiken**
40. Nate Coleman, c, Northwest HS, Omaha
41. Bruce Stanley, rhp, Shenandoah HS, Middletown, Ind.
42. Keith Finnerty, 2b, Rockland (N.Y.) CC
43. Robert Matlack, c, Madill (Okla.) HS
44. **Jeff Lutt, rhp, Wayne State (Neb.)**
45. Brian Harris, ss, Carmel (Ind.) HS
46. Robert Dulli, rhp, Fairfield (Ohio) HS
47. Tonka Maynor, of/1b, UNC Greensboro
48. Freddy Perez, c, Miami HS
49. Brandon Griffith, rhp, Sibley HS, Heflin, La.
50. Derek Mitchell, ss, Waukegan HS, Gurnee, Ill.
51. Justin Ludington, rhp, Sacramento CC
52. **Patrick Gosselin, ss, Montmorency HS, Sherbrooke, Quebec**
53. Steve Hueston, rhp, Skyline (Calif.) JC

ST. LOUIS CARDINALS

June—Regular Phase (16)

1. **Alan Benes, rhp, Creighton**
2. **Nate Dishington, 1b, Hoover (Calif.) HS** (Pick from Dodgers as compensation for Type B free agent Todd Worrell)
2. **Jay Witasick, rhp, Maryland-Baltimore County**
3. **Eli Marrero, c, Coral Gables (Fla.) HS**
4. Darrell Nicholas, of, New Orleans
5. **Marc Ottmers, rhp, Texas-Pan American**
6. **David Carroll, lhp, Manatee (Fla.) JC**
7. **Jeff Berblinger, 2b, Kansas**
8. **Otis Harper, of, Point Loma (Calif.) HS**
9. **Mike Windham, rhp, North Florida**
10. **Mike Martin, rhp, Walters (Tenn.) State CC**
11. **Scott Marquardt, rhp, Galveston (Texas) JC**
12. **Chris Christopher, of, Auburn**
13. **Anton French, of, Lafayette (La.) HS**
14. **Dave Madsen, 3b, Brigham Young**
15. **Dee Dalton, ss, Virginia Tech**
16. **Tom McMillan, of, Guaynabo, P.R.**
17. **Travis Welch, rhp, Sacramento CC**
18. **Jeremy Current, of, Mount Zion (Ill.) HS**
19. **Steven Santucci, of, Assumption (Mass.)**
20. **Osmel Garcia, of, Miami-Dade CC Wolfson**
21. **Armando Almanza, lhp, New Mexico JC**
22. Kristren Detmers, lhp, Lincoln Land (Ill.) CC

23. **Keith Conway, lhp, Gloucester County (N.J.) JC**
24. **Greg Almond, c, North Carolina State**
25. Ronald Johnson, lhp, Rice
26. **Greg Deares, of, George Mason**
27. Jeremy Ross, rhp, Dixie (Utah) JC
28. **Richard Lopez, of, Mount San Antonio (Calif.) JC**
29. **Joe Jumonville, 3b, Southwestern Louisiana**
30. **Cory Corrigan, rhp, Ohio**
31. **Daniel Pontes, rhp, Long Island**
32. **Michael Matvey, ss, Berry (Ga.)**
33. **Freddie Parker, rhp, Northeast HS, Clarksville, Tenn.**
34. **Ron Scott, lhp, Florida**
35. **Matt Arrandale, rhp, Illinois**
36. **Mark Dean, ss/of, Georgia Southern**
37. **Anthony Magnelli, rhp, Dominican (N.Y.)**
38. **Kevin Herde, c, San Diego**
39. **Robert Battles, rhp, Southern (Ga.) Tech**
40. **Sheldon Cain, rhp, Berry (Ga.)**
41. **Eric Alexander, rhp, Florida International**
42. **Joseph Henson, 1b/of, Lipscomb**
43. **Kurt Grashaw, rhp, Hartford**
44. **Troy Barrick, rhp, North Carolina Wesleyan**
45. **Mark Cruise, rhp, Fresno State**
46. **Curtis Williams, of, Connors State (Okla.) JC**
47. **Tighe Curran, lhp, Ventura (Calif.) JC**
48. Kortney Paul, c, Arkansas
49. **Chris Stewart, rhp, Memphis State**
50. **Edward Kehrli, rhp, Pace (N.Y.)**
51. Alfred Hughes, 1b, Vernon Regional (Texas) JC
52. Brad Gore, rhp, Oklahoma State
53. Matthew Leach, rhp, Long Island
54. Joshua Bradford, rhp, Hutchinson (Kan.) CC
55. Keith Bradley, ss, Connors State (Okla.) JC
56. Matt Johnson, 2b, South Park HS, Library, Pa.
57. Tim Bradley, rhp, Dixie (Utah) JC
58. Anthony Fisher, of, Cretin HS, Oakdale, Minn.
59. Mark Cridland, rhp, Ball HS, Galveston, Texas
60. Phillip Bailey, of, Westark (Ark.) CC
61. **Eric Iverson, of, Wilson HS, Fargo, N.D.**

SAN DIEGO PADRES

June—Regular Phase (14)

1. **Derrek Lee, 1b, El Camino HS, Sacramento**
2. **Matt LaChappa, lhp, El Capitan HS, Lakeside, Calif.**
3. **Matt Clement, rhp, Butler (Pa.) Area HS**
4. Tim Miller, rhp, Williamsport (Pa.) HS
5. **Hal Garrett, rhp, Brentwood (Tenn.) Academy**
6. **Greg Keagle, rhp, Florida International**
7. **Jason Schlutt, lhp, Central Florida**
8. **Derek Mix, rhp, San Bernardino Valley (Calif.) JC**
9. **Jason Thompson, 1b, Arizona**
10. Stacy Kleiner, c/3b, Taft HS, Tarzana, Calif.
11. Faruq Darcuiel, of, Fresno CC
12. **Darrick Duke, of, Texas**
13. **Gary Matthews Jr., of, Mission (Calif.) CC**
14. **DeVohn Duncan, rhp, Marist HS, Jersey City, N.J.**
15. Jose Colon, of, Eau Gallie HS, Melbourne, Fla.
16. **Brad Kaufman, rhp, Iowa State**
17. **Daniel Harpe, rhp, Serra HS, San Mateo, Calif.**
18. **Bryan Wolff, rhp, Oral Roberts**
19. Chris Logan, c, Southern Mississippi
20. Dan Cey, ss, El Camino Real HS, Woodland Hills, Calif.
21. Mark Hendrickson, lhp, Washington State
22. **Daniel Zanolla, ss, Purdue**
23. Chris Humphries, rhp, Cochise County (Ariz.) CC
24. **Chris Prieto, of, Nevada-Reno**
25. **Santiago Rivera, ss, Arizona State**
26. Mike Schiefelbein, rhp, Arizona
27. Frankie Sanders, ss, Riverview HS, Sarasota, Fla.
28. **Alan Meyer, rhp, Edison HS, Huntington Beach, Calif.**
29. **Chris West, 3b, East Carolina**
30. Nathan Koepke, 1b, Millikan HS, Long Beach
31. **Dickie Woodridge, 2b, LeMoyne**
32. **Leroy McKinnis, c, Jackson State**
33. **James Bostock, 2b, Eastern Michigan**
34. Corey Dillon, of, Franklin HS, Seattle
35. Dietrich Evans, c, Arizona Western JC
36. Travis Boyd, ss, UCLA
37. Kelan Washington, of, Lanier HS, Austin
38. Carlos Smith, ss, Anson County HS, Wadesboro, N.C.
39. Chris Havens, rhp, Central HS, Elkhart, Ind.
40. Ivan Loochkartt, of, Jordan HS, Long Beach
41. **Daniel Drewien, rhp, San Diego State**
42. **Obed Martinez, of, Rio Piedras, P.R.**
43. Brian Baklik, ss, El Campo (Texas) HS
44. Brent Bearden, rhp, Baylor
45. Brent Stentz, rhp, Hernando HS, Brooksville, Fla.
46. Etienne Hightower, of, Mount Lebanon (Pa.) HS
47. Brian Thompson, rhp, Northwest HS, Omaha
48. Robbie Reid, lhp, Spanish Fork (Utah) HS
49. William Bland, of, Dr. Phillips HS, Orlando
50. Oscar Hirschkorn, rhp, Kerman (Calif.) HS
51. Dexter Davis, ss, Jordan HS, Long Beach
52. Ken Wilson, c, South Mecklenburg HS, Charlotte
53. Brian Bejarano, ss, Alhambra HS, Laveen, Ariz.
54. Jason Kendler, Corona del Sol HS, Tempe, Ariz.
55. Greg Aiken, rhp, Temecula Valley (Calif.) HS
56. Rodrick Meyer, c, Stanford
57. Justin McConico, ss, Burke HS, Omaha
58. Gary Paul, 3b, Buena HS, Ventura, Calif.
59. Jonas Armenta, rhp, Bloomfield (N.M.) HS
60. Jeff Van Every, lhp, Benson HS, Omaha
61. Kyle Griffiths, c, Lake Michigan (Mich.) JC
62. Ryan Vandeweg, rhp, Grand Rapids (Mich.) JC
63. Kevin Coe, of, Simeon HS, Chicago
64. Russ Chambliss, of, Tucker HS, Glen Allen, Va.
65. Terry Adams, 3b, Eastern Commerce HS, Toronto
66. James Moore, ss, Sweetwater (Texas) HS
67. Byron Tribe, rhp, St. Thomas HS, Katy, Texas
68. Keith Dilgard, rhp, Raritan HS, Bridgewater, N.J.
69. Roger Main, 3b, Dundalk (Md.) CC
70. Larry Smith, c, DeMatha Catholic HS, Hyattsville, Md.
71. Donald Whitney, of, Cahokia (Ill.) HS
72. Scott Keithley, 2b, Alvin (Texas) HS
73. Isaac Byrd, of, Parkway Central HS, St. Louis
74. Stan Conti, of, Seneca Valley HS, Mars, Pa.
75. Keith Whitner, of, Lincoln HS, Los Angeles
76. David Yocum, lhp, Columbus HS, Miami
77. Donn Cunnigan, of, Southern California
78. Terrence Johnson, 1b/of, Guilford HS, Rockford, Ill.
79. **Byron Clark, lhp, Western New Mexico**
80. Chris Corn, rhp, Kansas
81. Joshua Gibbons, rhp, Lincoln Way HS, New Lenox, Ill.
82. Rob Bonanno, rhp, Florida
83. Larry Husted, 1b/of, Chaffey (Calif.) JC
84. Theodore Persell, of, East Los Angeles JC
85. Michael Brown, ss, Hazelwood West HS, Florissant, Mo.
86. Tim Farris, rhp, Newbury Park (Calif.) HS
87. Keith Evans, rhp, Crespi HS, Encino, Calif.
88. Eric Skaife, rhp, South HS, Torrance, Calif.
89. Jesse Shanon, 1b, Dos Pueblos HS, Goleta, Calif.
90. Mark Harriger, rhp, St. John Bosco HS, Lakewood, Calif.
91. Trevor Preston, rhp, Temecula Valley HS, Temecula, Calif.

SAN FRANCISCO GIANTS

June—Regular Phase (6)

1. **Steve Soderstrom, rhp, Fresno State**
2. **Chris Singleton, of, Nevada-Reno**
2. Macey Brooks, of, Kecoughtan HS, Hampton, Va. (Supplemental pick—71st—for loss of Type C free agent Mike Felder)
2. **Brett King, ss, South Florida** (Supplemental pick—72nd—for loss of Type C free agent Chris James)
3. **Don Denbow, of, Blinn (Texas) JC**
4. **Jay Canizaro, ss, Blinn (Texas) JC**
5. **Heath Altman, rhp, UNC Wilmington**
6. Pat Ryan, rhp, Apopka (Fla.) HS
7. **Keith Williams, of, Clemson**

8. **Brent Smith, rhp, Arizona State**
9. **Ivan Alvarez, lhp, Canoga Park, Calif.**
10. **Jason Myers, lhp, Chaffey (Calif.) JC**
11. **Brook Smith, lhp, Bradley**
12. **Kristin Franko, lhp, Ohio**
13. **Joel Galarza, c, Yabucoa, P.R.**
14. **Michael McMullen, rhp, Glendale (Calif.) JC**
15. **Bill Mueller, ss, Southwest Missouri State**
16. Mickey Callaway, rhp, Germantown (Tenn.) HS
17. **Chris Gump, 2b, Arizona**
18. **Doug Drumm, rhp, Rensselaer (N.Y.) Polytechnical Institute**
19. **Mark Gulseth, 1b, New Mexico**
20. **Robert Rector, rhp, Southwestern (Calif.) JC**
21. **Steve Bourgeois, rhp, Northeast Louisiana**
22. **Steven Day, lhp, Mesa State (Colo.)**
23. **Dan Barrett, c, Purdue**
24. Tim Conklin, rhp, Madison (Ore.) HS
25. Chris Ratliff, rhp, Laney (Calif.) JC
26. Tim Hicks, ss, Southwest HS, Macon, Ga.
27. Rodney Bonds, rhp, Union City (Tenn.) HS
28. Jason Grote, rhp, Centennial HS, Gresham, Ore.
29. Notorris Bray, of, Central Alabama CC
30. Rachaad Stewart, lhp, Triton (Ill.) JC
31. **David Tessicini, ss, Vermont**
32. **Brian Lootens, of, Arizona State**
33. **Matt Baumann, rhp, Maryland**
34. **Clark Anderson, rhp, George Fox (Ore.)**
35. **Brian Zaletel, 3b, Tampa**
36. Andrew Kalcounos, ss, DeMatha Catholic HS, Hyattsville, Md.
37. Daniel Fagley, c, Holy Cross HS, Riverton, N.J.
38. Jeff Tagliaferri, 1b, Kennedy HS, Granada Hills, Calif.
39. **Brian Benner, of, Capistrano Valley Christian HS, Mission Viejo, Calif.**
40. Chad Dube, rhp, Cambridge, Ontario
41. Anthony Hilde, of, Pendleton (Ore.) HS
42. Duane Stewart, of, Chino HS, Ontario, Calif.
43. Leonard McMillan, rhp, Crowder (Mo.) JC
44. Ryan Miller, ss/2b, JC of the Sequoias (Calif.)
45. William Dicken, ss, Bloomington (Ill.) HS
46. Tio Beall, rhp, South Salem (Ore.) HS
47. Stephen Logan, 3b, Oak Grove HS, Hattiesburg, Miss.
48. David Russell, c, Bishop McGuinness HS, Lewisville, N.C.
49. **Jon Sbrocco, 2b, Wright State**
50. **Todd Petering, of, Kansas State**
51. Micah Terrell, ss, Mitchell (Ind.) HS
52. **Chris Stasio, 1b, Barry (Fla.)**
53. **Michael Cecere, c, Rollins (Fla.)**
54. **Paul Reynolds, c, North Florida**
55. **Andrew Mason, of, Washington**

SEATTLE MARINERS

June—Regular Phase (1)

1. **Alex Rodriguez, ss, Westminster Christian HS, Miami**
2. (Pick to Brewers as compensation for Type A free agent Chris Bosio)
3. **Ed Randolph, 3b/of, Roosevelt HS, Dallas**
4. **Mike Collett, rhp, Southern California**
5. **David Cooper, rhp, Hesperia (Calif.) HS**
6. **Ken Cloude, rhp, McDonogh HS, Baltimore**
7. **Tim Schweitzer, lhp, Arizona**
8. Greg Hillengas, of, Seminole (Fla.) HS
9. **Rob Krueger, lhp, Western Michigan**
10. **Dean Crow, rhp, Baylor**
11. **Casey Craig, rhp, Napoleon HS, Jackson, Mich.**
12. **Randy Jorgensen, 1b, Washington**
13. **Rafael Carmona, rhp, Indian Hills (Iowa) CC**
14. **Brian Sosa, rhp, San Bernardino Valley (Calif.) JC**
15. **Chris Green, rhp, Grossmont (Calif.) JC**
16. **John Daniels, rhp, Mount San Antonio (Calif.) JC**
17. **Chad Dunavan, of, Howard (Texas) JC**
18. **Tim Bruce, rhp, Detroit Mercy**
19. Douglas Forde, lhp, Riverview HS, Sarasota, Fla.
20. Chris Dean, 2b, Seminole State (Okla.) JC
21. **Chris Dumas, of, Alabama Southern CC**
22. **Matt Apana, rhp, Hawaii**
23. **Mike Barger, of, Saint Louis**
24. **Joe Berube, c, Presbyterian (S.C.)**
25. **Daleon Isom, of, Benton Harbor (Mich.) HS**
26. **Russell Jacobs, rhp, Winter Haven (Fla.) HS**
27. **Joe Mathis, ss/of, Strom Thurmond HS, Johnston, S.C.**
28. **Jon Updike, rhp, Pensacola (Fla.) JC**
29. **Andy Augustine, c, Triton (Ill.) JC**
30. **Manny Patel, 2b, Yale**
31. Brandon Hoalton, rhp, Rancho Santiago (Calif.) JC
32. **John Tejcek, of, Arizona**
33. Chris Parker, rhp, Gonzalez Tate HS, Pensacola, Fla.
34. Grant Jondahl, rhp, Amador Valley HS, Pleasanton, Calif.
35. John White, c, University Christian HS, Jacksonville
36. **Willie Wilkins, of, Atlantic HS, Boynton Beach, Fla.**
37. Brad Brasser, rhp, Grand Rapids (Mich.) Christian HS
38. **Kelvin Mitchell, lhp, Choctaw County HS, Butler, Ala.**
39. Brandon Kleitch, of, Cibola HS, Rio Rancho, N.M.
40. Anibal Ramirez, ss, Miami-Dade CC Wolfson
41. Chris Champanois, c, Columbia Central (Mich.) HS
42. Heath Webster, rhp, Peninsula HS, Rancho Palo Verde, Calif.
43. Matt Wimmer, of, Washington
44. Thomas Redd, of, El Camino (Calif.) JC
45. Jeremy Morris, c, Monroe HS, Quincy, Fla.
46. **Johnny Cardenas, c, Texas Christian**
47. Marcus Jones, rhp, Esperanza HS, Yorba Linda, Calif.
48. Bryan Belflower, rhp, Oak Ridge HS, Orlando
49. Jeremy Reeves, lhp, Lincoln Trail (Ill.) JC
50. Jeff Harris, rhp, Contra Costa (Calif.) JC
51. **Roy Miller, ss, Washington State**
52. Ryan Mullen, rhp, Boca Ciega HS, St. Petersburg, Fla.
53. Kevin McCoy, rhp, Triton (Ill.) JC
54. Matt Wise, rhp, Bonita HS, La Verne, Calif.
55. **Jason Cook, ss, Virginia**
56. Chris Knowles, 1b, Blinn (Texas) JC
57. John Romero, rhp, San Fernando HS, Sylmar, Calif.
58. Chris Kelly, lhp, Hamilton HS, Inglewood, Calif.
59. Ricky Tutson, of, Willow Run HS, Ypsilanti, Mich.
60. Barret Markey, rhp, St. Petersburg (Fla.) HS
61. Robert Coddington, c, Grossmont HS, El Cajon, Calif.
62. Michael Rodgers, lhp, Olney (Ill.) HS
63. Arnold Brathwarte, ss, St. Joseph's HS, Frederiksted, Vt.
64. Justin Bice, rhp, Kentwood HS, Kent, Wash.
65. **Scott Smith, of, Texas A&M**
66. Aaron Keal, rhp, Labette County (Kan.) CC
67. George Rayborn, rhp, Purvis (Miss.) HS
68. Cirilo Cruz, 3b, Miami-Dade CC North
69. **Rob Ippolito, rhp, Arizona**
70. Jonathon Choate, of, Blinn (Texas) JC

TEXAS RANGERS

June—Regular Phase (15)

1. (Pick to Blue Jays as compensation lor Type A free agent Tom Henke)
1. **Mike Bell, 3b, Moeller HS, Cincinnati** (Supplemental pick—30th—for loss of Type A free agent Jose Guzman)
2. **Edwin Diaz, 2b, Vega Alta, P.R.** (Pick from Cubs as compensation for Guzman)
2. (Pick to Blue Jays as compensation for Type B free agent Manny Lee)
3. **Andrew Vessel, of, Kennedy HS, Richmond, Calif.**
4. **Toure Knighton, lhp, Tucson HS**
5. **Rod Walker, ss, Hyde Park HS, Chicago**
6. **Mark Ocasio, rhp, Carolina, P.R.**
7. **Dan Smith, rhp, Girard (Kan.) HS**
8. **Jack Stanczak, 3b, Villanova**
9. **Pete Hartmann, lhp, Oklahoma City**
10. **Brian Thomas, of, Texas A&M**
11. **James Franklin, rhp, Carson Newman (Tenn.)**
12. **Osmani Estrada, ss, Canoga Park, Calif.**
13. **Marc Sagmoen, of, Nebraska**
14. **Alexis Cabreja, of, Canoga Park, Calif.**
15. **Chris Unrat, c, Arkansas State**

16. **Tim Cossins, c, Oklahoma**
17. **Brian Clark, of, Houston**
18. **Ryan Falmier, rhp, Goreville HS, Tunnel Hill, Ill.**
19. **Wesley Sims, 2b, Austin Peay**
20. Cesar Cerda, c, Southridge HS, Miami
21. **Leland Macon, of, St. Louis CC-Meramec**
22. **Michael Jackson, rhp, Texas HS, Texarkana, Texas**
23. Jason Dyess, rhp, McLaurin HS, Florence, Miss.
24. **Eric Moody, rhp, Erskine (S.C.)**
25. **Larry Ephan, c, Hawaii Pacific**
26. **Eric Dominow, 1b, Western Michigan**
27. **Lonnie Goldberg, 2b, George Mason**
28. **Jeffrey Davis, rhp, Massasoit (Mass.) CC**
29. Michael Spence, rhp, South Gwinnett HS, Lithonia, Ga.
30. **Steve Ouimet, 1b, Glen Head North Shore HS, Glenwood Landing, N.Y.**
31. **Michael Hill, of, Harvard**
32. **Scott Smith, rhp, Kentucky**
33. Richard Collins, rhp/1b, Stockbridge (Ga.) HS
34. Jamie Phillips, c, Redan HS, Stone Mountain, Ga.
35. **Gardner O'Flynn, lhp, New Hampshire**
36. **Robert Kell, lhp, Temple**
37. **Gregory Lewis, of, New Hampshire**
38. **Dom Gatti, of, Adelphi (N.Y.)**
39. Ivan Zweig, rhp, Tulane
40. **Ray DeSimone, ss, Long Island**
41. **Mike Cather, rhp, California**
42. **Greg Willming, rhp, Evansville**
43. **Joe Morvay, rhp, Ohio**
44. Cajen Rhodes, 1b, Berkmar HS, Lilburn, Ga.
45. **Matt Huff, of, Northwestern**
46. Bryan Cunningham, rhp, Monte Vista HS, Spring Valley, Calif.
47. Rex Stevens, rhp, Wheeler HS, Marietta, Ga.
48. Michael Jackson, of, JC of Marin (Calif.)
49. Nicholas Caiazzo, c, Deering HS, Portland, Maine
50. Brian Tickell, rhp, Grand Prairie (Texas) HS
51. Juan Veras, ss, Palm Beach (Fla.) JC
52. Stephen Cardona, rhp, San Joaquin Delta (Calif.) JC
53. Daniel Schourek, rhp, Montgomery (Md.) CC
54. William Pepper, 1b, Houston (Miss.) HS
55. Kenneth Payne, 1b, St. Louis CC-Meramec
56. Robert Tucker, 1b, Robert E. Lee HS, Huntsville, Ala.
57. Steve Frascatore, rhp, C.W. Post (N.Y.)
58. Rayvon McGriff, of, Del Mar HS, San Jose
59. Frank Chapman, rhp, MacArthur HS, San Antonio

TORONTO BLUE JAYS

June—Regular Phase (26)

1. **Chris Carpenter, rhp, Trinity HS, Manchester, N.H.** (Pick from Rangers as compensation for Type A free agent Tom Henke)
1. (Pick to Brewers as compensation for Type A free agent Paul Molitor)
1. **Matt Farner, of, East Pennsboro HS, Enola, Pa.** (Supplemental pick—37th—for loss of Type A free agent David Cone)
1. **Jeremy Lee, rhp, Galesburg (Ill.) HS** (Supplemental pick—40th—for loss of Henke)
1. **Mark Lukasiewicz, lhp, Brevard (Fla.) CC** (Supplemental pick—41st—for loss of Type A free agent Jimmy Key)
2. **Anthony Medrano, ss, Jordan HS, Long Beach** (Pick from Royals as compensation for Cone)
2. **Ryan Jones, 1b, Irvine (Calif.) HS** (Pick from Rangers as compensation for Type B free agent Manny Lee)
2. (Pick to Athletics as compensation for Type A free agent Dave Stewart)
3. **Mike Romano, rhp, Tulane** (Pick from Yankees as compensation for Key)
3. **Joe Young, rhp, Ainlay HS, Fort McMurray, Alberta**
4. Thad Busby, c/of, Pace (Fla.) HS
5. **Charles Bourne, ss, Muir HS, Altadena, Calif.**
6. Rob DeBoer, c, South Carolina
7. Donny Barker, rhp, Leander (Texas) HS
8. **Matt Stone, lhp, Vista (Calif.) HS**
9. **Oreste Volkert, rhp, La Habra (Calif.) HS**
10. **Ruben Corral, rhp, Arroyo HS, El Monte, Calif.**
11. Larry Mohs, rhp, Nutley (N.J.) HS
12. **Brent Coe, lhp, Franklin Central HS, Indianapolis**
13. **Adam Melhuse, 3b, UCLA**
14. Chris Freeman, rhp, Tennessee
15. **Tyson Hartshorn, rhp, Lamar (Colo.) HS**
16. Shane Dennis, lhp, Wichita State
17. **Mike Johnson, rhp, Salisbury Composite HS, Edmonton**
18. **David Morgan, c, Harvard**
19. **David Sinnes, rhp, Notre Dame**
20. Aaron Gardin, of, Chaparral HS, Scottsdale, Ariz.
21. Daniel Crawford, rhp, Jersey Village HS, Houston
22. Steve Johnson, of, Michigan State
23. **Rob Steinert, rhp, North Carolina State**
24. **Brian Grant, lhp, Diablo Valley (Calif.) JC**
25. **William Daunic, 1b, Vanderbilt**
26. **Victor Davila, ss, Westchester (N.Y.) CC**
27. **Michael Toney, rhp, Cochise County (Ariz.) CC**
28. John Nape, rhp, Lewis (Ill.)
29. **Rob Mummau, ss, James Madison**
30. **Richard Lutz, c, Elizabethtown (Pa.)**
31. Brad Feldewerth, rhp, Fort Zumwalt North HS, Wentzville, Mo
32. James Bowman, lhp, Highline HS, Seattle
33. Jon Phillips, rhp, South Cobb HS, Austell, Ga.
34. Eric Booth, of, Bassfield (Miss.) HS
35. Michael Diebolt, lhp, Mayfield HS, Mayfield Village, Ohio
36. Scott Henderson, rhp, Villa Park (Calif.) HS
37. **Christian Roggendorf, 1b, Dowling (N.Y.)**
38. Ryan Brannan, rhp, Huntington Beach (Calif.) HS
39. James Smith, of, Greensboro HS, Quincy, Fla.
40. Adrian Poindexter, ss, Caldwell HS, Columbus, Miss.
41. David Sumner, of, Pittsburgh
42. Mane Gavric, of, Mather HS, Chicago
43. **Ivan Nobles, of, Brandon (Fla.) HS**
44. David Meyer, lhp, Kansas
45. Brian Haebig, lhp, Sahuaro HS, Tucson
46. Mark Macias, rhp, Ridgewood HS, Norridge, Ill.
47. Herman Gordan, of, El Camino HS, Oceanside, Calif.
48. Ronald Dempsey, of, Lufkin (Texas) HS
49. Jason Monk, rhp, Mississippi Gulf Coast JC
50. **David Fogle, rhp, Torrance HS, Lomita, Calif.**
51. Brian Thomas, rhp, Mount Pleasant (Texas) HS
52. Joseph Nelson, ss, Notre Dame HS, Alameda, Calif.
53. Jaime Roque, 2b, Vernon Regional (Texas) JC
54. Jim Mann, rhp, Massasoit (Mass.) CC
55. Michael Hannah, of, Bremen (Ga.) HS
56. **Victor Rodriguez, rhp, Okaloosa-Walton (Fla.) CC**

1994 Wilson ties bonus record after going No. 1, with Booty topping him weeks later

There was little suspense about who would be the No. 1 pick in the 1994 draft. For weeks, most everyone projected the Mets would take Florida State righthander Paul Wilson, and that's exactly what happened.

"I'm going to the Big Apple, baby," Wilson said, cameras flashing in his face, as the selection was announced in Omaha before the College World Series. "I'm going to the Big Apple."

After four weeks of amicable negotiations, the Mets signed Wilson to a contract that included a $1.55 million bonus, temporarily tying him with 1991 No. 1 pick Brien Taylor for the biggest bonus in draft history. But high school shortstop Josh Booty, the No. 5 pick, signed with the Marlins a few weeks later for $1.6 million.

The Mets' final considerations other than Wilson were outfielder Ben Grieve and righthander Dustin Hermanson, who went to the Athletics and Padres at Nos. 2 and 3.

Oakland decided at the last minute to pass on Hermanson for Grieve, whose father Tom was general manager of the Rangers at the time. Grieve became the first son of a first-round pick to be drafted in the opening round. Tom was the sixth overall pick in the June 1966 draft by the Washington Senators, but he never had a chance to draft his son because the Rangers' first pick didn't come until No. 56.

"I've tried to be objective, but sometimes the worst judge of talent is a player's own father," Tom said. "I can say, though, that he's a lot better ballplayer than I ever was. He's bigger and stronger and has a beautiful natural swing that I didn't have. The only thing I could do was run a little faster."

Grieve signed for $1.2 million and was American League rookie of the year by 1998. He went to the Devil Rays in a trade after the 2000 season, however, and his career went into a rapid decline. Neither Wilson nor Hermanson lived up to their promise, either. Wilson's career was dented by injuries, and while he had a few productive years with the Reds he compiled a 40-58, 4.86 record in just seven major league seasons. Hermanson pitched in 12 seasons, compiling 1,283 innings as both a starter and reliever, and finished with a 73-78, 4.21 record.

The most noted talent in the 1994 draft might have been Booty, though. And as it turned out, he was the biggest bust of all.

The Louisiana high school star was arguably the nation's best high school player in both baseball and football. He would have been a shortstop and quarterback at Louisiana State had he not signed.

Josh Booty (left) signed for $1.6 million weeks after Paul Wilson got $1.55 million

"You'd better be good," said Marlins owner Wayne Huizenga, smiling at Booty at a press conference soon after signing him.

"You feel a lot of emotions when you do this sort of thing," Booty said. "To get this deal . . . I hope I'm here a long time. I hope Miami is in my future soon."

Booty did reach Miami, but it was more an act of desperation by the Marlins than anything Booty did to merit the promotion. He ended up with seven hits in 26 career big league at-bats.

Booty's signing had been huge news in Louisiana, and the call of home eventually proved too much to resist. Frustrated with his progress in baseball, Booty dropped it after the 1998 season and went back to LSU to play football. His career .198 minor league average told the story. He had an up-and-down football career at LSU but eventually did hook on with the NFL's Cleveland Browns as a backup quarterback for a short time.

Led by Booty, bonuses jumped again in 1994, to an average of almost $796,000. Five first-round picks got $1 million or more, and bonus inflation continued along at a rate of about 30 percent. All told, 65 players got bonuses of at least $200,000 in 1994. That figure included $1.2 million paid in January by the Dodgers to South Korea pitcher Chan Ho Park, which was the largest bonus ever paid to a foreign player at the time.

Deja Vu For Varitek

It still wasn't enough for Jason Varitek, who knew that turning down $450,000 from the Twins in 1993 and returning to Georgia Tech for his senior season could leave him in a precarious position for the 1994 draft.

The end of his college eligibility left him little leverage, so the Mariners took him 14th overall and made him a $400,000 offer. Varitek wanted around $800,000. The major league strike put everything on hold for several months, and Varitek returned to class at Georgia Tech with no eligibility remaining to complete his degree. He argued that Seattle would hold his rights only until a week before the 1995 draft, when he would become a free agent able to negotiate with any club.

"It's a matter of wanting to be treated fairly in the market," said Varitek, who was represented by Scott Boras. "It's to the point where they're taking advantage of my position, saying I should get half of what I'm worth."

Varitek made his situation even murkier in January 1995 by signing a contract with the St. Paul Saints of the independent Northern League. Major League Baseball, though, ruled he would have to go through the draft again in 1995. A pivotal arbitration hearing was avoided when the Mariners and Varitek compromised on a $650,000 bonus.

The Mariners traded Varitek and Derek Lowe to the Red Sox in a deadline deal in July 1997 to acquire Heathcliff Slocumb. Varitek established himself as a fixture behind the plate for Boston by 1999.

The Red Sox scored more immediate returns from the '94 draft class when they got shortstop Nomar Garicaparra—another Georgia Tech product—with the 12th overall pick. Garciaparra was a five-time all-star in Boston before getting traded in the middle of the 2004 season.

The Astros made history by selecting catcher Ramon Castro with the 17th overall pick, making him the first Puerto Rican ever drafted in the first round.

Puerto Ricans were not subject to the draft until 1989. All three San Juan newspapers carried the news on their back pages.

And as usual the Astros were the last team to drop out of the draft, continuing until the 98th round.

DRAFT 94: FIRST-ROUND PICKS

No.	Club	Player, Pos.	School	Hometown	Ht.	Wt.	B-T	Age
1.	Mets	Paul Wilson, rhp	Florida State	Orlando	6-5	217	R-R	21
2.	Athletics	Ben Grieve, of	Martin HS	Arlington, Texas	6-4	195	L-R	18
3.	Padres	Dustin Hermanson, rhp	Kent	Springfield, Ohio	6-2	185	R-R	21
4.	Brewers	Antone Williamson, 3b	Arizona State	Torrance, Calif.	6-1	185	L-R	20
5.	Marlins	Josh Booty, ss	Evangel Christian HS	Shreveport, La.	6-3	215	R-R	19
6.	Angels	McKay Christensen, of	Clovis West HS	Fresno	5-11	175	L-L	18
7.	Rockies	Doug Million, lhp	Sarasota HS	Sarasota, Fla.	6-3	175	L-L	18
8.	Twins	Todd Walker, 2b	Louisiana State	Bossier City, La.	6-0	170	L-R	21
9.	Reds	C.J. Nitkowski, lhp	St. John's	Suffern, N.Y.	6-2	185	L-L	21
10.	Indians	Jaret Wright, rhp	Katella HS	Anaheim, Calif.	6-2	218	R-R	18
11.	Pirates	Mark Farris, ss	Angleton HS	Angleton, Texas	6-2	190	L-R	19
12.	Red Sox	Nomar Garciaparra, ss	Georgia Tech	Whittier, Calif.	6-0	162	R-R	20
13.	Dodgers	Paul Konerko, c	Chapparal HS	Scottsdale, Ariz.	6-2	195	R-R	18
14.	Mariners	Jason Varitek, c	Georgia Tech	Altamonte Springs, Fla.	6-2	215	B-R	22
15.	Cubs	Jayson Peterson, rhp	East HS	Denver	6-3	175	B-R	18
16.	Royals	Matt Smith, lhp	Grants Pass HS	Grants Pass, Ore.	6-4	225	L-L	18
17.	Astros	Ramon Castro, c	Rivera HS	Vega Baja, P.R.	6-3	195	R-R	18
18.	Tigers	Cade Gaspar, rhp	Pepperdine	Mission Viejo, Calif.	6-3	185	R-R	20
19.	Cardinals	Bret Wagner, lhp	Wake Forest	New Cumberland, Pa.	5-11	190	L-L	21
20.	Mets	Terrence Long, 1b	Stanhope Elmore HS	Millbrook, Ala.	6-1	180	L-L	18
21.	Expos	Hiram Bocachica, ss	Rexville HS	Bayamon, P.R.	5-11	168	R-R	18
22.	Giants	Dante Powell, of	Cal State Fullerton	Long Beach	6-2	185	R-R	20
23.	Phillies	Carlton Loewer, rhp	Mississippi State	Eunice, La.	6-4	204	R-R	20
24.	Yankees	Brian Buchanan, 1b/of	Virginia	Clifton, Va.	6-4	215	R-R	20
25.	Astros	Scott Elarton, rhp	Lamar HS	Lamar, Colo.	6-8	225	R-R	18
26.	White Sox	Mark Johnson, c	Warner Robins HS	Warner Robins, Ga.	6-0	185	L-R	18
27.	Braves	Jacob Shumate, rhp	Hartsville HS	Hartsville, S.C.	6-1	185	R-R	18
28.	Blue Jays	Kevin Witt, ss	Bishop Kenny HS	Jacksonville	6-4	185	L-R	18

1994

CLUB-BY-CLUB SELECTIONS

ATLANTA BRAVES

June—Regular Phase (27)

1. **Jacob Shumate, rhp, Hartsville (S.C.) HS**
2. **Corey Pointer, c, Waxahachie (Texas) HS** (Pick from Red Sox as compensation for Type B free agent Otis Nixon)
2. **George Lombard, of, Lovett HS, Atlanta**
3. **Joe Giuliano, rhp, Baden HS, Hamilton, Ohio**
4. **Eric Pickett, 1b/of, Independence HS, San Jose**
5. **Mike Russell, lhp, Nacogdoches (Texas) HS**
6. **Derek Foote, c, Wake Forest-Rolesville HS, Wake Forest, N.C.**
7. **Ron Wright, 1b, Kamiakin HS, Kennewick, Wash.**
8. **Billy Blythe, rhp, Bryan Station HS, Lexington, Ky.**
9. **Jason Bass, of, Fayette County HS, Fayette, Ala.**
10. **Wes Helms, ss/rhp, Ashbrook HS, Gastonia, N.C.**
11. **Joaquin Johnson, 1b/of, Oakland Tech HS, Oakland**
12. Scott Downs, lhp, Pleasure Ridge HS, Louisville
13. **William Wise, rhp, Sumter County HS, Plains, Ga.**
14. **Robert Duncan, of, Ellison HS, Killeen, Texas**
15. **Kendall Hill, rhp, Jefferson Davis (Ala.) JC**
16. Scott McAllister, lhp, Lovett HS, Atlanta
17. **Bennie Robbins, rhp, Pine Forest HS, Pensacola, Fla.**
18. **Derrin Ebert, lhp, Hesperia (Calif.) HS**
19. **Chris Gobert, lhp, Lee (Texas) JC**
20. **Ray McWhite, c/3b, Thomas (Maine)**
21. **Chris Gongora, lhp, Glendale (Ariz.) CC**
22. **Rich Spiegel, c, Anne Arundel (Md.) CC**
23. **Brett Newell, ss, Washington**
24. **Dwayne Jacobs, rhp, First Coast HS, Jacksonville**
25. **Tony Wood, 2b, Eastern Oregon State**
26. Jeff Garff, rhp, Viewmont HS, Bountiful, Utah
27. Jason Pozo, ss, Central Regional HS, Bayville, N.J.
28. Skip Ames, rhp, Howard (Texas) JC
29. Matt Herr, rhp, Hotchkiss HS, New Windsor, N.Y.
30. **Adam Mullen, c, Beaufort (S.C.) HS**
31. **Gus Kennedy, of, Nevada**
32. Mark Hendrickson, lhp, Washington State
33. Jeremy Salyers, rhp, Pound (Va.) HS
34. Doug Bridges, lhp, Spring Valley HS, Columbia, S.C.
35. **Antonio Williams, of, Tampa Bay Technical HS, Tampa**
36. **Ken Raines, lhp, Western Michigan**
37. **Sadiel Suarez, ss, Miami Senior HS, Miami**
38. Jim Egan, c, Champlin Park HS, Brooklyn Center, Minn.
39. **Brandon Hoalton, rhp, Rancho Santiago (Calif.) JC**
40. **Dwight Lewis, of, Long Beach (Calif.) CC**
41. **Colby Weaver, c, Florida State**
42. **Angel Espada, 2b, Salinas, P.R.**
43. Jim Sipkovich, lhp, Marina HS, Huntington Beach, Calif.
44. **Zach Collins, lhp, Essex (Md.) CC**
45. Matt Lubozynski, lhp, Choctawhatchee HS, Fort Walton Beach, Fla.
46. Drew Chaney, rhp, South HS, Springfield, Ill.
47. Pete Cuellar, lhp, Poly HS, Long Beach
48. Rich Hills, ss, Oklahoma
49. Fred Knox, of, Eldorado HS, Albuquerque
50. Bryan Senior, of, Brookstone HS, Columbus, Ga.
51. Larry Barnes, 1b, Bakersfield (Calif.) JC
52. Derrick Langford, of, Contra Costa (Calif.) JC
53. **Wilton Person, of, Florida A&M**
54. Troy Silva, rhp, Cuesta (Calif.) JC
55. **Charles Fritz, lhp, West Chester (Pa.)**
56. Jason Cook, of, Jefferson Davis (Ala.) JC
57. Marlin Hardy, of, Anderson HS, Austin, Texas

BALTIMORE ORIOLES

June—Regular Phase (20)

1. (Pick to Mets as compensation for Type A free agent Sid Fernandez)
2. **Tommy Davis, 1b, Southern Mississippi**
3. **Roger Worley, rhp, Quartz Hill (Calif.) HS**
4. **Jason Rogers, lhp, Nevada**
5. **Todd LaRocca, rhp/ss, Stanford**
6. **Brandon Huntsman, rhp, Pleasant Grove (Utah) HS**
7. **Noel Ramos, 1b, Isabela, P.R.**
8. Richard Welsh, ss, Germanton Academy, Blue Bell, Pa.
9. **Chris Fussell, rhp, Clay HS, Oregon, Ohio**
10. Jason Hairston, c, Jefferson HS, Portland, Ore.
11. **Brian Kerr, of, Farmington (N.M.) HS**
12. **Todd Dyess, rhp, Tulane**
13. **Sean Hugo, 1b/of, Oklahoma State**
14. **Kedric Porter, of, Hillsborough HS, Tampa, Fla.**
15. **Chris Kirgan, 1b, Northern Colorado**
16. **Rachaad Stewart, lhp, Triton (Ill.) JC**
17. **Michael Nadeau, 2b, George Fox (Ore.)**
18. John Sneed, rhp, Westfield HS, Houston, Texas
19. Matt Leviton, lhp, De Matha HS, Adelphi, Md.
20. **Rolando Avila, of, Long Beach State**
21. **Mike Wolff, 1b, Miami (Ohio)**
22. Ryan Young, rhp, Mississippi
23. **Tom D'Aguila, of, North Carolina Wesleyan**
24. **Shawn Bates, lhp, New Mexico JC**
25. Michael Young, of, Bishop Amat HS, Covina, Calif.
26. **Brad Crills, rhp, Mansfield (Pa.)**
27. **Matt Marenghi, rhp, Stanford**
28. **Frank Harmer, c, Brevard (Fla.) CC**
29. **Craig Daedelow, ss, Huntington Beach (Calif.) HS**
30. **Pedro Ortiz, of, Levittown, P.R.**
31. **Chris Sauritch, 2b, Southern Illinois**
32. **Tim Daigle, lhp, Nicholls State**
33. **Rick Short, 3b, Western Illinois**
34. Robert Conway, rhp, Tulane
35. Bradley Wagers, rhp, Parkland (Ill.) JC
36. Billy Oliver, rhp, Greenwood HS, Bowling Green, Ky.
37. Chris Kennedy, rhp, Quitman HS, Shubuta, Miss.
38. **Ryan Hendricks, 1b, St. Andrews (N.C.)**
39. **Todd Brown, of, Florida**
40. **Derek Brown, 2b, South Hagerstown HS, Hagerstown, Md.**
41. Steven Cook, rhp, Blair (Neb.) HS
42. Allen Sebold, c, Northern Garrett HS, Grantsville, Md.
43. Chris Blue, ss, Easton HS, Easton, Md.
44. Brian August, ss, St. Marks HS, Wilmington, Del.

BOSTON RED SOX

June—Regular Phase (12)

1. **Nomar Garciaparra, ss, Georgia Tech**
2. (Pick to Braves as compensation for Type A free agent Otis Nixon)
3. **Brian Rose, rhp, Dartmouth (Mass.) HS**
4. **Rob Welch, rhp, Twin Falls (Idaho) HS**
5. **Brian Barkley, lhp, Midway HS, Waco, Texas**
6. **Joe Mamott, rhp, Canisius**
7. **Denis McLaughlin, rhp, Old Dominion**
8. **Chad Barnhardt, c, Lake Wales (Fla.) HS**
9. **Chris Allison, 2b, Bradley**
10. **Damien Sapp, c, Pleasant Grove (Utah) HS**
11. **Donnie Sadler, ss, Valley Mills (Texas) HS**
12. **Antonio Santiago, lhp, Carolina, P.R.**
13. **Carl Pavano, rhp, Southington (Conn.) HS**
14. **Mike Jacobs, rhp, East Carolina**

15. **Matt Bazzani, c, UC Santa Barbara**
16. **Chuck Malloy, rhp, St. Joseph's**
17. Robert Moore, rhp, Hawaii
18. **Michael Coleman, of, Stratford HS, Nashville, Tenn.**
19. **Tony DeRosso, 1b, Colquitt County HS, Moultrie, Ga.**
20. **Bartt Carney, of, Indian Hills (Iowa) CC**
21. **Chris Westcott, rhp, New Orleans**
22. Shawn Rogers, of, Hawaii
23. Casey Child, of, Mountain View HS, Orem, Utah
24. **Robert Butler, lhp, Rend Lake (Ill.) JC**
25. **Marc Lewis, of, Calhoun (Ala.) CC**
26. **Jayson Black, rhp, Crestview HS, Convoy, Ohio**
27. **Rawlin Goodwin, of, Sulphur (La.) HS**
28. Torrance Miller, of, South Georgia JC
29. **Nathan Barns, of, Central HS, Rapid City, S.D.**
30. John McNeese, lhp, Mississippi
31. Dave Elliott, of, Western Michigan
32. Wayne Montgomery, rhp, Stratford Academy, Macon, Ga.
33. **John Raifstanger, 2b, Springfield (Mass.)**
34. Dave Maurer, lhp, Howard (Texas) JC
35. Derrick Lewis, rhp, Lanier HS, Montgomery, Ala.
36. Angel Diaz, c, Lake Gibson HS, Lakeland, Fla.
37. Jack Koch, rhp, Osceola HS, Kissimmee, Fla.
38. Joe Robinson, ss, Indian Hills (Iowa) CC
39. Tim Palmer, c, Fresno (Calif.) CC
40. Pat Daneker, rhp, Loyalsock Township HS, Williamsport, Pa.
41. Jessie Thompson, of, Hinds (Miss.) CC
42. Ken Arnold, 3b, Chipola (Fla.) JC
43. Dexter Battle, 1b, Hillsborough HS, Tampa, Fla.
44. Mike Whitley, rhp, Southwest Missouri State
45. **Rene Justiniano, rhp, Triton (Ill.) JC**
46. **Chris Kurek, c, St. Bonaventure**
47. Jamey Price, rhp, Mississippi

CALIFORNIA ANGELS

June—Regular Phase (6)

1. **McKay Christensen, of, Clovis West HS, Fresno**
2. **Norm Hutchins, of, Lincoln HS, Yonkers, N.Y.**
3. **Paul Failla, ss, Notre Dame**
4. **Matt Beaumont, lhp, Ohio State**
5. **Greg Morris, ss, UC Davis**
6. **Jason Dickson, rhp, Northeastern Oklahoma A&M JC**
7. **Richard Stuart, of, Arecibo, P.R.**
8. **Nick Skuse, rhp, Sonoma State (Calif.)**
9. **Jayson Sears, c, Henderson (Texas) HS**
10. **Rob Bonanno, rhp, Florida**
11. **Kevin Young, 3b/of, Central Michigan**
12. Derek Baker, 3b, Tustin (Calif.) HS
13. **Ariel Delgado, of, Carolina, P.R.**
14. **Bret Hemphill, c, Cal State Fullerton**
15. **Mike Freehill, rhp, San Diego State**
16. **George Parker, ss, Tennessee State**
17. **Mike Holtz, lhp, Clemson**
18. **Keith Coe, rhp, Old Dominion**
19. Todd Sears, 1b/rhp, Ankeny (Iowa) HS
20. Dustan Mohr, of, Oak Grove HS, Hattiesburg, Miss.
21. Brian Riley, rhp, Miami-Dade CC South
22. **Keith Volkman, lhp, Glen Burnie HS, Pasadena, Md.**
23. Corky Miller, c, Yucaipa (Calif.) HS
24. Carlos Vidal, c, Miami-Dade CC Wolfson
25. **Denny Van Pelt, 1b, Radford**
26. Paul Mintz, lhp, North Brunswick HS, Leland, N.C.
27. **Saul Rodriguez, ss, Southwestern (Calif.) JC**
28. Adam Walker, lhp, La Cueva HS, Albuquerque
29. Brian Blessie, rhp, Butler County (Kan.) CC
30. Winston Lee, rhp, Crescenta Valley HS, La Crescenta, Calif.
31. **Ryan Wheeler, ss/2b, Penn State**
32. **Mike Fontana, rhp, Long Beach State**
33. Rudy Rosales, rhp, Tucson (Ariz.) HS
34. **Dave Sick, rhp, San Jose State**
35. Michael Leach, rhp, Osceola HS, Seminole, Fla.
36. Tim Logan, of, Kennedy HS, Richmond, Calif.
37. Gary Thompson, of, Morse HS, San Diego
38. **Jeremy Ruby, 1b/lhp, Valley View HS, Eynon, Pa.**
39. Brian Nelson, c, Sarasota (Fla.) HS
40. **Don Nestor, rhp, South Florida**
41. Ryan Hammons, 1b, San Diego Mesa JC
42. Eric Knott, lhp, Edison (Fla.) CC
43. Kevin Nicholson, ss, Queen Elizabeth HS, Surrey, B.C
44. Steve Quinteros, rhp, Montgomery HS, San Diego
45. **Joey Jackson, 2b, Wichita State**

CHICAGO CUBS

June—Regular Phase (15)

1. **Jayson Peterson, rhp, East HS, Denver**
2. **Brian Stephenson, rhp, UCLA**
3. **Javier Martinez, rhp, Bayamon, P.R.**
4. **Jason Kelley, rhp, Suwanee HS, Live Oak, Fla.**
5. **Barry Fennell, lhp, Holy Cross HS, Pennsauken, N.J.**
6. **Ed Faulkner, rhp, Shoals (Ala.) CC**
7. Tim Spindler, rhp/ss, Washingtonville (N.Y.) HS
8. **Sean Bogle, rhp, Indiana State**
9. **Jason Ryan, rhp, Immaculata HS, Somerville, N.J.**
10. **Shawn Box, rhp, Schreiner (Texas)**
11. **David Crutchfield, of, Montgomery HS, Rockville, Md.**
12. **Marty Gazarek, of, Indiana**
13. **Michael McGehee, c, Browne HS, Phoenix, Ariz.**
14. **Kevin Coe, of, Laredo (Texas) JC**
15. **Ryan Casey, rhp, Virginia Wesleyan**
16. Joey Cranford, ss/2b, Stratford Academy, Macon, Ga.
17. **Jason Stevenson, rhp, Chattahoochee Valley (Ala.) CC**
18. **Roark Birsner, rhp, Edgewood Regional HS, Berlin, N.J.**
19. **Ricky Freeman, 1b, Houston**
20. **Andy Holin, c, Jacksonville**
21. **Jeff Havens, rhp, San Jacinto (Texas) JC**
22. Martin Barnett, rhp, Iowa Western CC
23. **Christian Jackson, of, Riverdale Baptist HS, Bowie, Md.**
24. Brad Hastings, lhp, South Georgia JC
25. **Joseph Montelongo, rhp, Truett-McConnell (Ga.) JC**
26. **Cortez Wyatt, rhp, West Georgia**
27. Courtney Stewart, of, Westlake HS, Atlanta
28. **Keith Pelatowski, lhp, Yale**
29. **Troy Ormonde, rhp, Taft (Calif.) JC**
30. **Saul Bustos, ss, Texas Tech**
31. **Michael Hartung, rhp, Brookdale (N.J.) CC**
32. **John Rehkopf, lhp, Northwood Institute (Texas)**
33. **David Blevins, of, Mississippi**
34. **Alex Barylak, rhp, Georgia**
35. Derek Mitchell, ss, Triton (Ill.) JC
36. **Chad Olinde, 2b/ss, Northeast Louisiana**
37. **Richie Barker, rhp, Quinsigamond (Mass.) CC**
38. Chad Helmer, rhp, Hillsborough (Fla.) CC
39. Robert Delpriore, rhp, Brookdale (N.J.) CC
40. **Ryan Opatkiewicz, ss/2b, Mount San Antonio (Calif.) JC**
41. Widd Workman, of, Gilbert, Ariz.
42. Dave Phillips, 2b, Washington Township (N.J.) HS
43. **Eric Hamm, rhp, California**
44. Kelly Armstead, ss/3b, Harlan HS, Chicago
45. **Larry Edens, of, North Carolina State**
46. Matt Williams, rhp, Lincoln-Sudbury HS, Sudbury, Mass.
47. **Kyle Farnsworth, rhp, Milton HS, Roswell, Ga.**
48. Allen Davis, lhp, Red Oak (Texas) HS
49. Jonathan Castro, rhp, Athens Christian HS, Athens, Ga.
50. John Subranni, rhp, St. Raymond HS, Bronx, N.Y.
51. **Michael Micucci, c, Montclair State (N.J.)**
52. Dean Vinson, ss, Valdosta (Ga.) HS
53. Rafael Rivera, rhp, Arecibo, P.R.
54. Jeffrey Astgen, 2b/of, Pierce (Calif.) JC
55. Rafael Corrales, rhp, Miami-Dade CC South
56. **Mike Lauterhahn, of, William Paterson (N.J.)**
57. Diego Rico, of, Sunnyside HS, Tucson, Ariz.
58. Brian Logan, c, Troy HS, Yorba Linda, Calif.
59. Galen Reeder, 1b/lhp, Shiloh HS, Snellville, Ga.
60. Travis Rapp, c, Polk (Fla.) CC
61. Doug Forde, lhp, Pasco Hernando (Fla.) CC
62. Eric Montross, rhp, North Carolina
63. David Bittler, lhp, Bridgewater Raritan HS, Bridgewater, N.J.
64. Jose Colon, of, Santa Fe (Fla.) JC

65. Lance Shannon, of, Newton County HS, Covington, Ga.
66. Donny Leon, ss, Ponce, P.R.
67. Dustin Brundage, c, Valley Central HS, Walden, N.Y.
68. James Wise, lhp, Effingham County HS, Springfield, Ga.
69. Eric Fuller, ss/rhp, LaMirada HS, Brea, Calif.
70. Ray Johnson, 1b/2b, Bayonne (N.J.) HS
71. Ryan Fuller, rhp, Corning East HS, Beaver Dams, N.Y.
72. Marcus Pearson, of, Hardaway HS, Columbus, Ga.
73. Theo Fefee, of, Lincoln Land (Ill.) CC
74. Steve Skrocki, lhp, Christian Brothers Academy, Howell, N.J.
75. Rodney Stevenson, rhp, Southern Union State (Ala.) JC

CHICAGO WHITE SOX

June—Regular Phase (26)

1. **Mark Johnson, c, Warner Robins (Ga.) HS**
1. **Chris Clemons, rhp, Texas A&M** (Supplemental pick—33rd—for loss of Type A free agent Ellis Burks)
2. **John Ambrose, rhp, Logan (Ill.) JC** (Pick from Rockies as compensation for Burks)
2. **Jerry Whittaker, of, Oklahoma**
3. **Carlos Castillo, rhp, Southwest HS, Miami**
4. **Jeff Abbott, of, Kentucky**
5. **Doug Bearden, ss, Lexington (S.C.) HS**
6. **Shane Buteaux, rhp, Houston**
7. **Dennis Crine, rhp, Saddleback (Calif.) JC**
8. **Ryan Helms, ss, Western Hills HS, Cincinnati**
9. **Sean Bagley, c, Gig Harbor (Wash.) HS**
10. **Tom McCaskey, rhp, San Marcos (Calif.) HS**
11. **Russell Herbert, rhp, Ohio**
12. **Carlos Chantres, rhp, Columbus HS, Miami**
13. **Brian Drent, of, Indian Hills (Iowa) CC**
14. **David Cancel, of, Indian Hills (Iowa) CC**
15. **Sean Duncan, lhp, Miami**
16. **Chernan Albert, of, Fernandina Beach (Fla.) HS**
17. **Brandon Moore, ss, Auburn**
18. John McConnell, lhp, La Salle HS, Fairfield, Ohio
19. Luis Garcia, of, Miami Senior HS, Miami
20. **Jeremy Griffith, rhp, Etowah HS, Atalla, Ala.**
21. Stephen Leonard, 3b/of, MacArthur HS, San Antonio, Texas
22. Charles Carter, 1b, Mount Pleasant (Texas) HS
23. Marvin Horn, 1b, El Camino (Calif.) JC
24. Adam Bernero, rhp, Kennedy HS, Sacramento, Calif.
25. Conan Horton, c, Sacramento CC
26. **Tom Koerick, c/3b, Villanova**
27. **James Nichols, rhp, St. Mark's HS, Bear, Del.**
28. Todd Johannes, c, Westminster Christian HS, Miami
29. David Harden, lhp, Shawnee Mission West HS, Overland Park, Kan.
30. Eric Gagne, rhp, Mascouche, Quebec
31. Robert Hicks, of, Milby HS, Houston
32. James Molina, of, Southridge HS, Miami
33. Kerron Bradford, of, Rancocas Valley HS, Mount Holly, N.J.
34. Chad Bradford, rhp, Hinds (Miss.) CC
35. Ryan Nicks, rhp, Gahr HS, Cerritos, Calif.
36. Clayton Stevens, of, Faulkner State (Ala.) JC
37. Darren Merrill, ss, Los Altos HS, Hacienda Heights, Calif.
38. Miles Campbell, lhp, Los Alamitos (Calif.) HS
39. Randy Hamilton, lhp, Simon Kenton HS, Independence, Ky.
40. John Pollard, of, Houston
41. Nate Forbush, 1b, Bingham HS, West Jordan, Utah
42. Eliot Montijo, 3b, Benson HS, Ponerene, Ariz.
43. Dustin Wright, rhp, Itawamba (Miss.) JC
44. Jason Olsen, rhp/3b, Napa Valley (Calif.) JC
45. Kevin Culmo, rhp, Sacramento CC
46. Tom Sullivan, rhp, Indian Hills (Iowa) CC
47. **Mike Tidick, of, Western Carolina**
48. Brian Horner, c/1b, Washington HS, Wenona, Md.
49. Nathan Koepke, 1b, Long Beach (Calif.) CC
50. **Edgar Malin, of, Memorial HS, West New York, N.J.**
51. Daniel McCluskey, c, King HS, Metairie, La.
52. Brett Bredensteiner, of, Duchesne HS, St. Charles, Mo.
53. Michael Bova, lhp, American HS, Miami
54. Chris Simonson, 1b, Claremont (Calif.) HS

CINCINNATI REDS

June—Regular Phase (9)

1. **C.J. Nitkowski, lhp, St. John's**
2. **Tony Terry, of, Abbeville (S.C.) HS**
3. **Aaron Boone, 3b, Southern California**
4. **Mike Hampton, 3b, Clemson**
5. **Clay Caruthers, rhp, Texas Christian**
6. **Clint Koppe, rhp, Texas**
7. **Decomba Conner, of, North Greenville (S.C.) JC**
8. Scott Brand, rhp, Monterey HS, Lubbock, Texas
9. **Eddie Priest, lhp, Southern Union (Ala.) JC**
10. Dustin Dabbs, c, Tupelo (Miss.) HS
11. Bryant Dickinson, ss/2b, Millbrook HS, Raleigh, N.C.
12. **Darron Ingram, of, Bryan Station HS, Lexington, Ky.**
13. **Brian Lott, rhp, McNeese State**
14. Clint Fair, lhp, Georgia Southern
15. **Jay Sorg, 3b, Morehead State**
16. Kevin Gryboski, rhp, Wilkes (Pa.)
17. **Tony Boyette, c, Santa Fe HS, Alachua, Fla.**
18. **Dan Masse, rhp, Northeastern Oklahoma A&M JC**
19. **Justin Smith, rhp, Gulf Coast (Fla.) CC**
20. **Wayne Ennis, 1b, Millbrook HS, Raleigh, N.C.**
21. **Scott Savary, of, Clarke (Iowa)**
22. **John Riedling, rhp, Ely HS, Pompano Beach, Fla.**
23. Terry Weaver, 3b, Liberty
24. Andrew Zwirchitz, rhp/ss, East HS, Appleton, Wis.
25. **Scott Sharp, c, George Washington**
26. **Marc Weiss, rhp, California Lutheran**
27. **Adam Bryant, rhp, Virginia Commonwealth**
28. **Ray Brown, 1b, Cal State Sacramento**
29. **Tony Nieto, rhp, Southern California**
30. **Nick Morrow, of, Vanderbilt**
31. **Jeff Andrews, c, Auburn-Montgomery**
32. **Cedric Allen, lhp, Mary Hardin-Baylor (Texas)**
33. **Brian Wilson, ss, Texas-San Antonio**
34. Paul Rigdon, rhp, Florida CC-Jacksonville
35. **Doyle Preston, 3b/1b, Arkansas**
36. Ed Flores, c, South HS, Bakersfield, Calif.
37. **Damon Callahan, rhp, Bradley Central HS, Cleveland, Tenn.**
38. Brandon Credeur, of, Southwestern Louisiana
39. Jeff Hutzler, rhp, Texas-San Antonio
40. **Marlon Allen, 1b, Columbus (Ga.)**
41. David Guthrie, ss, Southern Union State (Ala.) JC
42. Isaac Burton, of, Arizona State
43. Kevin Shipp, rhp, Meridian (Miss.) CC
44. Chad Angerhofer, lhp, Oak Hall Prep HS, Gainesville, Fla.
45. Patrick Zicka, rhp, Indian Hill HS, Cincinnati, Ohio
46. Tim Bell, rhp, Bakersfield (Calif.) HS
47. Malcolm King, 1b/of, Oak Hall Prep HS, Gainesville, Fla.

CLEVELAND INDIANS

June—Regular Phase (10)

1. **Jaret Wright, rhp, Katella HS, Anaheim, Calif.**
2. (Pick to Expos as compensation for Type A free agent Dennis Martinez)
3. **Rick Heiserman, rhp, Creighton**
4. **Danny Graves, rhp, Miami**
5. **Pepe McNeal, c, Armwood HS, Seffner, Fla.**
6. **Gonzalo Mojica, rhp, Yabucoa, P.R.**
7. **Russell Branyan, 3b, Stratford Academy, Warner Robins, Ga.**
8. **David Caldwell, lhp, Northeast Texas CC**
9. **Brad Tiller, ss, Sheldon Clark HS, Inez, Ky.**
10. **Jay Vaught, rhp, Texas**
11. **Blair Jensen, ss/3b, Kingsburg (Calif.) HS**
12. **Robert Oldham, rhp, Odessa (Texas) JC**
13. **Scott Kramer, rhp, Emory (Ga.)**
14. **Bryan Warner, of, Glendale (Calif.) JC**
15. **Quinn Murphy, ss, Assumption HS, Davenport, Iowa**
16. **Julius Matos, ss/2b, South Suburban (Ill.) JC**
17. Thomas Bennett, rhp, Alameda (Calif.) HS
18. Ronald Wallech, rhp, North Carolina State

19. **Darren Stumberger, 1b, South Florida**
20. **Jim Betzsold, of, Cal State Fullerton**
21. **Patrick Evans, c, Oklahoma Baptist**
22. Micah Stovall, lhp, Rancho Santiago (Calif.) JC
23. **Lenny Weber, rhp, New Orleans**
24. **Ted Warrecker, rhp, Arizona**
25. **Jonathan Choate, of, Blinn (Texas) JC**
26. **Arnold Santiago, 1b, Indian Hills (Iowa) CC**
27. Christian Parker, rhp, Eldorado HS, Albuquerque, N.M.
28. **Ricky Gutierrez, 2b, Oklahoma**
29. **Brian Duva, of, Florida**
30. **Bruce Aven, of, Lamar**
31. **Heath Hayes, 3b, San Diego State**
32. **Scot Donovan, rhp, Armstrong State (Ga.)**
33. Brad O'Malley, rhp, Canevin Catholic HS, Carnegie, Pa.
34. **Chris Granata, rhp, Ohio State**
35. William Hill, 2b, Muir HS, Altadena, Calif.
36. **Tony Dougherty, rhp, Slippery Rock (Pa.)**
37. **Chip Glass, of, Oklahoma**
38. Todd Abbott, rhp, Arkansas
39. Danny Ardoin, c, Texarkana (Texas) CC
40. Marty Heminger, rhp, Mira Mesa HS, San Diego
41. Mike Skeeles, lhp, McKinley HS, Canton, Ohio
42. **Matthew Culp, 1b, Murray State**
43. Nick De La Cruz, ss, Evergreen HS, Seattle, Wash.
44. **Chan Perry, 1b, Florida**
45. **Walter Owens, of, Miami**
46. **Mike Mastrullo, 2b, Billerica (Mass.) HS**
47. Denny Wagner, rhp, Castlewood (Va.) HS
48. Zane Gamewell, rhp, Tenino (Wash.) HS
49. Gary Anderson, rhp, Blinn (Texas) JC
50. Jimmy Jones, rhp, Irmo HS, Columbia, S.C.
51. **Steven Ortiz, lhp, McLennan (Texas) CC**
52. **James Lowry, lhp, Southeastern (N.C.) CC**
53. **Tyler Cheff, c, Hawaii**
54. **Jason Walker, lhp, Western Illinois**
55. Brian Wagner, c, Tokay HS, Lodi, Calif.
56. Joel Gallimore, rhp, Batavia (Ohio) HS
57. Brad Thomas, rhp, Northeast Texas CC
58. Jason Morones, lhp, Lower Columbia (Wash.) CC
59. Chris Enochs, rhp, Oak Glen HS, Newell, W.Va.
60. Robert O'Brien, 1b, Arcadia (Calif.) HS
61. Randy Crane, rhp, Linn-Benton (Ore.) CC
62. Juan Mussenden, 1b/of, Lake City (Fla.) CC
63. Brian Hincy, rhp, Federal Way (Wash.) HS
64. **Sean Murphy, 3b, St. Ambrose (Iowa)**
65. Jason Gooding, lhp, Seminole State (Okla.) JC

COLORADO ROCKIES

June—Regular Phase (7)

1. **Doug Million, lhp, Sarasota (Fla.) HS**
2. (Pick to White Sox as compensation for Type A free agent Ellis Burks)
3. (Pick to Marlins as compensation for Type B free agent Walt Weiss)
4. (Pick to Mets as compensation for Type B free agent Howard Johnson)
5. **John Slamka, lhp, Glendale (Ariz.) JC**
6. **Luther Hackman, rhp, Columbus (Miss.) HS**
7. **John Hallead, of, Ellensburg (Wash.) HS**
8. **Mike Kusiewicz, lhp, St. Pius HS, Nepean, Ontario**
9. **Arnold Gooch, rhp, Neshaminy HS, Levittown, Pa.**
10. **Brent Crowther, rhp, Simon Fraser (B.C.)**
11. **Mark Wells, of, North Carolina State**
12. **Mike Saipe, rhp, San Diego**
13. **Rasheed Rushdan, of, Cheraw (S.C.) HS**
14. **Pookie Jones, of, Kentucky**
15. **Matt Carpenter, c, Cleveland State**
16. **Matt Pool, rhp, UC Davis**
17. **Aaron Myers, ss/3b, Righetti HS, Santa Maria, Calif.**
18. **Arthur Waldrep, rhp, Union (Tenn.)**
19. **Jason Dietrich, rhp, Pepperdine**
20. Brady Wuestenhoefer, rhp, Mississippi Delta JC
21. **David Niles, of, Key West HS, Big Pine, Fla.**
22. **Link Jarrett, ss, Florida State**
23. **Jeff Twist, c, Oklahoma City**
24. **Chris Howard, lhp, Mobile (Ala.)**
25. Joe Germaine, rhp, Mountain View HS, Mesa, Ariz.
26. **Brian Rose, rhp, Cortland HS, Potsdam, N.Y.**
27. Ben Thomas, 1b/lhp, Central HS, Rapid City, S.D.
28. **Scott Warembourg, rhp, Fresno State**
29. **Scott Larock, rhp, Hartford**
30. **Jim Lezeau, of, Mesa State (Colo.)**
31. **Gary Jones, 2b, Ohio State**
32. **Mudcat Brewer, of, Middle Tennessee State**
33. **Joey DeAngelis, 1b, UNC Greensboro**
34. Rusty Loflin, c, Porterville (Calif.) JC
35. Brian Passini, lhp, Parkland (Ill.) JC
36. Jarret Daniel, of, Robinson HS, Tampa
37. **Chan Mayber, ss, Metro State (Colo.)**
38. Johnny Hunter, ss, Navarro (Texas) JC
39. Vincent Sanchez, rhp, Chaffey (Calif.) JC
40. Jeffery Hallock, c, La Mirada (Calif.) HS
41. James Slaughter, of, Lincoln HS, Stockton, Calif.
42. **Jonathan Mathews, 1b, New Orleans**
43. Brandon Hearn, ss, Beverly Hills (Calif.) HS
44. Caleb Brown, lhp, Wylie HS, Abilene, Texas
45. James Podjan, rhp, Lake Michigan (Mich.) JC
46. **Efrain Alamo, of, Canovanas, P.R.**
47. Todd Vickhammer, 3b, Flathead Christian HS, Kalispell, Mont.
48. William Peters, rhp, Palatine (Ill.) HS
49. Bart Miadich, rhp, Lakeridge HS, Lake Oswego, Ore.
50. Jerson Perez, ss, Lynn Tech HS, Lynn, Mass.
51. Brandon Knight, 2b, Ventura (Calif.) CC
52. Danny Delk, ss, Franklin-Simpson HS, Franklin, Ky.
53. Griffin Moore, ss, San Luis Obispo (Calif.) HS
54. Philip Davis, rhp, Central Arizona JC
55. Rusty Puffinbarger, c, Leedey HS, Camargo, Okla.
56. Freddie Jackson, of, Central Arizona JC
57. Gabriel Foster, rhp, Yuba City (Calif.) HS
58. Darren Baugh, ss, JC of San Mateo (Calif.)
59. Jason Romine, rhp, Mendocino (Calif.) CC

DETROIT TIGERS

June—Regular Phase (18)

1. **Cade Gaspar, rhp, Pepperdine**
2. **Mike Darr, of, Corona (Calif.) HS**
3. **Greg Whiteman, lhp, James Madison**
4. **Trad Sobik, rhp, Central Catholic HS, Clearwater, Fla.**
5. **Keith Smith, of, Newbury Park (Calif.) HS**
6. **Dave Kauflin, rhp, Chippewa Valley HS, Mount Clemens, Mich.**
7. **Neil Garcia, c, Nevada**
8. **Ryan Balfe, ss, Central HS, Cornwall, N.Y.**
9. **Darryl Monroe, of, Kansas**
10. Ryan Kjos, rhp, Texas
11. **Bubba Trammell, of, Tennessee**
12. **Michael Bajda, rhp, Sacred Heart (Conn.)**
13. **Chad Stevenson, c, Green Valley HS, Henderson, Nev.**
14. Matt King, rhp, Start HS, Toledo, Ohio
15. **Daryle Ward, 1b, Rancho Santiago (Calif.) JC**
16. Scott Winchester, rhp, Clemson
17. **Jason Jordan, rhp, Wichita State**
18. Rob Hauswald, ss/2b, Lafayette HS, Lexington, Ky.
19. **Kirk Hagge, ss, Crescenta Valley HS, La Crescenta, Calif.**
20. **Mac White, of, South Carolina**
21. Joshua Farrow, lhp, Dadeville HS, Camp Hill, Ala.
22. **Robert Balint, c, Valencia (Fla.) CC**
23. **Javier Cardona, c, Lake Land (Ill.) JC**
24. Erik Desrosiers, rhp, Mesa (Ariz.) CC
25. Greg Romo, rhp, Bakersfield (Calif.) JC
26. Brian Winders, rhp, Louisiana State
27. **Chris Newton, lhp, Michigan**
28. **Dave Roberts, of, UCLA**
29. **Jamie Borel, of, East Carolina**
30. Jeff Fryar, rhp, Fort Gibson (Okla.) HS
31. **Rivers Mitchell, of, Manatee (Fla.) CC**
32. Steven Elkins, rhp, Chesterton HS, Porter, Ind.

33. Brent Stentz, rhp, Pasco Hernando (Fla.) CC
34. **Mark Persails, rhp, Millington HS, Vassar, Mich.**
35. Bryan Jones, ss, Plantation (Fla.) HS
36. **Kelton Jacobson, rhp, Gonzaga**
37. Brent Sagedahl, rhp, Carthage (Wis.)
38. **Matt Ruess, rhp, Iowa State**
39. Jacob Freeman, 3b, Bakersfield (Calif.) JC
40. John Hayduk, rhp, Broken Arrow (Okla.) HS
41. Kiko Calero, rhp, Miami-Dade CC South
42. Derek Kopacz, of, Joliet (Ill.) JC
43. **Sean Freeman, 1b, Kent**
44. Brian Fuller, c, Northwestern
45. Manny Lutz, 3b, Monte Vista HS, Spring Valley, Calif.
46. DeAndre Cooper, of, St. Francis Cabrini HS, Detroit, Mich.
47. **Andy Kruger, of, Central Michigan**
48. **Eric Dinyar, rhp, Pittsburgh**
49. Michael Goralczyk, lhp, Lake Michigan (Mich.) JC
50. **Mike Martin, 2b, Boston College**
51. **Dale Dolejsi, rhp, Pacific**
52. John White, c, Gulf Coast (Fla.) CC
53. Derek Dixon, rhp, Chickasha (Okla.) HS
54. Aaron Anthony, 3b, Winder Barrow HS, Winder, Ga.
55. **Dan Driskill, rhp, Kansas Newman**
56. Michael Kujawa, rhp, Bowsher HS, Toledo, Ohio
57. Joe Eisen, of, Northmont HS, Englewood, Ohio
58. Dwayne Landry, ss, Gulf Coast (Fla.) CC
59. Rodney Archer, of, Hancock (Calif.) JC
60. Joel Hillebrand, rhp, Henry Ford (Mich.) CC
61. John Perry, rhp, Brazoswood HS, Lake Jackson, Texas
62. Stephen Berger, of, Clay HS, Oregon, Ohio
63. Nole Elizer, c, Seminole (Fla.) CC
64. Steven Williams, rhp, Seaholm HS, Birmingham, Mich.
65. Chris Champanois, c, Henry Ford (Mich.) CC
66. Reid Beucler, lhp, Georgetown Prep HS, Washington, D.C.
67. Brian Rios, ss, Riverside (Calif.) CC
68. Luis Rodriguez, of, Riverside (Calif.) CC

FLORIDA MARLINS

June—Regular Phase (5)

1. **Josh Booty, ss, Evangel Christian HS, Shreveport, La.**
2. **Victor Rodriguez, ss, Guayama, P.R.**
3. **Todd Cady, c, Arizona State**
3. **Brian Meadows, rhp, Henderson HS, Troy, Ala.** (Pick from Rockies as compensation for Type B free agent Walt Weiss)
4. **Chad Miles, lhp, Washington State**
5. **Jason Garrelts, rhp, Olivet Nazarene (Ill.)**
6. **Mike Parisi, rhp, Cal State Fullerton**
7. **Ryan Jackson, of, Duke**
8. **Hector Kuilan, c, Vega Alta, P.R.**
9. **Hayward Cook, of, UC Davis**
10. **Abdul Cole, of, CC of San Francisco**
11. **Jon Farmer, lhp, Porterville (Calif.) JC**
12. **Rob Stanifer, rhp, Anderson (S.C.) JC**
13. **Jose Camilo, of, Trujillo Alto, P.R.**
14. Rodney Getz, rhp, East Central HS, Lawrenceburg, Ind.
15. **Allan Hebbert, rhp, Cal State Los Angeles**
16. Seth Etherton, rhp, Dana Hills HS, Laguna Niguel, Calif.
17. **Kenyon West, rhp, Central HS, Miami**
18. **Jeremy Ross, rhp, Dixie (Utah) JC**
19. Kevin Tolan, rhp, Citrus (Calif.) JC
20. **Mark Gugino, of, South Carolina**
21. Brian Shackelford, lhp, McAlester (Okla.) HS
22. James Smith, rhp, Churchill HS, San Antonio
23. **Lionel Hastings, 2b, Southern California**
24. Wally Maynard, rhp, South Carolina
25. **Dan Vardijan, rhp, Glenbrook South HS, Glenview, Ill.**
26. **Michael Reyes, of, Wayland Baptist (Texas)**
27. **Sommer McCartney, c, UC Riverside**
28. Tim McClaskey, rhp, Wilton (Iowa) HS
29. Mark Hale, rhp, Central Arizona JC
30. Shawn O'Dell, 1b, Indian River HS, Chesapeake, Va.
31. Kirk Pierce, c, Long Beach State
32. Terry Bishop, lhp, Schenectady County (N.Y.) CC
33. Derrick Johnson, of, Mercer County (N.J.) CC
34. **Walter White, ss, Sonoma State (Calif.)**
35. Chadwick Mead, rhp, West Valley (Calif.) JC
36. Ali Samadini, rhp, Marin Catholic HS, Hamilton, Ga.
37. Derek Santiago, rhp, Aurora West HS, Aurora, Ill.
38. Mark Greenlee, lhp, Buffalo Grove HS, Arlington Heights, Ill.
39. Jay Gospodarek, rhp, Canyon Del Oro HS, Tucson
40. Jeremy Blaylock, rhp, Northeastern Oklahoma A&M JC
41. Quincy Foster, of, Hendersonville (N.C.) HS
42. Heath Askew, rhp, Connors State (Okla.) JC
43. Darren Mills, 3b, Key West (Fla.) HS
44. Aaron Cames, rhp, Woodland (Calif.) HS
45. Mike Evans, lhp, Wellington Community HS, Wellington, Fla.
46. Theron Truitt, of, Gordon (Ga.) JC
47. Randy Niles, rhp, Key West (Fla.) HS
48. **Randy Shagena, rhp, Aquinas (Mich.)**
49. **Joel Holland, lhp, Linfield (Ore.)**
50. Gaylon Dixon, lhp, Seminole State (Okla.) JC
51. Santos Cortez, of, Cerritos (Calif.) JC
52. Scott Dewitt, lhp, Lassen (Calif.) JC
53. John Arnold, c, Seward County (Kan.) CC
54. Shane Phillips, of, Culpepper County HS, Rixeyville, Va.
55. Chris Gorrell, rhp, Eldorado HS, Las Vegas, Nev.
56. Justin Fenus, rhp, Colorado Northwestern CC
57. Chris Windsor, rhp, Garden City (Kan.) CC
58. Philip Henderson, rhp, Ringgold (Ga.) HS
59. Peter Quitner, of, San Jose CC
60. Todd Moser, lhp, St. Thomas Aquinas HS, Davie, Fla.
61. Ryan Roberts, lhp, Chaffey (Calif.) JC
62. Tom Buckman, rhp, Edison (Fla.) CC
63. Curtis Hall, 3b, Orem, Utah
64. Tim Hicks, of/1b, Gordon (Ga.) JC
65. Greg McNeill, rhp, East Montgomery HS, Biscoe, N.C.
66. John Payne, rhp, Athens Drive HS, Raleigh, N.C.
67. **Jonathan Moores, rhp, Ithaca (N.Y.)**
68. Josh Deakman, rhp, Riverside (Calif.) CC
69. Ross Atkins, rhp, Wake Forest
70. Anthony Poindexter, of, Jefferson Forest HS, Forest, Va.
71. Beau Payne, rhp, Edmonds (Wash.) CC
72. Glenn Foley, 1b, Boston College
73. Hines Ward, of, Forest Park HS, Rex, Ga.
74. Troy Rauer, of, Arizona State
75. Tyler Nicol, of, Southern Arkansas
76. Douglas Bossert, rhp, Pitman (N.J.) HS
77. Brian Benefield, ss, Mesquite (Texas) HS
78. Ward White, c, Modesto (Calif.) JC
79. Peter Jezerinac, ss, Walton HS, Marietta, Ga.
80. Michael Howes, rhp, Jenks HS, Tulsa, Okla.

HOUSTON ASTROS

June—Regular Phase (17)

1. **Ramon Castro, c, Vega Baja, P.R.**
1. **Scott Elarton, rhp, Lamar (Colo.) HS** (Pick from Giants as compensation for Type A free agent Mark Portugal)
1. **Russ Johnson (Supplemental pick), ss, Louisiana State** (Supplemental pick—30th—for loss of Portugal)
2. **Dan Lock, lhp, Yale**
3. **Oscar Robles, ss, Montgomery HS, San Diego**
4. **Paul O'Malley, rhp, Illinois State**
5. **Mike Gunderson, rhp, North Dakota State**
6. **Shane Barksdale, of, Etowah HS, Gallant, Ala.**
7. **Tony Mounce, lhp, Kamiakin HS, Kennewick, Wash.**
8. **Derek Dace, lhp, Sullivan (Mo.) HS**
9. **Wes Pratt, of, North Carolina Wesleyan**
10. **Roy Marsh, of, Ohio State**
11. Bob Palithorpe, rhp, Santa Clara
12. **Hassan Robinson, of, Springfield (Mass.)**
13. **Victor Sanchez, c, Pacific**
14. **Anthony Rich, ss, Rollins (Fla.)**
15. **Billy Hall, rhp, Crowder (Mo.) JC**
16. **Chris Crawford, rhp, Marquette**
17. Donzell McDonald, of, Trinidad State (Colo.) JC
18. **Stephen Fuller, rhp, Triton (Ill.) JC**
19. **Mark Sacharko, rhp, Lancaster (Texas) HS**
20. Richard Rodrigues, 3b, De Anza (Calif.) JC

21. **John Smith, 3b, Auburn (N.Y.) HS**
22. **Donald Scolaro, 2b, Florida Southern**
23. **John Halama, lhp, St. Francis (N.Y.)**
24. Ruben Jurado, rhp, Chino HS, Ontario, Calif.
25. **Anthony Shaver, rhp, Jacksonville State**
26. Chris McFerrin, rhp, McLane HS, Fresno, Calif.
27. James Weaver, rhp, Clark HS, San Antonio
28. **James Lynch, rhp, Harrison HS, Evansville, Ind.**
29. James Whitehead, c, Franklin HS, Roxie, Miss.
30. Rosario Ortiz, rhp, Globe (Ariz.) HS
31. Ben Smith, rhp, Glebe Collegiate HS, Nepean, Ontario
32. Joe Valenti, 1b, Mendon HS, Pittsford, N.Y.
33. Joe Painich, rhp, Panola (Texas) JC
34. Kevin Burns, 1b, Texarkana (Texas) CC
35. **Stacy Chupailo, rhp, Mona Shores HS, Norton Shores, Mich.**
36. Michael Fee, rhp, Gibbs HS, St. Petersburg, Fla.
37. Cory Lusk, rhp, Dundee Crown HS, Carpentersville, Ill.
38. Rob Aronson, rhp, Eastern Connecticut State
39. Shane Gift, rhp, Central Arizona JC
40. Prenenyer Rodriguez, rhp, McCutcheon HS, Lafayette, Ind.
41. Peter Cervantes, rhp, East Los Angeles JC
42. Ralph Cadima, rhp, Mount San Antonio (Calif.) JC
43. **Julio Lugo, ss, Connors State (Okla.) JC**
44. Michael Eikenberry, rhp, Lincoln Trail (Ill.) JC
45. Erik Augustin, of, Norristown (Pa.) HS
46. Jay Spurgeon, rhp, Yosemite HS, Madera, Calif.
47. Kelly Johnson, rhp, Walla Walla (Wash.) CC
48. Robert Mills, 3b, Henderson (Texas) HS
49. Jonathan Black, rhp, Texarkana (Texas) CC
50. John Prestash, lhp, West Branch HS, Phillipsburg, Pa.
51. Casey Baker, of, Fresno (Calif.) CC
52. Trevor Zwaan, rhp, Prince Andrew HS, Dartmouth, Nova Scotia
53. John Rodriguez, of, Connors State (Okla.) JC
54. Scott Bronowicz, c, Shaler HS, Pittsburgh
55. Dustin Spencer, rhp, Cuesta (Calif.) JC
56. Stephen Dye, rhp, Butler HS, Augusta, Ga.
57. Petey Watts, of, Pike County HS, Molena, Ga.
58. Dale Davis, lhp, Trinity HS, Bedord, Texas (Selection voided)
59. Clint Weibl, rhp, Odessa (Texas) JC
60. Elvin Nina, rhp, Northeastern Oklahoma A&M JC
61. Kevin Parker, ss, Texarkana (Texas) CC
62. Chad Berryman, rhp, Brown HS, Kannapolis, N.C.
63. Reed Goemann, lhp, Elk Grove HS, Sacramento, Calif.
64. Paul Hoover, ss, Steubenville (Ohio) HS
65. Mark Manbeck, rhp, Galveston (Texas) JC
66. Justin Bowser, rhp, Seward County (Kan.) CC
67. Jeffrey Conner, c, Colonial HS, Orlando
68. Barney Albritton, rhp, Parklane Academy, McComb, Miss.
69. Brad Hardtke, 3b, Leland HS, San Jose
70. Daryl Jones, of, Bossier City (La.) HS
71. Johnny Estrada, c, Roosevelt HS, Fresno, Calif.
72. Brent Husted, ss, Santa Teresa HS, San Jose
73. Jim Chamblee, rhp, Odessa (Texas) JC
74. Brian Thompson, rhp, Howard (Texas) JC
75. Jason Middleton, rhp, Fort Myers (Fla.) HS
76. Ryan Anschuetz, rhp, Edison (Fla.) CC
77. Tim Worthen, 1b, Limestone Community HS, Peoria, Ill.
78. Canaan Price, ss, Palm Desert (Calif.) HS
79. **Jay Wright, rhp, New Mexico Highlands**
80. Derek Ballard, 1b, Moon Valley HS, Phoenix
81. Jeff Mathews, rhp, Vassar (Mich.) HS
82. Javier Encinia, rhp, Blinn (Texas) JC
83. Jonathan Echols, c, Connors State (Okla.) JC
84. Matt Reed, 2b, Mississippi Delta JC
85. Shane Howell, 1b, Andrew Hill HS, San Jose
86. Michael Constantino, rhp, Manatee HS, Bradenton, Fla.
87. Brian Slatkin, rhp, Lassen (Calif.) JC
88. Brian Tickell, rhp, McLennan (Texas) CC
89. Paul Powell, lhp, Texarkana (Texas) CC
90. James Sapp, of, Monroe (N.Y.) CC
91. Marcus Scott, of, Palm Springs HS, Desert Hot Springs, Calif.
92. Tyler Steketee, rhp, Jenison (Mich.) HS
93. Mike Glavine, 1b, Northeastern
94. Jeremie Durden, of, Huntington HS, Greenwood, La.
95. Karl Chatman, of, Galveston (Texas) JC
96. Juan Rivera, ss, Cypress Creek HS, Orlando
97. Doug Rummel, rhp, Lake Travis HS, Austin, Texas
98. Cameron Saska, lhp, Granite Hills HS, El Cajon, Calif.

KANSAS CITY ROYALS

June—Regular Phase (16)

1. **Matt Smith, lhp/1b, Grant Pass (Ore.) HS**
2. **Jed Hansen, 2b, Stanford**
3. **Jaime Bluma, rhp, Wichita State**
4. **Matt Treanor, c, Mater Dei HS, Santa Ana, Calif.**
5. **Tim Byrdak, lhp, Rice**
6. **Blaine Mull, rhp, Freedom HS, Morganton, N.C.**
7. **Javier Gamboa, rhp, Cuesta (Calif.) JC**
8. Todd Belitz, 1b, Edison HS, Huntington Beach, Calif.
9. Kris Didion, 3b, Poly HS, Riverside, Calif.
10. **Gary Coffee, 1b, Grady HS, Atlanta**
11. **Jacob Kringen, lhp, Elma (Wash.) HS**
12. **Jose Rosado, lhp, Galveston (Texas) JC**
13. **Eric Mooney, lhp, St. Mary's**
14. Ryan Bradley, rhp, Ayala HS, Chino, Calif.
15. **Ken Winkle, rhp, St. Leo (Fla.)**
16. **Sean McNally, 3b, Duke**
17. **Tyler Williamson, c, Biola (Calif.)**
18. **Dan Dillingham, of, Polk (Fla.) CC**
19. **Wayne Upchurch, rhp, Texas-Arlington**
20. **Scott Pinoni, 1b, Duke**
21. **Lance Carter, rhp, Manatee (Fla.) JC**
22. Nathan Ruhl, rhp, Lees Summit (Mo.) HS
23. **Tim Grieve, rhp, Texas Christian**
24. **James Welch, c, Tallahassee (Fla.) CC**
25. **Manuel Burciaga, rhp, Northwest Nazarene (Idaho)**
26. **Todd Thorn, lhp, Northwestern HS, Stratford, Ontario**
27. **Jason Ritter, rhp, Connors State (Okla.) JC**
28. Jaime Burton, lhp, Chemeketa (Ore.) CC
29. **Brent Kaysner, rhp, Green River (Wash.) CC**
30. **Mike Kurnik, rhp, Cal Poly Pomona**
31. **Shannon Coulter, ss, Texas Christian**
32. **Marc Phillips, lhp, Virginia Military Institute**
33. **Kortney Paul, c, Arkansas State**
34. **Rick Pitts, of, Franklin HS, Seattle**
35. Brian Scott, rhp, Ramona (Calif.) HS
36. **Ray Roberts, lhp, Napa Valley (Calif.) JC**
37. Thomas Stanton, c, Middleburg (Fla.) HS
38. **Duane Darby, lhp, West Middlesex (Pa.) Area HS**
39. **Victor Moreno, 3b, Flushing HS, Queens, N.Y.**
40. Stephen Rosen, rhp, Blue Springs (Mo.) HS
41. Steve Spille, lhp, Cincinnati
42. George Fergusson, of, Bronx (N.Y.) CC
43. Kimani Stafford, c, Swett HS, Richmond, Calif.
44. Eric Cole, 3b, Antelope Valley (Calif.) JC
45. Stephen Watson, rhp, Galveston (Texas) JC
46. J.J. Thomas, of, Wheeler HS, Marietta, Ga.
47. Derek Anderson, lhp, Lynwood (Wash.) HS
48. Dale Hill, lhp, Trinity HS, Bedford, Texas
49. Vincent Wells, 2b, MacKenzie HS, Detroit
50. Brandon Stanley, 3b/rhp, Texarkana (Texas) CC
51. Charles Schoenfeldt, 1b, Victor Valley (Calif.) CC
52. Dustin Wilson, rhp, Kiona Benton HS, Benton City, Wash.
53. Torrie Pinkins, c/2b, Mitchell-Baker HS, Camilla, Ga.
54. Will Schleuss, lhp, Hagerstown (Md.) JC
55. Dale Slater, rhp, Muscatine (Iowa) CC
56. Matt Montgomery, rhp, Western HS, Anaheim, Calif.
57. Dimitric Murph, rhp, Caldwell (Texas) HS
58. Michael Custer, rhp, Linn-Benton (Ore.) CC
59. Mario Olsen, rhp, Rowan (N.J.)
60. Kit Pellow, of, Johnson County (Kan.) CC
61. Matt Bailie, rhp, Hillsboro HS, Aloha, Ore.
62. Demond Thompkins, of, Nevada-Las Vegas
63. Brett Schafer, of, UCLA
64. Patrick Machado, 1b, Clovis West HS, Fresno, Calif.
65. **Ken Tipton, of, Dallas Baptist**
66. Eric Marks, 3b, Victor Valley (Calif.) CC
67. **Juan Rocha, of, Cerritos (Calif.) JC**

68. Justin Bowles, of, Galveston (Texas) JC
69. Richard Igou, lhp, Notre Dame HS, Sherman Oaks, Calif.
70. **Jose Santiago, rhp, Loiza, P.R.**
71. Casey Martin, c, Lakewood (Calif.) HS

LOS ANGELES DODGERS

June—Regular Phase (13)

1. **Paul Konerko, c, Chaparral HS, Scottsdale, Ariz.**
2. **Gary Rath, lhp, Mississippi State**
3. **Mike Metcalfe, ss, Miami**
4. **Ricky Stone, rhp, Hamilton (Ohio) HS**
5. **Chris Ochsenfeld, lhp, Bethel HS, Hampton, Va.**
6. Eric DuBose, lhp, Patrician Academy, Butler, Ala.
7. **Jamie Jaye, lhp, South Alabama**
8. Jason Huisman, ss, Thornwood HS, Thornton, Ill.
9. C.J. Ankrum, of, Saratoga (Calif.) HS
10. **Ron Hollis, rhp, Michigan**
11. Alex Fajardo, lhp, Coral Gables HS, Miami
12. **Greg Thompson, rhp/of, Goddard HS, Roswell, N.M.**
13. **Brian Harmon, of, Marist HS, Palos Heights, Ill.**
14. **Eddie Oropesa, lhp, Canoga Park, Calif.**
15. Alex Andreopoulos, c, Seton Hall
16. Ken Kilian, of, Wheaton Warrenville South HS, Warrenville, Ill.
17. **Kevin Zellers, ss/2b, Kent**
18. **J.P. Roberge, 1b, Southern California**
19. **Kyle Cooney, c, Connecticut**
20. Brett Tomko, rhp, Mount San Antonio (Calif.) JC
21. Justin Rumfield, ss/3b, Belton (Texas) HS
22. **Adam Riggs, 2b, South Carolina**
23. **Johnny Hilo, of, Cal State Los Angeles**
24. Zachary Hines, ss, DeKalb (Ga.) JC
25. Randy Wolf, lhp, El Camino Real HS, Canoga Park, Calif.
26. **Jason Reed, lhp, Grossmont (Calif.) JC**
27. George Dearborn, lhp, Mountain View HS, Vancouver, Wash.
28. Ben Butkus, ss, Dr. Phillips HS, Orlando
29. **Jeff Paluk, rhp, Saginaw Valley State**
30. **Eric Stuckenschneider, of, Central Missouri State**
31. Michael Wood, c, San Clemente (Calif.) HS
32. **Brian Majeski, of, Connecticut**
33. **Chip Sell, of, Pacific**
34. **Kevin Faircloth, ss, North Carolina State**
35. Robert Meyer, 2b, Kirkwood (Iowa) CC
36. **Ryan Sowards, 3b, Walla Walla (Wash.) CC**
37. Leonardo Matos, lhp, Utuado, P.R.
38. Eric Byrnes, c, St. Francis HS, Portola Valley, Calif.
39. Kirby Drube, of/rhp, Campbell County HS, Gillette, Wyo.
40. Aaron Miller, lhp, Middletown (Del.) HS
41. Jeff Bramlett, 1b, Bradley Central HS, Cleveland, Tenn.
42. Ryan Roskowski, 3b, Clovis West HS, Fresno, Calif.
43. Mark Shephard, rhp, Strathroy (Ontario) HS
44. Jermaine Clark, ss/2b, Wood HS, Vacaville, Calif.
45. Brad Block, rhp, Portage Central HS, Portage, Mich.
46. Charles Koone, of, McDowell HS, Marion, N.C.
47. Keith Graffagnini, of, De La Salle HS, New Orleans
48. Marc Charbonneau, lhp, Ottawa, Ontario
49. David Sloan, c, York Community HS, Elmhurst, Ill.
50. Jim Parque, lhp, Crescenta Valley HS, La Crescenta, Calif.
51. **Elias Tapia, rhp, South Gate, Calif.**
52. Clint Lawrence, lhp, White Oaks HS, Oakville, Ontario
53. Justin Atchley, lhp, Texas A&M
54. Frank Hinojosa, c, Ayala HS, Chino, Calif.
55. Thomas Cody, c, Lower Columbia (Wash.) JC
56. Adam Kiehl, of, East HS, Wauwatosa, Wis.
57. Tracy Johnson, of, Glendale (Ariz.) CC
58. Hector Esparza, 3b, Independence HS, San Jose
59. Anthony Cellers, of, Seminole (Okla.) CC
60. Jaime Decker, c, Fort Madison (Iowa) HS
61. Lucas Quaccia, 1b, Modesto (Calif.) JC
62. Josh Osborn, rhp, Butte (Calif.) JC
63. Joel Manfredi, 3b, Lincoln HS, Stockton, Calif.
64. Brandon Bowe, rhp, San Joaquin Delta (Calif.) JC
65. Calvin Tanton, c, Strathmore (Ala.) HS
66. Jesse Zepeda, ss, Cuesta (Calif.) JC
67. Eric Boisjoly, ss, Boucherville, Quebec
68. Lance Backowski, 2b, Fresno (Calif.) CC
69. Jaime Malave, 1b, Southeastern Illinois JC
70. Cordell Farley, of, Louisburg (N.C.) JC
71. **Greg Morrison, of, Medicine Hat, Alberta**
72. Shawn Painter, of, John Abbott (Quebec)
73. Chris Vollaro, rhp, Oak Ridge HS, Spring, Texas
74. Jeremy Meccage, rhp, West HS, Billings, Mont.
75. Otis Jasper, rhp, Quesnel (B.C.) HS
76. Justin Elsey, of, Casa Grande HS, Petaluma, Calif.
77. Ovidio Zepeda, of, King HS, Corpus Christi, Texas

MILWAUKEE BREWERS

June—Regular Phase (4)

1. **Antone Williamson, 3b, Arizona State**
2. **Doug Webb, rhp, San Diego State**
3. **Larry Barnes, rhp, Englewood HS, Jacksonville**
4. **Darrell Nicholas, of, New Orleans**
5. **Steve Woodard, rhp, Hartselle (Ala.) HS**
6. **Roberto Lopez, 2b, Oklahoma State**
7. **Chris Burt, rhp, Northern Illinois**
8. **Ronnie Belliard, ss, Central HS, Miami**
9. **Ed Collins, rhp, Union (N.J.) HS**
10. **Scott Krause, of, New Orleans**
11. Jason Franklin, ss/of, Winter Haven (Fla.) HS
12. Alan Johnson, of, Elizabeth (N.J.) HS
13. **Shane Moses, rhp, Riverside (Calif.) CC**
14. **Marc Fink, 1b, Memorial HS, Jackson, N.J.**
15. **Scott Nate, lhp, Lake Michigan (Mich.) JC**
16. **Robinson Cancel, 3b/c, Lajas, P.R.**
17. **Adrian Wilkerson, of, Coffee HS, Douglas, Ga.**
18. **Joseph Hiller, rhp, Columbus (Ga.)**
19. Mike Kinkade, c/of, Washington State
20. Trent Brown, lhp, San Manuel HS, Oracle, Ariz.
21. **Scott Huntsman, rhp, Wright State**
22. **Stephen Pritchard, ss, Western Carolina**
23. **Brian Titus, lhp, St. Bonaventure**
24. **Josh Tyler, 3b, Pittsburgh**
25. **Alfredo Gutierrez, rhp, Norte Vista HS, Riverside, Calif.**
26. Ben McGarvey, rhp, Indian Hills (Iowa) CC
27. Paul Chiaffredo, c, Leland HS, San Jose, Calif.
28. David Therneau, rhp, Denton (Texas) HS
29. **Robert Snook, c, Illinois Valley CC**
30. **Jeffrey Kramer, rhp, Emory (Ga.)**
31. Jamold Little, ss, Southeastern Illinois
32. **McKenzie Norris, rhp, Dobson HS, Mesa, Ariz.**
33. **Anthony Iapoce, of, Lamar**
34. **Greg Beck, rhp, West Florida**
35. **Ruberto Escalet, 2b, Mary Hardin-Baylor (Texas)**
36. **Brian Dalton, rhp, Florida Southern**
37. Mark Doubleday, ss, Faulkner State (Ala.) JC
38. William Rushing, lhp, Georgia Southern
39. Blair Murphy, rhp, Los Gatos (Calif.) HS
40. Corey Richardson, rhp, Millbrook HS, Raleigh, N.C.
41. Edmond Daniels, rhp, Seminole HS, Sanford, Fla.
42. Elliott Brown, rhp, George Wallace (Ala.) CC
43. Doug Wakefield, lhp, Apple Valley (Calif.) HS
44. Anthony Allen, of, Jefferson City HS, Keaneysville, W.Va.
45. Anthony Peters, c, Miami-Dade CC North
46. Beau Johnson, 1b/of, Ukiak (Calif.) HS
47. Bruce Lenhardt, rhp, Lake Michigan (Mich.) JC
48. David Glick, lhp, Palmdale (Calif.) HS
49. Tim Mullen, lhp, Malden Catholic HS, Reading, Mass.
50. Jorge Santiago, c, Vega Alta, P.R.
51. Javier Gomez, 1b, Moca, P.R.
52. Chris Donohoo, lhp, Notre Dame HS, Chattanooga, Tenn.
53. Ronrico Harris, of, Florida CC-Jacksonville
54. **Anthony Pavlovich, rhp, Middle Georgia JC**
55. Jeff Solomon, ss, Jackson HS, Miami
56. Ray Hughes, rhp/of, Aucilla Christian HS, Monticello, Fla.
57. Matt Erickson, ss, West HS, Appleton, Wis.
58. Bill Eaton, ss/rhp, Leonard HS, Lake Worth, Fla.
59. Etienne Hightower, of, Okaloosa Walton (Fla.) CC
60. Greg Cooper, rhp, Florida CC-Jacksonville
61. Javil Byron, 2b, Carol City HS, Miami

MINNESOTA TWINS

June—Regular Phase (8)

1. **Todd Walker, 2b, Louisiana State**
1. **Travis Miller** (Supplemental pick), lhp, Kent (Supplemental pick—34th—for failure to sign 1993 first-rounder Jason Varitek)
2. **Cleatus Davidson, ss, Lake Wales (Fla.) HS**
3. **A.J. Pierzynski, c, Dr. Phillips HS, Orlando**
4. **Tom Mott, rhp, Santa Clara**
5. **John Schroeder, of, Coeur d'Alene (Idaho) HS**
6. **Walker Chapman, rhp, Beall HS, Frostburg, Md.**
7. **Antuan Sunkley, 1b, Palm Beach Lakes HS, West Palm Beach, Fla.**
8. **Jerome Brown, ss, Smithville (Okla.) HS**
9. **Jeff Ferguson, 2b, Cal State Fullerton**
10. **Marcus Starling, lhp, Florida CC-Jacksonville**
11. David Dellucci, of, Mississippi
12. **Paul Pavicich, lhp, San Jose State**
13. **Jim McCalmont, 2b, Grand Canyon (Ariz.)**
14. **Brian Colburn, of, Central HS, La Crosse, Wis.**
15. **Eli Herdman, ss, Central Kitsap HS, Bremerton, Wash.**
16. **Kasey Richardson, lhp, Northern HS, Huntingtown, Md.**
17. **Robert Ruch, rhp, Millikin (Ill.)**
18. Glenn Davis, 1b, Malvern Prep HS, Aston, Pa.
19. **Paul Morse, rhp, Kentucky**
20. **Jason Meyhoff, lhp, Missouri**
21. **Rodney McBride, rhp, White Station HS, Memphis**
22. **Damon Irvis, of, Lake Wales (Fla.) HS**
23. Rob Neal, of, Cal Poly San Luis Obispo
24. **Nathan Craigue, ss, Concord (N.H.) HS**
25. Brian Tokarse, rhp, Fullerton (Calif.) JC
26. **Corey Koskie, 3b, Kwantlen (B.C.)**
27. **Brandon Puffer, rhp, Capistrano Valley HS, Mission Viejo, Calif.**
28. **Matt Leach, rhp, Long Island**
29. **Scott Hilt, c, Hartford**
30. Robert Quarnstrom, lhp, Hersey HS, Mount Prospect, Ill.
31. Frankie Sanders, rhp, Pasco Hernando (Fla.) CC
32. **Jim Champion, 1b, Oregon State**
33. **Joe Correia, lhp, St. Louis HS, Pearl City, Hawaii**
34. **Michael Raymondi, c, Watertown (S.D.) HS**
35. Richard Rowe, ss, Lake Wier HS, Summerfield, Fla.
36. Mike Narkter, rhp, Kent
37. Jacob Schaffer, ss, Holy Angels HS, Bloomington, Minn.
38. **Brannon Peters, lhp, Texas**
39. Brian Lawrence, rhp, Carthage (Texas) HS
40. Brad Winget, 1b, Murray (Utah) HS
41. Justin Lamber, lhp, Hackensack (N.J.) HS
42. Mark Gardner, lhp, Orange Coast (Calif.) JC
43. Landon Hessler, rhp, Pasco Hernando (Fla.) CC
44. Linus Williams, lhp, Stigler (Okla.) HS
45. Chris Traylor, lhp, Bartlesville (Okla.) HS
46. Ajani Carter, of, Oakland (Calif.) HS
47. **David Thompson, rhp, Dallas Baptist**
48. Julio Ayuso, of, Carolina, P.R.
49. Kelly Gage-Cole, lhp, Centennial HS, Coquitlam, B.C
50. William Munoz, of, Kofa HS, Yuma, Ariz.
51. Jose Marrero, 1b, Ponce, P.R.
52. Ray Ragland, rhp, Clemson

MONTREAL EXPOS

June—Regular Phase (21)

1. **Hiram Bocachica, ss, Bayamon, P.R.**
1. **Mike Thurman, rhp, Oregon State** (Supplemental pick—31st—for loss of Type A free agent Dennis Martinez)
2. **Jason Camilli, ss, Thunderbird HS, Phoenix** (Pick from Indians for loss of Martinez)
2. Kenny Henderson, rhp, Miami
3. **Paul Ottavinia, of, Seton Hall**
4. **Jeremy Powell, rhp/of, Highlands HS, Sacramento**
5. **Javier Vazquez, rhp, Ponce, P.R.**
6. **Scott Forster, lhp, James Madison**
7. **Geoff Blum, ss, California**
8. **Simon Pond, ss, Argyle HS, North Vancouver, B.C**
9. Brian Hervey, rhp, Spanish River HS, Boca Raton, Fla.
10. **Jason McCommon, rhp, Memphis State**
11. **Carl Hall, of, Wichita State**
12. **Jerald Stubbs, rhp, Alabama**
13. **Jake Benz, lhp, Oklahoma State**
14. **Mark Lewis, ss, Nevada**
15. **Kurt Alderman, c, Albertson (Idaho)**
16. Dan McKinley, of, Dobson HS, Mesa, Ariz.
17. Brent Peck, rhp, Gulf Coast (Fla.) CC
18. **Bob Hughes, of, Arkansas**
19. Jason Ryan, lhp, St. Thomas Aquinas HS, Davie, Fla.
20. Matt Jeckell, rhp, DeAnza (Calif.) JC
21. Jason Welch, of, Bishop Verot HS, Fort Myers, Fla.
22. Toby McDermott, lhp, Decatur HS, Federal Way, Wash.
23. **Cary Fenton, 2b, Memphis State**
24. Jason Walker, ss, Springville (Utah) HS
25. Jeremy Ware, of, Centennial Collegiate HS, Guelph, Ontario
26. Philip Derryman, rhp, Royal HS, Simi Valley, Calif.
27. Robert Everett, rhp, Monroe Area (Ga.) HS
28. Stephan Neill, rhp, Indian River (Fla.) CC
29. Damon Warren, rhp, Hudson's Bay HS, Vancouver, Wash.
30. Michael Young, lhp, Port Moody (B.C.) HS
31. **Edward Bady, of, Talledaga (Ala.)**
32. Michael Davis, rhp, Tallahassee (Fla.) CC
33. Joel Young, lhp, Ulster (N.Y.) CC
34. **Jay Cole, rhp, Alabama-Birmingham**
35. Raul Torres, of, Hialeah (Fla.) HS
36. **Ben Fleetham, rhp, Rollins (Fla.)**
37. **Thad Chaddrick, 3b, Oklahoma State**
38. Mike Brandley, lhp, Wichita State
39. Robert Price, rhp, Deer Valley HS, Glendale, Ariz.
40. Robert Vael, rhp, North Delta (B.C.) HS
41. **Matt Haas, c, Notre Dame**
42. Dennis Machado, lhp, Central HS, Kenai, Alaska
43. Ben Phillips, rhp, Sheridan (Wyo.) HS
44. Jonathan Zumwalt, rhp, South Kitsap HS, Port Orchard, Wash.
45. James Berger, rhp, Immanuel HS, Dinuba, Calif.
46. Kyle Duncan, rhp, Kalama (Wash.) HS
47. Garrett Neubart, of, Columbia

NEW YORK METS

June—Regular Phase (1)

1. **Paul Wilson, rhp, Florida State**
1. **Terrence Long, 1b/of, Stanhope Elmore HS, Millbrook, Ala.** (Pick from Orioles as compensation for Type A free agent Sid Fernandez)
1. **Jay Payton, of, Georgia Tech** (Supplemental pick—29th—for loss of Fernandez)
2. **Sean Johnston, lhp, Highland Park (Ill.) HS**
2. Matt LeCroy, c, Belton-Honea Path HS, Belton, S.C. (Supplemental pick—63rd—for loss of Type C free agent Charlie O'Brien)
3. **Bryon Gainey, 1b, Davidson HS, Mobile, Ala.**
4. **Kevin McCarthy, of, North Allegheny HS, Wexford, Pa.**
4. **Kenny Pumphrey, rhp, Old Mill HS, Millersville, Md.** (Pick from Rockies as compensation for Type B free agent Howard Johnson)
5. Brian Kukilck, rhp, Hatboro Horsham HS, Horsham, Pa.
6. **David Sanderson, of, Missouri**
7. Brett Nista, ss, Laguna Hills (Calif.) HS
8. **Kevin Manley, rhp, Frostproof (Fla.) HS**
9. **Robert Cox, 3b, Santa Monica (Calif.) JC**
10. Adam Piatt, ss, Bishop Verot HS, Fort Myers, Fla.
11. **John Kelly, rhp, Connecticut**
12. **Jeramie Simpson, of, Seward County (Kan.) CC**
13. **Steve Arffa, lhp, Arizona**
14. Travis Harper, rhp, Circleville HS, Riverton, W.Va.
15. **Melvin Poupart, rhp, Humaco, P.R.**
16. **Craig Cope, lhp, Brennan HS, Windsor, Ontario**
17. Jason Dellaero, ss, Brewster (N.Y.) HS
18. **Toby Larson, rhp, Alabama-Birmingham**
19. **Sammy Rodriguez, c, Mount St. Michaels HS, New York**
20. **Craig Jelsovsky, ss, Monte Vista HS, Spring Valley, Calif.**

21. **Don Spingola, rhp, Chabot (Calif.) JC**
22. Scott Haij, rhp, Columbia River HS, Vancouver, Wash.
23. **Scott Sauerbeck, lhp, Miami (Ohio)**
24. **Matt Koenig, rhp, Brookdale (N.J.) CC**
25. **Joe Lisio, rhp, New York Tech**
26. Matt Lytie, lhp, Wyomissing Area HS, Wyomissing Hills, Pa.
27. **William Santamaria, rhp, Lakewood (N.J.) HS**
28. **Rosloe Wicks, rhp, North HS, Eugene, Ore.**
29. Brad Kennedy, 2b, Neosho County (Kan.) CC
30. **Ryan Miller, ss, Long Beach State**
31. **Robert Borkowski, rhp, St. Mark's HS, Wilmington, Del.**
32. **Rocky Turner, of, Texas-Arlington**
33. **Luis Hernandez, 2b, Miami**
34. **Bo Haley, 1b, Wyoming**
35. **Ethan Burke, rhp, Baker HS, Baker City, Ore.**
36. Joe Mattingly, rhp, Indian River (Fla.) JC
37. Nate Laufer, rhp, Los Angeles Baptist HS, Sylmar, Calif.
38. Matt Simpson, c, California HS, Whittier, Calif.
39. **Noah Peery, rhp, Arizona State**
40. **Mark Guerra, rhp, Jacksonville**
41. Bryan Hebson, rhp, Central HS, Phenix City, Ala.
42. Calvin Whitekiller, rhp, Hulbert (Okla.) HS
43. Tracy Edmondson, 2b, Riverside (Calif.) CC
44. Samuel Mathis, rhp, Southern Arkansas
45. **Daniel Engle, c, Western Oklahoma State JC**
46. Darren Nordlund, of, Tacoma (Wash.) CC
47. Scott Schultz, rhp, Louisiana State
48. John Batts, 2b, Delaware
49. Mel Melehes, lhp, St. James HS, Guelph, Ontario
50. **Brian Mifflin, of, Lewes, Del.**
51. David Meng, rhp, New Mexico
52. Taylor Harris, 1b, DeKalb (Ga.) JC
53. Shawn McNally, rhp, Auburn
54. Maurice Bruce, ss, Connors State (Okla.) JC
55. Anthony Roossien, 3b/1b, Trinity Christian Academy, Plano, Texas
56. Carlos Morrison, of, Central Arizona JC
57. **Tim Bishop, of, Valparaiso (Ind.) HS**
58. John Garrison, rhp, San Joaquin Delta (Calif.) JC
59. Darren Dyt, of, Golden West HS, Tulare, Calif.
60. **Kyle Kessel, lhp, Mundelein (Ill.) HS**
61. Richard Lee, ss, Jackson (Miss.) Academy
62. Jeff Sonsoucie, lhp, Lebanon HS, Summerfield, Ill.
63. Harold Zdziarski, rhp, Lackawanna (Pa.) CC
64. **David Leonhad, lhp, Oklahoma Christian**
65. Kris Wilson, rhp, Tarpon Springs HS, Palm Harbor, Fla.
66. Brandon Villafuerte, rhp, West Valley (Calif.) JC
67. Matt Hopper, ss, Winder Barrow HS, Winder, Ga.
68. David Benham, 3b/of, Garland Christian Academy, Garland, Texas
69. Ted Cheatham, ss, Spring Hill (Kan.) HS
70. Heath Schesser, ss, Manhattan (Kan.) HS
71. **Hans Beebe, lhp, Camden County (N.J.) CC**
72. Greg Smyth, lhp, Rollins (Fla.)
73. Michael Terry, 1b/lhp, Edison HS, Tulsa, Okla.
74. **Paul LeClair, of, Livingston (Ala.)**
75. Jeromy Thomas, rhp, Kalama (Wash.) HS

NEW YORK YANKEES

June—Regular Phase (24)

1. **Brian Buchanan, 1b/of, Virginia**
2. **Rodriguez Smith, of, Lafayette HS, Lexington, Ky.**
3. **Garrett Butler, of, Northwest HS, Miami**
4. **Steve Shoemaker, rhp, Alabama**
5. **Ray Ricken, rhp, Michigan**
6. **Jose Velazquez, 1b, Guayama, P.R.**
7. **David Meyer, lhp, Kansas**
8. **Ryan Beeney, ss, Kent**
9. **Mike Mitchell, 1b, UCLA**
10. **Eric Kofler, 1b, Central Catholic HS, Clearwater, Fla.**
11. **Jake Robbins, rhp, Myers Park HS, Charlotte, N.C.**
12. **Marty Robinson, lhp, Cape Coral (Fla.) HS**
13. **Jason Jarvis, rhp, Bellevue (Neb.)**
14. **Eric Schaffner, rhp, Frank Phillips (Texas) JC**
15. **Dwaine Edgar, rhp, Southern**
16. **Brian Binversie, rhp, Iowa State**
17. Jason Grabowski, c, Morgan School, Clinton, Conn.
18. Charlie Ward, ss, Florida State
19. **Derek Dukart, 3b, Nebraska**
20. **Ben Ford, rhp, Indian Hills (Iowa) CC**
21. **Chris Corn, rhp, Kansas**
22. **Felix Mejia, rhp, American HS, Hialeah, Fla.**
23. Barry Patton, c, Kosciusko (Miss.) HS
24. Jason Grilli, rhp, Baker HS, Baldwinsville, N.Y.
25. **James Franklin, ss, Sarasota (Fla.) HS**
26. Patrick Dunham, rhp, Portage Central HS, Portage, Mich.
27. **Jeremy Benson, lhp, Delaware**
28. Corey Brittan, rhp, Hutchinson (Kan.) CC
29. Mitchell Henderson, of, Culver Military Academy, Lexington, Ky.
30. Michael Hughes, ss, Caruthers Union HS, Fresno, Calif.
31. Michael Karow, lhp, Tyler (Texas) JC
32. Fernando Rivero, 1b, Jackson HS, Miami
33. Mike Schnautz, lhp, Bryan (Texas) HS
34. Matthew Jones, rhp, Miami (Ohio)
35. Chris Halliday, c, Florida CC-Jacksonville
36. Sidney Newman, ss, Cosumnes River (Calif.) JC
37. Matt Blank, lhp, Martin HS, Arlington, Texas
38. Aaron Horton, lhp, Gulf Coast (Fla.) CC
39. Ben Tucker, rhp, Southern California
40. David Harper, rhp, McLennan (Texas) CC
41. **Carlos Yedo, 1b, Miami-Dade CC South**
42. David Trentine, c, Cypress (Calif.) JC
43. Casey Cunningham, lhp, Santa Rosa (Calif.) JC
44. Casey Hensley, 1b, Fort Scott (Ky.) CC
45. Steven Keen, rhp, Florida CC-Jacksonville
46. Darryl Craig, 1b, Kwantlen (B.C.)
47. Matt Schardt, rhp, Lake Brantley HS, Longwood, Fla.
48. Jason Deyell, rhp, Montcalm HS, London, Ontario
49. John Adams, of, South HS, Olathe, Kan.
50. Jeremy Lee, rhp, Apache (Okla.) HS
51. Todd Martin, rhp, South Florence HS, Florence, S.C.
52. Eric Carlisle, of, Rayburn HS, Pasadena, Texas
53. Zack McWhirter, rhp, Plano (Texas) HS
54. Jason Jordan, 1b, Alabama
55. Eddy Furniss, 1b, Nacogdoches (Texas) HS
56. Dan DeYoung, rhp, Lisbon (Iowa) HS
57. Robert Chrysler, lhp, Boca Ciega HS, St. Petersburg, Fla.
58. Jarred McAlvain, 1b, Eastern Oklahoma State JC
59. Shawn Onley, rhp, Northeast Texas CC
60. Jose Sevillano, of, Vega Alta, P.R.
61. Gerald Butt, c, Kwantlen (B.C.)
62. Erik Keech, c, Manatee (Fla.) JC
63. Erik Mattern, ss, Mater Dei HS, Fountain Valley, Calif.
64. Goefrey Tomlinson, of, Everman (Texas) HS
65. Michael Gil, c, Miami-Dade CC South
66. Kyle Heine, c, Scarborough HS, Houston, Texas
67. George Elmore, rhp, Louisburg (N.C.) JC
68. Anthony Edwards, rhp, Bartlesville (Okla.) HS
69. Dusty Rhodes, of, Madison (N.J.) HS
70. David Aldrich, rhp, Jefferson State (Ala.) CC
71. Keith Dilgard, rhp, Florida CC-Jacksonville
72. Clint Sauls, rhp, Evans HS, Martinez, Ga.
73. Chris Dickerson, 3b, Blinn (Texas) HS
74. Ryan Anholt, of, Moose Jaw (Saskatchewan) HS
75. Brandon James, 1b, Sacramento CC
76. Vernon Williams, of, Solano (Calif.) JC
77. Darren Bowleg, lhp, Indian River (Fla.) CC
78. Jose Cepeda, 2b/ss, Linn-Benton (Ore.) CC
79. Mike Schwamel, of, Holy Name HS, Seven Hills, Ohio
80. Jason Clark, 1b, Riverside (Calif.) CC
81. Thomas Carnes, rhp, Miami (Okla.) HS
82. Tyler Bain, 2b, Seward County (Kan.) CC
83. Derek Adair, rhp, Neosho County (Kan.) CC
84. **Monte Barnes, lhp, Indian River (Fla.) JC**
85. Jimmie Slaton, 3b, Barton County (Kan.) CC
86. Nathan Dighera, 3b, Hilltop HS, Chula Vista, Calif.
87. Wyley Steelmon, c, Cowley County (Kan.) CC

OAKLAND ATHLETICS

June—Regular Phase (2)

1. **Ben Grieve, of, Martin HS, Arlington, Texas**
2. **Brad Rigby, rhp, Georgia Tech**
3. **Bill King, rhp, Birmingham-Southern**
4. **Jason Beverlin, rhp, Western Carolina**
5. Ryan Drese, rhp, Bishop O'Dowd HS, Oakland
6. **Emil Brown, of, Indian River (Fla.) CC**
7. **Mike Maurer, rhp, Iowa State**
8. **Rob DeBoer, c, South Carolina**
9. Robert Harris, ss, Texas A&M
10. Stephen Randolph, lhp, Galveston (Texas) JC
11. Bubba Scarce, rhp, Tunstall HS, Danville, Va.
12. **Todd Weinberg, lhp, CC of Rhode Island**
13. **Al Gogolin, rhp, Georgia Tech**
14. **Chris Cochrane, rhp, Rutgers**
15. **Jon Valenti, 3b, Oklahoma City**
16. **Matt McDonald, lhp, Parkland (Ill.) JC**
17. **Eric Martins, 2b, Long Beach State**
18. **Manny DaSilva, c, North Carolina**
19. **Chad Rolish, lhp, Cal State Fullerton**
20. **John Smith, lhp, Old Dominion**
21. **Alex Miranda, 1b, Miami**
22. **Michael Rios, rhp, Pacific**
23. **Khris Law, of, Tunstall HS, Danville, Va.**
24. **Immanuel McDonald, of, Columbia State (Tenn.) CC**
25. Stacy Kelley, rhp, Milford Academy, Glastonbury, Conn.
26. **Mike Stamison, ss, Cumberland (Tenn.)**
27. **Stephen Holden, rhp, Shelby State (Tenn.) CC**
28. Damond Nash, rhp, Arkansas HS, Texarkana, Ark.
29. Michael Spence, rhp, Gordon (Ga.) JC
30. Aaron Gardin, of, Yavapai (Ariz.) JC
31. Terrance Freeman, ss, Edison (Fla.) CC
32. Daniel Crawford, rhp, San Jacinto (Texas) JC
33. Frank Chapman, rhp, San Jacinto (Texas) JC
34. David Plant, rhp, Davis HS, Modesto, Calif.
35. Tim Hudson, rhp, Chattahoochee Valley (Ala.) JC
36. **Chris Helfrich, rhp, Evansville**
37. Brent Whitlock, c, Jackson State (Tenn.) CC
38. Richard Collins, rhp, Southern Union State (Ala.) JC
39. Victor Chambers, 2b, Vallejo (Calif.) HS

PHILADELPHIA PHILLIES

June—Regular Phase (23)

1. **Carlton Loewer, rhp, Mississippi State**
2. **Ryan Nye, rhp, Texas Tech**
3. **Larry Wimberly, lhp, West Orange HS, Winter Garden, Fla.**
4. **Jason Sikes, rhp, Warner Robins (Ga.) HS**
5. **Scott Shores, of, Arizona State**
6. **Eric Schreimann, c, Jefferson City (Mo.) HS**
7. **Matt Beech, lhp, Houston**
8. **Jason Boyd, rhp, Logan (Ill.) JC**
9. **Joel Zamudio, rhp, Monroe HS, Sepulveda, Calif.**
10. **Rob Burger, rhp, Lampeter-Strasburg HS, Lampeter, Pa.**
11. **Mauricio Estavil, lhp, Pepperdine**
12. **Wendell Magee Jr., of, Samford**
13. **Torrey Pettiford, 2b, Pembroke State (N.C.)**
14. **Robert Dodd, lhp, Florida**
15. **Peter Nyari, rhp, Edinboro (Pa.)**
16. **Adrian Antonini, rhp, Louisiana State**
17. **James Northeimer, c, Tennessee**
18. **Jeff Jensen, 1b, Sam Houston State**
19. **John Torok, of, Toledo**
20. **Matt Guiliano, ss, Iona**
21. **Matt Williamson, 2b/ss, Rice**
22. **Brett Legrow, rhp, Southern Mississippi**
23. **Luis Andino, of, Carolina, P.R.**
24. **Bill Mobilia, ss, Minnesota**
25. Bobby Kahlon, rhp, California
26. **Shane Pullen, of, Southern Mississippi**
27. **Jason Valley, rhp, Washington State**
28. **Adan Millan, c, Cal State Fullerton**
29. **Stephan Paasch, rhp, Maryland**
30. **Ken Reed, rhp, Rolla (Mo.) HS**
31. **Kyle Karvala, lhp, Wisconsin-Whitewater**
32. **Larry Huff, ss, Cal State Los Angeles**
33. Ryan Hankins, 3b, Simi Valley (Calif.) HS
34. **Jose Flores, 3b, Texas**
35. **Aaron Royster, of, Northeast Missouri State**
36. **Courtney Mitchell, lhp, Grambling State**
37. **Bronson Heflin, rhp, Tennessee**
38. **Samuel Wampler, c, Hancock (Calif.) JC**
39. Brian Cooper, rhp, Citrus (Calif.) JC
40. Rob Galko, rhp, Oklahoma State
41. **David Stewart, lhp, Tulane**
42. Matt Kastelic, of, Rancho Santiago (Calif.) JC
43. **Johnny Beck, lhp, East Carolina**
44. **Leonard Manning, lhp, Wisconsin**
45. **Brian Stumpf, rhp, Delaware County (Pa.) CC**
46. **Chad Kearney, of, Brentwood HS, Central Islip, N.Y.**
47. Joe Winkelsas, rhp, South Carolina-Salkehatchie JC
48. Jeff Newkirk, of, Taft (Calif.) JC
49. **Jason Russell, 3b, Northeastern Oklahoma A&M JC**
50. Cameron Flower, of, Rincon HS, Tucson, Ariz.
51. Neal Presley, rhp, Opp (Ala.) HS
52. Jeff Andra, lhp, Northwest HS, Lenexa, Kan.
53. Blair Fowler, rhp, Walla Walla (Wash.) CC

PITTSBURGH PIRATES

June—Regular Phase (11)

1. **Mark Farris, ss, Angleton (Texas) HS**
2. **Roger Goedde, rhp, Reitz HS, Evansville, Ind.**
3. **Aaron France, rhp, Cypress (Calif.) JC**
4. **Bryan Farson, lhp, Kent**
5. **Eddie Brooks, 2b, Kentucky**
6. **Mike Asche, ss, Kearney State (Neb.)**
7. **Randy Viegas, lhp, Oakmont HS, Roseville, Calif.**
8. **Bo Springfield, of, Denison (Texas) HS**
9. **Jimmy Anderson, lhp, Western Branch HS, Chesapeake, Va.**
10. Jason Fry, rhp, Grand Island (Neb.) HS
11. **Richard Watts, c, UC Davis**
12. **Cordell Dunn, rhp/ss, Rosa Fort HS, Tunica, Miss.**
13. Thomas Hunter, of/1b, Eagan (Minn.) HS
14. **Anthony Robinson, ss, Diamond Bar (Calif.) HS**
15. **Jeff Kelly, lhp, McKee Tech HS, Staten Island, N.Y.**
16. Jason Krafft, rhp, Edison HS, Tulsa
17. **Richie Blackwell, lhp, East Carolina**
18. **Steve Thobe, 1b/of, Cal State Sacramento**
19. **Jonathan Sweet, c, Ohio State**
20. Andrew Van Wyk, rhp, Heritage HS, Littleton, Colo.
21. **Aaron Edwards, of, Cal Poly Pomona**
22. **Leotis Warren, 3b, Conroe (Texas) HS**
23. Minor Bond, rhp, Vanguard HS, Ocala, Fla.
24. Mark Dobson, rhp, Heritage HS, Littleton, Colo.
25. Pete Zamora, lhp, Capistrano Valley HS, Mission Viejo, Calif.
26. **Stan Schreiber, ss, Kimberly HS, Appleton, Wis.**
27. **Tonka Maynor, of/1b, UNC Greensboro**
28. **Matt Spade, rhp, Marshall**
29. **Paul McSparin, c, Southeastern Illinois**
30. **Matt Amman, c, Central Florida**
31. Matthew Noe, lhp, San Gorgonio HS, Highland, Calif.
32. **Richard Venezia, ss, California (Pa.)**
33. Jason Adamson, of, Moorpark (Calif.) HS
34. Kendrick Wallace, of, Carson (Calif.) HS
35. Kemuel Shipp, c, North Cobb HS, Kennesaw, Ga.
36. Clark Odom, of, Maclay HS, Quincy, Fla.
37. **Joe Maskivish, rhp, West Liberty State (W.Va.)**
38. Wayne Montgomery, ss/2b, Laney (Calif.) JC
39. **Albert Davis, of, Alcoa (Tenn.) HS**
40. **Leland McAfee, ss, Grossmont (Calif.) JC**
41. Jason Wright, rhp, Palomar (Calif.) JC
42. **Greg Chew, rhp, Gloucester (N.J.) CC**
43. **Curry Deutsch, lhp, Winona State (Minn.)**
44. Bryan Barber, lhp, Nogales HS, West Covina, Calif.
45. **Rick Paugh, lhp, Marshall**
46. Brandon Larson, ss, Holmes HS, San Antonio

ST. LOUIS CARDINALS

June—Regular Phase (19)

1. **Bret Wagner, lhp, Wake Forest**
2. **Carl Dale, rhp, Winthrop**
3. **Corey Avrard, rhp, Rummel HS, Metairie, La.**
4. **Yates Hall, rhp, Virginia**
5. **Curtis King, rhp, Philadelphia College of Textiles**
6. **Blake Stein, rhp, Spring Hill (Ala.)**
7. **Richard Mear, lhp, Rowland HS, Rowland Heights, Calif.**
8. **Ryan Foderaro, rhp, Brigham Young**
9. **Antonio Abell, of, Meade County HS, Ekron, Ky.**
10. Bruce Thompson, of, Miami
11. Dan Reichert, rhp, Turlock (Calif.) HS
12. John Bale, lhp, Jefferson Davis (Ala.) JC
13. Ryan Freel, ss, Englewood HS, Jacksonville
14. **Pete Ambrosina, 2b, Lincoln Memorial (Tenn.)**
15. Brandon Parker, rhp, Long Beach (Miss.) HS
16. **Sean Garman, 1b/3b, JC of Southern Idaho**
17. **Mark Roettgen, rhp, Jefferson City (Mo.) HS**
18. **Marcus Logan, rhp, Murray State**
19. **Placido Polanco, ss, Miami-Dade CC Wolfson**
20. Jerome Robinson, of, Taft (Calif.) JC
21. Kyle Wagner, c, Wake Forest
22. **Jose Leon, 3b, Cayey, P.R.**
23. **Ryan Hall, c, Brigham Young**
24. **Keith McDonald, c, Pepperdine**
25. **Kevin Lovingier, lhp, Oklahoma**
26. **Steve Reed, rhp, Palm Beach Lakes HS, North Palm Beach, Fla.**
27. **Manuel Mendez, lhp, Fresno (Calif.) CC**
28. **Richard Hartmann, rhp, Long Island**
29. **Steve Frascatore, rhp, C.W. Post (N.Y.)**
30. **Adam West, lhp, Pierce (Wash.) JC**
31. **Mike McDougal, 1b, Taft (Calif.) JC**
32. **Miguel Rivera, ss, Lincoln Memorial (Tenn.)**
33. **Hector Rodriguez, 3b, Florida Memorial**
34. **Kevin McNeill, lhp, McNeese State**
35. **Jody Crump, lhp, Volunteer State (Tenn.) CC**
36. **Efrain Contreras, of, Texas A&M**
37. **Scott Cunningham, rhp, Arkansas**
38. **Tommy Minor, rhp, Fresno State**
39. **Darren Tawwater, c, Texas Christian**
40. **Bo Johnson, lhp, Rice**
41. **Robert Helvey, lhp, Missouri Baptist**
42. **Keith Glauber, rhp, Montclair State (N.J.)**
43. Rodger Harris, 2b/of, Tulare (Calif.) Union HS
44. **Chris Arambula, 1b, Utah**
45. **Steve Abbs, of, Wyoming**
46. **Matthew Golden, rhp, Princeton**
47. **Dennis McCaffrey, rhp, Pemberton Township HS, Browns Mills, N.J.**
48. Jacob Whitfield, lhp, Florida HS, Tallahassee, Fla.
49. Nakia Hill, 2b, Crawford HS, San Diego
50. Andre Hall, c, St. Augustine HS, New Orleans
51. Robert Smoker, c, Central HS, Manheim, Pa.
52. **Calvin Coach, of, South Carolina-Aiken**
53. Mike Wolger, lhp, California
54. Mark McWilliams, rhp, UNC Charlotte
55. **Clarence Johns, rhp, Southern**
56. **Christian Reinheimer, lhp, Pacific**
57. Jack Moore, lhp, Zapata (Texas) HS
58. Jason Riley, c, Lee HS, Baytown, Texas
59. Duston Atkinson, c/of, Dixie (Utah) JC
60. Jarrod DeGeorgia, rhp, Santa Barbara (Calif.) CC
61. Eric Fuller, ss, Bakersfield (Calif.) JC
62. Michael Glendenning, 3b/of, Crespi HS, West Hills, Calif.
63. Gene Moseley, rhp, Deer Park (Texas) HS

SAN DIEGO PADRES

June—Regular Phase (3)

1. **Dustin Hermanson, rhp, Kent**
2. Troy Glaus, 3b, Carlsbad (Calif.) HS
3. **Heath Murray, lhp, Michigan**
4. **Gordon Amerson, of, San Gorgonio HS, San Bernardino, Calif.**
5. **Eric Newman, rhp, Texas Tech**
6. **Trajan Langdon, 3b/rhp, East HS, Anchorage, Alaska**
7. **Shane Dennis, lhp, Wichita State**
8. **David Ullan, c, Portland State (Ore.)**
9. **Jake Remington, rhp, Broken Arrow (Okla.) HS**
10. **Greg LaRocca, ss, Massachusetts**
11. **Keith Davis, rhp, Nicholls State**
12. **Rod Jackson, ss, Fairview HS, Camden, Ark.**
13. **Shawn Knight, ss, William & Mary**
14. **Bubba Dixon, lhp, Delta State (Miss.)**
15. **James Johnson, of, Nevada**
16. Pete Paciorek, 1b, San Marino HS, San Gabriel, Calif.
17. **Jon Morris, c, Northeastern Oklahoma A&M JC**
18. Kurt Blackmon, rhp, Northwestern HS, Rock Hill, S.C.
19. James Hyers, ss, Newton County HS, Covington, Ga.
20. **Scott Schroeder, rhp, Mount Hood (Ore.) CC**
21. **Jason Tyrus, of, Washington**
22. **Josh Davis, c, Locust Grove (Okla.) HS**
23. **Luis Torres, rhp, Manati, P.R.**
24. **Erik Martinez, ss, Pepperdine**
25. Rocky Biddle, rhp, Temple City HS, San Gabriel, Calif.
26. Rusty Sarnes, lhp, Havana (Ill.) HS
27. **Darren Grass, c, Minnesota**
28. Tim Jorgensen, ss, Wisconsin-Oshkosh
29. Alan Goudy, of, Kokomo (Ind.) HS
30. Jesse Coronado, rhp, Foothill HS, Bakersfield, Calif.
31. **Arthur Jenkins, rhp, Texas Southern**
32. **Dwain Koscielniak, 3b, Ferris State (Mich.)**
33. **Mark Merila, 2b, Minnesota**
34. Cruz Molina, rhp, Trinidad State (Colo.) JC
35. **Kenya Hunt, 1b, Master's (Calif.)**
36. Randy Bass, lhp, Crowder (Mo.) JC
37. **Jeff Conway, of, Texas**
38. **Jarman Leach, lhp, San Diego State**
39. **Rod Lindsey, of, Opelika (Ala.) HS**
40. David Robinson, of, Santa Fe (Fla.) CC
41. **Chris Clark, rhp, Otero (Colo.) JC**
42. Daryl Rutherford, 2b/of, Union (S.C.) HS
43. Tim Harrington, 1b, Glens Falls HS, Queensbury, N.Y.
44. **Mark Barrett, lhp, Maryland**
45. **Eliezer Rosario, ss, Cayey, P.R.**
46. Oscar Hirschkorn, rhp, Kings River (Calif.) JC
47. **Antonio Fernandez, 3b, New Mexico**
48. Adam Sisk, rhp, Riverdale HS, Mitchellville, Md.
49. Jason Michaels, of, Jesuit HS, Tampa
50. Steve Chavez, 3b, Carlsbad (N.M.) HS
51. Kevin Workman, ss, North Central HS, Spokane, Wash.
52. **Mark Desabrias, rhp, Lake Howell HS, Castleberry, Fla.**
53. Kevin Durham, rhp, Pendleton (S.C.) HS
54. Derek Mickelson, rhp, Arizona State

SAN FRANCISCO GIANTS

June—Regular Phase (25)

1. **Dante Powell, of, Cal State Fullerton** (Pick from Rangers as compensation for Type A free agent Will Clark)
1. (Pick to Astros as compensation for Type A free agent Mark Portugal)
1. **Jacob Cruz, of, Arizona State** (Supplemental pick—32nd—for loss of Clark)
2. **Andy Taulbee, rhp, Clemson**
3. **Alberto Castillo, 1b/lhp, Miami-Dade CC Wolfson**
4. **Troy Brohawn, lhp, Nebraska**
5. **Bobby Howry, rhp, McNeese State**
6. **Jesse Ibarra, 3b/rhp, Loyola Marymount**
7. **Pete Prater, rhp, Southwest Missouri State**
8. **Chad Frontera, rhp, Seton Hall**
9. **Keith Foulke, rhp, Lewis-Clark State (Idaho)**
10. Mike Littlefield, rhp, Mohave HS, Bullhead City, Ariz.
11. **Chad Dillon, rhp, Boone County HS, Florence, Ky.**
12. **Jeff Poor, c, Los Angeles Harbor JC**
13. **Ricardo Calderon, 1b, Iowa Western CC**
14. **Luis Rodriguez, lhp, Carolina, P.R.**

15. **Mike Schiefelbein, rhp, Arizona**
16. **Kevin Watson, of, George Fox (Ore.)**
17. **Ryan Hornbeck, lhp, El Camino (Calif.) JC**
18. **Kevin Lake, lhp, Nevada**
19. **Cory Lintern, rhp, Cal State Dominguez Hills**
20. J.D. Drew, of, Lowndes HS, Valdosta, Ga.
21. **Chad Hartvigson, lhp, Washington**
22. **Greg Keifer, of, Toledo**
23. Jacob Esteves, rhp, Sacramento CC
24. **Todd Wilson, 3b, Lewis-Clark State (Idaho)**
25. **Michael Villano, c, Saginaw Valley State (Mich.)**
26. **Scott Cook, rhp, Central Michigan**
27. **Dennys Gomez, rhp, William Penn (Iowa)**
28. **Anthony Mattos, rhp, Elon**
29. **Eric Martin, of, Cal State Dominguez Hills**
30. Greg White, rhp, Waynesboro (Pa.) Area HS
31. Tristan Paul, 3b, Los Angeles Harbor JC
32. Jack Witt, rhp, Hutchinson (Kan.) CC
33. **James Apicella, of, C.W. Post (N.Y.)**
34. **Brian Shepherd, c, Mesa State (Colo.)**
35. Angel Melendez, of, Labette (Kan.) CC
36. **Dan Schneider, c, UNC Greensboro**
37. Mike Lincoln, rhp, American River (Calif.) JC
38. Tim Conklin, rhp, Mount Hood (Ore.) CC
39. Daniel Sweet, rhp, Shasta HS, Redding, Calif.
40. Joel Greene, lhp, Madison HS, Portland, Ore.
41. Leroy McCauley, of, Central HS, Cape Girardeau, Mo.
42. Matt Schuldt, c, Washington HS, Sioux Falls, S.D.
43. Todd Eastin, c, South Mountain (Ariz.) CC
44. Brad Seare, lhp, West Jordan HS, Salt Lake City
45. Matt Woodward, 1b, Redmond (Wash.) HS
46. David Rivera, rhp, Toa Baja, P.R.
47. Richard Nye, rhp, Westark (Ark.) CC
48. Eric Smith, rhp, Butler County (Kan.) CC
49. Matt McGuire, c, Parkway West HS, Chesterfield, Mo.
50. Cody Barney, 3b, Chemeketa (Ore.) CC
51. Bryan Hule, lhp, Westark (Ark.) CC
52. Jason Thrower, ss, Yuma (Ariz.) HS
53. Brian Sailor, rhp, Marina HS, Huntington Beach, Calif.
54. Geoff Wilson, of, Fountain Valley (Calif.) HS
55. Alan Paisano, rhp, Burroughs HS, Ridgecrest, Calif.
56. **Dan Topping, c, St. Petersburg (Fla.) HS**
57. Geoff Williamson, rhp, West Jones HS, Laurel, Miss.
58. Robert Dillard, lhp, Huntington Beach (Calif.) HS

SEATTLE MARINERS

June—Regular Phase (14)

1. **Jason Varitek, c, Georgia Tech**
2. **Trey Moore, lhp, Texas A&M**
3. **Matt Wagner, rhp, Iowa State**
4. **Mike Burrows, of, American Fork (Utah) HS**
5. **Tom Szimanski, rhp, Florida Southern**
6. Joe Mays, rhp, Southeast HS, Bradenton, Fla.
7. **Chris Beck, rhp, Master's (Calif.)**
8. Dwayne Dobson, rhp, Clearwater (Fla.) HS
9. **James Rowson, lhp, Mount St. Michaels HS, Bronx, N.Y.**
10. **Doug Carroll, of, South Florida**
11. Carlos Rose, of, Cleveland (Miss.) HS
12. **Eric Clifford, rhp, Mesa (Ariz.) CC**
13. **Roy Smith, rhp, Dixie Hollins HS, Pinellas Park, Fla.**
14. Frank Sanders, of, Auburn
15. **Jason Ruskey, lhp, Arizona State**
16. Anthony Southern, of, Whiteville (N.C.) HS
17. Mike Martin, c, Florida State
18. **Colin Hinds, of, Loyola Marymount**
19. **Cy Simonton, of, Pittsburg (Calif.) HS**
20. Gus Ornstein, 1b, Fieldston HS, Bronx, N.Y.
21. **Eric Morgan, rhp, Miami**
22. **Osvaldo Fernandez, lhp, Mission (Calif.) JC**
23. Kevin Trimble, of, Mattoon (Ill.) HS
24. Adonis Harrison, ss, Muir HS, Pasadena, Calif.
25. **Matt Sachse, lhp, Ferris HS, Spokane, Wash.**
26. **Rick Ladjevich, 3b, Central Missouri State**
27. **Shane Thomason, ss, Chattanooga State (Tenn.) CC**
28. **Kyle Towner, of, Alabama-Birmingham**
29. **Shawn Buhner, 1b, Lewis-Clark State (Idaho)**
30. **Marcus Williams, rhp, Henry Ford HS, Detroit**
31. **Randy Vickers, ss, Glendale (Calif.) JC**
32. Jordan Zimmerman, lhp, Blinn (Texas) JC
33. Jason Hill, c, Cerritos (Calif.) JC
34. Todd Ozias, rhp, Taravella HS, Tamarac, Fla.
35. Chris Hayes, 3b, Jacksonville
36. Scott Atchison, rhp, McCollough HS, Woodlands, Texas
37. Johnathan Rose, lhp, Eastern Alamance HS, Haw River, N.C.
38. James Bowman, lhp, Green River (Wash.) CC
39. Michael Rooney, rhp, North Rockland HS, Stony Point, N.Y.
40. Matt Garrick, c, Duncanville (Texas) HS
41. **Shane Heams, of, Bedford HS, Lambertville, Mich.**
42. Brian Saltarelli, of, El Toro HS, Lake Forest, Calif.
43. Gus Rubio, c, El Camino (Calif.) CC
44. Greg Scheer, lhp, Jacksonville
45. Kyle Kennedy, rhp, Mississippi State
46. **Marvin Fowler, of, Palatka (Fla.) HS**
47. Greg Goligoski, of, Prescott (Ariz.) HS
48. Richard Nunez, rhp, Gulliver Prep HS, Miami
49. Brandon Butler, of, Hardin County HS, Selmer, Tenn.
50. Derek Nicholson, c, Torrance (Calif.) HS
51. Stephen Bagby, of, Glen Oaks (Ind.) CC
52. Brad Smith, 3b, Marina HS, Huntington Beach, Calif.
53. Saladin McCullough, of, Pasadena, Calif.
54. Warren Tisdale, rhp, Mandarin HS, Jacksonville
55. Brad Marshall, of, JC of San Mateo (Calif.)
56. Jermain Jordan, of, Vidalia (Ga.) HS
57. Scott Needham, c, Butler County (Kan.) CC
58. Tim Hill, rhp, Logan (Ill.) JC
59. Ramon Arias, 1b, Lompoc (Calif.) HS
60. Albert Derenches, lhp, Gaither HS, Tampa
61. Morgan Ensberg, ss, Redondo Union HS, Hermosa Beach, Calif.
62. Lucas Solomon, rhp, Canyon HS, Canyon Country, Calif.
63. Kevin High, of, Palm Desert (Calif.) HS
64. Richard Mora, rhp, Cypress Creek HS, Orlando
65. **Shelby Johnson, c/rhp, Holmes (Miss.) JC**
66. David Waites, rhp, McCullough HS, Spring, Texas
67. Jose Gonzales, c, Seminole State (Okla.) JC
68. Juan Romero, of, Carolina, P.R.
69. Kyle Rask, of, Redmond (Wash.) HS
70. Gerald Eady, of, Lee HS, Jacksonville
71. John Lauderdale, c, Tustin (Calif.) HS
72. Toby Sanchez, of, Rancho Santiago (Calif.) JC
73. Jose Montenegro, ss, South Gate (Calif.) HS
74. Leron Cook, of, Roosevelt HS, Fresno
75. Steve Rawson, 3b, Redondo HS, Redondo Beach, Calif.

TEXAS RANGERS

June—Regular Phase (22)

1. (Pick to Giants as compensation for Type A free agent Will Clark)
2. **Kevin Brown, c, Southern Indiana**
3. **Scott Podsednik, of, West (Texas) HS**
4. **Dan Hower, lhp, Creighton**
5. **Jason Johnson, of, Hogan HS, Vallejo, Calif.**
6. **Jim Brower, rhp, Minnesota**
7. **Bucky Buckles, rhp, Oklahoma**
8. **Mark Little, of, Memphis State**
9. **John Powell, rhp, Auburn**
10. **Stephen Larkin, 1b/of, Texas**
11. Terry Harvey, rhp, North Carolina State
12. **Matt Bokemeier, ss, UC Santa Barbara**
13. **Kevin Millican, c, Southeastern Louisiana**
14. **Carlos Simmons, rhp, Prince George's (Md.) CC**
15. **Chris Gogolewski, lhp, St. Mary's (Texas)**
16. **Craig McLendon, c, Jonesboro (Ga.) HS**
17. **Reid Ryan, rhp, Texas Christian**
18. Trey Salinas, c, Moody HS, Corpus Christi, Texas
19. **Erik Sauve, 2b, Virginia Commonwealth**
20. **Scott Stewart, lhp, East Gaston HS, Stanley, N.C.**
21. **Asbel Ortiz, ss, Cidra, P.R.**
22. Gerald Johnson, of, Menlo HS, Atherton, Calif.
23. **Ryan Rutz, 2b, Washington**

24. **Jason Miller, c, St. Rose (N.Y.)**
25. **Rodney Cook, rhp, Stephen F. Austin**
26. **Eddie Comeaux, of, California**
27. **Daniel Vasquez, of, Rockland (N.Y.) CC**
28. **Jaime Escamilla, lhp, Point Loma Nazarene (Calif.)**
29. **Mike Mortimer, rhp, Northwest Nazarene (Idaho)**
30. Gary MacKinlay, lhp, Hylton HS, Dumphries, Va.
31. **Joe Kail, 3b, Johns Hopkins (Md.)**
32. **Matthew Pauls, rhp/of, Odessa (Texas) JC**
33. **Joe Keusch, rhp, Eastern Illinois**
34. **Janos Briscoe, rhp, Western Kentucky**
35. **Matthew Buhs, lhp, Southern Illinois**
36. **Michael-Sean Ryan, rhp, Broadneck HS, Annapolis, Md.**
37. Jesse Brown, rhp, Kalaheo HS, Hailua, Hawaii
38. Buck Hall, lhp, Georgia Tech
39. James Matan, 1b, Gonzaga HS, Kensington, Md.

TORONTO BLUE JAYS

June—Regular Phase (26)

1. **Kevin Witt, ss, Bishop Kenny HS, Jacksonville**
2. **John Crowther, rhp, Coker (S.C.)**
3. **Chris McBride, rhp, UNC Wilmington**
4. Brad Freeman, ss, Oxford (Miss.) HS
5. **Tom Davey, rhp, Henry Ford (Mich.) JC**
6. **Michael Peeples, ss, Clay HS, Green Cove Springs, Fla.**
7. **Jose Maysonet, ss, Arecibo, P.R.**
8. **Chris Pettiet, rhp, San Ramon Valley HS, Danville, Calif.**
9. **Don Morris, c, North Clayton HS, Riverdale, Ga.**
10. **Mike Halperin, lhp, Central Florida**
11. **Billy Hibbard, rhp, Colonial HS, Orlando**
12. Tommy Fambrough, ss, South Florence HS, Florence, S.C.
13. **Joe Davenport, rhp, Santana HS, Santee, Calif.**
14. **Robert Hampton, of, Mount Pleasant (Texas) HS**
15. **Gary Glover, rhp, De Land (Fla.) HS**
16. **Willie Villa, of, Kamehameha HS, Nanakuli, Hawaii**
17. Ryan Cummings, rhp, Walton HS, Marietta, Ga.
18. **Mason Smith, rhp, Oregon State**
19. **Chris Freeman, rhp, Tennessee**
20. Matt Freeman, c, Indian River (Fla.) CC
21. **Shayne Timmons, c, Concord (W.Va.)**
22. Brandon Ward, rhp, Fontana (Calif.) HS
23. **Andy Thompson, ss, Sun Prairie (Wis.) HS**
24. **Brent Bearden, rhp, Baylor**
25. **Randy Smith, rhp, Northeastern Oklahoma A&M JC**
26. **Terry Adams, 3b, Eastern HS, Toronto**
27. **Brian Smith, rhp, UNC Wilmington**
28. **Mark Landers, 1b, West Virginia**
29. Brian Dahl, rhp, Connecticut
30. Preston White, of, Boys and Girls HS, Brooklyn, N.Y.
31. **Steve Soper, 2b, Tennessee**
32. Michael Pageler, rhp, Red Mountain HS, Mesa, Ariz.
33. Ryan Golisano, rhp, Fullerton (Calif.) HS
34. Jimmy Turman, rhp, Gordo (Ala.) HS
35. **Lester Henderson, lhp, Redlands (Calif.)**
36. **David Mendoza, rhp, El Camino HS, Oceanside, Calif.**
37. **Andy Shatley, 1b, Nettleton HS, Jonesboro, Ark.**
38. **Edward Budz, rhp, St. Xavier (Ill.)**
39. **Sean Strade, rhp, Portland**
40. Mike Kleckner, rhp, Sentinel HS, Missoula, Mont.
41. **Battle Holley, 3b, UNC Wilmington**
42. **Michael Zavershnik, lhp, St. Michael's HS, Mississauga, Ontario**
43. **Ben Lowe, lhp, Indian River (Fla.) CC**
44. **Eric Horton, rhp, Talledega (Ala.)**
45. Tracy Evridge, of, Midland Valley HS, North Augusta, S.C.
46. Jonathan Shank, rhp, Chaparral HS, Scottsdale, Ariz.
47. **Michael Strange, 2b, Santa Fe (Fla.) CC**
48. Kerry Collins, rhp, Penn State
49. Dustyn Edler, of, Eisenhower HS, Yakima, Wash.
50. **Brian Bowles, rhp, Peninsula HS, Manhattan Beach, Calif.**
51. David Steffler, rhp, St. Peter's HS, Keene, Ontario
52. Reginald Amos, ss, Grenada (Miss.) HS
53. D'Wayne Bates, of, Silver Bluff HS, Jackson, S.C.
54. **Chris Woodward, ss, Northview HS, Covina, Calif.**
55. Edward Taylor, rhp, Early County HS, Blakely, Ga.
56. Charles Mitchell, rhp, Jordan HS, Long Beach
57. Joe Nelson, ss, Seminole State (Okla.) JC
58. Jaime Alvarez, c, Franklin HS, Los Angeles
59. Michael Cochran, rhp, Brandon (Miss.) HS
60. Sidney Harden, rhp, Harris County HS, Hamilton, Ga.
61. Mike Hannah, of, Gordon (Ga.) JC
62. Rodney Hall, 2b, Clover (S.C.) HS
63. Alex Barbosa, of, Caguas, P.R.
64. William Carroll, rhp, Tallahassee (Fla.) CC

1995 CUBAN SENSATION GRABS HYPE, BUT ANGELS, ROCKIES, BLUE JAYS SCORE WITH COLLEGE SELECTIONS

For the first time in the draft's history, the player talked about most before the affair wasn't a strong-armed Texan, power-hitting Californian or any player from the United States. It was a Cuban refugee.

Ariel Prieto, a hard-throwing righthander, flew to the United States some six weeks before the draft. He didn't defect—he left with his government's permission by claiming he wanted to be with his wife's family in Florida—but he immediately sent scouting departments buzzing.

Some organizations said they would have chosen Prieto No. 1 overall. The Angels, who actually owned the pick, weren't among them.

Prieto ultimately went No. 5 to Oakland, and he made his major league debut four weeks later after signing a $1.2 million bonus contract. He became the 19th player in the draft era to enter the big leagues without any minor league experience and was the oldest first-rounder ever.

"I did this because this is what I have dreamed of doing for years," said Prieto, who claimed to be 25 but was believed to be 28. He finished the 1995 season with a 2-6 record and 4.97 ERA for the A's and ultimately won just 15 major league games in five seasons with Oakland. He spent the majority of his career pitching in Triple-A, with his last season coming in 2005.

Prieto's agent, Gus Dominguez, said that before the draft several clubs offered him $2.3 million to sign Prieto on the open market. But Major League Baseball ruled that because he had achieved temporary residency in the United States, Prieto was subject to the draft process.

Aside from Prieto, the first round unfolded with few surprises. Most encouraging to scouting staffs was the consensus that the 1995 draft pool was one of the deepest ever.

The Angels focused on Nebraska outfielder Darin Erstad all spring and didn't let Prieto's late presence dissuade them. Erstad, 21, was the consensus best player available. After two months of negotations, the Angels signed Erstad to a $1.575 million bonus. He was in the big leagues by 1996 and became a fixture in the Angels outfield for 11 seasons.

The pick following Erstad was just as much of a lock. The Padres had been infatuated with Ben Davis, widely considered the best high school catcher since Dale Murphy 21 years before, and snapped him up with the No. 2 selection. They signed him immediately for $1.3 million. He reached the big leagues in 1998, but ultimately the Padres tired of waiting for him to fulfill his potential and traded him to the Mariners after the 2001 season. He compiled 1,598 career major league at-bats but was never a significant contributor.

LARRY GOREN

Ariel Prieto was the talk of the draft but never lived up to his advance billing

The Cubs took the first pitcher in righthander Kerry Wood, the first time since 1978 that the first pitcher went as low as No. 4. The selection paid off for the Cubs, as Wood became a true big league power pitcher before injuries plagued his career. he experienced a rebirth as a reliever in 2008.

But the biggest scores in the 1995 class came beyond the top five. The Rockies found their first legitimate franchise cornerstone at No. 8, taking Tennessee outfielder Todd Helton, while the Blue Jays scored at No. 17 with righthander Roy Halladay, a Colorado high school product.

Helton was in the major leagues by 1997 and still manned first base in Colorado 12 years later. He had more than 2,000 career hits to his credit, as well as five All-Star Game appearances and three Gold Gloves.

Halladay, meanwhile, became one of the best pitchers in the game in Toronto. He reached the major league in 1998 but didn't fully establish himself until 2002. By 2003, though, he won the American League

Cy Young Award, and he had 148 career wins at the end of the 2009 season, with no sign that he'd be slowing down.

Strike Can't Stop Inflation

Because the draft took place in the wake of a strike, which sapped the industry of hundreds of millions of dollars in revenue, many executives predicted signing bonuses for draft picks would decrease in 1995. They were wrong, though bonuses did increase at a lower rate than in previous years. The average up-front payment for first-round picks climbed to $913,000, 15.6 percent higher than in 1994.

One player who surely would have raised the average was prep quarterback/righthander Chad Hutchinson, the No. 26 pick by the Braves, but he became the only 1995 first-rounder not to sign. He declined the Braves' $1.5 million offer and enrolled at Stanford to play football and baseball. He eventually signed with the Cardinals in 1998 and reached the big leagues, but he gave up baseball to return to football and played briefly for the Dallas Cowboys.

There were 1,666 players selected in 1995, over 87 rounds. Oakland was the first team to drop out, in the 45th round, and the Marlins were the last.

There were only two compensation picks between the first and second rounds, a reflection of the few free agents who were offered arbitration by their former clubs. Normally, if a Type A free agent signs with another club, his former club receives that club's first- or second-round draft pick and a supplemental pick at the end of the first round—unless arbitration is not offered. With the strike in full bloom, few clubs were willing to offer arbitration.

Owners also developed another plan to try to slow bonus inflation. This plan would have established an overall cap on bonus payments allowed for each team to sign both draft and international players during a calendar year. The proposal would have provided the team with the No. 1 pick in the draft $1.302 million for all its amateur signees. The second team would have $1.290 million, with caps decreasing down the line. In addition, teams would have specific spending limits for picks in the first five rounds of the draft—the precusor to bonus slots, which entered the draft lexicon in 2000.

Major League Baseball planned to negotiate the plan as part of the overall labor agreement with the union, but it was pushed aside by other issues and never got implemented.

DRAFT 95: FIRST-ROUND PICKS

No.	Club	Player, Pos.	School	Hometown	Ht.	Wt.	B-T	Age
1.	Angels	Darin Erstad, of	Nebraska	Jamestown, N.D.	6-2	195	L-L	21
2.	Padres	Ben Davis, c	Malvern Prep	Malvern, Pa.	6-2	175	B-R	18
3.	Mariners	Jose Cruz Jr., of	Rice	Houston	6-0	190	B-R	21
4.	Cubs	Kerry Wood, rhp	Grand Prairie HS	Grand Prairie, Texas	6-3	185	R-R	17
5.	Athletics	Ariel Prieto, rhp	Palm Springs	Marianao, Cuba	6-3	220	R-R	25
6.	Marlins	Jaime Jones, of	Rancho Bernardo HS	San Diego	6-3	180	L-L	18
7.	Rangers	Jonathan Johnson, rhp	Florida State	Ocala, Fla.	6-0	180	R-R	20
8.	Rockies	Todd Helton, 1b/lhp	Tennessee	Knoxville	6-2	190	L-L	21
9.	Brewers	Geoff Jenkins, of	Southern California	Rancho Cordova, Calif.	6-1	200	L-R	20
10.	Pirates	Chad Hermansen, ss	Green Valley HS	Henderson, Nev.	6-2	175	R-R	17
11.	Tigers	Mike Drumright, rhp	Wichita State	Valley Center, Kan.	6-3	210	R-R	21
12.	Cardinals	Matt Morris, rhp	Seton Hall	Montgomery, N.Y.	6-5	210	R-R	20
13.	Twins	Mark Redman, lhp	Oklahoma	Del Mar, Calif.	6-5	210	L-L	21
14.	Phillies	Reggie Taylor, of	Newberry HS	Newberry, S.C.	6-1	185	L-R	18
15.	Red Sox	Andy Yount, rhp	Kingwood HS	Kingwood, Texas	6-2	180	R-R	18
16.	Giants	Joe Fontenot, rhp	Acadiana HS	Lafayette, La.	6-2	180	R-R	18
17.	Blue Jays	Roy Halladay, rhp	West HS	Arvada, Colo.	6-5	200	R-R	18
18.	Mets	Ryan Jaroncyk, ss	Orange Glen HS	Escondido, Calif.	6-0	170	B-R	18
19.	Royals	Juan Lebron, of	Huyke HS	Arroyo, P.R.	6-4	185	R-R	18
20.	Dodgers	David Yocum, lhp	Florida State	Miami	6-1	180	L-L	20
21.	Orioles	Alvie Shepherd, rhp	Nebraska	Bellwood, Ill.	6-7	215	L-R	21
22.	Astros	Tony McNight, rhp	Arkansas HS	Texarcana, Ark.	6-5	210	R-R	17
23.	Indians	David Miller, 1b	Clemson	Philadelphia	6-4	200	L-L	21
24.	Red Sox	Corey Jenkins, of	Dreher HS	Columbia, S.C.	6-2	195	R-R	18
25.	White Sox	Jeff Liefer, 3b	Long Beach State	Upland, Calif.	6-3	185	L-R	20
26.	Braves	*Chad Hutchinson, rhp	Torrey Pines HS	Encinitas, Calif.	6-6	230	R-R	18
27.	Yankees	Shea Morenz, of	Texas	San Angelo, Texas	6-2	205	L-R	21
28.	Expos	Michael Barrett, ss	Pace Academy	Atlanta	6-2	185	R-R	18

*Did not sign

1995

CLUB-BY-CLUB SELECTIONS

ATLANTA BRAVES

June—Regular Phase (26)

1. Chad Hutchinson, rhp, Torrey Pines HS, San Diego
2. **Jim Scharrer, 1b, Cathedral Prep, Erie, Pa.**
3. **Rob Bell, rhp, Marlboro Central HS, Marlboro, N.Y.**
4. **Jimmy Osting, lhp, Trinity HS, Louisville**
5. **Kevin McGlinchy, rhp, Malden (Mass.) HS**
6. Matt Middleton, ss, Graham HS, Conover, Ohio
7. **Gerald Vecchioni, ss, Patapsco HS, Baltimore**
8. Chad Mead, lhp/1b, Woodward (Okla.) HS
9. **Ben Wyatt, lhp, Fair HS, Little Rock, Ark.**
10. **Ryan Schurman, rhp, Tualatin (Ore.) HS**
11. **Antone Brooks, lhp, Norfolk State**
12. **Joe Bauldree, rhp, Wake Forest-Rolesville HS, Wake Forest, N.C.**
13. **Charlie Cruz, lhp, Florida State**
14. **Steve Hacker, 1b, Southwest Missouri State**
15. **Matt McWilliams, rhp, UNC Charlotte**
16. Casey Crawford, of, O'Connell HS, Falls Church, Va.
17. **Jason Shy, c, Butte (Calif.) JC**
18. **Brian Rust, 3b, Lewis & Clark (Ore.)**
19. **Ben Fowler, rhp, Pace Academy, Alpharetta, Ga.**
20. Jason Hart, ss, Fair Grove (Mo.) HS
21. David Noyce, lhp, Marietta (Ga.) HS
22. **Oscar Otero, 3b, Cayey, P.R.**
23. **Keith Dougherty, 3b, Columbus (Ga.)**
24. **Watson Ellison, of, Dixie (Utah) JC**
25. **James Wise, lhp, Abraham Baldwin (Ga.) CC**
26. **Jerry McMullen, lhp, Portland State (Ore.)**
27. **Matt Taylor, ss, Cal State Hayward**
28. **Yan LaGrandeur, rhp, Granby, Quebec**
29. Jacob Ruotsinoja, of, Seminole (Fla.) HS
30. **Ariel Colon, 1b, Carolina, P.R.**
31. **Keith Mayhew, rhp, Ferrum (Va.)**
32. **Phillip Smith, of, Phillipsburg (N.J.) HS**
33. **Corey Walker, of, Teikyo Westmar (Iowa)**
34. **Randy Hodges, of, Florida State**
35. **Curt Schnur, rhp, Delaware**
36. Mike Goldstein, of, Cherry Creek HS, Englewood, Colo.
37. Donnie Thomas, lhp, Andrew (Ga.) JC
38. Troy Satterfield, lhp, Jonesboro (Ga.) HS
39. **Mike Mahoney, c, Creighton**
40. Nathan Bennett, lhp, Coastal Christian HS, Arroyo Grande, Calif.
41. **Walker Reynolds, rhp, Berry (Ga.)**
42. Craig Cozart, rhp, Central Florida
43. Darren Blakely, of, Pensacola (Fla.) HS
44. **Eric White, rhp, Enrico Fermi HS, Enfield, Conn.**
45. **Toby Anglen, 2b, Arkansas State**
46. Craig House, rhp, Christian Brothers HS, Memphis
47. **Zachery Hines, ss, DeKalb (Ga.) JC**
48. **Jason Shiell, rhp, Windsor-Forest HS, Savannah, Ga.**
49. Luther Salinas, rhp/1b, La Verne Lutheran HS, Whittier, Calif.
50. Robert Fishel, lhp, Pflugerville (Texas) HS
51. **Andrew Cochrane, lhp, Pacific Lutheran (Wash.)**
52. **Kevin Loewe, lhp, Maryland-Baltimore County**
53. Jamel McAdory, 1b, Jackson State
54. Craig Owens, of, Chowan (N.C.)
55. Charlie Curry, ss/2b, Centennial HS, Portland, Ore.
56. **Brian Jolliffe, lhp, Maine**

BALTIMORE ORIOLES

June—Regular Phase (21)

1. **Alvie Shepherd, rhp, Nebraska**
2. **Charles Alley, c, Palm Beach Lakes HS, West Palm Beach, Fla.**
3. **Darrell Dent, of, Montclair Prep, Panorama City, Calif.**
4. **Louis Fisher, rhp, Fremont HS, Oakland**
5. Luke Hudson, rhp, Fountain Valley (Calif.) HS
6. John Bale, lhp, Southern Mississippi
7. Kevin Miller, 3b, Ballard HS, Seattle
8. **Scott Eibey, lhp, Northern Iowa**
9. **Joel Stephens, of, Notre Dame HS, Elmira, N.Y.**
10. **David Dellucci, of, Mississippi**
11. **Greg Dean, rhp, Oklahoma State**
12. **Carlos Akins, of, Western Kentucky**
13. **Bob O'Toole, c, Providence**
14. **Chris Bryant, 3b, North Carolina Wesleyan**
15. **Tim Olszewski, rhp, Triton (Ill.) JC**
16. Zach Sorensen, ss, Highland HS, Salt Lake City
17. **Jason Lecronier, of, McNeese State**
18. Lawrence Adams, 1b, Creekside HS, Fairburn, Ga.
19. **Brion King, of, Oviedo (Fla.) HS**
20. Carlos Casillas, 1b, Santa Monica HS, Los Angeles
21. **Dan Reed, lhp, Stanford**
22. Doug Thompson, rhp, Mississippi Gulf Coast JC
23. Matthew Achilles, rhp, Black Hawk (Ill.) JC
24. Jason Albert, 2b, Central Connecticut State
25. Gaylon Dixon, lhp, Seminole State (Okla.) JC
26. **Joaquin Serra, ss, Beverly Hills, Calif.**
27. **Robert Morseman, lhp, Salem-Teikyo (W.Va.)**
28. **Johnny Isom, of, Texas Wesleyan**
29. **Tom Russin, 1b, Eckerd (Fla.)**
30. **Chris Bray, rhp, Mount Olive (N.C.) JC**
31. A.J. Marquardt, of, Columbia Basin (Wash.) CC
32. William Morstad, 3b, Windsor Academy, Macon, Ga.
33. Mike Cosgrove, rhp, Cypress (Calif.) JC
34. Darin Moore, rhp, Lodi HS, Acampo, Calif.
35. **Calvin Pickering, of/1b, King HS, Temple Terrace, Fla.**
36. John Santos, rhp, Corcoran HS, Tulare, Calif.
37. **Avery Taylor, ss, Long Beach (Miss.) HS**
38. Ken Sims, rhp, New Mexico JC
39. Craig Jones, rhp, La Quinta HS, Westminster, Calif.
40. Cory Scott, rhp, Currituck County HS, Knotts Island, N.C.
41. Josh Taylor, ss, Shawnee (Okla.) HS
42. Jerry Hairston Jr., 2b, Naperville (Ill.) North HS
43. Jason Glover, of, Georgia State
44. Mike Wooden, rhp, North County HS, Baltimore
45. **Chris Paxton, c, Palmdale (Calif.) HS**
46. Dan Keller, rhp, Fountain Valley (Calif.) HS
47. Corey Coil, rhp, Francis Scott Key HS, Taneytown, Md.
48. **Wess Winn, ss, Texas-Arlington**
49. Robert Williams, c, Edgewater HS, Winter Park, Fla.

BOSTON RED SOX

June—Regular Phase (15)

1. **Andy Yount, rhp, Kingwood (Texas) HS**
1. **Corey Jenkins, of, Dreher HS, Columbia, S.C.** (Pick from Reds as compensation for Type B free agent Damon Berryhill)
2. **Jose Olmeda, ss, Fajardo, P.R.**
3. **Jay Yennaco, rhp, Pinkerton Academy, Windham, N.H.**
4. **Mike Spinelli, lhp, Revere (Mass.) HS**
5. **Steve Lomasney, c, Peabody (Mass.) HS**
6. **Matt Kinney, rhp, Bangor (Maine) HS**
7. **Cole Liniak, ss, San Dieguito HS, Encinitas, Calif.**
8. **Luis Cardona, c, San Sebastian, P.R.**
9. **Paxton Crawford, rhp, Carlsbad (N.M.) HS**
10. **Lakevie Austin, rhp, Emmanuel (Ga.)**
11. **Jeff Sauve, rhp, Clemson**
12. **Jim Chamblee, ss, Odessa (Texas) JC**
13. **Andy Noffke, rhp, Ohio State**
14. Andrew Beinbrink, 3b, Scripps Ranch HS, San Diego
15. **Kevan Cannon, lhp, Ohio State**

16. **Rontrez Johnson, of, Marshall (Texas) HS**
17. **Bobby Rodgers, rhp, Wake Forest**
18. **Felipe Roman, of, Rio Piedras, P.R.**
19. **Ben Stallings, rhp, Apollo HS, Owensboro, Ky.**
20. **Dwight Ferguson, of, Miami-Dade Christian HS, Carol City, Fla.**
21. **Curtis Romboli, lhp, Boston College**
22. **Pete Prodanov, 3b/of, Oklahoma State**
23. Chuck Lopez, of, Gahr HS, Cerritos, Calif.
24. Chris Toomey, of/rhp, Dana Hills HS, Dana Point, Calif.
25. **Scott Jones, rhp, Miami (Ohio)**
26. **Moises Rojas, of, Brito Miami Private HS, Hialeah, Fla.**
27. **Juan Pena, rhp, Miami-Dade CC Wolfson**
28. Kaleb Harp, c, DeKalb (Texas) HS
29. **Bob Rauch, rhp/ss, Lamar**
30. **Mark Varriano, c, North Dakota**
31. Cliff Brand, rhp, Central Gwinnett HS, Lawrenceville, Ga.
32. Cordele Mincey, rhp, Dodge County HS, Milan, Ga.
33. Matt Burch, rhp, Edison HS, Horseheads, N.Y.
34. Bart Vaughn, rhp, Mount Dora Bible HS, Orlando
35. **Nick Gruber, c, Haddon Township HS, Westmont, N.J.**
36. Derrick Lewis, rhp, Central Alabama CC
37. Angel Diaz, c, Hillsborough (Fla.) JC
38. Tim Boeth, ss, Leon HS, Tallahassee, Fla.
39. Jason Wilson, rhp, South Broward HS, Hollywood, Fla.
40. **Jim Farrell, rhp, Kent**
41. Brian Messer, rhp, Northwest HS, Shawnee, Kan.
42. Juan Chaidez, c, Miami-Dade Christian HS, Hialeah, Fla.
43. Pat Burrell, 3b, Bellarmine Prep, San Jose
44. Bryan Wright, ss, Escambia HS, Pensacola, Fla.
45. Kris Brown, of, Central HS, Kalamazoo, Mich.

CALIFORNIA ANGELS

June—Regular Phase (1)

1. **Darin Erstad, of, Nebraska**
2. **Jarrod Washburn, lhp, Wisconsin-Oshkosh**
3. **Jeremy Blevins, rhp, Sullivan East HS, Bristol, Tenn.**
4. **Brian Cooper, rhp, Southern California**
5. **Justin Baughman, ss, Lewis & Clark (Ore.)**
6. **Ryan Kane, 3b, Presbyterian (S.C.)**
7. Chris Pine, rhp, Tualatin (Ore.) HS
8. **Brian Scutero, rhp, Central Florida**
9. **Jason Stockstill, lhp, Katella HS, Anaheim, Calif.**
10. **Brandon McGuire, rhp/ss, Coahoma (Texas) HS**
11. **Danny Buxbaum, 1b, Miami**
12. **Kyle Wagner, c, Wake Forest**
13. **Jon Vandergriend, of, Washington**
14. **Josh Deakman, rhp, Arizona State**
15. Darren Hooper, of, Aragon HS, San Mateo, Calif.
16. Mario Iglesias, rhp, Stanford
17. Michael Hughes, rhp, Fresno CC
18. Greg Jones, c, Seminole (Fla.) HS
19. **Jed Dalton, 3b/of, Nebraska**
20. **Bryan Graves, c, Southern**
21. Donnell Tate, ss/c, Oakland HS
22. **Jim O'Quinn, lhp, Florida CC**
23. Greg Millichap, of, Serra HS, Woodside, Calif.
24. **Gar Vallone, ss, UCLA**
25. **John Romero, rhp, Mission (Calif.) JC**
26. **Randy Betten, 2b, Arizona State**
27. **Thomas Darrell, rhp, Garrett (Md.) CC**
28. **Alex Llanos, 2b, Carolina, P.R.**
29. Scott Prather, lhp, Lassiter HS, Marietta, Ga.
30. **John McAninch, c, Lewis-Clark State (Idaho)**
31. **Ty Bilderback, of, Arkansas**
32. **E.J. t'Hoen, ss, Indian River (Fla.) CC**
33. Robb Quinlan, ss, Hill-Murray HS, Maplewood, Minn.
34. David Bittler, lhp, Florida CC-Jacksonville
35. Derrick Vargas, lhp, Memorial HS, Newark, Calif.
36. Douglas Hurst, rhp, Okaloosa Walton (Fla.) CC
37. Mike Gauger, lhp, Wakulla HS, St. Marks, Fla.
38. Bobby Bystrowski, 3b/of, Jesuit HS, Fair Oaks, Calif.
39. Jake Jensen, ss/2b, Washington Union HS, Fresno
40. **Steve Mikesell, c, Glendale (Calif.) JC**
41. Doug Blackman, c, Easton HS, New Orleans
42. John Opina, ss, La Sierra HS, Riverside, Calif.
43. Michael Clarke, rhp, St. Petersburg (Fla.) JC
44. **Esteban Barrios, of, Miami-Dade CC New World Center**
45. Widd Workman, rhp/of, Brigham Young
46. Antonio Diaz, ss, Gulf Coast (Fla.) CC
47. Sterling Bullock, 3b, Carson HS, Compton, Calif.
48. Matthew Koziara, rhp, Franklin (Pa.) HS
49. **Derek Ryder, c, Penn State**
50. **David Farfan, rhp, Fresno State**
51. Stanisles James, of, Shanks HS, Quincy, Fla.
52. **Joel Katte, 3b, North HS, Sheboygan, Wis.**
53. Khalif Jefferson, ss, Serra HS, Compton, Calif.
54. Javier Baretti, c, Caguas, P.R.
55. Fernando Sordo, rhp, Spanish River HS, Boca Raton, Fla.
56. Eddie Marquez, 2b/ss, Gurabo, P.R.
57. Steve Mans, ss/2b, Oak Hall HS, Gainesville, Fla.
58. Moses Herrera, rhp, Colton (Calif.) HS
59. Jason Townsell, rhp, Marianna (Fla.) HS
60. Kurt Bultmann, ss/2b, Seminole HS, Largo, Fla.

CHICAGO CUBS

June—Regular Phase (4)

1. **Kerry Wood, rhp, Grand Prairie (Texas) HS**
2. **Brian McNichol, lhp, James Madison**
3. **Jeff Yoder, rhp, Pottsville Area (Pa.) HS**
4. Adam Everett, ss, Harrison HS, Marietta, Ga.
5. **Ismael Villegas, rhp, Guaynabo, P.R.**
6. **Tony Ellison, of, North Carolina State**
7. **Dorian Speed, of, Florida International**
8. **Denny Bair, rhp, Northeast Louisiana**
9. **Chad Ricketts, rhp, Polk (Fla.) CC**
10. **Kasey Pressley, 1b, Dr. Phillips HS, Orlando**
11. **Matt Hammons, rhp, Mission Bay HS, San Diego**
12. **Barret Markey, rhp, St. Petersburg (Fla.) HS**
13. **Terry Joseph, of, Northwestern State**
14. **Don Kinnie, of, Livingston (Ala.)**
15. **Kris Stading, lhp, Browne HS, Phoenix**
16. **Brian Conley, ss/2b, Volunteer State (Tenn.) CC**
17. Chris Moller, 1b, Alabama
18. **Jerry Connell, of, Colonia HS, Avenel, N.J.**
19. **Buck Gordon, c, Bridgewater (Va.)**
20. **Chris Booker, rhp, Monroe County HS, Monroeville, Ala.**
21. **Brandon Hammack, rhp, Texas-San Antonio**
22. Andrew Mallory, rhp, Dixie Hollins HS, St. Petersburg, Fla.
23. **Jim Putko, 1b, Akron**
24. **Kevin Bentley, of, Southern Mississippi**
25. Dax Norris, c, Alabama
26. **Brian Greene, rhp, Indiana**
27. **Tim Mosley, rhp, Arkansas**
28. **Scott Vieira, c, Tennessee**
29. **Ashanti McDonald, ss/of, Olivet Nazarene (Ill.)**
30. **John McNeese, lhp, Mississippi**
31. **Ron Licciardi, lhp, Connecticut-Avery Point**
32. **Tom Maleski, 3b/c, Houston**
33. **Jason Martino, rhp, Vorhees HS, Pittstown, N.J.**
34. **Ryan Seidel, of, Southern California College**
35. Chris Humpert, of, Arcadia (Calif.) HS
36. Robert Kern, of, Central HS, Cape Girardeau, Mo.
37. Mark Taylor, lhp, Rice
38. Casey Burns, rhp, Hopewell Valley Central HS, Trenton, N.J.
39. Greg Strickland, of, Volunteer State (Tenn.) CC
40. Brandon Ward, rhp, Cerro Coso (Calif.) JC
41. Daniel Mooney, c, Monsignor Donovan HS, Forked River, N.J.
42. Michael Smosna, rhp, Burroughs HS, Ridgecrest, Calif.
43. Dave Phillips, 2b, Gloucester (N.J.) CC
44. David Kelly, rhp, Leon HS, Tallahassee, Fla.
45. Tim Currens, of, Volunteer State (Tenn.) CC
46. Lance Haver, c, Molalla Union HS, Molalla, Ore.
47. **Mickey Perez, 2b, Texas-San Antonio**
48. Brett Cornwell, rhp, Hobbs (N.M.) HS
49. Jerry Zaffis, rhp, Eustis HS, Mount Dora, Fla.
50. Aaron Anthony, 3b, Middle Georgia JC
51. Chris Grubbs, c, West Orange HS, Ocoee, Fla.

52. Jack Koch, rhp, Miami-Dade CC North
53. John Ogden, c, Palm Beach (Fla.) JC
54. Arturo Mata, ss/2b, New Mexico JC
55. **Justin Speier, c, Nicholls State**
56. Scott Stephens, lhp, Manatee (Fla.) JC
57. Steven Bechard, rhp, Onieda (N.Y.) HS
58. Seth Spiker, c, Blinn (Texas) JC
59. Bobby Sprague, c, Queen Of Peace HS, North Arlington, N.J.
60. Ryan Fuller, rhp, Monroe (N.Y.) CC
61. Kris Williams, rhp, Westfield (N.J.) HS

CHICAGO WHITE SOX

June—Regular Phase (25)

1. **Jeff Liefer, 3b, Long Beach State**
2. **Brian Simmons, of, Michigan**
3. J.J. Putz, rhp, Trenton (Mich.) HS
4. **Ryan Topham, of, Notre Dame**
5. **Tighe Brown, rhp, St. Xavier HS, Louisville**
6. **John Hunt, lhp, Ohio**
7. **Jason Lakman, rhp, Woodinville (Wash.) HS**
8. **Adam Virchis, rhp, San Diego State**
9. **Jason Secoda, rhp, Cal State Los Angeles**
10. **Chuck Klee, ss, Cardinal Gibbons HS, Fort Lauderdale**
11. **Kevin Beirne, rhp, Texas A&M**
12. **Daron Hollins, of, Sierra (Calif.) JC**
13. **Brian Downs, c, Riverside (Calif.) CC**
14. **Tom Buckman, rhp, Edison (Fla.) CC**
15. Eric Stanton, 1b, Newberry (S.C.) HS
16. **Erik Desrosiers, rhp, Grand Canyon (Ariz.)**
17. **Derek Hasselhoff, rhp, Towson State**
18. **Mike Vota, rhp, Towson State**
19. **Jeff Johnson, ss, Mississippi**
20. Chris Beck, of, El Dorado HS, Placentia, Calif.
21. **Barry Shelton, 3b, West Virginia State**
22. **Jason Gray, rhp, Coconut Creek (Fla.) HS**
23. **Frank Anderson, c, Southern Union State (Ala.) JC**
24. **Tim Kraus, rhp, Notre Dame**
25. **John Strasser, ss, Mesa (Ariz.) CC**
26. **Josh Fauske, c, Central Washington**
27. Aaron Gentry, ss, Labette (Kan.) CC
28. **Brent Wilhelm, 3b, Kansas**
29. **Kelly Kruse, rhp, Southwest Missouri State**
30. **Allen Halley, rhp, South Alabama**
31. Brian Bullock, rhp, Itawamba (Miss.) JC
32. **Joel Garber, lhp, Nevada-Las Vegas**
33. Chris Weekly, ss, Highland HS, Gilbert, Ariz.
34. Eric LeBlanc, rhp, St. Rose (N.Y.)
35. Nate Robertson, lhp, Maize (Kan.) HS
36. Aaron Randle, 2b/ss, Northeast HS, Fort Lauderdale
37. **Darren Hayes, of, Wingate (N.C.)**
38. Stephen Sparks, rhp, Faulkner State (Ala.) JC
39. Andrew Tellez, of, Fullerton (Calif.) JC
40. Matt Howe, ss, Mayde Creek HS, Houston
41. Kereon Clarke, of/2b, South Plantation HS, Plantation, Fla.
42. **Pete Demorejon, rhp, Miami**
43. Justin Rayment, lhp, San Diego State
44. David Harden, lhp, Allen County (Kan.) CC
45. **Jason Fennell, of, Baldwin HS, Pittsburgh**
46. Nestor Gonzales, c, Rio Grande HS, Albuquerque
47. David Hostetter, of, Fannett Metal HS, Fort Loudan, Pa.
48. Brian Thrash, of, Rising Sun HS, Elkton, Md.
49. Kris Conrad, rhp, Killian HS, Miami
50. Wade Sterling, c, Allen County (Kan.) CC
51. **Brian Bowness, 1b/3b, Villanova**
52. Peter Rodriguez, of, Broward (Fla.) JC
53. **Manny Lutz, 3b, Southwestern (Calif.) JC**
54. Mike Biasucci, 2b, South Broward HS, Hollywood, Fla.

CINCINNATI REDS

June—Regular Phase (54)

1. (Pick to Red Sox as compensation for Type B free agent Damon Berryhill)
2. **Brett Tomko, rhp, Florida Southern**
3. **Andre Montgomery, ss, Pleasure Ridge Park HS, Louisville**
4. **Mark Corey, rhp, Edinboro (Pa.)**
5. **Jason LaRue, c, Dallas Baptist**
6. **Andy Burress, c, Telfair County HS, McRae, Ga.**
7. **Herb Goodman, of, North Greenville (S.C.) JC**
8. **Ray King, lhp, Lambuth (Tenn.)**
9. Bobby Walters, of, Salisaw (Okla.) HS
10. **Ben Bailey, rhp, Glen Oaks (Mich.) CC**
11. **Rich Lawrence, rhp, Central Florida**
12. **Justin Atchley, lhp, Texas A&M**
13. Mike Daniel, rhp, Calhoun (Ala.) CC
14. Larfayette Stanley, rhp, Jordan HS, Columbus, Ga.
15. **Anthony Patellis, 3b, Kent**
16. **Lance Davis, lhp, Lake Gibson HS, Lakeland, Fla.**
17. **Todd Fehrenbach, c, Citrus HS, Inverness, Fla.**
18. **Justin Marine, rhp, Moorpark (Calif.) JC**
19. **Eric Mapp, of, Lamar**
20. **James Davis, c, Western Kentucky**
21. Jason Johnson, of, Montclair (Calif.) HS
22. **Gene Maddox, rhp, Florida CC-Jacksonville**
23. **Tony Cloud, rhp, Spartanburg Methodist (S.C.) JC**
24. **Jeff Sparks, rhp, St. Mary's (Texas)**
25. **Stephen Claybrook, of, Texas A&M**
26. **David Guthrie, ss, North Carolina State**
27. **Steve Goodhart, 2b, Ohio Wesleyan**
28. Andy Tracy, 1b, Bowling Green State
29. **Jason Parsons, 1b, Dallas Baptist**
30. Rob Mackowiak, ss/2b, South Suburban (Ill.) JC
31. Brian Willman, rhp, North Carolina
32. **Scott MacRae, rhp, Valdosta State (Ga.)**
33. Zach Frachiseur, rhp, Rockdale County HS, Conyers, Ga.
34. **Lamont Mason, 2b/ss, Lubbock Christian**
35. Jeffery Juarez, of, New Braunfels (Texas) HS
36. **Will Schleuss, lhp, Alabama**
37. **Thomas Scott, of, Linfield (Ore.)**
38. Jason Hubbard, lhp, Angelina (Texas) JC
39. Brian Loyd, c, Cal State Fullerton
40. **Chris Murphy, lhp, Cincinnati**
41. **Scott Wright, rhp, Missouri Southern State**
42. **Joe Montgomery, rhp, Jacksonville State (Ala.)**
43. Chad Truby, 3b, Yavapai (Ariz.) JC
44. **Dwayne Cushman, rhp, Valdosta State (Ga.)**

CLEVELAND INDIANS

June—Regular Phase (23)

1. **David Miller, 1b, Clemson**
2. **Sean Casey, 1b, Richmond**
3. **Chad Whitaker, of, St. Thomas Aquinas HS, Fort Lauderdale**
4. **Scott Harrison, rhp, Swett HS, Pinole, Calif.**
5. **Scott Schultz, rhp, Louisiana State**
6. **Jake Messner, of, Rio Americano HS, Sacramento**
7. **Scott Morgan, of, Gonzaga**
8. **Tim Jorgensen, ss, Wisconsin-Oshkosh**
9. **Mike Edwards, ss, Mechanicsburg (Pa.) Area HS**
10. **Jason Bennett, rhp, Shippensburg (Pa.)**
11. **Jewell Williams, of, Las Vegas HS**
12. **Brett Merrick, lhp, Washington**
13. **Frankie Sanders, rhp, Pasco Hernando (Fla.) CC**
14. **Scott Winchester, rhp, Clemson**
15. **Darren Loudermilk, rhp, Oklahoma City**
16. Luis Estrella, rhp, Rancho Santiago (Calif.) JC
17. **Terry Harvey, rhp, North Carolina State**
18. **Keith Horn, rhp, Arkansas State**
19. **Jason Minici, of, Long Beach State**
20. **Marc Deschenes, ss, Lowell (Mass.)**
21. **Mark Budzinski, of, Richmond**
22. **Mike Glavine, 1b, Northeastern**
23. **Jon Edwards, rhp, Whitman (Wash.)**
24. **Ken Wagner, rhp, Florida Atlantic**
25. **Jason Rakers, rhp, New Mexico State**
26. Frank Chapman, rhp, San Jacinto North (Texas) CC
27. Gary Rodriguez, of, Seminole State (Okla.) JC
28. Michael Bishop, of/c, Willis (Texas) HS

29. Corey Richardson, of, Daingerfield (Texas) HS
30. **Jason Adge, rhp, Miami**
31. **Richy Gonzalez, c, Miami**
32. Michael Custer, rhp, Linn-Benton (Ore.) CC
33. **Nathan Coats, c, CC of San Francisco**
34. Jamie Brown, rhp, West Lauderdale HS, Meridian, Miss.
35. **Bryan Hardy, 1b, Martin HS, Arlington, Texas**
36. **Jerry Taylor, of, Texas**
37. **Chad Thornhill, ss, Cal State Northridge**
38. **Ross Atkins, rhp, Wake Forest**
39. Thomas Blythe, c, North Little Rock (Ark.) HS
40. Randy Keisler, lhp, Navarro (Texas) JC
41. Mike Spiegel, lhp, Sacramento CC
42. **Dennis Martinez, rhp, St. Thomas (Fla.)**
43. Bryan Ransom, ss, South Mountain (Ariz.) CC
44. Albert Garza, rhp, Wapato (Wash.) HS
45. Kirk Irvine, rhp, Rancho Santiago (Calif.) JC
46. Rex Crosnoe, c, Southeast Missouri State
47. **Sam Mathis, rhp, Southern Arkansas**
48. Ryan Bailey, rhp, Rancho Bernardo HS, San Diego
49. Brian Anderson, rhp, East Tennessee State
50. Peter Lopez, rhp, Central HS, Manchester, N.H.
51. **Tony Fleetwood, lhp, Oklahoma State**
52. Michael Ploharz, rhp, Clovis (Calif.) HS
53. Kevin Eberwein, rhp, Green Valley HS, Henderson, Nev.
54. Damien Kolb, of, Capital HS, Olympia, Wash.
55. Brandon Driggers, rhp, Whitehouse (Texas) HS

COLORADO ROCKIES

June—Regular Phase (8)

1. **Todd Helton, 1b/lhp, Tennessee**
2. **Ben Petrick, c, Glencoe HS, Hillsboro, Ore.**
3. **Chris Macca, rhp, St. Leo (Fla.)**
4. **John Clark, ss, Clemens HS, Schertz, Texas**
5. **Mike Vavrek, rhp, Lewis (Ill.)**
6. **Chandler Martin, rhp, Portland**
7. **Cristy Rosa, rhp, Guanica, P.R.**
8. **Tal Light, 3b, Oklahoma State**
9. **Jamie Emiliano, rhp, Florida International**
10. **Gary Gordon, of, Willingboro (N.J.) HS**
11. **Scott Randall, rhp, Santa Barbara (Calif.) CC**
12. **Brian Kirkpatrick, ss, King City (Calif.) HS**
13. **John Lindsey, 1b, Hattiesburg (Miss.) HS**
14. **Pat Williams, rhp, Mount San Antonio (Calif.) JC**
15. **John Mahlberg, rhp, Douglas HS, Dillard, Ga.**
16. **Chris Druckery, rhp, Kankakee (Ill.) JC**
17. **Garrett Neubart, of, Columbia**
18. **Heath Bost, rhp, Catawba (N.C.)**
19. **John Clifford, c, Villanova**
20. **Bobby Bevel, lhp, Xavier**
21. **Blake Barthol, c, Eastern Kentucky**
22. **David Groseclose, ss, Virginia Military Institute**
23. **David Lee, rhp, Mercyhurst (Pa.)**
24. **Carlos Vidal, c, Miami-Dade CC New World Center**
25. **Reggie Douglas, rhp, Dorsey HS, Los Angeles**
26. **Matt Whitley, ss, Tennessee**
27. J.J. Moore, rhp, Burnsville (Minn.) HS
28. Rodney Nye, 3b, Cameron (Okla.) HS
29. **Marc Brzozoski, of, Shorter (Ga.)**
30. **Brett Elam, ss, McNeese State**
31. **Sean Murphy, rhp, North Carolina**
32. **Brad Reitzenstein, rhp, Portland**
33. **David Feuerstein, of, Yale**
34. Ryan Kohlmeier, rhp, Chase County HS, Cottonwood Falls, Kan.
35. Brian Bowman, c, Garces Memorial HS, Bakersfield, Calif.
36. Jeremy Jones, c, Raymore Peculiar HS, Raymore, Mo.
37. Josh Kalinowski, lhp, Natrona County HS, Casper, Wyo.
38. Scott Brent, of, Linden (Calif.) HS
39. Matt Montgomery, rhp, Rancho Santiago (Calif.) CC
40. Brandon Lenox, ss, Red Mountain HS, Mesa, Ariz.
41. Jason Pozo, rhp, Ocean County (N.J.) CC
42. Damione Merriman, of, Cheraw (S.C.) HS
43. Anthony Taylor, rhp, Pueblo HS, Tucson
44. Derek Corbett, rhp, Highland HS, Highley, Ariz.
45. Mike Medina, c, Moody HS, Corpus Christi, Texas
46. Brad Schwartzbauer, c/3b, White Bear Lake (Minn.) Area HS
47. Ali Samadani, rhp, JC of Marin (Calif.)
48. Kent Zweifel, 1b, Henley HS, Klamath Falls, Ore.
49. **Justin Drizos, 1b, Nevada-Reno**
50. Andres Mitchell, ss, Motlow State (Tenn.) CC
51. Rodney Friar, c, Temecula Valley HS, Temecula, Calif.
52. Chris Rodriguez, c, Modesto (Calif.) JC
53. Casey Kelley, 1b, Ellensburg (Wash.) HS
54. Dan Ledesma, ss, Moody HS, Corpus Christi, Texas
55. Derek Sawyer, ss, Paradise Valley HS, Phoenix
56. James Slaughter, of, San Joaquin Delta (Calif.) JC
57. John Garrison, rhp, San Joaquin Delta (Calif.) JC
58. Gabriel Foster, rhp, Santa Rosa (Calif.) JC

DETROIT TIGERS

June—Regular Phase (11)

1. **Mike Drumright, rhp, Wichita State**
2. **Brian Powell, rhp, Georgia**
3. Chuck Crowder, lhp, Crestwood HS, Mantua, Ohio
4. **Clay Bruner, rhp, Weatherford (Okla.) HS**
5. **Rosario Ortiz, rhp, Arizona Western JC**
6. **Jeremiah Lignitz, c, Davison (Mich.) HS**
7. **Chris Manser, rhp/of, Hillsborough HS, Tampa**
8. **Scott Weaver, of, Michigan**
9. Ron Marietta, lhp, Bishop Ford HS, Brooklyn
10. **John Foran, rhp, Central Florida**
11. **Dave Borkowski, rhp, Sterling Heights (Mich.) HS**
12. **Jason Lawrie, rhp, Independence HS, San Jose**
13. Kevin Jordan, ss, Lee HS, Midland, Texas
14. Steve Hartsburg, ss, Schaumburg (Ill.) HS
15. Justin Lehr, rhp/c, West Covina (Calif.) HS
16. Mark Hendrickson, lhp, Washington State
17. **Craig Caballero, c, Grand Canyon (Ariz.)**
18. **Brian Fuller, c, Northwestern**
19. Lawyer Milloy, of, Washington
20. **Ron Rojas, 2b, Northwestern**
21. Clint Bryant, 3b, Texas Tech
22. J.R. Webb, c, Texas
23. **Jay Waggoner, 1b/of, Auburn**
24. **Peter Durkovic, lhp, Fordham**
25. **Robert Gray, of, Embry-Riddle Aeronautical (Fla.)**
26. Eric Valent, of, Canyon HS, Anaheim
27. Matt Thornton, lhp, Centerville HS, Sturgis, Mich.
28. **Clausal Milord, of, New York Tech**
29. **Mike Miller, 3b, Hofstra**
30. Jason Haynie, lhp, South Carolina
31. Darrell Hussman, rhp, Quartz Hill HS, Lancaster, Calif.
32. **Derek Mitchell, ss, Triton (Ill.) JC**
33. **Derek Kopacz, 3b, Triton (Ill.) JC**
34. Luke Bonner, rhp, Divine Child HS, Dearborn, Mich.
35. Chris Clark, of, Arkansas
36. **Tom Shipman, c, River Ridge HS, New Port Richey, Fla.**
37. Greg Sprehn, rhp, Bangor (Wis.) HS
38. John Kremer, rhp, Chatard HS, Indianapolis
39. Josh Davis, rhp, Pensacola (Fla.) Catholic HS
40. Mike Davis, ss, Vocational HS, Chicago
41. Phil Rosengren, rhp, Day HS, Rye, N.Y.
42. Mike Whiteman, lhp, Potomac State (W.Va.) JC
43. Robert Fick, c, Cal State Northridge
44. Jeremy Giambi, of, Cal State Fullerton
45. Errick Lowe, of, Lake Worth (Fla.) HS
46. **Doug Engleka, ss, Ohio**
47. Pedro Flores, lhp, Sierra Vista HS, Baldwin Park, Calif.
48. Brian Justine, lhp, Dwyer HS, Palm Beach Lakes, Fla.
49. Judd Van Winkle, lhp, Spartanburg Methodist (S.C.) JC
50. Jose Nunez, 2b, Northeast Texas CC
51. Greg Ryan, lhp, Divine Child HS, Dearborn, Mich.
52. Maurice Watkins, rhp, Osser HS, Chicago
53. Bryan Houston, of, Escambia HS, Pensacola, Fla.
54. Chad Cook, rhp, Fallbrook (Calif.) HS
55. Mark Mulder, 1b, Thornwood HS, South Holland, Ill.
56. **Joe McFarlane, rhp, Anacortes (Wash.) HS**
57. **Gabe Kapler, 3b, Moorpark (Calif.) JC**

58. **Brian Cummins, lhp, Northwestern**
59. **David Reinfelder, lhp, Michigan State**

FLORIDA MARLINS

June—Regular Phase (6)

1. **Jaime Jones, of, Rancho Bernardo HS, San Diego**
2. **Nate Rolison, 1b, Petal (Miss.) HS**
3. **Randy Winn, of, Santa Clara**
4. **Mike Marriott, rhp, Spring (Texas) HS**
5. **Rene Rascon, of, Sonoma State (Calif.)**
6. **Michael Tejera, lhp, Southwest HS, Miami**
7. **Hansel Izquierdo, rhp, Southwest HS, Miami**
8. Mark Watson, lhp, Clemson
9. **Tony Enard, rhp, Fresno State**
10. **Bob Pailthorpe, rhp, Santa Clara**
11. **Gary Knotts, rhp, Brewer HS, Somerville, Ala.**
12. **Jonathan Widerski, rhp, Academy of the Holy Angels, Richfield, Minn.**
13. Jerrod Riggan, rhp, San Diego State
14. **David Miller, rhp, UNC Wilmington**
15. **Rick Garcia, rhp, Oklahoma City**
16. **Gabe Gonzalez, rhp, Long Beach State**
17. **Steve Goodell, ss, Arizona State**
18. **Travis Burgus, lhp, San Diego**
19. **Mike Duvall, lhp, Potomac State (W.Va.) JC**
20. **Mat Erwin, c, Nevada-Reno**
21. **Joe Funaro, 2b, Eastern Connecticut State**
22. **Swan Austin, rhp, Douglasville, Ga.**
23. Alex Morris, rhp, Westlake HS, Austin
24. Jim Detwiler, lhp, Valley Forge Military Academy, Pottsville, Pa.
25. Kevin Fitzmaurice, rhp, Silver Creek HS, San Jose
26. Ryan Tack, rhp, Durango HS, Las Vegas
27. David Therneau, rhp, Navarro (Texas) JC
28. Jorge Rodriguez, ss, Penuelas, P.R.
29. **Gary Santoro, rhp, Flagler (Fla.)**
30. **Euclides Rojas, rhp, Palm Springs/Western League**
31. Mike Rose, rhp, Southwood HS, Shreveport, La.
32. George Oleksik, rhp, Middle Tennessee State
33. Todd Bramble, ss, Sprague HS, Salem, Ore.
34. Kevin Green, of, Mohawk Valley (N.Y.) CC
35. **Jason Shanahan, 3b, Cal State Northridge**
36. Tim McClaskey, rhp, Muscatine (Iowa) CC
37. Brian Dallimore, 2b, Stanford
38. Ken Duebelbeis, lhp, De Anza (Calif.) JC
39. Dion Battee, of, St. Bernard HS, Los Angeles
40. Matt Blank, lhp, Galveston (Texas) JC
41. Dwaine Neal, of, Norland HS, Miami
42. Letarvius Copeland, of, Jackson HS, Miami
43. **Shannon Stephens, rhp, Cal Poly San Luis Obispo**
44. **Jason Garrett, 1b, Texas-Arlington**
45. **Rob Hernandez, c, Oklahoma State**
46. Jeff Cermak, of, Mesa (Ariz.) CC
47. Rhett Ingerick, rhp, Davidson
48. **Raymond Green, c, Sonoma State (Calif.)**
49. Rafael Riguiero, rhp, North HS, Riverside, Calif.
50. William Reed, of, Westchester HS, Inglewood, Calif.
51. Aaron Cames, rhp, Sacramento CC
52. Scott McKee, c, Riverdale Baptist HS, Bowie, Md.
53. Kerthatis Lovely, of, Glades Central HS, South Bay, Fla.
54. Howard Bell, rhp, Westchester HS, Los Angeles
55. Darin Baker, of, Fallon (Nev.) HS
56. Carl Jones, of, Andress HS, El Paso, Texas
57. Joel Atwater, of, Southern Alamance HS, Graham, N.C.
58. Richard Circuit, ss, La Jolla (Calif.) HS
59. Mark Greenlee, lhp, Triton (Ill.) JC
60. William Fleck, rhp, Mercer County (N.J.) CC
61. Scott Esker, 3b, JC of the Redwoods (Calif.)
62. Michael Laine, rhp, Connally HS, Waco, Texas
63. Druen Mahony, ss, Hillcrest HS, Fountain Inn, S.C.
64. Quincy Foster, of, Spartanburg Methodist (S.C.) JC
65. James Nederostek, lhp, St. Mary's HS, Lodi, Calif.
66. Robby Hammock, c, South Cobb HS, Marietta, Ga.
67. Matthew Pidgeon, ss, Eureka (Calif.) HS
68. **Andy Bair, lhp, Calvert Hall HS, Towson, Md.**
69. Jason Berry, rhp, Mountain View HS, Orem, Utah
70. William Tull, rhp, Gloucester County (N.J.) CC
71. Derek Rowan, of, Mesa (Ariz.) CC
72. William Boughey, rhp, Berkmar HS, Lawrenceville, Ga.
73. Jay Gospodarek, rhp, Pima (Ariz.) JC
74. Stephen Blevins, 1b, Spotsylvania (Va.) HS
75. Kevin Tolan, rhp, Citrus (Calif.) JC
76. Dustin Keppen, rhp, Central Gwinnet HS, Lawrenceville, Ga.
77. Eric Kalie, ss, Martin County HS, Stuart, Fla.
78. Brett Schreyer, rhp, Paul VI HS, Waterford, N.J.
79. Joel Sajiun, of, Miami Springs HS, Hialeah, Fla.
80. Timothy Hicks, of, Gordon (Ga.) JC
81. Shannon Carter, rhp, Gate City (Va.) HS
82. Brian Bush, of, Howland HS, Warren, Ohio
83. (Selection voided)
84. Ryan Roberts, ss, Brigham Young
85. Andrew Lecrone, 3b, Downers Grove (Ill.) North HS
86. John Schmitz, of, JC of San Mateo (Calif.)
87. Brian Haught, ss, Jesuit HS, Tampa

HOUSTON ASTROS

June—Regular Phase (22)

1. **Tony McKnight, rhp, Arkansas HS, Texarkana, Ark.**
2. **Eric Ireland, rhp, Millikan HS, Long Beach**
3. **Chad Alexander, of, Texas A&M**
4. **Brian Sikorski, rhp, Western Michigan**
5. **Mike Rose, c, Jesuit HS, Sacramento**
6. **Scott Chapman, c, Alexander HS, Albany, Ohio**
7. **Jason McCarter, rhp, Monterey Peninsula (Calif.) JC**
8. **Eric Smith, rhp, Butler County (Kan.) CC**
9. **Jason Adams, ss, Wichita State**
10. **Jeremy DeShazer, of, Lake Washington HS, Kirkland, Wash.**
11. **Ric Johnson, of, Indiana State**
12. **Eric Stachler, rhp, Bowling Green State**
13. **Marlon Mejia, ss, Westchester (N.Y.) CC**
14. **Barry Wesson, of, Brandon HS, Pearl, Miss.**
15. **Mike Corominas, lhp, Arizona State**
16. Aaron Vincent, rhp, Porterville (Calif.) JC
17. Charles Wheeler, lhp, Connors State (Okla.) JC
18. Derek Wallace, of, Neville HS, Monroe, La.
19. **Aaron Miles, 2b, Antioch (Calif.) HS**
20. **Eric Cole, 3b, Antelope Valley (Calif.) JC**
21. David Huggins, rhp, Galveston (Texas) CC
22. Shawn Sonnier, rhp, Chipola (Fla.) JC
23. **Nelson Ubaldo, of, Massachusetts**
24. **Jeriome Robertson, lhp, Exeter Union HS, Exeter, Calif.**
25. **Andy Bovender, 3b, UNC Charlotte**
26. James Alarcon, rhp, Jupiter (Fla.) Community HS
27. **Aaron McNeal, 1b, Castro Valley (Calif.) HS**
28. Adrian Taylor, ss, Tech HS, Oakland
29. Troy Stoppa, lhp, Havre (Mont.) HS
30. Robert Porter, lhp, McComb (Miss.) HS
31. Caleb Brown, lhp, Howard (Texas) JC
32. **Tim Hamulack, of/lhp, Edgewood (Md.) HS**
33. **Gregg Smyth, lhp, Rollins (Fla.)**
34. Bryan King, rhp, Brawley Union HS, Brawley, Calif.
35. Eric Eckenstahler, lhp, Antioch HS, Lindenhurst, Ill.
36. Brian Moon, c, Newton County HS, Mansfield, Ga.
37. Javier Contreras, rhp, Rio Piedras, P.R.
38. Scott Sandusky, c, Seward County (Kan.) CC
39. Corbett Leonard, c, Spring Grove (Pa.) HS
40. **Ryan Coe, c, Kennesaw State (Ga.)**
41. Marty Godwin, of, Osceola HS, Kissimmee, Fla.
42. Jason Welch, of, Edison (Fla.) CC
43. **Brett Brown, lhp, Delaware Tech JC**
44. Stephen Schwartz, rhp, Aurora (Ill.)
45. Brock Ashby, of, St. Francis Xavier HS, Edmonton
46. Troy Norrell, c, Brazoswood HS, Lake Jackson, Texas
47. Mark Burnett, ss, Bryant HS, Benton, Ark.
48. Luis Ramos, rhp, Rio Piedras, P.R.
49. Walter Harrington, rhp, Palomar (Calif.) JC
50. Ryan Channel, lhp, Satellite Beach (Fla.) HS
51. Jorge Mesa, c, Braddock HS, Miami

52. Ryan Block, rhp, Walla Walla (Wash.) HS
53. Corey Hart, 2b, Connors State (Okla.) JC
54. Mark Chambers, of, Navarro (Texas) JC
55. Stephen Dye, rhp, Middle Georgia JC
56. Brian Berryman, rhp, Union HS, Redford, Mich.
57. Chris Hargett, 1b, Jeffersonville (Ind.) HS
58. Juan Rivera, ss, Palm Beach (Fla.) JC
59. Chris Meyer, rhp, Dakota Collegiate HS, Winnipeg, Manitoba
60. Frank Bludau, rhp, Halletsville (Texas) HS
61. Mark Tomse, lhp, Central Catholic HS, Aurora, Ill.
62. Josh Pascarella, rhp, Rancho Bernardo HS, San Diego
63. Adam Bell, c, Helena (Mont.) HS
64. James Crossley, 3b, Chabot (Calif.) JC
65. Gabriel Garcia, c/rhp, Logan HS, Union City, Calif.
66. James Hawkins, rhp, Santa Margarita HS, Laguna Niguel, Calif.
67. Chris Oldham, c, Sullivan (Mo.) HS
68. Brian Jordan, rhp, Gordon (Ga.) JC
69. Blake Ricken, lhp, Fresno CC
70. Josh Maloney, rhp, Central HS, Butte, Mont.
71. Chris Hill, rhp, Long Beach CC
72. Michael Meyers, rhp, Annandale (Ontario) HS
73. Chris Castleberry, c, Americus (Ga.) HS
74. Peter Fukuhara, of, Canada (Calif.) JC
75. Brian Fritz, 1b, Santa Ynez HS, Solvang, Calif.
76. Roger Foltynowicz, 3b, Lakeside HS, Evans, Ga.
77. Wayne Chinapen, rhp/of, York Mills Collegiate Institute, Toronto
78. Scott Pasonage, rhp, Fullerton (Calif.) JC
79. Jason Von Haefen, rhp, Blinn (Texas) JC
80. Chris Sheldon, of, Glendale (Calif.) HS
81. Darren Brown, rhp, Brophy Jesuit HS, Scottsdale, Ariz.
82. Shawn Jacob, c, Brandon (Miss.) HS
83. Bill Eaton, ss/rhp, Indian River (Fla.) CC
84. Brian Issett, of, Kimball HS, Royal Oak, Mich.
85. Charles Carter, 1b, McLennan (Texas) CC
86. George Pickard, 1b, Hill (Texas) JC

KANSAS CITY ROYALS

June—Regular Phase (19)

1. **Juan Lebron, of, Arroyo, P.R.**
2. **Carlos Beltran, of, Manati, P.R.**
3. **Doug Blosser, 1b, Sarasota (Fla.) HS**
4. **Vic Radcliff, ss, North Augusta (S.C.) HS**
5. **Steve Medrano, ss, Bishop Amat HS, La Puente, Calif.**
6. **Melvin Dasher, of, Palatka (Fla.) HS**
7. **Allen Sanders, rhp, Lee (Texas) JC**
8. **Jeff Martin, rhp, Bishop Gorman HS, Las Vegas**
9. **Mike Robbins, lhp, Stanford**
10. **David Moore, rhp, Northeast HS, Oakland Park, Fla.**
11. **Mark Quinn, dh/rhp, Rice**
12. **Todd Meady, rhp, Milford (Conn.) Academy**
13. Steve Donaghey, rhp, Woburn (Mass.) HS
14. **Tony Penny, rhp, Newberry (S.C.) HS**
15. **Matt Saier, rhp, Georgia Tech**
16. **Jeremy Williamson, lhp, Southern Mississippi**
17. **Mark Melito, ss, Wake Forest**
18. **Patrick Hallmark, c, Rice**
19. Chad Schroeder, rhp, Northwestern
20. **Stephen Prihoda, lhp, Sam Houston State**
21. **Alonzo Aguilar, rhp, East Los Angeles JC**
22. **James Vida, 1b, Florida Southern**
23. **Randy Paulin, c, Pacific**
24. **Tony Miranda, of, Cal State Fullerton**
25. **Jeff Wallace, lhp, Minerva (Ohio) HS**
26. **Jon Albrecht, lhp, Kansas State**
27. **Steven Mullis, lhp, Brevard (N.C.) JC**
28. **William Hodge, lhp, Jacksonville State (Ala.)**
29. **Emiliano Escandon, ss, Pomona-Pitzer (Calif.)**
30. **Taylor Bales, c, Lee (Texas) JC**
31. **Scott Kortmeyer, of, Grand Canyon (Ariz.)**
32. **Bret Schafer, of, UCLA**
33. **Francis Key, rhp, Pensacola (Fla.) JC**
34. **Jesus Liz, lhp, Miami-Dade CC North**
35. **Craig Sanders, rhp, Nebraska**
36. **Adam Finnieston, of, Miami**
37. **Bobby Shannon, lhp, Shippensburg Area (Pa.) HS**
38. Jeremy Albritton, c, Parklane Academy, Bogue Chitto, Miss.
39. Brian Wiese, rhp, Central HS, Baton Rouge, La.
40. Cliff Wilson, 3b, Byrnes HS, Lyman, S.C.
41. Seth Tate, ss, Wenatchee (Wash.) HS
42. Jamison Powers, rhp, Sullivan East HS, Bluff City, Tenn.
43. Alan Bundy, rhp, Smith HS, Mansfield, Conn.
44. Adam Bolthouse, lhp, Spring Lake (Mich.) HS
45. Brandon Buckley, c, San Ramon HS, Danville, Calif.
46. James Scarborough, of, Elkins HS, Fort Bend, Texas
47. Dustin Wilson, rhp, Columbia Basin (Wash.) CC
48. Denton McDaniel, lhp, Lake Travis HS, Austin
49. Greg Arnold, lhp, Smithtown HS, Nesconset, N.Y.
50. Glen School, of, Brookdale (N.J.) CC
51. Rudy Bulgar, of, New Bedford (Mass.) HS
52. Brian Starcich, rhp, Blinn (Texas) JC
53. Paul Stryhas, 3b, Sarasota (Fla.) HS
54. Michael Cabales, rhp, East Islip (N.Y.) HS
55. Merrell Ligons, 2b, Palisades HS, Culver City, Calif.
56. Stephen Watson, rhp, Galveston (Texas) JC
57. Andy Lynch, lhp, Bridgton Academy, North Bridgton, Maine
58. Lance Aubrey, c, Sinagua HS, Flagstaff, Ariz.
59. Paul Phillips, c, West Lauderdale HS, Bailey, Miss.
60. Tommy Worthy, ss, Etowah HS, Attalla, Ala.
61. Jaime Bonilla, lhp, Villaalba, P.R.
62. Mike Rodriguez, ss, Chaffey HS, Ontario, Calif.
63. Courtney Thornton, rhp, Tallassee (Ala.) HS
64. Scott Ham, c, Palestine (Ill.) HS
65. Adam Reikowski, rhp, Providence HS, Charlotte
66. **Brian Winders, rhp, Louisiana State**
67. Michael Degruy, rhp, Harrison Central HS, Gulfport, Miss.
68. Robert Shabansky, lhp, Bishop Gorman HS, Las Vegas
69. Ralph Cadima, of, Mount San Antonio (Calif.) JC
70. Jason Van Curen, rhp, Monte Vista HS, San Ramon, Calif.

LOS ANGELES DODGERS

June—Regular Phase (20)

1. **David Yocum, lhp, Florida State**
2. **Darrin Babineaux, rhp, Southwestern Louisiana**
3. **Onan Masaoka, lhp, Waiakea HS, Hilo, Hawaii**
4. **Judd Granzow, of, Faith Baptist HS, Granada Hills, Calif.**
5. **Sef Soto, rhp, Palomar (Calif.) JC**
6. **Kevin Gibbs, of, Old Dominion**
7. **Trent Cuevas, ss, El Dorado HS, Placentia, Calif.**
8. **Jon Tucker, 1b, Chatsworth (Calif.) HS**
9. **Eric Brown, ss, East St. John HS, LaPlace, La.**
10. **Mike Carpentier, ss, Cal State Sacramento**
11. **Craig Taczy, lhp, Shepard HS, Crestwood, Ill.**
12. Kenny Miller, ss, Providence Catholic HS, New Lenox, Ill.
13. Brad Wilkerson, lhp, Apollo HS, Owensboro, Ky.
14. Spencer Micunek, rhp, Henry Ford (Mich.) CC
15. **J.J. Pearsall, lhp, South Carolina**
16. **Eric Flores, ss, Rio Mesa HS, Oxnard, Calif.**
17. **Antonio Mota, of, Miami Springs HS, Miami**
18. **Jay O'Shaughnessy, rhp, Northeastern**
19. David Ross, c, Florida HS, Tallahassee, Fla.
20. Jeffrey Rodriguez, c, Coral Gables HS, Miami
21. **Dennis Mauch, c, Cosumnes River (Calif.) JC**
22. **A.J. Walkanoff, c, Creighton**
23. **Brett Illig, 3b, Phoenixville (Pa.) HS**
24. **Travis Meyer, c, East Carolina**
25. **Peter Cervantes, rhp, East Los Angeles JC**
26. Peyton Warren, rhp, West Florence HS, Florence, S.C.
27. **Mike Sanchez, rhp, Chaffey (Calif.) JC**
28. **Ken Morimoto, of, Hawaii**
29. Greg Clark, c, Paradise Valley HS, Phoenix
30. **Mitch McNeely, lhp, Centenary**
31. **Pedro Feliciano, lhp, Dorado, P.R.**
32. **Andy Owen, of, UC Riverside**
33. Lazaro Gutierrez, lhp, Brito Miami Private HS, Hialeah, Fla.
34. **Scott Chambers, lhp, Logan (Ill.) JC**
35. **Jeff Keppen, rhp, Georgia Southern**
36. Trevor Bishop, rhp, Assiniboia (Saskatchewan) Composite HS

37. David Schmidt, c, Oregon State
38. **Terrence McClain, ss, Cumberland (Tenn.)**
39. Chad Roney, c, Jacksonville
40. Bobby Cripps, c, Cameron HS, Powell River, B.C
41. **John Davis, rhp, Bethune-Cookman**
42. Jason Smith, ss, Demopolis HS, Coatopa, Ala.
43. Saul Rivera, ss, Las Lomas, P.R.
44. Jeffrey Deno, lhp, Franklin HS, Los Angeles
45. Brad Block, rhp, Lake Michigan (Mich.) JC
46. **Michael Bourbakis, rhp, Roosevelt HS, Brooklyn**
47. Steve Green, rhp, Longueiul, Quebec
48. Xavier Curley, 3b, Marshall County HS, Lewisburg, Tenn.
49. Andrew Dougherty, c, Glassboro (N.J.) HS
50. Kevin Hodge, ss, Bryan (Texas) HS
51. Mark Paschal, of, Fontana HS, Bloomington, Calif.
52. Maurice Hightower, lhp, Arlington (Texas) HS
53. Christian Keating, rhp, Brother Rice HS, Country Club Heights, Ill.
54. Cesar Acosta, of, Yuma (Ariz.) HS
55. Justin Rumfield, ss/3b, McLennan (Texas) CC
56. Vance Cozier, rhp, Pickering HS, Ajax, Ontario
57. Joel Ainsworth, lhp, Sarnia (Ontario) Collegiate Institute
58. Cesar Castenada, 3b, Lincoln HS, Los Angeles
59. Jose Rijo-Berger, of, Walla Walla (Wash.) CC
60. Charles Koone, of, Spartanburg Methodist (S.C.) JC
61. **Cash Riley, of, Trinity Christian Academy, Irving, Texas**
62. Brian Oliver, ss, Antioch (Calif.) HS
63. Chris Vollaro, rhp, Alvin (Texas) CC
64. Mark Vallecorsa, lhp, Damien HS, San Dimas, Calif.
65. Stephen Dupont, rhp, Nicholls State
66. Gregory Conley, c, Sequim (Wash.) HS
67. Paul Auton, c, Ainlay HS, Edmonton
68. Brian Dawson, rhp, San Bernardino Valley (Calif.) JC
69. Tim Hackman, rhp, Vernon (B.C.) HS
70. Brian Wagner, c, Sacramento CC
71. Joseph Thomas, rhp, West Covina HS, La Puente, Calif.
72. Tony James, 2b, Chaffey (Calif.) JC
73. Ryan Cail, rhp, Kwantlen (B.C.)
74. Craig Allen, rhp, Notre Dame
75. Todd Sutton, of, Angola HS, Pleasant Lake, Ind.
76. Neal Atchison, rhp, Central Huron HS, Clinton, Ontario
77. Scott Oliver, rhp, Richland Northeast HS, Columbia, S.C.
78. Hal Featherstone, rhp, Hendersonville (N.C.) HS
79. **Larry Bethea, 1b, Red Springs (N.C.) HS**
80. Brandon Bowe, rhp, San Joaquin Delta (Calif.) CC
81. Michael Tablit, rhp, Yuba (Calif.) CC
82. Cary Stover, rhp, American River (Calif.) JC
83. Brad Brewer, ss, Sacramento CC
84. Mathew Randel, rhp, Ridgefield (Wash.) HS
85. Ryan Moskau, 1b/lhp, Sabino HS, Tucson

MILWAUKEE BREWERS

June—Regular Phase (9)

1. **Geoff Jenkins, of, Southern California**
2. **Mike Pasqualicchio, lhp, Lamar**
3. **Greg Schaub, rhp, Solanco HS, Oxford, Pa.**
4. Jeff Alfano, c, Mount Whitney HS, Visalia, Calif.
5. **Jared Camp, rhp, Indian River (Fla.) JC**
6. **Toby Kominek, of, Central Michigan**
7. **Sam Singleton, ss, DuPont HS, Rand, W.Va.**
8. **Ryan Ritter, 2b/of, Georgia Tech**
9. **Mike Kinkade, c/of, Washington State**
10. **Jason Dawsey, lhp, Clemson**
11. **Darren Berninger, rhp, Nicholls State**
12. **Chris Walther, of, Gaither HS, Tampa**
13. **Mickey Lopez, 2b, Florida State**
14. **Shawn Miller, rhp, Northeastern Illinois**
15. **Jonathan Guzman, lhp, Levittown, P.R.**
16. **Donald Moore, of, Dallastown HS, York, Pa.**
17. **Alex Andreopoulos, c, Seton Hall**
18. **Ledowick Johnson, of, North Carolina State**
19. **Travis Smith, rhp, Texas Tech**
20. **Sergio Guerrero, 2b, Laredo (Texas) JC**
21. **Brian Hommel, lhp, Louisville**
22. Brad Paulz, rhp, Reedsville (Wis.) HS
23. **Dave Elliott, of, Western Michigan**
24. **Jesse Richardson, lhp, Northern Illinois**
25. **Michael Roche, 2b, Brevard (Fla.) JC**
26. **Derek Torres, rhp, Miami-Dade CC North**
27. Beau Johnson, 1b/of, Mendocino (Calif.) CC
28. **Rick Smith, 1b, Central Michigan**
29. **Ryan Arevalos, ss, Texas-San Antonio**
30. **Scott Kirby, 3b, Lake Gibson HS, Lakeland, Fla.**
31. **Gerald Parent, of, Merrimack (Mass.)**
32. Travis Bailey, ss, Wellington Community HS, West Palm Beach, Fla.
33. Anthony Rodriguez, rhp, Cooper City HS, Pembroke Pines, Fla.
34. Eric Leiser, of, Antioch (Calif.) HS
35. Jonathan Rose, lhp, Brevard (N.C.) JC
36. Migues Rodriguez, ss, Sonora HS, Brea, Calif.
37. Doug Wakefield, lhp, Victor Valley (Calif.) CC
38. **Josh Bishop, rhp, Missouri**
39. Zane Curry, c, Ball HS, Galveston, Texas
40. Austin Lawes, of, North Miami HS, Miramar, Fla.
41. George Phillips, ss, Demopolis (Ala.) HS
42. Carlos Barbosa, c, Dinuba (Calif.) HS
43. Mark Cridland, of, Galveston (Texas) JC
44. Walter Ward, of, Northern HS, Chesapeake Beach, Md.
45. Blair Murphy, rhp, De Anza (Calif.) JC
46. Byron Tribe, rhp, Galveston (Texas) JC
47. Richard Cercy, rhp, Seabreeze HS, Ormond Beach, Fla.
48. Edward French, of, Seabreeze HS, Ormond Beach, Fla.
49. Michael Leach, rhp, Palm Beach (Fla.) CC
50. James Landingham, of, South Miami HS, Miami
51. Stanford Woods, of, Boone HS, Orlando
52. Alain Cruz, c, Miami-Dade CC North
53. Eric Armour, of, Palm Beach (Fla.) CC
54. Kenny Avera, rhp, Pace (Fla.) HS
55. Robert Cornett, c, North Hall HS, Gainesville, Ga.
56. Monty Ward, rhp, Monterey HS, Lubbock, Texas
57. Paul Turco, ss, Sarasota (Fla.) HS
58. Kip Wells, rhp, Elkins HS, Fort Bend, Texas
59. Charlie Hunter, rhp, Notre Dame HS, Ooltewah, Tenn.
60. Steven Lawson, rhp, Damien HS, La Verne, Calif.
61. Lance Jordan, rhp, Whittier Christian HS, La Habra, Calif.
62. James Leary, rhp, South Grand Prairie HS, Grand Prairie, Texas
63. Dirk Lewallen, 1b, Victor Valley (Calif.) JC
64. Ara Petrosian, rhp, Cypress (Calif.) JC
65. Jason Ross, of, Hawaii
66. Richard Jennings, ss, Overland HS, Aurora, Colo.
67. Kevin McDougal, of, West HS, Arvada, Colo.
68. Eric McMaster, 2b, West HS, Arvada, Colo.

MINNESOTA TWINS

June—Regular Phase (13)

1. **Mark Redman, lhp, Oklahoma**
2. **Jason Bell, rhp, Oklahoma State**
3. A.J. Hinch, c, Stanford
4. Jay Hood, ss, Germantown (Tenn.) HS
5. **Doug Mientkiewicz, 1b, Florida State**
6. **Shane Gunderson, c/1b, Minnesota**
7. **Mike Moriarty, ss, Seton Hall**
8. **Will Rushing, lhp, Georgia Southern**
9. **Joe McHenry, of, Oakland HS, Murfreesboro, Tenn.**
10. Kyle Kane, of, Linfield HS, Temecula Valley, Calif.
11. **Jamaal Harrison, 1b, Palo Alto (Calif.) HS**
12. **Jason McKenzie, rhp, Mississippi**
13. **Jamie Splittorff, rhp, Kansas**
14. Josh Holliday, c, Stillwater (Okla.) HS
15. **Brad Neidermaier, rhp, Northwestern**
16. **Alan Mahaffey, lhp, Arkansas**
17. Rob Ramsay, lhp, Washington State
18. **Freddy Reyes, 1b/3b, Levittown, P.R.**
19. **Carlisle Johnson, ss/of, Taylor HS, Pierson, Fla.**
20. **Jeff Smith, c, Stetson**
21. **David Orndorff, c, Shippensburg Area (Pa.) HS**
22. **Scott Tanksley, rhp, Mississippi State**
23. Jamie Vallis, lhp, Allen HS, Bedford, Nova Scotia

24. **John Blank, lhp, William Carey (Miss.)**
25. **Kevin Nelson, 1b, Bryant (Ark.) HS**
26. **Tim Peters, lhp, Baylor**
27. **Joe Fraser, 2b, Cal State Fullerton**
28. **Jeff Harris, rhp, San Francisco**
29. **Sean Reilly, lhp, Aldershot HS, Burlington, Ontario**
30. **Travis Johnson, of, North Dakota**
31. **Todd Bartels, rhp, Stanford**
32. **Lee Marshall, rhp, Enterprise (Ala.) HS**
33. Javier Mejia, rhp, Southern California
34. Matthew Noe, lhp, Riverside (Calif.) CC
35. **Ivory Jones, of, San Francisco State**
36. **Harold Boggs, rhp, West Virginia State**
37. Adam Danner, rhp, South Florida
38. John Chapman, lhp, St. Joseph's (Ind.)
39. Scott Dobson, rhp, West Potomac HS, Alexandria, Va.
40. **Matt Vanderbush, lhp, William Paterson (N.J.)**
41. Leo Torres, lhp, Cibola HS, Somerton, Ariz.
42. Edmond Daniels, rhp, Polk (Fla.) CC
43. Gary Forster, rhp, Montesano (Wash.) HS
44. **Jeff Garff, rhp, Dixie (Utah) JC**
45. Toby Wilmot, lhp, Oklahoma
46. **Andres Cruz, c, Salinas, P.R.**
47. Brian Mitchell, 3b, Iowa City (Iowa) HS
48. Edgar Oropeza, rhp, CC of San Francisco
49. Brian Bodwell, rhp, Ocosta HS, Westport, Wash.
50. Nelson Correa, 1b, Florida Air Academy HS, Melbourne, Fla.
51. (Selection voided)
52. Michael Brunet, rhp, Land O'Lakes (Fla.) HS
53. **Bryan Malko, rhp, Piscataway (N.J.) HS**
54. Craig Black, 2b, Palm Beach Lakes HS, West Palm Beach, Fla.
55. Paul Boykin, of, Columbine HS, Littleton, Colo.

MONTREAL EXPOS

June—Regular Phase (28)

1. **Michael Barrett, ss, Pace Academy, Atlanta**
2. **Henry Mateo, ss, Santurce, P.R.**
3. **Kenny James, of, Sebring (Fla.) HS**
4. **J.D. Smart, lhp, Texas**
5. **Brian Schneider, c, Northampton HS, Cherryville, Pa.**
6. **Ronney Daniels, of/lhp, Lake Wales (Fla.) HS**
7. **Peter Fortune, lhp, Rockland (N.Y.) JC**
8. **Trey Martin, rhp, Arcadia HS, Phoenix**
9. **Bienvenido Sanchez, rhp, Arecibo, P.R.**
10. Jeff Austin, rhp, Kingwood (Texas) HS
11. Jimmy Turman, rhp, Shelton State (Ala.) CC
12. **Robert Marquez, rhp, McNeese State**
13. **David Herr, rhp, Villanova**
14. **Tim Dixon, lhp, Cal State Fullerton**
15. **D.C. Olsen, 1b, Cal State Fullerton**
16. **Pete LaForest, ss/3b, Gatineau, Quebec**
17. **Wes Denning, of, Minnesota**
18. Tom Brady, c, Serra HS, San Mateo, Calif.
19. **Jake Steinkemper, c, Arizona State**
20. **Mike Bell, lhp, Florida State**
21. Stan Baston, of/3b, North Florida Christian HS, Tallahassee, Fla.
22. **Scott Mitchell, rhp, Pacific**
23. **Mo Blakeney, of, Elon (N.C.)**
24. **Mike Wolger, lhp, California**
25. **Jaime Garcia, c, New Mexico**
26. **Ryan Van Oeveren, ss, Michigan**
27. Noah Hall, of, Aptos (Calif.) HS
28. Jarrett Shearin, of, Wake Forest-Rolesville HS, Wake Forest, N.C.
29. **Jeremiah Colson, of, St. Paul's (N.C.) HS**
30. **James Lacey, rhp, Coconut Creek (Fla.) HS**
31. Toby McDermott, lhp, Tacoma CC
32. Joe Kerrigan, ss, Radnor HS, Rosemont, Pa.
33. Shawn Peterson, c/of, Orem (Utah) HS
34. Scott Porter, rhp, Middleburg (Fla.) HS
35. Mitch Wylie, rhp, North Scott HS, Princeton, Iowa
36. Aaron Underwood, rhp, Lehigh HS, Lehigh Acres, Fla.
37. Matt Dehner, 3b, El Dorado HS, Las Vegas
38. Brandon Gadke, of, Orange (Ohio) HS
39. Bruno Vaillancourt, lhp, Le Gardeur, Quebec
40. Shane Wright, rhp, Hayden HS, Topeka, Kan.
41. Robert Everett, rhp, Lake City (Fla.) CC
42. **Torrance Davis, of, Liberty Eylau HS, Texarkana, Texas**
43. Jesse Crespo, c, Camuy, P.R.
44. Phil Derryman, rhp, Moorpark (Calif.) JC
45. Adam Huxhold, lhp, Lindbergh HS, Maple Valley, Wash.
46. Daniel Prata, lhp, Repentigny, Quebec

NEW YORK METS

June—Regular Phase (18)

1. **Ryan Jaroncyk, ss, Orange Glen HS, Escondido, Calif.**
2. **Brett Herbison, rhp/ss, Central HS, Burlington, Ill.**
3. **Ryan Bowers, c, Pineview HS, St. George, Utah**
4. **Corey Erickson, ss, Lanphier HS, Springfield, Ill.**
5. **Jeff Parsons, ss, Arkansas**
6. Todd Cutchins, lhp, Tallahassee (Fla.) CC
7. Ryan Minor, 1b/rhp, Oklahoma
8. **A.J. Burnett, rhp, Central Arkansas Christian HS, North Little Rock, Ark.**
9. Tydus Meadows, of, Evans (Ga.) HS
10. **Dan Murray, rhp, San Diego State**
11. **Grant Roberts, rhp, Grossmont HS, El Cajon, Calif.**
12. **Mark Pileski, ss, Massachusetts**
13. **Erick Torres, rhp, Mayaguez, P.R.**
14. Eric McQueen, c, North Cobb HS, Alworth, Ga.
15. Anthony Johnson, c/of, Oakland HS
16. **Lindsay Gulin, lhp, Issaquah (Wash.) HS**
17. Scott Proctor, rhp, Martin County HS, Stuart, Fla.
18. Chris Adolph, of, Clovis West HS, Fresno
19. Damon Minor, 1b, Oklahoma
20. **Phil Olson, rhp, Florida State**
21. **Joey Pyrtle, rhp, UNC Wilmington**
22. **Andy Zwirchitz, rhp, Okaloosa Walton (Fla.) CC**
23. Brooks Stephens, 1b, Florida HS, Tallahassee, Fla.
24. **Jeff Howatt, rhp, UCLA**
25. Ben Hickman, rhp, Bryant (Ark.) HS
26. **Paul Yoder, of, Alvernia (Pa.)**
27. **Preston Ballew, lhp, Carlsbad (N.M.) HS**
28. **Chadwick Cooper, rhp, Potomac State (W.Va.) JC**
29. **Mark Enloe, lhp, Tarkington HS, Cleveland, Texas**
30. **Nelson Figueroa, rhp, Brandeis (Mass.)**
31. **Matt Ferullo, rhp, Michigan**
32. **Brandon Copeland, of, Washburn HS, Topeka, Kan.**
33. **Mike Blang, rhp, Southern Illinois**
34. **Brandon Black, of, Pensacola (Fla.) JC**
35. John Mattson, rhp, South Kitsap HS, Port Orchard, Wash.
36. Jacob Handy, rhp, Arvin HS, Bakersfield, Calif.
37. **Ryan Morrison, of, Onondaga (N.Y.) CC**
38. Clif Wren, c, Petal (Miss.) HS
39. **Richard Martinez, c, St. Mary's (Texas)**
40. Aaron Rowand, ss, Glendora (Calif.) HS
41. **Tim Tessmar, lhp, Eastern Michigan**
42. Donald Loland, rhp, Ascension Catholic HS, Donaldsonville, La.
43. **Casey Patterson, rhp, Fresno CC**
44. Randy Young, of, Wichita State
45. **Sean Gill, of, Wright State**
46. Taylor More, of, East HS, Cheyenne, Wyo.
47. Stephen Minus, rhp/c, Judson HS, San Antonio
48. Cory Patton, of, Olney Central (Ill.) JC
49. Jacob Bailey, rhp, Hutchinson (Kan.) CC
50. Clint Johnston, 1b, Carroll HS, Vero Beach, Fla.
51. Jaime Rodgers, rhp, Friendship Christian HS, Mount Juliet, Tenn.
52. **Chris Dewitt, rhp, St. Andrews Presbyterian (N.C.)**
53. Shawn Hannah, rhp, Clovis (Calif.) HS
54. Luis Castilio, c, American HS, Miami Lakes, Fla.
55. Chris Reinike, rhp, Long Beach (Miss.) HS
56. **Corey Brittan, rhp, Hutchinson (Kan.) CC**
57. Derek Daugherty, of, Kingfisher (Okla.) HS
58. Quinn Cravens, of, Valley Center (Kan.) HS
59. Jerrell Carver, 1b, Northeastern HS, Elizabeth City, N.C.
60. Tony Moreno, c, Riverside HS, El Paso, Texas
61. Robert Piercy, c, Crest HS, Shelby, N.C.
62. Hector Esparza, 3b, San Jose CC
63. Darren Dyt, of, Porterville (Calif.) JC

NEW YORK YANKEES

June—Regular Phase (27)

1. **Shea Morenz, of, Texas**
2. **Richard Brown, of, Nova HS, Fort Lauderdale**
2. **Brian Buchanan, lhp, Oviedo (Fla.) HS** (Supplemental pick—59th—for loss of Type C free agent Matt Nokes)
3. **Luke Wilcox, of, Western Michigan**
4. **Eric Boardman, rhp, Cerritos (Calif.) JC**
5. **Jason Wright, rhp, Martinsville (Ind.) HS**
6. **Brad Williams, lhp, Sabino HS, Tucson**
7. **Bob St. Pierre, rhp, Richmond**
8. **Scott Brand, rhp, McLennan (Texas) JC**
9. **Mike Judd, rhp, Grossmont (Calif.) JC**
10. **Jeff Saffer, of, Pima (Ariz.) CC**
11. **Darrell Einertson, rhp, Iowa Wesleyan**
12. **Cam Spence, rhp, Lake City (Fla.) CC**
13. Ryan Mills, lhp, Horizon HS, Scottsdale, Ariz.
14. **Cesar Verdin, lhp, Crawford HS, San Diego**
15. Josh Hochgesang, ss, Sunny Hills HS, Fullerton, Calif.
16. **Dana Davis, rhp, Rice**
17. **Jerry Lail, rhp, Wingate (N.C.)**
18. **Stephen Randolph, lhp, Texas**
19. **Jay Tessmer, rhp, Miami**
20. **Mike Lowell, 2b, Florida International**
21. **Scott Emmons, c, California**
22. **Donzell McDonald, of, Yavapai (Ariz.) JC**
23. **Cody McCormick, c, California**
24. Ryan Snellings, lhp, Seminole HS, Largo, Fla.
25. Dan Kanell, rhp, Florida State
26. Daunte Culpepper, of, Vanguard HS, Ocala, Fla.
27. **Patrick Antrim, ss, Saddleback (Calif.) CC**
28. **Les Dennis, ss, Portland**
29. Jason Ryan, lhp, Indian River (Fla.) CC
30. Michael Schnautz, lhp, San Jacinto North (Texas) JC
31. Chris Crawford, rhp, Wheeler HS, Marietta, Ga.
32. Tim Spindler, rhp/ss, Orange County (N.Y.) CC
33. Brian Aylor, of, Oklahoma State
34. Richard Cremer, lhp, West Frankfort (Ill.) HS
35. Orlando Carey, of, Motlow State (Tenn.) CC
36. Ben Phillips, rhp, Howard (Texas) JC
37. Travis Brummitt, rhp, Cleveland State (Tenn.) CC
38. Barry Brown, of, Grossmont (Calif.) JC
39. Lisnardo DeCastro, 1b/of, Florida Bible Christian HS, Sunrise, Fla.
40. Lateef Vaughn, ss, Southwestern (Calif.) JC
41. Ben Chestnut, of, Sacramento CC
42. Joe Horgan, lhp, Cordova HS, Rancho Cordova, Calif.
43. **Jason Imrisek, c, Evansville**
44. Jared Hoerman, rhp, Plainview HS, Armore, Okla.
45. Casey Blake, 3b, Wichita State
46. Denis Pujals, rhp, Miami
47. Jason Ellison, rhp, Navarro (Texas) JC
48. Scott Kingston, 1b, Columbus (Ga.) HS
49. Philip Haigler, rhp, Vanderbilt
50. Lance Hawkins, of, Lake Charles-Boston HS, Lake Charles, La.
51. Brandon James, of, Sacramento CC
52. Brian Hervey, rhp, Tallahassee (Fla.) CC
53. Chad Clements, ss, Centreville HS, Fairfax, Va.
54. Jason Becker, 2b, Bremen HS, Midlothian, Ill.
55. Michael Hamm, c, Shoals (Ala.) CC
56. Darryl Craig, lhp/1b, Douglas (B.C.)
57. Dorian Cameron, ss, Northern HS, Durham, N.C.
58. Jude Campbell, of, Chabot (Calif.) JC
59. Daniel Thomas, rhp, Poway (Calif.) HS
60. Nathan Koepke, of, Long Beach CC
61. Brandon Hemmings, of, Columbus (Ga.) HS
62. Charles Shipp, of, Vocational HS, Chicago
63. Jeremiah Johnson, rhp, Homer (Mich.) HS
64. Doug Dixon, rhp, Northside HS, Belhaven, N.C.
65. Scott Hardesty, rhp, Illinois-Chicago
66. Jake Zajc, rhp, Bradley-Bourbonnais HS, Bourbornais, Ill.
67. Justin Carpenter, rhp, Prague (Okla.) HS
68. Charles Thomas, of, Harlan (Ky.) HS
69. Peter Fisher, rhp, Stoneham (Mass.) HS
70. Daniel Washburn, rhp, Nova HS, Pembroke Pines, Fla.
71. William Duncan, c, Burlington-Edison HS, Burlington, Wash.

OAKLAND ATHLETICS

June—Regular Phase (5)

1. **Ariel Prieto, rhp, Palm Springs (Western League)**
2. **Mark Bellhorn, ss, Auburn**
3. Billy Brown, of, St. Thomas Aquinas HS, Fort Lauderdale
4. **Wayne Nix, rhp, Monroe HS, North Hills, Calif.**
5. **Danny Ardoin, c, McNeese State**
6. Jamey Price, rhp, Mississippi
7. **Tim Jones, of, Buena Park (Calif.) HS**
8. **Tom Bennett, rhp, Ohlone (Calif.) HS**
9. **Tom Knickerbocker, of, Kirkwood (Iowa) JC**
10. **Ryan Christenson, of, Pepperdine**
11. **Scott Rivette, rhp, Long Beach State**
12. **Troy Rauer, of, Arizona State**
13. **Willie Hilton, rhp, Eastern Illinois**
14. **Kevin Mlodik, rhp, Wisconsin-Oshkosh**
15. David Shepard, rhp, Mansfield (Pa.)
16. **Robert Harris, ss, Texas A&M**
17. **David Newhan, of, Pepperdine**
18. **Mike Klostermeyer, 1b, Louisiana State**
19. Jason Hill, c, Monte Vista HS, Danville, Calif.
20. **David Slemmer, ss/2b, Southwest Missouri State**
21. **Bill Knight, of, Massachusetts**
22. **T.J. Costello, lhp, Montclair State (N.J.)**
23. **Duane Filchner, of, Radford**
24. **Steve Connelly, rhp, Oklahoma**
25. Brian Callahan, rhp, The Citadel
26. **Jeff DaVanon, of/2b, San Diego State**
27. **Ryan Kjos, rhp, Texas**
28. **Victor Hernandez, of, Ciales, P.R.**
29. Stephen Bess, rhp, Montgomery Bell Academy, Nashville
30. **Bill Batchelder, rhp, New Hampshire**
31. **Kevin Gunther, rhp, Fresno State**
32. **Jace Johnson, of, Scottsdale (Ariz.) CC**
33. Byron Embry, rhp, Madison Central HS, Richmond, Ky.
34. **Chris Morrison, rhp, Auburn**
35. **Jon French, rhp, Arkansas State**
36. Ryan Gill, rhp, Woodlawn HS, Baton Rouge
37. Rodney Clifton, of, Elgin (Ill.) HS
38. Greg Halvorson, c, Canyon Del Oro HS, Tucson
39. Matthew Dornfeld, of, Arizona Western JC
40. Robert Norman, rhp, Columbia Academy, Mount Pleasant, Tenn.
41. **Chris Nelson, rhp, Oklahoma State**
42. **Brandon Welch, of, Texas Tech**
43. **Victor Chambers, 2b/of, CC of San Francisco**
44. **Todd Abbott, rhp, Arkansas**

PHILADELPHIA PHILLIES

June—Regular Phase (14)

1. **Reggie Taylor, of, Newberry (S.C.) HS**
1. **Dave Coggin, rhp, Upland (Calif.) HS** (Supplemental pick—30th—for loss of Type A free agent Danny Jackson)
2. **Marlon Anderson, 2b, South Alabama** (Pick from Cardinals as compensation for Jackson)
3. **Randy Knoll, rhp/3b, Corona (Calif.) HS**
4. **Steve Carver, 3b, Stanford**
5. Pee Wee Lopez, c, Westminster Christian HS, Miami
6. **Caleb Martinez, lhp, Florida Bible Christian HS, Miami**
7. Chris Bauer, rhp/ss, Wichita State
8. **Ricky Williams, ss, Patrick Henry HS, San Diego**
9. **Kirk Pierce, c, Long Beach State**
10. **Brian Mensink, rhp, Minnesota**
11. Jason Wallace, of, Callaway HS, Jackson, Miss.
12. **Jason Kershner, lhp, Saguaro HS, Scottsdale, Ariz.**
13. **Mark Raynor, ss, Barton (N.C.)**
14. **Marty Barnett, rhp, South Alabama**
15. **Walter Dawkins, of, Southern California**
16. **Melvin Pizarro, lhp, Carolina, P.R.**
17. Ryan Lentz, 3b, Woodinville (Wash.) HS

18. **Matt Buckles, c, Palatka (Fla.) HS**
19. **Christopher Snusz, c, Mercyhurst (Pa.)**
20. **Brian Miller, rhp, Marian College of Fond Du Lac (Wis.)**
21. **Tyson Kimm, ss, Creighton**
22. **Brian Ford, lhp, Methodist (N.C.)**
23. **Anthony Shumaker, lhp, Cardinal Stritch (Wis.)**
24. **Jared Janke, 1b, UC Santa Barbara**
25. Tim Walton, rhp, Oklahoma
26. **Todd Crane, of, Georgia**
27. **Gary Yeager, rhp, Elizabethton (Pa.)**
28. Casey Brookens, rhp, James Madison
29. **Zachary Elliot, 2b/ss, UC Santa Barbara**
30. **Kyle Kawabata, rhp, Washington State**
31. **Kevin Hooker, 2b, Oregon State**
32. **Kory Kosek, rhp, Mankato State (Minn.)**
33. **Brian Dunne, lhp, Kansas Newman**
34. **Richard O'Connor, ss, Valparaiso**
35. **Charles Cox, c, Texas-Pan American**
36. **Scott Tebbetts, rhp, UC Riverside**
37. **Bill Noone, rhp, Wilkes (Pa.)**
38. **Justin Kennedy, of, Bastrop (La.) HS**
39. **David Robinson, of, Rio Grande (Ohio)**
40. Courtney Moore, of, Shoals (Ala.) CC
41. **Rob Galko, rhp, Oklahoma State**
42. **Jonathon Cornelius, of, Cal State Los Angeles**
43. **Jeff Leaman, 3b, Indiana State**
44. **Clyde Livingston, c, Newberry (S.C.)**
45. Bryan Williamson, rhp, Kamiakin HS, Kennewick, Wash.
46. **Jaime Mendes, rhp, New Mexico State**
47. Josh Glenn, rhp, Riley HS, South Bend, Ind.
48. Marques Meshack, rhp, Lincoln HS, San Diego
49. Jason Bell, of, Atwater (Calif.) HS
50. Charles Marino, of, Kennedy HS, La Palma, Calif.
51. Jose Sandoval, ss, Poly HS, Sun Valley, Calif.
52. Benito Lemos, c, Royal HS, Simi Valley, Calif.
53. Mike Heidemann, 1b, Yavapai (Ariz.) JC

PITTSBURGH PIRATES

June—Regular Phase (10)

1. **Chad Hermansen, ss, Green Valley HS, Henderson, Nev.**
2. **Garrett Long, 1b, Bellaire HS, Houston**
3. **Bronson Arroyo, rhp, Brooksville-Hernando HS, Brooksville, Fla.**
4. **Alex Hernandez, of, Levittown, P.R.**
5. **Dawan Elliott, of, Long Branch (N.J.) HS**
6. **O.J. Cook, rhp, Liberty HS, Bethlehem, Pa.**
7. Josh Loggins, c, Harrison HS, West Lafayette, Ind.
8. Brad Weber, of, DeKalb HS, Auburn, Ind.
9. **Fred May, of, Kennedy HS, Seattle**
10. **Daniel Delgado, ss, Killian HS, Miami**
11. **Brian O'Connor, lhp, Redding (Ohio) HS**
12. Al Benjamin, of, Milby HS, Houston
13. **Brian Settle, rhp, Wilson HS, Portsmouth, Va.**
14. **Travis Gaerte, rhp, Fremont (Ind.) HS**
15. **Elton Pollock, of, Presbyterian (S.C.)**
16. Ian Rauls, of, Ewing HS, Trenton, N.J.
17. Jason Saenz, lhp, Mater Dei HS, Santa Ana, Calif.
18. **Ryan Gillispie, rhp, Rancho Bernardo HS, San Diego**
19. **Maika Symmonds, lhp, Old Dominion**
20. **Derek Bullock, rhp, Briar Cliff (Iowa)**
21. **Steven Flanigan, c, California (Pa.)**
22. **Chris Miyake, ss, UC San Diego**
23. **Cory Bigler, rhp, Wisconsin-Milwaukee**
24. **Tim Collie, rhp, UNC Charlotte**
25. **John Canetto, 3b, Coastal Carolina**
26. Chris Heck, lhp, Northeast Catholic HS, Philadelphia
27. **Jason Farrow, rhp, Houston**
28. George Hlodan, rhp, Forward HS, Elizabeth, Pa.
29. Neal McDade, rhp, Florida CC-Jacksonville
30. Brock Hundt, 3b, Logan (Ill.) JC
31. Chris Miller, rhp/3b, Winter Haven (Fla.) HS
32. Ronald Brooks, rhp, Leon HS, Tallahassee, Fla.
33. Travis Siegel, of, Choctaw HS, Midwest City, Okla.
34. Jacob Whitfield, lhp, Tallahassee (Fla.) CC
35. Matt Hoffman, rhp, Claremore (Okla.) HS
36. Ronald Ricks, rhp, Tallahassee (Fla.) CC
37. Michael Carney, lhp, Merritt Island (Fla.) HS
38. Brandon Larson, ss, Blinn (Texas) JC
39. Joseph Wroble, lhp, South Suburban (Ill.)
40. Arthur Young, of, New Rochelle (N.Y.) HS
41. Jason Wright, rhp, Palomar (Calif.) JC
42. **Scott Beach, rhp, Pittsburg State (Kan.)**
43. **Rob Thomas, lhp, Texas A&M**
44. Jason Shelley, ss, Plainfield (Ill.) HS

ST. LOUIS CARDINALS

June—Regular Phase (12)

1. **Matt Morris, rhp, Seton Hall**
1. **Chris Haas, 3b, St. Mary's HS, Paducah, Ky.** (Supplemental pick—29th—for loss of Type A free agent Gregg Jefferies)
2. (Pick to Phillies as compensation for Type A free agent Danny Jackson)
2. **Jason Woolf, ss, American HS, Hialeah, Fla.** (Pick from Phillies as compensation for Jefferies)
3. **Billy Deck, 1b, Potomac HS, Dumphries, Va.**
4. **Rodney Barfield, rhp, DeKalb (Ga.) JC**
5. Cody McKay, 3b, Arizona State
6. **Joe Freitas, of, Fresno State**
7. **Matt King, rhp, Galveston (Texas) JC**
8. **Jon Ward, rhp, Cal State Fullerton**
9. **Ryan McHugh, of, Florida Southern**
10. **Matt DeWitt, rhp/3b, Valley HS, Las Vegas**
11. **Robert Cooke, rhp, Mount Olive (N.C.) JC**
12. **Kevin Miedreich, rhp, St. Thomas Aquinas (N.Y.)**
13. **Shawn McNally, of/ss, Auburn**
14. **Ken Cameron, of, Washington State**
15. **Jason Lee, of, Burlington (Iowa) HS**
16. **Andy Hall, 2b, Cal Poly San Luis Obispo**
17. **Britt Reames, rhp, The Citadel**
18. **Lou Deman, c, Long Island**
19. **Chris Richard, of/1b, Oklahoma State**
20. **Adam Benes, rhp, Evansville**
21. **Tom Truselo, rhp, Delcastle HS, New Castle, Del.**
22. **Travis McClendon, c, Nevada-Las Vegas**
23. **Jorge Roque, rhp, Santurce, P.R.**
24. **Andy Schofield, of, Illinois State**
25. Mike Kimbrell, lhp, Southeastern Louisiana
26. **Darrell Betts, ss, Ball State**
27. **Matt Wagner, rhp, Lewis-Clark State (Idaho)**
28. Junior Spivey, 2b, Cowley County (Kan.) CC
29. Chris Mazur, lhp, East Bladen HS, Elizabethtown, N.C.
30. Rusty Sarnes, lhp, Lincoln Land (Ill.) CC
31. **Miguel Insunza, ss, Lewis-Clark State (Idaho)**
32. Gavin Brown, of, California
33. **Juan Munoz, of, Florida International**
34. **Kerry Robinson, of, Southeast Missouri State**
35. Dean Brueggemann, lhp, Belleville Area (Ill.) JC
36. Jeff Ryan, ss, Grand Prairie (Texas) HS
37. **Tony Falciglia, c, Farleigh Dickinson**
38. **Jose Villafana, rhp, Mission (Calif.) JC**
39. **Mike Swenson, lhp, South Florida**
40. Bryce Darnell, c, Missouri Southern State
41. **Scott Spaulding, rhp, Eastern Connecticut State**
42. Kyle West, ss, Pineview HS, St. George, Utah
43. Wade Jackson, 2b, Nevada-Reno
44. **Jason Lariviere, of/2b, Southern Maine**
45. Brian Clark, lhp, Mississippi State
46. **Bret Mueller, of, Cal Poly San Luis Obispo**
47. Michael Gray, rhp, North Florida JC
48. **Nick Deluca, ss, Bellevue (Neb.)**
49. **Ruben Cardona, 2b, Bellhaven (Miss.)**
50. **Brandon Folkers, 1b, Pasco-Hernando (Fla.) JC**
51. Michael Hogan, of, Middle Georgia JC
52. George Burgos, of, American HS, Miami
53. Brian Jorgensen, 3b, Missouri
54. **Cliff Politte, rhp, Jefferson (Mo.) JC**
55. Cheron Farley, 2b, Lincolnton (N.C.) HS
56. Nick Roberts, rhp, South Sevibic HS, Annabella, Utah

57. Michael Delano, lhp, North Hollywood (Calif.) HS
58. Nolan Vincent, 3b/of, Hollister (Mo.) HS
59. Ryan Gladwin, of, Martin County HS, Stuart, Fla.
60. **Nick Kast, lhp, Oral Roberts**
61. **Rob Donnelly, rhp, Fresno State**
62. James Birr, ss, North Florida
63. Ryan Pene, lhp, Grand County HS, Moab, Utah
64. Mike Glendenning, 3b/of, Pierce (Fla.) JC
65. Craig Moore, 3b, Bergail HS, Freemont, Neb.

SAN DIEGO PADRES

June—Regular Phase (2)

1. **Ben Davis, c, Malvern (Pa.) Prep**
2. **Gabe Alvarez, ss, Southern California**
3. **Ryan Van de Weg, rhp, Western Michigan**
4. **Brandon Kolb, rhp, Texas Tech**
5. **Kenny Henderson, rhp, Miami**
6. **Kevin Walker, lhp, Grand Prairie (Texas) HS**
7. **Jason Totman, 2b, Texas Tech**
8. **Sean Watkins, 1b, Bradley**
9. **Mike Martin, c, Florida State**
10. **James Sak, rhp, Illinois Benedictine**
11. **Mark Wulfert, of, New Mexico**
12. **Curt Lowry, of, McNeese State**
13. **Rick Gama, 2b, Miami**
14. **Andy Hammerschmidt, lhp, Minnesota**
15. Steven Hoff, lhp, Mills HS, San Bruno, Calif.
16. **John Rodriguez, ss, Miller HS, Corpus Christi, Texas**
17. **Michael Irvine, rhp, Northern Iowa**
18. Don Kirkendoll, lhp, Bacone (Okla.) JC
19. **Brandon Pernell, of, St. Bernard HS, Torrance, Calif.**
20. **Rich Hills, ss, Oklahoma., Okla.**
21. Aaron Looper, rhp, Byng HS, Ada, Okla.
22. **Anthony Marnell, c, Arizona**
23. **Matt Abernathy, of, Mississippi**
24. **James Moore, of, Ranger (Texas) JC**
25. Anthony Felston, of, Mississippi Delta JC
26. Damon Minor, of, Green River (Wash.) CC
27. Enrique Lazu, rhp, Trujillo Alto, P.R.
28. **Carmen Bucci, ss, Northwestern**
29. Clint Weibl, rhp, Odessa (Texas) JC
30. **Dusty Allen, of/1b, Stanford**
31. Joe Victery, rhp, Eastern Oklahoma State JC
32. **Damond Nash, rhp, Texarkana (Texas) JC**
33. **Ken Jones, c, Western Michigan**
34. Ryan Brown, rhp, Grapevine HS, Colleyville, Texas
35. **Andrew Hunter, of, Arlington (Texas) HS**
36. Jesse Cornejo, lhp, Wellington (Kan.) HS
37. Brandon Brown, lhp, Ranger (Texas) JC
38. Robert Gorr, ss, Rancho Buena Vista HS, Vista, Calif.
39. Chuck Crumpton, rhp, Poteet HS, Mesquite, Texas
40. **Brian Jacobus, of, Rogers HS, Puyallup, Wash.**
41. Scott Pratt, ss, Tooele (Utah) HS
42. William Alexander, rhp, Northwest Shoals (Ala.) CC
43. Rico Lagattuta, lhp, Nevada-Reno
44. John Robertson, rhp, Rockdale (Texas) HS
45. Brett Kondro, lhp, Fort Saskatchewan (Alberta) HS
46. Davis Kile, rhp, Friday Harbor (Wash.) HS
47. Wil Nieves, c, Condado, P.R.
48. Allen Goudy, of, Lake Michigan (Mich.) JC
49. Joel Vega, lhp, Cidra, P.R.
50. Chad Reynolds, rhp, Friendship HS, Lubbock, Texas
51. Justin Sellers, rhp, Evergreen HS, Vancouver, Wash.
52. Adrian Stewart, 1b, Claremont (Calif.) HS

SAN FRANCISCO GIANTS

June—Regular Phase (16)

1. **Joe Fontenot, rhp, Acadiana HS, Lafayette, La.**
2. **Jason Brester, lhp, Burlington-Edison HS, Burlington, Wash.**
3. **Darin Blood, rhp, Gonzaga**
4. **Russ Ortiz, rhp, Oklahoma**
5. **Jim Woodrow, rhp, Flagler (Fla.)**
6. **Joe Nathan, rhp, SUNY Stonybrook**
7. **Alex Morales, of, Central Florida**
8. **Ben Tucker, rhp, Southern California**
9. **Manny Bermudez, rhp, Antioch (Calif.) HS**
10. **Jeff Hutzler, rhp, Texas-San Antonio**
11. **Ian Rand, of, Helix HS, La Mesa, Calif.**
12. **Bruce Thompson, of, Miami**
13. **Philip Bailey, lhp, Central Arkansas**
14. **Jon Watson, 2b, Fairleigh Dickinson**
15. Nate Forbush, c/1b, Central Arizona JC
16. **Brian Knoll, rhp, Brigham Young**
17. Duane Eason, rhp, Brookdale (N.J.) CC
18. Rogelio Colon, rhp, Caguas, P.R.
19. **Kurt Takahashi, rhp, Fresno CC**
20. **Andy Norton, c, Gonzaga**
21. **Terry Weaver, ss, Liberty (Va.)**
22. Danny Harmon, rhp, Midland HS, Floral, Ark.
23. Mark Peer, of, St. Louis CC-Meramec
24. Toby Hall, c, American River (Calif.) JC
25. **Marc Mosman, rhp, Cal State Dominguez Hills**
26. Jeffrey Pohl, rhp, Three Rivers (Mo.) CC
27. Billy Coleman, rhp, Davidson (Okla.) HS
28. Jeremy Jackson, of, Indian Hills (Iowa) CC
29. Kelly Ireland, of, Mount Hood (Ore.) CC
30. John McMurray, 3b, Monticello (Ark.) HS
31. Shawn Lindsay, of, Franklin HS, Portland, Ore.
32. Brian Phelan, c, East Denver HS, Denver
33. Brian Little, 3b, Tulare Union HS, Tulare, Calif.
34. Justin Miller, rhp, Torrance (Calif.) HS
35. Matt Schuldt, c, Howard (Texas) JC
36. Brandon Hayes, rhp, McLane HS, Fresno
37. Jason Dewey, c, Brandon HS, Valrico, Fla.
38. LaJuan Rice, of, McNair HS, Atlanta
39. Tom Topaum, c, Centennial HS, Gresham, Ore.
40. Mike Lincoln, rhp, American River (Calif.) JC
41. Mike Littlefield, rhp, Central Arizona JC
42. Brad Lidge, rhp, Cherry Creek HS, Englewood, Colo.
43. Jason Huth, ss, Cherry Creek HS, Englewood, Colo.
44. Mike Davis, rhp, Tallahassee (Fla.) CC
45. Eric Thompson, rhp, Greenon HS, Fairborn, Ohio
46. Casey Bookout, 1b, Stroud (Okla.) HS
47. **Joe Blasingim, rhp, Southwest Missouri State**
48. Kirk Bolling, rhp, West Torrance HS, Torrance, Calif.
49. David Townsend, rhp, Delta State (Miss.)
50. **Edwards Guzman, 3b, Naranjito, P.R.**

SEATTLE MARINERS

June—Regular Phase (3)

1. **Jose Cruz Jr., of, Rice**
2. **Shane Monahan, of, Clemson**
3. **Greg Wooten, rhp, Portland State (Ore.)**
4. **Duan Johnson, ss, St. Paul's (N.C.) HS**
5. Gary Kinnie, rhp, Chippewa Valley HS, Clifton Township, Mich.
6. **Karl Thompson, c, Santa Clara**
7. **Branden Nogowski, lhp, Hood River (Ore.) Valley HS**
8. **Seth Brizek, ss, Clemson**
9. **Marty Weymouth, rhp, Brother Rice HS, Bloomfield Hills, Mich.**
10. **Ernest Tolbert, of, Lincoln HS, San Diego**
11. **Russ Koehler, rhp, Chemeketa (Ore.) CC**
12. **Dan Kurtz, rhp, LeMoyne**
13. **Andy Collett, rhp/1b, Loyola Marymount**
14. **Chad Sheffer, ss, Central Florida**
15. Lawrence Severence, c, Bryan HS, Archbold, Ohio
16. **Kevin Gryboski, rhp, Wilkes (Pa.)**
17. Aaron Myette, rhp, Johnston Heights HS, Surrey, B.C
18. Wynter Phoenix, of, UC Santa Barbara
19. **Justin Kaye, rhp, Bishop Gorman HS, Las Vegas**
20. **Greg Scheer, lhp, Jacksonville**
21. **Chad Soden, lhp, Arkansas State**
22. **Scott Maynard, c, Dana Hills HS, Laguna Niguel, Calif.**
23. Rob Morrison, rhp, Wellington Community HS, Loxahatchee, Fla.
24. Brett Laxton, rhp, Louisiana State

25. **Brian Fuentes, lhp, Merced (Calif.) JC**
26. Keith Law, ss, East Paulding HS, Hiram, Ga.
27. **Ramon Vazquez, ss, Indian Hills (Iowa) CC**
28. Greg Donahue, c, Rockland (N.Y.) CC
29. Charles Christianson, rhp, Chaffey (Calif.) JC
30. Juan Pierre, of, Alexandria (La.) HS
31. Adam Walker, lhp, Yavapi (Ariz.) JC
32. Harold Frazier, rhp, Oral Roberts
33. Yusef Hamilton, of, St. Martin Deporres HS, Detroit
34. Richard Sundstrom, rhp, Kennedy HS, La Palma, Calif.
35. Nathan Burnett, rhp, Rutherford HS, Panama City, Fla.
36. **Todd Niemeier, lhp, Southern Indiana**
37. Anthony Rice, 3b, CC of San Francisco
38. Joseph Hunt, of, Sante Fe (Fla.) CC
39. Brian Nelson, c, Edison (Fla.) CC
40. Michael Campbell, of, Coronado HS, Mesa, Ariz.
41. Shaylar Hatch, rhp, Gilbert (Ariz.) HS
42. Brian Grubbs, lhp, Cooper HS, Abilene, Texas
43. Travis Ray, rhp, Cairo (Ga.) HS
44. Leron Cook, of, Fresno CC
45. Joe DeVisser, ss, Mattawan HS, Schoolcraft, Mich.
46. Tim Burton, rhp, St. Thomas Aquinas HS, Fort Lauderdale
47. **Jeremy Palki, rhp, Clackamas (Ore.) CC**
48. James Pietraszko, c, Forest Heights HS, Kitchener, Ontario
49. Brian Smith, of, Granite Hills HS, El Cajon, Calif.
50. Zachary Tharp, 1b, Boone HS, Orlando
51. Jacob Hermann, lhp, Eagle Point (Ore.) HS
52. Joel Greene, lhp, Linn-Benton (Ore.) CC
53. Brandon McNab, 1b, Boerne HS, Fair Oaks Ranch, Texas
54. Jeffrey Hammond, of, Flomaton (Ala.) HS
55. Jason Balcom, of, Mount Desales HS, Macon, Ga.
56. Brian Cawaring, of, Alhambra HS, Martinez, Calif.
57. Roy Roundy, c, Coronado HS, Scottsdale, Ariz.
58. Todd Ozias, rhp, Miami-Dade CC Kendall
59. Jason Marr, rhp, Cerritos (Calif.) JC
60. Rafael Rivera, rhp, Miami-Dade CC New World Center
61. Ray Farmer, of, Duke
62. Eric Moten, of, Grant HS, Portland, Ore.
63. Joseph Seymour, c, Southside HS, Elmira, N.Y.
64. Damon Warren, rhp, Lower Columbia (Wash.) CC
65. Sean Hansen, 1b, Norco (Calif.) HS
66. **Isaac Burton, rhp, Arizona State**
67. Sean Kelley, rhp, Miramar HS, Miami
68. Steve Kokinda, 3b, Palm Beach (Fla.) JC
69. Gerald Eady, of, Seminole (Fla.) CC
70. Sean Hamilton, rhp, Dunedin (Fla.) HS
71. Eric Lloyd, rhp, Charlton County HS, Folkston, Ga.
72. Brian Shultz, of, Blinn (Texas) JC
73. Travis Knight, 2b, Kent Meridian HS, Kent, Wash.
74. Tim Hentey, of, Eastside HS, Gainesville, Fla.
75. Wendell Simmons, rhp, Southwest HS, Macon, Ga.
76. Michael Anderson, of, Jones County HS, Gray, Ga.
77. Shane Roland, of, Cook County HS, Adel, Ga.

TEXAS RANGERS

June—Regular Phase (7)

1. **Jonathan Johnson, rhp, Florida State**
2. Phil Lowery, lhp, Casa Grande HS, Petaluma, Calif.
3. **Ryan Dempster, rhp, Elphinstone HS, Gibson's, B.C**
4. **Ryan Glynn, rhp, Virginia Military Institute**
5. **Shawn Gallagher, 1b, New Hanover HS, Wilmington, N.C.**
6. **Dan Kolb, rhp, Sterling, Ill.**
7. **Jorge Carrion, rhp/ss, DeWitt Clinton HS, Bronx, N.Y.**
8. **Craig Monroe, ss, Texarkana (Texas) HS**
9. **Juan Rivera, c, Rio Grande, P.R.**
10. **Julio Mercado, of, Brooke Point HS, Stafford, Va.**
11. **Brian Martineau, rhp, Rancho Santiago (Calif.) JC**
12. **Bryan Link, lhp, Winthrop**
13. **Cliff Brumbaugh, 3b, Delaware**
14. **Brandon Knight, rhp, Ventura (Calif.) JC**
15. **Ryan Gorecki, 2b, Seton Hall**
16. **Nathan Vopata, 3b/2b, Lewis-Clark State (Idaho)**
17. **Brian Llibre, c, West Covina (Calif.) HS**
18. **Damian Rose, of, Overfelt HS, San Jose**
19. **Charles Bauer, rhp, St. Rose (N.Y.)**
20. **Joe Goodwin, c, George Mason**
21. **Ted Silva, rhp, Cal State Fullerton**
22. **Bobby Styles, rhp, East Henderson HS, Hendersonville, N.C.**
23. **Robert Moore, rhp, Hawaii**
24. Manny Torres, rhp, St Joseph's HS, Trumbull, Conn.
25. **Mike McHugh, lhp, Penn State**
26. **Chris Briones, c, Nevada-Reno**
27. David Brazeal, c, Mustang (Okla.) HS
28. Gary Johnson, of, East Los Angeles JC
29. **Mike Venafro, lhp, James Madison**
30. **Scott Mudd, rhp, Indiana**
31. **Kelly Stratton, of, Utah**
32. **Scooter Bryant, lhp, Sulphur (La.) HS**
33. Joe Garibaldi, lhp, Terra Nova HS, Pacifica, Calif.
34. **John McAulay, c, William Carey (Miss.)**
35. **Bobby Kahlon, rhp, California**
36. Joseph Williams, 3b, Chaffey HS, Ontario, Calif.
37. Emar Fleming, rhp, Allegany (Md.) CC
38. Russell Bratton, rhp, Central HS, Columbia, Tenn.
39. Danny Carrasco, rhp, Hayward (Calif.) HS
40. **Billy Reed, ss, Auburn**
41. **Manden Echols, of, William Carey (Miss.)**
42. **Brent Sagedal, rhp, Carthage (Wis.)**
43. Amury Leon, ss, Tucson (Ariz.) HS
44. **Tom Smith, rhp, Petaluma (Calif.) HS**
45. **Mark Draeger, rhp, Slippery Rock (Pa.)**
46. **Tim Codd, rhp, Edinboro (Pa.)**
47. Byan Haley, rhp, Loxahachee, Fla.

TORONTO BLUE JAYS

June—Regular Phase (17)

1. **Roy Halladay, rhp, West HS, Arvada, Colo.**
2. **Craig Wilson, c, Marina HS, Huntington Beach, Calif.**
3. **Jeff Maloney, ss, Ridge HS, Basking Ridge, N.J.**
4. **Mike Whitlock, 1b, San Lorenzo (Calif.) HS**
5. **Jay Veniard, lhp, Central Florida**
6. **Blaine Fortin, c, Lundar (Manitoba) HS**
7. **Jeremi Rudolph, of, Apopka (Fla.) HS**
8. Dave Marciniak, ss, Woodbridge (N.J.) HS
9. **Kyle Burchart, rhp, Bixby (Okla.) HS**
10. **Ryan Freel, 2b, Tallahassee (Fla.) CC**
11. Allen Levrault, lhp, Westport (Mass.) HS
12. **John Curl, 1b, Texas A&M**
13. Ted Lilly, lhp, Fresno CC
14. Jason Pomar, rhp, Vero Beach (Fla.) HS
15. Robert Corraro, rhp, Xavier (Conn.) HS
16. **Bill Brabec, rhp, Illinois State**
17. Johnny Byrd, rhp, University Christian HS, Jacksonville
18. Doug Dent, rhp, San Juan HS, Citrus Heights, Calif.
19. **Jaron Seabury, rhp, Bellevue (Wash.) CC**
20. James Whitehead, 1b/c, Meridian (Miss.) CC
21. **Logan Miler, c, Texas Tech**
22. **Scott Fitterer, rhp, Louisiana State**
23. **Brian Bejarano, 3b, Central Arizona JC**
24. Mark Curtis, lhp, Bellerose HS, St. Albert, Alberta
25. **John Mitchell, rhp, Cal State Fullerton**
26. **John Kehoe, 2b, Cumberland (Tenn.)**
27. **Robert Medina, c, Caguas, P.R.**
28. **Chris Hayes, 3b, Jacksonville**
29. **Brian Williams, c, Southwest Texas State**
30. Brandon Duckworth, rhp, JC of Southern Idaho
31. **John Douglas, ss, Catholic (Washington)**
32. Stanley Gay, lhp, Covington (Tenn.) HS
33. Todd Moser, lhp, Manatee (Fla.) JC
34. **Andrew McCormick, of, Grand Canyon (Ariz.)**
35. **Jonathan Herring, lhp, Alabama Christian Academy, Montgomery, Ala.**
36. Randy Albaral, of, Jesuit HS, River Ridge, La.
37. Thomas Taylor, ss, Tate HS, Gonzales, Fla.
38. Tyrone Gracia, 3b, Yarmouth Regional HS, Dennis, Mass.
39. Eduardo Marquez, of, Mater Dei HS, Orange, Calif.
40. Brian Leach, rhp, Osceola HS, Seminole, Fla.

41. Jesse Bechard, ss, Washington HS, Masillon, Ohio
42. **Thomas Peck, of, Rollins (Fla.)**
43. Justin Johnson, of, Diamond Bar (Calif.) HS
44. Brian Fitts, rhp, Gallatin (Tenn.) HS
45. Joe Pierson, ss, Huntington (W.Va.) HS
46. **Ryan Cisar, ss, Magnolia HS, New Martinsville, W.Va.**
47. Antonio Jackson, of, Parker HS, Birmingham
48. **Paxton Stewart, 1b, Florida International**
49. Derek Hines, of, West HS, Arvada, Colo.
50. Jeremy Satterfield, rhp, JC of Southern Idaho
51. Kyle Adams, lhp, Creighton Prep, Omaha
52. Albert Colon, of, Apopka (Fla.) HS
53. Ryan Bundy, c, Lake Stevens HS, Everett, Wash.
54. Claude Greene, 1b, O'Dea HS, Seattle
55. Travis Grant, rhp, Skyline HS, Salt Lake City
56. Sidney Harden, rhp, Middle Georgia JC
57. Pat Schultz, of, CC of Rhode Island
58. Doug Franklin, 2b, Pensacola (Fla.) JC
59. Andy Tarpley, rhp, California

1996 FOUR FIRST-ROUNDERS BECOME FREE AGENTS THROUGH LOOPHOLE, SENDING BONUSES INTO ORBIT

No matter what happens to the players from the draft of 1996, it's a year that will always be remembered for a loophole—a loophole that cost nearly $30 million.

A seemingly innocuous paragraph in the Professional Baseball Agreement would up turning the entire process upside down and made four prospects rich beyond their wildest dreams—and baseball executives' nightmares.

Because of violations to Rule 4(E) of the PBA, which required that teams make a formal contract offer to every pick within 15 days of the draft, Major League Baseball had to grant several premium players free agency and touched off unprecedented bidding wars.

The four players were first baseman Travis Lee (No. 2 overall, Twins), righthander John Patterson (No. 5, Expos), righthander Matt White (No. 7, Giants) and lefthander Bobby Seay (No. 12, White Sox). Most scouts agreed Lee was the top position player in the draft, and the three pitchers were the top high school arms.

Their draft positions had already been affected by their reported bonus demands. Hitting the open market meant the players got significantly more money than if they had been bound to the clubs that drafted them. They were helped even more by two new expansion clubs that had no player costs and were hungry for talent. Lee ($10 million) and Patterson ($6.075 million) ended up signing with the Diamondbacks, while White ($10.2 million) and Seay ($3 million) signed with the Devil Rays.

For nearly $30 million, the teams got precious little production. Lee made it to the big leagues first and had a promising start, but he tailed off and Arizona traded him to the Phillies before his career fizzled. Patterson battled through injuries to make the Diamondbacks rotation by 2003, though he ended up with just 18 wins over parts of six season. Seay made 261 appearances as a middle reliever, most of them with the Tigers, while White never even reached the major leagues.

The loophole had been part of the PBA since at least 1990, but no one had ever made it an issue. The rule first was challenged by Seay and his agent, Scott Boras, and the White Sox voluntarily relinquished their rights to Seay, setting a precedent that led other players to file.

Six players filed similar grievances, though three (Braden Looper, Cardinals; Eric Milton, Twins; A.J. Hinch, Athletics) signed with the teams that drafted them before Major League Baseball made a decision. Lee, Patterson and White were declared free agents Sept. 24, becoming the first U.S. players ever to gain free agency during the summer they were drafted. Previous snafus involving Tom Seaver (1966), Bill Bordley (1979) and Billy Cannon (1980) gave those players either limited free agency or access to a special lottery.

LARRY GOREN

Travis Lee cashed in with Arizona after a standout career at San Diego State

Boras, who represented White and Seay, said he noticed the rule when he was revising a draft guidebook he sent to his clients. While the loophole was closed, Boras used it in future years as an illustration of how the draft unfairly restricted the earning power of players.

"Baseball has made an admission that they're not paying for talent, they're paying for jurisdiction," Boras said, noting that most foreign players can sign with any club while American players are limited by the draft to one team. "That's where the draft is wrong."

Twins scouting director Mike Radcliff thought the loophole could lead to major changes, though the only lasting repercussion proved to be the continuing escalation of bonuses.

"You could view this as the first step toward a

major upheaval of the draft," Radcliff said. "The draft is designed to benefit all teams. I think you can show that it has."

By many estimates, at most only half of the 30 teams made proper offers to their first-round picks, and none of the four teams that lost their picks claimed they followed the rule to the letter. MLB closed the loophole after 1996, but the shockwaves were felt for years.

Oh Yeah, The No. 1 Pick

The rest of the draft almost became an afterthought. One of its only notable features was the consensus that the talent wasn't as strong as it had been in previous years, particularly in position players.

The clear No. 1 choice was Clemson righthander Kris Benson, who emerged as Baseball America's College Player of the Year in a stellar junior season. He went 14-2 with a 2.02 ERA and 204 strikeouts in 156 innings. The Pirates took him and signed him for a $2 million bonus, breaking the record of $1.6 million set by Marlins first-rounder Josh Booty in 1994.

The only big question was which team would draft White, who was regarded by some scouts as one of the best high school pitching prospects of the draft era but had steep bonus demands. White and Boras told at least 10 teams they shouldn't draft him. The Giants took him seventh overall and didn't seem likely to sign him even if he hadn't become a free agent.

And if the '96 draft didn't have enough twists, righthander R.A. Dickey's hope for a large signing bonus was knocked out by a magazine cover. Dickey, the 18th overall pick to the Rangers, had agreed to an $810,000 bonus, but subsequent physical revealed he was missing a ligament in his elbow.

The Rangers were tipped off when a team doctor saw the cover of Baseball America, which featured Dickey and four other pitchers from the U.S. Olympic team. The doctor didn't like the way Dickey's arm was hanging, which prompted the examination.

Dickey subsequently signed for $75,000, and in perhaps the best twist of all, persevered and made it to the big leagues with the Rangers as a middle reliever. In fact, he was still playing in 2009, long after the loophole players' careers had petered out.

DRAFT 96: FIRST-ROUND PICKS

No.	Club	Player, Pos.	School	Hometown	Ht.	Wt.	B-T	Age
1.	Pirates	Kris Benson, rhp	Clemson	Kennesaw, Ga.	6-4	190	R-R	21
2.	Twins	*Travis Lee, 1b	San Diego State	Olympia, Wash.	6-3	210	L-L	21
3.	Cardinals	Braden Looper, rhp	Wichita State	Mangum, Okla.	6-4	220	R-R	21
4.	Blue Jays	Billy Koch, rhp	Clemson	West Babylon, N.Y.	6-3	195	R-R	21
5.	Expos	*John Patterson, rhp	West Orange Stark HS	Orange, Texas	6-6	185	R-R	18
6.	Tigers	Seth Greisinger, rhp	Virginia	Falls Church, Va.	6-4	190	R-R	20
7.	Giants	*Matt White, rhp	Waynesboro Area HS	Waynesboro, Pa.	6-5	230	R-R	17
8.	Brewers	Chad Green, of	Kentucky	Mentor, Ohio	5-10	185	B-R	20
9.	Marlins	Mark Kotsay, of	Cal State Fullerton	Sante Fe Springs, Calif.	6-0	180	L-L	20
10.	Athletics	Eric Chavez, 3b	Mount Carmel HS	San Diego	6-1	190	B-R	18
11.	Phillies	Adam Eaton, rhp	Snohomish HS	Snohomish, Wash.	6-2	180	R-R	18
12.	White Sox	*Bobby Seay, lhp	Sarasota HS	Sarasota, Fla.	6-2	190	L-L	17
13.	Mets	Robert Stratton, of	San Marcos HS	Santa Barbara, Calif.	6-2	220	R-R	18
14.	Royals	Dermal Brown, of	Marlboro Central HS	Marlboro, N.Y.	6-1	210	L-R	18
15.	Padres	Matt Halloran, ss	Chancellor HS	Fredericksburg, Va.	6-2	185	R-R	18
16.	Blue Jays	Joe Lawrence, ss	Barbe HS	Lake Charles, La.	6-1	190	R-R	19
17.	Cubs	Todd Noel, rhp	North Vermillion HS	Maurice, La.	6-4	185	R-R	17
18.	Rangers	R.A. Dickey, rhp	Tennessee	Nashville, Tenn.	6-1	205	R-R	21
19.	Astros	Mark Johnson, rhp	Hawaii	Lebanon, Ohio	6-3	215	R-R	21
20.	Yankees	Eric Milton, lhp	Maryland	Bellefonte, Pa.	6-3	200	L-L	20
21.	Rockies	Jake Westbrook, rhp	Madison County HS	Danielsville, Ga.	6-3	180	R-R	18
22.	Mariners	Gil Meche, rhp	Acadiana HS	Lafayette, La.	6-3	185	R-R	17
23.	Dodgers	Damian Rolls, 3b	Schalgel HS	Kansas City, Kan.	6-2	205	R-R	18
24.	Rangers	Sam Marsonek, rhp	Jesuit HS	Tampa	6-6	225	R-R	17
25.	Reds	John Oliver, of	Lake-Lehman HS	Lehman, Pa.	6-3	190	R-R	18
26.	Red Sox	Josh Garrett, rhp	South Spencer HS	Richland, Ind.	6-4	190	R-R	18
27.	Braves	A.J. Zapp, 1b	Center Grove HS	Greenwood, Ind.	6-3	190	L-R	18
28.	Indians	Danny Peoples, 1b	Texas	Round Rock, Texas	6-0	210	R-R	21
29.	Devil Rays	Paul Wilder, of	Cary HS	Cary, N.C.	6-4	235	L-R	18
30.	Diamondbacks	Nick Bierbrodt, lhp	Millikan HS	Long Beach	6-4	180	L-L	18

*Signed as free agents with teams other than those that drafted them

1996

CLUB-BY-CLUB SELECTIONS

ARIZONA DIAMONDBACKS

June—Regular Phase (30)

1. **Nick Bierbrodt, lhp, Millikan HS, Long Beach**
2. **Jerry Proctor, of, Muir HS, Pasadena, Calif.**
3. **Mark Osborne, c, Lee County HS, Sanford, N.C.**
4. **Josh McAffee, c, Farmington (N.M.) HS**
5. **Brad Penny, rhp, Broken Arrow (Okla.) HS**
6. **Eric Putt, rhp, Deltona (Fla.) HS**
7. Casey Fossum, lhp, Midway HS, Waco, Texas
8. **Joe Verplancke, rhp, Cal State Los Angeles**
9. **Marc Van Wormer, rhp, Prescott (Ariz.) HS**
10. **George Oleksik, rhp, Middle Tennessee State**
11. **Ron Hartman, 3b, Maryland**
12. **Michael Boughton, ss, Northwood Institute (Texas)**
13. **Ben Norris, lhp, Westwood HS, Austin**
14. **Jamie Gann, of, Oklahoma**
15. **Reggie Davis, c, Augusta State (Ga.)**
16. Kevin Johnson, ss, St. Joseph's HS, Alameda, Calif.
17. **Jackie Rexrode, ss, Riverdale Baptist HS, Laurel, Md.**
18. **David Chapman, of, Alta Loma (Calif.) HS**
19. Jacob Brooks, rhp, East Lake HS, Palm Harbor, Fla.
20. **John Fleming, rhp, Bonita Vista HS, Chula Vista, Calif.**
21. Brian Crisorio, 3b, East Lake HS, Clearwater, Fla.
22. Jeffrey Nichols, rhp, Duncanville (Texas) HS
23. **Michael McCutchen, lhp, Modesto (Calif.) JC**
24. Eric Knott, lhp, Stetson
25. **Scott Glasser, 2b, Rancho Santiago (Calif.) JC**
26. **Rob Ryan, of, Washington State**
27. **Justin Bice, rhp, Grand Canyon (Ariz.)**
28. **Beau Baltzell, c, Purdue**
29. **Kevin Sweeney, of, Mercyhurst (Pa.)**
30. Michael Pesci, of, Detroit
31. **Jose Nunez, 3b/2b, Northeast Texas CC**
32. **Jason Conti, of, Pittsburgh**
33. **Dallas Anderson, rhp, Lethbridge (Alberta) CC**
34. Corey Hart, 2b, Connors State (Okla.) JC
35. **Brett Hardy, of, UC Santa Barbara**
36. **Junior Spivey, 2b, Cowley County (Kan.) CC**
37. **Jason Moore, c/1b, West Virginia State**
38. Curtis Johnson, of, St. Joseph's HS, Oakland
39. **Bert Hudson, c, Jay (Fla.) HS**
40. **Travis McCall, lhp, Ayala HS, Chino Hills, Calif.**
41. **Brad Allison, c, Morehead State**
42. **Erik Sabel, rhp, Tennesse Tech**
43. Charles Chungu, rhp, New Hampshire
44. James Harrison, rhp, William Penn HS, New Castle, Del.
45. Brett DeBoer, lhp, Lakeland HS, Rathdum, Idaho
46. **Matt Bell, rhp, Joplin (Mo.) HS**
47. Ryan Evans, c, Tuscaloosa County HS, Northport, Ala.
48. **Jorge Martinez, c, Newtown HS, New York**
49. Brent Wagler, rhp, Florida Southern
50. Casey Rowe, rhp, Bullard HS, Fresno
51. Patrick Coogan, rhp, Louisiana State
52. Jeff Remiliard, rhp, Memorial HS, Manchester, N.H.
53. **David Harper, rhp, Lubbock Christian (Texas)**
54. Jason Jennings, rhp, Poteet HS, Mesquite, Texas
55. Blake Ricken, lhp, Fresno CC
56. Andrew McCulloch, rhp, Western HS, Las Vegas
57. Eric O'Brien, rhp, Alton (N.H.) HS
58. **Bryce Darnell, c, Missouri Southern State**
59. **Carmen Panaro, c, Niagara**
60. **Mark Chavez, rhp, Cal State Fullerton**
61. Brandon Duckworth, rhp, JC of Southern Idaho
62. George Otero, 3b/c, Pace HS, Miami

ATLANTA BRAVES

June—Regular Phase (27)

1. **A.J. Zapp, 1b, Center Grove HS, Greenwood, Ind.**
1. **Jason Marquis, rhp, Tottenville HS, Staten Island, N.Y.** (Supplemental pick—35th—for failure to sign 1995 first-rounder Chad Hutchinson)
2. Eric Munson, c, Mount Carmel HS, San Diego
3. **Junior Brignac, of, Cleveland HS, Reseda, Calif.**
4. **Joe Nelson, rhp, San Francisco**
5. **Josh Pugh, c, Henry Clay HS, Lexington, Ky.**
6. **Shawn Onley, rhp, Rice**
7. **Mark DeRosa, 3b, Pennsylvania**
8. **A.D. Thorpe, ss, Southern HS, Durham, N.C.**
9. **Nathan Harden, rhp, Dripping Springs (Texas) HS**
10. **Winston Lee, rhp, Glendale (Calif.) JC**
11. **Aaron Taylor, rhp, Lowndes HS, Hahira, Ga.**
12. **Greg Ward, of, Avon (Conn.) HS**
13. **Jason Ross, of, Hawaii**
14. John Alkire, rhp, Tennessee
15. **Mike Hessman, 1b/rhp, Mater Dei HS, Westminster, Calif.**
16. **Earl Beasley, lhp, Lake City (Fla.) CC**
17. Dana Davis, rhp, Rice
18. **Donald Ceasar, rhp, LaGrange HS, Lake Charles, La.**
19. **Adam Milbum, lhp, Kentucky**
20. **John Arnold, c, Eastern New Mexico**
21. **Jesse Crespo, c, Camuy, P.R.**
22. Aaron Melebeck, ss, Clear Brook HS, Webster, Texas
23. **Dax Norris, c, Alabama**
24. Patrick Collins, rhp, Union (N.J.) HS
25. **Anthony Brooks, ss, Gulf Coast (Fla.) CC**
26. **Jason Katz, ss, New Mexico JC**
27. **Aaron Strangfeld, 1b, Grossmont (Calif.) JC**
28. Miguel Garcia, rhp, Cerritos (Calif.) JC
29. **Galen Reeder, lhp, DeKalb (Ga.) JC**
30. Fred Sanchez, ss, Burbank (Calif.) HS
31. Adam Love, rhp, Westlake HS, Austin
32. Dustin Franklin, lhp, Permian HS, Odessa, Texas
33. **Jerrod Wong, 1b, Gonzaga**
34. Adam Springston, rhp, Oxnard (Calif.) JC
35. Byron Embry, rhp, Indian Hills (Iowa) CC
36. Scott Frawley, c, South Suburban (Ill.) JC
37. Hunter Wenzel, lhp, Boerne HS, Fair Oaks Ranch, Texas
38. Randy Phillips, lhp, Olney Central (Ill.) JC
39. **Jeff Lindemann, rhp, Andrew HS, Lockport, Ill.**
40. Anthony Barrow, 1b, Blazer HS, Ashland, Ky.
41. **Justin Willoughby, lhp, Princeton (N.C.) HS**
42. **George Snead, rhp, Albany State (Ga.)**
43. Cory Simpson, rhp, Sumner HS, Kentwood, La.
44. Nate Fernley, rhp, Long Beach CC
45. **John Zydowsky, ss, Portage HS, Pardeeville, Wis.**
46. Joe Holzbauer, rhp, Palomar (Calif.) JC
47. Patrick Fuentes, ss, Logan HS, South San Francisco
48. Greg Dukeman, rhp, Millikan HS, Long Beach
49. **Mike Jones, lhp, UC Riverside**
50. Travis Richo, of, Fernandina Beach (Fla.) HS
51. Daniel Bell, of, University HS, Los Angeles
52. Brett Pierce, ss, Citrus (Calif.) JC
53. **Marcus Giles, 2b, Granite Hills HS, El Cajon, Calif.**
54. **Jeff Champion, of, Florida Memorial**
55. **Adam Johnson, of, Central Florida**
56. Bradley Green, ss, South Pittsburg (Tenn.) HS
57. **Juan Galban, lhp, Miami**
58. Baylor Moore, lhp, Friendswood (Texas) HS
59. Hector Gonzales, c, Scottsdale (Ariz.) CC
60. Ray Plummer, lhp, Point Loma Nazarene (Calif.)

BALTIMORE ORIOLES

June—Regular Phase (16)

1. (Pick to Blue Jays as compensation for Type A free agent Roberto Alomar)
2. **Brian Falkenborg, rhp, Redmond (Wash.) HS**
3. **Daren Hooper, of, Arizona**
4. **Mark Seaver, rhp, Wake Forest**
5. **Frank Figueroa, 1b/of, Florida Bible HS, Hialeah, Fla.**
6. **Josh McNatt, lhp, Motlow State (Tenn.) CC**
7. Brent Schoening, rhp, Columbus (Ga.) HS
8. **Chad Paronto, rhp, Massachusetts**
9. **Luis Ramirez, 1b, Arroyo, P.R.**
10. **Luis Matos, of, Bayamon, P.R.**
11. Bruce Stanley, rhp, Ball State
12. **Simeon Theodile, rhp, Acadiana HS, Lafayette, La.**
13. **Augie Ojeda, ss, Tennessee**
14. **Ryan Kohlmeier, rhp, Butler County (Kan.) CC**
15. **Josh Towers, rhp, Oxnard (Calif.) JC**
16. Josh Morris, ss, Motlow State (Tenn.) CC
17. **Tim DeCinces, c, UCLA**
18. Andrew Cheek, lhp, Beaver Creak HS, West Jefferson, N.C.
19. Gabe Crecion, rhp, Chaminade Prep, West Hills, Calif.
20. **Ashanti Davison, of, St. Mary's HS, Stockton, Calif.**
21. **Gabe Molina, rhp, Arizona State**
22. Mike MacDougal, rhp, Mesa (Ariz.) HS
23. **Jesse Perez, ss, Mayaguez, P.R.**
24. Jay Gehrke, rhp, North HS, Fargo, N.D.
25. **John Parrish, lhp, McCaskey HS, Lancaster, Pa.**
26. **Maleke Fowler, of, Nicholls State**
27. Robert Baker, rhp, Westwood HS, Austin
28. Cordell Lindsey, 3b, North Shore HS, Houston
29. Jason Johnson, lhp, Sacred Heart Academy, Winn, Mich.
30. **Johnny Morales, lhp, Central Arizona JC**
31. **Jeff Phipps, rhp, San Joaquin Delta (Calif.) JC**
32. **Todd Morgan, of, Deerfield Beach (Fla.) HS**
33. **Ryan Minor, 3b/1b, Oklahoma**
34. **DeShawn Ziths, of, Columbia-Greene (N.Y.) CC**
35. **Jeremiah Johnson, rhp, Kellogg (Mich.) CC**
36. **Jaime Escalante, c, Hagerstown (Md.) JC**
37. **Craig Ratliff, rhp, Paintsville HS, West Van Plear, Ky.**
38. Randall Benge, lhp, Fort Vancouver HS, Yacolt, Wash.
39. Eric Drew, rhp, Montello (Wis.) HS
40. Ben Christensen, rhp, Goddard HS, West Goddard, Kan.
41. Vanshan Renfroe, ss, McGavock HS, Hermitage, Tenn.
42. **Michael Kirkpatrick, of, St. Elizabeth HS, New Castle, Del.**
43. Tyson Martinez, rhp, Fort Madison (Iowa) HS
44. Daniel Allen, of, Perry (Okla.) HS
45. Josh Taylor, ss, Seminole State (Okla.) JC
46. Sean Gilchrist, of, Bigfork (Mont.) HS
47. Chad Anderson, of, Bigfork (Mont.) HS

BOSTON RED SOX

June—Regular Phase (26)

1. **Josh Garrett, rhp, South Spencer HS, Richland, Ind.**
1. **Chris Reitsma, rhp, Calgary Christian HS** (Supplemental pick—34th—for loss of Type A free agent Erik Hanson)
2. **Gary LoCurto, 1b, University HS, San Diego** (Pick from Blue Jays as compensation for Hanson)
2. **Jason Sekany, rhp, Virginia**
3. **Dernell Stenson, of, LaGrange (Ga.) HS**
4. **John Barnes, of, Grossmont (Calif.) JC**
5. **Bobby Brito, c, Cypress (Calif.) HS**
6. **Mike Perini, of, Carlsbad (N.M.) HS**
7. **Robert Ramsay, lhp, Washington State**
8. **Justin Duchscherer, rhp, Coronado HS, Lubbock, Texas**
9. **Marcus Martinez, lhp, Monterey HS, Lubbock, Texas**
10. **Shea Hillenbrand, ss, Mesa (Ariz.) CC**
11. **Brian Musgrave, lhp, Appalachian State**
12. **Dion Ruecker, ss, Texas Tech**
13. **Skipp Benzing, rhp, Indian Hills (Iowa) CC**
14. Justin Lynch, rhp, Marina HS, Huntington Beach, Calif.
15. Mark Robbins, 3b, Derry (Kan.) HS
16. **Jeff Keaveney, 1b/of, Southern Maine**
17. Justin Crisafulli, rhp, Arizona Western JC
18. **Mike McKinley, of, Scottsdale (Ariz.) CC**
19. **Mike Rupp, rhp, Monte Vista HS, Spring Valley, Calif.**
20. **Chuck Beale, rhp, Stetson**
21. **Javier Fuentes, ss/2b, Arizona State**
22. Aaron Harang, rhp, Patrick Henry HS, San Diego
23. Paul McCurtain, rhp, Mesa (Ariz.) CC
24. Robert Brandt, rhp, A&M Consolidated HS, College Station, Texas
25. Dominic Barrett, of, Trimble Tech HS, Fort Worth
26. **Chris Thompson, rhp, St. Leo (Fla.)**
27. Ryan Murray, rhp, Tampa Bay Tech HS, Tampa
28. **Erik Metzger, c, Samford**
29. Josh Stewart, lhp, Livingston Central HS, Ledbetter, Ky.
30. William Whitaker, lhp, First Coast HS, Jacksonville
31. Matt Frick, c, Yavapai (Ariz.) JC
32. Mike Bynum, lhp, Middleburg (Fla.) HS
33. **Adam Roller, rhp, Lakeland (Fla.) HS**
34. Jaime Bonilla, lhp, Lake City (Fla.) CC
35. Kasey Kuhlmeyer, lhp, San Pasqual HS, Escondido, Calif.
36. Ken Sarna, ss, Durango HS, Las Vegas
37. Jeremy Swindell, lhp, Clear Lake HS, Houston
38. Travis McRoberts, ss, El Capitan HS, El Cajon, Calif.
39. **Andre Thompson, of, Delta State (Miss.)**
40. Curtis Anthony, ss, Bishop Gorman HS, Las Vegas
41. (Selection voided)
42. Wesley Warren, of, Arcadia HS, Scottsdale, Ariz.
43. Jamaon Halbig, c, Southwestern (Calif.) JC
44. Bart Vaughn, rhp, Manatee (Fla.) CC

CALIFORNIA ANGELS

June—Regular Phase (20)

1. (Pick to Yankees as compensation for Type B free agent Randy Velarde)
2. **Chuck Abbott, ss, Austin Peay**
3. **Scott Schoeneweis, lhp, Duke**
4. **Brandon Steele, rhp, Huntington Beach (Calif.) HS**
5. Bobby Hill, ss, Leland HS, San Jose
6. Jason Verdugo, rhp, Arizona State
7. **Marcus Knight, of, Miramar HS, Pembroke Pines, Fla.**
8. **Jerrod Riggan, rhp, San Diego State**
9. **Jason Stephens, rhp, Arkansas**
10. **Eric Gillespie, 3b, Cal State Northridge**
11. **Pat Johnson, c, Brigham Young**
12. Mark Richards, rhp, Winthrop
13. Ken Polk, c, Howard (Texas) JC
14. Jaeme Leal, 1b, Poly HS, Riverside, Calif.
15. **Theo Fefee, of, Bethune-Cookman**
16. **Nate Murphy, of, Massachusetts**
17. Jason Cly, rhp, Arcadia (Calif.) HS
18. **Mark Harriger, rhp, San Diego State**
19. **Brian Ussery, c, Tampa**
20. **Cale Carter, of, Stanford**
21. **Scott Byers, 1b, Georgia Tech**
22. **Nathan Starkey, 3b/c, Modesto (Calif.) JC**
23. **John Margaritis, of, Treasure Valley (Ore.) CC**
24. **Eduardo Ferrer, 2b, Florida International**
25. **Jose Ortiz, rhp, Hayward (Calif.) HS**
26. **Jason Dewey, c, Indian River (Fla.) CC**
27. **Rob Neal, of, Cal Poly San Luis Obispo**
28. **Matt Curtis, c, Fresno State**
29. **Wade Jackson, 2b, Nevada**
30. **James Leach, lhp, Gibbs HS, Pinellas Park, Fla.**
31. William Robbins, rhp, Gulf Breeze (Fla.) HS
32. Greg Blum, c, Chino (Calif.) HS
33. Richard Stegbauer, c, Seminole (Fla.) HS
34. Kirk Asche, of, Edison (Fla.) CC
35. **Eric Plooy, rhp, JC of the Sequoias (Calif.)**
36. Jeremy Freitas, of, Fresno CC
37. Jack Taschner, lhp, Horlick HS, Racine, Wis.
38. Michael Carney, lhp, Indian River (Fla.) CC
39. Gary Forrester, rhp, Centralia (Wash.) JC
40. Dominic Repetti, ss, DeAnza (Calif.) JC
41. **Kris William, rhp, Brevard (Fla.) CC**

42. **Greg Jones, c, Pasco-Hernando (Fla.) CC**
43. **Marc Collier, ss, Lower Dauphin HS, Hummelstown, Pa.**
44. Richard Shaw, rhp, Marquette
45. Nathan Burnett, rhp, Gulf Coast (Fla.) CC
46. Michael Gauger, lhp, Tallahassee (Fla.) CC
47. Adrian Merkey, ss, Polk (Fla.) CC
48. Chris Finnegan, c, Millard North HS, Omaha
49. Kenny Avera, rhp, Pensacola (Fla.) JC
50. Anthony Lopresti, c, University HS, San Diego
51. Michael Abate, of, Norwalk (Conn.) HS
52. Elvis Hernandez, of, Aurora West HS, Montgomery, Ill.
53. **William Snellings, lhp, Pasco-Hernando (Fla.) CC**
54. Paul Poplin, rhp, South Stanly HS, Norwood, N.C.
55. Kevin Davis, ss, South Spencer HS, Rockport, Ind.
56. Orlando Sloan, of, Santa Monica HS, Westchester, Calif.

CHICAGO CUBS

June—Regular Phase (17)

1. **Todd Noel, rhp, North Vermillion HS, Maurice, La.**
2. **Quincy Carter, of, Southwest DeKalb HS, Ellenwood, Ga.**
3. **Skip Ames, rhp, Alabama**
4. **Chris Gissell, rhp, Hudson's Bay HS, Vancouver, Wash.**
5. **Chad Meyers, 2b/of, Creighton**
6. **Doug Hall, of, Alabama**
7. **Jon Cannon, lhp, Canada (Calif.) JC**
8. **Brian Connell, lhp, Dunedin (Fla.) HS**
9. **Nate Manning, 3b, Austin Peay**
10. **Phil Norton, lhp, Texarkana (Texas) JC**
11. Steve Sanberg, c, Midlothian (Texas) HS
12. Mark Ernster, ss, Ironwood HS, Glendale, Ariz.
13. Johnny Whitesides, rhp, Sarasota (Fla.) HS
14. Tim Lavery, lhp, Naperville (Ill.) Central HS
15. Freddie Young, of, Lyman HS, Longwood, Fla.
16. **Byron Tribe, rhp, Alabama**
17. **Brad King, c, Central Florida**
18. **Jim Crawford, rhp, Cowley County (Kan.) CC**
19. **Marcel Longmire, c/of, Vallejo (Calif.) HS**
20. **Courtney Duncan, rhp, Grambling State**
21. **Ryan Anderson, 2b, Dallas Baptist**
22. **John Nall, lhp, California**
23. **Jason Smith, ss, Meridian (Miss.) CC**
24. **Ronald Payne, of, Pitt (N.C.) CC**
25. Douglas Young, rhp, Sierra (Calif.)
26. **Courteney Stewart, of, DeKalb (Ga.) JC**
27. **Matthew Perry, rhp, Allegheny (Pa.) CC**
28. **Jeff Velez, rhp, Connecticut**
29. **Kyle Lohse, rhp, Hamilton Union HS, Glenn, Calif.**
30. **Casey Brookens, rhp, James Madison**
31. **Randy Crane, rhp, Linn-Benton (Ore.) CC**
32. Mike Miller, rhp/3b, Manatee (Fla.) CC
33. Nicholas Lee, rhp, Brockton (Mass.) HS
34. **Richard Powalski, lhp, Central Catholic HS, Clearwater, Fla.**
35. Keola Delatori, rhp, Schaumburg (Ill.) HS
36. David Regan, of, Brockton (Mass.) HS
37. **Lendon Hart, lhp, East Tennessee State**
38. Justin Lee, of, McLennan (Texas) CC
39. **Brad Ramsey, c, Gulf Coast (Fla.) CC**
40. Jeremy Smith, rhp, Needles (Calif.) HS
41. **Daniel Hodges, lhp, Liberty**
42. **Derrick Bly, 3b, Concordia (Calif.)**
43. Cameron Newitt, rhp, Northwest Shoals (Ala.) CC
44. John Guilmet, rhp, Merrimack (Mass.)
45. **Keith Lewis, 2b, Mississippi**
46. Mike Mainella, of, West Fairmont (W.Va.) HS
47. Joseph Tillmon, ss, Chatsworth HS, Winnetka, Calif.
48. **Dax Kiefer, of, Texas Lutheran**
49. Jacob Sutter, rhp, Celina (Ohio) HS
50. Rob Holmes, rhp, Creighton Prep, Omaha
51. Rahman Corbett, of, Princeton HS, Cincinnati
52. Harris Stanton, of, Spartanburg Methodist (S.C.) JC
53. Chris Bentley, rhp, Molalla Union HS, Mulino, Ore.
54. Cory Cattaneo, lhp, Sequoia HS, Redwood City, Calif.
55. **Shane Sullivan, rhp, Serrano HS, Pinon Hills, Calif.**
56. Ryan Blackmum, c, Mater Dei HS, Garden Grove, Calif.
57. John Halliday, 1b, Clearwater (Fla.) HS
58. Franklyn Bencosme, rhp, Miami-Dade CC North
59. Gene Richardson, rhp, Edison (Fla.) CC
60. Joseph Ortiz, c, Edison HS, San Antonio
61. Daniel Zisk, 3b, Pine Crest HS, Lighthouse Point, Fla.
62. Michael Thomson, rhp, Sulphur (La.) HS
63. Ryan Fien, rhp, Idaho

CHICAGO WHITE SOX

June—Regular Phase (12)

1. Bobby Seay, lhp, Sarasota (Fla.) HS
2. **Josh Paul, of, Vanderbilt**
3. **Jimmy Terrell, ss, Tri-City Christian HS, Blue Springs, Mo.**
4. **Mark Roberts, rhp, South Florida**
5. **Joe Crede, 3b, Fatima HS, Westphalia, Mo.**
6. **Dan Olson, of, Indiana State**
7. Kevin Knorst, rhp, Lake Howell HS, Winter Park, Fla.
8. Marcus Jones, rhp, Long Beach State
9. **Edwin Cochran, 2b, Arroyo, P.R.**
10. **Gene Forti, lhp, Del Valle HS, El Paso**
11. **Steve Schorzman, rhp, Gonzaga**
12. **Darren Baugh, ss, Nevada**
13. **Chad Bradford, rhp, Southern Mississippi**
14. **Joe Farley, lhp, Susquehanna (Pa.)**
15. **Tom Reimers, rhp, Stanford**
16. **Jeff Inglin, of, Southern California**
17. **Derek Wallace, of, Bossier Parish (La.) CC**
18. **Joe Sutton, c, West Virginia Wesleyan**
19. **Chris Heintz, 3b, South Florida**
20. **Mario Iglesias, rhp, Stanford**
21. Kevin Sadowski, rhp, Joliet (Ill.) Catholic Academy
22. **Reid Hodges, rhp, Columbus (Ga.)**
23. Mike Holmes, rhp, Wake Forest
24. **Sean Connolly, c, Rollins (Fla.)**
25. **Elvis Perez, lhp, Miami Lakes HS, Hialeah, Fla.**
26. **Pete Pryor, 1b, Kentucky**
27. Kenneth Ferguson, of, Issaquah (Wash.) HS
28. **Eloy Tellez, rhp, El Paso CC**
29. Robert Hatcher, lhp, Miami-Dade CC North
30. Marcos Munoz, rhp, North Rockland HS, Pomona, N.Y.
31. Juan Mendoza, lhp, Miami-Dade CC Wolfson
32. **Rick Heineman, rhp, UCLA**
33. **Kevin Stinson, rhp, Bellevue (Wash.) CC**
34. Chris Delgado, 1b, St. Thomas Aquinas HS, Fort Lauderdale
35. Ray Goirgolzarri, 3b, Columbus HS, Miami
36. Anthony Lofink, of, Salesianum HS, Bear, Del.
37. Tim McGhee, of, Crenshaw HS, Los Angeles
38. Michael Lindgren, rhp, Sandpoint (Idaho) HS
39. **Marcus Rodgers, lhp, Vigor HS, Saraland, Ala.**
40. Jose Arrieta, rhp, El Paso CC
41. Marshall McDougall, 2b, Buchholz HS, Gainesville, Fla.
42. Ken Trapp, rhp, Texas City (Texas) HS
43. Kenard Lang, 1b, Miami
44. Johnnie Thibodeaux, 3b, Barbe HS, Lake Charles, La.
45. **Allen Thomas, of, Wingate (N.C.)**
46. **Kirk Irvine, rhp, Cal State Fullerton**
47. Matt Watson, 3b/2b, McCaskey HS, Lancaster, Pa.
48. Levy Duran, 3b, George Washington HS, New York
49. Andres Martinez, c, St. Brendan HS, Miami
50. Mario Gianfortune, of, Elmwood Park (Ill.) HS
51. William Mauer, c, East HS, Mission Hills, Kan.
52. **Mike McDermott, 3b, Idaho**
53. Elio Borges, ss, American HS, Miami

CINCINNATI REDS

June—Regular Phase (25)

1. **John Oliver, of, Lake-Lehman HS, Lehman, Pa.**
1. Matt McClendon, rhp, Dr. Phillips HS, Orlando (Supplemental pick—33rd—for loss of Type A free agent Ron Gant)
2. **Buddy Carlyle, lhp, Bellevue (Neb.) East HS** (Pick from Cardinals as compensation for Gant)
2. **Randi Mallard, rhp, Hillsborough (Fla.) CC**

3. **David Shepard, rhp, Clemson**
4. **Phillip Merrell, rhp, Nampa (Idaho) HS**
5. **Nick Presto, ss, Florida Atlantic**
6. **Carl Caddell, lhp, Northwood (Texas)**
7. **Wylie Campbell, 2b, Texas**
8. **Kevin Marn, of, Kent**
9. **Desi Herrera, rhp, San Diego State**
10. Mike Vento, of, Cibola HS, Albuquerque
11. Kris Lambert, lhp, Baylor
12. **Corey Price, ss, North Central Texas JC**
13. **Chris Ward, c, Lubbock Christian (Texas)**
14. **Ted Rose, rhp, Kent**
15. Drew Roberts, lhp, Kent
16. **Jason Williams, ss, Louisiana State**
17. **Bubba Dresch, 1b/of, St. Mary's (Texas)**
18. Keith Dilgard, rhp, Mississippi State
19. **Bryan Zwemke, rhp, Trinidad State (Colo.) JC**
20. **Gene Altman, rhp, Hudgens Academy, Lynchburg, S.C.**
21. Travis Young, 2b, New Mexico
22. **Kevin Needham, lhp, Northwestern State**
23. **Scott Garrett, c, Appalachian State**
24. **Jeremy Keller, 3b/1b, Winthrop**
25. **Matt Buckley, rhp, Campbell**
26. **Josh Harriss, rhp, Smithson Valley HS, Canyon Lake, Texas**
27. **Doug Kirby, of, Victor Valley (Calif.) CC**
28. **Daniel Jenkins, of, Sam Houston State**
29. **Demond Denman, 1b, Dallas Baptist**
30. **Rod Griggs, of, Lambuth (Tenn.)**
31. **Brian Hucks, c, South Carolina**
32. **Brian Horne, rhp, Limestone (S.C.)**
33. **Jeremy Skeens, of, Lakota HS, Middletown, Ohio**
34. **Eric LeBlanc, rhp, St. Rose (N.Y.)**
35. Doug DeVore, lhp, Dublin (Ohio) HS
36. David Ferres, 2b, JC of the Redwoods (Calif.)
37. **John Clark, 2b, Jacksonville State**
38. **Brandon O'Hearn, of, Columbus (Ga.)**
39. **Stephan Smith, rhp, Southwest Texas State**
40. **Jon Phillips, rhp, Georgia Southern**
41. Nicholas Prater, c, Judson HS, Converse, Texas

CLEVELAND INDIANS

June—Regular Phase (28)

1. **Danny Peoples, 1b, Texas**
2. **Ryan McDermott, rhp, Alamogordo (N.M.) HS**
3. **Jarrod Mays, rhp, Southwest Missouri State**
4. **J.D. Brammer, rhp, Stanford**
5. **Grant Sharpe, 1b, Watkins HS, Laurel, Miss.**
6. **Paul Rigdon, rhp, Florida**
7. **Jim Hamilton, lhp, Ferrum (Va.)**
8. **Rob Stanton, of, Rollins (Fla.)**
9. **Sean DePaula, rhp, Wake Forest**
10. **William Jackson, of, Collin County (Texas) CC**
11. **Joe Horgan, lhp, Sacramento CC**
12. **John McDonald, ss, Providence**
13. **Cody Allison, c, Arkansas State**
14. **Troy Kent, ss/3b, Stanford**
15. Tonayne Brown, of, Godby HS, Tallahassee, Fla.
16. **Kaipo Spenser, rhp, Arizona State**
17. **Mark Taylor, lhp, Rice**
18. **Mike Bacsik, lhp, Duncanville (Texas) HS**
19. Dan Wright, rhp, Sullivan South HS, Kingsport, Tenn.
20. **Mike Huelsmann, of, Saint Louis**
21. **Jamie Brown, rhp, Okaloosa-Walton (Fla.) CC**
22. Tim Palmer, c, Fresno CC
23. **Adam Taylor, c, New Mexico**
24. **Aurelio Rodriguez, ss, Mesa State (Colo.)**
25. David Willis, c/1b, UC Santa Barbara
26. **Dennis Konrady, ss, Pepperdine**
27. **Bob Reichow, rhp, Bowling Green State**
28. **Brian Whitlock, ss, North Carolina**
29. **Mel Motley, of, Nebraska**
30. **Matt Koeman, rhp, Kansas State**
31. Chad Darnell, rhp, Carthage (Texas) HS
32. Jonathan McDonald, rhp, Edgewater HS, Orlando
33. Mitch Johnson, rhp, Meridian (Miss.) CC
34. Samuel Moses, rhp, Sacramento CC
35. Humberto Vargas, rhp, Connors State (Okla.) JC
36. Robert Aaron, rhp, McCallie HS, Chattanooga
37. Josh Walker, rhp, Lassen (Calif.) JC
38. Jeremy Jones, c, Mesa (Ariz.) CC
39. Marc Gwyn, rhp, McCullough HS, The Woodlands, Texas
40. Byron Watson, of, North Central (Texas) JC
41. Miles Bryant, of, Woodham HS, Pensacola, Fla.
42. Travis Veracka, lhp, Nashoba Regional HS, Stow, Mass.
43. Alfred Leatherwood, 1b, Woodham HS, Pensacola, Fla.
44. **Brian Bosch, c, Washington**
45. Scott Krause, 2b, Centralia (Wash.) HS
46. Brad Brenneman, rhp, Lane (Ore.) CC
47. Mark Zenk, ss, Mountlake Terrace HS, Edmonds, Wash.
48. **Ryan Siponmaa, c, Lowell (Mass.)**
49. Chris Hesse, of, Southern Mississippi
50. Anthony Wright, of, Hooks (Texas) HS
51. **Casey Smith, c, Hill (Texas) JC**
52. Mark Cridland, of, Texas
53. Joey Cole, rhp, Nacogdoches (Texas) HS
54. **Matt Minter, lhp, Lassen (Calif.) JC**
55. **Charles Roberson, rhp, Green River (Wash.) CC**
56. **David Riske, rhp, Green River (Wash.) CC**
57. Randy Keisler, lhp, Navarro (Texas) JC
58. Ovid Valentin, of, Oak Park-River Forest HS, Oak Park, Ill.

COLORADO ROCKIES

June—Regular Phase (21)

1. **Jake Westbrook, rhp, Madison County HS, Danielsville, Ga.**
2. **John Nicholson, rhp, Episcopal HS, Houston**
3. **Shawn Chacon, rhp, Greeley (Colo.) Central HS**
4. **Steve Matcuk, rhp, Indian River (Fla.) CC**
5. **Jeff Sebring, lhp, Iowa State**
6. **Dean Brueggeman, lhp, Belleville Area (Ill.) CC**
7. **Clint Bryant, 3b, Texas Tech**
8. **Alvin Rivera, rhp, Yabucoa, P.R.**
9. **Ryan Kennedy, rhp, Jones County (Miss.) JC**
10. **Tom Stepka, rhp, Le Moyne**
11. **Tim Christman, lhp, Siena**
12. **Travis Thompson, rhp, Madison (Wis.) Area Tech HS**
13. **Don Schmidt, rhp, Portland State (Ore.)**
14. Denny Gilich, rhp, Portland
15. **Scott Schroeffel, rhp/of, Tennessee**
16. **Rod Bair, of, Grand Canyon (Ariz.)**
17. **Doug Livingston, 2b, Clemson**
18. **Brian Keck, ss, Fort Hays State (Kan.)**
19. Steve Scarborough, rhp, Duncanville (Texas) HS
20. Jonathan Storke, ss, Douglas HS, Minden, Nev.
21. **Brian Hinchy, rhp, Green River (Wash.) CC**
22. **Bernard Hutchison, of, Montevallo (Ala.)**
23. **Blake Anderson, c, Mississippi State**
24. **Mark Hamlin, of, Georgia Southern**
25. **Brian Anthony, 1b, Nevada-Las Vegas**
26. **Mike Petersen, 1b, San Jacinto North (Texas) JC**
27. Lucas Anderson, rhp, Green Valley HS, Henderson, Nev.
28. **Jason Ford, lhp, Arizona**
29. Melvin Rosario, of, Carolina, P.R.
30. Steven Iannacone, rhp, Washington Township HS, Sicklerville, N.J.
31. Les Graham, 3b, Latta HS, Ada, Okla.
32. **Jake Kidd, rhp, Hesperia (Calif.) HS**
33. **Josh Kalinowski, lhp, Indian Hills (Iowa) CC**
34. Emmett Giles, ss, North Side HS, Jackson, Tenn.
35. **Brad Woodard, rhp, Palatka HS, San Mateo, Fla.**
36. Alex Fernandez, of, Hope HS, Providence
37. Eric Burris, of/1b, Carson (Calif.) HS
38. Adam Bernero, rhp, Sacramento CC
39. Daniel Viveros, rhp, JC of the Sequoias (Calif.)
40. **Ryan Price, rhp, Goddard HS, Roswell, N.M.**
41. Robby Shultz, rhp, University HS, Malibu, Calif.
42. Martin Rankin, lhp, Hill (Texas) JC
43. James Carroll, rhp, North Shore HS, Houston

44. David Christy, ss, Mount Hood (Ore.) CC
45. Ben Cortez, rhp, Santa Fe Springs (Calif.) HS
46. Jose Vasquez, lhp, Cerritos (Calif.) JC
47. Chris Robert, c, Soquel HS, Capitola, Calif.
48. James Munday, rhp, Hudson's Bay HS, Vancouver, Wash.
49. Mathew Bobo, ss, Longview (Texas) HS
50. Damon Thames, ss, San Jacinto North (Texas) JC
51. Jeremiah Harrington, of, Lowry HS, Winnemucca, Nev.

DETROIT TIGERS

June—Regular Phase (6)

1. **Seth Greisinger, rhp, Virginia**
2. **Matt Miller, lhp, Texas Tech**
3. **Antonio McKinney, of, Jefferson HS, Portland, Ore.**
4. **Kris Keller, rhp, Fletcher HS, Neptune Beach, Fla.**
5. **Robert Fick, c, Cal State Northridge**
6. **Chris Bauer, rhp, Wichita State**
7. **Scott Sollmann, of, Notre Dame**
8. **Craig Quintal, rhp, Southern**
9. **Keith Whitner, of, Los Angeles CC**
10. **Justin Hazleton, of, Philipsburg-Osceola HS, Philipsburg, Pa.**
11. **Aaron Alvord, rhp, Canton-Galva HS, Canton, Kan.**
12. **Jacques Landry, 3b, Rice**
13. Jeff Heaverlo, rhp, Ephrata (Wash.) HS
14. Dan Kelly, lhp, Niceville (Fla.) HS
15. **Chris Wakeland, of, Oregon State**
16. **Rick Kirsten, rhp/of, Rolling Meadows (Ill.) HS**
17. **George Restovich, c, Notre Dame**
18. **Brian Rios, ss, Oral Roberts**
19. **Derrick Neikirk, c, Mesa (Ariz.) CC**
20. **Don DeDonatis, ss, Eastern Michigan**
21. **David Lindstrom, c, Texas Tech**
22. **Jeff Tagliaferri, 1b, Long Beach State**
23. **Jesse Zepeda, 2b, Oklahoma**
24. **Chris Mitchell, rhp, Allentown (Pa.)**
25. **Tom Browning, lhp, Indiana State**
26. **David Darwin, lhp, Duke**
27. Matt Schuldt, rhp, Howard (Texas) JC
28. Drew Topham, 2b, Barbe HS, Lake Charles, La.
29. **Kurt Airoso, of, Cal State Northridge**
30. **Chad Schroeder, rhp, Northwestern**
31. **Nick Jamison, of, Center Grove HS, Greenwood, Ind.**
32. John Ogiltree, rhp, Kennedy HS, Mississauga, Ontario
33. Joe Kalczynski, c, Brother Rice HS, Farmington, Mich.
34. Daniel Cole, rhp, Monroe (Mich.) HS
35. Greg Bauer, rhp/ss, Jenks HS, Tulsa
36. **Tom Runnells, ss, Greeley (Colo.) West HS**
37. Michael Garner, lhp, Fullerton (Calif.) HS
38. K.O. Wiegandt, rhp, Westminster Christian HS, Miami
39. Harry Kenoi, rhp, Los Angeles Pierce JC
40. Brian Justine, lhp, Broward (Fla.) CC
41. Bryan Houston, rhp, Lake City (Fla.) CC
42. **Mike Seebode, lhp, Ichabod Crane HS, Valatie, N.Y.**
43. **Dave Malenfant, rhp, Central Michigan**
44. Ian Herweg, rhp, Redondo Union HS, Redondo Beach, Calif.
45. **Tris Moore, of, Miami**
46. **Mike Ciminiello, 1b, Princeton**
47. Kevin Robles, c, Dorado, P.R.
48. Durendell Daniels, of, Gulf Coast (Fla.) CC
49. Greg Sprehn, rhp, Triton (Ill.) JC
50. **Bruce Johnston, rhp, Nassau (N.Y.) CC**
51. Brandon Wheeler, rhp, Countryside HS, Clearwater, Fla.

FLORIDA MARLINS

June—Regular Phase (9)

1. **Mark Kotsay, of, Cal State Fullerton**
2. (Pick to Blue Jays as compensation for Type B free agent Devon White)
3. (Pick to Blue Jays as compensation for Type B free agent Al Leiter)
4. **Blaine Neal, rhp, Bishop Eustace HS, Pennsauken, N.J.**
5. **Brent Billingsley, lhp, Cal State Fullerton**
6. **David Townsend, rhp, Delta State (Miss.)**
7. **Chris Moore, rhp, Harlan Community HS, Chicago**
8. **Quantaa Jackson, of, Wharton (Texas) HS**
9. Vaughn Schill, ss, Audubon (N.J.) HS
10. **Cory Washington, of, Westover HS, Fayetteville, N.C.**
11. **Travis Wyckoff, lhp, Wichita State**
12. Skip Browning, rhp, Lakeview HS, Fort Oglethorpe, Ga.
13. Ryan Owens, ss, Sonora HS, La Habra, Calif.
14. Brian Tallet, lhp, Putnam City West HS, Bethany, Okla.
15. **David Wesolowski, rhp, Williamsville (N.Y.) North HS**
16. Simon Tafoya, 1b, Pittsburg (Calif.) HS
17. **Larry Kleinz, ss, Villanova**
18. Bryan Farkas, lhp, Varina HS, Sandston, Va.
19. **Shaw Casey, rhp, Nevada-Las Vegas**
20. **Steve Gagliano, rhp, Rolling Meadows (Ill.) HS**
21. **Matt Braughler, c, Indiana**
22. **Dan Ferrell, lhp, Indiana**
23. **Stephen Morales, c, Mayaguez, P.R.**
24. **Brad Farizo, rhp, Shaw HS, Marrero, La.**
25. **Jeff Venghaus, 2b, Rice**
26. Scott Dunn, rhp, Churchill HS, San Antonio
27. Brian Matzenbacher, rhp, Belleville Area (Ill.) CC
28. Justin Linquist, rhp, Palma HS, Salinas, Calif.
29. **Pete Arenas, ss, Georgia**
30. **Scott Conway, 1b, Lenape HS, Mount Laurel, N.J.**
31. Josh Laxton, rhp, Audubon (N.J.) HS
32. **Alain Diaz, of, Barry (Fla.)**
33. Rafael Rigueiro, rhp, Riverside (Calif.) CC
34. **Zak Ammirato, 3b/c, UCLA**
35. **Justin Foerter, 1b, Holy Cross HS, Bordentown, N.J.**
36. **Jay Jones, c, Alabama-Birmingham**
37. **Jason Alaimo, c, South Florida**
38. Jason Sharp, ss, Owen County HS, Owenton, Ky.
39. Jeff Bloomer, rhp, County HS, Pueblo, Colo.
40. Simon Young, lhp, West Hall HS, Flowery Branch, Ga.
41. Brian Forystek, lhp, Carl Sandburg HS, Palos Park, Ill.
42. Edwin Erickson, 1b, Eisenhower HS, Yakima, Wash.
43. Jimmy Frush, rhp, Texas Tech
44. **Patrick Pass, of, Tucker (Ga.) HS**
45. Mike Rose, rhp, Texarkana (Texas) CC
46. Steven Merrill, lhp, Sandy Union HS, Gresham, Ore.
47. **Mike Evans, lhp/1b, Palm Beach (Fla.) JC**
48. Harry Anderson, of, Virginia HS, Bristol, Va.
49. Kevin Kurilla, rhp, Virginia Tech
50. Eric Abshor, of, Heritage HS, Littleton, Colo.
51. **Kevin Zaleski, rhp, Indiana**
52. Daniel Torres, ss, Lenape HS, Mount Laurel, N.J.
53. David White, of, Water of Life Christian HS, Douglasville, Ga.
54. Joseph Hart, lhp, Walkersville (Md.) HS
55. Craig Lewis, rhp, Wallace State (Ala.) CC
56. Reece Borges, rhp, Lassen (Calif.) JC
57. Letarvius Copeland, of, Miami-Dade CC Wolfson
58. Travis Johnson, rhp, Snowflake HS, Taylor, Ariz.
59. Israel Pope, ss, Virginia HS, Bristol, Va.
60. Clayton Thomas, of, Central Senior HS, Victoria, Va.
61. Darius Gill, rhp, Columbia HS, Decatur, Ga.
62. Charles Walter, c, Lansdowne HS, Baltimore
63. Joel Sajiun, of, Miami-Dade CC North
64. Devon Younger, rhp, Lakota HS, West Chester, Ohio
65. Jorge Soto, c, Patillas, P.R.
66. Dustin Brisson, 1b, Wellington Community HS, West Palm Beach, Fla.
67. Juan Torres, rhp, Isabela, P.R.
68. Brian Partenheimer, lhp, Indiana
69. **Geoff Duncan, rhp, Georgia Tech**
70. Joshua Hoffpauir, ss, Vidalia (La.) HS
71. Gerald Perkins, 1b, Royalton Hartlant HS, Lockport, N.Y.
72. Dwayne Webb, of, Gallatin County HS, Warsaw, Ky.
73. Brian Pirazzi, ss, South San Francisco HS
74. **Matt Pidgeon, ss, JC of the Redwoods (Calif.)**
75. Scott Eskra, 3b, Lassen (Calif.) JC

HOUSTON ASTROS

June—Regular Phase (19)

1. **Mark Johnson, rhp, Hawaii**

2. **John Huber, rhp, Lakota HS, Cincinnati**
3. **Brandon Byrd, 3b, Trinity Presbyterian HS, Montgomery, Ala.**
4. **Bryan Braswell, lhp, Toledo**
5. **Tucker Barr, c, Georgia Tech**
6. **Michael Wheeler, ss, Oak Hills HS, Cincinnati**
7. **Esteban Maldonado, rhp, Lambuth (Tenn.)**
8. **Jason Hill, c, Mount San Antonio (Calif.) JC**
9. **Brian Dallimore, 2b, Stanford**
10. **John Blackmore, rhp, Plainville (Conn.) HS**
11. **Jay Mansavage, 2b, Southern Illinois**
12. **Jeff Cermak, of, Arizona State**
13. Joey Hart, c, Round Rock (Texas) HS
14. Ryan Oase, 3b/rhp, Lake Stevens HS, Everett, Wash.
15. **Jim Reeder, of, Northwestern**
16. **Randy Young, of, Wichita State**
17. **Matt Hyers, ss, Middle Georgia JC**
18. **David Bernhard, rhp, San Francisco**
19. Jake Eye, rhp/of, Ohio
20. **Wade Miller, rhp, Topton, Pa.**
21. **Geoff Robertson, of, Landrum (S.C.) HS**
22. Joe DiSalvo, of, New Orleans
23. **Roy Oswalt, rhp, Holmes (Miss.) JC**
24. Matt Dailey, lhp, Castro Valley (Calif.) HS
25. Paul Phillips, c, Meridian (Miss.) CC
26. Brian Grace, rhp, Mississippi Delta JC
27. Michael Meyers, rhp, Black Hawk (Ill.) JC
28. Jurrian Lobbezoo, lhp, Indian River (Fla.) CC
29. **Tom Shearn, rhp, Briggs HS, Columbus, Ohio**
30. Kevin Tillman, 3b, Leland HS, San Jose
31. Jed Fuller, rhp, St. Joseph Catholic HS, Renfrew, Ontario
32. Trey Hodges, rhp, Klein Oak HS, Spring, Texas
33. **Dru Nicely, 3b, Burley (Idaho) HS**
34. Brian Bishop, rhp, Crescenta Valley HS, La Crescenta, Calif.
35. Kevin Duck, 1b, Rancho Santiago (Calif.) JC
36. Eric Cooper, rhp, Chabot (Calif.) JC
37. Jason Davis, c, Woodbury (N.J.) HS
38. James Igo, rhp, West Columbia (Texas) HS
39. Chris Youmans, c, Seminole HS, Lake Mary, Fla.
40. Matt Gawer, lhp, Sullivan (Mo.) HS
41. Jim Hostetler, rhp, Fullerton (Calif.) JC
42. Jason Sinatra, rhp, Silver Creek HS, San Jose
43. Joseph Morrell, c, Elmira (N.Y.) Free Academy
44. Randy Brunette, ss, South Dade HS, Homestead, Fla.
45. Brad Payne, ss, Leacock HS, Agincourt, Ontario
46. Bruce Sutton, of, Seminole State (Okla.) JC
47. Derrick Vargas, lhp, Chabot (Calif.) JC
48. Chaz Eiguren, 1b, Seward County (Kan.) CC
49. Nathan King, of, Livingston (Texas) HS
50. Anthony Garcia, rhp, Belen Jesuit HS, Miami
51. Jason Chaney, lhp, Sacramento CC
52. Mark Burnett, ss, Northeast Texas CC
53. Resh Bondi, ss, Monterey HS, Seaside, Calif.
54. James Edelen, c, Eastern Oklahoma State JC
55. Jerymaine Beasley, of, Kamiakin HS, Kennewick, Wash.
56. Richard Terwilliger, rhp, Corning (N.Y.) East HS
57. Charles Harrington, rhp, Oxnard (Calif.) JC
58. Ferdinand Rivera, ss, Ranger (Texas) JC
59. Brian Jensen, lhp, St. Vincent's HS, Petaluma, Calif.
60. Steven Knotts, of, Parkway HS, Bossier City, La.
61. Stephen Neal, 1b, Pine Bluff (Ark.) HS
62. Todd Uzzell, rhp, Coronado HS, El Paso
63. Troy Norrell, c, Navarro (Texas) JC
64. Alexander Stencel, of, Mount San Antonio (Calif.) JC
65. Greg Peterson, of, CC of Morris (N.J.)
66. George Johnson, 1b/of, Conners State (Okla.) JC
67. Ben Keats, c, Faulkner State (Ala.) CC
68. Tyler Dunlap, ss, Pleasant Grove HS, Texarkana, Texas
69. Chris Hargett, 1b, Rend Lake (Ill.) JC
70. Johnnie Wheeler, lhp, Skiatook (Okla.) HS
71. Mike Rosamond, ss, Madison (Miss.) Central HS
72. Robbie White, lhp, Trinidad (Texas) HS
73. Daniel Duke, c, Leland HS, San Jose
74. Marcos Rios, c, Moreau HS, Hayward, Calif.
75. Jason Cox, c, Northeast Texas CC
76. Richard Roberts, 2b, Texarkana (Texas) CC
77. **Michael Janssen, rhp, Phoenix JC**
78. Noah Sweeters, rhp, Los Gatos (Calif.) HS
79. Robert Porter, lhp, Texarkana (Texas) JC
80. Jeremy Cunningham, rhp, Monte Vista HS, Cupertino, Calif.
81. Tim Neumark, of, Allegany (Md.) CC
82. Shawn Hancock, rhp, Monte Vista HS, Cupertino, Calif.
83. Luis Perez, rhp, Rancho Santiago (Calif.) JC

KANSAS CITY ROYALS

June—Regular Phase (14)

1. **Dee Brown, of, Marlboro (N.Y.) Central HS**
2. **Taylor Myers, rhp, Green Valley HS, Henderson, Nev.**
3. **Chad Durbin, rhp, Woodlawn HS, Baton Rouge**
4. **Corey Thurman, rhp, Texas HS, Wake Village, Texas**
5. **Jeremy Hill, c, W.T. White HS, Dallas**
6. **Jeremy Giambi, of, Cal State Fullerton**
7. **Scott Mullen, lhp, Dallas Baptist**
8. Javier Flores, c, Oklahoma
9. Jeremy Morris, of, Florida State
10. **Steve Hueston, rhp, Long Beach State**
11. **Mike Brambilla, c, Rancho Santiago (Calif.) JC**
12. **Ethan Stein, rhp, North Carolina**
13. **Cory Kyzar, rhp, South Jones HS, Ellisville, Miss.**
14. **Brandon Berger, of, Eastern Kentucky**
15. **Eric Sees, ss, Stanford**
16. **Mike Torres, rhp, Fontana (Calif.) HS**
17. **Roman Escamilla, c, Texas**
18. **Kris Didion, 3b, Riverside, Calif.**
19. **Brett Taft, ss, Alabama**
20. **Aaron Lineweaver, rhp, Dallas Baptist**
21. **Jason Simontacchi, rhp, Albertson (Idaho)**
22. **Kit Pellow, of, Arkansas**
23. **Richard Benes, 2b, Columbus HS, Bronx, N.Y.**
24. **Brandon Baird, lhp, Wichita State**
25. **Scott Harp, 2b, Dallas Baptist**
26. **Jake Chapman, lhp, St. Joseph's (Ind.)**
27. **Kiko Calero, rhp, St. Thomas (Fla.)**
28. **Gordon Alexander, lhp, Burnaby, B.C**
29. Robert Spangler, ss, Allegany (Md.) CC
30. Bryan Bealer, lhp, North Medford (Ore.) HS
31. **Steven Walsh, rhp, Wilson HS, Orleans, Ontario**
32. **Donald Quigley, rhp, Sonoma State (Calif.)**
33. Matt Guerrier, rhp, Shaker Heights (Ohio) HS
34. **Richard Boring, rhp, Texas A&M**
35. Gus Ornstein, 1b, Michigan State
36. Ryan Rupe, rhp, Texas A&M
37. Bryan Welch, rhp, Central Catholic HS, Salem, Mass.
38. Caleb Parmenter, of, Dinuba (Calif.) HS
39. John Janek, rhp, West HS, Abbott, Texas
40. William Cornish, rhp, Lucas HS, London, Ontario
41. Brent Gutierrez, of, Clovis West HS, Fresno
42. B.R. Cook, rhp, Sprague HS, Salem, Ore.
43. Ken Thomas, c, Pennsauken (N.J.) HS
44. **George Kauffman, rhp, Stetson**
45. William Ward, lhp, Rancho Santiago (Calif.) JC
46. Dennis Melendi, of, Pace HS, Miami
47. Daniel Fernandez, 3b, Braddock HS, Miami
48. Mario Ramos, lhp, Pflugerville (Texas) HS
49. Nikki Moses, of, Doyline HS, Minden, La.
50. Michael Bender, rhp, Vanden HS, Vacaville, Calif.
51. Tim Pittsley, rhp, Allegany (Md.) CC
52. David Meliah, ss, Walla Walla (Wash.) CC
53. Bret Halbert, lhp, Western HS, Buena Park, Calif.
54. James Blanchard, ss, Grants Pass (Ore.) HS
55. Macey Brooks, of, James Madison
56. Daniel Williams, 2b, Grand Canyon (Ariz.)

LOS ANGELES DODGERS

June—Regular Phase (23)

1. **Damian Rolls, 3b, Schlagel HS, Kansas City, Kan.**
2. **Josh Glassey, c, Mission Bay HS, San Diego**
3. **Alex Cora, ss, Miami**

4. **Peter Bergeron, of, Greenfield (Mass.) HS**
5. **Nick Leach, 1b, Madera (Calif.) HS**
6. **Jack Jones, ss, Cal State Fullerton**
7. **Ben Simon, rhp, Eastern Michigan**
8. **Chris Karabinus, lhp, Towson State**
9. **David Falcon, c, Bayamon, P.R.**
10. **Jeff Auterson, of, Norte Vista HS, Riverside, Calif.**
11. **Jason Walters, rhp, Meridian (Miss.) CC**
12. **Randy Stearns, of, Wisconsin-River Falls**
13. **Derrick Peoples, of, Ryan HS, Denton, Texas**
14. **Willie King, 1b, Roosevelt HS, Brooklyn**
15. **Casey Snow, c, Long Beach State**
16. **Matt Kramer, rhp, Moorpark (Calif.) JC**
17. **Mikal Richey, of, Columbia HS, Decatur, Ga.**
18. **Pedro Flores, lhp, East Los Angeles JC**
19. **Mickey Maestas, rhp, George Mason**
20. **Ismael Gallo, ss, Mount San Antonio (Calif.) JC**
21. **Kimani Newton, of, St. Joseph HS, St. Croix, Virgin Islands**
22. **Elvis Correa, rhp, South Division HS, Milwaukee**
23. **Ted Lilly, lhp, Fresno CC**
24. **Pat Kelleher, of, Paradise Valley, Ariz.**
25. **Scott Morrison, ss, Baylor**
26. **Monte Marshall, 2b, Birmingham-Southern**
27. **Steve Wilson, c, Georgia Southern**
28. **Brian Zaun, of, Butler**
29. **Toby Dollar, rhp, Texas Christian**
30. **Rick Saitta, 2b/ss, Rutgers**
31. **Brian Foulks, of, Benedict (S.C.)**
32. **Brian Sankey, 1b, Boston College**
33. **Brian Jacobson, lhp, California Baptist**
34. Brad Cresse, c, Marina HS, Huntington Beach, Calif.
35. Donnie Thomas, lhp, Andrew (Ga.) JC
36. **Wayne Franklin, lhp, Maryland**
37. Jim Fritz, c, Tennessee
38. **Jeff Kubenka, lhp, St. Mary's (Texas)**
39. Bryan Cranson, lhp, Bronson (Mich.) HS
40. **Frank Thompson, rhp, Embry-Riddle Aeronautical (Fla.)**
41. **Jason Weekley, of, St. Mary's**
42. **Jacob Allen, c, Southeastern Illinois JC**
43. **Kevin Culmo, rhp, Cal State Sacramento**
44. Eddie Sordo, rhp, Jacksonville
45. Erik Lazerus, ss, Cal State Chico
46. Bradley Turner, c, Belton (Texas) HS
47. Eric Lovinger, rhp, Oregon State
48. **Mike Hannah, rhp, Mercer**
49. Peter Brinjak, rhp, Power St. Joseph's HS, Etobicoke, Ontario
50. **Brian Paluk, rhp, Saginaw Valley State (Mich.)**
51. Doug Straight, rhp, Buckhannon-Upshur HS, Buckhannon, W.Va.
52. **Dean Mitchell, rhp, Texas A&M**
53. **Blake Mayo, rhp, Alabama-Birmingham**
54. James Jackson, of, Kankakee (Ill.) HS
55. Adam Flohr, lhp, Spokane Falls (Wash.) CC
56. Spencer Micunek, rhp, Kalamazoo Valley (Mich.) CC
57. Ryan Anholt, 2b, Kwantlen (B.C.)
58. Brian Little, 3b, JC of the Sequoias (Calif.)
59. Juan Huguet, c, Coral Park HS, Miami
60. Craig Jarvis, of, Claremont HS, Victoria, B.C
61. Kevin Sullivan, c, Pacelli HS, Stevens Point, Wis.
62. Mark Paschal, of, Chaffey (Calif.) JC
63. George Bailey, 3b, St. Joseph HS, St. Croix, Virgin Islands
64. Joseph Thomas, rhp, Mount San Antonio (Calif.) JC
65. Devin Helps, lhp, McClung Collegiate HS, Maniton, Manitoba
66. Travis Bolton, c, West Valley HS, Anderson, Calif.
67. Graig Merritt, c, Terry Fox Senior HS, Pitt Meadows, B.C
68. Samuel Shelton, rhp, Durango (Colo.) HS
69. Mike Meyer, ss, Sabino HS, Tucson
70. Matthew Mason, c, J.L. Crowe HS, Trail, B.C
71. Kevin Huff, rhp, Horizon HS, Scottsdale, Ariz.
72. Eric Bruntlett, ss, Harrison HS, Lafayette, Ind.
73. Edwin Rodriguez, 1b, Ponce, P.R.
74. Ryan Withey, ss, Mainland HS, Daytona Beach, Fla.
75. Paul Sirant, rhp, River East Collegiate HS, Winnipeg, Manitoba
76. Chad Zaniewski, of, John Leonard HS, West Palm Beach, Fla.
77. Richard Garner, c, Wade Hampton HS, Taylors, S.C.
78. Jim Davis, 1b, Berrien County HS, Nashville, Ga.
79. Saul Rivera, ss, Lake Land (Ill.) JC

MILWAUKEE BREWERS

June—Regular Phase (8)

1. **Chad Green, of, Kentucky**
2. **Jose Garcia, rhp, Baldwin Park (Calif.) HS**
3. **Kevin Barker, of, Virginia Tech**
4. Josh Hancock, rhp, Vestavia Hills (Ala.) HS
5. **Phil Kendall, c, Jasper (Ind.) HS**
6. **Paul Stewart, rhp, Garner (N.C.) HS**
7. **Mike Wetmore, ss, Washington State**
8. **Brian Passini, lhp, Miami (Ohio)**
9. **Doug Johnston, rhp, Millard South HS, Omaha**
10. **Josh Klimek, ss, Illinois**
11. Val Pascucci, rhp, Gahr HS, Cerritos, Calif.
12. **Garret Osilka, 3b, Edison (Fla.) CC**
13. **Allen Levrault, rhp, CC of Rhode Island**
14. Shawn Sonnier, rhp, Panola (Texas) JC
15. **Al Hawkins, rhp, Elizabeth (N.J.) HS**
16. **John Fulcher, lhp, George Mason**
17. Samone Peters, 1b, McKinleyville (Calif.) HS
18. **Maney Leshay, rhp, Palm Beach Atlantic**
19. **John Boker, rhp, Mount Vernon Nazarene (Ohio)**
20. **Jay Arnold, rhp, Glendale (Ariz.) CC**
21. Danny Bogeajis, rhp, Lyman HS, Longwood, Fla.
22. **Dan Thompson, of, Yale**
23. Monsantos Armstrong, of, Calhoun City (Miss.) HS
24. **Ross Parmenter, ss, Santa Clara**
25. Jeremy Ward, lhp, CC of Rhode Island
26. **Gio Cafaro, of, South Florida**
27. Derek Lee, lhp, Texas Christian
28. Kevin Candelaria, c, Page (Ariz.) HS
29. Tyler Vanpatten, c, Seabreeze HS, Ormond Beach, Fla.
30. **Jason Glover, of, Georgia State**
31. Antonio Garris, 3b/of, Anson County HS, Wadesboro, N.C.
32. **Travis Tank, rhp, Wisconsin-Whitewater**
33. Steven Truitt, 2b, Elkins HS, Missouri City, Texas
34. **Brad Richardson, lhp, Hill (Texas) JC**
35. **Michael Fieldbinder, rhp, Montevallo (Ala.)**
36. Brandon Backe, ss, Ball HS, Galveston, Texas
37. Jay Sitzman, of, Horizon HS, Scottsdale, Ariz.
38. **Adam Faurot, 3b/ss, Florida State**
39. **Brian Hedley, rhp, St. Mary's**
40. Greg Freetly, rhp, Orange Glen HS, San Marcos, Calif.
41. **Jason Washam, c, New Orleans**
42. **Ramon Fernandez, of, Cayey, P.R.**
43. Frank Valois, of, Good Counsel HS, Olney, Md.
44. Michel Dubreuil, rhp, Miami-Dade CC North
45. Todd Ludwig, c, Thomas More HS, Franklin, Wis.
46. James Morgan, rhp, Central HS, Chattanooga
47. Jack Keene, rhp, Gulf Coast (Fla.) CC
48. **Brian Moon, c, Southern Union State (Ala.) JC**
49. Tim Boeth, 3b/ss, Tallahassee (Fla.) CC
50. Brenton Kelley, rhp, Texarkana (Texas) JC
51. Kelley Love, rhp, Laredo (Texas) JC
52. Jose Camilo, ss, San Juan, P.R.
53. Daniel Prata, lhp, Seminole State (Okla.) JC
54. Brian Steinbach, rhp, Michigan
55. Robert Cornett, c, Young Harris (Ga.) JC
56. John Cornette, rhp, Seabreeze HS, Ormond Beach, Fla.
57. Eric McMaster, 2b, Seward County (Kan.) CC

MINNESOTA TWINS

June—Regular Phase (2)

1. Travis Lee, 1b, San Diego State
2. **Jacque Jones, of, Southern California**
3. **Dan Cey, ss, California**
4. **Chad Allen, of, Texas A&M**
5. **Michael Ryan, ss, Indiana (Pa.) HS**
6. **Tommy LaRosa, rhp, Nevada-Las Vegas**
7. **Chad Moeller, c, Southern California**
8. **Corey Spiers, lhp, Alabama**
9. **Nate Yeskie, rhp, Nevada-Las Vegas**

10. **Joe Cranford, 2b, Georgia**
11. **Tommy Peterman, 1b, Georgia Southern**
12. **Ryan Lynch, lhp, UCLA**
13. **Mike Lincoln, rhp, Tennessee**
14. **David Hooten, rhp, Mississippi State**
15. **Steve Huls, ss, Minnesota**
16. **Eric Brosam, 1b, Redwood Valley HS, Redwood Falls, Minn.**
17. William Gray, ss, Liberty Eylau HS, Texarkana, Texas
18. **Chris Garza, lhp, Nevada**
19. Ty Martin, ss, Melbourne (Fla.) HS
20. Matt Kata, rhp/ss, St. Ignatius HS, Willoughby Hills, Ohio
21. **Jake Jacobs, rhp, Pine Forest HS, Pensacola, Fla.**
22. **Mike Bauder, lhp, Nevada-Las Vegas**
23. **Richie Nye, rhp, Arkansas**
24. **Marcus Smith, of, Valencia (Fla.) CC**
25. **Phil Haigler, rhp, Vanderbilt**
26. **Charlie Gillian, rhp, Virginia Tech**
27. Shaun Berrow, lhp, Tumwater HS, Olympia, Wash.
28. **Brian Kennedy, of, Harrison HS, Lafayette, Ind.**
29. Dave Johnson, rhp, Kansas State
30. Dwayne Jones, c, Rockledge (Fla.) HS
31. Mike Lamb, c, Cal State Fullerton
32. **C.J. Thieleke, 2b, Iowa**
33. **Rick Loonam, rhp, Regis (Colo.)**
34. **Anthony Felston, of, Mississippi**
35. Josh Bard, c, Cherry Creek HS, Englewood, Colo.
36. Andrew Persby, 1b, Hill Murray HS, North St. Paul, Minn.
37. Richard Durrett, c, Farmington (N.M.) HS
38. **Tom Buchman, c, Missouri**
39. Ryan Brown, rhp, Northeast Texas CC
40. Anthony Denard, of, Emeryville HS, Oakland
41. Chris Shores, rhp, Beardstown (Ill.) HS
42. **Antonio Gholar, rhp, William Carey (Miss.)**
43. Clinton Bailey, of, Chemainus (B.C.) HS
44. **Rick Moss, 3b, Lewis (Ill.)**
45. Barry Lunney, lhp, Arkansas
46. Craig Munroe, 1b, The Crescent School, Thornhill, Ontario
47. Toby Franklin, of, Westwood HS, Fort Pierce, Fla.
48. Justin Pederson, rhp, Minnesota
49. Ryan Ferrell, rhp, Daviess County HS, Philpot, Ky.
50. Jacob Schaffer, ss, Bradley
51. Wilson Romero, of, Miami HS
52. Adam Robinson, 2b, Virginia
53. **Mario Opipari, rhp, Kansas**
54. Chris Alexander, rhp, Indian River (Fla.) CC
55. **John Mundine, rhp, Luling (Texas) HS**
56. Chris Adams, rhp, McGregor (Texas) HS

MONTREAL EXPOS

June—Regular Phase (5)

1. John Patterson, rhp, West Orange (Texas) Stark HS
2. **Milton Bradley, of, Poly HS, Long Beach**
3. **Joe Fraser, rhp, Katella HS, Anaheim**
4. **Christian Parker, rhp, Notre Dame**
5. Tony Lawrence, of, Louisiana Tech
6. **Karl Chatman, of, Dallas Baptist**
7. **Luis Rivera, c, Bayamon, P.R.**
8. **Keith Evans, rhp, California**
9. **Brian Matz, lhp, Clemson**
10. **Paul Blandford, 2b, Kentucky**
11. **Jeremy Salyers, rhp, Walters State (Tenn.) CC**
12. Greg Workman, lhp, Saddleback (Calif.) CC
13. Ray Casteel, rhp, Liberty Eylau HS, Texarkana, Texas
14. **Jamey Carroll, ss, Evansville**
15. **Tripp Mackay, 2b, Oklahoma State**
16. **Andy Tracy, 1b, Bowling Green State**
17. **Chris Stowers, of, Georgia**
18. **Matt Buirley, c, Ohio State**
19. **Tim Young, lhp, Alabama**
20. **Rod Stevenson, rhp, Columbus (Ga.)**
21. Kevin Jordan, 2b/ss, Blinn (Texas) JC
22. Jason Hoffman, of, Monte Vista HS, Danville, Calif.
23. Keith Dunn, rhp, Rosa Fort HS, Tunica, Miss.
24. **Shannon Swaino, c, Kent**
25. Thomas Pace, of, Mesa (Ariz.) HS
26. **Ethan Barlow, of, Vermont**
27. Ryan Luther, ss, Olympic (Wash.) JC
28. **Michael Rahilly, rhp, North Fort Myers HS, Cape Coral, Fla.**
29. Kevin Forbes, of, American River (Calif.) JC
30. **Eric Sparks, lhp, SUNY Cortland**
31. **Curtis Martin, lhp, Merritt Island HS, Melbourne, Fla.**
32. Darrick Edison, rhp, Cal Poly Pomona
33. Michael Schwam, rhp, Edison HS, Huntington Beach, Calif.
34. **Carl Sadler, lhp, Taylor County HS, Perry, Fla.**
35. Eric Cyr, lhp, Montreal
36. Rafael Erazo, rhp, Sabana Seca, P.R.
37. Joe Fretwell, c, Cardinal Gibbons HS, Overland Park, Fla.
38. Javier Sein, 1b, Aguadilla, P.R.
39. Jeremy Cook, rhp, Yuba City (Calif.) HS
40. Nathan Cook, 3b, Oakland HS
41. Robert Cope, rhp, JC of the Siskiyous (Calif.)
42. Daniel Custer, 3b, Dewey HS, Copar, Okla.
43. Jacob Smith, rhp, East Coweta HS, Newnan, Ga.
44. Jason Huth, ss, Howard (Texas) JC
45. Michael Brown, of, Saguaro HS, Scottsdale, Ariz.
46. Mike Sikorski, of, Knoch HS, Saxonburg, Pa.

NEW YORK METS

June—Regular Phase (13)

1. **Robert Stratton, of, San Marcos HS, Santa Barbara, Calif.**
2. **Brendan Behn, lhp, Merced (Calif.) JC**
3. **Ed Yarnall, lhp, Louisiana State**
4. **Jeromie Lovingood, lhp, McMinn County HS, Riceville, Tenn.**
5. **Patrick Burns, of, Ryan HS, Denton, Texas**
6. **Tom Johnson, of, Brookdale (N.J.) HS**
7. Tony Milo, lhp, Laguna Hills (Calif.) HS
8. **Rafael Lopez, c, Miami-Dade CC South**
9. **Willie Suggs, rhp, Mount Vernon (Ill.) HS**
10. **Scott Comer, lhp, Mazama HS, Klamath Falls, Ore.**
11. **Garrick Haltiwanger, of, The Citadel**
12. Geoff Linville, rhp, Redmond (Wash.) HS
13. David Walling, rhp, El Capitan HS, Lakeside, Calif.
14. **Tom Stanton, c, Florida CC-Jacksonville**
15. Jeff Rook, of, Badin HS, Fairfield, Ohio
16. **Dicky Gonzalez, rhp, Toa Baja, P.R.**
17. Kregg Talburt, rhp, Tahlequah (Okla.) HS
18. Eric Schmitt, rhp, Woodson HS, Fairfax, Va.
19. **Bailey Chancey, of, Alabama-Huntsville**
20. **Mike Lyons, rhp, Stetson**
21. **John Tamargo, ss, Florida**
22. **Jersen Perez, ss/2b, CC of Rhode Island**
23. **Brandon Mulvehill, of, Pell City (Ala.) HS**
24. Kendal Prather, rhp, Sweetwater HS, Erick, Okla.
25. **James Dougherty, lhp, Eastern HS, Voorhees, N.J.**
26. Dennis Anderson, c, Canyon Del Oro HS, Tucson
27. Jason Navarro, lhp, Tulane
28. Paul Ciofrone, of, Stony Brook School, Nesconset, N.Y.
29. Todd Meldahl, lhp, Butte (Mont.) HS
30. **Mike Queen, lhp, Gravette (Ark.) HS**
31. Joaquin Montada, rhp, Hialeah (Fla.) Senior HS
32. **Mike Meadows, 3b, Seminole (Fla.) HS**
33. Jim Magrane, rhp, Ottumwa (Iowa) HS
34. Aaron Vincent, rhp, Bakersfield (Calif.) JC
35. **Tim Carr, rhp, Westlake HS, Westlake Village, Calif.**
36. Randy Ruiz, 1b, Monroe HS, Bronx, N.Y.
37. **Adam Garmon, rhp, St. Augustine (Fla.) HS**
38. **Jeff Hafer, rhp, James Madison**
39. Zackery Usry, 1b, Hokes Bluff HS, Piedmont, Ala.
40. Josh Pearce, rhp, West Valley HS, Yakima, Wash.
41. Andrew Watt, of, St. Francis HS, Los Altos, Calif.
42. Daniel Nelson, rhp, Lackawanna (Pa.) CC
43. John Mattson, rhp, Tacoma (Wash.) CC
44. **Tim Corcoran, rhp, Jackson HS, Slaughter, La.**
45. Patrick Gorman, rhp, Rockland (N.Y.) CC
46. **William Payne, lhp, Rutherford HS, Panama City, Fla.**
47. Brian Holden, lhp, Palm Beach Lakes HS, West Palm Beach, Fla.

48. **B.J. Huff, of, Alabama-Birmingham**
49. Jason Gronert, c, Lyman HS, Longwood, Fla.
50. Michael Fierro, rhp, Merritt Island (Fla.) HS
51. **Mike Davis, rhp, Florida State**
52. Aaron Abram, of, Valley HS, West Des Moines
53. **Matt Splawn, rhp, Texas**
54. Ryan O'Toole, rhp, UCLA
55. **Jason Bohannon, lhp, Oklahoma City**

NEW YORK YANKEES

June—Regular Phase (24)

1. **Eric Milton, lhp, Maryland** (Pick from Angels as compensation for Type B free agent Randy Velarde)
1. (Pick to Rangers as compensation for Type A free agent Kenny Rogers)
2. **Jason Coble, lhp, Lincoln County HS, Fayetteville, Tenn.**
3. **Nick Johnson, 1b, McClatchy HS, Sacramento**
4. **Vidal Candelaria, c, Manati, P.R.**
5. **Zach Day, rhp, La Salle HS, Cincinnati**
6. **Brian Reith, rhp, Concordia Lutheran HS, Fort Wayne, Ind.**
7. **Brian Aylor, of, Oklahoma State**
8. **Allen Butler, 3b, Lincoln Memorial (Tenn.)**
9. Chris Fulbright, rhp, Libertyville (Ill.) HS
10. **Rudy Gomez, 2b, Miami**
11. Brant Ust, ss, Eastlake HS, Redmond, Wash.
12. **Eric Krall, lhp, Birmingham-Southern**
13. Andrew Helmer, rhp, Bishop Dwenger HS, New Haven, Ind.
14. **Yoiset Vale, lhp, Pace HS, Miami Lakes, Fla.**
15. Nick Stocks, rhp, Jesuit HS, Tampa
16. **Justin Rayment, lhp, San Diego State**
17. Matt Ginter, rhp, Clark HS, Winchester, Ky.
18. Chuck Hazzard, 1b, Florida
19. Brian Gilman, c/ss, Westview HS, Portland, Ore.
20. **Brandon Hendrixx, rhp, Rancho Santiago (Calif.) JC**
21. Kyle Brunen, Delisle Composite HS, Vanscoy, Saskatchewan
22. Joseph Pourron, rhp, Chattahoochee Valley (Ala.) CC
23. Kevin Overcash, ss, Collierville (Tenn.) HS
24. Fontella Jones, of, Mississippi Gulf Coast JC
25. Adam Ramos, of, Lehman HS, Bronx
26. Joshua Hawes, rhp, Toll Gate HS, Warwick, R.I.
27. **Jason McBride, rhp, Pensacola (Fla.) JC**
28. **Samuel Eavenson, rhp, Loganville, Ga.**
29. Ryan Tack, rhp, Saddleback (Calif.) CC
30. **Marcus Thames, of, East Central (Miss.) CC**
31. **Ryan Huffman, of, Texas A&M**
32. **Ryan Wheeler, 2b, Lincoln Memorial (Tenn.)**
33. **Blaine Phillips, c, Southwestern Louisiana**
34. Jared Hoerman, rhp, Eastern Oklahoma State JC
35. Dan Kerrigan, c, Northeast HS, St. Petersburg, Fla.
36. Noel Manley, c/1b, Louisburg (N.C.) JC
37. **Justin Carpenter, rhp, Seminole State (Okla.) JC**
38. Jarvis Larry, of, Parkway HS, Bossier City, La.
39. Eunique Johnson, 3b, Centennial HS, Compton, Calif.
40. **Dennis Twombley, c, Pepperdine**
41. Gavin Hare, c, Eastlake HS, Redmond, Wash.
42. **Alain Cruz, 3b, Miami-Dade CC North**
43. Migues Rodriguez, ss, Cypress (Calif.) JC
44. William Pieper, 3b, Kamenameha HS, Honolulu
45. Mark Hamilton, lhp, Bell HS, Hurst, Texas
46. Daryl Grant, 1b/lhp, Florin HS, Sacramento
47. Nathan Dighera, of/c, Southwestern (Calif.) JC
48. Samuel Norris, 1b, CC of San Francisco
49. Robert Simpson, c, Christian HS, El Cajon, Calif.
50. Charles Armstrong, lhp, Oakland
51. Caesar Castaneda, 3b, East Los Angeles JC
52. Russ Chambliss, of, Washington (Pa.)
53. Felix Lopez, 1b, Plant HS, Tampa
54. Jason Halper, of, Columbia
55. Derek Bauer, 2b, Clarkstown North HS, New City, N.Y.
56. **Bob Meier, c, Cinnaminson (N.J.) HS**
57. Hector Rivera, 3b, Jesuit HS, Tampa
58. Trevor Bishop, rhp, Lethbridge (Alberta) CC
59. Jay Foster, rhp, Birch Hills Composite HS, Birch Hills, Saskatchewan
60. Nathan Cadena, ss, Cerritos (Calif.) JC
61. Cedrick Harris, of, Ashdown (Ark.) HS
62. Jason Tisone, rhp, Seton Hall
63. Tony Gomes, rhp, Lodi HS, Galt, Calif.
64. Matt Wise, rhp, Cal State Fullerton
65. Mitchell Roth, c, Cleveland HS, Reseda, Calif.
66. Fred Smith, of, Bryan Station HS, Lexington, Ky.
67. Craig Hann, c, Walshe HS, Fort MacLeod, Alberta
68. Avante Rose, of, Centennial HS, Compton, Calif.
69. Ryan Suyama, ss, Sprague HS, Salem, Ore.
70. Amir Taylor, of, Lincoln HS, San Diego
71. Adrian Mora, 2b/ss, Southwestern (Calif.) JC
72. Aaron Kramer, rhp, Grand Canyon (Ariz.)
73. **Harold Frazier, lhp, Northeastern Oklahoma A&M JC**
74. William Duncan, c, Big Bend (Wash.) CC
75. **Mike Biehle, lhp, Ohio State**
76. Adam Danner, rhp, South Florida
77. **Rhett Ingerick, rhp, Davidson**
78. Bryan Green, 1b, Jasper (Texas) HS
79. Richard Bottomley, c, Ramona (Calif.) HS
80. Garry Templeton Jr., ss, Poway (Calif.) HS
81. Nicholas Herz, c, Poway (Calif.) HS
82. Corey Ward, of, Skyline HS, Dallas
83. Gustavo Alonso, c, Jordan HS, Long Beach
84. Chris Small, c, Punahou HS, Honolulu
85. Matt Martinez, ss, Big Bend (Wash.) CC
86. Adam Wilson, ss, Mission Bay HS, San Diego
87. Nathan Kaup, 3b, Camarillo (Calif.) HS
88. **Scott Seabol, 3b, West Virginia**
89. Damion Malott, of, Cosumnes River (Calif.) JC
90. Brad Gorrie, ss, Massachusetts
91. Michael Myers, c, Allentown (Pa.)
92. Ben Hickman, rhp, Northeast Texas CC
93. Errol Smith, of, St. Augustine HS, San Diego
94. Clay Condrey, rhp, Angelina (Texas) CC
95. Greg Donohue, c, Rockland (N.Y.) CC
96. Jose Garcia, lhp, Southwestern (Calif.) JC
97. Mark Copeland, rhp, Muscatine (Iowa) CC
98. **Todd Trunk, rhp, North Central (Ill.) JC**
99. Mike Amrhein, 3b, Notre Dame
100. Aron Amundson, 3b, Eastern Oklahoma State JC

OAKLAND ATHLETICS

June—Regular Phase (10)

1. **Eric Chavez, 3b, Mount Carmel HS, San Diego**
2. **Josue Espada, ss, Mobile (Ala.)**
3. **A.J. Hinch, c, Stanford**
4. Tom Graham, rhp, Beyer HS, Modesto, Calif.
5. **Julian Leyva, rhp, Arlington HS, Riverside, Calif.**
6. **Nick Sosa, 1b, Lake Mary (Fla.) HS**
7. Mike Paradis, rhp, Auburn (Mass.) HS
8. **Brad Blumenstock, rhp, Southern Illinois**
9. **Cody McKay, c/3b, Arizona State**
10. Eric Lee, of, Clear Lake HS, Houston
11. **Jake O'Dell, rhp, Texas**
12. **Todd Mensik, 1b, Mississippi**
13. **Doug Robertson, rhp, Bradley**
14. Chad Hawkins, rhp, Grapevine HS, Euless, Texas
15. **Kevin Gregg, rhp, Corvallis (Ore.) HS**
16. **Justin Bowles, of, Louisiana State**
17. Derek Rix, 3b, Bishop Kenny HS, Jacksonville
18. Joel Colgrove, rhp, Alabama
19. Joe Caruso, 2b, Alabama
20. **Eric Faulk, rhp, New Hanover HS, Wilmington, N.C.**
21. **Brian Luderer, c, Crespi HS, Tarzana, Calif.**
22. Scott Skeen, of, Mountain View HS, Bend, Ore.
23. **Frankey Jacobs, rhp, Jordan HS, Durham, N.C.**
24. **Brett Laxton, rhp, Louisiana State**
25. Randy Eversgerd, rhp, Kaskaskia (Ill.) CC
26. **Rico Lagattuta, lhp, Nevada**
27. **Flint Wallace, rhp, Texas Christian**
28. **Edward Marcinczyk, 1b, Miami**
29. **George Davis, 3b, Indian Hills (Iowa) CC**
30. **Peter Dellaratta, rhp, South Alabama**

31. **Ray Noriega, lhp, New Mexico Highlands**
32. **Bryan Garcia, rhp, Quartz Hill (Calif.) HS**
33. Ryan Gill, rhp, Galveston (Texas) JC
34. Joe Dusan, of, Bend (Ore.) HS
35. Ian Perio, lhp, Castle HS, Kaneohe, Hawaii
36. Danny Chavers, ss, Riverview HS, Sarasota, Fla.
37. Brent Spooner, c, Godby HS, Tallahassee, Fla.
38. Bryan King, rhp, Yavapai (Ariz.) JC
39. Anthony Taylor, rhp, Central Arizona JC
40. Gary Burnham, of/1b, Clemson
41. Graeme Brown, rhp, Avon Old Farms (Conn.) Prep School
42. Brent Miller, 3b, Butte (Calif.) JC
43. Michael Knight, of, Oakland HS

PHILADELPHIA PHILLIES

June—Regular Phase (11)

1. **Adam Eaton, rhp, Snohomish (Wash.) HS**
2. **Jimmy Rollins, ss, Encinal HS, Alameda, Calif.**
3. **Kris Stevens, lhp, Fontana (Calif.) HS**
4. **Ryan Brannan, rhp, Long Beach State**
5. **Ira Tilton, rhp, Siena**
6. Kevin Burford, of, Fountain Valley (Calif.) HS
7. **B.J. Schlicker, c/1b, North Montgomery HS, Crawfordsville, Ind.**
8. **David Francia, of, South Alabama**
9. **Brandon Marsters, c, Oral Roberts**
10. **Evan Thomas, rhp, Florida International**
11. **Salvatore Molta, rhp, Brookdale (N.J.) CC**
12. **Jason Johnson, of, Chaffey (Calif.) JC**
13. **Jason Knupfer, ss, Long Beach State**
14. **Mike Torti, 3b, Arizona State**
15. Brett Egan, ss, Royal HS, Simi Valley, Calif.
16. **Brandon Allen, lhp, Illinois-Chicago**
17. **Bob Van Iten, c, Truman HS, Independence, Mo.**
18. **Joe Cotton, rhp, Bowling Green State**
19. **Brad Crede, 1b, Central Missouri State**
20. **Jason Wesemann, ss, Wisconsin**
21. Greg Gregory, lhp, Pepperdine
22. **Rodney Batts, 2b, Delta State (Miss.)**
23. **Marty Crawford, 2b, Baylor**
24. **Shannon Cooley, of, Northeast Louisiana**
25. **Adam Shadburne, rhp, Kentucky**
26. **Javier Mejia, rhp, Southern California**
27. **Harry Kiil, of, Cal State Fullerton**
28. **Kevin Nichols, 1b/3b, Alabama**
29. **Nick Thompson, c, Elon (N.C.)**
30. **Jason Davis, lhp, San Jose State**
31. **Terry Bishop, lhp, St. Rose (N.Y.)**
32. **Kirby Clark, c, Auburn**
33. Brad Philley, of, Rogers HS, Puyallup, Wash.
34. **Tommy Ferrand, of, Southeastern Louisiana**
35. Richard Estep, rhp, Grand Canyon (Ariz.)
36. **Justin Fenus, rhp, North Alabama**
37. **Matt Buczkowski, c/3b, Butler**
38. Robert Voltz, 1b, Jesuit HS, Metairie, La.
39. **Tommy Worthy, ss, Gadsden State (Ala.) CC**
40. **Greg Taylor, ss, Arkansas-Little Rock**
41. **Jason Cafferty, rhp, Hastings (Neb.)**
42. **John Crane, lhp, Rider**
43. **Eddie Rivero, of, Miami**
44. David Campos, lhp, Kerman (Calif.) HS
45. Stephen Murphy, rhp, El Camino HS, South San Francisco
46. Lee Molaison, c, Terrebonne HS, Theriot, La.
47. **Keith Shockley, lhp, Allen County (Kan.) CC**
48. Clarence Hargrave, ss, Southern Union State (Ala.) JC
49. Chuck Crumpton, rhp, Northeast Texas CC
50. Rich Rodrigues, c, DeAnza (Calif.) JC

PITTSBURGH PIRATES

June—Regular Phase (1)

1. **Kris Benson, rhp, Clemson**
2. **Andy Prater, rhp, McCluer North HS, Florissant, Mo.**
3. **Luis Lorenzana, ss, Montgomery HS, San Diego**
4. **Lee Evans, c, Tuscaloosa County HS, Northport, Ala.**
5. **Tike Redman, of, Tuscaloosa (Ala.) Academy**
6. **Yustin Jordan, ss, Monticello (Ark.) HS**
7. **Andrew Hohenstein, rhp, Norte Vista HS, Riverside, Calif.**
8. **Bobby Vogt, lhp, Armwood HS, Tampa**
9. **Jess Siciliano, rhp, Rockland (N.Y.) CC**
10. **Carlos Rivera, 1b, Rio Grande, P.R.**
11. **Jason Haynie, lhp, South Carolina**
12. **Jeremy Rockow, of, Fort Myers (Fla.) HS**
13. **Xavier Burns, 3b, Central State (Ohio)**
14. **Ali Brooks, ss/of, Laney (Calif.) JC**
15. Nick Day, of, Green Valley HS, Las Vegas
16. **Michael Chaney, lhp, Bowling Green State**
17. **Mike Gonzalez, lhp, Faith Christian Academy, Pasadena, Texas**
18. **George Elmore, rhp, Lucama, N.C.**
19. **Garrett Larkin, ss, Merrimack (Mass.)**
20. **Jacob Jensen, ss, Fresno CC**
21. **Paul Ah Yat, lhp, Hawaii**
22. **Luis Gonzalez, rhp, New Mexico**
23. **Morgan Walker, 1b, Lamar**
24. Mark Freed, lhp, Pennsville (N.J.) HS
25. **Michael Gresko, lhp, Mercer County (N.J.) CC**
26. **Daniel Tobias, rhp, Oregon, Ohio**
27. Kendall Rhodes, rhp, Crockett (Texas) HS
28. Willie Harris, 2b/ss, Cairo (Ga.) HS
29. **Ender Classen, ss, Arecibo, P.R.**
30. **Wyatt Brooks, lhp, North Florida**
31. Makani Lum, c/3b, Kamehameha HS, Kaneohe, Hawaii
32. Chad Ciccone, c, Hopewell HS, Aliquippa, Pa.
33. **Carlton McKenzie, of/3b, Raritan Valley (N.J.) CC**
34. Mo Douglas, 1b, Eureka HS, Glenco, Mo.
35. **Joseph Hunt, of, Sante Fe (Fla.) CC**
36. Barry Johnson, lhp/1b, Hales Franciscan HS, Chicago
37. Brandon Schliinz, 3b/c, Orono HS, Loretto, Minn.
38. Jamaal Strong, of/ss, Pasadena HS, Altadena, Calif.
39. Josh Bonifay, ss/2b, Roberson HS, Arden, N.C.
40. Jesse Daggett, c, Crescenta Valley HS, La Crescenta, Calif.
41. **Scott May, c, Carson-Newman (Tenn.)**
42. James McAuley, c, Plant HS, Tampa
43. Jeremy Sickles, c, Millikan HS, Long Beach
44. Frank Moore, 2b, Coffee HS, Douglas, Ga.
45. Chris Capuano, lhp, Cathedral HS, West Springfield, Mass.
46. **Ricardo Finol, rhp, Navarro (Texas) JC**
47. Ian Rauls, of, Mercer County (N.J.) CC
48. Duane Eason, p, Troy State
49. Kevin Chapman, of, Bernards HS, Peapack, N.J.
50. Jason Bowers, ss, Laurel Highlands HS, Uniontown, Pa.
51. Francisco Lebron, 1b, Florida International
52. Dwight Edge, of, Apopka (Fla.) HS
53. **Rob Mackowiak, ss/2b, South Suburban (Ill.) JC**
54. J.D. Arteaga, lhp, Miami
55. Nathan Shepperson, 1b, Virginia Military Institute
56. Steven Yaeger, c, Thousand Oaks (Calif.) HS

ST. LOUIS CARDINALS

June—Regular Phase (3)

1. **Braden Looper, rhp, Wichita State**
2. (Pick to Reds as compensation for Type A free agent Ron Gant)
3. **Brent Butler, ss, Scotland County HS, Laurinburg, N.C.**
4. **Bryan Britt, of, UNC Wilmington**
5. Jeff Rizzo, 3b, La Jolla (Calif.) HS
6. **Jim Gargiulo, c, Miami**
7. **Kevin Sheredy, rhp, UCLA**
8. **Dave Schmidt, c, Oregon State**
9. **Shawn Hogge, rhp, Western HS, Las Vegas**
10. **Cordell Farley, of, Virginia Commonwealth**
11. **Isaac Byrd, of, Kansas**
12. Rodney Eberly, 3b, Highland Community (Kan.) JC
13. Lance Smith, rhp, Dickinson (Texas) HS
14. **Steve Norris, lhp, Tyler (Texas) JC**
15. **Greg Heffernan, rhp, St. Andrews Presbyterian (N.C.)**
16. **Stacy Kleiner, c, Nevada-Las Vegas**
17. **Keith Gallagher, rhp, Murray State**

18. William Goodson, lhp, Troup County HS, LaGrange, Ga.
19. **Keith Finnerty, 2b, St. John's**
20. **Ryan Darr, ss, Corona (Calif.) HS**
21. Randy Flores, lhp, Southern California
22. **Paul Tanner, ss, Nevada-Las Vegas**
23. Nathan Rice, lhp, Cal State Northridge
24. **Jason Pollock, rhp, West Liberty State (W.Va.)**
25. **Andrew Gordon, rhp, James Madison**
26. Patrick Driscoll, lhp, Nebraska
27. **Greg Montgomery, rhp, Central Arkansas**
28. **Tim Onofrei, rhp/of, Albertson (Idaho)**
29. **Mark Nussbeck, rhp, Bellevue (Neb.)**
30. Orvin Matos, c, Utuado, P.R.
31. **Brian Mazurek, 1b, St. Francis (Ill.)**
32. Steven Doherty, ss, Los Angeles CC
33. **Brad Kennedy, 3b, Southwest Missouri State**
34. **Ryan Kritscher, 2b/of, UC Santa Barbara**
35. **Paul Wilders, 3b, Siena**
36. **Stubby Clapp, 2b, Texas Tech**
37. **Clint Weibl, rhp, Miami**
38. Greg Johnson, rhp, Okeechobee (Fla.) HS
39. Daniel Pierce, of, Jurupa Valley HS, Mira Loma, Calif.
40. Clay Hawkins, c/of, Seminole State (Okla.) JC
41. **John Tuttle, rhp, San Marino (Calif.) HS**
42. **Ryan Roberts, 3b, Brigham Young**

SAN DIEGO PADRES

June—Regular Phase (15)

1. **Matt Halloran, ss, Chancellor HS, Fredericksburg, Va.**
2. **Vernon Maxwell, of, Midwest City (Okla.) HS**
3. **Widd Workman, rhp, Arizona State**
4. **Nathan Dunn, 3b, Louisiana State**
5. **Brian Loyd, c, Cal State Fullerton**
6. **Tom Szymborski, rhp, Illinois-Chicago**
7. **Brian Carmody, lhp, Santa Clara**
8. Chance Capel, rhp, Carroll HS, Southlake, Texas
9. **Jason Middlebrook, rhp, Stanford**
10. Tim Lanier, c, Louisiana State
11. **Brian McClure, 2b, Illinois**
12. **Ben Reynoso, ss, Fresno State**
13. Brennan Hervey, 1b, Florida Atlantic
14. **Francisco Gonzalez, rhp, Arecibo, P.R.**
15. Stephen Watkins, rhp, Lubbock (Texas) Christian HS
16. **Sandro Garcia, 2b, Pope John Paul II HS, Deerfield Beach, Fla.**
17. Craig Patterson, c, El Dorado HS, Placentia, Calif.
18. **Jacob Ruotsinoja, of, Manatee (Fla.) CC**
19. Kyle Holle, rhp, Blinn (Texas) JC
20. **James Alarcon, rhp, Jupiter, Fla.**
21. **John Powers, 2b, Arizona**
22. **Dominic Marino, rhp, Walnut (Calif.) HS**
23. **Ryan Thomas, rhp, Houston Baptist**
24. Jesse Cornejo, lhp, Seward County (Kan.) CC
25. Chris Spieth, of, Garfield HS, Seattle
26. **Brandon Sullivan, rhp, Stanford**
27. **Nick Witte, rhp, Ball State**
28. **Trey Dunham, c, Shattuck (Okla.) HS**
29. **Robbie Kent, 1b/2b, Arizona State**
30. Rufus French, of, Amory (Miss.) HS
31. **Danny Conroy, of, Fairleigh Dickinson**
32. **Shane Cronin, 1b/3b, Green River (Wash.) CC**
33. Keith Kubiak, c, Giddings (Texas) HS
34. Jake Epstein, 1b/c, Mount Carmel HS, San Diego
35. **Tyler Boulo, c, South Alabama**
36. Rich Park, rhp, Norman (Okla.) HS
37. **Travis Jones, lhp, Asher (Okla.) HS**
38. Al Thielemann, lhp, Vista HS, Oceanside, Calif.
39. Davis Kile, rhp, Tacoma (Wash.) CC
40. Paul Boykin, of, Odessa (Texas) JC

SAN FRANCISCO GIANTS

June—Regular Phase (7)

1. Matt White, rhp, Waynesboro (Pa.) Area HS
2. **Mike Caruso, ss, Stoneman Douglas HS, Parkland, Fla.**
3. **David Kenna, c, North Fort Myers (Fla.) HS**
4. **Ken Vining, lhp, Clemson**
5. **Matt Wells, lhp, Nevada**
6. **Bill Malloy, rhp, Rutgers**
7. **Brandon Leese, rhp, Butler**
8. **Ryan Jensen, rhp, Southern Utah**
9. **Brian Manning, of, Allentown (Pa.)**
10. **Mike Glendenning, 3b, Los Angeles Pierce JC**
11. **Tony Zuniga, ss, Rancho Santiago (Calif.) JC**
12. **Damon Minor, 1b, Oklahoma**
13. **Wynter Phoenix, of, UC Santa Barbara**
14. **Paul Galloway, 3b, Clemson**
15. **Mick Pageler, rhp, Odessa (Texas) JC**
16. **Mike Riley, lhp, West Virginia**
17. **Eric Johnson, rhp, Mount Hood (Ore.) CC**
18. Jeff Munster, rhp, Fresno CC
19. **Levi Miskolczi, of, Rider**
20. **Luis Estrella, rhp, Cal State Fullerton**
21. **Robby Crabtree, rhp, Cal State Northridge**
22. Kevin Tommasini, of, Arizona State
23. Tom Bartosh, of, Duncanville (Texas) HS
24. **Joel Fuentes, ss, Southeastern (Iowa) CC**
25. Lance Woodcock, ss, Ponderosa HS, Shingle Springs, Calif.
26. Chris Curry, c, Conway (Ark.) HS
27. **Art Baeza, 3b, Lewis-Clark State (Idaho)**
28. Craig Cozart, rhp, Central Florida
29. **Michael Sorrow, of, Georgia Tech**
30. **Mark Hutchings, rhp, Mineral Area (Mo.) CC**
31. **Richard Clark, of, Countryside HS, Clearwater, Fla.**
32. Michael Wright, lhp, Crete-Monee HS, Crete, Ill.
33. Michael Stevenson, rhp, Orange Coast (Calif.) JC
34. Jacob Joseph, rhp, San Juan HS, Citrus Heights, Calif.
35. Brad Garrett, of, Mountain View HS, Orem, Utah
36. Billy Coleman, rhp, North Central Texas JC
37. Donald Pearson, rhp, Foothill HS, Highlands, Calif.
38. Chuck Lopez, of, Cerritos (Calif.) JC
39. Matt Dempsey, 1b, Cypress (Calif.) JC
40. Andrew Beattie, ss, Clearwater (Fla.) HS
41. Chad Baum, c, Golden West (Calif.) JC
42. Chaz Johnson, of, Dr. Phillips HS, Orlando
43. Thomas Gessner, 3b, Thomas More HS, Milwaukee
44. Brandon Larson, ss, Blinn (Texas) JC
45. Don Gierke, of, Dr. Phillips HS, Orlando
46. Richard Dishman, rhp, Duke
47. Mark Williams, rhp, Cal State Sacramento
48. Justin Sherrod, ss, Santaluces HS, Lake Worth, Fla.
49. Robert Purvis, rhp, Tipton (Ind.) HS
50. **Angel Melendez, of, Caguas, P.R.**

SEATTLE MARINERS

June—Regular Phase (22)

1. **Gil Meche, rhp, Acadiana HS, Lafayette, La.**
2. **Jeff Farnsworth, rhp, Okaloosa-Walton (Fla.) CC**
3. **Tony DeJesus, lhp, Havelock (N.C.) HS**
4. **Denny Stark, rhp, Toledo**
5. **Chris Mears, rhp, Lord Byng HS, Vancouver, B.C.**
6. **Pat Williams, c, Nacogdoches (Texas) HS**
7. **Danny Garey, rhp, St. Joseph (Mich.) HS**
8. Willie Bloomquist, ss, South Kitsap HS, Port Orchard, Wash.
9. **Rob Luce, rhp, Nevada-Las Vegas**
10. **Matthew Noe, lhp, Riverside (Calif.) CC**
11. **Julio Ayala, lhp, Georgia Southern**
12. **Joe Victery, rhp, Oklahoma**
13. **Orin Kawahara, rhp, Rancho Santiago (Calif.) JC**
14. Dwayne Dobson, rhp, Manatee (Fla.) CC
15. **Don Beaver, rhp, East Rowan HS, Rockwell, N.C.**
16. **Mark Carroll, c, Coxsackie-Athens HS, Athens, N.Y.**
17. **Jason Bond, lhp, Arizona State**
18. Allan Westfall, rhp, Miami
19. Larry Haynes, of, Nogales HS, West Covina, Calif.
20. **Brian Fitzgerald, lhp, Virginia Tech**
21. **Kyle Kennison, rhp, Southern Maine**
22. **Brian Lindner, ss, William Paterson (N.J.)**

23. Devlon Davis, c, Pittsburg (Calif.) HS
24. Jeremy Pierce, rhp, Ventura (Calif.) JC
25. Matt Vincent, Floyd Central HS, Floyd's Knob, Ind.
26. Jacob Underwood, c, Hillsboro (Ore.) HS
27. **Josue Matos, rhp, Cabo Rojo, P.R.**
28. Donovan Ross, 3b, Columbia State (Tenn.) CC
29. Karmen Randolph, ss, Los Angeles CC
30. Jason Wilson, rhp, Broward (Fla.) CC
31. Chris McAdoo, rhp, Winnsboro (Texas) HS
32. Kevin Stewart, 3b, Corona HS, Newport Beach, Calif.
33. Patrick Williams, of, Blinn (Texas) JC
34. Joe Barnes, of, Old Mill HS, Severn, Md.
35. **Dallas Mahan, lhp, Greeley (Colo.) West HS**
36. Scott Harrison, lhp, Dixie (Utah) JC
37. Steven Rivera, lhp, Dundalk (Md.) CC
38. Laron McGee, ss/2b, Morse HS, San Diego
39. James McCoy, of, South Dade HS, Homestead, Fla.
40. **Sean Spencer, lhp, Washington**
41. William Allison, rhp, Central Florida CC
42. Brett Anderson, rhp, University HS, San Diego
43. Scott Starkey, lhp, Vista HS, Oceanside, Calif.
44. Noel Pelekoudas, 2b, Eastlake HS, Redmond, Wash.
45. Adam Walker, lhp, Yavapai (Ariz.) CC
46. Michael Campbell, of, Mesa (Ariz.) CC
47. Bret Nielsen, of, Grossmont HS, El Cajon, Calif.
48. Juan Pierre, of, Galveston (Texas) JC
49. Richard Sundstrom, rhp, Cypress (Calif.) JC
50. Jason Sutherland, c, Chuckey-Doak HS, Afton, Tenn.
51. **Jason Regan, 3b/2b, Blinn (Texas) JC**
52. Michael Albert, of, Carlsbad (Calif.) HS
53. Greg Dobbs, 3b, Canyon Springs HS, Moreno Valley, Calif.
54. Richard Snider, rhp, Byng HS, Ada, Okla.
55. Chad Schmidt, of, Skidmore (Texas) Tynan HS
56. Brandon Barnaby, rhp, Citrus (Calif.) JC
57. Tamar Turner, of, Liberty (Texas) HS
58. Brian Beinfest, lhp, Clayton (Calif.) Valley HS
59. Barry Zito, lhp, University HS, San Diego
60. Ryan Grimmett, of, Miami

TAMPA BAY DEVIL RAYS

June—Regular Phase (29)

1. **Paul Wilder, of, Cary (N.C.) HS**
2. **Doug Johnson, 1b/ss, Buchholz HS, Gainesville, Fla.**
3. **Ed Kofler, rhp, Tarpon Springs HS, Palm Harbor, Fla.**
4. **Cedrick Bowers, lhp, Chiefland (Fla.) HS**
5. **Alex Sanchez, of, Miami-Dade CC Wolfson**
6. **Elliot Brown, rhp, Auburn**
7. **Mickey Callaway, rhp, Mississippi**
8. **Matt Quatraro, c, Old Dominion**
9. **Denis Pujals, rhp, Miami**
10. **Chie Gunner, of, Grand View (Mo.) HS**
11. **Robert Cafaro, rhp, Southern Connecticut State**
12. **Scott Madison, lhp, Rutgers**
13. **Shawn Stutz, rhp, Florida International**
14. **Delvin James, rhp, Nacogdoches (Texas) HS**
15. **John Kaufman, lhp, Florida**
16. **Jared Sandberg, 3b, Capital HS, Olympia, Wash.**
17. **Michael DeCelle, of, Miami**
18. **Brad Weber, lhp, Indiana**
19. **Ryan Ledden, rhp, Parkview HS, Lilburn, Ga.**
20. **Jamie Ebling, 2b, Florida Southern**
21. **Trey Salinas, c, Texas**
22. **Luke Owens-Bragg, 2b, UC Riverside**
23. Russ Jacobson, c, Horizon HS, Scottsdale, Ariz.
24. **Matt Kastelic, of, Texas Tech**
25. **James Manias, lhp, Fairfield**
26. Jeff Jankowlak, rhp, Wayzata HS, Plymouth, Minn.
27. Kyle Snyder, rhp, Riverview HS, Sarasota, Fla.
28. Donny Barker, rhp, Texas
29. **R.J. Howerton, rhp, Southeastern Oklahoma State**
30. **Kyle Whitley, rhp, Southeastern Oklahoma State**
31. **Mark Hale, rhp, Carefree, Ariz.**
32. **Michael Brown, rhp, Walters State (Tenn.) CC**
33. Aaron Bouie, rhp, Albion (N.Y.) Central HS
34. **Dan Wheeler, rhp, Central Arizona JC**
35. Brian Packin, 1b, Randolph HS, Mendham, N.J.
36. Kevin Kay, c, Forest Park HS, Morrow, Ga.
37. **Derek Mann, ss, Columbus (Ga.) HS**
38. Walter Ward, of, Edison (Fla.) CC
39. Ryan Mottl, rhp, McCluer North HS, Florissant, Mo.
40. **Jared Verrall, 1b, Eastern Oregon State**
41. Lawrence Severence, c, Logan (Ill.) CC
42. Dayle Campbell, of, Lynwood HS, Carson, Calif.
43. Jason Smith, rhp, Palm Beach Lakes HS, West Palm Beach, Fla.
44. Jason Michaels, of, Okaloosa-Walton (Fla.) CC
45. **Michael Kimbrell, lhp, Southeastern Louisiana**
46. Robert Henker, rhp, Monte Vista HS, La Mesa, Calif.
47. Jeremy Robinson, lhp, St. Amant (La.) HS
48. Michael Barraza, lhp, Gladstone HS, Azusa, Calif.
49. Edward Lubbers, lhp, Forest Hill HS, West Palm Beach, Fla.
50. Bret Stewart, lhp, Leesburg HS, Fruitland Park, Fla.
51. Jason Briggs, rhp, Smithville (Texas) HS
52. Chris Lagrone, of, Seward County (Kan.) CC
53. **Scott Leon, rhp, Texas**
54. L.J. Yankosky, rhp, Georgia Tech
55. Ronnie Merrill, ss, Jesuit HS, Tampa
56. Joel de los Santos, 2b, Burncoat HS, Worcester, Mass.
57. Adrian Yother, rhp, Middle Georgia JC
58. Clint Kinsey, rhp, Fairland (Okla.) HS
59. Nathan Hilton, rhp, Boone (Iowa) HS
60. John Hensley, rhp, Fountain Central HS, Kingman, Ind.
61. **Nathan Ruhl, rhp, Johnson County (Kan.) CC**
62. **Mike King, of/2b, Duke**
63. **Tim Hill, rhp, St. Leo (Fla.)**
64. **Tony McCladdie, 2b, Middle Georgia JC**
65. Don Kivinemi, rhp, Bellevue (Neb.)
66. **Chris Anderson, c, Southeastern Oklahoma State**
67. Matt Hoffman, rhp, Seminole State (Okla.) JC
68. **Spencer Young, rhp, Mingus Union HS, Cottonwood, Ariz.**
69. Roger Carter, rhp, Fort Gibson (Okla.) HS
70. Juan Cruz, 3b, Jefferson HS, Lafayette, Ind.
71. Jason Kirk, of, Altus (Okla.) HS
72. Brad Smith, 1b, Edmond (Okla.) Memorial HS
73. Nicholas Rhodes, c, Danbury (Conn.) HS
74. Chad Pyle, ss, Christian County HS, Hopkinsville, Ky.
75. Michael O'Brien, 1b, Old Bridge (N.J.) HS
76. Zachary Roper, 3b, Tarpon Springs (Fla.) HS
77. Keith Brice, rhp, Westminster Christian HS, Miami
78. Rashard Casey, of, Hoboken (N.J.) HS
79. Emory Brock, of, Parkway West HS, St. Louis
80. Adrian Espino, 1b/of, Laredo (Texas) JC
81. David DeMarco, 1b, Marple Newtown HS, Newtown Square, Pa.
82. Victor Sauceda, 2b/ss, Laredo (Texas) JC
83. Layne Meyer, rhp, Parkway West HS, Ballwin, Mo.
84. Scott Diorio, rhp, Seward County (Kan.) CC
85. Justin Clements, ss, Manatee (Fla.) CC
86. Scott Neuberger, of, Tallahassee (Fla.) CC
87. David Taylor, rhp, Crossroads HS, Pacific Palisades, Calif.
88. Shannon Lovan, rhp, Christian County HS, Crofton, Ky.
89. **Travis Phelps, rhp, Crowder (Mo.) JC**
90. Jack Koch, rhp, Miami-Dade CC North
91. Dave Hoffman, lhp, Danville (Ill.) HS
92. Brian Newton, lhp, Juanita HS, Kirkland, Wash.
93. Willie Marin, rhp, Coral Gables (Fla.) HS
94. Blair Barbier, rhp, Brother Martin HS, Harvey, La.
95. Ryan Gripp, ss, Indianola (Iowa) HS
96. Jerrod Harris, c, Labelle (Fla.) HS
97. Michael Rose, of, Alter HS, Dayton, Ohio

TEXAS RANGERS

June—Regular Phase (18)

1. **R.A. Dickey, rhp, Tennessee**
1. **Sam Marsonek, rhp, Jesuit HS, Tampa** (Pick from Yankees as compensation for Type A free agent Kenny Rogers)
1. **Corey Lee, lhp, North Carolina State** (Supplemental pick—32nd—for loss of Rogers)
2. **Derrick Cook, rhp, James Madison**

3. **Derek Baker, 3b, Rancho Santiago (Calif.) JC**
4. **Kelly Dransfeldt, ss, Michigan**
5. **Warren Morris, 2b, Louisiana State**
6. **Tony Fisher, of, St. Thomas (Minn.)**
7. **Juan Pinella, of, North Stafford (Va.) HS**
8. **Luis Acevedo, ss, Isabela, P.R.**
9. Randy Rodriguez, lhp, Florida Air Academy HS, Melbourne, Fla.
10. **Doug Davis, lhp, CC of San Francisco**
11. Quenten Patterson, rhp, Killeen (Texas) HS
12. **Tony Dellamano, rhp, UC Davis**
13. **Justin Siegel, lhp, Long Beach State**
14. Chris Combs, 1b, North Carolina State
15. **Alex Vazquez, of, Westminster HS, Anaheim**
16. **Ron Nelson, rhp, Ohio State**
17. **John Kertis, rhp, Miami**
18. Brian Jackson, rhp, San Diego Mesa JC
19. Mark Hendrickson, lhp, Washington State
20. **John Ellis, c, Maine**
21. **Adrian Myers, of, William Carey (Miss.)**
22. **Tony Shourds, rhp, Norwalk (Conn.) CC**
23. Casey Davis, of, Wichita State
24. **Mike Zywica, of, Evansville**
25. John Santos, rhp, Cuesta (Calif.) JC
26. Joe Beimel, lhp, Alleghany (Pa.) CC
27. Todd Periou, lhp, Lassen (Calif.) JC
28. **Steve Smella, of, Indiana**
29. Grant Dorn, rhp, Derry Area (Pa.) HS
30. **Aaron Bond, rhp, JC of Southern Idaho**
31. **Travis Hafner, 3b, Cowley County (Kan.) CC**
32. Danny Meier, of, Northeast Texas CC
33. **Ryan Smith, lhp, San Diego State**
34. Kevin Smith, rhp, James Martin Senior HS, Texas
35. Ali Cepeda, of, Canada (Calif.) JC
36. Ryan Christenson, rhp, Normandale (Minn.) CC
37. Steve Wombacher, lhp, Mingus Union HS, Clarkdale, Ariz.
38. Scott Green, rhp, Navarro (Texas) JC
39. Craig Petulla, rhp, Philipsburg-Osceola HS, Philipsburg, Pa.
40. Jesse Smith, ss/of, American River (Calif.) JC
41. Fehlandt Lentini, of, Napa (Calif.) JC
42. Kyle Skinner, ss, Mount St. Joseph HS, Baltimore
43. Justin Wise, of, Westbrook HS, Beaumont, Texas
44. Jose Pimentel, 1b, Indio HS, Palm Springs, Calif.
45. **Francisco Jaramillo, ss, Southern Illinois**
46. **Rowan Richards, of, Notre Dame**
47. Curtis Young, of, Purvis (Miss.) HS
48. David Wigley, c, Pensacola (Fla.) HS
49. Kevin Colbourn, lhp, Hagerstown (Md.) JC
50. Ron Chiavacci, rhp, Lackawanna (Pa.) CC
51. Greg Horton, of, El Paso CC
52. Anthony Perlozzo, 1b, Athens HS, Sayre, Pa.

TORONTO BLUE JAYS

June—Regular Phase (4)

1. **Billy Koch, rhp, Clemson**
1. **Joe Lawrence, ss, Barbe HS, Lake Charles, La.** (Pick from Orioles as compensation for Type A free agent Roberto Alomar)
1. **Pete Tucci, 1b/of, Providence** (Supplemental pick—31st—for loss of Alomar)
2. (Pick to Red Sox as compensation for Type A free agent Erik Hanson)
2. **Brent Abernathy, ss, Lovett School, Atlanta** (Pick from Marlins as compensation for Type B free agent Devon White)
3. **Yan Lachapelle, rhp, Montreal**
3. **Clayton Andrews, lhp, Seminole HS, Largo, Fla.** (Pick from Marlins as compensation for White)
4. **Ryan Stromsborg, 2b, Southern California**
5. **John Bale, lhp, Southern Mississippi**
6. **Mike Rodriguez, c, Tarleton State (Texas)**
7. **Casey Blake, 3b, Wichita State**
8. **Davan Keathley, lhp, Johansen HS, Turlock, Calif.**
9. **Sam Goure, lhp, County HS, Pueblo, Colo.**
10. **Josh Phelps, c, Lakeland HS, Rathdrum, Idaho**
11. **Stan Baston, ss, Tallahassee (Fla.) CC**
12. **Ryan Meyers, rhp, Tennessee**
13. Lorenzo Ferguson, of, St. Martin de Porres HS, West Bloomfield, Mich.
14. **Sean McClellan, rhp, Oklahoma State**
15. **Josh Bradford, rhp, Xavier**
16. **Lorenzo Bagley, of, Central Florida**
17. **Jason Koehler, c, Rider**
18. Gary Johnson, of, East Los Angeles JC
19. Jason Ball, rhp, Los Alamitos (Calif.) HS
20. **Tim Giles, 1b, UNC Greensboro**
21. **Will Skett, of, Long Beach State**
22. **David Bleazard, rhp, Oklahoma City**
23. **Brad Moon, of, Hunting Hills HS, Red Deer, Alberta**
24. Darold Butler, 2b, Simeon HS, Chicago
25. Stephen Wood, 1b, Bishop Amat HS, West Covina, Calif.
26. **Lawrence Adams, 1b, Lake City (Fla.) JC**
27. Gary Peete, of, Munford HS, Brighton, Tenn.
28. Brian Leach, rhp, Palm Beach (Fla.) JC
29. **Ryan Zeber, c, Foothill HS, Tustin, Calif.**
30. Ryan Webb, 3b, Upland (Calif.) HS
31. **Clarence Watley, ss, Redan HS, Stone Mountain, Ga.**
32. Justin Brager, ss, Wenatchee Valley (Wash.) CC
33. Orlando Hudson, ss, Darlington (S.C.) HS
34. **Mark Curtis, lhp, Pensacola (Fla.) JC**
35. **James Landingham, of, Miami-Dade CC Wolfson**
36. Justin Montalbano, lhp, Mendocino (Calif.) CC
37. Craig Lariz, 1b, Key West (Fla.) HS
38. Cody Hartshorn, rhp, Lamar (Colo.) HS
39. Kyle Adams, lhp, Allen County (Kan.) CC
40. **Orlando Woodard, rhp, Franklin HS, Stockton, Calif.**
41. Anthony Novelli, rhp, Oak Grove HS, San Jose
42. Michael Galati, rhp, Connecticut
43. Derek Hines, of, Yavapai (Ariz.) CC
44. Greg Ferrell, of, Saddleback (Calif.) CC
45. Kevin Covington, of, Cherokee County HS, Centre, Ala.
46. Robert Gonzales, c, Castle Park HS, Chula Vista, Calif.
47. Michael Duperron, lhp, South Grenville HS, Prescott, Ontario
48. Harold Betts, c, Lakewood (Calif.) HS
49. Shaw Scovel, 3b, Foothill HS, Villa Park, Calif.
50. Joshua Glober, rhp, Upper Canada College, Toronto
51. Steven Lacy, rhp, Alhambra HS, Glendale, Ariz.
52. Michael Lopez, ss, Maryvale HS, Phoenix

1997 TEAMS TAKE CAUTIOUS APPROACH AFTER FALLOUT FROM '96 DRAFT, TALENT DOESN'T DRIVE DECISIONS

Fearful of more fallout from a draft system that sprang leaks in 1996, major league teams took an exceedingly cautious approach to the draft in 1997. In many cases players were chosen on the basis of signability, not ability. Several first-round picks reached contract agreements before the draft. Others were passed over because their asking price was deemed too steep.

Still, bonuses reached record numbers in 1997. Florida high school lefthander Rick Ankiel, selected 72nd overall by the Cardinals, signed a $2.5 million deal. All teams passed on Ankiel in the first round because they couldn't get a handle on his bonus demands. Rice righthander Matt Anderson, the No. 1 overall pick, held out through the fall but eventually signed for $2.505 million.

The whole process was complicated by the four draft picks from 1996 who became free agents because of a loophole in contract-tendering procedures. Major League Baseball tightened legislation to make sure the situation wouldn't repeat itself in 1997. But in many ways, the damage had been done. Clubs were in the position of having to defend themselves against the precedent of paying $10 million bonuses. Agent Scott Boras, who engineered Matt White's windfall from the Devil Rays, said the developments of 1996 proved conclusively that a draft system artificially stunts bonuses.

"Those were special circumstances involving expansion teams," Tigers general manager Randy Smith said. "Two million dollars is a lot of money. We're not interested in signing any of these players for $10 million. If we're going to spend that kind of money, we're going to spend it on a proven major leaguer, not on someone who is unproven."

J.D. Drew, the consensus top player in the 1997 draft, was adamant that his rights were being stifled under a system that allowed him to negotiate with only one team. He was represented by Boras, and set his price at a reported $10 million before the draft. He told every club not to draft him unless it was prepared to pay that amount, but the Phillies took him anyway with the No. 2 selection.

"What we've seen happen in the last two years, first internationally and then domestically, has given us a great barometer on the true worth of a select number of quality amateur players," Boras said. "The market has changed. I know from experience that there are many teams willing to pay optimum dollars for a premium talent."

STAN DENNY

Matt Anderson went No. 1 to the Tigers, but his career never really ignited

Drew sought to be declared a free agent on at least two occasions. First, he filed a grievance contending the Phillies sent his contract to an incorrect address. A second grievance was in response to a rules change by Major League Baseball that said amateur players were those who had not signed contracts with major league or National Association clubs. Drew signed with the independent Northern League's St. Paul Saints five weeks after being drafted and contended his signing with a professional team—albeit an independent one—meant he was not subject to rules as they applied to amateurs.

Drew ultimately lost his grievances, didn't sign with the Phillies and went back into the 1998 draft. The Cardinals made him their first-round pick and he signed relatively quickly.

The Tigers focused their last-minute scouting efforts on four players: Anderson, Drew, lefthander Ryan Anderson and outfielder Darnell McDonald. They settled on Matt Anderson, whose 98 mph fastball was the hardest in college baseball, because they believed he could make a contribution within a year or two in a position of need and because they thought he would be the easiest to sign.

Anderson did sign, but his big league career never lived up to the billing of a No. 1 pick. Of the four players the Tigers had considered, Drew clearly had the most productive career. McDonald got cups of coffee in the big leagues with the Orioles, Twins and Reds, while Ryan Anderson showed exceptional promise but never got out of the minors in an injury-plagued career.

Big Talent Gets Passed Over

Unlike the Phillies, several clubs decided not to gamble in the first round. As a result, premier players like Ryan Anderson, McDonald and Ankiel were passed over. Several clubs didn't want to become bogged down in negotiations or risk losing their first-round pick altogether and struck predraft deals. In many cases, a player was drafted earlier than expected to get him under contract for less than the going rate.

The Blue Jays were the first club to arrange such a deal. Selecting fifth, the Jays agreed to terms with Texas high school outfielder Vernon Wells on a $1.6 million deal. They were rewarded when Wells made it to the big leagues by 1999 and established himself in their outfield for the next decade.

UCLA All-American third baseman Troy Glaus, the third pick in the draft, held out until mid-September before signing a $2.25 million bonus with the Angels, ending a cordial stalemate.

The commissioner's office earlier nixed a deal that provided for a flexible bonus, where the final amount would be tied to a percentage increase in first-round bonuses from 1996 to 1997. That arrangement was similar to a contract signed a year earlier by lefthander Nick Bierbrodt, Arizona's first-round pick. Bierbrodt signed quickly and ended up doubling the size of his original bonus when all first-round picks were finally signed. Major league owners later voted to forbid flexible bonus amounts and vetoed Glaus' original $2 million deal.

While J.D. Drew struggled to get what he wanted from the Phillies, his younger brother Tim made out well as the Indians' first-round pick. Cleveland paid a surprising $1.6 million to sign the younger Drew, the 28th overall pick. It was the first time in draft history that siblings had been selected in the first round of the same draft.

DRAFT 97: FIRST-ROUND PICKS

No.	Club	Player, Pos.	School	Hometown	Ht.	Wt.	B-T	Age
1.	Tigers	Matt Anderson, rhp	Rice	Louisville, Ky.	6-4	195	R-R	20
2.	Phillies	*J.D. Drew, of	Florida State	Hahira, Ga.	6-1	200	L-R	21
3.	Angels	Troy Glaus, 3b	UCLA	Oceanside, Calif.	6-5	225	R-R	20
4.	Giants	Jason Grilli, rhp	Seton Hall	Baldwinsville, N.Y.	6-5	185	R-R	20
5.	Blue Jays	Vernon Wells, of	Bowie HS	Arlington, Texas	6-0	195	R-R	18
6.	Mets	Geoff Goetz, lhp	Jesuit HS	Tampa	6-0	170	L-L	18
7.	Royals	Dan Reichert, rhp	Pacific	Turlock, Calif.	6-3	165	R-R	20
8.	Pirates	J.J. Davis, of	Baldwin Park HS	Pomona, Calif.	6-6	230	R-R	18
9.	Twins	Michael Cuddyer, 3b	Great Bridge HS	Chesapeake, Va.	6-3	195	R-R	18
10.	Cubs	Jon Garland, rhp	Kennedy HS	Granada Hills, Calif.	6-5	200	R-R	17
11.	Athletics	Chris Enochs, rhp	West Virginia	Newell, W. Va.	6-3	210	R-R	21
12.	Marlins	Aaron Akin, rhp	Cowley County (Kan.) CC	Manhattan, Kan.	6-2	190	L-R	19
13.	Brewers	Kyle Peterson, rhp	Stanford	Elkhorn, Neb.	6-3	210	R-R	21
14.	Reds	Brandon Larson, ss	Louisiana State	San Antonio, Texas	5-11	190	R-R	21
15.	White Sox	Jason Dellaero, ss	South Florida	Brewster, N.Y.	6-2	195	B-R	20
16.	Astros	Lance Berkman, 1b	Rice	New Braunfels, Texas	6-1	205	B-L	21
17.	Red Sox	John Curtice, lhp	Great Bridge HS	Chesapeake, Va.	6-4	210	L-L	17
18.	Rockies	Mark Mangum, rhp	Kingwood HS	Kingwood, Texas	6-2	165	R-R	18
19.	Mariners	Ryan Anderson, lhp	Divine Child HS	Westland, Mich.	6-10	210	L-L	17
20.	Cardinals	Adam Kennedy, ss	Cal State Northridge	Riverside, Calif.	6-1	180	L-R	21
21.	Athletics	Eric DuBose, lhp	Mississippi State	Gilbertown, Ala.	6-3	215	L-L	21
22.	Orioles	Jayson Werth, c	Glenwood HS	Chatham, Ill.	6-5	191	R-R	18
23.	Expos	Donnie Bridges, rhp	Oak Grove HS	Purvis, Miss.	6-4	195	R-R	18
24.	Yankees	*Tyrell Godwin, of	East Bladen HS	Council, N.C.	5-11	190	L-R	17
25.	Dodgers	Glenn Davis, 1b	Vanderbilt	Aston, Pa.	6-1	205	B-L	21
26.	Orioles	Darnell McDonald, of	Cherry Creek HS	Englewood, Colo.	5-10	185	R-R	18
27.	Padres	Kevin Nicholson, ss	Stetson	Surrey, B.C.	5-10	190	B-R	20
28.	Indians	Tim Drew, rhp	Lowndes County HS	Hahira, Ga.	6-2	200	R-R	18
29.	Braves	Troy Cameron, ss	St. Thomas Aquinas HS	Fort Lauderdale, Fla.	5-11	185	B-R	18
30.	Diamondbacks	Jack Cust, 1b	Immaculata HS	Flemington, N.J.	6-1	195	L-R	18
31.	Devil Rays	Jason Standridge, rhp	Hewitt Trussville HS	Birmingham	6-4	205	R-R	18

*Did not sign

1997

CLUB-BY-CLUB SELECTIONS

ANAHEIM ANGELS

June—Regular Phase (3)

1. **Troy Glaus, 3b, UCLA**
2. (Pick to Mariners as compensation for Type B free agent Dave Hollins)
3. **Heath Timmerman, rhp, Northeastern Oklahoma A&M JC**
4. **Joe Gangemi, lhp, Seton Hall**
5. **Michael Brunet, rhp, Pasco-Hernando (Fla.) CC**
6. **Matt Wise, rhp, Cal State Fullerton**
7. **Matt Garrick, c, Texas A&M**
8. **Ryan Cummings, rhp, Georgia Southern**
9. **Dwayne Dobson, rhp, South Florida**
10. **Steve Green, rhp, Fort Scott (Kan.) CC**
11. **Brian Tokarse, rhp, Cal State Fullerton**
12. Felipe Alou Jr., of, Canada (Calif.) JC
13. **Doug Nickle, rhp, California**
14. **Adam Leggett, 2b, Georgia Tech**
15. Brent Wagler, rhp, Florida Southern
16. **Casey Child, of, Utah**
17. **Keith Medosch, ss, North Florida**
18. Mike O'Keefe, of, Notre Dame HS, Hamden, Conn.
19. **Bo Donaldson, rhp, Tampa**
20. **Jaymie Bane, lhp, Arizona State**
21. **Mike Colangelo, of, George Mason**
22. **Steve Fish, rhp, Nebraska**
23. Jake Brooks, rhp, Polk (Fla.) CC
24. **Ernie Miller, lhp, Methodist (N.C.)**
25. **Jeb Dougherty, of, San Diego**
26. **Tim Adams, 1b, UC Davis**
27. David Walling, rhp, Grossmont (Calif.) JC
28. Rogier Vandepohl, ss, Indian River (Fla.) CC
29. **Mike Condon, ss, Seton Hall**
30. **Oscar Betancourt, 3b, Cal Poly Pomona**
31. **Steve Hagins, of, San Diego State**
32. **Ben Talbott, 3b, Lehigh**
33. Eric Easton, rhp, East Lake HS, Tarpon Springs, Fla.
34. **Peter Quittner, of, San Francisco**
35. Graham McAllister, c/1b, Lyons (Kan.) HS
36. **Casey Martin, c, Long Beach State**
37. Richard Stegbauer, c, Edison (Fla.) CC
38. **Scot Shields, rhp, Lincoln Memorial (Tenn.)**
39. Ben Saxon, rhp, Chipola (Fla.) JC
40. Jullian Harris, lhp, West Valley (Calif.) JC
41. Josh Pearce, rhp, Centralia (Wash.) JC
42. **Jay Nunley, of, North Florida**
43. Ryan Bast, ss/2b, Sierra (Calif.) JC
44. **Brad Brewer, ss, Miami**
45. Wesley Crawford, lhp, Polk (Fla.) CC
46. Matthew Steele, rhp, Chipola (Fla.) JC
47. Jeff Kaita, rhp, Colfax HS, Applegate, Calif.
48. **Aaron Porter, rhp, St. Mary's**
49. Daniel Kerrigan, c, Manatee (Fla.) CC
50. **Sheldon Philip-Guide, of, Glendale (Calif.) CC**
51. William Hays, of, Garrett (Md.) CC
52. Ben Margalski, c, Northwest HS, Highridge, Mo.
53. **Steve Ahlers, ss, Livermore (Calif.) HS**
54. Shamar Cotton, rhp, Skyline HS, Oakland
55. Brian Sullivan, lhp, Booker HS, Sarasota, Fla.
56. **Gilberto Pichardo, of, South Shore HS, Brooklyn**
57. **Ron Ricks, rhp, West Florida**
58. Lamar Harvey, rhp, Fremont HS, Sunnyvale, Calif.
59. Jake Mapes, c, Hemet (Calif.) HS
60. Alexis Acosta, ss, Polk (Fla.) CC

ARIZONA DIAMONDBACKS

June—Regular Phase (29)

1. **Jack Cust, 1b, Immaculata HS, Flemington, N.J.**
2. **Jason Royer, rhp, Del City (Okla.) HS**
3. **Jeffrey Brooks, 1b, Solanco HS, Quarryville, Pa.**
4. Chase Voshell, ss, Milford (Ohio) HS
5. Matt Riethmaier, rhp, Arkadelphia (Ark.) HS
6. **Mike Rooney, rhp, St. John's**
7. **Brian Gordon, of, Round Rock (Texas) HS**
8. **Ron Calloway, of, Canada (Calif.) JC**
9. Justin Singleton, ss, St. Paul's HS, Lutherville, Md.
10. **Casey Cuntz, ss, Louisiana State**
11. **Jamie Sykes, of, Valparaiso**
12. **Doug Kohl, rhp, Green Valley HS, Henderson, Nev.**
13. Peter Nystrom, of, Dunedin (Fla.) HS
14. **Alvin Montilla, of, St. Raymond's HS, Bronx, N.Y.**
15. **Brian Fox, c, Grayson County (Texas) JC**
16. **David Haverstick, rhp, Bethel (Ind.)**
17. Steve Rowell, ss, Ridgewood HS, Kenner, La.
18. **Jason Jensen, lhp, Southern Maine**
19. Tony Hausladen, 1b, Saint Louis
20. Derek Michaelis, 1b, Midway HS, Waco, Texas
21. **Tutu Moye, ss, Rose HS, Greenville, N.C.**
22. **Keith Jones, 3b, Fullerton (Calif.) JC**
23. **Jared Martin, ss, Southern Mississippi**
24. **Jason Martines, rhp, Siena Heights (Mich.)**
25. Andrew Friedberg, lhp, Middleton (Wis.) HS
26. Ben Mitchell, rhp, Horizon HS, Scottsdale, Ariz.
27. **John Adams, of, Wichita State**
28. Jared Hoerman, rhp, Eastern Oklahoma State JC
29. **Jeffrey Wilson, lhp, Elon**
30. Daniel Hall, rhp, Plymouth (N.C.) HS
31. **Seth Tate, rhp, Wenatchee Valley (Wash.) CC**
32. **Scott Abeyta, lhp, Contra Costa (Calif.) JC**
33. **Lance Downing, 3b, Watson Chapel HS, Pine Bluff, Ark.**
34. Phillip McKaig, rhp, Corona Del Sol HS, Tempe, Ariz.
35. **Jeremy Quire, c, Murray State**
36. **Alex Cintron, ss, Institute of Mechanical Technology, Caguas, P.R.**
37. **Julio Guzman, of, Carson-Newman (Tenn.)**
38. **Charlie Jones, rhp, Florida Atlantic**
39. Kelly Martin, rhp, Arcadia HS, Phoenix
40. **Wyley Steelmon, 1b, Oklahoma State**
41. Jeremy Dameworth, of, Ramona (Calif.) HS
42. Jason Scobie, rhp, Westwood HS, Austin
43. **Jamie Puorto, lhp, Northeastern Illinois**
44. Jason Wiedmeyer, lhp, West Bend (Wis.) East HS
45. **Steve Doherty, 2b, Long Beach State**
46. **Chris Bloomer, rhp, Purdue**
47. **Jeff Santa, lhp, Winthrop**
48. Bryce Terveen, c, JC of the Desert (Calif.)
49. John Meyers, rhp, Boswell HS, Dallas
50. Tommy Murphy, rhp/ss, Charlotte (Fla.) HS
51. George Dixon, of, Stamford (Conn.) Catholic HS
52. Brandon Wells, lhp, Bagdad (Ariz.) HS
53. Ronnie Goodwin, rhp, North Little Rock HS, Sherwood, Ark.
54. Aaron Rifkin, 1b, Etwanda HS, Fontana, Calif.
55. Stuart Hunt, lhp, Memorial HS, Edmond, Okla.
56. Samuel Mendoza, rhp, Highland HS, Gilbert, Ariz.
57. Anthony Denard, of, Laney (Calif.) JC
58. Anthony Pena, rhp, Dallas Christian HS
59. Ronald Corona, rhp, Victor Valley HS, Victorville, Calif.
60. Robert Pierce, 2b, Green Valley HS, Henderson, Nev.

ATLANTA BRAVES

June—Regular Phase (28)

1. **Troy Cameron, ss, St. Thomas Aquinas HS, Fort Lauderdale**
2. **Joey Nation, lhp, Putnam City HS, Oklahoma City**
3. **Juan Velazquez, ss, Jose Campeche HS, San Lorenzo, P.R.**
4. **Cory Aldridge, of, Cooper HS, Abilene, Texas**
5. **Horacio Ramirez, lhp, Inglewood (Calif.) HS**
6. Brett Groves, ss, Tampa Bay Tech HS
7. **Bry Ewen, c, Belton (Texas) HS**
8. **Ryan Lehr, c/3b, Grossmont HS, La Mesa, Calif.**
9. Ryan Snare, lhp, East Lake HS, Palm Harbor, Fla.
10. Gary Loudon, rhp, Shippensburg (Pa.)
11. **Greg Strickland, of, Cumberland (Tenn.)**
12. Manny Crespo, of, Westminster Christian HS, Miami
13. **Doug Dent, rhp, Citrus Heights, Calif.**
14. Chris Frazier, rhp, Salado HS, Belton, Texas
15. **Jon Ciravolo, rhp, Kean (N.J.)**
16. **Jason Hairston, c, Washington State**
17. **Richard Thieme, lhp, Georgia Tech**
18. Brad Drew, lhp, Waterloo (Ontario) Collegiate Institute
19. **Stewart Smothers, of, San Diego State**
20. **Derrick Lewis, rhp, Florida A&M**
21. **Mike Roberts, rhp, Siena**
22. **Pat Schmidt, lhp, Bellefontaine (Ohio) HS**
23. **Richard Dishman, rhp, Duke**
24. Bill Scott, of, Bishop Alemany HS, Mission Hills, Calif.
25. **Robert Porter, lhp, Southwest Mississippi CC**
26. **Mark Burke, 1b, Portland State**
27. **Jason Bowers, lhp, Central Cabarrus HS, Concord, N.C.**
28. **Troy Allen, of, George Washington**
29. John Wright, lhp, Walton HS, Defuniak Springs, Fla.
30. Tyler Kemhus, 3b, Oregon City (Ore.) HS
31. **David Lebejko, rhp, Central Connecticut State**
32. **Collin Wissen, of, Southwest Texas State**
33. Craig Carter, ss, Lake Havasu (Ariz.) HS
34. Patrick Hannaway, rhp, Monsignor Farrell HS, Staten Island, N.Y.
35. Jeremy Hale, rhp, Lafayette HS, St. Joseph, Mo.
36. **Tim Lyons, rhp, Kansas**
37. Mike Dolan, rhp, Chattahoochee (Fla.) HS
38. Robert Medeiros, of, Hawaii
39. Sean Vann, of, Chaparral HS, Las Vegas
40. Charlie Thames, rhp, Humble (Texas) HS
41. **Will Fleck, rhp, La Salle**
42. **Paul Shanklin, rhp, West Virginia State**
43. Anthony Limbrick, of, Skyline HS, Oakland
44. Matt Price, lhp, Greater Atlanta Christian HS, Norcross, Ga.
45. Justin Dansby, rhp, Eastern Oklahoma State JC
46. Daniel Wright, of, Dixie HS, St. George, Utah
47. Cameron Hardy, rhp, Lake City (Fla.) CC
48. **Prinz Milton, of, West Torrance (Calif.) HS**
49. Michael Gray, lhp, Cuesta (Calif.) JC
50. Mike Robinson, rhp, Canby (Ore.) HS
51. Jason Westemeir, 3b/rhp, Bishop Alemany HS, Mission Hills, Calif.
52. Tyler Shelton, ss, Hillsboro HS, Donnellson, Ill.
53. Robert Coley, c, Irwin County HS, Fitzgerald, Ga.
54. Travis Wessel, lhp, Morningside (Iowa)
55. Shannon Royal, lhp, Mariner HS, Fort Myers, Fla.
56. Greg Dukeman, rhp, Long Beach CC
57. Anthony Purkiss, ss, Golden West HS, Visalia, Calif.
58. Jorge Guerrero, ss, Miller HS, Fontana, Calif.
59. Tony Piccotti, 1b, Capital HS., Boise, Idaho
60. Tyler Van Patten, 1b, Polk (Fla.) CC
61. Travis Harrington, ss, Columbia HS, Lake City, Fla.
62. Jerel Johnson, 3b, McNair HS, Decatur, Ga.
63. Joey Alvarez, c, Temple (Texas) HS
64. Lonnie Jaquez, c, Carlsbad (N.M.) HS
65. Daniel Bell, of, Los Angeles CC
66. Darryl Stephens, of, St. Pius X HS, Decatur, Ga.
67. Chris Carmichael, of, McNair HS, Decatur, Ga.
68. Adam Kepler, of, Riverwood HS, Atlanta
69. Justin Echols, of, Thatcher (Ariz.) HS

BALTIMORE ORIOLES

June—Regular Phase (21)

1. **Jayson Werth, c, Glenwood HS, Chatham, Ill.**
1. **Darnell McDonald, of, Cherry Creek HS, Englewood, Colo.** (Pick from Yankees as compensation for Type A free agent David Wells)
1. **Ntema Ndungidi, of, Edouard Montpetit HS, Montreal** (Supplemental pick—36th—for loss of Wells)
2. **Sean Douglass, rhp, Antelope Valley HS, Lancaster, Calif.**
3. **Matt Riley, lhp, Liberty Union HS, Oakley, Calif.**
4. **Shannon Carter, of, El Reno (Okla.) HS**
5. **Rick Bauer, rhp, Treasure Valley (Ore.) CC**
6. Caleb Balbuena, rhp, Cuesta (Calif.) JC
7. **Ricky Casteel, rhp, Northeast Texas CC**
8. **Jay Spurgeon, rhp, Hawaii**
9. Logan Cuellar, rhp, Wharton County (Texas) JC
10. **David Zwirchitz, rhp, East HS, Appleton, Wis.**
11. **Jerry Hairston Jr., ss, Southern Illinois**
12. **Darren Murphy, lhp, Grossmont (Calif.) JC**
13. **Mack Haman, of, Coastal Carolina**
14. **Sean Jones, rhp, Barton HS, Hamilton, Ontario**
15. **Jordan Romero, rhp, DeAnza (Calif.) JC**
16. **Cliff Wilson, 3b, Spartanburg Methodist (S.C.) JC**
17. Chris Thogersen, rhp, Newbury Park HS, Thousand Oaks, Calif.
18. Lance Surridge, rhp, UNC Greensboro
19. **Jason Ryba, rhp, Cuyahoga Heights HS, Brooklyn Heights, Ohio**
20. Joe Borchard, 1b, Camarillo (Calif.) HS
21. **Antoine Ide, of, Madison HS, Portland, Ore.**
22. **Juan Pacheco, ss, Rutgers**
23. **Tod Lee, c, Georgia Southern**
24. Jason Taylor, of, Billy Ryan HS, Denton, Texas
25. Roy Wells, rhp, Perry County Central HS, Hazard, Ky.
26. **D.J. Carrasco, rhp, Pima (Ariz.) CC**
27. Brian Harper, of, Hershey (Pa.) HS
28. Erick Eigenhuis, rhp/1b, Central Valley HS, Veradale, Wash.
29. Anthony Reed, rhp, Eisenhower HS, Walters, Okla.
30. Brian Schmitt, 1b, Monterey HS, Lubbock, Texas
31. Terry Byron, 3b, St. Joseph HS, St. Croix, Virgin Islands
32. Gavin Wright, of, Lufkin (Texas) HS
33. Andrew Beal, lhp, Reidland HS, Paducah, Ky.
34. Matthew Schwager, rhp, Indian Hills (Iowa) CC
35. Austin Bilke, 3b, Beaver Dam (Wis.) HS
36. Juan Bonilla, c, Crestview (Fla.) HS
37. Rodney Perry, of, Mater Dei HS, Irvine, Calif.
38. Sam Emerick, rhp, Lincoln Land (Ill.) CC
39. William Duplissea, c, San Mateo (Calif.) JC
40. **Tommy Martin, ss, Hillsdale (Mich.)**
41. **Shawn Curtis, rhp, Lexington, Ky.**

BOSTON RED SOX

June—Regular Phase (17)

1. **John Curtice, lhp, Great Bridge HS, Chesapeake, Va.**
1. **Mark Fischer, of, Georgia Tech** (Supplemental pick—35th—for loss of Type A free agent Roger Clemens)
2. **Aaron Capista, ss, Joliet Catholic HS, Joliet, Ill.** (Pick from Blue Jays as compensation for Clemens)
2. **Eric Glaser, rhp, Highlands HS, Fort Thomas, Ky.**
3. **Travis Harper, rhp, James Madison**
4. **Angel Santos, ss, Miguel Melendez HS, Cayey, P.R.**
5. **Greg Miller, lhp, Aurora HS, West Aurora, Ill.**
6. Kris Wilken, c, El Dorado HS, Albuquerque
7. **Jeff Taglienti, rhp, Tufts (Mass.)**
8. **Andrew Hazlett, lhp, Portland**
9. Justin Wayne, rhp, Punahou HS, Honolulu
10. **Marty McLeary, rhp, Mount Vernon Nazarene (Ohio)**
11. **Tom Miller, lhp, Ohio**
12. Billy Rich, of, Connecticut
13. **Charles Terni, ss, Montville HS, Uncasville, Conn.**
14. **Chad Alevras, c, New Mexico**
15. **Rick O'Dette, lhp, St. Joseph's**
16. **Jorge DeLeon, 3b, South Florida**
17. **Kenny Rayborn, rhp, South Alabama**

18. Danny Haas, of, Louisville
19. David Eckstein, 2b, Florida
20. Brian Partenheimer, lhp, Indiana
21. Joe Thomas, lhp, Marietta (Ohio)
22. Derek Rix, 1b, Florida CC-Jacksonville
23. Nate Bump, rhp, Penn State
24. Jason Fingers, rhp, Torrey Pines HS, San Diego
25. Chris Domurat, c, Sandwich HS, Forestdale, Mass.
26. Heath McMurray, rhp, Splendora (Texas) HS
27. Justin Fry, rhp, Ohio State
28. David Stickel, ss, Temple Heights HS, Tampa
29. Ryan Yeager, ss, Port St. Joe (Fla.) HS
30. Bret Prinz, rhp, Phoenix JC
31. Matt Kamalsky, rhp, Somerset (Pa.) HS
32. Robert Hardy, rhp, Countryside HS, Clearwater, Fla.
33. Patrick Santoro, ss, Fenwick HS, Elmwood Park, Ill.
34. Layne Meyer, rhp, Polk (Fla.) CC
35. Jason Berni, rhp, Rancho Bernardo HS, San Diego
36. Ryan Atkinson, rhp, Bellarmine Prep HS, San Jose
37. Donovan Marbury, ss, Southern Mississippi
38. Dennis Tankersley, rhp, St. Charles (Mo.) HS
39. Shawn Weaver, rhp, Bald Eagle-Nittany HS, Loganton, Pa.
40. Chad Zaucha, of, Mount Pleasant (Pa.) HS
41. Matthew Slagter, rhp, Jefferson HS, Tampa
42. Scott Candelaria, ss, La Cueva HS, Albuquerque
43. Nicholas Gray, ss, Florida HS, Tallahassee, Fla.
44. Todd Smith, 3b, Apopka (Fla.) HS
45. Joe Thurston, ss, Vallejo (Calif.) HS

CHICAGO CUBS

June—Regular Phase (10)

1. Jon Garland, rhp, Kennedy HS, Granada Hills, Calif.
2. (Pick to White Sox as compensation for Type A free agent Kevin Tapani)
3. Scott Downs, lhp, Kentucky
4. Nate Teut, lhp, Iowa State
5. Jaisen Randolph, of, Hillsborough HS, Tampa
6. Matt Mauck, 3b, Jasper (Ind.) HS
7. Paul Vracar, rhp, Orchard Park HS, Stoney Creek, Ontario
8. Ron Walker, 3b, Old Dominion
9. Gary Johnson, of, Nevada
10. Mike Amrhein, c, Notre Dame
11. Michael Wuertz, rhp, Austin (Minn.) HS
12. Randy Williams, lhp, Lamar
13. Tanner Ericksen, rhp, Bullard HS, Fresno
14. Antwaan Randle El, of, Thornton HS, Riverdale, Ill.
15. T.P. Waligora, rhp, William & Mary
16. Matthew Magers, lhp, South Dakota State
17. Deon Eaddy, ss, Norfolk State
18. John Massey, c, Adamsville (Tenn.) HS
19. Chris Piersoll, rhp, Fullerton (Calif.) JC
20. Gerald Johnson, of, Atherton, Calif.
21. Kevin Waldrum, rhp, Millsap HS, Weatherford, Texas
22. Cameron Likely, of, Port St. Joe (Fla.) HS
23. Greg Jacobs, of, Cypress (Calif.) JC
24. Kevin Hodge, ss, Blinn (Texas) JC
25. Nathan Batts, lhp, Souhegan HS, Mount Vernon, N.H.
26. Michael Meyers, rhp, Black Hawk (Ill.) JC
27. Michael Delano, lhp, Los Angeles CC
28. Brad Love, lhp, Meridian (Miss.) CC
29. Ryan Rupe, rhp, Texas A&M
30. George Arnott, c, Cabrillo (Calif.) JC
31. Anthony Calabrese, ss, Brunswick HS, Riverside, Conn.
32. Andrew Perry, rhp, Claremont (Calif.) HS
33. Ryan McKinley, rhp, Scottsdale (Ariz.) CC
34. Chris Williamson, of/1b, Westfield HS, Houston
35. Ken Conroy, rhp, East Gaston HS, Gastonia, N.C.
36. Todd Fereday, 3b, Kansas State
37. Brad Tucker, rhp, Fresno State
38. Clark Todd, c, Lufkin (Texas) HS
39. Peter Selden, rhp, Holley (N.Y.) HS
40. Robert Mitchell, lhp, Dixie Heights HS, Erlanger, Ky.
41. Jeff Duncan, of, Lamont HS, Frankfort, Ill.
42. Daren Bartula, rhp, McLennan (Texas) CC
43. Josh Benedict, lhp, South Salem HS, Keizer, Ore.
44. John Halliday, 1b, Pasco-Hernando (Fla.) CC
45. Tim Whitfield, rhp, Leland HS, San Jose
46. Tom Bernhardt, of, Louisiana State
47. Matt Bruback, rhp, Clements HS, Schertz, Texas
48. John Janek, of, McLennan (Texas) CC
49. Brad Hargreaves, c, Okaloosa-Walton (Fla.) CC
50. Matt Gunderson, rhp, Walla Walla (Wash.) CC
51. Coby Robinson, of, Enterprise State (Ala.) JC
52. Lester Galer, rhp, Acalanes HS, Lafayette, Calif.
53. Jeremy Taylor, rhp, Ankeny (Iowa) HS
54. Jeremy Smith, rhp, Cerro Coso (Calif.) CC
55. Matthew Murphy, lhp, Wallace State (Ala.) CC
56. Joshua Latimer, lhp, Kishwaukee (Ill.) JC
57. Morey Aldrup, ss, La Quinta HS, Santa Ana, Calif.
58. Michael Joyce, lhp, Fitch HS, Groton, Conn.
59. Shane Kelly, of, Meridian (Miss.) CC

CHICAGO WHITE SOX

June—Regular Phase (15)

1. Jason Dellaero, ss, South Florida
1. Kyle Kane, rhp, Saddleback (Calif.) CC (Supplemental pick—33rd—for loss of service-time free agent Alex Fernandez)
1. Brett Caradonna (Supplemental pick), of, El Capitan HS, San Diego (Supplemental pick—34th—for loss of Type A free agent Kevin Tapani)
1. Aaron Myette, rhp, Central Arizona JC (Supplemental pick—43rd—for loss of Fernandez)
1. Jim Parque (Supplemental pick), lhp, UCLA (Supplemental pick—46th—for loss of Fernandez)
1. Rocky Biddle (Supplemental pick), rhp, Long Beach State (Supplemental pick—51st—for failure to sign 1996 first-rounder Bobby Seay)
2. Jeff Weaver, rhp, Fresno State (Pick from Cubs—62nd—as compensation for Tapani)
2. (Pick to Indians as compensation for Type A free agent Albert Belle)
3. J.R. Mounts, of, Key West (Fla.) HS
4. Curtis Whitley, lhp, Mount Olive (N.C.)
5. Pat Daneker, rhp, Virginia
6. Brian Scott, rhp, San Diego State
7. Jake Meyer, rhp, UCLA
8. Tim Currens, rhp, Lindsey Wilson (Ky.)
9. Rolando Garza, ss, Coachella (Calif.) Valley HS
10. Jamie Smith, rhp/c, Texas A&M
11. Kevin Connacher, 2b, Florida Atlantic
12. Andrew Jacobson, rhp, Alma (Mich.)
13. Ryan Hankins, 2b, Nevada-Las Vegas
14. Chad Durham, 2b/of, Surry (N.C.) CC
15. Travis Rapp, c, North Florida
16. Adrean Acevedo, of, Miami-Dade CC South
17. Shawn Barksdale, rhp, Etowah HS, Gallant, Ala.
18. Tom Williams, rhp, Southern
19. Jason Bernard, rhp, Rutherford HS, Panama City, Fla.
20. Tyson Boston, 3b, Burlington-Edison HS, Burlington, Wash.
21. Jonathan Kvasnicka, rhp, Northeastern Illinois
22. Stuart Rohling, rhp, Northwest Shoals (Ala.) JC
23. Matt Berger, 1b, Louisville
24. Cormac Joyce, lhp, Burke HS, Washingtonville, N.Y.
25. Eric Thompson, 1b, Gardner (Kan.) Edge HS
26. Joshua Johnston, rhp, JC of Eastern Utah
27. Anthony Garcia, c, Miami-Dade CC Wolfson
28. Richardo Ramon, of, Miami HS, Hialeah, Fla.
29. Matthew Goldsmith, rhp, Rockwall (Texas) HS
30. Ray Goirgolzarri, 3b, Miami-Dade CC South
31. Michael Mallonee, lhp, Southwestern (Calif.) JC
32. Chadd Clarey, rhp, Des Moines Area (Iowa) CC
33. Mark Floersch, rhp, New Trier HS, Winnetka, Ill.
34. Jason Moates, rhp, Central HS, Columbia, Tenn.
35. Nelson Carreno, c/of, Miami Christian HS
36. Edward Scott, ss/of, Dominguez HS, Compton, Calif.
37. Kevin Provencher, rhp, Forest Hill HS, West Palm Beach, Fla.
38. John Newman, rhp/ss, Skyline HS, Idaho Falls

39. Luis Suarez, ss, Miami-Dade CC North
40. Darryll Rogue, rhp, Miami-Dade CC South
41. **Michael Hill, 3b/of, Bentley (Mass.)**
42. Richard Clover, rhp, Central Missouri State
43. Jeff Radziewicz, 1b, Easton (Md.) HS
44. Matt Smith, lhp, Bishop Gorman HS, Las Vegas
45. Jason Aspito, ss, Driscoll Catholic HS, Itasca, Ill.
46. **Francisco De Armas, c, Southridge HS, Miami**
47. David Siemon, 3b, Forest Hill HS, West Palm Beach, Fla.
48. Jackie Pettigrew, rhp, Sperry HS, Skiatook, Okla.
49. **J.J. Newkirk, of, Long Beach State**
50. James Lunsford, c, Central HS, San Angelo, Texas
51. Luke Albert, c, Chaminade Madonna Collegiate HS, Hollywood, Fla.
52. **Elio Borges, ss, Miami**

CINCINNATI REDS

June—Regular Phase (14)

1. **Brandon Larson, ss, Louisiana State**
2. **Gookie Dawkins, ss, Newberry (S.C.) HS**
3. **Thad Markray, 3b, Springhill (La.) HS**
4. **Monte Roundtree, lhp, Rose HS, Greenville, N.C.**
5. **Dewayne Wise, of, Chapin (S.C.) HS**
6. **Toby Sanchez, 1b, Long Beach State**
7. **Mike Frank, lhp/of, Santa Clara**
8. Matt Borne, rhp, Kentucky
9. **Scott Williamson, rhp, Oklahoma State**
10. **David Runk, rhp, Tussey Mountain HS, Saxton, Pa.**
11. **Clint Brewer, rhp, Blanchard HS, Dibble, Okla.**
12. **Dustin Robinson, rhp, Oklahoma Baptist**
13. **Fernando Rios, of, Glendale (Calif.) HS**
14. **Daniel Timm, rhp, Denver**
15. **Braxton Whitehead, c/1b, Southern Mississippi**
16. **David Tidwell, of, Alabama**
17. **Tye Levy, lhp, Juniata Valley HS, Alexandria, Pa.**
18. **Wesley Stumbo, rhp, Georgetown (Ky.)**
19. **Benny Craig, of, Loyola Marymount**
20. **Kevin Baderdeen, ss, Glen Oaks (Mich.) CC**
21. **Robert Averett, rhp, Florida A&M**
22. **Eric Welsh, 1b, Northern Illinois**
23. Brian Kirby, c, North Little Rock (Ark.) HS
24. Terence Senegal, of, Comeaux HS, Lafayette, La.
25. Samone Peters, 1b, Mendocino (Calif.) CC
26. Antjuan Mitchell, 1b, Mount Carmel HS, Chicago
27. Josh Holbrook, c/1b, San Marcos (Calif.) HS
28. Scott Sandusky, c, Texas A&M
29. **Zadrian Brown, rhp, Midland Valley HS, Warrenville, S.C.**
30. **Marc Suarez, c, Cumberland (Tenn.)**
31. Cody Stanley, rhp, Clark HS, San Antonio
32. Todd Holt, of, Manchester HS, Chesterfield, Va.
33. Chad Rogers, rhp, Pine Forest HS, Pensacola, Fla.
34. Mike Bomar, lhp, Prairie HS, Brush Prairie, Wash.
35. **John Whitesides, rhp, Santa Fe (Fla.) CC**
36. Jason Hubbard, lhp, White HS, Jacksonville
37. Cade Allison, rhp, Odessa (Texas) JC
38. Tim Godfrey, ss, Bacone (Okla.) JC
39. Brian Kennedy, c, North HS, Riverside, Calif.
40. Luis Munne, c, Miami Springs HS, Hialeah, Fla.

CLEVELAND INDIANS

June—Regular Phase (27)

1. **Tim Drew, rhp, Lowndes County HS, Hahira, Ga.**
1. **Jason Fitzgerald, of, Tulane** (Supplemental pick—41st—for loss of Type A free agent Albert Belle)
2. **Edgar Cruz, c, Vocational Tech, Juncos, P.R.** (Pick from White Sox as compensation for Belle)
2. **Rob Vael, rhp, JC of Eastern Utah**
3. **Rob Pugmire, rhp, Cascade HS, Snohomish, Wash.**
4. **Eric Thompson, of, Westover HS, Fayetteville, N.C.**
5. **Jonathan Hamilton, of/lhp, Ohlone (Calif.) JC**
6. **Brian Benefield, 2b, Texas A&M**
7. **Mark Turnbow, rhp, Hardin County HS, Saltillo, Tenn.**
8. **Johnnie Wheeler, lhp, Connors State (Okla.) JC**
9. **Dustan Mohr, of, Alabama**
10. **Joe Kilburg, 2b/of, Stanford**
11. Daniel Jahn, lhp, Franklin HS, Seattle
12. Brad Freeman, ss, Mississippi State
13. Chad Hawkins, rhp, Navarro (Texas) JC
14. **Mike Hughes, lhp, St. John's**
15. **Tyler Swinburnson, rhp, Oregon State**
16. Denny New, lhp, Panola (Texas) JC
17. Brian Shackelford, lhp, Oklahoma
18. **Troy Silva, rhp, Lewis-Clark State (Idaho)**
19. Devon Nicholson, rhp, Sacramento CC
20. Nicholas Waak, rhp, Chugiak (Alaska) HS
21. **Erick Rosa, c, Western Kentucky**
22. **Kelly Dampeer, ss, Radford**
23. **Heath Bender, 1b, Memphis**
24. Reggie Nelson, ss, Mission Bay HS, San Diego
25. **Ryan Upshaw, of, New Mexico State**
26. **Chris Jackson, c, Mountain Brook (Ala.) HS**
27. **Todd Harding, 2b, Lane (Ore.) CC**
28. Derek Wigginton, of, Father Ryan HS, Antioch, Tenn.
29. Courtney Hall, rhp, Meadowdale HS, Edmonds, Wash.
30. Francis Paiso, lhp, Encinal HS, Alameda, Calif.
31. Brandon Smith, 1b, Canyon HS, Anaheim
32. Jason Basil, c, St. Xavier HS, Westchester, Ohio
33. Anthony Jackson, of, Wilde Lake HS, Ellicott City, Md.
34. Jonathon Rouwenhorst, lhp, Brethren Christian HS, Anaheim
35. Kris McWhirter, rhp, Davidson Academy, Goodlettsville, Tenn.
36. Danny Borrell, lhp, Lee County HS, Sanford, N.C.
37. Ryan Satterwhite, c, Tate HS, Cantonment, Fla.
38. Austin Roberts, rhp, Elma (Wash.) HS
39. Brandon Wheeler, rhp, Hillsborough (Fla.) CC
40. Brandon Mauer, c, Lake Stevens HS, Everett, Wash.
41. Brad Drummond, rhp, Liberty HS, Renton, Wash.
42. **Ryan Haley, 2b, Central Oklahoma**
43. **Danny Alvarez, rhp, Florida International**
44. Joey Cole, rhp, Howard (Texas) JC
45. Brian Seever, of, Sacramento CC
46. Jeff Parker, rhp, Martin HS, Arlington, Texas
47. Justin Hutton, c, Tyee HS, Tukwila, Wash.
48. Mark Hamilton, lhp, Panola (Texas) JC
49. Richard Booth, of, Whiteville (N.C.) HS
50. Darnell Sanders, 1b, Warrensville HS, Twinsburgh, Ohio

COLORADO ROCKIES

June—Regular Phase (18)

1. **Mark Mangum, rhp, Kingwood (Texas) HS**
2. **Aaron Cook, rhp, Hamilton (Ohio) HS**
3. **Todd Sears, 1b, Nebraska**
4. **Chone Figgins, ss, Brandon (Fla.) HS**
5. **Justin Miller, rhp, Los Angeles Harbor JC**
6. **Sam Smith, ss, Jasper (Texas) HS**
7. **Jake Kringen, lhp, Washington**
8. **Jeremy Jackson, of, Arkansas**
9. **Dave Johnson, rhp, Kansas State**
10. **Derrick Vargas, lhp, Chabot (Calif.) JC**
11. **Tino Sanchez, of, Luis Munoz Marin HS, Yauco, P.R.**
12. **Ryan Seifert, rhp, Iowa State**
13. **Roger Little, rhp, Perry Central HS, Hazard, Ky.**
14. **Jose Gonzales, c, Southeastern Louisiana**
15. **Rodney Little, rhp, Perry Central HS, Hazard, Ky.**
16. **Jason Franklin, 3b, Cumberland (Tenn.)**
17. **Jerome Alviso, ss, Cal State Fullerton**
18. **Ara Petrosian, rhp, Long Beach State**
19. **Michael Johns, ss, Tulane**
20. Mark Woodyard, 1b, Grand Bay (Ala.) HS
21. **Armando Gonzalez, rhp, Cerritos (Calif.) JC**
22. Kendall Rhodes, rhp, Angelina (Texas) JC
23. Jacob Minter, 1b, Blanchet HS, Edmonds, Wash.
24. Melvin Rosario, of, Indian Hills (Iowa) CC
25. Trevor Kitsch, c, Kelowna (B.C.) HS
26. Jeremy Schultz, rhp, Mason City (Iowa) HS
27. Justin Lombardi, lhp, Coyle-Cassidy HS, Taunton, Mass.
28. Rocky Kirk, lhp, Viewmont HS, Casper, Wyo.
29. Dan Kelly, lhp, Okaloosa-Walton (Fla.) CC

30. Jerome Easter, of, Mount Union (Pa.) HS
31. Brian Putnam, rhp, Indianola (Miss.) HS
32. Braxton Batson, lhp, Mississippi Gulf Coast JC
33. Cody Trask, rhp, Riverside (Calif.) CC
34. Mark Scates, of, Coeur D'Alene (Idaho) HS
35. James McCoy, of, Miami-Dade CC South
36. Alfredo Amezaga, ss, Miami HS
37. Ronny Marmol, c, Southridge HS, Miami
38. **Chris Price, rhp, Eastern New Mexico**
39. Walcott Richardson, of, Dracut (Mass.) HS
40. Brandon Roberson, rhp, Hill (Texas) JC
41. Yamilke Ulloa, lhp, Hialeah (Fla.) HS
42. Matthew Ortiz, c, Grossmont (Calif.) JC
43. Shaun Wooley, lhp, Rancho Santiago (Calif.) JC
44. Chad Elliot, lhp, Rancho Santiago (Calif.) JC
45. Casey Lopez, 3b, Los Altos (Calif.) HS
46. Matthew Thomas, rhp, Weatherford (Texas) HS
47. Bobby Bass, of, Livermore (Calif.) HS

DETROIT TIGERS

June—Regular Phase (1)

1. **Matt Anderson, rhp, Rice**
2. **Shane Loux, rhp, Highland HS, Gilbert, Ariz.**
3. **Matt Boone, 3b, Villa Park (Calif.) HS**
4. **Alan Webb, lhp, Durango HS, Las Vegas**
5. **Heath Schesser, ss, Kansas State**
6. **Chris Parker, c, Westlake HS, Westlake Village, Calif.**
7. **Mike Diebolt, lhp, Minnesota**
8. **Dan Lauterhahn, 2b, William Paterson (N.J.)**
9. Bud Smith, of/lhp, St. John Bosco HS, Lakewood, Calif.
10. **Rick Roberts, lhp, Forest Hills HS, Summerhill, Pa.**
11. Leo Daigle, 1b, Monte Vista HS, Spring Valley, Calif.
12. **Darrell Pender, of, Miami Northwestern HS**
13. **John Alkire, rhp, Cal State Fullerton**
14. **Brennan Hervey, 1b, Florida Atlantic**
15. **Jason Howard, rhp, Purdue**
16. **Alex Steele, of, SUNY Cortland**
17. Chris Curry, c, Meridian (Miss.) CC
18. **Ryan Grimmett, of, Miami**
19. **Jeremy Sassanella, c, DeKalb HS, Auburn, Ind.**
20. **Craig Johnson, rhp, Siena**
21. **Nelson Alvarez, 1b, North Rockland HS, Haverstraw, N.Y.**
22. **Mandy Jacomino, of, Miami**
23. **Kevin Mobley, rhp, Georgia College & State**
24. Doyle Washington, of, Inglewood (Calif.) HS
25. Kelly Crosby, of, Wheaton (Ill.) Warrenville HS
26. **Maxim St. Pierre, c, Col de Levis HS, Montreal**
27. **William Snyder, rhp, Rensselaer Polytechnic (N.Y.) Institute**
28. **Jacob Schaffer, ss, Bradley**
29. Joseph Hall, of, Artesia HS, Lynwood, Calif.
30. **Richard Ozarowski, ss, Florida Atlantic**
31. Scott Martines, 1b, Punahou HS, Honolulu
32. Steve Rodriguez, of, East Los Angeles JC
33. **Joel Greene, lhp, William Penn (Iowa)**
34. **John Guilmet, rhp, Merrimack (Mass.)**
35. **Matthew Beck, rhp, Bradley**
36. Brian Cole, ss, Meridian (Miss.) HS
37. **Antonio Hasbun, ss, Briarcliff HS, New York**
38. Curtis Wickwire, 1b, Clovis West HS, Fresno
39. **Bernie Pedersoli, c, Illinois-Chicago**
40. **Clark Parker, 2b, Cal State Northridge**
41. Matthew Altagen, 1b, University HS, Malibu, Calif.
42. Carlos Hernandez, rhp, Columbus HS, Bronx, N.Y.

FLORIDA MARLINS

June—Regular Phase (12)

1. **Aaron Akin, rhp, Cowley County (Kan.) CC**
2. **Jeff Bailey, c, Kelso (Wash.) HS**
3. **Chris Aguila, 3b, McQueen HS, Reno, Nev.**
4. **Brandon Harper, c, Dallas Baptist**
5. Paul Avery, lhp, Fresno CC
6. **Brian Reed, of, Green Valley HS, Henderson, Nev.**
7. **Matt Erickson, 3b, Arkansas**
8. Clifton Lee, lhp, Benton (Ark.) HS
9. **Jon Heinrichs, of, UCLA**
10. **Kelley Washington, ss, Shenandoah HS, Stephens City, Va.**
11. **Jesus Medrano, 2b, Bishop Amat HS, La Puente, Calif.**
12. **Javon Walker, of, St. Thomas More HS, Lafayette, La.**
13. **Ross Gload, 1b, South Florida**
14. **Wes Anderson, rhp, Pine Bluff (Ark.) HS**
15. Travis Bailey, ss, Palm Beach (Fla.) CC
16. James Shook, rhp, Columbia-Greene (N.Y.) CC
17. **Rhodney Donaldson, of, Troy State**
18. **Drew Shields, rhp, Pima (Ariz.) CC**
19. **Robert Garvin, rhp, St. Andrew's Parish HS, Charleston, S.C.**
20. Howard Beard, of, Watkins HS, Laurel, Miss.
21. Eric Bernhardt, rhp, Pittsburg (Kan.) HS
22. **Alex Melconian, c, Seton Hall**
23. Andres Torres, of, Miami-Dade CC Wolfson
24. Jason Harrison, c, Allegany (Md.) CC
25. **Cory Lima, rhp, North Carolina A&T**
26. **Scott Henderson, rhp, Southern California**
27. **Matt Schnabel, of/1b, Southwest Texas State**
28. **James McGowan, rhp, Queensborough (N.Y.) CC**
29. **Blair Fowler, rhp, Washington**
30. **Gaige Thomas, rhp, Brenham (Texas) HS**
31. Jason Farmer, rhp, Indio (Calif.) HS
32. Bryant Hodges, rhp, Seminole HS, Donaldsonville, Ga.
33. Ronald Dorsey, of, Hammonton (N.J.) HS
34. **Chris Clark, of, Arkansas**
35. Josh Higgins, rhp, El Capitan HS, Santee, Calif.
36. Antwoine Anderson, lhp, Withrow HS, Cincinnati
37. Chris Louwsma, ss, Seminole HS, Sanford, Fla.
38. Eric Abshor, of, Howard (Texas) JC
39. Adam Spiker, 1b, Marina HS, Huntington Beach, Calif.
40. John Weis, lhp, Chipola (Fla.) JC
41. Billy Nofsinger, rhp, King HS, Tampa
42. Nicholas Carlson, rhp, Madison (Wis.) Area Tech JC
43. Glen Myers, lhp, South Charleston (W.Va.) HS
44. Esteben Elzy, c, Cochise County (Ariz.) CC
45. Jimmy Barndollar, rhp, Pacifica HS, Garden Grove, Calif.
46. Michael Wenger, lhp, Potomac State (W.Va.) JC
47. Michael Shumaker, 1b, Meyersdale (Pa.) Area HS
48. Aaron Lough, c, Potomac State (W.Va.) JC
49. Michael Nall, rhp, Schaumburg (Ill.) HS
50. Kyle Jenkins, rhp, Deptford HS, Woodbury, N.J.
51. Frank Valois, of, Montgomery (Md.) JC
52. Tim Strange, c, Eau Gallie HS, Melbourne, Fla.
53. Brian Middleton, rhp, Woodbury (N.J.) HS
54. Adrian Earles, of, Austin East HS, Knoxville
55. Nicholas Huntsman, rhp, Pleasant Grove (Utah) HS
56. William Baber, 3b, Western Albemarle HS, Crozet, Va.
57. Michael Kalchuk, rhp, Broward (Fla.) CC
58. Carl Lafferty, c, Pine Bluff (Ariz.) HS

HOUSTON ASTROS

June—Regular Phase (16)

1. **Lance Berkman, 1b, Rice**
2. **Camron Hahn, c, Male HS, Louisville**
3. Scott Barrett, lhp, Mayde Creek HS, Houston
4. Eric Byrnes, of, UCLA
5. Derek Stanford, rhp, Temple (Texas) HS
6. **Joe Messman, rhp, Oregon State**
7. **Rob Bystrowski, of, Sacramento CC**
8. **Ryan Dunn, of, Texas Christian**
9. **Don Thomas, lhp, Kennesaw State (Ga.)**
10. Scott Fredericks, rhp, Saguaro HS, Scottsdale, Ariz.
11. Javier Pamus, rhp, San Jose State
12. **Peter Sullivan, rhp, Limestone (S.C.)**
13. Barton Leahy, of, Ohio
14. Trey Hodges, rhp, Blinn (Texas) JC
15. **J.J. Thomas, 1b, Georgia Tech**
16. **Jim Wallace, rhp, North Carolina**
17. **Pat Cutshall, ss, Mercyhurst (Pa.)**
18. Simon Mitchell, of, West Seattle HS

19. **Brian Hecht, rhp, Illinois**
20. **Tim Redding, rhp, Monroe (N.Y.) CC**
21. Neal Maybin, of, Lake Howell HS, Castleberry, Fla.
22. **Jason Alfaro, rhp, Hill (Texas) JC**
23. **Kyle Logan, of/3b, Southern Mississippi**
24. Tim Judd, rhp, Dixon (Calif.) HS
25. Charlton Jimerson, of, Mount Eden HS, Hayward, Calif.
26. Jared Wood, rhp, St. Louis CC-Meramec
27. Derek Brewster, rhp, Carthage (Texas) HS
28. Graham Travis, rhp, Ballard HS, Seattle
29. **Joe Cathey, ss, Rice**
30. Chris Ross, rhp, Ringgold (Ga.) HS
31. Kris Clute, ss, Killian HS, Miami
32. Eric Armbruster, 1b, Central HS, Kalamazoo, Mich.
33. Lamont Matthews, of, Kiswaukee (Ill.) JC
34. John Skinner, rhp, Chabot (Calif.) JC
35. Kevin Marzion, rhp, Elk Grove (Calif.) HS
36. Jason Dill, 1b, Charlotte HS, Punta Gorda, Fla.
37. Jerymane Beasley, of, Olympic (Wash.) JC
38. John Colon, rhp, Molokai HS, Mauna Loa, Hawaii
39. Marcos Rios, c, Chabot (Calif.) JC
40. Garreth Perry, c, Service HS, Anchorage

KANSAS CITY ROYALS

June—Regular Phase (7)

1. **Dan Reichert, rhp, Pacific**
2. Dane Sardinha, c, Kamehameha HS, Kahuku, Hawaii
3. **Jeremy Affeldt, ss, Northwest Christian HS, Spokane, Wash.**
4. **Goefrey Tomlinson, of, Houston**
5. **Jason Gooding, lhp, Texas Tech**
6. Jason Anderson, rhp, Danville (Ill.) HS
7. **Joe Dillon, 1b, Texas Tech**
8. **Eric Yanz, rhp, Kansas State**
9. **Kris Wilson, rhp, Georgia Tech**
10. **David Willis, 1b, UC Santa Barbara**
11. **Joe Caruso, 2b, Alabama**
12. **Jason Gilfillan, rhp, Limestone (S.C.)**
13. **Ryan Douglass, rhp, Canevin Catholic HS, Pittsburgh**
14. **Tony Mancha, rhp, Las Cruces (N.M.) HS**
15. **Justin Pederson, rhp, Minnesota**
16. Rolando Geigel, rhp, Georgina Vaquaro HS, Canovanas, P.R.
17. **Justin Lamber, lhp, Richmond**
18. Bruce Stanley, rhp, Ball State
19. **Tarik Graham, of, Edgewater HS, Orlando**
20. **Carlos Pagan, c, Mobile (Ala.)**
21. **Rod Metzler, 2b, Purdue**
22. **James Woods, c, Muskegon (Mich.) HS**
23. **Rickey Crutchley, lhp, Etowan HS, Acworth, Ga.**
24. **Cameron Tillis, of, Lurleen Wallace State (Ala.) JC**
25. Ryan Hutchison, rhp, Vincennes (Ind.) HS
26. Michael Perkins, rhp, Charlotte HS, Punta Gorda, Fla.
27. Fontella Jones, rhp, Mississippi Gulf Coast JC
28. **Aaron Carter, rhp, St. Mary's (Texas)**
29. **David Ullery, c, Indiana State**
30. Robert Balazentis, rhp, Mercyhurst (Pa.)
31. George Petticrew, rhp, Lakeside HS, Nine Mile, Wash.
32. Kyle Turner, lhp, Antioch (Calif.) HS
33. Nelson Bellido, rhp, Brooklyn
34. Freddie Fincher, c, Galveston (Texas) JC
35. John Hale, rhp, Robert E. Lee HS, Midland, Texas
36. Donny Davis, rhp, El Cerrito HS, San Pablo, Calif.
37. John Majors, rhp, Flomaton HS, Brewton, Ala.
38. John Raymer, rhp, West Orange-Stark HS, Orange, Texas
39. Aaron Melebeck, ss, Galveston (Texas) JC
40. Ken Thomas, c, Gloucester County (N.J.) JC
41. Chris Sampson, ss, Lon Morris (Texas) JC
42. Chris Tallman, of, Rancho Santiago (Calif.) JC
43. Quentin Elder, rhp, Castlemont HS, Oakland
44. Daniel Martinez, lhp, Sweetwater HS, National City, Calif.
45. Bret Halbert, lhp, Cypress (Calif.) JC
46. Gary Schulz, lhp, Montgomery (Texas) HS
47. Mark Villarreal, c, John Foster Dulles HS, Missouri City, Texas
48. Matt Williams, 3b, Millikan HS, Long Beach
49. Carlos Spikes, of, North Florida Christian HS, Tallahassee, Fla.

LOS ANGELES DODGERS

June—Regular Phase (24)

1. **Glenn Davis, 1b, Vanderbilt**
2. Chase Utley, ss, Poly HS, Long Beach
2. **Steve Colyer, lhp, Fort Zumwalt South HS, St. Peters, Mo.** (Supplemental pick—83rd—for loss of Type C free agent Delino DeShields)
3. **Ricky Bell, ss, Moeller HS, Cincinnati**
4. **John Hernandez, c, Nogales HS, La Puente, Calif.**
5. **Kip Harkrider, ss, Texas**
6. **Will McCrotty, c, Russellville (Ark.) HS**
7. Miles Durham, of, Cooper HS, Abilene, Texas
8. **Beau Parker, rhp, Prairie HS, Brush Prairie, Wash.**
9. **Jamie Goudie, ss, Hardaway HS, Columbus, Ga.**
10. **Joe Patterson, of, Ontario (Calif.) HS**
11. Cory Vance, lhp, Butler HS, Vandalia, Ohio
12. David Lamberth, ss, Macon County HS, Montezuma, Ga.
13. **Matt Bornyk, rhp, Esquimalt HS, Victoria, British Columbia**
14. **Brent Husted, rhp, Nevada**
15. David Mittauer, rhp, Dade Christian HS, Cooper City, Fla.
16. Scott Walter, c, Loyola HS, Manhattan Beach, Calif.
17. Chad Cislak, rhp, Sabino HS, Tucson
18. **Michael Balbuena, 3b, Key West (Fla.) HS**
19. **Joel Allen, of, Glenns Ferry (Idaho) HS**
20. **Peter Zamora, 1b/lhp, UCLA**
21. **Stephen Verigood, lhp, Spartanburg Methodist (S.C.) JC**
22. **Matthew Montgomery, rhp, Long Beach State**
23. **Jared Moon, rhp, Redondo Union HS, Redondo Beach, Calif.**
24. **Michael Rawls, lhp, Bethune-Cookman**
25. David Detienne, 3b, Auburn Drive HS, Dartmouth, Nova Scotia
26. **Bill Everly, rhp, West Virginia Wesleyan**
27. **Aaron Dean, 1b, Lamar**
28. **Richard Bell, lhp, California Lutheran**
29. **Darin Schmalz, rhp, Notre Dame**
30. Sam Lopez, ss, Dinuba (Calif.) HS
31. **Wayne Slater, of, Bethune-Cookman**
32. Shaylar Hatch, rhp, Gilbert, Ariz.
33. Shaun Benzor, lhp, Redlands (Calif.) HS
34. Blake McGinley, lhp, North HS, Bakersfield, Calif.
35. Adam Thomas, of, Hazel Park HS, Troy, Mich.
36. Jesus Feliciano, of, Academia HS, Bayamon, P.R.
37. Tyler Renwick, rhp, New Mexico JC
38. Eliot Joyner, of, Mount San Antonio (Calif.) JC
39. Jahseam George, lhp, Buchanan HS, Clovis, Calif.
40. John Nelson, ss, Denton (Texas) HS
41. Ryan Beaver, rhp, Millikan HS, Long Beach
42. **Carlos Orozco, of, Montgomery HS, San Diego**
43. **Michael Hernandez, lhp, Carson (Calif.) HS**
44. Graig Merritt, c, Pitt Meadows, British Columbia
45. Shane Youman, lhp, New Iberia (La.) HS
46. Ryan Kellner, c, Spartanburg Methodist (S.C.) JC
47. Jean Emard, lhp, Edouard Montpetit HS, Montreal
48. Luis DeJesus, c, Miguel De Cervantes, Bayamon, P.R.
49. **Lance Warren, c, Richmond Hill (Calif.) HS**
50. Chris Howay, rhp, New Westminster (B.C.) HS
51. Eric Burris, 1b, Los Angeles Harbor JC
52. Russell Ivory, of, Grossmont (Calif.) JC
53. Ismael Garcia, 2b, Mount San Antonio (Calif.) JC
54. Michael Ford, of, Elk Grove (Calif.) HS
55. Melvin Anderson, 3b, North Iberville HS, Baton Rouge
56. Reggie LaPlante, rhp, Edouard Montpetit HS, Montreal
57. George Bailey, 3b, Indian River (Fla.) CC
58. James Howard, rhp, Orange Park, Fla.
59. Joshua Ridgway, ss, Delta HS, Ladner, British Columbia
60. Jason Ware, 1b, Long Beach CC
61. Javier Gonzalez, rhp, Mount San Antonio (Calif.) JC
62. Steve Holm, ss, McClatchy HS, Sacramento
63. Cedric Herbert, rhp, Grayson County (Texas) JC
64. Jeremy Loftice, rhp, Truett McConnell (Ga.) JC
65. Luis Fontanez, c, Juana Colon HS, Bayamon, P.R.

66. John Castellano, c, Indian River (Fla.) CC
67. Cory Stephen, c, Regina, Saskatchewan
68. Matt Ybarra, c, Encinal HS, Alameda, Calif.
69. **Luis Medina, c, Bayamon, P.R.**
70. Ryan Withey, of, Seminole (Fla.) CC

MILWAUKEE BREWERS

June—Regular Phase (13)

1. **Kyle Peterson, rhp, Stanford**
2. **Alvin Morrow, of, Kirkwood (Mo.) HS**
3. **Jeff Deardorff, 3b, South Lake HS, Clermont, Fla.**
4. **Tommy Warren, of, Westchester HS, Inglewood, Calif.**
5. **Frank Candela, of, Peabody (Mass.) HS**
6. **Jake Eye, rhp, Ohio**
7. **Bucky Jacobsen, of, Lewis-Clark State (Idaho)**
8. **Todd Incantalupo, lhp, Providence**
9. **Matt Childers, rhp, Westside HS, Augusta, Ga.**
10. **Chris Patton, ss, McClintock HS, Tempe, Ariz.**
11. **Jim Miller, rhp, Carthage (Wis.)**
12. **Kendall Guthrie, c, Northwood (Texas) Institute**
13. Brent Kelley, rhp, Arkansas State
14. **Chris Rowan, 3b, Mount Vernon (N.Y.) HS**
15. Romaro Miller, ss, Shannon (Miss.) HS
16. **Andrew Cavanagh, rhp, Young Harris (Ga.) JC**
17. **Mark Kirst, rhp, St. Norbert's (Wis.)**
18. **Jay Akin, lhp, Arkansas State**
19. **Shane Wooten, lhp, Birmingham-Southern**
20. Doug Clark, of, Massachusetts
21. Mark Cridland, of, Texas
22. Charles Manning, lhp, Winter Haven (Fla.) HS
23. **Kevin Priebe, lhp, Bradley**
24. Robbie Baker, rhp, Blinn (Texas) JC
25. Steve Beller, rhp, West Virginia
26. **Trad Sokol, lhp, Frederick (Md.) CC**
27. **Brian Mallette, rhp, Columbus (Ga.)**
28. **Marty Patterson, c, Michigan State**
29. Alfred Corbeil, c, Plantation HS, Margate, Fla.
30. Brian Fields, lhp, East Carolina
31. **Chauncey Jones, rhp, Briar Cliff (Iowa)**
32. Gary McConnell, rhp, North Florida CC
33. Arthur Garland, rhp, Magnolia HS, Anaheim
34. James Igo, rhp, Galveston (Texas) JC
35. Ryan Costello, lhp, Eastern HS, Voorhees, N.J.
36. **Chad Helmer, rhp, Florida Southern**
37. Landon Jacobsen, rhp, Howard HS, Canova, S.D.
38. Randy Rodriguez, lhp, Indian River (Fla.) CC
39. **Joel Arroyo, rhp, St. Leo (Fla.)**
40. **Robert Riggio, 3b, Lehman (N.Y.)**
41. Geoff Geary, rhp, Oklahoma
42. Justin Ames, lhp, Moorpark (Calif.) HS
43. **Ryan Pearson, of, Troy State**
44. Marcos Quinones, rhp, Lee (Texas) JC
45. **Nick Caiazzo, c, Maine**
46. Eric Tomlinson, of, Granbury (Texas) HS
47. Jeff Savage, rhp, Palm Beach Gardens (Fla.) HS
48. Oscar Ramirez, ss, Southridge HS, Miami
49. Nick Quinn, of, Atlantic HS, Boynton Beach, Fla.
50. Jimmy Smith, of, Lake Mary HS, Longwood, Fla.
51. Jose Camilo, 2b, North Florida CC
52. Michael Oiler, ss, Watertown (Wis.) HS
53. Bennie Harris, of, Myers Park HS, Charlotte

MINNESOTA TWINS

June—Regular Phase (9)

1. **Michael Cuddyer, ss, Great Bridge HS, Chesapeake, Va.**
1. **Matt LeCroy, c, Clemson** (Supplemental pick—50th—for failure to sign 1996 first-rounder Travis Lee)
2. **Michael Restovich, of, Mayo HS, Rochester, Minn.**
3. Greg Withelder, lhp, Strath Haven HS, Wallingford, Pa.
4. **Bob Davies, lhp, Marietta (Ohio)**
5. **Peter Blake, lhp, Indianola (Iowa) HS**
6. **Nate Melson, rhp, Rogers (Ark.) HS**
7. **Matt Carnes, rhp, Arkansas**
8. **Ben Thomas, lhp, Wichita State**
9. **Jon Schaeffer, c, Stanford**
10. **Josh Gandy, lhp, Georgia**
11. **Matt Jurgena, rhp, Hastings (Neb.)**
12. **Lateef Vaughn, ss, Long Beach State**
13. **Marques Southward, of, Pasco Comprehensive HS, Dade City, Fla.**
14. Eddy Furniss, 1b, Louisiana State
15. Jake Weber, of, North Carolina State
16. Jordan Gerk, lhp, KLO HS, Kelowna, British Columbia
17. Kevin Frederick, rhp/3b, Creighton
18. **Ray Underhill, rhp, DeLand (Fla.) HS**
19. Kevin Stuart, rhp, Golden West (Calif.) JC
20. **Billy Coleman, rhp, Western Michigan**
21. **J.C. Romero, lhp, Mobile (Ala.)**
22. Daniel Boyd, 3b, Pasco Comprehensive HS, Dade City, Fla.
23. **Tim Sturdy, rhp, La Cueva HS, Albuquerque**
24. Creston Whitaker, of, Jesuit Collegiate HS, Dallas
25. Adam Johnson, rhp, Torrey Pines HS, San Diego
26. Dan Morris, lhp, Ayersville HS, Defiance, Ohio
27. Daylan Holt, of, Mesquite (Texas) HS
28. David Shank, rhp, Miramonte HS, Orinda, Calif.
29. **Aaron Jaworowski, 1b, Missouri**
30. **Nate Stevens, ss, Keystone (Fla.) HS**
31. **Mike Cosgrove, rhp, Tennessee**
32. Trevor Mote, ss, Kingman (Ariz.) HS
33. Nick Punto, ss, Saddleback (Calif.) CC
34. Marques Tuiasosopo, 3b, Woodinville (Wash.) HS
35. Craig Hawkins, rhp, Notre Dame HS, Burlington, Ontario
36. **Brian Fitts, rhp, Volunteer State (Tenn.) CC**
37. **Patrick Stenger, rhp, St. Ignatius HS, Mentor, Ohio**
38. **Bryant Melson, c, North Florida**
39. Isaiah Haynes, of, Vanden HS, Fairfield, Calif.
40. Casey Fuller, lhp, Dixon (Calif.) HS
41. Corey Richardson, of, Northeast Texas CC
42. Russell Bratton, rhp, Memphis
43. Justin Smith, lhp, Seward County (Kan.) CC
44. Josh Reese, rhp, Lincoln County HS, Fayetteville, Tenn.
45. Matt Booth, lhp, Henry Clay HS, Lexington, Ky.
46. **Aaron Miller, lhp, Campbell**
47. **Joe Foote, rhp, Park View HS, Sterling, Va.**
48. **Jason McConnell, 2b, Arkansas**
49. David Justice, ss, Washington HS, Pensacola, Fla.
50. Tagg Bozied, c, Arvada (Colo.) West HS
51. Clint Bailey, rhp, Chemainus, British Columbia
52. Richard Durrett, 1b, El Paso (Texas) CC
53. Shawn Stiffler, lhp, Somerset (Pa.) HS

MONTREAL EXPOS

June—Regular Phase (22)

1. **Donnie Bridges, rhp, Oak Grove HS, Hattiesburg, Miss.**
1. **Chris Stowe, rhp, Chancellor HS, Fredericksburg, Va.** (Supplemental pick—37th—for loss of service-time free agent Mel Rojas)
1. **Scott Hodges, ss, Henry Clay HS, Lexington, Ky.** (Supplemental pick—38th—for loss of service-time free agent Moises Alou)
1. **Bryan Hebson, rhp, Auburn** (Supplemental pick—44th—for loss of Rojas)
1. **Thomas Pittman, 1b, East St. John HS, Garyville, La.** (Supplemental pick—45th—for loss of Alou)
1. **T.J. Tucker, rhp, River Ridge HS, New Port Richey, Fla.** (Supplemental pick—47th—for loss of Rojas)
1. **Shane Arthurs, rhp, Westmoore HS, Oklahoma City** (Supplemental pick—48th—for loss of Alou)
1. **Tootie Myers, of, Petal (Miss.) HS** (Supplemental pick—52nd—for failure to sign 1996 first-rounder John Patterson)
2. **Kris Tetz, rhp, Lodi (Calif.) HS**
3. **Josh Reding, ss, Rancho Santiago (Calif.) JC**
4. Ronte Langs, of, Whitehaven HS, Memphis
5. **Julio Perez, rhp, Brito Private HS, Miami**
6. **Scott Ackerman, c, Oregon City (Ore.) HS**
7. **Anthony Caracciolo, ss, Basic HS, Henderson, Nev.**
8. **Ryan Becks, lhp, West Valley (Calif.) JC**

9. **Talmadge Nunnari, 1b, Jacksonville**
10. **Scott Strickland, rhp, New Mexico**
11. **Matt Blank, lhp, Texas A&M**
12. **Ryan Van Gilder, rhp, Mankato State (Minn.)**
13. **Luis Rivera, c, Florida Southern**
14. **Scott Zech, 2b, Florida State**
15. **Lance Burkhart, c/3b, Southwest Missouri State**
16. **Ryan Saylor, rhp, Eastern Kentucky**
17. Spencer Nemer, rhp, Klein Forest HS, Houston
18. Josh Merrigan, lhp, Vermillion (S.D.) HS
19. Jonathan Boyett, 2b, Modesto (Calif.) JC
20. Marcus Bell, rhp, Pace (Fla.) HS
21. **Ray Plummer, lhp, Point Loma Nazarene (Calif.)**
22. **Michael Edge, of, North Brunswick HS, Winnabow, N.C.**
23. Matt Coleman, lhp, Centennial HS, Boring, Ore.
24. **Tobin Lanzetta, rhp, Santa Clara**
25. Shaun Poole, lhp, Hudson HS, Spring Hill, Fla.
26. Ralph Harrelson, rhp, Davis HS, Modesto, Calif.
27. Jason Hoffman, of, Ohlone (Calif.) JC
28. **Joseph Fretwell, rhp, Valencia (Fla.) CC**
29. Nathan Cook, 3b, Chabot (Calif.) JC
30. Derek Smith, ss, Tulare (Calif.) Union HS
31. Jeff Lincoln, rhp, American River (Calif.) JC
32. Cory Vandegriff, ss, Halls HS, Knoxville
33. Brandt Hayden, ss, South Salem (Ore.) HS
34. Joe Baldassano, rhp, Alta Loma (Calif.) HS
35. Arthur Anderson, ss, East St. John HS, LaPlace, La.
36. Sam Anderson, c, Mesquite (Texas) HS
37. David Vonah, 3b, Hoover HS, Fresno
38. Edwin Gomez, of, Teodoro Aguilar Mora HS, Yabucoa, P.R.
39. James McKnight, c, Washington HS, Phoenix
40. **John White, c, Jacksonville**
41. Luis Martinez, c, Jose Campeche HS, San Lorenzo, P.R.
42. Kevin Harmon, c, Palmdale HS, Acton, Calif.
43. Josh Laidlaw, of, Cheyenne HS, North Las Vegas
44. Matthew Baird, of, Burlington, Ontario
45. Mechel Elam, of, Eisenhower HS, San Bernardino, Calif.
46. Brian Oxley, ss, Los Medanos (Calif.) JC
47. Matthew Cody, c, Woodlawn HS, Baton Rouge
48. Chris Herman, ss, South Hills HS, Covina, Calif.
49. Dean Harper, c, Peoria, Ariz.

NEW YORK METS

June—Regular Phase (6)

1. **Geoff Goetz, lhp, Jesuit HS, Tampa**
2. **Tyler Walker, rhp, California**
3. **Cesar Crespo, ss, Notre Dame HS, Caguas, P.R.**
4. **Michael Yancy, of, Morse HS, San Diego**
5. **Brian Jenkins, c, Port St. Joe (Fla.) HS**
6. **Matt Lowe, rhp, Walhalla (S.C.) HS**
7. **Robert Weslowski, rhp, Marcellus (N.Y.) Central HS**
8. **Vicente Rosario, of, George Washington HS, New York**
9. **Kenny Miller, ss, Kentucky**
10. Garrett Atkins, 3b, University HS, Irvine, Calif.
11. **John Mangieri, rhp, St. Francis (N.Y.)**
12. **Nick Maness, rhp, North Moore HS, Robbins, N.C.**
13. **Eric Cammack, rhp, Lamar**
14. Craig Kuzmic, c, Cypress (Calif.) JC
15. Jeremy Guthrie, rhp, Ashland (Ore.) HS
16. **Mark Proctor, ss, Courtland HS, Fredericksburg, Va.**
17. **Bobby Hill, ss, Gainesville HS, Waldo, Fla.**
18. Dominic Rich, 2b, Line Mountain HS, Herndan, Pa.
19. **Nick Rains, of, John Carroll HS, Fort Pierce, Fla.**
20. **Jason Roach, 3b, UNC Wilmington**
21. **Jason Brett, ss, South Georgia JC**
22. Marcellus Presley, of, Hiram Johnson HS, Sacramento
23. Seth Davidson, ss, University HS, San Diego
24. **Jason Phillips, c, San Diego State**
25. Brandon Mayfield, rhp, Jefferson State (Ala.) CC
26. **J.D. Arteaga, lhp, Miami**
27. Matt Ardizzone, 2b, Delaware
28. Anthony Brown, of, DuPont HS, Hockessin, Del.
29. **Jose Rijo-Berger, of, Lewis-Clark State (Idaho)**
30. **Jason Shuck, ss, Carl Albert State (Okla.) JC**
31. **Randy Hamilton, lhp, Northern Kentucky**
32. **Jorge Santiago, ss, Marist**
33. **Shawn Mikkola, rhp, Largo (Fla.) HS**
34. Barry Paulk, of, Southridge HS, Miami
35. Miguel Miranda, ss, Academy HS, Rio Piedras, P.R.
36. Greg White, 1b, James Madison
37. Brandon Lyon, rhp, Taylorsville HS, Salt Lake City
38. Barry Wichert, lhp, Seminole State (Okla.) JC
39. Robert Scott, 2b, Cowley County (Kan.) CC
40. Randy Keisler, lhp, Navarro (Texas) JC
41. David Benham, c, Liberty
42. **David Lohrman, rhp, Rensselaer Polytechnic (N.Y.) Institute**
43. David DeJesus, of, Manalapan (N.J.) HS
44. Kevin Zaug, rhp, Carmel HS, Stormville, N.Y.
45. **Anthony Valentine, 2b, New Hampshire**
46. **Jason Bowring, 3b, Riverside (Calif.) CC**
47. Tanner Brock, rhp, Lake Brantley HS, Altamonte Springs, Fla.
48. Matt Whitehead, rhp, Athens (Texas) HS
49. Jeremy Jackson, lhp, Mississippi State
50. **Mark Maberry, rhp, Tennessee Tech**
51. Elvin Cannon, of, Northland HS, Columbus, Ohio
52. Mike Tonis, c, Elk Grove (Calif.) HS
53. **Mathias Fafard, 3b, Indian River (Fla.) CC**
54. Anthony Sutter, ss, Brookdale (N.J.) CC
55. Brian Kuklick, rhp, Wake Forest
56. **Joshua Taylor, ss, Cowley County (Kan.) CC**
57. **Clark Lambert, c, Lipscomb**
58. Ryan Lamattina, lhp, St. Bonaventure

NEW YORK YANKEES

June—Regular Phase (24)

1. Tyrell Godwin, of, East Bladen HS, Elizabethtown, N.C. (Pick from Rangers as compensation for Type A free agent John Wetteland)
1. (Pick to Orioles as compensation for Type A free agent David Wells)
1. **Ryan Bradley, rhp, Arizona State** (Supplemental pick—40th—for loss of Wetteland)
2. (Pick to Rangers as compensation for Type A free agent Mike Stanton)
2. **Jason Henry, rhp, Illinois-Chicago** (Supplemental pick—84th—for loss of Type C free agent Jimmy Key)
3. **Mike Knowles, rhp, Palatka (Fla.) HS**
4. **Dion Washington, of, JC of Southern Idaho**
5. **Randy Choate, lhp, Florida State**
6. **John Darjean, of, Dallas Baptist**
7. **Scott Wiggins, lhp, Northern Kentucky**
8. **Jeremy Morris, of, Florida State**
9. **Randy Flores, lhp, Southern California**
10. David Parrish, c, Esperanza HS, Yorba Linda, Calif.
11. **Cody Klein, lhp, Andrews (Texas) HS**
12. Ernie Villegas, of, Irving (Texas) HS
13. Brian Tallet, lhp, Hill (Texas) JC
14. **Chris Wallace, rhp, Wright State**
15. **Marc Mirizzi, ss, Southern California**
16. **Matt Purkiss, 3b, San Francisco**
17. Albert Jones, of, Pasco Comprehensive HS, Dade City, Fla.
18. **Brian August, 3b, Delaware**
19. Michael Shelley, lhp, Ashford (Ala.) HS
20. Paul Manning, of, Hunting Hill HS, Red Deer, Alberta
21. **Bill Bronikowski, c, Toledo**
22. Beau Hale, rhp, Little Cypress HS, Mauriceville, Texas
23. **David Langston, rhp, Ringgold (Ga.) HS**
24. **Jack Koch, rhp, Tampa**
25. **Stanton Wood, rhp, El Camino (Calif.) JC**
26. **Aaron Jones, 1b, Southern Illinois**
27. Robert Fischer, ss, Lyons Township HS, La Grange, Ill.
28. Adam Huddleston, 1b, Mississippi Gulf Coast JC
29. Matt Vincent, lhp, Logan (Ill.) JC
30. Keith Dunn, rhp, Grayson County (Texas) JC
31. Digno Torres, of, Jaime Collazo HS, Morovis, P.R.
32. Brandon Davis, c, George County HS, Lucedale, Miss.
33. Carlos Arvizu, 1b, Tucson HS

34. Jarrod Douglass, rhp, Briarcliff HS, Bayshore, N.Y.
35. Dustin Franklin, lhp, Odessa (Texas) JC
36. Chris Parrish, c, Jackson State (Tenn.) CC
37. Marshall McDougall, ss, Santa Fe (Fla.) CC
38. Nathan Kent, rhp, Motlow State (Tenn.) CC
39. Jeremy Lyon, of, Donelson Christian Academy, Old Hickory, Tenn.
40. **Mike Vento, of, New Mexico JC**
41. **Chris Spurling, rhp, Sinclair (Ohio) CC**
42. Robert Mapp, lhp, Turner HS, Burneyville, Okla.
43. David Rodriguez, of, Southridge HS, Miami
44. **Andy Smith, rhp, Bowling Green State**
45. **Jason Halper, of, Columbia**
46. Chad Conner, rhp, South Bend, Ind.
47. Matthew Berry, rhp, Christian HS, Lakeside, Calif.
48. Dylan Putnam, rhp, St. Mary's Prep, Ann Arbor, Mich.
49. Dan Seimetz, 1b, Ohio State
50. Blake Wilsford, 3b, Collierville (Tenn.) HS
51. Chad Harris, rhp, Jasper (Texas) HS
52. Anthony McNeal, 3b, Cosumnes River (Calif.) JC
53. Robert Fletcher, c, Southland Academy, Americus, Ga.
54. **Russ Chambliss, of, Washington (Mo.)**
55. Aaron Heilman, rhp, Logansport (Ind.) HS
56. Corey Ward, of, Dallas, Texas
57. Mark Gilliam, 1b, Grundy County HS, Pelham, Texas
58. Jeffrey Rossi, lhp, Skyline HS, Salt Lake City
59. Adam Manley, of, Clover Park HS, Tacoma
60. David Clark, of, Denham Springs (La.) HS
61. Eric Rodriguez, rhp, Aureo Quiles HS, Guanica, P.R.
62. Paul Schlosser, 3b, McCoy HS, Medicine Hat, Alberta
63. John Phillips, rhp, UCLA
64. Nicolas Alvarez, rhp, Socorro HS, El Paso
65. Javier Sein, 1b, Palm Beach (Fla.) CC
66. Nicholas Herz, c, Palomar (Calif.) JC
67. Rodney Friar, c, Mount San Jacinto (Calif.) JC
68. Scott Glaser, lhp, South Florida

OAKLAND ATHLETICS

June—Regular Phase (11)

1. **Chris Enochs, rhp, West Virginia**
1. **Eric DuBose, lhp, Mississippi State** (Supplemental pick—21st—for loss of service-time free agent Mike Bordick)
1. **Nathan Haynes, of, Pinole Valley HS, Hercules, Calif.** (Supplemental pick—32nd—for loss of Bordick)
1. **Denny Wagner, rhp, Virginia Tech** (Supplemental pick—42nd—for loss of Bordick)
2. **Chad Harville, rhp, Memphis**
3. **Marcus Jones, rhp, Long Beach State**
4. **Jason Anderson, lhp, Radford**
5. **Andy Kimball, rhp, Wisconsin-Oshkosh**
6. **Tim Hudson, rhp, Auburn**
7. **Roberto Vaz, of, Alabama**
8. **Adam Piatt, 3b, Mississippi State**
9. **Jared Jensen, rhp, Brigham Young**
10. **Javier Flores, c, Oklahoma**
11. **Mike Koerner, of, Louisiana State**
12. **Adam Robinson, ss, Virginia**
13. Jonathan Winterrowd, rhp, Germantown (Tenn.) HS
14. Ryan Drese, rhp, California
15. **Eric Meeks, rhp, West Orange HS, Orlando**
16. **Jamie Porter, of, Washington**
17. **Elvin Nina, rhp, Oklahoma State**
18. **Mike Holmes, rhp, Wake Forest**
19. Josh Canales, ss, Carson (Calif.) HS
20. **Randy Niles, rhp, Florida State**
21. **Brad Gorrie, ss, Massachusetts**
22. Forrest Johnson, c, Rialto (Calif.) HS
23. **Gary Thomas, 3b/of, Vanderbilt Catholic HS, Houma, La.**
24. **Jeremy Crawford, lhp, Glenwood HS, Chatham, Ill.**
25. Ronnie Williams, of, Booker HS, Sarasota, Fla.
26. **David Waites, rhp, New Mexico**
27. **Miguel Declet, ss, Eloisa Pascual HS, Caguas, P.R.**
28. **Ed Farris, 1b, Ball State**
29. Stephen Murphy, rhp, Canada (Calif.) JC
30. **Tim Manwiller, rhp, Radford**
31. Jon Weber, of, Los Angeles Harbor JC
32. Tim Newman, rhp, Davis HS, Yakima, Wash.
33. Ian Perio, lhp, Laney (Calif.) JC
34. Keith Foxton, of, Kirkwood (Iowa) CC
35. Brandon Pack, c, Esperanza HS, Yorba Linda, Calif.
36. **Jason Faust, lhp, New Orleans**
37. Marshall Rubens, rhp, Del Campo HS, Citrus Heights, Calif.
38. Matt Carlock, rhp, Armijo HS, Suisun City, Calif.
39. Tony Dawson, rhp, Laney (Calif.) JC
40. Will Lewis, of, Rialto HS, Adelanto, Calif.

PHILADELPHIA PHILLIES

June—Regular Phase (2)

1. J.D. Drew, of, Florida State
2. **Randy Wolf, lhp, Pepperdine**
3. **Shomari Beverly, of, Encinal HS, Alameda, Calif.**
4. **Nick Marchant, of, Capital HS, Boise, Idaho**
5. **Derrick Turnbow, rhp, Franklin (Tenn.) HS**
6. **Tom Jacquez, lhp, UCLA**
7. **Derek Adair, rhp, St. John's**
8. **Brian Harris, ss, Indiana**
9. Michael Schulte, rhp, Cleveland HS, Reseda, Calif.
10. **Bennie Bishop, of, Westchester HS, Inglewood, Calif.**
11. **Kevin Kurilla, ss, Virginia Tech**
12. **Mark Rutherford, rhp, Eastern Michigan**
13. Lance Niekro, ss, Jenkins HS, Lakeland, Fla.
14. **Geoff Zawatski, rhp, Virginia**
15. **Troy Norrell, c, Navarro (Texas) JC**
16. Brett Weber, rhp, Illinois
17. **Johnny Estrada, c/1b, JC of the Sequoias (Calif.)**
18. **Duane Johnson, of, Wooster HS, Reno, Nev.**
19. **Jimmy Frush, rhp, Texas Tech**
20. **Jeff Terrell, 2b, Missouri**
21. **Rusty McNamara, of/3b, Oklahoma State**
22. **Gary Burnham, of, Clemson**
23. **Brett Black, rhp, North Carolina State**
24. **Pat Driscoll, lhp, Nebraska**
25. **Jerry Valdez, c, Fort Hays State (Kan.)**
26. **Andy Dominique, 3b, Nevada**
27. **Adam Walker, lhp, Mississippi**
28. **Kevin Shipp, rhp, Louisiana State**
29. **Chad Albaugh, rhp, William Penn (Iowa)**
30. Kevin Leighton, c, Brewster (N.Y.) HS
31. **Mark Manbeck, rhp, Houston**
32. **Chris Humphries, rhp, Nevada-Las Vegas**
33. **Ed Fitzpatrick, c, Freed-Hardeman (Tenn.)**
34. **Lamonte Collier, ss, Southeast Missouri State**
35. **Calvin Key, rhp, Arkansas State**
36. **Jeff Hootselle, lhp, Mary Washington (Va.)**
37. **Uriel Casillas, ss, Cal State Los Angeles**
38. **Clay Eason, rhp, North Carolina State**
39. **Peter Mondello, rhp, Nicholls State**
40. **Ryan Cody, c, Fort Vancouver (Wash.) HS**
41. **Jim Fritz, c, Southwestern Louisiana**
42. John Marifan, lhp, Cerritos (Calif.) JC
43. David Walther, 2b, De Smet Jesuit HS, St. Louis
44. **Jonathan Bushman, of, Lindbergh HS, St. Louis**

PITTSBURGH PIRATES

June—Regular Phase (8)

1. **J.J. Davis, 1b/rhp, Baldwin Park HS, Pomona, Calif.**
2. **Jose Nicolas, of, Westminster Christian HS, Miami**
3. **John Grabow, lhp, San Gabriel (Calif.) HS**
4. **Maurice Washington, of, Chaparral HS, Las Vegas**
5. **Chris Combs, rhp/of, North Carolina State**
6. **Andy Bausher, lhp, Kutztown (Pa.)**
7. **Kory DeHaan, of, Morningside (Iowa)**
8. **Paul Stabile, lhp, Brookdale (N.J.) CC**
9. **Michael Parkerson, lhp, Columbus (Ga.) HS**
10. **Rico Washington, ss, Jones County HS, Gray, Ga.**
11. **Sam McConnell, lhp, Ball State**
12. Jeff Leuenberger, rhp, Canyon HS, Anaheim

13. **Kris Lambert, lhp, Baylor**
14. Ryan Carter, lhp, Beyer HS, Modesto, Calif.
15. Jason Moore, ss, Westminster Christian HS, Miami
16. **Jason Hardebeck, lhp, Carl Sandburg (Ill.) JC**
17. **Chris Luttig, lhp, Evansville**
18. Shawn Schumacher, c/3b, Panola (Texas) JC
19. **Andrew Jones, of, Mountain Point HS, Phoenix**
20. **Kevin Haverbusch, ss/rhp, Maryland**
21. **Keith Maxwell, of/c, Florida A&M**
22. **Alex Tolbert, 1b, Western Carolina**
23. Michael Smalley, lhp, Bishop Moore HS, Maitland, Fla.
24. Jeff Carlsen, rhp, North Kitsap HS, Poulsbo, Wash.
25. Jesse Daggett, c, JC of the Canyons (Calif.)
26. Michael Wiggs, ss, Mount Olive (N.C.)
27. **Brad Guy, rhp, Cal State Los Angeles**
28. Matt Wood, rhp, Cary (N.C.) HS
29. Ryan Earey, 3b, Laney HS, Wilmington, N.C.
30. **Mike Gonzalez, lhp, San Jacinto (Texas) JC**
31. Jeff LaRoche, lhp, Blinn (Texas) JC
32. Marcus Harris, lhp, Cabrillo HS, Lompoc, Calif.
33. Bill White, lhp, Benjamin Russell HS, Alexander City, Ala.
34. C.J. Steele, ss, Spiro (Okla.) HS
35. Jamal Strong, of/ss, Citrus (Calif.) JC
36. Jeff Phelps, ss, Kofa HS, Yuma, Ariz.
37. **Chris Clark, of, Stanford**
38. Mike Scarborough, of, Texas
39. Josh Newton, rhp, Springhill (La.) HS
40. **Peter Austin, of, Millsaps (Miss.)**
41. Kevin Brown, 3b, North Fort Myers (Fla.) HS
42. **Derrick Lankford, 3b, Carson-Newman (Tenn.)**
43. **Brett Kaplan, of, North Carolina**

ST. LOUIS CARDINALS

June—Regular Phase (20)

1. **Adam Kennedy, ss, Cal State Northridge**
2. **Rick Ankiel, lhp, Port St. Lucie (Fla.) HS**
3. **Patrick Coogan, rhp, Louisiana State**
4. Xavier Nady, ss, Salinas (Calif.) HS
5. **Jason Navarro, lhp, Tulane**
6. **Bryan Rupert, c, Limestone (S.C.)**
7. **Joe Secoda, 2b, Rancho Santiago (Calif.) JC**
8. **Jason Karnuth, rhp, Illinois State**
9. Seth Etherton, rhp, Southern California
10. **Finley Woodward, rhp, Auburn**
11. **Reynaldo Torres, 1b, Aurea Quiles HS, Guanica, P.R.**
12. **Aaron Gentry, ss, Berry (Ga.)**
13. **Derek Feramisco, of, Fresno State**
14. **Rob Macrory, 2b, Auburn**
15. Jason Michaels, of, Miami
16. **Jeremy Lambert, rhp, Kearns (Utah) HS**
17. **Tim Davis, of, Atkinson County HS, Pearson, Ga.**
18. **David Kim, of, Seton Hall**
19. Jeff Munster, rhp, Fresno CC
20. **Justin Brunette, lhp, San Diego State**
21. Wes McCrotty, lhp, Russellville (Ark.) HS
22. **Tristan Jerue, rhp, Georgia**
23. **Chris Martine, c, George Mason**
24. **Jose Rodriguez, lhp, Florida International**
25. **Michael Huffaker, rhp, Birmingham-Southern**
26. **Craig Hopson, rhp, Boylan Catholic HS, Rockford, Ill.**
27. **Luke Quaccia, 1b, Stanford**
28. **Neal Arnold, rhp, Nebraska-Kearney**
29. **Derek Gooden, rhp, Brewton-Parker (Ga.)**
30. **Taber Maier, ss, Cal Poly San Luis Obispo**
31. **Brady Gick, c, Ohio**
32. Andy Kroneberger, 2b, Camarillo (Calif.) HS
33. **Blake Ledbetter, c, Bertrand, Mo.**
34. **Michael Speckhardt, of, Marist**
35. **Robert Vazquez, 3b, Westmar (Iowa)**
36. **Andy Bevins, of, San Diego State**
37. Stephen Schaub, of, Cowley County (Kan.) CC
38. **Carl Gooden, of, MacArthur HS, Houston**
39. **Remer McIntyre, of, Hillsborough HS, Tampa**
40. **Scott Wilson, 3b/rhp, Tulane**
41. Doug Gant, lhp, Central HS, Macon, Ga.
42. Jeremy Weinburg, 3b, Sonora HS, La Habra, Calif.
43. Cody Getz, lhp, Wooster HS, Reno, Nev.
44. William Eyre, rhp, Snow (Utah) JC
45. Lionel Rogers, rhp, Fresno CC
46. Josh Dorminy, 1b, Middle Georgia JC

SAN DIEGO PADRES

June—Regular Phase (26)

1. **Kevin Nicholson, ss, Stetson**
2. **Ben Howard, rhp, Central Merry HS, Jackson, Tenn.**
3. **Jerry Darr, rhp, Glen Rose HS, Malvern, Ark.**
4. **Tony Lawrence, c, Louisiana Tech**
5. Tim Hummel, ss, Burke HS, Montgomery, N.Y.
6. **Brittan Motley, of, Hickman Mills HS, Kansas City, Mo.**
7. **Douglas Young, rhp, Sierra (Calif.) JC**
8. **Jason Dunaway, ss, Seward County (Kan.) CC**
9. **Junior Herndon, rhp, Moffat County HS, Craig, Colo.**
10. **Tony Cosentino, c, West Torrance (Calif.) HS**
11. **Dave Maurer, lhp, Oklahoma State**
12. **Pat Ryan, rhp, South Florida**
13. **Brent Horsman, of, Solano (Calif.) CC**
14. **Brian Dowell, rhp, Alvin (Texas) CC**
15. **Kevin Burford, of, Rancho Santiago (Calif.) JC**
16. **Shawn Camp, rhp, George Mason**
17. Michael Tejada, c, Provo (Utah) HS
18. **Brandon Hemmings, of, Abraham Baldwin (Ga.) JC**
19. **Karl Ryden, of, Alvin (Texas) CC**
20. Jonathon Stone, 2b, Lodi (Calif.) HS
21. **Johnny Hunter, of, Texas A&M**
22. **Ricky Guttormson, rhp, Edmonds (Wash.) CC**
23. **Scott Seal, 1b, Cal State Fullerton**
24. **Clay Snellgrove, ss, Middle Tennessee State**
25. **Brian Jergenson, of/1b, Northern Iowa**
26. Patrick Bourland, ss, Durango (Colo.) HS
27. Ron French, c, Northgate HS, Concord, Calif.
28. **Joe DeMarco, ss, Kansas**
29. Shawn Garrett, ss, South Central HS, Kinmundy, Ill.
30. **Todd Naff, rhp, St. Edward's (Texas)**
31. **Jon Oisseth, lhp, Kansas State**
32. Ryan O'Donnell, c, Casa Grande (Ariz.) HS
33. Chad Olszanski, ss, San Pasqual HS, Escondido, Calif.
34. **Jason Rakers, 3b, Quincy (Ill.)**
35. **Bryan DeLeon, rhp, Trujillo Alto, P.R.**
36. **Dustin Viator, rhp, Nicholls State**
37. Greg Bochy, rhp, Mount Carmel HS, Poway, Calif.
38. Josh France, c, Brophy Jesuit HS, Phoenix
39. **Jesse Curry, 1b, Gresham (Ore.) Union HS**
40. **Gus Ornstein, 1b, Michigan State**
41. Ryan Quinn, 3b, Brother Rice HS, Chicago
42. **Bryce Trudeau, rhp, San Bernardino HS, Redlands, Calif.**

SAN FRANCISCO GIANTS

June—Regular Phase (4)

1. **Jason Grilli, rhp, Seton Hall**
1. **Dan McKinley, of, Arizona State** (Supplemental pick—49th—for failure to sign 1996 first-rounder Matt White)
2. **Scott Linebrink, rhp, Southwest Texas State**
3. **Jeff Andra, lhp, Oklahoma**
4. Kevin McGerry, rhp, Father Judge HS, Philadelphia
5. **Giuseppe Chiaramonte, c, Fresno State**
6. **Kevin Joseph, rhp, Rice**
7. **Joe Farley, lhp, Capital HS, Olympia, Wash.**
8. **Brett Casper, of, Oral Roberts**
9. Todd Bellhorn, lhp, Central Florida
10. Joe Holland, lhp, Bowling Green State
11. **Travis Young, 2b, New Mexico**
12. **Jason Verdugo, rhp, Arizona State**
13. **C.J. Ankrum, 1b, Cal State Fullerton**
14. **William Otero, ss, Ohio Dominican**
15. **Mike Byas, of, Southwest Missouri State**
16. **Tom Nielsen, lhp, Fordham**
17. Scott Goodman, of, Cuesta (Calif.) JC

18. **Darin Cissell, of, Saint Louis**
19. **Nathan Rice, lhp, Cal State Northridge**
20. **Jesse Travis, rhp, Portland**
21. Paul Stryhas, 3b, Manatee (Fla.) CC
22. **Mark Hills, lhp, Chemeketa (Ore.) CC**
23. **Bryan Guse, c, Minnesota**
24. **Will Malerich, lhp, William & Mary**
25. Justin Lincoln, ss, Sarasota (Fla.) HS
26. Todd Uzzell, rhp, El Paso (Texas) CC
27. **Shawn Austin, lhp, Florida Southern**
28. George Crawford, of, Madison HS, Portland, Ore.
29. **Zachary Wells, of, Diablo Valley (Calif.) JC**
30. **Tim Flaherty, c, East Carolina**
31. **Clay Greene, 2b/of, Tennessee**
32. Luis Santiago, rhp, Adolfo Rivera HS, Penuelas, P.R.
33. Mike Stevenson, rhp, Orange Coast (Calif.) JC
34. Ty Burch, of, Cosumnes River (Calif.) JC
35. Shawn Lindsey, of, Lower Columbia (Wash.) JC
36. Dennis Anderson, c, Pima (Ariz.) CC
37. Jonathan Storke, ss, Cuesta (Calif.) JC
38. Lance Woodcock, ss, American River (Calif.) JC
39. Justin Thurman, lhp, Blue Mountain (Ore.) CC
40. Andy Neufeld, ss, Oviedo HS, Winter Springs, Fla.
41. Clifton Bowie, of, Alba HS, Bayou La Batre, Ala.
42. John Tatum, c, Forest Hill HS, West Palm Beach, Fla.
43. **Mark Mosier, 3b, Chicago**
44. **Jeremy Luster, 3b/1b, DeKalb (Ga.) JC**
45. **Chad Faircloth, of, UNC Asheville**

SEATTLE MARINERS

June—Regular Phase (19)

1. **Ryan Anderson, lhp, Divine Child HS, Westland, Mich.**
2. **Brandon Parker, rhp, Southern Mississippi** (Pick from Angels as compensation for Type B free agent Dave Hollins)
2. Patrick Boyd, of, Central Catholic HS, Clearwater, Fla.
3. **Patrick Dunham, rhp, Auburn**
4. **Scott Prouty, rhp, Pekin HS, Marquette Heights, Ill.**
5. **Jermaine Clark, 2b, San Francisco**
6. **Harvey Hargrove, 2b, Sacramento State**
7. **Sam Walton, lhp, W.W. Samuel HS, Dallas**
8. **Allan Simpson, rhp, Taft (Calif.) JC**
9. Frank Corr, c, Father Lopez HS, Deltona, Fla.
10. **Peter Duprey, lhp, Forest HS, Ocala, Fla.**
11. **Cip Garcia, c, La Cueva HS, Rio Rancho, N.M.**
12. **Joel Pineiro, rhp, Edison (Fla.) CC**
13. **Bret Soverel, rhp, Florida International**
14. Peter Bauer, rhp, Paint Branch HS, Silver Spring, Md.
15. Richard Sundstrom, rhp, Cypress (Calif.) JC
16. **Danny Delgado, rhp, Monsignor Pace HS, Miami**
17. **Clint Chrysler, lhp, Stetson**
18. Ryan Oase, rhp/1b, Edmonds (Wash.) CC
19. Jamie Clark, of, Brandon (Fla.) HS
20. **Mike Marchiano, of, Fordham**
21. **Emmanuel Ulloa, rhp, George Washington HS, Bronx, N.Y.**
22. **Hubert Parker, ss/2b, Eisenhower HS, Rialto, Calif.**
23. Jim Abbott, rhp, Caledonia (Mich.) HS
24. Jason Farren, rhp, Karns City (Pa.) Area HS
25. Ryan Reynolds, 3b, The Woodlands (Texas) HS
26. Glenn Murphy, lhp, Madison County (Fla.) HS
27. John Gabaldon, rhp, La Cueva HS, Albuquerque
28. Kirk Bolling, rhp, Saddleback (Calif.) CC
29. Matt Huntingford, of, West Vancouver (B.C.) HS
30. **Aaron Looper, rhp, Westark (Ark.) CC**
31. Matt Woodward, 1b, Florida State
32. Dave Garley, rhp, Glendale (Calif.) CC
33. Cordell Lindsey, 3b, Blinn (Texas) JC
34. Eric Mitchell, c, DuBois (Pa.) Area HS
35. Israel Torres, lhp, Dominguez HS, Compton, Calif.
36. Brian Ferreira, of, Barron Collier HS, Naples, Fla.
37. Mario Jackson, of, Pasadena (Calif.) CC
38. Ryan Webb, 3b, Citrus (Calif.) JC
39. Brian Spottsville, ss, Compton (Calif.) HS
40. Joseph Reyes, ss, Farmington (N.M.) HS
41. Kaazim Summerville, of, Burlingame (Calif.) HS
42. Andrew Padilla, ss, Highland HS, Bakersfield, Calif.
43. Bryan Krill, rhp, Rancho Santiago (Calif.) JC
44. Peter Graham, rhp, Brookdale (N.J.) CC
45. Shaun Stokes, rhp, Jefferson Township HS, Oak Ridge, N.J.
46. Barry Hawkins, rhp, Saddleback (Calif.) CC
47. Thomas Cunningham, c, Leesburg (Fla.) HS
48. Nick Padilla, rhp, St. Paul HS, Whittier, Calif.
49. Joe Barnes, of, Indian River (Fla.) CC
50. Jonathan Brandt, rhp, Palo Alto (Calif.) HS
51. Chris Silva, lhp, Queensborough (N.Y.) CC
52. Shah Bobonis, rhp, Southridge HS, Miami
53. Scott Starkey, lhp, Palomar (Calif.) JC
54. Kie Polard, of, Crenshaw HS, Los Angeles
55. D.J. Houlton, rhp, Servite HS, Yorba Linda, Calif.
56. Kevin Bice, rhp, Rancho Santiago (Calif.) JC
57. Kyle Albright, of, Palomar (Calif.) JC
58. Chris Mayberry, 3b, Saugus (Calif.) HS
59. Jamel White, of, Antelope Valley (Calif.) JC
60. Desmond Dailey, of, Eastern Arizona JC

TAMPA BAY DEVIL RAYS

June—Regular Phase (30)

1. **Jason Standridge, rhp, Hewitt Trussville HS, Trussville, Ala.**
2. **Kenny Kelly, of, Tampa Catholic HS**
3. **Barrett Wright, rhp, Myers Park HS, Charlotte**
4. **Todd Belitz, lhp, Washington State**
5. **Marquis Roberts, lhp/of, McLane HS, Fresno**
6. **Doug Mansfield, of, Jacksonville HS, Sherwood, Ark.**
7. **Eddy Reyes, rhp, Miami**
8. **Jack Joffrion, ss, Lamar**
9. **Toby Hall, c, Nevada-Las Vegas**
10. Carl Hutchens, rhp, Anderson HS, Austin
11. **Chris Wright, rhp, Cowley County (Kan.) CC**
12. **Carlos Vazquez, c, Caribbean HS, Ponce, P.R.**
13. **Kevin Price, rhp, Bingham HS, Riverton, Utah**
14. **Robert Davis, lhp, Boyd County HS, Ashland, Ky.**
15. **Jason Guerrero, ss, Pittsburg (Calif.) HS**
16. Lazaro Gutierrez, lhp, Miami
17. Chris Bootcheck, rhp, LaPorte (Ind.) HS
18. **Terry McCormick, lhp, Jesuit HS, Tampa**
19. Lavar Johnson, of, North Shore HS, Houston
20. Matt Kaffel, rhp, Blinn (Texas) JC
21. **Damian Scioneaux, of, Mississippi State**
22. **Dustin Carr, 2b, Houston**
23. **Paul Hoover, ss, Kent State**
24. **Travis Miller, of, Dallas Baptist**
25. Josh Davis, rhp, Tallahassee (Fla.) CC
26. Coty Cooper, rhp, Seward County (Kan.) CC
27. **Anthony Pigott, of, Elon**
28. **Jason Jimenez, lhp, San Jose State**
29. Ryan Jorgensen, c, Kingwood (Texas) HS
30. **Jon Cummins, rhp, Indiana (Pa.)**
31. Michael Meseberg, of, Royal HS, Othello, Wash.
32. Jeremy Murch, lhp, Sarasota (Fla.) HS
33. Daniel Firlit, ss, Rend Lake (Ill.) JC
34. Kris Ehmke, rhp, Thomas Stewart HS, Peterborough, Ontario
35. Ben Peterson, rhp, East Lake HS, Tarpon Springs, Fla.
36. **Chris Mason, rhp, Alabama-Birmingham**
37. **Heath McKoin, lhp, Watson Chapel HS, Pine Bluff, Ark.**
38. **Ryan Pandolfini, 1b, Rider**
39. Jim Munroe, rhp, Servite HS, Orange, Calif.
40. David Cash, rhp, Davis HS, Modesto, Calif.
41. John Hutchens, rhp, Fort Gibson (Okla.) HS
42. Lee Southard, rhp, Westmoore HS, Oklahoma City
43. Nicholas Rhodes, c, Norwalk (Conn.) CC
44. Alan Lowden, lhp, Hays HS, Kyle, Texas
45. Adam Luczycky, rhp, Labette Community (Kan.) JC
46. Marlyn Tisdale, rhp, Florida CC-Jacksonville
47. Fred Mitchell, of, Kathleen HS, Lakeland, Fla.
48. Josh Long, 3b, Northview HS, McDavid, Fla.
49. Jason Balkcom, rhp, Young Harris (Ga.) JC
50. **Chris Reynolds, rhp, North Lake (Texas) CC**
51. Ivar Wentzel, lhp, Flagler Palm Coast HS, Palm Coast, Fla.

52. Kyle Evans, rhp, El Dorado HS, Albuquerque
53. Dustin McKey, of, John Carroll HS, Alabaster, Ala.
54. Alan Keller, c, Mendocino (Calif.) CC
55. Tyler Tiesing, c, Butler County (Kan.) CC
56. Nick Lyon, of, Monroe (Wash.) HS
57. Jeremy Robinson, lhp, Okaloosa-Walton (Fla.) CC
58. David Berry, c, Pearce HS, Richardson, Texas
59. Cedric Razor, 2b, Pitt County (N.C.) CC
60. Richard McCabe, rhp, Camden HS, St. Mary's, Ga.
61. Ron Brooks, rhp, Tallahassee (Fla.) CC
62. Tavaris Keyes, rhp, Central HS, Fort Pierce, Fla.
63. Steve Gause, rhp, Jenkins HS, Lakeland, Fla.
64. Chris Wood, ss, Vanguard HS, Ocala, Fla.
65. Zachary Roper, 3b, Pasco-Hernando (Fla.) CC
66. Ray Nevels, of, Sarasota (Fla.) HS
67. Rafael Erazo, rhp, Labette Community (Kan.) JC
68. Dusty Hall, ss, Lincoln HS, Gahanna, Ohio
69. Heath Bell, rhp, Rancho Santiago (Calif.) JC
70. Kenny Baugh, rhp, Lamar HS, Houston
71. Carlos Perez, 2b, Roosevelt HS, Brooklyn
72. Julio Fortuna, rhp, Bushwick HS, Brooklyn
73. John Gillespie, rhp, Lake Washington HS, Redmond, Wash.
74. Jarrod Reineke, rhp, Grove HS, Joplin, Mo.
75. Brian Brown, ss, Olney Central (Ill.) JC
76. Brandon Brewer, rhp, Greely HS, Yarmouth, Maine
77. Jeff Dragg, of, Covington HS, Madisonville, La.
78. Rob Meyers, rhp, De La Salle HS, Concord, Calif.
79. Jon Smith, lhp, Ferris HS, Nuevo, Calif.
80. Clint Kinsey, rhp, Allen County (Kan.) CC
81. Jon Williams, c, Fox HS, Imperial, Mo.
82. Zach Lekse, ss, Sacramento CC
83. Blake Williams, rhp, San Marcos (Texas) HS
84. Mark Madsen, rhp, Quartz Hill HS, Lancaster, Calif.
85. Chad Ashlock, rhp, Seward County (Kan.) CC
86. Bryan Edwards, rhp, Bowie HS, Austin
87. Jon Benick, c, Greater Nanticoke HS, Glen Lyon, Pa.
88. **Bart Carter, 1b, William Carey (Miss.)**
89. Robby Hammock, c, DeKalb (Ga.) JC
90. William Harris, 2b/ss, Middle Georgia JC
91. Beau Barcus, 3b, San Lorenzo HS, Ben Lomond, Calif.
92. Andy Baxter, ss, Unicoi County HS, Erwin, Tenn.

TEXAS RANGERS

June—Regular Phase (23)

1. (Pick to Yankees as compensation for Type A free agent John Wetteland)
1. **Jason Romano, 3b, Hillsborough HS, Tampa** (Supplemental pick—39th—for loss of Type A free agent Mike Stanton)
2. **Jason Grabowski, c, Connecticut**
2. **Chris Tynan, rhp, Hudson's Bay HS, Vancouver, Wash.** (Pick from Yankees as compensation for Stanton)
3. **Brandon Warriax, ss, Purnell Swett HS, Pembroke, N.C.**
4. **Dave Elder, rhp, Georgia Tech**
5. **Trey Poland, lhp, Southwestern Louisiana**
6. **Dan DeYoung, rhp, Mississippi**
7. **Mike Lamb, c, Cal State Fullerton**
8. **Billy Diaz, rhp, Academia Adventista HS, Caguas, P.R.**
9. **Carlos Figueroa, lhp, Jose Lazaro HS, Carolina, P.R.**
10. **Kevin Harris, of, Tampa Bay Tech HS**
11. **Tom Sergio, 2b, North Carolina State**
12. **Corey Wright, of, Workman HS, La Puente, Calif.**
13. Robbie Milner, rhp, Deer Valley HS, Phoenix
14. **Jason Torres, c, John Carroll HS, Vero Beach, Fla.**
15. Karl Jernigan, ss, Milton HS, Navarre, Fla.
16. Kevin Ruedi, rhp, Sacramento CC
17. **Geronimo Cruz, of, Alfred State (N.Y.) JC**
18. Jaime Bubela, of, Cypress Falls HS, Houston
19. **Travis Hughes, rhp, Cowley County (Kan.) CC**
20. Jay Signorelli, rhp, Lake Brantley HS, Altamonte Springs, Fla.
21. **Jeff Ridenour, rhp, Southern Illinois-Edwardsville**
22. Curtis Gay, 1b, Cowley County (Kan.) CC
23. Quenten Patterson, rhp, Blinn (Texas) JC
24. Brian Shipp, ss, Central HS, Baton Rouge
25. **Alex Vazquez, of, Montgomery (Md.) JC**
26. **Spike Lundberg, rhp, San Diego Mesa JC**
27. Tanner Herrick, 1b, Show Low (Ariz.) HS
28. Mike Eskildsen, rhp, Maple Ridge (B.C.) HS
29. Jason Young, rhp, Berkeley (Calif.) HS
30. Derek Hines, of, Yavapai (Ariz.) JC
31. David Curtiss, ss, Havre (Mont.) HS
32. Jeff Fields, c, Alamogordo (N.M.) HS
33. Mitch Jones, 3b, Utah Valley State JC
34. Devon Younger, rhp, Meridian (Miss.) CC
35. Kelley Gulledge, c, Mansfield HS, Arlington, Texas
36. David Wigley, c, George Wallace (Ala.) CC
37. Blakely Allen, rhp, Russell HS, Alexander City, Ala.
38. **Jason Beitey, rhp, Olympic (Wash.) JC**
39. Pete Orr, ss, Newmarket HS, Hamilton, Ontario
40. Craig Mosher, lhp, McRoberts HS, Richmond, British Columbia
41. Josh Hawes, rhp, CC of Rhode Island

TORONTO BLUE JAYS

June—Regular Phase (5)

1. **Vernon Wells, of, Bowie HS, Arlington, Texas**
2. (Pick to Red Sox as compensation for Type A free agent Roger Clemens)
3. **Billy Brown, of, Florida Atlantic**
4. **Woody Heath, rhp, Green River (Wash.) CC**
5. **Michael Young, ss, UC Santa Barbara**
6. **Paul Chiaffredo, c, Santa Clara**
7. **Matt McClellan, rhp, Oakland (Mich.)**
8. **Joe Casey, rhp, Twin Valley HS, Elverson, Pa.**
9. **Carlos Ortiz, c, Loara HS, Anaheim**
10. Matt Bowser, 1b, Tarpon Springs HS, Palm Harbor, Fla.
11. **Ron Bost, lhp, Central Cabarrus HS, Harrisburg, N.C.**
12. **Randy Eversgerd, rhp, Eastern Illinois**
13. **Travis Hubbel, rhp, East Glen Composite HS, Edmonton, Alberta**
14. Cameron Reimers, rhp, Sentinel HS, Missoula, Mont.
15. **Colin Brackeen, lhp, St. Olaf (Minn.)**
16. **Dustin Seale, lhp, Safford (Ariz.) HS**
17. **Brian Barnett, ss, Linfield (Ore.)**
18. **Matt Weimer, rhp, Penn State**
19. **Erik Lorenz, rhp, Wisconsin-Whitewater**
20. **Mark Hendrickson, lhp, Mount Vernon, Wash.**
21. **David Huggins, rhp, McNeese State**
22. **John Sneed, rhp, Texas A&M**
23. Derek DeVaughan, rhp, Seminole State (Okla.) JC
24. **Anthony Salley, lhp, Wofford**
25. Perfecto Gaud, lhp, Luis Munoz Marin HS, Yauco, P.R.
26. Floyd Mack, of, Mays HS, Fairburn, Ga.
27. Fred Smith, of, Volunteer State (Tenn.) CC
28. **Andrew Barrett, ss, Stadium HS, Tacoma**
29. **Juan Santos, c/1b, Florida CC-Jacksonville**
30. **Tim Lacefield, rhp, Harding (Ark.)**
31. **Jermaine Davis, of, Chesnee (S.C.) HS**
32. Sean Green, rhp, Male HS, Louisville
33. **Taylor Smith, rhp, Green Valley HS, Henderson, Nev.**
34. Jamie Jenkins, rhp, Hill HS, Miramachi, New Brunswick
35. Josh Stevens, rhp, Jurupa Valley HS, Mira Loma, Calif.
36. Simon Stoner, rhp, Duchess Park HS, Prince George, British Columbia
37. Jason Burkley, c/3b, Lexington (Ky.) Catholic HS
38. **Chivas Clark, of, Northeast HS, Macon, Ga.**
39. Matt Easterday, 2b, Newton County HS, Covington, Ga.
40. Michael Ramsey, of, Columbus (Ga.) HS
41. Patrick Versluis, rhp, Saddleback (Calif.) CC
42. Andrew Beattie, ss, Pasco-Hernando (Fla.) CC
43. **Orlando Hudson, ss, Spartanburg Methodist (S.C.) JC**
44. Todd Thompson, rhp, Indian Hills (Iowa) CC
45. Brandon Long, lhp, Central Alabama CC
46. Brad Hawpe, lhp, Boswell HS, Fort Worth
47. Jesus Lebron, of, Orlando, Fla.
48. David Siboda, rhp, Southeast Missouri State
49. Anthony Novelli, rhp, West Valley (Calif.) JC
50. Michael Albert, ss, Grossmont (Calif.) JC
51. Chad Schmidt, of, Blinn (Texas) JC
52. Chad Qualls, rhp, Los Angeles Harbor JC

53. Jeff Nettles, 3b, Palomar (Calif.) JC
54. Craig Lariz, 1b, Indian River (Fla.) CC
55. Rashard Casey, of, Penn State
56. Arlyn Dozier, of, Vermillion Catholic HS, Abbeville, La.
57. Travis Cole, rhp, Lakeridge HS, Lake Oswego, Ore.
58. Billy Traber, lhp, El Segundo (Calif.) HS
59. Michael Willetts, rhp, Abraham Baldwin (Ga.) JC
60. Brandon Tellis, of, Charleston (Miss.) HS
61. Gary Peete, of, Itawamba (Miss.) JC
62. Matthew Dempsey, 1b, Cypress (Calif.) JC
63. Charles Lawrence, of, Lakeside HS, Decatur, Ga.
64. Jeremiah Barnes, rhp, Downey (Calif.) HS
65. William Wagner, of, Elmore County HS, Eclectic, Ala.
66. Cameron Newitt, rhp, Northwest Shoals (Ala.) JC
67. Dave Steffler, rhp, Winthrop

1998 After more than a year of headlines, Drew goes back into draft, then signs quickly

J.D. Drew was never the No. 1 pick, and his bonus record was short-lived, but discussion about the 1998 draft centered so much around him that the rest of the class sometimes appeared to be an afterthought.

Scouts talked about it, writers wrote about it. Even major league players such as prospective teammate Curt Schilling and future teammate Mark McGwire chimed in.

Drew was the second pick in the 1997 draft by the Phillies, even though he was regarded as the most talented player in the draft. But Drew's bonus demands were enough to worry teams, and he and the Phillies never came close to bridging their gap. Drew and agent Scott Boras sought a reported $11 million-$12 million.

Drew played for the independent Northern League's St. Paul Saints in the summer of 1997—the first notable draftee to do so—and then sought to be declared a free agent because the draft was for amateurs. Major League Baseball changed the wording of the draft rules to call it the "first-year player draft," but said it was merely a clarification of existing rules.

LINDA CULLEN

J.D. Drew's foray in St. Paul didn't make him a free agent, so he signed in 1998

The Players Association contended that because the commissioner's office unilaterally changed the rule, Drew should be declared a free agent. An arbitrator agreed on the principle but said he could not rule on Drew's status because he wasn't a member of the union. Both sides claimed victory, but the bottom line was that Drew went back into the 1998 draft pool.

On the high school and college fields, most scouts agreed that the Class of 1998 was above-average in overall talent depth but that no single player stood out. This created another predicament for the Phillies as the holders of the first pick.

Miami third baseman Pat Burrell had the best bat in the country but missed half of the college season with back problems. Lefthanders Mark Mulder of Michigan State and Ryan Mills of Arizona State were mature college pitchers who were thought to be able help the beleaguered Phillies staff quickly. Third baseman Sean Burroughs from Wilson High in Long Beach, son of former American League MVP Jeff Burroughs, rounded out the Phillies' short list.

The intrigue over who the first pick would be lost much of its momentum when Burrell returned from his back woes in time for the NCAA regionals and put on an awesome power display. So the intrigue shifted back to Drew, who had returned to the Northern League to keep his skills intact. The Athletics held the second pick and were considering selecting Drew as a bookend to outfielder Ben Grieve. Oakland scouting director Grady Fuson eventually decided on Mulder.

Where was Drew as the draft unfolded? Right where most predicted, available for the Cardinals in the No. 5 slot. The Cardinals had paid Boras client Rick Ankiel, a second-round choice in 1997, a $2.5 million bonus the previous summer, and they quickly came to terms with Drew on a four-year major league contract with a $3 million signing bonus and total value of $8.5 million.

Drew made all the contract negotiations appear almost anticlimatic after his long-awaited professional debut. He made quick three-week stops in Double-A and Triple-A before making his major league debut for the Cardinals the night McGwire hit his 61st home run. Aside from battling numerous injuries, he established himself as a solid player, though not a star, in St. Louis, then with the Dodgers and Red Sox.

The chain reaction to the Drew contract started almost immediately. Philadelphia quickly negotiated a five-year major league deal with Burrell that included a $3.15 million bonus and guarantees that brought the total value to $8 million.

The Burrell and Drew contracts introduced into negotiations the major league contract that allowed payments to be spread over several years. Boras, anticipating this change in the market, also demanded similar contracts for Stanford hurlers Jeff Austin and Chad Hutchinson. Mulder also asked for a major league deal.

Hutchinson was considered to have perhaps the top arm in the country, but slid to the No. 48 slot because of his desire to continue to play quarterback for Stanford. Hutchinson was also picked by the Cardinals and agreed to a $3.4 million contract, including a $2.3 million signing bonus. He agreed to give up his football career, though he eventually ditched baseball and returned to the gridiron, playing quarterback for the Dallas Cowboys.

Predraft Deals Proliferate

With signing bonuses skyrocketing, there were a significant number of teams who chose to negotiate deals before the draft contingent on the player being available. Such prearranged deals are specifically prohibited by major league rules but became part of the negotiating process for a large number of teams.

The first pick who was believed to have come to an agreement before the draft was Mills, the sixth selection by the Twins, who agreed to a $2 million signing bonus while pitching for Arizona State in the College World Series.

With signability an increasingly important and discussed aspect of the draft, it wasn't surprising that a number of players saw their draft position plummet based on their contract demands. The most notable was Severna Park, Md., third baseman Mark Teixeira. He turned down a predraft deal and slid until the Red Sox took a flier on him in the ninth round. He chose instead to attend Georgia Tech, and was a first-round pick of the Rangers in 2001.

The overall mood of the industry toward the draft at the end of the year was not positive. Bonuses continued to skyrocket and teams regarded them as out of control. But baseball's new vice president of baseball operations, Sandy Alderson, addressed the issue during his first day in office and would take action to bring things under control in the coming years.

The draft was also limited to a maximum of 50 rounds over two days, a departure from the unlimited-round, three-day format previously used. The change was voted in by the scouting directors in January 1998.

DRAFT 98: FIRST-ROUND PICKS

No.	Club	Player, Pos.	School	Hometown	Ht.	Wt.	B-T	Age
1.	Phillies	Pat Burrell, 3b/1b	Miami	Boulder Creek, Calif.	6-4	225	R-R	21
2.	Athletics	Mark Mulder, lhp	Michigan State	South Holland, Ill.	6-6	200	L-L	20
3.	Cubs	Corey Patterson, of	Harrison HS	Kennesaw, Ga.	5-10	175	L-R	18
4.	Royals	Jeff Austin, rhp	Stanford	Kingwood, Texas	6-0	185	R-R	21
5.	Cardinals	J.D. Drew, of	None	Hahira, Ga.	6-1	200	L-R	22
6.	Twins	Ryan Mills, lhp	Arizona State	Scottsdale, Ariz.	6-5	200	L-L	20
7.	Reds	Austin Kearns, of	Lafayette HS	Lexington, Ky.	6-3	215	R-R	18
8.	Blue Jays	Felipe Lopez, ss	Lake Brantley HS	Altamonte Springs, Fla.	6-0	175	B-R	18
9.	Padres	Sean Burroughs, 3b	Wilson HS	Long Beach	6-1	200	L-R	17
10.	Rangers	Carlos Pena, 1b	Northeastern	Haverhill, Mass.	6-2	210	L-L	20
11.	Expos	Josh McKinley, ss	Malvern Prep	Downington, Pa.	6-2	192	B-R	18
12.	Red Sox	Adam Everett, ss	South Carolina	Kennesaw, Ga.	6-1	176	R-R	21
13.	Brewers	J.M. Gold, rhp	Toms River North HS	Toms River, N.J.	6-5	225	R-R	18
14.	Tigers	Jeff Weaver, rhp	Fresno State	Simi Valley, Calif.	6-5	220	R-R	21
15.	Pirates	Clint Johnston, lhp	Vanderbilt	Vero Beach, Fla.	6-3	200	L-L	20
16.	White Sox	Kip Wells, rhp	Baylor	Sugar Land, Texas	6-3	195	R-R	21
17.	Astros	Brad Lidge, rhp	Notre Dame	Englewood, Colo.	6-3	200	R-R	21
18.	Angels	Seth Etherton, rhp	Southern California	Laguna Niguel, Calif.	6-1	205	R-R	21
19.	Giants	Tony Torcato, 3b	Woodland HS	Woodland, Calif.	6-1	200	L-R	18
20.	Indians	C.C. Sabathia, lhp	Vallejo HS	Vallejo, Calif.	6-6	240	L-L	17
21.	Mets	Jason Tyner, of	Texas A&M	Beaumont, Texas.	6-1	167	L-L	21
22.	Mariners	Matt Thornton, lhp	Grand Valley State	Centreville, Mich.	6-6	210	L-L	21
23.	Dodgers	Bubba Crosby, of	Rice	Houston	5-11	185	L-L	21
24.	Yankees	Andy Brown, of	Richmond HS	Richmond, Ind.	6-7	195	L-L	18
25.	Giants	Nate Bump, rhp	Penn State	Monroeton, Pa.	6-3	185	R-R	21
26.	Orioles	Rick Elder, of/1b	Sprayberry HS	Marietta, Ga.	6-6	230	L-L	18
27.	Marlins	Chip Ambres, of	Westbrook HS	Beaumont, Texas	6-1	190	R-R	18
28.	Rockies	Matt Roney, rhp	Edmond North HS	Edmond, Okla.	6-3	225	R-R	18
29.	Giants	Arturo McDowell, of	Forest Hill HS	Jackson, Miss.	6-1	175	L-L	18
30.	Royals	Matt Burch, rhp	Virginia Commonwealth	Elmira, N.Y.	6-3	185	R-R	21

1998

CLUB-BY-CLUB SELECTIONS

ANAHEIM ANGELS

June—Regular Phase (18)

1. **Seth Etherton, rhp, Southern California**
2. **Brandon Emanuel, rhp, Northwestern State**
3. Paul French, rhp, Northgate HS, Concord, Calif.
4. **Brian Oliver, ss, California**
5. **Darren Blakely, of, Hawaii**
6. **Jay Hood, ss, Georgia Tech**
7. **Jeff Hundley, lhp, Bowling Green State**
8. **Jason Hill, c, California**
9. **Kevin McClain, rhp, Central Florida CC**
10. Justin Lehr, rhp/c, UC Santa Barbara
11. **Bill Mott, of, Santa Clara**
12. **Ed Welch, of, Point Grey HS, Vancouver, B.C.**
13. **Greg Jacobs, lhp, Cal State Fullerton**
14. **Jason Huisman, ss, Mississippi**
15. Jaime Germain, 3b, Jose Campeche HS, San Lorenzo, P.R.
16. **Justin Ross, of, Tennessee**
17. **Doug Bridges, lhp, Embry-Riddle Aeronautical (Fla.)**
18. **Casey Kelley, 1b, Washington State**
19. Justin Stine, lhp, Missouri
20. **Ed Hurtado, rhp, UC Riverside**
21. **Oliver Harwas, rhp, Warner Southern (Fla.)**
22. **Chad Berryman, rhp, Virginia Commonwealth**
23. Ryan Braun, c/rhp, Edison HS, Fresno
24. **Chris Demouy, lhp, Louisiana State**
25. **Tommy Bond, rhp, Florida**
26. Josh Schaffer, 3b, Esperanza HS, Yorba Linda, Calif.
27. Simon Stoner, rhp, Pasco Hernando (Fla.) CC
28. Greg Moore, rhp, Ohlone (Calif.) JC
29. **Angel Diaz, c, Tampa**
30. Ronte Langs, of, Gulf Coast (Fla.) CC
31. **Mike Leach, rhp, Florida Southern**
32. Ryan Flanagan, rhp, Gulf Coast (Fla.) CC
33. **Kenny Corley, 1b, Arizona**
34. Bobby Crosby, ss, LaQuinta HS, Cypress, Calif.
35. Ben Margalski, c, Belleville Area (Ill.) CC
36. **Mike Christensen, 3b, Florida Southern**
37. Matt Tucek, rhp, Waxahachie (Texas) HS
38. **Chris Aronson, rhp, George Mason**
39. **Brad Downing, of, Cal Poly Pomona**
40. **Will Croud, of, Central Florida**
41. **Doug Wakefield, lhp, Cal State Dominguez Hills**
42. **Matt Lubozynski, lhp, Central Florida**
43. Josh Warren, rhp, Polk (Fla.) CC
44. Jon Steitz, rhp, Hopkins School, New Haven, Conn.
45. Cam Esslinger, rhp, Seton Hall
46. Mario Mendoza, rhp, Central Arizona JC
47. **Rudy Arguellas, of, Arizona State**
48. Brian Ferreira, of, Manatee (Fla.) JC
49. **Bryn Wade, 2b, Biola (Calif.)**
50. Edgardo Salgado, c, Florida Air Academy, Melbourne, Fla.

ARIZONA DIAMONDBACKS

June—Regular Phase (30)

1. (Pick to Royals as compensation for Type A free agent Jay Bell)
2. (Pick to Tigers as compensation for Type A free agent Willie Blair)
3. **Darryl Conyer, of, Mission Bay HS, San Diego**
4. **Javier Lopez, lhp, Virginia**
5. **J.D. Closser, c, Monroe HS, Alexandria, Ind.**
6. **Brock McCarty, of, Ouachita Parish HS, Monroe, La.**
7. **Jeff Pass, lhp, Chrysler HS, New Castle, Ind.**
8. **Andrew Good, rhp, Rochester HS, Rochester Hills, Mich.**
9. Brendan Fuller, rhp, Clearwater (Fla.) HS
10. **Tom Kail, of, Baldwin HS, Pittsburgh**
11. **Hector Cruz, ss, Florida College**
12. **Victor Hall, of, Monroe HS, Arleta, Calif.**
13. Brian Sager, rhp, Branford (Conn.) HS
14. **Dan Meier, of, Arizona State**
15. **Chris Cervantes, lhp, Pima (Ariz.) CC**
16. **Heath Corbett, of, McMinn County HS, Athens, Tenn.**
17. Lamar Sturdivant, of, Woodbury (N.J.) HS
18. **Bret Prinz, rhp, Phoenix JC**
19. **Jeff Barndollar, rhp, Saddleback (Calif.) CC**
20. **John Egly, 3b, Mountain View HS, Liberty, Mo.**
21. **Paul Giambalvo, rhp, South Florida**
22. Ryan Blake, c, Glenn HS, Kernersville, N.C.
23. **Robby Hammock, c, Georgia**
24. **Troy Niehaus, lhp, Eastern Michigan**
25. **Steve Neal, 1b, Pratt (Kan.) CC**
26. Jason Reuss, 1b, Canyon HS, Anaheim
27. **Mario Knorr, of, El Capitan HS, Lakeside, Calif.**
28. **Justin Santonocito, ss, Mercyhurst (Pa.)**
29. **Mike Koplove, rhp/ss, Delaware**
30. Charlie Manning, lhp, Polk (Fla.) CC
31. Carl Makowsky, rhp, Conroe (Texas) HS
32. Mario Glaser, rhp, Edmonds (Wash.) CC
33. Horace Lawrence, lhp, El Cerrito HS, Richmond, Calif.
34. **Justin Kees, rhp, Southern Illinois**
35. Russ Bayer, lhp, Naperville (Ill.) North HS
36. **James Rinne, of, Illinois Wesleyan**
37. **Matt White, rhp, Western Oregon**
38. **Justin Crivello, lhp, Edmonds (Wash.) CC**
39. **Kirk Bolling, rhp/3b, Saddleback (Calif.) CC**
40. John Gouzd, rhp, Fairmont (W.Va.) Senior HS
41. **Justin Beasley, c, Butler**
42. **Jody Fuller, rhp, Tennessee-Martin**
43. **Adam Neubart, of, Rutgers**
44. Courtney Hall, rhp, Edmonds (Wash.) CC
45. Wilton Reynolds, of, Monte Vista HS, Spring Valley, Calif.
46. Ben Mitchell, rhp, Scottsdale (Ariz.) CC
47. Cole Saben, rhp, Portland Lutheran HS, Portland, Ore.
48. Bryon Gribbons, rhp, Cooper City (Fla.) HS
49. Joe Bunton, 3b, Bell HS, Cudahy, Calif.
50. Lucas Gruner, c, Mayfair HS, Long Beach

ATLANTA BRAVES

June—Regular Phase (28)

1. (Pick to Rockies as compensation for Type A free agent Andres Galarraga)
2. **Matt Belisle, rhp, McCallum HS, Austin** (Pick from Padres as compensation for Type B free agent Greg Myers)
2. (Pick to Rockies as compensation for Type A free agent Walt Weiss)
3. **Ryan Langerhans, of, Round Rock (Texas) HS**
4. **Johnny McGinnis, rhp, Dacula (Ga.) HS**
5. **Damien Jones, of, Vigor HS, Whistler, Ala.**
6. Victor Menocal, ss, Gainesville (Ga.) HS
7. **Scott Sobkowiak, rhp, Northern Iowa**
8. Josh Karp, rhp, Bothell (Wash.) HS
9. **Matt Targac, lhp, Sacred Heart HS, Hallettsville, Texas**
10. Charlie Bilezikjian, of, Port Richmond HS, Staten Island, N.Y.
11. **L.J. Yankosky, rhp, Georgia Tech**
12. **Greg Donato, 3b, Clovis (Calif.) HS**
13. Steve Smyth, lhp, Cypress (Calif.) JC
14. **John Ennis, rhp, Monroe HS, Panorama City, Calif.**
15. **Tommy Clark, of, Brunswick (Ga.) HS**
16. Rob Moravek, rhp, Simsbury (Conn.) HS
17. **Daniel Curtis, rhp, Central HS, Chattanooga, Tenn.**
18. **Colin Stewart, of, Sonoma State (Calif.)**
19. **Zack Frachiseur, rhp, Georgia**
20. **Gregg Maluchnik, c, Duke**

21. **Aaron Garmong, lhp, Wayne State (Neb.)**
22. Sean Bischofberger, c, Granite Hills HS, El Cajon, Calif.
23. Jason Mikels, rhp, Rio Linda (Calif.) HS
24. **Derrick Truitt, rhp, Columbia State (Tenn.) JC**
25. Kregg Jarvais, c, Maine
26. **Brian Cox, of, Florida State**
27. **Bubba Scarce, rhp, North Carolina State**
28. Louis Angulo, lhp, Miami-Dade CC North
29. **Tim Spooneybarger, of, Pine Forest HS, Pensacola, Fla.**
30. **Drue James, c, Southeastern Oklahoma State**
31. Tim Lemke, c/3b, Immaculata HS, Belle Meade, N.J.
32. **Nick Green, 2b, DeKalb (Ga.) JC**
33. Derek Clifton, rhp, Clear Creek HS, League City, Texas
34. **Paul Burke, c, Bellarmine (Ky.)**
35. Marcus Hambrick, of, Robert E. Lee HS, Montgomery, Ala.
36. Philip Rosengren, rhp, Northwestern
37. Adrian Walker, lhp, Mission Bay HS, San Diego
38. Kevin Benson, of, Century HS, Bismarck, N.D.
39. **Casey Cheshier, 3b, San Jose State**
40. **Jerry Simmons, of, The Citadel**
41. Mike Perez, c, Palm Beach Lakes HS, West Palm Beach, Fla.
42. Eric Wise, rhp, Basic HS, Henderson, Nev.
43. Greg Birch, lhp, McArthur HS, Davie, Fla.
44. Dallas McPherson, rhp, Randleman (N.C.) HS
45. **Brad Voyles, rhp, Lincoln Memorial (Tenn.)**
46. Josh Carter, 3b, Fallbrook (Calif.) HS
47. Mike Gleason, rhp, Santa Fe Trail HS, Carbondale, Kan.
48. Jason King, ss, Englewood HS, Jacksonville
49. Micah Nodah, rhp, Columbia HS, Live Oak, Fla.
50. **Shaun Harper, of, Frederick Douglas HS, Atlanta**

BALTIMORE ORIOLES

June—Regular Phase (26)

1. **Rick Elder, of, Sprayberry HS, Marietta, Ga.**
1. **Mamon Tucker, of, Stephen F. Austin HS, Austin** (Supplemental pick—39th—for loss of Type A free agent Randy Myers)
2. **Ben Knapp, rhp, Oviedo (Fla.) HS** (Pick from Blue Jays as compensation for Myers)
2. Alex Hart, rhp, Chambersburg (Pa.) Area HS
3. **Steve Bechler, rhp, South Medford HS, Medford, Ore.**
4. **Chris Davidson, rhp, Western Carolina**
5. **Josh Yarno, rhp, Moscow (Idaho) HS**
6. **Tim Raines Jr., of, Seminole HS, Sanford, Fla.**
7. **Tim Nelson, 3b, Allen Hancock (Calif.) JC**
8. **Randy Perez, lhp, El Capitan HS, Lakeside, Calif.**
9. **Francisco Monzon, c, Lorenzo Vizcarrondo HS, Carolina, P.R.**
10. Dustin Emberley, rhp, Composite HS, Weyburn, Sask
11. **Eliot Tomaszewski, rhp, Sandia HS, Albuquerque**
12. **Derrick Gutierrez, ss, Sandalwood HS, Jacksonville**
13. John Kremer, rhp, Evansville
14. Jason Bellamy, rhp, Conway (S.C.) HS
15. Josh Doud, rhp, Round Rock, Texas
16. **Jason Pruitt, lhp, View Marana HS, Tucson**
17. Mike MacDougal, rhp, Wake Forest
18. **Denis Gratton, rhp, Kitchener, Ontario**
19. Ryan Smith, rhp, Lake Howell HS, Longwood, Fla.
20. Cliff Lee, lhp, Meridian (Miss.) CC
21. **Tony Mack, of, Boone HS, Orlando**
22. **Dustin Brewer, rhp, Granite City (Ill.) HS**
23. **Sam Berrien, 1b, Fort Meade (Fla.) HS**
24. **William Whitecotton, rhp, North County HS, Linthicum, Md.**
25. **Joey Hammond, ss, UNC Charlotte**
26. Jason Mandryk, rhp, Valley Heights HS, Langton, Ontario
27. Jared Jones, of, Walla Walla (Wash.) HS
28. Jason Botts, 1b, Paso Robles (Calif.) HS
29. Doug Slaten, lhp, Venice (Calif.) HS
30. **Richard Green, c, Coffee County HS, Tullahoma, Tenn.**
31. **Sean Fisher, lhp, Grand Rapids (Mich.) CC**
32. Troy Roberson, rhp, King's Academy, Boynton Beach, Fla.
33. Fred Brassfield, of, Bryan Station HS, Lexington, Ky.
34. Phil Cullen, rhp, Chelan (Wash.) HS
35. Jeffrey Gatch, rhp, Aquinas (Mich.)
36. Scott Moore, rhp, Cowley County (Kan.) CC
37. **Jason Benham, 3b, Liberty**
38. Mike Smith, lhp, Fletcher (Okla.) HS
39. **Marc Houle, rhp, Des Moines Area (Iowa) CC**
40. Matt Crandall, rhp, Allen Hancock (Calif.) JC
41. Cory Acklus, of, Cascade HS, Everett, Wash.
42. Matt Blethen, lhp/of, Havre de Grace (Md.) HS
43. Derek Eddie, c, Seward County (Kan.) CC
44. (Selection voided)
45. Brock Ralph, of, Raymond (Alberta) HS
46. Zack Lush, c, Florida Tech
47. **Sonny Garcia, rhp, Texas Southern**
48. Kevin Fox, lhp, Citrus (Calif.) JC
49. Mitch Jones, 3b, Utah Valley State JC
50. Scott Ridenour, rhp, Potomac State (W.Va.) JC

BOSTON RED SOX

June—Regular Phase (12)

1. **Adam Everett, ss, South Carolina**
2. (Pick to Cardinals as compensation for Type A free agent Dennis Eckersley)
3. **Mike Maroth, lhp, Central Florida**
4. **Jerome Gamble, rhp, Benjamin Russell HS, Alexander City, Ala.**
5. **Josh Hancock, rhp, Tupelo, Miss.**
6. **Rick Riccobono, rhp, Commack (N.Y.) HS**
7. Syketo Anderson, 2b, Prattville (Ala.) HS
8. **Frederick Silverthorn, lhp, Pearce HS, Richardson, Texas**
9. Mark Teixeira, 3b, Mount St. Joseph HS, Severna Park, Md.
10. Lenny DiNardo, lhp, Santa Fe HS, High Spring, Fla.
11. **Carlos Rodriguez, of, Louisville**
12. **David Benham, c, Liberty**
13. Mike Rabelo, c, Ridgewood HS, New Port Richey, Fla.
14. **Matt Phillips, rhp, Delaware**
15. **Lance Surridge, rhp, UNC Greensboro**
16. **Jason Norton, rhp, South Alabama**
17. **Benito Flores, lhp, Cal State Fullerton**
18. **Terrance Hill, lhp, Southern**
19. **Shon Norris, rhp, UNC Asheville**
20. **Tony James, 2b, San Jose State**
21. **Andrew Checketts, rhp, Oregon State**
22. **Tom Linarelli, rhp, Washington**
23. **Drew Larned, c, Fairfield**
24. **Josh Adeeb, of, Vanderbilt**
25. **John Hattig, ss, Piti, Guam**
26. Ben Kozlowski, lhp, Seminole (Fla.) HS
27. James Gates, of, Butler HS, Huntsville, Ala.
28. Jason Blanton, rhp, Brevard (Fla.) JC
29. Ryan Siebert, rhp, Germantown (Tenn.) HS
30. James Garcia, of, West Torrance HS, Torrance, Calif.
31. Robert Floyd, lhp, Satsuma (Ala.) HS
32. **Keith Hart, 1b, Lubbock Christian (Texas)**
33. Heath Heiberger, lhp, Putnam County HS, Hennepin, Ill.
34. **Chad Johnson, c, Bradley**
35. Mark Younk, c, Texas HS, Wake Village, Texas
36. **Tonayne Brown, of, Lurleen Wallace (Ala.) JC**
37. **Tony Caridi, c, Klein (Texas) HS**
38. **Dennis Tankersley, rhp, St. Louis CC-Meramec**
39. Rob Shabansky, lhp, Arizona
40. **Phil Ledesma, of, Rider**
41. Jason Fingers, rhp, Central Arizona JC
42. **Bryan Barnowski, c, Southwick-Tolland HS, Granville, Mass.**
43. Ron Bohinski, ss, Lakeland (Fla.) HS
44. John Parrado, c, Miami Lakes (Fla.) HS
45. Jon Smithers, 3b, Florida College
46. Chris Hart, c, Central Catholic HS, Clearwater, Fla.
47. Richie Smith, 2b, Liberty County HS, Marianna, Fla.
48. Darry Burgess, rhp, Alvin (Texas) HS

CHICAGO CUBS

June—Regular Phase (3)

1. **Corey Patterson, of, Harrison HS, Kennesaw, Ga.**

2. **David Kelton, ss, Troup County HS, LaGrange, Ga.**
2. **Jeff Goldbach, c, Princeton (Ind.) Community HS** (Pick from Astros as compensation for Type B free agent Dave Clark)
3. **Kevin Bass, 3b, Fayette County HS, Fayette, Ala.**
4. **Jeramy Gomer, lhp, Durant HS, Plant City, Fla.**
5. **Aaron Sams, lhp, James Madison**
6. **Tony Schrager, 2b, Stanford**
7. **Keola Delatori, rhp, Triton (Ill.) JC**
8. **Will Ohman, lhp, Pepperdine**
9. Stephen Reba, rhp, Concordia Lutheran HS, Fort Wayne, Ind.
10. **Nate Frese, ss, Iowa**
11. **Dustin Krug, rhp, Lassen (Calif.) JC**
12. **Tony Zamarripa, rhp, Texas A&M**
13. **David Ericks, rhp, Illiana Christian HS, Lansing, Ill.**
14. Tom Lipari, lhp, Indian Hills (Iowa) JC
15. Casey Grzecka, c, Santa Margarita HS, Laguna Niguel, Calif.
16. **Omar Rohena, 3b, Casiano Cepeda HS, Rio Grande, P.R.**
17. **Eric Hinske, 3b, Arkansas**
18. Carlton Wells, lhp, King HS, Tampa
19. **Joe Ohm, rhp, Wisconsin-La Crosse**
20. Dennis Cervenka, rhp, La Vernia (Texas) HS
21. **Larry Dant, rhp, Dana (Neb.)**
22. **Mikel Moreno, of, Arizona State**
23. Michael Carey, rhp, Westminster (Calif.) HS
24. Charles Redmond, of, Liberty Elyau HS, Texarkana, Texas
25. Nick Moran, rhp, Elk Grove (Calif.) HS
26. Eric Arnold, ss, LaPorte (Ind.) HS
27. **Tydus Meadows, of, Vanderbilt**
28. Adam Cox, of, Thomas County Central HS, Thomasville, Ga.
29. **Lawrence Alvarez, rhp, Nogales HS, Walnut, Calif.**
30. Justin Smith, c, Lake Brantley HS, Longwood, Fla.
31. **Leonardo Torres, lhp, Metro State (Colo.)**
32. **Matt Griffin, ss, Southern (Ga.) Tech**
33. **Chris Brown, rhp, Northwestern State**
34. Dustin Brentz, rhp, Moss Point HS, Pascagoula, Miss.
35. Matt Whitehead, rhp, Northeast Texas CC
36. Ben Johanning, 1b, Osceola HS, Kissimmee, Fla.
37. James Lunsford, c, Grayson County (Texas) CC
38. Chris Wood, ss, Central Florida CC
39. Keith Whatley, lhp, Atlanta (Texas) HS
40. Jonathan Macklin, lhp, Hallandale (Fla.) HS
41. Nate Beucler, rhp, Huntington Beach (Calif.) HS
42. **Kevin Boles, c, South Florida**
43. Jacob Pierce, rhp, Longview (Texas) HS
44. Juston Olson, rhp, Oak Park-River Forest HS, Oak Park, Ill.
45. **Chris Connally, of, Texas Christian**
46. Dustin Matthews, ss, Whitney Young HS, Chicago
47. Jon-Mark Sprowl, ss, Bay HS, Panama City Beach, Fla.
48. Chris Kellett, c, Deltona HS, Orange City, Fla.
49. Greg Eubanks, rhp, Wellington (Fla.) HS
50. Dan Jackson, rhp, South Suburban (Ill.) JC

CHICAGO WHITE SOX

June—Regular Phase (16)

1. **Kip Wells, rhp, Baylor**
1. **Aaron Rowand, of, Cal State Fullerton** (Supplemental pick—35th—for loss of Type A free agent Dave Martinez)
2. **Gary Majewski, rhp, St. Pius X HS, Houston**
3. **Josh Fogg, rhp, Florida**
3. **Dan Mozingo, lhp, Ashtabula Harbor HS, Ashtabula, Ohio** (Pick from Devil Rays as compensation for Martinez)
4. **Johnny Santamarina, 3b, Gulliver Prep, Miami**
5. Steve Kelly, rhp, Fairfield HS, Hamilton, Ohio
6. **Matt Borne, rhp, Kentucky**
7. **Eric Fischer, lhp, Moeller HS, Cincinnati**
8. **Mitch Wylie, rhp, St. Amrose (Iowa)**
9. **Gus Mosley, of, Wakulla HS, Crawfordville, Fla.**
10. Stephen Bess, rhp, Rice
11. **Mike Williams, rhp, Galveston (Texas) JC**
12. **Kai Freeman, rhp, Minnesota**
13. **Gerard McCall, c, Meridian (Miss.) HS**
14. **Solomon Johnson, lhp, Navarro (Texas) JC**
15. Nate Robertson, lhp, Wichita State
16. **Ernesto Lowe, of, American HS, Miami**
17. **Brannon Whatley, rhp, Kennesaw State**
18. Chris Hamblen, c, Highlands HS, Fort Thomas, Ky.
19. Jason Stovall, lhp, Battiest HS, Bethel, Okla.
20. Erik Lohse, rhp, Hamilton Union HS, Glenn, Calif.
21. **Andre Simpson, rhp, Mount Miguel HS, Lemon Grove, Calif.**
22. Carlos Castillo, 2b, Miami-Dade CC North
23. Todd Johannes, c, Florida
24. Caleb Reger, 1b, Bradshaw Mountain HS, Prescott, Ariz.
25. Mark Cochrane, c, Stoneman Douglas HS, Coral Springs, Fla.
26. **Edwin Almonte, rhp, St. Francis (N.Y.)**
27. **Eric Battersby, lhp/of, St. Mary's (Texas)**
28. Travis Edwards, of, Wilson HS, Long Beach
29. Nelson Lopez, 3b, Monsignor Pace HS, Miami
30. Jason Abreu, ss, Hialeah-Miami Lakes HS, Miami Lakes, Fla.
31. **Carlos Cline, 1b, Brookdale (N.J.) CC**
32. Todd Eames, rhp, JC of Eastern Utah
33. Paul Reuer, of, Schaumburg (Ill.) HS
34. **Terrell Merriman, of, Averett (Va.)**
35. Scott Atwood, 1b, North Florida CC
36. Dan Wells, c, Columbine HS, Littleton, Colo.
37. Jay Bernard, rhp, Gulf Coast (Fla.) CC
38. **Mark Buehrle, lhp, Jefferson (Mo.) CC**
39. Curtis Young, rhp, Grand Junction (Colo.) HS
40. Michael Baetzel, ss, Kishwaukee (Ill.) JC
41. Mike Mallonee, lhp, Southwestern (Calif.) JC
42. Kevin Cameron, rhp, Joliet Catholic HS, Joliet, Ill.
43. Mike Scioletti, 3b, Army
44. Julio Guerrero, of, San Angelo (Texas) HS
45. John Gusich, 3b, Deer Valley HS, Glendale, Ariz.
46. Vince Serafini, 1b, Lockport (Ill.) HS
47. Nathan Boyd, rhp, Allen Academy, Bryan, Texas
48. Ryan Costello, lhp, Milford Academy, Voorhees, N.J.
49. Ricardo Suarez, of, Miami-Dade CC North
50. Justin Hairston, 2b, JC of DuPage (Ill.)

CINCINNATI REDS

June—Regular Phase (7)

1. **Austin Kearns, of, Lafayette HS, Lexington, Ky.**
2. **Adam Dunn, of, New Caney (Texas) HS**
3. Greg Porter, ss, Keller (Texas) HS
4. **Darrell Hussman, rhp, Arizona**
5. **Jayson Larman, rhp, Wayne (Okla.) HS**
6. **Bobby Madritsch, lhp, Point Park (Pa.)**
7. **Josh Hall, rhp, Glass HS, Lynchburg, Va.**
8. **Clint Vaughn, 1b, Oklahoma Christian**
9. **Dave Therneau, rhp, Bellevue (Neb.)**
10. **Jacob Wallis, c, Paschal HS, Joshua, Texas**
11. **James Dehart, lhp, Texarkana (Texas) CC**
12. **John Koronka, lhp, South Lake HS, Clermont, Fla.**
13. **Damien Hart, lhp, Coastal Carolina**
14. **Dennis Russo, rhp, Santa Fe Catholic HS, Auburndale, Fla.**
15. **Blane Layton, of, Jacksonville**
16. **Casey McEvoy, rhp, Cincinnati**
17. **B.J. Ryan, lhp, Southwestern Louisiana**
18. **Gary Loudon, rhp, Shippensburg (Pa.)**
19. **Glen Joseph, rhp, King HS, Tampa**
20. **Duane Price, of, Texas Tech**
21. Alex Kellner, c, Freedom HS, Morganton, N.C.
22. Jason France, lhp, Chandler (Ariz.) HS
23. **Travis Copley, c, Tennessee**
24. **Eric Cooper, rhp, Texas Tech**
25. **Randy Stegall, ss, Cumberland (Tenn.)**
26. Vince LaCorte, rhp, Gavilan (Calif.) JC
27. **Cory Stewart, lhp, Boerne (Texas) HS**
28. Humberto Aguilar, 1b, Odessa (Texas) HS
29. John Nix, rhp, Kingwood (Texas) HS
30. **Tim Birdsong, rhp, Southeastern Oklahoma State**
31. Brad Salmon, rhp, Tate HS, Gonzalez, Fla.
32. **Roger Sellers, rhp, North Central Texas JC**
33. Paul Sanchez, of, Hubbard HS, Chicago
34. **James Matan, of, UNC Charlotte**
35. **Andrew Beattie, ss, St. Petersburg (Fla.) JC**
36. **Chris Toomey, of, Long Beach State**
37. Donald Caldwell, of, Jefferson HS, Tampa

38. Dave Jensen, 1b, Green Valley HS, Henderson, Nev.
39. **Randy Woodrum, lhp, Middle Tennessee State**
40. Lance Cormier, rhp, Lafayette (La.) HS
41. **Todd Coffey, rhp, Chase HS, Forest City, N.C.**
42. **Robert Jenkins, of, Valparaiso**
43. David Carr, of, Marquette HS, Milwaukee
44. David Martin, c, Katy (Texas) HS
45. Terrmel Sledge, of, Long Beach State
46. John Whiteside, rhp, Sunset HS, Beaverton, Ore.
47. Michael Grant, lhp, Charlotte Chritian HS, Charlotte
48. Gerald Butt, rhp, Mayville State (N.D.)

CLEVELAND INDIANS

June—Regular Phase (20)

1. **C.C. Sabathia, lhp, Vallejo (Calif.) HS**
2. **Zach Sorensen, ss, Wichita State**
3. **Scott Pratt, ss, Auburn**
4. **Ron Marietta, lhp, St. John's**
5. **Ryan Drese, rhp, California**
6. **Tyler Minges, of, Ross HS, Hamilton, Ohio**
7. **Brody Percell, lhp, Oregon State**
8. **Chris Reinike, rhp, Mississippi State**
9. **Paul Day, 3b, Long Beach State**
10. **Michael McPadden, rhp, Port St. Lucie (Fla.) HS**
11. **Jacob Reynolds, rhp, Giles County HS, Pulaski, Tenn.**
12. **Donnie Suttles, rhp, Western Carolina**
13. **Matt Wade, rhp, Parkview HS, Lilburn, Ga.**
14. **Brian Jackson, rhp, Southern Colorado**
15. **Matt White, lhp, Clemson**
16. **Richard Matsko, rhp, Shippensburg (Pa.)**
17. **Mark Koeth, rhp, Brookhaven HS, Carrollton, Texas**
18. **T.T. Gallaher, of, New Haven (Conn.)**
19. David Raymer, of, Sacramento CC
20. **Barry Patton, c, Mississippi State**
21. Mike DiRosa, c, Coral Gables HS, Miami
22. **Carey Novits, lhp, Cal State Northridge**
23. J.J. Sherrill, of, Monterey HS, Seaside, Calif.
24. Tom Bost, of, Louisiana Tech
25. **Eric Maleski, rhp, Benedictine (Ill.)**
26. **Chris MacMillan, 3b, Cal State Northridge**
27. **Jeff Depippo, c, Southern California**
28. **Rudolfo Rosales, rhp, Pima (Ariz.) CC**
29. **Ruben Escobar, rhp, Master's (Calif.)**
30. **Mike Pursell, 2b, Tulane**
31. **Marques Esquerra, ss, Point Loma Nazarene (Calif.)**
32. **Craig Brown, lhp, Tulane**
33. Brian Strelitz, rhp, Temple City (Calif.) HS
34. James Jurries, 3b, Brazoswood HS, Lake Jackson, Texas
35. Randon Ho, lhp, Hawaii
36. Matt Ramie, 1b, Castle HS, Kanoehe, Hawaii
37. Micah Simmons, ss, Paxon HS, Jacksonville
38. Brian Minks, lhp, Neosho County (Kan.) CC
39. **Darrel Berck, rhp, Palomar (Calif.) JC**
40. **Dan Guillory, rhp, Louisiana State**
41. Brian Sullivan, rhp, Port St. Lucie (Fla.) HS
42. Blake Whealy, ss, Oak Park-River Forest HS, Oak Park, Ill.
43. Dana Thomas, rhp, Fork Union (Va.) Military Academy
44. Miguel Hernandez, 3b, Nuestra Senora HS, Bayamon, P.R.
45. Eric Bush, lhp, Washington HS, Pensacola, Fla.
46. **Brandon Mauer, c, Bellevue (Wash.) CC**
47. Kevin Spaulding, rhp, Anacortes (Wash.) HS
48. Garth Blumberg, of, Hoquiam (Wash.) HS
49. Kevin Hooper, 2b, Wichita State
50. **Omar Moraga, 3b, Arizona**

COLORADO ROCKIES

June—Regular Phase (17)

1. (Pick to Astros as compensation for Type A free agent Darryl Kile)
1. **Matt Roney, rhp, Edmond North HS, Edmond, Okla.** (Pick from Braves as compensation for Type A free agent Andres Galarraga)
1. **Choo Freeman, of, Dallas Christian HS, Mesquite, Texas** (Supplemental pick—36th—for loss of Galarraga)
1. **Jeff Winchester, c, Archbishop Rummel HS, Metairie, La.** (Supplemental pick—40th—for loss of Type A free agent Walt Weiss)
2. **Jermaine Van Buren, rhp, Hattiesburg (Miss.) HS**
2. **Jody Gerut, of, Stanford** (Pick from Braves as compensation for Weiss)
3. **Kevin Gordon, rhp, Central Florida**
4. **Luke Hudson, rhp, Tennessee**
5. Ryan Shealy, 1b, Cardinal Gibbons HS, Fort Lauderdale
6. **Javier Guzman, of, University Garden HS, Rio Piedras, P.R.**
7. **Matt Holliday, 3b, Stillwater (Okla.) HS**
8. **Justin Lincoln, 3b/rhp, Manatee (Fla.) JC**
9. **Justin Carter, lhp, South Alabama**
10. Andrew Beinbrink, 3b, Arizona State
11. **Ryan Cameron, rhp, Massachusetts**
12. **Brian Brantley, rhp, Old Dominion**
13. **Juan Pierre, of, South Alabama**
14. **Vernand Morency, of, Northwestern HS, Miami**
15. **Mark DiFelice, rhp, Western Carolina**
16. **Brandon Garner, rhp, Central Merry HS, Jackson, Tenn.**
17. **Josh Etheredge, 1b/of, Auburn**
18. **Jase Wrigley, rhp, Georgia Tech**
19. **Doug Thompson, rhp, Louisiana State**
20. **Tom Whitehurst, of, South Alabama**
21. **Erik Johnson, c, Central Florida**
22. **Ryan Lamattina, lhp, St. Bonaventure**
23. **Richy Leon, 2b, Arizona State**
24. **Mike Mundy, rhp, Rutgers**
25. **Kevin Duck, 1b, Cal State Fullerton**
26. J.J. Durmanich, rhp, Merced (Calif.) JC
27. Manases Pabon, of, Hato Rey, P.R.
28. Jerry Johnson, of, Westark (Ark.) CC
29. Aaron Geralds, of, Madison-Central HS, Madison, Wis.
30. James Hymon, ss, Leo HS, Chicago
31. Mark Woodyard, 1b, Okaloosa Walton (Fla.) JC
32. Greg Colbrun, rhp, Skyview HS, Billings, Mon
33. Rocky Kirk, lhp, Cochise County (Ariz.) CC
34. Paul Miller, of, Pleasure Ridge Park HS, Louisville
35. Ryan Truxall, rhp, Miami-Dade CC North
36. Geoff Boutelier, rhp, Cypress (Calif.) JC
37. Ryan Wardinsky, ss, Flathead HS, Kalispell, Mon
38. T.J. Bird, of, Cloverdale (Calif.) HS
39. Dave Bernstine, c, Vallejo (Calif.) HS
40. Joe Simpson, rhp, Southeastern Illinois JC
41. Bryce Coppleters, of, Raymond (Alberta) HS
42. Nyjer Morgan, of, Willits, Calif.
43. Doug Baylor, of, Reagan HS, Austin
44. Alfredo Amezaga, ss, St. Petersburg (Fla.) JC
45. Frank Haase, lhp, Merced (Calif.) JC
46. John McCanne, 3b, Mammoth HS, Mammoth Lakes, Calif.

DETROIT TIGERS

June—Regular Phase (14)

1. **Jeff Weaver, rhp, Fresno State**
1. **Nate Cornejo, rhp, Wellington (Kan.) HS** (Supplemental pick—34th—for loss of Type A free agent Willie Blair)
2. **Brandon Inge, ss/rhp, Virginia Commonwealth**
2. **Adam Pettyjohn, lhp, Fresno State** (Pick from Diamondbacks as compensation for Blair)
3. **Tommy Marx, lhp, Brother Rice HS, West Bloomfield, Mich.**
4. **Andres Torres, of, Miami-Dade CC North**
5. **Greg Peterson, rhp/of, St. John's**
6. **Bobby Sismondo, lhp, Ohio**
7. **Clint Smith, rhp, Oklahoma**
8. **Barry Tolli, of, Newbury Park HS, Thousand Oaks, Calif.**
9. Donny Sevieri, of, El Dorado HS, Albuquerque
10. **Billy Rich, of, Connecticut**
11. Seth Taylor, ss, South Alabama
12. **Russ Cleveland, c, Chaparral HS, Las Vegas**
13. **Laz Gutierrez, lhp, Miami**
14. **Calvin Chipperfield, rhp, Mount San Antonio (Calif.) JC**
15. Doc Brooks, c, Central HS, Phenix City, Ala.
16. Greg Sain, 3b, West Torrance HS, Torrance, Calif.

17. **Reggie Nelson, ss, Santa Ana (Calif.) JC**
18. Andrew Earley, rhp, Shaker Heights (Ohio) HS
19. **Galen Shea, rhp, Houston Baptist**
20. **Jim Hostetler, rhp, Fullerton (Calif.) JC**
21. **Nate Forbush, c, Utah**
22. **Ryan Earl, lhp, Thousand Oaks (Calif.) HS**
23. **William Madson, rhp, Carthage (Wis.)**
24. **Thomas Koutrouba, lhp, Maine**
25. **Derek Besco, of, Michigan**
26. **Craig Daluz, 3b, Fresno State**
27. **Jason Colquitt, c, East Carolina**
28. **Lacarlo Moore, of, St. Xavier (Ill.)**
29. Scott Lawson, lhp, Logan (Ill.) JC
30. **Keith Law, ss, DeKalb (Ga.) JC**
31. Mack Paciorek, 3b, Los Angeles CC
32. **Ron Bush, ss, William & Mary**
33. **Brian McGowan, rhp, Queens (N.Y.)**
34. Robert Stiehl, c, West Torrance HS, Torrance, Calif.
35. **Joe Yingling, c, Camarillo (Calif.) HS**
36. Scott Stuck, rhp, Climax-Scotts HS, Climax, Mich.
37. Antoine Cameron, of, Ayala HS, Chino, Calif.
38. Edgar Varela, 3b, San Gabriel (Calif.) HS
39. Ryan Cox, rhp, Southern Illinois-Edwardsville
40. David Mendez, of, Lehman HS, Bronx, N.Y.
41. Chris Tiller, rhp, Panola (Texas) JC
42. Kevin Estrada, ss, El Segundo (Calif.) JC
43. Keith Perez, rhp, Holly (Mich.) HS
44. Craig Bowser, of, Lufkin (Texas) HS
45. Miles Luuloa, ss, Malokai HS, Kaunakakai, Hawaii
46. Patrick Gill, rhp, Grandville (Mich.) HS
47. Warren Trott, ss, West Torrance HS, Torrance, Calif.
48. Chris Curry, c, Meridian (Miss.) CC

FLORIDA MARLINS

June—Regular Phase (27)

1. **Chip Ambres, of, West Brook HS, Beaumont, Texas**
2. **Derek Wathan, ss, Oklahoma**
3. **David Callahan, 1b, Palm Bay (Fla.) HS**
4. **Heath Honeycutt, 3b, Georgia Tech**
5. **Matt Padgett, of, Clemson**
6. **Phillip Lowery, lhp, Arizona State**
7. **Ryan Harber, lhp, Butler**
8. **Marc Sauer, rhp, Bishop Eustace HS, Gloucester, N.J.**
9. Mike Trussell, rhp, Menchville HS, Newport News, Va.
10. Chris Heck, lhp, St. Joseph's
11. **Matt Demarco, ss, Gloucester Catholic HS, Gloucester City, N.J.**
12. **David Noyce, lhp, Furman**
13. **Paul McCurtain, rhp, Oklahoma**
14. **Eric Jupe, rhp, Schreiner (Texas)**
15. **Heath Kelly, 2b, Auburn**
16. **John Seaman, rhp, Northwestern**
17. Josh Hochgesang, 3b, Stanford
18. Adam LaRoche, lhp/1b, Fort Scott (Kan.) HS
19. Wendell Anderson, of, East Hartford (Conn.) HS
20. **David Campos, lhp, Fresno CC**
21. **Matt Frick, c, Alabama**
22. Mike Wright, c, San Jose State
23. Matt Krabbe, rhp, Larkin HS, Elgin, Ill.
24. **Terrence Smalls, 2b/ss, The Citadel**
25. Scott Murphy, rhp, Parkview HS, Lilburn, Ga.
26. **Kevin Olsen, rhp, Oklahoma**
27. **Willy Hill, of, Oklahoma**
28. Kevin Ryan, rhp, Morton (Ill.) JC
29. **Drew Niles, ss, Bowling Green State**
30. Vince Harrison, ss/2b, Princeton HS, Cincinnati
31. Jon Topolski, of, Baylor
32. **Randy Rigsby, 3b, East Carolina**
33. John Kocur, rhp, Cooper City (Fla.) HS
34. Adam Bragg, of, Bishop Verot HS, Cape Coral, Fla.
35. John Moylan, c, Sacred Heart HS, San Francisco
36. Chris Halgren, c, Mount Hood (Ore.) CC
37. Eric Bernhardt, rhp, Cowley County (Kan.) CC
38. Jorge Arceo, rhp, Lincoln HS, Stockton, Calif.
39. Jeffrey Wagner, of, San Jacinto (Texas) JC
40. **Julio Rivas, c, Washington & Lee HS, Arlington, Va.**
41. Bryan Lee, of, El Camino HS, Sacramento
42. Daniel Pettit, rhp, North Stafford HS, Stafford, Va.
43. Shawn Sabo, rhp, Oswego (Ill.) HS
44. Shawn Norris, ss, Alta HS, Draper, Utah
45. Pete Selden, rhp, Monroe (N.Y.) CC
46. Greg Mickles, of, Maple Shade (N.J.) HS
47. Aaron Alvarez, c, Chattahoochee HS, Duluth, Ga.
48. Rigo Orozco, c, Capuchino HS, San Bruno, Calif.
49. Rudy Simpson, of, Etiwanda HS, Alta Loma, Calif.

HOUSTON ASTROS

June—Regular Phase (19)

1. **Brad Lidge, rhp, Notre Dame** (Pick from Rockies as compensation for Type A free agent Darryl Kile)
1. (Pick to Giants as compensation for Type B free agent Doug Henry)
1. **Mike Nannini, rhp, Green Valley HS, Henderson, Nev.** (Supplemental pick—37th—for loss of Kile)
2. (Pick to Cubs as compensation for Type B free agent Dave Clark)
3. Brad Busbin, rhp, Dr. Phillips HS, Orlando
4. Jason Van Meetren, of, Bishop Gorman HS, Las Vegas
5. **Scott Barrett, lhp, San Jacinto (Texas) JC**
6. **Dave Matranga, ss, Pepperdine**
7. **John Buck, c, Taylorsville HS, Salt Lake City**
8. **Jesse Joyce, 3b, Cal State Los Angeles**
9. **Morgan Ensberg, 3b, Southern California**
10. **Keith Ginter, 2b, Texas Tech**
11. **Kevin Jordan, 3b/of, Texas Tech**
12. **Jeremy Ryan, rhp, Maple Woods (Mo.) CC**
13. **Doug Sessions, rhp, Armstrong Atlantic (Ga.) State**
14. Jacob Baker, 3b, Rice
15. **Chuck Carter, 1b, Baylor**
16. **Derek Nicholson, of, Florida**
17. **Colin Porter, of, Arizona**
18. **Rich Terwilliger, rhp, CC of the Finger Lakes (N.Y.)**
19. **Byron Wilkerson, rhp, Mary Hardin-Baylor (Texas)**
20. **Anthony Ramirez, 3b, Carson (Calif.) HS**
21. Brian Messer, rhp, New Mexico
22. **Garrett Zyskowski, lhp, West Virginia**
23. **Brandon Smith, rhp, Northeast Louisiana**
24. **Joshua Dimmick, c, Kansas**
25. **Jacob Whitney, lhp, Iowa State**
26. **Robert Cabrillo, 1b, Montgomery HS, San Diego**
27. Bobby Burns, c, Bingham HS, South Jordan, Utah
28. Chris Sheffield, rhp, Stephen F. Austin HS, Richmond, Texas
29. **Brandon Buckley, c, Texas Tech**
30. Jordan Hunt, rhp, Evergreen HS, Vancouver, Wash.
31. Alex Dvorsky, c, Marion (Iowa) HS
32. Bernie Gonzalez, of, Brito Miami Private HS, Miami
33. **Gavin Wright, of, Blinn (Texas) JC**
34. Ryan Humphrey, lhp, Indian River (Fla.) CC
35. Brett Kay, c, Mater Dei HS, Villa Park, Calif.
36. Benson Barrera, rhp, Skyview HS, Nampa, Idaho
37. Jeremy Frost, c, Oviedo (Fla.) HS
38. Bryan Edwards, rhp, Northeast Texas CC
39. Roberto Zaldivar, rhp, Arroyo HS, San Lorenzo, Calif.
40. Ray Leyba, lhp, Choctaw (Okla.) HS
41. Mike McHugh, rhp, Helix HS, La Mesa, Calif.

KANSAS CITY ROYALS

June—Regular Phase (4)

1. **Jeff Austin, rhp, Stanford**
1. **Matt Burch, rhp, Virginia Commonwealth** (Pick from Diamondbacks as compensation for Type A free agent Jay Bell)
1. **Chris George, lhp, Klein (Texas) HS** (Supplemental pick—31st—for loss of Bell)
2. **Robbie Morrison, rhp, Miami**
3. **Ben Cordova, of, Marian Catholic HS, Chula Vista, Calif.**
4. **Monty Ward, rhp, Texas Tech**
5. **Scott Chiasson, rhp, Eastern Connecticut State**
6. **Mike Curry, of, South Carolina**

7. **Jeremy Dodson, of, Baylor**
8. **Norris Hopper, ss, Shelby (N.C.) HS**
9. **Paul Phillips, of, Alabama**
10. **Jeremy Jackson, lhp, Mississippi State**
11. **Cary Ammons, lhp, Southeastern Oklahoma State**
12. **Emmanuel Santana, c, Maestro Ladi HS, Vega Alta, P.R.**
13. **Brian Shackelford, of, Oklahoma**
14. **Shawn Sedlacek, rhp, Iowa State**
15. Brock Griffin, c, Jesuit HS, Portland, Ore.
16. **Craig Jones, rhp, Southern California**
17. **Chuck Hamilton, rhp, Hollandale Simmons HS, Delta, Miss.**
18. **Ryan Hill, rhp, Wabash Valley (Ill.) JC**
19. Aaron Fausett, of, Beaverton (Ore.) HS
20. **Javier Pamus, rhp, San Jose State**
21. **James Shanks, of, Soloman HS, North Augusta, S.C.**
22. **John Lee, rhp, Washington**
23. **Corey Hart, 2b, Oklahoma**
24. **Ryan Fry, of, Missouri**
25. **Jeremy Freitas, of, Southern California**
26. Jeff Trzos, lhp, North Farmington HS, Farmington Hills, Mich.
27. **Yancy Ayres, c, Kansas State**
28. **Mike Russo, rhp, Queens (N.Y.)**
29. **Sean Bryan, 3b, Maple Woods (Mo.) JC**
30. Trevor Mote, ss, Yavapai (Ariz.) JC
31. Michael Denard, ss, Oakland (Calif.) Tech HS
32. **Jim Essian, c, Troy (Mich.) HS**
33. Jason Bartz, rhp, Manatee HS, Bradenton, Fla.
34. Damon Dombrowski, rhp, Truman HS, Independence, Mo.
35. Gabe Boruff, c, Ephrata (Wash.) HS
36. Shane Scoville, c, Ridge HS, Basking Ridge, N.J.
37. Jeffrey Jobe, rhp, Seward County (Kan.) CC
38. Lane Crews, rhp, Glades Day HS, Belle Glade, Fla.
39. Shawn Barksdale, rhp, Wallace State (Ala.) CC
40. Nathan Price, rhp, Cleveland, Miss.
41. Adam Lingenfelter, rhp, Buchholz HS, Gainesville, Fla.
42. **Felipe Alou Jr., of, Canada (Calif.) JC**

LOS ANGELES DODGERS

June—Regular Phase (23)

1. **Bubba Crosby, of, Rice**
2. **Mike Fischer, rhp, South Alabama**
3. Alex Santos, rhp, Miami
4. **Eric Riggs, ss, Central Florida**
5. **Scott Proctor, rhp, Florida State**
6. **Ryan Moskau, rhp/1b, Arizona**
7. **David Ross, c, Florida**
8. **Thomari Story-Hardin, 1b, El Cerrito HS, Richmond, Calif.**
9. **Joel Williams, rhp, Yoncalla (Ore.) HS**
10. **Lance Caraccioli, lhp, Northeast Louisiana**
11. **Christian Bridenbaugh, lhp, Central HS, Martinsburg, Pa.**
12. **J.K. Taylor, rhp, Louisa HS, Louisa City, Va.**
13. **Charles Thomas, of/rhp, McLane HS, Fresno**
14. **Robert Gorr, 1b/of, Southern California**
15. **Paul Avery, lhp, Pepperdine**
16. **Jim Goelz, ss, New York Tech**
17. **Alex Piedra, rhp, Southridge HS, Miami**
18. **Tony Richards, c, North Dakota State**
19. **Jeremy Meccage, rhp, Iowa**
20. **Tim Harrell, rhp, Liberty**
21. **Jacob Sampson, ss, Curtis HS, Tacoma**
22. **Tony Gomes, rhp, San Joaquin Delta (Calif.) JC**
23. **Jason Moody, lhp, Spartanburg Methodist (S.C.) JC**
24. **Allen Davis, lhp, Northwestern State**
25. **Scott Barnsby, rhp, Massachusetts**
26. **Matt Greer, c, Louisiana Tech**
27. **Nick Theodorou, 2b, UCLA**
28. Corry Parrott, of, Pasadena (Calif.) CC
29. David Baum, lhp, Martin County HS, Stuart, Fla.
30. Lloyd Turner, ss, Hephzibah (Ga.) HS
31. Paul Brown, lhp, Citrus (Calif.) JC
32. Darren Heal, c, Indian River (Fla.) JC
33. Herman Dean, of, Monrovia (Calif.) HS
34. Carlos Claudio, ss, Ora Wilma Chavez HS, Guaynabo, P.R.
35. Rashad Parker, ss, Crossroads HS, Santa Monica, Calif.
36. Curt Borland, rhp, Centaurus HS, Broomfield, Colo.
37. Joshua McMillen, of, West Virginia
38. Joshua Berndt, lhp, Oshkosh West HS, Oshkosh, Wis.
39. Marc-Andre Lagace, lhp, Louis Riel HS, Blackburn Hamlet, Ontario
40. Clint Hosford, rhp, Carson Graham HS, North Vancouver, B.C
41. Doug Vandecaveye, 3b, Tilbury (Ontario) District HS
42. Jahseam George, lhp, JC of the Sequoias (Calif.)
43. Jorge Roman, rhp, Jose de Diego HS, Aguadilla, P.R.
44. Joey Hart, c, Grayson County (Texas) CC
45. Brandon Smith, 1b, Cypress (Calif.) JC
46. Steve Andrade, rhp, American River (Calif.) JC
47. Harry Arocho, of, Benito Cerezo HS, Aguadilla, P.R.
48. Chad Marchand, rhp, Lethbridge (Alberta) CC
49. Wayne Stone, 3b, Miller HS, Rialto, Calif.
50. Blake McGinley, lhp, Bakersfield (Calif.) JC

MILWAUKEE BREWERS

June—Regular Phase (13)

1. **J.M. Gold, rhp, Toms River North HS, Toms River, N.J.**
2. **Nick Neugebauer, rhp, Arlington HS, Riverside, Calif.**
3. **Derry Hammond, of, West Point (Miss.) HS**
4. Rhett Parrott, rhp, Northwest Whitfield HS, Dalton, Ga.
5. **Chris Pine, rhp, Oregon State**
6. **Bill Hall, ss, Nettleton (Miss.) HS**
7. **Jason Fox, of, Florida Southern**
8. **Mike Penney, rhp, Southern California**
9. **Ryan Bordenick, c, South Carolina**
10. **James Johnson, lhp, Arizona**
11. **Jeff Pickler, 2b, Tennessee**
12. **Chris Barton, rhp, Connecticut**
13. Heath McMurray, rhp, San Jacinto (Texas) JC
14. Chuck Kegley, rhp, Middleburg (Fla.) HS
15. **Jose Montenegro, 3b, Oklahoma**
16. Hector Guadalupe, ss, Arundel HS, Gambrills, Md.
17. Steve Correa, lhp, Elk Grove (Calif.) HS
18. **Ricky Lewis, rhp, Mississippi Valley State**
19. **Scott Geitz, rhp, Southwest Missouri State**
20. Jeff Becker, 3b, Duke
21. **Ryan Poe, rhp, Saddleback (Calif.) CC**
22. Erik Smallwood, of, Tate HS, Gonzalez, Fla.
23. **Eric Ayala, 2b, Northeast Texas CC**
24. **Fontella Jones, rhp, Mississippi Valley State**
25. **Jack Krawczyk, rhp, Southern California**
26. **Dan Mathews, rhp, Indiana-Purdue Indianapolis**
27. **Jonathan Harraid, rhp, Sam Houston State**
28. **Tyrone Wayne, rhp, St. John's**
29. **Eduardo Figueroa, 1b, Tennessee**
30. **Casey Davis, of, Wichita State**
31. **Lee Jaramillo, c, Wisconsin-Milwaukee**
32. **Roberto Maysonet, rhp, Vega Baja, P.R.**
33. **Mac Mackiewitz, 1b, North Florida**
34. Curt Kautsch, rhp, Texas
35. Stephen York, of, Arizona Western JC
36. **Bill Eaton, of, South Florida**
37. Alfred Corbeil, c, Manatee (Fla.) CC
38. Jonathon Kuelz, rhp, West Lutheran HS, Minnetonka, Minn.
39. Dustin Wagoner, rhp, Corona (Calif.) HS
40. Ken Harold, c, Denham Springs HS, Baton Rouge
41. Brian Wojtkowski, of, Peoria (Ariz.) HS
42. Chris Vallette, rhp, Angelina (Texas) JC
43. Pedro Gavillan, 3b, Leonard HS, Lake Worth, Fla.
44. Jeff Eure, 3b, Upper Dauphin HS, Pillow, Pa.
45. Devin Butler, 1b, Key West (Fla.) HS
46. Nicholas Murphy, rhp, Central Florida CC
47. Landon Jacobsen, rhp, Trinidad State (Colo.) JC
48. Chad Christianson, lhp, Seabreeze HS, Ormond Beach, Fla.
49. Nick Wash, 3b, Picayune (Miss.) HS
50. Michael Wojtkowski, of, Peoria (Ariz.) HS

MINNESOTA TWINS

June—Regular Phase (6)

1. **Ryan Mills, lhp, Arizona State**
2. **Marcus Sents, rhp, Cookeville (Tenn.) HS**

3. **Brent Hoard, lhp, Stanford**
4. **Pete Fisher, rhp, Alabama**
5. **Mickey Blount, rhp, Kansas State**
6. Brad Pautz, rhp, Minnesota
7. Sam Taulli, lhp, Lafayette (La.) HS
8. **John Edwards, c, Triton (Ill.) JC**
9. **Saul Rivera, rhp, Mobile (Ala.)**
10. Ryan Lundquist, of, Arkansas
11. **Jon Pridie, rhp, Prescott (Ariz.) HS**
12. **Kareem Johnson, of, Crowe HS, Trail, B.C**
13. **Kyle Hawthorne, ss, Pensacola (Fla.) JC**
14. Mike Gosling, lhp, East HS, Salt Lake City
15. Brian Haskell, lhp, Canyon Springs HS, Moreno Valley, Calif.
16. **Jose Espinal, rhp, Canovanas, P.R.**
17. J.J. Putz, rhp, Michigan
18. Kevin Thompson, ss, Western Hills HS, Fort Worth
19. **Kevin Hodge, ss/3b, Rice**
20. **Brad Frazier, rhp, Mobile (Ala.)**
21. Marc Bluma, rhp, Wichita State
22. Rhett Riviere, rhp, St. Michael's Academy, Austin
23. **Andrew Butler, rhp, Bowling Green State**
24. **Juan Padilla, rhp, Jacksonville**
25. **Eric Sandberg, 1b, Ferris HS, Spokane, Wash.**
26. Jason Scobie, rhp, McLennan (Texas) JC
27. **Craig Selander, of, Minnesota**
28. **Dave Marciniak, 2b, Rutgers**
29. **Lester Victoria, lhp, Central Florida**
30. Jonathan Muller, 3b, Arapahoe HS, Littleton, Colo.
31. **Brian McMillan, of, Evansville**
32. **Todd Collura, c, Polk (Fla.) CC**
33. Bryan Gidge, rhp, Nevada-Las Vegas
34. **Kevin Frederick, rhp, Creighton**
35. Mack Lambert, rhp, Pearl River (La.) HS
36. **Richard Denholm, rhp, Edgewater HS, Orlando**
37. Ben Smith, rhp, Brownwood (Texas) HS
38. **Tommy Watkins, ss, Riverdale HS, Fort Myers, Fla.**
39. Nathan Kent, rhp, Motlow State (Tenn.) CC
40. Joe Maruffi, rhp, St. Pius X HS, Albuquerque
41. Kayzell Milton, of, Homestead HS, Fremont, Calif.
42. Andy Neufeld, ss, Manatee (Fla.) CC
43. Taylor Grant, lhp, Newport HS, Bellevue, Wash.
44. Robert Wood, rhp, Cherry Creek HS, Englewood, Colo.
45. Ernie Bascuas, rhp, Miami-Dade CC North
46. Mike Bradley, rhp, Dr. Phillips HS, Orlando
47. Wade Clark, rhp, Santa Ynez HS, Los Olivos, Calif.
48. Dan Olson, rhp, Loveland (Colo.) HS
49. Desmond Dailey, of, Eastern Arizona JC

MONTREAL EXPOS

June—Regular Phase (11)

1. **Josh McKinley, ss, Malvern Prep, Downington, Pa.**
1. **Brad Wilkerson, of/lhp, Florida** (Supplemental pick—33rd—for loss of Type A free agent Darrin Fletcher)
2. **Eric Good, lhp, Mishawaka (Ind.) HS**
3. **Clyde Williams, 1b, Seminole HS, Sanford, Fla.** (Pick from Blue Jays as compensation for Fletcher)
3. Kevin Kelly, 3b, Gloucester Catholic HS, Brooklawn, N.J.
4. **Rob Castelli, rhp, Eastern Illinois**
5. **Ryan Lentz, 3b, Washington**
6. **Wesley Chisnall, rhp, Etiwanda HS, Alta Loma, Calif.**
7. **Brad Piercy, c, North Carolina State**
8. **Scott Sandusky, c, Texas A&M**
9. **Juan Ortiz, of, Eastern District HS, Brooklyn**
10. **Ryan Grantham, rhp, Aldershot HS, Burlington, Ontario**
11. Jason Walker, lhp, Ontario (Calif.) HS
12. **Scott Dobson, rhp, North Carolina State**
13. **Jason Hendricks, of, Arizona**
14. **Kevin Hook, ss, Loyola Marymount**
15. Stephen Baker, of, Rome (N.Y.) Free Academy
16. **Derick Urquhart, of, South Carolina**
17. **Kyle Sheldon, rhp, Florida Southern**
18. **Jimmy Serrano, rhp, New Mexico**
19. **Omar Rosado, 2b, Toa Baja, P.R.**
20. **Brandon Agemennone, rhp, Maryland**
21. **Jason Kanovich, lhp, Shippensburg (Pa.)**
22. **Trevor Wamback, rhp, Dalhousie (Nova Scotia)**
23. **Jamie Hammond, ss, West Virginia**
24. Joe Clark, rhp, Chugiak HS, Eagle River, Alaska
25. Casey Fuller, lhp, Sacramento CC
26. **Brad Waldron, rhp, Iowa State**
27. **Steve Toriz, rhp, East Los Angeles JC**
28. Richard Lane, of, Tustin HS, Santa Ana, Calif.
29. Mike Castleberry, rhp, Batesville (Ark.) HS
30. Matt Romero, of, Spanish Fork (Utah) HS
31. Jeff Reboin, lhp, San Juan HS, Carmichael, Calif.
32. **Andrew Frierson, lhp, JC of San Mateo (Calif.)**
33. Josh Merrigan, lhp, Butler County (Kan.) JC
34. Charles Dubuc, lhp, St. Jean College HS, Iberville, Quebec
35. Jeff Lincoln, rhp, American River (Calif.) JC
36. Nathan Kershaw, of, Hoke County HS, Raeford, N.C.
37. Clint Dunbar, rhp, Norman (Okla.) HS
38. Chris Richards, of, Burlington (Vt.) HS
39. Anthony Watts, lhp, Lincoln HS, San Diego
40. Josh Laidlaw, of, Arizona Western JC
41. Alex Groleau, rhp, Edouard Montpetit HS, Longueil, Quebec
42. Ross Bennett, of, Central HS, Cape Girardeau, Mo.
43. Jace Brewer, ss, Washington (Okla.) HS
44. **Ron Chiavacci, rhp, Kutztown (Pa.)**
45. Tom Perez, ss, Burroughs HS, Burbank, Calif.

NEW YORK METS

June—Regular Phase (21)

1. **Jason Tyner, of, Texas A&M**
2. **Pat Strange, rhp, Central HS, Springfield, Mass.**
3. **Jason Saenz, lhp, Southern California**
4. Jason Moates, rhp, Meridian (Miss.) CC
5. **Craig Brazell, c, Jeff Davis HS, Montgomery, Ala.**
6. **Marvin Seale, of, Durango (Colo.) HS**
7. **Ryan Smith, c, Mifflinburg (Pa.) Area HS**
8. Vince Vazquez, rhp, Chaminade HS, Hollywood, Fla.
9. **Todd Bellhorn, lhp, Central Florida**
10. **Larnell Hamn, of, Potomac HS, Triangle, Va.**
11. **Josh Perich, of, Northwestern Lehigh HS, Slatington, Pa.**
12. Ryan Budde, c, Midwest City (Okla.) HS
13. **Andy Cook, rhp, William & Mary**
14. **Gil Velazquez, ss, Paramount (Calif.) HS**
15. **David Hunter, 1b, Porterville (Calif.) JC**
16. Scott Bikowski, of, Florida Southern
17. **Ty Wigginton, ss, UNC Asheville**
18. **Brian Cole, of, Navarro (Texas) JC**
19. **Frank Graham, rhp, Columbus State (Ohio) JC**
20. Jason Clements, ss, Riverside (Calif.) CC
21. **Roberto Lugo, 1b, Patria la Torres Ramirez HS, San Sebastian, P.R.**
22. Brian Shipp, ss, Meridian (Miss.) CC
23. **Jaime Cerda, lhp, Fresno CC**
24. **William Gobbel, ss, Presbyterian (S.C.)**
25. John Wesley, rhp, Clarke HS, Westbury, N.Y.
26. **Jason Osborn, c, Sehome HS, Bellingham, Wash.**
27. Justin Smith, lhp, Alabama
28. **Marc Ludvigsen, of, UNC Asheville**
29. **Alex Zardis, 2b, Edmonds (Wash.) CC**
30. **Alex Stoffels, c, Indian Hills (Iowa) CC**
31. **Rene Vega, lhp, Dominican (N.Y.)**
32. **Pedro Rodriguez, of, Rollins (Fla.)**
33. **Greg Halvorson, c/rhp, Arizona State**
34. **Billy Martin, 3b, Texas-Arlington**
35. Edwin Franco, lhp, Florida International
36. **Earl Snyder, 1b, Hartford**
37. Mike Wodnicki, rhp, Southington (Conn.) HS
38. **Gary Bohannon, rhp, Kennesaw State**
39. **Justin Kurtz, rhp, Brewton-Parker (Ga.)**
40. **Mike Prokop, rhp, Kennesaw State**
41. Joe Yarbrough, lhp, Hazel Green (Ala.) HS
42. Ben Leuthard, 1b, Mission Bay HS, San Diego
43. **Tom Paciorek, of, Southern (Ga.) Tech**
44. Ruben Feliciano, rhp, Bushwick HS, Brooklyn
45. Chris Nelson, of, Pasadena (Calif.) CC

46. **Ken Chenard, rhp, Fullerton (Calif.) JC**
47. Ben Vargas, rhp, El Monte HS, Azusa, Calif.
48. Chris Taylor, of, Riverside (Calif.) CC
49. Newton Hausmann, lhp, Red Bank Catholic HS, Colts Neck, N.Y.
50. **Aaron Hee, lhp, Taft (Calif.) JC**

NEW YORK YANKEES

June—Regular Phase (24)

1. **Andy Brown, of, Richmond (Ind.) HS**
1. Mark Prior (Supplemental pick), rhp, University HS, San Diego (Supplemental pick—43rd—for failure to sign 1997 first-rounder Tyrell Godwin)
2. **Randy Keisler, lhp, Louisiana State**
3. **Drew Henson, 3b/rhp, Brighton (Mich.) HS**
4. **Ivan Reyes, ss, Liceo Hispano Americano HS, Bayamon, P.R.**
5. **Brian Rogers, rhp, The Citadel**
6. **Brett Jodie, rhp, South Carolina**
7. **Ryan Ridenour, lhp, Texas Christian**
8. **David Fowler, of, McCluer North HS, Florissant, Mo.**
9. **Claude Greene, of, Notre Dame**
10. Damon Thames, ss, Rice
11. **Casey Degroote, 3b, West Vigo HS, West Terre Haute, Ind.**
12. **Jeffrey Sheffield, of, University HS, Spokane, Wash.**
13. Charlie Isaacson, rhp, Shawnee Mission West HS, Shawnee Mission, Kan.
14. **Brett Weber, rhp, Illinois**
15. **Justin Reisinger, rhp, Adena HS, Clarksburg, Ohio**
16. Gabriel Crecion, rhp, UCLA
17. **Jeff Shaddix, rhp, Texas Christian**
18. Danny Delmas, rhp, Odessa (Texas) JC
19. **Brad Elwood, c, West Virginia**
20. **Dusty Rhodes, of, Illinois**
21. **Neal Gregg, 1b, William Carey (Miss.)**
22. **Jeff Sziksai, 2b, Western Carolina**
23. **Mark Carek, ss, Ohio State**
24. Jason Willis, rhp, East Central (Miss.) JC
25. Mario Gandea, rhp, Odessa (Texas) HS
26. Javier Rodriguez, ss, Gulliver Prep, Miami
27. **Scott Massucco, c, St. Thomas Aquinas HS, Fort Lauderdale**
28. Lee Gwaltney, rhp, Aledo HS, Willow Park, Texas
29. Adam Manley, of, JC of Southern Idaho
30. Brian Conley, lhp, Gladewater (Texas) HS
31. **Elvis Corporan, ss, Espiritu Santo HS, Baja, P.R.**
32. Jay Signorelli, rhp, Manatee (Fla.) CC
33. Jeff Hunter, rhp, Meridian (Miss.) CC
34. **Brandon Claussen, lhp, Howard (Texas) JC**
35. Michael Gosz, ss, Treasure Valley (Ore.) CC
36. Eric Eckenstahler, lhp, Illinois State
37. Jarell McIntyre, ss, Laguna Creek HS, Elk Grove, Calif.
38. Chad Christian, lhp, Northeast Jones HS, Laurel, Miss.
39. Luke Miller, rhp, Rolla (Mo.) HS
40. Nook Logan, ss, Natchez (Miss.) HS
41. **David Kloes, rhp, West Virginia**
42. Justin Nash, rhp, Calvert Hall HS, Hunt Valley, Md.
43. Kris Ehmke, rhp, Hill (Texas) JC
44. Marc Love, of, Coldspring (Texas) HS
45. Jeff Moye, rhp, Hardin-Jefferson HS, Kountz, Texas
46. **Jeff Carlson, rhp, Quinnipiac**
47. **Jeff Nettles, 3b, Palomar (Calif.) JC**
48. Kyle Geswein, 1b, Carroll HS, Dayton, Ohio
49. Corey Lawson, rhp, Windsor (Mo.) HS
50. Joe List, rhp, Beechwood HS, Fort Mitchell, Ky.

OAKLAND ATHLETICS

June—Regular Phase (2)

1. **Mark Mulder, lhp, Michigan State**
2. **Gerald Laird, c, La Quinta HS, Westminster, Calif.**
3. **Kevin Miller, ss, Washington**
4. **Jeff Schultz, rhp, Cypress (Calif.) JC**
5. **Jason Hart, 1b, Southwest Missouri State**
6. **Gary Schneidmiller, ss, Don Lugo HS, Chino, Calif.**
7. **Donato Calandriello, lhp, College of Charleston**
8. **Eric Byrnes, of, UCLA**
9. **Jon Adkins, rhp, Oklahoma State**
10. **Bert Snow, rhp, Vanderbilt**
11. **Jay Pecci, ss, Stanford**
12. **Eric Thompson, rhp, Ohio State**
13. Jeff Bajenaru, rhp, Riverside (Calif.) CC
14. Mike Lockwood, of, Ohio State
15. **Rusty Keith, of, Portland State**
16. **Shane Bazzell, rhp, New Hope HS, Columbus, Miss.**
17. Elih Velazquez, lhp, Jose Campeche HS, San Lorenzo, P.R.
18. **Justin Hall, ss, Long Beach State**
19. **Justin Nixon, of, Walla Walla (Wash.) CC**
20. **DeWayne Betts, of, Lakewood (Calif.) HS**
21. Casey Bookout, 1b, Oklahoma
22. **Aaron Nieckula, c, Illinois**
23. **Tyler Yates, rhp, Hawaii-Hilo**
24. Bryan Williamson, of, Washington
25. **Jim Brink, rhp, Nevada**
26. **J.P. Schmidt, ss, Highland HS, Palmdale, Calif.**
27. **Jason Dobis, rhp, Minnesota**
28. **Matt Forbes, of, Muscatine (Iowa) CC**
29. **Matt Howe, 3b, Texas Christian**
30. **Anthony Taylor, rhp, Southern Colorado**
31. Mike Woods, 2b, Broadmoor HS, Baton Rouge
32. **Kurt Nantkes, rhp, Hibkley HS, Aurora, Colo.**
33. **Jose Negron, rhp, Southeastern (Iowa) CC**
34. Newt Parent, c, Phoenix (Ore.) HS
35. **Brad Moore, rhp, Northern Iowa**
36. Alex Torres, lhp, Cochise County (Ariz.) CC
37. Marshall Rubens, rhp, American River (Calif.) JC
38. Billy Green, of, Spring (Texas) HS
39. Bryan Ball, rhp, Taylorsville HS, Salt Lake City
40. Zack Riera, c, Florida HS, Tallahassee, Fla.
41. James Mears, rhp, Indian Hills (Iowa) CC
42. John Dean, of, Magnolia (Texas) HS
43. Mike Cervenak, 3b, Michigan

PHILADELPHIA PHILLIES

June—Regular Phase (1)

1. **Pat Burrell, 3b/1b, Miami**
1. **Eric Valent, of, UCLA** (Supplemental pick—42nd—for failure to sign 1997 first-rounder J.D. Drew)
2. **Brad Baisley, rhp, Land O' Lakes (Fla.) HS**
3. **Jorge Padilla, of, Florida Air Academy, Melbourne, Fla.**
4. **Jason Michaels, of, Miami**
5. **Kennon McArthur, c, Sylacauga (Ala.) HS**
6. Tommy Whiteman, ss, Midwest City (Okla.) HS
7. **Jarrod Lawson, rhp, Potosi (Mo.) HS**
8. **Mike Wilson, rhp, Granite Hills HS, El Cajon, Calif.**
9. **Ryan Madson, rhp, Valley View HS, Moreno Valley, Calif.**
10. **Ken Westmoreland, rhp, Alabama-Huntsville**
11. **Ben Jewson, 3b, Waukesha (Wis.) North HS**
12. **Ian Rauls, of, Old Dominion**
13. Adam Peterson, rhp, Oconto Falls (Wis.) HS
14. **Greg Kubes, lhp, Sam Houston State**
15. **Geoff Geary, rhp, Oklahoma**
16. **Chris Pilato, rhp, Villanova**
17. **Chip DeNure, ss, Ripon (Wis.)**
18. **Nate Espy, 1b, Lurleen Wallace State (Ala.) JC**
19. **Jeremy Salazar, c, Florida State**
20. **Jeremy Wedel, rhp, Armstrong Atlantic (Ga.) State**
21. **Nick Punto, ss, Saddleback (Calif.) JC**
22. **Matt Bailie, rhp, Oregon State**
23. **Cary Hiles, rhp, Memphis**
24. **Shayne Carnes, of, Alabama-Birmingham**
25. Aric LeClair, lhp, Crowder (Mo.) JC
26. **Mike Zipser, rhp, Nevada**
27. **Ron McGinnis, c, Texas-San Antonio**
28. **Chris Maness, rhp, Elon**
29. **Andrew Weidl, lhp, Winona State (Minn.)**
30. **Kurt Blackmon, rhp, North Carolina State**
31. **Len Hannahan, 2b, St. Thomas (Minn.)**
32. Abraham Ayala, 3b, Bayamon, P.R.

33. **Wes Rachels, 2b, Southern California**
34. **David Ciesla, lhp, Arkansas Tech**
35. Pete Montrenes, rhp, Ocean View HS, Fountain Valley, Calif.
36. **Roger Rodeheaver, 1b, Indiana**
37. **Ed Grammer, rhp, Union (Tenn.)**
38. Lance Cooley, ss, Killeen HS, Harker Heights, Texas
39. **Jeremy Deitrick, c, Penn State**
40. Todd Henry, rhp, Bakersfield (Calif.) JC
41. **Tom Donovan, rhp, Elon**
42. Kirk Nordness, ss, Beaverton (Ore.) HS
43. Earnest Graham, of, Mariner HS, Fort Myers, Fla.

PITTSBURGH PIRATES

June—Regular Phase (15)

1. **Clint Johnston, lhp/of, Vanderbilt**
2. **Jeremy Cotten, 3b/rhp, Fuquay-Varina (N.C.) HS**
3. **Jeremy Harts, of/lhp, Columbia HS, Decatur, Ga.**
4. **Eddy Furniss, 1b, Louisiana State**
5. **Rayner Cardona, c, Patria la Torres Ramirez HS, San Sebastian, P.R.**
6. **Brice Pelfrey, ss, Tate HS, Gonzalez, Fla.**
7. **James White, rhp, Chico (Calif.) HS**
8. Chuck Crowder, lhp, Georgia Tech
9. **Giovanni Gonzalez, rhp, Northwest Christian Academy, Miami**
10. **David Diaz, c, Hialeah-Miami Lakes HS, Hialeah, Fla.**
11. Chris Smith, lhp/of, Wantagh (N.Y.) HS
12. **Willie Burton, of, Lake Wales (Fla.) HS**
13. **Ben Levesque, rhp, Cary (N.C.) HS**
14. John Breck, rhp, Bridgewater-Raritan HS, Bridgewater, N.J.
15. Craig House, rhp, Memphis
16. Russ Rohlicek, lhp, College Park HS, Pleasant Hill, Calif.
17. **Dave Williams, lhp, Delaware Tech JC**
18. **Joe Beimel, lhp, Duquesne**
19. **Jeff Bennett, rhp, Gordonsville (Tenn.) HS**
20. **Mike Johnston, lhp, Garrett (Md.) CC**
21. **Mike Bumatay, lhp/of, Clovis (Calif.) HS**
22. **Josh Miller, c, Silver Bluff HS, Aiken, S.C.**
23. Tyson Thompson, of, Inglemoor HS, Bothell, Wash.
24. **David Hawk, lhp, Vista West HS, Bakersfield, Calif.**
25. Thom Ott, rhp, Greenbriar Christian Academy, Chesapeake, Va.
26. Jon Switzer, lhp, Clear Lake HS, Houston
27. **Casey Cloud, c, UCLA**
28. **Steve Sparks, rhp, South Alabama**
29. Scott Gardner, lhp, Cardinal Gibbons HS, Coral Springs, Fla.
30. Matt Vorwald, rhp, Freeport (Ill.) HS
31. Eric Tatum, lhp, Forest Hill HS, West Palm Beach, Fla.
32. Wyatt Allen, rhp, Brentwood Academy, Nashville
33. Marcus Nettles, of, Whitney Young HS, Chicago
34. Traviss Hodge, 1b, Highland HS, Agua Dulce, Calif.
35. Trevor Hutchinson, rhp, Torrey Pines HS, San Diego
36. Steve Wombacher, 1b, Yavapai (Ariz.) JC
37. Justin Fry, rhp, Ohio State
38. **Shaun Skrehot, ss, Houston**
39. **Veon Harris, rhp, East Mississippi JC**
40. Jeff Ellena, ss, Walnut HS, Diamond Bar, Calif.
41. Christian Ortiz, of, Arcadia (Calif.) HS
42. Scott Glaser, lhp, South Florida
43. **Eric Stanton, 3b, South Carolina**
44. Brian Walker, lhp, Westminster Christian HS, Miami
45. **Brian Cronk, 3b/of, Eastern New Mexico**
46. Jamie Shearin, c, East Wake HS, Knightdale, N.C.
47. Josh Renick, 2b, Manatee (Fla.) JC

ST. LOUIS CARDINALS

June—Regular Phase (5)

1. **J.D. Drew, of, St. Paul (Northern League)**
1. Ben Diggins, 1b/rhp, Bradshaw Mountain HS, Dewey, Ariz. (Supplemental pick—32nd—for loss of Type A free agent Dennis Eckersley)
2. **Chad Hutchinson, rhp, Stanford**
2. **Tim Lemon, of, La Mirada (Calif.) HS** (Pick from Red Sox as compensation for Eckersley)
3. **Gabe Johnson, c, Atlantic HS, Delray Beach, Fla.**
4. **Bud Smith, lhp, Los Angeles Harbor JC**
5. **Steve Stemle, rhp, Western Kentucky**
6. **Kris Rayborn, lhp, Purvis (Miss.) HS**
7. **Brad Freeman, ss/of, Mississippi State**
8. **Greg Clark, c, Arizona**
9. **Jack Wilson, ss, Oxnard (Calif.) JC**
10. **Pedro Zazueta, rhp, Amphitheater HS, Tucson**
11. Joel Vega, lhp, Ohio Dominican
12. Jeff Waldron, c, Boston College
13. **Les Walrond, lhp, Kansas**
14. **Jason Bowers, ss, Gulf Coast (Fla.) CC**
15. **John Hernandez, of, Xaverian HS, Brooklyn**
16. **Scott Prather, lhp, Georgia Tech**
17. **Matt Gargano, rhp, Dixie (Utah) JC**
18. **Esix Snead, of, Central Florida**
19. **Travis Held, rhp, Central Florida**
20. **Chris Kelly, 3b, Catawba (N.C.)**
21. **Jim Molina, of, Florida International**
22. Mike Rerick, lhp, North Dakota
23. **Andy Shibilo, rhp, Pepperdine**
24. **Richard Gonzales, rhp, New Mexico**
25. **Jon Hand, rhp, Virginia Tech**
26. Steve Parker, rhp, Key West (Fla.) HS
27. **Ryan Christianson, rhp, Nebraska-Omaha**
28. **Jason Marr, rhp, Long Beach State**
29. **Jeffrey Viles, rhp, Rockhurst (Mo.)**
30. **Eric Gutshall, rhp, Yale**
31. **Troy McNaughton, rhp, Brigham Young**
32. **Troy Farnsworth, 2b, Brigham Young**
33. **Tommy Kidwell, 2b, Yale**
34. John Boyer, ss, Bonneville HS, Ogden, Utah
35. Dustin Hawkins, of, Bonneville HS, Ogden, Utah
36. Andrew Ecklund, c, San Luis Obispo (Calif.) HS
37. Brent Cordell, c, Incline HS, Incline Village, Nev.
38. Seth Jerue, ss, Westfield (Mass.) HS
39. Vic Buttler, of, Westchester HS, Hawthorne, Calif.
40. Scott Neal, of, North HS, Bakersfield, Calif.
41. Justin Knoedler, c, Springfield (Ill.) HS
42. Brandon Tisher, 1b, Durango (Colo.) HS
43. Scott Sorensen, rhp, Fruita Monument HS, Grand Junction, Colo.
44. Matt Harvick, c, North HS, Bakersfield, Calif.
45. Matt Van Alsburg, of, Fort Collins (Colo.) HS

SAN DIEGO PADRES

June—Regular Phase (9)

1. **Sean Burroughs, 3b, Wilson HS, Long Beach**
2. (Pick to Braves as compensation for Type B free agent Greg Myers)
3. Beau Craig, c, Grossmont HS, La Mesa, Calif.
4. **Travis Devine, rhp, Dacula (Ga.) HS**
5. **Kevin Eberwein, 3b/of, Nevada-Las Vegas**
6. Dale Deveraux, rhp, American Fork (Utah) HS
7. **Brian Berryman, rhp, Michigan**
8. **Jeremy Owens, of, Middle Tennessee State**
9. **Sean Campbell, c, Nevada-Las Vegas**
10. **John Meyers, rhp, Grayson County (Texas) JC**
11. **Josh Loggins, of, Kentucky**
12. **Joe Dusan, 1b, Sacramento CC**
13. Thom Dreier, rhp, Oklahoma State
14. **Ryan Hawkins, rhp, Lurleen Wallace State (Ala.) JC**
15. **Casey Bell, rhp, Crowder (Mo.) JC**
16. **Steve Watkins, rhp, Lubbock Christian (Texas)**
17. **Brian Lawrence, rhp, Northwestern State**
18. **Aaron Kramer, rhp, Arizona State**
19. **Jeremy Fikac, rhp, Southwest Texas State**
20. Eron Morrow, 1b, Wilson HS, Tacoma
21. **Keith Forbes, rhp, Lurleen Wallace State (Ala.) JC**
22. **Jon Cook, of, San Francisco State**
23. **Jack Wickersham, 2b, Southwest Texas State**
24. Jerymaine Beasley, of, Spokane Falls (Wash.) CC
25. Jonathan Segarra, lhp, Frank Phillips (Texas) JC
26. **Ryan Bauer, rhp, Fontbonne (Mo.)**
27. Ralph Roberts, of, Cherryville (N.C.) HS

28. **Jeremy Reed, c, Lookout Valley HS, Chattanooga**
29. **Cliff Bartosh, lhp, Duncanville (Texas) HS**
30. **Eric Cyr, lhp, Seminole State (Okla.) JC**
31. **Michael Hazen, of, Princeton**
32. Geoffrey Jones, lhp, Montezuma-Cortez HS, Cortez, Colo.
33. **Bryan Schmidt, ss, Nebraska**
34. Simon Mitchell, of, Bellevue (Wash.) CC
35. Josh Barbarossa, 1b, Chesterton HS, Valparaiso, Ind.
36. Nathan Sturdivant, rhp, Westmoore HS, Oklahoma City
37. Felix Castillo, rhp, Rio Grande, P.R.
38. Trey Hodges, rhp, Blinn (Texas) JC
39. Jonathan Stone, c, Sacramento CC
40. Clint Kelley, rhp, Morton (Ill.) JC
41. Charis Britt, c, Gulf Coast (Fla.) CC
42. **Alex Pelaez, 3b, San Diego State**
43. Jason Jones, rhp, Kennesaw State
44. Jesse Gutierrez, c, Texas Southmost JC

SAN FRANCISCO GIANTS

June—Regular Phase (25)

1. **Tony Torcato, 3b, Woodland (Calif.) HS** (Pick from Astros as compensation for Type B free agent Doug Henry)
1. **Nate Bump, rhp, Penn State**
1. **Arturo McDowell, of, Forest Hill HS, Jackson, Miss.** (Pick from Devil Rays as compensation for Type A free agent Roberto Hernandez)
1. **Chris Jones, lhp, South Mecklenburg HS, Charlotte** (Supplemental pick—38th—for loss of Hernandez)
1. **Jeff Urban, lhp, Ball State** (Supplemental pick—41st—for loss of Type A free agent Wilson Alvarez)
2. **Sammy Serrano, c, Stetson**
2. **Chris Magruder, of, Washington** (Pick from Devil Rays as compensation for Alvarez)
3. **Mike Dean, c, Oral Roberts**
4. **Josh Santos, lhp, Connecticut**
5. **Ryan Vogelsong, rhp, Kutztown (Pa.)**
6. **Jake Esteves, rhp, Louisiana State**
7. **Doug Clark, of, Massachusetts**
8. **Todd Ozias, rhp, Miami**
9. **Cody Ransom, ss, Grand Canyon (Ariz.)**
10. **Chris Jackson, rhp, Wasson HS, Colorado Springs**
11. **Erasmo Ramirez, lhp, Cal State Fullerton**
12. **Randy Goodrich, rhp, Fresno State**
13. **John Summers, 1b, Utah**
14. **Mike Huller, lhp, George Mason**
15. **Jeff Allen, of, Illinois State**
16. **Erik Mattern, 2b/ss, Arizona**
17. **Joe Ojeda, rhp, St. Francis (N.Y.)**
18. **Dave Brous, lhp, Del Norte HS, Crescent City, Calif.**
19. Ben Quick, rhp, Riverside (Calif.) CC
20. Santiago Narciandi, 3b, Miami (Fla.) Senior HS
21. **Benji Miller, rhp, Liberty**
22. Theodore Sutton, lhp, Colton (Calif.) HS
23. Jake Mapes, c, Riverside (Calif.) CC
24. Ken Trapp, rhp, Alvin (Texas) CC
25. Oscar Vargas, ss, James Logan HS, Union City, Calif.
26. Jason Barrow, of, Canby Union HS, Canby, Ore.
27. **Steven Hill, ss, Oklahoma State**
28. Chad Ertel, rhp, Elmira (Ontario) District HS
29. Kyle Middleton, rhp, Escambia HS, Pensacola, Fla.
30. Grant Abrams, ss, Tarpon Springs HS, Palm Harbor, Fla.
31. Cade Sanchez, rhp, Texas-Arlington
32. Jackson Markert, rhp, Connors State (Okla.) JC
33. Ryan Gonzales, rhp, Riverside (Calif.) CC
34. Travis McGreal, rhp, Heritage HS, Littleton, Colo.
35. Matt Dryer, ss, McQuaid Jesuit HS, Rochester, N.Y.
36. Josh Souza, rhp, Turlock (Calif.) HS
37. Dan Kelly, lhp, Okaloosa Walton (Fla.) JC
38. Winston Woods, of, Coral Shores HS, Key Largo, Fla.
39. Joel Vasquez, of, Booker HS, Sarasota, Fla.
40. Bill Nahorodny, of, Clearwater (Fla.) HS
41. Marcellus Presley, of, Sacramento CC
42. **Carlos Frazier, of, Smackover (Ark.) HS**
43. Scott Goodman, of, Cuesta (Calif.) JC
44. Dorian Cameron, ss, Coastal Carolina
45. Cody Sudbeck, rhp, Tyler (Texas) JC

SEATTLE MARINERS

June—Regular Phase (22)

1. **Matt Thornton, lhp, Grand Valley State (Mich.)**
2. Jeff Verplancke, rhp, Cal State Los Angeles
3. **Andy Van Hekken, lhp, Holland (Mich.) HS**
4. **Jerry Amador, of, Luis Felipe Crespo HS, Camuy, P.R.**
5. **Corey Freeman, ss, King HS, Tampa**
6. **Jake Weber, of, North Carolina State**
7. **Shawn McCorkle, 1b, Montclair State (N.J.)**
8. **Craig Kuzmic, c/3b, Texas A&M**
9. **Neil Longo, rhp, Manhattan**
10. Jason Pomar, rhp, South Carolina
11. Jarrett Shearin, of, North Carolina
12. **Justin Dunning, rhp, Stanford**
13. **Israel Cruz, ss, Carolina, P.R.**
14. **Schuyler Doakes, ss, Jackson State**
15. **Wilfredo Quintana, of, Indian Hills (Iowa) CC**
16. **Patrick Barnes, lhp, Englewood HS, Jacksonville**
17. **Steve Wright, of, Liberty**
18. **Craig Willis, rhp, Pacific Lutheran (Wash.)**
19. **Rick Southall, 1b/of, Portland State**
20. Jon Nelson, ss, Timpanogos HS, Orem, Utah
21. Brandon DeJaynes, rhp, Quincy (Ill.) HS
22. Mike Myers, ss, Bishop Verot HS, Cape Coral, Fla.
23. Bryan Hartung, rhp, Sinton (Texas) HS
24. **Matt Woodward, 1b, Florida State**
25. Craig Helmandollar, lhp, North Stafford HS, Stafford, Va.
26. **Caleb Balbuena, rhp, Long Beach State**
27. **Jason Crist, lhp, Southwest Missori State**
28. **Bo Robinson, 3b, UNC Charlotte**
29. Derald Deason, of, Orange HS, Santa Ana, Calif.
30. John Rheinecker, lhp, Belleville Area (Ill.) CC
31. Roy Wells, rhp, Volunteer State (Tenn.) CC
32. Clay Bried, of, Apache Junction HS, Mesa, Ariz.
33. Brandon Pack, c, Cypress (Calif.) JC
34. Nick Padilla, rhp, Cerritos (Calif.) JC
35. Guarionez Rodriguez, 2b, Trujillo Alto, P.R.
36. Tim Dierkes, c, Mehlville HS, St. Louis
37. Michael Kashuba, rhp, Clarence Fulton HS, Vernon, B.C
38. Clint Patton, c, Sonora HS, Brea, Calif.
39. Aaron Kirkland, rhp, Lurleen Wallace State (Ala.) JC
40. Adam Thomas, rhp, North Miami (Fla.) HS
41. Nicholas Hobbs, of, Chaparral HS, Las Vegas
42. Geoff Comfort, of, Serra HS, Burlingame, Calif.
43. James Farris, c, Hattiesburg (Miss.) HS
44. Israel Torres, lhp, Cerritos (Calif.) JC
45. Drew Parkin, rhp, Aliso Niguel HS, Laguna Niguel, Calif.
46. Ernie Durazo, 3b, Pima (Ariz.) CC
47. Clayton McCullough, c, Rose HS, Greenville, N.C.
48. Greg Pines, c, Saddleback (Calif.) CC
49. Scott Atchison, rhp, Texas Christian
50. David Holliday, lhp, Anderson Shiro HS, Navasota, Texas

TAMPA BAY DEVIL RAYS

June—Regular Phase (29)

1. (Pick to Giants as compensation for Type A free agent Roberto Hernandez)
2. (Pick to Giants as compensation for Type A free agent Wilson Alvarez)
3. (Pick to White Sox as compensation for Type A free agent Dave Martinez)
4. **Josh Pressley, 1b/rhp, Westminster Academy, Fort Lauderdale**
5. **Aubrey Huff, 3b, Miami**
6. **Ryan Rupe, rhp, Texas A&M**
7. **John Jacobs, 3b, Marin Catholic HS, Kentfield, Calif.**
8. **Joe Kennedy, lhp, Grossmont (Calif.) JC**
9. **Brian Martin, c, Central Union HS, El Centro, Calif.**
10. Ben Keiter, rhp, Arvada (Colo.) West HS
11. **Steven Goodson, of, Cowley County (Kan.) CC**

12. **Adam Flohr, lhp, Portland State**
13. **Patrick Dickson, lhp, Dalton (Ga.) HS**
14. **Patrick Hertzel, rhp, Kansas State**
15. **Charles Armstrong, lhp, Contra Costa (Calif.) JC**
16. Neal Frendling, rhp, Lake Central HS, Dyer, Ind.
17. Mike Rodriguez, of, Cooper City (Fla.) HS
18. **Brandon Backe, ss, Galveston (Texas) JC**
19. Art Garland, of, Santa Ana (Calif.) JC
20. Preston Larrison, rhp, Aurora (Ill.) West HS
21. Darin Moore, rhp, Pacific
22. **Dan Grummitt, 1b, Shawnee State (Ohio)**
23. **Frank Moore, 2b, Middle Georgia JC**
24. Ryan Jorgensen, c, San Jacinto (Texas) JC
25. **Joe Haines, rhp, Freed-Hardeman (Tenn.)**
26. George Moran, rhp, Red Bluff (Calif.) HS
27. **James Lira, rhp, Laredo (Texas) HS**
28. Chad Cossette, c, Edmonds (Wash.) CC
29. Jeremy Manning, lhp, Pitt (N.C.) CC
30. Gary Welch, rhp, Howard (Texas) JC
31. Chris Wailand, rhp, Manatee HS, Bradenton, Fla.
32. **Sean Mahoney, of, Florida International**
33. Rudolph Frolish, lhp, Ansonia (Conn.) HS
34. **Matt Schuldt, rhp, Nebraska**
35. **Monte McGillivray, lhp, San Jacinto (Texas) JC**
36. Tim Olson, ss, Hutchinson (Kan.) JC
37. Brandon Medders, rhp, Hillcrest HS, Duncanville, Ala.
38. Andrew Cook, rhp, Antioch (Calif.) HS
39. Edwin Rodriguez, 1b, Ponce (P.R.) HS
40. Michael McCuan, rhp, Butler County (Kan.) JC
41. Jeff Bruksch, rhp, Beverly Hills (Calif.) HS
42. Dane Hutchens, rhp, McLennan (Texas) JC
43. Brandon Culp, rhp, Wallace State (Ala.) CC
44. Mark Carter, lhp, Hewitt-Trussville HS, Trussville, Ala.
45. Harold Godeill, of, Modesto (Calif.) JC
46. **Cody Getz, lhp, JC of Eastern Utah**
47. Brooks Stephens, 1b, Stetson
48. Mike Jacobs, c, Hilltop HS, Chula Vista, Calif.
49. Justin Hancock, ss, Bloomingdale HS, Valrico, Fla.
50. Luis Candelaria, of, Hill (Texas) JC

TEXAS RANGERS

June—Regular Phase (10)

1. **Carlos Pena, 1b, Northeastern**
2. **Cody Nowlin, of, Clovis (Calif.) HS**
3. Barry Zito, lhp, Los Angeles Pierce JC
4. **Antwon Rollins, of, Encinal HS, Alameda, Calif.**
5. **Ryan Dittfurth, rhp, Union HS, Tulsa**
6. **Frankie McGill, rhp, Tate HS, Gonzalez, Fla.**
7. **John Stewart, lhp, Western Michigan**
8. Brad Ticehurst, of, Southern California
9. **Andy Pratt, lhp, Chino Valley (Ariz.) HS**
10. **Justin Backsmeyer, rhp, DeSmet HS, St. Louis**
11. **Cesar Castaneda, 3b, Dallas Baptist**
12. **Dan Boublis, rhp, Villanova**
13. **Jeremiah Bullock, lhp, Kuna (Idaho) HS**
14. **Derek Ottevaere, 1b, Western Michigan**
15. **Ole Vigeland, rhp, Washington State**
16. **Domingo Valdez, rhp, Moody HS, Corpus Christi, Texas**
17. **Dave Meliah, ss, San Francisco**
18. **Michael Schaeffer, lhp, Saint Louis**
19. **Mike Daniel, rhp, Lambuth (Tenn.)**
20. Ryan Knox, of, Illinois State
21. **Matt Kosderka, rhp, Willamette (Ore.)**
22. John Shelley, 3b, Santa Margarita HS, Rancho Santa Margarita, Calif.
23. **Frank Marciante, 1b, Palm Beach (Fla.) JC**
24. **Jason Edgar, 2b, Connecticut**
25. Brandon Moorhead, rhp, Franklin County HS, Gainesville, Ga.
26. **Jimmie Romano, c, South Florida**
27. **Jeremy Jones, c, Arizona State**
28. **Rob LaMarsh, lhp, Southern Illinois-Edwardsville**
29. Ronnie Corona, rhp, Cypress (Calif.) JC
30. Jaime Bubela, of, Blinn (Texas) JC
31. **Marcos Quinones, ss, Dallas Baptist**
32. Greg Summers, of, Port St. Joe (Fla.) HS
33. Ryan Cullen, lhp, Satellite HS, Satellite Beach, Fla.
34. Josh Bolingbroke, c, Pleasant Grove (Utah) HS
35. **William Villamil, lhp, Carolina, P.R.**
36. **Eric Moore, rhp, Lambuth (Tenn.)**
37. Jon Harris, rhp, Maple Woods (Mo.) JC
38. Trent Pratt, c, Tooele (Utah) HS
39. **Greg Ryan, lhp/1b, Eastern Michigan**
40. Craig Mosher, lhp, JC of Southern Idaho
41. Scott Nicholson, lhp, Lower Columbia (Wash.) JC
42. Ross Peeples, lhp, Crisp Academy, Cordele, Ga.
43. Derrick Foster, rhp, Pell City (Ala.) HS
44. Josh Hollingsworth, ss, Dunedin (Fla.) HS
45. Greg Bochy, rhp, Palomar (Calif.) JC
46. Damon Sementilli, rhp, Norwalk (Conn.) CC
47. Roy York, of, Cowley County (Kan.) CC
48. Shaun Rudi, of, Baker HS, Baker City, Ore.
49. Marcis Hassell, of, Sam Houston HS, Arlington, Texas
50. Alberto Montes, rhp, Socorro HS, El Paso, Texas

TORONTO BLUE JAYS

June—Regular Phase (8)

1. **Felipe Lopez, ss, Lake Brantley HS, Altamonte Springs, Fla.**
2. (Pick to Orioles as compensation for Type A free agent Randy Myers)
3. (Pick to Expos as compensation for Type A free agent Darrin Fletcher)
4. **Ryan Bundy, c, Washington**
5. Lee Delfino, ss, Pickering (Ontario) HS
6. **Joe Orloski, rhp, Green Valley HS, Henderson, Nev.**
7. **Tyler Thompson, of, Indiana State**
8. **Mike Kremblas, c, Ohio State**
9. **Steve Murray, lhp, St. Peter HS, Peterborough, Ontario**
10. **Jarrod Kingrey, rhp, Alabama**
11. Ray Aguilar, lhp, South El Monte (Calif.) HS
12. **Eric Place, lhp, Western Michigan**
13. **Adam Huxhold, lhp, Lewis-Clark State (Idaho)**
14. **Jay Gibbons, 1b, Cal State Los Angeles**
15. **Richard Lee, 1b, Mississippi State**
16. **Brandon Jackson, ss, Southwest Missouri State**
17. **Reuben St. Amand, rhp, Capital HS, Olympia, Wash.**
18. **Ryan Fleming, of, Dayton**
19. **Bob File, 3b, Philadelphia College of Textiles**
20. **Auntawn Riggins, ss, Texas Southern**
21. **Franklyn Gracesqui, lhp, George Washington HS, New York**
22. Adam Stern, of, St. Thomas Aquinas HS, New Britain, Conn.
23. **Justin Davies, of, Queens (N.Y.)**
24. Maurice Murray, of, Hawkinsville (Ga.) HS
25. Nestor Rivera, ss, Josefa Pastrana HS, Aguas Buenase, P.R.
26. Matt Sorensen, rhp, Cerritos (Calif.) JC
27. Noel Daniel, ss, Northside HS, Jackson, Tenn.
28. Shawn Lynn, rhp, George Henry Academy, North York, Ontario
29. Jason Shelley, ss, Northeast Louisiana
30. Garris Gonce, c, Clay HS, Orange Park, Fla.
31. **Ryan Houston, rhp, Escambia HS, Pensacola, Fla.**
32. Jason Lind, lhp, Moon Valley HS, Phoenix
33. Ryan Smith, rhp, South Hills HS, West Covina, Calif.
34. Bob Cramer, lhp, Fullerton (Calif.) JC
35. **Cameron Reimers, rhp, JC of Southern Idaho**
36. Lee Southard, rhp, Seminole State (Okla.) JC
37. Justin Williams, of, Columbia Basin (Wash.) JC
38. **Aaron Dean, rhp, Canada (Calif.) JC**
39. Joel Alvarado, c, Miguel Melendez HS, Cayey, P.R.
40. Brian Hutchinson, lhp, Western Carolina
41. **Mike Stafford, lhp, Ohio State**
42. Justin Valente, of, Greenwich HS, Cos Cob, Conn.
43. Travis Beckham, rhp, Port Dover (Ontario) Composite HS
44. Greg Palmer, lhp, Clackamas (Ore.) JC
45. Brian Ackerson, rhp, Fountain Valley (Calif.) HS
46. D.J. Loland, rhp, Northeast Louisiana
47. Kenny Huff, of, Horizon HS, Scottsdale, Ariz.
48. Isaac Iorg, ss, Karns HS, Knoxville
49. Troy Wilkins, rhp, Mountain Home (Idaho) HS

1999 BASEBALL FINALLY GETS A DRAFT WITHOUT MAJOR CONTROVERSY, AS TEAMS HAND OUT BIG BONUSES

The 1999 draft will actually be remembered for . . . the players. There were no loophole free agents and $10 million contracts, no J.D. Drew style holdouts and few acrimonious negotiations. The commissioner's office attempted no last-minute rule changes and the word arbitrator was never whispered.

In fact, every player from the first round was under contract by the end of August, the first time that had happened since 1990. The underlying reason was the enormous amount of money spent on top amateur talent. The average bonus for first-round picks in 1999 was $1,809,767, easily surpassing the 1998 average of $1,637,667. It also topped the record first-round average of $1,794,383 set in 1996, when a draft loophole enabled four players to sign as free agents. Those players received contracts worth a total of $29.275 million.

Three players dominated speculation for the top pick all spring: high school righthander Josh Beckett, high school outfielder Josh Hamilton and Southern California catcher Eric Munson. Hamilton, 18, shocked scouts in preseason practice games in Raleigh, N.C., by hitting 95-96 mph from the mound—usually enough by itself to put a high school lefthander in the first round. But Hamilton's athleticism and power potential kept scouts focused on him as an outfielder.

Beckett, 19, came into the spring regarded as one of the most acclaimed high school pitchers in draft history and a candidate to become the first prep righthander ever to be selected first overall. He did nothing to discourage comparisons to past Texas schoolboy heroes Nolan Ryan, David Clyde and Kerry Wood.

Munson, 21, missed two months of the spring season at Southern California when he was crossed up by lefthander Barry Zito, a fellow first-rounder, and broke his right hand. The injury healed in time for Munson to return for NCAA tournament play before the draft, but he did not vault himself over the two high school players to the top of the draft.

When draft day came, it was obvious that Hamilton was Tampa Bay's choice. That there was a different climate for signing players become obvious when the Devil Rays announced Hamilton's signing hardly 48 hours after selecting him, for $3.96 million.

"We got ourselves a real old-fashioned ballplayer," Tampa Bay scouting director Dan Jennings said. "Besides all the obvious tools, Josh has all the intangibles you'd want to see in a ballplayer. He has a great natural rhythm and pace to his game."

Hamilton went on to become one of the most

MORRIS FOSTOFF

Josh Beckett paid huge dividends for the Marlins before leaving as a free agent

intriguing figures in draft history, getting off to a promising start in the minors before battling injuries and serious substance-abuse problems for several years. He was suspended by Major League Baseball and didn't play at all from 2003-2005, finally returning to the field at the end of the 2006 season. The Reds then took him in the Rule 5 draft in December, and he broke into the major leagues for the first time in 2007, hitting 19 home runs in 298 at-bats. He got traded to the Rangers and established himself as one of baseball's most dangerous power hitters—with 32 homers and 130 RBIs in 2008—though he continued to battle injuries.

Beckett, selected second by the Marlins, and Munson, picked third by the Tigers, both held firm on their predraft demands of a major league contract. Munson agreed to terms quickly on a four-year, $6.75 million deal. Beckett waited out the entire summer before the Marlins finally gave him a four-year, $7 million contract.

The Marlins were opposed initially to giving Beckett a major league deal, which required him to be in the big leagues for good by 2002. But on Aug. 26, four days before Beckett was scheduled to enroll at Blinn (Texas) Junior College, the Marlins gave him a $7 million major league deal that included a $3.625

million bonus.

Beckett was an almost immediate and unqualified success, debuting in the major leagues in 2001 and then helping the Marlins to a World Series title in 2003, as well as the Red Sox in 2007.

Unpleasant Surprise

The first and only major surprise of the first round was Arizona's selection of shortstop Corey Myers from nearby Desert Vista High with the fourth selection. Myers was one of several players in the first 10 picks to sign immediately, and his career proved to be a complete flop.

Outfielder B.J. Garbe, selected fifth by the Twins, was in on a slice of draft history. When Moses Lake (Wash.) High teammates Ryan Doumit (Pirates) and Jason Cooper (Phillies) were selected in the second round, it marked the first time that a single high school had produced three picks in the first two rounds in the same year. Overall, nine Washington state players were picked in the first two rounds, the most bountiful talent harvest in the state's history.

The usually conservative Cubs, picking in the No. 26 slot, endured controversy when they took Wichita State righthander Ben Christensen, who missed the final six weeks of the season after being suspended for hitting Evansville's Anthony Molina with a thrown ball before a game. The Cubs gave Christensen a bonus of $1.0625 million.

The Orioles, White Sox, Royals and Padres combined to make 21 picks before the second round started. The Orioles alone had seven of the first 50 picks and spent $8.1825 million to sign those players.

That the Orioles held so many extra picks highlighted what many regarded as a flaw in the system for awarding picks as compensation to teams that lose free agents. Because they finished in the bottom half of the American League standings in 1998, the Orioles didn't lose their first-round pick—even after signing four free agents. They lost their picks in the second, third, fourth and fifth rounds. But by losing three free agents to teams in the upper half of the 1998 standings, the Orioles raked in six extra picks before the second round began.

In all, there were 1,474 players drafted, including 256 from California, 186 from Florida, 126 from Texas, 48 from Arizona and 47 each from Oklahoma and Washington.

DRAFT 99: FIRST-ROUND PICKS

No.	Club	Player, Pos.	School	Hometown	Ht.	Wt.	B-T	Age
1.	Devil Rays	Josh Hamilton, of	Athens Drive HS	Raleigh, N.C.	6-4	200	L-L	18
2.	Marlins	Josh Beckett, rhp	Spring HS	Spring, Texas	6-4	200	R-R	18
3.	Tigers	Eric Munson, c	Southern California	San Diego	6-3	220	L-R	21
4.	Diamondbacks	Corey Myers, ss	Desert Vista HS	Pheonix	6-2	205	R-R	19
5.	Twins	B.J. Garbe, of	Moses Lake HS	Moses Lake, Wash.	6-1	195	R-R	18
6.	Expos	Josh Girdley, lhp	Jasper HS	Jasper, Texas	6-4	175	L-L	18
7.	Royals	Kyle Snyder, rhp	North Carolina	Sarasota, Fla.	6-8	215	R-R	21
8.	Pirates	Bobby Bradley, rhp	Wellington HS	Wellington, Fla.	6-1	170	R-R	18
9.	Athletics	Barry Zito, lhp	Southern California	La Mesa, Calif.	6-3	200	L-L	21
10.	Brewers	Ben Sheets, rhp	Northeast Louisiana	St. Amant, La.	6-2	195	R-R	20
11.	Mariners	Ryan Christianson, c	Arlington HS	Riverside, Calif.	6-2	210	R-R	18
12.	Phillies	Brett Myers, rhp	Englewood HS	Jacksonville	6-4	210	R-R	18
13.	Orioles	Mike Paradis, rhp	Clemson	Auburn, Mass	6-2	205	R-R	21
14.	Reds	Ty Howington, lhp	Hudson's Bay HS	Vancouver, Wash.	6-5	220	R-L	18
15.	White Sox	Jason Stumm, rhp	Centralia HS	Centralia, Wash.	6-2	200	R-R	18
16.	Rockies	Jason Jennings, rhp	Baylor	Mesquite, Texas	6-2	235	L-R	20
17.	Red Sox	Rick Asadoorian, of	Northbridge HS	Whitinsville, Mass.	6-2	180	R-R	18
18.	Orioles	Richard Stahl, lhp	Newton HS	Covington, Ga.	6-7	185	R-L	18
19.	Blue Jays	Alexis Rios, 3b/of	San Pedro Martin HS	Guaynabo, P.R.	6-5	185	R-R	18
20.	Padres	Vince Faison, of	Toombs County HS	Lyons, Ga.	5-11	185	L-R	18
21.	Orioles	Larry Bigbie, of	Ball State	Hobart, Ind.	6-4	187	L-R	21
22.	White Sox	Matt Ginter, rhp	Mississippi State	Winchester, Ky.	6-1	215	R-R	21
23.	Orioles	Keith Reed, of	Providence	Yarmouth Port, Mass.	6-4	215	R-R	20
24.	Giants	Kurt Ainsworth, rhp	Louisiana State	Baton Rouge, La.	6-4	178	R-R	20
25.	Royals	Mike MacDougal, rhp	Wake Forest	Mesa, Ariz.	6-5	187	R-R	22
26.	Cubs	Ben Christensen, rhp	Wichita State	Goddard, Kan.	6-4	185	R-R	21
27.	Yankees	David Walling, rhp	Arkansas	Lakeside, Calif.	6-5	195	R-R	20
28.	Padres	Gerik Baxter, rhp	Edmonds-Woodway HS	Edmonds, Wash.	6-2	185	R-R	19
29.	Padres	Omar Ortiz, rhp	Texas-Pan American	Edinburg, Texas	6-1	180	B-R	21
30.	Cardinals	Chance Caple, rhp	Texas A&M	Southlake, Texas	6-6	215	R-R	20

1999

CLUB-BY-CLUB SELECTIONS

ANAHEIM ANGELS

June—Regular Phase (17)

1. (Pick to Red Sox as compensation for Type A free agent Mo Vaughn)
2. **John Lackey, rhp, Grayson County (Texas) CC**
3. **Phil Wilson, rhp, Poway (Calif.) HS**
4. **Stan Bukowski, rhp, Dunedin (Fla.) HS**
5. **Vince LaCorte, rhp, San Jose State**
6. **Dusty Bergman, lhp, Hawaii**
7. **Alan Wawrzyniak, rhp, Philadelphia College of Textiles**
8. **Aaron Franke, rhp, Owens (Ohio) CC**
9. **Brian Specht, ss/2b, Doherty HS, Colorado Springs**
10. **Robb Quinlan, 1b, Minnesota**
11. **Chris Barski, c, New Mexico State**
12. **Mike O'Keefe, of, Providence**
13. **Alfredo Amezaga, ss, St. Petersburg (Fla.) JC**
14. **Jon Palmieri, 1b, Wake Forest**
15. **Sean Brummett, lhp, Indiana State**
16. **Brandon Jackson, of, Savannah State (Ga.)**
17. **Scott Bikowski, of, Florida Southern**
18. **Shayne Wright, rhp, Sacramento CC**
19. **Gary Johnson, of, Brigham Young**
20. **Brent Haworth, rhp, Rollins (Fla.)**
21. **Jeff Wagner, c, Notre Dame**
22. Pat Osborn, ss, Bakersfield (Calif.) HS
23. **Alcides Duverge, c, Norwalk (Conn.) CC**
24. **Ben Grezlovski, rhp, Florida**
25. **Shayne Ferrier, rhp, Southwest Missouri State**
26. **Palmer Ebanks, rhp, Jacksonville**
27. **Tom Gregorio, c, Troy State**
28. **Luke Sullivan, lhp, New Mexico State**
29. **Brett Schreyer, rhp, Florida Atlantic**
30. **Chip Gosewisch, 2b, Arizona State**
31. Kevin Tillman, 3b, Arizona State
32. **Chris Hills, of, Jackson State**
33. **Tim Boeth, 3b/ss, Central Florida**
34. **Patrick Bowen, rhp, St. Leo (Fla.)**
35. **Craig Glysch, rhp, Wisconsin-Oshkosh**
36. **Pete Orgill, c/1b, Washington**
37. Jason Farren, rhp, Gulf Coast (Fla.) CC
38. Jermie Fitzgerald, lhp, Cowley County (Kan.) CC
39. Robert Ellis, lhp, Mission (Calif.) JC
40. Ryan Smith, rhp, Chipola (Fla.) JC
41. **Brandon Martin, of, Riverside (Calif.) CC**
42. **David Wolensky, rhp, Chipola (Fla.) JC**
43. Jeremy Paul, c, Buffalo Grove (Ill.) HS
44. Moises Feliz, ss, Chipola (Fla.) JC
45. **Bill Curtis, of, Grand Canyon (Ariz.)**
46. George Malone, of, Victor Valley HS, Victorville, Calif.
47. **Adam Thomas, rhp, St Petersburg (Fla.) CC**
48. Klent Corley, rhp, Greenway HS, Phoenix
49. **Garry Templeton Jr., ss, North Carolina A&T**
50. **Jeff Nebel, rhp, Mercer**

ARIZONA DIAMONDBACKS

June—Regular Phase (4)

1. **Corey Myers, ss, Desert Vista HS, Phoenix**
1. **Casey Daigle, rhp, Sulphur (La.) HS** (Supplemental pick—31st—for loss of Type A free agent Devon White)
2. (Pick to Astros as compensation for Type A free agent Randy Johnson)
2. **Jeremy Ward, rhp, Long Beach State** (Pick from Dodgers as compensation for White)
3. (Pick to Red Sox as compensation for Type A free agent Greg Swindell)
4. (Pick to Rangers as compensation for Type A free agent Todd Stottlemyre)
5. (Pick to Padres as compensation for Type A free agent Steve Finley)
6. Justin Maureau, lhp, Highlands Ranch (Colo.) HS
7. **Ryan Owens, ss, Cal State Fullerton**
8. **Chris Capuano, lhp, Duke**
9. **Matt Kata, ss, Vanderbilt**
10. Matt Abram, 3b, Chaparral HS, Scottsdale, Ariz.
11. Ben King, lhp/of, Grapevine (Texas) HS
12. **Doug DeVore, of, Indiana**
13. Jesse Harper, rhp, Brazoswood HS, Clute, Texas
14. Todd Gelatka, rhp, Trabuco Hills HS, Lake Forest, Calif.
15. **Todd Kasper, c, Yale**
16. **Greg Perkin, rhp, Kingwood (Texas) HS**
17. **Shawn Lagana, ss, Lakewood HS, Cypress, Calif.**
18. **Lyle Overbay, 1b/of, Nevada**
19. **Jack Santora, ss, UCLA**
20. **Justin Graham, of, West Virginia State**
21. **Tim Stanton, lhp, Florida Southern**
22. **Mike Davis, rhp, Lyon County HS, Eddyville, Ky.**
23. **Evan Fahrner, rhp, Bradley**
24. **Toby Harris, rhp, Nevada**
25. **Travis Oglesby, c, Armstrong Atlantic State (Ga.)**
26. **Kevin Burns, of, Troy State**
27. **Dan Jackson, rhp, St Louis CC-Forest Park**
28. **Dan Williford, 1b, Mobile (Ala.)**
29. **Dale Deveraux, rhp, JC of Southern Idaho**
30. Hans Smith, lhp, Fresno State
31. **Joe Kalczynski, c, Michigan State**
32. Jim Kavourias, 1b, Pensacola (Fla.) JC
33. **Joe Yakopich, ss, St. Thomas of Villanova HS, Amherstburg, Conn.**
34. **Cody Sundbeck, rhp, Dallas Baptist**
35. **James Wollscheid, rhp, McMurry (Texas)**
36. **Steven Tomshack, c, Maryland**
37. **Derek Forbes, rhp, South Mountain (Ariz.) CC**
38. Erick Contreras, ss, Garden City (Kan.) CC
39. Carlton Wells, lhp, Hillsborough (Fla.) CC
40. Aaron Sobieraj, rhp, Dunedin (Fla.) HS
41. **Josh Goldfield, c, Moorpark (Calif.) JC**
42. **Brian Matzenbacher, rhp, Southern Illinois-Edwardsville**
43. **Todd Myers, rhp, Lamar**
44. Aaron Pullin, rhp, Midland (Texas) HS
45. Jered Liebeck, rhp, Mountain Ridge HS, Glendale, Ariz.
46. Scott Buffington, rhp, Lamar (Colo.) CC
47. **Chris Jorgenson, of, McCoy HS, New Brigden, Alberta**
48. Keith Schuttler, of, Agua Fria HS, Litchfield Park, Ariz.
49. Chris Churchill, c, Abilene (Texas) HS
50. Peter Hawley, of, Branford (Conn.) HS

ATLANTA BRAVES

June—Regular Phase (30)

1. (Pick to Cardinals as compensation for Type A free agent Brian Jordan)
2. **Matt Butler, rhp, Hattiesburg (Miss.) HS**
3. **Pat Manning, ss, Mater Dei HS, Anaheim Hills, Calif.**
4. **Alec Zumwalt, of, East Forsyth HS, Kernersville, N.C.**
5. **Matt McClendon, rhp, Florida**
6. **Andrew Brown, rhp, Trinity Christian Academy, Deltona, Fla.**
7. **Brett Evert, rhp, North Salem HS, Salem, Ore.**
8. Chris Spencer, rhp, Humble (Texas) HS
9. **Angelo Burrows, of, Killian HS, Miami**
10. **Bryan Cetani, lhp, Deep Valley Christian HS, Ukiah, Calif.**
11. **Chris Trevino, lhp, Andrews (Texas) HS**
12. **Ben Kozlowski, lhp, Santa Fe (Fla.) CC**
13. Shaud Williams, ss, Andrews (Texas) HS

14. **Garrett Jones, 1b, Andrew HS, Tinley Park, Ill.**
15. David Fiala, rhp, Orange Park (Fla.) HS
16. **Kevin Green, c, Georgia Perimeter JC**
17. Efren Lira, rhp, Walnut (Calif.) HS
18. **Tom Curtiss, lhp, Maryland**
19. Mike Wade, rhp, Sullivan South HS, Kingsport, Tenn.
20. **Collin Remekie, of, Martin County HS, Stuart, Fla.**
21. **Wes Rasmussen, ss, Moorpark (Calif.) HS**
22. **Bryce Terveen, c, Pacific**
23. **Kyle Colton, rhp, Bishop Moore HS, Longwood, Fla.**
24. **Alva Thompson, c, Southern**
25. **John Foster, lhp, Lewis-Clark State (Idaho)**
26. **Shanin Veronie, rhp, Chico State (Calif.)**
27. **Chris Chavez, rhp, Florida State**
28. Ryan Hubbard, ss, Huntington Beach (Calif.) HS
29. Travis Suereth, 1b, Buchholz HS, Gainesville, Fla.
30. **Jeff Rodriguez, c, Florida International**
31. Zach Parker, lhp, Westwood HS, Austin
32. **Joseph Francisco, of, Wagner (N.Y.)**
33. **Tommy Parrott, 3b, Merritt Island (Fla.) HS**
34. **Curt Fiore, 3b, Loyola Marymount**
35. Jeremy Barker, lhp, Willows (Calif.) HS
36. **Shaun Argento, c, New Mexico Highlands**
37. Jonathan Schuerholz, ss, Lovett School, Atlanta
38. **Anthony Sclafani, rhp, St. Peter's HS, Staten Island, N.Y.**
39. **Ryan Ewin, rhp, Monte Vista HS, Spring Valley, Calif.**
40. Josh Parker, rhp, Thompson HS, Alabaster, Ala.
41. Mike Gleason, rhp, Butler County (Kan.) CC
42. Klint Richardson, rhp, Lyons (N.Y.) HS
43. Michael Koppin, ss, Stephens County HS, Eastanollee, Ga.
44. **Toby Staveland, rhp, Mendocino (Calif.) CC**
45. **Grant Abrams, ss, St Petersburg (Fla.) CC**
46. J.C. Barnett, rhp, Fort Meade (Fla.) HS
47. James Anderson, c, North HS, Riverside, Calif.
48. August Marsala, 3b, Buffalo (Mo.) HS
49. **Nathan Kent, rhp, Kentucky**
50. Scott Leitz, lhp, Vanguard HS, Ocala, Fla.

BALTIMORE ORIOLES

June—Regular Phase (13)

1. **Mike Paradis, rhp, Clemson**
1. **Richard Stahl, lhp, Newton HS, Covington, Ga.** (Pick from Cardinals as compensation for Type A free agent Eric Davis)
1. **Larry Bigbie, of, Ball State** (Pick from Rangers as compensation for Type A free agent Rafael Palmeiro)
1. **Keith Reed, of, Providence** (Pick from Indians as compensation for Type A free agent Roberto Alomar)
1. **Josh Cenate, lhp, Jefferson HS, Shenandoah Junction, W.Va.** (Supplemental pick—34th—for loss of Alomar)
1. **Scott Rice, lhp, Royal HS, Simi Valley, Calif.** (Supplemental pick—44th—for loss of Davis)
1. **Brian Roberts, ss, South Carolina** (Supplemental pick—50th—for loss of Palmeiro)
2. (Pick to White Sox as compensation for Type A free agent Albert Belle)
3. (Pick to Mariners as compensation for Type A free agent Mike Timlin)
3. **Jon Kessick, c, Ball State** (Pick from Dodgers as compensation for Type B free agent Alan Mills)
4. (Pick to Cardinals as compensation for Type A free agent Delino DeShields)
5. (Pick to Rangers as compensation for Type A free agent Will Clark)
6. **Erik Bedard, lhp, Norwalk (Conn.) CC**
7. **David Farren, rhp, Texas HS, Texarkana, Texas**
8. **Matt Tate, rhp, Holmes County HS, Bonifay, Fla.**
9. **Pete Shier, ss, Hilliard HS, Columbus, Ohio**
10. **Octavio Martinez, c, Bakersfield (Calif.) JC**
11. Kraig Brinkman, rhp, Napa (Calif.) HS
12. **Brad Rogers, rhp, Wellington SS, Nanaimo, B.C**
13. **Drew Hassler, rhp, Arcadia HS, Phoenix**
14. **Matt Riordan, of, Loyola Marymount**
15. James Ralph, of, Wyoming
16. **Shaun Babula, lhp, Philadelphia College of Textiles**
17. Jason Tourangeau, rhp, South Carroll HS, Mount Airy, Md.
18. **Kyle Martin, c, Selah (Wash.) HS**
19. **Nick Garcia, ss, Desert View HS, Tucson**
20. **Steven Salargo, of, East Carolina**
21. Shane Waroff, rhp, Fullerton (Calif.) JC
22. Beau Kemp, rhp, Nathan Hale HS, Tulsa
23. **Aaron Rakers, rhp, Southern Illinois-Edwardsville**
24. **Willie Harris, 2b/ss, Kennesaw State (Ga.)**
25. Mitch Jones, 3b, Arizona State
26. **Mike Seestedt, c, Michigan**
27. **Rodney Ormond, rhp, North Carolina State**
28. Matt Larson, rhp, Corona Del Mar HS, Costa Mesa, Calif.
29. Martin LaRocca, rhp, Archbishop Rummel, Metaire, La.
30. Kyle Yudizky, of, Duncanville (Texas) HS
31. Kyle Roat, c, Coweta (Okla.) HS
32. Kevin Virtue, of, Lucas HS, London, Ontario
33. **James Phillips, rhp, Maysville HS, Zanesville, Ohio**
34. Doug Slaten, lhp, Glendale (Calif.) JC
35. **Kelvin Pickering, c, King HS, Tampa**
36. Andrew Corona, 1b, Moorpark (Calif.) CC
37. Ryan Rocheleau, lhp, Hemet (Calif.) HS
38. **Charles Dees, of, Chipola (Fla.) JC**
39. **Gary Cates, 2b, Brandon (Fla.) HS**
40. Matt Roy, rhp, Johnstown-Monroe HS, Johnstown, Ohio
41. Sean White, rhp, Mercer Island (Wash.) HS
42. Nicholas Vitielliss, rhp, Thomas Stone HS, Waldorf, Md.
43. **Terry Plank, rhp, Methodist (N.C.)**
44. **Doug Sowers, 3b, West Virginia State**
45. Brad Guglielmelli, 3b, Cuesta (Calif.) JC
46. Pat Tobin, c, Dun Barton SS, Pickering, Ontario
47. Judd Richardson, rhp, Country Day HS, Terra Cotta, Ontario
48. Michael Roga, rhp, Pine Ridge HS, Pickering, Ontario
49. Vince Perkins, rhp, Claremont SS, Victoria, B.C
50. Kyle Baumgartner, ss, Olympic HS, Bremerton, Wash.

BOSTON RED SOX

June—Regular Phase (25)

1. **Rick Asadoorian, of, Northbridge HS, Whitinsville, Mass.** (Pick from Angels as compensation for Type A free agent Mo Vaughn)
1. (Pick to Royals as compensation for Type A free agent Jose Offerman)
1. **Brad Baker, rhp, Pioneer Valley HS, Leyden, Mass.** (Supplemental pick—40th—for loss of Vaughn)
1. **Casey Fossum, lhp, Texas A&M** (Supplemental pick—48th—for loss of Type A free agent Greg Swindell)
2. **Mat Thompson, rhp, Timberline HS, Boise, Idaho**
3. **Rich Rundles, lhp, Jefferson County HS, New Market, Tenn.** (Pick from Diamondbacks as compensation for Swindell)
3. **Antron Seiber, of, Independence (La.) HS**
4. Rory Shortell, rhp, Madison HS, Portland, Ore.
5. **Greg Montalbano, lhp, Northeastern**
6. Jon Kail, of, Baldwin HS, Pittsburgh
7. Rich Carroll, 1b, Venice (Fla.) HS
8. Andrew Heimbach, rhp, Mount Vernon Nazarene (Ohio)
9. Hank Thoms, rhp, Mississippi State
10. **Brian Wiese, of, Mississippi State**
11. **Kregg Jarvais, c, Maine**
12. **Lew Ford, of, Dallas Baptist**
13. **Michael Dwyer, 1b, Richmond**
14. **B.J. Leach, rhp, Florida Southern**
15. Brian Wiley, rhp, The Citadel
16. Charlie Manning, lhp, Polk (Fla.) CC
17. Trae Duncan, 3b, Mississippi Gulf Coast JC
18. **Jeff Waldron, c, Boston College**
19. **Jason Bottenfield, rhp, Texas-Pan American**
20. **Dan Generelli, rhp, Quinsigamond (Mass.) CC**
21. Jason Henderson, rhp, Bishop Hendricken HS, Coventry, R.I.
22. Ellis Debrow, 1b/of, Woodham HS, Pensacola, Fla.
23. Nicolas Puckett, lhp, Timberline HS, Boise, Idaho
24. Rex Rundgren, ss, Mid-Pacific Institute, Honolulu, Hawaii
25. Tim McCabe, ss, North Catholic HS, Wexford, Pa.
26. Marshall McDougall, 2b, Florida State

27. Mark Kiger, 2b, Grossmont (Calif.) JC
28. **Jon Anderson, ss, Illinois**
29. **Bart Hollis, rhp, Lawrence County HS, Moulton, Ala.**
30. Charlie Frasier, 3b, Santa Rosa (Calif.) JC
31. Jaime Bubela, of, Baylor
32. David Flournoy, of, Deer Valley HS, Antioch, Calif.
33. **Perry Miley, of, William Carey (Miss.)**
34. **Dan Giese, rhp, San Diego**
35. **Ben Marbury, of, Rockford, Ala.**
36. John Brandon, of, Panola (Texas) JC
37. Chris Mabeus, rhp, Eastern Arizona JC
38. Jesse Cooksey, rhp, Port Neches-Groves HS, Port Arthur, Texas
39. Matt Ames, 1b, Stanhope Elmore HS, Millbrook, Ala.
40. Anthony Bass, of, Washington HS, Tulsa, Okla.
41. Justin Smetana, lhp, Cardinal HS, Huntsburg, Ohio
42. Bryan Rinehart, 2b, Southington (Conn.) HS
43. Ryan Coffin, rhp, Desert Vista HS, Phoenix
44. Alan Lindsey, of, Lee-Davis HS, Mechanicsville, Va.
45. **Brady Williams, 3b, Pasco-Hernando (Fla.) CC**
46. **Joe Kerrigan, ss, Temple**
47. James Burgess, of, Durango HS, Las Vegas
48. Joseph Kjose, rhp, Cochise County (Ariz.) CC
49. Jordan Remy, 2b, Weston (Mass.) HS
50. Brian Buscher, ss, Terry Parker HS, Jacksonville

CHICAGO CUBS

June—Regular Phase (26)

1. **Ben Christensen, rhp, Wichita State**
2. **Mike Mallory, of, Dinwiddie County HS, Dinwiddie, Va.**
3. **Ryan Gripp, 3b, Creighton**
4. **Steve Smyth, lhp, Southern California**
5. Todd Deininger, rhp, Joliet Township (Ill.) HS
6. **Ben Shaffar, rhp, Kentucky**
7. **Mike Dzurilla, 2b, St. John's**
8. **Dustin Pate, rhp, Daniel HS, Clemson, S.C.**
9. **Chris Curry, c, Mississippi State**
10. **Jim Deschaine, ss, Brandeis (Mass.)**
11. **Tim Lavery, lhp, Illinois**
12. **Condor Cash, of, Stephens County School, Toccoa, Ga.**
13. **Syketo Anderson, 2b, Chipola (Fla.) JC**
14. **Jandin Thornton-Murray, ss, St. Louis HS, Honolulu**
15. **Andrew Earley, rhp, Okaloosa Walton CC**
16. **Tony Gsell, 2b, Old Dominion**
17. **Derrick Cohens, of, Lake City (Fla.) CC**
18. **Jamie Eppeneder, lhp, Diablo Valley (Calif.) CC**
19. **John Webb, rhp, Manatee (Fla.) CC**
20. **Brandon Sing, ss/1b, Joliet Township (Ill.) HS**
21. Ron Ogle, lhp, Long Beach (Calif.) CC
22. Martin Calderon, ss, El Modena HS, Orange, Calif.
23. **Pete Zoccolillo, 1b/of, Rutgers**
24. **Kevin Collins, of, Land O'Lakes (Fla.) HS**
25. **Ryan Van Horn, c, Oklahoma**
26. **Ben Johnstone, of, Yale**
27. **Casey Kopitzke, c, Wisconsin-Oshkosh**
28. David Lemon, of, Eustis HS, Heathrow, Fla.
29. Ryan Jackson, c, McNeil HS, Austin
30. **Ray Sadler, of, Hill (Texas) JC**
31. Blake Melstrom, c, South Hills HS, West Covina, Calif.
32. Jorge Acevedo, of, Efrain Sanchez Hidalgo HS, Moca, P.R.
33. Greg Hanoian, of, Southern California
34. Stephen Solwick, rhp, Rio Rancho (N.M.) HS
35. **Eduardo Marquez, of, Nicholls State**
36. Jason Mackintosh, lhp, Cerro Coso (Calif.) CC
37. **Jeff Ryan, ss, Wichita State**
38. Cody Willis, rhp, Deweyville (Texas) HS
39. Federico Baez, 3b, Jose Alegria HS, Dorado, P.R.
40. Justin Valenti, of, Norwalk (Conn.) CC
41. Beau Benton, of, Central Florida CC
42. Donnie Bair, lhp/of, Merced (Calif.) HS
43. Bryan Golden, c, Potomac State (W.Va.) JC
44. Jeremy Mannin, lhp, Wenatchee (Wash.) HS
45. Michael Sims, of, Karns HS, Knoxville
46. **Chris Adams, rhp, McLennan (Texas) CC**
47. Dale Thayer, rhp, Edison HS, Huntington Beach, Calif.
48. Charles Talanoa, rhp, El Segundo (Calif.) HS
49. Ryan Johnson, of, Laguna Hills (Calif.) HS
50. Thomas Syc, rhp, Carl Sandburg HS, Orland Park, Ill.

CHICAGO WHITE SOX

June—Regular Phase (15)

1. **Jason Stumm, rhp, Centralia (Wash.) HS**
1. **Matt Ginter, rhp, Mississippi State** (Pick from Mets as compensation for Type A free agent Robin Ventura)
1. **Brian West, rhp, West Monroe HS, Monroe, La.** (Supplemental pick—35th—for loss of Type A free agent Albert Belle)
1. **Rob Purvis, rhp, Bradley** (Supplemental pick—45th—for loss of Ventura)
2. **Dan Wright, rhp, Arkansas** (Pick from Orioles as compensation for Belle)
2. Bobby Hill, ss, Miami
3. **Jon Rauch, rhp, Morehead State**
4. Brandon Sloan, rhp, Wichita State
5. **Josh Stewart, lhp, Memphis**
6. **David Sanders, lhp, Barton County (Kan.) CC**
7. **Scott Patten, rhp, Tecumseh (Okla.) HS**
8. **Dennis Ulacia, lhp, Monsignor Pace HS, Opa Locka, Fla.**
9. **Corwin Malone, lhp, Thomasville (Ala.) HS**
10. **Matt Guerrier, rhp, Kent**
11. **Alec Holifield, rhp, Stranahan HS, Fort Lauderdale, Fla.**
12. **Derek Stanley, of, North Florida JC**
13. **Casey Rogowski, of, Catholic Central HS, Livonia, Mich.**
14. **Spencer Oborn, of, Cal State Fullerton**
15. **Julio Reyes, 1b/of, Miami Senior HS**
16. Ben Birk, of, Minnesota
17. Ryan Childs, 3b/rhp, Damascus HS, Gaithersburg, Md.
18. Scott Hairston, ss, Canyon del Oro HS, Tucson
19. Che Done, rhp, Pace HS, Miami
20. David Brockman, rhp, Glendale (Ariz.) JC
21. **Daniel Martinez, lhp, Southwestern (Calif.) JC**
22. **Kris McWhirter, rhp, Volunteer State (Tenn.) CC**
23. **Joe Curreri, rhp, Long Island**
24. **Todd Holt, of, Louisburg (N.C.) JC**
25. **Rocky Hughes, lhp, Pratt (Kan.) CC**
26. **Joe Valentine, rhp, Jefferson Davis (Ala.) JC**
27. Dan Ortmeier, of/1b, Lewisville HS, Highland Village, Texas
28. **Wally Rosa, c, Brito Private HS, Miami**
29. **Jason Rummel, 2b, Towson State**
30. Jonathan Cavin, of, Connors State (Okla.) JC
31. Juan Gutierrez, of, Coral Park HS, Miami
32. Michel Valdez, of, Miami-Dade CC
33. Tony Neal, rhp, Faulkner State (Ala.) JC
34. **Matt Salvesan, 3b, Kishwaukee (Ill.) JC**
35. Greg Sandifer, rhp, Palomar (Calif.) JC
36. **Jeff Bajenaru, rhp, Oklahoma**
37. Kade Eady, of, West Ouachita HS, Eros, La.
38. **Trent Roehler, c, Fort Hays State (Kan.)**
39. Paul Beaudreau, c, El Modena HS, Orange, Calif.
40. Jeremy Castillo, of, Southridge HS, Miami
41. Eric Johnson, rhp, Southridge HS, Miami
42. John Koonig, rhp, Jefferson (Mo.) JC
43. Kris Gross, rhp, Lees Summit (Mo.) HS
44. Armando Perez, lhp, Montgomery HS, San Ysidro, Calif.
45. James Hymon, ss, Kishwaukee (Ill.) JC
46. Dustin Scheffel, rhp, Oak Ridge HS, Cameron Park, Calif.
47. Carlynn Steele, ss, Connors State (Okla.) JC
48. Mike Cox, c, Riverview HS, Sarasota, Fla.
49. Austin Rappe, of, Virginia Tech
50. Adam Heiden, rhp, Denison (Iowa) HS

CINCINNATI REDS

June—Regular Phase (14)

1. **Ty Howington, lhp, Hudson's Bay HS, Vancouver, Wash.**
2. **Ben Broussard, 1b, McNeese State**
3. **Brandon Love, rhp, Viola (Ark.) HS**
4. **Ken Lutz, rhp, Collinsville HS, Caseyville, Ill.**
5. Mike Esposito, rhp, Cimarron-Memorial HS, Las Vegas, Nev.

6. **Alex LeFlore, of, Pinellas Park (Fla.) HS**
7. **Okorie Barrow, of, Clarke Central HS, Athens, Ga.**
8. **Ryan Lundquist, c, Arkansas**
9. **Casey Bookout, 1b, Oklahoma**
10. **Scott Dunn, rhp, Texas**
11. **Paul Darnell, lhp, Tarleton State (Texas)**
12. **Joshua Spoerl, 3b, Texas**
13. Travis Wong, 1b, Timberline HS, Boise, Idaho
14. **David Bradley, rhp, Marietta (Ohio)**
15. **Rafael Erazo, rhp, Oklahoma Christian**
16. **Paco Escamilla, rhp, Lubbock Christian (Texas)**
17. **Kyle Moncrief, 1b, West Monroe HS, Monroe, La.**
18. **Matthew Dehner, ss, Oklahoma City**
19. **B.J. Hawes, ss, Augusta (Ga.) Christian School**
20. **Mark Burnett, 2b, Arkansas**
21. **Brad Salmon, rhp, Jefferson Davis (Ala.) CC**
22. Michael Fawcett, rhp, Central Michigan
23. **Matt Nanninga, rhp, Bellevue (Neb.)**
24. **Carlos Hines, rhp, Smithfield-Selma HS, Selma, N.C.**
25. **Kevin Schnall, c, Coastal Carolina**
26. **Jason Huth, ss, Texas Tech**
27. **Michael Landkammer, rhp, Mankato State (Minn.)**
28. **Tom Pike, rhp, McMurry (Texas)**
29. **Mike Neu, rhp, Miami**
30. Jon Sheaffer, of, South Mountain (Ariz.) CC
31. **Corey Ward, of, Odessa (Texas) JC**
32. Jack Arroyo, 2b, East Union HS, Prundale, Calif.
33. **Jason Howard, c, East Carolina**
34. **Stace Pape, rhp, Texas-San Antonio**
35. Evan Conley, ss, Manatee HS, Bradenton, Fla.
36. Richard Hill, lhp, Milton (Mass.) HS
37. **Jerymane Beasley, of, Eastern Washington**
38. Blake Bodenmiller, lhp, West Orange HS, Orlando
39. Josh Andrade, rhp, Sandalwood HS, Jacksonville
40. Matt Allen, rhp, Vernon Regional (Texas) JC
41. Garrett Alwert, lhp, Bethel HS, Puyallup, Wash.
42. Bryan Erstad, of, Jamestown (N.D.) HS
43. **Nate Rewers, 2b, Richmond**
44. Marlyn Tisdale, rhp, Tennessee
45. **Paul Brown, lhp, Citrus (Calif.) JC**
46. Matt Lynch, lhp, John Carroll HS, Fort Pierce, Fla.
47. **Leon Smith, of, Greenbrier HS, Appling, Ga.**
48. Scott Hindman, lhp, Fremd HS, Inverness, Ill.
49. Gerrit Simpson, rhp, Connors State (Okla.) CC
50. Cory Whitlock, ss, De Soto (Texas) HS

CLEVELAND INDIANS

June—Regular Phase (23)

1. (Pick to Orioles as compensation for Type A free agent Roberto Alomar)
2. **Will Hartley, c, Bradford County HS, Stark, Fla.**
3. **Eric Johnson, of, Western Carolina**
4. Jeff Baker, ss, Gar-Field HS, Woodbridge, Va.
5. **Curtis Gay, 1b, Oklahoma City**
6. **Shane Wallace, lhp, Newman Smith HS, Carrollton, Texas**
7. Daylon Monette, of, Miller HS, Fontana, Calif.
8. **Devin Rogers, rhp, Nicholls State**
9. **Stephen Cowie, rhp, Duke**
10. **Fernando Cabrera, rhp, Discipulus de Cristo HS, Bayamon, P.R.**
11. Monte Mansfield, rhp, Hesperia (Calif.) HS
12. **Francis Finnerty, c, Wellington (Fla.) Community HS**
13. **Adam Barr, lhp, South Williamsport Area HS, Williamsport, Pa.**
14. **Josh Martin, lhp, King Academy, Columbia, S.C.**
15. **Brody Lynn, ss, Kapaun-Mount Carmel HS, Wichita**
16. **Anthony Marini, lhp, Kennesaw State**
17. **Chris Kelley, rhp, William & Mary**
18. **Kyle Moyer, 1b, Mohawk HS, Tiffin, Ohio**
19. **Travis Santini, of, Lely HS, Naples, Fla.**
20. Louis Wieben, lhp, St. Mary HS, Secaucus, N.J.
21. **Jason Davis, rhp, Cleveland State (Tenn.) CC**
22. Jeff Reboin, lhp, Sacramento City CC
23. Anthony Tomey, rhp, Catholic Central HS, Northville, Mich.
24. **Philip Rosengren, rhp, Northwestern**
25. **Chris Lotterhos, 2b, Mississippi State**
26. **Kyle Denney, rhp, Oklahoma**
27. Jordan Olson, lhp, Crescenta Valley HS, La Crescenta, Calif.
28. Matt Spiess, rhp, Owosso (Mich.) HS
29. Roberto Vega, c, Adela Brenes Texidor HS, Guayama, P.R.
30. Willie McKenzie, rhp, Sullivan South HS, Kingsport, Tenn.
31. **Leyson Rivera, rhp, Calderon HS, Carolina, P.R.**
32. Ben Francisco, of, Servite HS, Fullerton, Calif.
33. Scott Thomas, rhp, Watervliet (Mich.) HS
34. Kerry Hodges, of, New Mexico JC
35. **Mike Byrd, rhp, Vanderbilt**
36. Jerad Doty, of, Rio Vista (Texas) HS
37. **Teddy Sullivan, rhp, Duke**
38. **John Christ, rhp, Johns Hopkins (Md.)**
39. **Byron Ewing, 1b, Howard (D.C.)**
40. Neil Dudkowski, lhp, Lassen (Calif.) JC
41. Royce Ring, lhp, Monte Vista HS, La Mesa, Calif.
42. Anthony Lunetta, ss, Arlington HS, Riverside, Calif.
43. Brad Harrison, of, Mandarin HS, Jacksonville
44. Michael Bishop, of/c, Kansas State
45. Doug Johnson, rhp, Pelham (N.H.) HS
46. **Jeff Becker, 3b, Duke**
47. **Samuel Button, lhp, Jacksonville State**
48. **Simon Young, lhp, Georgia Tech**
49. Neal Maybin, of, Brevard (Fla.) CC
50. John Gall, 1b, Stanford

COLORADO ROCKIES

June—Regular Phase (16)

1. **Jason Jennings, rhp, Baylor**
2. **Ryan Kibler, rhp, King HS, Tampa**
3. **Josh Bard, c, Texas Tech**
4. **Chuck Crowder, lhp, Georgia Tech**
5. **Chris Testa, of, Palmdale (Calif.) HS**
6. **Roney Johnson, rhp, Woodcreek HS, Antelope, Calif.**
7. **Carlos Figueroa, ss, Gilberto Concepcion HS, Carolina, P.R.**
8. **Greg Catalanotte, of, Florida**
9. **Colin Young, lhp, Fordham**
10. **Sean Daly, c, Golden West HS, Visalia, Calif.**
11. **Chris Moore, ss, Western Carolina**
12. **Craig House, rhp, Memphis State**
13. **Rick Cercy, rhp, Morehead State**
14. **Eric McQueen, c, Georgia Tech**
15. **Dan Phillips, 3b/of, Cal State Northridge**
16. **Cam Esslinger, rhp, Seton Hall**
17. **Billy Gasparino, ss, Oklahoma State**
18. Brandon Caraway, 2b, Houston
19. **David Mulqueen, 3b, Marquette HS, Milwaukee**
20. **Chris Warren, c, Howard (Texas) JC**
21. **Matt Hoffman, rhp, Oral Roberts**
22. Darin Naatjes, of, West Lyon HS, Alvord, Iowa
23. **Javier Lorenzo, rhp, Miami-Dade CC**
24. **Deryck Christensen, rhp, Eastside Catholic HS, Issaquah, Wash.**
25. **Ray Aguilar, lhp, Cypress (Calif.) JC**
26. Bobby Brownlie, rhp, Edison (N.J.) HS
27. **Michael Tejada, c, Brigham Young**
28. **Justin Hampson, lhp, Belleville Area (Ill.) CC**
29. Bryce Coppieters, of, Lethbridge (Alberta) CC
30. Rick Sander, rhp, Riverside (Calif.) CC
31. Andy Warren, rhp, Sam Houston State
32. Casey Kelly, 1b, Westview HS, Portland, Oregon
33. Darren Clarke, rhp, Plant HS, Tampa
34. Patrick Curran, lhp, Edmonds (Wash.) CC
35. Don Tolen, rhp, Orange Glen HS, Escondido, Calif.
36. Tom MacLane, lhp, St. Petersburg (Fla.) CC
37. Chad Liter, of, Madison (Ind.) Consolidated HS
38. Jason Kramer, lhp, Marcus HS, Flower Mound, Texas
39. Billy Dennis, of, Devine HS, Big Foot, Texas
40. Nicholas Gor, rhp, Esperanza HS, Yorba Linda, Calif.
41. Eli Lapka, ss, Dodge City (Kan.) HS
42. Grant Mullen, 1b, St. Christopher's SS, Corunna, Ontario
43. Cortney Inman, rhp, Parkview HS, Springfield, Mo.

44. Nick Loughren, rhp, Bishop Verot HS, Cape Coral, Fla.
45. Nick McCurdy, rhp, Jefferson Davis (Ala.) JC
46. **T.J. Bird, of, Mendocino (Calif.) CC**
47. Kendall Jones, c, Broken Arrow (Okla.) HS
48. Manases Pabon, of, Indian Hills (Iowa) CC
49. Billy Wheeler, rhp, Crown Point (Ind.) HS

DETROIT TIGERS

June—Regular Phase (3)

1. **Eric Munson, c, Southern California**
2. (Pick to Royals as compensation for Type A free agent Dean Palmer)
3. **Neil Jenkins, 3b, Dwyer HS, Jupiter, Fla.**
4. **Cody Ross, of, Carlsbad (N.M.) HS**
5. **Dayle Campbell, of, Los Angeles Pierce JC**
6. **Brant Ust, 3b, Notre Dame**
7. **Tim Kalita, lhp, Notre Dame**
8. **Anthony Ware, 3b, Hamilton HS, Los Angeles**
9. **Casey Rowe, rhp, Fresno State**
10. **Jerrod Fuell, rhp, Palo Verde HS, Tucson**
11. **Erick Burke, lhp, Houston**
12. **Daniel Davis, of, Osceola HS, Kissimmee, Fla.**
13. **Kevin Jackson, 3b, North Florida**
14. **Ross Garland, c, Walters State (Tenn.) CC**
15. **Corey Richardson, of, New Mexico State**
16. **Stephen Bess, rhp, Rice**
17. Brad Steele, rhp, California
18. **Randy Leek, lhp, William & Mary**
19. **Casey Williamson, of, Troy State**
20. **Dustin Bean, ss, Wright State**
21. **Corey McDonald, lhp, UNC Greensboro**
22. **Aaron Barnett, lhp, Middle Tennessee State**
23. **Jeremy Lewis, lhp, Central Cabarrus HS, Concord, N.C.**
24. Nathan Husser, 1b, Middletown HS, Newark, Del.
25. Ed Romprey, ss, Fullerton (Calif.) JC
26. **Greg Watson, rhp, Tampa**
27. **Johnny Gordon, of, Warner Southern (Fla.)**
28. Ryan Golem, rhp, Dearborn (Mich.) HS
29. Tim Leveque, rhp, Crespi HS, Northridge, Calif.
30. Joe Urban, of, Santa Ana (Calif.) JC
31. Randy Thurman, lhp, Ringling (Okla.) HS
32. **Eric Eckenstahler, lhp, Illinois State**
33. **Jason Frasor, rhp, Southern Illinois**
34. **Robert Hlousek, 3b, Missouri-St. Louis**
35. Dennis Wyrick, ss, Bishop Amat HS, Azusa, Calif.
36. **Jason Siegfried, c, Dayton**
37. **Miles Luuloa, ss, Laney (Calif.) CC**
38. Corey Loomis, ss, Eastwood HS, Pemberville, Ohio
39. Kaulana Kuhaulua, ss, Los Angeles CC
40. Francisco Arteaga, rhp, Roosevelt HS, Los Angeles
41. **John-Eric Hernandez, rhp, Chico State (Calif.)**
42. Pete Pirman, of, Triton (Ill.) JC
43. Phillip Mixter, rhp, Muskegon (Mich.) HS
44. **Jayson Drobiak, ss, Connecticut**

FLORIDA MARLINS

June—Regular Phase (2)

1. **Josh Beckett, rhp, Spring (Texas) HS**
2. **Terry Byron, rhp, Indian River (Fla.) JC**
3. **Josh Wilson, ss, Mount Lebanon HS, Pittsburgh**
4. **Dominic Woody, c, Washington**
5. **Nate Robertson, lhp, Wichita State**
6. **Charlie Frazier, of, Toms River (N.J.) South HS**
7. **Jake Laidlaw, ss, Cheyenne HS, Las Vegas**
8. **Kevin Hooper, 2b, Wichita State**
9. **Ben Hickman, rhp, Louisiana Tech**
10. **Scott Goodman, of, Arizona State**
11. **Randy Messenger, rhp, Sparks (Nev.) HS**
12. **Angel Sanchez, c, Vineland (N.J.) HS**
13. **Bryan Moore, rhp, Houston**
14. **Todd Moser, lhp, Florida Atlantic**
15. **Barry Schell, of, Palomar (Calif.) JC**
16. **Jared Wykoff, rhp, Kinder (La.) HS**
17. **Brad Haynes, rhp, Barren County HS, Glasgow, Ky.**
18. **David Johnston, rhp, Marshalltown (Iowa) HS**
19. **Kevin Perkins, 2b, UC Riverside**
20. **Shane Smuin, rhp, Utah Valley State JC**
21. **Joe Sergent, lhp, Lamar**
22. **James Close, of, Nevada-Las Vegas**
23. Jarrod Schmidt, 1b/rhp, Lassiter HS, Marietta, Ga.
24. **Bryan Morse, lhp, Mount Olive (N.C.)**
25. **Dennis Anderson, c, Arizona**
26. **Keith Herbert, ss, Boonsboro HS, Keedysvile, Md.**
27. **Tom Bell, rhp, George Marshall (Va.) HS**
28. **Matt Ward, lhp, Texas A&M**
29. **Matt Postell, 1b, North Carolina State**
30. **Brandon Bowe, rhp, Louisiana State**
31. Kenny Riley, c, Reed HS, Sparks, Nev.
32. Dustin Griffith, rhp, Dakota Ridge HS, Littleton, Colo.
33. **Mike Flannery, rhp, Gloucester County (N.J.) CC**
34. John Moylan, c, Canada (Calif.) JC
35. **Enrique Mendieta, of, Norfolk State**
36. Kevin Snowden, of, Roosevelt HS, Lanham, Md.
37. Derek Caraway, rhp, Andalusia (Ala.) HS
38. Robert Glaser, of, San Joaquin Delta (Calif.) JC
39. Chance Scott, ss, Pleasant Grove (Utah) HS
40. Matthew Krabbe, rhp, Triton (Ill.) JC
41. Jeff Nichols, rhp, Rice
42. Adam LaRoche, 1b, Fort Scott (Kan.) CC
43. Darin Phalines, rhp, Gloucester County (N.J.) CC
44. **Alonso Gomez, 3b, JC of San Mateo (Calif.)**
45. John Anderson, rhp, Pine Bluff (Ark.) HS
46. Ben Vannatter, c, Amelia (Ohio) HS
47. Jacob Robertson, of, Twin Falls (Idaho) HS
48. **Quian Davis, of, Buena Regional HS, Minotola, N.J.**
49. John Zamora, rhp, Cabrillo (Calif.) JC
50. Anthony Aceves, of, Howard HS, Columbia, Md.

HOUSTON ASTROS

June—Regular Phase (29)

1. (Pick to Padres as compensation for Type A free agent Ken Caminiti)
1. **Mike Rosamond, of, Mississippi** (Supplemental pick—42nd—for loss of Type A free agent Randy Johnson)
2. **Jay Perez, c, Seymour (Conn.) HS** (Pick from Diamondbacks as compensation for Johnson)
2. **Travis Anderson, rhp, Washington**
3. **Jimmy Barrett, rhp, Fort Hill HS, Cumberland, Md.**
4. **Jon Topolski, of, Baylor**
5. **Mike Gallo, lhp, Long Beach State**
6. **Jason Lane, of, Southern California**
7. **Nick Roberts, rhp, Southern Utah**
8. **Chris Sampson, ss, Texas Tech**
9. **Jon Helquist, ss, University Christian HS, Jacksonville**
10. Greg Dobbs, 3b, Long Beach State
11. **Kris Kann, rhp, Mansfield (Pa.)**
12. **Royce Huffman, 3b, Texas Christian**
13. **Garett Gentry, c, Victor Valley (Calif.) CC**
14. **Brian Schmitt, 1b, Blinn (Texas) JC**
15. Bryan Edwards, rhp, Northeast Texas CC
16. **Daniel Parker, rhp, Diablo Valley (Calif.) JC**
17. **Ryan Jamison, rhp, Missouri**
18. **Mike Hill, of/2b, Oral Roberts**
19. **Jon Andrianoff, ss, Portville (N.Y.) Central HS**
20. **Derrick Johnson, lhp, Wallace State (Ala.) CC**
21. Russ Morgan, lhp, Purdue
22. Stephen Ghutzman, c, Spring (Texas) HS
23. **Jason Maule, 2b, Central Connecticut State**
24. **Brian O'Connor, c, Valparaiso**
25. **Chris George, rhp, Missouri**
26. Lance Ericksen, rhp, Utah
27. Shane Hall, rhp, Sierra Vista HS, Hereford, Ariz.
28. Marc Gwyn, rhp, Rice
29. David Frame, rhp, Westfield HS, Houston
30. Steve Mortimer, 1b, Richland (Wash.) HS
31. Javier Andueza, rhp, West Valley (Calif.) JC
32. Billy Zbacnik, 1b, University HS, San Diego

33. **Steven Hoover, of, Cal State Stanislaus**
34. **John Ortiz, lhp, New Mexico**
35. Justin Toone, rhp, Kingwood (Texas) HS
36. **Jordan Hunt, rhp, Edmonds (Wash.) CC**
37. **Abraham Ayala, 3b, Miami Dade CC**
38. Deshain Beasley, of, Kamiakin HS, Kennewick, Wash.
39. **Jeffrey Blitstein, rhp, Chapman (Calif.)**
40. Darrick Bingham, rhp, Canada (Calif.) JC
41. Ray Leyba, lhp, Cowley County (Kan.) CC

KANSAS CITY ROYALS

June—Regular Phase (7)

1. **Kyle Snyder, rhp, North Carolina**
1. **Mike MacDougal, rhp, Wake Forest** (Pick from Red Sox as compensation for Type A free agent Jose Offerman)
1. **Jay Gehrke, rhp, Pepperdine** (Supplemental pick—32nd—for loss of Offerman)
1. **Jimmy Gobble, lhp, John Battle HS, Bristol, Va.** (Supplemental pick—43rd—for loss of Type A free agent Dean Palmer)
2. **Brian Sanches, rhp, Lamar** (Pick from Tigers as compensation for Palmer)
2. **Wes Obermueller, rhp, Iowa**
3. Kiki Bengochea, rhp, Columbus HS, Miami
4. **Mackeel Rodgers, ss, Jackson HS, Miami**
5. **Ken Harvey, 1b, Nebraska**
6. **Ryan Baerlocher, rhp, Lewis-Clark State (Idaho)**
7. **James McAuley, c, Louisville**
8. **Eric Nelson, 2b, Baylor**
9. **Mark Ellis, ss, Florida**
10. **Jesse Kurtz-Nicholl, lhp, Rice**
11. **Edwin Franco, lhp, Florida International**
12. **Tony Cogan, lhp, Stanford**
13. **G.J. Raymundo, 3b, Pepperdine**
14. **Jarrett Shearin, of, North Carolina**
15. **Casey Dunn, c, Auburn**
16. Sam Smith, rhp, Trinidad State (Colo.) JC
17. **Brad Stiles, lhp, Lamar (Colo.) HS**
18. Brandon Medders, rhp, Shelton State (Ala.) CC
19. **Jermaine Smiley, of, Bellevue (Wash.) CC**
20. Juan Figueroa, rhp, Juan Lazaro HS, Carolina, P.R.
21. Brian Nagore, c, Logan HS, Hayward, Calif.
22. **Chad Santos, 1b, St. Louis HS, Kaneohe, Hawaii**
23. Pat Magness, 1b, Wichita State
24. **Brian Johnson, c, Nebraska**
25. **Chris Cabaj, rhp, Ball State**
26. **Raul Garcia, rhp, Florida International**
27. Ben Carter, c, Bowie (Texas) HS
28. Brian Lockwood, rhp, Torrance (Calif.) HS
29. Lukas Guidroz, rhp, Enterprise State (Ala.) JC
30. Richard Frink, c, Mission Bay HS, San Diego
31. Jason Crear, of, King HS, Houston
32. Jason Arre, lhp, Toms River South HS, Beachwood, N.J.
33. **Mike Clay, ss/c, Southeastern Oklahoma State**
34. William Austin, rhp, Salina (Okla.) HS
35. Marcus Wyatt, of, Fontana (Calif.) HS
36. **Julian Gonzalez, of, Virginia**
37. Bryan Bullington, rhp, Madison (Ind.) Consolidated HS
38. Adam Lingenfelter, rhp, Florida CC-Jacksonville
39. **Abel Garcia, lhp, Laredo (Texas) JC**
40. Jason Fransz, of, Arlington HS, San Jacinto, Calif.
41. Herman Wright, of, Odem (Texas) HS
42. Anthony Mercado, rhp, Veve Calzada HS, Fajardo, P.R.
43. **Keronn Walker, c, Bluefield (Va.)**
44. Shane Menn, rhp, Calallen HS, Robstown, Texas
45. **Jacob Baker, 1b, Rice**
46. Jason Maloney, rhp, Stranahan HS, Fort Lauderdale
47. Greg Bauer, rhp, Wichita State
48. Lee Peach, rhp, Memorial HS, Newburgh, Ind.
49. **Kyle Middleton, rhp, Jefferson Davis (Ala.) JC**
50. **Byron Russell, of, Pamlico County HS, Bayboro, N.C.**

LOS ANGELES DODGERS

June—Regular Phase (20)

1. (Pick to Padres as compensation for Type A free agent Kevin Brown)
1. **Jason Repko, ss/of, Hanford HS, West Richland, Wash.** (Supplemental pick—37th—for loss of Type A free agent Scott Radinsky)
2. **Brennan King, ss, Oakland HS, Murfreesboro, Tenn.** (Pick from Cardinals as compensation for Radinsky)
2. (Pick to Diamondbacks as compensation for Type A free agent Devon White)
2. Drew Meyer, ss/of, Bishop England HS, Charleston, S.C. (Supplemental pick—83rd—for loss of Type C free agent Brian Bohanon)
3. (Pick to Orioles as compensation for Type B free agent Alan Mills)
4. **Joe Thurston, ss, Sacramento CC**
5. **Phil Devey, lhp, Southwestern Louisiana**
6. **Shane Victorino, of, St. Anthony's HS, Wailuku, Hawaii**
7. **Jose Escalera, of, Carlos Escobar Lopez HS, Loiza, P.R.**
8. **T.J. Nall, rhp, Schaumburg (Ill.) HS**
9. **Jon Berry, rhp, Newberry (S.C.)**
10. **Lamont Matthews, of, Oklahoma State**
11. **Eric Junge, rhp, Bucknell**
12. **Josh Dalton, ss, Louisiana State**
13. **Jon Hale, c, Southwest Missouri State**
14. **Randy Hadden, rhp, South Carolina**
15. **Wade Parrish, lhp, Washington State**
16. Tymber Lee, rhp, Wichita State
17. **Scott Martin, rhp, Central Connecticut State**
18. **John Rozich, c, Kutztown (Pa.)**
19. **Harold Eckert, rhp, Florida International**
20. Ryan Hamilton, rhp, San Diego
21. **Chris Snow, of, Desert Vista HS, Phoenix**
22. Tim Cunningham, lhp, Rocklin (Calif.) HS
23. **Reggie Abercrombie, of, Columbus (Ga.) HS**
24. Shane Nance, lhp, Houston
25. Clint Chauncey, c, Terry Parker HS, Jacksonville, Fla.
26. Traviss Hodge, 1b, Los Angeles Pierce JC
27. Luke Robertson, rhp, Butler County (Kan.) CC
28. **Mike Keirstead, rhp, St. Malachy's HS, St. John, New Brunswick**
29. Zachary Cates, 1b, Mesa (Ariz.) CC
30. Ryan Brnardic, rhp, Sandwich SS, LaSalle, Ontario
31. Justin Glenn, of, Sheridan HS, Little Rock, Ark.
32. Nolan McManus, rhp, Sierra (Calif.) JC
33. **Clif Wren, c, Mississippi State**
34. Nom Siriveaw, of, Eastern Oklahoma State JC
35. Kegan O'Toole, c, Jackson HS, Bothell, Wash.
36. Ryan Harris, rhp, Woodstock (New Brunswick) HS
37. Miguel Heredia, rhp, Eastern Oklahoma State JC
38. Chris Hunter, rhp, Mountain View HS, Lindon, Utah
39. Chris Hanne, lhp, Duluth (Ga.) HS
40. Michael Pelsnik, rhp, Horizon HS, Phoenix
41. **Keith Godbolt, of, Hillsborough HS, Tampa, Fla.**
42. Rob Harrand, rhp, Regina, Sask
43. Kyle Bateman, rhp, Coconino HS, Flagstaff, Ariz.
44. Robby Sumner, 1b, Pace (Fla.) HS
45. Erik Lohse, rhp, Butte (Calif.) JC
46. Chris Bell, rhp, Columbus HS, Miami
47. Joey Black, rhp, Bonneville HS, Ogden, Utah
48. Scott Wilson, c, Ellensburg (Wash.) HS
49. Jayson Casiano, 1b, Monserrate Leon de Irriza HS, Cabo Rojo, P.R.
50. Jonathan Morel, 1b, Colegio San Agustin HS, Cabo Rojo, P.R.

MILWAUKEE BREWERS

June—Regular Phase (10)

1. **Ben Sheets, rhp, Northeast Louisiana**
2. **Kade Johnson, c, Seminole State (Okla.) JC**
3. **Ruddy Lugo, rhp, Xaverian HS, Brooklyn, N.Y.**
4. **Travis Horne, lhp, First Coast HS, Jacksonville**
5. **Dustin Lansford, rhp, McLennan (Texas) CC**

6. **Mark Ernster, 2b, Arizona State**
7. **Jeff Robinson, rhp, Southwestern Louisiana**
8. **Dave Pember, rhp, Western Carolina**
9. **Bryan Tindell, c, Avon Park (Fla.) HS**
10. **Ben Hendrickson, rhp, Jefferson HS, Bloomington, Minn.**
11. **Will Ford, of, Rice**
12. **Frank Wagner, lhp, Minnesota**
13. **Terry Mayo, of, Eastern Guilford HS, Greensboro, N.C.**
14. **Steven Truitt, of, Texas A&M**
15. **Chris McGee, rhp, Mansfield (Pa.)**
16. Jason Tibesar, of, South Mountain (Ariz.) CC
17. **Chris Olean, rhp, St. Thomas (Minn.)**
18. **Steve Scarborough, ss, Texas A&M**
19. William Hudson, ss, Fountain Valley (Calif.) HS
20. **Kevin Grater, rhp, Wisconsin-Oshkosh**
21. **Ben Wallace, lhp, Quarbin HS, Hubbardston, Mass.**
22. Chad Clark, rhp, Glendora (Calif.) HS
23. Chad Sadowski, rhp, Wisconsin-Milwaukee
24. **Ryan Knox, of, Illinois State**
25. **Casey Trout, ss, Maryland**
26. **Anthony Forelli, 1b, Old Dominion**
27. **Brad Ralston, rhp, Texas Tech**
28. **Jeremy Durkee, lhp, Cuyahoga Falls (Ohio) HS**
29. **Darrell Gaston, rhp, Mobile (Ala.)**
30. **Robert Pregnolato, of, Palm Beach Atlantic (Fla.)**
31. **Corey Artieta, lhp, Northeast Louisiana**
32. **Justin Gordon, lhp, Massasoit (Mass.) CC**
33. **Chris Schilling, c, Daniel HS, Central, S.C.**
34. **Jason Kelley, rhp, Bowling Green State**
35. **Jeff Kenney, ss, Richmond**
36. **Jeremy Krismer, rhp, Oklahoma State**
37. Devin Butler, 1b, Hillsborough (Fla.) JC
38. Matt Gieble, lhp, Woodland (Calif.) HS
39. Sean Sivers, lhp, Kearny HS, San Diego
40. **Jeff House, rhp, Stetson**
41. **Javerro January, ss, Callaway HS, Jackson, Miss.**
42. **Brian Foster, c, Western Alamance HS, Burlington, N.C.**
43. **Chris Simonson, rhp, Wisconsin**
44. William Vazquez, rhp, Indian Hills (Iowa) CC
45. Jason France, lhp, Central Arizona JC
46. **Josh Lake, c, Buena HS, Ventura, Calif.**
47. Ryan Warpinski, rhp, Denmark HS, Maribel, Wis.
48. Amos Burgess, of, Lone Peak (Utah) HS
49. Blair Bourque, of, Taunton (Mass.) HS

MINNESOTA TWINS

June—Regular Phase (5)

1. **B.J. Garbe, of, Moses Lake (Wash.) HS**
2. **Rob Bowen, c, Homestead HS, Fort Wayne, Ind.**
3. **Justin Morneau, c, New Westminster (B.C.) SS**
4. **Jeff Randazzo, lhp, Cardinal O'Hara HS, Broomall, Pa.**
5. **Brent Schoening, rhp, Auburn**
6. **Brian Wolfe, rhp, Servite HS, Anaheim**
7. Darren Ciraco, of, Pelham (N.Y.) Memorial HS
8. **Matt Scanlon, 3b, Minnesota**
9. Grant Gregg, lhp, McLennan (Texas) CC
10. Jim Caine, rhp, St. Charles (Ill.) HS
11. Mike Prochaska, lhp, Leesville Road HS, Raleigh, N.C.
12. Kevin Johnson, rhp, California
13. Seth Morris, rhp/of, Hamilton (Ohio) HS
14. Brian Slocum, rhp, Iona Prep School, Eastchester, N.Y.
15. John Wilson, c/of, Kentucky
16. **Kevin West, of, Mendocino (Fla.) CC**
17. John Larson, rhp, Eastern Illinois
18. **Barry Quickstad, 2b, Waseca (Minn.) HS**
19. **Paul Poplin, rhp, UNC Charlotte**
20. **Travis Bowyer, rhp, Liberty HS, Bedford, Va.**
21. **Chad Wandall, ss, Auburn**
22. **Ricky Manning, of, Edison HS, Fresno**
23. **Willie Eyre, rhp, JC of Eastern Utah**
24. Danny Matienzo, c, Columbus HS, Miami
25. Craig Patterson, c, Cal State Fullerton
26. **Terry Tiffee, 1b, Pratt (Kan.) CC**
27. **Jess Turner, rhp, Centralia (Wash.) JC**
28. **Brad Weis, lhp, Auburn**
29. **Sherwin Lockridge, ss, Florida A&M**
30. **Matt Reed, ss, Haines City (Fla.) HS**
31. Ryan Miller, rhp, Evansville
32. Jeff Balser, rhp, Venice (Fla.) HS
33. Billy Keppinger, of, Lake City (Ga.) CC
34. John Thomman, of, Levelland (Texas) HS
35. **Jason Richardson, rhp, Polk (Fla.) CC**
36. Joey Monahan, ss, Wheeler HS, Marietta, Ga.
37. **Digno Torres, of, Lake City (Fla.) CC**
38. Scott Blackwell, rhp, Lincoln Land (Ill.) CC
39. Beau Vaughan, rhp, Mountain Ridge HS, Glendale, Ariz.
40. Richard Smart, lhp, Gulf Coast (Fla.) CC
41. Michael Stavey, 1b, Eustis (Fla.) HS
42. **Michael Wrenn, c, St. Leo (Fla.)**
43. **Bryan Williamson, of, Washington**
44. Chuck Campbell, rhp, Bay HS, Panama City, Fla.
45. Pat Neshek, rhp, Park Center HS, Brooklyn Park, Minn.
46. Maurice Powell, rhp, Upland HS, Alta Loma, Calif.
47. Luke Field, rhp, Barton County (Kan.) CC
48. Casey Rauschenberger, 3b, Oakland HS, Murfreesboro, Tenn.
49. David Slevin, ss, John Carroll HS, Port St. Lucie, Fla.
50. Joseph Ammirato, of, Marina HS, Long Beach

MONTREAL EXPOS

June—Regular Phase (6)

1. **Josh Girdley, lhp, Jasper (Texas) HS**
2. **Brandon Phillips, ss, Redan HS, Stone Mountain, Ga.**
3. **Drew McMillan, c, El Dorado HS, Placentia, Calif.**
4. **Matt Cepicky, of, Southwest Missouri State**
5. **Pat Collins, rhp, St. John's**
6. **Dominick Ambrosini, of, Connetquot HS, Ronkonkoma, N.Y.**
7. **Cletis Boyer, ss, Largo (Fla.) HS**
8. **Luke Lockwood, lhp, Silverado HS, Victorville, Calif.**
9. **Brandon Watson, 2b, Westchester HS, Los Angeles**
10. **Grant Dorn, rhp, North Carolina State**
11. **David Lutz, of, Monte Vista HS, Spring Valley, Calif.**
12. Brian Stavisky, of, Port Allegany (Pa.) HS
13. **Chris Humrich, rhp, Armstrong Atlantic State (Ga.)**
14. **Brian Preston, c, Wichita State**
15. **Val Pascucci, rhp, Oklahoma**
16. **Matt Watson, 3b/2b, Xavier**
17. **Josh Emmerick, c, Rancho Buena Vista HS, Oceanside, Calif.**
18. Pat Wyrick, rhp, Atoka (Okla.) HS
19. Neville Blount, of, Colton (Calif.) HS
20. Leonard Landeros, lhp, Hanford (Calif.) HS
21. **Mark Thomas, 1b, Youngstown State**
22. **Matt Brown, 3b, Eastern Randolph HS, Randleman, N.C.**
23. Israel Torres, lhp, Cerritos (Calif.) JC
24. **Eric Charron, rhp, Marie-Anne HS, Montreal**
25. **Chuck Crumpton, rhp, Arizona State**
26. **Lou Melucci, 2b, Pittsburgh**
27. Manuel Diaz, rhp, Glenn HS, Norwalk, Calif.
28. Mike Natale, rhp, Santa Ana (Calif.) JC
29. Francisco Chavez, rhp, Socorro HS, El Paso
30. Alex Groleau, rhp, Edouard Montpetit (Quebec)
31. **Jason Norderum, lhp, Shasta HS, Redding, Calif.**
32. Jason Stevenson, lhp, Foothill HS, Redding, Calif.
33. Victor Rosario, of, Sandalwood HS, Jacksonville, Fla.
34. **Eric Langill, c, Des Moines Area (Iowa) CC**
35. **Todd Johannes, c, Florida**
36. Jerry Alexander, ss, Westchester HS, Hawthorne, Calif.
37. Julio Acosta, c, Perkiomen School, Pennsburg, Pa.
38. Joe Clark, rhp, JC of Southern Idaho
39. Travis Edwards, of, Cerritos (Calif.) JC
40. Wes Cain, rhp, Marietta (Okla.) HS
41. Jonnie Mazzeo, rhp, LaSalle SS, Kingston, Ontario
42. Grant Oltjenbruns, of, Fresno (Calif.) CC
43. Chris Sieman, c, Blanchard (Okla.) HS
44. Chuck Rohr, rhp, Citrus (Calif.) JC
45. Chris Richard, of, Norwalk (Conn.) CC
46. Matt Alexander, c, Trinidad State (Colo.) JC
47. Matt Romero, of, Utah Valley State JC

48. **Antonio Garris, 3b/of, Pitt (N.C.) CC**

NEW YORK METS

June—Regular Phase (22)

1. (Pick to White Sox as compensation for Type A free agent Robin Ventura)
2. **Neal Musser, lhp, Benton Central HS, Otterbein, Ind.**
2. **Jake Joseph (Supplemental pick), rhp, Cosumnes River (Calif.) JC** (Supplemental pick—84th—for loss of Type C free agent Armando Reynoso)
3. **Jeremy Griffiths, rhp, Toledo**
4. **Angel Pagan, of, Republica De Colombia HS, Rio Piedras, P.R.**
5. **Nick James, rhp, Hancock (Calif.) JC**
6. Tyler Parker, c, Lassiter HS, Marietta, Ga.
7. **Rodney Nye, 3b, Arkansas**
8. **Forrest Lawson, of, Rogers HS, Puyallup, Wash.**
9. **Wayne Lydon, of, Valley View HS, Jessup, Pa.**
10. **Prentice Redman, of, Bevill State (Ala.) CC**
11. **Joe Cole, rhp, Texas-Pan American**
12. **Paul Viole, rhp, Seton Hall**
13. **Rob McIntyre, ss, Hillsborough HS, Tampa**
14. **John Hendricks, lhp, Wake Forest**
15. **Steven Elzy, c, New Mexico**
16. Gene Desalme, lhp, St. Louis CC-Meramec
17. **Kevin Ciarrachi, c, Northern Iowa**
18. **Matt Smith, rhp, Southwest Missouri State**
19. Jose Pabon, 2b, Potomac HS, Dumfries, Va.
20. Rob Henkel, lhp, UCLA
21. Adam Manley, of, JC of Southern Idaho
22. Kyle Woods, of, Washington
23. Terry Jackson, ss, Westside HS, Augusta, Ga.
24. Dustin Brisson, 1b, Central Florida
25. **Matt Dyer, c, Manchester (Ind.)**
26. **Brad Wright, of, UC Santa Barbara**
27. **Sam Lopez, ss, Fresno (Calif.) CC**
28. **Steve Bennett, rhp, Gonzaga**
29. Bryan Loeb, c, Baylor
30. **Matt Mize, 2b, Texas-Arlington**
31. **Orlando Roman, rhp, Indian Hills (Iowa) CC**
32. **Brian Williamson, rhp, Cornell**
33. **Lionel Rogers, rhp, Fresno (Calif.) CC**
34. **Patrick O'Sullivan, of, Austin Peay**
35. Jamie Gonzales, rhp, Porterville (Calif.) CC
36. Aaron Ledbetter, rhp, Cedarville HS, Fort Smith, Ark.
37. **Graeme Brown, rhp, Brown**
38. **Mike Jacobs, c, Grossmont (Calif.) JC**
39. Carrington Fisk, rhp, Keene (N.H.) HS
40. **Cory Harris, of, Pensacola (Fla.) JC**
41. Philip Perry, rhp, Walton HS, Marrietta, Ga.
42. Darius Shelby, of, Valley View HS, Moreno Valley, Calif.
43. Ryan Hay, c, St. Paul HS, Niagara Falls, Ontario
44. Brian Kelly, rhp, Southaven HS, Olive Branch, Miss.
45. **Ross Peeples, lhp, Middle Georgia JC**
46. Aaron Gureckis, of, Nashua (N.H.) HS
47. Andre DeCordova, ss, Pace HS, Hialeah, Fla.
48. Vincent White, of, John Abbott College HS, St. Anne de Bellevue, Quebec
49. Eric Bernier, of, Edouard Montpetit HS, Montreal
50. John Hoyos, lhp, San Gabriel HS, Rosemead, Calif.

NEW YORK YANKEES

June—Regular Phase (27)

1. **David Walling, rhp, Arkansas**
2. **Tommy Winrow, of, Bishop Verot HS, Fort Myers, Fla.**
3. **Alex Graman, lhp, Indiana State**
4. Robert Corrado, rhp, Oakwood HS, Dayton, Ohio
5. **Seth Taylor, ss, South Alabama**
6. **Reggie LaPlante, rhp, Ahuntsic College, Montreal**
7. **Andy Phillips, 3b, Alabama**
8. **Scott Oliver, rhp, College of Charleston**
9. **Jeff Leaumont, 1b, Louisiana State**
10. **Brad Ticehurst, of, Southern California**
11. Jeffrey Moye, rhp, Seminole State (Okla.) JC
12. **Lou Witte, rhp, Xavier**
13. **Brian Peeples, lhp, First Coast HS, Jacksonville**
14. **Todd Mitchell, ss, Illinois State**
15. **Casey Baker, ss, Towanda HS, Wysox, Pa.**
16. **Bryan Grace, rhp, Louisiana State**
17. **Ricky Spears, rhp, Gore (Okla.) HS**
18. **Dominic Correa, 2b, Southern California**
19. **John Kremer, rhp, Evansville**
20. Jesse Floyd, rhp, Nederland (Texas) HS
21. **Michael Aldridge, c, Eastern Michigan**
22. Chris Klosterman, 3b/of, Cypress (Calif.) JC
23. **Chad Sutter, c, Tulane**
24. **Josh McCloud, rhp, Bowsher HS, Holland, Ohio**
25. Brian Reed, rhp, Amory (Miss.) HS
26. Darin Davis, 2b, Palisades (Calif.) HS
27. John Dimercurio, c, Highlands Ranch (Colo.) HS
28. Chris Dobbins, rhp, Central Alabama CC
29. Sean Lichter, rhp, Deer Valley HS, Glendale, Ariz.
30. Sean Henn, lhp, Aledo (Texas) HS
31. **Kevin Thompson, ss, Grayson County (Texas) JC**
32. Ryan Fry, 3b, Nazareth Area HS, Stockertown, Pa.
33. Santiago Narciandi, c, Miami-Dade CC
34. Chad Bentz, lhp, Douglas HS, Juneau, Alaska
35. Larry Buckley, rhp, East Central (Mo.) JC
36. Nathan Bowden, 3b, Northwest Mississippi CC
37. Michael Hurd, lhp, Arapahoe HS, Littleton, Colo.
38. Mike Brown, of, Centreville HS, Dayton, Ohio
39. Jacob Pierce, rhp, Navarro (Texas) JC
40. Jonathan Habrack, lhp, Dallas Senior HS, Shavertown, Pa.
41. Rob Garibaldi, of, Santa Rosa (Calif.) JC
42. Bryan Hedgecock, rhp, Gaither HS, Tampa
43. **Jason Faigin, rhp, Rowan (N.J.)**
44. Jeremiah Porter, of, Columbia River HS, Vancouver, Wash.
45. Ruben Mancilla, 3b, Costa Mesa (Calif.) HS
46. Beau Dannemiller, rhp, Logan (Ill.) JC
47. John Perry, 1b, Arapahoe HS, Littleton, Colo.
48. David Lower, c, Culver Military Academy, Alexandria, Ind.
49. Henry Caban, rhp, Lehman HS, Bronx
50. Mark Cooper, 1b, Texas City (Texas) HS

OAKLAND ATHLETICS

June—Regular Phase (9)

1. **Barry Zito, lhp, Southern California**
2. **Ryan Ludwick, of, Nevada-Las Vegas**
3. **Jorge Soto, c/1b, Troy State**
4. **Keith Surkont, rhp, Williams (Mass.)**
5. **Darin Moore, rhp, Pacific**
6. **Mario Ramos, lhp, Rice**
7. **Josh Hochgesang, 3b, Stanford**
8. **Justin Lehr, rhp/c, Southern California**
9. **Kirk Asche, of, Jacksonville**
10. **Justin Sobchuk, rhp, Sehome HS, Bellingham, Wash.**
11. **Michael Wenner, of, Rider**
12. Jay Garthwaite, of, Kent Meridan HS, Kent, Wash.
13. **Jason Pomar, rhp, South Carolina**
14. **Alvyn Ellis, 1b, Clackamas (Ore.) CC**
15. Anthony Cicero, c, Cleveland HS, Van Nuys, Calif.
16. **Matt Allegra, of, Lake Mary (Fla.) HS**
17. **Bryan Mazur, lhp, UNC Wilmington**
18. **G.W. Keller, of, Alabama**
19. **Jason Clements, ss, Oral Roberts**
20. **Matt Gage, rhp, Eastern Illinois**
21. **Cade Sanchez, rhp, Texas-Arlington**
22. Edmund Muth, of, Stanford
23. **Mike Lockwood, of, Ohio State**
24. **Brad Henderson, 2b, Mississippi**
25. Fernando De Aza, rhp, Colegio Universario, Carolina, P.R.
26. **Jacob Beckman, rhp, Glen Oaks (Mich.) CC**
27. **Donald Atencio, rhp, Kirtland Central (N.M.) HS**
28. **Nathan Hilton, rhp, Iowa State**
29. Andre Marshall, of, Walla Walla (Wash.) CC
30. Jonathan Edge, of, Tampa
31. Kris Mancini, of, CC of Rhode Island

32. **Micah Dunphy, lhp, Sauk Valley (Ill.) CC**
33. Alex Coleman, of, Poly HS, Long Beach
34. Geoff Comfort, of, JC of San Mateo (Calif.)
35. **Darvin Withers, rhp, Spartanburg (S.C.) Methodist JC**
36. Jerry Knox, rhp, Oakland HS, Murfreesboro, Tenn.
37. **Jorge Ortiz, 3b, Miguel Melendez Munoz HS, Cayey, P.R.**
38. Frank James, lhp, Navarro (Texas) JC
39. Brandon Bahr, rhp, Gulf Coast HS, Marco Island, Fla.
40. Jared Joaquin, rhp, Lower Columbia (Wash.) CC
41. James Cole, lhp, Navarro (Texas) JC
42. Kellyn Shafer, rhp, Lane (Ore.) CC
43. Zach Gordon, ss, Moorpark (Calif.) JC
44. Eric Kitchen, 3b, Durango HS, Las Vegas
45. William Zeier, of, Laney (Calif.) JC

PHILADELPHIA PHILLIES

June—Regular Phase (12)

1. **Brett Myers, rhp, Englewood HS, Jacksonville**
2. Jason Cooper, of, Moses Lake (Wash.) HS
3. **Russ Jacobson, c, Miami**
4. **Brad Pautz, rhp, Minnesota**
5. Joe Saunders, lhp, West Springfield HS, Springfield, Va.
6. **Daniel Tosca, c, Durant HS, Seffner, Fla.**
7. Dave Gil, rhp, Miami
8. **Jesse Thrasher, rhp, Benton HS, St. Joseph, Mo.**
9. **Julio Collazo, ss, Mississippi Delta JC**
10. **Marlon Byrd, of, Georgia Perimeter JC**
11. **Allen Legette, rhp, Stratford HS, Goose Creek, S.C.**
12. **Brian Bush, of, Michigan**
13. **Frank Brooks, lhp, St. Peter's**
14. Jovanathan Clark, of, Vallejo (Calif.) HS
15. **Mark Outlaw, lhp, Baylor**
16. **Chris Keelin, rhp, Montclair State (N.J.)**
17. **Brad Tucker, rhp, Pepperdine**
18. **Rob Avila, c, Master's (Calif.)**
19. Trey Saye, rhp, Newberry (S.C.) HS
20. **Hector Serrano, c, Juan Ponce de Leon HS, Arecibo, P.R.**
21. **Aaron Merhoff, of, Texas Lutheran**
22. **Justin Duarte, 1b, Azusa Pacific (Calif.)**
23. **Todd Eagle, c, Albany (Calif.) HS**
24. **Joe Schley, of, Southern Illinois**
25. **Brian Hitchcox, ss, Samford**
26. **Justin Fry, rhp, Ohio State**
27. **Dan O'Neill, c, Illinois**
28. **Tom Batson, 3b, Northwestern State**
29. Randon Ho, lhp, Hawaii
30. **Chad Smith, rhp, Indiana**
31. **Wade Van Vark, of, Central (Iowa)**
32. **Jay Sitzman, of, Arizona State**
33. **Dean Muthig, 3b, Carthage (Wis.)**
34. **Charles Carey, lhp, Cuesta (Calif.) JC**
35. Chris Herman, ss, Mount San Antonio (Calif.) JC
36. Todd Simo, rhp, New Providence (N.J.) HS
37. **Ryan Brookman, rhp, Wisconsin-Whitewater**
38. Jon Uhl, rhp, Leto Comprehensive HS, Tampa
39. Kameron Loe, rhp, Granada Hills HS, Chatsworth, Calif.
40. Lawrence Alexander, of, Chandler (Okla.) HS
41. **Todd Oetting, c, Jefferson City (Mo.) HS**
42. **Erick Rivera, of, Luis Munoz Rivera HS, Utuado, P.R.**
43. Nicholas White, rhp, Arapahoe HS, Littleton, Colo.
44. Jordan Pickens, 3b, Atascadero (Calif.) HS

PITTSBURGH PIRATES

June—Regular Phase (8)

1. **Bobby Bradley, rhp, Wellington (Fla.) HS**
2. **Ryan Doumit, c, Moses Lake (Wash.) HS**
3. **Aron Weston, of, Solon (Ohio) HS**
4. **Justin Reid, rhp, UC Davis**
5. **J.R. House, c, Seabreeze HS, Ormond Beach, Fla.**
6. **B.J. Barns, of, Duquesne**
7. **Matt Schneider, of, North Florida**
8. **Jon Searles, rhp, Huntington (N.Y.) HS**
9. **Shane Wright, rhp, Texas Tech**
10. **Jeremy Sickles, c, Cal State Northridge**
11. Craig Munroe, 1b, Maryland
12. **Jay Langston, 3b/of, Georgia State**
13. **Josh Hudnall, ss, Ouachita Christian School, Monroe, La.**
14. **Daniel Hudson, of/rhp, Mississippi Gulf Coast JC**
15. **Joe Burruezo, rhp/of, Jesuit HS, Tampa**
16. **Justin Martin, 2b, Nevada**
17. **Cliff Reik, 3b, Cary (N.C.) HS**
18. **Ryan Dorsey, ss, Riverdale Baptist HS, Upper Marlboro, Md.**
19. Brian Tallet, lhp, Louisiana State
20. **Elliott Sarabia, ss, Nevada-Las Vegas**
21. Derek Ver Helst, lhp, Spearfish (S.D.) HS
22. Jason Wilson, of/rhp, San Augustine (Texas) HS
23. **Mike Piercy, of, Kean (N.J.)**
24. **Josh Bonifay, ss/2b, UNC Wilmington**
25. **Aaron Story, lhp, Lawrence County HS, Lawrenceburg, Tenn.**
26. Ja'mar Clanton, ss, Proviso West HS, Bellwood, Ill.
27. **Ken Henderson, lhp, New York Tech**
28. Andrew Green, rhp, Ouachita Parish HS, Monroe, La.
29. **Rodney Hancock, lhp, The Citadel**
30. **Derek Hurley, lhp, Seton Hall**
31. **Walter Young, 1b, Purvis (Miss.) HS**
32. **Jason Biddlestone, rhp, Columbus State (Ohio) CC**
33. **Michael Sabens, rhp, Berry (Ga.)**
34. **Kurt Bultmann, 2b, Clemson**
35. **Mo Douglas, 1b, Southwestern Louisiana**
36. Ryan Fillingim, c/of, Fairhope (Ala.) HS
37. **Troy Satterfield, lhp, Central Florida**
38. Ryan Stanek, c, New Providence (N.J.) HS
39. **Patrick O'Brien, rhp, Walsh Jesuit HS, Bath, Ohio**
40. Seth Hill, lhp/1b, Sandwich (Ill.) HS
41. **Brian Messer, rhp, New Mexico**
42. Frank Torre, lhp, Palm Beach Garden, Fla.
43. Daniel Stringer, rhp, Brazoswood HS, Clute, Texas
44. Michael Oehlberg, lhp, Guilford HS, Rockford, Ill.
45. Raul Nieves, ss, Mobile (Ala.)
46. **Chris Batcheller, c, Washington & Lee (Va.)**
47. Bryce Morrison, of, Leander (Texas) HS
48. Jude Voltz, 1b, Mississippi
49. **Brian Pollard, of, Florida**
50. **Landon Jacobsen, rhp, Trinidad State (Colo.) JC**

ST. LOUIS CARDINALS

June—Regular Phase (18)

1. (Pick to Orioles as compensation for Type A free agent Eric Davis)
1. **Chance Caple, rhp, Texas A&M** (Pick from Braves as compensation for Type A free agent Brian Jordan)
1. **Nick Stocks, rhp, Florida State** (Supplemental pick—36th—for loss of Jordan)
1. **Chris Duncan, 1b, Canyon del Oro HS, Tucson** (Supplemental pick—46th—for loss of Type A free agent Delino DeShields)
2. (Pick to Dodgers as compensation for Type A free agent Scott Radinsky)
2. **Josh Pearce, rhp, Arizona** (Supplemental pick—82nd—for loss of Type C free agent Tom Lampkin)
3. **B.R. Cook, rhp, Oregon State**
4. **Ben Johnson, of, Germantown (Tenn.) HS** (Pick from Orioles as compensation for DeShields)
4. **Jimmy Journell, rhp, Illinois**
5. **Charles Williams, of, Rice**
6. **Josh Teekel, rhp, Belaire HS, Greenwell Springs, La.**
7. **Coco Crisp, 2b, Los Angeles Pierce JC**
8. **Shawn Schumacher, c/3b, Texas A&M**
9. **Damon Thames, ss, Rice**
10. **Kevin Sprague, lhp, McNeese State**
11. Aaron Davidson, 2b, Cuesta (Calif.) CC
12. **Brent Spooner, c, Central Florida**
13. **Albert Pujols, 3b, Maple Woods (Mo.) CC**
14. **Matt Vincent, lhp, Lindsey Wilson (Ky.)**
15. **Travis Bailey, 3b, Florida Atlantic**

16. **Cheyenne Janke, rhp, Nicholls State**
17. **Michael Perkins, rhp, Manatee JC**
18. **Paul Fahs, rhp, Briar Cliff (N.Y.) JC**
19. Chris Beck, of, Cal State Fullerton
20. **Scotty Layfield, rhp, Valdosta State (Ga.)**
21. **Jeremy Cummings, rhp, West Virginia**
22. **Mike Floyd, of, Florida**
23. **Chris Fiora, rhp, Towson State**
24. **Mike Crudale, rhp, Santa Clara**
25. **Mark Penberthy, c, Master's (Calif.)**
26. Justin Berg, c, Rice
27. **Donovan Graves, rhp, Booneville (Mo.) HS**
28. **Brandon Peck, lhp, Kansas State**
29. **Justin Albertsen, of, El Camino (Calif.) JC**
30. **Mark Butler, rhp, Bellevue (Neb.)**
31. **Matt Parker, rhp, Mercer**
32. **Trevor Sansom, rhp, West Virginia State**
33. **Bo Hart, ss/2b, Gonzaga**
34. Jake Moon, rhp, Cypress (Calif.) JC
35. **Aaron Dinkel, rhp, JC of Eastern Utah**
36. Jeff Cruz, lhp, Fullerton (Calif.) CC
37. **Robert Yates, rhp, Arkansas**
38. **Chris Buckley, of, North Arkansas CC**
39. **Monte Lee, of, College of Charleston**
40. Ronnie Corona, rhp, Cypress (Calif.) JC

SAN DIEGO PADRES

June—Regular Phase (28)

1. **Vince Faison, of, Toombs County HS, Lyons, Ga.** (Pick from Dodgers for loss of Type A free agent Kevin Brown)
1. **Gerik Baxter, rhp, Edmonds-Woodway HS, Edmonds, Wash.**
1. **Omar Ortiz, rhp, Texas-Pan American** (Pick from Astros as compensation for Type A free agent Ken Caminiti)
1. **Casey Burns, rhp, Richmond** (Supplemental pick—41st—for loss of Brown)
1. **Mike Bynum, lhp, North Carolina** (Supplemental pick—49th—for loss of Caminiti)
1. **Nick Trzesniak, c, Andrew HS, Tinley Park, Ill.** (Supplemental pick—34th—for loss of Type A free agent Steve Finley)
2. Alberto Concepcion, c, El Segundo (Calif.) HS
3. **Josh Vitek, rhp, Fayetteville (Texas) HS**
4. **Jason Moore, ss, Texas**
5. **Chris Heck, lhp, Clemson** (Pick from Diamondbacks as compensation for Finley)
5. **Mike Thompson, rhp, Lamar (Colo.) HS**
6. **Blair DeHart, rhp, James Madison**
7. **John Scheschuk, 1b, Texas A&M**
8. **Todd Donovan, of, Siena**
9. **John Puccinelli, ss/3b, Notre Dame HS, Toluca Lake, Calif.**
10. **Todd Shiyuk, lhp, Alabama-Huntsville**
11. Brian Adams, lhp, Clemson
12. **Brian Ward, 2b, North Carolina State**
13. Tony Adler, rhp, Greenhill HS, Dallas
14. **Bobby Scales, 2b, Michigan**
15. **Jake Peavy, rhp, St. Paul's HS, Semmes, Ala.**
16. **Greg Ienni, of, Cal State Los Angeles**
17. Brandon Fahey, 3b, Duncanville (Texas) HS
18. **Andres Pagan, c, Luis Munoz Marin HS, Yauco, P.R.**
19. **Richard Huff, c, Mesa State (Colo.)**
20. Matt Moran, rhp, Cosumnes River (Calif.) JC
21. **Troy Schader, ss, Oregon State**
22. Kevin Howard, 3b, Westlake HS, Thousand Oaks, Calif.
23. Mike Mueller, rhp, West Bend East HS, West Bend, Wis.
24. Jeremy Alford, 3b, Benton (La.) HS
25. **Anthony Vandemore, of, Truman State (Mo.)**
26. Shawn Lynn, rhp, Seminole State (Okla.) JC
27. **Chris Adolph, of, Nevada-Las Vegas**
28. Chad Dias, c, Bellevue (Wash.) CC
29. B.J. Long, of, Evans HS, Martinez, Ga.
30. Jason Hammond, of, West Hills HS, Santee, Calif.
31. Jarrett Roenicke, of, Yuba (Calif.) CC
32. **Jeremy Webster, lhp, Salt Lake (Utah) CC**
33. Shawn Hill, rhp, Bishop Redding HS, Georgetown, Conn.
34. Michael Saunches, 1b, Argenta-Oreana HS, Decautur, Ill.
35. **Jeff Rizzo, 3b, Stanford**
36. Anthony Bianucci, of, Woodson HS, Fairfax, Va.
37. Kevin Okimoto, 1b, Santa Clara
38. Marcellus Dawson, of, Wauwatosa East HS, Milwaukee
39. Chris Wilkins, rhp, The Dalles (Ore.) HS
40. Jared Vance, rhp, Connorsville (Ind.) HS

SAN FRANCISCO GIANTS

June—Regular Phase (24)

1. **Kurt Ainsworth, rhp, Louisiana State**
1. **Jerome Williams, rhp, Waipahu HS, Honolulu** (Supplemental pick—39th—for loss of Type A free agent Jose Mesa)
2. **John Thomas, lhp, Righetti HS, Orcutt, Calif.** (Pick from Mariners as compensation for Mesa)
2. **Jack Taschner, lhp, Wisconsin-Oshkosh**
3. **Sean McGowan, 1b, Boston College**
4. **Jeremy Cunningham, rhp, Cal Poly San Luis Obispo**
5. **Ryan Cox, rhp, Southern Illinois-Edwardsville**
6. **Ryan Pene, of, Dixie (Utah) JC**
7. **Joe Jester, ss, Arkansas**
8. **Kevin Vent, rhp, Arkansas**
9. **Josh Cook, ss, Yuba (Calif.) CC**
10. **Anthony Yacco, rhp, Mahopac (N.Y.) HS**
11. **Jeff Verplancke, rhp, Cal State Los Angeles**
12. Ronnie Merrill, ss, Tampa
13. **Fletcher Lee, rhp, Lewis-Clark State (Idaho)**
14. Mike Meyer, rhp, Arizona
15. **Hal Featherstone, rhp, North Carolina A&T**
16. **Micah Holst, of, Southwest Missouri State**
17. **Vance Cozier, rhp, St. Bonaventure**
18. **Brian Meagher, lhp, JC of San Mateo (Calif.)**
19. Ryan Cheo, lhp, Saddleback (Calif.) CC
20. Anthony Turco, c, St. Petersburg (Fla.) JC
21. **Ryan Luther, ss, Lewis-Clark State (Idaho)**
22. Jason Barrow, of, Chemeketa (Ore.) CC
23. **Mike Zirelli, rhp, Cal Poly San Luis Obispo**
24. Bill Murphy, lhp, Arlington HS, Riverside, Calif.
25. Andrew Edwards, rhp, Christ The King HS, Queens, N.Y.
26. **Kevin Alexander, ss, Modesto (Calif.) JC**
27. **Troy Gustafson, of, Blaine (Minn.) HS**
28. **Lars Hansen, c, Hawaii**
29. **Troy Ransom, of, South Mountain (Ariz.) CC**
30. **Ryan Davis, of, Cosumnes River (Calif.) JC**
31. **Scott Daeley, of, Wake Forest**
32. Tim Gilhooly, c, San Ramon Valley HS, Danville, Calif.
33. Kavonski Chatman, lhp/of, Northeast Texas CC
34. Scott Shoemaker, rhp, Granite Hills HS, El Cajon, Calif.
35. Robert Lorona, ss, Hayden HS, Winkelman, Ariz.
36. Bryan Lang, of, Scottsdale (Ariz.) CC
37. Chris Norris, rhp, Central Arizona JC
38. Drew Endicott, rhp, Carthage (Mo.) HS
39. **Paul Turco, ss, Auburn**
40. Travis Veracka, lhp, Massachusetts
41. Winston Woods, of, Broward (Fla.) CC
42. Jason Hickman, lhp, Ball State
43. Brett Cayton, c, Fountain Valley (Calif.) HS
44. Daniel August, rhp, St. Petersburg (Fla.) JC
45. Chad Ashlock, rhp, Texas-Arlington
46. **Wes Faust, rhp, Oklahoma Baptist**
47. Oscar Vargas, ss, Chabot (Calif.) JC
48. Jamie Aloy, 1b, Hawaii
49. Josh Sousa, rhp, Modesto (Calif.) JC
50. **Brian Grochol, of, Canada (Calif.) CC**

SEATTLE MARINERS

June—Regular Phase (11)

1. **Ryan Christianson, c, Arlington HS, Riverside, Calif.**
1. **Jeff Heaverlo, rhp, Washington** (Supplemental pick—33rd—for loss of Type A free agent Mike Timlin)
2. (Pick to Giants as compensation for Type A free agent Jose

Mesa)
3. **Willie Bloomquist, ss, Arizona State**
3. **Sheldon Fulse, ss, George Jenkins HS, Bartow, Fla.** (Pick from Orioles as compensation for Timlin)
4. **Vaughn Schill, ss, Duke**
5. **Clint Nageotte, rhp, Brooklyn (Ohio) HS**
6. **J.J. Putz, rhp, Michigan**
7. Michael Davies, lhp, Westview HS, Beaverton, Ore.
8. **Terrmel Sledge, of, Long Beach State**
9. **Steve Kent, lhp, Florida International**
10. **Justin Smith, lhp, Alabama**
11. **Hawkeye Wayne, rhp, Columbia**
12. Larry Brown, of, San Fernando (Calif.) HS
13. **Justin Leone, ss, St. Martin's (Wash)**
14. **Oscar Ramirez, ss, St. Petersburg (Fla.) JC**
15. **Tim Burton, rhp, Florida Atlantic**
16. **Sean Parnell, of, Wisconsin-Oshkosh**
17. **Brian Hertel, 1b, Nevada-Las Vegas**
18. **Kris Gundrum, of, Western Michigan**
19. Brandon Roberson, rhp, Texas Tech
20. **Kevin Olore, rhp, Marist**
21. Craig Helmandollar, lhp, Potomac State (W.Va.)
22. Jason Edmonds, rhp/3b, De Anza HS, San Pablo, Calif.
23. Zeph Zinsman, 1b, Mission (Calif.) JC
24. Ryan Simon, rhp, Chamberlain HS, Tampa
25. Danny Davidson, lhp, Mosley HS, Lynn Haven, Fla.
26. Matt Walter, rhp, Brandon (Fla.) HS
27. Andrew Rempel, of, Mouat HS, Abbotsford, B.C
28. Jonathan Kuelz, rhp, Odessa (Texas) JC
29. William Gwaltney, rhp, McLennan (Texas) CC
30. Michael Squibb, lhp, South HS, Hagerstown, Md.
31. Travis Allen, rhp, Quartz Hill HS, Lancaster, Calif.
32. Andrew Wells, rhp, Mounds HS, Bixby, Okla.
33. **Chuck Lopez, of, Long Beach State**
34. Chris Bono, c, Brevard (Fla.) CC
35. Brian McDevitt, rhp, Waubonsie Valley HS, Naperville, Ill.
36. Eddie Menchaca, rhp, Westwood HS, Mesa, Ariz.
37. Glenn Tucker, rhp, Coral Shores HS, Tavenier, Fla.
38. Rich Harden, rhp, Claremont SS, Victoria, B.C
39. Derrik Dedge, ss, Suwannee HS, Jasper, Fla.
40. Jeff Thompson, 3b, Torrance HS, Lomita, Calif.
41. Guarionez Rodriguez, 2b, Miami-Dade CC
42. Tyson Munn, of, Earl Marriott SS, Surrey, B.C
43. Chris Snyder, c, Spring Woods HS, Houston
44. Steve Hassett, lhp, Sarasota (Fla.) HS
45. Jon Nelson, 3b, Dixie (Utah) JC
46. Ben Ashworth, rhp, Battle Ground Academy, Franklin, Tenn.
47. Jared Cudd, rhp, Sentinel (Okla.) HS
48. Shawn Brooks, rhp, Lamar (Colo.) CC
49. Mark Leith, rhp, David Thompson SS, Vancouver, B.C.
50. Nate Doorlag, 1b, Plainwell (Mich.) HS

TAMPA BAY DEVIL RAYS

June—Regular Phase (1)

1. **Josh Hamilton, of, Athens Drive HS, Raleigh, N.C.**
2. **Carl Crawford, of, Jefferson Davis HS, Houston**
3. **Doug Waechter, rhp, Northeast HS, St. Petersburg, Fla.**
4. **Alex Santos, rhp, Miami**
5. **Seth McClung, rhp, Greenbrier East HS, Lewisburg, W.Va.**
6. Eric Henderson, lhp, Santa Fe (Fla.) CC
7. **Andrew Beinbrink, 3b, Arizona State**
8. Ryan Gloger, lhp, Jesuit HS, Tampa
9. **Dan Ortiz, 1b, Hemet HS, Nuevo, Calif.**
10. **Nathan Cromer, lhp, Lincoln HS, Des Moines**
11. **Jason Cromer, lhp, Lincoln HS, Des Moines**
12. **Jorge Maduro, c, Monsignor Pace HS, Miami**
13. **Jason Pruett, lhp, Brookhaven (Texas)**
14. **Jeff Ridgway, lhp, Port Angeles (Wash.) HS**
15. **Scott Vandermeer, rhp, McMain HS, New Orleans**
16. Danny Lopaze, rhp/ss, Potomac HS, Lakeridge, Va.
17. **Matt Diaz, of, Florida State**
18. Ryan Raburn, ss, Durant HS, Dover, Fla.
19. **Oginga Aaron, 2b, Santa Ana (Calif.) JC**
20. **Chris Crawford, rhp, Georgia**
21. Mike Fontenot, 2b, Salmen HS, Slidell, La.
22. Cortney Jenkins, rhp, Lamar
23. **Travis Minix, rhp, Ball State**
24. Mark Carter, lhp, Wallace State (Ala.) CC
25. **Matt Dailey, lhp, UC Santa Barbara**
26. Aaron Sheffield, rhp, Pope HS, Marietta, Ga.
27. **Justin Schuda, c, Murietta Valley (Calif.) HS**
28. Scott Berney, rhp, Connecticut
29. Mike Hernandez, lhp, Central Union HS, Fresno
30. Ralph Harrelson, rhp, Modesto (Calif.) JC
31. Curtis White, lhp, Lindsay (Okla.) HS
32. Josh Nichols, lhp, Bradford HS, Starke, Fla.
33. Cortney Hill, 2b, Eastern Oklahoma State JC
34. Phil Klaiber, 3b, Schenectady County (N.Y.) CC
35. **Kevin O'Brien, 1b, Tarpon Springs HS, Dunedin, Fla.**
36. Ralph Roberts, of, Lenoir (N.C.) CC
37. Matt Lederhos, rhp, Westwood (Mass.) HS
38. Teryn Stanley, ss, Horizon Christian HS, San Diego
39. Kevin Beavers, lhp, Saddleback (Calif.) CC
40. Peter Bonifas, rhp, Marquette HS, Bellevue, Iowa
41. **Glenn Katz, of, Connecticut**
42. Ben Himes, of, Westlake HS, Austin, Texas
43. Trevor Tacker, rhp, Carroll HS, Southlake, Texas
44. Josh Radke, ss, Bozeman HS, Bozeman, Mont.
45. Chad Coder, of, East Lake HS, Redmond, Wash.
46. Bo Ashabraner, rhp, Esperanza HS, Yorba Linda, Calif.
47. Chadd Blasko, rhp, Mishawaka (Ind.) HS
48. Casey Blalock, rhp, Panola (Texas) JC
49. Randy Walter, of, Huntley Project HS, Ballantine, Mont.
50. Allen Nevels, rhp, Taloga HS, Putnam, Okla.

TEXAS RANGERS

June—Regular Phase (21)

1. (Pick to Orioles as compensation for Type A free agent Rafael Palmeiro)
1. **Colby Lewis, rhp, Bakersfield (Calif.) JC** (Supplemental pick—38th—for loss of Type A free agent Todd Stottlemyre)
1. **David Mead, rhp, Soddy Daisy HS, Chattanooga, Tenn.** (Supplemental pick—47th—for loss of Type A free agent Will Clark)
2. **Nick Regilio, rhp, Jacksonville**
3. **Hank Blalock, ss, Rancho Bernardo HS, San Diego**
4. **Kevin Mench, of, Delaware** (Pick from Diamondbacks as compensation for Stottlemyre)
4. **Chris Jaile, c, Columbus HS, Miami**
5. **Andy Cavazos, rhp, Brazoswood HS, Clute, Texas** (Pick from Orioles as compensation for Clark)
5. **Victor Hillaert, rhp, Shippensburg (Pa.)**
6. **Aaron Harang, rhp, San Diego State**
7. Luz Portobanco, rhp, Miami Senior HS
8. **John Rahrer, rhp, Emmett (Idaho) HS**
9. **Brett Cadiente, of, Arizona State**
10. **Jason Bryan, of, New Utrecht HS, Brooklyn**
11. **Justin Echols, rhp, Greenway HS, Phoenix**
12. **Mike Scuglik, lhp, Xavier**
13. **Jason Jones, of, Kennesaw State**
14. **Ernest Villegas, of, Northeast Texas CC**
15. Dennis Sarfate, rhp, Gilbert HS, Chandler, Ariz.
16. Joel Alvarado, c, Garden City (Kan.) CC
17. **Orlando Cruz, of, Jose Collazo Colon HS, Juncos, P.R.**
18. Raymond Knight, c, St. John's Prep, Jamaica, N.Y.
19. Noah Lowry, lhp, Ventura (Calif.) JC
20. Kevin Marshall, of, Martin HS, Arlington, Texas
21. Michael Falco, of, Agoura HS, Westlake Village, Calif.
22. Nick Devenney, rhp, Holmes (Miss.) JC
23. Denny Summerall, of, Armwood HS, Seffner, Fla.
24. Dan Sauer, rhp, Modesto (Calif.) JC
25. Matt Trepkowski, lhp, Killeen HS, Fort Hood, Texas
26. Jason Reuss, 1b, Orange Coast (Calif.) JC
27. Ryan Mottl, rhp, Clemson
28. J.T. Sherman, rhp, Durango (Nev.) HS
29. Erick Monzon, 2b, De Lourdes HS, Carolina, P.R.
30. Dustin Smith, c, Girard (Kan.) HS
31. Chuck Bowman, rhp, Pell City (Ala.) HS

32. Josue Lopez, 1b, El Toro HS, Trabuco Canyon, Calif.
33. Anthony Piazza, c, Fairview HS, Cody, Wyo.
34. Iggy Suarez, ss, John Bowne HS, Corona, N.Y.
35. Ed Erickson, 1b, Washington
36. J.R. Crider, rhp, Phoenix JC
37. Jared Hartness, rhp, Jonesboro (Ga.) HS
38. **Richard Gilbert, lhp, JC of Eastern Utah**
39. Chad Williams, lhp, Tucson HS, Arivaca, Ariz.
40. **Josh Hollingsworth, 3b, St. Petersburg (Fla.) JC**
41. Andrew Fryson, rhp, Shanks HS, Gretna, Fla.
42. **Adam Poe, of, South Carolina**
43. Michael Sills, lhp, Leon HS, Tallahassee, Fla.
44. Russel Reeves, lhp, Imperial (Calif.) HS
45. Brad Hertel, of, Clovis West HS, Fresno
46. **Jason Botts, 1b, Glendale (Calif.) JC**
47. Marty Hayes, rhp, San Diego
48. Nick Priest, 1b, El Capitan HS, El Cajon, Calif.
49. Nathan Neibauer, of, Overland HS, Aurora, Colo.
50. Clay Chesser, of, Golden West HS, Visalia, Calif.

TORONTO BLUE JAYS

June—Regular Phase (19)

1. **Alex Rios, 3b, San Pedro Martir HS, Guaynabo, P.R.**
2. **Michael Snyder, 3b, Ayala HS, Chino Hills, Calif.**
3. **Matt Ford, lhp, Taravella HS, Tamarac, Fla.**
4. **Brian Cardwell, rhp, Sapulpa (Okla.) HS**
5. **Scott Porter, rhp, Jacksonville**
6. **David Hanson, rhp, Richland (Wash.) HS**
7. **Derrick Nunley, rhp, Englewood HS, Jacksonville**
8. **Ryan McCullem, lhp, Hickman HS, Columbia, Mo.**
9. **Josh Holliday, c/3b, Oklahoma State**
10. **Rob Cosby, ss, Academie Bautista, San Juan, P.R.**
11. **Chuck Kegley, rhp, Okaloosa-Walton (Fla.) JC**
12. **Chris Weekly, ss, New Mexico State**
13. **Marc Bluma, rhp, Wichita State**
14. **Brandon Lyon, rhp, Dixie (Utah) JC**
15. **Tim Newman, rhp, Walla Walla (Wash.) CC**
16. **Jim Detwiler, lhp, Old Dominion**
17. **Reed Johnson, of, Cal State Fullerton**
18. **Peyton Lewis, rhp, Creighton**
19. **Ryan Spille, lhp, Southeast Missouri State**
20. **Thom Dreier, rhp, Oklahoma State**
21. **Rob Hamann, rhp, Wheaton (Ill.)**
22. **Justin Stine, lhp, Missouri**
23. Andre Monroe, of, Santa Monica HS, Palmdale, Calif.
24. Jeremy Cook, rhp, San Diego State
25. Joshua Berry, lhp, Lake Stevens HS, Everett, Wash.
26. **Doug Roper, rhp, Clemson**
27. Angel Molina, of, Colegio Cristo Rey, Santa Isabel, P.R.
28. Kirk Gosch, lhp, Coeur D'Alene (Idaho) HS
29. **Chris Baker, rhp, Oklahoma City**
30. Jerome McCoy, ss, Eastern Hills HS, Fort Worth
31. Charles Tasiaux, rhp, Ahuntsic (Quebec) JC
32. **Aaron Fera, of, Georgia College & State**
33. Collin Perschon, rhp, Bellevue, Wash.
34. **Lee Southard, rhp, Seminole State (Okla.) JC**
35. **Matt Bimeal, rhp, Conemaugh Township HS, Davidsville, Pa.**
36. **Douglas Dimma, lhp, Valdosta State (Ga.)**
37. Robbie Findlay, rhp, Power HS, Etobicoke, Ontario
38. Mike Tisdale, rhp, St. Peters SS, Peterborough, Ontario
39. Wilton Reynolds, of, Cosumnes River (Calif.) JC
40. **Brian Mitchell, 2b, Iowa**
41. Jeff Flegler, of, Gloucester, N.J.
42. Judson Jones, lhp, Meridian (Miss.) CC
43. Chad Scarbery, rhp, Clovis HS, Fresno
44. Jon Youngblood, ss, Arkansas HS, Texarkana, Ark.
45. Brendon Stafford, rhp, St. Mathews HS, Gloucester, Ontario
46. Brooks McNiven, rhp, Kalamalka SS, Vernon, B.C
47. Garris Gonce, c, Florida CC-Jacksonville
48. Jonathan Slack, of, Green Valley HS, Henderson, Nev.
49. Phil Banta, rhp, Bellevue (Wash.) CC
50. Derek Brehm, lhp, East Central HS, San Antonio

2000 COMMISSIONERS OFFICE TAKES FIRST ACTION TO SLOW BONUSES; TEAMS FOCUS ON SIGNABILITY

Signability had rivaled baseball ability as the most important criteria for first-round picks for several years, and in 2000 signability easily won.

Considering that veteran scouts called the 2000 draft the most unpredictable they had ever encountered, it unfolded exactly as expected. Several highly regarded players fell as money determined the players who went with the early selections. All but a few draftees in the top 11 picks agreed to bonus parameters before they were chosen.

The Marlins took San Diego high school first baseman Adrian Gonzalez with the No. 1 pick after agreeing on a $3 million signing bonus four days earlier, though predraft deals are technically prohibited by baseball rules.

If anything, though, Major League Baseball congratulated the Marlins. The commissioner's office held a negotiating seminar in Atlanta a month before the draft, and teams were urged to toe the line on bonuses. Gonzalez became the first No. 1 pick in eight years to receive less than his counterpart the year before.

Florida wanted to lock up a player before the draft and avoid spending the money it lavished on 1999's No. 2 pick. Texas high school righthander Josh Beckett held out for most of the summer before landing a $7 million big league deal.

After the Gonzalez choice, no one knew how the draft would play out. The consensus best prospect was California high school righthander Matt Harrington, who consistently threw 94-95 mph in the spring and topped out at 98.

It was a sign of the times that the Marlins never even approached Harrington about going No. 1. Harrington wouldn't commit to a dollar amount the night before the draft, and he lasted until the Rockies took him at No. 7. He and the Rockies went through some of the most acrimonious negotiations in draft history, and Harrington still hadn't signed after going through the draft four times. The Yankees selected him in the 36th round of the '04 draft, closing the final chapter of this draft saga—though Harrington would pitch for six seasons in independent ball.

All told, the 29 first-round picks who signed received an average of $1.873 million, just a 3 percent increase over the 1999 average of $1.810 million. That result put a smile on the face of MLB executive vice president Sandy Alderson, who came up with the idea for the negotiating seminar.

Alderson wasn't smiling on July 27, however, when

LARRY GOREN

Stanford two-sport star Joe Borchard set a new standard with a $5.3 million bonus

Stanford outfielder Joe Borchard, the No. 12 overall pick, came to terms with the White Sox—for $5.3 million. That shattered Josh Hamilton's record for a draftee signing with the team that selected him. Hamilton signed with the Devil Rays for $3.96 million as the '99 draft's first overall pick.

Chicago scouting director Duane Shaffer said Borchard was the top-rated player on the team's draft board, and he also had to be bought away from football. Borchard would have been the Cardinal's starting quarterback in the fall and was one of the top junior quarterbacks in the nation.

It's worth noting that Borchard never panned out, while Gonzalez established himself as a Gold Glove first baseman and one of baseball's better pure hitters. Gonzalez's success came only after the Marlins traded him away in 2003, however.

The Reds selected arguably the best shortstop (Miami high schooler David Espinosa at No. 23) and the top catcher (Pepperdine's Dane Sardinha at No. 46) after both slid because of signability concerns.

Getting them signed took a unique approach. Espinosa, who reportedly sought a $4 million bonus before the draft, accepted no bonus as part of an eight-year major league contract that guaranteed him $2.95 million and could be worth $5 million. Sardinha also signed for no bonus. He took a six-year major league contract worth between $1.95 million and $2.4 million. Neither of those players proved worth the trouble either.

Another Boras End-Run

Even with all the intrigue, the most unique draft-related event involved North Carolina high school catcher Landon Powell. Powell, a junior at Apex High, was Baseball America's No. 2-rated high school prospect for the 2001 draft class entering the spring.

Powell, who was represented by Scott Boras, became eligible for the 2000 proceedings by getting his GED diploma and applying to MLB for the draft. No teams realized he was available and he went unselected, which under draft rules should have made him a free agent.

The commissioner's office imposed a signing freeze on Powell while it investigated the situation. He was ruled a free agent Aug. 9, having lost two months of negotiating time. Fewer than half of the major league clubs attended his workouts as word spread that Powell's father compared his son to an early first-round talent who was a free agent.

The murky appraisal was interpreted by most clubs as meaning anywhere from $3 million to $6 million, which priced out all but the most free-spending teams in baseball.

The Powell case ultimately was much ado about nothing, as he ended up attending the University of South Carolina. Several club executives said Powell wasn't a premium first-round talent in the first place. The Athletics took him in the first round of the 2004 draft, and he reached the big leagues but was by no means a star.

Multiple agents mentioned the word collusion in regards to both the MLB-sponsored negotiating seminar and the Powell situation. However, baseball's collusion rules apply only to major league players. Clubs are free to set a common approach with respect to the draft.

Whether teams acted in concert can't be answered definitively. But it's obvious that the Atlanta meeting, and a mid-August one in Las Vegas to reinforce Alderson's message, had a pronounced effect on the 2000 draft.

DRAFT 00: FIRST-ROUND PICKS

No.	Club	Player, Pos.	School	Hometown	Ht.	Wt.	B-T	Age
1.	Marlins	Adrian Gonzalez, 1b	Eastlake HS	Chula Vista, Calif.	6-2	195	L-L	18
2.	Twins	Adam Johnson, rhp	Cal State Fullerton	San Diego	6-2	210	R-R	20
3.	Cubs	Luis Montanez, ss	Coral Park HS	Miami	6-0	170	R-R	18
4.	Royals	Mike Stodolka, lhp	Centennial HS	Corona, Calif.	6-2	205	R-L	18
5.	Expos	Justin Wayne, rhp	Stanford	Honolulu	6-4	205	R-R	21
6.	Devil Rays	Rocco Baldelli, of	Bishop Hendricken HS	Warwick, R.I.	6-4	180	R-R	18
7.	Rockies	*Matt Harrington, rhp	Palmdale HS	Palmdale, Calif.	6-3	180	R-R	18
8.	Tigers	Matt Wheatland, rhp	Rancho Bernardo HS	San Diego	6-5	215	R-R	18
9.	Padres	Mark Phillips, lhp	Hanover HS	Hanover, Pa.	6-3	190	L-L	18
10.	Angels	Joe Torres, lhp	Gateway HS	Kissimmee, Fla.	6-2	175	L-L	17
11.	Brewers	Dave Krynzel, of	Green Valley HS	Henderson, Nev.	6-1	180	L-L	18
12.	White Sox	Joe Borchard, of	Stanford	Camarillo, Calif.	6-5	220	B-R	21
13.	Cardinals	Shaun Boyd, of	Vista HS	Oceanside, Calif.	5-11	185	R-R	18
14.	Orioles	Beau Hale, rhp	Texas	Mauriceville, Texas	6-1	200	R-R	21
15.	Phillies	Chase Utley, 2b	UCLA	Long Beach	6-0	180	L-R	21
16.	Mets	Billy Traber, lhp	Loyola Marymount	El Segundo, Calif.	6-3	190	L-L	20
17.	Dodgers	Ben Diggins, rhp	Arizona	Pheonix	6-6	230	R-R	20
18.	Blue Jays	Miguel Negron, of	Manuela Toro HS	Caguas, P.R.	6-2	165	L-L	17
19.	Pirates	Sean Burnett, lhp	Wellington HS	Wellington, Fla.	6-1	172	L-L	17
20.	Angels	Chris Bootcheck, rhp	Auburn	LaPorte, Ind.	6-5	195	R-R	21
21.	Giants	Boof Bonser, rhp	Gibbs HS	Pinellas Park, Fla.	6-4	225	R-R	18
22.	Red Sox	Phil Dumatrait, lhp	Bakersfield (Calif.) JC	Bakersfield, Calif.	6-2	175	L-L	18
23.	Reds	David Espinosa, ss	Gulliver Prep	Miami	6-2	175	B-R	18
24.	Cardinals	Blake Williams, rhp	Southwest Texas State	San Marcos, Texas	6-5	210	R-R	21
25.	Rangers	Scott Heard, c	Rancho Bernardo HS	San Diego	6-2	190	L-R	18
26.	Indians	Corey Smith, ss	Piscataway HS	Piscataway, N.J.	6-0	200	R-R	18
27.	Astros	Robert Stiehl, rhp	El Camino (Calif.) JC	Torrance, Calif.	6-3	200	R-R	19
28.	Yankees	David Parrish, c	Michigan	Yorba Linda, Calif.	6-3	215	R-R	20
29.	Braves	Adam Wainwright, rhp	Glynn Academy	St. Simons Island, Ga.	6-7	195	R-R	18
30.	Braves	Scott Thorman, 3b	Preston HS	Cambridge, Ontario	6-3	210	L-R	18

*Did not sign

2000

CLUB-BY-CLUB SELECTIONS

ANAHEIM ANGELS

June—Regular Phase (10)

1. **Joe Torres, lhp, Gateway HS, Kissimmee, Fla.**
1. **Chris Bootcheck, rhp, Auburn** (Pick from Athletics as compensation for Type B free agent Mike Magnante)
2. **Jared Abruzzo, c, El Capitan HS, La Mesa, Calif.**
3. **Tommy Murphy, ss, Florida Atlantic**
4. **Charlie Thames, rhp, Texas**
5. **Bobby Jenks, rhp, Spirit Lake, Idaho**
6. **Brandon O'Neal, rhp, Kansas**
7. Aaron Hill, ss, Redwood HS, Visalia, Calif.
8. **Adam Pace, lhp, Dominican (N.Y.)**
9. **Jason Coulie, of, Bates (Maine)**
10. **Matt Hensley, rhp, Grossmont (Calif.) JC**
11. Garrett Patterson, lhp, McAlester (Okla.) HS
12. **Scott Schneider, rhp, Norfolk State**
13. **Josh Gray, of, Rock Creek HS, Durant, Okla.**
14. **Kevin Jenkins, of, Northwestern HS, Miami**
15. Geoff Smart, lhp, Kalamalka SS, Vernon, B.C
16. **Johnny Raburn, ss, South Florida**
17. **Mike Napoli, c, Flanagan HS, Cooper City, Fla.**
18. **Tony Socarras, c, Florida**
19. **Brandon Rogers, c, San Diego State**
20. **Brett Cimorelli, rhp, Zephyrhills (Fla.) HS**
21. **Rich Fischer, rhp, San Bernardino Valley (Calif.) JC**
22. **Jeremy Ward, lhp, Florida Southern**
23. Brian Finch, rhp, Columbia HS, Brazoria, Texas
24. **Ryan Withey, of, Florida Atlantic**
25. **Ransel Melgarejo, of, Miami Senior HS**
26. **James Warner, of, Missouri**
27. **Zach Roper, of, Florida Atlantic**
28. Leo Calderon, rhp, Killian HS, Miami
29. **Kevin Kay, c, North Florida**
30. **Larry Bowles, lhp, Virginia Tech**
31. **Jeff Stockton, ss, North Florida**
32. Clinton Hart, lhp, Florida CC-Jacksonville
33. **Adam Belicic, lhp, George Washington**
34. James Langham, of, Jones County HS, Gray, Ga.
35. **Tymber Lee, rhp, Wichita State**
36. Jon Chretien, rhp, LaGrange HS, Lake Charles, La.
37. **Gilbert Landestoy, rhp, Florida International**
38. Richard Brantley, lhp, Apopka (Fla.) HS
39. Casey Mutter, rhp, Rialto (Calif.) HS
40. David Marchbanks, lhp, Mauldin HS, Simpsonville, S.C.
41. Kellen Dupree, rhp, Baker County HS, Macclenny, Fla.
42. Adam Lesko, rhp, Cheyenne HS, Las Vegas
43. **Jeff Balser, rhp, Polk (Fla.) CC**
44. Ronald Ennis, lhp, Polk (Fla.) CC
45. Brian Nagore, c, Okaloosa-Walton (Fla.) CC
46. Robert Bellazetin, 3b, Miami Senior HS
47. Daniel Stillman, rhp, Central Florida
48. Andrew Daly, rhp, Indian River (Fla.) CC
49. Zack Matthews, of, Howard (Texas) JC
50. David Murphy, 1b, Klein HS, Spring, Texas

ARIZONA DIAMONDBACKS

June—Regular Phase (29)

1. (Pick to Braves as compensation for Type A free agent Russ Springer)
2. **Mike Schultz, rhp, Loyola Marymount**
3. **Bill White, lhp, Jacksonville State**
4. **Josh Kroeger, of, Scripps Ranch HS, San Diego**
5. **Brad Cresse, c, Louisiana State**
6. **Scott Barber, rhp, South Carolina**
7. **Tim Olson, of, Florida**
8. **Brandon Webb, rhp, Kentucky**
9. **Tanner Eriksen, rhp, Southern California**
10. **Cedrick Harris, of, Louisiana State**
11. **Rick Haydel, ss, Louisiana-Lafayette**
12. **Brian Bruney, rhp, Warrenton (Ore.) HS**
13. **Pete Sikaras, rhp, St. Francis (Ill.)**
14. **Jesus Cota, 1b, Pima (Ariz.) CC**
15. **JuJu Foreman, of, Augusta State (Ga.)**
16. **Will Rosellini, rhp, Dallas**
17. **Doug Slaten, lhp, Los Angeles Pierce JC**
18. **Vince Eppolito, rhp, Shippensburg (Pa.)**
19. **Aric Leclair, lhp, Indiana State**
20. **Chris Lesieur, rhp, New Haven (Conn.)**
21. **Jason Williams, ss, California**
22. **Corby Medlin, rhp, Katy (Texas) HS**
23. Brett Korth, rhp, Genoa-Kingston HS, Genoa, Ill.
24. **Andy Green, 2b, Kentucky**
25. James Gregg, rhp, George Wallace (Ala.) CC
26. **Greg Belson, rhp, Montclair State (N.J.)**
27. **Jonathan Sherlock, c, Hopkins (Minn.) HS**
28. **Matt Steele, rhp, Georgia**
29. Ian Kinsler, ss, Canyon del Oro HS, Tucson
30. Ryan Costello, lhp, Gloucester County (N.J.) CC
31. **John Massey, c, Tennessee**
32. Ralph Roberts, of/rhp, Lenoir (N.C.) CC
33. Khari Council, 1b, McClancy Memorial HS, Jamaica, N.Y.
34. **Steve Woodward, of, Cal State Fullerton**
35. **Joe Ricciardi, rhp, St. Leo (Fla.)**
36. **Joey Cramblitt, rhp, Mississippi**
37. Leonard Rice, lhp, Galveston (Texas) JC
38. Oscar Mattox, lhp, Phoenix JC
39. Brandon Simon, of, West Hills (Calif.) CC
40. Josh Perrault, rhp, Red Mountain HS, Mesa, Ariz.
41. **Orlando Delanvez, ss, Miami Springs (Fla.) HS**
42. Charles Parkinson, of, Blue Ridge HS, Lakeside, Ariz.
43. **Carlton Wells, lhp, Hillsborough (Fla.) CC**
44. **Marques Chilsom, of, Brandon (Fla.) HS**
45. Robert Ramsey, rhp, Bowie HS, Austin, Texas
46. Luis Trinidad, lhp, Long Beach CC
47. Andrew Wishy, of, Raytown (Mo.) South HS
48. Creighton Kahoalii, c, Newark Memorial HS, Fremont, Calif.
49. Eric Anderson, lhp, Lake Dallas HS, Corinth, Texas
50. Brian Buscher, 3b, Central Florida CC

ATLANTA BRAVES

June—Regular Phase (30)

1. **Adam Wainwright, rhp, Glynn Academy, St. Simons, Ga.** (Pick from Diamondbacks as compensation for Type A free agent Russ Springer)
1. **Scott Thorman, 3b, Preston HS, Cambridge, Ontario**
1. **Kelly Johnson, ss, Westwood HS, Austin, Texas** (Supplemental pick—38th—for loss of Type A free agent Jose Hernandez)
1. **Aaron Herr, ss, Hempfield HS, Lancaster, Pa.** (Supplemental pick—40th—for loss of Springer)
2. **Bubba Nelson, rhp, Riverdale Baptist HS, Fort Washington, Md.** (Pick from Brewers as compensation for Hernandez)
2. **Bryan Digby, rhp, McIntosh HS, Peachtree City, Ga.**
3. **Blaine Boyer, rhp, Walton HS, Marietta, Ga.**
4. **Zach Miner, rhp, Palm Beach Gardens (Fla.) HS** (Pick from Devil Rays as compensation for Type B free agent Gerald Williams)
4. Brian Montalbo, rhp, Dimond HS, Anchorage, Alaska
5. **Chris Waters, rhp, South Florida CC**
6. **Matt Merricks, lhp, Oxnard (Calif.) HS**
7. **Brian Almeida, rhp, Lemon Bay HS, Englewood, Fla.**
8. **Robert Perkins, c, Modesto (Calif.) JC**
9. **Ahmad Woods, of, Redan HS, Stone Mountain, Ga.**
10. **Rodric Douglas, rhp, Colmesneil (Texas) HS**

11. **Kevin Cust, c, Immaculata HS, Flemington, N.J.**
12. **Keoni DeRenne, ss, Arizona**
13. **Jonathan Rogers, rhp, Lee HS, Midland, Texas**
14. **Mike Machen, rhp, McGill-Toolen HS, Mobile, Ala.**
15. **Armando Tejero, 1b, Colon HS, Santa Isabel, P.R.**
16. **Andy Bent, rhp, Nebraska**
17. **Trey Hodges, rhp, Louisiana State**
18. Mike Davern, rhp, Brea-Olinda HS, Brea, Calif.
19. **Charles Thomas, of, Western Carolina**
20. **Kyle Roat, c, Connors State (Okla.) JC**
21. **Matt Wright, rhp, Robinson HS, Lorena, Texas**
22. **Josh Tillery, rhp, Dodge City (Kan.) CC**
23. **Mike Smalley, lhp, Florida**
24. **Robert Moose, 1b, Bridgewater (Va.)**
25. Tim McClendon, rhp, Dr. Phillips HS, Orlando
26. **Ralph Coleman, of, Texas Southern**
27. Josh Wyrick, of, Centennial HS, Bakersfield, Calif.
28. **Erick Contreras, ss, Culver-Stockton (Mo.)**
29. **Adam LaRoche, 1b, Seminole State (Okla.) CC**
30. **Quentin Jones, rhp, Norfolk State**
31. Delwyn Young, 2b, Little Rock HS, Lancaster, Calif.
32. Callix Crabbe, 2b, Stone Mountain (Ga.) HS
33. Tony Gwynn Jr., of, Poway (Calif.) HS
34. Adam Brandenburg, lhp, South Gwinnett HS, LaGrange, Ga.
35. William Hall, lhp, Evant HS, Hamilton, Texas
36. Efren Lira, rhp, Mount San Antonio (Calif.) JC
37. Josh Parker, rhp, Wallace State (Ala.) CC
38. **Francisco Arteaga, rhp, East Los Angeles JC**
39. Jimmy Rhodes, rhp, Jefferson HS, Shepherdstown, W.Va.
40. Adam Hilzendeger, rhp, Palmdale (Calif.) HS
41. Shane Hawk, lhp, Midwest City (Okla.) HS
42. Zachariah Watson, rhp, Columbus (Ga.) HS
43. Daniel Anderson, of, Temple (Texas) JC
44. Tanner Holecek, of, Temple (Texas) JC
45. Craig Bragg, of, Bellarmine Prep, San Jose
46. Brandon Green, ss, Adair (Okla.) HS
47. Justin Bergh, rhp, Oak Hall HS, Reddick, Fla.
48. Jason Herman, rhp, Marshfield (Mo.) HS
49. Billy Edwards, rhp, Evangelical Christian HS, Cordova, Tenn.
50. Drew Jackson, of, University HS, Morgantown, W.Va.

BALTIMORE ORIOLES

June—Regular Phase (14)

1. **Beau Hale, rhp, Texas**
1. **Tripper Johnson, 3b, Newport HS, Bellevue, Wash.** (Supplemental pick—32nd—for loss of Type A free agent Arthur Rhodes)
2. (Pick to Twins as compensation for Type A free agent Mike Trombley)
3. **Richard Bartlett, rhp, Kamiakin HS, Kennewick, Wash.**
3. **Tommy Arko, c, Cooper HS, Abilene, Texas** (Pick from Mariners as compensation for Rhodes)
4. Jon Skaggs, rhp, Rice
5. **Doug Gredvig, 1b, Sacramento CC**
6. **Brandon Spillers, rhp, Tattnall Square Academy, Roberta, Ga.**
7. **B.J. Littleton, of, Lamar**
8. **Jayme Sperring, rhp, Rice**
9. **Mike Russell, c, Bothell (Wash.) HS**
10. **Casey Cahill, rhp, Immaculata HS, New Brunswick, N.J.**
11. Darren Heal, rhp, Oklahoma State
12. **Kris Wilken, c/3b, Houston**
13. **Ryan Keefer, rhp, Southern Columbia Area HS, Catawissa, Pa.**
14. **Brian Forystek, lhp, Illinois State**
15. **Thomas Joyce, of, First Presbyterian HS, Macon, Ga.**
16. D.J. Jones, lhp, Texas
17. **Joel Crump, lhp, Yuma (Ariz.) HS**
18. Kyle Sleeth, lhp, Northglenn HS, Westminster, Colo.
19. **Shayne Ridley, ss, Ball State**
20. Ryan Mask, rhp, Garces Memorial HS, Bakersfield, Calif.
21. Fraser Dizard, lhp, Meadowdale HS, Edmonds, Wash.
22. **Aaron Bouie, rhp, St. Bonaventure**
23. Eric Walsh, rhp, El Toro HS, Mission Viejo, Calif.
24. **Jose Rodriguez, ss, Iowa Western CC**
25. Jeff Petersen, rhp, Kentwood HS, Covington, Wash.
26. **Dan Marchetti, rhp, Ohio Wesleyan**
27. Scott Koffman, rhp, Olympus HS, Salt Lake City
28. Robert Cheatwood, lhp, Allan Hancock (Calif.) JC
29. David Morrow, rhp, Sherman (Texas) HS
30. Donnie Poles, of, Harding HS, Charlotte, N.C.
31. Andy Hargrove, 1b, St. Ignatius HS, Cleveland
32. Brandon Fahey, 3b, Grayson County (Texas) CC
33. **Kurt Birkins, of, Los Angeles Pierce JC**
34. Josh Banks, rhp, Severna Park HS, Arnold, Md.
35. Jeff Salazar, of, Connors State (Okla.) JC
36. Tim Stauffer, rhp, Saratoga Central Catholic HS, Saratoga Springs, N.Y.
37. Ryan Newman, ss, Scottsdale (Ariz.) CC
38. Chaz Macklin, c, East St. Louis (Ill.) HS
39. Matt Harter, c, Penns Valley (Pa.) Area HS
40. Sean Patrick, c, John Logan (Ill.) CC
41. Justin Ruchti, c, San Jacinto (Texas) JC
42. Eric Fagan, lhp, Taft (Calif.) JC

BOSTON RED SOX

June—Regular Phase (22)

1. **Phil Dumatrait, lhp, Bakersfield (Calif.) JC**
2. **Manny Delcarmen, rhp, West Roxbury HS, Hyde Park, Mass.**
3. **Matt Cooper, 1b, Ripley HS, Stillwater, Okla.**
4. **Brandon Mims, lhp, Prattville (Ala.) HS**
5. **Brian Esposito, c, Connecticut**
6. **Kenny Perez, ss, South Miami HS, Miami**
7. **Tony Fontana, rhp, Bowling Green State**
8. **Brian Adams, lhp, Liberty**
9. **Patrick Johnson, of, William Carey (Miss.)**
10. Eric Doble, rhp, Arizona State
11. **Freddy Sanchez, ss, Oklahoma City**
12. **Shane Hall, rhp, Eastern Arizona JC**
13. Mike Quintana, of, Florida International
14. **Ian Perio, lhp, San Francisco**
15. **Dustin Brisson, 3b, Central Florida**
16. **Josh Thigpen, rhp, Rogers HS, Greenville, Ala.**
17. **Chris Elmore, lhp, North Carolina**
18. Haas Pratt, 3b, Rancho Bernardo HS, San Diego
19. **Justin Sherrod, 3b, Rollins (Fla.)**
20. **Brian Bentley, rhp, Louisville**
21. Ryan Carroll, rhp, Mississippi State
22. **Felix Villegas, rhp, Muscatine (Iowa) CC**
23. **Raul Nieves, ss, Mobile (Ala.)**
24. **Freddie Money, of, Wallace State (Ala.) CC**
25. Jon Gutierrez, lhp, Central Arizona JC
26. Marcellus Dawson, of, Muscatine (Iowa) CC
27. James Morrison, rhp, Beulah HS, Valley, Ala.
28. Travis Kaats, of, Desert Mountain HS, Scottsdale, Ariz.
29. **Kason Gabbard, lhp, Royal Palm Beach (Fla.) HS**
30. Jeremy Terni, ss, Montville HS, Uncasville, Conn.
31. Tommy Major, rhp, New London (Conn.) HS
32. Eric Rollins, rhp, Latta (Okla.) HS
33. Bart Braun, lhp, Vallejo (Calif.) HS
34. John Carreon, rhp, Arizona Western JC
35. **Dusty Brown, c, Bradshaw Mountain HS, Prescott Valley, Ariz.**
36. Mike Guerrero, of, South Mountain (Ariz.) CC
37. **Brett Bonvechio, 3b, Prospect HS, Saratoga, Calif.**
38. Daniel Coffee, of, St. Bernard's HS, Old Lyme, Conn.
39. Gabriel Roberti, rhp, West Hills (Calif.) HS
40. Brad Bettcher, rhp, Palo Verde HS, Tucson
41. Ferrari Miller, of, Castlemont HS, Oakland
42. Javi Herrera, c, Gulliver Prep, Miami
43. Chris Duffy, of, South Mountain (Ariz.) CC
44. Kevin Brown, 1b, Miami
45. Nathan Goodrich, lhp, Mercyhurst (Pa.)
46. Donald Benson, 3b, Mount San Jacinto (Calif.) JC

CHICAGO CUBS

June—Regular Phase (3)

1. **Lou Montanez, ss, Coral Park HS, Miami**
2. **Bobby Hill, ss, Newark (Atlantic League)**

3. **Aaron Krawiec, lhp, Villanova**
3. **Nic Jackson, of, Richmond** (Pick from Devil Rays as compensation for Type B free agent Steve Trachsel)
4. **Todd Wellemeyer, rhp, Bellarmine (Ky.)**
5. **Gary Banks, ss, Southern Choctaw HS, Gilbertown, Ala.**
6. **J.J. Johnson, ss, Greenbrier HS, Appling, Ga.**
7. **Ryan Jorgensen, c, Louisiana State**
8. **Dontrelle Willis, lhp, Encinal HS, Alameda, Calif.**
9. **Mark Freed, lhp, Mississippi State**
10. **Blake Blasi, 2b, Wichita State**
11. **Jon Leicester, rhp, Memphis**
12. **Antoine Cameron, of, Riverside (Calif.) CC**
13. **Jeremy Flanagan, rhp, San Lorenzo HS, Richmond, Calif.**
14. **Jason Dubois, of, Virginia Commonwealth**
15. Matt Tribble, of, South HS, Windsor, Ill.
16. Chad Corona, ss/3b, Santa Fe Christian HS, Carlsbad, Calif.
17. David Jablonski, rhp, Lord Beaverbrook HS, Calgary
18. **Buck Coats, ss, Valdosta (Ga.) HS**
19. **Nick Williamson, of, Benedictine HS, Richmond, Va.**
20. **Carmen Pignatiello, lhp, Providence Catholic HS, Frankfurt, Ill.**
21. **Lukas McKnight, c, Triton (Ill.) JC**
22. **Peter Graham, of, St. John's**
23. **John-Paul Glascock, rhp, Fullerton (Calif.) JC**
24. Lance Dawkins, ss, Caledonia HS, Columbus, Miss.
25. **Scott Fries, lhp, Nebraska**
26. Jonathan Anderson, of, Grace Prep Academy, Cedar Hill, Texas
27. **Jason Szuminski, rhp, MIT**
28. **Ryan Burnau, rhp, Huntington North HS, Markie, Ind.**
29. Matt Samuels, rhp, South Vigo HS, Terre Haute, Ind.
30. Pat Flynn, of, Providence Catholic HS, New Lenox, Ill.
31. **Weston O'Brien, rhp, Don Lugo HS, Chino Hills, Calif.**
32. Orlando Diaz, ss/2b, Downers Grove (Ill.) North HS
33. Larry Barnes, 3b, Pine Bluff (Ark.) HS
34. **Eric Albright, rhp/3b, Chapman (Calif.)**
35. Rocky Evans, rhp, Motlow State (Tenn.) CC
36. Brett Watkins, 1b, Petal (Miss.) HS
37. Donnie Bair, lhp/of, Merced (Calif.) JC
38. Jon Nourie, lhp, Munster (Ind.) HS
39. Joseph Catomer, rhp, Prospect HS, Mount Prospect, Ill.
40. Jeremy Mannin, lhp, Wenatchee Valley (Wash.) CC
41. Brad Blackwell, rhp, Broken Arrow (Okla.) HS
42. Federico Baez, 3b, Laredo (Texas) CC
43. Thomas Olejniczak, rhp, Fayetteville (Ark.) HS
44. Stephen Solwick, rhp, Belleville Area (Ill.) CC
45. **Sammy Cooper, ss, New Orleans**
46. Jason McIntyre, rhp, Plainville (Conn.) HS
47. Jamil Knight, rhp, Selma (Ala.) HS
48. Lance Laury, of, Lower Richland HS, Hopkins, S.C.
49. Jose Cruz, ss, Bellaire (Texas) HS
50. Nate Pendley, lhp, West Albany (Ore.) HS

CHICAGO WHITE SOX

June—Regular Phase (12)

1. **Joe Borchard, of, Stanford**
2. **Tim Hummel, ss, Old Dominion**
3. **Mike Morse, ss, Nova HS, Plantation, Fla.**
4. **Alvin Jones, rhp, Seguin (Texas) HS**
5. Tony Richie, c, Bishop Kenny HS, Jacksonville
6. **Bjorn Ivy, of, Shannon (Miss.) HS**
7. **Eddie Young, of, Jones County HS, Macon, Ga.**
8. **Chris Amador, ss, Luis Felipe Crespo HS, Camuy, P.R.**
9. **Jason Aspito, of, Loyola Marymount**
10. **Heath Phillips, lhp/1b, Central HS, Evansville, Ind.**
11. **Tommy Nicholson, 2b, Texas**
12. **Mike Spidale, ss, Nazareth Academy, Broadview, Ill.**
13. **Derek Wigginton, of, Alabama**
14. **James Sweeney, lhp, Holy Cross**
15. **John Lackaff, 2b, Miami (Ohio)**
16. **Brian Graham, rhp, Portland**
17. Ryan Liermann, 3b, Downers Grove (Ill.) South HS
18. **Curtis Young, rhp, Lamar (Colo.) CC**
19. Scott Perhla, lhp, Southridge HS, Miami
20. Etienne Ratte-Delorme, rhp, Edouard Montpetit HS, St. Hubert, Quebec
21. Joe Solis, rhp, Columbus HS, Miami
22. Gerron McGary, lhp, Nashville (Ark.) HS
23. **Rylan Reed, rhp/1b, Crossett (Ark.) HS**
24. Kyle Boyer, 3b, Temecula Valley HS, Temecula, Calif.
25. Travis Nesmith, lhp, Gulliver Prep, Miami
26. Victor Martinez, of, Barbara Goleman HS, Hialeah, Fla.
27. **Brad Murray, lhp, Embry-Riddle (Fla.)**
28. **Kyle Bohannan, rhp, Arkansas**
29. **Anthony Monegan, of, Kishwaukee (Ill.) JC**
30. Brian Keating, rhp, Lewis & Clark (Ill.) JC
31. **Darren Ciraco, of, Briarcliffe (N.Y.) JC**
32. **Brandon Bounds, of, Mansfield (Texas) HS**
33. Jeff Lundgren, c, Chaparral HS, Scottsdale, Ariz.
34. Richard Spivey, rhp, Glen Este HS, Cincinnati
35. Michael Oehlberg, lhp, Kishwaukee (Ill.) CC
36. **Armando Perez, lhp, Southwestern (Calif.) JC**
37. Matt Maley, of, Killian HS, Miami
38. Tom Gorzelanny, lhp, Marist HS, Orland Park, Ill.
39. **Tyrel Davis, 3b/of, Columbia Basin (Wash.) CC**
40. Jarod Tate, lhp, Lumberton (Texas) HS
41. Brian Barr, rhp, Arkansas HS, Texarkana, Ark.
42. Fernando Alvarez, of, Dodge City (Kan.) CC
43. Brian Schwelger, c, Fontana (Calif.) HS
44. Dustin Knight, c, North Little Rock (Ark.) HS
45. Danny Giraldo, of, Coral Park HS, Miami
46. John Grose, c, Green Valley HS, Henderson, Nev.
47. Corry Parrott, of, Long Beach State
48. **Jason Hutton, of, UNC Charlotte**
49. Tony Sterioti, rhp, Kishwaukee (Ill.) JC
50. Freddie Mitchell, of, UCLA

CINCINNATI REDS

June—Regular Phase (23)

1. **David Espinosa, ss, Gulliver Prep, Miami**
1. Dustin Moseley, rhp, Arkansas HS, Texarkana, Ark. (Supplemental pick—34th—for loss of Type A free agent Juan Guzman)
2. **Dane Sardinha, c, Pepperdine** (Pick from Devil Rays as compensation for Guzman)
2. **Ryan Snare, lhp, North Carolina**
3. **Dave Gil, rhp, Miami**
4. Marc Kaiser, rhp, Reno (Nev.) HS
5. Roydell Williams, of, East St. John HS, LaPlace, La.
6. **Ryan Mottl, rhp, Clemson**
7. **Daniel Fletcher, rhp, Bridge City (Texas) HS**
8. Dan Gooris, lhp, Creighton
9. **Bryan Edwards, rhp, Newark (Atlantic League)**
10. **Noochie Varner, 3b, St. Catharine (Ky.) JC**
11. **Chris Williams, 1b, McNeese State**
12. **Brad George, rhp, Canyon HS, New Braunfels, Texas**
13. **Omar Lopez, rhp, Blanca Malaret HS, Sabana Grande, P.R.**
14. Eric Sultemeier, of/ss, New Braunfels (Texas) HS
15. **Brian Ross, lhp, Old Dominion**
16. Jason Arnold, rhp, Central Florida
17. **Adam Sheefel, lhp, Ball State**
18. **Jeff Schachleiter, rhp, Colerain HS, Cincinnati**
19. Danny Eisentrager, rhp/ss, Sacramento CC
20. **Matt Bynum, rhp, Chipola (Fla.) JC**
21. Matt Moyer, rhp, Shelton State (Ala.) CC
22. **Clint Collins, rhp, South Carolina**
23. **Stephen Smitherman, of, Arkansas-Little Rock**
24. **Todd Stone, c, Southeastern Oklahoma State**
25. **Josh Tomsu, rhp, Southwest Texas State**
26. **Brandon Culp, rhp, Jacksonville State**
27. **Ryan Smith, of, Texas-San Antonio**
28. Jason Moates, rhp, Middle Tennessee State
29. **Andy Boutwell, rhp, Valdosta State (Ga.)**
30. Ron Hayward, of, Bishop State (Ala.) JC
31. Danny Touchet, rhp, Palm Beach Lakes (Fla.) HS
32. **Nathan Culwell, c, Wayland Baptist (Texas)**
33. Gerrit Simpson, rhp, Connors State (Okla.) JC
34. Rod Allen, 3b, Desert Vista HS, Phoenix
35. Andrew Murray, ss, Tyler (Texas) HS
36. Bo Dickerson, lhp, Roberson HS, Asheville, N.C.

37. **Sean Patterson, 1b, Cascade HS, Everett, Wash.**
38. Jason John, rhp, Calallen HS, Corpus Christi, Texas
39. Brendon Davis, rhp, Richland (Texas) JC
40. **Mike Wagnon, rhp, Calallen HS, Corpus Christi, Texas**
41. Herman Rogers, rhp, Athens (Texas) HS
42. Eric Mitchell, c, George Washington
43. **Mike Laesch, rhp, Iowa State**
44. **Bryan Anderson, ss, Southwest Texas State**
45. **Eric Spadt, 2b, Penn State**
46. Chris Schroder, rhp, Oklahoma City
47. **Stacy Sparks, c, East Tennessee State**
48. John Garcia, rhp, Uvalde (Texas) HS
49. Brandon Pyles, rhp, Kennedale HS, Arlington, Texas
50. Jude Auzenne, rhp, Humble (Texas) HS

CLEVELAND INDIANS

June—Regular Phase (26)

1. **Corey Smith, ss, Piscataway (N.J.) HS**
1. **Derek Thompson, lhp, Land O'Lakes (Fla.) HS** (Supplemental pick—37th—for loss of Type A free agent Mike Jackson)
2. **Brian Tallet, lhp, Louisiana State** (Pick from Phillies as compensation for Jackson)
2. **Mark Folsom, of, West Orange HS, Winter Garden, Fla.**
3. **Sean Swedlow, c, San Dimas (Calif.) HS**
4. **Adam Cox, of, Darton (Ga.)**
5. **Rashad Eldridge, of, First Presbyterian HS, Macon, Ga.**
6. **Kyle Evans, rhp, Baylor**
7. **Victor Kleine, lhp, Logan (Ill.) JC**
8. **Joe Inglett, of, Nevada**
9. Gary Tolbert, rhp, Madison County HS, Danielsville, Ga.
10. **Tom Canale, rhp, California Lutheran**
11. **Scott Threinen, 3b, Kasson-Mantorville HS, Mantorville, Minn.**
12. Jason Colson, rhp, Winthrop
13. **Jeff Haase, c, Cleveland State**
14. **Ryan Church, of, Nevada**
15. **Nate Janowicz, of, South Carolina**
16. **Luke Field, rhp, Arizona State**
17. **Brandon Matheny, lhp, Emory & Henry (Va.)**
18. Jeremy Rogelstad, rhp, San Jose State
19. **Chad Cislak, rhp, UCLA**
20. **Ryan Larson, rhp, Sacramento CC**
21. **Steve Fugarino, rhp, Iona**
22. **Vance Pietro, 3b, Creighton**
23. Brandon Harmsen, rhp, Jemison (Mich.) HS
24. Chris Houser, 3b, Texas
25. Andy Helmer, rhp, Purdue
26. **Rodney Choy Foo, ss, Kailua (Hawaii) HS**
27. **Johri Litman, rhp, Yavapai (Ariz.) JC**
28. Jeff Opalewski, rhp, Heritage HS, Saginaw, Mich.
29. **Jon Van Every, of, Itawamba (Miss.) JC**
30. Brian Wilson, rhp, Londonderry (N.H.) HS
31. Conor Jackson, 3b, El Camino Real HS, Woodland Hills, Calif.
32. **Scott Thomas, rhp, Lake Michigan (Mich.) JC**
33. Ashley Dunlap, lhp, Palomar (Calif.) JC
34. **Steve Fitch, rhp, Kutztown (Pa.)**
35. Willie McKenzie, rhp, Walters State (Tenn.) CC
36. J.T. Schultz, lhp, East HS, Appleton, Wis.
37. **Damon Katz, 2b, Pepperdine**
38. **Robert Sierer, rhp, Bluffton (Ohio)**
39. Curtis Ledbetter, c, Lawrence (Kan.) HS
40. Jon Hooker, rhp, Kentucky
41. **Eric Crozier, 1b, Norfolk State**
42. Silas Ah Sui, 3b, JC of the Siskiyous (Calif.)
43. **Ron Colvard, rhp, The Citadel**
44. Joe Little, lhp, Arvada (Colo.) HS
45. Mark Carroll, ss, Arcadia (Calif.) HS
46. Chris Appuhn, rhp, Millard North HS, Omaha

COLORADO ROCKIES

June—Regular Phase (7)

1. Matt Harrington, rhp, Palmdale (Calif.) HS
2. **Jason Young, rhp, Stanford**
3. **Chris Buglovsky, rhp, College of New Jersey**
4. **Cory Vance, lhp, Georgia Tech**
5. **Garrett Atkins, 1b, UCLA**
6. **Scott Dohmann, rhp, Louisiana-Lafayette**
7. **Edmund Muth, of, Stanford**
8. **Dan Conway, c, Wake Forest**
9. **Nick Webb, lhp, Louisiana-Lafayette**
10. **Clint Barmes, ss, Indiana State**
11. **Brad Hawpe, 1b, Louisiana State**
12. **Sean Green, rhp, Louisville**
13. **William Vazquez, rhp, Indian Hills (Iowa) CC**
14. Bob Zimmermann, rhp, DeSmet HS, St. Louis
15. **Justin Huisman, rhp, Mississippi**
16. **Jose Vasquez, of, Booker HS, Sarasota, Fla.**
17. **Charles Merricks, lhp, UCLA**
18. **Scott Berney, rhp, Clemson**
19. **Joe Abell, rhp, New Mexico**
20. **Ross Pilkington, ss, Loveland HS, Fort Collins, Colo.**
21. **Zach Parker, lhp, San Jacinto (Texas) JC**
22. **Bryan Peck, 3b, Middle Tennessee State**
23. **Josh Pride, 3b, Middle Tennessee State**
24. **Eric Storey, 3b, Butler**
25. **Kevin Blocker, ss, Wofford**
26. Darin Davis, 2b, Cypress (Calif.) JC
27. Patrick Curran, lhp, Edmonds (Wash.) CC
28. Steve Guthrie, 3b, Palomar (Calif.) JC
29. Marcus Townsend, of, Waller (Texas) HS
30. Michael Vick, of, Virginia Tech
31. Adam Heether, ss, Ripon (Calif.) Christian HS
32. Chris Netwall, c, Penn State
33. Nick McCurdy, rhp, Jefferson Davis (Ala.) CC
34. Grant Mullen, 1b, Gordon (Mass.)
35. **Darren Clarke, rhp, South Florida CC**
36. Michael Perdomo, of, Barbara Goleman HS, Miami
37. Jason Frome, of, Indiana State
38. **Jentry Beckstead, rhp, Salt Lake (Utah) CC**
39. **Michael Davies, lhp, Mount Hood (Ore.) CC**
40. Joshua Bryant, rhp, South Cobb HS, Austell, Ga.
41. Sean Johnson, rhp/ss, Clinton (Iowa) HS
42. Chad Liter, of, Wabash Valley (Ill.) JC
43. Seth McCauley, c, Three Forks (Mont.) HS
44. Matt Farnum, rhp, Dakota Ridge HS, Littleton, Colo.
45. Chad Reeves, of, Pomona HS, Arvada, Colo.
46. Matt Barker, 2b, Niwot HS, Longmont, Colo.
47. Don Rogers, 3b, DeSmet Jesuit HS, St. Louis
48. David Rose, of, El Cerrito HS, Richmond, Calif.
49. Jason Kramer, lhp, Vernon (Texas) JC
50. Daniel Bria, rhp, Lassen (Calif.) JC

DETROIT TIGERS

June—Regular Phase (8)

1. **Matt Wheatland, rhp, Rancho Bernardo HS, San Diego**
2. **Chad Petty, lhp, Chalker HS, West Farmington, Ohio**
3. **Nook Logan, ss, Copiah-Lincoln (Miss.) CC**
4. **Mark Woodyard, rhp, Bethune-Cookman**
5. **Miles Durham, of, Texas Tech**
6. **Matt Parris, rhp, Highland HS, Palmdale, Calif.**
7. **Ronnie Merrill, ss, Tampa**
8. **Andy Warren, rhp, Sam Houston State**
9. Steven Hofius, 1b, Lakewood (Calif.) HS
10. **Tom Rodney, rhp, Kennesaw State (Ga.)**
11. **Jeremy Johnson, rhp, Mooresville (N.C.) HS**
12. **Nate Tekavec, rhp, Miami (Ohio)**
13. **Forrest Johnson, c, UCLA**
14. Kevin Johnson, rhp, California
15. Cole Bruce, 3b, Brazoswood HS, Clute, Texas
16. Ryan Schroyer, rhp, Canyon del Oro HS, Tucson
17. **Matthew Birkett, of, West Torrance (Calif.) HS**
18. **Emmanuel Valentin, rhp, Landron HS, Guayama, P.R.**
19. **Antoine Tellis, of, Harlan HS, Chicago**
20. **Jeremy Swindell, lhp, Houston**
21. **Jeff Leuenberger, rhp, Long Beach State**
22. **Ryan Neill, 1b/of, Oral Roberts**
23. **Tom Muldoon, rhp, Eckerd (Fla.)**

24. **Tapley Holland, of, Dallas**
25. **Hugh Quattlebaum, 3b, Amherst (Mass.)**
26. **Mark Moccia, 2b, Concordia (N.Y.)**
27. **Joe Gerber, 1b, Oregon State**
28. Scott Sturkie, rhp, Coastal Carolina
29. **Mike Steele, rhp, Central Michigan**
30. **Shawn Lambert, 1b, Buchanan HS, Clovis, Calif.**
31. **Demetrius Heath, 2b, Louisburg (N.C.) JC**
32. Brian Eck, rhp, Blinn (Texas) JC
33. **Joshua Vanvessen, lhp, Point Loma Nazarene (Calif.)**
34. **Jared Pitney, rhp, North Carolina Wesleyan**
35. Ryan Cremeans, lhp, Adrian (Mich.) HS
36. **Jerry Dunn, rhp, Spartanburg Methodist (S.C.) JC**
37. **Matt Walker, of, George Washington**
38. Chris Langlois, rhp, River Ridge HS, New Port Richey, Fla.
39. Luis Alicea, rhp, Osceola HS, Kissimmee, Fla.
40. Josh Bishop, rhp, Permian HS, Odessa, Texas
41. **Jordan Gerk, lhp, Oral Roberts**
42. **Shawn Hannah, rhp, Fresno State**
43. Rafael Mojica, rhp, Amalia Marin HS, San Juan, P.R.

FLORIDA MARLINS

June—Regular Phase (1)

1. **Adrian Gonzalez, 1b, Eastside HS, Chula Vista, Calif.**
2. **Jason Stokes, 1b, Coppell (Texas) HS**
3. **Rob Henkel, lhp, UCLA**
4. **Anthony Brewer, of, Simeon HS, Chicago**
5. **Jim Kavourias, of, Tampa**
6. **Will Smith, of, Palo Verde HS, Tucson**
7. **Brandon Sloan, rhp, Wichita State**
8. **Matt Massingale, rhp, Washington**
9. Jesse Kozlowski, rhp, Westlake HS, Thousand Oaks, Calif.
10. Bill Clayton, rhp, Glenwood HS, Chatham, Ill.
11. **Steve Sawyer, rhp, Southeastern Louisiana**
12. **Pat Magness, 1b, Wichita State**
13. **Phil Akens, rhp, Fallston HS, Bel Air, Md.**
14. **Robert Jones, lhp, William & Mary**
15. **Tim Schilling, lhp, Elon**
16. **Daniel Hicks, 1b, Lake Sumter (Fla.) CC**
17. **Josh Willingham, ss, North Alabama**
18. **Chris Key, lhp, San Jose State**
19. **Brian Rogers, c, William & Mary**
20. **Adam Sterrett, rhp, Lee HS, Staunton, Va.**
21. **Matt Easterday, 2b, Georgia Southern**
22. David Gresky, of, St. Ignatius HS, North Royalton, Ohio
23. Daniel Moore, lhp, North Rowan HS, Spencer, N.C.
24. **Ben Birk, lhp, Minnesota**
25. **Mike McNutt, rhp, Mount St. Joseph (Ohio)**
26. Nate Staggs, rhp, University HS, San Diego
27. Josh Muecke, lhp, Scripps Ranch HS, San Diego
28. Patrick Green, ss, Milton HS, Alpharetta, Ga.
29. Casey Hoorelbeke, of/rhp, North Idaho JC
30. **Dustin Griffith, rhp, Seward County (Kan.) CC**
31. **Jon Asahina, rhp, Fresno CC**
32. Derek Mills, rhp, Fresno CC
33. Jim Samolovitch, of, West Mifflin (Pa.) HS
34. Joey Sexton, lhp, Johnson HS, Savannah, Ga.
35. J.T. Sherman, rhp, Dixie (Utah) JC
36. Erik Dean, ss, Wilcox HS, Santa Clara, Calif.
37. Josh Barton, rhp, Millington (Tenn.) HS
38. Anthony Aceves, of, Dundalk (Md.) CC
39. Nathan Kopszywa, rhp, D'Iberville (Miss.) HS
40. Christian Larsen, ss, San Mateo HS, Foster City, Calif.
41. Jared Brite, rhp, Centennial HS, Bakersfield, Calif.
42. Justin Knapp, ss, Arlington Country Day HS, Jacksonville
43. Steve Ramsey, 1b, Eastlake HS, Redmond, Wash.
44. Levi Webber, 1b, Glide (Ore.) HS
45. **Jeff Stevens, of, UC Riverside**

HOUSTON ASTROS

June—Regular Phase (27)

1. **Robert Stiehl, rhp, El Camino (Calif.) JC**
2. **Chad Qualls, rhp, Nevada**
3. **Tony Pluta, rhp, Las Vegas HS**
4. Eric Keefner, 3b, De La Salle HS, Bridgeview, Ill.
5. **Jake Whitesides, of, Hickman HS, Columbia, Mo.**
6. **Tommy Whiteman, ss, Oklahoma**
7. **Joe Lydic, 3b, Pittsburgh**
8. **Cory Doyne, rhp, Land O'Lakes (Fla.) HS**
9. **Eric Bruntlett, ss, Stanford**
10. **Nate Nelson, 3b, Louisiana-Lafayette**
11. Bob McCrory, rhp, Columbus (Miss.) HS
12. **Ryan Hamilton, rhp, San Diego**
13. **Anthony Acevedo, of, Fresno State**
14. **Anthony Angel, 2b, Loyola Marymount**
15. **Todd Self, of, Louisiana-Monroe**
16. **Monte Mansfield, rhp, Riverside (Calif.) CC**
17. **Ralph Hicks, lhp, Centenary (N.J.)**
18. **Eric Lee, of, Houston**
19. Michael Bourn, of/ss, Nimitz HS, Humble, Texas
20. **Jory Coughenour, rhp, Pittsburgh**
21. Steve Mortimer, 1b, Yakima Valley (Wash.) CC
22. Jorge Ruiz, 2b, Notre Dame HS, Caguas, P.R.
23. **Mark Hamilton, lhp, Texas Christian**
24. **Paul Lockhart, of, San Diego State**
25. **Craig Petulla, rhp, Slippery Rock (Pa.)**
26. **Jon Krysa, rhp, Rockhurst (Mo.)**
27. Andy Hutchings, rhp, Alfred State (N.Y.) JC
28. **Damon Yee, rhp, Vanderbilt**
29. Mike Johnson, c, Bellevue (Wash.) HS
30. **Mike Burns, rhp, Cal State Los Angeles**
31. **T.J. Soto, 2b, Louisiana Tech**
32. **Mickey McKee, c/1b, Tulane**
33. Weston Burnette, rhp, Owen HS, Swannanoa, N.C.
34. Jesse Floyd, rhp, San Jacinto (Texas) JC
35. David Frame, rhp, Blinn (Texas) JC
36. Chris Spencer, rhp, San Jacinto (Texas) JC
37. George Drusina, rhp, El Paso (Texas) CC
38. Chris Sawyers, rhp/ss, Evergreen HS, Ariel, Wash.
39. Darryl Chever, of, Delaware Tech JC
40. Deshain Beasley, of, Bellevue (Wash.) CC
41. Aaron Coiteux, 2b, Evergreen HS, Vancouver, Wash.
42. Jason Godkin, lhp, Chabot (Calif.) JC
43. Jason Windsor, rhp, Leigh HS, San Jose

KANSAS CITY ROYALS

June—Regular Phase (4)

1. **Mike Stodolka, lhp, Centennial HS, Corona, Calif.**
2. **Mike Tonis, c, California**
3. **Scott Walter, c, Loyola Marymount**
4. **David DeJesus, of, Rutgers**
5. **Zach McClellan, rhp, Indiana**
6. **Brian Bass, rhp, Lee HS, Montgomery, Ala.**
7. **Jason Kaanoi, rhp, Kamehameha HS, Kaneohe, Hawaii**
8. **Luis Cotto, ss, Institutio Cumbre, Carolina, P.R.**
9. **Luis Escobar, c, Fernando Callejo HS, Manati, P.R.**
10. **Jason Fingers, rhp, Arizona State**
11. **Ryan Bukvich, rhp, Brandon, Miss.**
12. **Darren Fenster, ss, Rutgers**
13. **Jon Metzger, lhp, Virginia**
14. **Justin Gemoll, 3b, Southern California**
15. Adam Peterson, rhp, Wichita State
16. **Joey Baker, rhp, San Jose State**
17. **Billy Keppinger, of, Cumberland (Tenn.)**
18. **Trey Saye, rhp, Newberry, S.C.**
19. **Aaron Melebeck, ss, Houston**
20. **Justin Cowan, c, Nebraska**
21. **Ian Ferguson, rhp, Regis (Colo.)**
22. **Mike Natale, rhp, Lewis-Clark State (Idaho)**
23. Robert Mosby, rhp, East St. Louis (Ill.) HS
24. **Mike Matthews, of, Columbia State (Tenn.) CC**
25. Billy Brian, rhp, Louisiana State
26. **Dusty Wrightsman, rhp, Faulkner State (Ala.) JC**
27. **Marco Cunningham, of, Texas Tech**
28. Louis Wieben, lhp, Pitt County (N.C.) CC
29. Daniel McKinney, lhp, White Station HS, Memphis, Tenn.
30. **Jeb Thomas, rhp, Montreat (N.C.)**

31. **Ruben Gotay, 2b/ss, Indian Hills (Iowa) CC**
32. Rich Carroll, 1b, St. Petersburg (Fla.) JC
33. Jason Cierlik, lhp, Kirkwood (Iowa) CC
34. Luca Petrocelli, rhp, Hackensack (N.J.) HS
35. Brad Knox, rhp, Cypress Falls HS, Houston
36. Darnell Suber, of, Laurens (S.C.) HS
37. Marland Williams, of, Williston (Fla.) HS
38. John Caruso, c, Chaparral HS, Las Vegas
39. Bill Hooten, rhp, Evangel HS, Waskor, Texas
40. Mike Abdalla, rhp, Youngstown State
41. Dustin Timm, rhp, Yutan (Neb.) HS
42. **Odannis Ayala, of, Frank Phillips (Texas) JC**
43. Britt Bearden, ss/2b, Lexington (S.C.) HS
44. Steve Nielsen, rhp, Joliet (Ill.) Catholic HS
45. Reinaldo Colon, rhp, Ramirez HS, San Sebastian, P.R.
46. Seth Davidson, ss, Southern California
47. Brandon Bird, rhp, Northwest HS, Omaha
48. Reeves Smith, rhp, Cleveland (Miss.) HS
49. Clint Mokry, rhp, Taylor HS, Coupland, Texas
50. **Hector Rosado, lhp, Hill (Texas) JC**

LOS ANGELES DODGERS

June—Regular Phase (17)

1. **Ben Diggins, rhp, Arizona**
2. **Joel Hanrahan, rhp, Norwalk (Iowa) Community HS**
3. **Jeff Tibbs, rhp, Davis HS, Farmington, Utah**
4. **Koyie Hill, c/3b, Wichita State**
5. **Heath Totten, rhp, Lamar**
6. **Greg Withelder, lhp, Wilmington (Del.)**
7. **Jared Price, c, Minico HS, Rupert, Idaho**
8. **Jason Hickman, lhp, Ball State**
9. Humberto Sanchez, rhp, South Bronx (N.Y.) HS
10. Andrew Toussaint, c, Centennial HS, Los Angeles
11. **Shane Nance, lhp, Houston**
12. **Travis Ezi, of, Southwestern HS, Baltimore**
13. **Ronte Langs, of, Oklahoma State**
14. **Jonathan Lorenzen, rhp, Katella HS, Anaheim**
15. **Derek Michaelis, 1b, Rice**
16. **Adrian Mendoza, 1b, Cal State Northridge**
17. **Jason Olson, rhp, Armstrong Atlantic State (Ga.)**
18. **Casey Kennedy, rhp, Central Florida**
19. Kevin Poenitzsch, rhp, Galveston (Texas) CC
20. Aaron Rice, c, Miller HS, Fontana, Calif.
21. **Steve Langone, rhp, Boston College**
22. **Greg Bauer, rhp, Wichita State**
23. **Victor Martinez, 3b, Ranum HS, Westminster, Colo.**
24. **Zach Lekse, ss, Oklahoma**
25. **Nathan Lipowicz, of, Central Missouri State**
26. **Nick Alvarez, of, St. Thomas (Fla.)**
27. **Brian Steffek, rhp, Houston Baptist**
28. **Aron Andrews, rhp, Auburn-Montgomery**
29. Ryan Sadowski, rhp, Western HS, Davie, Fla.
30. **Clifton Glidewell, lhp, Northwestern State**
31. Frank Esposito, lhp, Sierra (Calif.) JC
32. **Ryan Johansen, rhp, South Florida CC**
33. Brad Jalbert, of, St. Joseph's HS, Saskatoon, Saskatchewan
34. Patrick Hicklen, rhp, Oakland HS, Murfreesboro, Tenn.
35. Erik Lohse, rhp, Sacramento CC
36. Dustin Schroer, of, Johnston Heights HS, Surrey, B.C
37. **Victor Diaz, 2b, Roberto Clemente HS, Chicago**
38. Brian Barton, of, Westchester HS, Los Angeles
39. Demetrick Drumming, 2b, Spartanburg Methodist (S.C.) JC
40. Kyle Bateman, rhp, Central Arizona JC
41. Michael Lynch, c, Oak Forest (Ill.) HS
42. Timi Moni, of, Columbus (Ga.) HS
43. Danny Desclouds, rhp, Sir Robert Borden HS, Nepean, Ontario
44. Josh Mayo, ss, Sacramento CC
45. Justin Glenn, of, Cowley County (Kan.) CC
46. Marcus Davila, rhp, Key West (Fla.) HS
47. Jason Blejwas, rhp, Vernon Regional (Texas) JC
48. Jayson Berrios, rhp, Discipulos de Cristo HS, Bayamon, P.R.
49. Shaun Kott, rhp, Miller Comprehensive HS, Nipawin, Saskatchewan
50. Brooks Bollinger, 3b, Wisconsin

MILWAUKEE BREWERS

June—Regular Phase (11)

1. **Dave Krynzel, of, Green Valley HS, Henderson, Nev.**
2. (Pick to Braves as compensation for Type A free agent Jose Hernandez)
3. **Dane Artman, lhp, Westminster Academy, Fort Lauderdale**
4. **Eric Henderson, lhp, North Carolina**
5. **Jason Belcher, c, Walnut Ridge (Ark.) HS**
6. **Brian Hicks, of, Natchitoches (La.) Central HS**
7. **Gerry Oakes, rhp, Archbishop Carroll HS, Upper Darby, Pa.**
8. **Bill Scott, of, UCLA**
9. **Ryan Miller, rhp, Evansville**
10. **Brian Nielsen, lhp, Seminole HS, Sanford, Fla.**
11. **Corey Hart, of, Greenwood HS, Bowling Green, Ky.**
12. **Heath McMurray, rhp, Louisiana State**
13. **Matt Yeatman, rhp, Tomball (Texas) HS**
14. **Todd West, ss, Texas**
15. **Dan Hall, rhp, Campbell**
16. Scott Roehl, rhp, Shoreland Lutheran HS, Somers, Wis.
17. **Daryl Clark, 3b, UNC Charlotte**
18. **Jonah McClanahan, of, Monterey (Calif.) HS**
19. **Zach Thompson, of, Callaway HS, Jackson, Miss.**
20. Troy Pickford, rhp, Fresno CC
21. **Jeremy Shorey, rhp, Lisbon (Maine) HS**
22. **Scott Candelaria, ss, New Mexico**
23. Brent Lewis, 3b, Germantown (Tenn.) HS
24. **Jude Voltz, 1b, Mississippi**
25. Luis Alvarado, lhp, Luis Matos HS, Bayamon, P.R.
26. Michael Reiss, rhp, Vaughan HS, Thornhill, Ontario
27. **Travis Hake, ss/2b, Carson-Newman (Tenn.)**
28. **Todd Gelatka, rhp, Golden West (Calif.) JC**
29. Drew Friedberg, lhp, Arizona State
30. Casey Myers, c, Arizona State
31. Mike Kabel, c, Denham Springs (La.) HS
32. **Kelly Werner, lhp, Minnesota**
33. Jon Coutlangus, of, Indian River (Fla.) CC
34. Walter Sevilla, ss/2b, Palm Beach (Fla.) JC
35. Michael Oiler, rhp, Wisconsin-Milwaukee
36. Barry Paulk, of, Florida International
37. **Shaun Gragg, c, Central Michigan**
38. Markum King, 1b, Laney (Calif.) JC
39. **Ryan Trytten, rhp, Ottumwa HS, Agency, Iowa**
40. Alan Abram, of, West Des Moines (Iowa) HS
41. David Walczak, 1b, CC of Rhode Island
42. **Byron Batson, rhp, Campbell**
43. **Kevin Shrout, rhp, Virginia**
44. **Mike Shwam, rhp, Cal State San Luis Obispo**
45. Steve Bray, rhp, Norwalk (Conn.) CC
46. Steve Tracey, rhp, Columbus State (Ohio) CC
47. Jason Henderson, rhp, CC of Rhode Island
48. Matt Mahoney, rhp, North Dakota
49. **Ryan Nohr, of, Diablo Valley (Calif.) JC**
50. Aaron Rowe, lhp, Novi (Mich.) HS

MINNESOTA TWINS

June—Regular Phase (2)

1. **Adam Johnson, rhp, Cal State Fulleton**
1. Aaron Heilman, rhp, Notre Dame (Supplemental pick—31st—for loss of Type A free agent Mike Trombley)
2. Tagg Bozied, 1b, San Francisco
2. **J.D. Durbin, rhp, Coronado HS, Scottsdale, Ariz.** (Pick from Orioles as compensation for Trombley)
3. **Colby Miller, rhp, Weatherford (Okla.) HS**
4. **Jason Miller, lhp, Sarasota (Fla.) HS**
5. **Edgardo Lebron, ss, Ramon Power HS, Las Piedras, P.R.**
6. **Ronnie Corona, rhp, Cal State Fullerton**
7. **James Tomlin, of, St. Bernard HS, Los Angeles**
8. **Henry Bonilla, rhp, Tulane**
9. **Ken Holubec, lhp, Louisiana-Monroe**
10. **Kelley Gulledge, c, Alabama**
11. **Josh Rabe, of, Quincy (Ill.)**
12. **Jason Kubel, of, Highland HS, Palmdale, Calif.**

13. Shane Boyd, rhp, Henry Clay HS, Lexington, Ky.
14. **Cory Agar, c, Dunedin (Fla.) HS**
15. **Jeff Lincoln, rhp, Western Kentucky**
16. **Daniel Decola, c, Slippery Rock (Pa.)**
17. Paul Maholm, lhp, Germantown (Tenn.) HS
18. **Andrew Persby, rhp, Minnesota**
19. **Bruce Dohrman, of, Garrett (Ind.) HS**
20. T.J. Prunty, rhp, St. Paul Academy HS, Inner Grove Heights, Minn.
21. Mark Michael, 3b/rhp, Gloucester Catholic HS, Gloucester City, N.J.
22. Brett Groves, ss, Florida State
23. Jered Goodwin, rhp, Oviedo (Fla.) HS
24. **J.R. Taylor, ss, Skyline HS, Oakland**
25. **Joseph Hamer, c, Newbury Park (Calif.) HS**
26. Jeremy Fortner, rhp, Venice (Fla.) HS
27. Steven Reiss, rhp, Vaughan HS, Thornhill, Ontario
28. Danny Davidson, lhp, Gulf Coast (Fla.) CC
29. **Tom Sullivan, lhp, Slippery Rock (Pa.)**
30. **Shawn Cline, c, Baker County HS, Macclenny, Fla.**
31. **Beau Kemp, rhp, Saddleback (Calif.) CC**
32. **Cody Kimball, rhp, MacArthur HS, Irving, Texas**
33. David Nowak, of, Arcadia HS, Scottsdale, Ariz.
34. **Luke Martin, lhp, Embry-Riddle (Fla.)**
35. **Gregory Stokes, 3b, Slippery Rock (Pa.)**
36. **Pedro Sanchez, lhp, Du Puig HS, Toa Baja, P.R.**
37. **Chad Pylate, rhp, Vancleave (Miss.) HS**
38. John Lynch, lhp, Elk River HS, Rogers, Minn.
39. Marco Gonzales, c, Eastlake HS, Chula Vista, Calif.
40. **Scott Suraci, of, Hawaii Pacific**
41. **Terry Corn, rhp, Florida Southern**
42. Steve Garrabrants, 2b, Moon Valley HS, Phoenix
43. Jeff Marquez, rhp, Brito Private HS, Miami
44. Brian Poetschlag, rhp, Magnolia HS, Anaheim
45. Austin Polk, rhp, Coppell (Texas) HS
46. **Brian Baron, 2b, UCLA**
47. Peter Eberhardt, c, Whittier (Calif.) Christian HS
48. Tanner Munsey, c, Oyster River HS, Durham, N.H.
49. Ben Riley, lhp, Iowa Western CC
50. John Garrard, ss, Brownsburg (Ind.) HS

MONTREAL EXPOS

June—Regular Phase (5)

1. **Justin Wayne, rhp, Stanford**
2. (Pick to Blue Jays as compensation for Type A free agent Graeme Lloyd)
3. **Grady Sizemore, of, Cascade HS, Mill Creek, Wash.**
4. **Cliff Lee, lhp, Arkansas**
5. **Thomas Mitchell, rhp, Bladenboro (N.C.) HS**
6. **Shawn Hill, rhp, Bishop Reding HS, Georgetown, Ontario**
7. Wes Littleton, rhp, Vista HS, Oceanside, Calif.
8. **Phil Seibel, lhp, Texas**
9. **Benji Dequin, lhp, Gavilan (Calif.) JC**
10. **Darryl Jenkins, ss, Plainfield (Ill.) HS**
11. **Seth Johnson, 3b, Kelso (Wash.) HS**
12. **Jason Stevenson, lhp, Sacramento CC**
13. **Craig Kerner, of, Cortland State (N.Y.)**
14. **Ben Washburn, rhp, UC Riverside**
15. **Mike Rose, rhp, Oral Roberts**
16. **Phil Downing, of, Arizona State**
17. **Derrick DePriest, rhp, North Carolina**
18. **Jordan Griswold, lhp, Shiloh HS, Lilburn, Ga.**
19. **Justin Estel, rhp, Mississippi State**
20. Fred Lewis, of, Mississippi Gulf Coast JC
21. **Josh Vaughn, lhp, Cowley County (Kan.) CC**
22. **Jason Bay, of, Gonzaga**
23. Reid Santos, lhp, Castle HS, Kaneohe, Hawaii
24. **Eric Miller, ss, Florida International**
25. **Mike Bolson, rhp, Wisconsin-Whitewater**
26. **Scott Russo, lhp, Penn State**
27. Leonard Landeros, lhp, JC of the Sequoias (Calif.)
28. **Ryan Ellis, 2b, Point Park (Pa.)**
29. Jim Brauer, rhp, Carmel (Ind.) HS
30. **Dan Sauer, rhp, Modesto (Calif.) JC**
31. **Nick Schnabel, 2b, East Carolina**
32. **Chris Bye, rhp, St. Mary's**
33. Justin Pouk, ss, Streator Township (Ill.) HS
34. Nick Currin, rhp/of, Rex Putnam HS, Milwaukie, Ore.
35. Russell Martin, 3b, Edouard Montpetit HS, Montreal
36. Chad Scarbery, rhp, Fresno CC
37. Derek Adams, rhp, Sultana HS, Hesperia, Calif.
38. **Luis Rosas, ss, Dr. Pila HS, Bayamon, P.R.**
39. Johnny King, of, Teutopolis (Ill.) HS
40. Ivan Naccarata, ss, Edouard Montpetit HS, Longueil, Quebec
41. Toby Barnett, c, JC of Southern Idaho
42. Zach Brooks, rhp, Columbia Basin (Wash.) CC
43. Alex Groleau, rhp, Seminole State (Okla.) JC
44. **Anthony Ferrari, lhp, Lewis-Clark State (Idaho)**
45. Jeff Karstens, c, Mount Miguel HS, San Diego
46. Scott Jensen, rhp, Clovis West HS, Fresno
47. Jimmy Gulden, rhp, Lewisburg (Pa.) HS
48. Neville Blount, of, Riverside (Calif.) CC
49. Victor Rosario, of, Lake City (Fla.) CC
50. Bob Brethauer, lhp, Bishop O'Dowd HS, Oakland

NEW YORK METS

June—Regular Phase (25)

1. **Billy Traber, lhp, Loyola Marymount** (Pick from Mariners as compensation for Type A free agent John Olerud)
1. (Pick to Rangers as compensation for Type A free agent Todd Zeile)
1. **Bob Keppel, rhp, DeSmet HS, St. Louis** (Supplemental pick—36th—for loss of Olerud)
2. **Matt Peterson, rhp, Rapides HS, Alexandria, La.**
3. **Josh Reynolds, rhp, Central Missouri State**
4. **Brandon Wilson, c, Christian Life Academy, Baton Rouge**
5. **Quenten Patterson, rhp, Oklahoma State**
6. **Chris Basak, ss, Illinois**
7. **Jeff Duncan, of, Arizona State**
8. **Chad Bowen, rhp, Gallatin (Tenn.) HS**
9. **Nick Mattioni, rhp, Florida Atlantic**
10. Travis Veracka, lhp, Massachusetts
11. **John Wilson, c, Kentucky**
12. Todd Faulkner, 1b, Auburn
13. Collin Perschon, rhp, Bellevue (Wash.) CC
14. Luis Robles, c, Rialto (Calif.) HS
15. **Wayne Ough, rhp, Trinidad State (Colo.) JC**
16. B.J. Benik, rhp, Seton Hall
17. Mike Nunez, rhp, Cal State Fullerton
18. **Mike Cox, lhp, Texas-Pan American**
19. Travis Rios, rhp, Eustis HS, Leesburg, Fla.
20. **Chad Elliott, lhp, Sacramento State**
21. Scott Shoemaker, rhp, Grossmont (Calif.) JC
22. Todd Nicholas, lhp, Fort Dale Academy, Greenville, Ala.
23. **Tony Coyne, ss, Yale**
24. Jonathan Craig, rhp, Young Harris (Ga.) JC
25. Skyler Fulton, of, Capital HS, Olympia, Wash.
26. **Bubba Castaneda, c, Texas-San Antonio**
27. **John Raffo, 1b/of, Florida Atlantic**
28. **Justin Wendt, 3b, St. David Catholic HS, Waterloo, Ontario**
29. Chris Davis, rhp, Reedley (Calif.) JC
30. **Tim Flannigan, 3b, St. Xavier (Ill.)**
31. Thomas Hepworth, lhp, Carteret (N.J.) HS
32. **Tim Lavigne, rhp, Virginia**
33. Freddy Jimenez, of, Monsignor Pace HS, Miami
34. **Tanner Osberg, rhp, River Glen HS, Red Deer, Alberta**
35. **David Byard, rhp, Mount Vernon (Ohio) Nazarene**
36. **Luz Portobanco, rhp, Miami-Dade CC**
37. Nathen Vicari, lhp, Yuba (Calif.) CC
38. **Ryan Danly, lhp, Jefferson HS, Cedar Rapids, Iowa**
39. Brendan Winn, of, Merritt Island (Fla.) HS
40. **Joe Jiannetti, 3b, St. Petersburg (Fla.) HS**
41. Verissimo Pereira, c, Edouard Montpetit HS, Montreal
42. Greg Burke, rhp, Gloucester Catholic HS, Gloucester City, N.J.
43. Cristian Cajigas, ss, Dr. Carlos Gonzalez HS, Aguada, P.R.
44. Justin Harris, ss, Manatee (Fla.) JC
45. **Brett Harper, 3b, Desert Mountain HS, Scottsdale, Ariz.**
46. Jody Roughton, 3b, Maple Woods (Mo.) CC
47. **David Housel, 2b, Mendham HS, Chester, N.J.**
48. Danny Rubino, rhp, Coconut Creek (Fla.) HS

49. Eddie Cannon, rhp, Sebring (Fla.) HS
50. Jamar Hill, 3b/of, Bartlett HS, Anchorage

NEW YORK YANKEES

June—Regular Phase (28)

1. **David Parrish, c, Michigan**
2. **Danny Borrell, lhp, Wake Forest**
3. **Jason Grove, of, Washington State**
4. **Matt Smith, lhp, Oklahoma State**
5. **Andrew Beal, lhp, Vanderbilt**
6. **Jeremy King, rhp, DeSoto HS, Nocatee, Fla.**
7. **Mitch Jones, of, Arizona State**
8. **Sam Bozanich, 2b, Alabama**
9. **Eric Reynolds, lhp, Itawamba (Miss.) JC**
10. **Jason Anderson, rhp, Illinois**
11. **Jason Smith, rhp, Kamiakin HS, Kennewick, Wash.**
12. **Kyle Stanton, rhp, Ohio Wesleyan**
13. **Mike Wombacher, 1b, Louisiana-Monroe**
14. Nic Touchstone, lhp, Sumter (S.C.) HS
15. **Eric Mosley, rhp, Bishop Kelly HS, Tulsa**
16. **Clint Chauncey, c, Florida CC-Jacksonville**
17. **Ryan Gill, rhp, Louisiana-Lafayette**
18. Josh Smith, rhp, Crawford HS, McGregor, Texas
19. Brad Halsey, lhp, Hill (Texas) JC
20. Darric Merrell, rhp, Temecula Valley HS, Temecula, Calif.
21. **Tony Calabrese, ss, Seton Hall**
22. **Eric Olson, 3b, Boston College**
23. **Jeff Segar, 3b, Montevallo (Ala.)**
24. Scott Barber, rhp, Kishwaukee (Ill.) JC
25. **Eric Schmitt, rhp, Wake Forest**
26. **Sean Henn, lhp, McLennan (Texas) JC**
27. Shaun O'Connor, rhp, Navarro (Texas) JC
28. **Trevor Tacker, rhp, McLennan (Texas) JC**
29. David Lindsay, rhp, Itawamba (Miss.) JC
30. **Tommy Rojas, c, Silverado HS, Henderson, Nev.**
31. Robert Edmiston, lhp, Mississippi Delta JC
32. Chris Dickerson, of, Notre Dame HS, Van Nuys, Calif.
33. Daniel Mead, lhp, Worthington (Ohio) HS
34. Luke Carroll, c, Northwest Mississippi CC
35. **John Ramistella, of, Santa Barbara (Calif.) CC**
36. **Jeff Gates, c, Cal State Fullerton**
37. Justin Whitlock, rhp, Ryan HS, Denton, Texas
38. Joe Bunton, 3b, Cerritos (Calif.) JC
39. Aaron Edwards, c, Marshall County HS, Benton, Ky.
40. **Jeff Kennard, rhp, Centerville (Ohio) HS**
41. Peter Stonard, ss, Clayton (Mo.) HS
42. David Ryan, ss, Coppell (Texas) HS
43. Andrew Ogelsby, c, Denham Springs (La.) HS
44. Jacob Willett, of, Latexo HS, Huntsville, Texas
45. **Ryan Clark, lhp, Owens (Ohio) CC**
46. Steve Pickerell, c, Norwood (Okla.) HS
47. **Tim Nettles, 3b, UNC Asheville**
48. Brandon Chreene, of, Sibley HS, Minden, La.
49. Angel Rios, c, Berdecia HS, Barranquitas, P.R.
50. Joe Powers, rhp, Wright State

OAKLAND ATHLETICS

June—Regular Phase (20)

1. (Pick to Angels as compensation for Type B free agent Mike Magnante)
2. **Freddie Bynum, ss, Pitt County (N.C.) CC**
3. **Daylan Holt, of, Texas A&M**
4. **Kevin McGerry, rhp, St. John's**
5. Kenny Baugh, rhp, Rice
6. **Beau Craig, c, Southern California**
7. **Marc Gwyn, rhp, Rice**
8. **Kyle Crowell, rhp, Houston**
9. **Marshall McDougall, 3b, Florida State**
10. **Derell McCall, rhp, Tate HS, Gonzalez, Fla.**
11. **Matt Bowser, of, Central Florida**
12. Steve Ellis, rhp, Bradley
13. Larry Grayson, of, Oviedo (Fla.) HS
14. **Mike Ziegler, rhp, Florida State**
15. **Kevin Barry, rhp, Rider**
16. **Chris Scarcella, rhp, Texas A&M**
17. **Rich Harden, rhp, Central Arizona JC**
18. **Matt O'Brien, lhp, Washington State**
19. **Chris Tritle, of, Center Point-Urbana HS, Center Point, Iowa**
20. John Hudgins, rhp, Mission Viejo (Calif.) HS
21. Kip Bouknight, rhp, South Carolina
22. **John Suomi, c, Cariboo (B.C.)**
23. **Dan Jackson, rhp, Florida Atlantic**
24. **Steve Fischer, rhp, Pacific**
25. **T.J. Gilpatrick, rhp, Mesa State (Colo.)**
26. **Conor Brooks, rhp, Dartmouth**
27. Tripp Kelly, 1b, South Carolina
28. Sammy Hewitt, rhp, Lenoir (N.C.) CC
29. **Ron Flores, lhp, Southern California**
30. **Joe Cirone, of, Rutgers**
31. Dan Valentin, rhp, Liberty
32. Bryan Moore, 1b, Indian River (Fla.) CC
33. Anthoney Bennett, rhp, Blue Mountain (Ore.) CC
34. Robbie Findlay, rhp, Seminole State (Okla.) JC
35. Shannon Telles, of, Waianae (Hawaii) HS
36. Mike Serrata, of, Hueneme HS, Oxnard, Calif.
37. Derek Wilson, rhp, Mount San Jacinto (Calif.) JC
38. Domanic Roses, rhp, Mount Hood (Ore.) CC
39. James Garvey, rhp, La Quinta HS, Westminster, Calif.
40. **Richie Rodarmel, rhp/3b, Shippensburg (Pa.)**
41. Karl Jernigan, of/rhp, Florida State
42. Jeff Carlsen, rhp, Washington
43. Jon Shirley, rhp, California
44. Jordan DeVoir, 3b, Southridge HS, Kennewick, Wash.
45. John Voita, c, Granada Hills HS, Northridge, Calif.
46. Fernando De Aza, rhp, Wabash Valley (Ill.) JC

PHILADELPHIA PHILLIES

June—Regular Phase (15)

1. **Chase Utley, 2b, UCLA**
2. (Pick to Indians as compensation for Type A free agent Mike Jackson)
3. **Keith Bucktrot, rhp, Claremore (Okla.) HS**
4. **Danny Gonzalez, ss, Florida Air Academy HS, Melbourne, Fla.**
5. **Matt Riethmaier, rhp, Arkansas**
6. **Taylor Buchholz, rhp, Springfield (Pa.) HS**
7. **Tony Cancio, 1b, Plant HS, Tampa**
8. **Ryan Carter, lhp, UCLA**
9. **Felix Ortega, c, Medardo Carazo HS, Trujillo Alto, P.R.**
10. **Scott Youngbauer, ss, Georgia State**
11. **Brandon Mayfield, rhp, Auburn**
12. **Brandon Caraway, of, Houston**
13. **Carlos Rivera, 1b, Santo Tomas de Aquina HS, Toa Baja, P.R.**
14. **Mark McRoberts, 3b/of, Granite Hills HS, San Diego**
15. **Todd Meldahl, lhp, Washington State**
16. Jeremy Hudson, rhp, Jefferson State (Ala.) CC
17. **Travis Chapman, 3b, Mississippi State**
18. **Reggie Griggs, 1b, Florida A&M**
19. Dave Hoffman, lhp, Bradley
20. **Anthony Hensley, of, Baylor**
21. **Julio Campos, ss, Missouri Baptist**
22. **Jamie Bennett, lhp, Tennessee**
23. **Chad Sadowski, rhp/1b, Wisconsin-Milwaukee**
24. **Melvin Anderson, ss, Southern**
25. **Doug Stasio, rhp, New York Tech**
26. **Brad Steele, rhp, California**
27. **Trevor Bullock, lhp, Nebraska**
28. **Kevin Donovan, lhp, Mississippi State**
29. Ryan Myers, rhp, CC of Southern Nevada
30. Chad White, lhp, Prattville (Ala.) HS
31. **Preston Underdown, 2b/3b, Baylor**
32. **Kevin Sullivan, c, Carthage (Wis.)**
33. **Dan Adams, rhp, Kent**
34. Mike Mueller, rhp, Triton (Ill.) JC
35. Jason Sugden, of, Central Dauphin HS, Harrisburg, Pa.
36. **Andrew Elskamp, rhp, Wisconsin-La Crosse**
37. Kyle Bakker, lhp, Millard West HS, Omaha

38. Jason Fransz, of, Riverside (Calif.) CC
39. Jason Martinez, lhp, Central HS, Grand Junction, Colo.

PITTSBURGH PIRATES

June—Regular Phase (19)

1. **Sean Burnett, lhp, Wellington (Fla.) Community HS**
2. **David Beigh, rhp, Harrison HS, Battle Ground, Ind.**
3. **Chris Young, rhp, Princeton**
4. Patrick Boyd, of, Clemson
5. **Jason Sharber, rhp, Oakland HS, Mufreesboro, Tenn.**
6. **Josh Shortslef, lhp, Hannibal Central HS, Sterling, N.Y.**
7. **Cole Burzynski, rhp, Navasota (Texas) HS**
8. **Kurt Shafer, rhp, Land O'Lakes (Fla.) HS**
9. **Chris Bass, ss, Madison (Ind.) HS**
10. **Brandon Chaves, ss, Hawaii-Hilo**
11. Kyle Parcus, lhp, Rosebud-Lott HS, Rosebud, Texas
12. **Jason Keyser, rhp, Boyd County HS, Ashland, Ky.**
13. **Troy Veleber, of, Jacksonville**
14. **Vic Buttler, of, El Camino (Calif.) JC**
15. **Sean Smith, 3b/of, Joliet West HS, Joliet, Ill.**
16. **David Baum, lhp, Okaloosa-Walton (Fla.) CC**
17. Daylon Monette, of, Cypress (Calif.) JC
18. **Jon Pagan, 1b, El Camino (Calif.) CC**
19. **Mike Connolly, lhp, Oneonta (N.Y.) HS**
20. **Jose Bautista, 3b, Chipola (Fla.) JC**
21. John Larson, rhp, Eastern Illinois
22. **Shannon Cabell, lhp, West Virginia State**
23. **Josh Higgins, rhp, Master's (Calif.)**
24. Ryan Kanekeberg, rhp, Kamiak HS, Everett, Wash.
25. **Nate McLouth, 2b, Whitehall (Mich.) HS**
26. **Ian Snell, rhp, Caesar Rodney HS, Camden, Del.**
27. **Alex Cruz, ss, Pasco Comprehensive HS, Ridge Manor, Fla.**
28. Brian Hall, ss, Carlsbad (N.M.) HS
29. Denver Kitch, ss, Yukon (Okla.) HS
30. Chris Gale, rhp, Oyster River HS, Durham, N.H.
31. Jeremy Blaylock, rhp, North Hall HS, Gainesville, Ga.
32. Danny Mackey, rhp, McQuaid Jesuit HS, Rochester, N.Y.
33. **Mike Cockrell, ss, Los Angeles Harbor JC**
34. **Mike Fortin, rhp, American International (Mass.)**
35. **Victor Ramos, c, Cayey, P.R.**
36. Scott Baker, rhp, Captain Shreve HS, Shreveport, La.
37. Joe McBride, ss, El Cerrito (Calif.) HS
38. **Kevin Lee, rhp, Wheaton North HS, Wheaton, Ill.**
39. **Tristan Johnson, 1b, Woonsocket (R.I.) HS**
40. Adam Blair, rhp, Okaloosa-Walton (Fla.) CC
41. **Mike Collum, ss, Indian River (Fla.) CC**
42. Jasha Balcom, 2b, Dublin (Ga.) HS
43. Jason Wilson, of/rhp, Eastern Oklahoma State JC
44. Landon Kersey, lhp, Caruthersville (Mo.) HS
45. Garrett Greer, c, Memorial HS, Peabody, Mass.
46. Seth Hill, lhp/1b, Kishwaukee (Ill.) CC
47. Matt Lindenmeyer, c, Butler County (Kan.) CC
48. Andrew Kasparek, c, Weimar (Texas) HS
49. **Marc Love, of, Galveston (Texas) JC**
50. **Josh Shackleford, lhp, South Grand Prairie (Texas) HS**

ST. LOUIS CARDINALS

June—Regular Phase (13)

1. **Shaun Boyd, of, Vista HS, Oceanside, Calif.**
1. **Blake Williams, rhp, Southwest Texas State** (Pick from Rangers as compensation for Type B free agent Darren Oliver)
2. **Chris Narveson, lhp, Roberson HS, Arden, N.C.**
3. **Chase Voshell, ss, Wake Forest**
4. **Yadier Molina, c, Maestro Ladi HS, Vega Alta, P.R.**
5. **Josh Axelson, rhp, Michigan State**
6. **Justin Woodrow, of, Knoch HS, Saxonburg, Pa.**
7. **Shaun Stokes, rhp, William Paterson (N.J.)**
8. **Dan Moylan, c, North Carolina**
9. **John Novinsky, rhp, Iona**
10. **Carmen Cali, lhp, Florida Atlantic**
11. **John Gall, 1b, Stanford**
12. **Rodney Friar, c, Southern Colorado**
13. **Matt Galante, 2b, St. John's**
14. **Dee Haynes, of, Delta State (Miss.)**
15. **Chris Morris, of, The Citadel**
16. **Justin Hileman, ss, Palmyra Area (Pa.) HS**
17. Kaulana Kuhaulua, ss, Los Angeles CC
18. Marc Lamacchia, rhp/ss, East Lake HS, Palm Harbor, Fla.
19. **Chet Medlock, rhp, McNeese State**
20. **Landon Brandes, 3b, Missouri**
21. **Bryan Schultz, rhp, Nevada**
22. **Billy Schmitt, 3b, Green Valley HS, Henderson, Nev.**
23. **Mike Meyer, rhp, Arizona**
24. **John Lockhart, rhp, Centenary (N.J.)**
25. **Ryan Hamill, c, UCLA**
26. **Matthew Dogero, c, Santa Barbara (Calif.) CC**
27. Derek Roper, rhp, Hutchinson (Kan.) CC
28. **Bryan Grassing, rhp, St. Leo (Fla.)**
29. **David Lindsey, rhp, Loyola (La.)**
30. Mailon Kent, of, Auburn
31. **Dan Firlit, ss, Southwest Missouri State**
32. **Dallas Pallaro, 2b, Dixie (Utah) JC**
33. **Richie Burgess, rhp, San Bernardino Valley (Calif.) JC**
34. **Tyler Johnson, lhp, Moorpark (Calif.) JC**
35. **John Santor, 1b, Highland HS, Palmdale, Calif.**
36. Troy Grimmer, rhp, Rex Putnam HS, Milwaukie, Ore.
37. **Matt Vriesenga, rhp, Western Michigan**
38. Bruce Nelson, c, Rockhurst (Mo.)
39. **Preston Harriman, 3b, North Arkansas CC**
40. **Nate Meza, rhp, Palomar (Calif.) JC**
41. **Brian Fatur, of, Moorpark (Calif.) CC**
42. Ty Soto, ss, Centennial HS, Bakersfield, Calif.
43. Adam Pritchard, of, Griffin (Ga.) HS
44. Chad Cummings, rhp, Saddleback (Calif.) CC
45. **Kelly Johnson, rhp, Yavapai (Ariz.) CC**
46. Matt Pender, rhp, Middle Georgia JC
47. Felipe Tetelboin, ss, Grant HS, Van Nuys, Calif.

SAN DIEGO PADRES

June—Regular Phase (9)

1. **Mark Phillips, lhp, Hanover (Pa.) HS**
2. **Xavier Nady, 3b, California**
3. **Omar Falcon, c, Southridge HS, Miami**
4. **Mewelde Moore, of, Belaire HS, Baton Rouge, La.**
5. **Jon Huber, rhp, North Fort Myers (Fla.) HS**
6. **Ryan Earey, rhp, North Carolina**
7. **Lee McCool, ss, North Florida**
8. **David Giorgis, of, Rancho Bernardo HS, San Diego**
9. **J.K. Scott, rhp, Ramona (Calif.) HS**
10. **Kevin Nulton, ss, El Capitan HS, Lakeside, Calif.**
11. **Joel Klatt, 3b, Pomona HS, Arvada, Colo.**
12. Juan Valle, lhp, Efrain Hidalgo HS, Moca, P.R.
13. **Justin Germano, rhp, Claremont (Calif.) HS**
14. **J.P. Woodward, 1b, Houston**
15. **John DiBetta, ss, CC of Southern Nevada**
16. **Chuck Lawton, rhp, Palatka (Fla.) HS**
17. **Jarrett Roenicke, of, Yuba (Calif.) JC**
18. Corey Alexander, of, Forest Brook HS, Houston
19. Drew Jenson, 1b, El Capitan HS, Lakeside, Calif.
20. **Nick Day, of, Brigham Young**
21. Mike Adams, lhp, Cherokee HS, Canton, Ga.
22. **J.J. Furmaniak, 3b/ss, Lewis (Ill.)**
23. **Craig Thompson, 1b/of, Stanford**
24. **Edgardo Laureano, rhp, Vizcarrondo HS, Bayamon, P.R.**
25. **Jack Cassel, rhp, Los Angeles Pierce JC**
26. Chad Cordero, rhp, Don Lugo HS, Chino, Calif.
27. **Kevin Reese, of, San Diego**
28. **John Herbert, rhp, San Francisco**
29. **Denny Chapman, rhp, Towson**
30. **Jesse Bussard, rhp, Sonoma State (Calif.)**
31. Noah Grubenhoff, rhp, Selah (Wash.) HS
32. Jamie Franey, rhp, Ascension (La.)
33. **Jarrod Bitter, c, Houston**
34. **Marc Dulkowski, rhp, Andrew HS, Tinley Park, Ill.**
35. **Claiborne Daniels, of, Stephen F. Austin HS, Richmond, Texas**
36. Mike Brown, of, Chipola (Fla.) JC
37. Alshawn Rodgers, of, Jordan HS, Long Beach

38. Hunter Brown, ss, Galveston (Texas) JC
39. **Justin Williams, rhp, Seward County (Kan.) CC**
40. **Andre Gomez, c, Cal Poly Pomona**
41. Matt Pollard, rhp, Poteau (Okla.) HS
42. Jose Garcia, 2b, Edison HS, Caguas, P.R.
43. David Sanders, lhp, Jenks (Okla.) HS
44. Jason Hammond, of, Grossmont (Calif.) JC
45. Daniel Shanahan, rhp, Wright HS, Mobile, Ala.

SAN FRANCISCO GIANTS

June—Regular Phase (21)

1. **Boof Bonser, rhp, Gibbs HS, Pinellas Park, Fla.**
2. **Lance Niekro, 3b, Florida Southern**
3. **Brion Treadway, rhp, UNC Charlotte**
4. **Ryan Hannaman, lhp, Murphy HS, Mobile, Ala.**
5. **Kyle Gross, rhp, Cuesta (Calif.) JC**
6. **Chad Ashlock, rhp, Southern Nazarene (Okla.)**
7. **Erick Threets, lhp, Modesto (Calif.) JC**
8. **Nick Wilfong, of, Missouri**
9. **Edwin Maldonado, ss, Oklahoma Christian**
10. **Adam Shabala, of, Nebraska**
11. **Jackson Markert, rhp, Oral Roberts**
12. **Elliot Strankman, ss, Lewis-Clark State (Idaho)**
13. Justin Knoedler, c, Lincoln Land (Ill.) CC
14. **Jason Farmer, rhp, Riverside (Calif.) CC**
15. **Matt Faas, rhp, Florida Southern**
16. **Anthony Pannone, rhp, Seward County (Kan.) CC**
17. **Rafael Rigueiro, rhp, Southern Nazarene (Okla.)**
18. **Luke Anderson, rhp, Nevada-Las Vegas**
19. **Dan Padgett, lhp, Northwestern**
20. **Jeff Clark, rhp, Connecticut**
21. Steve Gendron, ss, Berkeley Prep, Tampa
22. **Jason Ellison, of, Lewis-Clark State (Idaho)**
23. **Markus King, rhp, Modesto (Calif.) JC**
24. **Jim Harrelson, rhp, Modesto (Calif.) JC**
25. **Danny Trumble, of, San Francisco**
26. Matt Larson, rhp, Golden West (Calif.) JC
27. Jino Gonzalez, lhp, Cimarron-Memorial HS, Las Vegas
28. Alex Hinshaw, lhp, Claremont (Calif.) HS
29. Denny Hernandez, lhp, Brito Private HS, Miami
30. **Jason Pekar, of, Houston**
31. **Brian Burres, lhp, Mount Hood (Ore.) CC**
32. **Todd Uzzell, rhp, New Mexico State**
33. **Trey Lunsford, c, Texas Tech**
34. Jonathan Albaladejo, rhp, Colegio Janil, Vega Alta, P.R.
35. **Matt Keating, 1b, Northeastern**
36. Matt Gibson, 1b, Sarasota (Fla.) HS
37. Jeremy Schmidt, rhp, Manatee (Fla.) CC
38. **Elgin Graham, lhp, Bethune-Cookman**
39. Greg Stone, ss, Connors State (Okla.) JC
40. **Mark Walker, of, Miami**
41. Michael Cox, c, St. Petersburg (Fla.) JC
42. **Bryan Carter, of, Embry-Riddle (Fla.)**
43. Craig Molldrem, rhp, Boscobel (Wis.) HS
44. Jason Daily, rhp, San Luis Obispo (Calif.) HS
45. Calvin Fugett, 3b, Montebello HS, Aurora, Colo.
46. Austin Allen, ss, Beaverton (Ore.) HS
47. **Bryan Gann, 2b, Oral Roberts**
48. Lou Colletti, ss, Timothy Christian HS, Wood Dale, Ill.
49. Nick Conte, c, Serra HS, San Carlos, Calif.
50. Bennett Elder, c, Lakeside HS, Martinez, Ga.

SEATTLE MARINERS

June—Regular Phase (16)

1. (Pick to Mets as compensation for Type A free agent John Olerud)
2. (Pick to Rangers as compensation for Type A free agent Aaron Sele)
3. (Pick to Orioles as compensation for Type A free agent Arthur Rhodes)
4. **Sam Hays, lhp, Waco (Texas) HS**
5. **Derrick Van Dusen, lhp, Riverside (Calif.) CC**
6. **Jamal Strong, of, Nebraska**
7. **Jaime Bubela, of, Baylor**
8. **Rett Johnson, rhp, Coastal Carolina**
9. Charlie Manning, lhp, Tampa
10. **Ryan Ketchner, lhp, John Leonard HS, Lantana, Fla.**
11. **Blake Bone, 3b, Alabama-Huntsville**
12. **Erick Swanson, lhp, Oakland (Mich.)**
13. **Skip Wiley, rhp, Chaminade-Madonna HS, Pembroke Pines, Fla.**
14. **Manny Crespo, of, Miami**
15. **Jake Daubert, 3b, Rutgers**
16. **Jared Jones, of, Florida State**
17. Steven Moore, of, Dominguez HS, Culver City, Calif.
18. Jon Douillard, c, Harrison HS, Kennesaw, Ga.
19. **Tanner Watson, rhp, Arnprior (Ontario) District HS**
20. **Miguel Martinez, lhp, Maria Auxiliadora HS, Carolina, P.R.**
21. Robbie Van, lhp, Silverado HS, Las Vegas
22. **Larry Brown, of, JC of the Canyons (Calif.)**
23. Jason Hammel, rhp, South Kitsap HS, Port Orchard, Wash.
24. William Corbin, c, Jefferson HS, Lafayette, Ind.
25. Kyle Pawelczyk, lhp, Elkins (W.Va.) HS
26. Jose Cruz, of, Florida Air Academy HS, Melbourne, Fla.
27. **Theo Heflin, lhp, Hutchinson (Kan.) CC**
28. Thomas Williams, of, McCallum HS, Austin
29. Brandon Espinosa, rhp, Mater Dei HS, Santa Ana, Calif.
30. Chip Ambres, rhp, Ranger (Texas) JC
31. Jason Looper, ss, Sentinel (Okla.) HS
32. **Phil Cullen, rhp, Utah**
33. Ben Hudson, c, Truett McConnell (Ga.) JC
34. Chris E. Way, rhp, Groves HS, Sylvan Lake, Mich.
35. Chris S. Way, rhp, Ridgewood HS, Spring Hill, Fla.
36. Ben Williams, ss, Calloway HS, LaGrange, Ga.
37. Billy Sadler, rhp, Pensacola (Fla.) Catholic HS
38. Colby Summer, ss, Mountain View HS, Bend, Ore.
39. John Nelson, ss/rhp, Kansas
40. Justin Ottman, lhp, North Rockland HS, Garnersville, N.Y.
41. Ryan Welborn, of, Yukon (Okla.) HS
42. Ronnie Brown, of, Cartersville (Ga.) HS
43. Craig Moreland, of, Trousdale County HS, Hartsville, Tenn.
44. **Dennis Cervenka, lhp, McLennan (Texas) CC**
45. **Alejandro Cadena, c, Galveston (Texas) JC**
46. Derrell Smith, ss, Palm Beach Lakes (Fla.) HS
47. **Chris Collins, c, South Mountain (Ariz.) CC**
48. Philip Perry, of, Lakewood (Calif.) HS
49. Isaac Johnson, of, Willcox HS, Thatcher, Ariz.
50. Matt Armstrong, c/1b, Eustis (Fla.) HS

TAMPA BAY DEVIL RAYS

June—Regular Phase (6)

1. **Rocco Baldelli, of, Bishop Hendricken HS, Warwick, R.I.**
2. (Pick to Reds as compensation for Type A free agent Juan Guzman)
3. (Pick to Cubs as compensation for Type A free agent Steve Trachsel)
4. (Pick to Braves as compensation for Type A free agent Gerald Williams)
5. **Jace Brewer, ss, Baylor**
6. **Dan Massiatte, c, Louisiana-Lafayette**
7. **Mike Krga, ss, St. Ignatius HS, Chicago**
8. **Mark Malaska, lhp, Akron**
9. **John Dischiavo, rhp, Las Vegas HS**
10. **John Benedetti, rhp, Augustana (Ill.)**
11. **Hans Smith, lhp, Fresno State**
12. **Kelly Eddlemon, 3b, Sam Houston State**
13. **Rich Dorman, rhp, Western Baptist (Ore.)**
14. **Tim Coward, rhp, Guilford (N.C.)**
15. **Nate Dion, of, Yukon (Okla.) HS**
16. **James Shields, rhp, Hart HS, Valencia, Calif.**
17. **Adam Bonner, of, Jefferson State (Ala.) CC**
18. **Matthew Martunas, lhp, Presbyterian (S.C.)**
19. **Brian Lockwood, rhp, Los Angeles Harbor JC**
20. Nick Lyon, of, UCLA
21. Mark Weinmunson, lhp, De La Salle HS, New Orleans
22. **Daniel Marsh, c, UNC Wilmington**
23. **Julius Anderson, rhp, Bishop State (Ala.) JC**

24. **Shawn Riggans, c, Indian River (Fla.) CC**
25. **Elliott Shaw, rhp, San Jose CC**
26. Ryan Mulhern, 1b, Trinidad State (Colo.) JC
27. **Alex Marconi, c, Kent**
28. **Benito Gomez, lhp, Laredo (Texas) JC**
29. **Chad Hill, of, Mississippi**
30. **Edgar Gonzalez, ss, San Diego State**
31. Danny Muegge, rhp, McLennan (Texas) CC
32. Taylor George, rhp, St. Mary's
33. Keeyon Sanders, of, Belaire HS, Baton Rouge
34. Robert Blackburn, rhp, Del City HS, Norman, Okla.
35. Brett Davis, 1b, Lovejoy HS, Hampton, Ga.
36. Colt Morton, c, Kings Academy, West Palm Beach, Fla.
37. Shane Costa, of, Golden West HS, Visalia, Calif.
38. Steven Jackson, rhp, Summerville (S.C.) HS
39. Griffin Zarbough, lhp, Wallace State (Ala.) CC
40. **Jason Habel, of, CC of Southern Nevada**
41. Jon Dobyns, rhp, Desert Vista HS, Phoenix
42. Edwar Gonzalez, of, South Miami HS
43. Vince Davis, lhp, Harlan HS, Chicago
44. Micah Hoffpauir, of, Lon Morris (Texas) JC
45. Luke Scott, of, Oklahoma State
46. Curtis White, lhp, Seward County (Kan.) CC
47. **Juan Renteria, rhp, Driscoll, Texas**
48. Chad Christy, of, Trinidad State (Colo.) JC
49. Andrew Martin, lhp, University HS, San Diego
50. Corey Hicks, rhp, Lakewood (Calif.) HS

TEXAS RANGERS

June—Regular Phase (24)

1. (Pick to Cardinals as compensation for Type A free agent Darren Oliver)
1. **Scott Heard, c, Rancho Bernardo HS, San Diego** (Pick from Mets as compensation for Type A free agent Todd Zeile)
1. Tyrell Godwin, of, North Carolina (Supplemental pick—35th—for loss of Type A free agent Aaron Sele)
1. **Chad Hawkins, rhp, Baylor** (Supplemental pick—39th—for loss of Zeile)
2. **Jason Bourgeois, ss, Forest Brook HS, Houston** (Pick from Mariners as compensation for Sele)
2. **Randy Truselo, rhp, Delcastle Tech, Wilmington, Del.**
3. **Chris Russ, lhp, Towson**
4. **Laynce Nix, of, Midland (Texas) HS**
5. **Greg Runser, rhp, Houston**
6. **Matt Meisenheimer, rhp, Greenville (Texas) HS**
7. Virgil Vasquez, rhp, Santa Barbara (Calif.) HS
8. **Nick Masset, rhp, Pinellas Park HS, Largo, Fla.**
9. **Edwin Encarnacion, 3b, Manuela Toro HS, Caguas, P.R.**
10. **Billy Montgomery, of, San Diego State**
11. Mike Moat, rhp, Niwot HS, Longmont, Colo.
12. **Branden Pack, c, South Carolina**
13. Chris Wailand, rhp, Manatee (Fla.) CC
14. Myron Leslie, 3b, Brandon HS, Valrico, Fla.
15. Scott Nicholson, lhp, Oregon State
16. **Anthony Mongeluzzo, 3b, Florida Atlantic**
17. Andrew Myette, rhp, Guildford Park HS, Surrey, B.C
18. **Keith Stamler, rhp, St. John's**
19. **A.J. Murray, lhp, Uintah HS, Vernal, Utah**
20. **Ty Martin, 2b/ss, Mississippi State**
21. **Matt Gleason, rhp, Bountiful (Utah) HS**
22. Caleb Crosby, rhp, Chipola (Fla.) JC
23. **Tyler Evans, of, Pepperdine**
24. **Timothy Riley, 2b/of, James Madison**
25. **Frank Sansonetti, of, Staten Island (N.Y.)**
26. **Jason Gray, of, Rice**
27. Sean Thompson, lhp, El Camino (Calif.) JC
28. Ryan Heath, rhp, Midvale HS, Mesa, Idaho
29. Justin Quaempts, rhp, Linn-Benton (Ore.) CC
30. **Nick Devenney, rhp, Delgado (La.) CC**
31. Joe Lane, rhp, Osbourn HS, Manassas, Va.
32. **Casey Berry, rhp, Cowley County (Kan.) CC**
33. Michael Vargo, rhp, Fountain Hills (Ariz.) HS
34. Garrett Bauer, lhp, Lafayette HS, St. Louis
35. Worth Scott, of/lhp, Hendersonville (Tenn.) HS
36. Daniel Ellison, rhp, Houston HS, Woodland, Miss.
37. Chris Pillsbury, rhp, Arlington Country Day HS, Jacksonville
38. **Dustin Smith, c, Cowley County (Kan.) CC**
39. Mike Steller, rhp, George Mason
40. Brian Pecor, lhp, Overton HS, Memphis
41. Ben Ashworth, rhp, St. Petersburg (Fla.) JC
42. Juan Serrato, rhp, Norte Vista HS, Riverside, Calif.
43. Erik Thompson, rhp, Pine Forest HS, Pensacola, Fla.
44. Julian Davis, 1b, Brandon HS, Valrico, Fla.
45. James Radford, rhp, Bartow (Fla.) HS
46. Matt Kline, of, Arroyo Grande HS, Pismo Beach, Calif.
47. **Jason Guy, of, Charlotte HS, Fort Myers, Fla.**
48. Ryan Lupul, lhp, North Idaho JC
49. Shane Reedy, rhp, Kearns (Utah) HS
50. **Ruben Feliciano, rhp, Kingsborough (N.Y.) CC**

TORONTO BLUE JAYS

June—Regular Phase (18)

1. **Miguel Negron, of, Manuela Toro HS, Caguas, P.R.**
1. **Dustin McGowan, rhp, Long County HS, Ludowici, Ga.** (Supplemental pick—33rd—for loss of Type A free agent Graeme Lloyd)
2. **Peter Bauer, rhp, South Carolina** (Pick from Expos as compensation for Lloyd)
2. **Dominic Rich, 2b, Auburn**
3. **Morrin Davis, of, Hillsborough HS, Tampa**
4. **Raul Tablado, ss, Southridge HS, Miami**
5. **Mike Smith, rhp, Richmond**
6. **Rich Thompson, of, James Madison**
7. **Aaron Sisk, 3b, New Mexico**
8. **Dave Abbott, rhp, Arizona**
9. **Nom Siriveaw, 3b/of, Eastern Oklahoma State JC**
10. **Jerrod Payne, rhp, North Florida**
11. **Tracy Thorpe, rhp, Melbourne (Fla.) HS**
12. **Vinnie Chulk, rhp, St. Thomas (Fla.)**
13. **Shawn Fagan, 3b, Penn State**
14. **Charles Talanoa, rhp, Los Angeles Harbor JC**
15. **Eric Stephenson, lhp, Triton HS, Benson, N.C.**
16. **Rich Brosseau, ss, Minnesota**
17. **Josh McMillan, lhp, Riverside (Calif.) CC**
18. **Vince Perkins, rhp, Lake City (Fla.) CC**
19. **John Blackburn, c, Lucas SS, London, Ontario**
20. **Andrew McCulloch, rhp, Nevada-Las Vegas**
21. **Jesse Harper, rhp, Galveston (Texas) JC**
22. **Ron Davenport, ss, Leesville Road HS, Raleigh, N.C.**
23. **Scott Cavey, rhp, Notre Dame**
24. **Kurt Keene, 2b, Florida**
25. **William Rivera, ss, Turabo (P.R.)**
26. **Jeremy Johnson, of, Southeast Missouri State**
27. **Brian Sellier, of, Grand Canyon (Ariz.)**
28. **Chris Small, c, Princeton**
29. Chris Neuman, lhp, Western Hills HS, Fort Worth
30. **Lanny Patten, rhp, Allan Hancock (Calif.) JC**
31. **Will Morris, rhp, Cal Poly Pomona**
32. **Kris Kozlowski, lhp, Fordham**
33. **Tommy Callen, 2b, California**
34. **Jeremy Ridley, 2b, Ball State**
35. Blake Gill, 2b, Manatee HS, Bradenton, Fla.
36. **Steve Wood, 1b, Cal State San Luis Obispo**
37. **Jeromie Spillman, lhp, Grand Canyon (Ariz.)**
38. **Dan Huesgen, rhp, Southeast Missouri State**
39. **Neesan Zieour, 2b, Sacramento CC**
40. Tom McLane, lhp, St. Petersburg (Fla.) JC
41. Kirk Gosch, lhp, Spokane (Wash.) CC
42. Matt Sorensen, rhp, Cal State Fullerton
43. Matt Kniginyzky, rhp, Lorne Park SS, Mississauga, Ontario
44. Derek McNeil, 2b, Land O'Lakes (Fla.) HS
45. Dennis Robinson, rhp, Lakeland HS, Putnam Valley, N.Y.
46. Pat Breen, of, Servite HS, Santa Ana, Calif.
47. **Casey Martinez, c, Sacramento State**
48. Cody Clark, c, Fayetteville (Ark.) HS
49. Jacob Bailey, rhp, Indian River (Fla.) CC
50. !Stuart McFarland, lhp, Florida

2001

Twins stay away from Prior's huge price tag, come away with franchise talent in Mauer

The Twins owned the No. 1 overall pick in the 2001 draft, which could have been interpreted as either a blessing or a curse.

The last time Minnesota led off the draft, it chose Tim Belcher in 1983 but couldn't sign him. The Twins traditionally struggled as much as any team to bring in first-round picks, and they also had been unable to get first-rounders Jason Varitek (1993) and Travis Lee (1996) under contract in recent drafts. Just one year earlier, they let supplemental first-rounder Aaron Heilman and second-rounder Tagg Bozied get away.

Come draft day in 2001, the Twins made the best of their situation. Unable to get a firm grasp as to what it would take to sign Southern California righthander Mark Prior, the consensus top prospect, they played it safe and took Cretin-Derham Hall catcher Joe Mauer.

Cretin-Derham is in St. Paul, just eight miles from the Metrodome. But Mauer wasn't picked because he's a hometown favorite. He was the top high school prospect in the nation and the national high school football player of the year, a coveted quarterback recruit of Florida State.

Besides Prior and Mauer, the Twins also considered Georgia Tech third baseman Mark Teixeira and Middle Tennessee State righthander Dewon Brazelton for the top choice.

Twins scouting director Mike Radcliff said the Twins went to great lengths to determine if they could sign Prior, whose camp never divulged a bonus request but reportedly was looking at Drew Henson money. They Yankees gave Henson, a Michigan quarterback projected as a possible No. 1 pick in the 2002 NFL draft, a $17 million contract when he left football behind in the spring of 2001.

As it turned out, the Twins had the last laugh. Prior went to the Cubs and made a fast impact in the big leagues, but injuries sent his career into a steep decline. Mauer, meanwhile, reached Minnesota in 2004 and quickly established himself as the best all-around catcher in the game. He led the American League in batting in 2006, '08 and '09 and had already won a Gold Glove, just as he was entering what should be the peak years of his career.

The selection of Mauer kicked off a development that had to rank as stunning, when the top five prospects in the draft actually went in the first five picks. That scenario hadn't unfolded since the 1995 draft. Since then, many early picks had been determined by a player's willingness to sign a predraft deal.

BILL SETLIFF

Joe Mauer signed quickly and then established himself as a hero in Minnesota

Some scouts considered Prior the best college pitcher of all time. Teixeira had more to offer than any recent slugger. Maryland high school righthander Gavin Floyd, who came from the same high school that produced Teixeira, headlined an exceptional group of prep righthanders. Brazelton wasn't expected to require much of an apprenticeship in the minors.

Like the Twins, the Cubs also were uncertain as to what Prior would cost, but they decided they couldn't pass him up. Baseball America's 2001 College Player of the Year, Prior overmatched hitters all spring with his 94-97 mph fastball and sharp curveball.

Of course, selecting these players was easier than signing them. Though Mauer had the leverage of football—he might have emerged as the Seminoles' successor to fellow Cretin-Derham alum and 2000 Heisman Trophy winner Chris Weinke—he was by far the quickest to agree to terms, accepting a $5.15 million bonus on July 17.

None of the other top five picks signed in time to debut in 2001. The Cubs didn't begin negotiating in earnest with Prior until August 5, and signed him 17 days later. He got a five-year major league contract worth $10.5 million—the largest guaranteed payout ever to a drafted player—and he quickly proved worth it, making his big league debut in 2002 and getting the Cubs to the brink of the World Series in 2003. But injuries essentially ended his career in 2006.

Teixeira signed on the same day that Prior did, getting a four-year major league deal worth a guaranteed $9.5 million from the Rangers, including a $4.5 million signing bonus and easily attainable roster bonuses. Right after the Phillies announced that his team had concluded negotiations with Floyd, who was set to attend the University of South Carolina, he signed at the last minute for a $4.2 million bonus.

Another New Bonus Record

Meanwhile, cash-strapped Tampa Bay was trying to come up with a creative way to land Brazelton. Ultimately, the lure of an immediate big league callup got him into the fold. He accepted a five-year, $4.8 million major league contract, which included a $4.2 million bonus spread over the length of the deal.

Twenty-eight of the first 30 picks turned pro for an average signing bonus of $2,162,723, a new record and a 15 percent increase over the 2000 average of $1,872,586.

Two first-round picks went unsigned in the same draft for the first time since 1997. Lefthander Jeremy Sowers, the 20th overall selection, chose Vanderbilt over the Reds, while righty Alan Horne, chosen 27th, turned down the Indians for the University of Mississippi.

A Cincinnati club official acknowledged the Reds took Sowers because they knew they couldn't sign him. Sowers, who comes from a well-to-do family that wanted him to attend college, set an asking price in the neighborhood of $3 million. The Reds never offered him more than $1.4 million and were content to save first-round bonus money and get a supplemental first-rounder in the 2002 draft.

Matt Harrington, the consensus top prospect in the 2000 draft who went seventh overall to the Rockies, didn't sign as negotiations turned ugly. He ultimately turned down a $3.75 million bonus and signed with the independent Northern League's St. Paul Saints to showcase himself for the 2001 draft. The Padres took him in the second round, but he never signed with them either.

DRAFT 01: FIRST-ROUND PICKS

No.	Club	Player, Pos.	School	Hometown	Ht.	Wt.	B-T	Age
1.	Twins	Joe Mauer, c	Cretin-Derham Hall	St. Paul, Minn.	6-4	215	L-R	18
2.	Cubs	Mark Prior, rhp	Southern California	San Diego	6-5	225	R-R	20
3.	Devil Rays	Dewon Brazelton, rhp	Middle Tennessee State	Tullahoma, Tenn.	6-4	205	R-R	21
4.	Phillies	Gavin Floyd, rhp	Mount St. Joseph HS	Severna Park, Md.	6-6	210	R-R	18
5.	Rangers	Mark Teixeira, 3b	Georgia Tech	Severna Park, Md.	6-2	215	B-R	21
6.	Expos	Josh Karp, rhp	UCLA	Bothell, Wash.	6-5	195	R-R	20
7.	Orioles	Chris Smith, lhp	Cumberland (Tenn.)	Wantagh, N.Y.	5-11	190	B-L	21
8.	Pirates	John VanBenschoten, 1b	Kent State	Milford, Ohio	6-4	215	R-R	21
9.	Royals	Colt Griffin, rhp	Marshall HS	Marshall, Texas	6-4	198	R-R	18
10.	Astros	Chris Burke, ss	Tennessee	Louisville	5-11	190	R-R	21
11.	Tigers	Kenny Baugh, rhp	Rice	Houston	6-4	195	R-R	22
12.	Brewers	Mike Jones, rhp	Thunderbird HS	Phoenix	6-5	210	R-R	18
13.	Angels	Casey Kotchman, 1b	Seminole HS	Seminole, Fla.	6-3	210	L-L	18
14.	Padres	Jake Gautreau, 3b	Tulane	McAllen, Texas	5-11	185	L-R	21
15.	Blue Jays	Gabe Gross, of	Auburn	Dothan, Ala.	6-3	205	L-R	21
16.	White Sox	Kris Honel, rhp	Providence Catholic HS	New Lenox, Ill.	6-5	190	R-R	18
17.	Indians	Dan Denham, rhp	Deer Valley HS	Antioch, Calif.	6-1	195	R-R	18
18.	Mets	Aaron Heilman, rhp	Notre Dame	Logansport, Ind.	6-5	225	R-R	22
19.	Orioles	Mike Fontenot, 2b	Louisiana State	Slidell, La.	5-8	180	L-R	21
20.	Reds	*Jeremy Sowers, lhp	Ballard HS	Louisville	6-1	165	L-L	18
21.	Giants	Brad Hennessey, rhp	Youngstown State	Toledo	6-2	180	R-R	21
22.	Diamondbacks	Jason Bulger, rhp	Valdosta State	Snellville, Ga.	6-4	205	R-R	22
23.	Yankees	John-Ford Griffin, of	Florida State	Sarasota, Fla.	6-2	195	L-L	21
24.	Braves	Macay McBride, lhp	Screven County HS	Sylvania, Ga.	5-11	185	L-L	18
25.	Athletics	Bobby Crosby, ss	Long Beach State	Cypress, Calif.	6-3	195	R-R	21
26.	Athletics	Jeremy Bonderman, rhp	Pasco HS	Pasco, Wash.	6-1	210	R-R	18
27.	Indians	*Alan Horne, rhp	Marianna HS	Marianna, Fla.	6-3	170	R-R	18
28.	Cardinals	Justin Pope, rhp	Central Florida	Lake Worth, Fla.	6-0	180	B-R	21
29.	Braves	Josh Burrus, ss	Wheeler HS	Marietta, Ga.	6-0	180	R-R	17
30.	Giants	Noah Lowry, lhp	Pepperdine	Ojai, Calif.	6-2	190	L-L	20

*Did not sign

2001

CLUB-BY-CLUB SELECTIONS

ANAHEIM ANGELS

June—Regular Phase (13)

1. **Casey Kotchman, 1b, Seminole (Fla.) HS**
1. **Jeff Mathis, c, Marianna (Fla.) HS** (Supplemental pick—33rd—for loss of Type A free agent Mark Petkovsek)
2. **Dallas McPherson, 3b, The Citadel**
3. **Steven Shell, rhp, El Reno (Okla.) HS** (Pick from Rangers for loss of Type A free agent Mark Petkovsek)
3. **Jake Woods, lhp, Bakersfield (Calif.) JC**
4. **Mike Nickoli, rhp, Birmingham-Southern**
5. **Brad Pinkerton, lhp, Elon**
6. **Quan Cosby, of, Mart (Texas) HS**
7. Rich Hill, lhp, Michigan
8. **Justin Turner, 3b, Warner Southern (Fla.)**
9. Devin Ivany, c, Cardinal Gibbons HS, Fort Lauderdale
10. **Matt Brown, 3b, Cour d'Alene (Idaho)**
11. **Jonathan Shull, rhp, Eastside HS, Butler, Ind.**
12. **Ryan Budde, c, Oklahoma State**
13. **Lloyd Arthor, lhp, Arkansas State**
14. **Jason Dennis, lhp, California**
15. **Micah Posey, rhp, North Florida Christian HS, Tallahassee, Fla.**
16. **Alfred Corbeil, c, Florida Southern**
17. Bruce Gallaway, lhp, Allen (Texas) HS
18. **Edward Tolzien, 1b, Illinois State**
19. **Nick Gorneault, of, Massachusetts**
20. Justin Nelson, of, Rancho Buena Vista HS, Vista, Calif.
21. **James Gates, of, Alabama-Huntsville**
22. Brock Keffer, rhp, LaSalle-Peru HS, LaSalle, Ill.
23. **Mitchell Arnold, rhp, New Mexico JC**
24. William Robbins, rhp, Lockhart HS, Sharon, S.C.
25. **Mark O'Sullivan, rhp, Rollins (Fla.)**
26. Jason Durbin, of, Atwater (Calif.) HS
27. **Kelly Sisco, lhp, Connors State (Okla.) JC**
28. **Ryan Nevins, ss, New York Tech**
29. Carlos Corporan, 1b, Francisco Oller HS, Catano, P.R.
30. **Kristopher Sutton, rhp, Tampa**
31. **Ryan Bailey, rhp, Utah**
32. **Steve Andrade, rhp, Cal State Stanislaus**
33. Scott Lewis, lhp, Washington HS, Washington Court House, Ohio
34. **Casey Smith, 2b, Troy State**
35. **Blake Allen, rhp, Alabama-Birmingham**
36. Steve Trosclair, rhp, Southeastern Louisiana
37. James Morris, lhp, Eldorado (Ill.) HS
38. Tom Sgueglia, 2b, Mount St. Michael HS, Bronx, N.Y.
39. **Edward Steward, lhp, LeMoyne**
40. Alan Crigger, rhp, Okaloosa Walton (Fla.) CC
41. **Brent Del Chiaro, c, Kansas**
42. **Ryan Webb, 3b, Chico State (Calif.)**
43. David Bartelt, rhp, Jesuit HS, Odessa, Fla.
44. **Mike Eylward, 3b, South Florida**
45. **Greg Porter, 3b, Texas A&M**
46. Alberto Marrero, c, Luis Pales Matos HS, Bayamon, P.R.
47. Jorge Marrero, of, Jose Collazo Colon HS, Juncos, P.R.
48. Collin Mahoney, c, Mount St. Michael HS, Bronx, N.Y.
49. Steve Nielsen, rhp, Triton (Ill.) JC
50. Kevin Letz, rhp, Hanks HS, El Paso, Texas

ARIZONA DIAMONDBACKS

June—Regular Phase (22)

1. **Jason Bulger, rhp, Valdosta State (Ga.)**
2. **Mike Gosling, lhp, Stanford**
3. **Scott Hairston, 2b, Central Arizona JC**
4. **Justin Wechsler, rhp, Ball State**
5. **Richie Barrett, of, Ursinas (Pa.)**
6. Matt Fox, rhp, Stoneman Douglas HS, Parkland, Fla.
7. **Chad Tracy, 3b, East Carolina**
8. **Brandon Medders, rhp, Mississippi State**
9. **Jared Ball, of, Tomball (Texas) HS**
10. Matt Durkin, rhp, Willow Glen HS, San Jose
11. **Dan Uggla, 2b, Memphis**
12. **Eric Macha, 2b/ss, Texas Christian**
13. **Shane Waroff, rhp, Cal State Fullerton**
14. **Josh Clark, rhp, Southern Illinois-Edwardsville**
15. **Sam Taulli, lhp, Chipola (Fla.) JC**
16. **Mike DiRosa, c, Miami**
17. **Jay Belflower, rhp, Florida**
18. **Michael Gaber, lhp, San Diego State**
19. **Dustin Vugteveen, of, Grand Valley State (Mich.)**
20. Eddie Bonine, rhp, Glendale (Ariz.) CC
21. Brett Smith, rhp, Sonora HS, La Habra, Calif.
22. **Ryan Holsten, rhp, Fairfield**
23. **Scott Hilinski, ss, Warner Southern (Fla.)**
24. **Phil Avlas, c, Kennedy HS, North Hills, Calif.**
25. Chase Bassham, lhp, Western Hills HS, Benbrook, Texas
26. Ian Kinsler, ss/2b, Central Arizona JC
27. **Cliff McMachen, lhp, CC of Southern Nevada**
28. **Clark Mace, of, Miami (Ohio)**
29. **Ryan Coffin, rhp, Chandler Gilbert (Ariz.) CC**
30. **Alex Frazier, of, Lurleen B. Wallace State (Ala.) JC**
31. Jason Bingham, lhp, Pima (Ariz.) CC
32. **Jeramy Janz, of, San Francisco**
33. Daniel Morris, lhp, Mosley HS, Southport, Fla.
34. Trent Pratt, c, Auburn
35. Chad Halbert, lhp, Cypress HS, Buena Park, Calif.
36. **Marland Williams, of, North Florida CC**
37. Brett Dowdy, 3b, Manatee (Fla.) JC
38. Quinn Stewart, of, Dallas Christian HS, Rowlett, Texas
39. Brian Cooper, ss, Bakersfield (Calif.) HS
40. Cary Nelson, of, Channelview (Texas) HS
41. Jesse Torborg, of, Connetquot HS, Ronkonkoma, N.Y.
42. **Michael Thiessen, of, Air Force Academy**
43. Matt Raguse, rhp, St. Louis CC Forest Park
44. Jon Felfoldi, lhp, La Jolla, Calif.
45. **Matt Wilkinson, rhp, Southern Illinois Edwardsville**
46. Jake Hanen, of, North HS, Phoenix
47. Matt Grooms, of, St. James HS, Montgomery, Ala.
48. Seth Smith, of, Hillcrest Christian HS, Jackson, Miss.
49. Troy Pickford, rhp, Fresno CC
50. Scott Foresman, rhp, American Heritage HS, Miramar, Fla.

ATLANTA BRAVES

June—Regular Phase (29)

1. **Macay McBride, lhp, Screven County HS, Sylvania, Ga.** (Pick from Dodgers as compensation for Type A free agent Andy Ashby)
1. **Josh Burrus, ss, Wheeler HS, Marietta, Ga.**
1. **Richard Lewis, 2b, Georgia Tech** (Supplemental pick—40th—for loss of Ashby)
2. J.P. Howell, lhp, Jesuit HS, Sacramento (Pick from Pirates as compensation for Type B free agent Terry Mulholland)
2. **Cole Barthel, 3b, Decatur (Ala.) HS**
3. **Adam Stern, of, Nebraska**
4. **Kyle Davies, rhp, Stockbridge (Ga.) HS**
5. **Matt Esquivel, of, McArthur HS, San Antonio**
6. **Billy McCarthy, of, Rutgers**
7. **Raymond Nieves, rhp, Ileana de Gracia HS, Vega Alta, P.R.**
8. **Alonzo Ruelas, c, Grayson County (Texas) CC**
9. **Donnie Furnald, rhp/3b, Cal Poly Pomona**
10. **Willie Collazo, lhp, Florida International**
11. **Anthony Lerew, rhp, Northern Senior HS, Wellsville, Pa.**
12. **Mailon Kent, of, Auburn**

13. **Bryon Jeffcoat, 2b, South Carolina**
14. **Kevin Barry, rhp, Rider**
15. **Dexter Cooper, rhp, Etowah HS, Woodstock, Ga.**
16. **Roberto Santana, of, Colon HS, Las Piedras, P.R.**
17. Tony Mandel, rhp, Pensacola (Fla.) Catholic HS
18. **Justin Parker, lhp, Tennessee**
19. **Kevin Brown, 1b, Miami**
20. **Greg Miller, of, James Madison**
21. **Adam Sokoll, rhp, Oakland (Mich.)**
22. **Dewayne Jones, c, Jackson State**
23. **Brian Strong, c, Ferrum (Va.)**
24. **Frederick Wray, rhp, UNC Wilmington**
25. **Travis Anderson, c, Burney, Calif.**
26. Alexander Trommelen, rhp, Pace (Fla.) HS
27. Cesar Montes De Oca, rhp, Bethune-Cookman
28. **Dominique Partridge, of, Northgate HS, Newnan, Ga.**
29. Delwyn Young, 2b, Riverside (Calif.) CC
30. Tyler Jones, rhp, Martin HS, Arlington, Texas
31. Justin Willis, of, Parkland (Ill.) JC
32. Jeff Howell, c, Merritt Island (Fla.) HS
33. Ken Livesley, rhp, Stagg HS, Stockton, Calif.
34. Andy Alvarado, rhp, James Logan HS, Union City, Calif.
35. John Grose, c, Chandler-Gilbert (Ariz.) JC
36. Jesse Craig, rhp, Basic HS, Henderson, Nev.
37. **Robert Mason, lhp, Walnut (Calif.) HS**
38. Matt Mercurio, ss, Avon Park (Fla.) HS
39. Matt Campbell, lhp, Hillcrest HS, Simpsonville, S.C.
40. Brandon Williams, c, Cour d'Alene (Idaho)
41. Ryan Morgan, 3b, Boston College HS, Weymouth, Mass.
42. Paco Figueroa, ss, Gulliver Prep, Miami
43. Tim McClendon, rhp, Valencia (Fla.) CC
44. Adam Horner, 3b, University HS, Irvine, Calif.
45. Andrew Bowdish, rhp, St. Michaels Prep, San Jose
46. Dallas Braden, lhp, Amos Alonzo Stagg HS, Stockton, Calif.
47. Curtis White, lhp, Seward County (Kan.) CC
48. Danny Figueroa, of, Gulliver Prep, Miami
49. Adam Hilzendeger, rhp, Moorpark (Calif.) JC
50. **Vontrez Wilson, of, Southern Colorado**

BALTIMORE ORIOLES

June—Regular Phase (7)

1. **Chris Smith, lhp, Cumberland (Tenn.)**
1. **Mike Fontenot, 2b, Louisiana State** (Pick from Yankees as compensation for Type A free agent Mike Mussina)
1. **Bryan Bass, ss, Seminole (Fla.) HS** (Supplemental pick—31st—for loss of Mussina)
2. (Pick to Indians as compensation for Type A free agent David Segui)
3. **David Crouthers, rhp, Southern Illinois-Edwardsville**
4. **Rommie Lewis, lhp, Newport HS, Bellevue, Wash.**
5. **Jim Johnson, rhp, Endicott-Union HS, Endicott, N.Y.**
6. **Eli Whiteside, c, Delta State (Miss.)**
7. **Joe Coppinger, rhp, Seminole State (Okla.) JC**
8. **Chris Britton, rhp, Plantation (Fla.) HS**
9. **Dustin Yount, 1b, Chaparral HS, Phoenix**
10. **Woody Cliffords, of, Pepperdine**
11. John Hardy, ss, Centennial HS, Boise, Idaho
12. **T.W. Mincey, lhp, The Citadel**
13. **Richard Salazar, lhp, Miami-Dade CC**
14. **Cory Keylor, of, Ohio**
15. **Cory Morris, rhp, Dallas Baptist**
16. **Mike Edwards, lhp, Indiana**
17. **James Tiller, rhp, Elysian Field (Texas) HS**
18. Trevor Caughey, lhp, San Luis Obispo (Calif.) HS
19. **Adam Thomas, of, Abilene Christian**
20. Andrew Perkins, lhp, Cal Poly Pomona
21. Donald Hahn, of, Galena HS, Reno, Nev.
22. Adam Larson, rhp, Mississippi State
23. **Josh Potter, rhp, Philipsburg Osceola HS, Philipsburg, Pa.**
24. **Adam Manley, 1b, Missouri Valley**
25. **Richard Hackett, of, Pacific**
26. Brent Burger, rhp, Paso Robles (Calif.) HS
27. Antoan Richardson, of, American Heritage School, Delray Beach, Fla.
28. Adam Dunavant, lhp, Prince George HS, Disputania, Va.
29. Kyle Schmidt, rhp, Dunedin (Fla.) HS
30. Coby Mavroulis, of, Cooper HS, Abilene, Texas
31. Evan Seibly, lhp, Moorpark (Calif.) HS
32. Lorenzo Mack, of, Larue County HS, Hodgenville, Ky.
33. Daniel Hanna, c, Eastern Arizona JC
34. Michael Coles, of, Hammond (Ind.) HS
35. Joshua Wilkening, rhp, Green River (Wash.) CC
36. **Jeff Montani, rhp, SUNY Binghamton**
37. Dwayne Carter, rhp, East Bakersfield (Calif.) HS
38. Sean Letsinger, rhp, Glen Oaks (Mich.) CC
39. Jesse Saunders, lhp, Eastside Catholic HS, Seattle
40. Robert Done, 3b, Washington
41. Eric Blevins, rhp, Sullivan East HS, Bluff City, Tenn.
42. Josh Palm, rhp, Conneaut Lake (Pa.) HS
43. Justin Maxwell, of, Sherwood HS, Olney, Md.
44. **Doug Brubaker, rhp, Hill (Texas) JC**
45. Tabor Woolard, rhp, Antonian HS, San Antonio
46. Jonathon Fowler, lhp, Kirk Academy, Grenada, Miss.
47. Anthony Cupps, rhp, University Christian HS, Madison, Miss.
48. Bryan Johnson, lhp, Selah (Wash.) HS
49. Oscar Serrato, rhp, Riverside (Calif.) CC

BOSTON RED SOX

June—Regular Phase (17)

1. (Pick to Indians as compensation for Type A free agent Manny Ramirez)
2. **Kelly Shoppach, c, Baylor** (Pick from Phillies as compensation for Type B free agent Rheal Cormier)
2. Matt Chico, lhp, Fallbrook (Calif.) HS
3. **Jonathan Devries, c, Irvine (Calif.) HS**
4. **Stefan Bailie, 1b, Washington State**
5. **Eric West, ss, Southside HS, Gadsden, Ala.**
6. Justin James, rhp, Yukon (Okla.) HS
7. **Rolando Viera, lhp, Cuba**
8. **Kevin Youkilis, 3b, Cincinnati**
9. **Billy Simon, rhp, Wellington (Fla.) Community HS**
10. Ben Crockett, rhp, Harvard
11. **Shane Rhodes, lhp, West Virginia**
12. **Ryan Brunner, of, Northern Iowa**
13. **Alec Porzel, ss, Notre Dame**
14. **Chris Farley, rhp, Mahar Regional HS, Orange, Mass.**
15. Ryan Carroll, rhp, Mississippi State
16. Tony Gonzalez, of, Framingham (Mass.) HS
17. **Michael Grant, rhp, Danville Area (Ill.) JC**
18. **Brian Lane, rhp, Richmond**
19. Jeremy Brown, c, Alabama
20. **Devoris Williams, ss, Greensboro (Ala.) HS**
21. **Charlie Weatherby, rhp, UNC Wilmington**
22. **Gerald Rogers, rhp, Boston College**
23. **Pedro Suarez, rhp, Mount Miguel HS, Spring Valley, Calif.**
24. Jason Ramos, ss, Braddock HS, Miami
25. **Kris Coffey, of, Dallas Baptist**
26. **Ken Trapp, rhp, Dallas Baptist**
27. **Bryan Kent, 2b, Southwest Texas State**
28. Steven Ponder, lhp, Texas A&M
29. **Mario Campos, 3b, Trevecca Nazarene (Tenn.)**
30. **Richard Sander, rhp, Cal State San Bernardino**
31. **Brett Rudrude, rhp, Cal State San Bernardino**
32. **Kyle Jackson, rhp, Alvirne HS, Litchfield, N.H.**
33. Christopher Honsa, rhp, Corona del Sol HS, Chandler, Ariz.
34. Eron Brown, 3b, Auburn (Ala.) HS
35. Koley Kolberg, rhp, Coppell (Texas) HS
36. Adam Sabari, 1b, Cardinal Mooney HS, Sarasota, Fla.
37. Emmanuel Lopez, 1b, Globe (Ariz.) HS
38. Jacob Almestica, rhp, Medardo Carazo HS, Trujillo Alta HS, P.R.
39. Ricky Bauer, rhp, Mid-Pacific Institute, Honolulu, Hawaii
40. Josh Bolen, of, Illinois Central JC
41. Bart Braun, lhp, Napa Valley (Calif.) JC
42. Tommy Major, rhp, Briarcliffe (N.Y.) JC
43. Tanner Wootan, ss, Mountain View HS, Mesa, Ariz.
44. Terrence Taylor, of, JC of Marin (Calif.)
45. **Brent Tarbett, of, CC of Southern Nevada**
46. Chris Keeran, of, Eastlake HS, Chula Vista, Calif.

47. **Donald Benson, 3b, Mount San Jacinto (Calif.) JC**

CHICAGO CUBS

June—Regular Phase (2)

1. **Mark Prior, rhp, Southern California**
2. **Andy Sisco, lhp, Eastlake HS, Sammamish, Wash.**
3. **Ryan Theriot, ss, Louisiana State**
4. **Ricky Nolasco, rhp, Rialto (Calif.) HS**
5. **Brendan Harris, ss, William & Mary**
6. **Adam Wynegar, lhp, James Madison**
7. **Sergio Mitre, rhp, San Diego CC**
8. **Warren Hanna, c, South Alabama**
9. Alan Bomer, rhp, Iowa State
10. **Corey Slavik, 3b, Wake Forest**
11. **Geovany Soto, c, American Military Academy, Rio Piedras, P.R.**
12. **Jason Blanton, rhp, North Carolina State**
13. **Tony Garcia, ss, Pepperdine**
14. Khalil Greene, ss, Clemson
15. **Kevin Hairr, of, UNC Wilmington**
16. **Dwaine Bacon, of, Florida A&M**
17. **Nick Martin, lhp, Rice**
18. **Steve Ellis, rhp, Bradley**
19. **Mark Carter, lhp, Alabama**
20. **Joshua Arteaga, ss, Virginia Commonwealth**
21. **Brad Bouras, 1b, Columbus State (Ga.)**
22. **Jeff Carlsen, rhp, Washington**
23. **B.J. Benik, rhp, Seton Hall**
24. **Luis Reyes, rhp, East Central (Mo.) JC**
25. **Eric Servais, 3b, Wisconsin-Oshkosh**
26. Jesse Krause, rhp, Columbia City (Ind.) HS
27. Chad Farr, lhp, Christian Brothers HS, Memphis
28. Tony Sipp, lhp, Moss Point (Miss.) HS
29. **Rick Devinney, c, Western HS, Fullerton, Calif.**
30. Kyle Dubois, rhp, Cox HS, Virginia Beach
31. **Dan Foli, rhp, Walters State (Tenn.) CC**
32. Jeff Larish, ss, McClintock HS, Tempe, Ariz.
33. Brian Stavisky, of, Notre Dame
34. Charlie Isaacson, rhp, Arkansas
35. Justin McCarty, of, Wichita State
36. Aaron O'Dell, rhp, Bend (Ore.) HS
37. Edwar Gonzalez, of, Seminole State (Okla.) JC
38. Jeff Teasley, rhp, Grossmont HS, La Mesa, Calif.
39. Jesse Chavez, rhp, A.B. Miller HS, Fontana, Calif.
40. Matt Pagnozzi, c, Highland HS, Gilbert, Ariz.
41. Wes Whisler, lhp, Noblesville (Ind.) HS
42. Mark Jecmen, rhp, Diamond Bar (Calif.) HS
43. Kevin Culpepper, lhp, Stephens County School, Toccoa, Ga.
44. Jared Eichelberger, rhp, Marian Catholic HS, San Diego
45. Jamil Knight, rhp, Shelton State (Ala.) CC
46. Chris Niesel, rhp, St. Thomas Aquinas HS, Fort Lauderdale
47. Taylor Gartz, lhp, Clear Lake HS, Seabrook, Texas
48. Kevin Randel, ss, Riverside (Calif.) CC
49. Mike Pete, lhp, Armwood HS, Brandon, Fla.
50. Patrick McIntyre, c, Vallivue HS, Caldwell, Idaho

CHICAGO WHITE SOX

June—Regular Phase (27)

1. **Kris Honel, rhp, Providence Catholic HS, New Lenox, Ill.** (Pick from Marlins as compensation for Type A free agent Charles Johnson)
1. (Pick to Indians as compensation for Type A free agent Sandy Alomar)
1. **Wyatt Allen, rhp, Tennessee** (Supplemental pick—39th—for loss of Johnson)
2. **Ryan Wing, lhp, Riverside (Calif.) CC**
3. Jon Zeringue, c, E.D. White HS, Thibodeaux, La.
4. Jay Mattox, of, Conway (Ark.) HS
5. **Andy Gonzalez, ss, Florida Air Academy HS, Melbourne, Fla.**
6. **Stevie Daniel, 2b/ss, Tennessee**
7. Brandon Camardese, lhp, Chaminade-Madonna HS, Cooper City, Fla.
8. **Andrew Fryson, rhp, Wallace State (Ala.) CC**
9. **Jim Bullard, lhp, UC Santa Barbara**
10. **Tim Bittner, lhp, Marist**
11. **Tim Huson, 3b, Central Arizona JC**
12. **Chris Stewart, c, Riverside (Calif.) CC**
13. **Brian Sager, rhp, Georgia Tech**
14. Matt Mitchell, rhp, JC of Lake County (Ill.)
15. **Anthony Webster, of, Riverside HS, Parsons, Tenn.**
16. **Chris Young, of, Bellaire (Texas) HS**
17. **Jason McCurdy, lhp, South Dade HS, Miami**
18. **Justin Dowdy, lhp, Rancho Bernardo HS, San Diego**
19. Wes Swackhamer, of, Delbarton HS, Morristown, N.J.
20. Brian Miller, rhp, Charlotte (Mich.) HS
21. Lou Palmisano, c, St. Thomas Aquinas HS, Fort Lauderdale
22. **Andrew Salvo, 2b, Delaware**
23. **Joshua Fields, rhp, Mesa (Ariz.) CC**
24. **Charlie Lisk, c, Fort Mill (S.C.) HS**
25. **Charlie Haeger, rhp, Catholic Central HS, Plymouth, Mich.**
26. Dustin Roddy, c, Searcy (Ark.) HS
27. **Tom Collaro, of, Piper HS, Sunrise, Fla.**
28. Jonathan Forest, rhp, Edouard Montpetit HS, St. Hubert, Quebec
29. Matthew Sibigtroth, ss, Hampshire (Ill.) HS
30. **Heath Dobyns, rhp, Northern Colorado**
31. **Nikolas Lubisch, lhp, Willamette (Ore.)**
32. Heath Castle, lhp, St. Catharine (Ky.) JC
33. Sean Kramer, lhp, Cornwall HS, New Windsor, N.Y.
34. **Tim Tisch, lhp, Mesa (Ariz.) JC**
35. Michael Moljewski, lhp, De La Salle Collegiate HS, Shelby, Mich.
36. Brent Speck, lhp, Broward (Fla.) JC
37. Juan Razzo, rhp, San Diego CC
38. Kenyatta Davis, of, Harlem Community Academy, Chicago
39. **J.D. Johnson, rhp, Del Norte HS, Moriarty, N.M.**
40. Christopher Roque, 3b, Monsignor Pace HS, Opa Locka, Fla.
41. Chris Martinez, of, Florida Christian HS, Miami
42. Nick McMillan, rhp, El Dorado HS, Placentia, Calif.
43. **Freddie Lebron, 2b, New Mexico JC**
44. Kenneth Pridgeon, rhp, Cy Fair HS, Cypress, Texas
45. **Gerron McGary, lhp/of, Texarkana (Texas) JC**
46. Roy Irle, rhp, Anderson (Ind.) Madison Heights HS
47. Adrian Casanova, c, Coral Park HS, Miami
48. Josh Crede, 3b, Fatima HS, Westphalia, Mo.
49. Richard Morman, of, Fayetteville (Ark.) HS
50. Zach Jackson, lhp, Seneca Valley HS, Cranberry Township, Pa.

CINCINNATI REDS

June—Regular Phase (20)

1. Jeremy Sowers, lhp, Ballard HS, Louisville
2. **Justin Gillman, rhp, Mosley HS, Panama City, Fla.**
3. **Alan Moye, of, Pine Tree HS, Longview, Texas**
4. **Steve Kelly, rhp, Georgia Tech**
5. **Daylan Childress, rhp, McLennan (Texas) CC**
6. **Scott Light, rhp, Elon**
7. **Bobby Basham, rhp, Richmond**
8. Jose Rodriguez, c, Warren HS, Downey, Calif.
9. **Junior Ruiz, of/2b, San Jose State**
10. **Bryan Prince, c, Georgia Tech**
11. Keith Ramsey, lhp, Florida
12. Craig Bartosh, of, Duncanville (Texas) HS
13. Tanner Brock, rhp, Mississippi State
14. **Dave Molidor, 3b, UC Santa Barbara**
15. **Matt McWilliams, lhp, Cumberland (Tenn.)**
16. **Jason Vavao, 1b, Los Angeles Harbor CC**
17. **Richard Bartel, rhp, Grapevine (Texas) HS**
18. **Jeff Bannon, ss, UC Santa Barbara**
19. **Justin Davis, of, Cal Poly Pomona**
20. **Jesse Gutierrez, c, St. Mary's (Texas)**
21. John Palmer, rhp, Georgia Perimeter JC
22. **Ryan Fry, c, Young Harris (Ga.) JC**
23. **Joe Powers, rhp, Wright State**
24. **Jay Adams, rhp, Pepperdine**
25. **Curtus Moak, lhp, Cincinnati**
26. Will Crouch, 1b, Westlake HS, Austin

27. **Weston Burnette, rhp, Young Harris (Ga.) JC**
28. Brian Martin, lhp, Texas City (Texas) HS
29. Seth Epstein, lhp, JC of the Canyons (Calif.)
30. Darin Blackburn, rhp, Fort Myers (Fla.) HS
31. Aaron Trolia, rhp, Edmonds (Wash.) CC
32. **David Shafer, rhp, Central Arizona JC**
33. David Asher, lhp, University HS, Orlando
34. **Domonique Lewis, 2b, Southwest Texas State**
35. Nick Markakis, lhp, Woodstock (Ga.) HS
36. Isaac Dillon, of, Nettleton HS, Jonesboro, Ark.
37. Erik Meyer, rhp, La Mirada (Calif.) HS
38. Justin Myers, rhp, Symmes Valley HS, Scottown, Ohio
39. **Miles Carpenter, rhp, Pickens (Ga.) HS**
40. Ben Rulon, lhp, Columbus (Ga.) HS
41. Douglas Curley, c, Granite Bay HS, Roseville, Calif.
42. Mike Moorhead, rhp, Georgia
43. Kyle Broussard, ss, Carencro (La.) HS
44. Francis Poni, c, Carson (Calif.) HS
45. Mark Schramek, rhp/3b, Texas-San Antonio
46. Bart Hunton, c, Dublin (Ohio) Coffman HS
47. Raymond Gonzalez, of, Jose Campeche HS, San Lorenzo, P.R.
48. Jeff Crinklaw, c, Ohlone (Calif.) JC
49. Trey Hearne, of, Lufkin (Texas) HS
50. Clay Alarcon, ss, Sequoia HS, Redwood City, Calif.

CLEVELAND INDIANS

June—Regular Phase (21)

1. **Dan Denham, rhp, Deer Valley HS, Antioch, Calif.** (Pick from Red Sox as compensation for Type A free agent Manny Ramirez)
1. (Pick to Giants as compensation for Type A free agent Ellis Burks)
1. Alan Horne, rhp, Marianna (Fla.) HS (Pick from White Sox as compensation for Type A free agent Sandy Alomar)
1. **J.D. Martin, rhp, Burroughs HS, Ridgecrest, Calif.** (Supplemental pick—35th—for loss of Ramirez)
1. **Mike Conroy, of, Boston College HS, Dorchester, Mass.** (Supplemental pick—43rd—for loss of Type A free agent David Segui)
2. **Jake Dittler, rhp, Green Valley HS, Henderson, Nev.** (Pick from Orioles as compensation for Segui)
2. (Pick to Tigers as compensation for Type A free agent Juan Gonzalez)
3. **Nicholas Moran, rhp, Fresno State**
4. **Travis Foley, rhp, Butler HS, Louisville**
5. **Marcos Mendoza, lhp, San Diego State**
6. **Jim Ed Warden, rhp, Tennessee Tech**
7. **Josh Noviskey, of, Newton (N.J.) HS**
8. **Mike Quintana, of, Florida International**
9. **Luke Scott, of, Oklahoma State**
10. Brian Harrison, rhp, Dalton (Ga.) HS
11. **Brad Guglielmelli, c, Allan Hancock (Calif.) JC**
12. **Scott Sturkie, rhp, Coastal Carolina**
13. **Matt Knox, of, Millersville (Pa.)**
14. **Doug Lantz, rhp, Kansas**
15. Martin Vergara, rhp, DePaul HS, Wayne, N.J.
16. Sean Smith, rhp, College Park HS, Pleasant Hill, Calif.
17. Dave Jensen, 1b, Brigham Young
18. T.J. Burton, rhp, Notre Dame HS, Ottawa, Ontario
19. **Luis Alvarado, lhp, Puerto Rico**
20. **Michael Rogers, rhp, Oral Roberts**
21. **Richard Spaulding, lhp, Lexington (Ky.) CC**
22. **Jimmy Schultz, rhp, Klein Forest HS, Houston**
23. **Kenton Myers, c, Mesa State (Colo.)**
24. **Matt Blethen, lhp, West Virginia**
25. **Rickie Morton, of, Pacific**
26. **Bryce Uegawachi, ss, Hawaii Pacific**
27. Josh Lex, c, Sacramento CC
28. Brandon Harmsen, rhp, Grand Rapids (Mich.) CC
29. Chris Hunter, rhp, Lindon, Utah
30. **Keith Lillash, 2b, Cleveland State**
31. **Brian Kirby, c, Arkansas**
32. **Andrew Baxter, 1b, East Tennessee State**
33. **Chad Peshke, 2b, UC Santa Barbara**
34. Aaron Mardsen, lhp, Hutchinson (Kan.) CC
35. **Chris Cooper, lhp, New Mexico**
36. Jose Cruz, of, Metropolitan (P.R.)
37. **Todd Culp, rhp, Pacific**
38. Neto Quiroz, lhp, Saddleback (Calif.) CC
39. **Brian Farman, rhp, Pacific Lutheran (Wash.)**
40. Aaron Russell, rhp, Cerro Coso (Calif.) CC
41. Ross Lewis, rhp/of, University Christian HS, Jacksonville, Fla.
42. Kyle Allen, lhp, Trabuco Hills HS, Rancho Santa Margarita, Calif.
43. Vince Davis, lhp, New Mexico JC
44. Garrett Mock, rhp, North Shore HS, Houston
45. Brett Ashmun, rhp, Modesto (Calif.) JC
46. **Jeffery Pennington, rhp, Southeast Missouri State**
47. Billy Brian, rhp, Louisiana State
48. Doug Brooks, rhp, Henry Ford (Mich.) CC
49. Jason Columbus, 1b, New Mexico JC
50. James Burok, rhp, Valley View HS, Archbald, Pa.

COLORADO ROCKIES

June—Regular Phase (18)

1. (Pick to Mets as compensation for Type A free agent Mike Hampton)
1. **Jayson Nix, ss, Midland (Texas) HS** (Supplemental pick—44th—for failure to sign 2000 first-rounder Matt Harrington).
2. (Pick to Yankees as compensation for Type A free agent Denny Neagle)
2. Trey Taylor, lhp, Mansfield (Texas) HS (Supplemental pick—75th—for loss of Type C free agent Julian Tavarez)
3. **Jason Frome, of, Indiana State**
4. **Jay Mitchell, rhp, LaGrange (Ga.) HS**
5. **Gerrit Simpson, rhp, Texas**
6. **Jamie Tricoglou, rhp, Kennesaw State**
7. **Cory Sullivan, of, Wake Forest**
8. **Scott Nicholson, lhp, Oregon State**
9. **James Sweeney, c, Bellaire (Texas) HS**
10. **Tony Miller, of, Toledo**
11. **Jason Fardella, rhp, St. Francis (N.Y.)**
12. **Bryan Ingram, c, Oregon State**
13. **Kip Bouknight, rhp, South Carolina**
14. **Levi Frary, rhp, Texas-Pan American**
15. **David Burkholder, 1b, Grand View (Iowa)**
16. **Beau Dannemiller, rhp, Kent State**
17. **Judd Songster, rhp, Southern Colorado**
18. **Shawn Gallagher, lhp, Rutgers**
19. **Ashley Freeman, 3b, Vanderbilt**
20. Matt Palmer, rhp, Southwest Missouri State
21. Roberto Martinez, rhp, Riverview HS, Brandon, Fla.
22. **Trey George, of, Bellaire HS, Houston**
23. Eric Patterson, ss, Harrison HS, Kennesaw, Ga.
24. **Casey Lambert, ss, Alabama**
25. Mike Huggins, 1b, Baylor
26. Jake Glanzmann, lhp, West Springfield (Va.) HS
27. **Jeff Cruz, lhp, Long Beach State**
28. Adam Heether, 3b, Modesto (Calif.) JC
29. **Peter Greenbush, rhp, Massachusetts College**
30. **Jonathan Varcarcel, lhp, Margarita Janer HS, Guaynabo, P.R.**
31. Jino Gonzalez, lhp, CC of Southern Nevada
32. Joshua Merino, rhp, Kirkwood (Iowa) CC
33. Sean Hofferd, of, Bend (Ore.) HS
34. Chris Gimenez, c, Gilroy (Calif.) HS
35. Jeff MacDonald, rhp, Lethbridge (Alberta) CC
36. Brandon Freese, rhp, Skyview HS, Vancouver, Wash.
37. Chris Buechner, rhp, Little Cypress-Mauriceville HS, Orange, Texas
38. Vern Sterry, rhp, Cypress (Calif.) JC
39. Lucas Gaskamp, lhp, Northeast Texas CC
40. **Pedro Diaz, rhp, Seminole State (Okla.) JC**
41. Duke Sardinha, 3b, Pepperdine
42. Colby Hughes, of, Branson HS, Walnut Shade, Mo.
43. Kelly Castles, rhp, McLaughlin HS, Milton Freewater, Ore.
44. Joshua Bryant, rhp, Wallace State (Ala.) CC
45. Brandon Young, of, Springfield (Ohio) North HS
46. Sergio Silva, rhp, JC of the Sequoias (Calif.)

47. John Toffey, rhp, St. Sebastian's HS, Barnstable, Mass.
48. Andrew York, c, JC of the Siskiyous (Calif.)
49. J.R. Revere, of, Georgia Southern
50. Mike Marksbury, rhp, Miami (Ohio)

DETROIT TIGERS

June—Regular Phase (11)

1. **Kenny Baugh, rhp, Rice**
1. **Michael Woods, 2b, Southern** (Supplemental pick—32nd—for loss of Type A free agent Juan Gonzalez)
2. **Preston Larrison, rhp, Evansville**
2. **Matt Coenen, lhp, Charleston Southern** (Pick from Indians as compensation for Gonzalez)
3. **Jack Hannahan, 3b, Minnesota**
4. **Mike Rabelo, c, Tampa**
5. **Ryan Raburn, 3b, South Florida CC**
6. **Jason Knoedler, of, Miami (Ohio)**
7. **Tom Farmer, rhp, Miami**
8. **Don Kelly, ss, Point Park (Pa.)**
9. **David Mattle, of, Kent State**
10. **Vincent Blue, of, Lamar HS, Houston**
11. Eric Thomas, rhp, Briarcliffe (N.Y.) JC
12. **James Gonzalez, rhp, UC Santa Barbara**
13. **Landon Stockman, rhp, Kennesaw State**
14. **Matthew Williams, of, Fontana (Calif.) HS**
15. **Kevin McDowell, lhp, Bucknell**
16. Joey Metropoulos, 3b, Monte Vista HS, Jamul, Calif.
17. **Dan Smith, rhp, Miami**
18. **Alex Trezza, c, Stony Brook**
19. **William Ryan, 3b, Briarcliffe (N.Y.) JC**
20. **Jason Moates, rhp, Middle Tennessee State**
21. Tim Dorn, 1b, Monrovia (Calif.) HS
22. **Francisco Rosado, of, Antelope Valley (Calif.) JC**
23. **Mike Scott, of, Connecticut**
24. John Schneider, c, Delaware
25. **Chris Kolodzey, of, Delaware**
26. **Herman Dean, of, Citrus (Calif.) JC**
27. **Mike Kobow, rhp, Minnesota**
28. **Jon Connolly, lhp, Oneonta (N.Y.) HS**
29. **Garth McKinney, of, Walters State (Tenn.) CC**
30. **John Birtwell, rhp, Harvard**
31. **Humberto Sanchez, rhp, Rockland (N.Y.) CC**
32. **Trevor Leu, of, Oral Roberts**
33. **Michael Howell, rhp, SUNY Binghamton**
34. **Ian Ostlund, lhp, Virginia Tech**
35. **Charles Lombardy, rhp, Ohio**
36. **Jed Stringham, of, UC Santa Barbara**
37. Kevin Miller, lhp, Cuesta (Calif.) JC
38. Adam Harben, rhp, Central Arkansas Christian HS, Little Rock
39. Robert White, lhp, Spartanburg Methodist (S.C.) JC
40. **Thomas Lyons, rhp, Downers Grove (Ill.) North HS**
41. Geoffrey Holloway, lhp, Booneville (Ark.) HS
42. Coby Judd, lhp, Simi Valley (Calif.) HS
43. Sean Richardson, c, Vista (Calif.) HS
44. Brent Hale, rhp, Peninsula HS, Rancho Palos Verde, Calif.
45. Lonnie Patterson, rhp, Harlan HS, Chicago
46. Lonnie Patterson, p, Harlan HS, Chicago, Ill.

FLORIDA MARLINS

June—Regular Phase (16)

1. (Pick to White Sox as compensation for Type A free agent Charles Johnson)
2. **Garrett Berger, rhp, Carmel (Ind.) HS**
3. **Allen Baxter, rhp, Varina HS, Sandston, Va.**
4. **Chris Resop, rhp/of, Barron Collier HS, Naples, Fla.**
5. Tyler Lumsden, lhp, Cave Spring HS, Roanoke, Va.
6. **Adam Bostick, lhp, Greensburg-Salem HS, Greensburg, Pa.**
7. **Lincoln Holdzkom, rhp, Arizona Western JC**
8. **Jeff Fulchino, rhp, Connecticut**
9. **Dustin Kupper, rhp, Pima (Ariz.) CC**
10. **Kody Naylor, rhp, Western Michigan**
11. **Rex Rundgren, ss, Sacramento CC**
12. **Nic Ungs, rhp, Northern Iowa**
13. **Lance Davis, rhp, George County HS, Lucedale, Miss.**
14. **Michael Tucker, 3b, Florida Southern**
15. Doug Boone, c, Ball State
16. **Hunter Wyant, ss, Virginia**
17. **Kevin Cave, rhp, Xavier**
18. **Josh Coffey, c, Lee-Davis HS, Mechanicsville, Va.**
19. **Lou Evans, lhp, San Jose (Calif.) CC**
20. Carl Lafferty, c, Mississippi (Contract voided)
21. Dane Mason, rhp, Cherokee HS, Marlton, N.J.
22. **Jason Helps, ss, Central Michigan**
23. **Wes McCrotty, lhp, Arkansas**
24. **John Skinner, rhp, San Diego State**
25. **Philip Hartig, 1b, The Citadel**
26. Adam Russell, rhp, North Olmsted (Ohio) HS
27. **Franco Blackburn, of, Southern**
28. Jon Hunton, rhp, North Plainfield (N.J.) HS
29. **Gooby Gerlits, c/of, Stoneman Douglas HS, Parkland, Fla.**
30. Nick Pesco, rhp, Tokay HS, Lodi, Calif.
31. Chris Johnston, rhp, Smoky Hills HS, Aurora, Colo.
32. Sergio Roman, c, Bishop Carroll HS, Wichita
33. **Torik Harrison, rhp, Southern**
34. **Steve Thomas, rhp, Nova Southeastern**
35. **Marc Rittenhouse, 2b, Washington**
36. **Kevin Halamicek, rhp, Cal State Dominguez Hills**
37. **Kris Clute, 2b, Miami**
38. **Ronnie Goodwin, rhp, Mississippi**
39. Justin Ottman, lhp, Rockland (N.Y.) CC
40. **Tyson Graham, of, North Gaston HS, Dallas, N.C.**
41. Eric Otero, 2b, Monignor Pace HS, Miami
42. Josh Perrault, rhp, South Mountain (Ariz.) CC
43. Isaac Garza, rhp, Odem (Texas) HS
44. Cliff Dancy, of, Pine Forest HS, Pensacola, Fla.
45. Nick Blasi, of, Butler County (Kan.) CC
46. Andrew Vansickle, of, Senatobia (Miss.) HS
47. Chuck Taylor, rhp, Westlake HS, Austin
48. Derek Hutton, ss, Palm Beach Gardens (Fla.) HS
49. Phil Coke, lhp, Sonora HS, Twain Harte, Calif.
50. Steve Stanley, of, Notre Dame

HOUSTON ASTROS

June—Regular Phase (10)

1. **Chris Burke, 2b/ss, Tennessee**
2. **Mike Rodriguez, of, Miami**
3. **Kirk Saarloos, rhp, Cal State Fullerton**
4. **Philip Barzilla, lhp, Rice**
5. **Charlton Jimerson, of, Miami**
6. **Russ Rohlicek, lhp, Long Beach State**
7. **Ryan Stegall, ss, Missouri**
8. **Brooks Conrad, 2b, Arizona State**
9. **Kerry Hodges, of, Texas Tech**
10. Lance Cormier, rhp, Alabama
11. **D.J. Houlton, rhp, Pacific**
12. **Carmen Little, lhp, St. Louis CC-Forest Park**
13. **Kendall Jones, c, Texarkana (Texas) CC**
14. **Clint Hoover, 1b, California**
15. **Trevor Mote, 2b, Baylor**
16. **Brian Rodaway, lhp, Nebraska**
17. **Tom Bayrer, rhp, Campbell**
18. **Jose DeLeon, rhp, Nixon-Smiley HS, Nixon, Texas**
19. **Ryan Kochen, ss, Western Michigan**
20. **Mark Obradovich, c, Gadsden State (Ala.) CC**
21. Jeffery Derrickson, c, Bryan Station HS, Lexington, Ky.
22. **Justin Humphries, c, Episcopal HS, Richmond, Texas**
23. **Matt Albers, rhp, Clements HS, Sugar Land, Texas**
24. **Cameron Likely, of, South Alabama**
25. **Chad Durham, rhp, Texas Christian**
26. **Steve Checksfield, of, Albany**
27. Henry Colbert, rhp, Columbia Basin (Wash.) CC
28. **Seth Bobbitt, rhp, Birmingham-Southern**
29. Raymar Diaz, of, Luis Hernaiz Verone HS, Canovanas, P.R.
30. **Jjallil Sandoval, ss, Cal State Los Angeles**
31. **Brian Middleton, rhp, West Viginia State**
32. **Billy Jacobson, of, Rice**

33. **John Fagan, 1b, San Jose State**
34. **Brandon Macchi, of, San Jose State**
35. Travis Teeter, rhp, Rensselaer Polytechnic (N.Y.) Institute
36. **Andrew Perry, rhp, Cal State Pomona**
37. Jared Gothreaux, rhp, McNeese State
38. Ryan McKeller, rhp, Pflugerville (Texas) HS
39. Paul Hazeres, rhp, Carolina Forest HS, Conway, S.C.
40. Osvaldo Diaz, rhp, Cuba
41. Christopher Saywers, rhp/ss, Edmonds (Wash.) CC
42. Patrick Wells, lhp, West Jordan (Utah) HS
43. **James McNair, rhp, Virginia Commonwealth**
44. Lance Dawkins, ss, Meridian (Miss.) CC
45. Kyle Thompson, rhp, Valley Center HS, Escondido, Calif.
46. Justin Ard, of, Clear Lake HS, Houston
47. Eric Turnbow, ss, Jordan HS, Sandy, Utah
48. Ben Leuthard, of, San Diego State
49. Kevin House, of, Alabama Southern CC

KANSAS CITY ROYALS

June—Regular Phase (9)

1. **Colt Griffin, rhp, Marshall (Texas) HS**
2. **Roscoe Crosby, of, Union HS, Buffalo, S.C.**
3. **Matt Ferrera, 3b, Westminster Academy, Fort Lauderdale**
4. **John Draper, c, Cal State Los Angeles**
5. **Chamar McDonald, 1b, Madison (Miss.) Central HS**
6. **Clint Frost, rhp, Jordan HS, Columbus, Ga.**
7. **Chris Tierney, lhp, Lockport (Ill.) HS**
8. **Ira Brown, rhp, Willis (Texas) HS**
9. **Justin Nelson, of/lhp, Platte Valley HS, Kersey, Colo.**
10. **Danny Tamayo, rhp, Notre Dame**
11. **Angel Sanchez, of, Florencia Garcia HS, Las Piedras, P.R.**
12. **Victor Rosario, of, Lake City (Fla.) CC**
13. **Cedric Watkins, of, Bassett (Va.) HS**
14. **Devon Lowery, rhp, South Point HS, Belmont, N.C.**
15. Danny Zell, lhp, Angelina (Texas) JC
16. **Mel Stocker, of, Arizona State**
17. **Marcus Chandler, of, Southern**
18. **Alexis Alexander, of, Medical Lake (Wash.) HS**
19. **Mervin Williams, of, East St. John HS, Garyville, La.**
20. **Peter Gunny, of, Los Angeles Pierce JC**
21. **Brian Melnyk, lhp, Point Park (Pa.)**
22. **Chris Fallon, 1b, St. John's**
23. Jermaine Johnson, of, Glynn (Ga.) Academy
24. **J.D. Alleva, c, Duke**
25. **Richard Zary, rhp, Limestone (S.C.)**
26. Derek DeCarlo, rhp, Southridge HS, Miami
27. **Derrik Lytle, of, Mesa (Ariz.) CC**
28. **Lucas Palmer, rhp, Baker HS, Baker City, Ore.**
29. Bryan McCaulley, rhp, Barbe HS, Lake Charles, La.
30. Zeke Parraz, ss, Green Valley HS, Henderson, Nev.
31. **Jacob Guzman, c, Palomar (Calif.) JC**
32. Julio Medina, rhp, Elk Grove (Ill.) HS
33. **John Barnett, rhp, Arizona Western JC**
34. **Erik Dean, ss, West Valley (Calif.) JC**
35. Barry Richardson, rhp, Lake City (Fla.) CC
36. Chris Washington, rhp, Port St. Lucie (Fla.) HS
37. Brad Knox, rhp, Blinn (Texas) JC
38. James Dayley, rhp, Utah Valley CC
39. Taylor Tankersley, lhp, Warren Central HS, Vicksburg, Miss.
40. Jason Snyder, rhp, Alta HS, Sandy, Utah
41. Rene Pablos, lhp, Cochise County (Ariz.) CC
42. Nick Cadena, c, Apollo HS, Glendale, Ariz.
43. Stephen Green, of, Moahalua HS, Honolulu
44. Brady Everett, c, Federal Way HS, Kent, Wash.
45. **Curtis Legendre, 3b/c, Angelina (Texas) JC**
46. Bret Berglund, 3b, Kent Denver HS, Englewood, Colo.
47. Caleb Irwin, rhp, Temple (Texas) JC
48. Ryan Coiner, rhp, Las Vegas HS
49. Ryan Patterson, of, Rowlett (Texas) HS
50. **Bo Baker, rhp, Eastern Arizona JC**

LOS ANGELES DODGERS

June—Regular Phase (24)

1. (Pick to Braves as compensation for Type A free agent Andy Ashby)
2. **Brian Pilkington, rhp, Santiago HS, Garden Grove, Calif.**
3. **David Taylor, rhp, Southlake HS, Clermont, Fla.**
4. **Kole Strayhorn, rhp, Shawnee HS, Seminole, Okla.**
5. **Steve Nelson, rhp, Cole Harbour District HS, Dartmouth, Nova Scotia**
6. **Edwin Jackson, of, Shaw HS, Columbus, Ga.**
7. **David Cuen, lhp, Cibola HS, Somerton, Ariz.**
8. **David Cardona, of, San Jose de Calasanza HS, Trujillo Alta, P.R.**
9. **Sean Pierce, of, San Diego State**
10. **Thom Ott, rhp, Nebraska**
11. **Luis Gonzalez, lhp, Florida Air Academy HS, Melbourne, Fla.**
12. **Cedric Benson, of, Lee HS, Midland, Texas**
13. **Matt Kauffman, lhp, San Jose State**
14. **Ryan Carter, of, Riverdale HS, Fort Myers, Fla.**
15. **Jimmy Stewart, rhp, Sabino HS, Tucson**
16. **Josh Canales, ss, UCLA**
17. **Jerry Johnson, of, Arkansas-Little Rock**
18. **Vance McCracken, rhp, West Virginia**
19. John Urick, 1b, Cowley County (Kan.) CC
20. **William Malone, 2b, Robert Morris (Ill.)**
21. **Jereme Milons, of, Starkville (Miss.) HS**
22. **Scott Gillitzer, 2b, Wisconsin-Milwaukee**
23. James Dykes, lhp, Parklane Academy, McComb, Miss.
24. Ryan Lennerton, lhp, Brookswood SS, Langley, B.C
25. Garrett Murdy, rhp, Mission Viejo HS, Laguna Hills, Calif.
26. Jay Sadlowe, rhp, Farragut HS, Knoxville
27. Christopher Hutcheson, lhp, Florala HS, Lockhart, Ala.
28. Kyle Crist, rhp, Granite Bay HS, Grant, Calif.
29. Dennis Bigley, 1b, Dallas Christian HS, Lancaster, Texas
30. Tom Wilson, lhp, Central Cabarrus HS, Concord, N.C.
31. David Parker, rhp, Sisler HS, Winnipeg, Manitoba
32. Michael Hollimon, ss, Jesuit Prep, Dallas
33. **Jason Stefani, lhp, Albertson (Idaho)**
34. Brian Devereaux, rhp, Hollywood (Fla.) Christian HS
35. Christopher Casey, lhp, Hunstville (Texas) HS
36. Brian Cleveland, ss, San Jose CC
37. Dustin Schroer, of, Surrey, B.C
38. Ryan Hamilton, ss, Klein HS, Spring, Texas
39. William Johnson, 1b, North Springs HS, College Park, Ga.
40. Cameron Feightner, rhp, Beaverton HS, Portland, Ore.
41. Jim Gregory, lhp, Crockett (Texas) HS
42. Jordan Kissock, of, Delphi Academy, Surrey, B.C
43. Clint Sammons, c, Parkview HS, Stone Mountain, Ga.
44. Clay Wehner, c, Thomasville (Ga.) HS
45. **Mike Rodriguez, rhp, Sierra (Calif.) JC**
46. **Michael Lynch, c, South Suburban (Ill.) JC**
47. Devin Monds, rhp, Nepean HS, Ottawa, Ontario
48. Danny Desclouds, rhp, Connors State (Okla.) JC
49. Jason Schuler, c, JC of Lake County (Ill.)
50. Brooks Bollinger, 3b, Wisconsin

MILWAUKEE BREWERS

June—Regular Phase (12)

1. **Mike Jones, rhp, Thunderbird HS, Phoenix**
2. **J.J. Hardy, ss, Sabino HS, Tucson**
3. **Jon Steitz, rhp, Yale**
4. **Brad Nelson, 1b, Bishop Garrigan HS, Algona, Iowa**
5. **Judd Richardson, rhp, Miami (Ohio)**
6. **Calvin Carpenter, rhp, Natchitoches (La.) Central HS**
7. **Taylor McCormack, 3b, Dunedin (Fla.) HS**
8. **Brandon Gemoll, 1b, Fresno State**
9. **Dennis Sarfate, rhp, Chandler-Gilbert (Ariz.) CC**
10. **Greg Moreira, rhp, Lake Brantley HS, Apopka, Fla.**
11. David Slevin, 2b, Indian River (Fla.) JC
12. Ray Liotta, lhp, Archbishop Rummel HS, Metairie, La.
13. **Travis Hinton, 1b, Chandler-Gilbert (Ariz.) CC**
14. **Aaron Sheffield, rhp, Young Harris (Ga.) JC**

15. Tim Dillard, c, Saltillo (Miss.) HS
16. **Gene Desalme, lhp, Northwestern State (La.)**
17. Justin Wilson, lhp, Chandler (Ariz.) HS
18. **Jeff Eure, c, Old Dominion**
19. **Joel Alvarado, c, Texas-Arlington**
20. Josh Smith, rhp, Lake Havasu (Ariz.) City HS
21. **Orlando Viera, of, Cuevas HS, Gurabo, P.R.**
22. Damarius Bilbo, of, Moss Point (Miss.) HS
23. **David Nolasco, rhp, Riverside (Calif.) CC**
24. **Danny Kolb, rhp, Manatee (Fla.) CC**
25. **Chris Barnwell, ss, Flagler (Fla.)**
26. **Manny Parra, lhp, American River (Calif.) JC**
27. **Dan Boyd, of, South Florida**
28. **Chris Saenz, rhp, Pima (Ariz.) CC**
29. Jamie McAlister, rhp, Clearwater HS, Piedmont, Mo.
30. **Christopher Gittlings, rhp, De Sales HS, Louisville**
31. Andy Sigerich, rhp, Downers Grove (Ill.) North HS
32. Jon Calmes, rhp, Eastlake HS, Sammamish, Wash.
33. Greg Esteves, ss, River Ridge HS, New Port Richey, Fla.
34. Fuarieuir Miller, of, Laney (Calif.) JC
35. **Stephen Hunt, of, Chandler-Gilbert (Ariz.) CC**
36. **Richard Huggins, lhp, Central Florida CC**
37. **Tom Carrow, of, Tampa**
38. Ross Hawley, rhp, Augustana (S.D.)
39. Travis Johnson, of, Shannon (Miss.) HS
40. Jeremy Wilson, c, Catholic Central HS, Burlington, Wis.
41. Hubert Pruett, rhp, Kamehameha (Hawaii) HS
42. **Ralph Santana, ss, Lake Sumter (Fla.) CC**
43. **Matt Serafini, c, Evansville**
44. **Corry Parrott, of, Long Beach State**
45. Jason Costello, lhp, Clearwater (Fla.) HS
46. Jordan Szabo, of, Carlsbad (Calif.) HS
47. Joseph Costentino, of, Bishop Gorman HS, Henderson, Nev.
48. Brian Harper, lhp, North Little Rock (Ark.) HS
49. Nick Stillwagon, c, Biloxi (Miss.) HS
50. **Chris Haggard, c, Oklahoma**

MINNESOTA TWINS

June—Regular Phase (1)

1. **Joe Mauer, c, Cretin-Derham Hall, St. Paul, Minn.**
2. **Scott Tyler, rhp, Downingtown (Pa.) HS**
3. **Jose Morales, ss, Academie la Providencia HS, Rio Piedras, P.R.**
4. **Angel Garcia, rhp, Nicolas Sevilla HS, Dorado, P.R.**
5. **Jeremy Brown, rhp, Georgia**
6. **Vince Serafini, lhp, Evansville**
7. **Matt Vorwald, rhp, Illinois**
8. **Jared Hemus, lhp, Grossmont (Calif.) JC**
9. **Dusty Gomon, 1b, Terry Parker HS, Jacksonville**
10. **Garrett Guzman, of, Green Valley HS, Henderson, Nev.**
11. **Josh Renick, ss, Middle Tennessee State**
12. **Kaulana Kuhaulua, 2b, Long Beach State**
13. **Kevin Cameron, rhp, Georgia Tech**
14. Ryan Anderson, lhp, Gaither HS, Tampa
15. **Brett Lawson, rhp, Northwestern Oklahoma State**
16. Brian Stitt, rhp, Wellington Community (Fla.) HS
17. Matt Macri, ss, Dowling HS, Clive, Iowa
18. **Robert Guzman, of, Cal State Fullerton**
19. **Scott Whitrock, of, Madison (Wis.) Area Tech CC**
20. Anthony Albano, of, Brother Rice HS, Chicago
21. **Felix Molina, 2b, Eugenio Maria de Hostos HS, Trujillo Alto, P.R.**
22. **Ryan Smith, c, Citrus (Calif.) JC**
23. **Jake Mauer, 2b, St. Thomas (Minn.)**
24. **Bryan Kennedy, c, Long Beach State**
25. **Josh Johnson, c, Ridgway (Pa.) HS**
26. John Herrera, rhp, Redlands (Calif.) HS
27. **Justin Elliott, c, Lake Gibson HS, Lakeland, Fla.**
28. **Brian Gates, rhp, Tennessee**
29. **Nick Blackburn, rhp, Seminole State (Okla.) JC**
30. **Josh Daws, rhp, Jacksonville**
31. Ben Thomas, 3b, Central HS, Rapid City, S.D.
32. Jason Wilmes, lhp, Somerset (Wis.) HS
33. Ryan Gehring, lhp, Burlington (Wis.) Catholic Central HS
34. Marshall Hendon, lhp, Christian Brothers HS, Sacramento
35. Bookie Gates, 2b, Washington State
36. **Kenny Huff, of, Arizona**
37. **Shawn Tarkington, rhp, Seton Hall**
38. **Matt Abram, 2b/of, Arizona**
39. **Nick Niedbalski, lhp, East Central (Mo.) JC**
40. **Erik Lohse, rhp, Sacramento CC**
41. **Ryan Spataro, of, St. Peters SS, Barrie, Ontario**
42. **Pat Tingley, lhp, Indiana State**
43. Jason Vargas, lhp, Apple Valley (Calif.) HS
44. **Jacob Hader, lhp, Belton (Mo.) HS**
45. Josh Smith, of, Canyon Springs HS, Moreno Valley, Calif.
46. Mitch Pruemer, rhp, Rend Lake (Ill.) CC
47. Daniel Smith, of, Eau Gallie HS, Melbourne, Fla.
48. William Guzman, ss, Northwest Christian Academy, Miami
49. Jason Paul, rhp, Ball State
50. Robert Strickland, 2b, Frostproof (Fla.) HS

MONTREAL EXPOS

June—Regular Phase (6)

1. **Josh Karp, rhp, UCLA**
2. **Don Levinski, rhp, Weimar (Texas) HS**
3. **Mike Hinckley, lhp, Moore (Okla.) HS**
4. **Nick Long, rhp, Shaw HS, Columbus, Ga.**
5. **Reggie Fitzpatrick, of, McNair HS, Atlanta**
6. **Josh Labandeira, ss, Fresno State**
7. **Chad Bentz, lhp, Long Beach State**
8. **Greg Thissen, 3b, Triton (Ill.) JC**
9. **Shawn Norris, 3b, Cal State Fullerton**
10. **Eddie Diaz, rhp, Colonial HS, Orlando**
11. Kyle Pawelczyk, lhp, Chipola (Fla.) JC
12. **Daniel Kahr, c, Durango HS, Las Vegas**
13. **Tyler Kirkman, rhp, Mount Carmel (Ill.) HS**
14. **Jason Walker, lhp, Pacific**
15. **Tory Imotichey, lhp, Purcell (Okla.) HS**
16. **Warmar Gomez, rhp, Casiano Cepeda HS, Rio Grande, P.R.**
17. **David Maust, lhp, West Virginia**
18. **Rob Caputo, rhp, Alabama-Birmingham**
19. **Chris Schroder, rhp, Oklahoma City**
20. **Jason Greene, ss, Minford (Ohio) HS**
21. Tim Wood, rhp, Sabino HS, Tucson
22. Arlandus Brown, of, Copiah-Lincoln (Miss.) JC
23. **Ja'mar Clanton, ss, Triton (Ill.) JC**
24. James Treece, rhp, Riverside (Calif.) Poly HS
25. Zach Lerch, rhp, Prairie HS, Cedar Rapids, Iowa
26. Jerrell Jackson, of, Altoona (Pa.) Area HS
27. Daniel Smith, rhp, Sacramento CC
28. Michael Richardson, rhp, Richland (Wash.) HS
29. Mark Rodrigues, rhp, Kauai HS, Koloa, Hawaii
30. Jared Brown, lhp, Notre Dame Catholic HS, Milford, Conn.
31. Jamieson Boulanger, lhp, Concordia (Quebec)
32. Jean-Sebastien Varney, rhp, Edouard Montpetit HS, St. Hubert, Quebec
33. Jeremey White, lhp, Victor Valley (Calif.) CC
34. Henry Gutierrez-Portalatin, c, Florida Air Academy HS, Melbourne, Fla.
35. Michael Springsteen, rhp, Marshalltown (Iowa) CC
36. Micah Zumbro, rhp, Franklin (Miss.) HS
37. P.J. Connelly, lhp, Beloit (Wis.) Memorial HS
38. David Leclerc, lhp, Laval, Quebec
39. Jecorey Matthews, of, Northwest Classen HS, Oklahoma City
40. Frederick Perkins, of, Brookhaven (Miss.) HS
41. Travis Becktel, of, Capistrano Valley HS, Mission Viejo, Calif.
42. John Taylor, lhp, Northside HS, Northport, Ala.
43. Joe Gullion, ss, Johnson County (Kan.) CC
44. Brian Hipps, of, San Diego Mesa CC
45. Franklyn Jimenez, 2b, Muscatine (Iowa) CC
46. Joshua Ranson, of, Chatfield HS, Littleton, Colo.
47. Ross Wolf, rhp, Newton HS, Wheeler, Ill.
48. Chris Jones, c, Edison HS, Fresno
49. Matt Hayes, lhp, Effingham (Ill.) HS
50. Chad Scarbery, rhp, Fresno CC

NEW YORK METS

June—Regular Phase (26)

1. **Aaron Heilman, rhp, Notre Dame** (Pick from Rockies as compensation for Type A free agent Mike Hampton)
1. (Pick to Athletics as compensation for Type A free agent Kevin Appier)
1. **David Wright, 3b, Hickory HS, Chesapeake, Va.** (Supplemental pick—38th—for loss of Hampton)
2. **Alhaji Turay, of, Auburn (Wash.) HS**
2. **Corey Ragsdale, ss, Nettleton HS, Jonesboro, Ark.** (Supplemental pick—76th—for loss of Type C free agent Bobby Jones)
3. **Lenny DiNardo, lhp, Stetson**
4. **Brian Walker, lhp, Miami**
5. **Danny Garcia, 2b, Pepperdine**
6. **Jason Weintraub, rhp, Jefferson HS, Tampa**
7. **Tyler Beuerlein, c, Grand Canyon (Ariz.)**
8. **Brett Kay, c, Cal State Fullerton**
9. **Jayson Weir, lhp, Boone HS, Orlando**
10. **Ryan Olson, lhp, Nevada-Las Vegas**
11. **D.J. Mattox, rhp, Anderson (S.C.)**
12. **Derran Watts, of, British Columbia**
13. **Jay Caligiuri, 3b, Cal State Los Angeles**
14. Kyle Larsen, 1b, Eastlake HS, Sammamish, Wash.
15. **Jason Scobie, rhp, Louisiana State**
16. **Joe Hietpas, c, Northwestern**
17. **Frank Corr, of, Stetson**
18. Justin Barnes, ss, Merritt Island (Fla.) HS
19. Josh Alliston, rhp, Long Beach State
20. Trevor Hutchinson, rhp, California
21. **Blake McGinley, lhp, Texas Tech**
22. **Dave Bacani, 2b, Cal State Fullerton**
23. **John Toner, of, Western Michigan**
24. Josh Deel, rhp, Wolfson HS, Jacksonville
25. Nathaniel Craft, lhp, Palm Harbor (Fla.) University HS
26. **Justin Sassanella, of, De Kalb HS, Auburn, Ind.**
27. **Eric Templet, rhp, Louisiana-Lafayette**
28. **Ron Ogle, lhp, UC Santa Barbara**
29. **Domingo Acosta, rhp, Palm Beach (Fla.) JC**
30. **Chris Sherman, rhp, San Jose State**
31. Newton Hausmann, lhp, Seton Hall
32. Cole Armstrong, c, Delphi Academy, Surrey, B.C
33. **Taylor George, rhp, Cypress (Calif.) JC**
34. **Richard Pittman, ss/2b, North Georgia College & State**
35. Wayne Foltin, rhp, Centennial HS, Bakersfield, Calif.
36. Phillip Tyson, rhp, Katella HS, Anaheim
37. Jose Torres, c, Centennial HS, Corona, Calif.
38. Luis Roberts, lhp, Dartmouth (Nova Scotia) HS
39. Michael Almand, lhp, Stockbridge (Ga.) HS
40. Jay Sawatski, lhp, Westark (Ark.) CC
41. **Sean Farrell, lhp, Briarcliffe (N.Y.) JC**
42. Chris Davis, rhp, Fresno CC
43. Michael Schaeffer, rhp, Wilson HS, Sinking Springs, Pa.
44. Randy Wells, c, Southwestern Illinois JC
45. Eddie Cannon, rhp, South Florida CC
46. Karnie Vertz, rhp, Porterville (Calif.) JC
47. Michael Hawkins, of, Eisenhower HS, Rialto, Calif.
48. Jamar Hill, 3b, Santa Ana (Calif.) JC
49. Paul Labiche, rhp, Reserve Christian HS, LaPlace, La.
50. DeWayne Carver, rhp, Santa Fe (Fla.) CC

NEW YORK YANKEES

June—Regular Phase (19)

1. (Pick to Orioles as compensation for Type A free agent Mike Mussina)
1. **John-Ford Griffin, of, Florida State** (Pick from Mariners as compensation for Type A free agent Jeff Nelson)
1. **Bronson Sardinha, ss, Kamehameha HS, Honolulu** (Supplemental pick—34th—for loss of Type A free agent Denny Neagle)
1. **Jon Skaggs, rhp, Rice** (Supplemental pick—42nd—for loss of Nelson)
2. **Shelley Duncan, of, Arizona**
2. **Jason Arnold, rhp, Central Florida** (Pick from Rockies as compensation for Neagle)
3. **Chase Wright, lhp, Iowa Park (Texas) HS**
4. **Aaron Rifkin, 1b, Cal State Fullerton**
5. **Jeff Christensen, of, Tennessee**
6. **Rik Currier, rhp, Southern California**
7. **Andy Cannizaro, ss, Tulane**
8. Adam Peterson, rhp, Wichita State
9. **Charlie Manning, lhp, Tampa**
10. **Jared Pitney, 1b, Pepperdine**
11. **Brian Strelitz, rhp, Texas A&M**
12. **Chris Russ, rhp, Texas A&M**
13. **Adam Wheeler, rhp, Campbell HS, Smyrna, Ga.**
14. Trenton Henderson, rhp, Pratt (Kan.) CC
15. **John Picco, lhp, Villanova HS, LaSalle, Ontario**
16. Nic Touchstone, lhp, Okaloosa-Walton (Fla.) JC
17. Quinton Robertson, rhp, Texarkana (Texas) JC
18. Josh Smith, rhp, Navarro (Texas) JC
19. Mike McGowan, rhp, Newman Smith HS, Carrollton, Texas
20. Jason McMillan, lhp, Dundee Crown HS, Carpentersville, Ill.
21. **Omir Santos, c, East Central (Mo.) JC**
22. **Todd Faulkner, 1b, Auburn**
23. **Kaazim Summerville, of, St. Mary's**
24. **Robert Wood, rhp, Michigan**
25. Harold Edwards, c, Midland (Texas) HS
26. Andrew Marcus, rhp, Tyler (Texas) JC
27. Jeff Tuttle, of, Cypress (Calif.) JC
28. Brandon Jones, of, Liberty Eylau HS, Texarkana, Texas
29. Philip Humber, rhp, Carthage (Texas) HS
30. Daniel Schwab, 1b, Arvada (Colo.) West HS
31. Ricky Stover, lhp, Navarro (Texas) JC
32. Aaron Edwards, c, John A. Logan (Ill.) JC
33. Chris Weakley, ss, Albany HS, El Cerrito, Calif.
34. **Chris Kemlo, rhp, McLaughlin HS, Oshawa, Ontario**
35. **Kevin Goodrum, lhp, Ohio State**
36. Fernando Fuentes, c, Weehawken (N.J.) HS
37. **Josh Kerschen, rhp, CC of Southern Nevada**
38. Brent Jackson, lhp, Henderson (Texas) HS
39. Tate Wallis, rhp, Ennis (Texas) HS
40. Edward Gleason, of, El Modena HS, Orange, Calif.
41. Jonathan Mercer, of, Jefferson (Mo.) JC
42. Gregory Taylor, ss, St. Louis CC-Forest Park
43. Michael Bass, rhp, Santana HS, Santee, Calif.
44. Eric Hullinger, rhp, Oak Forest (Ill.) HS
45. Jose Robles, rhp, East Central (Mo.) JC
46. Domenic Ficco, lhp, Regis Jesuit HS, Aurora, Colo.
47. Chad Borek, rhp, Northmont HS, Dayton, Ohio
48. Brian Carpenter, of, Fairfield (Ohio) HS
49. Aneury Pichardo, ss, Miramar (Fla.) HS
50. Brandon Boggs, of, Pope HS, Marietta, Ga.

OAKLAND ATHLETICS

June—Regular Phase (25)

1. **Bobby Crosby, ss, Long Beach State**
1. **Jeremy Bonderman, rhp, Pasco (Wash.) HS** (Pick from Mets as compensation for Type A free agent Kevin Appier)
1. **John Rheinecker, lhp, Southwest Missouri State** (Supplemental pick—37th—for loss of Appier)
2. **Neal Cotts, lhp, Illinois State**
3. **J.T. Stotts, ss, Cal State Northridge**
4. **Marcus McBeth, of, South Carolina**
5. **Jeff Bruksch, rhp, Stanford**
6. **Austin Nagle, of, Barbe HS, Lake Charles, La.**
7. **Dan Johnson, 1b, Nebraska**
8. **Michael Frick, rhp, Cal State Northridge**
9. **Casey Myers, c, Arizona State**
10. **Mike Wood, rhp, North Florida**
11. **J.R. Crider, rhp, Lewis-Clark State (Idaho)**
12. **Jeff Christy, of, Stetson**
13. **Chris Mabeus, rhp, Lewis-Clark State (Idaho)**
14. **Brett Price, lhp, South Carolina**
15. **Jason Basil, of, Georgia Tech**
16. Steve Reba, rhp, Clemson
17. Pete Montrenes, rhp, Mississippi

18. Jacob Dixon, 1b, Rowva HS, Oneida, Ill.
19. **Justin Peirce, of, Wayland Baptist (Texas)**
20. **Jeff Muessig, rhp, Briarcliffe (N.Y.) JC**
21. **Jeff Coleman, rhp, Hawaii**
22. **Harold Holbert, 2b, Locke HS, Los Angeles**
23. **Kory Wayment, ss, Salt Lake CC**
24. Dylan Putnam, rhp, Michigan State
25. **Andy Neufeld, 3b, Georgia**
26. **Chris Gill, rhp/3b, Phoenix JC**
27. **Bryan Simmering, rhp, Towson State**
28. **Matt Groff, of, Tulane**
29. **Leonard Landeros, lhp, JC of the Sequoias (Calif.)**
30. Thomas Braun, rhp, Kingwood (Texas) HS
31. **Brian Rooke, of, Hawaii-Hilo**
32. Mark Hilde, 3b, Woodway HS, Edmonds, Wash.
33. Dan Fyvie, rhp, Fenton (Mich.) HS
34. Adolfo Garza, rhp, Walla Walla (Wash.) CC
35. Trenton Froehlich, lhp, Lompoc (Calif.) HS
36. Cooper Fouts, c, Bishop Gorman HS, Las Vegas
37. Andre Ethier, of, Chandler-Gilbert (Ariz.) CC
38. Robert Lacheur, rhp, Prairie Baseball Academy, Lethbridge, Alberta
39. Nic Crosta, of, Highline HS, Seattle

PHILADELPHIA PHILLIES

June—Regular Phase (4)

1. **Gavin Floyd, rhp, Mount St. Joseph HS, Baltimore**
2. (Pick to Red Sox as compensation for Type B free agent Rheal Cormier)
3. (Pick to Mariners as compensation for Type B free agent Jose Mesa)
4. **Terry Jones, ss, Upland (Calif.) HS**
5. **Ryan Howard, 1b, Southwest Missouri State**
6. **Bryan Hansen, of, Longwood HS, Coram, N.Y.**
7. **Vinnie DeChristofaro, lhp, Richmond Hill (Ga.) HS**
8. **Taft Cable, rhp, UNC Greensboro**
9. **Chris Roberson, of, Feather River (Calif.) JC**
10. Rocky Cherry, rhp, Oklahoma
11. **Matt Sweeney, rhp, Steinert HS, Yardville, N.J.**
12. **Rod Perry, of, Penn State**
13. **Andre Marshall, of, Washington**
14. **Mario Delgado, of, Oklahoma City**
15. **Tim Davis, lhp, South Alabama**
16. **Ben Margalski, c, Southwest Missouri State**
17. **Ryan Hutchison, rhp, Western Kentucky**
18. **Ben Ally, rhp, Warner Southern (Fla.)**
19. **Matt Squires, lhp, Whitworth (Wash.)**
20. **Vince Vukovich, of, Delaware**
21. Julian Williams, of, Upland (Calif.) HS
22. **Mike Floyd, of, South Carolina**
23. **Josh Cisneros, c, West Virginia**
24. **Kris Lammers, lhp, Middle Tennessee State**
25. **Josh Scott, lhp, Baylor**
26. **Carl Dawson, rhp, Memphis**
27. **Jay Bernard, rhp, Troy State**
28. **Michael Nall, rhp, Northwestern**
29. Jeremy Kurella, ss, Central Florida
30. **Kris Bennett, 3b, Tennessee**
31. **Gabrial Johnston, c, Sonoma State (Calif.)**
32. **Josh Miller, rhp, North Carolina State**
33. **Daniel McCall, lhp, Penn State**
34. **Brian Schriner, rhp, Louisiana-Monroe**
35. **Nick Glaser, rhp, Clemson**
36. **Jeff Phelps, 3b, Arizona State**
37. **Wes Carroll, ss, Evansville**
38. Jaime Martinez, 1b, Hueneme HS, Oxnard, Calif.
39. Jason Jaramillo, c, Racine Case HS, Franksville, Wis.
40. Arnold Hughey, lhp, Venice (Fla.) HS
41. Dustin Miller, rhp, Diamond Bar (Calif.) HS
42. Will Thompson, 1b, Loyola Sacred Heart HS, Missoula, Mont.
43. Andy Lytle, rhp, Highlands Ranch (Colo.) HS
44. Humberto Gonzales, ss/2b, Rainier Beach HS, Seattle
45. Jared Birrenkott, c, Granite Hills HS, El Cajon, Calif.
46. Allen Hicks, of, King HS, Tampa
47. **Sean Walsh, 3b/of, North Carolina State**
48. **Maximo Reyes, rhp, St. Petersburg (Fla.) JC**

PITTSBURGH PIRATES

June—Regular Phase (8)

1. **John Van Benschoten, rhp/1b, Kent State**
2. (Pick to Braves as compensation for Type B free agent Terry Mulholland)
3. Jeremy Guthrie, rhp, Stanford
4. **Jeff Keppinger, ss, Georgia**
5. **Travis Chapman, 1b, Indian River (Fla.) CC**
6. **Drew Friedberg, lhp, Arizona State**
7. **Mike McCuistion, c, Yucaipa (Calif.) HS**
8. **Chris Duffy, of, Arizona State**
9. Jason Fellows, 1b, Berkmar HS, Lawrenceville, Ga.
10. Aaron Bulkley, ss, Port Byron (N.Y.) HS
11. Stephen Drew, ss, Lowndes HS, Valdosta, Ga.
12. **Tim Brown, 1b, Sheldon HS, Eugene, Ore.**
13. **Jeff Dutremble, lhp, Dartmouth**
14. **Jason Kiley, rhp, St. Charles (Ill.) East HS**
15. **Jeff Miller, rhp, New Orleans**
16. Jon Smith, lhp, Cal State Fullerton
17. Tim Morley, lhp, Stevenson HS, Buffalo Grove, Ill.
18. **Lino Mariot, ss, Woodbridge (N.J.) HS**
19. **Jonathan Albaladejo, rhp, Miami-Dade CC**
20. **Zach Duke, lhp, Midway HS, Clifton, Texas**
21. Tim Pahuta, c/1b, Hunterdon Central HS, Whitehouse Station, N.J.
22. Jon Koch, rhp, Berrien Springs (Mich.) HS
23. **Casey Shumaker, rhp, Jacksonville**
24. **Marcus Davila, rhp, Tallahassee (Fla.) CC**
25. Robert Coomer, rhp, John Logan (Ill.) JC
26. **Morel Tjosandy, lhp, Emerson HS, Union City, N.J.**
27. **Dan D'Amato, lhp, North Carolina State**
28. **Claudell Clark, lhp, Norfolk State**
29. **Scott Tower, lhp, Temple (Texas) JC**
30. **Kody Kirkland, 3b, Pocatello (Idaho) HS**
31. **Brady Borner, lhp, Wayne State (Neb.)**
32. Chris Torres, c, Vero Beach (Fla.) HS
33. **Chris Shelton, c, Utah**
34. Brett Korth, rhp, Kishwaukee (Ill.) JC
35. Renardo Pitts, of, Jones County HS, Gray, Ga.
36. Adam Riddle, of, New Mexico JC
37. Eduardo Elias, rhp, Brito Private HS, Miami
38. **Rajai Davis, 2b, Connecticut-Avery Point**
39. Taylor Johnson, of, Skyview HS, Vancouver, Wash.
40. Jase Turner, 1b, Skyline HS, Oakland
41. Scott Wearne, 2b, Chipola (Fla.) JC
42. Preston Simms, rhp, Bethany HS, Oklahoma City
43. **Shane Youman, lhp, Louisiana State**
44. Joe Martinez, rhp, Seton Hall Prep HS, West Orange, N.J.
45. Brent Sportsman, rhp, Elgin (Ill.) CC
46. Matthew Davis, lhp/of, Terry Parker HS, Jacksonville
47. Josh MacDonald, rhp, Notre Dame HS, Milford, Conn.
48. Tony Cekovsky, rhp, Southington (Conn.) HS
49. Jeb Gibbs, rhp, Pope HS, Villa Ricca, Ga.
50. **Justin Rethwisch, of, Antelope Valley (Calif.) JC**

ST. LOUIS CARDINALS

June—Regular Phase (28)

1. **Justin Pope, rhp, Central Florida**
2. **Dan Haren, rhp, Pepperdine**
3. **Joe Mather, ss, Mountain Pointe HS, Phoenix**
4. **Josh Brey, lhp, Liberty**
5. **Skip Schumaker, of, UC Santa Barbara**
6. **John Killalea, lhp, Seminole (Fla.) HS**
7. **Tyler Adamczyk, rhp, Westlake HS, Westlake Village, Calif.**
8. **John Nelson, ss, Kansas**
9. **Rhett Parrott, rhp, Georgia Tech**
10. **Seth Davidson, ss, Southern California**
11. **Jesse Roman, 1b, Rice**
12. **Ben Julianel, rhp, San Diego State**
13. **Chris Netwall, c, Penn State**

14. **Jordan Robinson, of, Northwestern State (La.)**
15. **Matt Williams, 3b, Baylor**
16. **Mike Wodnicki, rhp, Stanford**
17. **Josh Merrigan, lhp, Oklahoma State**
18. **Neil Simoneaux, ss, Louisiana-Lafayette**
19. Shane Komine, rhp, Nebraska
20. Bryce Kartler, lhp, Arizona State
21. **Cody Gunn, c, Brewster (Wash.) HS**
22. **Bryan Moore, 1b, Louisiana State**
23. Kevin Correia, rhp, Cal Poly San Luis Obispo
24. **Aaron Ledbetter, rhp, Westark (Ark.) CC**
25. **Dan Kantrovitz, 2b, Brown**
26. **Aaron Russelburg, rhp, Murray State**
27. Lee Gwaltney, rhp, Louisiana Tech
28. **Blake Hawksworth, rhp, Eastlake HS, Sammamish, Wash.**
29. **Pilar Amaya, ss, San Diego State**
30. **Jeffrey Jones, of, Long Beach State**
31. Marcus Markray, lhp, Springhill (La.) HS
32. **John Davie, 1b, Central Arkansas Christian HS, Little Rock, Ark.**
33. Jake Nowlen, rhp, Arkansas-Monticello
34. **Matt Pearl, of, UCLA**
35. Mike Cust, of, Immaculata HS, Whitehouse Station, N.J.
36. Billy Biggs, rhp, West Virginia
37. Richard Quihuis-Bell, 1b, Central Arizona JC
38. **Jared Blasdell, rhp, Cal Poly San Luis Obispo**
39. **Dan Shouse, lhp, Saint Louis**
40. **Steven Green, of, Arkansas-Monticello**
41. **Travis Palmer, rhp, Utah**
42. **Anthony Rawson, lhp, Southern Mississippi**
43. Jesse Kozlowski, rhp, Los Angeles Pierce JC
44. **Shane Reedy, rhp, Utah Valley State JC**
45. Billy Paganetti, of, Galena HS, Reno, Nev.
46. Drew Davidson, of, Dowling HS, West Des Moines
47. **Terry Evans, 3b, Middle Georgia JC**
48. **Mike Levy, c, Dartmouth**
49. Samuel Fisher, rhp, Dayton
50. **Mike Fox, ss, Central Florida**

SAN DIEGO PADRES

June—Regular Phase (14)

1. **Jake Gautreau, 3b, Tulane**
2. Matt Harrington, rhp, St. Paul (Northern League)
3. Tagg Bozied, 1b/3b, San Francisco
4. **Josh Barfield, 2b, Klein HS, Spring, Texas**
5. **Greg Sain, c/3b, San Diego**
6. **Jason Weidmeyer, lhp, Memphis**
7. **Doc Brooks, of, Georgia**
8. **David Pauley, rhp, Longmont (Colo.) HS**
9. **John Benick, 1b, Virginia**
10. **Ben Fox, lhp, Dixie State (Utah) JC**
11. **Marcus Nettles, of, Miami**
12. **Jordan Pickens, 1b, Cuesta (Calif.) JC**
13. **Jason Bartlett, ss, Oklahoma**
14. **Josh Carter, of, Oregon State**
15. Carlos Fisher, of, Duarte (Calif.) HS
16. **Jon Brandt, rhp, UCLA**
17. **Trevor Brown, c, Lewis-Clark State (Idaho)**
18. Scott Shapiro, rhp, St. Augustine HS, Oceanside, Calif.
19. **Jason Anderegg, rhp, Belmont**
20. Jeremy Slayden, of, Oakland HS, Murfreesboro, Tenn.
21. **Rusty Tucker, lhp, Maine**
22. Drew Macias, of, Alta Loma HS, Rancho Cucamonga, Calif.
23. Kyle Cullinan, 3b, Fullerton (Calif.) HS
24. **Joseph Hastings, 1b, East Carolina**
25. **Scott Kelly, lhp, Missouri Valley**
26. **Matt Hellman, of, Lewis-Clark State (Idaho)**
27. Elliot Singletary, 2b, North Fort Myers (Fla.) HS
28. Michael Watson, lhp, Midland (Texas) JC
29. Brendan Katin, c, Fort Myers (Fla.) HS
30. Matt Hobbs, lhp, Missouri
31. Hunter Brown, 3b, Rice
32. **Irving Falu, 2b, Angel P. Millan HS, Carolina, P.R.**
33. Rashad Smith, of, Lambuth (Tenn.)
34. **Zach Wykoff, rhp, Oxford, Ga.**
35. Chad Etheridge, of, Friendship Christian HS, Old Hickory, Tenn.
36. Shawn Leblanc, rhp, Bourgeois HS, Gray, La.
37. John Coker, of, Muskogee (Okla.) HS
38. **Anthony Lester, of, Hillsborough (Fla.) CC**
39. Nick Walter, of, Hun School, Princeton, N.J.
40. Josh Archer, c, Henry County HS, Paris, Tenn.
41. Marcos Martinez, 1b, Chaffey (Calif.) JC

SAN FRANCISCO GIANTS

June—Regular Phase (30)

1. **Brad Hennessey, rhp, Youngstown State** (Pick from Indians as compensation for Type A free agent Ellis Burks)
1. **Noah Lowry, lhp, Pepperdine**
1. **Todd Linden, of, Louisiana State** (Supplemental pick—41st—for loss of Burks)
2. **Jesse Foppert, rhp, San Francisco**
3. **Julian Benavidez, 3b, Diablo Valley (Calif.) CC**
4. **Josh Cram, rhp, Clemson**
5. **Justin Knoedler, rhp, Miami (Ohio)**
6. **David Cash, rhp, California**
7. **Jamie Athas, ss, Wake Forest**
8. **Jason Waddell, lhp, Riverside (Calif.) CC**
9. T.J. Large, rhp, Seminole (Fla.) HS
10. **Wes Hutchinson, rhp, Lewis-Clark State (Idaho)**
11. **Derin McMains, 2b, Arkansas-Little Rock**
12. **Alberto Montez, rhp, Texas**
13. **Juan Serrato, rhp, Riverside (Calif.) CC**
14. Jeffrey Timmons, c, Nova HS, Hollywood, Fla.
15. **Tyler Von Schell, 1b, UC Santa Barbara**
16. **Craig James, rhp, Killian HS, Miami**
17. **Steven Holm, ss/c, Oral Roberts**
18. **Dayton Buller, c, Fresno CC**
19. **Robbie Meyer, of, California**
20. Richard Giannotti, of, St. Thomas Aquinas HS, Fort Lauderdale
21. **Miguel Miranda, ss, Arkansas-Little Rock**
22. Karl Jernigan, of, Florida State
23. **Petersen Benjamin, rhp, Florida Atlantic**
24. Peter Healey, rhp, Cardinal Gibbons HS, Fort Lauderdale
25. **Ryan Meaux, lhp, Lamar (Colo.) CC**
26. Bobby Wilson, c, Seminole (Fla.) HS
27. **Keith Anderson, c/3b, Cal Poly San Luis Obispo**
28. **David Hixson, rhp, Gonzaga**
29. **Matt Huntingford, of, Florida International**
30. Joe Mercer, c, American River (Calif.) JC
31. **Chris Ciesluk, ss, Taunton (Mass.) HS**
32. **Brian Stirm, rhp, West Valley (Calif.) JC**
33. **Randall Spiehs, rhp, Nebraska**
34. **Aaron Hornostaj, 2b, St. Thomas of Villanova HS, Waterloo, Ontario**
35. Chris Hamblen, c, Cincinnati
36. Matt Hopper, rhp/1b, Nebraska
37. Todd Mittauer, rhp, Dade Christian HS, Cooper City, Fla.
38. Lamont Jordan, 2b, Dinwiddie (Va.) HS
39. Matthew Somnis, rhp, Tumwater HS, Olympia, Wash.
40. **Ruddy Garcia, rhp, Lake Worth (Fla.) HS**
41. Austin Allen, ss, Mount Hood (Ore.) CC
42. P.J. Hiser, rhp, Hagerstown (Md.) JC
43. Kevin Bulger, ss, Brookwood HS, Snellville, Ga.
44. **Jon Williams, c, Missouri**
45. Karl Amonite, 1b, Connors State (Okla.) JC
46. Mike Adcock, rhp, Lebanon HS, Watertown, Tenn.
47. **Scott Munter, rhp, Butler County (Kan.) CC**
48. Paul O'Toole, c, Notre Dame
49. Brian Bulger, rhp, South Georgia JC
50. P.J. McGinnis, rhp, Central Missouri State

SEATTLE MARINERS

June—Regular Phase (23)

1. (Pick to Yankees as compensation for Type A free agent Jeff Nelson)
1. **Michael Garciaparra, ss, Don Bosco HS, La Habra Heights, Calif.** (Supplemental pick—36th—for loss of Type A free

agent Alex Rodriguez)
2. **Rene Rivera, c, Papa Juan XXIII HS, Bayamon, P.R.** (Pick from Rangers as compensation for Rodriguez)
2. **Mike Wilson, of, Booker T. Washington HS, Tulsa**
3. **Lazaro Abreu, c, Southridge HS, Miami** (Pick from Phillies as compensation for Type B free agent Jose Mesa)
3. **Tim Merritt, ss, South Alabama**
4. **Bobby Livingston, lhp, Trinity Christian HS, Lubbock, Texas**
5. **John Cole, 2b/of, Nebraska**
6. **Justin Ockerman, rhp, Garden City (Mich.) HS**
7. John Axford, rhp, Assumption College SS, Brantford, Ontario
8. **Jeff Ellena, ss, Cal Poly Pomona**
9. **Justin Blood, lhp, Franklin Pierce (N.H.)**
10. **Beau Hintz, lhp, Fresno State**
11. **Josh Ellison, of, Westminster Academy, Fort Lauderdale**
12. **Mike Hrynio, 3b, Dover HS, Mine Hill, N.J.**
13. **Jason Van Meetren, of, Stanford**
14. **Blake Woods, ss, Grand Canyon (Ariz.)**
15. **Chris Colton, of, Newnan (Ga.) HS**
16. **Sean Peless, 1b, Edmonds (Wash.) CC**
17. **Ramon Royce, rhp, Lewis-Clark State (Idaho)**
18. **John Williamson, of, East Carolina**
19. **Brian Sabourin, rhp, Dakota Collegiate HS, Winnipeg, Manitoba**
20. David Purcey, lhp, Trinity Christian Academy, Dallas
21. **Matt Ware, of, Loyola HS, Malibu, Calif.**
22. Ladd Hall, rhp, Buena HS, Hereford, Ariz.
23. Aaron Braithwaite, of, Killian HS, Miami
24. Garry Bakker, rhp, Suffern HS, Sloatsburg, N.Y.
25. **Eddie Olszta, c, Butler**
26. Jon Nelson, 3b, Dixie State (Utah) JC
27. **Tim Bausher, rhp, Kutztown (Pa.)**
28. **David Morrow, rhp, Grayson County (Texas) CC**
29. Kyle Aselton, lhp, West HS, Chehalis, Wash.
30. Billy Sadler, rhp, Pensacola (Fla.) JC
31. **Jason Rainey, of, Texas Tech**
32. Bryan Vickers, c, Perrysburg (Ohio) HS
33. Tom Keefer, rhp, Byng HS, Sasakwa, Okla.
34. Trevor Heid, of, Dixie State (Utah) JC
35. Todd Holliday, lhp, South Charleston (W.Va.) HS
36. **Ben Hudson, c, Truett-McConnell (Ga.) JC**
37. **Miguel Martinez, lhp, Miami-Dade CC**
38. Bob Cramer, lhp, Long Beach State
39. Justin Ruchti, c, Klein Forest HS, Houston
40. Marquis Pettis, of, Diablo Valley (Calif.) JC
41. Kevin Guyette, rhp, Chaparral HS, Paradise Valley, Ariz.
42. Ryan Brincat, of, Mira Costa HS, Manhattan Beach, Calif.
43. Bradley Pahs, c, Chesterton HS, Porter, Ind.
44. William Keyes, rhp, St. James (Md.) HS
45. Brandon Fusilier, of, Navarro (Texas) JC
46. Alan Gannaway, rhp, Bessemer Academy, McCalla, Ala.
47. Ethan Katz, rhp, University HS, Los Angeles
48. Luis DeJesus, ss, Teodoro Aguilar Mora HS, Yabucoa, P.R.
49. Nick Hamilton, of, West Lowndes HS, Starkville, Miss.
50. Brandon Espinosa, rhp, Santa Ana (Calif.) JC

TAMPA BAY DEVIL RAYS

June—Regular Phase (3)

1. **Dewon Brazelton, rhp, Middle Tennessee State**
2. **Jon Switzer, lhp, Arizona State**
3. **Chris Flinn, rhp, Stony Brook**
4. Dave Bush, rhp, Wake Forest
5. **Chris Seddon, lhp, Canyon HS, Santa Clarita, Calif.**
6. **Matt Rico, of, Fresno CC**
7. **Tim King, lhp, Deer Park (Texas) HS**
8. **Aaron Clark, of, Alabama**
9. **Fernando Cortez, ss, Grossmont (Calif.) JC**
10. **Jason St. Clair, ss, Desert Vista HS, Phoenix**
11. Mark Worrell, rhp, John I. Leonard HS, Boynton Beach, Fla.
12. **Neville Blount, of, Chaffey (Calif.) JC**
13. **Vince Harrison, 2b, Kentucky**
14. **Tommy Nichols, 1b, Armijo HS, Fairfield, Calif.**
15. **Eric Miller, lhp, Gulf Coast HS, Naples, Fla.**
16. Tim Layden, lhp, Deer Park (N.Y.) HS
17. **Mike Navaroli, rhp, Indian River (Fla.) CC**
18. **Jonny Gomes, of, Santa Rosa (Calif.) CC**
19. Jason Hammel, rhp, Treasure Valley (Ore.) CC
20. **Jared Carney, rhp, Dallas**
21. Jarod Matthews, rhp, Yelm HS, Olympia, Wash.
22. **John-Paul Davis, 1b, Arkansas Tech**
23. **Brent Cordell, c, Cosumnes River (Calif.) JC**
24. **Brian Wolotka, of, Valparaiso**
25. Daron Roberts, c, Westview HS, Portland, Ore.
26. Josh Asanovich, 2b, Highland HS, Gold Canyon, Ariz.
27. Gaby Martinez, 1b, Blanca Malaret HS, Sabana Grande, P.R.
28. Mumba Rivera, rhp, Marshalltown (Iowa) CC
29. **Josh Parker, rhp, Wallace State (Ala.) CC**
30. Matt Wilkerson, of, Santa Margarita HS, Trabuco Canyon, Calif.
31. Diego Lopez, rhp, Calexico (Calif.) HS
32. Joey Gathright, of, LaPlace, La.
33. **Tyson Thompson, rhp, Washington State**
34. **Chad Gaudin, rhp, Crescent City Baptist HS, Harahan, La.**
35. Bryan Banks, rhp, Dunedin (Fla.) HS
36. Michael White, lhp, Countryside HS, Clearwater, Fla.
37. Michael Rider, rhp, Armijo HS, Fairfield, Calif.
38. Thomas Diamond, rhp, Archbishop Rummel HS, Metairie, La.
39. Greg Dini, c, Bishop Moore School, Orlando
40. Brett Davis, 1b, Southern Union State (Ala.) JC
41. Derek Acosta, rhp, Capistrano Valley HS, Mission Viejo, Calif.
42. Kevin Bertrand, rhp, JC of the Sequoias (Calif.)
43. Griffin Zarbough, lhp, Wallace State (Ala.) CC
44. **Danny Van Ruiten, 3b, St. John Bosco HS, LaMirada, Calif.**
45. Matt Lukevics, 2b, Jesuit HS, Tampa
46. Chris Eickhorst, c, Kean (N.J.)
47. Eric Beattie, rhp, Riverview HS, Valrico, Fla.
48. Brad Davis, c, Capistrano Valley HS, Mission Viejo, Calif.
49. Darwin Pittman, 1b, East St. John HS, Garyville, La.
50. **Nick Aiello, lhp, Oklahoma Christian**

TEXAS RANGERS

June—Regular Phase (5)

1. **Mark Teixeira, 3b, Georgia Tech**
2. (Pick to Mariners as compensation for Type A free agent Alex Rodgriguez)
3. (Pick to Angels as compensation for Type A free agent Mark Petkovsek)
4. Josh Baker, rhp, Memorial HS, Houston
5. **C.J. Wilson, lhp, Loyola Marymount**
6. **Ben Keiter, rhp, Wichita State**
7. **Patrick Boyd, of, Clemson**
8. **Masjid Khairy, of, Los Angeles CC**
9. **Gerald Smiley, rhp, Rainier Beach, Seattle**
10. **Rob Moravek, rhp, Georgia**
11. **Greg Buscher, 3b, Terry Parker HS, Jacksonville**
12. **Paul Abraham, rhp, Shippensburg (Pa.)**
13. **Michael Paustian, rhp, Fresno CC**
14. **Chris Bradshaw, rhp, Texas Christian**
15. Ryan Dixon, rhp, Seminole (Fla.) HS
16. **Royce Hampton, lhp, Lehi (Utah) HS**
17. **Randall Shelley, 3b, UCLA**
18. **Nathan Bright, rhp, Northern Colorado**
19. **Craig Frydendall, lhp, Cowley County (Kan.) CC**
20. **Jason Patty, ss, Fort Hays (Kan.) State**
21. Chad Oliva, c, Jacksonville
22. **Brad Stockton, of, Georgia Tech**
23. Scott Beerer, rhp, Orange Coast (Calif.) CC
24. Richie Gardner, rhp, Santa Rosa (Calif.) JC
25. Ryan Rote, rhp, Kettle Moraine HS, Delafield, Wis.
26. **Dustin Scheffel, rhp, Sacramento CC**
27. Timothy Lloyd, of, Christian Brothers HS, Memphis
28. Troy Roberson, rhp, Miami
29. Ryan Mask, rhp, Bakersfield (Calif.) JC
30. **Andrew Campbell, lhp, Linn-Benton (Ore.) CC**
31. Brandon Alford, lhp, Marshall (Texas) HS
32. Brandon Cornwell, rhp, James Madison
33. **Jeff Moye, rhp, Cowley County (Kan.) CC**
34. Dane DeLaRosa, rhp, Elsinore HS, Wildomar, Calif.

35. Jarvis Hicks, rhp, Durant HS, Plant City, Fla.
36. Tony Irvin, rhp, Chamberlain HS, Tampa
37. Jason Ward, rhp, Spanish Fork (Utah) HS
38. Drake Wade, of, George Jenkins HS, Lakeland, Fla.
39. Jeremy Zick, rhp, Riverside (Calif.) CC
40. Jose Romo, lhp, Riverside HS, El Paso
41. Clay Timpner, lhp/of, LaBelle HS, Alva, Fla.
42. Reid Santos, lhp, Saddleback (Calif.) JC
43. Jason Windsor, rhp, West Valley (Calif.) JC
44. Andrew Myette, rhp, JC of Southern Idaho
45. Luke Steidlmayer, rhp, UC Davis
46. Jarle Brooks, rhp, Puyallup (Wash.) HS
47. **Joldy Watts, rhp, JC of Eastern Utah**
48. Joseph Martinson, rhp, Payson (Utah) HS
49. Travis Kassebaum, of, Auburn (Wash.) HS
50. Joseph Garrett, 3b, Murray (Utah) HS

TORONTO BLUE JAYS

June—Regular Phase (15)

1. **Gabe Gross, of, Auburn**
2. **Brandon League, rhp, St. Louis HS, Honolulu**
3. **Tyrell Godwin, of, North Carolina**
4. **Chris Sheffield, rhp, Miami**
5. **Mike Rouse, ss, Cal State Fullerton**
6. **Lee Delfino, ss, East Carolina**
7. **Jason Colson, rhp, Winthrop**
8. **Sean Grimes, lhp, Saunders SS, London, Ontario**
9. **Luke Hetherington, of, Kentwood HS, Covington, Wash.**
10. **Ryan Costello, lhp, Montclair State (N.J.)**
11. Sean Gamble, of, Jefferson Davis HS, Montgomery, Ala.
12. **Ernie Durazo, 1b, Arizona**
13. **Brendan Fuller, rhp, South Florida**
14. **David Corrente, c, Chatham-Kent SS, Chatham, Ontario**
15. Nick Thomas, rhp, Laguna Creek HS, Elk Grove, Calif.
16. Rock Mills, c, Pepperdine
17. **Chris Neylan, lhp, Steinert HS, Trenton, N.J.**
18. **Aaron McEachran, 3b, Northern Iowa**
19. **Isaac Iorg, ss, Knoxville**
20. **Jon Ashford, of, Covington (Tenn.) HS**
21. Jeff Fiorentino, of, Nova HS, Davie, Fla.
22. **Darren Heal, rhp, Oklahoma State**
23. Garrick Evans, of, Lake Braddock HS, Burke, Va.
24. **Dave Gassner, lhp, Purdue**
25. **Mark Comolli, rhp, Delaware Tech JC**
26. **Nick Tempesta, ss, Eastern Connecticut State**
27. Adam Daniels, lhp, North Vancouver, B.C
28. Joel Kirsten, lhp, Los Angeles Pierce JC
29. Mark McDonald, rhp, Robinson HS, Burlington, Ontario
30. Arturo Lopez, of, Northwest Christian Academy, Miami
31. Robert Grana, c, Cimarron Memorial HS, Las Vegas
32. Adam Sanabria, lhp, Lake Mary HS, Longwood, Fla.
33. Kellen Ludwig, rhp, Lee County HS, Leesburg, Ga.
34. Brian Ennis, rhp, Harding University HS, Charlotte
35. Nicholas Gor, rhp, Saddleback (Calif.) CC
36. Brian McFadden, of, Lake City (S.C.) HS
37. Felix Peguero, of, Bladensburg (Md.) HS
38. **Timothy Whitaker, c, South Carolina**
39. Adam Rodgers, c, Grapevine (Texas) HS
40. Alex Castellvi, c, Plant HS, Tampa
41. Ryan Olivo, 2b, Grapevine (Texas) HS
42. Jared Sanders, rhp, Mount Hood (Ore.) CC
43. P.J. McDonald, rhp, Robinson HS, Burlington, Ontario
44. Kevin Johnston, rhp, Matheson HS, Surrey, B.C
45. Lawrence Best-Berfet, 2b, CC of Morris County (N.J.)
46. Sean Barker, inf, Louisiana State
47. Chris Jones, 1b, Heritage HS, Colleyville, Texas
48. Scott Shoemaker, rhp, Grossmont (Calif.) JC
49. Kenny Holmberg, 2b, Dunedin (Fla.) HS
50. **Floyd Albert, lhp, Kernohan Park HS, St. Catharines, Ontario**

2002 TAMPA BAY GETS STEAL IN UPTON AS BONUSES DECREASE FOR FIRST TIME IN MORE THAN A DECADE

For a change, the biggest news involving the draft didn't concern which prospects were taken by which teams. The most significant developments in 2002 were the curbing of first-round bonus inflation.

After Baseball America started tracking bonuses in 1989, the average first-round bonus always rose from one year to the next. Increases of 25 percent or more were commonplace. Inflation slowed to an annual average of 10 percent in 1999-2001, then hit the wall in 2002.

Significant alterations to draft rules were also discussed. While talk of a worldwide draft and other extensive changes to the process were tabled when the owners and players narrowly averted a strike by agreeing to a Basic Agreement on Aug. 30, the sides did agree to adjust the rules eventually. Those changes had not happened yet, but by 2009 bonus inflation had taken off again to such a degree that draft changes became a front and center issue.

A joint committee of MLB representatives, union officials and possibly owners planned to revisit the rules changes and work toward the formation of a worldwide draft. Officials considered shortening the draft from its existing 50 rounds to somewhere between 20 and 38. The committee also planned to consider allowing teams to trade picks, which has been forbidden since the draft started in 1965.

The Pirates owned the No. 1 pick in the 2002 draft. Their decision went down to the wire, as they whittled their list of candidates down to three: Ball State righthander Brian Bullington, Virginia high school shortstop B.J. Upton and Canadian prep lefthander Adam Loewen.

Bullington, tabbed as a future first-round pick since his freshman year, pushed his velocity to a consistent 92-94 mph and refined a hard slider as a junior. He was the Pirates' man. They made courtesy calls to the teams picking behind them, the Devil Rays and Reds, to let them know of their intent.

The next step was to contact Bullington's advisers at IMG to discuss bonus parameters before the draft. (While this technically violates MLB rules, virtually every team does this while MLB looks the other way.) Several sources said the Pirates floated a $4 million deal.

When IMG declined and countered with $6 million, the Pirates' plans weren't concrete any longer. Pittsburgh made offers to Upton and Loewen, but were rebuffed in both cases. The Pirates also sounded out Texas high school lefthander Scott Kazmir, though they didn't regard him as highly as some other teams did and didn't mention a specific dollar figure.

BILL SETLIFF

B.J. Upton turned out much better than No. 1 overall pick Bryan Bullington

That led them back to Bullington. They decided to take him and let negotiations unfold as they may. He finally signed in October for a bonus of $4 million.

Upton, the top position player available, went No. 2 overall to the Devil Rays. He didn't sign until Sept. 11. Like Dewon Brazelton did after Tampa Bay selected him third overall in 2001, Upton balked at the Rays' first offers because they contained relatively little up-front money. Upton eventually agreed to $4.6 million over five years, with $250,000 payable immediately.

The Reds had no such trouble with the No. 3 pick. Cincinnati officials were split on Kazmir and California prep righthander Chris Gruler, both of whom had bullpen sessions at Cinergy Field the weekend prior to the draft. Word quickly spread that Gruler's workout was lackluster while Kazmir's was spectacular. The assumption was that Cincinnati would go with Kazmir.

But the Reds never talked money with Kazmir, apparently using him to leverage Gruler into signing for a club-record $2.5 million bonus, an agreement announced shortly after teams finished drafting.

Neither Gruler nor Bullington worked out, while both Upton and Kazmir became solid major leaguers and potential stars.

Ability, Not Signability

Loewen, the No. 4 overall selection by the Orioles, decided to attend Chipola (Fla.) Junior College, making him the highest-drafted player ever to take the draft-and-follow route. He got to negotiate with the Orioles until a week before the 2003 draft, and ultimately signed a major league contract worth a shade more than $4 million.

Loewen, too, didn't pan out, and he was trying to resurrect his career with the Blue Jays as a position player.

For the most part, teams went after ability and didn't let signability dictate their first-round selections. After Bullington, the rest of the top 10 unfolded mostly as expected, though Kazmir's name was notably absent.

Kazmir was believed to want a bonus in the $3.5 million range, and there were few teams with early picks who had the desire and the resources to spend more than MLB-recommended money on their first-round pick. The Mets pounced on him at No. 15, and he agreed to a $2.15 million deal two months after the draft. He was a prep teammate of Clint Everts, and they made Houston's Cypress Falls High the fourth high school to produce two first-round picks in a single draft.

Interestingly, Kazmir also fell into the Devil Rays' laps, though it was through a trade and not through the draft. Some Mets officials doubted him because of his small frame, so they included him in a 2004 deadline deal for Victor Zambrano—to Mets fans' eternal chagrin.

Two of the best college pitchers available also slid because of signability concerns. Bobby Brownlie was considered the top overall prospect in the 2002 draft class before he came down with biceps tendinitis and didn't pitch well for Rutgers down the stretch. He went 21st overall to the Cubs. Stanford's Jeremy Guthrie, who like Brownlie was advised by Scott Boras, went one pick later to the Indians. Guthrie became the 18th player in draft history to receive a major league contract, signing a four-year, $4 million deal.

DRAFT 02: FIRST-ROUND PICKS

No.	Club	Player, Pos.	School	Hometown	Ht.	Wt.	B-T	Age
1.	Pirates	Bryan Bullington, rhp	Ball State	Madison, Ind.	6-5	212	R-R	21
2.	Devil Rays	B. J. Upton, ss	Greenbrier Christian Acad.	Chesapeake, Va.	6-2	170	R-R	17
3.	Reds	Chris Gruler, rhp	Liberty HS	Brentwood, Calif.	6-3	200	R-R	18
4.	Orioles	Adam Loewen, lhp	FraserValley Christian HS	Surrey, B. C.	6-6	210	L-L	18
5.	Expos	Clint Everts, rhp	Cypress Falls HS	Houston	6-2	170	B-R	17
6.	Royals	Zack Greinke, rhp	Apopka HS	Orlando	6-2	185	R-R	18
7.	Brewers	Prince Fielder, 1b	Eau Gallie HS	Melbourne, Fla.	5-11	250	L-R	18
8.	Tigers	Scott Moore, ss	Cypress HS	Cypress, Calif.	6-2	170	L-R	18
9.	Rockies	Jeff Francis, lhp	British Columbia	Vancouver, B. C.	6-5	195	L-L	21
10.	Rangers	Drew Meyer, ss	South Carolina	Charleston, S. C.	5-11	183	L-R	20
11.	Marlins	Jeremy Hermida, of	Wheeler HS	Marietta, Ga.	6-3	180	L-R	18
12.	Angels	Joe Saunders, lhp	Virginia Tech	Springfield, Va.	6-3	195	L-L	20
13.	Padres	Khalil Greene, ss	Clemson	Key West, Fla.	5-10	190	R-R	22
14.	Blue Jays	Russ Adams, 2b	North Carolina	Laurinburg, N. C.	6-1	170	L-R	21
15.	Mets	Scott Kazmir, lhp	Cypress Falls HS	Houston	6-0	170	L-L	18
16.	Athletics	Nick Swisher, 1b/of	Ohio State	Parkersburg, W. Va.	6-0	200	B-L	21
17.	Phillies	Cole Hamels, lhp	Rancho Bernardo HS	San Diego	6-2	185	L-L	18
18.	White Sox	Royce Ring, lhp	San Diego State	San Diego	6-0	215	L-L	21
19.	Dodgers	James Loney, 1b	Elkins HS	Missouri City, Texas	6-3	190	L-L	18
20.	Twins	Denard Span, of	Tampa Catholic HS	Tampa	6-1	175	L-L	18
21.	Cubs	Bobby Brownlie, rhp	Rutgers	Edison, N. J.	6-1	195	R-R	21
22.	Indians	Jeremy Guthrie, rhp	Stanford	Ashland, Ore.	6-1	195	R-R	23
23.	Braves	Jeff Francoeur, of	Parkview HS	Lilburn, Ga.	6-4	205	R-R	18
24.	Athletics	Joseph Blanton, rhp	Kentucky	Brownsville, Ky.	6-2	210	R-R	21
25.	Giants	Matt Cain, rhp	Houston HS	Germantown, Tenn.	6-3	185	R-R	17
26.	Athletics	John McCurdy, ss	Maryland	Crofton, Md.	6-2	195	R-R	21
27.	Diamondbacks	Sergio Santos, ss	Mater Dei HS	Hacienda Heights, Calif.	6-3	190	R-R	18
28.	Mariners	John Mayberry, 1b	Rockhurst HS	Kansas City, Mo.	6-4	195	R-R	18
29.	Astros	Derick Grigsby, rhp	Northeast Texas CC	Marshall, Texas	6-0	200	R-R	19
30.	Athletics	Ben Fritz, rhp	Fresno State	San Jose	6-4	220	R-R	21

2002

CLUB-BY-CLUB SELECTIONS

ANAHEIM ANGELS

June—Regular Phase (12)

1. **Joe Saunders, lhp, Virginia Tech**
2. **Kevin Jepsen, rhp, Bishop Manogue HS, Sparks, Nev.**
3. **Kyle Pawelczyk, lhp, Chipola (Fla.) JC**
4. **Jordan Renz, of, Tulsa Union HS, Broken Arrow, Okla.**
5. **Javy Rodriguez, ss, Miami**
6. **Chris Walston, 1b, El Capitan HS, Lakeside, Calif.**
7. Jeff Leise, of, Nebraska
8. **James Holcomb, rhp, Nevada**
9. **Caleb Maher, of, Ceres (Calif.) HS**
10. **Howie Kendrick, 2b, St John's River (Fla.) CC**
11. **Aaron Peel, of, Seminole (Texas) HS**
12. **Ryan Kenning, of, New Mexico State**
13. **Osvaldo Lugo, rhp, Florida International**
14. **Ronnie Ray, rhp, Pacific (Mo.) HS**
15. **Justin Hancock, 3b, Florida Southern**
16. **Tommy Duenas, c, Florida International**
17. Tony Mandel, rhp, Chipola (Fla.) JC
18. **Nic Touchstone, lhp, Okaloosa-Walton (Fla.) JC**
19. **Mike Perdomo, of, Broward (Fla.) CC**
20. Ryan Broderick, of, Palm Desert HS, Rancho Mirage, Calif.
21. **Matt McCarthy, lhp, Yale**
22. **Scott Hindman, lhp, Princeton**
23. Andrew Slorp, rhp, Bellarmine Prep, Morgan Hill, Calif.
24. **Brett Martinez, c, Redlands (Calif.) East Valley HS**
25. **Michel Simard, rhp, St. Petersburg (Fla.) JC**
26. **Alex Dvorsky, c, Northern Iowa**
27. **Bryan Williams, rhp, Jacksonville**
28. **Jake Mathis, 3b, Alabama-Huntsville**
29. Ryan Rote, rhp, Kishwaukee (Ill.) JC
30. **Jeff Marquez, rhp, Broward (Fla.) CC**
31. **Ross Lewis, rhp/of, Central Florida CC**
32. Chris Hunter, rhp, Utah Valley State JC
33. **Chris Roque, rhp, Broward (Fla.) CC**
34. Jeremy King, lhp, Itawamba (Miss.) JC
35. **Jason Sugden, of, Harrisburg, Pa.**
36. Matt Byrd, c, Hunt HS, Kenly, N.C.
37. Trevor Weedon, c, Nordhoff HS, Ojai, Calif.
38. Buck Shaw, rhp, Wagoner (Okla.) HS
39. Taylor McIntyre, lhp, Edmond Santa Fe HS, Oklahoma City
40. Adam Rodgers, c, Grayson County (Texas) CC
41. **Jason Cox, 1b, Lamar (Colo.) CC**
42. Brad Beaman, of, Northglenn HS, Thornton, Colo.
43. Steven Delabar, rhp, Volunteer State (Tenn.) CC
44. **Wayne Hedden, rhp, Hillsborough (Fla.) CC**
45. Shawn McGill, c, South Kingstown HS, Wakefield, R.I.
46. Brock Keffer, rhp, Illinois Valley CC
47. **Karl Gelinas, rhp, Edouard Montpetit (Quebec)**
48. **Bobby Wilson, c, St. Petersburg (Fla.) CC**
49. **Jason Corbett, rhp, Palm Harbor (Fla.) University HS**
50. Cody Dickens, rhp, Forbush HS, East Bend, N.C.

ARIZONA DIAMONDBACKS

June—Regular Phase (27)

1. **Sergio Santos, ss, Mater Dei HS, Hacienda Heights, Calif.**
2. **Chris Snyder, c, Houston**
3. **Jared Doyle, lhp, James Madison**
4. **Lance Cormier, rhp, Alabama**
5. **Mark Rosen, lhp, Salisbury (Conn.) Prep**
6. **Brian Barden, 3b, Oregon State**
7. **Matt Henrie, rhp, Clemson**
8. Ryan Mahoney, c, Carmel HS, Patterson, N.Y.
9. **Klent Corley, rhp, Grand Canyon (Ariz.)**
10. Mike Pierce, c, Clovis (Calif.) HS
11. **Nebasset Brown, 2b, Oklahoma State**
12. **Mitch Douglas, lhp, Augusta State (Ga.)**
13. **Adam Haley, ss, Louisville**
14. **Jay Garthwaite, of, Washngton**
15. **Dustin Nippert, rhp, West Virginia**
16. **Bryan Johnson, 1b, Washington**
17. **Donnie Saba, of, Utah**
18. **Matt Morgan, ss, Lewis-Clark State (Idaho)**
19. **Sam Smith, rhp, South Alabama**
20. **Jeff Stanek, 1b, Southern Illinois**
21. **Dan Callahan, of, Tufts (Mass.)**
22. Kenneth Parker, 1b, Henry Foss HS, Tacoma
23. **Jared Bonnell, rhp, Nevada-Las Vegas**
24. **Matt Incinelli, rhp, North Florida**
25. **Bookie Gates, 2b, Washington State**
26. **Wes Gilliam, lhp, Illinois-Chicago**
27. **Josh Kranawetter, rhp, Polk (Fla.) CC**
28. **Sean Luellwitz, 1b/c, Vanderbilt**
29. Mike Buss, rhp, Wellington (Fla.) Community HS
30. Anthony Isabella, of, Chemeketa (Ore.) CC
31. **Clint Goocher, lhp, San Jacinto (Texas) JC**
32. T.J. Large, rhp, Chipola (Fla.) JC
33. Donta Warfield, ss, Riverview HS, Sarasota, Fla.
34. Jesus Albino, rhp, Northwest Mississippi CC
35. Jake Hanen, of, Scottsdale (Ariz.) CC
36. Nicholas Richardson, c, Elgin (Ill.) CC
37. Kirk Gross, rhp, San Ramon Valley HS, Danville, Calif.
38. Matt Falk, rhp, Dana Hills HS, San Juan Capistrano, Calif.
39. **Grady Symonds, c, Hawaii**
40. **Billy Biggs, rhp, West Virginia**
41. **Keith Whatley, lhp, Houston**
42. Mike Ridgway, lhp, Tacoma (Wash.) CC
43. Kris Krise, rhp, Crescenta Valley HS, La Crescenta, Calif.
44. Conor Lalor, rhp, Houston HS, Germantown, Tenn.
45. Jon Crosby, rhp, Christian Brothers HS, Germantown, Tenn.
46. Ryan Gloger, lhp, South Florida
47. **Robert Ferns, rhp, Darton (Ga.) CC**
48. Ron Lowe, lhp, Ridgewood HS, New Port Richey, Fla.
49. Matt Raguse, rhp, St. Louis CC-Forest Park
50. Kyle Reynolds, ss, Second Baptist HS, Houston

ATLANTA BRAVES

June—Regular Phase (23)

1. **Jeff Francoeur, of, Parkview HS, Lilburn, Ga.**
1. **Dan Meyer, lhp, James Madison** (Supplemental pick—34th—for loss of Type A free agent Steve Karsay)
2. **Brian McCann, c, Duluth (Ga.) HS**
2. Tyler Greene, ss, St. Thomas Aquinas HS, Plantation, Fla. (Pick from Yankees as compensation for Karsay)
3. **Charlie Morton, rhp, Joel Barlow HS, Redding, Conn.**
4. **Steve Russell, rhp, Cimarron Memorial HS, Las Vegas**
5. Kris Harvey, c, Bandys HS, Catawba, N.C.
6. **James Jurries, 1b, Tulane**
7. Pat Clayton, rhp, Walton HS, Marietta, Ga.
8. **Jon Schuerholz, ss, Auburn**
9. Nick Starnes, rhp, Graham HS, Haw River, N.C.
10. **Yaron Peters, 1b, South Carolina**
11. **Mike Grasso, 2b, Albany**
12. **Wes Timmons, ss, Bethune-Cookman**
13. **Daniel Mead, lhp, Manatee (Fla.) JC**
14. **Michael Reiss, rhp, Seminole State (Okla.) CC**
15. J.P. Lowen, c, Lassiter HS, Marietta, Ga.
16. **Mike Mueller, rhp, Auburn**
17. **Brad David, lhp, Louisiana State**
18. **Josh Adams, lhp, Franklin (Ind.)**
19. **Fernando Tadefa, lhp, St. Mary's (Texas)**
20. **Chuck James, lhp, Chattahoochee Valley (Ala.) CC**
21. **Aaron Parker, rhp, Sonoma State (Calif.)**

22. Trey Shields, rhp, Bay HS, Panama City, Fla.
23. Tim Cunningham, lhp, Stanford
24. **Paul Bush, rhp, Georgia Southwestern**
25. **Steven Reiss, rhp, Seminole State (Okla.) CC**
26. Chris Maher, rhp, Pensacola (Fla.) JC
27. Travis Stanton, rhp, Lake City (Fla.) CC
28. **Devin Anderson, lhp, West Orange HS, Ocoee, Fla.**
29. Mark Wagner, c, Mayfair HS, Lakewood, Calif.
30. Cooper Osteen, ss, Indian River (Fla.) CC
31. Brandon Nall, rhp, George Wallace (Ala.) CC
32. Darrell Qualls, ss, Middleburg (Fla.) HS
33. Jacob Eckley, lhp, Burke HS, Omaha
34. Ryan Patterson, of, Texarkana (Texas) CC
35. Ken Brock, lhp, Lane (Ore.) CC
36. Buzz Vargas, rhp, Bay City (Texas) HS
37. Matt Dale, lhp, Walton HS, Marietta, Ga.
38. Jeffrey Timmons, c, Manatee (Fla.) CC
39. Brett Young, 1b, Gloucester County (N.J.) CC
40. Kevin Kotch, c, Middlesex (N.J.) HS
41. David Hayes, rhp, American Heritage HS, Sunrise, Fla.
42. Ryan Paul, lhp, Moorpark (Calif.) HS
43. Ken Livesley, rhp, Cosumnes River (Calif.) CC
44. Chris Tyndall, rhp, Armstrong (Ill.) HS
45. **Daniel Collins, lhp, Indian River (Fla.) CC**
46. Brandon Judge, rhp, Santa Margarita HS, Rancho Santa Margarita, Calif.
47. **Rick Aguilar, lhp, Cypress (Calif.) JC**
48. Christopher Widing, lhp, East Paulding HS, Dallas, Ga.
49. Christopher Dunbar, of, La Conner HS, Camana Island, Wash.
50. Matt Handley, lhp, Greater Atlanta Christian HS, Duluth, Ga.

BALTIMORE ORIOLES

June—Regular Phase (4)

1. **Adam Loewen, lhp, Fraser Valley Christian HS, Surrey, B.C**
2. **Corey Shafer, of, Choctaw (Okla.) HS**
3. **Val Majewski, of, Rutgers**
4. **Tim Gilhooly, of, Pacific**
5. **Hayden Penn, rhp, Santana HS, Santee, Calif.**
6. **John Maine, rhp, UNC Charlotte**
7. **Paul Henry, rhp, Ball State**
8. **Ryan Hubele, c, Texas**
9. **Trevor Caughey, lhp, Cuesta (Calif.) JC**
10. **Matt Bolander, rhp, Pendleton Heights HS, Anderson, Ind.**
11. Mark McCormick, rhp, Clear Creek HS, Clear Lake Shores, Texas
12. **Brandon Fahey, 3b, Texas**
13. **Mike Huggins, 1b, Baylor**
14. **Matthew Rohr, lhp, Cal State San Bernardino**
15. **Matthew Howerton, of, Riverdale HS, Fort Myers, Fla.**
16. **Gerardo Alvarez, ss, Texas Tech**
17. **Neal Stephenson, of, Texas A&M**
18. **Carl Makowsky, rhp, Northwestern State**
19. **Mike Patitucci, lhp, Oklahoma State**
20. **George Cox, c, Central Florida**
21. **Gregg Davies, of, Towson**
22. **Zach Sutton, rhp, Central Florida**
23. **Jason Cierlik, lhp, Minnesota State-Mankato**
24. Ryan Soehlig, 3b, North Florida
25. **Tim Thurman, 1b, Cal Poly Pomona**
26. **Erik Smallwood, of, South Alabama**
27. Antoan Richardson, of, Palm Beach (Fla.) JC
28. **Zach Davis, of, J.A. Fair HS, Little Rock, Ark.**
29. **Edward Colbert, of, Catonsville (Md.) CC**
30. **Mel Spivey, rhp, South Alabama**
31. **Justin Nash, rhp, Penn State**
32. **Whitney Robinson-Pierce, c, Cuesta (Calif.) JC**
33. **Ryan Childs, rhp, Clemson**
34. **Levi Robinson, ss, Texas Christian**
35. **Nick McCurdy, rhp, Oklahoma State**
36. Jordan Compton, lhp, Haysi (Va.) HS
37. **Russell Petrick, lhp, Bellevue (Wash.) CC**
38. Alex Muszynski, 1b, Alpena (Mich.) HS
39. **Henry Lozado, rhp, Adolfina Irizarry de Puig HS, Toa Baja, P.R.**
40. Steven Guerra, rhp, Paso Robles (Calif.) HS
41. Chuck White, c, Overlea HS, Baltimore
42. Barry Roe, rhp, Heath (Okla.) HS
43. Randy Youtsey, 2b, Coolidge (Ariz.) HS
44. Brad Wiggins, of, Arlington Heights HS, Fort Worth
45. **Jim Cooney, lhp, Florida Atlantic**
46. David Mittelberger, lhp, Righetti HS, Santa Maria, Calif.
47. Andre Psaradelis, of, Bellevue (Wash.) CC
48. **Mark Wahl, c, Dayton**
49. Gabe Somarriba, of, Florida Atlantic
50. Allen Ponder, rhp, Lee-Scott Academy, Auburn, Ala.

BOSTON RED SOX

June—Regular Phase (16)

1. (Pick to Athletics as compensation for Type A free agent Johnny Damon)
2. **Jon Lester, lhp, Bellarmine Prep, Puyallup, Wash.**
3. **Scott White, 3b, Walton HS, Marietta, Ga.**
4. **Chris Smith, rhp, UC Riverside**
5. **Chad Spann, ss, Southland Academy, Buena Vista, Ga.**
6. Barrett Browning, lhp, Wayne County HS, Jesup, Ga.
7. Jason Neighborgall, rhp, Riverside HS, Durham, N.C.
8. **Brandon Moss, ss, Loganville HS, Monroe, Ga.**
9. **Tyler Pelland, lhp, Mount Abraham HS, Bristol, Vt.**
10. **Greg Stone, ss, Bacone (Okla.)**
11. **Mike Goss, of, Jackson State**
12. Dustin Majewski, of, Texas
13. Stoney Stone, rhp, Ruston (La.) HS
14. **Andy Priola, rhp, Faulkner (Ala.)**
15. **Ian Cronkhite, of, Westmoore HS, Oklahoma City**
16. **Peter Ciofrone, ss, Smithtown HS, Nesconset, N.Y.**
17. **Arian Alcala, 3b, St. Thomas (Fla.)**
18. **Brandon Smith, rhp, Southeast Missouri State**
19. **Tom MacLane, lhp, Florida Atlantic**
20. **Luis Villarreal, lhp, Northwood (Texas)**
21. **Alberto Concepcion, c, Southern California**
22. John Anderson, rhp, Arkansas State
23. **Dave Pahucki, rhp, Siena**
24. **Pat Boran, ss, Princeton**
25. **Jim Buckley, c, Siena**
26. Adam Davis, rhp, Metter HS, Pulaski, Ga.
27. Mike Armstrong, of, Chabot (Calif.) JC
28. **Mike Barclay, of, South Florida**
29. Matt Clarkson, c, Broken Arrow (Okla.) HS
30. Jonathan Williams, rhp, Opelika (Ala.) HS
31. Steve Boggs, of, San Diego HS
32. Brock Hunton, rhp, Dublin Coffman HS, Dublin, Ohio
33. Luke Taylor, rhp, Lowndes HS, Valdosta, Ga.
34. Mitchell Woolf, rhp, Madison HS, Rexburg, Idaho
35. **Jose Vaquedano, rhp, Vernon Regional (Texas) JC**
36. Don Powers, rhp, Shawnee (Okla.) HS
37. Ricky Romero, lhp, Roosevelt HS, Los Angeles
38. Koley Kolberg, rhp, Navarro (Texas) JC
39. Tyler Jacobson, rhp, Auburn River HS, Sumner, Wash.
40. Dustin Roddy, c, Northeast Texas CC
41. Matt Inouye, c, Mid-Pacific HS, Honolulu
42. Rosalino Valenzuela, rhp, Marcos de Niza HS, Guadalupe, Ariz.
43. Lance Schartz, c, Garden City (Kan.) CC
44. David Baker, c, Rogers HS, Puyallup, Wash.
45. Brian Bannister, rhp, Southern California
46. West Harris, lhp, Lone Oak HS, Paducah, Ky.
47. **Anthony Bianucci, of, Daytona Beach (Fla.) CC**
48. Sergio Roman, c, Allen County (Kan.) CC
49. Robert Caruso, 1b, Chaminade-Madonna Prep, Pembroke Pines, Fla.
50. Seth Dhaenens, ss, Mountain Pointe HS, Chandler, Ariz.

CHICAGO CUBS

June—Regular Phase (21)

1. **Bobby Brownlie, rhp, Rutgers**
1. **Luke Hagerty, lhp, Ball State** (Supplemental pick—32nd—for loss of Type A free agent David Weathers)
1. **Chadd Blasko, rhp, Purdue** (Supplemental pick—36th—for loss of Type A free agent Rondell White)

1. **Matt Clanton, rhp, Orange Coast (Calif.) JC** (Supplemental pick—38th-for loss of Type A free agent Todd Van Poppel)
2. **Brian Dopirak, 1b, Dunedin (Fla.) HS** (Pick from Mets as compensation for Weathers)
2. **Justin Jones, lhp, Kellam HS, Virginia Beach**
3. **Billy Petrick, rhp, Morris (Ill.) HS**
3. **Matt Craig, ss, Richmond** (Pick from Yankees as compensation for White)
4. **Rich Hill, lhp, Michigan** (Pick from Rangers as compensation for Van Poppel)
4. **Alan Rick, c, Palatka (Fla.) HS**
5. Shawn Scobee, of, Rio Linda (Calif.) HS
6. **Chris Walker, of, Georgia Southern**
7. **Joey Monahan, ss, Liberty**
8. **Jason Fransz, of, Oklahoma**
9. **Adam Greenberg, of, North Carolina**
10. **Keith Butler, of, Liberty**
11. **Chris Miller, c, UC Irvine**
12. **Jason Wylie, rhp, Utah**
13. **Micah Hoffpauir, of, Lamar**
14. **Rocky Cherry, rhp, Oklahoma**
15. **C.J. Medlin, c, Seminole State (Okla.) JC**
16. **Jemel Spearman, ss, Georgia Southern**
17. Forrest Beverly, lhp, Conway (S.C.) HS
18. **Donnie Hood, ss, Kennesaw State (Ga.)**
19. **Rick Atlee, rhp, Lamar**
20. **Matthew Hines, rhp, Olivet Nazarene (Ill.)**
21. **Paul O'Toole, c, Notre Dame**
22. Taylor Teagarden, c, Creekview HS, Carrollton, Texas
23. **Steve O'Sullivan, ss, Marist**
24. Ben Thurmond, rhp, Winthrop
25. **Bear Bay, rhp, Angelina (Texas) JC**
26. Jeff Jacobsen, rhp, Durango HS, Las Vegas
27. **Travis Welsch, ss/2b, Northern Iowa**
28. Evan Seibly, lhp, Los Angeles Pierce JC
29. Brett Lewis, rhp, Georgia Southern
30. Kyle Emmons, ss, Chaparral HS, Scottsdale, Ariz.
31. Kurt Steele, rhp/ss, Crescent Valley HS, Corvallis, Ore.
32. Jose Rios, ss, Pablo Gonzalez Bendecia HS, Barranquitas, P.R.
33. Adam Harvey, c, Celina (Texas) HS
34. Grant Staniszewski, c, Marquette HS, Chesterfield, Mo.
35. Anthony McLin, c, McLaurin HS, Florence, Miss.
36. Kalen Gibson, rhp, Webster HS, Slaughters, Ky.
37. Kyle Dubois, rhp, Manatee (Fla.) JC
38. **Randy Wells, c, Southwestern Illinois JC**
39. Danny DeSouza, of, Xaverian HS, Brooklyn
40. Collin Walker, rhp, Minooka HS, Channahon, Ill.
41. Mark Holliman, rhp, Germantown (Tenn.) HS
42. Geoff Orr, ss, Carl Sandburg HS, Orland Park, Ill.
43. Cory Anderson, rhp, Chaparral HS, Scottsdale, Ariz.
44. Jose Cortez, c, Pomona-Pitzer (Calif.)
45. Chris Ericksen, lhp, Joliet (Ill.) Catholic Academy
46. **Patrick McIntyre, c, Walla Walla (Wash.) CC**
47. Josh Morgan, c, Thomasville (Ala.) HS
48. Clemon Bailey, of, Southern HS, Durham, N.C.
49. Gary Kerschke, rhp, Bartlett HS, Hanover Park, Ill.
50. Bryan Kayser, 1b, Bartlesville (Okla.) HS

CHICAGO WHITE SOX

June—Regular Phase (18)

1. **Royce Ring, lhp, San Diego State**
2. **Jeremy Reed, of, Long Beach State**
3. **Josh Rupe, rhp, Louisburg (N.C.) JC**
4. **Ryan Rodriguez, lhp, Keller (Texas) HS**
5. **B.J. LaMura, rhp, Clemson**
6. Chris Getz, ss, Grosse Pointe South HS, Grosse Pointe Farms, Mich.
7. **Micah Schnurstein, 3b, Basic HS, Henderson, Nev.**
8. **Sean Tracey, rhp, UC Irvine**
9. **Todd Deininger, rhp, Texas A&M**
10. **Orionny Lopez, rhp, Forest Hill HS, West Palm Beach, Fla.**
11. **Matt Herring, 1b/of, Georgia Southern**
12. Jayson Ruhlman, lhp, L'Anse Creuse North HS, Macomb, Mich.
13. **Demetrius Banks, lhp, Chattahoochee Valley (Ala.) CC**
14. Christian Madson, rhp, Bloomingdale HS, Valrico, Fla.
15. **Adam Larson, rhp, Middle Tennessee State**
16. **Daniel Haigwood, lhp, Midland HS, Batesville, Ark.**
17. **Brandon McCarthy, rhp, Lamar (Colo.) CC**
18. **Shane Scoville, c, South Alabama**
19. Paul Keck, c, Granada HS, Pleasanton, Calif.
20. **Boone Logan, lhp, Sandra Day O'Connor HS, Helotes, Texas**
21. **Seth Morris, of, Kentucky**
22. **Eric Keefner, 1b, Mesa (Ariz.) CC**
23. David Beasley, lhp, Cooper City (Fla.) HS
24. **Thomas Brice, 1b/of, Faulkner State (Ala.) JC**
25. **Jay Marshall, lhp, Jefferson (Mo.) JC**
26. Kris Dufner, ss, Delaware
27. **Michael Bohlander, 1b, Pace (N.Y.)**
28. Hector Ambriz, rhp, Valencia HS, Placentia, Calif.
29. Neil Giesler, 3b, Jasper (Ind.) HS
30. **Jake Nowlen, rhp, Arkansas-Monticello**
31. **Edgar Varela, 3b, Long Beach State**
32. **Rick Hummel, rhp, Indianapolis**
33. Tony Sipp, lhp, Okaloosa-Walton (Fla.) CC
34. Brandon Durden, lhp, Cook (Ga.) HS
35. Eric Everly, lhp, Seagoville (Texas) HS
36. Jason Pilkington, lhp, Central Arizona JC
37. **Jamin Hutchingson, rhp, Fayetteville (Ark.) HS**
38. D.J. Wabick, of, Stagg HS, Palos Park, Ill.
39. Gabriel Casanova, 2b, Coral Park HS, Miami
40. Dennis Pawelek, rhp, Snow (Utah) JC
41. Daniel Barone, rhp, Monterey Peninsula (Calif.) JC
42. Ian Ganzer, rhp, Wellington (Fla.) Community HS
43. Matthew Sibigtroth, ss, Kishwaukee (Ill.) JC
44. Ramon Castro, 2b/ss, George Washington HS, Manhattan
45. Jorge Mico, c, Hialeah (Fla.) HS
46. Jeremy Paul, c, Trinity International (Ill.)
47. Tim Grogan, ss, Covington (Ky.) Catholic HS
48. Anthony Manuel, 2b, Kishwaukee (Ill.) JC
49. **Fernando Hernandez, rhp, Miami Southwest HS**
50. **Matt Payne, rhp, California**

CINCINNATI REDS

June—Regular Phase (3)

1. **Chris Gruler, rhp, Liberty Union HS, Brentwood, Calif.**
1. **Mark Schramek, 3b, Texas-San Antonio** (Supplemental pick—40th—for failure to sign 2001 first-rounder Jeremy Sowers)
2. **Joey Votto, c, Richview Collegiate Institute, Toronto**
3. **Kyle Edens, rhp, Baylor**
4. **Camilo Vazquez, lhp, Hialeah (Fla.) HS**
5. **Kevin Howard, 3b, Miami**
6. **Walter Olmstead, 1b, Texas Christian**
7. **Corey Wachman, rhp, Valdosta State (Ga.)**
8. **O.J. King, rhp, Northwestern State (La.)**
9. **Steve Booth, c, San Francisco**
10. **Frankie Keller, lhp, Abilene (Texas) Christian**
11. **Mike Bassett, of, George Washington**
12. **Don Gemmell, rhp, San Jose State**
13. Jose Enrique Cruz, ss, Rice
14. **Joe Curran, lhp, Fort Hays State (Kan.)**
15. Glenn Kamis, rhp, Elgin (Ill.) CC
16. **Jon George, rhp, Camden Catholic HS, Pennsauken, N.J.**
17. Trey Lavender, c, Pelham (Ala.) HS
18. Zach McCormack, lhp, Sacramento CC
19. **Chris Denorfia, of, Wheaton (Mass.)**
20. Tyler Coon, lhp, Silverado HS, Las Vegas, Nev.
21. Mike Causey, rhp, Moorpark (Calif.) JC
22. Matt Luca, rhp, Ball HS, Galveston, Texas
23. Nick Markakis, lhp, Young Harris (Ga.) JC
24. **Jarrod Schmidt, c/rhp, Clemson**
25. **Robert Mosby, 1b, Northeastern Oklahoma A&M JC**
26. Chris Dunn, ss, Chaparral HS, Parker, Colo.
27. Juan Velazquez, rhp, Montgomery HS, San Diego
28. Jay Tust, 2b, Stadium HS, Tacoma
29. **Brad Correll, ss, Limestone (S.C.)**
30. **Justin Knoff, rhp, Siena**

31. **Mayque Quintero, rhp, Sonoma County (Western League)**
32. Gerald Smith, of, Thomas Jefferson HS, Tampa
33. Bart Braun, lhp, Diablo Valley (Calif.) JC
34. Cody McAllister, rhp, Snohomish (Wash.) HS
35. Stantrel Smith, of, Towers HS, Decatur, Ga.
36. **Matt Krimmel, 3b, George Washington**
37. **Shawn Aichele, rhp, Western Hills HS, Cincinnati**
38. Hardy Hutto, rhp, Garden City (Kan.) CC
39. **Calvin Medlock, rhp, Westbury HS, Houston**
40. **Chris Bell, rhp, Miami-Dade North JC**
41. Marcus Townsend, of, Texas-Brownsville
42. Danny Kelly, ss, Durango HS, Las Vegas
43. **Derek Hawk, rhp, Mendocino (Calif.) CC**
44. Jason Baca, rhp, Sweeny (Texas) HS
45. Dennis Leduc, rhp, Cuesta (Calif.) JC
46. **Troy Cairns, ss, New Mexico**
47. **Mike Bryant, rhp, Sam Rayburn HS, Pasadena, Texas**
48. **Travis Wong, 1b, Texas A&M**
49. Billy Dennis, of, Incarnate Word (Texas) (Contract voided)
50. Ben Himes, of, Texas A&M

CLEVELAND INDIANS

June—Regular Phase (22)

1. **Jeremy Guthrie, rhp, Stanford**
1. **Matt Whitney, 3b, Palm Beach Gardens (Fla.) HS** (Supplemental pick—33rd—for loss of Type A free agent Juan Gonzalez)
1. **Micah Schilling, 2b, Silliman Institute, Clinton, La.** (Supplemental pick—41st—for failure to sign 2001 first-rounder Alan Horne)
2. **Brian Slocum, rhp, Villanova**
2. **Pat Osborn, 3b, Florida** (Supplemental pick—72nd—for loss of Type B free agent Marty Cordova)
3. **Jason Cooper, of, Stanford** (Pick from Rangers as compensation for Gonzalez)
3. **Dan Cevette, lhp, Elkland (Pa.) HS**
4. **Fernando Pacheco, 1b, Montgomery HS, San Ysidro, Calif.**
5. **Ben Francisco, of, UCLA**
6. **Mike Hernandez, lhp, Fresno State**
7. **Brian Wright, of, North Carolina State**
8. **Blake Allen, lhp, Union (Tenn.)**
9. **Shaun Larkin, 2b, Cal State Northridge**
10. **Keith Ramsey, lhp, Florida**
11. **Bill Peavey, 1b, Southern California**
12. **Chad Longworth, of, J.J. Kelly HS, Wise, Va.**
13. **Reid Santos, lhp, Saddleback (Calif.) CC**
14. Mike Mitchell, rhp, St. Charles (Mo.) JC
15. **Nathan Panther, of, Muscatine (Iowa) CC**
16. **Omar Casillas, c, Ana J. Candelas HS, Cidra, P.R.**
17. Jeff Ostrander, lhp, Patrick Henry HS, Montpelier, Va.
18. **Jahseam George, lhp, San Jose State**
19. Curt Mendoza, of, Redlands (Calif.) HS
20. **Chris White, lhp, Kent State**
21. Zeke Parraz, ss, CC of Southern Nevada
22. **Clayton McCullough, c, East Carolina**
23. Aaron Tennyson, lhp, Milan (Mich.) HS
24. Dan Donaldson, lhp, Memorial HS, Houston
25. **Nick Pesco, rhp, Cosumnes River (Calif.) JC**
26. Jose Cardona, lhp, American Military Academy, Guaynabo, P.R.
27. Derek Dunne, rhp, Sullivan (Mo.) HS
28. Tim Sabo, rhp, Don Bosco Prep, Suffern, N.Y.
29. Ruben Flores, rhp, Riverside HS, El Paso
30. **Daniel Eisentrager, rhp, Long Beach State**
31. **Jeff Davis, rhp, Kansas**
32. **Shea Douglas, lhp, Southern Mississippi**
33. Jensen Lewis, rhp, Anderson HS, Cincinnati
34. Chris Williams, c, Marcus HS, Flower Mound, Texas
35. Kevin Hawkins, rhp, Embry-Riddle (Fla.) Aeronautical
36. Aaron Braithwaite, of, Indian River (Fla.) CC
37. Luis DeJesus, ss, New Mexico JC
38. John Moran, ss, Southaven (Miss.) HS
39. **Blake Taylor, rhp, South Carolina**
40. Shea McFeely, ss, Federal Way (Wash.) HS
41. Andrew Knight, lhp, Maize (Kan.) HS
42. Chris Rosario, of, Pine Ridge HS, Deltona, Fla.
43. Matt Paz, rhp, Long Beach State
44. Richard Wells, 3b, Glendale (Calif.) JC
45. Truan Mehl, of, Hutchinson (Kan.) CC
46. **Aaron Davidson, 2b, Florida**
47. Jimmy Mayer, ss, Somerset (Pa.) Area HS
48. Bryce Kartler, lhp, Arizona State
49. Daniel Lindner, rhp, Potomac State (W.Va.) JC
50. Ricardo Concepcion, of, Petra Corretser HS, Manati, P.R.

COLORADO ROCKIES

June—Regular Phase (9)

1. **Jeff Francis, lhp, British Columbia**
2. Micah Owings, rhp, Gainesville (Ga.) HS
3. **Ben Crockett, rhp, Harvard**
4. **Jeff Baker, 3b, Clemson**
5. **Neil Wilson, c, Vero Beach (Fla.) HS**
5. **Doug Johnson, rhp, Bryant (R.I.)** (Pick from Rangers as compensation for Type B free agent Jay Powell)
6. **Sean Barker, of, Louisiana State**
7. **Ryan Spilborghs, of, UC Santa Barbara**
8. **Jeff Salazar, of, Oklahoma State**
9. **John Tetuan, rhp, Wichita State**
10. **Isaac Pavlik, lhp, Seton Hall**
11. **Ryan Shealy, 1b, Florida**
12. **Mike Esposito, rhp, Arizona State**
13. **Brian Barre, of, Southern California**
14. **Bernie Gonzalez, of, Florida International**
15. **Andy Bushey, c/3b, Notre Dame**
16. Brad Corley, of, Pleasure Ridge Park HS, Louisville
17. **Steven Ponder, rhp, Texas A&M**
18. **Chris Young, rhp, Mississippi State**
19. **Duke Sardinha, 3b, Pepperdine**
20. **Dan Street, 3b, Virginia**
21. **Steve Reba, rhp, Clemson**
22. **Pete Montrenes, rhp, Mississippi**
23. **Carson White, 2b, California**
24. **Mitsuru Sakamoto, of, Arizona Western JC**
25. **Rock Mills, c, Pepperdine**
26. **K.J. Hendricks, ss, Texas-Arlington**
27. Lance Beus, lhp, Cochise County (Ariz.) CC
28. Jose Lado, lhp, Delgado (La.) JC
29. **Richard Cartier, rhp, Cuesta (Calif.) JC**
30. Aaron Gamboa, lhp, Bakersfield (Calif.) JC
31. Dan Lonsberry, rhp, Northeast Texas CC
32. Derek Patterson, lhp, Evangel Christian Academy, Keithville, La.
33. **Mike Watson, rhp, Penn State**
34. Ryan Mattheus, rhp, Galt (Calif.) Union HS
35. Robert Madsen, rhp, McLennan (Texas) CC
36. Clayton Trenary, of, Crystal River (Fla.) HS
37. Victor Alvarez, ss, Chipola (Fla.) JC
38. Steve Sutton, ss, Texarkana (Texas) CC
39. **Tomas Santiago, rhp, Pikeville (Ky.)**
40. Matthew Albidrez-Garza, rhp, Washington Union HS, Fresno
41. Johnny DeFendis, of, Xaverian HS, Brooklyn
42. **Jason Dooley, rhp, Bethune-Cookman**
43. Justin Hoyman, rhp, Brevard (Fla.) CC
44. Ryan Earnest, rhp, Hardaway HS, Columbus, Ga.
45. Tyler Littlehales, of, Boulder (Colo.) HS
46. **Joshua Merino, rhp, Kirkwood (Mo.) CC**
47. John Brownell, rhp, Butler County (Kan.) CC
48. Jim Popp, rhp, Duquesne
49. Jared Theodorakos, lhp, Baylor
50. Andrew York, c, JC of the Siskiyous (Calif.)

DETROIT TIGERS

June—Regular Phase (8)

1. **Scott Moore, ss, Cypress HS, Long Beach**
2. **Brent Clevlen, of, Westwood HS, Cedar Park, Texas**
3. **Curtis Granderson, of, Illinois-Chicago**
3. **Matt Pender, rhp, Kennesaw State (Ga.)** (Pick from Mets as compensation for Type B free agent Roger Cedeno)

4. **Robbie Sovie, of, Stratford Academy, Macon, Ga.**
5. **Bo Flowers, of, Walter Lutheran HS, Maywood, Ill.**
6. **Chris Maples, rhp, North Carolina**
7. **Wilton Reynolds, of, Oral Roberts**
8. **Troy Pickford, rhp, Oral Roberts**
9. **Marcos Hernandez, rhp, Juan Ponce de Leon HS, San Juan, P.R.**
10. **Luke Carlin, c, Northeastern**
11. **Joel Zumaya, rhp, Bonita Vista HS, Chula Vista, Calif.**
12. **Corey Hamman, lhp, Montclair State (N.J.)**
13. Anthony Reyes, rhp, Southern California
14. **Jason Graham, rhp, Central Florida**
15. **Jesse Carlson, lhp, Connecticut**
16. **Michael Smith, lhp, Valdosta State (Ga.)**
17. **Rob Watson, ss, Oklahoma State**
18. Jacob Coash, lhp, Canyon HS, Saugus, Calif.
19. **Rafael Mendez, c, Notre Dame HS, Caguas, P.R.**
20. **Jason Kennedy, of, Minnesota**
21. **Corey Loomis, 2b, Bowling Green State**
22. Cameron McGuire, c, South Grand Prairie (Texas) HS
23. **Drew Caravella, 1b, Ohio Wesleyan**
24. **Jody Roughton, 3b, Missouri**
25. Dan Nelson, ss, Crenshaw HS, Los Angeles
26. **Billy Kieninger, rhp, Miami (Ohio)**
27. **Damian Myers, lhp, Concordia (N.Y.)**
28. **Everett Hancock, lhp, UNC Greensboro**
29. Miguel Donate, 1b, Morell HS, Vega Alta, P.R.
30. **David Garcia, ss, Santa Ana (Calif.) JC**
31. Chris McCuiston, of, Michigan State
32. Douglas Webb, rhp, Newbury Park (Calif.) HS
33. Jose Rodriguez, c, Cypress (Calif.) JC
34. **Jason Allec, c, Cal State Northridge**
35. Brandon McCormick, rhp, W.W. King Academy, Batesburg, S.C.
36. **Chris Steinborn, lhp, Lakeland (Ohio) CC**
37. Ronnie Baron, rhp, Blinn (Texas) JC
38. **Ed Romprey, ss, Bellevue (Neb.)**
39. **Kevin McDonald, c, Maryland**
40. Matt Taylor, lhp, Antioch (Tenn.) HS
41. **Edgar Ortiz, 1b, Compton (Calif.) CC**
42. Travis Simmons, 3b, Cleveland (Tenn.) HS
43. Corey McCoy, of, Pine Bluff (Ark.) HS
44. Sean Richardson, c, Palomar (Calif.) JC

FLORIDA MARLINS

June—Regular Phase (11)

1. **Jeremy Hermida, of, Wheeler HS, Marietta, Ga.**
2. **Robert Andino, ss, Southridge HS, Miami**
3. **Trevor Hutchinson, rhp, California**
4. **Josh Johnson, rhp, Jenks HS, Tulsa**
5. Nick Hundley, c, Lake Washington HS, Redmond, Wash.
6. **Scott Olsen, lhp, Crystal Lake (Ill.) South HS**
7. **Xavier Arroyo, of, Antilles HS, Fort Buchanan, P.R.**
8. **Ryan Warpinski, rhp, Texas A&M**
9. **Eric Reed, of, Texas A&M**
10. **Robert Word, 1b, Virginia**
11. **Patrick Arlis, c, Illinois**
12. **Jimmy deMontel, rhp, Bellevue (Neb.)**
13. **Kevin Randel, ss, Long Beach State**
14. **Travis Chick, rhp, Whitehouse (Texas) HS**
15. **Tom Merkle, 3b, New York Tech**
16. Chris Goodman, rhp, Georgia Tech
17. **Evan Greusel, rhp, Oklahoma**
18. **Ross Wolf, rhp, Wabash Valley (Ill.) CC**
19. **Jordan Baker, of, Zane Trace HS, Chillicothe, Ohio**
20. **Jason Iehl, rhp, Downers Grove (Ill.) North HS**
21. Waylon Byers, lhp, Nebraska
22. **Shaun O'Connor, rhp, Pasco Hernando (Fla.) CC**
23. **Carl Primus, rhp, Southern**
24. **Andy Rohleder, of, Evansville**
25. **Eric Ordorica, 2b, Azusa Pacific (Calif.)**
26. Brae Wright, lhp, Southaven (Miss.) HS
27. **Casey Blalock, rhp, Louisiana Tech**
28. Aaron Gabriel, rhp, Lake City HS, Coeur d'Alene, Idaho
29. **Chris Gabriel, rhp, Chaffey (Calif.) JC**
30. Kurt Koehler, rhp, Pinole Valley HS, Pinole, Calif.
31. **Kyle Eazor, lhp, Chandler-Gilbert (Ariz.) CC**
32. Dan Olson, rhp, Kansas (Contract voided)
33. **Joseph Apotheker, of, Barry (Fla.)**
34. Kyle Dickson, rhp, Granada HS, Livermore, Calif.
35. Greg Goetz, lhp, Newport HS, Bellevue, Wash.
36. Neal Warchol, rhp, St. Laurence HS, Burbank, Ill.
37. Ryan Anderson, lhp, St. Petersburg (Fla.) JC
38. P.J. Connelly, lhp, Cowley County (Kan.) CC
39. Matt Miller, of, Modesto (Calif.) JC
40. Bradley Pahs, c, Triton (Ill.) JC
41. Rob Johnson, c, Saddleback (Calif.) CC
42. **Zach Lerch, rhp, Muscatine (Iowa) CC**
43. Tyler Williams, c, North Delta (B.C.) SS
44. **Tim Wood, rhp, Pima (Ariz.) CC**
45. Shany Carle, rhp, Quebec
46. **Nicholas Ewen, of, Triton (Ill.) JC**
47. Jacob Manning, of, Mineral Area (Mo.) JC
48. Matt Hayes, lhp, Parkland (Ill.) JC
49. Mike Gaffney, ss, New York Tech
50. Dusty Hughes, c, Northgate HS, Walnut Creek, Calif.

HOUSTON ASTROS

June—Regular Phase (29)

1. **Derick Grigsby, rhp, Northeast Texas CC**
2. **Mitch Talbot, rhp, Canyon View HS, Cedar City, Utah**
3. **Rory Shortell, rhp, San Diego State**
4. **Mark McLemore, lhp, Oregon State**
5. Pat Misch, lhp, Western Michigan
6. **J.P. Duran, rhp, St. Mary's (Texas)**
7. **Scott Robinson, 1b/of, Rancho Bernardo HS, San Diego**
8. **Bill Westhoff, rhp, Dallas**
9. **Andy Topham, ss, Stanford**
10. Brad Chedister, rhp, Panola (Texas) JC
11. **Jason Reuss, of, Nevada-Las Vegas**
12. **Chance Douglass, rhp, Randall HS, Amarillo, Texas**
13. **Nick Covarrubias, of, Long Beach State**
14. B.J. Boening, rhp, Yoakum HS, Portland, Texas
15. **Jeff Mackor, c, Boston College**
16. **Jared Gothreaux, rhp, McNeese State**
17. **Daniel Freeman, rhp, Texarkana (Texas) CC**
18. **Brent Long, rhp, Brevard (N.C.)**
19. **Aaron Heitzman, lhp, Minnesota State-Mankato**
20. Justin Glover, of, Grant HS, Portland, Ore.
21. Ivan Naccarata, 2b, Chipola (Fla.) JC
22. **Sam Fischer, rhp, Dayton**
23. **Jesse Harrington, ss, Concordia (Ore.)**
24. Nick Tisone, rhp, Mandeville HS, Covington, La.
25. Ethien Santana, of, Colegio Bautista, Carolina, P.R.
26. **Randy McGarvey, c, Coastal Carolina**
27. Shawn Burris, lhp, Poteet HS, Mesquite, Texas
28. **Kevin Davidson, c, Rollins (Fla.)**
29. **Sean Kramer, rhp, Hill (Texas) JC**
30. Ladd Hall, rhp, Eastern Arizona JC
31. **Andy Salmela, 1b, Augustana (S.D.)**
32. Tyson Olson, of, Dixie (Utah) JC
33. **Pat Peavey, 3b, Santa Clara**
34. **Mike Lorsbach, of, Rice**
35. Shawn Williams, of, Clearwater (Fla.) Central Catholic HS
36. **Adam Seuss, of, UC Riverside**
37. **Dustin Hawkins, of, Wichita State**
38. **Ryan Larson, 3b, UC San Diego**
39. Nick Stavinoha, of, San Jacinto (Texas) JC
40. Adam Yesalusky, lhp, Minersville (Pa.) Area HS
41. Scott Feldman, rhp, JC of San Mateo (Calif.)
42. Chase Medford, lhp/of, Richland (Texas) HS
43. Freddie Thon, 1b, Baldwin HS, Guaynabo, P.R.
44. William Mac-Holmes, rhp, Northwest HS, Omaha
45. **Ryan McKeller, rhp, McLennan (Texas) CC**
46. Eric Brock, rhp, Santa Margarita HS, Laguna Niguel HS, Calif.
47. **Raymar Diaz, of, Laredo (Texas) CC**
48. Kyle Thompson, rhp, Palomar (Calif.) CC

KANSAS CITY ROYALS

June—Regular Phase (6)

1. **Zack Greinke, rhp, Apopka HS, Orlando**
2. **Adam Donachie, c, Timber Creek HS, Orlando**
3. **Dave Jensen, 1b, Brigham Young**
4. **Daniel Christensen, lhp, Xaverian HS, Brooklyn**
5. **Donnie Murphy, ss, Orange Coast (Calif.) JC**
6. Brandon Jones, ss, Wewahitchka (Fla.) HS
7. **Jonah Bayliss, rhp, Trinity (Conn.)**
8. **Kenard Springer, 3b, Nettleton (Miss.) HS**
9. **Matt Tupman, c, Massachusetts-Lowell**
10. **Greg Atencio, rhp, Lamar (Colo.) CC**
11. Kainoa Obrey, 3b, Brigham Young
12. **Adam Keim, ss, Coastal Carolina**
13. **Rusty Meyer, c, Texas A&M**
14. **Steve Chamberlain, rhp, Portland**
15. **Kila Ka'aihue, 1b, Iolani HS, Honolulu**
16. **Eric Ackerman, lhp, Pittsburgh**
17. Jason Bartz, rhp, South Florida (Contract voided)
18. **Donnie Poles, of, Pitt (N.C.) CC**
19. Alex Crooks, 1b, Sierra Vista HS, Azusa, Calif.
20. **Nate Zettler, rhp, Union (Ky.)**
21. Steve Mena, 3b, South Miami HS
22. Nick Bates, rhp, Michigan State
23. **Tim Frend, of, Davidson**
24. **Mike Aguilar, rhp, Franklin HS, Portland, Ore.**
25. **Carlos Caballero, of, Ines Maria Mendoza HS, Cabo Rojo, P.R.**
26. J.J. Brown, of, Vicksburg (Miss.) HS
27. Michael Hernandez, of, Xaverian HS, Brooklyn
28. **Robert Grana, c, CC of Southern Nevada**
29. Mike Honce, rhp, Bridgeport (W.Va.) HS
30. Clinton Johnson, rhp, Murrah HS, Jackson, Miss.
31. Matt Castillo, of, Mesa (Ariz.) CC
32. **Leon Stephens, of, Virginia State**
33. Cesar Carrillo, rhp, Mount Carmel (Ill.) HS
34. **Eric Lonnquist, ss, Minnesota State-Mankato**
35. Tyler Kimmons, rhp, Mandeville (La.) HS
36. Chris Turner, c, El Dorado (Ark.) HS
37. Jason Ward, rhp, Utah Valley State JC
38. **Justin Taylor, rhp, Baylor**
39. Eric Hullinger, rhp, Kishwaukee (Ill.) JC
40. Vince Berry, of, Triton (Ill.) JC
41. **Drew Endicott, rhp, Missouri**
42. Odell Cosby, of, Paris (Ky.) HS
43. **David Nelson, lhp, North Carolina A&T**
44. Bryan McCaulley, rhp, San Jacinto (Calif.) JC
45. Andrew Scholl, of/1b, Lamar (Colo.) CC
46. Devan Ewell, of, Osborne HS, Manassas, Va.
47. Ty Wallace, c, Newman Smith HS, Carrollton, Texas
48. Lenny Bays, rhp, Northern Kentucky (Contract voided)
49. Luis Rivera, ss, Carvin School, Carolina, P.R.
50. Matt Hobbs, lhp, Missouri

LOS ANGELES DODGERS

June—Regular Phase (19)

1. **James Loney, 1b, Elkins HS, Missouri City, Texas**
1. **Greg Miller, lhp, Esperanza HS, Yorba Linda, Calif.** (Supplemental pick—31st—for loss of Type A free agent Chan Ho Park)
2. **Zach Hammes, rhp, Iowa City HS, Iowa City** (Pick from Rangers as compensation for Park)
2. **Jonathan Broxton, rhp, Burke County HS, Waynesboro, Ga.**
3. **Mike Nixon, c, Sunnyslope HS, Phoenix**
4. **Delwyn Young, 2b, Santa Barbara (Calif.) CC**
5. **Mike Megrew, lhp, Chariho Regional HS, Hope Valley, R.I.**
6. **Marshall Looney, lhp, La Pine (Ore.) HS**
7. **David Bagley, 3b, San Diego**
8. **Jamaal Hamilton, lhp, Monterey HS, Lubbock, Texas**
9. Denver Kitch, ss, Oklahoma
10. **Ryan Williams, rhp, Old Dominion**
11. **James McDonald, 1b, Poly HS, Long Beach**
12. **Ryan Owen, c, Wichita State**
13. **Julio LaSalle, rhp, Palm Beach Atlantic (Fla.)**
14. Karl Mejlholm, rhp, Dover Bay HS, Nanaimo, B.C
15. **Eric Stults, lhp, Bethel (Ind.)**
16. **Sambu Ndungidi, of, St. Georges HS, Montreal**
17. **Russell Martin, 2b, Chipola (Fla.) JC**
18. Curtis Hudson, c, Yuba City (Calif.) HS
19. **Michael White, lhp, St. Petersburg (Fla.) JC**
20. Andrew Walker, rhp, Cowley County (Kan.) CC
21. Ryan Tracy, rhp, Claremont (Calif.) HS
22. **Brett Wayne, ss, St. Mary's**
23. Josh Bartusick, 1b, Fountain Valley (Calif.) HS
24. **Derry Jackson, of, Jesuit HS, Portland, Ore.**
25. **Alvin Hayes, rhp, Alabama Southern CC**
26. **Jarod Plummer, rhp, South Garland (Texas) HS**
27. **Mike Potoczny, rhp, North Marion HS, Farmington, W.Va.**
28. Robert Ray, rhp, Lufkin (Texas) HS
29. Dominique Laurin, ss/2b, Eastern Oklahoma State JC
30. Edward Roberts, rhp, Key West (Fla.) HS
31. **Ross Hawley, rhp, Kansas State**
32. Richie Robnett, of, Santa Barbara (Calif.) CC
33. Eddy Baeza, rhp, Poly HS, Sun Valley, Calif.
34. Doug Mathis, rhp, Show Low (Ariz.) HS
35. Matt Long, rhp, Granville (Ohio) HS
36. **Bryan Goelz, of, New York Tech**
37. Jon Riggleman, 3b, Hillsborough (Fla.) CC
38. Danny Forrer, lhp, Jefferson Davis HS, Montgomery, Ala.
39. Luke Hochevar, rhp, Fowler (Col.) HS
40. Eric Wolfe, 1b, York Mills HS, Willowdale, Ontario
41. Ryan Lennerton, p, Eastern Oklahoma State JC
42. Nathan Warrick, of, Belton (Texas) HS
43. **David Parker, rhp, Eastern Oklahoma State JC**
44. James Bailie, c, Kodiak (Alaska) HS
45. Justin Estrada, ss, Jesuit HS, Tampa
46. **Mickey Jordan, of, Armstrong Atlantic State (Ga.)**
47. **Chad Bailey, lhp, North Idaho JC**
48. Andre Trahan, of, Yuba (Calif.) CC
49. Jeffrey Cristy, c, Southeast HS, Lincoln, Neb.
50. Jason Farrand, c, Conway (S.C.) HS

MILWAUKEE BREWERS

June—Regular Phase (7)

1. **Prince Fielder, 1b, Eau Gallie HS, Melbourne, Fla.**
2. **Josh Murray, ss, Jesuit HS, Tampa**
3. **Eric Thomas, rhp, South Alabama**
4. **Nic Carter, of, Campbell**
5. Jarrad Page, ss, San Leandro (Calif.) HS
6. **Khalid Ballouli, rhp, Texas A&M**
7. **Tom Wilhelmsen, rhp, Tucson Magnet HS, Tucson**
8. Stephen Kahn, rhp, Servite HS, Anaheim
9. **Edwin Walker, lhp, Highland HS, San Antonio**
10. **Jeremy Frost, c, Central Florida**
11. Brian Hernandez, c, John I. Leonard HS, Boynton Beach, Fla.
12. **Callix Crabbe, 2b, Manatee (Fla.) CC**
13. Tila Reynolds, ss, Washington
14. **Kennard Bibbs, of, Oklahoma City**
15. **Justin Barnes, rhp, Manatee (Fla.) CC**
16. **Dana Eveland, lhp, Hill (Texas) JC**
17. **Adam Mannon, of, Hamilton HS, Chandler, Ariz.**
18. Steven White, rhp, Baylor
19. **Bo Hall, rhp, Central Florida**
20. **Tyler Shepple, rhp, Washington**
21. **Josh Alliston, rhp, Long Beach State**
22. **Lenden Willis, 3b, Motlow State (Tenn.) CC**
23. **Keith Bohanan, 3b, Oklahoma City**
24. **Arturo Bravo, c, Montgomery HS, San Ysidro, Calif.**
25. **John Vanden Berg, c, Wisconsin-Milwaukee**
26. **Craig Breslow, lhp, Yale**
27. **Dallas Bates, of, Chandler (Ariz.) HS**
28. **Eric Thomas, rhp, Southern**
29. **Steve Moss, of, Notre Dame HS, Sherman Oaks, Calif.**
30. **Justin Gabriel, lhp, Louisiana-Lafayette**
31. **Jason Baker, rhp, George Washington**
32. **Simon Beresford, rhp, Tyler (Texas) JC**
33. **Jeff Housman, lhp, Cal State Fullerton**

34. **Tim Dillard, c, Itawamba (Miss.) CC**
35. Emmanuel Cividanes, of, Colegio San Antonio, San Juan, P.R.
36. Daniel Carter, rhp, Tallahassee (Fla.) CC
37. Stephen Bryant, c, Warren Central HS, Indianapolis
38. David Hancox, rhp, Pasco Hernando (Fla.) CC
39. Juan Herrera, lhp, Arizona Western JC
40. Hunter Pence, of, Texarkana (Texas) CC
41. Jonathan Shapland, of, St. Petersburg (Fla.) JC
42. Neil Avery, of, Dartmouth HS, North Dartmouth, Mass.

MINNESOTA TWINS

June—Regular Phase (20)

1. **Denard Span, of, Tampa Catholic HS**
2. **Jesse Crain, rhp, Houston**
3. Mark Sauls, rhp, Bay HS, Panama City, Fla.
4. **Alex Merricks, lhp, Oxnard (Calif.) HS**
5. Clete Thomas, of, Mosley HS, Lynn Haven, Fla.
6. **Pat Neshek, rhp, Butler**
7. **Ricky Barrett, lhp, San Diego**
8. Adam Lind, 1b, Highland HS, Anderson, Ind.
9. **Doug Deeds, of, Ohio State**
10. **Kyle Phillips, c, El Capitan HS, Lakeside, Calif.**
11. **Evan Meek, rhp, Inglemoor HS, Bothell, Wash.**
12. Jeff Clement, c, Marshalltown (Iowa) HS
13. Bo Pettit, rhp, Louisiana State
14. Garrett Mock, rhp, Grayson County (Texas) CC
15. **Adam Harben, rhp, Westark (Ark.) CC**
16. **K.C. Jones, rhp, Eatonville (Wash.) HS**
17. Adam Hawes, rhp, St. Theresa's Catholic HS, Victoria Harbour, Ontario
18. **Arturo Lopez, of, Galveston (Texas) JC**
19. Adam Daniels, lhp, North Vancouver, B.C.
20. Ryan Schreppel, lhp, Lincoln HS, Stockton, Calif.
21. **T.J. Prunty, rhp, Miami**
22. **Justin Sims, of, Middle Tennessee State**
23. **Danny Matienzo, c, Miami**
24. Josh Petersen, 1b, Jupiter (Fla.) HS
25. **Justin Keeling, lhp, California Lutheran**
26. Jared Johnson, rhp, Cimarron Memorial HS, Las Vegas
27. **Ron Perodin, of, El Camino (Calif.) CC**
28. Hasan Rasheed, of, White's Creek HS, Nashville
29. James Avery, rhp, Central Collegiate HS, Moose Jaw, Saskatchewan
30. Roberto Martinez, rhp, St. Petersburg (Fla.) CC
31. **Terry Killion, rhp, Bowie HS, Austin**
32. **Jon Koch, rhp, Lake City (Fla.) CC**
33. Tom Ferrara, rhp, Brevard (Fla.) CC
34. Christian Castorri, rhp, Thomas County Central HS, Thomasville, Ga.
35. **Terrence Patterson, of, Bartow HS, Lakeland, Fla.**
36. **John Cahill, rhp, Lakewood (Calif.) HS**
37. Mike Costantino, 3b, Somerset (Mass.) HS
38. Toby Gardenhire, ss, Westark (Ark.) CC
39. Brandon Doddo, c, Cooper City (Fla.) HS
40. Rodney Story, lhp, Gulf Coast (Fla.) CC
41. Chris Brown, 2b, Cooper City (Fla.) HS
42. **Kyle Geiger, c, Rend Lake (Ill.) JC**
43. Jacob Jean, lhp, Cosumnes River (Calif.) CC
44. Chris Beatty, ss, Kokomo (Ind.) HS
45. John Stocco, rhp, Academy of Holy Angels HS, Richfield, Minn.
46. Wayne Renfrow, rhp, Kellam HS, Virginia Beach
47. Brandon Carlton, lhp, Bay HS, Panama City, Fla.
48. Brandon Cohen, of, River Dell HS, Oradell, N.J.
49. **Brock Peterson, 3b, West HS, Chehalis, Wash.**
50. Mike Ballard, lhp, Ocean Lakes HS, Virginia Beach

MONTREAL EXPOS

June—Regular Phase (5)

1. **Clint Everts, rhp, Cypress Falls HS, Houston**
2. **Darrell Rasner, rhp, Nevada**
3. **Larry Broadway, 1b, Duke**
4. **Jon Felfoldi, lhp, Glendale (Calif.) CC**
5. **Anthony Pearson, rhp, Jackson State**
6. **Chad Chop, 1b, Vanguard (Calif.)**
7. **Mike O'Connor, lhp, George Washington**
8. Friedel Pinkston, rhp, Hart County HS, Hartwell, Ga.
9. **Chris Barlow, rhp, Le Moyne**
10. Justin Azze, lhp, Orange Coast (Calif.) JC
11. **Jason Bergmann, rhp, Rutgers**
12. **Danny Rueckel, rhp, Furman**
13. **Brett Nyquist, lhp, St. Scholastica (Minn.)**
14. **Erik Fiedler, rhp, San Diego State**
15. **Isaiah Wright, rhp, Dover (Del.) HS**
16. **Brian Ellerson, ss, Montclair State (N.J.)**
17. **Jason Conlisk, ss, Fordham**
18. **Anthony Brown, of, George Washington**
19. **Franklyn Jimenez, 2b, Muscatine (Iowa) CC**
20. **Tim Sweeney, ss, Rutgers**
21. **Stockton Davis, rhp, Oral Roberts**
22. Marcus Davis, rhp, Luray (Va.) HS
23. **Nathan Weese, of, Utah**
24. **Matt Swope, of, Maryland**
25. **Adrian Urquhart, of, Alabama State**
26. **Maurice Cobb, of, Rocky Mount (N.C.) HS**
27. Matt Bonovich, c, Southern California
28. Tony Irvin, rhp, Hillsborough (Fla.) CC
29. Tim Hudnall, 1b, Lake Michigan (Mich.) JC
30. Robert Rohrbaugh, lhp, Littlestown (Pa.) Area HS
31. Ruben Kerbs, lhp, Wichita State
32. Cam O'Donnell, rhp, Middle Georgia JC
33. Andrew Wells, lhp, St. Stephens-St. Agnes HS, Alexandria, Va.
34. Jack Lyons, lhp, Maret HS, Washington, D.C.
35. Sean White, rhp, Washington
36. Jeff Miller, 1b, Pine Grove (Pa.) Area HS
37. Jarvis Hicks, rhp, South Florida CC
38. Nick Ponomarenko, rhp, Cuesta (Calif.) JC
39. Jon Hunton, rhp, Miami-Dade CC North
40. Bryan Coffey, rhp, Culpepper HS, Rixeyville, Va.
41. Michael Romeo, 3b, Lindenhurst (N.Y.) HS
42. Randy Dicken, rhp, Allegany (Md.) CC
43. Brody Taylor, lhp, Louisburg (N.C.) CC
44. Michael Gibbs, rhp, Roxborough HS, Philadelphia
45. Jon Link, rhp, Chantilly (Va.) HS
46. Marc Nunez, rhp, Countryside HS, St. Petersburg, Fla.
47. Ronald Ball, rhp, John F. Kennedy HS, Buena Park, Calif.
48. **Ken Beck, rhp, Maryland**
49. James Treece, rhp, Orange Coast (Calif.) CC
50. Joe Gregory, rhp, Western HS, Davie, Fla.

NEW YORK METS

June—Regular Phase (15)

1. **Scott Kazmir, lhp, Cypress Falls HS, Houston**
2. (Pick to Cubs as compensation for Type A free agent David Weathers)
3. (Pick to Tigers as compensation for Type B free agent Roger Cedeno)
4. **Bobby Malek, of, Michigan State**
5. **Jon Slack, of, Texas Tech**
6. **Adam Elliott, rhp, Clayton Valley HS, Concord, Calif.**
7. **Jim Anderson, c, UC Riverside**
8. **Tyler Davidson, of, Washington**
9. Christian Colonel, ss, JC of Southern Idaho
10. **Matt Lindstrom, rhp, Ricks (Idaho) JC**
11. **Kelvin Garay, lhp, Santa Cruz HS, Trujillo Alta, P.R.**
12. **Shawn Bowman, 3b, Dr. Charles Best SS, Coquitlam, B.C**
13. **Blake Whealy, 2b, Evansville**
14. **Jeff Brewer, rhp, British Columbia**
15. Elvys Quezada, rhp, Seton Hall
16. **Zachary Clements, c, Christian Brothers (Tenn.)**
17. **Laron Wilson, of, Longwood (Va.)**
18. **Ivan Maldonado, rhp, Indian Hills (Iowa) CC**
19. **Bryan King, rhp, Mesa State (Colo.)**
20. **Will Hudson, ss, Oregon State**
21. Brendan Winn, of, Brevard (Fla.) CC
22. **Tim McNab, rhp, Florida Atlantic**
23. **Rashad Parker, of, UCLA**
24. **Robert Paulk, rhp, North Florida JC**

25. Nathan Kiser, 1b, Lebanon (Va.) HS
26. Kyle Cullinan, 3b, Fullerton (Calif.) JC
27. Ricky Steik, rhp, John F. Kennedy HS, La Palma, Calif.
28. Chris Munn, rhp, St. Thomas Aquinas HS, Fort Lauderdale
29. Tim Didjurgis, rhp, Pima (Ariz.) JC
30. Chris Robinson, c, Lord Dorchester SS, Dorchester, Ontario
31. **Marcos Cabral, ss/2b, Southwest Miami HS, Miami**
32. **Todd Dulaney, 2b, Wabash Valley (Ill.) JC**
33. Timmy Jones, of, Morristown (N.J.) HS
34. **Chase Lambin, ss, Louisiana-Lafayette**
35. John Findley, rhp, Nettleton HS, Jonesboro, Ark.
36. Joey Huskins, c, Fountain Valley (Calif.) HS
37. **Billy Weitzman, rhp, Briarcliffe (N.Y.) JC**
38. Derek Antelo, rhp, Broward (Fla.) JC
39. DeWayne Carver, rhp, Daytona Beach (Fla.) CC
40. Jon Malo, ss, Montmorency (Quebec)
41. Steven Romero, rhp, South Hills HS, Walnut, Calif.
42. Ryan DiPietro, lhp, Berlin HS, Kensington, Conn.
43. Jeremy Brown, of, Sylvan Hills HS, Sherwood, Ark.
44. **Ian Bladergroen, 1b, Lamar (Colo.) CC**
45. Brian Rabbitt, rhp, Brookdale (N.J.) CC
46. Doug Fink, rhp, Southington (Conn.) HS
47. Troy Roberson, rhp, Miami
48. Alfred Profeet, c, Delaware Tech JC
49. Steven Lopez, c, Chandler (Ariz.) HS
50. Jack Spradlin, lhp, Eastlake HS, Chula Vista, Calif.

NEW YORK YANKEES

June—Regular Phase (24)

1. (Pick to Athletics as compensation for Type A free agent Jason Giambi)
2. (Pick to Braves as compensation for Type A free agent Steve Karsay)
2. **Brandon Weeden, rhp/ss, Santa Fe HS, Edmond, Okla.** (Pick from Cardinals as compensation for Type B free agent Tino Martinez)
3. (Pick to Cubs as compensation for Type A free agent Rondell White)
4. **Alan Bomer, rhp, Texas**
5. **Matt Carson, of, Brigham Young**
6. **Brandon Harmsen, rhp, Grand Rapids (Mich.) JC**
7. **Ross Michelsen, 1b, Lamar (Texas) HS**
8. **Brad Halsey, lhp, Texas**
9. **Eric Verbryke, of, Cal State Northridge**
10. **Gary Bell, lhp, South Carolina**
11. **Scott McClanahan, of, Alabama**
12. **Matt Mamula, 1b, Point Loma Nazarene (Calif.)**
13. **Blake Blase, 1b, Jefferson (Mo.) JC**
14. **Ray Clark, rhp, Texas**
15. **Philip Tribe, rhp, Rice**
16. **Jared Koutnik, ss, Michigan State**
17. **Gabe Lopez, 2b, San Jose State**
18. **Luis Robles, c, Riverside (Calif.) CC**
19. **Jon Sheaffer, of, Arizona State**
20. **Ben King, lhp, Texas**
21. **Hector Zamora, 3b, San Jose State**
22. Skyler Fulton, of, Skagit Valley (Wash.) JC
23. **Eric Hacker, rhp, Duncanville (Texas) HS**
24. **Dane de la Rosa, rhp, Riverside (Calif.) CC**
25. **Josh Neitz, rhp, St. Leo (Fla.)**
26. **Phil Coke, lhp, San Joaquin Delta (Calif.) JC**
27. **Mike Knox, rhp, Jesuit College Prep, Dallas**
28. **Nathan Kopp, lhp, Wright State**
29. **Charlie Isaacson, rhp, Arkansas**
30. Kyle Marlatt, rhp, San Jacinto (Texas) JC
31. **Paul Thorp, rhp, Baylor**
32. **Justin Meccage, rhp, Oklahoma State**
33. David Smith, lhp, Parkland (Ill.) JC
34. **Nathan Bowden, ss, North Alabama**
35. Mike Brown, rhp, Owasso (Okla.) HS
36. **Doug Boone, c, Ball State**
37. **Richard Cowan, rhp, Navarro (Texas) JC**
38. Justin Keadle, rhp, Cypress (Calif.) JC
39. Randy Gattis, rhp, Mesquite HS, Dallas
40. **Joe DiFranco, rhp, St. Thomas (Fla.)**
41. **Mike Miehls, c, Tennessee Tech**
42. Matt Goodson, rhp, Galveston (Texas) JC
43. Jason Maes, lhp, Folsom HS, Elk Grove, Calif.
44. **Matthew Brumit, rhp, Youngstown State**
45. Matt Yost, 1b, Elk City (Okla.) HS
46. **Jared Treadway, of, Wooster (Ohio)**
47. Ryan Jennings, rhp, James Monroe HS, Lindside, W.Va.
48. Billy Carnline, rhp, New Caney (Texas) HS
49. Levi Dartt, lhp, Denton (Texas) HS
50. Arthur Christal, of, Ennis (Texas) HS

OAKLAND ATHLETICS

June—Regular Phase (26)

1. **Nick Swisher, 1b/of, Ohio State** (Pick from Red Sox as compensation for Type A free agent Johnny Damon)
1. **Joe Blanton, rhp, Kentucky** (Pick from Yankees as compensation for Type A free agent Jason Giambi)
1. **John McCurdy, ss, Maryland**
1. **Ben Fritz, rhp, Fresno State** (Pick from Cardinals as compensation for Type A free agent Jason Isringhausen)
1. **Jeremy Brown, c, Alabama** (Supplemental pick—35th—for loss of Giambi)
1. **Steve Obenchain, rhp, Evansville** (Supplemental pick—37th—for loss of Isringhausen)
1. **Mark Teahen, 3b, St. Mary's** (Supplemental pick—39th—for loss of Damon)
2. **Steve Stanley, of, Notre Dame**
3. **Bill Murphy, lhp, Cal State Northridge**
4. **John Baker, c, California**
5. **Mark Kiger, ss, Florida**
6. **Brian Stavisky, of, Notre Dame**
7. **Brant Colamarino, 1b, Pittsburgh**
8. **Jared Burton, rhp, Western Carolina**
9. **Shane Komine, rhp, Nebraska**
10. **J.R. Pickens, rhp, Mississippi**
11. **Justin Crowder, lhp, Rice**
12. **Kirk Nordness, of, Armstrong Atlantic State (Ga.)**
13. **Tyler Klippenstein, 3b, Lethbridge (Alberta)**
14. **Brad Knox, rhp, Central Arizona JC**
15. **Chris Dunwell, rhp, San Diego State**
16. **Lloyd Turner, 2b, Kennesaw State**
17. **David Harriman, c, Armstrong Atlantic State (Ga.)**
18. **Jose Corchado, rhp, Hilberto Domenech, Isabela, P.R.**
19. Dusty Barnard, rhp, Moore (Okla.) HS
20. Trevor Crowe, ss, Westview HS, Portland, Ore.
21. Wally Pontiff, 3b, Louisiana State
22. **Shawn Kohn, rhp, Washington**
23. **Chris Shank, rhp, Franklin Pierce (N.H.)**
24. **Daniel Gibbons, of, Central Michigan**
25. **Steve Schilsky, rhp, Illinois Wesleyan**
26. **Ty Bubalo, c, Beaverton (Ore.) HS**
27. Greg Dupas, rhp, Arlington HS, Riverside, Calif.
28. **Andy Dickinson, lhp, Illinois**
29. **Daniel Barnett, rhp, Salt Lake (Utah) CC**
30. Brian Rodgers, of, Berkmar HS, Lilburn, Ga.
31. Brad Ziegler, rhp, Southwest Missouri State
32. J.R. Towles, c, Crosby (Texas) HS
33. Nate Nelson, 1b, Holy Name Central Catholic HS, Worcester, Mass.
34. Rene Quintana, ss, Patria la Torres HS, San Sebastien, P.R.
35. Robby Jacobson, c, Durango HS, Las Vegas
36. **Jed Morris, c, Nebraska**
37. Mark Rodrigues, rhp, Los Medanos (Calif.) JC
38. Jason Williams, rhp, Cactus Shadows HS, Cave Creek, Ariz.
39. Joel Evans, rhp, Columbia Basin (Wash.) CC
40. Jonathan Papelbon, rhp, Mississippi State
41. Don Sutton, 1b, Durango HS, Las Vegas
42. Joe Ryan, rhp, Assumption HS, Davenport, Iowa
43. Curtis White, lhp, Oklahoma
44. Ty Taubenheim, rhp, Edmonds (Wash.) CC
45. Matt Elfeldt, rhp, Boston College

PHILADELPHIA PHILLIES

June—Regular Phase (17)

1. **Cole Hamels, lhp, Rancho Bernardo HS, San Diego**
2. **Zack Segovia, rhp, Forney (Texas) HS**
3. **Kiel Fisher, 3b/of, Riverside Poly (Calif.) HS**
4. **Nick Bourgeois, lhp, Tulane**
5. **Jake Blalock, 3b, Rancho Bernardo HS, San Diego**
6. **Lee Gwaltney, rhp, Louisiana Tech**
7. **Robby Read, rhp, Florida State**
8. Steven Doetsch, of, Dunedin (Fla.) HS
9. **Rob Harrand, rhp, San Diego State**
10. **Ryan Barthelemy, 1b, Florida State**
11. T.J. Beam, rhp, Mississippi
12. **Trent Pratt, c, Auburn**
13. **Brian Manfred, c, San Diego State**
14. **Darin Naatjes, rhp, Stanford**
15. **Victor Menocal, ss, Georgia Tech**
16. **Leslie Bramasco, ss, Long Beach CC**
17. **Scott Mathieson, rhp, Aldergrove (B.C.) SS**
18. **Chad Oliva, c, Jacksonville**
19. **Bobby Korecky, rhp, Michigan**
20. **Karl Nonemaker, of, Vanderbilt**
21. Brett McMillan, 3b, Ponderosa HS, Shingle Springs, Calif.
22. Brad McCann, 3b, Gulf Coast (Fla.) CC
23. Jason Fletcher, rhp, Indian River (Fla.) CC
24. **Whit Bryant, lhp, Elon**
25. **Zach Minor, rhp, Fresno State**
26. **Erik Winegarden, c, New Mexico State**
27. **Brad Busbin, rhp, Central Florida**
28. **Derek Brewster, rhp, Louisiana Tech**
29. **Adam Steen, rhp, Minnesota State-Mankato**
30. **Ryan Wardinsky, ss, Texas A&M**
31. **Jeremy Isenhower, 2b, Southwest Missouri State**
32. **Rob Cafiero, 1b, Villanova**
33. **Jeremy Rogelstad, rhp, San Jose State**
34. **Beau Richardson, lhp, Tulane**
35. **Josh Paddock, rhp, Aurora (Ill.)**
36. Keahi Rawlins, rhp, Molokai HS, Kaunakakai, Hawaii
37. **Tim Gradoville, c, Creighton**
38. Corey Carter, of, West Point (Miss.) HS
39. Daniel Lewis, rhp, Folsom (Calif.) HS
40. Brandon Joseph, of, A.J. Dimond HS, Anchorage
41. McCay Green, rhp, Edgewater HS, Orlando
42. Clay Dirks, lhp, Hernando (Miss.) HS
43. Byron Cragg, rhp, Galena HS, Reno
44. Jacob Habsieger, lhp, Festus (Mo.) HS
45. Sam LeCure, rhp, Helias HS, Centertown, Mo.
46. Dusty Ryan, c, Golden Valley HS, Merced, Calif.
47. Ryan Greives, rhp, Benton Central HS, Otterbein, Ind.
48. Dennis Winn, ss, Bowling Green, Ky.

PITTSBURGH PIRATES

June—Regular Phase (1)

1. **Bryan Bullington, rhp, Ball State**
2. **Blair Johnson, rhp, Washburn HS, Topeka, Kan.**
3. **Taber Lee, ss, San Diego State**
4. **Wardell Starling, rhp, Elkins HS, Missouri City, Texas**
5. **Alex Hart, rhp, Florida**
6. **Brad Eldred, 1b, Florida International**
7. **Matt Capps, rhp, Alexander HS, Douglasville, Ga.**
8. **Bobby Kingsbury, of, Fordham**
9. **Joe Hicks, of, Forest Brook HS, Houston**
10. **Dave Davidson, lhp, Denis Morris HS, Thorold, Ontario**
11. **Anthony Bocchino, of, Marist**
12. **Brian Holliday, lhp, Moon Area HS, Moon Township, Pa.**
13. Chris Cunningham, c, Arizona
14. **John Smith, 2b, Middle Georgia JC**
15. **Jonathan Schneider, rhp, Liberty**
16. **John Hummel, lhp, Schaumburg (Ill.) HS**
17. **Chris DeMaria, rhp, Long Beach State**
18. Jeff Watchko, rhp, Georgia Tech
19. Herbert Andres, rhp, W.J. Mouat HS, Abbotsford, B.C
20. **Russ Bayer, lhp, Miami (Ohio)**
21. **Chris Holt, rhp, Flagler (Fla.)**
22. Paul Harp, rhp, Middle Georgia JC
23. **Dean Devine, 3b/2b, South Dakota**
24. **Sam Christensen, 1b, Southern Colorado**
25. Matt Cundiff, rhp, Cooper City (Fla.) HS
26. Calvin Beamon, of, Smoky Hill HS, Aurora, Colo.
27. Gene Filyaw, ss, Jasper (Texas) HS
28. **Anthony Stevens, ss, South Doyle HS, Knoxville**
29. **Francis Poni, c, Los Angeles Harbor JC**
30. Chris Toneguzzi, rhp, Markville SS, Thunder Bay, Ontario
31. William Webster, c, Moon Valley HS, Phoenix
32. Angel Colon, of, San Vicente de Paul HS, Toa Baja, P.R.
33. **Nyjer Morgan, of, Walla Walla (Wash.) CC**
34. Adam Howard, rhp, Ooltewah (Tenn.) HS
35. Eric King, 2b, Los Medanos (Calif.) JC
36. Ryan Aldridge, rhp, Wayne County HS, Jesup, Ga.
37. Tony Snow, rhp, Cascade HS, Everett, Wash.
38. Phillip Stillwell, rhp, North Florida JC
39. Chase Moore, of, St. Mary's College HS, Albany, Calif.
40. Matt Maropis, ss, Franklin Regional HS, Murrysville, Pa.
41. Rollie Gibson, lhp, Buchanan HS, Fresno
42. **Chaz Lytle, of, Georgia**
43. Mike Hicks, lhp, St. Stephens HS, Hickory, N.C.

ST. LOUIS CARDINALS

June—Regular Phase (30)

1. (Pick to Athletics as compensation for Type A free agent Jason Isringhausen)
2. (Pick to Yankees as compensation for Type B free agent Tino Martinez)
3. **Calvin Hayes, ss, East Rowan HS, Salisbury, N.C.**
4. **Kyle Boyer, ss, Dixie (Utah) JC**
5. Josh Bell, c, North Side HS, Jackson, Tenn.
6. **Cody Haerther, 3b, Chaminade Prep, Chatsworth, Calif.**
7. **David Williamson, lhp, Massachusetts-Lowell**
8. **Tyler Parker, c, Georgia Tech**
9. **Travis Hanson, ss, Portland**
10. **Matt Lemanczyk, of, Sacred Heart (Conn.)**
11. **David Brockman, rhp, Grand Canyon (Ariz.)**
12. **Bob Runyon, rhp, Fresno State**
13. **Reid Gorecki, of, Delaware**
14. **Joe Van Gorder, lhp, West Virginia**
15. **Daylon Monette, of, Oklahoma State**
16. **Brad Thompson, rhp, Dixie (Utah) JC**
17. Chad Clark, rhp, Southern California
18. **Scott Schweitzer, lhp, Kentucky Wesleyan**
19. Ryan Mulhern, of, South Alabama
20. **Hal Chafey, lhp, Francis Marion (S.C.)**
21. **Gabe Veloz, 2b, New Mexico State**
22. **Andy Davidson, lhp, Cal State Northridge**
23. **Rich Scalamandre, rhp, Dominican (N.Y.)**
24. **Kevin Coleman, rhp, Florida**
25. **Kyle McClellan, rhp, Hazelwood West HS, Hazlewood, Mo.**
26. **Mitch Maio, rhp, Utah**
27. Matt Elliott, rhp, Basic HS, Henderson, Nev.
28. **Melvin Falu, 2b, Southern Arkansas**
29. **Wes Jaillet, rhp, Saint Louis**
30. **Zach Cates, 1b, Oklahoma State**
31. **Garris Gonce, of, South Carolina**
32. Sean Kasmar, ss, Las Vegas HS
33. **Josh Bridges, c, Martin Methodist (Tenn.)**
34. **Mike McCoy, 2b, San Diego**
35. Julian Williams, of, Long Beach CC
36. **James Mondesir, rhp, Dominican (N.Y.)**
37. **Tyler Durham, 2b, Northwestern State**
38. Matt Varner, rhp, Angelina (Texas) JC
39. **Jeff Tolotti, of, Nevada**
40. **Brian Flynn, rhp, St. Thomas Aquinas (N.Y.)**
41. **Jonathan Estes, rhp, Freed-Hardeman (Tenn.)**
42. **Kevin Estrada, ss, Pepperdine**
43. **Joey Vandever, of, Evansville**
44. **Brock Jacobsen, of, Dixie (Utah) JC**
45. Sean Clark, rhp, Chaminade Prep, Chatsworth, Calif.
46. **Jason Galbraith, lhp, Concordia (N.Y.)**

47. Chris Gibson, 1b/of, Bellevue East HS, Bellevue, Neb.
48. Philip Perry, rhp, Georgia Tech
49. David Dennis, lhp, Valhalla HS, El Cajon, Calif.
50. John Powell, rhp, McGehee HS, Tillar, Ark.

SAN DIEGO PADRES

June—Regular Phase (13)

1. **Khalil Greene, ss, Clemson**
2. **Michael Johnson, 1b, Clemson**
3. **Kennard Jones, of, Indiana**
4. **Aaron Coonrod, rhp, John A. Logan (Ill.) JC**
5. **Sean Thompson, lhp, Thunder Ridge HS, Denver**
6. **Adam Shorsher, c, San Jose State**
7. Matt Lynch, lhp, Florida State
8. **Luke Steidlmayer, rhp, UC Davis**
9. **Brian Burgamy, 2b, Wichita State**
10. **L.J. Biernbaum, of, Florida Atlantic**
11. **Brandon Wilson, rhp, Okaloosa-Walton (Fla.) JC**
12. **Paul McAnulty, 1b, Long Beach State**
13. Lance Pendleton, rhp, Kingwood (Texas) HS
14. **Gabe Ribas, rhp, Northwestern**
15. **Rolando Agosto, ss, Union (Tenn.)**
16. **Kevin Beavers, lhp, Pepperdine**
17. **Rashad Smith, of, Lambuth (Tenn.)**
18. Bruce Gallaway, lhp, Grayson County (Texas) CC
19. Spencer Grogan, lhp, Okaloosa-Walton (Fla.) CC
20. **George Kottaras, c, Connors State (Okla.) JC**
21. Andy LaRoche, ss, Grayson County (Texas) CC
22. **David Krisch, lhp, Cal Poly Pomona**
23. **Rusty Moore, of, Bethune-Cookman**
24. **Adam Montarbo, rhp/3b, Chico State (Calif.)**
25. Chuck Bechtel, rhp, Marist
26. **E.J. Laratta, rhp, Ohio State**
27. **Brian Whitaker, rhp, UNC Wilmington**
28. **Mike Richardson, of/c, Sonoma State (Calif.)**
29. **Stephen Baker, of, Liberty**
30. **Danny de la O, lhp, Fresno CC**
31. **Jared Wells, rhp, Tyler (Texas) JC**
32. Jesse Estrada, rhp, Socorro HS, El Paso
33. Bo Banach, 3b, Lakewood (Calif.) HS
34. Bill Silvestri, rhp, Dixie (Utah) JC
35. **Drew Macias, of, Chaffey (Calif.) JC**
36. **Greg Bochy, rhp, Cal Poly**
37. Corey Hall, rhp, Seminole State (Okla.) JC
38. Brendan Katin, c, Okaloosa-Walton (Fla.) JC
39. Scott Lonergan, rhp, Poway (Calif.) HS
40. Daniel Fitch, c, Mount Carmel HS, San Diego
41. Ryan Werner, c, San Diego CC
42. **Brian Wahlbrink, of, UC Riverside**
43. Jason Catala, of, Margarita Janer HS, Guaynabo, P.R.
44. Marcus Barriger, rhp, Kaskaskia (Ill.) CC
45. **Chad Etheridge, of, Columbia State (Tenn.) CC**
46. Craig Bartosh, of, Grayson County (Texas) CC
47. Stephen Nam, 1b/2b, Mississauga, Ontario
48. Matt Morizio, rhp/ss, Waltham (Mass.) HS
49. John Parscal, lhp, Northglenn HS, Denver
50. Chris Regan, 1b/of, Earl Wooster HS, Reno, Nev.

SAN FRANCISCO GIANTS

June—Regular Phase (25)

1. **Matt Cain, rhp, Houston HS, Germantown, Tenn.**
2. **Fred Lewis, of, Southern**
3. **Dan Ortmeier, of, Texas-Arlington**
4. **Kevin Correia, rhp, Cal Poly**
5. **Kevin Kelly, ss, Duke**
6. **Jesse English, lhp, Rancho Buena Vista, Vista, Calif.**
7. **Mike Musgrave, rhp, Forest HS, Ocala, Fla.**
8. **Clay Hensley, rhp, Lamar**
9. **Randy Walter, of, Wichita State**
10. **Glenn Woolard, rhp, Kutztown (Pa.)**
11. **Jake Wald, ss, George Washington**
12. Kellen Ludwig, rhp, Chipola (Fla.) JC
13. **Aaron Sobieraj, 3b, Florida**
14. **Josh Habel, lhp, Northern Iowa**
15. **Matt Dryer, 1b, Miami**
16. **Greg Bruso, rhp, UC Davis**
17. **Luke Nelson, rhp, Southern Illinois**
18. **Bryan Millikan, rhp, Black Hills HS, Olympia, Wash.**
19. David Timm, lhp, Seminole (Fla.) CC
20. **Ben Mitchell, rhp, Grand Canyon (Ariz.)**
21. **Travis Ishikawa, 1b/of, Federal Way (Wash.) HS**
22. **Nelson Lopez, rhp, Florida Atlantic**
23. Neil Walton, ss, Santa Cruz (Calif.) HS
24. **Jay Knowlton, ss, Lewis-Clark State (Idaho)**
25. Justin Gee, rhp, Sarasota (Fla.) HS
26. Sean Rierson, rhp, Arizona
27. **Ryan McGovern, lhp, W.J. Mouat HS, Abbotsford, B.C**
28. Philip Tapley, rhp, Greenbrier HS, Evans, Ga.
29. Alex Hinshaw, lhp, Chaffey (Calif.) JC
30. Matt Somnis, rhp, Lassen (Calif.) HS
31. **Matt Palmer, rhp, Southwest Missouri State**
32. **Joe Bateman, rhp, Massachusetts College**
33. Brett Cooley, 1b/of, Houston
34. Phil Monte, lhp, Cosumnes River (Calif.) JC
35. Ryan Stevenson, of, Chabot (Calif.) JC
36. **David Stone, of, Virginia**
37. Chris Sweet, rhp, Virginia
38. Randal Hodge, lhp, Pearl-Cohn HS, Nashville
39. **Anthony Moreno, rhp, South Mountain (Ariz.) CC**
40. Mike Redford, rhp, Woodland HS, Sacramento
41. Danny Muegge, rhp, Texas
42. **Andrew Jefferson, lhp, Southwest Missouri State**
43. Jason Chavez, rhp, Mineral Area (Mo.) JC
44. Tim Torres, ss, Diablo Valley (Calif.) JC
45. Matt Berezay, of, Sierra HS, Manteca, Calif.
46. Matt Ircandia, lhp, Semiahmoo HS, Surrey, B.C
47. Scott Dodge, of, Cuesta (Calif.) JC
48. Dante Brinkley, of, Southwest Missouri State
49. Zach Borowiak, ss, Southeast Missouri State
50. Robert Davis, c, Greenbrier HS, Evans, Ga.

SEATTLE MARINERS

June—Regular Phase (28)

1. John Mayberry Jr., of, Rockhurst HS, Kansas City, Mo.
2. **Josh Womack, of, Crawford HS, San Diego**
3. Eddy Martinez-Esteve, of, Westminster Christian HS, Miami
4. **Randy Frye, rhp, Lake Orion (Mich.) HS**
5. **Kendall Bergdall, lhp, Cimarron HS, Layhoma, Okla.**
6. **Troy Cate, lhp, Ricks (Idaho) JC**
7. **Evel Bastida-Martinez, 2b, Miami**
8. **Brandon Perry, lhp, Graham (N.C.) HS**
9. **Terry Forbes, rhp, Auburn Drive HS, Halifax, Nova Scotia**
10. **Brian Stitt, rhp, Indian River (Fla.) CC**
11. **Jared Thomas, lhp, Oakland (Mich.)**
12. **Matt Hagen, 3b, Liberty**
13. **T.A. Fulmer, rhp, The Citadel**
14. **Theiborh Almanzar, c, Bronx (N.Y.) CC**
15. Gaby Sanchez, 3b, Brito Private HS, Miami
16. Ryan Leaist, rhp, Montreat (N.C.)
17. **Corey Harrington, ss, New Mexico State**
18. **Gary Harris, of, Georgia College & State**
19. **Chris Kroski, c, St. Petersburg (Fla.) CC**
20. **David Viane, rhp, Oakland (Mich.)**
21. **Eric Blakeley, 2b, Indiana**
22. **Hunter Brown, 3b, Rice**
23. Travis Buck, ss, Richland (Wash.) HS
24. Johnnie Bassham, lhp, Grayson County (Texas) CC
25. Cory Vanderhook, c, Edison HS, Fountain Valley, Calif.
26. **David Bernat, rhp, South Miami HS, Miami**
27. Royce Dickerson, of, Central HS, Kalamazoo, Mich.
28. **Vance Hall, lhp, Allderdice HS, Pittsburgh**
29. **Michael Nesbitt, of, Los Angeles Pierce JC**
30. **T.J. Bohn, of, Bellevue (Neb.)**
31. Clayton Stewart, rhp, San Jacinto (Texas) JC
32. Dane Awana, lhp, Waianae (Hawaii) HS
33. Kyle Patrick, rhp, Apopka (Fla.) HS
34. Brady Burrill, c, Michigan State

35. Patrick Pfeiffer, rhp, Brentwood School, Los Angeles
36. Jermaine Smith, ss, King HS, Tampa
37. **Brad Rose, rhp, Walters State (Tenn.) JC**
38. Deandre Green, of, Encinal HS, Alameda, Calif.
39. **Bryan LaHair, of, St. Petersburg (Fla.) JC**
40. Josh Cooper, rhp, South HS, Pueblo, Colo.
41. Andrew Edwards, rhp, Florida International
42. Brandon Jones, 1b, Grayson County (Texas) CC
43. Adam Pernasilici, of/1b, St. Anne HS, Tecumseh, Ontario
44. Omar Borges, of, Brito Private HS, Miami
45. Ray Lockhart, of, Compton (Calif.) HS
46. Roberto Mena, 2b, Pedro Falu HS, Rio Grande, P.R.
47. Jason Godin, rhp, North Stafford HS, Stafford, Va.
48. **Cardoza Tucker, rhp, Bullard HS, Fresno**
49. Aaron Ruchti, c, San Jacinto (Texas) JC
50. Oliver Arias, rhp, CC of Rhode Island

TAMPA BAY DEVIL RAYS

June—Regular Phase (2)

1. **B.J. Upton, ss, Greenbrier Christian Academy, Chesapeake, Va.**
2. **Jason Pridie, of, Prescott (Ariz.) HS**
3. **Elijah Dukes, of, Hillsborough HS, Tampa**
4. **Wes Bankston, of, Plano East HS, Plano, Texas**
5. Mark Romanczuk, lhp, St. Mark's HS, Newark, Del.
6. Cesar Ramos, lhp, El Rancho HS, Pico Rivera, Calif.
7. **Scott Autrey, rhp, North Carolina**
8. **Joey Gomes, of, Santa Clara**
9. Chris Leroux, c, St. Joseph's SS, Mississauga, Ontario
10. **Jason Hammel, rhp, Treasure Valley (Ore.) JC**
11. **Adam Moreno, rhp, Fresno HS**
12. **Blair Irvin, of, Patterson (La.) HS**
13. Matt Harrington, rhp, Long Beach (Western League)
14. **Nick DeBarr, rhp, Lassen (Calif.) JC**
15. Mike Pelfrey, rhp, Wichita Heights HS, Wichita
16. **Mike Prochaska, lhp, North Carolina State**
17. **Ernest Woodruff, c, Gulf Coast (Fla.) CC**
18. **Romelio Lopez, rhp, Conroe (Texas) HS**
19. **Cole Smith, rhp, Rockwall (Texas) HS**
20. **Jarred Farrell, rhp, Hahnville HS, Boutte, La.**
21. Chris Garcia, rhp, Xaverian HS, Brooklyn
22. Travis Ingle, rhp, Cal State Fullerton
23. Jacoby Ellsbury, of, Madras (Ore.) HS
24. **Adam Nikolic, of, Cal State Northridge**
25. **Brian Bulger, rhp, Georgia College & State**
26. **Jarrad LaVergne, lhp, Westgate HS, New Iberia, La.**
27. **Brandon Mann, lhp, Mount Rainier HS, Des Moines, Wash.**
28. Adam Olerio, rhp, North Kingston (R.I.) HS
29. Mike McGowan, rhp, Navarro (Texas) JC
30. Mike Geddes, rhp, Jenison (Mich.) HS
31. **Isiah Garner, lhp, Arkansas-Pine Bluff**
32. Rodney Keener, lhp, Minden (La.) HS
33. **Coltyn Simmons, c, Durango HS, Las Vegas**
34. John-Austin Emmons, of, Wharton County (Texas) JC
35. Luke Cosmos, rhp, McAteer HS, San Francisco
36. Jake Muyco, c, Richland (Wash.) HS
37. **Shane Shelley, ss, Belle Chasse (La.) HS**
38. **Matt Cobb, lhp, Shelton State (Ala.) CC**
39. Brandon Rousseve, ss, Holy Cross HS, New Orleans
40. Justin Hopes, rhp, Jeanerette (La.) HS
41. Daron Roberts, c, Cosumnes River (Calif.) JC
42. Brandon Federici, lhp, Riverview HS, Oakmont, Pa.
43. **Steve Skinner, 2b, Santa Rosa (Calif.) JC**
44. Rolando Quinonez, c, San Juan, P.R.
45. Justin Standridge, rhp, Clay Chalkville HS, Pinson, Ala.
46. **Jino Gonzalez, lhp, CC of Southern Nevada**
47. Adam Dalby, c, Daingerfield HS, Hughes Spring, Texas
48. Jason Urquidez, rhp, Central Arizona JC
49. **Shane Sanders, rhp, Alabama**
50. Bryan Banks, rhp, St. Petersburg (Fla.) JC

TEXAS RANGERS

June—Regular Phase (10)

1. **Drew Meyer, ss, South Carolina**
2. (Pick to Dodgers as compensation for Type A free agent Chan Ho Park)
3. (Pick to Indians as compensation for Type A free agent Juan Gonzalez)
4. (Pick to Cubs as compensation for Type A free agent Todd Van Poppel)
5. (Pick to Rockies as compensation for Type B free agent Jay Powell)
6. **J.C. Barnett, rhp, Florida Southern**
7. **Andrew Tisdale, rhp, Chapman (Calif.)**
8. **Chris O'Riordan, 2b, Stanford**
9. Steven Herce, rhp, Rice
10. **Nate Gold, 1b, Gonzaga**
11. **Kiki Bengochea, rhp, Miami**
12. **Erik Thompson, rhp, Pensacola (Fla.) JC**
13. **Chris Hamblen, c, Cincinnati**
14. **Charlie Bilezikjian, of, St. John's**
15. **Sam Narron, lhp, East Carolina**
16. **Josh Kreuzer, 1b, West Valley (Calif.) JC**
17. Chris Wilson, 3b, Redlands (Calif.) HS
18. **Cameron Coughlan, 2b, Brigham Young**
19. Jesus Maldonado, rhp, Manuel Negron HS, Humacao, P.R.
20. **Kameron Loe, rhp, Cal State Northridge**
21. **Jason Mann, c, Central Alabama CC**
22. Bobby Andrews, of, Rancho Buena Vista HS, Vista, Calif.
23. **Craig Ringe, ss, Central Missouri State**
24. Chad Decker, lhp, Valley View HS, Moreno Valley, Calif.
25. **Joel Kirsten, lhp, Los Angeles Pierce JC**
26. **Julius Smith, lhp, Lewiston (Idaho) HS**
27. John McCarthy, of, St. Rita HS, Palos Park, Ill.
28. Jake Tompkins, rhp, Louisiana State
29. **Nick Shields, c, Wright State**
30. **Rob Corrado, rhp, Kentucky**
31. Mike Tamulionis, rhp, St. John's
32. **Gary Hogan, rhp, Arkansas**
33. **Larry Grayson, of, Manatee (Fla.) CC**
34. Charles Fletcher, of, North Springs HS, Atlanta
35. Ken Pokryfke, lhp, Union HS, Wilmot, Wis.
36. Frans Meyer, 3b, Northridge HS, Layton, Utah
37. Dion McDaniel, of, Hales Franciscan HS, Chicago
38. Robbie Wachman, rhp, Middle Georgia JC
39. Paul Sandoval, rhp/3b, Trabuco Hills HS, Mission Viejo, Calif.
40. Jared Gaston, ss/of, Cleveland (Tenn.) HS
41. Andy Myette, rhp, Kwantlen (B.C.) JC
42. **Jesse Chavez, rhp, Riverside (Calif.) CC**
43. Ronald Harris, c, George Washington HS, Denver
44. Ryan Mieszala, of, Greenway HS, Glendale, Ariz.
45. Tom Zimmerman, rhp, Whitnall HS, Milwaukee
46. Josh Hernandez, c/3b, Los Lunas (N.M.) HS
47. Paul Oseguera, lhp, La Costa Canyon HS, Carlsbad, Calif.
48. Steven Friend, ss/of, Kishwaukee (Ill.) JC
49. Brad Burkhead, of, Northwest Mississippi CC
50. Will Peterson, of, Valdosta (Ga.) HS

TORONTO BLUE JAYS

June—Regular Phase (14)

1. **Russ Adams, ss, North Carolina**
2. **Dave Bush, rhp, Wake Forest**
3. **Justin Maureau, lhp, Wichita State**
4. **Adam Peterson, rhp, Wichita State**
5. **Chad Pleiness, rhp, Central Michigan**
6. **Jason Perry, of, Georgia Tech**
7. **Brian Grant, rhp, C.B. Aycock HS, Goldsboro, N.C.**
8. **Chris Leonard, lhp, Miami (Ohio)**
9. **Russ Savickas, rhp, Johnston (R.I.) HS**
10. **Eric Arnold, 2b, Rice**
11. **Jason Waugh, of, St. Mary's**
12. **Michael Roga, rhp, Armstrong Atlantic State (Ga.)**
13. **John Schneider, c, Delaware**
14. **Michael Galloway, 1b/of, Miami (Ohio)**

15. **David Smith, of, West Virginia State**
16. Aric Van Gaalen, lhp, Harry Ainlay HS, Edmonton
17. **Randy Braun, of, Belton (Mo.) HS**
18. **Jordan De Jong, rhp, Cal State Fullerton**
19. **Brad Hassey, ss, Arizona**
20. Jesus Carnevale, lhp, Fernando Chavez HS, Arecibo, P.R.
21. Melvin Burkhalter, 1b, Seminole (Fla.) CC
22. **Eric Rico, of, Cornell**
23. **Bubbie Buzachero, rhp, Tennessee Tech**
24. Matt Farnum, rhp, Texas A&M
25. **Zeph Zinsman, 1b, Lewis-Clark State (Idaho)**
26. **Dewon Day, rhp, Southern**
27. Jared Odom, rhp, Vero Beach (Fla.) HS
28. **Paul Richmond, c, Baylor**
29. **Erik Kratz, c, Eastern Mennonite (Va.)**
30. **A.J. Porfirio, of, Rice**
31. Jeff Terrell, lhp, Tennessee
32. **Michael Seifert, lhp, Rend Lake (Ill.) JC**
33. **Carlo Cota, 2b, San Diego State**
34. **Justin Owens, of, Coastal Carolina**
35. **Andy Torres, rhp, Lewis-Clark State (Idaho)**
36. **Scott Dragicevich, ss, Stanford**
37. Ross Swisher, lhp, Hudson's Bay HS, Vancouver, Wash.
38. Bryan Hansen, lhp, Fontana (Calif.) HS
39. **Nick Thomas, rhp, Sacramento CC**
40. Danny Anderson, of, San Joaquin Delta (Calif.) JC
41. Adam Carr, rhp, San Lorenzo (Calif.) HS
42. Dirk Kleinmann, lhp, King (Tenn.)
43. Chris Nicoll, rhp, Righetti HS, Santa Maria, Calif.
44. **Ben Harrison, lhp, Colleyville Heritage HS, Colleyville, Texas**
45. Brandon Bailey, c/of, Sacramento CC
46. Justin Tordi, ss, Dr. Phillips HS, Orlando
47. Tim Maloney, of, Kansas State
48. Drew Butera, c, Bishop Moore HS, Orlando
49. James Jewell, of, Roosevelt HS, Gary, Ind.
50. J.B. Cox, rhp, Bay City (Texas) HS

2003 Baseball drives down bonuses dramatically, while signing players at a record rate

Devil Rays scouting director Cam Bonifay knew for several days that he wanted to choose Delmon Young with the No. 1 pick in the 2003 draft. After three days of organization meetings, general manager Chuck LaMar came to the same conclusion.

Tampa Bay finalized its decision the night before the draft, but Young, a Camarillo (Calif.) High outfielder, didn't learn his fate until he heard his name called on the Web draft broadcast. His father Larry knew beforehand but kept it a secret.

Young said he had thought the Devil Rays were going with Southern second baseman Rickie Weeks. He had the requisite Rays cap and T-shirt on hand for photo opportunities, but he also had Brewers paraphernalia on hand in case he lasted until the second pick.

Few teams had any questions about Young, the most accomplished high school hitter in the draft. At 6-foot-3 and 205 pounds, he projected as a slugging right fielder. He set a U.S. junior national team record with 16 homers in 2002, when he topped all players at the World Junior Championship with nine homers and 18 RBIs in seven games.

Young and his brother Dmitri, a Tigers outfielder, became the highest-drafted siblings ever. Dmitri, who went fourth overall to the Cardinals in 1991, also had been drafted by the Devil Rays. Tampa Bay selected him in the November 1997 expansion draft, then traded him to Cincinnati in a prearranged deal.

Because the Tigers were in San Diego to play the Padres, Dmitri was able to surprise his brother by arriving via limousine for the draft-day celebration. Delmon sounded relaxed and confident afterward, saying he wasn't going to put pressure on himself and comparing his game to Vladimir Guerrero's. He also said he hoped to reach Tampa Bay quickly.

Young did reach the big leagues in 2006, but he became known more for his churlish behavior than for his performance, most notably throwing a bat at an umpire during a Triple-A game in 2006. Tampa Bay traded him to the Twins after the 2007 season.

Despite Tampa Bay's outfield depth and glaring weaknesses elsewhere, LaMar said Young's position was not a consideration. The Devil Rays were determined to get the best player available. They signed him for a $3.7 million bonus (as part of a major league deal) as MLB's concerted efforts to drive bonuses down had even more success than in 2002.

In 2003, the average first-round pick signed for

LARRY GOREN

Delmon Young's career got off to a good start, but the Rays later traded him away

$1,766,667, the cheapest cost since 1998 and down a whopping 16.2 percent from 2002. That exceeded even MLB's hopes, as its predraft guidelines for the first round averaged $1,855,833.

"If you're not willing to sign for slot money," one agent said, "you're going to start sliding through the draft."

Just six first-rounders exceeded their predraft slots, and for the first time in draft history every player selected in the first two rounds came to terms. Just 16 of the 307 players from the first 10 rounds went unsigned, which also was unprecedented. The previous low had been 24 in 2000.

After Young, the top of the first round played out as expected. The Brewers took Weeks, whose career .473 average is the NCAA Division I record, and the Tigers and Padres snapped up the top college pitchers available, Wake Forest's Kyle Sleeth and Richmond's Tim Stauffer. Picking fifth, the Royals went with Pennsylvania high school outfielder Chris Lubanski.

Stauffer forever wrote himself into the annals of draft history, revealing to the Padres a shoulder problem after the team had offered him a $2.6 million bonus. After Stauffer's revelation, he signed for $750,000. Neither Sleeth nor Stauffer panned out, with Stauffer spending most of his career in Triple-A and Sleeth already out of baseball due to injuries.

At No. 7, the Orioles were the wild card in the top 10 picks. They signed a blue-chip talent a week before the draft, agreeing to a five-year, $4.02 million major league contract with Chipola (Fla.) Junior College lefthander Adam Loewen shortly before they would have lost his rights. Baltimore picked Loewen fourth overall in 2002, but negotiations bogged down and he became a draft-and-follow, setting a record for the process when he agreed to his deal on the eve of the closed period.

Orioles Success Story

Looking to save money after signing Loewen, the Orioles tried to get Tulane first baseman Michael Aubrey to accept a predraft deal. When he declined, they opted for Young Harris (Ga.) JC two-way star Nick Markakis. Markakis ranked right behind Loewen among draft-and-follows from 2002. Drafted twice by the Reds, Markakis turned down $1.5 million from the Reds. He agreed to a $1.85 million bonus from the Orioles.

While Baltimore's decision to take Markakis wasn't surprising, its choice for his future was. Most teams preferred him as a lefthander and some clubs were split, but the Orioles liked his bat more and made him a full-time outfielder. He reached the big leagues in 2006 and had been one of the most successful players from the draft class.

When major league owners and players reached accord on a new Basic Agreement on Aug. 30, 2002, they agreed to adjust the draft rules. But they later failed to agree on what they had agreed to when it came down to putting those changes in writing, so the alterations were tabled and the draft remained largely unchanged for the remainder of the decade.

A total of 1,480 players were selected in 2003. Arizona State led all colleges with 12 draftees, starting with outfielder Andre Ethier (Athletics, second round). Cal State Fullerton had 11, including righthander Chad Cordero in the first round. Miami's Brito Private High, with an enrollment of just over 100 students, tied a prep record set by Seminole (Fla.) High in 2001 with six draftees, though none higher than 23rd-round catcher Danny Santin (Mariners). While Seminole won the 2001 national high school title, Brito went 30-6 and finished the season unranked in Baseball America's poll.

DRAFT 03: FIRST-ROUND PICKS

No.	Club	Player, Pos.	School	Hometown	Ht.	Wt.	B-T	Age
1.	Devil Rays	Delmon Young, of	Camarillo HS	Camarillo, Calif.	6-2	200	R-R	17
2.	Brewers	Rickie Weeks, 2b	Southern	Altamonte Springs, Fla.	6-0	195	R-R	20
3.	Tigers	Kyle Sleeth, rhp	Wake Forest	Westminster, Colo.	6-5	205	R-R	21
4.	Padres	Tim Stauffer, rhp	Richmond	Saratoga Springs, N.Y.	6-2	205	R-R	21
5.	Royals	Chris Lubanski, of	Kennedy-Kendrick HS	Schwenksville, Pa.	6-3	180	L-L	18
6.	Cubs	Ryan Harvey, of	Dunedin HS	Palm Harbor, Fla.	6-5	192	R-R	18
7.	Orioles	Nick Markakis, lhp/of	Young Harris (Ga.) JC	Woodstock, Ga.	6-1	170	L-L	19
8.	Pirates	Paul Maholm, lhp	Mississippi State	Holly Springs, Miss.	6-2	215	L-L	20
9.	Rangers	John Danks, lhp	Round Rock HS	Round Rock, Texas	6-2	190	L-L	18
10.	Rockies	Ian Stewart, 3b	La Quinta HS	Garden Grove, Calif.	6-3	200	L-R	18
11.	Indians	Michael Aubrey, 1b	Tulane	Shreveport, La.	6-1	195	L-L	21
12.	Mets	Lastings Milledge, of	Lakewood Ranch HS	Palmetto, Fla.	6-1	180	R-R	18
13.	Blue Jays	Aaron Hill, ss	Louisiana State	Visalia, Calif.	5-11	195	R-R	21
14.	Reds	Ryan Wagner, rhp	Houston	Yoakum, Texas	6-4	210	R-R	20
15.	White Sox	Brian Anderson, of	Arizona	Tucson, Ariz.	6-2	205	R-R	21
16.	Marlins	Jeff Allison, rhp	Veterans Memorial HS	Peabody, Mass.	6-2	195	R-R	18
17.	Red Sox	David Murphy, of	Baylor	Spring, Texas	6-3	195	L-L	21
18.	Indians	Brad Snyder, of	Ball State	Bellevue, Ohio	6-3	210	L-L	21
19.	Diamondbacks	Conor Jackson, 1b	California	Woodland Hills, Calif.	6-3	210	R-R	21
20.	Expos	Chad Cordero, rhp	Cal State Fullerton	Chino, Calif.	6-0	195	R-R	21
21.	Twins	Matt Moses, 3b	Mills Godwin HS	Richmond, Va.	6-0	210	L-R	18
22.	Giants	David Aardsma, rhp	Rice	The Woodlands, Texas	6-5	200	R-R	21
23.	Angels	Brandon Wood, ss	Horizon HS	Scottsdale, Ariz.	6-2	180	R-R	18
24.	Dodgers	Chad Billingsley, rhp	Defiance HS	Defiance, Ohio	6-2	195	R-R	18
25.	Athletics	Brad Sullivan, rhp	Houston	Nederland, Texas	6-1	190	R-R	21
26.	Athletics	Brian Snyder, 3b	Stetson	Wellington, Fla.	5-11	195	R-R	21
27.	Yankees	Eric Duncan, 3b	Seton Hall Prep	Florham Park, N.Y.	6-1	205	L-R	18
28.	Cardinals	Daric Barton, c	Marina HS	Huntington Beach, Calif.	5-11	195	L-R	17
29.	Diamondbacks	Carlos Quentin, of	Stanford	Chula Vista, Calif.	6-2	215	R-R	20
30.	Royals	Mitch Maier, c	Toledo	Novi, Mich.	6-2	195	L-R	20

2003

CLUB-BY-CLUB SELECTIONS

ANAHEIM ANGELS

June—Regular Phase (23)

1. **Brandon Wood, ss, Horizon HS, Scottsdale, Ariz.**
2. **Anthony Whittington, lhp, Buffalo HS, Putnam, W.Va.**
3. **Sean Rodriguez, ss, Braddock HS, Miami**
4. **Bob Zimmermann, rhp, Southwest Missouri State**
5. **Blake Balkcom, of, Florida State**
6. **Jesse Smith, rhp, Illinois Valley CC**
7. **Reggie Willits, of, Oklahoma**
8. **Josh Cowles, of, East Valley HS, Redlands, Calif.**
9. **Von Stertzbach, rhp, Central Florida**
10. **Patrice Lepage, c, Edouard Montpetit College HS**
11. **Adam Pavkovich, ss, Alabama**
12. **Andy Hill, rhp, Brewster (Wash.) HS**
13. **Danny Davidson, lhp, Florida State**
14. **Kelly Shearer, lhp, Elkins HS, Missouri City, Texas**
15. **David Austen, rhp, South Florida**
16. **Stantrel Smith, of, North Florida CC**
17. **Matt Pali, of, Florida Atlantic**
18. **Fernando Rodriguez, rhp, El Paso (Texas) CC**
19. **Billy Boyer, 2b, Enumclaw (Wash.) HS**
20. Jason Donald, ss, Buchanan HS, Clovis, Calif.
21. Josh Land, of, Milton (Fla.) HS
22. **B.J. Brown, lhp, Oakland (Mich.)**
23. Brett Douglas, rhp, Westminster (Calif.) HS
24. **Chad Hauseman, of, Jacksonville**
25. Justin Brashear, c, Barbe HS, Lake Charles, La.
26. Joseph Rowe, rhp, Central Alabama CC
27. Jimmy Durette, lhp, Ahuntsic College HS, Matine, Quebec
28. Nick Roxby, 2b, North Florida JC
29. Drew Fiorenza, rhp, Okaloosa-Walton (Fla.) CC
30. Adam Frank, c, Lamar (Colo.) CC
31. David Huff, lhp, Edison HS, Huntington Beach, Calif.
32. Keith Williams, of, Gulf Coast (Fla.) CC
33. Ricky Bambino, c, Foothill HS, Redding, Calif.
34. Jason Blackey, rhp, Malaspina (B.C.) CC
35. Jay Mattox, of, Chipola (Fla.) JC
36. **Brandon Doddo, 3b, Broward (Fla.) CC**
37. Tommy Baumgardner, lhp, Indian River (Fla.) CC
38. Ron Lowe, lhp, Pasco-Hernando (Fla.) CC
39. Nate Boman, lhp, Patrick Henry HS, San Diego
40. Brandon Morrow, rhp, Rancho Cotate HS, Rohnert Park, Calif.
41. Chris Hunter, rhp, Utah Valley State JC
42. Cody Nelson, ss, Chabot (Calif.) JC
43. Caleb Hatfield, rhp, Red Bluff (Calif.) HS
44. John Mariotti, rhp, Chaminade College HS, Toronto
45. Chris Noonan, lhp, Seton Hall
46. Hank Lanto, c, Modesto (Calif.) HS
47. Ryan Anderson, lhp, St. Petersburg (Fla.) CC
48. Jeremy Labigano, lhp, Westwood HS, Fort Pierce, Fla.
49. Evan Bailey, rhp, Westsyde SS, Kamloops, B.C
50. Kris Johnson, lhp, Blue Springs (Mo.) HS

ARIZONA DIAMONDBACKS

June—Regular Phase (29)

1. **Conor Jackson, 3b, California** (Pick from Mariners as compensation for Type B free agent Greg Colbrunn)
1. **Carlos Quentin, of, Stanford**
2. **Jamie D'Antona, 3b, Wake Forest**
3. **Matt Chico, lhp, Palomar (Calif.) JC**
4. **Chris Kinsey, rhp, Sacramento State**
5. **Jeff Cook, of, Southern Mississippi**
6. **Orlando Mercado, c, Antonio Luchetti HS, Arecibo, P.R.**
7. **Dustin Glant, rhp, Purdue**
8. **Robbie Van, lhp, Nevada-Las Vegas**
9. **Steve Garrabrants, 2b, Arizona State**
10. **Adam Bass, rhp, Alabama-Huntsville**
11. **Tila Reynolds, ss, Washington**
12. **Jon Kaplan, of, Tulane**
13. **Todd Buchanan, 1b, Western Carolina**
14. **Brian Rose, c, Florida**
15. **Ben Krantz, rhp, Pennsylvania**
16. **Ruben Kerbs, lhp, Wichita State**
17. **Jayson Santiago, of, Maestro Ladi HS, Vega Alta, P.R.**
18. Chris Coghlan, c, East Lake HS, Tarpon Springs, Fla.
19. **Danny Muegge, rhp, Texas**
20. **Joe Carque, rhp, San Diego State**
21. **Chad Clark, rhp, Azusa Pacific (Calif.)**
22. **Walt Novosel, lhp, Ohio**
23. **Travis McAndrews, of, Southern California**
24. **Allen Mottram, c, Massachusetts-Lowell**
25. **Kellen Raab, lhp, Wisconsin-Parkside**
26. **Travis Van Zile, of, Wisconsin-Whitewater**
27. **Jason McStoots, ss, Missouri Baptist**
28. **Brian Viafore, 1b, Central Washington**
29. Tony Festa, 3b, UC Riverside
30. **Greg Mathis, of, Southwest Missouri State**
31. **Tim Vaillancourt, rhp, Delaware State**
32. **Andrew McCreery, 3b, Pennsylvania**
33. Brandon Belcher, lhp, Ruston (La.) HS
34. **Gabe Rio, lhp, Florida Southern**
35. **Alex Cremidan, rhp, UC San Diego**
36. **Derik Nippert, rhp, Ohio Valley (W.Va.)**
37. Ryan LaCross, lhp, Lakewood Ranch HS, Bradenton, Fla.
38. **Shane Dove, lhp, Spartanburg Methodist (S.C.) JC**
39. **Cristobal Melendez, of, Missouri Baptist**
40. Connor Rapkoch, c, Bellarmine Prep, Tacoma, Wash.
41. Kevin Stiehl, lhp, West Torrance HS, Torrance, Calif.
42. **Mike Guerrero, of, Arizona State**
43. Matt Mammen, lhp, St. Charles (Mo.) CC
44. Jacob Coash, lhp, JC of the Canyons (Calif.)
45. Joshua Terrell, 1b, Lurleen B. Wallace State (Ala.) JC
46. Lester Contreras, ss, Champagnat Catholic HS, Hialeah, Fla.
47. Brody Taylor, lhp, Louisburg (N.C.) JC
48. Ben Colton, rhp, Reno (Nev.) HS
49. Juan Velazquez, rhp, Grossmont (Calif.) JC
50. Jeff Manship, rhp, Ronald Reagan HS, San Antonio

ATLANTA BRAVES

June—Regular Phase (30)

1. (Pick to Royals as compensation for Type B free agent Paul Byrd)
1. **Luis Atilano, rhp, Gabriela Mistral HS, San Juan, P.R.** (Supplemental pick—35th—for loss of Type A free agent Tom Glavine)
1. **Jarrod Saltalamacchia, c, Royal Palm Beach HS, West Palm Beach, Fla.** (Supplemental pick—36th—for loss of Type A free agent Mike Remlinger)
2. **Jo-Jo Reyes, lhp, Riverside Poly HS, Riverside, Calif.** (Pick from Cubs as compensation for Remlinger)
2. **Paul Bacot, rhp, Lakeside HS, Atlanta**
3. **Jake Stevens, lhp, Cape Coral (Fla.) HS** (Pick from Mets as compensation for Glavine)
3. **Matt Harrison, lhp, South Granville HS, Creedmoor, N.C.**
4. **Jamie Romak, 3b, A.B. Lucas SS, London, Ontario**
5. **Chris Vines, rhp, Pelham (Ala.) HS**
6. **Asher Demme, rhp, South Lakes HS, Reston, Va.**
7. **Ryan Basner, rhp, Western Carolina**
8. **Sean White, rhp, Washington**
9. **Adam Stanley, lhp, Garner (N.C.) HS**
10. **Brad Nelson, rhp, Lenoir (N.C.) CC**
11. **Glenn Tucker, rhp, East Carolina**
12. Casey Spanish, of, Kansas
13. **Mark Jurich, of, Louisville**

14. **Steven Doetsch, of, Indian River (Fla.) CC**
15. **Ben Thomas, 3b, Midland (Texas) JC**
16. **Cole Armstrong, c, Chipola (Fla.) JC**
17. **Keith Eichas, 1b, Temple (Texas) JC**
18. Keith Weiser, lhp, Talawanda HS, Hamilton, Ohio
19. **Andy Barden, c, Virginia Military Institute**
20. **Kyle Bakker, lhp, Georgia Tech**
21. Brooks Brown, rhp, Portal (Ga.) HS
22. **Jacob Blakeney, rhp, Mississippi State**
23. **Jamie Hemingway, of, UNC Wilmington**
24. **Brandon Jones, of, Tallahassee (Fla.) CC**
25. Quintin Berry, of, Morse HS, San Diego
26. **C.J. Bressoud, c, North Cobb HS, Kennesaw, Ga.**
27. Brandon Berdoll, lhp, Temple (Texas) JC
28. Kyle Perry, rhp, Ball HS, Galveston, Texas
29. Drew Shetrone, rhp, Apopka (Fla.) HS
30. **Jonny Venters, lhp, Lake Brantley HS, Altamonte Springs, Fla.**
31. **Jon Schaus, rhp, East Lake HS, Palm Harbor, Fla.**
32. **Larry Williams, 1b, Hawthorne HS, Lawndale, Calif.**
33. Daniel Stange, rhp, Elsinore HS, Wildomar, Calif.
34. Michael Gibbs, rhp, Chipola (Fla.) JC
35. Daniel Rios, 1b, Mount Whitney HS, Visalia, Calif.
36. Justin Phillips, ss, Louisburg (N.C.) JC
37. Cody Pyle, 3b, Smithson Valley HS, Spring Branch, Texas
38. Eric Chown, rhp, Massachusetts
39. Eugene Edwards, 1b, Mayfair HS, Bellflower, Calif.
40. Joey Doan, rhp, Baker HS, Mobile, Ala.
41. John Ray, c, Monarch HS, Louisville, Colo.
42. Marcus Covington, rhp, East Rutherford HS, Forest City, N.C.
43. Zech Zinicola, rhp, Arlington HS, San Bernardino, Calif.
44. Tony Portugal, rhp, Northeast HS, Fort Lauderdale, Fla.
45. David Crook, lhp, Monte Vista HS, Spring Valley, Calif.
46. Lyall Foran, c, Delta SS, Ladner, B.C
47. Joe Northrup, rhp, West Covina (Calif.) HS
48. **Tony Harris, lhp, Surry (N.C.) CC**
49. Kyle Price, 2b, Green Valley HS, Henderson, Nev.
50. John Scaglione, rhp, Palm Beach Gardens HS, Lake Park, Fla.

BALTIMORE ORIOLES

June—Regular Phase (7)

1. **Nick Markakis, of, Young Harris (Ga.) JC**
2. **Brian Finch, rhp, Texas A&M**
3. **Chris Ray, rhp, William & Mary**
4. **Bob McCrory, rhp, Southern Mississippi**
5. **Nate Spears, ss, Charlotte HS, Port Charlotte, Fla.**
6. **Eric Sultemeier, of, Texas**
7. **Justin Azze, lhp, Hawaii**
8. Nate Nery, lhp, Moon Area HS, Moon Township, Pa.
9. **Jarod Rine, of, West Virginia**
10. **Jacob Duncan, of, Texas Christian**
11. **Matt Houston, c, Oklahoma City**
12. **Matt Pulley, 3b, Woodland (Calif.) HS**
13. **Jim Hoey, rhp, Rider**
14. **Brian Bock, c, Hawaii**
15. Jordan Timm, lhp, Wisconsin-Oshkosh
16. **Alan Beck, of, Western Carolina**
17. **Lorenzo Scott, of, Ball State**
18. **Jason Furrow, lhp, Judson (Texas) HS**
19. Matt Tolbert, 2b, Mississippi
20. **Tony Neal, rhp, South Alabama**
21. David Cash, ss, Northside Christian HS, St. Petersburg, Fla.
22. **Zach Dixon, lhp, Texas A&M**
23. **Dennis Wyrick, 3b, Arizona State**
24. **Josh McCurdy, of, Niagara**
25. Richard Hummell, of, Tombstone HS, Sierra Vista, Ariz.
26. Brian LeClerc, of, Northside Christian HS, Clearwater, Fla.
27. **Travis Brown, ss, Western Kentucky**
28. **Russ Brocato, rhp, Pennsylvania**
29. Jason Ward, rhp, Utah Valley State JC
30. **Chris Osentowski, rhp, Texas Christian**
31. **Ryan Brnardic, rhp, Southeastern Oklahoma State**
32. **Landon Wareham, 2b, Mesa State (Colo.)**
33. Jake Muyco, c, Columbia Basin (Wash.) CC
34. Brad Wiggins, of, Howard (Texas) CC
35. Richard Orange, of, Greenville (Texas) HS
36. Danny Martin, of, Dunedin (Fla.) HS
37. David Smith, rhp, Chrysler HS, New Castle, Ind.
38. Matthew Garnett, lhp, Stockdale HS, Bakersfield, Calif.
39. Shaun Corning, lhp, Madison Area (Wis.) Tech JC
40. Joe Welsh, lhp, Grand Rapids (Mich.) CC
41. Aaron Feterl, rhp, Crescenta Valley HS, La Crescenta, Calif.
42. Chad Boudon, of, Washington
43. **Kyle George, ss, Maryland**
44. Scott Houin, of, Rampart HS, Colorado Springs
45. Brett Jensen, rhp, Iowa Central CC
46. Greg Young, of, Old Mill HS, Millersville, Md.
47. Roy Irle, rhp, Rend Lake (Ill.) JC
48. Cameron McGuire, c, McLennan (Texas) JC
49. Casey Janssen, rhp, UCLA
50. Adam Ricciardulli, of, Mission Bay HS, San Diego

BOSTON RED SOX

June—Regular Phase (17)

1. **David Murphy, of, Baylor**
1. **Matt Murton, of, Georgia Tech** (Supplemental pick—32nd—for loss of Type A free agent Cliff Floyd)
2. **Abe Alvarez, lhp, Long Beach State** (Pick from Mets as compensation for Floyd)
2. **Mickey Hall, of, Walton HS, Marietta, Ga.**
3. **Beau Vaughan, rhp, Arizona State**
4. **Jonathan Papelbon, rhp, Mississippi State**
5. **Brian Marshall, lhp, Virginia Commonwealth**
6. **Jessie Corn, rhp, Jacksonville State**
7. **Jeremy West, c, Arizona State**
8. **Lee Curtis, 2b, College of Charleston**
9. **John Wilson, rhp, Northeastern (Colo.) JC**
10. **Chris Durbin, of, Baylor**
11. **Barry Hertzler, rhp, Central Connecticut State**
12. **Justin Sturge, lhp, Coastal Carolina**
13. **Zach Basch, rhp, Nevada**
14. **Zach Borowiak, ss, Southeast Missouri State**
15. **Chris Turner, of, Texarkana (Texas) JC**
16. **Kevin Ool, lhp, Marist**
17. **William Newton, lhp, Mountain View HS, Orem, Utah**
18. **Tom Cochran, lhp, Middle Georgia JC**
19. **Jarrett Gardner, rhp, Arkansas**
20. Josh Morris, of, Cartersville (Ga.) HS
21. **Mike Dennison, rhp, Wichita State**
22. Kala Ka'aihue, c, Iolani HS, Kailua, Hawaii
23. **David Coffey, of, Georgia**
24. **Iggy Suarez, ss, Southwest Texas State**
25. Drew Moffitt, of, Wichita State
26. **Jason Ramos, ss, St. Petersburg (Fla.) JC**
27. Andrew Sharpe, ss, Los Angeles Pierce JC
28. **Davey Penny, rhp, East Carolina**
29. **Doug Fink, rhp, Manatee (Fla.) JC**
30. **David Sanders, lhp, Wichita State**
31. Greg Schilling, lhp, Taravella HS, Coral Springs, Fla.
32. Matt Pike, rhp, Centennial HS, Pueblo, Colo.
33. **Scooter Jordan, of, Texas Tech**
34. **Arthur Santos, rhp, Florida International**
35. **Erich Cloninger, c, Liberty**
36. Ben Sosebee, rhp, Truett McConnell (Ga.) JC
37. Chris Johnson, ss, Bishop Verot HS, Fort Myers, Fla.
38. Mike McBryde, of, Palm Beach Gardens HS, North Palm Beach, Fla.
39. Jeff Culpepper, of, Gonzaga
40. Michael Rutledge, ss, Cullman (Ala.) HS
41. **Lance Schartz, c, Garden City (Kan.) CC**
42. Dallas Williams, of, Pike HS, Indianapolis
43. Scott Thomas, c, Chaminade College Prep, St. Louis
44. Tom Caple, of, San Diego
45. Terrence Cramer, rhp, Palm Beach (Fla.) JC
46. Victor Rodriguez, c, Cape Coral (Fla.) HS
47. A.J. Lloyd, of, Bishop Carroll HS, Wichita, Kan.
48. Adam Davis, rhp, Middle Georgia JC
49. **Jason Smith, rhp, Bourne (Mass.) HS**
50. **Mitch Stachowsky, c, JC of Southern Idaho**

CHICAGO CUBS

June—Regular Phase (6)

1. **Ryan Harvey, of, Dunedin (Fla.) HS**
2. (Pick to Braves as compensation for Type A free agent Mike Remlinger)
3. **Jake Fox, c, Michigan**
4. **Tony Richie, c, Florida State**
5. **Darin Downs, lhp, Santaluces HS, Boynton Beach, Fla.**
6. **Sean Marshall, lhp, Virginia Commonwealth**
7. **Kyle Boyer, of, Cal State Fullerton**
8. Matt Lincoln, lhp, Santa Ana (Calif.) JC
9. **Drew Larsen, ss, Salt Lake CC**
10. **Casey McGehee, 3b, Fresno State**
11. **Nick Jones, 2b, Virginia Commonwealth**
12. **Chuck Hickman, ss, Nicholls State**
13. Ryan Coultas, ss, UC Davis
14. Matt LaPorta, c, Charlotte HS, Port Charlotte, Fla.
15. **Tony McQuade, of, Florida State**
16. **Matt Weber, rhp, Boylan Catholic HS, Rockford, Ill.**
17. **Ryan Kalita, rhp, Notre Dame**
18. **Trey Johnston, 3b, Schaumburg (Ill.) HS**
19. **Brian Carter, lhp, Washington**
20. **Lance Dawkins, ss, McNeese State**
21. **Reid Willett, rhp, Rhode Island**
22. **Craig Green, rhp, Bakersfield (Calif.) JC**
23. **Robert Ransom, rhp, Vanderbilt**
24. Sam Fuld, of, Stanford
25. Landon Powell, c, South Carolina
26. Barrett Browning, lhp, Middle Georgia JC
27. **Jose Rios, ss, Barranquitas, P.R.**
28. **Adam Tidball, c, Richmond**
29. Matt Brown, rhp, California
30. Corteze Armstrong, of, Hiwassee (Tenn.) JC
31. Chris Ortmeier, rhp, Marcus HS, Flower Mound, Texas
32. Adam Tobler, rhp, Rochelle (Ill.) HS
33. **Jasha Balcom, of, Georgia**
34. Adam Harvey, c, Grayson County (Texas) CC
35. **Sean Overholt, rhp, Utah**
36. Jason Fellows, 1b, Georgia Perimeter JC
37. Chris Ericksen, lhp, South Suburban (Ill.) CC
38. Skyler Southwick, rhp, Dixie (Utah) JC
39. **David Gresky, of, Northwestern**
40. **Danny Lopaze, 1b, Virginia Commonwealth**
41. Doug Low, c, Foothill HS, Henderson, Nev.
42. Danny Calvert, rhp, Grain Valley HS, Blue Springs, Mo.
43. Brandon Harmon, rhp, Shadle Park HS, Spokane, Wash.
44. Cyle Hankerd, 1b, South Hills HS, Covina, Calif.
45. Jose Sanchez, c, West Covina (Calif.) HS
46. Jefferies Tatford, 3b, St. Thomas More HS, Lafayette, La.
47. Justin Simmons, lhp, Texas
48. Tim Lincecum, rhp, Liberty HS, Renton, Wash.
49. Brian Cleveland, ss, Tennessee
50. Kris Rochelle, c, Mills Godwin HS, Richmond, Va.

CHICAGO WHITE SOX

June—Regular Phase (15)

1. **Brian Anderson, of, Arizona**
2. **Ryan Sweeney, of, Xavier HS, Cedar Rapids, Iowa**
3. **Clint King, of, Southern Mississippi**
4. **Robert Valido, ss, Coral Park HS, Miami**
5. **Matt Nachreiner, rhp, Round Rock (Texas) HS**
6. **Chris Kelly, of, Pepperdine**
7. **James Casey, rhp, Azle (Texas) HS**
8. **John Russ, rhp, Frank Phillips (Texas) JC**
9. **David Cook, of, Miami (Ohio)**
10. **Fraser Dizard, lhp, Southern California**
11. Ricky Brooks, rhp, North Tonawanda (N.Y.) HS
12. Donald Veal, lhp, Buena HS, Hereford, Ariz.
13. Wes Hodges, ss, Baylor School, Chattanooga
14. **Ricardo Nanita, of, Florida International**
15. Greg Moviel, lhp, St. Ignatius HS, Cleveland
16. Cody Dickens, rhp, Surry (N.C.) CC
17. Guillermo Martinez, ss, Coral Park HS, Miami
18. **Cory Haggerty, 2b, Cortland State (N.Y.)**
19. **Mike Moat, rhp, San Diego State**
20. **Jeff Schmidt, ss, Mira Mesa HS, San Diego**
21. **Matt Lenderman, c, Plano (Texas) East HS**
22. Travis Doyle, lhp, Grand Rapids (Mich.) CC
23. **John Hurd, rhp, JC of Southern Idaho**
24. Burke Baldwin, lhp, Neuqua Valley HS, Naperville, Ill.
25. **Antoin Gray, 3b, Southern**
26. Logan Williamson, lhp, Penscola (Fla.) Catholic HS
27. **Dwayne Pollok, rhp, Texas A&M**
28. Van Pope, 3b, Meridian (Miss.) CC
29. Gerardo Cabrera, of, Miami-Dade CC South
30. Brandon Lowe, 1b, Vidalia HS, Mount Vernon, Ga.
31. Robbie Grinestaff, c, Jeffersonville (Ind.) HS
32. Josh Morgan, of, Meridian (Miss.) CC
33. Alex Acevedo, ss, Dr. Carlos Gonzales HS, Aguada, P.R.
34. **Scott Martin, of, Delaware State**
35. **Sean Thompson, lhp, UC Santa Barbara**
36. **Paul Moviel, rhp, Kishwaukee (Ill.) JC**
37. Neil Giesler, 1b, Okaloosa-Walton (Fla.) JC
38. Michael Mendrin, lhp, Central HS, Fresno, Calif.
39. Jason Sullivan, rhp, Joplin (Mo.) HS
40. **Matt Deuchler, c, James Madison**
41. **Rolando Acosta, ss, Pima (Ariz.) CC**
42. **Eric Everly, lhp, Olney Central (Ill.) JC**
43. **Dustin Shafer, ss, Russell HS, Flatwoods, Ky.**
44. **Brandon Johnson, 2b, Crowder (Mo.) JC**
45. Mitchell Woolf, rhp, JC of Southern Idaho
46. Greg Del George, ss, Monsignor Farrell HS, Staten Island, N.Y.
47. Richard O'Brien, c, Catholic HS, Little Rock, Ark.
48. Mike Alvarez, rhp, Monsignor Pace HS, Opelika, Fla.
49. Tim Edmeades, 3b, Buena Regional HS, Weymouth, N.J.
50. Sean Gaston, c, Brownsburg (Ind.) HS

CINCINNATI REDS

June—Regular Phase (14)

1. **Ryan Wagner, rhp, Houston**
2. **Thomas Pauly, rhp, Princeton**
3. **Jose Ronda, ss, Gabriela Mistral HS, San Juan, P.R.**
4. **Kenny Lewis, of, Washington HS, Danville, Va.**
5. Marc Cornell, rhp, Ohio
6. **Richie Gardner, rhp, Arizona**
7. **Carlos Guevara, rhp, St. Mary's (Texas)**
8. **Damian Ursin, rhp, Southern**
9. **Ben Himes, of, Oklahoma City**
10. Andy D'Alessio, 1b, Barron Collier HS, Naples, Fla.
11. **Blake Hendley, rhp, Oklahoma City**
12. **James Paduch, rhp, Concordia (Ill.)**
13. **Matt Gray, of, Butler County (Kan.) CC**
14. Marcus Townsend, of, Southern
15. Jo Jo Batten, of, Telfair County HS, McRae, Ga.
16. **Chris Dickerson, of, Nevada**
17. **Brock Till, rhp, Bradley**
18. **Kyle Smith, of, Houston Baptist**
19. Charles Benoit, lhp, Carroll HS, Southlake, Texas
20. Dennis Dixon, of, San Leandro (Calif.) HS
21. Todd Nicholas, lhp, Mississippi State
22. Brian Barr, rhp, Southern Arkansas
23. **Chad Ziemendorf, c, UC Santa Barbara**
24. Matt Harrington, rhp, Fort Worth (Central League)
25. Jack Harris, 3b, Ronald Reagan HS, San Antonio
26. **Jeff Urgelles, c, Savannah State**
27. Zac Stott, rhp, Dixie (Utah) JC
28. Dustin Evans, rhp, Adairsville HS, Taylorsville, Ga.
29. **Philip Gentry, of, Texas-San Antonio**
30. Michael Brown, rhp, Grayson County (Texas) JC
31. Josh Newman, lhp, Ohio State
32. German Duran, ss, Paschal HS, Fort Worth
33. **David Talamantez, rhp, Lamar**
34. **Evan Conley, c, Jacksonville State**
35. **Matt Trepkowski, lhp, Incarnate Word (Texas)**
36. Nick Vaughn, rhp, Oak Ridge HS, El Dorado Hills, Calif.
37. Bart Braun, lhp, Southeastern Louisiana
38. Adam Hicks, 3b, Scottsdale (Ariz.) CC
39. **Clay Cleveland, 1b, Savannah State**
40. Jake McCarter, rhp, Tivy HS, Kerrville, Texas

41. **Jordan Belcher, of, Augusta (Ga.) Christian HS**
42. David Scott, c, Northside Christian HS, Pinellas Park, Fla.
43. Nick Devito, 1b, Hingham (Mass.) HS
44. Carlyle Holliday, of, Notre Dame
45. **Rusty Beale, ss, Stetson**
46. Brian Wyatt, rhp, Vernon Regional (Texas) JC
47. Dane Mason, rhp, Gloucester County (N.J.) JC
48. Johntavis Character, of, McNair HS, Decatur, Ga.
49. Jordan Mayer, 1b, Alexandria (La.) HS
50. Colin Curtis, of, Issaquah (Wash.) HS

CLEVELAND INDIANS

June—Regular Phase (11)

1. **Michael Aubrey, 1b, Tulane**
1. **Brad Snyder, of, Ball State** (Pick from Phillies as compensation for Type A free agent Jim Thome)
1. **Adam Miller, rhp, McKinney (Texas) HS** (Supplemental pick—31st—for loss of Thome)
2. **Javi Herrera, c, Tennessee**
3. **Ryan Garko, c, Stanford**
4. Ben Harrison, of, Florida
5. **Juan Valdes, of, Fernando Callejo HS, Manati, P.R.**
6. **Kevin Kouzmanoff, 3b, Nevada**
7. **Matt Davis, rhp, Ohio State**
8. **Bo Ashabraner, rhp, Long Beach State**
9. **Anthony Lunetta, ss, Southern California**
10. **Scott Roehl, rhp, Arkansas**
11. **Ryan Mulhern, of, South Alabama**
12. **Brandon Pinckney, ss, Sacramento CC**
13. Steven Reinhold, 2b, Tuscola HS, Waynesville, N.C.
14. Chase Williams, of, A&M Consolidated HS, College Station, Texas
15. **Ryan Spilman, c, Mount Vernon (Ind.) HS**
16. **Aaron Laffey, lhp, Allegany HS, Foxburg, Md.**
17. **Jeff Pry, rhp, Franklin HS, Portland, Ore.**
18. Dusty Barnard, rhp, Connors State (Okla.) JC
19. Joseph Huskins, c, Cypress (Calif.) JC
20. Shane Mathews, rhp, St. Stephens HS, Conover, N.C.
21. **Adam Brandenburg, lhp, Kennesaw State (Ga.)**
22. Matt Elliot, rhp, Dixie (Utah) JC
23. Tim Montgomery, of, Hawaii
24. **Ryan Goleski, 1b, Eastern Michigan**
25. Travis DeBondt, lhp, Bakersfield (Calif.) JC
26. Andrew Johnston, rhp, Jefferson (Mo.) JC
27. Mike Felix, rhp, Rutherford HS, Panama City, Fla.
28. Jason James, of, Kishwaukee (Ill.) JC
29. **Brett Parker, ss, South Alabama**
30. James Smith, rhp, Merced (Calif.) JC
31. **Mark Harris, rhp, William & Mary**
32. Steven Jackson, rhp, Clemson
33. Joe Reid, rhp, St. John's
34. **Roger Lincoln, lhp, Stetson**
35. Bart Babineaux, of, El Camino (Calif.) JC
36. Jared Goedert, 3b, Concordia (Kan.) HS
37. Zach Wallis, lhp, Enid (Okla.) HS
38. Neall French, c, Grand Rapids (Mich.) CC
39. Jim Rapoport, of, Chaminade Prep, Westlake Village, Calif.
40. Adrian Schau, rhp, Villanova
41. Jake Leonhardt, rhp, Cypress Fairbanks HS, Cypress, Texas
42. **Adam Hanson, rhp, Wake Forest**
43. **Joe Weaver, rhp, Oklahoma State**
44. Kyle Muschara, rhp, Lassiter HS, Marietta, Ga.
45. Rafael Cotto, of, Miguel Such HS, Rio Piedras, P.R.
46. James O'Neill, lhp, Milford HS, Highland, Mich.
47. Chad Corona, 3b, San Diego State
48. Jordan Karnofsky, of, Christian Brothers HS, Sacramento
49. David Horlacher, rhp, Dixie (Utah) JC
50. Seth Button, of, Elk Lake HS, Meshoppen, Pa.

COLORADO ROCKIES

June—Regular Phase (10)

1. **Ian Stewart, 3b, La Quinta HS, Garden Grove, Calif.**
2. **Scott Beerer, rhp, Texas A&M**
3. **Aaron Marsden, lhp, Nebraska**
4. **Rick Guarno, c, Arkansas-Little Rock**
5. **Christian Colonel, ss, Texas Tech**
6. **Randy Blood, 2b, UC Riverside**
7. **Larry Robles, rhp, Cal State Dominguez Hills**
8. **Darric Merrell, rhp, Cal State Fullerton**
9. **Gene Reynolds, ss, Tampa**
10. **Marc Kaiser, rhp, Lewis-Clark State (Idaho)**
11. **John Restrepo, of, Santa Ana (Calif.) JC**
12. **Joe Gaetti, of, North Carolina State**
13. **Matt Brinson, 1b, Mississippi State**
14. **J.P. Gagne, rhp, Notre Dame**
15. **Mark Ion, rhp, Lamar**
16. **Mike Wiley, lhp, Stetson**
17. Jim Brauer, rhp, Michigan
18. Friedel Pinkston, rhp, Chipola (Fla.) JC
19. **Ryan Mattheus, rhp, Sacramento CC**
20. **Scott Anderson, ss, Cal Poly**
21. **Ryan Fox, of, Arkansas**
22. Adam Daniels, lhp, Eastern Oklahoma State JC
23. **Brian Lynch, rhp, Ball State**
24. **Jeff Watchko, rhp, Georgia Tech**
25. **Jordan Czarniecki, of, Tennessee**
26. Cole Garner, of, La Quinta HS, Westminster, Calif.
27. **Jason DiAngelo, rhp, West Virginia**
28. Ricardo Rivas, rhp, El Paso (Texas) CC
29. David Hernandez, rhp, Elk Grove (Calif.) HS
30. **Eric Young Jr., 2b, Piscataway (N.J.) HS**
31. Aaron George, rhp, Scottsdale (Ariz.) CC
32. Kyle Allen, lhp, Orange Coast (Calif.) JC
33. Garret Baker, 3b, Modesto (Texas) JC
34. Stoney Stone, rhp, Texarkana (Texas) JC
35. Kyle Wright, rhp, Columbia Basin (Wash.) CC
36. Derek Patterson, lhp, Northeast Texas CC
37. Jesse Litsch, rhp, Dixie Hollins HS, St. Petersburg, Fla.
38. Ryan Snell, rhp, Skyline HS, Sammamish, Wash.
39. Don Powers, rhp, Seminole State (Okla.) JC
40. David Hurst, lhp, Florida CC-Jacksonville
41. Brandon Anderson, of, Wayland (Mass.) HS
42. Carlos Moreno, rhp, Odessa (Texas) CC
43. Justin Jameson, of, Creekside HS, Fairburn, Ga.
44. Robert Rose, rhp, Cleveland State (Tenn.) CC
45. Josh Banda, c, Artesia HS, Lakewood, Calif.
46. **Jason Van Kooten, ss, Regis Jesuit HS, Aurora, Colo.**
47. Jose Cardona, lhp, San Juan, P.R.
48. Ryan Flavell, c, Clarendon (Texas) JC
49. Jason Martinez, lhp, Mesa State (Colo.)
50. Michael Jenkins, 3b, Hiwassee (Tenn.) CC

DETROIT TIGERS

June—Regular Phase (3)

1. **Kyle Sleeth, rhp, Wake Forest**
2. **Jay Sborz, rhp, Langley HS, McLean, Va.**
3. **Tony Giarratano, ss, Tulane**
4. **Josh Rainwater, rhp, DeRidder (La.) HS**
5. **Danny Zell, lhp, Houston**
6. **Cody Collet, c, Newbury Park (Calif.) HS**
7. **Virgil Vasquez, rhp, UC Santa Barbara**
8. Adam Trent, rhp, Ooltewah (Tenn.) HS
9. **Eric Rodland, 2b, Gonzaga**
10. Sean Henry, of, Armijo HS, Suisun City, Calif.
11. **Brian Rogers, rhp, Georgia Southern**
12. **Jeramy Laster, of, Hunters Lane HS, Nashville, Tenn.**
13. **Michael Brown, of, William & Mary**
14. **Luis Sabino, of, Wabash Valley (Ill.) JC**
15. **Andy Baldwin, rhp, Western Kentucky**
16. **Jordan Tata, rhp, Sam Houston State**
17. Ronnie Martin, lhp, St. Mary's HS, St. Louis
18. Josh Wahpepah, rhp, Cowley County (Kan.) CC
19. **Andrew Graham, c, Armstrong Atlantic State (Ga.)**
20. **Nick McIntyre, 2b, Purdue**
21. **Jacob Ford, 3b, Spalding (Ky.)**
22. **Richie Burgos, 1b, Cal State Fullerton**
23. **Bobby Huddleston, c, Auburn**
24. **Chris Homer, rhp, Marist**

25. **Nathan Doyle, ss, James Madison**
26. **Lavon Lewis, rhp, Northeastern Oklahoma A&M JC**
27. **Aaron McRae, c, LSU-Shreveport**
28. Steven Alexander, 1b, Rocklin (Calif.) HS
29. **Kelly Hunt, 1b, Bowling Green State**
30. **Anthony Tomey, rhp, Eastern Michigan**
31. **Justin Justice, of, Tavares HS, Leesburg, Fla.**
32. **Justin Barnes, c, Alabama-Huntsville**
33. **Kenon Ronz, lhp, Harvard**
34. Chaz Schilens, of, Highland HS, Mesa, Ariz.
35. Ryan Muller, rhp, Live Oak HS, Morgan Hill, Calif.
36. **John McGorty, 1b, Marist**
37. Cirilo Cruz, 3b, Chandler (Ariz.) HS
38. John Juergens, c, Bradley Bourbonnais HS, Bourbonnais, Ill.
39. Dustin Richardson, lhp, Cowley County (Kan.) CC
40. Emmanuel Vasquez, rhp, Nicholas Rodriguez HS, Corozal, P.R.
41. **Ezequiel Perez, rhp, Missouri Baptist**
42. **Daniel Spring, rhp, Brown**
43. **Brian Santo, rhp, Mount St. Mary's**
44. **Kurt Piantek, 1b, Trinity (Conn.)**
45. Josh Tarnow, c, Carona del Sol HS, Chandler, Ariz.
46. Clay Britton, of, Canyon HS, Canyon Country, Calif.
47. Travis Simmons, 3b, Cleveland State (Tenn.) CC
48. **Dusty Ryan, c, Merced (Calif.) JC**
49. **William Baez, rhp, Northwood (Texas)**
50. Brandon McCormick, rhp, Spartanburg Methodist (S.C.) JC

FLORIDA MARLINS

June—Regular Phase (16)

1. **Jeff Allison, rhp, Veterans Memorial HS, Peabody, Mass.**
2. **Logan Kensing, rhp, Texas A&M**
3. **Jonathan Fulton, ss, Washington HS, Danville, Va.**
4. **Jai Miller, of, Selma (Ala.) HS**
5. **Cole Seifrig, 3b, Heritage Hills HS, Lincoln City, Ind.**
6. **Lee Mitchell, 3b, Georgia**
7. **David Marchbanks, lhp, South Carolina**
8. **Tanner Rogers, c, Columbine HS, Littleton, Colo.**
9. **David Humen, rhp, Bethel (Ind.)**
10. **J.T. Restko, 3b, Marist HS, Tinley Park, Ill.**
11. **Zach McCormack, lhp, Sacramento CC**
12. **Joe Mazzuca, ss, Northern Illinois**
13. **Chris Pillsbury, rhp, Florida Atlantic**
14. **Scott Nestor, rhp, Chaffey (Calif.) JC**
15. **Mikela Olsen, of, Sacramento State**
16. **Jon Nickerson, lhp, Stanhope Elmore HS, Millbrook, Ala.**
17. **Kurt Koehler, rhp, Sacramento CC**
18. **Craig Lybarger, lhp, Jefferson State (Ala.) CC**
19. **Nathan Nowicki, rhp, Colorado State**
20. Seferino Encarnacion, of, Orange Park, Fla.
21. Brandon Tripp, of, Los Alamitos (Calif.) HS
22. **Ryan Blake, c, North Carolina**
23. Tony Watson, lhp, Dallas Center-Grimes HS, Grimes, Iowa
24. **Scott Dierks, of, Santa Clara**
25. Alex Hinshaw, lhp, Chaffey (Calif.) JC
26. **Ben Schroeder, of, Ball State**
27. Toddric Johnson, of, Provine HS, Jackson, Miss.
28. **Greg Bartlett, lhp, Pheonix JC**
29. **Stu Alexander, rhp, Windsor (Calif.) HS**
30. **Ryan Bear, of, Central Florida**
31. **Spencer Wyman, c, Oklahoma**
32. **Kris Thedorf, of, Elgin (ill.) CC**
33. **Roy Friesen, rhp, Columbia Basin (Wash.) CC**
34. **Antonio Orozco, rhp, California Baptist**
35. **Justin Mattison, of, Virginia Commonwealth**
36. Rodney Rutherford, of, Shaw HS, Columbus, Ga.
37. **Nick Lovato, lhp, Cal State Fullerton**
38. Chris Bodishbaugh, rhp, Freedom HS, Oakley, Calif.
39. Neal Warchol, rhp, Triton (Ill.) JC
40. Geoff Rottmayer, of, Countryside HS, Clearwater, Fla.
41. Randall Clay, ss, Rattan (Okla.) HS
42. **Jim Adduci, of, Columbus HS, Bronx, N.Y.**
43. Jared Johnson, rhp, Kelowna, B.C
44. Ben Hodges, ss, Allan Hancock (Calif.) JC
45. Chris Allen, c, South Williamsport Area HS, Duboistown, Pa.
46. Angel Flores, c, Petra Corret O'Neill HS, Manati, P.R.
47. Chilion Stapleton, rhp, Mississippi Delta JC
48. Ashkelon Stapleton, rhp, Mississippi Delta JC
49. Kyle Dickson, rhp, Sacramento CC
50. George Otero, ss, Hialeah (Fla.) HS

HOUSTON ASTROS

June—Regular Phase (22)

1. (Pick to Giants as compensation for Type A free agent Jeff Kent)
2. **Jason Hirsh, rhp, California Lutheran**
3. Drew Stubbs, of, Atlanta (Texas) HS
4. **Josh Anderson, of, Eastern Kentucky**
5. **Josh Muecke, lhp, Loyola Marymount**
6. **Cliff Davis, rhp, Eupora (Miss.) HS**
7. **Jeff Jorgensen, of, Rice**
8. **Mike Collar, rhp, Maine**
9. **Brock Koman, 3b, Michigan**
10. **Beau Hearod, of, Alabama**
11. Nick Green, rhp, Darton (Ga.) JC
12. **Wade Robinson, ss, Louisiana Tech**
13. **Jimmy Barthmaier, rhp, Roswell (Ga.) HS**
14. Mike Dunn, of, Cimarron Memorial HS, Las Vegas, Nev.
15. **Bo Edmiston, rhp, Mississippi College**
16. **Jamie Merchant, rhp, Vermont**
17. **Pat O'Brien, c, Kent State**
18. **Kevin Vital, 1b, Southern**
19. **Edwin Maysonet, 2b, Delta State (Miss.)**
20. **Brian Skaug, 2b, California Lutheran**
21. **Kerri Fair, of, Jacksonville State**
22. **Lance Koenig, 2b, Monmouth**
23. **Mark Saccomanno, 3b, Baylor**
24. **Ryan Yurek, rhp, Loyola Marymount**
25. **Mario Garza, c, Florida**
26. **Robert Ramsey, rhp, Texas A&M**
27. Omar Arif, lhp, Poteet HS, Mesquite, Texas
28. **Chad Prosser, ss, North Carolina**
29. **Jason Corapci, 2b, Cal State Fullerton**
30. Scott Bradley, 2b, Chabot (Calif.) JC
31. Brandon McDougall, ss, Diablo Valley (Calif.) CC
32. Justin O'Bannon, rhp, Kingwood (Texas) HS
33. **Michael Walls, 3b, St. Joseph's**
34. Shawn Burris, lhp, North Central Texas JC
35. John Slusarz, rhp, Connecticut-Avery Point
36. Logan Ondrusek, rhp, St. Paul HS, Shriner, Texas
37. Ethien Santana, of, Laredo (Texas) JC
38. Victor Ferrante, rhp, Benicia HS, Vallejo, Calif.
39. Josh Smith, rhp, Riverside (Calif.) CC
40. David Roberts, of, The Woodlands (Texas) HS
41. Ray Stokes, 2b, San Leandro (Calif.) HS
42. Shane Buschini, 1b, California HS, San Ramon, Calif.

KANSAS CITY ROYALS

June—Regular Phase (5)

1. **Chris Lubanski, of, Kennedy-Kenrick HS, Schwenksville, Pa.**
1. **Mitch Maier, c, Toledo** (Pick from Braves as compensation for Type B free agent Paul Byrd)
2. **Shane Costa, of, Cal State Fullerton**
3. **Brian McFall, 1b, Chandler-Gilbert (Ariz.) JC**
4. **Miguel Vega, 3b, Carmen B. Huyke HS, Arroyo, P.R.**
5. **Chris Goodman, rhp, Georgia Tech**
6. **Ryan Braun, rhp, Nevada-Las Vegas**
7. **Mike Aviles, ss, Concordia (N.Y.)**
8. **Brandon Powell, 2b, Coastal Carolina**
9. **John Gragg, lhp, Bethune-Cookman**
10. **Luis Cota, rhp, Sunnyside HS, Tucson**
11. **Dusty Hughes, lhp, Delta State (Miss.)**
12. **Robbie McClellan, rhp, Arizona State**
13. **Mike Gaffney, ss, New York Tech**
14. **Steve Bray, rhp, New Haven (Conn.)**
15. **Jake Mullis, rhp, UNC Wilmington**
16. **Bryan Graham, of, William Paterson (N.J.)**
17. Keoni Ruth, ss, Kamehameha HS, Honolulu
18. **Jeff Barry, of, Vermont**

19. Nick Tisone, rhp, Pearl River (Miss.) CC
20. Michael Hernandez, of, Daytona Beach (Fla.) CC
21. **Irving Falu, 2b, Indian Hills (Iowa) CC**
22. Phillip Andersen, rhp, Chandler-Gilbert (Ariz.) CC
23. Pat Bresnehan, rhp, Dover Sherborn HS, Dover, Mass.
24. Wayne Daman, rhp, Forks (Wash.) HS
25. Jim West, rhp, River Valley HS, Fort Mohave, Ariz.
26. **Mitch Goins, rhp, New Mexico JC**
27. Kendall Thurman, rhp, Angelina (Texas) JC
28. Derrick Thomas, rhp, Captain Shreve HS, Shreveport, La.
29. Derrick Arnold, ss, Tallahassee (Fla.) CC
30. Austin Pride, c, Lake Mary (Fla.) HS
31. D'Antonio Warren, rhp, Woodham HS, Pensacola, Fla.
32. **Darrell Qualls, 3b, Lake City (Fla.) CC**
33. Adam Miller, rhp, Knoxville (Iowa) HS
34. **Walter Sevilla, 2b, Tennessee**
35. **John Sokoll, lhp, Solon (Iowa) HS**
36. Chris Malone, rhp, San Joaquin Delta (Calif.) CC
37. Clay Young, lhp, St. Francis HS, La Canada, Calif.
38. Jeff Ostrander, lhp, Louisburg (N.C.) JC
39. **Eddie Solis, 3b, Eastlake HS, San Diego**
40. Todd Redmond, rhp, Northside Christian HS, St. Petersburg, Fla.
41. Andy Underwood, rhp, Madera (Calif.) HS
42. Josh Hernandez, 2b, El Paso (Texas) CC
43. Matt Mallory, rhp, Central HS, Grand Junction, Colo. HS
44. Vince Berry, of, Triton (Ill.) JC
45. Andy Groves, rhp, John Glenn HS, Walkerton, Ind.
46. Robert Coello, c, Lake Region HS, Winter Haven, Fla.
47. Jimmy Wallace, rhp, Bossier Parish (La.) CC
48. Zach Weidenaar, of, Bozeman (Mont.) HS
49. Gered Mochizuki, ss, Baldwin HS, Wailuku, Hawaii
50. Keven Whalen, 3b, Mid-Pacific Institute, Honolulu

LOS ANGELES DODGERS

June—Regular Phase (24)

1. **Chad Billingsley, rhp, Defiance (Ohio) HS**
2. **Chuck Tiffany, lhp, Charter Oak HS, Covina, Calif.**
3. Cory VanAllen, lhp, Clements HS, Sugar Land, Texas
4. **Xavier Paul, of, Slidell (La.) HS**
5. **Jordan Pratt, rhp, Central HS, Independence, Ore.**
6. **Matt Kemp, of, Midwest City (Okla.) HS**
7. **Wesley Wright, lhp, Goshen (Ala.) HS**
8. **Lucas May, 3b, Parkway West HS, Chesterfield, Mo.**
9. **Brett Dowdy, 2b, Florida**
10. **Phil Sobkow, rhp, Central Missouri State**
11. **Tony Harper, c, Oak Creek HS, South Milwaukee**
12. **Cody White, lhp, Pleasant Grove HS, Texarkana, Texas**
13. Derik Olvey, rhp, Pelham (Ala.) HS
14. **David Pfeiffer, lhp, Lincoln Park Academy, Fort Pierce, Fla.**
15. **Russ Mitchell, ss, Cartersville (Ga.) HS**
16. **James Peterson, 1b, Indian Hills (Iowa) CC**
17. **Steven Sapp, of, West Torrance HS, Los Angeles**
18. **A.J. Ellis, c, Austin Peay**
19. Matt Antonelli, ss, St. John's Prep, Danvers, Mass.
20. Chad Barben, 3b, Taylorsville (Utah) HS
21. **Travis Denker, 2b, Brea Olinda HS, Brea, Calif.**
22. Doug Frame, lhp, Tomball (Texas) HS
23. **Taylor Slimak, c, California Lutheran**
24. Ben Snyder, lhp, Bellevue (Ohio) HS
25. Kevin Skogley, lhp, Hermiston (Ore.) HS
26. **Thomas Piazza, c, Palm Beach Atlantic (Fla.)**
27. **Jesus Castillo, rhp, Tuscon (Ariz.) HS**
28. Adam Moore, c, Northeast Texas CC
29. Adam Parliament, of, Penticton (B.C.) SS
30. Mark Melancon, rhp, Golden HS, Arvada, Colo.
31. Garrett Kohler, rhp, Cimarron-Memorial HS, Las Vegas, Nev.
32. Kyle Reichert, rhp, Porterville (Calif.) JC
33. Ryan Zaft, rhp, Yuba (Calif.) CC
34. Brett Lawler, 1b, A&M Consolidated HS, College Station, Texas
35. Antonio Anderson, of, Greene County HS, Leakesville, Miss.
36. Drew Jeffcoat, lhp, Martin HS, Arlington, Texas
37. **Michael Ludwig, 1b, St. Olaf (Minn.)**
38. Justin Ferreira, of, Stoneman Douglas HS, Parkland, Fla.
39. **Andy LaRoche, ss, Grayson County (Texas) CC**
40. D.J. Lewis, 1b, San Fernando (Calif.) HS
41. Matt Votaw, 3b, Brea Olinda HS, Brea, Calif.
42. Cory Vanderhook, c, Golden West (Calif.) JC
43. Clayton Van Hook, ss, Brenham (Texas) HS
44. Travis Check, c, Logan HS, La Crosse, Wis.
45. Cass Rhynes, c, Bluefield HS, Cornwall, Prince Edward Island
46. Steven Paddock, of, Milford (Mass.) HS
47. Matt Chase, rhp, Naaman Forest HS, Garland, Texas
48. Kyle Rapp, of, Milford HS, Cincinnati
49. Clarence Farmer, of, Arizona
50. Curtis Hudson, c, Yuba (Calif.) JC

MILWAUKEE BREWERS

June—Regular Phase (2)

1. **Rickie Weeks, 2b, Southern**
2. **Tony Gwynn Jr., of, San Diego State**
3. **Lou Palmisano, c, Broward (Fla.) CC**
4. **Charlie Fermaint, of, Jose S. Alegria HS, Dorado, P.R.**
5. **Bryan Opdyke, c, Catalina Foothills HS, Tucson**
6. **Robbie Wooley, rhp, Taylor HS, Kokomo, Ind.**
7. **Brian Montalbo, rhp, California**
8. **Ryan Marion, rhp, Glenn HS, Kernersville, N.C.**
9. **Greg Kloosterman, lhp, Bethel (Ind.)**
10. **Tyler Morrison, rhp, Glendora (Calif.) HS**
11. **Adam Heether, 3b, Long Beach State**
12. **Carlos Corporan, 1b, Lake City (Fla.) CC**
13. Luke Cannon, of, North Central Texas JC
14. Garrett Bussiere, c, Northglenn HS, Thornton, Colo.
15. **Joel Rivera, of, Hoboken (N.J.) HS**
16. **Mitch Stetter, lhp, Indiana State**
17. **Tommy Hawk, rhp, Cabrillo HS, Lompoc, Calif.**
18. Oscar Montes, rhp, Flanagan HS, Cooper City, Fla.
19. **Ty Taubenheim, rhp, Edmonds (Wash.) CC**
20. **Nick Slack, rhp, Lake City (Fla.) CC**
21. Taylor Meier, rhp, Orangewood Christian HS, Maitland, Fla.
22. **Terry Trofholz, of, Texas Christian**
23. Jon Mungle, of, Mississippi State
24. **Drew T. Anderson, of, Nebraska**
25. **Jared Theodorakos, lhp, Baylor**
26. **Hasan Rasheed, of, Lake City (Fla.) CC**
27. **Daniel McKenna, rhp, Rutgers-Camden**
28. **Kenny Durost, rhp, Lubbock Christian**
29. **Ricky Stover, lhp, Texas-Arlington**
30. **Robby Deevers, of, Texas-Arlington**
31. Sheldon Catchot, lhp, North Shore HS, Slidell, La.
32. **Will Lewis, 2b, Texas Christian**
33. Chad Miller, 1b, Mesquite HS, Gilbert, Ariz.
34. **Dan Grybash, rhp, Carthage (Wis.)**
35. **Phil Hendrix, rhp, Virginia Military Institute**
36. Joe Ayers, ss, Juneau (Alaska) HS
37. **Justin Wilson, lhp, Chandler-Gilbert (Ariz.) CC**
38. Brent Weaver, rhp, Midwest City (Okla.) HS
39. Wes Yeary, rhp, Leon HS, Tallahassee, Fla.
40. **Robert Hinton, rhp, Riverview HS, Sarasota, Fla.**
41. Evan Baubles, c, Wall HS, Wall Township, N.J.
42. Zach Kohan, ss, Juneau-Douglas HS, Juneau, Alaska
43. Daryl Maday, rhp, Westocha Central HS, Bristol, Wis.
44. Raynel Robles-Encarnacion, 2b, Florida Air Academy HS, Melbourne, Fla.
45. Tim Grubbs, rhp, Lake City (Fla.) CC
46. **Clay Blevins, c, Cowley County (Kan.) CC**
47. Ryan Zink, rhp, La Follette HS, Madison, Wis.
48. Calvin Thompson, of, Shaw HS, East Cleveland, Ohio
49. Justin Sarka, rhp, Englewood HS, Jacksonville, Fla.
50. Luis Pardo, rhp, Westminster Christian HS, Miami

MINNESOTA TWINS

June—Regular Phase (21)

1. **Matt Moses, 3b, Mills Godwin HS, Richmond, Va.**
2. **Scott Baker, rhp, Oklahoma State**
3. **Johnny Woodard, 1b, Cosumnes River (Calif.) JC**
4. **David Shinskie, rhp, Mount Carmel Area HS, Kulpmont, Pa.**
5. Brandon McArthur, ss, Armwood HS, Seffner, Fla.

6. **Errol Simonitsch, lhp, Gonzaga**
7. **Chris Schutt, rhp, Cornell**
8. **Brandon McConnell, rhp, Foothill HS, Red Bluff, Calif.**
9. **Kevin Culpepper, lhp, Georgia Southern**
10. **Chris Marini, lhp, Glendale (Ariz.) CC**
11. Ryan Schroyer, rhp, Arizona State
12. **Steven Duguay, rhp, Gulf Coast (Fla.) CC**
13. **David Winfree, 1b, First Colonial HS, Virginia Beach, Va.**
14. **Levale Speigner, rhp, Auburn**
15. Trey Shields, rhp, Gulf Coast (Fla.) CC
16. **Michael Rogers, lhp, Del City (Okla.) HS**
17. Danny Vais, rhp, Seward County (Kan.) CC
18. **Eli Tintor, c, Hibbing (Minn.) HS**
19. **Jon Uhl, rhp, South Florida**
20. **Gregory Najac, c, Mons, Belgium**
21. Scott Leffler, c, Dunedin (Fla.) HS
22. **Joe Gault, rhp, Canyon HS, Canyon Country, Calif.**
23. Chuck Smith, rhp, Casa Roble HS, Orangevale, Calif.
24. **Patrick Ortiz, ss, Alfonso Casta Martinez HS, Maunabo, P.R.**
25. John Gaub, lhp, South St. Paul (Minn.) HS
26. **Jason Bowlin, rhp, Volunteer State (Tenn.) CC**
27. Peter Taraskevich, rhp, American Heritage HS, Sunrise, Fla.
28. Josh Oslin, rhp, Mora (Minn.) HS
29. **Bo Pettit, rhp, Louisiana State**
30. **Josh Gray, lhp, Lamar**
31. **Kris Lankford, rhp, Western Oklahoma State JC**
32. Nicholas Bleau, lhp, St. Elizabeth-Anne HS, Mercier, Quebec
33. Yvenson Bernard, of, Boca Raton (Fla.) Community HS
34. Quentin Andes, rhp, Cibola HS, Albuquerque, N.M.
35. Phillip Utley, rhp, Central-Merry HS, Jackson, Tenn.
36. Marquez Smith, 3b, Forest HS, Ocala, Fla.
37. **Heath Anderson, c, Pensacola (Fla.) JC**
38. Travis Metcalf, 3b, Kansas
39. **Jesse Collins, c, North Florida**
40. **Adam Hawes, rhp, Connors State (Okla.) JC**
41. **John Rumsey, of, San Diego Mesa JC**
42. **Mitchell Zamojc, of, British Columbia**
43. **Travis Kalin, ss, Bishop Moore HS, Orlando, Fla.**
44. **Larry Jones, of, Baldwin County HS, Minette, Ala.**
45. Steve Pearce, ss, Indian River (Fla.) CC
46. Brant Rustich, rhp, Grossmont HS, San Diego
47. Clayton Trenary, of, Central Florida CC
48. Jared Swart, rhp, Cimmarron HS, Ames, Okla.
49. Michael Hollimon, ss, Texas
50. Andy De La Garza, lhp, Norwell HS, Ossian, Ind.

MONTREAL EXPOS

June—Regular Phase (20)

1. **Chad Cordero, rhp, Cal State Fullerton**
2. **Jerry Owens, of, Master's (Calif.)**
3. **Kory Casto, of, Portland**
4. **Edgardo Baez, of, Jose S. Alegria HS, Dorado, P.R.**
5. **Trey Webb, ss, Baylor**
6. **Josh Whitesell, 1b, Loyola Marymount**
7. **Devin Perrin, rhp, Grand Canyon (Ariz.)**
8. **Daryl Thompson, rhp, La Plata HS, Mechanicsville, Md.**
9. **Gabriel Sosa, lhp, Lino Padron Rivera HS, Vega Baja, P.R.**
10. **Victor Hamisevicz, 1b, Gonzaga College HS, Dunn Loring, Va.**
11. **A.J. Wideman, lhp, Streetsville HS, Mississauga, Ontario**
12. **Mike St. Martine, c, Monmouth**
13. **Brad Ditter, 2b, New Mexico State**
14. **Larry York, 2b, Liberty**
15. **Brett Reid, rhp, Avila (Mo.)**
16. **Rickey Jenkins, rhp, South Carolina-Aiken**
17. **Luke Montz, c, Hill (Texas) JC**
18. **Eduardo Nunez, ss, American Military Academy, Guaynabo, P.R.**
19. **Jeremy Plexico, lhp, Winthrop**
20. **Terry Engles, rhp, St. Peter's Boys HS, Staten Island, N.Y.**
21. Joe Bisenius, rhp, Iowa Western CC
22. **Gus Hlebovy, rhp, Kent State**
23. Brett Cooley, rhp, Houston
24. Jon Hunton, rhp, Hutchinson (Kan.) JC
25. **James Russell, rhp, Villanova**
26. **Jim Henderson, rhp, Tennessee Wesleyan**
27. **Bret Pignatiello, c, Eastern Illinois**
28. **Oscar Bernazard, 2b, Lindenwood (Mo.)**
29. **James Lehman, rhp, Notre Dame HS, Brompton, Ontario**
30. Matt Buck, lhp, Cactus Shadows HS, Cave Creek, Ariz.
31. Chris Hufft, rhp, West Hills HS, Santee, Calif.
32. B.J. Weidenbach, of, Fresno CC
33. Gabe Suarez, ss, Arcadia HS, Scottsdale, Ariz.
34. Matt Montgomery, rhp, Watkins Mill HS, Gaithersburg, Md.
35. **Doug Vroman, of, New Haven (Conn.)**
36. Konrad Thieme, rhp, Westlake HS, Westlake Village, Calif.
37. Brendan Murphy, 1b, Grace Baptist Academy, Chattanooga, Tenn.
38. **Seth Bynum, ss, Indiana**
39. Trent Kline, c, West York Area HS, York, Pa.
40. Jacob Cook, lhp, Lee Davis HS, Mechanicsville, Va.
41. Jonathan Kalkau, rhp, Holy Trinity HS, Hicksville, N.Y.
42. Scott Rogowski, rhp, White County HS, Doyle, Tenn.
43. Anthony Savio, rhp, American River (Calif.) JC
44. Michael Ambort, c, South Side HS, Rockville Centre, N.Y.
45. Sean O'Brien, 1b, Horace Greeley HS, Chappaqua, N.Y.
46. **Alex Morales, rhp, Oakton (Ill.) CC**
47. Steven Romero, rhp, Mount San Antonio (Calif.) JC
48. Lance Zawadzki, ss, St. John's HS, Ashland, Mass.
49. Kyle Nicholson, rhp, A&M Consolidated HS, College Station, Texas
50. Michael James, rhp, Connecticut

NEW YORK METS

June—Regular Phase (12)

1. **Lastings Milledge, of, Lakewood Ranch HS, Palmetto, Fla.**
2. (Pick to Red Sox as compensation for Type A free agent Cliff Floyd)
3. (Pick to Braves as compensation for Type A free agent Tom Glavine)
4. **Shane Hawk, lhp, Oklahoma State**
5. **Corey Coles, of, Louisiana-Lafayette**
6. **Mateo Miramontes, rhp, Nevada-Reno**
7. **Brian Bannister, rhp, Southern California**
8. **Seth Pietsch, of, Oregon State**
9. **Vince Cordova, rhp, Loyola Marymount**
10. **David Reaver, ss, Richmond**
11. **Andy Sides, rhp, De Soto (Mo.) HS**
12. **Anthony Piazza, c, Southwest Missouri State**
13. **Carlos Muniz, rhp, Long Beach State**
14. **Stacy Bennett, 3b, Armstrong Atlantic State (Ga.)**
15. Harold Mozingo, rhp, Essex HS, Tappahannock, Va.
16. **David Smith, lhp, Pfeiffer (N.C.)**
17. **Ryan Meyers, rhp, Round Valley HS, Springerville, Ariz.**
18. Kyle McCulloch, rhp, Bellaire HS, Houston
19. **Ryan Harvey, of, UC Riverside**
20. Trip Mealor, rhp, Oconee County HS, Bishop, Ga.
21. **Travis Garcia, ss, Iona**
22. **Greg Ramirez, rhp, Pepperdine**
23. **Dante Brinkley, of, Southwest Missouri State**
24. **Troy Fry, rhp, Berry (Ga.)**
25. **Evan MacLane, lhp, Feather River (Calif.) CC**
26. **Kevin Rios, ss, Concordia (Calif.)**
27. Deunte Heath, rhp, Newton County HS, Decatur, Ga.
28. **Cory Wells, of, Plant City (Fla.) HS**
29. Justin Valdes, rhp, Dunedin (Fla.) HS
30. Adam Carr, rhp, West Valley (Calif.) JC
31. Jordan Newton, c, Larue County HS, Hodgenville, Ky.
32. **Humberto Gonzalez, ss, Feather River (Calif.) JC**
33. Abel Newton, rhp, Arkansas-Fort Smith JC
34. Drew Johnson, rhp, Wylie (Texas) HS
35. Patrick Howe, lhp, Faith Baptist HS, Longmont, Colo.
36. **Jim Wallace, c, Santa Clara**
37. Alex Turner, of, Catonsville (Md.) CC
38. Simon Gagnon, lhp, Montmorency (Quebec)
39. Garrett Young, 3b, Edison HS, Fountain Valley, Calif.
40. Dan Fischer, rhp, Los Angeles Pierce JC
41. Mike Bartley, rhp, Alleghany HS, Covington, Va.
42. Brian Baugher, rhp, Brunswick HS, Frederick, Md.
43. Mike Chambless, c, Round Rock (Texas) HS
44. **Tom Sgueglia, 3b, Rockland (N.Y.) CC**
45. Jean-Michel Rochon-Salvas, rhp, Edouard Montpettit College HS, Longueuil, Quebec

46. Joel Thorney, rhp, Leaside HS, Toronto
47. **David Torres, rhp, Central Florida**
48. **Jonathan Malo, ss, Miami-Dade JC**
49. Grover Benton, of, Webber (Fla.)
50. Lester Aragon, c, Brito Private HS, Miami

NEW YORK YANKEES

June—Regular Phase (27)

1. **Eric Duncan, 3b, Seton Hall Prep, Florham Park, N.J.**
2. **Estee Harris, of, Islip HS, Central Islip, N.Y.**
3. **Tim Battle, of, McIntosh HS, Peachtree City, Ga.**
4. **Steven White, rhp, Baylor**
5. **Cory Stuart, rhp, British Columbia**
6. **Jay Stephens, rhp, Tallmadge (Ohio) HS**
7. **Jose Perez, of, Oceanside (Calif.) HS**
8. **Josh Smith, rhp, Texas**
9. **Tyler Clippard, rhp, J.W. Mitchell HS, Trinity, Fla.**
10. **T.J. Beam, rhp, Mississippi**
11. **Bryce Kartler, lhp, Arizona State**
12. **Brad Blackwell, rhp, North Carolina State**
13. **Michael Gardner, rhp, Miami (Ohio)**
14. **Jose Enrique Cruz, 2b, Rice**
15. **Elvys Quezada, rhp, Seton Hall**
16. **Heath Castle, lhp, Kentucky**
17. David Purcey, lhp, Oklahoma
18. **Michael Wagner, lhp, Lincoln Park Academy, Fort Pierce, Fla.**
19. **Jeff Karstens, rhp, Texas Tech**
20. Daniel Bard, rhp, Charlotte Christian HS, Charlotte, N.C.
21. Richard Brindle, rhp, Peru (Ind.) HS
22. **John Urick, 1b, Oklahoma State**
23. Josh Smith, rhp, Central Arizona JC
24. Jeremiah Shepherd, rhp, Kilgore (Texas) HS
25. Kevin Smith, 3b, Cypress (Calif.) JC
26. Ryan Aldridge, rhp, Middle Georgia JC
27. **Andrew Edwards, rhp, Florida International**
28. Scott Kelly, rhp, St. Louis CC-Forest Park
29. **Adam Unger, 2b, Great Neck (N.Y.) South HS**
30. Grant Duff, rhp, JC of the Sequoias (Calif.)
31. Joe Larman, c, Purcell (Okla.) HS
32. Jeff Jacobsen, rhp, CC of Southern Nevada
33. Gary Keithley, rhp, Cleburn (Texas) HS
34. Robbie Widlansky, 3b, Taravella HS, Coral Springs, Fla.
35. **Hector Gonzalez, 2b, Brito Private HS, Miami**
36. Jose Hernandez, rhp, Oceanside (Calif.) HS
37. Blake Murphy, c, Tuscola HS, Waynesville, N.C.
38. David Welch, lhp, Texarkana (Texas) CC
39. Mikel McIntyre, of, Antioch (Calif.) HS
40. Brandon Kintzler, rhp, Pasadena (Calif.) CC
41. Carleton Hargrove, lhp, San Diego CC
42. **Taylor Mattingly, 1b, Evansville (Ind.) Central HS**
43. **Justin Berg, rhp, Indian Hills (Iowa) CC**
44. Mike Martinez, rhp, Cal State Fullerton
45. **Andre Randolph, 2b, Felecian (N.J.)**
46. Jonathan Bertschinger, of, Fossil Ridge HS, Keller, Texas
47. Daniel McCutchen, rhp, Grayson County (Texas) JC
48. Eric Schaler, rhp, Cherry Creek HS, Englewood, Colo.
49. David Ferazza, c, American River (Calif.) JC
50. Mike Muscato, c, Glendale (Ariz.) CC

OAKLAND ATHLETICS

June—Regular Phase (25)

1. **Brad Sullivan, rhp, Houston**
1. **Brian Snyder, 3b, Stetson** (Pick from Giants as compensation for Type A free agent Ray Durham)
1. **Omar Quintanilla, ss, Texas** (Supplemental pick—33rd—for loss of Durham)
2. **Andre Ethier, of, Arizona State**
3. **Dustin Majewski, of, Texas**
4. **Eddie Kim, 1b, James Madison**
5. **Trent Peterson, lhp, Florida State**
6. **Luke Appert, 2b, Minnesota**
7. **David Castillo, c, Oral Roberts**
8. **Mike McGirr, rhp, Richmond**
9. **Grant Reynolds, rhp, Kennesaw State**
10. **Matt Lynch, lhp, Florida State**
11. **Vasili Spanos, 3b, Indiana**
12. **Brian Ingram, ss, Elon**
13. **Eddie Cornejo, ss, Oklahoma**
14. **Anthony Zambotti, rhp, Indiana (Pa.)**
15. **Steve Bondurant, lhp, South Carolina**
16. Vern Sterry, rhp, North Carolina State
17. **Ryan France, rhp, Chapman (Calif.)**
18. Billy Becher, 1b, New Mexico State
19. Graham Harrison, c, Tulare Union HS, Tulare, Calif.
20. **Gordon Corder, 1b, Gonzaga**
21. Braedyn Pruitt, ss, King's Academy, West Palm Beach, Fla.
22. Brian Peacock, c, Palmetto (Fla.) HS
23. J.R. Towles, c, Collin County (Texas) CC
24. Cory Hahn, rhp, Tulane
25. **Sean Farrell, of, North Carolina**
26. Brian Horwitz, of, California
27. **James Heuser, lhp, Illinois Valley CC**
28. **Jared Trout, rhp, Rhode Island**
29. Alex Woodson, lhp, Stella Marquez HS, Salinas, P.R.
30. Justin Cassel, rhp, Chatsworth (Calif.) HS
31. Joel Fountain, rhp, Feather River (Calif.) CC
32. Steve Sollmann, 2b, Notre Dame
33. **Eric Macha, 3b, Case Western Reserve (Ohio)**
34. Broc Coffman, lhp, Rainier (Ore.) HS
35. Mike Mitchell, rhp, St. Charles (Mo.) CC
36. Matt Ryals, rhp, Wilson HS, Hacienda Heights, Calif.
37. Sean Kazmar, ss, CC of Southern Nevada
38. Zach Simons, rhp, Glenns Ferry (Idaho) HS
39. Josh Rodriguez, 2b, South Houston HS, Houston
40. Chris Westervelt, c, Stetson

PHILADELPHIA PHILLIES

June—Regular Phase (18)

1. (Pick to Indians as compensation for Type A free agent Jim Thome)
2. (Pick to Giants as compensation for Type B free agent David Bell)
3. **Tim Moss, 2b, Texas**
4. **Michael Bourn, of, Houston**
5. **Javon Moran, of, Auburn**
6. Jordan Parraz, rhp, Green Valley HS, Henderson, Nev.
7. **Kyle Kendrick, rhp, Mount Vernon (Wash.) HS**
8. **Matt Linder, rhp, Winston Churchill HS, Thunder Bay, Ontario**
9. **Jason Crosland, 3b, Lamar (Colo.) CC**
10. **Matt Hopper, 1b, Nebraska**
11. Myron Leslie, 3b, South Florida
12. **Kyle Parcus, lhp, Texas A&M**
13. **Joe Wilson, lhp, Maryland-Baltimore County**
14. **Jose Cortez, c, Pomona-Pitzer (Calif.)**
15. **Joe Brunink, 1b, Grand Valley State (Mich.)**
16. **Nate Cabrera, rhp, Trinidad State (Colo.) JC**
17. **Derek Griffith, lhp, Birmingham-Southern**
18. Rob Johnson, c, Saddleback (Calif.) JC
19. **Joe Diefenderfer, lhp, Santa Clara**
20. **Brad Ziegler, rhp, Southwest Missouri State**
21. **Caleb McConnell, rhp, Louisiana-Monroe**
22. **Marc Tugwell, 2b, Virginia Tech**
23. **Charlie Waite, c, Mississippi**
24. **Justin Foust, of, Toledo**
25. **C.J. Woodrow, rhp, Minnesota**
26. **Dan Hodges, lhp, Florida State**
27. **Brad Overton, rhp, UNC Wilmington**
28. Blair Erickson, rhp, Jesuit HS, Fair Oaks, Calif.
29. **Justin Cerrato, rhp, North Florida**
30. **Ryan Harris, ss, Eisenhower HS, Rialto, Calif.**
31. **Matt Padilla, rhp, American River (Fla.) JC**
32. Jake Tompkins, rhp, Louisiana State
33. **Justin Libey, rhp, Manchester (Ind.)**
34. **Justin Riley, c, North Carolina State**
35. **Jason Pritchard, rhp, Baylor**
36. Brett Amyx, 3b, Coppell (Texas) HS
37. **Jesse Torborg, of, Suffolk County (N.Y.) CC-Ammerman**

38. Edgar Mercado, ss, Stoneman Douglas HS, Parkland, Fla.
39. Eddie Romero, lhp, Central Union HS, Fresno
40. **Andy Barb, c, Juanita HS, Kirkland, Wash.**
41. Greg Reynolds, rhp, Terra Nova HS, Pacifica, Calif.
42. Matt Lambeth, of, Mesa (Ariz.) CC
43. Cole Buchanan, lhp, Santiago HS, Corona, Calif.
44. Cal Stanke, rhp, St. Mary Central HS, Neenah, Wis.
45. Jerod Estey, of, Moffat County HS, Craig, Colo.
46. Ryan Tabor, lhp, Green Valley HS, Henderson, Nev.
47. Mike Crotta, rhp, Martin County HS, Stuart, Fla.
48. Kyle Nash, rhp, Mater Dei HS, Huntington Beach, Calif.
49. Adam Sorgi, ss, Capistrano Valley HS, Mission Viejo, Calif.
50. Tad Reida, ss, Western HS, Kokomo, Ind.

PITTSBURGH PIRATES

June—Regular Phase (8)

1. **Paul Maholm, lhp, Mississippi State**
2. **Tom Gorzelanny, lhp, Triton (Ill.) JC**
3. **Steve Lerud, c, Galena HS, Reno**
4. **Kyle Pearson, rhp, Mosley HS, Panama City, Fla.**
5. **Craig Stansberry, 3b, Rice**
6. C.J. Smith, 1b, Florida
7. **Russell Johnson, rhp, Benjamin Russell HS, Alexander City, Ala.**
8. **Sergio Silva, rhp, Pacific**
9. **Kent Wulf, 2b, Quartz Hill HS, Lancaster, Calif.**
10. **John Peabody, of, Rancho Bernardo HS, San Diego**
11. **John Santiago, 3b, Nuestra Senora Del Carmen HS, Trujillo Alta, P.R.**
12. **Adam Boeve, of, Northern Iowa**
13. Lee Land, rhp, Riverside HS, Durham, N.C.
14. **Jake Cuffman, rhp, Butler Area HS, Butler, Pa.**
15. **Dustin Molleken, rhp, Lethbridge (Alberta) CC**
16. **Justin Harris, ss, South Carolina**
17. Steven Herce, rhp, Rice
18. **Pedro Powell, of, Middle Georgia JC**
19. Dallas Buck, rhp, Newberg (Ore.) HS
20. **Brett Holmes, of, Auburn-Montgomery**
21. Clay Hamilton, rhp, Penn State
22. **Chris Hernandez, rhp, South Carolina**
23. **Greg Picart, ss, Adela Brenes Texidor HS, Guayama, P.R.**
24. **Josh Sharpless, rhp, Allegheny (Pa.)**
25. Matt Downs, rhp, Shelton State (Ala.) CC
26. Owen Williams, lhp, Edmonds (Wash.) CC
27. Clegg Snipes, rhp, Lincoln HS, Tallahassee, Fla.
28. Matthew Creighton, lhp, Meridian (Miss.) CC
29. Jimmy Van Ostrand, of, Allan Hancock (Calif.) JC
30. Joey Friddle, ss, Young Harris (Ga.) JC
31. Cody Doonan, rhp, Kirkwood (Iowa) CC
32. Sean Coughlin, c, Golden (Colo.) HS
33. Nicholas Palmisano, 1b, Broward (Fla.) CC
34. Jeremy Horst, lhp, Des Lacs-Burlington HS, Des Lacs, N.D.
35. Nick Colborn, rhp, Blue Mountain (Ore.) CC
36. Andy Mudd, of, Scotland HS, Laurinburg, N.C.
37. Daniel Brown, lhp, Bakersfield (Calif.) CC
38. Bobby Felmy, of, Georgia Perimeter JC
39. Peter Wiggins, rhp, Patterson HS, Morgan City, La.
40. Christian Romple, c, West Valley HS, Yakima, Wash.
41. Chandler Miller, rhp, Young Harris (Ga.) JC
42. Tony Snow, rhp, Edmonds (Wash.) CC
43. Lance Scoggins, lhp, Bolton HS, Memphis, Tenn.
44. Troy Harrington, rhp, Palmdale (Calif.) HS
45. Domingo Reyes, lhp, Brito Private HS, Miami
46. Cody Lovejoy, c, Cypress (Calif.) HS
47. Bryan Henry, rhp, Florida HS, Tallahassee, Fla.
48. **Antonio Westfield, of, Cleveland (Tenn.) HS**
49. Raul Torres, rhp, Puerto Rico Advance College HS, Bayamon, P.R.
50. Rhyne Hughes, 1b, Pearl River (Miss.) CC

ST. LOUIS CARDINALS

June—Regular Phase (28)

1. **Daric Barton, c, Marina HS, Huntington Beach, Calif.**
2. **Stuart Pomeranz, rhp, Houston HS, Collierville, Tenn.**
3. **Dennis Dove, rhp, Georgia Southern**
4. **Mark Michael, rhp, Delaware**
5. **Brandon Yarbrough, c, Richmond HS, Ellerbe, N.C.**
6. **Matt Weagle, rhp, Franklin Pierce (N.H.)**
7. **Brendan Ryan, ss, Lewis-Clark State (Idaho)**
8. **Matt Pagnozzi, c, Central Arizona JC**
9. **Justin Garza, rhp, Seminole State (Okla.) JC**
10. **Buddy Blair, lhp, Oklahoma**
11. **Nathan Kopszywa, rhp, Crichton (Tenn.)**
12. Calvin Beamon, of, CC of Southern Nevada
13. **Kainoa Obrey, 3b, Brigham Young**
14. Ian Kennedy, rhp, La Quinta HS, Huntington Beach, Calif.
15. **Anthony Reyes, rhp, Southern California**
16. **Omar Pena, ss, Northeastern**
17. **Kevin House, of, Memphis**
18. **Jose Virgil, of, Oklahoma State**
19. **Jason Motte, c, Iona**
20. **Jordan Pals, rhp, Eastern Illinois**
21. **Jason Burch, rhp, Nebraska**
22. Derik Drewett, rhp, Watson Chapel HS, Sherrill, Ark.
23. **Matt Blanton, lhp, Hendrix (Ark.)**
24. **Temetric Thomas, 2b, Mississippi Valley State**
25. **Tavaris Gary, of, Cumberland (Tenn.)**
26. **Levi Webber, of, Oregon State**
27. **Jason John, rhp, Grayson County (Texas) JC**
28. **Tanner Wootan, 2b, Chandler-Gilbert (Ariz.) JC**
29. **Brantley Jordan, lhp, Texas**
30. Matt Lane, rhp, Iowa Western CC
31. **Mike Tamulionis, rhp, St. John's**
32. **Derek Roper, rhp, Missouri**
33. **Casey Grimm, of, Seton Hall**
34. Kevin Mulvey, rhp, Bishop Ahr HS, Edison, N.J.
35. Peter Eberhardt, rhp, Cerritos (Calif.) JC
36. John Powell, rhp, Carl Albert State (Okla.) JC
37. **Sal Frisella, of, Southern Illinois**
38. Brett Sinkbeil, rhp, Charles Page HS, Sand Springs, Okla.
39. T.J. Brewer, rhp, Bloomington South HS, Bloomington, Ind.
40. **Peter Soteropoulos, lhp, Connecticut**
41. Ryan Castellanos, 3b, Silverado HS, Las Vegas, Nev.
42. Roy Merritt, of, Nimitz HS, Houston
43. Max Scherzer, rhp, Parkway Central HS, St. Louis
44. Ryan Reichelderfer, 1b, Arkansas-Fort Smith JC
45. **Joshua Markham, lhp, Riverdale HS, Murfreesboro, Tenn.**
46. Kam Mickolio, rhp, JC of Eastern Utah
47. Tobirus Bell, of, John Wood (Ill.) CC

SAN DIEGO PADRES

June—Regular Phase (4)

1. **Tim Stauffer, rhp, Richmond**
2. **Daniel Moore, lhp, North Carolina**
3. **Colt Morton, c, North Carolina State**
4. **Peter Stonard, ss, San Diego State**
5. **Billy Hogan, ss, Chandler-Gilbert (Ariz.) JC**
6. Cory Patton, of, Texas A&M
7. **Clark Girardeau, rhp, South Alabama**
8. **Dirk Hayhurst, rhp, Kent State**
9. **Matt Lauderdale, c, College of Charleston**
10. **Fernando Valenzuela Jr., 1b, Nevada-Las Vegas**
11. **Justin Smyres, ss, Cal State Fullerton**
12. **Jeff Leise, of, Nebraska**
13. **Ryan Johnson, of, Wake Forest**
14. Steve Gendron, ss, Mississippi State
15. **Chuck Bechtel, rhp, Marist**
16. Zane Carlson, rhp, Baylor
17. Justin Sokol, rhp, Iowa Central CC
18. **Greg Conden, rhp, George Washington**
19. Jesse Estrada, rhp, Grayson County (Texas) CC
20. **Leo Rosales, rhp, Cal State Northridge**
21. **Brett Burnham, ss, Connecticut**
22. **Brandon Kaye, 1b, Oklahoma City**
23. **Eddie Bonine, rhp, Nevada**
24. **Ronnie Robinson, rhp, Georgia State**
25. Chuck Caufield, of, Seminole State (Okla.) JC
26. Steven Wright, rhp, Valley View HS, Moreno Valley, Calif.

27. John Banach, 3b, Los Angeles Harbor (Calif.) JC
28. Corey McCoy, of, Arkansas-Fort Smith JC
29. **Steven Delabar, rhp, Volunteer State (Tenn.) CC**
30. Ben Cox, rhp, San Jacinto (Texas) JC
31. Alan Tungate, rhp, St. Catharines (Ky.) JC
32. Chad Catalano, rhp, Pearl River (Miss.) CC
33. Colin Carter, lhp, Liberty Christian HS, Frisco, Texas
34. **Chris Rayborn, rhp, Meridian (Miss.) CC**
35. Dean Turner, rhp, Bellevue (Wash.) CC
36. Josh Sawatzky, rhp, W.C. Miller Collegiate HS, Altona, Manitoba
37. Thomas Skipper, of, Sandy Union (Ore.) HS
38. **Ryan Klatt, rhp, Biola (Calif.)**
39. Ryan McGraw, of, Coastal Carolina
40. Zach Shadle, rhp, Bethel HS, Spanaway, Wash.
41. Pat Warfle, of, Eau Gallie HS, Melbourne, Fla.
42. Nigel Goodwin, rhp, Spokane Falls (Wash.) CC
43. **Nathan Rogers, lhp, Connors State (Okla.) JC**
44. Justin Wichert, rhp, Cowley County (Kan.) CC
45. Clay Collier, c, Edmond North HS, Edmond, Okla.
46. **Brian Edwards, of, Metro State (Colo.)**
47. Bryan Eubanks, rhp, Meridian (Miss.) CC
48. **Tom Vincent, of, McKellar, Australia**
49. Nate Simms, c, Central HS, Grand Junction, Colo.
50. Sean Rierson, rhp, Arizona

SAN FRANCISCO GIANTS

June—Regular Phase (26)

1. **David Aardsma, rhp, Rice** (Pick from Astros as compensation for Type A free agent Jeff Kent)
1. (Pick to Athletics as compensation for Type A free agent Ray Durham)
1. **Craig Whitaker, rhp, Lufkin (Texas) HS** (Supplemental pick—34th—for loss of Kent)
2. **Todd Jennings, c, Long Beach State**
2. **Nate Schierholtz, 3b, Chabot (Calif.) JC**
3. **Brian Buscher, 3b, South Carolina**
4. **Brooks McNiven, rhp, British Columbia**
5. **Mike Wagner, of, Washington**
6. **Billy Sadler, rhp, Louisiana State**
7. **Pat Misch, lhp, Western Michigan**
8. **Tim Hutting, ss, Long Beach State**
9. **Kellen Ludwig, rhp, Chipola (Fla.) JC**
10. **Jesse Schmidt, of, Cal State Sacramento**
11. **Jeff Petersen, rhp, Washington**
12. **Ryan Sadowski, rhp, Florida**
13. **Nick Conte, c, St. Mary's**
14. **Sean Martin, rhp, Cal State Fullerton**
15. **Ben Thurmond, rhp, Arizona State**
16. **Mike Mooney, of, JC of San Mateo (Calif.)**
17. **Marcus Sanders, ss, Sarasota (Fla.) HS**
18. **Patrick Dobson, of, Nevada-Las Vegas**
19. **Jon Coutlangus, of, South Carolina**
20. Raul Rodriguez, c, Florida Christian HS, Miami
21. Sean Watson, rhp, Florida Christian HS, Miami
22. Nate Fogle, rhp, Mount Hood (Ore.) CC
23. **Mike Kunes, lhp, UCLA**
24. **Brian Wilson, rhp, Louisiana State**
25. Nolan Mulligan, rhp, Chaminade-Madonna Prep, Hollywood, Fla.
26. Tyler Coon, lhp, CC of Southern Nevada
27. Omar Aguilar, rhp, Livingston (Calif.) HS
28. Roberto Gonzalez, of, Sunny Hills HS, Fullerton, Calif.
29. **Danny DeSouza, of, Connors State (Okla.) JC**
30. **Derek Barrows, 3b, Campbell**
31. Eddy Baeza, rhp, Mission (Calif.) JC
32. O.D. Gonzalez, of, American HS, Miami
33. **Travis NeSmith, lhp, Florida Atlantic**
34. Cody McAllister, rhp, Edmonds (Wash.) CC
35. Tyson Brummett, rhp, Spanish Fork (Utah) HS
36. **Tim Alvarez, lhp, Southeast Missouri State**
37. Shannon Wirth, lhp, Mount Hood (Ore.) CC
38. Jordan Hafer, 1b, Deerfield Beach (Fla.) HS
39. Mike Pierce, c, Fresno CC
40. Dylan Gonzalez, rhp, American Heritage HS, Plantation, Fla.
41. Mike Johnston, lhp, Ball State
42. Luis Martinez, c, Coral Park HS, Miami
43. Mike Bell, c, Red Bluff (Calif.) HS
44. **John Odom, rhp, Tallahassee (Fla.) CC**
45. James Braden, rhp, Manatee (Fla.) JC
46. Brandon Federici, lhp, Polk (Fla.) CC
47. Thomas Correa, ss, Florin HS, Sacramento, Calif.
48. Matt Berezay, of, Modesto (Calif.) JC
49. Doug Fister, rhp, Merced (Calif.) JC
50. Jim Popp, rhp, Duquesne

SEATTLE MARINERS

June—Regular Phase (19)

1. (Pick to Diamondbacks as compensation for Type B free agent Greg Colbrunn)
1. **Adam Jones, ss/rhp, Morse HS, San Diego** (Supplemental pick—37th—for failure to sign 2002 first-rounder John Mayberry Jr.)
2. **Jeff Flaig, 3b, El Dorado HS, Placentia, Calif.**
3. **Ryan Feierabend, lhp, Midview HS, Grafton, Ohio**
4. **Paul Fagan, lhp, Bartram Trail HS, Jacksonville**
5. **Casey Abrams, lhp, Wright State**
6. **Eric O'Flaherty, lhp, Walla Walla (Wash.) HS**
7. **Jeremy Dutton, 3b, North Carolina State**
8. **Tom Oldham, lhp, Creighton**
9. **Justin Ruchti, c, Rice**
10. **Mike Cox, 3b, Florida Atlantic**
11. **Joe Woerman, rhp, San Diego CC**
12. **Ruben Flores, rhp, El Paso (Texas) CC**
13. **Shawn Nottingham, lhp, Jackson HS, Canton, Ohio**
14. **Tim Dorn, rhp, East Los Angeles JC**
15. Scott Maine, lhp, Dwyer HS, Palm Beach Gardens, Fla.
16. **Brian Schweiger, c, Cal State San Bernardino**
17. **Jason Snyder, rhp, Dixie (Utah) JC**
18. **James Hymon, ss, Rust (Miss.)**
19. **Aaron Jensen, rhp, Springville (Utah) HS**
20. Carroll Gaddis, of, Hoke County HS, Raeford, N.C.
21. **Casey Craig, of, Granite Hills HS, La Mesa, Calif.**
22. **Sam Bradford, of, Gardner-Webb**
23. **Danny Santin, c, Brito Private HS, Miami**
24. **Kenneth Falconer, rhp, Kansas**
25. Jason Cable, lhp, Palmdale (Calif.) HS
26. Dwayne Lynah, of, Spartanburg Methodist (S.C.) JC
27. Richard Breshears, rhp, Hutchinson (Kan.) CC
28. Daniel McDonald, lhp, Theodore (Ala.) HS
29. Chris Garcia, rhp, Brooklyn, N.Y.
30. Steve Santos, rhp, Los Medanos (Calif.) JC
31. Doug Mathis, rhp, Central Arizona JC
32. Adam Poole, lhp, Lincoln Trail (Ill.) JC
33. Blake Rampy, rhp, Tomball (Texas) HS
34. Paul Keck, c, Sacramento CC
35. Andy Reichard, rhp, State College (Pa.) HS
36. Alex Baboulas, lhp, Birchmount Park Collegiate Institute, Toronto
37. Joel Allin, lhp, Stockbridge (Ga.) HS
38. Yusuf Carter, c, Canarsie HS, Brooklyn, N.Y.
39. Trevor Heid, of, Dixie (Utah) JC
40. Mark Tourangeau, rhp, Queen Elizabeth Park HS, Scarborough, Ontario
41. Dane Awana, lhp, Saddleback (Calif.) CC
42. Danny Santiesteban, of, Brito Private HS, Miami
43. Harold Williams, lhp, Cerritos (Calif.) CC
44. Edwin Totesault, ss, Brito HS, Miami
45. McCay Green, rhp, Lake Sumter (Fla.) CC
46. Mike Hofius, 1b, Long Beach State
47. Dan Kapala, rhp, Shrine HS, Royal Oak, Mich.
48. Markus Roberts, ss, Deer Valley HS, Antioch, Calif.
49. Jose Laffitte, of, Miami Senior HS
50. Tim Turner, of, East Tennesee State

TAMPA BAY DEVIL RAYS

June—Regular Phase (1)

1. **Delmon Young, of, Camarillo (Calif.) HS**
2. **James Houser, lhp, Sarasota (Fla.) HS**
3. Andrew Miller, lhp, Buchholz HS, Gainesville, Fla.
4. **Travis Schlichting, 3b, Round Rock (Texas) HS**

5. **Jon Barratt, lhp, Hillcrest HS, Springfield, Mo.**
6. **Christian Lopez, c, Hialeah HS, Miami Lakes, Fla.**
7. **Brian Henderson, lhp, Houston**
8. **Matt Maniscalco, ss, Mississippi State**
9. Billy Buckner, rhp, Young Harris (Ga.) JC
10. **Shaun Cumberland, of, Pace HS, Milton, Fla.**
11. **Chad Cooper, 2b, Middle Tennessee State**
12. **John Jaso, c, Southwestern (Calif.) JC**
13. **Chad Orvella, rhp, North Carolina State**
14. **Aaron Gangi, lhp, Akron**
15. **Andy Weimer, rhp, LeMoyne**
16. Jared Hughes, rhp, Santa Margarita HS, Laguna Niguel, Calif.
17. **Chris Gustafson, of, Kamiak HS, Granite Falls, Wash.**
18. **Jason Cayton, rhp, Cerritos (Calif.) JC**
19. Josh Geer, rhp, Navarro (Texas) JC
20. **Mark Schleicher, 2b, Pfeiffer (N.C.)**
21. Casey Hudspeth, rhp, Sarasota (Fla.) HS
22. Rod Allen, of, Arizona State
23. **Ryan McCally, rhp, Stanford**
24. Chris Shaver, lhp, William & Mary
25. **Stephen Jones, of, Alabama-Birmingham**
26. **Joe Little, lhp, Arizona**
27. Adam Roos, 3b, Hamarskjeld HS, Thunder Bay, Ontario
28. Andrew Swanson, rhp, Galesburg (Ill.) HS
29. **Fernando Puebla, ss, Southern**
30. Adam Ottavino, rhp, Berkeley Carroll HS, Brooklyn, N.Y.
31. **Tom Lagreid, c, Everett (Wash.) CC**
32. **Matt Travis, lhp, Santa Clara**
33. **Jordan Olson, lhp, Southern California**
34. Travis Fuller, lhp, Hayesville (N.C.) HS
35. Gus Jacobson, rhp, Cactus Shadows HS, Cave Creek, Ariz.
36. Wade LeBlanc, lhp, Barbe HS, Lake Charles, La.
37. Kris Medlen, ss, Garh HS, Cerritos, Calif.
38. **Kris Dufner, ss, Deleware**
39. Kevin Allen, of, West Henderson HS, Hendersonville, N.C.
40. Graham Baxter, rhp, McQueen HS, Reno, Nev.
41. Leon Johnson, of, Thatcher (Ariz.) HS
42. **Travis Beech, 2b, Austin Peay**
43. Grant Theophilus, lhp, Ocean View HS, Huntington Beach, Calif.
44. **Josh Kendrick, 1b, Mobile (Ala.)**
45. **Brandon Rousseve, ss, Meridian (Miss.) CC**
46. **Josh Bolen, of, Louisville**
47. Brad Matthews, 2b, Surry (N.C.) CC
48. Derrick Shaw, ss, Benton HS, Bossier City, La.
49. Lars Davis, c, Grand Prairie Composite HS, Grande Prairie, Albert
50. **Brent Speigner, rhp, Vestavia Hills, Ala.**

TEXAS RANGERS

June—Regular Phase (9)

1. **John Danks, lhp, Round Rock (Texas) HS**
2. **Vince Sinisi, 1b, Rice**
3. **John Hudgins, rhp, Stanford**
4. **Wes Littleton, rhp, Cal State Fullerton**
5. **Matt Lorenzo, rhp, Kent State**
6. **Adam Bourassa, of, Wake Forest**
7. **Matt Farnum, rhp, Texas A&M**
8. **Jeremy Cleveland, of, North Carolina**
9. **Tim Cunningham, lhp, Stanford**
10. **Adam Fox, 3b, Ohio**
11. **Cody Clark, c, Wichita State**
12. **Andrew Wishy, of, Arkansas**
13. **Emerson Frostad, 3b, Lewis-Clark State (Idaho)**
14. **Brian Mattoon, lhp, LeMoyne**
15. **Chris Alexander, 1b, New Mexico**
16. **Kevin Altman, rhp, Rubidoux HS, Riverside, Calif.**
17. **Ian Kinsler, ss, Missouri**
18. **Cain Byrd, rhp, Southwood HS, Shreveport, La.**
19. **Charles Bowman, rhp, Jacksonville**
20. **Micah Furtado, 2b, Lewis-Clark State (Idaho)**
21. **Marc LaMacchia, rhp, Florida State**
22. **Dane Bubela, of, Rice**
23. **Jonathan Ramos, rhp, Tomas C Ongay HS, Bayamon, P.R.**
24. Ben Rowe, rhp, Oregon State
25. **Justin Hatcher, c, Texas Christian**
26. **Ian Gac, 1b, Edmonds-Woodway HS, Seattle**
27. **Johnny Washington, ss, Mount San Jacinto (Calif.) JC**
28. Brad Lincoln, rhp, Brazoswood HS, Clute, Texas
29. **Chris Cordeiro, rhp, UCLA**
30. **Scott Feldman, rhp, JC of San Mateo (Calif.)**
31. Rosalino Valenzuela, rhp, Central Arizona JC
32. Colby Paxton, rhp, Auburn
33. **Scott Welch, ss, Minnesota**
34. Sammy Hewitt, 3b, North Carolina
35. Austin Faught, lhp, Louisiana-Lafayette
36. Dwayne White, of, Cowley County (Kan.) CC
37. Loren Deans, of, Capistrano Valley HS, Mission Viego, Calif.
38. Paul Sandoval, rhp, Saddleback (Calif.) JC
39. Josh Lansford, 3b, St. Francis HS, Santa Clara, Calif.
40. Matt Vogel, 2b, East Los Angeles JC
41. Francisco Mora, rhp, Eastlake HS, Chula Vista, Calif.
42. Charles Hesseltine, lhp, Maloney HS, Meriden, Conn.
43. Hunter Harrigan, c, Cowley County (Kan.) CC
44. Curtis White, lhp, Oklahoma

TORONTO BLUE JAYS

June—Regular Phase (13)

1. **Aaron Hill, ss, Louisiana State**
2. **Josh Banks, rhp, Florida International**
3. **Shaun Marcum, rhp, Southwest Missouri State**
4. **Kurt Isenberg, lhp, James Madison**
5. **Justin James, rhp, Missouri**
6. **Christian Snavely, of, Ohio State**
7. **Danny Core, rhp, Florida Atlantic**
8. **Chad Mulholland, rhp, Southwest Missouri State**
9. **Jamie Vermilyea, rhp, New Mexico**
10. **Jayce Tingler, of, Missouri**
11. **Tom Mastny, rhp, Furman**
12. **Jayson Rodriguez, rhp, Indian River (Fla.) CC**
13. **Matt Foster, lhp, Navy**
14. **Jeremy Harper, rhp, Virginia Military Institute**
15. **Vito Chiaravalloti, 1b, Richmond**
16. **Joey Reiman, c, Grand Canyon (Ariz.)**
17. **Jordy Templet, rhp, Louisiana-Lafayette**
18. **Ryan Roberts, 3b, Texas-Arlington**
19. **Adrian Martin, rhp, South Fork HS, Stuart, Fla.**
20. Brad DePoy, rhp, The Woodlands (Texas) HS
21. **Mark Sopko, rhp, Arizona State**
22. **Vinny Esposito, 3b, Rutgers**
23. **Jeremy Acey, 2b, Skyline (Calif.) JC**
24. Nick Evangelista, rhp, Pittsburgh
25. **Brian Patrick, 2b, Duke**
26. **Kyle Thousand, of, Iowa**
27. **Brian Reed, rhp, Alabama**
28. Pat Breen, of, Cal Poly
29. Ben Nieto, lhp, Riverside (Calif.) CC
30. **Billy Wheeler, rhp, South Suburban (Ill.) JC**
31. **Joaquin Canizal, rhp, Union (Ky.)**
32. **Brad Mumma, lhp, Western Michigan**
33. **Joey Wolfe, c, Louisiana-Monroe**
34. Jeremy Noegel, rhp, West Florida
35. Jim Burt, 1b, Miami
36. Matt Trink, rhp, Horizon HS, Scottsdale, Ariz.
37. Aric Van Gaalen, lhp, St. Petersburg (Fla.) JC
38. Jack Ryser, of, Santa Ana (Calif.) JC
39. William Blackmon, lhp, Arlington Heights HS, Fort Worth, Texas
40. James Coker, lhp, Spartanburg (Methodist (S.C.) JC
41. Scott Tolbert, rhp, Georgia Southern
42. **Jeremy Knicely, c, Longwood (Va.)**
43. Ryan Gordon, lhp, UNC Greensboro
44. Brent Johnson, of, Nevada-Las Vegas
45. Paul Franko, 1b, Horizon, HS, Scottsdale, Ariz.
46. Paul Marlow, rhp, Elgin Park HS, White Rock, B.C
47. Jeff Walker, lhp, Vernon Regional (Texas) JC
48. Bryan Hansen, lhp, Kishwaukee (Ill.) JC
49. **Michael Rider, rhp, Cosumnes River (Calif.) JC**
50. Angel Hernandez, of, Champagnat Catholic HS, Hialeah, Fla.

2004 PADRES GO WITH HOMETOWN PLAYER FOR NO. 1 OVERALL PICK, WITH HISTORICALLY BAD RESULTS

Move over, Steve Chilcott.

The catcher the Mets took No. 1 overall in 1966—one spot ahead of Reggie Jackson—has long gone down in draft history as the worst No. 1 overall pick ever.

But as time passes since the 2004 draft, it becomes apparent that the Padres surpassed the Mets when they selected Matt Bush No. 1 overall. Chilcott at least had some positive outcomes in his minor league career. Furthermore, Chilcott never had repeated run-ins with authorities, as Bush did even before his professional career got under way.

San Diego general manager Kevin Towers told reporters in the weeks leading up to the draft that the Padres had narrowed their choices to three college players: Florida State shortstop Stephen Drew and righthanders Jeff Niemann of Rice and Jered Weaver of Long Beach State.

He went to owner John Moores a week before the draft, Towers later recalled, the GM told his owner it could take as much as $7 million as part of a big league contract to sign Drew. When Moores asked if he was worth it, Towers said no. At that point, the Padres' plans began to unravel.

First, they ruled out taking Drew, and then they also ruled out Niemann and Weaver as being too expensive. That left the club short on information, as it had been bearing down on those three top picks. When Bush, a local product of San Diego's Mission Bay High, called area scout Tim McWilliam to express his desire to play for the Padres, the club sent a large contingent to watch him in a playoff game.

The 5-foot-10, 170-pound Bush was considered a first-round talent, and BA ranked him as the No. 8 overall prospect heading into the draft. His arm earned 80 grades on the 20-80 scouting scale, so despite some questions about his bat, he was considered a fine defender at shortstop. The Padres quickly commenced negotiations with Bush, took him No. 1 overall and signed him for $3.15 million.

Before playing in his first pro game, Bush and his friends trashed a suite at Petco Park, and he was arrested after fighting with a bouncer at an Arizona nightclub. More trouble followed, including Tommy John surgery that followed his move in 2007 from shortstop to the mound. An assault arrest in February 2009 in El Cajon, Calif., prompted the Padres to trade Bush to the Blue Jays. In between his run-ins with the law, Bush hit .219/.294/.276 and made 76 errors in 204 games, and he never pitched for the Jays organization, which released him out of spring training.

Detroit scored a coup when Justin Verlander fell to the No. 2 overall pick

All three players the Padres passed on have gone on to productive big league careers, but the Tigers' No. 2 overall pick—righthander Justin Verlander—has had the most success. Verlander signed in October 2004 after his father stepped in to help with the negotiations, and he reached Detroit after only one minor league season. He was BA's Rookie of the Year in 2006 and helped lead the Tigers to the American League pennant.

Drew and Weaver fell in the draft as signability concerns dropped their stock. Drew landed at No. 15 overall. The Diamondbacks wound up signing him a week before the 2005 draft, just beating the May 30 deadline that would have required Drew to re-enter the draft. He received a $4 million bonus as part of a major league contract that guaranteed him $5.5 million after a short turn with the Camden Riversharks of the independent Atlantic League.

Weaver went 12th overall to the Angels and wound up signing with Camden as well, though he never appeared in a game. He also received a $4 million bonus, which was the same offer the Angels and scouting director Eddie Bane made when they first drafted Weaver, who was coming off an impressive 15-1, 1.63 season at Long Beach State.

"Now everybody's happy," Bane said. "We can just

talk about baseball now. We're pretty excited."

Bonuses Tick Back Upward

When Weaver and Drew signed, they brought the average first-round bonus up to $1,958,448, a 10.9 percent increase on the 2003 average. Teams were efficient signing high school players,

Another holdout in the 2004 first-round didn't have the same happy ending. Rice righthander Wade Townsend teamed with Niemann (who went No. 4 overall to Tampa Bay) and fellow righthander Philip Humber (No. 3 overall, Mets) to be the highest drafted trio of college teammates in draft history. The trio led Rice to the 2003 College World Series championship. Humber and Niemann wound up signing in January 2005, while Townsend rejected the Orioles' below-slot offer of $1.7 million at the No. 8 overall spot.

He petitioned Major League Baseball for the right to continue negotiating with the Orioles, despite attending class at Rice. MLB denied Townsend's proposal to rewrite the existing draft rules, and the righthander went back into the '05 draft pool. He wound up going in the first round again, to the Devil Rays at No. 8 overall again, but never got past Double-A before retiring in 2009.

All the top players didn't come out of the first round in the '04 draft. Texas righthander Huston Street went 40th overall to the Athletics, and one year later he earned BA Rookie of the Year honors as one of the American League's top closers. Second-rounder Dustin Pedroia (Arizona State) stormed through the Red Sox farm system en route to being named AL Rookie of the Year in 2007 and MVP a year later.

The Rockies and Angels made splashes in the 17th round with players who fell in the draft. Colorado signed outfielder Dexter Fowler away from a Miami baseball scholarship for a $925,000 bonus, while the Angels nabbed righthander Nick Adenhart for $710,000. Adenhart had entered the spring as the nation's top-ranked prep pitcher before requiring Tommy John surgery to repair an elbow injury, but the Angels signed him anyway, and the gamble paid off when Adenhart emerged as their top pitching prospect in short order. A member of the big league roster, Adenhart died in an April 2009 auto accident.

DRAFT 04: FIRST-ROUND PICKS

No.	Club	Player, Pos.	School	Hometown	Ht.	Wt.	B-T	Age
1.	Padres	Matt Bush, ss	Mission Bay HS	San Diego	5-10	170	R-R	18
2.	Tigers	Justin Verlander, rhp	Old Dominion	Manakin-Sabot, Va.	6-5	200	R-R	21
3.	Mets	Philip Humber, rhp	Rice	Carthage, Texas	6-4	220	R-R	21
4.	Devil Rays	Jeff Niemann, rhp	Rice	Houston	6-9	260	R-R	21
5.	Brewers	Mark Rogers, rhp	Mt. Ararat HS	Topsham, Maine	6-2	205	R-R	18
6.	Indians	Jeremy Sowers, lhp	Vanderbilt	Louisville	6-1	165	L-L	21
7.	Reds	Homer Bailey, rhp	LaGrange HS	LaGrange, Texas	6-4	185	R-R	18
8.	Orioles	*Wade Townsend, rhp	Rice	Dripping Springs, Texas	6-4	225	R-R	21
9.	Rockies	Chris Nelson, ss	Redan HS	Stone Mountain, Ga.	5-11	176	R-R	18
10.	Rangers	Thomas Diamond, rhp	New Orleans	Metairie, La.	6-3	230	R-R	21
11.	Pirates	Neil Walker, c	Pine Richland HS	Gibsonia, Pa.	6-3	205	B-R	18
12.	Angels	Jered Weaver, rhp	Long Beach State	Simi Valley, Calif.	6-7	205	R-R	21
13.	Nationals	Bill Bray, lhp	William & Mary	Virginia Beach	6-3	215	L-L	21
14.	Royals	Billy Butler, 3b	Wolfson HS	Jacksonville, Fla.	6-2	225	R-R	18
15.	Diamondbacks	Stephen Drew, ss	Florida State	Valdosta, Ga.	6-0	185	L-R	21
16.	Blue Jays	David Purcey, lhp	Oklahoma	Addison, Texas	6-5	240	L-L	22
17.	Dodgers	Scott Elbert, lhp	Seneca HS	Seneca, Mo.	6-2	190	L-L	19
18.	White Sox	Josh Fields, 3b	Oklahoma State	Stillwater, Okla.	6-2	210	R-R	21
19.	Cardinals	Chris Lambert, rhp	Boston College	Manchester, N.H.	6-1	205	R-R	21
20.	Twins	Trever Plouffe, ss	Crespi Carmelite HS	Encino, Calif.	6-1	175	R-R	18
21.	Phillies	Greg Golson, of	Connally HS	Connally, Texas	6-0	190	R-R	18
22.	Twins	Glen Perkins, lhp	Minnesota	Stillwater, Minn.	6-0	200	L-L	21
23.	Yankees	Phil Hughes, rhp	Foothill HS	Santa Ana, Calif.	6-5	220	R-R	18
24.	Athletics	Landon Powell, c	South Carolina	Apex, N.C.	6-3	225	B-R	22
25.	Twins	Kyle Waldrop, rhp	Farragut HS	Knoxville, Tenn.	6-4	190	R-R	18
26.	Athletics	Richie Robnett, of	Fresno State	Visalia, Calif.	5-10	195	L-L	20
27.	Marlins	Taylor Tankersley, lhp	Alabama	Vicksburg, Miss.	6-1	220	L-L	21
28.	Dodgers	Blake DeWitt, 2b	Sikeston HS	Sikeston, Mo.	5-11	175	L-R	18
29.	Royals	Matt Campbell, lhp	South Carolina	Simpsonville, S.C.	6-2	170	L-L	21
30.	Rangers	Eric Hurley, rhp	Wolfson HS	Jacksonville, Fla.	6-4	195	R-R	18

*Did not sign

2004

CLUB-BY-CLUB SELECTIONS

ANAHEIM ANGELS

June—Regular Phase (12)

1. **Jered Weaver, rhp, Long Beach State**
2. (Pick to White Sox as compensation for Type A free agent Bartolo Colon)
3. (Pick to Blue Jays as compensation for Type A free agent Kelvim Escobar)
4. Patrick White, of, Daphne (Ala.) HS
5. **Luis Rivera, of, Ramon Vila Mayo HS, Rio Piedras, P.R.**
6. **Josh LeBlanc, 2b, Southern**
7. **Bill Layman, rhp, North Florida**
8. **Freddy Sandoval, 3b, San Diego**
9. **Hainley Statia, ss, Trinity Christian Academy, Boynton Beach, Fla.**
10. **Doug Reinhardt, 3b, Santa Margarita Catholic HS, Laguna Beach, Calif.**
11. **Clifton Remole, 1b, Georgia Tech**
12. **Tyler Johnson, of, Haskell (Okla.) HS**
13. **Andrew Toussaint, 3b, Southern**
14. **Nick Adenhart, rhp, Williamsport (Md.) HS**
15. Adam Crabtree, rhp, Phillips Academy, Andover, Mass.
16. **Chris Waters, rhp, North Florida**
17. **Ryan Aldridge, rhp, Middle Georgia JC**
18. **Mark Trumbo, rhp, Villa Park HS, Orange, Calif.**
19. **David Hernandez, rhp, Miami-Dade CC**
20. **D.T. McDowell, of, Tucker HS, Atlanta**
21. Stan Posluszny, of, West Virginia
22. Matt Moore, 3b, Newhall, Calif.
23. **Ben Johnson, c, Washington**
24. **Nate Sutton, 2b, UC Santa Barbara**
25. **Casey Mutter, rhp, Cal State San Bernardino**
26. **Jaime Douglas, lhp, Central Florida**
27. **Martin Maldonado, c, Dr. Juan J. Nunez HS, Naguabo, P.R.**
28. Cristen Tapia, 1b, Tuscon (Ariz.) Magnet HS
29. **Billy Edwards, rhp, Memphis**
30. Alan Horne, rhp, Chipola (Fla.) JC
31. Ricky Bambino, c, Sierra (Calif.) JC
32. **Brooks Shankle, 3b, Texas-San Antonio**
33. **Frederic Carney, rhp, Regis (Colo.)**
34. **Bobby Cassevah, rhp, Pace (Fla.) HS**
35. **Nick Green, rhp, Darton (Ga.) JC**
36. John Mariotti, rhp, Gulf Coast (Fla.) JC
37. Clayton Trenary, of, Central Florida CC
38. **Richard Giannotti, of, Miami**
39. **Mike Sweeney, lhp, St. Petersburg (Fla.) CC**
40. **Stephen Marek, rhp, San Jacinto (Texas) JC**
41. William Cooper, rhp, Shelton State (Ala.) JC
42. Pat Warfle, of, Daytona Beach (Fla.) CC
43. Chris Lombardo, rhp, Etiwanda (Calif.) HS
44. **Grant Harper, of, San Pedro (Calif.) HS**
45. Andrew Colon, rhp, Choctawhatchee HS, Fort Walton Beach, Fla.
46. Marquez Smith, 3b, Daytona Beach (Fla.) JC
47. Erik Davis, rhp, Mountain View (Calif.) HS
48. Julian Laurean, 2b, Chandler-Gilbert (Ariz.) CC
49. Nick Dashnaw, rhp, Santa Clarita (Calif.) Christian HS
50. **Abel Nieves, 2b, Middle Georgia JC**

ARIZONA DIAMONDBACKS

June—Regular Phase (15)

1. **Stephen Drew, ss, Florida State**
2. **Jon Zeringue, of, Louisiana State**
3. **Garrett Mock, rhp, Houston**
4. **Ross Ohlendorf, rhp, Princeton**
5. **Cesar Nicolas, 1b, Vanderbilt**
6. **Brandon Burgess, of, Sonoma State (Calif.)**
7. **Koley Kolberg, rhp, Arizona**
8. Jimmy Shull, rhp, Cal Poly
9. **A.J. Shappi, rhp, UC Riverside**
10. **Steven Jackson, rhp, Clemson**
11. **Darryl Lawhorn, of, East Carolina**
12. **Richard Mercado, c, Arizona**
13. Antoan Richardson, of, Vanderbilt
14. **Lester Contreras, ss, St. Petersburg (Fla.) JC**
15. **Dan Pohlman, c, Northwestern**
16. **Mark Reynolds, ss, Virginia**
17. **Chris Carter, 1b/of, Stanford**
18. **Vince Davis, lhp, Southern**
19. **Derek Bruce, ss, Lewis-Clark State (Idaho)**
20. Edwin Roman, of, Princeton (Ind.) Community HS
21. **Chris Thompson, rhp, Mississippi**
22. Luis Lajara, of, Santo Domingo, D.R
23. **Travis Gulick, of, Michigan State**
24. **Trey Hendricks, 1b, Harvard**
25. **Todd Stein, lhp, Illinois State**
26. **Eric Schindewolf, 2b, Texas A&M**
27. **Garrett Bauer, lhp, Missouri Baptist**
28. **Ramon Downing, 2b, Wabash Valley (Ill.) CC**
29. Christopher Bowen, lhp, Maryland
30. **Kevin Williams, of, South Alabama**
31. **Marcus Townsend, of, Southern**
32. **Josh Buhagiar, of, Long Beach State**
33. Joseph Campbell, 3b, Fremd HS, Palatine, Ill.
34. David Hernandez, rhp, Cosumnes River (Calif.) JC
35. **Jo Jo Batten, 2b, Middle Georgia JC**
36. Craig Heyer, rhp, Coronado HS, Scottsdale, Ariz.
37. **Billy Lockin, ss, Loyola Marymount**
38. **Lorenzo Church, rhp, Mission Bay HS, San Diego**
39. Michael Jarman, lhp, Edmond North HS, Edmond, Okla.
40. Ulrich Snijders, c, Trinity Christian Academy, West Palm Beach, Fla.
41. **Frank Curreri, c, Massachusetts**
42. Brandon Pullen, lhp, Idaho Falls (Idaho) HS
43. Brandon White, 3b, Surry (N.C.) CC
44. **Adam Howard, rhp, Walters State (Tenn.) CC**
45. Ryan McKibben, rhp, Aliso Niguel HS, Aliso Viejo, Calif.
46. Ryan Castellanos, 3b, CC of Southern Nevada
47. **Eddy Baeza, rhp, Mission (Calif.) JC**
48. Ryan Mooradian, lhp, Essex (Md.) CC
49. Carlos Soto, of, Wabash Valley (Ill.) JC
50. **Kyler Newby, rhp, Mesa (Ariz.) CC**

ATLANTA BRAVES

June—Regular Phase (30)

1. (Pick to Rangers as compensation for Type B free agent John Thomson)
2. **Eric Campbell, 3b, Gibson Southern HS, Owensville, Ind.**
3. **J.C. Holt, 2b, Louisiana State**
4. **James Parr, rhp, La Cueva HS, Albuquerque, N.M.**
5. **Van Pope, 3b, Meridian (Miss.) JC**
6. **Clint Sammons, c, Georgia**
7. **Trae Wiggins, lhp, Brewton-Parker (Ga.)**
8. **Derrick Arnold, ss, Tallahassee (Fla.) CC**
9. **Jeff Katz, rhp, Cheshire (Conn.) HS**
10. **Brady Endl, lhp, Wisconsin-Whitewater**
11. **Wes Letson, lhp, Birmingham-Southern**
12. **Jeff Long, rhp, Gardner-Webb**
13. **Todd Blackford, rhp, Triton HS, Bourbon, Ind.**
14. **Mike Rozema, ss, St. John's**
15. **Jason Paul, rhp, Southern New Hampshire**
16. **Zach Schreiber, rhp, Duke**
17. **Jon Owings, of, Gainesville (Ga.) HS**
18. Brad Emaus, ss, East Coweta HS, Sharpsburg, Ga.

19. **Scott Brazeale, ss, Berkeley HS, Moncks Corner, S.C.**
20. Christian Marrero, of, Monsignor Pace HS, Miami
21. **Tyler Wilson, lhp, Andalusia (Ala.) HS**
22. **Gary Harp, c, Middle Tennessee State**
23. Austin Hyatt, rhp, Marietta (Ga.) HS
24. Josh Flores, of, Lincoln-Way Central HS, New Lenox, Ill.
25. Judson Norton, rhp, Manatee (Fla.) CC
26. **Adam Parliament, of, El Paso (Texas) CC**
27. Tyler Flowers, c/1b, Blessed Trinity HS, Marietta, Ga.
28. Joey Leiberman, 1b, Meridian (Miss.) CC
29. **Trevion Griffin, of, Lurleen B. Wallace (Ala.) JC**
30. Kurt Houck, rhp, Boyertown (Pa.) HS
31. **Jamie Richmond, rhp, Cawthraw SS, Mississauga, Ontario**
32. Clay Caulfield, rhp, Lawrence Park Collegiate HS, Toronto
33. Brian Murphy, rhp, Torrey Pines HS, Carmel Valley, Calif.
34. Luis Sanchez, ss, Puerto Rico Baseball Academy, Caguas, P.R.
35. Shawn Lee, c, Gosnell (Ark.) HS
36. **Phillip Britton, c, Olney Central (Ill.)**
37. **Josh Ward, rhp, Seminole HS, Donalsonville, Ga.**
38. Ryan Horton, lhp, Bishop Moore School, Orlando, Fla.
39. Sean Doolittle, lhp, Shawnee HS, Medford, N.J.
40. **Jared Shaffer, ss, Kiski Area HS, Vandergrift, Pa.**
41. Steven Creswell, lhp, Rim of the World HS, Lake Arrowhead, Calif.
42. Eric Farris, ss, Hamilton HS, Chandler, Ariz.
43. Adam Myers, rhp, Herbet Hoover HS, Clendenin, W.Va.
44. Daniel Rios, 1b, JC of the Sequoias (Calif.)
45. **Jesse Warren, lhp, Western Alamance HS, Elon College, N.C.**
46. **Marcus Covington, rhp, Louisburg (N.C.) JC**
47. Kevin Camacho, rhp, Santa Fe Springs (Calif.) HS
48. Eric Evans, lhp, UMS Wright HS, Mobile, Ala.
49. William Tanner, rhp, White Knoll HS, Lexington, S.C.
50. Eric Gonzalez, rhp, Cochise County (Ariz.) CC

BALTIMORE ORIOLES

June—Regular Phase (8)

1. Wade Townsend, rhp, Rice
2. (Pick to Athletics as compensation for Type A free agent Miguel Tejada)
3. **Jeff Fiorentino, c/1b, Florida Atlantic**
4. **Brad Bergesen, rhp, Foothill HS, Pleasanton, Calif.**
5. **C.J. Smith, of, Florida**
6. **Bryce Chamberlin, rhp, Washington State**
7. Seth Johnston, 2b, Texas
8. **David Haehnel, lhp, Illinois-Chicago**
9. **Joey Howell, of, Santaluces HS, West Palm Beach, Fla.**
10. **Drew Moffitt, of, Wichita State**
11. **Kevin Hart, rhp/1b, Maryland**
12. **Dan Puente, c, Bradley**
13. **Denver Kitch, ss, Oklahoma City**
14. **Kyle Schmidt, rhp, South Florida**
15. Will Venable, of, Princeton
16. **Andy Schindling, rhp, St. John's Collegiate HS, Bowie, Md.**
17. **Kyle Boehm, rhp, Oakland**
18. **Trent Baysinger, lhp, Washington**
19. Matt McGuirk, of, Arlington Heights HS, Fort Worth
20. **Jonathan Tucker, 2b, Florida**
21. **Ryan Finan, 1b, Lamar**
22. **Rob Marconi, 3b, Northern Illinois**
23. **Ryan Schwabe, lhp, Louisiana-Monroe**
24. Dale Mollenhauer, ss, Pine Richland HS, Gibsonia, Pa.
25. **Zach Minor, lhp, Northern Illinois**
26. **Kevin Kotch, c, Cecil (Md.) CC**
27. **Cody Wargo, c, Indiana**
28. Alex Graham, rhp, Pacific
29. Marc Young, lhp, Riverside HS, Greer, S.C.
30. Jaime Garcia, lhp, Sharyland (Texas) HS
31. Matthew Garnett, lhp, Bakersfield (Calif.) JC
32. Jeff Jeffords, rhp, Spartanburg Methodist (S.C.) JC
33. Jared Elmore, rhp, Raymond (Miss.) HS
34. Nick Burns, c, Palomar (Calif.) CC
35. Drew Crisp, ss, Riverside HS, Greer, S.C.
36. Derik Drewett, rhp, Arkansas-Fort Smith JC
37. Ian Harrington, lhp, Bellevue (Wash.) CC
38. Adam Crisp, of, Riverside HS, Greer, S.C.
39. Larry Hill, lhp, Smithson Valley HS, Spring Branch, Texas
40. Jason Roach, lhp, Sacramento CC
41. Demetrios Marinos, c, Steinert HS, Hamilton, N.J.
42. Brian Blackburn, c, Kellogg (Mich.) CC
43. Bryan Casey, c, Kofa HS, Yuma, Ariz.
44. Leonardo Calderon, lhp, Puerto Rico Baseball Academy, Loiza, P.R.
45. **Samuel Basta, lhp, Marquette University HS, Milwaukee**
46. Casey Larson, of, Paso Robles (Calif.) HS
47. Bailey Daniels, rhp, Manteo (N.C.) HS
48. Matt Lane, rhp, Iowa Western CC
49. **Alex Turner, of, CC of Baltimore-Catonsville**
50. Michael Banks, rhp, Lake Michigan (Mich.) JC

BOSTON RED SOX

June—Regular Phase (24)

1. (Pick to Athletics as compensation for Type A free agent Keith Foulke)
2. **Dustin Pedroia, ss, Arizona State**
3. **Andrew Dobies, lhp, Virginia**
4. **Tommy Hottovy, lhp, Wichita State**
5. **Ryan Schroyer, rhp, San Diego State**
6. **Cla Meredith, rhp, Virginia Commonwealth**
7. **Pat Perry, c, Northern Colorado**
8. **Kyle Bono, rhp, Central Florida**
9. **Matt Vanderbosch, of, Oral Roberts**
10. Steve Pearce, 1b, South Carolina
11. **Ryan Phillips, lhp, Barton County (Kan.) CC**
12. **Mike Rozier, lhp, Henry County HS, Stockbridge, Ga.**
13. **Matt Ciaramella, of, Utah**
14. **R.J. Swindle, lhp, Charleston Southern**
15. **Dustin Kelly, ss, Cuesta (Calif.) JC**
16. Matt Clarkson, c, Arkansas-Fort Smith JC
17. Jeremy Haynes, of, Madison County HS, Madison, Fla.
18. **Randy Beam, lhp, Florida Atlantic**
19. **Logan Sorensen, 1b, Wichita State**
20. Brian Van Kirk, c, Westminster Academy, Fort Lauderdale
21. **Chuck Jeroloman, ss, Auburn**
22. **John Burgess, 1b, Georgia State**
23. **Matt Goodson, rhp, Texas**
24. Matt Spencer, 1b, Morristown West HS, Morristown, Tenn.
25. **Michael Jones, of, Arizona Western JC**
26. Jake Renshaw, rhp, Ventura (Calif.) CC
27. Justin Phillabaum, rhp, Royal Palm Beach HS, West Palm Beach, Fla.
28. **Michael James, rhp, Connecticut**
29. **David Seccombe, rhp, Nevada-Las Vegas**
30. **Drew Ehrlich, rhp, Stanford**
31. Brendan Winn, of, South Carolina
32. Brad Hertzler, lhp, East Providence (R.I.) HS
33. **John Wells, lhp, Timber Creek HS, Orlando**
34. **Andrew Pinckney, 3b, Emory (Ga.)**
35. Bo Lanier, rhp, Georgia
36. **Cooper Eddy, rhp, New Mexico**
37. Glenn Swanson, lhp, UC Irvine
38. Colby Summer, rhp, Hawaii
39. Zak Farkes, ss, Harvard
40. Nick Francona, lhp, Lawrenceville HS, Yardley, Pa.
41. Steven Edlefsen, ss, Barton County (Kan.) CC
42. Kyle Peter, of, Archbishop O'Hara HS, Kansas City, Mo.
43. Tyler Latham, rhp, Hewitt-Trussville HS, Trussville, Ala.
44. Beau Mills, 3b, Golden West HS, Visalia, Calif.
45. Adam Campbell, 3b, British Columbia
46. **Tom Caple, of, San Diego**
47. **Austin Easley, 1b, Florida**
48. Felipe Garcia, c/1b, Cal State Fullerton
49. Blake Tillett, lhp, Brandon (Fla.) HS
50. Raudel Alfonso, rhp, Hialeah (Fla.) HS

CHICAGO CUBS

June—Regular Phase (25)

1. (Pick to Twins as compensation for Type A free agent LaTroy

Hawkins)
2. **Grant Johnson, rhp, Notre Dame**
3. **Mark Reed, c, Bonita HS, La Verne, Calif.**
4. **Chris Shaver, lhp, William & Mary**
5. Adrian Ortiz, of, Puerto Rico Baseball Academy, Caguas, P.R.
6. **Tim Layden, lhp, Duke**
7. **Mitch Atkins, rhp, Northeast Guilford HS, Browns Summit, N.C.**
8. **Eric Patterson, 2b, Georgia Tech**
9. **Ryan Norwood, 1b, East Carolina**
10. **Sam Fuld, of, Stanford**
11. **Jon Hunton, rhp, Lamar**
12. **Sean Gallagher, rhp, St. Thomas Aquinas HS, Fort Lauderdale, Fla.**
13. Ryan Moorer, rhp, Veterans Memorial HS, Peabody, Mass.
14. Eli Iorg, of, Tennessee
15. **Alfred Joseph, of, Foy H. Moody HS, Corpus Christi , Texas**
16. **J.R. Mathes, lhp, Western Michigan**
17. **Jerry Blevins, lhp, Dayton**
18. **Jake Marsello, rhp, Boston College**
19. Micah Owings, rhp, Georgia Tech
20. Trey Taylor, lhp, Baylor
21. **Will Fenton, rhp, Washington**
22. Walter Diaz, ss, Braddock HS, Miami
23. **Chris Gaskin, 1b, Manhattan**
24. **Jeff Culpepper, of, Gonzaga**
25. Casey Erickson, rhp, Glenwood HS, Chatham, Ill.
26. Paul Cinder, rhp, Lake Mary HS, Longwood, Fla.
27. **Jason Kosow, rhp, Babson (N.H.)**
28. **Jon Douillard, c, Vanderbilt**
29. **Mike Svetlic, 2b, UCLA**
30. **Russ Canzler, 3b, Hazleton Area HS, Conyngham, Pa.**
31. Jesse Estrada, rhp, Grayson County (Texas) JC
32. Cody Gilbert, 3b, Lincoln HS, Vincennes, Ind.
33. **Randy Brown, of, Jonesboro (Ga.) HS**
34. Dustin Bamberg, c, Winter Haven (Fla.) HS
35. Drew O'Connell, rhp, Barrington HS, South Barrington, Ill.
36. Colby Wark, rhp, Redmond (Ore.) HS
37. Michael Hyle, rhp, Georgia
38. Kurt Eichorn, of, Kent State
39. Trent Luyster, lhp, Ohio State
40. Marcus Crockett, of, St. Bernard HS, Inglewood, Calif.
41. Kenn Kasparek, rhp, Weimar (Texas) HS
42. **Ryan Morgan, 3b, Boston College**
43. Adam Daniels, lhp, Eastern Oklahoma State JC
44. **Zane Green, of, Clemson**
45. Christopher Dunkin, c, La Porte (Texas) HS
46. Greg Fudacz, lhp, Cle Elum-Roslyn HS, Cle Elum, Wash.
47. Andrew Liebel, rhp, Damien HS, Pomona, Calif.
48. **Olin Wick, c, Puget Sound (Wash.)**
49. Brandon Harmon, rhp, Columbia Basin (Wash.) JC
50. **Gerald Miller, of, Prairie View A&M**

CHICAGO WHITE SOX

June—Regular Phase (18)

1. **Josh Fields, 3b, Oklahoma State**
1. **Tyler Lumsden, lhp, Clemson** (Supplemental pick—34th—for loss of Type A free agent Bartolo Colon)
1. **Gio Gonzalez, lhp, Monsignor Pace HS, Miami** (Supplemental pick—38th—for loss of Type A free agent Tom Gordon)
2. **Wes Whisler, lhp, UCLA** (Pick from Angels as compensation for Colon)
2. **Donny Lucy, c, Stanford**
2. **Ray Liotta, lhp, Gulf Coast (Fla.) CC** (Pick from Yankees as compensation for Gordon)
3. **Grant Hansen, rhp, Oklahoma City**
4. **Lucas Harrell, rhp, Ozark (Mo.) HS**
5. **Brandon Allen, of, Montgomery (Texas) HS**
6. **Adam Russell, rhp, Ohio**
7. **Tim Murphey, lhp, Glacock County HS, Gibson, Ga.**
8. **Nick Lemon, rhp, Brigham Young**
9. **Ryan McCarthy, 3b, UCLA**
10. **Adam Ricks, 2b, Miami**
11. **Garry Bakker, rhp, North Carolina**
12. **Daron Roberts, of, Cal State San Bernardino**
13. **Jack Egbert, rhp, Rutgers**
14. **Michael Swain, 3b, Wabash Valley (Ill.) JC**
15. **Carlos Torres, rhp, Kansas State**
16. **Fernando Alvarez, of, Florida International**
17. Jake Wild, rhp, Bakersfield (Calif.) JC
18. Brett Scarpetta, rhp, Hononegah HS, Rockton, Ill.
19. **Caleb Cooper, 3b, Cal State Hayward**
20. Michael Dubee, rhp, Riverview HS, Sarasota, Fla.
21. Brian Flores, lhp, Carlsbad (N.M.) HS
22. Matt Mansilla, ss, American Heritage HS, Pembroke, Fla.
23. **Derek McNeil, ss, St. Leo (Fla.)**
24. **Josh Hansen, c, San Diego**
25. Justin Sincock, rhp, Millikan HS, Long Beach, Calif.
26. Danny Jordan, 3b, Gulliver Prep, Miami
27. **Logan Williamson, lhp, Pensacola (Fla.) JC**
28. Greg Young, of, Delaware Tech JC
29. Frank Viola, rhp, Florida CC-Jacksonville
30. **Matt Zaleski, rhp, Indiana State**
31. **Nick Walters, lhp, Mountain Ridge HS, Desert Hills, Ariz.**
32. Eric Sheridan, rhp, Saddleback (Calif.) JC
33. Brandon Cooney, rhp, Broward (Fla.) CC
34. **Mario Suarez, 3b, Florida International**
35. **Evan Tartaglia, of, Elon**
36. Kenny Williams Jr., of, Plainfield (Ill.) HS
37. Robert Grinestaff, c, Okaloosa-Walton (Fla.) CC
38. Shaun Spearman, ss, St. Pius X HS, Atlanta, Ga.
39. James Leigh, lhp, Bryant (Ark.) HS
40. **Justin Roelle, lhp, Iowa Western CC**
41. Matthew Rozier, rhp, Meridian (Miss.) CC
42. Michael Schower, lhp, Riverview HS, Sarasota, Fla.
43. Ian Murray, rhp, Jefferson (Mo.) JC
44. Steven Muck, rhp, Covington Catholic HS, Park Hills, Ky.
45. Jason Sullivan, rhp, Crowder (Mo.) JC
46. Jason Rodriguez, ss, Alta Loma (Calif.) HS
47. Richard O'Brien, c, Connors State (Okla.) JC
48. **Peter Vuckovich, c, Clarion (Pa.)**
49. **Dennis Guest, 2b, St. Joseph's (Ind.)**
50. Bryan Wagner, rhp, Thunderbird HS, Phoenix

CINCINNATI REDS

June—Regular Phase (7)

1. **Homer Bailey, rhp, La Grange (Texas) HS**
2. **B.J. Szymanski, of, Princeton**
3. **Craig Tatum, c, Mississippi State**
4. **Rafael Gonzalez, rhp, George Washington HS, Bronx, N.Y.**
5. **Paul Janish, ss, Rice**
6. **Lonny Roa, c, Puerto Rico Baseball Academy, San Juan**
7. **Philippe Valiquette, lhp, Eduard Montpetit HS, Montreal**
8. **Greg Goetz, lhp, Bellevue (Wash.) CC**
9. **Trevor Lawhorn, 2b, East Carolina**
10. **Terrell Young, rhp, Grenada (Miss.) HS**
11. Jason Urquidez, rhp, Arizona State
12. **Cody Strait, of, Evansville**
13. **Drew M. Anderson, 2b, Ohio State**
14. **Jared Sanders, rhp, Oregon State**
15. **J.D. Reininger, 3b, Texas**
16. **Travis Kaats, of, Grand Canyon (Ariz.)**
17. Milton Loo, ss, Molokai HS, Hoolehua, Hawaii
18. **Charles O'Neal, lhp, Chipola (Fla.) JC**
19. **Drew Jenson, lhp, San Diego State**
20. **Robert Coello, c, Okaloosa-Walton (Fla.) CC**
21. **Blake Honey, ss, Lafayette County HS**
22. **Matt Levering, 3b, Regis (Colo.)**
23. **Pedro Hawkins, of, Green River (Wash.) CC**
24. **Adam Gillihan, rhp, Crowder (Mo.) JC**
25. Robbie Nickols, lhp, Sabino HS, Tucson
26. **Johnny Dillard, rhp, Southwestern Oklahoma State**
27. **James Langham, of, Georgia College & State**
28. Donnie Ecker, of, Los Altos (Calif.) HS
29. **Terrance Sparks, lhp, Prairie View A&M**
30. **David Griffin, lhp, Fresno State**
31. Jake Arrieta, rhp, Plano East HS, Plano, Texas

32. **Robbie Wachman, rhp, Valdosta State (Ga.)**
33. Dylan Moseley, rhp, Arkansas HS, Texarkana, Ark.
34. **Drew Phillips, ss, Northwestern Oklahoma State**
35. Robert Palencia, rhp, Monsignor Pace HS, Opa Locka, Fla.
36. **T.J. Johnson, lhp, Central Michigan**
37. Andrew Wells, of, Union HS, Tulsa, Okla.
38. Robert Orton, c, Florida Atlantic
39. Mario Colletto, 1b, Simi Valley (Calif.) HS
40. **Brad Morenko, rhp, Oakland**
41. Scott Mueller, rhp, Greenway HS, Phoenix
42. Ben Price, ss, Terra Linda HS, San Rafael, Calif.
43. **Ben Parker, rhp, Huston-Tillotson (Texas)**
44. Jacob Long, c, Johansen HS, Modesto, Calif.
45. **J.D. Roberts, of, Michigan**
46. Justin Glover, 1b, Westside HS, Houston
47. Bradley Jarrell, 1b, Denham Springs (La.) HS
48. **Brad Key, 3b, South Carolina-Aiken**
49. Tyler Cales, rhp, James Madison HS, San Antonio
50. Juan Buck, of, East HS, Anchorage, Alaska

CLEVELAND INDIANS

June—Regular Phase (6)

1. **Jeremy Sowers, lhp, Vanderbilt**
2. **Justin Hoyman, rhp, Florida**
3. **Scott Lewis, lhp, Ohio State**
4. **Chuck Lofgren, lhp, Serra HS, Burlingame, Calif.**
5. **Mike Butia, of, James Madison**
6. **Cody Bunkelman, rhp, Itasca (Minn.) CC**
7. **Mark Jecmen, rhp, Stanford**
8. **Justin Pekarek, lhp, Nebraska**
9. **Chris Niesel, rhp, Notre Dame**
10. Reinaldo Alicano, of, Josefina Barcelo HS, Guaynabo, P.R.
11. Brian Logan, lhp, Varina HS, Richmond, Va.
12. Jordan Chambless, rhp, Calallen HS, Corpus Christi, Texas
13. **Jason Denham, of, Deer Valley HS, Antioch, Calif.**
14. Jeff Sues, rhp, Vanderbilt
15. **Brian Finegan, ss, Hawaii**
16. Josh Williamson, rhp, Columbia Basin (Wash.) CC
17. **Marshall Szabo, 2b, Georgia**
18. Danny Calvert, rhp, Hutchinson (Kan.) CC
19. **Chris Gimenez, of, Nevada**
20. **Derrick Peterson, 3b, Eastern Michigan**
21. **Carlton Smith, rhp, Piscataway (N.J.) HS**
22. Jeff Corsaletti, of, Florida
23. **Michael Storey, lhp, Bellevue West HS, Bellevue, Neb.**
24. **Wyatt Toregas, c, Virginia Tech**
25. David Newmann, lhp, San Jacinto (Texas) JC
26. **Justin Holmes, ss, Georgia**
27. **Adrian Schau, rhp, Villanova**
28. **Doodle Hicks, lhp, Virginia HS, Bristol, Va.**
29. **P.J. Hiser, of, Pittsburgh**
30. **Alfred Ard, of, Southern**
31. Doug Pickens, c, Brother Rice HS, West Bloomfield, Mich.
32. **Kyle Collins, rhp, San Diego**
33. **Paul Lubrano, lhp, Georgia**
34. Ashton Shewey, lhp, Payson (Ariz.) HS
35. **Ryan Knippschild, lhp, Kansas**
36. Jeff Kamrath, rhp, Virginia
37. Blake Gill, 2b, Louisiana State
38. **Jose Amaya, rhp, San Jose State**
39. Preston Clark, c, Rockwall (Texas) HS
40. **Dustin Roddy, rhp, Nicholls State**
41. David Coulon, lhp, Hanford (Calif.) HS
42. **Josh Harris, rhp, Lamar**
43. Trevor Mortensen, of, Santa Ana (Calif.) JC
44. Phil Shirek, rhp, Nebraska
45. **Tony Sipp, lhp, Clemson**
46. Chris Sosa, of, West Hills (Calif.) JC
47. Tyler Beranek, 1b, Waukesha (Wis.) South HS
48. Brian Winings, rhp, Pennsylvania
49. **Jose Chavez, ss, Santa Ana (Calif.) JC**
50. Tim Battaglia, rhp, Minnesota-Duluth

COLORADO ROCKIES

June—Regular Phase (9)

1. **Chris Nelson, ss, Redan HS, Decatur, Ga.**
2. **Seth Smith, of, Mississippi**
3. **Steven Register, rhp, Auburn**
4. **Chris Iannetta, c, North Carolina**
5. **Matt Macri, 3b, Notre Dame**
6. **Joe Koshansky, 1b, Virginia**
7. **Jake Postlewait, lhp, Oregon State**
8. **Jim Miller, rhp, Louisiana-Monroe**
9. **Dustin Hahn, 3b, Sacramento CC**
10. **Jarrett Grube, rhp, Memphis**
11. **Chris Buechner, rhp, Lamar**
12. **David Patton, rhp, Green River (Wash.) CC**
13. **Matt Miller, of, Texas State**
14. **Dexter Fowler, of, Milton HS, Alpharetta, Ga.**
15. **Justin Nelson, of, California**
16. **Patrick Stanley, rhp, Pace (N.Y.)**
17. Dominick Foster, rhp, Buchanan HS, Clovis, Calif.
18. **Jeff Dragicevich, ss, California**
19. **Josh Newman, lhp, Ohio State**
20. Rene Garcia, rhp, Sunnyside HS, Tuscon, Ariz.
21. **Matt Prendergast, rhp, Virginia Commonwealth**
22. **Stephen Edsall, rhp, Rollins (Fla.)**
23. **Jason Metzger, lhp, UNC Greensboro**
24. **Rob Hosgood, of, Central Connecticut State**
25. Aaron Lovett, rhp, Brownstown (Ill.) HS
26. **Kyle Wilson, c, Fresno State**
27. Andrew Koubek, lhp, Eau Gallie HS, Melbourne, Fla.
28. **Steven Thomas, rhp, Texas Tech**
29. Kyle Foster, lhp, Castle Rock (Wash.) HS
30. Michael Criswell, lhp, Lincoln HS, Tallahassee, Fla.
31. **Xavier Cedeno, lhp, Asuncioan Rodriguez HS, Desal, P.R.**
32. Jackie Davidson, rhp, Richland (Texas) CC
33. Justin Jameson, of, Southern Union (Ala.) JC
34. Richard Crowell, of, East Los Angeles JC
35. Josiah Cowden, rhp, Cypress Community Christian HS, Kingwood, Texas
36. **Jeremey White, lhp, Cal Poly Ponoma**
37. Todd Frazier, of, Toms River (N.J.) South HS
38. Rei Gonzalez, rhp, St. Petersburg (Fla.) JC
39. Jonathan Santos, ss, Puerto Rico Baseball Academy, Caguas, P.R.
40. Gary McKissick, lhp, Itawamba (Miss.) JC
41. Chris Henry, lhp, San Joaquin Delta (Calif.) JC
42. Colt Sedbrook, 2b, Broomfield (Colo.) HS
43. Tony Snow, rhp, Edmonds (Wash.) CC
44. Justin Keadle, rhp, Wake Forest
45. Colby Lehman, lhp, Bishop (Calif.) HS
46. Kody Keroher, rhp, Solano (Calif.) JC
47. Josh Banda, of, Cypress (Calif.) JC
48. J.T. LaFountain, c, Louisville
49. Brian Brohm, of, Trinity HS, Louisville
50. Andy Goff, 2b, Mount Lebanon HS, Pittsburgh

DETROIT TIGERS

June—Regular Phase (2)

1. **Justin Verlander, rhp, Old Dominion**
2. **Eric Beattie, rhp, Tampa**
3. **Jeff Frazier, of, Rutgers**
4. **Collin Mahoney, rhp, Clemson**
5. **Andrew Kown, rhp, Georgia Tech**
6. **Brent Dlugach, ss, Memphis**
7. Chris Carpenter, rhp, Bryan (Ohio) HS
8. **Luke French, lhp, Heritage HS, Littleton, Colo.**
9. **Brandon Timm, of, Broken Arrow (Okla.) HS**
10. **Cory Middleton, ss, Escambia HS, Pensacola, Fla.**
11. **Josh Kauten, rhp, Illinois State**
12. **Cole Miller, c, JC of the Siskiyous (Calif.)**
13. **Brooks Colvin, ss, Southwest Missouri State**
14. **James Skelton, c, West Covina (Calif.) HS**
15. **Matt O'Brien, rhp, Florida Atlantic**
16. **Steve Young, 2b, Princeton**
17. **Dan Konecny, rhp, Northwestern**

18. Chris Martin, rhp, Arlington (Texas) HS
19. **Tyler Jacobson, rhp, Central Arizona JC**
20. **Ed Clelland, lhp, Gonzaga**
21. **Matthew Righter, rhp, Johns Hopkins (Md.)**
22. **Thomas Royals, rhp, Pearl River (Miss.) CC**
23. **Vince Berry, of, Triton (Ill.) JC**
24. **Jordan Foster, of, Lamar**
25. **Robbie Tulk, rhp, UC Davis**
26. Thad McBurrows, lhp, Lake Wales (Fla.) HS
27. **Dominic Carmosino, lhp, Oakland**
28. **Brian Hensen, lhp, Elon**
29. **Octavio Amezquita, ss, Pacific**
30. **Josh Lee, 1b, McMurray (Texas)**
31. **Leonardo Grullon, of, South Florida**
32. **Nate Bumstead, rhp, Louisiana State**
33. **Kevin Brower, rhp, North Carolina**
34. **Dallas Trahern, rhp, Owasso (Okla.) HS**
35. Clay Britton, of, Weatherford (Texas) JC
36. Travis DeBondt, of, Bakersfield (Calif.) CC
37. Ramon Navarro, ss, Triton (Ill.) JC
38. **Jamaal Peoples, of, Philadelphia (Miss.) HS**
39. Adrian Bowens, ss, Lumberton (Miss.) HS
40. Kevin McAtee, 1b, Regis Jesuit HS, Littleton, Colo.
41. Bryan Sheffield, of, Williston (Fla.) HS
42. Trenton Lare, lhp, Coffeyville (Kan.) CC
43. Chris Schwinden, rhp, Golden West HS, Visalia, Calif.
44. Tyler Fockler, rhp, Scotts Valley (Calif.) HS
45. **Lionel Roberts, 1b, John McDonogh HS, New Orleans**
46. Alec Sheppard, rhp, Colorado Springs (Colo.) Christian School
47. Rene Recio, rhp, Oral Roberts
48. Bernard Williams, of, East Marion HS, Columbia, Miss.
49. Dominic De La Osa, ss, Archbishop Carroll HS, Coral Gables, Fla.
50. Maxwell Leon, 2b, South Mountain (Ariz.) JC

FLORIDA MARLINS

June—Regular Phase (27)

1. **Taylor Tankersley, lhp, Alabama**
2. **Jason Vargas, lhp, Long Beach State**
3. **Greg Burns, of, Walnut HS, West Covina, Calif.**
4. **Jamar Walton, of, Greensville County HS, Emporia, Va.**
5. **Brad Davis, c, Long Beach State**
6. **Brad McCann, 3b, Clemson**
7. **Jared Gaston, ss, Walters State (Tenn.) CC**
8. **Craig Molldrem, rhp, Minnesota**
9. **Joe Pietro, of, New Orleans**
10. **Brett Carroll, 3b, Middle Tennessee State**
11. **Daniel Barone, rhp, Sonoma State (Calif.)**
12. **Jeff Gogal, lhp, Montclair State (N.J.)**
13. **Steve Gendron, ss/3b, Mississippi State**
14. **Patrick Hogan, rhp, Clemson**
15. **Brandon Verley, of, Columbia HS, White Salmon, Wash.**
16. **Brian Cleveland, ss, Tennessee**
17. Barry Gunther, c, Mississippi
18. **Nathan Messner, 3b, Muncy (Pa.) HS**
19. John Wilson, c, Hoover (Ala.) HS
20. **Rhett James, rhp, Florida State**
21. Marcus Davis, of, East Central (Miss.) JC
22. **Chris Mobley, rhp, Middle Tennessee State**
23. **Ted Ledbetter, of, Oklahoma City**
24. **Jeff Lacher, rhp, Mississippi State**
25. Agustin Montanez, ss, Ramon Vila Mayo HS, Rio Piedras, P.R.
26. Kevin Turmail, rhp, St. Louis CC-Forest Park
27. **Brian Hoff, rhp, UC Riverside**
28. Charlie Blackmon, lhp, North Gwinnett HS, Suwanee, Ga.
29. **Aaron Easton, rhp, Lowell (Mass.)**
30. Joseph Munn, lhp, Foothill HS, Pleasonton, Calif.
31. **Parrish Castor, lhp, St. Anselm (N.H.)**
32. Jared Petrovich, lhp, Shamokin Area HS, Coal Township, Pa.
33. **Clay Westmoreland, rhp, Utah**
34. **Jarrett Santos, rhp, UNC Greensboro**
35. Drew Shetrone, rhp, Seminole (Fla.) CC
36. Sebastien Vendette, rhp, Ahuntsic College HS, Laval, Quebec
37. **Juan Figueroa, 1b, Bethune-Cookman**
38. Zach Barrett, of, Reitz Memorial HS, Evansville, Ind.
39. **Beau McMillan, 2b, Lynn (Fla.)**
40. Gerald Watson, 2b, Central Catholic HS, Morgan City, La.
41. Jacob Taylor, 3b, Canyon Springs HS, Moreno Valley, Calif.
42. Steve Santos, rhp, Diablo Valley (Calif.) CC
43. Reyes Dorado, rhp, A.B. Miller HS, Fontana, Calif.
44. Charles Jestice, rhp, Memorial HS, Tulsa, Okla.
45. Matt Bates, rhp, Illinois Valley CC
46. Jared Johnson, rhp, Central Arizona JC
47. Michael Mulholland, lhp, Lincoln Trail (Ill.) JC
48. Brady Decker, rhp, Red Hill HS, Bridgeport, Ill.
49. Chris Kirkland, c, South Doyle HS, Knoxville, Tenn.
50. Saunders Ramsey, rhp, Mississippi State

HOUSTON ASTROS

June—Regular Phase (23)

1. (Pick to Astros as compensation for Type A free agent Andy Pettitte)
2. **Hunter Pence, of, Texas-Arlington**
3. **Jordan Parraz, of, CC of Southern Nevada**
4. **Lou Santangelo, c, Clemson**
5. **Mitch Einertson, 2b, Rancho Buena Vista HS, Oceanside, Calif.**
6. **Ben Zobrist, ss, Dallas Baptist**
7. **Andy Alvarado, rhp, Chabot (Calif.) JC**
8. **Evan Englebrook, rhp, Shippensburg (Pa.)**
9. **Troy Patton, lhp, Tomball HS, Magnolia, Texas**
10. **Eric Cavers, c, Franklin Pierce (N.H.)**
11. **Jonny Ash, 2b, Stanford**
12. **Bryan Triplett, ss, South Carolina**
13. **Chad Reineke, rhp, Miami (Ohio)**
14. **Ole Sheldon, 1b, Oklahoma**
15. **Drew Sutton, ss, Baylor**
16. **Garrett Murdy, rhp, Texas A&M-Kingsville**
17. **Beau Torbert, of, Faulkner (Ala.) JC**
18. **Chris Clark, c, Eastern Kentucky**
19. Jared Clark, rhp, Valencia (Calif.) HS
20. **J.R. Towles, c, North Central Texas JC**
21. **Ryan Reed, of, Louisiana State-Eunice JC**
22. **Matt Brown, rhp, California**
23. **Jeff Wigdahl, lhp, St. Mary's (Texas)**
24. **Brandon Averill, 3b, UCLA**
25. Andrew Darnell, of, Castro Valley (Calif.) HS
26. **Jared Brite, rhp, Kansas State**
27. **Casey Brown, rhp, Oklahoma**
28. **Chris Sotro, rhp, Cal Poly Ponoma**
29. **Brad James, rhp, North Central (Texas) JC**
30. **Brandon Barganier, of, Temple (Texas) JC**
31. **Christopher Uhle, ss, Eastern Illinois**
32. **Neil Sellers, 3b, Eastern Kentucky**
33. **James Cooper, of, Grambling State**
34. Nick Cobler, lhp, Strake Jesuit College Prep, Houston
35. Kyle Woodruff, rhp, Leland HS, San Jose, Calif.
36. **Anthony DeWitt, rhp, Southern Mississippi**
37. **Brad Chedister, rhp, Louisiana Tech**
38. Brandon Todd, rhp, Central Florida CC
39. Zachary Williams, rhp, Lindsay (Okla.) HS
40. Dane Ponciano, c, Mount Miguel HS, Grossmont, Calif.
41. Casey McCleskey, of, Burkburnett (Texas) HS
42. Josh Smith, rhp, Riverside (Calif.) CC
43. Tommy Rafferty, of, Temple (Texas) JC
44. Vladimir Frias, ss, Chipola (Fla.) JC
45. Chris Siewert, ss, CC of Southern Nevada
46. **Anthony Adler, rhp, Texas-Dallas**
47. **Corey Bass, rhp, Pearl River (Miss.) CC**
48. Eric Epperson, of, Arlington Heights HS, Fort Worth, Texas
49. Matthew Gardner, c, Andrews (Texas) HS
50. Victor Ferrante, rhp, Solano (Calif.) JC

KANSAS CITY ROYALS

June—Regular Phase (14)

1. **Billy Butler, 3b, Wolfson HS, Jacksonville**
1. **Matt Campbell, lhp, South Carolina** (Pick from Giants as

compensation for Type B free agent Michael Tucker)
1. **J.P. Howell, lhp, Texas** (Supplemental pick—31st—for loss of Type A free agent Raul Ibanez)
2. **Billy Buckner, rhp, South Carolina**
2. **Erik Cordier, rhp, Southern Door HS, Sturgeon Bay, Wis.** (Pick from Mariners as compensation for Ibanez)
3. **Josh Johnson, ss, Middleton HS, Tampa**
4. **Nate Moore, rhp, Troy State**
5. **Henry Barrera, rhp, Rosemead (Calif.) HS**
6. **Chad Blackwell, rhp, South Carolina**
7. **Patrick Green, rhp, Louisiana-Lafayette**
8. **Ed Lucas, ss, Dartmouth**
9. **Chris McConnell, ss, Delsea HS, Franklinville, N.J.**
10. **Bobby Beeson, lhp, Southern Arkansas**
11. **Josh Haney, 2b, Texas Tech**
12. **Brad Hayes, 3b, Arkansas State**
13. **Travis Trammell, rhp, Arkansas-Little Rock**
14. Kyle Howe, rhp, North Kitsap HS, Poulsbo, Wash.
15. **Gilbert De La Vara, lhp, Pima (Ariz.) CC**
16. **Patrick Hicklen, rhp, Tennessee**
17. Adam Trent, rhp, Ooltewah, Tenn.
18. **Andrew Coffey, lhp, Mingus Union HS, Cottonwood, Ariz.**
19. Kade Keowen, 1b, Central HS, Baton Rouge, La.
20. **Adam Rowe, lhp, Mount Vernon Nazarene (Ohio)**
21. Andrew Underwood, rhp, Fresno CC
22. **Ethien Santana, of, Laredo (Texas) CC**
23. **O.D. Gonzalez, of, Broward (Fla.) CC**
24. Myles Ioane, lhp, Waiakea HS, Hilo, Hawaii
25. Garrick Evans, of, Clemson
26. **Nick Cerulo, of, Rutgers**
27. **Zane Carlson, rhp, Baylor**
28. Marty Beno, rhp, Horn Lake HS, Lake Cormorant, Miss.
29. Riley Hollingsworth, rhp, Minden (La.) HS
30. Kris Krise, rhp, JC of the Canyons (Calif.)
31. Kevin Clark, of, Armwood HS, Seffner, Fla.
32. Tyler Hogan, of, Servite HS, Anaheim
33. Jimmy Wallace, rhp, Pratt (Kan.) CC
34. **Kyle Crist, rhp, California**
35. Vincent Biancamano, ss, Cactus HS, Glendale, Ariz.
36. Eric Krebs, rhp, Alvin (Texas) CC
37. Kyle Hartz, of, De Anza (Calif.) JC
38. David Herndon, rhp, A Crawford Mosely HS, Lynn Haven, Fla.
39. Will Jostock, rhp, Lapeer West HS, Lapeer, Mich.
40. Johnnie Santangelo, rhp, Bossier Parish (La.) CC
41. Kendall Thurman, rhp, Angelina (Texas) JC
42. Anthony Marbry, rhp, Jackson State (Tenn.) CC
43. Tyler Brown, rhp, Lane (Ore.) CC
44. Ty Sarchet, rhp, Kalani HS, Honolulu
45. Jacob Myking, c, Kalaheo HS, Kailua, Hawaii
46. Randy Rundgren, ss, Mid-Pacific Institute, Honolulu, Hawaii
47. Mark Serrano, rhp, Downey (Calif.) HS
48. Ernie Medina, rhp, San Jacinto (Calif.) HS
49. Tyler Jennings, of, Daphne (Ala.) HS
50. **Jefferson Infante, c, Ramapo (N.J.)**

LOS ANGELES DODGERS

June—Regular Phase (17)

1. **Scott Elbert, lhp, Seneca (Mo.) HS**
1. **Blake DeWitt, ss, Sikeston (Mo.) HS** (Pick from Yankees as compensation for Type A free agent Paul Quantrill)
1. **Justin Orenduff, rhp, Virginia Commonwealth** (Supplemental pick—33rd—for loss of Quantrill)
2. **Blake Johnson, rhp, Parkview Baptist HS, Baton Rouge**
3. **Cory Dunlap, 1b, Contra Costa (Calif.) JC**
4. **Javy Guerra, rhp, Denton Ryan HS, Denton, Texas**
5. **Anthony Raglani, of, George Washington**
6. **Daniel Batz, 1b, Rhode Island**
7. **Barry Richmond, of, Spartanburg (S.C.) Methodist JC**
8. **Carlos Medero-Stullz, c, Barbara Goleman HS, Hialeah, Fla.**
9. **David Nicholson, 3b, California**
10. **Cory Wade, rhp, Kentucky Wesleyan**
11. **Chris Westervelt, c, Stetson**
12. **Sam Steidl, of, Minnesota**
13. Jeff Larish, of, Arizona State
14. **Brian Akin, rhp, Davidson**
15. Joe Savery, lhp, Lamar HS, Bellaire, Texas
16. Chase Dardar, rhp, Delgado (La.) CC
17. Danny Forrer, lhp, Chipola (Fla.) JC
18. **Matt Paul, 2b, Southern**
19. David Price, lhp, Blackman HS, Murfreesboro, Tenn.
20. **Mark Alexander, rhp, Missouri**
21. **Justin Simmons, lhp, Texas**
22. **Kyle Wilson, rhp, UCLA**
23. **Kenny Plaisance, rhp, Louisiana State-Eunice JC**
24. Kody Kaiser, ss, Santa Fe HS, Edmond, Okla.
25. **Justin Ruggiano, of, Texas A&M**
26. Ben Petralli, c, Weatherford (Texas) HS
27. Levander Graves, c, Dillon (S.C.) HS
28. Brett Lawler, 1b, San Jacinto (Texas) JC
29. Ryan Strieby, 1b, Edmonds (Wash.) CC
30. Paul Gran, ss, Bothell (Wash.) HS
31. Ryan Koch, rhp, Osceola HS, Pinellas Park, Fla.
32. Mike Stutes, rhp, Lake Oswego (Ore.) HS
33. **James Gilbert, rhp, Chabot (Calif.) JC**
34. Chris LeMay, lhp, Kwantlen (B.C.)
35. Lynn Henry, of, Buras (La.) HS
36. Mike Burgher, of, Shorecrest HS, Seattle
37. **Jeremy Brown, of, Pratt (Kan.) CC**
38. **Justin Crist, 2b, Chandler-Gilbert (Ariz.) CC**
39. Michael Branham, rhp, Jesuit HS, Tampa
40. **Brandon Carter, ss, Old Dominion**
41. Troy Grundy, rhp, Carbon HS, North Price, Utah
42. Chris Johnson, rhp, Cabell-Midland HS, Huntington, W.Va.
43. Davis Bilardello, lhp, Vero Beach (Fla.) HS
44. Kyle Rapp, lhp, Wabash Valley (Ill.) CC
45. Michael Hernandez, of, Connors State (Okla.) CC
46. Andrew Brewer, rhp, Metro Christian Academy, Tulsa, Okla.
47. Bobby Bratton, ss, Columbia (Tenn.) Central HS
48. **Joey Norrito, rhp, Nova Southeastern**
49. Scott Bates, c, Salado HS, Belton, Texas
50. Ross Hoffman, 1b, Bakersfield (Calif.) CC

MILWAUKEE BREWERS

June—Regular Phase (5)

1. **Mark Rogers, rhp, Mount Ararat HS, Orr's Island, Maine**
2. **Yovani Gallardo, rhp, Trimble Tech, Fort Worth**
3. **Josh Wahpepah, rhp, Cowley County (Kan.) CC**
4. **Josh Baker, rhp, Rice**
5. **Angel Salome, c, George Washington HS, Bronx, N.Y.**
6. **Stephen Chapman, of, Marianna (Fla.) HS**
7. **Craig Langille, rhp, Charles Allen HS, Bedford, Nova Scotia**
8. **Brandon Parillo, lhp, Marina HS, Huntington Beach, Calif.**
9. **Derek DeCarlo, rhp, Florida International**
10. **Steve Sollmann, 2b, Notre Dame**
11. **Lenny Leclercq, ss, West Vigo HS, Terra Haute, Ind.**
12. Andrew Albers, lhp, John Paul II HS, North Battleford, Sask
13. **Angel Ayala, 1b, Lino Padron Rivera HS, San Juan, P.R.**
14. **Grant Richardson, 1b, Washington State**
15. **David Johnson, rhp, UCLA**
16. **Alex Periard, rhp, Poly Deux-Montagnes HS, St. Eustache, PQ**
17. **Lorenzo Cain, of, Madison County HS, Madison, Fla.**
18. **Darren Ford, of, Vineland (N.J.) HS**
19. **Josh Brady, of, Texas Tech**
20. Jose Garcia, rhp, Indian Hills (Iowa) CC
21. Drew Bowman, lhp, Dakota Ridge HS, Morrison, Colo.
22. **Matt Kretzschmar, rhp, San Pedro (Calif.) HS**
23. **Tony Festa, 3b, UC Riverside**
24. Jose Delgado, rhp, Puerto Rico Baseball Academy, Caguas, P.R.
25. Sean Morgan, rhp, Fort Bend Clements HS, Sugar Land, Texas
26. Dustin Timm, rhp, Nebraska
27. Ty Pryor, rhp, Olympia HS, Orlando
28. Ronnie Prettyman, 3b, Cal State Fullerton
29. Ryan Paterson, rhp, Lake Cowichan HS, Duncan, B.C
30. Brian Johnson, rhp, East Islip (N.Y.) HS
31. Kanekoa Texeira, rhp, Kamehameha HS, Kula, Hawaii

32. **Joel Needham, rhp, UC Davis**
33. **Luis Bernal, rhp, Pima (Ariz.) CC**
34. Kris Dabrowiecki, rhp, Ursula Franklin Academy, Toronto
35. Chris Copot, c, John Diefenbaker HS, Prince Albert, Sask
36. Stephen Barnes, rhp, First Coast HS, Jacksonville
37. Sean McCraw, c, Alvin (Texas) HS
38. Donald Jordat, rhp, Summit Christian HS, Fort Myers, Fla.
39. Jeremy Bloor, lhp, Grand Rapids (Mich.) CC
40. Chris Rickey, lhp, Reno (Nev.) HS
41. James Coker, lhp, Spartanburg Methodist (S.C.) JC
42. **Josh Louis, rhp, Temple (Texas) JC**
43. Brandon Jasper, 1b, Newport Harbor HS, Newport Beach, Calif.
44. Jon Mungle, of, Mississippi State
45. Deik Scram, of, Cowley County (Kan.) CC
46. Louis Metzner, rhp, Langley, B.C
47. **Derek Miller, lhp, Vermont**
48. Brandon Glover, of, McKinney (Texas) HS
49. Shane Buriff, lhp, Sickles HS, Tampa
50. Chad Miller, 1b, Chandler-Gilbert (Ariz.) CC

MINNESOTA TWINS

June—Regular Phase (20)

1. **Trevor Plouffe, ss, Crespi HS, Northridge, Calif.**
1. **Glen Perkins, lhp, Minnesota** (Pick from Mariners as compensation for Type A free agent Eddie Guardado)
1. **Kyle Waldrop, rhp, Farragut HS, Knoxville** (Pick from Cubs as compensation for Type A free agent LaTroy Hawkins)
1. **Matt Fox, rhp, Central Florida** (Supplemental pick—35th—for loss of Guardado)
1. **Jay Rainville, rhp, Bishop Hendricken HS, Pawtucket, R.I.** (Supplemental pick—39th—for loss of Hawkins)
2. **Anthony Swarzak, rhp, Nova HS, Ft. Lauderdale**
3. **Eduardo Morlan, rhp, Coral Park HS, Miami**
4. **Mark Robinson, of, Mountain View HS, El Monte, Calif.**
5. **Jeff Schoenbachler, lhp, Reno (Nev.) HS**
6. **Patrick Bryant, rhp, Pensacola Catholic HS, Gulf Breeze, Fla.**
7. **John Williams, lhp, Middle Tennessee State**
8. **Jay Sawatski, lhp, Arkansas**
9. **J.P. Martinez, rhp, New Orleans**
10. **Jeremy Pickrel, of, Illinois State**
11. **Kyle Aselton, lhp, Oregon State**
12. Shane Boyd, rhp, Kentucky
13. **Walter Patton, rhp, Lincoln Land (Ill.) CC**
14. **Javi Sanchez, c, Notre Dame**
15. **Juan Portes, ss, Malden, Mass.**
16. **Matt Tolbert, ss, Mississippi**
17. Eammon Portice, rhp, Fort Lauderdale HS
18. Josh Rose, rhp, Mariner HS, Cape Coral, Fla.
19. Tate Casey, rhp, Longview (Texas) HS
20. **Tim Lahey, c, Princeton**
21. **Joseph Abellera, 3b, Hopkins HS, Minnetonka, Minn.**
22. Vincent Scarduzio, lhp, Jupiter Community HS, Jupiter, Fla.
23. Tim Arnold, lhp, Fallbrook (Calif.) HS
24. Garrett White, lhp, San Jacinto (Texas) JC
25. Joe Welsh, lhp, Grand Rapids (Mich.) CC
26. **Deacon Burns, of, Northern State (S.D.)**
27. **Landon Burt, of, San Diego State**
28. **Aaron Craig, rhp, Century HS, Rochester, Minn.**
29. **Ricky Prady, of, Sebastian River HS, Sebastian, Fla.**
30. **Daniel Berg, 3b, Texarkana (Texas) JC**
31. Jason Laird, rhp, Henry County HS, Hampton, Ga.
32. Nolan Mulligan, rhp, Broward (Fla.) JC
33. Sean Kalmen, rhp, Katella HS, Anaheim
34. Rene Tosoni, of, Terry Fox SS, Port Coquitlam, B.C.
35. **Jeff Mousser, rhp, Arizona State**
36. John Thies, lhp, St. Louis CC-Meramec
37. Greg D'Oleo, c, Puerto Rico Baseball Academy, Toa Baja, P.R.
38. **Josh Land, of, Okaloosa-Walton (Fla.) CC**
39. **Danny Santiesteban, of, Palm Beach (Fla.) CC**
40. Justin Otto, rhp, Chandler (Okla.) HS
41. Eric Sweeney, rhp, Mount Carmel HS, San Diego
42. Greg Schilling, lhp, Broward (Fla.) CC
43. **Robbie Hebert, rhp, Nicholls State**
44. Tony Joiner, of, Haines City (Fla.) HS
45. Lance Lofton, 3b, Connally HS, Waco, Texas
46. Matt Rizzotti, 1b, Archbishop Molloy HS, Jamiaca, N.Y.
47. Chris Petrie, of, Lake City (Fla.) CC
48. Ryne Nelson, rhp, Dickinson (Texas) HS
49. Nicholas Bleau, lhp, Gulf Coast (Fla.) CC
50. Taylor Cameron, rhp, Cypress (Calif.) JC

MONTREAL EXPOS

June—Regular Phase (13)

1. **Bill Bray, lhp, William & Mary**
2. **Erick San Pedro, c, Miami**
3. **Ian Desmond, ss, Sarasota (Fla.) HS**
4. **Collin Balester, rhp, Huntington Beach (Calif.) HS**
5. **Greg Bunn, rhp, East Carolina**
6. **Devin Ivany, c, South Florida**
7. **Marvin Lowrance, of, Golden West (Calif.) JC**
8. **Leonard Davis, 3b, Fresno (Calif.) CC**
9. **Brandon Conway, ss, Frederick (Md.) CC**
10. **Duron Legrande, of, North Carolina A&T**
11. **David Trahan, rhp, Alvin (Texas) JC**
12. **Bobby Mosebach, of, Hillsborough (Fla.) CC**
13. **David Travis, 2b, Southern Wesleyan (S.C.)**
14. **Lyndsey Simmons, c, New York Tech**
15. Mike Wlodarczyk, lhp, Boston College
16. **Thomas Wilson, lhp, Catawba (N.C.)**
17. **John Poppert, c, East Carolina**
18. **Matt Perks, rhp, Mercer County (N.J.) CC**
19. **Ben Cox, rhp, Lamar**
20. **Gene Yost, lhp, Averett (Va.)**
21. Ibrahim Lopez, of, Puerta Rico Baseball Academy, Carolina, P.R.
22. **Aaron Jackson, rhp, St. Augustine (Fla.) HS**
23. **Ryan Harrison, rhp, South Carroll HS, Woodbine, Md.**
24. Steven Hornostaj, ss, St. David Catholic HS, Waterloo, Ont
25. **Steven Cook, rhp, UNC Asheville**
26. **Gabe Suarez, ss, South Mountain (Ariz.) CC**
27. Ladd Hall, rhp, Arizona State
28. **Chris Lugo, rhp, Hudson Catholic School, Hoboken, N.J.**
29. Steven Hirschfeld, rhp, Grand County HS, Moab, Utah
30. Brendan Murphy, 1b, Garden City (Kan.) CC
31. P.J. Treadaway, rhp, Archbishop Hannan HS, Meraux, La.
32. Matt Averitt, rhp, New Mexico JC
33. Chris Whisenhunt, lhp, Fort Worth Christian HS, North Richland Hills, Texas
34. **Brett Campbell, rhp, Kennesaw State (Ga.)**
35. **Rudy Garza, rhp, Hill (Texas) JC**
36. Todd Nicholas, lhp, Troy State
37. Jamie Gant, rhp, Mississippi State
38. Daniel Cooper, rhp, Costa Mesa (Calif.) HS
39. Brian Peacock, c, Manatee (Fla.) JC
40. **Melvin Perez, 3b, George Washington HS, Bronx, N.Y.**
41. Joe Dunigan, of, St. Ignatius Prep, Chicago
42. Brent Gaphardt, lhp, Dundalk (Md.) CC
43. Andy Gale, rhp, Philips Exeter Academy, Exeter, N.H.
44. Phillip Vale, ss, Bellevue Christian HS, Clyde, Wash.
45. Austin Reilly, ss, Fort Worth (Texas) Country Day HS
46. Robert Molinaro, ss, American Heritage HS, Boca Raton, Fla.
47. Jonathan Del Franco, rhp, Bridgewater (N.J.) Raritan HS
48. Carlos Ceron, rhp, Miami-Dade CC
49. Patrick Kanakevich, rhp, Georgetown Prep, Rockville, Md.
50. Joel Collins, c, Cardinal Carter School, Richmond Hill, Ontario

NEW YORK METS

June—Regular Phase (3)

1. **Philip Humber, rhp, Rice**
2. **Matt Durkin, rhp, San Jose State**
3. **Gaby Hernandez, rhp, Belen Jesuit HS, Miami**
4. **Aaron Hathaway, c, Washington**
5. **Nick Evans, 3b, St. Mary's HS, Phoenix**
6. **Ryan Coultas, ss, UC Davis**
7. **Scott Hyde, rhp, George Fox (Ore.)**
8. Neil Jamison, rhp, Long Beach State
9. **Mike Carp, 1b, Lakewood (Calif.) HS**

10. **Brahiam Maldonado, of, St. Francis HS, Carolina, P.R.**
11. **Josh Wyrick, of, Porterville (Calif.) CC**
12. **Jeff Landing, rhp, Virginia Tech**
13. Martinez Allen, of, Dunnellon (Fla.) HS
14. Brad Meyers, rhp, Servite HS, Yorba Linda, Calif.
15. **Grant Psomas, ss, West Virginia**
16. **Parris Austin, of, Douglas County HS, Douglasville, Ga.**
17. **Joe Williams, lhp, St. Xavier (Ill.)**
18. **Kyle Brown, of, LeMoyne**
19. **Jim Burt, 1b, Miami**
20. **Sean Henry, ss, Diablo Valley (Calif.) CC**
21. Tim Smith, of, Birchmount Park HS, Scarborough, Ont
22. **Caleb Stewart, of, Kentucky**
23. **Michael Devaney, rhp, Concordia (Ore.)**
24. **Bryan Zech, 2b, Florida State**
25. **Jonathan Castillo, rhp, Miami-Dade CC**
26. **Rafael Arroyo, c, Cal State Los Angeles**
27. **Bryant Suggs, of, Hillsborough (Fla.) CC**
28. **Armand Gaerlan, ss, San Francisco**
29. **Mike Swindell, rhp, Oklahoma**
30. **Blake Eager, rhp, Metropolitan State (Colo.)**
31. Erin Jones, rhp, Francis Marion (S.C.)
32. Jason James, of, Kishwaukee (Ill.) JC
33. **Matt Fisher, 2b, UC Irvine**
34. Jeremiah Lokken, of, Eagle View Academy, Jacksonville, Fla.
35. Garret Holleran, rhp, Central Arizona JC
36. **Jake Harrington, rhp, Northeastern (Colo.) JC**
37. Brad Burns, rhp, Lookeba Sickles HS, Gracemont, Okla.
38. Zack Sterner, rhp, Franklin (Pa.) Regional HS
39. Bryan Lee, rhp, Cuesta (Calif.) JC
40. Julio Rodriguez, of, Manuel Mendez Liceaga HS, San Juan, P.R.
41. **Jake Ruckle, rhp, Mohave HS, Bullhead City, Ariz.**
42. Jim Brauer, rhp, Michigan
43. Ian Thurman-Kelly, lhp, Eastern New Mexico
44. Lance Scoggins, lhp, Okaloosa-Walton (Fla.) CC
45. Dan McDonald, rhp, Morris Hills HS, Rockaway, N.J.
46. Jeremy Hefner, rhp, Perkins (Okla.) Tryon HS
47. Ryan Paul, lhp, Los Angeles Pierce JC
48. Morgan Carlile, lhp, Three Oaks HS, Summerside, Prince Edward Island
49. Daniel Buller, lhp, Fresno CC
50. Sean Cunningham, lhp, Bullard HS, Fresno

NEW YORK YANKEES

June—Regular Phase (28)

1. **Phil Hughes, rhp, Foothill HS, Santa Ana, Calif.** (Pick from Astros as compensation for Type A free agent Andy Pettitte)
1. (Pick to Dodgers as compensation for Type A free agent Paul Quantrill)
1. **Jon Poterson, c, Chandler (Ariz.) HS** (Supplemental pick—37th—for loss of Pettitte)
1. **Jeff Marquez, rhp, Sacramento CC** (Supplemental pick—41st—for loss of Type A free agent David Wells)
2. **Brett Smith, rhp, UC Irvine** (Pick from Padres as compensation for Wells)
2. (Pick to White Sox as compensation for Type A free agent Tom Gordon)
3. **Christian Garcia, rhp, Gulliver Prep, Miami**
4. **Jason Jones, rhp, Liberty**
5. **Jesse Hoover, rhp, Indiana Tech**
6. **Nate Phillips, ss, Grace Prep Academy, Arlington, Texas**
7. Alex Garabedian, c, Columbus HS, Miami
8. **Mike Martinez, rhp, Cal State Fullerton**
9. **Grant Plumley, ss, Oral Roberts**
10. **Ben Scheinbaum, lhp, Nevada-Las Vegas**
11. **Cody Ehlers, 1b, Missouri**
12. **Rod Allen, of, Oklahoma State**
13. **P.J. Pilittere, c, Cal State Fullerton**
14. **Ben Jones, 1b, Louisiana-Monroe**
15. **Robert Villanova, of, Iona (N.Y.)**
16. **Ryan Haag, 2b, Fresno State**
17. **Evan Tierce, of, Texas State**
18. **Yosvany Almario-Cabrera, 3b, Miami-Dade CC South**
19. **Jordan DeVoir, ss, Illinois-Chicago**
20. **Jose Tadeo, rhp, Culver-Stockton (Mo.)**
21. **Scott Rich, of, Rider**
22. Patrick Caldwell, lhp, Yavapai (Ariz.) JC
23. Jamarkus James, of, Grand Prairie (Texas) HS
24. Ryan Tabor, lhp, CC of Southern Nevada
25. Gary Campfield, rhp, Navarro (Texas) JC
26. **Sean Kramer, lhp, Iona**
27. Jeremiah Shepherd, rhp, Texarkana (Texas) JC
28. Jake McCarter, rhp, Navarro (Texas) JC
29. Kyle Ginley, rhp, Dunnellon (Fla.) HS
30. Jonathan Lindenberger, rhp, San Jacinto (Texas) JC
31. **Grant Duff, rhp, JC of the Sequoias (Calif.)**
32. Clint Preisendorfer, lhp, La Jolla (Calif.) Country Day HS
33. **Mike Dunn, 1b, CC of Southern Nevada**
34. Jonathan Bertschinger, of, Navarro (Texas) JC
35. Michael Hale, lhp, Ball State
36. Matt Harrington, rhp, Fort Worth (Central League)
37. Ryan Rote, rhp, Vanderbilt
38. Joseph Krebs, lhp, Navarro (Texas) JC
39. Tim LeMaster, of, Perry Meridian HS, Indianapolis
40. **Nathan Griffin, c, Oral Roberts**
41. Mike Lomba, lhp, Sacramento CC
42. Ronald Ball, rhp, Cypress (Calif.) JC
43. Keaton Hougen, rhp, Wylie (Texas) HS
44. Harrison Ashmore, rhp, Mansfield HS, Arlington, Texas
45. Drew Fiorenza, rhp, Middle Georgia
46. **Juan Velazquez, rhp, Grossmont (Calif.) JC**
47. Justin O'Bannon, rhp, San Jacinto (Texas) JC
48. Erik Morrison, ss, Arroyo Grande (Calif.) HS
49. Andrew Spaulding, of, Purcell Marian HS, Cincinnati
50. Chris Davis, 3b, Longview (Texas) HS

OAKLAND ATHLETICS

June—Regular Phase (26)

1. **Landon Powell, c, South Carolina** (Pick from Red Sox as compensation for Type A free agent Keith Foulke)
1. **Richie Robnett, of, Fresno State**
1. **Danny Putnam, of, Stanford** (Supplemental pick—36th—for loss of Foulke)
1. **Huston Street, rhp, Texas** (Supplemental pick—40th—for loss of Type A free agent Miguel Tejada)
2. **Michael Rogers, rhp, North Carolina State** (Pick from Orioles as compensation for Tejada)
2. **Kurt Suzuki, c, Cal State Fullerton**
3. **Jason Windsor, rhp, Cal State Fullerton**
4. **Ryan Webb, rhp, Clearwater Central Catholic HS, Palm Harbor, Fla.**
5. **Kevin Melillo, 2b, South Carolina**
6. **Derek Tharpe, lhp, Tennessee**
7. **Jarod McAuliff, rhp, Oklahoma**
8. **Myron Leslie, 3b, South Florida**
9. **Chad Boyd, of, El Camino Real HS, West Hills, Calif.**
10. **Tommy Everidge, 1b, Sonoma State (Calif.)**
11. **Steve Sharpe, rhp, Central Missouri State**
12. **Nick Blasi, of, Wichita State**
13. **Scott Drucker, rhp, Tennessee**
14. Jorge Charry, rhp, Puerto Rico Baseball Academy, Fajardo, P.R.
15. **Ryan Ford, lhp, Eastern Michigan**
16. **Tyler Best, c, Lewis-Clark State (Idaho)**
17. **Clay Tichota, rhp, Regis (Colo.)**
18. Jeremy Slayden, of, Georgia Tech
19. **Ryan Ruiz, ss, Nevada-Las Vegas**
20. **Rob Semerano, rhp, Fordham**
21. **Chalon Tietje, of, Cal Poly**
22. Ryan Jones, of, East Carolina
23. **Shawn Martinez, rhp, Colorado State-Pueblo**
24. **Dallas Braden, lhp, Texas Tech**
25. Jim Conroy, rhp, Illinois
26. **Steven Carter, rhp, Coastal Carolina**
27. Clayton Turner, rhp, Northwestern State
28. **Andre Piper-Jordan, of, Everett (Wash.) CC**
29. **Wesley Long, ss, Alabama-Huntsville**
30. **Haas Pratt, 1b, Arkansas**
31. **Connor Robertson, rhp, Birmingham-Southern**

32. **Jeff Gray, rhp, Southwest Missouri State**
33. **Scott Fairbanks, rhp, Lewis-Clark State (Idaho)**
34. Yusuf Carter, of, El Paso (Texas) CC
35. Broc Coffman, lhp, Lower Columbia (Wash.) JC
36. Matt Cassel, rhp, Southern California
37. Beau Seabury, c, Skajit Valley (Wash.) CC
38. Drew Saberhagen, 1b, Calabasas (Calif.) HS
39. Joseph Florio, 2b, Blair Academy, Blairstown, N.J.
40. Danny Figueroa, of, Miami

PHILADELPHIA PHILLIES

June—Regular Phase (21)

1. **Greg Golson, of, John Connally HS, Austin**
2. **Jason Jaramillo, c, Oklahoma State**
3. **J.A. Happ, lhp, Northwestern**
4. **Lou Marson, c, Coronado HS, Scottsdale, Ariz.**
5. **Andy Baldwin, lhp, Oregon State**
6. **Sean Gamble, of, Auburn**
7. **John Hardy, 2b, Arizona**
8. **Sam Orr, ss, Biola (Calif.)**
9. **Andy Macfarlane, of, Treasure Valley (Ore.) CC**
10. **Reece Creswell, c, Perryton (Texas) HS**
11. **Carl Galloway, 1b, Biola (Calif.)**
12. **Joe Bisenius, rhp, Oklahoma City**
13. James Adkins, lhp, Wilson Central HS, Mount Juliet, Tenn.
14. **Jason Martinez, lhp, Mesa State (Colo.)**
15. **Zac Cline, lhp, West Virginia**
16. **Kyle Allen, lhp, Lewis-Clark State (Idaho)**
17. **Ryan Frith, of, Southern Mississippi**
18. **Greg Isaacson, 2b, Washington**
19. **Jacob Barrack, rhp, Pepperdine**
20. **Nathan Johnson, rhp, Iowa**
21. **Buck Shaw, 1b, Connors State (Okla.) JC**
22. **Anthony Buffone, 3b, Maryland**
23. **Kevin Rose, rhp, San Francisco**
24. **Aaron Wilson, rhp, San Diego**
25. **Joe Dirnberger, 3b, Mesa State (Colo.)**
26. **Nick Evangelista, rhp, Pittsburgh**
27. Jason Appel, of, John F. Kennedy HS, Plainview, N.Y.
28. **Chris Raulinaitis, rhp, Sacramento CC**
29. **Josh Mader, ss, New Mexico**
30. **Kevin Shepard, lhp, Boston College**
31. Jesse Kovacs, ss, Pacific
32. **Nick Shimer, 3b, George Mason**
33. **Clary Carlsen, rhp, Hawaii**
34. **Alex McEnaney, rhp, Royal Palm Beach HS, West Palm Beach, Fla.**
35. **Derek Brant, c, Grand View (Iowa)**
36. Andrew Romine, ss, Trabuco Hills HS, Mission Viejo, Calif.
37. Steve Marquardt, 3b, Kennewick (Wash.) HS
38. Jay Brown, rhp, Brunswick (Ga.) HS
39. Dusty Brabender, rhp, Oregon (Wis.) HS
40. **Michael Mihalik, rhp, Delaware**
41. Bryce Massanari, c, Centennial HS, Las Vegas
42. **Curt Miaso, of, Chaparral HS, Scottsdale, Ariz.**
43. Jerome Wooley, of, Columbia HS, Decatur, Ga.
44. Erik Morris, c, Michigan State
45. Lucas Miranda, 3b, Ferndale (Calif.) HS
46. Aaron Brown, rhp, Clear Creek HS, League City, Texas
47. Brendan Lafferty, lhp, Poly HS, Riverside, Calif.
48. Steven Lopez, c, Yavapai (Ariz.) JC
49. Willie Mays, of, Bryan Station HS, Lexington, Ky.
50. Matt Johnson, 1b, Bryan HS, Omaha

PITTSBURGH PIRATES

June—Regular Phase (11)

1. **Neil Walker, c, Pine Richland HS, Gibsonia, Pa.**
2. **Brian Bixler, ss, Eastern Michigan**
3. **Eddie Prasch, 3b, Milton HS, Alpharetta, Ga.**
4. **Joe Bauserman, rhp, Lincoln HS, Tallahassee, Fla.**
5. **Kyle Bloom, lhp, Illinois State**
6. **A.J. Johnson, of, Tallahassee (Fla.) CC**
7. **Jason Quarles, rhp, Southern**
8. **Eric Ridener, rhp, Taravella HS, Coral Springs, Fla.**
9. **Christopher Covington, of, Brookwood HS, Snellville, Ga.**
10. **Derek Hankins, rhp, Memphis**
11. **Matt Guillory, rhp, Louisiana-Monroe**
12. J.P. Padron, 3b, Clear Creek HS, League City, Texas
13. **Brett Grandstrand, 2b, Coastal Carolina**
14. **Jermel Lomack, 2b, Prairie View A&M**
15. John Slone, c, Miami (Ohio)
16. **Ryan Herbort, rhp, Northwest Whitfield HS, Dalton, Ga.**
17. **Matt Bishop, rhp, East Carolina**
18. Cory Luebke, lhp, Marion (Ohio) HS
19. **Brad Clapp, rhp, Juanita HS, Kirkland, Wash.**
20. **Brandon Reddinger, c, Washington State**
21. **Derek Drage, rhp, Southwest Missouri State**
22. **Mike Hofius, 1b, Long Beach State**
23. **Dustin Craig, rhp, Sam Houston State**
24. **Joe Salas, lhp, New Mexico**
25. **Kevin Miller, rhp, Bucknell**
26. Jason Tweedy, ss, Newark (Calif.) Memorial HS
27. Scott Leffler, c, Lake City (Fla.) CC
28. Pat McAnaney, lhp, Westhill HS, Syracuse, N.Y.
29. Christian Romple, c, Big Bend (Wash.) CC
30. **Issael Gonzalez, 2b, Edouard Montpetit HS, Quebec, Canada**
31. Oliver Marmol, ss, Dr. Phillips HS, Orlando
32. Chris Palma, rhp, JC of the Canyons (Calif.)
33. Justin Byler, c, Harding HS, Warren, Ohio
34. Nick Beghtol, c, Mountainview HS, Fort Collins, Colo.
35. Jeff Robinson, rhp, Roswell (Ga.) HS
36. Jose Nunez, ss, Puerto Rico Baseball Academy, Caguas, P.R.
37. Tim Rice, lhp, Richmond
38. Keith Pedersen, lhp, Glide (Ore.) HS
39. **Todd Redmond, rhp, St. Petersburg (Fla.) CC**
40. Jeremy Horst, lhp, Iowa Western CC
41. **Dan Schwartzbauer, ss, Duquesne**
42. Mikel McIntyre, of, Diablo Valley (Calif.) CC
43. Stephen Ashcraft, of, Brentwood (Tenn.) HS
44. Sean Setzer, 1b, Woodrow Wilson HS, Portland, Ore.
45. Corey Kemp, c, Centennial HS, Franklin, Tenn.
46. Josh Scofield, lhp, Newport HS, Bellevue, Wash.
47. Zach Phillips, rhp, Lee County HS, Sanford, N.C.
48. Ricardo Rivas, rhp, El Paso (Texas) CC
49. **Patrick Wandtke, lhp, West Orange HS, Winter Garden, Fla.**
50. Brock Lindeke, c, Soquel (Calif.) HS

ST. LOUIS CARDINALS

June—Regular Phase (19)

1. **Chris Lambert, rhp, Boston College**
2. **Mike Ferris, 1b, Miami (Ohio)**
3. **Eric Haberer, lhp, Southern Illinois**
4. **Donnie Smith, rhp, Old Dominion**
5. **Wes Swackhamer, of, Tulane**
6. **Jarrett Hoffpauir, 2b, Southern Mississippi**
7. Buck Cody, lhp, Texas
8. **Matt Shepherd, ss, Southern Mississippi**
9. **Mike Parisi, rhp, Manhattan**
10. **Brady Toops, c, Arkansas**
11. **Simon Williams, of, Maine**
12. **Mark Worrell, rhp, Florida International**
13. **Dan Nelson, ss, Los Angeles Pierce JC**
14. **Jake Mullinax, 2b, Nebraska**
15. **Jeremy Zick, rhp, Mississippi**
16. **Matt Scherer, lhp, LeMoyne**
17. **Chris Noonan, lhp, Seton Hall**
18. Cameron Blair, ss, Texas Tech
19. **Das Jesson, 3b, Cal State Los Angeles**
20. **Chad Gabriel, of, Santa Ana (Calif.) JC**
21. **Mike Sillman, rhp, Nebraska**
22. **Billy Becher, 1b, New Mexico State**
23. **Phillip Andersen, rhp, Chandler-Gilbert (Ariz.) CC**
24. **Jose Delgado, 2b, Texas Tech**
25. **Mike Miller, of, Cal State Los Angeles**
26. **Steven Sherman, of, UNC Asheville**

27. Christian Reyes, c, Jose M. Pestrana HS, Aguas Buenas, P.R.
28. **Chris Della Rocco, rhp, Monmouth (N.J.)**
29. **Cory Taillon, c, Cal Poly**
30. **Brandon Marcelli, c, Fresno State**
31. **Daniel Baysinger, rhp, Cornell**
32. **Austin Tubb, rhp, Southern Mississippi**
33. **Michael Gross, rhp, North Carolina**
34. **Brett Cooley, 1b, Houston**
35. **Brian Parish, rhp, Iona**
36. **Chris Bova, rhp, Ohio**
37. **Chris Patrick, ss, Fresno State**
38. **Adam Burton, c, Arkansas-Monticello**
39. **Sam Herbert, of, Cal Poly**
40. **Sean Dobson, of, Toledo**
41. **Mark Broome, 3b, Delta State (Miss.)**
42. **Matt Rigoli, 1b, Parsippany (N.J.) HS**
43. **Jessen Grant, rhp, Columbia**
44. **Quinton Robertson, rhp, Nebraska**
45. **Gregg Pleeter, rhp, Fairleigh Dickinson**
46. Matt Johnson, rhp, Eupora (Miss.) HS
47. Nicholas Dinapoli, of, Buena HS, Ventura, Calif.

SAN DIEGO PADRES

June—Regular Phase (1)

1. **Matt Bush, ss, Mission Bay HS, El Cajon, Calif.**
2. (Pick to Yankees as compensation for Type A free agent David Wells)
3. **Billy Killian, c, Chippewa Hills HS, Stanwood, Mich.**
4. **Daryl Jones, 1b, Westchester HS, Los Angeles**
5. **Sean Kazmar, ss, CC of Southern Nevada**
6. **Jonathan Ellis, rhp, The Citadel**
7. **Ricky Steik, rhp, Golden West (Calif.) JC**
8. **Vern Sterry, rhp, North Carolina State**
9. **David O'Hagan, rhp, Stanford**
10. **Chris Kolkhorst, of, Rice**
11. **Matt Varner, rhp, Houston**
12. **Mike Ekstrom, rhp, Point Loma Nazarene (Calif.)**
13. **Jake Vose, rhp, Nevada-Las Vegas**
14. Matt Montgomery, rhp, Okaloosa-Walton (Fla.) JC
15. Brandon Thomson, lhp, Gilbert (Ariz.) HS
16. **Ben Krosschell, rhp, Highlands Ranch (Colo.) HS**
17. **Clay Hamilton, rhp, Penn State**
18. Michael Moon, 3b, Southern California
19. **Craig Johnson, of, Sacramento State**
20. **Brian Fryer, of, New Mexico Highlands**
21. **Gary Gallegos, lhp, Biola (Calif.)**
22. **Kyle Stutes, lhp, Lamar**
23. **Rielly Embrey, 1b, San Diego State**
24. **Jodam Rivera, ss, Puerto Rico Baseball Academy, Caguas, P.R.**
25. **Brian Burks, rhp, Georgia Tech**
26. **Kelvin Vazquez, ss, Indian Hills (Iowa) CC**
27. **Orlando Diaz, 3b, Jacksonville**
28. **B.J. Jenkins, rhp, Trevecca Nazarene (Tenn.)**
29. **E.J. Shanks, rhp, Oklahoma City**
30. **Adam Kroft, rhp, Albany**
31. **Matt Thayer, of, UCLA**
32. Toddric Johnson, of, Meridian (Miss.) JC
33. Adam Miller, rhp, Indian Hills (Iowa) CC
34. Gary Moran, rhp, Fresno CC
35. Josh Bartusick, 1b, Golden West (Calif.) JC
36. Chorye Spoone, rhp, Catonsville (Md.) CC
37. Erik Lovett, of, Louisburg (N.C.) JC
38. Michael Lorentson, lhp, Malvern (Pa.) Prep School
39. Bobby Spain, 3b, Norman (Okla.) HS
40. **Brandon Kintzler, rhp, Dixie State (Utah) JC**
41. Taylor Bennett, rhp, Okaloosa-Walton (Fla.) CC
42. **Kyle Blanks, 1b, Moriarty HS, Edgewood, N.M.**
43. Zach Shadle, rhp, Tacoma (Wash.) JC
44. Omar Kadir, rhp, Lethbridge (Alberta) CC
45. Cameron Nickell, of, Columbia State (Tenn.) CC
46. Aaron Breit, rhp, Thomas More Prep HS, Hays, Kan.
47. Sean Cunningham, 3b, Sinclair SS, Whitby, Ontario
48. David Minor, of, South Hagerstown (Md.) HS
49. Brandon Tuten, rhp, Mount Pleasant (Tenn.) HS
50. Brian Joynt, 1b, Indian Hills (Iowa) CC

SAN FRANCISCO GIANTS

June—Regular Phase (29)

1. (Pick to Royals as compensation for Type A free agent Michael Tucker)
2. **Eddy Martinez-Esteve, of, Florida State**
3. **John Bowker, of, Long Beach State**
4. **Clay Timpner, of, Central Florida**
5. **Garrett Broshuis, rhp, Missouri**
6. **Justin Hedrick, rhp, Northeastern**
7. **Will Thompson, 1b, Santa Clara**
8. Omar Aguilar, rhp, Merced (Calif.) JC
9. Jamie Arneson, lhp, Liberty HS, Bakersfield, Calif.
10. **Spencer Grogan, lhp, Oklahoma State**
11. **Darren Sack, rhp, Sonoma State (Calif.)**
12. **Kevin Frandsen, 2b, San Jose State**
13. Thomas Martin, lhp, Richmond
14. **Geno Espineli, lhp, Texas Christian**
15. **Jeff Palumbo, ss, George Mason**
16. **Emmanuel Cividanes, of, Broward (Fla.) CC**
17. **Jordan Thomson, rhp, Northeastern**
18. **Jeremiah Luster, ss, Oceanside (Calif.) HS**
19. **Nate Pendley, lhp, Oregon State**
20. **Rickey Putnam, rhp, Houston**
21. **Simon Klink, 3b, Purdue**
22. **Doug MacKay, rhp, Utah**
23. **Brad Groth, ss, Elmhurst (Ill.)**
24. **Matt Raguse, rhp, Miami (Ohio)**
25. **John Acha, 3b, Sacramento State**
26. **Trevor Wohlgemuth, rhp, Northern Illinois**
27. **Jonathan Sanchez, lhp, Ohio Dominican**
28. **Charlie Babineaux, of, Mississippi**
29. **Ryan Shaver, rhp, Lower Columbia (Wash.) JC**
30. **Kevin Jenson, rhp, Loyola Marymount**
31. **Kyle Haines, ss, Eastern Illinois**
32. **Morgan Brinson, rhp, Walnut Grove HS, Langley, B.C**
33. **Judson Richards, 1b, Point Loma Nazarene (Calif.)**
34. Jacob Coash, lhp, JC of the Canyons (Calif.)
35. **Tim Grant, rhp, Dartmouth**
36. **Buster Lussier, rhp, Diman Vocational HS, Fall River, Mass.**
37. Erik Meyer, rhp, Eastern Washington
38. Tyson Brummett, rhp, Central Arizona JC
39. Brad Schwarzenbach, rhp, St. John Bosco HS, Bellflower, Calif.
40. Mac Nelson, c, Timpanogas HS, Orem, Utah
41. **Chase Smith, rhp, Central Oklahoma**
42. Ryan Addition, rhp, Western HS, Davie, Fla.
43. Jack Spradlin, lhp, Southwestern (Calif.) JC
44. **T.J. Gornati, rhp, Pittsburgh**
45. Kris Gibson, 1b, San Francisco State
46. **David Quinowski, lhp, Redlands (Calif.) HS**
47. **Matt Minor, rhp, Nevada-Las Vegas**
48. **Benny Cepeda, rhp, Ohio Dominican**
49. **Michael Santoro, of, Northern Illinois**
50. Garrett Lingle, 2b, Mission Bay HS, San Diego

SEATTLE MARINERS

June—Regular Phase (22)

1. (Pick to Twins as compensation for Type A free agent Eddie Guardado)
2. (Pick to Royals as compensation for Type A free agent Raul Ibanez)
3. **Matt Tuiasosopo, ss, Woodinville (Wash.) HS**
4. **Rob Johnson, c, Houston**
5. **Mark Lowe, rhp, Texas-Arlington**
6. **Jermaine Brock, of, Ottawa Hills HS, Grand Rapids, Mich.**
7. **Sebastien Boucher, of, Bethune-Cookman**
8. **Marshall Hubbard, 1b, North Carolina**
9. **Jeff Dominguez, ss, Puerto Rico Baseball Academy, Carolina, P.R.**
10. **Eric Carter, rhp, Delaware State**
11. **Michael Saunders, 3b, Lambrick Park HS, Victoria, BC**

12. **Steve Uhlmansiek, lhp, Wichita State**
13. Kris Kasarjian, of, Los Angeles Pierce JC
14. **Brent Johnson, of, Nevada-Las Vegas**
15. Brent Thomas, of, Bellevue (Wash.) CC
16. **Chad Fillinger, rhp, Santa Clara**
17. J.P. Arencibia, c, Westminster Christian HS, Miami
18. **Jack Arroyo, 2b, Sacramento State**
19. **Brandon Green, ss, Wichita State**
20. Brian Chavez, ss, Quartz Hill HS, Palmdale, Calif.
21. **Mumba Rivera, rhp, Bethune-Cookman**
22. **David Hall, of, San Diego State**
23. Ben Summerhays, 1b, Stanford
24. **Greg Slee, c, Huntington (Ind.)**
25. **Joe Jacobitz, c, San Francisco**
26. Zach Ashwood, lhp, The Colony (Texas) HS
27. **Aaron Trolia, rhp, Washington State**
28. **Adam Brandt, lhp, Otterbein (Ohio)**
29. **Mike Ciccotelli, lhp, Villanova**
30. **Rollie Gibson, lhp, Fresno CC**
31. Chad Rothford, 1b, Fresno CC
32. **Don Clement, rhp, Colorado State-Pueblo**
33. **Marquise Liverpool, of, Don Bosco Prep, Ramsey, N.J.**
34. Duke Welker, rhp, Woodinville (Wash.) HS
35. Brandon Javis, ss, Cross Creek HS, Augusta, Ga.
36. Nick Hagadone, lhp, Sumner (Wash.) HS
37. James Russell, lhp, Heritage HS, Colleyville, Texas
38. **Harold Williams, lhp, Mount San Jacinto (Calif.) JC**
39. Jake Opitz, ss, Heritage HS, Littleton, Colo.
40. **Michael Schilling, rhp, Fresno CC**
41. Garrett Parcell, rhp, Norco (Calif.) HS
42. **Erwin Jacobo, 3b, Braddock HS, Miami**
43. Luis Coste, of, Puerto Rico Baseball Academy, Caguas, P.R.
44. Felix Martinez, of, Broward (Fla.) CC
45. Dwayne Lynah, of, Spartanburg Methodist (S.C.) JC
46. Daniel Martin, of, Indian River (Fla.) CC
47. Andrew McDonald, c, Sahuaro HS, Tucson, Ariz.
48. Zachary Walden, c, Stockbridge HS, McDonough, Ga.
49. Andy Reichard, rhp, Seminole (Fla.) CC
50. Leighton Autrey, of, Navarro (Texas) JC

TAMPA BAY DEVIL RAYS

June—Regular Phase (4)

1. **Jeff Niemann, rhp, Rice**
2. **Reid Brignac, ss, St. Amant (La.) HS**
3. **Wade Davis, rhp, Lake Wales (Fla.) HS**
4. **Matt Spring, c, Dixie State (Utah) JC**
5. **Jake McGee, lhp, Edward Reed HS, Sparks, Nev.**
6. **Ryan Royster, of, Churchill HS, Eugene, Ore.**
7. **Fernando Perez, of, Columbia**
8. **Rhyne Hughes, 1b, Pearl River (Miss.) CC**
9. **Joseph Muro, rhp, Mount San Antonio (Calif.) JC**
10. **Matt Walker, rhp, Central HS, Baton Rouge, La.**
11. **Josh Asanovich, 2b, Arizona State**
12. **Chris Cunningham, of, South Suburban (Ill.) JC**
13. **Andy Sonnanstine, rhp, Kent State**
14. **Woods Fines, rhp, Northwood HS, Pittsboro, N.C.**
15. **Ken Brock, lhp, Lane (Ore.) CC**
16. Cale Iorg, ss, Karns HS, Knoxville, Tenn.
17. **Marcus Barriger, rhp, Armstrong Atlantic State (Ga.)**
18. **Jimmy Scholzen, ss, Hurricane (Utah) HS**
19. **Chris Nowak, 3b, South Carolina-Spartanburg**
20. Matt Duryea, lhp, Marshfield HS, North Bend, Ore.
21. **Pat Breen, of, Houston**
22. **Ryan Bitter, rhp, Siena**
23. **Logan Wiens, 1b, Merced (Calif.) HS**
24. **Francisco Leandro, of, Central Missouri State**
25. Deunte Heath, rhp, Lake City (Fla.) CC
26. **Alex Crooks, 1b, East Los Angeles CC**
27. Matt Goyen, lhp, Georgia College & State
28. **Nick Wagner, rhp, Georgia Tech**
29. Daniel McCutchen, rhp, Oklahoma
30. **Aaron Walker, lhp, Georgia Tech**
31. John Rodriguez, lhp, Pearl River (Miss.) CC
32. Matt Rainey, rhp, Odessa (Texas) JC
33. **Patrick Cottrell, ss, West Florida**
34. Grant Theophilus, lhp, Cypress (Calif.) JC
35. **Billy Evers, rhp, Eckerd (Fla.)**
36. Ryan Davis, 3b, Chaparral HS, Scottsdale, Ariz.
37. Brian McCormick, c, Arundel Senior HS, Gambrills, Md.
38. Ryan Conan, ss, Archbishop Mity HS, San Jose, Calif.
39. **Drew Bigda, lhp, Holy Cross**
40. Jason Dean, of, Sacramento CC
41. **J.T Hall, of, Southwest Mississippi JC**
42. Matt Ware, lhp, Quartz Hill HS, Lancaster, Calif.
43. **John Price, lhp, Mobile**
44. **Matt Fields, 1b, Rainier Beach HS, Seattle**
45. **John Bouman, ss, Tusculum (Tenn.)**
46. **Chris Kelly, rhp, Jacksonville**
47. Ben Lanier, ss, Kinston (N.C.) HS
48. Andrew Gray, 1b, Holy Spirit HS, Tuscaloosa, Ala.
49. Patrick Mahoney, c, Lincoln HS, Des Moines, Iowa
50. Jerrylee Scott, ss, Livonia (La.) HS

TEXAS RANGERS

June—Regular Phase (10)

1. **Thomas Diamond, rhp, New Orleans**
1. **Eric Hurley, rhp, Wolfson HS, Jacksonville** (Pick from Braves as compensation for Type B free agent John Thomson)
2. **K.C. Herren, of, Auburn (Wash.) HS**
3. **Michael Schlact, rhp, Wheeler HS, Marietta, Ga.**
4. **Brandon Boggs, of, Georgia Tech**
5. **Mike Nickeas, c, Georgia Tech**
6. **Bill Susdorf, of, UCLA**
7. **Ben Harrison, of, Florida**
8. **Mark Roberts, rhp, Oklahoma**
9. **Jim Fasano, 1b, Richmond**
10. Justin Maxwell, of, Maryland
11. **Travis Metcalf, 3b, Kansas**
12. Kevin Ardoin, rhp, Louisiana-Lafayette
13. **Kyle Rogers, rhp, Ball HS, Galveston, Texas**
14. **Tug Hulett, 2b, Auburn**
15. **John Lujan, rhp, New Mexico JC**
16. **Jarrad Burcie, rhp, Tarleton State (Texas)**
17. Nic Crosta, of, Santa Clara
18. **Freddie Thon, 1b, Brevard (Fla.) CC**
19. **Marc Cornell, rhp, Ohio**
20. **Shawn Phillips, rhp, Delaware State**
21. **Bobby Lenoir, ss, Richmond**
22. **Ryan Griffith, c, Birmingham-Southern**
23. **Zach Phillips, lhp, Galt Union HS, Galt, Calif.**
24. **Charles Isbell, rhp, Temescal Canyon HS, Lake Elsinore, Calif.**
25. **Ben Foster, lhp, Tennessee Temple**
26. **J.D. Cockroft, lhp, Miami**
27. **Marlon Melendez, rhp, Chemeketa (Ore.) CC**
28. **Brett Zamzow, rhp, Navarro (Texas) JC**
29. Justin Klipp, rhp, Cuesta (Calif.) JC
30. **Wally Backman II, ss, Crook County HS, Prinveille, Ore.**
31. **Nicholas Casanova, rhp, Canyon HS, Corona, Calif.**
32. **Michael Mask, of, Texas Tech**
33. **Luis Rodriguez, ss, New Mexico JC**
34. **Clint Brannon, lhp, Arkansas**
35. Sam Demel, rhp, Spring (Texas) HS
36. **Jesse Ingram, rhp, California**
37. **Justin Lensch, lhp, Louisiana-Monroe**
38. **Craig Hurba, c, Mount Olive (N.C.)**
39. **Jose Torres, of, East Los Angeles JC**
40. **Tony Irvin, rhp, Hillsborough (Fla.) JC**
41. **Clayton Jerome, rhp, Texas Christian**
42. **Joe Kemp, of, Indiana**
43. Austin Faught, lhp, Louisiana-Lafayette
44. Joe Franklin, 3b, Dawson (Mont.) CC
45. Jeffrey Hoffner, rhp, Yavapai (Ariz.) JC
46. Arthur Hill, rhp, Mount San Jacinto (Calif.) JC
47. **Kellan McConnell, rhp, Santa Clara**
48. Brian Capon, c, Saddleback (Calif.) JC
49. Adam Resendez, of, Boswell HS, Fort Worth
50. **Ivan Ramirez, lhp, UC Santa Barbara**

TORONTO BLUE JAYS

June—Regular Phase (16)

1. **David Purcey, lhp, Oklahoma**
1. **Zach Jackson, lhp, Texas A&M** (Supplemental pick—32nd—for loss of Type A free agent Kelvim Escobar)
2. **Curtis Thigpen, c, Texas**
3. **Adam Lind, 1b, South Alabama** (Pick from Angels as compensation for Escobar)
3. **Danny Hill, rhp, Missouri**
4. **Casey Janssen, rhp, UCLA**
5. **Ryan Klosterman, ss, Vanderbilt**
6. **Cory Patton, of, Texas A&M**
7. **Randy Dicken, rhp, Shippensburg (Pa.)**
8. **Chip Cannon, 1b, The Citadel**
9. **Joey Metropoulos, 1b, Southern California**
10. **Brian Hall, 2b, Stanford**
11. **Kristian Bell, rhp, Blinn (Texas) CC**
12. **Eric Nielsen, of, Nevada-Las Vegas**
13. **Kyle Yates, rhp, Texas**
14. **Jordan Timm, lhp, Wisconsin-Oshkosh**
15. **Michael MacDonald, rhp, Maine**
16. Jose Castro, ss, Puerto Rico Baseball Academy, Caguas, P.R.
17. Michael Cooper, rhp, Santa Ana (Calif.) JC
18. **Joey McLaughlin, rhp, Oklahoma City**
19. **Aaron Mathews, of, Oregon State**
20. Bobby Scott, rhp, Stelly's SS, Saanich, B.C
21. **Scott Roy, rhp, Hartford**
22. **Joe Wice, lhp, Dixie State (Utah) CC**
23. **Daryl Harang, lhp, San Diego State**
24. **Jesse Litsch, rhp, South Florida CC**
25. **Jason Armstrong, ss, Trinity (Texas)**
26. **Brian Bormaster, c, Tulane**
27. **Casey McKenzie, rhp, Tampa**
28. **Josh Lex, c, Oral Roberts**
29. **Michael Macaluso, ss, South Florida**
30. **Cory Hahn, rhp, Tulane**
31. **Paul Franko, 3b, Scottsdale (Ariz.) CC**
32. **Aaron Tressler, rhp, Penn State**
33. **Greg Powers, 3b, UC Santa Barbara**
34. **Derek Tate, lhp, San Francisco**
35. **Charles Anderson, of, Detroit**
36. **David Hicks, 1b, North Carolina State**
37. **Anthony Garibaldi, 3b, Southeastern Louisiana**
38. Ben Humphrey, 1b, Olney Central (Ill.)
39. Matt Trink, rhp, Yavapai (Ariz.) JC
40. Jacob Vasquez, 1b, Santa Ana (Calif.) JC
41. Derek Feldkamp, rhp, Michigan
42. Jon Hesketh, lhp, Brookswood SS, Langley, B.C.
43. Chad Beck, rhp, Panola (Texas) JC
44. **Eddie Cannon, rhp, Florida State**
45. Rodrick Ratliff, rhp, Labette (Kan.) CC
46. Brok Butcher, rhp, Santa Barbara (Calif.) CC
47. Colin Quarles, rhp, Melbourne (Fla.) HS
48. Ryan Harris, ss, San Bernardino (Calif.) Valley CC
49. Brad Miller, 1b, Ball State
50. Jordan Lennerton, 1b, Brookswood SS, Langley, B.C.

2005

Another Upton one-ups his brother, heading up strong class led by college hitters

The 2005 draft figures to go down as the best of the decade, and perhaps one of the best of all time when all is said and done.

Scouts liked the draft class early in the year and didn't change their mind as the spring wound down. The biggest reason was a strong contingent of college hitters, rare in this era when clubs do such a strong job of signing the top high school talent available. The draft class also had a definite No. 1 prospect in Virginia prep infielder Justin Upton, whose older brother B.J. was drafted No. 2 overall in 2002.

The younger Upton had played with and against such Tidewater area talents as B.J. Upton, David Wright and Ryan Zimmerman growing up, and scouts had a longer track record on him than they had on any high school player in memory. He'd been on the radar since before high school, and stamped himself as the draft's top player early with his five-tool talent at shortstop. The only question was whether or not he could stay at shortstop, prompting more comparisons to Ken Griffey Jr., than to his brother.

The Diamondbacks drafted Upton first overall and had just signed 2004 first-rounder Stephen Drew on May 30, eight days before the '05 draft. Signing Upton, who was represented by Larry Reynolds, was thought to be a tough process, and it took more than six months to get done. Finally, in January 2006, Upton signed for a then-record $6.1 million bonus. Just two years after being picked, Upton stormed to the majors and helped the Diamondbacks win the 2007 National League West division title. Now a right fielder, Upton reached his first All-Star Game berth in 2009, batting .300/.366/.532 with 26 home runs and 20 stolen bases.

Once Upton signed, the '05 first round wound up with an average signing bonus of $2.018 million, a three percent increase over the previous year.

The rest of the first round was full of premium college bats. The Royals took Nebraska's Alex Gordon, BA's 2005 College Player of the Year, No. 2 overall, and the first mild surprise came at the No. 3 spot, where Seattle drafted Southern California catcher Jeff Clement. Third baseman Zimmerman, the first first-round pick in Washington Nationals history, was a no-brainer at No. 4 overall as a local choice whose polish would help him move quickly. He was the second player from the draft to reach the majors, debuting Sept. 1, 2005.

The Brewers got an all-star of their own at No. 5 with third baseman Ryan Braun of Miami, who

DAVID STONER

Justin Upton didn't take long to reach the big leagues with the Diamondbacks

wound up moving to left field. The Blue Jays, picking sixth, made a choice that helped define the J.P. Ricciardi era, selecting Cal State Fullerton lefthander Ricky Romero over Long Beach State shortstop Troy Tulowitzki. Ricciardi's Jays had drafted lefthanded college pitchers with two first-round picks in 2004 but went that route again in '05 despite the organization's need at shortstop. Tulowitzki, No. 4 on BA's Top 200 Prospects list, fell to the Rockies at No. 7 and helped lead the team to the World Series just two years later.

Maybin, who ranked just behind Upton among high school hitters in the '05 class, wound up signing in September for a $2.65 million bonus. That left Upton and Gordon as the lone hitters holding out, while Scott Boras Corporation clients Mike Pelfrey (No. 9 overall, Mets) and Luke Hochevar (40th overall, Dodgers) were the top pitchers unsigned.

Hochevar's holdout soon became one of the top stories in the draft. Over Labor Day weekend, the Tennessee All-America righthander switched advisers, leaving the Boras Corp. to sign with the Sosnick-Cobbe Sports agency. He then negotiated a $2.98 signing bonus in a phone call with Sosnick and Dodgers scouting director Logan White. Between the phone call and the time when a Dodgers scout showed up with a contract for Hochevar to sign, Boras had convinced Hochevar to return to the fold, turn down the Dodgers offer and remain a holdout.

The negotiations then turned ugly, as Boras first accused White of lying, trying to drive a wedge between White and new general manager Paul DePodesta. DePodesta responded by holding firm by White, and the Dodgers soon withdrew their offer to Hochevar. Because his agent switch had become so public, Hochevar had little hope of returning to college as a senior and wound up pitching in the independent American Association the following May.

But his holdout wound up paying off. Hochevar threw very well for the Fort Worth Cats, and the Royals eventually drafted him No. 1 overall in 2006.

Red Sox Bonanza

The strong first round also included 2009 BA Rookie of the Year Andrew McCutchen, drafted 11th overall by the Pirates; Reds outfielder Jay Bruce, the 2007 Minor League Player of the Year; and Twins selection Matt Garza, the Fresno State righthander who was an instrumental part of Tampa Bay's AL pennant in 2008 after being traded for Delmon Young after the 2007 season.

No team had as good of a draft as Boston, though. Coming off their first World Series championship in 86 years, the Red Sox had a mini-bonanza of picks, with five of the first 47 selections. All five—outfielder Jacoby Ellsbury (picked 23rd overall); righthanders Craig Hansen (26), Clay Buchholz (42) and Michael Bowden (47); and shortstop Jed Lowrie (45)—have reached the majors. Ellsbury helped ignite the Red Sox in '07 in their second World Series title run, while Buchholz no-hit the Orioles that year. Lowrie and Bowden were still with Boston through 2009, while Hansen was used in a trade with the Pirates that brought Jason Bay to Boston.

Hansen wound up reaching the majors third among all draftees, making his debut Sept. 19 for Boston. The Braves' Joey Devine, though, beat everyone to the majors, as the 27th overall pick got to Atlanta on Aug. 20 after just 22 minor league appearances. Devine, the first college pitcher the Braves had drafted in the first round since 1987, gave up a game-losing grand slam to Xavier Nady in his big league debut. He made the Braves' playoff roster and wound up giving up a walk-off, series-ending solo home run to Houston rookie Chris Burke in the 18th inning of Game Four of the Division Series, a 7-6 Astros victory.

DRAFT 05: FIRST-ROUND PICKS

No.	Club	Player, Pos.	School	Hometown	Ht.	Wt.	B-T	Age
1.	Diamondbacks	Justin Upton, ss	Great Bridge HS	Chesapeake, Va.	6-1	195	R-R	17
2.	Royals	Alex Gordon, 3b	Nebraska	Lincoln, Neb.	6-1	210	L-R	21
3.	Mariners	Jeff Clement, c	Southern California	Marshalltown, Iowa	6-1	210	L-R	21
4.	Nationals	Ryan Zimmerman, 3b	Virginia	Virginia Beach	6-2	210	R-R	20
5.	Brewers	Ryan Braun, 3b	Miami	Granada Hills, Calif.	6-2	200	R-R	21
6.	Blue Jays	Ricky Romero, lhp	Cal State Fullerton	Los Angeles	6-1	195	R-L	20
7.	Rockies	Troy Tulowitzki, ss	Long Beach State	Sunnyvale, Calif.	6-3	205	R-R	20
8.	Devil Rays	Wade Townsend, rhp	No School	Dripping Springs, Texas	6-4	225	R-R	22
9.	Mets	Mike Pelfrey, rhp	Wichita State	Wichita, Kan.	6-7	210	R-R	21
10.	Tigers	Cameron Maybin, of	T.C. Roberson HS	Asheville, N.C.	6-3	200	R-R	18
11.	Pirates	Andrew McCutchen, of	Fort Meade HS	Fort Meade, Fla.	5-11	175	R-R	18
12.	Reds	Jay Bruce, of	West Brook HS	Beaumont, Texas	6-3	195	L-L	18
13.	Orioles	Brandon Snyder, c	Westfield HS	Chantilly, Va.	6-2	210	R-R	18
14.	Indians	Trevor Crowe, of	Arizona	Beaverton, Ore.	6-0	190	B-R	21
15.	White Sox	Larry Broadway, rhp	Texas Christian	Wellington, Fla.	6-4	190	R-R	21
16.	Marlins	Chris Volstad, rhp	Palm Beach Gardens HS	Palm Beach Gardens, Fla.	6-7	190	R-R	18
17.	Yankees	C.J. Henry, ss	Putnam City HS	Oklahoma City	6-3	205	R-R	19
18.	Padres	Cesar Carrillo, rhp	Miami	Chicago	6-3	177	R-R	21
19.	Rangers	John Mayberry Jr., of	Stanford	Kansas City	6-6	230	R-R	21
20.	Cubs	Mark Pawelek, lhp	Springville HS	Springville, Utah	6-3	190	L-L	18
21.	Athletics	Cliff Pennington, ss	Texas A&M	Corpus Christi, Texas	5-11	180	B-R	21
22.	Marlins	Aaron Thompson, lhp	Second Baptist HS	Houston	6-3	195	L-L	18
23.	Red Sox	Jacoby Ellsbury, of	Oregon State	Madras, Ore.	6-1	185	L-L	21
24.	Astros	Brian Bogusevic, lhp	Tulane	Chicago	6-3	215	L-L	21
25.	Twins	Matt Garza, rhp	Fresno State	Easton, Calif.	6-4	185	R-R	21
26.	Red Sox	Craig Hansen, rhp	St. John's	Glen Cove, N.Y.	6-6	210	R-R	21
27.	Braves	Joey Devine, rhp	North Carolina State	Junction City, Kan.	5-11	195	R-R	21
28.	Cardinals	Colby Rasmus, of	Russell County HS	Seale, Ala.	6-1	175	L-L	18
29.	Marlins	Jacob Marceaux, rhp	McNeese State	Crowley, La.	6-1	195	R-R	21
30.	Cardinals	Tyler Greene, ss	Georgia Tech	Fort Lauderdale	6-2	185	R-R	21

2005

CLUB-BY-CLUB SELECTIONS

ARIZONA DIAMONDBACKS

June—Regular Phase (1)

1. **Justin Upton, ss, Great Bridge HS, Chesapeake, Va.**
1. **Matt Torra, rhp, Massachusetts** (Supplemental pick—31st—for loss of Type A free agent Richie Sexson)
2. **Matt Green, rhp, Louisiana-Monroe**
3. **Jason Neighborgall, rhp, Georgia Tech**
3. **Micah Owings, rhp, Tulane** (Pick from Mariners as compensation for Sexson)
4. **Mark Romanczuk, lhp, Stanford**
5. **Chris Rahl, of, William & Mary**
6. **Greg Smith, lhp, Louisiana State**
7. **Anthony Cupps, rhp, Mississippi**
8. **Ryan Schreppel, lhp, Cal State Fullerton**
9. **Josh Ford, c, Baylor**
10. **Cody Evans, rhp, Long Beach State**
11. Brett Jacobson, rhp, Cactus Shadows HS, Carefree, Ariz.
12. **Bryan Byrne, 1b, St. Mary's**
13. Daniel Roberts, lhp, Chipola (Fla.) JC
14. **Rusty Ryal, 3b, Oklahoma State**
15. **Greg Thomson, of, St. John's**
16. **Craig Pfautz, lhp, Darton (Ga.) JC**
17. **Jason Urquidez, rhp, Arizona State**
18. **Jake Elder, c, Minnesota**
19. **Kyle Wright, rhp, Lewis-Clark State (Idaho)**
20. **Peter Duda, rhp, Stanford**
21. **Matt Krohe, lhp, Webber International (Fla.)**
22. **Maels Rodriguez, rhp, Hialeah, Fla.**
23. **Travis Tully, of, Houston**
24. **Vince Bongiovanni, rhp, Miami**
25. Dave Williams, of, Rutgers
26. Brian Chavez, ss, JC of the Canyons (Calif.)
27. **Matt Fowles, rhp, Illinois State**
28. **Joel Melendez, of, Southeastern (Iowa) CC**
29. Trevor Pippin, 1b, McIntosh HS, Peachtree City, Ga.
30. Reinaldo Alicano, of, Seminole (Fla.) CC
31. Craig Heyer, rhp, CC of Southern Nevada
32. Rene Garcia, rhp, South Mountain (Ariz.) CC
33. J.B. Paxson, c, Center Grove HS, Greenwood, Ind.
34. Kevin Hammons, lhp, Cleveland State (Tenn.) CC
35. Ray Kruml, of, Indian Hills (Iowa) JC
36. Jonathan Runnels, lhp, San Jacinto (Texas) JC
37. Scott Mueller, rhp, South Mountain (Ariz.) CC
38. Tom Calahan, lhp, Saddleback (Calif.) CC
39. Dustin Renfrow, rhp, Jefferson (Mo.) JC
40. Eric Lawrence, rhp, Grand Rapids (Mich.) CC
41. Cheyne Hann, rhp, San Jose (Calif.) CC
42. Forrest Beverly, lhp, South Carolina
43. **Eric Butler, rhp, Tusculum (Tenn.)**
44. T.J. Peabody, rhp, Rancho Bernardo HS, San Diego
45. Drew Thomas, c, Neville HS, Monroe, La.
46. Brandon Thomson, lhp, Chandler-Gilbert (Ariz.) CC
47. **Houston Summers, c, Northeast Guilford HS, Summerfield, N.C.**
48. **Aaron Gamboa, lhp, Mill Valley, Calif.**
49. Joseph Campbell, rhp, Wabash Valley (Ill.) JC
50. Ritchie Franklin, ss, Thompson HS, Alabaster, Ala.

ATLANTA BRAVES

June—Regular Phase (27)

1. **Joey Devine, rhp, North Carolina State**
1. **Beau Jones, lhp, Destrehan (La.) HS** (Supplemental pick—41st—for loss of Type A free agent Jaret Wright)
2. **Yunel Escobar, ss, Miami, Fla.**
2. **Jeff Lyman, rhp, Monte Vista HS, Alamo, Calif.** (Pick from Yankees as compensation for Wright)
3. **Jordan Schafer, of, Winter Haven (Fla.) HS**
4. **Mike Broadway, rhp, Pope County HS, Golconda, Ill.**
5. **Will Startup, lhp, Georgia**
6. **Tyler Bullock, rhp, Baylor**
7. **Brandon Monk, 2b, LaGrange (Ga.) HS**
8. **Kyle Cofield, rhp, Southside HS, Rainbow City, Ala.**
9. **Steven Garcia, c, Temecula Valley HS, Temecula, Calif.**
10. Colin Carter, lhp, Grayson County (Texas) CC
11. **Michael Nix, rhp, Auburn**
12. **Rudy Quinonez, rhp, Fresno State**
13. **Quentin Davis, of, Francis Marion (S.C.)**
14. **Willie Cabrera, of, Los Angeles Pierce JC**
15. Mason Tobin, rhp, Kentridge HS, Renton, Wash.
16. **Jaye Chapman, rhp, Mosley HS, Lynn Haven, Fla.**
17. Clay Caulfield, rhp, Pensacola (Fla.) JC
18. Zac Oliver, lhp, Midway HS, Waco, Texas
19. **Cole Miles, ss, Viewmont HS, Bountiful, Utah**
20. Andrew Cashner, rhp, Conroe HS, Montgomery, Texas
21. Kris Cichoski, rhp, Durango HS, Las Vegas, Nev.
22. **Tommy Hanson, rhp, Riverside (Calif.) CC**
23. Brian O'Dell, rhp, Osceola Senior HS, Kissimmee, Fla.
24. Justin Reynolds, of, Central HS, Independence, Ore.
25. Matt Miller, of, Redmond (Wash.) HS
26. Michael Ryan, rhp, Lake City (Fla.) CC
27. Kyle Miller, 3b, Terry Parker HS, Jacksonville, Fla.
28. Louis Coleman, rhp, Pillow Academy HS, Greenwood, Miss.
29. Tyler Musselwhite, rhp, Gainesville (Ga.) HS
30. Brett Wiggins, lhp, Cross Creek HS, Augusta, Ga.
31. Cole McCurry, lhp, Surry (N.C.) CC
32. Brad Schwarzenbach, rhp, Cerritos (Calif.) JC
33. **Tyler Flowers, 1b, Chipola (Fla.) JC**
34. Blake Holt, of, Belton HS, Salado, Texas
35. Blake Guthrie, c, Dan River HS, Ringgold, Va.
36. Lou Green, rhp, Logan HS, Madison, W.Va.
37. **David Williams, rhp, Surry (N.C.) CC**
38. Brett Scarpetta, lhp, Madison Area (Wis.) Tech CC
39. Austin Fleet, rhp, Edmond Santa Fe HS, Edmond, Okla.
40. **James Curtis, rhp, Manatee (Fla.) JC**
41. Michael Robbins, lhp, Meridian (Miss.) CC
42. Thomas Alexander, c, Santa Barbara (Calif.) CC
43. Ryan Littlejohn, of, Verdigris HS, Broken Arrow, Okla.
44. Ben Jeffers, rhp, Madison County HS, Danielsville, Ga.
45. Mike Griffith, rhp, Issaquah (Wash.) HS
46. Luis Sanchez, ss, Lake City (Fla.) CC
47. Aaron Brady, rhp, CC of Southern Nevada
48. **Nate Weidenaar, of, Bozeman (Mont.) HS**
49. Jesse Simpson, rhp, Zachary (La.) HS
50. **Derick Himpsl, lhp, Johnstown (N.Y.) HS**

BALTIMORE ORIOLES

June—Regular Phase (13)

1. **Brandon Snyder, c, Westfield HS, Centreville, Va.**
1. **Garrett Olson, lhp, Cal Poly** (Supplemental pick—48th—for failure to sign 2004 first-rounder Wade Townsend)
2. **Nolan Reimold, of, Bowling Green State**
3. **Brandon Erbe, rhp, McDonough School, Baltimore**
4. **Kieron Pope, of, East Coweta HS, Gay, Ga.**
5. **Reid Hamblet, rhp, Biola (Calif.)**
6. **Blake Owen, rhp, Belmont**
7. **Bobby Andrews, of, Cal State Fullerton**
8. **Chorye Spoone, rhp, Catonsville (Md.) JC**
9. **Paco Figueroa, 2b, Miami**
10. **Ryan Stadanlick, rhp, St. Joseph's**
11. **Bruce Gallaway, lhp, Missouri Valley**
12. John Raynor, of, UNC Wilmington
13. **Kyle Dahlberg, c, Texas Christian**
14. **Mark Fleisher, 1b, Radford**

15. Brandon Kendricks, of, De Soto HS, Ovilla, Texas
16. **David Hernandez, rhp, Cosumnes River (Calif.) JC**
17. **Jeff Moore, rhp, UNC Wilmington**
18. Michael Whitney, rhp, Cypress-Fairbanks HS, Houston
19. D.J. Lidyard, rhp, Lower Columbia (Wash.) JC
20. **Ryan Steinbach, ss, Indiana-Purdue Fort Wayne**
21. Brian Logan, lhp, Louisburg (N.C.) CC
22. **Paul Chmiel, 1b, Pittston Area HS, Pittston, Pa.**
23. Elvin Vargas, of, Connors State (Okla.) JC
24. **Stuart Musslewhite, ss, Texas Christian**
25. **Dan Lonsberry, rhp, Northwestern State**
26. Carlos Hernandez, lhp, Santa Clara (Calif.) HS
27. **Chad Thall, lhp, Jefferson (Mo.) JC**
28. **Miguel Abreu, 2b, East Central (Okla.)**
29. Tanner Scheppers, rhp, Dana Hills HS, Laguna Niguel, Calif.
30. **Greg Young, of, Anne Arundel (Md.) CC**
31. Arik Hempy, lhp, South Carolina
32. Josh Faiola, rhp, Dartmouth
33. Tyrone Anu, of, Colonial HS, Orlando
34. Matthew Sopic, rhp, Seward County (Kan.) CC
35. Pat Egan, rhp, Quinnipiac
36. Shawn Ferguson, rhp, Texas Christian
37. Stephen Foster, lhp, Auburn (Wash.) HS
38. **Chris Vinyard, c, Chandler-Gilbert (Ariz.) CC**
39. Caleb Annesley, c, Blanchard (Okla.) HS
40. Harrison Bishop, rhp, Edmonds (Wash.) CC
41. **Tag Horner, lhp, Oklahoma City**
42. **Bryan Lee, rhp, Cuesta (Calif.) JC**
43. **Daniel Figueroa, of, Miami**
44. **Brian Bent, c, Catonsville (Md.) CC**
45. Brad Rifkin, 1b, Park School HS, Columbia, Md.
46. Benjamin Brian, of, Wayne HS, Waynesville, Ohio
47. Craig Johnson, rhp, Bellevue (Wash.) CC
48. Brent Davis, rhp, Clear Lake HS, Houston
49. Ryan Saldivar, c, Ryan High, Denton, Texas
50. Jeremy Bloor, lhp, Grand Rapids (Mich.) CC

BOSTON RED SOX

June—Regular Phase (28)

1. **Jacoby Ellsbury, of, Oregon State** (Pick from Angels as compensation for Type A free agent Orlando Cabrera)
1. **Craig Hansen, rhp, St. John's** (Pick from Dodgers as compensation for Type A free agent Derek Lowe)
1. **Clay Buchholz, rhp, Angelina (Texas) JC** (Supplemental pick—42nd—for loss of Type A free agent Pedro Martinez)
1. **Jed Lowrie, 2b, Stanford** (Supplemental pick—45th—for loss of Cabrera)
1. **Michael Bowden, rhp, Waubonsie Valley HS, Aurora, Ill.** (Supplemental pick—47th—for loss of Lowe)
2. **Jon Egan, c, Cross Creek HS, Hephzibah, Ga.** (Pick from Mets as compensation for Martinez)
2. (Pick to Padres as compensation for Type A free agent David Wells)
3. (Pick to Cubs as compensation for Type B free agent Matt Clement)
4. **Scott Blue, rhp, Morro Bay (Calif.) HS**
5. **Reid Engel, of, Lewis-Palmer HS, Monument, Colo.**
6. **Jeff Corsaletti, of, Florida**
7. **Yahmed Yema, of, Florida International**
8. **J.T. Zink, rhp, Everett (Wash.) CC**
9. **Mark Wagner, c, UC Irvine**
10. **Kevin Guyette, rhp, Arizona**
11. **Ismael Casillas, rhp, Benedictine (Kan.)**
12. **Kyle Fernandes, lhp, Massasoit (Mass.) CC**
13. **Jay Johnson, of, Xavier**
14. Pedro Alvarez, ss, Horace Mann HS, Bronx, N.Y.
15. P.J. Thomas, rhp, Jeffersonville (Ind.) HS
16. **Matt Mercurio, 3b, Florida Southern**
17. **Dominic Ramos, ss, Texas State**
18. Nick Criaris, c, St. Peter's Prep, Jersey City, N.J.
19. **Jim Baxter, lhp, Villanova**
20. Charlie Blackmon, lhp, Young Harris (Ga.) JC
21. Drew Johnson, rhp, Navarro (Texas) JC
22. Orvil Aviles, lhp, Fernando Callejo HS, Manati, P.R.
23. **Carl Lipsey, 2b, Jackson State**
24. **Jason Twomley, of, Massachusetts**
25. **Ricardo Sanchez, c, Barry (Fla.)**
26. Kirby Yates, rhp, Kauai HS, Koloa, Hawaii
27. **Matt Hancock, lhp, Oral Roberts**
28. Ryan Hinson, lhp, Northwestern HS, Rock Hill, S.C.
29. **Chris Jones, rhp, Indiana State**
30. **Ryan Colvin, rhp, Carroll HS, Southlake, Texas**
31. **Luis Exposito, c, Champagnat Catholic HS, Hialeah, Fla.**
32. **Jeff Natale, 2b, Trinity (Conn.)**
33. John Hester, c, Stanford
34. Allan Dykstra, 1b, Rancho Bernardo HS, Poway, Calif.
35. Jason Determann, lhp, Louisiana State
36. Mark McClure, rhp, Hillsborough HS, Tampa
37. Jason Schnitzer, rhp, Los Alamitos (Calif.) HS
38. **Levi Tapia, c, Ralston Valley HS, Arvada, Colo.**
39. **Bubba Bell, of, Nicholls State**
40. **Blake Maxwell, rhp, Methodist (N.C.)**
41. Eddie Degerman, rhp, Rice
42. Miguel Alicea, of, Manuela Toro HS, Caguas, P.R.
43. Jason Castro, c, Castro Valley (Calif.) HS
44. Chris Garcia, 1b, Xaverian HS, Brooklyn, N.Y.
45. Dustin Bamberg, c, Tallahassee (Fla.) CC
46. **T.J. Large, rhp, Alabama**
47. Alex Wolfe, c, Timpanogos HS, Payson, Utah
48. **Matt Sheely, of, Palm Beach Gardens (Fla.) HS**
49. Erik Turgeon, rhp, Dunedin (Fla.) HS
50. Colin Arnold, of, King's Academy, Palm Beach Gardens, Fla.

CHICAGO CUBS

June—Regular Phase (20)

1. **Mark Pawelek, lhp, Springville (Utah) HS**
2. **Donald Veal, lhp, Pima (Ariz.) CC**
3. **Mark Holliman, rhp, Mississippi**
3. **Mike Billek, rhp, Central Florida** (Pick from Red Sox as compensation for Type B free agent Matt Clement)
4. **Dylan Johnston, ss, Hamilton HS, Chandler, Ariz.**
5. **Scott Taylor, rhp, Hermitage High, Richmond, Va.**
6. **Kyle Reynolds, ss, Baylor**
7. **Trey Taylor, lhp, Baylor**
8. **Jake Muyco, c, North Carolina State**
9. **Matt Avery, rhp, Virginia**
10. **Joe Simokaitis, ss, Nebraska**
11. **Michael Phelps, rhp, Central Missouri State**
12. **Yusuf Carter, c, El Paso (Texas) CC**
13. **Brett Jackson, rhp, Modesto (Calif.) JC**
14. Tyler Graham, of, Oregon State
15. **Roger Evenson, rhp, Northwest Nazarene (Idaho)**
16. Jon Mueller, rhp, Minnesota
17. **Brandon Taylor, 3b, Brigham Young**
18. **Victor Liriano, of, El Paso (Texas) CC**
19. **Kyle Holden, rhp, Cal State San Bernardino**
20. L.V. Ware, of, North Atlanta HS, Atlanta
21. **Peter Farina, c, Virgina Commonwealth**
22. **Michael Hyle, rhp, Georgia**
23. **Jayson Ruhlman, lhp, Central Michigan**
24. **Scott Hode, ss, Arkansas**
25. **D.J. Lewis, of, Los Angeles Valley CC**
26. **Nikolaus Crouch, 1b, Vanguard (Calif.)**
27. **Davy Gregg, of, South Carolina**
28. **Michael Greenhouse, lhp, Evansville**
29. **Johnny Defendis, of, Rutgers**
30. Matt Liuzza, c, Louisiana State
31. Brad DePoy, rhp, San Jacinto (Texas) JC
32. Colby Wark, rhp, Lower Columbia (Wash.) JC
33. Ben Ferguson, rhp, Cottonwood HS, Salt Lake City
34. **Cody Gilbert, 3b, Lincoln Trail (Ill.) JC**
35. Drew O'Connell, rhp, John A. Logan (Ill.) JC
36. Needham Jones, lhp, Old Dominon
37. Kyle Keen, of, Georgia
38. **Ryan Episcopo, of, Andrew (Ga.) JC**
39. **Justin Morgan, c, Louisiana-Lafayette**
40. **Ryan Chambers, lhp, Brigham Young**
41. Chris Rollins, rhp, Winslow Township HS, Blue Anchor, N.J.

42. Noah Garza, rhp, Nolan HS, Burleson, Texas
43. Michael Brenly, c, Notre Dame HS, Scottsdale, Ariz.
44. Eddie Rush, of, Westlake HS, McDonough, Ga.
45. Corey Madden, rhp, St. Mary's
46. **Luther Murphy, 1b, Hialeah Miami Lakes (Fla.) HS**
47. Mario Williams, c, Hillsborough HS, Tampa
48. Andy Hawranick, c, Georgia Tech
49. Kyle Mura, 3b, Loyola Marymount
50. Steven Morlock, rhp, UC Santa Barbara

CHICAGO WHITE SOX

June—Regular Phase (15)

1. **Lance Broadway, rhp, Texas Christian**
2. (Pick to Yankees as compensation for Type B free agent Orlando Hernandez)
3. **Ricky Brooks, rhp, East Carolina**
4. **Chris Getz, 2b, Michigan**
5. **Ryan Rote, rhp, Vanderbilt**
6. **Aaron Cunningham, of, Everett (Wash.) CC**
7. **Dan Cortes, rhp, Garey HS, Pomona, Calif.**
8. **Clayton Richard, lhp, Michigan**
9. **Joe Winn, rhp, Delgado (La.) JC**
10. **Israel Chirino, lhp, Miami**
11. **Jason Rice, rhp, Chaffey (Calif.) JC**
12. **Sheldon Catchot, lhp, Delgado (La.) JC**
13. Joey Fernandez, 1b, Braddock HS, Miami
14. **Derek Rodriguez, rhp, Nevada-Las Vegas**
15. **Chris Carter, 3b, Sierra Vista HS, Las Vegas**
16. **Alex Woodson, lhp, Porterville (Calif.) CC**
17. Enrique Garcia, rhp, Potomac State (W.Va.) JC
18. **Tim Sabo, rhp, Seton Hall**
19. Jordan Danks, of, Round Rock (Texas) HS
20. **Josh Morgan, of, South Alabama**
21. **Raleigh Evans, lhp, Lake City (Fla.) CC**
22. **Christian Marrero, of, Broward (Fla.) JC**
23. Bobby LaFromboise, lhp, Rio Hondo (Calif.) JC
24. Tyler Wright, of, Charlotte HS, Punta Gorda, Fla.
25. Andrew Beatty, lhp, West High, Aurora, Ill.
26. **Anthony Carter, rhp, Georgia Perimeter JC**
27. **Daniel Jordan, c, Broward (Fla.) CC**
28. Justin Sincock, rhp, Golden West (Calif.) JC
29. Aljay Davis, 2b, Northeastern Oklahoma A&M JC
30. Brandon Langston, rhp, Cleveland State (Tenn.) CC
31. Lucas Luetge, lhp, Bellville HS, Industry, Texas
32. Matt Headley, lhp, San Jacinto (Texas) JC
33. Scott Savastano, ss, Plymouth (Mass.) North HS
34. **Tim Day, rhp, Michigan State**
35. **Marcos Causey, of, South Florida CC**
36. Nate Templeton, rhp, Valley HS, Des Monies, Iowa
37. Brian Flores, lhp, New Mexico JC
38. **Enrique Escolano, rhp, Kell HS, Kennesaw, Ga.**
39. Jovan Rosa, ss, East Hartford (Conn.) HS
40. Rafael Vera, 2b, Sarasota (Fla.) HS
41. **Kris Welker, c, Iowa**
42. Michael Kelly, lhp, Lafayette HS, Mayo, Fla.
43. Brooks Dunn, lhp, Mississippi State
44. Drew George, ss, Lower Columbia (Wash.) CC
45. Cody Wright, lhp, Bountiful, Utah
46. Brendon O'Donnell, of, Santa Barbara (Calif.) CC
47. John Wolff, 2b, Harvard
48. Chris Cassidy, lhp, Claremont (Calif.) HS
49. **Steven Squires, rhp, Wayne State (Mich.)**
50. Kyle Landers, lhp, Noblesville (Ind.) HS

CINCINNATI REDS

June—Regular Phase (12)

1. **Jay Bruce, of, West Brook HS, Beaumont, Texas**
2. **Travis Wood, lhp, Bryant HS, Alexander, Ark.**
3. **Zach Ward, rhp, Gardner-Webb**
4. **Sam LeCure, rhp, Texas**
5. **James Avery, rhp, Niagara**
6. **Jeff Stevens, rhp, Loyola Marymount**
7. **Brandon Roberts, of, Cal Poly**
8. **Michael Jones, ss, Wayne County HS, Jesup, Ga.**
9. **Milton Loo, 3b, Yavapai (Ariz.) CC**
10. **Bo Lanier, rhp, Georgia**
11. **Carlos Fisher, rhp, Lewis-Clark State (Idaho)**
12. **Adam Rosales, ss, Western Michigan**
13. **Logan Ondrusek, rhp, McLennan (Texas) CC**
14. **Michael Griffin, 2b, Baylor**
15. **Michael DeJesus, 2b, Coastal Carolina**
16. **Jason Vecchio, rhp, Texas-San Antonio**
17. **David Wilson, lhp, Lander (S.C.)**
18. **Kevyn Feiner, ss, Sun Prairie (Wis.) HS**
19. **Eric Eymann, ss, Kansas State**
20. **Ben Mummy, 1b, Nevada**
21. **Ben Blumenthal, c, Erskine (S.C.)**
22. **Robbie Nickols, lhp, Pima (Ariz.) CC**
23. **James Morris, lhp, Illinois**
24. Kyle Ginley, rhp, St. Petersburg JC
25. **Taylor Johnson, of, Washington**
26. Matthew Salmon, of, South Aiken HS, Aiken, S.C.
27. Kenny Smalley, rhp, St. Charles (Ill.) HS
28. Henry-Judsen Smith, rhp, Phoenix JC
29. **Russ Haltiwanger, rhp, Newberry (S.C.)**
30. **Mark Rodriguez, c, Texas-Pan American**
31. **Abe Woody, rhp, Baylor**
32. **Chris Denove, c, UCLA**
33. Leroy Hunt, of, Linden HS, Stockton, Calif.
34. **Brandon Camardese, lhp, Miami**
35. **Angel Colon, 3b, Iowa Wesleyan**
36. Lorenzo Douglas, rhp, Sachse HS, Garland, Texas
37. **Jacob Long, c, Modesto (Calif.) JC**
38. Kuyaunnis Miles, of, Russell County HS, Phenix City, Ala.
39. Edwin Quirarte, rhp, Oxnard (Calif.) HS
40. **Angel Cabrera, ss, Connors State (Okla.) JC**
41. **Justin Tordi, ss, Florida**
42. John Axford, rhp, Notre Dame
43. Clay Long, rhp, Chipola (Fla.) JC
44. Jason Erickson, rhp, White River HS, Buckley, Wash.
45. Andre Lamontagne, rhp, Righetti HS, Santa Maria, Calif.
46. J.W. Brown, 1b, Howard (Texas) JC
47. **Matt Garrett, of, Grand Rapids (Mich.) CC**
48. Gary Poynter, rhp, Marcus HS, Flower Mound, Texas
49. Cody Allen, of, Coleman (Mich.) HS
50. Jacob Christensen, of, Lockport Township (Ill.) HS

CLEVELAND INDIANS

June—Regular Phase (14)

1. **Trevor Crowe, of, Arizona**
1. **John Drennen, of, Rancho Bernardo HS, San Diego** (Supplemental pick—33rd—for loss of Type A free agent Omar Vizquel)
2. **Stephen Head, 1b, Mississippi**
3. **Nick Weglarz, 1b, Lakeshore Catholic HS, Stevensville, Ontario**
3. **Jensen Lewis, rhp, Vanderbilt** (Pick from Giants as compensation for Vizquel)
4. **Jordan Brown, 1b, Arizona**
5. **Kevin Dixon, rhp, Minnesota State-Mankato**
6. **Joe Ness, rhp, Ball State**
7. **James Deters, rhp, Calvin (Mich.)**
8. **Ryan Edell, lhp, College of Charleston**
9. **Roman Pena, of, Mongomery HS, San Diego**
10. **Jason Schutt, rhp, Central Missouri State**
11. **Nick Petrucci, 3b, JC of the Canyons (Calif.)**
12. **Matt Fornasiere, ss, Minnesota**
13. Barry Laird, rhp, Lee HS, Baytown, Texas
14. **Mike Finocchi, rhp, Louisburg (N.C.) JC**
15. Chase Phillips, rhp, Monterey HS, Lubbock, Texas
16. Aaron Shafer, rhp, Troy Buchanan HS, Moscow Mills, Mo.
17. Eric Barrett, lhp, Marion (Ill.) HS
18. Desmond Jennings, of, Pinson Valley HS, Pinson, Ala.
19. Tim Dennehy, lhp, Oak Park-River Forest HS, Oak Park, Ill.
20. **Scott Sumner, rhp, Louisiana College**
21. **Neil Wagner, rhp, North Dakota State**
22. Clint Storr, of, Key West (Fla.) HS

23. Dexter English, of, Encinal HS, Suisun City, Calif.
24. Willie Hale, rhp, Alexander HS, Albany, Ohio
25. **Andy Lytle, ss, Iowa**
26. **Thomas Cowley, lhp, Oklahoma State**
27. Brandon Laird, 1b, La Quinta HS, Garden Grove, Calif.
28. Angel Claudio, rhp, Puerto Rico Baseball Academy, Caguas, P.R.
29. John Curtis, c, Cal State Fullerton
30. Joel Martin, lhp, Marion Center HS, Homer, Pa.
31. **Matt Loberg, rhp, Minnesota**
32. **Brent Thomas, of, Texas Tech**
33. **Trevor Mortensen, of, Cal State Fullerton**
34. Arshwin Asjes, rhp, Gloucester County (N.J.) CC
35. Levi Laughlin, rhp, Connors State (Okla.) JC
36. Matt Yokley, rhp, Collierville (Tenn.) HS
37. Cody Satterwhite, rhp, Hillcrest Christian HS, Jackson, Miss.
38. Daniel Lima, ss, Florida Christian HS, Miami
39. Jessie Mier, c, Irvine Valley (Calif.) JC
40. DeWayne Carver, rhp, Oklahoma State
41. Ashton Shewey, lhp, Chandler-Gilbert (Ariz.) CC
42. Tim Lincecum, rhp, Washington
43. Chadd Hartman, of, Olympia HS, Windermere, Fla.
44. Travis Turek, rhp, Westlake HS, Westlake Village, Calif.
45. Drew Fiorenza, rhp, Clemson
46. Blake Davis, ss, Cal State Fullerton
47. Gus Milner, of, Kansas
48. Joseph Hunter, of, Mississippi State
49. Ryan Wood, ss, Hylton HS, Woodbridge, Va.
50. Cameron Satterwhite, of, Moeller HS, Cincinnati

COLORADO ROCKIES

June—Regular Phase (7)

1. **Troy Tulowitzki, ss, Long Beach State**
1. **Chaz Roe, rhp, Lafayette HS, Lexington, Ky.** (Supplemental pick—32nd—for loss of Type A free agent Vinny Castilla)
2. **Daniel Carte, of, Winthrop** (Pick from Nationals as compensation for Castilla)
2. **Zach Simons, rhp, Everett (Wash.) CC**
3. **Kyle Hancock, rhp, Rowlett (Texas) HS**
4. **Brandon Durden, lhp, Georgia College & State**
5. **Josh Sullivan, rhp, Auburn**
6. **Corey Wimberly, 2b, Alcorn State**
7. **Geoff Strickland, ss, Florida Southern**
8. **James Burok, rhp, Old Dominion**
9. **Andrew Johnston, rhp, Missouri**
10. **Garner Wetzel, ss, Millsaps (Miss.)**
11. **Chris Frey, of, Arizona**
12. Dominick Foster, rhp, Fresno (Calif.) CC
13. **Mike Paulk, of, Cal State Northridge**
14. **Kyle Blumenthal, c, Cal Poly**
15. **Travis Becktel, of, San Jose State**
16. **Bret Berglund, of, Cal Poly**
17. **Jimmy Freeman, lhp, Washington State**
18. **Brett Strickland, rhp, Georgia State**
19. **Byron Binda, rhp, Coastal Carolina**
20. **Andrew Kreidermacher, rhp, Minnesota State-Mankato**
21. Chris Martin, rhp, McLennan (Texas) CC
22. **Radames Nazario, ss, Pimentel HS, Naguabo, P.R.**
23. **Phil Cuadrado, 3b, Cumberland (Tenn.)**
24. Sean Toler, rhp, Parkway South HS, Manchester, Mo.
25. **Steven Hirschfeld, rhp, CC of Southern Nevada**
26. **Ethan Katz, rhp, Cal State Sacramento**
27. **Sean Ruthven, rhp, Georgia**
28. **David Bechtold, lhp, Liberty**
29. Reese Havens, ss, Bishop England HS, Charleston, S.C.
30. **Michael Milliron, ss, Penn State**
31. Sean Halton, 1b, Fresno (Calif.) HS
32. Jarrad Page, of, UCLA
33. Jordan Jarvis, rhp, Arcadia HS, Phoenix
34. Kyle Beitey, lhp, Lower Columbia (Wash.) JC
35. Tim Brewer, rhp, Kean HS, St. Thomas, Virgin Islands
36. **Chris Cook, 1b, Grand Canyon (Ariz.)**
37. C.J. Belanger, of, Cypress HS, Stanton, Calif.
38. Barret Browning, lhp, Florida State
39. Rod Scurry, rhp, Sierra (Calif.) JC
40. Joseph Servais, c, Garden City (Kan.) CC
41. Jeremy Farrell, 3b, St. Ignatius HS, Cleveland
42. Maikol Gonzalez, ss, Louisburg (N.C.) JC
43. Jordan Rogers, rhp, Dayton (Texas) HS
44. Philip Myers, lhp, Ballard HS, Louisville
45. Chris Bell, of, Johnson HS, Gainesville, Ga.
46. Garrett Vaughan, c, Sibley (La.) HS
47. Brent Weiss, 2b, St. Joseph Regional HS, Suffern, N.Y.
48. Spencer Schuh, rhp, Harrison (Ark.) HS
49. Jordan Moore, lhp, Spokane Falls (Wash.) CC
50. James Pollack, c, North Broward Prep, Parkland, Fla.

DETROIT TIGERS

June—Regular Phase (10)

1. **Cameron Maybin, of, T.C. Roberson HS, Arden, N.C.**
2. (Pick to Angels as compensation for Type A free agent Troy Percival)
3. **Chris Robinson, c, Illinois**
4. **Kevin Whelan, rhp, Texas A&M**
5. **Jeff Larish, 1b, Arizona State**
6. **Clete Thomas, of, Auburn**
7. **P.J. Finigan, rhp, Southern Illinois**
8. **Brendan Wise, rhp, Pratt (Kan.) JC**
9. Paul Coleman, lhp, Pepperdine
10. **Kevin Ardoin, rhp, Louisiana-Lafayette**
11. **Anthony Claggett, rhp, UC Riverside**
12. **Matt Joyce, of, Florida Southern**
13. **Louis Ott, ss, Sacramento CC**
14. **Casper Wells, of, Towson**
15. Ben Petralli, c, Sacramento CC
16. **Michael Hollimon, ss, Oral Roberts**
17. Warner Jones, 2b, Vanderbilt
18. **Agustin Guzman, 2b, Baton Rouge (La.) CC**
19. **Burke Badenhop, rhp, Bowling Green State**
20. **Erik Averill, lhp, Arizona State**
21. David Adams, ss, Grandview Prep, Boca Raton, Fla.
22. **Matt Norfleet, rhp, Tennessee Wesleyan**
23. **Mark Haske, ss, Cincinnati**
24. Brett Bordes, lhp, Arizona State
25. **Jacob Baxter, rhp, Texas-Arlington**
26. **Schuyler Williamson, c, U.S. Military Academy**
27. **Will Rhymes, 2b, William & Mary**
28. Ryan Paul, lhp, Los Angeles Pierce JC
29. Eric Fry, of, Barbe HS, Lake Charles, La.
30. **Ryan Roberson, 1b, George Washington**
31. **Tim Robertson, rhp, Oral Roberts**
32. **Chris Torres, c, Cumberland (Tenn.)**
33. **Loren Fraser, rhp, UC Santa Barbara**
34. Alex Avila, 3b, Archbishop McCarthy HS, Pembroke Pines, Fla.
35. **Jeffrey Hahn, rhp, Clemson**
36. **Gibbs Wilson, rhp, Weatherford (Texas) JC**
37. Jeff Kunkel, c, Michigan
38. Zach Putnam, rhp, Pioneer HS, Ann Arbor, Mich.
39. Kiel Renfro, rhp, Texarkana (Texas) CC
40. Kyle Peter, of, Cloud County (Texas) CC
41. Tony Pechek, c, South HS, Pueblo, Colo.
42. Ben Rodewald, rhp, East Kenwood (Mich.) HS
43. Ryan Perry, ss, Rocklin (Calif.) HS
44. Adrian Casanova, c, Clemson
45. Tyson Jaquez, 3b, Loyalton (Calif.) HS
46. David Mattox, rhp, North Arkansas CC
47. Albert Gonzalez, 2b, American Senior HS, Hialeah, Fla.
48. Kevin Hammons, rhp, Sierra (Calif.) JC
49. Anthony Capra, lhp, Arvada West High, Arvada, Colo.
50. Jeff Whitlow, of, Detroit Country Day HS, Southfield, Mich.

FLORIDA MARLINS

June—Regular Phase (16)

1. **Chris Volstad, rhp, Palm Beach Gardens (Fla.) HS**
1. **Aaron Thompson, lhp, Second Baptist HS, Houston** (Pick from Giants as compensation for Type A free agent Armando Benitez)

1. **Jacob Marceaux, rhp, McNeese State** (Pick from Yankees as compensation for Type A free agent Carl Pavano)
1. **Ryan Tucker, rhp, Temple City (Calif.) HS** (Supplemental pick—34th—for loss of Benitez)
1. **Sean West, lhp, Captain Shreve HS, Shreveport, La.** (Supplemental pick—44th—for loss of Pavano)
2. **Kris Harvey, of, Clemson**
2. **Brett Hayes, c, Nevada** (Supplemental pick—79th—for loss of Type C free agent Mike Redmond)
3. **Matt Goyen, lhp, Georgia College & State**
4. **Gaby Sanchez, c, Miami**
5. **Kyle Winters, rhp, Pomona HS, Arvada, Colo.**
6. **James Guerrero, 2b, San Diego State**
7. **Chris Leroux, rhp, Winthrop**
8. Aaron Bates, 1b, North Carolina State
9. **Jim Brauer, rhp, Michigan**
10. **Cody Allen, 3b, Elk Grove (Calif.) HS**
11. **Andy Jenkins, c, Oregon State**
12. Kyle Marlatt, rhp, Texas A&M
13. **Jeff Van Houten, of, Arizona**
14. **Travis Talbott, lhp, California**
15. **Paul Witt, ss, Baylor**
16. **Jonathon Lewis, rhp, Stony Brook**
17. **Zac McCamie, rhp, South Carolina**
18. **Kyle Padgett, ss, William & Mary**
19. **Adam Wood, lhp, South Alabama**
20. **Rafael Galbizo, rhp, Miami**
21. **Colin Roberson, of, Virginia Wesleyan**
22. **Logan Morrison, 1b, Northshore HS, Slidell, La.**
23. **Justin Webb, c, North Carolina**
24. **Matt Kutler, of, Brown**
25. **Blake Jones, rhp, Northwestern State**
26. **Scott Lindeen, rhp, La Verne (Calif.)**
27. **Jason Jarrett, rhp, Virginia Wesleyan**
28. Michael Thomasson, of, Laney (Calif.) JC
29. Jared Wesson, lhp, Itawamba (Miss.) CC
30. **Chris Haupt, c, Central Columbia HS, Bloomsburg, Pa.**
31. Matt Jones, lhp, Guildford Park SS, Surrey, B.C
32. **Adalberto Flores, rhp, Gurabo, P.R.**
33. **Adam Howard, c, St. Louis CC-Meramec**
34. Adam Abraham, 3b, Grosse Point (Mich.) South HS
35. Jacob Taylor, c, Chaffey (Calif.) JC
36. Sean Boatright, of, Long Beach State
37. **Josh Short, of, Marysville-Pilchuck HS, Marysville, Wash.**
38. Steven Pujol, lhp, San Fernando (Calif.) HS
39. Jonathan Prevost, of, Ahunstic (Quebec) JC
40. Eric Basurto, rhp, Chabot (Calif.) JC
41. Luis Ramos, of, Jose de Diego HS, Mayaguez, P.R.
42. David Woods, c, West Lauderdale HS, Bailey, Miss.
43. Zach Barrett, 3b, Olney Central (Ill.) JC
44. Ryan Pollard, lhp, Illinois Central JC
45. Brady Decker, rhp, Olney (Ill.) Central CC
46. Stephen Schneider, 1b, Orange Coast (Calif.) CC
47. Dustin Kaats, 2b, Desert Mountain HS, Scottsdale, Ariz.
48. Chris Bodishbaugh, rhp, Los Medanos (Calif.) JC
49. James Wallace, rhp, Benicia (Calif.) HS
50. Jared Banks, rhp, Los Medanos (Calif.) JC

HOUSTON ASTROS

June—Regular Phase (24)

1. **Brian Bogusevic, lhp, Tulane**
1. **Eli Iorg, of, Tennessee** (Supplemental pick—38th—for loss of Type A free agent Carlos Beltran)
2. **Ralph Henriquez, c, Key West (Fla.) HS**
3. **Tommy Manzella, ss, Tulane** (Pick from Mets as compensation for Beltran)
3. Josh Lindblom, rhp, Harrison HS, West Lafayette, Ind.
4. **Josh Flores, of, Triton (Ill.) JC**
5. **Billy Hart, 3b, Southern California**
6. **Brandon Barnes, of, Cypress (Calif.) JC**
7. **Tim Johnson, ss, Wissahickon HS, Penllyn, Pa.**
8. **Koby Clemens, 3b, Memorial HS, Houston**
9. Jordan Meaker, rhp, Flower Mound (Texas) HS
10. **Allen Langdon, of, Eagle HS, Boise, Idaho**
11. **Cory Lapinski, lhp, Illinois Wesleyan**
12. **Tip Fairchild, rhp, Southern Maine**
13. **Eric King, ss, Tennessee**
14. **Mark Ori, 1b, Northwestern**
15. **Eric Sheridan, rhp, Saddleback (Calif.) CC**
16. **Aaron Bulkley, of, Le Moyne**
17. **Andy Kroeker, c, Biola (Calif.)**
18. Brian Needham, rhp, John Foster Dulles HS, Sugar Land, Texas
19. **Drew Himes, rhp, Illinois Wesleyan**
20. **Ryan Mitchell, rhp, Magnolia (Texas) HS**
21. **Scott Sarver, lhp, Cal State Fullerton**
22. T.J. Steele, of, Canyon del Oro HS, Oro Valley, Ariz.
23. **Chris Blazek, lhp, Vermont**
24. **Sean Walker, rhp, Baylor**
25. **Jacob Hurry, lhp, Coastal Carolina**
26. **Michael Thompson, 3b, Santa Clara**
27. Matt Luca, rhp, Nevada-Las Vegas
28. Eric Baker, 2b, Mansfield (Pa.)
29. **Jamie Gant, rhp, Mississippi State**
30. **Matt Hirsh, rhp, California Lutheran**
31. Brad Stone, rhp, Quincy (Ill.)
32. **Cole Graham, 1b, Triton (Ill.) JC**
33. **Reid Kelly, rhp, Desert Mountain HS, Scottsdale, Ariz.**
34. **Nathan Warrick, of, Texas-Arlington**
35. **Andy Darnell, of, Chabot (Calif.) JC**
36. **Matt Cunningham, of, UC Riverside**
37. Matt Bishop, rhp, Endicott (Mass.)
38. Mike Colla, rhp, Clovis West HS, Fresno, Calif.
39. Zachary Williams, rhp, Seminole State (Okla.) CC
40. Collin Fanning, of, Clarendon (Texas) JC
41. Casey McCleskey, of, Temple (Texas) JC
42. **Brandon Stricklen, rhp, Texas Southern**
43. Jacob Hower, rhp, American River (Calif.) JC
44. Nicholas Cobler, lhp, Northeast Texas CC
45. Craig Herrforth, rhp, Arrowhead Union HS, Hartland, Wis.
46. Wes Musick, lhp, Hudson HS, Lufkin, Texas

KANSAS CITY ROYALS

June—Regular Phase (2)

1. **Alex Gordon, 3b, Nebraska**
2. **Jeff Bianchi, ss, Lampeter-Strasburg HS, Lancaster, Pa.**
3. **Chris Nicoll, rhp, UC Irvine**
4. **Joe Dickerson, of, Esperanza HS, Yorba Linda, Calif.**
5. **Shawn Hayes, ss, Franklin Pierce (N.H.)**
6. **Ryan DiPietro, lhp, Eastern Connecticut State**
7. **Brent Fisher, lhp, Tolleson Union HS, Goodyear, Ariz.**
8. **Nick Doscher, c, Moore Catholic HS, Staten Island, N.Y.**
9. **Kiel Thibault, c, Gonzaga**
10. **Jeff Howell, c, Florida Southern**
11. **Michael Penn, rhp, Michigan**
12. **Cody Harkcom, rhp, New Mexico JC**
13. **Andrew Larsen, of, Stony Brook**
14. **Antonio Sabatini, of, Erskine (S.C.)**
15. **Brady Everett, c, Washington State**
16. **Mario Santiago, rhp, Baton Rouge (La.) CC**
17. Miguel Vasquez, ss, Dewitt Clinton HS, Bronx, N.Y.
18. **Paul Raglione, rhp, Grant HS, Portland, Ore.**
19. Zane Chavez, c, Fallbrook (Calif.) HS
20. **Bryan Casey, rhp, Arizona Western JC**
21. **David Henninger, rhp, Messiah (Pa.)**
22. Justin Bristow, ss, Mills Godwin HS, Richmond, Va.
23. **Matt Kniginyzky, rhp, High Point (N.C.)**
24. **Josh Colafemina, ss, St. Rose (N.Y.)**
25. **Kevin Bulger, rhp, College of Charleston**
26. Jake McLintock, rhp, San Diego State
27. **Jase Turner, 1b, Pomona-Pitzer (Calif.)**
28. **Felix Peguero, of, Oklahoma Baptist**
29. **Brandon Brantley, rhp, Science and Arts of Oklahoma**
30. **Jeremy Jirschele, 2b, Wisconsin-Oshkosh**
31. **Pedro Lopez, ss, Universidad del Turabo HS, Toa Baja, P.R.**
32. Michael Dubee, rhp, Okaloosa-Walton (Fla.) CC
33. **Danny Gutierrez, rhp, Rubidoux HS, Riverside, Calif.**
34. **Oscar Marrero, c, Juan Antonio Corretjer HS, Ciales, P.R.**
35. Luke Burnett, rhp, Carthage (Texas) HS

36. Matt Klimas, c, Broken Arrow (Okla.) HS
37. Nickolas Love, of, Enterprise (Ala.) HS
38. Jacob Myking, c, San Joaquin Delta (Calif.) JC
39. Steve Teno, lhp, St. Thomas of Villanova HS, LaSalle, Ontario
40. Nick Romero, ss, Eastlake HS, Chula Vista, Calif.
41. Anthony Rodriguez, ss, Puerto Rico Baseball Academy, Vega Baja, P.R.
42. David McClain, rhp, North Shore HS, Houston
43. Tyler Backus, rhp, Mingus Union HS, Cottonwood, Ariz.
44. Mark Serrano, rhp, Cypress (Calif.) CC
45. Eric Martinez, rhp, Eastlake HS, Chula Vista, Calif.
46. Bryan Paukovits, rhp, El Capitan HS, Lakeside, Calif.
47. Kip Masuda, c, Mid-Pacific Institute, Kaneohe, Hawaii
48. Chester Wilson, 1b, St. Louis HS, Honolulu
49. Matthew Gibbs, rhp, Modesto (Calif.) JC
50. Juan Perez, rhp, Jose Rojas Cortez HS, Orocovis, P.R.

LOS ANGELES ANGELS

June—Regular Phase (23)

1. (Pick to Red Sox as compensation for Type A free agent Orlando Cabrera)
1. **Trevor Bell, rhp, Crescenta Valley HS, La Crescenta, Calif.** (Supplemental pick—37th—for loss of Type A free agent Troy Percival)
2. **Ryan Mount, ss, Ayala HS, Chino Hills, Calif.** (Pick from Tigers as compensation for Percival)
2. **P.J. Phillips, ss, Redan HS, Stone Mountain, Ga.**
3. **Sean O'Sullivan, rhp, Valhalla HS, El Cajon, Calif.**
4. Brian Matusz, lhp, St. Mary's HS, Cave Creek, Ariz.
5. **Tommy Mendoza, rhp, Monsignor Pace HS, Miami**
6. **Jerome Moore, of, North Caddo HS, Vivian, La.**
7. **Robert Romero, rhp, Grayson County (Texas) CC**
8. Matt Hall, ss, Horizon HS, Scottsdale, Ariz.
9. **Bobby Mosebach, rhp, Hillsborough (Fla.) CC**
10. **Peter Bourjos, of, Notre Dame HS, Scottsdale, Ariz.**
11. Tim Murphy, of, Rancho Buena Vista HS, Vista, Calif.
12. **Greg Dini, c, Tulane**
13. Bryce Cox, rhp, Rice
14. Stephen Brock, rhp, Chipola (Fla.) JC
15. **Brad Coon, of, Trevecca Nazarene (Tenn.)**
16. **Darrell Sales, 1b, West Valley (Calif.) CC**
17. **Ryan Pressley, 1b, Evans HS, Martinez, Ga.**
18. **Jim West, rhp, Chandler-Gilbert (Ariz.) CC**
19. **Anthony Sullivan, rhp, St. John's**
20. Martinez Allen, of, North Florida JC
21. Bradley Suttle, 3b, Boerne (Texas) HS
22. Chris Nash, 1b, Marquette HS, Chesterfield, Mo.
23. Deunte Heath, rhp, Lake City (Fla.) CC
24. **Dallas Morris, 3b, Louisiana-Lafayette**
25. **Brok Butcher, rhp, Oxnard (Calif.) JC**
26. **Kevin Lynch, rhp, Florida State**
27. **Colby Overstreet, 1b, Oklahoma City**
28. Blair Brejtfus, rhp, Arcadia HS, Phoenix
29. Vincent Scarduzio, 1b, Broward (Fla.) CC
30. Neil Medchill, c, Lake Orion HS, Oxford, Mich.
31. **Tim Didjurgis, rhp, Regis (Colo.)**
32. Braden Wells, of, Dixie State (Utah) JC
33. **Marco Albano, ss, Boston College**
34. Brian Schlitter, rhp, Lake City (Fla.) CC
35. Chris Davis, 3b, Navarro (Texas) JC
36. **Jacob Dixon, rhp, North Florida**
37. **Jeremy Haynes, rhp, Tallahassee (Fla.) CC**
38. **Flint Wipke, c, Georgia Southern**
39. Brent Milleville, c, Maize HS, Wichita, Kan.
40. Rian Kiniry, of, Chaminade-Madonna Prep, Hollywood, Fla.
41. Joseph Klein, rhp, Patuxent HS, Lusby, Md.
42. Carlos Del Rosario, of, George Washington HS, New York
43. Brent Solich, lhp, Manatee (Fla.) JC
44. Michael Bunton, lhp, Tallahassee (Fla.) CC
45. Shay Conder, c, American Fork (Utah) HS
46. Julian Laurean, 2b, Chandler-Gilbert (Ariz.) CC
47. **Seth Loman, 1b, Lamar (Colo.) CC**
48. **Cody Fuller, of, Texas Tech**
49. Anthony Vasquez, of, Ronald Reagan HS, San Antonio
50. Buster Posey, rhp, Lee County HS, Leesburg, Ga.

LOS ANGELES DODGERS

June—Regular Phase (26)

1. (Pick to Red Sox as compensation for Type A free agent Derek Lowe)
1. Luke Hochevar, rhp, Tennessee (Supplemental pick—40th—for loss of Type A free agent Adrian Beltre)
2. **Ivan DeJesus Jr., ss, Puerto Rico Baseball Academy, Guaynabo, P.R.** (Pick from Mariners as compensation for Beltre)
2. **Josh Wall, rhp, Central Private HS, Walker, La.**
3. **Sergio Pedroza, of, Cal State Fullerton**
4. **Josh Bell, 3b, Santaluces HS, Lantana, Fla.**
5. **John Meloan, rhp, Arizona**
6. **Brent Leach, lhp, Delta State (Miss.)**
7. **Chris Hobdy, rhp, Monterey HS, Lubbock, Texas**
8. **David Horlacher, rhp, Brigham Young**
9. Michael Davitt, rhp, Davidson HS, Mobile, Ala.
10. **Trayvon Robinson, of, Crenshaw HS, Los Angeles**
11. **Adam Godwin, of, Troy**
12. **Kris Krise, rhp, Chico State (Calif.)**
13. **Steve Johnson, rhp, St. Paul's HS, Brooklynville, Md.**
14. **Scott Van Slyke, of, John Burroughs HS, Ladue, Mo.**
15. **Wilfredo Diaz, lhp, Puerto Rico Baseball Academy, Caguas, P.R.**
16. George McDonald, c, Westchester HS, Playa Del Rey, Calif.
17. Kyle Henson, c, Oak Ridge HS, Conroe, Texas
18. Kevin Carby, ss, Booker T. Washington HS, Tulsa, Okla.
19. **Drew Locke, of, Boston College**
20. **Schuyler Tripp, lhp, Davis County HS, Drakesville, Iowa**
21. **Shane Justis, ss, Towson**
22. Travis DeBondt, of, Oral Roberts
23. Jayson Whitehouse, of, Spartanburg Methodist (S.C.) JC
24. **Jon Dutton, lhp, Rancho Bernardo HS, San Diego**
25. Kyle Foster, lhp, Lower Columbia (Wash.) JC
26. Jordy Mercer, ss, Taloga (Okla.) HS
27. Matthew Coburn, rhp, Humble (Texas) HS
28. Timothy Segelke, lhp, Green River (Wash.) CC
29. Kent Williamson, rhp, Hayden HS, Topeka, Kan.
30. Kyle Morgan, of, Bakersfield (Calif.) JC
31. Jonathan Forest, rhp, British Columbia
32. Nathan Hammons, lhp, Fort Cobb (Okla.) Broxton HS
33. Chris Lemay, lhp, Kwantlen (B.C.) JC
34. Shawn Loglisci, rhp, JC of Southern Idaho
35. **Rick Taloa, 1b, Santa Ana (Calif.) JC**
36. Andrew Marquardt, rhp, St. Francis HS, Sierra Madre, Calif.
37. Justin Wilson, lhp, Buchanan HS, Clovis, Calif.
38. Stephen Hermann, c, Penn Trafford HS, Harrison City, Pa.
39. Jake Debus, lhp, Victor J. Andrew HS, Tinley Park, Ill.
40. **Jason Mooneyham, 1b, Chapman (Calif.)**
41. Chris Johnson, rhp, John A. Logan (Ill.) JC
42. Arnoldi Cruz, c, Okaloosa-Walton (Fla.) CC
43. Brandon Rocha, c, Los Alamitos (Calif.) HS
44. Chase D'Arnaud, ss, Los Alamitos (Calif.) HS
45. **Brian Mathews, 3b, Newton County HS, Covington, Ga.**
46. Anthony Benner, 3b, Eastlake HS, Chula Vista, Calif.
47. Mark Sunga, 3b, Notre Dame HS, Van Nuys, Calif.
48. Paul Wourms, c, Thompson River (B.C.)
49. Garet Hill, rhp, Biola (Calif.)
50. Mitch Houck, lhp, Cypress Bay HS, Weston, Fla.

MILWAUKEE BREWERS

June—Regular Phase (5)

1. **Ryan Braun, 3b, Miami**
2. (Pick to Athletics as compensation for Type A free agent Damian Miller)
3. **Will Inman, rhp, Tunstall HS, Dry Fork, Va.**
4. **Mat Gamel, 3b, Chipola (Fla.) JC**
5. **Kevin Roberts, rhp, Houston**
6. **Steve Hammond, lhp, Long Beach State**
7. **Michael Brantley, of, Fort Pierce Central HS, Port St. Lucie, Fla.**

8. Jemile Weeks, ss, Lake Brantley HS, Altamonte Springs, Fla.
9. **Carlos Hereaud, 2b, Elkins HS, Missouri City, Texas**
10. **Steve Garrison, lhp, The Hun School, Princeton, N.J.**
11. Brent Allar, rhp, Weatherford (Texas) JC
12. **John Alonso, 1b, Polk (Fla.) CC**
13. Ryan Babineau, c, Etiwanda HS, Alta Loma, Calif.
14. **Mark James, rhp, Sinclair SS, Whitby, Ontario**
15. **Michael Bell, 3b, Grayson County (Texas) CC**
16. Andrew Bailey, rhp, Wagner
17. Tim Smith, of, Midland (Texas) CC
18. **Zach Braddock, lhp, Gloucester Catholic HS, Southampton, N.J.**
19. **Patrick Ryan, rhp, Embry-Riddle (Fla.)**
20. **David Welch, lhp, Texarkana (Texas) CC**
21. Justin Stires, rhp, Saddleback (Calif.) CC
22. **Kenny Holmberg, 2b, Embry-Riddle (Fla.)**
23. **Brendan Katin, of, Miami**
24. Mike Ramlow, lhp, Owens (Ohio) CC
25. **Taylor Green, 2b, Cypress (Calif.) JC**
26. Jake Arrieta, rhp, Weatherford (Texas) JC
27. **Brad Willcutt, c, Southern Mississippi**
28. **Scott McKnight, ss, Saddleback (Calif.) CC**
29. **Dane Renkert, rhp, Washington State**
30. **Omar Aguilar, rhp, Merced (Calif.) JC**
31. Patrick Murray, 1b, Marina HS, Huntington Beach, Calif.
32. Spencer Pennington, of, Alabama
33. Jorge Core, rhp, Puerto Rico Baseball Academy, Bayamon, P.R.
34. **Brock Kjeldgaard, rhp, Indian Hills (Iowa) CC**
35. Sebastien Vendette, rhp, Northeastern Oklahoma A&M JC
36. Stephen Barnes, rhp, Lake City (Fla.) CC
37. Chris Hopkins, of, Sierra (Calif.) JC
38. **Christopher Jean, rhp, Texas State**
39. **Brad Miller, ss, Cowley County (Kan.) CC**
40. **Ryan Crew, ss, Texas-San Antonio**
41. Jordan Lennerton, 1b, El Paso (Texas) CC
42. Chris Copot, c, Lethbridge (Alberta) CC
43. Kyle Eveland, 2b, Palmdale (Calif.) HS
44. George Washington, of, Demopolis HS, Boligee, Ala.
45. **Ulrich Snijders, c, St. Petersburg (Fla.) JC**
46. Alex Lowrey, of, Monsignor Pace HS, Opa Locka, Fla.
47. Matt Broughton, rhp, Triton Central HS, Indianapolis
48. Frederick Lewis, lhp, Buchholz HS, Gainesville, Fla.
49. Cory Large, lhp, Bell HS, Bedford, Texas
50. Garret Regan, of, Sir Winston Churchill HS, Calgary, Alberta

MINNESOTA TWINS

June—Regular Phase (25)

1. **Matt Garza, rhp, Fresno State**
1. **Hank Sanchez, 1b, Mission Bay HS, San Diego** (Supplemental pick—39th—for loss of Type A free agent Corey Koskie)
2. **Paul Kelly, ss, Flower Mound (Texas) HS** (Pick from Blue Jays as compensation for Koskie)
2. **Kevin Slowey, rhp, Winthrop**
2. **Drew Thompson, ss, Jupiter Community HS, Tequesta, Fla.** (Supplemental pick—80th—for loss of Type C free agent Henry Blanco)
3. **Brian Duensing, lhp, Nebraska** (Pick from Nationals as compensation for Type B free agent Cristian Guzman)
3. **Ryan Mullins, lhp, Vanderbilt**
4. **Caleb Moore, c, East Tennessee State**
5. **Steven Tolleson, ss, South Carolina**
6. **J.W. Wilson, of, Midland (Texas) HS**
7. **Greg Yersich, c, Andrean HS, Merrillville, Ind.**
8. **Danny Powers, rhp, Central Missouri State**
9. **Erik Lis, 1b, Evansville**
10. **Matt Betsill, 3b, Furman**
11. **Brian Kirwan, rhp, Santa Fe Christian HS, Del Mar, Calif.**
12. **Alex Burnett, rhp, Ocean View HS, Huntington Beach, Calif.**
13. **Michael Allen, rhp, Arlington Country Day HS, Jacksonville**
14. David Duncan, lhp, New Richmond (Ohio) HS
15. Mike Hacker, lhp, Cosumnes River (Calif.) JC
16. Yonder Alonso, c, Coral Gables HS, Miami
17. Robert Lara, c, Nova HS, Davie, Fla.
18. Matt Morgal, rhp, Edmond (Okla.) Santa Fe HS
19. **Sean Richardson, c, Kansas**
20. Eric Santiago, ss, Natividad Rodriguez Gonza HS, Arroyo, P.R.
21. Chris Kelley, rhp, San Jacinto (Texas) JC
22. **Curtis Leavitt, rhp, Vasquez HS, Acton, Calif.**
23. David Herndon, rhp, Gulf Coast (Fla.) CC
24. Gustavo Duran, rhp, George Washington HS, Bronx, N.Y.
25. Aaron Lovett, rhp, Kaskaskia (Ill.) JC
26. Michael Mopas, lhp, Iolani HS, Mililani, Hawaii
27. Evan Frederickson, lhp, Oakton HS, Oak Hill, Va.
28. Josh Brink, rhp, Mennonite Educational Institute SS, Abbotsford, B.C
29. Steve Hernandez, rhp, Redwood HS, Visalia, Calif.
30. Kiko Vazquez, 1b, Sebring (Fla.) HS
31. Kyle Carr, lhp, Linton (N.D.) HS
32. **David Bromberg, rhp, Palisades HS, Los Angeles**
33. Brandon Trodick, of, Cimmaron-Memorial HS, Las Vegas, Nev.
34. Danny Cox, ss, W.F. West HS, Chehalis, Wash.
35. Lukas Thomason, rhp, Brook Hill HS, Jacksonville, Texas
36. **Rene Tosoni, of, Chipola (Fla.) JC**
37. James Leigh, lhp, Texarkana (Texas) CC
38. Carlos Rodriguez, c, Puerto Rico Baseball Academy, Vega Baja, P.R.
39. Charles Duffey, rhp, Westminster (Calif.) HS
40. Charlie Leesman, lhp, Elder HS, Cincinnati
41. **Toby Gardenhire, ss, Illinois**
42. Jacob Cox, c, Lakeland (Fla.) HS
43. Justin Parker, rhp, Fort Wayne (Ind.) HS
44. Jose Cordero, rhp, Miami
45. Michael Kinsel, ss, Cretin-Derham Hall, St. Paul, Minn.
46. Denver Wynn, rhp, Valleyview SS, Kamloops B.C
47. Mike Ballard, lhp, Virginia
48. Juan Rodriguez, c, Bayamon (P.R.) Military Academy
49. Dane Ponciano, c, CC of Southern Nevada
50. Justin Otto, rhp, Cowley County (Kan.) CC

NEW YORK METS

June—Regular Phase (9)

1. **Mike Pelfrey, rhp, Wichita State**
2. (Pick to Red Sox as compensation for Type A free agent Pedro Martinez)
3. (Pick to Astros as compensation for Type A free agent Carlos Beltran)
4. **Hector Pellot, 2b, Puerto Rico Baseball Academy, Cidra, P.R.**
5. **Drew Butera, c, Central Florida**
6. **Greg Cain, of, Gahr HS, Cerritos, Calif.**
7. **Jon Niese, lhp, Defiance (Ohio) HS**
8. **Sean McCraw, c, San Jacinto (Texas) JC**
9. **Bobby Parnell, rhp, Charleston Southern**
10. **Courtney Billingslea, of, Sinclar (Ohio) CC**
11. Luis Martinez, c, Jackson State (Tenn.) CC
12. **Matthew Spath, of, Flagler Palm Coast HS, Bunnell, Fla.**
13. **Josh Thole, c, Mater Dei HS, Breese, Ill.**
14. Ian Marshall, rhp, Gaithersburg (Md.) HS
15. Daniel Martin, rhp, Harleton HS, Marshall, Texas
16. **Eric Domangue, lhp, Alvin (Texas) JC**
17. Pedro Beato, rhp, Xaverian HS, Queens, N.Y.
18. **Eric Brown, rhp, Wingate (N.C.)**
19. **Tim Grogan, 3b, Western Kentucky**
20. Cody Railsback, rhp, Ryan HS, Denton, Texas
21. **Joe Holden, of, Molloy (N.Y.)**
22. Petey Paramore, c, Allen (Texas) HS
23. **Joe D'Alessandro, rhp, College of New Jersey**
24. **Kyle Risinger, rhp, Galveston (Texas) CC**
25. **D.J. Wabick, 1b, College of Charleston**
26. **Kevin Tomasiewicz, lhp, Wisconsin-Whitewater**
27. **David Koons, rhp, St. Leo (Fla.)**
28. **Greg Gonzalez, of, Chico State (Calif.)**
29. **Sal Aguilar, rhp, Lewis-Clark State (Idaho)**
30. **Steven Holquin, rhp, Porterville (Calif.) JC**
31. **Matt Anderson, 3b, UC Irvine**

32. **Jose Castro, ss, Miami-Dade CC North**
33. **Daniel Arizmendi, lhp, Santa Ana (Calif.) JC**
34. **Joseph Mihalics, 2b, Buffalo**
35. **Michael Sharpe, of, St. Thomas Aquinas**
36. **Jeramy Simmons, rhp, South Alabama**
37. **Alex Beras, rhp, Scranton (Pa.)**
38. Pierre Miville-Deschenes, rhp, Edouard Montpetit HS
39. Colin Thomson, rhp, Mountain View HS, Tucson
40. Jake Blackwood, 2b, Maplewoods (Mo.) CC
41. **Nick Carr, rhp, Twin Falls (Idaho) HS**
42. Jared Barkdoll, c, Greencastle-Antrim HS, Greencastle, Pa.
43. Javier Brown, ss, Valhalla HS, El Cajon, Calif.
44. Phillip Pursino, c, St. Dominic HS, Stewart Manor, N.Y.
45. **Anthony Manuel, 2b, Biola (Calif.)**
46. Pete Tountas, ss, Maine South HS, Park Ridge, Ill.
47. Samuel Lane, rhp, Pedro Menendez HS, Elkton, Fla.
48. Jeremy Hefner, rhp, Seminole State (Okla.) JC
49. **Will Jostock, rhp, Pensacola (Fla.) JC**
50. Julio Rodriguez, of, Wabash Valley (Ill.) JC

NEW YORK YANKEES

June—Regular Phase (29)

1. **C.J. Henry, ss, Putnam City HS, Oklahoma City** (Pick from Phillies as compensation for Type B free agent Jon Lieber)
1. (Pick to Marlins as compensation for Type A free agent Carl Pavano)
2. **J.B. Cox, rhp, Texas** (Pick from White Sox as compensation for Type B free agent Orlando Hernandez)
2. (Pick to Braves as compensation for Type A free agent Jaret Wright)
3. **Brett Gardner, of, College of Charleston**
4. **Lance Pendleton, rhp, Rice**
5. **Zach Kroenke, lhp, Nebraska**
6. Doug Fister, rhp, Fresno State
7. **Garrett Patterson, lhp, Oklahoma**
8. **Austin Jackson, of, Ryan HS, Denton, Texas**
9. **James Cooper, of, Loyola Marymount**
10. **Kyle Anson, 3b, Texas State**
11. **Alan Horne, rhp, Florida**
12. **Joe Muich, c, Wichita State**
13. Karl Amonite, 1b, Auburn
14. **Joel Perez, of, Miami, Fla.**
15. **Josh Schmidt, rhp, Pacific**
16. **Chris Malec, 2b, UC Santa Barbara**
17. **Keaton Everitt, rhp, Washington**
18. **Joe Burke, c, St. John's**
19. **Jim Conroy, rhp, Illinois**
20. **Bryan Rueger, lhp, Southern Illinois**
21. **Hanseld Diaz, c, Miami-Dade (Fla.) CC**
22. Michael Lee, rhp, Skyline HS, Issaquah, Wash.
23. Matt Wallach, c, Cypress (Calif.) JC
24. Justin Phillabaum, 1b, Indian River (Fla.) CC
25. **Brad Canada, c, Bradley**
26. Patrick Caldwell, lhp, Yavapai (Ariz.) JC
27. **Josh Morgan, rhp, Missouri-St. Louis**
28. Derek Duclos, rhp, Richmond
29. Justin Turner, 2b, Cal State Fullerton
30. **Cameron Johnson, of, CC of Southern Nevada**
31. Clint Preisendorfer, lhp, Palomar (Calif.) JC
32. Jared Souza, lhp, Navarro (Texas) JC
33. **Michael Mlotkowski, rhp, Oklahoma City**
34. **Felipe Garcia, 1b, Cal State Fullerton**
35. **Andy Carter, rhp, Davidson**
36. Brett Summers, rhp, Lake Central HS, Dyer, Ind.
37. **Jesse Bahr, lhp, Missouri Baptist**
38. Clayton Young, lhp, Glendale (Calif.) JC
39. Miguel Ruiz, rhp, South Hills HS, Fort Worth, Texas
40. Michael Roskopf, 1b, CC of Southern Nevada
41. **Chris Valencia, of, Westchester HS, Los Angeles**
42. Josh Styes, rhp, Clay-Chalkville HS, Birmingham
43. **Brady Salter, rhp, Aurora**
44. Justin Keadle, rhp, Wake Forest
45. Brett Pill, 1b, Cal State Fullerton
46. **Eric Wordekemper, rhp, Creighton**
47. Eric Hanlon, of, James Martin HS, Arlington, Texas
48. Andrew Rice, of, Itawamba (Miss.) CC
49. Diallo Fon, of, Las Lomas High, Walnut Creek, Calif.
50. Blake Heym, c, Grayson County (Texas) CC

OAKLAND ATHLETICS

June—Regular Phase (21)

1. **Cliff Pennington, ss, Texas A&M**
1. **Travis Buck, of, Arizona State** (Supplemental pick—36th—for loss of Type A free agent Damian Miller)
2. **Craig Italiano, rhp, Flower Mound (Texas) HS** (Pick from Brewers as compensation for Miller)
2. **Jared Lansford, rhp, St. Francis HS, Santa Clara, Calif.**
3. **Vin Mazzaro, rhp, Rutherford (N.J.) HS**
4. **Jimmy Shull, rhp, Cal Poly**
5. **Scott Deal, rhp, Curtis HS, University Place, Wash.**
6. **Justin Sellers, ss, Marina HS, Huntington Beach, Calif.**
7. **Kevin Bunch, rhp, Serrano HS, Victorville, Calif.**
8. **Jason Ray, rhp, Azusa Pacific (Calif.)**
9. **Trey Shields, rhp, Alabama**
10. **John Herrera, rhp, Lubbock Christian**
11. **Steve Kleen, rhp, Pepperdine**
12. **Jeff Baisley, 3b, South Florida**
13. **Mike Massaro, lhp, Colorado State-Pueblo**
14. **Brad Davis, lhp, Lewis-Clark State (Idaho)**
15. **Jeff Bieker, of, Fort Hays State (Kan.)**
16. Justin Smoak, 1b, Stratford HS, Goose Creek, S.C.
17. **Isaac Omura, 2b, Hawaii**
18. **Anthony Recker, c, Alvernia (Pa.)**
19. **Julio Rivera, c, Puerto Rico Baseball Academy, Toa Alta, P.R.**
20. **Stephen Bryant, rhp, Hawaii**
21. **Michael Madsen, rhp, Ohio State**
22. **Shawn Callahan, c, Central Missouri State**
23. James Bennett, of, Louisiana-Monroe
24. **Ben Ingold, ss, Wake Forest**
25. **Zeke Parraz, ss, Nevada-Las Vegas**
26. **Ron Madej, lhp, Bellevue (Neb.)**
27. **Jess Lacasse, rhp, Bellevue (Neb.)**
28. **Michael Klug, 2b, North Alabama**
29. **Brad Kilby, lhp, San Jose State**
30. **T.J. Franco, rhp, San Francisco**
31. **Josh Kay, rhp, Cincinnati**
32. Jake Hammons, c, Snohomish (Wash.) HS
33. Matt Singleton, c, Ball State
34. Edwin Mieles, rhp, Patria La Torres Ramirez HS, San Sebastian, P.R.
35. Steve Braun, ss, Los Angeles Pierce JC
36. **Shane Keough, ss, Northwood HS, San Jose, Calif.**
37. A.J. Huttenlocker, lhp, Edmonds (Wash.) CC
38. Nicholas Pulos, c, Pennsylvania

PHILADELPHIA PHILLIES

June—Regular Phase (17)

1. (Pick to Yankees as compensation for Type B free agent Jon Lieber)
2. **Mike Costanzo, 3b, Coastal Carolina**
3. **Matt Maloney, lhp, Mississippi**
4. **Mike Durant, 3b, Berkeley (Calif.) HS**
5. **Brett Harker, rhp, College of Charleston**
6. **Justin Blaine, lhp, San Diego**
7. **Jermaine Williams, of, Los Angeles HS**
8. **Jeremy Slayden, of, Georgia Tech**
9. **Clay Harris, 2b, Louisiana State**
10. **Josh Outman, lhp, Central Missouri State**
11. **Tuffy Gosewisch, c, Arizona State**
12. **Mike Zagurski, lhp, Kansas**
13. **Matt Olson, rhp, Western Branch HS, Chesapeake, Va.**
14. Aja Barto, of, Stratford HS, Spring Branch, Texas
15. **P.J. Antoniato, ss, St. John's**
16. **Matt Edwards, 1b, Notre Dame**
17. **Ronald Hill, rhp, UNC Wilmington**
18. **Darren Byrd, rhp, Pine Forest HS, Cantonment, Fla.**

19. David Huff, lhp, Cypress (Calif.) JC
20. Vance Worley, rhp, McClatchy HS, Sacramento
21. **Aaron Rawl, rhp, South Carolina**
22. **Pat Overholt, rhp, Santa Clara**
23. **Derrick Mitchell, ss, Paw Paw (Mich.) HS**
24. **Dennis Diaz, 2b, Florida International**
25. **Joseph Frazee, of, Loyola Marymount**
26. **Brett Dalton, 2b, UC Irvine**
27. **Steven Alexander, of, Sacramento CC**
28. **Clayton Stewart, rhp, Texas**
29. **Aaron Cheesman, c, Florida State**
30. Charles Benoit, lhp, Grayson County (Texas) CC
31. **Cooper Osteen, 2b, Mississippi**
32. Tim Sherlock, of, Chaparral HS, Scottsdale, Ariz.
33. Andrez Ibarz, rhp, Champagnat Catholic HS, Hialeah, Fla.
34. Osvaldo Torres, 1b, Wabash Valley (Ill.) JC
35. Aaron Greer, c, North Eugene (Ore.) HS
36. Nick Monett, c, Granite Hills HS, El Cajon, Calif.
37. Kyle Bredenkamp, rhp, Millikan HS, Long Beach, Calif.
38. Micah Sales, rhp, Madison County HS, Danielsville, Ga.
39. Bobby Kennedy, lhp, Trinity Catholic HS, Ocala, Fla.
40. Travis Jones, 2b, Lake City (Fla.) CC
41. Ryan Selden, ss, Canyon Springs HS, Moreno Valley, Calif.
42. John Dischert, lhp, St. Marks HS, Wilmington, Del.
43. Ryan Verdugo, lhp, Lake Stevens (Wash.) HS
44. Luis Alvarez, of, Pedro Falu Oreliano HS, Rio Grande, P.R.
45. Mike Modica, lhp, Washington Township HS, Sewell, N.J.
46. Jason Stacy, rhp, Westview HS, Phoenix
47. **Ben Blanton, ss, William Jewel (Mo.)**
48. Ben Hornbeck, lhp, Sunnyslope HS, Phoenix
49. Shane Erb, rhp, Father Judge High, Lewes, Del.
50. **Tyler Gooch, rhp, Oklahoma**

PITTSBURGH PIRATES

June—Regular Phase (11)

1. **Andrew McCutchen, of, Fort Meade (Fla.) HS**
2. **Brad Corley, of, Mississippi State**
3. **James Boone, of, Missouri**
4. **Brent Lillibridge, ss, Washington**
5. **Jeff Sues, rhp, Vanderbilt**
6. **Cameron Blair, 2b, Texas Tech**
7. **Justin Vaclavik, rhp, Houston**
8. **Steve Pearce, 1b, South Carolina**
9. **Derrik Moeves, rhp, Northern Kentucky**
10. **Derek Antelo, rhp, Nova Southeastern (Fla.)**
11. **Chris Jones, c, Long Beach State**
12. **Jason Delaney, of, Boston College**
13. **Matt Swanson, rhp, California**
14. **Albert Laboy, of, John I. Leonard HS, West Palm Beach, Fla.**
15. Jarred Bogany, of, George Bush HS, Houston
16. **Eric Krebs, rhp, Alvin (Texas) JC**
17. **Darren Newlin, rhp, Central Florida**
18. **Ryan Searage, of, Eckerd (Fla.)**
19. **Daniel Rios, 1b, JC of the Sequoias (Calif.)**
20. Ryan Lollis, of, Houston Christian HS
21. Elias Otero, ss, Puerto Rico Baseball Academy, Toa Alta, P.R.
22. David DiNatale, of, Stoneman Douglas HS, Parkland, Fla.
23. **Juan Mesa, of, Miami, Fla.**
24. **Jared Brown, lhp, Cumberland (Tenn.)**
25. Michael Wanamaker, rhp, Nyack HS, Valley Cottage, N.Y.
26. **Tony Mansolino, 3b, Vanderbilt**
27. **Nash Robertson, rhp, UC Irvine**
28. Clayton McMillan, lhp, Carthage (Texas) HS
29. Iain Sebastian, rhp, Columbus (Ga.) HS
30. Chad Povich, rhp, Dixie State (Utah) JC
31. **Jason Herman, rhp, West Alabama**
32. **Duke Acors, rhp, Virginia Military Institute**
33. Michael Klindt, of, Centennial HS, Roswell, Ga.
34. Gary Bucuren, 3b, Ambridge Area HS, Sewickley, Pa.
35. Lyndon Estill, of, Sammamish HS, Bellevue, Wash.
36. **Justin Byler, c, Gulf Coast (Fla.) CC**
37. Eric Marshall, rhp, Barrington (Ill.) HS
38. Carl Uhl, of, Serrano HS, Phelan, Calif.
39. Jason Brock, lhp, Lipscomb HS, Nolansville, Tenn.
40. Ken Wieda, rhp, John Hersey HS, Arlington Heights, Ill.
41. Nick Beghtol, c, Dixie State (Utah) JC
42. Kyle Sweat, rhp, Apopka (Fla.) HS
43. Scott Kuhns, rhp, John Hersey HS, Arlington Heights, Ill.
44. Jordan Latham, rhp, Centennial HS, Boise, Idaho
45. Philip Riley, rhp, Jackson State (Tenn.) CC
46. Kody Hinze, 1b, Nimitz HS, Houston
47. Ryan Lormand, ss, McLennan (Texas) CC
48. Paul Dickey, rhp, Lake Washington HS, Redmond, Wash.
49. Francisco Ortiz, rhp, Puerto Rico Baseball Academy, Toa Alta, P.R.
50. Stephen Merino, 3b, American Senior HS, Miami

ST. LOUIS CARDINALS

June—Regular Phase (30)

1. **Colby Rasmus, of, Russell County HS, Phenix City, Ala.** (Pick from Red Sox as compensation for Type A free agent Edgar Renteria)
1. **Tyler Greene, ss, Georgia Tech**
1. **Mark McCormick, rhp, Baylor** (Supplemental pick—43rd—for loss of Renteria)
1. **Tyler Herron, rhp, Wellington (Fla.) Community HS** (Supplemental pick—46th—for loss of Type A free agent Mike Matheny)
2. **Josh Wilson, rhp, Whitehouse HS, Tyler, Texas** (Pick from Giants as compensation for Matheny)
2. **Nick Webber, rhp, Central Missouri State**
3. **Daryl Jones, of, Spring (Texas) HS**
4. **Bryan Anderson, c, Simi Valley (Calif.) HS**
5. **Mitchell Boggs, rhp, Georgia**
6. **Wilfrido Pujols, of, Fort Osage HS, Independence, Mo.**
7. **Nick Stavinoha, of, Louisiana State**
8. **Jason Cairns, rhp, Central Michigan**
9. **Zach Zuercher, lhp, Rhode Island**
10. **Randy Roth, c, Southeastern Lousiana**
11. **Steve Gonzalez, c, Programa Alcase, San Juan, P.R.**
12. Daniel McCutchen, rhp, Oklahoma
13. **Malcolm Owens, of, San Bernadino Valley (Calif.) JC**
14. **Michael Repole, rhp, Birmingham-Southern**
15. **Adam Daniels, lhp, Oklahoma State**
16. **Matt Lane, rhp, Louisiana-Monroe**
17. **Michael Cooper, rhp, Fresno State**
18. **Brandon Garner, ss, Yale HS, Melvin, Mich.**
19. Miers Quigley, lhp, Roswell (Ga.) HS
20. **Shaun Garceau, rhp, Royal Palm Beach (Fla.) HS**
21. Ryan Rohlinger, ss, Oklahoma
22. **Jaime Garcia, lhp, Mission, Texas**
23. **A.J. Van Slyke, 1b, Kansas**
24. **David Phillips, rhp, El Paso (Texas) CC**
25. **Adam Rodgers, 1b, Rice**
26. Steven Blackwood, of, Georgia Tech
27. **Chuck Carter, of, Texas A&M-Corpus Christi**
28. **Trey Hearne, rhp, Texas A&M-Corpus Christi**
29. **Reid Price, lhp, College of Charleston**
30. **Matthew Trent, rhp, Wingate (N.C.)**
31. **Christian Lopez, ss, Juana Colon HS, Comerio, P.R.**
32. **Casey Rowlett, of, Arkansas**
33. **Scott Vander Weg, rhp, Lamar**
34. **Kyle Sadlowski, rhp, Kutztown**
35. **Cory Meacham, rhp, Alabama Southern CC**
36. **Armando Carrasco, rhp, Saddleback (Calif.) CC**
37. **Kenny Maiques, rhp, Rio Hondo (Calif.) CC**
38. Steve Junker, lhp, Valley Forge HS, Parma Heights, Ohio
39. **Tyler Leach, rhp, Kings Mountain (N.C.) HS**
40. Jesse Schoendienst, 2b, Old Dominion
41. David Fonseca, ss, Thousand Oaks (Calif.) HS
42. **Josh Schwartz, lhp, Rowan (N.J.)**
43. **Michael Meagher, lhp, Maryland**
44. **Blake King, rhp, Bishop Kelley HS, Tulsa, Okla.**
45. **Kevin Fitzgerald, rhp, Stony Brook**
46. Danny Feldman, rhp, Gloucester Catholic HS, West Deptford, N.J.
47. **Adam Morris, 3b, Rice**

SAN DIEGO PADRES

June—Regular Phase (18)

1. **Cesar Carrillo, rhp, Miami**
1. **Cesar Ramos, lhp, Long Beach State** (Supplemental pick—35th—for loss of Type A free agent David Wells)
2. **Chase Headley, 3b, Tennessee**
2. **Nick Hundley, c, Arizona** (Pick from Red Sox as compensation for Wells)
3. **Josh Geer, rhp, Rice**
4. **Mike Baxter, of, Vanderbilt**
5. **Seth Johnston, ss, Texas**
6. **Neil Jamison, rhp, Long Beach State**
7. **Will Venable, of, Princeton**
8. **John Madden, rhp, Auburn**
9. **Casey Smith, 1b, Erskine (S.C.)**
10. **Josh Alley, of, Tennessee**
11. Josh Tomlin, rhp, Angelina (Texas) JC
12. **Aaron Breit, rhp, Garden City (Kan.) CC**
13. **Arnold Hughey, lhp, Auburn**
14. **Billy Richardson, ss, East Carolina**
15. Josh Romanski, lhp, Norco HS, Corona, Calif.
16. **Brent Carter, lhp, Alabama**
17. **Chad Decker, lhp, UC Riverside**
18. **Mike Sansoe, of, St. Mary's**
19. Gabriel Fargas, rhp, Puerto Rico Baseball Academy, Caguas, P.R.
20. **Chad Steiner, 3b, Lamar (Colo.) CC**
21. **Brian Cavanaugh, of, East Carolina**
22. **Drew Davidson, of, Illinois**
23. Josh Conover, rhp, Washington
24. **John Slone, c, Miami (Ohio)**
25. **Grant Varnell, rhp, Texas-Arlington**
26. **Jon Link, rhp, Bluefield (VA.)**
27. **Ray Gill, 1b, Brevard (N.C.)**
28. **Brandon Higelin, lhp, Cal State Los Angeles**
29. **Rey Garramone, rhp, Denver North HS, Denver**
30. Todd Conerly, rhp, Angelina (Texas) JC
31. Tae Kwon, rhp, Hoover HS, Glendale, Calif.
32. Tyson Ford, rhp, Timpanogos HS, Orem, Utah
33. **Adam Gold, rhp, California**
34. **Geoff Vandel, lhp, Shaw HS, Columbus, Ga.**
35. Andrew Morgan, c, Norcross HS, Atlanta
36. Gary Moran, rhp, Fresno CC
37. **Drew Miller, rhp, Seminole State (Okla.) JC**
38. Jeremy McBryde, rhp, Midwest City (Okla.) HS
39. Patrick Norris, of, Butler County (Kan.) CC
40. Donnie Snow, lhp, Grossmont (Calif.) HS
41. Bret Bochsler, lhp, Inglemoor HS, Redmond, Wash.
42. Terrence Dayleg, ss, North Surrey SS, Surrey, B.C
43. Justin Worby, c, Georgetown District HS, Acton, Ontario
44. Troy Dawe, rhp, Cardinal Newman Catholic SS, Toronto
45. Daniel Towe, c, Charlotte (Mich.) HS
46. Jeremy Shelby, of, Tates Creek HS, Lexington, Ky.
47. Mark Letchworth, of, Louisburg (N.C.) JC
48. Carson Bryant, rhp, JC of Southern Idaho
49. **Josh Thomas-Dotson, of, Oregon**
50. Jason Ogata, ss, Westview HS, Portland, Ore.

SAN FRANCISCO GIANTS

June—Regular Phase (22)

1. (Pick to Marlins as compensation for Type A free agent Armando Benitez)
2. (Pick to Cardinals as compensation for Type A free agent Mike Matheny)
3. (Pick to Indians as compensation for Type A free agent Omar Vizquel)
4. **Ben Copeland, of, Pittsburgh**
5. **Daniel Griffin, rhp, Niagara**
6. Brad Cuthbertson, rhp, Lethbridge (Alberta) CC
7. **Joey Dyche, of, Lewis-Clark State (Idaho)**
8. Scotty Bridges, 2b, Arkansas
9. **Anthony Contreras, ss, San Jose State**
10. **Nick Pereira, rhp, San Francisco**
11. **Henry Gutierrez, c, Troy**
12. **Joe Martinez, rhp, Boston College**
13. **Taylor Wilding, rhp, Cal Poly Pomona**
14. **Brian Anderson, rhp, Long Beach State**
15. **Alex Hinshaw, lhp, San Diego State**
16. **Buck Cody, lhp, Texas**
17. **Mark Minicozzi, 3b, East Carolina**
18. Chad Wagler, rhp, Kent State
19. Brandon Grabham, rhp, Grayson County (Texas) JC
20. Jon Gaston, of, Borah HS, Boise, Idaho
21. **Robert Grace, rhp, JC of the Desert (Calif.)**
22. **Taylor Creswell, of, Deer Valley HS, Antioch, Calif.**
23. **David Maroul, 3b, Texas**
24. **James Simmons, of, Vernon Regional (Texas) JC**
25. **Barry Gunther, c, Mississippi**
26. **Ivan Rusova, rhp, Oasis Alternative HS, Toronto**
27. Johnny Monell, c, Christopher Columbus HS, Bronx, N.Y.
28. **Sergio Romo, rhp, Mesa State (Colo.)**
29. Angel Nicolas, ss, Killian HS, Miami
30. Erik Meyer, rhp, Eastern Washington
31. **Wayne Foltin, rhp, Nevada-Las Vegas**
32. Damon Brewer, lhp, Lake City (Fla.) CC
33. **Chris Todd, 2b, Coastal Carolina**
34. Matt Long, rhp, Miami (Ohio)
35. **Antoan Richardson, of, Vanderbilt**
36. **Thomas Neal, of, Poway (Calif.) HS**
37. **David Newton, rhp, West Valley (Calif.) CC**
38. **Ben Nieto, lhp, Riverside (Calif.) CC**
39. Melvin Blackmon, lhp, Temecula Valley (Calif.) HS
40. Kurt Lipton, of, Pine Crest HS, Boca Raton, Fla.
41. Bo Merrell, ss, Perryton (Texas) HS
42. Tony Snow, rhp, Edmonds (Wash.) CC
43. **Chris Stanton, 1b, Virginia Tech**
44. Reggie Fuller, lhp, Diablo Valley (Calif.) JC
45. **Eric Dworkis, rhp, California**
46. Jared Cranston, lhp, Seward County (Kan.) CC
47. George Snyder, rhp, Chaffey (Calif.) JC
48. Adam Ortiz-Jusino, rhp, Brookdale (N.J.) CC
49. Curtis Partch, rhp, Merced (Calif.) HS
50. Justin Robertson, rhp, Nipomo (Calif.) HS

SEATTLE MARINERS

June—Regular Phase (3)

1. **Jeff Clement, c, Southern California**
2. (Pick to Dodgers as compensation for Type A free agent Adrian Beltre)
3. (Pick to Diamondbacks as compensation for Type A free agent Richie Sexson)
4. **Justin Thomas, lhp, Youngstown State**
5. **Stephen Kahn, rhp, Loyola Marymount**
6. Lance Lynn, rhp, Brownsburg (Ind.) HS
7. **Robert Rohrbaugh, lhp, Clemson**
8. **David Asher, lhp, Florida International**
9. **Bryan Sabatella, 3b, Quinnipiac**
10. **Ronnie Prettyman, 3b, Cal State Fullerton**
11. Brian Contreras, of, P.R. Baseball Academy, Caguas, P.R.
12. **Anthony Varvaro, rhp, St. John's**
13. **Reed Eastley, ss, Niagara**
14. Brad Boyer, 2b, Arizona
15. John Holdzkom, rhp, Rancho Cucamonga (Calif.) HS
16. Grant Gerrard, of, Southern Illinois
17. **James Russell, lhp, Navarro (Texas) JC**
18. **Curtis Ledbetter, 1b, Nebraska**
19. **Brett Bannister, rhp, Southern California**
20. **Travis Scott, c, Lincoln Land (Ill.) CC**
21. **Nick Allen, rhp, Villanova**
22. **Alex Gary, of, Virginia Commonwealth**
23. Ryan Lindgren, rhp, Stillwater Area (Minn.) HS
24. **Kevin Gergel, c, Kennesaw State (Ga.)**
25. **Will Brown, lhp, Downey HS, Modesto, Calif.**
26. **Ari Kafka, rhp, Quinnipiac**
27. Jeremy Hill, rhp, Ohlone (Calif.) JC
28. **Lance Beus, lhp, Brigham Young**
29. Eric Thomas, of, Buchholz HS, Gainesville, Fla.

30. Aric Van Gaalen, lhp, Lethbridge (Alberta) JC
31. **Jeff Gilmore, rhp, Stanford**
32. **Corby Heckman, 2b, Indiana**
33. **Julian Henson, c, Cordova (Tenn.) HS**
34. Andrew Schneider, rhp, Franklin (Texas) HS
35. Blake Amador, of, Modesto (Calif.) JC
36. Max Kwan, c, Seattle Prep, Bellevue, Wash.
37. Jesse Costa, rhp, Magnolia HS, Anaheim, Calif.
38. **Joe Agreste, 1b, Greenbrier Christian Academy, Chesapeake, Va.**
39. Duke Welker, rhp, Seminole State (Okla.) JC
40. Eugene Edwards, of, Long Beach (Calif.) CC
41. **Joe White, 1b, Georgia Perimeter JC**
42. Kevin Reynolds, of, Quincy
43. Philip Roy, rhp, Southridge HS, Miami
44. Paul Patterson, rhp, Northern Kentucky
45. Luis Coste, of, Cochise County (Ariz.) CC
46. **Worth Lumry, lhp, Princeton**
47. **Andy Hargrove, 1b, Kent State**
48. Matthew Gardner, rhp, Grayson County (Texas) CC
49. Dennis Raben, 1b, St. Thomas Aquinas HS, Fort Lauderdale
50. Xavier Scruggs, 1b, Poway (Calif.) HS

TAMPA BAY DEVIL RAYS

June—Regular Phase (8)

1. **Wade Townsend, rhp, Dripping Springs, Texas**
2. **Chris Mason, rhp, UNC Greensboro**
3. Bryan Morris, rhp, Tullahoma (Tenn.) HS
4. **Jeremy Hellickson, rhp, Hoover HS, Des Moines, Iowa**
5. **Mike McCormick, 3b, Marist HS, Eugene, Ore.**
6. **Greg Reinhard, rhp, Wisconsin-Whitewater**
7. **Mike Wlodarczyk, lhp, Boston College**
8. **Andrew Lopez, of, Elk Grove (Calif.) HS**
9. **Derek Feldkamp, rhp, Michigan**
10. **John Matulia, of, Eustis (Fla.) HS**
11. **Jeff Kamrath, rhp, Virginia**
12. **Ryan Zimmerman, rhp, Salt Lake CC**
13. **Ryan Morse, lhp, Southwest Minnesota State**
14. Henry Wrigley, 1b, JC of San Mateo (Calif.)
15. **Matt Fisher, rhp, Franklin Pierce (N.H.)**
16. **Neil Walton, ss, Cal State Fullerton**
17. Jared Edwards, c, Rummel HS, New Orleans
18. Tommy Hunter, rhp, Cathedral HS, Indianapolis
19. Ike Davis, 1b/lhp, Chaparral HS, Scottsdale, Ariz.
20. Wade Miley, lhp, Loranger (La.) HS
21. Jared Bradford, rhp, Shelton State (Ala.) CC
22. Adam Hall, rhp, Pacific HS, Gray Summit, Mo.
23. Danny Dorn, of, Cal State Fullerton
24. **Neal Frontz, rhp, Jacksonville**
25. Clay Mortensen, rhp, Treasure Valley (Ore.) CC
26. Jeff Urlaub, lhp, Horizon HS, Scottsdale, Ariz.
27. Rylan Ostrosky, rhp, Salisbury Composite HS, Edmonton, Alberta
28. **Matt Falk, rhp, San Diego**
29. **Chad Pendarvis, lhp, Southeastern Louisiana**
30. **Chris Fessler, rhp, Yavapai (Ariz.) JC**
31. Jordan Brown, ss, Hahnville HS, Luling, La.
32. **Ryan Bethel, ss, Grand Canyon (Ariz.)**
33. Tyler Reves, c, Wharton County (Texas) JC
34. **Matt Devins, ss, Stony Brook**
35. Damien Mazzetti, 1b, North Mecklenburg HS, Huntersville, N.C.
36. John Maschino, rhp, Edmond North HS, Edmond, Okla.
37. **Carnell Parker, of, Mobile**
38. **Ben Rulon, lhp, Georgia State**
39. Michael McClaren, rhp, Durango HS, Las Vegas
40. Matt Gaudet, 1b, Archbishop Rummel HS, Metairie, La.
41. **Garrett Groce, of, Columbus State (Ga.)**
42. Taylor Cobb, rhp, Central Florida
43. Joshua Stewart, c, Bowling Green State
44. Rashad Taylor, of, Riordan HS, San Francisco
45. Leon Johnson, of, Thatcher, Ariz.
46. William Oliver, rhp, San Pasqual HS, Escondido, Calif.
47. Eli Diaz, rhp, Baton Rouge (La.) CC
48. **Brad Matthews, 2b, Wallace State (Ala.) CC**
49. Casey Coleman, rhp, Mariner HS, Cape Coral, Fla.
50. Matt Duryea, lhp, Edmonds (Wash.) CC

TEXAS RANGERS

June—Regular Phase (19)

1. **John Mayberry Jr., of, Stanford**
2. **Johnny Whittleman, 3b, Kingwood (Texas) HS**
3. **Taylor Teagarden, c, Texas**
4. **Shane Funk, rhp, Arnold HS, Panama City Beach, Fla.**
5. **Michael Kirkman, lhp, Columbia HS, Lake City, Fla.**
6. **German Duran, 2b, Weatherford (Texas) JC**
7. **Jacob Rasner, rhp, Earl Wooster HS, Reno, Nev.**
8. Brad Barragar, rhp, Golden West (Calif.) JC
9. **R.J. Anderson, of, Armwood HS, Seffner, Fla.**
10. **Matt Nevarez, rhp, San Fernando (Calif.) HS**
11. **Nate Fogle, rhp, Oregon State**
12. Dexter Carter, rhp, Greenbrier Christian Academy, Chesapeake, Va.
13. **Doug Mathis, rhp, Missouri**
14. **Steve Murphy, of, Kansas State**
15. **Kea Kometani, rhp, Pepperdine**
16. **Jesse Hall, lhp, Yavapai (Ariz.) JC**
17. Chris Dominguez, 3b, Gulliver Prep, Miami
18. Chase Fontaine, ss, Daytona Beach (Fla.) CC
19. **Brian Valichka, c, Delaware**
20. **Joey Hooft, 2b, Arizona State**
21. **Brandon James, rhp, Carlisle (Pa.) HS**
22. Jarrod Dumont, lhp, Riverside (Calif.) CC
23. **Steve Marquardt, 3b, Columbia Basin (Wash.) CC**
24. Zach Borba, of, Columbia Basin (Wash.) CC
25. **Brian Spielmann, rhp, Bradley**
26. **Ben Crabtree, c, Ohio**
27. **Jon Wilson, rhp, Winthrop**
28. Sergio Morales, of, Hollywood Hills HS, Hollywood, Fla.
29. **Matt Hawke, 1b, Lousiana-Lafayette**
30. **Truan Mehl, of, Maryland**
31. Austin Faught, lhp, Louisiana-Lafayette
32. Renny Osuna, ss, New Mexico JC
33. **Kevin Gossage, c, Coronado HS, Colorado Springs, Colo.**
34. Shooter Hunt, rhp, Ramapo HS, Wyckoff, N.J.
35. Chris Hicks, rhp, Milton HS, Alpharetta, Ga.
36. Steven Farris, rhp, Langham Creek HS, Houston
37. **Tim Rodriguez, of, Centennial HS, Gresham, Ore.**
38. Jeffrey Murphy, rhp, Yavapai (Ariz.) JC
39. David Makim, rhp, Monte Vista HS, Spring Valley, Calif.
40. **Thomas Van Buskirk, rhp, Santa Clara**
41. **Warren Rosebrock, rhp, Cal State Sacramento**
42. Travis Hill, rhp, Seminole State (Okla.) JC
43. Shawn Keil, of, Seminole (Fla.) HS
44. **Roberto Valiente, of, Tampa**
45. Frank Lonigro, c, Fullerton (Calif.) JC
46. **Thomas Berkery, c, Mississippi State**
47. Marc Nobriga, rhp, Hartnell (Calif.) JC
48. **Broc Coffman, lhp, Lower Columbia (Wash.) JC**
49. **Glenn Swanson, lhp, UC Irvine**
50. **Joe Napoli, of, Bradley**

TORONTO BLUE JAYS

June—Regular Phase (6)

1. **Ricky Romero, lhp, Cal State Fullerton**
2. (Pick to Twins as compensation for Type A free agent Corey Koskie)
3. **Brian Pettway, of, Mississippi**
4. **Ryan Patterson, of, Louisiana State**
5. **Eric Fowler, lhp, Mississippi**
6. **Josh Bell, c, Auburn**
7. **Robert Ray, rhp, Texas A&M**
8. **Jacob Butler, of, Nevada**
9. **Paul Phillips, rhp, Oakland**
10. **Josh Sowers, rhp, Yale**
11. **Wesley Stone, ss, A.B. Miller HS, Rialto, Calif.**
12. **Billy Carnline, rhp, Texas Tech**

13. **Anthony Hatch, 3b, Nicholls State**
14. **Sean Stidfole, rhp, Penn State**
15. **Sean Shoffit, 2b, Cosumnes River (Calif.) JC**
16. **Kyle Bohm, c, Michigan**
17. Tyler Norrick, lhp, Southern Illinois
18. Rob Hogue, lhp, St. Joseph HS, Edmonton, Alberta
19. **Rei Gonzalez, rhp, St. Petersburg (Fla.) JC**
20. **Zach Kalter, of, Southern California**
21. **Chris Martinez, c, St. Thomas (Fla.)**
22. **Dennis Bigley, rhp, Oral Roberts**
23. Manuel Garcia, rhp, Puerto Rico Baseball Academy, Toa Baja, P.R.
24. **Alex McRobbie, rhp, UC Santa Barbara**
25. Philip Carey, ss, A.B. Lucas HS, London, Ontario
26. **Marshall Bernhard, ss, Central Florida**
27. Bobby Nicoll, rhp, Connecticut-Avery Point
28. **Scott Byrnes, rhp, Purdue**
29. John Roberts, of, Pryor (Okla.) HS
30. Trent Luyster, lhp, Ohio State
31. Jason Riley, c, North HS, Riverside, Calif.
32. **Matt Cooksey, of, George Mason**
33. Jeff Tobin, lhp, British Columbia
34. Mace Thurman, lhp, Westlake HS, Austin
35. Derek Tarapacki, rhp, Yavapai (Ariz.) JC
36. **Hector Delgadillo, rhp, Incarnate Word**
37. **Chris Looze, 1b, George Mason**
38. Adam Demichaele, rhp, Okaloosa-Walton (Fla.) CC
39. **Joshua Celigoy, 1b, Lewis-Clark State (Idaho)**
40. **Al Quintana, c, Cal State Northridge**
41. Eric Oxio, of, Puerto Rico Baseball Academy, Ponce, P.R.
42. Brett Wallace, 1b, Justin-Siena HS, Sonoma, Calif.
43. Connor Falkenbach, rhp, Florida
44. Eric Larson, of, Brown
45. **Michael Barbara, rhp, St. Petersburg (Fla.) JC**
46. Corey Weglin, rhp, Sacramento CC
47. Kyle Thornton, rhp, Odessa (Texas) JC
48. Kevin Denis-Fortier, 1b, Edouard Montpetit HS, Quebec City, Quebec
49. Nicholas Nordgren, of, Jefferson HS, Cedar Rapids, Iowa
50. Brian Mooney, lhp, Walt Whitman HS, Huntington Station, N.Y.

WASHINGTON NATIONALS

June—Regular Phase (4)

1. **Ryan Zimmerman, 3b, Virginia**
2. (Pick to Rockies as compensation for Type A free agent Vinny Castilla)
3. (Pick to Twins as compensation for Type B free agent Cristian Guzman)
4. **Justin Maxwell, of, Maryland**
5. **Ryan DeLaughter, of, Ryan HS, Denton, Texas**
6. **Marco Estrada, rhp, Long Beach State**
7. **Mike Daniel, of, North Carolina**
8. **Jack Spradlin, lhp, Southern California**
9. **John Howell, of, Central Florida**
10. **Dee Brown, of, Central Florida**
11. **John Lannan, lhp, Siena**
12. **Craig Stammen, rhp, Dayton**
13. **Andre Enriquez, rhp, Le Moyne**
14. **Deryck Johnson, of, Cypress Creek HS, Orlando, Fla.**
15. **Michael Wadkins, rhp, William E. Tolman HS, Pawtucket, R.I.**
16. **Josh Palm, rhp, Penn State**
17. **Eduardo Pichardo, rhp, Southridge HS, Miami**
18. **Tim Pahuta, 1b, Seton Hall**
19. **Bradley Clark, rhp, Hillsborough HS, Tampa**
20. **Ricky Shefka, rhp, Coastal Carolina**
21. **Coby Mavroulis, rhp, Texas A&M**
22. **Antonio Evangelista, rhp, Seminole State (Okla.) JC**
23. Brett Jensen, rhp, Nebraska
24. **Jeffrey Taylor, rhp, Missouri Southern State**
25. Jose Peley, ss, Edouard Montpetit HS, Montreal
26. Doug Thennis, 3b, American River (Calif.) JC
27. **Andrew Lane, 2b, Grand Canyon (Ariz.)**
28. Hunter Pace, of, Hamilton HS, Chandler, Ariz.
29. Pat Barnes, of, Southwest Mississippi JC
30. Brian Pruitt, 3b, Florida Christian HS, Miami
31. Clayton Conner, 3b, Pensacola (Fla.) Catholic HS
32. Daniel Schuh, of, Bishop Kenny HS, Jacksonville, Fla.
33. **Ryan Buchter, lhp, Highland Regional HS, Blackwood, N.J.**
34. Jordan Thibodeaux, lhp, San Jacinto (Texas) JC
35. Matt Averitt, rhp, New Mexico JC
36. Brett McMillan, 1b, UCLA
37. Brandon Hamilton, of, Woodlawn HS, Shreveport, La.
38. Marcus Jones, of, Landon School, Washington, D.C.
39. Jake McCarter, rhp, Navarro (Texas) JC
40. Anthony Williams, of, Mission Bay HS, San Diego
41. Tyler Moore, 1b, Northwest Rankin HS, Brandon, Miss.
42. Paul Treadaway, rhp, Pearl City River (Miss.) CC
43. Scott Barnes, lhp, Cathedral HS, Springfield, Mass.
44. Steven Hensley, rhp, Owen HS, Black Mountain, N.C.
45. Anthony Shawler, rhp, Oscar Smith HS, Chesapeake, Va.
46. Ibrahim Lopez, of, Lake City (Fla.) CC
47. Luis Feliz, of, New Brunswick (N.J.) HS
48. Will Cherry, of, George Jenkins HS, Lakeland, Fla.
49. Terrance Brown, rhp, Bullard HS, Fresno
50. Jake Leonhardt, rhp, Angelina (Texas) JC

2006 Assortment of talented arms leads off draft, with Longoria, Lincecum topping class

After the 2005 draft, which featured a group of heavy-hitting college infielders and a plethora of talented prep outfielders, college pitching took center stage in 2006.

The only hitter to crack BA's Top 10 draft prospects was Long Beach State's Evan Longoria, who checked in at No. 4. For teams that wanted pitchers, they had plenty of variety to choose from.

Need a lefthander? No. 1 prospect Andrew Miller and No. 6 Clayton Kershaw were the best the college and prep ranks had to offer.

Looking for a big-bodied righthander with premium stuff? Teams had their pick, from Stanford's 6-foot-7, 225-pound Greg Reynolds and Nebraska's 6-foot-3, 225-pound Joba Chamberlain to indy ball's Luke Hochevar, the former Tennessee righthander whose negotiations fell apart with the Dodgers in 2005. Need pure velocity? Righthanders Max Scherzer of Missouri and Brandon Morrow of California both had reached the upper 90s. Willing to gamble on shorter righthanders? Washington's Tim Lincecum and Houston's Brad Lincoln ranked second and third on our board.

Tim Lincecum quickly made teams regret not taking him with their first-round pick

The Royals had the top overall pick and narrowed their choices down to three pitchers, with Hochevar, Lincoln and Miller all under consideration. Complicating matters, the Royals fired general manager Allard Baird during the spring and replaced him with Braves farm director Dayton Moore, though Moore wasn't able to leave the Braves until after the draft. Word filtered out that Moore favored Texas outfielder Drew Stubbs, the consensus No. 2 hitter on most draft boards.

Ultimately, they decided on Hochevar, whom BA had ranked No. 8 on its board. And the rest of the first round continued apace, with teams selecting players based as much on signability as on ability.

The Rockies wanted to take Longoria at No. 2 but couldn't pull the trigger only a year after taking Troy Tulowitzki in 2005, and wound up taking Reynolds. The Rays jumped on Longoria with the third pick and signed him quickly, and he had as good a debut as any player in the draft class. He hit .315/.360/.597 with 18 home runs while reaching Double-A, and he quickly established himself as a fixture at third base in Tampa Bay, playing a key role in the Rays' run to the World Series in 2008.

Miller fell to the sixth spot to Detroit, while nine teams wound up passing on Lincecum, who was listed at 6-foot, 165 pounds but confounded some scouts with his unique delivery and rubber arm. The two-time Pacific-10 Conference pitcher of the year was a 41st-round pick in 2005, when he put out a $1 million price tag as an eligible sophomore. He returned to school after dominating the Cape Cod League in the summer and put up a monster season, leading NCAA Division I with 14.3 strikeouts per nine innings. The Giants signed him for the highest bonus in franchise history, $2.025 million, and watched him emerge as the face of the franchise in the post-Barry Bonds era.

Miller, BA's 2006 College Player of the Year, signed in August for a $3.55 million bonus on a contract that guaranteed him $5.45 million. He wound up being the first member of the '06 draft class to reach the majors, debuting Aug. 30 for the Tigers. He nearly was named to Detroit's playoff roster as a relief pitcher, but the Tigers wound up trading him to the Marlins after the 2007 season in a deal to acquire Dontrelle Willis and Miguel Cabrera.

Other than Lincecum falling, the biggest surprise of the first round happened with the 13th overall selection. The Cubs picked there, then didn't pick again until the fifth round thanks to a slew of free-agent signings. Chicago's new scouting director, veteran Tim Wilken, selected Clemson outfielder Tyler Colvin, who heated up late to jump to the front of a thin class of college hitters. Colvin ranked 170th on BA's Top 200.

The Cubs made much more noise later in the draft, though. Lacking picks until the fifth round, they went for a riskier high-ceiling selection with their second choice, Notre Dame righthander Jeff Samardzija.

Better known at the time as a wide receiver for the Fighting Irish's football team, Samardzija went 8-2, 4.33 for the Irish baseball team that spring, and the Cubs couldn't resist his power sinker, which they saw register in the mid-to-upper 90s. Samardzija signed a lucrative contract, initially for a bonus of $250,000, but eventually he signed a five-year, $10 million contract to give up football, a deal that included a $2.5 million bonus.

The Cubs weren't done. In the 11th round, they drafted Florida prep pitcher Chris Huseby, a 6-foot-7 righthander who was committed to Auburn and who had pitched just six innings in the spring after Tommy John surgery. Nevertheless, the Cubs gave Huseby a $1.3 million bonus, a record for the 11th round.

Sons Also Rise

Another storyline of the draft involved sons of big leaguers. The most prominent example was Texas prep righthander/shortstop Kyle Drabek, who entered the season as one of the draft's top prospects. Drabek's father Doug won the 1990 Cy Young Award and Kyle was on the draft radar from early in his teenage years. However, he also had significant maturity issues, and wound up falling to the 18th overall pick, where the Phillies took him as a pitcher.

Thirteen picks later, the Dodgers stunned most clubs by taking Preston Mattingly, the son of 1985 AL MVP Don Mattingly, with the 31st overall pick. Mattingly signed for $1 million as the Dodgers took him 10 spots before the Yankees' supplemental pick. New York was widely believed to be considering Mattingly at No. 41, but instead took righthander Joba Chamberlain, No. 7 on BA's draft board but available in the supplemental round as teams had late medical concerns about the Cornhuskers' ace.

Another Midwestern talent who wound up falling in the draft was lefthander Brett Anderson, son of Oklahoma State coach Frank. Anderson wound up going 55th overall, with the 11th pick of the second round to the Diamondbacks. He was traded to the Athletics in December, 2007.

DRAFT 06: FIRST-ROUND PICKS

No.	Club	Player, Pos.	School	Hometown	Ht.	Wt.	B-T	Age
1.	Royals	Luke Hochevar, rhp	None	Fowler, Colo.	6-5	205	R-R	22
2.	Rockies	Greg Reynolds, rhp	Stanford	Pacifica, Calif.	6-7	220	R-R	20
3.	Devil Rays	Evan Longoria, 3b	Long Beach State	Bellflower, Calif.	6-2	213	R-R	20
4.	Pirates	Brad Lincoln, rhp	Houston	Clute, Texas	6-0	200	L-R	21
5.	Mariners	Brandon Morrow, rhp	California	Rohnert Park, Calif.	6-3	190	R-R	21
6.	Tigers	Andrew Miller, lhp	North Carolina	Gainesville, Fla.	6-6	195	L-L	21
7.	Dodgers	Clayton Kershaw, lhp	Highland Park HS	Dallas	6-3	220	L-L	18
8.	Reds	Drew Stubbs, of	Texas	Atlanta, Texas	6-4	200	R-R	21
9.	Orioles	Billy Rowell, 3b	Bishop Eustace HS	Pennsauken, N.J.	6-5	215	L-R	17
10.	Giants	Tim Lincecum, rhp	Washington	Renton, Wash.	5-11	170	L-R	21
11.	Diamondbacks	Max Scherzer, rhp	Missouri	Chesterfield, Mo.	6-2	210	R-R	21
12.	Rangers	Kasey Kiker, lhp	Russell County HS	Seale, Ala.	5-11	185	L-L	18
13.	Cubs	Tyler Colvin, of	Clemson	North Augusta, S.C.	6-3	190	L-L	20
14.	Blue Jays	Travis Snider, of	Jackson HS	Mill Creek, Wash.	5-11	230	L-L	18
15.	Nationals	Chris Marrero, of	Monsignor Pace HS	Opa Locka, Fla.	6-3	210	R-R	21
16.	Brewers	Jeremy Jeffress, rhp	Halifax County HS	South Boston, Va.	6-0	175	R-R	18
17.	Padres	Matt Antonelli, 3b	Wake Forest	Danvers, Mass.	6-1	195	R-R	21
18.	Phillies	Kyle Drabek, rhp	The Woodlands HS	The Woodlands, Texas	6-1	190	R-R	18
19.	Marlins	Brett Sinkbeil, rhp	Missouri State	Sand Springs, Okla.	6-3	195	R-R	21
20.	Twins	Chris Parmelee, of	Chino Hills HS	Chino Hills, Calif.	6-1	205	L-L	18
21.	Yankees	Ian Kennedy, rhp	Southern California	Westminster, Calif.	6-0	195	R-R	21
22.	Nationals	Colton Willems, rhp	Carroll HS	Fort Pierce, Fla.	6-4	175	R-R	17
23.	Astros	Max Sapp, c	Bishop Moore HS	Orlando	6-2	220	L-R	18
24.	Braves	Cody Johnson, of	Mosley HS	Lynn Haven, Fla.	6-4	195	L-R	17
25.	Angels	Hank Conger, c	Huntington Beach HS	Huntington Beach, Calif.	6-0	205	B-R	18
26.	Dodgers	Bryan Morris, rhp	Motlow St. (Tenn.) CC	Tullahoma, Tenn.	6-3	175	L-R	19
27.	Red Sox	Jason Place, of	Wren HS	Piedmont, S.C.	6-3	205	R-R	18
28.	Red Sox	Daniel Bard, rhp	North Carolina	Charlotte	6-4	200	R-R	21
29.	White Sox	Kyle McCulloch, rhp	Texas	Houston	6-3	185	R-R	21
30.	Cardinals	Adam Ottavino, rhp	Northeastern	Brooklyn	6-5	215	R-R	20

2006

CLUB-BY-CLUB SELECTIONS

ARIZONA DIAMONDBACKS

June—Regular Phase (11)

1. **Max Scherzer, rhp, Missouri**
1. **Brooks Brown, rhp, Georgia** (Supplemental pick—34th—for loss of Type A free agent Tim Worrell)
2. **Brett Anderson, lhp, Stillwater (Okla.) HS**
3. **Dallas Buck, rhp, Oregon State** (Pick from Giants as compensation for Worrell)
3. **Cyle Hankerd, of, Southern California**
4. **Bryant Thompson, rhp, Pensacola (Fla.) JC**
5. **Hector Ambriz, rhp, UCLA**
6. **Joey Side, of, Georgia**
7. **Daniel Stange, rhp, UC Riverside**
8. **Chase Christianson, rhp, South Alabama**
9. **Eddie Romero, lhp, Fresno State**
10. **Tony Barnette, rhp, Arizona State**
11. **Daniel Fournier, rhp, Franklin Pierce (N.H.)**
12. **Andrew Fie, 3b, Trinity Christian Academy, Jacksonville, Fla.**
13. **John Hester, c, Stanford**
14. **Chad Beck, rhp, Louisiana-Lafayette**
15. **Matthew Oxendine, ss, North Florida**
16. **Blake Sharpe, 2b, Southern California**
17. **Brett Reynolds, rhp, Missouri**
18. **Brad Miller, 1b, Ball State**
19. **Tyler Jones, of, South Alabama**
20. Enrique Garcia, rhp, Potomac State (W.Va.) JC
21. **Sean Smith, 2b, UCLA**
22. **Daniel Perales, of, Southern California**
23. **Derrick Walker, of, Wabash Valley (Ill.) JC**
24. **Andrew Beshenich, of, Norristown (Pa.) HS**
25. **Shane Byrne, of, East Tennessee State**
26. Frank Corolla, rhp, Magnolia (Texas) HS
27. **Connor Janes, of, British Columbia**
28. **Shea McFeely, 3b, Oregon State**
29. Andrew Hayes, ss, McKenzie (Tenn.) HS
30. **Clay Zavada, lhp, Southern Illinois-Edwardsville**
31. Kiel Roling, c, Central Arizona JC
32. Osmany Masso, ss, Miami, Fla.
33. **Osbek Castillo, rhp, Encino, Calif.**
34. **Roberto Cruz, c, Long Beach State**
35. Casey Whitmer, rhp, Kilgore (Texas) HS
36. Jason Durst, rhp, Lake Sumter (Fla.) CC
37. Tyler Kmetko, 2b, Utah
38. Michael Guerrero, of, Meridian (Miss.) CC
39. Riley Etchebarren, of, Paradise Valley HS, Phoenix
40. Nick Cejka, c, Columbia Basin (Wash.) CC
41. Quinton Marsh, lhp, Wickenburg (Ariz.) HS
42. Sean Coughlin, c, Kentucky
43. Jason Stidham, ss, Melbourne (Fla.) HS
44. **Justin Brashear, c, Mississippi**
45. **Clayton Conner, 3b, Okaloosa-Walton (Fla.) CC**
46. Rene Garcia, rhp, Pima (Ariz.) CC
47. David Mixon, rhp, Louisiana-Monroe
48. Michael Solbach, rhp, Liberty
49. Dominic Piazza, c, Notre Dame
50. Kendal Volz, rhp, Smithson Valley HS, Spring Branch, Texas

ATLANTA BRAVES

June—Regular Phase (24)

1. **Cody Johnson, of, Mosley HS, Lynn Haven, Fla.**
1. **Cory Rasmus, rhp, Russell County HS, Seale, Ala.** (Supplemental pick—38th—for loss of Type A free agent Kyle Farnsworth)
1. **Steve Evarts, lhp, Robinson HS, Tampa** (Supplemental pick—43rd—for loss of Type A free agent Rafael Furcal)
2. **Jeff Locke, lhp, Kennett HS Conway, N.H.** (Pick from Dodgers as compensation for Furcal)
2. **Dustin Evans, rhp, Georgia Southern**
2. **Chase Fontaine, ss, Daytona Beach (Fla.) CC** (Pick from Yankees as compensation for Farnsworth)
3. **Chad Rodgers, lhp, Walsh Jesuit HS, Stow, Ohio**
4. **Lee Hyde, lhp, Georgia Tech**
5. **Kevin Gunderson, lhp, Oregon State**
6. **Steven Figueroa, rhp, Edgewater HS, Orlando**
7. **Adam Coe, 3b, Russell County HS, Seale, Ala.**
8. **Casey Beck, rhp, San Jacinto (Texas) JC**
9. **Tim Gustafson, rhp, Georgia Tech**
10. **Kris Medlen, rhp, Santa Ana (Calif.) JC**
11. **Mike Mehlich, rhp, Bishop Moore HS, Orlando**
12. **Josh Morris, 1b, Georgia**
13. **Joe Johnson, rhp, Louisburg (N.C.) JC**
14. **Matt Small, rhp, Ipswich (Mass.) HS**
15. **Stephen Shults, 3b, Walters State (Tenn.) CC**
16. Jack Tilghman, rhp, Walters State (Tenn.) CC
17. **Clayton McMillan, lhp, Texarkana (Texas) CC**
18. J.B. Paxson, c, Walters State (Tenn.) CC
19. **Deunte Heath, rhp, Tennessee**
20. Jonathan Cluff, of, Bingham HS, South Jordan, Utah
21. Jordan Brown, rhp, Meridian (Miss.) CC
22. **Cole Rohrbough, lhp, Western Nevada CC**
23. Blake Guthrie, c, Louisburg (N.C.) JC
24. Zac Oliver, lhp, Paris (Texas) JC
25. Kyle Witten, rhp, Liberty HS, Bakersfield, Calif.
26. **Ryne Reynoso, rhp, Boston College**
27. Jake Rodriguez, rhp, Whittier (Calif.) HS
28. Adam Milligan, of, Hardin County HS, Savannah, Tenn.
29. Andrew Dunn, rhp, Logan (Ill.) JC
30. **David Berres, of, South Suburban (Ill.) JC**
31. **Eric Barrett, lhp, Logan (Ill.) JC**
32. Brendon Porch, rhp, East Union HS, Blue Springs, Miss.
33. Jordan Poirrier, ss, Riverside Academy, Coushatta, La.
34. Matt Morgal, rhp, Seminole State (Okla.) JC
35. Aroyo Fleming, rhp, Central HS, Baton Rouge, La.
36. Samson Williams, of, Laney HS, Wilmington, N.C.
37. Eric Broberg, 1b, Bishop Moore HS, Orlando
38. Josh Ashton, of, Rose HS, Greenville, N.C.
39. Danny Davidson, rhp, Southern Union State (Ala.) CC
40. Tyreace House, of, Palmdale (Calif.) HS
41. Keegan Dennis, rhp, White County HS, Carmi, Ill.
42. Ralph West, lhp, Gar-Field HS, Woodbridge, Va.
43. **L.V. Ware, of, Okaloosa-Walton (Fla.) CC**
44. Kris Cichoski, rhp, CC of Southern Nevada
45. Mason Tobin, rhp, Western Nevada CC
46. Tyler Musselwhite, rhp, Chipola (Fla.) JC
47. John Kessick, rhp, Lake Michigan (Mich.) JC
48. Travis Tucker, 2b, McLennan (Texas) CC
49. Blake Holt, of, Temple (Texas) CC
50. Matt Jordan, lhp, Hinds (Miss.) CC

BALTIMORE ORIOLES

June—Regular Phase (9)

1. **Bill Rowell, 3b, Bishop Eustace Prep, Pennsauken, N.J.**
1. **Pedro Beato (Supplemental pick), rhp, St. Petersburg (Fla.) JC** (Supplemental pick—32nd—for loss of Type A free agent B.J. Ryan)
2. (Pick to Padres as compensation for Type A free agent Ramon Hernandez)
2. **Ryan Adams, 3b, Jesuit HS, New Orleans** (Pick from Blue Jays as compensation for Ryan)
3. **Zach Britton, lhp, Weatherford (Texas) HS**
4. **Blake Davis, ss, Cal State Fullerton**
5. **Tyler Henson, ss, Tuttle (Okla.) HS**

6. **Jason Berken, rhp, Clemson**
7. **Josh Tamba, rhp, Cypress (Calif.) JC**
8. **Jedidiah Stephen, ss, Ohio State**
9. **Brett Bordes, lhp, Arizona State**
10. Emeel Salem, of, Alabama
11. **Anthony Martinez, 1b, Louisburg (N.C.) JC**
12. **Brandon Tripp, of, Cal State Fullerton**
13. **Ryan Ouellette, rhp, Indian River (Fla.) CC**
14. **Brent Allar, rhp, Texas Christian**
15. **Dustin Black, c, Cleveland State (Tenn.) CC**
16. **Justin Johnson, c, Illinois-Chicago**
17. Tony Watson, lhp, Nebraska
18. **Nate Nery, lhp, Stetson**
19. **Todd Davison, ss, Delaware**
20. **Zach Dillon, c, Baylor**
21. **Luis Lopez, of, Dra Maria Cadilla de Martinez HS, Arecibo, P.R.**
22. **Chris Salberg, lhp, Florida Atlantic**
23. **Aubrey Miller, rhp, Arkansas Tech**
24. **Josh Faiola, rhp, Dartmouth**
25. Donnie Anderson, rhp, Southwestern (Calif.) JC
26. Kipp Schutz, of, Harrison HS, Evansville, Ind.
27. **Zach Jevne, rhp, Northern Iowa**
28. **Mike Pierce, c, Fresno Pacific (Calif.)**
29. Brandon Kimbrel, rhp, Yoe HS, Cameron, Texas
30. Chris Cassidy, lhp, Riverside (Calif.) CC
31. Zach Gerler, ss, Howell Central HS, St. Charles, Mo.
32. B.J. Dail, rhp, Millbrook HS, Raleigh, N.C.
33. **Drew Conklin, rhp, South Mountain (Ariz.) CC**
34. Tyler Blandford, rhp, Daviess County HS, Owensboro, Ky.
35. Matt Drummond, lhp, Paso Robles (Calif.) HS
36. **Pat Egan, rhp, Quinnipiac (Conn.)**
37. Michael Lane, of, Daviess County HS, Owensboro, Ky.
38. Adam Urnberg, rhp, JC of Southern Idaho
39. Neal Davis, lhp, Catonsville HS, Baltimore
40. **David Cash, 2b, Florida**
41. Scott Migl, rhp, St. Pius X HS, Houston
42. Jordan Durrance, lhp, Sierra HS, Manteca, Calif.
43. **Jose Kianes, of, Martin County HS, Stuart, Fla.**
44. Travis Lamar, rhp, Harrison HS, Evansville, Ind.
45. Isaiah Stanback, of, Washington
46. Vin DiFazio, c, Indian River (Fla.) CC
47. Troy Burki, lhp, Gig Harbor (Wash.) HS
48. **Jason Mills, rhp, George Mason**
49. Dan Watson, rhp, Manatee (Fla.) HS
50. Orlando Rodriguez, c, Domenech HS, Isabela, P.R.

BOSTON RED SOX

June—Regular Phase (27)

1. **Jason Place, of, Wren HS, Piedmont, S.C.**
1. **Daniel Bard, rhp, North Carolina** (Pick from Yankees as compensation for Type A free agent Johnny Damon)
1. **Kris Johnson (Supplemental pick), lhp, Wichita State** (Supplemental pick—40th—for loss of Damon)
1. **Caleb Clay (Supplemental pick), rhp, Cullman (Ala.) HS** (Supplemental pick—44th—for loss of Type A free agent Bill Mueller)
2. **Justin Masterson, rhp, San Diego State**
3. **Aaron Bates, 1b, North Carolina State** (Pick from Dodgers as compensation for Mueller)
3. **Bryce Cox, rhp, Rice**
4. **Jon Still, c, North Carolina State**
5. **Dustin Richardson, lhp, Texas Tech**
6. **Zach Daeges, 3b, Creighton**
7. **Kris Negron, ss, Cosumnes River (Calif.) JC**
8. **Rafael Cabreja, of, Monroe HS, New York**
9. **Ryan Kalish, of, Red Bank (N.J.) Catholic HS**
10. Kyle Snyder, rhp, Wellington (Fla.) Community HS
11. Brandon Belt, of, Hudson HS, Lufkin, Texas
12. **Ryan Khoury, ss, Utah**
13. **Jordan Craft, rhp, Dallas Baptist**
14. Matt LaPorta, 1b, Florida
15. **Jorge Jimenez, 3b, Porterville (Calif.) JC**
16. **Ty Weeden, c, Santa Fe HS, Edmond, Okla.**
17. **Josh Reddick, of, Middle Georgia JC**
18. **Lars Anderson, 1b, Jesuit HS, Carmichael, Calif.**
19. **Richie Lentz, rhp, Washington**
20. Kyle Gilligan, ss, Etobicoke Collegiate Institute, Toronto
21. **Brian Steinocher, rhp, Stephen F. Austin**
22. Mike Christl, rhp, Bradley
23. **Paul Smyth, of, San Diego State**
24. Robert Phares, rhp, Shelton State (Ala.) CC
25. Sean Gleason, rhp, Lamar (Colo.) CC
26. Chad Gross, 1b, Claremont (Calif.) HS
27. **Brantley New, rhp, Mercer**
28. Carmine Giardina, lhp, Durant HS, Plant City, Fla.
29. Devin Foreman, 1b, Hales Franciscan HS, Chicago
30. **Ryne Lawson, rhp, West Alabama**
31. Logan Shafer, of, Cuesta (Calif.) JC
32. **Mike Chambers, 2b, Franklin Pierce (N.H.)**
33. Jeffrey Rea, 2b, Mississippi State
34. Bryan Morgado, lhp, Florida Christian HS, Tallahassee, Fla.
35. Jeremy Rahman, of, Hazelwood Central HS, Florissant, Mo.
36. **Darren Blocker, 3b, Connors State (Okla.) JC**
37. Justin Marks, lhp, Owensboro (Ky.) Catholic HS
38. **Travis Beazley, rhp, Randolph-Macon (Va.)**
39. Jordan Abruzzo, c, San Diego
40. Corey Davisson, c, West HS, Fresno, Calif.
41. Pete Tountas, ss, Jefferson (Mo.) CC
42. Doug Graybill, lhp, Sarasota (Fla.) HS
43. **Jeff Vincent, of, Niagara**
44. Andrew Leary, rhp, Sierra Vista HS, Las Vegas
45. Jake McCarter, rhp, Alabama
46. Junior Rodriguez, 3b, Coral Gables (Fla.) HS
47. Nick Hill, lhp, Army
48. **Josh Papelbon, rhp, North Florida**
49. P.J. Thomas, rhp, Wabash Valley (Ill.) CC
50. Darrell Fisherbaugh, rhp, Hawaii

CHICAGO CUBS

June—Regular Phase (13)

1. **Tyler Colvin, of, Clemson**
2. (Pick to Indians as compensation for Type A free agent Bob Howry)
3. (Pick to Giants as compensation for Type A free agent Scott Eyre)
4. (Pick to Twins as compensation for Type B free agent Jacque Jones)
5. **Jeff Samardzija, rhp, Notre Dame**
6. **Josh Lansford, 3b, Cal Poly**
7. **Steve Clevenger, ss, Chipola (Fla.) JC**
8. **Billy Muldowney, rhp, Pittsburgh**
9. **Cliff Andersen, of, Cottonwood HS, Salt Lake City**
10. **Jake Renshaw, rhp, Ventura (Calif.) CC**
11. **Chris Huseby, rhp, Martin County HS, Stuart, Fla.**
12. **Kitt Kopach, rhp, Illinois State**
13. **Matt Camp, of, North Carolina State**
14. **Drew Rundle, of, Bend (Ore.) HS**
15. **Matt Canepa, c, Cal Poly**
16. **Blake Parker, c, Arkansas**
17. Keoni Ruth, 2b, San Diego
18. Jose Hernandez, rhp, Edgewater HS, Orlando
19. **Jeremy Papelbon, lhp, North Florida**
20. **Kevin Kreier, rhp, Foothill HS, Henderson, Nev.**
21. **Taylor Parker, lhp, Missouri**
22. **Jovan Rosa, 3b, Lake City (Fla.) CC**
23. **Chuckie Platt, rhp, Lamar**
24. **Matt Matulia, ss, The Citadel**
25. Jamie Bagley, rhp, Hargrave HS, Huffman, Texas
26. **Michael Cooper, rhp, California**
27. **Cedric Redmond, rhp, Joliet (Ill.) Township HS**
28. Brett Summers, rhp, South Suburban (Ill.) CC
29. **Jordan Latham, rhp, JC of Southern Idaho**
30. **Donny Walters, rhp, Richland (Texas) JC**
31. Bryan Collins, rhp, Alvin (Texas) CC
32. **Cesar Valentin, ss, Catalina Morales de Flore HS, Moca, P.R.**
33. **Brad Clipp, rhp, Point Loma Nazarene (Calif.)**

34. **Nate Samson, ss, Ocala Forest HS, Ocala, Fla.**
35. Marquez Smith, 3b, Clemson
36. **Miguel Cuevas-Novas, rhp, Los Angeles Pierce JC**
37. David Francis, rhp, St. Joseph SS, Mississauga, Ontario
38. Ben Feltner, of, Temple (Texas) JC
39. **Marcus Hatley, of, Mission Hills HS, San Marcos, Calif.**
40. **Eli Diaz, rhp, Texarkana CC**
41. Jonathan Negron, rhp, Puerto Rico Baseball Academy, Guaynabo, P.R.
42. Ben Ornelas, of, Cypress (Calif.) JC
43. Anthony Morel, ss, Riverside (Calif.) CC
44. Dan Berlind, rhp, Calabasas (Calif.) HS
45. Elliott Shea, of, Franklin Pierce (N.H.)
46. Ryan Shook, lhp, Valley Christian Academy, Roseville, Calif.
47. **Andrew McCormick, rhp, Pikeville (Ky.)**
48. Kenneth Goodline, rhp, North Monterey County HS, Castroville, Calif.
49. **Ryne Malone, 3b, Florida State**
50. Ryan Davis, lhp, East Lake HS, Sammamish, Wash.

CHICAGO WHITE SOX

June—Regular Phase (29)

1. **Kyle McCulloch, rhp, Texas**
2. **Matt Long, rhp, Miami (Ohio)**
3. **Justin Edwards, lhp, Olympia HS, Orlando**
4. **Tyler Reves, c, Texas Tech**
5. **John Shelby, 2b, Kentucky**
6. **Brian Omogrosso, rhp, Indiana State**
7. **Justin Cassel, rhp, UC Irvine**
8. **Kent Gerst, of, Fort Zumwalt West HS, O'Fallon, Mo.**
9. Chris Duffy, 3b, Cypress Creek HS, Orlando
10. **Lee Cruz, of, Tampa**
11. **Andrew Urena, rhp, Mercer**
12. **Sergio Morales, of, Broward (Fla.) CC**
13. **Tyson Corley, rhp, South Mountain (Ariz.) CC**
14. **Mike Grace, 1b, Florida Southern**
15. Yasser Clor, rhp, Wilcox HS, Santa Clara, Calif.
16. Jose Jimenez, 3b, Monsignor Edward Pace HS, Opa Locka, Fla.
17. **Kylee Hash, c, Basic HS, Henderson, Nev.**
18. Lucas Luetge, lhp, San Jacinto (Texas) JC
19. Jeff Dunbar, c, UC Riverside
20. Wade Kapteyn, rhp, Illiana Christian HS, Lansing, Ill.
21. **Matt Inouye, c, Hawaii**
22. **Kanekoa Texeira, rhp, Saddleback (Calif.) CC**
23. Brandon Villalobos, lhp, Chaffey (Calif.) JC
24. **Michael Rocco, rhp, Cal State San Bernardino**
25. **Joseph Hunter, of, Mississippi State**
26. **David Wasylak, rhp, Lubbock Christian (Texas)**
27. Tyler Herriage, lhp, Marcus HS, Flower Mound, Texas
28. **Jedon Matthews, 3b, Horizon HS, San Diego**
29. **Garrett Johnson, lhp, Orme HS, Mayer, Ariz.**
30. **Hector Santiago, lhp, Essex County Vocational Technical HS, Bloomfield, N.J.**
31. **Stefan Gartrell, of, San Francisco**
32. Alex Curry, rhp, Canyon HS, Anaheim
33. Chris Ulrey, of, New Palestine (Ind.) HS
34. Tyler Wright, of, South Florida CC
35. Adam Heisler, of, Baker HS, Mobile, Ala.
36. **Matt Enuco, 2b, Rowan (N.J.)**
37. Adam Severino, of, Broward (Fla.) CC
38. Jake Petricka, rhp, Faribault (Minn.) HS
39. Clint Cisper, rhp, Northeastern State (Okla.)
40. **Andy Mead, of, SUNY Cortland**
41. Mike Bolsenbroek, rhp, Santa Ana (Calif.) CC
42. Jose Jackson, 2b, South Florida CC
43. **Jordan Cheatham, of, Pike HS, Indianapolis**
44. Andy Fernandez, rhp, Hialeah (Fla.) HS
45. Raul Duran, of, Saddleback HS, Santa Ana, Calif.
46. Michael Cerda, 3b, Beyer HS, Modesto, Calif.
47. Kyle Williams, 2b, Chaparral HS, Scottsdale, Ariz.
48. Rafael Reyes, c, Palmer Trinity HS, Miami
49. Rafael Vera, 2b, Manatee (Fla.) CC
50. **Brendon O'Donnell, of, Texas-Permian Basin**

CINCINNATI REDS

June—Regular Phase (8)

1. **Drew Stubbs, of, Texas**
2. **Sean Watson, rhp, Tennessee**
3. **Chris Valaika, ss, UC Santa Barbara**
4. **Justin Reed, of, Hillcrest Christian HS, Jackson, Miss.**
5. **Josh Ravin, rhp, Chatsworth (Calif.) HS**
6. **Jordan Smith, rhp, CC of Southern Nevada**
7. **Justin Turner, 2b, Cal State Fullerton**
8. **Travis Webb, rhp, Washington State**
9. **Jeremy Burchett, rhp, California**
10. **Josh Roenicke, rhp, UCLA**
11. **Brandon Rice, rhp, Spalding HS, Griffin, Ga.**
12. **Logan Parker, 1b, Cincinnati**
13. **Kevin Gunter, rhp, Old Dominion**
14. **Carson Kainer, of, Texas**
15. **Rafael Sanchez, 3b, Queensborough (N.Y.) CC**
16. **Jamie Arneson, lhp, Bakersfield (Calif.) CC**
17. **Chris Heisey, of, Messiah (Pa.)**
18. Ryan Wehrle, ss, Nebraska
19. **Derrik Lutz, rhp, George Washington**
20. **Eddy Rodriguez, c, Miami**
21. **Chris White, rhp, Texas A&M-Kingsville**
22. **Adam Pointer, rhp, Alvin (Texas) CC**
23. **Tony Brown, of, Crestview (Fla.) HS**
24. **Anthony Esquer, c, Cal Poly Pomona**
25. **Mike McKennon, of, Texas-San Antonio**
26. **Anthony Gressick, rhp, Ohio**
27. **Kel Jones, of, Darton (Ga.) JC**
28. **Tyler Hauschild, c, Edmonds (Wash.) CC**
29. **Jason Louwsma, 3b, Florida Gulf Coast**
30. **Lee Tabor, lhp, Francis Marion (S.C.)**
31. **Eric Schaler, rhp, Dallas Baptist**
32. **Danny Dorn, of, Cal State Fullerton**
33. Justin Curry, rhp, Buford (Ga.) HS
34. Ben Ihde, 1b, Neenah (Wis.) HS
35. John Touchton, rhp, Kingwood (Texas) HS
36. **Nick Wandless, rhp, South Carolina-Aiken**
37. Jarrod Gaskey, of, Azle (Texas) HS
38. Trevor Coleman, c, Dripping Springs (Texas) HS
39. **Todd Waller, 3b, Cape Coral (Fla.) HS**
40. Tyler Dewitt, of, Ponderosa HS, Shingle Springs, Calif.
41. Jeremy Erben, rhp, New Braunfels (Texas) HS
42. John Housey, rhp, Nova HS, Davie, Fla.
43. Geraldo Leal, rhp, Mission (Texas) HS
44. Jason Chapman, of, Truckee (Calif.) HS
45. Mike Lachapelle, lhp, Sahuaro HS, Tuscon, Ariz.
46. Jordan Tiegs, rhp, Sauk Valley (Ill.) CC
47. Freuny Parra, c, Connors State (Okla.) JC
48. Jordan Shadle, ss, Green River (Wash.) CC
49. Cameron Bayne, rhp, St. Louis HS, Honolulu
50. Blake Benveniste, 3b, Chaminade Prep, West Hills, Calif.

CLEVELAND INDIANS

June—Regular Phase (25)

1. (Pick to Angels as compensation for Type B free agent Paul Byrd)
1. **David Huff, lhp, UCLA** (Supplemental pick—39th—for loss of Type A free agent Bob Howry)
2. **Steven Wright, rhp, Hawaii** (Pick from Rangers as compensation for Type B free agent Kevin Millwood)
2. **Josh Rodriguez, 2b, Rice** (Pick from Cubs as compensation for Howry)
2. **Wes Hodges, 3b, Georgia Tech**
2. **Matt McBride, c, Lehigh** (Supplemental pick—75th—for loss of Type C free agent Scott Elarton)
3. **Adam Davis, ss, Florida**
4. **Ryan Morris, lhp, South Mecklenburg HS, Charlotte, N.C.**
5. **Chris Archer, rhp, Clayton (N.C.) HS**
6. **Austin Creps, rhp, Texas A&M**
7. **Robbie Alcombrack, c, Bear River HS, Grass Valley, Calif.**
8. **Mike Eisenberg, rhp, Marietta (Ohio)**
9. **Jared Goedert, 2b, Kansas State**

10. **Paolo Espino, rhp, Pendleton School, Bradenton, Fla.**
11. **Kelly Edmundson, c, Tennessee**
12. **Dan Frega, rhp, Illinois State**
13. Brant Rustich, rhp, UCLA
14. **William Delage, lhp, Lamar**
15. **Matt Meyer, lhp, Boston College**
16. **Stephen Douglas, of, East Tennessee State**
17. **Kyle Harper, rhp, Orange Coast (Calif.) CC**
18. **Daryl King, of, Benicia (Calif.) HS**
19. **Josh Tomlin, rhp, Texas Tech**
20. **Vinnie Pestano, rhp, Cal State Fullerton**
21. **John Gaub, lhp, Minnesota**
22. **Chuck Hargis, ss, East Tennessee State**
23. **Derrick Loop, lhp, Cal State Los Angeles**
24. **Chris Nash, 1b, Johnson County (Kan.) CC**
25. Alex Jordan, rhp, Cypress (Calif.) JC
26. Ty Pryor, rhp, Tennessee
27. Chris Roberts, of, West HS, Oshkosh, Wis.
28. **Dustin Realini, 3b, Santa Clara**
29. Thomas Benton, rhp, UNC Wilmington
30. **Brett Carlin, lhp, Fullerton (Calif.) JC**
31. Easton Gust, 2b, Cottonwood HS, Salt Lake City
32. **David Uribes, 2b, Pepperdine**
33. Jarett Jackson, of, Jefferson HS, Auburn, Wash.
34. Mike Bolsinger, rhp, McKinney North HS, McKinney, Texas
35. **Alan Brech, lhp, Bowling Green State**
36. **Ryan Miller, lhp, Blinn (Texas) JC**
37. **Brett Kinning, 2b, Arkansas State**
38. **Nate Bunton, rhp, Midland Lutheran (Texas)**
39. **Jimmy Brettl, lhp, Cal State Northridge**
40. Josh Yates, c, Arkansas State
41. Kyle Paul, c, Vernon (Texas) CC
42. Roderick Barcelo, of, Rivera HS, Vega Baja, P.R.
43. **Mike Pontius, rhp, Holt HS, Wentzville, Mo.**
44. Brad Reid, rhp, Decatur HS, Federal Way, Wash.
45. Zach Barger, of, Grossmont (Calif.) JC
46. **Dan Miltenberger, rhp, UCLA**
47. Eric McKinney, of, Spiro (Okla.) HS
48. **Travis Turek, rhp, Santa Barbara (Calif.) CC**
49. Ryan Mottern, rhp, Oklahoma
50. Vinnie Catricala, 3b, Jesuit HS, Carmichael, Calif.

COLORADO ROCKIES

June—Regular Phase (2)

1. **Greg Reynolds, rhp, Stanford**
2. **David Christensen, of, Douglas HS Parkland, Fla.**
3. **Keith Weiser, lhp, Miami (Ohio)**
4. **Craig Baker, rhp, Cal State Northridge**
5. **Helder Velazquez, ss, Puerto Rico Baseball Academy, Gurabo, P.R.**
6. **Kevin Clark, of, Manatee (Fla.) CC**
7. **Michael McKenry, c, Middle Tennessee State**
8. **Brandon Hynick, rhp, Birmingham-Southern**
9. **Will Harris, rhp, Louisiana State**
10. **David Arnold, rhp, Lincoln Trail (Ill.) CC**
11. Aaron Miller, of, Channelview (Texas) HS
12. **Austin Rauch, c, El Capitan HS, Lakeside, Calif.**
13. **Spence Nagy, ss, Tallahassee (Fla.) CC**
14. **Jeff Kindel, of, Georgia Tech**
15. **Victor Ferrante, of, Solano (Calif.) JC**
16. **Anthony Jackson, of, Pacific**
17. **Michael Gibbs, rhp, Virginia Commonwealth**
18. Andrew Cashner, rhp, Angelina (Texas) JC
19. **Zack Murry, ss, Chanute (Kan.) HS**
20. **Sean Jarrett, rhp, Oral Roberts**
21. **Andy Graham, rhp, UC Santa Barbara**
22. **Jay Cox, of, North Carolina**
23. Scott Maine, lhp, Miami
24. Shane Dyer, rhp, Eaton (Colo.) HS
25. Jeremy Jones, of, North Carolina A&T
26. **Devin Collis, lhp, Arkansas**
27. **Matt Repec, ss, Winthrop**
28. **Tommy Baumgardner, lhp, Mississippi**
29. **Shane Lowe, ss, New Bloomfield (Mo.) HS**
30. **Scott Robinson, of, Henry County HS, McDonough, Ga.**
31. Curtis Dupart, of, Woodinville (Wash.) HS
32. Miguel Valcarcel, rhp, Perkiomen School, Pennsburg, Pa.
33. **Drew Shetrone, rhp, Cumberland (Tenn.)**
34. Jamie Niley, lhp, Elk Grove (Calif.) Sr. HS
35. **Josh Banda, 1b, California Baptist**
36. Michael Diaz, c, Luis Munoz Marin HS, Barranquitas, P.R.
37. Zach Helton, 2b, Central HS, Knoxville, Tenn.
38. Jon Hesketh, lhp, Vernon (Texas) JC
39. Jason Fuqua, lhp, Sterling HS, Houston
40. David Luna, c, Piedmont Hills HS, San Jose, Calif.
41. Jay Taylor, rhp, West Seattle HS
42. Sean Halton, 1b, Fresno (Calif.) CC
43. Bryan Jaeger, of, Louisiana State-Eunice JC
44. Scott Bachman, lhp, Rocky Mountain HS, Fort Collins, Colo.
45. Jamie Manning, rhp, Wallace State (Ala.) CC
46. Damion Carter, of, Southern Mississippi
47. Justin Miller, rhp, Bakersfield (Calif.) JC
48. Jesus Cebollero, rhp, Puerto Rico Baseball Academy, San Sebastian, P.R.
49. Paul Dickey, rhp, Lower Columbia (Wash.) CC
50. Jamie Johnson, of, West Ouachita HS, West Monroe, La.

DETROIT TIGERS

June—Regular Phase (6)

1. **Andrew Miller, lhp, North Carolina**
2. **Ron Bourquin, 3b, Ohio State**
3. **Brennan Boesch, of, California**
4. **Ryan Strieby, 1b, Kentucky**
5. **Scott Sizemore, 2b, Virginia Commonwealth**
6. **Jordan Newton, c, Western Kentucky**
7. **Jonah Nickerson, rhp, Oregon State**
8. **Chris Cody, lhp, Manhattan**
9. **Zach Piccola, lhp, South Alabama**
10. **L.J. Gagnier, rhp, Cal State Fullerton**
11. **Hayden Parrott, 2b, Desert Mountain HS, Scottsdale, Ariz.**
12. **Joe Bowen, c, Vanguard HS, Ocala, Fla.**
13. **Angel Castro, rhp, Western Oklahoma State JC**
14. **Brett Jensen, rhp, Nebraska**
15. Franco Valdes, c, Monsignor Edward Pace HS, Opa Locka, Fla.
16. **Jeff Gerbe, rhp, Michigan State**
17. Ben Petralli, c, Sacramento CC
18. **Deik Scram, of, Oklahoma State**
19. **Duane Below, lhp, Lake Michigan (Mich.) JC**
20. **Casey Fien, rhp, Cal Poly**
21. **Tom Thornton, lhp, Notre Dame**
22. **Chris Krawczyk, rhp, Missouri State**
23. **Aaron Fuhrman, lhp, Pleasant Valley HS, Brodheadsville, Pa.**
24. **Joe Tucker, of, Kent State**
25. Casey Weathers, rhp, Vanderbilt
26. Daniel Renfroe, of, Tattnall Square Academy, Macon, Ga.
27. Ryan Lindgren, rhp, Seminole State (Okla.) JC
28. **Derek Witt, rhp, Ohio**
29. **Chris Carlson, 1b, New Mexico**
30. Philip Ortez, of, Scottsdale (Ariz.) CC
31. **Mike Sullivan, of, Ball State**
32. **Rudy Darrow, rhp, Nicholls State**
33. Kodiak Quick, rhp, Kansas
34. **Brandon Johnson, rhp, Butler County (Kan.) CC**
35. **Paul Hammond, lhp, Michigan**
36. Chad Nading, rhp, East HS, Anchorage, Alaska
37. Ryan LaMotta, rhp, Baylor
38. **Dana Arrowood, rhp, Old Dominion**
39. **Michael Bertram, 3b, Kentucky**
40. **Adrian Casanova, c, Clemson**
41. Taylor Freeman, c, Carney (Okla.) HS
42. Kevin Chapman, lhp, Westminster Academy, Fort Lauderdale, Fla.
43. David Mattox, rhp, Connors State (Okla.) JC
44. Ryan Kilmer, of, Midwest City (Okla.) HS
45. Lance Durham, of, Bacon HS, Cincinnati
46. Kent Williamson, rhp, Cowley County (Kan.) CC
47. **Alec Shepherd, rhp, South Mountain (Ariz.) CC**

48. Matthew McDonald, rhp, Ulster County (N.Y.) CC
49. Kyle Peter, of, Cloud County (Kan.) CC
50. Alan Oaks, of, Divine Child HS, Dearborn, Mich.

FLORIDA MARLINS

June—Regular Phase (19)

1. **Brett Sinkbeil, rhp, Missouri State**
1. **Chris Coghlan, 3b, Mississippi** (Supplemental pick—36th—for loss of Type A free agent A.J. Burnett)
2. **Tom Hickman, of, Pepperell HS, Lindale, Ga.**
3. **Torre Langley, c, Alexander HS, Douglasville, Ga.** (Pick from Blue Jays as compensation for Burnett)
3. **Scott Cousins, of, San Francisco**
4. **Hector Correa, rhp, Lorenzo Coballes Gandia HS, Hatillo, P.R.**
5. **Chris Hatcher, c, UNC Wilmington**
6. **Justin Jacobs, ss, Chino (Calif.) HS**
7. **Don Czyz, rhp, Kansas**
8. **Dan Garcia, ss, Nogales HS, La Puente, Calif.**
9. **John Raynor, of, UNC Wilmington**
10. **Graham Taylor, lhp, Miami (Ohio)**
11. **Ozzie Martinez, ss, Porterville (Calif.) JC**
12. **Brad Stone, rhp, Quincy (Ill.)**
13. **Drew Saylor, 2b, Kent State**
14. **Jay Buente, rhp, Purdue**
15. **Guillermo Martinez, ss, South Alabama**
16. **Jake Blackwood, 3b, Maplewoods (Mo.) CC**
17. **Hunter Mense, of, Missouri**
18. **Ross Liersemann, rhp, Akron**
19. **Jordan Davis, rhp, Alabama**
20. Steven Sultzbaugh, of, Westwood HS, Austin, Texas
21. **Corey Madden, rhp, St. Mary's**
22. **Kevan Kelley, lhp, Cal State San Bernardino**
23. Rylan Hanks, lhp, Cal State San Bernardino
24. Ernesto Rivera, of, Puerto Rico Baseball Academy, Canovanas, P.R.
25. **Joel Fountain, rhp, St. Mary's**
26. **Andy Jackson, lhp, Central Arkansas**
27. Jeremy Hall, rhp, East Tennnessee State
28. **Kedrick Martin, lhp, Meridian (Miss.) CC**
29. **Jonathan Van Looy, lhp, John Swett HS, Crockett, Calif.**
30. Quinn Harris, ss, Elizabethtown (Ky.) HS
31. William Mays, of, Sinclair (Ohio) CC
32. **Alejandro Sanabia, rhp, Castle Park HS, Chula Vista, Calif.**
33. **Eric Basurto, rhp, Chabot (Calif.) CC**
34. T.J. Kelly, rhp, Bakersfield (Calif.) JC
35. Chris Evans, c, Serrano HS, Phelan, Calif.
36. Dave Williams, of, Rutgers
37. James Wallace, rhp, JC of Southern Idaho
38. Jeremie Tice, 3b, Tallahassee (Fla.) CC
39. **Spike McDougall, of, UC Irvine**
40. **Tony Suarez, rhp, Southeastern Louisiana**
41. Kyle Barry, rhp, Madison Area (Wis.) Tech CC
42. Ryan Kussmaul, rhp, Madison Area Tech (Wis.) CC
43. **William Jackel, rhp, Tallahassee (Fla.) CC**
44. T.J. Forrest, rhp, Haughton (La.) HS
45. Kyle Price, 2b, Eastern Oklahoma State JC
46. **Mitch MacDonald, 3b, Monterey Peninsula (Calif.) JC**
47. Brooks Martin, rhp, Streator (Ill.) HS
48. Lance Hanmer, ss, Greensburg (Ind.) HS
49. Michael Hubbard, of, Arkansas-Fort Smith JC
50. Andrew Raponi, 1b, Monte Vista HS, Danville, Calif.

HOUSTON ASTROS

June—Regular Phase (23)

1. **Max Sapp, c, Bishop Moore HS, Orlando**
2. **Sergio Perez, rhp, Tampa**
3. **Nick Moresi, of, Fresno State**
4. **Chris Johnson, 3b, Stetson**
5. **Casey Hudspeth, rhp, South Florida**
6. **Bud Norris, rhp, Cal Poly**
7. **David Qualben, lhp, Pace (N.Y.)**
8. **Jimmy Van Ostrand, of, Cal Poly**
9. **Greg Buchanan, 2b, Rice**
10. Nathan Karns, rhp, Martin Senior HS, Arlington, Texas
11. **Tom Vessella, lhp, Whittier (Calif.)**
12. **Bryan Hallberg, rhp, Pace (N.Y.)**
13. **Chris Salamida, lhp, Oneonta State (N.Y.)**
14. **Justin Tellam, c, Pepperdine**
15. **Kevin Fox, lhp, Biola (Calif.)**
16. **Drew Holder, of, Dallas Baptist**
17. **Justin Stiver, rhp, Florida Gulf Coast**
18. **Colt Adams, rhp, Dixie State (Utah) JC**
19. **Orlando Rosales, of, Tampa**
20. Mark Sobolewski, ss, Sarasota (Fla.) HS
21. **Anthony Bello, lhp, Nova Southeastern (Fla.)**
22. **Chad Wagler, rhp, Kent State**
23. **Tim Torres, ss, Oral Roberts**
24. John Wiedenbauer, lhp, Seabreeze HS, Daytona Beach, Fla.
25. Jamaal Hollis, rhp, Whitney Young HS, Chicago
26. Lenell McGee, 3b, Mount Carmel (Ill.) HS
27. **Cirilo Cruz, 1b, Cumberland (Tenn.)**
28. **Brandon Caipen, 3b, Youngstown State**
29. **Rafael Parks, of, Greenbrier HS, Evans, Ga.**
30. **Eric Taylor, 3b, UCLA**
31. **Kyle DeYoung, rhp, Florida Southern**
32. **Adam Hale, rhp, Texas A&M**
33. Codi Harshman, of, Sabino HS, Tucson
34. John Anderson, rhp, Captain Shreve HS, Shreveport, La.
35. Patrick Allen, of, Everett (Wash.) CC
36. Johnathan Moore, c, Lamar HS, Arlington Texas
37. Trent Henderson, ss, Newport (Wash.) HS
38. Casey Anderson, c, West Quacita HS, West Monroe, La.
39. Will Kline, rhp, Mississippi
40. Steven Detwiler, ss, San Rafael (Calif.) HS
41. **Axel Gonzalez, of, Martinez HS, Guaynabo, P.R.**
42. Kevin Sullivan, c, York HS, Elmhurst, Ill.
43. Greg Joseph, of, Mount San Jacinto (Calif.) CC
44. Adam Pilate, of, Sylacauga (Ala.) HS
45. Cody Madison, of, Vista Del Lago HS, Moreno Valley, Calif.
46. Joey Wong, ss, Sprague HS, Salem, Ore.
47. Mike Pericht, c, Providence Catholic HS, New Lenox, Ill.
48. Jerry Quinones, lhp, Compton (Calif.) CC
49. **Andy Launier, 1b, Sierra (Calif.) JC**
50. Tyler Henley, of, Rice

KANSAS CITY ROYALS

June—Regular Phase (1)

1. **Luke Hochevar, rhp, Fort Worth (American Association)**
2. **Jason Taylor, ss, Kellam HS, Virginia Beach**
3. **Blake Wood, rhp, Georgia Tech**
4. **Derrick Robinson, of, Yonge HS, Gainesville, Fla.**
5. **Jason Godin, rhp, Old Dominion**
6. **Harold Mozingo, rhp, Virginia Commonwealth**
7. **Brett Bigler, of, UC Riverside**
8. **Josh Cribb, rhp, Clemson**
9. **Marc Maddox, 2b, Southern Mississippi**
10. **Nick Van Stratten, of, St. Louis CC-Meramec**
11. **Tyler Chambliss, rhp, Florida State**
12. **Everett Teaford, lhp, Georgia Southern**
13. **Kurt Mertins, 2b, JC of the Desert (Calif.)**
14. **Daniel Best, rhp, Southern Mississippi**
15. **Nick Francis, of, Pensacola (Fla.) JC**
16. **Tyrone Wilson, ss, Southern HS, Durham, N.C.**
17. **Matt Morizio, c, Northeastern**
18. Chase Larsson, of, Kitsilano SS, Vancouver, B.C.
19. Jeff Inman, rhp, Garces Memorial HS, Bakersfield, Calif.
20. Brad Boxberger, rhp, Foothill HS, Santa Ana, Calif.
21. **Burke Baldwin, lhp, Elgin (Ill.) CC**
22. Romas Hicks, rhp, Georgia State
23. **Aaron Hartsock, rhp, California Baptist**
24. Tyler Moyneur, c, Arizona Western JC
25. Rafael Valenzuela, ss, Nogales (Ariz.) HS
26. Darrell Lockett, of, Weatherford (Texas) HS
27. Colby Killian, rhp, Warren County HS, McMinnville, Tenn.
28. Michael Wheeler, of, Walters State (Tenn.) CC
29. Steve Rinaudo, ss, American River (Calif.) JC

30. Tyler Pearson, rhp, Northern Colorado
31. **Brandon Lance, c, New Mexico State**
32. Fernando Garcia, 2b, Immaculada HS, Arecibo, P.R.
33. Harold Smith, of, Palmetto (Fla.) HS
34. Jared Grace, 1b, Pensacola (Fla.) JC
35. Anthony Stovall, rhp, Kailua (Hawaii) HS
36. Manuel Garcia, rhp, Cochise (Ariz.) JC
37. Kaleb Harst, c, St. Thomas More HS, Lafayette, La.
38. Mike Dabbs, of, Cowley County (Kan.) CC
39. Steven Moore, rhp, Thomasville (Ga.) HS
40. Chris Snipes, lhp, Warner Robins (Ga.) HS
41. Jeremy Toole, rhp, Huntsville (Texas) HS
42. Todd McBride, of, The Dalles (Ore.)-Wahtonka Union HS
43. Brennan Thorpe, rhp, Saddleback (Calif.) CC
44. **Bryan Paukovits, rhp, Southwestern (Calif.) JC**
45. Eric Martinez, rhp, Southwestern (Calif.) JC
46. Chase Lehr, rhp, Centennial HS, Peoria, Ariz.
47. Ryan Cisterna, c, Chandler-Gilbert (Ariz.) CC
48. Colby Ho, 3b, Kaiser HS, Honolulu
49. Rocky Gale, c, North Salem HS, Salem, Ore.
50. **Jarrod Dyson, of, Southwest Mississippi JC**

LOS ANGELES ANGELS

June—Regular Phase (26)

1. **Hank Conger, c, Huntington Beach (Calif.) HS** (Pick from Indians as compensation for Type B free agent Paul Byrd)
1. (Pick to Dodgers as compensation for Type A free agent Jeff Weaver)
2. (Pick to Nationals as compensation for Type B free agent Hector Carrasco)
3. Russ Moldenhauer, of, Boerne (Texas) HS
4. **Clay Fuller, of, Smithson Valley HS, Spring Branch, Texas**
5. **David Herndon, rhp, Gulf Coast (Fla.) CC**
6. **Robert Fish, lhp, Miller HS, San Bernardino, Calif.**
7. Jarrad Page, of, Cal State Los Angeles
8. **Matt Sweeney, 1b, Magruder HS, Rockville, Md.**
9. **Nate Boman, lhp, San Diego**
10. **Leonardo Calderon, lhp, Lake City (Fla.) CC**
11. **David Pellegrine, rhp, Northeastern**
12. **Jordan Walden, rhp, Mansfield (Texas) HS**
13. **Blake Holler, lhp, Stanford**
14. **Chris Armstrong, lhp, Owasso (Okla.) HS**
15. **Scott Knazek, c, Rider**
16. Scott Carroll, rhp, Missouri State
17. **Tadd Brewer, 2b, Lipscomb**
18. Charles Brewer, rhp, Chaparral HS, Scottsdale, Ariz.
19. **Chris Pettit, of, Loyola Marymount**
20. J.D. Reichenbach, lhp, Central Bucks East HS, Doylestown, Penn
21. John Vincent, of, New Mexico State
22. Michael Thomas, rhp, Marshall HS, Missouri City, Texas
23. **Tim Schoeninger, rhp, Nevada**
24. John Curtis, c, Cal State Fullerton
25. Jason Jarvis, rhp, Chaparral HS, Scottsdale, Ariz.
26. Ryan Kelley, lhp, Indian River (Fla.) CC
27. **Matt Reilly, rhp, Pace (N.Y.)**
28. **Barret Browning, lhp, Florida State**
29. **Michael Davitt, rhp, Okaloosa-Walton (Fla.) CC**
30. Kevin Skogley, lhp, Nevada-Las Vegas
31. **Dylan Lindsey, rhp, Broward (Fla.) CC**
32. **Chris Lewis, 2b, Stanford**
33. **Wilberto Ortiz, ss, Dowling (N.Y.)**
34. Bobby Wagner, of, Douglas (B.C.) JC
35. **Aaron Cook, rhp, Tampa**
36. **Alex Fonseca, ss, Florida Atlantic**
37. Ronnie Welty, of, Mesquite HS, Gilbert, Ariz.
38. **Eduardo Chile, rhp, Rollins (Fla.)**
39. **Rian Kiniry, of, Broward (Fla.) CC**
40. Jake Locker, rhp, Ferndale (Wash.) HS
41. Brian Hobbs, of, Chipola (Fla.) JC
42. Jonathan Conaster, rhp, Tallahassee (Fla.) CC
43. **Doug Brandt, lhp, Cal State San Bernardino**
44. **Lou Green, rhp, Chipola (Fla.) JC**
45. Matt McCracken, lhp, Florida CC-Jacksonville
46. Ryan Lipkin, c, Solano (Calif.) JC
47. Jon Plefka, rhp, Texas Tech
48. Abraham Gonzalez, rhp, Coachella Valley HS, Thermal, Calif.
49. **Gordie Gronkowski, 1b, Jacksonville**
50. Tim Brewer, lhp, Kean HS, St. Thomas, Virgin Islands

LOS ANGELES DODGERS

June—Regular Phase (7)

1. **Clayton Kershaw, lhp, Highland Park HS, Dallas**
1. **Bryan Morris, rhp, Motlow State (Tenn.) CC** (Pick from Angels as compensation for Type A free agent Jeff Weaver)
1. **Preston Mattingly, ss, Evansville (Ind.) Central HS** (Supplemental pick—31st—for loss of Weaver)
2. (Pick to Braves as compensation for Type A free agent Rafael Furcal)
3. (Pick to Red Sox as compensation for Type A free agent Bill Mueller)
4. **Kyle Orr, 1b, Lambrick Park SS, Victoria, B.C.**
5. **Kyle Smit, rhp, Spanish Springs HS, Sparks, Nev.**
6. **Garrett White, lhp, Mississippi**
7. **Jaime Ortiz, 1b, San Alfonso de Ligorio HS, Guayama, P.R.**
8. **Tommy Giles, of, Miami**
9. **Bridger Hunt, 3b, Central Missouri State**
10. Andy D'Alessio, 1b, Clemson
11. **Justin Fuller, ss, Lewis-Clark State (Idaho)**
12. **Paul Coleman, lhp, Pepperdine**
13. Nick Akins, ss, Los Angeles HS
14. Alex White, rhp, Conley HS, Greenville, N.C.
15. **Gorman Erickson, c, Westview HS, San Diego**
16. Justin Coats, ss, Texas HS, Texarkana, Texas
17. **Michael Rivera, 2b, Tennessee**
18. **Joe Jones, rhp, Portland**
19. Martin Beno, rhp, Mississippi Gulf Coast JC
20. Billy Bullock, rhp, Riverview (Fla.) HS
21. **Matt Berezay, of, Pacific**
22. **Chris Jensen, of, UCLA**
23. **Eric Thompson, rhp, Roseburg (Ore.) HS**
24. **John Martin, c, Emporia State (Kan.)**
25. **Esteban Lopez, c, Hawaii**
26. Kody Kaiser, 2b, Oklahoma
27. A.J. Casario, c, Overbrook Senior HS, Pine Hill, N.J.
28. Taylor Lewis, rhp, Canyon del Oro HS, Oro Valley, Ariz.
29. Roberto Perez, c, Eugenio Maria de Hostos HS, Mayaguez, P.R.
30. Alex Burkard, lhp, Milton HS, Alpharetta, Ga.
31. Jonathan Wilson, 3b, St. Charles (Mo.) HS
32. Jordan Kopycinski, c, St. Thomas HS, Houston
33. Kurt Bradley, 2b, Northern Iowa
34. Luke Yoder, of, Liberty HS, Bakersfield, Calif.
35. Nick Buss, of, San Diego Mesa JC
36. Robert Taylor, c, Laredo (Texas) CC
37. Anthony Benner, 3b, Southwestern (Calif.) JC
38. Kameron Forte, c, Texas HS, Texarkana, Texas
39. Jake Debus, lhp, Moraine Valley (Ill.) CC
40. Chris Jones, ss, Redan HS, Stone Mountain, Ga.
41. Todd McCraw, c, St. James HS, Myrtle Beach, S.C.
42. Joe Dispensa, of, St. Rita HS, Chicago
43. Jordan Chambless, rhp, Texas A&M
44. Aaron Barrett, rhp, Central HS, Evansville, Ind.
45. Greg Hendrix, lhp, North Atlanta HS
46. Ryan Aguayo, 2b, Servite HS, Anaheim
47. Brett Sowers, 3b, Cherry Creek HS, Englewood, Colo.
48. Tanner Biagini, 3b, Conley HS, Greenville, N.C.
49. Paul Goldschmidt, 1b, The Woodlands (Texas) HS
50. Kurt Benton, rhp, West Stanly HS, Oakboro, N.C.

MILWAUKEE BREWERS

June—Regular Phase (16)

1. **Jeremy Jeffress, rhp, Halifax County HS, South Boston, Va.**
2. **Brent Brewer, ss, Sandy Creek HS, Tyrone, Ga.**
3. **Cole Gillespie, of, Oregon State**
4. **Evan Anundsen, rhp, Columbine HS, Littleton, Colo.**
5. **Chris Errecart, of, California**

6. **Brae Wright, lhp, Oklahoma State**
7. **Andy Bouchie, c, Oral Roberts**
8. **Shane Hill, rhp, Florida Christian HS, Miami**
9. **Shawn Ferguson, rhp, Texas Christian**
10. **Mike McClendon, rhp, Seminole (Fla.) CC**
11. **Zach Clem, of, Washington**
12. **Chad Robinson, rhp, Silverado HS, Las Vegas**
13. **Chris Toneguzzi, rhp, Purdue**
14. **Hector Bernal, ss, El Paso (Texas) CC**
15. **Brett Whiteside, c, Mesquite HS, Gilbert, Ariz.**
16. **R.J. Seidel, rhp, Central HS, La Crosse, Wis.**
17. Aaron Tullo, rhp, St. Peterburg (Fla.) HS
18. Andrew Clark, 1b, New Palestine (Ind.) HS
19. **Lee Haydel, of, Riverside Academy, Coushatta, La.**
20. Mehdi Djebbar, lhp, Ahuntsic (Quebec) JC
21. **Jesse Damico, c, Mohawk HS, Bessemer, Pa.**
22. **J.T. King, rhp, Northeastern Oklahoma A&M JC**
23. Scott Shuman, rhp, Tift County HS, Tifton, Ga.
24. **Travis Wendte, rhp, Missouri**
25. **Mike Goetz, of, Wisconsin-Milwaukee**
26. Marc Lewis, lhp, Creighton
27. T.J. Macy, rhp, Scottsdale (Ariz.) CC
28. Terrell Alliman, of, Bluevale Collegiate Institute, Waterloo, Ontario
29. David Newmann, lhp, Texas A&M
30. **Jordan Swaydan, c, San Diego State**
31. **Rob Bryson, rhp, William Penn HS, New Castle, Del.**
32. **Nick Tyson, rhp, Timber Creek Regional HS, Erial, N.J.**
33. **Eric Newton, 2b, Santa Clara**
34. **Stuart Sutherland, rhp, Dallas Baptist**
35. Sanduan Dubose, 3b, Stillman (Ala.)
36. Clay Jones, c, Bibb County HS, Centreville, Ala.
37. Wes Munson, ss, Fond du Lac (Wis.) HS
38. Todd Fitzgerald, lhp, San Jose (Calif.) CC
39. **Chuck Caufield, of, Oklahoma**
40. Alex Koronis, rhp, Monsignor Edward Pace HS, Opa Locka, Fla.
41. John Poulk, 3b, UNC Wilmington
42. Matt Peck, rhp, Cowley County (Kan.) CC
43. **D.J. Lidyard, rhp, Lower Columbia (Wash.) JC**
44. **Bryan Crosby, 3b, William Blount HS, Maryville, Tenn.**
45. Matt Thompson, ss, Aztec (N.M.) HS
46. Aaron Johnson, c, Lethbridge (Alberta) CC
47. Matthew Coburn, rhp, San Jacinto (Texas) JC
48. Brandon Owens, rhp, Heritage HS, Conyers, Ga.
49. Nick Spears, ss, Poway (Calif.) HS
50. Ricky Alvernaz, 3b, Tamanawis SS, Vancouver, B.C.

MINNESOTA TWINS

June—Regular Phase (20)

1. **Chris Parmelee, of, Chino Hills (Calif.) HS**
2. **Joe Benson, of, Joliet (Ill.) Catholic HS**
3. **Tyler Robertson, lhp, Bella Vista HS, Fair Oaks, Calif.**
4. **Whit Robbins, 1b, Georgia Tech** (Pick from Cubs as compensation for Type B free agent Jacque Jones)
4. **Garrett Olson, 3b, Franklin Pierce (N.H.)**
5. Devin Shepherd, of, Oxnard (Calif.) HS
6. **Jeff Christy, c, Nebraska**
7. **Jon Waltenbury, 1b, Henry Street HS, Whitby, Ontario**
8. **Brian Dinkelman, 2b, McKendree (Ill.)**
9. **Sean Land, lhp, Kansas**
10. Jared Mitchell, of, Westgate HS, New Iberia, La.
11. **Steve Singleton, ss, San Diego**
12. **Kevin Harrington, of, Royal HS, Simi Valley, Calif.**
13. Aaron Senne, of, Mayo HS, Rochester, Minn.
14. **Jeff Manship, rhp, Notre Dame**
15. **Mark Dolenc, of, Minnesota State-Mankato**
16. Shayne Willson, of, Earl Marriott SS, Surrey, B.C
17. Andy Oliver, lhp, Vermillion (Ohio) HS
18. **Chris Anderson, lhp, Northern Essex (Mass.) CC**
19. **Danny Valencia, 3b, Miami**
20. **Gilbert Buenrostro, c, Cuesta (Calif.) JC**
21. **Eric Santiago, ss, Miami Dade CC South**
22. Aaron Tennyson, lhp, Kentucky
23. **Thomas Wright, rhp, McGavock HS, Nashville**
24. **Nick Papasan, ss, Granbury (Texas) HS**
25. Dillon Baird, 3b, Prescott (Ariz.) HS
26. Kyle Mitchell, rhp, Mosley HS, Panama City, Fla.
27. Joe Tribou, c, Northeast HS, St. Petersburg, Fla.
28. Dustin Williams, c, Woodlawn HS, Rison, Ark.
29. Braxton Chisholm, c, St. Cloud (Fla.) HS
30. **Michael Mopas, lhp, Golden West (Calif.) JC**
31. Kyle Thornton, rhp, Cowley County (Kan.) CC
32. Andres Diaz, c, Santaluces HS, Palm Beach, Fla.
33. Alberto Espinosa, c, Brito HS, Miami
34. Marcel Champagnie, ss, Kaskaskia (Ill.) CC
35. Robby Donovan, rhp, Royal Palm Beach HS, West Palm Beach, Fla.
36. J.D. Martinez, of, Flanagan HS, Pembroke Pines, Fla.
37. Aaron Baker, c, Denton (Texas) HS
38. Randy Boone, rhp, Texas
39. **Anthony Slama, rhp, San Diego**
40. **Michael Cowgill, 2b, James Madison**
41. Joan Ortiz, rhp, Juan Ponce de Leon HS, San Juan, P.R.
42. Robert Anderson, rhp, Rider HS, Wichita Falls, Texas
43. Frank Berry, rhp, First Colonial HS, Virginia Beach
44. Isaac Castillo, 2b, Waimea HS, Kauai, Hawaii
45. Brandon Trodick, rhp, CC of Southern Nevada
46. Richard Breton, of, Keystone Heights (Fla.) HS
47. Josh Chester, of, Cypress Bay HS, Weston, Fla.
48. Steve Vento, rhp, Palm Beach (Fla.) CC
49. Calvin Culver, of, Quartz Hill HS, Lancaster, Calif.
50. Derek McCallum, ss, Hill-Murray HS, St. Paul, Minn.

NEW YORK METS

June—Regular Phase (18)

1. (Pick to Phillies as compensation for Type A free agent Billy Wagner)
2. **Kevin Mulvey, rhp, Villanova**
3. **Joe Smith, rhp, Wright State**
4. **John Holdzkom, rhp, Salt Lake CC**
5. **Steve Holmes, rhp, Rhode Island**
6. **Scott Schafer, rhp, Memorial HS, Pasadena, Texas**
7. **Daniel Stegall, of, Greenwood (Ark.) HS**
8. **Nathan Hedrick, rhp, Barton County (Kan.) CC**
9. Jeremy Barfield, of, Klein HS, Spring, Texas
10. **Phillips Orta, rhp, Western Nebraska CC**
11. Andrew Moye, rhp, Alpharetta (Ga.) HS
12. **Nick Giarraputo, 3b, Simi Valley (Calif.) HS**
13. **Daniel Murphy, 3b, Jacksonville**
14. **Todd Privett, lhp, JC of Southern Idaho**
15. Justin Dalles, c, Park Vista Community HS, Boynton Beach, Fla.
16. **Tobi Stoner, rhp, Davis & Elkins (W.Va.)**
17. **Stephen Puhl, c, St. Edward's (Texas)**
18. **Ritchie Price, ss, Kansas**
19. Justin Woodall, lhp, Lafayette HS, Oxford, Miss.
20. **Jason Jacobs, c, Georgia**
21. Joel Wells, 1b, Abilene Christian (Texas)
22. **Tim Stronach, rhp, Worcester State (Mass.)**
23. **Nick Waechter, rhp, Western Oregon**
24. **Valentin Ramos, 1b, Sallisaw (Okla.) HS**
25. **Steven Cheney, rhp, Gulf Coast (Fla.) CC**
26. **Dustin Martin, of, Sam Houston State**
27. **Tim Haines, rhp, Texas-Pan American**
28. **Will Bashelor, of, Dartmouth**
29. **Jake Eigsti, ss, Indiana State**
30. **Ricky Sparks, rhp, Dallas Baptist**
31. **Jeremy Hambrice, of, Southern Arkansas**
32. **B.J. Roper-Hubbert, c, Alcorn State**
33. **Teddy Dziuba, c, Babson (Mass.)**
34. **J.R. Voyles, 2b, Texas-San Antonio**
35. **James Newman, 2b, Erskine (S.C.)**
36. **Edgar Ramirez, rhp, Louisiana State**
37. **Josh Stinson, rhp, Northwood HS, Shreveport, La.**
38. **J.J. Leaper, rhp, Sentinel (Okla.) HS**
39. **Donald Green, of, Texas Southern**
40. Tyler Binkley, rhp, St. Mary's HS, Sault Ste. Marie, Ontario
41. Victor Black, rhp, Amarillo (Texas) HS
42. Terrell Stringer, rhp, Smith Station HS, Smiths, Ala.

43. Albert Cartwright, 2b, American Heritage Boca-Delray HS, Delray Beach, Fla.
44. Brad Schwarzenbach, rhp, Cerritos (Calif.) CC
45. Beau Pender, rhp, Gulf Coast (Fla.) CC
46. **Kyle Johnson, rhp, Chapman (Calif.)**
47. Shay Conder, c, CC of Southern Nevada
48. **Jon Koller, rhp, Oregon State**
49. Johnny Monell, c, Seminole (Fla.) CC
50. Ryan Wolfe, lhp, Winter Park (Fla.) HS

NEW YORK YANKEES

June—Regular Phase (28)

1. **Ian Kennedy, rhp, Southern California** (Pick from Phillies as compensation for Type A free agent Tom Gordon)
1. (Pick to Red Sox as compensation for Type A free agent Johnny Damon)
1. **Joba Chamberlain, rhp, Nebraska** (Supplemental pick—41st—for loss of Gordon)
2. (Pick to Braves as compensation for Type A free agent Kyle Farnsworth)
3. **Zach McAllister, rhp, Illinois Valley Central HS, Chillicothe, Ill.**
4. **Colin Curtis, of, Arizona State**
5. **George Kontos, rhp, Northwestern**
6. **Mitch Hilligoss, ss, Purdue**
7. **Tim Norton, rhp, Connecticut**
8. **Dellin Betances, rhp, Grand Street HS, New York**
9. **Mark Melancon, rhp, Arizona**
10. **Casey Erickson, rhp, Springfield (Ill.) JC**
11. **Seth Fortenberry, of, Baylor**
12. **Nick Peterson, rhp, Tampa**
13. **Daniel McCutchen, rhp, Oklahoma**
14. **D.J. Hollingsworth, of, UC Riverside**
15. **Gabriel Medina, rhp, Emporia State (Kan.)**
16. **Paul Patterson, rhp, Northern Kentucky**
17. **David Robertson, rhp, Alabama**
18. Del Howell, lhp, American Christian Academy, Tuscaloosa, Ala.
19. **Chris Kunda, 2b, Oregon State**
20. **Kevin Russo, 2b, Baylor**
21. **Russell Raley, 2b, Oklahoma**
22. **Brian Aragon, of, North Carolina State**
23. **Brandon Thomson, lhp, Chandler-Gilbert (Ariz.) CC**
24. **Brian Baisley, c, South Florida**
25. Kevin Carby, ss, Texarkana (Texas) CC
26. **Tim Dennehy, lhp, Chandler-Gilbert (Ariz.) CC**
27. Michael Lee, rhp, Bellevue (Wash.) CC
28. Barrett Bruce, lhp, Flower Mound (Texas) HS
29. Orlando Torres, c, Puerto Rico Baseball Academy, Santa Isabell, P.R.
30. **Brock Ungricht, c, San Diego State**
31. Zak Presley, of, Carroll HS, Southlake, Texas
32. Tommy Palica, lhp, Golden West (Calif.) JC
33. **Luke Trubee, rhp, Dayton**
34. Tyler Ladendorf, ss, Maine West HS, Des Plaines, Ill.
35. David Van Ostrand, 3b, Hancock (Calif.) JC
36. Jared Rogers, rhp, Duncanville (Texas) HS
37. **Tim O'Brien, 3b, San Diego State**
38. **Nicholas Diyorio, of, Florida Southern**
39. **Kevin Smith, 1b, Oklahoma**
40. Tanner Chitwood, lhp, Sulphur (Okla.) HS
41. Ohmed Danesh, of, Dr. Phillips HS, Orlando
42. Dan Duffy, ss, Mountain Ridge HS, Glendale, Ariz.
43. Eric Erickson, lhp, Sarasota (Fla.) HS
44. **James Lasala, c, Iona**
45. Nathan Albert, rhp, Bakersfield (Calif.) JC
46. Jeff Ludlow, rhp, Palm Harbor (Fla.) University HS
47. Charles Smith, c, Second Baptist HS, Houston
48. Jeffrey Loveys, rhp, Ball State
49. **Chase Odenreider, of, Creighton**
50. Sam Honeck, 1b, Grayson County (Texas) CC

OAKLAND ATHLETICS

June—Regular Phase (22)

1. (Pick to Nationals as compensation for Type B free agent Esteban Loaiza)
2. **Trevor Cahill, rhp, Vista (Calif.) HS**
3. **Matt Sulentic, of, Hillcrest HS, Dallas**
4. **Chad Lee, rhp, Barton County (Kan.) CC**
5. **Jermaine Mitchell, of, UNC Greensboro**
6. **Andrew Bailey, rhp, Wagner**
7. Mike Leake, rhp, Fallbrook (Calif.) Union HS
8. **Angel Sierra, of, Puerto Rico Baseball Academy, Cayey, P.R.**
9. Danny Hamblin, 1b, Arkansas
10. **Christian Vitters, ss, Fresno State**
11. **Jason Fernandez, rhp, Louisiana-Lafayette**
12. **Shane Presutti, rhp, Franklin Pierce (N.H.)**
13. **Ben Jukich, lhp, Dakota Wesleyan (S.D.)**
14. **Toddric Johnson, of, Southern Mississippi**
15. **Kyle Christensen, rhp, Millikan HS, Long Beach**
16. **Branden Dewing, lhp, San Jose State**
17. **Michael Affronti, ss, Le Moyne**
18. Michael Ambort, c, Lamar
19. **Greg Dowling, 1b, Georgia Southern**
20. **Josh McLaughlin, rhp, College of Charleston**
21. **Jacob Smith, c, East Carolina**
22. **Patrick Currin, rhp, UNC Greensboro**
23. **Scott Moore, rhp, Texas State**
24. **Earl Oakes, rhp, Pace (N.Y.)**
25. Aaron Odom, lhp, Texas Tech
26. **Derrick Gordon, lhp, Lamar**
27. **Larry Cobb, of, College of Charleston**
28. **Lorenzo Macias, of, Mount San Antonio (Calif.) JC**
29. **Matt Manship, rhp, Stanford**
30. **Josh Morgan, rhp, Missouri-St. Louis**
31. Jonathan Pigott, of, Seabreeze HS, Daytona Beach, Fla.
32. Nick Hernandez, lhp, Hialeah (Fla.) Senior HS
33. Burke Lieppman, 1b, Prescott (Ariz.) HS
34. Steve Cochrane, c, Mission Viejo (Calif.) HS
35. **Carlos Hernandez, lhp, West Valley (Calif.) JC**
36. Jean Diaz, 3b, Perpetuo Socorro HS, San Juan, P.R.
37. David Fry, of, Bishop Gorman HS, Las Vegas
38. Rylan Sandoval, inf, Chabot (Calif.) JC
39. **Dante Love, c, San Diego CC**
40. Goldy Simmons, rhp, Monta Vista HS, Spring Valley, Calif.
41. Jeremy Weih, c, Wilton (Iowa) HS

PHILADELPHIA PHILLIES

June—Regular Phase (21)

1. **Kyle Drabek, rhp, The Woodlands (Texas) HS** (Pick from Mets as compensation for Type A free agent Billy Wagner)
1. (Pick to Yankees as compensation for Type A free agent Tom Gordon)
1. **Adrian Cardenas, ss, Monsignor Pace HS, Opa Locka, Fla.** (Supplemental pick—37th—for loss of Wagner)
2. **Drew Carpenter, rhp, Long Beach State**
3. **Jason Donald, ss, Arizona**
4. **D'Arby Myers, of, Westchester HS, Los Angeles**
5. **Quintin Berry, of, San Diego State**
6. **Daniel Brauer, lhp, Northwestern**
7. **Charlie Yarbrough, 1b, Eastern Kentucky**
8. **T.J. Warren, of, Bethel HS, Vallejo, Calif.**
9. **Andrew Cruse, rhp, South Carolina**
10. **Sam Walls, rhp, North Carolina State**
11. **Jarrod Freeman, rhp, Alta HS, Sandy, Utah**
12. **Darin McDonald, of, Cherry Creek HS, Englewood, Colo.**
13. **Zach Penprase, ss, Mississippi Valley State**
14. **Gus Milner, of, Kansas**
15. Riley Cooper, of, Clearwater (Fla.) Central Catholic HS
16. **Cody Montgomery, 3b, Dallas Baptist**
17. **Jay Miller, of, Washington State**
18. **Michael Dubee, rhp, Okaloosa-Walton (Fla.) CC**
19. **Robert Roth, rhp, Lewiston (Idaho) HS**
20. **Domonic Brown, rhp, Redan HS, Stone Mountain, Ga.**

21. **Jacob Dempsey, of, Winthrop**
22. **Ben Pfinsgraff, rhp, Maryland**
23. **Shawn McGill, c, Boston College**
24. **Garet Hill, rhp, Biola (Calif.)**
25. Billy Mohl, rhp, Tulane
26. **Will Savage, rhp, Oklahoma**
27. **John Brownell, rhp, Oklahoma**
28. **Herman Demmink, 3b, Clemson**
29. **Michael Fuentes, c, Coastal Carolina**
30. **Brian Capps, of, Texas Tech**
31. Bruce Billings, rhp, San Diego State
32. **Alan Robbins, c, Winthrop**
33. **Mike Deveaux, ss, Georgia College & State**
34. Josh Thrailkill, rhp, Roberson HS, Asheville, N.C.
35. Rashad Taylor, of, Skyline (Calif.) JC
36. Kyle Gibson, rhp, Greenfield (Ind.) Central HS
37. Shawn Epps, rhp, Northern Oklahoma JC
38. Bobby Haney, ss, Kings Park (N.Y.) HS
39. Gerard Mohrmann, rhp, Manitou Springs (Colo.) HS
40. Nathan Solow, lhp, La Cueva HS, Albuquerque, N.M.
41. Mike Antonini, lhp, Georgia College & State
42. Daniel Faulkner, rhp, Bishop Noll Institute, Hammond, Ind.
43. Yazy Arbelo, 1b, John Carroll HS, Fort Pierce, Fla.
44. Mike Petello, of, Saguaro HS, Scottsdale, Ariz.
45. Patrick Murray, 1b, Santa Ana (Calif.) JC
46. Trayvone Johnson, c, Community Harvest Charter School, Los Angeles
47. Tylien Manumaleuna, 3b, Dixie HS, St. George, Utah
48. Nick Morreale, c, Vernon Hills (Ill.) HS
49. Olivier Routhier-Pare, lhp, Ahuntsic (Quebec) JC
50. Matt Adams, 2b, King's Academy, West Palm Beach, Fla.

PITTSBURGH PIRATES

June—Regular Phase (4)

1. **Brad Lincoln, rhp, Houston**
2. **Mike Felix, lhp, Troy**
3. **Shelby Ford, 2b, Oklahoma State**
4. **Jared Hughes, rhp, Long Beach State**
5. **Pat Bresnehan, rhp, Arizona State**
6. **Jim Negrych, 2b, Pittsburgh**
7. **Austin McClune, of, Santa Fe HS, Edmond, Okla.**
8. **Alex Presley, of, Mississippi**
9. **Steve Macfarland, rhp, Lamar**
10. **Charles Benoit, lhp, Oklahoma State**
11. Lonnie Chisenhall, 3b, West Carteret HS, Morehead City, N.C.
12. **Kent Sakamoto, 1b, Fresno State**
13. **Brandon Holden, rhp, Douglas HS, Parkland, Fla.**
14. **Greg Smith, 1b, Fordham**
15. **James Barksdale, of, North Alabama**
16. **Kris Watts, c, Santa Clara**
17. **Mike Crotta, rhp, Florida Atlantic**
18. **Francisco Ortiz, rhp, Puerto Rico Baseball Academy, Toa Alta, P.R.**
19. Jason Moseby, of, Newport HS, Bellevue, Wash.
20. **Matt Clarkson, c, Oklahoma State**
21. Kody Paul, rhp, Glynn Academy, Brunswick, Ga.
22. **Miles Durham, of, Northwestern State**
23. Preston Claiborne, rhp, Newman Smith HS, Carrolton, Texas
24. **Scott Massey, rhp, Southern Mississippi**
25. **Adam Simon, rhp, San Diego State**
26. **Ryan Kelly, rhp, Hilton Head (S.C.) HS**
27. Cache Breedlove, 3b, Santa Fe HS, Edmond, Okla.
28. **Rudy Owens, lhp, Mesa (Ariz.) HS**
29. **Brandon Williams, rhp, South Carolina-Upstate**
30. Alphonso Owens, of, Dillon (S.C.) HS
31. **Jared Keel, 3b, Troy**
32. **Jorge Charry, rhp, Lake City (Fla.) CC**
33. **Victor Alvarez, ss, Cumberland (Tenn.)**
34. Pernell Halliman, rhp, West Hills (Calif.) JC
35. **Jose Peley, ss, Seminole State (Okla.) JC**
36. Chadwick Arnold, rhp, Southridge HS, Kennewick, Wash.
37. **Damian Walcott, of, Brookdale (N.J.) CC**
38. **Matt McCullen, rhp, Western Carolina**
39. **Tom Hagan, of, Virginia**
40. Philip Brannon, rhp, Broome HS, Spartanburg, S.C.
41. Scott Kuhns, rhp, Parkland (Ill.) CC
42. Jonathan Harmston, lhp, Bullard HS, Fresno, Calif.
43. **Devin Copley, rhp, Gulf Coast (Fla.) CC**
44. Tanner Hines, ss, Hudson HS, Lufkin, Texas
45. Paul-Michael Klingsberg, 1b, Notre Dame HS, Sherman Oaks, Calif.
46. Ryan Groth, of, Indian River (Fla.) CC
47. Brandon Wilkerson, ss, Lamar HS, Arlington, Texas
48. Ken Wieda, rhp, Vernon (Texas) JC
49. Carson Middleton, rhp, Lindale (Texas) HS
50. Marquise Zachery, of, Lake City (Fla.) CC

ST. LOUIS CARDINALS

June—Regular Phase (30)

1\. **Adam Ottavino, rhp, Northeastern**
1\. **Chris Perez, rhp, Miami** (Supplemental pick—42nd—for loss of Type A free agent Matt Morris)
2\. **Brad Furnish, lhp, Texas Christian** (Pick from Giants as compensation for Morris)
2\. **Jon Jay, of, Miami**
2\. **Mark Hamilton, 1b, Tulane** (Supplemental pick for loss of Type C free agent Abraham Nunez)
3\. **Gary Daley, rhp, Cal Poly**
4\. **Eddie Degerman, rhp, Rice**
5\. **Shane Robinson, of, Florida State**
6\. **Tyler Norrick, lhp, Southern Illinois**
7\. **Luke Gorsett, of, Nebraska**
8\. **Allen Craig, ss, California**
9\. **Matthew North, rhp, Deer Valley HS, Antioch, Calif.**
10\. Blair Erickson, rhp, UC Irvine
11\. **P.J. Walters, rhp, South Alabama**
12\. **David Carpenter, c, West Virginia**
13\. **Travis Mitchell, of, Parkway Central HS, Chesterfield, Mo.**
14\. **Jon Edwards, of, Keller (Texas) HS**
15\. Lance Zawadzki, ss, San Diego State
16\. **Tommy Pham, ss, Durango HS, Las Vegas**
17\. **Nathan Southard, of, Tulane**
18\. **Amaury Cazana Marti, of, Miami, Fla.**
19\. **Brandon Buckman, 1b, Nebraska**
20\. Brandon Cooney, rhp, Florida Atlantic
21\. **Mark Diapoules, rhp, Martin County HS, Stuart, Fla.**
22\. **Casey Mulligan, rhp, Valencia (Calif.) HS**
23\. **LaCurtis Mayes, rhp, Poly HS, Riverside, Calif.**
24\. Roberto Gomez, lhp, Texas-Pan American
25\. **D'Marcus Ingram, of, North Little Rock (Ark.) HS**
26\. **Garrett Bussiere, c, California**
27\. **Christian Reyes, c, Porterville (Calif.) JC**
28\. **Luke Gregerson, rhp, St. Xavier (Ill.)**
29\. **Will Groff, 2b, SUNY Cortland**
30\. **Jared Schweitzer, 3b, Kansas**
31\. **Mark Shorey, of, High Point (N.C.)**
32\. Ross Smith, of, Dodge County HS, Eastman, Ga.
33\. **Brian Schroeder, lhp, UCLA**
34\. **Isaias Garcia, 2b, Houston**
35\. **Jim Rapoport, of, Stanford**
36\. Adrian Alaniz, rhp, Texas
37\. **Logan Collier, rhp, Guilford (N.C.)**
38\. **Scott Thomas, c, Missouri Baptist**
39\. **Matt Michael, lhp, Grand Canyon (Ariz.)**
40\. Tyler Mach, 3b, Oklahoma State
41\. Mitch Canham, c, Oregon State
42\. **Kyle Mura, rhp, Loyola Marymount**
43\. Gabe Torres, ss, St. Peter's Prep, Jersey City, N.J.
44\. Cameron Grant, of, Hermitage HS, Richmond, Va.
45\. John Goodman, rhp, Georgia Tech
46\. Robert Woodard, rhp, North Carolina
47\. **Nick Additon, lhp, Western HS, Davie, Fla.**
48\. Garry Thomas, lhp, Pine Bluff (Ark.) HS
49\. Gary Taylor, of, Holmes (Miss.) JC
50\. Charles Matthews, rhp, Athens (Ga.) Academy

SAN DIEGO PADRES

June—Regular Phase (17)

1. **Matt Antonelli, 3b, Wake Forest**
1. **Kyler Burke, of, Ooltewah (Tenn.) HS** (Supplemental pick—35th—for loss of Type A free agent Ramon Hernandez)
2. **Chad Huffman, 2b, Texas Christian** (Pick from Orioles as compensation for Hernandez)
2. **Wade LeBlanc, lhp, Alabama**
3. **Cedric Hunter, of, King HS, Decatur, Ga.**
4. **Nathan Culp, lhp, Missouri**
5. **Andy Underwood, rhp, Fresno State**
6. Tim Bascom, rhp, Central Florida
7. **Craig Cooper, 1b, Notre Dame**
8. **Tom King, ss, Troy**
9. **David Freese, 3b, South Alabama**
10. **Kody Valverde, c, Alabama**
11. **Mat Latos, rhp, Coconut Creek (Fla.) HS**
12. **Stephen Faris, rhp, Clemson**
13. **Mike Epping, of, New Orleans**
14. Grant Green, ss, Canyon HS, Carlsbad, Calif.
15. **Matt Buschmann, rhp, Vanderbilt**
16. **Ray Stokes, 2b, Cal State East Bay**
17. **Tyler Mead, rhp, Skyview (Wash.) HS**
18. **Garner Wetzel, of, Millsaps (Miss.)**
19. **Brian Hernandez, c, Vanderbilt**
20. **Michael Campbell, of, South Carolina**
21. **Luke Cannon, of, Texas State**
22. **Justin Pickett, 1b, Walters State (Tenn.) CC**
23. **Brooks Dunn, lhp, Mississippi State**
24. **Nick Tucci, rhp, Connecticut**
25. **Nick Kliebert, 2b, Pepperdine**
26. **Jeremy McBryde, rhp, Rose State (Okla.) JC**
27. **Matt Huff, rhp, Regis (Colo.)**
28. **Jeremy Hunt, 1b, Villanova**
29. **A.J. Davidiuk, 3b, Furman**
30. Joe Cates, rhp, Palomar (Calif.) JC
31. **Jon Kirby, rhp, Lee (Tenn.)**
32. Jordan Rogers, rhp, San Jacinto (Texas) JC
33. Sean Finefrock, rhp, Blanchard (Okla.) HS
34. Casey Haerther, 1b, Chaminade Prep HS, Chatsworth, Calif.
35. Joe Cruz, rhp, South Hills HS, West Covina, Calif.
36. Dan Johansen, rhp, Woodinville (Wash.) HS
37. Miguel Flores, rhp, St. John Bosco HS, Bellflower, Calif.
38. Ben Francis, rhp, Mosley HS, Lynn Haven, Fla.
39. Chance Deason, lhp, Piedmont (Okla.) HS
40. Josh Casas, lhp, South El Monte (Calif.) HS
41. Mike Freeman, ss, Edgewater HS, Orlando
42. Luke Stewart, 3b, Normal (Ill.) Community West HS
43. Jeff Ramirez, ss, El Camino HS, South San Francisco
44. Jeff Hart, ss, Puyallup (Wash.) HS
45. Bryce Lefebvre, 3b, Scottsdale (Ariz.) CC

SAN FRANCISCO GIANTS

June—Regular Phase (10)

1. **Tim Lincecum, rhp, Washington**
1. **Emmanuel Burriss, ss, Kent State** (Supplemental pick—33rd—for loss of Type A free agent Scott Eyre)
2. (Pick to Cardinals as compensation for Type A free agent Matt Morris)
3. (Pick to Diamondbacks as compensation for Type A free agent Tim Worrell)
3. **Clayton Tanner, lhp, De La Salle HS, Concord, Calif.** (Pick from Cubs as compensation for Eyre)
4. **Ben Snyder, lhp, Ball State**
5. **Mike McBryde, of, Florida Atlantic**
6. **Ryan Rohlinger, ss, Oklahoma**
7. **Brett Pill, 1b, Cal State Fullerton**
8. **Matt Klimas, c, Texarkana (Texas) JC**
9. **Brian Bocock, ss, Stetson**
10. **Ryan Paul, lhp, Cal State Fullerton**
11. **Gib Hobson, rhp, North Carolina State**
12. **Matt Weston, of, Houston**
13. **Brad Boyer, 2b, Arizona**
14. **Eric Stolp, rhp, Pacific**
15. Andrew Barbosa, lhp, Riverview HS, Sarasota, Fla.
16. **Paul Oseguera, lhp, UCLA**
17. **Kevin Pucetas, rhp, Limestone (S.C.)**
18. Jeff Stallings, rhp, North Carolina State
19. **Tyler Graham, of, Oregon State**
20. **Adam Paul, rhp, UNC Wilmington**
21. **Steven Calicutt, lhp, East Tennessee State**
22. **Bobby Felmy, of, Georgia**
23. E.B. Crow, rhp, Sitka (Alaska) HS
24. Jeff Walters, rhp, Olympia HS, Orlando
25. Joseph Moos, ss, Williston (Fla.) HS
26. Shane Mathews, rhp, East Carolina
27. **Sean Van Elderen, of, Mesa State (Colo.)**
28. Dusty Harvard, of, Natrona County HS, Casper, Wyo.
29. Nick Liles, 2b, Scotland HS, Laurinburg, N.C.
30. **Daryl Maday, rhp, Arkansas**
31. **Matt McMurtry, lhp, Minnesota State-Mankato**
32. Matt Fairel, lhp, Winter Haven (Fla.) HS
33. Chris Siewert, c, Tennessee
34. **Jared Cranston, lhp, Nebraska**
35. **Adam Cowart, rhp, Kansas State**
36. **Matt Downs, 3b, Alabama**
37. **Lance Salsgiver, of, Harvard**
38. Ryan Butner, rhp, Hialeah (Fla.) Senior HS
39. Lee Darracott, ss, Vernon (Texas) JC
40. Jon Amaya, of, Diamond Bar (Calif.) HS
41. Bo Merrell, ss, Seward County (Kan.) CC
42. Brandon Grabham, rhp, Grayson County (Texas) CC
43. Kevin Boggan, rhp, Boston College
44. Bronco Lafrenz, c, Marshalltown (Iowa) CC
45. Matt Speake, rhp, New Mexico JC
46. Taylor Hammack, lhp, Angleton (Texas) HS
47. Ryan Bradley, lhp, Mattoon (Ill.) HS
48. **Evan Bush, 2b, Alabama**
49. Jonathan Batts, c, UNC Wilmington
50. **Robert Davis, c, South Carolina-Aiken**

SEATTLE MARINERS

June—Regular Phase (5)

1. **Brandon Morrow, rhp, California**
2. **Chris Tillman, rhp, Fountain Valley (Calif.) HS**
3. **Tony Butler, lhp, Oak Creek (Wis.) HS**
4. **Ricky Orta, rhp, Miami**
5. **Nathan Adcock, rhp, North Hardin HS, Elizabethtown, Ky.**
6. **Adam Moore, c, Texas-Arlington**
7. **Doug Fister, rhp, Fresno State**
8. **Steve Richard, rhp, Clemson**
9. **Justin Souza, rhp, Sacramento CC**
10. **Chris Minaker, ss, Stanford**
11. **Aaron Solomon, rhp, Cumberland (Tenn.)**
12. **Gavin Dickey, of, Florida**
13. **Joe Kantakevich, rhp, William & Mary**
14. Jared Baehl, 3b, North Posey HS, Poseyville, Ind.
15. **Drew Fiorenza, rhp, Clemson**
16. **Austin Bibens-Dirkx, rhp, Portland**
17. Dan Runzler, lhp, UC Riverside
18. **Kam Mickolio, rhp, Utah Valley State**
19. Cam Nobles, rhp, Jackson HS, Mill Creek, Wash.
20. **Johan Limonta, 1b, Miami Dade CC South**
21. **Brent Gaphardt, lhp, Delaware**
22. **Fabian Williamson, lhp, Kennedy HS, Granada Hills, Calif.**
23. **Marcos Villezcas, ss, Brigham Young**
24. **Kyle Parker, rhp, Washington**
25. **Tyson Gillies, of, Mountain HS, Vancouver**
26. **Greg Moviel, lhp, Vanderbilt**
27. **Bryan Ball, rhp, Florida**
28. **Rocky Collis, rhp, Cornell**
29. **Greg Nesbitt, lhp, James Madison**
30. **Matt Vogel, ss, Lewis-Clark State (Idaho)**
31. David McClain, rhp, San Jacinto (Texas) JC
32. Joe Agreste, 1b, Potomac State (W.Va.) JC
33. **Rob Harmon, rhp, Arkansas-Little Rock**
34. **Stan Posluszny, of, West Virginia**

35. **Alex Meneses, ss, Barry (Fla.)**
36. Kyle Haas, rhp, Douglas (B.C.) CC
37. Chris Walden, rhp, Bellefontaine (Ohio) HS
38. Mike Drake, of, Consumnes River (Calif.) JC
39. **Philip Roy, rhp, Miami Dade CC South**
40. **Haley Winter, rhp, UC Riverside**
41. **Brandon Fromm, 1b, San Jose State**
42. Shane Cox, rhp, Alvin (Texas) CC
43. Clint Straka, rhp, Northern Oklahoma JC
44. Bryan Earley, rhp, Elder HS, Cincinnati
45. Jeremy Camacho, ss, Eagle Rock HS, Los Angeles
46. **Robbie Dominguez, rhp, Cerritos (Calif.) JC**
47. Sean Ward, of, Evans (Ga.) HS
48. Jeremy Beeching, lhp, Volunteer State (Tenn.) CC
49. Ryne Tacker, rhp, Rice
50. Tyler Sanford, c, Saguaro HS, Scottsdale, Ariz.

TAMPA BAY DEVIL RAYS

June—Regular Phase (3)

1. **Evan Longoria, 3b, Long Beach State**
2. **Josh Butler, rhp, San Diego**
3. Nick Fuller, rhp, Kell HS, Marietta, Ga.
4. **Alex Cobb, rhp, Vero Beach (Fla.) HS**
5. **Shawn O'Malley, ss, South Ridge HS, Kennewick, Wash.**
6. **Nevin Ashley, c, Indiana State**
7. **Ryan Reid, rhp, James Madison**
8. **Tyree Hayes, rhp, Tomball (Texas) HS**
9. **Eli Sonoqui, 1b, Chavez HS, Laveen, Ariz.**
10. **Desmond Jennings, of, Itawamba (Miss.) CC**
11. **Heath Rollins, rhp, Winthrop**
12. Teddy Hubbard, rhp, Hooks (Texas) HS
13. Mikie Minor, lhp, Forrest HS, Lewisburg, Tenn.
14. **Travis Barnett, rhp, Salt Lake CC**
15. **K.D. Kang, of, Parkview HS, Lilburn, Ga.**
16. **Ryan Owen, lhp, Cal State Dominguez Hills**
17. Ryan Thornton, of, American River (Calif.) JC
18. Jay Brown, rhp, Young Harris (Ga.) JC
19. **Robi Estrada, ss, El Segundo (Calif.) HS**
20. **Erik Walker, rhp, UNC Charlotte**
21. **Joey Callender, 2b, Texas Tech**
22. **Mark Thomas, c, Alpharetta (Ga.) HS**
23. Matt McCarney, of, Holy Trinity Catholic HS, Kanata, Ontario
24. **Angel Chapa, rhp, Treasure Valley (Ore.) CC**
25. Blaine Howell, rhp, Reynolds HS, Asheville, N.C.
26. Johnathon Parker, rhp, Lord Tweedsmuir SS, Surrey, B.C
27. Luis Lopez, of, St. Francis HS, Carolina, P.R.
28. Andrew Hagins, of, Oak Park (Ill.) River Forest HS
29. Leon Johnson, of, Thatcher, Ariz.
30. **Jimmy Mayer, ss, Pittsburgh**
31. **Justin Reynolds, of, Mount Hood (Ore.) CC**
32. Emmanuel Morales, of, Puerto Rico Baseball Academy, Aguas Buenas, P.R.
33. Brooks Lindsay, 2b, Mount Hood (Ore.) CC
34. Stephen McCray, rhp, Parkview HS, Lilburn, Ga.
35. **Michael Ross, 2b, Northwest Mississippi CC**
36. Walter Marciel, lhp, Iolani HS, Honolulu
37. Kalvin Johnson, 1b, Iowa Western CC
38. Chris Dennis, 1b, St. Thomas of Villanova SS, LaSalle, Ontario
39. Matt Miraldi, of, Bear River HS, Grass Valley, Calif.
40. Brando Casalicchio, rhp, Cold Spring Harbor HS, Long Island, N.Y.
41. Michael Dufek, of, Desert Mountain HS, Scottsdale, Ariz.
42. Brandon Vernon, c, Overton HS, Nashville
43. Victor Ramos, of, Miami Senior HS
44. Neil Hardon, of, Saguaro HS, Scottsdale, Ariz.
45. Chris Wilson, rhp, Trinidad State (Colo.) JC
46. Candy Maldonado, of, Porterville (Calif.) JC
47. Brandon Brown, 3b, Tate HS, Cantonment, Fla.
48. Alex McRee, lhp, Chestatee HS, Gainesville, Ga.
49. Ryan Fraser, rhp, Walker Valley HS, Cleveland, Tenn.
50. Travis Tartamella, c, Los Osos HS, Rancho Cucamonga, Calif.

TEXAS RANGERS

June—Regular Phase (12)

1. **Kasey Kiker, lhp, Russell County HS, Seale, Ala.**
2. (Pick to Indians as compensation for Type B free agent Kevin Millwood)
3. **Chad Tracy, c, Pepperdine**
4. **Marcus Lemon, ss, Eustis (Fla.) HS**
5. **Chris Davis, 1b, Navarro (Texas) JC**
6. **Jake Brigham, rhp, Central Florida Christian Academy, Ocoee, Fla.**
7. **Grant Gerrard, of, Southern Illinois**
8. **Josh Bradbury, of, Orange Coast (Calif.) CC**
9. **Brennan Garr, rhp, Northern Colorado**
10. **Craig Gentry, of, Arkansas**
11. **Craig Crow, rhp, Rice**
12. **Matt Jaimes, 3b, Chino (Calif.) HS**
13. Kevin Angelle, lhp, Bridge City (Texas) HS
14. **Mike Ballard, lhp, Virginia**
15. **Cody Himes, ss, JC of San Mateo (Calif.)**
16. **Cody Podraza, of, Tomball (Texas) HS**
17. John Maschino, rhp, Seminole State (Okla.) JC
18. **Mike Wagner, rhp, Washington State**
19. Miguel Velazquez, of, Gabriel Mistral HS, San Juan, P.R.
20. Tyler Fleming, rhp, Cowley County (Kan.) CC
21. Brandt Walker, rhp, St. Stephen's Episcopal HS, Austin
22. Cory Luebke, lhp, Ohio State
23. **Jay Heafner, ss, Davidson**
24. Robert McClain, lhp, Walters State (Tenn.) CC
25. **Derek Holland, lhp, Wallace State (Ala.) CC**
26. Ken Gregory, 1b, Immaculata HS, Sommerville, N.J.
27. Jared Olson, 3b, Frederick (Md.) CC
28. Shaeffer Hall, lhp, Lee's Summit (Mo.) HS
29. **Dan Hoben, lhp, Chandler-Gilbert (Ariz.) CC**
30. **Nick Cadena, 3b, Florida International**
31. **Adam Schaecher, rhp, Creighton**
32. **Shannon Wirth, rhp, Lewis & Clark (Ore.)**
33. **Eric Fry, of, San Jacinto (Texas) JC**
34. **Austin Weilep, rhp, Lewis-Clark State (Idaho)**
35. **Brian Nelson, of, Corban (Ore.)**
36. **John Slusarz, rhp, Connecticut**
37. John Lambert, lhp, Chesterton (Ind.) HS
38. **Jon Hollis, rhp, Yale**
39. Gary Poynter, rhp, Weatherford (Texas) JC
40. **Chris Dennis, rhp, Auburn**
41. Brandon Gribbin, rhp, Golden West (Calif.) CC
42. Lance West, of, Captain Shreve HS, Shreveport, La.
43. Shawn Sanford, rhp, Cinnaminson (N.J.) HS
44. **Dan Sattler, rhp, Purdue**
45. **Daniel Ray Herrera, lhp, New Mexico**
46. Clifton Thomas, of, El Cajon (Calif.) Valley HS
47. Joey Norwood, 3b, Modesto (Calif.) JC
48. Rylan Ostrosky, rhp, Lethbridge (Alberta) CC
49. Clint Stubbs, of, Atlanta (Texas) HS
50. **Patrick Donovan, lhp, Gonzaga**

TORONTO BLUE JAYS

June—Regular Phase (14)

1. **Travis Snider, of, Jackson HS, Everett, Wash.**
2. (Pick to Orioles as compensation for Type A free agent B.J. Ryan)
3. (Pick to Marlins as compensation for Type A free agent A.J. Burnett)
4. **Brandon Magee, rhp, Bradley**
5. **Luke Hopkins, 1b, New Mexico State**
6. **Brian Jeroloman, c, Florida**
7. **Jon Baksh, of, Florida Tech**
8. **Dan O'Brien, lhp, Western Michigan**
9. Cole Figueroa, ss, Lincoln HS, Tallahassee, Fla.
10. **Scott Campbell, 2b, Gonzaga**
11. **Matt Lane, c, Washington**
12. **Jonathan Diaz, ss, North Carolina State**
13. **Mikal Garbarino, of, San Dimas (Calif.) HS**
14. **Shawn Scobee, of, Nevada**

15. **Seth Overbey, rhp, Maryland**
16. **Chase Lirette, rhp, South Florida**
17. **Kyle Ginley, rhp, St. Petersburg (Fla.) JC**
18. **Kyle Walter, lhp, Bucknell**
19. **Matt Liuzza, c, Louisiana State**
20. **Jonathan Del Campo, ss, Cibola HS, Yuma, Ariz.**
21. **Ron Lowe, lhp, St. Leo (Fla.)**
22. Brad Mills, lhp, Arizona
23. **Adam Calderone, of, Florida Southern**
24. Keith Demorgandie, rhp, Orange Coast (Calif.) JC
25. **Luis Fernandez, ss, Cervantes HS, San Juan, P.R.**
26. **Chris Emanuele, of, Northeastern**
27. **Pat McGuigan, rhp, San Francisco**
28. **Zach Dials, rhp, Kentucky**
29. Ryan Basham, of, Michigan State
30. **Raul Barron, ss, Pasadena (Calif.) CC**
31. **Adam Rogers, rhp, Evansville**
32. **Noah Tritz, rhp, Texas-San Antonio**
33. Greg Lopez, ss, Notre Dame
34. **Graham Godfrey, rhp, College of Charleston**
35. **John Zinnicker, lhp, St. Bonaventure**
36. Domonique Rodgers, of, Sacramento CC
37. **Ben Zeskind, of, Richmond**
38. **Kevin Denis-Fortier, 1b, Crowder (Mo.) JC**
39. Luke Tucker, rhp, Florida State
40. **Ted Serro, rhp, Franklin & Marshall (Pa.)**
41. **C.J. Ebarb, c, Lamar**
42. Justin Figueroa, 2b, Lincoln HS, Tallahassee, Fla.
43. **Nate Melek, rhp, New Mexico**
44. **Kelly Sweppenhiser, 3b, Virginia Military Institute**
45. Lee Verweel, lhp, Malvern Collegiate Institute, Toronto
46. Mace Thurman, lhp, McLennan (Texas) CC
47. Wilberto Morales, 1b, Arizona Western JC
48. Jonathan Fernandez, ss, American Heritage HS, Delray Beach, Fla.
49. **Brad Cuthbertson, rhp, Midland (Texas) JC**
50. **Baron Frost, of, Southern California**

WASHINGTON NATIONALS

June—Regular Phase (15)

1. **Chris Marrero, of, Monsignor Pace HS, Opa Locka, Fla.**
1. **Colton Willems, rhp, John Carroll Catholic HS, Fort Pierce, Fla.** (Pick from Athletics as compensation for Type B free agent Esteban Loiaza)
2. Sean Black, rhp, Lenape HS, Medford, N.J.
2. **Stephen Englund, of, Bellevue (Wash.) HS** (Pick from Angels as compensation for Type B free agent Hector Carrasco)
3. **Stephen King, ss, Winter Park (Fla.) HS**
4. **Glenn Gibson, lhp, Center Moriches (N.Y.) HS**
5. **Cory VanAllen, lhp, Baylor**
6. **Zech Zinicola, rhp, Arizona State**
7. Sam Brown, rhp, Millbrook HS, Raleigh, N.C.
8. **Sean Rooney, c, Saddleback (Calif.) CC**
9. Joey Rosas, lhp, Yavapai (Ariz.) JC
10. Marcus Salmon, rhp, Sunset HS, Miami
11. **Desmond Jones, rhp, Middle Georgia JC**
12. **Cole Kimball, rhp, Centenary**
13. **Hassan Pena, rhp, Palm Beach (Fla.) CC**
14. **Brett McMillan, 1b, UCLA**
15. Dustin Dickerson, 3b, Midway HS, Henrietta, Texas
16. **Patrick Nichols, c, Old Dominion**
17. **Erik Arnesen, rhp, Grove City (N.J.)**
18. **Adam Carr, rhp, Oklahoma State**
19. Sam Dyson, rhp, Jesuit HS, Tampa
20. **Alberto Tavarez, rhp, Western Oklahoma State JC**
21. **Chris French, of, New Mexico JC**
22. **Robby Jacobsen, 1b, George Mason**
23. Forrest Beverly, lhp, South Carolina
24. **Ricky Caputo, 3b, Hofstra**
25. Jim Birmingham, lhp, Overbrook HS, Pine Hill, N.J.
26. **Brett Logan, c, Houston**
27. **Dan Pfau, lhp, George Washington**
28. Michael Robbins, lhp, Meridian (Miss.) CC
29. Khris Davis, of, Deer Valley HS, Glendale, Ariz.
30. Burt Reynolds, ss, Essex County Vocational Technical HS, Bloomfield, N.J.
31. **Zach Baldwin, lhp, West Virginia State**
32. **Joe Welsh, lhp, Toledo**
33. Tyler Moore, 1b, Meridian (Miss.) CC
34. Taylor Kinzer, of, Homestead HS, Fort Wayne, Ind.
35. D'Vontrey Richardson, of, Lee County HS, Leesburg, Ga.
36. **Jeremy Goldschmeding, ss, Dallas Baptist**
37. Austin Hudson, rhp, Boone HS, Orlando
38. Zach Von Tersch, rhp, Cedar Falls (Iowa) HS
39. Andrew Doyle, rhp, Alleman HS, Rock Island, Ill.
40. Nick Pearce, rhp, DeMatha Catholic HS, Hyattsville, Md.
41. **Brad Peacock, rhp, Palm Beach Central HS, Wellington, Fla.**
42. Javier Martinez, rhp, Fordham
43. **Cory Anderson, rhp, U.S. Coast Guard Academy (Conn.)**
44. Chad Jenkins, lhp, Caravel Academy HS, Bear, Del.
45. Adam Kramer, rhp, New Mexico JC
46. Jayson Brugman, ss, South Mountain (Ariz.) CC
47. Josh Rodriguez, c, Red Mountain HS, Mesa, Ariz.
48. Kyle Page, of, Brevard County (Fla.) CC
49. Jarred Holloway, lhp, Russellville (Ark.) HS
50. J.J. Pannell, rhp, George Mason

2007 SOUTHPAW PRICE GOES TO DEVIL RAYS AT NO. 1 AS DRAFT GOES ON TELEVISION FOR FIRST TIME

In some ways, the first round of Major League Baseball's 2007 draft went exactly as scripted.

As expected, Vanderbilt lefthander David Price went No. 1 overall to the Devil Rays. He was one of a record-tying seven lefthanded pitchers drafted in the first round, as the strongest position of the draft class was in full evidence. And as predicted, the strongest high school draft class in years reversed a recent trend, as more prep players (17) were picked in the first round than collegians (13).

It all went down for the first time ever on TV, as the draft's first round was shown live on ESPN2.

"It's a great day for us and this is such an important day," commissioner Bud Selig said. "This is a special event and we want to communicate that as best as possible to all of our fans. This is really a dramatic manifestation of how the sport has improved. This will get bigger and bigger."

Price going first overall was no surprise, after he dominated the Southeastern Conference for Vanderbilt. BA's College Player of the Year led the nation with 194 strikeouts and just 31 walks in 133 innings while going 11-1, 2.63.

DAVID STONER

David Price was drafted in 2007 and pitched in the playoffs in 2008

The real drama came two months later, when clubs for the first time faced a signing deadline. All clubs had to sign their players by 11:59 p.m. Aug. 15 or lose their rights to sign those players. Many of the biggest contracts were signed that day, as clubs waited until the last minute to sign large, over-slot contracts and try to escape scrutiny from the commissioner's office.

Price waited until the 15th and wound up signing a backloaded contract that included a $5.6 million bonus and $8.25 million in guaranteed money. Much of the drama involved Scott Boras Corporation clients. The Royals had to go to the last minute with the No. 2 overall pick, California prep infielder Mike Moustakas. After setting state records for single-season and career home runs, Moustakas had his bags packed and nearly left home to attend Southern California before signing at the deadline for a $4 million bonus.

The top college hitter on most boards, Georgia Tech switch-hitting catcher Matt Wieters, went fifth overall to the Orioles. He also was a Boras client, and in 2008 he became BA's Minor League Player of the Year. That followed his last-minute signing, as he agreed to a $6 million bonus just three minutes before the deadline. It was the second-largest bonus in draft history at the time, behind only the $6.1 million the Diamondbacks gave 2005 No. 1 overall pick Justin Upton. However, Upton's bonus was a two-sport deal spread out over five years, so Wieters' was the largest up-front bonus.

Two righthanders who were Boras clients, New Jersey prep Rick Porcello and North Carolina State 7-footer Andrew Brackman, signed record-setting contracts at the deadline. Porcello was No. 4 on BA's Top 200 entering the draft, while Brackman ranked seventh. Shortly after the list was compiled, however, Brackman was shut down at N.C. State with an elbow injury that ultimately required Tommy John surgery.

Nevertheless, the Yankees drafted Brackman with the 30th overall selection, the last one in the first round. Porcello went three spots ahead of him to the Tigers after scaring off many clubs with a price tag rumored to be in the neighborhood of Josh Beckett's 1999 contract, the highest for any prep pitcher. Ultimately, that's exactly what the Tigers gave Porcello—a major league contract guaranteeing him $7 million, with a bonus of $3.58 million. The guarantee matched Beckett's record.

Brackman ultimately got the draft's richest contract, though. Despite his injury, the Yankees signed him the afternoon of Aug. 15 for a $3.35 million bonus. The biggest surprise was the major league contract that guaranteed Brackman $4.55 million, with roster bonuses—designed to keep the former Wolfpack basketball player from bolting for the

NBA—that could drive the total value of the contract to $13 million over seven years.

Soon after signing, Brackman had Tommy John surgery, and due to that and an emergency appendectomy he had in July 2008, he didn't make his debut until the 2008 Hawaii Winter Baseball season. Then in his first action in an affiliated minor league, in 2009, Brackman had a forgettable season, going 2-12, 5.91 with 26 wild pitches, 76 walks and 10 hit batters in 107 innings while striking out 103.

End Of An Era

The new signing deadline also ended the 20-year draft-and-follow era, as 2007 was the last year that teams could draft players and still sign them the following spring after a junior-college season. The final draft-and-follow crop was significant, as the Angels signed righthander Jordan Walden for $1 million and the Padres locked up righty Matt Latos for $1.25 million. The Rangers also got a future big leaguer in the last class, signing Wallace State (Ala.) lefthander Derek Holland for $200,000.

The lefthanded pitching angle was prominent in the first round with Price leading the way. Three other southpaws went in the top 10 with the Pirates taking Clemson closer Daniel Moskos No. 4 overall, followed by the Nationals drafting Missouri State's Ross Detwiler sixth overall and the Giants taking Madison Bumgarner, a prep pitcher from North Carolina, at the 10 spot. Three more college lefties also went in the first round in Rice's Joe Savery (Phillies), Arkansas' Nick Schmidt (San Diego) and San Francisco's Aaron Poreda (White Sox).

Moskos' selection was the most intriguing, as the Pirates took him ahead of Wieters. Dave Littlefield, in what turned out to be his final year as general manager in Pittsburgh, said it was the Pirates' evaluation that Moskos was the better prospect, but most in the industry doubted the Pirates had the stomach to negotiate with Boras and meet Wieters' asking price. The Pirates shifted Moskos into a starting pitching role, a role he filled 10 times as a junior for Clemson, and he had a difficult first full pro season, going 7-7, 5.95 at high Class A Lynchburg. Moskos did make significant progress in 2009, going 11-10, 3.74 at Double-A Altoona, but he was not seen as a future franchise cornerstone as Wieters was, making his selection a decision that may haunt the Pirates for years.

DRAFT 07: FIRST-ROUND PICKS

No.	Team	Player, Pos.	School	State	Ht.	Wt.	B-T	Age
1.	Rays	David Price, lhp	Vanderbilt	Murfreesboro, Tenn.	6-5	215	L-L	21
2.	Royals	Mike Moustakas, ss	Chatsworth HS	Chatsworth, Calif.	6-0	185	L-L	18
3.	Cubs	Josh Vitters, 3b	Cypress HS	Cypress, Calif.	6-3	195	R-R	17
4.	Pirates	Daniel Moskos, lhp	Clemson	Greenville, S.C.	6-1	200	R-L	21
5.	Orioles	Matt Wieters, c	Georgia Tech	Goose Creek, S.C.	6-5	230	B-R	21
6.	Nationals	Ross Detwiler, lhp	Missouri State	Wentzville, Mo.	6-4	175	R-L	21
7.	Brewers	Matt LaPorta, 1b	Florida	Port Charlotte, Fla.	6-1	215	R-R	22
8.	Rockies	Casey Weathers, rhp	Vanderbilt	Elk Grove, Calif.	6-1	200	R-R	21
9.	Diamondbacks	Jarrod Parker, rhp	Norwell HS	Ossian, Ind.	6-2	175	R-R	18
10.	Giants	Madison Bumgarner, lhp	South Caldwell HS	Hudson, N.C.	6-5	220	R-L	17
11.	Mariners	Phillippe Aumont, rhp	Ecole Du Versant HS	Gatineau, Quebec	6-7	225	R-R	18
12.	Marlins	Matt Dominguez, 3b	Chatsworth HS	Chatsworth, Calif.	6-2	185	R-R	17
13.	Indians	Beau Mills, 1b	Lewis-Clark (Idaho) State	Visalia, Calif.	6-3	205	L-R	20
14.	Braves	Jason Heyward, of	Henry County HS	McDonough, Ga.	6-2	198	L-L	17
15.	Reds	Devin Mesoraco, c	Punxsutawney HS	Punxsutawney, Pa.	6-1	195	R-R	18
16.	Blue Jays	Kevin Ahrens, 3b	Memorial HS	Houston	6-2	180	B-R	18
17.	Rangers	Blake Beaven, rhp	Irving HS	Irving, Texas	6-7	210	R-R	18
18.	Cardinals	Pete Kozma, ss	Owasso HS	Owasso, Okla.	6-1	180	R-R	19
19.	Phillies	Joe Savery, lhp	Rice	Houston	6-3	215	L-L	21
20.	Dodgers	Chris Withrow, rhp	Midland Christian HS	Midland, Texas	6-3	195	R-R	18
21.	Blue Jays	J.P. Arencibia, c	Tennessee	Knoxville	6-1	195	R-R	21
22.	Giants	Tim Alderson, rhp	Horizon HS	Scottsdale, Ariz.	6-7	208	R-R	18
23.	Padres	Nick Schmidt, lhp	Arkansas	Kirkwood, Mo.	6-5	230	L-L	21
24.	Rangers	Michael Main, rhp	Deland HS	Deland, Fla.	6-1	171	R-R	18
25.	White Sox	Aaron Poreda, lhp	San Francisco	San Francisco	6-6	240	L-L	20
26.	Athletics	James Simmons, rhp	UC Riverside	Yorba Linda, Calif.	6-4	215	R-R	20
27.	Tigers	Rick Porcello, Rhp	Seton Hall Prep	West Orange, N.J.	6-5	188	R-R	18
28.	Twins	Ben Revere, of	Lexington Catholic HS	Lexington, Ky.	5-9	152	L-R	19
29.	Giants	Wendell Fairley, of	George Co.-Lucedale HS	Lucedale, Miss.	6-0	190	L-R	19
30.	Yankees	Andrew Brackman, rhp	North Carolina State	Cincinnati	6-10	240	R-R	21

2007

CLUB-BY-CLUB SELECTIONS

ARIZONA DIAMONDBACKS

June—Regular Phase (9)

1. **Jarrod Parker, rhp, Norwell HS, Ossian, Ind.**
1. **Wes Roemer, rhp, Cal State Fullerton** (Supplemental pick—50th—for loss of Type B free agent Craig Counsell)
1. **Ed Easley, c, Mississippi State** (Supplemental pick—61st—for loss of Type B free agent Miguel Batista)
2. **Barry Enright, rhp, Pepperdine**
3. **Reynaldo Navarro, ss, Puerto Rico Baseball Academy, Guaynabo, P.R.**
4. **Sean Morgan, rhp, Tulane**
5. **Tyrell Worthington, of, South Central HS, Winterville, N.C.**
6. **Scott Maine, lhp, Miami**
7. **Bryan Augenstein, rhp, Florida**
8. **Taylor Harbin, 2b, Clemson**
9. **Mark Hallberg, ss, Florida State**
10. **Evan Frey, of, Missouri**
11. **Josh Ellis, rhp, Wake Forest**
12. **Bryan Henry, rhp, Florida State**
13. **Sean Coughlin, c, Kentucky**
14. Bobby LaFromboise, lhp, New Mexico
15. **Josh Collmenter, rhp, Central Michigan**
16. **Mike Mee, of, Minnesota**
17. **Chance Wheeless, 1b, Texas**
18. Sammy Solis, lhp, Agua Fria HS, Litchfield Park, Ariz.
19. Michael Solbach, rhp, Liberty (Contract voided)
20. **Pete Clifford, of, Jacksonville**
21. **Anthony Smith, of, St. John's**
22. **Ty Davis, rhp, Vanderbilt**
23. **Ian Harrington, lhp, Hawaii**
24. **Luke Prihoda, rhp, Sam Houston State**
25. **Billy Spottiswood, rhp, Chico State (Calif.)**
26. **Tom Layne, lhp, Mount Olive (N.C.)**
27. Austin Garrett, lhp, Pensacola (Fla.) JC
28. **Evan Scribner, rhp, Central Connecticut State**
29. **Omar Arif, lhp, Long Beach State**
30. **Bill Musselman, c, Saint Louis**
31. Gary Bulman, rhp, Greenbrier Christian Academy, Chesapeake, Va.
32. Joey Stevens, c, Pensacola (Fla.) JC
33. Chuck Huggins, lhp, UC Santa Barbara
34. Chris Kelley, rhp, Rice
35. **Josh Blake, lhp, Auburn**
36. Tyler Conn, lhp, Southern Mississippi
37. **Jimmy Principe, of, Brookdale (N.J.) CC**
38. **Aaron Hanke, of, UC Davis**
39. **Eli Rumler, ss, Kansas State**
40. Torrey Jacoby, 2b, Notre Dame Prep, Scottsdale, Ariz.
41. **Danny Rosen, rhp, Florida State**
42. Golden Tate, of, Pope John Paul II HS, Hendersonville, Tenn.
43. Andrew Allen, 1b, Desert Vista HS, Phoenix
44. Nick Ewing, rhp, Oakmont HS, Roseville, Calif.
45. Garrett Bullock, lhp, Wake Forest
46. Josh Garcia, 1b, Brophy Prep, Phoenix
47. Mike Greco, 3b, Notre Dame Prep, Scottsdale, Ariz.
48. **Joe Ayers, ss, Boston College**
49. Matt Newman, of, Brophy Prep, Phoenix
50. Dylan Moseley, rhp, Louisiana Tech

ATLANTA BRAVES

June—Regular Phase (14)

1. **Jason Heyward, of, Henry County HS, McDonough, Ga.**
1. **Jon Gilmore, 3b, Iowa City (Iowa) HS** (Supplemental pick—33rd—for loss of Type A free agent Danys Baez)
2. Joshua Fields, rhp, Georgia (Pick from Orioles as compensation for Baez)
2. **Freddie Freeman, 1b/rhp, El Modena HS, Orange, Calif.**
3. **Brandon Hicks, ss, Texas A&M**
4. **Cory Gearrin, rhp, Mercer**
5. **Dennis Dixon, of, Oregon**
6. **Michael Fisher, ss, Georgia Tech**
7. **Travis Jones, 2b, South Carolina**
8. Colby Shreve, rhp, CC of Southern Nevada
9. **Tim Ladd, lhp, Georgia Tech**
10. **Tommy Palica, lhp, Golden West (Calif.) JC**
11. Brandon Belt, lhp, San Jacinto (Texas) JC
12. **Nick Fellman, rhp, Minnesota State-Mankato**
13. **Chad Maddox, of, Tennessee**
14. **Caleb Brewer, rhp, Harris County HS, Hamilton, Ga.**
15. Paul Demny, rhp, East Bernard (Texas) HS
16. Eddie Burns, rhp, Georgia Tech
17. **Benji Johnson, c, North Carolina**
18. **Randy Gress, ss, Quinnipiac**
19. **Brett Butts, rhp, Auburn**
20. **C.J. Lee, of, East Tennessee State**
21. **Kuyaunnis Miles, of, Chattahoochee Valley (Ala.) CC**
22. Lyle Allen, of, Cartersville (Ga.) HS
23. Edmond Sparks, c, Lovejoy HS, Hampton, Ga.
24. Mitch Harris, rhp, Navy
25. **Rico Reid, rhp, East Coweta HS, Sharpsburg, Ga.**
26. **Daniel Elorriaga-Matra, c, Douglas HS, Parkland, Fla.**
27. Adam Milligan, of, Walters State (Tenn.) CC
28. **Rashod Henry, of, Lumberton (Miss.) HS**
29. Gary Gillheeney, rhp, Bishop Hendricken HS, Warwick, R.I.
30. Rene Escobar, 1b, Riverside (Calif.) CC
31. **Benino Pruneda, rhp, San Jacinto (Texas) JC**
32. **T.J. Wohlever, lhp, Western Nevada CC**
33. Craig Kimbrel, rhp, Wallace State (Ala.) CC
34. Robert Maddox, 1b, Villa Angela-St. Joseph HS, Cleveland
35. Chris Moon, of, Tucson (Ariz.) HS
36. Vernell Warren, 2b, Grant HS, Portland, Ore.
37. Randy Yard, rhp, Palm Desert (Calif.) HS
38. Will Casey, lhp, Kennesaw Mountain HS, Kennesaw, Ga.
39. Elliott Armstrong, of, Harlan Community HS, Chicago
40. Taylor Whitenton, ss, Heritage HS, Conyers, Ga.
41. Sheldon Johnson, rhp, Deptford (N.J.) HS
42. Bryson Rahler, c, Cajon HS, San Bernardino, Calif.
43. Ryan Chaffee, rhp, Chipola (Fla.) JC
44. Dock Doyle, c, Coastal Carolina
45. Tarus Thomas, of, St. Dominic HS, Oyster Bay, N.Y.
46. Brett Krill, of, Aliso Niguel HS, Aliso Viejo, Calif.
47. Goldy Simmons, rhp, San Diego CC
48. Joe Lincoln, c, Tipton (Mo.) HS
49. Tyreace House, of, JC of the Canyons (Calif.)
50. Andrew Armstrong, lhp, Ashby HS, Bridgewater, Va.

BALTIMORE ORIOLES

June—Regular Phase (5)

1. **Matt Wieters, c, Georgia Tech**
2. (Pick to Braves as compensation for Type A free agent Danys Baez)
3. (Pick to Mets as compensation for Type A free agent Chad Bradford)
4. **Tim Bascom, rhp, Bradenton (South Coast)**
5. **Jake Arrieta, rhp, Texas Christian**
6. **Joe Mahoney, 1b, Richmond**
7. **Matt Angle, of, Ohio State**
8. **Shane Mathews, rhp, East Carolina**
9. **Malcolm Crowley, ss, Galveston (Texas) JC**
10. Eryk McConnell, rhp, North Carolina State
11. **Robbie Widlansky, of, Florida Atlantic**
12. **Wally Crancer, of, Georgia Tech**
13. **Jordan Wolf, c, Xavier**
14. **Hank Williamson, rhp, San Jacinto (Texas) JC**

15. Tyrone Hambly, 3b, Grayson County (Texas) CC
16. **Tyler Kolodny, 3b, El Camino Real HS, Woodland Hills, Calif.**
17. **Jason White, ss, Iowa**
18. **John Mariotti, rhp, Coastal Carolina**
19. **Brian Parker, rhp, Lewis-Clark State (Idaho)**
20. **Sean Gleason, rhp, St. Mary's**
21. **Scott Mueller, rhp, Arizona State**
22. **Colin Allen, rhp, Lamar (Colo.) CC**
23. **Tony Kirbis, rhp, Point Loma Nazarene (Calif.)**
24. Dan Klein, rhp, Servite (Calif.) HS
25. **Cliff Flagello, rhp, Shorter (Ga.)**
26. **Justin Moore, rhp, Chancellor HS, Fredericksburg, Va.**
27. **Kraig Binick, of, New York Tech**
28. **Stephen Procner, lhp, Cleveland State**
29. **Danny Heller, of, Pierce (Calif.) JC**
30. **Brandon Cooney, rhp, Florida Atlantic**
31. **Matt Tucker, 3b, Dallas Baptist**
32. Pete Andrelczyk, rhp, Coastal Carolina
33. **Jacob Julius, of, Arkansas**
34. **Kyle Touchatt, rhp, Wichita State**
35. **Eric Perlozzo, 2b, Shippensburg (Pa.)**
36. **Calvin Lester, of, Prairie View A&M**
37. Merrill Kelly, rhp, Desert Mountain HS, Scottsdale, Ariz.
38. Michael Harrington, of, Charleston
39. Joe Yermal, rhp, McDonogh HS, Bel Air, Md.
40. **Aaron Odom, lhp, Texas Tech**
41. Russell Wilson, 2b/ss, Collegiate HS, Richmond, Va.
42. **Joe DiGeronimo, ss, Wagner**
43. **Cole McCurry, lhp, Tennessee Wesleyan**
44. Travis Dirk, rhp, Navarro (Texas) JC
45. **Jacob Smith, lhp, Brescia (Ky.)**
46. **Lee Ellis, of, California Lutheran**
47. **Preston Pehrson, c, Towson**
48. **Nick Ray, of, Northwest Nazarene (Idaho)**
49. Tyler Newsome, of, Marist HS, Chicago
50. **Mike Gioioso, ss, Mount St. Mary's**

BOSTON RED SOX

June—Regular Phase (20)

1. (Pick to Dodgers as compensation for Type A free agent Julio Lugo)
1. **Nick Hagadone, lhp, Washington** (Supplemental pick—55th—for loss of Type B free agent Alex Gonzalez)
1. Ryan Dent, ss/2b, Wilson HS, Long Beach (Supplemental pick—62nd—for loss of Type B free agent Keith Foulke)
2. Hunter Morris, 1b, Grissom HS, Huntsville, Ala.
3. **Brock Huntzinger, rhp, Pendleton Heights HS, Pendleton, Ind.**
4. **Chris Province, rhp, Southeastern Louisiana**
5. **Will Middlebrooks, 3b/rhp, Liberty-Eylau HS, Texarkana, Texas**
6. **Anthony Rizzo, 1b/lhp, Douglas HS, Parkland, Fla.**
7. **David Mailman, 1b, Providence HS, Charlotte, N.C.**
8. **Adam Mills, rhp, UNC Charlotte**
9. **Kade Keowen, of, Louisiana State-Eunice JC**
10. **Kenneth Roque, ss, Puerto Rico Baseball Academy, Guaynabo, P.R.**
11. **Ryan Pressly, rhp, Marcus HS, Flower Mound, Texas**
12. **Eammon Portice, rhp, High Point (N.C.)**
13. Justin Grimm, rhp, Virginia HS, Bristol, Va.
14. Jake Cowan, rhp, Roswell (Ga.) HS
15. Scott Green, rhp, Kentucky
16. **Austin Bailey, rhp, Prattville (Ala.) HS**
17. Jaren Matthews, 1b/of, Don Bosco Prep, Teaneck, N.J.
18. **Hunter Strickland, rhp, Pike County HS, Zebulon, Ga.**
19. **David Marks, of, Edmonds (Wash.) CC**
20. **Dan Milano, c, Northeastern**
21. **Aaron Reza, ss, Oklahoma**
22. **Will Latimer, lhp, Trinidad State (Colo.) JC**
23. **Drake Britton, lhp, Tomball (Texas) HS**
24. Matt Presley, 3b, Cheyenne Mountain HS, Colorado Springs
25. Seth Garrison, rhp, Texas Christian
26. **Deshaun Brooks, 3b, Benedict (S.C.)**
27. Yasmani Grandal, c, Miami Springs (Fla.) HS
28. Nick Tepesch, rhp, Blue Springs (Mo.) HS
29. Juan Carlin, lhp, Riverview HS, Sarasota, Fla.
30. **Will Vazquez, c, Kent State**
31. **Daniel Buller, lhp, Fresno (Calif.) CC**
32. Ridge Carpenter, of, Kalani HS, Honolulu, Hawaii
33. Garrett Larsen, rhp, Navarro (Texas) JC
34. **Tony Bajoczky, rhp, Duke**
35. Sean Tierney, lhp, Clover Hill HS, Midlothian, Va.
36. Scott Lyons, ss, Mount San Antonio (Calif.) JC
37. **Scott Lonergan, rhp, Rice**
38. Derrick Stultz, rhp, Wharton HS, Tampa
39. Jonathan Roof, ss, St. Mary's HS, Paducah, Ky.
40. Ryan Fischer, rhp, Lodi (Calif.) HS
41. Mike Bourdon, c, Northwest Catholic HS, West Hartford, Conn.
42. **Chad Povich, rhp, Dixie State (Utah)**
43. Scott Cure, lhp, Idalia (Colo.) HS
44. **Emmanuel Solano, ss, Miami-Dade (Fla.) CC**
45. **Pete Gilardo, c, Dominican (N.Y.)**
46. Garrett Young, of, Liberty

CHICAGO CUBS

June—Regular Phase (3)

1. **Josh Vitters, 3b, Cypress (Calif.) HS**
1. **Josh Donaldson, c, Auburn** (Supplemental pick—48th—for loss of Type B free agent Juan Pierre)
2. (Pick to Nationals as compensation for Type A free agent Alfonso Soriano)
3. **Tony Thomas, 2b, Florida State**
4. **Darwin Barney, ss, Oregon State**
5. **Brandon Guyer, of, Virginia**
6. **Casey Lambert, lhp, Virginia**
7. **Ty Wright, of, Oklahoma State**
8. **Marquez Smith, 3b, Clemson**
9. **Clark Hardman, of, Cal State Fullerton**
10. **Leon Johnson, of, Brigham Young**
11. **Chris Siegfried, lhp, Portland**
12. **Ryan Acosta, rhp/ss, Clearwater (Fla.) Central Catholic HS**
13. **Jonathan Wyatt, of, Georgia**
14. **James Russell, lhp, Texas**
15. **Marc Sawyer, 1b, Yale**
16. **Zach Ashwood, lhp, Kansas**
17. **Arik Hempy, lhp, South Carolina**
18. **Jeffrey Rea, 2b, Mississippi State**
19. Kyle Day, c, Michigan State
20. **Jose Made, ss, Dominican (N.Y.)**
21. **Dustin Sasser, lhp, East Carolina**
22. **Craig Muschko, rhp, La Salle**
23. **Steve Vento, rhp, Palm Beach (Fla.) CC**
24. **Scott Meyer, rhp, Lamar**
25. Victor Sanchez, 3b/c, Gahr HS, Norwalk, Calif.
26. **Michael Bunton, lhp, College of Charleston**
27. Clayton Suss, rhp, Cooper City (Fla.) HS
28. **Bill Moss, 2b, Memphis**
29. Andrew Cashner, rhp, Angelina (Texas) JC
30. **Luke Sommer, of, San Francisco**
31. **Brian Leclerc, of, Florida**
32. **Luis Bautista, c, Florida International**
33. Preston Clark, c, Texas
34. Enrique Garcia, rhp, Miami
35. J.C. Casey, rhp, Kickapoo HS, Springfield, Mo.
36. **Billy Mottram, 3b, Dowling (N.Y.)**
37. Mike McGee, rhp, Port St. Lucie (Fla.) HS
38. **Yuri Higgins, rhp, South Florida**
39. **Roberto Sabates, c, Miami, Fla.**
40. **Corey Bachman, rhp, Virginia Military Institute**
41. Jordan Herr, of, Pittsburgh
42. Colt Sedbrook, inf, Arizona
43. Garrett Clyde, rhp, San Jacinto (Texas) JC
44. **Bryan Jost, 1b, Minnesota**
45. Ryan Lewis, of, Yakima Valley (Wash.) CC
46. Tyler Clark, rhp, Springfield (Mo.) Catholic HS
47. Josh Walter, rhp, Texas State
48. Carlos Rivera, of, East Aurora (Ill.) HS

49. Jordan Rogers, rhp, San Jacinto (Texas) JC
50. Blake Murphy, c, Western Carolina

CHICAGO WHITE SOX

June—Regular Phase (25)

1. **Aaron Poreda, lhp, San Francisco**
2. **Nevin Griffith, rhp, Middleton HS, Tampa**
3. **John Ely, rhp, Miami (Ohio)**
4. **Leroy Hunt, rhp, Sacramento (Calif.) CC**
5. **Nathan Jones, rhp, Northern Kentucky**
6. **Johnnie Lowe, rhp, Point Loma Nazarene (Calif.)**
7. **Jimmy Gallagher, of, Duke**
8. **Lyndon Estill, of, Lower Columbia (Wash.) CC**
9. **Ken Gilbert, of, DeSoto (Texas) HS**
10. Brian Guinn, ss, Berkeley (Calif.) HS
11. **Jordan Kendall, of, Contra Costa (Calif.) JC**
12. **Kevin Skogley, lhp, Nevada-Las Vegas**
13. **Sergio Miranda, ss, Virginia Commonwealth**
14. **John Curtis, c, Cal State Fullerton**
15. **Greg Paiml, ss, Alabama**
16. **Nick Mahin, of, Cal State Fullerton**
17. **Dale Mollenhauer, ss, East Carolina**
18. **Levi Maxwell, rhp, West Virginia**
19. **Henry Mabee, rhp, Morehead State**
20. **Logan Johnson, 2b, Louisville**
21. Mitch Delaney, 1b, St. Thomas of Villanova HS, LaSalle, Ontario
22. **Justin Klipp, rhp, Cal State Fullerton**
23. **Charlie Shirek, rhp, Nebraska**
24. Kevin Patterson, 1b/c, Oak Mountain HS, Birmingham
25. **Dan Albritton, rhp, Florida Southern**
26. Mike Bolsenbroek, rhp, Santa Ana (Calif.) JC
27. Caleb Hurst, rhp, Beyer HS, Modesto, Calif.
28. Chris Epps, of/rhp, Dunwoody (Ga.) HS
29. Jabari Blash, of, Amalie HS, St. Thomas, Virgin Islands
30. John Flanagan, lhp, Belleville (Ill.) HS
31. Eduardo Orozco, rhp, Rubidoux HS, Riverside, Calif.
32. Andre Lamontagne, rhp, Long Beach State
33. Mitch LeVier, of, Fullerton (Calif.) JC
34. Ryan Sharpley, rhp, Marshall (Mich.) HS
35. Zach Babbit, 2b, Albany HS, Richmond, Calif.
36. **Oney Guillen, 2b, North Park (Ill.) JC**
37. Alex Rodriguez, 3b, La Salle HS, Miami
38. Grant Monroe, rhp, Schaumburg (Ill.) HS
39. Roddy Jones, of, Chamblee (Ga.) HS
40. Austin King, 2b, Gallia Academy HS, Gallipolis, Ohio
41. Devon Shines, 1b, Westwood (Texas) HS
42. Mike Jones, of, Arizona State
43. Baldwin Vargas, rhp, New Jersey City
44. John Grim, 1b, John Hersey HS, Arlington Heights, Ill.
45. **Ronnie Morales, lhp, Wichita State**

CINCINNATI REDS

June—Regular Phase (15)

1. **Devin Mesoraco, c, Punxsutawney (Pa.) HS**
1. **Todd Frazier, 3b, Rutgers** (Supplemental pick—34th—for loss of Type A free agent Rich Aurilia)
1. **Kyle Lotzkar, rhp, South Delta (B.C.) SS** (Supplemental pick—53rd—for loss of Type B free agent Scott Schoeneweis)
2. **Zack Cozart, ss, Mississippi**
3. **Scott Carroll, rhp, Missouri State** (Pick from Giants as compensation for Aurilia)
3. **Neftali Soto, 3b, Colegio Marista HS, Manati, P.R.**
4. Blake Stouffer, 3b/of, Texas A&M
5. **Drew Bowman, lhp, Nebraska**
6. **Evan Hildenbrandt, rhp, Mennonite Educational Institute SS, Abbotsford, B.C**
7. **Brandon Waring, 3b, Wofford**
8. Drew O'Neil, rhp, Penn State
9. **Alex Oliveras, of, Puerto Rico Baseball Academy, Guaynabo, P.R.**
10. **Harris Honeycutt, rhp, South Carolina**
11. **Jordan Wideman, c, Streetsville SS, Mississauga, Ontario**
12. **Scott Gaffney, rhp/ss, Penn State**
13. **Brandon Menchaca, of, Delaware**
14. **Joseph Krebs, lhp, Texas**
15. **Matt Klinker, rhp, Furman**
16. **Shea Snowden, lhp, Brandon (Miss.) HS**
17. Jesse Craig, rhp, Brigham Young
18. Taylor Jordan, rhp, Merritt Island (Fla.) HS
19. **Jeff Jeffords, rhp, South Carolina**
20. **Jake Kahaulelio, ss, Oral Roberts**
21. **Jeremy Horst, lhp, Armstrong Atlantic State (Ga.)**
22. **Tyler Rhoden, rhp, Vanderbilt**
23. **Jason Bour, c, George Mason**
24. **Frank Meade, c, Rutgers**
25. **Eli Rimes, 1b, Sonoma State (Calif.)**
26. **Curtis Partch, rhp, Merced (Calif.) JC**
27. Jason Roenicke, rhp, Cuesta (Calif.) JC
28. **Derrick Conatser, rhp, Tallahassee (Fla.) CC**
29. **Steven Otterness, lhp, Embry-Riddle (Fla.)**
30. **Brett Bartles, 3b, Duke**
31. **Jordan Hotchkiss, rhp, Brevard (N.C.)**
32. Brandon Douglas, ss, Northern Iowa
33. **Brodie Pullen, 3b, Calhoun (Ga.) HS**
34. **Jeremy Vinyard, rhp, Boaz (Ala.) HS**
35. Thad Weber, rhp, Nebraska
36. Leon Landry, 3b, Baker (La.) HS
37. Scott Alexander, lhp, Cardinal Newman HS, Santa Rosa, Calif.
38. Ari Ronick, lhp, Portland
39. Jimmy Nelson, rhp, Niceville (Fla.) HS
40. Ross Hopkins, c, Tyee HS, Seatac, Wash.
41. **Kevin Hickey, of, Concordia (N.Y.)**
42. Sean Bierman, lhp, Kinnelon (N.J.) HS
43. Austin Taylor, 3b, Thomas County Central HS, Thomasville, Ga.
44. **Josh Beal, rhp, Independence (Kan.) CC**
45. Jordan Brown, rhp, Meridian (Miss.) CC
46. Mike McGuire, rhp, Delaware
47. Drew Benes, 3b, Westminster Christian Academy, St. Louis
48. **Mike Henry, rhp, St. Patrick's HS, Ottawa, Ontario**
49. Cameron Gray, rhp, Silverthorn Collegiate HS, Toronto
50. Jordan Chambless, rhp, Texas A&M

CLEVELAND INDIANS

June—Regular Phase (13)

1. **Beau Mills, 1b/3b, Lewis-Clark State (Idaho)**
2. (Pick to Mets as compensation for Type A free agent Roberto Hernandez)
3. (Pick to Phillies as compensation for Type A free agent David Dellucci)
4. **T.J. McFarland, lhp, Stagg HS, Palos Heights, Ill.**
5. **Jonathan Holt, rhp, Tampa**
6. **Bo Greenwell, of, Riverdale HS, Fort Myers, Fla.**
7. Cole St. Clair, lhp, Rice
8. **Mark Thompson, ss, Lewis-Clark State (Idaho)**
9. **Adam White, of, West Virginia**
10. **Heath Taylor, lhp, Oklahoma**
11. Matt Hague, of/rhp, Washington
12. **Gary Campfield, rhp, Texas A&M**
13. **Matt Brown, of, Wichita State**
14. **Daniel Morales, rhp, San Francisco**
15. **Chris Jones, lhp, Gaither HS, Tampa**
16. Doug Hogan, c, Clemson
17. Miles Morgan, rhp, Texas Tech
18. **Kyle Landis, rhp, Pittsburgh**
19. Bobby Coyle, of, Chatsworth (Calif.) HS
20. **Jeff Hehr, ss, Eastern Michigan**
21. Jared Clark, of/rhp, Cal State Fullerton
22. Stihl Sowers, rhp, North Lenoir HS, Wheat Swamp, N.C.
23. Shaeffer Hall, lhp, Jefferson County (Mo.) CC
24. Adam Zornes, c, Rice
25. Kyle Leiendecker, lhp, Homestead HS, Fort Wayne, Ind.
26. **Michael Valadez, c, Lee (Tenn.)**
27. Daniel Edwards, rhp, Kansas State
28. Scott Savastano, 3b/ss, Franklin Pierce (N.H.)
29. **Garrett Rieck, lhp, Chico State (Calif.)**
30. Bryce Brentz, rhp, South-Doyle HS, Knoxville, Tenn.
31. Jason Hessler, rhp, St. Joseph's

32. **Joey Mahalic, rhp/3b, Wilson HS, Portland, Ore.**
33. Tyler Kuhn, 3b/ss, West Virginia
34. **Josh Judy, rhp, Indiana Tech**
35. **Brian Juhl, c, Stanford**
36. **P.J. Zocchi, rhp, Clemson**
37. Dean Kiekhefer, lhp, Oldham County HS, Buckner, Ky.
38. **Johnny Williams, rhp, Tampa**
39. Eric Jokisch, lhp, Virginia (Ill.) HS
40. **Dallas Cawiezell, rhp, Valparaiso**
41. Tommy Luce, rhp, Seminole State (Okla.) JC
42. Bryce Tafelski, c, Santa Ynez (Calif.) HS
43. Travis Howell, c, Long Beach State
44. Ryan Royster, of, UC Davis
45. Dan Evatt, of, Grapevine (Texas) HS
46. **Brock Simpson, of, Kansas**
47. **Kevin Rucker, of, Pioneer Valley HS, Santa Maria, Calif.**
48. **Walter Diaz, ss, Miami**
49. **Matt Willard, ss, Arkansas**
50. **Doug Pickens, c, Michigan**

COLORADO ROCKIES

June—Regular Phase (8)

1. **Casey Weathers, rhp, Vanderbilt**
2. **Brian Rike, of, Louisiana Tech**
3. **Lars Davis, c, Illinois**
4. **Isaiah Froneberger, lhp, Forest Park HS, McDonough, Ga.**
5. **Connor Graham, rhp, Miami (Ohio)**
6. **Cory Riordan, rhp, Fordham**
7. **Jeff Cunningham, 1b, South Alabama**
8. **Parker Frazier, rhp, Bishop Kelley HS, Tulsa, Okla.**
9. **Jordan Pacheco, 2b, New Mexico**
10. **Jeff Fischer, rhp, Eastern Michigan**
11. **Andy Groves, rhp, Purdue**
12. **Darin Holcomb, 3b, Gonzaga**
13. **Beau Seabury, c, Virginia**
14. Kentrail Davis, of, Theodore (Ala.) HS
15. **Kenny Durst, lhp, West Virginia**
16. **Mitch Lively, rhp, Cal State Sacramento**
17. **Austin Chambliss, rhp, Middle Georgia JC**
18. **Brian Lapin, of, Fresno State**
19. Evan Chambers, of, Lakeland (Fla.) HS
20. **Matt Reynolds, lhp, Austin Peay**
21. Chris Sale, lhp, Lakeland (Fla.) HS
22. **Bo Bowman, 1b, Louisiana-Monroe**
23. **Don Taylor, rhp, Dallas Baptist**
24. **Brandon Miller, lhp, Fresno State**
25. **Mike Mitchell, of, Virginia**
26. **Stephen Shao, lhp, Vanderbilt**
27. **James Sims, of, Jackson State**
28. **Craig Rodriguez, lhp, Mississippi**
29. **Andres Marrero, rhp, Puerto Rico Baseball Academy, Guaynabo, P.R.**
30. **Bruce Billings, rhp, San Diego State**
31. Israel Troupe, of, Tift County HS, Tifton, Ga.
32. Kenny Williams Jr., of, Wichita State
33. Wayman Gooch, rhp, Ohlone (Calif.) JC
34. Travis Lawler, rhp, A&M Consolidated HS, College Station, Texas
35. Dan Renken, rhp, Orange (Calif.) Lutheran HS
36. **Joey Williamson, rhp, Notre Dame**
37. Nick Gallego, 2b, Esperanza HS, Anaheim
38. **Warren Schaeffer, ss, Virginia Tech**
39. **Chris Vasami, 1b, Elon**
40. Richie Rowland, c, Cloverdale (Calif.) HS
41. **Johnny Bowden, c, Southern California**
42. David Coulon, lhp, Arizona
43. Devin Lohman, ss, Righetti HS, Santa Maria, Calif.
44. **Chad Lembeck, of, Rice**
45. Zach Jones, c, Jordan HS, Sandy, Utah
46. Kyle Saukko, rhp, Granite Bay (Calif.) HS
47. Logan Schafer, of, Cal Poly
48. Chris Morton, 3b, Bellevue (Wash.) HS
49. **Brandon Reichert, inf, Florida State**
50. Billy McHenry, 2b, Cheyenne (Wyo.) East HS

DETROIT TIGERS

June—Regular Phase (27)

1. **Rick Porcello, rhp, Seton Hall Prep, West Orange, N.J.**
1. **Brandon Hamilton, rhp, Stanhope Elmore HS, Millbrook, Ala.** (Supplemental pick—60th—for loss of Type B free agent Jamie Walker)
2. **Danny Worth, ss, Pepperdine**
3. **Luke Putkonen, rhp, North Carolina**
4. **Charlie Furbush, lhp, Louisiana State**
5. **Casey Crosby, lhp, Kaneland HS, Maple Park, Ill.**
6. **Cale Iorg, ss, Alabama**
7. **Devin Thomas, c, Brown**
8. **Manny Miguelez, lhp, Miami**
9. **Justin Henry, 2b, Mississippi**
10. Dominic De La Osa, of, Vanderbilt
11. **Gary Perinar, rhp, Minnesota**
12. **Christopher White, of, Sacramento (Calif.) CC**
13. **Londell Taylor, of, Vian (Okla.) HS**
14. Chris Hernandez, lhp, Monsignor Pace HS, Opa Locka, Fla.
15. **Kody Kaiser, of, Oklahoma City**
16. **Mark Brackman, rhp, William Jewell (Mo.)**
17. **Noah Krol, rhp, Wichita State**
18. Kevin Rhoderick, rhp, Horizon HS, Scottsdale, Ariz.
19. **Andrew Hess, rhp, Michigan**
20. **Erik Crichton, rhp, Oral Roberts**
21. Kyle Brule, rhp, Marcos de Niza HS, Tempe, Ariz.
22. **Kris Rochelle, c, UNC Charlotte**
23. **Brandon Harrigan, c, Oklahoma City**
24. Barret Loux, rhp, Stratford (Texas) HS
25. Colin Kaline, 2b, Groves HS, Beverly Hills, Mich.
26. **Matt Hoffman, lhp, Owasso (Okla.) HS**
27. Steve Susdorf, of, Fresno State
28. Warren McFadden, of, Tulane
29. **Wade Lamont, 1b, Flagler (Fla.)**
30. **Jon Kibler, lhp, Michigan State**
31. **Paul Nardozzi, rhp, Pittsburgh**
32. Forrest Moore, lhp, Parkview Baptist HS, Baton Rouge, La.
33. **Shawn Roof, ss, Illinois**
34. **Kyle Peter, of, Washburn (Kan.)**
35. **Sean Finefrock, rhp, Butler County (Kan.) CC**
36. Tanner Rindels, of, Seward County (Kan.) CC
37. Toby Matchulat, rhp, Redford Union HS, Redford, Mich.
38. Austin Woodard, lhp, Bishop Carroll HS, Wichita, Kan.
39. Jake Oberlechner, ss, Arkansas City (Kan.) HS
40. **D'Andrea Vaughn, of, Tavares (Fla.) HS**
41. D.J. Lemahieu, 3b, Brother Rice HS, Bloomfield Hills, Mich.
42. Matt Robertson, rhp, Valley Center (Kan.) HS
43. **Richard Zumaya, rhp, Bonita Vista HS, Chula Vista, Calif.**
44. Kolby Wood, rhp, Berrien Springs (Mich.) HS

FLORIDA MARLINS

June—Regular Phase (12)

1. **Matt Dominguez, 3b, Chatsworth (Calif.) HS**
2. **Mike Stanton, 1b/of, Notre Dame HS, Sherman Oaks, Calif.**
3. **Jameson Smith, c, Fresno (Calif.) CC**
4. **Bryan Petersen, of, UC Irvine**
5. **Steven Cishek, rhp, Carson-Newman (Tenn.)**
6. Taiwan Easterling, of, Oak Grove HS, Hattiesburg, Miss.
7. **Andrew Paulauskas, rhp, Tremper HS, Kenosha, Wis.**
8. **Jay Voss, lhp, Kaskaskia (Ill.) JC**
9. **Marcus Crockett, of, Compton (Calif.) CC**
10. **Brandon Barrow, lhp, Zachary (La.) HS**
11. **Brett Durand, rhp, Delta State (Miss.)**
12. **Garrett Parcell, rhp, San Diego State**
13. **Chris Shafer, rhp, Cajon HS, San Bernardino, Calif.**
14. **Lucas Waters, 3b, Eastern Kentucky**
15. **Ryan Anetsberger, 3b, Illinois State**
16. **Adam Campbell, rhp, New Orleans**
17. **Mike Pasek, ss, Apple Valley (Calif.) HS**
18. **Chris Ingoglia, lhp, Stetson**
19. Charley Williams, of, Itawamba (Miss.) CC
20. **Marc Lewis, lhp, Creighton**

21. **Ryan Curry, 2b, Bradley**
22. **Chaz Gilliam, rhp, Cyril (Okla.) HS**
23. **Daniel Prieto, lhp, Long Beach (Calif.) CC**
24. **Kevin Hammons, lhp, Tusculum (Tenn.)**
25. **Kyle Kaminska, rhp, Naperville (Ill.) Central HS**
26. Bryan Hagerich, of, Delaware
27. **Ray White, ss, Compton (Calif.) CC**
28. Virgil Hill, ss, Valencia (Calif.) HS
29. **Ben Lasater, 3b, Charleston**
30. **A.J. Battisto, rhp, Georgia Southern**
31. Justin Harper, rhp, Yavapai (Ariz.) JC
32. Josh Thompson, c, Mercer
33. **Derek Blacksher, rhp, McNeese State**
34. **Stephen Flake, rhp, Southern Poly State (Ga.)**
35. **Josh Roberts, rhp, Portland**
36. **Matt Mallory, rhp, Science and Arts of Oklahoma**
37. Kellen St. Luce, lhp, All Saints Cathedral HS, St. Thomas, Virgin Islands
38. Tyler Waldron, rhp, Golden Sierra HS, Garden Valley, Calif.
39. Ricky Rossman, of, Claremont (Calif.) HS
40. Mike McCravey, lhp, JC of the Canyons (Calif.)
41. Skyler Crawford, rhp, Hartnell (Calif.) JC
42. **Brett Lawler, c, Arkansas-Little Rock**
43. Stephen Kohlscheen, rhp, Norman (Okla.) North HS
44. **Ernie Banks, 1b, Norfolk State**
45. Kevin Stanley, c, Las Lomas HS, Walnut Creek, Calif.
46. John Hellweg, rhp, St. Dominic HS, O'Fallon, Mo.
47. Mitch Rider, c, North Gwinnett HS, Suwanee, Ga.
48. Jacob Elmore, 2b, Wallace State (Ala.) CC
49. Kyle Rose, of, Lee HS, Huntsville, Ala.
50. Rafael Carlot, 3b, Southeastern (N.C.) CC

HOUSTON ASTROS

June—Regular Phase (17)

1. (Pick to Rangers as compensation for Type A free agent Carlos Lee)
2. (Pick to Padres as compensation for Type A free agent Woody Williams)
3. Derek Dietrich, 3b, St. Ignatius HS, Cleveland
4. Brett Eibner, rhp, The Woodlands (Texas) HS
5. **Collin DeLome, of, Lamar**
6. **David Dinelli, rhp, Sierra (Calif.) JC**
7. **Russell Dixon, 2b, Auburn**
8. Chad Bettis, rhp, Monterey HS, Lubbock, Texas
9. **Luis Pardo, rhp, Florida Gulf Coast**
10. **Matt Cusick, 2b/3b, Southern California**
11. **Robert Bono, c/rhp, Waterford (Conn.) HS**
12. **Brian Pellegrini, 1b, St. Bonaventure**
13. Chad Jones, of/lhp, Southern Lab HS, Baton Rouge, La.
14. **Craig Corrado, 3b, Tampa**
15. Matt Fitts, rhp, Lewis-Clark State (Idaho)
16. **Devon Torrence, of, Canton (Ohio) South HS**
17. **Mason Roberts, rhp, Cisco (Texas) JC**
18. **Brian Espersen, rhp, Mercyhurst (Pa.)**
19. **Jon Fixler, c, Indiana**
20. **Kyle Greenwalt, rhp, Souderton (Pa.) HS**
21. **Kyle Miller, c, Central Florida CC**
22. **Drew Anderson, of, New Orleans**
23. **Charlie Gamble, 3b, North Carolina A&T**
24. **Philip Stringer, ss, Auburn**
25. **Kevin Carkeek, c, Oakland**
26. **Sal Iacono, c, Princeton**
27. **Brett Robinson, rhp, Florida Southern**
28. **Jared Pitts, of, Stephen F. Austin State**
29. **Travis Sweet, 3b, Iowa**
30. **Danny Gil, rhp, Miami**
31. **Jason Dominguez, rhp, Pepperdine**
32. **David Miller, rhp, Stephen F. Austin State**
33. **Cody Phipps, of, Vauxhall HS, Crows Nest Pass, Alb**
34. **Brian Wabick, rhp, Oakton (Ill.) CC**
35. **Jordan Powell, rhp, Southern Illinois**
36. **Albert Cartwright, of, Polk (Fla.) CC**
37. **Jake Leonhardt, rhp, Stephen F. Austin State**
38. Robbie Weinhardt, rhp, Oklahoma State
39. Brian Fletcher, 3b/of, Starr's Mill HS, Fayetteville, Ga.
40. Kyle Erdman, lhp, Oakton (Ill.) CC
41. **Colton Pitkin, lhp, Sterling HS, Baytown, Texas**
42. **Chris Turner, of, Brandon (Fla.) HS**
43. **Marques Williams, of, Compton (Calif.) CC**
44. **Cat Everett, ss, Tulane**

KANSAS CITY ROYALS

June—Regular Phase (2)

1. **Mike Moustakas, ss, Chatsworth (Calif.) HS**
2. **Sam Runion, rhp, Reynolds HS, Asheville, N.C.**
3. **Danny Duffy, lhp, Cabrillo HS, Lompoc, Calif.**
4. **Mitch Hodge, rhp, Prince of Wales SS, Vancouver, B.C.**
5. **Adrian Ortiz, of, Pepperdine**
6. **Fernando Cruz, ss, Dorado, P.R.**
7. **Hilton Richardson, of, Lake Washington HS, Kirkland, Wash.**
8. **Casey Feickert, rhp, Antelope Valley (Calif.) JC**
9. Zach Kenyon, rhp, Davenport (Iowa) Central HS
10. **Greg Holland, rhp, Western Carolina**
11. **David Lough, of, Mercyhurst (Pa.)**
12. **Sean McCauley, c, Osbourn HS, Manassas, Va.**
13. **Alex Caldera, rhp, Chaffey (Calif.) JC**
14. **Matt Mitchell, rhp, Barstow (Calif.) HS**
15. **Ryan Eigsti, c, Bradley**
16. **Patrick Norris, of, Oklahoma City**
17. **Ivor Hodgson, of, Mount St. Mary's**
18. Stephen Dodson, rhp, Georgia
19. **Joe Billick, c, Southern Poly State (Ga.)**
20. **Mike Lehmann, rhp, Pearl River Central HS, Carriere, Miss.**
21. Josh Billeaud, rhp, Louisiana State-Eunice JC
22. **Jake Rodriguez, rhp, East Los Angeles JC**
23. Geoff Brown, lhp, Jackson HS, Mill Creek, Wash.
24. **Ben Norton, rhp, Evansville**
25. **Clint Robinson, 1b, Troy**
26. **Nat Lovell, rhp, Fresno CC**
27. **Dane Secott, rhp, Minnesota State-Mankato**
28. **Fernando Garcia, 2b, Manatee (Fla.) CC**
29. **Kyle Martin, ss, Texas Tech**
30. **Brett Amyx, 1b, Texas-Tyler**
31. **Keaton Hayenga, rhp, Eastlake (Wash.) HS**
32. **Jake Lane, 1b, Austin Peay**
33. **Will Tucker, of, Belmont**
34. **Tom Hill, c, Albany**
35. Garrett Weber, ss, Clovis (Calif.) HS
36. **Mike Bionde, 2b, Rutgers**
37. **Derek Rodriguez, of, Ignacio (Colo.) HS**
38. Brian Leach, rhp, Northwest Mississippi CC
39. Trevor Feeney, rhp, Northern Illinois
40. **Clegg Snipes, rhp, Troy**
41. Tyler Topp, rhp, Riverside (Calif.) CC
42. Doug Antilla, rhp, MidAmerica Nazarene (Kan.)
43. Chris Snipes, lhp, Middle Georgia JC
44. Chris Hopkins, of, Oregon State
45. **Brandon Fowler, c, Westview HS, San Diego**
46. Scott Boley, 3b, Toledo
47. John Anderson, rhp, Bossier Parish (La.) CC
48. **Devery Van De Keere, 3b, Louisiana-Lafayette**
49. Joe Vierra, 3b, Quartz Hill (Calif.) HS
50. Brandon Van Riper, c, Farmington (N.M.) HS

LOS ANGELES ANGELS

June—Regular Phase (24)

1. (Pick to Rangers as compensation for Type A free agent Gary Matthews Jr.)
1. **Jon Bachanov, rhp, University HS, Orlando, Fla.** (Supplemental pick—58th—for loss of Type B free agent Adam Kennedy)
2. (Pick to Blue Jays as compensation for Type A free agent Justin Speier)
3. Matt Harvey, rhp, Fitch HS, Groton, Conn.
4. **Trevor Pippin, of, Middle Georgia JC**
5. **Andrew Romine, ss, Arizona State**

6. **Ryan Brasier, rhp, Weatherford (Texas) JC**
7. **Baron Short, rhp, Southern**
8. **Trevor Reckling, lhp, St. Benedict's Prep, Newark, N.J.**
9. **Tyler Mann, of, Princess Anne HS, Virginia Beach, Va.**
10. **Milan Dinga, rhp, Army**
11. Martin Viramontes, rhp, Bullard HS, Fresno, Calif.
12. **Mike Anton, lhp, Virginia Military Institute**
13. David Clark, rhp, Southern Mississippi
14. Tanner Robles, lhp, Cottonwood HS, Salt Lake City
15. **Chris Garcia, 3b, St. Petersburg (Fla.) JC**
16. **Mason Tobin, rhp, Everett (Wash.) CC**
17. **Eddie McKiernan, rhp, Monrovia (Calif.) HS**
18. Zack Martin, 3b, Andrew (Ga.) JC
19. **Ryan Kennedy, 2b, Tampa**
20. **Tremayne Holland, rhp, Brewton-Parker (Ga.)**
21. **Justin Bass, 2b, Clements HS, Sugar Land, Texas**
22. Steven Salas, rhp, Chandler-Gilbert (Ariz.) CC
23. Mike Bianucci, 3b/of, Auburn
24. **DeAndre Miller, of, Loyola Marymount**
25. **Jordan Towns, rhp, West Georgia**
26. **Michael Wing, ss, Upland (Calif.) HS**
27. Patrick White, of, West Virginia
28. Ty Pryor, rhp, North Florida
29. **Brian Walker, c, Arkansas**
30. Matt Davis, rhp, Jacksonville
31. **Derek Schlecker, rhp, Western Michigan**
32. **Richard Bohlken, 2b, La Cueva HS, Albuquerque**
33. **Donato Giovanatto, of, San Jose State**
34. Carlos Ramirez, c, Chandler-Gilbert (Ariz.) CC
35. **Luke Gordon, of, Georgia State**
36. **Jay Brossman, 3b, Utah**
37. **Cephas Howard, rhp, Augusta, Ga.**
38. **Cory Page, rhp, Huntingtown (Md.) HS**
39. Jayson Brown, rhp, Barry (Fla.)
40. **Hector Estrella, 2b, Southern California**
41. Matt Scioscia, 1b, Crespi HS, Encino, Calif.
42. Jeremy Thorne, rhp, Florida Southern
43. **Terrell Alliman, of, Bluevale Collegiate Institute, Waterloo, Ontario**
44. Alex Hale, rhp, Richmond
45. Chris Bullard, of, Harris County HS, Hamilton, Ga.
46. Brandon Lodge, ss, Tesoro HS, Las Flores, Calif.
47. Billy Falasco, rhp, Seminole (Fla.) HS
48. Sean Loggins, c, McCluer North HS, Florissant, Mo.
49. Chris Vitus, rhp, Sheldon HS, Eugene, Ore.
50. **Efren Navarro, 1b/lhp, Nevada-Las Vegas**

LOS ANGELES DODGERS

June—Regular Phase (22)

1. **Chris Withrow, rhp, Midland (Texas) Christian HS** (Pick from Red Sox as compensation for Type A free agent Julio Lugo)
1. (Pick to Giants as compensation for Type A free agent Jason Schmidt)
1. **James Adkins, lhp, Tennessee** (Supplemental pick—39th—for loss of Lugo)
2. **Michael Watt, lhp, Capistrano Valley HS, Mission Viejo, Calif.**
3. **Austin Gallagher, 3b, Manheim Township HS, Lancaster, Pa.**
4. **Andrew Lambo, 1b/of, Newbury Park (Calif.) HS**
5. Kyle Blair, rhp, Los Gatos (Calif.) HS
6. **Justin Miller, rhp, Johnson County (Kan.) CC**
7. **Danny Danielson, rhp, Russell County HS, Seale, Ala.**
8. **Alex Garabedian, c, College of Charleston**
9. **Jaime Pedroza, ss, UC Riverside**
10. **Erik Kanaby, of, Lamar**
11. **Paul Koss, rhp, Southern California**
12. **Jessie Mier, c, Lewis-Clark State (Idaho)**
13. **Bobby Blevins, rhp, Le Moyne**
14. Devin Fuller, rhp, Gilbert (Ariz.) HS
15. **Cal Stanke, rhp, Wisconsin-Oshkosh**
16. **Andres Santiago, rhp, Colegio Carmen Sol, Bayamon, P.R.**
17. **Chris Jacobs, 1b, Glenn HS, Kernersville, N.C.**
18. **Given Kutz, rhp, Portland**
19. **Joris Bert, of, Frank Phillips (Texas) JC**
20. Sean Koecheler, rhp, Palm Beach Gardens (Fla.) HS
21. Terry Doyle, rhp, Boston College
22. **Matt Wallach, c, Cal State Fullerton**
23. Nathan Carter, ss, De La Salle HS, Concord, Calif.
24. **Parker Dalton, ss, Texas A&M**
25. **Tim Sexton, rhp, Miami-Dade CC**
26. Taylor Cole, rhp, Bishop Gorman HS, Las Vegas
27. Rob Rasmussen, lhp, Poly HS, Pasadena, Calif.
28. Nathan Woods, of, Xavier HS, Cedar Rapids, Iowa
29. Chad Keefer, 1b, North Central Texas JC
30. Justin Coats, ss, Seminole State (Okla.) JC
31. Rafael Thomas, of, Lufkin (Texas) HS
32. Matt Gardner, rhp, Oklahoma State
33. Jonathan Gonzalez, rhp, Cardinal Hayes HS, Bronx, N,Y,
34. Garrett Poe, 1b, Silver City (N.M.) HS
35. Ryan Christenson, lhp, Arnett (Okla.) HS
36. Tim Jones, rhp, Redan HS, Stone Mountain, Ga.
37. **Gabriel Casanova, 2b, Barry (Fla.)**
38. Matt Szczur, c, Lower Cape May (N.J.) HS
39. John Hay, of, JC of the Canyons (Calif.)

MILWAUKEE BREWERS

June—Regular Phase (7)

1. **Matt LaPorta, 1b, Florida**
2. (Pick to Cardinals as compensation for Type A free agent Jeff Suppan)
3. **Jonathan Lucroy, c, Louisiana-Lafayette**
4. **Eric Farris, 2b/ss, Loyola Marymount**
5. **Caleb Gindl, of/lhp, Pace HS, Milton, Fla.**
6. **Daniel Merklinger, lhp, Seton Hall**
7. **Efrain Nieves, lhp, Puerto Rico Baseball Academy, Gurabo, P.R.**
8. **David Fonseca, ss, Pierce (Calif.) JC**
9. **Kristian Bueno, lhp, Calallen HS, Corpus Christi, Texas**
10. **Eric Fryer, c, Ohio State**
11. **Cody Scarpetta, rhp, Guilford HS, Rockford, Ill.**
12. **Wes Etheridge, rhp, UC Irvine**
13. **Chris Dennis, of, St. Thomas of Villanova SS, LaSalle, Ontario**
14. **Donovan Hand, rhp, Jacksonville State**
15. **Joey Paciorek, 3b, Blaine (Wash.) HS**
16. **Joel Morales, rhp, Puerto Rico Baseball Academy, Guaynabo, P.R.**
17. **Erik Miller, of, Scottsdale (Ariz.) CC**
18. **Bobby Bramhall, lhp, Rice**
19. **Zelous Wheeler, 3b, Wallace State (Ala.) CC**
20. **Cameron Robulack, 1b, Silverthorn Collegiate Institute, Toronto**
21. Connor Hoehn, rhp, St. John's HS, Washington, D.C.
22. **Matt Cline, ss, Long Beach State**
23. Cody Hawn, 3b, South-Doyle HS, Knoxville, Tenn.
24. Jonathan White, of, Vanderbilt
25. Chad Bell, lhp, South-Doyle HS, Knoxville, Tenn.
26. Ben Feltner, of, Texas A&M
27. **Josh Trejo, lhp, Logan HS, Union City, Calif.**
28. **Steffan Wilson, 3b, Harvard**
29. **Travis Nevakshonoff, of, Humphries SS, Castlegar, B.C**
30. **Corey Frerichs, rhp, Temple (Texas) JC**
31. Jon Clarence, lhp, Colombus North (Ind.) HS
32. **Miguel Vasquez, ss, Seminole (Fla.) CC**
33. **Ryan Jensen, of, Langley, B.C.**
34. **Casey Baron, lhp, Maryland**
35. **Curt Rindal, 1b, Washington**
36. **Curtis Pasma, lhp, Pacific**
37. Rick Hague, ss, Klein Collins HS, Spring, Texas
38. **Kurt Crowell, of, Cal State Los Angeles**
39. Joe Scott, ss, Cal State Fullerton
40. Jordan Tanner, rhp, Neshannock (Pa.) HS
41. **Adam Arnold, rhp, Thompson Rivers (B.C.)**
42. Chase Reid, rhp, Carroll HS, Southlake, Texas
43. Cullen Sexton, rhp, Stevens Point (Wis.) HS
44. **Shawn Zarraga, c/3b, Trinity Christian HS, Boynton Beach, Fla.**
45. Matt Sergey, rhp, South Plantation HS, Plantation, Fla.

46. Stewart Ijames, of, Owensboro (Ky.) Catholic HS
47. Aaron Tullo, rhp, St. Petersburg (Fla.) JC

MINNESOTA TWINS

June—Regular Phase (28)

1. **Ben Revere, of, Lexington (Ky.) Catholic HS**
2. **Danny Rams, c/1b, Gulliver Prep, Miami**
3. **Angel Morales, of, Puerto Rico Baseball Academy, Guaynabo, P.R.**
4. **Reggie Williams, 3b, Bellflower (Calif.) HS**
5. Nate Striz, rhp, Santa Fe Catholic HS, Lakeland, Fla.
6. **Mike McCardell, rhp, Kutztown (Pa.)**
7. **Dan Berlind, rhp, Pierce (Calif.) JC**
8. **Danny Lehmann, c, Rice**
9. **Steven Hirschfeld, rhp, San Diego State**
10. **Blair Erickson, rhp, UC Irvine**
11. **Andrew Schmiesing, of, St. Olaf (Minn.)**
12. **Mike Tarsi, lhp, Connecticut**
13. Elliot Soto, ss, Dundee-Crown HS, Carpentersville, Ill.
14. **Dan Rohlfing, c, Oakville HS, St. Louis**
15. **Daniel Latham, rhp, Tulane**
16. **Nelvin Fuentes, lhp, Puerto Rico Baseball Academy, Guaynabo, P.R.**
17. Jose Rodriguez, of/1b, Hialeah (Fla.) HS
18. **Lee Martin, rhp, Southern Arkansas**
19. **Ben Petsch, c, Belmont**
20. Tom Farmer, rhp, Akron
21. **Ozzie Lewis, of, Fresno State**
22. Mickey Storey, rhp, Florida Atlantic
23. Josh Workman, 2b, Wichita State
24. **Charles Nolte, rhp, San Diego State**
25. **Spencer Steedley, of/lhp, UNC Charlotte**
26. Kyle Witten, rhp, Bakersfield (Calif.) JC
27. Kyle Heyne, rhp, Ball State
28. Seth Rosin, rhp, Mounds View HS, Arden Hills, Minn.
29. Fred Atkins, of, JC of Marin (Calif.)
30. Josh Adams, ss, Eagle's View Academy, Jacksonville, Fla.
31. Mike Kvasnicka, of, North HS, Lakeville, Minn.
32. Johnny Bromberg, rhp, Palisades HS, Mission Viejo, Calif.
33. Evan Danieli, rhp, Seton Hall Prep, West Orange, N.J.
34. Stephen Branca, ss, Newsome HS, Lithia, Fla.
35. Ryan Strauss, rhp, Florida State
36. **Dominique Rodgers, rhp, Kent State**
37. Julien Pollard, 2b, Washington HS, Tacoma, Wash.
38. **Chris Cates, ss, Louisville**
39. Joe Leftridge, of, Duncanville (Texas) HS
40. Chase Anderson, rhp, North Central Texas JC
41. Jon Griffin, rhp, Lakewood Ranch HS, Bradenton, Fla.
42. Troy Scott, 1b, Auburn (Ala.) HS
43. **Andres Diaz, c, Palm Beach (Fla.) CC**
44. Zach Barger, of, Long Beach State
45. Kevin Arico, rhp, Hunterdon Central HS, Flemington, N.J.
46. John Williams, 3b, Niles North HS, Skokie, Ill.
47. Chris Heston, rhp, Seminole (Fla.) CC
48. Ken Smalley, rhp, Logan (Ill.) JC
49. Nick Cobler, lhp, Butler (Kan.) CC
50. Chris Freshcorn, c, Alonso HS, Tampa

NEW YORK METS

June—Regular Phase (29)

1. (Pick to Giants as compensation for Type A free agent Moises Alou)
1. **Eddie Kunz, rhp, Oregon State** (Supplemental pick—42nd—for loss of Type A free agent Roberto Hernandez)
1. **Nathan Vineyard, lhp, Woodland HS, Cartersville, Ga.** (Supplemental pick—47th—for loss of Type A free agent Chad Bradford)
2. **Scott Moviel, rhp, St. Edward HS, Berea, Ohio** (Pick from Indians as compensation for Hernandez)
2. **Brant Rustich, rhp, UCLA**
3. **Eric Niesen, lhp, Wake Forest** (Pick from Orioles as compensation for Bradford)
3. **Stephen Clyne, rhp, Clemson**
4. **Richard Lucas, 3b, Wolfson HS, Jacksonville, Fla.**
5. **Zach Lutz, 3b, Alvernia (Pa.)**
6. **Guillaume Leduc, rhp, Montpetit HS, Montreal**
7. **Lucas Duda, 1b, Southern California**
8. **Dan McDonald, rhp, Seton Hall**
9. **Michael Olmsted, rhp, Cypress (Calif.) JC**
10. **Brandon Richey, ss, Northwestern State**
11. **Matt Bouchard, ss, Georgetown**
12. **Will Morgan, rhp, Lewis-Clark State (Idaho)**
13. **Jordan Abruzzo, c, San Diego**
14. **Robert Carson, lhp, Hattiesburg (Miss.) HS**
15. **Jefferies Tatford, c, Louisiana-Lafayette**
16. **Chris Fournier, of, George Mason**
17. Brandon Efferson, rhp, Zachary (La.) HS
18. **Mike Antonini, lhp, Georgia College & State**
19. **Ernesto Gonzalez, ss, George Wallace (Ala.) CC**
20. **Dylan Owen, rhp, Francis Marion (S.C.)**
21. **Dillon Gee, rhp, Texas-Arlington**
22. **Tyler Vaughn, 3b, UC Irvine**
23. Norberto Navarro, c, Pasco-Hernando (Fla.) CC
24. **Michael Parker, 2b, George Washington**
25. **Cole Abbott, rhp, Weber HS, Ogden, Utah**
26. **Brad Burns, rhp, Oklahoma**
27. **Kyle Catto, rhp, Southern Illinois**
28. Kyle Maxie, c, Pearl River (Miss.) CC
29. **Roy Merritt, lhp, Southern**
30. Rylan Sandoval, 2b, Chabot (Calif.) JC
31. Tony Peraza, lhp, La Mirada (Calif.) HS
32. **Juan Centeno, c, Antonio Lucchetti HS, Arecibo, P.R.**
33. Nicholas Abshire, ss, Lake Charles, La.
34. **Terry Johnson, ss, William Carey (Miss.)**
35. **Jason Lavorgna, rhp, Eastern Connecticut State**
36. Glen Johnson, ss/3b, South Fork HS, Hobe Sound, Fla.
37. **Jose Alvarez, 3b, Otay Ranch HS, Chula Vista, Calif.**
38. **Brandon Kawal, of, Concordia (Calif.)**
39. **Alonzo Harris, ss, McComb (Miss.) HS**

NEW YORK YANKEES

June—Regular Phase (30)

1. **Andrew Brackman, rhp, North Carolina State**
2. **Austin Romine, c, El Toro HS, Lake Forest, Calif.**
3. **Ryan Pope, rhp, Savannah College of Art and Design (Ga.)**
4. **Bradley Suttle, 3b, Texas**
5. **Adam Olbrychowski, rhp, Pepperdine**
6. **Chase Weems, c, Columbus (Ga.) HS**
7. **Damon Sublett, 2b/rhp, Wichita State**
8. **Taylor Grote, of, The Woodlands (Texas) HS**
9. **Austin Krum, of, Dallas Baptist**
10. **Carmen Angelini, ss, Barbe HS, Lake Charles, La.**
11. **Isaiah Howes, of, Louisville**
12. **Manuel Barreda, rhp, Sahuarita (Ariz.) HS**
13. **Nick Chigges, rhp, Charleston**
14. **Braedyn Pruitt, 3b, Stetson**
15. **Dave Williams, of, Rutgers**
16. Dan Mahoney, rhp, Cushing Academy, Ashburnham, Mass.
17. **Ryan Zink, rhp, Illinois-Chicago**
18. Chris Carpenter, rhp, Kent State
19. **Taylor Holiday, of, UC Irvine**
20. **Ryan Wehrle, ss, Nebraska**
21. **Justin Snyder, 2b, San Diego**
22. **Craig Heyer, rhp, Nevada-Las Vegas**
23. **Matt Morris, of, UC Irvine**
24. Greg Peavey, rhp, Hudson's Bay HS, Vancouver, Wash.
25. **Jason Kiley, rhp, Florida Gulf Coast**
26. **Gary Gattis, of, Yavapai (Ariz.) JC**
27. **Brandon Laird, 3b, Cypress (Calif.) JC**
28. **Jeff Livek, rhp, Carthage (Wis.)**
29. Matt Pilgreen, rhp, Louisiana-Lafayette
30. **Chris Carrara, 2b, Winthrop**
31. Chad Dawson, rhp, Indiana State
32. **Brian Chavez, ss, San Francisco**
33. **Fred Jones, rhp, Evansville**
34. Drew Storen, rhp, Brownsburg (Ind.) HS
35. Greg Holle, rhp, Christian Brothers HS, Loudonville, N.Y.

36. **Danny Cox, ss, Washington**
37. **Steve Strausbaugh, of, Western Carolina**
38. Erik Komatsu, of, Oxnard (Calif.) JC
39. Eric Thames, of, Pepperdine
40. Luke Murton, 1b, Georgia Tech
41. **Jake Shafer, rhp, Missouri State**
42. **Chris Raber, 1b, Coastal Carolina**
43. Jason Chowning, rhp, Texarkana (Texas) JC
44. Tyler Herriage, lhp, Weatherford (Texas) JC
45. Pat Venditte, rhp/lhp, Creighton
46. **Daniel Kapala, rhp, Notre Dame**
47. Colin Arnold, of, Daytona Beach (Fla.) CC
48. Scott Bittle, rhp, Mississippi
49. Ken Toves, lhp, Carlsbad (Calif.) HS
50. **Larry Day, c, Connecticut**

OAKLAND ATHLETICS

June—Regular Phase (26)

1. **James Simmons, rhp, UC Riverside**
1. **Sean Doolittle, 1b/lhp, Virginia** (Supplemental pick—41st—for loss of Type A free agent Barry Zito)
1. **Corey Brown, of, Oklahoma State** (Supplemental pick—59th—for loss of Type B free agent Frank Thomas)
2. **Grant Desme, of, Cal Poly** (Pick from Giants as compensation for Zito)
3. **Sam Demel, rhp, Texas Christian**
4. **Travis Banwart, rhp, Wichita State**
5. **Andrew Carignan, rhp, North Carolina**
6. **Scott Hodsdon, rhp, Azusa Pacific (Calif.)**
7. **Lance Sewell, lhp, San Diego State**
8. Daniel Schlereth, lhp, Arizona
9. Eric Berger, lhp, Arizona
10. **Danny Hamblin, 1b, Arkansas**
11. **Michael Richard, ss, Prairie View A&M**
12. Gary Brown, of/2b, Diamond Bar HS, Walnut, Calif.
13. **Justin Friend, rhp, Oklahoma State**
14. **Matt Smith, c, Texas Tech**
15. **Brad Hertzler, lhp, Maine**
16. **Brent Lysander, rhp, Sonoma State (Calif.)**
17. Stephen Hunt, lhp, Jesuit HS, Tampa
18. **Matt Ray, ss, Middle Tennessee State**
19. **Dusty Napoleon, c, Iowa**
20. **Dan Wentzell, of, George Fox (Ore.)**
21. Stephen Porlier, rhp, Oklahoma
22. **Aaron Jenkins, lhp, Northern Iowa**
23. **J.D. Pruitt, of, Montevallo (Ala.)**
24. **Raymond Rodriguez, c, Puerto Rico Baseball Academy, Guaynabo, P.R.**
25. **Jareck West, of, Delta State (Miss.)**
26. Tobias Streich, c, Johnsonburg (Pa.) HS
27. **Justin Frash, 3b, Hawaii**
28. **Lee Land, rhp, UNC Greensboro**
29. Collin Cowgill, of, Kentucky
30. **Chad Kerfoot, rhp, Delaware**
31. **Fabian Gomez, lhp, Rockford (Ill.)**
32. **Bryan Collins, rhp, Central Missouri State**
33. **John Quine, rhp, San Francisco**
34. Ryne Tacker, rhp, Rice
35. **Herbert Hudson, of, Mount San Jacinto (Calif.) JC**
36. Trent Abbott, rhp, Fullerton (Calif.) JC
37. Nick Longmire, of, Grossmont HS, El Cajon, Calif.
38. Kevin Rath, lhp, Silverado HS, Las Vegas
39. Stan Widmann, ss, Clemson
40. Daniel Magnante, c, Campbell Hall HS, North Hollywood, Calif.
41. James Wernke, lhp, Troy HS, Fullerton, Calif.
42. Jonathan Johnston, c, Navy
43. Stephen Cochrane, c, Yavapai (Ariz.) JC
44. **Ben Barrone, c, Winona State (Minn.)**
45. J.T. Wise, 1b/3b, Louisiana State
46. Conner Bernatz, of, Mater Dei HS, Santa Ana, Calif.
47. Seth Blair, rhp, Rock Falls (Ill.) HS
48. **Adam Klein, of, Cal State Los Angeles**
49. Josh Bowman, rhp, Northeast HS, St. Petersburg, Fla.
50. Steve Hagen, 3b, Peninsula HS, Gig Harbor, Wash.

PHILADELPHIA PHILLIES

June—Regular Phase (19)

1. **Joe Savery, lhp, Rice**
1. **Travis D'Arnaud, c, Lakewood (Calif.) HS** (Supplemental pick—37th—for loss of Type A free agent David Dellucci)
2. **Travis Mattair, ss/3b, Southridge (Wash.) HS**
3. Brandon Workman, rhp, Bowie (Texas) HS (Pick from Indians as compensation for Dellucci)
3. **Matt Spencer, of/lhp, Arizona State**
4. **Tyler Mach, 3b, Oklahoma State**
5. **Michael Taylor, of, Stanford**
6. **Matt Rizzotti, 1b, Manhattan**
7. **Tyson Brummett, rhp, UCLA**
8. **Chance Chapman, rhp, Oral Roberts**
9. **Chris Kissock, rhp, Lewis-Clark State (Idaho)**
10. **Joe Rocchio, rhp, Cal State Northridge**
11. **Justin De Fratus, rhp, Ventura (Calif.) JC**
12. **Julian Sampson, rhp, Skyline (Wash.) HS**
13. **Luke Wertz, rhp, Nebraska**
14. **Jesus Villegas Andino, ss, Porterville (Calif.) JC**
15. **Karl Bolt, 1b, Air Force**
16. **Brian Schlitter, rhp, College of Charleston**
17. **Zack Sterner, rhp, Tennessee Wesleyan**
18. Mark Adzick, lhp, William Penn Charter HS, Haverford, Pa.
19. Cedric Johnson, of, Thatcher (Ariz.) HS
20. Carlos Moncrief, of, Hillcrest Christian HS, Jackson, Miss.
21. **Adam Sorgi, 2b, Stanford**
22. **Jiwan James, rhp, Williston (Fla.) HS**
23. **Gerard Breslin, rhp, La Salle**
24. **Caleb Mangum, c, North Carolina State**
25. William Harris, lhp, Delaware
26. **Nolan Mulligan, rhp, Lynn (Fla.)**
27. **Rick Austin, rhp, Seton Hill (Pa.)**
28. **Chris Rhoads, rhp, Arkansas**
29. Derek Hall, c, El Dorado HS, Placentia, Calif.
30. **Jacob Diekman, lhp, Cloud County (Kan.) CC**
31. Jeff Richard, rhp, Central Michigan
32. **Kirk Bacsu, c, Evansville**
33. **Rich Prall, c, La Salle**
34. Brett Hambright, c, Temescal Canyon HS, Lake Elsinore, Calif.
35. Zach Cleveland, rhp, Golden (Colo.) HS
36. Kyle Benoit, rhp, Cardinal Leger SS, Brampton, Ontario
37. **Kyle Slate, rhp, Christian Brothers Academy, Lincroft, N.J.**
38. Joseph Paylor, of, Hillcrest HS, Dallas
39. Michael Branham, rhp, Florida
40. John Hinson, of/2b, Reynolds HS, Asheville, N.C.
41. Tyler Glider, rhp, Butte (Mont.) HS
42. James Mahler, rhp, Jordan HS, Sandy, Utah
43. Cory Vaughn, of, Jesuit HS, Carmichael, Calif.
44. Brandon Bonner, rhp, Lakewood HS, St. Petersburg, Fla.
45. Mike Morrison, 1b, Bishop Luers HS, Fort Wayne, Ind.
46. Damien Seguen, rhp, North Bergen (N.J.) HS
47. Joey Manning, of, Bartow (Fla.) HS
48. Cody Winiarski, rhp, Union Grove (Wis.) HS
49. Navarro Hall, of, Kennesaw Mountain HS, Kennesaw, Ga.
50. Jeremy Penn, rhp, All Saints Cathedral HS, St. Thomas, Virgin Islands

PITTSBURGH PIRATES

June—Regular Phase (4)

1. **Danny Moskos, lhp, Clemson**
2. **Duke Welker, rhp, Arkansas**
3. **Brian Friday, ss, Rice**
4. **Quincy Latimore, of, Middle Creek HS, Apex, N.C.**
5. **Andrew Walker, c, Texas Christian**
6. **Matt Foust, rhp, Nebraska**
7. **Juan Garcia, c, Puerto Rico Baseball Academy, Guaynabo, P.R.**
8. **Maurice Bankston, rhp, Texarkana (Texas) JC**
9. **Tony Watson, lhp, Nebraska**
10. **Sean Giblin, rhp, Pearl River (N.Y.) HS**
11. Runey Davis, of, Georgetown (Texas) HS
12. **Erik Huber, of, Eastern Illinois**
13. **Butch Biela, c, Palatine (Ill.) HS**

14. **Kyle McPherson, rhp, Mobile (Ala.)**
15. Rey Cotilla, rhp, Miami Springs (Fla.) HS
16. **Zac Oliver, lhp, Paris (Texas) JC**
17. **Harrison Bishop, rhp, Washington**
18. **Marcus Davis, of, Alcorn State**
19. **Bobby Spain, 3b, Oklahoma City**
20. **Brian Tracy, rhp, UC Santa Barbara**
21. **Matt Cavagnaro, 2b, Penn State**
22. Nikko Navarro, c, Flanagan HS, Pembroke Pines, Fla.
23. Luis Penate, ss, Flanagan HS, Pembroke Pines, Fla.
24. **Chad Rice, ss, Virginia Military Institute**
25. **Keanon Simon, of, Oklahoma State**
26. Steven Neff, lhp, Lancaster (S.C.) HS
27. Bob Revesz, lhp, Grove City (Pa.) HS
28. Matt Clark, 3b, Riverside (Calif.) CC
29. Brian Harrison, ss, Hilton Head (S.C.) HS
30. Josh Hula, c, Miami (Ohio)
31. **Taylor Cameron, rhp, Point Loma Nazarene (Calif.)**
32. **Daniel Forrer, lhp, Auburn-Montgomery**
33. **Caleb Fields, 2b, Northwestern**
34. Cedric Pomerlee, lhp, Gentry HS, Indianola, Miss.
35. **Tom Boleska, rhp, High Point (N.C.)**
36. Drew Crisp, ss, South Carolina
37. Cody Springer, rhp, Montgomery (Texas) HS
38. Pat McAnaney, lhp, Virginia
39. J.C. Menna, rhp, Red Bank (N.J.) Catholic HS
40. Chad Poe, rhp, Bossier Parish (La.) CC
41. Demetrius Washington, of, Silver Bluff HS, New Ellenton, S.C.
42. **Daniel Bomback, 2b, Florida Atlantic**
43. Cameron Rupp, c/1b, Prestonwood Christian Academy, Plano, Texas
44. Dustin Emmons, rhp, Crescenta Valley HS, La Crescenta, Calif.
45. Pernell Halliman, rhp, West Hills (Calif.) JC
46. Reyes Dorado, rhp, Riverside (Calif.) CC
47. Robbie Broach, rhp, Archbishop Rummel HS, Metairie, La.
48. **Gary Amato, rhp, Penn State**
49. Erik Morrison, ss, Kansas
50. Brandon Glover, of, San Diego State

ST. LOUIS CARDINALS

June—Regular Phase (18)

1. **Pete Kozma, ss, Owasso (Okla.) HS**
1. **Clay Mortensen, rhp, Gonzaga** (Supplemental pick—36th—for loss of Type A free agent Jeff Suppan)
2. **David Kopp, rhp, Clemson** (Pick from Brewers as compensation for Suppan)
2. **Jess Todd, rhp, Arkansas**
3. **Daniel Descalso, 3b, UC Davis**
4. Kyle Russell, of, Texas
5. **Thomas Eager, rhp, Cal Poly**
6. **Oliver Marmol, ss, Charleston**
7. **Deryk Hooker, rhp, Mira Mesa HS, San Diego**
8. **Tyler Henley, of, Rice**
9. Mike Stutes, rhp, Oregon State
10. **Beau Riportella, of, JC of the Sequoias (Calif.)**
11. **Adam Reifer, rhp, UC Riverside**
12. **Brett Zawacki, rhp, LaSalle-Peru HS, LaSalle, Ill.**
13. **Steven Hill, 1b, Stephen F. Austin State**
14. **Josh Dew, rhp/1b, Troy**
15. **Chuck Fick, rhp, Cal State Northridge**
16. **Antonio DeJesus, of, Kentucky**
17. **Matt Arburr, 1b/3b, Pace (N.Y.)**
18. **Andrew Brown, of, Nebraska**
19. **Nick Peoples, 2b, Texas**
20. **Bryan Cartie, 3b, McNeese State**
21. **Brian Broderick, rhp, Grand Canyon (Ariz.)**
22. **Charlie Kingrey, of, McNeese State**
23. **Joey Hage, of, Douglas HS, Parkland, Fla.**
24. Sam Freeman, lhp, North Central Texas JC
25. **J.D. Stambaugh, lhp, Brigham Young**
26. **Arnoldi Cruz, 3b, Palm Beach (Fla.) CC**
27. **Brian Buck, of, Santa Barbara (Calif.) CC**
28. **Ross Oeder, 2b, Wright State**
29. **Charlie Pelt, 1b, Georgia State**
30. **Nick Derba, c, Manhattan**
31. **Dylan Gonzalez, rhp, Pepperdine**
32. **Nick Vera, 3b, Trinity (Texas)**
33. **Josh Fritsche, lhp, Oklahoma State**
34. **Steve Hill, rhp, Southeastern (Fla.)**
35. **Michael Blazek, rhp, Arbor View HS, Las Vegas**
36. **Collin Fanning, of, Brigham Young**
37. C.J. Ziegler, 1b, Arizona
38. **Adron Chambers, of, Pensacola (Fla.) JC**
39. **Rigoberto Lugo, rhp, Puerto Rico Baseball Academy, Guaynabo, P.R.**
40. Justin Dalles, c, St. Petersburg (Fla.) JC
41. **Ramon Delgado, rhp, Pima (Ariz.) CC**
42. **Mike Folli, 2b, Buffalo**
43. **Davis Bilardello, lhp, South Florida**
44. Dan Thomas, rhp, South Florida
45. **Jameson Maj, rhp, Abilene Christian (Texas)**
46. **Robert Sanzillo, c, Johns Hopkins (Md.)**
47. **Mateo Marquez, of, Cal State Dominguez Hills**
48. Jason King, of, Jerome HS, Dublin, Ohio
49. **Ronald Russell, rhp, Harmony Grove HS, Camden, Ark.**
50. Stephen McCray, rhp, Young Harris (Ga.) JC

SAN DIEGO PADRES

June—Regular Phase (23)

1. **Nick Schmidt, lhp, Arkansas**
1. **Kellen Kulbacki, of, James Madison** (Supplemental pick—40th—for loss of Type A free agent Woody Williams)
1. **Drew Cumberland, ss, Pace HS, Milton, Fla.** (Supplemental pick—46th—for loss of Type A free agent Dave Roberts)
1. **Mitch Canham, c, Oregon State** (Supplemental pick—57th—for loss of Type B free agent Chan Ho Park)
1. **Cory Luebke, lhp, Ohio State** (Supplemental pick—63rd—for loss of Type B free agent Alan Embree)
1. **Danny Payne, of, Georgia Tech** (Supplemental pick—64th—for loss of Type B free agent Ryan Klesko)
2. **Eric Sogard, 2b, Arizona State** (Pick from Astros as compensation for Williams)
2. **Brad Chalk, of, Clemson**
3. Tommy Toledo, rhp, Alonso HS, Tampa
4. **Corey Kluber, rhp, Stetson** (Pick from Giants as compensation for Roberts)
4. **Lance Zawadzki, ss, Lee (Tenn.)**
5. **Jeremy Hefner, rhp, Oral Roberts**
6. **Emmanuel Quiles, c, Delgado HS, Sabana Hoyo, P.R.**
7. **Justin Baum, 3b, Pacific**
8. **Matt Teague, lhp, Carson-Newman (Tenn.)**
9. **Wynn Pelzer, rhp, South Carolina**
10. Christian Colon, ss/2b, Canyon HS, Canyon Country, Calif.
11. **Shane Buschini, of, San Diego**
12. **Luis Martinez, c, Cumberland (Tenn.)**
13. **Allen Harrington, lhp, Lamar**
14. **Keith Conlon, of, Texas Christian**
15. **Ryan Hill, of, Rutgers**
16. **Robert Perry, of, Long Beach State**
17. **Brandon Gomes, rhp, Tulane**
18. **Robbie Blauer, 1b, UC Santa Barbara**
19. **Adam McDaniel, rhp, Georgia**
20. **Robert Woodard, rhp, North Carolina**
21. **Tyler Davis, rhp, Hawaii**
22. **Keoni Ruth, 2b, Concordia (Calif.)**
23. **Angel Mercado, of, Bethune-Cookman**
24. **Bryan Oland, rhp, Sonoma State (Calif.)**
25. Hunter Ovens, of, Cardinal Mooney HS, Bradenton, Fla.
26. **Andy Parrino, 2b, Le Moyne**
27. **Zach Brown, of, The Citadel**
28. **Shawn Olsen, rhp, Southern California**
29. **Brian Joynt, 3b, Oklahoma City**
30. **Dylan Axelrod, rhp, UC Irvine**
31. **Colt Hynes, lhp, Texas Tech**
32. Anthony Renteria, ss, Great Oaks HS, Temecula, Calif.
33. A.J. Schugel, 3b, Mountain Vista HS, Highlands Ranch, Colo.
34. Joseph Pagan, 1b, Archbishop Curley-Notre Dame HS, Miami
35. Ross Wilson, ss, Hoover (Ala.) HS

SAN FRANCISCO GIANTS

June—Regular Phase (10)

1. **Madison Bumgarner, lhp, South Caldwell HS, Hudson, N.C.**
1. **Tim Alderson, rhp, Horizon HS, Scottsdale, Ariz.** (Pick from Dodgers as compensation for Type A free agent Jason Schmidt)
1. **Wendell Fairley, of, George County-Lucedale (Miss.) HS** (Pick from Mets as compensation for Type A free agent Moises Alou)
1. **Nick Noonan, 2b, Parker HS, San Diego** (Supplemental pick—32nd—for loss of Alou)
1. **Jackson Williams, c, Oklahoma** (Supplemental pick—43rd—for loss of Schmidt)
1. **Charlie Culberson, 2b/ss, Calhoun (Ga.) HS** (Supplemental pick—51st—for loss of Type B free agent Mike Stanton)
2. (Pick to Athletics as compensation for Type A free agent Barry Zito)
3. (Pick to Reds as compensation for Type A free agent Rich Aurilia)
4. (Pick to Padres as compensation for Type A free agent Dave Roberts)
5. **Chance Corgan, rhp, Texas Christian**
6. **Michael Ambort, c, Lamar**
7. **Kyle Nicholson, rhp, Texas A&M**
8. **Daniel Turpen, rhp, Oregon State**
9. **Dan Runzler, lhp, UC Riverside**
10. **Joe Paterson, lhp, Oregon State**
11. **Evan McArthur, 3b, Cal State Fullerton**
12. **Andrew Davis, 3b, Kent State**
13. **Andy Reichard, rhp, Georgia College & State**
14. **Craig Clark, lhp, Penn State**
15. **Bruce Edwards, of, Auburn**
16. **Steve Edlefsen, rhp, Nebraska**
17. **John King, rhp, Lipscomb**
18. **Andy De La Garza, lhp, Coastal Carolina**
19. **Andy D'Alessio, 1b, Clemson**
20. **David Mixon, rhp, Louisiana-Monroe**
21. **Danny Otero, rhp, South Florida**
22. **Oliver Odle, rhp, Oklahoma State**
23. **Drew Bowlin, rhp, Chattanooga State Tech (Tenn.) CC**
24. **Brock Bond, 2b, Missouri**
25. **Casey Bond, of, Lipscomb**
26. **Ramon Corona, ss/2b, North Carolina State**
27. **Myles Schroder, of, Diablo Valley (Calif.) JC**
28. Dan McDaniel, rhp, Chabot (Calif.) JC
29. **Lars Knepper, rhp, Hawaii-Hilo**
30. **Johnny Monell, c, Seminole (Fla.) CC**
31. **Josh Lopez, ss, Lehigh (Fla.) Senior HS**
32. **Dom Duggan, of, Coastal Carolina**
33. **Mike Loberg, of, Augustana (S.D.)**
34. Tyler Ladendorf, ss, Howard (Texas) JC
35. **T.J. Brewer, rhp, Arkansas State**
36. Paul Clemens, rhp, Louisburg (N.C.) JC
37. **Jason Neitz, lhp, East Carolina**
38. **J.J. Pannell, rhp, George Mason**
39. **Tim Egart, rhp, Arkansas State**
40. **Ben Wilshire, rhp, Austin Peay**
41. **Brandon Grabham, rhp, Grayson County (Texas) CC**
42. **Chad Rothford, 1b, Oral Roberts**
43. **Shane Jordan, of, Stetson**
44. **Joseph Edens, rhp, Samford**
45. Phil Disher, c, South Carolina
46. Jack Rye, of, Florida State
47. Ryan Verdugo, lhp, Skagit Valley (Wash.) CC
48. Andrew Barbosa, lhp, South Florida CC
49. **Trent Kline, c, South Carolina**
50. **Mike Loree, rhp, Villanova**

SEATTLE MARINERS

June—Regular Phase (11)

1. **Phillippe Aumont, rhp, Ecole Du Versant, Gatineau, Quebec**
1. **Matt Mangini, 3b, Oklahoma State** (Supplemental pick—52nd—for loss of Type B free agent Gil Meche)
2. **Denny Almonte, of, Florida Christian HS, Miami**
3. **Danny Carroll, of, Valley View HS, Moreno Valley, Calif.**
4. **Nolan Gallagher, rhp, Stanford**
5. **Joe Dunigan, of, Oklahoma**
6. **Jamie McOwen, of, Florida International**
7. **Nick Hill, lhp, Army**
8. **Donnie Hume, lhp, San Diego State**
9. **Aaron Brown, rhp, Houston**
10. **Keith Renaud, rhp, Franklin Pierce (N.H.)**
11. **Jeff Dunbar, c, UC Riverside**
12. **Ryan Moorer, rhp, Maryland**
13. **Shawn Kelley, rhp, Austin Peay**
14. **Brandon McKerney, rhp, Washington**
15. **Keith Meyer, rhp, Duquesne**
16. **Colin Buckborough, rhp, Stamford Collegiate SS, Niagara Falls, Ontario**
17. **Ryan Rodriguez, rhp, Nevada**
18. **Guy Welsh, 3b, UNC Greensboro**
19. **Roberto Mena, ss, Tampa**
20. Stephen Penney, rhp, UC Riverside
21. **Travis Mortimore, lhp, Wayne State (Neb.)**
22. **Bryan Harris, rhp, Cal State Fullerton**
23. **Brodie Downs, rhp, Modesto (Calif.) JC**
24. **Matt Renfree, rhp, Nevada**
25. Conrad Flynn, rhp, Lee HS, Midland, Texas
26. **Jake Wild, rhp, Pacific**
27. **Brooks Mohr, rhp, Elida (Ohio) HS**
28. Josh Satow, lhp, Arizona State
29. **Javier Martinez, rhp, Fordham**
30. Jason Nance, 1b, Blackford HS, Hartford City, Ind.
31. Rod Scurry, rhp, Nevada
32. **Blake Trinkler, 2b, Modesto (Calif.) JC**
33. Chris Pecora, of, North Carolina Wesleyan
34. **John DuRocher, rhp, Washington**
35. Trent Rothlin, rhp, Foard HS, Newton, N.C.
36. Cole Cook, rhp, Palisades Charter HS, Pacific Palisades, Calif.
37. Donald Brown, of, Pepperdine
38. Chris Kupillas, rhp, Central Michigan
39. Michael Beltran, ss, St. John Bosco, Lakewood, Calif.
40. Josh Liles, c, Jackson (Tenn.) HS
41. Matthew Thomas, rhp, Chino Hills (Calif.) HS
42. Jack Peterson, 2b, La Jolla (Calif.) HS
43. Jason Buursma, rhp, Bucknell
44. Forrest Snow, rhp, Lakeside HS, Seattle
45. Clay Van Hook, 2b, Texas
46. **Kyle Haas, rhp, Northeastern Oklahoma A&M JC**
47. Brett Oberholtzer, lhp, Penn HS, New Castle, Del.
48. Eric Maupin, rhp, Galena HS, Reno, Nev.
49. David Carpenter, rhp, New Mexico JC
50. Nick Purdy, of, St. Mary SS, Hamilton, Ontario

TAMPA BAY DEVIL RAYS

June—Regular Phase (1)

1. **David Price, lhp, Vanderbilt**
2. **Will Kline, rhp, Mississippi**
3. **Nick Barnese, rhp, Simi Valley (Calif.) HS**
4. **David Newmann, lhp, Texas A&M**
5. **Dustin Biell, of, Inglemoor HS, Kenmore, Wash.**
6. **Emeel Salem, of, Alabama**
7. **Reid Fronk, 3b/of, North Carolina**
8. **Matt Moore, rhp, Moriarty (N.M.) HS**
9. **Cody Cipriano, 2b, UC Irvine**
10. **Greg Sexton, 3b, William & Mary**
11. **D.J. Jones, of, Gulf Shores (Ala.) HS**
12. **Stephen Vogt, 1b, Azusa Pacific (Calif.)**
13. **Brian Flores, lhp, Arizona State**
14. **Kyle Ayers, rhp, Oswego (Ill.) HS**
15. **Mike Southern, rhp, West Hills (Calif.) JC**
16. **Josh Johnson, rhp, Mississippi State**
17. Will Harvil, rhp, Young Harris (Ga.) JC
18. **Julius Dettrich, lhp, Arlington (Wash.) HS**
19. **Kevin Boggan, rhp, Boston College**

20. **Chris Luck, rhp, South Granville HS, Creedmoor, N.C.**
21. **Kevin Brophy, rhp, UCLA**
22. Ryan Turner, rhp, Richland (Texas) HS
23. Joel Carranza, c, Flanagan HS, Pembroke Pines, Fla.
24. **John Baird, rhp, Cincinnati**
25. **Justin Garcia, rhp, Western Nevada CC**
26. Grimes Medlin III, lhp, Young Harris (Ga.) JC
27. **John Mollicone, c, Fordham**
28. **Ben Humphrey, 1b, Central Michigan**
29. Robert Morey, rhp, Cape Henry HS, Virginia Beach
30. **Joe Cruz, rhp, East Los Angeles JC**
31. Stephen Sauer, rhp, Western Nevada CC
32. Thad Griffen, c, Barbe HS, Lake Charles, La.
33. R.J. Preach, rhp, Brophy Prep, Phoenix
34. **Kevin Chavez, rhp, St. Michaels HS, Santa Fe, N.M.**
35. Joe Terdoslavich, c, Sarasota (Fla.) HS
36. Travis Stortz, lhp, Countryside HS, Clearwater, Fla.
37. **Robert Della Grotta, rhp, Pepperdine**
38. **Jesse Darcy, rhp, Manhattan**
39. Joe Staley, c, Decatur (Texas) HS
40. Will Smith, lhp, Northgate HS, Newnan, Ga.
41. **Austin Hinkle, rhp, Coastal Carolina**
42. Sean Green, rhp, Chesterton (Ind.) HS
43. Brad Buehler, rhp, St. Pius X HS, Festus, Mo.
44. Braden Degamo, c, Mariner HS, Everett, Wash.
45. Brett Miller, rhp, Montgomery HS, San Diego
46. Elliot Glynn, lhp, Wilson HS, Long Beach
47. Brad Decater, of, Bellevue (Wash.) CC
48. Matt Evers, lhp, Stratford (Texas) HS
49. Ken Burdi, of, Kishwaukee (Ill.) CC
50. Mark Peterson, lhp, Lincoln Park Academy, Fort Pierce, Fla.

TEXAS RANGERS

June—Regular Phase (16)

1. (Pick to Blue Jays as compensation for Type A free agent Frank Catalanatto)
1. **Blake Beavan, rhp, Irving (Texas) HS** (Pick from Astros as compensation for Type A free agent Carlos Lee)
1. **Michael Main, rhp/of, Deland (Fla.) HS** (Pick from Angels as compensation for Type A free agent Gary Matthews Jr.)
1. **Julio Borbon, of, Tennessee** (Supplemental pick—35th—for loss of Lee)
1. **Neil Ramirez, rhp, Kempsville (Va.) HS** (Supplemental pick—44th—for loss of Matthews)
1. **Tommy Hunter, rhp, Alabama** (Supplemental pick—54th—for loss of Type B free agent Mark DeRosa)
2. **Matt West, 3b, Bellaire (Texas) HS**
3. **Evan Reed, rhp, Cal Poly**
4. Garrett Nash, ss/of, Jordan HS, Draper, Utah
5. John Gast, lhp, Lake Brantley HS, Altamonte Springs, Fla.
6. **Bobby Wilkins, rhp, Valhalla HS, El Cajon, Calif.**
7. **Tim Smith, of, Arizona State**
8. **Jonathan Greene, c, Western Carolina**
9. **Davis Stoneburner, inf, James Madison**
10. **Andrew Laughter, rhp, Louisiana-Lafayette**
11. Anthony Ranaudo, rhp, St. Rose HS, Ocean Township, N.J.
12. Drew Pomeranz, lhp, Collierville (Tenn.) HS
13. **Kyle O'Campo, rhp, Poly HS, Riverside, Calif.**
14. **Matt Lawson, 2b, Missouri State**
15. **Hector Nelo, rhp, St. Thomas (Fla.)**
16. **Josh Lueke, rhp, Northern Kentucky**
17. **Mitch Moreland, 1b/lhp, Mississippi State**
18. **Ryan Tatusko, rhp, Indiana State**
19. **Kyle Murphy, of, Kansas**
20. **Kenny Smith, 2b, Western Carolina**
21. Erik Davis, rhp, Stanford
22. **Donnie Ecker, of, Lewis-Clark State (Idaho)**
23. **Jake Kaase, ss, Texas Lutheran**
24. **Chris Gradoville, c, Creighton**
25. Andy Wilkins, 3b/1b, Broken Arrow (Okla.) HS
26. Kevin Keyes, of, Connally HS, Austin, Texas
27. Drew Gray, c, Longview (Mo.) CC
28. **Mike Ortiz, 1b, Miami Palmetto Senior HS**
29. **Ryan Falcon, lhp, UNC Greensboro**
30. **Ben Henry, rhp, Loris (S.C.) HS**
31. **Anton Maxwell, lhp, Oregon State**
32. Gaspar Santiago, lhp, Puerto Rico Baseball Academy, Gurabo, P.R.
33. **Jared Hyatt, rhp, Georgia Tech**
34. Chase Huchingson, lhp, Fayetteville (Ark.) HS
35. Jeff Schaus, of, Barron Collier HS, Naples, Fla.
36. Brian Dupra, rhp, Greece Athena HS, Rochester, N.Y.
37. B.J. Salsbury, rhp, San Jacinto (Calif.) HS
38. Hunter Hill, rhp, Prestonwood Christian Academy, Plano, Texas
39. Tyler Fleming, rhp, Cowley County (Kan.) CC
40. Sean Meehan, rhp, Centralia (Wash.) HS
41. Tom Edwards, 1b, Rutgers
42. **Jason Sowers, 1b, Cowley County (Kan.) CC**
43. Joey Rosas, lhp, Yavapai (Ariz.) JC
44. Kris Jiggitts, rhp, Colby (Kan.) CC
45. **Ryan Turner, lhp, Georgia Tech**
46. Yoandy Barroso, of, Miami Springs (Fla.) HS
47. Ben Petralli, c, Sacramento (Calif.) CC
48. Dillon Baird, ss, Yavapai (Ariz.) JC
49. Brandon Hayes, of, Sheldon HS, Eugene, Ore.
50. Paul Zarlengo, 1b, Marian Catholic HS, Chicago Heights, Ill.

TORONTO BLUE JAYS

June—Regular Phase (21)

1. **Kevin Ahrens, 3b, Memorial HS, Houston** (Pick from Rangers as compensation for Type A free agent Frank Catalanatto)
1. **J.P. Arencibia, c/1b, Tennessee**
1. **Brett Cecil, lhp, Maryland** (Supplemental pick—38th—for loss of Type A free agent Justin Speier)
1. **Justin Jackson, ss, Roberson HS, Asheville, N.C.** (Supplemental pick—45th—for loss of Catalanatto)
1. **Trystan Magnuson, rhp, Louisville** (Supplemental pick—56th—for loss of Type B free agent Ted Lilly)
2. **John Tolisano, 2b/of, Estero (Fla.) HS**
2. **Eric Eiland, of, Lamar HS, Houston** (Pick from Angels as compensation for Speier)
3. **Alan Farina, rhp, Clemson**
4. **Brad Mills, lhp, Arizona**
5. **Marc Rzepczynski, lhp, UC Riverside**
6. **Mike McDade, 1b, Silverado HS, Las Vegas**
7. **Randy Boone, rhp, Texas**
8. **Scott Leffler, rhp, Tampa**
9. **Marcus Walden, rhp, Fresno (Calif.) CC**
10. **Joel Collins, c, South Alabama**
11. **Brad Emaus, 2b, Tulane**
12. **Steve Condotta, ss, Florida Tech**
13. **Jon Talley, c, Carlsbad (Calif.) HS**
14. **Cody Crowell, lhp, Vanderbilt**
15. **Nate Jennings, rhp, Texas-Tyler**
16. **Darin Mastroianni, 2b, Southern Indiana**
17. Adalberto Santos, 2b, New Mexico JC
18. Chris Corrigan, rhp, San Jacinto (Texas) JC
19. **Brian Letko, lhp, Embry-Riddle (Fla.)**
20. Jake Hale, rhp, Ohio State
21. Cody Dunbar, rhp, Texas Christian
22. Matt Thomson, rhp, Santa Rosa (Calif.) JC
23. **Frank Gailey, lhp, West Chester (Pa.)**
24. **Jimmy Dougher, rhp, SUNY Cortland**
25. **Jay Monti, rhp, Sacred Heart (Conn.)**
26. **Ross Buckwalter, rhp, Shippensburg (Pa.)**
27. **Kyle Gilligan, ss, Connors State (Okla.) JC**
28. Xorge Carrillo, c, McClintock HS, Tempe, Ariz.
29. Jonathan Runnels, lhp, Rice
30. Dave Kaye, rhp, Riverview HS, Oakmont, Pa.

WASHINGTON NATIONALS

June—Regular Phase (6)

1. **Ross Detwiler, lhp, Missouri State**
1. **Josh Smoker, lhp, Calhoun (Ga.) HS** (Supplemental pick—31st—for loss of Type A free agent Alfonso Soriano)
1. **Michael Burgess, of, Hillsborough HS, Tampa**

(Supplemental pick—49th—for loss of Type B free agent Jose Guillen)

2. **Jordan Zimmermann, rhp, Wisconsin-Stevens Point** (Pick from Cubs as compensation for Soriano)
2. **Jake Smolinski, 3b, Boylan Catholic HS, Rockford, Ill.**
3. **Steven Souza, 3b, Cascade HS, Everett, Wash.**
4. **Derek Norris, c, Goddard (Kan.) HS**
5. **Brad Meyers, rhp, Loyola Marymount**
6. **Jack McGeary, lhp/1b, Roxbury Latin HS, West Roxbury, Mass.**
7. **P.J. Dean, rhp, New Caney (Texas) HS**
8. **Adrian Alaniz, rhp, Texas**
9. **Mark Gildea, of, Florida State**
10. **Patrick McCoy, lhp, Sahuaro HS, Tucson, Ariz.**
11. **Bill Rhinehart, of, Arizona**
12. **Craig Stinson, c, Texas A&M**
13. **Steven Shepard, rhp, Franklin Pierce (N.H.)**
14. **Dan Lyons, ss, Minnesota**
15. **Patrick Arnold, rhp, Huntington (W.Va.) HS**
16. **Chris Blackwood, of, Gloucester County (N.J.) JC**
17. **Luke Pisker, rhp, Virginia Commonwealth**
18. Sawyer Carroll, 1b, Kentucky
19. **Jeff Mandel, rhp, Baylor**
20. Dan Cook, of, Florida Atlantic
21. **Anthony Benner, 3b, Southwestern (Calif.) JC**
22. **Jake Rogers, ss, South Dakota State**
23. David Duncan, lhp, Georgia Tech
24. **Rick Nolan, c, St. Leo (Fla.)**
25. Chris Berroa, of, Pennsauken (N.J.) HS
26. Kelvin Clark, of, Redan HS, Stone Mountain, Ga.
27. **Aaron Seuss, of, California Baptist**
28. **Boomer Whiting, of, Louisville**
29. **Justin Phillabaum, rhp, Florida Atlantic**
30. Zach Pitts, rhp, Louisville
31. Dave Stewart, of, St. John Vianney HS, St. Louis
32. Dan Killian, c, Chippewa Hills HS, Remus, Mich.
33. **Jeff McCollum, rhp, Southern**
34. Kenn Kasparek, rhp, Texas
35. Alex Floyd, of, Hillsborough (Fla.) CC
36. **Martin Beno, rhp, Oklahoma State**
37. **Devin Drag, rhp, Chapman (Calif.)**
38. **Shane Erb, rhp, Hillsborough (Fla.) CC**
39. **Caleb Staudt, rhp, St. Mary's (Texas)**
40. **Kai Tuomi, lhp, Evansville**
41. Iden Nazario, of/lhp, Southridge HS, Miami
42. **Garrett Bass, of, Jacksonville State**
43. Michael Martinez, lhp, Columbus HS, Miami
44. **Clint Pridmore, 3b, Santa Rosa (Calif.) JC**
45. **Travis Reagan, c, Rice**
46. Ryan Cisterna, c, Chandler-Gilbert (Ariz.) CC
47. Jeff Walters, rhp, St. Petersburg (Fla.) JC
48. **Kyle Gunderson, rhp, Rice**
49. **Jake Dugger, of, Arkansas**
50. **Lindon Bond, of, Texas Southern**

2008 Beckham goes No. 1 to Rays, while baseball runs afoul of own rules again with Alvarez

The 2008 draft produced some outcomes no baseball draft ever has seen, starting with the No. 1 overall selection.

The newly renamed Tampa Bay Rays drafted first overall in '07, then again in '08, the first time in draft history that the same team picked No. 1 overall in back to back years, and the fourth time in their 13 years of drafting that Tampa Bay picked first overall.

Of course, the first three times it picked first overall—selecting Josh Hamilton (1999), Delmon Young (2003) and David Price (2007)—the team was known as the Devil Rays. And on June 5, the day they kicked off the '08 draft with the first pick, the Rays entered the day a half-game behind the Red Sox in the American League East, and eventually the Rays passed the Red Sox, beat them in the AL Championship Series—with Price closing out Game Seven out of the bullpen—and became the first team to pick first in the draft and play in the World Series in the same year.

With less pressure to go for instant gratification in the draft, the Rays opted for upside and raw talent over polish and experience in their top pick. After considering Florida State catcher Buster Posey (the 2008 College Player of the Year) and Vanderbilt third baseman Pedro Alvarez, as well as San Diego lefthander Brian Matusz and Florida prep first baseman Eric Hosmer, the Rays were more than satisfied taking the top-rated high school talent on the board, shortstop Tim Beckham. They also quickly signed Beckham, giving him a bonus valued at $6.15 million, paid over five years due to his two-sport ability. Beckham stood out to scouts and to the Rays for his combination of smooth tools, power potential and middle-of-the-diamond potential.

Pittsburgh followed, with a new administration including general manager Neal Huntington and scouting director Greg Smith making the selection. The Pirates began a trend by taking the top talent on the board without great regard for signability, selecting third baseman Pedro Alvarez out of Vanderbilt.

Alvarez's signing came down to the Aug. 15 deadline, like many others. Many of the top picks went down to the last minute—and, apparently, beyond. Alvarez was among the last players who agreed to terms, with the Pirates, Alvarez and agent Scott Boras apparently agreeing to a $6 million bonus.

But more than a week later, Alvarez still had yet to go to Pittsburgh for a physical, or for an introductory press conference. On Aug. 27, the Pirates released a press release in which team president Frank

DAVID STONER

Picking first for the second year in a row, the Rays took shortstop Tim Beckham

Coonelly—who worked in the commissioner's office and was heavily involved in the draft before joining the Pirates—announced the club had requested Alvarez be placed on the restricted list.

"Regrettably, we are not surprised that Mr. Boras would attempt to raise a meritless legal claim in an effort to compel us to renegotiate Pedro's contract to one more to his liking," Coonelly said in a statement.

The Players Association filed a grievance, arguing that the Pirates had signed Alvarez after the midnight deadline. Union general counsel Michael Weiner said in a statement, "The Players Association learned from several sources that the commissioner's office had extended the deadline for negotiating and reporting signings with drafted players."

The grievance sucked in No. 3 overall pick Hosmer, who had played three games with the Royals but was pulled off the field due to the grievance. Pressure from MLB prompted the Pirates to agree to re-open negotiations with Alvarez. The grievance was resolved Sept. 24, and a day later Alvarez signed a major league contract worth $6.355 million.

Coonelly said later that the deadline had been extended Aug. 15 because the Pirates "begged." In settling the Alvarez/Hosmer grievance, MLB changed its draft rules, and the commissioner's office no longer can unilaterally extend the deadline past 11:59 p.m.

An arbitrator will have the authority to void any deals signed after the deadline.

Crow, Cole Head Unsigned

Coonelly was part of MLB's informal slotting system, an effort that started in 2000 to establish specific bonuses for every pick in the first five rounds of the draft. But with the exception of 2006, the average first-round signing bonus increased every year after 2002. The introduction of draft rules changes in 2007 that included the Aug. 15 signing deadline was an effort to exert more control over signing bonuses, but it backfired and led to an 8.5 percent increase.

Clubs that adhered to the slotting system were losing out on talent to teams that were willing to take on the commissioner's office and spend for top talent. The commissioner's office responded, and for 2008, MLB relaxed its enforcement of the slotting system, telling clubs in a predraft memo to take players based on ability, not signability.

First-round bonuses went up accordingly, even though two first-rounders failed to sign, the first time that had happened since 2001. Righthander Aaron Crow was one of the 10 unsigned first-round picks entering the Aug. 15 deadline, and he and the Nats were far apart on a potential deal.

The difference of opinion was one problem, but the contract Matusz got from the Orioles with the No. 4 overall pick also changed things. Matusz was generally regarded as the top pitcher in the class, followed by Crow. When Matusz signed a major league deal with a $3.2 million bonus and $3,472,500 guaranteed, the Nationals made what general manager Jim Bowden termed a "take it or leave it" offer of $3 million. Over the final hour of the negotiations, the Nats came up to $3.5 million, while Crow and the Hendricks came down to $4 million. The last-minute compromises weren't enough to bridge the gap, and Crow didn't get signed.

The Yankees also failed to sign their first-rounder, prep righthander Gerrit Cole, as Cole warmed up to the idea of going to college as the summer progressed and wound up turning down New York so he could attend UCLA. Cole and Dodgers first-rounder Ethan Martin were the only two high school pitchers drafted in the first round, an all-time draft low.

DRAFT 08: FIRST-ROUND PICKS

No.	Team	Player, Pos.	School	State	Ht.	Wt.	B-T	Age
1.	Rays	Tim Beckham, ss	Griffin HS	Griffin, Gla.	6-1	180	R-R	18
2.	Pirates	Pedro Alvarez, 3b	Vanderbilt	New York City	6-2	225	L-R	21
3.	Royals	Eric Hosmer, 1b	American Heritage HS	Cooper City, Fla.	6-4	215	L-L	18
4.	Orioles	Brian Matusz, lhp	San Diego	Phoenix	6-4	193	L-L	21
5.	Giants	Buster Posey, c	Florida State	Leesburg, Ga.	6-1	205	R-R	21
6.	Marlins	Kyle Skipworth, c	Patriot HS	Riverside, Calif.	6-3	195	L-R	18
7.	Reds	Yonder Alonso, 1b	Miami	Coral Gables, Fla.	6-2	215	L-R	18
8.	White Sox	Gordon Beckham, ss	Georgia	Atlanta	6-0	185	R-R	21
9.	Nationals	*Aaron Crow, rhp	Missouri	Topeka, Kan.	6-2	205	R-R	21
10.	Astros	Jason Castro, c	Stanford	Castro Valley, Calif.	6-3	215	L-R	20
11.	Rangers	Justin Smoak, 1b	South Carolina	Goose Creek, S.C.	6-4	215	B-L	21
12.	Athletics	Jemile Weeks, 2b	Miami	Altamonte Springs, Fla.	5-10	175	B-R	21
13.	Cardinals	Brett Wallace, 3b	Arizona State	Napa, Calif.	6-2	235	L-R	21
14.	Twins	Aaron Hicks, of	Wilson HS	Long Beach	6-2	175	B-R	18
15.	Dodgers	Ethan Martin, rhp	Stephens County HS	Toccoa, Ga.	6-2	195	R-R	18
16.	Brewers	Brett Lawrie, c	Brookswood SS	Langley, B.C.	5-11	200	R-R	18
17.	Blue Jays	David Cooper, 1b	California	Lodi, Calif.	6-1	210	L-L	21
18.	Mets	Ike Davis, 1b	Arizona State	Scottsdale, Ariz.	6-4	215	L-L	21
19.	Cubs	Andrew Cashner, rhp	Texas Christian	Lufkin, Texas	6-5	185	R-R	21
20.	Mariners	Joshua Fields, rhp	Georgia	Hull, Ga.	6-0	180	R-R	22
21.	Tigers	Ryan Perry, rhp	Arizona	Marana, Ariz.	6-4	200	R-R	21
22.	Mets	Reese Havens, ss	South Carolina	Charleston, S.C.	6-1	195	L-R	21
23.	Padres	Allan Dykstra, 1b	Wake Forest	San Diego	6-4	230	L-R	21
24.	Phillies	Anthony Hewitt, ss	Salisbury (Conn.) School	New York City	6-1	195	R-R	19
25.	Rockies	Christian Friedrich, lhp	Eastern Kentucky	Wilmette, Ill.	6-3	210	R-L	20
26.	Diamondbacks	Daniel Schlereth, lhp	Arizona	Anchorage, Alaska	6-1	210	L-L	22
27.	Twins	Carlos Gutierrez, rhp	Miami	Miami	6-3	205	R-R	21
28.	Yankees	*Gerrit Cole, rhp	Lutheran HS	Orange, Calif.	6-3	200	R-R	17
29.	Indians	Lonnie Chisenhall, ss	Pitt (N.C.) CC	Morehead City, N.C.	6-1	200	L-R	19
30.	Red Sox	Casey Kelly, rhp/ss	Sarasota HS	Sarasota, Fla.	6-3	195	R-R	18

*Did not sign

2008

CLUB-BY-CLUB SELECTIONS

ARIZONA DIAMONDBACKS

June—Regular Phase (26)

1. **Daniel Schlereth, lhp, Arizona**
1. **Wade Miley, lhp, Southeastern Louisiana** (Supplemental pick—43rd—for loss of Type B free agent Livan Hernandez)
2. **Bryan Shaw, rhp, Long Beach State**
3. **Kevin Eichhorn, rhp, Aptos (Calif.) HS**
4. **Ryne White, of, Purdue**
5. **Collin Cowgill, of, Kentucky**
6. **Justin Parker, ss, Wright State**
7. **Miles Reagan, rhp, El Capitan HS, Lakeside, Calif.**
8. **Pat McAnaney, lhp, Virginia**
9. **Brett Moorhouse, rhp, Indian River (Fla.) CC**
10. Danny Hultzen, lhp, St. Alban's HS, Washington, D.C.
11. **Kyle Greene, 3b, Lewis-Clark State (Idaho)**
12. Daniel Webb, rhp, Heath HS, Paducah, Ky.
13. **Ollie Linton, of, UC Irvine**
14. **Trevor Harden, rhp, New Mexico JC**
15. **Bobby Stone, of, Montgomery (Texas) HS**
16. Ryan Hughes, lhp, Chabot (Calif.) JC
17. **Ryan Babineau, c, UCLA**
18. Sam Brown, rhp, North Carolina State
19. **Joseph Gautier, lhp, Bethune-Cookman**
20. **Jordan Meaker, rhp, Dallas Baptist**
21. **Bryan Woodall, rhp, Auburn**
22. Justin LaTempa, rhp, Golden West (Calif.) JC
23. Matt Long, of, Santa Clara
24. **Nelson Gomez, 3b, Keystone (Pa.)**
25. Josh Spence, lhp, Central Arizona JC
26. Alex Sogard, lhp, North Carolina State
27. **Ryan Cook, rhp, Southern California**
28. Adam Smith, ss, Klein HS, Spring, Texas
29. Travis Meiners, ss, Des Moines Area (Iowa) CC
30. **Daniel Rodriguez, of, Miami-Dade CC**
31. Taylor Cole, rhp, CC of Southern Nevada
32. Riccio Torrez, 2b, Brophy Prep, Phoenix
33. Luke Murton, 1b, Georgia Tech
34. **Jake Elmore, ss, Arizona State**
35. **Chris Davis, c, Central Arkansas**
36. **T.J. Hose, rhp, East Carolina**
37. Sanders Commings, of, Westside HS, Augusta, Ga.
38. **Jesse Orosco Jr., rhp, Grossmont (Calif.) JC**
39. Kyle Godfrey, lhp, Wabash Valley (Ill.) CC
40. Taylor Wall, lhp, Westside HS, Houston
41. **Brendan Duffy, of, Oral Roberts**
42. Erik Stewart, rhp, Chabot (Calif.) JC
43. **Clayton Suss, rhp, Miami-Dade CC**
44. **David Cooper, ss, Mount Olive (N.C.)**
45. Jeremy Rathjen, of, Memorial HS, Houston
46. **Dan Kauffman, 1b, Juniata (Pa.)**
47. Andrew Maggi, ss, Brophy Prep, Phoenix
48. Cecil Richardson, of, Sacramento CC
49. Willie Argo, of, Assumption HS, Davenport, Iowa
50. Sean Koecheler, rhp, Palm Beach (Fla.) CC

ATLANTA BRAVES

June—Regular Phase (18)

1. (Pick to Mets as compensation for Type A free agent Tom Glavine)
1. **Brett DeVall, lhp, Niceville (Fla.) HS** (Supplemental pick—40th—for loss of Type B free agent Ron Mahay)
2. **Tyler Stovall, lhp, Hokes Bluff (Ala.) HS**
2. **Zeke Spruill, rhp, Kell HS, Marietta, Ga.** (Supplemental pick—70th—for failure to sign 2007 second-round pick Joshua Fields)
3. **Craig Kimbrel, rhp, Wallace State (Ala.) CC**
4. **Braeden Schlehuber, c, CC of Southern Nevada**
5. **Jacob Thompson, rhp, Virginia**
6. **Adam Milligan, of, Walters State (Tenn.) CC**
7. **Paul Clemens, rhp, Louisburg (N.C.) JC**
8. **Brett Oberholtzer, lhp, Seminole (Fla.) CC**
9. **Kyle Farrell, rhp, Western Nevada CC**
10. **J.J. Hoover, rhp, Calhoun (Ala.) CC**
11. **Richard Sullivan, lhp, Savannah College of Art and Design (Ga.)**
12. **David Francis, rhp, Walters State (Tenn.) CC**
13. **Travis Adair, ss, Cleveland State (Tenn.) CC**
14. **Jake Hanson, 3b, Sabino HS, Tucson**
15. **Layton Hiller, of, Blinn (Texas) JC**
16. Billy Burns, of, Walton HS, Marietta, Ga.
17. Mark Pope, rhp, Walton HS, Marietta, Ga.
18. Michael Palazzone, rhp, Lassiter HS, Marietta, Ga.
19. Zac Fuesser, lhp, York (S.C.) HS
20. **Robert Brooks, ss, Wallace State (Ala.) CC**
21. **Tyler Barnett, ss, Eastern Kentucky**
22. Dane Carter, 3b, Texas A&M
23. **Casey Hodges, rhp, Mount Olive (N.C.)**
24. **Shayne Moody, ss, Charlotte**
25. Nick Fuller, rhp, Walters State (Ala.) CC
26. **Calvin Culver, of, Los Angeles Pierce JC**
27. Anthony Rendon, ss, Lamar HS, Houston
28. Quentin Cate, c, Cuesta (Calif.) JC
29. Josh Moody, lhp, Western Nevada CC
30. **Chris Shehan, of, Georgia Southern**
31. Jason Stolz, ss, Kell HS, Marietta, Ga.
32. Pat Lenton, rhp, Minnesota State-Mankato
33. Justin Fowler, rhp, Texarkana (Texas) CC
34. Matthew Price, rhp, Walker School, Augusta, Ga.
35. Zack Osborne, rhp, New Mexico JC
36. Cecil Tanner, rhp, Ware County HS, Waycross, Ga.
37. Lucas Hileman, of, Anna-Jonesboro HS, Anna, Ill.
38. Jeffrey Richard, rhp, Coastal Carolina
39. Taylor Wulf, rhp, Alvin (Texas) CC
40. Jesse Wierzbicki, c, Walters State (Tenn.) CC
41. Ian Gilley, ss, Northside HS, Fort Smith, Ark.
42. Stephen Foster, lhp, Bellevue (Wash.) CC
43. **Adam Bullard, rhp, Gardner-Webb**
44. Taylor Hart, rhp, Madison County HS, Danielsville, Ga.
45. Nick Croce, c, Mission Bay (Calif.) HS
46. Matt Harrison, ss, Green Valley HS, Henderson, Nev.
47. David Walters, rhp, Francis Marion (S.C.)
48. David Holman, rhp, Andale (Kan.) HS
49. Josh Adams, rhp, Midland Valley HS, Graniteville, S.C.
50. Dylan Lightell, rhp, West Hills (Calif.) CC

BALTIMORE ORIOLES

June—Regular Phase (4)

1. **Brian Matusz, lhp, San Diego**
2. **Xavier Avery, of, Cedar Grove HS, Ellenwood, Ga.**
3. **L.J. Hoes, 2b, St. John's HS, Washington**
4. **Kyle Hudson, of, Illinois**
5. **Greg Miclat, ss, Virginia**
6. **Rick Zagone, lhp, Missouri**
7. **Caleb Joseph, c, Lipscomb**
8. **Bobby Bundy, rhp, Sperry (Okla.) HS**
9. **Nick Haughian, lhp, Washington**
10. Chris Herrmann, 3b, Alvin (Texas) CC
11. **Nathan Moreau, lhp, Georgia**
12. **Jason Rook, of, Appalachian State**
13. **Corey Thomas, 3b, Middleton HS, Tampa**
14. **Jesse Beal, rhp, South County SS, Lorton, Va.**
15. **Jason Gurka, lhp, Angelina (Texas) JC**
16. **Bobby Stevens, ss, Northern Illinois**

17. **Brian Conley, of, Towson**
18. Keith Landers, lhp, St. Peter-Marian HS, Worcester, Mass.
19. Jarret Martin, lhp, Centennial HS, Bakersfield, Calif.
20. **Ronnie Welty, of, Chandler-Gilbert (Ariz.) CC**
21. **Eddie Gamboa, rhp, UC Davis**
22. **Pat Kantakevich, rhp, William & Mary**
23. **Edwin Cintron, of, Antonio Luchetti HS, Arecibo, P.R.**
24. **T.J. Baxter, of, New Orleans**
25. **Xavier Lopez, c, Isabel Flores HS, Juncos, P.R.**
26. **Jose Barajas, rhp, Western Nevada CC**
27. **Ryan O'Shea, rhp, New Orleans**
28. **Tom Edwards, 3b, Rutgers**
29. **Dennis Perez, c, Puerto Rico-Arecibo**
30. Jeremy Dobbs, lhp, Daviess County HS, Owensboro, Ky.
31. **Tyler Sexton, lhp, Western Carolina**
32. Brandon Loy, ss, Rowlett (Texas) HS
33. Art Charles, 1b, Ridgeview HS, Bakersfield, Calif.
34. **Travis Keating, rhp, Northern Colorado**
35. **Buck Britton, 2b, Lubbock Christian (Texas)**
36. **Dan Eastham, rhp, Nevada**
37. **Chad Durakis, c, Maryland**
38. **Thomas Phelps, rhp, Whittier (Calif.)**
39. **Lance West, of, Bossier Parish (La.) CC**
40. Kirk Singer, ss, Los Alamitos (Calif.) HS
41. Peter Birdwell, rhp, Riverside (Calif.) CC
42. **Chase Phillips, rhp, Western Oklahoma State JC**
43. **Oliver Drake, rhp, Navy**
44. Kevin Brady, rhp, Gaithersburg (Md.) HS
45. **Zach Petersime, rhp, Rend Lake (Ill.) JC**
46. Michael Mudron, lhp, King HS, Riverside, Calif.
47. Jared Eskew, lhp, Cal Poly
48. Chris Garrison, rhp, Rocklin (Calif.) HS
49. Hector Morales, of, Puerto Rico-Carolina
50. Wes Soto, 2b, Riverview HS, Sarasota, Fla.

BOSTON RED SOX

June—Regular Phase (30)

1. **Casey Kelly, rhp/ss, Sarasota (Fla.) HS**
1. **Bryan Price, rhp, Rice** (Supplemental pick—45th—for loss of Type B free agent Eric Gagne)
2. **Derrik Gibson, ss, Seaford (Del.) HS**
3. **Stephen Fife, rhp, Utah** (Supplemental pick—85th—for failure to sign 2007 second-round pick Hunter Morris)
3. **Kyle Weiland, rhp, Notre Dame**
4. **Pete Hissey, of, Unionville (Pa.) HS**
5. **Ryan Westmoreland, of, Portsmouth (R.I.) HS**
6. **Ryan Lavarnway, c, Yale**
7. **Tim Federowicz, c, North Carolina**
8. **Michael Lee, rhp, Oklahoma City**
9. **Christian Vazquez, c, Puerto Rico Baseball Academy, Gurabo, P.R.**
10. **Pete Ruiz, rhp, Santa Barbara (Calif.) CC**
11. **Bryan Peterson, of, West Valley HS, Spokane, Wash.**
12. **Lance McClain, lhp, Cumberland (Tenn.)**
13. **Tyler Wilson, rhp, Armuchee HS, Rome, Ga.**
14. **Tyler Yockey, of, Acadiana HS, Lafayette, La.**
15. John Lally, lhp, Santa Margarita HS, Rancho Santa Margarita, Calif.
16. **Mitch Herold, lhp, Central Florida**
17. Jordan Cooper, rhp, Shawnee Heights HS, Tecumseh, Kan.
18. Brian Flynn, lhp, Owasso (Okla.) HS
19. Brian Humphries, of, Granite Hills HS, El Cajon, Calif.
20. Alex Meyer, rhp, Greensburg (Ind.) HS
21. **Jonathan Hee, 2b, Hawaii**
22. Anthony DeSclafani, rhp, Colts Neck (N.J.) HS
23. **Seth Garrison, rhp, Texas Christian**
24. Ricky Oropesa, 1b, Etiwanda (Calif.) HS
25. Justin Parker, lhp, Jesuit HS, Carmichael, Calif.
26. Navery Moore, rhp, Battle Ground Academy, Franklin, Tenn.
27. **Hunter Cervenka, lhp, Sterling HS, Baytown, Texas**
28. Matt Marquis, of, Immaculata HS, Somerville, N.J.
29. Jake Rogers, 3b, Dunedin (Fla.) HS
30. **Alex Hale, rhp, Richmond**
31. **Andrew Frezza, of, Barry (Fla.)**
32. Travis Shaw, 3b, Washington HS, Washington Court House, Ohio
33. Brandon Miller, c, Woodward Academy, College Park, Ga.
34. Zak Sinclair, rhp, West Allegheny HS, Imperial, Pa.
35. **Carson Blair, ss, Liberty Christian HS, Argyle, Texas**
36. **Richie Wasielewski, lhp, Brunswick (Ga.) HS**
37. **Tom DiBenedetto, ss, Trinity (Conn.)**
38. Bobby Hernandez, rhp, Barry (Fla.)
39. Yan Gomes, c/inf, Tennessee
40. Sam Stafford, lhp, Klein Collins HS, Spring, Texas
41. **Dustin Mercadante, rhp, San Diego CC**
42. Caleb Brown, of, Central Kitsap HS, Silverdale, Wash.
43. John Killen, lhp, Blue Valley HS, Stilwell, Kan.
44. Ben Whitmore, lhp, Fresno (Calif.) CC
45. Jon Griffin, 1b, Manatee (Fla.) CC
46. Jeremy Heatley, rhp, North Lake (Texas) CC
47. **Jeremy Kehrt, rhp, Southern Indiana**
48. Kevin Hoef, 3b, Iowa
49. **Zach Gentile, 2b, Western Michigan**
50. **Kyle Stroup, rhp, Grant HS, Fox Lake, Ill.**

CHICAGO CUBS

June—Regular Phase (19)

1. **Andrew Cashner, rhp, Texas Christian**
1. **Ryan Flaherty, ss, Vanderbilt** (Supplemental pick—41st—for loss of Type B free agent Jason Kendall)
2. **Aaron Shafer, rhp, Wichita State**
3. **Chris Carpenter, rhp, Kent State**
4. **Matt Cerda, ss, Oceanside (Calif.) HS**
5. **Justin Bristow, rhp, East Carolina**
6. **Josh Harrison, 2b, Cincinnati**
7. **Luis Flores, c, Oklahoma State**
8. **James Leverton, lhp, Texas Tech**
9. **Jay Jackson, rhp, Furman**
10. Alex Wilson, rhp, Texas A&M
11. **Toby Matchulat, rhp, Wabash Valley (Ill.) CC**
12. **Jake Opitz, 2b, Nebraska**
13. **Tony Campana, of, Cincinnati**
14. **Dan McDaniel, rhp, Chabot (Calif.) JC**
15. **Casey Coleman, rhp, Florida Gulf Coast**
16. **Ryan Keedy, 1b, Alabama-Birmingham**
17. **Jon Nagel, rhp, Independence (Kan.) CC**
18. **Jeff Beliveau, lhp, Florida Atlantic**
19. **David Macias, of, Vanderbilt**
20. **Jericho Jones, of, Louisiana Tech**
21. **Logan Watkins, ss, Goddard (Kan.) HS**
22. **Tarlandas Mitchell, rhp, Alto (Texas) HS**
23. **Ryan Sontag, of, Arizona State**
24. **David Cales, rhp, St. Xavier (Ill.)**
25. **Rebel Ridling, 1b, Oklahoma State**
26. **Josh Whitlock, rhp, West Virginia**
27. Sonny Gray, rhp, Smyrna (Tenn.) HS
28. **TeWayne Willis, of, Lincoln Memorial (Tenn.)**
29. Sean Buckley, 3b, King HS, Tampa
30. Matt White, rhp, Paris (Texas) JC
31. Kyle Wilson, 3b, Hill (Texas) JC
32. **Kurt Calvert, of, Missouri**
33. **Sean Hoorelbeke, 1b, Central Michigan**
34. **Bubba O'Donnell, rhp, High Point (N.C.)**
35. Ross Vagedes, rhp, Wright State
36. **Michael Brenly, c, Nevada-Las Vegas**
37. **Erik Hamren, rhp, Saddleback (Calif.) CC**
38. Sean McNaughton, of, Brigham Young
39. Jordan Brown, rhp, Louisiana State
40. Jared McDonald, ss, Pima (Ariz.) CC
41. Jordan Petraitis, ss, Miami (Ohio)
42. Derek Riley, rhp, Chandler-Gilbert (Ariz.) CC
43. Jesse Ginley, rhp, Dunnellon (Fla.) HS
44. David Doss, c, South Alabama
45. Ashton Florko, lhp, British Columbia
46. Tony Zych, rhp, St. Rita of Cascia HS, Chicago
47. Chad Cregar, of, Western Kentucky
48. Dylan Moseley, rhp, Louisiana Tech
49. Hunter Scantling, rhp, Episcopal HS, Jacksonville, Fla.

50. Pete Levitt, rhp, Pitt (N.C.) CC

CHICAGO WHITE SOX

June—Regular Phase (8)

1. **Gordon Beckham, ss, Georgia**
2. (Pick to Brewers as compensation for Type A free agent Scott Linebrink)
3. **Brent Morel, 3b, Cal Poly**
4. **Drew O'Neil, rhp, Penn State**
5. **Dan Hudson, rhp, Old Dominion**
6. **Kenny Williams Jr., of, Wichita State**
7. **Jordan Danks, of, Texas**
8. **Kevin Dubler, c, Illinois State**
9. **Ryan Strauss, rhp, Florida State**
10. **Stephen Sauer, rhp, Arizona State**
11. **Charlie Leesman, lhp, Xavier**
12. **Steven Upchurch, rhp, Faith Academy, Mobile, Ala.**
13. **Dexter Carter, rhp, Old Dominion**
14. Jorden Merry, rhp, Washington
15. **Tyler Kuhn, ss, West Virginia**
16. Brett Basham, c, Mississippi
17. Jonathan Weaver, rhp, East Leyden HS, Franklin Park, Ill.
18. **Josh Billeaud, rhp, Southern Mississippi**
19. **Justin Kuehn, rhp, Santa Clara**
20. **Justin Greene, of, Francis Marion (S.C.)**
21. **Drew Garcia, 2b, UC Riverside**
22. **Jose Vargas, 3b, Ventura (Calif.) JC**
23. Kyle Long, lhp, St. Anne's-Belfield School, Charlottesville, Va.
24. **Brett Graffy, rhp, Notre Dame**
25. Taylor Thompson, rhp, Auburn
26. **Jorge Castillo, 1b, Florida International**
27. **Doug Thennis, 1b, Texas Tech**
28. **Brandon Short, of, St. John's River (Fla.) CC**
29. Randall Thorpe, of, Heritage HS, Colleyville, Texas
30. **Kevin Asselin, rhp, Sonoma State (Calif.)**
31. James McCann, c, Dos Pueblos HS, Santa Barbara, Calif.
32. Justin Marrero, 2b, Reynoldsburg (Ohio) HS
33. Eddie Young, inf, Christian HS, El Cajon, Calif.
34. Marcus Semien, ss, St. Mary's HS, Berkeley, Calif.
35. Harold Riggins, 1b, Normal (Ill.) West HS
36. Jordan Keegan, of, Silverado HS, Las Vegas
37. **Terry Doyle, rhp, Boston College**
38. Steve Domecus, c, Moorpark (Calif.) JC
39. Rusty Shellhorn, lhp, Central Valley HS, Spokane Valley, Wash.
40. Mark Hawkenson, rhp, Red Mountain HS, Mesa, Ariz.
41. Mason Radeke, rhp, Santa Barbara (Calif.) HS
42. Steve Sabatino, lhp, Lockport (Ill.) Township High
43. Cory Farris, c, Boone County HS, Florence, Ky.
44. C.J. Cron, c, Mountain Pointe HS, Phoenix
45. Julian Kenner, ss, Whitney Young HS, Chicago
46. **Lee Fischer, ss, Missouri**
47. Dan Hayden, c, Xavier
48. Ricardo Alvarez, 2b, San Fernando (Calif.) HS
49. Travis Otto, 1b, Wheaton (Ill.) North HS
50. Steve Florence, ss, Simeon Career Academy, Chicago

CINCINNATI REDS

June—Regular Phase (7)

1. **Yonder Alonso, 1b, Miami**
2. (Pick to Brewers as compensation for Type A free agent Francisco Cordero)
3. **Zach Stewart, rhp, Texas Tech**
4. **Tyler Cline, rhp, Cass HS, Cartersville, Ga.**
5. **Clayton Shunick, rhp, North Carolina State**
6. **Alex Buchholz, 2b, Delaware**
7. **Pedro Villarreal, rhp, Howard (Texas) JC**
8. **Cody Puckett, ss, Cal State Dominguez Hills**
9. **David Sappelt, of, Coastal Carolina**
10. **Sean Conner, of, Palm Beach (Fla.) CC**
11. **Andrew Means, of, Indiana**
12. **Kyle Day, c, Michigan State**
13. **Blaine Howell, lhp, Pensacola (Fla.) JC**
14. **Lance Janke, rhp, San Diego Christian**
15. Eric Pfisterer, lhp, Don Bosco Prep, Ramsey, N.J.
16. **Carter Morrison, of, Clayton Heights SS, Surrey, B.C**
17. **Frank Pfister, 3b, Emory (Ga.)**
18. **Chris McMurray, c, UC Santa Barbara**
19. **Mace Thurman, lhp, Baylor**
20. **Tyler Stovall, of, Central Michigan**
21. **Theodis Bowe, of, Milford (Del.) HS**
22. **Byron Wiley, of, Kansas State**
23. **Will Hudgens, rhp, Memphis**
24. **Enrique Garcia, rhp, Miami**
25. **Raul Rodriguez, rhp, Simi Valley (Calif.) HS**
26. **Michael Bohana, rhp, Kennesaw State (Ga.)**
27. **Matt Stiffler, of, Ohio**
28. Bryce Bandilla, lhp, Bella Vista HS, Fair Oaks, Calif.
29. Ben Hunter, rhp, Wake Forest
30. **Juan Carlos Sulbaran, rhp, American Heritage HS, Plantation, Fla.**
31. Joey Housey, rhp, Nova HS, Davie, Fla.
32. **Justin Freeman, rhp, Kennesaw State (Ga.)**
33. Taylor Wrenn, 2b, Lakeland (Fla.) HS
34. **Bryan Gardner, lhp, Ithaca (N.Y.)**
35. **Matt Fairel, lhp, Florida State**
36. Erik Gregersen, rhp, Stephen F. Austin State
37. **Randall Linebaugh, rhp, Baylor**
38. Ricky Bowen, rhp, Mississippi State
39. **Mike Konstanty, 1b, Albany**
40. Dave Peterson, rhp, Los Lomas HS, Walnut Creek, Calif.
41. **Justin Walker, lhp, Lamar**
42. Benson Merritt, rhp, South Lincoln HS, Smithville, Ontario
43. Bronson Gagner, rhp, Parkview HS, Lilburn, Ga.
44. **Kevin Coddington, c, Illinois-Chicago**
45. Brendan Lobban, lhp, St. Joseph Regional HS, Montvale, N.J.
46. Grant Hogue, of, Mississippi State
47. **David Torcise, lhp, South Florida**
48. Kenny Monteith, rhp, Morristown-Beard School, Morristown, N.J.
49. Patrick White, of, West Virginia
50. Kevin Leslie, of, Faulkner (Ala.)

CLEVELAND INDIANS

June—Regular Phase (29)

1. **Lonnie Chisenhall, ss, Pitt (N.C.) CC**
2. **Trey Haley, rhp, Central Heights HS, Nacogdoches, Texas**
3. **Cord Phelps, 2b, Stanford**
4. **David Roberts, rhp, Long Beach State**
5. **Zach Putnam, rhp, Michigan**
6. **Jeremie Tice, 3b, College of Charleston**
7. **Tim Fedroff, of, North Carolina**
8. **Eric Berger, lhp, Arizona**
9. **Clayton Cook, rhp, Amarillo (Texas) HS**
10. **Donnie Webb, of, Oklahoma State**
11. **Matt Langwell, rhp, Rice**
12. **Guido Fonseca, rhp, Northern Iowa**
13. **Adam Abraham, 3b, Michigan**
14. **Carlos Moncrief, rhp, Chipola (Fla.) JC**
15. **Jason Rodriguez, 3b, Nevada**
16. **T.J. House, lhp, Picayune (Miss.) Memorial HS**
17. Mitch Mormann, rhp, Des Moines Area (Iowa) CC
18. **Kaimi Mead, lhp, Hawaii Pacific**
19. **Nate Recknagel, 1b, Michigan**
20. **Marty Popham, rhp, Union (Ky.)**
21. **Ryan Blair, of, Sacramento State**
22. **Bryce Stowell, rhp, UC Irvine**
23. Otto Roberts, rhp, Belleville (Ill.) West HS
24. **Kevin Fontanez, ss, Puerto Rico Baseball Academy, Gurabo, P.R.**
25. **Steve Smith, rhp, Ouachita Baptist (Ark.)**
26. **Moises Montero, c, Chipola (Fla.) JC**
27. Michael Goodnight, rhp, Westside HS, Houston
28. **Russell Young, lhp, Dartmouth**
29. Ryan McCarney, rhp, JC of the Canyons (Calif.)
30. Jeff Walters, rhp, St. Petersburg (Fla.) JC
31. Trevor Cousineau, lhp, Davison (Mich.) HS
32. Nick Christiani, rhp, Vanderbilt

33. **Roberto Perez, c, Lake City (Fla.) CC**
34. Collin Brennan, rhp, Bradley
35. Eagan Smith, lhp, CC of Southern Nevada
36. Adam Warren, rhp, North Carolina
37. Chad Bell, lhp, Walters State (Tenn.) CC
38. **Brian Grening, rhp, Cal Poly**
39. **Eddie Burns, rhp, Georgia Tech**
40. **Tim Palincsar, of, Texas-San Antonio**
41. Adam Matthews, of, White Knoll HS, Lexington, S.C.
42. Logan Thompson, ss, Jupiter (Fla.) HS
43. **Mike McGuire, rhp, Delaware**
44. Cory White, rhp, Rend Lake (Ill.) JC
45. Dean Lagonosky, of, Haverford (Pa.)
46. Matt Ramsey, rhp, Farragut HS, Knoxville, Tenn.
47. Randon Henika, ss, Garber HS, Essexville, Mich.
48. Troy White, 3b, Whitney Young HS, Chicago
49. Devin Jones, rhp, Eupora (Miss.) HS
50. Hector Acosta-Carillo, of, Junction City (Kan.) HS

COLORADO ROCKIES

June—Regular Phase (25)

1. **Christian Friedrich, lhp, Eastern Kentucky**
2. **Charlie Blackmon, of, Georgia Tech**
3. **Aaron Weatherford, rhp, Mississippi State**
4. **Ethan Hollingsworth, rhp, Western Michigan**
5. Chris Dominguez, 3b, Louisville
6. **Kiel Roling, c, Arizona State**
7. **Dan Houston, rhp, Boston College**
8. **Kurt Yacko, rhp, Chapman (Calif.)**
9. **Craig Bennigson, lhp, California**
10. **Stephen Dodson, rhp, Georgia**
11. **Kyle Walker, lhp, Texas**
12. **Ryan Peisel, 3b, Georgia**
13. **Erik Wetzel, 2b, Fresno State**
14. **Tyler Massey, of, Baylor School, Chattanooga, Tenn.**
15. **Juan Rodriguez, rhp, Universidad del Turabo (P.R.) JC**
16. **Chad Rose, rhp, Broward (Fla.) CC**
17. **Alan Deratt, rhp, UNC Asheville**
18. **Chad Jacobsen, 1b, South Carolina-Aiken**
19. Ben Orloff, 2b, UC Irvine
20. Nate Lape, of, Marshall
21. **Tyler Trice, rhp, North Carolina**
22. **Nick Schnaitmann, rhp, Cosumnes River (Calif.) JC**
23. Sam Elam, lhp, Notre Dame
24. **Thomas Field, ss, Texas State**
25. Andy Burns, ss, Rocky Mountain HS, Fort Collins, Colo.
26. **Adam Jorgenson, rhp, Cal State Fullerton**
27. Tim Matthews, rhp, Baylor
28. **Mike Zuanich, of, UC Santa Barbara**
29. **Matt Baugh, lhp, San Francisco**
30. **Carlos Luna, rhp, Oral Roberts**
31. **Rod Scurry, rhp, Nevada**
32. Will Scott, of, Kell HS, Marietta, Ga.
33. Aaron Gates, lhp, Orange (Calif.) Lutheran HS
34. Ryan Radcliff, c, Fairview HS, Fairview Park, Ohio
35. **Maikol Gonzalez, 2b, Tusculum (Tenn.)**
36. **Patrick Rose, of, UC Santa Barbara**
37. **Delta Cleary, of, Louisiana State-Eunice JC**
38. Tyler Pill, rhp, Covina (Calif.) HS
39. Kyle Ottoson, lhp, Eaton (Colo.) HS
40. Kemer Quirk, of, Rockhurst HS, Kansas City
41. Dean Espy, ss, Red Mountain HS, Mesa, Ariz.
42. Taylor Hightower, c, Cartersville (Ga.) HS
43. **Alex Feinberg, 2b, Vanderbilt**
44. Jordan Swagerty, rhp, Prestonwood Christian Academy, Plano, Texas
45. **Brad McAtee, rhp, UC Davis**
46. **Jimmy Cesario, 2b, Houston**
47. Mark Lincoln, rhp, American River (Calif.) JC
48. Austin Nola, ss, Catholic HS, Baton Rouge, La.
49. Roy Uhl, of, UC Riverside
50. Josh Hungerman, lhp, Cleveland State

DETROIT TIGERS

June—Regular Phase (21)

1. **Ryan Perry, rhp, Arizona**
2. **Cody Satterwhite, rhp, Mississippi**
3. **Scott Green, rhp, Kentucky**
4. **Brett Jacobson, rhp, Vanderbilt**
5. **Alex Avila, c, Alabama**
6. **Tyler Stohr, rhp, North Florida**
7. **Jade Todd, lhp, Shades Valley HS, Birmingham, Ala.**
8. **Andy Dirks, of, Wichita State**
9. **Anthony Shawler, rhp, Old Dominion**
10. **Robbie Weinhardt, rhp, Oklahoma State**
11. **Brandon Douglas, ss, Northern Iowa**
12. **Brett Anderson, ss, Bristol (Conn.) Eastern HS**
13. **Jared Gayhart, rhp, Rice**
14. **Tyler Conn, lhp, Southern Mississippi**
15. **Alden Carrithers, 2b, UCLA**
16. **Thad Weber, rhp, Nebraska**
17. **Robb Waite, rhp, UC Riverside**
18. Scott Weismann, rhp, Acton-Boxborough (Mass.) Regional HS
19. **Ben Guez, of, William & Mary**
20. Ryan Lollis, of, Missouri
21. **Adam Frost, ss, St. Norbert (Wis.)**
22. Zach MacPhee, ss, O'Connor HS, Phoenix
23. **Mike Gosse, 2b, Oklahoma**
24. **Carmelo Jaime, 2b, Miami-Dade CC**
25. **Billy Nowlin, c, Golden West (Calif.) JC**
26. **Brent Wyatt, ss, Lewis-Clark State (Idaho)**
27. James Young, rhp, Southridge HS, Miami
28. **David Stokes, rhp, Liberty**
29. **Keith Stein, of, Sam Houston State**
30. **Tyler Weber, c, Wichita State**
31. **Trevor Feeney, rhp, Northern Illinois**
32. **Mark Sorensen, rhp, Michigan State**
33. **Jordan Lennerton, 1b, Oregon State**
34. **Bryan Pounds, 3b, Houston**
35. **Dan DeLucia, lhp, Ohio State**
36. **Steve Gilman, rhp, Yale**
37. **Nick Cassavecchia, rhp, Baylor**
38. **Josh Workman, 2b, Wichita State**
39. Chris Gloor, lhp, Quinnipiac (Conn.)
40. Bryan Bingham, rhp, Navarro (Texas) JC
41. **Eric Broberg, rhp, Seminole (Fla.) CC**
42. Paul Hoenecke, 3b, West Bend (Wis.) East HS
43. Tyler Grimes, ss, North HS, Wichita, Kan.
44. Brian Wheeler, of, Childersburg (Ala.) HS
45. Edward Linseman, lhp, Our Lady of Lourdes HS, Guelph, Ontario
46. Eric Roof, c, Michigan State
47. Alan Avila, 2b, Archbishop McCarthy HS, Fort Lauderdale, Fla.
48. Casey Moore, c, Saint Louis
49. Matt Robertson, rhp, Barton County (Kan.) CC
50. Landon Hernandez, c, Hawaii

FLORIDA MARLINS

June—Regular Phase (6)

1. **Kyle Skipworth, c, Patriot HS, Rubidoux, Calif.**
2. **Brad Hand, lhp, Chaska (Minn.) HS**
3. **Edgar Olmos, lhp, Birmingham HS, Van Nuys, Calif.**
4. **Curtis Petersen, rhp, Ryan HS, Denton, Texas**
5. **Pete Andrelczyk, rhp, Coastal Carolina**
6. **Graham Johnson, rhp, Westlake HS, Westlake Village, Calif.**
7. **Paul Gran, 3b, Washington State**
8. **Isaac Galloway, of, Los Osos HS, Rancho Cucamonga, Calif.**
9. **Dan Jennings, lhp, Nebraska**
10. Trevor Holder, rhp, Georgia
11. **Blake Brewer, rhp, Sandy Creek HS, Tyrone, Ga.**
12. **Brandon Turner, 2b, Mississippi State**
13. **Danny Pertusati, 2b, Damien HS, La Verne, Calif.**
14. **Bryan Evans, rhp, UC Davis**
15. **Johnny Dorn, rhp, Nebraska**

16. **Andy Loomis, lhp, Purdue**
17. Ben Soignier, ss, Louisiana-Monroe
18. **Tom Koehler, rhp, SUNY Stony Brook**
19. **Justin Bass, of, Stetson**
20. **Wade Korpi, lhp, Notre Dame**
21. **Lonnie Lechelt, 2b, Oregon State**
22. **Jared Yecker, rhp, St. John's**
23. **Konrad Thieme, c, Sonoma State (Calif.)**
24. **Zach Moore, c, Dundalk (Md.) CC**
25. **Robert Taylor, c, Arkansas-Little Rock**
26. **Jason Peacock, 1b, Florida Gulf Coast**
27. **Elih Villanueva, rhp, Florida State**
28. **Kevin Mattison, of, UNC Asheville**
29. **Ricky Orton, 3b, UNC Greensboro**
30. **Skyler Crawford, rhp, Hartnell (Calif.) JC**
31. Marvin Campbell, 1b, Las Vegas HS
32. **Wayman Gooch, rhp, Lewis-Clark State (Idaho)**
33. Moses Munoz, lhp, Bossier Parish (La.) CC
34. **Matt Lokken, 3b, St. Helens (Ore.) HS**
35. **Brian Schultz, of, Florida Southern**
36. **Brandon Todd, rhp, South Carolina**
37. **Drew Clothier, rhp, Army**
38. Joey DeBernardis, 3b, Lake Zurich (Ill.) HS
39. Mikie Mahtook, of, St. Thomas More HS, Lafayette, La.
40. Trent Fuller, ss, Fairfield (Calif.) HS
41. Alan Williams, of, Mangham (La.) HS
42. **Jeremy Synan, of, North Carolina State**
43. Kess Carter, of, Ravenwood HS, Brentwood, Tenn.
44. **Joel Staples, 3b, St. Mary's**
45. Fred Atkins, of, JC of Marin (Calif.)
46. **Casey Fry, lhp, Los Angeles Pierce JC**
47. Jeff Urlaub, lhp, Nevada-Las Vegas
48. Barrett Serrato, ss, Community HS, West Chicago, Ill.
49. Taylor Davis, c, Jupiter (Fla.) HS
50. Colin Hoffman, of, St. Augustine HS, San Diego

HOUSTON ASTROS

June—Regular Phase (10)

1. **Jason Castro, c, Stanford**
1. **Jordan Lyles, rhp, Hartsville (S.C.) HS** (Supplemental pick—38th—for loss of Type B free agent Trever Miller)
2. **Jay Austin, of, North Atlanta HS, Atlanta**
3. Chase Davidson, 1b, Milton (Ga.) HS
3. **Ross Seaton, rhp, Second Baptist HS, Houston** (Supplemental pick—109th—for failure to sign 2007 third-round pick Derek Dietrich)
4. **T.J. Steele, of, Arizona**
5. **David Duncan, lhp, Georgia Tech**
6. **J.B. Shuck, of, Ohio State**
7. **Jon Gaston, of, Arizona**
8. **Brad Dydalewicz, lhp, Lake Travis HS, Austin**
9. **Luis Cruz, lhp, Academia Santa Monica, San Juan, P.R.**
10. **Jarred Holloway, lhp, St. Petersburg (Fla.) JC**
11. **Jacob Priday, of, Missouri**
12. **Jeff Hulett, ss, Okaloosa-Walton (Fla.) CC**
13. **Kyle Godfrey, rhp, Hiwassee (Tenn.) JC**
14. **Chris Hicks, rhp, Georgia Tech**
15. **Phil Disher, c, South Carolina**
16. Josh Poythress, lhp, Fowler (Calif.) HS
17. **Andy Simunic, 2b, Tennessee**
18. **David Flores, 3b, Sacramento State**
19. **Ashton Mowdy, rhp, Eastern Oklahoma State JC**
20. Shea Robin, c, Vanderbilt
21. Rodarrick Jones, of, St. John HS, Plaquemine, La.
22. Terrance Jackson, lhp, North Central Texas JC
23. Chase Huchingson, lhp, Arkansas-Fort Smith JC
24. **Danny Meier, of, Portland**
25. **Mike Hacker, lhp, Cosumnes River (Calif.) CC**
26. **Shane Wolf, lhp, Ithaca (N.Y.)**
27. **Nate Pettus, rhp, Western Oklahoma State JC**
28. **Zach Grimmett, rhp, Beggs (Okla.) HS**
29. **Chris Jackson, ss, Virginia Commonwealth**
30. **Mike Diaz, 2b, Southern Connecticut State**
31. **Philip Rummel, rhp, Kutztown (Pa.)**
32. Bryan Vollmuth, ss, Biloxi (Miss.) HS
33. Shawn Armstrong, rhp, West Craven HS, Vanceboro, N.C.
34. Jordan Jankowski, c, Peters Township HS, McMurray, Pa.
35. **Rene Garcia, c, Colegio Sagrada Familia HS, Corozal, P.R.**
36. Austin Wood, rhp, Niceville (Fla.) HS
37. **Kirkland Rivers, lhp, Texas A&M**
38. Kris Castellanos, lhp, Newsome HS, Lithia, Fla.
39. Tyson Van Winkle, c, Gonzaga
40. Scott Lawson, 2b, Grayson County (Texas) CC
41. Tony McClendon, of, Damien HS, La Verne, Calif.
42. Ryan Danbury, of, North Florida CC
43. Austin Green, c, Henry HS, San Diego
44. Edmond Sparks, c, Chipola (Fla.) JC
45. Grayson Garvin, lhp, Wesleyan School, Norcross, Ga.
46. Mike Modica, lhp, George Mason
47. **Nathan Metroka, of, Compton (Calif.) CC**
48. **Danny Meszaros, rhp, College of Charleston**
49. **Chase Lehr, rhp, Glendale (Ariz.) CC**
50. Jamal Austin, of, Harrison HS, Kennesaw, Ga.

KANSAS CITY ROYALS

June—Regular Phase (3)

1. **Eric Hosmer, 1b, American Heritage HS, Plantation, Fla.**
1. **Mike Montgomery, lhp, Hart HS, Newhall, Calif.** (Supplemental pick—36th—for loss of Type B free agent David Riske)
2. **Johnny Giavotella, 2b, New Orleans**
3. **Tyler Sample, rhp, Mullen HS, Denver**
4. **Tim Melville, lhp, Holt HS, Wentzville, Mo.**
5. **John Lamb, lhp, Laguna Hills (Calif.) HS**
6. **Alex Llanos, of, Westlake HS, Westlake Village, Calif.**
7. Jason Esposito, lhp, Amity Regional HS, Woodbridge, Conn.
8. **Malcolm Culver, rhp, William Paterson (N.J.)**
9. **J.D. Alfaro, of/lhp, St. John Bosco HS, Lakewood, Calif.**
10. **Mauricio Matos, lhp, Forest Hills HS, Summerhill, Pa.**
11. Malcolm Bronson, of, Monte Vista HS, Spring Valley, Calif.
12. **Keven Caldwell, of, Miami Northwestern HS**
13. **John Flanagan, rhp, Southwestern Illinois JC**
14. **Chase Hentges, rhp, Shakopee (Minn.) HS**
15. **Alberto Espinosa, rhp, Broward (Fla.) CC**
16. **Derrick Saito, lhp, SUNY Cortland**
17. **Jake Kuebler, 3b, Meridian (Miss.) CC**
18. **Carlo Testa, of, Belmont**
19. **Miguel Moctezuma, c, DeKalb HS, Auburn, Ind.**
20. **Shawn Griffin, rhp, Tennessee**
21. **Jake Theis, rhp, North Rockland HS, Haverstraw, N.Y.**
22. **Blaine Hardy, lhp, Lewis-Clark State (Idaho)**
23. **Dale De Schepper, rhp, Georgia College & State**
24. **Jason Morales, 3b, Inglewood (Calif.) HS**
25. **Carson Bryant, rhp, Wheaton (Ill.) Warrenville HS**
26. **Ryan Morgan, rhp, Col de Levis HS, Montreal**
27. **Tim Huber, rhp, Rensselaer Polytechnic (N.Y.) Institute**
28. **Greg Billo, rhp, Sandburg HS, Orland Park, Ill.**
29. Beau Brett, 1b, Artesia HS, Lynwood, Calif.
30. Rick Dodridge, lhp, Ogemaw Heights HS, West Branch, Mich.
31. Ryan Curl, of, Punahou HS, Honolulu
32. Rey Cotilla, rhp, Miami-Dade CC
33. Eric Swegman, lhp, William Penn (Iowa)
34. **Brett Richardson, rhp, Merrimack (Mass.)**
35. Chris Balcom-Miller, rhp, West Valley (Calif.) JC
36. Nick Purdy, rhp, Meridian (Miss.) HS
37. Bradin Hagens, rhp, Briarcliff HS, New York
38. **James Thompson, rhp, Clovis West HS, Fresno**
39. Ryan Modglin, rhp, Scott City (Mo.) HS
40. **Pernell Halliman, rhp, Jackson State**
41. Doug Joyce, c, University HS, Malibu, Calif.
42. Marc Oslund, rhp, West HS, Torrance, Calif.
43. Cory Kiefer, rhp, Valley View HS, Moreno Valley, Calif.
44. Patrick Johnson, of, Colony HS, Ontario, Calif.
45. Ray Anderson, of, Lassiter HS, Marietta, Ga.
46. William Beckwith, 1b, West Lowndes HS, Columbus, Miss.
47. **Steve Gilgenbach, lhp, Arkansas-Little Rock**
48. Terrence Buchanan, ss, Mount Carmel HS, San Diego
49. Alan Salgado, 3b, San Ysidro HS, San Diego

50. **Travis Jones, c, Sabino HS, Tucson**

LOS ANGELES ANGELS

June—Regular Phase (27)

1. (Pick to Twins as compensation for Type A free agent Torii Hunter)
2. **Tyler Chatwood, rhp, Redlands (Calif.) East Valley HS**
3. **Ryan Chaffee, rhp, Chipola (Fla.) JC**
3. Zach Cone, of, Parkview HS, Lilburn, Ga. (Supplemental pick—112th—for failure to sign 2007 third-round pick Matt Harvey)
4. **Buddy Boshiers, lhp, Calhoun (Ala.) CC**
5. Khiry Cooper, of, Calvary Baptist Academy, Shreveport, La.
6. **Josh Blanco, lhp, Franklin HS, El Paso**
7. **Will Smith, lhp, Gulf Coast (Fla.) CC**
8. **Chris Scholl, rhp, Green River (Wash.) CC**
9. **Nick Farnsworth, 1b, Union HS, Tulsa, Okla.**
10. **Gabe Jacobo, 3b, Sacramento State**
11. **Rolando Gomez, ss, Flanagan HS, Pembroke Pines, Fla.**
12. **Braulio Pardo, c, St. Leo (Fla.)**
13. **Michael Kohn, rhp, College of Charleston**
14. **Reyes Dorado, rhp, Arizona State**
15. **Marcel Champagnie, of, Arizona State**
16. **John Hellweg, rhp, Florida CC-Jacksonville**
17. Jamie Mallard, 1b, Middleton HS, Tampa
18. **Adam Younger, ss, Oral Roberts**
19. Marshall Burford, c, Manor HS, Austin
20. **Beau Brooks, c, Troy**
21. **Dwayne Bailey, 2b, Central Florida**
22. **Ryan Groth, of, Oral Roberts**
23. **Matt Crawford, of, Mercer**
24. Taylor Jungmann, rhp, Georgetown (Texas) HS
25. **Roberto Lopez, of, Southern California**
26. **Kevin Nabors, rhp, South Alabama**
27. **Tim Kiely, rhp, Trinity (Conn.)**
28. **Mike Kenney, rhp, Loyola Marymount**
29. **Jeremy Thorne, rhp, Florida Southern**
30. **Jayson Miller, lhp, Washington State**
31. John Hicks, c, Goochland (Va.) HS
32. Miguel Starks, rhp, Mundy's Mill HS, Jonesboro, Ga.
33. Jose Jimenez, 1b, Tampa
34. **Drew Taylor, lhp, North Carolina State**
35. **Demetrius Washington, of, Middle Georgia JC**
36. **Kyle Hurst, rhp, South Mountain (Ariz.) CC**
37. Evan Scott, rhp, Battlefield HS, Haymarket, Va.
38. **John Rickard, c, Bishop Gorman HS, Las Vegas**
39. Kyle Hendricks, rhp, Capistrano Valley HS, Mission Viejo, Calif.
40. Donnie Roach, rhp, Bishop Gorman HS, Las Vegas
41. Josh Edmondson, rhp, Florida
42. Chandler Griffin, rhp, Central Arizona JC
43. **Kevin Ferguson, lhp, Tampa**
44. David Fischer, rhp, Ballston Lake HS, Burnt Hills, N.Y.
45. Jared Clark, 1b, Cal State Fullerton
46. Ryan Hege, c, Maize (Kan.) HS
47. Josh Copeland, rhp, Alabama
48. Chris Vitus, rhp, Mount Hood (Ore.) CC
49. Will Roberts, rhp, Walker Governor's School, Richmond
50. Joey Belviso, of, American Heritage HS, Plantation, Fla.

LOS ANGELES DODGERS

June—Regular Phase (15)

1. **Ethan Martin, rhp, Stephens County HS, Toccoa, Ga.**
2. **Josh Lindblom, rhp, Purdue**
3. **Kyle Russell, of, Texas**
4. **Dee Gordon, ss, Seminole (Fla.) CC**
5. **Jon Michael Redding, rhp, Florida CC-Jacksonville**
6. **Tony Delmonico, ss, Florida State**
7. **Cole St. Clair, lhp, Rice**
8. **Nick Buss, of, Southern California**
9. **Steven Caseres, 1b, James Madison**
10. Chris Joyce, lhp, Dos Pueblos HS, Goleta, Calif.
11. **Nathan Eovaldi, rhp, Alvin (Texas) HS**
12. **Austin Yount, 3b, Stanford**
13. **Lenell McGee, of, Oakton (Ill.) CC**
14. **Clay Calfee, of, Angelo State (Texas)**
15. **Albie Goulder, 1b, Louisiana Tech**
16. Kyle Conley, of, Washington
17. Danny Coulombe, lhp, Chaparral HS, Scottsdale, Ariz.
18. **Allen Webster, rhp, McMichael HS, Madison, N.C.**
19. David Rollins, lhp, First Baptist Academy, Carthage, Texas
20. Zack Cox, 3b, Pleasure Ridge Park HS, Louisville
21. Dave Sever, rhp, Saint Louis
22. **Matt Smith, rhp, Wichita State**
23. **Brian Ruggiano, 2b, Texas A&M**
24. **Roberto Feliciano, lhp, Puerto Rico Baseball Academy, Gurabo, P.R.**
25. **Jerry Sands, of, Catawba (N.C.)**
26. Cody Weiss, rhp, Parkland HS, Allentown, Pa.
27. **Clayton Allison, rhp, Fresno State**
28. **Jordan Roberts, lhp, Embry-Riddle (Fla.)**
29. **Jonathan Runnels, lhp, Rice**
30. **Garett Green, 2b, San Diego State**
31. **Matt Magill, rhp, Royal HS, Simi Valley, Calif.**
32. **Shan Sullivan, 3b, Angelo State (Texas)**
33. **Melvin Ray, of, North Florida Christian HS, Tallahassee, Fla.**
34. Andrew Darwin, of, San Jacinto (Calif.) HS
35. Adam Westmoreland, lhp, Brookland-Cayce HS, Cayce, S.C.
36. **Jake New, of, Tennessee Tech**
37. Will Clinard, rhp, East Robertson HS, Cross Plains, Tenn.
38. Tommy Nurre, 1b, Miami (Ohio)
39. Matt Murray, rhp, Roberts HS, Pottstown, Pa.
40. Jimmy Parque, of, Skyline (Calif.) JC
41. Jett Bandy, c, Thousand Oaks (Calif.) HS
42. Adam Moskowitz, 2b, Valley HS, Des Moines, Iowa
43. Greg Zebrack, of, Campbell Hall HS, North Hollywood, Calif.
44. Matt Reed, lhp, West Stanly HS, Oakboro, N.C.
45. **Ryan Arp, c, Iowa**

MILWAUKEE BREWERS

June—Regular Phase (16)

1. **Brett Lawrie, 3b/c, Brookswood SS, Langley, B.C.**
1. **Jake Odorizzi, rhp, Highland (Ill.) HS** (Supplemental pick—32nd—for loss of Type A free agent Francisco Cordero)
1. **Evan Frederickson, lhp, San Francisco** (Supplemental pick—35th—for loss of Type A free agent Scott Linebrink)
2. **Seth Lintz, rhp, Marshall County HS, Lewisburg, Tenn.** (Pick from Reds as compensation for Cordero)
2. **Cutter Dykstra, of, Westlake HS, Westlake Village, Calif.** (Pick from White Sox as compensation for Linebrink)
2. **Cody Adams, rhp, Southern Illinois**
3. **Logan Schafer, of, Cal Poly**
4. **Josh Romanski, lhp, San Diego**
5. **Maverick Lasker, rhp, O'Connor HS, Phoenix**
6. **Jose Duran, ss, Texas A&M**
7. **Trey Watten, rhp, Abilene Christian (Texas)**
8. **Erik Komatsu, of, Cal State Fullerton**
9. **Michael Bowman, rhp, Virginia Military Institute**
10. **Greg Miller, rhp, Seton Hall**
11. **Michael Marseco, ss, Samford**
12. **Garrett Sherrill, rhp, Appalachian State**
13. **Rob Wooten, rhp, North Carolina**
14. **Corey Kemp, c, East Carolina**
15. **Mark Willinsky, rhp, Santa Clara**
16. **Stosh Wawrzasek, rhp, Walnut Grove SS, Langley, B.C**
17. **Damon Krestalude, rhp, Port St. Lucie (Fla.) HS**
18. **Nick Bucci, rhp, St. Patrick's HS, Sarnia, Ontario**
19. **Blake Billings, rhp, Hillcrest HS, Tuscaloosa, Ala.**
20. **Liam Ohlmann, rhp, Manchester (Conn.) CC**
21. **Lucas Luetge, lhp, Rice**
22. **Ben Jeffers, rhp, Chipola (Fla.) JC**
23. Marcus Knecht, of, St. Michael's College School, Toronto
24. **Brandon Ritchie, lhp, Grand Rapids (Mich.) CC**
25. **John Delaney, ss, Quinnipiac (Conn.)**
26. **Derrick Alfonso, c, Louisville**
27. Austin Adams, ss, Faulkner (Ala.)
28. Brandon Garcia, c, Bishop Gorman HS, Las Vegas

29. Tommy Collier, rhp, Cypress-Fairbanks HS, Cypress, Texas
30. **Wayne Dedrick, of, Hillcrest HS, Tuscaloosa, Ala.**
31. **Brandon Rapoza, rhp, Flagler (Fla.)**
32. Colton Farrar, rhp, First Baptist Academy, Dallas
33. Michael White, rhp, Anderson County HS, Clinton, Tenn.
34. Calvin Drummond, rhp, Huntington Beach (Calif.) HS
35. **Mike Vass, of, Chapman (Calif.)**
36. Evan Bronson, lhp, Trinity (Texas)
37. Kyle Winkler, rhp, Kempner HS, Sugar Land, Texas
38. **Michael Roberts, c, Virginia Military Institute**
39. Eric Decker, of, Minnesota
40. Nicholas Fogarty, lhp, Thornlea SS, Thornhill, Ontario
41. Joe Scott, ss, Cal State Fullerton
42. Ryan Wood, ss, East Carolina
43. Dexter Price, rhp, Air Academy HS, Colorado Springs
44. Kaleb Herren, rhp, North Central Texas JC
45. James Kottaras, 2b, Milliken Mills HS, Markham, Ontario
46. **Carlos George, ss, Monroe HS, Bronx, N.Y.**
47. Kayvon Bahramzadeh, rhp, Catalina Foothills HS, Tucson
48. **Marcus Salmon, rhp, Miami-Dade CC**
49. **Dan Meadows, lhp, Temple (Texas) JC**
50. Sean Nolin, lhp, Seaford (N.Y.) HS

MINNESOTA TWINS

June—Regular Phase (14)

1. **Aaron Hicks, of, Wilson HS, Long Beach**
1. **Carlos Gutierrez, rhp, Miami** (Pick from Angels as compensation for Type A free agent Torii Hunter)
1. **Shooter Hunt, rhp, Tulane** (Supplemental pick—31st—for loss of Hunter)
2. **Tyler Ladendorf, ss, Howard (Texas) JC**
3. **Bobby Lanigan, rhp, Adelphi (N.Y.)**
4. **Danny Ortiz, of, Harrison HS, Cayey, P.R.**
5. **Nick Romero, 3b, San Diego State**
6. **B.J. Hermsen, rhp, West Delaware HS, Manchester, Iowa**
7. **Dan Osterbrock, lhp, Cincinnati**
8. **Jeff Lanning, c, New Orleans**
9. **Mike Gonzales, 1b, Diablo Valley (Calif.) JC**
10. **Evan Bigley, of, Dallas Baptist**
11. **Dominic De La Osa, 2b, Vanderbilt**
12. **Kyle Carr, lhp, Minnesota**
13. **Michael Harrington, of, College of Charleston**
14. **Blayne Weller, rhp, Key West (Fla.) HS**
15. **David Coulon, lhp, Arizona**
16. Kolten Wong, 2b, Kamehameha HS, Hilo, Hawaii
17. **Blake Martin, lhp, Louisiana State**
18. Matt Nohelty, of, Minnesota
19. **Bruce Pugh, rhp, Hillsborough (Fla.) CC**
20. Aaron Barrett, rhp, Wabash Valley (Ill.) CC
21. **Steve Blevins, rhp, Marshall**
22. Kyle Witten, rhp, Bakersfield (Calif.) JC
23. Chris Odegaard, rhp, Minnesota State-Mankato
24. Lionel Morrill, of, Vauxhall HS, Crows Nest Pass, Alb
25. **Alex Curry, rhp, Cypress (Calif.) JC**
26. **Adan Severino, of, Miami**
27. Jerico Weitzel, 2b, Ridgway (Pa.) HS
28. **Nate Hanson, 3b, Minnesota**
29. Joe Loftus, 3b, Academy of the Holy Angels, Richfield, Minn.
30. **Mike Tonkin, rhp, Palmdale (Calif.) HS**
31. Lee Ridenhour, rhp, Shawnee Mission (Kan.) West HS
32. Adam Conley, lhp, Olympia (Wash.) HS
33. Luke Yoder, of, Cal Poly
34. Adam Purdy, rhp, Pell City (Ala.) HS
35. Sam Ryan, c, Tartan Senior HS, Oakdale, Minn.
36. Miers Quigley, lhp, Alabama
37. **Javier Brown, ss, Grossmont (Calif.) JC**
38. Alex Mendez, lhp, Bishop Moore HS, Orlando
39. Steve Proscia, 3b, Don Bosco Prep, Ramsey, N.J.
40. Wade Kapteyn, rhp, Evansville
41. Pat Lehman, rhp, George Washington
42. Riley Boening, lhp, Texas
43. Jeff Pickering, lhp, Nitro (W.Va.) HS
44. Colby Sokol, of, Emerald Ridge HS, Puyallup, Wash.
45. Mike Spina, 3b, Cincinnati
46. Lyndon Eusea, of, Hahnville HS, Boutte, La.
47. Tom Farmer, rhp, Akron
48. George Springer, of, Avon (Conn.) Old Farms School
49. Johnny Bromberg, rhp, Los Angeles Pierce JC
50. Tyler Anderson, lhp, Valley HS, Las Vegas

NEW YORK METS

June—Regular Phase (22)

1. **Ike Davis, 1b, Arizona State** (Pick from Braves as compensation for Type A free agent Tom Glavine)
1. **Reese Havens, ss, South Carolina**
1. **Brad Holt, rhp, UNC Wilmington** (Supplemental pick—33rd—for loss of Glavine)
2. **Javier Rodriguez, of, Puerto Rico Baseball Academy, Gurabo, P.R.**
3. **Kirk Nieuwenhuis, of, Azusa Pacific (Calif.)**
4. **Sean Ratliff, of, Stanford**
5. **Dock Doyle, c, Coastal Carolina**
6. **Josh Satin, 2b, California**
7. **Mike Hebert, rhp, Saugus (Calif.) HS**
8. **Eric Campbell, 3b, Boston College**
9. **Eric Beaulac, rhp, Le Moyne**
10. **Brian Valenzuela, lhp, Vista Murrieta HS, Murrieta, Calif.**
11. **Jeff Kaplan, rhp, Cal State Fullerton**
12. **Mark Cohoon, lhp, North Central Texas JC**
13. **Scott Shaw, rhp, Illinois**
14. **Brandon Moore, rhp, Indiana Wesleyan**
15. Jamie Bruno, 1b, Mandeville (La.) HS
16. **Travis Babin, rhp, Sonoma State (Calif.)**
17. **Mitch Houck, lhp, Central Florida**
18. **Collin McHugh, rhp, Berry (Ga.)**
19. **Zach Rosenbaum, rhp, UNC Charlotte**
20. **Michael Moras, c, New Haven (Conn.)**
21. **Jim Fuller, lhp, Southern Connecticut State**
22. **Chris Schwinden, rhp, Fresno Pacific (Calif.)**
23. **Evan LeBlanc, of, Santa Clara**
24. **Kyle Allen, rhp, Pendleton School, Bradenton, Fla.**
25. **Erik Turgeon, rhp, Connecticut**
26. **John Servidio, of, Barry (Fla.)**
27. **Jeff Flagg, 1b, Mississippi State**
28. **Jimmy Johnson, lhp, Biola (Calif.)**
29. Mike Giuffre, 2b, Tottenville HS, Staten Island, N.Y.
30. **Mike Lynn, rhp, College of Charleston**
31. **Michael Powers, rhp, Michigan**
32. Mark Grbavac, rhp, Oregon State
33. Neil Medchill, of, Oklahoma State
34. **Justin Garber, of, Shippensburg (Pa.)**
35. **Kyle Suire, 2b, Louisiana-Monroe**
36. **Jake Goldberg, rhp, College of Charleston**
37. **Tim Erickson, lhp, Lamar**
38. **Chris Hilliard, lhp, Itawamba (Miss.) CC**
39. **Charlie Hinojosa, c, Don Lugo HS, Chino, Calif.**
40. **Seth Williams, of, North Carolina**
41. **Tyler Howe, c, Kentucky**
42. **Tim Smith, rhp, Catawba (N.C.)**
43. **Mark McGonigle, of, New Orleans**
44. Jean-Francois Ricard, lhp, Ahuntsic (Quebec) JC
45. David Phillips, 1b, Texarkana (Texas) CC
46. Brian Gump, of, UC Santa Barbara
47. Matt Bischoff, rhp, Purdue
48. Tyler Baisley, of, Gateway (Ariz.) CC
49. **Doug McNulty, 1b, Akron**
50. Kameron Brunty, of, Gulf Breeze (Fla.) HS

NEW YORK YANKEES

June—Regular Phase (28)

1. Gerrit Cole, rhp, Orange (Calif.) Lutheran HS
1. **Jeremy Bleich (Supplemental pick), lhp, Stanford** (Supplemental pick—44th—for loss of Type B free agent Luis Vizcaino)
2. Scott Bittle, rhp, Mississippi
3. **David Adams, 2b, Virginia**
4. **Corban Joseph, ss, Franklin (Tenn.) HS**

5. **Chris Smith, of, Centennial HS, Compton, Calif.**
6. **Brett Marshall, rhp, Sterling HS, Baytown, Texas**
7. **Kyle Higashioka, c, Edison HS, Huntington Beach, Calif.**
8. **Dan Brewer, of, Bradley**
9. **Mikey O'Brien, rhp, Hidden Valley HS, Roanoke, Va.**
10. **D.J. Mitchell, rhp, Clemson**
11. **Ray Kruml, of, South Alabama**
12. **Luke Greinke, rhp, Auburn**
13. **Jack Rye, of, Florida State**
14. **David Phelps, rhp, Notre Dame**
15. **Matt Richardson, rhp, Lake Mary (Fla.) HS**
16. Luke Anders, 1b, Texas A&M
17. **Addison Maruszak, ss, South Florida**
18. **Brandon Braboy, rhp, Indianapolis**
19. **Mitch Abeita, c, Nebraska**
20. **Pat Venditte, rhp/lhp, Creighton**
21. **Mitch Delaney, 1b, Western Texas JC**
22. **Cory Arbiso, rhp, Cal State Fullerton**
23. **Ryan Wilkes, ss, Kentucky**
24. **Mike Lyon, 3b, Northeastern**
25. **Jeff Nutt, c, Arkansas**
26. Blake Monar, lhp, South Spencer HS, Rockport, Ind.
27. **Garrison Lassiter, ss, West Forsyth HS, Clemmons, N.C.**
28. **Chad Gross, of, Cuesta (Calif.) JC**
29. **Mike Jones, of, Arizona State**
30. Ben McMahan, c, Bishop Moore HS, Orlando
31. **Spencer Lucian, 2b, Princeton**
32. Andy Suiter, lhp, UC Davis
33. **Tommy Baldridge, of, Coastal Carolina**
34. **Brad Rulon, rhp, Georgia Tech**
35. **Andrew Shive, rhp, Azusa Pacific (Calif.)**
36. Chris Dwyer, lhp, Salisbury (Conn.) School
37. Justin Harper, rhp, Yavapai (Ariz.) JC
38. Clay Caulfield, rhp, College of Charleston
39. **Erik Lovett, 1b, Mount Olive (N.C.)**
40. Sam Mende, ss, Clearwater (Fla.) Central Catholic HS
41. Mykal Stokes, of, Tustin (Calif.) HS
42. **Clint Preisendorfer, lhp, San Diego Christian**
43. Matt Summers, rhp, Chaparral HS, Scottsdale, Ariz.
44. Evan Ocheltree, of, Wake Forest
45. Creede Simpson, ss, Auburn (Ala.) HS
46. Matt Veltmann, rhp, San Diego CC
47. **Ryan Flannery, rhp, Fairleigh Dickinson**
48. Rob Scahill, rhp, Bradley
49. John Folino, rhp, Connecticut
50. **Nik Turley, lhp, Harvard-Westlake School, North Hollywood, Calif.**

OAKLAND ATHLETICS

June—Regular Phase (12)

1. **Jemile Weeks, 2b, Miami**
2. **Tyson Ross, rhp, California**
3. **Petey Paramore, c, Arizona State**
4. **Anthony Capra, lhp, Wichita State**
5. **Jason Christian, ss, Michigan**
6. **Tyreace House, of, JC of the Canyons (Calif.)**
7. **Brett Hunter, rhp, Pepperdine**
8. **Jeremy Barfield, of, San Jacinto (Texas) JC**
9. **Mitch LeVier, of, Fullerton (Calif.) JC**
10. **Rashun Dixon, of, Terry (Miss.) HS**
11. **Chris Berroa, of, Chipola (Fla.) JC**
12. Zac Elgie, 1b, Minot (N.D.) HS
13. **Dan Thomas, rhp, South Florida**
14. **David Thomas, of, Catawba (N.C.)**
15. **Nino Leyja, ss, Houston Christian HS**
16. **Matt Fitts, rhp, Lewis-Clark State (Idaho)**
17. Brad Glenn, 3b, Arizona
18. Rayan Gonzalez, rhp, Luchetti HS, Arecibo, P.R.
19. **Michael Hart, rhp, Texas State**
20. **Rodney Rutherford, 3b, Columbus State (Ga.)**
21. **Mathieu LeBlanc Poirier, rhp, Ahuntsic (Quebec) JC**
22. Preston Guilmet, rhp, Arizona
23. Chris Rusin, lhp, Kentucky
24. **Ken Smalley, rhp, Delta State (Miss.)**
25. **Trey Barham, lhp, Virginia Military Institute**
26. **Ryan Doolittle, rhp, Cumberland (N.J.) CC**
27. Brent Warren, of, Xavier HS, Cedar Rapids, Iowa
28. **Dusty Coleman, ss, Wichita State**
29. **Justin Murray, rhp, Kansas State**
30. **Ryne Jernigan, 2b, South Alabama**
31. **Mickey Storey, rhp, Florida Atlantic**
32. **Ben Hornbeck, lhp, Kansas State**
33. **Shawn Haviland, rhp, Harvard**
34. Riley Welch, rhp, Desert Mountain HS, Scottsdale, Ariz.
35. Virgil Hill, of, Mission (Calif.) JC
36. Jon Berti, ss, Troy (Mich.) HS
37. Ryan Doiron, rhp, Barbe HS, Lake Charles, La.
38. Bobby Crocker, of, Aptos (Calif.) HS
39. Danny Clement, rhp, Cascia Hall Prep, Tulsa, Okla.
40. Jeff Dennis, lhp, SUNY Binghamton
41. Cody Hawn, 3b, Walters State (Tenn.) CC
42. Kent Walton, 2b, Brigham Young
43. Nick Maronde, lhp, Lexington (Ky.) Catholic HS
44. Jimmy Messer, rhp, South Caldwell HS, Hudson, N.C.
45. Derek Benny, rhp, Roseville (Calif.) HS
46. J.R. Graham, rhp, Livermore (Calif.) HS
47. Coley Crank, c, Pinole Valley HS, Pinole, Calif.
48. Brett Holland, rhp, Texas-Tyler
49. Matt Bowman, 2b, Nevada
50. Derek Wiley, 1b, Belmont

PHILADELPHIA PHILLIES

June—Regular Phase (24)

1. **Anthony Hewitt, ss, Salisbury (Conn.) School**
1. **Zach Collier, of, Chino Hills (Calif.) HS** (Supplemental pick—34th—for loss of Type A free agent Aaron Rowand)
2. **Anthony Gose, of, Bellflower (Calif.) HS** (Pick from Giants as compensation for Rowand)
2. **Jason Knapp, rhp, North Hunterdon HS, Annandale, N.J.**
3. **Vance Worley, rhp, Long Beach State**
3. **Jon Pettibone, rhp, Esperanza HS, Anaheim** (Supplemental pick—110th—for failure to sign 2007 third-round pick Brandon Workman)
4. **Trevor May, rhp, Kelso (Wash.) HS**
5. **Jeremy Hamilton, 1b, Wright State**
6. **Colby Shreve, rhp, CC of Southern Nevada**
7. Johnny Coy, 3b, Benton HS, St. Joseph, Mo.
8. **Julio Rodriguez, rhp, Puerto Rico Baseball Academy, Gurabo, P.R.**
9. **Cody Overbeck, 3b, Mississippi**
10. **Jean Carlos Rodriguez, c, Washington HS, New York**
11. **Mike Stutes, rhp, Oregon State**
12. Ryan Weber, rhp, Clearwater (Fla.) Central Catholic HS
13. **B.J. Rosenberg, rhp, Louisville**
14. **Michael Schwimer, rhp, Virginia**
15. **Damarii Saunderson, of, Northville (Mich.) HS**
16. **Troy Hanzawa, ss, San Diego State**
17. **Jim Murphy, 1b, Washington State**
18. **Tyler Cloyd, rhp, Bellevue, Neb. (no school)**
19. **Steve Susdorf, of, Fresno State**
20. **Eryk McConnell, rhp, North Carolina State**
21. **Sean Grieve, lhp, William & Mary**
22. **Daniel Hargrave, 2b, UNC Wilmington**
23. **Brandon Haislet, of, Hawaii**
24. **Korey Noles, lhp, Columbus State (Ga.)**
25. Daniel Edwards, rhp, Kansas State
26. **Ryan Bergh, rhp, Old Dominion**
27. **Chad Poe, rhp, Bossier Parish (La.) CC**
28. **Jordan Ellis, rhp, Villanova**
29. Keon Broxton, 3b, Lakeland (Fla.) HS
30. Dwayne Henderson, ss, Southeastern HS, Detroit
31. **Spencer Arroyo, lhp, Modesto (Calif.) JC**
32. **Sean Ellis, rhp, Polk (Fla.) CC**
33. Jamie Simpson, 1b, Dowagiac (Mich.) Union HS
34. Blaine O'Brien, rhp, Scituate (Mass.) HS
35. **Ruddy Rio-Nunez, of, Eduardo Montpetit HS, Montreal**
36. **Mike Cisco, rhp, South Carolina**
37. Matt Johnson, of, North HS, Riverside, Calif.

38. **Jarred Cosart, rhp, Clear Creek HS, League City, Texas**
39. Joe Pond, rhp, Judge Memorial HS, Salt Lake City
40. Daniel Marrs, rhp, James River HS, Midlothian, Va.
41. Mike Petello, of, Scottsdale (Ariz.) CC
42. **Mike Bolsenbroek, rhp, Ageldoorn, Netherlands**
43. **Bryan Frew, of, Nebraska-Omaha**
44. Charlie Law, rhp, Mainland Regional HS, Linwood, N.J.
45. Justin Zumwalde, 1b, Sabino HS, Tucson
46. Giovany Soto, lhp, Advanced Central College HS, Carolina, P.R.
47. **Nate Fike, lhp, Potomac State (W.Va.) JC**
48. Mark Ginther, ss, Jenks (Okla.) HS
49. Michael Russo, rhp, Hun School, Princeton, N.J.
50. Josh Hake, rhp, Park (Ariz.)

PITTSBURGH PIRATES

June—Regular Phase (2)

1. **Pedro Alvarez, 3b, Vanderbilt**
2. Tanner Scheppers, rhp, Fresno State
3. **Jordy Mercer, ss, Oklahoma State**
4. **Chase D'Arnaud, ss, Pepperdine**
5. **Justin Wilson, lhp, Fresno State**
6. **Robbie Grossman, of, Cypress-Fairbanks HS, Cypress, Texas**
7. **Benji Gonzalez, ss, Puerto Rico Baseball Academy, Gurabo, P.R.**
8. **Jeremy Farrell, 3b, Virginia**
9. **Matt Hague, 3b, Oklahoma State**
10. Drew Gagnon, rhp, Liberty HS, Brentwood, Calif.
11. **David Rubinstein, of, Appalachian State**
12. **Calvin Anderson, 1b, Southern**
13. Seth Gardner, of, Highland Park HS, Dallas
14. **Mike Colla, rhp, Arizona**
15. **Chris Aure, lhp, North Pole (Alaska) HS**
16. **Wes Freeman, of, All Saints Academy, Lakeland, Fla.**
17. Jaron Shepherd, of, Navarro (Texas) JC
18. **Jarek Cunningham, ss, Mount Spokane HS, Spokane, Wash.**
19. Jason Haniger, c, Georgia Tech
20. **Quinton Miller, rhp, Shawnee HS, Medford, N.J.**
21. **Brent Klinger, rhp, Glendale (Ariz.) CC**
22. Patrick Palmeiro, 3b, Heritage HS, Colleyville, Texas
23. Austin Wright, lhp, Conant HS, Hoffman Estates, Ill.
24. Brian Litwin, 3b, St. Stephens HS, Hickory, N.C.
25. **Brian Leach, rhp, Southern Mississippi**
26. Zach Wilson, 3b, Wilson HS, Long Beach
27. **Edwin Roman, of, Puerto Rico Baseball Academy, Gurabo, P.R.**
28. **Kyle Saukko, rhp, Sierra (Calif.) JC**
29. Kevin Komstadius, 1b, East Valley HS, Yakima, Wash.
30. Daniel Martin, rhp, Panola (Texas) JC
31. Ryan Hinson, lhp, Clemson
32. T.J. Forrest, rhp, Bossier Parish (La.) CC
33. **Mark Carver, 1b, UNC Wilmington**
34. **Matt Payne, 3b, North Carolina State**
35. **Tyler Cox, lhp, Illinois State**
36. **Kyle Morgan, of, San Francisco**
37. Matt Curry, 1b, Howard (Texas) JC
38. **Alan Knotts, rhp, Louisiana Tech**
39. **Albert Fagan, rhp, Yonkers, N.Y. (no school)**
40. Beau Didier, 3b, Bellarmine Prep, Tacoma, Wash.
41. **Chris Simmons, c, Army**
42. **Cole White, of, Army**
43. Johnny Gunter, rhp, Chattahoochee Valley (Ala.) CC
44. **Mike Williams, lhp, Mount Olive (N.C.)**
45. **Allen Ponder, rhp, Auburn-Montgomery**
46. Scott McGough, ss, Plum HS, Pittsburgh
47. Jordan Craft, of, Kennesaw Mountain HS, Kennesaw, Ga.
48. **Owen Brolsma, rhp, Texas Tech**
49. **Zach Foster, rhp, Pittsburgh-Bradford**
50. **Craig Parry, of, South Dakota State**

ST. LOUIS CARDINALS

June—Regular Phase (13)

1. **Brett Wallace, 1b, Arizona State**
1. **Lance Lynn (Supplemental pick), rhp, Mississippi** (Supplemental pick—39th—for loss of Type B free agent Troy Percival)
2. **Shane Peterson, of, Long Beach State**
3. **Niko Vasquez, ss, Durango HS, Las Vegas**
4. **Scott Gorgen, rhp, UC Irvine**
5. **Jermaine Curtis, 3b, UCLA**
6. **Eric Fornataro, rhp, Miami-Dade CC**
7. **Anthony Ferrara, lhp, Riverview HS, Sarasota, Fla.**
8. **Ryan Kulik, lhp, Rowan (N.J.)**
9. **Aaron Luna, of, Rice**
10. **Alex Castellanos, 2b, Belmont Abbey (N.C.)**
11. **Devin Shepherd, of, CC of Southern Nevada**
12. **Michael Swinson, of, Coffee County HS, Douglas, Ga.**
13. Mitch Harris, rhp, Navy
14. **Charlie Cutler, c, California**
15. **Scott McGregor, rhp, Memphis**
16. **Miguel Flores, rhp, Cerritos (Calif.) JC**
17. **Josh Hester, rhp, Freed Hardeman (Tenn.)**
18. **Jared Bradford, rhp, Louisiana State**
19. **Xavier Scruggs, 1b, Nevada-Las Vegas**
20. **Luis Mateo, ss, Jose Rojas Cortez Superior HS, Orocovis, P.R.**
21. **Matt Rigoli, 1b, Pace (N.Y.)**
22. **Colt Sedbrook, ss, Arizona**
23. **Jonny Bravo, lhp, Azusa Pacific (Calif.)**
24. **Zach Pitts, rhp, Louisville**
25. **Jason Buursma, rhp, Bucknell**
26. **Chris Swauger, of, The Citadel**
27. **George Brown, lhp, St. John's**
28. **Matt Frevert, rhp, Missouri State**
29. **Brett Lilley, 2b, Notre Dame**
30. Brett Bruening, rhp, Grayson County (Texas) CC
31. Justin Leith, lhp, Collier HS, Naples, Fla.
32. **Sam Freeman, lhp, Kansas**
33. **Kevin Thomas, rhp, Stephen F. Austin State**
34. **Jack Cawley, c, Pace (N.Y.)**
35. Shane Boras, 2b, Serra HS, San Mateo, Calif.
36. **Chris Notti, rhp, Moorpark (Calif.) JC**
37. Danny Jimenez, lhp, St. Charles (Ill.) North HS
38. **Dan Richardson, rhp, Delaware**
39. **Curt Smith, 1b, Maine**
40. **Paul Cruz, of, Tampa**
41. **Kevin Siegrist, lhp, Palm Beach (Fla.) CC**
42. **Blake Murphy, c, Western Carolina**
43. **Joe Babrick, of, King HS, Tampa**
44. **Santo Maertz, rhp, St. Peter's (N.J.)**
45. Chris Taylor, c, Charlotte
46. Brandon Sizemore, 2b, Charleston
47. Ray Asaro, of, UC Irvine
48. **Adam Prange, rhp, South Mountain (Ariz.) CC**
49. **Adam Veres, rhp, St. Petersburg (Fla.) JC**
50. Danny Miranda, lhp, Miami Killian HS

SAN DIEGO PADRES

June—Regular Phase (23)

1. **Allan Dykstra, 1b, Wake Forest**
1. **Jaff Decker, of, Sunrise Mountain HS, Peoria, Ariz.** (Supplemental pick—42nd—for loss of Type B free agent Doug Brocail)
1. **Logan Forsythe, 3b, Arkansas** (Supplemental pick—46th—for loss of Type B free agent Mike Cameron)
2. **James Darnell, 3b, South Carolina**
3. **Blake Tekotte, of, Miami**
3. Sawyer Carroll, 1b, Kentucky (Supplemental pick—111th—for failure to sign 2007 third-round pick Tommy Toledo)
4. Jason Kipnis, of, Arizona State
5. **Anthony Bass, rhp, Wayne State (Mich.)**
6. **Cole Figueroa, ss, Florida**
7. **Adam Zornes, c, Rice**

8. **Beamer Weems, ss, Baylor**
9. Kyle Thebeau, rhp, Texas A&M
10. **Andrew Albers, lhp, Kentucky**
11. **Tyson Bagley, rhp, Dallas Baptist**
12. **Matt Clark, 1b, Louisiana State**
13. **Erik Davis, rhp, Stanford**
14. **Rob Musgrave, lhp, Wichita State**
15. Brett Mooneyham, lhp, Buhach Colony HS, Atwater, Calif.
16. **Tom Davis, rhp, Fordham**
17. **Derek Shunk, ss, Villanova**
18. **Nick Vincent, rhp, Long Beach State**
19. **Robert Lara, c, Central Florida**
20. **Jason Codiroli, of, West Valley (Calif.) JC**
21. **Joey Railey, 2b, San Francisco**
22. **Chris Wilkes, rhp, Dr. Phillips HS, Orlando**
23. Nick Conaway, rhp, Walnut Cove, N.C. (no school)
24. **Eric Gonzalez, rhp, South Alabama**
25. Logan Power, of, Mississippi
26. **Dean Anna, ss, Ball State**
27. **Aaron Murphree, of, Arkansas**
28. **Nick Schumacher, rhp, Wayne State (Neb.)**
29. **Omar Gutierrez, rhp, Texas A&M-Corpus Christi**
30. **Bobby Verbick, of, Sam Houston State**
31. Sean Gilmartin, of, Crespi Carmelite HS, Encino, Calif.
32. **Kyle Heyne, rhp, Ball State**
33. **Dan Robertson, of, Oregon State**
34. **Matt Gaski, 2b, UNC Greensboro**
35. **Logan Gelbrich, c, San Diego**
36. Jake Shadle, rhp, Graham-Kapowsin HS, Graham, Wash.
37. **Matt Means, lhp, Sonoma State (Calif.)**
38. **Zach Herr, lhp, Nebraska**
39. **Gary Poynter, rhp, Lubbock Christian (Texas)**
40. **Colin Lynch, rhp, St. John's**
41. Zach Dascenzo, c, Laurel Highlands HS, Uniontown, Pa.
42. **Brad Brach, rhp, Monmouth**
43. James Tunnell, of, Oklahoma City, Okla. (no school)

SAN FRANCISCO GIANTS

June—Regular Phase (5)

1. **Buster Posey, c, Florida State**
1. **Conor Gillaspie, 3b, Wichita State** (Supplemental pick—37th—for loss of Type B free agent Pedro Feliz)
2. (Pick to Phillies as compensation for Type A free agent Aaron Rowand)
3. **Roger Kieschnick, of, Texas Tech**
4. **Brandon Crawford, ss, UCLA**
5. **Edwin Quirarte, rhp, Cal State Northridge**
6. **Eric Surkamp, lhp, North Carolina State**
7. **Aaron King, lhp, Surry (N.C.) CC**
8. **Scott Barnes, lhp, St. John's**
9. **Ryan Verdugo, lhp, Louisiana State**
10. Ryan O'Sullivan, rhp, Valhalla HS, El Cajon, Calif.
11. **Justin Fitzgerald, rhp, UC Davis**
12. **Ari Ronick, lhp, Portland**
13. **Juan Carlos Perez, of, Western Oklahoma State JC**
14. **Caleb Curry, of, Iowa**
15. **Dan Cook, 2b, Florida Atlantic**
16. **C.J. Ziegler, 1b, Arizona**
17. **Brian Irving, rhp, Yale**
18. **Brooks Lindsley, ss, Lower Columbia (Wash.) JC**
19. **Ryan Mantle, of, Missouri State**
20. Trey Sutton, 2b, Southern Mississippi
21. **Mike Eifel, rhp, Dominican (Ill.)**
22. Carter Bell, 3b, Vanier SS, Toronto
23. **Jason Jarvis, rhp, Lincoln Saltdogs (American Association)**
24. Wes Musick, lhp, Houston
25. **Damon Wright, of, Dartmouth**
26. **Ryan Lormand, 2b, Houston**
27. **Kyle Woodruff, rhp, Chico State (Calif.)**
28. **Shane Kaufman, rhp, San Diego State**
29. **Rob Flanigan, 1b, North Georgia College & State**
30. **Vladimir Frias, ss, Tennessee Wesleyan**
31. **Aaron Davidson, rhp, Arkansas-Fort Smith JC**
32. John Blake, rhp, Lake Sumter (Fla.) CC
33. **Ryne Price, of, Kansas**
34. Francois Lafreniere, rhp, Ahuntsic (Quebec) JC
35. Dan Black, 3b, Purdue
36. Matt Way, lhp, Washington State
37. Jeremy Penn, rhp, Western Oklahoma State JC
38. **Chris Wilson, rhp, Trinidad State (Colo.) JC**
39. Braden Kapteyn, 3b, Illiana Christian HS, Lansing, Ill.
40. Austin Stadler, 1b, James River HS, Midlothian, Va.
41. Corey Figueroa, 2b, St. Petersburg (Fla.) JC
42. Tyler Thompson, of, Jupiter (Fla.) HS
43. Zack Thornton, rhp, Ventura (Calif.) JC
44. **Aaron Lowenstein, c, UC Irvine**
45. Kenneth Villines, 2b, Riverside HS, Durham, N.C.
46. Joey Hainsfurther, ss, Highland Park HS, Dallas
47. Abe Ruiz, 3b, Pacific Grove (Calif.) HS
48. **Leo Ochoa, 2b, St.-Amable, Quebec (no school)**
49. Dalton Hicks, 1b, Lake Brantley HS, Altamonte Springs, Fla.
50. Chase Ware, rhp, Arkansas State

SEATTLE MARINERS

June—Regular Phase (20)

1. **Josh Fields, rhp, Georgia**
2. **Dennis Raben, of, Miami**
3. **Aaron Pribanic, rhp, Nebraska**
4. **Steven Hensley, rhp, Elon**
5. **Brett Lorin, rhp, Long Beach State**
6. **Jarrett Burgess, of, Florida Christian HS, Miami**
7. **Nate Tenbrink, 3b, Kansas State**
8. **Bobby LaFromboise, lhp, New Mexico**
9. Billy Morrison, rhp, Western Michigan
10. Nate Newman, rhp, Pepperdine
11. Matt Jensen, 2b, Clovis (Calif.) East HS
12. **Kenn Kasparek, rhp, Texas**
13. **Ryan Royster, of, UC Davis**
14. **Luke Burnett, rhp, Louisiana Tech**
15. **Jake Shaffer, of, Northern Kentucky**
16. **Ben Billingsley, 2b, Lenoir (N.C.) CC**
17. Mike Dennhardt, rhp, Don Bosco Prep, Ramsey, N.J.
18. **Travis Howell, c, Long Beach State**
19. **Taylor Lewis, rhp, Yavapai (Ariz.) JC**
20. **Fred Bello, ss, Cerro Coso (Calif.) CC**
21. **Jordan Alvis, rhp, Middle Tennessee State**
22. **Blake Nation, rhp, Georgia Southern**
23. **Brandon Maurer, rhp, Orange (Calif.) Lutheran HS**
24. **Henry Contreras, c, Cal State Los Angeles**
25. Paul Robinson, 2b, Paris (Texas) JC
26. **Taylor Stanton, rhp, Diablo Valley (Calif.) JC**
27. **Tommy Johnson, c, Marshall**
28. **Scott Savastano, ss, Franklin Pierce (N.H.)**
29. **Stephen Penney, rhp, UC Riverside**
30. **Brad Reid, rhp, Bellevue (Wash.) CC**
31. **Randy Castillo, rhp, Aiea (Hawaii) HS**
32. **Nick Love, rhp, Bellevue (Neb.)**
33. **Kyle Brown, lhp, UC Santa Barbara**
34. Ty Tostenson, of, Oak Ridge HS, El Dorado Hills, Calif.
35. **Nick Czyz, lhp, Kansas**
36. **Chris Kirkland, rhp, Memphis**
37. **Brandon Pullen, lhp, San Diego State**
38. **Andres Esquibel, rhp, Kansas**
39. **Christian Staehely, rhp, Princeton**
40. Troy Channing, c, Foothill HS, Pleasanton, Calif.
41. **Henry Cotto, of, Gateway (Ariz.) CC**
42. **Randy Molina, 1b, Stanford**
43. Mike Kindel, of, Springboro (Ohio) HS
44. **Donny Jobe, 2b, Elon**
45. Andrew Kittredge, rhp, Ferris HS, Spokane, Wash.
46. Alvin Rittman, of, Germantown (Tenn.) HS
47. Rich O'Donald, rhp, Dickinson HS, Wilmington, Del.
48. D.J. Mauldin, rhp, Cal Poly
49. **Josh Rodriguez, c, South Mountain (Ariz.) CC**
50. Walker Kelly, lhp, Arlington Heights HS, Fort Worth, Texas

TAMPA BAY RAYS

June—Regular Phase (1)

1. **Tim Beckham, rhp, Griffin (Ga.) HS**
2. **Kyle Lobstein, lhp, Coconino HS, Flagstaff, Ariz.**
3. **Jake Jefferies, c, UC Davis**
4. **Ty Morrison, of, Tigard (Ore.) HS**
5. **Mike Sheridan, 1b, William & Mary**
6. **Shane Dyer, rhp, South Mountain (Ariz.) CC**
7. **Jason Corder, of, Long Beach State**
8. **Anthony Scelfo, 2b, Tulane**
9. **Shawn Smith, lhp, Saugus (Calif.) HS**
10. **Matt Hall, 2b, Auburn**
11. **Brad Furdal, rhp, Ancaster HS, Ancaster, Ontario**
12. **Brian Bryles, rhp/of, North Little Rock (Ark.) HS**
13. **Jason McEachern, rhp, St. Stephens HS, Hickory, N.C.**
14. **Mike McKenna, of, Florida Atlantic**
15. Brandon Meredith, 1b, Montgomery HS, San Diego
16. **Matt Gorgen, rhp, California**
17. **Jeremy Beckham, 2b, Georgia Southern**
18. **David Genao, c, Oral Roberts**
19. **Trevor Shull, rhp, Central Valley HS, Spokane, Wash.**
20. **Jason Tweedy, 2b, Long Beach State**
21. Ryan Carpenter, lhp, Cactus HS, Peoria, Ariz.
22. **Jason Appel, of, UNC Wilmington**
23. **Neil Schenk, lhp, Memphis**
24. **Marquis Fleming, rhp, Cal State Stanislaus**
25. **Josh Satow, lhp, Arizona State**
26. **Michael Jarman, lhp, Oral Roberts**
27. **Luis Marchena, ss, Otay Ranch HS, San Diego**
28. **Tommy Rafferty, rhp, Arizona State**
29. Brandon Magee, of, Centennial HS, Corona, Calif.
30. Ryan Turner, rhp, Midland (Texas) JC
31. Greg Williams, lhp, Moeller HS, Cincinnati
32. Kyle Gaedele, of, Rolling Meadows (Ill.) HS
33. Kyle Hunter, lhp, Galesburg (Ill.) HS
34. **Matt Long, rhp, Cal State San Bernardino**
35. **Jamie Bagley, rhp, San Jacinto (Texas) JC**
36. Jordan Leyland, 1b, Sam Dimas (Calif.) HS
37. Kramer Champlin, rhp, Olympia (Wash.) HS
38. Anthony Haase, rhp, Rio Rancho (N.M.) HS
39. Andrew Gans, of, Coronado HS, Henderson, Nev.
40. Sam Gaviglio, rhp, Ashland (Ore.) HS
41. Brett Parsons, of, Navarro (Texas) JC
42. Tim Clubb, rhp, Missouri State
43. Robbie Ross, lhp, Saddleback (Calif.) CC
44. Philip Pohl, c, Cooperstown (N.Y.) Central HS
45. Royce Bolinger, of, Chaparral HS, Scottsdale, Ariz.
46. Jeff Lease, lhp, American River (Calif.) JC
47. Chris Matulis, lhp, Park Vista HS, Lake Worth, Fla.
48. Lath Guyer, rhp, Mercer
49. Kash Kalkowski, rhp, Grand Island (Neb.) HS
50. Kyle Peterson, c, Hamilton HS, Chandler, Ariz.

TEXAS RANGERS

June—Regular Phase (11)

1. **Justin Smoak, 1b, South Carolina**
2. **Robbie Ross, lhp, Lexington (Ky.) Christian Academy**
3. **Tim Murphy, lhp, UCLA**
4. **Joe Wieland, rhp, Bishop Manogue HS, Reno, Nev.**
5. **Clark Murphy, 1b, Fallbrook (Calif.) HS**
6. **Richard Bleier, lhp, Florida Gulf Coast**
7. **Matt Thompson, rhp, Grace Prep Academy, Arlington, Texas**
8. **Mike Bianucci, of, Auburn**
9. **Jared Bolden, of, Virginia Commonwealth**
10. Kevin Castner, rhp, Cal Poly
11. **Cliff Springston, lhp, Arkansas**
12. **Corey Young, lhp, Seton Hall**
13. **Ed Koncel, ss, Joliet (Ill.) JC**
14. **Justin Gutsie, rhp, St. John's**
15. **Joey Butler, of, New Orleans**
16. **Justin Miller, rhp, Fresno State**
17. **Dennis Guinn, 1b, Florida State**
18. **Doug Hogan, c, Clemson**
19. Harold Martinez, ss, Braddock HS, Miami
20. **Michael Hollander, ss, Louisiana State**
21. **Dustin Brader, rhp, Arizona State**
22. **Trevor Hurley, rhp, Kansas State**
23. **Eric Evans, lhp, Radford**
24. **Adam Cobb, of, Louisiana Tech**
25. **Tanner Roark, rhp, Southern Illinois Miners (Frontier)**
26. **Chris Dove, of, Elon**
27. Charlie Lowell, lhp, Winfield (Mo.) HS
28. Nate Freiman, 1b, Duke
29. Charlie Robertson, rhp, Bella Vista HS, Fair Oaks, Calif.
30. **Justin King, rhp, Jacksonville State**
31. **Kyle Higgins, ss, Monmouth**
32. **Tyler Tufts, rhp, Indiana**
33. **Ben Petralli, c, Oral Roberts**
34. **Ryan Schlecht, rhp, Mount Olive (N.C.)**
35. John Ruettiger, of, Joliet (Ill.) Catholic Academy
36. Jack Armstrong, rhp, Jupiter (Fla.) HS
37. Matt Andriese, rhp, Redlands (Calif.) East Valley HS
38. **Jason Ogata, 2b, Oregon State**
39. Brad Miller, ss, Olympia HS, Orlando
40. **Jamie McGraw, of, Corban (Ore.)**
41. Brian Feekin, lhp, Iowa Western CC
42. Stephen Pryor, rhp, Cleveland State (Tenn.) CC
43. **Cody Eppley, rhp, Virginia Commonwealth**
44. Alex Pepe, lhp, Florida Atlantic
45. **Kevin Torres, c, Puerto Rico Baseball Academy, Gurabo, P.R.**
46. **Erik Morrison, ss, Kansas**
47. **Lejuan Hill, of, Austin Peay**
48. Daniel Bowman, of, Ashby HS, Bridgewater, Va.
49. Matt Sample, rhp, Crowder (Mo.) JC
50. Josh Rosecrans, c, Santa Fe HS, Edmond, Okla.

TORONTO BLUE JAYS

June—Regular Phase (17)

1. **David Cooper, 1b, California**
2. **Kenny Wilson, of, Sickles HS, Tampa**
3. **Andrew Liebel, rhp, Long Beach State**
4. **Mark Sobolewski, 3b, Miami**
5. **Tyler Pastornicky, ss, Pendleton School, Bradenton, Fla.**
6. **Markus Brisker, of, Winter Haven (Fla.) HS**
7. **Eric Thames, of, Pepperdine**
8. **Evan Crawford, lhp, Auburn**
9. **A.J. Jimenez, c, Discipulos De Cristo HS, Bayamon, P.R.**
10. **Danny Farquhar, rhp, Louisiana-Lafayette**
11. **Dustin Antolin, rhp, Mililani (Hawaii) HS**
12. **Matt Wright, lhp, Shippensburg (Pa.)**
13. **Matt Daly, rhp, Hawaii**
14. **Chris Holguin, rhp, Lubbock Christian (Texas)**
15. **Scott Gracey, rhp, New Mexico**
16. **Michael Crouse, of, Centennial SS, Coquitlam, B.C.**
17. **Jonnathan Valdez, c, Puerto Rico Baseball Academy, Gurabo, P.R.**
18. **Bobby Bell, rhp, Rice**
19. **Jason Roenicke, rhp, UC Santa Barbara**
20. **Ryan Page, lhp, Liberty**
21. **Brian Van Kirk, of, Oral Roberts**
22. **Karim Turkamani, c, Miami-Dade CC**
23. **Chuck Huggins, lhp, UC Santa Barbara**
24. **Chris Hopkins, of, Oregon State**
25. **Brad McElroy, of, UNC Charlotte**
26. Justin Dalles, c, St. Petersburg (Fla.) JC
27. **Bryan Kervin, ss, Texas Christian**
28. **John Anderson, lhp, Chabot (Calif.) JC**
29. **Justin Cryer, rhp, Mississippi**
30. **Cody Dunbar, rhp, Texas Christian**
31. Justin Betts-Robinson, lhp, New Mexico JC
32. Ryan Scott, c, Chaparral HS, Scottsdale, Ariz.
33. **Justin McClanahan, 2b, Louisville**
34. **Austin Armstrong, rhp, Palm Beach (Fla.) CC**
35. **Hunter Moody, lhp, Louisiana-Lafayette**
36. **Ryan Koch, rhp, Florida Southern**

37. Dallas Beeler, rhp, Jenks (Okla.) HS
38. Quentin Williams, of, Pittsburgh Central Catholic HS
39. Jordan Flasher, rhp, George Mason
40. **Nate Nelson, 1b, Worcester State (Mass.)**
41. Kyle Petter, lhp, West HS, Torrance, Calif.
42. Andrew Durden, of, Indian River (Fla.) CC
43. **Tyler Ybarra, lhp, Wellington (Kan.) HS**
44. George Agyapong-Mensah, of, Western Texas JC

WASHINGTON NATIONALS

June—Regular Phase (9)

1. Aaron Crow, rhp, Missouri
2. **Destin Hood, of, St. Paul's Episcopal HS, Mobile, Ala.**
3. **Danny Espinosa, ss, Long Beach State**
4. **Graham Hicks, lhp, Jenkins HS, Lakeland, Fla.**
5. **Adrian Nieto, c, American Heritage HS, Plantation, Fla.**
6. **Paul Demny, rhp, Blinn (Texas) JC**
7. **Dan Killian, c, Kellogg (Mich.) CC**
8. **Ricardo Pecina, lhp, San Diego**
9. **J.R. Higley, 1b, Sacramento CC**
10. **Tom Milone, lhp, Southern California**
11. **Marcus Jones, of, North Carolina State**
12. **Will Atwood, lhp, South Carolina**
13. **Blake Stouffer, 2b, Texas A&M**
14. Louis Coleman, rhp, Louisiana State
15. **J.P. Ramirez, of, Canyon HS, New Braunfels, Texas**
16. **Tyler Moore, 1b, Mississippi State**
17. **Jose Lozada, ss, Bethune-Cookman**
18. **Bobby Hansen, lhp, Lewis-Palmer HS, Monument, Colo.**
19. **Steve Lombardozzi, ss, St. Petersburg (Fla.) JC**
20. Nick Akins, of, Riverside (Calif.) CC
21. **Michael Guerrero, of, Mississippi**
22. **Chris Curran, 2b, Miami-Dade CC**
23. **Derrick Phillips, of, Westminster Christian Academy, St. Louis**
24. **Chris Kelley, rhp, Rice**
25. **Austin Garrett, lhp, College of Charleston**
26. Cory Mazzoni, rhp, Seneca Valley HS, Harmony, Pa.
27. **Chris Solis, c, Incarnate Word (Texas)**
28. **Nick Arata, ss, Florida Atlantic**
29. Chris Heston, rhp, Seminole (Fla.) CC
30. **Casey Whitmer, rhp, Texas**
31. Bryan Harper, lhp, Las Vegas HS
32. Scott Silverstein, lhp, St. John's HS, Washington, D.C.
33. Billy Cather, of, Maine
34. **Brian Pruitt, of, Stetson**
35. **Clayton Dill, lhp, Missouri Baptist**
36. John Lambert, lhp, Santa Fe (Fla.) CC
37. Casey Selsor, lhp, Reagan HS, San Antonio
38. **Ronnie Labrie, 3b, Lynchburg (Va.)**
39. **James Keithley, ss, Texas-San Antonio**
40. Avery Barnes, of, Florida
41. Mike Rayl, lhp, Palm Beach (Fla.) CC
42. Naoya Washiya, of, JC of the Desert (Calif.)
43. Anthony Meo, rhp, Cranston (R.I.) West HS
44. **J.P. Padron, 1b, Rice**
45. Colin Rooney, ss, Saddleback (Calif.) CC
46. Robbie Brantly, c, Chaparral HS, Scottsdale, Ariz.
47. Anthony Coletti, lhp, South Broward HS, Hollywood, Fla.
48. Alex Dickerson, of, Poway (Calif.) HS
49. B.J. Zimmerman, of, Osceola HS, Kissimmee, Fla.
50. Fernando Frias, of, Washington HS, New York

2009 Strasburg draws new levels of hype before signing record $15.1 million deal with Nats

The 2009 draft will be long remembered as the Season of Strasburg.

The San Diego State righthander burst on the scene as a closer in 2007, his freshman year, and ranked as the No. 1 prospect in the New England Collegiate League that summer. The next year, Stephen Strasburg went national, setting a Division I record with 23 strikeouts against Utah, and later earning a spot on the U.S. Olympic team. While he took a loss against Cuba, Strasburg's profile was already higher than any college player in recent memory, and he got into Mark Prior/Jered Weaver/Mark Teixeira territory in 2009.

Strasburg dominated college baseball, going 13-1, 1.32 and leading the nation in ERA and strikeouts (195, an absurd 16.1 K's per nine innings) while reaching 100 mph regularly on radar guns. After he capped his regular season in late May with a no-hitter with 17 strikeouts against Air Force, the only question was whether the Nationals, drafting No. 1 overall, would be able to afford Strasburg. Put another way, could they afford *not* to draft him?

A Scott Boras Corp. client, Strasburg was rumored to have a price tag approaching the $50 million that free-agent righty Daisuke Matsuzaka got from the Red Sox after the 2006 season. But Strasburg wasn't a free agent, and the Nationals' interim general manager Mike Rizzo had plenty of experience dealing with Boras from his days as the Diamondbacks' scouting director. Rizzo and the Nats took Strasburg, then agreed to terms with him just before the deadline on a major league contract with a record $7.5 million bonus and record $15.1 million guarantee.

Strasburg was the dominant storyline of the draft, and his record-setting contract helped a record-setting draft. The Nationals had two picks in the top 10, a first in draft history thanks to having a compensation pick at No. 10 overall for failing to sign 2008 first-rounder Aaron Crow. While Stanford closer Drew Storen signed a below-slot deal, it was still a second seven-figure bonus to go with Strasburg's record, and the Nats wound up spending $11,194,500 just on players in the first 10 rounds and two six-figure signings after the 10th round. That surpassed the Royals' 2008 record total of $11,148,000.

It was the longest first round in draft history, as for the first time two teams had compensation picks in the first round added after they failed to sign their picks in 2008. The Nats had the 10th pick, and the Yankees picked 29th overall after failing to sign Gerrit Cole. That led to 32 first-round picks, and the same will happen in 2010 after the Rays failed to sign Florida high school outfielder LeVon Washington and the Rangers couldn't agree with Texas prep lefthander Matthew Purke.

LARRY GOREN

Stephen Strasburg becomes the latest college ace to try to deliver on his hype

Washington was not a consensus first-rounder, though he is a true burner with top-of-the-scale speed and excellent hitting tools. He wound up going 30th overall, but the Boras Corp. client and the Rays didn't come particularly close to a deal. The Rays also failed to sign their second-round selection, infielder Kenny Diekroger, who chose to attend Stanford.

Purke entered the spring in consideration to be the top prep pitcher on the draft board and had a strong spring, showing a 92-95 mph fastball, hard, mid-80s slider and projectable 6-foot-3, 180-pound frame. However, rumors about his price tag scared some teams off and he fell to the Rangers with the 14th pick.

The Rangers had bigger problems, though, as owner Tom Hicks' financial problems began to hamstring the organization. Major League Baseball had significant input on Rangers decisions in 2009 as it helped keep the club functioning through Hicks' troubles and the search for a new owner. As a result, Texas' $4 million offer to Purke the night of the deadline wound up being too little, too late, and he chose to attend Texas Christian and go into the 2011 draft.

The Rangers made up for losing Purke a bit by signing supplemental first-rounder Tanner Scheppers in September, just before the Royals signed their first-rounder, Aaron Crow. With no college eligibility remaining, Scheppers and Crow were not bound by the deadline. Crow was a first-rounder for a second consecutive season and wound up getting a $1.5 million bonus as part of a major league contract.

Scheppers figured to be a top 10 pick in 2008 before he came down with a shoulder injury in May while pitching for Fresno State. He missed the Bulldogs' amazing College World Series championship run and fell to the second round, where the Pirates drafted him. He didn't sign with Pittsburgh and re-entered the draft, prepping with a four-start stint with the St. Paul Saints of the independent American Association. Scheppers wound up signing for a $1.25 million bonus.

More Draft Records

■ For the first time ever, all 30 teams signed at least one player over MLB's slot recommendations. In 2008, the only time in the decade the commissioner's office gave clubs the go-ahead to value ability over signability, the Blue Jays, Cardinals, Mets and Tigers still toed the line.

■ MLB recommends specific bonuses for each slot in the first five rounds. In '09, teams spent $134.7 million on bonuses in that range, 24 percent above the $108.8 million total for all the slots. Last year, clubs shelled out $137.6 million in the top five rounds, 14 percent above the $120.9 million slot total.

■ The 29 first-round picks who signed averaged $2,467,034 in bonuses, just ahead of the record of $2,458,714 set a year ago.

■ Strasburg set new standards for the biggest bonus ($7.5 million) and largest guarantee ($15.1 million) in draft history. The bonus marks for a high school draftee (Donavan Tate, Padres, $6.25 million) and a high school pitcher (Jacob Turner, Tigers, $4.7 million bonus in major league deal) also were erased.

DRAFT 09: FIRST-ROUND PICKS

No.	Club	Player, Pos.	School	Hometown	Ht.	Wt.	B-T	Age
1.	Nationals	Stephen Strasburg, rhp	San Diego State	San Diego	6-5	225	R-R	21
2.	Mariners	Dustin Ackley, of	North Carolina	Walnut Cove, N.C.	6-1	190	L-R	21
3.	Padres	Donavan Tate, of	Cartersville HS	Cartersville, Ga.	6-2	184	R-R	18
4.	Pirates	Tony Sanchez, c	Boston College	Miami	6-0	215	R-R	21
5.	Orioles	Matt Hobgood, rhp	Norco HS	Norco, Calif.	6-4	245	R-R	18
6.	Giants	Zack Wheeler, rhp	East Paulding HS	Dallas, Ga.	6-3	180	R-R	19
7.	Braves	Mike Minor, lhp	Vanderbilt	Chapel Hill, Tenn.	6-3	200	R-L	21
8.	Reds	Mike Leake, rhp	Arizona State	Fallbrook, Calif.	6-0	180	R-R	21
9.	Tigers	Jacob Turner, rhp	Westminster Christian Acad.	St. Louis, Mo.	6-4	205	R-R	18
10.	Nationals	Drew Storen, rhp	Stanford	Brownsburg, Ind.	6-1	175	B-R	21
11.	Rockies	Tyler Matzek, lhp	Capistrano Valley HS	Mission Viejo, Calif.	6-3	210	L-L	18
12.	Royals	Aaron Crow, rhp	None	Topeka, Kan.	6-2	205	R-R	22
13.	Athletics	Grant Green, ss	Southern California	Anaheim Hills, Calif.	6-3	185	R-R	21
14.	Rangers	*Matt Purke, lhp	Klein HS	Klein, Texas	6-3	175	L-L	18
15.	Indians	Alex White, rhp	North Carolina	Greenville, N.C.	6-4	190	R-R	20
16.	Diamondbacks	Bobby Borchering, 3b	Bishop Verot	Fort Myers, Fla.	6-4	195	B-R	18
17.	Diamondbacks	A.J. Pollock, of	Notre Dame	Hebron, Conn.	6-2	200	R-R	21
18	Marlins	Chad James, lhp	Yukon HS	Yukon, Okla.	6-3	190	L-L	18
19.	Cardinals	Shelby Miller, rhp	Brownwood HS	Browndwood, Texas	6-3	195	R-R	18
20.	Blue Jays	Chad Jenkins, rhp	Kennesaw State	Canton, Ga.	6-4	235	R-R	21
21.	Astros	Jiovanni Mier, ss	Bonita HS	La Verne, Calif.	6-2	175	R-R	18
22.	Twins	Kyle Gibson, rhp	Missouri	Greenfield, Ind.	6-6	210	R-R	21
23.	White Sox	Jared Mitchell, of	Louisiana State	New Iberia, La.	6-0	190	L-L	20
24.	Angels	Randal Grichuk, of	Lamar Consolidated HS	Rosenberg, Texas	6-0	195	R-R	17
25.	Angels	Mike Trout, of	Millville HS	Millville, N.J.	6-1	200	R-R	17
26.	Brewers	Eric Arnett, rhp	Indiana	Pataskala, Ohio	6-5	230	R-R	21
27.	Mariners	Nick Franklin, ss	Lake Brantley HS	Altamonte Springs, Fla.	6-1	170	B-R	18
28.	Red Sox	Reymond Fuentes, of	Fernando Callejo HS	Manati, P.R.	6-0	160	L-L	18
29.	Yankees	Slade Heathcott, of	Texas HS	Texarkana, Texas	6-1	190	L-L	18
30.	Rays	*LeVon Washington, 2b	Buchholz HS	Gainesville, Fla.	5-11	170	L-R	17
31.	Cubs	Brett Jackson, of	California	Orinda, Calif.	6-2	210	L-R	20
32.	Rockies	Tim Wheeler, of	Sacramento State	Sacramento	6-4	205	L-R	21

*Did not sign

2009

CLUB-BY-CLUB SELECTIONS

ARIZONA DIAMONDBACKS

June—Regular Phase (15)

1. **Bobby Borchering, 3b, Bishop Verot HS, Fort Myers, Fla.**
1. **A.J. Pollock, of, Notre Dame** (Pick from Dodgers as compensation for Type A free agent Orlando Hudson)
1. **Matt Davidson, 3b, Yucaipa (Calif.) HS** (Supplemental pick—35th—for loss of Hudson)
1. **Chris Owings, ss, Gilbert (S.C.) HS** (Supplemental pick—41st—for loss of Type A free agent Juan Cruz)
1. **Mike Belfiore, lhp, Boston College** (Supplemental pick—45th—for loss of Type B free agent Brandon Lyon)
2. **Eric Smith, rhp, Rhode Island** (Pick from Royals as compensation for Cruz)
2. **Marc Krauss, of, Ohio**
3. **Keon Broxton, 3b, Santa Fe (Fla.) CC**
4. **David Nick, ss, Cypress (Calif.) HS**
5. **Ryan Wheeler, 1b, Loyola Marymount**
6. **Bradin Hagens, rhp, Merced (Calif.) JC**
7. **Matt Helm, 3b, Hamilton HS, Chandler, Ariz.**
8. **Paul Goldschmidt, 1b, Texas State**
9. **Chase Anderson, rhp, Oklahoma**
10. **Tyson Van Winkle, c, Gonzaga**
11. **Scottie Allen, rhp, Lyman HS, Longwood, Fla.**
12. **Charles Brewer, rhp, UCLA**
13. **Patrick Schuster, lhp, Mitchell HS, New Port Richey, Fla.**
14. **Brent Greer, ss, Western Carolina**
15. **David Narodowski, ss, Kansas**
16. **Ryan Robowski, lhp, Ohio Dominican**
17. **Andrew Wolcott, rhp, Duke**
18. **Roidany Aguila, c, Colegio Nuestra Senora de la Providencia HS, Rio Piedras, P.R.**
19. **Randy Hamrick, ss, Brewton-Parker (Ga.)**
20. **Adam Worthington, rhp, Illinois-Chicago**
21. **Dan Taylor, lhp, Central Michigan**
22. **Evan Button, ss, Mississippi**
23. **Chris Odegaard, rhp, Minnesota State-Mankato**
24. **Brad Gemberling, rhp, Princeton**
25. Taylor Wrenn, ss, Manatee (Fla.) CC
26. **Dan Kaczrowski, ss, Hamline (Minn.)**
27. **Jake Hale, rhp, Ohio State**
28. **Brian Budrow, rhp, Utah**
29. Jake Williams, 1b, Brophy Prep, Scottsdale, Ariz.
30. Jack Marder, ss, Newbury Park (Calif.) HS
31. **Keith Cantwell, rhp, Seton Hall**
32. **Will Harvil, rhp, Georgia**
33. **Brad Wilson, rhp, Cal Poly Pomona**
34. Patrick Cooper, rhp, Des Moines Area CC
35. Zach Morgan, rhp, Shasta (Calif.) JC
36. Mike Freeman, ss, Clemson
37. Chris Jacobs, of, Westchester HS, Los Angeles
38. Trevon Prince, lhp, Oakland, Calif.
39. Ryan Jones, of, Wichita State
40. **Tim Sherlock, of, Duke**
41. Cade Kreuter, 3b, Hart HS, Newhall, Calif.
42. Zach Hendrix, 2b, Emerald Ridge HS, Puyallup, Wash.
43. Brooklyn Foster, c, Walnut Grove SS, Langley, B.C
44. **Zach Varnell, c, Arkansas-Pine Bluff**
45. Beau Amaral, of, Huntington Beach (Calif.) HS
46. Matt Ozanne, of, Notre Dame Prep, Scottsdale, Ariz.
47. Mario Gallardo, lhp, West Los Angeles JC
48. Juan Avila, of, Narbonne HS, Harbor City, Calif.
49. Jordan Luvisi, of, Notre Dame Prep, Scottsdale, Ariz.
50. Frank Abbl, rhp, Mesa (Ariz.) CC

ATLANTA BRAVES

June—Regular Phase (7)

1. **Mike Minor, lhp, Vanderbilt**
2. (Pick to Dodgers as compensation for Type A free agent Derek Lowe)
3. **David Hale, rhp, Princeton**
4. **Mycal Jones, ss, Miami Dade CC**
5. **Thomas Berryhill, rhp, Newberry (S.C.)**
6. Ryan Woolley, rhp, Alabama-Birmingham
7. **Robert Hettlinger, of, Georgia Perimeter JC**
8. **Kyle Rose, of, Northwest Shoals (Ala.) CC**
9. **Matt Weaver, ss, Burlington (N.J.) CC**
10. **Aaron Northcraft, rhp, Mater Dei HS, Santa Ana, Calif.**
11. **Chris Masters, lhp, Western Carolina**
12. **Chris Lovett, ss, Columbia State (Tenn.) CC**
13. **Jordan Kreke, 3b, Eastern Illinois**
14. **Cory Harrilchak, of, Elon**
15. Bennett Pickar, c, Eaton (Colo.) HS
16. **Riaan Spanjer-Furstenburg, 1b, Nova Southeastern (Fla.)**
17. **Jace Whitmer, c, Kennesaw State**
18. **Jakob Dalfonso, 3b, Middle Georgia JC**
19. **Ty'Relle Harris, rhp, Tennessee**
20. **Jeff Lorick, lhp, Virginia**
21. **Matt Crim, lhp, The Citadel**
22. **Ryan Weber, rhp, St. Petersburg (Fla.) JC**
23. **Lucas LaPoint, rhp, Knight HS, Palmdale, Calif.**
24. Casey Upperman, rhp, Notre Dame Prep, Scottsdale, Ariz.
25. Ethan Icard, rhp, Wilkes (N.C.) CC
26. Will Scott, rhp, Walters State (Tenn.) CC
27. Joey Leftridge, of, Howard (Texas) JC
28. Eric Swegman, rhp, Young Harris (Ga.) JC
29. **Bobby Rauh, of, Daytona Beach (Fla.) CC**
30. Vince Howard, of, Sikeston (Mo.) HS
31. **Derek Wiley, 1b, Belmont**
32. Jake Montgomery, rhp, Pope HS, Marietta, Ga.
33. Tyler Stubblefield, ss, Kennesaw State
34. Arby Fields, of, Los Osos HS, Rancho Cucamonga, Calif.
35. Matt Hartunian, c, Montclair Prep, Van Nuys, Calif.
36. **Andrew Wilson, rhp, Liberty**
37. Matt Moynihan, of, Cathedral Catholic HS, San Diego
38. Tripp Faulk, of, North Myrtle Beach HS, Little River, S.C.
39. Joey Bourgeois, rhp, Louisiana State-Eunice JC
40. Antonio Carrillo, of, San Ysidro HS, San Diego
41. Kyle Petter, lhp, El Camino (Calif.) JC
42. Josh Conway, of, Smithburg (Md.) HS
43. Alan Walden, rhp, Red Bank HS, Chattanooga
44. Corey Newsom, rhp, Bay HS, Panama City, Fla.
45. Nathan Dorris, lhp, Marion (Ill.) HS
46. George Farmer, rhp, Rockdale County HS, Conyers, Ga.
47. Colby Holmes, rhp, Conway (S.C.) HS
48. **Jamie Hayes, rhp, Rider**
49. Gabe Gutierrez, rhp, Apollo HS, Glendale, Ariz.
50. Josh Edgin, lhp, Francis Marion (Pa.)

BALTIMORE ORIOLES

June—Regular Phase (5)

1. **Matt Hobgood, rhp, Norco (Calif.) HS**
2. **Mychal Givens, ss, Plant HS, Tampa**
3. **Tyler Townsend, 1b, Florida International**
4. **Randy Henry, rhp, South Mountain (Ariz.) CC**
5. **Ashur Tolliver, lhp, Oklahoma City**
6. **Justin Dalles, c, South Carolina**
7. **Aaron Wirsch, lhp, El Toro HS, Lake Forest, Calif.**
8. Devin Harris, of, East Carolina
9. **Ryan Berry, rhp, Rice**
10. **Jacob Cowan, rhp, San Jacinto (Texas) JC**

11. **Michael Ohlman, c, Lakewood Ranch HS, Bradenton, Fla.**
12. **Steve Bumbry, of, Virginia Tech**
13. **Ty Kelly, 2b, UC Davis**
14. **David Baker, rhp, Hemet (Calif.) HS**
15. Garrett Bush, rhp, Stanton College Prep HS, Jacksonville
16. **Ryan Palsha, rhp, Diablo Valley (Calif.) JC**
17. Jeff Walters, rhp, Georgia
18. **Jarret Martin, lhp, Bakersfield (Calif.) JC**
19. **Kipp Schutz, of, Indiana**
20. **James Brandhorst, rhp, Lamar**
21. **Kevin Landry, rhp, William & Mary**
22. **Cameron Coffey, lhp, Houston Christian HS**
23. **Mike Mooney, ss, Florida**
24. **Justin Anderson, lhp, Louisiana-Monroe**
25. Jay Johnson, lhp, Lethbridge (Alberta) CC
26. **Blake Mechaw, lhp, Shelton State (Ala.) CC**
27. **Mike Planeta, of, Glendale (Ariz.) CC**
28. **Kyle Hoppy, of, Orchard Park (N.Y.) HS**
29. Brandon Alexander, of, Oakville HS, St. Louis
30. **Brenden Webb, of, Palomar (Calif.) JC**
31. **Mike Flacco, 3b, Catonsville (Md.) CC**
32. Matt Nadolski, lhp, Casa Grande HS, Petaluma, Calif.
33. Tyler Naquin, of, Klein Collins HS, Spring, Texas
34. Malcolm Clapsaddle, rhp, Oviedo (Fla.) HS
35. Jeremy Lucas, c, West Vigo HS, Terre Haute, Ind.
36. Scott Firth, rhp, Stevenson HS, Lincolnshire, Ill.
37. Taylor Rogers, lhp, Chatfield HS, Littleton, Colo.
38. **Josh Dowdy, rhp, Appalachian State**
39. Kevin Alexander, rhp, Taravella HS, Coral Springs, Fla.
40. Bobby Shore, rhp, Palomar (Calif.) JC
41. Mason Magleby, rhp, Del Oro HS, Loomis, Calif.
42. Joe Valleggia, c, Old Dominion
43. Brad Decater, of, Cuesta (Calif.) JC
44. Kyle Westwood, rhp, Palm Harbor (Fla.) University HS
45. **David Rivera, of, Francisco Oller HS, Catano, P.R.**
46. Scott Swinson, rhp, Maryland
47. Nolan Martz, rhp, McKendree (Ill.)
48. Ryan Burnaman, 3b, San Jacinto (Texas) JC
49. Ashley Bulluck, rhp, South Broward HS, Hollywood, Fla.
50. **Tim Berry, lhp, San Marcos (Calif.) HS**

BOSTON RED SOX

June—Regular Phase (27)

1. **Reymond Fuentes, of, Fernando Callejo HS, Manati, P.R.**
2. **Alex Wilson, rhp, Texas A&M**
3. **David Renfroe, ss, South Panola HS, Batesville, Miss.**
4. **Jeremy Hazelbaker, of, Ball State**
5. **Seth Schwindenhammer, of, Limestone Community HS, Bartonville, Ill.**
6. Branden Kline, rhp, Johnson HS, Frederick, Md.
7. **Madison Younginer, rhp, Maudlin (S.C.) HS**
8. **Shannon Wilkerson, of, Augusta State (Ga.)**
9. **Kendal Volz, rhp, Baylor**
10. **Brandon Jacobs, of, Parkview HS, Lilburn, Ga.**
11. **Jason Thompson, ss, Germantown (Tenn.) HS**
12. **Michael Thomas, c, Southern**
13. **Chris McGuiness, 1b, The Citadel**
14. **Willie Holmes, of, Chaffey (Calif.) JC**
15. **Michael Bugary, lhp, California**
16. Luke Bard, rhp, Charlotte Christian HS
17. Kraig Sitton, lhp, Oregon State
18. **Renny Parthemore, rhp, Cedar Cliff HS, Camp Hill, Pa.**
19. **Tom Ebert, rhp, Florida International**
20. **Alex Hassan, rhp, Duke**
21. Randall Fant, lhp, Texas HS, Texarkana, Texas
22. **Jordan Flasher, rhp, George Mason**
23. **Chris Court, rhp, Stephen F. Austin State**
24. Dan Kemp, ss, Tantasqua Regional HS, Fiskdale, Mass.
25. Austin House, rhp, La Cueva HS, Albuquerque
26. **Miles Head, 3b, Whitewater HS, Fayetteville, Ga.**
27. Reed Gragnani, ss, Godwin HS, Richmond
28. **Eric Curtis, rhp, Miami Dade CC**
29. Cody Stubbs, 1b, Tuscola HS, Waynesville, N.C.
30. **Jeremiah Bayer, rhp, Trinity (Conn.)**
31. **Tim Webb, lhp, Palm Beach (Fla.) CC**
32. Mike Clark, lhp, American Heritage HS, Plantation, Fla.
33. Blaze Tart, rhp, Pendleton School, Bradenton, Fla.
34. Jimmy Patterson, lhp, Central Arizona JC
35. Matt Milroy, rhp, Marmion Academy, Aurora, Ill.
36. Mike Yastrzemski, of, St. John's Prep, Danvers, Mass.
37. Matt Koch, rhp, Washington HS, Cherokee, Iowa
38. Zeke DeVoss, of, Astronaut HS, Titusville, Fla.
39. Frank McCourt, of, Harvard-Westlake HS, Los Angeles
40. Jimmy Dykstra, rhp, Rancho Bernardo HS, San Diego
41. **Kyle Rutter, rhp, North Carolina State**
42. Gera Sanchez, rhp, New Mexico JC
43. Luke Maile, c, Covington Catholic HS, Park Hills, Ky.
44. Derrick Thomas, of, Roswell (Ga.) HS
45. Kyle Arnsberg, c, Lamar HS, Arlington, Texas
46. John Pivach, rhp, New Orleans
47. **Jordan Sallis, 2b, Arkansas-Fort Smith JC**
48. Brian Heere, of, Kansas
49. Chris Constantino, 3b, Bishop Hendricken HS, Warwick, R.I.
50. **Drew Hedman, 1b, Pomona-Pitzer (Calif.)**

CHICAGO CUBS

June—Regular Phase (29)

1. **Brett Jackson, of, California**
2. **D.J. Lemahieu, 2b, Louisiana State**
3. **Austin Kirk, lhp, Owasso (Okla.) HS**
4. **Chris Rusin, lhp, Kentucky**
5. **Wes Darvill, ss, Brookswood SS, Langley, B.C.**
6. **Brooks Raley, lhp, Texas A&M**
7. **Blair Springfield, ss, MacArthur HS, Decatur, Ill.**
8. **Robert Whitenack, rhp, SUNY Old Westbury**
9. **Richard Jones, c, The Citadel**
10. **Charles Thomas, 3b, Edward Waters (Fla.)**
11. **John Mincone, lhp, Suffolk County (N.Y.) CC-Grant**
12. **Runey Davis, of, Howard (Texas) JC**
13. Chad Taylor, ss, Jefferson HS, Tampa
14. **Danny Keefe, rhp, Tampa**
15. **Cody Shields, of, Auburn-Montgomery**
16. Keenyn Walker, of, Judge Memorial HS, Salt Lake City
17. B.J. Dail, rhp, Mount Olive (N.C.) (Contract voided)
18. **Matt Williams, c, Duke**
19. **Sergio Burruel, c, Browne HS, Phoenix**
20. Eric Erickson, lhp, Miami
21. **Greg Rohan, 1b, Kent State**
22. **D.J. Fitzgerald, 2b, Dyersburg State (Tenn.) CC**
23. Jeff Pruitt, of, Cal State Northridge (Contract voided)
24. Gerardo Esquivel, rhp, De La Salle Institute, Chicago
25. **Justin Bour, 1b, George Mason**
26. **Steve Grife, rhp, Mercyhurst (Pa.)**
27. **Corey Martin, rhp, Western Carolina**
28. **Jordan Petraitis, 3b, Miami (Ohio)**
29. **Tim Clubb, rhp, Missouri State**
30. Danny Sheppard, c, Downers Grove (Ill.) North HS
31. Andrew Clark, 1b, Louisville
32. **Trey McNutt, rhp, Shelton State (Ala.) CC**
33. John Lambert, lhp, North Carolina State
34. Rett Varner, rhp, Texas-Arlington
35. Kevin David, c, Oklahoma State
36. **Brandon May, 2b, Alabama**
37. Peter Mooney, ss, Palm Beach (Fla.) CC
38. **Bobby Wagner, 3b, Panola (Texas) JC**
39. **Nick Struck, rhp, Mount Hood (Ore.) CC**
40. Eric Whaley, rhp, Cardinal Gibbons HS, Fort Lauderdale
41. **Jake Schmidt, rhp, Concordia (Minn.)**
42. Trey Ford, ss, Chaparral HS, Scottsdale, Ariz.
43. Colin Kaepernick, rhp, Nevada
44. Frank DeJiulio, rhp, Daytona Beach (Fla.) CC
45. Addison Dunn, rhp, Warren (Pa.) Area HS
46. **Glenn Cook, of, Miami**
47. Joe Jocketty, 3b, Watkins HS, St. Louis
48. John Nasshan, rhp, Niles West HS, Skokie, Ill.
49. Christian Segar, of, McQuaid Jesuit HS, Rochester, N.Y.
50. Zach Cleveland, rhp, Central Arizona JC

CHICAGO WHITE SOX

June—Regular Phase (22)

1. **Jared Mitchell, of, Louisiana State**
1. **Josh Phegley, c, Indiana** (Supplemental pick—38th—for loss of Type A free agent Orlando Cabrera)
2. **Trayce Thompson, of, Santa Margarita Catholic HS, Rancho Santa Margarita, Calif.** (Pick from Athletics as compensation for Cabrera)
2. **David Holmberg, lhp, Port Charlotte (Fla.) HS**
3. Bryan Morgado, lhp, Tennessee
4. **Matt Heidenreich, rhp, Temescal Canyon HS, Lake Elsinore, Calif.**
5. **Kyle Bellamy, rhp, Miami**
6. **Justin Collop, rhp, Toledo**
7. Justin Jones, lhp, Oakdale (Calif.) HS
8. **Ryan Buch, rhp, Monmouth**
9. **Matt Hopps, rhp, Cal State Dominguez Hills**
10. **Nick Ciolli, of, Indiana State**
11. **J.R. Ballinger, rhp, Southern Mississippi**
12. **Kyle Colligan, of, Texas A&M**
13. **Cameron Bayne, rhp, Concordia (Calif.)**
14. **Dan Black, 1b, Purdue**
15. Dane Williams, rhp, Archbishop McCarthy HS, Fort Lauderdale
16. **Daniel Wagner, 2b, Belmont**
17. Brian Goodwin, of, Rocky Mount (N.C.) HS
18. **Phil Negus, rhp, Wake Forest**
19. **Brady Shoemaker, of, Indiana State**
20. Nate Reed, lhp, Pittsburgh
21. **Jared McDonald, ss, Arizona State**
22. **Zach Kayne, ss, Davidson**
23. **Goldy Simmons, rhp, San Diego State**
24. **Jeff Tezak, 2b, Nebraska**
25. Mike Strong, lhp, Iowa Western CC
26. **Matt Harughty, 2b, Oklahoma**
27. **Kyle Davis, 2b, Delaware**
28. **Robby Cummings, 3b, UC Santa Barbara**
29. **Trey Delk, rhp, Clemson**
30. **Rob Vaughn, c, Kansas State**
31. **Ryan Hamme, of, Campbell**
32. **Jake Wilson, rhp, New Mexico State**
33. **Chase Cooney, rhp, Volunteer State (Tenn.) CC**
34. **Alex Farotto, lhp, South Carolina**
35. **Danny Wiltz, rhp, Tennessee**
36. Ryan Crowley, lhp, Morton West HS, Berwyn, Ill.
37. **Joe Serafin, lhp, Vermont**
38. **A.J. Casario, of, Maryland**
39. **Paul Burnside, rhp, Auburn**
40. **Leighton Pangilinan, 1b, Escalon (Calif.) HS**
41. **Ryan Lee, of, Cal Poly**
42. **Chris Zagyi, rhp, Middlesex (N.J.) CC**
43. Tyler Williams, 3b, Chaparral HS, Scottsdale, Ariz.
44. **Taylor Thompson, rhp, Auburn**
45. **Harold Baines Jr., of, McDaniel (Md.)**
46. Grant Monroe, rhp, Northwest Florida State JC
47. Jordan Yallen, of, Golden Valley HS, Santa Clarita, Calif.
48. Matthew Little, lhp, Bryan (Texas) HS
49. Theron Geith, lhp, Scottsdale (Ariz.) CC
50. Kevin Chapman, lhp, Florida

CINCINNATI REDS

June—Regular Phase (8)

1. **Mike Leake, rhp, Arizona State**
1. **Brad Boxberger, rhp, Southern California** (Supplemental pick—43rd—for loss of Type B free agent Jeremy Affeldt)
2. **Billy Hamilton, ss, Taylorsville (Miss.) HS**
3. **Donnie Joseph, lhp, Houston**
4. **Mark Fleury, c, North Carolina**
5. **Daniel Tuttle, rhp, Randleman (N.C.) HS**
6. **Mark Serrano, rhp, Oral Roberts**
7. **Josh Fellhauer, of, Cal State Fullerton**
8. **Juan Silva, of, Puerto Rico Baseball Academy, Gurabo, P.R.**
9. **Brian Pearl, rhp, Washington**
10. **Tucker Barnhart, c, Brownsburg (Ind.) HS**
11. **Jacob Johnson, rhp, Trinity Christian Academy, Lake Worth, Fla.**
12. **Josh Garton, of, Volunteer State (Tenn.) CC**
13. **Nick Christiani, rhp, Vanderbilt**
14. **Tim Crabbe, rhp, Westmont (Calif.)**
15. **Jamie Walczak, rhp, Mercyhurst (Pa.)**
16. Chase Fowler, c, South Forsythe HS, Cumming, Ga.
17. Deven Marrero, ss, American Heritage HS, Plantation, Fla.
18. Steven Perez, ss, Gulliver Prep HS, Miami
19. **Mitchell Clarke, lhp, Forest Heights Collegiate Institute, Kitchener, Ont**
20. Matt Valaika, 2b, UC Santa Barbara
21. Jon Reed, rhp, Memorial HS, Tulsa
22. **Dave Stewart, 1b, Grayson County (Texas) CC**
23. **Chris Richburg, 1b, Texas Tech**
24. **Derrick Lowery, 1b, Young Harris (Ga.) JC**
25. Mike Monster, rhp, Rutland SS, Kelowna, B.C.
26. **Trey Manz, c, South Florida**
27. Stefan Del Pino, lhp, Dorman HS, Roebuck, S.C.
28. Derek Poppert, ss, San Francisco
29. **Jason Braun, rhp, Corban (Ore.)**
30. **Yovan Gonzalez, c, Wabash Valley (Ill.) CC**
31. **Adian Kummet, rhp, St. Scholastica (Minn.)**
32. **Shane Carlson, ss, UC Santa Barbara**
33. **Will Stramp, 3b, Lubbock Christian (Texas)**
34. **Forest Cannon, rhp, UC Santa Barbara**
35. **Oliver Santos, 3b, South Carolina-Salkehatchie JC**
36. **Chris Burleson, ss, Southern Maine**
37. **Dayne Read, of, Chipola (Fla.) JC**
38. **Tommy Nurre, 1b, Miami (Ohio)**
39. Paul Barton, rhp, Kwalikum SS, Qualicum Beach, B.C
40. Michael Robertson, of, Bellevue (Wash.) CC
41. **Jake Wiley, rhp, Marist**
42. **Blair Carson, rhp, Anderson (S.C.)**
43. **Ricky Bowen, rhp, Mississippi State**
44. Jaron Shepherd, of, Navarro (Texas) JC
45. Brian Adams, of, South Forysth HS, Cumming, Ga.
46. Tim Dunn, rhp, Trevecca Nazarene (Tenn.)
47. Jason Hampton, rhp, Rocklin (Calif.) HS
48. Kenny Swab, c, Young Harris (Ga.) JC
49. Darion Hamilton, of, Taylorsville (Miss.) HS
50. Chris Page, 1b, Genesee (N.Y.) CC

CLEVELAND INDIANS

June—Regular Phase (14)

1. **Alex White, rhp, North Carolina**
2. **Jason Kipnis, of, Arizona State**
3. **Joe Gardner, rhp, UC Santa Barbara**
4. **Kyle Bellows, 3b, San Jose State**
5. **Austin Adams, rhp, Faulkner (Ala.)**
6. **Ben Carlson, 1b, Missouri State**
7. **Jordan Henry, of, Mississippi**
8. **Cory Burns, rhp, Arizona**
9. **Preston Guilmet, rhp, Arizona**
10. **Brett Brach, rhp, Monmouth**
11. **Kirk Wetmore, lhp, Bellevue (Wash.) CC**
12. **Joseph Colon, rhp, Caguas, P.R.**
13. **Jeremy Johnson, rhp, Washington State**
14. **Kyle Smith, ss, Cal Poly**
15. **Mike Rayl, lhp, Palm Beach (Fla.) CC**
16. **Dale Dickerson, rhp, Nicholls State**
17. **Casey Frawley, of, Stetson**
18. **Dwight Childs, c, Arizona**
19. **Nick Kirk, lhp, Northern Iowa**
20. **Kyle Smith, rhp, Kent State**
21. Jeff Rowland, of, Georgia Tech
22. Merrill Kelly, rhp, Yavapai (Ariz.) JC
23. **Danny Jimenez, lhp, Logan (Ill.) CC**
24. Michael Hamann, rhp, Danbury HS, Lakeside, Ohio
25. Blake Hauser, rhp, Manchester HS, Midlothian, Va.
26. **Antwonie Hubbard, rhp, Oklahoma**
27. **Tyler Sturdevant, rhp, New Mexico State**
28. **Nick Sarianides, rhp, Chattahoochee Valley (Ala.) JC**
29. Xorge Carrillo, c, Central Arizona JC

30. Bryson Smith, 3b, Young Harris (Ga.) JC
31. Raynor Campbell, 3b, Baylor
32. **Matt Packer, lhp, Virginia**
33. **Chris Kersten, 3b, Louisiana Tech**
34. Westley Moss, of, Nevada
35. Chris Beck, rhp, Jefferson (Ga.) HS
36. Austin Evans, rhp, Alabama
37. Steve Ewing, lhp, University HS, Orlando
38. Robert Sabo, rhp, Kent State
39. Brian Hernandez, 3b, UC Irvine
40. **Greg Folgia, ss, Missouri**
41. Max Muncy, c, Keller (Texas) HS
42. Jonathan Kountis, rhp, Ohio Dominican
43. D.J. Gentile, dh, Cal Poly
44. Jose Madrid, c, Memorial HS, Victoria, Texas
45. James Jones, rhp, Logan (Ill.) CC
46. Scott Sommerfeld, of, Parkway South HS, Ballwin, Mo.
47. Christian Powell, rhp, Greenwood (S.C.) HS
48. **Vidal Nuno, lhp, Baker (Kan.)**
49. Burch Smith, rhp, Howard (Texas) JC
50. Tyler Joyner, lhp, Northern Nash HS, Rocky Mount, N.C.

COLORADO ROCKIES

June—Regular Phase (10)

1. **Tyler Matzek, lhp, Capistrano Valley HS, Mission Viejo, Calif.**
1. **Tim Wheeler, of, Sacramento State** (Pick from Angels as compensation for Type A free agent Brian Fuentes)
1. **Rex Brothers, lhp, Lipscomb** (Supplemental pick—34th—for loss of Fuentes)
2. **Nolan Arenado, 3b, El Toro HS, Lake Forest, Calif.**
3. **Ben Paulsen, 1b, Clemson**
4. **Kent Matthes, of, Alabama**
5. **Joseph Sanders, 3b, Auburn**
6. **Chris Balcom-Miller, rhp, West Valley (Calif.) JC**
7. **Erik Stavert, rhp, Oregon**
8. **Rob Scahill, rhp, Bradley**
9. **Wes Musick, lhp, Houston**
10. **Charlie Ruiz, rhp, Long Beach State**
11. **Avery Barnes, of, Florida**
12. **Jared Clark, 1b, Cal State Fullerton**
13. **Paul Bargas, lhp, UC Riverside**
14. **Jeff Squier, ss, Mississippi Valley State**
15. **Tyler Gagnon, rhp, Diablo Valley (Calif.) JC**
16. **Dominic Altobelli, 3b, Illinois**
17. **Josh Hungerman, lhp, Cleveland State**
18. **Ricky Testa, rhp, Lamar**
19. **Dustin Garneau, c, Cal State Fullerton**
20. **Dallas Tarleton, c, Elon**
21. **Chandler Laurent, of, Delgado (La.) JC**
22. **David Born, lhp, Long Beach State**
23. **Jose Rivera, 2b, Universidad Interamericana (P.R.)**
24. **Joey Wong, ss, Oregon State**
25. **Trevor Gibson, rhp, San Jose State**
26. **Rhett Ballard, rhp, Virginia Tech**
27. **Dan Perkins, rhp, Delaware State**
28. **David DiNatale, of, Miami**
29. Corey Dickerson, of, Meridian (Miss.) CC
30. **Bryce Massanari, c, Georgia**
31. **Clint Tilford, rhp, Kentucky**
32. **Steve Junker, lhp, Bellevue (Neb.)**
33. **Coty Woods, rhp, Middle Tennessee State**
34. **Brandon Whitby, c, Prairie View A&M**
35. Tym Pearson, of, Thurston HS, Springfield, Ore.
36. Jarrett Higgins, of, Bellaire (Texas) HS
37. Brandon Thomas, of, Pace Academy, Atlanta
38. Brett Hambright, c, Riverside (Calif.) CC
39. **Eric Federico, rhp, Cal State Stanislaus**
40. Jason Bagoly, c, Fitch HS, Austintown, Ohio
41. **Matt Sanders, 3b, Clemson**
42. **Joe Scott, 2b, Cal State Fullerton**
43. Franco Broyles, of, Fayetteville (Ark.) HS
44. Micah Green, of, Cherokee Trail HS, Aurora, Colo.
45. Heath Holliday, c, Bixby (Okla.) HS
46. Tyler Wallace, 3b, Eaton (Calif.) HS
47. Sterling Monfort, 1b, Eaton (Colo.) HS
48. **Clint McKinney, rhp, Clemson**
49. Mark Tracy, c, Duquesne
50. **Nathan Hines, of, Middle Tennessee State**

DETROIT TIGERS

June—Regular Phase (9)

1. **Jacob Turner, rhp, Westminster Christian Academy, St. Louis**
2. **Andrew Oliver, lhp, Oklahoma State**
3. **Wade Gaynor, 3b, Western Kentucky**
4. **Edwin Gomez, ss, Puerto Rico Baseball Academy, Gurabo, P.R.**
5. **Austin Wood, lhp, Texas**
6. **Daniel Fields, ss, University of Detroit Jesuit HS**
7. **Jamie Johnson, of, Oklahoma**
8. Craig Fritsch, rhp, Baylor
9. **John Murrian, c, Winthrop**
10. **Chris Sedon, 2b, Pittsburgh**
11. **Adam Wilk, lhp, Long Beach State**
12. Matt Thompson, rhp, San Diego
13. **Michael Rockett, of, Texas-San Antonio**
14. **Kevan Hess, rhp, Western Michigan**
15. Mark Appel, rhp, Monte Vista HS, Danville, Calif.
16. **Kenny Faulk, lhp, Kennesaw State**
17. **Nathan Newman, rhp, Pepperdine**
18. **Eric Roof, c, Michigan State**
19. **Rawley Bishop, 3b, Middle Tennessee State**
20. **Jimmy Gulliver, ss, Eastern Michigan**
21. **Giovanni Soto, lhp, Carolina, P.R.**
22. **Matt Mansilla, of, College of Charleston**
23. **Cory Hamilton, rhp, UC Irvine**
24. **Wade Kapteyn, rhp, Evansville**
25. Victor Roache, of, Lincoln HS, Ypsilanti, Mich.
26. **Edgar Corcino, 3b, Adolfina Irizarry De Puig HS, Toa Baja, P.R.**
27. **Pat McKenna, ss, Bryant (R.I.)**
28. Tobin Mateychick, rhp, Enid (Okla.) HS
29. **Michael Morrison, rhp, Cal State Fullerton**
30. **James Robbins, 1b, Shorecrest HS, Shoreline, Wash.**
31. Andrew Walter, rhp, Cactus HS, Glendale, Ariz.
32. Parker Markel, rhp, Mountain Ridge HS, Glendale, Ariz.
33. Cody Keefer, of, Davis (Calif.) HS
34. Derek Kline, rhp, Millersville (Pa.)
35. Patrick Biondi, of, Divine Child HS, Dearborn, Mich.
36. Ben Crumpton, ss, Lakeside HS, Hot Springs, Ark.
37. Danny Canela, c, Florida Christian HS, Miami
38. Tarran Senay, of, South Park (Pa.) HS
39. Chad Duling, ss, Bishop Carroll HS, Wichita
40. Ben Bechtol, c, Neshannock HS, New Castle, Pa.
41. Larry Balkwill, c, Ursuline College Chatham SS, Chatham-Kent, Ontario
42. Nick Avila, rhp, Central Florida CC
43. Andrew Allen, 3b, Central Arizona JC
44. Charlie Markson, of, Whitefish Bay (Wis.) HS
45. Jimmy Brennan, of, Suffern (N.Y.) HS
46. Nate Goro, 3b, Lafayette HS, Wildwood, Mo.
47. Kevin Chambers, lhp, Capistrano Valley HS, Mission Viejo, Calif.
48. Jake Porcello, rhp, Seton Hall Prep, West Orange, N.J.
49. Cameron Giannini, rhp, Hargrave Military Academy, Chatham, Va.
50. Nico Rosthenhausler, of, South Mountain (Ariz.) CC

FLORIDA MARLINS

June—Regular Phase (17)

1. **Chad James, lhp, Yukon (Okla.) HS**
2. **Bryan Berglund, rhp, Royal HS, Simi Valley, Calif.**
3. **Marquise Cooper, of, Edison HS, Huntington Beach, Calif.**
4. **Dan Mahoney, rhp, Connecticut**
5. **Chase Austin, ss, Elon**
6. **Dustin Dickerson, 1b, Baylor**
7. **Josh Hodges, rhp, Ingomar HS, New Albany, Miss.**

8. **Stephen Richards, lhp, Arkansas**
9. **Jobduan Morales, c, Jose S. Alegria HS, Dorado, P.R.**
10. **Matt Montgomery, rhp, UC Riverside**
11. **Chris Wade, ss, Kentucky**
12. **Kyle Jensen, of, St. Mary's**
13. Tyler Curtis, rhp, JC of Southern Idaho
14. **Sequoyah Stonecipher, of, Grossmont (Calif.) JC**
15. **Chad Cregar, of, Western Kentucky**
16. **David Peters, c, Lakewood (Calif.) HS**
17. **Brent Keys, of, Simi Valley (Calif.) HS**
18. **Brett Bukvich, lhp, Mississippi**
19. **Erick Carrillo, rhp, Cal State San Bernardino**
20. **Rand Smith, of, Appalachian State**
21. **A.J. Ramos, rhp, Texas Tech**
22. **Terrence Dayleg, ss, Western Kentucky**
23. **Tommy Peale, rhp, Lewis-Clark State (Idaho)**
24. **Mike Brady, ss, California**
25. **Sean Teague, rhp, Southern Polytechnic State (Ga.)**
26. **Brent Weaver, 3b, Oklahoma City**
27. **Nate Simon, 2b, Pepperdine**
28. **Holden Sprague, rhp, Fresno State**
29. **Jared Eskew, lhp, Cal Poly**
30. **Harold Brantley, of, Connecticut**
31. **Joey O'Gara, rhp, Indiana**
32. **Dallas Hord, c, Missouri State**
33. Tom Buske, rhp, Minnesota
34. **Isaac Morales, lhp, Cal State Los Angeles**
35. **Tyler Topp, rhp, Long Beach State**
36. Kaleth Fradera, rhp, Puerto Rico Baseball Academy, Gurabo, P.R.
37. Keith Glenn, of, Henry County HS, McDonough, Ga.
38. Kevin Johnson, lhp, Cincinnati
39. **Noah Perio, ss, De La Salle HS, Concord, Calif.**
40. Mitch Patito, rhp, Patriot HS, Riverside, Calif.
41. Darnell Sweeney, ss, American Heritage HS, Plantation, Fla.
42. Jordan Poyer, of, Astoria (Ore.) HS
43. Donovan Gonzales, rhp, Twentynine Palms (Calif.) HS
44. Kenny Giles, rhp, Rio Grande HS, Albuquerque
45. Zach Hurley, of, Ohio State
46. Nick Ammirati, c, Seton Hall Prep, West Orange, N.J.
47. Cody Miller, c, River Valley HS, Yuba City, Calif.
48. Ryan Gibson, lhp, Yukon (Okla.) HS
49. **Alan Williams, lhp, Meridian (Miss.) CC**
50. **Adam Kam, 1b, Douglas HS, Parkland, Fla.**

HOUSTON ASTROS

June—Regular Phase (20)

1. **Jiovanni Mier, ss, Bonita HS, La Verne, Calif.**
2. **Tanner Bushue, rhp, South Central HS, Farina, Ill.**
3. **Telvin Nash, of, Griffin (Ga.) HS**
3. **Jonathan Meyer, 3b, Simi Valley (Calif.) HS** (Supplemental pick—111th—for failure to sign 2008 third-rounder Chase Davidson)
4. **B.J. Hyatt, rhp, South Carolina-Sumter JC**
5. **Brandon Wikoff, ss, Illinois**
6. **Enrique Hernandez, ss, American Military Academy, Toa Baja, P.R.**
7. **Dallas Keuchel, lhp, Arkansas**
8. **Brandt Walker, rhp, Stanford**
9. **Ben Orloff, ss, UC Irvine**
10. **Erik Castro, 3b, San Diego State**
11. **Bubby Williams, c, Crowder (Mo.) JC**
12. Geoff Thomas, rhp, Stephenson HS, Stone Mountain, Ga.
13. **Jake Goebbert, of, Northwestern**
14. **David Berner, lhp, San Jose State**
15. **Ryan Humphrey, of, St. Louis CC-Meramec**
16. **Ronald Sanchez, 1b, Manuela Toro Morice HS, Caguas, P.R.**
17. **Justin Harper, rhp, Oklahoma City**
18. **J.B. MacDonald, rhp, Boston College**
19. **Brian Kemp, of, St. John's**
20. **Julio Martinez, of, Nova Southeastern (Fla.)**
21. **Barry Butera, 2b, Boston College**
22. **Mark Jones, rhp, Manheim Township HS, Lititz, Pa.**
23. **Robby Donovan, rhp, Stetson**
24. **Mike Modica, lhp, George Mason**
25. **Nick Stanley, 1b, Florida Southern**
26. Matt Watson, 1b, Pompano Beach (Fla.) HS
27. **Aaron Bray, 3b, Charlotte**
28. Eric Anderson, rhp, Mountain Vista HS, Highlands Ranch, Colo.
29. **Garen Wright, of, Putnam City HS, Oklahoma City**
30. Brandon Petite, rhp, Vauxhall Academy, Edmonton
31. **Travis Smink, lhp, Virginia Military Institute**
32. Greg Peavey, rhp, Oregon State
33. **Brenden Stines, rhp, Ball State**
34. **Scott Migl, rhp, Texas A&M**
35. **Grant Hogue, of, Mississippi State**
36. Tyler Saladino, ss, Palomar (Calif.) JC
37. Raul Rivera, rhp, Colegio San Vicente de Paul HS, Santurce, P.R.
38. **Sean Barksdale, of, Temple**
39. Rory Young, rhp, Mountain SS, Langley, B.C
40. **Dan Sarisky, rhp, Oglethorpe (Ga.)**
41. Carlos Escobar, c, Chatsworth (Calif.) HS
42. Ivory Thomas, of, Downey (Calif.) HS
43. Anthony Tzamtzis, rhp, La Salle HS, Miami
44. **Mike Schurz, rhp, Iowa**
45. Adrian Morales, 2b, Miami Dade CC
46. Justin Gonzalez, ss, Columbus HS, Miami
47. Matt Branham, rhp, South Carolina-Upstate
48. Paco Rodriguez, lhp, Gulliver Prep, Miami
49. Matt Smith, 1b, Mississippi
50. **Spencer Hylander, lhp, Oklahoma Baptist**

KANSAS CITY ROYALS

June—Regular Phase (11)

1. **Aaron Crow, rhp, Fort Worth (American Association)**
2. (Pick to Diamondbacks as compensation for Type A free agent Juan Cruz)
3. **Wil Myers, c/3b, Wesleyan Christian Academy, High Point, N.C.**
4. **Chris Dwyer, lhp, Clemson**
5. **Louis Coleman, rhp, Louisiana State**
6. **Cole White, rhp, New Mexico**
7. **Buddy Baumann, lhp, Missouri State**
8. **Dusty Odenbach, rhp, Connecticut**
9. **Ben Theriot, c, Texas State**
10. **Geoff Baldwin, 1b, Grand Junction (Colo.) HS**
11. **Ryan Wood, rhp, East Carolina**
12. **Nick Wooley, rhp, William Woods (Mo.)**
13. **Lane Adams, of, Red Oak (Okla.) HS**
14. **Crawford Simmons, lhp, Statesboro (Ga.) HS**
15. **Scott Lyons, ss, Arkansas**
16. **Eric Diaz, lhp, New Mexico JC**
17. **Ben Tschepikow, 2b, Arkansas**
18. **Brendan Lafferty, lhp, UCLA**
19. **Ryan Stovall, 3b, Thomas (Ga.)**
20. **Patrick Keating, rhp, Florida**
21. **Chanse Cooper, of, Belhaven (Miss.)**
22. **Ryan Dennick, lhp, Tennessee Tech**
23. **Scott Kelley, rhp, Penn State**
24. Zach Jones, rhp, Santa Teresa HS, San Jose
25. **Richard Folmer, rhp, Stephen F. Austin State**
26. Matt Frazer, 1b, Nitro (W.Va.) HS
27. **Gabe MacDougall, of, Lynn (Fla.)**
28. Eric Peterson, inf, Liberty HS, Spangle, Wash.
29. Nick Zaharion, of, South Fork HS, Stuart, Fla.
30. **Josh Worrell, rhp, Indiana Wesleyan**
31. **Brian Peacock, lhp, Santa Ana (Calif.) JC**
32. Luke Voit, c, Lafayette HS, Wildwood, Mo.
33. **Claudio Bavera, lhp, Cochise (Ariz.) JC**
34. **Justin Trapp, ss, Fairfield Central HS, Winnsboro, S.C.**
35. Levi Cartas, of, Marysville-Pilchuck HS, Marysville, Wash.
36. Fabian Roman, rhp, Marist HS, Bayonne, N.J.
37. Tanner Poppe, rhp, Girard (Kan.) HS
38. Arthur Owens, ss, Sandy Creek HS, Tyrone, Ga.
39. Art Charles, 1b, Bakersfield (Calif.) JC
40. Mike Morin, rhp, Shawnee Mission South HS, Overland Park, Kan.

41. **Joey Lewis, c, Georgia**
42. **Jonathon Keck, lhp, Bethel (Tenn.)**
43. Jeff Soptic, rhp, Shawnee Mission East HS, Prairie Village, Kan.
44. Derrick Hudgins, ss, Middleton HS, Tampa
45. Derek Spencer, 3b, Bowling Green State
46. Hudson Randall, rhp, Dunwoody (Ga.) HS
47. **Anthony Howard, of, Quince Orchard HS, Gaithersburg, Md.**
48. Kevin Kuntz, ss, Union HS, Tulsa
49. Zac Fisher, c, Miller HS, Fontana, Calif.
50. **Anthony Scirrotto, ss, Penn State**

LOS ANGELES ANGELS

June—Regular Phase (30)

1. **Randal Grichuk, of, Lamar Consolidated HS, Rosenberg, Texas** (Pick from Mets as compensation for Type A free agent Francisco Rodriguez)
1. **Mike Trout, of, Millville (N.J.) HS** (Pick from Yankees as compensation for Type A free agent Mark Teixeira)
1. (Pick to Rockies as compensation for Type A free agent Brian Fuentes)
1. **Tyler Skaggs, lhp, Santa Monica (Calif.) HS** (Supplemental pick—40th—for loss of Teixeira)
1. **Garrett Richards, rhp, Oklahoma** (Supplemental pick—42nd—for loss of Rodriguez)
1. **Tyler Kehrer, lhp, Eastern Illinois** (Supplemental pick—48th—for loss of Type B free agent Jon Garland)
2. **Pat Corbin, lhp, Chipola (Fla.) JC**
3. Josh Spence, lhp, Arizona State
4. **Wes Hatton, 2b, Norco (Calif.) HS**
5. **Casey Haerther, 1b, UCLA**
6. **Danny Reynolds, rhp, Durango HS, Las Vegas**
7. **Jon Karcich, ss, Santa Clara**
8. **Carlos Ramirez, c, Arizona State**
9. **David Carpenter, rhp, Paris (Texas) JC**
10. **Jake Locker, of, Washington**
11. **Dillon Baird, 3b, Arizona**
12. **Travis Witherspoon, of, Spartanburg Methodist (S.C.) JC**
13. **Jeremy Cruz, of, Stetson**
14. Sam Selman, lhp, St. Andrew's Episcopal HS, Austin
15. Mike Nesseth, rhp, Nebraska
16. Andrew Del Colle, rhp, Newark Academy, Livingston, N.J.
17. **Jeremy Gillan, c, Jacksonville**
18. **Jamie Mallard, 1b, Hillsborough (Fla.) CC**
19. Adam Hornung, of, Baylor
20. **Dan Eichelberger, of, East Central (Miss.) CC**
21. **Rich Cates, of, Cal State Northridge**
22. **Stephen Locke, lhp, Florida**
23. **Jordan Drake, of, Elsinore HS, Wildomar, Calif.**
24. **Taylor Kinzer, rhp, Taylor (Ind.)**
25. **Michael Demperio, 2b, Georgia**
26. Garrett Cannizaro, 2b, Mandeville (La.) HS
27. Devon Zenn, of, Benicia (Calif.) HS
28. **Carson Andrew, rhp, Jacksonville**
29. **William Nichols, rhp, JC of Southern Idaho**
30. **Matt Long, of, Santa Clara**
31. Jordan Whatcott, rhp, Utah
32. Raoul Torrez, 2b, Arizona State
33. Ben Dew, rhp, Seminole (Fla.) CC
34. **Ryan Cisterna, rhp, Arkansas**
35. Robbie Harris, ss, Cardinal Gibbons HS, Baltimore
36. **Eric Oliver, 1b, UC Santa Barbara**
37. Erik Gregersen, rhp, Stephen F. Austin State
38. Justin Bellez, rhp, Mira Mesa (Calif.) HS
39. Ryan Hege, c, Cowley County (Kan.) CC
40. Asaad Ali, c, Niles (Mich.) HS
41. Joey Rapp, of, Chipola (Fla.) JC
42. Sam Wolff, rhp, Stevens HS, Rapid City, S.D.
43. Seth Harvey, rhp, Washington State
44. R.J. Santigate, 3b, Bishop Gorman HS, Las Vegas
45. **Phil Bando, 2b, JC of the Canyons (Calif.)**
46. Jonathan Paquet, rhp, Cardinal Roy SS, Ancienne-Lorette, Quebec
47. **Jose Jimenez, 1b, Tampa**
48. **Jake Rife, of, Washington**
49. Chunner Nyberg, rhp, Dixie HS, St. George, Utah
50. **Alibay Barkley, 1b, Washington HS, New York**

LOS ANGELES DODGERS

June—Regular Phase (16)

1. (Pick to Diamondbacks as compensation for Type A free agent Orlando Hudson)
1. **Aaron Miller, lhp, Baylor** (Supplemental pick—36th—for loss of Type A free agent Derek Lowe)
2. **Blake Smith, of, California** (Pick from Braves as compensation for Lowe)
2. **Garrett Gould, rhp, Maize (Kan.) HS**
3. **Brett Wallach, rhp, Orange Coast (Calif.) CC**
4. **Angelo Songco, of, Loyola Marymount**
5. **J.T. Wise, c, Oklahoma**
6. **Jan Vazquez, c, Puerto Rico Baseball Academy, Gurabo, P.R.**
7. **Brandon Martinez, rhp, Fowler (Calif.) HS**
8. **Jonathan Garcia, of, Luis Munoz Marin HS, Yauco, P.R.**
9. **Bryant Hernandez, ss, Oklahoma**
10. **Andy Suiter, lhp, UC Davis**
11. Connor Powers, 1b, Mississippi State
12. **Brian Cavazos-Galvez, of, New Mexico**
13. **J.B. Paxson, rhp, Western Kentucky**
14. **Casio Grider, ss, Newberry (S.C.)**
15. **Jeff Hunt, 3b, St. Benedict Catholic SS, Cambridge, Ont**
16. **Mike Pericht, c, St. Joseph's (Ind.)**
17. **Steven Ames, rhp, Gonzaga**
18. **Greg Wilborn, lhp, Louisiana-Lafayette**
19. **Nick Akins, of, Vanguard (Calif.)**
20. Daniel Palo, rhp, Houston HS, Germantown, Tenn.
21. **Chris Henderson, 3b, George Mason**
22. **Stetson Banks, of, Brigham Young**
23. **Jimmy Marshall, rhp, Florida State**
24. Chad Kettler, ss, Coppell (Texas) HS
25. Richie Shaffer, 3b, Providence HS, Charlotte
26. Alex McRee, lhp, Georgia
27. Brian Johnson, lhp, Cocoa Beach (Fla.) HS
28. **John Hernandez, rhp, Barry (Fla.)**
29. Reshawn Payne, 2b, Middle Georgia JC
30. **Nick Gaudi, rhp, Pepperdine**
31. **Austin King, of, Jackson State (Tenn.) CC**
32. **Paul Miller, lhp, Master's (Calif.)**
33. **Stephen Cilladi, c, Kansas Wesleyan**
34. **Justin Dignelli, rhp, George Washington**
35. **David Iden, 2b, California Lutheran**
36. **K.J. Childs, rhp, Culver-Stockton (Mo.)**
37. Joel Effertz, rhp, Ladysmith (Wis.) HS
38. Kirby Pellant, 2b, Corona Del Sol HS, Tempe, Ariz.
39. Ryan Hander, rhp, Lincoln HS, Sioux Falls, S.D.
40. Ryan Christenson, lhp, South Mountain (Ariz.) CC
41. **Chris Handke, rhp, Cornell**
42. Tony Renda, ss, Serra HS, San Mateo, Calif.
43. Chad Gough-Fortenberry, c, Northshore HS, Slidell, La.
44. R.C. Orlan, lhp, Deep Run HS, Glen Allen, Va.
45. Stephen Piscotty, ss, Amador Valley HS, Pleasanton, Calif.
46. James Smith, 2b, Second Baptist HS, Houston
47. Cole Pembroke, of, Desert Vista HS, Phoenix
48. Travis Burnside, of, Laurens (S.C.) District HS
49. Christian Walker, 3b, Kennedy-Kenrick Catholic HS, Limerick, Pa.
50. David Garcia, ss, Kennedy HS, Granada Hills, Calif.

MILWAUKEE BREWERS

June—Regular Phase (25)

1. **Eric Arnett, rhp, Indiana**
1. **Kentrail Davis, of, Tennessee** (Supplemental pick—39th—for loss of Type A free agent C.C. Sabathia)
1. **Kyle Heckathorn, rhp, Kennesaw State** (Supplemental pick—47th—for loss ot Type B free agent Brian Shouse)
2. **Max Walla, of, Albuquerque Academy** (Pick from Yankees as compensation for Sabathia)

2. **Cameron Garfield, c, Murrieta (Calif.) Valley HS**
3. **Josh Prince, ss, Tulane**
4. **Brooks Hall, rhp, Hanna HS, Anderson, S.C.**
5. **D'Vontrey Richardson, of, Florida State**
6. **Hiram Burgos, rhp, Bethune-Cookman**
7. **Khris Davis, of, Cal State Fullerton**
8. **Chad Stang, of, Midland (Texas) CC**
9. **Jon Pokorny, lhp, Kent State**
10. **Tyler Roberts, c, Jones County HS, Gray, Ga.**
11. **Andre Lamontagne, rhp, Oral Roberts**
12. **Rob Currie, rhp, Tusculum (Tenn.)**
13. **Sean Halton, 1b, Lewis-Clark State (Idaho)**
14. **Mike Brownstein, 2b, New Mexico**
15. **Del Howell, lhp, Alabama**
16. **Scooter Gennett, ss, Sarasota (Fla.) HS**
17. **Tyler Cravy, rhp, Napa Valley (Calif.) CC**
18. **Caleb Thielbar, lhp, South Dakota State**
19. **Scott Krieger, of, George Mason**
20. **Franklin Romero, of, Cerro Coso (Calif.) CC**
21. Brian Vigo-Suarez, ss, Fossil Ridge HS, Keller, Texas
22. **Michael Fiers, rhp, Nova Southeastern (Fla.)**
23. Austin Pressley, rhp, Franklin Monroe HS, Arcanum, Ohio
24. **Peter Fatse, 2b, Connecticut**
25. **Demetrius McKelvie, of, East Columbus HS, Lake Waccamaw, N.C.**
26. Lex Rutledge, lhp, Tupelo (Miss.) HS
27. **Ryan Platt, rhp, UC Riverside**
28. Geno Escalante, c, Rodriguez HS, Fairfield, Calif.
29. Chandler McLaren, of, Guelph (Ontario) Collegiate Vocational Institute
30. **Brandon Sizemore, 2b, Charleston**
31. **Jose Oviedo, rhp, Miami Dade CC**
32. **Chris Ellington, of, Texas Christian**
33. Jacobbi McDaniel, 3b, Madison (Fla.) County HS
34. Mike Ojala, rhp, Rice
35. **Matt Costello, lhp, Valdosta State (Ga.)**
36. Josh Turley, lhp, Texas HS, Texarkana, Texas
37. Cullen Sexton, rhp, Minnesota
38. Casey Stevenson, 2b, UC Irvine
39. Brady Rodgers, rhp, Lamar Consolidated HS, Rosenberg, Texas
40. Kyle Hansen, rhp, St. Dominic HS, Oyster Bay, N.Y.
41. Steven Sultzbaugh, of, Rice
42. Brad Schreiber, rhp, Kimberly (Wis.) HS
43. **Kyle Dhanani, 3b, Thompson Rivers (B.C.)**
44. Andrew Morris, rhp, Gulf Coast (Fla.) CC
45. Richard Stock, c, Agoura HS, Agoura Hills, Calif.
46. Jordan Wong, rhp, Vauxhall Academy, Edmonton
47. Trevor Kirk, of, CC of Southern Nevada
48. Reynaldo Cotilla, rhp, Miami Dade CC
49. John Altobelli, ss, Woodbridge HS, Irvine, Calif.
50. Darren Farmer, c, West Lauderdale HS, Collinsville, Miss.

MINNESOTA TWINS

June—Regular Phase (21)

1. **Kyle Gibson, rhp, Missouri**
1. **Matt Bashore, lhp, Indiana** (Supplemental pick—46th—for loss of Type B free agent Dennys Reyes)
2. **Billy Bullock, rhp, Florida**
3. **Ben Tootle, rhp, Jacksonville State**
4. **Derek McCallum, 2b, Minnesota**
5. **Tobias Streich, c, West Virginia**
6. **Chris Herrmann, c, Miami**
7. **Brad Stillings, rhp, Kent State**
8. **Brian Dozier, ss, Southern Mississippi**
9. **Nick Lockwood, ss, Jesuit HS, Tampa**
10. Blake Dean, of, Louisiana State
11. Ronnie Richardson, of, Lake Region HS, Eagle Lake, Fla.
12. **Tony Davis, lhp, Florida**
13. Clarence Davis, ss, Campbell HS, Smyrna, Ga.
14. **Matt Tone, lhp, SUNY Cortland**
15. **Steven Liddle, of, Vanderbilt**
16. **Dakota Watts, rhp, Cal State Stanislaus**
17. **Nick Tindall, c, O'Fallon (Ill.) HS**
18. Beau Stoker, ss, Bishop Ward HS, Kansas City, Kan.
19. John Stilson, rhp, Texarkana (Texas) CC
20. Tommy Mackoul, lhp, UC Riverside
21. **Kane Holbrooks, rhp, Texas State**
22. **Buddy Munroe, c, Florida**
23. Eduardo Encinosa, rhp, Coral Park HS, Miami
24. Mario Hollands, lhp, UC Santa Barbara
25. Tony Bryant, rhp, Kennewick (Wash.) HS
26. Mike Giovenco, rhp, North Park (Ill.)
27. Eric Decker, of, Minnesota
28. Pat Light, rhp, Christian Brothers Academy, Lincroft, N.J.
29. Beau Wright, lhp, Los Alamitos (Calif.) HS
30. **Trayvone Johnson, c, Los Angeles, Calif.**
31. Cody Martin, 3b, Stephens County HS, Toccoa, Ga.
32. Aaron Senne, of, Missouri
33. **Nick Freitas, of, Southern Utah**
34. Ricky Claudio, rhp, American HS, Hialeah, Fla.
35. David Hurlbut, lhp, Diablo Valley (Calif.) JC
36. Jason Zylstra, rhp, Jacksonville State
37. David Gutierrez, rhp, Miami
38. **Peter Kennelly, rhp, Fordham**
39. Ryan Sadler, rhp, Naples (Fla.) HS
40. Ryan Abrahamson, of, Tartan HS, Oakdale, Minn.
41. Pat Butler, rhp, Chatham (N.J.) HS
42. Marc Bourgeois, of, Chipola (Fla.) JC
43. Jon Hedges, 1b, Olney Central (Ill.) CC
44. **Tyler Herr, rhp, Katy (Texas) HS**
45. **Eddie Ahorrio, rhp, Jesus Silverio Delgado HS, Arecibo, P.R.**
46. Jake Kretzer, of, Benton HS, St. Joseph, Mo.
47. **Richard Calcano, rhp, Dr. Jose M. Lazaro HS, Carolina, P.R.**
48. Cody Dordan, rhp, Newport (Ore.) HS
49. **Paul-Michael Klingsberg, 1b, Cal State Dominguez Hills**
50. Alberto Cardenas, rhp, Palmetto Ridge HS, Naples, Fla.

NEW YORK METS

June—Regular Phase (23)

1. (Pick to Angels as compensation for Type A free agent Francisco Rodriguez)
2. **Steve Matz, lhp, Melville HS, East Setauket, N.Y.**
3. **Robbie Shields, ss, Florida Southern**
4. **Darrell Ceciliani, of, Columbia Basin (Wash.) CC**
5. Damien Magnifico, rhp, North Mesquite HS, Mesquite, Texas
6. David Buchanan, rhp, Chipola (Fla.) JC
7. **Darin Gorski, lhp, Kutztown (Pa.)**
8. **Taylor Freeman, c, McNeese State**
9. **Jeff Glenn, c, Winter Haven (Fla.) HS**
10. **Nick Santomauro, of, Dartmouth**
11. **Sam Honeck, 1b, Tulane**
12. **James Ewing, 2b, Southern Mississippi**
13. **Zach Dotson, lhp, Effingham County HS, Springfield, Ga.**
14. **R.J. Harris, of, Northwood (Mich.)**
15. Casey Schmidt, rhp, San Diego
16. **Jeff Greene, of, West Boca Raton (Fla.) Community HS**
17. **Alex Gregory, of, Radford**
18. **Cody Holliday, of, Wilmington (Del.)**
19. **Nelfi Zapata, c, English HS, Jamaica Plain, Mass.**
20. **Joey August, of, Stanford**
21. **Joe Bonfe, 3b, Sierra (Calif.) JC**
22. **Zach Von Tersch, rhp, Georgia Tech**
23. **John Church, rhp, West Florida**
24. **Michael Johnson, rhp, Concordia (Texas)**
25. **Josh Dunn, 3b, Sickles HS, Tampa**
26. **John Semel, of, Chapman (Calif.)**
27. **Kurt Steinhauer, of, Point Loma Nazarene (Calif.)**
28. **Brian Needham, rhp, Lamar**
29. **ZeErika Hall, of, East Central (Miss.) CC**
30. Jordan Harrison, lhp, New Caney (Texas) HS
31. Mitch Haniger, of, Archbishop Mitty HS, San Jose
32. **T.J. Chism, lhp, La Salle**
33. **James Schroeder, 3b, Southern Arkansas**
34. **Cam Maron, c, Hicksville (N.Y.) HS**
35. **Wes Wrenn, rhp, The Citadel**
36. **Lance Hoge, lhp, Kansas State**
37. **Brandon Sage, lhp, South Alabama**
38. **Will Cherry, of, Florida Southern**

39. **Taylor Whitenton, rhp, Darton (Ga.) JC**
40. Jerome Pena, 2b, Western Nevada CC
41. **Travis Ozga, 1b, Florida Atlantic**
42. Ryan Gunhouse, c, Clear Creek HS, League City, Texas
43. Bobby Rinard, of, Yavapai (Ariz.) JC
44. James Wooster, lhp, Alvin (Texas) CC
45. Jake Johansen, rhp, Allen (Texas) HS
46. Trey Pilkington, rhp, Oxford (Ala.) HS
47. **Ryan Mollica, 2b, Florida International**
48. Joe Mantiply, lhp, Tunstall HS, Dry Fork, Va.
49. Josh Easley, rhp, Weatherford (Texas) HS
50. Zack Godley, rhp, Bamberg-Ehrhardt HS, Bamberg, S.C.

NEW YORK YANKEES

June—Regular Phase (24)

1. (Pick to Angels as compensation for Type A free agent Mark Teixeira)
1. **Slade Heathcott, of, Texas HS, Texarkana, Texas** (Supplemental pick—29th—for failure to sign 2008 first-rounder Gerrit Cole)
2. (Pick to Brewers as compensation for Type A free agent C.C. Sabathia)
2. **J.R. Murphy, c, Pendleton School, Bradenton, Fla.** (Supplemental pick—76th—for failure to sign 2008 second-rounder Scott Bittle)
3. (Pick to Blue Jays as compensation for Type A free agent A.J. Burnett)
4. **Adam Warren, rhp, North Carolina**
5. **Caleb Cotham, rhp, Vanderbilt**
6. **Rob Lyerly, 3b, Charlotte**
7. **Sean Black, rhp, Seton Hall**
8. **Sam Elam, lhp, Notre Dame**
9. **Gavin Brooks, lhp, UCLA**
10. Tyler Lyons, lhp, Oklahoma State
11. **Neil Medchill, of, Oklahoma State**
12. **Brett Gerritse, rhp, Pacifica HS, Garden Grove, Calif.**
13. **DeAngelo Mack, of, South Carolina**
14. **Graham Stoneburner, rhp, Clemson**
15. **Shane Greene, rhp, Daytona Beach (Fla.) CC**
16. **Bryan Mitchell, rhp, Rockingham County HS, Hamlet, N.C.**
17. Chad Thompson, rhp, El Toro HS, Lake Forest, Calif.
18. **Hector Rabago, c, Southern California**
19. **Luke Murton, 1b, Georgia Tech**
20. Thomas Keeling, lhp, Oklahoma State
21. **Joe Talerico, of, Brookdale (N.J.) CC**
22. Ben Soignier, ss, Louisiana-Monroe
23. **Kevin Mahoney, 3b, Canisius**
24. **Isaac Harrow, 2b, Appalachian State**
25. **Shaeffer Hall, lhp, Kansas**
26. Steve Bruno, ss, Gloucester Catholic HS, Gloucester City, N.J.
27. **Jeff Farnham, c, New Mexico State**
28. Aaron Meade, lhp, Missouri State
29. Scott Matyas, rhp, Minnesota
30. Kyle McKenzie, rhp, Thayer Academy, Braintree, Mass.
31. **Judd Golsan, of, Mountain Brook (Ala.) HS**
32. Nick Ebert, 1b, South Carolina
33. Andrew Aplin, of, Vanden HS, Fairfield, Calif.
34. Jake Petricka, rhp, Indiana State
35. Brett Bruening, rhp, Grayson County (Texas) CC
36. Kyle Ottoson, lhp, South Mountain (Ariz.) CC
37. **Justin Milo, of, Vermont**
38. Adam Bailey, of, Nebraska
39. Cody Stiles, rhp, Taravella HS, Coral Springs, Fla.
40. **Ben Watkins, rhp, Pittsburgh-Johnstown (Pa.)**
41. **Mariel Checo, rhp, Thomas HS, New York**
42. Danny Black, ss, Feather River (Calif.) JC
43. **Isaiah Brown, of, Paradise Valley (Ariz.) CC**
44. **Evan DeLuca, lhp, Immaculata HS, Somerville, N.J.**
45. Jeremy Baltz, of, Vestal (N.Y.) HS
46. Tony Plagman, 1b, Georgia Tech
47. Shane Brown, c, Central Florida
48. Patrick White, of, West Virginia
49. Xavier Esquivel, rhp, Loyola Marymount
50. Stephen Kaupang, 1b, Cypress (Calif.) JC

OAKLAND ATHLETICS

June—Regular Phase (12)

1. **Grant Green, ss, Southern California**
2. (Pick to White Sox as compensation for Type A free agent Orlando Cabrera)
3. **Justin Marks, lhp, Louisville**
4. **Max Stassi, c, Yuba City (Calif.) HS**
5. **Steve Parker, 3b, Brigham Young**
6. **Ryan Ortiz, c, Oregon State**
7. **Ian Krol, lhp, Neuqua Valley HS, Naperville, Ill.**
8. **Rob Gilliam, rhp, UNC Greensboro**
9. **Myrio Richard, of, Prairie View A&M**
10. Sam Dyson, rhp, South Carolina
11. **Mike Spina, 3b, Cincinnati**
12. **Connor Hoehn, rhp, St. Petersburg (Fla.) JC**
13. **Murphy Smith, rhp, SUNY Binghamton**
14. Drew Gagnier, rhp, Oregon
15. **Anthony Aliotti, 1b, St. Mary's**
16. **Josh Leyland, c, San Dimas (Calif.) HS**
17. Pat Stover, of, Rocklin (Calif.) HS
18. **Max Peterson, lhp, San Jose State**
19. **Daniel Tenholder, rhp, Austin Peay**
20. Tyler Bernard, ss, Valley Center (Calif.) HS
21. Mike Faulkner, of, Germantown (Tenn.) HS
22. **Ryan Quigley, lhp, Northeastern**
23. **Kent Walton, of, Brigham Young**
24. **Dan Straily, rhp, Marshall**
25. **Chris Mederos, rhp, Georgia Southern**
26. **Nathan Long, rhp, Texas-Arlington**
27. **Michael Gilmartin, 2b, Wofford**
28. **Conner Crumbliss, 2b, Emporia State (Kan.)**
29. Michael Zunino, c, Mariner HS, Cape Coral, Fla.
30. **Royce Consigli, of, Notre Dame HS, Welland, Ontario**
31. Ian Texidor, 3b, Centro Especializado de Educacion Avanzada, Rio Piedras, P.R.
32. Garett Claypool, rhp, UCLA
33. Mike Bolsinger, rhp, Arkansas
34. Dylan Brown, of, Oklahoma State
35. **Paul Smyth, rhp, Kansas**
36. **Jeremy Wells, 2b, Patten (Calif.)**
37. Colin Bates, rhp, North Carolina
38. Tristan Archer, rhp, Sullivan South HS, Blountville, Tenn.
39. Ryan Lockwood, of, South Florida
40. Chris O'Dowd, c, Regis Jesuit HS, Aurora, Colo.
41. Justin Hilt, of, Elon
42. **Blake Crosby, 1b, Sacramento State**
43. Ryan Lipkin, c, San Francisco
44. **A.J. Huttenlocker, lhp, Missouri Western State**
45. **Anthione Shaw, of, St. Augustine's (N.C.)**
46. **Joel Eusebio, 3b, Northeastern Oklahoma A&M JC**
47. Kyle Roller, 1b, East Carolina
48. Addison Johnson, of, Clemson
49. Anthony Giansanti, of, Siena
50. Tanner Biagini, 3b, Virginia Military Institute

PHILADELPHIA PHILLIES

June—Regular Phase (26)

1. (Pick to Mariners as compensation for Type A free agent Raul Ibanez)
2. **Kelly Dugan, of, Notre Dame HS, Sherman Oaks, Calif.**
3. **Kyrell Hudson, of, Evergreen HS, Vancouver, Wash.**
4. **Adam Buschini, 2b, Cal Poly**
5. **Matt Way, lhp, Washington State**
6. **Steven Inch, rhp, Vauxhall Academy, Edmonton**
7. **Brody Colvin, rhp, St. Thomas More HS, Lafayette, La.**
8. **Jonathan Singleton, 1b, Millikan HS, Long Beach**
9. **Aaron Altherr, of, Agua Fria HS, Avondale, Ariz.**
10. **Josh Zeid, rhp, Tulane**
11. **Jeremy Barnes, ss, Notre Dame**
12. **Nick Hernandez, lhp, Tennessee**
13. **Ryan Sasaki, lhp, Connally HS, Austin**
14. Jake Stewart, of, Rocky Mountain HS, Fort Collins, Colo.
15. **Austin Hyatt, rhp, Alabama**

16. Andrew Susac, c, Jesuit HS, Carmichael, Calif.
17. **Micheal Dabbs, of, Oklahoma State**
18. **Carl Uhl, of, UC Riverside**
19. **Stephen Batts, 1b, East Carolina**
20. **Darin Ruf, 1b, Creighton**
21. **Chase Johnson, rhp, South Mountain (Ariz.) CC**
22. **Bronco Lafrenz, c, Indiana State**
23. **Evan Porter, ss, Nebraska-Omaha**
24. **Justin Long, rhp, Bellevue (Neb.)**
25. **Eric Massingham, rhp, Cal Poly**
26. **Brian Gump, of, UC Santa Barbara**
27. **Marlon Mitchell, c, Hillsborough HS, Tampa**
28. **Justin Beal, rhp, Missouri Southern State**
29. **Mark Doll, rhp, Southern Polytechnic State (Ga.)**
30. Stephen Kohlscheen, rhp, Cowley County (Kan.) CC
31. **David Doss, c, South Alabama**
32. **Kevin Angelle, lhp, San Jacinto (Texas) JC**
33. **Colin Kleven, rhp, Mountain SS, Langley, B.C**
34. A.J. Griffin, rhp, San Diego
35. **Phil Aviola, c, Wilmington (Del.)**
36. **Matt McConnell, 2b, Metro State (Colo.)**
37. Brodie Greene, 2b, Texas A&M
38. **Cory Wine, 1b, Penn State**
39. Sam Kidd, rhp, Ohio County HS, Hartford, Ky.
40. Rob Amaro, 3b, Penn Charter HS, Philadelphia
41. Jeff Gelalich, of, Bonita HS, La Verne, Calif.
42. Matt Laney, lhp, Miami Dade CC
43. Francois Lafreniere, rhp, Ahuntsic (Quebec) JC
44. Brian Feekin, lhp, Iowa Western CC
45. Richard Bain, of, Trinity Christian Academy, Jacksonville
46. Jeff Ames, rhp, Skyview HS, Vancouver, Wash.
47. **Ryan Bollinger, 1b, Magic City HS, Minot, N.D.**
48. Wander Nunez, of, Frankford HS, Philadelphia
49. Chris Gosik, 3b, Malvern (Pa.) Prep HS
50. **David Hissey, of, Emory (Ga.)**

PITTSBURGH PIRATES

June—Regular Phase (4)

1. **Tony Sanchez, c, Boston College**
1. **Victor Black, rhp, Dallas Baptist** (Supplemental pick—49th—for failure to sign 2008 second-rounder Tanner Scheppers)
2. **Brooks Pounders, rhp, Temecula (Calif.) Valley HS**
3. **Evan Chambers, of, Hillsborough (Fla.) CC**
4. **Zack Dodson, lhp, Medina Valley HS, Castroville, Texas**
5. **Nate Baker, lhp, Mississippi**
6. **Zack Von Rosenberg, rhp, Zachary (La.) HS**
7. **Trent Stevenson, lhp, Brophy Prep, Phoenix**
8. **Colton Cain, lhp, Waxahachie (Texas) HS**
9. **Brock Holt, 2b, Rice**
10. **Joey Schoenfeld, c, Santiago HS, Garden Grove, Calif.**
11. **Aaron Baker, 1b, Oklahoma**
12. **Jeff Inman, rhp, Stanford**
13. **Walker Gourley, 3b, Eastern Wayne HS, Goldsboro, N.C.**
14. Marcos Reyna, rhp, Bakersfield (Calif.) JC
15. Peter Bako, rhp, Connors State (Okla.) JC
16. Matt den Dekker, of, Florida
17. Jordan Cooper, rhp, Central HS, Shelbyville, Tenn.
18. **Ryan Beckman, rhp, Grayson County (Texas) CC**
19. Josh Urban, rhp, Dripping Springs (Texas) HS
20. Sam Spangler, rhp, Hawaii
21. **Phillip Irwin, rhp, Mississippi**
22. Carmine Giardina, lhp, Tampa
23. **Jose Hernandez, inf, Texas-San Antonio**
24. **Jason Erickson, rhp, Washington**
25. Aaron LaFountaine, of, North HS, Riverside, Calif.
26. Matt Dermody, lhp, Norwalk (Iowa) HS
27. Wes Luquette, c, Newman HS, New Orleans
28. Kyle Hooper, rhp, Saugus (Calif.) HS
29. Michael Heller, rhp, Cardinal Mooney HS, Bradenton, Fla.
30. **Ty Summerlin, ss, Southeastern Louisiana**
31. Zach Taylor, of, Statesboro (Ga.) HS
32. Niko Spezial, lhp, Don Bosco Prep, Ramsey, N.J.
33. **Pat Irvine, of, Elon**
34. **Zac Fuesser, lhp, Walters State (Tenn.) CC**
35. Chris McKenzie, rhp, San Jacinto (Texas) JC
36. Bobby Doran, rhp, Seward County (Kan.) CC
37. Zach Nuding, rhp, Weatherford (Texas) JC
38. Jake Lamb, 3b, Bishop Blancet HS, Seattle
39. Keifer Nuncio, rhp, Katy (Texas) HS
40. Brett Lee, lhp, West Florida HS, Pensacola, Fla.
41. Tyler Cannon, ss, Virginia
42. **Marc Baca, rhp, Nevada-Las Vegas**
43. **Teddy Fallon, rhp, South Carolina-Upstate**
44. Dexter Bobo, lhp, Georgia Southern
45. Kevin Gelinas, lhp, Central Arizona JC
46. Parker Bangs, rhp, South Carolina
47. Justin Earls, lhp, Georgia
48. Blake Brown, of, Normal (Ill.) West HS
49. Yasser Clor, rhp, California
50. Matt Taylor, lhp, Columbus (Ga.) HS

ST. LOUIS CARDINALS

June—Regular Phase (18)

1. **Shelby Miller, rhp, Brownwood (Texas) HS**
2. **Robert Stock, c, Southern California**
3. **Joe Kelly, rhp, UC Riverside**
4. **Scott Bittle, rhp, Mississippi**
5. **Ryan Jackson, ss, Miami**
6. **Virgil Hill, of, Mission (Calif.) JC**
7. **Kyle Conley, of, Washington**
8. **Jason Stidham, ss, Florida State**
9. **Nick McCully, rhp, Coastal Carolina**
10. **Hector Hernandez, lhp, Puerto Rico Baseball Academy, Gurabo, P.R.**
11. **Alan Ahmady, 1b, Fresno State**
12. **Pat Daugherty, lhp, Pearl River (Miss.) CC**
13. **Matt Carpenter, 3b, Texas Christian**
14. **Ross Smith, of, Middle Georgia JC**
15. **David Washington, 1b, University City HS, San Diego**
16. Daniel Bibona, lhp, UC Irvine
17. **Jonathan Rodriguez, 1b, Manatee (Fla.) CC**
18. **Anthony Garcia, c, San Juan Educational HS, San Juan, P.R.**
19. **Travis Tartamella, c, Cal State Los Angeles**
20. **Scott Schneider, rhp, St. Mary's**
21. **Trevor Rosenthal, rhp, Cowley County (Kan.) CC**
22. Joey Bergman, 2b, College of Charleston
23. **Matt Adams, c, Slippery Rock (Pa.)**
24. **Keith Butler, rhp, Wabash Valley (Ill.) CC**
25. **Josh Squatrito, rhp, Towson**
26. **C.J. Beatty, of, North Carolina A&T**
27. **John Folino, rhp, Connecticut**
28. **Justin Edwards, lhp, Kennesaw State**
29. **Daniel Calhoun, lhp, Murray State**
30. **Chris Corrigan, rhp, Mississippi**
31. **Tyler Bighames, ss, Estero (Fla.) HS**
32. **Travis Lawler, rhp, Midland (Texas) JC**
33. **Devin Goodwin, ss, Delta State (Miss.)**
34. **David Kington, rhp, Southern Illinois**
35. **Andy Moss, rhp, Lincoln (Mo.)**
36. **Justin Smith, rhp, Utah Valley**
37. **Rich Racobaldo, 3b, Mount Olive (N.C.)**
38. **John Durham, lhp, Warner (Fla.)**
39. Taylor Terrasas, ss, Santa Fe (Texas) HS
40. **Jesse Simpson, rhp, Charleston**
41. **Cale Johnson, rhp, McKendree (Ill.)**
42. **Aaron Terry, rhp, Southern Arkansas**
43. **Manuel de la Cruz, lhp, Imperial Valley (Calif.) JC**
44. **Kyle Heim, lhp, Iowa**
45. Adam Heisler, of, South Alabama
46. Jim Klocke, c, Southeast Missouri State
47. **Michael Thompson, rhp, Bellarmine (Ky.)**
48. **Jason Novak, rhp, UCLA**
49. Andy Hillis, rhp, Brentwood (Tenn.) HS
50. **Tyler Lavigne, rhp, San Diego State**

SAN DIEGO PADRES

June—Regular Phase (3)

1. **Donavan Tate, of, Cartersville (Ga.) HS**
2. **Everett Williams, of, McCallum HS, Austin**
3. **Jerry Sullivan, rhp, Oral Roberts**
4. **Keyvius Sampson, rhp, Forest HS, Ocala, Fla.**
5. **Jason Hagerty, c, Miami**
6. **James Needy, rhp, Santana HS, Santee, Calif.**
7. **Miles Mikolas, rhp, Nova Southeastern (Fla.)**
8. **Nate Freiman, 1b, Duke**
9. **Chris Fetter, rhp, Michigan**
10. **Ryan Hinson, lhp, Clemson**
11. Drew Madrigal, rhp, Mount San Jacinto (Calif.) JC
12. **Brayden Drake, 3b, Missouri State**
13. **Matt Vern, 1b, Texas Christian**
14. **Nick Greenwood, lhp, Rhode Island**
15. **Matt Lollis, rhp, Riverside (Calif.) CC**
16. **Griffin Benedict, c, Georgia Southern**
17. **Jorge Reyes, rhp, Oregon State**
18. Shuhei Fujiya, rhp, Northern Iowa
19. **Chris Tremblay, ss, Kent State**
20. John Wooten, 3b, Eastern Wayne HS, Goldsboro, N.C.
21. **Kendall Korbal, rhp, Blinn (Texas) JC**
22. **Cody Decker, 1b, UCLA**
23. **Jeff Ibarra, lhp, Lee (Tenn.)**
24. **Bo Davis, of, Southern Mississippi**
25. **Ty Wright, of, Georgia Southern**
26. **Kevin Winn, 2b, Louisiana Tech**
27. **Cameron Monger, of, New Mexico**
28. **Vince Belnome, 2b, West Virginia**
29. **Robert Poutier, rhp, Virginia**
30. **Wande Olabisi, of, Stanford**
31. **Matt Jackson, rhp, South Alabama**
32. **David Erickson, rhp, Connecticut**
33. **Jon Berger, rhp, San Diego State**
34. Josh Cephas, rhp, Southern Nazarene (Okla.)
35. Adalberto Santos, of, Oregon State
36. **Dylan Tonneson, c, California**
37. Gaspar Santiago, lhp, Ranger (Texas) JC
38. **Kyle Loretelli, of, Cal State Stanislaus**
39. **Chris Ahearn, ss, Catawba (N.C.)**
40. **Tom Porter, rhp, Elon**
41. Dane Hamilton, 2b, New Mexico
42. Rey Delphey, rhp, Alonso HS, Tampa
43. **Chadd Hartman, of, Central Florida**
44. **Ryan Skube, 2b, Mountain Ridge HS, Glendale, Ariz.**
45. Derek Landis, rhp, Iowa Western CC
46. Mykal Stokes, of, Orange Coast (Calif.) CC
47. Zach Thomas, lhp, Cypress-Fairbanks HS, Cypress, Texas
48. Andrew Ruck, of, Sinclair SS, Whitby, Ontario
49. **Brett Holland, rhp, Texas-Tyler**
50. **Brett Basham, c, Mississippi**

SAN FRANCISCO GIANTS

June—Regular Phase (6)

1. **Zack Wheeler, rhp, East Paulding HS, Dallas, Ga.**
2. **Tommy Joseph, c, Horizon HS, Scottsdale, Ariz.**
3. **Chris Dominguez, 3b, Louisville**
4. **Jason Stoffel, rhp, Arizona**
5. **Brandon Belt, 1b, Texas**
6. **Matt Graham, rhp, Oak Ridge HS, Spring, Texas**
7. **Nick Liles, 2b, Western Carolina**
8. **Gus Benusa, of, Riverview HS, Oakmont, Pa.**
9. **Evan Crawford, of, Indiana**
10. **Jeremy Toole, rhp, Brigham Young**
11. **John Eshleman, ss, Mount San Jacinto (Calif.) JC**
12. **Chris Heston, rhp, East Carolina**
13. **Shawn Sanford, rhp, South Florida**
14. **B.J. Salsbury, rhp, Mount San Jacinto (Calif.) JC**
15. **Kyle Vazquez, rhp, Franklin Pierce (N.H.)**
16. **Ryan Cavan, ss, UC Santa Barbara**
17. **Chris Gloor, lhp, Quinnipiac**
18. Jonathan Walsh, of, Coppell (Texas) HS
19. **Jason Walls, rhp, Troy**
20. Mitch Mormann, rhp, Des Moines Area CC
21. Zach Wasserman, 1b, Lake Shore HS, St. Clair Shores, Mich.
22. **Drew Biery, 3b, Kansas State**
23. Adam Champion, lhp, Arkansas-Little Rock
24. **Alex Burg, c, Washington State**
25. **Taylor Rogers, rhp, Tulane**
26. **Luis Munoz, of, Puerto Rico Baseball Academy, Gurabo, P.R.**
27. **Kyle Mach, 3b, Missouri**
28. Jamaine Cotton, rhp, Western Oklahoma State JC
29. Luke Demko, rhp, Rhode Island (Contract voided)
30. **Craig Westcott, rhp, Bellhaven (Miss.)**
31. Diego Seastrunk, c, Rice
32. **Luke Anders, 1b, Texas A&M**
33. **Jake Dunning, rhp, Indiana**
34. Brandon Kirby, of, Lake Wales (Fla.) HS
35. **Brandon Graves, lhp, Valdosta State (Ga.)**
36. **Ryan Scoma, of, UC Davis**
37. **Ryan Lollis, of, Missouri**
38. **A.J. Proszek, rhp, Gonzaga**
39. **Kyle Henson, c, Mississippi**
40. **Jonathan White, of, Vanderbilt**
41. **Gary Moran, rhp, Sonoma State (Calif.)**
42. Nick Schwaner, 3b, New Orleans
43. Matt Jansen, lhp, Purdue
44. Joe Lewis, 1b, Pittsburg (Calif.) HS
45. Kyle Kramp, rhp, Westfield (Ind.) HS
46. **Juan Martinez, ss, Oral Roberts**
47. Michael Ness, rhp, Duke
48. Randolph Oduber, of, Western Oklahoma State JC
49. Austin Goolsby, c, Embry-Riddle (Fla.)
50. **Kaohi Downing, rhp, Point Loma Nazarene (Calif.)**

SEATTLE MARINERS

June—Regular Phase (2)

1. **Dustin Ackley, of, North Carolina**
1. **Nick Franklin, ss, Lake Brantley HS, Altamonte Springs, Fla.** (Pick from Phillies as compensation for Type A free agent Raul Ibanez)
1. **Steve Baron, c, Ferguson HS, Miami** (Supplemental pick—33rd—for loss of Ibanez)
2. **Rich Poythress, 1b, Georgia**
3. **Kyle Seager, 2b, North Carolina**
4. **James Jones, of, Long Island**
5. **Tyler Blandford, rhp, Oklahoma State**
6. **Shaver Hansen, 3b, Baylor**
7. **Brian Moran, lhp, North Carolina**
8. **Jimmy Gilheeney, lhp, North Carolina State**
9. **Trevor Coleman, c, Missouri**
10. **Vinnie Catricala, 3b, Hawaii**
11. **Tim Morris, 1b, St. John's**
12. **Andrew Carraway, rhp, Virginia**
13. **Matt Cerione, of, Georgia**
14. Adam Nelubowich, 3b, Vauxhall Academy, Edmonton
15. Blake Keitzman, lhp, Western Oregon
16. Tillman Pugh, of, Gateway (Ariz.) CC
17. Joe Terry, 2b, Cerritos (Calif.) CC
18. **Anthony Vasquez, lhp, Southern California**
19. **Eric Thomas, rhp, Bethune-Cookman**
20. **John Hesketh, lhp, New Mexico**
21. **Daniel Cooper, rhp, Southern California**
22. Drew Hayes, rhp, Vanderbilt
23. David Rollins, lhp, San Jacinto (Texas) JC
24. **Carlton Tanabe, c, Pearl City (Hawaii) HS**
25. **Brandon Josselyn, rhp, Yale**
26. **Chris Sorce, rhp, Troy**
27. **Austin Hudson, rhp, Central Florida**
28. Regan Flaherty, 1b, Deering HS, Portland, Maine
29. **Brandon Haveman, of, Purdue**
30. **Brandon Bantz, c, Dallas Baptist**
31. Clint Dempster, lhp, Mississippi Gulf Coast JC
32. Bennett Whitmore, lhp, Oregon
33. **Hawkins Gebbers, 2b, Biola (Calif.)**

34. Scott Griggs, rhp, San Ramon Valley HS, Danville, Calif.
35. **Eric Valdez, rhp, Indiana State**
36. **John Housey, rhp, Miami**
37. **Chris Kessinger, rhp, Nebraska-Omaha**
38. Matt Nohelty, of, Minnesota
39. **Greg Waddell, of, Florida International**
40. **Jorden Merry, rhp, Washington**
41. **Kyle Witten, rhp, Cal State Fullerton**
42. Steve Hagen, 3b, Eastern Oklahoma State JC
43. Cameron Perkins, of, Southport HS, Indianapolis
44. **Mark Angelo, of, East Stroudsburg (Pa.)**
45. **Kevin Mailloux, 2b, Canisus**
46. Clay Cederquist, 1b, Fowler HS, Fresno
47. David Holman, rhp, Hutchinson (Kan.) CC
48. Sean Nolin, lhp, San Jacinto (Texas) JC
49. Dane Phillips, c, Central Heights HS, Nacogdoches, Texas
50. **Evan Sharpley, 3b, Notre Dame**

TAMPA BAY RAYS

June—Regular Phase (28)

1. LeVon Washington, 2b, Buchholz HS, Gainesville, Fla.
2. Kenny Diekroeger, ss, Menlo HS, Atherton, Calif.
3. **Todd Glaesmann, of, Midway HS, Waco, Texas**
4. **Luke Bailey, c, Troup County HS, LaGrange, Ga.**
5. **Jeff Malm, 1b, Bishop Gorman HS, Las Vegas**
6. **Devin Fuller, rhp, Chandler-Gilbert (Ariz.) CC**
7. **Cody Rogers, of, Panola (Texas) JC**
8. **Brett Nommensen, of, Eastern Illinois**
9. **Kevin James, lhp, Whitefish Bay HS, Milwaukee**
10. Derek Dennis, ss, Forest Hills Central HS, Grand Rapids, Mich.
11. **Alex Koronis, rhp, Tampa**
12. **Andrew Bellatti, rhp, Steele Canyon HS, Spring Valley, Calif.**
13. **Hunter Hill, rhp, Howard (Texas) JC**
14. **Zach Quate, rhp, Appalachian State**
15. Pierce Johnson, rhp, Faith Christian Academy, Arvada, Colo.
16. **Tyler Bortnick, 2b, Coastal Carolina**
17. **Alex Diaz, of, Puerto Rico Baseball Academy, Gurabo, P.R.**
18. **Jacob Partridge, lhp, Rogers HS, Puyallup, Wash.**
19. **Scott Shuman, rhp, Auburn**
20. Dylan Floro, rhp, Buhach Colony HS, Atwater, Calif.
21. **Matt Swilley, rhp, El Camino HS, Oceanside, Calif.**
22. **Jake Sullivan, lhp, Arkansas-Little Rock**
23. Trevor Petersen, rhp, Hallsville (Texas) HS
24. Andrew Heaney, lhp, Putnam City HS, Oklahoma City
25. **Ryan Wiegand, 1b, Gonzaga**
26. **Dan Rhault, ss, Rhode Island**
27. Brady Wager, rhp, Globe (Ariz.) HS
28. **Zach Rosscup, lhp, Chemeketa (Ore.) CC**
29. **Gabe Cohen, of, UCLA**
30. **Marcus Proctor, rhp, Pinnacle HS, Phoenix**
31. **Aaron Dott, lhp, Wisconsin-Whitewater**
32. Alex Besaw, rhp, Skagit Valley (Wash.) CC
33. Ryan McCarney, rhp, Cal State Northridge
34. **Kyle Spraker, ss, Loyola Marymount**
35. **Chris Murrill, of, Nicholls State**
36. **Jeff Cinadr, rhp, Toledo**
37. Austin Maddox, c, Eagle's View HS, Jacksonville
38. Drew Hillman, 3b, Orange Coast (Calif.) CC
39. **Dan April, lhp, Mercer**
40. James Pazos, lhp, Highland HS, Gilbert, Ariz.
41. **Matt Stabelfeld, lhp, Lewis-Clark State (Idaho)**
42. **Bennett Davis, 3b, Elon**
43. **Geno Glynn, 3b, Minnesota State-Mankato**
44. Kalani Brackenridge, ss, Kapolei (Hawaii) HS
45. Cole Nelson, lhp, Des Moines Area CC
46. Aaron Oates, 3b, Skyline HS, Oakland
47. **Jason Patton, of, Kent State**
48. Nate Roberts, of, Parkland (Ill.) JC
49. Vince Spilker, rhp, Raytown (Mo.) HS
50. **David Wendt, c, Dowling (N.Y.)**

TEXAS RANGERS

June—Regular Phase (13)

1. Matt Purke, lhp, Klein (Texas) HS
1. **Tanner Scheppers, rhp, St. Paul (American Association)** (Supplemental pick—44th—for loss of Type B free agent Milton Bradley)
2. **Tommy Mendonca, 3b, Fresno State**
3. **Robbie Erlin, lhp, Scotts Valley (Calif.) HS**
4. **Andrew Doyle, rhp, Oklahoma**
5. **Nick McBride, rhp, Ragsdale HS, Jamestown, N.C.**
6. **Ruben Sierra Jr., of, San Juan Educational HS, San Juan, P.R.**
7. **Braxton Lane, of, Sandy Creek HS, Tyrone, Ga.**
8. **Braden Tullis, rhp, Skagit Valley (Wash.) CC**
9. Jabari Blash, of, Miami Dade CC
10. Thomas Lemke, rhp, Northwest Christian HS, Phoenix
11. **Johnny Gunter, rhp, Chattahoochee Valley (Ala.) CC**
12. **Vin DiFazio, c, Alabama**
13. **Justin Jamison, rhp, Strongsville (Ohio) HS**
14. **Chad Bell, lhp, Walters State (Tenn.) CC**
15. **Keith Campbell, rhp, Everett (Wash.) CC**
16. Mike Revell, 3b, Florida HS, Tallahassee, Fla.
17. **Paul Strong, lhp, Marina HS, Huntington Beach, Calif.**
18. Mike Schaaf, rhp, Hill HS, Saginaw, Mich.
19. David Boyd, 3b, Tate HS, Cantonment, Fla.
20. Jerome Werniuk, rhp, Neil McNeil HS, Toronto
21. **Chris Matlock, rhp, Central Missouri State**
22. **Sam Brown, rhp, North Carolina State**
23. **Danny Lima, ss, Barry (Fla.)**
24. **Shawn Blackwell, rhp, Clear Creek HS, League City, Texas**
25. **Riley Cooper, of, Florida**
26. **Kevin Castner, rhp, Cal Poly**
27. Aaron Barrett, rhp, Mississippi
28. Derek Law, rhp, Seton LaSalle Catholic HS, Pittsburgh
29. C.C. Watson, lhp, Cleburne County HS, Heflin, Ala.
30. Bryan Fogle, of, Erskine (S.C.)
31. **Shon Landry, ss, McNeese State**
32. Reggie Williams Jr., of, Brooks-DeBartolo Collegiate HS, Tampa
33. **Kyle Rhoad, of, Eastern Michigan**
34. **Jared Prince, of, Washington State**
35. Tim Butler, rhp, Greenbrier Christian Academy, Chesapeake, Va.
36. Matt Carasiti, rhp, Berlin (Conn.) HS
37. Chad Nading, rhp, Nevada-Las Vegas
38. Anthony Hutting, of, Tesoro HS, Rancho San Margarita, Calif.
39. Jabari Henry, of, Olympia HS, Orlando
40. **Taylor Vail, 3b, Cabrillo (Calif.) JC**
41. Forrest Garrett, lhp, Norcross (Ga.) HS
42. **Shane Zagarac, lhp, St. Joseph's (Ind.)**
43. **Joe Bonadonna, of, Illinois**
44. Tyler Christman, rhp, South Carolina-Sumter JC
45. Dale Anderson, c, JC of Southern Idaho
46. Jerad Grundy, lhp, Johnsburg (Ill.) HS
47. Tyler Higgins, rhp, Mount Pleasant (Mich.) HS
48. Cole Frenzel, 3b, Dickinson (N.D.) HS
49. Cat Kendrick, rhp, Northgate HS, Newnan, Ga.
50. Ronald Melendez, of, Cowley County (Kan.) CC

TORONTO BLUE JAYS

June—Regular Phase (19)

1. **Chad Jenkins, rhp, Kennesaw State**
1. James Paxton, lhp, Kentucky (Supplemental pick—37th—for loss of Type A free agent A.J. Burnett)
2. Jake Eliopoulos, lhp, Sacred Heart Catholic HS, Newmarket, Ont
3. Jake Barrett, rhp, Desert Ridge HS, Mesa, Ariz.
3. **Jake Marisnick, of, Poly HS, Riverside, Calif.** (Pick from Yankees as compensation for Burnett)
4. **Ryan Goins, ss, Dallas Baptist**
5. **Ryan Schimpf, 2b, Louisiana State**
6. **K.C. Hobson, of, Stockdale HS, Bakersfield, Calif.**
7. **Egan Smith, lhp, CC of Southern Nevada**
8. **Brian Slover, rhp, Cal State Northridge**

9. **Aaron Loup, lhp, Tulane**
10. **Yan Gomes, c, Barry (Fla.)**
11. **Sean Ochinko, c, Louisiana State**
12. **Bryson Namba, 3b, Pearl City (Hawaii) HS**
13. **Matt Morgal, rhp, Southern Nazarene (Okla.)**
14. **Lance Durham, 1b, Cincinnati**
15. **Drew Hutchison, rhp, Lakeland (Fla.) HS**
16. **Dave Sever, rhp, Saint Louis**
17. **Steve Turnbull, rhp, Iowa**
18. **Daniel Webb, rhp, Northwest Florida State JC**
19. **Ryan Tepera, rhp, Sam Houston State**
20. **Kevin Nolan, ss, Winthrop**
21. Kurt Giller, rhp, Manhattan (Kan.) HS
22. **Matt Fields, rhp, Gonzaga**
23. **Brad Glenn, of, Arizona**
24. **Matt Nuzzo, ss, Brown**
25. **Sam Strickland, lhp, Texas A&M-Kingsville**
26. **Lance Loftin, rhp, Texas State**
27. **Brian Justice, rhp, St. Mary's**
28. **Zach Outman, rhp, Saint Louis**
29. **Zach Anderson, rhp, Buffalo**
30. Tim McDonald, of, Edison HS, Fresno
31. **Jack Murphy, c, Princeton**
32. **Ryan Shopshire, rhp, San Jose State**
33. Robert Benincasa, rhp, Armwood HS, Seffner, Fla.
34. **Jonathan Fernandez, ss, Guilford Tech (N.C.) CC**
35. **Evan Teague, lhp, Western Kentucky**
36. **Alex Pepe, lhp, Florida Atlantic**
37. **Shawn Griffith, rhp, George Mason**
38. **Yudelmis Hernandez, 1b, Barry (Fla.)**
39. Josh Lucas, rhp, Lakeland (Fla.) HS
40. Jonathan Gilbert, of, Ahuntsic (Quebec) JC
41. Zach Kirksey, of, Louisiana State-Eunice JC
42. Michael Reeves, c, St. Peter's SS, Peterborough, Ontario
43. Maxx Tissenbaum, ss, York Mills Collegiate Institute, Toronto
44. Nick Wagner, of, Santa Margarita HS, Rancho Santa Margarita, Calif.
45. Brandon Kaye, rhp, Douglas (B.C.)
46. Carlos Castro, 3b, Lon Morris (Texas) JC
47. John Rigg, of, St. Petersburg (Fla.) JC
48. Jeff Gibbs, rhp, Birchmount Park Collegiate Institute, Scarborough, Ontario
49. Tommy Collier, rhp, San Jacinto (Texas) JC
50. Burke Seifrit, rhp, Semiahmoo SS, Surrey, B.C

WASHINGTON NATIONALS

June—Regular Phase (1)

1. **Stephen Strasburg, rhp, San Diego State**
1. **Drew Storen, rhp, Stanford** (Supplemental pick—10th—for failure to sign 2008 first-rounder Aaron Crow)
2. **Jeff Kobernus, 2b, California**
3. **Trevor Holder, rhp, Georgia**
4. **A.J. Morris, rhp, Kansas State**
5. Miguel Pena, lhp, La Joya HS, Mission, Texas
6. **Michael Taylor, ss, Westminster Academy, Fort Lauderdale**
7. **Dean Weaver, rhp, Georgia**
8. **Roberto Perez, ss, Dorado Academy, Dorado, P.R.**
9. **Taylor Jordan, rhp, Brevard (Fla.) CC**
10. **Paul Applebee, lhp, UC Riverside**
11. **Justin Bloxom, of, Kansas State**
12. **Nathan Karns, rhp, Texas Tech**
13. **Pat Lehman, rhp, George Washington**
14. **Naoya Washiya, of, JC of the Desert (Calif.)**
15. Corey Davis, 1b, Coffee HS, Douglas, Ga.
16. **Sean Nicol, ss, San Diego**
17. **Chad Jenkins, lhp, Cecil (Md.) CC**
18. Marcus Stroman, ss, Patchogue-Medford HS, Medford, N.Y.
19. **Frank Corolla, rhp, Houston**
20. **Jack Walker, 3b, Concordia (Ill.)**
21. **Mitchell Clegg, lhp, Massachusetts**
22. **Danny Rosenbaum, lhp, Xavier**
23. **Kyle Breault, ss, Northville (Mich.) HS**
24. **Dustin Crane, rhp, Snead State (Ala.) CC**
25. Matt Ridings, rhp, Western Kentucky
26. **Gianison Boekhoudt, ss, Carroll HS, Southlake, Texas**
27. **Brandon King, rhp, Martinsburg (W.Va.) HS**
28. **Matt Swynenberg, rhp, Black Hawk (Iowa) JC**
29. **Evan Bronson, lhp, Trinity (Texas)**
30. **Rob Wort, rhp, Jefferson (Mo.) JC**
31. **J.J. Sferra, of, Nevada-Las Vegas**
32. **Kyle Morrison, rhp, Wagner**
33. Nick DeSantiago, c, Hays HS, Kyle, Texas
34. **Shane McCatty, rhp, Oakland**
35. Jacob Morris, of, Coppell (Texas) HS
36. Josh Miller, lhp, O'Connor HS, Helotes, Texas
37. **Josh Elander, c, Round Rock (Texas) HS**
38. Chris Manno, lhp, Duke
39. Kyle Martin, rhp, St. Michael's Academy, Austin
40. Joseph Hughes, rhp, McMichael HS, Mayodan, N.C.
41. Dane Opel, of, Edwardsville (Ill.) HS
42. Daniel Cropper, rhp, Columbus HS, Bronx, N.Y.
43. Cohl Walla, rhp, Lake Travis HS, Austin
44. Hoby Milner, lhp, Paschal HS, Fort Worth
45. Michael Ratterree, ss, Memorial HS, Houston
46. Seth Greene, rhp, Deep Run HS, Glen Allen, Va.
47. Darius Rudoph, 2b, Snead State (Ala.) CC
48. Zach Dygert, c, Ball State
49. Jose Sermo, of, Ileana de Gracia HS, Vega Alta, P.R.
50. Alvin Hines, of, Pelham (Ala.) HS